Dictionary of

WOMEN ARTISTS

VOLUME 2

Dictionary of

WOMEN ARTISTS

VOLUME 2

Artists, J–Z

Editor
DELIA GAZE

Picture Editors
MAJA MIHAJLOVIC
LEANDA SHRIMPTON

FITZROY DEARBORN PUBLISHERS
LONDON AND CHICAGO

FITZROY DEARBORN PUBLISHERS
70 East Walton Street
Chicago, Illinois 60611
USA

or

11 Rathbone Place
London W1P 1DE
England

British Library Cataloguing in Publication Data
Dictionary of women artists
    1. Women artists – Dictionaries
    I. Gaze, Delia
    709.2'2

ISBN 1-884964-21-4

Library of Congress Cataloging in Publication Data is available.

First published in the USA and UK 1997

Typeset by Lorraine Hodghton, Radlett, Herts, UK
Printed in Great Britain by the Bath Press

Cover illustration:
Self-Portrait in Profile Facing Left, Drawing by Käthe Kollwitz, 1933

Frontispieces:
vol.1: Jacoba van Heemskerck in her studio, 1915
vol.2: *In the Studio* by Asta Nørregaard, 1883

CONTENTS

ALPHABETICAL LIST
OF ARTISTS

VOLUME I

Magdalena Abakanowicz
Louise Abbéma
Berenice Abbott
Carla Accardi
Eileen Agar
Anni Albers
Gretchen Albrecht
Helen Allingham
Laura Alma-Tadema
Tarsila do Amaral
Anna Ancher
Sophie Anderson
Sofonisba Anguissola
Rita Angus
Eleanor Antin
Ida Applebroog
Diane Arbus
Pauline Auzou
Josefa d'Ayala de Óbidos
Gillian Ayres

Harriet Backer
Caroline Bardua
Hannah and Florence Barlow
Wilhelmina Barns-Graham
Jennifer Bartlett
Glenys Barton
Marie Bashkirtseff
Hester Bateman
Gudrun Baudisch
Mary Beale
Lady Diana Beauclerk
Cecilia Beaux
Clarice Beckett
María Eugenia de Beer
Vanessa Bell
Benedetta
Lynda Benglis
Teresa Benincampi
Mme Benoist
Charlotte Berend-Corinth
Ella Bergmann-Michel

Sarah Bernhardt
Mme Léon Bertaux
Elsa Beskow
Henryka Beyer
Aenne Biermann
Anna Bilińska-Bohdanowicz
Vivienne Binns
Isabel Bishop
Dorrit Black
Elizabeth Blackadder
María Blanchard
Tina Blau
Lucienne Bloch
Sandra Blow
Anna Blunden
Anna Boch
Barbara Leigh Smith Bodichon
Bona
Rosa Bonheur
Lee Bontecou
Gesina ter Borch
Marie-Geneviève Bouliar
Louise Bourgeois
Margaret Bourke-White
Joanna Boyce
Olga Boznańska
Marie Bracquemond
Norah Braden
Marianne Brandt
Louise-Catherine Breslau
Eleanor Fortescue Brickdale
Elena Brockmann
Romaine Brooks
Lucy Madox Brown
Henriette Browne
Trude Brück
Jaroslava Brychtová
Beverly Buchanan
Kate Bunce
Lady Butler

Margherita Caffi
Claude Cahun
Julia Margaret Cameron

Gabrielle Capet
Anne Marie Carl Nielsen
Margaret Carpenter
Emily Carr
Rosalba Carriera
Carrington
Leonora Carrington
Maria Caspar-Filser
Mary Cassatt
Elizabeth Catlett
Hanna Cauer
Marie Cazin
Vija Celmins
Emilie Charmy
Constance Charpentier
Barbara Chase-Riboud
Elisabeth-Sophie Chéron
Judy Chicago
Chryssa
Fanny Churberg
Lygia Clark
Edna Clarke Hall
Camille Claudel
Franciska Clausen
Florence Claxton
Joyce Clissold
Prunella Clough
Marie-Anne Collot
Ithell Colquhoun
Susie Cooper
Maria Cosway
Louisa Courtauld
Suor Maria Eufrasia della Croce
Lena Cronqvist
Imogen Cunningham

Louise Dahl-Wolfe
Anne Seymour Damer
Natalya Danko
Hanne Darboven
Anna Julia De Graag
Dorothy Dehner
Elaine de Kooning
Mary Delany
Sonia Delaunay
Virginie Demont-Breton
Evelyn De Morgan
Siri Derkert
Maria Oakey Dewing
Teresa Díaz
Barbara Regina Dietzsch
Jessica Dismorr
Suor Maria de Dominici
Rita Donagh
Marion Dorn
Victoria Dubourg
Ruth Duckworth
Natalia Dumitrescu
Susanna Duncombe
Françoise Duparc

Amalia Duprè
Susan Durant
Sofya Dymshits-Tolstaya

Susan Macdowell Eakins
Joan Eardley
Abastenia St Leger Eberle
Mary Beth Edelson
Marie Ellenrieder
Rebeccah Emes
Ende
Gutte Eriksen
Eléonore Escallier
Alexandra Exter

Jacqueline Fahey
Claire Falkenstein
Félicie de Fauveau
Sheila Fell
Sonja Ferlov
Jackie Ferrara
Lucrina Fetti
Leonor Fini
Janet Fish
Audrey Flack
Gerda Flöckinger
Mathilde Flögl
Mary Sargant Florence
Lavinia Fontana
Anne Forbes
Elizabeth Forbes
Raquel Forner
Gela Forster
Ethel Fox
Fernanda Francés y Arribas
Helen Frankenthaler
Elizabeth Frink
Harriet Whitney Frishmuth
Elizabeth Fritsch
Meta Vaux Warrick Fuller

Wanda Gág
Fede Galizia
Elizabeth Gardner
Anna Maria Garthwaite
Giovanna Garzoni
Wilhelmina Geddes
Artemisia Gentileschi
Marguerite Gérard
Margaret Gillies
Caterina Ginnasi
Gluck
Elizabeth Godfrey
Hilde Goldschmidt
Anna Golubkina
Natalya Goncharova
Eva Gonzalès
Dora Gordine
Sylvia Gosse
Mary Grant

Nancy Graves
Norah Neilson Gray
Kate Greenaway
Gertrude Greene
Marion Greenwood
Majlis Grotell
Lea Grundig
May Guinness
Elena Guro

Ellen Day Hale
Alice Halicka
Maggi Hambling
Letitia Hamilton
Harmony Hammond
Nina Hamnett
Frida Hansen
Gwyn Hanssen Pigott
Grace Hartigan
Sella Hasse
Margareta Haverman
Clementina, Viscountess Hawarden
Jacoba van Heemskerck
Margaretha de Heer
Katharina Heise
Catharina van Hemessen
Louise Henderson
Florence Henri
Grace Henry
Barbara Hepworth
Gertrude Hermes
Herrad
Eva Hesse
Joy Hester
Sheila Hicks
Hildegard of Bingen
Susan Hiller
Hanna Hirsch Pauli
Sigrid Hjertén
Diana Hobson
Hannah Höch
Frances Hodgkins
Malvina Hoffman
Evie Hone
Rebecca Horn
Harriet Hosmer
Anita Hoy
Valentine Hugo
Anna Vaughn Hyatt Huntington
Ulrica Hydman-Vallien

Adelaide Ironside
María Izquierdo

VOLUME 2

Lotte Jacobi
Tess Jaray
Valerie Jaudon
Mainie Jellett

Elisabeth Jerichau Baumann
Lisbet and Gocken Jobs
Gwen John
Frances Benjamin Johnston
Dorothy Johnstone
Joan Jonas
Lois Mailou Jones
Louise Jopling
Grethe Jürgens

Frida Kahlo
Gertrude Käsebier
Angelica Kauffman
Mary Kelly
Lucy Kemp-Welch
Ida Kerkovius
Nadia Khodossievitch
Kitty Kielland
Jessie M. King
Erika Giovanna Klien
Hilma af Klint
Anna Klumpke
Laura Knight
Katarzyna Kobro
Ghisha Koenig
Käthe Kollwitz
Joyce Kozloff
Lee Krasner
Oda Krohg
Barbara Kruger
Elizaveta Kruglikova

Adélaïde Labille-Guiard
Betty LaDuke
Maria Margaretha La Fargue
Giulia Lama
Dorothea Lange
Marie-Anne Lansiaux
Lotte Laserstein
Else Lasker-Schüler
Maria Lassnig
Marie Laurencin
Sarra Lebedeva
Madeleine-Jeanne Lemaire
Marie-Victoire Lemoine
Tamara de Lempicka
Thérèse Lessore
Edmonia Lewis
Judith Leyster
Liliane Lijn
Maria Likarz-Strauss
Kim Lim
Amalia Lindegren
Anna Rosina Lisiewska
Anna Dorothea Lisiewska-Therbusch
Elfriede Lohse-Wächtler
Marie Anne Loir
Barbara Longhi
Gillian Lowndes
Alexandra Luke

Helen Lundeberg
Vivian Lynn

Dora Maar
Molly Macalister
Frances Macdonald
Margaret Macdonald
Norah McGuinness
Loren MacIver
Isabel McLaughlin
Mary Louise McLaughlin
Mary Fairchild MacMonnies
Bessie MacNicol
Anne Madden
Bea Maddock
Elena Makovskaya-Luksch
Marie von Malachowski
Anita Malfatti
Maruja Mallo
Jeanne Mammen
Sylvia Plimack Mangold
Diana Mantuana
Marcello
Marevna
Marisol
Theresa Concordia Maron-Mengs
Agnes Martin
Mary Martin
Maria Martins
Jacqueline Marval
Enid Marx
Alice Trumbull Mason
Louisa Matthiasdóttir
Constance Mayer
Else Meidner
Margaret Mellis
Louisa Anne Meredith
Maria Sibylla Merian
Anna Lea Merritt
Annette Messager
Lee Miller
Lizinka de Mirbel
Mary Miss
Joan Mitchell
Lisette Model
Paula Modersohn-Becker
Tina Modotti
Lucia Moholy
Louise Moillon
Marg Moll
Berthe Morisot
Jacqueline Morreau
May Morris
Ree Morton
Mary Moser
Anna Mary Robertson Moses
Marlow Moss
Marie-Louise von Motesiczky
Vera Mukhina
Gabriele Münter

Elizabeth Murray

Hanna Nagel
Alice Neel
Plautilla Nelli
Louise Nevelson
Jessie Newbery
Elisabet Ney
Winifred Nicholson
Vera Nilsson
Astrid Noack
Asta Nørregaard
Elizabeth Nourse
Gunnel Nyman
Jenny Nyström

Georgia O'Keeffe
Maria van Oosterwijck
Meret Oppenheim
Olga Oppenheimer
Princess Marie Christine d'Orléans
Chana Orloff
Emily Mary Osborn
Anna Ostroumova-Lebedeva
Gerta Overbeck

Ana Maria Pacheco
María Luisa Pacheco
Gina Pane
Lygia Pape
Isabella Catanea Parasole
Mimi Parent
Vilma Parlaghy
Ulrica Fredrica Pasch
Magdalena van de Passe
Anna Claypoole and Sarah Miriam Peale
Clara Peeters
Amelia Peláez
Beverly Pepper
I. Rice Pereira
Lilla Cabot Perry
Deanna Petherbridge
Howardena Pindell
Eunice Pinney
Katharine Pleydell-Bouverie
Elena Polenova
Lyubov Popova
Beatrix Potter
Mary Potter
Jane Poupelet
Alexandra Povorina
Lotte B. Prechner
Margaret Preston
Hans Anton Prinner
Dod Procter
Sarah Purser

Henrietta Rae
Alice Rahon
Yvonne Rainer

Carol Rama
Wendy Ramshaw
Clara von Rappard
Gwen Raverat
Katharine Read
Vinnie Ream
Anne Redpath
Anita Rée
Ruth Reeves
Regina
Paula Rego
Anne Estelle Rice
Germaine Richier
Lucie Rie
Bridget Riley
Clara Rilke-Westhoff
Faith Ringgold
Coba Ritsema
Christina Robertson
Suze Robertson
Adelaide Alsop Robineau
Marietta Robusti
Dorothea Rockburne
Emy Roeder
Geertruydt Roghman
Luisa Roldán
Henriëtte Ronner-Knip
Margaretha Roosenboom
Martha Rosler
Properzia de' Rossi
Susan Rothenberg
Olga Rozanova
Sophie Rude
Rachel Ruysch
Hannah Ryggen

Betye Saar
Kay Sage
Niki de Saint Phalle
Kyllikki Salmenhaara
Charlotte Salomon
Josefa Sánchez
Susanna Maria von Sandrart
Angeles Santos Torroella
Augusta Savage
Miriam Schapiro
Mira Schendel
Helene Schjerfbeck
Carolee Schneemann
Anna Maria van Schurman
Ethel Schwabacher
Thérése Schwartze
Kathleen Scott
Janet Scudder
Louise Seidler
Zinaida Serebryakova
Ellen Wallace and Rolinda Sharples
Aleksandra Shchekatikhina-Pototskaya
Amrita Sher-Gil
Elizabeth Eleanor Siddal

Renée Sintenis
Elisabetta Sirani
Monica Sjöö
Marta Skulme
Sylvia Sleigh
Clarissa Sligh
Agnes Slott-Møller
Grace Cossington Smith
Jaune Quick-to-See Smith
Pamela Colman Smith
Joan Snyder
Rebecca Solomon
Marie Spartali
Jo Spence
Lilly Martin Spencer
Nancy Spero
Louisa Starr
Emma Stebbins
Milly Steger
Pat Steir
Varvara Stepanova
Alice Barber Stephens
Irma Stern
Florine Stettheimer
May Stevens
Margaret Olrog Stoddart
Marianne Stokes
Gunta Stölzl
Zofia Stryjeńska
Michelle Stuart
Jane Sutherland
Júlíana Sveinsdóttir
Betty Swanwick
Mary Swanzy
Annie Swynnerton

Sophie Taeuber-Arp
Agnes Tait
Dorothea Tanning
Lenore Tawney
Janice Tchalenko
Levina Teerlinc
Ellen Thesleff
Alma W. Thomas
Mary Thornycroft
Anna Ticho
Charley Toorop
Toyen
Phoebe Traquair
Nína Tryggvadóttir
Tilsa Tsuchiya

Nadezhda Udaltsova

Suzanne Valadon
Nanine Vallain
Anne Vallayer-Coster
Remedios Varo
Gertrud Vasegaard
Pablita Velarde

Paule Vézelay
Maria Elena Vieira da Silva
Elisabeth Vigée-Lebrun
Caterina Vigri
Anna Roemersdochter and Maria Tesselschade
Visscher
Bessie Onahotema Potter Vonnoh
Ursula von Rydingsvard
Charmion von Wiegand

Ethel Walker
Kay WalkingStick
Cecile Walton
Henrietta Ward
Louisa, Marchioness of Waterford
Caroline Watson
June Wayne
Bertha Wegmann
Ruth Weisberg
Rosario Weiss
Clara Pauline Barck Welles
Marianne Werefkin

Candace Wheeler
Anne Whitney
Gertrude Vanderbilt Whitney
Joyce Wieland
Vally Wieselthier
Maria Wiik
Hannah Wilke
Evelyn Williams
Jackie Winsor
Ann Wolff
Marta Worringer
Michaelina Woutier
Denise Wren

Marya Yakunchikova
Vera Yermolayeva

Dana Zámečniková
Eva Zeisel
Marguerite Thompson Zorach
Unica Zürn

CHRONOLOGICAL LIST OF ARTISTS

1786–1866	Louise Seidler
1791–1863	Marie Ellenrieder
1791–1878	Anna Claypoole Peale
1793–1872	Margaret Carpenter
1793–1838	Rolinda Sharples
1796–1849	Lizinka de Mirbel
1796–1854	Christina Robertson
1797–1867	Sophie Rude
1800–1885	Sarah Miriam Peale
1801–1886	Felicie de Fauveau
1803–1887	Margaret Gillies
active 1808–c.1829	Rebeccah Emes
1809–1895	Mary Thornycroft
1812–1895	Louisa Anne Meredith
1813–1839	Princess Marie Christine d'Orléans
1814–1891	Amalia Lindegren
1814–1843	Rosario Weiss
1815–1879	Julia Margaret Cameron
1815–1882	Emma Stebbins
1818–1891	Louisa, Marchioness of Waterford
1819–1881	Elisabeth Jerichau Baumann
1821–1909	Henriëtte Ronner-Knip
1821–1915	Anne Whitney
1822–1899	Rosa Bonheur
1822–1865	Clementina, Viscountess Hawarden
1822–1902	Lilly Martin Spencer
1823–1903	Sophie Anderson
1825–1909	Mme Léon Bertaux
1827–1891	Barbara Leigh Smith Bodichon
1827–1888	Eléonore Escallier
1827–1923	Candace Wheeler
1829–1915	Anna Blunden
1829–1901	Henriette Browne
1829–1862	Elizabeth Eleanor Siddal
1830–1908	Harriet Hosmer
1831–1861	Joanna Boyce
1831–1908	Mary Grant
1831–1867	Adelaide Ironside
1832–1886	Rebecca Solomon
1832–1924	Henrietta Ward
1833–1907	Elisabet Ney
1834–after 1908	Emily Mary Osborn
1836–1879	Marcello
1837–1922	Elizabeth Gardner
1840–1916	Marie Bracquemond
1840–after 1879	Florence Claxton
1840–1926	Victoria Dubourg
1841–1895	Berthe Morisot
1842–1928	Amalia Duprè
1843–1894	Lucy Madox Brown
1843–1933	Louise Jopling
1843–1914	Kitty Kielland
1843–1896	Margaretha Roosenboom
1843–1927	Marie Spartali
1844–1923	Sarah Bernhardt
1844–1926	Mary Cassatt
1844–1924	Marie Cazin
1844–1930	Anna Lea Merritt
1844–1933	Annie Swynnerton
c.1844–after 1911	Edmonia Lewis
1845–1932	Harriet Backer
1845–1916	Tina Blau
1845–1892	Fanny Churberg
1845–1927	Maria Oakey Dewing
1845–1909	Louisa Starr
1846–1933	Lady Butler
1846–1901	Kate Greenaway
1846–1928	Madeleine-Jeanne Lemaire
1847–1939	Mary Louise McLaughlin
1847–1914	Vinnie Ream
1847–1926	Bertha Wegmann
active 1847–73	Susan Durant
1848–1926	Helen Allingham
1848–1936	Anna Boch
1848–1933	Lilla Cabot Perry
1848–1943	Sarah Purser
1849–1883	Eva Gonzalès
1850–1898	Elena Polenova
1851–1916	Hannah Bolton Barlow
1851–1938	Susan Macdowell Eakins
1851–1918	Thérèse Schwartze
1852–1909	Laura Alma-Tadema
1852–1934	Gertrude Käsebier
1852–1936	Phoebe Traquair
1853–1933	Asta Nørregaard
1853–1928	Jane Sutherland
1853–1928	Maria Wiik
1854–1946	Jenny Nyström
1855–1909	Florence Elizabeth Barlow
1855–1942	Cecilia Beaux
1855–1919	Evelyn De Morgan
1855–1940	Ellen Day Hale
1855–1931	Frida Hansen
1855–1922	Suze Robertson
1855–1927	Marianne Stokes
1856–1927	Louise-Catherine Breslau
1856–1927	Kate Bunce
1856–1942	Anna Klumpke
1857–1893	Anna Bilińska-Bohdanowicz
1857–1954	Mary Sargant Florence
1857–1912	Clara von Rappard
1858–1927	Louise Abbéma
1858–1946	Mary Fairchild MacMonnies
1858–1932	Alice Barber Stephens
1859–1935	Anna Ancher
1859–1935	Virginie Demont-Breton
1859–1912	Elizabeth Forbes
1859–1938	Elizabeth Nourse
1859–1928	Henrietta Rae
1860–1884	Marie Bashkirtseff
1860–1935	Oda Krohg
1860–1961	Anna Mary Robertson Moses
1860–1938	Marianne Werefkin
1861–1951	Ethel Walker
1862–1944	Hilma af Klint
1862–1939	Fernanda Francés y Arribas
1862–1938	May Morris
1862–1946	Helene Schjerfbeck
1862–1937	Agnes Slott-Møller
1863–1945	Anne Marie Carl Nielsen

1863–1955	May Guinness	1879–1979	Edna Clarke Hall
1863–1923	Vilma Parlaghy	1879–1970	Ida Kerkovius
1864–1943	Camille Claudel	1880–1967	Charlotte Berend-Corinth
1864–1927	Anna Golubkina	1880–1980	Harriet Whitney Frishmuth
1864–1940	Hanna Hirsch Pauli	1880–1943	Marie von Malachowski
1864–1952	Frances Benjamin Johnston	1881–1932	María Blanchard
1864–1933	Margaret Macdonald	1881–1962	Natalya Goncharova
1864–1948	Jessie Newbery	1881–1968	Sylvia Gosse
1865–1940	Olga Boznańska	1881–1948	Milly Steger
1865–1941	Elizaveta Kruglikova	1881–1965	Marta Worringer
1865–1929	Adelaide Alsop Robineau	1882–1949	Alexandra Exter
1865–1934	Margaret Olrog Stoddart	1882–1931	Norah Neilson Gray
1865–1938	Suzanne Valadon	1882–1978	Mary Swanzy
1866–1932	Jacqueline Marval	1883–1976	Imogen Cunningham
1866–1943	Beatrix Potter	1883–1956	Marie Laurencin
1867–1945	Käthe Kollwitz	1884–1945	Thérèse Lessore
1867–1940	Janet Scudder	1884–1977	Marg Moll
1868–1953	Grace Henry	1884–1967	Zinaida Serebryakova
1868–1965	Clara Pauline Barck Welles	1885–1979	Sonia Delaunay
1869–1947	Frances Hodgkins	1885–1939	Jessica Dismorr
1869–1958	Lucy Kemp-Welch	1885–1948	Sigrid Hjertén
1869–1945	Else Lasker-Schüler	1885–1966	Malvina Hoffman
1869–1904	Bessie MacNicol	1885–1963	Alexandra Povorina
1869–1954	Ellen Thesleff	1885–1957	Gwen Raverat
1870–1902	Marya Yakunchikova	1885–1933	Anita Rée
1871–1945	Emily Carr	1886–1973	Tarsila do Amaral
1871–1955	Anna Ostroumova-Lebedeva	1886–1963	Sofya Dymshits-Tolstaya
1871–1944	Florine Stettheimer	1886–1941	Olga Oppenheimer
1872–1945	Eleanor Fortescue Brickdale	1886–1918	Olga Rozanova
1872–1952	Ethel Fox	1886–1961	Nadezhda Udaltsova
1872–1955	Bessie Onahotema Potter Vonnoh	1887–1935	Clarice Beckett
1873–1921	Frances Macdonald	1887–1955	Wilhelmina Geddes
1874–1953	Elsa Beskow	1887–1968	Valentine Hugo
1874–1970	Romaine Brooks	1887–1986	Georgia O'Keeffe
1875–1949	Jessie M. King	1887–1968	Marguerite Thompson Zorach
1875–1963	Margaret Preston	active 1887–96	Elena Brockmann
1875–1942	Gertrude Vanderbilt Whitney	1888–1973	Siri Derkert
1876–1923	Jacoba van Heemskerck	1888–1979	Vera Nilsson
1876–1973	Anna Vaughn Hyatt Huntington	1888–1954	Astrid Noack
1876–1939	Gwen John	1888–1968	Chana Orloff
1876–1907	Paula Modersohn-Becker	1888–1965	Renée Sintenis
1876–1961	Coba Ritsema	1889–1978	Hannah Höch
1877–1924	Anna Julia De Graag	1889–1964	Anita Malfatti
1877–1968	Meta Vaux Warrick Fuller	1889–1953	Vera Mukhina
1877–1913	Elena Guro	1889–1924	Lyubov Popova
1877–1970	Laura Knight	1889–1966	Júlíana Sveinsdóttir
1877–1962	Gabriele Münter	1889–1943	Sophie Taeuber-Arp
1877–1967	Lotte B. Prechner	1890–1956	Nina Hamnett
1877–1959	Anne Estelle Rice	1890–1976	Jeanne Mammen
1878–1968	Maria Caspar-Filser	1890–1958	Marlow Moss
1878–1974	Emilie Charmy	1890–1971	Emy Roeder
1878–1942	Abastenia St Leger Eberle	1890–1962	Marta Skulme
1878–1964	Letitia Hamilton	1891–1951	Dorrit Black
1878–1963	Sella Hasse	1891–1964	Katharina Heise
1878–1967	Elena Makovskaya-Luksch	1891–1976	Zofia Stryjeńska
1878–1932	Jane Poupelet	1891–1978	Alma W. Thomas
1878–1954	Clara Rilke-Westhoff	1891–1955	Charley Toorop
1878–1947	Kathleen Scott	1891–1956	Cecile Walton
1878–1951	Pamela Colman Smith	1891–1979	Denise Wren
1879–1961	Vanessa Bell	1892–1942	Natalya Danko

1892–1957	Gela Forster	1900–1988	Louise Nevelson
1892–1980	Dorothy Johnstone	1900–1981	Mary Potter
1892–1967	Sarra Lebedeva	1900–1983	Charmion von Wiegand
1892–1984	Marevna	1901–	Norah Braden
1892–1972	Dod Procter	1901–1994	Dorothy Dehner
1892–1966	Ruth Reeves	1901–1983	Gertrude Hermes
1892–1962	Augusta Savage	1901–1967	Alexandra Luke
1892–1967	Aleksandra Shchekatikhina-Pototskaya	1901–1987	Else Meidner
1892–1984	Grace Cossington Smith	1901–1983	Lisette Model
1892–1984	Paule Vézelay	1902–1988	Isabel Bishop
1893–1983	Marianne Brandt	1902–1992	Trude Brück
1893–1932	Carrington	1902–1989	Hanna Cauer
1893–1958	Mathilde Flögl	1902–1995	Susie Cooper
1893–1946	Wanda Gág	1902–1987	Raquel Forner
1893–1982	Florence Henri	1902–1994	Louise Henderson
1893–1971	Maria Likarz-Strauss	1902–1995	Maruja Mallo
1893–1981	Winifred Nicholson	1902–	Enid Marx
1893–1938	Vera Yermolayeva	1902–1971	I. Rice Pereira
1894–1954	Claude Cahun	1902–1983	Hans Anton Prinner
1894–1955	Evie Hone	1902–1959	Germaine Richier
1894–1989	Lucia Moholy	1902–1995	Lucie Rie
1894–1974	Regina	1902–1980	Toyen
1894–1970	Hannah Ryggen	c.1902–1955	María Izquierdo
1894–1958	Varvara Stepanova	1903–1982	Joyce Clissold
1894–1966	Irma Stern	1903–1975	Barbara Hepworth
1894–1981	Agnes Tait	1903–1980	Norah McGuinness
1894–1980	Anna Ticho	1903–	Isabel McLaughlin
1895–1971	Ella Bergmann-Michel	1903–1984	Ethel Schwabacher
1895–1989	Louise Dahl-Wolfe	1904–1971	Margaret Bourke-White
1895–1978	Gluck	1904–1956	Gertrude Greene
1895–1975	Alice Halicka	1904–1982	Nadia Khodossievitch
1895–1965	Dorothea Lange	1904–1971	Alice Trumbull Mason
1895–1985	Katharine Pleydell-Bouverie	1904–1987	Alice Rahon
1895–1965	Anne Redpath	1905–	Lois Mailou Jones
1895–1945	Vally Wieselthier	1906–1988	Ithell Colquhoun
1896–1964	Marion Dorn	1906–1977	Lea Grundig
1896–1990	Lotte Jacobi	1906–1996	Marie-Louise von Motesiczky
1896–1942	Tina Modotti	1906–	Eva Zeisel
1896–1968	Amelia Peláez	1907–1982	Gudrun Baudisch
1897–1977	Benedetta	1907–1954	Frida Kahlo
1897–1980	Hilde Goldschmidt	1907–	Dora Maar
1897–1944	Mainie Jellett	1907–1969	Mary Martin
1897–1983	Gunta Stölzl	1907–1977	Lee Miller
1898–1991	Berenice Abbott	1907–1975	Hanna Nagel
1898–1933	Aenne Biermann	1907–	Lenore Tawney
1898–1951	Katarzyna Kobro	1908–1970	Rita Angus
1898–1993	Lotte Laserstein	1908–	Claire Falkenstein
1898–1980	Tamara de Lempicka	1908–1996	Leonor Fini
1898–1977	Gerta Overbeck	1908–1984	Lee Krasner
1898–1963	Kay Sage	1908–	Helen Lundeberg
c.1898–1991	Dora Gordine	1908–1963	Remedios Varo
1899–1991	Eileen Agar	1908–1992	Maria Elena Vieira da Silva
1899–1994	Anni Albers	1909–	Lucienne Bloch
1899–1986	Franciska Clausen	1909–1970	Marion Greenwood
1899–1973	Majlis Grotell	1909–1961	Lisbet Jobs
1899–1981	Grethe Jürgens	1909–	Loren MacIver
1899–1940	Elfriede Lohse-Wächtler	1909–1948	Gunnel Nyman
1900–1957	Erika Giovanna Klien	1910–	Dorothea Tanning
1900–1973	Maria Martins	1911–	Louise Bourgeois
1900–1984	Alice Neel	1911–1984	Sonja Ferlov

1912–	Wilhelmina Barns-Graham
1912–	Agnes Martin
1912–	Angeles Santos Torroella
1913–1988	Marie-Anne Lansiaux
1913–1985	Meret Oppenheim
1913–1941	Amrita Sher-Gil
1913–1968	Nína Tryggvadóttir
1913–	Gertrud Vasegaard
1914–	Anita Hoy
1914–1996	Gocken Jobs
1914–	Margaret Mellis
1915–	Elizabeth Catlett
1915–	Natalia Dumitrescu
1915–1981	Kyllikki Salmenhaara
1915–1989	Betty Swanwick
1916–	Sylvia Sleigh
1916–1970	Unica Zürn
1917–	Leonora Carrington
1917–	Louisa Matthiasdóttir
1917–1943	Charlotte Salomon
1918–	Gutte Eriksen
1918–	Carol Rama
1918–	Pablita Velarde
1918–	June Wayne
1919–	Prunella Clough
1919–1989	Elaine de Kooning
1919–	Ruth Duckworth
1919–	Maria Lassnig
1919–1982	María Luisa Pacheco
1919–1988	Mira Schendel
1920–1988	Lygia Clark
1920–1960	Joy Hester
1920–1979	Molly Macalister
1921–1963	Joan Eardley
1921–1993	Ghisha Koenig
1922–	Grace Hartigan
1923–1971	Diane Arbus
1923–	Miriam Schapiro
1924–	Carla Accardi
1924–	Jaroslava Brychtová
1924–	Mimi Parent
1924–	Beverly Pepper
1924–	May Stevens
1925–	Sandra Blow
1926–	Bona
1926–1992	Joan Mitchell
1926–	Jacqueline Morreau
1926–	Betye Saar
1926–	Nancy Spero
1927–	Gerda Flöckinger
1928–	Helen Frankenthaler
1929–	Ida Applebroog
1929–	Jacqueline Fahey
1929–	Jackie Ferrara
1929–	Evelyn Williams
1930–	Magdalena Abakanowicz
1930–	Gillian Ayres
1930–1993	Elizabeth Frink
1930–	Marisol
1930–	Faith Ringgold

1930–	Niki de Saint Phalle
c.1930–	Lygia Pape
1931–	Elizabeth Blackadder
1931–	Lee Bontecou
1931–1979	Sheila Fell
1931–	Audrey Flack
1931–	Vivian Lynn
1931–	Bridget Riley
1931–	Joyce Wieland
1932–	Anne Madden
1932–1984	Tilsa Tsuchiya
1933–	Chryssa
1933–	Betty LaDuke
1933–	Michelle Stuart
1934–	Sheila Hicks
1934–	Bea Maddock
1934–	Yvonne Rainer
1934–	Dorothea Rockburne
1934–1992	Jo Spence
c.1934–	Mary Beth Edelson
1935–	Eleanor Antin
1935–	Gwyn Hanssen Pigott
1935–	Paula Rego
1935–	Kay WalkingStick
1936–1970	Eva Hesse
1936–	Joan Jonas
1936–	Kim Lim
1936–	Gillian Lowndes
1936–1977	Ree Morton
1937–	Tess Jaray
1937–	Ann Wolff
1938–	Vija Celmins
1938–	Lena Cronqvist
1938–	Janet Fish
1938–	Ulrica Hydman-Vallien
1938–	Sylvia Plimack Mangold
1938–	Monica Sjöö
1939–	Barbara Chase-Riboud
1939–	Judy Chicago
1939–	Rita Donagh
1939–	Liliane Lijn
1939–1990	Gina Pane
1939–	Deanna Petherbridge
1939–	Wendy Ramshaw
1939–	Carolee Schneemann
1939–	Clarissa Sligh
1940–	Vivienne Binns
1940–	Beverly Buchanan
1940–	Elizabeth Fritsch
1940–1995	Nancy Graves
1940–	Elizabeth Murray
1940–	Jaune Quick-to-See Smith
1940–	Joan Snyder
1940–	Pat Steir
1940–1993	Hannah Wilke
1941–	Jennifer Bartlett
1941–	Lynda Benglis
1941–	Hanne Darboven
1941–	Mary Kelly
1941–	Jackie Winsor

1942–	Susan Hiller	1943–	Martha Rosler
1942–	Joyce Kozloff	1944–	Glenys Barton
1942–	Janice Tchalenko	1944–	Harmony Hammond
1942–	Ursula von Rydingsvard	1944–	Rebecca Horn
1942–	Ruth Weisberg	1944–	Mary Miss
1943–	Gretchen Albrecht	1945–	Maggi Hambling
1943–	Diana Hobson	1945–	Valerie Jaudon
1943–	Annette Messager	1945–	Barbara Kruger
1943–	Ana Maria Pacheco	1945–	Susan Rothenberg
1943–	Howardena Pindell	1945–	Dana Zámečniková

J

Jacobi, Lotte
German photographer, 1896–1990

Born Johanna Alexandra Jacobi in Thorn, West Prussia, 17 August 1896, into a Jewish family of photographers. Studied art history and literature at the Posen Academy, 1914–16. Married Fritz Honig, 1916; son born 1917; divorced 1926. Studied photography and film at Bayerische Staatliche Fachschule für Phototechnik and art history at Munich University, 1925–7. Took over her father's studio in Berlin, 1927. Trip to Soviet Union, 1932–3. Emigrated to USA and opened own studio in New York, 1935; naturalised US citizen, 1944. Married publisher Erich Reiss, 1940; he died 1951. Moved to Deering, New Hampshire, 1955; established own studio and gallery, 1963. Studied art history, French, gardening and television at University of New Hampshire, Durham, 1961–2. Trip to Europe, 1962–3; attended etching classes at Stanley W. Hayter's Studio 17, Paris. Honorary curator of photography, Currier Gallery of Art, Manchester, New Hampshire, 1972–8. Recipient of silver medal, Royal Photography Salon, Tokyo, 1931; first prize, British War Relief Photography Competition (*Life* magazine), New York, 1941; first prize, New Hampshire Art Association, 1970; Governor's Award for the Arts, New Hampshire, 1980; Erich Salomon prize, Deutsche Gesellschaft für Photographie, Berlin, 1983; honorary doctorates from University of New Hampshire, Durham, 1974; New England College, Henniker, 1978; Colby-Sawyer College, New London, 1982; New Hampshire College, Manchester, 1982; University of Maryland, Baltimore, 1983; Rivier College, Nashua, New Hampshire, 1984. Died in Concord, New Hampshire, 6 May 1990.

Selected Individual Exhibitions
Lotte Jacobi Studio, New York: 1937, 1941, 1955
Direction Gallery, New York: 1941
Norlyst Gallery, New York: 1948
Boston Camera Club: 1957
Currier Gallery of Art, Manchester, NH: 1959–61 (touring retrospective), 1984
303 Gallery, New York: 1964 (retrospective)
University of Chicago: 1965
Community Church Art Gallery, New York: 1967
Staatliche Landesbildstelle, Hamburg: 1972
Museum Folkwang, Essen: 1973 (touring), 1990 (retrospective)
Light Gallery, New York: 1974
Washington Gallery of Photography, Washington, DC: 1974
Kimmell-Cohn Gallery, New York: 1977
Kiva Gallery, Boston: 1977, 1978
Allan Frumkin Gallery, Chicago: 1977
Manchester Institute of Arts and Sciences, NH: 1977 (touring)
University of Maryland Library, Baltimore: 1978
Galerie Taube, Berlin: 1979, 1983
Alfred University, Alfred, NY: 1980
Münchner Stadtmuseum, Munich: 1981
Catskill Center for Photography, Woodstock, NY: 1981
Ledel Gallery, New York: 1984
Das Verborgene Museum, Berlin: 1989

Bibliography
Emma Bugbee, "New York enchanting to artist with camera, says Lotte Jacobi", *New York Herald Tribune*, 1 November 1937
"Photogenics", *Aperture*, x/1, 1962, pp.4–16
Fotografinnen, exh. cat., Museum Folkwang, Essen, 1970
Menschen von Gestern und Heute: Fotografische Portraits, Skizzen und Dokumentationen von Lotte Jacobi, exh. cat., Museum Folkwang, Essen, 1973
Women of Photography, exh. cat., San Francisco Museum of Art, 1975
Jacobi Place: Portrait of a Photographer, exh. cat., Manchester Institute of Arts and Sciences, NH, 1977
Künstlerinnen international, 1877–1977, exh. cat., Schloss Charlottenburg, Berlin, 1977
Kelly Wise, ed., *Lotte Jacobi*, Danbury, NH: Addison House, 1978
Vicki Goldberg, "Lotte Jacobi", *American Photographer*, ii, March 1979, pp.22–31
Light Abstractions, exh. cat., University of Missouri, St Louis, 1979
Margaretta K. Mitchell, *Recollections: 10 Women of Photography*, New York: Viking, 1979
Avant-Garde Photography in Germany, 1919–1939, exh. cat., San Francisco Museum of Modern Art, 1980
Kelly Wise, ed., *Portrait: Theory*, New York: Lustrum Press, 1981
Berlin – New York: Schriftsteller in den 30er Jahren, Marbach am Neckar: Marbacher Schriften, Deutsches Literaturarchiv, 1982 (with foreword by Ludwig Greve)
Theater and Dance Photographs, Woodstock, VT: Countryman Press, 1982 (introduction by Cornell Capa)
Lotte Jacobi: A Selection of Vintage and Modern Photographs, exh. cat., Stephen White Gallery of Photography, Beverly Hills, CA, 1986
Deutsche Lichtbildner, exh. cat., Museum Ludwig, Cologne, 1987
William A. Ewing, *The Fugitive Gesture: Masterpieces of Dance Photography*, London: Thames and Hudson, 1987
Nine Masters, exh. cat., Photographic Resource Center, Boston, 1987

Jacobi: *Claire Bauroff, Dancer,* 1928, Berlin; Lotte Jacobi Archives, Dimond Library, University of New Hampshire, Durham

Helmut Pfanner and Gary Samson, "Lotte Jacobi: German photographer and portraitist in exile", *Germanic Review*, lxii/3, 1987, pp.109–17

Marion Beckers and Elisabeth Moortgat, *Russland 1932/33: Moskau Tadschikistan Usbekistan*, Berlin: Nishen, 1988

Lotte Jacobi, 1896–1990: Berlin-New York-Deering, exh. cat., Museum Folkwang, Essen, 1990

Floris M. Neusuess, *Das Fotogramm in der Kunst des 20. Jahrhunderts*, Cologne: DuMont, 1990

Photo-Sequenzen: Reportagen, Bildgeschichten, Serien aus dem Ullstein Bilderdienst von 1925 bis 1944, exh. cat., Haus am Waldsee, Berlin, 1992

Fotografieren hiess teilnehmen, exh. cat., Museum Folkwang, Essen, 1994

Naomi Rosenblum, *A History of Women Photographers*, New York: Abbeville Press, 1994

Marion Beckers and Elisabeth Moortgat, *Atelier Lotte Jacobi: Berlin New York*, Berlin: Nicolai, 1997

Lotte Jacobi Collection (negative archives, correspondence and biographical material) is in the University of New Hampshire, Durham.

As a photographer and artist engaged with contemporary politics, Lotte Jacobi led a diversely creative and ambitious life. Always full of ideas, which she carried out with astonishing purposefulness even in difficult times, she was never content with photography alone. She valued exchanging ideas and suggestions at social gatherings, and after her move to the USA she gave both male and female artists the opportunity to exhibit at her studio.

After completing her studies in Munich, Jacobi returned to Berlin to take over her father's photography studio. She was the fourth generation to practise the trade: the studio was founded by her great-grandfather Samuel Jacobi, who had acquired a camera and a licence from Louis Daguerre in Paris around 1840. The Atelier Jacobi, in the Joachimstalerstrasse near the Kurfürstendamm in the Neuer Westen, was a traditional portrait studio, but Lotte Jacobi turned to press photography, seeking clients from the emerging newspaper market. Until 1935 she worked mainly for magazines and newspapers of the famous Ullstein Verlag, such as *Berliner Illustrirte Zeitung*, *Uhu*, *Querschnitt* and *Tempo*, as well as for many other publications, including *Der Tanz*, *Das Theater*, *Die schaffende Frau*, *Münchner Illustrierte Presse* and *Das Magazin*. Her greatest success came through her portraits, and it is fair to say that she helped to establish the image of many personalities. In her carefully composed portrait of *Lotte Lenya*, for example, taken in 1928 during rehearsals for Brecht's *Dreigroschenoper* (Threepenny Opera), the viewer is captivated by the gaze of the actress. Her face immaculate, the apparently stylised Lenya appears as the "new woman" she had embodied in her life. The work's subtle arrangement of black and grey and its unusual combination of the hand with a cigarette and the close-up of the head connect it to the Neues Sehen (New Vision), in which, through the alienation of the familiar, the aesthetic impression becomes more important than the subject. The portrait of *Lenya* shows Jacobi's special ability to capture personalities and situations, even amidst the hectic activity of the stage. The expression "being completely with oneself" is characteristic of her portraits, whether of *Kurt Weill* (1928), *René Clair* (1929), *Käthe Kollwitz* (1929) or *Peter Lorre* (1932). "My style is the style of the people I photograph", Jacobi emphasised repeatedly; she realised her role behind the camera, trying to come as "close" as possible to the person opposite.

Using an Ermanox 9 × 12 cm. camera with a lens of 1:1.8, Jacobi was well-equipped for her special passion, theatre and dance photography. The camera made it possible to take pictures during performances; the viewpoint was set in advance and empathy alone decided the right moment of exposure. Here the art is to summarise, to sum up the entire action in one picture. This ability is also expressed in Jacobi's dance photographs. The famous study of the expressive dancer *Claire Bauroff* (see illustration) was created in her studio in 1928. It shows the dancer in a play of endless movements, completely self-absorbed. Motion and suppleness, combined with the highest discipline, produce a figure reminiscent of a classical pose that captures all dimensions, with limbs fully stretched and rounded. The dancer seems to float in the whirl of movement, yet she is not bodiless, and the impression of lightness is echoed by her shadow. With the depiction of this moment, in which the elegance of the motion reaches its peak, Jacobi concentrated the high art of photographic composition of space, time and movement.

By the end of the 1920s Jacobi had made the Atelier Jacobi into one of the best-known studios in Berlin. The pictures sought after by the press were not so much from the glamorous world of film, but portraits of the famous without make-up, often private. The photograph of the writer *Carl Zuckmayer and Family* on their roof garden is of this kind: the two daughters are posed acrobatically on their parents' shoulders, an allusion to Zuckmayer's piece about acrobats, *Katharina Knie*, which had brought him great success in 1928–9.

A commission for a portrait of *Ernst Thaelmann*, the chairman of the Communist Party (KPD), on the occasion of the Reichstag election in March 1932, led to the fulfilment of Jacobi's fervent wish to visit the Soviet Union. Instinctively opposed to inhumanity, she had become increasingly involved in politics of the left during the 1920s and wanted to experience for herself post-revolutionary Russia and the Soviet idea of the "new man". Permission to photograph there was obtained only via political backing. For half a year she travelled around the Soviet Union, photographing towns, everyday life and portraits from Moscow, Tadzhikistan and Uzbekistan. She drew a fine picture of the "other", not seeking the sensational but inspired by human curiosity. In this way she created surprisingly natural portraits, without self-conscious poses, often close-ups of heads, in which the self-confident individual is far more important than the foreign typology. This was also true of her cityscapes, like the ones she had made earlier in Berlin, and in 1934 in Hamburg. They concentrate on a detail such as a building or a street, everyday situations in which the living space of people is emphasised more than the architecture, thus they are never without human beings.

Jacobi returned to Berlin in February 1933 when the Nazis were already in power. Employment opportunities for Jews were increasingly limited, and state control of the press ended her work for newspapers. In 1935 she emigrated to New York via London; her mother and son followed later. There she opened a photographic studio and attempted to re-establish her business, with only partial success, however. The press in the USA had firmly held ideas and concepts, and cooperation proved difficult. For *Life* magazine, for example, she produced a totally unpretentious portrait of *Albert Einstein* in a leather jacket (1938), showing the unconventional scientist lost in thought, identified by the equations in his notebook. Considered insufficiently serious, the photograph was not published. It became clear that in the USA, more than in Berlin, she could produce powerful, lasting photographs only by working independently, on subjects she chose herself, a freedom she enjoyed only rarely. A number of her New York portraits have retained their importance, however, for example *Alfred Stieglitz* (1938), *Marc Chagall* (1942), *Berenice Abbott* (1943) and *Karen Horney* (1947). She roamed the city, where she quickly felt at home, taking pictures of Central Park, streets of houses and the destruction of buildings.

In the 1940s and 1950s Jacobi experimented with camera-less photography and created her own "photogenics", unique works made in the darkroom that she titled *Adventures in the World of Light*. These luminous figures were planned compositions, created from memory with the help of cellophane, which she moved, and a mobile light source. Taken on army-surplus photo paper, they are creations of fine tones of grey that appear somewhere between abstraction and suggested corporeality. Several "photogenics" were shown in the exhibition *In and Out of Focus* at the Museum of Modern Art in New York in 1948 and in *Subjektive Fotografie 2* in Saarbrucken in 1955. With the "photogenics" Jacobi for the first time attracted public attention in America.

After her move to Deering, New Hampshire, in 1955, Jacobi took photographs inspired by nature, although portraits were still important, as well as the dialogue with friends. As she had in New York in 1952–5, she presented exhibitions of new work in her studio by many colleagues including Frances Flaherty, F.G. Kuttner, Rudi Lesser, Louise Nevelson (q.v.), Josef Scharl and Minor White.

Lotte Jacobi's portrait photographs are among the most impressive produced in the 20th century. They cannot be classified as a particular style, but rather result from her perception of a humanistic, democratic world, a standard she applied equally to her photographic and political actions. In her last years she became increasingly engaged in cultural, social and environmental politics. She campaigned publicly against nuclear energy and the war in Vietnam in the 1970s, and her persistent advocacy of photography as an art resulted in the establishment of a photographic department at the museum in Manchester, New Hampshire, in 1970–71.

MARION BECKERS

Jakunchikova, Marja *see* Yakunchikova

Jaray, Tess

British painter and public artist, 1937–

Born in Vienna, 31 December 1937; came to Britain, 1938. Studied at St Martin's School of Art, London, 1954–7; Slade

School of Fine Art, London, 1957–60. Awarded Abbey Minor travelling scholarship to Italy, 1960; French Government scholarship to France, 1961. Taught at Hornsey College of Art, London, 1964–8; subsequently at Slade School of Fine Art (now head of Graduate Painting). Visited Australia, 1980. Recipient of RSA Art for Architecture award, 1992; "The Arts – Working for Cities", Arts Council of Great Britain and British Gas award for Wakefield Cathedral Precinct, 1993; Civic Trust, Wordhouse Landscape award, Centenary Square jointly with Victoria Square, 1994; Brick Design award, 1994; Jerwood Art for Architecture award, 1994. Lives in London.

Selected Individual Exhibitions

Grabowski Gallery, London: 1963
Hamilton Gallery, London: 1965, 1967
Richard Demarco Gallery, Edinburgh: 1967
Axiom Gallery, London: 1969
Graves Art Gallery, Sheffield: 1972
City Art Gallery, Bristol: 1972
Whitechapel Art Gallery, London: 1973 (with Marc Vaux)
Angela Flowers Gallery, London: 1973
Adelaide Festival Centre, Australia: 1980
Whitworth Art Gallery, Manchester: 1984
Ashmolean Museum, Oxford: 1984
Serpentine Gallery, London: 1988
Todd Gallery, London: 1993

Bibliography

Gene Baro, "Tess Jaray's mural for Expo 67", *Studio International*, clxxiii, 1967, pp.150–51
Robert Kudielka, "Tess Jaray: New paintings", *Art International*, xiii, Summer 1969, pp.40–42
Tess Jaray, exh. cat., Whitechapel Art Gallery, London, 1973
Hayward Annual '78, exh. cat., Arts Council of Great Britain, London 1978
Helena Drysdale, "Tess Jaray: In pursuit of perfection", *The Artist*, xcvii, 12 December 1980, pp.28–31
Tess Jaray: Prints and Drawings, 1964–84, exh. cat., Ashmolean Museum, Oxford, 1984
Dave Lee, "Tess Jaray", *Arts Review*, xxxvi, 11 May 1984, p.241
Helena Drysdale, "Tess Jaray", *Artscribe*, no.46, May–July 1984, pp.49–52
Tess Jaray: Paintings and Drawings from the Eighties, exh. cat., Serpentine Gallery, London, 1988
M. Miles, "Speakeasy", *New Art Examiner*, xvi, Summer 1989, pp.13–14
Rebecca Fortnum, "Living perspective: Tess Jaray and inner city design", *Women Artists Slide Library Journal*, no.30, October–November 1989, pp.9–11
Tanya Harrod, "Bravura answer to brutalism", *Independent on Sunday*, 2 June 1991
"Paving on a higher plane", *Brick Bulletin*, Brick Design award, Winter 1993–4
Richard Cork, "Praise be to All Saints", *The Times*, 23 February 1995
Michaela Crimmin, "First Jerwood Art for Architecture award", *RSA Journal*, cxliii, April 1995, pp.8–9

Tess Jaray first gained recognition in the mid-1960s with her geometric abstract paintings, and she has continued to draw inspiration from geometric structures found in architecture, landscaped gardens, Islamic art and from natural forms such as plant cells and fossils. Characteristically, the surfaces of the paintings are executed with immaculate precision – colour is strictly orchestrated and the imagery rigorously reduced. The work is dependent upon restriction, and Jaray adopts simple but necessary rules based on elementary geometry or number sequences. Jaray is also an experienced public artist, gaining recognition in the 1990s for her vast floors and decorative brick pavements.

Jaray's large minimalist paintings can be identified within a universal humanist tradition (see Griselda Pollock, "Painting, feminism and history", *Destabilizing Theory: Contemporary Feminist Debates*, ed. Anne Phillips and Michele Barrett, Stanford, CA: Stanford University Press, and Cambridge: Polity Press, 1992, p.148). Her formal explorations have been praised for their consistency, for pursuing a single line of development and for never radically departing from their governing principles (Fortnum 1989, p.10). One of the characteristics of Jaray's art is that whenever a given problem seems to have been resolved a new question appears. In this way she produces bodies of work that consist of slowly shifting focal points contained within an ever-changing set of self-imposed boundaries. It was the form, or pattern, that linked her work of the 1960s with Op and Systems art, although Jaray herself never saw her work as being so prescriptive. Because of the spiritual aspect of her painting, critics have drawn comparisons with Mondrian and Kandinsky and more recently with the subtle and tense variations of paintings by Agnes Martin (q.v.).

Jaray's early paintings are characterised by their symmetrical centralised compositions. *Minuet* (1966; Graves Art Gallery, Sheffield), for example, suggests the grandeur of a Gothic or Renaissance interior – perhaps a vaulted ceiling or elaborate church window. This airtight linear structure was later abandoned in favour of an open constellation of forms suspended in a state of latent tension, as illustrated by *Quadrille* (1967; Granada Television, Manchester).

Jaray's paintings entice the viewer to look at delicate, imperceptible shifting patterns that reveal the currents at work under the smooth surface of life: "I would like to echo in my work certain qualities of life: the understated, the mysterious, the events-below-the-surface, the ungraspable, the un-understandable" (London 1973). Her paintings are distillations of the simplest possible forms of her own experiences, of everyday things, of living, of relationships and change executed with a classical restraint.

Between 1981 and 1983 Jaray made the curve paintings, which play on groups of receding shapes: the curve always appears to be on the point of breaking and the group about to disintegrate as the units hover in open space. In *Always Now* (1981; Arts Council Collection) a series of pink and beige rectangular units glides across the lower section of a pale canvas. The units reduce in size and number and increase in density of colour as the form curves vertically across the canvas and recedes back into the picture plane. Light penetrates from the left and almost drains the form of colour. The weightlessness and light together have a dynamically uplifting effect: "Jaray's work shows an artist whose pursuit of light and movement is as scrupulous in its measure and feeling as it is exact in its execution" (Alister Warman in London 1988, p.4). *Minaret* (1984; Whitworth Art Gallery, Manchester) is the first of a series that departs from the curve cycle. Here the image, a complex collection of pale blue lozenge shapes, appears to roll across and in front of the canvas, implying a curve around the

Jaray: *Six Red Steps*, 1987; 195.6 × 119.4 cm.; artist's collection

back of a cylinder. The painting is influenced by Islamic decorative brickwork, in which the intricate surface is not merely a form of ornamentation but reveals and unites the structure.

An important characteristic of Jaray's work is her alertness to the vitality inherent within archetypal rhythms and patterns. Architecture, a prime source of her imagery, is seen as confirming enduring sensations within human experience. In later works, such as *Six Red Steps* (1987; see illustration) and *Red Pyramid* (1987; artist's collection), Jaray acknowledges her preoccupation with the motif in the titles of the paintings.

The manipulation of space on a two-dimensional canvas has in her public commissions been translated into actual space. Since the mid-1980s Jaray has concentrated on major urban landscape commissions for public locations. With an individual approach to urban design, which continues to reflect a commitment to both function and purity of form, this new move comes at the height of her career and shows a determination not to "go stale". Her work covers all aspects of planning a public space from designing the paving right through to the seating, lighting and planting areas. Jaray is responsible for the terrazzo paving at Victoria Station, London (1985), and the intricate brick floor at the Midland Art Centre, Birmingham (1987). In 1988 Jaray made a major impression on the public arts scene with her design and landscaping of Centenary Square, Birmingham. Her fine art sensibility was given full rein in the design of the square, in particular in the wonderful oriental carpet of red and blue brick paving. The project succeeded in unifying an area enclosed by a disparate collection of 20th-century buildings. In 1991 Jaray was commissioned to redesign the pedestrian areas in the city centre surrounding Wakefield Cathedral. She was given complete artistic freedom to develop the overall design concept for the pedestrian area surrounding the building, working closely with a team of engineers and architects to develop practical solutions for her design.The creation of flights of York stone steps in front of the cathedral and paved terraces linking it to the pedestrian area, together with new seating, lighting and street furniture, has given Wakefield a completely new public space. Currently Jaray is working on the design for the refurbishment of Pontefract town centre.

A reciprocal and fruitful relationship exists between Jaray's studio paintings and her public commissions, yet a clear distinction is maintained between them. The paintings had already shown a development of Jaray's concerns before she moved into the public sphere while at the same time they deal with preoccupations far larger than architecture alone. The paintings are not studies for Jaray's floor designs. The act of moving through space, however, whether upwards or across, within the realms of the canvas or public sphere, has always been important to Jaray in her attempts to encompass and articulate lived experiences.

LESLEY HALLIWELL

Jaudon, Valerie
American painter, 1945–

Born in Greenville, Mississippi, 6 August 1945. Studied at Mississippi State College for Women, Columbus, 1963–5; Memphis Academy of Art, Tennessee, 1965; University of the Americas, Mexico City, 1966–7; St Martin's School of Art, London, 1968–9. Moved to New York, 1969. Married artist Richard Kalina, 1969. Appointments as visiting artist include Aspen Institute for Humanistic Studies, Baca, Colorado, 1982; Art Institute of Chicago, 1983; School of Visual Arts, New York, 1983, 1984 and 1993; Maryland Institute, College of Art, Baltimore, 1985; Vermont Studio School, Johnson, 1991; Yale University Summer School of Music and Art, Norfolk, Connecticut, 1991; Echo Press, Bloomington, 1993. Associate professor, 1986, and professor of art, 1992, Hunter College, New York. Recipient of Creative Artists Public Service (CAPS) grant, New York State Council for the Arts, 1980; Mississippi Institute of Arts and Letters art award, 1981; Special Commendation, 1987, and Excellence in Design award, 1988, for Police Plaza, Art Commission of the City of New York; National Endowment for the Arts (NEA) grant, 1988; merit award, American Society of Landscape Architects, Alabama Chapter, for Charles Ireland

Memorial Sculpture Garden of the Birmingham Museum of Art, 1994. Lives in New York.

Selected Individual Exhibitions
Holly Solomon Gallery, New York: 1977, 1978, 1979, 1981
Pennsylvania Academy of the Fine Arts, Philadelphia: 1977
Galerie Bischofberger, Zürich: 1979
Galerie Hans Strelow, Düsseldorf: 1980
James Corcoran Gallery, Los Angeles: 1981
Sidney Janis Gallery, New York: 1983, 1985, 1986, 1988, 1990, 1993, 1995, 1996
Quadrat Museum, Bottrop, and Amerika Haus, Berlin: 1983
Dart Gallery, Chicago: 1983
Fay Gold Gallery, Atlanta: 1985
McIntosh/Drysdale Gallery, Washington, DC: 1985
Barbara Scott Gallery, Bay Harbor Islands, FL: 1994
Mississippi Museum of Art, Jackson: 1996

Selected Writings
"Art hysterical notions of art history", *Heresies*, no.4, Winter 1978, pp.38–42 (with Joyce Kozloff); reprinted in *Theories and Documents of Contemporary Art: A Sourcebook of Artists Writings*, ed. Kristine Stiles and Peter Selz, Berkeley: University of California Press, 1996
"Limited immunity", *New Observations*, no.68, June 1989, pp.8–9
"Figuring abstraction", *Tema Celeste*, no.34, January–March 1992, p.91
"Rappresentare l'astrazione", *Tema Celeste*, no.35, April–June 1992, p.71
"The question of gender in art", *Tema Celeste*, no.37–8, Autumn 1992, p.57

Bibliography
Jeff Perrone, "Approaching the decorative", *Artforum*, xv, December 1976, pp.26–30
——, "Review", *Artforum*, xvi, September 1977, pp.75–6
John Perreault, "Issues in pattern painting", *Artforum*, xvi, November 1977, pp.32–6
Amy Goldin, "The body language of pictures", *Artforum*, xvi, March 1978, pp.54–9
John Yau, "Review", *Art in America*, lxvii, May–June 1979, pp.144–5
Carrie Rickey, "Decoration, ornament, pattern and utility", *Flash Art*, no.90–91, June–July 1979, pp.19–23
Jacqueline Brody, "Prints and photographs published: Valerie Jaudon", *Print Collector's Newsletter*, xi, 1980, pp.101–2
E.A. Carmean, "American abstraction and decorative painting", *The Morton Neumann Family Collection*, exh. cat., National Gallery of Art, Washington, DC, 1980
Grace Glueck, "Review", *New York Times*, 1 May 1981
Constance Mallison, "Valerie Jaudon at James Corcoran", *Images and Issues*, Summer 1981, pp.55–6
Robert Jensen and Patricia Conway, *Ornamentalism: The New Decorativeness in Architecture and Design*, New York: Potter, 1982; London: Allen Lane, 1983
Valerie Jaudon, exh. cat., Quadrat Museum, Bottrop, and Amerika Haus, Berlin, 1983
Grace Glueck, "Review", *New York Times*, 22 April 1983, p.25
Kay Larson, "Freezing expressionism", *New York Magazine*, 25 April 1983, p.95
John Perreault, "Allusive depths: Valerie Jaudon", *Art in America*, lxxi, October 1983, pp.162–5
H. Harvard Arnason, *History of Modern Art*, 3rd edition, Englewood Cliffs, NJ: Prentice Hall, 1986
Making Their Mark: Women Artists Move into the Mainstream, 1970–1985, exh. cat., Cincinnati Art Museum, and elsewhere, 1989

Whitney Chadwick, *Women, Art and Society*, London and New York: Thames and Hudson, 1990

Robert Mahoney, "Valerie Jaudon", *Flash Art*, xxiii, Summer 1990, p.146

Shirley Kaneda, "Painting and its others: In the realm of the feminine", *Arts Magazine*, lxvi, Summer 1991, pp.58–64

Demetrio Paparoni, "Valerie Jaudon", *Tema Celeste*, no.36, Summer 1992, pp.72–3

Shirley Kaneda, "Valerie Jaudon", *Bomb*, no.38, Winter 1992, pp.40–45

Marjorie Welish, "Valerie Jaudon", *Tema Celeste*, no.39, Winter 1993, p.76

Norma Broude and Mary D. Garrard, eds, *The Power of Feminist Art: The American Movement of the 1970s*, New York: Abrams, and London: Thames and Hudson, 1994

Valerie Jaudon, exh. cat., Mississipi Museum of Art, Jackson, 1996

To call Valerie Jaudon a Pattern and Decoration painter is to underestimate her ambition to prove that "abstraction speaks representationally". Her rigorously composed paintings of bands and curves in a limited colour range are more cerebral than works by other "P and D" artists, and she prefers the term "decorative". Although her early works on grids have affinities with Minimalism, their light-catching buttery brush-work, repeating patterns and sensitivity to architectural space link them to the ornamental. Hers is a feminist art that is directed outward towards public discourse, welcoming scanning, seductively inviting interpretation.

Jaudon left Mississippi to become an artist; in the mid-1960s she travelled through Mexico where she was deeply moved by Mayan architecture. After studying with Gillian Ayres (q.v.) at St Martin's School of Art in London, painting Matisse-inspired abstractions, she moved to New York in 1969, where Minimalism was the dominant style. She married the artist Richard Kalina, whose critical approach contrasted with her controlled yet intuitive method of painting.

Seeking to define painting, Jaudon conceived of its fundamental elements as brush stroke and colour, which led to *Toomsuba* (1973; acrylic; repr. Jackson 1996, p.49). To see how far she could go with the simplest of means, working from the centre of the canvas, she used a compass to draw concentric circles, overlapping them with diagonal and rectilinear grids and painting the shapes with 250 colours – so many that the effect of the colour was neutralised. Subsequent paintings, executed in oil with colour restricted to black, white and metallics, were derived from the *Toomsuba* matrix drawing, which she expanded outwards geometrically in mirror-image modules. A reticulated ribbon of unpainted canvas surrounds the painted forms, contributing to the over-under spatial ambiguity of the interlace created (*Yazoo City*, 1975; oil on canvas; Aldrich Museum of Contemporary Art, Ridgefield, CT). The monochrome interlaces, pulsing with reflected light, superficially resemble Celtic or Islamic patterns, or even lace, but the patterns were Jaudon's own invention (*Jackson*, 1976; Hirshhorn Museum and Sculpture Garden, Washington, DC; *Ingomar*, 1979; National Museum of Women in the Arts, Washington, DC).

Following the strictures of pure abstraction, she worked against the grain of modernism and subversively produced work that was not autonomous but engaged representationally with the viewer. By using minimalist devices, the grid, subdued colour and also decorative strategies, she quietly challenged male-dominated Minimalism; her repeated use of a single motif generated by *Toomsuba* recalled Conceptual art, but the central focus, sensuous paint application and repetitive and obsessive patterning were typical of feminist art of the early 1970s. Circular motifs have a long history, whether as symbols of Platonic perfection or as used in Pop Art and Color-Field painting, and Jaudon's paintings take aim at Kenneth Noland's target-like images. To separate the paintings from illusionistic suggestion, she titled them after towns in Mississippi; the earliest were named for towns on the road from her mother's house to her grandmother's. After 1985 she chose words of double purpose, noun and verb, and is currently raiding lists of film titles available on video.

By the 1980s Jaudon had simplified her drawing process, enlarging and, ultimately, separating the geometric shapes of the interlace, as if breaking a code (*Aberdeen*, 1981; repr. Broude and Garrard 1994, p.220). Retaining the netlike tracery, she introduced limited colour (such as two shades of red and black) and gold leaf, emphasising the architectural and spatial character of the paintings with Gothic and Romanesque arch forms, but the compositions go beyond a representation of religious architecture, narrating visually the bodily experience of moving through space shaped by design (*Tallahatchee*, 1984; repr. Arnason 1986, p.601). The paintings recall, abstractly, the cultural contexts of building.

Moving away from the architectural in the late 1980s, Jaudon floated geometric shapes – circles, arcs, ellipses, bars and bands – in asymmetrical compositions on backgrounds of a single colour inscribed with a double-banded grid (*Sound*, 1986; Collection Henkel, Düsseldorf), increasing the assonance and dynamic charge with "dashed" lines in black and white (*Constant*, 1988; Albright-Knox Art Gallery, Buffalo, NY) and vertical arrangements of ornamental forms that began to read as figures (*Eastern Standard*, 1990–91; mural, 1675 Broadway, New York).

Jaudon was associated with the Pattern and Decoration movement in the 1970s, attending meetings and participating in panel discussions. While other P and D artists challenged modernism by using non-Western art and women's crafts as subject matter, she pursued the self-effacing properties of the decorative to question formalism. Searching for a socio-political activism to replace her earlier anti-Vietnam War involvements in California, Jaudon attended planning meetings of the feminist magazine *Heresies*, collaborating with Joyce Kozloff (q.v.) to defend the "decorative" from aspersions of feminine "inferiority" in the still-pertinent polemic on the sexual politics of aesthetics in "Art hysterical notions in art history" (1978), which revealed the sexist and racist biases of canonical Western male writers.

In addition to her involvement with feminist issues and the decorative, Jaudon was influenced by collaborative work with the architect Romaldo Giurgola. Between 1975 and 1980 she received informal lessons in the history and theory of architecture while working on projects with the Philadelphia firm of Mitchell/Giurgola (*Untitled*, 1977; ceiling mural, INA Building, Philadelphia). Going outside art, she found the same language of form and structure in abstract painting and modern architecture. Her public art melds utility and decoration, feminist collaborative practice and architecture, sympathetically combining simply fabricated materials with

Jaudon: *Foreign Correspondent*, 1994; oil and alkyd on canvas; 121.9 × 91.4 cm.

their location to narrate symbolically the site's function. In *Long Division* (1988; welded steel; l. 18.3 m.; IRT Subway, Lexington Avenue and 23rd Street, New York, repr. Laurie Schneider Adams, *A History of Western Art*, 1994, p.480) a sculptural security fence of ornamental bars and arches in Jaudon's signature patterns separates the fare-paying and unpaid zones. She wanted the work to be "a sort of transparent lens through which people can see where they are going and where they have been" (artist's statement, Arts for Transit Program, Metropolitan Transportation Authority). In *Blue Pools Courtyard* (1993; bluestone, brick, ceramic-tiled pools, plantings; Birmingham Museum of Art, AL) she fused "nests of knowledge" – art, architecture and landscape architecture – with social discourse. Brought up in the Deep South, she instantly reconnected with local interests to create an oasis where geometric order converses with ever-changing nature, stimulating and soothing human response.

The early 1990s brought changes in Jaudon's painting. She rearranged the alphabet of forms of her interlaces into vertically oriented chains of symmetrical and syncopated figures in dance-like movement on striped or chequered backgrounds in colour progressions; the semaphore-like signs are isolated from the polychrome field by narrow bands of unpainted canvas, a reminder of her architectural compositions of the 1970s and early 1980s (*Concordance*, 1992; Sidney Janis Gallery, New York). Subsequently, Jaudon suppressed the main elements of

her youthful work – brushwork and colour – to generate new relationships of form and space (*Back Street*, 1995; oil and alkyd on canvas; 213 × 152 cm.; Sidney Janis Gallery; *Foreign Correspondent*, 1994; see illustration). The stencil-like figures, executed in a new method, are drawn on the canvas, masked and painted in. Then, in an uncharacteristic release of control, Jaudon pours on the background colour over the painted shapes. The black paint contains so much alkyd medium that as it flows down over the white-gessoed canvas it separates into gauzy streaks, yet dries to a seamless glossy surface, sealing in the figures and its own drips, the language of the painting's process. In a darkly luminous field the familiar alphabet of forms dissected from the interlaces spin out of time, suspended in infinite space without visible architectural structure, new life made from ancestral strands of DNA.

JANE NECOL

Jellett, Mainie
Irish painter, 1897–1944

Born Mary Harriet Jellett in Dublin, 20 April 1897. Enrolled at the Metropolitan School of Art, Dublin, 1915. Studied under Walter Sickert at the Westminster School of Art, London, 1917–19. Awarded two prizes in Dublin, enabling her to study in Paris; joined Evie Hone (q.v.) at Académie Lhôte, then studied with Hone in the studio of Albert Gleizes, 1921–2; again in Paris, winter 1922–3. Lived in Dublin from 1923, but visited Gleizes each summer in France until 1932. Visited the Baltic States and Germany, 1931; Amsterdam, 1933. Member, Society of Dublin Painters, 1920; founder-member, Abstraction-Création group, Paris, 1931; associate member, White Stag Group, 1940. First Chair, Irish Exhibition of Living Art, 1943. Died in Dublin, February 1944.

Principal Exhibitions

Individual
Mills Hall, Dublin: 1920 (with Lilian Davidson)
Dublin Painters' Gallery, Dublin: 1924 (with Evie Hone), 1925, 1926, 1927, 1928, 1929, 1931, 1933, 1935, 1937, 1939, 1941, 1944 (retrospective)
Waddington Gallery, Dublin: 1944 (retrospective)

Group
Royal Hibernian Academy: 1918–21, 1930–37
Salon des Indépendants, Paris: 1922
Society of Dublin Painters: from 1923
L'Art d'Aujourd'hui, Paris: 1925
London Group, London: 1925–6
Seven and Five Society, London: 1926
Palais des Beaux-Arts, Brussels: 1930 (*L'Art irlandais*)
Salon des Surindépendants, Paris: 1930–38
Abstraction-Création, Paris: 1931–6
New York World's Fair: 1939
Contemporary Picture Galleries, Dublin: 1940 (*Académie Lhôte Irish Students*), 1943 (*Watercolours*)

Selected Writings
"An approach to painting", *Irish Art Handbook*, Dublin: Cahill, 1943, pp.17–18

The Artist's Vision: Lectures and Essays on Art, ed. Eileen
  MacCarvill, Dundalk: Dundalgan Press, 1959

Bibliography

James White, "The art of Mainie Jellett", *The Studio*, cxxix, 1945,
  pp.192–3
Stella Frost, ed., *A Tribute to Evie Hone and Mainie Jellett*, Dublin:
  Browne and Nolan, 1957
*Mainie Jellett, 1897–1944: A Retrospective Exhibition of Paintings
  and Drawings*, exh. cat., Municipal Gallery, Dublin, 1962
Mainie Jellett, 1897–1944, Neptune Gallery, Dublin, 1974
Irish Art, 1900–50, exh. cat., Municipal Art Gallery, Crawford, 1975
Abstraction-Création, 1931–1936, exh. cat., Westfälisches
  Landesmuseum für Kunst und Kulturgeschichte, Münster, and
  elsewhere, 1978
Mainie Jellett: Abstracts, exh. cat., Neptune Gallery, Dublin, 1980
Irish Women Artists from the Eighteenth Century to the Present Day,
  exh. cat., National Gallery of Ireland, Dublin, and elsewhere,
  1987
S. B. Kennedy, *Irish Art and Modernism, 1880–1950*, Belfast:
  Institute of Irish Studies, 1991
Bruce Arnold, *Mainie Jellett and the Modern Movement in Ireland*,
  New Haven and London: Yale University Press, 1991
Mainie Jellett, exh. cat., Irish Museum of Modern Art, Dublin, 1991

Mainie Jellett is the leading modernist Irish painter of the 20th
century, and a significant figure in the international movement
of pure abstract art that was led by the French painter Albert
Gleizes. She worked closely with Gleizes during the crucial
years of 1921–4, during which he formulated his principles
and ideas on pure abstract painting and wrote his seminal
works on the subject. She remained in close contact with him
thereafter, and with others associated with the movement,
including Robert and Sonia Delaunay (q.v.), Robert Pouyaud
and her compatriot Evie Hone (q.v.). But in 1923 she returned
to Dublin, exhibiting her first pure abstract works, and
followed this in 1924 with a solo exhibition of abstract painting, provoking an artistic controversy that pushed her to the
forefront of the modern movement in Ireland. She led it, and
was its most outspoken proponent from then until her death.
She influenced many younger artists, and she taught painting,
but she did not develop any school of abstraction, though she
lectured widely on the subject.

Jellett's work went through several stages of development.
Her background was the conventional one of the eldest child
in a prominent Unionist and Protestant family in Dublin. Her
ancestors, on both sides of the family, had distinguished forebears tracing their involvement in Dublin life back to the 17th
century. Her father, a successful barrister, was also a Unionist
Member of Parliament, representing Trinity College. She was
given an education entirely at home, and was a remarkably
gifted musician. She was a pupil, in her childhood, of Elizabeth
Yeats, the sister of the painter Jack Yeats and the writer W.B.
Yeats. She studied at art school in Dublin, and briefly under
William Orpen, before going to London, where she became a
star pupil of Walter Sickert. She was, and is, much admired for
her drawings, watercolours and oils in his manner. She was the
leading figure of her time at the Westminster School, and won
the Taylor and other prizes in Dublin after her return.

In 1920 she went to Paris, and was a pupil of André Lhôte
for almost a year, producing a surprisingly large body of Cubist
work, including landscapes, nudes and classical studies based
on Poussin and other artists. Towards the end of the following
year she and Evie Hone called on Albert Gleizes and, against
his will – which was not strong – persuaded him that they had
to become pupils. The association led to regular visits to
France from Dublin, and direct involvement in the Gleizes-
inspired experiment in artistic commune-living, at Moly
Sabata in the 1930s. But both women were dedicated to their
own city of Dublin and to the development of modern methods
and beliefs among Irish artists. Jellett was successful in this.
Ten years before Ben Nicholson introduced abstraction to an
English public, Jellett had established a following for such
work in Dublin, and had steadily developed the theories of
"translation" and "rotation" and the later theories of colour in
abstract art that were central to the methods of the followers
of Gleizes. They have since become fundamental to abstract
theory, and are widely and increasingly recognised for their
central importance in 20th-century art.

Jellett was a founder-member of Abstraction-Création, and
exhibited in a number of European cities with other modernist
painters, as well as being represented in the early shows of that
movement. There were notable stylistic developments during
the 1920s. Her earliest abstract works had great simplicity and
purity, leading to comparisons with Juan Gris and the
Delaunays. A more decorative style followed, and dominated
her earliest public exhibitions in Dublin, which began after her
return to the city in 1923, and continued, usually at two-year
intervals, throughout the 1920s and 1930s. Greater expression
of rational and structured composition is evident in her paintings into the 1930s, and in 1936 she moved towards a form of
semi-abstract realism and produced a succession of great
canvases on religious themes, including several Pietàs,
Crucifixions, and representations of the Virgin and of Christ
on the Cross. It is difficult to cite individual works by name,
since she eschewed titles and often used only such words as
Abstract Study or Abstract Painting. But the *Ninth Hour*
(1941; Hugh Lane Municipal Gallery of Modern Art, Dublin)
and *Madonna of Spring* (1939; private collection, Ireland, repr.
Arnold 1991, fig.224) are notable examples of the later
manner.

Jellett befriended many refugee artists at the beginning of
World War II, and became an increasingly influential figure
during the war years, when artistic life flourished in neutral
Ireland. She was associated with one of the dominant groups
of the period, the White Stag Group, and in 1943 she was a
leading activist in setting up the Irish Exhibition of Living Art,
a modernist forum that quickly became the main rival to the
academic school of the Royal Hibernian Academy. In the
autumn of that year she contracted cancer of the pancreas, and
died early in 1944. A full retrospective was not held until
1962. There were several shows of her work put on in Dublin
in the 1960s and 1970s by a private gallery, and in 1991 a
major solo exhibition was held at the Irish Museum of Modern
Art.

Mainie Jellett is widely regarded as the leading Irish woman
artist of the 20th century, if not of all centuries. Her command
of colour and composition is outstanding. Her courage, in
facing early indifference and then the ignorant disdain of critics
in Dublin, paid off handsomely, and largely through the strong
support and encouragement of other women, including both
painters and women working in other fields of art. She had
a natural sympathy with all the arts, and believed in their

Jellett: *Virgin and Child*, 1936; National Gallery of Ireland, Dublin

collective promotion and in the common bond of understanding required by the theory and practice of modernist beliefs.

BRUCE ARNOLD

Jerichau Baumann, Elisabeth
German painter, 1819–1881

Born Elisabeth Anna Maria Baumann near Warsaw, Poland, 27 November 1819. After a short period in Berlin, studied at the Düsseldorf Academy under Wilhelm von Schadow and others, c.1840–45. Went to Rome, 1845. Married Danish sculptor Jens Adolf Jerichau in Rome, 1846; nine children (sons Harald, 1851–78, and Holger, 1861–1900, both became painters). Set up home in Denmark in 1849, when husband became a member of the Copenhagen Academy, but retained a studio in Rome, where she frequently spent long periods alone. Travelled widely, visiting Greece, Egypt, Persia and Constantinople. Member, Royal Danish Academy of Fine Arts, Copenhagen, 1861; Accademia di Raffaello, Bramante, Italy. Recipient of first-class Academy medal, Copenhagen, 1858. Died in Copenhagen, 11 July 1881.

Principal Exhibitions

Individual
142 New Bond Street, London: 1871
Pilgeram and L.H. Lefevre Gallery, London: 1873

Group
Charlottenborg, Copenhagen: 1849–82 (salons), 1872 (*Den Nordiske udstilling* [Nordic exhibition])
Royal Academy of Fine Arts, Stockholm: 1850, 1860, 1866, 1870
Royal Academy, London: 1859–60, 1863–9

Selected Writings

Jugenderinnerungen, 1874 (memoirs)
Til erendring om Harald Jerichau [In memory of Harald Jerichau], 1879
Brogede rejsebilleder [Travel images of many colours], 1881

Bibliography
M. Müller, *Düsseldorfer Künstler*, 1854, pp.315–17
"The works of M. and Madame Jerichau", *Art Journal*, 1863, p.152
Illustreret Tidende, 1867–8, pp.189–91, 297–9; 1877–8, pp.353–4; 1880–1, pp.533–5
"The works of Madame Jerichau", *Art Journal*, 1871, p.165
"Paintings by Madame Jerichau", *Art Journal*, 1873, pp.254–5
Ellen C. Clayton, *English Female Artists*, 2 vols, London: Tinsley, 1876
Niemirowski, *Elżbieta Jerichau-Baumann*, 1882, pp.67, 92–3, 99–100
Nicolai Bøgh, *Elisabeth Jerichau-Baumann*, 1886
L. Dietrichson, *Svundne tider* [Times gone by], ii, 1899, pp.268–79
John Paulsen, *Nye erindringer* [New recollections], 1901, pp.1–59
Emma Kraft, *Brogede blade* [Mottled pages], 1905, pp.274–80
Axelline Lund, *Spredte erindringer* [Scattered recollections], 1917, pp.137–43
Fanny Lewald, *Römisches Tagebuch, 1845–46*, 1927
Jette Kjaerboe, "'Du sjael har i havfruens øjne lagt': Et studie over et billede af Elisabeth Jerichau Baumann" ["You have put soul into the eye of the mermaid": A study of a painting by Elisabeth Jerichau Baumann], *Cras: Tidsskrift for Konst og Kultur*, xxxv, 1983, pp.53–63
Artystki polskie [Polish women artists], exh. cat., National Museum, Warsaw, 1991
I Halvmånens skær [In the light of the half-moon], exh. cat., Davids Samling, Copenhagen, 1996

Elisabeth Baumann was born near Warsaw to German parents and grew up in comfortable wealth. Her first artistic training took place in Berlin, then around 1840 she moved on to study in Düsseldorf, where she remained until 1845. Under the direction of Wilhelm von Schadow, the Düsseldorf Academy had moved from the provision of an efficient training for history painters in the 1830s to genre paintings of an anecdotal character and with painstaking details in the 1840s. The colour scheme was mellow, close to the uncleaned works of old masters with their darkened varnishes that could be studied in museums. At the time of Baumann's arrival in Düsseldorf, the Academy was frequented by a great many Norwegian and Swedish art students, while the Finns were to follow a little later. Contrarily, the Danish artists were vehemently urged not to go to Düsseldorf, where the teaching was claimed to foster the artificial and the superficial, as opposed to a thorough study after nature. That Baumann was firmly rooted in the German tradition came to tell against her until the very end in Danish art circles.

In 1844 she exhibited two paintings with Polish themes in Düsseldorf, and in 1845 she moved to Rome, where she met the Danish sculptor Jens Adolf Jerichau. They were married at the Capitol in 1846, and Elisabeth was to live for the rest of her life alternately in Rome and in Copenhagen. She found no tranquillity in marriage; her husband was of a nervous constitution, and rejected his position as head of the family. As Jerichau Baumann gradually became the mother of nine, her economic responsibilities were a determining factor in her art: she herself wrote that she had to compromise in order to paint works that would appeal to art buyers. She lost two daughters at an early age, while two others spent their lives in mental institutions. The two sons, the dearly beloved but short-lived Harald Jerichau and Holger Jerichau, both became painters.

Portraiture and genre painting were the fields cultivated by Jerichau Baumann. Her early work is full of picturesque detail and of a certain unconvincing sweetness that rather conforms with one part of her complex and sometimes contradictory character, as can be seen from her autobiographical writing and prolific letter writing. In Denmark she was considered odd and exuberant, or whimsical as she grew on in years. Her flamboyant and bohemian manners contrasted strongly with the prim and proper ideals of the provincial capital that was Copenhagen in the latter part of the 19th century. Especially after the Danish war with Germany of 1848–51, artists were called upon to give evidence of patriotism in their paintings and sculptures. Jerichau Baumann tried her best by producing a number of folkloristic genre paintings from rural Denmark, but neither she nor her husband was committed to the nationalistic formulas; they belonged to the "European" (termed "the Brunettes"), as against the "Nationals" (or "Blonds"). Neither of them was entirely ostracised, however, and Jerichau Baumann continued to exhibit at the Charlottenborg Salon, the only annual art show open exclusively to members of the

Jerichau Baumann: *Hans Christian Andersen Reading Aloud to a Sick Child*, 1865; Hans Christian Andersens Hus, Odense Bys Museer, Denmark

Royal Academy of Fine Arts. The total sum of her paintings shown there between 1849 and 1882 was 172.

Jerichau Baumann painted portraits of prominent Danish writers as well as the likeness of the national-liberal politician *Orla Lehmann* (1848; Frederiksborg Castle), probably a patriotic gesture. Her portrait of the *prima donna assoluta* of Danish 19th-century theatre, *Johanne Louise Heiberg*, dated 1852, is in the Teatermuseet, Copenhagen. She was friendly with Hans Christian Andersen, whom she portrayed reading aloud to a sick child (1865; see illustration), a composition based on a personal memory, as well as in a rather elegant, flattering likeness (Frederiksborg Castle). As she commanded high prices for her work, her clients were often to be found among the landed gentry or various royal families in Europe, from Copenhagen to Athens.

Apart from her portraits, her most popular work was genre paintings with Italian subjects, probably the most stereotyped part of her work, with a strong taste of the painter's studio. In

order to secure the finances of her large family, Jerichau Baumann travelled widely across Europe in order to find affluent sitters and clients for her genre scenes, as well as to show her work at prestigious exhibitions, such as the Royal Academy in London. In Germany she executed a portrait of the *Brothers Grimm* (1855; Nationalgalerie, Berlin) and she is represented at the Kunstmuseum, Düsseldorf, by *An Italian Girl* (1845–6) and at the Niedersächsisches Landesmuseum, Hannover, by the sketch *An Italian Woman at a Well* (1845–9). A painting of an Icelandic woman in national costume was de-accessioned from the Kunsthalle, Hamburg, early in the 20th century. The major Scandinavian museums all possess works by her, whereas the numerous paintings sold in Britain and France have not as yet been traced. *Girl Mending Her Stockings* was acquired by Empress Eugénie of France and *David as a Shepherd* by the German Kaiser. Napoleon III paid a large sum for *Devotion at Home*, and in Britain Sir Morton Peto and Baron Hambro were among her clients. In order to benefit to the full from her happier inventions, she would often repeat her favourite compositions several times. *The Devotion* thus ran into nine versions, *Woman of Iceland* was painted five times and the *Mermaid* three times (one version in Ny Carlsberg Glyptotek, Copenhagen). Jerichau Baumann also sold works to the Empress of Russia, King George of Greece and Princess Anna of Hesse.

Of particular interest are the paintings Jerichau Baumann executed in the Middle East. In 1869–70 she travelled by way of Athens, where she portrayed *Queen Olga*, to Cairo, and in 1875 she worked in Constantinople. As a woman she had access to a world forbidden to her male contemporaries, and at the Charlottenborg exhibition of 1876 she presented *Selim Pasha's Harem in Stamboul Zennab-Hannum* (her *Princess Nazili Hanum*, 1895, is in the collection of the Sultan of Brunei). Her lively impressions from the Orient were also given literary form in the book *Brogede rejsebilleder* (1881). Her Danish biographer Bøgh noted that her printed reminiscences are the result of careful weeding by her friends ahead of publication, being too "unruly" in the raw. Her autobiographical work is full of poems, which she composed easily in six languages, and among her unpublished literary attempts is a five-act drama with a female nihilist as its protagonist, as well as a "Night novel", so termed as it was written after normal bedtime.

Although Elisabeth Jerichau Baumann painted one of the emblems of Danish patriotism, *Denmark* (1851; Ny Carlsberg Glyptotek), a figure represented in folk costume and carrying the national banner, the foreign character of her paintings has relegated her to the position of a footnote in the histories of Danish art. There has been a recent re-evaluation of Jens Adolf Jerichau's work, but the dispersal of Elisabeth's paintings all over Europe makes the reassessment of her art extremely difficult. No modern monograph or major exhibition has made the attempt to take a closer look at the work of Elisabeth Jerichau Baumann.

CHARLOTTE CHRISTENSEN

Jessica *see* Dismorr

Jobs, Lisbet, 1909–1961, and Gocken, 1914–1996
Swedish ceramists, textile designers and printmakers

Both sisters born in Falun, Dalarna; father an organist, composer and teacher, mother a painter and embroiderer. Moved to Stockholm after parents' divorce, 1925; followed a similar path throughout their careers. Lisbet studied at the Technical School, Stockholm, 1925–31 (two years in department for women artists, three years in higher school for industrial art). Made study trip to Hegnetslund earthenware factory, Køge, Denmark, after receiving a Swedish Craft Association bursary, 1931. Set up workshop with electric kiln on return to Sweden, 1931. Further grants funded subsequent study trips to Germany, Austria and France. Gocken finished studies at Stockholm Technical School in 1935; subsequently studied at Hegnetslund earthenware factory in Denmark, then returned to Sweden and entered the firm Jobs keramik, set up by Lisbet. The sisters sold work in the gallery opened by their mother Elisabet Wisén-Jobs in 1930, and participated in numerous exhibitions at home and abroad in the 1930s, receiving international recognition. Took up textile design during World War II, working with their brother, Peer, who had invented a new silkscreen printing technique. Moved from Stockholm back to Dalarna in 1942; bought large farm in Västanvik and converted it into a family compound with ceramic studios, textile workshop and retail outlet, 1944. Three generations of the Jobs family have lived and worked there.

Principal Exhibitions
Galerie Moderne, Stockholm: 1935
Exposition Internationale, Paris: 1937
New York World's Fair: 1939
Golden Gate International Exposition, San Francisco: 1939
Nordiska Kompaniet, Stockholm: 1945 (*När skönheten kom till byn* [When beauty came to the village])
Nationalmuseum, Stockholm: 1986 (*Jobs keramik och textil* [Jobs ceramics and textiles])

Selected Writings
Lisbet Jobs, text in *Svensk Nyttokonst*, 1937

Bibliography
Gunnel Persson, *Jobs Handtryck – firman och hantverket* [Jobs Handtryck – The firm and the craft], dissertation, Uppsala, n.d.
Svante Svärdström, "Ung keramik: Jobs verkstad i Stockholm" [Young ceramics: The Jobs workshop in Stockholm], *Svensk Nyttokonst*, 1935
Gotthard Johansson, "Generalrepetition för Paris" [General rehearsal for Paris], *Svenska Dagbladet*, 24 February 1937
J. Hodin, "Jobs", *Form*, no.9, 1941
Marita Lindgren-Fridell, "När Skönheten kom till byn ..." [When beauty came to the village], *Form*, no.4, 1954
Gunvor Björkman, *Från keramik till textil* [From ceramics to textiles], dissertation, Stockholm, 1984
——, *Keramiskt 30-tal* [The ceramic 1930s], dissertation, Stockholm, 1984
Inez Svensson, *Tryckta tyger från 30-tal till 80-tal* [Printed cloth from the 1930s to the 1980s], Stockholm, 1984
Jobs Keramik och textil [Jobs ceramics and textiles], exh. cat., Nationalmuseum, Stockholm, 1986
Michelle Facos, "New designs, old techniques: The Jobs family workshop", *Scandinavian Review*, Spring–Summer 1994, pp.43–8

The Jobs sisters were pivotal figures in the evolution of Swedish modernism in the decorative arts. Considered the most typically Swedish of contemporary Swedish textile producers, their handprinted fabrics are found in Swedish embassies and corporate boardrooms throughout the world. While their charming prints reminiscent of an earlier, more tranquil era are often likened to the fabrics of the British designer Laura Ashley, Jobs textiles are produced by hand through a painstakingly slow and laborious process, whereas Laura Ashley material is machine-made.

They began as ceramists, having received their training at the Technical School in Stockholm during the 1920s; Lisbet

Jobs: Textile, *Aurora*, 1958; Nationalmuseum, Stockholm

was the first independent woman ceramist in Sweden. Inspiration for their designs came first from the floral embroideries for which their mother was famous among a select group of Stockholm collectors. Receptiveness to, and appreciation of, handicrafts was nurtured by a revival initiated at the end of the 19th century, which continued to gain momentum until World War II. At the turn of the 19th and 20th centuries, Sweden's intellectual elite was staunchly populist and concerned with preserving the country's folk culture. It established several groups such as the Friends of Handicraft in the 1880s in order to teach native handicrafts such as knitting, embroidery and birch-bark weaving. In the late 1880s August Strindberg even remarked on the importance of the handicraft revival in the formation of a Swedish national identity.

The Jobs family came from Dalarna, the province of Sweden with the strongest peasant traditions, and grew up in an environment permeated by folk artisans. But embroidery was also a traditionally middle-class female activity, and it was to this class that Elisabet Jobs's designs appealed. She sold them in a fashionable shop in Stockholm, and stocked the ceramics of her daughters when they began to produce functional, decorative pieces in the early 1930s. The drawing style of the Jobs sisters was simple, linear and naive. The motifs were simple – a barefoot girl in a solid colour shift kneeling

and gazing at her reflection in a lily pond, a field of flowers. Their ceramics were exhibited in Paris in 1937 and in San Francisco in 1939. An American critic proclaimed Lisbet "one of the best potters in the world" (*Arts and Decoration*, 1939).

Lisbet and Gocken experimented avidly with glazes and relied heavily upon materials imported from Germany. With the onset of World War II, these compounds became inaccessible, and their ceramic production dwindled. They spent increasing amounts of time designing and fewer producing. They turned to their brother, Peer, who had occasionally translated their ceramic designs into printed fabrics. An unusual sibling collaboration resulted, with the Jobs sisters adopting for their own designs the silk-screen printing technique developed by Peer Jobs and Edgar Lundsten.

The Jobs siblings returned to Dalarna, where they established their textile workshop in a small village on the edge of Lake Siljan. While some of their designs are more complicated, Lisbet and Gocken are best known for their small designs with frequent repeats and few colours. Lisbet tended to create rows of simple objects – hearts, roosters, stylised trees, bows, bowls – frequently using only one colour, with either the objects or background in white. Another type designed by Lisbet and Gocken was inspired by the floral richness of their surroundings – mushrooms, ferns, flowers and leaves are distilled to their essential contours and printed in solid blocks of local colour. Of the two, Gocken was the more inclined to produce figural or narrative designs, slightly larger in scale than those of her sister. Frolicking children emerge in her work more frequently than they do in Lisbet's. Their production was not limited to bolts of fabric, however. Lisbet was particularly active in producing larger scale, individual scenes as independent works of art. In these, she was especially inspired by the 18th-century folk paintings that adorned the church and farmstead interiors of Dalarna. Lisbet translated religious and secular images – the Virgin and Child as well as soldiers on horseback – to textile. Sometimes she adhered to the palette of the original work, sometimes she experimented by producing it in several different colour variants.

Their breakthrough came with an exhibition in Stockholm's largest and most fashionable department store, Nordiska Kompaniet, in 1945. The sisters displayed "rooms" of Swedish modern furniture using their fabrics for curtains and upholstery. Not only did this bring their art to a wider public, but it showed the decorative possibilities of Jobs textiles. Jobs fabric became *the* fabric for upholstering Scandinavian modern furniture among Sweden's affluent classes. Like other works of art, each Jobs pattern has a name. Sometimes these are merely descriptive, *Small Pottery*, *Ladybugs*; at other times they pay tribute to the family – "Stina" was named after Lisbet's daughter. Some patterns refer to specific occasions such as *Midsummer* or *Wedding*. Because the designs are so popular and so costly, there are a host of imitators emulating the designs of Lisbet and Gocken. The imitations are immediately recognisable because of the disparity in the quality of materials and production techniques. The workshop, where production techniques and materials have not changed, is now overseen by Lisbet's daughter-in-law Eva, also a gifted designer.

MICHELLE FACOS

John, Gwen

British painter, 1876–1939

Born Gwendolen Mary John in Haverfordwest, Wales, 22 June 1876; older sister of the painter Augustus John. Grew up in Tenby, Wales, from 1884. Studied at Slade School of Fine Art, London, under Frederick Brown and Henry Tonks, 1895–8 (won Melvill Nettleship prize, 1897); Académie Carmen, Paris, under James McNeill Whistler, 1898–9. Lived in London, 1899–1903; Paris 1904–11 (worked as artist's model); Meudon, near Paris, 1911–39. Converted to Catholicism, 1913. Died in Dieppe, France, 18 September 1939.

Principal Exhibitions

New English Art Club, London: 1900–03, 1908–11
Carfax & Co., London: 1903 (with Augustus John)
International Exhibition of Modern Art, "Armory Show", New York: 1913
Penguin Club, New York: 1918
Salon d'Automne, Paris: 1919–20, 1923
Société Nationale des Beaux-Arts, Paris: 1920, 1924–5
Paris Salon: 1920
Sculptors Gallery, New York: 1922
Salon des Tuileries, Paris: 1924
New Chenil Galleries, London: 1926 (individual)
Art Center, New York: 1926 (*Representative Works Selected from the John Quinn Collection*)
Carnegie Institute, Pittsburgh: 1930
Deffett Francis Art Gallery, Swansea: 1935
National Eisteddfod, Fishguard: 1936
Matthiesen Ltd, London: 1946 (retrospective)
Arts Council of Great Britain, London: 1946 (touring retrospective)

Bibliography

Anthony Bertram, "The Johns", *Saturday Review*, cxli, 5 June 1926, pp.676–7
M. Chamot, "Gwen and Augustus John", *Country Life*, lix, 5 June 1926, pp.771–3
——, "An undiscovered artist: Gwen John", *ibid*, 19 June 1926, pp.884–5
William Rothenstein, *Men and Memories: Recollections of William Rothenstein*, 3 vols, London: Faber, 1931–9; New York: Coward McCann, 1931–40; revised edition, ed. Mary Lago, Columbia: University of Missouri Press, 1978
Augustus John, "Gwendolen John", *Burlington Magazine*, lxxxi, 1942, pp.236–40
Gwen John Memorial Exhibition, exh. cat., Matthiesen Ltd, London, 1946
Gwen John, exh. cat., Arts Council of Great Britain, London, 1946
Wyndham Lewis, "The art of Gwen John", *The Listener*, xxxvi, 1946, p.484
Denys Sutton, "Gwen John", *Country Life*, c, 25 October 1946, p.762
J. Wood Palmer, "Gwen John", *The Studio*, cxxxiv, 1947, pp.138–9
Augustus John, *Chiaroscuro: Fragments of Autobiography: First Series*, London: Cape, 1952
Ethel Walker, Frances Hodgkins, Gwen John: A Memorial Exhibition, exh. cat., Tate Gallery, London, 1952
J. Wood Palmer, "Gwen John", *Connoisseur*, cli, October 1962, pp.88–92
Jacques Maritain, *Carnet des notes*, Paris: De Brouwer, 1965
Gwen John: A Retrospective Exhibition, exh. cat., Arts Council of Great Britain, London, 1968
B. L. Reid, *The Man from New York: John Quinn and His Friends*, New York: Oxford University Press, 1968
Annela Twitchin, *Gwen John: Her Art and Her Religion*, MA thesis, Courtauld Institute of Art, University of London, 1972
Gwen John: A Retrospective Exhibition, exh. cat., Davis & Long Co., New York, 1975
Raïssa Maritain, *Raïssa's Journal*, ed. Jacques Maritain, Albany, NY: Magi, 1975
Michael Holroyd, *Augustus John*, 2 vols, 2nd edition, London: Penguin, 1976
Richard Shone, "Gwen John at Anthony d'Offay", *Burlington Magazine*, cxviii, 1976, pp.175–6
Christopher Neve, "In empty rooms: Gwen John (1876–1939)", *Country Life*, clix, 11 March 1976, pp.620–21
"The Noble Buyer": John Quinn: Patron of the Avant-Garde, exh. cat., Hirshhorn Museum and Sculpture Garden, Washington, DC, 1978
Susan Chitty, *Gwen John, 1876–1939*, London: Hodder and Stoughton, 1981
Gwen John, exh. cat., Anthony d'Offay, London, 1982
Gwen John: Paintings and Drawings from the Collection of John Quinn and Others, exh. cat., Stanford University Museum of Art, CA, 1982
Sara John, "Shades of meaning: Gwen John (1876–1939)", *Country Life*, clxxii, 12 August 1982, pp.462–4
A Very Private View, film, BBC Wales, 25 April 1984 (repeat), written and produced by Herbert Williams
Journey into the Shadows: A Portrait of Gwen John, 1876–1939, film, BBC2, 27 May 1984, written by Elaine Morgan, produced and directed by Anna Benson-Gyles
Cecily Langdale and David Fraser Jenkins, *Gwen John: An Interior Life*, Oxford: Phaidon, 1985; New York: Rizzoli, 1986
Mary Taubman, *Gwen John: The Artist and Her Work*, London: Scolar Press, and Ithaca, NY: Cornell University Press, 1985
Cecily Langdale, *Gwen John: With a Catalogue Raisonné of the Paintings and a Selection of the Drawings*, New Haven and London: Yale University Press, 1987
Ceridwen Lloyd-Morgan, *Gwen John Papers at the National Library of Wales*, Aberystwyth: National Library of Wales, 1988
Alicia Foster, "She shopped at the Bon Marché", *Women's Art Magazine*, no.65, July–August 1995, pp.10–14

Gwen John Papers are in the National Library of Wales, Aberystwyth; her correspondence with John Quinn is in the John Quinn Collection, New York Public Library; her letters to Auguste Rodin are in the Musée Rodin, Paris.

Gwen John did fewer than 200 paintings, and some several thousand drawings. From first to last, her pictures appear modest and unassuming. The pictures are invariably muted in palette, small in size and restrained in mood. The repertoire of subject matter is extremely limited: an impassive woman or girl; small groups of children and nuns viewed from behind; the occasional austere interior or still-life arrangement; an infrequent landscape. None the less, they evoke from the viewer a powerful emotional response out of all proportion to their reticence.

Again and again John's art is described as "reticent", "private", "quiet". She herself wrote: "As to whether I have anything worth expressing ... I may never have anything to express except this desire for a more interior life" (letter of 4 September 1912(?) to Ursula Tyrwhitt). The viewer is drawn into that interior life, into an intensely private communion with the artist. Because of the intimacy of that communion, one forgets how public her art has become. More than a third of John's paintings are now in public collections; more than 1000 of her drawings belong to the National Museum of Wales in Cardiff; most of her letters and papers are preserved in

John: *Young Woman Holding a Black Cat*, 1914–15; Tate Gallery, London

various public collections. Her following is large and passionately devoted to her art. Once known primarily as the sister of the celebrated painter and flamboyant personality Augustus John, Gwen John is now widely recognised as one of the most important British artists of the 20th century. Augustus's own prophecy, "Fifty years after my death I shall be remembered as Gwen John's brother" (Holroyd 1976, p.61), has been fulfilled.

To understand John's art, one must remember that she was Anglo-French. Brought up in Wales, she lived in London until the age of 27. She then went to France, where she lived until her death 36 years later. She consciously distanced herself from her family and background, returning to Britain only very rarely, declaring it "quite a foreign country" (letter postmarked 3 December 1914 to Ursula Tyrwhitt). Nevertheless, her art always retained certain British traits. Its tonalism and intimist subject matter are legacies of her Slade School training and New English Art Club associations, while the patterned brushwork, dry surfaces and subdued colour of her mature paintings recall the work of such Camden Town contemporaries as Walter Sickert, Frederick Spencer Gore, Malcolm Drummond and Robert Bevan. Yet John had a vivid appreciation of avantgarde Parisian art and was by no means untouched by her French experience; her mature work also shows hints of affinities with Cézanne, Modigliani, Picasso, Puvis de Chavannes and Rouault, among others.

John's instruction at the Slade School was in the academic tradition; her teachers there, Frederick Brown and Henry Tonks, painted somewhat Victorian intimist views. James McNeill Whistler, her teacher during her brief studies at the Académie Carmen in Paris, commented that her work had "a fine sense of *tone*" (John 1952, p.48). Her first mature oil compositions reflect this training. The portrait of *Mrs Atkinson* (Metropolitan Museum of Art, New York), *Landscape at Tenby, with Figures* (private collection, USA, repr. Langdale 1987, pl.6) and *Interior with Figures* (National Gallery of Victoria, Melbourne) are carefully executed tonal paintings of rather detailed genre subjects.

After the Académie Carmen, the artist returned to London for several years of "subterranean life" (Augustus John, "Introduction", London, Arts Council, 1946, p.7). In 1904 she left Britain permanently for an independent and comparatively isolated existence in Paris. Living in a series of modest Montparnasse rooms, she painted, supporting herself by working as an artist's model. It was then that she met the great sculptor Auguste Rodin, for whom she posed, and with whom she immediately fell profoundly in love. Like her pictures, John herself appeared self-effacing; but her quiet exterior hid enormous passion, a passion she fixed upon Rodin obsessively for nearly a decade. Although she now complained that "everything interests me more than painting" (letter of 4 February (1910?) to Ursula Tyrwhitt), she did continue to work, and some of her best-known paintings date from this period. They include *La Chambre sur la cour* (collection of Mr and Mrs Paul Mellon, repr. Langdale 1987, pl.47), *A Corner of the Artist's Room in Paris* (Sheffield City Art Galleries) and *Girl Reading at the Window* (Museum of Modern Art, New York), all meticulously rendered interiors still in the Slade tradition. In two other paintings, both monochromatic and both entitled *Woman Sewing* (both private collection, *ibid.*, pls 57 and 184),

the emaciated, stylised figures clearly reveal a familiarity with Picasso's Blue Period pictures. Equally celebrated are certain drawings of this time: her watercolours of a tortoiseshell cat (e.g. *Cat*; Tate Gallery, London) and her eloquent and assured pencil and wash drawings of Chloë Boughton-Leigh (e.g. *Bust of a Woman*; Albright-Knox Art Gallery, Buffalo, NY), and of "a lady" (e.g. *Portrait of a Lady*; Borough of Thamesdown-Swindon Permanent Art Collection). The ease and spontaneity of these sheets are reminiscent of Rodin's drawings of much the same time.

During the early 1910s several significant changes occurred in John's life. Her obsession with Rodin waned, freeing her to turn more fully to her art. In 1910 she met John Quinn, the distinguished American lawyer and collector. Their relationship endured until his death in 1924, and precisely paralleled her time of greatest artistic productivity, a productivity due in no small part to his influence. Quinn became her patron and most enthusiastic supporter. He ultimately acquired about a dozen of her paintings, and numerous drawings. His provision of a stipend gave her a modest financial security; his attention and encouragement stimulated her to work.

In 1911 John moved to the Paris suburb of Meudon (where Rodin also lived), where she was to stay for the rest of her life. Her studio at 29 rue Terre Neuve is the subject of a number of paintings, including *Interior, Rue Terre Neuve* (Manchester City Art Galleries). As her relationship with Rodin diminished, she found comfort in religion, and was received into the Catholic Church in early 1913. She spent considerable time in the local church, where she saw the children and nuns who appear in hundreds of her watercolours (e.g. *Nun with a Group of Orphans*; collection of Mr and Mrs Paul Mellon, *ibid.*, pl.83). For those Dominican nuns, she did a famous series of paintings of their order's founder (e.g. *Mère Poussepin*; Southampton Art Gallery).

By the end of the decade, John's style had reached full maturity. Most of her paintings are of female sitters, usually anonymous, most often of the woman known as "the convalescent" (e.g. *Young Woman Holding a Black Cat*, see illustration; *Seated Girl Holding a Piece of Sewing*, Aberdeen Art Gallery and Museums). For the artist, the model was not of interest as an individual, but as "an affair of volumes" (undated letter of 1936 to Ursula Tyrwhitt). These paintings are rigorously edited: detail is suppressed both in the monumental, impassive figure and in the background. Surfaces are chalky and opaque; pigment is applied in small rhythmic strokes to a thinly primed canvas; and the predominantly cool-grey palette and range of tonal values are severely limited. John's often-expressed admiration for Cézanne is evident in these pictures; the compositions and proportions of the figures – small heads set on massive, pyramidal bodies – are akin to those in his late portraits. Also from this time is a series of eleven paintings of a convalescent (e.g. *Convalescent*, Tate Gallery; *The Letter*, Manchester City Art Galleries), which exemplify a curious feature of John's art: the repetition again and again of a composition with very little change indeed. Although not evident to the viewer, presumably a process of refinement was occurring for the artist; the repetition is surely also an expression of the obsessiveness that was such a notable attribute of John's character.

After about 1923 John's paintings change subtly but distinctly. They are still usually portraits of women in simple interiors, but the palette, proportions and silhouettes change. Paint application is bolder and more vigorous; the palette is more varied, with a new mauvish cast; and there are stronger contrasts between light and dark. Forms are now sometimes reduced to flat patterned passages. The figures are more slender, their silhouettes more irregular, their features more stylised (e.g. *Girl with a Blue Scarf*; Museum of Modern Art, New York). There is a resemblance to the women in Modigliani's portraits of the late 1910s: the proportions and simple poses are similar; the sitters' eccentric features (for which Modigliani was indebted to African masks) are strikingly alike.

Of John's drawings, among the most moving are a group of charcoal and wash studies of children done during the late 1910s (e.g. *Elisabeth de Willman Grabowska*; Victoria and Albert Museum, London). They are clearly done from life, and the draughtsmanship is fluid and economical. The same sitters appear repeatedly, but always in slightly altered poses; this is the one area of her mature work in which there are no repetitions.

From the early 1910s until the end of her working life most of John's watercolours are of women and children in church. These intimate, reticent studies typically show figures seen from the rear, and their setting is summarily indicated by an occasional prie-dieu. Compositions are repeated again and again, sometimes with alterations in palette or size. The earlier watercolours tend to be muted and translucent (e.g. *Seated Woman*; Stanford University Museum of Art, CA); the later ones are increasingly colourful and opaque (e.g. *A Girl Wearing a Hat and Coat with a Fur Collar, Seated in Church*; National Museum of Wales, Cardiff).

The portrait of *Miss Bridget Sarah Bishop* (1929; Johannesburg Art Gallery) is John's last known finished oil, but she continued to work in watercolour and gouache for several more years. Her last works on paper are opaque, brightly coloured and increasingly abstract; these stylised decorative images (e.g. *Seated Girl Holding a Child*; private collection, *ibid.*, pl.377) have real similarities to the art of Chagall and Rouault. She also made vast numbers of tiny ink sketches, often a dozen to a page; these nervous, angular drawings seem almost like unconscious jottings. There is no evidence that she did anything at all after about 1933.

Quinn's death in 1924 broke John's strongest connection to the art world, and in her later years she became increasingly solitary. She did maintain certain old friendships, and she formed one final passionate attachment to Véra Oumancoff, sister-in-law of the eminent neo-Thomist philosopher Jacques Maritain, and her neighbour in Meudon. This attachment was entirely one-sided, and was ended by Véra around 1930, when she found the artist's attentions unbearable. John's last decade was marked by growing self-neglect. A visitor in 1937 described her as living "like a feminine St Gerome" (letter of 6 May 1946 from Maynard Walker to Edwin John), and her niece believed that she "gave up … (it) may have been her unconscious that was trying to get her to die" (Vivien John in *A Very Private View* 1984). In September 1939 John drew up her will before travelling to Dieppe where she died eight days later, at the age of 63.

The idea that before her final years John lived in isolation is a mistaken one. Rodin, John Quinn, Rainer Maria Rilke and Arthur Symons were all close friends; and at one time or another she also met Picasso, Braque, Wyndham Lewis, Brancusi, de Segonzac, Ezra Pound, Lady Gregory, Maud Gonne and Henri-Pierre Roche. Nor did she refuse to exhibit or sell her work. Although she had only one large exhibition during her lifetime, in London at the New Chenil Galleries in 1926 (a show that was notably well received), she showed in London from 1900 until before World War I, once at Carfax & Co. and a number of times at the New English Art Club. In 1913 she was included in the famous "Armory Show" in New York. After the war, until 1924, she exhibited repeatedly at various Paris salons. Her pictures received considerable attention and were frequently sold out at these shows. In 1919 *Nude Girl* (Tate Gallery) became the first of John's pictures to enter a public collection. By 1930 there were several works at the Tate, several at the City of Manchester Art Galleries and others at the Whitworth Art Gallery, University of Manchester; Hugh Lane Municipal Gallery of Modern Art, Dublin; Albright-Knox Art Gallery, Buffalo, New York; and the Art Institute of Chicago. The first major exhibition after her death was a retrospective at Matthiesen in London; since that time her reputation has steadily grown, and she is now one of the most profoundly admired of all British artists.

Gwen John is a particular feminist heroine. It must be said, however, that she was probably far less constrained by her gender than most women of her generation or, indeed, later. It is true that, as a girl, she was kept at home while her younger brother was allowed to attend a Tenby art school, but from the time she entered the Slade she lived as independently as she wished. Because of her unhappy relationship with Rodin, she is often viewed as a victim, but in fact she was ruthlessly self-willed. She once said: "I think if we are to do beautiful pictures we ought to be free from family conventions & ties … I think the family has had its day. We don't go to Heaven in families now but one by one" (undated letter of about 1910 to Ursula Tyrwhitt), and she lived by that belief.

CECILY LANGDALE

Johnston, Frances Benjamin
American photographer, 1864–1952

Born in Grafton, West Virginia, 15 January 1864. Graduated from Notre Dame of Maryland Collegiate Division, Govanston, 1883; studied art at Académie Julian, Paris, 1883–5; Art Students League, Washington, DC, 1885–8; studied photography under Thomas William Smillie, Smithsonian Institution Division of Photography, Washington, DC, 1890. Opened professional studio in Washington, 1890; specialised in documentary work and portraiture of political and society celebrities. Served as member of jury for Philadelphia Photographic Society annual exhibition, 1899. Championed photography as a career for women. Organised exhibition of prints by 28 American women photographers for the Exposition Universelle, Paris, 1900; the display was also seen in St Petersburg and Moscow (autumn 1900) and at the Photo Club of Paris (1901). Received first architectural commission to photograph the New Theatre, New York, 1909. Studio on Fifth Avenue, New York, with Mattie Edwards Hewitt, 1913–17; specialised in architectural commissions. Took photographs of gardens and estates from 1917. Received seven consecutive grants from the Carnegie Corporation to photograph American colonial architecture in nine southern states, 1933–40. Moved to New Orleans, 1940. Associate member, Photo-Secession, 1904; member, New York Camera Club; honorary member, American Institute of Architects, 1945. Donated prints, negatives and correspondence to Library of Congress, 1947. Died in New Orleans, 1952.

Principal Exhibitions

New York Camera Club: 1898
Exposition Universelle, Paris: 1900 (gold medal)
Library of Congress, Washington, DC: 1929, 1947 (both individual)

Selected Writings

"What a woman can do with a camera", *Ladies Home Journal*, September 1897, pp.6–7
"The foremost women photographers in America", *Ladies Home Journal*, May 1901–January 1902 (series of seven articles)

Bibliography

Mammoth Cave by Flash-Light, Washington, DC: Gibson, 1893
The White House, Washington, DC: Gibson, 1893
Jaun Abel, "Women photographers and their work", *Delineator*, October 1901, pp.574–9
Henry Irving Brock, *Colonial Churches in Virginia*, Richmond: Dale Press, 1930; reprinted Port Washington, NY: Kennikat Press, 1972 (photographs)
Thomas Tileston Waterman, *The Early Architecture of North Carolina: A Pictorial Survey*, Chapel Hill: University of North Carolina Press, 1941
Samuel Gaillard Stoney, *Plantations of the Carolina Low Country*, Charleston, SC: Carolina Art Association, 1945
Paul Vanderbilt, "Frances Benjamin Johnston, 1864–1952", *Journal of American Institute of Architects*, xviii, 1952, pp.224–8
Frederick Doveton Nichols, *The Early Architecture of Georgia*, Chapel Hill: University of North Carolina Press, 1957
Lincoln Kirstein, ed., *The Hampton Album: 44 Photographs from an Album of Hampton Institute*, New York: Museum of Modern Art, 1966
Pete Daniel and Raymond Smock, *A Talent for Detail: The Photographs of Miss Frances Benjamin Johnston, 1889–1910*, New York: Harmony, 1974
Frances Benjamin Johnston: Women of Class and Station, exh. cat., University Art Museum and Galleries, California State University, Long Beach, 1979
Toby Quitslund, "Her feminine colleagues: Photographs and letters collected by Frances Benjamin Johnston in 1900", *Women Artists in Washington Collections*, exh. cat., University of Maryland Art Gallery, College Park, 1979
Amy S. Doherty, "Frances Benjamin Johnston, 1864–1952", *History of Photography*, iv, 1980, pp.97–111
Frances Benjamin Johnston: What a Woman Can Do with a Camera, exh. cat., Impressions Gallery of Photography, York, 1984
C. Jane Gover, *The Positive Image: Women Photographers in Turn of the Century America*, Albany: State University of New York Press, 1988
Lamia Doumato, *Frances Benjamin Johnston, Architectural Photographer: A Bibliography*, Monticello, IL: Vance, 1990
Dolores Mitchell, "The 'new woman' as Prometheus: Women artists depict women smoking", *Woman's Art Journal*, xii/1, 1991, pp.3–9
Naomi Rosenblum, *A History of Women Photographers*, London and New York: Abbeville, 1994

Frances Benjamin Johnston is best known for her documentary photographs of the American Scene of the turn of the century, but she also earned renown for her portraits, landscapes and architectural work. An advocate of photography as a career for women of her generation, Johnston wrote articles for the *Ladies Home Journal* in which she offered practical advice and encouragement to novices ("What a woman can do with a camera") and highlighted and promoted the work of prominent women colleagues both by writing about them ("The foremost women photographers in America") and by organising an important exhibition of their prints as part of the US Government exhibit for the Paris Exposition Universelle of 1900.

Like many women photographers, Johnston began as a student of drawing and painting, at the Académie Julian in Paris and at the Art Students League of Washington, DC (later part of the Corcoran Gallery School). She planned to become an illustrator, but after briefly working in that career, realised that the photograph would soon replace illustration in newspapers and magazines, and decided to become a professional photographer. She learned her craft as an apprentice to commercial photographers and later to Thomas William Smillie, head of the Division of Photography at the Smithsonian Institution. She later admitted candidly: "I entered upon my new vocation with an ignorance of photography that was as dense as my self-confidence was unbounded" (Long Beach 1979, p.11). Johnston "seems to have enjoyed immediate success, artistically and financially" (Kirstein 1966, p.53). Social position, family connections and parental encouragement no doubt helped. Her father worked for the US Treasury Department, she was distantly related to Frances Folsom, the wife of President Grover Cleveland, and her parents not only built a studio for her located – with Victorian propriety – in the rose garden behind their Washington home, but also helped to manage her business correspondence as well as supervise the work of her darkroom assistant (Gover 1988, p.38).

Johnston set high professional standards for herself and had an independent spirit: "I've learned not to depend on the Lord, I'll make the changes myself" (Daniel and Smock 1974, p.34), which enabled her to accept several daunting assignments requiring not only an adventurous nature but also physical stamina. Johnston was to photography what Ida Tarbell was to reference journalism. For *Demorest's Family Magazine* (March 1892), she did photographic essays of Pennsylvania coalfields, which entailed going down into mineshafts with heavy photographic equipment. She also gamely photographed America's natural wonders: *Mammoth Cave by Flashlight* (1892) and *Yellowstone by Stagecoach* (1903; both Library of Congress, Washington, DC). Writing the accompanying explanatory text, Johnston did several notable series focusing on American workers: in the United States Mint in Philadelphia; in the Bureau of engraving and printing in Washington (*Demorest's Family Magazine*, 1889); on Iron Workers; and also on women workers (*Women Workers at the Lynn Massachusetts Shoe*

Lynn

Johnston: *Women Workers Leaving the Lynn Massachusetts Shoe Factory*, 1895; Library of Congress, Washington, DC (neg. LC-USZ-62-81152)

Factory, 1895; see illustration), their private lives and standards of living.

By the 1890s Johnston had become known as the "photographer of the American Court" (Daniel and Smock 1974, p.5); she had easy access to the White House and photographed the administrations of presidents Cleveland, Harrison, McKinley, Theodore Roosevelt and Taft. Mrs Cleveland, Mrs McKinley and the wives of Cabinet members posed for Johnston in her studio. With the help of Roosevelt (then Secretary of the Navy) and on commission from a news syndicate, she got permission to photograph Admiral George Dewey on his flagship, the *USS Olympia* (1899), while it was anchored in the Bay of Naples soon after his triumphant victory in Manila Bay during the Spanish-American war (1898). She also recorded several world's fairs: the World's Columbian Exposition in Chicago (1893), the Pan-American Exposition in Buffalo (1901) and the Louisiana Purchase Exposition in St Louis (1904).

Johnston's photographic essay on the public school system of Washington, DC, attracted considerable attention and led to

what is probably her most famous body of work: a suite of photographs of the Hampton Institute, Virginia (1899). A progressive and experimental institution, Hampton was founded in 1868 "to train selected Negro youth who should go out and teach and lead their people" (Kirstein 1966, p.6). In the hope of interesting patrons in the work of the Institute, a bound presentation album of Johnston's prints was prepared, and was part of the Negro exhibit at the Paris Exposition of 1900.

Johnston found her personal vision and style early and rarely deviated from it. Her work is generally sober, austere, static and quiet. Her images are always thoughtfully composed – little is left to chance – and the carefully arranged figures that inhabit them seem hypnotically frozen in time and possess a monumental dignity. The photographer may well have found inspiration in the work of the American painters William Sidney Mount and Thomas Eakins, both for her compositions and for the solemn and respectful treatment of her subjects (see the Hampton Album studies *Poor Black Family at Mealtime*,

Black Farm Hands: Tending the Horse and *Stacking Pumpkins in Barn*, 1899). The occasional Impressionist influence can also be found in the photographer's work (*Rainy Day, the Pan-American Exposition*, 1901). One of Johnston's most interesting and provocative photographs is a *Self-Portrait* (c.1896; Library of Congress), in which the photographer sits in a no-nonsense and, for the time, shocking manner – her legs are crossed and her skirts hiked up to reveal not only a petticoat but also well-turned calves and ankles. By holding a cigarette in one hand and a large beer stein in the other, the young woman flaunts typically masculine attributes outrageously, thereby proclaiming her status as an independent "New Woman", albeit in the safety and seclusion of her properly Victorian and artfully appointed "bohemian" studio.

HELEN GOODMAN

Johnstone, Dorothy

British painter, 1892–1980

Born in Edinburgh, 25 December 1892. Studied at Edinburgh College of Art, 1908–10 (diploma). Awarded travelling scholarship to Italy, 1910; also visited Paris and London in pre-war years. Appointed to teaching staff of Edinburgh College of Art, 1914. Opened studio at 36 Torhichen Street, Edinburgh, and made first of many visits to Kirkcudbright, 1915. Joined the re-formed Edinburgh Group, 1919. Travelled to Vienna, 1923. Married D.M. Sutherland, 1924 (obliged to give up teaching post); son born 1925, daughter born 1928. Moved to Aberdeen on husband's appointment as principal of Gray's School of Art, 1933. Associate, Royal Scottish Academy, 1962. Died at Glanclwyd Hospital, North Wales, 15 July 1980.

Principal Exhibitions

Royal Scottish Academy, Edinburgh: occasionally 1912–81
Royal Academy, London: 1915, 1921, 1923
New Gallery, Edinburgh: 1919–21 (all with Edinburgh Group)
Edinburgh: 1924 (with Cecile Walton)
Aberdeen Art Gallery: 1982–3 (touring retrospective)

Bibliography

E.A. Taylor, "The Edinburgh Group", *The Studio*, lxxix, 1920, pp.88–98
J.W.S., "Studio-talk", *The Studio*, lxxxi, 1923, pp.162–4
Jessica Walker Stephens, "Cecile Walton and Dorothy Johnstone", *The Studio*, lxxxviii, 1924, pp.80–87
Dorothy Johnstone ARSA, 1892–1980, exh. cat., Aberdeen Art Gallery and elsewhere, 1982
The Edinburgh Group, exh. cat., City Art Museum, Edinburgh, and elsewhere, 1983
Scottish Art since 1900, exh. cat., Scottish National Gallery of Modern Art, Edinburgh, and elsewhere, 1989
Duncan Macmillan, *Scottish Art, 1460–1990*, Edinburgh: Mainstream, 1990
John Kemplay, *The Two Companions: The Story of Two Scottish Artists, Eric Robertson and Cecile Walton*, Edinburgh: Crowhurst, 1991
Duncan Macmillan, *Scottish Art in the Twentieth Century*, Edinburgh: Mainstream, 1994

Johnstone: *September Sunlight*, 1916; University of Edinburgh, Talbot-Rice Gallery

Dorothy Johnstone was born in Edinburgh on Christmas Day in 1892. Her father, George Whitton Johnstone RSA, was a painter, and at the age of 16 she was among the first students enrolled at the newly founded Edinburgh College of Art. She won a travelling scholarship from the College in 1910 which took her to Italy and to Paris. There she met Jessie M. King (q.v.), one of a lively group of Scottish artists resident in the city. King also befriended Cecile Walton (q.v.) and seems to have had an important role in encouraging these younger women. In 1914 Johnstone was appointed to the teaching staff of Edinburgh College of Art.

During these years she produced some very fine figure paintings, including a series of studies of girls in informal poses, such as *Broken String* (1912; artist's estate), the first work that she exhibited at the Royal Scottish Academy, *September Sunlight* (1916; see illustration), *Cecile Walton* (1918; artist's estate) and *Rest Time in the Life Class* (1923; Edinburgh City Art Centre). This last picture includes in the background a self-portrait of Johnstone engaged in teaching a group of students.

Cecile Walton is a portrait of one of her closest friends. It shows her reclining on a haystack chewing a straw. She is wearing a fine pair of pink-, white- and blue-striped pantaloons with a matching turban, white blouse and orange stockings. The informality of the pose is typical of Johnstone's approach, but the picture also discreetly reflects the easy-going, rather bohemian life-style and flamboyant dress of the circle of friends to which she belonged in Edinburgh. In 1920 Johnstone painted a fine portrait of another mutual friend in an equally colourful costume, but it was the clothes of Johnstone herself that her friend Mary Newbery recalled, as being: "… individual in colour and design, [and] outstandingly different to the uniformly conventional woman's dress of the day." *September Sunlight* was painted in Kirkcudbright where Johnstone went to work regularly for several years from 1915, renewing her friendship with King and staying in Greengate Close, studios attached to the house owned by King and her husband E.A. Taylor and lent to young painters. The picture is a study of a young girl at a sunlit window wearing an orange smock and sitting on a blue cloth against a white wall. Like all Johnstone's best paintings, especially those painted during these periods in Kirkcudbright, this picture is broadly handled and characterised by fresh light and brilliant colour. The colour scheme bears some relationship to King's palette at the time, but it also endorses the memory of one of Johnstone's students at Edinburgh College of Art, who recalled being told to use a very simple palette: "White, yellow ochre, light red and cobalt blue, on no account burnt sienna, raw sienna or fancy colours".

In 1919 Johnstone joined the Edinburgh Group, a small exhibiting society of young painters and close friends who had first shown in Edinburgh before World War I. They included Cecile Walton, Eric Robertson, Mary Newbery and David Macbeth Sutherland. In 1924 Johnstone had a joint show in Edinburgh with Walton, with whom she had spent a period in Vienna the previous year. In the same year she married D.M. Sutherland. He also taught at Edinburgh College of Art, but according to the rules of the time, her marriage meant that she had to give up her teaching post. In 1933 she moved with her family to Aberdeen, where her husband had been appointed principal of Gray's School of Art. She lived for the rest of her life in Aberdeen. She herself felt that her most productive years were those when she was teaching in Edinburgh, but in Aberdeen she continued to paint and to exhibit, carrying out a number of portrait commissions and more informal portraits of her own children and family. She also continued to paint landscapes, often working in the summer at Plockton on the west coast of Scotland. Throughout her life she exhibited at the Royal Scottish Academy, and was elected an Associate in 1962. This was a tribute to her enduring reputation, as she was among the first half dozen women to be elected to the Academy either as Associates or as Academicians. She died in 1980 at Glanclwyd Hospital, North Wales. A memorial exhibition was held in Aberdeen and in Edinburgh in 1983, when most of the work shown was from her studio.

DUNCAN MACMILLAN

Jonas, Joan

American performance artist, 1936–

Born Joan Amerman Edwards in New York, 13 July 1936. Studied at Mount Holyoke College, South Hadley, Massachusetts, 1954–8 (BFA); School of the Museum of Fine Arts, Boston, 1958–61; Columbia University, New York, 1963–4 (MFA). Married Gerald Jonas, 1959. Taught art to children in workshops and schools in Boston and New York, 1958–65. Visiting artist, Video School of Visual Arts, New York, 1972; San Diego State University, California, 1975; Otis Art Institute, Los Angeles, 1975; Kent State University, Ohio, 1977; guest lecturer, Princeton University, 1974; Yale University, New Haven, 1974; Minneapolis College of Art, 1974; artist-in-residence, TV Lab, WNET-TV, 1976; Television Workshop, WXXI-TV, 1980. Recipient of Creative Artists Public Service (CAPS) grants, 1971 and 1974; Deutscher Akademischer Austauschdienst (DAAD) grant, Berlin, 1971; National Endowment for the Arts (NEA) grants, 1973, 1975, 1978, 1980 and 1983; Guggenheim fellowship, 1976; prize for *Upside Down and Backwards*, International Video Art Festival, Tokyo, 1981; Rockefeller fellowship, 1981. Lives in New York.

Selected Individual Exhibitions

The Kitchen, New York: 1974, 1977
Contemporanea, Rome: 1974
Walker Art Center, Minneapolis: 1974
Institute of Contemporary Art, Los Angeles: 1975
Womanspace, Los Angeles: 1975
Institute of Contemporary Art, Philadelphia: 1976, 1977
Whitechapel Art Gallery, London: 1979
Stedelijk van Abbemuseum, Eindhoven: 1979
University Art Museum, Berkeley, CA: 1980–82 (touring retrospective)
Solomon R. Guggenheim Museum, New York: 1980
Contemporary Art Museum, Houston: 1981
Whitney Museum of American Art, New York: 1983 (touring)
Museum of Modern Art, New York: 1984
De Appel, Amsterdam: 1985
Stedelijk Museum, Amsterdam: 1994–5 (touring retrospective)

Selected Writings

"Seven years", *Drama Review*, xix, March 1975, pp.13–17 (with Rosalind Krauss)
"He saw her burning", *Illuminating Video: An Essential Guide to Video Art*, ed. Doug Hall and Sally Jo Fifer, New York: Aperture, 1990, pp.366–74

Bibliography

Constance de Jong, "Organic honey's visual telepathy", *Drama Review*, xvi, June 1972, pp.63–5
Douglas Crimp, "Joan Jonas's performance works", *Studio International*, cxcii, July–August 1976, pp.10–12
Rosalind Krauss, "Video: The aesthetics of narcissism", *October*, no.1, 1976, pp.50–63
Douglas Crimp, ed., *Joan Jonas: Scripts and Descriptions, 1968–1982*, Berkeley: University Art Museum, 1983
Kathy O'Dell, "Performance, video and trouble in the home", *Illuminating Video: An Essential Guide to Video Art*, ed. Doug Hall and Sally Jo Fifer, New York: Aperture, 1990, pp.135–51
Joan Jonas: Works, 1958–1994, exh. cat., Stedelijk Museum, Amsterdam, and elsewhere, 1994
Joan Simon, "Scenes and variations: An interview with Joan Jonas", *Art in America*, lxxxiii, July 1995, pp.72–9, 100–01

Joan Jonas began employing mirrors and closed-circuit television in her performances and video tapes of the 1970s as a way of creating disjunction between audiences and performers and severing actions from images. An active participant in the performance scene of lower Manhattan, she staged works for an audience of peers who attended each other's events on an almost nightly basis. She referred to the environment as "a laboratory" because feedback could be incorporated as the pieces were repeated in different venues. While the terms performance and video are used to describe her work, Jonas's art defies easy classification. She selects materials and techniques that are useful to her investigations of perception, time and memory, incorporating several media within each piece and borrowing ideas and images from a wide range of sources and cultures.

After receiving her MFA from Columbia University in 1964, Jonas began her professional career by abandoning the traditional techniques of sculpture – in which she had been trained – in order to create her own idiosyncratic practice: "I gave up making sculpture", she said, "and I walked into the space" (Simon 1995, p.75). In 1965, as an assistant to Richard Bellamy at the Green Gallery, Jonas saw her first Happenings and performance work, which had a significant impact on the direction of her art. She was also inspired by Yvonne Rainer (q.v.) and the other dancers associated with the Judson Church, participating in their workshops and incorporating their use of everyday gestures and task-oriented movement into her own work. Later, Jonas borrowed gestures and rituals from Noh and Kabuki theatre that she saw on a trip to Japan in 1970.

In her earliest work Jonas shattered the illusion of the "real" by fracturing the performing space. Her interest in illusion resulted from both her training in art history, which emphasised the representation of deep space through perspective, and her love of magic and film, which create the illusion of reality through other kinds of trickery. Using mirrors and video cameras to displace images from their sources, Jonas consistently resisted the resolution of the figure in space. For example, in *Mirror Piece I*, performed at three different locations (Loeb Student Center, New York University; Gilles Larraine's loft, 66 Grand Street, New York; Bard College, Annandale-on-Hudson), women in short dresses moved in choreographed patterns while holding full-length mirrors. Although the performers traversed the entire performing area – a common theatrical device employed to define the performing space – the mirrors interrupted that space by simultaneously reflecting the area beyond it.

In addition to altering the perception of space, *Mirror Piece I* denied the conventional relationship between performer and spectator. When the audience looked at the performers in front of them, instead of an unimpaired view of the female body, their own image was reflected back to them. Thus, observers became the observed, caught in the act of looking. It was a device that Jonas repeated in her work throughout the 1970s. By rejecting the traditional structure of the theatre, where performers work in a defined space and the audience is allowed to behold them from a comfortable distance, Jonas upset subject/object relations and obstructed the clear path of vision and pleasure associated with both theatre and the visual arts.

In addition to mirrors, Jonas often used closed-circuit television, again to undermine the direct relationship between spectator and art work. In her video *Left Side Right Side* (1972) the viewer sees two reflections of Jonas, one in a mirror and the other on a closed-circuit video monitor. It is immediately apparent that each image relays only partial information. On the one hand, the mirror allows a broader view, exposing more of Jonas's body than the video monitor. On the other hand, that the mirror's image is always in reverse is made clear by the contrasting view in the monitor. Towards the end of *Left Side Right Side*, Jonas moves directly in front of the camera, offering a third view of the artist and further creating a disjunction between the source of the images (Jonas) and the way they are perceived through the distancing devices of camera and mirror.

In *Delay Delay* (1972) Jonas extended the displacement of source and perception to sound by creating distance between audience and action. In the original version spectators watched the performance from the roof of a five-storey loft building in lower Manhattan. The piece began with several performers clapping wooden blocks together, which was first seen and then heard after a slight delay. Jonas refers to her practice of separating action and perception as de-synchronisation.

In 1972 Jonas used both mirror and closed-circuit television in what are perhaps her best-known performances: *Organic Honey's Visual Telepathy* and *Organic Honey's Vertical Roll*. In these works she not only continued her investigation of audience/performer relationships by reflecting the audience back to itself and splitting object and image via the video monitor, but she also undermined the construction of identity through role-playing and costume. At the beginning of *Organic Honey's Vertical Roll*, Jonas examined her nude body, piece by piece, with a small hand mirror. Her clinical (as opposed to erotic) presentation of the body then gave way to a masquerade of gender as Jonas became her *alter ego* Organic Honey, who wore a sequin jacket, a feather head-dress and a mask purchased at an erotica shop. In this demonstration of the production of gender, Jonas clearly separated femininity from the body and located it in culture (O'Dell 1990, pp.148–9). In *Organic Honey's Visual Telepathy* she shifted identities again by changing into a blue satin robe mid-way through the performance. This second persona moved the mirror around the stage, drew messages on a blackboard and performed for both mirror and video camera. Organic Honey became a sorcerer – a conjurer of images – revealing representation to be a game of manipulation and artifice.

Jonas's most radical critique of vision and pleasure occurs in her video *Organic Honey's Vertical Roll* (1972). In this tape the viewer is denied an easy view of the performer (Jonas). Costumed as Organic Honey, with mask, head-dress and belly-dancing attire, Jonas performs a series of actions before the camera. The monitor rarely reveals her entire body, however. The viewer can only guess at her actions by piecing together the fragments. At one moment we see her hands, at another her back and so on. Further disturbing any pleasure in seeing is the vertical roll (a result of two un-synchronised frequencies) continually running down the screen, like a television set whose vertical hold adjustment has gone awry. Also contributing to the disjointed effect are the metallic throb of a spoon hitting a mirror followed by wooden blocks clapping together. The vertical roll and its attendant noise create a staccato rhythm, never allowing the eye, the ear or the mind to rest.

In 1976 Jonas moved in a new direction when she became interested in story-telling. Inspired by a commission to create a performance for children for the Institute for Contemporary Art in Boston, she based her subsequent performances and related videos on legends and fairy tales. As the stories were told in narrative sequence, action and images interpreted rather than illustrated the texts. These works have a dreamlike quality. Stories are often told in haunting, monotone voices, while scenes and images appear and reappear, seeming to shift in and out of time. In accordance with the shift in the work, mirrors, masks and closed-circuit television were replaced by spoken texts and colour video images. Jonas's video tapes also became more technologically sophisticated, often including several frames within a larger frame.

As her travels took her to different places, she often incorporated local stories into her work. While she was living in Berlin in 1982, she created a performance and a related video based on two separate news stories that she intercut. In *He Saw Her Burning* an account of an American soldier who drove a stolen tank through the city of Mannheim is interwoven with the testimony of a man who saw a woman spontaneously burst into flames. Each story is told by a different narrator who seems to be an eyewitness to the event. The format is that of the nightly newscast, but because the strange events are made even stranger by the astonished expressions of the narrators, the reports take on a surreal quality.

In 1989 Jonas completed her most complex work, *Volcano Saga*, which was both a performance with a video component and an independent video tape. The text is based on a 13th-century Icelandic saga in which a woman tells her dreams to a male dream interpreter. Jonas depicts the man and woman sitting in the water, their bodies visible from the shoulders up. Throughout the performance and video, she intersperses their conversations with dream images and various Icelandic myths. With the assistance of a computer, she was able to superimpose and layer images, animate still photographs of Iceland and place actors within photographic landscapes. The resulting footage suggests time-lapse and altered memory. Jonas appears in *Volcano Saga* as the narrator, and begins the tape with her own true story of being blown off the road by the wind while driving by herself in an Icelandic rainstorm. The effect is to link past and present. "What I found fascinating about Iceland", she commented, "was the closeness between the present and the past – as if all the mythic stories happened yesterday" (Simon 1995, p.100).

In 1994, in conjunction with her retrospective exhibition at the Stedelijk Museum in Amsterdam, Jonas staged a performance combining aspects of both phases of her work. *Sweeney Astray* is based on a medieval Irish poem about a pagan king who, because of a curse, was forced to wander in the country. In the poem he both laments his condition and praises nature. While Jonas was interested in the dichotomies of this story – order and brutality, nature and culture – she also wanted to address Sweeney's misogyny, which she did by interweaving poems from the same period that were by or about women. She worked with professional actors and used narrative to structure the event, a practice common to her late work. She also reintroduced techniques from her work of the early 1970s, including a mirror and a suspended video screen for live transmission.

Throughout her career Jonas has played the roles of both director and performer. Although she has created several solos

for herself, she has often appeared as one among several elements in a production. In her most recent work she usually enters the action near the end of the performance, announcing her authorship and identifying herself as a performer. In *Sweeney Astray* she used an actor to play Joan Jonas, which was a way of simultaneously directing and being in the piece. When Jonas herself jumped in and joined the other performers at the end of the performance, however, she reaffirmed her desire not to stand outside her art as she once again walked into the space of the work.

SAUNDRA GOLDMAN

Jones, Lois Mailou
American painter and designer, 1905–

Born in Boston, Massachusetts, 3 November 1905. Apprenticed to Grace Riley, costume designer and professor of Rhode Island School of Design, then employed by Ripley Studios to make costumes and masks for Ted Shawn School of Dance. Studied at School of the Museum of Fine Arts, Boston, 1923–7 (diploma in design); Boston Normal Art School, 1926–7 (certificate); Designers Art School of Boston, 1927–8 (diploma); Harvard University, 1927; Columbia University, New York, 1934–6; Howard University, Washington, DC (AB in art education 1945). Freelance textile designer, especially for F.A. Foster Company, Boston, and Schumacher Company, New York, 1927–8. Chair and instructor, Palmer Memorial Institute, Sedalia, North Carolina, 1928–30; instructor and professor of art, Howard University, Washington, DC, 1930–77. Studied at Académie Julian during sabbatical year in Paris, 1937–8; exhibited at Société des Artistes Français and Salon des Indépendants, 1938. Married Haitian graphic designer Louis Vergniaud Pierre-Noël in Cabris, France, 1953; he died 1982. Taught at Centre d'Art and Foyer des Arts Plastiques, Port-au-Prince, Haiti, 1954. Worked on Howard University Black Visual Arts project, travelling widely to collect data on Haitian, African and African-American art and artists, 1968–71; lectured on African-American art in several African countries as cultural ambassador for the United States Information Service, 1970. Recipient of numerous honours and awards, including diplôme and décoration, Ordre National d'Honneur et Mérite, Haitian government, 1954; Candace award, Metropolitan Museum of Art, New York, 1983; Outstanding Achievement in the Visual Arts award, Women's Caucus for Art, 1986; honorary doctorates from Colorado Christian College, Lakewood, 1973; Suffolk University, Boston, 1981; Massachusetts College of Art, Boston, 1986; Howard University, 1987; Findlay University, Ohio, 1993; Tougaloo College, Mississippi, 1994. First African-American artist to be elected honorary member of Society of Washington Artists, 1954; fellow, Royal Society of Arts, London, 1962; honorary member, Art Association, Washington, DC, 1972. Lives in Washington, DC.

Selected Individual Exhibitions
Hampton University, Hampton, VA: 1935

Howard University Gallery of Art, Washington, DC: 1937, 1948,
    1972 (retrospective), 1987, 1988, 1989
Robert C. Vose Galleries, Boston: 1939
Barnett-Aden Gallery, Washington, DC: 1946
Centre d'Art, Port-au-Prince, Haiti: 1954
Pan-America Union Building, Washington, DC: 1955
Galerie International, New York: 1961, 1968
Galerie Soulanges, Paris: 1966
Association for the Presentation and Preservation of the Arts,
    Washington, DC: 1968 (retrospective)
Museum of Fine Arts, Boston: 1973 (retrospective)
Phillips Collection, Washington, DC: 1979
Harbor Gallery, University of Massachusetts, Boston: 1985
Musée d'Art Haitien, Port-au-Prince, Haiti: 1986
Brody Gallery of Art, Washington, DC: 1988
Meridian House International, Washington, DC: 1990–94 (touring)

Selected Writings

Lois Mailou Jones: Peintures, 1937–1951, Tourcoing: Presses Georges
    Frère, 1952

Bibliography

Alain Locke, *The Negro in Art*, Washington, DC: Associates in
    Negro Folk Education, 1940; reprinted New York: Hacker, 1968
James A. Porter, *Modern Negro Art*, New York: Dryden Press, 1943;
    reprinted New York: Arno, 1969
Samella S. Lewis and Ruth G. Waddy, *Black Artists on Art*, i, Los
    Angeles: Contemporary Crafts, 1969
J. Edward Atkinson, ed., *Black Dimensions in Contemporary
    American Art*, New York: New American Library, 1971
Lois Mailou Jones: Retrospective Exhibition, 1932–1972, exh. cat.,
    Howard University Art Gallery, Washington, DC, 1972
Elsa Honig Fine, *The Afro-American Artist: A Search for Identity*,
    New York: Holt, Rinehart and Winston, 1973
Reflective Moments: Lois Mailou Jones: Retrospective, 1930–1972,
    exh. cat., Museum of Fine Arts, Boston, 1973
Robert Taylor, "Lois Jones achieves identity in retrospective art
    show", *Boston Globe*, 26 March 1973
Juliette H. Bowles, "Lois Mailou Jones: Portrait of an artist", *New
    Directions* (Howard University), iv/3, July 1977, pp.4–23
Women Artists in Washington Collections, exh. cat., University of
    Maryland Art Gallery, College Park, 1979
Forever Free: Art by African-American Women, 1862–1980, exh.
    cat., Illinois State University, Normal, 1980
Lois and Pierre: Two Master Artists, exh. cat., Museum of the
    National Center of Afro-American Artists, Boston, 1983
Keith Morrison, *Art in Washington and Its Afro-American Presence,
    1940–1970*, Washington, DC: Washington Project for the Arts,
    1985
Betty LaDuke, "Lois Mailou Jones: The grande dame of African-
    American art", *Woman's Art Journal*, viii/2, 1987–8, pp.28–32
*American Women Artists: The 20th Century, in Celebration of
    Woman's Art Journal's 10th Anniversary*, exh. cat., Knoxville
    Museum of Art, 1989
Romare Beardon and H.A. Henderson, *A History of African-
    American Art from 1792 to the Present*, New York: Pantheon,
    1993
Tritobia Hayes Benjamin, *The Life and Art of Lois Mailou Jones*, San
    Francisco: Pomegranate, 1994 (contains extensive bibliography)
——, "Lois Mailou Jones", *Gumbo ya ya: Anthology of
    Contemporary African-American Women Artists*, ed. Leslie King-
    Hammond, New York: Midmarch Arts Press, 1995, pp.126–9

Lois Mailou Jones has had a long and productive career as
painter, educator, designer and illustrator. Her influence as an
artist and teacher has been felt by several generations of
African-American students and colleagues in the USA, and also
in Haiti and Africa where she has exhibited, taught and
lectured. She has been a shining example of an artist who
successfully followed an original talent and vision, undeterred
by issues of prejudice against women artists or those of
African-American descent. Throughout her career Jones has
found new subjects in African, Haitian and African-American
themes and has expressed her perceptions in bold and unique
ways.

Jones was influenced in the choice of career by her friendship with the African-American sculptor Meta Vaux Warrick
Fuller (q.v.), whom she met at Martha's Vineyard where Jones's
family owned property and spent their summers. In 1923 she
won a four-year scholarship to the School of the Museum of
Fine Arts, Boston, where she was the only black student. After
graduating from the Designers Art School of Boston she
became a successful freelance designer, but decided to become
a painter because her work would then be recognised as her
own. At the same time she developed her career as a teacher,
first at the Palmer Memorial Institute, a junior college in
Sedalia, North Carolina, and then from 1930 at Howard
University in Washington, DC. While teaching painting, Jones
was also a freelance illustrator for Associated Publishers of
Washington, DC, from 1936 to 1963.

The breakthrough in Jones's painting came in 1937 when
she was awarded an Education Board Fellowship to study at
the Académie Julian in Paris for the next academic year. In her
education and new-found freedom abroad she was following
the steps of illustrious African-American artists such as Fuller,
who had lived in Paris and studied with Rodin, and Henry
Ossawa Tanner, a distinguished expatriate who lived and
exhibited his paintings in Paris during most of his career.
Sharing a studio at 23 rue Campaigne Première with Céline
Tabary, who became a valued friend, Jones adopted plein-air
painting, which she continued all her life. Her early still-life
paintings such as *Cauliflower and Pumpkin, Paris* (1938;
Metropolitan Museum of Art, New York) show a thorough
understanding of academic technique, combined with fluid
brush strokes and vibrant colour. Jones's mastery of volumetric form is frequently displayed in a number of Paris street
scenes, such as *Rue St Michel* (1938; artist's collection) and
Place du Tertre (1938; Phillips Collection, Washington, DC).
Here the underlying structure of the buildings reveals her interest in Cézanne's techniques. She exhibited her works at the
Salon de Printemps of the Société des Artistes Français and also
at the Salon des Indépendants in Paris in 1938.

Another important revelation of her Paris period was the
interest in African art, dance and music. "When I arrived in
Paris, African art was just the thing. All the galleries and
museums were featuring African sculptures, African designs,
and I sketched, sketched everything", Jones recounted
(Benjamin 1994, pp.ix–x). Her response to this stimulus was
Les Fétiches (1938; National Museum of American Art,
Smithsonian Institution, Washington, DC), a painting that
interprets the dynamic rhythms of African culture in an
angular, semi-abstract collage of masks, both completely
modern and in the tradition of African culture.

Jones returned to Howard University to resume her teach-
ing there in 1938. Her friend Céline Tabary came to
Washington for a visit in 1940, and stayed with Jones in the
USA for seven years. Tabary would often deliver Jones's

Jones: *Ubi Girl from the Tai Region*, 1972; acrylic on canvas; 110 × 150 cm.; Museum of Fine Arts, Boston, Hayden Collection

paintings to museum and gallery competitions where they would not have been accepted or won prizes if they were known to have been painted by an African-American artist. During the 1940s Alain Locke encouraged Jones to use African-American experience as subject matter. Her most moving painting of this period is *Mob Victim (Meditation)* (1944; artist's collection). This three-quarter view of a bearded, grey-headed African-American man with bound hands done with a muted palette of browns and greys is an eloquent testimony to fortitude in the face of racial violence.

Jones's marriage to Louis Vergniaud Pierre-Noël, a Haitian citizen and graphic designer, in 1953 opened a new chapter in her artistic as well as her personal life. Her annual trips to Haiti from 1954 onwards resulted in a period of Haitian subject matter with new locales, flattened forms and brilliant colour. In 1954 she was invited by the President of Haiti to teach at the Centre d'Art and at the Foyer des Arts Plastiques. This produced such paintings as *Peasant Girl, Haiti* (1954; Wadsworth Atheneum, Hartford, CT), a brilliant study of a seated girl in orange, brown and green in which the coiled energy of the girl's body contrasts with the cubic volume of the block against which she rests. In a later Haiti painting, *Les Vendeuses de tissus* (1961; Johnson Publishing Company Art Collection), forms have become more abstract, spread out in a long horizontal line.

In 1970 Jones visited eleven African countries on a grant from Howard University to research African art and culture. Her experiences ignited a series of paintings on African themes between 1971 and 1989, her most original contributions to American art. In these large-scale acrylic paintings on canvas Jones juxtaposed three-dimensional African figures on a flat background of native patterns, masks, carvings and textiles. She combined art forms from different regions to suggest the underlying unity of the African continent. An example of this is *Ubi Girl from the Tai Region* (1972; see illustration), which was in her solo exhibition in Boston in 1973. Here masks from Zaïre and a heddle pulley from the Ivory Coast are combined with the three-dimensional portrait head of the Ubi girl silhouetted against an African textile, creating tensions of form versus colour and Western-style portraiture versus African symbols and designs. This breakthrough in style, subject matter and design moved Jones's paintings into a new stage and resulted in new recognition of her art in solo exhibitions and honorary degrees.

Lois Mailou Jones has worked in a wide array of media and subject matter. Although social comment can be found in such paintings as *Mob Victim (Meditation)* (1944) and *We Shall Overcome* (1988; commissioned by the *Washington Post*), Jones's primary concern is to use her African and Western heritage to create original works on African, Haitian, American and European themes in which women often play a prominent role. Her superb technique and imaginative juxtapositions, especially in her Haitian and African works, show an artist creatively combining new themes and styles in a vision sensitive to the unique aspects of place, persons and culture on an international scale.

ALICIA CRAIG FAXON

Jopling, Louise
British painter, 1843–1933

Born Louise Goode in Manchester, 16 November 1843; father a railway contractor. Married (1) civil servant Frank Romer, 1861; three children; separated from husband, 1871; he died 1873; (2) watercolour painter Joseph Middleton Jopling, 1874; one son; husband died 1884; (3) lawyer G.W. Rowe, 1887. Entered State Technical School and studied in Charles Chaplin's studio, Paris, 1867. Settled in London, attending Leigh's School of Art, Newman Street, 1869; spent a brief period in Paris, 1871. Set up an art school in Clareville Grove, London, to train women as professional artists, 1887. Published articles for *Punch* and wrote journalism, poems and stories. Member, Society of Women Artists; Pastel Society; Women's International Art Club; founder-member, Society of Portrait Painters, 1891; first woman member, Royal Society of British Artists, 1902; founder and president, Society of the Immortals. Died in Amersham, Buckinghamshire, 19 November 1933.

Principal Exhibitions

Paris Salon: 1869
Royal Academy, London: occasionally 1870–1916
Centennial Exposition, Philadelphia: 1876
Royal Hibernian Academy, Dublin: occasionally 1876–1905
Grosvenor Gallery, London: 1877–90
Exposition Universelle, Paris: 1878, 1889
Lyceum Club, London: 1906 (individual)

Selected Writings

Hints to Amateurs: A Handbook on Art, London: Chapman and Hall, 1891; as *Hints to Students and Amateurs*, London: Rowney, 1911; abridged as *Hints and Tips*, London: Artist Publishing, 1953
(as Louise Jopling Rowe) *Poems*, London: Elkin Mathews, 1913
(as Louise Jopling Rowe) *The Tête à Tête Bridge*, London: Lamley, 1916
Twenty Years of My Life, 1867–87, London: Lane, and New York: Dodd Mead, 1925

Bibliography

Ellen C. Clayton, *English Female Artists*, 2 vols, London: Tinsley, 1876
Clara Erskine Clement and Laurence Hutton, *Artists of the Nineteenth Century*, 2 vols, Boston: Houghton Osgood, 1879; reprinted New York: Arno Press, 1969
Wilfrid Meynell, *Some Modern Artists and Their Works*, London, Paris and New York, 1883
"Chronicle", *Magazine of Art*, March 1891, p.xxiii
Royal Academy Pictures, London, 1891, p.98; 1892, p.136; 1894, p.72; 1896, p.158; 1897; 1902, p.3
Tessa MacKenzie, *The Art Schools of London*, London, 1895
Alfred Lys Baldry, "Private schools of art: No.1, the schools of Mr W.J. Donne and Mrs Jopling-Rowe", *The Studio*, vii, 1896, pp.40–46
A Record of Art in 1898, London: Studio, 1898, p.66
John Guille Millais, *The Life and Letters of Sir John Everett Millais*, 2 vols, London: Methuen, and New York: Stokes, 1899
Clara Erskine Clement, *Women in the Fine Arts*, Cambridge, MA: Houghton Mifflin, 1904; reprinted New York: Hacker, 1974
Walter Shaw Sparrow, *Women Painters of the World*, London: Hodder and Stoughton, and New York: Stokes, 1905; reprinted New York: Hacker, 1976

Windsor Magazine, xxiv, June–November 1906 (photograph of Jopling at work)

Jeremy Maas, *The Victorian Art World in Photographs*, London: Barrie and Jenkins, 1984 (photograph of Jopling, p.62)

Pamela Gerrish Nunn, *Canvassing: Recollections by Six Victorian Women Artists*, London: Camden, 1986

——, *Victorian Women Artists*, London: Women's Press, 1987

Paula Gillett, *The Victorian Painter's World*, Gloucester: Sutton, 1990

Deborah Cherry, *Painting Women: Victorian Women Artists*, London and New York: Routledge, 1993

Wendy Slatkin, *The Voices of Women Artists*, Englewood Cliffs, NJ: Prentice Hall, 1993

Gordon Millais, *Louise Jopling* (in preparation)

Louise Jopling began studying art in Paris in 1867, encouraged by Baroness de Rothschild. Despite being "heavily handicapped ... by [her] duties of wife and mother", Jopling, then Mrs Romer, studied anatomy and attended Charles Chaplin's classes for women and nude life classes, where the emphasis was on drawing. She continued her training in London when the family settled there. Deploring the exclusion of women from the nude classes of the Royal Academy – "it is no shock to a girl student to study from life" (*Twenty Years of My Life* 1925, p.6) – she attended Leigh's School of Art instead.

A woman of charm and wit, Jopling led a fashionable life in literary and artistic circles in London, with friends including Frith, Val Prinsep, Pettie, du Maurier, Leighton and Kate Perugini. She wrote poetry as well as short stories, and designed initials for *Punch*, where her first published drawing, *A Sketch from Nursery History*, appeared on 13 March 1869 (signed L.R.). In 1871 she separated from her husband, a compulsive gambler. Determined to achieve independence, she hired a studio and a nurse for the children. She spent a brief period in Paris, where she met Alfred Stevens and Jacques Tissot, whose glossy portraiture she admired. Ill health, however, as well as the death of her husband and of two of her children, inclined her to "pathetic subjects" (*ibid.*, p.43). Her launch into subject painting was particularly well received. Friends posed in Japanese robes for *Five O'Clock Tea* (exh. Royal Academy 1874; *ibid.*, p.92), which was bought by Agnew's and brought her to "the very front rank of women artists" (*Art Journal*, 1874, p.199).

In 1874 she married Joseph Jopling, a watercolour painter. As an artist he was less successful than his wife, but he was Superintendent of the Fine Arts for the Philadelphia International Exhibition in 1876, to which she sent *Five Sisters of York*, based on Charles Dickens's novel *Nicholas Nickleby*. In 1876 her painting *Lorraine*, exhibited at the Royal Academy, was purchased by the Art Union. From 1877 she exhibited at the Grosvenor Gallery at the invitation of Sir Coutts Lindsay. Joe Jopling introduced his wife to Whistler, who painted her in 1877 (*Harmony in Flesh Colour and Black*, Hunterian Art Gallery, University of Glasgow, repr. Andrew McLaren Young and others, *The Paintings of James McNeill Whistler*, New Haven: Yale University Press, 1980, no.191). Her chief mentor, John Everett Millais, painted a striking portrait of her in 1879 (National Portrait Gallery, London).

Jopling's paintings included some landscapes, but her main area of expertise was portraiture. Family and friends modelled for sentimental portraits, which were well received. The need to customise her work for the market led her to produce "disguised" portraits with emotive titles, such as her self-portrait exhibited as *Bud and Bloom* (exh. Royal Academy 1870; Manchester City Art Gallery, repr. *Twenty Years of My Life* 1925, p.16) and a charming profile head in the classical mode popularised by Leighton, called *Phyllis* (1883; Rothesay Museum). She excelled in oil portraits of well-dressed women, such as *Mrs Cockell* and *Mrs Alexander* (*ibid.*, opposite pp.136 and 212), and emphasised the importance of unifying background and figure. "If done quickly, a portrait has more truth and life in it, because the effect of the whole has never been lost sight of", she said. Her brushwork was careful, sometimes enlivened by broader, sketchy areas, but always controlled.

Jopling worked extensively in pastel, which suited her delicate touch and appreciation of subtle colour harmonies. She rarely drew men, and her chalk portrait of *Samuel Smiles* (National Portrait Gallery, London) is superficial compared to the rapport evident in her portraits of intelligent and fashionable women, such as the journalist *Mabel Collins* (1886; *ibid.*, opposite p.278), who formed her chief clientele. Among her few prints was an etching of *Walter Sickert* (*ibid.*, opposite p.226) and a boldly competent lithograph, *Study of Head* (1892–5; Victoria and Albert Museum, London), printed and probably inspired by Frederick Goulding.

An exotic air was given to some of Jopling's models by the use of fabrics and accessories, for example *A Spanish Beauty* (Christie's, London, 3 November 1989, lot 130), *An Indian Princess* and *Far-away Heart* (repr. *Twenty Years of My Life* 1925, opposite pp.250 and 142). Blue and white oriental porcelain surrounds two female figures in *Home Bright, Hearth Light* (1896; see illustration); the stiff poses and uncertain perspective do not obscure the decorative charm of this tribute to Whistler and the Pre-Raphaelites. A theatrical costume provides the interest in *St Bride* (exh. Royal Academy 1902; *ibid.*, opposite p.204). Her theatrical portraits included *Ellen Terry as Portia* (exh. Grosvenor Gallery 1883, Royal Glasgow Institute 1885; repr. Clement 1904, p.176), which was bought by Sir Henry Irving for the Alhambra Theatre. "It is a great help to an artist to paint a celebrity", she commented, "The picture is certain of being talked about, either in praise or the reverse" (*Twenty Years of My Life* 1925, p.232). The technical skill of her later works is sometimes marred by a cloying sweetness, although an attempt at social comment, *Song of the Shirt* (*ibid.*, opposite p.310), was not overly sentimentalised.

Frustrated by the constraints of her sex ("Painting is so difficult, it discourages me dreadfully – besides I hate being a woman. Women never do anything", letter to Joe Jopling in *ibid.*, p.64), Jopling began teaching and giving demonstrations. In 1887 she set up an art school to train women as professional artists. "Every girl should have a vocation", she wrote. Students drew and painted from nature – nude and clothed models – studied perspective and anatomy from models and casts, and modelled in clay. They visited the National Gallery, the countryside and even the zoo (see the competent drawings of a lion and a girl, each with a mane, by two pupils, Miss Austin and Lady Alix Egerton, in Baldry 1896, pp.44–5). Jopling was assisted at first by the draughtsman Dudley Hardy and later by four teachers. Annual fees by 1895 were £31.10.0. "I found teaching intensely interesting. I learned so much myself", she wrote (*Twenty Years of My Life* 1925, p.307; photographs of the school, pp.267 and 309). Her *Hints to*

Jopling: *Home Bright, Hearth Light*, 1896; Lady Lever Art Gallery, Port Sunlight, Merseyside

Amateurs (1891) outlines basic techniques and materials in drawing, painting, photography, modelling, anatomy, colour and perspective: "Perspective is to the draughtsman what grammar is to the writer". She encouraged students to develop their visual memory, to work fast and "never patch it up".

Jopling was the first woman to be elected a member of the Royal Society of British Artists, and she asserted her right to vote, despite opposition, at the Society of Portrait Painters: "There is no sex in art" (*Twenty Years of My Life* 1925, p.307). She supported the National Union of Women's Suffrage and signed the *Declaration in Favour of Women's Suffrage* in 1889. "What I know I chiefly learned alone. Hard work and the genius that comes from infinite pains, the eye to see nature, the heart to feel nature – these are the best qualifications for the artist who would succeed" (Jopling, quoted in Clement 1904, p.177).

MARGARET F. MACDONALD

Jürgens, Grethe

German painter, illustrator and graphic artist, 1899–1981

Born in Holzhausen, near Osnabrück, 15 February 1899; grew up in Wilhelmshaven. Studied interior design for one semester at the Technische Hochschule (Technical High School), Berlin, until its forced closure during the November Revolution in 1918; returned to Wilhelmshaven. Studied graphics under Fritz Burger-Mühlfeld at the Hannover Handwerker- und Kunstgewerbeschule, Hannover, 1919–22. Associated with artists of the Hannover Neue Sachlichkeit group. Began to practise art professionally, 1928. Member of GEDOK (Gemeinschaft Deutscher und Österreichischer Künstlerinnen) from 1928. Forbidden to exhibit by the National Socialists, 1938. Died in Hannover, 8 May 1981.

Principal Exhibitions

Individual
Galerie Abels, Cologne: 1933
GEDOK, Hannover: 1935
Wilhelm-Busch Museum, Hannover: 1951 (retrospective)

Group
GEDOK, Hannover: from 1929
Grosse Kunstausstellung, Hannover: 1929, 1931
Herzog Anton Ulrich Museum, Braunschweig: 1932 (*Die Neue Sachlichkeit in Hannover*)
Grosse Frühjahrsausstellung, Hannover: 1933–7
Kunstverein Hannover: 1962 (*Die zwanziger Jahre in Hannover*), 1974 (*Neue Sachlichkeit in Hannover*)
Kunst- und Museumsverein, Wuppertal: 1967 (*Magischer Realismus in Deutschland, 1920–1933*)
Galerie Hasenclever, Munich: 1973, 1976 (*Realismus der zwanziger Jahre*)
Hayward Gallery, London: 1978 (*Neue Sachlichkeit and German Realism of the Twenties*)

Selected Writings
"Eine Stimme der Maler", *Der Wachsbogen*, i, November 1931, p.5
"Rezepte zum erspriesslichen Besuch einer Kunstausstellung", *Der Wachsbogen*, no.5–6, January 1932, pp.8–10
Das Atelier, 1944

Bibliography

Die zwanziger Jahre in Hannover, exh. cat., Kunstverein Hannover, 1962
Wieland Schmied, *Neue Sachlichkeit und Magischer Realismus in Deutschland, 1918–1933*, Hannover: Fackeltrager, 1969
Christa Sobe, "Sicherheit und Gleichmass nicht gefragt: Besuch bei Grethe Jürgens", *Hannoversche Allgemeine Zeitung*, 4 May 1972, p.13
Neue Sachlichkeit in Hannover, exh. cat., Kunstverein Hannover, 1974
Realismus und Sachlichkeit: Aspekte deutscher Kunst, exh. cat., Nationalgalerie (Ost), Staatliche Museen zu Berlin, 1974
Ursula Horn, "Zum Schaffen einer progressiven Künstlergruppe der zwanziger Jahre in Hannover", *Bildende Kunst*, xxiii, 1975, pp.172–6
Neue Sachlichkeit: 12 Maler zwischen den Kriegen, exh. cat., Galerie von Abercron, Cologne, 1975
Harald Seiler, *Grethe Jürgens*, Göttingen: Musterschmidt, 1976
Künstlerinnen international, 1877–1977, exh. cat., Schloss Charlottenburg, Berlin, 1977
Der Realismus der Zwanziger Jahre, exh. cat., Niedersächsische Landesgalerie, Hannover, 1977
Wem gehört die Welt: Kunst und Gesellschaft in der Weimarer Republik, exh. cat., Staatliche Kunsthalle, Berlin, 1977
L'altra metà dell'avanguardia, 1910–1940: Pittrici e scultrici nei movimenti delle avanguardie storiche, exh. cat., Palazzo Reale, Milan, and elsewhere, 1980
Grethe Jürgens, Gerta Overbeck: Bilder der zwanziger Jahre, exh. cat., Bonner Kunstverein, Bonn, 1982
Domesticity and Dissent: The Role of Women Artists in Germany, 1918–1938, exh. cat., Leicester Museum and Art Gallery, and elsewhere, 1992
Marsha Meskimmon, *Women Artists and the Neue Sachlichkeit: Grethe Jürgens and Gerta Overbeck*, PhD dissertation, Leicester University, 1992
Marsha Meskimmon and Shearer West, eds, *Visions of the "Neue Frau": Women and the Visual Arts in Weimar Germany*, Aldershot: Scolar Press, 1995
Marsha Meskimmon, *The Art of Reflection: Women Artists' Self-Portraiture in the Twentieth Century*, London: Scarlet Press, and New York: Columbia University Press, 1996

Grethe Jürgens's career spanned nearly six decades, but she is best known for her realist paintings from the 1920s and 1930s when she was associated with the Neue Sachlichkeit (New Objectivity) in Hannover. At that time, her works were characteristically sober and figurative, concentrated on working-class subjects and local themes. In the 1950s Jürgens changed from the realist style with which she had become associated before World War II and began to produce abstract pieces. Additionally, she produced a number of illustrated books.

Jürgens was brought up in Wilhelmshaven, began her art education in Berlin (1918), but finally went to Hannover in 1919 to study in the graphics class of Fritz Burger-Mühlfeld at the Hannover Handwerker- und Kunstgewerbeschule. This was to begin her lifelong association with the city, which she left only for short holidays before her death. Hannover's working-class districts and art politics were critical to the work of Jürgens. Many of her works, including the *Textile Workers* (1932), *Flower Seller* (1931), *Labour Exchange* (1929; see illustration; all Sprengel Museum, Hannover) and her self-portraits of 1932 and 1944, show recognisable districts in the city. More significantly, by associating herself with the Neue Sachlichkeit and representing these local scenes, Jürgens placed

Jürgens: *Labour Exchange*, 1929; oil on canvas; 66 × 50 cm.; Sprengel Museum, Hannover

herself in opposition to the middle-class art patrons of the city who favoured international versions of abstraction.

Within the Hannoverian art scene of the 1920s and 1930s, the young realist painters of the Neue Sachlichkeit (who included Hans Mertens, Ernst Thoms, Erich Wegner and Gerta Overbeck, q.v.) were relatively marginal figures, who were considered neither modern nor fashionable. Their representations of Hannover's poor and unemployed, banal street scenes and domestic interiors of the Liststadt (the working-class district of Hannover in which they set up their attic studios) remained outside the patronage of such avant-garde Hannoverian institutions as the Kestner-Gesellschaft. Thus the group developed anti-bourgeois cultural politics, summed up by Jürgens's assessment of the group as vulgar painters who simply worked very hard. They remained aloof from high theory and maintained their associations with art practice as work; their paradigm was the artist as a worker who produced representations that were accessible and relevant to the people.

In this context Jürgens's works are particularly interesting. As a young working woman in the period, she represented aspects of women's lives and occupations more often ignored in the works of her male contemporaries. For example, in the *Labour Exchange* the artist represented the controversial scene of the long dole queue that would have been an embarrassment to the city's establishment. In addition, the variety of unemployed workers included both a woman with a perambulator and a back view of the artist walking away. The young, single women and the married mothers who formed such a significant part of the labour market are shown here, rather than left unrepresented as was more commonly the case. Furthermore, in such works as the *Flower Seller*, Jürgens placed the labour of women into the context of the control of production and consumption. In this work the artist set the figure of the young woman with her basket of flowers in front of the greenhouses of the Bahlsen Gardens. By insisting on this clever juxtaposition, Jürgens removed the romantic overtones of the flower seller on the street and located her labour precisely in a set of relationships between wealthy capitalists and their exploited workers.

Jürgens's situation as a woman artist integrally placed within the Neue Sachlichkeit group in Hannover was unique. Besides her obvious anti-bourgeois politics, from 1928 Jürgens was also a member of the Hannover branch of GEDOK, a fact that clearly indicates her own awareness of the difficulties facing women who chose to practise professionally in the period. Her focus on women workers and her self-portraits from the period are critical comments on the realities behind the myths of the *neue Frau* (New Woman). In her *Self-Portrait* of 1928 (private collection, repr. Leicester 1992), for example, Jürgens painted herself in the unflinchingly sober style with which she was associated, but also played with the androgyny of her figure in ways that query the assumption of a masculine, professional role by a woman. In her small illustrated volume of 1944, *Das Atelier*, she further explored the difficulties facing someone who attempted to combine their roles as both "woman" and "artist" in the period into a meaningful union. The book described her studio space (which was, significantly, simultaneously domestic and professional) and the ways in which she was marginalised by critics and institutions. Moreover, she also considered in the text the ways in which she would have been seen as inadequate in terms of fulfilling a domestic role.

In the years after World War II Jürgens moved away from the realism of the Neue Sachlichkeit and towards abstraction because she was afraid that her realist works might be confused, stylistically, with the art of the Nazis. Throughout the 1950s and 1960s she illustrated a variety of books, both by other authors and herself. A number of these were children's books (*Der Wechselbalg*, 1947; *Omkbr-geschichte eines freunden Sterns*, 1955–9). Her later work differs from her work in the Weimar Republic more than just stylistically; the later work is lighter in its themes, as the lyrical and amusing children's books reveal. This shift marks the double path Jürgens's career took over the course of her life and, like so many other German artists of this time, the change in direction came with the traumas of the Third Reich and the tragedy of World War II.

MARSHA MESKIMMON

K

Kahlo, Frida
Mexican painter, 1907–1954

Born in Coyoacán, a suburb of Mexico City, 6 July 1907. Permanently injured after a streetcar accident, 1925; taught herself to paint during convalescence. Joined Young Communist League, 1927. Married mural painter Diego Rivera, 1929; divorced 1939; remarried 1940. With Rivera travelled to USA, living in San Francisco, Detroit and New York, 1930–33. Met André Breton in Mexico, 1938. Trip to New York, 1938; to Paris, 1939. Appointed painting professor, La Esmeralda, the Education Ministry's School of Painting and Sculpture, 1943. Began diary, charting her physical decline, c.1945. Recipient of National Prize of Arts and Sciences, Education Ministry, Mexico, 1946. Hospitalised for several months after a spine operation, 1950; gangrenous right leg amputated, 1953. Died in the Casa Azul, Coyoacán, 13 July 1954.

Principal Exhibitions
Julien Levy Gallery, New York: 1938 (individual)
Galerie Renau et Colle, Paris: 1939 (*Mexique*)
Galería de Arte Mexicano, Mexico City: 1940 (*Exposición internacional del surrealismo*, touring)
Galería de Arte Contemporáneo, Mexico City: 1953 (individual)

Selected Writings
"Portrait of Diego", *Calyx*, v/2–3, October 1980, pp.93–107 (Spanish original in *Hoy*, xxii, January 1949)
The Diary of Frida Kahlo: An Intimate Self-Portrait, ed. Carlos Fuentes and Sarah M. Lowe, New York: Abrams, 1995

Bibliography
Bertram D. Wolfe, "Rise of another Rivera", *Vogue*, xcii, October–November 1938, pp.64, 131
W[alter] P[ach], "Frida Rivera: Gifted canvases by an unselfconscious Surrealist", *Art News*, xxxvii, 12 November 1938, p.13
Frida Kahlo: Exposición nacional de homenaje, exh. cat., Palacio de Bellas Artes, Mexico City, 1977
Raquel Tibol, *Frida Kahlo: Crónica, Testimonios y Aproximaciones*, Mexico City: Ediciones de Cultura Popular, 1977
Frida Kahlo and Tina Modotti, exh. cat., Whitechapel Art Gallery, London, and elsewhere, 1982
Rupert Garcia, *Frida Kahlo: A Bibliography*, Berkeley: University of California Chicano Studies Library Publications Unit, 1983
Hayden Herrera, *Frida: A Biography of Frida Kahlo*, New York: Harper, 1983; London: Bloomsbury, 1989
Terry Smith, "From the margins: Modernity and the case of Frida Kahlo", *Block*, no.8, 1983, pp.11–23
—, "Further thoughts on Frida Kahlo", *Block*, no.9, 1983, pp.34–7
Susan B. Laufer, "Kahlo's gaze", *Poetics Journal*, iv, May 1984, pp.124–9
Whitney Chadwick, *Women Artists and the Surrealist Movement*, Boston: Little Brown, and London: Thames and Hudson, 1985
Helga Prignitz-Poda, Salomón Grimberg and Andrea Kettenmann, eds, *Frida Kahlo: Das Gesamtwerk*, Frankfurt: Neue Kritik, 1988
The Art of Frida Kahlo, exh. cat., Art Gallery of South Australia, Adelaide, and elsewhere, 1990
Joan Borsa, "Frida Kahlo: Marginalization and the critical female subject", *Third Text*, no.12, 1990, pp.21–40
Martha Zamora, *Frida Kahlo: The Brush of Anguish*, San Francisco: Chronicle, 1990 (Spanish original, 1987)
Janice Helland, "Aztec imagery in Frida Kahlo's paintings: Indigenity and political commitment", *Woman's Art Journal*, xi/2, 1990–91, pp.8–13
Oriana Baddeley, "'Her dress hangs here': De-frocking the Kahlo cult", *Oxford Art Journal*, xiv, 1991, pp.10–17
Hayden Herrera, *Frida Kahlo: The Paintings*, New York: HarperCollins, and London: Bloomsbury, 1991
Sarah M. Lowe, *Frida Kahlo*, New York: Universe, 1991
Janice Helland, "Frida Kahlo: The politics of confession", *Latin American Art*, iii, December 1991, pp.31–4
Edward J. Sullivan, "Frida Kahlo", *ibid.*, pp.34–6
David Lomas, "Body languages: Kahlo and medical imagery", *Body Imaged: The Human Form and Visual Culture since the Renaissance*, ed. Marcia Pointon and Kathleen Adler, Cambridge and New York: Cambridge University Press, 1993, pp.5–19, 191–2
Raquel Tibol, *Frida Kahlo: An Open Life*, Albuquerque: University of New Mexico Press, 1993 (Spanish original, 1983)
Paula M. Cooey, *Religious Imagination and the Body: A Feminist Analysis*, New York: Oxford University Press, 1994
Renée Riese Hubert, *Magnifying Mirrors: Women, Surrealism and Partnership*, Lincoln: University of Nebraska Press, 1994

Frida Kahlo's career spanned less than three decades, from 1926 when she painted *Self-Portrait Wearing a Velvet Dress*, until 1954, the year of her death and the date of *Marxism will Heal the Sick*. She produced about 130 paintings, some 30 drawings and a handful of watercolours; she made around 30 portraits and as many still-life paintings. The balance of her oeuvre is marked by a preponderance of images in which she appears – either in formal, bust-length self-portraits or larger, tableau images. Kahlo is primarily remembered for her obsessive rendering of herself, a preoccupation that achieved worldwide recognition decades after her death. The feminist

Kahlo: *Self-Portrait with Thorn Necklace and Hummingbird*, 1940; Harry Ransom Humanities Research Center, University of Texas at Austin

movement of the 1980s was largely responsible for her sudden burst on to an international scene, specifically, the publication of her biography (Herrera 1989).

Kahlo worked in the years following the Mexican Revolution, a period of cultural renaissance when the visual arts were in ascendancy, enlisted as a tool in the government's massive social reforms. Thus although Kahlo's paintings are seen as highly personal, in part because the literature on Kahlo focuses on her dramatic and traumatic life, her work resonates with international and national artistic concerns and styles of the time. She was skilled at fusing an astounding variety of visual forms – many of them Mexican in origin – with her own symbolism, and her oeuvre establishes her as an inventive and effective artist.

Kahlo encouraged the perception that she was *sui generis*, a notion strengthened by her naive painting style. She had limited artistic training, beginning in the studio of her father Guillermo Kahlo, a successful photographer, who taught her the painstaking technique of touching up hand-coloured photographs. One characteristic of her own work are tiny, indivisible brush strokes. Kahlo attended the prestigious National Preparatory School in Mexico City from 1922 until 1925, following a course of study that would have led to a medical career. There she took two required art classes: two-dimensional drawing and three-dimensional clay modelling. During the first half of 1925 Kahlo studied drawing with Fernando Fernández, a commercial engraver, who had her copy reproductions of etchings by Anders Zorn, nudes and portraits of *fin-de-siècle* intellectuals. She performed the task easily with free-hand replication. A number of watercolours from the 1920s indicate Kahlo's innate ability for verisimilitude, and she considered using this aptitude for a profession in scientific illustration.

Later, after they married in 1929, Kahlo's husband, Diego Rivera, was an influence on her art-making. He was a passionate, dedicated and driven artist. Rivera was a prominent player in Mexico's mural movement and a proponent of using Mexican culture and history as both source and subject in his art, and Kahlo saw him as a painter of his time and of his country. She followed his example of rejecting European abstraction and adapting a descriptive realism, although she favoured the intimate rather than the large-scale style that was the hallmark of muralism. Both artists turned to Mexico's rich artistic heritage as a visual resource. Kahlo followed a road independent of Rivera, however; whereas he peopled his frescoes with anonymous masses who symbolised the material condition of "humanity", Kahlo concentrated on images of herself, which transcend her personal story and speak of the emotional and spiritual aspects of the human condition.

Kahlo's focus on her own body and the vivid, sometimes gruesome imagery of many of her self-portraits are understandable in the light of a series of physical misfortunes she endured. She contracted polio as a child, and in 1925 nearly died in a horrendous traffic accident. By her own count, she underwent at least 22 operations (some therapeutic abortions). Her inability to bear a child was a continual torment to her, and a leitmotif in her work. In her unremitting preoccupation with her body and "selves", Kahlo undertook to position herself at various levels of being, exploring her condition as Mexican, as woman and as artist.

Kahlo's earliest works were self-portraits and portraits of friends, in which the figures are presented in a shallow space, sometimes with a token signifying an interest of theirs. These works are reminiscent of Italian Renaissance portraiture, a source evident in Kahlo's first painting, *Self-Portrait Wearing a Velvet Dress* (1926; private collection, repr. Herrera 1991, p.43), which is modelled after a work by the 16th-century Mannerist painter Bronzino. A year after her marriage, Kahlo travelled with Rivera to the USA where they lived in San Francisco, Detroit and New York. They moved in art circles and Kahlo met a number of artists, among them Edward Weston, Imogen Cunningham (q.v.), Georgia O'Keeffe (q.v.) and Louise Nevelson (q.v.), and had the opportunity to visit a great many museums. Her reaction to America, which she called "Gringolandia", was largely negative and fuelled her already heightened nationalism.

Following a miscarriage in 1932, Kahlo painted *Henry Ford Hospital* (1932; Fundación Dolores Olmedo, Mexico), a painting that marks the beginning of the style and content she would develop over the next 20 years. Here she fuses her own experience with a formal construction based on the specifically Mexican conventions found in the tiny ex-voto paintings done on tin. Kahlo made use of an extensive variety of visual references, culled from a myriad of sources. In particular, art forms distinctive to Mexico are expressly evident in much of her work, and add a powerful dimension to her autobiographical oeuvre. Elements of Aztec culture are conspicuous in a number of paintings, for example, *My Nurse and I* (1937; Fundación Dolores Olmedo). Kahlo paints the face of her wet nurse as a mask resembling the stone heads from Pre-Columbian Teotihuacán culture, while the figure itself is copied from a Jalisco funerary figure of a nursing mother in Kahlo's collection (Helland 1990–91). Kahlo thus makes visible her Mexican ancestry.

Kahlo's self-conscious disregard of traditional rules of academic painting, especially of linear perspective, allies her with a number of visual traditions in Mexico. She admired the provincial painters of Mexico's colonial period, such as José María Estrada, José Agustín Arrieta and Hermenegildo Bustos. Child mortuary portraiture, for example, was a genre that provided income to itinerant artists, and is the macabre subject matter of the *Deceased Dimas* (1937; Fundación Dolores Olmedo). Kahlo's hyper-realist approach gives the image a somewhat surreal appearance, but the subject itself was also taken up by her contemporaries, among them David Alfaro Siqueiros, María Izquierdo (q.v.) and Juan Soriano.

Another source of inspiration for Kahlo was the work of the turn-of-the-century printmaker José Guadalupe Posada, whose political prints were peopled by *calaveras* (skeletons), the ever-present Mexican symbol of death. Many of Kahlo's paintings share with his prints the mingling of the grotesque with the ordinary, as, for example, Kahlo's *A Few Small Nips* (1935; Fundación Dolores Olmedo). The muralists also championed Posada as a home-grown source who developed independent of European influence.

Kahlo consciously emulated the style of unschooled retablo or ex-voto painters. She collected hundreds of these tiny images rendered to commemorate some divine intervention in the lives of individuals who, having experienced a miraculous recovery from an accident or illness, would commission a local artist to execute a votive offering. The coexistence of fact and fantasy – the journalistic verity of the incident with the patron saint's intercession – is a prominent feature of many of Kahlo's paintings, for example, *Henry Ford Hospital*. Kahlo found this blending of the visible and the invisible a useful means to express the physical manifestations of feelings and of sensation, a bio-psychological mapping that merges the scientific with the emotional. In *The Broken Column* (1944; Fundación Dolores Olmedo) Kahlo depicts her pain using X-ray vision, showing the viewer where she hurts, and underscoring her agony with pins as large as nails pricking her entire naked body.

In her visualisation of experience, the painting of feelings not otherwise articulable, Kahlo's approach resembles that of the Surrealist René Magritte. Kahlo has been linked to the Surrealist movement, in part because its leader André Breton championed her work. Breton and his wife, the painter Jacqueline Lamba, visited Mexico in 1938. Breton wrote an enthusiastic essay to accompany Kahlo's first one-person show, held at the Julien Levy Gallery in New York (English translation in London 1982, p.36), and then arranged for her to exhibit her work in Paris early the following year. Breton also had a hand in the organisation of the International Surrealist Exhibition in Mexico City in 1940, in which Kahlo showed her two largest canvases.

Kahlo travelled to New York in October 1938 to help organise her November show, and sailed for Europe in January, staying with the Bretons in Paris. There she met many of the Surrealists, all of whom, with the exception of Marcel Duchamp, she disdained. After her sojourn in Paris, Kahlo was ambivalent about being labelled a Surrealist, even though her work, in some respects, shares many of its aspects. While her paintings most resemble such imagists as Magritte and Salvador Dalí, Kahlo's diary demonstrates her use of automatic drawing, a method advocated in the Manifesto of Surrealism (1924). Its proponents – Max Ernst, André Masson and Joan Miró – relied on automatism, accident and biomorphism as means of expression (see *The Diary of Frida Kahlo* 1995). Kahlo's formal innovations, like her subject matter, sprang from Mexican sources, however, and not the intellectual constructions that motivated Breton and his circle.

During the 1940s Kahlo enjoyed a good deal of professional success. Her work was shown steadily in numerous exhibitions internationally and her signature self-portraits were much sought after. *Self-Portrait with Thorn Necklace and Hummingbird* (1940; see illustration) is an especially deft example of Kahlo's ability to merge various artistic sources. Here she draws from native sources and imported Catholic symbolism to create a truly syncretic image. The severe frontality of the pose casts the portrait as a secular icon, while her pets, a monkey and black cat, act as religious attributes. In Aztec belief, however, animals were thought to be alter egos for their owners. The necklace of thorns refers most obviously to Christ's crown, but the humming-bird, as well as the butterflies, are Aztec symbols.

In 1943 Kahlo was appointed a painting professor at the Education Ministry's La Esmeralda art school, where she was extremely popular. Four students with whom she worked especially closely – Fanny Rabel, Arturo García Bustos, Guillermo Monroy and Arturo Estrada – became known as "Los Fridos".

The decade was also one of personal loss and physical decline, and Kahlo charted the last years of her life in a diary she began in the mid-1940s, shortly after her father's death and her divorce and remarriage to Rivera. Over the next 12 years she endured numerous tests and medical procedures, including confinement in a series of 30 plaster and steel corsets and countless operations on her back and leg, as well as lengthy hospital stays.

As Kahlo's health deteriorated, her production of self-portraits subsided, and she began to make still lifes, a subject that had interested her since the 1930s. Between 1951 and 1954, the years immediately preceding her death, Kahlo painted 13 extremely disturbing works in this genre. There is a quality about these pictures that suggests Kahlo has replaced her obsession with her own visage with images of strange fruits, some deteriorating, and that this new preoccupation parallels her own disintegration. At the same time she both displaced her own image and anthropomorphised inanimate objects, as in *Looks – Still Life – Coconuts* (1951; Museo de Arte Moderna, Mexico City), where the coconut has tears rolling down its "face".

Kahlo's last work, *Marxism will Heal the Sick* (1954; Museo de Frida Kahlo, Mexico City), brings together several themes that are evident throughout her work. The image amounts to a political ex-voto, Marx functioning as the divine being, intervening to protect and strengthen her. Throughout her life Kahlo was politically active. She joined the Young Communist League in 1927; ten years later, she worked in support of Mexicans fighting on the side of the Spanish Loyalists during the Spanish Civil War; and she gave Leon Trotsky and his wife refuge in her home when the exiled leader found asylum in Mexico in 1938. Later, Kahlo disavowed her association with Trotsky, opting instead to put her faith in Marx and his dream of a political utopia, a deliverance depicted in this last painting.

SARAH M. LOWE

Käsebier, Gertrude
American photographer, 1852–1934

Born Gertrude Stanton in Fort Des Moines (now Des Moines), Iowa, 18 May 1852; grew up in Colorado; moved to Brooklyn, New York, 1864. Married Eduard Käsebier, a shellac importer from Germany, 1874; three children (one son, two daughters), born 1875, 1878 and 1880; husband died 1909. Studied at Pratt Institute, Brooklyn, 1889–96; taught photography by a priest, Father Wenzel, late 1880s. First visited Europe, 1894; studied under Frank Vincent Dumond at Crécy-en-Brie, near Paris, and at Académie Julian; apprenticed to a photographic chemist in Germany. Began career as commercial portrait photographer, 1896; opened first New York studio, winter 1897–8; new studio at 273 Fifth Avenue, 1899; students included Alice Austin and Alvin Langdon Coburn. Met Alfred Stieglitz, 1898. Joined Camera Club of New York, 1899; Alfred Stieglitz's Photo-Secession, 1902 (resigned 1912); Professional Photographers of New York, 1906. Co-founder, Women's Federation of the

Photographers' Association of America; taught women photographers under its auspices, 1909–10. Honorary vice president, Pictorial Photographers of America (PPA), 1915. Died in New York, 13 October 1934.

Principal Exhibitions

Individual

Boston Camera Club: 1896, 1900
Camera Club of New York: 1899 (organised by Alfred Stieglitz)
Little Galleries of the Photo-Secession, New York: 1906 (with Clarence H. White)
Brooklyn Institute of Arts and Sciences (now Brooklyn Museum), NY: 1929 (retrospective)

Group

Philadelphia Photographic Salon: 1898–1900
Exposition Universelle, Paris: 1900 (display of prints by American women photographers organised by Frances Benjamin Johnston; also shown in St Petersburg, Moscow and Photo-Club de Paris)
Royal Photographic Society, London: 1900–01 (*New School of American Photography*, touring, organised by F. Holland Day)
National Arts Club, New York: 1902 (*American Pictorial Photography Arranged by the Photo-Secession*)
International Photography Exhibition, Dresden: 1909
Albright Art Gallery (now Albright-Knox Art Gallery), Buffalo, NY: 1910 (*International Exhibition of Pictorial Photography*)

Selected Writings

"Studies in photography", *Photographic Times*, xxx, June 1898, pp.269–72; reprinted in *A Photographic Vision: Pictorial Photography, 1889–1923*, ed. Peter C. Bunnell, Salt Lake City: Peregrine Smith, 1980

Bibliography

Joseph T. Keiley, "Mrs Käsebier's prints", *Camera Notes*, iii, July 1899, p.34
"Some Indian portraits", *Everybody's Magazine*, iv, 1901, pp.3–24
Charles H. Caffin, "Mrs Käsebier and the artistic-commercial portrait", *Everybody's Magazine*, iv, 1901, pp.480–95; included in *Photography as Fine Art*, New York: Doubleday, 1901; reprinted Hastings-on-Hudson, NY: Morgan and Morgan, 1971, and New York: Amphoto, 1972
Frances Benjamin Johnston, "Gertrude Käsebier: Professional photographer", *Camera Work*, no.1, January 1903, p.20
Mary Fanton Roberts [Giles Edgerton], "Photography as an emotional art: A study of the work of Gertrude Käsebier", *Craftsman*, xii, April 1907, pp.80–93; reprinted in *Image*, xv, December 1972, pp.9–12
"Threescore years and sixteen is ardent exponent of photography", *New York Sun*, 5 January 1929, p.21; reprinted as "Gertrude Käsebier is interviewed", *Photo-Era*, lxii, March 1929, pp.129–30
A Pictorial Heritage: The Photographs of Gertrude Käsebier, exh. cat., Delaware Art Museum, Wilmington, and elsewhere, 1979
Barbara L. Michaels, *Gertrude Käsebier: The Photographer and Her Photographs*, New York: Abrams, 1992 (contains extensive bibliography)
Naomi Rosenblum, *A History of Women Photographers*, New York: Abbeville, 1994

Gertrude Käsebier's correspondence is in the Alfred Stieglitz Archive, Collection of American Literature, Beinecke Rare Book and Manuscript Library, Yale University, New Haven.

From the late 1890s until the 1920s Gertrude Käsebier was the pre-eminent woman among the international group of pictorial photographers who considered photography to be a fine art. Her portraits, as well as expressive scenes on themes of womanhood, motherhood and family life, inspired other photographers, including Edward Steichen and Imogen Cunningham (q.v.).

Around 1900 Käsebier's sensitive portraits helped her to reach the highest levels of the photographic world, both as a founding member of Alfred Stieglitz's Photo-Secession and as a commercial photographer on Fifth Avenue, New York. In taking likenesses of celebrities, including *Mark Twain*, *Booker T. Washington*, *Jacob Riis* (published in the magazine *World's Work*, 1900–01) and the French sculptor *Auguste Rodin* (1905; Musée Rodin, Paris), Käsebier endeavoured to capture each sitter's temperament or personality. By dispensing with the fancy backdrops and furnishings that conventional photographers considered *de rigueur*, Käsebier concentrated attention on the sitter. Her plain backgrounds are especially effective in the many portraits of Sioux men (1898–1901; Division of Photographic History, National Museum of American History, Smithsonian Institution, Washington, DC) who toured with Buffalo Bill's "Wild West" show. They posed in Käsebier's studio during several visits that Buffalo Bill's troupe made to New York. Most of the pictures show them in full regalia with feathered head-dresses, but Käsebier prized the few pictures in which she was able to show the men in simpler garb, as she remembered the Indians she had known during her childhood in Colorado.

The photographer's informal and conversational manner helped her to achieve the relaxed poses for which she was noted. In 1899 Alfred Stieglitz, the noted American photographer and tastemaker, called her "beyond dispute the leading portrait photographer in this country" (*Camera Notes*, July 1899, p.24). Käsebier's ideas about individualised portraiture came from her painting studies at Pratt Institute in Brooklyn, which she began after her son and two daughters were past primary school. She studied photography on her own and as a studio apprentice, adapting concepts of composition that she had learned from Arthur W. Dow and others during her years at Pratt.

Many of her portraits illustrate her friendships with other advanced photographers of her era, including *Fred Holland Day* (c.1900; Metropolitan Museum of Art, New York), *Alvin Langdon Coburn* (c.1902) and *Baron de Meyer* (1903; both International Museum of Photography at George Eastman House, Rochester, NY), *Edward Steichen* ([1901]) and *Alfred Stieglitz* (1902; both Museum of Modern Art, New York). Some of these pictures were taken out of doors, during holidays in Newport, Rhode Island, and in France. Even when working away from her studio, however, Käsebier tended to support her camera on a tripod and to use $6^{1}/_{2} \times 8^{1}/_{2}$-inch (16.5 × 21.5 cm.) glass plate negatives. Her prints were usually about that size or enlarged to about 9 × 12 inches (23 × 30cm.).

Two portraits of her colleague Clarence H. White and his family demonstrate Käsebier's skill at group portraiture, as well as her stylistic development. In the earlier portrait she depicted the Whites and their sons at home, in evenly lit shallow space (*Clarence H. White and Family*, 1908; print from negative of 1902; Metropolitan Museum of Art). *Sunshine in the House* (1913; Museum of Modern Art, New York) portrays the Whites in a furnished, sun-streaked room, using a composition typical of the deeper, light-accented

Käsebier: *"Blessed Art Thou Among Women"*, 1899;
platinum print; Metropolitan Museum of Art, New York,
Alfred Stieglitz Collection

formats that Käsebier adopted around 1909 in scenes of her
own family, including one of her daughter, *Gertrude Käsebier
O'Malley* (c.1909; J. Paul Getty Museum, Malibu), shown
playing billiards at the Käsebier home in Oceanside, Long
Island.

Beginning at the Philadelphia Photographic Salons in 1898
and 1899, Käsebier won acclaim for her tender representations
of motherhood, especially *The Manger* (1899; Museum of
Modern Art, New York) and *"Blessed Art Thou Among
Women"* (1899; see illustration), both of which Stieglitz reproduced in the first issue of *Camera Work* (January 1903), which
featured Käsebier's photographs. *"Blessed Art Thou Among
Women"* remains a prime example of Käsebier's imagery, as it
is an environmental portrait of her friend Agnes Lee, the poet
and author of children's books, as well as a memorable depiction of motherhood. The photograph's title derives from the
biblical inscription surrounding Selwyn Image's print of the

Annunciation hanging behind the figures. The photograph,
which was taken at the Lee home in Boston, stands for the Lee
family's dedication to both Christianity and the Arts and
Crafts movement. In *The Sketch* and *The Picture-Book* (both
1903; Metropolitan Museum of Art) Käsebier alludes to
another friend's career as an artist and illustrator, by showing
Beatrice Baxter (Ruyl) drawing or helping Käsebier's grandson,
Charles O'Malley, to draw. On the other hand, in *Miss N.*
([1902]; National Gallery of Canada, Ottawa) the photographer portrayed the well-known model and showgirl, Evelyn
Nesbit, as a temptress in an off-the-shoulder gown.

Although Käsebier played down the importance of technique to her work, many of her platinum prints (her most
usual medium) are now considered exemplary for their velvety
quality and subtle tonalities. From around 1901 she also began
to use the gum-bichromate process to create pictures with a
more textured or painterly appearance. She often used whatever combination of media seemed to suit her expressive needs.
For instance, in two versions of the *Road to Rome*, a picture
of her three-year-old grandson, Charles O'Malley, approaching
a long, winding path, she painted over parts of a gelatin silver
print, re-photographed it on to a new glass plate negative and
made a gum-bichromate exhibition print from that negative
(both prints 1903; Art Museum, Princeton University). The
picture is a metaphor for a child's – and an artist's – imagination and creativity. Käsebier also used gum bichromate effectively to simulate the grainy intensity of charcoal in *Labor*
(c.1902), a scene of men shovelling, and in the poster-like landscape, *Bungalows* (c.1907; both Museum of Modern Art, New
York). Towards the end of her career (and as an aftermath to
her own unhappy marriage and the break-up of her daughter
Hermine Turner's marriage) she turned a country scene of a
boy and girl gazing at yoked oxen into an ironical commentary
on wedlock by darkening the original version with handwork,
printing the picture in gum bichromate and titling the
completed image *Yoked and Muzzled – Marriage* (1915 or
earlier; Library of Congress, Washington, DC).

Käsebier never became a modernist photographer, but the
landscapes she took during a visit to Newfoundland in 1912
(International Museum of Photography) show a responsiveness
to geometric forms that may have been influenced directly or
indirectly by Cubism. Although her work fell out of critical
favour during the period of high modernism, the revival of
interest in Käsebier's images since the 1970s confirms her belief
that: "The key to artistic photography is to work out your own
thoughts, by yourselves ... New ideas are always antagonized.
Do not mind that. If a thing is good it will survive" ("Studies
in photography", 1898).

BARBARA L. MICHAELS

Kauffman [Kauffmann], Angelica
Swiss painter, printmaker and designer, 1741–1807

Born in Chur (Coire), 30 October 1741, to Johann Josef
Kauffman, a painter from Bregenz, Austria, and his wife
Cleofa Lucin (d. 1757). Living with her family in Como,
north Italy, 1752; in Milan, 1754. Travelled with her father

to Modena and Parma, 1759. Elected member of Accademia Clementina, Bologna, and Accademia del Disegno, Florence, 1762. Moved to Rome, 1763; stayed in Naples, 1763–4; in Rome, 1764–5. Elected member of Accademia di San Luca, Rome, 1765. Travelled to England via Bologna, Venice and Paris, arriving in London in June 1766. Married an impostor, the "Count de Horn", 1767; marriage annulled 1768. Founder-member of Royal Academy, London, 1768. Began collaborating with printmaker W.W. Ryland, 1770. Spent six months in Ireland, 1771. Married painter Antonio Zucchi, 1781; he died 1795. Left England for Italy, 1781. Settled in Rome, 1782; toured Italy, 1805. Died in Rome, 5 November 1807; buried in Sant'Andrea delle Fratte.

Principal Exhibitions

Free Society of Artists, London: 1765–6, 1783
Society of Artists of Great Britain, London: 1768 (special exhibition for King Christian VII of Denmark)
Royal Academy, London: 1769–82, 1786, 1788, 1791, 1796–7

Bibliography

Giovanni Gherardo De Rossi, *Vita di Angelica Kauffmann, pittrice*, Florence: Molini Landi, 1810; reprinted London: Cornmarket, 1970

Frances A. Gerard, *Angelica Kauffmann: A Biography*, London: Ward and Downey, and New York: Macmillan, 1893

Lady Victoria Manners and G.C. Williamson, *Angelica Kauffmann RA: Her Life and Her Works*, London: Bodley Head, 1924; reprinted New York: Hacker, 1976

Adeline Hartcup, *Angelica: The Portrait of an Eighteenth-Century Artist*, London: Heinemann, 1954

Eugen Thurnher, *Angelika Kauffmann und die deutsche Dichtung*, Bregenz: Vorarlberger, 1966

Claudia Helbok, *Miss Angel: Angelika Kauffmann: Eine Biographie*, Vienna: Rosenbaum, 1968

Angelika Kauffmann und ihr Zeitgenossen, exh. cat., Vorarlberger Landesmuseum, Bregenz, and elsewhere, 1968

Peter Walch, *Angelica Kauffmann*, Ph.D. dissertation, Princeton University, 1969

Women Artists, 1550–1950, exh. cat., Los Angeles County Museum of Art, and elsewhere, 1976

Peter Walch, "An early Neoclassical sketchbook by Angelica Kauffman", *Burlington Magazine*, cxix, 1977, pp.98–111

Angelika Kauffmann und ihre Zeit: Graphik und Zeichnungen von 1760–1810, exh. cat., C.G. Boerner, Düsseldorf, 1979

Arthur S. Marks, "Angelica Kauffman and some Americans on the Grand Tour", *American Art Journal*, xii/2, 1980, pp.5–24

Anthony Clark, "'Roma mi è sempre in pensiero'", *Studies in Roman Eighteenth-Century Painting*, ed. E.P. Bowron, Washington, DC: Decatur House Press, 1981, pp.125–38

Wendy Wassyng Roworth, "The gentle art of persuasion: Angelica Kauffman's *Praxiteles and Phryne*", *Art Bulletin*, lxv, 1983, pp.488–92

—, "Angelica Kauffman's 'Memorandum of Paintings'", *Burlington Magazine*, cxxvi, 1984, pp.629–30

Ellen Spickernagel, "'Helden wie zarte Knaben oder verkleidete Mädchen': Zum Begriff der Androgynität bei Johann Joachim Winckelmann und Angelika Kauffmann", *Frauen-Weiblichkeit-Schrift*, new series, xiv, ed. Renate Berger and others, Berlin: Argument, 1985, pp.99–118

Ellis Waterhouse, "Reynolds, Angelica Kauffmann and Lord Boringdon", *Apollo*, cxxii, 1985, pp.270–74

Sabine Hammer, *Angelica Kauffmann*, Vaduz: Haas, 1987

Wendy Wassyng Roworth, "Artist/model/patron in Antiquity: Interpreting Ansiaux's *Alexander, Apelles and Campaspe*", *Muse*, xxii, 1988, pp.92–106

—, "Biography, criticism, art history: Angelica Kauffman in context", *Eighteenth-Century Women and the Arts*, ed. Frederick M. Keener and Susan E. Lorsch, New York: Greenwood, 1988, pp.209–23

Bettina Baumgärtel, "Freeheit-Gleichheit-Schwesterkeit: Der Freundschaftskult der Malerin Angelika Kauffmann", *Sklavin oder Bürgerin Französische Revolution und Neue Weiblichkeit, 1760–1838*, exh. cat., Historisches Museum, Frankfurt am Main, 1989, pp.325–39

—, *Angelika Kauffmann (1741–1807): Bedingungen weiblicher Kreativität in der Malerei des 18. Jahrhunderts*, Weinheim and Basel, 1990

Angela Rosenthal, "Die Zeichnungen der Angelika Kauffmann im Vorarlberger Landesmuseum, Bregenz", *Jahrbuch der Vorarlberger Landesmuseumsvereins. 1990*, Bregenz, 1990, pp.139–81

Bettina Baumgärtel, "'Ich zeichne beständig …': Unbekannte Zeichnungen und Olskizzen von Angelika Kauffmann (1741–1807)", *Weltkunst*, no.19, 1991, pp.2832–4; no.22, 1991, pp.3542–4

Malise Forbes Adam and Mary Mauchline, "*Ut Pictura Poesis*: Angelica Kauffman's literary sources", *Apollo*, cxxxii, 1992, pp.345–9

Hommage au Angelika Kauffman, exh. cat., Liechtensteinische Staatliche Kunstsammlung, Vaduz, and Palazzo della Permanente, Milan, 1992

Angelika Kauffmann (1741–1807)/Marie Ellenrieder (1791–1863), exh. cat., Rosengartenmuseum, Konstanz, 1992

Angela Rosenthal, "Angelika Kauffman ma(s)king claims", *Art History*, xv, 1992, pp.38–59

Wendy Wassyng Roworth, ed., *Angelika Kauffman: A Continental Artist in Georgian England*, London: Reaktion, 1992

"… ihr werten Frauenzimmer, auf!": Malerinnen der Aufklärung", exh. cat., Roselius Haus, Bremen, 1993

Angela Rosenthal, "Double-writing in painting: Strategien der Selbstdarstellung von Künstlerinnen im 18. Jahrhundert", *Kritische Berichte: Zeitschrift für Kunst- und Kulturwissenschaften*, iii/3, 1993, pp.21–36

Wendy Wassyng Roworth, "Anatomy is destiny: Regarding the body in the art of Angelica Kauffman", *Femininity and Masculinity in Eighteenth-Century Art and Culture*, ed. Gill Perry and Michael Rossington, Manchester: Manchester University Press, 1994, pp.41–62

—, "Painting for profit and pleasure: Angelica Kauffman and the art business in Rome", *Eighteenth-Century Studies*, xxix, 1995–6, pp.225–8

Angela Rosenthal, *Angelika Kauffmann: Bildnismalerei im 18. Jahrhundert*, Berlin: Reimer, 1996

Throughout her life Angelica Kauffman enjoyed admiration for her considerable talents and acclaim for her professional accomplishments. This exceptionally prolific artist earned large sums of money from the sale of pictures, commissions and the reproduction of her compositions in a variety of media. These included etchings, engravings, book illustrations and designs for ceramics, fans, textiles and furniture. She painted fashionable oil portraits for a large international clientele and created a broad range of mythological, religious and literary paintings. Kauffman's delicate Neo-classical compositions were especially suitable for the interior designs of the architect Robert Adam, and while she provided drawings for some of his projects, recent research has shown that almost all the decorative compositions attributed to her were executed after her designs by copyists (Forbes Adam and Mauchline in Roworth 1992).

Kauffman's ability to please a varied audience from aristocratic patrons to such intellectuals as the German antiquarian

Johann Joachim Winckelmann (*Winckelmann*, 1764; Kunsthaus, Zürich), her friend during her early years in Rome, and the poet Johann Wolfgang von Goethe (*Goethe*, 1787; Goethe-Wohnhaus, Weimar), whom she met during his travels in Italy in the late 1780s, to the wider public taste for her decorative work secured her a place within the mainstream of artistic developments during the latter half of the 18th century. As a result of her extensive activities and critical acclaim, Kauffman stands out as one of the few female artists whose name never entirely disappeared from the history of art and design.

Kauffman first made her name as a portrait painter, but some of her most popular pictures were Classical allegories (*Beauty Directed by Prudence Rejects with Scorn the Solicitations of Folly* and *Cupid Bound by the Graces*, repr. Roworth 1992, pp.130 and 160) and versions of sentimental scenes from Shakespeare, Homer, Ovid and other literary sources such as *Rinaldo and Armida* (Iveagh Bequest, Kenwood) from Tasso's *Gerusalemme liberata*, *Poor Maria* (1777; Burghley House, Stamford) from Laurence Sterne's *Sentimental Journey* and Alexander Pope's *Eloisa to Abelard* (*c*.1778; Burghley House).

While Kauffman produced many types of art, she identified herself primarily as a history painter, an unusual designation for a woman artist in the 18th century when portraiture and flower painting were still considered more appropriate for women. History painting, as defined in academic art theory, was classified as the most elevated category. Its subject matter, the representation of human actions based on themes from history, mythology, literature and scripture, required extensive learning in biblical and Classical literature, knowledge of art theory and a practical training that included the study of anatomy from the male nude. Most women were denied access to such training, especially the opportunity to draw from nude models; yet Kauffman managed to cross the gender boundary to acquire the necessary skills to build a reputation as a successful history painter who was admired by colleagues and eagerly sought by patrons.

Several factors contributed to Kauffman's success. One was her arrival in England in 1766 shortly before the establishment of the Royal Academy of Arts. During the 1760s British artists had been trying to cultivate a public taste and potential patrons for historical and mythological subjects. Kauffman originally came to England because of the well-established market for portraits, but she also had experience as a history painter. That background, combined with a clever business sense and winning personality, paved the way for professional recognition. The fact that she was a woman probably helped, for she was less likely to be seen as a serious rival by British artists. Kauffman found a receptive public, admiring friends of both sexes and the support of influential figures among artists and patrons such as Joshua Reynolds, one of the strongest advocates for history painting, Lady Spencer and Lord Exeter, for whom she made a number of important pictures (*Cleopatra Adorning the Tomb of Mark Antony*, 1770; Burghley House).

Kauffman and Reynolds became close friends. Her engaging portrait of *Reynolds* (1767; National Trust, Saltram), made within a year of her arrival, was well received, and soon Kauffman was in great demand for portraits of men, women and children. One of her popular portrait types depicted aris-tocratic women dressed in pseudo-Turkish dress (*Mary, 3rd Duchess of Richmond*, 1775; Goodwood House, Sussex) and engaged in solitary domestic pursuits such as needlework. Other portraits from the 1770s include *John, Lord Althorp, with His Sisters* (1774; Spencer Collection, Althorp) and *Frances Anne Hoare with a Bust of Clio* (*c*.1770–75; National Trust, Stourhead). Kauffman's six months in Ireland in 1771 resulted in a number of large family portraits (*Henry Loftus, Earl of Ely, His Wife and Nieces*, 1771; National Gallery of Ireland, Dublin).

Kauffman's remarkable popularity does not mean that she was universally admired or without detractors. Some contemporaries criticised the "effeminacy" of her male figures and other deficiencies. Her relationship with Reynolds was mocked in a painted satire by Nathaniel Hone (*The Conjuror*, 1775; National Gallery of Ireland), which she succeeded in having removed from public display. After her death, as the taste for Neo-classicism and allegorical subjects declined during the 19th century, her work fell out of fashion. In more recent histories of art she has often been dismissed as a mere "decorative" painter of lesser stature than her celebrated contemporaries Jacques-Louis David, Joshua Reynolds and Benjamin West. Nevertheless, her influence has persisted.

Kauffman's keen practical sense of how to succeed as a woman artist within the male art establishment served her well. As revealed in correspondence, financial records, biographies and the observations of her contemporaries, she worked hard at promoting her career. This evidence suggests that she supervised most aspects of her professional life and arranged her studios, both in London where she lived from 1766 to 1781 and in Rome where she settled in 1782, to show herself and her work to the greatest advantage. She was aided by her father, whom she supported through her work, and when at the age of 40 she married the older artist Antonio Zucchi, her husband took over the day-to-day management of her business affairs. On the occasion of this marriage they signed an agreement that ensured Kauffman's continuing control of her own considerable wealth. David Alexander's research has shown that she was directly involved in the production and marketing of prints after her work and the selling of compositions for mechanical paintings ("Kauffman and the print market in eighteenth-century England" in Roworth 1992). Throughout her years in England she collaborated with engravers and publishers in the production and sale of stipple prints and mezzotints after her paintings and drawings. She was one of the few contemporary artists whose works were used in the production of "mechanical paintings", a new process of colour reproduction invented in the mid-1770s. Kauffman's profitable involvement in what were considered the "minor" arts, as well as the higher categories of portraiture and grand-style history painting, reveals an important aspect of her shrewd and practical nature. She did not affect the temperament that had come to be associated with the idea of artistic genius, that heroic, masculine quality, cultivated by most academicians, and which Kauffman, as a woman, could not adopt. Instead she managed a successful balance between the desirable feminine traits of modesty and charm, polite society's ideal of an 18th-century woman of accomplishment, and her ambition to be accepted at the highest level of academic achievement.

Kauffman: *Self-Portrait Hesitating Between Music and Painting*, 1794; National Trust, Nostell Priory, Wakefield

Kauffman's awareness of the constraints on women artists may have contributed to her motivation to provide generous financial as well as moral support to younger women artists. She assisted Maria Cosway (q.v.) in her career, encouraged the talent of Georgiana Keate, the daughter of her friend the poet George Keate, and her own cousin Rosa Florini, who married the architect Joseph Bonomi.

According to her biographer and friend, Giovanni Gherardo De Rossi (1810), as a young woman Kauffman was equally talented as a painter and musician, and she faced the hard choice of which career to pursue. Thirty years later she commemorated this choice in a well-known allegorical portrait, which exists in two versions (1791; Pushkin Museum, Moscow; 1794; see illustration). She portrayed herself as a youthful woman between female personifications of the sister arts, Music and Painting. The composition was based on the Classical story of "The Choice or Judgement of Hercules" (Xenophon, *Memorabilia*, II, i, 22). Hercules, an exemplar of heroic virtue, had to choose between the easy joys of Pleasure and the hard, rocky path of Virtue that led to the Temple of Fame. In a deliberate gender shift, Kauffman played the role of the mythical hero and portrayed herself hesitating between gentle Music and powerful Painting. This story of Kauffman's decision to follow what was considered to be the more rigorous and intellectually challenging art must be based on some truth, but the fact that her biographer chose to relate it at length and the artist herself to memorialise it in a major self-

portrait is noteworthy. This characterisation of Kauffman in both biography and portrait ensured that she would be recognised as not only intelligent, hard-working and ambitious, but also remembered as a proper woman of virtue, the female equivalent of the masculine hero.

In addition, Kauffman's abandonment of Music represented a deliberate departure from a tradition of Italian Renaissance self-portraits of women artists, such as those by Lavinia Fontana (1578), Sofonisba Anguissola (1561) and Marietta Robusti (c.1580) (all q.v.), who had portrayed themselves with keyboard instruments, which associated them with Music, an art considered a proper feminine accomplishment (although this had more to do with class and decorum than their status as either musicians or painters). Kauffman, despite the coy playfulness of her self-portrait, demonstrated through the rejection of Music her desire to be recognised within the noble tradition of history painting, the most public and "masculine" of all genres. Her knowledge of history and literature was obtained, according to her biographer, through extensive reading. Instead of attending to amusements or the distractions of love, she devoted herself studiously to reading history, as well as the Italian, French and German poets. These sources provided ideas for painting and stimulated her lively imagination (De Rossi 1810, pp.14–15).

After her initial training with her father, a provincial painter, Kauffman followed the established practice for artistic education by travelling throughout Italy. She copied paintings

Kauffman: *Penelope Sacrificing to Minerva for the Safe Return of Telemachus,* 1774; National Trust, Stourhead

by the Renaissance and 17th-century masters in the galleries of Milan, Parma, Bologna, Rome, Florence and Naples, and drew from the great works of Classical antiquity. It was through studies of statues and paintings that she learned human anatomy and the representation of figures in action. According to De Rossi, she sometimes worked from live male models, but her father was present and they were always properly covered except for their limbs. Kauffman was accepted as a member of the Accademia Clementina in Bologna (1762), the Accademia del Disegno in Florence (1762) and the Accademia di San Luca in Rome (1765). As a female prodigy, she attracted attention and received many visitors to her studio. By the mid-1760s she was producing large history paintings of Classical subjects (*Penelope at Her Loom*, 1764; Hove Museum and Art Gallery; *Bacchus and Ariadne*, 1764; Rathaus, Bregenz) and portraits for British visitors on the Grand Tour, such as the actor *David Garrick* (1764; Burghley House). She became friends with many artists who were involved in the development of the Neo-classical style such as the American Benjamin West, the Scotsman Gavin Hamilton, and Nathaniel Dance, to whom she was briefly engaged.

Soon after her arrival in England Kauffman nearly ruined her developing career when in 1767 she married a man who turned out to be an impostor, the Swedish "Count de Horn". This very brief and apparently unconsummated marriage ended when the truth came to light – he had at least one other wife – and Kauffman paid him to leave. It is remarkable that what could have been a disaster and was certainly the subject for much gossip did not affect her career. Ironically, it may have been this illegal marriage that allowed her to maintain her freedom and control of her career. Whether through poor judgement, rashness or innocence, Kauffman in effect exempted herself from the traditional expectation of marriage and motherhood, a situation that would probably have curtailed the high aspirations and heavy workload she maintained. After this episode she retained a peculiar status: neither spinster nor virgin, widow nor wife, and not quite a fallen woman, a situation that seems to have kept further suitors at bay and turned attention to her work rather than her person.

In 1768 Kauffman became one of the founding members of the Royal Academy of Arts, one of two women – Mary Moser (q.v.) was the other – within that elite group. Her earliest history paintings exhibited at the Royal Academy in 1769 were among the first Classical subjects shown in public by any artist in England: *Penelope Taking Down the Bow of Ulysses*, *Hector Taking Leave of His wife Andromache*, *Aeneas and Achates Meeting Venus Disguised as a Hunting Maiden* and *Achilles among the Daughters of Lycomedes* (National Trust, Saltram Park). All four subjects from the Trojan legend were bought by Reynolds's old friend John Parker for his country seat at Saltram, Devon, to be installed in the Grand Saloon designed by Robert Adam. As a group they represented the conflicts between love and war, personal desire and civic duty, male and female roles, and employed gender reversals and disguises. Kauffman frequently chose subjects that allowed for the treatment of women in prominent roles as a way to draw attention to her unique status as a female history painter and in order to attract patronage, especially from a female clientele. In fact, she received support from Queen Charlotte (*Queen Charlotte Raising the Genius of the Fine Arts*, engraved by Burke, 1772)

in England, and in her later years she counted the Empress Catherine of Russia, Maria Theresa of Austria and her daughter Queen Carolina of Naples (*King Ferdinand IV and Queen Carolina of Naples and His Family*, 1783; Capodimonte, Naples) among her most important patrons.

Most notable of Kauffman's female subjects is Penelope, the crafty and wise heroine of the Odyssey, the embodiment of feminine virtue under the guidance of Minerva: patient, faithful, devoted to husband and son, and adept at the female art of weaving. Kauffman was the first artist to exploit the image of Penelope, and the subject became something of a speciality. Some were shown at the Royal Academy exhibitions and many were reproduced as popular engravings: *Penelope Sacrificing to Minerva for the Safe Return of Telemachus* (1774; see illustration), *Penelope Awakened by Euryclea with the News of Ulysses' Return* (engraved by Burke, 1773), *Return of Telemachus* (1775; Lord Derby, Knowsley) and *Penelope Weeping over the Bow of Ulysses* (1777; Burghley House).

The choice of female characters was practical in terms of the moralising purpose of history painting and her own strategies for success, but it also allowed her to avoid the depiction of active nude or semi-nude male figures. In fact, Kauffman's paintings were more likely to represent subjects in which gender roles are ambiguous, reversed, masked or disguised, such as *Achilles Disguised as a Maiden Discovered by Ulysses* (1768; Saltram), the young *Telemachus at the Court of Sparta Weeping for the Loss of His Father* (engraved by Ryland, 1773) and *Imbaca Disguised as a Warrior, Revealing Herself as a Maiden to Trenmor from "Ossian"* (1773; private collection, repr. Bregenz 1968, fig.30).

Two other large history paintings (also at Saltram) were the first subjects from British history exhibited at the Royal Academy: *Vortigern, King of Britain Enamoured of Rowena at the Banquet of Hengist* (1770) and *Interview of King Edgar and Elfrida after Her Marriage with Aethelwold* (1771), the first known pictorial representation of this subject. Kauffman continued to exhibit regularly at the annual Royal Academy exhibitions. Other important paintings of Classical and historical subjects from this period include *Sappho and Cupid* (1775; John and Mable Ringling Museum, Sarasota), *Andromache Fainting at the Unexpected Sight of Aeneas* (1775; Walker Art Gallery, Liverpool), *Tender Eleanora Sucking the Venom out of the Wound of Edward I* (1776; engraved by Ryland, 1780) and *Lady Elizabeth Grey Imploring Edward IV for the Restitution of Her Deceased Husband's Lands* (engraved by Ryland, 1780). These are treated in similar Neo-classical fashion with figures arranged near the picture plane in eloquent interaction of gestures and expressions based on Classical reliefs and Renaissance paintings. The sources for Kauffman's British subjects are David Hume's and Nicholas Rapin's histories of England, although Reynolds or someone else may have suggested some of the specific subjects. Many of her Classical scenes, but not all, were taken from the Comte de Caylus's book *Tableaux tirés de l'Iliade, de l'Odyssée d'Homère et de l'Enéide de Virgile* (Paris, 1757).

In 1773 Kauffman was one of five painters commissioned to paint the dome of St Paul's Cathedral in London with historical subjects, although this project was never carried out. When the Royal Academy moved into new premises at Somerset House in 1780, Kauffman made four oval ceiling paintings of allegorical subjects (now Burlington House, London) as part of the didactic decoration for the Council Chamber. These represented the four parts of the art of painting: *Invention*, *Composition*, *Drawing* (Design) and *Colouring*.

After a highly successful career in England, Kauffman returned to Italy to take advantage of the wider and more sophisticated Continental market. She and Zucchi, her husband, were soon established in a large house in Rome with their impressive collection of paintings, engravings and books by Classical and modern authors, and she quickly became one of the stars of the international community. In 1788 she was honoured by the acceptance of her self-portrait into the Medici collection of artists' portraits (Uffizi, Florence). Her studio became a popular stop on the Grand Tour for fashionable visitors and clients, agents and dealers, painters and engravers, poets and princes from Britain, Germany, Russia and Poland who wished to have their portraits made, to order history paintings or simply to participate in the evenings of conversation, poetry reading and music. Her work of this period is recorded in the *Memorandum of Paintings* kept by Zucchi until his death in 1795.

Kauffman also continued to produce pictures for British patrons, most notably George Bowles, who owned many of her most interesting Classical and allegorical works. These included *Zeuxis and the Maidens of Crotona* (c.1778; Annmary Brown Collection, Brown University, Providence), which contained a cleverly masked self-portrait, and *Self-Portrait in the Character of Design Embraced by Poetry* (1782; Iveagh Bequest). Three of her most severely Neo-classical and serious moralising paintings for Bowles were exhibited at the Royal Academy in 1786. These represent *Cornelia, Mother of the Gracchi Showing Her Sons as Her Treasures* (Virginia Museum of Fine Arts, Richmond), *Pliny the Younger with His Mother at Misenum* (Art Museum, Princeton) and *Vergil Writing His Own Epitaph at Brundisium* (private collection, repr. Los Angeles 1976, p.177).

Despite the turmoil that engulfed Europe during the French Revolution and its aftermath, and her failing health in later years, Kauffman remained busy making paintings for such patrons as the King of Poland, Prince Poniatowski, the Emperor Franz Joseph and Frederick, Prince of Wales. Among works of this period are portraits of *Lady Hamilton*, the novelist *Cornelia Knight* (1793; Manchester City Art Galleries), *Thomas Noel Hill, 2nd Lord Berwick* (1793; National Trust, Attingham) and *Ludwig I of Bavaria* (1805–7; Bayerische Staatsgemaldesammlungen, Munich). She turned increasingly to religious subjects, for example the *Holy Family*, the *Annunciation*, *Christ and the Woman of Samaria* (1795; Bayerische Staatsgemaldesammlungen) and *David Reproached by Nathan* (1797; untraced, engraved by Ryland, 1773). The last two pictures were carried in the elaborate funeral procession held in Rome at her death in 1807. Her will records that she left considerable wealth and property to her family and to the poor of her father's home parish in Bregenz, Austria, but Kauffman left an even greater legacy in her role as one of the most successful and influential women artists, whose image continued to inspire later generations of women painters.

WENDY WASSYNG ROWORTH

See also Academies of Art and Printmakers surveys

Kelly, Mary

American artist, 1941–

Born in Minneapolis, Minnesota, 1941. Studied at College of St Teresa, Winona (BA 1963); Pius XII Institute, Florence, Italy, 1963–5 (MA); St Martin's School of Art, London, 1968–70 (diploma). Taught at American University of Beirut, 1965–8. Married British artist Ray Barrie; son born, 1973. Joined editorial board of *Screen* magazine, 1979. Returned to New York to teach on Independent Study Program, Whitney Museum of American Art, New York, 1989, and became Director of Studios. Artist-in-residence, New Hall, Cambridge University, England, 1985–6. Recipient of Arts Council of Great Britain award, 1977; Lina Garnade Memorial Foundation award, 1978; National Endowment for the Arts (NEA) fellowship, 1987. Lives in New York.

Selected Individual Exhibitions

South London Art Gallery: 1975 (*Women and Work*, with Kay Hunt and Margaret Harrison)
Institute of Contemporary Arts, London: 1976
Museum of Modern Art, Oxford: 1977
Fruitmarket Gallery, Edinburgh: 1985 (*Interim*, touring)
New Museum of Contemporary Art, New York: 1990–91 (*Interim*, touring)
Herbert F. Johnson Museum of Art, Ithaca, NY: 1992 (*Gloria Patri*, touring)

Selected Writings

"Re-viewing modernist criticism", *Screen*, no.22, Autumn 1981, pp.41–62
Post-Partum Document, London: Routledge, 1983
"Desiring images/imaging desire", *Wedge*, vi, Winter 1984, pp.4–9
"Beyond the purloined image", *Framing Feminism: Art and the Women's Movement, 1970–1985*, ed. Rozsika Parker and Griselda Pollock, London: Pandora, 1987, pp.249–53
"On sexual politics and art", *ibid.*, pp.303–12
"On representation, sexuality and sameness: Reflections on the 'Difference Show'", *Screen*, no.28, Winter 1987, pp.102–7
"From Corpus", *Taking Our Time: Feminist Perspectives on Temporality*, ed. Frieda Forman, Oxford: Pergamon, 1989, pp.153–9
"Re-presenting the body", *Psychoanalysis and Cultural Theory: Thresholds*, ed. James Donald, London: Macmillan, and New York: St Martin's Press, 1991
"(P)age 49: on the *subject* of history", *New Feminist Art Criticism: Critical Strategies*, ed. Katy Deepwell, Manchester: Manchester University Press, 1995, pp.147–52
Imaging Desire, Cambridge: Massachusetts Institute of Technology Press, 1997

Bibliography

Hayward Annual '78, exh. cat., Arts Council of Great Britain, London, 1978
Griselda Pollock and Rozsika Parker, *Old Mistresses: Women, Art and Ideology*, London: Routledge, and New York: Pantheon, 1981
Jo-Anna Isaak, "Our mother tongue: The *Post-Partum Document*", *Vanguard*, xi, April 1982, pp.14–17
Mary Kelly: Interim, exh. cat., Fruitmarket Gallery, Edinburgh, and elsewhere, 1985
"Mary Kelly and Laura Mulvey in conversation", *Afterimage*, xiii, March 1986, pp.6–8
Griselda Pollock, *Vision and Difference: Femininity, Feminism and the Histories of Art*, London and New York: Routledge, 1988

Laura Mulvey, *Visual and Other Pleasures*, Bloomington: Indiana University Press, and London: Macmillan, 1989

Mary Kelly: Interim, exh. cat., New Museum of Contemporary Art, New York, and elsewhere, 1990

John Roberts, *Postmodernism, Politics and Art*, Manchester: Manchester University Press, 1990

Charlotte Streifer Rubinstein, *American Women Sculptors*, Boston: Hall, 1990

Parveen Adams, "The art of analysis: Mary Kelly's *Interim* and the discourse of the analyst", *October*, no.58, 1991, pp.81–96

Emily Apter, "Fetishism and visual seduction in Mary Kelly's *Interim*", *ibid.*, pp.97–108

Cassandra Langer, "Mary Kelly's *Interim*", *Woman's Art Journal*, xiii/1, 1992, pp.41–5

Judith Mastai, ed., *Mary Kelly and Griselda Pollock in Conversation at the Vancouver Art Gallery, June 1989*, Vancouver: Vancouver Art Gallery, 1992

"Mary Kelly and Margaret Iversen in conversation", *Talking Art 1*, ed. Adrian Searle, London: Institute of Contemporary Arts, 1993

Mara R. Witzling, ed., *Voicing Today's Visions: Writings by Contemporary Women Artists*, New York: Universe, 1994

Helaine Posner, "The masculine masquerade: Masculinity represented in recent art", *The Masculine Masquerade: Masculinity and Representation*, ed. Andrew Perchuk and Helaine Posner, Cambridge: Massachusetts Institute of Technology Press, 1995, pp.21–30

Mary Kelly's entrance into the international art scene of the mid-1970s was nothing short of audacious. The first three sections of *Post-Partum Document* (see illustration) were exhibited at the London Institute of Contemporary Arts in 1976 and were given a noisy reception by the tabloid press: "Dirty nappies!", they shrieked. In fact, Part I of the *Document*, which is concerned with the mother's anxieties over the months of weaning her baby from the breast, consists of analysed faecal stains (or their simulation) on nappy liners and are exhibited with pristine elegance. The liners are fixed flat within recessed frames like precious prints on some rare, hand-made paper and the stains themselves form shadowy images reminiscent of the Shroud of Turin. An obsessively careful daily diary of the infant's solid food intake is printed at the bottom of each liner.

The tabloid press represents one extreme reaction to the work that deemed it scatological. But Kelly's work met with another negative reaction, which judged it to be too cerebral and obscure. This split response is eloquent testimony to a deep ambivalence that inhabits all her work. Her "style" evokes the precision and restraint of Minimalism and her use of language and diagrams that record and analyse the results of extended research projects links her to the strategies of Conceptualism. But what Conceptualist would have thought of inserting a mother and baby into that art discourse? Even some feminists were a bit surprised since they were busy asserting their right to be free from the demands of reproduction, which was thought to hamper women's creative production. The mother-artist was an oxymoron both within Patriarchy and within the movements that sought to challenge it.

Kelly's work shares with Conceptualism a political commitment to reflect on cultural discourses, but she exchanges the tools of linguistic analysis for those of psychoanalysis. Her "content" or raw material is subjectivity, the body, fears and desires, and the cultural forms that condition them. The systematic lucidity of Kelly's art is set against powerful emotion and it sometimes tips over into anxious repetition. *Post-Partum Document* marks a highly significant turn towards the subject in art practice and theory prompted mainly by feminists. Kelly was well placed to take the lead. Although born in the USA and now returned there, she spent formative years in the 1960s and 1970s in London in close contact with Juliet Mitchell (*Psychoanalysis and Feminism*, New York: Pantheon, and London: Allen Lane, 1974) and Laura Mulvey ("Visual pleasure and narrative cinema", 1975; reprinted in Mulvey 1989, pp.14–26). She has maintained this incisive cutting-edge. In the following discussion of this great installation work, made readily available in book form, and the two other major works to date, *Interim* and *Gloria Patri*, the three terms – art practice, feminism and psychoanalysis – must be kept in play if the full measure of Kelly's astuteness, inventiveness and audacity is to be appreciated.

The tension or ambivalence at the heart of *Post-Partum Document* (1973–8) is summed up succinctly by Kelly's statement that it concerns "my lived experience as a mother and my analysis of that experience". In it she explores, with the aid of psychoanalysis, the way biological sex difference is made to conform to patriarchal social norms of gender difference that are "sealed", so to speak, in the woman's experience of maternity. Her status as the gender that lacks a penis is momentarily absolved by the birth of a baby. But separation, anxiety and loss mark even the early months of motherhood. She re-experiences the symbolic castration she underwent as a little girl. Understanding these psychic processes through which women internalise their oppression was thought to be a crucial first step towards liberation.

How are these processes to be represented? Actual pictures of mother and child, an icon of love and tenderness in the history of art, could now only be sentimental and kitsch and, in any case, would lack explanatory power. Kelly's "modernist" eschewal of figurative representation is also motivated by the vulnerability of the woman's body to appropriation and exploitation within patriarchal culture. Instead, one finds a division in the work between gestural marks, traces, moulds (what C.S. Peirce called indexical signs) and writing, diagrams, symbols. The index, to some extent, resists verbalisation and is related to the sense of touch, so these signs invoke the sensuous, emotive quality of the mother's lived experience. The mute immediacy of this experience is relieved through the other register of Lacanian theory and diagrams in which these experiences are situated and put in perspective. These antagonistic registers of signification are used very effectively in the pre-document series that consists of four tiny undershirts in a row, each one adding a line to complete a Lacanian diagram. The piece suggests that the mother's intense attachment to these objects is now mediated by an explanatory theory.

The "beauty" of the undershirts or of the plaster casts of the child's hand in Documentation IV raises another issue explored in the work: maternal fetishism. According to psychoanalytic theory, fetishism is an exclusively male perversion, but Kelly suggests that if a baby fulfils in fantasy the lack carved out in the woman by a phallo-centric society, then the loss of the maturing child must represent a castration threat. As a consequence, the mother preserves little fetishes – shoes, photographs, locks of hair, school reports – that both memorialise the loss and defend against it. The small scale and

 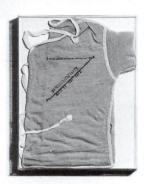 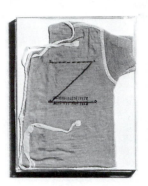 

Kelly: *Post-Partum Document*, introduction, 1973; four units, 25.4 × 20.3 cm.

box-like dimensions of the individually framed units allude to this fetishisation, yet they also combine to form "cinematic" frames recording the passage of time and the changes occurring in the mother's relationship with her child. Kelly calls this latter strategy "the narrativization of space" (Kelly and Iversen 1993, p.103) and it is crucial to her ongoing explorations of complex social realities and theories.

With *Post-Partum Document* Kelly broke the taboo surrounding maternity in contemporary critical art practice. She followed this up with an equally provocative topic: women and middle age. *Interim* (1984–9) explores the crisis of identity experienced by the older, post-maternal woman. What are the social roles, the self-images, the expectations in circulation for her? The work is truly monumental in scale: it filled the New Museum of Contemporary Art in New York when it was exhibited there in 1990. But it might also be considered monumental in other senses since it is so reflexive about the past and concerned with memory, both personal and collective. It has been suggested that "middle age" is also metaphorically the position of the women's movement itself, which is in the process of redefining itself.

The work consists of four parts that focus on the Body, Money, History and Power (with the Latin titles *Corpus*, *Pecunia*, *Historia* and *Potestas*). In the same way that the earlier work proposed maternal fetishism as a specifically feminine "aesthetic", *Interim* turns on the issue of identification and dis-identification in relation to representations as well as

to other people. Kelly began her project by sifting through pop-cultural artefacts (such as women's magazines) and by recording conversations with many women in order to find out what positions they habitually take up or what ones are fantasised. Part I, *Corpus*, consists of photographs of garments arranged in different postures: Menacé, Erotisme, Extase – which are paired with first person, anecdotal text panels. Charcot's practice of documenting photographically his hysterical patients and his classification of *attitudes passionelles* are invoked here but not uncritically. In an interview with Hal Foster, Kelly remarked that "*Interim* proposes not one body but many bodies, shaped within a lot of different discourses. It doesn't refer to an anatomical fact or to a perceptual entity, but to the dispersed body of desire" (quoted in New York 1990, p.55). The absence of iconic images of the woman's body in Kelly's work is in response to the special requirements of the female spectator: it prevents her "hysterical" identification with the male voyeur and the use of writing helps to open up a gap: "to distance the spectator from the anxious proximity of her body" (*idem*).

Interim is addressed to a female spectator as the subject of desire. How does it propose to do this? By representing the maternal body as lost and therefore as an object of desire. The "middle-aged" or post-maternal woman is ideally placed to make this transition to sublimated pleasure, for at that moment the stability and pleasure of identification with the mother's body in maternity give way to shifting instability that can be experienced as pleasurable loss. Perhaps this is why the garments in *Corpus* have a ghostly presence – they are semi-transparent photo-laminates affixed to sheets of raised Perspex so that they "float" and cast a shadow. The beautiful image of a summer dress, for example, with its tiny waist was apparently inspired by shop-window displays that frequently show impossible anatomies. But, through the text panel, Kelly links the image to the fantasies of romantic fiction with their excess of desire and straining for release from normative strictures.

Although Part II is called *Pecunia* (Latin: money), it is less about money than the way that a culture dominated by commodities and the imperative of professional or business success inflects our most intimate desires. We see these desires in turn refracted through four social positions – mother, daughter, sister and wife. The series is made up of cleverly folded "pop-up" pieces of galvanised steel, treated in such a way that they have the glitzy iridescence of greeting cards. The narratives printed inside the "cards" are scenes from the everyday life of everywoman. Some of them are horribly familiar: there is the self-sacrificing mother who has "postponed her life" and the housewife whose idea of happiness is a perfectly clean toilet bowl, emblem of her independent identity – "Now everything would be her way".

The first-person fictional narratives of *Corpus* contrast with the "true stories" of *Historia*. Identification in the latter case is about the assumption of a political identity in the women's movement. Here, again, Kelly presents not a monolith of the collectivity of women, but four consecutive and parallel personal histories told by four generations of feminists since 1968. The texts in this section offer a utopian vision of political, ethnic and age differences subsumed within a jubilant common gender identity, and they also question this aspiration. Formally, the *Historia* series looks like open books and newspaper galleys recording what might otherwise have been hidden from history, and also like tombstones, monuments to the courage of those who have gone before. The last Part, *Potestas* or Power, is made up of contrasting metal bars that evoke, for men, the work of the Abstract Expressionist sculptor David Smith and, for women, the rusted surfaces of Richard Serra's much-maligned minimalist prop pieces. Although the work as a whole is deeply informed by psychoanalytic and Foucauldian theory, it does not rest content with representing the circumstances of women's oppression. Self-transcendence is presented as a possibility within the history of the women's movement.

One of the most striking images of *Corpus* is a glossy black leather jacket, the artist's equivalent of the businesswoman's tailored suit, which mimes male attire and points to the importance of identification with the father. One of the paths through the Oedipal complex in girls as described by Freud is the "masculinity complex" in which she stubbornly resists the imputation that she has not got the Phallus. In fantasy, she does and so presumably do men whose penis inevitably falls far short of the Phallus.

In *Gloria Patri* (1992) Kelly analyses the masculinity complex in men and women. The work was also sparked by the media coverage of the Gulf War and the quite sinister spectacle of violent aggression set against a weakened national position following the end of the Cold War. The polished aluminium shields that make up part of the installation are meant, first, to evoke a pathological, armoured, masculine ideal and, second, to show this up as a façade. The narratives printed on the shields do the same; they are scenarios of failed masculinity taken, not from war, but from everyday life.

The other elements of the installation, all in polished aluminium, are 20 discs silk-screened with re-configured military logos and two-dimensional trophies topped by male figurines in an archaic "deco" style. Its forbidding visual quality, heightened by "search-beam" up-lighting, is in fact counterpointed by the narratives themselves, which are sympathetic. There are ironic rhymes between the snatches of Gulf War rhetoric printed on the trophies and the downbeat stories – for example, Schwarzkopf's stated strategy for liquidating the Iraqi army, "cut it off and kill it", is echoed in the reflections of a lone fisherman stalking a brook trout: "He could do whatever he wanted: cut it up and eat it or throw it back". The common element of sadistic pleasure is underscored in both. Yet the fisherman's puffed-up, confident mastery is punctured at the end of the story by the mere quizzical gaze of a Great Blue heron; the man suddenly sees his own muddled reflection in the water. The other stories concern different fantasies of mastery: a man witnesses his son's birth with mixed emotions; an adolescent boy's nascent masculinity rebels at the sight of greens on his plate, emblem of the mother and of femininity generally. The last story is about a woman on a body-building machine attacking her soft feminine flesh: if only she could "cut off her sequacity and kill it". In each case an armour-like shell of an ego defends against a sense of bodily fragmentation and the distress of helplessness. Have women unconsciously incorporated a masculine ego ideal? And if so, what price Glory?

Works by the artist in public collections are to be found at the Arts Council of Great Britain; Tate Gallery, London; Vancouver Art Gallery; New Museum of Contemporary Art, New York; Kunsthaus, Zürich; Helsinki City Museum; and the National Gallery of Australia, Canberra.

MARGARET IVERSEN

Kemp-Welch, Lucy (Elizabeth)

British painter and illustrator, 1869–1958

Born in Poole Hill, Dorset, 20 June 1869; father a Bournemouth solicitor. Attended art classes at Bournemouth School of Art; studied at Hubert von Herkomer's School of Art, Bushey, Hertfordshire, from 1891. Lived at Kingsley House, Bushey, with sister Edith. Principal of von Herkomer's school from 1900; purchased the school, 1907; sold it, 1926. Visited France, 1909, Italy, 1914. Member, Royal Society of British Artists, 1902; Royal Institute of Painters in Watercolour, 1917; Pastel Society, 1917; Women's International Art Club; Royal British and Colonial Society; Royal Cambrian Academy. First president, Society of Animal Painters, 1914. Died in Watford, 28 November 1958. Lucy Kemp-Welch Memorial Gallery founded at Church House, Bushey, 1967 (now closed).

Principal Exhibitions

Royal Academy, London: 1895–1920, 1923–5, 1930, 1938–9, 1949
Fine Art Society, London: 1905 (individual)
Dudley Gallery, London: 1912 (individual)
Arlington Gallery, London: 1938 (individual)

Bibliography

Walter Shaw Sparrow, *Women Painters of the World*, London: Hodder and Stoughton, and New York: Stokes, 1905; reprinted New York: Hacker, 1976
Edward F. Strange, ed., *In the Open Country: Studies and Sketches by Lucy Kemp-Welch*, London: Hodder and Stoughton, 1905
Paintings and Drawings by Some Women War Artists, exh. cat., Imperial War Museum, London, 1958
David Messum, *The Life and Work of Lucy Kemp-Welch*, ed. Laura Wortley, Woodbridge, Suffolk: Antique Collectors' Club, 1976
Grant Longman, *The Herkomer Art School and Subsequent Developments, 1901–1918*, Bushey Reference Paper, no.2, March 1981

Lucy Kemp-Welch, painter of horses, could be described as the British Rosa Bonheur (q.v.). In 1897 the Chantrey Bequest bought her picture *Colt Hunting in the New Forest* (see illustration) for the Tate Gallery, London, a work whose achievement can be compared with the French artist's great canvas the *Horse Fair* (National Gallery, London). Although she painted other subjects, principally landscapes, Kemp-Welch dedicated herself to a lifelong exploration of depictions of horses, demonstrating the same kind of rigorous application to study and similarly ambitious working methods as those employed by Rosa Bonheur and by the battle painter Lady Butler (q.v.). Like Bonheur, Kemp-Welch never married, and as a child she enjoyed the support of an artistic and intellectual family. Her mother encouraged Lucy and her sister Edith (also an artist, a painter of landscapes and portraits) to paint and draw from an early age, and her father, a keen amateur naturalist, took her on drawing expeditions in the New Forest near Bournemouth where she grew up. Horse-riding was her passion from childhood.

Kemp-Welch exhibited prolifically, and her oils, watercolours and drawings can be found in many public collections. In 1923 the Walker Art Gallery, Liverpool, bought her contribution to the Liverpool Autumn Exhibition, *Low Tide at St Ives*, a watercolour of two carts and horses being driven along the water's edge at the Cornish seaside town. Completing the "Biographical particulars" requested by the gallery, Kemp-Welch jotted down brief details of her numerous honours, refused to give her age – "I do not put the date as it's frequently made unfair use of" – and under "Education and Training" wrote: "The Herkomer School Bushey. 1892 for three or four years, afterwards lived in Bushey and was in constant touch with Sir Hubert Herkomer, who never ceased to be the most helpful friend and critic any young painter could have."

Hubert von Herkomer was an autocratic principal who despised what he called "gigantic wholesale tuition" in art schools and laid great importance on individual tuition and lively extra-curricular activities, including film-making: in one production, the *Hunt Breakfast*, Kemp-Welch appears riding Baden-Powell's horse, Black Prince. Clearly, Kemp-Welch won Herkomer's particular attention. Curiously, she omitted to mention in her Liverpool *curriculum vitae* that she took over Herkomer's school after his resignation, and ran it until 1926. Lucy's school specialised in animal painting and did not welcome women: "Only such Students are accepted as intend to make Art a profession. Students under 18 and married ladies, and ladies above the age of 28, are not eligible for admission." Art was Kemp-Welch's vocation, not teaching, and apparently she had little patience with what she assumed to be dilettante female pupils.

Kemp-Welch: *Colt Hunting in the New Forest*, purchased 1897; Tate Gallery, London

From Herkomer, Kemp-Welch learned the importance of making studies from life and the confidence to work on a large scale. She wrote: "On the advice of Prof. Herkomer, the painting of the splendid subject of 'Colt Hunting' was delayed for two years as he did not want me to attempt it until I had at least passed into the 'Life Class' at the School. (It was sound advice.)" Her love and knowledge of animals informed her art and invested it with a sense of movement and life that was much admired: "Miss Kemp-Welch has developed a talent such as is uncommon in a man and quite rare in a woman for animal painting" (*Bazaar*, 1 May 1896). She derided the use of photographs and instead used what she called her "mental photography". For the Tate picture she herself rode a rough course on horseback through the New Forest and studied at a horse hospital in Christchurch. To facilitate painting large pictures in the open air, she devised a large wooden packing-case box with "barn-doors" opening outwards to protect her canvas. *Colt Hunting in the New Forest* took three months to paint, outside at a suitable spot in the forest. Another large-scale horse subject is *The Riders* (2.4 × 2.1 m.; Graves Art Gallery, Sheffield), inspired by lines from Robert Browning's poem "The Last Ride Together": "What if we still ride on we two,/With love forever old – forever new".

In 1914 Kemp-Welch enjoyed the honour of becoming first president of the newly formed Society of Animal Painters, with such illustrious members as Briton Rivière and Alfred Munnings, and in the same year she suffered the grief of Herkomer's death. In the years of World War I, Kemp-Welch diversified into book illustration, providing, for example, colour plates and line drawings for a limited edition of Anna Sewell's *Black Beauty*. Eager to play an active part in the war effort, she combined ambulance driving in London with her war art. She produced a propaganda poster *Forward* depicting a charging horse and rider, and her wartime painting *Forward the Guns!* (1.5 × 3.06 m.) was bought by the Tate Gallery. This picture was painted from studies made at manoeuvres at Bulford Camp on Salisbury Plain, where the artist joined camp training for several weeks. Kemp-Welch's obituary in *The Times* recorded: "For this picture she sat with her easel on Salisbury Plain while eight batteries of horse artillery were driven towards her so that she could sketch the general outline of their movement." After the war Kemp-Welch was commissioned to paint *Women's Work in the Great War, 1914–1918* for the Empress Club, a women's club in the Royal Exchange in London, for which she balanced on a scaffolding platform to paint a panel nearly 6 metres high.

In the 1920s and 1930s, when she was in her fifties and sixties, Kemp-Welch continued her career in customary intrepid fashion, at one time travelling with a circus to paint the animals, just as Laura Knight (q.v.) had done, only in her case to study the performers. Kemp-Welch fits into the mould of the feisty, single-minded professional British woman artist, not dissimilar to Knight in that she found success within the art establishment by combining her vigour with a fundamentally traditional technique and subject matter. Unlike Knight, and even with Herkomer's backing, Kemp-Welch did not win Associate membership of the Royal Academy, even though the barriers were beginning to erode before the end of her lifetime.

JANE SELLARS

Kennet, Lady *see* Scott

Kerkovius, Ida
Latvian painter and textile artist, 1879–1970

Born in Riga, 31 August 1879. Studied painting at a private art school in Riga, 1899. Visited Italy then studied painting under Adolf Hölzel in Dachau, 1903. In Latvia, 1904–7. Studied painting under Adolf Mayer in Berlin, then under Hölzel again at the Stuttgart Academy, 1908. Worked as a freelance artist in Stuttgart and taught at the Academy as Hölzel's assistant from 1911. Exhibited at Der Sturm, Berlin, 1911. Student in the Bauhaus weaving workshop, Weimar, 1920–23. Freelance artist in Stuttgart, 1924–34; exhibited with Novembergruppe, Berlin, 1925; at Salon de l'Art d'Aujourd'hui, Paris: 1926. Denounced as a "degenerate" artist and forbidden to work or exhibit by the National Socialists, 1933. Left Germany, and travelled in Norway, Italy, Bulgaria, France and Belgium, with stays in Riga, 1934–9. Returned to Stuttgart, 1939; studio and much of her work destroyed by bombing, 1944. Freelance painter and weaver, 1950–70; often travelled abroad. Recipient of painting prize, State of Baden-Württemberg, 1954; Distinguished Service medal, first class, of the Federal Republic of Germany, 1954. Member, 1950, and honorary board member, 1963, Deutscher Künstlerbund; honorary member, Stuttgart Academy, 1962. Died in Stuttgart, 8 June 1970.

Selected Individual Exhibitions
Leopold-Hoesch Museum, Düren: 1929
Württembergischer Kunstverein, Stuttgart: 1930 (retrospective), 1948, 1954, 1959, 1969
Galerie Valentien, Stuttgart: 1933, 1964
Frankfurter Kunstkabinett, Frankfurt am Main: 1948, 1962
Galerie Günther Franke, Munich: 1958, 1963, 1966
Museum am Ostwall, Dortmund: 1961
Badischer Kunstverein, Karlsruhe: 1961 (with Alfred Lörcher)
Galerie Maercklin, Stuttgart: 1962, 1964, 1969
Galerie Vömel, Düsseldorf: 1963
Residenz, Salzburg: 1963
Nassauischer Kunstverein, Wiesbaden: 1964
Museum, Düsseldorf: 1964
Galerie Bremer, Berlin: 1965
Kunstnernes Hus, Oslo: 1966
Heidelberger Kunstverein, Heidelberg: 1966

Bibliography
Edouard Roditi, *Ida Kerkovius*, Constance: Simon-Koch, 1961
Kurt Leonhard, *Ida Kerkovius: Leben und Werk*, Cologne: DuMont-Schauberg, 1967
Hans Kinkel, *14 Berichte: Begegnungen mit Malern und Bildhauern*, Stuttgart: Goverts, 1967
Ida Kerkovius, exh. cat., Württembergischer Kunstverein, Stuttgart, 1969
Ernst Schremmer, *Ida Kerkovius: Landschaften*, Munich: Delp'sche, 1975
Ida Kerkovius, 1879–1970, Gesichter: Bilder und Zeichnungen aus Sieben Jahrzehnten, exh. cat., Galerie der Stadt, Stuttgart, 1979
L'altra metà dell'avanguardia, 1910–1940: Pittrici e scultrici nei movimenti delle avanguardie storiche, exh. cat., Palazzo Reale, Milan, and elsewhere, 1980

Ida Kerkovius, 1879–1970, exh. cat., Galerie Orangerie-Reinz, Cologne, 1981

Das Verborgene Museum I: Dokumentation der Kunst von Frauen in Berliner öffentlichen Sammlungen, exh. cat., Akademie der Künste, Berlin, 1987

Ida Kerkovius, exh. cat., Frankfurter Kunstkabinett, Frankfurt am Main, 1988

Ida Kerkovius: Bilder, Aquarelle, Zeichnungen und Graphik, exh. cat., Galerie Vömel, Düsseldorf, 1989

Sigrid Wortmann Weltge, *Bauhaus Textiles: Women Artists and the Weaving Workshop*, London: Thames and Hudson, 1993; as *Women's Work: Textile Art from the Bauhaus*, San Francisco: Chronicle, 1993

"She is all art", said Alexej Jawlensky of the painter and craftswoman Ida Kerkovius. Respected equally by her fellow artists and by art critics and collectors, Kerkovius created a remarkable body of work in 70 years of artistic activity. Kerkovius, who came from Riga, produced paintings and prints; she also worked in textiles (weaving) and designed stained-glass windows.

At the age of 24, Kerkovius left Riga to study at Adolf Hölzel's private art school (she had become aware of his work through an exhibition held by one of his pupils). Hölzel's artistic and didactic ideas were to remain an important reference for her for the rest of her life. At first, the classes in Dachau lasted only a few months. Five years later she became Hölzel's star pupil at the Stuttgart Academy. Over the years, the teacher-pupil relationship developed into a working association of mutual inspiration. The most important tenets of Hölzel's teaching for Kerkovius's work were the "primacy of the medium" and the "primacy of perception", his theory of the construction of works of art. The only system he recognised was that of the artist's "organs of perception". Accordingly, works of art are generated by the dynamics of the artistic medium itself in the hand of the creative artist. On the occasion of an exhibition at the Württembergischer Kunstverein in 1969, Kerkovius described her concept of art thus, under the title "My life, my creative work":

> My work is determined by two diametrically opposed opposites. On the one side, finding the creative means of expression for the inner experience, giving one's imagination free rein, primarily beginning with the play of the medium from the material. From this the living artistic organism develops, which occupies me most of all in the opposing play of colour and form. These prerequisites also apply when I start with objective things, when I want to paint a still life or a landscape [Stuttgart 1969].

Kerkovius's influence on Adolf Hölzel is primarily noticeable in the surprisingly intense colours of his later works.

After working for nearly ten years as an independent artist and as Hölzel's assistant, at the age of 41 Kerkovius decided to study at the Bauhaus in Weimar. Among others, she worked under Johannes Itten, Paul Klee, Kandinsky and Oskar Schlemmer, who had previously been her pupil at Hölzel's school in Stuttgart. She had already taught herself to work with textiles, and now her apprenticeship in the weaving workshops was the starting point for her growing interest in this art form. From 1920 onwards she started to make her first rugs and wall hangings featuring purely abstract compositions, which she took up in her paintings more than ten years later,

Kerkovius: *Self-Portrait*, 1929; oil; 80 × 61 cm.; Galerie der Stadt, Stuttgart

for example, *Abstract Still Life* (c.1935; Staatsgalerie Stuttgart). The artistic quality of her weaving is apparent, for example, in the rugs entitled *Vegetable Composition* (1932) and *Symphonic Composition* (date unknown; both Staatsgalerie Stuttgart).

However homogeneous and organic the overall effect of Kerkovius's work may appear, when her works are examined separately they are seen to vary greatly as regards the application of the particular medium. A strict division into different phases is not possible, because it would not do justice to the artist's complexity. It is possible, however, to form groups of works, even though these were often produced decades apart. Kerkovius's artistic disagreement with her teachers and colleagues was not limited to the phases in which the contact was particularly intensive. Thus her association with Paul Klee is much clearer in pictures from the 1950s than in those from her time at the Bauhaus (e.g. the watercolour *Turkey*, 1955; Galerie der Stadt Esslingen).

"I do not lay claim to any artistic school, to any trend; I have always tried to find a form, a quality and an expression for the feelings that move me" (Düsseldorf 1989). This lifelong search is reflected in the heterogeneity of Kerkovius's work. The artist described her method of work, her experimenting with a diversity of forms, colours and line, as "construction". She "constructed" her works out of motifs of objects or abstract forms, geometric or organic elements, cool or warm colours, transparent structures or dense, plain expanses of colour. Good examples of the last technique are the paintings *Annunciation* (1932; Westfälisches Landesmuseum für Kunst und Kulturgeschichte, Münster) and *Self-Portrait* (1929; see illustration), which show Kerkovius's interest in Schlemmer's work.

Kerkovius also chose dense compositions with expanses of colour for her landscapes, for example, the painting *Stuttgart Landscape* (1924; Wiesbaden Museum). The landscapes that she painted on her travels of 1934–9 are, however, more representational; the rigid forms are loosened by the flowing application of colour. This is visible in the pastels *Rising Sea on Riga Beach* (1938; Staatsgalerie Stuttgart) and *Evening Sun on the Sea (Riga Beach)* (1935–8; Museum Ostdeutsche Galerie, Regensburg).

In a further group of works – from around 1930 until her death – Kerkovius introduced narrative elements into her paintings. In these exceptionally colourful pictures she refers to "naïve" peasant art, as, for example, in *Large Polish Landscape* (1943; Staatsgalerie Stuttgart), which depicts a peasant couple working in idyllic natural surroundings. The exciting tension in her work becomes apparent when these paintings are juxtaposed with her later abstract works, which are very freely constructed. An example of the latter is *Seated Figures in Landscape* (1965; gouache and chalk; Preussischer Kulturbesitz, Staatliche Museen zu Berlin).

With her unstoppable artistic energy, Kerkovius carried on creating vigorous works to a very advanced age. Even when she was over 80, she had a horror of stagnation. She is among the very few artists of her generation who managed to overcome social opposition through ability and resolve and to live as an independent artist. She also succeeded in doing so during the difficult years of the "inner emigration" that the Nazi ban on painting and exhibiting imposed on her, and then in 1944 when her Stuttgart studio was destroyed in a bombing raid and many of her works were lost.

ANKE MÜNSTER

Khodossievitch, Nadia

Russian artist, 1904–1982

Born in Gorno, near Vitebsk, 1904. Studied at the Soviet Palace of the Arts, Below, 1917. Worked with Wladyslaw Streminski in Smolensk, 1919. Studied at the School of Fine Arts in Warsaw, 1922. Left for Paris with her Polish husband Stanislas Grabowski, 1924; separated from him after the birth of her daughter, 1927. Studied at the Académie Moderne under Fernand Léger and Amédée Ozenfant, 1924; subsequently taught there. Married Léger, 1952; he died 1955. Died 1982.

Selected Individual Exhibitions

Galerie Bernheim-Jeune, Paris: 1953
Pushkin Museum, Moscow: 1963 (with Fernand Léger and Georges Bauquier)
Centre d'Art International, Paris: 1971–2 (touring)
Musée National Fernand Léger, Biot: 1992 (retrospective)

Selected Writings

"Ce sont des frangines?" *Cahiers d'Art*, December 1971 (special issue: "Hommage à Fernand Léger")

Bibliography

Nadia Khodossievitch, exh. cat., Galerie Bernheim-Jeune, Paris, 1953
Bruce Gregory, "Léger's atelier", *Art Journal*, Fall 1962, pp.40–41
Fernand Léger, Georges Bauquier, Nadia Léger, exh. cat., Pushkin Museum, Moscow, 1963
Nadia Léger: Evolution première, 1920–1926, exh. cat., Centre d'Art International, Paris, 1971
Jean-Jacques Lévêque, "Hommage de Nadia Léger à son premier maître", *Cahiers d'Art*, December 1971 (special issue: "Hommage à Fernand Léger")
Christophe Czwiklitzer, *Suprématisme de Nadia Khodossievitch-Léger*, Paris: Editions Art-CC, 1972
André Verdet, *Nadia Léger: Mosaïques monumentales: Portraits*, Paris: Editions du Centre d'Art International, 1972
Gladys Fabre, "L'atelier de Fernand Léger, période 1937–1955", *Paris-Paris, 1937–1957: Créations en France*, exh. cat., Centre Georges Pompidou, Paris, 1981
Hommage à Nadia Léger: Retrospective, 1967–1992, exh. cat., Musée National Fernand Léger, Biot, 1992

Nadia Khodossievitch, a talented artist, had a flamboyant career, definitively oriented by her encounter with Fernand Léger in 1924. Born in Gorno near Vitebsk in 1904, into poverty, she enrolled at the new Soviet Palace of the Arts in Below in 1917, learned the rudiments of drawing and composition and "idolised" Malevich. She left for Smolensk in 1919 to work with Wladyslaw Streminski and met her hero, who alas was already rejecting Suprematism. Discovering the journal *L'Esprit Nouveau*, Nadia resolved to work in Paris under Fernand Léger. Her *Self-Portrait* (1920) and *Young Girl with Plaits* (1921) show her already developing self-portraiture, arguably her most successful genre (e.g. *Self-Portrait*, 1941). Leaving for Warsaw, she studied at the School of Fine Arts in 1922 and persuaded her new Polish husband, Stanislas Grabowski, to leave for Paris, where in 1924 she enrolled in the Académie Moderne Fernand Léger-Amédée Ozenfant. In 1925 the Comtesse de Noailles bought her Cubist/purist portrait. In 1927, after the birth of her daughter Wanda, Khodossievitch separated from her husband.

According to some sources, in 1931 the local Communist party cell held its meetings in the cellars of the atelier, which closed in July. As the Académie de l'Art Contemporain it reopened at 23 rue du Moulin Vert in 1933–4, with Nadia moving from the position of pupil to teaching assistant, subsequently running the atelier for Léger during his trips to America. Paradoxically, her work responded to the Communist call for realism that Léger roundly rejected. She frequented the militant Maison de la Culture, exhibiting such works in 1936 as a female figure, signed "Kodassievitch" and inscribed in Russian with the words: "Down with Impressionism in proletarian painting!" (see *Commune*, May 1936, p.1145).

During the German occupation of Paris, Nadia, proud of her Russian nationality, worked in the Resistance on behalf of Russian prisoners of war. The Académie Léger, under Nadia's supervision and with Georges Bauquier as director, reopened in January 1946, one month before Léger's return, at 40 Place Jules Ferry, Montrouge, close to Robert Doisneau, André

Fougeron and the resistant Front National des Arts community. Léger's status as a Communist was linked to a cultivated "proletarian" image but remained bright, optimistic and resolutely modernist; Khodossievitch and Bauquier, however, while his epigones, often espoused deliberately politicised themes; as "Nadia Petrova" she exhibited *Peace*, depicting three Soviet peasant women with doves and peace slogans in French and Russian, at the notorious Salon d'Automne of 1951, where Bauquier's protest painting about armaments shipped to Indochina was taken down by the police (see *Les Lettres françaises: Editions speciale du Salon d'Automne*, no.387, 7 November 1951; she is called "Nina Petrova" here). From the mid-1940s the atelier, now the Académie Montmartre, in boulevard de Clichy, was run by "M. et Mme Bauquier". Khodossievitch married Léger in 1952, and in November 1953 more than 100 of her paintings and sketches of this period were shown at the Galerie Bernheim-Jeune. From 1952 to 1955 she assisted Léger on his stained-glass projects for the Eglise de Courfaivre in Switzerland, Caracas University, Venezuela, and the mosaic of the Gaz de France building in Alfortville, continuing with the last project and the Saint-Lô hospital after Léger's death in August 1955. Her influence on his last works, the unfinished "realist" portrait of *Mayakovsky and Lili Brik* (1955), remains an open question – as indeed do her Soviet affiliations as an "égerie russe" in this fraught Cold War period.

Between 1957 and 1960 she was involved with Bauquier in the construction of the Musée Fernand Léger at Biot, with Léger's mosaic-design façade. During the short-lived USSR thaw period, she exhibited her finely-drawn portrait of *Fernand Léger* (1955) among other works in the exhibition with Bauquier and Léger at the Pushkin Museum, Moscow, in January 1963 (see Pierre Descargues, "Fernand Léger en USSR", *XXe siècle*, 1971, p.104). In 1967 André Malraux accepted the donation of 348 of Léger's most important works to the state, as well as the buildings and land of the new Musée National Fernand Léger. Between 1965 and 1970 Léger's farm at Gisors in Normandy was transformed into the Ferme-Musée Fernand Léger and refurbished.

Beginning in 1969 from a series of highly finished preparatory gouaches, and working in Biot with the Italian artist Melano, Nadia Léger created a remarkable portrait gallery in large-scale mosaics of the heroes of "La France Stalinienne", ranging from Tolstoy, Lenin and the cosmonauts to Thorez, Duclos, Picasso and "La République Française" against biomorphic abstract backgrounds. These coincided with her astonishing re-launch as a latter-day Suprematist artist. Yuri Gagarin's first orbits around the earth in 1959 apparently inspired her to take out her old folders of drawings from the Smolensk and Warsaw period: works signed "N. Kh. Léger" were given double datings, as in *Geometric Forms in Movement Against the Moon* (1924–68). These were exhibited in Paris and Milan in 1971 as were her tapestries and jewellery at the Espace Cardin. In 1972 her monumental mosaics were shown in Paris, while the paintings travelled to the Fondation Legninani near Milan. She continued to manage Léger's affairs and the Biot museum until her death in 1982.

SARAH WILSON

Kielland, (Christine) Kitty (Lange)
Norwegian painter, 1843–1914

Born in Stavanger, 8 October 1843. Studied under Fanny Zeuthen in Stavanger, 1860s; under Morten Müller in Christiania (Oslo), c.1870. Studied in Karlsruhe, at the Kunstschule and under Norwegian painter Hans Gude, 1873–5; in Munich under Norwegian painter Eilif Peterssen, 1875–8, and Hermann Baisch, c.1876. Usually spent summers in Jären, Norway, after 1876. Lived in Paris, 1878–89; studied at Académie Julian, under Tony Robert-Fleury, 1879; private studies under Léon Pelouse in Cernay-la-Ville and Brittany, intermittently 1880–86; attended Académie Colarossi, 1883 and 1886–7. Member of Norwegian art committee for Exposition Universelle, Paris, 1889. Lived in Christiania from 1889, with frequent trips abroad, often with Harriet Backer (q.v.). Active participant in Norwegian debates on art and the women's movement, late 1880s. Recipient of King's gold medal of merit, 1908. Honorary member, Norwegian Students Society. Died in Oslo, 1 October 1914.

Principal Exhibitions

Individual
Blomqvist, Christiania: 1899
Christiania Kunstforening: 1904
Trondheim Kunstforening: 1904
Diorama Gallery, Christiania: 1911

Group
Drammens Kunstforening (Art Association), Christiania: from 1878
Paris Salon: 1879–83, 1887
Christiania Kunstforening (Art Association): from 1880
Göteborg: 1881 (*Nordisk konstutställningen* [Nordic exhibition])
Høstutstillingen (Autumn Salon), Christiania: 1882–92, 1894–1908
Charlottenborg, Copenhagen: 1883 (*Den Nordiske udstilling* [Nordic exhibition]); 1888 (*Den Nordiske udstilling* [Nordic exhibition])
Exposition Universelle d'Anvers, Antwerp: 1885
Valand, Göteborg: 1886 (*Nordisk konstutställningen* [Nordic exhibition])
Exposition Universelle, Paris: 1889 (silver medal), 1900
World's Columbian Exposition, Chicago: 1893
Venice Biennale: 1897, 1899, 1907
Blomqvist, Christiania: 1910 (*Malerindeforbundets utstilling* [Society of Women Painters exhibition])

Selected Writings
"Et indlæg i kvindesagen" [A plea for the women's movement], *Luthersk Ugeskrift*, 1885, pp.209–15
"Mors kjæledægge" [Mother's pet], *Nyt Tidsskrift*, 1885, pp.282–99
Kvindespørgsmaalet [The woman question], Christiania, 1886
"Et par ord i diskussionen" [A few words in the discussion], *Nyt Tidsskrift*, 1887, pp.714–20
"Svar til Gina Krog" [Reply to Gina Krog], *Nylænde*, 1887, pp.341–6
"Kunstkritik" [Art criticism], *Dagbladet*, 1 May 1887 (signed "en maler", "a painter")
"Nogle betragtninger over stiftsmødets forhandlinger angaaende kvindens deltagelse i Guds ords forkyndelse" [Some thoughts on the diocesan meeting's negotiations regarding women's participation in the spreading of God's word], *Morgenbladet*, 12 December 1888
"Lidt om norsk kunst" [Something about Norwegian art], *Samtiden*, 1890, pp.223–8

"Svar til Andreas Aubert" [Reply to Andreas Aubert], *Dagbladet*, 17 November 1890

"Lidt om eller mod Le Bons artikel" [Something about or against Le Bon's article], *Samtiden*, 1891, pp.161–7

"Hafdan Egedius", *Samtiden*, 1899, pp.83–7

"Jæderen", *Norge i det nittende aarhundrede* [Norway in the 19th century], ii, Christiania, 1900, pp.158–65

Bibliography

Andreas Aubert, *Det nye Norges malerkunst* [Painting of the new Norway], Christiania, 1904

Jen Thiis, *Norske malere og billedhuggere* [Norwegian painters and sculptors], Bergen, i, 1904, pp.185, 311; ii, 1907, pp.311–16

E. Lone, *Harriet Backer*, Oslo, 1924

B. Kielland, *Min far Alexander L. Kielland* [My father Alexander L. Kielland], Oslo, 1929

H. Aars, "På Fleskum i Bærum" [At Fleskum in Bærum], *Kunst og Kultur*, 1942, pp.93–110

A. Durban, *Malerskikkelser fra 80-årene* [Figures in painting from the 1880s], Trondheim, 1943

E. Christie Kielland, "Kitty L. Kielland", *Urd*, 1943, pp.376–8

G.S. Hidle, *Profiler og paletter i Rogalands kunst* [Profiles and palettes in Rogland's art], Stavanger, 1965

U. Hamran, "Harriet Backer og Kitty L. Kielland på Bosvik sommeren 1885" [Harriet Backer and Kitty L. Kielland in Bosvik in the summer of 1885], *Aust-Agder arv: Aust-Agder Museum Årbok*, 1977, pp.117–26

Marit Lange, "Fra den hellige lund til Fleskum: Kitty L. Kielland og den nordiske sommernatt" [From the holy grove to Fleskum: Kitty L. Kielland and the Nordic summer night], *Kunst og Kultur*, 1977, pp.69–92

——, "Kitty Lange Kielland", *Norske mesterverker i Nasjonalgalleriet* [Norwegian masterpieces in the National Gallery], Oslo, 1981, pp.56–8

Anne Wichstrøm, "Blant likemenn: Søkelys på Harriet Backers og Kitty L. Kiellands karrierer" [Among equals: Spotlight on the careers of Harriet Backer and Kitty L. Kielland], *Den skjulte tradisjon* [The hidden tradition], Bergen, 1982, pp.172–91

Harriet Backer, 1845–1932, Kitty L. Kielland, 1843–1914, exh. cat., Stiftelsen Modums Blaafarvevaerk, Drammen, 1983

Anne Wichstrøm, *Kvinner ved staffeliet: Kvinnelige malere i Norge før 1900* [Women at the easel: Women painters in Norway before 1900], Oslo: Universitetsforlaget, 1983 (revised edition in preparation)

1880-årene i nordisk maleri [The 1880s in Nordic painting], exh. cat., Nasjonalgalleriet, Oslo, and elsewhere, 1985

Dreams of a Summer Night: Scandinavian Painting at the Turn of the Century, exh. cat., Arts Council of Great Britain, London, 1986

De drogo till Paris: Nordiska konstnärinnor på 1880-talet [They went to Paris: Nordic women artists in the 1880s], exh. cat., Liljevalchs Konsthall, Stockholm, 1988

Kirk Varnedoe, *Northern Light: Nordic Art at the Turn of the Century*, New Haven and London: Yale University Press, 1988

Alessandra Comini, "Nordic luminism and the Scandinavian recasting of Impressionism", *World Impressionism: The International Movement, 1860–1920*, ed. Norma Broude, New York: Abrams, 1992, pp.274–313

Knut Berg, "Naturalisme og nyromanrikk" [Naturalism and Neoromanticism], *Norges Malerkunst*, ed. Knut Berg, Oslo: Gyldendal, 1993

Tradisjon og fornyelse [Tradition and innovation], exh. cat., Nasjonalgalleriet, Oslo, 1994

Anne Wichstrøm, "At century's end: Harriet Backer, Kitty Kielland, Asta Nørregaard", *At Century's End: Norwegian Artists and the Figurative Tradition, 1880/1990*, exh. cat, Henie-Onstad Art Center, Høvikodden, and National Museum of Women in the Arts, Washington, DC, 1995, pp.21–67

Best known for her landscapes of the Jæren region, Kitty Kielland was an integral member of Norway's National Romantic generation of painters. There were several women in this group, and they worked with their male colleagues as peers and equals, developing a distinctive group style that won them immediate and continuing popularity. While the urge to define a national identity distinct from Denmark (which had ruled Norway prior to 1815) and Sweden (which ruled Norway until 1906) had fuelled ethnographic pursuits and permeated literature and music since the beginning of the century, it was not until the 1880s that the impulse to manifest a Norwegian identity in painting appeared. Kielland, always devoted to an exacting observation and experience of nature as part of the creative process, was an important link between Naturalism and Nordic Symbolism.

Kielland was the only member of this group trained by a woman; her first studies in her home town of Stavanger were given by Fanny Zeuthen. While Zeuthen was a painter of purely local significance, the fact that women painters functioned as teachers in the 1850s and 1860s indicates the relatively high stature of women artists in the Nordic countries. Kielland spent most of the 1870s in Germany, primarily in Munich, where she pursued plein-air landscape painting. Rather than studying with a local artist, she relied on the critique of fellow Norwegian artist Eilif Petersson, who began his career as a history painter, turning to landscape only in the 1880s during his residence in Paris. Since Kielland was a leading proponent of Naturalistic landscape painting from the very beginning, she exerted an influence on Petersson and other Norwegians who turned to landscape painting as the National Romantic movement escalated.

Kielland's small-format compositions typically involved a detailed foreground and a broadly delineated background. In the Naturalist tradition, her images were unpretentious. Narrative was reduced to a minimum, forcing the viewer's concentration on subtleties of light, shadow and atmosphere. Often the only figure in her landscapes is a lone woman, quietly engaged in a leisure activity, as in *After Sunset* (1885; Slottet, Oslo), where a woman rows on a placid lake in front of a manor house, and *Jærtun, Kvalbein* (1904; Breidablikk Foundation, Stavanger), where a peasant woman draws water from a well on a rural Norwegian farm. While Kielland's sketchy brushwork conveys the impression of an image executed in plein air, there is a methodical and unhurried quality about it that conveys a sense of tranquillity rather than agitation.

One of Kielland's best known-works, *Summer Night* (1886; see illustration), was produced during her residence at the summer artists' colony flourishing at Fleskum Farm, near Oslo. Amidst the invigorating company of more than a half dozen Norwegian National Romantic painters, all of whom had resided in Munich and Paris during the previous decade, Kielland painted one of her largest landscapes (1 × 1.35 m.), which must be understood as a major declaration of her artistic intentions. Here the pervasive sense of tranquillity in nature found in much of Kielland's production attains its most emphatic expression. She chose as her subject the unusual atmospheric conditions of summer nights in the northernmost latitudes, where, for a brief period, darkness never falls. The darkness of the earth contrasts dramatically with the silvery

Kielland: *Summer Night*, 1886; oil on canvas; 100.5 × 135.5 cm.; Nasjonalgalleriet, Oslo

blue sky, reflected on the water, but the dominance of a cool palette restrains the emotional tenor to one of quiet contemplation. A lone figures rows towards the distant shore, creating a slight ripple in the otherwise static surface. Conceptualising this painting as a kind of visual "tone poem" makes explicit the urge of National Romantic painters to achieve a form of musical harmony in their works. They were interested in producing paintings that had the evocative potential of music in order to create an emotional bridge between the artist and the viewer.

In *Summer Night* Kielland places the viewer among the reeds near, but not on, the shore. The low vantage point suggests that the artist/viewer is situated on a boat (it is too low to be a dock), furthering the sense of immersion in and identity with the landscape that National Romantic painters sought to convey. Their intent was to create a pictorial analogue for the symbiotic relationship they felt existed between Norwegians and Nordic nature. The decorative patterning of the lily pads evidences the simplification and stylisation utilised by Kielland to represent her subject more emphatically, and points towards the evolution of a highly stylised, Art Nouveau style that would emerge in other Norwegian painters (particularly Gerhard Munthe) towards

the end of the 19th century. *Summer Night* was immediately acclaimed a key National Romantic work, and appeared at the Paris Salon of 1887, the Nordic exhibition in Copenhagen in 1888 and at the Paris Exposition Universelle of 1889 before being purchased by the Norwegian government in 1890. While most of Kielland's works remain in private collections in Norway, examples can also be found in the Nasjonalgalleriet, Oslo, the Faste Galleri, Stavanger, and the Lillehammer Bys Malerisamling.

MICHELLE FACOS

Killigrew, Anne *see* Court Artists survey

King, Jessie M(arion)
British illustrator, painter and designer, 1875–1949

Born in Bearsden, Dunbartonshire, 20 March 1875; father the Revd James W. King, DD. Took foundation course in anatomy at Queen Margaret College, Glasgow, 1891–2. Studied at Glasgow School of Art under Francis Newbery, 1892–7 (Queen's prize and studentship, 1897); appointed tutor in book decoration and design, 1899, tutor in ceramic decoration, 1906. Visited Germany and Italy, 1902, France, 1904. Married painter and designer Ernest Archibald Taylor, 1908; daughter born 1909. Lived first in Salford near Manchester, then moved to Paris in 1910, when Taylor was appointed professor at Tutor Hart's studio and Paris correspondent for *The Studio*. The couple established the Shealing Atelier, a studio for fine and applied art, in 1911 (closed 1920), and began running summer sketching schools on the island of Arran, Scotland. Returned to Scotland at outbreak of World War I, settling in Kirkcudbright; retained a studio in Paris until 1928. Recipient of silver medal, Department of Science and Art National Competition, 1898. Member, Glasgow Society of Lady Artists, 1905. Died in Kirkcudbright, 3 August 1949.

Principal Exhibitions

Individual

Bruton Street Galleries, London: 1905
T. & R. Annan and Sons, Glasgow: 1907, 1909, 1912
Lady Artists Club, Glasgow: 1931 (*Spring in Three Rooms*), 1932, 1935 (all with Helen Paxton Brown)
Pearson and Westergard Gallery, Glasgow: 1935

Group

Esposizione Internazionale d'Arte, Venice: 1899
Royal Glasgow Institute of the Fine Arts: occasionally 1901–48
Glasgow Society of Lady Artists: from 1901 (Lauder award 1921)
Royal Scottish Academy, Edinburgh: occasionally 1902–44
Esposizione Internazionale d'Arte Decorativa Moderna, Turin: 1902 (gold medal for book design)
Royal Society of Arts, London: from 1902
Paris Salon: 1912

Bibliography

Walter R. Watson, "Miss Jessie M. King and her work", *The Studio*, xxvi, 1902, pp.177–88
E. A. Taylor, "Miss Jessie M. King", *Book-Lover's Magazine*, vii, 1908, pp.195–201
Jessie M. King, 1875–1949, exh. cat., Scottish Arts Council Gallery, Glasgow, and elsewhere, 1971
The Glasgow Style, 1890–1920, exh. cat., Glasgow Museums and Art Gallery, 1984
Colin White, *The Enchanted World of Jessie M. King*, Edinburgh: Canongate, 1989
Jude Burkhauser, ed., *Glasgow Girls: Women in Art and Design, 1880–1920*, 2nd edition, Edinburgh: Canongate, and Cape May, NJ: Red Ochre, 1993
Colin White, "The bookplate designs of Jessie M. King", *Bookplate Journal*, xiii, March 1995, pp.2–29

Like many other late 19th-century Glaswegian women artists, Jessie King began her career as a student at the Glasgow School of Art (GSA), taught at that institution, and was an active member of the Glasgow Society of Lady Artists. The relationship between the GSA and the Society had been established in 1882 when the founder-members met in the studio of Robert Greenlees, the principal of the GSA, with the intention of promoting the study of art and of holding "periodical exhibitions, open to the public" (*Glasgow Herald*, 5 December

1893). King joined the Society early in 1905 and exhibited with them until her death.

In 1902 *The Studio* referred to King as "a pure product of what may be called the Glasgow School of Decorative Art" (Watson 1902, p.177). As such she "coupled" beauty with utility, and persisted in "seeing things and representing them entirely with her own vision, and absolutely in her own way" (p.178). Ten years later, in 1912, when King had a solo exhibition at Annans' in Glasgow, the *Glasgow Herald* indicated her success as a watercolour painter: "while containing much in the old vein" the exhibition revealed "the artist in a new phase". King was lauded for the "cleanliness" of her design, her "deft draughtsmanship" and her "consummate power"; at the same time her work was considered "mystical and elusive", but without the "decadence" and "morbidity" found in much of the decorative art of the time, and which, according to the *Glasgow Herald*, was "most conspicuous in the work of women artists" (5 October 1912). Certainly, while King is still most known for illustrative work such as *The Little Princess* and *The Little Princess and the Peacock* (repr. Watson 1902, pp.178 and 180), the exhibition of 1912 included watercolour landscapes. Typically, it is her illustrations that are seen in *The Studio*; the pictures are composed rhythmically with a thin, delicate line interspersed with the dot-constructed shapes characteristic of her black-and-white drawings. The images are fairy-tale-like: armoured knights, young long-haired women, gentle, graceful animals, exquisite plant-life and dreamlike architecture. This is usually our impression of King the illustrator, and rarely do art historians reach beyond this to find more. Her "Book-Plate" for William Rowat (father of Jessie Newbery, q.v.) and a "Book-Cover" (*ibid.*, pp.186 and 178; see illustration), however, clearly demonstrate the strength and clarity of her designs, her elegant use of space and the confidence of her line; in other words King was an outstandingly accomplished designer.

In addition, King worked in collaboration with other artists on design projects, most frequently with Helen Paxton Brown. Brown and King had become friends as students at the Glasgow School of Art, and for nine years during the 1890s shared a studio on St Vincent Street, living in adjacent apartments next door. During the 1930s King collaborated on three exhibition projects with Brown. The first of these opened in the gallery of the Lady Artists Club in April 1931. Appropriately called *Spring in Three Rooms*, the artists divided the gallery and arranged art and craft work to fit each interior. The first room, in "bright and cheerful colours" functioned as an entrance hall that led into a "dining-room" with a breakfast table set for four and a dinner table set for six; the tables were laid with pottery and china designed and painted by King (*Glasgow Herald*, 10 April 1931). The third room was designed as a bedroom for two children with two sets of furniture, one designed by King, the other by Paxton Brown. Landscapes by both artists graced the walls of all the rooms. While this kind of "installation" is rarely discussed in literature on King, it represents her entire oeuvre, not only her illustrations, and it speaks to us of her large collaborative projects. In May 1932 the artists exhibited together again at the Lady Artists Club; although not arranged in "rooms", the work included pictures, "gay" embroidery, hand-made dresses and painted pottery (*Glasgow Herald*, 6 May 1932). The last

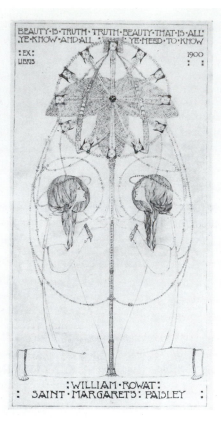

King: Book-cover design in *The Studio*, vi, August 1902, p.186; Metropolitan Toronto Reference Library

exhibition of this kind done by the women together was *Youth's the Stuff* in 1935, which included newly designed children's toys, thus continuing an interest that, for King, had begun in the early part of the 20th century.

In her perceptive catalogue essay for the King exhibition organised by the Scottish Arts Council in 1971, Cordelia Oliver attributed to the artist a "double focus". Oliver suggested that the "top" of King's mind scanned "some hazy, improbable never-land of romance and legend, while her eye was fixed on small natural phenomena which she was able to set down with minute exactitude" (Glasgow 1971, p.8). Much earlier, E.A. Taylor, Jessie King's husband, wrote of her that she was "the seer and the poet's artist" (Taylor 1908, p.201). While King's perceived romantic idealism may deter certain late 20th-century viewers from looking closely at her work, an examination of her entire production will reveal a diligent, thoughtful and productive decorative artist and watercolour painter who succeeded at teaching and art-making, and left a legacy that requires analysis and discussion.

JANICE HELLAND

Klien, Erika Giovanna

Austrian painter, 1900–1957

Born in Borgo di Valsugano, Trentino, 12 April 1900. Studied ornamental design under Franz Cižek at the Kunstgewerbe-schule, Vienna, 1919–24 (New York prize). Taught trial course at newly founded Elisabeth Duncan School, Klessheim, Salzburg, 1925; full-time teacher, 1926. Son born 1928. Invited to USA, 1928. Began teaching at Stuyvesant Neighborhood House, New York, 1928; taught architecture course, 1931; retired, 1932. Taught at New School for Social Research, New York, 1931–6. Employed by Dalton School in New York, 1932; resigned 1935. Director of art department at Spence School, New York, 1935; arranged successful annual summer exhibitions until 1940, when forced to leave. Became US citizen, 1938. Taught at Walt Whitman School, New York, 1946–51. Died in New York, 19 July 1957.

Principal Exhibitions

Museum für Kunst und Industrie, Vienna: 1920 (*Erneuerung der geistigen Grundlagen des rhythmischen Gestaltens*)
Netherlands: 1922–4 (touring exhibition of work by Cižek's students)
Fichtegasse, Vienna: 1923, 1924 (Cižek school exhibitions)
Österreichisches Museum, Vienna: 1923 (*Ausstellung von Arbeiten des modernen österreichischen Kunsthandwerks – Dagobert Peche zum Gedächtnis*), 1926 (*Internationale Ausstellung moderner künstlerischer Schrift*), 1928 (Klien school of Klessheim), 1929 (*Kunstgewerbeschule Wien: 60. Bestandsjahr*)
USA: 1923–6 (touring exhibition of work by Cižek's students)
Exposition Internationale des Arts Décoratifs et Industriels Modernes, Paris: 1925
Brooklyn Museum, NY: 1926 (*International Exhibition of Modern Art*)
Landesgewerbemuseum, Stuttgart: 1928 (Klien school)
Gewerbemuseum, Basel: 1928 (Klien school)

Schloss Klessheim: 1929 (Klien school)
New School for Social Research, New York: 1930 (individual), 1932 (Klien school), 1934 (individual)
Stuyvesant House, New York: 1930 (*Works by Klien School*)
Galerie Vaudemont, Paris: 1931 (works by Klien/Duncan school)
New York Art Center: 1931 (individual, with students)
Dalton School, New York: 1934 (*Constructive Woodwork*), 1935 (Klien school)
Progressive Education Association, New York: 1934

Bibliography

L.W. Rochowanski, *Der Formwille der Zeit*, Vienna: Burg, 1922
Max Ermers, "Rhythmical art", *Der Tag* (Vienna), 2 July 1924
L.W. Rochowanski, "Das kinetische Marionettentheater der Erika Giovanna Klien", *Die Neue Schaubühne*, i/5, January 1925, pp.47f
International Exhibition of Modern Art, exh. cat., Brooklyn Museum, NY, and Société Anonyme, 1926
"Industrial art in Austria", *Christian Science Monitor*, 24 January 1927
Exhibition review in *Art Center Bulletin of the National Alliance of Art and Industry*, New York, May 1931
"Erika Klien's pupils exhibit", *New York Times*, 12 May 1932
Erika Giovanna Klien, exh. cat., Galerie Michael Pabst, Vienna, 1975
Bernhard Leitner, "Kinetismus: Eine Wiener Erfindung", *Die Presse* (Vienna), 7 January 1975
Österreichs Avantgarde, 1900–1938, exh. cat., Galerie nächst St Stephan, Vienna, and elsewhere, 1976
Léger et l'esprit moderne, exh. cat., Musée d'Art Moderne de la Ville de Paris, 1982
Marietta Mautner Markhof, "Der Wiener Kinetismus und Erika Giovanna Klien, 1900–1957", *Schwarz/Weiss*, exh. cat., Galerien Maximilianstrasse and Galerie Michael Pabst, Munich, 1983, pp.2–3; revised in *Künstlerinnen*, exh. cat., Neue Galerie der Stadt, Linz, 1983
——, "Franz Cižek und der Wiener Kinetismus", *Bildende Kunst*, ii, 1984. pp.81ff
——, "Franz Cižek und die Moderne Kunst", *Franz Cižek: Pionier der Kunsterziehung*, exh. cat., Historisches Museum der Stadt Wien, Vienna, 1985, pp.15ff
Dieter Bogner, "Une modernité optimiste: La voie abstraite", *Vienne, 1880–1938: L'Apocalypse joyeuse*, exh. cat., Centre Georges Pompidou, Paris, 1986, pp.646–54
Wiener Kinetismus/E.G. Klien, exh. cat., Galerie Michael Pabst, Munich, 1986
Erika Giovanna Klien, 1900–1957, exh. cat., Museum Moderner Kunst, Vienna, 1987
The Life and Work of Erika Giovanna Klien: A Retrospective Through Drawing, exh. cat., Rachel Adler Gallery, New York, 1989
Marietta Mautner Markhof, "Konstruktive Tendenzen", *Die Ungewisse Hoffnung: Österreichische Malerei und Graphik zwischen 1918 und 1938*, ed. Christoph Bertsch and Markus Neuwirth, Salzburg and Vienna: Residenz, 1993, pp.188ff

Of the many gifted artists who trained in Austria after the end of the Habsburg monarchy in 1918, Erika Giovanna Klien was one of the few to transcend the provincial style and develop an artistic language of international relevance. The crucial formative influence in her remarkable development was the teaching of Franz Cižek, whose classes she attended from 1919 to 1924 at the Kunstgewerbeschule, Vienna. Cižek, the promoter of what he called Kinetismus (from Kinetism, the art of movement), was a rare teacher among the heroic reformers of the

Klien: *Winter Landscape*, 1925; charcoal and gouache on paper, laid down on tag board; Yale University Art Gallery, New Haven, Gift from the Estate of Katharine S. Dreier, Photo Joseph Szaszfai (1953.6.54)

Secession. Although he was a distinguished professor, he was open-minded enough to keep a vital interest in the European and American avant-garde. While Austrian painting ranged from Secessionist formalism, expressionist and naturalistic realism to half-hearted versions of Cézanne, he taught his students about the evolution of modern art from the abstraction of feelings and spatial perception to the construction of movement. Deeply influenced by the social and cultural revolutions of the time and by his experience of teaching art to children, he encouraged his adult students to develop an art language expressive of modern times. The early work of Klien, like that of her colleagues Elisabeth Karlinsky and Marianne Ullmann, reflected the evolution to which Cižek's teaching was directed. After three years study with Cižek, around 1922–3 Klien found her own way to Constructivism. Her drawings, which evolve from Cubo-Futurist studies of moving figures, plants and architecture (e.g. *Moving Figure*, 1921–2; Historisches Museum, Vienna, repr. Vienna 1987, p.77) influenced by the Hungarian MA ("Today") group and possibly Johannes Itten, convey movement through spatial and geometrical rhythms (*Nude Series*, 1922–3; *ibid.*, pp.24–5; *Das Lied der Goldamsel*, 1923; Historisches Museum, *ibid.*, p.80).

In 1924 the Viennese public was introduced to the European avant-garde with the international art exhibitions held at the Secession and the Konzerthaus. After this, Klien's art reflected some of the sobriety of the purist conception typical of Esprit Nouveau and De Stijl artists (*Winter Landscape*, 1925; see illustration). As if to counter this loss of vivacity she began experimenting with the laws of infantile expression in drawings. Throughout her life she continued to return to the source of primitive creativity for help in negotiating the constraints of abstraction (*The Walk*, 1924–5; *Riders*, 1925; both Historisches Museum, *ibid.*, pp.36 and 90).

From 1925 Klien was in charge of the art classes at the Elisabeth Duncan School in Klessheim Castle near Salzburg. Some of her works on paper were collected by Katherine Dreier for the Société Anonyme in New York and for the *International Exhibition of Modern Art* at the Brooklyn Museum in 1926. Invited to the USA in 1928, Klien spent the rest of her life in New York, earning her living as an art teacher. Despite some disillusionment with the USA as the "promised land", she vividly expressed the spirit and reality of her new country in her mature work. The dichotomy of abstraction and primitivism persisted, although her work underwent important changes around 1932–4. Her seemingly naive depictions of everyday life were not so much derived from children's drawings as from American muralists such as Thomas Hart Benton. Benton completed murals for the new building of the New School for Social Research in New York in 1931, just before Klien began teaching there, and her murals reflect this influence (e.g. *Men at Work*, 1931; private collection, Frankfurt am Main, *ibid.*, p.44). The abstractionist aspect of her kinetism became quite conceptual and free, as in her diagrammatic series, *Bird Flight Motion* (1933; most in private collection, Vienna, and Galerie Michael Pabst, Munich, *ibid.*, pp.96 and 122–3). Another, purely abstract series on expanding and concentric movements (1935–6; most in private collection, Vienna, and Galerie Michael Pabst, Munich, *ibid.*, pp.47, 99 and 124–5) was based on the geometrical-machinist murals that Klien designed for the staircase of the Stokowski apartment near Central Park in 1932 (studies at Museum moderner Kunst, Vienna, and some private collections, *ibid.*, pp.94–5).

These highly conceptual works were again counterbalanced by groups of primitivist figure studies. Here the depiction of movement was based on the rhythmical scansion of line and form, as in early kinetism, but also on the forms and additive rhythms of American folk art (*Man at the Crank*, c.1936; Galerie Michael Pabst, Munich; *Grief*, 1934; private collection, Düsseldorf; *ibid.*, pp.97–8). There are virtually no datable records of Klien's activity during the war years, and she seems to have had a period of crisis with the incorporation of Austria into National Socialist Germany in 1938, the outbreak of war in Europe, the deterioration of relations between her native and her new country, and the entry of the USA into the war in 1941. In addition, in 1940 she lost her job at the Spence School, where she had directed the art department since 1935. Her creativity returned when she renewed contact with her son in Austria after the war and made efforts to earn money with applied art, design and short stories. Towards the end of her life, a period of teaching at the Walt Whitman School gave her the security to produce new series: *Racing Lights (Subway)*, *Rhythm of Bird Flight* and *Rhythm of Walking* (1950–56; most in private collections and Galerie Michael Pabst, Munich, *ibid.*, pp.49, 103–4 and 112) are outstanding examples of the synthesis of the abstract and primitivist conceptions of Klien's art of motion.

MARIETTA MAUTNER MARKHOF

af Klint, Hilma

Swedish painter, 1862–1944

Born in Stockholm, 26 October 1862. Attended the Technical School, Stockholm, and studied privately under portrait painter Kerstin Cardon, c.1880; studied at the Royal Academy of Fine Arts, Stockholm, 1882–7. Professional portrait and landscape painter, 1887–1908. Seriously involved in spiritualism by 1879. Formed a spiritualist group with four other women, called the Friday Group or The Five, 1890s. Met social philosopher Rudolf Steiner, 1908. Ceased painting, 1908–12. Moved to Helsingborg, southern Sweden, and made first of many visits to Steiner in Dornach, Switzerland, 1920. Became increasingly interested in theosophy and anthroposophy after 1922. Died in Djursholm, 21 October 1944.

Selected Writings

"Anteckningsböcker" [Notebooks], manuscript, 1882–1944, Hilma af Klint Foundation, Stockholm

"Avskrifter ur föredrag av Rudolf Steiner" [Transcripts of speeches by Rudolf Steiner], manuscript, Hilma af Klint Foundation, Stockholm

"Studier över själslivet" [Soul studies], manuscript dictated by Hilma af Klint to Dr Anna Ljungberg, 1917–18, typed in 1941–2, Hilma af Klint Foundation, Stockholm

Bibliography

Åke Fant, "Synpunkter på Hilma af Klints måleri" [Points of view about Hilma af Klint's painting], *Studier i konstvetenskap tillägnade Brita Linde* [Studies in art history dedicated to Brita Linde], Stockholm: Konstvetenskapliga Institutionen, 1985, pp.45–54

——, *Kring Hilma af Klints sekelskiftesmåleri* [Around Hilma af Klint's turn-of-the century paintings], Helsinki, 1986

The Spiritual in Art: Abstract Painting, 1890–1985, exh. cat., Los Angeles County Museum of Art, and elsewhere, 1986

T. Dijkhuis and others, *Het mysterie van de abstracten: Het onzichtbare zichtbaar gemakt* [The mystery of the Abstracts: The invisible made visible], Utrecht, 1987

T. Ekbom, *Bildstorm* [Picture storm], Uppsala, 1987

Het Mystere van de Abstracten, 1890–1985 [The mystery of the Abstracts, 1890–1985], exh. cat., Haags Gemeentemuseum, The Hague, 1987

Hilma af Klints hemliga bilder [Hilma af Klint's secret pictures], exh. cat., Nordiskt Konstcentrums, 1988

Konkret i Norden/Scandinavian Concrete Art, exh. cat., Amos Andersson Museum, Helsinki, and elsewhere, 1988

Brooks Adams, "Contemplating the rose hip", *Art in America*, lxxvii, December 1989, pp.164–7

J. Clair and others, *Wunderblock: Eine Geschichte der modernen Seele*, Vienna: Messepalast, 1989

Hilma af Klint: Ockult målarinna och abstrakt pionjär [Hilma af Klint: Occult painter and abstract pioneer], exh. cat., Museum Moderna Kunst, Stockholm, 1989 (contains extensive bibliography)

Nancy G. Heller, *Women Artists: An Illustrated History*, 2nd edition, New York: Abbeville, 1991

Okkultismus und Abstraktion: Die Malerin Hilma af Klint (1862–1944), exh. cat., Graphische Sammlung Albertina, Vienna, and elsewhere, 1991

The oeuvre of the Swedish painter Hilma af Klint can be divided into two distinct groups. During her studies at the Royal Academy of Fine Arts in Stockholm in the 1880s and just after, she devoted herself to landscape and portrait painting. In their fresh, naturalistic rendering of nature and great sensitivity to colour and light, such works as *View over Mälaren* (1903; Hilma af Klint Foundation, Stockholm) are linked to the practice of the time. Although af Klint continued to produce this type of naturalistic painting throughout her artistic career, it was the second and very extensive group of works, begun in earnest in 1906, that was to be of much greater significance. A secret occupation that was made known to the public only in the 1980s, this group of works moves away completely from contemporary forms of expression, and is of particular interest for its originality. The style of painting is strange, full of symbols that can be difficult to interpret. The high degree of abstraction in the paintings aroused great interest when the works were first exhibited. Under the influence of a sort of inner spiritual guide, af Klint executed such paintings as *Swan No.16* and *Swan No.17* (both 1914–15; see illustration), both of which went far in their exquisite reduction of colour and form. Yet such pictures were already emerging in the *Urkaos* series of 1906 (Hilma af Klint Foundation). In these af Klint abolished natural forms, thereby anticipating some of modernism's great male artists in abandoning the representation of external reality. Af Klint executed this work secretly within a small circle of women, and apparently without any influence from the nascent Scandinavian modernism.

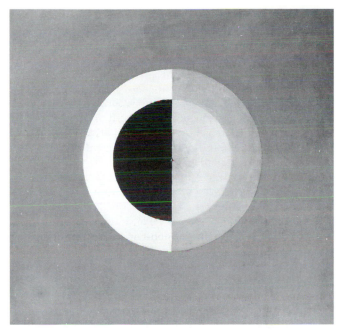

af Klint: *Swan No.17*, 1914–15; oil on canvas; 155 × 152 cm.; Hilma af Klint Foundation, Stockholm

In her autobiographical notes or "Soul studies" ("Studier över själslivet", 1917–18) af Klint wrote:

> In order to execute work that is extremely important I have been obliged to give up that which during my youth my heart yearned for: to be able to represent external forms and colours. In other words, I have frankly been held back from a sphere of activity, and laboriously clambered up the steps …

This task, which came from a spirit named Amaliel by af Klint in her notes, resulted in a series of works emerging from processes that occasionally overlap one another chronologically. In 1905 "Amaliel" gave her a commission that resulted in the *WU Series/The Rose* (1906–7), the *WUS Series/Seven Stars* (1908), the *SUW Series/The Swan*, the *UW Series/The Dove and Altar Pictures* (1915) and finished with the summary painting *Human Chastity* (1915; all Hilma af Klint Foundation). The next period began with the *Parsifal* series (1916) and continued until 1920 with another series *The Atom: Series II–VIII* (all Hilma af Klint Foundation). Thereafter there was some reduction in af Klint's productivity, but up to her death she executed works that can be linked as much to the naturalistic as to the abstract part of her artistic make-up.

The first series, from 1906, the *WU Series/The Rose*, are small-format paintings (50 × 38 cm.) on the theme of Urkaos (Original chaos). They are all executed with expressive brushwork contrasting with more massed shapes: embryo, star or snail forms. The paintings are completely free of the careful representation of nature that distinguishes af Klint's earlier paintings, and seem to derive their form from apparently uncontrolled hand movements on a canvas only partially visible. Af Klint characterises these as an exercise in anticipation of future commissions. After a series of smaller paintings, the *Series II*, in which, against an overall light background, she executed forms with marked contours and combinations of letters and symbols that are difficult to interpret, she began to paint in much larger formats.

Human figures appear in the *Large Figure Paintings* of 1907. These were made while af Klint "was without consciousness", according to her notes. In several of them (such as nos 3, 4, 6 and 7A) the figure of a man or woman occurs in different symbolic compositions, not infrequently accompanied by a third, prophet-like figure. In her notebooks af Klint writes about the *Large Figure Painting No.3*: "Devan (natural spirit) is represented as a middle-aged man. Free from karma he supports humankind's imprisoned children." In the picture the prophet-like man sits in a yellow cloak, with a female figure kneeling beside him and a standing male figure turning towards him, his hands clasped behind his back. The figures are painted here without great attention to proportions and angles, against a ground that is reminiscent of the *Urkaos Series*: the gesticulating paint strokes against a black background create a cell-like double form. In the next series, *Ten Largest*, which are as large as 328 × 240 centimetres, the lines become more loaded, the forms ever larger and flower-like, with some of them even completely geometrical. According to af Klint these forms represent evolution: "It was the leader's intention to give the world an insight into the systematisation of the four departments of people's lives. Ardent childhood, adolescence as well as old age". Here the colours are clear, and unified in fields of blue, green, orange and red-pink as backgrounds.

The *Swan* series dates from after the completion of the *Ten Largest* series. *Swan No.24* is typical in the way in which the picture is built up from symmetries, or occasionally in geometrical planes divided in four. Here a white and a black swan are joined in an embrace. Their beaks meet in a kiss, also comprising a hook and eye, which according to af Klint are the symbols for woman and man respectively. The background is made up of four square fields. The degree of abstraction culminates, as mentioned above, in the beautiful *Swan No.16* and *Swan No.17* (1914–15). In these paintings the divided circular form rests against a monochrome background, with a triangle in the centre. The compositional austerity and use of colour are very sophisticated. Within the limits of the secret commissions that af Klint received, *The Dove* and *Altar Pictures* stand out as high points in conveying religious meaning.

In order to get closer to an understanding of af Klint's work, one can regard her painting and the texts she and her female friends wrote as two aspects of the same oeuvre, although the writings are insufficient tools for the interpretation of the pictures. The texts register the creation of the pictures: she formulated the spiritual guide's commission as it appeared to her, describing her own emotions during its execution.

Throughout her career af Klint appears to have strongly identified with the female sex. She grew up during a time and in a social milieu – she came from a prominent naval family – when a clear distinction between the characteristics and areas of activity of the two genders was constantly maintained. Af Klint experienced love during her youth but remained unmarried. Throughout her life she sought solidarity exclusively with women, in groups in which she was often the central figure. She was a strong believer, but also enterprising, an organiser who inspired confidence. From 1879 to 1882 she participated in organised seances. She appears not to have been interested in either the Swedish opponent movement or later in the dawning modernism of the 1910s. She joined the Association of Swedish Women Artists when it was founded in 1910.

Af Klint was well acquainted with the ideas of the period's theosophical and spiritual teachers. Rudolf Steiner, whom she met in Stockholm, was a great role-model for her. She visited him in Dornach, hoping to gain acknowledgement and an explanation of her life's work. But Steiner, who stressed the importance of the conscious development of the soul, considered her working methods unsuitable. This became a conflict for af Klint, and she was disappointed by his lack of appreciation of her work. Her own working method was spiritual; during the working process she experienced the fact that her work was conceived and directed by external intelligences.

Af Klint's world of thought and conception of life was constructed dualistically. She had experience of a male opposite, Gidro, whom she never met in her real life. She saw her life's task as being the intermediary between what she called "dual knowledge", a platonically coloured understanding emanating from the fact that each person belongs with a particular individual of the opposite sex. In her "Studier över själslivet", dictated in 1917–18 and recorded in a typescript of 2058 pages in 1941–2, she returns repeatedly to the dual thought. It is a detailed vision of the different functions of the souls of men and women and of the positive strength contained in the struggle between them.

It is possible to interpret the abstract qualities of Hilma af Klint's paintings as resting on a dichotomy. The symmetry or the divided halves are the recurring compositional models, which point towards a correspondence between her understanding of the world and her painting. Through her extensive and innovative life's work she was to overcome the gender order of her period, at the same time as having a deep conviction of this order's fundamental significance. Af Klint allowed no-one outside a small circle of women to see this part of her work. She stated in her will that her paintings should be kept together, and not be exhibited publicly for 20 years after her death.

ANNIKA ÖHRNER

Klumpke, Anna (Elizabeth)
American painter, 1856–1942

Born in San Francisco, 1856. Moved with mother and four siblings to Europe after parents' divorce, 1870; settled in Lausanne, Switzerland, receiving treatment for childhood knee injury that left her permanently disabled. Moved to Paris with her family, 1877; copied at the Louvre then entered the Académie Julian. Career as portraitist in USA, 1890–98. Returned to France to paint portrait of Rosa Bonheur (q.v.), 1898; bequeathed Bonheur's entire estate at her death in 1899. Converted Bonheur's Château de By into a convalescent hospital during World War I. Established Musée Rosa Bonheur at Fontainebleau, 1924. Returned to San Francisco with surviving sisters, 1937. Recipient of silver medal, La Reconnaissance Française, Versailles, 1920.

Chevalier, 1924, and Officier, 1936, Légion d'Honneur, France. Died 1942.

Principal Exhibitions

Individual
St Botolph's Club, Boston: 1892
Albany Historical Society, NY: 1898
Doll and Richards Gallery, Boston: 1932
M.H. De Young Museum, San Francisco: 1933
San Francisco Museum of Art: 1939

Group
Paris Salon: occasionally 1882–1937 (honourable mention 1885)
American Exhibition, London: 1886
Pennsylvania Academy of the Fine Arts, Philadelphia: 1889 (Temple gold medal)
Art Institute of Chicago: 1889
World's Columbian Exposition, Chicago: 1893
Carnegie Institute, Pittsburgh: 1907

Selected Writings
Rosa Bonheur: Sa vie, son oeuvre, Paris: Flammarion, 1908
Memoirs of an Artist, ed. Lilian Whiting, Boston: Wright and Potter, 1940

Bibliography
George William Sheldon, *Recent Ideals of American Art*, New York: Appleton, 1888; reprinted New York: Garland, 1977

M.P. Handy, *Woman's Building*, xiv of *The Official Directory of the World's Columbian Exposition*, Chicago: Conkey, 1893

Theodore Stanton, ed., *Reminiscences of Rosa Bonheur*, London: Melrose, and New York: Appleton, 1910; reprinted New York: Hacker, 1976

The National Cyclopedia of American Biography, xxxi, New York: James T. White, 1944 (essays on Klumpke family)

Doreen Bolger Burke, "Anna Elizabeth Klumpke (1856–1942)", *American Paintings in the Metropolitan Museum of Art*, iii, New York: Metropolitan Museum of Art, 1980

Dore Ashton, *Rosa Bonheur: A Life and Legend*, New York: Viking, and London: Secker and Warburg, 1981

Lois Marie Fink, *American Art at the Nineteenth-Century Paris Salons*, Washington, DC: Smithsonian Institution Press, and Cambridge: Cambridge University Press, 1990

Anna Klumpke (1856–1942): Duty and the Dedicated Spirit, exh. cat., University Art Museum, Arizona State University, Tempe, 1993

Mary Jo Aagerstoun, *Gender, Nationality, Agency and the Art of the Fin de Siècle Woman Artist: The Example of Anna Elizabeth Klumpke (1856–1942)*, MA thesis, George Washington University, Washington, DC, 1994

Tamar Garb, *Sisters of the Brush: Women's Artistic Culture in Late Nineteenth-Century Paris*, New Haven and London: Yale University Press, 1994

Anna Klumpke lived most of her life in Europe and was an active member of the American expatriate community in Paris for more than 40 years. From an extraordinary family in which achievement by the female siblings was aggressively encouraged by an unusually independent and courageous mother, Klumpke sought – and received – recognition from American and European collectors and art institutions at a time when professional women artists were regarded with suspicion. One of her early portraits was of the 19th-century founder of modern feminism, *Elizabeth Cady Stanton* (1889; National Portrait Gallery, Washington, DC). Several one-woman exhibitions of her work were held in the USA during her career there

in the 1890s. She was the first woman to win the Temple gold medal, the most prestigious art prize in the USA, for her monumental genre painting *In the Washhouse* (1888; Pennsylvania Academy of the Fine Arts, Philadelphia). In France, she exhibited at the conservative Paris Salon almost every year, a reflection of her support for traditional values in art at a time when these were under attack by the Impressionists and other artists of the avant-garde.

Like her American contemporaries, Klumpke followed the American market and taste for art. Her early style emphasised a dark, monochrome palette, strong chiaroscuro and a polished surface (*Portrait of the Artist's Mother*, 1889; Mueller Collection, USA). Later, as Impressionism made inroads into American taste, her palette lightened and her brushwork became more free and gestural (*Portrait of the Artist's Father*, 1912; M.H. De Young Museum, San Francisco). The sombre early portraits have a palpable power, and in contrast most of her later, lighter works seem frivolous and unconvincing.

Klumpke's most famous portrait is of the distinguished animal painter *Rosa Bonheur* (1898; for illustration, see p. 90). It was painted shortly before Bonheur's death, and was donated to the Metropolitan Museum of Art by the artist. Klumpke also painted several other life-size portraits of Bonheur (e.g. Musée Nationale du Château de Fontainebleau; Rosa Bonheur Studio Museum, Château de By, Thoméry-sur-Seine), one posthumously. These perceptive portraits convey Bonheur's instantly recognisable, individualistic self-presentation and confident air, in darkly lyrical, dignified depictions, lovingly and meticulously crafted. The Metropolitan version of 1898 shows her holding a sketch and a pencil, with the edge of an oil sketch of running horses visible on an easel in the background. Bonheur wears her "feminine costume", composed of masculine and feminine elements: the skirt of a peasant woman, heavy, plain and uncrinolined; the uncorseted torso relaxed in a braid-defined soldier's jacket. Klumpke's naturalistic treatment suggests a powerful "saint of art", with the free, short hair of a modern Joan of Arc, in the white collar of a cleric, and the red ribbon of the Légion d'Honneur symbolising official recognition of her dedication to her art and the credit her fame brought to France.

Considered historically, the 1898 portrait of Bonheur resonates with politico-cultural overtones. It was painted a year after women were finally admitted to the Ecole des Beaux-Arts, after long and often acrimonious debate. The conservative Union des Femmes Peintres et Sculpteurs had cannily elected Bonheur as its honorary life president and advanced her as a sponsor of the admission of women to the Ecole because she used traditional technique and subject matter in her art. Bonheur supported the Union's contention that the admission of talented women, with "woman's special inborn sensitivity", would help to "save" French art from the degradations of experimentation, especially Impressionism. To join the battle to save the French Neo-classical tradition, female recruits needed to be armed with the rigorous academic art training of the Ecole (Garb 1994, p.219). Thus, Klumpke's portrait can be seen as documenting the canonisation of Bonheur by the women artists who venerated her and her adherence to traditional approaches to art.

Other layers of meaning in the portrait emerge when the circumstances of its execution are known. Bonheur agreed to

Klumpke's request to paint her ten years after they first met. For seven years their friendship had developed by correspondence, as Klumpke was pursuing her career as a portrait painter in the USA. When she returned to France to paint Bonheur's portrait, she did not plan an extended stay, but during the weeks she lived at Bonheur's château the bond between them grew and they determined to form what was, in effect, a "Boston marriage". This is supported by Bonheur's letters to Klumpke's mother, stating her "honourable intentions" and her decision to make Klumpke her heir (*Memoirs of an Artist* 1940, p.44).

In addition to portraying Bonheur as a saintly female warrior of art, Klumpke's portrait may refer to the personal, emotional and artistic bonding of two artists dedicated to naturalistic depictions and classical French painting technique. The fragment of the oil sketch is from Bonheur's unfinished *Wild Horses* (Rosa Bonheur Studio Museum), a picture inspired by Buffalo Bill Cody's Wild West Show, which was at the Paris Exposition Universelle of 1889. According to Klumpke, at her second meeting with Bonheur, just before she left to begin her career in America, Bonheur asked her to gather prairie plants – weeds and sagebrush – to ensure authenticity for this painting. *Wild Horses* could represent the wild white horses of France's marshy Camargue as well as the mustangs of the American prairies, and it is significant that the portion of the Bonheur painting Klumpke chose to include shows the white and the bay horses that lead the herd. They are unrestrained, at full gallop, a vision of freedom that in life can be experienced only fleetingly. Klumpke's selection of this work not only alludes to one of the first acts to bond the two artists together – the collection of American prairie plants for the painting – but may also refer to their shared love for France and America.

MARY JO AAGERSTOUN

Knight, Laura

British painter and graphic artist, 1877–1970

Born Laura Johnson in Long Eaton, Derbyshire, 4 August 1877. Studied at Nottingham School of Art, 1891–7 (several awards). Exhibited at Royal Academy from 1903. Married portrait painter Harold Knight, 1903; he died 1961. Lived in Staithes on the Yorkshire coast and in Laren, Netherlands, before settling in Cornwall, 1907, in Newlyn then Lamorna. Moved to London after World War I, but retained studios in Cornwall. Stayed in USA, 1922 and 1926–7; acted as judge for international art exhibition at Carnegie Institute, Pittsburgh, 1922. Commissioned by the War Artists' Advisory Committee during World War II; painted Nuremberg trials, 1946. Recipient of honorary doctorates from University of St Andrews, 1931; University of Nottingham, 1951. Member, Royal Watercolour Society, 1928; Royal Society of Painter-Etchers and Engravers, 1932; President, Society of Women Artists. Associate, 1927, and member, 1936 (the first woman since the 18th century), Royal Academy. Dame Commander of the British Empire (DBE), 1929. Died in London, 7 July 1970.

Selected Individual Exhibitions

Leicester Galleries, London: 1906, 1907, 1912 (all with Harold Knight), 1918, 1920, 1926, 1928 (with Mark Gertler), 1932, 1934, 1939
Alpine Club Galleries, London: 1922, 1930
Cleveland Art Institute, Chicago: 1931 (touring)
Usher Art Gallery, Lincoln: 1931
Laing Art Gallery, Newcastle upon Tyne: 1933
Museum and Art Gallery, Leicester: 1934 (with Harold Knight)
Castle Museum, Nottingham: 1934 (with Harold Knight), 1970 (retrospective)
Ian MacNichol's Galleries, Glasgow: 1946
Worthing Art Gallery, Sussex: 1963
Upper Grosvenor Galleries, London: 1963, 1967 (with Harold Knight), 1968, 1969 (retrospective)
Royal Academy, London: 1965 (retrospective)
Aquascutum Ltd, London: 1970

Selected Writings

Oil Paint and Grease Paint: Autobiography of Laura Knight, London: Nicholson and Watson, and New York: Macmillan, 1936
"Nuremberg diary", manuscript, 1947, Nottingham Record Office
"An artist's experience", *The Studio*, cxlviii, 1954, pp.129–35
A Proper Circus Omie, London: Davies, 1962
The Magic of a Line: The Autobiography of Laura Knight, London: Kimber, 1965

Bibliography

Norman Garstin, "The art of Harold and Laura Knight", *The Studio*, lvii, 1913, pp.183–200
Charles Marriott, ed., *A Book of Drawings*, London: Lane, 1923
M.C. Salaman, *Laura Knight*, London: Studio, and New York: Rudge, 1932
Janet Dunbar, *Laura Knight*, London: Collins, 1975
Meirion and Susie Harries, *The War Artists*, London: Joseph, 1983
Painting in Newlyn, 1880–1930, exh. cat., Barbican Art Gallery, London, 1985
Caroline Fox, *Dame Laura Knight*, Oxford: Phaidon, 1988
On with the Show: Drawings by Dame Laura Knight (1877–1970), exh. cat., David Messum, London, 1988
Teresa Grimes, Judith Collins and Oriana Baddeley, *Five Women Painters*, London: Lennard, 1989
The Staithes Group, exh. cat., Nottingham Castle Museum, and elsewhere, 1993
G. Fredric Bolling and Valerie A. Withington, *The Graphic Work of Laura Knight Including a Catalogue Raisonné of Her Prints*, Aldershot: Scolar Press, 1993

Laura Knight's artistic career spanned some 70 years and was in many respects exceptional. The scope of her subject matter displays enormous versatility, although the portrayal of women and their lives is a recurring motif. During the late 1920s and early 1930s she achieved great popular success with her ballet and circus paintings and, in 1927, was only the second woman, after Annie Swynnerton (q.v.), to be elected an Associate of the Royal Academy since its foundation. Her election was probably due to the efforts of her friend Alfred Munnings, who had submitted her name several times before 1927 without success, but her autobiography also acknowledges the part played by Swynnerton in breaking down prejudice against women painters within the Academy. She became a full member in 1936 and served on the council for the following two years. Thirty years later she was the first woman to be honoured with a solo exhibition at the Royal Academy Diploma Gallery. Ironically it was her allegiance to the Royal

Academy and the conservative, academic tradition that led to critical attacks on her lack of emotional and intellectual rigour and to the decline of her reputation since her death.

Laura Johnson received her training at the Nottingham School of Art, where she met her future husband, Harold Knight. Under the life master, Wilson Foster, teaching at the school emphasised an exact understanding of the model and little beyond. Several of her charcoal portrait studies submitted for the annual South Kensington examinations are in the collection of Nottingham Castle Museum and Art Gallery. They reveal a precocious technical proficiency and confidence in line drawing. According to the artist, she was continually upbraided for making her lines too heavy and for "drawing like a man" – from the shoulder rather than the wrist – and encouraged to develop her "feminine" side, something she felt unable to do. She was critical of the limitations of her art-school training and particularly of the fact that women were barred from working from the nude model. None the less, she was a successful student and won several awards, including, in 1894, the Princess of Wales scholarship for the female student with the most awards, and the Queen's prize in 1896.

Around 1898 Laura and Harold left Nottingham and settled in the north Yorkshire fishing village of Staithes, which had been recommended to them by a master at the School of Art. Since the 1880s Staithes and the neighbouring village of Runswick had been the focus for a growing colony of artists, drawn largely from the Midlands and the North, attracted there by the unspoilt lifestyle of the local fishing communities. Laura had been deeply impressed by an exhibition of Newlyn School artists held at Nottingham Castle Museum in 1894, and her early pictures painted at Staithes reflect her allegiance to the tenets of plein-air realism. She made numerous watercolour studies of children playing on the beach that display an increasing spontaneity in her figure painting. It was a period of enthusiastic experimentation, and much of the work was subsequently destroyed.

Knight's most ambitious painting to survive from the early years at Staithes, and signed with her maiden name, is the *Fishing Fleet* (Bolton Museum and Art Gallery). Painted in a muted palette of grey and brown that also characterised Harold's work at this time, it exemplifies a preoccupation in both artists' work with the harsh and tragic lifestyle of the local fishing community and, in mood, is reminiscent of some of the Newlyn paintings of Walter Langley and Frank Bramley. Laura had particularly admired Bramley's *A Hopeless Dawn* at the Nottingham exhibition of Cornish painters in 1894. While at Staithes Laura received some instruction in colour theory from the Scottish painter Charles Hodge Mackie, who taught her the laws of complementary colours and how, by using a restricted palette of earth pigments, a colour might be suggested in a neutral grey through the presence of its complementary.

Between 1904 and 1907 the Knights (who had married in 1903) made three visits to the Netherlands to work amid a colony of artists at Laren, a location popularised by the Dutch realist painter Anton Mauve. Laura painted almost exclusively genre subjects of peasant interiors in a limited range of predominantly grey tones that perhaps owed something to the influence of the Hague school artists (e.g. *Peeling Potatoes*, c.1904–7; Castle Museum and Art Gallery, Nottingham).

These were shown alongside those of Harold at their first London exhibition, *Dutch Life and Landscape*, held at the Leicester Galleries in 1906. They had first met Ernest Brown of the Leicester Galleries in 1904 and were to exhibit there together again in 1907 and 1912; Laura had several further exhibitions at the galleries before World War II.

The artist achieved something of a breakthrough with her painting *Dressing the Children* (Ferens Art Gallery, Hull), exhibited at the Royal Academy in 1906. Although painted at Staithes, it shares many of the preoccupations of contemporary Dutch works. She painted many such domestic scenes of mothers and their children in dimly lit interiors illuminated by a single window. Avoiding Harold's dramatic use of light and silhouette, she concentrates instead on the unremarkable action of a daily chore. Her paintwork is animated by a swift outlining of contour and drapery folds, a characteristic more pronounced in her watercolour work.

In 1907 the Knights moved to Newlyn in Cornwall, where Stanhope Forbes had founded a School of Painting, and were introduced to his pupils Dod Shaw (later Dod Procter, q.v.), Ernest Procter and Charles Simpson, who formed part of a thriving artists' community. In Cornwall Laura continued painting children as she had done in Staithes, but the canvases exhibited at the Royal Academy in 1909 (*The Beach*; Laing Art Gallery, Newcastle upon Tyne) and 1910 reveal a marked change of direction. She was now working on a much larger scale with broad, confident brushwork and a lighter, more colourful palette that captured the fall of the bright Cornish sunlight on her subjects. The angst and grim realism of the Staithes work is replaced by a vigour and *joie de vivre* that reflects the Knights' new-found pleasure in their carefree, bohemian lifestyle in Cornwall.

In 1911 Laura Knight's subject matter changed and she began painting hired models, both clothed and naked, in the open air at Lamorna, again observing the fall of natural light on flesh. Her willingness to flout convention is poignantly expressed in *Self-Portrait with Nude* (1913; National Portrait Gallery, London) where she portrays herself, brush in hand, before a posed naked female model, subverting the traditional iconography of the male artist and his muse. The subject of women posed in the open air and on cliff tops culminated around 1917 in a group of paintings that were characterised by high horizons, a certain flattening of illusionistic space and broad, unmodulated blocks of bright colour (e.g. *Lamorna Cave*, c.1917; private collection, Sotheby's, repr. Fox 1988, pl.30). Similarities were drawn with the work of Augustus John, to whom she had been introduced by Munnings in 1913. As the art critic Paul Konody pointed out, however (*Country Life*, February 1918), Knight's intention was fundamentally different to John's and she remained essentially attached to a realist tradition, absorbed by effects of light and atmosphere.

The Knights' move to London after World War I occasioned another change in Laura's subject matter, when she gained permission to work backstage with Diaghilev's Ballets Russes. Whereas Sickert and Gore, in their music-hall paintings, had focused attention on what was happening on the stage and in the audience, Knight's interest lay in the more informal moments of theatre that she witnessed in the dressing rooms or waiting in the wings, both at the ballet and at the productions of the Birmingham Repertory Theatre. She made studies of the

Knight: *Fine Feathers (Gypsy Splendour)*, 1939; oil on canvas; 127 × 101.6 cm.; City of Nottingham, Castle Museum and Art Gallery famous ballerinas Lydia Lopokova and, later, Anna Pavlova, but perhaps the most significant introduction for the development of her work was to the Maestro, Cecchetti, at whose dance classes she learned to execute swift, economic line drawings at great speed to capture the movement and stance of her models.

A new emphasis on line is also evident in the etchings and aquatints she began to produce in 1923, apparently working directly on to the plate with no preliminary drawings or tracing. She received much technical help from an artist friend, John Everett, and also took advice from Gerald Brockhurst. The subjects of her printed works mirrored her obsessions during the 1920s and early 1930s with the ballet, theatre and circus; the years 1923 and 1925–6 were particularly productive. Despite Brockhurst's advice to concentrate on pure line, she preferred the combination of etching and aquatint. In two aquatints of Diaghilev's Spanish dancers, produced in 1923 (repr. Bolling and Withington 1993, nos 8 and 19), and much indebted to Goya's *Los caprichos*, she created highly decorative surfaces using a three-tone ground. The rhythmic use of line and dramatic silhouette were entirely new to her work but very much in keeping with the medium and subject. She experimented later with drypoint, engraving and soft ground etching. In the early 1930s the market for prints slumped and her printmaking activities largely ceased around 1935.

A number of nudes and ballet subjects, exhibited at the Royal Academy in the late 1920s and featuring strong, solid-limbed women, reveal something of the influence of Dod Procter and the spirit of new realism on Knight's work at that time. In these works a cool studio light gives strong, sculptural form and an impressive, physical presence to the model even when in an outdoor setting. The artist Eileen Mayo, who was a favourite model of both Laura and Harold, posed for several of her nudes but it is in an uncharacteristically restrained portrayal of a young girl in *Susie and the Washbasin* (1929; Harris Museum and Art Gallery, Preston) that she is perhaps closest in spirit to Dod Procter's work.

The circus paintings for which Knight became best known and loved by the British public were exhibited at the Royal Academy between 1928 and 1938. She sketched backstage at Fossett's "old-fashioned" circus in Islington and with Bertram Mills's circus at Olympia in the early 1920s, capturing the movement and agility of the performers as she had those of the corps de ballet. The life of the circus was to become an obsession, and in the early 1930s she joined Carmo's on two separate tours of the country. Although popular, her circus pictures did not meet with critical success, and she herself admitted that she had probably found the whole experience too entertaining to produce her best work. Too often the spectacle of costume and circus paraphernalia dominate at the expense of any deeper feeling for her subjects, and we are rarely given any insight into the personalities behind the grease paint. *Charivari; or, Grand Parade* (1928; Newport Museum and Art Gallery, Gwent), exhibited at the Royal Academy in 1929 and parodied in *Punch*, is perhaps an extreme example of this tendency and was significantly excluded from her choice of pictures for her retrospective exhibition in Nottingham in 1970.

Executed in the late 1930s and early 1940s and rather more successful in their depth of characterisation were her portraits of Gypsies. At Munnings's suggestion she went to the horse races at Epsom and Ascot and several spirited crowd scenes resulted from these visits. It was the Gypsies "working the crowd", however, who really engaged her attention, and her best work was produced at the Gypsy camp at Iver, Buckinghamshire, following an invitation there from one of her models. The enigmatic features of a Gypsy girl called Beulah, of whom she made several portraits, and the proud bearing of a beplumed doyenne in *Fine Feathers (Gypsy Splendour)* (1939; see illustration) reveal the very real talent Knight possessed for portraiture. In 1938, in some particularly prickly correspondence regarding his resignation from the Royal Academy and in which he accused Knight of siding with the forces of conservatism, Augustus John, another great devotee of Gypsy life, complimented her on her portraits of Romany girls exhibited that year. Knight appears to have preferred painting women and children – she made a number of sensitive portraits of black children in a Baltimore hospital in 1927 (e.g. *The Piccaninny*, c.1927; private collection, Pyms Gallery, London, repr. Fox 1988, pl.49) – and her Gypsy work is unusual in that it includes several revealing paintings and studies of a Gypsy man on his sick bed (e.g. *A Gypsy*, 1938–9; Tate Gallery, London).

Knight's popular success and objective, academic style of painting were no doubt what commended her to the propagandist ends of the War Artists' Advisory Committee chaired by Kenneth Clark during World War II. She was commissioned to paint several portraits of women with distinguished service in the Women's Auxiliary Air Force (WAAF), and a number of paintings emphasising the importance of women workers to the war effort. A portrait of a young munitions factory worker, *Ruby Loftus Screwing a Breech-ring* (1943; Imperial War Museum, London), was exhibited at the Royal Academy to particular acclaim. In 1946, at her own suggestion, she flew to Germany to record the trial of Nazi war criminals at Nuremberg. Given the unpromising subject matter, the resulting canvas, *The Dock, Nuremberg* (1946; Imperial War Museum), manages to achieve both a factual account of the courtroom with an imaginative composition incorporating scenes of the concentration camp atrocities and the destruction of Nuremberg.

Despite the gradual eclipse of Laura Knight's reputation in the post-war period, there has been a re-evaluation of her early paintings made at Staithes and Newlyn within the context of exhibitions surveying English Impressionism, notably *Painting in Newlyn* (Barbican Art Gallery, London, 1985) and *The Staithes Group* (Castle Museum and Art Gallery, Nottingham, 1993).

NEIL WALKER

Knip, Henriëtte *see* Ronner-Knip

Knip, Henriëtte Geetruij *see* Training and Professionalism survey 5

Kobro, Katarzyna
Polish sculptor, 1898–1951

Born in Moscow, 26 January 1898. Studied at the Moscow School of Painting, Sculpture and Architecture, then at Svomas (State Free Art Workshops), 1917–20. Married Wladyslaw Strzeminski, 1920; daughter born 1936; separated from husband, c.1945. Head of visual arts department, IZO (People's Commissariat), Smolensk, Poland, 1920–22. Moved to Vilna (Vilnius), 1922, then to Szczekociny, where she taught at the School of Industry; also taught in Koluszki, near Lódz. Moved to Lódz and taught at the School of Industry for Women, 1931. Co-publisher of the magazine *Forma*, Lódz. Left Poland in 1939, leaving most of her work behind; this was later destroyed by the National Socialists on grounds of "degeneracy". Returned to Lódz after World War II; taught drawing and Russian, 1949–50. Member of Unovis (Affirmers of the New Art); Blok, 1924–5; Praesens, 1926–9; Abstraction-Création, Paris, 1933; co-founder of a.r. (artyski revolucyni-avangarda rzeczyvista, Revolutionary Artists Real Avant-Garde); also contacts with the Society of Young Artists, 1920–22. Died in Lódz, 26 February 1951.

Principal Exhibitions
Artists Association, Lódz, Kraków, Warsaw and Lemberg: 1932
Dom Plastyków, Kraków: 1935 (with Wladyslaw Strzeminski and Grupa Krakowska)

Selected Writings
"Die Skulptur und der Körper", *Europa* (Warsaw), no.2, 1929, p.60 (English translation in Essen and New York 1973)
Komposition des Raumes, Berechnungen des raumzeitlichen Rhythmus, Lódz, 1931 (with Wladyslaw Strzeminski)
"L'action de sculpteur, un nu donne des émotions d'ordre psychologique ou sexuel", *Abstraction-Création*, no.2, 1933, p.7
"Bemerkungen", *Forma* (Lódz), no.3, 1935, p.14 (English translation in Odense 1985)
"Der Funktionalismus", *Forma* (Lódz), no.4, 1936, pp.9–13
"Die Skulptur ist ein Teil des Raumes", *Glos Plastików*, no.1–7, 1937, pp.42–3
L'Espace uniste: Ecrits du constructivisme polonais, ed. Antoine Baudin and Pierre-Maxime Jedryka, Lausanne: L'Age d'Homme, 1977 (with Wladyslaw Strzeminski)

Bibliography
Constructivism in Poland, 1923–1936: BLOK – Praesens – a.r., exh. cat., Museum Folkwang, Essen, Museum of Modern Art, New York, and elsewhere, 1973
Die 20er Jahre in Osteuropa, exh. cat., Galerie Gmurzynska, Cologne, 1975
Merle Schipper, "Katarzyna Kobro: Innovative sculptor of the 1920s", *Woman's Art Journal*, i/2, 1980–81, pp.19–24
Andrzej Turowski, *Constructivism in Poland: An Attempted Reconstruction of the Trend, 1921–1934*, Wroclaw: PAN, 1981 (Polish original)
Présences polonaises: Witkiewicz, Constructivisme, les contemporains: L'Art vivant autour du Musée de Lódz, exh. cat., Centre Georges Pompidou, Musée National d'Art Moderne, Paris, 1983
Yves-Alain Bois, "Polarization: 'Polish presences', an exhibition mounted last fall by the Pompidou Center", *Art in America*, lxxii, April 1984, pp.152–61 (French original in *Critique*, no.440–41, 1984)
Janusz Zagrodzki, *Katarzyna and Composition of Space*, Warsaw, 1984
Tre Pionérer for Polsk Avant-Garde/Three Pioneers of Polish Avant-garde, exh. cat., Fyns Kunstmuseum, Odense, and elswhere, 1985
Urszula Grzecha, *Kobro und die konstruktivistische Bewegung*, dissertation, Münster, 1986
Sophie Taeuber-Arp und ihre Künstlerfreunde: a.r., exh. cat., Internationale Sammlung Moderner Kunst, Museum Sztuki, Lódz, and elsewhere, 1989
Künstlerinnen des 20. Jahrhunderts, exh. cat., Museum Wiesbaden, 1990
Artystki polskie [Polish women artists], exh. cat., National Museum, Warsaw, 1991
Katarzyna Kobro, 1898–1951, exh. cat., Städtisches Museum Abteiberg, Mönchengladbach, 1991
Voices of Freedom: Polish Women Artists and the Avant-Garde, 1880–1990, exh. cat., National Museum of Women in the Arts, Washington, DC, 1991
Europa, Europa: Das Jahrhundert der Avantgarde in Mittel- und Osteuropa, exh. cat., Kunst- und Ausstellungshalle der Bundesrepublik Deutschland, Bonn, 1994

The influence of Suprematism and Constructivism is marked in the early Russian work of Katarzyna Kobro. Under the influence of Vladimir Tatlin she began to use combinations of industrial materials, creating spatial structures from, for example, glass and metal with other elements such as screws. Yet her aim, to create forms in space with different materials – "space sculptures" and "space compositions", as she called them – transcended mere material assemblage. This clearly distinguishes her from Tatlin, who felt visual art should be devoted to utilitarian ends, including architecture, design, typography and, not least, social revolution.

In 1920 Kobro moved with her husband Wladyslaw Strzeminski to Poland, where they were active in artistic life and became pioneers of the Polish avant-garde. There, Kobro distanced herself from art with a direct social function, although not with the same intensity as Kazimir Malevich. In her theoretical essay "Die Skulptur und der Körper" (1929) she stressed the need to accept absolutely "that a sculpture is neither literature nor symbolism nor an individual, psychological emotion". Art should not be informative or propagandistic, but nevertheless should be functional in a wider sense, in the form with the greatest economic use, for example in architecture or social relations (see "Der Funktionalismus", 1936). This view reflects two opposing positions within Russian Constructivism, represented by Malevich and Tatlin. Both tendencies were regarded as the official art of the Russian revolution, many of whose representatives emigrated due to the political situation in Russia in 1922, as Kobro and Strzeminski had done two years earlier.

The sculptures Kobro created in Poland in 1920–25 have a graphic quality: *Suspended Composition 1* (1924; 20 × 40 × 40cm.; destroyed, replica in Museum Sztuki, Lódz), made of epoxy resin, fibre glass, wood and metal, is like a composition of line and dot (points of contact) in transition from plane to space. The various materials of the individual interconnected forms support the effect of rhythm in the composition, and their different emphases lend it a certain dynamism. A metal bar, about 25 centimetres long, is attached to the underside of a white, highly polished egg form, suspended horizontally, continuing the vertical line of the wire. The point of suspension is not the centre but in the right-hand third. A rectangular wooden block, in black, is fastened to the longer end. The

with her insistence that sculpture should reflect the organisational and technical possibilities of its time. In "Bemerkungen" (1935) she stressed that the fundamental task of sculpture is space and its arrangement: "Sculpture should be an architectonic problem, a laboratory-like organisation of traffic, town planning as a functional organism; it should result from realisable possibilities of modern art, science and technology; it should be an expression of the longing for a supra-individual organisation of society." Eager to design sculptures in the form of an organised rhythm of proportions, she adopted the golden section, combining the ratios of 3:5:8:13. Yet she was opposed to an exclusively architectural use for her sculptures.

After an extended fallow period from about 1936 to 1948, Kobro produced small nude figures using Cubist forms; they were her last works. The sculptures she created in the 1920s reveal her as a precursor of the artistic avant-garde that reached its peak in the movements of De Stijl and the Bauhaus.

ANNE GANTEFÜHRER

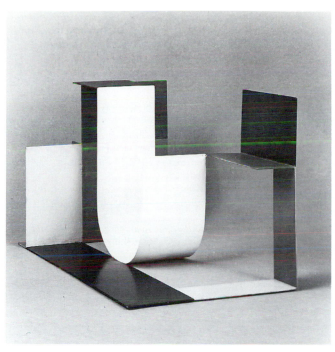

Kobro: *Spatial Composition 4*, 1929; coloured steel; 40 × 64 × 40 cm.; Muzeum Sztuki, Lódz, Poland

weighty appearance of the dark wooden object contrasts with the lightness of the white egg and the reflective metal. A small cube, also in black, is attached to the opposite side as a counterbalance. The smaller *Suspended Composition 2* (1921–2; replica in Museum Sztuki) is made up of a variety of metal elements welded together, some linear and some distinctly three-dimensional, including a saw blade, a ring, a cross and a cord. A steel ring is fixed to one end of the metal cord, a twisted circular cord to the other, with the cross shape approximately in the centre. These works show Kobro's intensive examination of the phenomenon of space. Thus the impact of a self-contained body like the egg in *Suspended Composition 1* is extended by means of its reflecting surface and other attached forms. The distinction between interior and exterior is no longer possible in *Suspended Composition 2*. The hanging sculpture enters the viewer's space and becomes part of it. In her essay "Die Skulptur und der Körper" Kobro indicated that she wanted to abolish not only interior-exterior boundaries but also those between the reality of the art and that of the viewer: "The sculpture is a part of the space surrounding it. One must not be separated from the other. The sculpture penetrates the space and the space penetrates the sculpture."

Signs of Malevich's Suprematism appear in many of Kobro's suspended compositions until 1925, when she completely abandoned the style. From this point she examined the construction and order of sculptural structures as well as their spatial penetration. Concentrating on a formal language of line and plane, she produced steel sculptures in white or primary colours, and such works as *Spatial Composition 4* (1929; see illustration) approach architectonic models. The Polish artists' groups to which Kobro belonged – Blok, Praesens and a.r. – advocated the integration of visual art in the organisation of everyday life. Kobro contributed to the definition of this goal

Koenig, Ghisha

British sculptor, 1921–1993

Born in London, 8 December 1921. Won scholarship to Hornsey School of Art, 1939, but studies interrupted by World War II. Served in the Auxiliary Territorial Service (ATS), 1942–6. Studied at Chelsea School of Art under Henry Moore, 1946–9; Slade School of Fine Art under F.E. McWilliam, 1949–50. Married physician Emanuel Tuckman, 1950; daughter born 1955. Lived in St Mary Cray, Kent, 1950–67; Sidcup, Kent, 1967–81; London from 1981. Visited Mexico to study Pre-Columbian terracotta sculpture, 1963. Recipient of Arts Council of Great Britain major award, 1978. Died in London, 15 October 1993.

Selected Individual Exhibitions

Grosvenor Gallery, London: 1966
Gallery 359, Nottingham: 1973
Bedford House Gallery, London: 1974
Midland Group Gallery, Nottingham: 1977
Galerie d'Eendt, Amsterdam: 1978 (touring)
Wylma Wayne Fine Art, London: 1981
Serpentine Gallery, London: 1986 (touring retrospective, organised by Arts Council of Great Britain)
Boundary Gallery, London: 1986, 1994 (retrospective)

Bibliography

Charles S. Spencer, "Gisha [sic] Koenig", *The Studio*, clix, 1960, pp.22–3
Ghisha Koenig: Sculpture, 1968–74, exh. cat., Bedford House Gallery, London, 1974
Art for Society, exh. cat., Whitechapel Art Gallery, London, and elsewhere, 1978
Ghisha Koenig: Sculpture, 1968–86, exh. cat., Serpentine Gallery, London, 1986
Writing on the Wall: Women Writers on Women Artists, exh. cat., Tate Gallery, London, 1993
Ghisha Koenig, 1921–1993: Memorial Exhibition, exh. cat., Boundary Gallery, London, 1994

Koenig: *Machine Minders*, 1956; Tate Gallery, London

Ghisha Koenig's work was based on a direct observation of industry. Her choice of working people as subject matter and her preference for figurative, realist work to some extent reflected her socialist beliefs. Yet, for all this, she did not identify herself with the "kitchen-sink" painters of the 1950s; her work is not overburdened by social realism, and documentary and social concerns never supersede sculptural ones.

The strongest influence on her work was probably not Henry Moore, her teacher at Chelsea, but her father Leo Koenig, a Russian émigré and Yiddish writer. He had known Marc Chagall in Paris, and when he moved to London his home became a meeting place for a circle of Jewish artists including David Bomberg, Mark Gertler, Jankel Adler and Joseph Herman. It was from this background that Koenig gained her first grounding in the worlds of art and politics.

There is a great consistency in Koenig's work. Once she had found her main subject matter and way of working, she adhered strictly to them, changing only her technique during more than 40 years. The men and women whom she observed working in factories in southeast England provided Koenig with the principal focus for her work. The most notable exceptions to her factory subjects are *Ezekiel (Survival)* (1956; bronze; private collection, repr. London 1986), *The Crucifixion* (1961; terracotta; private collection, repr. London 1994) and the *Blind School* reliefs (1987; bronze; New Hall, Cambridge). The last comprised groups of individuals at work, although not in an industrial setting. She also made a series of *Studies of Miners* (repr. London 1986) after observing miners underground at Chislet Colliery near Canterbury in 1958.

Koenig's first experience of factories came as part of her war service, when she worked for the *London Educational Bulletin* and visited factories to investigate job opportunities for demobilised service workers. Her move to St Mary Cray in Kent in 1950 brought her into contact with the new light industries that had been developed there for Londoners relocated from areas destroyed in the Blitz. It was here that she embarked on her enduring preoccupation with the subject of human labour. Koenig has explained her reasons for working in factories as a combination of ready models, political motives and a desire for a certain anonymity. "I find that in using a factory as the starting point for my work I can use it on many levels, the level of human beings, relationships to space, movement" (London 1974). Once she had located a factory and obtained permission to draw there, her method of working was to spend weeks or months clocking in with the workers and sketching on the factory floor.

Simultaneously being part of the workforce and yet maintaining a degree of isolation, she gained a certain insight into factory life. For the workers, she felt, the factories became more than a production line; they formed a community. Long before artists' placements were to become fashionable, Koenig instigated a working process that she was to maintain throughout her career. She drew without any preconceived idea of a particular sculpture and made studies recording her subjects' numerous variations in posture. After this intensive study, she would return to her studio and work directly from her sketchbooks on to large sheets. She would then translate her ideas into three-dimensional forms. Although she based her sculpture on specific people whom she had observed, she was able to draw on her vast store of images to create sculptures that were not necessarily literal representations of a particular moment. Koenig had observed the industrial methods of working with materials, but in her own work she modelled rather than carved to create small-scale reliefs and free-standing sculptures in plaster, terracotta and bronze.

In the course of her career, Koenig worked at seven factories. These were not chosen on the basis of specific types of work, although they tended to involve tasks that veered more towards traditional skills, which have now, with new technology, largely become history. The factories in which she worked were: Coates, St Mary Cray, Kent, ink factory (1956–7); Morphy Richards, electrical equipment (1962–4); J. & E. Hall, Dartford-APV Products Ltd, a heavy industrial plant making escalators and water salination systems (1968–9 and 1972–3); Klingers, plastics (1970–71); ITT, telephone switchboards (1974–5); Black and Edgingtons, London, makers of tents, sleeping bags and other military and leisure camping gear (1978); and United Glass Containers, makers of miniature liquor bottles and fishpaste jars (1983).

With its detailed treatment of the workers, *Machine Minders* (1956; see illustration) is particularly characteristic of her sculpture of the 1950s. This work, which represents two half-life-size figures, was unusually made of "Astex" and is one of the largest of her sculptures (130 × 106 × 60 cm.). Koenig's work is generally small in scale, and she explained her reason for choosing to work at this size: "you can't go very large with terracotta in the round ... I've had to accept the limitations on size imposed by materials" (London 1974).

In her later work, the subjects' features are less modelled and more integrated with the mass of their surrounding environment. In a work such as the relief sculpture *Tentmakers 4* (1981; terracotta; repr. London 1986) the people and inanimate objects are locked together to form a whole. Although each figure was based on an actual individual, they are to a large degree anonymous, with their facial features hidden and their individuality expressed through bodily gestures. The emphasis in these works is on the routine gestures induced by repetitive physical tasks. The rhythms of individuals at work are caught up in a greater whole. While each figure is part of a collective unit, they nevertheless manage to retain a strong sense of human individuality.

ANN JONES

Kollwitz, Käthe

German graphic artist and sculptor, 1867–1945

Born Käthe Schmidt in Königsberg (now Kaliningrad, Russia), 8 July 1867. First art lessons with engraver Rudolf Maurer in Königsberg, 1881–2. Visited Switzerland, Berlin and Munich with mother and sister Lise, 1884. Studied painting under Karl Stauffer-Bern at the Zeichen- und Malschule des Vereins der Künstlerinnen und Kunstfreundinnen zu Berlin, 1885–6; taught etching and painting there from 1898. Studied under Emil Neide in Königsberg, 1886, then under Ludwig Herterich in Munich, 1888–9. Rented a studio in Königsberg, 1890. Settled in Berlin after marriage to physician Karl Kollwitz, 1891; two sons, born 1892 and 1896; husband died 1942. Member of Berlin Secession, 1899. Studied sculpture at Académie Julian and met Rodin during stay in Paris, 1904. Studied in Florence after winning the Villa Romana prize, established by Max Klinger, 1907. Elected member of the Prussian Academy and named professor, 1919; director of the master studio for graphic arts, 1928; forced to resign by National Socialists, 1933. Visited Moscow with husband, 1927. Recipient of Ordre pour le Mérite for peace work, 1929. Unofficially forbidden to exhibit by the National Socialists, 1936. Evacuated to Nordhausen to escape bombing, 1943; much of her work destroyed in an air raid in Berlin later that year. Died in Moritzburg, near Dresden, 22 April 1945.

Principal Exhibitions

Individual
Galerie Cassirer, Berlin: 1917
Kunsthalle, Bremen: 1917
Berlin Secession: 1917
Civic Club, New York: 1925
Kupferstichkabinett, Basel: 1929
Moscow and Leningrad: 1932
Jake Zeitlin Bookshop and Galleries, Los Angeles: 1937
Kleemann Galleries, New York: 1938
Berner Kunstmuseum, Bern: 1946 (retrospective)

Group
Freie Kunstausstellung, Berlin: 1893
Galerie Gurlitt, Berlin: 1897 (*Kunstlerinnen Ausstellung*)
Grosse Berliner Kunstausstellung, Berlin: 1898
Dresden: 1899 (*Deutsche Kunstausstellung*, small gold medal)
Freie Secession, Berlin: 1916

Selected Writings

Ich will wirken in dieser Zeit, ed. Friedrich Ahhlers-Hestermann, Frankfurt am Main, 1952; 2nd edition, edited by Hans Kollwitz, 1981
The Diary and Letters of Käthe Kollwitz, ed. Hans Kollwitz, Chicago, 1955; 2nd edition, Evanston, IL: Northwestern University Press, 1988 (German original, 1948)
Briefe der Freundschaft und Begegnungen, ed. Hans Kollwitz, Munich, 1966
Bekenntnisse, Leipzig, 1981 (with appendix by Volker Frank)
Ich sah die Welt mit liebevollen Blicken: Käthe Kollwitz, Ein Leben in Selbstzeugnissen, ed. Hans Kollwitz, Wiesbaden: Fourier, 1988
Die Tagebücher, ed. Jutta Bohnke-Kollwitz, Berlin, 1989
Briefe an den Sohn, 1904 bis 1945, ed. Jutta Bohnke-Kollwitz, Berlin, 1992

Bibliography

Julius Elias, "Käthe Kollwitz", *Kunst und Künstler*, xvi, 1917, pp.540–49
Alfred Kuhn, *Käthe Kollwitz: Graphiker der Gegenwart*, vi, Berlin, 1921
Kurt Glaser, "Käthe Kollwitz", *Die Graphik der Neuzeit vom Anfang des 19. Jahrhunderts bis zur Gegenwart*, Berlin, 1923, pp.466–70
Arthur Bonus, *Das Käthe-Kollwitz-Werk*, Dresden, 1925
Elizabeth McCausland, "Käthe Kollwitz", *Parnassus*, ix, February 1937, pp.20–25
Carl Zigrosser, *Käthe Kollwitz*, New York: Bittner, 1946; reprinted 1961
Beate Bonus-Jeep, *Sechzig Jahre Freundschaft mit Käthe Kollwitz*, Boppard: Rauch, 1948; reprinted 1963
August Klipstein, *The Graphic Work of Käthe Kollwitz: Complete Illustrated Catalogue*, Bern: Klipstein, and New York: Galerie St Etienne, 1955 (catalogue raisonné of prints; German original)
Glaubrecht Friedrich, "Käthe Kollwitz als Zeichnerin", *Dresdner Kunstblätter*, iv, 1960, pp.148–50
Harri Nündel, *Käthe Kollwitz*, Leipzig, 1964
Otto Nagel, *Die Selbstbildnisse der Käthe Kollwitz*, Berlin, 1965
Käthe Kollwitz, exh. cat., Akademie der Künste, Berlin, 1967
Leopold Reidemeister, *Käthe Kollwitz: Das plastische Werk*, Hamburg, 1967
Carl Zigrosser, *Prints and Drawings of Käthe Kollwitz*, New York: Dover, 1969
Otto Nagel, *Käthe Kollwitz*, London: Studio Vista, and Greenwich, CT: New York Graphic Society, 1971 (German original, 1963)
Otto Nagel and Werner Timm, *Käthe Kollwitz: Die Handzeichnungen*, Berlin and Stuttgart, 2 vols, 1972–80 (catalogue raisonné of drawings)
Käthe Kollwitz, exh. cat., Frankfurter Kunstverein, Frankfurt am Main, 1973
Werner Timm, *Käthe Kollwitz*, Welt der Kunst, Berlin, 1974
Mina C. Klein and H. Arthur Klein, *Käthe Kollwitz: Life in Art*, New York: Holt Rinehart, 1975
Martha Kearns, *Käthe Kollwitz: Woman and Artist*, Old Westbury, NY: Feminist Press, 1976
Käthe Kollwitz, exh. cat., Galerie St Etienne and Kennedy Galleries, New York, 1976
John A. Walker, "Art and the peasantry 2", *Art and Artists*, xiii, February 1979, pp.14–17
Alessandra Comini, "State of the field, 1980: The women artists of German Expressionism", *Arts Magazine*, November 1980, pp.147–53
Ilse Kleberger, *"Eine Gabe ist eine Aufgabe": Käthe Kollwitz*, Berlin: Klopp, 1980
Renate Hinz, ed., *Käthe Kollwitz: Graphics, Posters, Drawings*, New York: Pantheon, and London: Writers and Readers, 1981 (German original, 1980)
Käthe Kollwitz, 1867–1945: The Graphic Works, exh. cat., Kettle's Yard, Cambridge, 1981

Catherine Krahmer, *Käthe Kollwitz in Selbstzeugnissen und Bilddokumenten*, Reinbek bei Hamburg: Rowohlt, 1981

German Expressionist Sculpture, exh. cat., Los Angeles County Museum of Art, 1983

France Roussillon, *La Sculpture de Käthe Kollwitz*, PhD dissertation, Paris-Sorbonne, 1983

The Print in Germany, 1880–1933: The Age of Expressionism, exh. cat., British Museum, London, 1984

Käthe Kollwitz Handzeichnungen, Cologne: Käthe Kollwitz Museum, 1985

Ateliergemeinschaft Klosterstrasse: Vom Stillen Kampf der Künstler, exh. cat., Galerie Mitte, Berlin, 1988

Tom Fecht, ed., *Käthe Kollwitz: Works in Color*, New York: Schocken, 1988 (German original, 1987)

Elmar Jansen, *Ernst Barlach – Käthe Kollwitz: Die Geschichte einer verborgenen Nähe*, Berlin, 1988

Die Kollwitz-Sammlung des Dresdner Kupferstich-Kabinettes: Graphik und Zeichnungen, 1890–1912, exh. cat., Käthe Kollwitz Museum, Cologne, 1988

Alexandra von dem Knesebeck, "Die Bedeutung von Zolas Roman 'Germinal' für den Zyklus 'Ein Weberaufstand' von Käthe Kollwitz", *Zeitschrift für Kunstgeschichte*, iii, 1989, pp.402–22

Zwischen den Kriegen: Druckgraphische Zyklen von Kollwitz, Dix, Pechstein, Masereel u.a., exh. cat., Käthe Kollwitz Museum, Berlin, 1989

"Käthe Kollwitz Museum Köln", *Kölner Museums-Bulletin*, i–ii, 1991 (special issue)

Mara R. Witzling, ed., *Voicing Our Visions: Writings by Women Artists*, New York: Universe, 1991; London: Women's Press, 1992

Käthe Kollwitz, exh. cat., National Gallery of Art, Washington, DC, 1992

Angela Moorjani, *The Aesthetics of Loss and Lessness*, New York: St Martin's Press, 1992

Käthe Kollwitz, exh. cat., Fondation Neumann, Gingins, 1994

Käthe Kollwitz: Artist of the People, exh. cat., South Bank Centre, London, and elsewhere, 1995

Schmerz und Schuld, exh. cat., Käthe Kollwitz Museum, Berlin, 1995

Celebrated and beloved throughout the world, the graphic artist and sculptor Käthe Kollwitz (*Self-Portrait in Profile Facing Left, Drawing*, 1933; see illustration) is known for her powerful treatment of the themes of mothers and children, of solidarity among human beings, and of protest against suffering and social injustice. Spanning the turn of a century, two world wars and the turbulent Weimar Republic, Kollwitz's life was as rich as her art and is well documented in letters, in accounts by friends and family and in the extensive diaries she kept from 1910 to 1943.

Critics and the public appreciated Kollwitz's art from the time it was first exhibited in 1893; its accessible style and humanitarian subject matter ensured a wide audience both during her lifetime and to this day. Yet Kollwitz is a somewhat anomalous figure of the modern period because she was a woman working in a male-dominated field, because she depicted socially engaged subjects when this was unfashionable and because she steadfastly adhered to a figurative style in the era of abstraction. For these reasons, Kollwitz and her work (which includes five published graphic cycles and numerous single-sheet prints, as well as sculptures) have always been studied from the perspectives of politics and feminism (understood from a late 20th-century viewpoint) and this during an age when formalism dominated critical discourse. The newest scholarship, by contrast, has devoted attention to the technical and aesthetic aspects of her oeuvre, because too little has been known about Kollwitz as a technically brilliant graphic artist as well as a virtuosic visual rhetorician.

Kollwitz's preoccupation with socially engaged subjects grew out of her family background. She was born in Königsberg to a solidly middle-class, highly cultivated family, in which the tone was set by her maternal grandfather Julius Rupp, a dissident Protestant minister who founded a Free Congregation emphasising morality, duty and the intellect. Her family was supportive of her artistic ambitions and sent her to art classes both in her home town and in Berlin. In the Prussian capital, she studied under the Swiss artist Karl Stauffer-Bern, who encouraged her to pursue drawing; she also encountered the work of Stauffer-Bern's friend Max Klinger, whose etched cycle, *A Life*, and treatise *Malerei und Zeichnung* of 1891 would deeply influence her eventual decision to abandon painting in favour of the graphic arts. Klinger believed that the graphic arts, far more than painting, were capable of exploring ideas and social issues, partly because they were, according to his definition, executed exclusively in black and white and therefore not subject to the "pure enjoyment" that colour provided. He also valued the reproducible quality of the print and saw it as a more democratic art.

Kollwitz perfected her drawing skills in Berlin, and then in Munich under the direction of Ludwig Herterich, frequently using herself as a model, something she would do throughout her life (*Self-Portrait en face, Laughing*, c.1888–9; Käthe-Kollwitz-Museum Berlin; *Self-Portrait*, 1891; Art Institute of Chicago). She gradually began to synthesise her interest in socially engaged subject matter with the notion of graphic media as understood by Klinger. Kollwitz had long been attracted to what she perceived as the beauty and romance of the lives of workers as opposed to the middle classes; only later would she depict the poor and suffering out of direct observation and social conviction. In Munich she decided to create a visual narrative based on Emile Zola's naturalist mining novel, *Germinal*, which had appeared in 1885. Her *Scene from Germinal* (1891; private collection, repr. Washington 1992, p.20), which depicts the character of Catherine being fought over by two men, was much praised by her art school classmates and Kollwitz felt that with this work her career had taken a definitive turn. In 1893, in Berlin, she attended a performance of Gerhart Hauptmann's play *The Weavers*. This was such a transformative experience for the young woman that she immediately abandoned the Zola novel as the subject of her proposed graphic cycle and began work on the series that she would entitle *A Weavers' Rebellion* (*Ein Weberaufstand*).

As Kollwitz began work on the cycle that would win her both critical and popular success nationally, her circumstances were much changed. No longer a free young art student, she had married Dr Karl Kollwitz, a friend of her brother Conrad, and had moved with him to the working-class Prenzlauer Berg district of Berlin where her husband set up a practice caring for the industrial poor. Her first son, Hans, was born in 1892; her second, Peter, would be born four years later. The artist faced a challenging moment as she confronted the dual responsibilities of family and career.

At the beginning of the 1890s Kollwitz began to pursue the graphic arts seriously. Given her technical and expressive brilliance, it is remarkable to realise that she was virtually self-

Kollwitz: *Self-Portrait in Profile Facing Left, Drawing*, 1933; charcoal on brown laid paper; 47.7 × 63.5 cm.; National Gallery of Art, Washington, DC, Rosenwald Collection

taught as a printmaker. She had received some training in Königsberg from a copper engraver and then in Berlin laboured to teach herself how to etch. Her letters of the early 1890s document her experiments with the difficult intaglio media. Yet with the firm foundation of her drawing talent (and her protests to the contrary), the artist soon became familiar with the graphic techniques, and her first etched self-portrait of 1891 (Klipstein 1955, no.8) reveals her increasing ambition and mastery. Kollwitz also learned lithography, a more straightforward process. With these tools, she was ready to embark upon *A Weavers' Rebellion*.

In 1893 Kollwitz began work on the six images of the series: *Poverty*, *Death*, *Council*, *March of the Weavers*, *Storming the Gate* and *End*. Unusually, the cycle combined different media: the first three images were lithographs, the last three were etchings. These six prints comprise a loose narrative that only roughly relates to Hauptmann's play. The product of extensive preliminary studies in different media and different compositional formats (*Storming the Gate*, 1897; private collection, courtesy Galerie St Etienne, New York, repr. Washington 1992, p.143; *End*, 1897; Staatliche Kunstsammlungen, Dresden),

they recount the miserable conditions of cottage industry weavers who rise up against the boss and are slaughtered. In the dense, often claustrophobic images, Kollwitz eloquently yet unsentimentally communicated the plight of these people: a mother mourns her dead child; men and women rip up cobblestones to fling through the ornate gate of the boss's estate; and the dead are ignominiously carried back to the dark huts where the looms take up more space than the people.

The cycle received great attention and praise when it was exhibited in 1897 at the *Kunstlerinnen Ausstellung* at the Galerie Gurlitt and then at the Grosse Berliner Kunstausstellung. It was also a *succès de scandale*: in the cycle, the artist succeeded in combining an essentially academic style with a topic that was considered so unconventional and subversive in the repressive, philistine Prussian era that Kaiser Wilhelm II was advised by his ministers to prevent the artist from receiving the Berlin Salon's small gold medal. He is said to have remarked: "I beg you, gentlemen, a medal for a woman, that would really be going too far ... Orders and medals of honor belong on the breasts of worthy men!" (Alessandra Comini in *ibid.*, p.100).

Kollwitz was nevertheless greatly encouraged by the reception of *A Weavers' Rebellion*, and in the ensuing 15-year period she created some of her finest images, including the *Peasants' War* cycle and the series of images of *Woman with Dead Child*. In them, she experimented with increasingly inventive graphic techniques, including complex soft-ground etching processes. Kollwitz also made her images larger; the scale of the motifs grew along with the artist's ambition and desire to convey important messages. This was true for her more socially oriented subjects as well as for her more symbolic images; indeed, Kollwitz was as interested in the ideal as the real (*From Many Wounds You Bleed, O People*, 1896; Städelsches Kunstinstitut, Frankfurt am Main; *The Downtrodden*, 1900; Staatliche Kunstsammlungen, Dresden). This creative period coincided with a love affair (roughly 1905–9) between the artist and the Viennese publisher Hugo Heller. Probably related to this affair is a series of some ten erotic drawings executed by the artist and entitled the *Sekreta* (*c*.1910; Käthe-Kollwitz-Museum Berlin). At this time, too, Kollwitz began to place her art at the service of society in such posters as the *Poster for the German Home Workers Exhibition* (1906; National Gallery of Art, Washington, DC). Kollwitz also explored the use of colour in her prints: in *Female Nude with Green Shawl Seen from Behind* (1903; Kunsthalle, Bremen; Staatliche Kunsthalle, Dresden) and *Woman Arranging Her Hair* (1900; Staatliche Kunstsammlungen, Dresden) the artist moved away from social and emotional themes to indulge herself in some isolated, and non-recurring, moments of lyrical aestheticism.

One of the most compelling motifs of this period is that of the *Woman with Dead Child*. The artist was always influenced by Renaissance art and by traditional Christian iconography, and with her interest in mothers and children it is no surprise that she should have concentrated on that theme. After executing a series of large drawings and lithographs of a theme she called *Pietà* (1903; Käthe Kollwitz Museum, Cologne; Staatliche Museen zu Berlin; National Gallery of Art), which focused on a seated mother bent over and clasping a dead child, Kollwitz slightly altered the motif. In *Woman with Dead Child* (1903; National Gallery of Art) she used the process of direct and soft-ground etching to create, through rough, passionately scratched lines, the highly simplified scene of a naked woman who, seated cross-legged in an indeterminate space, sinks her head into the lifeless body of her child. The image was of such raw grief that it terrified her best friend, who immediately recognised the child as Kollwitz's son Peter (who indeed had been the model) and thought that he must actually have died. Kollwitz printed many versions of this motif, so revelatory of her sense of tragedy and empathy, and of her gift for conveying deep emotions in visual form. Among them are experimental impressions that she hand-coloured and printed with gold backgrounds (1903; British Museum, London).

Around 1903 Kollwitz undertook her second graphic cycle. *Peasants' War* was based on a historical event, the peasants' revolt of 1522–5, which Kollwitz had read about in an account of 1841–2 by the Swabian theologian and historian Wilhelm Zimmermann. The seven large images of the cycle – they are the size of small easel paintings – were made out of order and later arranged to fashion a rough narrative continuity. The artist depicted humans ploughing the land as if they were animals (*The Ploughers*, 1906); a peasant woman raped by a feudal lord (*Raped*, 1907); the peasants preparing for revolt (*Whetting the Scythe*, 1905; *Arming in a Vault*, 1906); charging into battle (*Outbreak*, 1903); their defeat (*Battlefield*, 1907); and the taking of prisoners (*The Prisoners*, 1908; all Staatliche Kunstsammlungen, Dresden). Typical of the artist's approach, she never once portrayed the perpetrators of injustice, preferring to give voice to the suffering of the victims. Further, she avoided specifying a particular time or place for the events, aiming for the expression of human universals.

The plates of *Peasants' War* are among the most technically unusual of her works. She explored new surface textures through the use of soft-ground etching, sometimes placing a cloth over the plates to create a canvas-like background on the print (*Outbreak*). The scope of her invention may be witnessed in the numerous states of each motif, created as the artist searched for the most expressive configurations. With the *Woman with Dead Child* and the colour lithographs, the sheets of the *Peasants' War* represent one of the most creative moments in Kollwitz's career, from the perspective of technique as well as compositional power. This was the last time she worked so intensely with intaglio methods. The technical complexity of the copper-plate images would no longer seem suitable for her goals of the succeeding decades, which required a poster-like immediacy and accessibility. Later, other media such as woodcut and sculpture would challenge as well as trouble her, but never again did the artist pursue technique with the same joy in materials and pure experimentation.

As Kollwitz became increasingly committed to using her art for social ends, she turned to lithography, and particularly transfer lithography, as her medium of choice, rather than etching. The more spontaneous handling evident in her work after 1908 may be seen in the drawings she contributed for reproduction in the political-satirical magazine *Simplicissimus*, such as *Out of Work* (1909; National Gallery of Art, Washington, DC), which portrays an unemployed man sitting dejectedly beside the sick-bed of his wife and children. At this time the artist also abandoned the practice of making studies from life; her simplified and concentrated images were now often made from memory and imagination.

The commitment that Kollwitz had always felt to social causes became urgent with the onset of World War I. A turning point was the death in combat of her younger son Peter at the age of 18 in October 1914. Like many young men across Europe, Peter Kollwitz had enlisted in the army as a volunteer, and Kollwitz's diaries chronicle her dilemma between disgust for the endless fighting and numerous casualties, and the fear that her son's death was meaningless. The death cast a pall over the artist's life; from then on much of her work, especially in sculpture, was an attempt to come to terms with the notions of sacrifice and loss. The war and the violent establishment of the Weimar Republic also precipitated a shift in Kollwitz's attitude towards the function of art. In 1922, in a now-famous diary entry, she observed: "Actually my art is not *pure* art … But still art. Each works as he can … my art has *purpose*. *I want to have an effect on this time*, in which human beings are so much at a loss and so in need of help" (4 December 1922).

Kollwitz: *The Volunteers, War: Plate 2*, 1922–3; woodcut; National Gallery of Art, Washington, DC, Rosenwald Collection

Kollwitz's more political orientation may be seen in the *Memorial Sheet to Karl Liebknecht* (1919; National Gallery of Art, Washington, DC), which commemorated the Spartacist leader who was assassinated on 15 January 1919 in the midst of the juggling for power as the Weimar Republic was formed. An acquaintance of the Liebknecht family, the artist visited the morgue and made drawings of the dead man. After many unsatisfactory drawings, trial etchings and lithographs depicting Liebknecht surrounded by mourners (1920; Käthe-Kollwitz-Museum, Berlin), Kollwitz, inspired by her recent viewing of woodcuts by the sculptor and printmaker Ernst Barlach, decided that woodcut was the very medium in which to realise her idea. Woodcut had been a popular medium in Germany since c.1905, when Die Brücke group, especially Ernst Ludwig Kirchner, adopted it to achieve a new primitive and expressive language. Although the loose, somewhat abstract handling of the woodcut, with its broad planes of black and white, might initially seem unsuited to Kollwitz's far more naturalistic style, throughout the 1920s she exploited its qualities in her rendering of more universal themes as well as for some of her self-portraits (*Self-Portrait*, 1924; National Gallery of Art). By contrast, she continued to make her anecdotal images and posters in the more narrative medium of lith-

ography. When the *Memorial Sheet* was completed, its stark monumentality accounted for its success; the woodcut went into two editions and was sold very cheaply at an Arbeiter Kunstausstellung in Berlin in 1920.

This was a wrenching time for Kollwitz. She had never before been programmatically political but soon felt that the chaotic events at the end of the war and the beginning of the Weimar Republic were forcing her into a role that she hesitated to fill. In a diary entry of October 1920 she noted that, because of her previous work, she was being praised as an artist of the proletariat and of the November Revolution, but that in fact, out of cowardice, she did not belong to any political party, and certainly not to the Communist Party. Yet at the same time, she did wish her art to serve a social function. Her stance was further complicated by the fact that in 1919 she was appointed the first woman professor at the Prussian Academy, an establishment position. The artist was torn between her wish for social reform and her deployment of her work to that end, and the forces of the establishment art world. Although she was committed to engaged art, she felt that the role of "standard bearer" had been thrust upon her at the price of some of her artistic freedom and of much personal ambivalence.

Recognising that the simplicity and readability of the

expressionist woodcut style had a unique potential to convey ideas quickly and powerfully, Kollwitz chose it for her third graphic cycle, *War* (1922–3). This seven-sheet portfolio comprises *The Sacrifice, The Volunteers* (see illustration), *The Parents, The Widow I, Widow II, The Mothers* and *The People* (published 1924; National Gallery of Art). As with *Peasants' War*, and unlike any other war portfolios such as Otto Dix's, Kollwitz portrayed no scenes of combat, only images of mothers and children, widows, parents and volunteers. Drastically reductive, transcending time and place, the *War* series, in its iconic abstraction, captures the full horror of loss and the equivocal nature of sacrifice.

In the years between the wars, Kollwitz was occupied with teaching at the Academy, with her family (her remaining son Hans married in 1920 and he and his wife had four children between 1921 and 1930) and with social concerns. She lithographed many posters such as *Never Again War!* (1924), executed for a pacifist organisation, and images such as *Municipal Shelter* (1926; both National Gallery of Art), in which a homeless mother bearing Kollwitz's own features huddles over her two sleeping children. In 1925 she made a three-sheet woodcut cycle called *Proletariat*; the eight sheets of her last series, entitled *Death*, were lithographed in 1934–5. In the most famous of the *Death* images, *Call of Death* (1934; National Gallery of Art), the artist herself receives the touch of a disembodied hand, calling her away from earthly existence. A concrete expression of Kollwitz's lifelong dialogue with death, the lithograph reveals the artist's mastery of expressive draughtsmanship and her astonishing economy of means.

Although Kollwitz continued to pursue her graphic work until 1942, three years before her death, sculpture was her main interest in the last decades of her life. It is surprising how little is known about this aspect of her oeuvre. For example, one account lists 25 works; another lists 19. Not all of their dates are known. The artist received her first introduction to the medium during a sojourn in Paris in 1904; she visited Rodin's studio and took some sculpture lessons at the Académie Julian. She returned to sculpture in 1909. Kollwitz was a modeller, working in clay and plaster, as in *Lovers* (1913; Museum of Fine Arts, Boston), leaving the bronze casting or stone cutting to other hands. Kollwitz made most of her sculptures during the 1930s and early 1940s after she signed an appeal to unify leftist party candidates against the Nazis and was dismissed from her professorship and directorship of the master studio for graphic arts at the Prussian Academy. In that year, 1933, Kollwitz joined a number of young artists in a communal studio building in the Klosterstrasse and, unofficially forbidden to exhibit her work, found solace during her internal exile, as she called it, in working in three dimensions. The artist's longest ongoing project was the two figures of the mourning father and mother, her monument to her son Peter. She discussed it at length in her diaries and agonised over it for some two decades before the finished plasters were translated into granite and finally put into place in 1932 in the military cemetery at Dixmuiden, Belgium, where Peter was buried. In their enclosed, inward-looking, blocky forms, these works convey a simplicity, self-contained apartness and quiet pathos that may be seen as well in some of the bronze relief sculptures, such as her plaque for her family grave *Rest in the Peace of His Hands* (1935; National Gallery of Art) and *Lamentation: In Memory of Ernst Barlach, Who Died in 1938* (1938; Hirshhorn Museum and Sculpture Garden, Washington, DC).

Kollwitz was devastated when World War II broke out in 1939. Her husband Karl died in 1942, the same year that her grandson Peter was killed on the Eastern Front. In response, Kollwitz made her last lithograph, an anti-war statement entitled *Seed Corn Must Not Be Ground* (1942; Staatliche Museen zu Berlin), after a phrase from Goethe, in which a mother encircles her children protectively. In the summer of 1943 the artist was evacuated to escape the bombing of Berlin; later that year her home was destroyed. In 1944 Kollwitz accepted the invitation of Prince Ernst Heinrich of Saxony to live on the grounds of his Schloss Moritzburg outside Dresden. She died the following year and was ultimately buried in the Central Cemetery in Berlin.

By the time Kollwitz died at the age of 78, she was already one of the best-known German artists. Her work had been sought after since the 1890s by major figures of the art world such as Max Lehrs, director of the world-famous Dresden Kupferstichkabinett, as well as by numerous German private collectors. The prints gained an even wider audience through the inexpensive reproductions that were published from 1913 onwards. By the 1920s, one could find reproductions, if not original examples of her images, in millions of homes throughout Germany. In 1927 she visited the Soviet Union, where she was already well-known and appreciated. Since then, her fame has spread throughout the world. By the late 1950s and 1960s, the German Art Council was sending exhibitions of her work to cities as distant as Paris and Cape Town, South Africa. During and after World War II, German refugees brought Kollwitz prints to America and elsewhere. More recently, with the aid of the artist's grandchildren, two museums entirely devoted to her art have been established in Berlin and Cologne, and a new one has opened in Moritzburg.

Kollwitz's art has not always been admired, however. Critics, especially modernists, have objected to its retardatory naturalism, its privileging of theme over style, and what some view as its bathetic sentimentalism. Käthe Kollwitz, however, who in many ways was far more a 19th-century naturalist than a 20th-century modernist, on the whole considered that she had served the world by fulfilling her grandfather Rupp's dictum "a talent is a duty" ("Eine Gabe ist eine Aufgabe"). Because of the accessibility of her style and the universal humanitarianism of her imagery, her art can be understood by all. Indeed, Kollwitz has come to be regarded by Germans as well as by other citizens of the world as a "symbol of [that] nation's 'good conscience in its darkest times', and 'the embodiment of the good Germany'" (Gunther Thiem, quoted by Hildegard Bachert in Washington 1992, p.125). More than any of her contemporaries, she was, as individual and as artist, truly the conscience of her age.

ELIZABETH PRELINGER

Kooning, Elaine de *see* de Kooning

Kozloff, Joyce
American painter and public artist, 1942–

Born Joyce Blumberg in Somerville, New Jersey, 14 December 1942. Studied at Art Students League, New York, 1959; Rutgers University, New Brunswick, New Jersey, 1962; Università di Firenze, Italy, 1963; Carnegie Institute of Technology, Pittsburgh (BFA 1964); Columbia University, New York (MFA 1967). Married Max Kozloff, 1967; one son. Held teaching positions in elementary and secondary schools, then at Queens College, New York, 1972–3; School of Visual Arts, New York, 1973–4; Art Institute, Chicago, 1975; Syracuse University, New York, 1977; University of New Mexico, Albuquerque, 1978; Brooklyn Museum Art School, New York, 1978–9; Washington University, St Louis, 1986; Cooper Union, New York, 1990; International Art Workshop, Teschemakers, New Zealand, 1991; Rutgers University, 1992. Recipient of Tamarind Lithography Institute grant, Albuquerque, 1972; Creative Artists Public Service (CAPS) grants, 1972 (New York State Council on the Arts) and 1975; National Endowment for the Arts (NEA) grant, 1977. Member of the Board of Directors, College Art Association, 1985–9. Lives in New York.

Selected Individual Exhibitions
Tibor de Nagy Gallery, New York: 1970, 1971, 1973, 1974, 1976, 1977
Mabel Smith Douglass Library, Rutgers University, New Brunswick: 1973
Everson Museum, Syracuse, NY: 1979–81 (*An Interior Decorated*, touring)
Joslyn Art Museum, Omaha, NE: 1982
Institute of Contemporary Art, University of Pennsylvania, Philadelphia: 1983 (with Keith Haring, Jenny Holzer and Rich Paul)
Lincoln Center for the Performing Arts, New York: 1983 (with Judith Murray and Elizabeth Murray)
Boston University Art Gallery: 1986–7 (*Visionary Ornament*, touring retrospective)
Lorence-Monk Gallery, New York: 1990–93 (*Patterns of Desire*, touring)
Tile Guild, Los Angeles: 1995

Selected Writings
"The Women's Movement: Still a 'source of strength' or 'one big bore'?", *Art News*, lxxv, April 1976, pp.49–50 (with Barbara Zucker)
"Art hysterical notions of art history", *Heresies*, no.4, Winter 1978, pp.38–42 (with Valerie Jaudon); reprinted in *Theories and Documents of Contemporary Art: A Sourcebook of Artists Writings*, ed. Kristine Stiles and Peter Selz, Berkeley: University of California Press, 1996
Patterns of Desire, New York: Hudson Hills Press, 1990 (introduction by Linda Nochlin)

Bibliography
Joseph Masheck, "Joyce Kozloff", *Artforum*, xii, September 1973, pp.76–7
Nancy Foote, "Joyce Kozloff at de Nagy", *Art in America*, lxiii, May 1975, pp.88–9
John Perreault, "Issues in pattern painting", *Artforum*, xvi, November 1977, pp.32–6
Amy Goldin, "Pattern and print", *Print Collector's Newsletter*, ix, 1978, pp.10–13
Carrie Rickey, "Joyce Kozloff", *Arts Magazine*, lii, January 1978, pp.2, 29
Joyce Kozloff: An Interior Decorated, exh. cat., Everson Museum, Syracuse, NY, and elsewhere, 1979
Jeff Perrone, "Joyce Kozloff", *Artforum*, xviii, November 1979, pp.78–9
Robin White, "Joyce Kozloff", *View*, Oakland, CA: Crown Point Press, 1981 (interview)
Jeff Perrone, "Two ethnics sitting around talking about Wasp culture", *Arts Magazine*, lix, March 1985, pp.78–83 (interview)
Joyce Kozloff: Visionary Ornament, exh. cat., Boston University Art Gallery, and elsewhere, 1986
Sally Webster, "Pattern and decoration in the public eye", *Art in America*, lxxv, February 1987, pp.118–25
Peggy Phelan, "Crimes of passion", *Artforum*, xxviii, May 1990, pp.173–7
Charlotte Streifer Rubinstein, *American Women Sculptors*, Boston: Hall, 1990
Hermine Freed, *Joyce Kozloff: Public Art Works*, video, New York, 1996

Joyce Kozloff creates walls of decorative colour. Trained in the Hard Edge minimalist vocabulary that dominated the eastern seaboard of the USA in the 1960s, she was inspired by her feminist studies to fuse geometric compositions with specific historical content that honours the ethnically and racially diverse, often female makers. Kozloff's first solo exhibition (New York, 1970) featured large acrylics of rectilinear patterns derived from Greek temple façades. By the mid-1970s, after having spent time in Mexico and the American Southwest, she began to look to native textile and architectural designs for inspiration. *Mitla* (1974; Massachusetts Institute of Technology, Cambridge) is a gouache and coloured pencil recollection of the fine stone mosaic façades of the stunning Zapotec Indian site in Oaxaca, Mexico. Six horizontal bands animate the composition, each a brilliant ribbon of colour marked with a variation of the Zapotec step-fret pattern. Although Kozloff derived the *Mitla* image from architectural sources, the stone mosaics themselves were originally derived from Zapotec textile patterns. Aware of this, Kozloff realised that many of the fabric, ceramic and basketry forms she admired had been made by women, and that most of these women had been lost to anonymity in the dominant historical discourse. The artist then determined to use her painting and pattern-making to honour such "disappeared" artists and their art forms.

When Kozloff exhibited such Mexican works as *Mitla*, she was praised for the rich elaboration of colour and pattern, but criticised for the "literalism" of her work. As, however, Patricia Johnston, curator of Kozloff's retrospective at the Boston University Art Gallery, asserted:

> Kozloff's fidelity to her sources may be the most radical aspect of her art. Pattern is not secondary … [it] functions as both the form and the subject matter of her painting; its associations constitute its meaning. The specificity of her motifs forces the viewer to confront its content: the aesthetic strength and cultural value of the decorative arts [Boston 1986, p.4].

Since the 1970s Kozloff has travelled the planet (both literally and figuratively) to mine a multitude of artistic traditions for decorative sources. She has explored these sources in formats that range from intimate watercolours to immense public

Kozloff: *Underwater Landscapes*, 1989; marble and glass mosaic; Atrium of Home Savings of America Headquarters, Irwindale, California

works, but she has remained consistent in her "literal" interpretations and in her assertion that decorative and popular art traditions are worthy of aesthetic investigation.

In the late 1970s Kozloff worked on a large installation that she entitled *An Interior Decorated*. First exhibited at the Everson Museum, Syracuse, in the autumn of 1979 and later at the Renwick Gallery of the National Museum of American Art, Smithsonian Institution, Washington, DC (August 1980), *An Interior Decorated* marks Kozloff's move from painted canvas to work applied directly to the wall. An elaborate environment combining ceramic tile "rugs" with silkscreened and lithographed fabric wall works, *An Interior Decorated* embodies what Kozloff called her

> personal anthology of the decorative arts [with motifs derived from] American Indian pottery, Moroccan ceramics, Viennese Art Nouveau book ornament, American quilts, Berber carpets, Caucasian kilims, Egyptian wall paintings, Iznik and Catalan tiles, Islamic calligraphy, Art Deco design, Sumerian and Romanesque

> carvings, Pennsylvania Dutch designs, Chinese painted porcelain, French lace patterns, Celtic illuminations, Turkish woven and brocaded silks, Seljuk brickwork, Persian miniatures and Coptic textiles [Syracuse 1979, p.8].

It is, as the critic Carrie Rickey wrote in the catalogue: "where painting meets architecture, where art meets craft, where personal commitment meets public art" (*ibid.*).

Even as she was working on *An Interior Decorated*, Kozloff was also beginning her foray into public art. Each of her public art projects has been initiated by research into the popular and folk art traditions germane to the site and each has placed locally relevant decorative motifs in architectural arenas, often the large walls that commuters see as they hurry from one train or subway stop to another. Kozloff intends the complexity of her compositions to allow multiple "reads" to be "discovered" over time, as viewers pass her work repeatedly. To date, she has completed 12 major public art commissions: Harvard Square Subway Station, Boston, and Amtrak Station, Wilmington (both 1979–85); California Airport, San Francisco (1982–3); Humboldt-Hospital Subway Station, Buffalo (1983–4); Suburban Train Station, Philadelphia (1985); Financial Station, Detroit, Michigan (1985); Home Savings Tower, Los Angeles (1989); Home Savings of America Headquarters, Irwindale (1989; see illustration); Plaza Las Fuentes, Pasadena (1990); Intermediate School 218, New York (1991); Seventh & Flower Metro Station, Los Angeles, (1993); and Memorial Library foyer, Mankato State University (1995).

Kozloff's Mankato project is one of her most complex and successful. She entitled it *Around the World on the 44th Parallel*, because she began with the library's latitudinal position and circled the globe to locate other cities on the same parallel, selecting Nice, Ravenna, Florence and Sarajevo from Europe; Urumqi, Changchun, Sapporo and Vladivostok from Asia; and Burlington, Eugene, Toronto and, of course, Mankato from North America. Her compositions began with strips from each city map, over which she laid patterns derived from the local art traditions. There were Northwest coast Native American images for Eugene, golden mosaics for Ravenna, tile work and carpets from the Ottoman Empire for Sarajevo. All these images were painted on majolica ceramic tiles made at the Tile Guild in Los Angeles. The tile panels encircle large open bays in the library, inviting viewers to consider the confluence of architecture and geography that produces the patterns of maps and the smaller folk and popular art patterns created by the inhabitants of those cities. A scintillating kaleidoscope of visionary decoration, Kozloff's Mankato project reveals the consistency and validity of her compelling patchworks of colour, design, image and pattern.

BETTY ANN BROWN

Krasner, Lee
American painter, 1908–1984

Born Lena Krassner in Brooklyn, New York, 27 October 1908. Studied in New York at Women's Art School of Cooper Union, 1926–8; Art Students League, 1928; National Academy of Design, 1928–32; City College and Greenwich House, 1933; Hans Hofmann's School of Fine Arts, 1937–40. Employed on Public Works of Art Project (PWAP), 1934; Temporary Emergency Relief Administration, 1934–5; Mural Division of Works Progress Administration Federal Arts Project (WPA/FAP), 1935–43, all in New York. Member of American Abstract Artists (AAA) from 1939. Married painter Jackson Pollock, 1945; he died 1956. Moved to The Springs, East Hampton, New York, 1945. Recipient of Augustus Saint-Gaudens medal, Cooper Union Alumni Association, 1974; Lowe Fellowship for Distinction, Barnard College, New York, 1974; Outstanding Achievement in the Visual Arts award, Women's Caucus for Art, 1980. Died in New York, 19 June 1984.

Selected Individual Exhibitions
Betty Parsons Gallery, New York: 1951
Stable Gallery, New York: 1955
Martha Jackson Gallery, New York: 1958

Signa Gallery, East Hampton, NY: 1959
Howard Wise Gallery, New York: 1960, 1962
Whitechapel Art Gallery, London: 1965–6 (touring, organised by Arts Council of Great Britain)
University Art Gallery, University of Alabama, Tuscaloosa: 1967
Marlborough Gallery, New York: 1968, 1969, 1973
Whitney Museum of American Art, New York: 1973
Corcoran Gallery of Art, Washington, DC: 1975 (touring)
Pace Gallery, New York: 1977, 1979, 1981
Janie C. Lee Gallery, Houston: 1978, 1981
Guild Hall Museum, East Hampton, NY: 1981 (with Jackson Pollock)
Grey Art Gallery and Study Center, New York University: 1981 (*A Working Relationship*, with Jackson Pollock)
Robert Miller Gallery, New York: 1982
Museum of Fine Arts, Houston: 1983–5 (touring retrospective, accompanied by *The Education of an Artist*)

Bibliography
Paintings, Drawings and Collages, exh. cat., Whitechapel Art Gallery, London, and elsewhere, 1965
Lawrence Campbell, "Of Lilith and lettuce", *Art News*, lxvii, March 1968, pp.42–3, 61–4
Emily Wasserman, "Lee Krasner in mid-career", *Artforum*, vi, March 1968, pp.38–43
Lee Krasner: Large Paintings, exh. cat., Whitney Museum of American Art, New York, 1973
Bryan Robertson, "The nature of Lee Krasner", *Art in America*, lxi, November–December 1973, pp.83–7
Cindy Nemser, "Lee Krasner's paintings, 1946–49", *Artforum*, xii, December 1973, pp.61–5
—, *Art Talk: Conversations with 12 Women Artists*, New York: Scribner, 1975
—, "The indomitable Lee Krasner", *Feminist Art Journal*, iv, Spring 1975, pp.4–9
Barbara Rose, "Lee Krasner and the origins of Abstract Expressionism", *Arts Magazine*, li, February 1977, pp.96–100
Abstract Expressionism: The Formative Years, exh. cat., Herbert F. Johnson Museum of Art, Ithaca, NY, and elsewhere, 1978
Elsa Honig Fine, *Women and Art*, Montclair, NJ: Allenheld and Schram, and London: Prior, 1978
Eleanor Munro, *Originals: American Women Artists*, New York: Simon and Schuster, 1979
Barbara Cavaliere, "An interview with Lee Krasner", *Flash Art*, no.94–5, January–February 1980, pp.14–16
The Abstract Expressionists and Their Precursors, exh. cat., Nassau County Museum of Fine Arts, Roslyn Harbor, NY, 1981
Amei Wallach, "Lee Krasner out of Jackson Pollock's shadow", *Newsday*, 23 August 1981, pp.10–15, 29–31, 33–4
Ellen G. Landau, "Lee Krasner's early career", *Arts Magazine*, lvi, October 1981, pp.110–22; November 1981, pp.80–89
Charlotte Streifer Rubinstein, *American Women Artists from Early Times to the Present*, Boston: Hall, 1982
Lee Krasner: A Retrospective, exh. cat., Museum of Fine Arts, Houston, and elsewhere, 1983
Ellen G. Landau, "Lee Krasner's past continuous", *Art News*, lxxxiii, February 1984, pp.68–76
Marcia E. Vetrocq, "An independent tack: Lee Krasner", *Art in America*, lxxii, May 1984, pp.136–45
Michael Cannell, "An interview with Lee Krasner", *Arts Magazine*, lix, September 1984, pp.87–9
John Bernard Myers, "Naming pictures: Conversations between Lee Krasner and John Bernard Myers", *Artforum*, xxiii, November 1984, pp.69–73
Lee Krasner: Collages, 1939–1984, exh. cat., Robert Miller Gallery, New York, 1986
Abstract Expressionism: The Critical Developments, exh. cat., Albright-Knox Art Gallery, Buffalo, NY, 1987

Robert Hobbs, "Lee Krasner: A retrospective", *Woman's Art Journal*, viii/1, 1987, pp.42–5

Lee Krasner, Jackson Pollock: Künstlerpaare-Künstlerfreunde/Dialogues d'artistes-résonances, exh. cat., Kunstmuseum, Bern, 1989

Steven Naifeh and Gregory White Smith, *Jackson Pollock: An American Saga*, New York: Potter, 1989; London: Barrie and Jenkins, 1990

Anne M. Wagner, "Lee Krasner as L.K.", *Representations*, no.25, Winter 1989, pp.42–57; reprinted in Norma Broude and Mary D. Garrard, eds, *The Expanding Discourse: Feminism and Art History*, New York: Icon, 1992, pp.425–36

Stephen Polcari, "In the shadow of an innovator", *Art International*, August 1990, pp.105–7

——, *Abstract Expressionism and the Modern Experience*, Cambridge and New York: Cambridge University Press, 1991

Robert Hobbs, *Lee Krasner*, New York and London: Abbeville, 1993

Lee Krasner: Umber Paintings, 1959–1962, exh. cat., Robert Miller Gallery, New York, 1993

Anne M. Wagner, "Fictions: Krasner's presence, Pollock's absence", *Significant Others: Creativity and Intimate Partnership*, ed. Whitney Chadwick and Isabelle de Courtivron, New York and London: Thames and Hudson, 1993, pp.222–43

Ellen G. Landau and Jeffrey D. Grove, *Lee Krasner: A Catalogue Raisonné*, New York: Abrams, 1995

Anne M. Wagner, *Three Artists (Three Women): Modernism and the Art of Hesse, Krasner and O'Keeffe*, Berkeley: University of California Press, 1996

Recognised at the time of her death in 1984 as a "pioneering Abstract Expressionist", "a major force in the art world" and "an artist's artist", Lee Krasner is today viewed as a visionary Abstract Expressionist painter. However, the dual stigma that she bore both as a female artist and as the wife and widow of one of the 20th century's most infamous painters, Jackson Pollock, led to an "odd mixture of fame and obscurity" (London 1965, p.5) that plagued Krasner's own development and reception as an independent artist during most of her life.

Pursuing her vocation with unwavering dedication (her nephew stated that she believed in art the way other people believed in God), as a teenager Krasner commuted daily from Brooklyn to Manhattan to study at Washington Irving High School (1922–6), the only public high school where a girl could study art. She then graduated to the Women's Art School of the Cooper Union and the National Academy of Design. Her work from this period is discursive, embracing developments in Social Realism, Surrealism and Cubism, arriving ultimately at a reverence for Picasso and Matisse. While working as an artist for the Public Works of Art Project in 1937, Krasner joined Hans Hofmann's School of Fine Arts, an experience she described as "opening a new world for me". Working from the model, Krasner created figure studies that echo the structure of still-life arrangements and developed a private language of cubo-abstraction stressing spatial relationships of colour and structure. *Composition* (*c*.1940–43; National Museum of American Art, Smithsonian Institution, Washington, DC) illustrates her quest at this time to follow Matisse by eliminating ordinary perspective, creating an illusion of depth through colour and formal organisation.

In 1939 Krasner joined the American Abstract Artists (AAA), a group of politically concerned artists dedicated to the principles of non-objective painting. While involved with the group, Krasner painted several canvases influenced by her hero Piet Mondrian's Neo-Plasticism (repr. Laudau 1981, fig.23).

Concurrently, Krasner was employed by the Mural Division of the Federal Arts Project of the Works Progress Administration, and much of her output between 1940 and 1943 grew out of ideas for mural projects. Becoming progressively more abstract, these biomorphic and geometric designs still belie their derivation from the still-life arrangements that Krasner first drew at the Hofmann school.

In 1942 Krasner became involved with Pollock and for the next three years virtually abandoned her own art-making, stymied by her admitted struggle to "lose Cubism" and "absorb Pollock". Shortly after their marriage in late 1945 and move to rural East Hampton, Krasner commandeered the living room of their rustic home as a studio where she began turning out her signature "Little Images". Purely abstract, the Little Images took three typical forms: thickly impastoed dabs (*Shattered Color*, 1947; Guild Hall Museum, East Hampton, NY), thin skeins with an all-over patterning (*Untitled*, 1948; Metropolitan Museum of Art, New York) and serial hieroglyphs (*Untitled*, 1949; Museum of Modern Art, New York). These discreetly proportioned paintings allowed Krasner to develop a typology of devices that she reiterated in larger paintings throughout her career.

In 1950, moving her studio to the upstairs bedroom, Krasner broke the Little Image cycle and created her first large-scale works: a series of automist-inspired, quasi-figural works dubbed the "personage paintings". These large-scale, thickly painted canvases prefigured the strong verticality manifested in Krasner's canvases of the mid-1950s (see Nemser 1975). Now destroyed, they are known only through photographs taken by Hans Namuth (repr. Rose 1977, fig.64). In a now characteristic move, Krasner radically shifted styles to create next a series of thinly painted canvases concerned with "holding the vertical" (Nemser 1975). Although only two paintings remain intact (*Number 3 [Untitled]*, 1951; Museum of Modern Art), the rest served as backdrops for collages shown at the Stable Gallery in 1955. Clearly, their tonal, reductive surfaces had more in common with the colour field abstractions of later Rothko, Still and Newman than with Pollock's own frenzied skeins of paint.

In 1953, as the conflicts in their relationship increased, Krasner began creating large-scale collages reflecting a renewed attention to natural elements rather than academic styles. Using fragments of drawings and canvas, torn and shorn from her own as well as Pollock's rejected works, Krasner's art began to disclose a new confidence and mastery of form. 1955 was a break-out year. The large, stylistically sophisticated collages Krasner showed that year at the Stable Gallery constituted a revolutionary development in her career: not only a unique recontextualisation of old paintings, new materials, cloth, canvas and paint, these surfaces seemed to function as a direct outlet for the friction Krasner was experiencing with Pollock at this time. Perceiving the organic metaphors embedded in Krasner's materials, Fairfield Porter compared the surface of one painting to a "messed-up beach of pebbles" and noted that such works as *Milkweed* (1955; Albright-Knox Art Gallery, Buffalo, NY) resembled "nature photographs magnified" (Fairfield Porter, "Art news of one year: November, Lee Krasner", *Art News*, November 1955, pp.66–7).

After Pollock's death in 1956, Krasner, refocusing on her own creativity and ambition, worked on an escalated scale and with increased ferocity. Taking over Pollock's large studio, she created her first series of large, Abstract Expressionist canvases. An early example from this group, *The Seasons* (1957; for illustration, see p.141), is one of the largest she ever painted. In this work Krasner developed an exuberantly expressionistic composition dominated by rhythmically interactive, sexually suggestive organic forms; allusions to specific anatomical parts (heart, buttocks, penis, eyes, mouths, labia) are cleverly combined with other natural forms (leaves, fruit, etc.). Natural processes of growth and change are suggested through her gestural and painterly technique, through emphasis on the spherical and curvilinear, and through the use of fresh greens and bright pinks modulated by cream and black. In 1981 John Russell of the *New York Times* declared *The Seasons* "one of the most remarkable American paintings of its date" ("Delights, surprises – and gaps", 8 March 1981, section 2, p.D31).

In the early 1960s Krasner created the *Umber and White* series, a group of more than 30 enormous canvases characterised by the poet Richard Howard as psychoanalytically motivated "mourning" pictures of which *Gothic Landscape* (1961; Tate Gallery, London) is a prime example (see Howard in New York 1993). Ferocious and lyrical, these canvases disclose Krasner's investigation of Jungian precepts that she had previously held in suspicion. These tumultuous canvases, worked from left to right in violent, slashlike rhythms, seem to express turmoil and rage, perhaps over Pollock's or her mother's death.

It was during the late 1960s to mid-1970s that feminist-oriented art historians and critics first began to take note of Krasner and re-evaluate her position within the history of modern art, particularly the Abstract Expressionist movement. In the late 1960s Krasner returned to more foliate schemes in which she experimented with highly keyed colour and regenerative, biotic forms. Interestingly, works like these, exemplified by *Pollination* (1968; Dallas Museum of Art), were the first to be interpreted along the lines of feminist rhetoric. Describing *Pollination*, Cindy Nemser remarked on its "thrusting phallic, pistil-like shapes, ejecting fructifying splinters of paint, evok[ing] the plant, animal, and human processes of regeneration" ("In the galleries: Lee Krasner", *Arts Magazine*, April 1968, p.59). Although Krasner once claimed: "I have very little patience with clubby attitudes toward it [feminism]", she approved of and encouraged the movement's role in elevating consciousness of female artists, and in late 1972 she even joined the group Women in the Arts to picket the Museum of Modern Art for its neglect of female artists. Newly "radicalised", and an example to a new generation of "feminist" artists, Krasner again made an abrupt switch in both scale and form in her art of the 1970s. From 1970 to 1973, to a certain degree recapitulating and magnifying the vocabulary of marks and gestures initiated in the "Little Images", Krasner created a group of large paintings that embraced concurrent developments in Color Field and Op Art. Such works as *Rising Green* (1972; Metropolitan Museum of Art) demonstrate that at the age of 62 Krasner was clearly intent on positioning herself as a forward-looking artist.

Krasner's most significant late-career contribution came in 1976 when she once again chose to cannibalise her own past, cutting up her own Hofmann School charcoal drawings from the 1930s and 1940s and recontextualising them into eleven stunning collages based on a linguistic system suggesting time and its conditions. The group, entitled *Eleven Ways to Use the Words to See*, was characterised by Grace Glueck as "the present ingesting the past" ("How to recycle your drawings", *New York Times*, 25 February 1977, p.C18). Indeed, such works as *Past Continuous* (1976; Solomon R. Guggenheim Museum, New York), with its repetition of expressionistically deformed female figures, signifies Krasner's quest to explore in this series "in what ways I, as an artist, differed now from then" (Myers 1984). Underlying Krasner's re-evaluation of her own career was her inclusion as the sole female artist in two important revisionist studies of Abstract Expressionism's early years: *Abstract Expressionism: The Formative Years* (Ithaca, NY, 1978) and *The Abstract Expressionists and Their Precursors* (Roslyn Harbor, NY, 1981). Krasner once claimed: "I certainly was there through the formative years of Abstract Expressionism and I have been treated like I wasn't", and it took shows like these, her retrospective of more than 150 works in 1983–4 and her rediscovery by feminist writers and art historians to ensure her position today as "one of the handful of important abstract expressionists" (Mark Stevens, "The American masters", *Newsweek*, 2 January 1984).

JEFFREY D. GROVE

See also Training and Professionalism survey 10

Krohg, Oda

Norwegian painter, 1860–1935

Born Othilia Lasson in Åsgårdstrand, 11 June 1860; father a government lawyer. Studied under Christian Krohg in Christiania (Oslo) from 1883; attended painting school run by Krohg, H. Heyerdahl and Erik Werenskiold, Christiania, from 1885; studied under Willem Geets in Mechelen, Belgium, 1885. Married businessman Jørgen Engelhardt, 1881; daughter born 1882, son born 1883; separated 1883; divorced 1888. Daughter Nana (also an artist) by Christian Krohg born 1885; married Krohg, 1888; son Per (also an artist) born 1889; husband died 1925. Associated with Christiania bohemians, particularly their leader, the writer Hans Jæger. In Berlin, winter 1893. Moved to Paris with dramatist Gunnar Heiberg, 1897; attended Académie Julian and Académie Colarossi. Reconciled with husband, moving to Montparnasse, Paris, 1901. Returned to Oslo when Krohg became first director of the Norwegian Art Academy, 1909. Died in Oslo, 19 October 1935.

Principal Exhibitions

Individual
Studentersamfundet, Christiania: 1890 (with Christian Krohg)
Fritzners Pavilion, Christiania: 1892 (with Christian Krohg)
Trondheim Kunstforening: 1905 (with Christian Krohg)
Christiania Kunstforening: 1906 (with Christian Krohg)
Blomqvist, Christiania: 1909 (with Christian and Per Krohg)

Group
Høstutstillingen (Autumn Salon), Christiania/Oslo: occasionally 1886–1930

Copenhagen: 1888 (*Den Nordiske udstilling* [Nordic exhibition]),
   1906 (*Den Norske udstilling* [Norwegian exhibition]), 1915 (*Den
   Norske kunstudstilling* [Norwegian art exhibition])
World's Columbian Exposition, Chicago: 1893
Internationale Kunstausstellung, Berlin: 1896
Royal Academy of Fine Arts, Stockholm: 1904 (*Norska konstnärers
   arbeten* [The work of Norwegian artists])
Internationale Kunstausstellung, Düsseldorf: 1904
Christiania Kunstforening (Art Association): 1905–15
Bergens Kunstforening (Art Association): 1905
Venice Biennale: 1907
Blomqvist, Christiania/Oslo: 1910 (*Malerindeforbundets utstilling*
   [Society of Women Painters exhibition]), 1914
   (*Malerindeforbundets portretutstilling* [Society of Women Painters
   portrait exhibition])
Esposizione Internazionale, Rome: 1911
Brighton: 1913 (*Modern Norwegian Artists*)
Glaspalast, Munich: 1913

Bibliography

Bokken Lasson, *Slik var det dengang* [That was the way it was],
   Oslo: Gyldendal, 1938 (autobiography of Oda Krohg's sister)
H. Gran and R. Revold, *Kvinneportretter i norsk malerkunst* [Female
   portraits in Norwegian painting], Oslo, 1945, pp.45–50, no.56
Per Krohg, "Oda Krohg", *Kunst og Kultur*, 1953, pp.5–10
——, *Memoarer, minner og meninger* [Reminiscences, memories and
   opinions], Oslo, 1966
Anne Wichstrøm, *Kvinner ved staffeliet: Kvinnelige malere i Norge
   før 1900* [Women at the easel: Women painters in Norway before
   1900], Oslo: Universitetsforlaget, 1983 (revised edition in prepa-
   ration)
*Kvindelige kunstnere på Skagen: Anna Ancher, Oda Krohg, Marie
   Krøyer* [Women artists at Skagen: Anna Ancher, Oda Krohg,
   Marie Krøyer], exh. cat., Skagens Museum, Skagen, and else-
   where, 1987
De drogo till Paris: Nordiska konstnärinnor på 1880-talet [They
   went to Paris: Nordic women artists in the 1880s], exh. cat.,
   Liljevalchs Konsthall, Stockholm, 1988
Anne Wichstrøm, *Oda Krohg: Et kunstnerliv* [Oda Krohg: An artist's
   life], Oslo: Gyldendal, 1988
Billy Klüver and Julie Martin, *Kiki's Paris: Artists and Lovers,
   1900–1930*, New York: Abrams, 1989
Anne Wichstrøm, "Oda Krohg: A turn-of-the-century Nordic artist",
   Woman's Art Journal, xii/2, 1991–2, pp.3–8
Alessandra Comini, "Nordic luminism and the Scandinavian recast-
   ing of Impressionism", *World Impressionism: The International
   Movement, 1860–1920*, ed. Norma Broude, New York: Abrams,
   1992, pp.274–313
Tradisjon og fornyelse [Tradition and renewal], exh. cat.,
   Nasjonalgalleriet, Oslo, 1994

Othilia, or Oda, Lasson was the daughter of a prominent
lawyer, Christian Lasson, and his half-Russian wife of aristocratic descent, Alexandra von Munthe af Morgenstierne.
Belonging to a family of two sons and eight daughters, she
made herself known to her home town of Christiania (today's
Oslo) quite early: the "Lasson sisters" had striking beauty and
artistic gifts. Alexandra married the Norwegian painter Fritz
Thaulow, Bokken pursued a career as a singer, and the thrice-
married Soffi had for her second husband the mercurial Danish
poet and playwright Holger Drachmann. Oda herself played
the piano and, according to Bokken, later in life sang in a deep,
nasal voice *à la* Yvette Guilbert.

Married in 1881 to Jørgen Engelhardt she bore a daughter,
Sascha, in 1882 and a son, Frederik, in 1883, but after her
husband's bankruptcy she left home with the two children. In
1884, with Thaulow, she became the student of Christian
Krohg, who had initiated a private academy for women four
years earlier, to which male students were admitted by 1882
(among them Edvard Munch). Christian Krohg had studied
law before turning to painting and therefore knew Oda's
husband. Oda went on to pursue her studies at the second art
school founded by Krohg in 1885, with the painters Hans
Heyerdahl and Erik Werenskiold as co-directors. When she
became pregnant by Krohg, she had to retire to Belgium where
their daughter was born in 1885 and left to foster parents until
Oda could remarry.

Her first show was at the Høst (Autumn) Salon of 1886,
where Edvard Munch showed *Sick Girl*, which he later
presented to Krohg. Oda's paintings were quite remarkable, in
particular the study of sophisticated light effects, as in *At the
Fjord of Christiania*, also called *Japanese Lanterns*
(Nasjonalgalleriet, Oslo) and *My Boy* (untraced). An extraordinary feature of the latter painting was its frame, decorated
with a collage of her son's toys, a gilded flute, a trumpet and
tin soldiers. Her divorce from Engelhardt was finalised in 1888
and in the same year she married Krohg. They set up home in
various parts of Europe: at Skagen in Denmark in 1888,
Copenhagen in 1889–90, Berlin in 1893 – where they could
find other nomadic artists such as August Strindberg and
Holger Drachmann – and Copenhagen again in 1894. Paris
became the more or less fixed abode of Oda Krohg between
1895 and 1901, and she became acquainted with Oscar Wilde
at the Thaulows' house in Dieppe in 1897. She undertook
some further travelling in Italy in 1920–21, and in 1926 went
to Rio de Janeiro to visit the two children of her first marriage,
who had emigrated with their father in 1898 after she went to
live with the writer Gunnar Heiberg in Paris.

Oda Krohg's early paintings are related to the naturalism of
Christian Krohg, himself trained in Germany and friendly with
Max Klinger in Berlin. Her compositions occasionally may be
more daring than those of her husband. She was one of the first
Norwegian artists to seek inspiration in Japanese art, as
evidenced in the striking painting *Aftenposten* (a Norwegian
daily paper, hostile to Christian Krohg), where the child cuts
into the newspaper (1887; see illustration). The floor is tilted
and the child is viewed from above and behind at a most
unusual angle. Oda Krohg's brush strokes at this early period
are often very free and thin, resembling translucent watercolours. Her homely subject matter, though, is idyllic
compared to the crass realism of Christian Krohg's paintings of
the slums of Christiania (e.g. *Struggle for Life*, 1887;
Nasjonalgalleriet). During the time that Oda's relationship to
Krohg was still, in terms of law, adulterous, he was turning
into an "enemy of society" in his attacks on conventional
marriage and what he saw as one of its consequences, prostitution. In his novel *Albertine* of 1886, and a series of paintings
based upon its story of a working-class girl, raped by a police
officer and thereupon sliding into streetwalking, he brought
down upon himself sequestration of the book and a major fine,
in spite of his own brilliant advocacy in court.

Linked with Krohg and flamboyantly bohemian in her
lifestyle, Oda also brought herself into the public eye – even
more so when she entered into a *ménage à trois* with the anti-
Establishment writer Hans Jæger as the third party. It was he
who named Oda "une vraie princesse de la Bohème" (a pun

Krohg: *Aftenposten*, 1887; oil on canvas; 46.5 × 54.5 cm.; Nasjonalgalleriet, Oslo

upon Balzac's "un prince de la Bohème"). Jæger, Christian Krohg's best friend, also had visions of a utopian, anarchic society. The three of them were to keep separate diaries but Oda decreed that hers was to be destroyed at her death. Jæger, however, published his version of the story, based also upon letters, in his novels *Syk kjærlihet* (Diseased love; 1893), *Bekjendelser* (Confessions; 1902) and *Fængsel og fortvilelse* (Prison and despair; 1893). Sequestration and imprisonment followed on the publication of the first of the three parts of the book, but Oda and Christian Krohg had already considered that Jæger had not kept his side of the bargain.

In the years 1892 to 1900 Oda Krohg painted very little, although she worked with compositions in coloured leather, some of which she exhibited at the Høstutstillingen of 1901. After 1900 she turned to portraiture, as witnessed in the likeness of her companion *Gunnar Heiberg* (1900; Nationalmuseum, Stockholm), her portrait of *Christian Krohg* (1904; City Museum of Oslo) and her image of the Swedish

painter *Ivar Arosenius* (1905; Nasjonalgalleriet). Her portraiture is intense and psychologically convincing, often with a dramatic play of chiaroscuro. Particularly interesting is the almost disturbing likeness of the Danish-born *Margrethe Vullum* (Nasjonalgalleriet). Krohg also painted her sister Bokken Lasson, as well as the *grande dame* of Norwegian theatre, the actress *Johanne Dybwad* (1912; National Theatre, Oslo).

Oda Krohg was chosen to represent her country at several major exhibitions abroad, such as the Esposizione Internazionale at Rome in 1911 and the Brighton show *Modern Norwegian Artists* in 1913. She exhibited at the Glaspalast in Munich in 1913 and two years later in Copenhagen. After World War I she gradually fell into oblivion outside Norway, while her son Per Lasson Krohg became the better-known painter of the family. In recent years she has been reassessed by art historians as well as by Norwegian novelists and playwrights. As Christian Krohg said about the

"Lasson sisters": "Never indifference! Always strength! ... such a sum of rich noble feelings these sisters have laid down in all of us ... a hint of the 'troll' there was in each and every one of them ...". The fascination both of Oda Krohg's art and her eccentric personality as a woman who led her life according to her own rules has lived on.

CHARLOTTE CHRISTENSEN

Kruger, Barbara
American photographer and artist, 1945–

Born in Newark, New Jersey, 26 January 1945. Studied at Syracuse University, New York, 1964–5; Parsons School of Design, New York, under Diane Arbus (q.v.) and Marvin Israel, 1965–6. Subsequently designer for *Mademoiselle* magazine, Condé Nast Publications; also freelance graphic designer. Independent artist and photographer from 1972. Visiting artist, California Institute of the Arts, Valencia; Art Institute of Chicago; University of California, Berkeley. One of the few women to be included in Documenta VII art fair, Kassel, 1982. Recipient of Creative Artists Public Service (CAPS) grant, 1976; National Endowment for the Arts (NEA) grant, 1982. Lives in New York.

Selected Individual Exhibitions

Artists Space, New York: 1974
Fischbach Gallery, New York: 1975
PS 1, Long Island City, NY: 1980
Institute of Contemporary Arts, London: 1983–4 (touring)
Kunsthalle, Basel: 1984
Rhona Hoffman Gallery, Chicago: 1984, 1986, 1990
Los Angeles County Museum of Art: 1985
Krannert Art Museum, University of Illinois, Urbana: 1986
Mary Boone Gallery, New York: 1987, 1989, 1991, 1994
National Art Gallery, Wellington, New Zealand: 1988
Kölnischer Kunstverein, Cologne: 1994

Selected Writings

Editor, *TV Guides: A Collection of Thoughts about Television*, New York: Kuklapolitan Press, 1987
My Pretty Pony, New York: Knopf, 1989 (with Stephen King)
Editor, *Remaking History*, Albany, CA: Bay Press, 1989 (with Phil Mariani)
Remote Control: Power, Cultures and the World of Appearances, Cambridge: Massachusetts Institute of Technology Press, 1993 (collected essays)

Bibliography

Hal Foster, "Subversive signs", *Art in America*, lxx, November 1982, pp.88–92
Craig Owens, "The discourse of others: Feminists and postmodernism", *The Anti-Aesthetic: Essays on Postmodern Culture*, ed. Hal Foster, Port Townsend, WA: Bay Press, 1983; London: Pluto, 1985, pp.57–77
We Won't Play Nature to Your Culture: Works by Barbara Kruger, exh. cat., Institute of Contemporary Arts, London, and elsewhere, 1983
Howard N. Fox, Miranda McClintic and Phyllis Rosenzweig, *Content: A Contemporary Focus, 1974–1984*, Washington, DC: Smithsonian Institution Press, 1984

Kunst mit Eigen-Sinn: Aktuelle Kunst von Frauen, Vienna and Munich: Locher, 1985
Kate Linker, "Barbara Kruger", *Flash Art*, no.121, 1985, pp.36–7 (interview)
Slices of Life, exh. cat., Krannert Art Museum, University of Illinois, Urbana, 1986
Anders Stephanson, "Barbara Kruger", *Flash Art*, no.136, 1987, pp.55–9 (interview)
Carol Squiers, "Diversionary (syn)tactics: Barbara Kruger has her way with words", *Art News*, lxxxvi, February 1987, pp.76–85
Jeanne Siegel, "Barbara Kruger: Pictures and words", *Arts Magazine*, lxi, Summer 1987, pp.17–21; reprinted in *Art Talk: The Early 80s*, New York: Da Capo Press, 1990, pp.299–312
Anne Le Schreiber, "You can look at Oliver North and listen to him speak and wonder how a nation doesn't know a sociopath when it sees one", *Vogue*, October 1987, pp.260–62
Nancy D. Campbell, "The oscillating embrace: Subjection and inter-apellation in Barbara Kruger's art", *Genders*, no.1, 1988, pp.56–74
Barbara Kruger, exh. cat., National Art Gallery, Wellington, 1988
Laura Mulvey, *Visual and Other Pleasures*, Bloomington: Indiana University Press, and London: Macmillan, 1989
Kate Linker, *Love for Sale: The Words and Pictures of Barbara Kruger*, New York: Abrams, 1990
W.J.T. Mitchell, "An interview with Barbara Kruger", *Critical Inquiry*, xvii, 1991, pp.434–48
David Deitcher, "Barbara Kruger: Resisting arrest", *Artforum*, xxix, February 1991, pp.84–92
Mignon Nixon, "You thrive on mistaken identity", *October*, no.60, 1992, pp.58–81
Mara R. Witzling, ed., *Voicing Today's Visions: Writings by Contemporary Women Artists*, New York: Universe, 1994
Jill Diane Ball, *The Effects of Public Representation upon the Identity of the Subject: Two Case Studies in Public Art*, PhD dissertation, University of California at Los Angeles, 1995
Melissa Harris, ed., *On Location with Henri Cartier-Bresson, Graciela Iturbide, Barbara Kruger, Sally Mann, Andres Serrano, Clarissa Sligh*, New York: Aperture Foundation, 1995

Eleven years' work as a graphic designer for Condé Nast publications and as a free-lance picture editor taught Barbara Kruger that if the viewer did not look at the design: "you were fired". Before her commercial career, Kruger spent a year at Syracuse University and a year at Parsons School of Design, where she studied under Marvin Israel and the photographer Diane Arbus (q.v.), who once assigned her to photograph the exterior of buildings and to imagine the lives lived inside. Her first solo show at Artists Space in New York in 1974 did not, however, feature photography, but abstract painting and fibre work (*Two A.M. Cookie*, 1973), reflecting the then-prevalent taste for both abstraction and the fibre arts on the New York art scene. The decorative style of these pieces coincided with the Pattern and Decoration movement that flourished in California during the mid-1970s. In these years, Kruger was active with Artists for Cultural Change, which strengthened her personal interest in feminism and its criticism, and in the relationship between art and politics, pivotal issues in her later work.

In 1976 Kruger began using language in a performance piece – for her a major shift in style and content. The *Hospital Series* followed in 1977. Combining photographs taken in New York hospitals with patients' voices ("No don't/Not now/Go away/Not that") and other texts ("The technology of early death/The providing of consumer goods to a dying populace"), Kruger began to probe social ideology through the incisive juxtaposition of image and text. A self-published collection of photographs paired with invented narratives entitled *Picture/Readings* followed in 1978. Since then she has marshalled the skills of the graphic designer and advertiser to deconstruct media culture through black-and-white photographs paired with short, evocative texts. Together they become insidious critiques of the established cultural narrative. Echoes of the early modernists' exploration of poster design and the photo-montages of the Dadaists Hannah Höch (q.v.) and John Heartfield underlie her work, although as Kruger emphasises, their impact on advertising and graphic art were her direct sources of influence; she did not discover Heartfield's work until 1981.

Kruger's subjects range from stereotypes of social roles to feminist deconstructive criticism of the gaze, as in *Untitled (Your Gaze Hits the Side of My Face)* (1981; for illustration, see p.156). Her use of text resonates with the linguistic theory of the French Post-structuralist philosopher Roland Barthes and his analysis of "language as legislation", and also the writings of Jean Baudrillard, such as his essays on fashion and its territorial scope, "Design and environment", and other essays on the commodification of the art object: "The art auction" and "Gesture and signature". Discovered by artists of the later 1970s, these writings were also widely discussed by avant-garde critics. Congruent with her generation's concern with art in the public sphere, Kruger dispersed her works on matchbooks, T-shirts, postcards and billboards, echoing the strategies used by her contemporary and friend, Jenny Holzer. Under the auspices of the US Public Art Fund, in 1983 she produced *I AM NOT TRYING TO SELL YOU ANYTHING* for the Spectacolor board in Times Square, New York, which was followed that year by the *Sign on a Truck* project to coincide with the re-election campaign of President Ronald Reagan. In 1985 she began producing public billboards: in the USA they appeared in Minneapolis, Berkeley, Chicago and Los Angeles, and 30 billboards were designed for Las Vegas. She designed more than 80 others in England, Scotland and Northern Ireland.

Stylistically, the art that Kruger created during the early 1980s was dominated by black-and-white media photographs from the post-war years, often culled from the photo archives of the New York Public Library, paired with short phrases or narrative texts, and framed by a trademark red border. Such works, which were transferred to paper and sometimes to vinyl or mirrored glass through photo-silkscreen, reflect the dominance of photography and absence of expressionistic handling that typified the "image scavenger" artists who came to dominate the New York scene in the early 1980s, including Ross Bleckner, Sherrie Levine and Richard Prince, as well as the Neo-expressionist David Salle. These friends shared with Kruger a fascination with the photographic and cinemagraphic dimensions of contemporary media culture, as well as its social impact, its structures of representation and codes of public speech. Kruger's concern with such issues also finds an outlet in the film and television criticism she first began writing in 1976, while teaching at the University of California, Berkeley, and which she continues to contribute to such magazines as *Artforum*.

In 1986 she began experimenting with colour photography, as in *Untitled (Give Me All You've Got)* (1986; Dennis and Ellen Schweber Collection), and also with innovative techniques, such as lenticular imagery. This process – popular in the USA during the 1950s for gifts distributed in boxes of cereal – consists of dual pictures covered by a lenticular lens. Tilting the picture brings the secondary image into focus. In *Untitled (Read My Lips: My Tongue is in Your Cheek)* (1986; repr. Wellington 1988, cat.19) Kruger combines a photographic image with an insidious and haunting sub-text. More recently, she has used 19th-century photo-engraved plates for her works. Perhaps due to her experience as a graphic artist, Kruger has often worked collaboratively, with Jenny Holzer, Keith Haring and other artists for the *Sign on a Truck* project, and published illustrated books (with Stephen King, *My Pretty Pony*, 1989). Her recent projects have included installations, such as *Untitled (Pledge)* (1989) for the Museum of Contemporary Art, Los Angeles, curating exhibitions, such as *Picturing Greatness* for the Museum of Modern Art, New York, in 1988, and also organising critical symposia, such as *Remaking History* for the Dia Art Foundation in 1989, whose proceedings she also edited.

"I'm interested in making art that displaces the powers that tell us who we can be and who we can't be", she observed in an interview in 1989 (Deitcher 1991, p.90). Barbara Kruger continues to challenge the role that women play in society through her photographic imagery, her billboards, her film and television criticism, and her exhibitions.

PHYLIS FLOYD

Kruglikova, Elizaveta (Sergeevna)

Russian graphic artist, 1865–1941

Born in St Petersburg (later Petrograd/Leningrad), 6 January (Old Style calendar)/19 January (New Style calendar) 1865. Attended the Moscow School of Painting, Sculpture and Architecture, 1890–95; studied under Adam Arkhipov, Ilarion Pryanishnikov and Sergei Korovin. Travelled to Constantinople, Greece and Venice, 1892; Italy and Paris, 1894. Lived in Paris, making annual trips to Russia, 1895–1914; studied under Edmond François Aman-Jean, Luc-Olivier Merson and R. Collin; founded "Monparnas" society, 1903; taught etching at La Palette, 1906–8. Returned to Petrograd, 1914; taught in Graphics Faculty, Svomas/Vkhutemas/Vkhutein (Free State Art Workshops/Higher State Artistic and Technical Workshops/Higher State Artistic and Technical Institute), 1918–29. Member, Mir Iskusstva (World of Art); Société de la Gravure Originale en Couleur, 1904; Leonardo da Vinci Society, Moscow, 1906; NOKh (New Society of Artists), Petrograd; Dom Iskusstv (House of the Arts), Petrograd. Founding member, Union of Artist-Engravers, Moscow, 1917. Exhibiting member, Zhar-Tsvet (Fire-Colour); Leningrad Society of Ex-Librists; Association of Artists-Graphic Artists of the House of Printing, Moscow; Association of Artists-Graphic Artists, Leningrad. Died in Leningrad, 21 July 1941.

Principal Exhibitions

Individual

Moscow: 1899

Galerie d'Art Décoratif, Paris: 1907
St Petersburg/Leningrad: 1913, 1940 (retrospective)
Kazan: 1925

Group
Salon des Indépendants, Paris: from 1897
Mir Iskusstva (World of Art): 1900, 1911–24
Izdebsky Salon, Odessa: 1909–10 (*International Exhibition*, touring)
Petrograd/Leningrad: 1919 (*First State Free Exhibition of Artworks*),
    1923 (*Pictures by Petrograd Artists of All Trends, 1919–1923*),
    1927 (*Jubilee Exhibition of Fine Arts*), 1927 (*Graphic Art in the
    USSR, 1917–1927*), 1927 (*Russian Stage Design, 1917–1927*),
    1928 (*The Artistic Ex-Libris, 1917–1928*)
Moscow: 1919 (*VI State Exhibition: The Print*), 1927 (*All-Union
    Polygraphic Exhibition*), 1927 (*Printmaking in the USSR over 10
    Years*)
Grand Central Palace, New York: 1923–4 (*Russian Art*, touring)
Exposition Internationale des Arts Décoratifs et Industriels
    Modernes, Paris: 1925
Venice Biennale: 1928
Leningrad and Moscow: 1932–3 (*Artists of the RSFSR over 15 Years,
    1917–1932*)

Bibliography

Parizh nakanune voyny v monotipyakh E.S. Kruglikovoy [Paris on
    the eve of war, in the monotypes of E.S. Kruglikova], Petrograd,
    1916
V.Ya. Adaryukov, "Russkiye gravyory: E.S. Kruglikova" [Russian
    engravers: E.S. Kruglikova], *Pechat i revolyutsiya*, Moscow, 1923,
    no.4, Kn.1, pp.103–14
E.S. Kruglikova, exh. cat., Kazan, 1925
Vyacheslav Polansky, ed., *Mastera sovremennoy gravyury i grafiki:
    Sbornik materialov* [Masters of contemporary engraving and
    graphic arts: Anthology of materials], Moscow: Gosizdat, 1928
Aleksei Alekseyevich Sidorov, *E.S. Kruglikova*, Leningrad: izdat.
    LSSKh, 1936
75 let so dnya rozhdeniya E.S. Kruglikovoy, 1865–1940 [75 years
    from the birth of E.S. Kruglikova], exh. cat., Leningrad, 1940
E.S. Kruglikova: Zhizn i tvorchestvo [E.S. Kruglikova: Life and
    works], Leningrad, 1969
S.S. Pererve, "Vozrozhdyonnoye iskusstvo silueta" [The revived art
    of the silhouette], *Leningradskaya panorama*, no.1, 1987,
    pp.29–31
Ekaterina Vasilevna Grishina, *Elizaveta Sergeyevna Kruglikova*,
    Leningrad: Khudozhnik RSFSR, 1989

Elizaveta Kruglikova was well known for her skill in the field
of colour engraving and an innovator in the techniques of
monotype and the silhouette. While resident in Paris, she gathered in her atelier the elite of the intellectual, literary and artistic Russian émigré community. Her silhouette portraits of these
intimates and of later public figures provide a record of the
age; these and her etchings and silhouettes of Paris earned her
the sobriquet "Singer of Paris's streets". After returning to
Russia at the outset of World War I, she turned her observation
to the construction of a new society.

Kruglikova was born into a cultivated St Petersburg family,
from whom she inherited a lifelong interest in the arts.
Although her mother was an accomplished pianist and her
father sketched, they were not enthusiastic about their daughter's determination to take up a career as an artist.
Nevertheless, after some initial training in Moscow with the
painter N.A. Martynov, Kruglikova entered the Moscow
School of Painting, Sculpture and Architecture in 1890. On
graduating in 1895, at the age of 30, she moved to Paris.

Kruglikova: *Self-Portrait*, 1934; silhouette; 21.3 × 17 cm.;
State Russian Museum, St Petersburg

Kruglikova began taking lessons at the Académie Vitti, but
by 1903 was teaching etching herself from her atelier on the
rue Boissonade. During her residence in Paris, she made annual
trips to Russia, as well as frequent journeys to Brittany,
Normandy, Belgium, Spain and Corsica. She made copious
sketches from nature on these trips, gathering material for later
prints (*Work in Pont-Aven, Brittany*, colour aquatint; and
Swine: Belgium, colour aquatint with soft-ground etching;
both 1908; Pushkin Museum, Moscow). Her aquatints and
etchings on Breton themes, in particular, show a strong formal
resemblance to Gauguin's landscape and genre paintings.

Kruglikova's studio soon became a gathering place for
writers, musicians and poets. She was particularly close to
Anatole France, the poet Maksimilian Voloshin and the writer
Aleksei Tolstoy. In 1903 she and the artist O.N. Mechnikova
founded Monparnas, an association dedicated to disseminating
information to Russian artists arriving in Paris. The association was made up of regular visitors to Kruglikova's studio,
who gathered there during the day while classes were held,
and in the evenings when concerts and literary readings took
place. Members included the artists Anna Golubkina
(q.v.), Venyamin Belkin, Matvei Dobrov, Ivan Efimov,
Konstantin Kostenko, Anna Ostroumova-Lebedeva (q.v.),
E.N. Rossinskaya, Margarita V. Sabashnikova and Aleksei
Yakimchenko and the writers Konstantin Balmont, Valery
Bryusov, Nikolai Gumilyov, Nikolai Minsky and Tolstoy.

Other visitors included Nicholas Roerich, Kuzma Petrov-Vodkin, Martiros Sarian, Anatoly Lunacharsky and Prince Pyotr Kropotkin. Most of these figures appeared later in Kruglikova's portraits and prints of Paris life. Like Kruglikova, artists attracted to her circle tended to be modernist, even Post-Impressionist, but not formally experimental; they were not drawn to Cubism nor were they contributors to abstraction in the Russian avant-garde movement.

Beginning in 1909, Kruglikova combined her work in coloured printmaking and painting in the production of monotypes. A process that yields one original print, rather than multiple impressions, monotype involves painting in ink on a plate, then impressing the image on paper. Unless combined with another technique, such as engraving or drawing, monotypes are characterised by unbounded areas and strokes of colour, and are therefore an agreeable medium for the impressionist or fauvist artist. Few artists of her time made such extensive use of the technique, which Kruglikova pursued for the next three decades. Her personal show of prints in St Petersburg in 1913 was the first time that monotypes had been exhibited in Russia. Landscapes and urban scenes were her most frequent subjects; the most famous of these was *Tango in Luna Park* (1914; Pushkin Museum), a lively scene invigorated by light colours and swirling shapes. She also created expressive still lifes of flowers (*White Roses*, 1914; State Russian Museum, St Petersburg) and about 100 works on the theme of "colours".

At the outbreak of World War I Kruglikova returned to Russia, where her apartment on Ostrovsky Street in Petrograd soon became another gathering place for the creative world. From the streets of Paris, she turned her attention to scenes of Moscow and Petrograd (*A Corner of Moscow*, 1916; colour aquatint; Pushkin Museum). In 1916 she published *Parizh nakanune voyny* (Paris on the eve of war), containing monotypes of Paris and essays by Balmont, illustrated by silhouettes of Paris scenes and many portraits. This marked the first publication of Kruglikova's silhouettes, a technique she adopted around 1914. The silhouette, an image cut from black paper, usually against a white background, enjoyed a revival in Russia among artist-illustrators associated with the World of Art. A medium that attracted many admirers, particularly among women, the silhouette was primarily used for portraiture; although in some artists' hands it achieved a lace-like delicacy, it was usually seen as presenting an "outlined shadow". In Kruglikova's silhouettes, forcefully represented in her café and street scenes in *Paris*, white accents let into black masses give the impression of different colours, of patterns and energised space. Frequently white areas are outlined in black, giving the silhouette the flexibility of line, rather than shadow. After the Revolution, Kruglikova adapted her silhouettes to poster and postcard reproduction. Typical of these (in several variations) is the literacy-drive poster of a peasant woman and her daughter: *Woman! Learn to Read and Write!* (1923; State Museum of the Revolution, Moscow), one version of which has the daughter complaining: "Ach, Mama! if you had learned to read and write, you could help me!"

Kruglikova executed about 1000 silhouettes, most of them portraits of leading artists, literary figures, musicians and some political leaders. Many were simple but sensitive profiles, such as the portrait of *Marina Tsvetaeva* (1920); others were full-figure scenes, such as *Mikhail Vasilevich Nesterov Painting My Portrait* (1934; both State Russian Museum). She also made a number of self-portraits, some of which showed her at work in her studio. A collection of portraits, one of an anticipated series, was published in *Siluety sovremennikov: I. Poety* (Silhouettes of contemporaries: I. Poets; Moscow, 1922). In addition, she designed *ex libris* plates and illustrations for many journals and books issued by State publishing companies. In the 1920s she illustrated and sometimes wrote accompanying text for children's picture books (*Skazochki* [Little tales], Moscow, 1924), and in 1921 published *Moskva v siluetakh* (Moscow in silhouettes). In the 1930s, when she was in her sixties, Kruglikova travelled to regional mining centres and factories. Her resulting print series on themes such as "Public Power Supply" and individual etchings and aquatints such as *Azneft* (1934) and *Baku: Black City* (1933; both State Russian Museum), contributed to an emerging area of Socialist Realism, the industrial landscape.

KATHLEEN M. FRIELLO

L

Labille-Guiard, Adélaïde

French painter, 1749–1803

Born Adélaïde Labille in Paris, 11 April 1749; father a haberdasher. Trained by the miniaturist François-Elie Vincent, by the pastellist Maurice Quentin de la Tour, and subsequently by the academician François-André Vincent. Taught art, c.1779–93. Admitted to the Académie Royale des Beaux-Arts, 1783. Awarded the title of Peintre de Mesdames (the king's aunts), 1787. Married (1) financial clerk Louis-Nicolas Guiard, 1769; legally separated, 1779; divorced 1793; (2) François-André Vincent, 1800. Died in Paris, 24 April 1803.

Principal Exhibitions

Académie de Saint-Luc, Paris: 1774
Salon de la Correspondance, Paris: 1782–3
Paris Salon: 1783, 1785, 1787, 1789, 1791, 1795, 1798–1800

Bibliography

Roger Portalis, "Adélaïde Labille-Guiard (1749–1803)", *Gazette des Beaux-Arts*, 3rd series, xxvi, 1901, pp.353–67, 477–94; xxvii, 1902, pp.100–18, 325–47

Les Femmes peintres au XVIIIe siècle, exh. cat., Musée Goya, Castres, 1973

Anne-Marie Passez, *Adélaïde Labille-Guiard (1749–1803): Biographie et catalogue raisonné de son oeuvre*, Paris: Arts et Métiers Graphiques, 1973

Women Artists, 1550–1950, exh. cat., Los Angeles County Museum of Art, and elsewhere, 1976

Elsa Honjg Fine, *Women and Art: A History of Women Painters and Sculptors from the Renaissance to the 20th Century*, Montclair, NJ: Allanheld and Schram, and London: Prior, 1978

Germaine Greer, *The Obstacle Race: The Fortunes of Women Painters and Their Work*, London: Secker and Warburg, and New York: Farrar Straus, 1979

La Femme artiste d'Elisabeth Vigée-Lebrun à Rosa Bonheur, exh. cat., Musée Despiau-Wlerick, Donjon Lacataye, Mont-de-Marsan, 1981

Vivian Cameron, *Woman as Image and Image-Maker in Paris During the French Revolution*, PhD dissertation, Yale University, 1983

Danielle Rice, "Vigée-Lebrun vs Labille-Guiard: A rivalry in context", *Proceedings of the XIth Annual Meeting of the Western Society for French History: Riverside, 1983*, pp.130–38

Diaconoff Suellen, "Ambition, politics and professionalism: Two women painters", *Eighteenth-Century Women and the Arts*, ed. Frederick M. Keener and Susan E. Lorsch, New York: Greenwood, 1988, pp.201–8

Viktoria Schmidt-Linsenhoff, "Gleichheit für Künstlerinnen?", *Sklavin oder Bürgerin? Französische Revolution und Neue Weiblichkeit, 1760–1830*, exh. cat., Historisches Museum, Frankfurt am Main, 1989, pp.114–32

Marie-Jo Bonnet, "La révolution d'Adélaïde Labille-Guiard et Elisabeth Vigée-Lebrun ou deux femmes en quête d'un espace dans la société", *Les Femmes et la Révolution française*, ed. Marie-France Brive, Toulouse: Presses Universitaires du Mirail, 1991, pp.337–44

As one of four female members of the French Académie Royale des Beaux-Arts, Adélaïde Labille-Guiard is famous for her accomplished portraits in pastels and oils. In her teens she was trained by the miniaturist François-Elie Vincent. One of her first known works, a *Self-Portrait* in miniature (untraced, repr. Passez 1973, pl.I), which was exhibited at the Académie de Saint-Luc in 1774, demonstrates a fairly finicky, nervous touch, with a concern for the details of setting and dress that would remain with Labille-Guiard throughout her life. After her marriage in 1769, and before 1774, she became a student of Maurice Quentin de la Tour for instruction in the technique of pastels. The attention to veracity in representing both the character of the sitter as well as the details of costume and surroundings, so characteristic of Quentin de la Tour's work, was also a hallmark of Labille-Guiard's, as in the portrait of the *Marquise de Montciel* (untraced, *ibid.*, pl.XVII). Ever ambitious, she decided to study oil painting after 1777 and became an apprentice of François-André Vincent, *agrée* at the Academy in 1777 and eldest son of her first teacher. During her training she continued to execute pastels and miniatures. She also separated from her husband, and shortly thereafter opened an atelier for students to supplement her income. Teaching had a high priority in her life, and she continued instruction until 1793.

After the Académie de Saint-Luc had been dissolved in 1776, Labille-Guiard found a new site to exhibit at the Salon de la Correspondance, first showing numerous works there in June 1782, including her portrait of the *Comte de Clermont-Tonnerre* (Anzy-le-France, *ibid.*, pl.XIX, oil replica), dressed in the costume of a "Dragon de la Reine", which shows a skilful rendering of costume and sensitivity to different textures, as well as the accomplished placement of the figure in space. Also exhibited there was a *Head of Cleopatra* (untraced, *ibid.*, pl.XXIII), which depicts the heroine in the style of Guido Reni, eyes raised to the skies, left breast exposed to

Labille-Guiard: *Madame Adélaïde de France*, exhibited 1787; Palais de Versailles, Paris

receive the bite of the asp, and which shows Labille-Guiard's early interest in history painting. She was exceptionally productive during this year and the next, creating numerous pastels of various members of the Academy, including those of *Voiriot* (private collection, Brussels, *ibid.*, pl.XXII), *Bachelier* (Louvre, Paris), *Vien* (Musée Fabré, Montpellier), *Pajou* and *Beaufort* (both Louvre). Exhibited first during various months at the Salon de la Correspondance, most of these pastels were re-exhibited at the Salon of 1783 after her acceptance into the Academy on 31 May 1783. For her reception pieces, she submitted the portrait of *Pajou* as well as an oil painting of the sculptor *Gois* (untraced). She also exhibited a sensitive portrayal of maternity in the group picture of *Madame Mitoire and Her Children* (private collection, Paris, *ibid.*, pl.XXXIII), representing the granddaughter of Carle van Loo nursing a baby, with her young son. With the accessories of the small round table, the painting formally balances the round form of the mother, the heads of the two children and the oval of the table top. Socially, the work documents a contemporary fashionable attitude about nursing promoted earlier by Rousseau (see Carol Duncan, "Happy mothers and other new ideas in French art", *Art Bulletin*, lv, 1973, pp.470–83). It may well have been this work that attracted the notice of the Comtesse de Flahaut, sister-in-law to d'Angiviller, Directeur Général des Bâtiments, who commissioned her own portrait with her young son gazing at a medallion representing d'Angiviller's wife, an oil painting exhibited at the Salon of 1785 (private collection, Jersey, repr. Passez 1973, pl.XLIV). Indeed, Madame d'Angiviller herself had earlier commissioned a portrait of the poet *Ducis* (Comédie Française, Paris, *ibid.*, pl.XXXVII) from the new academician. Other commissions from nobility, such as the *Princesse de la Trémoïlle* (private collection, France, *ibid.*, pl.XLI), followed.

It was at the Salon of 1785 that Labille-Guiard exhibited her brilliant *Self-Portrait with Two Students* (Metropolitan Museum of Art, New York), a work possibly inspired by Vigée-Lebrun's *Self-Portrait with a Straw Hat* (private collection, Switzerland). The names of Elisabeth Vigée-Lebrun (q.v.) and Labille-Guiard were frequently paired by the critics, starting with their first exhibition at the Académie de Saint-Luc (*ibid.*, pp.12–13). Both women were accepted into the Academy on the same day, and both exhibited at the Salon in 1783. Reviewers of that Salon generally favoured Vigée-Lebrun with lengthier and more laudatory reviews, which must have caused particular dismay to Labille-Guiard, who was sometimes even ignored. Such evaluations may well have spurred her to reassess her production critically, with the *Self-Portrait with Two Students* as a result. It was her most complex effort to date. On the one hand, she demonstrated her virtuosity as a technician in the fine rendering of textures (she had copied ter Borch, for instance). On the other, while the painting is part of the tradition of the artist and his family, Labille-Guiard, through her rich costume, elevated herself above the class of ordinary academician, showing an ambition to rise in social status. At the same time she affirmed that she was a producer of paintings, depicting herself absorbed in the act of creating, gazing at her model (the viewer). Further, the presence of the statue of a Vestal Virgin alludes to her role as a teacher, keeping the flames of creativity burning. The work won much critical acclaim, and also earned her the admiration

of Madame Adélaïde, aunt to Louis XVI. Indeed, this interest helped Labille-Guiard in her straitened circumstances in 1785 to obtain a government pension of 1000 livres.

Both aunts, Mesdames Adélaïde and Victoire, as well as the king's sister, Madame Elisabeth, subsequently commissioned portraits. That of *Madame Adélaïde de France* (see illustration), exhibited in 1787, was intended to be more than a capturing of the physiognomy of the sitter. Labille-Guiard's largest and most complicated portrait to date, the work represented the life-sized figure of Madame Adélaïde standing in front of an easel, on which rests a composite portrait in profile of her father Louis XV, her mother and brother, the dauphin, all deceased. Decorating the architectural background is a relief showing the presence of the Princess at her father's deathbed, when he was ill with smallpox. Filial piety, loyalty and devoutness (a plan of a convent rests on a stool) are conveyed in the painting, which is intended not only to indicate qualities of this princess, but also meant to be part of royalist propaganda to support the weakened throne of Louis XVI. The attention to the rendering of specific textures is even more refined here, as Labille-Guiard captured everything from gilded wood to marble, paper to satin, painted bronze to flesh. The pendant to the work, *Madame Victoire* (Château, Versailles), exhibited at the following Salon of 1789, was equally meticulously painted, showing the Aunt on the terrace of the property at Bellevue. Like many of the Vestals seen in earlier French paintings, the virginal aunt pays homage to a sculpture of Friendship. A vase of lilies gave Labille-Guiard the opportunity to demonstrate her talents as a still-life painter, while the background, claimed by one critic to be by a M. Hue not by her (*ibid.*, p.210), gave her a chance to show her skills as a landscapist.

Labille-Guiard's opportunity to win acclaim as a history painter came in 1788 when she was commissioned by the king's brother, the Comte de Provence, to paint a large work (4.26 × 5.18 m.) depicting the *Reception of a Chevalier de Saint-Lazare by Monsieur, Grand Master of the Order*, on which she worked for two and a half years before the emigration of the count in June 1791. The incomplete painting was rolled up; in 1793 she received the order to destroy the work.

While Labille-Guiard was labouring on this large painting, she was also active in the reforms of the Academy. Attempting to throw open the doors of the Academy to women and gain status for her students, in September 1790 she proposed that the number of women accepted into the Academy be indeterminate and that those who were accepted be given an honorary academic distinction of Conseiller only. Although the proposal was passed by the moderates, the conservative academicians turned it down and called her a "Jeanne d'Arc", "a hen amongst roosters", spreading dissension among them (see Cameron 1983, pp.86–8). The radicals, who formed the Commune des Arts, equally condemned her.

Ever pragmatic, with the loss of her royalist patrons, Labille-Guiard continued to paint portraits, first that of her friend *Madame Genlis* (Bethesda, MD, repr. Passez 1973, pl.LXXXIX), through whose salon she was probably introduced to various political members. At the Salon of 1791, she exhibited portrait busts, some in pastel, some in oil, of deputies of various political persuasions of the National Assembly, from Robespierre to the Duc d'Aiguillon. She was equally active as an advocate for women, presenting the National Assembly with a mémoire about the education of young women deprived of fortune (now lost), to which Talleyrand referred as a model. Indeed, although the Academy may not have been amenable to the rights of female artists, the government commissioned Labille-Guiard, as well as Jacques-Louis David, to paint a work representing the king giving the Constitution to the dauphin. All sketches for this work have been lost.

During the Terror, Labille-Guiard obtained a divorce. She remained installed in a country home in Pontault-en-Brie with François-André Vincent (whom she married in 1800), but in 1795, with the support of Joachim Lebreton, chief of the bureaux of the Museums of Public Instruction, she obtained a lodging at the Louvre as well as a pension of 2000 livres. She continued to exhibit portraits at the Salons until 1800. In such works as the portrait of her student, *Gabrielle Capet* (private collection, Paris, *ibid.*, pl.CVII), exhibited in 1798, she maintained her high technical standards and also offered a sensitive portrayal of another serious woman artist.

VIVIAN P. CAMERON

See also Academies of Art survey and Lemoine

LaDuke, Betty

American painter and printmaker, 1933–

Born Betty Bernstein in the Bronx, New York, 13 January 1933. Studied at Denver University, Colorado, 1950–51; Cleveland Institute of Art, Ohio, 1951–2; Instituto Allende, San Miguel de Allende, Mexico, 1953–4; California State University, Los Angeles, 1960–63 (MA). Director of art program, Grand Street Settlement House, New York, 1957. Married (1) Native American Sunbear (Vincent LaDuke); one daughter; divorced; (2) agricultural scientist Peter Westigard, 1965; one son. Taught at Stevenson Junior High, Los Angeles, 1961–4. Professor of art, Southern Oregon State College, Ashland, 1964–92 (Faculty award of excellence 1986). Travelled to India, China and Indonesia between 1972 and 1978; Papua New Guinea, Australia and Borneo, between 1978 and 1980; Chile, Nicaragua, Bolivia, Peru, Brazil, Mexico, Guatemala, Cuba, Haiti, Grenada, the San Blas Islands, Ecuador and Puerto Rico, between 1981 and 1985; and subsequently to Nigeria, the Ivory Coast, Cameroon, Ghana, Senegal, Mali, Egypt, Morocco, Togo, Benin and Burkina Faso. Curated the exhibitions *Compañeras: Women, Art and Social Change in Latin America* (1986–96), *Africa: Between Myth and Reality* (1992–3) and *Africa Through the Eyes of Women Artists* (1993–6), all organised by Exhibit Touring Service. Recipient of Governor's Award for the Arts, Portland, 1993; Academic Specialist grant to Eritrea, Africa, from United States Information Service, 1995. Lives in Ashland, Oregon.

Selected Individual Exhibitions

Galeria de Arte Moderno, Mexico City: 1956
Crocker Art Museum, Sacramento, CA: 1972
Cheney Cowles Museum, Spokane, WA: 1979
Museum of Art, University of Arizona, Tucson: 1981
University of Texas, Austin: 1983
Casa Fernando Gordillo, Managua, Nicaragua: 1984
San José State University, CA: 1985
Maier Museum of Art, Lynchburg, VA: 1993
African American Caribbean Cultural Center, Fort Lauderdale, FL: 1993
Crealde School of Art, Orlando, FL: 1994
In Her Image Gallery, Portland, OR: 1994
University Art Galleries, University of South Dakota, Vermillion: 1995

Selected Writings

Compañeras: Women, Art and Social Change in Latin America, San Francisco: City Lights, 1985
Africa Through the Eyes of Women Artists, Trenton, NJ: Africa World Press, 1991
Women Artists: Multi-Cultural Visions, Trenton, NJ: Red Sea Press, 1992
Africa: Women's Art and Lives, Trenton, NJ: Africa World Press, 1995
An Artist's Journey from the Bronx to Timbuctu (in preparation)

Bibliography

Contemporary Graphic Artists, Detroit: Gale, 1989
Elinor Gadon, *The Once and Future Goddess: A Symbol for Our Time*, San Francisco: Harper, and Wellingborough: Aquarian, 1989
Northwest Originals: Oregon Women and Their Art, In Unison, 1989
Gloria Feman Orenstein, *The Reflowering of the Goddess*, Oxford: Pergamon Press, 1990
Karen Foss and Sonya Foss, *Women Speak: The Eloquence of Women's Lives*, Prospect Heights, IL: Waveland Press, 1991
Gloria F. Orenstein, *Multi-Cultural Celebrations: The Paintings of Betty LaDuke, 1972–1992*, Petaluma, CA: Pomegranate, 1993

From the 1970s to the 1990s, Betty LaDuke's art has been based on her visionary understanding of the fine arts, popular arts, folk arts, traditional ceremonies, myths and mores of indigenous women around the world. Her travels in order to understand the lives and art of women from a global perspective have taken her to Asia, Oceania, Latin America and Africa. What LaDuke has expressed through painting, printmaking and photography is the way in which women's arts and lives around the world embody the close interconnections between human lives, non-human nature and the spirit world. She then relates the cosmogonic myths and ethos of a particular culture's understanding of the interrelated webs of human, ecological and spiritual forces to the roles of women in the workplace in different societies.

Africa: Creation Myth (1988; see illustration), for example, depicts a Senegalese woman selling fish in the marketplace. The Senegalese woman also exemplifies the image of a Mother Goddess. Using a technique based on X-ray vision (seeing the insides of things), LaDuke enables us to observe how the flora, fauna and seeds of the vegetal world flow through the woman's body. We also realise that our own bodies are composed of the water that keeps the fish alive, just as the fish that the woman is selling nourish our own bodies as well. The painting reveals how, in a sacred way, we become what we eat, and that a humble woman selling fish in the marketplace is performing sacred work. Human bodies flow through the fish, and a spirit bird emerges from the woman's head/mind/vision/imagination in a glowing yellow aura. The bird on the foreheads, hands or

LaDuke: *Africa: Creation Myth*, 1988; acrylic

faces of LaDuke's women is always a symbol of hope and the possibility of soaring on the wings of female spiritual power.

LaDuke's art is always political as well as spiritual. In *Latin America: Homage to the Mothers of the Disappeared* (1984; artist's collection) she depicts the powerful life-force of mothers who, despite their deep sorrow (over the political kidnappings and torture of their children), open themselves to love again, move through their darkness and bring forth more souls into life. This particular mother has many loving couples flowing through her thighs and a new child's face in her womb. She is offering a bird of hope to the future.

As a child, LaDuke spent summers at a camp whose art directors were the African-American artists Charles White and Elizabeth Catlett (q.v.). They encouraged her art, and taught her important values related to dignity, strength and cultural diversity. Later she attended the High School of Music and Art near Harlem, New York, and she began to explore the city's ethnic neighbourhoods, sketchbook in hand. It was during the summer of 1951 that her journeying began. She left Denver University and hitch-hiked south. She travelled down the Mississippi River on a river boat that tugged barges, and she hoed weeds in the cotton fields. Eventually she landed in New Orleans, where she became involved in jazz and the blues. In 1953 LaDuke was awarded a scholarship to attend the Instituto Allende in San Miguel de Allende, Mexico, and the following year she moved to Guanajuato, where she visited the market-places and attended traditional celebrations – sketchbook at the ready. During the next two years she had five one-person government-sponsored shows, and was considered one of Mexico's "new generation" of artists. LaDuke, however, was more involved with her larger quest than with seeking fame and fortune, so she went to live with the Otomi Indians in Mexico. At that time she witnessed many rites of passage:

births, deaths and saint's day celebrations. Most of all she learned about the enduring strength of the Otomi Indians, who had managed to preserve their cultural heritage despite government efforts to bring them into the mainstream.

Betty LaDuke's children, her daughter Winona LaDuke, a well-known Native American activist, and her son Jason, appear in several of her paintings (*Oregon: Jason's Journey*, 1972, and *Oregon: Winona, The Parting*, 1976; both artist's collection). When she paints her own children, however, she suggests comparisons and contrasts with children's lives in other parts of the world. For LaDuke, most children of the world are a colonised, marginalised people. Many live under political oppression. In her work children are depicted as having a political drama of their own. Children in Central America (*Central America: Children in Transition*, 1982; artist's collection) may be robbed of their adolescence by war. In *Chile: Children of the Disappeared* (1982; artist's collection) LaDuke depicts the suffering on the faces of children who have no food, clothing or shelter. A more joyous observation of the lives of children is found in her painting *Africa: Goat Boys* (1989; artist's collection), which shows the fertility and life-force of youth who are raised in harmony with nature. We see how their torsos and minds are filled with images of the spiritual powers of the animals, birds and plants with which they interact daily.

LaDuke can be called an Eco-feminist artist, for she always shows how the Earth's survival is intimately and reciprocally connected to human survival and to that of women, as well as to a political and spiritual vision that comprehends the ways in which the Earth is threatened when humans are endangered (wars, natural disasters, pollution, etc.) and vice versa. LaDuke emphasises the burdens placed upon the land and the people by the demands of Western culture and development in its exploitation of natural resources and its indifference to the sacredness of the Earth and its creatures. In *India: Spring Ritual* (1973; artist's collection) ploughing the soil is done with a sense of the sacred nature, both of the work performed and of all the participants – human, animal and spiritual. In *Africa: On the Farm* (1990; artist's collection) women and men work the millet fields together and their movements undulate with the rhythms of the Earth and the dance of creation.

LaDuke uses a bright palette for her paintings, which radiate a vibrant energy-field. Although her work has evolved in its themes ever since she began her journeys to the women of the world (whose traditional and fine arts she has written about in her books), her guiding quest has always been that of depicting a larger vision of the multi-dimensional, multi-cultural realities of women's lives – one that integrates the spiritual, the mythic, the political, the social and the cultural into the economic contexts in which they live everywhere on Earth. Her most important artistic technique is one that could be called shamanic clairvoyance – the ability to see the inside of everything via a radar-like, X-ray vision, which renders the invisible visible. In the summer of 1995 LaDuke was involved with a major project with the organisation Freedom from Hunger. She visited women's projects in Africa, and made drawings and photography for a planned book. As always, her art, spirituality and politics are intimately intertwined.

GLORIA F. ORENSTEIN

La Fargue, Maria Margaretha
Dutch amateur artist, 1743–1813

Baptised in The Hague, 29 December 1743, daughter of the notary and pamphlet writer Jean Thomas La Fargue, sister of the artists Isaac Lodewijk La Fargue van Nieuwland, Paulus Constantijn La Fargue, Jacob Elias La Fargue and Karel La Fargue. Took drawing lessons from her older brothers Paulus Constantijn and Jacob Elias. Gave drawing lessons herself from 1792. Never married. Died in poverty in The Hague, 21 April 1813.

Selected Writings

"Godes lof geeft juichens stof" [Praise of God makes one shout for joy], manuscript, 1789, Archives of the Haagsch Genootschap, Municipal Archives, The Hague, inv. no.13 (a collection of prose and poetry dedicated to the members of the Genootschap ter Verdediging des Christelijken Godsdienst [Society for the Defence of Christian Service])

Bibliography

J. W. M. Klomp, "De kunstenaarsfamilie La Fargue" [The La Fargues: A family of artists], *Jaarboek Die Haghe*, 1960, pp.43–66

L. J. van der Haer, "Levensbeschrijving van Maria Margaretha La Fargue" [Biography of Maria Margaretha La Fargue], *Jaarboek Die Haghe*, 1965, pp.56–61

Charles Dumas, *Haagse stadsgezichten, 1550–1800: Topografische schilderijen van het Haags Historisch Museum* [City views of The Hague, 1550–1800: Topographical paintings of the Historical Museum of The Hague], Zwolle: Waanders, 1991, pp.417–28

Maria Margaretha La Fargue, who never became a member of the Confrerie Pictura (the local society of painters in The Hague) and thus must be considered an amateur artist, was the youngest child of an unusually artistic family. Of her four older brothers, who drew, painted and etched primarily topographical subjects, landscapes and portraits, Paulus Constantijn was the most versatile and productive. He was really the driving force and the principal breadwinner of the family, and after his

La Fargue: *The Lyre-Player*, 1772; drawing, pen in brown, grey and black, brush in colour, over traces of black chalk; 29.8 × 36.6 cm.; Kupferstichkabinett, Städelsches Kunstinstitut, Frankfurt am Main

death in 1782 the surviving members fell on hard times. In 1808 Maria Margaretha was taken into the charitable care of the Dutch Reformed Poor-Relief Board and at her death five years later she was residing in its hospital and care facility.

Both paintings and drawings (on paper and on parchment), all in a relatively small format, are known from Maria Margaretha's hand (most in private collections; others in Haags Historisch Museum and Municipal Archives, The Hague; Museum Boijmans Van Beuningen, Rotterdam; Prentenkabinet der Rijksuniversiteit, Leiden; Museum Mr Simon van Gijn, Dordrecht; Städelsches Kunstinstitut, Frankfurt am Main; Philadelphia Museum of Art; John and Mable Ringling Museum of Art, Sarasota; and Spaans Gouvernement Museum, Maastricht). The earliest work dates from 1761, the latest from 1792. Her oeuvre could not have been very extensive – at present only about 50 works are known. They consist primarily of genre scenes, which may be divided into four types. In the first place there are interiors of the affluent middle class, which are usually peopled with a mother with her children and a serving maid. Sometimes there is reference to domestic pursuits; sometimes a visit to a cradle is depicted. From this interior a vista is generally provided into a room beyond or out through a window. La Fargue also depicted outdoor scenes with a woman selling fish, shellfish, eggs or vegetables at the door. These little pictures were often intended as pendants, one showing an urban environment, and the other a more rural one. Variations on these are the scenes in which the saleswoman is replaced by a knife-grinder or a youth playing on a lyre, sometimes accompanied by a little dressed-up dancing dog. A third type employs an arched niche, through which we see the interior of a kitchen, where a woman is busy peeling potatoes, polishing copper pans or other such activity. Finally there are the scenes in which only one person, usually a fish-seller, a Savoyard or a lyre-player, is depicted in a landscape.

The architecture rendered in La Fargue's street scenes is usually imaginary, but on a few occasions recognisable buildings in The Hague are included, as in her two paintings in the Haags Historisch Museum. In contrast to her brothers, she never made true topographical representations – with one exception: in 1780 she executed, on commission from the well-to-do Hague banker Jacques Bergeon, four drawings of his country home of Brittenrust near Alphen aan den Rijn (Museum Boijmans Van Beuningen, Rotterdam), three of which were made into prints by Dirk de Jong in 1782.

At the end of the 1780s La Fargue executed a few portraits, including a drawing of *Friedrich Wilhelm II of Prussia, Elector of Brandenburg* (Prentenkabinet der Rijksuniversiteit, Leiden), and, in the years 1787–9, seven drawings of contemporary events that were engraved by Mattheus de Sallieth and Theodorus Koning for the *Haagsche Princelyke en Koninglyke Almanach* (Hague Princely and Royal Almanac). Her last known work is an etching – her only one – from 1792 (only a proof of it exists; Municipal Archives, The Hague). It depicts the distribution of prizes to students of the Latin school in what was then the English Church in The Hague. La Fargue, as a fervent supporter of the House of Orange, dedicated this work to Princess Wilhelmina of Prussia, the wife of the *stadhouder* Willem V.

La Fargue was influenced by the work of such 17th-century genre painters as Emanuel de Witte, Pieter de Hooch and Jacob Ochtervelt, but she also looked at artists of her own era, such as Willem van Mieris, Frans van Mieris the Younger, Hieronymus van der Mij and Cornelis Troost. From this last, for example, she borrowed the theme of a cradle visit, and of a man playing a lyre in front of a house. The painter cannot be seen as a great talent, but her genre scenes – while limited in choice of subject – do nevertheless have an undeniable charm.

CHARLES DUMAS

Lama, Giulia
Italian painter, 1681–1747

Born in the parish of Santa Maria Formosa, Venice, 1 October 1681, to Agostino Lama, painter, and his wife Valentina (not surnamed Jugali, as sometimes stated). Died in Venice, 7 October 1747.

Bibliography
Antonio Maria Zanetti, *Descrizione di tutte le pubbliche pitture della città di Venezia*, Venice, 1733; reprinted Bologna: Forni, 1980

Giuseppe Fiocco, "Il ritratto di Giulia Lama agli Uffizi", *Rivista d'Arte*, xi, 1929, pp.113–17

Ugo Ruggeri, *Disegni Piazzetteschi ... di raccolte bergamasche*, Bergamo: Monumenta Bergomensia, 1967

Rodolfo Pallucchini, "Per la conoscenza di Giulia Lama", *Arte Veneta*, xxiv, 1970, pp.161–72

Don Gino Bortolan, "Per una 'più completa' conoscenza di Giulia Lama", *Ateneo Veneto*, ii/2, 1973, pp.183–9

—, "S. Maria Formosa nel '700", *Bollettino dei Musei Civici Veneziani*, xviii, 1973, pp.10–17

Ugo Ruggeri, *Dipinti e disegni di Giulia Lama*, Bergamo: Monumenta Bergomensia, 1973

Leslie Jones, *The Paintings of Giovanni Battista Piazzetta*, PhD dissertation, Institute of Fine Arts, New York, 1981

Adriano Mariuz, *L'opera completa del Piazzetta*, Milan: Rizzoli, 1982

Ugo Ruggeri, "Giulia Lama", *Giambattista Piazzetta: Il suo tempo, la sua scuola*, exh. cat., Palazzo Vendramin-Calergi, Venice, 1983, pp.119–29

Peter Krückmann, *Federico Bencovich, 1677–1753*, Hildesheim: Olms, 1988

George Knox, *Giambattista Piazzetta, 1682–1754*, Oxford: Clarendon Press, 1992

Giulia Lama is known principally for her two large altarpieces in the Venetian churches of Santa Maria Formosa and San Vidal, both of the 1720s. Since Fiocco published her *Self-Portrait* (1725; Uffizi, Florence) in 1929, and identified the celebrated Piazzetta in the Thyssen collection as a portrait of *Giulia Lama as "Painting"*, her name has been linked, even mildly romantically, with the Venetian artist Piazzetta: it was once even suggested that they were cousins, on the basis of an error in the interpretation of documents. Since Don Gino Bortolan established the date of her birth and death in the registers of Santa Maria Formosa, it has become clear that she was some four and a half months older than Piazzetta, and a contemporary rather than a pupil or follower of his.

Lama: *Virgin and Child with Saints*, altarpiece, commissioned 1722; Santa Maria Formosa, Venice

A unique contemporary description of the painter survives, contained in a letter from the Abate Conti to Mme de Caylus, dated 1 March 1728:

> I have just found here a woman who paints better than Rosalba [Carriera], so far as large compositions are concerned ... this woman excels as much in (poetry) as in painting, and I find in her poems the turn of phrase of Petrarch: she is named Giulia Lama, and in her youth she studied mathematics under the celebrated p. Maffei: the poor girl is persecuted by the painters, but her virtue triumphs over her enemies. It is true that she is as ugly as she is witty but she speaks with grace and precision, so one easily forgives her her face. She works in lace ... [quoted in Ruggeri 1983, p.120].

Sadly, we have no further evidence of Lama's skills as a mathematician and her gifts as a poet, nor do we know anything further of the hostility of her male fellow artists, except to note that she does not appear to figure in the guild lists of the "Fraglia dei pittori", as is also the case with the celebrated Rosalba Carriera (q.v.), some five years her senior. As for her appearance, to which Conti ungallantly refers, the Uffizi portrait, which of itself testifies to her professional standing in 1725, depicts a woman of 45, while the Piazzetta portrait, a passionate and sensuous study, now generally thought to be at least ten years earlier in date, shows a woman far from ugly.

As children of artists, Piazzetta and Lama probably knew each other from childhood, and by the time of his marriage in 1724 he was known as a resident of the parish of San Lio, adjacent to Giulia's parish of Santa Maria Formosa. It is possible that she shared in some degree his education in the school of Antonio Molinari. Around 1715, the supposed date of Piazzetta's portrait of her, she appears to have been closely associated with him and with Federico Bencovich in the production of a series of small canvases on the theme of *St Mary Magdalene in the Desert*, all closely related in style and character, which must have been executed before Bencovich went to Vienna in 1716. A painting from this series attributed to Lama, the *Penitent Magdalene*, appeared on the Milan art market in 1970 (Finarte sale, Milan, 21 May 1970; see Knox 1992, p.71, note 18). The first secure date for Lama's work, 1719, marks the publication of a portrait of *Pietro Grimani*, engraved by Andrea Zucchi after a drawing by Lama. In 1722 she secured the important commission to paint the high altarpiece for her parish church, the beautiful and prominent Santa Maria Formosa in the Sestiere of Castello. This now hangs on the back wall of the church, where it can be seen through the arch of the high altar that originally contained it, in better light but in a rather cramped space. The painting (see illustration) depicts the Virgin and Child above, St Matthew below to the left, his attribute, an angel, in the centre and St Joseph on the right. In the lower foreground on the left is a richly dressed woman, sometimes identified as Ecclesia (Church). The composition, which appears to be highly original, has dignity and assurance; the paint surface is boldly handled, with the touch that will become characteristic of the artist, and one feels that her fellow parishioners must have been more than satisfied with this important addition to their church.

The *Crucifixion*, painted for the central altar on the left side of San Vidal, facing a sculptured altar of the *Annunciation* by Antonio Tarsia on the right, indicates that Lama played a leading role in a scheme of decoration in which she was surrounded by a group of distinguished painters. Over the high altar hangs a great work by Carpaccio; to the left hangs the *Immaculate Conception* by Sebastiano Ricci, opposite is the *Guardian Angel with SS Anthony of Padua and Gaetano Thiene* by Piazzetta; by the door, on the left, *SS Sebastian and Roch* by Angelo Trevisan, and on the right, the *Trinity with SS Joseph and Francis of Paola* by Antonio Pellegrini, documented to 1727, giving an approximate date for the whole scheme. Again, the *Crucifixion* is a work of astonishing originality, the figure of Christ offcentre to the right, balanced by two weeping putti; the Almighty and the Holy Dove above, almost suggesting (so invisible is the Cross) an Assumption rather than a Crucifixion. The off-centre axis of the picture is taken up in the fine figure of St John, lower left, with his right hand circling the Cross by the terrible nail piercing Christ's feet, while the Virgin swoons (lower right) into a luminescent mass of drapery with two gesticulating Apostles above her. This is one of the great paintings of its time, and one of the most neglected.

It is perhaps less surprising that Lama's third great religious work in the vicinity of Venice should also be neglected and completely misunderstood, for the parish church at Malamocco on the Lido is well off the beaten track. It was first noticed by Fiocco in 1927, and since then has always been referred to as *A Saint in Glory*. So bold and original is the conception of this painting that no-one has noticed that it in fact represents the *Assumption of the Virgin*. The canvas is almost square, and has probably lost the lower half of the composition, with the Twelve Apostles and the empty Tomb. The Virgin is shown kneeling on a cloud (as canonical usage requires), slightly off-centre, in the upper half of the canvas. She is supported by three angels: one steadies her with outstretched arm as she gazes up to heaven; one supports the cloud with back and another outstretched arm; a third strikes a balletic pose on the right. The work is generally dated to the 1730s, which appears to be right, but if it is compared with the great monumental versions of this theme by Ricci in Vienna, and by Piazzetta in Paris and in Parma, the extraordinarily vivid and personal quality of Giulia Lama's achievement is immediately and brilliantly manifest. Other works attributed to Giulia Lama are *Judith and Holofernes* (Accademia, Venice), the *Martyrdom of St John the Evangelist* (Musée des Beaux-Arts, Quimper) and *Christ on the Road to Calvary* (Eremo Camaldolesi, Monte Rua).

GEORGE KNOX

Lange, Dorothea
American photographer, 1895–1965

Born Dorothea Margaretha Nutzhorn in Hoboken, New Jersey, 25 May 1895; took mother's family name of Lange, 1918. Moved to New York with her family as a child. Attended New York Training School for Teachers, 1914–17; during this period was also apprenticed to photographers Arnold Genthe and Charles H. Davis; studied under Clarence H. White at Columbia University, New York, 1917–18. Settled in San Francisco, 1918. Opened own portrait studio after working as a photo finisher, 1919. Married (1) painter Maynard Dixon, 1920; two sons, born 1925 and 1928; divorced 1935; (2) Paul Schuster Taylor, an agricultural economist at the University of California, 1935. Began taking documentary photographs of conditions resulting from the Depression, 1933. Worked for various state and federal agencies, including the State Emergency Relief Administration, Federal Emergency Relief Administration, Resettlement Administration, Farm Security Administration, Bureau of Agricultural Economics, War Relocation Authority and Office of War Information, 1935–45. Resumed photography after a five-year break due to illness, 1951. Subsequent work included photo-essays on Mormon towns in Utah (1953–4), on Ireland (1954–5), and the Public Defender (1955).

Travelled extensively with Taylor to Asia, South America and the Middle East, 1958–63. Recipient of Guggenheim fellowship, 1941. Died of cancer in Marin County, California, 11 October 1965.

Principal Exhibitions
Willard Van Dyke studio, 683 Brockhurst Street, Oakland, CA: 1934 (individual)
Museum of Modern Art, New York: 1955 (*Family of Man*, touring), 1962 (*The Bitter Years: FSA Photographs, 1935–41*, touring), 1966 (touring retrospective)

Selected Writings
An American Exodus: A Record of Human Erosion, New York: Reynal and Hitchcock, 1939 (with Paul Schuster Taylor)
"Fortune's wheel", *Fortune*, xxxi/2, 1945 (with Ansel Adams)
"Miss Lange's counsel: Photographer advises use of picture themes", *New York Times*, 7 December 1952
"Photographing the familiar", *Aperture*, i, 1952, pp.4–15, 68–72 (with Daniel Dixon)
Death of a Valley, Rochester, NY: Aperture, 1960 (with Pirkle Jones)

Bibliography
Dorothea Lange, exh. cat., Museum of Modern Art, New York, and elsewhere, 1966
Suzanne Riess, *The Making of a Documentary Photographer*, Berkeley: Bancroft Library Regional Oral History Office, 1969 (interview)
Celebrating a Collection: The Work of Dorothea Lange, exh. cat., Oakland Museum, CA, 1978
Milton Meltzer, *Dorothea Lange: A Photographer's Life*, New York: Farrar Straus and Giroux, 1978
Howard M. Levin and Katherine Northrop, eds, *Dorothea Lange: Farm Security Administration Photographs, 1935–1939*, 2 vols, Glencoe, IL: Texte-Fiche Press, 1980
Karin Becker Ohrn, *Dorothea Lange and the Documentary Tradition*, Baton Rouge: Louisiana State University Press, 1980
Robert Coles, *Dorothea Lange: Photographs of a Lifetime*, Millerton, NY: Aperture, and Oxford: Phaidon, 1982
Penelope Dixon, *Photographers of the Farm Security Administration: An Annotated Bibliography, 1930–1980*, New York: Garland, 1983
John Rogers Puckett, *Five Photo-Textual Documentaries from the Great Depression*, Ann Arbor: UMI Research Press, 1984
Jan Arrow, *Dorothea Lange*, London: Macdonald, 1985
Christopher Cox, ed., *Dorothea Lange*, Millerton, NY: Aperture, 1987
James Curtis, *Mind's Eye, Mind's Truth: FSA Photography Reconsidered*, Philadelphia: Temple University Press, 1989
Dorothea Lange: American Photographs, exh. cat., San Francisco Museum of Modern Art, and elsewhere, 1994
Elizabeth Partridge, ed., *Dorothea Lange: A Visual Life*, Washington, DC: Smithsonian Institution Press, 1994
Karen Tsujimoto, *Dorothea Lange: Archive of an Artist*, Oakland, CA: Oakland Museum, 1995
Charles Wollenberg, *Photographing the Second Gold Rush: Dorothea Lange and the East Bay at War, 1941–1945*, Berkeley, CA: Heyday, 1995
Keith F. Davis, *The Photographs of Dorothea Lange*, New York: Abrams, 1996
Gerry Mullins and Daniel Dixon, *Dorothea Lange's Ireland*, Washington, DC: Elliott and Clark, and London: Aurum Press, 1996
Betsy Fahlman, "Cotton culture: Dorothea Lange in Arizona", *Southeastern College Art Conference Review*, xiii/1, 1996, pp.32–41

Lange: *Migratory Cotton Picker, Eloy, Arizona*, 1940; Dorothea Lange Collection, Oakland Museum of California, Gift of Paul S. Taylor

One of the most important documentary photographers of the 20th century, Dorothea Lange made images during the years of the American Depression that remain emblematic of that era. She was part of a group of photographers employed by Roy Stryker to make a historical record of the work of several government agencies: the Resettlement Administration (RA, 1935–7), the Farm Security Administration (FSA, 1937–42) and the Office of War Information (OWI, 1942–3). While these photographers were hired to make official records, their considerable skills as artists brought a high level of aesthetic quality to their work. Lange's strong humanitarian concerns, which are evidenced in her photographs, were deeply rooted in her personal history.

Lange's childhood was not an easy one. Her father's desertion of his family when she was 12 was traumatic, and resulted in her parents' divorce in 1907. A bout with polio at the age of seven left her with a permanent limp. These events had a strong emotional impact on her, though she rarely discussed them, even with those closest to her. By her late teens she had determined to become a photographer. With a friend, she left New York in 1918 with the intention of travelling around the world. But when her funds were stolen in San Francisco she decided to settle there, and for the remainder of her career established herself as one of California's leading photographers. Opening her own portrait studio in 1919, she embarked on what would be a successful 14-year career in commercial work. Working in a pictorialist style and favouring imaginative poses, she photographed many prominent residents of the community, and was also part of a lively group of artists and writers, many of whom visited her studio, including the painter Maynard Dixon, who became her first husband. Travelling together throughout the Southwest, he sketched subjects for later canvases and she took her first photographs outside the studio, making prints of the Native Americans she saw and the environment in which they lived. Her work in this period is rather stereotypical and romantic, and contrasts both with her portraiture and her later documentary work.

The beginning of the Depression in 1929 brought widespread unemployment and plunged America into economic crisis. In 1933, no longer able to ignore the conditions of dislocation she witnessed just outside her fashionable studio, Lange turned from portraiture to subjects of strong social content.

Emblematic of the shift in her work is *White Angel Breadline* (1933), one of her most powerful photographs. Here she drew on a long art-historical tradition of image-making, as she isolates a single figure from a crowd of men who face in the other direction; his eyes are shielded by his hat, his hands folded as if in prayer. She first exhibited her new documentary photographs in 1934, when they were seen by Paul Schuster Taylor, an agricultural economist from the University of California whose speciality was migrant labour. They soon married and embarked on a productive intellectual collaboration that continued for the rest of Lange's career. Their work for state agencies came to the attention of Roy Stryker, the head of the Resettlement Administration's Historical Section, who employed Lange in 1935. Remaining based in California, she continued her government-sponsored work under several other agencies, including the Farm Security Administration and the Bureau of Agricultural Economics. Although she photographed a wide range of conditions suffered by the rural poor, many driven west by Dust Bowl conditions, migrant labour was a particular focus, and she travelled widely around the country on assignments, producing a series of memorable images, of which *Migrant Mother* (1936), taken in Nipomo, California, remains the most famous. Flanked by two of her children, and holding a third, this destitute 32-year-old woman in a squatter camp vividly evokes iconography of the Virgin and Child. The image *Migratory Cotton Picker, Eloy, Arizona* (1940; see illustration) was part of a study undertaken for the Bureau of Agricultural Economics. While the identity of the figure remains anonymous, he is emblematic of many such workers. Lange frames her shot up close, recording the subject as he pauses for a moment. The labour in which he is engaged is exhausting and his economic situation unpromising; his hand shields him from the hot sun as well as from the intrusive camera.

At the outbreak of World War II Lange worked for the War Relocation Authority (photographs in National Archives), recording the forcible removal of Japanese-Americans from the San Francisco Bay area to internment camps away from the coast, and she photographed them once resettled at Manzanar, one of the California camps. Work for the Office of War Information permitted her to record changed conditions during the war years. Although almost all of the work she did for this agency has been lost, with Ansel Adams she recorded wartime shipbuilding industries in Richmond (just north of her Berkeley home) on assignment for *Fortune* magazine.

With the end of the World War II in 1945, serious illness made Lange inactive as a photographer. She did not resume work again until 1951, and did not travel until 1953. An assignment from *Life* in 1953 permitted her to collaborate with her old friend Ansel Adams to produce a series on several Mormon towns in Utah. This and her photographic essays on *The Public Defender* (1954) and *Death of a Valley* (1956) are among her best work of the 1950s. Although she took pictures throughout her travels with Taylor to developing countries, they lack the sensibility of deeply personal experience and the humanitarian grounding in difficult social conditions in need of change that marked her work of the 1930s and 1940s. Among the strongest work of her later years is a highly personal visual diary of the activities of family (especially grandchildren) and friends at her home in Berkeley and at a cabin she and Taylor acquired in 1955 at Steep Ravine in Marin County about 32 kilometres north of San Francisco. Although continuing health problems (ulcers, esophagitis, malaria, chronic fatigue) reduced Lange's productivity during the last two decades of her life, the keen visual intelligence that informs her most perceptive work remained alert to the end, even as she was working on the retrospective of her work at the Museum of Modern Art, which opened after her death.

Lange's work for the FSA is in the Prints and Photographs Division of the Library of Congress; that for the Bureau of Agricultural Economics is in the National Archives. Most of her non-governmental photographs are in the Dorothea Lange Collection, Oakland Museum, California.

BETSY FAHLMAN

Lansiaux, Marie-Anne

French painter, 1913–1988

Born in Reims, 20 March 1913. Studied at the Ecole Régionale des Arts Industriels, Reims; Ecole Nationale Supérieure des Beaux-Arts, Paris; also attended classes given by Jean Pierné. Worked as graphic designer, 1936–42; as teacher of advertising drawing, 1944–5. Married photo-journalist Willy Ronis, 1946. Spent time each year in Gordes, Provence, from 1948. Ran the Atelier "Peinture et Joie de Vivre", Paris, for art teachers, 1958–72; subsequently retired to Provence. Recipient of city of Paris prize, 1953. Died 15 April 1988.

Principal Exhibitions

Individual
Galerie Roux-Hentschel, Paris: 1946
Galerie Bénézit, Paris: 1956
Atelier, rue de la Foire, Villeneuve-les-Avignon: 1971

Group
Salon de l'Imagerie, Paris: 1947
Salon des Indépendants, Paris: 1948–9, 1954, 1961, 1963
Salon d'Automne, Paris: 1949–51
Biennale de France, Menton: 1953
Salon de "La Cigale", Bollène: 1954
Union des Arts Plastiques, Paris: 1955
Musée d'Art Moderne de la Ville de Paris: 1957 (*Salon "Comparaisons"*), 1962 (*Salon du dessin et de la peinture à l'eau*)

Bibliography
Lansiaux, peintures, exh. cat., Galerie Roux-Hentschel, Paris, 1946

Marie-Anne Lansiaux's oeuvre is little known, and almost never seen, despite numerous official purchases – illustrative of the supportive policy of the French State and the municipality of Paris to French artists in the 1950s. Yet she is significant as a well-known artist of the French Socialist Realist tendency of the 1940s and 1950s. In particular, as the wife of the photographer Willy Ronis, whose photographs of this period are now extensively exhibited. Her work raises interesting questions about the status of photography and "realism" in those highly politicised times.

Lansiaux was born in Reims in 1913; her family was from Flanders. She interrupted her secondary education to attend the Ecole Régionale des Arts Industriels in Reims and then the Ecole Nationale Supérieure des Beaux-Arts in Paris, as well as additional classes given by Jean Pierné. She was initially a graphic designer, making posters, graphics and so on from 1936 to 1942, and in 1944–5 she worked as a teacher of *dessin publicitaire* – drawing for advertisements. Her first important exhibition was at the Galerie Roux-Hentschel, Paris, in 1946, the catalogue of which was prefaced by Anatole Jakowsky, the expert on naive art:

> Eyes. Immense, boundless, eager, never big enough, as though they were horrified at being unable to contain what they say. Those eyes that have drunk so much of the unhappiness of our times … Ah! Those dolorous maternities, those pallid bodies, those tortured and suffering bodies! … This is also why, when torment has passed, sun and flowers, frocks and lips take up their rightful place again …

Jakowsky saw Lansiaux as an *imagier* – an illustrator of the "Book of Hours" of contemporary life.

Lansiaux began to exhibit regularly at the Salon des Indépendants in 1948, and exhibited at the Salon d'Automne in 1949, 1950 and 1951. Once the birthplace of Fauvism, since 1948 the Salon d'Automne had become the forum for a politically committed and increasingly violent Socialist Realist art. In 1950 Lansiaux joined a team under the direction of André Fougeron to decorate a model kindergarten in the Cité-jardin, rue Karl Marx, Champigny-sur-Marne. In 1951 she was one of six artists to have her work removed from the Salon d'Automne by the police. The works ranged from the most stereotypical and anodyne Socialist Realism: Jean Milhau's painting showing the image of Maurice Thorez, the French Communist Party leader, reproduced on copies of *L'Humanité* and waved before groups of children holding bunches of flowers; George Bauquier's painting of striking dockers, *Les Dockers*, indebted to Fernand Léger and inscribed "Pas un bateau pour Indochine"; and paintings by Boris Taslitzky and Gérard Singer on a similar Indo-China theme. Lansiaux's work taken down at the Salon, *May 1st, 1951*, painstakingly painted in gouache, showed the traditional procession of 1 May, sacred in the Communist calendar, with groups of veteran Resistance fighters joined by military groups from Algeria. Her husband, Willy Ronis, is depicted in the foreground. The banished canvases were shown in the rue d'Astorg, in the tradition of the Salon des Refusés. An unusual handwritten note demonstrates Lansiaux's convictions:

> Yes, I'm in my canvas [here] as I was indeed on the Faubourg Saint-Antoine on May 1st. I did not go there as a spectator searching for inspiration for a work of art. I was in the procession, shoulder to shoulder with the workers and all the good people, republicans, Catholics, Communists, who fought honestly, with calm and courage for peace and for better living conditions. I was among them because, quite simply, I am one of them and such is my sole pride.
>
> After the manifestation everyone resumed their work and their political struggle in the factory, the office or the studio. I, too, and on returning to my studio I did what I had to do for my art. The most important thing in my art, for me that year, was this canvas which I painted laboriously through the four or five summer months. Most important for me was to express to my best ability the joyous reality that I had experienced so profoundly: the people of France, united on May 1st under a blue sky, beneath the burgeoning green plane trees; a people trusting in the power of their unity, marching forward to reconquer their national independence and to achieve a better life, in Paris which wins all the peoples of the world to its side.

After 1953 and Stalin's death the impetus for a French Socialist Realism ceased, although the humanistic preoccupations and the class militancy of the Communist Party and its members continued. Lansiaux showed variously at the Salons Comparaisons, Populiste, Biennale de Menton, etc. Several of her works were bought by the State and the city of Paris (including the *Fisherman's Garden at Mont-Saint-Michel*, which won the city of Paris prize of 1953), by the Communist municipalities of Drancy, Bollène and the Musée de Saint-Denis. Further solo shows were held in Valence and Bollène in 1954, and at the Galerie Bénézit in the rue de Seine, Paris, in 1956. From 1958 to 1972 Lansiaux ran the Atelier "Peinture et Joie de Vivre" for teachers of art. This involved drawing in the morning followed by nine afternoon classes, on colour, lettering, an introduction to art history, rapid composition exercises, drawing from memory and training visual memory, different conceptions of drawing and, of course, practical work: modelling, ceramics, mosaics, flower arranging, collage, making linocuts, drawing as therapy and, finally, a discussion of photography. From 1948 onwards she spent part of every year in Provence, in Gordes. This led to several summer exhibitions, from Moret-sur-Loing outside Paris to Provence: Valence, Bollène, Gordes, Meaux and Villeneuve-les-Avignon. Tragically, after some years of complete retirement in Provence and increasing depression, Marie-Anne Lansiaux died of Alzheimer's disease in 1988.

SARAH WILSON

Laserstein, Lotte

German painter, 1898–1993

Born in Pr-holland, Prussia, 28 November 1898. Moved to Danzig (now Gdańsk, Poland) with her family, 1903, to Berlin, 1912. Received first training at an aunt's art school. Studied at the Berlin Academy, 1919–25 (gold medal 1925); also studied art history and philosophy at Berlin University. Studio in the Kaiserdamm, Berlin, 1925–35; taught groups of students; began lifelong collaboration with model Traute Rose. Visited Paris, Rome and Sweden, 1936. Forced to leave Nazi Germany due to part-Jewish ancestry. Settled in Stockholm, 1937. Spent summers in Provence, France, 1950s. Visited USA, 1958. Died 21 January 1993.

Principal Exhibitions

Individual

Galerie Fritz Gurlitt, Berlin: 1930
Galleri Modern, Stockholm: 1937
Agnew and Belgrave Galleries, London: 1987
Agnew Gallery, London: 1990 (with Erich Wolfsfeld and Gottfried Meyer)

Group

Exposition Internationale, Paris: 1937

Bibliography

Lotte Laserstein: Paintings and Drawings from Germany and Sweden, 1920–70, exh. cat., Agnew and Belgrave Galleries, London, 1987

Caroline Stroude and Adrian Stroude, "Lotte Laserstein and the German Naturalist tradition", *Woman's Art Journal*, ix/1, 1988, pp.35–8

Domesticity and Dissent: The Role of Women Artists in Germany, 1918–1938, exh. cat., Leicester Museum and Art Gallery, and elsewhere, 1992

Friedrich Rothe, "Lotte Laserstein und Charlotte Salomon: Zwei künstlerische Entwicklungen unter den Bedingungen der NS-Zeit", *Profession ohne Tradition: 125 Jahre Verein der Berliner Künstlerinnen*, exh. cat., Berlinische Galerie, Berlin, 1992, pp.151–8

Marsha Meskimmon and Shearer West, eds, *Visions of the "Neue Frau": Women and the Visual Arts in Weimar Germany*, Aldershot: Scolar Press, 1995

Marsha Meskimmon, *The Art of Reflection: Women Artists' Self-Portraiture in the Twentieth Century*, London: Scarlet Press, and New York: Columbia University Press, 1996

Lotte Laserstein was a successful realist painter in Berlin during the 1920s and 1930s who, because of her part-Jewish background, was forced to emigrate to Sweden in 1937 where she remained for the rest of her life. Her career, therefore, can be viewed in two parts: the German years during which she was a flourishing student at the Berlin Academy and a young professional painter associated with the Neue Sachlichkeit (New Objectivity), and the years in Sweden, when she made a name for herself as a portraitist. It is for her work in Berlin that she is today best known.

Laserstein's early career was marked by academic success. She won the Berlin Academy gold medal in 1925; she subsequently ran her own studio; she had her first one-woman show in 1930 at Fritz Gurlitt's gallery; and, in 1937, she showed at the Paris Exposition Internationale (though not in the German Pavilion). She was described positively by critics of the day, and even the city of Berlin attempted to purchase one of her works. Her works of this period tended to be monumental figure paintings in the sober realism that flourished during the Weimar Republic. Works such as *Roof Garden, Potsdam* (1928; private collection, England, repr. London 1987) and *Eve and the Knight* (1930; whereabouts unknown, *ibid.*) typify her aspirations as a serious academic painter. These works are large-scale scenes that evoke in their style the fine art figural traditions of the Renaissance.

Despite these links to straightforward academic realism, Laserstein's oeuvre from the 1920s and 1930s was

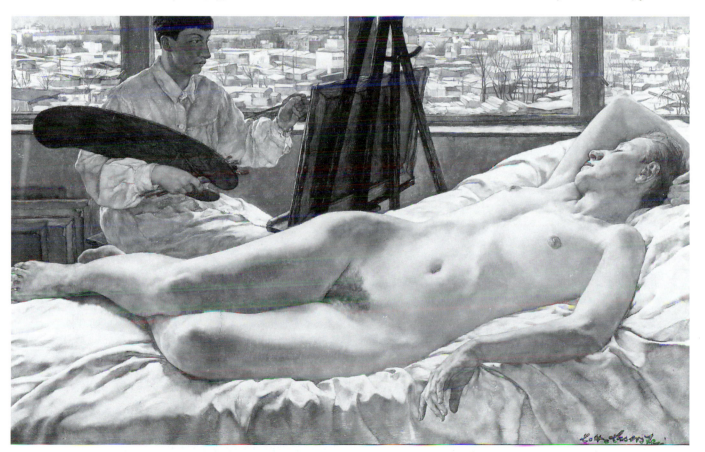

Laserstein: *Artist and Model in the Studio, Berlin, Wilmersdorf*, 1928; oil on panel; 70.5 × 97.5 cm.; private collection, Montreal Museum of Fine Arts

characterised by the attention paid to the *neue Frau* (New Woman) as a theme. This is hardly surprising when one considers her own position as an independent, professional young woman artist in the period – she epitomised this New Woman. Her numerous self-portraits identify her as such and raise a number of fascinating issues to do with the representation of women and their new roles in the Weimar Republic.

In *Self-Portrait with Cat* (1925; Leicestershire Museums, Arts and Records Service), for example, the artist played with the fashionable and empowering image of the androgynous young woman. Laserstein is represented in a smock at her easel, sporting the latest "men's haircut" (*Herrenschnitt*). Her features have been exaggerated to enhance their "masculinity"; the work permits gender boundaries to be obscured and explored. The fact that Laserstein had chosen not to marry in order to further her professional career clearly indicates that the artist was concerned with definitions of "woman" that assumed domesticity and acted to marginalise the practice of women artists. Her official career achievements in these years were ways in which she negotiated her roles as both "woman" and "artist"; her self-portraiture with its studied androgyny was another.

The work *Artist and Model in the Studio, Berlin, Wilmersdorf* (1928; see illustration), in which the androgynous self-portrait of Laserstein is merely the backdrop against which a large nude female figure is shown reclining, explores the problematics of women's representation in the period. On the one hand, the work demonstrates Laserstein's well-honed skills as an artist and her ability to paint the nude. The work was very well received in this context. Furthermore, the androgynous self-portrait and the fact that the woman artist is shown working, and in control of the work, are powerful assertions of the artist's independence and status. However, the displayed female nude in the foreground exemplifies the difficulties facing a woman artist who seeks to present new images of women; the ubiquity of "woman" as a sign both in and of fine art made it very difficult for women artists to move from object to subject in representation.

The model in the work was Traute Rose, a woman with whom Laserstein worked for the whole of her career, even continuing into the years in Sweden. Traute Rose and Laserstein were lifelong friends, and the number of works in which the model is actually named is testimony to this (see, for example, the *Artist and Traute*, c.1930; *Traute in Evening Dress*, *Traute with White Gloves* and *Traute – A Head Study*, all undated; whereabouts unknown, repr. London 1987). Furthermore, Rose was Laserstein's tennis coach and herself, as a sporty, independent woman, the model of the New Woman. Rose was represented by Laserstein in the guise of the sporting *neue Frau* in the *Tennis Player* (1930; whereabouts unknown, *ibid.*). Thus, despite Laserstein's assumption of the rather traditional role of the academic painter in her early career, the fact that she was a woman artist when the position of women was in flux meant that her works entered into dialogues with gender roles and definitions.

After 1937 Laserstein's work centred more particularly on commissioned portraiture. These works are marked by a slightly looser handling, but were, yet again, well received. She continued producing self-portraits until the end of her career, though the ones from Sweden do not focus on the androgyny

of the artist or her activity as a painter as much as they do on closely observed renderings of her likeness (e.g. *Self-Portrait in Green*, 1966; *ibid.*).

MARSHA MESKIMMON

Lasker-Schüler, Else

German poet and artist, 1869–1945

Born Else Schüler in Elberfeld, Westphalia, 11 February 1869, into a large and well-to-do Jewish family. Completed education at home with a private tutor after being unhappy at school. Sensitive nature affected by many deaths and disappointments: death of brother Paul in 1883, mother in 1890. Married Dr Berthold Lasker, 1894; son born, 1899 (d. 1927); separated from husband, 1899. Close friendship with the mystical poet Peter Hille, who became her mentor until his death in 1904. Met Georg Levin (whom she renamed Herwarth Walden), 1901; married him, 1903; divorced 1912. Met Franz Marc, 1911; Gottfried Benn, 1912; Georg Trakl, 1914. Emigrated to Switzerland, 1933; trip to Alexandria and Palestine, 1934; Palestine again, 1937; final journey to Palestine, 1940–41. Recipient of Kleist prize, 1932. Died in Palestine, 22 January 1945.

Selected Individual Exhibitions
Galerie Haas-Heyer, Berlin: 1928
Nationalgalerie, Berlin: 1931
Matthieson Gallery, London: 1939

Selected Writings
Styx: Gedichte, Berlin: Juncker, 1902 (poetry)
Der siebente Tag, Gedichte, Berlin: Amelang, 1905 (poetry)
Das Peter Hille-Buch, Berlin: Juncker, 1906 (poetry)
Die Nächte der Tino von Bagdads, Stuttgart: Juncker, 1907 (poetry)
Die Wupper, Berlin: Oesterhold, 1909 (play)
Meine Wunder, Gedichte, Leipzig: Dreililien, 1911 (poetry)
Mein Herz: Ein Liebesroman, Munich: Bachmair, 1912 (fiction)
Gesichte: Essays, Leipzig: Wolff, 1913
Hebräische Balladen, Berlin: Meyer, 1913 (poetry)
Der Prinz von Theben: Ein Geschichtenbuch, Leipzig: Weissen Bücher, 1914 (fiction)
Die Gesammelten Gedichte, Leipzig: Weissen Bücher, 1917; reprinted Munich: Wolfs, 1920 (poetry)
Der Malik, eine Kaisergeschichte (collection of letters to Franz Marc, first published in *Die Aktion*, *Der Brenner* and *Die neue Jugend*), Berlin: Cassirer, 1919
Der Prinz von Theben: Ein Geschichtenbuch (Mit 13 Abbildungen nach Zeichnungen der Verfasserin), Berlin: Cassirer, 1920 (fiction)
Essays, Berlin: Cassirer, 1920
Der Wunderrabbiner von Barcelona: Erzählung, Berlin: Cassirer, 1921 (fiction)
Theben: Gedichte und Lithographien (auf d. Stein geschrieben und gezeichnet), Frankfurt am Main: Guersehuitt, 1923 (poetry)
Ich räume auf! Meine Anklage gegen meine Verleger, Zürich: Lago, 1925 (fiction)
Arthur Aronymus, Die Geschichte meines Vaters, Berlin: Rowohlt, 1932 (fiction)
Arthur Aronymus und seine Väter, Berlin: Fischer, 1932 (play)
Joseph und seine Brüder, 1932 (play, lost)
Das Hebräerland, Zürich: Oprecht, 1937 (fiction)
Mein blaues Klavier, Jerusalem: Jerusalem Press, 1943 (poetry)

Gesammelte Werke in drei Banden, ed. F. Kemp and W. Kraft, Munich: Kösel, 1959–62

Briefe, ed. Margarete Kupper, Munich: Kösel, 1969

Ichundich, eine theatralische Tragödie, ed. Margarete Kupper, Munich: Kösel, 1980 (play; excerpts first published in *hortulus* 43, February 1960)

Bibliography

Margarete Kupper, *Die Weltanschauung Else Lasker-Schülers in ihren poetischen Selbstzeugnissen*, dissertation, Julius-Maximilians-Universität, Würzburg, 1963

Michael Schmid, ed., *Lasker-Schüler: Ein Buch zum 100. Geburtstag der Dichterin*, Wuppertal: Hammer, 1969

Hans W. Cohn, *Else Lasker-Schüler: The Broken World*, Cambridge: Cambridge University Press, 1974

Else Lasker-Schüler: Drawings, exh. cat., Israel Museum, Jerusalem, 1975

Sigrid Bauschinger, *Else Lasker-Schüler: Ihr Werk und ihre Zeit*, Heidelberg: Stiehm, 1980

Jakob Hessing, *Else Lasker-Schüler: Biographie einer deutsch-jüdischen Dichterin*, Karlsruhe: Loeper, 1988

Ruth Schwertfeger, *Else Lasker-Schüler: Inside This Deathly Solitude*, New York and Oxford: Berg, 1991

Leon I. Yudkin, *Else Lasker-Schueler: A Study in German Jewish Literature*, Northwood: Science Reviews, 1991

Heinz Ludwig Arnold, ed., *Else Lasker-Schüler*, Munich: Text + Kritik, 1994

Sonja M. Hedgepeth, *Überall blicke ich nach einem heimatlichen Boden aus: Exil im Werk Else Lasker-Schülers*, New York: Lang, 1994

Calvin N. Jones, *The Literary Reputation of Else Lasker-Schüler: Criticism, 1901–1993*, Columbia, SC: Camden House, 1994

"Sieh in mein verwandertes Gesicht": Else Lasker-Schüler: Ihr Leben – ihr Werk – ihre Zeit, exh. cat., Kunsthalle Barmen, Wuppertal, and Museum Strauhof, Zürich, 1995

Archive Lasker-Schüler is in the Hebrew University, Jerusalem.

Else Lasker-Schüler was a gifted artist whose whimsical sketches, often simply drawn with graphite, coloured pencil or pen and ink, were sometimes included in her lyric or prose work. Lasker-Schüler is today known chiefly for her beautiful if idiosyncratic poetry. Nevertheless, she had an uncle and older brother who were both artists, and she herself resorted to selling her drawings in times of financial hardship, which were frequent in spite of the generosity of friends and admirers. Her most characteristic art work appears in *Theben: Gedichte und Lithographien* (1923; see illustration), in which ten poems are illustrated with ten lithographs of Lasker-Schüler herself as the boyish Prince Jussuf striding through his (her) imaginary world. The Holy Land that Lasker-Schüler would visit 14 years later is evoked in these lithographs, with Eastern-style houses and a barren hinterland. Lasker-Schüler's mother is never far away – she is the topic of the second poem, and the lithograph depicts Jussuf the sculptor re-creating the life-size figure of the mother, complete with star on her forehead. Stars and sickle moons were the hallmarks of Lasker-Schüler's sketches. The poem begins by asking whether the mother is an angel and concludes by asserting that Jussuf will always be alone, like the angel beside him. The androgynous illustrations of Jussuf remind us that Lasker-Schüler herself dressed in baggy Eastern trousers and wore waistcoats and gaudy cheap jewellery, creating a bizarre impression that was certainly enough to put off many men (such as Franz Kafka and Walter Benjamin) even if they liked her poetry. But others found her intoxicatingly erotic

and she had many love affairs with some of the most creative men of the time, including Gottfried Benn. Lasker-Schüler's life story, which is nearly always the topic of both her art and poetry, was exotic, nomadic and frequently touched by tragedy, the chief loss she sustained being the death of her son Paul in 1927 after a two-year battle with tuberculosis.

Lasker-Schüler's talents were first brought to the fore by the poet Peter Hille, who gave her the persona of Tino of Baghdad and who introduced her to Julius Hart's circle (the Neue Gemeinschaft or New Society) in Berlin after the break-up of her first marriage in 1899. Hart's group were Nietzscheans, dabbling in mysticism and seeking a unity of man within his environment; such a unity is described in the love-poem "Ein alter Tibetteppich" (An old Tibetan carpet; 1910; republished in *Theben*, where – somewhat problematically – three figures are seated on a sofa). The carpet is a symbol for boundlessness: it is "heaven-long" (*himmellang*). Such oblique religious references have led critics to describe Lasker-Schüler's work as ultimately a quest for God. More recently, her attempt to become

Lasker-Schüler: *Reconciliation (Versöhnung)*, plate 3 of *Theben: Gedichte und Lithographien*, 1923; Los Angeles County Museum of Art, Robert Gore-Rifkind Center for German Expressionist Studies, purchased with funds from Anna Bing Arnold, Museum Associates Acquisition Fund and de-accession funds

a spokesperson for the Jews through her collection of poems *Hebräische Balladen* (1913) and the prose work *Das Hebräerland* (1937), which contains eight illustrations inspired by the Holy Land, has been acknowledged and researched.

A frequenter of the Café des Westens in pre-war Berlin, Lasker-Schüler mixed with those at the forefront of literary productivity, such as Georg Heym, and was invited to give poetry readings in Berlin and other major European cities, readings that were highly charged with the intensity of both her personality and her material. Even so, Lasker-Schüler's bohemian homelessness was never overcome: she referred to the Café itself as her "Gypsy tent" or "oasis". In spite of a lifestyle that often gave the impression of rootlessness, however, Lasker-Schüler kept up a barrage of correspondence with friends and relatives and it is often here – on envelopes or postcards – that colourful miniature sketches appear, hinting at a talent that constantly had to bow to her poetic creativity. Ruth Schwertfeger is right to stress that "the relationship between her verse and her art cannot be overlooked" (Schwertfeger in Arnold 1994, p.57). Paradoxically, though, the drawings are mainly black and white, while the brightest colours are reserved for the poems, which have their own colour symbolism, as did those of Lasker-Schüler's friend Georg Trakl and, of course, the paintings of her close friend Franz Marc. Significantly, the book dedicated to him, *Der Malik* (1919), contains the largest number of illustrations of any of her works – 28, of which four are in colour. The frontispiece, entitled *Schloss Réal*, depicts a stag-hunt with, of course, a blue huntsman on a blue horse in the foreground; in the top right of the picture is a forest of blue trees in true Blaue Reiter mode. Sketches of artefacts such as crowns and head-dresses deck out the imaginary exotic soliloquy with Marc (dubbed Ruben). The 23rd letter reads: "Ruben, think of me, love me, so I won't be alone". An illustration of the profiles of Jussuf and Ruben at the end of the 46th letter shows them cheek by jowl, but Marc was happily married during his friendship with Lasker-Schüler and fell during World War I. It is typical of Lasker-Schüler that she sought comfort from dead loved ones. Her sense of alienation is all too apparent in the drawings of herself in whichever persona she chose, as in her self-portrait as Jussuf that Kurt Pinthus included in his *Menschheitsdämmerung* (Twilight of mankind; 1920), a collection of poems and drawings from Expressionist artists and poets.

Wisely, Lasker-Schüler fled into exile in Switzerland in 1933. Her choice of the Holy Land as final resting place was unintentional: she had meant to return to Switzerland after her second visit to Palestine. Her final cycle of poems, *Mein blaues Klavier* (c.1943), shows her to have remained disillusioned, still longing for her mother and the happy home in which she grew up. The dangers that such a "Peter Pan" attitude can have in terms of encouraging flights of fancy is only too apparent, but so, too, is the fact that as a Jew and as a woman Lasker-Schüler really was a waif and stray in the chauvinistic Wilhelmine society into which she had been thrust. In an illustration dated both 1933 and 1942 entitled the *Scared-Away Poetess* (coloured chalks on graphite; Archive Lasker-Schüler, Hebrew University, Jerusalem), we see a grieving woman supported by an Oriental nurse. The writing underneath reads:

"If I knew a river as deep as my life, I would flow with its water".

CAROL DIETHE

Lassnig, Maria

Austrian painter, graphic artist and film-maker, 1919–

Born in Kappel am Krappfeld, Carinthia, 8 September 1919. Taught at a primary school, 1940–41. Studied at the Vienna Academy, 1941–4 and 1954. Moved to Klagenfurt, 1944; returned to Vienna, 1951. Scholarship for study in Paris, 1951 and 1952. Moved to Paris, 1961; to New York, 1968. Studied at School of Visual Arts, Pratt Graphic Center, New York, 1970. Worked in Berlin, 1978–9. First female professor of painting, 1980–90, and professor of animated cartoon, 1981, Vienna Academy. Co-founder of Hundsgruppe, 1951; member of Exil group, 1954–5; active member of Millennium film workshops and women film-makers, from 1971. Recipient of Deutscher Akademischer Austauschdienst (DAAD) scholarship, 1978; Great Austrian State Prize, 1988. Lives in Vienna.

Selected Individual Exhibitions

Galerie Kleinmayr, Klagenfurt: 1949
Galerie Würthle, Vienna: 1956, 1966
Galerie St Stephan, Vienna: 1960
Landesmuseum Kärnten, Klagenfurt: 1961
Galerie La Case d'Art, Paris: 1965
Neue Galerie am Landesmuseum Joanneum, Graz: 1970 (touring)
Galerie nächst St Stephan, Vienna, and Galerie im Taxispalais, Innsbruck: 1973
Green Mountains Gallery, New York: 1974
Graphische Sammlung Albertina, Vienna: 1977 (touring)
Haus am Lützowplatz, Berlin: 1978
Austrian Pavilion, Venice Biennale: 1980
Kunstverein, Mannheim: 1982–4 (touring retrospective)
Museum Moderner Kunst im Schweizergarten, Vienna: 1985 (touring retrospective)
Galerie Barbara Gross, Munich: 1988, 1995
Galerie Ulysses, Vienna and New York: 1988, 1992
Kärntner Landesgalerie, Klagenfurt: 1988–9 (touring)
Galerie Klewan, Munich: 1989, 1992
Kunstmuseum, Lucerne: 1989–90 (touring)
Stedelijk Museum, Amsterdam: 1994–5 (touring)

Selected Writings

"Chancen des Kreativen", *Protokolle 68: Wiener Jahresschrift für Literatur, bildende Kunst und Musik*, Vienna and Munich: Jugend und Volk, 1968, pp.130–35
"Statement: Für den Katalog der Ausstellung Magna", *Magna Feminismus: Kunst und Kreativität*, exh. cat., Galerie nächst St Stephan, Vienna, 1975, p.8
"Über das Malen von Körpergefühlen", *Körperzeichen Österreich*, exh. cat., Kunstmuseum, Winterthur, 1982, p.64

Bibliography

Otto Breicha, "Angelegentliches über Maria Lassnig", *Protokolle 68: Wiener Jahresschrift für Literatur, bildende Kunst und Musik*, Vienna and Munich: Jugend und Volk, 1968, pp.135–8

Maria Lassnig: Paintings – Graphics/Gemälde – Graphik, exh. cat., Neue Galerie am Landesmuseum Joanneum, Graz, and elsewhere, 1970

Maria Lassnig: Zeichnungen, 1948–1950, exh. cat., Galerie Ariadne, Vienna, 1975

Maria Lassnig: Zeichnungen, exh. cat., Graphische Sammlung Albertina, Vienna, 1977

Maria Lassnig, exh. cat., Haus am Lützowplatz, Berlin, 1978 (text by Peter Gorsen reprinted in "Konstruktion der weiblichen Kultur", *Frauen in der Kunst*, ii, Frankfurt am Main: Suhrkamp, 1980, pp.17–99)

Ruth Labak, *Zur Malerei von Maria Lassnig*, diploma thesis, Hochschule für angewandte Kunst, Vienna, 1979

Maria Lassnig, exh. cat., Österreichischer Pavillon, Biennale, Venice, 1980

Maria Lassnig: Zeichnungen, Aquarelle, Gouachen, 1949–1982, exh. cat., Kunstverein, Mannheim, and elsewhere, 1982

Maria Lassnig, exh. cat., Museum Moderner Kunst im Schweizergarten, Vienna, and elsewhere, 1985 (abridged English version of essay by Wolfgang Drechsler in *Maria Lassnig*, exh. cat., Galerie Ulysses, Vienna and New York, 1988, pp.8–11)

Johanna Bolkart, *Bei Leibe und von Sinnen: Körper und Körpererfahrung: Versuch einer Annäherung an das Schaffen der Künstlerin Maria Lassnig*, MA thesis, Hildesheim, 1987

Maria Lassnig: Aquarelle, exh. cat., Kärntner Landesgalerie, Klagenfurt, and elsewhere, 1988

Maria Lassnig: Werkverzeichnis der Druckgraphik, 1949–1987, exh. cat., Galerie Barbara Gross, Munich, 1988

Maria Lassnig: Mit dem Kopf durch die Wand: Neue Bilder, exh. cat., Kunstmuseum, Lucerne, and elsewhere, 1989

Sabina Lessmann, "Selbstakt: Frauen-Akt-Darstellungen und deren Leibhaftigkeit", *Der Weibliche Blick*, exh. cat., Haus Opherdicke, Unna, 1990, pp.51–6

Christa Murken, "Das Selbstporträt der Künstlerin als Akt in der Malerei des 20. Jahrhunderts", *ibid.*, pp.57–60

——, *Maria Lassnig: Ihr Leben und ihr malerisches Werk: Ihre kunstgeschichtliche Stellung in der Malerei des 20. Jahrhunderts*, Herzogenrath: Murken-Altrogge, 1990 (contains extensive bibliography and catalogue raisonné of paintings to 1987)

Donald Kuspit, "The hospital of the body: Maria Lassnig's body ego portraits", *Arts Magazine*, lxiv, September 1990, pp.68–73

Maria Lassnig: Bilder, Zeichnungen, Aquarelle, Grafik, 1946–1986, exh. cat., Galerie Klewan, Munich, 1992

Birgit Thiemann, "*Von Anfang an mit dabei gewesen ... und doch gern übersehen!*" Zur Rezeption von Maria Lassnig, MA thesis, Philipps Universität, Marburg, 1992 (contains extensive bibliography)

Silvia Eiblmayr, "Der 'Schauplatz Körper' bei Maria Lassnig", *Die Frau als Bild: Der weibliche Körper in der Kunst des 20. Jahrhunderts*, Berlin: Reimer, 1993, pp.169–81

Birgit Thiemann, "Über Maria Lassnig: Aschaffenburg – Paris – New York und Wien – verblüffende Strategien wider die eigene Fremdheit", *Avantgarde in Aschaffenburg*, ii, exh. cat., Neuer Kunstverein, Aschaffenburg, 1993, pp.18–20

Maria Lassnig: Bilder/Schilderijen/Paintings, exh. cat., Stedelijk Museum, Amsterdam, and elsewhere, 1994

Hanne Weskott, ed., *Maria Lassnig: Zeichnungen und Aquarelle, 1946–1995*, Munich, 1995

Maria Lassnig is one of the major figures of post-war Austrian art. She played a decisive role in the propagation of Informell art in the early 1950s (see the exhibition *Unfigurative Malerei* at the Künstlerhaus und Kunstverein für Kärnten, Klagenfurt, organised by herself and Arnulf Rainer in 1951, and *Anfänge des Informell in Österreich, 1949–53: Maria Lassnig, Oswald Oberhuber, Arnulf Rainer* at the Museum des 20. Jahrhunderts, Vienna, in 1971, repeated there in 1975 and at the Kulturhaus, Graz). Her chief contribution,

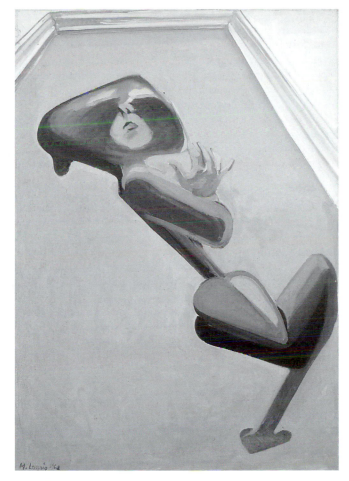

Lassnig: *Self-Portrait in Green Room*, 1968; private collection, Galerie Klewan, Munich

however, is in extending the conventional boundaries of the self-portrait genre. Apart from portraits and isolated still lifes, most from the 1970s, her central subject was self-perception and its differentiation between the interior and exterior world. Like numerous younger Austrian colleagues – Renate Bertelmann, Günter Brus, Friederike Pezold, Arnulf Rainer, Valie Export – she chose as a starting point her own body, an ever-available and ever-changing model. The representation of her exterior appearance was of secondary importance; rather, her aim lay in the visual transformation of her body awareness. Her pictures were always created through introspection, they "documented" the condition of her body, and often also her pose, during the process of their creation.

Lassnig considers herself primarily a painter. From the 1960s onwards she executed mainly life-size paintings, usually in oil on canvas; since the 1980s she has used watercolour more often, especially when travelling. She also constantly made drawings, particularly in the 1970s when she produced animated films with her "body-awareness" drawings. In 1965 she began working in various graphic techniques: until 1968 on a series of intaglio prints that in form and content are closely linked to her contemporary paintings; in the *Serigraphien*, executed in New York between 1968 and 1971, she united her own pictorial language with the poster language of Pop Art; and in the 1980s she again made intaglio prints (repr. Munich 1988).

Lassnig rejects the traditional artistic subject matter of the idealised female body. Her use of deformed or alienated bodies requires an emotional response from the viewer, a demand that initially limited the acceptance of her work. Her attempts to elucidate her work for the viewer by means of literary statements were only partially successful. Often quotations from her texts replaced the viewer's personal analysis, or the term "body-awareness-painting", coined by Lassnig in 1970, was used as a label. Critically, Lassnig's works were seen in isolation, without an enlightening context, until 1975 when she began to participate in exhibitions of female artists, beginning with *Magna Feminismus: Kunst und Kreativität* at the Galerie nächst St Stephan, Vienna. Although she does not approve of her work being subsumed under the term "feminist art", she must be considered one of its pioneers: in her work she repeatedly and explicitly declares her gender-specific situation as a woman and as a female artist, thus thematising the "problem of the representation of the female body" and "the problem of the 'woman as representation'"(Eiblmayr 1993). She achieved official artistic recognition only in 1980 when she represented Austria at the Venice Biennale, sharing the pavilion with Valie Export.

In the isolated art scene of post-war Austria, when she executed expressive-colouristic and cubist figure paintings (see Vienna 1985), Lassnig, like many of her female colleagues, longed to join the international art world. The figurative drawings of her surreal phase in the late 1940s already show several of the decisive pictorial strategies of her future subject matter: distortion and fragmentation of the body, as well as self-depiction by means of identification with objects, for example *Self-Portrait as Lemon* (1949; *ibid.*, p.122). In addition, she executed – sometimes with her eyes closed – abstract automatic drawings, like *Body Consciousness* (1949; *ibid.*, p.124), thus for the first time transforming her body awareness optically.

Lassnig's own Informell works were introduced in the exhibition *Vehémences confrontés* at the Galerie Nina Dausset, Paris, in 1951. In these she attempted on an abstract level what later became important in her body-conscious paintings: the relation of (body-)mass to its surroundings and marking the border between interior and exterior. Drawings with humorous-surreal titles such as *Informal Dumpling Self-Portrait* (1951; repr. Vienna 1977) or paintings such as *Informal* (1951; Museum Moderner Kunst, Vienna) show her gestural working method, at this time linked to *Ecriture automatique*. In the following years she tended to use clearer, constructed lines and forms, as in *Static Meditation III* (1952; repr. Vienna 1985, p.30). These led to the strongly abstracted figures of the mid-1950s, divided into few colour planes, such as *Head* (c.1956; Österreichische Galerie, Vienna). The painting *Body Awareness* of 1958 (*ibid.*, p.40) combines earlier experiments with form and colour and marks the beginning of a continuing visualisation of inner emotional states.

After Lassnig moved from Vienna to Paris, in 1961, her compact creations, breaking through the boundaries of the pictures, are replaced by "airy" *Line Pictures* on over-life-size canvases. This series, with its allusive body contours, marks her return to figurative work, as in *Figuration of Tension* (1961; *ibid.*, p.49). Metamorphoses to robot-like figures, animals, monsters or objects followed, as in her *Armchair Self-Portraits*, which, from 1963, often bore her own caricatured facial features. Also typical of this period are pictures of several figures in which Lassnig comments on the relationship of the sexes in a humorous-ironical way, for example in *Training* (1965; *ibid.*, p.63), *Dream of Wedded Bliss* (1965; G. Lang Collection, Traun, repr. *Maria Lassnig*, exh. cat., Galerie Klewan, Munich, 1989), or focuses on the mother-daughter relationship; the work dealing with mourning for her own mother is particularly impressive, *Mother and Daughter* (1966; Kunsthandlung Kalb, Vienna).

From 1969 the introspective body pictures such as *Whitsun Self-Portrait* (1969; repr. Vienna 1985, p.73) increasingly gave way to realistic depictions of exterior appearance, culminating in the *Double Self-Portrait with Camera* (1974; Österreichische Galerie). However, none of these paintings shows a complete, realistic body: the heads consist only of faces, the back of the head with hair and often also the eyes are missing; single body parts are depicted as felt and thus deformed, as in *Burden of the Flesh* (1973; IAKW Collection, Vienna), the self-portraits with animals and *Woman Laocoön* (1976; *ibid.*, p.88). Here Lassnig supplied the discussion of the patriarchal "image of women" with a possibility of female self-representation, withdrawn from voyeurism by means of her use of heroic male figures, such as Laocoön. Equally, with the animation films produced in the years 1970–76, she contributed to discussions of female identity (see *Self-Portrait*, 1971; five minutes, colour), role clichés (*Couples*, 1972, and *Palmistry*; each ten minutes, colour) and patriarchal patterns in art history (*Art Education*, 1976; ten minutes, colour).

Lassnig's body pictures became more introverted in the late 1970s and her technique more expressive and colour intensive, for example *Hermit* (1979; repr. Vienna 1985, p.92). This was not influenced by her successes and the long-overdue official recognition by Austria – the Venice Biennale nomination and her appointment at the Vienna Academy. Such paintings as *Compulsion to Speak* (1980; *ibid.*, p.113) testify instead to the psychic demands of her new role. The fact that she entered a male domain as the first female professor of painting at a German-speaking art academy suggests the context for her gender crossing to a female *Samson* (1983; *ibid.*, p.130) or her appearance in a male *Traditional Chain* (1983; *ibid.*, p.133), alongside such "painters of genius" as Velázquez and van Gogh.

In parallel with her numerous exhibition successes from 1985 Lassnig reflected on her relation as a painter to the image/depiction in the series *Inside and Outside of the Canvas* (1984/5–7; repr. Lucerne 1989). Since 1987 a playful recourse to methods of depiction of the 1950s and 1960s can be detected in both her paintings and drawings. The bodily effects of ageing and repeatedly also death are at the centre of her latest works, such as *Tha, Tha, Tha* (1990; repr. Amsterdam 1994, p.52) and *Grim Reaper* (1991; *ibid.*, p.55). Lassnig gave an extremely humorous retrospective view of her life in the short film *Cantata*, premièred at the Berlinale in 1993.

BIRGIT THIEMANN

Laurencin, Marie

French painter and designer, 1883–1956

Born in Paris, 31 October 1883; mother from a Creole family, father unknown. Started training as a porcelain painter at École de Sèvres, 1902; studied art at the Académie Humbert, Paris, from 1904; met Georges Braque, who introduced her to Picasso and his circle. Exhibited at Salon des Indépendants from 1907. Lived with writer and critic Guillaume Apollinaire, 1907–12. Included in *Section d'Or* exhibition at Galerie La Boétie, Paris, 1912. Married German artist Otto van Wätjen, 1914; divorced 1921. Lived in Spain during World War I; while in Madrid, co-edited the Dada magazine *391* with Picabia, Gleizes and Arthur Cravan. Spent a year in Düsseldorf at end of war, returning to Paris in 1920. Designed costumes and décor for Francis Poulenc's ballet *Les Biches*, commissioned by Diaghilev, 1923. Visited Italy, 1928. Taught at Académie du XVIe, Paris, founded by Laboureur, 1933. Died in Paris after a heart attack, 8 June 1956.

Selected Individual Exhibitions

Galerie Berthe Weill, Paris: 1908 (with Jacqueline Marval)
Galeries Paul Rosenberg, Paris: 1921, 1936
Galerie Alfred Flechtheim, Berlin: 1925 (with Renée Sintenis)
Galerie H. Clovis Sagot, Paris: 1944
Gimpel Fils, London: 1947
Librairie Paul Morihien Paris: 1949
Kunsthalle, Düsseldorf: 1957 (retrospective)

Selected Writings

Les Carnets des nuits, Brussels: Nouvelle Revue Belgique, 1942; revised Geneva: Cailler, 1956

Bibliography

Roger Allard, *Marie Laurencin*, Paris: Nouvelle Revue Française, 1921
Marcel Jouhandeau, *Marie Laurencin*, Paris: Quatre Chemins, 1928
George Day, *Marie Laurencin*, Paris: Dauphin, 1947
René Gimpel, *Diary of an Art Dealer*, New York: Farrar Straus, and London: Hodder and Stoughton, 1966 (French original)
Charlotte Gere, *Marie Laurencin*, London: Academy, and New York: Rizzoli, 1977
Daniel Marchesseau, *Catalogue raisonné de l'oeuvre gravé de Marie Laurencin*, Tokyo: Kyuryodo, and San Francisco: Alan Wofsy Fine Arts, 1981
——, *Catalogue Raisonné of the Paintings of Marie Laurencin*, San Francisco: Alan Wofsy Fine Arts, 1986 (French original)
Flora Groult, *Marie Laurencin*, Paris: Mercure de France, 1987
Julia Fagan-King, "United on the threshold of the twentieth-century mystical ideal: Marie Laurencin's integral involvement with Guillaume Apollinaire and the inmates of the Bateau Lavoir", *Art History*, xi, March 1988, pp.88–114
Marie Laurencin: Artist and Muse, exh. cat., Birmingham Museum of Art, AL, and elsewhere, 1989 (contains extensive bibliography)
Ute Brandenburger and Petra Welzel, "Marie Laurencin (1883–1956): Die 'Dernière femme des 18. Jahrhunderts' und die 'Frau von heute'", *Profession ohne Tradition*, exh. cat., Berlinische Galerie, Berlin, 1992, pp.249–58
Marie Laurencin: Cent oeuvres des collections du Musée Marie Laurencin au Japon, exh. cat., Fondation Pierre Gianadda, Martigny, 1993
Elisabeth Couturier, "Marie Laurencin: Mémoires d'une jeune fille rangée", *Beaux Arts*, no.118, December 1993, pp.96–101
Gill Perry, *Women Artists and the Parisian Avant-Garde*, Manchester: Manchester University Press, and New York: St Martin's Press, 1995
Diane Radycki, "Pretty/ugly: Morphing Paula Modersohn-Becker and Marie Laurencin", *Make: The Magazine of Women's Art*, no.72, 1996, pp.19–21

Of all the women artists associated with the Cubist movement, it is Marie Laurencin whose name is now best known, and whose work is best documented. Her (marginal) position in many histories of the movement was encouraged by the support of the critic Guillaume Apollinaire, who described her works in the Salon des Indépendants of 1910 as *cubiste*. While studying art at the Académie Humbert, a private Parisian art school, Laurencin became friendly with the Cubist painter Georges Braque. In 1907 he introduced her to the circle of artists and writers who gathered regularly in Picasso's studio, the Bateau Lavoir on the rue Ravignon. This group is commemorated by Laurencin in two versions of the painting *Apollinaire and His Friends* of 1908. In the first version, titled *Group of Artists* (Baltimore Museum of Art), Laurencin places herself between the two male protagonists, Picasso and Apollinaire, as if to suggest some comparable status. However, in the larger version, *Apollinaire and His Friends* or *Country Reunion* (see illustration), Laurencin is dressed in a pale blue dress and is seated to the far right, conspicuously separated off from the central group of artists around Apollinaire and Picasso. This self-representation on the margins of the avant-garde may partly reflect Laurencin's view of herself as a separate "feminine" artist, practising a quintessentially "feminine" art. It has also been suggested that this work is steeped in quasi-religious ideas about the roles of art and artists that were fashionable at the time. According to Julia Fagan-King (1988, p.88), Apollinaire, with whom Laurencin was having a relationship at the time, pursued such ideas with a characteristic missionary zeal. Fagan-King has suggested that Laurencin may have cast her protagonists in ambitious symbolic roles in this painting, echoing the mystical ideology with which some members of the group identified. Thus the central figure of Apollinaire, crowned with a halo-like shape, may represent Christ; Picasso may be symbolically cast as John the Baptist, and Laurencin, dressed in blue, as the Virgin Mary.

Laurencin's peripheral involvement with Cubism continued during the years leading up to the outbreak of World War I, when her work was included in several Cubist shows, and in 1914 she contributed to the decorations for the Maison Cubiste, an experiment in interior design led by Raymond Duchamp-Villon and André Mare. Throughout her career she continued to work on decorative and applied designs and book illustration, a division of labour often associated in contemporary criticism with "feminine" artistic pursuits.

Laurencin is perhaps best known for her work from the 1920s and 1930s, when her paintings sold well and she benefited from a business relationship with the dealer Paul Rosenberg. Her work from this period, examples of which can now be found in French public collections, included many portraits and portrait commissions of women and children, painted in soft pastel tones with delicate features. Her delicately painted, fashionably dressed adolescent women provided contemporary critics with an idealised image of contemporary femininity, or what the critic Louis Vauxcelles

Laurencin: *Apollinaire and His Friends*; or, *Country Reunion*, 1908; oil on canvas; 82 × 124 cm.; Musée National d'Art Moderne, Centre Georges Pompidou, Paris

called "un Marie Laurencin". This feminine type proved highly marketable, and was itself appropriated as an image of fashionable modernity. In 1924, after seeing the ballet *Les Biches*, for which Laurencin had designed the sets, the art dealer René Gimpel wrote:

> the whole ballet comes to look like the figures she paints. In the corridor I heard a woman say to a man: "Look around the house, all the women look as though they were by Marie Laurencin; she has fashioned a type just as Boldini created the eel look fifteen years ago" [Gimpel 1966, entry for 17 May 1924].

Moreover, such images of women were often identified by contemporary critics as mirror images of the artist herself, thus helping to establish a contemporary notion of a woman artist narcissistically reproducing an idealised image of her own femininity (see also entry on Jacqueline Marval). Laurencin welcomed such popular interpretations of her imagery of women, and encouraged critical representations of her work as quintessentially feminine. In the 1920s and 1930s such images were also claimed by critics such as Vauxcelles and André Salmon as revealing a national identity. In his *L'Histoire générale de l'art histoire français de la Révolution à nos jours* (vol.ii, Paris, 1922, p.321), Vauxcelles described Laurencin's ideal feminine type as revealing "une sensibilité racée" (a thoroughbred sensibility) – an essential Frenchness. While such associations may be more troubling to a modern audience, during the inter-war period Laurencin's fashionably dressed adolescent women were easily appropriated as marketable symbols of modernity and desirable French femininity.

GILL PERRY

Lebedeva, Sarra (Dmitriyevna)

Russian sculptor, 1892–1967

Born Sarra Dmitriyevna Darmolatova in St Petersburg (later Petrograd/Leningrad), 11 December (Old Style calendar)/23 December (New Style calendar) 1892. Briefly attended the Drawing School of the Society for the Encouragement of the Arts, St Petersburg, 1906; studied sculpture under Leonid Sherwood (Leonty Shervud) at M.D. Bernshtein's school, St Petersburg, 1910–12; transferred to Sherwood's school as a sculpture student, 1912–14. Student, then assistant to Vasily Kuznetsov, 1914. Formed close friendship with Vladimir Tatlin. Married Vladimir Lebedev, 1915. Studio assistant to Aleksandr Matveyev at time of Revolution; taught sculpture at Petrograd Free State Art Educational Workshops, then at Stieglitz Institute, Petrograd, 1918–20. Worked in ceramics and stage design, 1920–24. Travelled to Paris and Berlin,

1928. Designed tableware and pottery for Konakovsky Factory (porcelain factory), 1931–5. Member, ORS (Society of Russian Sculptors), 1926–31. Named Honoured Arts Worker of the RSFSR (Russian Republic), 1945; Corresponding Member, Academy of Arts of the USSR. Donated large collection of Tatlin's papers and work to the nation, 1960. Died in Moscow, 7 March 1967.

Principal Exhibitions

Individual

State Museum of Western Art, Moscow: 1941
Tretyakov Gallery, Moscow, and State Russian Museum, Leningrad: 1969 (retrospective)

Group

Mir Iskusstva (World of Art), Petrograd: 1918
Petrograd: 1922 (*New Tendencies in Art*)
Moscow: 1926 (*State Art Exhibition of Contemporary Sculpture*), 1928 (*Exhibition for the Tenth Anniversary Jubilee of the October Revolution*), 1935 (with Vera Mukhina, Vladimir Favorsky, Iosif Chaikov and others)
ORS (Society of Russian Sculptors), Moscow: 1926, 1929, 1931
Venice Biennale: 1928, 1932, 1934, 1938
Grand Central Palace, New York: 1929 (*Contemporary Art of Soviet Russia*, touring)
Park of Culture and Rest (Gorky Park), Moscow: 1931 (*"Alley of Shock-Workers": Sculpture Portraits of Heroes of Labour*)
Leningrad and Moscow: 1932–3 (*Artists of the RSFSR over 15 Years, 1917–1932*)
Exposition Internationale, Paris: 1937 (silver medal)
Paris: 1948 (*Woman, Her Life and Aspirations*)
Exposition Universelle et Internationale, Brussels: 1958 (silver medal)

Selected Writings

"Neskolko slov k portretu F. Dzerzhinskogo", [Some words on the portrait of F. Dzerzhinsky], *Prozhektor*, no.17, 1926; reprinted in Ternovets 1940 (excerpts in English in Yablonskaya 1990)
"Portrety geroyev" [Portraits of heroes] in "Sovetskiye khudozhniki v dni voyny" [Soviet artists during wartime], *Iskusstvo*, part 5, 1983, pp.46–9

Bibliography

B[oris] N[ikolayevich] Ternovets, "Sarra Lebedeva", *Iskusstvo*, 1935, no.3, pp.62–84.
B.N. Ternovets, *Sarra Lebedeva*, Moscow-Leningrad: Gosizdat "Iskusstvo", 1940
Sarra Lebedeva: Vystavka khudozhestvennykh proizvedeniy [Sarra Lebedeva: Exhibition of artistic works], exh. cat., Moscow Union of Soviet Artists, State Museum of Western Art, Moscow, 1941
M.L. Neiman, *Sarra Dmitriyevna Lebedeva: Album*, Moscow-Leningrad: "Sovetskiy khudozhnik", 1960
Posmertnaya vystavka proizvedeniy S.D. Lebedevoy, 1892–1967 [Posthumous exhibition of the works of S.D. Lebedeva], exh. cat., Tretyakov Gallery, Moscow, and elsewhere, 1969
Trois sculpteurs soviétiques: A.S. Goloubkina, V.I. Moukhina, S.D. Lebedeva, exh. cat., Musée Rodin, Paris, 1971
M[ikhail] V[ladimirovich] Alpatov and others, *Sarra Lebedeva: Album*, Moscow: Sov. Khudozhnik, 1973
A.V. Kuprin, *S.D. Lebedeva, N.P. Ulyanov*, exh. cat., Moscow, 1978
M.N. Yablonskaya, *Women Artists of Russia's New Age, 1900–1935*, New York: Rizzoli, and London: Thames and Hudson, 1990

Sarra Lebedeva's sculpture portraits were celebrated in the Soviet Union for their expression of individual life and character, their formal beauty and humanity. She was known primarily as a creator of monumental sculpture – official or memorial works for public display, usually life- or over-life-sized. This field, in which a number of women artists distinguished themselves, was enlarged under the goals of the State-sanctioned arts ideology of Socialist Realism. In spite of the often deadening strictures of prescribed realism, Lebedeva's sensitive handling of surfaces, manipulation of light and shadow and rendition of facial details resulted in energetic works that captured the intelligence, nervous energy and shifting expressions of her subjects. She worked primarily in bronze.

Lebedeva was born into a wealthy, intellectual household in St Petersburg, one of three sisters. Until the age of 14, she was privately educated at home, where she demonstrated an early talent for drawing. Her first serious commitment to sculpture came under the instruction of Leonid Sherwood (Leonty Shervud), an admirer of Rodin and Impressionism. At Bernshtein's school she encountered Vladimir Tatlin and the graphic artist Vladimir Lebedev, whom she married in 1915. Although she was personally acquainted with members of the avant-garde art community, Lebedeva did not seek out exhibitions of contemporary art, either in Russia or abroad. On European travels with her family before World War I, she was drawn to the work of Renaissance sculptors, particularly Donatello. Her only significant sculpture showing the influence of Cubism (as well as ancient sculpture) is *Bull* (1922; Tretyakov Gallery, Moscow), unusual also for its subject matter and material, sheet iron.

During the first few years following the Revolution, Lebedeva worked less in sculpture, lacking a private studio and materials. She was briefly active in stage design and created her first porcelain efforts, coloured statuettes, at the State Porcelain Factory, Petrograd. She also provided illustrations for a number of journals. Alone and in collaboration with Lebedev, she designed agitprop street decorations and posters for the ROSTA windows propaganda programme (1920). Lebedeva's most important work of this period were her designs for Lenin's Plan for Monumental Propaganda, an ambitious project for disseminating public monuments to revolutionary heroes. In 1920 she designed plaster monumental busts and bas-reliefs of Marx, Danton, Aleksandr Herzen and Robespierre. The only work to survive was her bronze plaque of *Maximilien Robespierre* (1920; Tretyakov Gallery), which combined sharply delineated facial details and stylised framing elements drawn from the formal lexicon of the non-objective avant-garde to communicate a heroic determination and thrust towards the future.

Lebedeva followed this public work with a series of portraits of State officials, beginning with the diplomat and family friend *L.B. Krasin* (1924; private collection). In 1925 she moved to Moscow, following the relocation of the central Soviet government from Leningrad. Her goal was a portrait of *Feliks Dzerzhinsky* (1925; State Museum of the Revolution, Moscow), the head of the Cheka, the first Soviet secret police. Unwilling to resort to photographs, Lebedeva begged sessions in Dzerzhinsky's office, which she later described as her first studio in Moscow, modelling her maquette as he worked. Success and recognition came quickly. She continued to sculpt portraits of officials and military commanders: *Semyon Budyonny* (1926), *Aleksandr Tsyurupa* (1927; both State

Lebedeva: *Sailor Vlasov, Red Fleet Shockworker*, 1931; State Russian Museum, St Petersburg

Russian Museum, St Petersburg) and *Kliment Voroshilov* (1933) are typical. These were interspersed with depictions of writers and dramatists, also from life, and noted for their depth of expression and inner identity, as in *Vsevolod Ivanov* (1925; Tretyakov Gallery) and *Aleksandr Serafimovich* (1936; State Painting Gallery, Perm). Contemporaries remarked on Lebedeva's ability to capture the recognisable character of her subjects, and imbue even those sitters they did not know with a lively, human quality. Her portrait of *Solomon Mikhoels* (1939; Tretyakov Gallery), the actor and director of GOSET, the State Jewish Theatre, nine years before his execution, shows great humour and dignity. As with most of her portraits, Lebedeva modelled the head carefully with her fingertips, leaving a softly textured and visibly manipulated surface scored by her nails and modelling tools.

In the 1930s Lebedeva created a number of portraits of "worker-heroes", including *Sailor Vlasov, Red Fleet Shockworker* (1931; see illustration), *Textile Worker-Shockworker Lena Trubnikova* (1931–7) and *Hero of the Soviet Union Pilot V.P. Chkalov* (1936–9; both Tretyakov Gallery). The first of these was done in 1931, when she was commandeered by the government to Sevastapol as an artist-observer to record figures and deeds of the Navy stationed in the Black Sea. Her portrait of the gunner Vlasov is less individual and more evocative of the worker "type", an approach favoured by the artists and officials then developing the tenets of Socialist Realism. This series was followed in the 1940s by portraits of artists, musicians, writers and other cultural figures, including her fellow sculptor *Vera Mukhina* (1939), *Anatoly Mariengof* (1944), *Lavinia A. Bajbeouk-Melikian* (1946), *Vladimir Tatlin* (1943–4; all Tretyakov Gallery) and the writer *Lieutenant-General A.A. Ignatiyev* (1943; State Russian Museum). Although none was realised, Lebedeva completed commissioned designs for memorials to *Dzerzhinsky* (1940), *Aleksandr Pushkin* (1937) and *Anton Chekhov* (1944–5).

Lebedeva produced figures for fountains, exhibition pavilions and genre figures for outdoor display. The most famous of these was her *Girl with Butterfly* (1936; later forged-copper version in the State Russian Museum), which was placed in the Central Park of Rest and Culture (Gorky Park), Moscow. These works, as well as her many sculptures of nudes and young girls, were smoother and more serene than her portraits. Their compact, classical poses, heavy, rounded bodies and reflective faces are more evocative of Maillol and Matveyev than Rodin. For a few years, Lebedeva investigated faience, finding it a perfect medium for the free and light expression of the figure. While working with the Konakovsky ceramic factory, she designed many figurines, as well as pottery that was not put into production; the most famous of these, the *Hen* tea set (1934–6; State Museum of Ceramics), for which she won a silver medal at the Paris Exposition Internationale of 1937, featured a teapot in the form of a stylised chicken. From the beginning, Lebedeva sketched and drew, producing studies of nudes, portraits and sketches for prospective monuments and projects. Many of her nudes are fresh and freely rendered, some of them appearing to be quick notations of a model in motion, as practised by Rodin; others are studio drawings of standing and reclining figures.

Despite her lifelong dedication to realism, Lebedeva formed a close friendship with Tatlin, the great founder of Russian Constructivism. Although he wrote in a letter to Anna, Lebedeva's sister, that she had declared his early pictures "an abomination" (1914), biographers of Tatlin claim that she ultimately understood his work more fully than anyone else. She was one of a handful of people who attended Tatlin's funeral in 1953 and was responsible for the preservation of his private papers and some important works, including a wing of *Letatlin*. In 1960 she donated this collection to the State.

KATHLEEN M. FRIELLO

le Hay, Elisabeth-Sophie *see* Chéron

Léger, Nadia *see* Khodossievitch

Lemaire, Madeleine-Jeanne
French painter and illustrator, 1846–1928

Born Madeleine-Jeanne Coll in Sainte-Rosseline, near Fréjus, Var, 28 May 1846. Studied in Paris under her aunt Jeanne-Mathilde Herbelin, and then under Charles Chaplin. Married M. Lemaire, 1865; exhibited under this surname from 1869. Sociétaire, Société Nationale des Beaux-Arts, 1890. Chevalier, Légion d'Honneur, 1906. Died in Paris, 8 April 1928.

Principal Exhibitions
Paris Salon: occasionally 1864–78 (honourable mention 1877)
Société des Aquarellistes, Paris: from 1879
Exposition des Beaux-Arts, Nantes: 1886
Société Nationale des Beaux-Arts, Paris: from 1890
World's Columbian Exposition, Chicago: 1893
Woman's Art Club, New York: 1894
Exposition Universelle, Paris: 1900 (silver medal)
Galerie Georges Petit, Paris: 1905 (individual)

Bibliography
Gérald Schurr, *Les Petits Maîtres de la peinture, valeurs de demain*, ii, Paris, 1875, pp.63–4
"Madeleine Lemaire", *Le Figaro*, 16 May 1901
Dominique [pseudonym of Marcel Proust], "Le salon de Madame Lemaire", *Le Figaro*, 11 May 1903
Jacques Patin, "Mme Madeleine Lemaire", *Le Figaro*, 10 April 1928
Proust et les peintres, exh. cat., Musée des Beaux-Arts, Chartres, 1991

From her aunt Jean-Mathilde Herbelin, née Habert, Madeleine Lemaire acquired not only the first stirrings of her passion for art, but above all the art of conducting a salon. She filled it with all the personalities of the art world, and these people have contributed as much to the memory of her name as has her prolific but somewhat forgotten oeuvre.

Lemaire's first submissions to the Paris Salon went unnoticed and most of the paintings she exhibited are no longer known to us, but their titles enable us to discern from an early stage the main subjects of her inspiration and of her work. From 1864 onwards she was interested in portraiture, with the portrait of *Baroness H …* (Salon cat. 1864, no.424; untraced), followed in 1870 by the portrait of *Prince J. Poniatowski, Senator* (Salon cat. 1870, no.1706; private collection). In 1865 she exhibited one portrait, seemingly her only work of orientalist inspiration, *Jamma Bent-Assem, Young Girl of Blidah* (Salon cat. 1865, no.487; untraced). After that it was not until 1877 and 1878 that she again exhibited portraits, including that of the painter *Jules-Emile Saintin* (Salon cat. 1878, no.1399; untraced). She seems subsequently to have abandoned this subject for many years. Genre scenes occupied her attention from 1866, when she exhibited *Child Playing with a Dog* (Salon cat. 1866, no.431; untraced). The following year she showed *Have You Eaten?* (Salon cat. 1867, no.356; untraced). Under literary titles she painted charming, flowery scenes in bright colours: *Columbine* (Salon cat. 1875, no.1168), *Corinna* (Salon cat. 1876, no.127), *Manon* (Salon

cat. 1877, no.1315), *Ophelia* (Salon cat. 1878, no.1398; all untraced) and *Two Fairies* (Musée des Beaux-Arts, Sens). Finally, in 1870, Lemaire's main subject of inspiration appeared, one that, throughout her career, she would work out in oils, in watercolour, gouache and pencil: the depiction of flowers. The series begins with *Flowers and Peaches* (Salon cat. 1870, no.1707; untraced). From 1872 to 1876, due to the limit imposed on the number of works accepted at the Salon, she contented herself with showing just two works: a flower picture and a genre scene. After 1877 she submitted watercolours in addition to oils (*Oranges and Chrysanthemums*, Salon cat. 1877, no.3033; and *Roses and Peaches*, Salon cat. 1878, no.316; both untraced). Two famous phrases are linked with the many flower paintings she produced: Alexandre Dumas *fils* said that "she created more flowers than anyone except God" (*Le Figaro*, 16 May 1901, p.1), and Marcel Proust is credited with the line that named her "the inspiration of roses". Two of her flower paintings appeared on the art market in 1995: *Roses in a Vase* (sold Sotheby's, London, 14 June 1995) and *Vase of Flowers* (sold Calais, 19 March 1995).

Lemaire took part in the Salon for the last time in 1878 but was to be found among the founder-members of the Société des Aquarellistes, alongside artists as diverse as Edouard Detaille, Gustave Doré and Eugène Isabey. At the first exhibition (1879), held at 16 rue Lafitte, she continued her practice of submitting genre scenes and floral compositions. Each year's exhibition catalogue includes one or two illustrations per artist, which enables us to get a better understanding of the pictures she was painting at the time, which were heavily imbued with the spirit of the Rococo style, full of light and tranquillity. At the seventh exhibition in 1885 four works listed under the one entry were painted in gouache, a medium that Lemaire was to use regularly from then on. In the same year she returned to portraiture with *Gabrielle Réjane* (Musée Carnavalet, Paris), a small watercolour depicting the actress full-length in theatrical costume. The Musée Carnavalet also holds a number of her other portraits of actors, *Coquelin Cadet*, *Jeanne Granier* and others. In 1887 her submission included six watercolours (cat. no.220; untraced) for the illustrations of the *Abbé Constantin*, written by Ludovic Halévy, which belonged at that time to the publisher Bussod and, among the drawings under entry no.229, some *Illustrations Intended for a Novella by M. Marcel Ballot for the Journal Les Lettres et Les Arts* (untraced).

Throughout this time Lemaire was conducting gatherings in her little town house at 31 rue Monceau, which attracted the prominent figures of the day. The accounts of these soirées mention the names of Alexandre Dumas *fils*, Robert de Montesquiou, Anatole France, Jules Lemaître, Marcel Proust, Edmond de Rothschild and of many painters and sculptors:

> Lemaire's was the liveliest and most crowded of the bourgeois *salons*, counting many of the *gratin* who rolled up in their carriages to view, as in a zoo, such talent. The receptions took place in a large studio giving on to a small lilac-hung garden, where by day Mme Lemaire painted her popular rose pictures [William Sansom, *Proust and His World*, London, 1973, p.53].

These connections led to her receiving commissions for illustrations. For Paul Hervieu she painted the watercolours for

Lemaire: *Sleep of Manon*, exhibited 1906; Musée d'Orsay, Paris

Peints par eux-mêmes (1893) and *Flirt* (1890). In 1896 Marcel Proust entrusted her with the illustrations for the collection *Les Plaisirs et les jours*, with its preface by Anatole France, texts by Proust, previously published in *Le Banquet* and the *Revue Blanche* from 1892 on, and for four pieces for piano by Reynaldo Hahn. The result of this collaboration was published by Calmann-Lévy.

In 1890 Lemaire was a founder-member of the Société Nationale des Beaux-Arts and took part regularly in its exhibitions. Until 1900 she concentrated on flower painting almost exclusively, whatever the subject matter might be, as for example *St Roseline, the Miracle of the Roses* (1898 cat., no.744; untraced), which she showed in the same year as a decorative piece composed of four panels and two overdoors in which she returned to the subject of the seasons (nos 717–22). She still produced some genre scenes, however, such as *Five o'clock* (1891 cat., no.581; Musée des Arts Décoratifs, Paris) and *Sleep of Manon* (1906; see illustration). After 1900 the success of her work declined and she found herself obliged to extend her repertoire to include once again portraiture, landscapes, which she painted in Normandy (*Varengeville, Landscape*; 1901 cat., no.561; untraced), and genre scenes (*Woman Selling Herrings, Dieppe*; 1903 cat., no.822; untraced), which she was by then treating in a more sombre, brooding manner. From 1904 onwards, to bring in some money, Lemaire resorted to regular sales of her work, first in

Paris (40 watercolours on 28 December 1904, 30 watercolours on 28 December 1906), then in the provinces (21 works at Reims on 28 December 1911, 49 at Angers on 17 December 1913). Like many artists who had had a successful Salon career in the 1870s, and despite efforts to re-animate her subject matter and her technique, Madeleine Lemaire died in 1928 in relative obscurity.

DOMINIQUE LOBSTEIN

Lemoine, Marie-Victoire

French painter, 1754–1820

Born in Paris, 1754. Studied under François Menageot in Paris. Died in Paris, 1820.

Principal Exhibitions

Salon de la Correspondance, Paris: 1779, 1785
Paris Salon: 1796, 1798, 1802, 1804, 1814

Bibliography

Les Femmes peintres au XVIIIe siècle, exh. cat., Musée Goya, Castres, 1973
Women Artists, 1550–1950, exh. cat., Los Angeles County Museum of Art, and elsewhere, 1976

Lemoine: *Interior of the Atelier of a Woman Painter,* exhibited Salon of 1796; 116.5 × 88.9 cm.; Metropolitan Museum of Art, New York; Gift of Mrs Thorneycroft Ryle, 1957 (57.103)

Mary O'Neill, *Les Peintures de l'Ecole française des XVIIe et XVIIIe siècles, Musée des Beaux-Arts d'Orléans*, doctoral dissertation, Université de Paris-Sorbonne, 1980

Marie-Victoire Lemoine remains a shadowy figure in the history of women artists. Few of her works have been identified, there is scant documentary evidence of her career, and she has been the subject of little research. Born in Paris in 1754, Lemoine was a contemporary of Elisabeth Vigée-Lebrun (q.v.), Marguerite Gérard (q.v.) and Adélaïde Labille-Guiard (q.v.). Although she never entered the French Academy, she is said to have first trained in the studio of the academic history painter François Menageot. It is likely that Lemoine was a student in the early 1770s, when Menageot lived and worked in a house on the rue de Cléry owned by Vigée-Lebrun's husband, the collector and dealer Jean-Baptiste Lebrun. The Lebruns also resided in this house, and it was there that Vigée-Lebrun had her atelier. These associations may in part account for the painting that is today Lemoine's best-known work, the *Interior of the Atelier of a Woman Painter* (see illustration), which appeared in the Salon of 1796. The painting has been generally accepted as some sort of tribute to Vigée-Lebrun, and the depicted artist's costume suggests that reputedly worn by her. Older traditions identified the pupil at work under her tutelage as a self-portrait of Lemoine. The discrepancy in the ages of pupil (who is shown as an adolescent) and teacher makes this unlikely. Lemoine was a year older than Vigée-Lebrun, and in her self-portrait done some time in the 1780s showed herself as a young, yet mature, woman (*Self-Portrait*, signed and dated, last digit of the date illegible; Musée des Beaux-Arts, Orléans). The closeness in age between the two artists does not, however, preclude the possibility that Lemoine might have worked in Vigée-Lebrun's atelier at the rue de Cléry. Vigée-Lebrun trained several women students in the 1770s, most of whom – according to the artist's *Souvenirs* – were older than she (among those students Vigée-Lebrun records only by name Emilie Roux de La Ville (sic), later Mme Benoist, q.v.). If we accept the identification of the master artist depicted in Lemoine's *Interior* as Elisabeth Vigée-Lebrun, even if the pupil is not a literal self-portrait of Lemoine, the image could hint at some direct, even formative, contact between the two women artists. At the very least, we can imagine Lemoine visiting Vigée-Lebrun's studio, or Menageot directing her there.

Lemoine's image of a woman artist in her atelier shares several motifs with her self-portrait made in the 1780s, the only other of her works now hanging in a public collection. Both images focus on women painters holding the tools of their trade, and both represent them before canvases on which a composition is sketched in white chalk. Not only do these represented canvases depict studio practice, they also show Classical themes. The presence of a sketched-out history painting in the atelier of a woman painter bears some explanation – especially since it occurs in both self-portraits by Lemoine, for whom no history paintings are recorded. The subjects by Lemoine listed in exhibition records are portraits, portrait miniatures and genre subjects. Many of the last – for example, a young girl holding a dove, a small boy playing the violin, a girl cutting lilacs – suggest sentimental scenes far from the sort of image projected on the canvases visible within the paintings in New York and Orléans.

It would be easy to suggest that the self-portrait in Orléans is either an allegory of painting or combines an allegory with a self-portrait. The figure is sufficiently idealised to sustain such a reading and the traditional attributes of painting – the palette, brushes, maulstick – are on display. With its emphasis on the transmission of art from woman to woman, the *Atelier* is less readily interpreted in this way. This aspect recalls Labille-Guiard's *Self-Portrait with Two Pupils* (1785; Metropolitan Museum of Art); indeed, the figure of the pupil in Lemoine's painting recalls in its profile expression and dress the portrait of Gabrielle Capet (q.v.) in Labille-Guiard's famous work. Yet the works differ significantly in the setting of the imagined art training. The interior of Lemoine's atelier is decorated with a floral rug, a curtain hangs over the entryway, and the artist leans on the end of a harpsichord covered with a carpet. It is a setting that combines the suggestion of domestic life with a representation of professional space. In Labille-Guiard's image, the bare wooden floor, the plaster busts, the darkened and unrelieved wall surfaces locate the image in a setting that emphasises the professional and eschews any hint of domesticity. In this respect, Labille-Guiard's self-portrait is similar to representations of the male artist's atelier produced in the late 1790s and early 1800s by such artists as Boilly.

Located in a space at once both domestic and professional, Lemoine's image may more faithfully suggest the actual situation of most women artists in the 18th century. The professional woman artist such as Vigée-Lebrun conducted her business in her home (only one woman artist, the privileged Anne Vallayer-Coster, q.v., was allowed a studio in the Louvre); the academician's artist-wife, for example Mme Suvée, taught women students in the domestic spaces of the family's Louvre lodgings, safely locked away from her husband's atelier and male students; women amateurs taught by other women practised art at home as an "accomplishment". Lemoine's image signals this doubled space both in the furnishings of the atelier and in the image sketched on the canvas depicted within it. That image shows a young girl kneeling before a statue of Athena placed on an altar while an older priestess or vestal virgin oversees her devotions. Athena would seem an appropriate deity here, as she was both patron of the arts (in her association with the Muses) and goddess of household crafts. The doubled setting and devotion to Athena are thus also metaphoric of the artist's position as a woman living her life between the domestic and professional worlds.

The *Atelier* was among the first works that Lemoine showed at the official art Salons five years after that professional space had been opened to all comers. Hanging this image in a public space previously closed to the vast majority of women artists makes Lemoine's mixing of the domestic and professional both poignant and pointed. Because she was excluded from this public arena and thereby sheltered from published criticism for so much of her artistic life, for Lemoine the opportunity to exhibit in this symbolic location was probably both exhilarating and frightening.

Referring to at least two well-known women artists and including the sketch for a history painting (which itself demonstrates in miniature the artist's ability to compose such a work and her knowledge of the procedures for making one), Lemoine's *Atelier* can be read as articulating the woman artist's position at the end of the 18th century; it is as much a representation of the situation that "ordinary" women artists faced as it is a tribute to a woman – Elisabeth Vigée-Lebrun – who in many ways was exceptional among them. The scanty information about Lemoine's career and the loss of her paintings make her presence in this dictionary of women artists an appropriate parallel to her *Atelier*. For if she can be taken to depict the ambiguous professional situation of most women artists in late 18th-century France, our ignorance about her career only reinforces their equivocal status as practitioners of the fine arts.

MARY D. SHERIFF

Lempicka, Tamara de
Polish painter, 1898–1980

Born Tamara Gorska in Warsaw, 16 May 1898. Travelled to Italy with her grandmother, 1911; educated in Lausanne; went to live with an aunt in Petrograd, Russia, 1914. Married lawyer Tadeusz Lempicki in Petrograd, 1916; one daughter; divorced 1928. Emigrated to Paris via Copenhagen, 1918. Studied painting at Académie de la Grande Chaumière and Académie Ranson, Paris; instructors included Maurice Denis and André Lhôte. Exhibited at Salon des Indépendants and Salon d'Automne, Paris, from 1923; at Salon des Femmes Artistes Modernes, Paris, 1924. Visited Italy, 1925; met poet Gabriele D'Annunzio. Married Hungarian Baron Raoul Kuffner, 1933; he died 1962. Emigrated to USA, 1939, settling in Beverly Hills, California. Moved to New York, 1943; Houston, Texas, to live near her daughter Kizette, 1963; Cuernavaca, Mexico, 1974. Recipient of first prize, Exposition Internationale, Bordeaux, 1927; bronze medal, International Exhibition, Poznań, 1929. Died in Cuernavaca, 18 March 1980.

Selected Individual Exhibitions
Galerie Colette Weill, Paris: 1923
Bottega di Poesia, Milan: 1925
Galeria Zacheta, Warsaw: 1928
Galerie Zak, Paris: 1928
Carnegie Institute, Pittsburgh: 1929
Galerie du Cygne, Paris: 1934
Galerie Charpentier, Paris: 1938
Julien Levy Gallery, New York: 1941
Galerie du Luxembourg, Paris: 1972 (retrospective)

Bibliography
Tamara de Lempicka, exh. cat., Galerie du Luxembourg, Paris, 1972
Giancarlo Marmori, *Tamara de Lempicka* [with] *The Journal of Aelis Mazoyer, Gabriele D'Annunzio's Housekeeper*, Milan: Ricci, 1977
Tendenzen der Zwanziger Jahre: 15 Europäische Kunstaustellung, exh. cat., Neuen Nationalgalerie, Akademie der Künste and Grossen Orangerie des Schlosses Charlottenburg, Berlin, 1977
Giancarlo Marmori, *The Major Works of Tamara de Lempicka, 1925–1935*, Milan: Idea, 1978
Szymon Bojko, "Tamara de Lempicka", *Art and Artists*, xv, June 1980, pp.6–9
Geneviève Bréerette, "The strange life and work of Tamara de Lempicka", *The Guardian*, 12 October 1980
Françoise Gilot, "Tamara: The mystery of a great artist, and perhaps a greater tease", *Art and Antiques*, January 1986, pp.64–9, 88
Alberto Arbasino, "Tamara in Hollywood", *FMR*, no.18, February–March 1986, pp.99–100
Giancarlo Marmori, "Tamara: Painting the beau monde", *ibid.*, pp.77–97
Baroness Kizette de Lempicka-Foxhall and Charles Phillips, *Passion by Design: The Art and Times of Tamara de Lempicka*, New York: Abbeville, and Oxford: Phaidon, 1987
Vivienne Heines, "My mother the artist: Houstonian recalls life of Tamara de Lempicka", *Houston Chronicle*, 22 September 1987
Szymon Bojko, "Tamara de Lempicka, 1898–1980", *Pro Arte*, Winter 1987, pp.84–97
Agnieszka Morawińska, *Autoportret w zielonym Bugatti* [Self-portrait in Green Bugatti], Warsaw: Centrum Sztuki STUDIO, 1990 (published to accompany performance of the play *Tamara*, written by John Krizanc and directed by Richard Rose)
—, "Tamara Lempicka, 1927", *Dialog*, nos 5–6, 1991, pp.158–61
Artystki polskie [Polish artists], exh. cat., National Museum, Warsaw, 1991
Voices of Freedom: Polish Women Artists and the Avant-Garde, 1880–1990, exh. cat., National Museum of Women in the Arts, Washington, DC, 1991
Gilles Néret, *Tamara de Lempicka, 1898–1980*, Cologne: Taschen, 1992
Ellen Thormann, *Tamara de Lempicka: Kunstkritik und Künstlerinnen in Paris*, Berlin: Reimer, 1993
Maurizio Calvesi and Alessandra Borghese, *Tamara de Lempicka: Tra eleganza e trasgressione*, 4th edition, Milan: Arte, 1994

Above all other artists, Tamara de Lempicka has come to symbolise the painting style of Art Deco in the inter-war period. Hard-edged and controlled, de Lempicka's art was that of gesture and theatrical display rather than emotional statement, decorative rather than profound, reflecting the often desperate, frantic spirit of the times. In 1925, the year that the Exposition Internationale des Arts Décoratifs et Industriels Modernes – popularly known as Art Deco – opened in Paris, a self-portrait, *Tamara in the Green Bugatti* (1925; private collection), appeared on the cover of the magazine *Die Dame*, the caption describing her as a "symbol of women's liberation 1925". The tight, precise composition of the painting, the carefully selected range of colours, the inscrutable look of the artist viewing the world from beneath lowered eyelids and the racy, expensive sports car were all vital elements of the art and image of de Lempicka. *Tamara in the Green Bugatti* is also a ruthless portrait of an independent woman, self-possessed and self-assured, symbolising the move towards female emancipation.

Born in Warsaw at the turn of the century to well-to-do parents, at the age of 14 she declared her passion for Count Lempicki, a handsome aristocrat, and married him two years later in Petrograd. In 1917 Count Lempicki was arrested in the city by the Bolsheviks, but the resourceful and determined Tamara de Lempicka succeeded in securing his release. After a visit to London, she and her husband followed her parents to Paris, and though she gave birth to a daughter, Kizette, the romance of the marriage was over, and de Lempicka sought to establish her career as an artist. She enrolled at the Académie de la Grande Chaumière and also studied the work of the old masters, in particular the paintings of such Mannerists as Bronzino and Pontormo. Later she studied in the studio of the successful Symbolist artist Maurice Denis, who taught her to simplify line and colour. More significantly, she worked in the

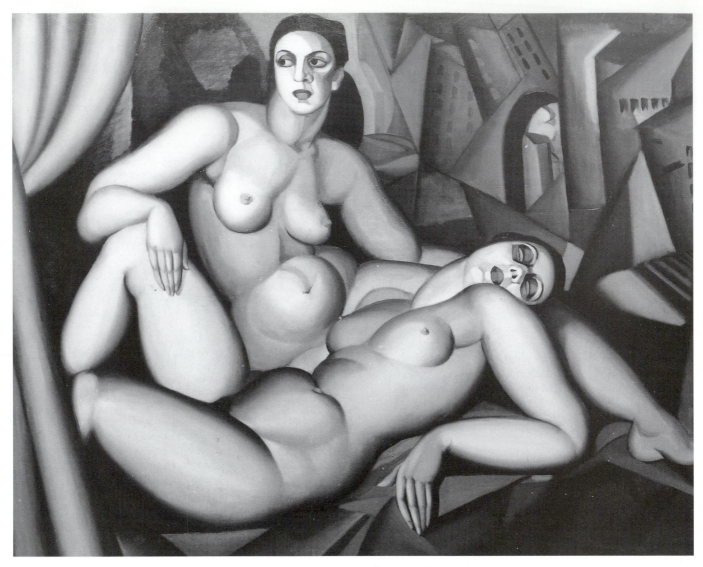

Lempicka: *Two Friends*, 1923; oil on canvas; 130 × 160 cm.; Musée du Petit Palais, Geneva

atelier of the Cubist artist and theoretician André Lhôte, who in his own paintings sought to combine Cubism with the avant-garde experiments of Juan Gris and Georges Braque. Through Lhôte she also learned to appreciate the precise and sensuous work of Ingres, which later inspired her to paint seductive harem compositions of voluptuous naked women.

By 1923 Tamara de Lempicka was showing paintings in galleries in Paris, including Galerie Colette Weill, the Salon des Indépendants, the Salon d'Automne and the Salon des Mins de Trente Ans. The de Lempicka style of the inter-war years is characterised by a hard, enamel-like handling of paint, the use of a loosely Cubist approach of small planes to build up the composition – identified as Synthetic Cubism – a controlled palette that restricted the range of colours to achieve maximum visual impact rather than convey a sense of naturalism, and tight, often photographically inspired compositions.

Tamara de Lempicka's paintings, both in their choice of subject matter – single and double portraits and flower paintings – and in their ordered compositions, epitomise the style, mood and excitement of the inter-war years in cities such as

Paris and Berlin. They also reflected an interest in the sort of authoritarian control offered by Fascist ideology, which was welcomed by many as a resolution to escalating inflation and apparent aimlessness. In tune with her own acquired aristocratic background, de Lempicka took her family and friends as her subject matter, portraying them to suggest wealth, glamour and sophistication. Sitters also included deposed Russian nobility, aristocrats, famous writers, distinguished scientists and industrialists, as well as male and female lovers. Notable examples are *Portrait of a Man (Baron Kuffner)* (1929; Musée National d'Art Moderne, Paris) and *Adam and Eve* (1932; Musée du Petit Palais, Geneva). As a successful and fashionable portrait painter, de Lempicka painted, among others, the *Duchesse de la Salle* (1925; Galerie du Luxembourg, Paris), *Young Girl in Green* (c.1928; Centre Georges Pompidou, Paris), *Queen Elizabeth of Greece* (private collection), *Suzy Solidor* (1922; Musée de Cagnes sur Mer), the owner of a lesbian nightclub, and the eminent chemist and his wife, *Dr and Mme Boucard* (1931; Collection Boucard, Paris).

In 1929 de Lempicka visited New York to carry out a

commission, and while in the USA arranged an exhibition of her work at the Carnegie Institute, Pittsburgh. In 1933 she married Baron Raoul Kuffner, and six years later, as the German armies rolled across Europe, they moved to America, settling first in Hollywood and then New York. With the change of country and the outbreak of war, the persona of Tamara de Lempicka, the Parisian artist, was abandoned in favour of the more subdued Baroness Kuffner.

Although for a time she continued to paint in the familiar hard-edged style, with the subject matter of figures from high society replaced by still lifes (examples in Centre Georges Pompidou), stilted portraits (*Mexican Girl*, Musée des Beaux-Arts, Nice) and mythical and religious figures (examples in Musée de l'Oise, Beauvais), the life and vigour in her art had gone, and her work seemed dated and irrelevant in a climate in which Abstract Expressionism was the favoured style. Experiments with abstraction in the 1950s fail to carry conviction. In the 1960s she adopted a freer, more relaxed style, characterised by closely toned pastel colours and the dry use of paint applied with a palette knife, taking as her subject matter cityscapes, figure studies and flower arrangements. Again they failed to carry the conviction and assurance of the paintings from the inter-war period, and attempts to exhibit them met with little success. (While most of her paintings remain in private collections, public collections not already referred to include the Metropolitan Museum of Art, New York, and Musée des Beaux-Arts, Le Havre.) Out of favour and out of fashion, Tamara de Lempicka's work was all but forgotten until the success of a retrospective exhibition at the Galerie du Luxembourg in 1972 introduced her work to a new generation. She remains an artist quintessentially associated with Art Deco, with all its excess, theatricality and power.

EMMANUEL COOPER

Leroulx-Delaville, Marie Guillemine *see* Benoist

Lessore, Thérèse
British painter, 1884–1945

Born in Brighton, 1884, into an artistic family of French origin. Trained at the Slade School of Fine Art, London, 1904–9 (Melville Nettleship prize). Lived in or around London, except for some years in Bath, 1938–42, and brief excursions abroad, mainly to France. Married (1) painter Bernard Adeney, 1913; divorced; (2) painter Walter Sickert, 1926; he died 1942. Died 10 December 1945.

Principal Exhibitions
Individual
Eldar Gallery, London: 1918, 1919
Leicester Galleries, London: 1924, 1946 (retrospective)
Savile Gallery, London: 1926
R.E.A. Wilson's Ryder Street Gallery, London: 1931

Beaux-Arts Gallery, London: 1936
Reid and Lefevre Gallery, London: 1938

Group
Brighton Art Gallery: 1913 (*Camden Town Group*)
London Salon of the Allied Artists Association: 1913–20
London Group: from 1914
Whitechapel Art Gallery, London: 1914 (*Twentieth-Century Art*)
New English Art Club, London: from 1920

Bibliography
Robert Emmons, *The Life and Opinions of Walter Richard Sickert*, London: Faber, 1941; reprinted London: Lund Humphries, 1992
Walter Sickert, *A Free House; or, The Artist as Craftsman*, ed. Osbert Sitwell, London: Macmillan, 1947
Marjorie Lilly, *Sickert: The Painter and His Circle*, London: Elek, 1971
Wendy Baron, *Sickert*, London: Phaidon, and New York: Praeger, 1973
The Sickert Women and the Sickert Girls, exh. cat., Michael Parkin Fine Art, London, 1974
Wendy Baron, *Miss Ethel Sands and Her Circle*, London: Owen, 1977
Late Sickert: Paintings, 1927 to 1942, exh. cat., Arts Council of Great Britain, London, 1981
Richard Shone, *Walter Sickert*, Oxford: Phaidon, 1988
Sylvia Gosden, *The Paintings of Thérèse Lessore*, M.Phil. dissertation, Leeds Metropolitan University, 1995

From the outset of her career as an easel painter Thérèse Lessore followed an independent artistic direction, which was influenced by her training at the Slade. Lessore entered the school at the relatively late age of 20 and, it may be inferred, brought with her a degree of confidence and maturity deriving from the professional artistic orientation of her family. Her grandfather, the painter Emile Lessore, came to Britain in 1858 and subsequently became well known as a decorator of Wedgwood ceramics; her father was the painter Jules Lessore; and her older siblings also followed artistic careers, her sister Louise as an applied artist and her brother, Frederick, as a sculptor. The Slade was regarded as the most progressive art school in Britain. The painting classes were conducted by Philip Wilson Steer, who adopted a non-didactic approach to teaching. He expected his students, including Lessore, to struggle to find their own individual mode of expression, thus leaving them open to new formal ideas. Lessore excelled at the Slade and was awarded its prestigious Melville Nettleship prize for figure composition.

There was also a growing acceptance in Britain of the formal innovations inspired by the artists who became known as Post-Impressionists: van Gogh, Cézanne and Gauguin. Their work led to the recognition that a painting was not an illusion of actuality, but should be understood in terms not only of its content but also and primarily of its form. Throughout Lessore's known work this concern with form is demonstrated by the use of individual formal elements for both decorative and illusionistic effects. At its most successful, this approach creates a balance between plane and recession that serves to distance the spectator from the content of a painting so that it is seen as a distinct entity that can be appreciated for its form. In the case of Lessore's oils, this effect is enhanced when seen at normal viewing distance by the relatively small dimensions of the canvases.

Lessore: *The Dare-Devils*, *c*.1932; oil on canvas; Hastings Museum and Art Gallery, Kent

One example of this formal approach is the oil painting *The Dare-Devils* (*c*.1932; see illustration), which depicts three spot-lit acrobats seated on a trapeze hanging beneath the massive roof of a large, darkened auditorium, in which only the highest tier of the audience is faintly visible behind an arcade. The low viewpoint and theatrical lighting of the scene not only provide the possibility of surface pattern but also permit the minimal use of tonal gradation. The pattern consists of the shapes of the acrobats and their repeat as shadows together with the geometry of the internal architecture and the areas of light and dark. The effect is enhanced through the application of relatively flat areas of differing but harmoniously related colour to each of these constituents, blue white for the two intersecting beams of light in the upper half of the painting and various cool tones of blue and green for most of the remaining areas, the whole enlivened by small patches of pink and orange. The result is a composition that remains intelligible to the viewer while presenting formal interest.

The Dare-Devils also illustrates a further essential characteristic of Lessore's art. Like the work of most artists of her time, the painting remains within the figurative tradition and is concerned with contemporary life. In Lessore's case a major part of her known work relates to aspects that have obvious visual appeal, including scenes of public entertainment and recreation: music halls, theatres, cafés, cinemas, circuses, dance

halls, fairs, public parks and the seaside. Of the 120 paintings in British public collections 71 represent such scenes (examples are included among the more representative selections of Lessore's work at Bradford City Art Gallery, Glasgow Museums and Art Gallery, Islington Borough Libraries, London, Manchester City Art Galleries and Portsmouth City Museum and Art Gallery). Even where Lessore depicts commercial activities, the more serious connotations of economic life and work are neutralised by her choice of subjects with a potential for decorative treatment: open-air markets, hop-pickers, washerwomen and fishermen rather than factory or office life. In *My Little Piccaninny* (1936; Manchester City Art Galleries), for instance, prominence is given to the arabesques of hop bines surrounding the figure of a woman who, though apparently hard at work picking hops, is seated and accompanied by an infant child. Lessore's iconography distils her social location. The choice of title *My Little Piccaninny* (describing a white child) is indicative of contemporary racial and class attitudes, as is her avoidance of manual labour, while the leisure pursuits Lessore favours are those to which a respectable middle-class woman would have legitimate access.

Lessore's iconographic and formal concerns were established within the context of independent artists' groups that provided mutual support for those interested in new kinds of art and in creating a market for it. She was a member of the Allied Artists Association and her first public showing was at one of its non-selective and large exhibitions. During the early years of her career Lessore also became associated with a group of her contemporaries in Sickert's circle, in particular the painters Sylvia Gosse (q.v.) and Malcolm Drummond. At the same time her developing relationship with her future first husband, the painter Bernard Adeney, brought her into contact with another group initiated by the painter Vanessa Bell (q.v.), known as the Friday Club. In 1914 Lessore also exhibited at the newly established and select London Group. She therefore had access to the most progressive English artistic thinking and the opportunity for the mutual exchange of ideas as well as the possibility of following an economically independent career. These networks were an advantage to women artists, providing relative freedom from the gender-based discrimination of the established art market.

The critical reception accorded Lessore's work, however, did not escape gendered judgements. During the course of her career there was a growing tendency to interpret her work as expressive of her gender. Reviews began auspiciously with supportive commentary from Sickert who was then at his most influential as an art critic. In an article on the large group show, *Twentieth-Century Art*, held at the Whitechapel Art Gallery in 1914, Sickert singled out Lessore as "... the most interesting and masterful personality of them all" (*New Age*, 28 May 1914); and in 1918 he described her as "... a designer of genius" whose economy of means was "... the surest source of artistic enjoyment" (*Art and Letters*, 31 January 1918). Unfortunately, Sickert's early promotion of Lessore's work, and her developing relationship with him, which ended in marriage, appears to have encouraged subsequent critics to describe her painting as merely derivative of his. This is not altogether true, for, despite inevitable similarities, there are marked differences of palette, drawing and subject matter. It has also been suggested by Wendy Baron (London 1981, pp.97–8) that the influence was not entirely one way. This seems very probable. Sickert himself believed that progress in painting was achieved by the mutual interaction of ideas among groups of artists and was founded on the achievements of their predecessors. He was a keen admirer of Lessore's work and, from c.1918, they often worked closely together when Lessore acted as one of his studio assistants. Following their marriage, Lessore's involvement in the preparation of Sickert's painting increased to the point at which, in his later years, he is said to have done no more than direct operations and add his signature together with a few touches of colour (ibid.). None the less, on those rare occasions it has been mentioned since her death, Lessore's painting continues to be seen as derivative. There has been no attempt to evaluate her contribution alongside that of her contemporaries. Although it achieved a degree of recognition and some commercial success during her lifetime, the work of Thérèse Lessore has been relegated to the margins of traditional art history.

SYLVIA GOSDEN and SUE CLEGG

Lewis, Edmonia

American sculptor, c.1844–after 1911

Probably born in Ohio or New York State, c.1844, of mixed African-American and Chippewa Indian parentage. Entered Oberlin College, Ohio, 1859; left before graduation after being accused of poisoning two white room-mates and of theft. Moved to Boston, 1863; became involved with abolitionists and began to study sculpture under Edward Brackett. Sailed to Europe, 1865, visiting London, Paris and Florence; established studio in Rome, winter 1865–6. Occasionally revisited USA. Converted to Catholicism, c.1868. Last recorded living in Rome in 1911.

Principal Exhibitions

San Francisco Art Association: 1873
Memorial Hall, Centennial Exposition, Philadelphia: 1876
World's Columbian Exposition, Chicago: 1893

Bibliography

Henry T. Tuckerman, Book of the Artists: American Artists Life, New York: Putnam, 1867; reprinted New York: Carr, 1966

Clara Erskine Clement and Laurence Hutton, Artists of the Nineteenth Century, 2 vols, Boston: Houghton Osgood, 1879; reprinted New York: Arno Press, 1969

Lorado Taft, The History of American Sculpture, 3rd edition, New York: Macmillan, 1930

James A. Porter, Modern Negro Art, New York: Dryden Press, 1943; reprinted New York: Arno, 1969

Van Wyck Brooks, The Dream of Arcadia: American Artists and Writers in Italy, 1760–1915, New York: Dutton, and London: Dent, 1958

Margaret Farrand Thorp, The Literary Sculptors, Durham, NC: Duke University Press, 1965

The White Marmorean Flock: Nineteenth Century American Women Neoclassical Sculptors, exh. cat., Vassar College Art Gallery, Poughkeepsie, 1972

William H. Gerdts, American Neo-Classic Sculpture: The Marble Resurrection, New York: Viking, 1973

Marcia Goldberg, "A drawing by Edmonia Lewis", American Art Journal, ix, November 1977, p.104

J.T., "More information on the Edmonia Lewis drawing", American Art Journal, x, May 1978, p.112

John S. Crawford, "The classical tradition in American sculpture: Structure and surface", American Art Journal, xi, July 1979, pp.38–52

Forever Free: Art by African-American Women, 1862–1980, exh. cat., Illinois State University, Normal, 1980 (includes extensive bibliography and lists of collections and exhibitions)

Wayne Craven, Sculpture in America, 2nd edition, Newark: University of Delaware Press, 1984

Cynthia D. Nickerson, "Artistic interpretations of Henry Wadsworth Longfellow's The Song of Hiawatha, 1855–1900", American Art Journal, xvi, Summer 1984, pp.49–77

Sharing Traditions: Five Black Artists in Nineteenth-Century America, exh. cat., National Museum of American Art, Smithsonian Institution, Washington, DC, and elsewhere, 1985

Marilyn Richardson, "Vita. Edmonia Lewis: A brief life of a neo-classical sculptor", Harvard Magazine, March–April 1986, p.40

American Women Artists, 1830–1930, exh. cat., National Museum of Women in the Arts, Washington, DC, 1987

Ron Grossman, "Two savoirs vie for 'Cleopatra'", Chicago Tribune, 20 June 1988

Charlotte Streifer Rubinstein, American Women Sculptors, Boston: Hall, 1990

The Lure of Italy: American Artists and the Italian Experience, 1760–1914, exh. cat., Museum of Fine Arts, Boston, 1992

Romare Bearden and Harry Henderson, A History of African-American Artists from 1792 to the Present, New York: Pantheon, 1993

L. Frapiselli, "Una scultrice afro-indiana dall'America a Roma al tempo di Pio IX", Strenna dei Romanisti, 18 April 1994, pp.213–22

Edmonia Lewis was the first professional American sculptor of colour, and was quickly identified with the conditions of her societal marginalisation by contemporary critics. Henry James noted that one of the "white, marmorean flock" of American women sculptors in Rome "was a negress, whose colour, picturesquely contrasting with that of her plastic material, was the pleading agent of her fame" (William Wetmore Story and His Friends, 1903). Henry Tuckerman described Lewis "[i]n her coarse but appropriate attire, with her black hair loose, and grasping in her tiny hand the chisel with which she does not disdain – perhaps with which she is obliged – to work", and suggested that "with her large, black, sympathetic eyes brimful of simple, unaffected enthusiasm, Miss Lewis is unquestionably the most interesting representative of our country in Europe" (Tuckerman 1867, pp.603–4). As Lynda Roscoe Hartigan remarked, however, Lewis was seen as "triply disadvantaged as a black, Indian woman" and "offered a tempting opportunity to those eager to demonstrate their support of human rights" (Hartigan in Washington 1985, p.88). Accordingly, her works have typically been read through a "trivialising elision" with both her racial background and her gender (a phenomenon in art criticism of women artists elucidated by Claudine Mitchell in "Intellectuality and sexuality: Camille Claudel, the fin de siècle sculptress", Art History, xii, 1989, pp.419–47).

Lewis's first works, of 1864–5 – portrait busts of abolitionist leaders such as William Lloyd Garrison, Senator Charles Sumner, Wendell Phillips (president of the Anti-Slavery Society in America) and *Colonel Robert Gould Shaw*, leader of a black regiment in the Civl War – were well received among progressive New Englanders who hoped to assist the cause of emancipation by supporting the emerging artist (later abolitionist portraits included *Abraham Lincoln*, Municipal Library, San Jose, CA; *Ulysses S. Grant* and *Maria Weston Chapman*, head of the Boston Female Anti-Slavery Society). Lewis, however, initially seems to have identified herself more with her mother's Indian heritage than with her father's African-American one, perhaps a response to the ranking of Native Americans over African Americans in the American racial hierarchy, where African Americans were perceived as inferior for having "submitted" to slavery, while Native Americans had the dubious distinction of representing the "Noble Savage".

While tracing the roots of her creativity to her Chippewa mother's inventive embroidery patterns, Lewis qualified this heritage by suggesting: "perhaps the same thing is coming out in me in a more civilized form" (Lydia Maria Child, "Edmonia Lewis", *Broken Fetter*, 3 March 1865, p.25, quoted in Washington 1985, p.88). She described her first work made in Italy, the *Freed Woman and Her Child* (1866; untraced), as "a humble one, but my first thought was for my poor father's people, how I could do them good in my small way" (*The Revolution*, 20 April 1871). Thus Lewis simultaneously claimed and rejected her racial identity, an ambivalence further evidenced by her early busts of white – rather than of black – abolitionist men.

There was also ambivalence among Lewis's supporters, who frequently perceived her as impetuous and lacking in good business judgement. While Lewis was sculpting the portrait bust of *Colonel Robert Gould Shaw* (marble copy of 1867 made in Rome; Museum of Afro-American History in Boston), the sale of which funded her trip to Rome, the abolitionist Lydia Maria Child, sceptical of Lewis's ability to model the Boston hero's features adequately, neglected to show the photographs she owned of Shaw to the artist in an attempt to dissuade her from what she considered an overly ambitious undertaking. Only the actress Charlotte Cushman, herself a maverick, expatriate in Rome, and particular patron of the pioneering women sculptors there, seems to have recognised the "fight" in Lewis's character as a determination to succeed in her career (see Rubinstein 1990).

Lewis completed the necessary Neo-classical apprenticeship by studying with the sculptor Edward Augustus (also known as Edwin C. or E.) Brackett in Boston, but neither these credentials nor the pathos of her racial and economic position paved the way for easy integration into the Roman artistic community. Despite a warm reception by Harriet Hosmer (q.v.) and Charlotte Cushman, among others, Lewis was all too aware of her vulnerability to prejudices against her gender and colour. She reportedly refused to employ artisans to carve her works according to the accepted practice of the day for fear of being accused of not producing her own work – charges that had been levelled against Harriet Hosmer and Vinnie Ream (q.v.). The sculptor Anne Whitney (q.v.) related that for the same reason Lewis rejected recourse to the instruction and criticism of her peers. It should be noted that early American sculptors, with no true art Academy available at home, frequently pursued and succeeded in their profession with little or no

formal instruction. Thus Lewis's choice to remain outside the "Academy" was neither uncommon nor a sign of amateurism.

Lewis seems to have decided soon after her arrival in Rome that it was to be her permanent home. Around 1868 she was received into the Catholic Church and shortly thereafter executed a marble altarpiece of the *Virgin and Child with Angels* for the Marquis of Bute and, in 1883, an *Adoration of the Magi* for a church in Baltimore (both works untraced). As was the case with many 19th-century women sculptors, the Classical and classicising works on view in Rome were sources for both art and anatomy instruction. Among Lewis's study copies was a marble *Moses* (1875; National Museum of American Art, Smithsonian Institution, Washington, DC), a small-scale version of the *Moses* of Michelangelo. Another copy, the bust of *Young Octavian* (c.1873; National Museum of American Art) after the ancient original in the Capitoline Museums, had great success with a visiting American tourist, Elisabeth Buffum Chase. Chase purchased the head, pronouncing it the "best reproduction of the original then offered by any artist in Rome" (Porter 1943, pp.60–61).

Lewis's faithful study of Michelangelo's *Moses* may have inspired the long, twisting curls of another life-sized figure of the same year, *Hagar* (1875; National Museum of American Art). Although there is nothing in the rendering of Hagar's features to associate her with an African slave, she is represented after her expulsion into the wilderness by her jealous mistress, Sarah. Hagar is represented as looking up in midstride with her hands clasped in prayer, and the agitated movement of her drapery and the overturned pitcher at her feet testify to her desperation. Long, coarse locks of hair repeat the highly textured patterns of light and shadow in her gown and lend the whole figure a sense of movement that defies both the rigidly vertical Neo-classical pose of the body and the Neo-classical preference for figures in idealised, "transcendental" repose.

Critics have frequently identified Lewis's Native American background as the reason for her affinity with the story of *Hiawatha*, from which, in 1865, she modelled three small groups in clay – the *Wooing of Hiawatha* (untraced), *Marriage of Hiawatha* (destroyed) and *Departure of Hiawatha and Minnehaha* (untraced) – which bear a strong resemblance in size and sentiment to the celebrated small anecdotal "parlour groups" of her contemporary John Rogers, and small busts of *Minnehaha* (Detroit Institute of Arts; Kennedy Galleries, New York) and *Hiawatha* (Kennedy Galleries), executed in marble in 1866–7. Her versions were, however, mediated by the poem *The Song of Hiawatha* (1855) by H.W. Longfellow, whom she sculpted in 1871 during a visit to Rome (bust in Harvard University Portrait Collection, Cambridge, MA). A later group, the *Old Arrow Maker*, also known as *"Old Indian Arrow Maker and His Daughter"* (two copies, dated 1872 and c.1872; National Museum of American Art), also recalls stories that Lewis told of a nomadic childhood spent with her mother's tribe, making baskets and embroidering moccasins. Many contradictory stories have been reported about Lewis's childhood that have obfuscated her origins, but what has emerged consistently from these tales has been an affectionate and proud, though problematically picturesque view of the Native American (the most deeply researched account of

Lewis: *Forever Free*, 1867; marble; Howard University Gallery of Art, Washington, DC

Lewis's background to date is given in Bearden and Henderson 1993). Perhaps the Indian cycle works represent a further move by the artist to identify herself with a Native American ancestry that was to be read as admirable and artistic, not as savage or dangerous.

While Lewis's selection of these subjects seems to have followed many of the sentimental conventions of the period, her renderings of the *Old Arrow Maker* and, to a lesser extent, of *Minnehaha* are unusual in that their facial features do not repeat the European ideal preferred by the Neo-classical style. Laura Curtis Bullard praised this realism in Lewis's treatment of these figures in a letter to the *New National Era* in May 1871, reporting:

> In both, the Indian type of feature is carefully preserved, and every detail of dress, etc., is true to nature; the sentiment is equal to the execution. They are charming bits, poetic, simple and natural, and no happier illustrations of Longfellow's most original poem were ever made than these by the Indian sculptor [quoted in Craven 1984, p.334].

Crawford (1979) has related Lewis's developing realism to "structural classicism", a willingness to experiment with the Neo-classical idiom in freely adapting its traditional poses and forms to non-European figural types. The strength, and indeed the appeal, of structurally classical works lay in their "democratic, *American* spirit" of independence and innovation with respect to their European roots. Without much exposure to the European cultural vocabulary, Americans could appreciate structurally classical works as addressing themes and representing people of importance to them.

Crawford identified Lewis's representation of the freed man in her life-sized marble group *Forever Free* (1867; see illustration) as a reference to the Montorsoli restoration of the *Laocoön*, and the kneeling female figure as a possible adaptation of Doidalsas's *Crouching Aphrodite* (ibid., pp.46–8). The basic forms of these ancient works have been made contemporary by the use of modern dress, unclassical racial types, unidealised proportions and reference to contemporary events. As Crawford observed, Lewis made the bold move of rewriting the captive Trojan priest as a modern African-American slave, finally "forever free" (ibid., p.46). Indeed, Lewis seems more willing here to re-fashion the classical tradition than to question modern gender iconographies in the two figures of *Forever Free*. The contrast between the erect, active male figure, triumphant in having broken his fetters, and the passive female figure, kneeling in prayerful gratitude for having been liberated, is as much a representation of 19th-century concepts of sexual difference as it is of racial emancipation. Freeman Murray, the first African-American art historian, sent a photograph of Lewis's *Forever Free* to the contemporary African-American woman sculptor, Meta Vaux Warrick Fuller (q.v.), who interpreted the piece thus: "The man accepts it [freedom] as a glorious victory, while the woman looks upon it as a precious gift" (Freeman H.M. Murray, *Emancipation and the Freed in American Sculpture: A Study in Interpretation*, Washington, DC: privately printed, 1916, p.225).

Another gender distinction in *Forever Free* as well as in the *Hagar* and, to a lesser extent, in the Indian cycle works, is made according to the convention seen in Greek vase paintings, Etruscan tomb paintings and the like, whereby females are painted in a lighter colour than males. Lewis reproduced the painterly effect in marble by making her male figures noticeably more "ethnic" in their facial features than their female counterparts. As her studies of Michelangelo, the *Laocoön* and the *Octavian*, among others, indicate, Lewis gave particular attention to the historical and art-historical research of her works (her first known work was a pencil drawing of the *Muse Urania* done as a wedding present for a classmate at Oberlin College, 1862; Oberlin College Archives) and could probably have learned of this convention from Roman art collections such as the celebrated Albani collection of Greek vases, held in the Capitoline Museums in the 19th century.

Lewis did try her hand at three works in the popular "conceit" mode, treating light-hearted themes from popular literature, legend and mythology. Lewis's "conceits" or "fancy-pieces" directly reference successful works on the same theme by contemporaries. Her *Poor Cupid* (1876; National Museum of American Art) recalls in particular Horatio Greenough's *Love Prisoner to Wisdom* (1836; Museum of Fine Arts, Boston). The companion pieces of infants *Asleep* (1871) and *Awake* (1872; both San Jose Public Library) evoke both Harriet Hosmer's impish putti, the *Puck* (1856) and *Will-o'-the-Wisp* (1858; copies of both in Watertown Free Public Library and National Museum of American Art), and sleeping figures of children by William Rinehart and Thomas Crawford.

The Classical world provided Lewis with the subjects for two more of her most important works, the marble *Death of Cleopatra* (Historical Society of Forest Park, IL), exhibited at the Philadelphia Centennial Exposition in 1876, and *Hygeia*, a monument for the grave of Dr Hariot Kezia Hunt in Mount Auburn Cemetery, Cambridge, Massachusetts. Of the *Cleopatra*, William J. Clark wrote:

> This was not a beautiful work, but it was a very original and striking one, and it deserved particular comment, as its ideals were so radically different from those adopted by Story and Gould in their statues of the Egyptian Queen. ... The effects of death are represented with such skill as to be absolutely repellent. Apart from all questions of taste, however, the striking qualities of the work are undeniable, and it could only have been reproduced by a sculptor of genuine endowments [*Great American Sculptures*, Philadelphia: Gebbie and Barrie, 1878; reprinted New York: Garland, 1977, pp.141–2].

While Lewis's *Cleopatra* has fortunately been brought back to light, the *Hygeia*, monument to one of America's first female physicians, is slowly eroding in Mount Auburn Cemetery. Despite the obviously lamentable damage, the weather has given the marble *Hygeia* a strikingly ancient-looking patina and surface texture that reveals, perhaps just as well as its pristine state, Lewis's classicising touch.

NANCY PROCTOR

Leyster, Judith

Dutch painter, 1609–1660

Baptised in the Grote Kerk, Haarlem, 28 July 1609, the eighth child of Jan Willemsz and his wife Trijn Jaspers. Enrolled in the guild of St Luke, Haarlem, 1633; had three pupils in 1635. Moved to Amsterdam after marriage to painter Jan Miense Molenaer, 1636; at least five children (three sons, two daughters), born 1637, 1639, 1643, 1646 and 1650. Moved back to Haarlem by 1649. Buried in nearby Heemstede, 10 February 1660.

Bibliography

Samuel van Ampzing, *Beschrijvinge ende Lof der stad Haerlem in Holland* [Description and praise of the town of Haarlem in Holland], Haarlem, 1628

Theodorus Schrevelius, *Harlemias, Ofte, om beter te seggen, De eerste stichtinghe der Stadt Haerlem* [Harlemias; or, that is to say, the first foundation of the town of Haarlem], Haarlem, 1648

Cornelis Hofstede de Groot, "Judith Leyster", *Jahrbuch der Königlich Preussischen Kunstsammlungen*, xiv, 1893, pp.190–98, 232

Juliane Harms, "Judith Leyster: Ihr Leben und ihr Werk", *Oud Holland*, xliv, 1927, pp.88–96, 112–26, 145–54, 221–42, 275–9

Frima Fox Hofrichter, *Judith Leyster: A Woman Painter in Holland's Golden Age*, Doornspijk: Davaco, 1989

Judith Leyster: A Dutch Master and Her World, exh. cat., Frans Halsmuseum, Haarlem, and Worcester Art Museum, MA, 1993 (contains extensive bibliography)

Judith Leyster was one of the few master women painters of Holland's golden age and the only female member of the painters' guild known to have had a workshop. Her work, which consists primarily of scenes from daily life, reflects the interest of ordinary Dutch citizens who at the time were replacing the Church and State as the chief client of artists.

Leyster had a remarkable career in a male-dominated profession. Unlike most women artists of her day, she was not born into an artistic family. Her father was involved in both cloth manufacturing and brewing, two of the major industries in Haarlem, her home town. It is not certain with whom Leyster studied, though she may have first trained in the studio of Frans Pieter de Grebber, a well-established Haarlem master who specialised in portrait and history painting in a traditional manner. It is in connection with the de Grebber family that Leyster was first cited in 1628 – when she was still a teenager – as one who painted with "a good, keen sense" (Ampzing 1628, p.370). Yet, by 1629, the date of her earliest known signed paintings, *Jolly Toper* (Rijksmuseum, Amsterdam; on loan to Frans Halsmuseum, Haarlem) and *Serenade* (Rijksmuseum), Leyster was clearly influenced by Haarlem's most innovative painter, Frans Hals. Like Hals, she incorporated spontaneous poses and bold brushwork to impart a life-like quality to contemporary subjects. Recent technical examination of Leyster's work suggests that, like Hals, she sketched the composition directly on the primed panel or canvas and often revised it in the painting process. If Leyster was associated with Hals's workshop early in her career, she was already asserting her independence by signing her paintings with her monogram, which features a star, a reference to her family name, which translates as "lodestar" or "leading star".

Leyster was also attracted to the work of Frans Hals's younger brother Dirck, who was the leading exponent of small-scale genre scenes of full-length figures. Another artist who influenced Leyster and who was also influenced by Dirck Hals was Jan Miense Molenaer, the man she eventually married. Leyster appears to have been in close contact with both of these artists, even sharing studio props with Molenaer long before their marriage. Although she was clearly influenced by several of her male colleagues, Leyster developed her own style that was crystallised in small, intimate scenes such as *Man Offering Money to a Young Woman* (see illustration), *Young Woman with a Lute* (private collection, London, repr. Haarlem and Worcester 1993, p.83) and *A Game of Tric-Trac* (Worcester Art Museum, MA). In these works Leyster focuses on one or only a few figures with little attention to the interior setting. By carefully orchestrating the artificial light on the figures, who are set against a dark, shadowy background, she creates an intimate mood and an air of mystery.

Leyster's oeuvre is small – only about 20 works are attributed to her – yet in subject and style her captivating scenes of everyday life compose a microcosm of Haarlem genre painting at its height. These so-called realistic scenes, which at the time were referred to as "modern figures" (*moderne beelden*), often incorporate symbolic elements that reflect the moral values of 17th-century Dutch society. For example, in Leyster's *Last Drop* (Philadelphia Museum of Art), two young men are joined by a skeleton holding an hourglass to demonstrate the dire consequences of excessive drinking.

Leyster's focus on paintings of moderate scale and price suggests that she was responding to popular taste. She was among the majority of Haarlem artists who made their living by painting primarily for the open market, then a relatively new form of art patronage that was to transform the art world. In fact, only two of Leyster's surviving works, *Portrait of a Woman* of 1635 and a watercolour of a tulip dated 1643 (both Frans Halsmuseum), may have been commissions.

Leyster's acceptance into the Guild of St Luke in 1633 confirmed her status as a professional artist. Because her father was not a member of the painters' guild, nor was she married to a guild member at the time, she had to join it to receive its benefits, which included the right to sell art in the local market. Guild membership also enabled Leyster to establish a workshop and take on students. She is known to have had at least three male pupils.

Leyster appears to have painted most of her pictures between 1629 and 1635 when she was single. After her marriage to Molenaer in 1636 she appears to have spent her time bringing up their children and helping with her husband's business, which included both painting and art dealing. Only one of her known works, the watercolour of a tulip, bears a date after her marriage. And yet in 1648, just before she and Molenaer settled back in Haarlem after spending a decade in Amsterdam, she was still referred to in her home town as "the true leading star in art" (Schrevel 1648, pp.384–5), which suggests the community's pride in its women artists.

In spite of her fame during her lifetime, Leyster was virtually forgotten from the time of her death until the end of the 19th century. During this time many of her works were attributed to Frans Hals, including two of her most celebrated paintings, *Self-Portrait* (National Gallery of Art, Washington, DC)

Leyster: *Man Offering Money to a Young Woman*, 1631; Mauritshuis Museum, The Hague

and *Young Flute Player* (Nationalmuseum, Stockholm). It was the discovery of Leyster's monogram on her *Carousing Couple* (Louvre, Paris) that led to the first study on her in 1893 written by Cornelis Hofstede de Groot. One hundred years later, in 1993, the Frans Halsmuseum and the Worcester Art Museum co-organised the first retrospective exhibition of Leyster's work.

JAMES A. WELU

See also Guilds and the Open Market survey

Liebe, Marianne *see* Brandt

Liepiṇa-Skulme, Marta *see* Skulme

Lijn, Liliane

American sculptor, 1939–

Born Liliane Segall in New York, 22 December 1939; adopted the name Lijn, 1961. Moved to Switzerland with her family, mid-1950s. Studied archaeology at the Sorbonne, Paris, 1958–9; history of art at Ecole du Louvre, Paris, 1959–60; interrupted studies to teach herself to draw. Married the artist Takis, 1961; two children; divorced 1967. Lived in New York, 1961–2; Paris, 1963–4; Athens, 1964–6; London from 1966. Recipient of Arts Council of Great Britain awards, 1976 and 1981; Alecto award, Bradford Print Biennale, 1976; Arts Council bursary for holograph *Crossing Map*, 1982. Lives in London.

Selected Individual Exhibitions

La Librairie Anglaise, Paris: 1963
Indica Gallery, London: 1967
Hanover Gallery, London: 1970
Galerie Germain, Paris: 1972
Bill Jordan Gallery, London: 1973
Serpentine Gallery, London: 1976–7 (*Beyond Light*, touring, organised by Arts Council of Great Britain)
Alecto Gallery, London: 1977
Central Art Gallery, Wolverhampton: 1979
Eagle Walk Gallery, Milton Keynes: 1980
Roundhouse Gallery, London: 1980
Aberdeen Art Gallery: 1983
Paton Gallery, London: 1983
Galerie Peter Ludwig, Cologne: 1985
Fischer Fine Art, London: 1987
National Art Library, Victoria and Albert Museum, London: 1993

Selected Writings

Six Throws of the Oracular Keys, Paris: De la Nepe, 1982
Crossing Map, London: Thames and Hudson, 1983
"Imagine the Goddess! A rebirth of the female archetype in sculpture", *Leonardo*, xx, 1987, pp.123–30

Bibliography

Cyril Barrett, "Art as research", *Studio International*, clxxiii, 1967, pp.314–16
Vera Lindsay, "Liliane Lijn", *Studio International*, clxxvii, 1969, pp.219–23 (interview)
Jeremy Rees, "Public sculpture", *Studio International*, clxxxiv, 1972, pp.10–15, 26
Beyond Light: Liliane Lijn, Bill Culbert, exh. cat., Arts Council of Great Britain, London, 1976
Cyril Barrett, "Liliane Lijn, Bill Culbert", *Art Monthly*, February 1977, pp.19–20
Hayward '78, exh. cat., Arts Council of Great Britain, London, 1978
Prism Figures, Prism Stones, Public Projects, exh. brochure, Aberdeen Art Gallery, 1983
Cathy Courtney, "Liliane Lijn: Headpieces exhibited at the Venice Biennale", *Crafts*, no.83, November–December 1986, p.57
Imagine the Goddess: Liliane Lijn, exh. cat., Fischer Fine Art, London, 1987
"Liliane Lijn", *Contemporary Artists*, ed. Colin Naylor, 3rd edition, London and Chicago: St James Press, 1989, pp.561–4
Liliane Lijn: Poem Machines, 1962–1968, exh. cat., National Art Library, Victoria and Albert Museum, London, 1993
Frank Popper, *Art of the Electronic Age*, London: Thames and Hudson, and New York: Abrams, 1993
The Sixties Art Scene in London, exh. cat., Barbican Art Gallery, London, 1993

Liliane Lijn has been most readily associated with the international Kinetic art movement that was becoming prominent during the early 1960s when she first started to exhibit. Her work, however, has been diverse and interdisciplinary. She has produced sculptures, poetry, performances, a video, a film and artist's books. Her central aims are comparable with those of her former husband, the Greek Kinetic sculptor Takis: that is, a fundamental concern with natural forces and the sub-atomic energy that animates all matter. Lijn emphasises the fact that she had no formal artistic education and she draws upon diverse formative influences. Typically, these combine the poetic with a love of mathematical structure and precision. In the visual arts she cites ancient Greek and Egyptian statuary, Hieronymus Bosch and Piet Mondrian. She also draws on an interest in science – in particular physics. Her working process is typically one of experimentation with materials, likened to research in a quasi-scientific mode. Ideas and research are translated into precise drawings from which technicians can work.

During the early 1960s Lijn turned away from painting, rejecting its fine art associations. She believed that "images block reality" (Aberdeen 1983) and underwent a period of experimentation with processes and materials – plastics, Perspex, fire and acid – that developed into her earliest moving mechanism, *Vibrographe*. *Poem Machines* of 1962–8 (e.g. *Sky Never Stops*, 1965; National Art Library, Victoria and Albert Museum, London) evolved from this spinning cylinder and were produced collaboratively with a poet friend. Evocative words were cut out of poems and applied in Letraset to motorised cylinders or cones. As the cylinder spins the words become lines and patterns, jump and read non-sequentially, and create "after-colours". Placement and size of text and the speed of rotation all enhance this effect. The intention was consistent throughout: "I want the word to be seen in movement splitting itself into a pure vibration until it becomes the energy of sound" ("Imagine the Goddess!", 1987, p.128).

Liquid Reflections (1967–8; made as a multiple; example in Tate Gallery, London) consolidated Lijn's experiments with reflected or refracted light and motion. A combination of water and oil creates droplets of condensed water that act as natural lenses. The liquid droplets are sandwiched behind a clear Perspex turntable on which rest two or more Perspex balls. A light is trained on the disc and a motor revolves it slowly, setting the balls in a random pattern of motion across its surface. The water "lenses" are magnified and refracted within the balls, and the combination of motion and light creates a hypnotic effect.

During the 1970s Lijn continued to work with the vocabulary of forms and materials that she had established with her early machines. Her working process during this time was systematic as she explored a limited range of forms: cones (or koans), light columns and prisms. Sculptures such as *White Koan* (1972; City Sculpture Project, Peter Stuyvesant Foundation; now University of Warwick, Coventry) are characterised by their creation of optical illusions through slow movement and light. As the Koan spins slowly, the solidity of the form is dematerialised as the eye focuses on the undulations of the lines of light. Lijn's spelling of Koan indicates her intention: Koan is a Zen Buddhist term meaning a question without an answer.

Throughout the 1970s Lijn balanced monumental public commissions and projects with more intimate works made for gallery exhibition. *Thru Another Eye* (1974–5; whereabouts unknown, repr. London 1976, cover) developed Lijn's interest in the manipulation of the spectator's visual experience. A precise alignment of lenses and a light column meant that the refraction of light could be seen only from a particular point, by one person. The spectator's movement altered the distortion of the light – magnifying or refracting it. Increasingly, Lijn concentrated on the optical transformations and perceptual experience of the spectator rather than the actual motion of her sculptures. These concerns were resolved in the monumental public project *Split Spiral Spin* (1980), commissioned by the Warrington Development Corporation, Birchwood Science Park, Warrington. In this case it is the spectator's movement around and between the two spiral parabolas that creates an optical illusion. Overlapping screens of steel mesh create patterns of interference as the spectator moves, and the direction of natural light transforms the sculpture from an opaque structure to one that is transparent and open.

From the late 1970s there was a marked diversification in Lijn's work and an increased self-awareness of her position as a woman artist. A shift towards figuration can be seen in *Queen of Hearts – Queen of Diamonds* (1981; repr. "Imagine the Goddess!", 1987, p.129) and about this time Lijn started to introduce new materials and techniques with overtly feminine associations. *Feathered Lady* (1979; *idem*) combines a prism and aluminium frame with feathers and glass beads. For *Heshe* (1979; *ibid.*, p.128), she used a technique of weaving highly coloured synthetic fibres to create luxurious tresses and velvety bristle. Lijn explains her earlier use of industrial materials, geometric form and restrained colour as a perceived need to "efface any trace of myself" (*ibid.*, p.130).

The turning point in Lijn's imagery is encapsulated in her book *Crossing Map* (1983), which presents an oblique autobiography in the form of a poetic account of a woman artist's

Lijn: *Electric Bride*, 1990; mixed media, sculpture drama

process of self-discovery and creativity. While still referring to energy, light and matter, the expression of ideas about natural forces are translated into terms of the feminine and the masculine. Since the 1980s Lijn has developed her exploration of archetypes in a series of larger-than-life sculptures of goddesses. *Lady of the Wild Things* (1983) and *Woman of War* (1984–5; both artist's collection) are triggered by human proximity and perform a dramatic ritual involving song, light, a laser beam and a smoke machine. Similarly, *The Bride* and *Electric Bride* (1990; see illustration) combine sculpture and performance. Where *Woman of War* represented a triumphant, warrior-like aspect of the feminine, the *Brides* concern themselves with a narrative of sacrifice and surrender. Collectively, they are entirely unconventional images of female power, combining science fiction technology, futuristic armour, vivid "plumage" and translucent "veils". Their inspiration lies in non-Western and pre-Christian mythologies and rituals. Lijn's aim was to create the essential image of powerful and sexual womanhood – the archetypal Goddess in her "genetic memory" (*idem*). The Goddess sculptures relate to and extend Lijn's fundamental interest in energy and mutability. The reconciliation of dualisms – transparency and opacity, light and dark, positive and negative – has been a consistent feature of her work and these ideas are re-interpreted on a metaphorical level.

Lijn's current projects have an autobiographical focus. She is working on a personal history, initially concentrating on her mother's memories. Experiments for new sculptures include fragmented body casts, and Lijn hopes to combine both projects to explore aspects of her own femininity. Broadly speaking, Lijn's work concerns itself with transformation on many levels: literal, metaphorical and spiritual. She stated: "I intend the final 'object' to be a SUBJECT, in other words an active transformer and emittor of energies received" (Naylor 1989). This implies the active participation of the spectator and a manipulation of their responses. Visually, Liliane Lijn's work is distinct by virtue of its precision. The tendency to give her sculptures an industrial finish and her use of man-made materials give an aesthetic sophistication to her mature works. Although the sheer diversity of Kinetic art makes it difficult to make useful comparisons between artists, Lijn's work distinguishes itself by subtle subversion: the irony of a woman creating poetic and idealistic objects from materials associated with a "man's world" of technology and warfare.

SIOBHAN DOUGHERTY

Likarz-Strauss, Maria

Austrian textile artist, designer and painter, 1893–1971

Born in Przemyśl, Poland, 18 March 1893. Studied at the Kunstschule für Frauen und Mädchen, Vienna, under Otto Friedrich, 1908–10; Kunstgewerbeschule, Vienna, under Anton von Kenner and Josef Hoffmann, 1911–c.1915. Member of the Wiener Werkstätte, Vienna, 1912–14 and 1920–31; head of fashion department, 1924–5. Member of Österreichischer Werkbund and Wiener Frauenkunst, Vienna. Taught at the Kunstgewerbeschule Burg Giebichenstein, Halle an der Saale, c.1915–20. Moved to Italy, November 1918. Fled with her Jewish husband to a Yugoslavian island owned by the family, 1938. Worked for a ceramics factory in Rome, 1950s–60s. Died in Rome, March 1971.

Principal Exhibitions

Deutscher Werkbund, Cologne: 1914
Österreichisches Museum für Kunst und Industrie, Vienna: 1915 (*Modeausstellung*), 1923 (*Modernes, österreichisches Kunsthandwerk*), 1925 (*Christliche Kunst*), 1930 (*Werkbundausstellung*)
Kunstschau, Vienna: 1920
Deutsche Gewerbeschau, Munich: 1922
Exposition Internationale des Arts Décoratifs et Industriels Modernes, Paris: 1925 (gold medal)
Wiener Frauenkunst, Künstlerhaus, Vienna: 1927–33

Bibliography

Alex Koch, *Deutsche Werkkunst: Arbeiten deutscher und österreichischer Künstler auf der Werkbund-Ausstellung, Köln*, Darmstadt: Koch, 1916
E. Hofmann, "Die malerin Maria Strauss-Likarz", *Deutsche Kunst und Dekoration*, lxviii, Darmstadt, 1931
H. Ankwicz-Kleehoven, "Die Wiener Werkstätte", *Alte und Moderne Kunst*, xii/92, 1967
Die Wiener Werkstätte: Modernes Kunsthandwerk von 1903–1932, exh. cat., Österreichisches Museum für angewandte Kunst, Vienna, 1967
Waltraud Neuwirth, *Die Keramik der Wiener Werkstätte*, i: *Originalkeramiken, 1920–1931*, Vienna: Neuwirth, 1981
Isabelle Anscombe, *A Woman's Touch: Women in Design from 1860 to the Present Day*, London: Virago, and New York: Viking, 1984
Traude Hansen, *Wiener Werkstätte: Mode, Stoffe, Schmuck, Accessoires*, Vienna: Brandstatter, 1984
Werner J. Schweiger, *Wiener Werkstätte: Designs in Vienna, 1903–1932*, New York: Abbeville, and London: Thames and Hudson, 1984 (German original, 1982)
Angela Völker, *Wiener Mode und Modefotographie: Die Modeabteilung der Wiener Werkstätte, 1911–1932*, Munich: Schneider-Henn, 1984 (catalogue of the Österreichisches Museum für angewandte Kunst, Vienna)
Astrid Gmeiner and Gottfried Pirhofer, *Der Österreichische Werkbund*, Salzburg: Residenz, 1985
Elisabeth Schmuttermeier, "Die Wiener Werkstätte", *Traum und Wirklichkeit, Wien, 1870–1930*, exh. cat., Historisches Museum der Stadt Wien, Vienna, 1985
Jane Kallir, *Viennese Design and the Wiener Werkstätte*, New York: Braziller, and London: Thames and Hudson, 1986
Schmuck von 1900–1925, exh. cat., Österreichisches Museum für angewandte Kunst, Vienna, 1986
Wiener Werkstätte: Atelier viennois, 1903–1932: Europalia, exh. cat., Brussels, 1987
Wien um 1900, exh. cat., Sezon Museum of Art, Tokyo, and elsewhere, 1989
E. Michitsch, *Frauen-Kunst-Kunsthandwerk: Künstlerinnen der Wiener Werkstätte*, diploma dissertation, University of Vienna, 1993
Japonismus, exh. cat., Sezon Museum of Art, Tokyo, 1994
S. Plakolm-Forsthuber, *Künstlerinnen in Österreich, 1897–1938*, Vienna: Picus, 1994
Angela Völker, *Textiles of the Wiener Werkstätte, 1910–1932*, London: Thames and Hudson, 1994; as *The Wiener Werkstätte Textiles*, New York: Rizzoli, 1994 (German original, 1990)

Manuscript collection is in the Archiv der Wiener Werkstätte, Österreichisches Museum für angewandte Kunst, Vienna.

Maria Likarz's artistic education began in 1911 at the Kunstgewerbeschule in Vienna, where she was particularly impressed by the enamelling classes taken by Anton von Kenner and the design classes for fashion, fabrics, graphics and stencils taken by Josef Hoffmann. At this time, the Kunstgewerbeschule was working closely with the Kaiserlich-Königlich Museum für Kunst und Industrie. Each of these institutions passed on to her its own, very specific ideology, which emphasised a training in craft skills as well as aesthetic taste. A successful artistic career was guaranteed only by combining both these aspects and applying them to all the areas of the arts and crafts that surround our daily lives. The pupils thus had their own training workshops, and any division in the school between the artists who designed objects and those who made them was avoided.

Likarz must have impressed Hoffmann right from the start, because by 1912 she was already working at the Wiener Werkstätte. The Werkstätte had been founded in 1903 by two professors at the Kunstgewerbeschule, Hoffmann and Koloman Moser, and by the industrialist Fritz Wärndorfer, who acted as financier. On 19 May 1903 the Wiener Werkstätte Produktiv Genossenschaft von Kunsthandwerkern in Wien (Wiener Werkstätte Cooperative Association of Arts and Crafts Workers of Vienna) was incorporated. The purpose of the Association was

the promotion of the economic interests of its members through training and education of the same in arts and crafts, by manufacturing objects from all genres of arts and crafts to the designs of other artist members, by establishing workshops, and by the sale of the work produced by the members [extract from the companies register in Vienna].

The Werkstätte not only made the highest artistic demands on its members; it also insisted on great flexibility in working with a wide variety of different materials.

Likarz's earliest designs – independent, elegant versions of the style of the time – may well have coloured her whole career. Attenuated and distorted figures mixed with geometric motifs are scattered over the surfaces. The faces are reminiscent of designs that became popular in the 1950s. Her debut was probably at the great Deutscher Werkbund exhibition in Cologne in 1914. Eduard Josef Wimmer-Wisgrill, head of the fashion department, where she was working at the time, designed the Werkstätte's exhibition space and planned a whole wall of "costume sketches", including some by Likarz. Although in France the use of fashion sketches in publicity was a well-established practice even before World War I, in Vienna they were only now being used, despite the high quality of the designs to be promoted. Immediately afterwards, the first port-folio edition appeared: *Mode Wien 1914/15*, featuring work by Likarz and other leading lights of the Werkstätte such as Dagobert Peche and Wimmer-Wisgrill. She went on to do even more to fill this gap in the market by producing numerous fashion designs for postcards (more than 80 of them before she left the Werkstätte).

Despite her initial success, from 1915/16 to 1920 Likarz took a teaching post at the Kunstgewerbeschule in Halle, where she taught mainly enamelling. She kept up her contact with the Werkstätte during this time, however, and from 1918 designed boxes, snuff-boxes, caskets, clocks and other objects in enamelled silver. While the forms are characterised by extreme simplicity, the style of the figures and ornament reveals Likarz's modernist interests and her leaning towards Expressionism, a tendency that was always present at the Werkstätte.

In 1920, the year she returned to work at the Werkstätte, Likarz took part in the Kunstschau. The journal *Deutsche Kunst und Dekoration* (DKD) singled out the "charm of the humour of her painting and the inventive arrangement of the space" of her painted boxes and glasses for special praise. On account of Likarz's liking for surface decoration, Hoffmann allowed her to work on a "lady's rest-room", which was on display at the exhibition of Austrian craft at the Österreichis-ches Museum für Kunst und Industrie and at the Paris Exposition of 1925. Appropriate to the brief, Likarz painted the centre of the wall above the large bed with a coquettish Venus and other scenes in simulated marquetry.

Like Peche, Likarz favoured fantastic, bizarre decoration. Following his famous example, in 1925 she designed a second wallpaper collection for the firm Flammersheim & Steinmann in Cologne. That same year the *DKD* praised her work: "The artist has taken old patterns from the eighteenth and nine-teenth centuries and freely recreated them." In 1927, with Hoffmann, she decorated the Vienna flat of Director-General Bauer. For the walls, she returned to the traditional medium of painting in an abstract design that covered only part of the otherwise blank surfaces, creating a very transparent effect (a predilection for large empty spaces can also be seen in

Likarz-Strauss: *Ireland*, 1910–12; textile

Hoffmann's work from his earlier Secession period). The versa-tility apparent in Likarz's designs is typical of the pluralism of style that the Werkstätte publicised for their different types of work.

Right from the start, however, her *métier* at the Werkstätte was fashion and fabrics. From 1912 onwards Likarz designed a vast range of beautiful patterns in varied styles, some of which broke new ground, such as *Ireland*, a fabric pattern of 1910–12 (see illustration); its bold geometric design, reflecting the international trend towards abstraction, was exceptional even then. Only the Russian artists Varvara Stepanova (q.v.) and Sonia Delaunay (q.v.) were creating comparable work at this time. Likarz designed almost 200 patterns. Influenced by Peche, some consisted of stylised flowers, others were purely geometric. They are all designs of their time, yet they possess a timeless air. This quality is typical of all her work, including her fashion designs.

Likarz's designs for clothes that were actually manufactured are documented from 1918 onwards. The papers reported: "Mrs Strauss-Likarz's clothes are simple and yet tasteful, making allowances for the personal stamp". From 1922 onwards the extant fashion sketches from the Werkstätte's fashion department are virtually all dated by Likarz. In the late 1920s she more or less took over the running of the fashion department, and had a major influence on the styles produced there until its closure in 1931. Völker said that the Werkstätte's achievements in fashion constituted a "leap from a purely artistic 'rational dress' to practical, generally fashionable clothing", and emphasised that these achievements were made "by designers who were not in any way trained as creators of fashion, but regarded themselves as craft workers – such as Maria Likarz". The only thing known about Likarz-Strauss's artistic career after she left the Wiener Werkstätte is that she worked in Rome as a potter – a medium she had hardly touched while at the Werkstätte.

GABRIELE FABIANKOWITSCH

Lim, Kim
British sculptor and printmaker, 1936–

Born in Singapore, 1936. Studied at St Martin's School of Art, London, 1954–6; Slade School of Fine Art, London, 1956–60. Married sculptor William Turnbull, 1960. Lives in London.

Selected Individual Exhibitions
Axiom Gallery, London: 1966, 1968
Waddington Galleries, London: 1973, 1990
Alpha Gallery, Singapore: 1974
Museum of Modern Art, Oxford: 1975
Felicity Samuel Gallery, London: 1975
Tate Gallery, London: 1977
Roundhouse Gallery, London: 1979 (retrospective)
Southampton Museum and Art Gallery: 1981
Nicola Jacobs Gallery, London: 1982, 1984, 1985
Arcade Gallery, Harrogate, Yorkshire: 1983
National Museum of Art Gallery, Singapore: 1984
Yorkshire Sculpture Park, Wakefield: 1995

Bibliography
Kim Lim, exh. cat., Axiom Gallery, London, 1966
Gene Baro, "The work of Kim Lim", Studio International, clxxvi, 1968, pp.186–9
Kim Lim: Graphics, exh. cat., Tate Gallery, London, 1977
"Kim Lim", The Tate Gallery, 1974–6: Illustrated Catalogue of Acquisitions, London: Tate Gallery, 1978, pp.125–7
Kim Lim, exh. cat., Nicola Jacobs Gallery, London, 1982
Margaret Garlake, "Kim Lim at Nicola Jacobs", Art Monthly, no.61, November 1982, pp.13–14
Denise Hooker, "Kim Lim: Nicola Jacobs Gallery", Arts Review, xxxiv, 5 November 1982, p.581 Martin Holman, "Kim Lim at Nicola Jacobs", Artscribe, no.38, December 1982, pp.55–6
Kim Lim, exh. cat., National Museum of Art Gallery, Singapore, 1984
Larry Berryman, "Kim Lim: Nicola Jacobs Gallery", Arts Review, xxxviii, 8 November 1985, pp.569–70
Mel Gooding, "Kim Lim", Art Monthly, no.92, December 1985–January 1986, pp.19–20
Penelope Curtis, Modern British Sculpture from the Collection, Liverpool: Tate Gallery Publications, 1988
Kim Lim, exh. cat., Waddington Galleries, London, 1990
British Abstract Art: Part 2: Sculpture, exh. cat., Flowers East, London, 1995
Kim Lim: Sculpture and Works on Paper, exh. cat., Yorkshire Sculpture Park, Wakefield, 1995

In 1954, when Kim Lim moved to London from Singapore to attend St Martin's School of Art, she concentrated from the start on sculpture, attracted by the immediate physical connection between artist and medium. Her generation of young British sculptors rejected the figurative, expressionistic style prevalent in the post-war years, seeking instead a reiteration of the basic formal properties of the sculpture as autonomous object. Lim executed her first works in wood, sometimes whitened to emphasise the natural texture of the material. They reveal the interest in the surfaces of forms over volumetric shapes that continues in Lim's mature work. Throughout her career, she has worked on an intimate, human scale, distinguishing her from others who participated in the redefinition of abstract sculpture in the 1960s. Her more recent works display an affiliation with the natural world, especially the shifting effects of light and shadow. A preoccupation with space and rhythm also informs Lim's prolific output of prints, which complement her work in sculpture.

While studying at the Slade, Lim frequented museums and art libraries in London, where she was attracted by the sculpture of Brancusi, and travelled to Greece, encountering Cycladic sculptures for the first time: "These things seemed a great gift; they excited my own feelings and brought me closer to finding a sculptural form for those feelings" (Baro 1968, p.187). Samurai (1961; Arts Council of Great Britain), an asymmetric construction of rough wood with the presence of a primitive, ritualistic object, predicts the balance between heavy material and delicate appearance in Lim's totems of two decades later.

After the Slade, Lim made larger but flatter sculptures in laminated wood and steel, for example, Borneo II (1964; painted steel; repr. London 1966, no.8), Candy (1965; painted wood; ibid., no.10) and Day (1966, painted steel; repr. Baro 1968, p.187). These early works share a vocabulary of convex and concave curves that, combined with their flat silhouettes, stresses the edges of forms. They demonstrate Lim's urge towards simplification and the implication of volume without massiveness, that is, to "give the experience of more than is there" (ibid., p.188). R.R. (1965; painted steel; repr. London 1966, no.9) marks her first use of receding planes: a thin arc mounted flat side on a base reads against a slightly bigger arc that, in turn, sits before a vertical post crowned with a circle. The strict frontal orientation underlines the stepped progression of each element, as in Step (1966; painted steel; repr. Baro 1968, p.187). Several works of the 1960s explore form in relation to negative space, for example, the three upright slats in Split (1966; anodised aluminium; ibid., p.186). Echo (1967; painted steel; ibid., p.187) resembles an odd vessel; two curves cut into its sides focus attention on the space contained within. By painting surfaces, Lim achieves uniform textures and, depending on the reflectivity of colour, controls the impression of mass.

During the same period, Lim began placing identical elements directly on the ground in repetitive formations. The three bent steel rectangles of One and a Half (1967; repr. Baro 1968, p.188) may be interpreted as fanning out or converging in. Unlike R.R., this piece invites the viewer to walk around it – each vantage point contributes to the perception of a centre. Another aspect of the patterning of units is the tension between spaces, as seen in the fibreglass Trengannu series (ibid., p.189). In Trengannu II (1967) the alignment of six biomorphic blocks in two rows produces the inverse of the shapes in the intervals between them. Four amorphous rings, more outlines than forms, arranged in a gently curving line in Trengannu III

Lim: *Wind-Stone*, 1989; rose Aurora marble;
97.2 × 70.5 × 28.8 cm.

(1968) almost seem capable of levitating. This floating quality also informs three related drawings (1968).

For her wood sculptures of the 1970s, Lim provided specific instructions for various installations, each manifesting different configurations of light and shadow. *Intervals I and II* (1973; Tate Gallery, London) may be shown individually or together. *Intervals I*, a pine board with rungs protruding from either side, hangs vertically on the wall or leans against it at a slight diagonal. The two parts comprising *Intervals II* either rest vertically against the wall with prongs facing out or in, flat on the floor with prongs facing in, or on the floor with both sets of prongs intersecting. The *Ladder Series* etchings (1972; Flowers Graphics, London) illustrate how Lim often develops her ideas for sculpture and prints simultaneously. Prescribed distances between element and support for *Interstices I, II and III* (1974–5, 1977), planks with cut-out linear sections, and *Link I, II and III* (1975; all artist's collection), narrow wood and acrylic structures, also result in multiple combinations of verticals, horizontals and angles.

Contemplating the body of work on view at her retrospective at the Roundhouse Gallery in 1979, Lim resolved to merge her two successive interests in contour and organised precision by adopting stone as a new material. Whereas her earlier works remained purely self-referential, the sectioning of smooth versus rough textures and flowing incisions carved into the stone suggest the weathering effects of wind or water (*Quadrifed*, 1985; marble; repr. Gooding 1985, no.5; *Source II*, 1988, granite; repr. London 1990, no.7; *Wind-Stone*, 1989; see illustration) and the growth and movement of plants (*Frond*, 1983; Portland stone; and *Padma I*, 1983; French stone; *ibid.*, nos 3 and 6). These allusions to nature find parallels in her prints. In the etching *Spring* (1979; Flowers Graphics) two triangles of fine cross-hatching almost meet to form a square. The stark white line dividing them serves the same structural function as the dark striations in the white irregular slabs, *Oblique* (1980–81; Portland stone) and *Trace II* (1982; limestone; both repr. London 1982). The diagonally rippling lines in the aquatint *Wind/Water Series* (1985; repr. *Ninth British International Print Biennale*, Bradford, 1986, no.14) recall those carved into the marble *Wind/Water Series I* (1983; Collection Mildred Tao Ong, Singapore) and *Breeze* (1985; repr. *Black and White*, exh. cat., Nicola Jacobs Gallery, London, 1987, no.16).

Lim selects stones that she can manoeuvre on her own without an assistant. This smallness of scale combined with the modulations of surface uphold her early desire to express weightlessness. When combined in multiples, the flat white horizontal blocks become stepping stones (*Flow*, 1982; Portland stone; repr. London 1982; *Naga*, 1984; Portland stone; repr. Gooding 1985, no.10) or bench-like components of a Japanese garden (*Spiral III*, 1983; Portland stone; Collection Alistair McAlpine). The quiet, meditative mood that they impart has often been ascribed to Lim's Asian heritage.

Lim's columnar works, usually just one metre high, endow static material with a sense of rising from the ground. *Column(s)* (1982; Portland stone; repr. London 1982) and *Stele* (1985; Portland stone; repr. Gooding 1985, no.11) are each constructed from three stacked slabs, one totem-like and the other stepped. Both *Caryatid* (1985; Portland stone; Collection E.J. Power) and *Langkawi* (1988; white Sicilian marble; repr. London 1990, no.9) consist of one block engraved with vertically sweeping lines. A pair of upright slabs compare with screens (*Dyad*, 1985; Portland stone; repr. Gooding 1985, no.9), while four are attached to the wall as reliefs (*Stone-cuts*, 1985; Portland stone; *ibid.*, no.8). Several prints superimpose diagonals over a rectangle in similar references to a screen or window (*Time Shift*, 1993; set of six screen prints; Flowers Graphics).

Lim's sculptures have more recently become increasingly monolithic and less frontal. In place of incisions, they bear subtle indentations (*Eve*, 1987; Carrara marble; repr. London 1990, no.11), gradations in height (*Kudah*, 1989; Rose Aurora marble; *ibid.*, no.2) or deep cuts on all four sides (*Gingko*, 1989; Rose Aurora marble; *ibid.*, no.1). A revisitation of the themes of budding flowers appears in *Padma IV and V* (1987 and 1988; white marble and Rose Aurora marble; *ibid.*, nos 5 and 10) and of the erosion of rocks swept over by water in *Sea Stone* (1989; Rose Aurora marble; *ibid.*, no.4). The semicircular shape of her metal sculptures recurs in the three sections of *Segments* (1988; Rose Aurora marble; *ibid.*, no.8) swelling over their base. There exists a greater interplay of abraded and smooth planes, highlighting the flecks of grey, brown or pink in the marble (*River-Stone*, 1991–2; Calacatta Siena marble;

repr. *Sculpture*, exh. cat., Waddington Galleries, London, 1992, no.41). Lim's central concern with the ephemeral effects of light on the refined surfaces of her sculptures remains constant; their seeming response to the transient passage of natural elements lends her works an aura of timelessness.

MARY CHAN

Lindegren, Amalia (Euphrosyne)
Swedish painter, 1814–1891

Born in Stockholm, 23 May 1814, the illegitimate daughter of a Swedish nobleman; brought up with her father's family. Studied under Sophie Adlersparre, a portrait painter and copyist, from 1842. Gained admission to the Antique School of the Royal Academy of Fine Arts, Stockholm, with the help of sculptor Carl Gustaf Qvarnström, 1847; studied in the Lower Antique School at the Academy, 1849. Awarded a government scholarship to study in Paris, 1850; studied first at the women's atelier of Léon Cogniet, then under Ange Tissier, c.1851–3. Subsequently visited Munich and spent a year working in Rome, 1854–5. Returned to Stockholm, 1856. Trip to Dalarna, a backward region of Sweden, 1857; further trips to Paris, 1859, and Düsseldorf, 1861. Recipient of Litteris et Artibus medal, Royal Academy of Fine Arts, Stockholm, 1866. Associate member, 1850, and member, 1856, Royal Academy of Fine Arts, Stockholm; honorary member, Society of Women Artists, London. Died in Stockholm, 27 December 1891.

Principal Exhibitions

Royal Academy of Fine Arts, Stockholm: occasionally 1843–85
Paris Salon: 1853
International Exhibition, London: 1862
International Exhibition, Dublin: 1865
Exposition Universelle, Paris: 1867
Weltausstellung, Vienna: 1873

Bibliography

Amalia Fahlstedt, "Amalia Lindegren: Några intryck" [Amalia Lindegren: A few impressions], *Dagny*, i, 1892
G. Nordensvan, "Amalia Lindegren", *Idun*, no.2, 1892
Clara Erskine Clement, *Women in the Fine Arts*, Boston: Houghton Mifflin, 1904; reprinted New York: Hacker, 1974
A. Roosval, *Svenska kvinnor i bild* [Pictures of Swedish women], 1936
Kvinnor som målat [Women who painted], exh. cat., Nationalmuseum, Stockholm, 1975
Ingrid Ingelman, "Women artists in Sweden: A two-front struggle", *Woman's Art Journal*, v/1, 1984, pp.1–7
Eva-Lena Bengtsson, "Amalia Lindegren: Aspects of a 19th-century artist", *Woman's Art Journal*, v/2, 1984–5, pp.16–20

Born in the early 19th century, Amalia Lindegren belonged to the pioneer generation of women artists in Sweden. Her artistic talents were discovered and promoted by Carl Gustaf Qvarnström, a professor at the Royal Academy of Fine Arts in Stockholm, who saw to it that she got an opportunity to study at its Antique School, together with two other women. The 1848 review of the Royal Academy for the previous year singled out "Demoiselle Lindegren, who is already making portraits rather cleverly", and goes on to say that if she had been a regular pupil of the Academy she would most probably have received an award. In 1848 Lindegren was admitted to the Lower Antique School of the Academy, where she drew from plaster casts of antique sculpture. Altogether 26 students were trained here, six of them women. Again Lindegren was mentioned for her talents, together with her fellow-students Elise Brandt and Mathilda Brandström, all of them a good deal older than the male students. In 1850 Lindegren received an official travel grant from the Board of the Academy that took her to Paris, Germany, Italy and back to Paris, where her principal teacher was Ange Tissier. Although she studied in Paris, her paintings show a strong resemblance to the style of the Düsseldorf Academy. The anecdotal genre painting of this school was immensely popular and attracted a great many Norwegian, Swedish and Finnish painters, whereas Danish artists were dissuaded from studying in Düsseldorf, which was considered to be a harmful artistic influence.

During her time in Paris Lindegren produced her own genre paintings in the traditional vein, for example *Old Man and Two Orphans*, also called *Grandfather's Teaching* (exh. Paris Salon 1853; Nasjonalgalleriet, Oslo), which shows an old grandfather seated deep in thought under the portrait of his dead daughter, while his two grandchildren wait for him to speak. From Paris she sent home a jolly *Drinking Scene*, or, *Merry Company* (1852), depicting two men and a woman seated at a table laden with fruit, which created great interest. She was praised for her careful execution, and the subject, which was derived from Dutch 17th-century painting, was remarked upon as an unusually audacious one for a woman artist. Paintings inspired by her Italian trip include *Italian Mother and Child* (1854–5; private collection, repr. Bengtsson 1984, fig.2), showing the influence of Raphael, *Italian Beggar* (1855; Göteborgs Konstmuseum, Göteborg) and *Girl with an Orange* (Nationalmuseum, Stockholm), which was purchased by the Swedish government in 1856.

On her return to Sweden in 1856, Lindegren became a member of the Royal Academy of Fine Arts in Stockholm, which did not open its department for women students until 1864. She found it comparatively easy to make a living as a portrait painter, executing some excellent portraits and receiving royal commissions (e.g. *Queen Lovisa*, 1859; Gripsholm Castle; *Princess Lovisa*, 1869); she also depicted one of the most influential of the Scandinavian "Düsseldorfers", the painter of Norwegian folklore *Adolph Tidemand* (1862; Göteborgs Konstmuseum). She found in addition a market for her genre paintings, and some of her most popular themes were derived from the province of Dalarna, a picturesque region of Sweden with colourful folk costumes, to which Anders Zorn gave immense fame at the Salons at the end of the 19th century. Amalia Lindegren can be very coy in her saccharine treatment of the lowly life (e.g. *Sunday Afternoon in a Dalecarlian Farmhouse*, 1860; repr. Ingelman 1984; *Peasants in Dalarna Mourning Their Dead Child*, wood engraving from *Ny Illustrerad Tidning*, 1866; repr. Bengtsson 1984, fig. 3; and *Jumping Jack*, 1879; see illustration), but her paintings had great popular appeal, and many were mass-produced in a variety of media.

CHARLOTTE CHRISTENSEN

Lindegren: *Jumping Jack*, 1879; oil on canvas; 92 × 75.5 cm.; Göteborgs Konstmuseum, Sweden

Lisiewska, Anna Rosina

German painter, 1713–1783

Born in Berlin, 10 July 1713; elder sister of Anna Dorothea Lisiewska-Therbusch (q.v.). Trained by her father, George Lisiewski. Married Berlin portrait painter David Matthieu, 1741; daughter Rosina Ludovica born 1748, son Leopold born 1750 (both became painters); also stepmother and teacher of Georg David Matthieu; husband died 1755. Married Ludwig de Gasc, 1760. Moved to Braunschweig, c.1764; appointed court painter, 1777. Travelled to the Netherlands, where her son was a student at the academy of drawing in The Hague, 1766–7. Applied for membership of the Dresden Academy, 1769. Died in Dresden, 1783.

Bibliography

Johann Georg Meusel, *Miscellaneen artistischen Inhalts*, Erfurt, 1783

Heinrich Mack and Johannes Lochner, eds, *Leisewitzens Tagebücher*, 2 vols, Weimar, 1916

Lothar Brieger, *Das Pastell*, Berlin, 1921

Elfriede Ferber, "Ein Selbstbildnis der Anna Rosina de Gasc im Provinzialmuseum zu Hannover", *Jahrbuch des Provinzialmuseums zu Hannover*, new series, ii, 1927, pp.87–8

Ludwig Goldscheider, *Five Hundred Self-Portraits from Antique Times to the Present Day*, Vienna: Phaidon, and London: Allen and Unwin, 1937 (German original, 1934)

H. Hardenberg, "De schilderes Rosine de Gasc en haar Haagse relaties" [The painter Rosine de Gasc and her relations in The Hague], *Die Haghe Jaarboek*, 1948–9, pp.139–61

Höfische Bildnisse des Spätbarock, exh. cat., Schloss Charlottenburg, Berlin, 1966

Germaine Greer, *The Obstacle Race: The Fortunes of Women Painters and Their Work*, London: Secker and Warburg, and New York: Farrar Straus, 1979

Helmut Börsch-Supan, *Die Kunst in Brandenburg-Preussen*, Berlin: Mann, 1980

Selbstbildnisse und Künstlerportraits von Lucas van Leyden bis Anton Raphael Mengs, exh. cat., Herzog Anton Ulrich-Museum, Braunschweig, 1980

Helmut Börsch-Supan, *Die Gemälde Antoine Pesnes in den Berliner Schlössern*, Berlin, 1982

Ekhart Berckenhagen, "Anna Dorothea Therbusch", *Zeitschrift des Deutschen Vereins für Kunstwissenschaft*, xli, 1987, pp.118–60

Ekhart Berckenhagen and others, *Antoine Pesne*, Munich, 1987

Das Verborgene Museum I: Dokumente von Frauen in Berliner öffentlichen Sammlungen, exh. cat., Akademie der Künste, Berlin, 1987

Die deutschen Gemälde des 17. und 18. Jahrhunderts, exh. cat., Herzog Anton Ulrich-Museum, Braunschweig, 1989

Die deutschen, französischen und englischen Gemälde des 17. und 18. Jahrhunderts, exh. cat., Niedersächsisches Landesmuseum, Hannover, 1990

Gabriele Armenat, *Frauen aus Braunschweig*, Braunschweig, 1991

Ekhart Berckenhagen, "Anna Rosina Lisiewska-Matthieu-de Gasc", *Niederdeutsche Beiträge zur Kunstgeschichte*, xxxi, 1992, pp.77–114

Menschen-Bilder: Das Bildnis zwischen Spiegelbild und Rollenspiel, exh. cat., Herzog Anton Ulrich-Museum, Braunschweig, 1992

Edith Schoeneck, *Anna Rosina Lisiewska-Matthieu-de Gasc*, dissertation (in preparation)

Like her sister Anna Dorothea Lisiewska-Therbusch (q.v.) and her brother Christian Friedrich Reinhold, Anna Rosina was instructed early on in childhood in portrait painting by her father, the Polish portrait and miniature painter Georg Lisiewski, who worked at the Berlin court and had come to the city in 1692. The meticulous drawing, severity and sometimes a certain stiffness – characteristics of Lisiewski's manner of painting – seen in her early work reveal this training. Her precise rendering of lace and fabric is often in contrast to the seemingly rigid appearance of physiognomy and bodies, which can be seen in the portrait of *Frau von Platen* (c.1734; private collection) as a shepherdess and in the group portrait with a dancing Barbarina (1748; private collection). According to Meusel (1783) she also painted a portrait of her brother, *Christian Friedrich Reinhold* (untraced), when she was only ten years old. When she was 14 she followed her father to Stettin, where she painted a portrait of *Princess Johanna Elisabeth von Anhalt-Zerbst* (untraced) in the same year. She had become an indispensable assistant in her father's studio, the reason she apparently rejected an appointment in Dresden in 1734. Her father's oeuvre was influenced by Adam Manjoki and especially Antoine Pesne, whose works Anna Rosina, like Anna Dorothea, had initially copied. Both in composition and colour, the paintings of her early and middle period up to c.1758 show connections with Pesne's work. In the portrait of *Anna Elisabeth Louise of Prussia* (c.1756; Schloss Charlottenburg, Berlin) Anna Rosina copied one of Pesne's compositions exactly. The three-quarter-length portrait shows the princess with a Moor on her right offering her a bowl of flowers and holding a parasol. She had earlier, around 1733, painted an exact copy of Pesne's portrait of *Princess Anna Friderike of Anhalt Köthen* (Schloss Wernigerode; Pesne's portrait in Schloss Mosigkau). Whether Lisiewska actually had access to Pesne's studio is uncertain.

In 1741 Anna Rosina married the painter David Matthieu, the widower of her sister Dorothea Elisabeth, who had died young. (Matthieu had been appointed court painter and "portrait copyist" at the Berlin court in 1736.) Through the marriage she became the stepmother and teacher of the painter Georg David Matthieu, whose artistic development she substantially supported. Her own children, Rosina Ludovica and Leopold, also turned to painting under her instruction. The extent of artistic co-operation between Lisiewska and Matthieu has not been entirely understood and needs further investigation.

After Matthieu's early death in 1755, Lisiewska took on a commission to create a gallery of beauties in the east wing of Zerbst Castle (destroyed in World War II), with around 70 portraits. Of these, however, only 40 were executed in ten years, and today only one is known, from a slide in the Georgium, Dessau. In the 1740s and early 1750s she received a number of portrait commissions from the royal house of Anhalt-Zerbst. In 1752 she created an impressive, full-length portrait of *Princess Johanna Elisabeth of Anhalt-Zerbst*, which depicts her in a silver-grey dress with the red ribbon of the Russian order of St Anna. She also painted a number of portraits of the princess's daughter, *Sophia Augusta*, the future Empress Catherine the Great. Of those painted in 1740, one portrait could be seen in the St Petersburg Academy and two in the public library in Weimar (untraced). One three-quarter-length portrait (formerly in Zerbst) depicted Catherine while still a Russian grand-princess. A magnificent full-length portrait of the grand-prince and princess from 1756 with a kneeling white pageboy and a little dog is now in Schloss Gripsholm.

Lisiewska: *Self-Portrait*, 1782; 95.8 × 74.4 cm.; Niedersächsisches Landesmuseum, Hannover

The quality of Anna Rosina's oeuvre varies, as does that of other female portrait painters of the 18th century. Numerous copies of particularly successful paintings had to be made for clients, and some of these were very conventional portraits with sitters that were of neither artistic nor picturesque interest to the artist. Her marriage to the much older David Matthieu and the bringing up of her children on her own after her husband's death made it necessary for her to earn a living through a large number of portrait commissions, which inhibited her artistic development. Her second marriage, in 1760, was to the graduate civil servant (*Assessor*) Ludwig de Gasc, who entered the service in Braunschweig around 1766 and finally became a professor at the Carolinum in 1779. From 1764 onwards Lisiewska's name appears in the Braunschweig records, where she was finally appointed court painter in 1777. Through Ludwig de Gasc's friendship with the writer Gotthold Ephraim Lessing, Anna Rosina had access to an enlightened literary circle, which is reflected in her later works executed in Braunschweig. In many of her portraits – especially those of *Philippine Charlotte of Braunschweig-Wolfenbüttel* (Herzog Anton Ulrich-Museum, Braunschweig; Braunschweigisches Landesmuseum, Braunschweig) from the 1770s – Lisiewska achieves a matter-of-fact characterisation of the sitter that probably derives from the notion of naturalness in early classicism. She created remarkable portraits that capture the sitter in a psychologically sensitive way, as in the portrait of *Madame Branconi* (1770; Herzog Anton Ulrich-Museum). The portrait of *Princess Thérèse Natalie of Braunschweig-Wolfenbüttel as Abbess of Gandersheim* (1770; Schloss Charlottenburg, Berlin) mixes the stiffness and severity of a courtly representation with the cosiness of the ambience, characteristic of a time of radical spiritual change.

Anna Rosina's work shows a distinct talent for the precise recording and masterly rendering of shot silks, precious frothy lace and gleaming velvets. A perfect example of this is the full-length portrait of *Thérèse Nathalie of Braunschweig-Wolfenbüttel* (1773; Schloss Ambras, Innsbruck), again depicted as Abbess of Gandersheim. She wears a splendid dark blue velvet dress set off with ermine and sleeves lavishly decorated with lace, painted with great virtuosity. She also wears the ribbon and decoration of the diocese and her left hand rests on the gospel of Gandersheim. The artist depicted with sobriety and slavish precision the gospel and the decoration as well as the medallion that the abbess wears on her right wrist, but at the same time the work is marked by remarkable expressiveness.

Anna Rosina's activity in Braunschweig was interrupted by a journey to the Netherlands in 1766–7 to visit her son, who was studying at The Hague Academy. The journey did not, however, have much influence on her work; only in her *Self-Portrait* (1767; Herzog Anton Ulrich-Museum) are Netherlandish influences, in colouring and subject, visible. Her use of colour shows a typical north German coolness. A cold blue set off with points of white or a cool red with grey shading to a cold blue-green are favourite colour combinations in her painting. She was more inclined towards the sober expression of the Danish painter Johann Georg Ziesenis, whom she knew through the family connections between the courts of Braunschweig and Hannover, than towards the soft elegance of Graff.

A year before her death, a period that was marked by illness, Anna Rosina Lisiewska created her last *Self-Portrait* (1782; see illustration). Her hands placed in her lap, she looks out at the viewer with a melancholy and resigned expression. The composition of her last self-portrait is constructed in large and clearly defined areas. The simplicity of the structure is underlined by the plainness of the dress, simplicity of line and the absence of any peripheral or decorative detail. Like her sister Anna Dorothea, Anna Rosina anticipated the realistic tendency of the 19th-century bourgeois notion of portraiture, which can probably be explained by her contact, through her husband, with the Braunschweig scholarly circle around Lessing. Her circle of clients included the courts of Prussia, von Anhalt-Zerbst and Braunschweig-Wolfenbüttel. In many of the north and middle German courts and galleries the names of Lisiewska and Matthieu appear again and again, and thus provide an example of a typical family and studio business. Anna Rosina Lisiewska-Matthieu-de Gasc was a productive artist whose works were engraved by Haid and Gericke. The recognition received by her sister Anna Dorothea, who had become a member of the Paris and Berlin academies early on, was, however, denied to her. She tried more than once to be accepted into the Dresden Academy, where she was admitted as an "Agréé" in 1769. She probably spent the last years of her life in Dresden, where she died in 1783.

EDITH SCHOENECK

See also Court Artists survey

Lisiewska-Therbusch, Anna Dorothea
German painter, 1721–1782

Born Anna Dorothea Lisiewska in Berlin, 23 July 1721, into a Polish family of artists; younger sister of Anna Rosina Lisiewska (q.v.). Pupil of her father, Georg Lisiewski. Married Berlin inn proprietor Ernst Friedrich Therbusch, 1742; at least three children; husband died 1772. Ceased working professionally after her marriage until 1760. Invited to the court of Duke Karl Eugen von Württemberg in Stuttgart, 1761. Appointed court painter to Elector Palatine Karl Theodor in Mannheim, 1763. Returned to Berlin, 1764. Travelled to Paris, 1765; elected member of the Académie Royale, 1767. Left Paris, 1768, returning to Berlin via Brussels and the Netherlands. Member, Vienna Academy, 1776. Died in Berlin, 9 November 1782.

Principal Exhibitions
Paris Salon: 1767

Bibliography
Johann Georg Meusel, "Lebensumstände der im Jahre 1782 zu Berlin verstorbenen Madame Therbusch", *Miscellaneen artistischen Inhalts*, Erfurt, 1783, pp.266–7

Leopold Reidemeister, *Anna Dorothea Therbusch: Ihr Leben und ihr Werk*, PhD dissertation, Berlin, 1924

Ludwig Goldscheider, *Five Hundred Self-Portraits from Antique Times to the Present Day*, Vienna: Phaidon, and London: Allen and Unwin, 1937 (German original, 1934)

Jean Adhémar and Jean Seznac, eds, *Diderot Salons (1759–1779)*, iii, Oxford: Clarendon Press, 1963

Höfische Bildnisse des Spätbarock, exh. cat., Schloss Charlottenburg, Berlin, 1966

Anna-Dorothea Therbusch, 1721–1782, exh. cat., Kulturhaus Hans Marchwitza, Potsdam-Sanssouci, 1971

Women Artists, 1550–1950, exh. cat., Los Angeles County Museum of Art, and elsewhere, 1976

Germaine Greer, *The Obstacle Race: The Fortunes of Women Painters and Their Work*, London: Secker and Warburg, and New York: Farrar Straus, 1979

Helmut Börsch-Supan, *Die Kunst in Brandenburg-Preussen*, Berlin: Mann, 1980

Ekhart Berckenhagen, "Anna Dorothea Therbusch", *Zeitschrift des Deutschen Vereins für Kunstwissenschaft*, xli, 1987, pp.118–60

Ekhart Berckenhagen and others, *Antoine Pesne*, Munich, 1987

Das Verborgene Museum I: Dokumente von Frauen in Berliner öffentlichen Sammlungen, exh. cat., Akademie der Künste, Berlin, 1987

Die deutschen Gemälde des 17. und 18. Jahrhunderts, exh. cat., Herzog Anton Ulrich Museum, Braunschweig, 1989

"… Ihr werten Frauenzimmer auf!" Malerinnen der Aufklärung, exh. cat., Roselius-Haus, Bremen, 1993

Anna Dorothea Lisiewska-Therbusch was the seventh child of the portrait painter Georg Lisiewski from Olesko in Poland and his wife Maria Elisabetha (née Kahlow). Besides Anna Dorothea, two more of the nine children from this marriage became artists: Anna Rosina Lisiewska (q.v.) and Christian Friedrich Reinhold. Christian's activities in Berlin in the years 1772–9 were of great importance for Anna Dorothea's work. Like her siblings, she was first a pupil of her father. This is apparent in the graphic elements in her work, which are characteristic of Lisiewski's painting technique. She counteracted the characteristic stiffness of Lisiewski's portraits, however, with a sometimes seemingly exaggerated agility, thus showing her interest in figurative compositions. His oeuvre of realistic and conventional portraits of members of the princely family of Anhalt Dessau, Prussian officers and civil servants is influenced by Adam Manjoki and especially Antoine Pesne, whose works Anna Dorothea initially copied, as well as those of Watteau. Whether she actually had access to Pesne's Berlin studio is not known, although the relationship to his work is unmistakable. Like Pesne, she tried to probe as deeply as possible into the sitter's personality. It was the emphasis on the individual that was important to her; she achieved this through a differing density of painting in the figure and the surroundings, as well as by striving to convey the face and hands in three dimensions by modelling. She also achieved a fine representation of the different materials (e.g. *Anna Elisabeth von Arnim*, c.1741; Neues Palais, Potsdam).

Her first period of work can be identified by two conversation pieces that form a pair: *The Swing* and *Game of Shuttlecock* (Neues Palais, Potsdam), the latter being signed and dated 1741. Watteau was clearly the model for these two park scenes. It is not only the subjects that are similar to his, but the figures on the swing are almost identical to those in his paintings and the works of his follower, Nicolas Lancret. The subjects are taken from paintings that were in the collection of Frederick II. It can thus not be ruled out that she was able to copy from the originals, as was common for prospective artists in the 18th century, and which was permitted in the royal collections as part of training. It is, however, more likely that the artist knew of Watteau's work and that of his followers through engravings, which were widely available.

Anna Dorothea's first period of work came before her marriage to the Berlin inn proprietor Ernst Friedrich Therbusch in 1742. He is sometimes described as a painter as well, but this has not yet been substantiated. Her marriage and the birth of her children initially limited her artistic activity. It was not until 1760 that she returned to her career, with a more vigorous style, after a period in which she taught herself. In 1761 she was called to the court of Duke Karl Eugen von Württemberg in Stuttgart, where she painted 18 decorative works for the hall of mirrors and a series of decorative wall paintings above doors. It was in Stuttgart that an important phase of her development started. The study of Pesne and perhaps also the influence of Lesueur and van Loo led her to a softer and more sketchy manner of painting. In 1763 she was called to Mannheim, where she painted portraits of the Elector Palatine Karl Theodor and was promoted to court painter. She soon returned to Berlin, and from there set off to Paris, where she managed to be elected a member of the Académie Royale. She sent several works to the Salon, including her reception piece for the Academy, *The Drinker* (Ecole Nationale des Beaux-Arts, Paris), which shows a young man sitting at a table, holding a glass of wine in his left hand, lit by candlelight. The portrait of the painter *Jacob Philipp Hackert* (1768; Gemäldegalerie, Vienna), painted in Paris, also brought her the membership of the Vienna Academy (1776).

Despite these successes and her acquaintance with Diderot, her stay in Paris was rather unpleasant. The French public – used to the sophisticated courtly taste of the Rococo – found her works too realistic and she did not receive large commissions. She left Paris as early as 1768, and returned to Berlin via Brussels and the Netherlands.

The artistic advantages of these travels became apparent in her final and most prolific period of work. Since her husband died in 1772, it is likely that economic reasons lay behind her productivity. From this time on she signed her works "Peintre du Roi de France". Lisiewka-Therbusch probably began to conduct colour experiments at this time, possibly with her brother, with whom she shared a studio. The essential result of these experiments was the invention of a glossy red paint, which, when made lighter only with the addition of white, she thought perfect for flesh colours. This unbroken pink is the surest sign for the attribution of paintings to her.

Besides commissions for mythological scenes for Frederick II (e.g. *Anakreon*, 1771; *Toilet of Venus*, 1772; *Diana and Her Nymphs*, 1772; all Neues Palais, Potsdam), Anna Dorothea also painted portraits of Frederick and of other members of the royal family, but these did not lead to an appointment as court painter. In 1772 she received a commission from the Tsar's family to paint eight life-size portraits of the royal family (portrait of *Princess Friederike von Preussen*, Neues Palais, Potsdam; others in Hermitage, St Petersburg). For this commission there is evidence of her brother's collaboration. Her manner of painting had become lighter; a few brush strokes and areas of light would often be enough to characterise a certain material. Her realistic portraits of middle-class sitters are excellent and advanced for their time, but her outstanding achievements in both colour and ideas can also be seen in her large paintings.

Lisiewska-Therbusch: *Self-Portrait with Eyeglass*, 1780; Germanisches Nationalmuseum, Nuremberg

Anna Dorothea's self-portraits should surely be counted among her best works. Two years before her death she painted a *Self-Portrait with Eyeglass* (1780; see illustration), in which she rejected the traditional role of the beautiful and desirable woman – depicted again and again by the French painters of the Rococo – and created instead an image of a distinguished woman. The full-length portrait shows her sitting at a table reading. She looks up incidentally, but still seems to be deep in thought. A monocle held on a leather cord can be seen as an attribute of her rationality and at the same time as a reference to the importance of sight and recognition for her artistic work. It obscures her face and thus intentionally creates a moment of irritation for the viewer. Lisiewska-Therbusch describes her own mature and intellectually alert personality in a rational and sober way. Her self-portrait symbolises and foretells the step for women across the boundaries from the simply beautiful to the intellectual. The combination of the splendour of the Rococo with conscious self-reflection creates a tension, apparent in the figure of this admirable woman, who managed to overcome the barriers set for her person and sex.

EDITH SCHOENECK

See also Court Artists survey and Training and Professionalism survey 3

Lizarraga, Remedios *see* Varo

Lloyd, Mary *see* Moser

Lohse-Wächtler, Elfriede

German painter and graphic artist, 1899–1940

Born Elfriede Wächtler in Dresden, 4 December 1899; father a commercial clerk. Studied at the Kunstgewerbeschule, Dresden, 1915–19. Married singer Kurt Lohse, 1921. Lived in Hamburg, 1925–31; spent two months in Friedrichsberg psychiatric hospital after a nervous breakdown, 1929. Returned to Dresden, 1931. Patient in Arnsdorf psychiatric hospital, 1932–40; diagnosed schizophrenic. Divorce and compulsory sterilisation, 1935. Gassed during the National Socialist T4 euthanasia programme in Pirna-Sonnenstein; official cause of death stated as "pneumonia and myocarditis", 31 July 1940.

Principal Exhibitions

Bund der Hamburgischen Künstlerinnen und Kunstfreundinnen, Stadtbundclub, Hamburg: 1928 (*Osterausstellung*), 1930 (individual), 1930 (*Vom Weltverkehr und seinen Mitteln*, Arts and Crafts exhibition)
Graphisches Kabinett Maria Kunde, Hamburg: 1929 (with Friedrichsberger Köpfe and August Glemmer), 1932 (with Ralf Volkner)

Altonaer Kunstverein, Hamburg-Altona: 1929 (*Grosse Altonaer Kunstausstellung*)
Kunsthalle, Hamburg: 1930 (*Hamburger Künstler*)

Bibliography

Conrad Felixmüller, "Porträt (genannt Laus)", *Die Aktion*, ed. Franz von Pfemfert, no.26, 30 June 1917, p.352
Anna Banaschewski, "Friedrichsberger Köpfe", *Der Kreis: Zeitschrift für künstlerische Kultur* (Hamburg), no.5–6, 1929, pp.307ff
Bericht über die Neuerwerbungen des Jahres 1930/31: Justus Brinckmann Gesellschaft, Hamburg, 1931, pp.4, 6
Raabe Paul, ed., *Expressionismus und Politik in Franz Pfemferts Aktion*, dtv-Dokumente, no.4, 1964, p.279
Gerhart Söhn, ed., *Conrad Felixmüller: Das Graphische Werk, 1912–1977*, Düsseldorf: Söhn, 1975; revised 1987
Grossstadt und Grossstadtleben um 1926, exh. cat., BAT-Cigaretten-Fabrik, Hamburg, 1976
Künstlerinnen international, 1877–1977, exh. cat., Schloss Charlottenburg, Berlin, 1977
Ulrika Evers, *Deutsche Künstlerinnen des 20. Jahrhunderts: Malerei-Bildhauerei-Tapisserie*, Hamburg: Schultheis, 1983
Otto Griebel, *Ich war ein Mann der Strasse*, Frankfurt am Main: Röderberg, 1986
Überblick 1986, exh. cat., Galerie Hasenclever, Munich, 1986
Reinhold Heller, *Art in Germany, 1909–1936: From Expressionism to Resistance*, Munich: Prestel, 1990
Die Sammlung Frank Brabant: Deutsche Malerei und Graphik des 20. Jahrhunderts: Expressionismus, Neue Sachlichkeit, Moderne, exh. cat., Schwerin, 1993
Der weibliche Blick: Käthe Kollwitz, Else Lasker-Schüler, Paula Modersohn-Becker, Gabriele Münter, Hannah Höch, Jeanne Mammen, Elfriede Lohse-Wächtler, Else Bertha Fischer-Ginsburg, Hanna Nagel: Gemälde, Zeichnungen, Druckgraphik, 1897–1947, exh. cat., Galerie der Stadt Aschaffenburg, 1993
Sergiusz Michalski, *New Objectivity: Painting, Graphic Art and Photography in Weimar Germany, 1919–1933*, Cologne: Taschen, 1994 (German original, 1992)
Winfried Reichert and Rita E. Täuber, *Wider die Erwartung: Elfriede Lohse-Wächtler, 1899–1940*, Rothenbuch bei Aschaffenburg, 1994
Neue Sachlichkeit: Bilder auf der Suche nach der Wirklichkeit: Figurative Malerei der zwanziger Jahre, exh. cat., Kunsthalle, Mannheim, 1994
Hildegard Reinhardt, "'... fort muss ich, nur fort': Elfriede Lohse-Wächtler", *Malerinnen des XX. Jahrhunderts*, ed. Bernd Küster, Bremen: Donat, 1995
Anne Peters, ed., *Paula Lauenstein – Elfriede Lohse-Wächtler – Alice Sommer: Drei Dresdener Künstlerinnen in den zwanziger Jahren*, Albstadt, 1996
Georg Reinhardt, ed., *Im Malstrom des Liebens versunken: Elfriede Lohse-Wächtler, 1899–1940: Leben und Werk*, Cologne: Wienand, 1996

The daughter of a commercial clerk in Dresden, Elfriede Wächtler trained at the Dresden Kunstgewerbeschule. As a student she was associated with the Spartakusbund, the Dresden Secession: Gruppe 1919 and the Pfemfert circle through fellow students including Otto Dix, Conrad Felixmüller and Otto Griebel. Wächtler financed her studies with art and craft objects: batik, lithographed greeting cards and illustrations. She became friendly with the Dada artist Johannes A. Baader, probably while he was performing in Dresden. Through Dix and Griebel she met Kurt Lohse, a painter and singer, whom she married in 1921. The couple left Dresden for Hamburg in 1925 when Lohse accepted an engagement at the Stadttheater there.

During her years in Hamburg Lohse-Wächtler developed

Lohse-Wächtler: *Time Out for a Smoke*, 1930; private collection

her own artistic language, a generous late-Expressionist figurative style, and participated in solo and group exhibitions. Marital and economic difficulties contributed to a nervous breakdown, and she was hospitalised in Friedrichsberg for two months in 1929. Her drawings of other mental patients, the *Friedrichsberg Heads*, already show the "eminent talent for psychological intuition" noted by the critic Anna Banaschewski (1929). Despite ill-health, Lohse-Wächtler created the main body of her work in Hamburg: portraits of relatives, friends and lower-class inhabitants of Altona during the great Depression, views of houses and the harbour of Altona, and scenes of the bar and prostitute milieu of Hamburg, where she herself lived. Her impressions of working life and amusements in Altona occupy a wide iconographic range (*Pleasures of St Pauli*, 1930; pastel; private collection, repr. Reichert and Täuber 1994; *In the Launch*, 1930; pastel; *Lissy*, 1931; watercolour; both private collections, repr. Heller 1990). Reflections on the pleasures and conflicts of relationships, both general and personal, run through her oeuvre (*A Flower*, 1930; pastel; Schleswig-Holsteinisches Landesmuseum, Schleswig; *Three Drinkers*, 1930; pastel; private collection, repr. Reichert and Täuber 1994). Without doubt the quality of her work is most evident in her series of self-portraits, in which she mercilessly documented her own development: a pause in work (*Time Out for a Smoke*, 1930; see illustration), the confession of erotic dependencies (*Self-Portrait and a Shadow*, 1930; pastel) to the uncompromising registration of her own mental and physical deterioration (*Self-Portrait*, 1931; watercolour; repr. Reinhardt 1995).

The difficulties of her life in Hamburg drove Lohse-Wächtler to return to live with her parents in Dresden in 1931. Diagnosed as a schizophrenic, at the request of her father she was committed to a psychiatric sanatorium in nearby Arnsdorf. In her first years there she returned to the theme of her Friedrichsberg period, capturing the mental and physical deterioration of fellow patients in stunningly precise head and figure studies. As well as executing mainly small-scale portrait drawings of patients and nurses she made landscape sketches during trips to the surrounding area. In 1935 she was divorced and was subjected to compulsory sterilisation under legislation introduced by the National Socialists. Despite repeated requests to her family to obtain her release, she remained in Arnsdorf until she was transported to Pirna-Sonnenstein, where she died on 31 July 1940. The cause of her death was recorded as pneumonia, but she was gassed as part of the National Socialists' T4 euthanasia programme.

The effects of the Depression, the rise of National Socialism and the danger and misery of individual lives formed the background of Elfriede Lohse-Wächtler's personal and artistic biography. From the 1970s a renewed interest in realism and women's art brought her posthumous recognition. Her works are in museums of the cities in which she lived: the Staatliche Kunstsammlungen, Dresden; the Kunsthalle and Altonaer Museum, Hamburg; and the Schleswig-Holsteinisches Landesmuseum, Schleswig. However, the majority of her oeuvre – mainly large portraits, and figure and landscape studies in pastel and watercolour – is in private collections in Germany.

HILDEGARD REINHARDT

Loir, Marie Anne
French painter, active 1737–79

Born in Paris to Nicolas Loir, royal official, and Marie-Anne Gérin; sister of Alexis Loir III, painter to the king and member of the Académie Royale. Received payments for portraits from the Duc de Bourbon, 1737 and 1738. Pupil of Jean François de Troy, who was appointed director of the French Academy in Rome in 1738; possibly followed him to Rome (her brother Alexis was there by 1739). Working for patrons in Pau, southern France, 1760s. Member, Marseille Academy, 1762. Last recorded work, 1779. Dates of birth and death unknown.

Bibliography

Paul Lafond, "Alexis Loir – Marianne Loir", *Réunion des Sociétés des Beaux-Arts des Départements*, 1892, pp.365–77

Les Femmes peintres au XVIIIe siècle, exh. cat., Musée Goya, Castres, 1973

Women Artists, 1550–1950, exh. cat., Los Angeles County Museum of Art, and elsewhere, 1976

Les Peintures de l'Ecole française des XVII et XVIII siècles, Musée des Beaux-Arts, Orléans, 1980

National Museum of Women in the Arts: Selections from the Permanent Collection, New York: Abrams, 1987

Little is known of the personal life and circumstances of Marie Anne Loir although she seems to have worked exclusively as a portraitist for wealthy and mostly aristocratic patrons. She belonged to an artistic family that had been active as silversmiths in Paris since the 17th century, but several of her last recorded works were made for patrons in Pau, and she was elected to the Marseille Academy in 1762. This seems to suggest that she had strong links to the south of France and may even have worked there.

The ten dated portraits that have been attributed to Loir can be associated with the style of Jean Marc Nattier and Louis Tocqué, and they also show the influence of her training in the studio of the leading French academician, Jean François de Troy. Her sitters do not appear in fashionable mythological disguise, but most include flowers to ornament, embellish and prettify. A representative example of her work is the portrait of *Antoine Vincent Louis Barbe Duplaa at the Age of 9* (1763; Musée des Beaux-Arts, Tours). This is of a boy who is still really a child; he holds a rake and is surrounded by flowers. His hat is set at a rakish angle and the work as a whole has a deliberately playful, colourful and artful superficiality about it. It does not document the boy's features as an accurate record for posterity but instead presents us with a pretty image of childhood. The false rusticity and pseudo-simplicity of its conceit herald the highly sophisticated return to nature in which leisured members of the aristocracy and of the high nobility indulged before the coming of the French Revolution.

The portrait of *Gabrielle-Emilie le Tonnelier de Breteuil, Marquise du Châtelet* (1745–9; see illustration) presents something of a contrast to this. The sitter here is justly being celebrated for her scientific erudition, mathematical pursuits and intellectual achievements. The Marquise du Châtelet produced three major publications: the *Institutions de physique* (1740), which helped to make the ideas of Leibniz known in France,

Loir: *Gabrielle-Emilie le Tonnelier de Breteuil, Marquise du Châtelet,* 1745–9; oil on canvas; 102 × 80 cm.; Musée des Beaux-Arts, Bordeaux

the *Discours sur la nature et la propagation du feu* (1744) and a translation of Newton's *Principia Mathematica*. In the portrait by Loir she is shown sitting and elegantly leaning on a table on which stand a celestial globe, a set-square and paper with calculations; behind her is a row of books. These are all clear tributes to the scholarly interests and achievements of the Marquise du Châtelet, which are further evoked by the pair of dividers she holds out in one hand. In her other hand, however, she holds out a carnation – a symbol of true love.

The Marquise du Châtelet also achieved fame because of her friendship with Voltaire, with whom she lived almost continuously from 1734 until her death in 1749. The portrait is one of high fashion and of artifice and it is thus also a record of the sitter's putative beauty as well as of her evident intellect. The three-quarter-length seated pose, the slightly turning contrapposto, the extended graceful gesturing of hands and arms are all highly conventional. The fashionable décolleté of the sitter's dress, the fine lace and ribbons at her elbows, the sheen and fur of the draperies are those of contemporary high society portraits, in which women were generally celebrated only on account of a beauty that was of a highly stereotyped and idealised elegance. In opposition to this is the frankness of the sitter's gaze that indicates the knowing intelligence of a specific individual beyond the establishment of a recognisably beautiful type. The dark eyes, the long nose and the lips of the slightly smiling mouth intimate an independence of spirit and of passion. It would, however, be quite wrong to consider such a portrait as in any way an accurate or authentic record of the minutiae of a named individual's well-defined facial features or of a highly particular and personal psychology.

Loir's portraits of men are of similarly contrived and highly conventionalised types and they have comparatively little specific detail or penetrating characterisation. The undated portrait of *Jean de Lacroix-Laval* (Musée Lyonnais des Arts Décoratifs, Lyon), attributed to Loir, shows, seated at a desk, the aristocratic patron of a lavish hôtel. A book lies open before him, but it is not being studied. Instead the sitter, fashionably clad in an elegantly trimmed jacket, looks out at the viewer smilingly and with confidence. The portrait painter contributed and provided further support to the status of her aristocratic sitters and patrons, although this woman artist had, herself, at best an extremely limited public profile. Other works attributed to Loir include a portrait of *Président Bayard* (1769; Musée des Beaux-Arts, Pau) and two portraits of male sitters (Musée des Beaux-Arts, Orléans). A print by J.N. Tardieu after her portrait of *Mme Dubocage* was published in *Recueil des Oeuvres*, Paris, 1762.

VALERIE MAINZ

Longhi, Barbara

Italian painter, 1552–1638

Born in Ravenna, 1552; father the painter Luca Longhi, brother the painter and poet Francesco Longhi. Died in Ravenna, 1638.

Bibliography

Giorgio Vasari, *Le vite de' più eccellenti pittori, scultori ed architettori*, Florence, 1568; ed. Gaetano Milanesi, vii, Florence: Sansoni, 1881; as *Lives of the Most Eminent Painters, Sculptors and Architects*, 10 vols, London: Macmillan-Medici Society, 1912–15; reprinted New York: AMS, 1976 (life of Luca Longhi)

Francesco Beltrami, "Il forestiere instruito delle cose notabili della città di Ravenna e suburbane della medesima", Ravenna, 1791; Archivio di Stato, Bologna, MS A91

F. Nanni, *Il forestiero in Ravenna*, Ravenna, 1821

Gaspare Ributti, *Guida di Ravenna*, 1835, 1866 and 1885

Jadranka Bentini, ed., *Luca Longhi e la pittura su tavola in Romagna nel '500*, Bologna: Alfa, 1982

Liana De Girolami Cheney, "Barbara Longhi of Ravenna", *Woman's Art Journal*, ix/1, 1988, pp.16–21

The daughter of Luca Longhi, a provincial Mannerist painter, Barbara Longhi trained with her father and assisted him on his large altarpieces. She was also inspired by the Emilian painters Correggio and Parmigianino, the Roman engravers Marcantonio Raimondi and Agostino Veneziano, and Raphael, particularly his Florentine period (1506–8), when he registered the impact of the works of Leonardo and Fra Bartolommeo. Assimilating these influences, she developed her own recognisable style: in the delicate modelling of the arms and necks of her madonnas, the saints who are no more corporeal than their rippling garments, and her warm and subtle golden palette. Her works won the esteem of contemporary connoisseurs such as Giorgio Vasari and Munzio Manfredi.

Although Longhi was especially admired for her portraits, only one is certainly known. The *Camaldolese Monk* (1570 or 1573; Pinacoteca, Ravenna), one of her few paintings to bear a date, though the last digit is unclear, is also the only one to depict a male subject. The pose of the figure, seated at a table, suggests a Raphaelesque model such as *Leo X and His Nephews* (c.1515; Palazzo Pitti, Florence); the books in the background emphasise the sitter's learning. On the basis of its resemblance to the probable depiction of Longhi as St Barbara in her father's *Virgin and Child Enthroned with Saints* (1570), the *St Catherine of Alexandria* (1589; both Pinacoteca, Ravenna), painted for the monastery of Classe in Ravenna, has been identified as a self-portrait. Several copies are known.

Longhi's paintings reflect the authoritarian ideas of the Counter Reformation, according to which religious images should be simple and unambiguous to elicit a devotional response from the viewer. The element of empathy was crucial. Of the 15 paintings by her that have been identified, 12 depict the Virgin and Child. As the chronology is unclear, they are organised here according to stylistic development. In her earliest works (c.1570–90) Longhi simplified the composition, limited modelling to emphasise linearity of design, used a limited palette and gave her themes a lyrical, intimate treatment, for example in two versions of the *Virgin with Sleeping Child* (both c.1570; Pinacoteca, Ravenna; Grohs-Collison Collection, Birmingham, AL). The *Madonna del Baldacchino* (c.1570–73; Pinacoteca, Ravenna) has an elaborate canopy and floating angels recalling Raphael's painting of this subject (1506–7; Palazzo Pitti), which Longhi may have known from engravings.

The muted palette and gentle rhythms of the *Reading Madonna* (c.1570–75; Pinacoteca, Ravenna) reveal what

Longhi: *Virgin and Child with St John the Baptist,* c.1598–1600; oil on canvas; 88.5 × 71 cm.

Vasari called Longhi's "grace and style". It is signed with her initials B.L.F. (Barbara Longhi Fecit). The pose of the Christ Child, resting on a globe, is reminiscent of works by Mannerist painters such as Parmigianino. Inspiration from another Emilian Mannerist, Correggio, is suggested by her *Virgin and Child with St John the Baptist* (c.1589–90; private collection, repr. Cheney 1988, fig.3), in which the family scene is set off from the landscape by dramatic drapery.

The period c.1590 to c.1605 must be considered Longhi's maturity, as no work that can be attributed to a later period has been discovered. Here her compositional devices include a draped column and a background view showing a scene from nature. The figures have a monumental quality, and the colour is more brilliant. A deeper devotional element is added to the lyrical treatment of the theme. In the *Virgin and Child with SS Agatha and Catherine* (c.1590–95; Pinacoteca, Ravenna) the Virgin is depicted as aloof, in a formal, frontal pose. Longhi depicted these saints in other altarpieces, for example, the *Healing of St Agatha*, painted for San Vitale, Ravenna (c.1595; now Santa Maria Maggiore, Ravenna).

Her *Cappuccini Altarpiece* (c.1595; Brera, Milan), a "sacra conversazione" in an elaborate architectural setting, shows Venetian influence, particularly of Giovanni Bellini's altarpiece for San Zaccaria, Venice (1505). As there is no documentation about Longhi's patrons, the identification of saints in her pictures is often speculative. For example, in the *Virgin and Child with Saint* (c.1590–95; Louvre, Paris) the Franciscan

habit of the figure being crowned by Christ suggests she may be St Elizabeth of Hungary, who belonged to the order.

Counter-Reformation themes are evident in the *Virgin and Child with St John the Baptist* (c.1598–1600; Pinacoteca, Ravenna): in the foreground, a small cross at the feet of the Baptist recalls his role forecasting the coming of Christ and is also a reminder of Christ's fate. The painting, which shows the brilliance and variety of her colour, is signed B.L.F. Another version of the same subject (c.1595–1600; see illustration) represents the culmination of Longhi's style: the tender expressions and soft modelling of the children; the *sfumato* treatment of the landscape in the tradition of Leonardo; and the Emilian Mannerist motif of the draped column. In these two works Longhi assimilated the dominant styles of the mid-16th century and added her own intimate and gentle touch.

Longhi's mature style emphasised grace and softness of contour, as in the *Mystical Marriage of St Catherine, with St John the Baptist* (c.1600; Museo Biblioteca, Bassano del Grappa). The scene exemplifies Counter Reformation ideas about Christ as an active participant in the lives of saints and about the importance of presenting saints' lives as models for the faithful to emulate. In this picture Longhi visually integrated these didactic religious elements with the artistic quest of Mannerism.

Of the latest-known examples of Longhi's paintings of the Virgin and Infant Christ, the *Virgin with Sleeping Child* (c.1600–05; Walters Art Gallery, Baltimore) is perhaps the most intensely devotional. The figures occupy an extremely confined interior space, with a draped column and a window view of heavenly clouds. Mary gazes in adoration at the Child, whose sleep also presages his death. Although the composition recalls works by Bellini (c.1505; Isabella Stewart Gardner Museum, Boston) and Lavinia Fontana, q.v. (1603; Prado, Madrid), Longhi has moved away from Bellini's classicism and the Mannerist elaboration of Fontana to focus instead on the intimate spiritual relationship between mother and viewer, both adoring the divine Child. The monumentality of the forms is an analogue for the directness and mysticism expressed in the painting. The *Nursing Madonna* (c.1600–05; Brera, Milan) depicts a theme derived from Early Christian art that became particularly popular in Italy in the 14th century. During the Counter-Reformation, however, nudity in sacred figures was not acceptable, and Longhi's Madonna only partially reveals her breast, while Christ gently embraces his mother. The unity of femininity and motherly love expressed in the image are characteristic of her mature style.

Like Fede Galizia (q.v.), Elisabetta Sirani (q.v.) and Artemisia Gentileschi (q.v.), Longhi painted *Judith with the Head of Holofernes* (c.1570–75; Pinacoteca, Ravenna). Her Judith shows none of the violence of Gentileschi's versions, however, but looks to heaven as if seeking forgiveness. The acceptance of guilt and faith in divine absolution reflect Counter-Reformation ideas. In her lifetime Longhi's fame did not extend beyond Ravenna, which may be why little is known of her life, and few of her works have been identified. Nevertheless, she was a productive member of the family workshop, and her paintings give some idea of the regional expression of the artistic aims of the Counter-Reformation.

LIANA DE GIROLAMI CHENEY

Low, Mary Fairchild MacMonnies *see* MacMonnies

Lowndes, Gillian
British potter and sculptor, 1936–

Born in Cheshire, 19 June 1936. Studied at Central School of Arts and Crafts, London, 1957–9 (diploma); Ecole des Beaux-Arts, Paris, 1960. Set up workshop in London with Robin Welch, 1960; shared a workshop with future husband Ian Auld in Chippenham, Wiltshire, 1966–71; spent two years in Nigeria with Auld, 1971–2. Established workshop in Camberwell, London, 1975; in Toppesfield, Essex, 1989. Taught part-time at Camberwell School of Arts and Crafts from 1975, at Central School of Arts and Crafts from 1976. Recipient of silver medal, International Ceramics, Geneva, 1964; World Crafts Council silver medal, 1967. Has one son. Lives in Halstead, Essex.

Selected Individual Exhibitions
Primavera, London: 1966
British Crafts Centre, London: 1976 (with Ian Auld)
Crafts Council Shop, Victoria and Albert Museum, London: 1983
Amalgam Gallery, Barnes, London: 1985 (*Three from Camberwell*)
Crafts Council Gallery, London: 1987 (retrospective)
Contemporary Applied Arts, London: 1994

Bibliography
Tony Birks, *The Art of the Modern Potter*, London: Country Life, 1967
Michael Casson, *Pottery in Britain Today*, London: Tiranti, and New York: Transatlantic Arts, 1967
Five Studio Potters, exh. brochure, Victoria and Albert Museum, London, 1968
Sue Harley, "Ian Auld and Gillian Lowndes", *Ceramic Review*, no.44, 1977, pp.4–6
Elisabeth Cameron, "Gillian Lowndes", *Ceramic Review*, no.83, 1983, pp.9–11
Robert A. Saunders, *The Studio Ceramics Collection at Paisley Museum and Art Galleries*, Paisley, 1984
Angus Suttie, "The dangerous edge of things", *Crafts*, no.75, July–August 1985, pp.49–50
Gillian Lowndes: New Ceramic Sculpture, exh. cat., Crafts Council Gallery, London, 1987
Henry Pim, "Uncertain echoes", *Ceramic Review*, no.103, 1987, pp.10–12
Tanya Harrod, "Transcending clay", *Crafts*, no.84, January–February 1987, pp.16–21
The Raw and the Cooked: New Work in Clay in Britain, exh. cat., Barbican Art Gallery, London, and elsewhere, 1993
Oliver Watson, *Studio Pottery: Twentieth-Century British Ceramics in the Victoria and Albert Museum Collection*, London: Phaidon, 1993 (originally published as *British Studio Pottery*, Oxford: Phaidon, 1990)
Gillian Lowndes, exh. cat., Contemporary Applied Arts, London, 1994
Victor Margrie, "Gillian Lowndes", *Studio Pottery*, no.9, June–July 1994, pp.35–8

Gillian Lowndes is a sculptor principally working with clay who makes relatively small-scale, fascinating objects redolent with references to the natural and industrial world. In size, they are always relevant to the domestic environment, and they often incorporate objects found in and around the home that serve as a starting point for the discourse offered in her work. Lowndes was part of a small, but highly influential group of ceramists studying in the 1950s who were more concerned with the possibilities of exploring the versatility of clay as a means for making sculptural forms rather than utilitarian objects. Rejecting the use of the wheel, Lowndes made use of a wide range of making and forming techniques, which are relatively slow, and allow time for contemplation. These methods range from pinching and hand-building to slip-casting. In her most recent work (e.g. *Form*, 1994; artist's collection) Lowndes often incorporates materials such as wire; other pieces have included stones and fired pieces of commercially produced ceramic as part of a commentary on waste, industrial culture and the environment. While many of her objects are aware of and use the idea of inner space, none has any utilitarian function.

As a student at the Central School of Arts and Crafts in the late 1950s, Lowndes first studied sculpture before transferring to what was at that time a lively ceramic department, where the mood was one of experiment and exploration, with students looking more to Picasso's bold use of colour and decoration than to the sombre and earnest work produced by Bernard Leach and his followers. In keeping with the mood of expansion and experiment, emphasis was on ideas and innovation, rather than adopting a ready-made aesthetic. A period in Paris, studying at the Ecole des Beaux-Arts, provided a further broadening experience.

Despite being primarily concerned with the formal qualities of sculpture, Lowndes's interest and knowledge of clay is apparent from her earliest work. A group of small containers made by pinching out balls of clay, shown in the early 1960s, demonstrated a determination to explore the plastic and informal qualities of the material as an expressive medium. A set of standing pipe forms, which twist and curl in their vertical ascent, could only be made in clay (*Three Standing Pipe Forms*, 1968; Victoria and Albert Museum, London). The use of the geometric, tubular form, manipulated and articulated into intriguing forms, works both as metaphor and as an exercise in the control and understanding of formal relationships. Clay was also used to imitate such qualities as the softness of cushions, or to build forms by "weaving" clay twigs to create structures that were both "open" in that they could be seen through, and "closed" because they formed a regular shape.

The most significant shift in Lowndes's work came after a two-year period spent in Nigeria. Here she was particularly impressed by the freedom with which materials were used, the inventive improvisation, and by the combining of different materials in a single object. As a consequence, she started to call on a wider and more diffuse range of influences for her own work, in which the more formal and ordered aesthetic of the West gave way to a more sensual use of form and texture. For one memorable series, experiments were made using fibreglass sheets of fabric dipped in porcelain casting slip, which were then draped over metal forms and fired. The distorted forms that came out of the kiln carried a memory of the original construction, but were so disrupted and metamorphosed as

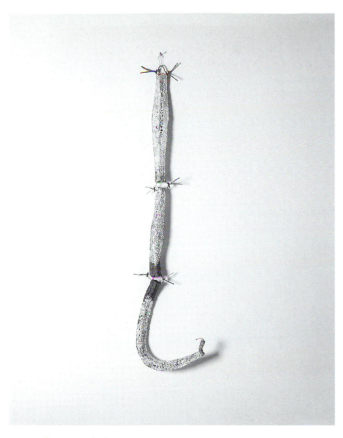

Lowndes: Untitled

a result of the firing that they take on an independent life of their own

Her later work became even more free and inventive. In such pieces as *Tail of the Dog* (1983; Crafts Council, London) the clay was rolled to make thin, pastry-like slabs, and then folded to form a long tube joined along an obvious seam. One end stands vertical at an angle of 90 degrees providing an allusion to an animal form, but the object retains a mystery about its origins and references. More dramatic are objects made up of assemblies incorporating parts of what look like mattress springs, broken pieces of commercially made tiles and bits of brightly coloured pottery and clay. During the firing in the kiln, the objects soften, distort and fuse to form an intricate collage that can be seen as a meditation on the detritus of urban life.

With an acute understanding of how clay behaves, and the sort of magic that materials undergo in the heat of the firing, Lowndes has developed a highly distinctive language. This is both intrinsic to clay and to heat, and the processes of ceramics. It offers a commentary on change, on decay, and on the way familiar fragments, such as broken parts of coloured tiles and cups, can spark off a series of ideas, thoughts and emotions. Her work, in such collections as the Crafts Council and Victoria and Albert Museum, London; Buckinghamshire County Museum, Aylesbury; Landesmuseum, Stuttgart; Shigaraki Cultural Park, Japan; and the Newark Museum, New Jersey, is relatively small in size but intense in feeling, retaining its domestic scale, although its intention is large and ambitious. It is work that, while having roots within the

processes of craft, uses these as starting points for objects that successfully and imaginatively link the worlds of art and craft to become pieces with sculptural resonance.

EMMANUEL COOPER

Luke, Alexandra
Canadian painter, 1901–1967

Born in Montreal, Quebec, 14 May 1901. Lived in Oshawa, Ontario, from 1914. Married C. Ewart McLaughlin, 1928 (second marriage); son born 1926, daughter born 1930. Studied at Banff School of Fine Arts, Alberta, under A.Y. Jackson of the Group of Seven and Jock Macdonald, 1945; under Hans Hofmann in Provincetown, Massachusetts, 1947–52. Awarded diploma of honour, Vichy Salon, 1961. Member of Painters Eleven, 1953–60; Canadian Society of Painters in Water Colour, 1958; Canadian Group of Painters, 1959; Ontario Society of Artists, 1962–7. Fellow of the International Institute of Arts and Letters, 1960. Died in Oshawa, 1 June 1967.

Principal Exhibitions
YWCA (Adelaide House), Oshawa: 1946 (with Isabel McLaughlin), 1952 (*Canadian Abstract Show*, touring)
Riverside Museum, New York: 1947 (*Canadian Women Painters*)
Picture Loan Society, Toronto: 1952 (individual)
Simpson's department store, Toronto: 1953 (*Abstracts at Home*)
Riverside Museum, New York: 1956 (*20th Annual Exhibition of American Abstract Artists, with "Painters Eleven" of Canada*)
Robert McLaughlin Gallery, Oshawa: 1977, 1987 (both retrospectives)

Bibliography
Alexandra Luke: A Tribute, exh. cat., Robert McLaughlin Gallery, Oshawa, 1977
Joan Murray, "Foreword: The Collection and Alexandra Luke", *Permanent Collection Catalogue*, Oshawa: Robert McLaughlin Gallery, 1978
Alexandra Luke: Continued Searching, exh. cat., Robert McLaughlin Gallery, Oshawa, 1987
Margaret Rogers, *Locating Alexandra*, Toronto: ECW Press, 1995

In the 1950s Alexandra Luke became one of the two women members of the first abstract painting group in Ontario, Painters Eleven. Her work differed from that of her male colleagues: from her training with Hans Hofmann, she had developed a personal calligraphy (as Tom Hodgson, one of the other members of the group, recalled in 1977). The refinements of design that he, Oscar Cahén, Harold Town and Jack Bush learned through advertising clouded their individuality to a certain degree, he felt; not so Luke. Kazuo Nakamura, another member, considered her work, unlike that of many of the others, spontaneous. Hofmann's concepts intrigued Luke: the study of space, filling the surface so that it contained no meaningless passages; plasticity; forces and counterforces, his "push and pull" theory; his rhetoric of "plastic sensing" (he related the object to the shape of the paper or the outside picture plane); his colour intervals; and colour as form. She understood quickly his essentials of a good abstract movement,

Luke: *Journey Through Space*, 1956; oil on canvas; 210.7 × 148.5 cm.

shape or negative space, rhythm, the injunction that the work "breathe a life of its own", so that it contains the "mystery of creation". Like Hofmann, Luke believed that the model or still life was a way of exploring space. Through his teaching she found a way to organise her material. In her first days of study with him in 1947, a student next to her said that he had never known anyone "to get it so quickly". By "it" he meant Hofmann's idea of reducing form to a series of "shifting planes moving in space" to express plastic, three-dimensional form.

That Hofmann helped Luke to move away from realism can be seen from the landscape work she did at Lake Rosseau in Ontario in the late summer of 1947. On the back of one sketch, *Rocky Shoreline* (1947), she wrote: "stressing shifting planes and texture". This small panel is far more abstract than her earlier work (e.g. *Chalk Lake Road*; oil and graphite on panel; 1936). With its expressive, dramatic colour, it is a harbinger of later paintings. Colour was something about which Luke continued to take notes. With Hofmann's aid, she sought to understand colour as a plastic means, a way of organising volume. Eventually, Hofmann's theories formed the underpinnings of her art and life. Her studies were also important for other Canadian artists, because she conveyed Hofmann's importance to her peers, urging others to join her in her annual visits to Provincetown (many made the trip, including Jock Macdonald, William Ronald, Isabel McLaughlin (q.v.) and Yvonne McKague Housser).

Luke's initial attraction to abstraction came through the Banff School of Fine Arts and Jock Macdonald. Macdonald told her about "automatic" painting, which he had learned in turn from Dr Grace Pailthorpe in Vancouver. By the spring of 1948 Luke was experimenting with small, loosely painted ink-blot-like works using this method (e.g. *Adventure*, 1962; watercolour and ink on paper). What she found in these fantasies was a rich, evocative power, fresh compositions and forms.

Many of her paintings expand a still-life theme. Later, she often tried for a more fiery effect, as in *Journey Through Space* (1956; see illustration). Here she charted new discoveries in science or the cosmic energy about which she may have learned through her reading books by the mathematician and mystic P.D. Ouspensky, such as *Tertium Organum* (1922), *In Search of the Miraculous* (1949) and *The Fourth Way* (1957) (in the latter two books he explained his years with G.I. Gurdjieff, his teacher). Through one member of an Oshawa group studying *In Search of the Miraculous*, Luke learned of the Gurdjieff Foundation and in 1957–8 began to attend meetings regularly in Toronto and New York.

There was always a strong element of playfulness in her painting, especially evident in work of the 1960s (e.g. *Yellow Space*, 1961; watercolour on paper; *Bythwood*, 1964; collage, watercolour, india ink on hand-made paper). She used different materials in the medium, sometimes sand or torn papers, even feathers or birch bark. She let the watercolour form pools and interrupted these with black spots of ink. Her enjoyment and amusement appear in every work she did. Often too, she introduced her own sense of colour – a glowing combination of golds and oranges. Her work is also remarkable for its large scale (ranging from 210×148 to 246×208 cm.), coming as it did at an early moment of abstraction in Canada.

Painters Eleven existed as a group for only seven years. By 1960 their primary role – to provide an arena for exhibitions of abstract art – was finished, due to the opening up of commercial galleries in Toronto. The paintings that Luke had bought from her friends in the group were left in her will to the city of Oshawa until such time as a suitable gallery could be built. After her death in 1967, her husband Ewart McLaughlin gave the funds for an art gallery to be built by the then Art Gallery of Oshawa. He named it after his grandfather, Robert McLaughlin, an amateur painter, and the man who had started the carriage trade that developed into General Motors of Canada. Most of Luke's works in public galleries are in this collection.

JOAN MURRAY

Luksch-Makowsky, Elena *see* Makovskaya-Luksch

Lundeberg, Helen
American painter, 1908–

Born in Chicago, 24 June 1908. Studied at Pasadena Junior College, 1927–30, then at Stickney Memorial School of Art, Pasadena, under modernist painter Lorser Feitelson, 1930. Subsequently married Feitelson; he died 1978. Moved to Los Angeles and participated in Federal Public Works of Art Project (PWAP), 1933. Included in *Progressive Painters of Southern California* at Fine Arts Gallery of San Diego, 1933. Exhibited with Post-Surrealist artists from 1934, and participated in *Fantastic Art, Dada, Surrealism* at Museum of Modern Art, New York, 1936. Worked for the California Works Progress Administration Federal Art Project (WPA/FAP), 1936–42. Recipient of Vesta award, Woman's Building, Los Angeles, 1987; honorary degree, Otis Arts Institute of Parsons School of Design, New York, 1990; Purchase award, American Academy of Arts and Letters, 1993. Named "Woman of the Year" by Palm Springs Desert Museum, 1988. Lives in Los Angeles.

Selected Individual Exhibitions
Stanley Rose Gallery, Los Angeles: 1933, 1935 (with Lorser Feitelson)
Pasadena Art Institute, CA: 1953 (retrospective)
Scripps College, Claremont, CA: 1958 (retrospective, with Lorser Feitelson)
Paul Rivas Gallery, Los Angeles: 1959, 1960, 1961, 1962
La Jolla Museum of Contemporary Art, CA: 1971 (retrospective)
Los Angeles Municipal Art Gallery: 1979 (retrospective)
San Francisco Museum of Modern Art: 1980–81 (touring retrospective, with Lorser Feitelson)
Graham Gallery, New York: 1982 (retrospective)
Palm Springs Desert Museum, CA: 1983
Tobey C. Moss Gallery, Los Angeles: 1983, 1985, 1987, 1989, 1992, 1995
Sesnon Art Gallery, University of California at Santa Cruz: 1988 (retrospective)
Los Angeles County Museum of Art: 1988 (retrospective)

Selected Writings
New Classicism, 1934

Bibliography

Americans 1942/18 Artists from 9 States, exh. cat., Museum of
Modern Art, New York, 1942

Geometric Abstraction in America, exh. cat., Whitney Museum of
American Art, New York, 1962

Helen Lundeberg: A Retrospective Exhibition, exh. cat., La Jolla
Museum of Contemporary Art, CA, 1971

Fidel Danieli, *Helen Lundeberg Interviewed*, Los Angeles: UCLA
Oral History Program, 1977

Helen Lundeberg: A Retrospective Exhibition, exh. cat., Los Angeles
Municipal Art Gallery, 1979

Eleanor Munro, *Originals: American Women Artists*, New York:
Simon and Schuster, 1979

Diane Moran, "Helen Lundeberg: The sixties and seventies", *Art
International*, xxiii, May 1979, pp.35–43

Lorser Feitelson and Helen Lundeberg: A Retrospective Exhibition,
exh. cat., San Francisco Museum of Modern Art, and elsewhere,
1980

Painting and Sculpture in Los Angeles, 1900–1945, exh. cat., Los
Angeles County Museum of Art, 1980

Charlotte Streifer Rubinstein, *American Women Artists from Early
Times to the Present*, Boston: Hall, 1982

Diane Moran, "Post-Surrealism: The art of Lorser Feitelson and
Helen Lundeberg", *Arts Magazine*, lvii, December 1982,
pp.124–8

Rena Hansen, "Helen Lundeberg: Paintings through five decades",
Women Artists News, viii, Winter 1982–3, p.11

Mitchell Douglas Kahan, *Subjective Currents in American Painting of
the 1930s*, PhD dissertation, City University of New York, 1983

Helen Lundeberg since 1970, exh. cat., Palm Springs Desert
Museum, CA, 1983

Prudence Carlson, "Deep space", *Art in America*, lxxi, February
1983, pp.104–7

80th: A Birthday Salute to Helen Lundeberg, exh. cat., Los Angeles
County Museum of Art, 1988

Generation of Mentors, exh. cat., National Museum of Women in the
Arts, Washington, DC, and elsewhere, 1994

*Pacific Dreams: Currents of Surrealism and Fantasy in Early
Californian Art*, exh. cat., Armand Hammer Museum, University
of California at Los Angeles, and elsewhere, 1995

Helen Lundeberg and Lorser Feitelson Papers are on deposit at the
Archives of American Art, Smithsonian Institution, Washington, DC.

Helen Lundeberg's paintings traverse the nuances of space.
While it was the interior spaces of the psyche that she charted
in her early works of the 1930s, it is the ranges of physical
space – from the subtle illumination of architectural interiors
to veils of clouds draped over horizons – that she has explored
since the 1950s. Always restrained, always refined, always
classical in her pictorial expression, Lundeberg is a formidable
presence in the history of art in the USA.

Born in Chicago, Lundeberg moved to Southern California
as a young child. She met Lorser Feitelson in 1930, when she
attended his figure drawing class at the Stickney Memorial
School of Art in Pasadena. Feitelson soon became her husband
and together they founded what they called New Classicism or
Subjective Classicism, a movement that became known as
Post-Surrealism. Unlike much European Surrealism, which
emphasised the accidental and irrational aspects of the
(Freudian) subconscious, Lundeberg's Post-Surrealism dealt
with the poetic association of apparently unrelated objects and
images presented in landscapes of reverie. Rather than recall-

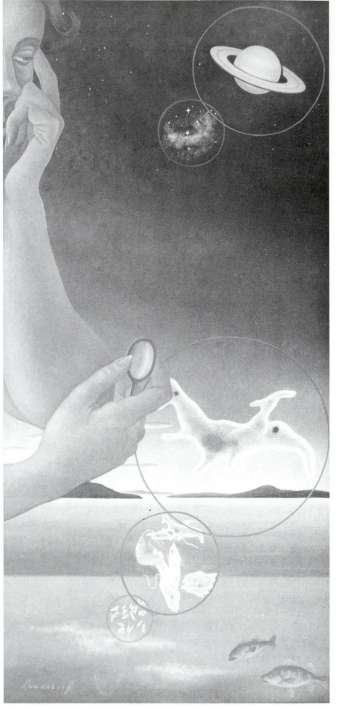

Lundeberg: *Microcosm & Macrocosm*, 1937; oil on
masonite; 72.4 × 35.6 cm.

ing Salvador Dalí or Max Ernst, her works are more likely to
evoke the metaphysical paintings of Giorgio de Chirico or
Morandi. Like many of her works from that period, *Double
Portrait of the Artist in Time* (1935; National Museum of
American Art, Washington, DC) contains specific references to
the painter herself. A blonde baby dressed in starched white –
the artist aged two and a quarter years – sits at a covered table
and holds a budding stem. On top of the table is a clock with
the hands at 2.15, a reference to the age of the child. The baby

casts a lavender shadow of the artist as an adult across the wall behind her, where there hangs a framed painting of the adult artist sitting at another table and gazing at an opened globe. Recognising that "the thoughts of youth are long, long thoughts", Lundeberg looks to duration, to eternity, in her exploration of self and identity.

Microcosm & Macrocosm (1937; see illustration) includes a fragmentary self-portrait. At the upper edge of the frame the artist rests her head on her hand and contemplates a tiny magnifying glass. Behind her stretches a translucent seascape. Rising up from ocean to darkening sky are five bubble-like spheres containing, in order of ascendance: a cluster of tiny plankton, several biomorphic creatures with whipping, thread-like tails, then a sensuous amoeba apparently on the verge of bisection into two beings. Floating as it does over the distant mountains, the amoeba also appears cloud-like. Above it are spheres encapsulating a ringed planet and a luminous band of distant stars. A meditation on unity in diversity, on the absolute and intimate connection of "all things great and small", *Microcosm & Macrocosm* embodies the quiet, reflective nature characteristic of so many of Lundeberg's works.

From the 1950s Lundeberg began to eliminate overt references to herself and to narrative objects in her expansive landscapes. Culling away literary allusions, she created spare, silent spaces that invite dream-bound exegesis. *Shadow of the Bridge* (1962; Los Angeles County Museum of Art) is a study of the rhythmic repetitions of angular arches in meditative tonalities. *Arches No.4* (1962; private collection, California) presents the viewer with an adamant pillar bifurcating the large canvas. An arch opens behind the pillar, avoiding the golden blankets of light that angle back towards it, to remain hushed and deeply darkened. The crisp, curving edges of the arch echo the silhouettes of the shaft of light but stand in counterpoint to the quietly insistent verticals. Lundeberg creates a hypnotically ambivalent geometric fugue. Uncertain of their position vis-à-vis the arena of representation, viewers are led to phenomenological musings. In the catalogue for the artist's retrospective in 1979, Diane Moran compared the works of this period to the writings of Gaston Bachelard, who "pondered the phenomenology of such imagery, noting that inside and outside create a dialectic of division which multiplies with countless diversified nuances: Here, There; the Measurable, the Immeasurable; the Beginning and the End, to list a few" (Los Angeles 1979).

Lundeberg returned briefly in the mid-1960s to the planetary theme seen in earlier works such as *Microcosm & Macrocosm*. *Among the Planets* (1965; Hirshhorn Museum, Washington, DC) captures the darkened void between two immense blue spheres. Occasionally, she also painted still lifes reminiscent of the biomorphic ruminations of Post-Surrealism (*Still Life with Folded Paper*, 1961; oil on canvas; Long Beach Museum of Art, CA), but most of her work of the last three decades has presented expansive vistas abstracted from the land- and seascapes of Southern California. The gentle curves of cloud, mountain and sea undulate beyond the angular bracketing of window, arch and doorway. Works such as *Night Flying In* (1984; artist's collection) have a sustained, seemingly eternal, balance and harmony. Lundeberg's most recent paintings are so pristine in treatment and so stilled in tone that they embody a kind of peace rarely seen in contemporary art. We can say of Helen Lundeberg's work, as May Sarton did of de Chirico's:

> Here space, time, peace are given a habitation,
> Perspective of pillar and arch, shadow on light,
> A luminous evening where it can never be night.
> This is the pure splendor of imagination

["These pure arches", reprinted in Oriole Farb Feschbach and others, *Parallels: Artists/Poets*, New York: Midmarch Arts Press, 1993, p.120].

BETTY ANN BROWN

Lynn, Vivian
New Zealand artist, 1931–

Born Vivian Robertson in Wellington, 30 November 1931. Studied at Canterbury University School of Fine Arts, 1949–51 (DFA 1952); Auckland Teachers College, 1952 (diploma 1954). Lived on a farm after marriage to Eric Charles Lynn in 1956; two children; divorced 1977. Travelled extensively in Europe, USA, Egypt and the Pacific. Co-ordinator, Women's Art Archive, National Art Gallery, Wellington, 1983–4. Part-time lecturer in design, 1974–91, and lecturer in basic design studies, 1992–6, Wellington Polytechnic School of Design. Recipient of Queen Elizabeth II Arts Council awards, 1980, 1981, 1982 and 1983. Lives in Wellington.

Principal Exhibitions

Individual

Woodware Gallery, Christchurch: 1966
Bett-Duncan Studio Gallery, Wellington: 1971
New Vision Gallery, Auckland: 1980
City Art Gallery, Wellington: 1982, 1986
Janne Land Gallery, Wellington: 1982, 1984
National Art Gallery, Wellington: 1983
Govett-Brewster Art Gallery, New Plymouth: 1986
Southern Cross Gallery, Wellington: 1989
Museum of New Zealand, Wellington: 1993

Group

Auckland City Art Gallery: 1963 (*Contemporary New Zealand Painting*), 1976 (*New Zealand Drawing*)
Wairarapa Arts Centre, Masterton: 1968
Galerie Legard, Wellington: 1979
ANZART-in-Hobart, Tasmania: 1983 (*Lamella-Lamina*)
Dunedin: 1984 (*Art in Dunedin*)
Brooker Gallery, Wellington: 1996

Bibliography

Anne Kirker, "Vivian Lynn's Guarden Gates", *Art New Zealand*, no.26, 1983, pp.40–41
Anxious Images: Aspects of Recent New Zealand Art, exh. cat., Auckland City Art Gallery, 1984
New Art in New Zealand: Artists from the 1984 Art in Dunedin Project, exh. cat., Dunedin, 1984, pp.38–9
Content/Context: A Survey of Recent New Zealand Art, exh. cat., National Art Gallery, Wellington, 1986
Elizabeth Eastmond and Merimeri Penfold, *Women and the Arts in New Zealand: Forty Works, 1936–86*, Auckland: Penguin, 1986

Alexa M. Johnston, "Vivian Lynn", *Sculpture 1986: Aspects of Recent New Zealand Art*, exh. cat., Auckland City Art Gallery, 1986

Nobodies: Adventures of the Generic Figure, exh. cat., National Art Gallery, Wellington, 1989

Alter Image: Feminism and Representation in New Zealand Art, 1973–1993, City Gallery, Wellington, and elsewhere, 1993

Anne Kirker, *New Zealand Women Artists: A Survey of 150 Years*, 2nd edition, Tortola, BVI: Craftsman House, 1993

Painter, printmaker, installation and conceptual artist, Vivian Lynn is a crucial figure in the history of feminist art in New Zealand. Her practice derives from her ongoing and evolving critique of Western metaphysics, especially its phallo-centric privileging of male over female, culture over nature, that has led her to investigate the ways in which the values of dominant culture are enforced. During a career spanning 40 years she has produced a body of work that, while refusing the notion of an essential femininity, celebrates the female and nature by means of her invocation of what she calls the "sensuous" or "erotic" body.

Lynn began her career as a painter and printmaker. By the late 1960s she had developed a formal language whereby abstract shapes and structures (the grid and arabesque, for example) were manipulated as metaphors for her philosophical investigations. Thus in colour prints from the series *Breaking the Code* (c.1960–69; artist's collection) an interplay of geometrical structure and free organicism was set up as a means to debunk binary oppositions (order/chaos, surface/depth, structure/ornament) and to undercut the values such dichotomies inscribe.

By the early 1970s Lynn had begun to introduce figurative elements as a better means to reveal her social, political and philosophical intent. As a result of this and her developing interest in the processes of art-making, narrative and seriality increasingly became a feature of her work. The *Book of Forty Images* (1974; artist's collection) is an important example of

Lynn: *Eyes of Life, Eyes of Death*, from *Guarden Gates* series, 1982; real and artificial hair, satin, galvanised steel; Museum of New Zealand Te Papa Tongarewa, Wellington (F2800/12)

her work at this time. A series of screen-prints combining images and texts that explore life in New Zealand, the book operates on multiple representational registers, serving to elucidate Lynn's views on the social and political situation for New Zealand women. Unfolding through time, it suggests an alternative narrative to that of official history. Lynn's prints, drawings and paintings of the 1970s were featured in *Anxious Images: Aspects of Recent New Zealand Art*, held at Auckland City Art Gallery in 1984. This exhibition identified a figurative tradition that explored the human condition from a dark and anguished perspective. Unlike some of her contemporaries, however, Lynn did not adopt the position of "outsider", because her work, despite its use of mythological and personal iconographies, was always engaged with critical philosophical and political issues that were of broadly social import.

Lynn's commitment to a critical practice has not only affected the content of her work. It has also meant that she has refused to adopt conventional artistic roles or to meet traditional expectations. Thus her preference for the activity of making, over the formal or aesthetic resolution of her work, has led her to move freely between various media, making it difficult to define her artistic evolution in terms of stylistic development alone. It has also led to her exploring various methods of working, including that of collaborative art-making. Proposals such as that conceived while she was undertaking research at the Bauhaus in Dessau (1992), and her *Gore Project* – in which Lynn worked with residents of the small town of Gore using photographs and texts to create a community map of the life space of the town – for the South Island Art Projects Public Practices event (1993), have seen the artist working as a facilitator with local communities to encourage participants to investigate individual and shared responses to the architectural, historical and cultural significances of their respective sites.

In the 1980s Lynn undertook a number of large-scale installations that are central to her oeuvre. They signal a renewed interest in working with a wide range of non-traditional media, now in site-specific contexts, to achieve her ambition of combining personal expression with formal concerns and socio-political content. These are also the outcome of her desire to work towards establishing a non-dichotomous relationship between nature and culture and of her interest in and knowledge of the goddess cultures that Lynn sees as the suppressed underpinnings of Western culture. These works were commissioned for public gallery projects (*Lamella-*

Asherim, 1983; Dowse Art Museum; *Asherim*, 1984; CSA Gallery; *Gates of the Goddess*, 1986; Govett-Brewster Art Gallery and Auckland City Art Gallery; and *Caryatid*, 1986; Wellington City Art Gallery), and were undertaken in alternative venues, for example in a factory as part of the F1 Sculpture Project (1982) and at the artist-initiated event, ANZART-in-Hobart (1983), as well as in dealer galleries and other contexts, notably Lynn's own garden (*Taupataumu*, 1978–82).

The *Guarden Gates* series (1982; see illustration) is recognised as one of the key examples of feminist art in New Zealand. The installation consists of seven steel gates that have been woven with hair and, in one, caked with clay. According to Lynn, they describe a spiritual journey (reconstituting the Stations of the Cross) that is a female alternative to orthodox Christian narrative and a personal odyssey marking significant moments of change through life. Despite its sculptural form and installational function, this work harks back to Lynn's early prints and paintings. Here a grid is interwoven with organic material and nature and culture again entwine.

Guarden Gates is one of a number of works in which hair is used as a medium (others include *Self-Portrait*, *Hair Trigger*, *Caryatid*, *Gates of the Goddess*, *Twist* and *Stain*). Lynn is attracted to this material because of its evocative symbolic potential. She draws on its many cultural meanings, knowingly referring to it as fetish, talisman and taboo. She has used other substances similarly – including skin-like paper, clay and tapa cloth – drawing on both Western and non-Western traditions to imbue her works with personal, female and local (Pacific) significance.

Lynn has contributed as an artist, lecturer and active participant in the art world to the development of a feminist practice in New Zealand. While reclaiming materials and subjects specific to women, she has always used these as artefacts with cultural and not natural significance to women. Strongly independent and fiercely analytical, Lynn is perhaps the first New Zealand artist to develop a critical practice based on the precepts of cultural feminism. Yet her work is neither programmatic nor conventionally political. Enriched by her complex reference to cultural history, Lynn seeks to reinscribe a positive notion of the female erotic into the discourses of Western art and philosophy. Although an important area of activity has been her site-specific and temporary installations, Lynn's less ephemeral work is held in major public collections in New Zealand, the USA and Germany.

CHRISTINA BARTON

M

Maar, Dora
French photographer and painter, 1907–

Born Henrietta Théodora Markovič in Tours, 22 November 1907; changed name to Dora Maar early in life. Studied painting in Paris, at the Ecole des Arts Décoratifs, Académie de Passy, Académie Julian and under André Lhôte; also attended Ecole de Photographie. Lived with the writer Georges Bataille, early 1930s. Shared photographic studio with Pierre Keffer in Neuilly, 1931–4, then temporarily one with Brassaï. Introduced to the Surrealists by Paul Eluard, 1934; exhibited with them in Tenerife (1935), London (1936), New York (1936), Tokyo (1937) and Amsterdam (1938). Met Picasso and joined him at Mougins, 1936; suffered nervous collapse after the affair ended in 1945; ceased working for 10 years. Lives in Ménerbes, Vaucluse.

Selected Individual Exhibitions
Galerie Vanderberg, Paris: 1932
Galerie de Beaune, Paris: 1934
Galerie Jeanne Bucher, Paris: 1944
Galerie René Drouin, Paris: 1945
Galerie Pierre Loeb, Paris: 1946
Galerie Berggruen, Paris: 1957
Leicester Galleries, London: 1958
Standler Gallery, Paris: 1983
Galerie 1900–2000, Paris: 1990
Centre Cultural Bancaixa, Barcelona: 1995

Bibliography
Salvador Dalí, "Objets psycho-atmosphériques-anamorphiques", *Le Surréalisme au service de la Révolution*, no.5, May 1933, pp.45–8
Fantastic Art, Dada, Surrealism, exh. cat., Museum of Modern Art, New York, 1936
Dora Maar, exh. cat., Leicester Galleries, London, 1958
Jean-Paul Crespelle, *Picasso and His Women*, London: Hodder and Stoughton, 1969 (French original)
Roland Barthes, "The photographic message", *Image, Music, Text*, ed. Stephen Heath, London: Fontana, and New York: Hill and Wang, 1977
Walter Benjamin, "A small history of photography" (1931), *One-Way Street*, London: New Left, 1979, pp.240–57 (German original)
L'Amour fou: Photography and Surrealism, exh. cat., Corcoran Gallery of Art, Washington, DC, and elsewhere, 1985
Whitney Chadwick, *Women Artists and the Surrealist Movement*, Boston: Little Brown, and London: Thames and Hudson, 1985
Roy MacGregor-Hastie, *Picasso's Women*, Luton: Lennard, 1988
Dora Maar: Oeuvres anciennes, exh. cat., Galerie 1900–2000, Paris, 1990
Ginger Danto, "Dora Maar: Galerie 1900", *Art News*, lxxxix, November 1990, pp.183–5
James Lord, *Picasso and Dora: A Personal Memoir*, London: Weidenfeld and Nicolson, and New York: Farrar Straus, 1993
Picasso and the Weeping Women: The Years of Marie-Thérèse Walter and Dora Maar, exh. cat., Los Angeles County Museum of Art, and elsewhere, 1994
Dora Maar: Fotógrafa, exh. cat., Centre Cultural Bancaixa, Barcelona, 1995 (with English translation)
Julie L'Enfant, "Dora Maar and the art of mystery", *Woman's Art Journal*, xvii/2, 1996–7, pp.15–20

The artistic career of Théodora Markovič, or Dora Maar as she is better known, has been overshadowed by her personal life. As the model for Pablo Picasso's *Weeping Woman* (Tate Gallery, London), her iconic face has masked an artistic career that has been both varied and fruitful, beginning and ending with painting but being most notable for photography.

Maar took classes in both painting and photography as a student in Paris in the 1920s. Establishing herself as a photographer in 1931 in her own studio at Neuilly with Pierre Keffer, she quickly earned fame with her photographic portraits, still lifes and advertisements. Her talents extended to the film camera, for she worked with Louis Chavance in 1930 and with Jean Renoir in 1935 on his film *Le Crime de Monsieur Lange*. She also produced archaeological photographs in collaboration with Germain Bazin, and after the closure of her studio in 1934, she temporarily shared a studio with another eminent artist – Brassaï.

Maar's studies of Arums (*Arums*, 1930; see illustration; *Bouquet d'Arums*, 1933; Centre Georges Pompidou, Paris) are not merely still lifes, they must be viewed – in the light of Roland Barthes's terminology – as "photogenia", that is, embellished images wherein reality is sublimated by techniques of lighting, exposure and printing. It is this quality that brings photography into the realm of aesthetics. Transposing petals and stalks into voluptuous compositions, using light to create a painterly chiaroscuro, juxtaposing fleshy petals with powdery stamens, her *Arums* are posed so that they imply "signifieds of connotation" – namely spirituality, fragility, eroticism.

A comparison of Man Ray's portrait of *Dora Maar* (1936) and her portrait of *Nusch Eluard* (1935; Centre Georges

Maar: *Arums*, 1930; Musée National d'Art Moderne, Centre Georges Pompidou, Paris

Pompidou) highlights the exciting development of photography as an artistic medium in Paris in the 1930s. While Man Ray's image reduces Maar to a mask-like fetish, Maar's study of Nusch Eluard is seductive, but actively so. While fellow male Surrealists removed woman or the *femme-enfant* from the real, logical world, Maar rejected this mythologising of woman and presented Nusch as an autonomous being, emphasising her strongly lit hands in such a way as to reinforce her concreteness.

It was through Paul Eluard that Maar was first introduced to the Surrealists in 1934. Her composition *29 rue d'Astorg* of 1936 was reproduced in the Surrealist publication *Cartes postales surréalistes* (1937), and her photographs were exhibited in the *Fantastic Art, Dada, Surrealism* exhibition of that year at the Museum of Modern Art, New York. *The Simulator* (1936; Centre Georges Pompidou) exemplifies her surreal blend of eroticism and collage-like juxtapositions, creating a dislocation of meaning. This photomontage challenges the distinction between the real and the feigned in a Freudian scene of a wanderer rapt in a Tower-of-Babel-like turret: lacking fixity, he sways before his unconscious imagination. Maar's image of Alfred Jarry's *Père Ubu* (1936; Collection Arturo Schwarz, Milan) is even more nightmarish. Here she uses virtuoso techniques to distort reality so that the blurring of lines and close-up of surface create a monstrous image in a Poe-like manner. It is also reminiscent of Salvador Dalí's "psycho-atmospheric-anamorphic object".

Maar's relationship with Picasso from 1936 to 1945 marked a traumatic turn in her artistic and mental well-being. Artistically it heralded a turn to reportage photography with her lengthy documentation of Picasso's *Guernica* in its evolv-

ing stages, her study of Giacometti's *La Femme invisible* and of the fur-lined *Objet* by Meret Oppenheim (q.v.), capturing it from a Freudian-womb angle to emphasise its erotic potency. Maar did not merely capture these art works on film, she contributed to their historical production by re-presenting them. She was the catalyst behind Picasso's rare venture into political imagery, suggesting symbols for *Guernica* and inspiring the wailing woman figure bearing her dead child.

For Picasso she was always the weeping woman. In an interview with James Lord, Picasso claimed: "I gave her a tortured appearance, not out of Sadism ... but in obedience to a vision that had imposed itself upon me ... She was anything you wanted, a dog, a mouse, a bird, an idea, a thunderstorm" (quoted in Lord 1993). Evidently her peculiar (for the time and for a lover of Picasso) blend of femininity and intellectuality threatened Picasso, who admitted: "she made my brain work, it was sometimes very tiring". Maar saw that with each lover came a new period in his oeuvre, a new colour scheme, a new self-portrait. She would parody this artist-model relationship in her own Cubist portrait of the master: *Picasso* of 1938 (repr. Paris 1990). Their relationship ended with the arrival of Françoise Gilet, the "Florentine Virgin" in 1945. Maar suffered a nervous breakdown, and was reported to have been found naked in the stairway of her apartment building, hysterical. She was committed to the psychiatric hospital of Sainte-Anne in Paris where she was subjected to electric shock therapy. Eluard was appalled at such treatment – there is no mention of Picasso – and ensured that she was placed under the private analysis of Jacques Lacan instead. This led to mental recovery but her self-image had suffered a heavy blow. She would not produce art for another ten years.

Maar's subsequent move from photography to painting has been attributed to her involvement with Picasso. Her still-life exhibition of 1945 in Paris marked a turn towards bleak palettes and macabre juxtapositions that seemed to match her black-clad image. By 1957 a move from Paris to sunny Provence inspired a series of landscapes that combined her new-found Catholicism with a Buddhist approach to nature. Her *Paysage* (1957; *ibid*), exhibited in Paris and London, marks a renewed confidence in its translation of photographic lyricism into paint. A rolling mountainside, which evokes depth through flat brush strokes and bands of earthy hues, this image is majestic in its worship of nature and yet ominous in its marked lack of human life. In the accompanying catalogue Douglas Cooper noted the influence of Turner and Courbet (London 1958). Apart from vague links with the sublime and the rural this is a tenuous if not mistaken comparison. Maar's dramatic use of colour, surface play and denial of symbolism are better viewed in the light of contemporary Abstract Expressionism.

The lyrical but economic style of Maar's art permeated her exhibition at the Galerie 1900–2000 in 1990. In his catalogue entry Edouard Jaguer described her landscapes as "automatic landscapes", and quoted the artist's artistic intention to "say what I say with authenticity" (Paris 1990). This Surrealist automatism permeates all her art: the orientation of art away from the pictorial, the framed world, and towards the poetic, the indulgence in what Walter Benjamin termed the "optical unconscious". In an interview with James Lord, Maar stated in true Surrealist language, endorsing Barthes's theory of photogenia: "Art after all only embellishes truth. It is not truth itself" (Lord 1993). This conviction has been the constant principle on which all her work is based.

ALYCE MAHON

Macalister, Molly
New Zealand sculptor, 1920–1979

Born in Invercargill, New Zealand, 18 May 1920. Studied at Canterbury University College School of Art under sculptor Francis Shurrock, 1938–40. Worked as a land girl on a Southland farm, under wartime regulations, 1941. Went to work at the Otago Museum, making models of animals for agricultural displays, 1942. Moved north to Auckland, 1943. Married Hungarian immigrant George Haydn, 1945; son born 1947. Lived at Takapuna, North Shore, Auckland. First left New Zealand, travelling to USA and Europe, 1961. After a second trip to Europe in 1969, initiated an international sculpture symposium, which took place in Auckland in 1971. Visited the Zen Centre in San Francisco, 1972; later joined the Auckland Zen Buddhist group. Founder-member, 1961, and honorary life member, 1976, New Zealand Society of Sculptors and Painters. Died in Auckland, 12 October 1979.

Principal Exhibitions
Auckland Society of Arts: 1944–9
Tate Gallery, London: 1953 (*Entries for Unknown Political Prisoner Sculpture*)
Auckland City Art Gallery: 1955 (*New Zealand Contemporary Sculpture*), 1957 (*Freyburg Place Rediscovered*, New Zealand Institute of Architects Conference), 1959 (*Three Auckland Sculptors*, with Alison Duff and Ann Severs), 1966 (*Recent New Zealand Sculpture*), 1982 (retrospective)
Commonwealth Institute, London: 1962 (*Commonwealth Art Today*)
Elam School of Fine Arts, Auckland: 1963 (*Elam Sculpture*)
Mildura Arts Festival, Australia: 1973 (*Sculpturscape*)
New Vision Gallery, Auckland: 1975 (*New Zealand Women Sculptors and Printmakers*)

Bibliography
Year Book of the Arts in New Zealand, no.1, 1945, p.94; no.3, 1947, p.93; no.5, 1949, pp.98–9
Michael Nicholson, "New Zealand contemporary sculpture", *Home and Building*, July 1955, pp.44–7
Gerhard Rosenberg, "Two Auckland sculpture exhibitions", *Landfall*, xiii, 1959, pp.267–9
—, "An exhibition of sculpture in Auckland", *Home and Building*, November 1959, pp.52, 81–4
I.V. Porsolt, "Festival exhibition of sculpture at Elam School of Art", *Home and Building*, August 1963, pp.52–3, 69
P.A. Tomory, "New Zealand sculpture", *Art and Australia*, iii, 1965, pp.108–13
—, "Art", *The Pattern of New Zealand Culture*, ed. A.C. McLeod, Ithaca, NY: Cornell University Press, 1968
Peter Cape, *Artists and Craftsmen in New Zealand*, London: Collins, 1969
Charles Fearnley, "Sculptures and murals in public buildings", *New Zealand Institute of Architects Journal*, September 1973, p.240
Michael Dunn, "Aspects of New Zealand sculpture, 5: The art schools, 1890–1976", *Education*, xxvi/5, 1977, p.26
Molly Macalister: A Memorial Exhibition, exh. cat., Auckland City Art Gallery, 1982
Robin Woodward, "The sculpture of Molly Macalister", *Art New Zealand*, no.26, 1983, pp.32–3
Elizabeth Eastmond and Merimeri Penfold, *Women and the Arts in New Zealand: Forty Works, 1936–86*, Auckland: Penguin, 1986
Anne Kirker, *New Zealand Women Artists: A Survey of 150 Years*, 2nd edition, Tortola, BVI: Craftsman House, 1993

Molly Macalister was primarily a sculptor of human figures, heads and animals, in attitudes of stillness and repose. Her best works convey power, presence, a deep respect for her subject, and monumental scale whatever their physical size. Her large public sculptures combine to an unusual degree sculptural excellence with general popularity.

Macalister began her training as a sculptor at a time when modelling in clay and casting in plaster were the norms in New Zealand art schools. She excelled at these academic exercises, but quickly developed skills in carving wood and local Oamaru limestone. Several early works demonstrate her knowledge of and admiration for Maori and Oceanic traditions in wood carving: *Head* (1941–2; jarrah), which depicts a Maori woman, and *Mask* (1948–50; kauri; both Haydn Family Collection, Auckland) were described by Peter Tomory (1965) as the two strongest works of New Zealand sculpture of the 1940s.

Opportunities to exhibit work were scarce in Auckland before the late 1950s, when the first professional dealer galleries were established. Macalister was one of a small group of artists at that time who attempted to increase public interest in sculpture. In 1952 she entered an international competition for a sculpture of the Unknown Political Prisoner, organised by the Institute of Contemporary Arts in London. Her maquette (destroyed), a standing figure with hands clasped above the head, was selected as the New Zealand entry and was exhibited at the Tate Gallery, London, in 1953. Macalister's political commitment to the cause of oppressed and suffering people was the impetus for other works, such as the *Last of the Just* (1960; concrete; University of Waikato, Hamilton) and *Victim* (1966; see illustration).

In 1955 seven of her works were selected for the first exhibition of contemporary New Zealand sculpture at the Auckland City Art Gallery (now Auckland Art Gallery). This was a landmark exhibition, featuring the work of artists who had made a conscious break with the prevailing academic style. Most of Macalister's works were in wood or plaster, but she also showed a small bronze piece, *Birds* (1954; Haydn Family Collection), and a kneeling figure of a man, *Concrete Figure for Bronze* (1953; private collection, Auckland, repr. Auckland 1982, p.34). At this time there were no facilities for casting bronze on a large scale in Auckland.

In 1956 the Auckland City Art Gallery mounted an exhibition of Henry Moore's sculpture and drawings, which attracted 36,000 visitors – a world record for a Moore show – as well as outraged comments in the local press. Macalister responded to Moore's emphasis on the fundamental importance of the human figure for sculpture. Further developments in her work were precipitated by the arrival in New Zealand in 1957 of Ann Severs, a British sculptor who had worked in Italy with Marino Marini. The two women became friends and practised life drawing together. In July 1959 Macalister and Severs had an exhibition at the Auckland City Art Gallery with Alison Duff, who had returned to New Zealand from

Macalister: *Victim*, 1966; Auckland Art Gallery Collection

Australia. This exhibition marked the beginning of a flowering of sculpture in Auckland. The three women sculptors all began using concrete as a final material with intrinsic qualities and merits – no longer an interim stage on the way to bronze casting. Concrete had none of the preciousness nor academic history of bronze; it was tough and modern. The women had to invent their own techniques, and experimented with mixing and colouring the concrete, which they then built up over steel armatures or cast in plaster moulds. The resulting works were vigorously modelled and physically strong, and Macalister's figures became more compact and solidly grounded. Critical response was enthusiastic, and Macalister showed other works in concrete at successive contemporary exhibitions at the Auckland City Art Gallery in 1960 and 1962. One of these was *Bird Watcher* (1961; McCahon Family Collection), a figure of a woman. Colin McCahon, himself a major New Zealand painter, later wrote:

> Molly gave us our Bird Watcher who sits in the garden and watches birds on our grapefruit tree and a privet. She never looks down. She is a calm and detached figure who watches beyond the birds and the trees to something even more rewarding. It could be the sunset or rainbows lacing a passing storm or the world of clouds that hang heavily in the Auckland sky most times – a feeling of peace [*Art New Zealand*, no.14, 1979].

In February 1964 the Auckland City Council commissioned Macalister to make a large sculpture of a Maori chief to stand at the lower end of Queen Street looking out over the port and Waitemata Harbour. She consulted the local Maori, Ngati

Whatua o Orakei, and gained their support for the work. After a year of working on small models, Macalister began making the final plaster model, which was built over reinforced steel in a plastic tent in her garden. The work, 3 metres high, was then cast in bronze and finally unveiled on 2 July 1967. It is an imposing figure of a chief wearing a *kaitaka* (full-length ceremonial cloak), a feather ear ornament and holding a *mere* (short, flat hand club). In 1967 Macalister won a competition for a bronze sculpture for public gardens in Hamilton, the city at the centre of the rural Waikato region south of Auckland. Her aim was a work of public sculpture that adults could enjoy and children play on. *Little Bull* is a strong, almost archaic work that arouses affection through its approachability. In the early 1970s she made a number of abstract works based on the shapes and shards of hollow broken vessels. These included a commission for a crematorium on Auckland's North Shore. In her last work, however, Macalister returned to solid, simplified forms made from the hard, volcanic basalt of the Takapuna reef near her home. They included the *Buddha* (1976–7; vesicular basalt; ht 15.5 cm.; Collection of the Auckland Zen Buddhist Group), a sheep, a bird and a fish – small, self-contained and serene. Although she did not make a large number of works, Macalister is an important figure in 20th-century New Zealand sculpture. In a discussion of Macalister's *Maori Youth with Child* (1959; concrete; Victoria University of Wellington) Peter Tomory quoted Paul Gauguin, and his words could apply to all of Molly Macalister's oeuvre: "Let everything about you breathe the calm and peace of the soul".

ALEXA M. JOHNSTON

Macdonald, Frances
British painter and designer, 1873–1921

Born in Kidsgrove, Staffordshire, 24 August 1873, younger sister of Margaret Macdonald (q.v.); father a colliery manager. Moved frequently with her family during early years, settling in father's home town of Glasgow by 1890. Studied at Glasgow School of Art under Francis Newbery, 1890–94. Collaborated with Margaret at their Glasgow studio, mid-1890s. Worked with the group that became known as "The Four": Frances and Margaret Macdonald, architect Charles Rennie Mackintosh and designer James Herbert McNair. Married McNair, 1899; son born 1900. Moved to Liverpool after marriage, and taught with McNair at the School of Architecture and Applied Art. Returned to Glasgow, 1908; taught design in the enamelling and embroidery departments, Glasgow School of Art, until 1910. Won bronze medal for a design for a majolica plate, Department of Science and Art National Competition, 1892. Died in Glasgow, 12 December 1921; McNair destroyed most of her work after her death.

Principal Exhibitions
Glasgow Institute of Fine Arts: 1895
Arts and Crafts Exhibition Society, London: 1896
Liverpool Autumn Exhibition: 1896
International Society of Sculptors, Painters and Gravers, London: 1899

Frances Macdonald: *Girl in the East Wind with Ravens Passing the Moon (Ill Omen)*, 1893; Glasgow University: Hunterian Museum

Vienna Secession: 1900
Esposizione Internazionale d'Arte Decorativa Moderna, Turin: 1902
Sandon Society of Artists, Liverpool: from 1905
London Salon of the Allied Artists Association: 1908
Baillie Gallery, London: 1911 (with Herbert McNair)

Bibliography

The Studio, ix, 1896, pp.202–3
Gleeson White, "Some Glasgow designers and their work", *The Studio*, xi, 1897, pp.86–100
Anthea Callen, *Angel in the Studio: Women in the Arts and Crafts Movement, 1870–1914*, London: Astragal, 1979; as *Women Artists of the Arts and Crafts Movement, 1870–1914*, New York: Pantheon, 1979
Jude Burkhauser, ed., *Glasgow Girls: Women in Art and Design, 1880–1920*, 2nd edition, Edinburgh: Canongate, and Cape May, NJ: Red Ochre, 1993
Janice Helland, "Frances Macdonald: The self as *fin-de-siècle* woman", *Woman's Art Journal*, xiv/1, 1993, pp.15–22
——, "Collaborative work among 'The Four'", *Charles Rennie Mackintosh*, ed. Wendy Kaplan, New York: Abbeville, 1996
——, *The Studios of Frances and Margaret Macdonald*, Manchester: Manchester University Press, 1996

Frances Macdonald studied at the Glasgow School of Art (GSA), and with her sister Margaret Macdonald (q.v.) opened a studio in the mid-1890s. Most of the collaborative studio production was decorative art, such as the *Vanity* mirror (1895; Hunterian Art Gallery, University of Glasgow) made with her future husband James Herbert McNair and her sister Margaret, and the silver clock designed and made by the sisters and exhibited first at the Arts and Crafts Exhibition (London) of 1896, then later at the Vienna Secession of 1900. Although Frances collaborated extensively with her sister during the 1890s (particularly on metalwork), she moved away from such production after her marriage and focused on watercolour painting. The exception to this was the work that she designed and exhibited at the Esposizione Internazionale d'Arte Decorativa Moderna, Turin, in 1902 (e.g. a carpet, a table cover and an embroidered curtain for a settle, *The Studio*, 1902, p.98).

Macdonald's early watercolour pictures, such as *Girl in the East Wind with Ravens Passing the Moon (Ill Omen)* (1893; see illustration), *A Pond* (1894; Glasgow School of Art) and her early metalwork such as *Day* (untraced, repr. *Dekorative Kunst*, iii, 1899, p.72), a beaten metal sconce paired with Margaret Macdonald's *Night*, exemplify the non-traditional direction she took in her production. In *Ill Omen* Frances Macdonald's strong vertical line enhanced the unconventional representation of a 19th-century female, and made the picture a visual articulation of a solitary woman. The picture conveys a pervasive sense of distance, aloneness and aloofness. The severe elongation of the closed-eyed woman with her large, powerful hands folded across her pubic area assures the impenetrability of her space. Far from being a desirable object, she exists as an independent subject in her own world. The androgynous figures in *A Pond* also speak of a "different kind" of woman; they represent a sardonic mockery of the languid, sensuous Pre-Raphaelite woman, and the figures become a caricature of a type of Victorian woman. By the 1890s the languid, melancholy Pre-Raphaelite woman was a recognisable type that existed in contradistinction to the "new woman". Frances Macdonald's naked figures effectively deny Victorian Puritanism and, at the same time, eliminate the seductiveness evoked by the form-hugging Pre-Raphaelite drapery. The smiling "ghosts" floating above the figures observe the knobby-kneed hermaphrodites with glee and, while the picture has usually been called hideous, its humour is also evident. The elongated nude figure that stretches up through the centre of her beaten metal sconce, powerfully holding up a portion of the sky, reinforces Macdonald's conception of woman as strong, independent and solitary.

After having her membership nomination rejected by the Royal Scottish Society of Painters in Watercolours in 1898, Macdonald turned to newer, less traditional exhibiting venues such as the International Society of Sculptors, Painters and Gravers, the Sandon Studios in Liverpool (she also did some teaching in Liverpool, first for the University, then for Sandon) and the London Salon. Her decorative work after 1899 was limited to the decorating of her own home (photographed for *Modern British Domestic Architecture: Special Number of The Studio*, 1901, pp.116–19); her exhibited work after this date consisted largely of watercolour paintings.

Pictures such as *Birth of the Rose* (c.1908; Dublin Municipal Art Gallery) and *Sleep* (c.1908; private collection, repr. Christie's, Glasgow, 13 May 1993, p.23) are typical of her work after the turn of the century. The tall, lone, white figure dominating the left side of *Sleep* covers her eyes in order to banish from her view "a sequence of dreams, where three couples, perhaps depicting courtship, marriage and death, form a narrative against a linear chimerical background strewn with hearts, petals and bubbles" (*idem*). This speaks to the viewer of isolation from the "coupled" world in which the early 20th-century woman was located on marriage. *Birth of the Rose* reinforces childbirth and child-raising as women-centred activities; the male is notably absent.

Macdonald's later watercolour pictures continue to question the role of "woman"; they were never exhibited and speak poignantly of the relationship between the sexes. For example, *Man Makes the Beads of Life but Woman Must Thread Them* (after 1912; Hunterian Art Gallery) is a clear and direct representation of woman's role and her inability to transcend it. The picture shows a nude male, sex organs explicitly depicted, holding an egg-like circle containing a child. He offers this "gift" to a woman. She faces the viewer straight-on; her hair, recalling that of the "girl in the east wind", streaks out in a strong horizontal away from her head. The woman covers her pubic area with a large circle containing a child. Her hands intrude into the circle; her long, thin fingers wrap around the baby. Both the male and the female figures are elongated and emaciated. Like Frances Macdonald's earlier work, the predominant colours are blue, mauve and green. Also like some of her early work, this picture is unsettling, disturbing. According to Frances's title, pregnancy is caused by the male while responsibility for the child's care and tending belongs to the female. Once again Macdonald confronts female desire, suggesting that motherhood, rather than being desired by women, is thrust upon them. Like her sister Margaret, Frances depicted women, but unlike her sister, she introduced pathos, frustration, futility and despair into her visual descriptions of women and their constructed roles.

JANICE HELLAND

Macdonald, Margaret

British painter and designer, 1864–1933

Born in Tipton, near Wolverhampton, Staffordshire, 5 November 1864; older sister of Frances Macdonald (q.v.). Studied at the Glasgow School of Art under Francis Newbery. Set up studio in Glasgow with Frances by 1896. Worked with the group that became known as "The Four": Frances and Margaret Macdonald, architect Charles Rennie Mackintosh and designer James Herbert McNair. Married Mackintosh, 1900; he died 1928. Lived in Chelsea, London, 1914–23. Moved to the south of France, 1923; lived in Collioure in the French Pyrenees, then in Port Vendres, Provence. Stayed in London while Mackintosh received treatment for cancer, 1927–8; settled in England after his death. Member, Royal Scottish Society of Painters in Watercolours, 1898 (served on Council, 1907–13). Died in Chelsea studio, London, 7 January 1933.

Principal Exhibitions

Arts and Crafts Exhibition Society, London: 1896, 1899, 1916
Royal Scottish Society of Painters in Watercolours: occasionally 1898–1922
International Society of Sculptors, Painters and Gravers, London: 1899, 1909 (special *Fair Women* exhibition)
Esposizione Internazionale d'Arte, Venice: 1899
Vienna Secession: 1900
Esposizione Internazionale d'Arte Decorativa Moderna, Turin: 1902 (diploma of honour, with Charles Rennie Mackintosh)

Bibliography

The Studio, ix, 1896, pp.202–3
Gleeson White, "Some Glasgow designers and their work", *The Studio*, xi, 1897, pp.86–100
Anthea Callen, *Angel in the Studio: Women in the Arts and Crafts Movement, 1870–1914*, London: Astragal, 1979; as *Women Artists of the Arts and Crafts Movement, 1870–1914*, New York: Pantheon, 1979
Margaret Macdonald Mackintosh, 1864–1933, exh. cat., Hunterian Art Gallery, University of Glasgow, 1983
Jude Burkhauser, ed., *Glasgow Girls: Women in Art and Design, 1880–1920*, 2nd edition, Edinburgh: Canongate, and Cape May, NJ: Red Ochre, 1993
Janice Helland, "The critics and the Arts and Crafts: The instance of Margaret Macdonald and Charles Rennie Mackintosh", *Art History*, xvii, 1994, pp.205–23
——, *The Studios of Frances and Margaret Macdonald*, Manchester: Manchester University Press, 1996

In the autumn of 1890 Margaret Macdonald and her younger sister Frances Macdonald (q.v.) enrolled as students at the progressive Glasgow School of Art. The securely middle-class Macdonald sisters studied as day students at the school; young women studying in the evening classes tended to be from working-class homes and followed courses that would lead to careers in teaching or industrial design. The sisters, however, followed courses in drawing, design, metalwork and modelling, and by the beginning of their second year of study registered themselves as design students, thus preparing themselves for careers as decorative artists as well as exhibitors of watercolour paintings.

Margaret Macdonald's career included the production of collaborative art (first with her sister and James Herbert McNair, then with her husband, Charles Rennie Mackintosh), as well as the production of her own decorative art and the making of watercolour pictures. The bold and striking design made to advertise Joseph Wright's umbrella manufacture, *Drooko* (1895; repr. *Dekorative Kunst*, 1899), represents the first commissioned work that the sisters made from their studio in Hope Street. Although the poster was criticised in the *Glasgow Evening News* (February 1895), it established the sisters' reputations as "the only 'new' poster designers" working in Glasgow, and by the spring of the same year their "clever" metalwork was commended by the press when it appeared in a Glasgow Arts and Crafts exhibition.

Following successes in Glasgow, the group of artists who came to be known as "The Four" (Margaret and Frances Macdonald, Mackintosh and McNair) achieved critical acclaim in Europe with their contributions to the Vienna Secession (1900) and the Esposizione Internazionale d'Arte Decorativa Moderna in Turin (1902). In both exhibitions the four artists were responsible for the unusual decoration of spaces set aside as "rooms", considered by German critics to be elegant, magical and bizarre (*Dekorative Kunst*, vii, 1901, p.171). The Scottish section at the Turin exhibition was called "quaint and curious" and Margaret Macdonald's panels were singled out for their elongation and "chimerical character" (*Journal of Decorative Art and British Decorator*, July 1902, p.195).

Macdonald's gesso panels are most representative of her production and bring together the imagery that she used repeatedly in design projects as well as in watercolour painting. A panel made for Kate Cranston's Ingram Street tea rooms, the *May Queen* (Glasgow Museums and Art Galleries), which was also exhibited at the Vienna Secession, is characteristic. Woman becomes a round, enclosed shape, a head emerging from a large blossom, or a narrow, armless and footless shape. Like almost all of Macdonald's representations of women, these figures are decorative, confined and denied movement. The two panels that she exhibited at Turin, *Heart of the Rose* and *The White Rose and the Red Rose*, both of which were purchased by the Viennese art patron Fritz Wärndorfer, are typical of Macdonald's production in two ways: they depict women and they are not one-of-a-kind productions.

Macdonald continually represented a restricted and limited woman in her gessos and watercolours. In 1901 she made a duplicate *Heart of the Rose* panel for R. Wylie Hill, which was incorporated into a fireplace designed by Mackintosh. The commission probably came to Macdonald through her friend Jessie Newbery (q.v.). The panel takes as its theme the female experience of childbirth (nativity) shared with another woman. Thus the rose motif, favoured by Newbery, becomes the foil around which to build an image of motherhood and childbirth and, given the time the design for the panel was first made (*c*.1900), it might represent Frances Macdonald's recent nativity (she gave birth to her only child, Sylvan, in 1900). During the 19th and early 20th centuries sisters often aided each other during childbirth as well as during the subsequent recovery period. In the panel, responsibility for the infant is shared by two women; there is no man present. And while the luxurious surface and sensuous line transfer the image from the material world into the ideal, the sharing of the "rose child" pulls the viewer back into an environment of kinship, support and harmony.

The exquisite panels *Heart of the Rose* and *The White Rose and the Red Rose* represent a decorative motif that Macdonald

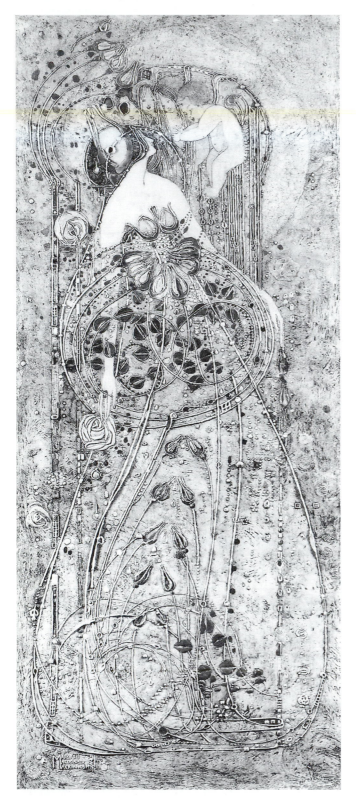

Margaret Macdonald: *Summer*, 1904; National Museum of Antiquities, Edinburgh

used as a trademark during the early years of the century. Thus, as with earlier work from the sisters' studio in Hope Street, these two works can be read as highly developed, thought-out designs, recognisable as Margaret's and usually made to interact with commissioned interiors. While reading them hermetically for meanings that might be ascribed to women, one must also read them practically as decorative work made to harmonise with and beautify specific environments. The design prototype or "signature stamp" for the completed projects can be found on the cover of *Deutsche Kunst und Dekoration* (May 1902). The drawing represents woman as rose in full bloom. The three white roses near the top of the drawing, one of which is in the woman's hair, the seven red roses in the composition, the peacock in the upper right-hand corner and the two round purple shapes signal Macdonald's design pattern. The pattern appeared first in her gesso panel *May Queen* and was subsequently repeated in her commissions. This design is not meant as a precious and one-of-a-kind piece but rather as an individualised kind of work-shop production in which the hand of a particular author can be read clearly.

Macdonald's long discussed but "missing" panel of the *Seven Princesses*, which was commissioned by Wärndorfer for the Music Room of his Viennese home around 1900, was recently found locked away in a wooden crate behind a partition wall in the Österreichisches Museum für angewandte Kunst, Vienna. It reveals, as do her other panels, the exquisite sense of detail and elegantly textured surface that characterise the work she did for interiors ("A lost masterpiece is found in Vienna: Margaret Macdonald's triptych resurfaces after fifty years", *Architectural Digest*, October 1995, pp.66–72). This panel was inspired by Maeterlinck's play *The Seven Princesses* (probably at Wärndorfer's request) and, like earlier panels, helped to compose a total environment, a room or rooms designed by Mackintosh and Margaret Macdonald.

In 1909 Macdonald exhibited three of these gesso panels at the International Society of Sculptors, Painters and Gravers' special exhibition of *Fair Women*; they were *In Willow Wood* (1903; Glasgow Art Gallery and Museum), *Summer* (1904) and *The White Rose and the Red Rose* (c.1909; Hunterian Art Gallery, University of Glasgow). According to *Building News*, a "good deal of attention" was claimed by these "three large exhibits in gesso". The critic saw them as "studies of fine-line decoration" in which the female figure had been "introduced merely as something round with which to weave these decorated forms" (*Building News*, 26 February 1909, p.4). The figure in *The White Rose and the Red Rose*, however, is not "something round" but is enveloped in the same tear-drop-shaped shroud that enclosed the women in a set of embroidered panels that Macdonald had designed for the Vienna Secession. *The White Rose and the Red Rose* had hung above the studio fireplace in her own home, and was a duplicate of the panel that had been part of the *Rose Boudoir* at the Turin exhibition of 1902. *Summer* (1904; see illustration) was probably similar to two earlier pieces: a metal-framed watercolour of the same name from 1897 (Glasgow Art Gallery and Museums) and her watercolour picture, *June Roses* (1898; Neue Galerie in der Stallburg, Vienna); *In Willow Wood* had been lent by Cranston from the Sauchiehall Tea Rooms. The *Building News* selected for discussion the two panels in which the female figure is more obviously female and implicitly "fair", and ignored the narrow, oblong figure in *The White Rose and the Red Rose*, which, while perhaps less fair than the other representations, does represent a consistent aspect of Macdonald's work – a woman unable to move, restricted and bound. Her watercolour pictures presented the same image of women to their viewers and although her watercolour production represents a smaller part of her work than does her decorative art, it enhances an understanding of it and elaborates upon the theme of all her images: women.

Three watercolour pictures, all exhibited with the Royal Scottish Society of Painters in Watercolours, clearly represent her oeuvre: *Mysterious Garden*, (1911; private collection, repr. Helland 1996, p.150), *Pool of Silence* (1913; private collection, *ibid.*, p.153) and *Legend of the Blackthorns* (1922; Hunterian Art Gallery). All three pictures depict solemn, introspective women who represent a kind of shrouded stillness. Contemporary critics read these pictures as mysterious, strange and decorative (*The Times*, 6 April 1911, p.10; *Glasgow Herald*, 31 March 1911, p.9); to a present-day viewer they might be considered as images that eschew sexual subservience by eradicating desire. Whatever meaning they represent for a viewer they are technically exquisite.

All Macdonald's projects, whether collaboratively made with her sister or her husband, or made alone, speak of intelligence, thoughtfulness and craftsmanship. They represent a caring about her subject matter and a concern for an elegant and precise presentation that has continuing power to fascinate viewers.

JANICE HELLAND

Macdowell, Susan *see* Eakins

McGuinness, Norah

Irish painter, 1903–1980

Born in Derry, 1903. Studied at Metropolitan College of Art, Dublin, under Patrick Tuohy, Oswald Reeves and Harry Clarke, 1921–4; Chelsea School of Art, London, 1924. Married the poet Geoffrey Phibbs (better known as Geoffrey Taylor), 1925; divorced 1931. Through Phibbs became involved with literary and theatrical activities in Ireland, which led to illustrating and set and costume designing. Studied at Académie Lhôte, Paris, 1929–31; exhibited at Galerie Zac, 1932. Lived in London, 1931–7; exhibited with Seven and Five Society and London Group, 1933, and at Zwemmer Gallery, 1934. Moved to New York, 1937; began designing shop-window displays; exhibited in Ireland's Historical and Cultural Pavilion, New York World's Fair, 1939. Returned to Dublin 1939 or 1940. President, Irish Exhibition of Living Art, 1944–72; honorary member, Royal Hibernian Academy, 1957. Recipient of honorary doctorate, Trinity College, Dublin, 1973. Died in Dublin, 22 November 1980.

Selected Individual Exhibitions

Wertheim Gallery, London: 1933
Painters' Gallery, Dublin: 1936, 1938, 1941
Sullivan Gallery, New York: 1938
Victor Waddington Gallery, Dublin: 1938, 1940, 1943
Paul Reinhart Gallery, New York: 1939
Leicester Galleries, London: 1947, 1951, 1957, 1963
Venice Biennale: 1950 (with Nano Reid)
Dawson Gallery, Dublin: 1964, 1977
Mercury Gallery, London: 1967
Douglas Hyde Gallery, Trinity College, Dublin: 1968 (touring retrospective)
Keys Gallery, Derry: 1976
Taylor Galleries, Dublin: 1979

Bibliography

Twelve Irish Painters, exh. cat., Art Centre of the New School for Social Research, New York, 1963
Norah McGuinness: A Retrospective Exhibition, exh. cat., Trinity College, Dublin, 1968
Marianne Hartigan, "The commercial design career of Norah McGuinness", *Irish Arts Review*, iii/3, 1986, pp.23–5
Irish Women Artists from the Eighteenth Century to the Present Day, exh. cat., National Gallery of Ireland, Dublin, and elsewhere, 1987
Kenneth McConkey, *A Free Spirit: Irish Art, 1860–1960*, Woodbridge: Antique Collectors Club-Pyms Gallery, 1990
S.B. Kennedy, *Irish Art and Modernism, 1880–1950*, Belfast: Institute for Irish Studies, 1991

Norah McGuinness belongs to a second generation of Irish women artists of the modern movement. Trained like many of them in Paris under André Lhôte, she developed a painting style characterised by richness of colour and brushwork, which in its generalised abstraction fits in with the work of other Irish artists of the mid-20th century. Certainly, McGuinness provided leadership and opportunities for Irish artists. The first Irish Exhibition of Living Art was held in September and October of 1943 as part of a reaction to the conservatism of the Royal Hibernian Academy and the need for a venue for avant-garde artists. McGuinness played an important role of leadership and within the year she took over as director, serving until early 1972. Her handling of this annual event is admired even more than her paintings.

McGuinness began her career as a commercial artist. In 1926 she provided set and costume designs for the Abbey Theatre and in 1927 for the Peacock Theatre. She continued to supplement her income with such work throughout her life. She also illustrated books by W.B. Yeats, Laurence Sterne, Maria Edgeworth, Elizabeth Bowen and Elizabeth Hamilton and did fashion illustrations for the *Bystander*, *Vogue* and *Harper's Bazaar*. In the USA in the late 1930s she began shop-window display designs for such New York stores as B. Altman and Bonwit Teller. On her return to Dublin she resumed design work for the Abbey Theatre and undertook window displays for the Dublin store Brown Thomas.

By the late 1920s, however, painting was her main occupation. In 1929 she studied under Lhôte in Paris but initially was little influenced by Cubism. She worked largely with gouache in a Fauvist manner reminiscent of Vlaminck. Among her best and most admired works is a series of the Thames in London, done in the early 1930s. Here, using bold strokes, she invokes

McGuinness: *Garden Green*, 1952; Hugh Lane Municipal Gallery of Modern Art, Dublin

illustration) is a strong, indeed monumental study of still life, window and garden. She creates a stable frame with chair, window frame and blinds, against which is set a Cubist study of pots and bottles. The background is a beautifully painted garden with trees, roses and a human figure. The bright greens and strength of forms make it a dominant painting. A similar but less dynamic work is *Still Life* (oil on canvas; 51 × 76 cm.; Allied Irish Banks) with a Cubist foreground composition of chair, plants and pots set against a snowy mountain landscape. Norah McGuinness produced a delightful series of paintings dealing with images that she could see easily. Nature, birds, the sea were the basis of her art, and she approached them with a sure sense of colour and form. Her leadership of the Irish Exhibition of Living Art was of inestimable value to Irish artists. The most important public collections of her work are the Hugh Lane Municipal Gallery of Modern Art, Dublin, the Ulster Museum, Belfast, and the Hirshhorn Museum and Sculpture Garden, Washington, DC.

MARTHA B. CALDWELL

the broad river and its setting (e.g. *Thames*, private collection, repr. Dublin 1987, fig.27).

Her delight in waterscapes continued throughout her career, but she also painted still-life scenes, mountain and domestic views. She turned from gouache to oils, and her late work is more Cubist than Fauvist but with a strong lyrical quality. One of her favourite subjects was Dublin Bay, focusing on light, patterns of sand and sea-birds. *Wet Patches, No.3* (1965; gouache on paper; 33.6 × 49.5 cm.; Hirshhorn Museum and Sculpture Garden, Washington, DC) is a painting with strong contrasts of image and brushwork. The sand, with the wet patches done in grey with black outlines, is very different from the rough, white-capped water. Except for the water, McGuinness used a subdued palette largely composed of greys and browns. Bold colours and brushwork and strong angular compositions dominate another work, *Summer Morning* (76 × 56 cm.; Allied Irish Banks, Dublin). Paintings of this type show the influence of Georges Braque, whom McGuinness admired more than any other artist (Kennedy 1991). Similarities can be found in the subdued colours and the fascination with object and setting.

McGuinness also painted her immediate surroundings, especially her garden and its birds. *Garden Green* (1952; see

MacIver, Loren

American painter, 1909–

Born Loren Newman in New York, 2 February 1909; adopted her mother's maiden name of MacIver. Attended Saturday classes at Art Students League, New York, 1919. Married poet and critic Lloyd Frankenberg, 1929; he died 1975. Lived in New York; spent time each year at North Truro, Cape Cod, Massachusetts, 1931–40; stayed for several months at Key West, Florida, 1939–40. Worked on Works Progress Administration Federal Art Project (WPA/FAP), New York, 1936–9. First trip to Europe, visiting France, Italy, Britain and Ireland, 1948. Returned to France, 1966, remaining in Paris for four years, spending winters in Provence. Recipient of first prize, Corcoran Biennial, 1957; Ford Foundation grant, 1960; Frank G. Logan medal, Art Institute of Chicago annual exhibition, 1962; Urbana Purchase prize, Krannert Art Museum, University of Illinois, Champaign-Urbana, 1963; Mark Rothko Foundation grant, 1972; Guggenheim fellowship, 1976; Lee Krasner award, 1992. Member, National Institute of Arts and Letters, 1959. Lives in New York.

Selected Individual Exhibitions

East River Gallery, New York: 1938
Pierre Matisse Gallery, New York: 1940, 1944, 1949, 1956, 1961, 1966, 1970, 1981, 1987
Art Institute of Chicago: 1941, 1953
Baltimore Museum of Art: 1945
Vassar College Art Gallery, Poughkeepsie, NY: 1950
Phillips Collection, Washington, DC: 1951, 1965 (both touring)
Whitney Museum of American Art, New York: 1953 (touring retrospective, with Irene Rice Pereira)
Corcoran Gallery of Art, Washington, DC: 1958
American Pavilion, Venice Biennale: 1962 (with Louise Nevelson, Jan Muller and Dimitri Hadzi)
Musée des Beaux-Arts, Lyon: 1968 (touring)
Montclair Art Museum, NJ: 1975

Newport Harbor Art Museum, Newport Beach, CA: 1983 (retrospective)

Terry Dintenfass Gallery, New York: 1993, 1995

Selected Writings
"How I work", *Art News*, xlvi, September 1947, p.26

Bibliography

MacIver, exh. cat., East River Gallery, New York, 1938

Loren MacIver, exh. cat., Pierre Matisse Gallery, New York, 1940

Fourteen Americans, exh. cat., Museum of Modern Art, New York, 1946

Renée Arb, "Loren MacIver", *Magazine of Art*, xli, 1948, pp.12–15

Contemporary Painters, exh. cat., Museum of Modern Art, New York, 1948

MacIver, exh. cat., Pierre Matisse Gallery, New York, 1949

Loren MacIver/I. Rice Pereira, exh. cat., Whitney Museum of American Art, New York, and elsewhere, 1953

James Thrall Soby, "Again to the ladies", *Saturday Review of Literature*, xxxvi, 7 February 1953, pp.50–51

XXXI Biennale: 2 Pittori, 2 Scultori (Stati Uniti d'America), exh. cat., Venice Biennale, 1962

Paintings by Loren MacIver, exh. cat., Phillips Collection, Washington, DC, and elsewhere, 1965

Loren MacIver, exh. cat., Montclair Art Museum, NJ, 1975

Sarah Phillips, *Loren MacIver: A Bibliography of Criticism from 1939 to 1973*, Wollaston, MA: Phillips, 1975

Loren MacIver: Recent Paintings, exh. cat., Pierre Matisse Gallery, New York, 1981

Charlotte Streifer Rubinstein, *American Women Artists from Early Times to the Present*, Boston: Hall, 1982

Loren MacIver: Five Decades, exh. cat., Newport Harbor Art Museum, Newport Beach, CA, 1983

Sandra Garbrecht, *Loren MacIver: The Painter and the Passing Stain of Circumstance*, Washington, DC: Georgetown University Press, 1987

Loren MacIver, exh. cat., Terry Dintenfass Gallery, New York, 1993

Robert G. Edelman, "MacIver's luminous visions", *Art in America*, lxxxii, February 1994, pp.80–82, 117

From her early paintings of the 1930s Loren MacIver distinguished herself as an artist painting with the sensitivity of a poet – transforming the details of the world around her. When receiving her only art training at the age of ten, in Saturday classes that she took for a year at the Art Students League, she preferred to wander from one studio to another. Essentially a self-taught artist, she never felt compelled to work from tradition or within any art movement. With an original vision, she painted commonplace images from the city and nature in a flat, iconic and abstract style. Her oil paintings are luminous and atmospheric in their combination of vaporous layers of thin glazes and stippled brush strokes that approximate pastel – a technique that she also pursued alongside her painted work. The intimacy and quietness of her paintings prompted the critic James Thrall Soby to describe her work as "shy, tiptoe art" (New York 1948, p.56). MacIver has been compared to Odilon Redon in her poetic and dreamlike quality, and has also been called a romantic, and even a Surrealist because of her subconscious responses to nature (Rubinstein 1982, p.251). She herself cites the influence of Paul Klee.

MacIver's small to medium-size paintings from the 1930s often portray their subjects from unnaturalistic and conceptual angles in a seemingly naive manner. *Shack* (1934; Museum of Modern Art, New York) depicts the summer cottage in Cape Cod that she built from driftwood with her husband, the late poet and critic Lloyd Frankenberg. Seen from a bird's-eye perspective, the four walls fold out to form a cross, like the ground-plan of a Byzantine church or a schematic architectural drawing. This two-dimensional iconic image is surrounded by a mystical aura of yellow, white and light blue. In *Strunsky House* (1935; artist's collection) MacIver also looks into the interior of another building, her home in Greenwich Village. This time she has omitted the outside walls to reveal the interior with pictographic forms symbolising its contents. By bleeding soft colours into each other, she introduces a stylistic feature that enhances the painting's mysteriousness.

In 1940 MacIver reached her mature style with a direct and fresh treatment of her subject matter. She explained her method in 1946: "Quite simple things can lead to discovery. This is what I would like to do with painting: starting with simple things to lead the eye by various manipulations of colors, objects and tensions toward a transformation and a reward" (New York 1946, p.28). While at first glance *Hopscotch* (1940; see illustration) appears to be an organic abstraction, the subject is a close-up view of a child's hopscotch game on cracked and blistered asphalt. MacIver focuses on the eroded pavement, which seems to throb with life, overwhelming the fading pink chalk marks cropped on the right, and suggesting the ephemerality of the game. The close-up view of a floating ginko leaf in *Puddle* (1945; Wellesley College Museum, Wellesley, MA) brings her closest to such contemporaries as Barnett Newman and William Baziotes, who also concentrated on biomorphic forms in their primal works of this period. During these years MacIver painted murals for the liner *SS Argentina* of the Moore-McCormack Lines (1947), and for *SS Excalibur, Exeter, Exochorda* and *Excambion* of the American Export Lines (1948); she also designed the lighting and décor for four Coffee Concerts at the Museum of Modern Art, New York (1941).

MacIver is not only fascinated in reflected light on wet surfaces but also its iridescent effects. *Window Shade* (1948; Phillips Collection, Washington, DC), with its utterly simplified parallel bands of colour, not only relates to the Color-Field painting being developed simultaneously, but is also a precursor of Jasper Johns's paintings of flat, commonplace objects aligned with the picture plane. In MacIver's painting the dark blue battered shade emits the piercing light of the sky through its cracks and glowing button. In *Subway Lights* (1959; Smith College Museum of Art, Northampton, MA) a grid of modulated glass discs seen from above glows against the dark ground of the pavement. This painting's frieze-like composition echoes that of her frontal views of flickering votive lights – a favourite subject (*Red Votive Lights*, 1943; Museum of Modern Art; *Blue Votive Lights*, 1944; Museum of Contemporary Art, Chicago; *Green Votive Lights*, 1946; private collection, repr. Newport Beach 1983, p.24). Other images are seen from below, like her numerous views of the skylight in her studio, as in *Thunder* (1957; private collection, New York, *ibid.*, p.22). In this bold, blue-violet diagonal composition, streaks of hazy white, lavender and yellow rain hit the glass. In *Skylight Storm* (1985; Terry Dintenfass Gallery, New York) from almost 30 years later, MacIver looks at the same skylight but in a much more abstract manner.

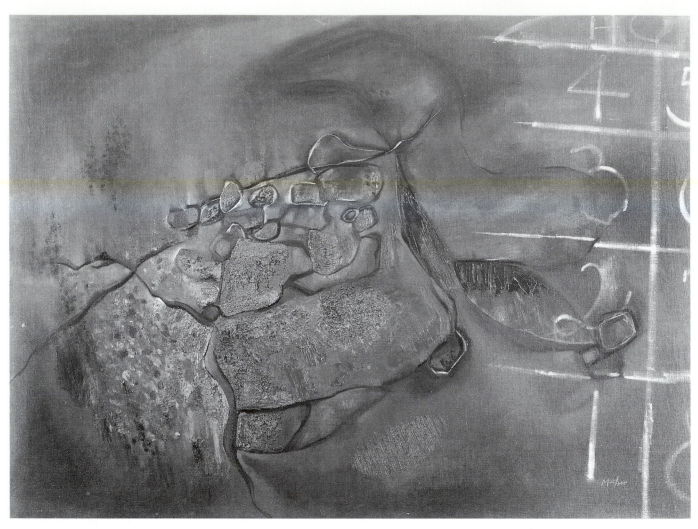

MacIver: *Hopscotch*, 1940; 68.6 × 91.1 cm.; Museum of Modern Art, New York; Purchase

In contrast to her earlier work, many of MacIver's paintings of the 1960s show bright and expansive spaces, like views seen from a distance, as in the rectilinear canvas *Byzantium* (1965; Art Museum, Princeton University), where a mosaic veils a frieze of domes and towers bordering a flowing river in the foreground. This recalls the format of her earlier painting *Venice* (1949; Whitney Museum of American Art, New York), with its high horizon line that pushes the tiny buildings lining the canal to the top margin of the canvas. Another foreign scene is *Bretagne* (1965; Terry Dintenfass Gallery), showing a roadside shrine at night, which recalls Paul Gauguin's *Yellow Christ* (1889; Albright-Knox Gallery, Buffalo, NY). But instead of using bright colours like the French artist, MacIver paints the mottled background of blue and black lichen with a smoky effect achieved through blotting and scraping the canvas (see Edelman 1994, p.117). On the other hand, MacIver also maintains the focused style that she developed in the 1940s. In the iconic *Le Thon* (1968; Terry Dintenfass Gallery) she captures a glistening fish with fins spread like wings that she saw lying on ice in a market window.

MacIver's interest in nature, which was forecast in her earliest works, is seen in her paintings of the 1980s. In a style reminiscent of Claude Monet's late work, *Paris Spring* (1985; Terry Dintenfass Gallery) continues the theme of trees found in her work of the 1940s (*The Tree*, 1945; Museum of Modern Art). In *Lilacs* (1985; Terry Dintenfass Gallery) she paints the flowers as bursts of yellow and white in an impressionistic manner, in which the oil seems to be transformed into pastel. Her poetic vision still informs her view of the world.

DEBORAH A. GOLDBERG

Mackintosh, Margaret *see* Macdonald, Margaret

McLaughlin, Isabel
Canadian painter, 1903–

Born in Oshawa, Ontario, 10 October 1903. Studied under Louise Saint in Paris, 1921–4; studied at Ontario College of Art, Toronto, 1925–7; Art Students League, Toronto,

1927–8; Scandinavian Institute, Paris, 1929–30. Subsequently worked with Emile Bisttram in New Mexico, 1938–9; Hans Hofmann in Provincetown, Massachusetts, 1947 and 1952. Founder-member, 1933, and President, 1937–44, Canadian Group of Painters; member, Ontario Society of Artists, 1963. Awarded Order of Ontario, 1993. Lives in Toronto.

Principal Exhibitions

Art Gallery of Toronto: 1931 (*Group of Seven*), 1933 (*Young Canadians*), occasionally 1933–62 (*Canadian Group of Painters*)
International Art Center, Roerich Museum, New York: 1932 (*Contemporary Canadian Artists*)
Scott and Sons, Montreal: 1934 (with Prudence Heward and Sarah Robertson)
National Gallery of Canada, Ottawa: 1936–9 (*Southern Dominions*, touring)
YWCA (Adelaide House), Oshawa: 1946 (with Alexandra Luke)
Riverside Museum, New York: 1947 (*Canadian Women Painters*)
Hart House, Toronto: 1948 (individual)
Robert McLaughlin Gallery, Oshawa: 1983 (touring retrospective)

Bibliography

Isabel McLaughlin: Recollections, exh. cat., Robert McLaughlin Gallery, Oshawa, and elsewhere, 1983
Part 1: The Isabel McLaughlin Gift, exh. cat., Robert McLaughlin Gallery, Oshawa, 1987
Part 2: The Isabel McLaughlin Gift, exh. cat., Robert McLaughlin Gallery, Oshawa, 1990

Isabel McLaughlin is one of the important early modernists of Canada. Her special contribution was the adaptation to her country of an art internationally oriented towards painters such as Wassily Kandinsky and Lyonel Feininger rather than towards the mid-Edwardian painters she knew as she grew up. Although she was always to be preoccupied with the study of tangible space, her paintings are highly subjective. Bold direct handling was her strength. To transform nature into art she relied on pattern, bright colour and a flat two-dimensional surface. The metaphors created by the landscape counted most to her, and her work was defined by an extraordinary ability to design.

After an early introduction to art in Paris from the painter Louise Saint, McLaughlin returned to Canada. Her training and formative years as a painter spanned the seminal period between two of the best-known groups in Canadian art – from the formation of the Group of Seven in 1920 to that of Painters Eleven in 1953. She studied at the Ontario College of Art, then

Isabel McLaughlin: *Flying Impressions*, c.1945–50; oil on canvas; 68 × 91.9 cm.; Robert McLaughlin Gallery, Oshawa, Ontario

moved on to Toronto's independent art school, the Art Students League, in 1927. Her early career was nurtured by the Group of Seven, particularly by Arthur Lismer (who taught at the College and then at the League) and by Lawren Harris and A.Y. Jackson, both of whom came to the League to provide criticism. The League also provided McLaughlin with a lively group of friends, among them Yvonne McKague Housser, Lismer's assistant at the college. Although her background was academic, instruction from Lismer and help from other members of the Group influenced her subsequent direction. She became a strong exponent of progressive developments, remarkable for her powerful handling, originality of expression and fine structural sense, as the early champion of the Group, Frederick B. Housser, wrote ("The amateur movement in Canadian painting", *Yearbook of the Arts in Canada, 1928–1929*, ed. Bertram Brooker, Toronto: Macmillan, 1929, p.89). Further study followed in Paris and Vienna in 1929–30 (on the latter trip she was accompanied by Yvonne Housser).

With the Group and Housser, Luke was one of the first to focus on the industrial landscape in Canadian art. By contrast to the work of Franklin Carmichael of the Group, her mine paintings are filled with a rollicking energy (e.g. *Nipissing Mine, Cobalt*, c.1931; *Goldmine, Kirkland Lake*, c.1932). Over the years, she imbued her semi-abstracted oil paintings, watercolours, collages and drawings with her own dynamism and intensity. Nature often provided the stimulus for her work – particularly in the form of a certain intimate landscape space (e.g. *Magic Memory*, c.1962). Yet "it's *how* you paint, not so much *what* you paint", she wrote to Jackson in 1954.

McLaughlin also often chose contemporary subjects, such as the ferry boat that ran between Toronto and Central Island. In *Flying Impressions* (c.1945–50; see illustration) she used bold, rhythmic patterns to evoke the speed of flight. A growing individualism was in part a negative reaction – a direct response to her study with Hans Hofmann. In the spring of 1947 her friend Alexandra Luke (q.v.) had talked her into studying with him. Luke found Hofmann immensely stimulating, and learned quickly from him. McLaughlin by contrast, found that Hofmann both confused her and made her think. He wasn't *her* teacher, despite Luke's unwavering enthusiasm. She did not understand positive and negative space, the search for the real, or Hofmann's famous theory of push and pull, but she did enjoy watching him. Sometimes, she recalled later, he would tear a drawing in half or again the other way, then reassemble it to get a totally different feeling of composition and arrangement. "It stirred me up but I kept doing things that were perhaps more and more cubistic …", she said later (interview with author, 21 October 1979).

Hofmann's only immediate lesson for McLaughlin was increased freedom of handling. In the 1950s she achieved a more decorative treatment in her painting. In the same years transcendental qualities entered her work. A rhythm and a mood of joyous comprehension flows in her landscapes and still lifes alike (e.g. *Cape Cod Boats*, c.1950; *South Shore, Beruda*, 1953). Flight still fascinated her as a subject, but more often she turned to draughtsmanship, and specific lessons from this discipline, as a way of renewing her apprenticeship in painting. Many of her works of the 1960s with their all-over patterns resemble big coloured drawings (e.g. *Early Spring, Haliburton*, c.1962; *Milkweed Pod, No.2*, 1964). The subjects

fulfil the imagery of her works of the 1940s, using earlier themes writ large deliberately to replay the past, but she handles her ideas with more freedom. Her landscapes are all mood, vortex and fantasy, her still lifes of leaves or milkweed pods a way of imaging the complex journey of life.

In her work there is the repeated feeling of a beginning, of constant, stubborn self-renewal – that continues to make the whole body of her work meaningful (examples in National Gallery of Canada, Ottawa, Art Gallery of Ontario, Toronto, and McMichael Canadian Art Collection, Kleinburg, Ontario). McLaughlin has often said self-deprecatingly that once she took a pupil, taught him "all she knew in one lesson and automatically put an end to that career" (quoted by Thelma LeCocq, "4 women who paint", *Chatelaine*, September 1948, p.106). In fact, her work's internal strength, the immensely personal visual language she created from elements of nature, her mastery of colour, her verve as a draughtswoman and, above all, her ongoing capacity for discovery, are compelling lessons for today's painters.

JOAN MURRAY

McLaughlin, Mary Louise

American ceramist, woodcarver, metalworker, painter and printmaker, 1847–1939

Born in Cincinnati, Ohio, 29 September 1847. Studied drawing at a private academy, then drawing and woodcarving under Benn Pitman, and china painting under Marie Eggers, at McMicken School of Design, Cincinnati, 1873–7; studied etching under Henry Farny as a member of the Cincinnati Etching Club; also studied privately under Frank Duveneck. Member, Cincinnati Etching Club; Woman's Art Club of Cincinnati; The Crafters; Porcelain League of Cincinnati; American Ceramic Society; Society of Arts, London; National League of Mural Painters. Founder-member and first president, Cincinnati Pottery Club, 1879; founder-member, Associated Artists of Cincinnati, 1890. Died in Cincinnati, 17 January 1939.

Principal Exhibitions

Women's Pavilion, Centennial Exposition, Philadelphia: 1876
Exposition Universelle, Paris: 1878 (honourable mention, underglaze decoration), 1889 (silver medal, overglaze decoration), 1900
Cincinnati Industrial Exposition: 1879, 1882, 1883
Museum of Fine Arts, Boston: 1880 (*Works of Living American Artists*), 1881 (*American Etchings*), 1887 (*Women Etchers of America*), 1892 (*Technical Methods of the Reproductive Arts*), 1893 (*American Engravings and Etchings*)
Cincinnati Art Museum: 1881 (*First Exhibition*), 1882 (*Cincinnati Decorated Pottery*), 1898–9, 1904–5, 1916, 1918 (American Art annuals)
Society of American Artists, New York: 1882
Howell and James Art Pottery Galleries, London: 1884
Union League Club, New York: 1888 (*Women Etchers of America*)
Frederick Keppel & Co., New York: 1892 (individual)
Art Department and Woman's Building, World's Columbian Exposition, Chicago: 1893 (honourable mention, ceramic decoration)
Cotton States and International Exposition, Atlanta: 1895 (gold medal, ceramic decoration)

Pan-American Exposition, Buffalo, NY: 1901 (bronze medal, Losanti ware)

Selected Writings

China Painting: A Practical Manual for the Use of Amateurs in the Decoration of Hand Porcelain, Cincinnati: Clarke, 1877
Etching: A Practical Manual for Amateurs, Cincinnati: Clarke, 1880
Pottery Decoration under the Glaze, Cincinnati: Clarke, 1880
"Hints to china painters", *Art Amateur*, viii, 1882–3, pp.19, 41, 71–2, 88, 111, 139; ix, 1883, pp.18, 37, 64, 83, 105, 123
Suggestions to China Painters, Cincinnati: Clarke, 1884
Painting in Oil: A Manual for the Use of Students, Cincinnati: Clarke, 1890
The China Painter's Handbook, Cincinnati, 1917
"Mary Louise McLaughlin", *Bulletin of the American Ceramic Society*, xvii, 1938, pp.217–25 (paper read at the Porcelain League, 25 April 1914)

Bibliography

"Cincinnati art pottery", *Harper's Weekly*, xxiv, 1880, pp.341–2
Mrs Aaron F. Perry, "Decorative pottery of Cincinnati", *Harper's New Monthly Magazine*, lxii, 1881, pp.834–5
Catalogue of an Exhibition of Paintings in Oil, Watercolours, Wood Carvings, Etchings, Drypoints, Art Pottery and Etched Decoration on Metal: The Work of Miss Mary Louise McLaughlin of Cincinnati, exh. cat., Frederick Keppel & Co., New York, 1892
"Work by a talented lady", *New York Times*, 27 October 1892, p.7
Mrs Aaron F. Perry, "The work of Cincinnati women in decorated pottery", *Art and Handicraft in the Woman's Building of the World's Columbian Exposition, Chicago, 1893*, ed. Maud Howe Elliott, Chicago and New York: Rand McNally, 1894, pp.101–6
Irene Sargent, "Some potters and their products", *Craftsman*, iv, 1903, pp.328–37
Edwin A. Barber, *Pottery and Porcelain of the United States: An Historical Review of American Ceramic Art from the Earliest Times to the Present Day*, 2nd edition, New York and London: Putnam, 1909
Clara C. Newton, "The Cincinnati Pottery Club", *Bulletin of the American Ceramic Society*, 1940, pp.345–53
"Overture of Cincinnati ceramics", *Cincinnati Historical Society Bulletin*, xxv, 1967, pp.70–84
Herbert Peck, "The amateur antecedents of Rookwood pottery", *Cincinnati Historical Society Bulletin*, xxvi, 1968, pp.317–37
Paul Evans, *Art Pottery of the United States: An Encyclopedia of Producers and Their Marks*, New York: Scribner, 1974
The Ladies, God Bless 'Em: The Women's Art Movement in Cincinnati in the Nineteenth Century, exh. cat., Cincinnati Art Museum, 1976
Anthea Callen, *Angel in the Studio: Women in the Arts and Crafts Movement, 1870–1914*, London: Astragal, 1979; as *Women Artists of the Arts and Crafts Movement, 1870–1914*, New York: Pantheon, 1979
The Golden Age: Cincinnati Painters of the Nineteenth Century Represented in the Cincinnati Art Museum, exh. cat., Cincinnati Art Museum, 1979
Elaine Levin, "Mary Louise McLaughlin and the Cincinnati art pottery movement", *American Craft*, xlii, December 1982–January 1983, pp.28–31, 82–3
In Pursuit of Beauty: Americans and the Aesthetic Movement, exh. cat., Metropolitan Museum of Art, New York, 1986
Phyllis Peet, *The Emergence of American Women Printmakers in the Late Nineteenth Century*, PhD dissertation, University of California at Los Angeles, 1987
American Women of the Etching Revival, exh. cat., High Museum of Art, Atlanta, 1988
Susan Waller, *Women Artists in the Modern Era: A Documentary History*, Metuchen, NJ: Scarecrow Press, 1991

Mary Louise McLaughlin Papers, 1906–33, are in the Cincinnati Historical Society.

Mary Louise McLaughlin earned a national reputation as an innovator in America's Art Pottery movement while also working in many other media. Although her speciality was ceramic decorative glazing, she experimented with wood, metal, printmaking, watercolour and oil painting, and textiles, having been trained in both arts and crafts at the McMicken School of Design. She was inspired and supported by the artistic climate of Cincinnati in the 1870s when a group of women was organising the Cincinnati Art Museum and Academy.

In 1876, while McLaughlin was still a student, her work in woodcarving and ceramics was exhibited in the Women's Pavilion at the Centennial Exposition in Philadelphia. She designed and built a hanging cabinet (Don Burke Collection, Cincinnati) in walnut and ebony, carving acanthus leaves and other foliage, rosettes, birds, butterflies and turkey finials to decorate it. She applied hand-painted tiles (which she later replaced with etched copper plaques) and elaborate bronze hinges and locks to the doors. Inside the cabinet she exhibited her hand-painted ceramic pieces. The design of the piece was inspired by medieval handcraft traditions that lay behind the Arts and Crafts movement.

McLaughlin had begun to study overglaze china painting in 1875 with Marie Eggers at McMicken School of Design. After the Centennial Exposition she began to experiment with underglaze painting on her own. She painted with underglaze cobalt blue on porcelain blanks, finally achieving success in 1877 with a plate on which she portrayed reeds surrounded by a rim decorated with tree branches (see illustration). In 1878 she exhibited her underglaze faience painting, realistic plant

Mary Louise McLaughlin: *Plate*, 1877; ironstone; diameter 20.32 cm.; Cincinnati Art Museum, gift of the artist through the Women's Art Museum Association

and flower images at the Exposition Universelle in Paris, where she was one of only three exhibitors in ceramics from the USA.

McLaughlin then worked to duplicate the secret Haviland "Limoges" faience underglaze painting technique and came up with an underglaze method of her own. She used unfired clay slip with the minerals for colour mixed into it, then painted her designs on the damp porcelain vessel before it was fired. The coral and cream roses with green leaves in low relief on a bowl (1878; Cincinnati Art Museum) demonstrate this use of coloured slips. Obviously anxious to share her findings, she published a detailed description in 1880. Her process of decorating ceramics, often referred to as "Cincinnati faience" or "Cincinnati Limoges", was adopted by Rookwood and many other potteries throughout the USA. She experimented with underglaze painting on wet clay until 1885, when she turned to overglaze work for the next ten years because she lacked access to the kilns she needed.

McLaughlin began to work in metal in the 1870s in order to produce by hand all the components of her furniture, such as the hanging cabinet described above. At some point she replaced the painted ceramic tiles on the cabinet with copper plaques etched with portraits of a girl and boy. She etched natural forms into decorative copper plaques and vessels. A covered bowl (1884; Cincinnati Art Museum), with a design of sunburst daisies and spider webs covering every surface, reflects in its overall patterning the medieval inspiration for the Arts and Crafts movement.

In the late 1870s, using an embossed or etched copper plate to print, McLaughlin began to work in drypoint and etching with Henry Farny and members of the Cincinnati Etching Club. Her earliest etchings were tightly drawn, probably influenced by her teacher Farny's careful realism. During the 1880s, however, her prints became bolder and more individualistic. Landscapes such as *Beeches in Burnet Woods* (1883; Cincinnati Art Museum) were both dramatically expressive and decorative, with a heavy, linear quality similar to her work on ceramics during this period. One of her best known and most exhibited works is *Portrait of a Girl* (1884; New York Public Library), which she printed from a heavily scored and etched copper plate. The portrayal of the girl's hair is richly textured and heavily inked, creating an almost tangible presence, as if it were sculpted on a vase.

In the 1890s McLaughlin returned to experiment in pottery decoration. In 1894 she invented and patented "American Faience", a process of painting the interior of a plaster mould with coloured slip and then casting the piece in a different coloured clay. The piece came out of the mould with decorative colours creating an inlaid design. In further experiments she produced in 1898 a fine, creamy-white, translucent porcelain into which she carved decoration, tinting it in monochrome blues, pinks and greens. A cylindrical vase (1903; Worcester Art Museum, MA) decorated with large, carved leaves represents the simple curvilinear designs from nature that she used to decorate the spare, classical forms of Losanti ware. Deriving from Cincinnati's original name, Losantiville, this was an important contribution to American Art Nouveau. She made her last ceramic pieces in 1914.

McLaughlin is perhaps least known for the oil and watercolour portrait and landscape paintings that she produced throughout her career, but most actively during the 1880s, while she was writing her book on oil painting. She exhibited paintings more frequently in 1882 and 1883. Too few of her paintings have been saved to be able to describe an evolution in style. The portrait of *Elizabeth Haven Appleton* (1890; Cincinnati Art Museum), one of the founders of the Museum, demonstrates the thoughtful, direct realism that was the basis for all McLaughlin's image-making. Related to her paintings are the colour monotype landscapes that McLaughlin produced in the early 20th century. *Sunset* (Library of Congress, Washington, DC) combines the expressive, painterly qualities of her oils with the less controlled transfer process of "American Faience" pottery decoration. The technique of painting an image with colours directly on to the copper plate, then transferring the image to paper to create a monotype is similar to painting colours with slip on to the interior of a mould to create "American Faience" ceramic decoration. McLaughlin also continued to work in glass mosaic, and to make jewellery and embroidered panels well into the 20th century, bringing women's culture into the professional art world.

PHYLLIS PEET

MacMonnies, Mary Fairchild

American painter, 1858–1946

Born Mary Louise Fairchild in New Haven, Connecticut, 11 August 1858; grew up in New Orleans and St Louis. Schoolteacher for five years. Studied at St Louis School of Fine Arts, winning a three-year scholarship for study in Paris in 1885; studied at Académie Julian, 1885–7, and in women's class of Carolus-Duran, 1887–8. Married American sculptor Frederick William MacMonnies, 1888; two daughters born 1895 and 1897, son born 1899 (d. 1901); divorced 1909. Lived in Paris; rented a house in Giverny, north of Paris, from 1894; moved to Giverny, 1898. Married artist Will Hicok Low, 1909. Returned to USA, 1910; settled in Bronxville suburb of Lawrence Park, New York. Associée, Société Nationale des Beaux-Arts, Paris, 1898; president, American Women's Art Club of Paris, 1900–03; associate member, National Academy of Design, New York, 1906. Died in Bronxville, New York, 23 May 1946.

Principal Exhibitions

Paris Salon: from 1886
Art Institute of Chicago: from 1888
Exposition Universelle, Paris: 1889 (bronze medal), 1900 (gold medal)
World's Columbian Exposition, Chicago: 1893 (medal)
Société Nationale des Beaux-Arts, Paris: from 1895
Internationale Kunstausstellung, Dresden: 1901 (gold medal)
Pan-American Exposition, Buffalo, NY: 1901 (gold medal)
Society of American Artists, New York: 1902 (Julia M. Shaw memorial prize)
Normandy Exposition, Rouen: 1903 (gold medal)
Centennial Exhibition, National Academy of Design, New York: 1925

Selected Writings

"Mrs R.L.S.: Impressions", *Villager* (Bronxville), December 1933, pp.14–16

"Memoirs", manuscript, 1938, MacMonnies family papers, Archives of American Art, Washington, DC

Bibliography
Eleanor E. Greatorex, "Mary Fairchild MacMonnies", *Godey's*, cxxvi, 1893, pp.624–32
Will H. Low, "In an old French garden", *Scribner's*, xxxii/1, July 1902, pp.3–19
Bronxville Review (pictorial supplement), xxiv, May 1925, p.2
"Mary Fairchild Low, ANA", *Villager* (Bronxville), December 1929; reprinted in *Villager*, xl, January 1968, p.13
Mary Smart, "Sunshine and shade: Mary Fairchild MacMonnies Low", *Woman's Art Journal*, iv/2, 1983–4, pp.20–25
Frederick William MacMonnies, Mary Fairchild MacMonnies: *Deux artistes americains à Giverny*, exh. cat., Musée Municipal A.G. Poulain, Vernon, 1988
Loretta Hoagland, *Lawrence Park: Bronxville's Turn-of-the-Century Art Colony*, Bronxville: Lawrence Park Hilltop Association, 1992
Mary Smart, *A Flight with Fame: The Life and Art of Frederick MacMonnies*, Madison, CT: Sound View Press, 1996

Born in New Haven to Sidney and Mary Lines Fairchild, both descendants of the city's 17th-century founders, the painter Mary Louise Fairchild herself pioneered in the world of art, in an age that severely handicapped women artists. Determinedly pursuing her goals, both at home and in France, she achieved many of her objectives in a long and productive life. She moved to St Louis as a child, and for five years she dutifully taught at a school – the only career available to unmarried women at the time. When the local university opened a new art department, which became the St Louis School of Fine Arts, she enrolled in its first classes and escaped into her true vocation. Discovering that women students were denied access to the life class, she led a rebellion that convinced the authorities that drawing from the nude was as essential in training women as men – but that women should not simply pose for each other, as the school had at first assumed. Working determinedly for three years, she was rewarded in 1885 when the director, Halsey C. Ives, created a three-year scholarship for her to study art in Paris. She stayed there for 25 years.

In Paris she found that women students, who were not yet admitted to the prestigious Ecole Nationale des Beaux-Arts where the tuition was free, worked in crowded private schools – at double the fees charged in the men's classes. Choosing the Académie Julian over Colarossi's, which was cheaper but provided less distinguished teachers, MacMonnies concentrated on painting or drawing, mostly from the nude, from eight o'clock until five, six days a week, from autumn to spring. Three visiting professors alternated in giving cursory criticisms twice weekly. At the end of her first year at Julian's, MacMonnies's portrait of a friend, the art agent *Sara Tyson Hallowell* (Robinson College, Cambridge), was accepted at the Salon of 1886. By turning the face of her sitter into the shadows she emphasised her elegance in dress and ease of manner.

Investigating the methods of the Barbizon school, MacMonnies worked during the summer recess in Picardy with the British painter Harry Thompson. Although preferring less dreary scenes, she used her country sketches to develop, during her second year at Julian's, a dramatically lighted genre painting entitled *Les Confidences* (untraced). It was accepted by the Salon of 1887, the first of her many sunny, flower-filled

MacMonnies: *Fanny Stevenson*, 1912–13; Lady Stair's House, Edinburgh

garden scenes to appear there almost annually. Not satisfied with the minimal criticisms given at Julian's, she enrolled in the autumn of 1887 in the intensive women's class of the portrait painter Carolus-Duran, whose most famous pupil had been John Singer Sargent. She and a friend from Julian's, Eurilda Loomis, also took an attic apartment together at 53 rue Bonaparte, both to economise and to overcome their total segregation from male students, not only in classes but by the impropriety of their entering the cafés where men furthered their art education in serious discussions. Among their earliest visitors was an impoverished sculpture student at Falguière's class at the Beaux-Arts, the American Frederick MacMonnies. He and Mary instantly fell in love.

Halsey Ives refused to release her from the stipulation in her contract that she could not marry until her scholarship expired in August 1888, so she and MacMonnies became engaged until that time. Sharing her workroom at 16 Impasse du Maine, he developed a lithe statue of *Diana*, while she joined his classical mood by producing a large painting, *Young Juno* (untraced), which at the time of their marriage Hallowell sent to the Chicago Art Institute's annual autumn exhibition. The hoped-for turn in their fortunes occurred the following spring. Not only did the Salon of 1889 accept another of her decorative garden scenes, *June Morning* (untraced, ex-St Louis Art Museum), but the following week at the Paris Exposition Universelle she won a bronze medal and much notice for a dramatic *Self-Portrait* (untraced, repr. Smart 1983), in which she is swathed in a feather boa, her oval, olive-complexioned face shadowed by dark brown hair and an enormous, flower-piled hat. Gratifying though her achievements were, however, it was Frederick MacMonnies's honourable mention in the Salon, the highest award yet given to an American sculptor, that enabled the firm of McKim, Mead and White and his influential American teacher Augustus Saint-Gaudens to recommend him for a flood of commissions, including $50,000 for the central fountain at the World's Columbian Exposition of 1893.

Earning substantial amounts herself by skilfully copying a series of old masters at the Louvre for an American client, as she would for the new Knickerbocker Hotel, New York, in 1906, Mary also enterprisingly copied Botticelli's two frescoes from the Villa Lemmi in the Louvre, which so impressed Hallowell that she secured for her the challenging commission of painting a semi-elliptical panel, *Primitive Woman* (18.2 × 4.5 m.), for the Woman's Building at the coming Chicago fair. Mary journeyed alone to Chicago to install it and its companion mural, Mary Cassatt's *Modern Woman* (both untraced), high beneath the roof, and received much publicity as well as critical acclaim for her cool, clear colours and the unified design of her enormous work. MacMonnies joined her in Chicago just before the opening to finish his popular *Columbian Fountain*, which established him as America's best-known sculptor.

Returning to France the couple began a newly luxurious life, with a Paris town house and homes in the medieval village of Giverny where Monet lived – first a villa and then a three-hectare walled estate, The Priory. With a large staff of servants, Mary was free to paint full time. Most often she worked outdoors, her style influenced by Monet and other Impressionist neighbours, whom she dubbed "plein-airtistes". Her husband worked in his Giverny sculpture studio on small projects, but for his massive public monuments was kept busy in four Paris studios. When their three children arrived, Berthe Hélène (Betty) in 1895, Marjorie in 1897 and Ronald (who died before the age of two) in 1899, she filled her canvases with their portraits.

Always open to experiments, however, in 1895 Mary MacMonnies sent to the Société Nationale des Beaux-Arts two large decorative panels in the Art Nouveau style: *Diana* (untraced), a figure in profile in a short red tunic drawing a bow against a uniform background of pale gold, and the more fantastic *La Brise* (untraced), a grisaille dancer in swirling draperies "on a blue background uniformly studded with silver lines". On visits to Paris during 1900–03 while she was president of the American Women's Art Club of Paris, she also painted a small jewel-like interior, *Gallery of Apollo of the Louvre* (untraced), shown at the Salon of 1901, and at the Salon of 1904 exhibited an actual miniature on ivory, *Le Masque* (untraced).

Usually separated from his wife in Paris and on his frequent months-long business trips to the USA, MacMonnies decided at last to end their part-time marriage; by January 1909 he had obtained a divorce, retaining custody of his daughters but

supporting Mary as well as them in a Paris apartment on the Ile de la Cité. Here she painted views of the Seine until the arrival within months of her old admirer, the artist and writer Will Hicok Low. Mary, now aged 50, chose security with Low over the free life she had been living, and married him in November 1909, departing for the USA the following January accompanied by her two young daughters, whom MacMonnies had reluctantly decided he could not separate from their mother.

The respected Low was one of three artists for whom the developer of Lawrence Park, Bronxville, had built attractive homes and studios, to raise the tone of his exclusive community. Adapting quickly to her new role of artist-in-residence, Mary, with her experience of painting large canvases, helped her husband to enlarge his mural commissions, even indicating the colours he should use. Soon she began accepting portrait commissions herself from the admiring neighbours who flocked to the weekly receptions she instituted, in the Paris fashion. Drawing on her thorough training and decades of award-winning work, she soon demonstrated her ability to suggest the character of a sitter rather than merely catch a likeness.

Among the distinguished portraits that she produced during these years were a bold depiction of *Fanny Stevenson* (1912–13; see illustration), widow of Low's friend Robert Louis Stevenson; a sensitive impression of her 16-year-old daughter *Marjorie* with a lute; and a richly detailed portrait of her other daughter in her twenties. This dark, controlled canvas, sent to the National Academy's Centennial Exhibition in 1925 as *Portrait of a Lady* (private collection), demonstrates the effect on her painting style of her years of studio portraits since the days of Impressionist flamboyance used when the same sitter was aged two, among the flowers of Giverny. Continuing to paint until the invalidism of her last few years, visited by her daughters and grandchildren, Mary MacMonnies lived to be almost 88, dying at Bronxville in 1946.

MARY SMART

McNair, Frances *see* Macdonald, Frances

MacNicol, Bessie
British painter, 1869–1904

Born in Glasgow, 15 July 1869, the elder of twin girls; father a headmaster. Studied at St George's School; Glasgow School of Art, 1887–92, under Francis Newbery; Académie Colarossi, Paris, c.1892. Acquired own studio in Glasgow, 1895; also spent time in Kirkcudbright, Scotland, 1896–7. Married Dr Alexander Frew, gynaecologist and painter, 1899; lived in Hillhead, Glasgow. Died in childbirth, 4 June 1904.

Principal Exhibitions
Royal Academy, London: 1893
Royal Glasgow Institute of the Fine Arts: 1893–1905

MacNicol: *Autumn*, 1898; Aberdeen Art Gallery

Glaspalast, Munich: occasionally 1895–1903
Munich Secession: 1896
Royal Scottish Academy, Edinburgh: occasionally 1897–1901
Carnegie Institute, Pittsburgh: 1897–1901
International Society of Sculptors, Painters and Gravers, London: occasionally 1898–1904
Vienna Secession: 1898
Stephen T. Gooden Art Rooms, Glasgow: 1899 (individual)
Glasgow Society of Artists: 1902–5
Craibe Angus, Glasgow: 1905 (retrospective)

Bibliography

Percy Bate, "'In memoriam': Bessie MacNicol", *Scottish Art and Letters*, iii/3, 1904, pp.197–208
Ailsa Tanner, "Portrait of a portrait", *Scots Magazine*, new series, cxxxiv, November 1990, pp.192–202
Jude Burkhauser, ed., *Glasgow Girls: Women in Art and Design, 1880–1920*, 2nd edition, Edinburgh: Canongate, and Cape May, NJ: Red Ochre, 1993

Letters from Bessie MacNicol to E.A. Hornel, December 1896–December 1897, are at Broughton House, Kirkcudbright (National Trust of Scotland).

In her working life at the turn of the 19th and 20th centuries, Bessie MacNicol was a "new woman" of the period. With her Scottish headmaster father and English mother she and her two sisters enjoyed a relatively emancipated upbringing in Glasgow, then a thriving commercial city. More importantly, she enjoyed the privilege of studying at the Glasgow School of Art under the charismatic Francis Newbery, who treated his women students as equals to men. He encouraged her to further her studies at the Académie Colarossi in Paris. The first exhibited works by MacNicol to be noticed were her assured *Self-Portrait* (Glasgow Art Gallery), in which she appears to be studying the viewer, and *A French Girl* (1895; private collection, repr. Burkhauser 1993, fig.265), both dark-toned oil paintings, which show her interest in the old masters that she had studied at the Louvre in preference to the teaching at Colarossi's, which she found oppressive.

In 1896 MacNicol spent some time in Kirkcudbright in southwest Scotland, and painted the portrait of *E.A. Hornel*, one of the younger Glasgow Boys, in his studio. This painting still hangs in Broughton House (National Trust of Scotland), to which Hornel moved in 1900. It is a strong and richly textured painting of an artist, palette in hand, the colours of which are echoed in a Japanese hanging behind him. Exhibited at the Glasgow Institute the following year, it was given hurtful notices as if the critics found a portrait of a well-known artist by a woman to be an impertinence. Hornel's influence on MacNicol's work at this time, and that of his friend George Henry, was considerable. Her palette lightened and brightened, and her brushwork became more assured and painterly. She painted in plein air young girls dappled by the sun shining through foliage (e.g. *Under the Apple Tree*, 1896–9; Glasgow Museums and Art Galleries). These paintings were not necessarily portraits but rather evocations of youth and beauty in painterly terms; the main object was not to render a likeness, even if it existed, but to create a unity of design, form and colour, and to paint a picture. Such paintings were called "fancy portraits" at that time. The effect of warm colours of sunlight and of cool colours in shade had been brilliantly explored by James Guthrie in his *Midsummer* (1892; Royal

Scottish Academy Diploma Collection, Edinburgh), and studies of young girls under foliage were painted by another Glasgow Boy, David Gauld, but MacNicol added her own interpretation and feeling. Very often the figures hold posies of flowers, which were often used to avoid the necessity of painting hands, never her strong point.

It may be claimed legitimately that MacNicol was a fringe member of the Glasgow Boys at this period. The Glasgow Boys were a loosely knit group of young artists, mainly from Glasgow, who exhibited in Britain and abroad from 1880 to 1895. They favoured rural scenes with farm workers, influenced by the work of Jules Bastien-Lepage and Dutch painters of The Hague school, and admired the rich painterly qualities and tonal values in the work of Whistler. MacNicol was certainly on friendly terms with Glasgow painters, and would have been elected a member of the Glasgow Art Club if membership had been open to women. She was never a member of the Glasgow Society of Lady Artists, and preferred to sign her work B. MacNicol. As a critic noted in the *Scots Pictorial* of April 1902: "... it might be Benjamin or Barney and it need not necessarily be Bessie. She is *bon camarade*, and can talk art with the best of the mere male painters."

The girls in MacNicol's paintings were often dressed in fashions of the past, or in theatrical costume. Her grandfather was a master tailor, and MacNicol was always interested in dress. She was entranced with the costumes, set in the 1860s, of Arthur Wing Pinero's play *Trelawny of the "Wells"*, which came to Glasgow in 1898. In 1900 she exhibited *A Girl of the "Sixties"* (1899; Glasgow Art Galleries), a girl with her hair in a chignon, black choker ribbon round her neck and wearing a "pork pie" hat. *Autumn* (1898; see illustration) is a "fancy portrait" of a girl in a costume that MacNicol may have worn to a fancy dress ball in 1896.

Autumn was sent to the first exhibition in London of the International Society of Sculptors, Painters and Gravers in 1898. The first president of the Society was James McNeill Whistler, and the influence of his work can be seen in her paintings from this time (e.g. *Motherhood*, 1902; private collection, repr. Burkhauser 1993, fig.268). As well as exhibiting in Britain, works by MacNicol were sent to exhibitions in Ghent, Munich, Vienna and to Pittsburgh and St Louis, with paintings by the Glasgow Boys.

In 1899 MacNicol married Alexander Frew, a medical man with many interests, who had given up medicine for painting, but who resumed his practice as consultant in gynaecology on his marriage. They moved into a terrace house in Glasgow with a large studio at the rear designed by the previous owner, D.Y. Cameron. In this studio MacNicol was able to paint larger works such as *Vanity* (1902; private collection, *ibid.*, fig. 309), a virtuoso study of the back view of a draped nude looking at herself in a mirror. One is reminded of Velázquez's *Toilet of Venus* (National Gallery, London); as in that painting, the colours are dark-toned and rich in contrast to the luminous flesh tones. *Vanity* was one of 17 works by MacNicol at the first exhibition in 1902 of the Glasgow Society of Artists, a group under the leadership of Alexander Frew that broke away in protest at the way the Glasgow Institute was then run. Nevertheless she also showed at the Institute exhibition, running concurrently, two paintings including a tender study of a baby, *Baby Crawford* (1902; City of Edinburgh Art Centre), which one critic thought was her masterpiece. Another baby, her nephew George, can be seen with his mother in *Motherhood*, which was exhibited at the second exhibition of the Glasgow Society of Artists in 1903. It is all the more poignant that Bessie MacNicol lost her own life in childbirth the following year. Obituaries mourn the loss of the finest Scottish woman artist of her time.

AILSA TANNER

M[a]cPherson, Margaret Rose *see* Preston

Madden, Anne

Irish painter, 1932–

Born in London, 1932, of Irish and Anglo-Chilean parentage; grew up in Chile, but subsequently lived in England; often spent childhood holidays in Ireland, and later travelled widely in France, Spain and Italy. Attended Chelsea School of Arts and Crafts, London, 1950–52. Lived for a time in Co. Clare, Ireland, 1950s; career interrupted by a series of spinal operations, which resulted in long periods of immobilisation, 1953–7. Married Irish painter Louis le Brocquy, 1958; moved to France; two sons. Represented Ireland at the Paris Biennale, 1965. Recipient of Carroll's award, Irish Exhibition of Living Art, Dublin, 1964. Lives in France, spending part of each year in Ireland.

Selected Individual Exhibitions

Leicester Galleries, London: 1959, 1961, 1967
Dawson Gallery, Dublin: 1960, 1964, 1968, 1970, 1974
New Art Centre, London: 1970, 1972, 1974, 1978, 1990
Gimpel Weitzenhoffer Gallery, New York: 1970
Demarco Gallery, Edinburgh: 1971
Ulster Museum, Belfast: 1974
Galerie Darthea Speyer, Paris: 1976, 1979
Galerie le Dessin, Paris: 1978, 1980
Arts Council of Northern Ireland, Belfast: 1979
Taylor Galleries, Dublin: 1979, 1982, 1987
Fondation Maeght, Saint-Paul, Alpes-Maritimes: 1983
Galeria Maeght, Barcelona: 1985
Galerie Joachim Becker, Cannes: 1985
Armstrong Gallery, New York: 1986
Galerie Jeanne Bucher, Paris: 1989
Kerlin Gallery, Dublin: 1990, 1992
RHA Gallagher Gallery, Dublin: 1991 (touring retrospective)
Galerie Sapone, Nice: 1993

Selected Writings

Seeing His Way: Louis le Brocquy, A Painter, Dublin: Gill and Macmillan, 1994

Bibliography

Bruce Arnold, *A Concise History of Irish Art*, London: Thames and Hudson, and New York: Praeger, 1969
Jacques Dupin, *L'Espace autrement dit*, Paris: Galilee, 1982
Roderick Knowles, ed., *Contemporary Irish Art*, Dublin: Wolfhound Press, 1982
Dorothy Walker, "Anne Madden", *Irish Arts Review*, iii, Autumn 1986, pp.37–40
Marcelin Pleynet and Michel Ragon, *L'Art abstrait 5, 1970–1987*, Paris: Maeght Editeur, 1989
Anne Madden: A Retrospective Exhibition, exh. cat., RHA Gallagher Gallery, Dublin, and elsewhere, 1991

Madden: *Pompeian Openings VII* (triptych), 1982; oil and pastel on paper; 110 × 225 cm.; Hugh Lane Municipal Gallery of Modern Art, Dublin

Images and Insights, exh. cat., Hugh Lane Municipal Gallery of Modern Art, Dublin, 1993

Among Irish artists, and those with close associations with Ireland, Anne Madden is one of the most internationally oriented painters of her generation. This is no doubt a result of the cosmopolitan nature of her background, but it also results from her life with Louis le Brocquy, whom she married in 1958, for together they divide their time between the south of France and Ireland. Madden has also travelled widely and has exhibited in numerous solo and mixed exhibitions throughout Europe and in the USA and Japan.

Initially inspired by Italian Renaissance painters, Madden later turned to Cézanne, Matisse and the American Abstract Expressionists for stimulus. Her main interest lies in the very act of painting – and she might be termed a "painter's painter". This interest is borne out in her technique, which, despite her changing subject matter, places emphasis on the medium itself. Even in early works, such as the splendidly expansive *Slievecarran* (1963; Ulster Museum, Belfast), in which she worked with a combination of grit and flint chippings mixed with oil paint, one's attention is drawn to the tactile nature of the surface of the painting, and hence to her handling of the medium, and only then does one begin to explore other themes such as the landscape *per se*, place and context. Yet despite this emphasis on technique, Madden is never boldly expressionist, as one might expect, but rather manages to combine a freedom of technique with an otherwise cerebral approach to picture making. Thus her work, whatever the subject matter, is always tightly controlled and carefully thought out.

The *Slievecarran* picture, like others similar to it, is in fact a panoramic landscape, although the precise setting remains unimportant to our reading of the work. Rather, the rocky structure of the barren hillside dominates the whole picture plane and one is acutely aware of the centuries of weathering and human activity that have combined to create the present scene. This treatment of the landscape resulted, no doubt, from Madden's experience of the Burren, that fascinating landscape of karsts so well known to geologists, botanists and antiquarians, situated on Ireland's west coast. Later, in the 1970s, she made a number of works that draw upon archaeological remains for their subject matter and these, too, as in *Megalith 14* (1971; Bank of Ireland, Dublin), *Alignment II* (1972; Fondation Maeght, Saint-Paul) and *Monolith 3* (1972; Allied Irish Banks, Dublin), explore man's eternal relationship with the landscape. In these works her emphasis on the tactile nature of surface is less accentuated than in previous paintings, although her range of colours, often restricted to permutations of reds, ochres and umbers, and her use of light have strong landscape connotations.

In the early 1980s, stimulated by a visit to Pompeii, Madden began a number of paintings based on the idea of what she terms "openings", wherein she created openings, or vistas, as metaphors for some of the contradictions and opposites that confront us in life - day/night, life/death, male/female, interior/exterior space and so on. "I see these openings as thresholds, windows of the mind, metaphors of the artist's vision. Openings into a possible space, both psychic and physical, of the mind and of matter", she has said (Dublin 1993, p.152). In Pompeii she sensed "layers of meaning and significance",

which, because of the apocalyptic end of the city, captured her imagination in human terms. *Pompeian Openings VII* (1982; see illustration) emerged from this experience. Here, the composition is divided vertically into three equal openings, each separated by uprights, a device that harks back to the structure of her megalithic pictures. The imagery beyond each opening is largely indiscernible (there is, however, a sense of holocaust), but the brightly painted uprights recall the colours of the murals that have survived in Pompeii.

The bright colours prevalent in her Pompeian pictures have been carried over into Madden's most recent works, *Chemins eclairés* (1988; private collection), *Le Jardin* (1988; Ulster Museum), *Night Garden* (1990; private collection) and others, and these show her to be a colourist of considerable merit. The subject matter remains essentially landscape, and traces of human activity are never far away, but her brushwork has become much more delicate, the paint less heavily impastoed and the emphasis on expression, which characterises her early work, has returned. These late works suggest a painter at ease with herself and developing into a rich maturity.

S.B. KENNEDY

Maddock, Bea
Australian painter and printmaker, 1934–

Born in Hobart, Tasmania, 13 September 1934. Studied painting at Hobart Technical College, 1952–6 (diploma of fine art); postgraduate painting and printmaking at the Slade School of Fine Art, London, under William Coldstream, Anthony Gross and Ceri Richards, 1959–61; also travelled in Europe, studying for a short time in Perugia, Italy. Returned to Australia, 1962. Subsequently lecturer in art, Launceston Teachers College, Tasmania, 1962–3; lecturer in ceramics and printmaking, Launceston Technical College, 1965–9; lecturer in printmaking, National Gallery School, Melbourne, 1970–72; senior lecturer in printmaking, School of Art, Victoria College of the Arts, Melbourne, 1973–81 (acting Dean, 1979–80); Creative Arts fellow, Australian National University, Canberra, 1976; artist-in-residence, University of Alberta, Edmonton, Canada, 1978, and Sydney College for the Arts, 1979; part-time lecturer in printmaking, Bendigo College of Advanced Education, Victoria, 1982–3; lecture tour of New Zealand, 1983; head of School of Art, Tasmanian College of Advanced Education, Launceston, 1983–4; chair, Ritchies Mills Arts Centre, Launceston, 1984–5 (also ran papermaking workshop). Worked full-time in studios in Launceston from 1985, Dunolly, Victoria, 1985–90, and Oatlands, Tasmania, from 1993. Visited Antarctica through the "Artists in Antarctica" programme, 1987. Recipient of Tasmanian Drawing prize, 1968; F.E. Richardson print prize, Geelong, Victoria, 1969; fourth prize, International Print Biennale, Poland, 1974; Alice prize, Alice Springs, Northern Territory, 1979; Queensland Art Gallery purchase prize, 1982; Joan and Peter Clemenger award, Triennial Exhibition of Contemporary Australian Art, National Gallery of Victoria, Melbourne, 1993. Member, Visual Arts Board, Australia Council, 1979–80; Council of the Australian National Gallery, Canberra, 1985–8. Member of the Order of Australia, 1994. Lives in Launceston, Tasmania.

Selected Individual Exhibitions

Ingles Building, Launceston, Tasmania: 1964
Crossley Gallery, Melbourne: 1967, 1968, 1971
Queen Victoria Museum and Art Gallery, Launceston, Tasmania: 1970
Gallery A, Sydney: 1974, 1978
National Gallery of Victoria, Melbourne: 1975 (*Three Printmakers*), 1980
National Art Gallery of New Zealand, Wellington: 1982–3 (touring retrospective)
Stuart Gerstman Galleries, Melbourne: 1988
Tasmanian Museum and Art Gallery, Hobart: 1988 (*Antarctic Journey*, with John Caldwell and Jan Senbergs), 1990 (*Australian Printmakers*, with Ray Arnold and Rod Ewins)
Australian National Gallery, Canberra: 1992–3 (*Being and Nothingness*, touring retrospective)

Selected Writings

"Decoy: A lithograph by Jasper Johns", *Art Bulletin of Victoria*, no.15, 1973–4, pp.42–3
"The makings of a trilogy", *Art Bulletin of Victoria*, no.31, 1990, pp.44–51

Bibliography

Survey II: Bea Maddock, exh. cat., National Gallery of Victoria, Melbourne, 1980
Bea Maddock Prints, 1960–1982, exh. cat., National Art Gallery of New Zealand, Wellington, 1982
Pat Gilmour, "Unravelling history: Parallel searches for cultural identity", *Print News*, vi/3, 1984, pp.4–7
Antarctic Journey: Three Artists in Antarctica, exh. cat., Tasmanian Museum and Art Gallery, Hobart, 1988
Sue Backhouse, *Tasmanian Artists of the Twentieth Century*, Hobart: Pandani Press, 1988
Australian Printmakers: Ray Arnold, Rod Ewins, Bea Maddock, exh. cat., Tasmanian Museum and Art Gallery, Hobart, 1990
Janine Burke, *Field of Vision: A Decade of Change: Women's Art in the Seventies*, Ringwood, Victoria: Viking, 1990
Being and Nothingness: Bea Maddock: Work from Three Decades, exh. cat., Australian National Gallery, Canberra, and elsewhere, 1992
Julie Ewington, "After Being and Nothingness: Reconsidering Bea Maddock", *Binocular*, ed. Ewen McDonald, Moët and Chandon Contemporary Edition, 1992
Sasha Grishin, *Contemporary Australian Printmaking: An Interpretative History*, Roseville East, NSW: Craftsman House, 1994

The significance of Bea Maddock has long been recognised in Australia; her elusive, compelling work has been the subject of several survey exhibitions since 1968, with the most comprehensive in 1992. The single largest collection of her work resides at the National Gallery of Australia, Canberra. During the early part of her career, the artist was recognised primarily as an innovative printmaker, challenging easy decorative formulas with imagery that stressed the private and personal within a fragmented and increasingly dislocated world. Some 30 years later, she is acclaimed as much for her series of encaustic paintings with collage, which reconstruct the notion of landscape.

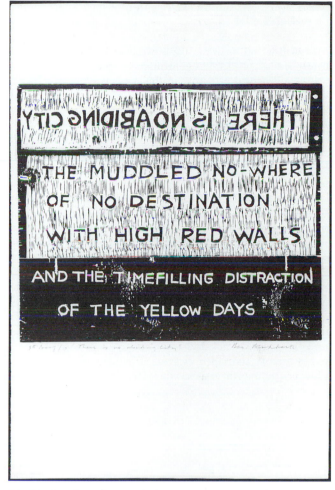

Maddock: *There Is No Abiding City*, 1964; woodcut; National Gallery of Australia, Canberra

Maddock trained in Hobart in the mid-1950s before embarking on a postgraduate course in painting and printmaking at the Slade School in London. Exposed to the wealth of public art collections in London and continental Europe, Maddock sharpened her understanding of past masters and was particularly drawn towards the uncompromising intensity and emphatic gesture of Georges Rouault's work and that of the German Expressionists. The small oil paintings and etchings she produced at the Slade echoed their approach, as did the stark, intentionally crude woodcuts she produced in the mid-1960s on her return to Australia.

Based in Melbourne, the artist faced one of the most solitary and testing times of her life, deriving solace from the existentialist writings of Jean-Paul Sartre. The subject matter she chose echoed her struggle, for example, *There Is No Abiding City* (1964; see illustration) and *Self-Portrait with Icarus* (1964), which were both editioned woodcuts. There were also small drypoints that acted as visual notations of a day's familiar patterns and that extended to screenprints when Maddock became an art teacher in Launceston in the late 1960s. Her role as an influential educator was consolidated in Melbourne from 1970, when the artist was employed at the prestigious National Gallery School. Here, she began experimenting with photographic imagery, finding in it a new stimulus for her graphic work, and in turn she was instrumental in promoting the practice of photo-screen printing and photo-etching in Australian art schools.

Maddock's prints of the 1970s were conceptually and technically brilliant, which has contributed to the belief that as an artist she is skilled primarily in this area. Photography-based source material brought an immediate world of tragedy and disquieting incident into play with Maddock's continuing themes of solitary introspection. The serial nature of her work became increasingly important, paralleling the sequential nature of personal diaries as much as news reportage. Using the dot-screen rather than the woodcut tool and etching or drypoint needle, she found a language through which to communicate readily with an audience deluged by mass media. References to "disasters" and human calamities characterised these prints of the mid-1970s. The artist intentionally avoided presenting any logical and direct "reading" of her subjects, which were often culled from newspaper clippings. The companion photo-etchings of 1974, *No-where* and *Now-here*, for instance, are deliberately ambiguous as one senses the familiar and recognisable without being able fully to pin the subject down. *No-where* provides barely enough evidence to indicate survivors of the *Titanic* adrift in a lifeboat. Above this potently symbolic black-and-white image is a passage of "lost" text, a blurred and faded message. It is haunting and memorable, reminding one of the transitory and fragile nature of earthly existence.

The written word and its extension into a series of large encaustic (wax) paintings marked the late 1970s. For Bea Maddock the act of writing is closely allied to her art production. Both forms of creativity are serial and convey a sense of narrative, the unfolding of a theme. In many ways she can be described as having a poet's sensibility, chronicling with fearless honesty the different stages of her personal growth and the alert perceptions she has of humankind. The interdependence of text and image operates almost as a leitmotif throughout her work.

Among the commanding word paintings is *Mutable* (1978; Art Gallery of South Australia, Adelaide), which re-articulates and extends the dictionary definition of the term. A matrix of words overlaying a photographic image that documented the opening of the first High Court of Australia in 1903 was Maddock's solution to a major commission for the new High Court in Canberra. Completed in 1980, the 12 panels "read" as tablets of text abutting one another and hung in a continuous line. Numerals sometimes replaced the emblematic presence of words in the artist's paintings and drawings of the late 1980s and they invariably had religious connotations. Although Maddock continued to produce editions of prints, this activity was integrated with her work in other media and she matched the more ambitious visual statements with a number of artist's books.

The project that she focused on in the late 1980s was a trilogy of panoramic paintings and a suite of etchings resulting from a 40-day voyage to Antarctica in January 1987. Antarctica presented Maddock with a vast, remote continent that readily served as a starkly appropriate reflection of human isolation. Landscape, rather than the figure as such, became a vehicle for expressing existentialist themes; not surprisingly, the artist's first painting in the trilogy was entitled *We Live in*

the Meanings We Are Able to Discern (1987; National Gallery of Australia, Canberra). This multi-panelled work combined pigment wash and encaustic on canvas with cibachrome photographs. The seven panels comprise three distinct layers, the top portion recording a continuous vista of land forms and glaciers, with one or two remnants of human habitation. Like the associated prints, landscape is rudimentarily described by a sensitive exploratory line and accompanied by text flowing as a rhythmic frieze through each panel. The second painting in the trilogy was based on the ancestral lands of the Tasmanian Aborigines and the third on Melbourne and its surrounds.

In the past few years Bea Maddock has continued to work on reconstructed landscapes using the encaustic technique. For instance, the four-panel painting TROUWERNER … *The White Ships Came from the West and the Sea of Darkness* (1992–3; Tasmanian Museum and Art Gallery, Hobart) is developed from sketchbook drawings that have been modified substantially to evoke a land mass of no specific time, and one configured with Aboriginal place names from pre-settlement tribal areas of Tasmania. It is as much about early expeditions to Australia, resulting in colonisation and ensuing racial injustice, as it is a metaphor for the artist's own journey in unveiling self-deception and the paradoxes endemic to contemporary life.

ANNE KIRKER

Madox Brown, Lucy *see* Brown

Mailou, Lois *see* Jones

Makovskaya-Luksch, Elena
Russian artist, 1878–1967

Born in St Petersburg, 1 November (Old Style calendar)/13 November (New Style calendar) 1878; daughter of painter Konstantin Makovsky, niece of painters Nikolai and Vladimir Makovsky, elder sister of art critic Sergei Makovsky, founder of *Apollon* periodical. Studied at Tenisheva School, St Petersburg, 1894–6; St Petersburg Academy under Ilya Repin and Vladimir Beklemishev, 1896–7; studied in Anton Ažbè's studio in Munich, 1898. Married Austrian sculptor Richard Luksch and moved to Vienna, 1900. Member, Wiener Kunst im Hause, 1902; Wiener Werkstätte, 1905; Mir Iskusstva (World of Art), 1911. Settled permanently in Hamburg, 1907; taught at the Kunstgewerbeschule. Died in Hamburg, 15 September 1967.

Principal Exhibitions
Vienna Secession: 1901–3
SRKh (Union of Russian Artists), St Petersburg: 1904–5
Wiener Werkstätte, Berlin: 1904
Wiener Werkstätte, Vienna: 1905
Venok (The Wreath), St Petersburg: 1908
Kunstschau Wien, Vienna: 1908

Internationale Baukunstausstellung, Vienna: 1908
Hamburg: 1910 (individual)
Mir Iskusstva (World of Art), St Petersburg: 1912

Bibliography

Joachim Heusinger von Waldegg, "Richard Luksch und Elena Luksch-Makowsky: Ein Künstlerpaar der Wiener Jahrhundertwende", *Alte und Moderne Kunst*, xvii/124–5, 1972, pp.40–47
Joachim Heusinger von Waldegg and Helmut R. Leppien, *Richard Luksch, Elena Luksch-Makowsky*, Hamburg: Christian, 1979

The Russian artist Elena Makovskaya-Luksch was one of the leading contributors to the Secession style in *début-de-siècle* Vienna, having moved there after her marriage to the Austrian sculptor Richard Luksch in 1900. In the spirit of the times she worked in several fields, establishing herself as a painter, sculptor, applied and graphic artist. Her approach was marked by considerable diversity, encompassing realism, symbolism and primitivism. The first, which was to be expressed in the oil *Turkeys* (1896; repr. Waldegg and Leppien 1979, pl.45) and the bas-relief *Future War* (1898; ex-Museum of War and Peace, Lucerne), followed from the tradition in which her father Konstantin Makovsky had attained renown, and her training at the St Petersburg Academy, in the painting and sculpture studios of Ilya Repin and Vladimir Beklemishev respectively. The critical realist emphasis of the bas-relief, which she completed with the sculptor Sergei Konyonkov, was apparent through its depiction of the corpse of a soldier, hit by a shell in the trenches and then thrown out undignifiedly on to the battlefield by his comrades. Commissioned by the eminent pacifist Jan Gotlib Bloch, it was intended for a Peace Pavilion (unrealised) that he proposed for the Paris Exposition Universelle of 1900.

Bloch's patronage led to the installation of the bas-relief in his Museum of War and Peace in Lucerne (1902) and to Makovskaya-Luksch's studies in Munich. It was from there that she moved to Vienna to become one of the earliest female participants in the Secession's exhibitions, to join the early design co-operative Wiener Kunst im Hause, and to become a member of the Wiener Werkstätte. Among her contributions to the Secession were two square painted panels inlaid with metal for the seminal experiment in *Raumkunst*, the Beethoven Exhibition of 1902. The stylised images of youth, the flowing and radiant forms and the progression of life of these were in accord with the Promethean and cosmic musicality of the friezes by Klimt, Böhm, Andri and others and were integrated cohesively into Josef Hoffmann's ensemble. Yet Makovskaya-Luksch's works were unique for their association with Russian folklore and philosophy: one represented the climactic scene from the *bylina* (epic song) Sadko where the hero, a musician and merchant, selects his bride in the undersea kingdom in order to return to his beloved city of Novgorod; the other illustrated a messianic verse on "the rule of death and time" and the "constancy of the sun of love" by the philosopher Vladimir Solovyov. Appropriately, given the subject of the exhibition, in both there is a fusion of the fantastic and the real, a sense of mortal struggle conjoined with enlightenment and salvation.

Throughout the mid-1900s Makovskaya-Luksch was to continue her collaboration with Hoffmann through her design of artefacts (including fans, painted caskets, Neo-rococo venti-

Makovskaya-Luksch: *Gargantua's Youth and Exploits*, 1907; Hamburger Kunsthalle, Hamburg

lator covers and panels in embossed brass or silver) and ornamental sculptures for the Wiener Werkstätte and its major architectural projects such as the Palais Stoclet, Brussels. In addition, she created three large faience reliefs depicting *Melpomene and Her Choir* (1905; Museum für Kunst und Gewerbe, Hamburg) for the façade of the Vienna Bürger-Theater. The simplified, expressive forms of the Muse of tragedy and her sombre cohorts with masks and wreaths flow together against the ochre ground in a self-contained, homogeneous manner that Makovskaya-Luksch was to repeat in her watercolour and gouache illustrations to Rabelais's *Gargantua* (1906–8; Kunsthalle, Hamburg). Her decision to illustrate the vulgar scenes coincided with the revival of interest in folk customs, popular festivities, proverbs, children's games and comic theatre, mixed with a new love of folly and fantasy unreined, that occurred across Europe at the start of the 20th century, and which was particularly strong in Russia following the revolution of 1905. She created at least four scenes of Gargantua's life – the drunken party of his birth, his youth and exploits, the battle of the common people and the languorous amusements at the magnificent Thélème Abbey. The pictures are compressed compilations of figures, overtly primitivised with crude anatomical and spatial distortions, and engaged in various activities, mostly unseemly. This is in keeping with the lack of central plot and conclusion to the tale, its temporal ambiguities, disparities of size, mixture of the real and fictitious, and its emphasis on anecdotal interludes. Hence in *Gargantua's Youth and Exploits* (1907; see illustration) the giant is depicted reading from a book held by several tiny monks, gorging himself, taking his "post-prandial piss" which becomes a river capturing six pilgrims, experimenting to find the best material to wipe his "arse" on, and spitting up a dog's bottom.

At the same time Makovskaya-Luksch created a series of designs for modern *lubki* (broadsheets) and a cycle of sketches illustrating Russian proverbs, which was in keeping with the Wiener Werkstätte's programme of publication of such graphic designs. The return to native folk themes, however, was also symptomatic of the move being made by several of her compatriots, not least Bilibin and Kandinsky, who had studied with her at Ažbè's in Munich, and anticipates the more radical Neo-Primitivism of Malevich, Larionov and Goncharova (q.v.). For her *lubki* she utilised many of the stylisations found in the widely circulated printed sheets of the 18th and 19th centuries – figures in peasant dress pushed up against the picture plane, a restricted palette, ambiguous treatment of space and light, simplified and often distorted forms, and the inclusion of script. Such features characterised the depiction of a drunken brawl in *To Drink. To Be. Russia Is Merriment. It Can't Do Without It* and the cosmic dream world that illustrated the *Fish Have the Sea, the Birds the Air, but Mankind's Home Is the Whole of the Universe* (both 1908; *ibid.*, pls 74 and 75), with its idyll of fish, birds and young maidens in touch with nature combined with modern steamships and an airship. With their boldly delineated forms, they also typified the less complex, deliberately naive visualisations of old proverbs and were eventually printed as a set of 12 postcards by the Wiener Werkstätte in 1912. In the majority of her works from her most fruitful period (1900–12) Makovskaya-Luksch expressed a laconic, generalised interpretation of human fate and foibles, which culminated in her elegant, life-size ceramic statue *A Woman's Lot* (1910–12; Stadtpark, Hamburg), which, with classical idealisation and some self-identification, revealed a young woman as mother and protectress of children.

JEREMY HOWARD

Malachowski, (Clara Anna) Marie von

German painter and graphic artist, 1880–1943

Born in Hannover, 3 May 1880; father an army officer. Moved to Dresden with her family, 1890s; studied under Wilhelm C.H. Claudius, who also taught at the Dresden Academy, 1899. Moved to Stuttgart and received private tuition in printmaking from Leopold von Kalckreuth, then director of the Stuttgart Academy, 1900. Moved to Berlin, 1902. Married painter Heinrich Nauen in Dresden, 1905; children. Lived in Paris, 1905–6; Berlin, 1906–11; Dilborn near Brüggen on the Lower Rhine, 1911–31; Neuss, 1931–8; Kalkar, 1938–43. Husband appointed professor at the Düsseldorf Academy, 1922; forced to resign by the National Socialists, 1937. Malachowski's work in the Gelsenkirchen museum declared "degenerate" and confiscated, 1937; some

further work destroyed by a fire bomb during World War II. Died in Kalkar, 9 November 1943.

Principal Exhibitions

Internationale Kunstausstellung, Dresden: 1901
Grosse Kunstausstellung, Dresden: 1904
Kunstsalon Cohen, Bonn: 1913 (*Rheinische Expressionisten*)
Galerie Alfred Flechtheim, Düsseldorf: 1913, 1919 (*Frauen*)
Kölnischer Kunstverein, Cologne: 1918
Kunsthalle, Düsseldorf: 1919, 1921 (both *Das Junge Rheinland*)
Galerie Cassirer, Berlin: 1919 (*Jüngere Künstler*)
Barmen: 1919 (*Das Junge Rheinland*, touring)
Grosse Berliner Kunstausstellung, Berlin: 1920
Messepalast, Cologne: 1924 (*Grosse Düsseldorfer Kunstausstellung*)
Kunstverein, Barmen: 1929

Bibliography

Dresslers Kunsthandbuch, ii, *Das Buch der lebenden deutschen Künstler: Altertumsforscher, Kunstgelehrten und Kunstschriftsteller*, Berlin, 1930
Die Rheinischen Expressionisten: August Macke und seine Malerfreunde, exh. cat., Städtisches Kunstmuseum, Bonn, 1979
Shulamith Behr, *Women Expressionists*, Oxford: Phaidon, and New York: Rizzoli, 1988
Anke Münster, "Künstlerinnen in Köln und Düsseldorf von 1918 bis 1933", typescript, Giessen, 1991
Die Rheinischen Expressionisten, 1913: Der Schock der Moderne in Bonn, Schriftenreihe Verein August Macke Haus, no.8, Bonn, 1993
Rheinische Expressionistinnen, Schriftenreihe Verein August Macke Haus, no.10, Bonn, 1993
Unbekannte Druckgraphik des Rheinischen Expressionismus: Texte und Kurzbiographien zur Ausstellung, typescript, August Macke Haus, Bonn, 1993

The inclusion of four watercolours by Marie von Malachowski in the *Rheinische Expressionisten* exhibition held in Bonn in 1913 went almost unnoticed at the time. It was this participation, however, that first brought her to the attention of art historians, in 1979, 36 years after her death. Initiated by August Macke, the exhibition of works by 16 artists, including Max Ernst, Franz Henseler, Heinrich Nauen and Olga Oppenheimer (q.v.), the other female artist, at the Städtisches Kunstmuseum, Bonn, emphasised the independent nature of Rhenish Expressionist art.

The first full examination of Malachowski's life and work took place in connection with the exhibition of female Rhenish Expressionist artists (*Rheinische Expressionistinnen*) at the August Macke Haus, Bonn, in 1993, based on a study and catalogue raisonné (unpublished). Most of the works listed (48 paintings, 4 watercolours, 21 drawings, 29 prints and 1 painting on glass) are in private collections and have not been exhibited or published, so the characterisation of her oeuvre is based only on the few works in public collections.

Among the earliest known works by Malachowski is a small drypoint engraving, *Canal Work* (1900; Kupferstichkabinett, Dresden), which brought her success at the beginning of her career. In 1901, as a 21-year-old private pupil of Leopold von Kalckreuth, Director of the Stuttgart Academy, she showed this and other prints at the Internationale Kunstausstellung in Dresden. Three years later, *Canal Work* was bought by the Dresden Kupferstichkabinett, thus she was represented in a public collection at a very young age. The engraving, which is

Malachowski: *Girl with Blue Apron (Margarethe Loibl)*, 1928; oil on canvas on paper; 67.5 × 47.5 cm.; Städtisches Museum Abteiberg, Mönchengladbach

flat, without expressive contrasts, was influenced by the formal language of Art Nouveau. At first it appears to be a landscape, because the true subject matter – people at physical work – blends with the background detail. Only after intense scrutiny do the small shadows in the canal emerge as about two dozen labourers, and the impressive scale of the project becomes apparent. It is Malachowski's sole surviving work based on the theme of man and work, or industrialisation.

The promising start of Malachowski's career contrasts with the dominance from 1905 of her husband Heinrich Nauen, whom she met at Kalckreuth's. Apart from the usual obstacles for a female artist – housekeeping and bringing up children – the marriage of two artists is full of conflicts. It is telling that Malachowski, who deliberately kept her maiden name, is almost invariably referred to as Marie Nauen.

Malachowski did not exhibit between 1904 and 1913, and only two works from this period are known. Although a year's study in Paris (1905–6) provided good working conditions, her artistic activity declined after the couple's return to Berlin, with the death of her first child and birth of a daughter in 1908. Yet, presumably through Nauen, she became acquainted with the paintings of the Dresden artists' group Die Brücke that influenced her colour compositions. The move to Castle Dilborn, near Brüggen on the Lower Rhine, and the improvement in the family's economic situation enabled Malachowski to resume regular artistic work. Apart from landscapes and still lifes, she executed mainly portraits of women and children from the region. In 1924 the portrait of *Johanna Wingen* was bought by the Städtisches Museum, Gelsenkirchen; it was confiscated as degenerate by the National Socialists in 1937 and is untraced. The portraits of children show her admiration for the work of Paula Modersohn-Becker (q.v.), whom she had met in Paris shortly before the artist's death. This influence is especially obvious in the oil painting *Girl with Blue Apron (Margarethe Loibl)* (1928; see illustration), one of her few works in public collections. The subject, shown three-quarter length and seated on a chair, was about nine years old, the daughter of the forester of Dilborn, and the portrait conveys the sense of an immensely wilful personality. The girl faces the viewer, her eyes disproportionately large, her head bowed and hands folded in her lap, and the absence of any attribute concentrates the viewer's attention on her individuality. The expressive power of the picture is enhanced by the use of complementary colours: the red of the chair is set off by the dark green background, the orange blouse contrasts with the blue of the apron. Another strong reductive portrait is of *Katharina Smeets* (c.1911; August Macke Haus, Bonn), a shop owner from Brüggen aged about 60.

A series of 19 woodcuts made by Malachowski in the years 1922–4 was bought by the Kunstmuseum, Bonn, in 1980. In subject matter and technique these forceful, expressive works are without comparison in her surviving oeuvre. The studio she used from 1921 was unheated, and it is likely that during the winter months she turned increasingly to creating woodcuts at home. For the first time she depicted religious motifs, such as *Resurrection* and *Damnation* (both 1922; Kunstmuseum, Bonn).

Although Malachowski liked Dilborn and found most of her subject matter in the landscape and people of the Lower Rhine, her life there was also isolated. Her husband spent much of his time in Düsseldorf (he became professor at the Academy in 1922), participating in the artistic life there. In a letter of 1941 she referred to this loneliness as a "still world of thoughts", in which she felt increasingly confined. Between 1918 and 1921 Malachowski exhibited frequently as a member of the artists' group Das Junge Rheinland. Her last documented participation in an exhibition was 15 years before her death. Her reasons for not exhibiting are unknown.

ANKE MÜNSTER

Malfatti, Anita
Brazilian painter, 1889–1964

Born in São Paulo, 2 December 1889. Educated at Mackenzie College, São Paulo, 1904–6. Went to Berlin, 1910; studied at the Berlin Academy and under Fritz Burger and Expressionist painter Lovis Corinth, 1913. Returned to Brazil via Paris, 1914, leaving for New York later that year. Studied briefly at the Art Students League, New York, then under Homer Boss at the Independent School of Art; began to produce illustrations for *Vogue*, *Vanity Fair* and other magazines. Returned to Brazil, 1916. Founder member, Grupo dos Cinco, São Paulo, 1922. Lived in Paris, 1923–8; visited Italy, 1924. Returned to São Paulo, 1928. President, Sindicato dos Artístas Plásticos, 1940. Contributed articles to the journal *Deutsche Nachrichten*, São Paulo, from 1955. Died in São Paulo, 6 November 1964.

Principal Exhibitions

Individual
26 rua 15 de Novembro, São Paulo: 1914
111 rua Líbero Badaró, São Paulo: 1917
Galerie André, Paris: 1926
Museu de Arte, São Paulo: 1949 (retrospective), 1955
Clubinho, São Paulo: 1957
São Paulo Bienal: 1963 (retrospective)
Museu de Arte Brasileira, São Paulo: 1971 (retrospective)

Group
Teatro Municipal, São Paulo: 1922 (*Semana de arte moderna*)
Maison de l'Amérique Latine, Paris: 1923
Salon d'Automne, Paris: 1924, 1926–7
Salon des Indépendants, Paris: 1926–8
Roerich Museum, New York: 1930 (*First Representative Collection of Paintings by Contemporary Brazilian Artists*)
Exposição Geral de Belas Artes, Rio de Janeiro: 1931
Exposiçao de Arte Moderna da SPAM, São Paulo: 1933
Salão Paulista de Belas Artes, São Paulo: 1934–6
Salão da Familia Artística Paulista, São Paulo: 1937, 1939–40
Salão do Sindicato dos Artístas Plásticos (SPBA), São Paulo: 1938–9, 1941, 1944, 1946
Galeria Itá, São Paulo: 1946 (*Exposição de pintura moderna em homenagem póstuma a Mário de Andrade*)
São Paulo Bienal: 1951
Museu de Arte Moderne de São Paulo: 1952 (*Exposição comemorativa da Semana de Arte Moderna de 1922*)
Museo Nacional de Bellas Artes, Buenos Aires: 1957 (*Arte moderno en Brasil*)

Bibliography

Monteiro Lobato, "A propósito da exposição Anita Malfatti", *O estado de São Paulo*, 20 December 1917

Oswald de Andrade, "A exposição Anita Malfatti", *Jornal do Comércio*, 11 January 1918

Aracy Amaral, *Artes plasticas na Semana de 22*, São Paulo: Perspectiva, 1970

Paulo Mendes de Almeida, *De Anita ao Museu*, São Paulo: Perspectiva, 1976

Anita Malfatti, 1889–1964, exh. cat., Museu de Arte Contemporānea, Universidade de São Paulo, 1977 (contains bibliography and full exhibition list)

Marta Rossetti Batista, *Anita Malfatti no tempo e no espaço*, São Paulo: IBM, 1985

Modernidade: Art brésilien du 20e siècle, exh. cat., Musée d'Art Moderne de la Ville de Paris, 1987

Mario de Andrade, *Cartas a Anita Malfatti*, Rio de Janeiro: Forense Universitaria, 1989

Art in Latin America, exh. cat., Hayward Gallery, London, 1989

Edward Lucie-Smith, *Latin American Art of the 20th Century*, London and New York: Thames and Hudson, 1993

The role of Anita Malfatti as the absolute pioneer of Brazilian modern art marked both her career and her work. The artist was 28 years old when her solo show of modern paintings in São Paulo in 1917 provoked the furore of the press and the public in the cosmopolitan, and yet in many ways provincial, state capital. In the early decades of the 20th century São Paulo was a rapidly developing industrial city and the most important business centre of Brazil. In one sense Malfatti's early works reflected the spiritual energies of the place. She was the daughter of immigrants in a city marked by large-scale immigration – her father was Italian, an engineer by profession, her mother, a North American of German descent, was an amateur painter. Of a relatively stable, middle-class family, Malfatti followed the traditional educational path of aspiring artists in Brazil that included a period of study in Europe, whether funded by public grants through annual competitions or by private patronage. The specific difference in her case was not only her young age at the time of her departure to Europe but the fact that the trip, a personal and familial enterprise, combined an educational and professional goal with the private aspect of a visit to the continent of her ancestors. In 1910 she went to Germany, the country of her maternal forebears, to study painting at the Berlin Academy, and at the end of 1914, after a brief period back in São Paulo, she departed for New York.

Her formative years as a young artist, therefore, were spent outside Brazil, and nothing, apart from her own personal sensibility and initiative, and especially nothing in her previous educational experience, prepared her for the artistic choices she made while in Germany, which determined the path of development of her art. In Berlin she felt dissatisfied with the rigidity of the traditional instruction at the Academy and gravitated towards the experimental and innovative works of the German avant-garde. She studied under Lovis Corinth and something of the influence of the German painter, a search for immediacy of form and colour, could be seen in her first (and rather inconspicuous) solo exhibition in São Paulo in 1914, aspects of which were identified by contemporary critics as a lack of mastery and technical crudeness. Uncompromisingly, she reaffirmed her avant-garde leanings in New York, where she studied for a brief period at the Art Students League and with more concentration at the Independent School of Art under the American painter Homer Boss. During her period in New York she met, among other American and European avant-garde artists, Francis Picabia and Marcel Duchamp, and produced the greater part of her works for her exhibition of 1917 in São Paulo. Her New York period was indeed a confirmation of the expressionist disposition she had defined in direct contact with the works of the German avant-garde artists in Europe.

The most effective works of Malfatti's New York period concentrated on the isolated human figure painted directly, emotionally, emphatically, with a firm, vigorous delineation of form and a use of colour that reverberated the subjective tones, the emotional energies of the encounter of artist and sitter in the space of the canvas. In *Yellow Man* and *The Japanese* painted in 1915–16, and in *The Idiot* of 1917, the half-figure confronts the viewer against a background of broken diagonals or of raw surfaces of colour created with rapid, energetic brush strokes. These concentrated and self-absorbed individuals are the masks of the artist's subjectivity.

These were the very works that at first met with incomprehension in São Paulo and then with universal condemnation and ridicule after the show was harshly criticised by the writer Monteiro Lobato in a newspaper article whose title, "Paranoia or hoax?", intended to define not only Malfatti's works but modern art in general as the natural product of a deranged mind or, in the absence of a mental condition, the fruit of a malicious intent to deceive the credulous. The immediate result of Lobato's attack was an atmosphere of public scandal surrounding the exhibition and the sudden notoriety of the young painter. To others, however, the initial feelings of discomfort in front of those "distorted" images and unusual colour harmonies gave way to interest and soon to the positive evaluation of the quality and the importance of the paintings. Such was the case of the writer and poet Mario de Andrade, later one of the leading figures of modern Brazilian literature, for whom the works of Malfatti had the effect of a sudden revelation, of a new artistic universe in the making. Andrade was part of a group of (mostly young) artists and writers that congregated informally in defence of Malfatti's works and of modern art – a group that was to give impulse to the celebrations of the *Semana de Arte Moderna* in São Paulo in 1922. The *Semana* repeated in a larger dimension the scandals associated with modern art in the mind of the Brazilian public since Malfatti's show, but this time as a collective and organised effort of the artists with the deliberate aim of "upsetting the bourgeois". The *Semana* consolidated Modernismo (modernism) as a growing and vital movement in Brazilian art, in a sense bringing to realisation what Malfatti started on a purely individual basis in 1917.

To Malfatti, however, the immediate results of her exhibition were isolation, the loss of sales and the loss of students, a solitary struggle for professional and artistic survival in which the confident experimental character and subjective emotional dimension of her expressionist paintings gave way gradually to an eclecticism of pure aesthetic experimentation on the one hand and the search for stylistic "syntheses" between modern and traditional concepts on the other. Her contact with modern French art in Paris from 1923 to 1928 also contributed to this synthesis. After 1922 the consolidation of Brazilian modernism occurred in the creation of a modern and national art thanks to the efforts of painters such as Tarsila do Amaral (q.v.), Rego Monteiro and Di Cavalcanti and writers such as Mario de Andrade and Oswald de Andrade. The writers developed the ideological basis and theoretical foundations of the Movimento Modernista in manifestoes and critical works as well as fiction and poetry.

The contributions of Anita Malfatti to modern Brazilian art never attained the intensity of the heroic years. At times her later paintings alluded to the achievements of the early years. In a general way, however, Malfatti tended towards an individualised thematic elaboration of, or a response to, some of the nationalist and popular preoccupations of the modernists and their successors in the 1930s and 1940s. Without achieving either the formal or the ideological impact of the avant-garde artists, her works tended more and more towards a somewhat idiosyncratic "return to innocence", a sort of artistic quietism, exemplified in some of the paintings of landscapes of rural Brazil and the depictions of peasant life of her later years.

MARCELO LIMA

Mallo, Maruja

Spanish painter, 1902–1995

Born in Vigo, Galicia, 5 January 1902. Moved to Madrid with her family in 1922, and entered the Academia de Bellas Artes de San Fernando alongside her brother Cristino, a sculptor. Attended the drawing classes of Julio Moisés, where she met Salvador Dalí, José Moreno Villa and others, 1924. Worked in Paris and met André Breton, 1931–2. Taught drawing at Instituto de Arévalo, Instituto Escuela de Madrid and Escuela de Cerámica, early 1930s; taught at Escuela de Artes y Oficios, Vigo, 1936. Left Spain at outbreak of Civil War due to political convictions; lived in Buenos Aires, Argentina, with stays in Chile and Uruguay, until 1961. Returned to Madrid, 1962. Recipient of Estrada Saladrich prize, Barcelona, 1967; gold medal in fine arts, Ministry of Culture, 1982; gold medal, County of Madrid, 1990; gold medal, Council of Galicia, 1991. Died in Madrid, February 1995.

Principal Exhibitions

Individual
Galería de la *Revista de Occidente*, Madrid: 1928
Galerie Pierre, Paris: 1932
Salas Adlan, Centro de la Construcción, Madrid: 1936
Carroll Carstairs Gallery, New York: 1948
Galerie Silvagni, Paris: 1950
Galería del Este, Punta del Este, Uruguay: 1952
Galería Compte, Buenos Aires: 1955
Galería Ruiz Castillo, Madrid: 1979
Galería Guillermo de Osma, Madrid: 1992
Centro de Arte Contemporáneo de Galicia, Santiago de Compostela: 1993–4 (touring retrospective)

Group
Sociedad de Artistas Ibéricos, San Sebastián: 1931

Salón de Otoño, Madrid: 1933 (*Grupo constructivo*)
Musée du Jeu de Paume, Paris: 1936 (*L'Art espagnol contemporain*)
Galería D'Art Catalonia, Barcelona: 1936 (*Exposición Lógicofobista*, organised by ADLAN, Barcelona)
Galería Multitud, Madrid: 1975 (*El surrealismo en España*)

Selected Writings
"Plástica escenográfica", *Gaceta de Arte* (Tenerife), March 1935
"La plástica", *U.O. Revista de Cultura Moderna* (Mexico), August–September 1936
"Proceso histórico de la forma en las artes plásticas", *Grafos* (Havana), November–December 1937; reprinted in *Maruja Mallo*, Buenos Aires: Losada, 1942
"Lo popular en la plástica española a través de mi obra", *Sur* (Buenos Aires), April 1938
"Integración de la forma en las artes plásticas", *Sur* (Buenos Aires), February 1939
"Una sala cinematográfica", *Arquitectura* (Buenos Aires), March 1946
"La ciencia de la medida", *Nuevo Continente*, i, 1947 (signed Buenos Aires, April 1946)
"El surrealismo a través de mi obra", *El surrealismo*, ed. Antonio Bonet Correa, Madrid: Cátedra, 1983 (text of lecture given at Santander University, September 1981)

Bibliography
Ernesto Giménez Caballero, "Notre Dame de la Aleluya", *Papel de Aleluyas* (Seville), March 1928
Melchor Fernández Almagro, "María Mallo", *Verso y Prosa* (Murcia), June 1928
Francisco Alcántara, "María Mallo en la *Revista de Occidente*", *El Sol* (Madrid), 13 June 1928
Antonio Espina, "Arte 'Nova Novorum': Maruja Mallo", *La Gaceta Literaria* (Madrid), 15 June 1928
Manuel Abril, "María Mallo", *Revista de Occidente* (Madrid), July 1928
Sebastián Gasch, "Els pintors nous: Maruja Mallo", *L'Amie de les Arts* (Sitges), 31 September 1928
Rafael Alberti, "La primera ascensión de Maruja Mallo al subsuelo", *La Gaceta Literaria* (Madrid), 1 July 1929
Luis Gómez Mesa, "Cinema y arte nuevo: Originalidad de Maruja Mallo", *Popular Film* (Barcelona), 15 May 1930
Benjamín Jarnes, "Sobre una definición pictórica del hombre", *La Vanguardia*, 12 April 1931
Jean Cassou, "Maruja Mallo", *Revue Hebdomadaire*, May 1932
Maruja Mallo, exh. cat., Salas Adlan, Centro de la Construcción, Madrid, 1936
Margarita Nelken, "La vida artística: Exposición Maruja Mallo", *Claridad* (Madrid), 11 June 1936
Ernesto Giménez Caballero, "El arte y la guerra", *Levante*, 21 July 1939
Alfonso de Sayons, "Maruja Mallo y lo popular en la plástica española", *Conducta al servicio del pueblo* (Buenos Aires), September–October 1939
Ramón Gómez de la Serna, *Maruja Mallo*, Buenos Aires: Losada, 1942
—, "Nueva actualidad de Maruja Mallo", *Atlántida* (Buenos Aires), May 1956
Francisco Rivas, "Homenaje de Maruja Mallo a *Revista de Occidente*", *El País*, 12 April 1976
Maria Escribano, "Las fantásticas criaturas de Maruja Mallo", *Arteguia*, Madrid, 1979
Juan Manuel Bonet, "Maruja Mallo: Pura y genial paradoja", *El País*, 25 October 1979
Consuelo de la Gandara, "Maruja Mallo en la *Revista de Occidente*", *Ya* (Madrid), 4 November 1979
Francisco Calvo Serraller, "Maruja Mallo: Invencible en su sueño", *El País*, 25 September 1983

Estrella de Diego, "Los paisajes del límite: Frida Kahlo y Maruja Mallo a partir de un retrato", *La balsa de la Medusa*, Madrid, 1991

Maruja Mallo, exh. cat., Galería Guillermo de Osma, Madrid, 1992

Maruja Mallo, exh. cat., Centro de Arte Contemporáneo de Galicia, Santiago de Compostela, and elsewhere, 1993

Estrella de Diego, "María, Maruja, Mallo", *Revista de Occidente*, May 1995

Maruja Mallo is perhaps one of the most interesting female painters of the Spanish avant-garde, both in terms of her pictorial contribution and because of her personality, which was very unusual within the somewhat closed Spanish society of the 1930s, particularly as regards female behaviour. From many points of view she is the type of artist who falls within the definition of the avant-garde; in fact, her most interesting work was produced during the 1920s and 1930s. The friend of, among others, Salvador Dalí, Benjamín Palencia, Federico García Lorca, Miguel Hernández, Rafael Alberti, Pablo Neruda and Rafael Barradas, she represents the ideal of the modern woman, which was frequently opposed to the more restrictive expectations of a "middle-class young lady".

Mallo moved from Galicia to Madrid with her family in 1922, when she was 20. There she met the philosopher and writer José Ortega y Gasset, founder of the magazine *Revista de Occidente*, who would affect her career in many ways. When he saw her paintings, Ortega decided to support her by means of an exhibition in the magazine's gallery in 1928 as well as by commissioning a series of cover illustrations for the magazine, which reveal the geometric style that would characterise Mallo's work throughout her career.

Mallo showed about 30 works in this exhibition – both oil paintings and coloured prints – which attracted the interest and admiration of Madrid intellectuals. The city was then living through the final years of the collapsing dictatorship of Primo de Rivera and was enjoying a period of intensely animated cultural activity. Mallo's work at this time centred on two series which denote a passion for modernity very much in keeping with the spirit of the time and with that of Mallo herself: the *Fairs* and *Sporting Elements*. The first series comprises four large paintings in which parts of the city and its leisure activities are depicted in a vertiginous manner within the picture space. Without abandoning a certain kind of realism that predominates throughout Mallo's work, the style of these pictures uses futuristic, almost *simultaneist* devices in a manner similar to that of Barradas to create the idea of speed, fragmentation and simultaneously occurring events. *The Fair* (1928; see illustration) portrays two Amazonian women characteristic of Mallo's work, together with sailors, puppets, civil guards, magicians – and everything that years later in a lecture given by the artist in Santander in 1981 she defined as an allegory of popular and pagan leisure. The universe that she presents in this series is the world of her journeys through the city – soldiers, maids, policemen, shawls, along the lines of popular cinematographic productions such as those of the writer Ernesto Giménez Caballero – and at the same time a territory of subverted values, as shown by the Three Magi – one white and two black – in *Easter Procession* (1927; private collection, New York, repr. Santiago de Compostela 1993, p.62) or the pigs replacing the fairground horses in *The Fair* (1928; Centre Georges Pompidou, Paris, *ibid.*, p.65). It may

have been these unexpected associations that have led to the frequent use of the label Surrealist to describe the painter.

The same type of strange associations and taste for urban life is evident in some of the works belonging to the second series referred to above, *Sporting Elements* (1926–7), in which Mallo uses her typical style, at once realist and fragmented. The paintings depict objects related to a kind of open-air life. *Sporting Elements* (1927; private collection, Madrid, *ibid.*, p.61), in which a racquet, a fan, a chess board and a miniature aeroplane share the picture space with other artefacts, may speak, like the woman in a bathing costume cycling on the beach in *Cyclist* (1927; untraced, repr. Gómez de la Serna 1942), of some of the photographs of modern life that fascinated the entire Art Deco generation.

Another series dating from 1927 is *Kinetic Prints*, in which angels and mannequins, skyscrapers and businessmen in top hats and suits live together in the recurring theme of the metropolis, as in perhaps the most popular of these works *Print* (1927; private collection, Barcelona, repr. Santiago de Compostela 1993, p.68). The most striking aspect of this series is the almost total absence of colour and the use of mannequins, a favourite pictorial motif of the Surrealists. This may in part be explained by Mallo's meeting Dalí at the Residencia de Estudiantes in Madrid during these years; he had already become very familiar with André Breton's definition of Surrealism through his trips to Paris. Be that as it may, and despite the use of mannequins, the Surrealist elements here are isolated traits. The cut legs, feet, torsos, wigs and long hair that define the world of Mallo's cities in the late 1920s are painted in an identical, fragmented style. Besides, in contrast to the work of some of the women artists associated with Surrealism, such as Claude Cahun (q.v.) and Ithell Colquhoun (q.v.), Mallo's work of these years reveals no attempt to revise the Surrealist vocabulary from a female point of view.

Mallo also met Federico García Lorca and Rafael Alberti at the Residencia de Estudiantes. She worked with Alberti on a production of *La pajara pinta*, producing figurines and decorations for the scenery, as well as on other projects, also unrealised but which nevertheless demonstrated her passionate search for other forms of artistic expression beyond strictly pictorial ones. In fact, in the early 1930s, Mallo strengthened her interest in stage design through a project to execute the theatrical decorations for a play about García Lorca's bullfighter friend Ignacio Sánchez Mejía; the Ampliación de Estudios, associated with the same Residencia de Estudiantes and the Institución Libre de Enseñanza, progressive bodies of the period, awarded her a grant to study scenography.

In 1931, shortly before leaving for Paris for several months with her father, Mallo took part in the II Exposición de los Ibéricos in San Sebastián, in which a good selection of Spain's avant-garde artists were included. Mallo's style underwent a radical transformation during her stay in Paris, becoming more dramatic and less vital. The world of fairs was replaced by horrifying visions of a world submerged in catastrophe. Bones and dead birds, as in *Rooks and Excrements* (1931; private collection, Madrid, *ibid.*, p.74), and devastated lands, as in *Land and Excrements* (1932; Museo Nacional Centro de Arte Reina Sofía, Madrid, *ibid.*, p.81) are among the works of this period in which the colours are also darker, closer to earth pigments. The 16 works that Mallo exhibited in the Galerie

Mallo: *The Fair*, 1928; Museo Nacional Centro de Arte Reina Sofía, Madrid

Pierre in Paris in 1932 form part of this series. Some of the most celebrated international artists of the time visited the show, which again aroused great interest; not only did Picasso and Jean Cassou see the exhibition, but Breton himself seems to have bought a work, *Scarecrow*, reproduced in the book that Ramón Gómez de la Serna wrote during his exile in Argentina in the 1940s (Gómez de la Serna 1942).

Breton's fascination may have been the cause of Mallo's slightly forced inclusion among the Surrealists, added to the isolated elements in her work previously mentioned. Whatever the reasons, the series *Sewers and Bell Towers* is usually considered to be the most Surrealist of her works, partly due to its reception by Breton and partly due to Mallo's lecture of 1981 in which the painter acknowledged the series as Surrealist. In any case, if these works are compared with Mallo's later interests, her growing fascination with nature and its internal order made visible in such series as *Mineral Architectures* and *Vegetal Architectures*, dating from these same years, it is perhaps possible to read *Sewers and Bell Towers* from a perspective that is not strictly, or at least not only, Surrealist. In fact, this period also coincides with Mallo's friendship with some of the painters of the so-called Vallecas School, outstanding among whose members were Benjamín Palencia and

Alberto Sánchez. Seen from this perspective, *Sewers and Bell Towers* inserts itself within her interest in nature and the changes that occur within it, while also bearing a relationship to Dalí's "putrefactions", if one recalls the photograph in which Mallo is represented as the high priestess of a cult of rubbish (date unknown; repr. Madrid 1992, p.110). The materials used for the colour and the texture itself, compared with *Architectures*, enable reference to be made to the influence of Alberto and Palencia in journeys through the south of Madrid rather than to that of Surrealism itself. On the other hand, some of these works, such as *Vegetal Architectures* (1933; private collection, Madrid), testify to the painter's growing interest in geometry with her adoption of the golden section and the meticulous study of mathematics that she undertook in 1933 in the little-known Madrid circle of Torres García, who included her in the *Grupo Constructivo* that he showed at the XVI Salón de Otoño in Madrid.

Following her passion for artistic forms other than painting, Mallo continued to execute some of her scenographic experiments, most of which are preserved only through reproductions in magazines of the period, such as the *Gaceta de Arte* (Canary Islands). In the mid-1930s she executed some ceramics that, together with geometric designs, used humorous figures belonging to popular Spanish traditions as shown by a cartoon representing a bullfighter (1935; private collection, Madrid).

Mallo's inclusion in the exhibition *L'Art espagnol contemporain* at the Musée du Jeu Paume in Paris, as well as her participation in the *Exposición Lógicofobista* in Barcelona, reveal an increasingly mature artist who presents herself as such in one of her most spectacular works, the *Wheat's Surprise* (1936; private collection, Madrid, repr. Santiago de Compostela 1993, p.105). The impressive painting manifest in Mallo's best pieces appears here united with a metamorphic passion – evident in the hands from which the wheat springs – that the artist always related to the Castilian landscapes through which she had travelled with the poet Miguel Hernández.

This work was one of the last paintings she executed in Spain; when the Spanish Civil War erupted in July 1936, Mallo was teaching at the Escuela de Artes y Oficios in Galicia and, given her political convictions, she left for Argentina via Portugal, thanks to an invitation from the Amigos del Arte of Buenos Aires. During the ensuing years in the Americas, Mallo alternated her activities as a lecturer with working on her series *Work*, in which elements of the sea are united with those of the land. In this series executed between 1936 and 1938, Mallo returned to the Amazonian type of woman first seen in such early works as *Cyclist*, and which may be analysed from a feminist perspective: doubles (mirror images), metamorphosis. A second glance also makes it possible to connect Mallo's passion for strong women manifested in her particular taste for convincing, solid forms with the geometries in which the "doubles" can also be included, such as *Song to the Ear of Grain* (1939; Museo Nacional Centro de Arte Reina Sofía).

Mallo's portraits from the early 1940s can be included within this same line and perhaps constitute the last truly interesting works by the artist. Some of the paintings in this series – feminine full-face and profile portraits of white and black women, generally preserved in Argentinian museums or private collections, such as *Woman's Head* (1941; Museo Provincial de Bellas Artes, Santa Fé) – precede mysterious and lively works such as *Human Hind* (1948; private collection, Buenos Aires, *ibid.*, pp.134–5), in which Mallo's taste for metamorphosis and forms generating forms reappears.

Mallo also executed works such as the series *Still/Moving Life* and *The Grapes* (1944; whereabouts unknown, repr. Madrid 1992) during her exile in Argentina, which she interspersed with journeys to Chile and Uruguay and with meetings with such Latin American intellectuals as Pablo Neruda. A preparatory drawing for *The Grapes* reveals the geometric process the artist used. The *Mask* series, in which geometric masks alternate with fashionable beaches where bathers play with sunshades or dance, dates from these same years.

While in Buenos Aires Mallo received a commission to paint a mural in the Los Angeles Cinema. She also received other offers to paint murals during her visit to New York in 1947 – the Rockefeller Foundation and the Metro-Goldwyn-Meyer Studios – although none was executed. Three years later she held another exhibition in Paris, at the Galerie Silvagni. In 1951 *Human Hind* was shown in Madrid at the Primera Bienal Hispano-Americana de Arte. During these years she began

several studies of dancers that testify to Mallo at her most vital.

After spending several years withdrawn from the world, in 1961 Mallo decided to return to Spain. Several exhibitions were organised on her return in various cities, and she received awards and prizes. She again produced illustrations for the *Revista de Occidente* and began the series *Inhabitants of Space*, totally submerged in a type of composition without reference to anything beyond pure geometric forms, and fascinated by word play, as shown by *Geonautic Almotron* (1975; Guillermo de Osma Collection, Madrid). In the early 1980s Mallo became ill and remained in a clinic until her death in 1995. In one way, until very recently Mallo remained one of the great forgotten figures of Spanish art and it is only in the last few years that retrospective exhibitions of her work have been mounted: at the Galería Guillermo de Osma in Madrid in 1992 and the retrospective held in Galicia in 1993.

ESTRELLA DE DIEGO

Mammen, Jeanne
German graphic artist and painter, 1890–1976

Born in Berlin, 21 November 1890. Moved to Paris with her family, 1895. Studied at Académie Julian, Paris, 1906; Académie des Beaux-Arts, Brussels, 1908–10; Scuola Libera Accademica, Villa Medici, Rome, 1911. Left Paris for the Netherlands at the outbreak of World War I; moved to Berlin, 1916. Worked on cinema posters for the Ufa film studio. Moved into a studio on the Kurfürstendamm, Berlin, initially sharing it with her older sister Adeline, also a painter, 1919. Provided illustrations for fashion magazines and satirical journals, 1922–34. Visited Soviet Union, 1929. Ceased exhibiting under the National Socialist regime, 1933–45. Visited Morocco, 1969. Died in Berlin, 22 April 1976.

Principal Exhibitions
Individual
Galerie Gurlitt, Berlin: 1930
Galerie Gerd Rosen, Berlin: 1947
Galerie Anja Bremer, Berlin: 1954
Senator für Volksbildung, Akademie der Künste, Berlin: 1960
Neuer Berliner Kunstverein, Berlin: 1970
Galerie Brockstedt, Hamburg: 1971
Landesmuseum für Kunst- und Kulturgeschichte, Oldenburg: 1971
Galerie Wolfgang Gurlitt, Munich: 1972
Gallery La Boëtie, New York: 1972
Galerie G.A. Richter, Stuttgart: 1974
Berlinische Galerie, Berlin: 1978
Fischer Fine Art, London: 1980
Bonner Kunstverein, Bonn: 1981 (retrospective)

Group
Salon des Indépendants, Paris: 1912
Salon des Indépendants, Brussels: 1913
Abteilung für Volksbildung, Berlin-Steglitz: 1946
  (*Frühjahrsausstellung in der Kamillenstrasse*)
Stadthalle, Dresden: 1946 (*Allgemeine Deutsche Kunstausstellung*)
Jahrhunderthalle, Frankfurt am Main-Hoechst: 1971–2 (*Liebespaare in der deutschen Graphik des 20. Jahrhunderts*, touring)

Mammen: *Masked Ball*, 1932; watercolour and pencil; 46 × 35.5 cm.; Des Moines Art Center, Iowa

Bibliography

Kurt Tucholsky, "Antwort an Jeanne Mammen", *Weltbühne*, xxv, 6 August 1929, p.225

Jeanne Mammen, exh. cat., Galerie Gurlitt, Berlin, 1930

Jeanne Mammen, exh. cat., Senator für Volksbildung, Akademie der Künste, Berlin, 1960

Jeanne Mammen, exh. cat., Neuer Berliner Kunstverein, Berlin, 1970

Künstlerinnen international, 1877–1977, exh. cat., Schloss Charlottenburg, Berlin, 1977

Jeanne Mammen, 1890–1976, exh. cat., Berlinische Galerie, Berlin, 1978

Jeanne Mammen, Hans Thiemann, exh. cat., Staatliche Kunsthalle, Berlin, 1979

Jeanne Mammen, 1890–1976: Works from 1914–1930, exh. cat., Fischer Fine Art, London, 1980

Jeanne Mammen, 1890 bis 1976: Retrospektive, exh. cat., Bonner Kunstverein, Bonn, 1981

Hildegard Reinhardt, "Jeanne Mammen (1890–1976): Gesellschaftsszenen und Porträtstudien der zwanziger Jahre", *Niederdeutsche Beitrage für Kunstgeschichte*, xxi, 1982, pp.163–88 (contains extensive bibliography)

Annelie Lütgens, "Jeanne Mammen, 1890–1976", *Tendenzen*, xxvi/152, 1985, pp.34–9

Das Verborgene Museum I: Dokumentation der Kunst von Frauen in Berliner öffentlichen Sammlungen, exh. cat., Akademie der Künste, Berlin, 1987

Katharina Sykora, "Jeanne Mammen", *Woman's Art Journal*, ix/2, 1988–9, pp.28–31

Annelie Lütgens, *"Nur ein Paar Augen sein …": Jeanne Mammen: Eine Künstlerin in ihrer Zeit*, Berlin: Reimer, 1991

Jeanne Mammen: Köpfe und Szenen, 1920–1933: Berlin 1920 bis 1933, exh. cat., Kunsthalle, Emden, and elsewhere, 1991

Domesticity and Dissent: The Role of Women Artists in Germany, 1918–1938, exh. cat., Leicester Museum and Art Gallery, and elsewhere, 1992

Annelie Lütgens, "Jeanne Mammen und die Berliner Kunstszene der Nachkriegszeit, 1945–1950", *Profession ohne Tradition: 125 Jahre Verein der Berliner Künstlerinnen*, exh. cat., Berlinische Galerie, Berlin, 1992, pp.183–91

Three Berlin Artists of the Weimar Era: Hannah Höch, Käthe Kollwitz, Jeanne Mammen, exh. cat., Des Moines Art Center, IA, 1994

Marsha Meskimmon and Shearer West, eds, *Visions of the "Neue Frau": Women and the Visual Arts in Weimar Germany*, Aldershot: Scolar Press, 1995

Jeanne Mammen had a long and varied career in Berlin, spanning the period from the 1920s to the 1970s. She is best known today for her work from the 1920s and 1930s, when she was producing painting and graphics associated with the Neue Sachlichkeit (New Objectivity). Significantly, Mammen was as well known for her graphics and illustrations during the period as for her "fine art" production.

After studying in Paris, Brussels and Rome, Mammen settled permanently in Berlin, and her works are intimately tied to the atmosphere of that city during the "Golden Twenties". Her works for such journals as *Simplicissimus* and *Uhu* as well as the fashion illustrations she produced for such women's magazines as *Die Dame* placed her at the centre of the current debates about the changing roles for women in the period and especially about the *neue Frau* (New Woman). There was a marked increase in popular press publication during the years of the Weimar Republic, particularly journals that sought the newly independent young women as their market. Mammen's illustrations directly addressed the New Woman, both as a consumer and as a type. Her fashion illustrations displayed the latest styles for women, including bobbed hair, boyish "flapper" dresses and androgynous suits. Her satirical works for such journals as *Simplicissimus* confronted the stereotypical image of the New Woman with humour and searing wit. Mammen's success as a graphic artist indicates the currency of her themes and her incisive approach to them.

Clearly, the theme of the New Woman was central to Mammen, but she did not merely parody the type. Her works showed the range of roles and situations in which the new young woman of the day might find herself; Mammen did not flinch from showing the negative aspects of the "Golden Twenties" in Berlin. She tackled the issue of drug and alcohol abuse by women, prostitution (*In the "Kaschemme"*) and the tedium of urban life with such works as *Boredom* (both 1920s; Jeanne Mammen Gesellschaft, Berlin) and *Boring Dollies* (c.1927–30; Hausweddel und Nolte, Hamburg). She also showed the poverty of many personal relationships, from the estrangement of the heterosexual couple in *Young Woman with Cat* to the isolation of the two figures in *Mother and Daughter* (both 1920s; Jeanne Mammen Gesellschaft).

Probably the most striking feature of Mammen's work, and the one that causes most critical comment, is its "woman-centredness". The women depicted in Mammen's graphics and paintings are the central figures, rather than the attributes of male figures. Mammen's representations of women place them and their situations at the heart of the image. Indeed, the representations of male figures in Mammen's oeuvre tend to marginalise their experience; in a complete reversal of the norm, the men are mere props in the women's lives. Furthermore, many of Mammen's works show women together, at home, in the shops or hairdressers' salons, in cafés and bars and as mothers and daughters, friends and lovers. Women's relationships with other women, in all their range and intensity, were scrutinised by Mammen in her art.

Mammen documented the flourishing lesbian night-life of Berlin in the Weimar years. In works such as *Masked Ball* (1932; see illustration) the artist explored the excitement of the underground scene – the gay and lesbian scene was nicknamed "Eldorado". The ways in which fashionable, urban lesbians were able to manipulate the androgyny of the New Woman as an image are explored; the central figure is a strutting woman in a man's suit and top-hat, dangling a cigarette from her lips and looking at us straight out of the picture frame. This is not one of those bitter caricatures of "masculinised" women that were used in the period to frighten girls back into the kitchen – this is an empowered woman, using masquerade to challenge strict gender boundaries and find a place for herself. Between 1931 and 1932 Mammen was commissioned to produce ten lithographs on the theme of lesbian love for Pierre Louÿs's book *The Songs of Bilitis*. When the Nazis banned its publication, some of these lithographs were lost (and a portion of Mammen's other work was destroyed), but the remaining images (Jeanne Mammen Gesellschaft) are stunning in the range of emotions they represent. *Jealousy*, for example, with its representation of the woman on her knees clinging desperately to the figure who shuns her, delineates all the sexual desire and frustration of one woman for another who scorns her. In complete contrast, both *In the Morning* and *Siesta* show women in tender, private moments. Their gentleness, and the fact that Mammen does not make them into displays for heterosexual titillation, reinforces their sense of "woman-centredness".

Mammen remained in Berlin during the Third Reich and World War II, despite harassment from the Nazis. In the 1950s she turned towards abstract work. These paintings are most often constructed through layers of thin washes out of which emerge shapes and images (e.g. *Contemplation*, 1960s; repr. Berlin 1978). Towards the very end of her life, when the realism of the Weimar period became of interest to scholars, critical acclaim attended Mammen yet again. After her death, the Jeanne Mammen Gesellschaft was set up in her former studio in Berlin to maintain her works and notebooks for posterity.

MARSHA MESKIMMON

Mancoba, Sonja Ferlov *see* Ferlov

Mandiargues, Bona de *see* Bona

Mangold, Sylvia Plimack
American painter, 1938–

Born Sylvia Plimack in the Bronx, New York, 18 September 1938. Studied at Cooper Union School of Art, New York, 1956–9 (certificate); Yale University School of Art, New Haven, 1959–61 (BFA). Married painter Robert Mangold, 1961; two sons, born 1963 and 1971. Part-time instructor of painting and drawing, School of Visual Arts, New York, 1974–84. Recipient of National Endowment for the Arts (NEA) grant, 1974. Lives in Washingtonville, Orange County, New York.

Selected Individual Exhibitions
Fischbach Gallery, New York: 1974, 1976
Daniel Weinberg Gallery, San Francisco: 1975
Droll/Kolbert Gallery, New York: 1978, 1979, 1980
Annemarie Verna Galerie, Zürich: 1978, 1991
Matrix Gallery, Wadsworth Atheneum, Hartford, CT: 1980
Brooke Alexander, New York: 1982, 1984, 1985, 1986, 1989, 1992, 1995
Madison Art Center, WI: 1982–3 (touring retrospective)
University of Michigan Museum of Art, Ann Arbor: 1992–3 (touring retrospective)
Albright-Knox Art Gallery, Buffalo, NY: 1994–5 (touring retrospective)

Selected Writings
Inches and Field, ed. Amy Baker, New York: Lapp Princess, 1977

Bibliography
Michael André, "New editions: Sylvia Mangold," *Art News* , lxxiv, September 1975, pp.55–6
Gregory Battcock, ed., *Super Realism: A Critical Anthology*, New York: Dutton, 1975

Ruth Bass, "Sylvia Plimack Mangold (Droll/Kolbert)", *Art News*, lxxix, April 1980, p.181
Contemporary American Realism since 1960, exh. cat., Pennsylvania Academy of the Fine Arts, Philadelphia, and elsewhere, 1981
Sylvia Plimack Mangold: Paintings, 1965–1982, exh. cat., Madison Art Center, WI, and elsewhere, 1982
John T. Paoletti, "Sylvia Plimack Mangold: Uses of the past", *Arts Magazine*, lvii, May 1983, pp.90–93
John B. Ravenal, "Sylvia Plimack Mangold: Framework", *ibid.*, pp.94–6
Margaret Mathews, "Sylvia Plimack Mangold," *American Artist*, March 1984, pp.52–6, 84–8
Sylvia Plimack Mangold: Works on Paper, 1968–1991, with a Catalogue Raisonné of the Prints, exh. cat., University of Michigan Museum of Art, Ann Arbor, and elsewhere, 1992 (contains bibliography)
The Paintings of Sylvia Plimack Mangold, exh. cat., Albright-Knox Art Gallery, Buffalo, NY, and elsewhere, 1994

Although she has worked with a variety of materials and techniques, it is Sylvia Plimack Mangold's paintings that have recently been the subject of critical investigation. As with her drawings and prints, the paintings are meticulously rendered representational images taken from the immediate environment of home and studio. Because her paintings of floors, landscapes and other aspects of these surroundings have a high degree of verisimilitude, she is typically described as a realist. However, to categorise her work as representative of a particular style is to impose limitations when, in fact, she has explored a broad range of expressive possibilities.

Mangold concentrated on developing and refining her technical skills in spite of the dominance of non-representational painting during the 1950s and 1960s. She insisted that, although she was drawn to the energy integral to Abstract Expressionism, it did not demand the concentration on recognisable subject matter that she equated with quality in art. She could understand wanting to make a Franz Kline, but could not understand wanting to look at it. To be an artist, she insisted, was to paint like Thomas Eakins, but that demanded a high level of courage and commitment. It also required the determination to pursue illusionist realism when it seemed that few critics or galleries had an interest in supporting it.

She married the Minimalist painter Robert Mangold in 1961, the year they both graduated from Yale University with degrees in art, but she did not mimic the eccentric shapes and industrial surfaces that characterise his work. Rather, her close-up studies of the interior of her home have a literal austerity that exceeds the documentation of photography. Her *Floor No.1* (1968; 99 × 132 cm.; Collection Rachele and Larry Sullivan), one of her first precisely rendered sections of wood floors, was described by the art historian Linda Nochlin as providing: "… a sense of an intensely personal vantage point which is at the same time very cool and non-committal". Mangold then propped a wood-framed mirror against one wall of her studio and painted the reflected illusion of a confined space. *Absent Image* (1973; 142 × 111 cm.; Feiwel Collection, New York) reflects an extension of the plane of the floor that extends to take in a corner of the opposite wall, a view that is further complicated by the addition of a window through which a landscape is visible.

Tapes, rulers and masking tape were inclusions in the interior paintings of 1974–7. These exist as still-life objects that

Mangold: *Elm Tree*, 1993–4; oil on linen; 228.6 × 114.3 cm.

assert a quantifiable reality within the carefully concocted illusions of space. For example, a pencil and watercolour study, *Flexible and Stainless* (1974; 58.6 × 73.5 cm.; private collection), includes a highly detailed ruler that is treated much like a still-life element. When meticulously rendered rulers are combined with floors, as in *Two Rules, One Exact, One Diminished* (1975; 45.9 × 61 cm.; Collection Robert Mangold), they energise the space in which they are placed by questioning interpretations of measurement. Further investigation of reality versus illusion is seen in paintings of tiled floors, in some of which a ruler asserts itself both as flat object and denial of the

artifice of one-point linear perspective, as in *In Memory of My Father* (1976; 76 × 183 cm.; private collection) and *Taped-Over Twenty-Four-Inch Exact Rule on Light Floor* (1976; 51 × 61 cm.; private collection). *In Memory of My Father* is a sensitive investigation of how one's perspective determines perception, and since perspective is determined by one's age and position, the rule in the painting is ended at 66 3/4 inches, her father's age at the time of his death.

Mangold's concerns with measurement appear throughout her works on paper, a support that allowed her to experiment with creating contrasts between abstraction and the exact replication of rulers. If a ruler can be interpreted as measuring truth, then abstraction is allowed to exist as imaginary pictorial space. Some of her drawings and prints on paper are preparatory works for later paintings, such as *Where a 38-Inch Vanishing Point Is Along the Right Ruler (Eighteen-Inch Chase)* (1976; private collection), which is a study for the acrylic painting *Two Exact Rules on a Diminishing Floor Plane* (1976; Collection Nancy and Martin Melzer). Others, however, depend on drawn imagery for their identity, such as *Paint the Tape, Paint the Paper, Paint the Tape* (1975; private collection), a meticulous replication of a page seemingly torn from a spiral-ringed notebook.

Masking tape and measuring devices continued to be important elements in Mangold's drawings and paintings of 1977 and 1978, in which she explored landscape imagery superimposed on grid patterns and cropped by implied tape. In *Changing Colors* (1977; 76 × 91 cm.; Collection Allied Signal) a central landscape image is bordered and enhanced by numerous layers of tape that extend beyond the edges of the canvas. While the landscape is contained by the tape, the tape itself suggests unlimited space. In this way, Mangold investigated ideas about process, a concept that dominated much artistic expression during the late modern period, including that of her husband and others categorised as Minimalists. Process, for Mangold, consists of assimilation of ideas, which combines intellect and emotion with the pleasurable physical activity of painting.

She continues to conceptualise experiences of her immediate environment by visiting the same site repeatedly in order to accumulate information. Since 1990 Mangold has concentrated on the various nearby trees that change with the seasons. Illusionist tapes persisted in her earlier tree paintings, but disappeared after 1991 as she resolved some of her self-imposed struggles with the depiction of nature in geometric terms. Acknowledging Cézanne's advice to revive instincts and sensations of art that dwell within us all, she has recorded the varied and changing characteristics of the elm trees on her property on numerous occasions. *Elm Tree, Winter* (1990–93; Brooke Alexander, New York) and *Elm Tree* (1993–4; see illustration) are examples of the problems that she has assigned herself. Like the meticulously rendered floors, the trees challenge her ability to replicate, on a geometrised flat surface, the feelings they evoke. Living and working in Washingtonville, New York, Mangold continues to examine numerous facets of a single motif until she is compelled to explore another aspect of her immediate environment.

MARY F. FRANCEY

Mantuana [Mantovana; Ghisi; Scultori], Diana

Italian printmaker, c.1547–1612

Born in Mantua, c.1547, to the engraver and stucco-worker Giovanni Battista Mantuano and his wife Osanna de Aquanegra; younger sister of the engraver and print publisher Adamo Scultori. Moved to Rome at the time of her marriage to the architect Francesco Capriani da Volterra, 1575; one son, Giovanni Battista Capriani, born 2 September 1578; husband died 1594. Received honorary Volterran citizenship with her husband, 1579. Joined the religious confraternity of Roman artists and craftworkers, the Compagnia di San Giuseppe di Terra Santa, 10 April 1580. Married the architect Giulio Pelosi, 1596. Buried in San Lorenzo in Lucina, Rome, 5 April 1612.

Bibliography

Giorgio Vasari, *Le vite de' più eccellenti pittori, scultori ed architettori*, Florence, 1568; ed. Gaetano Milanesi, vi, Florence: Sansoni, 1881; as *Lives of the Most Eminent Painters, Sculptors and Architects*, 10 vols, London: Macmillan-Medici Society, 1912–15; reprinted New York: AMS, 1976 (lives of Benvenuto Garofalo and Girolamo da Carpi)

Giovanni Francesco Peranda, *Lettere del Signor Gio. Francesco Peranda*, Venice, 1621

Giovanni Baglione, *Le vite de' pittori, scultori et architetti dal Pontificato di Gregorio XIII del 1572 in fino a' tempi di Papa Urbano Ottavo nel 1642*, Rome: Fei, 1642; reprinted Bologna: Forni, 1975–6

Carlo D'Arco, *Di cinque valenti incisori mantovani*, Mantua, 1840 (as Diana Ghisi)

A. Cinci, "Francesco Capriano e Diana Mantovana", *Dall'Archivio di Volterra, memorie e documenti*, Volterra, 1885

G.F. Hill, *Portrait Medals of Italian Artists of the Renaissance*, London: Warner, 1912

J.A.F. Orbaan, "Virtuosi al Pantheon: Archivalische Beitrag zur römischen Kunstgeschichte", *Repertorium für Kunstwissenschaft*, xxxvii, 1914, pp.17–52

Adam von Bartsch, *Le Peintre-graveur*, xv, Würzburg, 1920 (as Diana Ghisi)

Incisori mantovani del '500, exh. cat., Istituto Nazionale per la Grafica-Calcografia, Rome, 1980 (as Diana Scultori)

Loránd Zentai, "Portrait inconnu de Diana Scultori", *Bulletin du Musée Hongrois des Beaux-Arts*, no.62–3, 1984, pp.43–51

Suzanne Boorsch and J.T. Spike, *Italian Artists of the Sixteenth Century* (Illustrated Bartsch, xxxi), New York: Abaris, 1986 (as Diana Scultori)

Paolo Bellini, *L'opera incisa di Adamo e Diana Scultori*, Vincenza: Pozza, 1991

Laura Marcucci, *Francesco da Volterra*, Rome: Multigrafica, 1991

Valeria Pagani, "A *lunario* for the years 1584–1586 by Francesco da Volterra and Diana Mantovana", *Print Quarterly*, viii, 1991, pp.140–45

——, "Adamo Scultori and Diana Mantuana", *Print Quarterly*, ix, 1992, pp.72–87

Evelyn Lincoln, *Printing and Visual Culture in Italy, 1470–1575*, PhD dissertation, University of California, Berkeley, 1994

——, "Making a good impression: Diana Mantuana's printmaking career", *Renaissance Quarterly* (in preparation)

Diana Mantuana was the only female engraver of the 16th century who signed her prints with her own name. She was also, possibly not coincidentally, one of only five professional craftswomen mentioned by name in the second edition (1568) of Vasari's *Vite* (the other four are Properzia de' Rossi, Sofonisba Anguissola, Suor Plautilla Nelli, all q.v., and Lucrezia Quistelli). He noted that Diana "engraves so well that it is a wonderful thing and … is a very well-bred and charming young lady", having met her on a trip to Mantua in 1566. Like many Renaissance artists and almost every Renaissance woman in the arts, Diana learned her trade from her father and brother. For her father, a draughtsman and decorator working for the Gonzaga court from designs by Giulio Romano and Giovanni Battista Bertani, printmaking represented a much-needed independent income for his family (*Lettere di artisti italiani ad Antonio Perrenot di Granvelle*, Madrid: Istituto Italiano di Cultura di Madrid, 1977, and Lincoln 1994). Diana's brother Adamo preceded her to Rome where he engraved for several publishers and tried publishing himself (G.L. Masetti-Zannini, *Stampatori e librai a Roma nella seconda metà del cinquecento*, Rome, 1980). Diana followed him there in 1575 after the death of her father and her marriage to the architect Francesco da Volterra, but there is no record of professional links between Diana's printing and that of her brother.

In Rome, in June 1575, Diana requested and obtained a papal privilege that protected her rights to print and market images from the copper plates that she had brought from Mantua. She was then able to operate freely, signing her prints Diana Mantuana (or Mantovana), a form of her name that identified her with the Mantuan court and with a printing tradition that had begun with Andrea Mantegna and continued through her family. This kind of signature, consisting of a first name with a surname that identified the provenance or profession of the bearer, was a common form of self-identification for people of non-noble birth. Diana's father used the name Giovanni Battista Mantuano, Scultor (Giovanni Battista, Mantuan sculptor); her brother adopted Scultori as a surname, although it was professionally descriptive as well. Diana never used that name, but identified herself on her earliest prints by first name only, then after arriving in Rome usually as "Diana Mantuana", often appending some written connection identifying herself as the wife of Francesco da Volterra. After her husband obtained honorary Volterran citizenship in 1579 which extended to her (Cinci 1885), she often signed her prints "Diana Mantovana, civis volaterrana". She never used the surname "Scultori", which was assumed for her by art historians of the 19th century (for a fuller discussion of Diana's name, see Ugo Bazzotti and M.G. Savoia, "Uno scritto del giugno 1592", *La Gazzetta di Mantova*, 24 November 1981, and for a discussion of the significance of signing, Lincoln 1994). Diana's first dated engraving is marked 1575 and the last is marked 1588, but since she did not always date her prints the exact time-span of her engraving career is not certain. She was already engraving well before Vasari's visit to Mantua in 1566, and there is no reason to believe that she did not produce undated engravings after 1588. During her lifetime her prints were published by herself, Antonio Lafreri, Claudio Duchet and Orazio Pacifico. Some of the plates later entered the stock of the de' Rossi family, and from there passed into the collection that became the core of the Calcografia Nazionale in Rome (some of her plates still exist at the Calcografia, see Bellini 1991). Other publishers who printed her plates include Antonio Carenzano (possibly working during Diana's lifetime),

Carlo Losi, Calisto Ferranti, Vincente Billy, Hendrick van Schoel and Giovanni Orlandi. (A complete list of her known engravings may be found by consulting Bellini 1991 with the addition of Pagani 1991.)

The Roman market for engravings after inventions by other artists provided Diana with many opportunities to make prints. She engraved several drawings by her father and Giulio Romano, and continued with decorative architectural drawings by her husband. She also collaborated with Francesco on a calendar, or "Lunario", illustrated with motifs from the

Mantuana: *Feast of the Gods*, engraving; British Museum, London

painted rooms of the Mantuan palaces on which Diana's father worked, and presumably for which she had access to drawings (for a recently discovered impression of this print, see Pagani 1991). She also made engravings after the works of such earlier artists as Correggio and Salviati, and copied an engraving by Marcantonio Raimondi. Likewise, her own engraving after Daniele da Volterra (Bellini 1991, p.25) was used for a painting by Lavinia Fontana (q.v.; see also M.T. Cantaro, *Lavinia Fontana bolognese*, Rome, 1989, cat. 4a. 30, and Lincoln 1994).

It is unlikely that Diana had much formal training in drawing, but it seems on the evidence of the prints that she was trained to engrave drawings on to copper plates with a good deal of fidelity. She based her engraving technique on the later 16th-century Roman school, incorporating a northern style much like that of Cornelis Cort or her fellow Mantuan, Giorgio Ghisi, but with less emphasis on chiaroscuro and texture and more on clarity of subject matter. She was also adept at elegant forms of address, and several of her earlier Roman engravings bear long, complicated and courtly dedications designed to win favour for her work and, used as gifts, to obtain employment for her husband in Rome (Lincoln 1994).

Although she became well known in the 19th and 20th centuries as one of the few Renaissance female artists to sign her work, in the 16th century she seemed to enjoy a certain amount of fame both in her own right and as a member of a successful artistic family. Besides being mentioned by Vasari, her work was noted with praise during her lifetime by Giovanni Francesco Peranda, the secretary to the Caetani family who employed Diana's husband. Among his published letters is one in which he thanks Francesco for the gift of Diana's engraving of the *Feast of the Gods* (see illustration) after Giulio Romano. Both socially and professionally she was part of an active artistic circle in Rome: the painter Durante Alberti was her son's godfather, and portrait medals were made of both her and Francesco da Volterra by the Medallist T.R. (repr. Hill 1912 and Pagani 1991). Diana's portrait was also engraved by Cherubino Alberti and drawn by Federico Zuccaro (repr. Zentai 1984).

Neither Diana's social connections nor her entry into the artists' confraternity of San Giuseppe provided her with a public voice on the Roman art scene, however. Women were recruited to enlarge the pool of dues-paying members, active mainly in choosing brides to be dowered on the confraternity feast day. They had no say in confraternity government and did not attend the plenary meetings. Neither could she belong to Federico Zuccaro's newly re-formed Accademia di San Luca, of which her husband was a founding member (R. Alberti, *Origine e progresso dell'Accademia del disegno de' pittori, scultori e architetti in Roma*, Pavia, 1604). Here again she was excluded because of her sex. As a printmaker, however, Diana mobilised her name, her position and her access first to the Mantuan images of Giulio Romano, then to the wider circle of her Roman friends (including Durante and Cherubino Alberti, Federico Zuccaro, Raffaellino da Reggio and others) in order to publicise her own and her husband's presence in Rome, his skill as an architect and the willingness of both of them to work in their adoptive city.

EVELYN LINCOLN

Marcello
Swiss sculptor and painter, 1836–1879

Born Adèle d'Affry in Fribourg, 6 July 1836, into the aristocratic family of the Comtes d'Affry; lived in Fribourg and in Nice, France, after her father's death in 1841. Visited Rome, and studied under the Swiss sculptor Imhoff, 1853–4. Adopted pseudonym "Marcello". Married Don Carlo Colonna, Duke of Castiglione-Aldovrandi, 5 April 1856; he died October 1856. Subsequently divided her time between Fribourg, Rome and Paris. Died of tuberculosis at Castellamare, near Naples, 14 July 1879.

Principal Exhibitions
Paris Salon: 1863, 1865–6, 1869–70, 1876
Royal Academy, London: 1865–7
Cercle de l'Union Artistique, Paris: 1867
Exposition Universelle, Paris: 1867
Weltausstellung, Vienna: 1873

Bibliography
Frédéric Loliée, *Les Femmes du Second Empire*, Paris: Juven, 1906
Comtesse d'Alcantara, *Marcello, Adèle d'Affry, duchesse Castiglione Colonna*, Geneva, 1961
Henriette Bessis, *Adolphe Thiers et la duchesse Colonna*, doctoral thesis, Paris I, 1972
——, *Marcello sculpteur*, Fribourg: Musée d'Art et d'Histoire, 1980 (contains extensive bibliography)
Marcello: Adèle d'Affry, duchesse Castiglione Colonna, exh. cat., Musée Rodin, Paris, 1980
Marcello (1836–1879): Adèle d'Affry, duchesse de Castiglione Colonna, exh. cat., Musée d'Art et d'Histoire, Fribourg, 1980
Henriette Bessis and Anne Clancier, "Psychanalyse des arts de l'image", *Colloquium: Cerisy, 1980*, Paris: Clancier-Guénaud, 1981
La Femme artiste d'Elisabeth Vigée-Lebrun à Rosa Bonheur, exh. cat., Musée Despiau-Wlerick, Donjon Lacataye, Mont-de-Marsan, 1981
Michel Terrapon, "Questions de métier: A propos de l'oeuvre sculpté de Marcello", *Zeitschrift für Schweizerische Archäologie und Kunstgeschichte*, xxxviii, 1981, pp.135–40
Henriette Bessis, "Pourquoi une telle résonance de la *Bianca Capello* de Marcello dans les dernières années du XIXe siècle?", *Gazette des Beaux-Arts*, 6th series, c, 1982, pp.183–7
Ghislain de Diesbach, *La Double Vie de la duchesse Colonna, 1836–1879*, Paris: Perrin, 1988

Born into an aristocratic family, the Duchess of Castiglione Colonna, known by her pseudonym Marcello, faced many obstacles due to her social rank – to which she remained attached – and her position as a woman artist, hoping for recognition of her work on a par with that of male colleagues. Her father died when she was five, a wound from which she never fully recovered, and her interest in art seems to have filled a vacuum. She received a refined and moral education appropriate to her social status and from childhood anticipated "a remarkable and active destiny", although she regretted having been born a woman. At the age of 17 she studied art in Rome, becoming a pupil of the sculptor Imhoff. She married the Italian nobleman Don Carlo Colonna, who died shortly afterwards, and to distract herself from grief she devoted herself to sculpture, executing his portrait from memory. It is from this point that she really became an artist, dividing her time between Fribourg, Rome and Paris.

Marcello: *Pythian Sibyl*, 1870; bronze; Opéra, Paris

In Paris, Marcello moved in both artistic and political circles, forming friendships with Thiers and Cousin, as well as Delacroix and Gounod. Mainly, however, she worked in her studio. That some of her works were labelled "virile" accorded with her view of herself as "somewhat masculine" in relation to sculpture, which she called her "wife". Marcello was a prolific writer, of letters, intimate notes, memoirs (incomplete and as yet unpublished). Her writings are at once elegant and restrained, tremulous and troubled, not given to overstatement, sometimes detached and penetrating. They offer insight into her nature as a woman and above all as an artist. Her motto: to love only "an art in which thought flows within the outward form, like blood beneath the skin".

The work that most completely embodies Marcello's art, her favourite "daughter", is without question the *Pythian Sibyl* (1870; Opéra, Paris, from 1875; see illustration). This large statue (ht 2.9 m. with tripod) she regarded as her *magnum opus*. In it she is master of her technique, which one must control "sufficiently to transcend it, to forget it if need be" (Delacroix), as the sculptor's task is to find solutions for the material problems posed by the medium. Her technical accomplishment is revealed in her letters and working notebooks, in which she ponders the choice of materials and the mathematical calculations needed to achieve correct proportion. Calipers, bradawls, chisels were tools enabling her to manipulate the planes and surfaces in order to "seize the harmony of form, line and relief". Dissatisfied with the bas-reliefs on the plinth of the Sibyl, she began remodelling, revising the armature and making use of a "flexible lead fountain pipe" for the twisting serpent. For the bust, a problem as much of characterisation as of form, she decided to cast her own body. Thus the *Pythian Sibyl* can be seen to represent the artist on two levels: simultaneously her outward form and her inner being, pulsating with controlled emotion. Technique alone is insufficient; it must be combined with the personal expression of an individual artistic talent. The *Pythian Sibyl*, a bravura work, unites all the elements of style and technique. Although in general critics were not inclined to praise her, indeed some were hostile, Charles Garnier, the architect of the Opéra, reasserted his admiration for her talent by confirming the commission.

Marcello's artistic credentials were secure from her sensational official début at the Salon of 1863. The three sculptures she exhibited demonstrated full command of her craft, if not of the personal style evident in the Sibyl. Her bust of *Bianca Capello*, a revenant from the Renaissance, won general approval. The severe and introverted expression of the Tuscan Grand Duchess, wife of Francesco de' Medici, hints at dire passions within. The taste for drama, inherited from Romanticism, allied to a felicitous illustrative presentation, entirely in harmony with the taste of the time, explains the response to the work. Marble and bronze versions of the bust were produced, and purchasers included a dealer (Beurdeley), a collector (Chauchat), a friend (Fould) and the Emperor himself. The bust was used to demonstrate his "numerical aesthetic" in a booklet published by Eugène Lagout. The well-known photographer Nadar produced many images of the work, which appeared in such journals as *L'Artiste*, *L'Illustration* and *L'Illustrateur des Dames*.

A friend of Nadar, Marcello was a passionate collector of photographs and used them for her work, especially portraits.

The sculptures she exhibited at the Salon, which were unanimously approved by the jury, show respect for both the spirit and forms of the past, reviving the "forgotten style of the great school of Florence". Although she was never an artistic outcast, Marcello never again enjoyed such critical success, perhaps due to the exclusion of so many other artists from the official Salon. As a result of this exclusion Napoleon III instituted the Salon des Refusés, in which artists could exhibit paintings of a different type from that promoted by the establishment.

Marcello worked tirelessly throughout her life, studying, drawing, sculpting, painting, engraving and reading. She frequented the Bibliothèque Nationale to draw after Piranesi or Bibiena, or Lavater for physiognomy. Among her innumerable drawings in various techniques are studies for sculpture, life sketches and copies of works by old masters and contemporary artists. She made lithographs and etchings, as well as drypoint, which she learned from Desboutins. Increasingly drawn to painting, she studied with Andrieu, a follower of Delacroix, then Regnault, Clairin and, later, Bonnat. Nevertheless, to her chagrin, the *Fieschi Conspiracy* (oil on canvas; Musée d'Art et d'Histoire, Fribourg) was refused by the jury for the Salon of 1874. There is nothing revolutionary about this painting, however; its subject taken from Schiller, in an almost classical Venetian setting.

In sculpture, Marcello's predominant concern was the representation of the female form: portraits, of the more conventional kind, of celebrities, family, friends or anonymous models. Some are fancy-dress or allegorising portraits, for example *Mélanie de Pourtalès as Phoebe* (1875; marble; Musée d'Art et d'Histoire, Fribourg), bringing to portraiture the qualities of such mythological figures as *Hecate* (1866; marble group; Montpellier), a private commission from the Emperor, or the *Tired Bacchante* (1869; marble; Musée d'Art et d'Histoire, Fribourg). Other works were inspired by her reading: *Paolo and Francesca* (c.1862; terracotta; Musée d'Art et d'Histoire, Fribourg) reflects her "profound impression" from reading Dante, "this being the way artistic creation should spring forth". After she read Faust, it blossomed into *Goethe's Marguerite* (1867; marble; Fondation Marcello, Fribourg), and, after seeing Rossini's *Barber of Seville*, into *Rosina* (1869; terracotta; Fondation Marcello). Among other remarkable portraits, the *Smiling Moorish Woman* (1869; marble and bronze; private collection, Paris), executed while she was working on the *Pythian Sibyl*, shows a free handling and ardent sensuality that contrasts with the high-strung sensitivity and greater reserve of the *Arab Sheikh* (1869; marble; Musée d'Orsay, Paris). Here, as in her other sculptures, one is aware of the importance for her of the subject's inner state. This concern is also evident in her male portraits: *Carpeaux* (1875; plaster), his features marked by physical suffering; *Milan del Bosc* (1868; pink plaster), all verve, brilliance and spontaneity; *Liszt* (1869; plaster); and *Thiers* (1872; marble; all Fondation Marcello).

Marcello's style, for all its eclecticism, reveals an unusual personality, with the nerve to keep projecting itself and occasionally to display an ever-responsive feminine sensibility. In works such as the *Sibyl* and the *Smiling Moorish Woman* she anticipates Art Nouveau. Carpeaux, her friend and admirer, wrote to her: "Be proud of your works … Yours is the future, yours the glory: because you possess the power, the wisdom and the genius of the arts."

HENRIETTE BESSIS

Marevna
Russian painter, 1892–1984

Born Maria Vorobyov in Cheboksary near Kazan, 14 February 1892; mother an actress; adopted as an infant by Bronislav Stebelski, a Polish nobleman. Studied art at the Tiflis academy, then at the School of Decorative Arts and Free Academy, Moscow. Left Russia to study painting in Italy, 1910; met the poet Maxim Gorky who named her "Marevna"; stayed on Capri and visited Rome. Went to Paris, 1912; studied at Académie Zuluaga, Académie Russe and Académie Colarossi; exhibited at Salon des Indépendants, 1913. Travelled to Portofino, Biarritz and Spain after father's suicide in 1914. Returned to Paris, 1915. Exhibited at Salon d'Automne, 1919; Salon des Tuileries, 1919 and 1923. Lived with the artist Diego Rivera; daughter Marika, also an artist, born 1919; Rivera returned to Mexico, 1921. Moved to Côte d'Azur for daughter's health, 1936; remained in southern France during World War II, then moved to England to live near her daughter, 1949. Painted in Malaga, Spain, 1969–70. Died in Ealing, London, 4 May 1984.

Selected Individual Exhibitions

Le Quotidien, Paris: 1929
D'Audreth Gallery, The Hague: 1934
Galerie Zborowski, Paris: 1936
Galerie Serguy, Cannes: 1946
Galerie Selection, Tunis: 1946
Lefevre Gallery, London: 1951
Galerie Claude, Paris: 1953
Musée du Petit Palais, Geneva: 1970 (retrospective)
Festival Gallery, Leicester: 1976
Lyric Theatre, Hammersmith, London: 1980
Galerie Leticia, Lugarno: 1981
Musée Bourdelle, Paris: 1985 (retrospective)
Wildenstein, London: 1992 (retrospective)

Selected Writings

(as Marevna Vorobëv)
Life in Two Worlds, London: Abelard Schuman, 1962
Life with the Painters of La Ruche, London: Constable, 1972; New York: Macmillan, 1974 (Russian original)
Mémoires d'une nomade, Paris: Encre, 1979

Bibliography

Marevna, exh. cat., Musée du Petit Palais, Geneva, 1971
L'altra metà dell'avanguardia, 1910–1940: Pittrici e scultrici nei movimenti delle avanguardie storiche, exh. cat., Palazzo Reale, Milan, and elsewhere, 1980
Marevna: Paintings and Works on Paper, 1915–1975, exh. cat., England & Co., London, 1989
Marevna and Montparnasse: A Centenary Tribute, exh. cat., Wildenstein, London, 1992
Gill Perry, *Women Artists and the Parisian Avant-Garde*, Manchester: Manchester University Press, and New York: St Martin's Press, 1995

Marevna was one of several women artists, including Maria Blanchard (q.v.), Sonia Delaunay (q.v.) and Alice Halicka (q.v.), who worked on the fringes of the Cubist movement during the 1910s. She first came to Paris in 1912, where she studied at several private academies, including the Académie Colarossi and the Académie Russe. Although her work from this period reveals a close engagement with some of the technical concerns of Cubist painting and collage, it is less well documented than that of her male colleagues working on the fringes of the movement. Her canvases often include figures and objects broken down into geometric forms, and are clearly influenced by Synthetic Cubism. Among her subjects are still lifes and many figure groups, some of which draw on themes from her Russian background or evoke allegorical meanings (e.g. *Woman and Death* or *Prostitute and Dead Soldier*, 1917; private collection, repr. Perry 1995, colour pl.23). She found it difficult to make a living from the sale of such works, and after the death of her adoptive father in 1914 she was left without financial support.

In her autobiography *Life in Two Worlds* (1962) Marevna provides a dramatic account of the difficulties that she encountered as a woman artist seeking the support of a dealer, especially after she became a single parent in 1919, when she gave birth to her daughter Marika, fathered by Diego Rivera. She describes the double standards that many independent women artists had to confront in their pursuit of professional status comparable to that of their male colleagues:

> If I am asked why I held aloof from the circle of contemporary artists who have all achieved universal recognition, my answer is that my exhibitions were always followed by long blanks, because I had to fight fearfully hard to bring up my child, devote much time to commercial art and decorative art, and give up exhibiting for lack of money. By force of circumstances, money has come between me and my work. In order to paint, a woman must enjoy a certain security, even if she has only quite a small family to support. For a man the problem is easier to solve: he nearly always has a woman, wife or mistress, who earns money: she works for "her man". She is devoted, and sacrifices herself until the man becomes celebrated [p.183].

Marevna's book describes her participation in the social and artistic culture that flourished around the bars of Montparnasse during the 1910s and 1920s. It projects a self-image of a vulnerable yet stubbornly independent woman struggling in a "bohemian" world that is both professionally hostile and sexually exploitative. The unsatisfactory terms of her relationship with the better-known artist Rivera, and the effect of that relationship on her career, are almost painfully revealed, and may have influenced her decision to abandon Cubist practices around 1920. She became increasingly involved with Neo-Impressionist techniques, a change of style that was less easily identified with avant-garde interests, and which contributed to her difficulties in selling work. However, some paintings from the 1920s, 1930s and 1940s combine Cubist and Neo-Impressionist techniques, and attracted the interest of dealers such as Gustav Kahn and Zborowski, who both held shows of her work. Examples of both

Marevna: *Homage to Friends from Montparnasse*, 1961; oil on canvas; 160 × 305 cm.; Musée du Petit Palais, Geneva

Neo-Impressionist and Cubist works can be found in the collection of the Musée du Petit Palais, Geneva.

After moving to England in the late 1940s she produced many canvases in which geometric forms, broken space and strong diagonal planes and lines recall the influence of Cubist and Futurist conventions, and became increasingly preoccupied with the pursuit of a "poetic" force in her work, with the representation of what she called "the fourth dimension". During the 1950s and 1960s she painted many retrospective portraits and group portraits of artists with whom she had been closely associated in Paris in the pre-war period, including several versions of *Homage to Friends from Montparnasse*. These are large-scale, frieze-like paintings in which Marevna represents groups of famous artists, writers and dealers who gathered in and around the cafés of Montparnasse. In one variation on the theme (which is in two versions) she paints herself and her daughter to one side of a group that includes Modigliani, Rivera, Soutine, Kisling, Max Jacob and Zborowski (1961; see illustration). The only other woman in the painting is Marevna's friend Jeanne Hébuterne, the young artist and long-suffering partner of Modigliani who killed herself shortly after his death in 1920.

Marevna's work and career stand as exemplars of the ambivalent and sometimes contradictory relationship that many women artists negotiated with so-called avant-garde styles and group activities during the first half of the 20th century. Although engaged with Cubist practices, she rarely exhibited with the male-dominated groups associated with that label, and increasingly sought to separate her work from what she saw as "fashionable" concerns. Ironically, perhaps, her own bid for independence has encouraged the retrospective separation of her work from that of her better-known male colleagues, and from the histories that feature them.

GILL PERRY

Maria *see* Martins

Marisol
Venezuelan sculptor and graphic artist, 1930–

Born Marisol Escobar in Paris, 22 May 1930, to Venezuelan parents. Grew up in Europe, the USA and Caracas. Studied at Ecole des Beaux-Arts and Académie Julian, Paris, 1949–50; Art Students League, New York, 1950; New School for Social Research and Hans Hofmann School, New York, 1951–4. Subsequently travelled widely. Represented Venezuela at Venice Biennale, 1968. Recipient of honorary doctorates from Moore College of Art, Philadelphia, 1969; Rhode Island School of Design, Providence, 1986; State University of New York, Buffalo, 1992. Member, American Academy of Arts and Letters, 1978. Lives in New York.

Selected Individual Exhibitions
Leo Castelli Gallery, New York: 1958
Stable Gallery, New York: 1962, 1964
Arts Club of Chicago: 1965
Sidney Janis Gallery, New York: 1966, 1967, 1973, 1975, 1981, 1984, 1989
Hanover Gallery, London: 1967
Museum Boymans-van Beuningen, Rotterdam: 1968
Moore College of Art, Philadelphia: 1970 (retrospective)
Worcester Art Museum, MA: 1971 (retrospective)
New York Cultural Center: 1973
Estudio Actual, Caracas: 1974
Contemporary Arts Museum, Houston: 1977
Boca Raton Museum of Art, FL: 1988
Galerie Tokoro, Tokyo: 1989
National Portrait Gallery, Smithsonian Institution, Washington, DC: 1991 (retrospective)

Bibliography

Lawrence Campbell, "Marisol's magic mixtures", *Art News*, lxiii, March 1964, pp.38–41, 64–5

Marisol, exh. cat., Arts Club of Chicago, 1965

Grace Glueck, "It's not Pop, it's not Op – it's Marisol", *New York Times Magazine*, 7 March 1965, pp.34–5, 45–9

Lucy R. Lippard, *Pop Art*, New York: Praeger, and London: Thames and Hudson, 1966

José Ramon Medina, *Marisol*, Caracas: Armitano, 1968

Marisol, exh. cat., Moore College of Art, Philadelphia, 1970

Marisol, exh. cat., Worcester Art Museum, MA, 1971

Marisol: Prints, 1961–1973, exh. cat., New York Cultural Center, 1973

Cindy Nemser, *Art Talk: Conversations with 12 Women Artists*, New York: Scribner, 1975

Jeff Goldberg, "Pop artist Marisol – 20 years after her first fame – recalls her life and loves", *People*, 24 March 1975, pp.40–43

Robert Creeley, *Presences: A Text for Marisol*, New York: Scribner, 1976

Roberta Bernstein, "Marisol as portraitist: Artists and artistes", *Arts Magazine*, lv, May 1981, pp.112–15

——, "Marisol's self-portraits: The dream and the dreamer", *Arts Magazine*, lix, March 1985, pp.86–9

Paul Gardner, "Who is Marisol?", *Art News*, lxxxviii, 1989, pp.146–51

Carol Anne Mahsun, ed., *Pop Art: The Critical Dialogue*, Ann Arbor: UMI Research Press, 1989

Marisol: Recent Sculpture, exh. cat., Galerie Tokoro, Tokyo, 1989

Charlotte Streifer Rubinstein, *American Women Sculptors*, Boston: Hall, 1990

Marisol: *Women and Dog*, 1964; wood, plaster, synthetic polymer, taxidermed dog head and miscellaneous items; installed dimensions: 183.5 × 185.4 × 78.6 cm.; Whitney Museum of American Art, New York; purchased with funds from the Friends of the Whitney Museum of American Art

Magical Mixtures: Marisol Portrait Sculpture, exh. cat., National Portrait Gallery, Smithsonian Institution, Washington, DC, 1991 (contains extensive bibliography)

Born of Venezuelan parents in Paris, the artist known since the 1950s as Marisol (meaning "sea and sun" in Spanish) decided to become an artist by the age of 16. During her childhood her family lived in Europe and then commuted between the USA and Caracas. In 1946 her family moved to Los Angeles, where her father supported her desire to study art with Howard Warshaw at the Jepson School. In 1949 Marisol returned to Paris to study at the Ecole des Beaux-Arts, but remained there only a year before returning to the USA, where she has subsequently resided apart from periods spent travelling or living abroad (e.g. in Rome from 1958 to 1960 and to Asia and elsewhere in 1968). In New York she studied at the Art Students League, the New School for Social Research, then worked with the noted abstract German expressionist Hans Hofmann at the school he founded.

From the outset, Marisol received some favourable attention from the art world. Her work was included in many group shows of the 1950s, and her first solo exhibition was held in New York in 1958 at the Castelli Gallery. She also contributed to the Venice Biennale in 1968 as well as many group shows at the Museum of Modern Art and the Whitney Museum of American Art in New York, the Los Angeles County Museum, innumerable private galleries, the Tate Gallery, London, and elsewhere. A full-scale retrospective was mounted in 1971 by the Worcester Art Museum and in the Moore College of Art, Philadelphia, the previous year, although earlier, smaller exhibitions of her work had also been shown at the Arts Club in Chicago in 1965. Currently her works can be found in many private as well as public collections, from the Museum of Modern Art in New York to the Hadone Open-Air Museum in Japan and the Wallraf-Richartz Museum in Cologne, Germany.

In the early 1950s, inspired by Pre-Columbian art as well as South American folk art, Marisol turned her attention from painting to sculpture. In 1961 she began to create life-size wooden constructions (to which plaster casts and real objects were sometimes affixed) with provocative titles such as *The Family*, *The Generals*, *The Wedding*, *The Party*, *Dinner Date*, *The Kennedys*, *The Royal Family*, *Women and Dog* (see illustration) and *The Dealers*. This artist's unique, mostly figurative sculpture uses diverse materials and techniques and blends highly illusionistic images with often two-dimensional surfaces such as wood (often pine or mahogany). Marisol also incorporates Plexiglas, plastic, steel, bronze and other materials alongside ready-made objects such as a car, a sofa or a rug. By her own admission, her unique interpretation of "realism" is also indebted to important American painters such as Jasper Johns and Robert Rauschenberg. In the early 1960s Marisol's unique imagery was associated with Pop Art, mostly because her subjects – like those of Andy Warhol and others – often derived from mass-media images of contemporary society, popular celebrities and everyday objects or activities such as sunbathing, bicycle riding, riding in a car and enjoying a party. Works such as *The Family* (1963; Milwaukee Art Museum) also wittily parody the middle-class concept of the family, its function and its individual members.

Marisol's singular style of sculpture also created a new direction for modern sculpture; like Warhol, she drew many of her sitters from the realms of entertainment and the mass media. Her portraits from the late 1960s include those of *Bob Hope*, *Mao Tse-tung*, *Harold Wilson*, *Generalissimo Francisco Franco*, *Hugh Hefner*, *John Wayne*, *Charles de Gaulle* and *Lyndon B. Johnson*. Members of the British royal family in her "figures of state" sculpture, for example, elicited some indignation from critics and viewers when it was exhibited at the Hanover Gallery in London in 1967. In such assemblages she forged a new modernist aesthetic for the heroic and political potential of sculpture. There is also a highly personal element in many works, since she frequently used herself as a model (her face, hands or body parts) for convenience as well as artistic reasons. For example, in *The Party*, a large work with 13 figures and two servants, all the figures derive from Marisol's own features.

In appearance, her inventive, highly original images evoke multiple associations with Gothic wooden saints, early American folk art and Surrealist imagery. In addition, her multi-figure assemblages combine autobiography with sometimes revealing commentary on gender roles and issues, notably in her group constructions of families and also her works of 1965–6 dealing almost exclusively with females and their features.

Following her travels to Asia, South America and Europe in 1968, Marisol returned to New York in 1970 and discovered a changing art scene no longer dominated by Pop Art. The artist shifted her focus from cultural icons to organic subjects such as fish, although she occasionally produced a portrait (such as a cover for *Time* magazine in 1972). In 1975 her new graphic art was on view at the Sidney Janis Gallery, with various wall pieces such as *I Have Been Here 24 Years*. At about this time she ceased using her face as part of her sculpture. Instead she produced a series of roughly carved portraits of "artists and artistes" (as she called them), older artists whom she personally respected. The resulting rather hieratic figures paid homage to *Picasso*, *Georgia O'Keeffe*, *Louise Nevelson* and *Marcel Duchamp*. Marisol also returned somewhat to the theme of the family, transformed, however, by a new use of rough carving, uncoloured wood and occasional religious allusions. In the early 1980s she explored other avenues of portraiture in images of *Mark Twain*, *Abraham Lincoln* and other important figures from American history and literature. Later in the decade she produced powerful portrait sculptures of *Bishop Desmond Tutu* and the *Emperor Hirohito with Empress Nagako*.

SUSAN P. CASTERAS

Maron-Mengs, Theresa Concordia
German painter, 1725–1808

Born Theresa Concordia Mengs at Aussig, Bohemia, 1725, to Ismaël Mengs and Charlotte Bormann. Trained by her father, alongside her brother Anton Raphael Mengs and her sister Juliane Charlotte. In Rome with her father and siblings, 1741–4; returned to Rome with her family, June 1746.

Married Anton von Maron, who was studying under Anton Raphael in Rome, 1765. Member, Accademia di San Luca, Rome, 1766. Died in Rome, 1808.

Bibliography

G.K. Nagler, *Neues Allgemeines Künstler Lexikon*, ix, 1840

John W. Bradley, *A Dictionary of Miniaturists, Illuminators, Calligraphers and Copyists*, ii, London: Quaritch, 1888; reprinted New York: Burt Franklin, 1958

Ulrich Thieme and Felix Becker, *Allgemeines Lexikon der bildenden Künstler von der Antike bis zur Gegenwart*, 37 vols, Leipzig: Seeman, 1907–50

Women Artists, 1550–1950, exh. cat., Los Angeles County Museum of Art, and elsewhere, 1976

Edith Krull, *Women in Art*, London: Studio Vista, 1986 (German original)

Harry Blättel, *International Dictionary of Miniature Painters, Porcelain Painters, Silhouettists*, Munich: Arts & Antiques, 1992

Sherry Piland, *Women Artists: An Historical, Contemporary and Feminist Bibliography*, 2nd edition, Metuchen, NJ: Scarecrow, 1994

Theresa Concordia was born into a highly artistic environment. Her father, Ismaël Mengs, a gifted portraitist, was court painter in Dresden and undertook the artistic education of his three children. Her brother Anton Raphael Mengs, with whom she studied, was one of the earliest exponents of Neo-classicism, and was to become one of the most celebrated artists of his time. Her sister Juliane Charlotte (d. 1789) was also an accomplished miniaturist and pastellist, who worked for the court at Dresden, but who later withdrew into religious life. Her niece Anna Maria Mengs, Anton Raphael's daughter, married the Spanish engraver Manuel Salvador Carmona and was a well-known portrait miniaturist and pastellist in Spain, becoming a member of the Academia di San Fernando, Madrid, in 1790.

We can be sure that Ismael, who insisted on a very rigorous routine for all his children, would have put a strong emphasis on the study of the great masters of the Renaissance; his enthusiasm for them is seen in the naming of his son Anton Raphael after two of the most famous 16th-century Italian painters, Raphael and Antonio Correggio. Theresa Concordia would have copied famous compositions by Renaissance artists regularly, not only as an artistic exercise, but also as an end in itself. Such copies were very much in mode and were particularly suited to the miniature medium. Clients liked to commission small-scale, highly finished copies of their favourite works, which in many cases, unlike a copy made to the original size, could be easily fitted into domestic interiors. All members of the family made copies after famous compositions (Anton Raphael's copy after a Raphael *Holy Family*, for example, is in the Gemäldegalerie, Dresden), and Theresa Concordia painted copies after Correggio's *Giorno* and *Notte*, in watercolour laid down on copper (each 24.7 × 18.4 cm.; Pinacoteca Nazionale, Parma; Gemäldegalerie, Dresden, respectively). Two pastel portraits by Theresa Concordia, her *Self-Portrait* and a *Portrait of the Artist's Sister, Julia Mengs* (both c.1750; Gemäldegalerie, repr. Los Angeles 1976, figs 18 and 19), show the careful, highly finished technique of Anton Raphael. Little is known about her patrons, although she must have worked for August III, because he paid her a sum of 300 thaler before she left for Rome in 1746; given the family's connection with the court at

Dresden, it is likely that many commissions for her miniatures and portraits arose directly from the court or from those associated with it.

EMILY BLACK

Martin, Agnes
Canadian painter, 1912–

Born in Maklin, Saskatchewan, 22 March 1912; grew up in Vancouver. Emigrated to USA, 1931; naturalised 1950. Studied at Western Washington College of Education, Bellingham, 1934–7 (teaching certificate); Teachers College, Columbia University, New York, 1941–2 (BS), 1951–2 (MA); University of New Mexico, Albuquerque, 1946–8. Painting instructor, University of New Mexico, 1947–8; Eastern Oregon College, La Grande, 1952–3. Lived in Taos, New Mexico, 1954–7; returned to New York, 1957; settled in New Mexico, 1967. Abandoned painting for seven years, 1967–74. Recipient of Alexej von Jawlensky prize, Wiesbaden, Germany, 1991; Oskar Kokoschka prize from Austrian government, 1992. Presented work to Taos Museum, 1993. Member, American Academy and Institute of Arts and Letters, New York, 1989. Lives in New Mexico.

Selected Individual Exhibitions

Betty Parsons Gallery, New York: 1958, 1959, 1961
Robert Elkon Gallery, New York: 1962, 1963, 1965, 1966, 1970, 1972, 1974, 1976, 1978
Institute of Contemporary Art, University of Pennsylvania, Philadelphia: 1973 (touring retrospective)
Galerie Yvon Lambert, Paris: 1973, 1987
Kunstraum, Munich: 1973–4 (touring)
Museum of Fine Arts, Santa Fe: 1974, 1979, 1994
Pace Gallery, New York: 1975, 1976, 1977, 1978, 1979, 1980, 1981, 1982, 1984, 1985, 1986, 1989, 1990, 1991, 1995 (Pace Wildenstein)
Hayward Gallery, London: 1977 (touring retrospective, organised by Arts Council of Great Britain)
Wichita State University, Wichita, KS: 1980–81 (touring, organised by Pace Gallery, New York)
Waddington Galleries, London: 1986, 1990
Annemarie Verna Galerie, Zürich: 1986
Akira Ikada Gallery, Tokyo: 1989
Stedelijk Museum, Amsterdam: 1991–2 (touring retrospective)
Whitney Museum of American Art, New York: 1992–4 (touring retrospective)
Serpentine Gallery, London: 1993

Selected Writings

"On the perfection underlying life", lecture given at Institute of Contemporary Art, Philadelphia, 14 February 1972; published in Munich 1973
"Untroubled mind", ed. Ann Wilson, *Studio International*, clxxxvi, 1973, pp.63–4
We Are in the Midst of Reality Responding with Joy, Santa Fe: Museum of New Mexico, 1979 (lecture)
"Beauty is the mystery of life", *El Palacio*, xcv/1, Fall–Winter 1989 (lecture given in April 1989 at the Museum of Fine Arts, Santa Fe)
Hiljaisuus Taloni Lattialla [The silence on the floor of my house], Helsinki: Vapaa Taidekoulu, 1990 (in Finnish and English)

Writings/Schriften, ed. Dieter Schwarz, Winterthur: Kunstmuseum, 1991

La Perfection inhérente à la vie, ed. Dieter Schwarz, Paris: Ecole Nationale Supérieure des Beaux-Arts, 1993

Bibliography

Dore Ashton, "Agnes Martin", *Quadrum 20*, 1966, pp.148–9

Ann Wilson, "Linear webs", *Art and Artists*, i, October 1966, pp.46–9

Lucy R. Lippard, "The silent art", *Art in America*, lv, January–February 1967, p.61

—, "Diversity in unity: Recent geometricizing styles in America", *Art since Mid-Century*, i, ed. Jean Leymarie, Greenwich, CT: New York Graphic Society, 1971, pp.231–3

Agnes Martin, exh. cat., Institute of Contemporary Art, University of Pennsylvania, Philadelphia, 1973

Agnes Martin, exh. cat., Kunstraum, Munich, and elsewhere, 1973

Lawrence Alloway, "Formlessness breaking down form: The paintings of Agnes Martin", *Studio International*, clxxxv, 1973, pp.61–3

—, "Agnes Martin", *Artforum*, xi, April 1973, pp.32–7

Lizzie Borden, "Early work", *Artforum*, xi, April 1973, pp.39–44

Carter Ratcliff, "Agnes Martin and the 'artificial infinite'", *Art News*, lxxii, May 1973, pp.26–7

Susan Moss Galloway, "Agnes Martin: Master artist", *Womanspace Journal*, Summer 1973

Douglas Crimp, "Agnes Martin: Numero, misura, apporto", *Data*, iii, Winter 1973, p.83

John Gruen, "Agnes Martin: 'Everything, everything is about feeling ... feeling and recognition'", *Art News*, lxxv, September 1976, pp.91–4

Agnes Martin: Paintings and Drawings, 1957–1975, exh. cat., Arts Council of Great Britain, London, 1977

William Peterson, "Agnes Martin: The islands", *Artspace*, Summer 1979, pp.36–41

Kate Horsfield, "On art and artists: Agnes Martin", *Profile*, i, March 1981, pp.1–24

Dore Ashton, *American Art since 1945*, New York: Oxford University Press, 1982

Thomas McEvilley, "'Grey Geese Descending': The art of Agnes Martin", *Artforum*, xxv, Summer 1987, pp.94–9

Mark Stevens, "Thin gray line", *Vanity Fair*, March 1989, pp.50–56

Agnes Martin: Paintings and Drawings/Schilderijen en Tekeningen/Gemälde und Zeichnungen/Peintures et Dessins, 1974–1990, exh. cat., Stedelijk Museum, Amsterdam, and elsewhere, 1991

Eva Schmidt, "Agnes Martin", *Kunstforum International*, no.114, 1991, pp.316–25

Marja Bloem, "Agnes Martin: The late works", *Forum International*, no.7, March–April 1991

Agnes Martin, exh. cat., Whitney Museum of American Art, New York, and elsewhere, 1992

Holland Cotter, "Agnes Martin: All the way to heaven", *Art in America*, lxxxi, April 1993, pp.88–97, 149

Mara R. Witzling, ed., *Voicing Today's Visions: Writings by Contemporary Women Artists*, New York: Universe, 1994

Joan Simon, "Perfection is in the mind: An interview with Agnes Martin", *Art in America*, lxxxiv, May 1996, pp.82–9, 124

During the late 1950s, at a time when painting was very much involved with the gestural and representational, Agnes Martin developed an intuitive type of painting that can be characterised as "mental". The intentions behind Martin's work, which draws on resources within herself and not on outside impressions, is to develop an "awareness of a perfection, that which is forever known in the mind". She would like her work to be recognised as being in the "classic" tradition (Coptic, Egyptian, Greek, Chinese), it being not based on the observation of nature but on the representation of the Ideal in the mind ("On the perfection underlying life", 1972). Her thinking is influenced by the Chinese philosophers Chuang-tzu and Lao-tzu, who exalt an ego-less abstraction, preach detachment, humility and the need to listen to one's own mind, and the Buddhist doctrine of the wheel of life.

Martin belongs to the generation of the Abstract Expressionists to whom she feels kinship because of their shared spiritual values. They also have in common the holistic character of the composition and the idea of originality. But because she was a woman she was not taken as seriously as her male contemporaries. And although she was highly respected, she had to wait until late in life for recognition in terms of major museum exhibitions. Because of her later work, with its geometrical, repetitive structures, Martin is also compared to Minimalist artists. Although she reduces her means to attain the essence of painting, however, there is no relation to Minimalist art because her paintings are more emotional and expressionistic and are not machine-made.

Martin began to paint seriously when she was 25. Most of the early work grew from realistic, Rouault-inspired portraits and landscapes, into a kind of surrealistic painting with biomorphic or flat geometrical forms and, later, to a more abstract style. She destroyed all these works because for her they only represented stages along the way to discovering her own form and content. *Landscape-Taos* (1947; watercolour on paper; 29.9×38.6 cm.; Jonson Gallery, University of New Mexico, Albuquerque) shows a strong linearity, simple forms and strong contrast between shadow and light. *Untitled* (1955; oil on canvas; 83.8×134.6 cm.; whereabouts unknown), a surrealistic painting with linear, vaguely descriptive forms floating in a weightless, frontally conceived space, still seems to contain a horizon line. The work reminds one of Ashile Gorky. *Drift of Summer* (1957; oil on canvas; $c.160 \times 100$ cm.; private collection) is a more abstract painting in matching tones of sienna and ochre.

In her search for simplicity and the non-representational Martin became involved in systems, repetition and the suppressing of hierarchical order. Around 1960 she arrived at her characteristic form: the grid. The grid is flat, anti-nature and anti-reality, a result of aesthetic considerations, not of observation. In *Untitled* (1962; gesso, graphite and brass nails on canvas; 30.4×30.4 cm.; San Diego Museum of Contemporary Art, La Jolla) the horizontal and vertical lines of the grid continue to the edge of the canvas, but the point of focus is formed by the regularity of the nails. The work is very literal and does not allude to something outside itself. The eye and mind grasp at the same time the ground and the image. The image occupies the entire surface, is totally frontal and is void of a hierarchic order.

After living for about 10 years in New York – where she had moved at the request of Betty Parsons who showed her work regularly with that of other Abstract Expressionist artists, Martin left the city in 1967 and stopped painting until 1974. During this period she re-thought her work and spent time travelling and living in primitive conditions in the American Southwest. This self-imposed exile contributed to her becoming a kind of legendary figure. When she started painting again in 1974 – the only work she had produced in the interim was

Agnes Martin: *Untitled*, 1955; oil on canvas; 83.82 × 134.62 cm.

a series of prints in 1971 – she continued where she had left off in 1967. The format that she chose when she started painting again is similar to a work of 1967, *Grass* (acrylic, pencil, canvas; 180 × 180 cm.; Stedelijk Museum, Amsterdam), a grid on square canvas. From 1974 onwards the format is always square, on a human scale of 1.8 × 1.8 metres (although when she was in her eighties the format became smaller, 1.5 × 1.5 m.). Her works are no longer painted in oil paint, but in gesso, acrylics, Indian ink and pencil. Her grids are never absolutely square, they are rectangles, as she says: "in order to lighten the weight of the square, to destroy its power" ("Homage to the square", *Art in America*, July–August 1967, p.55).

Martin's work, although there is a preconceived plan for every painting which is jotted down with numbers, is not at all mechanical, for any irregularity in the canvas, a trembling of her hand, the pressure of pencil, brush or knife and ruler are all visible; measure and order, scale and colour, proportions and rhythms, the atmospheric oscillating between ground and lines, are important for the impact of the image, but at the same time they also express something about process, time and concentration. In order to see the work, to see the illusions of changing textures, the viewer has to come close and then increase the distance.

Martin accepts the canvas as the bounds of the image; there is indeed neither a beginning nor an end – what matters is the tension between the square canvas and the lines traced on it.

The pencil lines determine where the colour is found and indicate divisions, but it is not clear if they confine the colour or merely provide an indication for the paint strokes. The lines sometimes continue right up to the edge of the canvas and sometimes end several centimetres short of the edge, thereby creating a floating effect. Through the length of the lines aspects of time and space figure in the content of the work.

The works from the 1970s on have mostly horizontal divisions – vertical lines no longer appear – and the colours are soft, with a frequent use of grey and white. The paint is invariably applied in one direction. *Untitled No.9* (1990; acrylic and graphite on canvas; Whitney Museum of American Art, New York) is built up from three different tones of grey in horizontal bands of different height. An exceptional group of works of this late period, the *Black Paintings* (Pace Gallery, New York), are canvases thickly painted in dark grey acrylic, which seem weightless.

Even though in certain periods works have been given titles that refer to nature, the paintings are not abstractions from nature. The titles, which come later through looking at the work, are not descriptions or allusions. The paintings are reflections of Martin's desire for, and of her actual experience of, the potential peace, rhythm and beauty of the universe. It is this universal quality that makes her paintings feel familiar, thereby evoking a sense of nature.

In her texts and lectures, which parallel her paintings, Martin makes her position as an artist clear by going her own way and sticking to her own concerns. She is not involved in feminist issues; her artistic language is modernistic if one assumes that geometry is a typical male vocabulary; and she feels that it is important to give the young artist advice about the morality of painting. Martin is as unambiguous about the theme of her work as she is about its form:

> Art without a theme is meaningless ... I think I will say my oldest paintings are about joy. And the middle ones I did in 1974 and 1975 were about happiness and innocence ... But now [c.1990] I know what I am going to paint about and I discovered it when I was making a print. I am going to be painting a lot about praise ["Art as art", *Art International*, December 1992, p.37].

Her whole oeuvre in fact is, as she says, "a celebration of life".

MARJA BLOEM

Martin, Mary

British artist, 1907–1969

Born Mary Balmford in Folkestone, Kent, 16 January 1907. Studied at Goldsmiths' School of Art, London, 1925–9; Royal College of Art, London, 1929–32. Married sculptor Kenneth Martin, 1930; two sons, born 1944 and 1946. Exhibited with Artists International Association from 1934; with London Group from 1949. Joint first prizewinner, with Richard Hamilton, John Moore's exhibition, Liverpool, 1969. Died in London, 9 October 1969.

Selected Individual Exhibitions

Heffer Gallery, Cambridge: 1954 (with Kenneth Martin)
Institute of Contemporary Arts, London: 1960 (with Kenneth Martin)
Molton and Lords, London: 1964
Axiom Gallery, London: 1968
Museum of Modern Art, Oxford: 1970 (touring retrospective, with Kenneth Martin; organised by Arts Council of Great Britain)

Selected Writings

"Reflections", *Data: Directions in Art, Theory and Aesthetics*, ed. Anthony Hill, London: Faber, 1968; Greenwich, CT: New York Graphic Society, 1969, pp.95–6
"Constructivism and architecture: Art is anti-convention", *Towards Another Picture: An Anthology of Writings by Artists Working in Britain, 1945–1977*, ed. Andrew Brighton and Lynda Morris, Nottingham: Midland Group, 1977, pp.57, 231–2

Bibliography

Lawrence Alloway, *Nine Abstract Artists: Their Work and Theory*, London: Tiranti, 1954
Alan Bowness, "The constructive art of Mary Martin", *Studio International*, clxxv, 1968, pp.120–25
Mary Martin, Kenneth Martin, exh. cat., Museum of Modern Art, Oxford, and elsewhere, 1970
Alastair Grieve, "Constructivism after the Second World War", *British Sculpture in the Twentieth Century*, exh. cat., Whitechapel Art Gallery, London, 1981, pp.155–64
Mary Martin, exh. cat., Tate Gallery, 1984 (contains list of writings and extensive bibliography)
Kenneth and Mary Martin, exh. cat., Annely Juda Fine Art, London, 1987

During the 1950s and 1960s Mary Martin was a leading figure within the group of British Constructivist artists whose principal members included Victor Pasmore, Anthony Hill and her husband Kenneth Martin. They were concerned with the production of a non-figurative, constructed art characterised by geometric forms and a concern with sequence, rhythm and repetition, light and physical space. Martin shared their notion of an art analogous to nature that was constructed from the same systems found in nature. A notable source for this idea was the American artist Charles Biederman, who suggested in his book *Art as the Evolution of Visual Knowledge* (1948) that the role of the artist was "to penetrate into the natural laws that govern the world from which his art inevitably originates". The origins of Martin's work can be found in Bauhaus, De Stijl, Russian Suprematism and Constructivism. It is often architectural in feeling and, indeed, Martin regarded her working process as "nuclear building". Describing this method she wrote: "one commences with a single cell, or unit, a logical process of growth is applied and, as with kinetic and optical art, which are branches of construction, the whole, or the effect, is unforeseen until the work is complete" ("Statement", December 1967, in Bowness 1968, p.121).

Although she did not work as a full-time artist until her early forties, she exhibited at the Artists International Association from 1934 using her maiden name, Mary Balmford. The main subjects of her pre-war works are landscapes and still lifes. One of her last figurative paintings is *Houses and Trees* (1949; oil on canvas; artist's estate), which can be seen as a transitional work between the earlier figurative works and her first abstract painting. It depicts Hampstead, London, viewed from Primrose Hill, and is unique among Martin's work in the extent to which the image is abstracted from nature. The composition is based on harmonious proportions using the golden section. The image is predominantly grey, black and white with roofs and windows rendered in triangular and rectangular patterns.

In 1950 Martin rejected figuration and painted her first abstract work. By the following year she had abandoned painting and had begun to make metal, wood and Perspex reliefs. She wrote:

> The logic by which I became an abstract painter in 1950 was set in motion among many other things (e.g. traditional uses of laws of proportion and pictorial composition) by a study of the Cubists' use of the 'moving format'. I saw that it could be used as an inventing element in its own right as a geometric shape; non-mimetically [quoted in London 1984, p.12].

Martin's early abstract reliefs were often white. This rejection of colour was linked to her interest in Cubism and to what she perceived as the dominance of sculpture in contemporary art. At this point she felt that colour should be restricted or eliminated in order to free the work from association. In *Columbarium* (1951; plaster original version; artist's estate) Martin established the formal language that was to characterise her subsequent work. The relief is composed of incised squares and rectangles arranged in harmonious proportions. Some of the squares are cut on the hypotenuse to form slopes that catch the light. The cube sliced diagonally in two was to be one of Martin's favourite units, with the square, rectangle,

Mary Martin: *Spiral*, 1963; Tate Gallery, London

cube and occasionally the circle. She explained how another early relief, *Spiral Movement* (1951; oil relief on board; Tate Gallery, London), was created: "I took a simple element (in this case a parallelepiped) and subjected it to a system of changes, not knowing what would happen to it, and without any knowledge of the final appearance of the work. I think all my work has been based on this kind of curiosity" (letter to the Tate Gallery, 21 May 1963). Starting with a drawing, often suggested by a mathematical idea, the reliefs and all their parts were hand-made by the artist, although in the mid-1960s she did have an assistant to help with the finishing of works.

The period 1956–66 was one of close collaboration with architects. Martin was interested in the relation between art and architecture and the possible social function of art, and in 1957 wrote: "The abstract relief, or three-dimensional work, is concerned with architectonic values, therefore it appears to come very close to architecture" ("Artist and architect", 1957, in London 1984, p.26). She believed that the artist could be part of contemporary society by working with architects and by using new materials such as Perspex. Her first architectural project, in collaboration with Kenneth Martin and the architect John Weeks, was to construct one of the pavilions for the exhibition, *This Is Tomorrow*, held at the Whitechapel Art Gallery, London, in 1956. For this she made a number of reliefs that were integral to the environment they created. *Black Relief* (plastic and painted wood on painted wood; Tate Gallery) is unique in Martin's oeuvre in that she made a number of significant changes to it between 1957 and c.1966–9. The work was one of a set of four constructed reliefs made between 1957 and 1959 that exemplify her distinctive combination of following a logical system and allowing for a degree of intuition, for instance in the use of colour. These were followed by a series of pierced reliefs based on minimal drawings, such as *Pierced Relief* (c.1959; wood, Perspex and Formica; Drs J.M. and M. Morris), in which an off-centre circle is cut out of a rectangle shape. In 1962 Martin started to

use half-cubes, cut diagonally and faced with stainless steel to build up a structure of "superpatterns". She continued to be concerned with the internal logic of the constructions based on permutations of number, and by introducing the reflected surface she was able to intensify the reflection of light. David Sylvester described one such relief, *Spiral* (1963; see illustration), as: "a preponderance of reflecting surfaces jut out towards us, the feeling is aggressive, menacing" (David Sylvester, "Introduction", *Mary Martin*, exh. cat., Molton and Lords, London, 1964).

Between 1966 and 1969 Martin returned to using the open plane and began to focus on colour, volume and space. She increasingly employed brightly coloured plastics, red, orange and blue, as in *Dispersal on Blue* (1967; stainless steel and painted wood on Perspex and wood; repr. London 1987, p.43). In contrast, one of her last works, *Three Group* (1969; painted wood; artist's estate), is a free-standing work – she had made her first free-standing construction in 1956 – made of rough wood that emphasises the sculpture's tactile quality. Martin wrote: "Works of art are not memories, temporal like a performance. They are physical, material presences meant to be handled, gazed upon and lived with. To possess them, both privately and publicly, is a primitive human urge; food for the mind and the spirit" ("Statement", October 1968, in *ibid.*, p.57).

ROSEMARY HARRIS

Martin, Mrs *see* Blunden

Martins, Maria

Brazilian sculptor, 1900–1973

Born Maria de Lourdes Alves in Campanha, Minas Gerais, Brazil, 7 August 1900. Educated at Colégio Sion, a private French school in Petrópolis, Rio de Janeiro. Studied art at Académie des Beaux-Arts, Rio de Janeiro, and Académie des Beaux-Arts, Paris; studied sculpture under Catherine Barjanski in Paris, Oscar Jespers in Brussels and Jacques Lipchitz in New York; printmaking under Stanley William Hayter, Atelier 17, New York. Married diplomat Carlos Martins Pereira e Sousa, 1926 (second marriage); three daughters. Exhibited with the Surrealists at Galerie Maeght, Paris, 1947. Founder-member, Museu de Arte Moderna, Rio de Janeiro, 1952. Newspaper columnist for *Correio de Manhã*, Rio de Janeiro, and author. Recipient of second prize, 1953, and first prize, 1955, São Paulo Bienal. Died in Rio de Janeiro, 26 March 1973.

Selected Individual Exhibitions

Corcoran Gallery of Art, Washington, DC: 1941
Valentine Gallery, New York: 1942, 1943, 1944, 1946
Julien Levy Gallery, New York: 1947
Galerie René Drouin, Paris: 1949
Museu de Arte Moderna, São Paulo: 1950
Museu de Arte Moderna, Rio de Janeiro: 1956

Selected Writings

Asia Maior: O Planêta China, Rio de Janeiro: Civilização Brasileira, 1958 (preface by Oswaldo Aranha)

Deuses Malditos: I. Nietzsche, Rio de Janeiro: Civilização Brasileira, 1965

Bibliography

C. Powell Minnigerode, "Sculptures by Maria Martins", *Pan American Union Bulletin*, lxxv, 1941, pp.682–5

Amazonia, exh. cat., Valentine Gallery, New York, 1943

A.C. Callado, "Brazilian sculpture: A very vague outline", *The Studio*, cxxvi, 1943, pp.132–4

Vogue, April 1943

Religious Art Today, no.70, Dayton Art Institute, OH, 1944

Vogue, July 1944

"Madame Martins is a gifted sculptress", *Brazil*, xix/11, 1945, pp.8–9

Maria 1946, exh. cat., Valentine Gallery, New York, 1946 (limited edition)

Maria: Recent Sculptures, exh. cat., Julien Levy Gallery, New York, 1947 (essay by André Breton reprinted in *Surrealism and Painting*, London: Macdonald, 1972, pp.318–21)

Le Surréalisme en 1947: Exposition International du Surréalisme, exh. cat., Galerie Maeght, Paris, 1947

Les Statues magiques de Maria, exh. cat., Galerie René Drouin, Paris, 1949 (contains texts by André Breton and Michel Tapié, and anonymous writings by Maria Martins)

Maria, exh. cat., Museu de Arte Moderna, Rio de Janeiro, 1956

Surrealist Intrusion in the Enchanter's Domain, exh. cat., D'Arcy Galleries, New York, 1960

Clarice Lispector, "Maria Martins: A juventude sempre tem razão", *Manchete*, 21 December 1968, pp.174–5

Sarane Alexandrian, *Surrealist Art*, New York and Washington, DC: Praeger, 1970 (French original, 1970)

Arturo Schwarz, *The Complete Works of Marcel Duchamp*, revised edition, New York: Abrams, 1970

Sarane Alexandrian, "Sculpture surréaliste: Première explication suivie d'un repertoire", *Connaissance des Arts*, no.245, July 1972, pp.53–9

Dicionário Brasileiro de Artistas Plásticos, iii, Brasilia: Instituto Nacional do Livro, 1973–7

Alfred H. Barr, Jr, ed., *Painting and Sculpture in the Museum of Modern Art, 1929–1967*, New York: Museum of Modern Art, 1977

René Passeron, *Phaidon Encyclopedia of Surrealism*, New York: Phaidon, 1978 (French original, 1975)

Adam Biro and René Passeron, eds, *Dictionnaire générale du surréalisme et de ses environs*, Paris: Presses Universitaires de France, 1982

Anne d'Harnoncourt and Walter Hopps, *Etant donnés: 1) la chute d'eau: 2) le gaz d'éclairage: Reflections on a New Work by Marcel Duchamp*, Philadelphia: Philadelphia Museum of Art, 1987

Imaginários Singulares, exh. cat., Bienal de São Paolo, 1987

Roberto Pontual, "Entre dois sécolos", *Arte Brasileira do sécolo XX na Coleção Gilberto Chateaubriand*, Rio de Janeiro: JB, 1987

Francis Naumann, "The bachelor's quest", *Art in America*, lxxxi, September 1993, pp.73–81, 67, 69,

Sculptor, writer, diplomat's wife, muse, Maria Martins – or Maria, the name she used as a sculptor – lived a worldly life, largely outside Brazil. Her bronze sculptures, extravagantly crafted in the lost wax method, evoke poetically, through mythic transformation, the inner recesses of the legends of the Amazon and nature's erotic pulse, transmuting the sinuous, writhing forms of vegetal undergrowth and the denizens of the river into primordial beings that embody a pre-conscious world. She played up her Brazilian origins exuberantly in a nostalgic, illusory creation of Surrealist fantasy – earthy, whimsical, erotic: "I have the blood of the equatorial star coursing in my veins ..." (New York 1946). Working formally with the Surrealist tenets of metamorphosis, fantasy, the unconscious and the literary, she created intimate bronze figures of "sensual and barbarous" goddesses and monsters derived from legends of Amazonia, which attracted the attention of André Breton in 1943. Possessed by the palpable sexuality and tropical allure of her works – "at the very roots of the *sacred*" – Breton wrote about Martins in *Surrealism and Painting*, in one of the few essays devoted to a woman artist. In the sophisticated use of folklore and exploitation of rhythms of Afro-Brazilian cults through Surrealist techniques, her works may be compared to the "chôros" of Heiter Villa-Lobos or the poetry of Ismael Nery and Raul Bopp. Although not directly part of the Brazilian anthropophagy (cannibalism) movement of the 1920s, her work nevertheless embraces notions of contradiction and *digesão universal*, "digesting" Western ideas to create a modern Brazilian art; in her case, a movement of one (*Macumba*, 1943–4; bronze; ht 79 cm.; San Francisco Museum of Modern Art).

Born in the richly wooded state of Minas Gerais, Martins was educated in French and trained as a pianist before taking up wood sculpture in Ecuador. After the failure of an early marriage, she went to Paris, where her father, a lawyer, lived in political exile. There she met the Brazilian diplomat Carlos Martins Pereira e Sousa, whom she married in 1926. The couple lived in Ecuador, Denmark, Japan, Belgium, the USA (1939–48) and France, before returning to Brazil. In Brussels, Martins studied with the Belgian Expressionist Oscar Jespers, whose influence is evident in her large, simplified figures passionately hewn from Brazilian woods (e.g. *Christ*, 1941; jacaranda; ht 23 cm.; Museum of Modern Art, New York; *St Francis*, 1941; jacaranda; ht 185 cm.; Metropolitan Museum of Art, New York). Exploring the expressive potential of the female body, working in wood, bronze and terracotta (learned in Japan), she made smaller female figures in a rhythmic naturalistic style, dancing the samba, the Brazilian native dance, and also several figures of *Salome*, the biblical temptress, foreshadowing the devouring passions of her Amazon goddesses.

In the 1940s, commuting between Washington, DC, and New York, where she met exiled European artists including Marcel Duchamp, Yves Tanguy, Max Ernst, André Masson and Piet Mondrian, Martins developed her new Surrealist style. Adopting a Surrealist idiom steeped in poetry, metamorphosis, the erotic and the unconscious, she began retelling the Amazon legends in text and bronze, retaining the myths' quicksilver transformations between mind and material. She showed the bronzes in 1943, at the Valentine Gallery, New York.

The diminutive but voluptuous figures of her *Amazonia* series, with a dripping canopy of leafy vines and creepers, evoke a dreamlike, transgressive state of fanciful eroticism. *Iacy*, the Amazon Indian virgin who avenged her defilement by male "perfidy", is shown ecstatic, standing on a tumescent mound (c.1940; bronze; ht 76 cm.; Museum of Fine Arts, Houston). *Yara*, "siren of the Amazon", rises from the river, luring men with the "kiss of death" (repr. New York 1943; version, c.1940; Philadelphia Museum of Art). Others in the series are more phallic in form. Cobra Norato, the

Martins: *The Road; The Shadow; Too Long, Too Narrow,* 1946; bronze, 143.4 × 179.7 × 59.4 cm.; Museum of Modern Art, New York, Brazil Fund

embodiment of the Amazon, who must have an annual female sacrifice, a "morena wild with love and fright", so that the forest may live another year, is represented as a thick snake, with skin textured by a network of distended veins, coiling upward towards a female figure in the title work, *Amazonia* (1942; *ibid.*). In *Cobra Grande* (1942; *ibid.*), the snake goddess of all the deities, Breton saw a metaphor of undulating desire; Martins made an ominously swelling serpentine form suspended between underwater reeds.

Martins's more abstract works, combining snake, vine and human forms in compositions that slither between polished and roughly finished bronze, have the Freudian impact of the sinister – terrifying and attractive – and show increasing insight into the human condition. Her primordial beings ("sêres"), which so moved Benjamin Péret, rise from the formless alluvial mud, writhing in anaconda-like movements towards consciousness, humanoid hands extending from serpentine coils (*Sem Eco*, 1943; Jean Boghici collection, Rio di Janeiro), or stir more amorphously, symbolic of a waking, inchoate state (*Sem Titulo*, n.d.; Torquato Saboia Pessoa collection, São

Paulo). Rocked by Eros, figures starkly reveal unconscious desires in two major works. A blind female is "shadowed" by a male from whom writhing snakes protrude in looping twists (*The Road; The Shadow; Too Long, Too Narrow*, 1946; bronze; edition of two, see illustration; Palácio do Itamaraty, Brasilia). In *The Impossible III* (1946; bronze; ht 79 cm.; edition of two, Museum of Modern Art, New York; Museu de Arte Moderna, Rio de Janeiro) two anthropomorphic figures bristle dangerously with magnetic attraction.

Martins's ambivalent love affair with the serpent is also expressed in other sculptures. Snakes in a matt green patina coil around an elongated female body in a shiny gold finish (*However*, 1944; several versions: with leaf head, Nora Martins Lobo collection, São Paulo); in another, snakes flicker from the eyes of a seated girl (*Eighth Veil*, 1949; Ana Maria Martins Jones collection, Rio de Janeiro). In a later public sculpture, she grafted the language of international Constructivism on to her earlier metamorphic animal-vegetal forms; in the monumental *Ritual de Ritmo* (Gardens, Palacio da Alvorado, Brasilia) of the early 1960s, spiky open forms thrust upwards like a synthetic plant rooted on a hump-backed, quadrupedal form.

In a doubly clandestine relationship with Marcel Duchamp, Martins modelled for the sprawling female nude of his voyeuristic last work, created in secrecy (*Etant donnés: 1) la chute d'eau: 2) le gaz d'éclairage*, 1946–66; Philadelphia Museum of Art), and inspired his sexual passion. An effusion of his affection is included in the de-luxe edition of *Box in a Valise* that Duchamp dedicated to her; the cloudy forms of the customised "original" are made of seminal fluid. Traces of their creative contact may also be glimpsed in Martins's work of the mid-1940s.

Conscientiously aware of her position, Martins made a radio speech pleading for world peace through art and noting that art is not a Western prerogative; this was read into the US Congressional Record in 1947 (A3129; by Senator Jacob Javits). In Brazil she helped to organise the first São Paulo Bienal, of 1951, and was a founding member of the Museu de Arte Moderna in Rio de Janeiro in 1952, donating her own Mondrian.

Martins also maintained a public presence through writing. She was a newspaper columnist in Rio, wrote about the French poets Arthur Rimbaud and Paul Verlaine and published books on Nietzsche and on her travels. In the chapter on women in *Asia Maior* (1958) she wrote that the major creation of the Chinese revolution, evolving from the subservient "brick" underfoot to active participant, is the "Eve of new China who wears the identical blue uniform as the men … a free being, body and soul". Yet the peripatetic Martins concluded her book with the enigmatic query: "Valera a pena?" (at what price?).

JANE NECOL

Marval, Jacqueline
French painter, 1866–1932

Born Marie-Josephine Vallet in Quaix, near Grenoble, 19 October 1866. Qualified as a school teacher and began to paint under the name Marie Jacques, 1884. Married Albert Valentin, a travelling salesman, 1886; separated after death of baby son, 1891. Moved to Paris, 1895; lived in Montparnasse with the painter Jules Flandrin, and attended classes in Gustave Moreau's studio. Adopted the name Jacqueline Marval, 1900. Separated from Flandrin, 1919. Died of cancer at Hôpital Bichat, Bichat, 28 May 1932.

Principal Exhibitions

Individual
Galerie Berthe Weill, Paris: 1902, 1908 (with Marie Laurencin)
Galerie Druet, Paris: 1908, 1912, 1924 (with Gimmi)
Musée de Rouen, Paris: 1929 (with Kees van Dongen)
Salon d'Automne, Paris: 1932 (retrospective)

Group
Salon des Indépendants, Paris: from 1901
Salon d'Automne, Paris: from 1902
Société Nationale des Beaux-Arts, Paris: 1904
St Petersburg: 1912 (*La Centenale de l'art français*)
Salon de Mai, Marseille: 1912

International Exhibition of Modern Art, "Armory Show", New York: 1913
Salon de la Triennale, Paris: 1916
Galerie Bernheim-Jeune, Paris: 1916
Salon des Tuileries, Paris: 1923–31

Bibliography
Andry-Farcy, *Jacqueline Marval*, Paris: Morancé, 1929
Jean Hesse, *Jacqueline Marval: Extrait du Bulletin de l'Académie Delphinale, 1944–1946*, Grenoble: Allier, 1948
Guillaume Apollinaire, *Chroniques d'art, 1902–1918*, ed. L.C: Breunig, Paris: Gallimard, 1960
François Roussier, *Jacqueline Marval, 1866–1932*, Grenoble: Didier Richard, 1987
Jacqueline Marval (1866–1932), exh. cat., Crane Gallery, London, 1989
Gill Perry, *Women Artists and the Parisian Avant-Garde*, Manchester: Manchester University Press, and New York: St Martin's Press, 1995

In recent art history, Marval's work has either been ignored or seen as a variation on the soft-toned canvases of Marie Laurencin (q.v.), peopled with supposedly "feminine" women. But this impression is at least partly conditioned by limited knowledge of the range of Marval's work and interests, because many of her works are now in private collections. By 1903 her art had already been supported by the dealers Ambroise Vollard and Berthe Weill, and she was beginning to establish a reputation as a "modern" artist influenced by Impressionism and the Nabis. She was showing regularly at the Salon des Indépendants and the Salon d'Automne, where her painting on the theme of an oriental harem, *Les Odalisques* (1903; see illustration), attracted critical attention. In 1912 the writer Guillaume Apollinaire described *Les Odalisques* as "an important work for modern painting", and the following year it was included among the French exhibits at the New York Armory Show. Marval was closely associated with the so-called Fauve group whose controversial works were featured in the Salon des Indépendants and the Salon d'Automne of 1904–7, and there are many canvases from this period in which she employs bold brushwork and rich colour. However, these canvases, like those of several other women artists engaged with Fauve techniques (see entry on Emilie Charmy), were hung separately from those of Matisse and his colleagues, and therefore did not usually qualify for the group label "les fauves". A later critic, Henry Nesme, wrote of her "fauvisme marvalian", a term used to describe what he saw as the distinctive tonal qualities and the "voluptuous impasto" of her work (Nesme in Roussier 1987, p.9). According to Nesme, then, hers was a separate and qualified form of Fauvism.

From 1911 onwards Marval participated in annual shows at the Galerie Druet, where she held a successful one-woman show in 1912. Shortly afterwards, Apollinaire wrote an article in which he identified the emergence of a new style of art by women, which he saw as opposed to the "technical innovation" associated with male painters. He wrote: "Men usually come unstuck in compositions in which good taste is allied with delicacy … Charm is the really French artistic quality that women like Mme Marval and Mlle Laurencin have been able to preserve in art …" (*Le Petit Bleu*, April 1912). Apollinaire was one of several contemporary critics to group together Marval and Laurencin as exponents of a supposedly

Marval: *Les Odalisques*, 1903; oil on canvas; 194 × 230 cm.; Musée de Grenoble

"feminine" art distinguished by its Frenchness, "delicacy" and "charm".

Marval's show of 1912 at the Galerie Druet included many paintings of the female nude, an important theme in her work. According to Berthe Weill, an exhibition of her *Grands nus* in a group show at Weill's gallery in 1906 had scandalised at least one client, although Marval's representation of the theme rarely produced threatening or unorthodox images of female sexuality. *Les Odalisques*, one of her earliest large-scale canvases on the subject of the female nude, gained popular appeal partly because it was seen to be clearly rooted in a French, postIngres tradition of an oriental harem and *odalisque* paintings. Vauxcelles's claim for the "modern" status of this work is presumably derived from Marval's use of unconventional techniques – bright tones, loose brushwork and somewhat stiff poses – in combination with a relatively conventional art-historical theme. Many of her nudes from the 1910s and 1920s rework variations on the "bathers" or reclining nude themes, and are painted in soft flesh tones, with sensual, elongated bodies (see, for example, Roussier 1987, pl. 5), a style of painting often associated with the male painters of the broadly labelled School of Paris, such as van Dongen, Modigliani and Foujita. Like many so-called *femmes peintres* of her era, among them Emilie Charmy (q.v.) and Suzanne Valadon (q.v.), Marval adopted and reworked a theme that has (mistakenly) been seen as largely the prerogative of the early 20th-century male avant-garde.

Portraits and still-life, especially flower painting, also featured prominently in Marval's oeuvre, although her enduring interest in flower painting has often been cited as evidence of her "feminine" form of art, apparently engaged with an iconography different from that of many male colleagues. Accounts of her work, much like those of Laurencin's oeuvre, often identify a distinctive "feminine" type, a particular image of woman that recurs throughout her career. Thus Lucien Manissieux wrote that Marval had produced an "essentially feminine" type, "a large affected woman with a pointed nose, languorous eyes, outrageously painted lips", whom he identified as a mirror-image of the artist herself (quoted in Roussier 1987, p.50). The notion of the woman artist narcissistically reproducing a fantasised (fantasy?) image of herself was rooted in some complex contemporary ideas about women's roles as artists, fashionable icons and symbols of French modernity, and is often to be found in the critical discourses that surrounded the work of so-called *femmes peintres* in the 1920s and 1930s. Despite a critical tendency to exaggerate or misrepresent the significance of Marval's imagery, there is ample evidence from her paintings to suggest that she often represented (consciously or unconsciously) a female type based on an ideal self-image.

GILL PERRY

Marx, Enid (Crystal Dorothy)
British painter and designer, 1902–

Born in London, 20 October 1902. Studied at Central School of Arts and Crafts, London, 1921–2; Royal College of Art, London, 1922–5. First freelance studio-workshop, Hampstead, London, 1926; later moved to St John's Wood, London. Worked in advertising and as book illustrator (including eleven children's books) from 1925; designed moquette fabrics for London Passenger Transport Board, 1936–9 (in production to mid-1950s); cotton tapestries, vinyls and laminates for Board of Trade Utility Furniture Panel, 1943–8. Taught wood engraving, Ruskin School of Art, Oxford, 1931–3; subsequently instructor in design, Bromley School of Art and Maidstone School of Art, both Kent; head of department of dress, textiles and ceramics, Croydon College of Art, 1961–5. Subsequently freelance lecturer and writer. Co-curator, *Popular Art* exhibition, Reading University, 1958; *Scottish Popular Art*, Scottish Arts Council, 1959. Founder-member, National Register of Industrial Designers, Central Institute of Art and Design, 1937. Fellow, Royal Society of Arts; Royal Designer for Industry (RDI), pattern design, 1944; fellow, Society of Industrial Artists and Designers, 1946; Society of Wood Engravers, 1955; honorary fellow, Royal College of Art, 1982. Lives in London.

Principal Exhibitions
American Federation of Arts, Boston: 1929–30 (*Industrial Art*, touring)
Zwemmer Gallery, London: 1932 (*Room and Book*)
Burlington House, London: 1935 (*British Art and Industry*), 1948 (*Design at Work; Royal Designers for Industry*, RSA/COID)
Department of Overseas Trade, Paris: 1937 (*Arts and Crafts*)
Victoria and Albert Museum, London: 1946 (*Britain Can Make It*)
Royal Pavilion, South Bank, London: 1951 (*Festival of Britain*)
Het Nederlanse Post Museum, Antwerp: 1955 (*L'Artiste et le timbre-poste*)
National Book League, London: 1950s–70s
Red Rose Guild, Manchester: 1950s–70s
Society of Wood Engravers, London: 1950s–70s
Camden Arts Centre, London: 1979 (retrospective)
Sally Hunter Fine Art, London: 1988, 1990, 1992 (all individual)

Selected Writings
"'Design in industry': A talk about women's prospects, 2: Textile design", *Journal of Careers*, November 1936, pp.625–9
"Fabrics for hard wear", *Architectural Review*, xcv, 1944, pp.53–5
English Popular and Traditional Art, London: Collins, 1946 (with Margaret Lambert)
"Furnishing fabrics", *Design '46: A Survey of British Industrial Design as Displayed at the "Britain Can Make It" Exhibition*, ed. W.H. Newman, London, Council of Industrial Design, 1946, pp.87–8
"New furniture design in Great Britain", *Blick in die Welt*, no.10, 1949
"Pattern papers", *Penrose Annual*, xliv, 1950, pp.51–3
English Popular Art, London: Batsford, 1951 (with Margaret Lambert); revised London: Merlin, 1989
"Manuscript for Mr Coutts: The war years", unpublished, London, Victoria and Albert Museum Print Department, April 1984

Bibliography
Christian Barman, "Enid Marx", *Signature*, no.4, November 1936, pp.47–53
Misha Black, "The problem of art in industry: Design in everyday things", *Picture Post*, 6 January 1945, pp.14–17
"Design at work", *Ambassador*, no.10, 1948, pp.135–9
Kay Smallshaw, "Beauty in a teapot", *John Bull*, 23 October 1948, pp.8–9
R. Amos, "RAs of industry", *Everybody's*, 13 November 1948, p.4
Malcolm Logan, "Design at work", *Art and Industry*, xlv, December 1948, pp.203–8
Noel Ward, "Look for good design", *Modern Woman*, February 1949, pp.72–5
"The Royal Pavilion at the South Bank", *Royal Society of Arts Journal*, 28 February 1951, pp.125–6
Stamp Design, exh. cat., Design Centre, London, 1962
Enid Marx: A Retrospective Exhibition, exh. cat., Camden Arts Centre, London, 1979
The Thirties: British Art and Design Before the War, exh. cat., Hayward Gallery, London, and elsewhere, 1979
Cynthia Weaver, transcript of taped interview with Enid Marx, 26 July 1986 (author's possession)
—, *Enid Marx: Textile Designer for Industry*, MA thesis, University of Central England in Birmingham, 1987
—, "Enid Marx: Designing fabrics for the London Passenger Transport Board in the 1930s", *Journal of Design History*, ii, 1989, pp.35–46
Helen Salter, "Enid Marx RDI: An interview", *Women Designing: Redefining Design in Britain Between the Wars*, exh. cat., University of Brighton Gallery, 1994, pp.89–93

In 1925 Enid Marx failed her final assessment at the Royal College of Art. The principal, William Rothenstein, commented that it was always the most outstanding students who were likely to fail. And according to the RCA student magazine: "Among all the Misses who flirt with Art [Marx] alone woos it seriously ... she is the Cassandra who prophesies the doom of the old régime of design" (*Gallimaufry*, June 1925). Nearly 60 years later, in 1982, Marx was made an honorary fellow of the Royal College. The product of an inspirational family (her father died leaving 50 patents in his name) in terms of her future career, Marx says it never occurred to her to do anything else.

It was her education at Roedean School in Sussex that introduced her to the individual, intrinsic qualities of materials: wood, paper, fabric. And there, inspired by Japanese tradition, Marx cut her first stencil, to print a scarf. This interest in time-honoured crafts and the arts of other cultures has marked all her work. An enforced intermediate year at the Central School of Arts and Crafts proved fruitful, despite the fact that textile design was taught there only as a paper exercise. At her second attempt, Marx entered the flourishing Royal College of Art painting school. Already avant-garde in style and attitude, she was refused admission to Sir Frank Short's wood-engraving class on the grounds that she drew so badly. A friend of Barnett Freedman and the "Queensgate Common Room Set" surrounding him, Marx was "one of the Fauves", as opposed to the traditional Italianate group. Marx, Edward Bawden and Eric Ravilious (who taught her wood-engraving) also formed the nucleus of that coterie of enthusiastic students who surrounded Paul Nash, a part-time teacher in the design school.

Marx acknowledges the debt to Nash that is evident in her work. Her hand-block-printed *Arches* fabric of 1928 (repr. *Third International Exhibition of Industrial Art*, American Federation) can be compared with his undated block-printed fabric designed for Allan Walton Textiles Ltd (repr. Herbert Read, *Art and Industry*, London: Faber, 1934, p.156), and her engraved landscape, *Kenwood, Hampstead Heath* (see illustration), the cover for a *Handbook of Evening Drives* of c.1930, with Nash's *Arches* wood-engraving of 1926 (repr. *Paul Nash as Designer*, exh. cat., Victoria and Albert Museum, London, 1975, p.13). Marx rejoiced at Nash's love of all around him: "One looked through Paul's spectacles with great enjoyment: he saw pattern in the movement of the waves" (Weaver 1986). But the relationship between their works goes further than shared themes: Marx inherited Nash's sensitivities to working in both two and three dimensions and she epitomises his belief that artists and designers could – and should – design in all media and for all purposes.

Following her apprentice year with the hand-block fabric printers, Barron and Larcher, Marx established four consecutive independent studio workshops (1926–39), usually working alone and cutting blocks for printing both on fabric and on paper. Wartime shortages of materials prompted her to concentrate on works on paper. Such works – and those on canvas – were rarely intended to be hung: they were usually executed in a spirit of self-development and genuine enjoyment. In terms of subject matter, Marx's work shows a synthesis of Nash's love of *objets trouvés*, her mother's fondness for antiquities and flowers, and her sister's taste for *imagerie populaire*. Recognised as the author of many designs fundamental to people's everyday lives, Marx always returned to the discipline of painting and drawing that she had learned as a student. In *Who's Who* she describes herself first as a painter, secondly a designer. She protested to *The Times* (30 June 1956, p.7) that to remove fine art from applied arts courses was like being asked to write free verse without knowing the alphabet.

In 1944 Marx was honoured as Royal Designer for Industry (see *Eye for Industry, 1936–86*, exh. cat., Victoria and Albert Museum, London, 1986), a recognition of her proselytising efforts to marry art with industry, as demonstrated by her prestigious commissions: upholstery fabrics – and later poster designs – for the London Underground (repr. *Women Designers Associated with London Transport*, exh. cat., Transport Museum, London, 1985); furniture-cladding for the Government's Utility Scheme (repr. *CC41: Utility Furniture and Fashion, 1941–51*, exh. cat., Geffrye Museum, London,

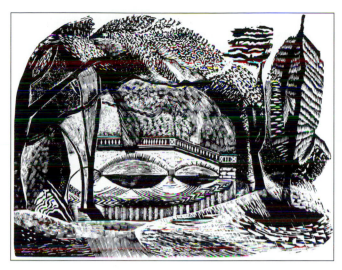

Marx: *Kenwood, Hampstead Heath, c.1930; engraving*

1974); and, from 1951, stamp design for home and abroad, which heralded a new simplicity and clarity, notably her Definitive Stamps issued on the accession of Elizabeth II (1952) and in use until 1967, and her Christmas special issue stamps of 1976 (a range of Marx's designs, many unused, can be seen at the National Postal Museum; see also Douglas Latto, "The romance of British postage stamps", *Great Britain Journal*, nos 1–6, 1979).

From 1925 Marx worked on advertising leaflets, *belles-lettres*, book illustrations, book jackets and decorative devices for the leading printers and publishers of her day. Her twin seraphim trademark for Chatto and Windus, re-worked by Marx several times over the years, surely ranks among her best-known works. She also provided designs for Insel Verlag, Oxford University Press, Faber and Penguin, among others (*Designers in Britain*, i–iii, London: Wingate, 1947, 1949 and 1951; v, London: Deutsch, 1957). Colour is always sparing, but Marx achieves an impressive range and quality of line, tone and texture, as in her jacket and engravings for Francesca Allinson's *A Childhood* (London: Hogarth Press, 1937), and the jacket and bulldog device for *The Pick of Punch: An Annual Selection* (London: Chatto, 1951).

It was productions such as these that realised Marx's desire to bring "art and aesthetics" to a wider public, harnessing advances in technology. She has always battled indefatigably with errant manufacturers and publishers unfaithful to original design sketches. Perhaps the ultimate synthesis of Marx's design philosophy is expressed through her pattern papers of 1925 onwards, in which hand-crafted key units were multiplied on lithographic plates (for papers designed and engraved for Curwen Press, see Oliver Simon, *Printer and Playground*, London: Faber, 1951, fig.14) – here was the marriage of art and mass-production of which her father had spoken.

Marx's watercolours and wood-engravings (she was still cutting blocks in 1990) combine consummate skill with artistic flair. Metal pins are sometimes added to print blocks, extending their textural range. Her mastery of the craft is as evident in her illustrative work as it is in her textile and wallpaper designs. In Marx's linocuts of the 1950s her typically extensive exploration of technique led to experimental over-printing and to an exploitation of the properties of the transparent water-based inks used.

A major concern of Marx's throughout her career has been to elevate the status of the British folk heritage. Traditional motifs, historical references and a deceptive simplicity characterise her work, as in her use of the cornucopia motif (repr. *World of Interiors*, March 1988, p.138, and Enid Marx's *A Book of Nursery Rhymes*, reprinted Oldham: Incline Press, 1993, title page). Marx's assessment failure at the Royal College had centred on her painting inspired by the fairground – the subject was thought vulgar and her inclination towards pattern was seen as unacademic.

In 1942 Marx was commissioned to document features of Britain's heritage endangered by war (e.g. *Clarence Terrace, Regent's Park*; Pilgrim Trust; pencil and watercolour). And in 1946 she illustrated *English Popular and Traditional Art*, co-authored with Margaret Lambert. As an author she also made a less usual contribution to the war effort with four illustrated children's books, including *Bulgy the Barrage Balloon* (Oxford University Press, 1941), *Nelson the Kite of the King's Navy* (London: Chatto, 1942) and *The Pigeon Ace* (London: Faber, 1943).

After World War II Marx accompanied the British Government teams sent out to investigate German and Scandinavian progress in industrial design and design education. During the succeeding decades Marx again developed her work in a wide range of media. The respect she enjoys as an authority on the arts and crafts of many eras and cultures is evident in the breadth and depth of her commissioned writings, spanning half a century, as well as in her teaching activities. For *The Maker's Eye* exhibition at the Crafts Council in 1981, Marx selected a harvest loaf and an Eileen Gray table to stand alongside a book design of her own: these apparently disparate artefacts exemplify all that she considers good in art and design. It is tempting to apply Marx's description of Diaghilev as "the magician, perfectly blending the classic, with the ultra-modern – without ever seeming *outré*" (Enid Marx to Mr Coutts, manuscript, London, April 1984, p.7) to the artist herself. Marx is a paradigm of the British multi-disciplinary artist-designer, with a career spanning most of the 20th century, and her work shows an unfailing reverence for the past, combined with a tireless zest for the new. Works by her are held by the Crafts Study Centre, Bath; Sheffield Art Gallery; Scottish Arts Council; Victoria and Albert Museum, London; Musée des Arts Décoratifs, Paris; and the Museum of Fine Arts, Boston.

CYNTHIA R. WEAVER

Mason, Alice Trumbull

American painter and printmaker, 1904–1971

Born Alice Bradford Trumbull in Litchfield, Connecticut, 1904. Lived in Italy with her family, 1921–2; attended classes at the British Academy, Rome. Studied at National Academy of Design, New York, and under the painter Charles W. Hawthorne, 1923–7. Attended classes taught by Arshile Gorky at Grand Central Art Galleries, New York, 1927–8.

Visited Italy and Greece, 1928. Married merchant seaman Warwood E. Mason, 1930; daughter Emily, also an artist, born 1932, son John born 1933 (d. 1958). Studied printmaking at Stanley William Hayter's Atelier 17, New York, 1944–7. Recipient of Charles M. Lea prize, Print Club of Philadelphia, 1946; Treasurer's prize, Society of American Graphic Artists, 1948; Longview Foundation purchase prize, Walker Art Center, Minneapolis, 1963. Founder member, 1936, treasurer, 1939, secretary, 1940–45, president, 1959–63, American Abstract Artists (AAA), New York. Member, Federation of Modern Painters and Sculptors. Died in New York, 1971.

Selected Individual Exhibitions
Museum of Living Art, New York: 1942
Rose Fried Gallery, New York: 1948
USA: 1950–51 (prints, touring)
Wittenborn & Co., New York: 1952
Hansa Gallery, New York: 1959
Fire House Gallery, Nassau Community College, New York: 1967
The 20th Century Gallery, New York: 1967
Whitney Museum of American Art, New York: 1973 (touring retrospective)

Selected Writings
"Concerning plastic significance", *American Abstract Artists Yearbook*, 1938, pp.19–20

Bibliography
Alice Trumbull Mason Retrospective, exh. cat., Whitney Museum of American Art, New York, and elsewhere, 1973
Three American Purists: Mason/Miles/von Wiegand, exh. cat., Museum of Fine Arts, Springfield, MA, 1975
Women Artists, 1550–1950, exh. cat., Los Angeles County Museum of Art, and elsewhere, 1976
Jan Butterfield, "Replacing women artists in history", *Art News*, lxxiv, March 1977, pp.40–44
Robert Hughes, "Rediscovered: Women painters", *Time*, 10 January 1977, p.60
Alice Trumbull Mason, Emily Mason: Two Generations of Abstract Painting, exh. cat., Art Department Gallery, Newcomb College, Tulane University, New Orleans, and elsewhere, 1982
Charlotte Streifer Rubinstein, *American Women Artists from Early Times to the Present*, Boston: Hall, 1982
Marilyn R. Brown, "Three generations of artists: Anne Train Trumbull, Alice Trumbull Mason and Emily Mason", *Woman's Art Journal*, iv/1, 1983, pp.1–8
William Zimmer, "American works of the 30s in Stamford", *New York Times*, 21 August 1983
Una E. Johnson, *Alice Trumbull Mason: Etchings and Woodcuts*, New York: Taplinger, 1985
Stephen Westfall, "Alice Trumbull Mason: Home-grown abstraction", *Art in America*, lxxiv, October 1985, pp.146–9

Alice Trumbull Mason Papers are in the Archives of American Art, New York.

Born to a mother who had been trained in Paris as an academic painter, and herself the recipient of comparable training in Europe and New York, Alice Trumbull Mason was to spend some four decades as a painter and printmaker in pursuit of a very different approach to art-making, that of abstraction. An early and frequent executive member of the American Abstract Artists (AAA) association, founded in 1936, she was one of only two women to have a statement published by the group in its first yearbook. There she elaborated upon her understanding of abstraction, in which the "magic in the work itself" was the primary goal: "Today a sense of wonder is alive again. The abstract painter finds it, essentially, in his materials, and deals with the magic of textures, colors juxtaposed to force intensities which thus show movement somewhat as the sculptor shapes the air with his constructions" ("Concerning plastic significance", 1938).

Mason's commitment to abstraction, without which Ad Reinhardt is alleged to have said "we should not be here in such strength, nor in such numbers" (*New York Times*, 13 February 1977, p.D33), began in 1929. According to the artist, this shift followed a year of liberating studies with Arshile Gorky and a trip to Europe that brought to her maturing attention Archaic Greek, Byzantine and 14th-century Italian art. A work such as *Springtime* (1931; oil on canvas; repr. *Alice Trumbull Mason: Paintings from 1930 to 1950*, pamphlet, Washburn Gallery, New York, 1979, cover) attests to her interest in establishing links between the abstract elements in earlier art and more contemporary experiments. The painting, with its dominating colours of yellow and burnished gold, puts one in mind of her comments of 1938 on the mosaics of Ravenna, in which the use of gold backgrounds was said to be "almost an abstraction of colour, being unrelated to nature and working well with the stylized lines of the figures." At the same time, the sophisticated combination in *Springtime* of oddly shaped planes of non-prismatic colour, straight and erratic linear elements and a sprinkling of tiny dots moved the work out of any historicising context and placed Mason in the company of such lyric abstractionists as Arthur Dove.

Marriage, followed rapidly by the mothering of two children, led to a three-year break in Mason's painting, during which time she turned to poetry, receiving encouragement from William Carlos Williams and Gertrude Stein for her exploration of the abstract potential of words and sounds, but only one opportunity to publish ever materialised. When she resumed painting in 1934, she actively sought exhibition venues, and as a result was the only abstract artist included in the Washington Square Art Show of 1935, a fact that was reported on the front page of the *New York Times* (see Brown 1983, p.3). Quickly a more resolute biomorphism began to characterise her work, which on the surface seemed to identify her painting with "the look" of such AAA colleagues and friends as Ilya Bolotowsky, Balcomb Greene and Gertrude Greene (q.v.). However, a careful viewing and reviewing of *Untitled* (c.1938) and *Untitled* (c.1939; both oil on masonite; repr. Westfall 1985) reveal a thoroughly independent "deadpan wit" that urged viewers, through vestiges of such representational elements as a duck/decoy and an umber moon, to reflect upon the compositional complexities of what Mason would call throughout her life "true realism".

Several abstract options were investigated in the early 1940s. The mosaic *Untitled Abstraction* (1941; repr. *The Patricia and Philip Frost Collection: American Abstraction, 1930–1945*, 1989, p.129) , an exuberant, curvaceous explosion of shells and brightly coloured tesserae set into a field of grey, was created not long after *Untitled* (c.1940; oil on masonite; repr. *Alice Trumbull Mason: Paintings from 1930 to 1950*, op. cit.), in which defined geometric elements were beginning to assert themselves. Existing alongside these "opposites" were further biomorphic exercises, pictures such as *Necessity of Yellow* (1941; oil on masonite; repr. *Art News*, April 1988, p.145), which referred, perhaps even ironically, to the most decisive element to cross the boundaries of her stylistic experimentations at the time.

Geometry, though rarely of the grid-bound sort, was to win the day with Mason by the end of the decade. This settling down, as it were, was unquestionably aided by the presence of Mondrian in the USA, and was one that, upon rare occasions after his death in 1944, led her to create works that "could have been certified by the master himself" (*New York Times*, 3 June 1973, p.D22). Nevertheless, her interest in Mondrian was generally anything but servile, rejecting as it did any significant ties with spiritual content and the use of primary colours. Instead, it reflected, in her own words, the "need of a greater potential in governing the allotted space and at the same time of creating a lyrical statement" (*ibid.*). This search, sometimes more of a struggle, for balance can be witnessed most clearly in the printmaking she did during and after her participation in Stanley William Hayter's Atelier 17 (1944–7); a soft-ground etching such as *White Scaffolding* (1946; repr. Johnson 1985, p.19), while stunning in its textural play, almost gave way to the very trap she sought to avoid: "the ... almost irresistible ... temptation to drown in a sea of textures" (cited in New Orleans 1982, p.28). The "controlling structure of the space", which ultimately drew her back from that shore, was a simplified geometry, as can be observed in the woodcut *9 Triangles* (1952; *ibid.*, p.38). In retaining a degree of texture appropriate to the medium, this woodcut demonstrated a deep rather than superficial understanding of Mondrian's formal values.

Throughout the rest of her career, and to the detriment of her once positive positioning within the American art world, Mason subscribed to the control offered by sagely and often dynamically placed geometric forms. Attention swirled around the Abstract Expressionists, while such works as *Magnetic Field* (1951; repr. *Arts Magazine*, October 1982, p.23), as always small in size and painted with the oils she made herself, consigned the artist to the ranks of the almost forgotten, propelling her, some believe, into a long-term depression and dependency on alcohol. For those few who continued to watch, it must have been obvious that her art encompassed emotions just as intense as those exhibited by the new "extroverted" monarchs. The death by drowning of her son, John, in 1958 initiated a series of works based on the Trinity motif: the most striking of these, *Memorial* (1958–9; oil on board; Whitney Museum of American Art, New York), was a poignant, indeed painful composition of light, potentially ascending forms tied to the bottom of the picture plane by large passages of dark blue and black. Nevertheless, it was not until the early 1970s, when her daughter Emily Mason and son-in-law Wolf Kahn – both painters – actively began to bring forth some of the 200 paintings left by Mason, that attempts were made to examine her career. She began to be seen as a leading woman in the positing of alternatives to the representational art felt by so many to be the appropriate response to the economic devastation of the 1930s, and a reclusive, though never silenced, advocate of a controlled lyricism during the hegemony of the Abstract Expressionists. An exhibition in the summer of 1996 at the Washburn Gallery, which juxtaposed Mason's work of the 1950s with the paintings of Agnes Martin (q.v.) and the collages of her friend, Anne Ryan, augurs well for a consideration, in the near future, of the artist's production that will move beyond the obvious.

CATHERINE MACKENZIE

Matthiasdóttir, Louisa
Icelandic painter and sculptor, 1917–

Born in Reykjavik, 1917. Studied at the College of Industrial Design, Copenhagen, 1934–7; studied under Marcel Gromaire in Paris, 1938–9. Returned to Iceland, 1939. Moved to New York, 1941, to study under Hans Hofmann, 1942–4. Married painter Leland Bell, 1943; one daughter, Temma, also a painter. Lives in New York.

Selected Individual Exhibitions
Jane Street Gallery, New York: 1948
Tanager Gallery, New York: 1958
University of Connecticut, Storrs: 1960
Robert Schoelkopf Gallery, New York: 1964, 1966, 1968, 1969,
    1972, 1974, 1976, 1978, 1980, 1982, 1984, 1987, 1989, 1991
Litchfield Art Center, CT: 1972
Windham College, Putney, VT: 1972
University of New Hampshire, Durham: 1978
Mount Holyoke College Art Museum, South Hadley, MA: 1982
Bryggens Museum, Norway: 1987
Meredith Long, Houston: 1988
Donald Morris Gallery, Birmingham, MI: 1988, 1994
Municipal Art Museum, Reykjavik: 1993
Salander-O'Reilly Galleries, New York: 1994

Bibliography
Martica Sawin, "Louisa Matthiasdóttir: A painter of the figure", *Arts Magazine*, November 1961, pp.26–33
Hilton Kramer, "Realists and others", *Arts Magazine*, xxxviii, January 1964, pp.18–23
Leland Bell, Louisa Matthiasdóttir, exh. cat., Austin Art Center, Trinity College, Hartford, CT, 1969
John Ashbery, "North light", *Art News*, lxx, February 1972, pp.44–5
Leland Bell, Louisa Matthiasdóttir, Temma Bell: A Family of Painters, exh. cat., Canton Art Institute, OH, 1973
Deborah Rosenthal, "Louisa Matthiasdóttir", *Arts Magazine*, l, April 1976, p.12
Ruth Gilbert Bass, *Five Realist Painters*, PhD dissertation, New York University, 1978
Gerrit Henry, "Louisa Mattiasdóttir", *Art News*, lxxvii, April 1978, p.149
Harry Rand, "Louisa Matthiasdóttir", *Arts Magazine*, lii, April 1978, p.4
Janet Hobhouse, "Independent Icelander", *Quest*, April 1979, pp.98–100
Jim Monte, "Louisa Matthiasdóttir at Schoelkopf", *Art in America*, lxviii, May 1980, p.156
Deborah Rosenthal and Jed Perl, "Louisa Matthiasdóttir", *Arts Magazine*, liv, May 1980, p.4
Louisa Matthiasdóttir, exh. cat., Robert Schoelkopf Gallery, New York, 1982
"Louisa Matthiasdóttir", *Art News*, lxxxi, January 1982, p.170
Mark Strand, ed., *Art of the Real: Nine American Figurative Painters*, New York: Potter, 1983; as *Art of the Real: Nine Figurative Painters*, London: Aurum Press, 1984
Adalsteinn Ingolfsson, "A solid and serene world", *Iceland Review 3*, xxiii, 1984, pp.18–24
Hearne Pardee, "The new American landscape", *Arts Magazine*, lviii, April 1984, pp.116–17
Deborah Rosenthal, "Louisa Matthiasdóttir at Robert Schoelkopf", *Art in America*, lxxii, November 1984, pp.164–5
Jed Perl, Deborah Rosenthal and Nicholas Fox Weber, *Louisa Matthiasdóttir: Small Paintings*, New York: Hudson Hills Press, 1986 (contains bibliography)
Jed Perl, "Art", *New Criterion*, v, March 1987, pp.60–61
Scandinavian Review, lxxv, Spring 1987, pp.61–5
Becky Brimacombe in *Arts Magazine*, lxiii, Summer 1989, p.78
G. Laderman, "In the galleries", *Art and Antiques*, vi, Summer 1989, p.37
Jed Perl, "Art", *New Criterion*, ix, November 1990, pp.66–7
John Russell, "An artist looks at other people's paintings: Art view", *New York Times*, 9 August 1992

On the surface, Louisa Matthiasdóttir's paintings are reticent and unadorned – silent landscapes inhabited only by the occasional figure, farm animal or horse and rider; empty cityscapes that have been compared to the work of both Giorgio de Chirico and Edward Hopper; sparse arrangements of still-life elements; faceless portraits and strong, unyielding self-portraits. They are also astonishingly consistent paintings. Neither the subjects nor their presentation have changed much in 50 years. Where there is change, it is in the direction of ever greater simplicity and economy: fewer colours and broader brush strokes. The key to Matthiasdóttir's work lies in her decision, whether conscious or not, to confine herself to these few, apparently mundane subjects. When linked to her preferred method of working – she seldom, if ever, reworks a painting, but will move on readily to re-examine (but not repeat) the same subject on a fresh canvas – the result is a grasp of content and form that is intimate and sure. The subjects are so well known, the process so regularly rehearsed, that they have become second nature. The magic is that each remaking is a new birth – spontaneous, fresh and full of wonder.

The constancy of her work is mirrored in Matthiasdóttir's life. She has lived in New York, at the same address, and painted in the same studio there, since 1954. Yet there are no traces of the life of the metropolis in her work. The landscapes are rooted firmly in memories (renewed through regular visits) of Iceland, a land of such singular beauty and character as to provide inexhaustible inspiration. Sometimes they bear specific place names, like *Olafsvik* or *View from Hverfisgata*, but these are merely points of reference and most titles are spare and descriptive: *Three Sheep*, *Black Horse* or *Red Roof, Yellow House*. Over and over again the basic elements – sky, mountains, lakes and treeless meadows – are deftly arranged and rearranged in carefully overlapped planes. Painted in brilliant colours with lush brush strokes, they are simultaneously both completely unaffected renderings of the real world and skilful painterly abstractions.

In *House and Sheep* (1982; see illustration) blue mountains extend into the upper corners of the picture format on either side, creating bands of intense, barely modulated colour. In the centre their contours slope down to meet gently and overlap. The inverted triangle thus formed between the two overlapping mountain masses is painted a lighter shade of blue and broken by a few brush strokes that signal white clouds. With this restrained gesture, the sky ceases to be an abstraction and becomes a completely convincing, infinitely receding space. Below, or in front of the mountains, a broad horizontal band

Matthiasdóttir: *House and Sheep*, 1982; 33 × 52 cm.

of dark olive green is tipped by delicate yellow and reddish brush strokes. Paint becomes tangible reality as the viewer senses the sun casting a glow over the meadow through a break in the cloudy sky. Such effects of light and dark, the result of the most skilful manipulations and colour juxtaposition, continue towards the foreground through a stretch of water, past simplified and colourful pink and green, yellow and red, windowless "Monopoly houses", over gently rolling hills and around the stolid forms of one black and two white sheep. A whole world, all at once crystal clear yet silent and mysterious, animated yet frozen, is made visible. Tensions like these, set up between the real and the painted forms, the obvious and the hidden content, give Matthiasdóttir's work its arresting power. Spread around her studio, a group of canvases produce a linked sequence, like the frames of a film. Disclaiming, however, the grandiose scale of a cinema screen, many of these panoramas compress vast stretches of landscape into formats that are often quite small – no more than 25 or 30 centimetres in both dimensions. At other times the scale is expanded to five or six times this size. Some have wide, low, frieze-like formats, others are more regularly rectangular. Seen as a group, the shifts and manipulations of scale and format demand a constant adjustment of eye and mind, so that the viewer is prevented from settling into a complacent and repetitive mode. As the eye moves from canvas to canvas, the spaces between and beyond the paintings dissolve, and the fresh, pulsating Icelandic landscape becomes a tangible presence on a New York street.

As the landscapes are reduced in size and compressed, so the still lifes (by convention usually quiet and intimate subjects) are astonishingly and provocatively exploded in canvases of up to 1.5 or 1.8 metres wide. These still lifes are set up by Matthiasdóttir in the studio. Characteristically they contain a tabletop, wholly or partially covered by a cloth, on which are placed, at strategic intervals, vegetables and occasionally fruits – squashes of all shapes and colours, eggplants and peppers seem most favoured – and often a bottle or other glass or ceramic vessel. Separated from one another, marking out the space, the objects are so vividly painted that they appear not so much real, as *present*, in a most compelling and tangible way. Matisse's statement "Exactitude is not truth", intended to explicate his own work, equally elucidates the realism of Matthiasdóttir's paintings. Matisse eloquently pointed out that truth in painting does not "... depend on the exact copying of natural forms, nor on the patient assembling of exact details, but on the profound feeling of the artist before the objects which he has chosen, on which his attention is focused, and the spirit of which he has penetrated" (Alfred H. Barr, Jr, *Matisse: His Art and His Public*, New York, 1951, p.561).

Although she is almost exclusively recognised as a painter, Louisa Matthiasdóttir has also produced some remarkable, though seldom seen sculptures. These are worked in plaster over rough metal or wire armatures and have an unfinished quality, as though created as aids to realising three-dimensional form in her paintings. The unstudied immediacy of these works – mostly heads or partial torsos, but including at least one life-size female figure – their rough surfaces enlivened by traces of the artist's shaping hands, is a revelation. They reiterate in a most persistent way the complex understanding of reality that underlies all of this artist's work.

BRENDA DANILOWITZ

Matthieu, Anna Rosina de *see* Lisiewska

Mayer (de la Martinière), (Marie Françoise) Constance
French painter, 1775–1821

Born in Paris, 1775; father a customs official. Convent education in Paris. Studied under Jean-Baptiste Greuze and Joseph-Benoît Suvée, then for a brief period in 1801 under Jacques-Louis David. Became pupil of Pierre-Paul Prud'hon, 1802; collaborated with him, and shared care of his children and helped to run household after his wife's mental collapse. Given lodgings in the Louvre in recognition of achievement as an artist, 1816. Committed suicide in Paris, 26 May 1821.

Principal Exhibitions
Paris Salon: 1796, 1798–1802, 1804, 1806, 1808, 1810, 1812, 1814, 1817, 1819
Paris: 1822 (memorial, organised by Prud'hon)

Bibliography
Charles Clément, *Prud'hon: Sa vie, ses oeuvres et sa correspondance*, Paris: Didier, 1872

Charles Guellette, "Mademoiselle Constance Mayer et Prud'hon", *Gazette des Beaux-Arts*, 2nd series, xix, 1879, pp.476–90; xx, 1879, pp.337–57, 525–38

Jeanne Doin, "Constance Mayer", *Revue de l'Art Ancien et Moderne*, xxix, 1911, pp.49–60, 139–50

Edmond Pilon, *Constance Mayer (1775–1821)*, Paris: Delpleuch, 1927

Carol Duncan, "Happy mothers and other new ideas in French art", *Art Bulletin*, lv, 1973, pp.570–83

Women Artists, 1550–1950, exh. cat., Los Angeles County Museum of Art, and elsewhere, 1976

Helen Weston, "The case for Constance Mayer", *Oxford Art Journal*, iii/1, 1980, pp.14–19

La Femme artiste d'Elisabeth Vigée-Lebrun à Rosa Bonheur, exh. cat., Musée Despiau-Wlerick, Donjon Lacataye, Mont-de-Marsan, 1981

At the end of the reign of Terror, a return to family values under the bourgeois French republic brought a demand in the late 1790s for portraits and miniatures. Constance Mayer was then in her early twenties and converting a hobby of painting portraits and genre scenes into a profession. She was one of an increasing number of women artists who found new opportunities to exhibit work in the Paris Salons. She exhibited at every Salon from 1796, including miniatures of her father, large self-portraits, portraits of women and children and domestic genre scenes. These showed the influence of her first teachers, Joseph-Benoît Suvée and Jean-Baptiste Greuze, in the choice of themes and the use of soft brushwork. They represented popular sentimental subjects of young girls holding pigeons, being caught in a storm and children with portfolios of drawings. Two portraits, however, were of herself as an artist, and these indicated the interest that was developing among women artists from the studios of David, Elisabeth Vigée-Lebrun (q.v.) and Adélaïde Labille-Guiard (q.v.) to assert professional identity. The first represented a *Self-Portrait of Citizenness Mayer Pointing to a Sketch for a Portrait of Her Mother* (exh. 1796 Salon; untraced) and the second a full-length *Self-Portrait with Artist's Father: He Points to a Bust of Raphael, Inviting Her to Take This Celebrated Painter as a Model* (exh. 1801 Salon; see illustration). In common with other women artists of her time, Mayer found strategies for ensuring that her work would be acceptable, by masking this public self-assertion and professional aspiration with an acceptance of parental protection and control within the image, and by submitting this work as by a pupil of Suvée and Greuze. She could thus be seen as dutiful daughter and subordinate pupil. In fact, in 1801 she worked briefly in David's studio and this may account for the new simplicity, incisiveness and the reference to Raphael and the antique to be seen in this self-portrait. On the other hand, David's women pupils were often expected to emphasise their dependence on the master by including in their self-portraits copies after David's works which they were seen to be copying. By avoiding this configuration of the master-pupil relationship and by placing herself standing with her own portfolio of works, Mayer expressed a sense of ambition and separateness as an artistic identity.

Although she attempted allegorical subjects after this date, which would come into the category of history painting, these still bore the imprint of Greuze's sentimentalism. In 1802 she became a pupil of Prud'hon, and this quickly developed into friendship and mutual devotion, as Mayer took on the roles of housekeeper and child-minder, following Mme Prud'hon's mental breakdown and transfer to a nursing home in 1803. From this point Mayer and Prud'hon worked collaboratively, Prud'hon producing the early drawings and sketches and Mayer working them up into paintings with his assistance. A case in point is *Innocence Preferring Love to Wealth* (exh. 1804 Salon; Hermitage, St Petersburg), finally exhibited under her name. *Innocence Drawn by Love and Followed by Regret* (exh. 1810 Salon; private collection), for which Prud'hon had done studies in Rome in the 1780s, was a reprise of a Greuzian subject, begun by Mayer but finished by Prud'hon and catalogued under his name. This collaborative process has led to many confusions. The *Sleep of Venus and Cupid, Disturbed by Zephyrs* (Wallace Collection, London), for example, was commissioned from Mayer by Empress Josephine and exhibited under Mayer's name in the Salon of 1806. With its pendant it was sold as a Mayer for a modest sum but later attributed to Prud'hon and sold for a grossly inflated price. Catalogued by the Goncourts as a Prud'hon and displayed in the Wallace Collection until 1911 as a Prud'hon, this work has suffered the fate of many at the hands of dealers and misogynist historians, and Mayer's reputation with it.

During her lifetime Mayer's Salon submissions of genre scenes and mythologies incurred the familiar scorn of critics who saw them as a violation of nature and of "all the laws of modesty (*pudeur*)". She and her female colleagues were

Mayer: *Self-Portrait with Artist's Father: He Points to a Bust of Raphael, Inviting Her to Take This Celebrated Painter as a Model*, exhibited Salon of 1801; Wadsworth Atheneum, Hartford, Connecticut; Ella Gallup Sumner and Mary Catlin Sumner Collection Fund

advised to limit themselves to flower painting and family portraits. What many of them in fact took up was the subject of motherhood, which had been popularised by the *philosophes* of the 18th century and by politicians of the Revolution. In the early 19th century there was continuing interest in painting the joys of breast feeding, observing the child's first steps, the importance of inoculations and the grief at the loss of a child. Mayer produced the *Happy Mother* (exh. 1810 Salon) and the *Unfortunate Mother* (exh. 1812 Salon; both Louvre, Paris), the latter in the tradition of personifications of Melancholia and sepulchral gloom that women artists, in particular, had produced in the wake of the revolutionary and Napoleonic wars. The *Unfortunate Mother* shows a solitary, luminous figure in a mysterious moonlit landscape, of a type that had gained currency in the work of Girodet-Trioson, Gros and Prud'hon.

Mayer continued to paint portraits, mostly of her circle of female artists and friends (*Mme Voïart*, exh. 1814 Salon; Musée des Beaux-Arts, Nancy), in a style that was softer and less dramatic than Prud'hon's, but she persisted with more ambitious genre and allegorical works despite adverse critical comment, focusing on subjects of poverty and wretchedness, such as the *Unfortunate Family* (begun 1821; private collection) and *Dream of Happiness* (exh. 1819 Salon; Louvre). These lugubrious subjects are again close to those of Greuze, but have nothing of the melodramatic appeal and theatricality of his works, nor the overt moralising nature. The *Unfortunate Family* does not preach filial duty in a rustic family, and the happiness in the *Dream of Happiness* is not that of the village bride. The mood is sinister and the happiness threatened. Mayer's work has a seriousness, an inwardness, that locate it firmly within the early Romantic tradition of the 19th century. She was becoming increasingly melancholic herself even though she had gained a reputation as an artist and had been given lodgings in the Louvre in 1816. Unhappy with her personal life, and the more so when Prud'hon refused to remarry in the event of his wife's death, Mayer committed suicide, using his razor to cut her throat, in 1821. The following year Prud'hon organised an exhibition of her works in tribute to her talent.

HELEN WESTON

Meidner, Else

German painter and graphic artist, 1901–1987

Born Else Meyer in Berlin, 2 September 1901, into a Jewish family. Studied at the Kunstgewerbeschule, Berlin, and in Lewin-Funcke's Studien-Atelier für Malerei und Plastik, Berlin-Charlottenburg, 1918–25. Married the artist Ludwig Meidner, 1927; son born, 1929. Prohibited from exhibiting by the National Socialists, 1933. Moved to Cologne, 1935; emigrated to London, 1939; British citizenship, 1953. Won second prize in "best etching of the year" competition, *Die Schaffenden* magazine, 1929. Died in London, 5 May 1987.

Principal Exhibitions

Individual
Juryfreie Kunstschau, Berlin: 1932
Ben Uri Gallery, London: 1949 (with Ludwig Meidner), 1964 (retrospective), 1972
Kunstkabinett Hannah Bekker vom Rath, Frankfurt am Main: 1955
Matthiesen Gallery, London: 1956
Beaux Arts Gallery, London: 1959
Justus-Liebig-Haus, Darmstadt: 1969 (touring)
Mishkan Le'Omanut Museum of Art, Ein Harod, Israel: 1992 (retrospective)

Group
Ben Uri Gallery, London: 1961 (*Opening Exhibition*)
Leicester Gallery, London: 1966 (*New Year Exhibition of Paintings, Drawings and Sculpture of 19th- and 20th-Century Artists*)

Bibliography

Max Hermann Neisse, "Meine Erlebnisse mit der bildenden Kunst", *Das Kunstblatt*, no.3, 1929, pp.78–80
Max Osborn, "Bei den Juryfreien", *Vossische Zeitung*, 11 May 1932
Joseph Paul Hodin, "Else Meidner", *Art News and Review*, xxiv, October 1959
——, "Else Meidner", *The Studio*, clix, 1960, pp.164ff
Else Meidner: Retrospective Exhibition, exh. cat., Ben Uri Gallery, London, 1964
Thomas Grochowiak, *Ludwig Meidner*, Recklinghausen, 1966
Else Meidner: Zeichnungen, 1927–1962, exh. cat., Justus-Liebig-Haus, Darmstadt, 1969
Else Meidner, exh. cat., Ben Uri Gallery, London, 1972
Joseph Paul Hodin, *Aus den Erinnerungen von Else Meidner*, Darmstadt: Leibig, 1979
Gerda Breuer and Ines Wagemann, *Ludwig Meidner: Maler, Zeichner, Literat, 1884–1966*, Stuttgart: Hatje, 1991
Vom Expressionismus zum Widerstand: Kunst in Deutschland, 1909–1936: Die Sammlung Marvin und Janet Fishman, exh. cat., Kunsthalle Schirn, Frankfurt am Main, 1991
Else Meidner, exh. cat., Mishkan Le'Omanut Museum of Art, Ein Harod, Israel, 1992
Jutta Dick and Marina Sassenberg, eds, *Jüdische Frauen im 19. und 20. Jahrhundert: Lexikon zu Leben und Werk*, Reinbek bei Hamburg: Rowohlt, 1993

Else Meidner's name was established in Germany in 1932 with her first solo show at the Juryfreie in Berlin, where she exhibited oil paintings and drawings. By the time her second German exhibition was held, at the Frankfurter Kunstkabinett in 1955, Meidner – who had emigrated to London in 1939 – had lived through a period of abject poverty, illness and loneliness in a hopeless struggle for recognition in a country that was used to accepting only what originated in Paris, or later the USA, and rejected "Expressionism", the blanket term for everything German. Meidner never experimented with the various "isms" and hated everything abstract (letter to Joseph Paul Hodin of 6 October 1969, quoted in Hodin 1979, p.54). At her death in 1987 she left a rich oeuvre as a painter and graphic artist. Apart from a small number of still lifes and landscapes, her works are mainly of figures – portraits, self-portraits and nudes.

Meidner's earlier works are ostensibly influenced by Rembrandt, who combined deep religious feeling with outstanding artistry and the compelling urge to tell a human story. *Praying Woman* (oil; artist's estate, Kibbutz Shluchot, Israel, repr. London 1972, cover), her hands tightly clasped, her head bowed in deep respect, is completely removed from this world. This very private picture might be understood as a confession about the real nature of her work: "I am an admirer of the perfection in creation. In giving expression to this admiration in my work, I praise the Creator. When I concentrate, when I feel my work intensely, then painting acquires a quality for me which comes near to prayer" (letter to Hodin). Whereas *Mother and Child* (1946; charcoal; artist's estate, Kibbutz Shluchot, repr. Ein Harod 1992) explores the loving and contented mother and child bond, *Diaspora* (charcoal; artist's estate, Kibbutz Shluchot) describes its ache and fear. Covering her eyes in utter despair, the mother tightly holds her child, who innocently tries to console her. The sadness and melancholy are skilfully captured.

Meidner gave an account of herself at different moments in her life in numerous self-portraits. *Self-Portrait, Laughing* (1927; charcoal; repr. Darmstadt 1969, p.2) shows a radiant young woman; another *Self-Portrait with Book*, of the same year (charcoal; artist's estate, Kibbutz Shluchot, repr. Hodin 1979, p.17), a coy, studious woman, clutching a small book, who is timidly engaging with the viewer. The older, mature Meidner is seen in the powerful *Self-Portrait* (1947; see illustration) with a white, almost ghostlike face. Having started to use strong colours as a primary means of expression after she came to London, she shows here supreme confidence in handling brilliant colour with deep psychological insight.

In contrast to the rejection Meidner experienced in her surroundings, the heat of the colours seems to assert her power and vitality. The multi-coloured *Reclining Nude* (oil; John Denham Gallery) is set against a flat, vibrant, startling orange background. Her closed eyes make her appear mysterious and withdrawn. Yet there are a tenderness, a vibration of light and a sensuous *joie de vivre* in this painting, which are not present in *Nude* (1956) and *Nude* (1958; both charcoal; artist's estate, Kibbutz Shluchot). Both seem unaware of being observed, one turns her body away from the viewer, her face invisible; the other crouches on the floor, her face hidden by a shock of hair, completely self-absorbed. Although Meidner brings out the three-dimensionality of the figures, she does not beautify them. Both *Nudes* convey eroticism touching on the fragile beauty of human existence.

Meidner often signed her works with two "M"s, one on top of the other, to distinguish herself from her husband Ludwig Meidner, an established painter who had been her teacher at Lewin-Funcke's in Berlin. Although she suffered from her husband's greater artistic prominence, Else was described by Ludwig in 1966 as highly gifted and among the most important European female graphic artists of the 1930s. (He admitted, however, that she had had no luck and would always be in the shade: letter quoted in Breuer and Wagemann 1991, p.487.) He often served as her model (*Ludwig Meidner*, 1930; charcoal; artist's estate, Kibbutz Shluchot, repr. Ein Harod 1992). He is shown reading at the family dinner table in the small and claustrophobic apartment (*Ludwig Meidner and Son at the Table, Reading*, 1944; charcoal; Jüdisches Museum, Frankfurt am Main) or as an artist, working at an improvised table (*Ludwig, Drawing*, charcoal; Städtische Kunstsammlung, Darmstadt). Although Ludwig claimed it was purely accidental if Else's portraits resembled her sitters, *Portrait of a Woman* (1953; charcoal; artist's estate, Kibbutz Shluchot) shows a strong objectivity towards the subject and makes no

Meidner: *Self-Portrait*, 1947; oil on canvas; 50.8 × 40.6 cm.

concession to prettiness, presenting with expressive realism a Jewish matron who quietly submits to the law of ageing.

Meidner's lifelong fascination with demons, devils and death reveals a preoccupation with the realm of the supernatural. Her paintings of masks mainly show heads (*The Devil*), only exceptionally whole figures (*Two Devil Women*, both oil; John Denham Gallery). Painted in primary colours, coarse and grim, they do not possess Ensor's mild humour and all-too-human attraction, but uncover the distorted, often brutal, sometimes ridiculous features of human nature. They are expressions of human fear, cruelty and tragi-comedy. *The Devil* shows a bizarre and dehumanised mask, not carnivalesque, but sombre and frightening.

The masks led to the depiction of death itself. In *Death and the Maiden* (1950; pencil and watercolour; John Denham Gallery) a winged skeletal death comforts a naked woman crouching in desperation at his feet. In the lyrical *Kiss of Death* (1946; charcoal; artist's estate, Kibbutz Shluchot, repr. Ein Harod 1992) death and a beautiful young woman are seen in a passionate embrace, the maiden having surrendered happily. Death is welcomed as a relief. It is as if an inner reservation was forbidding Meidner to conceive life as too pure a song of joy and beauty. The mood of her work might be summarised as "life in the shadow of death" with a profound awareness of the poetic sadness and transience of life, a tender resignation that is only occasionally slightly bitter.

INES SCHLENKER

Mellis, Margaret
British painter and sculptor, 1914–

Born in Wu-Kung-Fu, China, to Scottish parents, 22 January 1914; came to Britain as an infant. Studied at Edinburgh College of Art under S.J. Peploe, 1929–33; won travelling scholarship, enabling her to study in Paris under André Lhôte, 1933; subsequently travelled to Spain and Italy. Fellowship at Edinburgh College of Art, 1935–7. Worked at Euston Road School, London, 1937–8. Included in *New Movements in Art* at London Museum, 1942; exhibited with St Ives Society of Artists, 1946. Married (1) writer and painter Adrian Stokes, 1938; one son; divorced; (2) collage artist Francis Davison, 1948; he died 1984. Lived in St Ives, Cornwall, 1939–46; Cap d'Antibes, southern France, 1947–50; Syleham, Suffolk, 1950–76; moved to Southwold, Suffolk, 1976. Lives in Southwold.

Selected Individual Exhibitions
AIA Gallery, London: 1958
Scottish Gallery, Edinburgh: 1959
Bear Lane Gallery, Oxford: 1968
Grabowski Gallery, London: 1969
Richard Demarco Gallery, Edinburgh: 1970
Basil Jacobs Gallery, London: 1972
Compass Gallery, Glasgow: 1976
Pier Arts Centre, Stromness, Orkney: 1982
New '57 Gallery, Edinburgh: 1982
Redfern Gallery, London: 1987 (retrospective), 1990, 1994
Peter Pears Gallery, Aldeburgh (Festival Exhibition): 1991

Bibliography
Margaret Mellis, 1940–80: Constructions, Paintings, Reliefs, exh. cat., Pier Arts Centre, Stromness, Orkney, 1982
St Ives, 1939–64: Twenty-Five Years of Painting, Sculpture and Pottery, exh. cat., Tate Gallery, London, 1985
Margaret Mellis, 1940–1987: Constructions in Wood and Paintings, exh. cat., Redfern Gallery, London, 1987
Mel Gooding, "Margaret Mellis", *Art Monthly*, no.107, June 1987, pp.16–17
Scottish Art since 1900, exh. cat., Scottish National Gallery of Modern Art, Edinburgh, and elsewhere, 1989
Margaret Mellis: Relief Constructions and Envelope Drawings, exh. cat., Redfern Gallery, London, 1990
Margaret Mellis, exh. cat., Peter Pears Gallery, Aldeburgh, 1991
Ena Kenday, "A room of my own", *The Observer*, 9 June 1991, magazine
Jean Walsh, "Women's work", *Art Quarterly* (National Art Collections Fund), no.10, Summer 1992, pp.27–31

Margaret Mellis was closely associated with the St Ives group of artists in the years 1939–45. During this period Ben Nicholson, the major pioneer of abstract painting in Britain, influenced her to make non-figurative collages and reliefs that eventually led on after 1978 to the found driftwood constructions that are now recognised as her most significant work.

Mellis's early training at the Edinburgh College of Art under S.J. Peploe, followed by a period working with the Cubist artist André Lhôte in Paris, concentrated her mind on the exploration of colour and form. Her early paintings were chiefly still lifes and landscapes, influenced by the French artists Matisse, Bonnard and Cézanne. A typical work, influenced by Bonnard, is *Regent's Park, London* (artist's collection), in which the landscape, with various coloured elements of trees, path and figure, is tightly constructed from a series of oblongs, vertical and horizontal, in various shades of green. In 1937–8 Mellis spent a year at the Euston Road School but soon realised that its "realistic" approach to landscape and interiors was entirely contrary to the direction she wished to pursue.

In 1939 she moved with her husband Adrian Stokes to St Ives in Cornwall. At the outbreak of World War II they were joined by their friends Ben Nicholson and Barbara Hepworth (q.v.), who together with Peter Lanyon and the Russian Constructivist artist Naum Gabo formed the nucleus of what was later to become the St Ives school. Gabo and Nicholson motivated Mellis to experiment with non-figurative works; and in the period 1940 to 1944 she made about 50 reliefs and collages. The shallow reliefs of geometrical form were made of a variety of materials, and were unpainted, stressing the natural colour and textures of cardboard, wood, marble and slate. The finest and largest piece from this period is *Relief Construction in Wood* (1941; Scottish National Gallery of Modern Art, Edinburgh). The collages incorporated colours and words, pencil and ink, and labels from bottles and other packaging; an example is *Sobranie Collage* (1942; mixed media on board; Tate Gallery, London). Two collages were included in the Constructivist section of the London Museum exhibition *New Movements in Art* in 1942. Featuring chiefly abstract works by St Ives artists as well as Gabo and Mondrian, it was the major avant-garde exhibition of its period in Britain.

After World War II, Mellis abandoned Constructivism in order to concentrate once more on colourful still lifes and landscapes. She moved to the south of France and then with her second husband Francis Davison to Syleham near Diss, Suffolk. In addition to bold flower paintings she began a new series known as "Dead flower" studies. Examples are *Blue Anemones* (Tate Gallery, London) and *Seeding Flowers* (Arts Council of Great Britain), both oil on Essex board, dated 1957. *Seeding Flowers* features simplified poppy heads with erect and drooping stalks forming a rhythmic pattern silhouetted against the flat abstract shapes of the glasses and table. The sombre, elegiac mood reappears in a totally different form in the later *Resurrection* wood constructions, demonstrating Mellis's ability to articulate both melancholy and joyful cadences from simple arrangements of shapes and colours.

In 1963 Mellis began making abstract colour structures, some very large, in pure colours with soft edges in oils, first on hardboard and afterwards on canvas, for example, *Two Circles (Red, Blue, Yellow, Violet and White)* (1964; Arts Council of Great Britain), where the composition is composed of bright patches of colour and white in square, triangular and semicircular shapes. In the earlier works colour was used intuitively, but Mellis then experimented with deliberate colour arrangements in hard-edged style. The works of this period were related to the current trends of Op Art and American Abstract Expressionism. They were followed in the early 1970s by the attempt to make small compositions as powerful as large ones. For these, Mellis returned to relief and colour, building out from a small area using shallow layers of wood and paint in a development from the Constructivist works of the 1940s.

The move with Francis Davison to Southwold by the sea in Suffolk in 1976 led to Mellis's discovery of the ideal medium

Mellis: *Drowned Head*, 1989; driftwood construction; 58.4 × 39.4 × 10.16 cm.; artist's collection, Manor House Museum, Bury St Edmunds, Suffolk

in which to express her feelings for colour and form. Finding a knob of driftwood painted bright red on the beach in 1978 resulted in the idea for driftwood constructions, on which she began to concentrate more seriously in 1980. Several were exhibited for the first time at the Pier Art Centre, Stromness, in 1982. Pieces are selected for their size, shape and texture, but also for their colour, particularly the remnants of fishing vessels, which reveal various layers of brightly coloured peeling paint. The artist selects, always intuitively, the pieces required, which are then screwed together to form the construction. Some pieces are designed to be wall-hung, and others viewed in the round. In the conception period Mellis is concerned solely with arrangements of colour and form, solid and void, and the earliest pieces were simply given number titles, for example, the large, mainly blue *Number Thirty-Five* (1982; Tate Gallery). Increasingly, however, the works have been given figurative connotations, often allusions to the seascape from which they have come.

Mellis has described her working method in connection with *Bog Man* (1990; artist's collection, repr. London 1990). It was constructed from the remains of a boat skeleton that she observed over a period of time as it lay in her studio. Having eventually conceived the abstract form it should take, she worked fast screwing the component parts together, and then realised that it "looked like a kind of man ... I had no idea he would be a Bog Man when I started". Conversely, some "found" pieces are spontaneously recognised for the form they will eventually take. *Drowned Head* (1989; see illustration) resulted from a walk on the beach when the artist suddenly saw "two strange eyes with protruding pupils staring at me from the bottom of a pool".

After the death of her husband in 1984, Mellis began a new type of wood construction, now termed the *Resurrection* series. These also combine natural and painted pieces of driftwood but feature saints and angels, simplified "skittle" shapes, the figures often juxtaposed against the void in the wood from which they have been cut out with an electric saw. Unlike some of the other more complex and zestful constructions, they display a stillness and simplicity reminiscent of early Italian art, for example, *Temptation* (1986; Arts Council of Great Britain). Apart from the wood constructions from 1987, Mellis produced the series of "Envelope" drawings that consist of chalk drawings of flowers on opened-out envelopes. The different sizes, shapes, colours and patterns of the envelopes, and the fact that the flowers are always changing, have provided an unending source of inspiration, for example, *Purple Colchicum – Purple Envelope* (1989; artist's collection, repr. Aldeburgh 1991). Summing up her career to date, Patrick Heron commented: "the great optimism which dedication to sheer colour and form always generates in painting is a permanent characteristic of all Margaret's work of whatever period" (London 1987).

CHRISTOPHER REEVE

Mengs, Theresa Concordia *see* Maron-Mengs

Meredith, Louisa Anne
Australian painter, illustrator and writer, 1812–1895

Born Louisa Anne Twamley in Birmingham, England, 20 July 1812. Received some tuition in the painting of miniature portraits from Sir Thomas Lawrence. Supported herself by writing and illustrating books by age 21; also took over father's job as Corn Inspector for Birmingham after his death in 1835. Married Charles Meredith, a cousin, in Edgbaston, 1839; four sons, three surviving infancy, born 1840, 1841, 1844 and 1847; husband died 1880. Emigrated to Australia, 1839, staying in New South Wales before settling at Swan Vale in the Swan Port district of Van Diemen's Land (now Tasmania). Helped support husband in his subsequent political career with the income from her books. Granted an annual pension of £100 by Tasmanian government for distinguished literary and artistic services to colony, 1884. Subsequently retired to Melbourne after financial losses. Member of the Royal Birmingham Society of Artists; honorary member, Royal Society of Tasmania. Died in Melbourne, 21 October 1895.

Principal Exhibitions
Royal Birmingham Society of Artists: occasionally 1829–38
Great Exhibition, London: 1851 (prize)
International Exhibition, London: 1862 (bronze medal)
Intercolonial Exhibition, Melbourne: 1866 (silver medal, "art combined with literature"), 1880
Intercolonial Exhibition, Sydney: 1870 (bronze medal)
International Exhibition, Calcutta: 1884 (award)

Selected Writings
(as Twamley, afterwards Meredith)
Poems, 1835
The Romance of Nature; or, the Flower Seasons Illustrated, 1836
Notes and Sketches of New South Wales During a Residence in that Colony from 1839 to 1844, London: Murray, 1844
My Home in Tasmania During a Residence of Nine Years, 2 vols, London: Murray, 1852
Some of My Bush Friends in Tasmania: Native Flowers, Berries and Insects, London: Day, 1860 (first series), *Bush Friends in Tasmania*, 1891 (second series)
Over the Straits: A Visit to Victoria, London: Chapman and Hall, 1861
Tasmanian Friends and Foes, Feathered, Furred and Finned, London: Ward, 1880

Bibliography
Mercury, 8 January 1885; 7 July 1886 (G.T. Stilwell)
M. Swann, "Mrs Meredith and Miss Atkinson, writers and naturalists", *Journal of the Royal Australian Historical Society*, xv/1, 1929, pp.1–29
Early Art in Tasmania: Souvenir of Art, Antique and Historical Exhibition, exh. cat., Hobart, 1931
J.M. Buchanan, *Mrs Charles Meredith: A Biography, 1812–1895*, MA thesis, University of Melbourne, 1950
K.R. von Stieglitz, *Six Pioneer Women of Tasmania*, Launceston: Telegraph, 1956
Australian Art in the 1870s, exh. cat., Art Gallery of New South Wales, Sydney, 1976
Marcie Muir, *Australian Children's Book Illustrators*, Melbourne: Sun Books, 1977
Vivienne Rae Ellis, *Louisa Anne Meredith: A Tigress in Exile*, Sandy Bay, Tasmania: Blubber Head Press, 1979 (contains bibliography)

Janine Burke, *Australian Women Artists, 1840–1940*, Collingwood, Victoria: Greenhouse, 1980

Nicolette Scourse, *The Victorians and Their Flowers*, London: Croom Helm, and Portland, OR: Timber Press, 1983

Bernard Smith, *European Vision and the South Pacific*, 2nd edition, New Haven and London: Yale University Press, 1985

Shades of Light: Photography and Australia, exh. cat., Australian National Gallery, Canberra, 1988

Caroline Clemente, "Artists in society: A Melbourne circle, 1850s–1880s", *Art Bulletin of Victoria*, no.30, 1989, pp.40–57

Louisa Anne Meredith's importance to colonial Australia lies in her many creative abilities. She was not only a miniaturist, watercolourist, engraver and illustrator but also a poet, writer, botanist and early conservationist. Her contribution to the development of cultural life in the colonies can hardly be overestimated, because Meredith approached everything with the energy and determination of ten people.

Despite the financial and social difficulties of her family situation, Louisa, when only a child of ten, could paint a competent miniature of her aunt Sara (a copy after Peat, private collection) as well as drawing, painting, writing poetry and stories and playing the piano. She evidently took lessons in miniature painting from Sir Thomas Lawrence, possibly a family friend, shortly before his death in 1830, and by the time she was 18 had entered the world of blue-stocking Birmingham, claiming such friends as William and Mary Howitt and W.G. Lewis, the editor of the radical paper, the *Birmingham Journal*. Although at the time she described her career derogatorily as "artist and scribbler", she was able to support herself through her portrait painting with additional income from reviewing new novels and writing articles for the *Birmingham Journal*. Her extant miniatures (private collection, repr. Ellis 1979, p.50) from this early period are precociously good and it seems likely that this medium was later abandoned by her only because of the excessive demands it made on her already weakened sight. In February 1835, while also earning an income as Corn Inspector of Birmingham (a position her uncle held in name), her first book, *Poems*, was published. It contained six copper engravings of picturesque views around Tintern Abbey and Kenilworth Castle, as well as 40 poems in the Romantic style popularised by Wordsworth. Less than a year later this was followed by a second book of poems, *The Romance of Nature*, which contained no fewer than 26 coloured illustrations of flowers, a publishing feat that set new standards. The book sold well and went into three editions.

Altogether in this period Louisa published three more books, though some included previously published poems. During this time she also regularly exhibited her miniature paintings with the Royal Birmingham Society of Artists, though suffering more and more with eye problems that were no doubt exacerbated by the close work. At the height of her fame, Leigh Hunt, the writer and critic, wrote glowingly of her talented etchings and later dedicated a verse of his poem entitled *Blue Stocking Revels* of the *Feast of the Violets* to "young Twamley/nice sensitive thing/whose pen and whose pencil/give promise like spring", while the critic for the London *Athenaeum* wrote that "the poems are sweet and elegant, and some of them possess much originality of manner, and glow of language ..." (4 April 1835, p.264).

On the brink then of what seemed a brilliant literary and artistic career, Louisa accepted a proposal of marriage from her cousin Charles Meredith and went with him to Van Diemen's Land (now Tasmania). Many years later she would write of this decision: "I was born under an evil star, or put myself under one, in quitting England in the first instance" (Louisa Anne Meredith to Sir Henry Parkes, 18 June 1893, Mitchell Library, Sydney). After settling in Australia, Charles lost most of his money in the economic depression of the 1840s and Louisa turned once again to her own talents to make money for the family, publishing a book with the slightly misleading title of *Notes and Sketches of New South Wales During a Residence in that Colony from 1839 to 1844*. A carefully observed book, it was highly critical of Sydney society and caused something of a publishing sensation, being reprinted three times in the next few years. Although she did not illustrate this volume, she went on to publish a further 14 books, a mixture of travel writing, poetry, fiction and natural history, most of them illustrated by Louisa alone or in collaboration with others. Nevertheless, she considered herself to be a writer first and artist second and was always modest about her illustrative abilities. Her writing is not only an invaluable source of information on the colonies at that time but paved the way for the popularity of women's autobiographical writing – her travel stories, rich as they are in the detailed observation of human behaviour, are equally so in their personal disclosure and use of memoir as a literary device. Fastidious about accuracy, Meredith was frequently disappointed by the errors in the illustrations in many of the books after they had been sent back from their London publishers – the distance only adding to the frustration. They remain, however, among the best examples of a lavish era in illustrated books. For example, *Some of My Bush Friends in Tasmania* (1860 and 1891) was dedicated to Queen Victoria and was sumptuously bound, exceeding all previous publishing in the colony. And, despite her own views of her work, her botanical drawings continued to improve in both their accuracy and composition and by the 1860s Meredith was regularly winning medals at the large intercolonial and international exhibitions for her botanical watercolours. At their best, they are witty as well as accurate, incorporating her keen observations of human behaviour with often quite beautiful drawing and colouring. *A Cool Debate* (see illustration), from the 1891 edition of *Bush Friends*, for example, illustrates four frogs, perched on lily pads in a pond, croaking out a question-and-answer spoof of a political kind to which, no doubt, Meredith was no stranger. Examples of her work may be found in Hobart (Allport Library and Museum of Fine Arts; Van Diemen's Land Folk Museum; Royal Society of Tasmania; Meredith collection in Tasmanian Museum and Art Gallery), Launceston (Queen Victoria Museum and Art Gallery) and Sydney (Mitchell Library).

As well as being occupied with her family and her work, Meredith participated in the local theatrical scene, producing and performing in plays, concerts, masques and poetry readings, for the entertainment of the people and the benefit of local charities. She was still giving public recitals – to great acclaim – well into her eighties. This may seem a small achievement but in fact was vital to life in such a new and raw society. She brought an intellectualism that was otherwise lacking. She was a designer, lyricist and may even have been active as a

Meredith: *A Cool Debate, c.*1891; watercolour highlighted with gold and Chinese white; 27 × 38 cm.; Tasmanian Museum and Art Gallery, Hobart; Royal Society of Tasmania Collection

photographer, although there is no evidence of this. Having witnessed, however, a demonstration of "sun-printing" in 1839 in Oxford, she remained interested in the process and was instrumental in organising the many photographs of the disappearing tribes of Tasmanian Aborigines being taken in the 1860s and 1870s. An enthusiastic naturalist, she corresponded with notable scientists in Britain and Europe about the speci-mens she had collected (her collection of seaweeds is held at the University of Tasmania); and she continued to raise public awareness of the need to protect and cherish the environment and native animals, although, like many of her generation, she held to deeply racist views on indigenous people all her life.

By her own admission, ambitious and determined, she had a restless energy that drove her on through all the hardships of her life. In 1884 Meredith was granted a special government pension of £100 a year for her services to science, literature and art. In 1832, while she was busily engaged in preparing for her first publication, her uncle George, her future father-in-law, had written to Louisa inviting her to come to Van Diemen's Land as governess to his children. Aghast at the notion she had replied:

> Where would my literature be in Van Diemen's Land? Writing sonnets to whales and porpoises, canzonets to kangaroos, madrigals to 'prime merinos' and dirges to

black swans, illustrated by portraits of the engaging and lovely natives? [Where] would be all the literary papers, periodicals, new music, new engravings, etc. etc. with which I am now enlivened, amused and excited to "go and do likewise"? [Louisa Ann Twamley to George Meredith, 18 May 1833].

CANDICE BRUCE

Merian, Maria Sibylla
German painter, 1647–1717

Born in Frankfurt am Main, 2 April 1647, youngest daughter of the draughtsman, printmaker and publisher Matthäus Merian the Elder (d. 1650). Taught the art of flower painting by her stepfather, the still-life painter Jacob Marell, and his assistants Johann Andreas Graff and Abraham Mignon. Married Graff, 16 May 1665; two daughters, Johanna Helena, baptised in Frankfurt, 5 May 1668, and Dorothea Maria, baptised in Nuremberg, 2 February 1678. Moved to Nuremberg, 1670; taught the art of flower painting to unmarried women. Returned to Frankfurt, 1682. Separated from husband in 1685; with her daughters and mother joined half-brother Caspar Merian in the Labadist community of Den Bosch castle in Wieuwerd, West Friesland, Netherlands, 1685–6. Settled in Amsterdam with her daughters, 1691; lived by selling natural history paintings, colouring copies of the caterpillar book and providing illustrations for books, including Agnes Block's *Groot Konst Boek* and Georg Everhard Rumpf's *D'Amboinsche Rariteitkamer*, Amsterdam, 1705. Sailed with Dorothea Maria to Dutch colony of Surinam, South America, where they studied the metamorphoses of tropical insects on their fodder plants, June 1699–September 1701. Died in Amsterdam, 13 January 1717.

Selected Writings

Neues Blumenbuch, 3 vols, Nuremberg, 1675–80; facsimile edition with text by Helmut Deckert, Leipzig, 1966

Der Raupen wunderbare Verwandelung und sonderbare Blumennahrung, 3 vols, 1679–1717; part facsimile edition with text by Armin Geus, Dortmund, 1982

Metamorphosis insectorum surinamensium, Amsterdam: G. Valk, 1705; facsimile editions, Leipzig, 1975 (commentary by Helmut Deckert); 2 vols, London: Pion, 1980–82 (commentary by Elisabeth Rücker); Frankfurt am Main: Insel, 1991

Erucarum ortus: Alimentum et paradoxa metamorphosis ..., Amsterdam, 1718

Butterflies, Beetles and Other Insects: The Leningrad Book of Notes and Studies, ed. Wolf-Dietrich Beer and others, New York: McGraw Hill, 1976 (German original)

Bibliography

Joachim von Sandrart, *L'Academia todesca della architectura, scultura e pittura: Oder Teutsche Academie der edlen Bau-, Bild- und Mahlerey-künste*, Nuremberg, i, 1675, p.339; ii, 1679, p.85; ed. A.R. Peltzer, Munich, 1925; reprinted Farnborough: Gregg, 1971

Arnold Houbraken, *De groote Schouburgh der Nederlantsche Konstschilders en Schilderessen*, iii, Amsterdam, 1721, pp.173–6

Johann Gabriel Doppelmayr, *Historische Nachricht von den Nürnbergischen Mathematicis und Künstlern*, Nuremberg, 1730, pp.255, 268–70

Heinrich Sebastian Hüsgen, *Artistisches Magazin*, Frankfurt am Main, 1790, pp.263–73

Friedrich Carl Gottlob Hirsching, *Historisch-Literarisches Handbuch berühmter und denkwürdiger Personen*, v, Leipzig, 1800–01, pp.271–8

Philipp Friedrich Gwinner, *Kunst und Künstler in Frankfurt am Main*, Frankfurt am Main, 1862, pp.168–74

Max Adolf Pfeiffer, "Das neue Blumenbuch der M.S. Merian", *Philiobiblon*, ix, 1936, pp.97–102

Jantje Stuldreher-Nienhuis, *Verborgen Paradijzen: Het leven en de werken van Maria Sibylla Merian, 1647–1717*, Arnhem, 1944; 2nd edition, 1945; abridged edition, Arnhem and Amsterdam, 1952

Margarete Pfister-Burkhalter, "Florum Fasciculi Tres", *Stultifera Navis*, iv, 1947, pp.114–25

"A Surinam portfolio", *Natural History*, lxxi/10, 1962, pp.30–41

Maria Sibylla Merian, 1647–1717, exh. cat., Germanisches Nationalmuseum, Nuremberg, 1967

Ernst Ullmann and others, eds, *Maria Sibylla Merian: Leningrad Watercolors*, 2 vols, New York: Harcourt Brace, 1974 (German original)

William T. Stearn, ed., *The Wondrous Transformation of Caterpillars: Fifty Engravings Selected from Erucarum Ortus*, London: Scolar Press, 1978

A. Tatiana Lukina, *Maria Sibylla Merian, 1647–1717*, Leningrad: Nauka, 1980

Margarete Pfister-Burkhalter, *Maria Sibylla Merian: Leben und Werk, 1647–1717*, Basel: GS Verlag, 1980

Maria Sibylla Merian (1647–1717), exh. cat., Rosenborg Slot, Copenhagen, 1983

Ingrid Guentherodt, "Maria Cunitz und Maria Sibylla Merian: Pionierinnen der deutschen Wissenschaftssprache im 17. Jahrhundert", *Zeitschrift für Germanistische Linguistik*, xiv/1, 1986, pp.23–49

Charlotte Kerner, *Seidenraupe, Dschungelblüte: Die Lebensgeschichte der Maria Sibylla Merian*, Basel: Weinheim, 1988

Flowers, Butterflies and Insects, New York: Dover, and London: Constable, 1991

Natalie Zemon Davis, *Women on the Margins: Three Seventeenth-Century Lives*, Cambridge, MA: Harvard University Press, 1995

Heidrun Ludwig, "Von der Betrachtung zur Beobachtung: Die künstlerische Entwicklung der Blumen- und Insektenmalerin M.S. Merian in Nürnberg (1670–1682)", *Der Franken Rom*, ed. John Roger Paas, Wiesbaden, 1995, pp.95–113

The importance of Maria Sibylla Merian is based on a specific, perhaps feminine synthesis of natural history and art, of an observant and at the same time contemplative view of nature. During her years in Amsterdam and in the course of the 18th century, Merian's accomplishments were seen mainly as contributing to the field of entomology. In the 19th and early 20th centuries her discoveries no longer attracted attention, and the interest in her shifted from science to art. The image of a harmless and gentle flower painter, absorbed in the meditation of butterflies and flowers, concealed her merits as a natural historian. More recently, historians, natural scientists and linguists have tried to see Merian in her historical context and have rediscovered her achievements in the field of natural history as well as in the history of art of the second half of the 17th century.

As a member of a family of artists, Merian had access to a workshop where she received basic training as a painter – although as a woman she was severely restricted in her education by guild regulations. Joachim von Sandrart mentioned oil paintings by Merian but none has as yet come to light. Since only licensed painters were allowed to paint in oil, it is probable that Merian was restricted to body- and watercolour painting, a technique that was then regarded as appropriate for amateur painters and for women who were not able to receive an official training. Like her stepfather, Jacob Marell, Merian specialised in still lifes. That she was also an expert in the textile arts, in painted and embroidered fabrics with designs of flowers and the metamorphoses of insects, sheds light on her early work. In the manner of embroiderers she composed her pictures by adding and arranging motifs that she had copied from engravings or drawn from life; as a result, motifs are often repeated in her early works. The close affinity that Merian saw between painting and embroidery is expressed in her first publication, the *Neues Blumenbuch*, a pattern book containing 36 engravings of flowers.

Merian painted pictures of flowers and fruits, enlivening them with butterflies and insects, as was customary in Dutch and German still-life painting. In Nuremberg she started to develop the art of natural history painting. It now seemed insufficient merely to copy natural objects and to place them into artificially composed art works. Like the Dutch still-life painter Otto Marseus van Schrieck, she started to breed her models. With the assistance of her husband Johann Andreas

Merian: *Blue Hyacinth (Arctia caja Linnaeus)* (Book of Prints 198* b.6., Bibl.Sloane 5276 PLUT); British Museum, London

Graff she collected native insects, fed them and observed their metamorphoses. In 1679 she published some of her observations in the first part of the caterpillar book, *Der Raupen wunderbare Verwandelung und sondebare Blumennahrung*, which contains 50 plates with descriptions. The phenomena of metamorphosis had already been discovered and explored, but Merian's book for the first time showed the metamorphoses on those plants from which caterpillars drew their nourishment. By depicting plants and insects, Merian was able to combine her experience as a flower painter with her interest in natural history. Her approach to the observation of nature was not limited to the single phenomenon or to dried specimens. Instead, she tried to understand the overall correlation of living nature and its relation to God.

Scholars received Merian's caterpillar book and her insect and flower paintings favourably. Although the extraordinary beauty and the careful rendering of nature in her works attracted admiration, they were far from causing a sensation. Merian's international reputation as a learned woman and as a natural historian was founded largely on her expedition to Surinam, a Dutch colony in South America. Many European collectors owned dried specimens from Surinam, but the fauna and flora of this tropical country were barely explored. Merian and her younger daughter Dorothea Maria took the risk of the

voyage and used the opportunity to observe the beautiful exotic insects and their fodder plants. Furthermore, they studied the customs of the native people, and tried to improve their conditions by looking at their plants and finding an economic use for them. After two years Merian, who suffered from malaria, had to return to Amsterdam. There she started to work on a book about the metamorphoses of the Surinam insects. Investing large amounts of money in the publication, she employed professional engravers for the large-sized plates done after her paintings. She wrote the descriptions herself, but the director of the Amsterdam botanical garden, Caspar Commelin, determined the species of the plants. The appearance of the *Metamorphosis insectorum surinamensium* in 1705 caused a sensation. The beautiful, life-size plates showed the exotic insects in previously unpublished states and in their natural surroundings. The 62 plates and the careful descriptions kindled the imagination of natural history collectors, who knew the species only from dried specimens.

As an artist and as a natural historian, Merian devoted her art and experience to an aim that she shared with many artists and scientists of the time. She believed that natural phenomena could only be understood with regard to God. While she observed nature, admired its beauty and was astonished by its wonders, she always set her observations in relation to men and to God. She shared the Protestant view of her time that God had created the beauties of nature not only for its reproduction, but also for humankind, in order to make men respect and praise him. From this point of view Merian's paintings might be considered Protestant adoration pictures.

Early flower pieces by Merian are kept in the Kupferstichkabinett, Staatliche Preussischer Kulturbesitz, Berlin, and in Rosenborg Castle, Copenhagen. The Academy of Sciences in St Petersburg possesses Merian's entomological study book, as well as a large collection of her flower paintings. There are insect pieces by her and by her daughter Johanna Helena Graff in the British Museum, London. Paintings from Surinam that relate to the published book can be found in the British Museum and in the Royal Collection, Windsor Castle. The Fitzwilliam Museum, Cambridge, the Städelsches Kunstinstitut, Frankfurt am Main, and the Albertina, Vienna, own smaller collections of her gouaches.

HEIDRUN LUDWIG

Merritt, Anna Lea
American painter and printmaker, 1844–1930

Born Anna Massey Lea in Philadelphia, 1844, into a Quaker family. Studied anatomy at Women's Medical College, Philadelphia. Moved to Europe with her family, 1865; stayed in Florence and Rome, then Paris; took private lessons in Dresden with Heinrich Hoffman, professor at the Dresden Academy, winter 1869–70; left Dresden due to outbreak of Franco-Prussian war, and settled in London. Took a studio in Devonshire Street and studied under Henry Merritt, c.1871. Married Merritt, April 1877; he died July 1877. Lived in Britain for the rest of her life, making frequent return visits to USA, and visiting Ireland, Belgium and Egypt. Moved to

Hurstbourne Tarrant, Dorset, 1890–91. Member, Royal Society of Painters and Etchers. Died in Hurstbourne Tarrant, 7 April 1930.

Principal Exhibitions

Pennsylvania Academy of the Fine Arts, Philadelphia: occasionally 1867–1924
Royal Academy, London: occasionally 1871–1917
Centennial Exposition, Philadelphia: 1876 (diploma and medals)
Grosvenor Gallery, London: 1879, 1881, 1883–4
National Academy of Design, New York: 1881
Paris Salon: 1883
New Gallery, London: 1887–90
Union League Club, New York: 1888 (*Women Etchers of America*)
Exposition Universelle, Paris: 1889 (honourable mention)
World's Columbian Exposition, Chicago: 1893 (award and medal)
Pan-American Exposition, Buffalo, NY: 1901 (award)
Royal Society of British Artists, London: 1902–5

Selected Writings

Henry Merritt: Art Criticism and Romance, 2 vols, 1879
"A talk about painting", *St Nicholas*, xii/1, 1884, pp.85–92
"Mural painting by the aid of soluble silicates and metallic oxides, with examples chiefly from St Martin's, Wonersh", *Journal of the Society of Arts*, xliv, 5 December 1895, pp.39–51 (with Professor Roberts-Austen)
"A letter to artists: Especially women artists", *Lippincott's Monthly Magazine*, lxv, 1900, pp.463–9; reprinted in *Love Locked Out* 1982
A Hamlet in Old Hampshire, 1902
An Artist's Garden: Tended, Painted, Described, 1908
"My journey through life from 1844 to 1924", manuscript, 1924, Victoria and Albert Museum, London
Love Locked Out: The Memoirs of Anna Lea Merritt, ed. Galina Gorokhoff, Boston: Museum of Fine Arts, 1982

Bibliography

Walter Shaw Sparrow, ed., *Women Painters of the World*, London: Hodder and Stoughton, and New York: Stokes, 1905; reprinted New York: Hacker, 1976
Austin Chester, "The art of Anna Lea Merritt", *Windsor Magazine*, xxxviii, 1913, pp.605–20
New York Times, 9 April 1930 (obituary)
Winchester Magazine, June 1930 (obituary)
Galina Gorokhoff, "Anna Lea Merritt: Expatriate American painter", *Magazine Antiques*, cxxiii, 1983, pp.1221–7
Pamela Gerrish Nunn, ed., *Canvassing Women: Recollections by Six Victorian Women Artists*, London: Camden, 1986
——, *Victorian Women Artists*, London: Women's Press, 1987
Wendy Slatkin, *The Voices of Women Artists*, Englewood Cliffs, NJ: Prentice Hall, 1993

Born into an affluent as well as prominent Quaker family from Philadelphia, Anna Lea was the eldest of six sisters. Well-educated for a female of the period, she studied both at the progressive Eagleswood School in Bryn Mawr, Pennsylvania, and later in a pre-collegiate setting at the Agassiz School in Cambridge, Massachusetts. She started drawing lessons at the age of seven, although she did not receive much formal art instruction. As a child she saw William Holman Hunt's *Light of the World*, a version of which was shown in a touring exhibition of British Art in 1857–8, and this influenced her work entitled *I Will Give You Rest* (1890; untraced). Before leaving for Europe with her family in 1865 after the end of the American Civil War, she enrolled in a special class at the

Women's Medical College in Philadelphia in order to learn more about anatomy. Lea travelled extensively throughout Europe and received private critiques of her work (due to the exclusion of women students in art academies) both in Dresden from Heinrich Hoffman and in Florence from Stefano Ussi. Largely self-taught, she worked briefly with Léon Cogniet in Paris before fleeing from the Franco-Prussian War and coming via Basel to Britain. There Lea also took some private lessons from Alphonse Legros. Like many Victorian women artists, her training/output included a stint as a copyist, an endeavour encouraged by the Pre-Raphaelite artist John Everett Millais, to whom Lea had been given an introduction.

At about this time, in 1871, Lea met and became the pupil of a British painter and picture restorer named Henry Merritt, who first served as her mentor and then became her husband. Henry Merritt exclusively oversaw her studies and the direction of her work, recommending, for example, that she produce only portraits, not genre pictures, although in time the latter would earn her success and a measure of fame and fortune. His influence was powerful, almost suffocating, and Anna Lea considered abandoning her career after their marriage. His death only three months after they wed altered these circumstances, however, and in widowhood she began to produce prolifically and intensely. In homage to her deceased husband, she wrote *Henry Merritt: Art Criticism and Romance* (1879), an idolising biography (plus some of her spouse's writings) illustrated with 23 of her etchings. She later continued working in this medium and was praised by the art critic Mariana van Rensselaer, S.R. Koehler and others for her talent as an etcher.

By the 1870s Merritt was thus an expatriate in her adopted homeland, although she regularly returned to Philadelphia for visits, sometimes with a sister. She continued to exhibit in both countries and found American as well as British sitters and patrons of her work. Elected a member of the Royal Society of Painters and Etchers, she executed numerous portrait commissions, especially earlier in her career. Portraiture served as a financial mainstay at this time, and her distinguished subjects included Oliver Wendell Holmes, Ellen Terry, James Russell Lowell, Sir William Boxall, Horace Howard Furness, Henry Gurdon Marquand, Mary Tileston Hemenway, General John Adams Dix and Hugh McCullough.

In America her art was on view with some regularity at the renowned Pennsylvania Academy of the Fine Arts, which purchased *Piping Shepherd* of 1896. The Avery Galleries in New York also displayed her works and in 1888 she exhibited 33 etchings in New York at an exhibition entitled *Work of the Women Etchers of America* sponsored by the Union League Club. (She also travelled to Ottawa, Canada, in 1876 to execute a portrait commission of the *Countess of Dufferin*.) More importantly, however, in America her art was included both in the Centennial Exposition in Philadelphia (1876) and at the World's Columbian Exposition in Chicago (1893). *St Genevieve* (untraced) and *A Patrician Mother* (Hudson River Museum, Yonkers, NY), both of 1875, won accolades for the artist at the Centennial. One of her portraits for that venture was praised by a critic in *Frank Leslie's Illustrated Historical Register* (1876, p.185) for its evidence of "absolute genius" and "forceful mastery of technique". In 1893 Merritt blended her personal allegiances by exhibiting *Eve Overcome by*

Merritt: *Love Locked Out*, 1889; Tate Gallery, London

primarily from 1878 to 1893, although her first work was accepted in 1871 and her last in 1917. She also sporadically contributed to the Grosvenor Gallery and the New Gallery in London, both avant-garde sites where many women artists were invited to participate, confirming the success and stature that Merritt had attained as a professional in her field. Living in London at various addresses (at one point on Cheyne Walk, Chelsea), Merritt was able to meet many of the most celebrated contemporary artists, notably William Holman Hunt, Edward Burne-Jones, Lawrence Alma-Tadema, Charles W. Cope, George F. Watts, James McNeill Whistler, Frederic Leighton, George Henry Boughton, Frank Dicksee, William Powell Frith, George Cruikshank and fellow expatriate Edwin Austin Abbey, as well as innumerable writers and critics.

In 1890 *Love Locked Out* (1889; see illustration) became the first painting by a woman artist to be purchased by the Chantrey Bequest for the national collection. At about the same time, for health reasons Merritt settled into a thatched cottage called The Limes, which was situated in the Hampshire village of Hurstbourne Tarrant. It was only after she moved to Hampshire that the artist began to paint landscapes, primarily views of the region. Her flower garden also inspired at least one still life, although many of the landscapes of her later years included floral elements. Merritt wrote and illustrated two books about this picturesque village. *A Hamlet in Old Hampshire* (1902) chronicled her life in Hurstbourne Tarrant, while *An Artist's Garden* of six years later focused on its garden environment. She lived and went to church in this area until the end of her life, ceasing to exhibit in London after World War I and becoming blind in her final years.

In 1900 her article entitled "A letter to artists: Especially women artists" offered some telling advice about the challenges facing women in the profession. Noting financial insecurity and other hardships, Merritt cited that "the great obstacles to [women's] success" were "thriftiness, industry, altruism – these qualities are not art qualities". Despite her unwillingness to acknowledge bias against "lady painters", she none the less mused about how different life might be if women artists had wives as helpmates or, as she succinctly commented: "The chief obstacle to a woman's success is that she can never have a wife". On whether women's talents equalled those of men, she remarked: "The inequality observed in women's work is generally the result of untoward domestic accidents". In general, however, her opinions (also, for example, about Post-Impressionist canvases) reflected a conservative viewpoint and comments about her own achievements tended to be self-deprecating, both in published accounts and in the unpublished autobiographical manuscript entitled "My journey through life from 1844 to 1924" (Victoria and Albert Museum, London) that she wrote in 1924.

Among her women patrons was Mrs Warren de la Rue, who commissioned *Romeo and Juliet* (untraced) in 1883. Merritt also received some mural commissions, for example to provide a series of religious subjects (completed 1895) for St Martin's, Chilworth, near Wonersh in Surrey. Besides her most famous painting, *Love Locked Out*, Merritt's other notable work was *War* (Bury City Museum and Art Gallery) of 1883, a critically acclaimed canvas that indicts war through its focus on the suffering women left behind to deal with the consequences. Stylistically, Merritt's work was not avant-garde but typically

Remorse (which won a medal) in the British section at the Exposition, and a portrait and a replica of *Love Locked Out* in the American section. Perhaps her greatest achievement at this event was the three decorative panels on the theme of women's occupations (needlework, education, charity) that she executed for the foyer of the Woman's Building. That edifice and its contents were a benchmark and symbol of female creativity that included the works of hundreds of women, from Mary Cassatt (q.v.) and Mary Fairchild MacMonnies (q.v.) to anonymous contributors of handicrafts. This opportunity, moreover, enabled her to meet other women artists, such as Annie Swynnerton (q.v.), who shared the mural commission with her. Merritt also sent paintings to other world's fairs: *Camilla, a Nymph of Diana* (1882; untraced), for example, received an honourable mention at the Paris Exposition Universelle of 1889.

In Britain Merritt exhibited at the Royal Academy

academic in look and content. Some of her portraits offer quite solid characterisations of men and especially women of the period, and *Love Locked Out* reveals a handling of anatomical detail and modelling of the nude male child that is outstanding among her works. While some of Merritt's classicising images could be rather lacklustre, *War* (1883) and its "masculine" subject reveal an unusual (if covert) awareness of contemporary political issues, that is, presenting female responses to war at a time when Britain was waging a military campaign and had occupation forces in Egypt. Other significant paintings include the *Pied Piper of Hamelin* (1872; Cheltenham Ladies' College), *Ophelia* (1880; Robert P. Coale Collection, Chicago), *Watchers of the Straight Gate* (1894; La Salle College Art Museum, Philadelphia) and the *Shipley Sisters* (1902; Shipley School, Bryn Mawr, PA). In general, Merritt's career and art have been better known in Britain than in America, largely due to the greater number of individual paintings there, but recent scholarship has begun to re-examine her paintings as well as her place in the history of 19th-century art.

SUSAN P. CASTERAS

Messager, Annette
French artist, 1943–

Born in Berck-sur-Mer, 30 November 1943. Studied at the Ecole Nationale Supérieure des Arts Décoratifs, Paris, 1962–6. Recipient of first prize, Kodak Photography International, 1964; Grand Prix, Ville de Paris, and Grand Prix des Arts Plastiques, 1994. Teaches at Ecole Nationale des Beaux-Arts, Paris. Lives in Paris.

Selected Individual Exhibitions
Musée de Peinture et de Sculpture, Grenoble: 1973, 1989–90 (touring retrospective)
Musée d'Art Moderne de la Ville de Paris: 1974, 1984 , 1995
Rheinisches Landesmuseum, Bonn: 1976, 1978
Holly Solomon Gallery, New York: 1978
Galerie Gillespie-Laage Salomon, Paris: 1979, 1985
Fine Arts Gallery, University of California, Berkeley: 1981
PS 1, Long Island City, NY: 1981
Artists' Space, New York: 1981
Musée des Beaux-Arts, Calais: 1983
Riverside Studios, London: 1985
Artspace Visual Arts Centre, Surrey Hills, Australia: 1986
Vancouver Art Gallery, Vancouver: 1987, 1991
Centre d'Art Contemporain, Dijon: 1988
Galerie Crousel-Robelin Bama, Paris: 1990
Mercer Union, Toronto: 1991 (*Making Up Stories/Faire des histoires*, touring)
Arnolfini, Bristol: 1992 (*Telling Tales*, touring)
Josh Baer Gallery, New York: 1992, 1993
Monika Sprüth Galerie, Cologne: 1992, 1994
Foksal Gallery, Warsaw: 1995
Los Angeles County Museum of Art: 1995 (touring)

Bibliography
Barbara Radice, "Annette Messager", *Flash Art*, June 1974 (interview)

Annette Messager: Chimères, 1982–1983, exh. cat., Musée des Beaux-Arts, Calais, 1983
Annette Messager: Les Pièges à chimères, exh. cat., Musée d'Art Moderne de la Ville de Paris, 1984
Annette Messager: Comédie, Tragédie, 1971–1989, exh. cat., Musée de Peinture et de Sculpture, Grenoble, and elsewhere, 1989
Mona Thomas, "Les ficelles d'Annette", *Beaux Arts Magazine*, no.74, 1989, pp.58–63
Lynn Gumpert, "Annette Messager: Comédie, tragédie", *Galeries Magazine*, no.35, 1990, pp.86–9
Annelie Pohlen, "The utopian adventures of Annette Messager", *Artforum*, xxix, September 1990, pp.111–16
Mo Gourmelon, "Arbitrated dissections: The art of Annette Messager", *Arts Magazine*, lxv, November 1990, pp.66–71
Gianni Romano, "Talk dirt: Interview with Annette Messager", *Flash Art*, no.159, 1991, p.102
Eric Troncy, "Annette Messager", *ibid.*, pp.103–5
Annette Messager: Telling Tales, exh. cat., Arnolfini, Bristol, and elsewhere, 1992
Annette Messager, exh. cat., Los Angeles County Museum of Art and elsewhere, 1995
Penelope Rowlands, "Art that annoys", *Art News*, xciv, October 1995, pp.132–5

Self-confessed collector, artist, handy-woman, trickster and peddler, Annette Messager has emerged as the chameleon of French contemporary art over the past 20 years. When in 1989 the newspaper *Le Monde* declared her a "sensational new discovery", Messager had been exhibiting nationally and internationally for more than 15 years. Her oeuvre reflects a compelling, sometimes morbid, fascination with the fragmented or absent body and a rejection of painting and sculpture in favour of "bricolage". Due to the resurgence of interest in artists concerned with the body (such as Kiki Smith, Robert Gober and Geneviève Cadieux) in the 1990s, Messager's work has been identified as a significant contribution to recent debates on the body as the site of struggle over identity, gender and race.

Messager studied traditional fine art in Paris during the turbulent years of the late 1960s, a period of intense reconsideration of political, social and cultural beliefs, epitomised in the work of French post-modern thinkers such as Lyotard and Foucault and feminist philosophers such as Hélène Cixous, Julia Kristeva and Luce Irigaray. It was this social and political climate that formed the critical context for Messager's developing creative imagination.

Rejecting traditional high art values, Messager first became an avid collector. During the 1970s she produced a plethora of albums, sketchbooks and boxes, designed to be hand-held for intimate viewing. In these works she combined the media of painting, drawing and photography with those skills traditionally ascribed to a so-called feminine sensibility – needlework, knitting and collage. *My Collection of Proverbs* (1974; private collection, repr. Grenoble 1989, pp.26–7), for example, comprises a set of tissues embroidered with homilies. While North American and British women artists such as Miriam Schapiro (q.v.) and Joyce Kozloff (q.v.) were criticised for essentialising "women's art", in France Messager was also reproached for reinforcing the notion of women's art as merely "decorative". It is possible, however, to read her collections as intentionally deconstructive in their dissection and examination of established visual languages and codes.

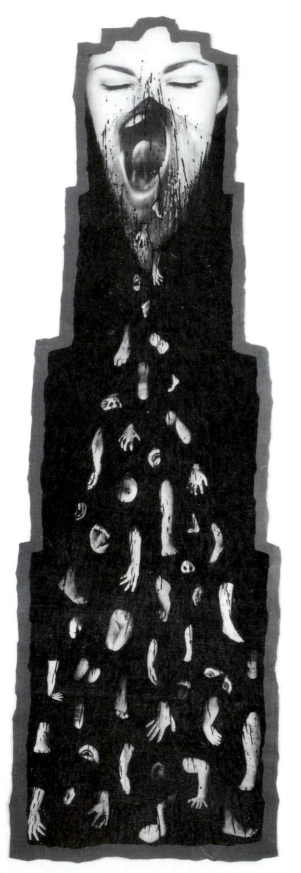

Messager: *Mounted Piece*, 1986; acrylic and oil, black-and-white photograph on canvas; 265 × 83 cm.

In more than 56 albums comprising two years' work, Messager sought to document, categorise and display the everyday. What emerges is a fascination with 19th-century methods of taxonomy and the study of physiognomical features, seen in the collection of 86 photographs, *Voluntary Tortures* (1972; Fonds Régional d'Art Contemporain de Rhône-Alpes, Dijon). Here, by isolating images of masochistic beauty treatments through which women seek to transform their bodies into the socially acceptable ideal, Messager refuses to supply a celebratory, positive image of female power. Rather she confronts the viewer with meanings that oscillate between the grotesque and the beautiful, between death and desire, and she sets in motion an unnerving and equivocal voyeurism that is found throughout her career. This work also marks her subversion of the sign of the female body as the cipher of desire epitomised in Surrealist works (see René Magritte's *L'Evidence éternelle*, 1930; Menil collection, Houston).

During the 1970s Messager expanded and developed this "taxidermy of desire". In *Happiness Illustrated* (1975–6; Musée Departmental d'Art Contemporain de Rochechouart) she drew together miniature paintings and drawings based on the clichéd images in tourist brochures; in *My Clichés* (1976–7, private collection, *ibid.*, p.59) she used reproductions of film stills to explore further the spaces between fiction and reality into which viewers project their own fantasies.

Photography, historically bound to criminal anthropology, became for Messager the primary medium through which to immobilise and isolate the objects of her fascination. Her *Chimèras* (1982–4; Fonds National d'Art Contemporain, Paris), for example, were shaped from torn photographs of enlarged body parts into monstrous shapes – spiders, knives and dragons – and then mounted on to canvas. The colouring of these motifs served to heighten their haunting quality, rendering them bewitching shadows of the everyday. Messager developed this iconography in *Mounted Piece* (1986; see illustration). The screaming mouth of *Mounted Piece*, from which fragmented limbs descend, draws strongly on Charcot's study (and construction) of female hysteria at the Salpêtrière hospital in the late 1880s, which had a profound effect on Messager's artistic sensibility.

What emerges in Messager's practice during the mid- to late 1980s is a funereal mood epitomised in *My Little Effigies* (1988; Musée National d'Art Moderne, Centre Georges Pompidou, Paris). Strongly influenced by the custom of pilgrimage offerings, Messager pinned cuddly toys to the wall of the gallery, hanging pictures of bodily parts around their necks. Not only do these objects seem like ex-voto offerings, they also take on the violent associations of trophies. They recall the unnerving impact of the *Sleep of the Boarders* (1971–2; Musée National d'Art Moderne), in which Messager displayed a collection of dead sparrows in baby clothes. These haunting and repulsive configurations reflect Messager's continuing fascination with childhood fears and taboos, but also mark the expansion of her work into the gallery space in the form of installation, relating to the work of Mike Kelly.

Histories of Dresses (1991; Fond Regional d'Art Contemporain de Languedoc-Roussillon) were composed of a series of glass coffins in which the remnants of a life – clothes pinned with charms and tokens – narrate the absence of their female owners. They are testimonies to the rites of passage for women in society and expose the hollowness of exterior appendages and adornments. In particular they relate to the narrative process of Messager's contemporary Sophie Calle and to the Catholicism of Messager's earlier veneration pieces. Messager's feminist consciousness can be seen to develop further in *My Wishes* (1988–91; Fonds Regional d'Art Contemporain de Corse), in which the body is reconstituted into a cluster of images hung from the ceiling. As tongue is juxtaposed with belly button and female mouths with male hands, this body is rendered non-hierarchical and disintegrates. The polished, complete female body of consumer culture is smashed by this work into tiny pieces and the objectification of the female body is destroyed through the denial of the mastery of the viewer's gaze.

The idea that began with the glimpse of private albums and developed through the fragmented forms of the body and the disturbing juxtapositions of cuddly toys and dead birds culminates in an exploration of the relationship between fetish object and voyeur. "I still find myself working on the same idea of hiding while showing, stimulating curiosity, suggesting that what lies underneath is more important than what you actually see", Messager says. "In this way, there is always the idea of secrecy even if it is a false secrecy because it ends up being put on exhibition" (Romano 1991).

CLAIRE DOHERTY

Miller, Lee

American photographer, 1907–1977

Born in Poughkeepsie, New York, 23 April 1907. Travelled to Europe on a school trip, staying on alone in Paris to study art, 1925; forced home by her father, and enrolled in Art Students League, New York, 1926. Pursued a successful career as a fashion model in New York, 1927–9. Worked with the photographer Man Ray in Paris, and associated with the Surrealists, 1929–32. Opened own studio in New York, 1932. Married Egyptian businessman Aziz Eloui Bey, 1934; lived in Egypt until separation in 1937; divorced 1947. Returned to Paris, 1937; travelled extensively with old Surrealist friends and met painter and art critic Roland Penrose. Settled in London with Penrose and began work as staff photographer for *Vogue*, 1940; war correspondent for US Armed Forces during World War II. Married Penrose, 1947; son born later that year. Moved to Farley Farm, Sussex, 1949. Died there of cancer, 27 July 1977.

Principal Exhibitions

Galerie de la Pléiade, Paris: 1931 (*Groupe annuel des photographes*)
Julien Levy Gallery, New York: 1932 (*Modern European Photography*), 1933 (individual)
Museum of Modern Art, New York: 1955 (*The Family of Man*, touring)

Selected Writings

Grim Glory: Pictures of Britain under Fire, ed. Ernestine Carter, London: Lund Humphries, 1941
Wrens in Camera, London: Hollis and Carter, 1945

Lee Miller's War: Photographer and Correspondent with the Allies in Europe, 1944–45, ed. Antony Penrose, Boston: Little Brown, and London: Condé Nast, 1992

Bibliography

Mario Amaya, "My Man Ray: An interview with Lee Miller Penrose", *Art in America*, lxiii, May–June 1975, pp.54–61
Roland Penrose, *Scrap Book, 1900–1981*, London: Thames and Hudson, and New York: Rizzoli, 1981
Atelier Man Ray, Berenice Abbott, Jacques-André Boiffard, Bill Brandt, Lee Miller, 1920–1935, exh. cat., Centre Georges Pompidou, Paris, 1982
L'Amour Fou: Photography and Surrealism, exh. cat., Corcoran Gallery of Art, Washington, DC, and elsewhere, 1985
Whitney Chadwick, *Women Artists and the Surrealist Movement*, Boston: Little Brown, and London: Thames and Hudson, 1985
Antony Penrose, ed., *The Lives of Lee Miller*, London: Thames and Hudson, and New York: Holt Rinehart, 1985
La Femme et le surréalisme, exh. cat., Musée Cantonal des Beaux-Arts, Lausanne, 1987
Jane Livingston, *Lee Miller: Photographer*, London and New York: Thames and Hudson, 1989
Renée Riese Hubert, *Magnifying Mirrors: Women, Surrealism and Partnership*, Lincoln: University of Nebraska Press, 1994
Val Williams, *Warworks: Women, Photography and the Iconography of War*, London: Virago, 1994

Unpublished material, prints and negatives are in the Lee Miller Archive, Chiddingly, Sussex.

To examine Lee Miller's photography is to examine Lee Miller's history, because her biography is bound to the striking images that divulge her talent and the tales of her varied life as a model, a muse, a Surrealist, a fashion photographer and a photo-journalist.

Miller's artistic career is often described through photographs of her rather than by her, perhaps because she took up photography while modelling. After leaving her home town of Poughkeepsie, she lived in New York and attended the Art Students League, studying theatrical design and lighting. In 1927 she was befriended by the magazine publishing magnate Condé Nast, who offered her modelling work; soon, Miller had a successful career as a high fashion model. Photographers such as Edward Steichen, Arnold Genthe and Horst P. Horst frequently photographed Miller, and her image was often featured in *Vogue*.

Miller's first work as a photographer came in 1929 when a *Vogue* designer sent her to Europe to make detailed drawings of Renaissance ornamentation. Rather than drawing them, Miller experimented with capturing the details on film. Her photographic interest came not only from modelling, but also from her father, Theodore Miller, an avid amateur photographer. Her past experiences, as well as her exposure to European art and culture, motivated Miller to pursue a career as a professional photographer. Armed with a letter of introduction from Edward Steichen and determined to learn photography, Miller made her way to the Paris studio of Man Ray, the American Surrealist.

Miller worked with Man Ray and the Surrealist circle from 1929 to 1932. Ultimately, she became Man Ray's student, model, muse, lover and collaborator. Since Surrealist photography often employed depictions of the female body, Miller appears frequently in the canon of Surrealist art, as in Man Ray's *Neck* (1929; Lee Miller Archives, Sussex). This

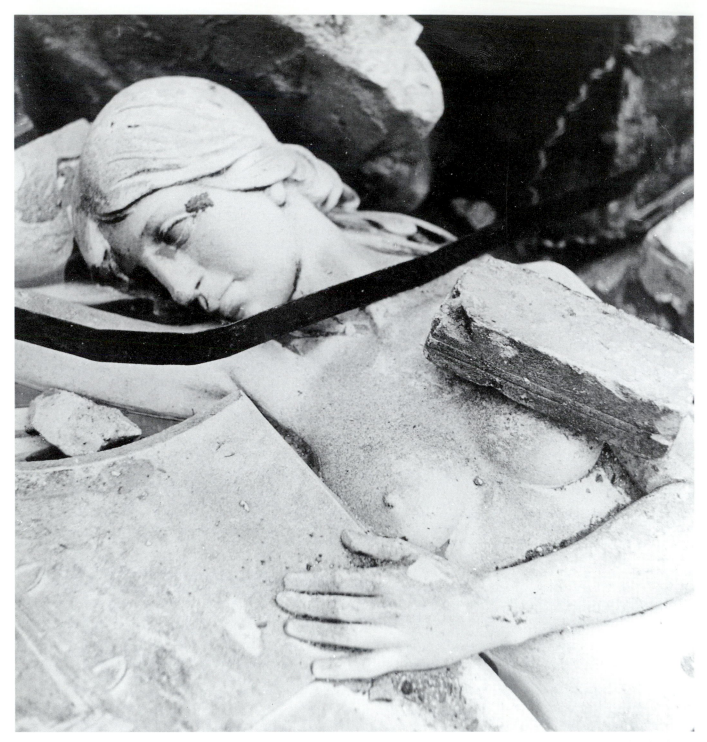

Miller: *Revenge on Culture*, London 1940, from *Grim Glory: Pictures of Britain under Fire* © Lee Miller Archives, Chiddingly, England

photograph shows only the smooth curves of Miller's neck and cheek, demonstrating the Surrealists' fetishistic visual representation of the female body. Although she submitted her body to Man Ray's dissecting camera lens, Miller appears to have been the first woman to enter the Surrealist circle with the aim of receiving an aesthetic education and producing her own art. Although the visual language of Surrealism informs her photography, Miller developed her own distinctive style. Using simple techniques of "straight" photography (photographically unaltered negatives and prints that are not subjected to double exposure or montage), such as camera angle and lens framing capacity, Miller achieved the Surrealist idea of "convulsive beauty" (André Breton's notion that a shocking sense of beauty is inherent in the accidental or decontextualised). Her photograph *Exploding Hand* (1930; Lee Miller Archives) uses these techniques to create an image that looks like a woman's hand smashing through a glass door. In *Untitled (Hand Reaching for Umbrella Fringe)* (1929; Art Institute of Chicago) Miller makes a simple subject haunting with her use of framing, angle and light. Miller's collaboration with Man Ray led to her accidental discovery of "solarisation" (the practice of exposing negatives to sharp bursts of light to achieve heightened contrast between subject and background). Man Ray later refined this darkroom process to use as his own signature technique. Miller continued to implement solarisation as well in such images as *Dorothy Hill, Solarized Portrait* (1933; Lee Miller Archives). In this extreme close-up, the solarisation creates a distinct, almost glowing boundary between the subject's translucent skin and the dark background.

Miller severed her romantic ties with Man Ray and returned to New York in 1932. Here she opened her own studio with her younger brother, Erik, as assistant. From 1932 to 1934 she maintained her studio with fashion, advertising and portrait shoots. *Scent Bottles* (1933; Lee Miller Archives), which shows a row of perfume bottles perfectly doubled by their mirrored reflection, exemplifies Miller's ability to enhance ordinary subject matter with her unique vision. Her most creative work appears in her portrait photography of clientèle consisting mostly of New York actors, artists and socialites. The portrait of *Joseph Cornell* (1933; Lee Miller Archives) typifies her interesting style of portraiture, depicting the artist's profile emerging from one of his whimsical, three-dimensional creations.

Miller left New York and her studio on her marriage to Aziz Eloui Bey in 1934. After moving to Egypt, she ceased photographing until 1936, when she began shooting desert landscapes. *Portrait of Space, Near Siwa* (1937; Lee Miller Archives) shows a very deep dimensional view of the desert plains through a ripped screen. This photograph of the open desert paradoxically creates a sense of claustrophobia, perhaps representing Miller's own feelings about Egypt. Unhappy and bored by her life as a businessman's wife, she separated from her husband in 1937 to rejoin her Surrealist friends in Europe. Her photography from this period consists mostly of snapshots of her travelling companions, as in *Picnic* (1937; Lee Miller Archives), which portrays Paul and Nusch Eluard, Man Ray and his lover Ady, and Roland Penrose (whom Miller would later marry) lounging decadently at a picnic in Mougins, France.

Miller's return to professional photography came with the outbreak of World War II. In 1940 she settled in London with Roland Penrose. As a staff photographer for British *Vogue*, she initially carried out routine fashion assignments. On her own, Miller began shooting the devastating effects of the blitz on London. These photographs became part of a book project entitled *Grim Glory: Pictures of Britain under Fire*, which Miller co-produced with American journalists Ernestine Carter and Edward R. Murrow. Her photographs disturb powerfully and beautifully. In *Revenge on Culture* (1940; see illustration), for instance, Miller photographed the image of a fallen, Venus-like statue whose broken, upper torso is obscured by debris and seemingly dismembered by a fallen power line that brutally marks the statue's marble skin. Eventually *Vogue* began publishing Miller's war coverage in addition to her fashion photography. In 1942 her accreditation as an official US Forces War Correspondent enabled her to pursue photojournalism actively.

Miller landed in France shortly after D-Day in 1944. Following the Allied advance until the American forces connected with the Russians, she was the only woman photographer on this front. Her written texts and photographs documenting such events as the siege of St Malo, the liberation of Paris and the concentration camps were published in both American and British *Vogue*. Miller's coverage of the concentration camps especially reflects her keen Surrealist eye. *Murdered Prison Guard, Dachau* (1945; Lee Miller Archives) shows a dead SS guard clearly visible in his rippled, sun-dappled watery grave. The photograph simultaneously horrifies and tantalises the viewer.

Miller essentially gave up professional photography after marrying Roland Penrose and giving birth to her son Antony in 1947. After Miller's death, her son and husband found thousands of negatives and prints that she had packed away from her brief photographic career. As a result, Lee Miller's family established an archive to house and collect her photography, enabling a rediscovery of her work and her talent.

JEANA K. FOLEY

Mirbel, Lizinka de

French painter, 1796–1849

Born Lizinka Aimée Zoë Rue in Cherbourg, 26 July 1796; father a naval official. Introduced to Parisian society through her uncle, General Bailly de Monthion. Studied under Jean-Baptiste Augustin. Appointed "Miniature Painter to the King", 1818. Married botanist Charles-François Brisseau de Mirbel, member of the Académie Royale des Sciences, 1824. Died of cholera in Paris, 29 August 1849.

Principal Exhibitions

Paris Salon: occasionally 1819–49 (second-class medal 1822, first-class medals 1828 and 1848)

Selected Writings

"De la peinture: Du portrait", *Revue de Paris*, viii, 1829, pp.91–100

Bibliography

Auguste Jal, *Esquisses, croquis, pochades ou tout ce qu'on voudra sur le Salon de 1827*, Paris: Dupont, 1828

Charles Blanc, *Histoire des peintres de toutes les écoles: Ecole française*, 4 vols, Paris: Renouard, 1861–76

Auguste Jal, *Dictionnaire critique de biographie et d'histoire*, Paris: Plon, 1872

Henri Bouchot, "Le portrait miniature en France", *Gazette des Beaux-Arts*, 3rd series, xiii, 1895, pp.243–6

René Jean, "Madame de Mirbel", *Gazette des Beaux-Arts*, 3rd series, xxxv, 1906, pp.131–46

Leo R. Schidlof, *La Miniature en Europe*, iv, Graz, 1964

Albert-P. de Mirimonde, "Un document inédit sur le portrait d'Ingres par Mme de Mirbel", *Bulletin de la Société de l'Histoire de l'Art Français*, 1968, 1970, pp.159–61

Graham Reynolds, *Wallace Collection: Catalogue of Miniatures*, London: Wallace Collection, 1980

John Ingamells, *The Wallace Collection Catalogue of Pictures: French Nineteenth Century*, London: Wallace Collection, 1986

Mirbel: *Louis XVIII*, 1819; oil on ivory (miniature); 15.1 × 12.1 cm.; Wallace Collection, London

Madame Lizinka de Mirbel, née Rue, was a leading painter of portrait miniatures and watercolours from the reign of Louis XVIII to the Revolution of 1848, portraying the major political, aristocratic and artistic figures of her day. She began with the miniature tradition as practised by her teacher Jean-Baptiste Augustin, but soon developed a freer and broader approach to her art. In addition to painting, she wrote with erudition on the theory and history of portraiture. Mirbel, a powerful figure in the Parisian art world in the early 19th century, also hosted an important salon and trained many of the noted miniaturists of the next generation.

Mirbel's career as a court painter during the Restoration and July Monarchy began with a successful portrait of *Louis XVIII* in 1818 (untraced), which earned her the title "Miniature Painter to the King". A year later she created a second likeness of the monarch (1819; see illustration), indebted stylistically to the tightly painted and highly detailed surfaces of Augustin. She presented the official image of the king, dressed in a blue uniform with gold epaulettes and sporting medals, in a formal, half-length pose in a rectangular format. The monarch's favour encouraged aristocratic patronage of her art, and in 1823 Caroline, Duchess of Berry, and the widow of Charles X's second son, sat for her portrait (Wallace Collection, London). The artist, employing her preferred oval format, captured a vibrant figure wearing a black dress and sitting in front of simple red curtains. The loosely painted highlights in the jewellery and hair energise the portrait and prefigure Mirbel's second mature style, evident in her portrait of the *Mademoiselles de Pourtalès* (1830; repr. Bouchot 1895, p.244). Typical of her images of women from 1830, Mirbel replaced a plain background with a broadly painted landscape, influenced by English portraiture and by her friend Charles-Emile Champmartin. She combined draped and landscape backgrounds in the portrait of *Madame Bouclier* (1840; repr. Schidlof 1964, p.405) and developed further her loose brushwork in the earth and sky.

In addition to her work for the *haute société*, Mirbel painted many significant writers, artists and critics of the Romantic period to great acclaim. She captured the likeness of the Scottish novelist *Sir Walter Scott* (1826) and the American writer *James Fenimore Cooper* (1827; both Wallace Collection) in watercolour during their respective visits to Paris. Scott, who reported a "most affectionate parting with wet cheeks on the lady's side", seems to have greatly impressed Mirbel (Ingamells 1986, p.185). She also requested Ingres to sit for her, though his miniature remained only a sketch (1834; Louvre, Paris); she nearly completed his face, but only roughed in his clothing. Perhaps none of her works is as penetrating as her portrayal of the worldly *Fanny Elssler* (n.d.; Musée de l'Opéra, Paris), a popular dancer in the first half of the 19th century. Mirbel also depicted the two most influential art critics of the Romantic period – Etienne Delécluze and Auguste Jal – both of whom praised her work. Jal, for example, exclaimed: "Madame de Mirbel is a woman of great talent. Energy and finesse, grace and science, she embodies the most precious qualities that a miniaturist should possess" (Jal 1828, p. 294).

At the foundation of Mirbel's art was a sophisticated understanding of the theory and history of the portrait. In an article in the *Revue de Paris* (1829) she argued "an almost universal need for portraiture", comparing it with history painting. The portrait offers the public "for contemplation the representation of great characters who do honour to humanity" and affords the private individual the image of a loved one that is "precious during life and an invaluable treasure once they are gone" (pp.91–2). Moreover, she expressed a gendered notion of portraiture: "Men should be painted as they are, women as they want or could be" (p.95). Images of Mirbel, in light of these views, present a complex and multi-faceted woman. Jean-Hilaire Belloc captured a graceful and well-dressed miniaturist at her painting table (c.1830; Musée d'Art et d'Histoire, Rochefort), while in contrast to this image of the professional, Champmartin's portrait (1831; Château, Versailles) depicts Mirbel standing in a landscape filled with vegetation and holding a bouquet of flowers, linking her with the profession of her husband, the botanist Charles-François Mirbel.

From 1830 Mirbel consolidated her position in the Parisian art world as the hostess of an important salon and as an influential teacher. Regular visitors to her soirées included the Comtesse de Bassanville and Madame Ancelot, literary women, Comte Jean de Castellane and the Marquis d'Aligre, millionaires, and Comte Auguste Forbin, director of the Louvre. From this influential group, the artists attending Mirbel's gatherings, Paul Delaroche, Baron Gérard, Paul Gavarni and Champmartin among others, found distinguished patrons and supporters. Mirbel also trained many successful miniaturists, both women and men. Among her outstanding female students were Madame Herbelin, Sidonie Berthon, Herminie Mutel and Louise Besnard, mother of the painter Albert Besnard. She counted as her male pupils Gabriel-Aristide Passot, who portrayed the theatrical personalities and high-level bureaucrats of his day, Maxime David, who carried forth Mirbel's highly detailed first style, and Pierre-Paul Pommayrac, who developed her loosely painted second style.

JOHN P. LAMBERTSON

Miss, Mary

American public artist, 1944–

Born in New York, 27 May 1944. Studied at University of California, Santa Barbara, 1962–6 (BA); Rhinehart School of Sculpture, Maryland Institute College of Art, Baltimore, 1966–8 (MFA). Married sculptor Bruce Colvin, 1967. Moved to New York, 1968. Taught at Sarah Lawrence College, Bronxville, New York, 1976–83; at School of Visual Arts, New York, from 1983. Recipient of Creative Artists Public Service (CAPS) grants, New York State Council on the Arts, 1973 and 1976; National Endowment for the Arts (NEA) grants, 1974, 1975 and 1984; Brandeis University Creative Arts award, 1982; Guggenheim fellowship, 1986; Medal of Honor, American Institute of Architects, 1990; Philip N. Winslow Landscape Design award, Parks Council, New York City, 1992; Urban Design award (in collaboration with Studio Works), *Progressive Architecture Magazine*, 1992. Member of Board of Directors, American Academy in Rome (artist-in-residence 1989). Lives in New York.

Selected Individual Exhibitions

55 Mercer Gallery, New York: 1971, 1972
Museum of Modern Art, New York: 1976
Nassau County Museum of Fine Arts, Roslyn, NY: 1978
Fogg Art Museum, Cambridge, MA: 1980
Max Protetch Gallery, New York: 1980
Brown University, Providence, and University of Rhode Island, Kingston, RI: 1981
Laumeier Sculpture Park, St Louis: 1982 (with Jackie Ferrara)
Institute of Contemporary Arts, London: 1983
Harvard University, Graduate School of Design, Cambridge, MA: 1990
Freedman Gallery, Albright College, Reading, PA: 1991

Selected Writings

"Statement" in Nancy Foote, "Monument-sculpture-earthwork", *Artforum*, xviii, October 1979, pp.32–7
"From autocracy to integration: Redefining the objectives of public art", *Insights/On Sites: Perspectives on Art in Public Places*, ed. Stacy P. Harris, Washington, DC: Partners for Livable Spaces, 1984, pp.61–71
"On a redefinition of public sculpture", *Perspecta 21: Yale Architectural Journal*, 1984, pp.52–70
"Statement" in Lilly Wei and others, "Making art, making money: 13 artists comment", *Art in America*, lxxviii, July 1990, pp.134–5, 178

Bibliography

Marjorie Wellish, "Material extension in new sculpture", *Arts Magazine*, xlv, Summer 1971, pp.24–6
Laurie Anderson, "Mary Miss", *Artforum*, xii, November 1973, pp.64–5
Lucy R. Lippard, "Mary Miss: An extremely clear situation", *Art in America*, lxii, March–April 1974, pp.76–7; reprinted in Lucy R. Lippard, *From the Center: Feminist Essays on Women's Art*, New York: Dutton, 1976
—, "Art outdoors: In and out of the public domain", *Studio International*, cxciii, 1977, pp.83–90
Nancy D. Rosen, "A sense of place: Five American artists", *ibid.*, pp.115–21
April Kingsley, "Six women at work in the landscape", *Arts Magazine*, lii, April 1978, pp.108–12
Ronald J. Onorato, "Illusive spaces: The art of Mary Miss", *Artforum*, xvii, December 1978, pp.28–33
Rosalind Krauss, "Sculpture in the expanded field", *October*, no.8, Spring 1979, pp.31–44
Mary Miss, exh. cat., Fogg Art Museum, Cambridge, MA, 1980
Nancy Foote, "Situation esthetics: Impermanent art and the seventies audience", *Artforum*, xviii, January 1980, pp.22–9
Kate Linker, "An anti-architectural analog", *Flash Art*, January–February 1980, pp.19–25
Mary Miss: Interior Works, 1966–1980, exh. cat., Brown University, Providence, RI, and elsewhere, 1981
Kate Linker, "Public sculpture", *Artforum*, xix, March 1981, pp.64–73; Summer 1981, pp.37–42
Connections: Bridges/Ladders/Ramps/Staircases/Tunnels, exh. cat., Institute of Contemporary Art, University of Pennsylvania, Philadelphia, 1983
Mary Miss, exh. cat., Institute of Contemporary Arts, London, 1983
Deborah Nevins, "An interview with Mary Miss", *Princeton Journal*, ii, 1985, pp.96–104
Mary Miss: Projects, 1966–1987, exh. cat., Architectural Association, London, 1987
Site Sculpture at Laumeier: Jackie Ferrara and Mary Miss, exh. cat., Laumeier Sculpture Park, St Louis, 1987
Nancy Princenthal, "On the lookout", *Art in America*, lxxvi, October 1988, pp.158–61
Joan M. Marter, "Collaborations: Artists and architects on public sites", *Art Journal*, xlviii, 1989, pp.315–20
Mary Miss: Photographs/Drawings, exh. cat., Freedman Gallery, Albright College, Reading, PA, 1991

Mary Miss has made a career of pushing the boundaries of sculpture and architecture. Her art is neither easy nor simple, but it is anti-elitist, and her public environmental works reach an audience that might be disinclined to visit a traditional gallery or museum milieu. Miss began working as a sculptor in the mid-1960s, making objects that rejected the dominant idiom, Minimalism, by eschewing monumental scale and industrial fabrication, and by embracing the theatricality that high modernist minimal art was supposed to oppose (see Michael Fried, "Art and objecthood", *Artforum*, v, Summer 1967, pp.12–23). *Glass* (1967; repr. London 1987, p.40), made of prosaic materials, derives meaning from the associations its form inspires: the ropes suspended from a sheet of glass suggest the mooring lines of boats at anchor. The early objects privilege a single point of view; no additional meanings come into play when the viewer walks around the piece. In *Filter* (1967; *ibid.*, p.44) Miss first raises other issues that dominate her later projects. The viewer can look through the metal screens hinged to form a V-shape, and the open form shapes space as well as occupying it.

Miss's outdoor installations of the late 1960s take time to experience. The viewer must walk through or around them, accumulating multiple perspectives in order to formulate a complex interpretation. No single point of view provides enough information to understand *Stake Fence* (c.1968; *ibid.*, p.42), an arrangement of wooden stakes linked by ropes, set on a grassy incline. From a distance, the piece is calligraphic, white lines against the ground; up close, the work's three dimensions are more evident, and from the top of the incline the stakes become the dominant elements. *Vs in a Field* (1969; repr. Anderson 1973, p.64) controls the viewer's experience of space with three V-shaped wooden markers placed at intervals of 75 feet (22.9 m.) in a field. The markers frame the landscape and shape space by playing with conventions of perspective: the vista seems to telescope when sighted along the Vs.

In the 1970s Miss attempted to conform her conceptions to the limitations of a gallery space. *Sapping* (1975; repr. London 1987, p.48) reiterates the manipulation of space and perspectival play of *Vs in a Field*. Seen from the side, *Sapping* looks like a large wooden crate, which inhibits movement through the room. From the end, it is a dead-end corridor, wider at the open end with three interior levels and orders of width, which exaggerate the sense of distance. Entering the work, the viewer experiences progressive constriction of space.

In a statement for *Art in America* (July 1990) on the subject "Making art, making money", Miss said that she realised early on that she was not interested in making objects for sale through the gallery system. Instead, she pursued the direction she had established with *Vs in a Field*, making temporary outdoor site sculptures. During the 1970s and 1980s she aimed to make her work accessible to an audience put off by the elitism of modernist art. Extended scale and multiple parts disguised the fact that one was encountering an art object. That the meaning of a work was completed in the viewer's mind, through memory, association and the physical experi-

Miss: *Pool Complex: Orchard Valley*, 1983–5; Laumeier Sculpture Park, St Louis

ence of moving through the installation, made the work accessible on many levels. *Battery Park Site Piece* (1973; temporary, repr. London 1987, pp.50–51) was situated on an abandoned lot and consisted of five rough wooden barriers pierced by circular holes. The spatial extension of the elements subverts any sense of monumentality despite the piece's overall scale. It invites the viewer to participate in the construction of meaning by permitting various physical viewing positions. The viewer can stand so as to line up the five apertures to frame a view, or can stand off to the side, which produces the illusion of a circular form rising or setting.

Miss's works from the mid-1970s focus on the viewer's process of approaching and moving through them. Miss conceived *Blind Set* (1976; Artpark, Lewiston, NY) as a film set, thus a suggestive environment incomplete without the layer of meaning supplied by the individual viewer. Yet the structure contains clues that indicate how it ought to be experienced. It is a circular pit with four concentric levels, with retaining walls made of steel painted to match the gravel at the site. Four concrete troughs radiate from the pit at ground-level, directing the viewer's gaze to specific vistas. The viewer ought to suspend drawing conclusions about *Blind Set* until he or she has reached the lowest level and climbed back out after sighting along the V-shaped troughs. *Blind Set* articulates space, and directs the audience's experience of the site.

Crucial to understanding Miss's later works is the apprehension of the layers of meaning built into the structures. Her sources are as often literary as architectural or art historical in the preliminary stages of her conceptualising a project, sources that she brings to bear on the particular geography of the site, and which tacitly inform the viewer's meditation on the work. Her installation of 1978 at the Nassau County Museum in New York, *Perimeters/Pavilions/Decoys*, is physically complex, extending above and below ground by more than four acres. There are five discrete elements: three unclimbable wood and screen towers of different heights (pavilions), a semicircular grassy mound and a subterranean area (the decoy) that is deceptive in its extension beyond the area suggested by the opening through which one descends. Miss's literary source here is the explorer Richard Burton's account of visiting Mecca and Al-Madinah, a hidden allusion since the structures are not orientalising, although the visitor's traversing of the site amounts to an exploration in pursuit of knowledge.

A narrative of nostalgia is one of the layers of *Pool Complex: Orchard Valley* (1983–5; see illustration). Miss designed a sequence of walks and pavilions around a dry sunken pool, the remains of a private estate that once occupied the site. The ruins that she incorporates evoke memories of a past era, which are articulated in the viewer's mind as he or she navigates the structures, entering the pavilions and traversing the walkways that outline the shape of the ruined pool. Even more theatrical than *Perimeters/Pavilions/Decoys* and *Blind Set*, *Pool Complex* is also the most architectural of the projects cited so far; it barely reads as a sculptural object.

Miss's most public commission is the *South Cove* project of 1988, designed in collaboration with an architect and landscape architect to revitalise three acres of shoreline in Battery Park City, lower Manhattan. A winding walkway of various materials, it is practically invisible as an art object, but directs the public's experience of the landscape. It effectively transforms the site; it articulates the relation of water to shore and requires the visitor to take in the site over time. The visitor has an aesthetic experience almost without realising it, which in Miss's terms marks the project as a success, reaching as it does a public larger than the audience for high art.

MARGO HOBBS THOMPSON

Mitchell, Joan
American painter, 1926–1992

Born in Chicago, Illinois, February 1926. Studied at Smith College, Northampton, Massachusetts, 1942–4; Art Institute of Chicago, 1944–7 (BFA) and 1950 (MFA); Columbia University, New York, 1950. Lived in France on Edward L. Ryerson fellowship, 1948–9. Married publisher Barney Rosset, 1950; divorced 1952. Returned to New York, 1950; established studio at St Mark's Place; invited by members of Artists' Club and by dealer Leo Castelli to exhibit in *Ninth Street Show*, 1951. Met Canadian painter Jean-Paul Riopelle in Paris, 1955; lived with him until 1979. Settled in Paris, 1959; moved to Vétheuil, 1968. Recipient of Premio Lissone, Milan, 1961; Brandeis University Creative Arts medal, 1973; Grand Prix National de Peinture, French Ministry of Culture, 1989; Grand Prix des Arts (Peinture) of the city of Paris, 1991; honorary doctorates from Miami University, Oxford, Ohio, 1971; School of the Art Institute of Chicago, 1987; Rhode Island School of Design, Providence, 1992. Member, American Institute of Arts and Letters. Died in Paris, 30 October 1992.

Selected Individual Exhibitions

Saint Paul Gallery, St Paul, MN: 1950
New Gallery, New York: 1952
Stable Gallery, New York: 1953, 1954, 1955, 1957, 1958, 1961, 1965
Southern Illinois University, Carbondale: 1961
New Gallery, Massachusetts Institute of Technology, Cambridge: 1962
Galerie Jean Fournier, Paris: 1967, 1969, 1971, 1978, 1980, 1984, 1987, 1990, 1992
Martha Jackson Gallery, New York: 1968, 1971, 1972
Everson Museum of Art, Syracuse, NY: 1972
Arts Club of Chicago: 1974
Whitney Museum of American Art, New York: 1974 (retrospective), 1992
Xavier Fourcade Inc., New York: 1976, 1977, 1980, 1981, 1983, 1985, 1986
Musée d'Art Moderne de la Ville de Paris: 1982
Herbert F. Johnson Museum of Art, Cornell University, Ithaca, NY: 1988–9 (touring retrospective)
Robert Miller Gallery, New York: 1989, 1991, 1993, 1994
Musée des Beaux-Arts, Nantes, and Galerie Nationale du Jeu de Paume, Paris: 1994 (retrospective)

Bibliography

Irving Sandler, "Mitchell paints a picture", *Art News*, lvi, October 1957, pp.44–7, 69–70
"My Five Years in the Country": An Exhibition of Forty-Nine Paintings by Joan Mitchell, exh. cat., Everson Museum of Art, Syracuse, NY, 1972
James Harithas, "Weather paint", *Art News*, lxxi, May 1972, pp.40–43, 63
Joan Mitchell, exh. cat., Whitney Museum of American Art, New York, 1974
Cindy Nemser, "An afternoon with Joan Mitchell", *Feminist Art Journal*, Spring 1974, pp.5–6, 24
Lucy R. Lippard, *From the Center: Feminist Essays on Women's Art*, New York: Dutton, 1976
Eleanor Munro, *Originals: American Women Artists*, New York: Simon and Schuster, 1979
Barbara Rose, ed., *Bedford Series: A Group of Ten Color Lithographs*, Bedford, NY: Tyler Graphics, 1981
Joan Mitchell: Choix de peintures, 1970–1982, exh. cat., Musée d'Art Moderne de la Ville de Paris, 1982
Charlotte Streifer Rubinstein, *American Women Artists from Early Times to the Present*, Boston: Hall, 1982
Linda Nochlin, "Joan Mitchell: Art and life at Vétheuil", *House and Garden* (USA), clvi, November 1984
Stephen Westfall, "Then and now: Six of the New York School look back", *Art in America*, lxxiii, June 1985, pp.112–21
Joan Mitchell: New Paintings, exh. cat., Xavier Fourcade Inc., New York, 1986
Judith E. Bernstock, *Joan Mitchell*, New York: Hudson Hills Press, 1988 (contains bibliography)
Martica Sawin, "A stretch of the Seine: Joan Mitchell's paintings", *Arts Magazine*, lxii, March 1988, pp.29–31
Harry Gaugh, "Dark victories", *Art News*, lxxxvii, Summer 1988, pp.154–9
Ora Lerman, "The elusive subject: Joan Mitchell's reflections on van Gogh", *Arts Magazine*, lxv, September 1990, pp.42–6
Joan Mitchell: A Portrait of an Abstract Painter, film by Marion Cajori, New York: Christian Blackwood Productions, 1992
Michel Waldberg, *Joan Mitchell*, Paris: Editions de la Différence, 1992
Klaus Kertess, "Joan Mitchell: The last decade", *Art in America*, lxxx, December 1992, pp.94–101
Joan Mitchell: Prints and Illustrated Books: A Retrospective, exh. cat., Susan Sheehan Gallery, New York, 1993
Joan Mitchell, exh. cat., Musée des Beaux-Arts, Nantes, and Galerie Nationale du Jeu de Paume, Paris, 1994 (with English translation)
Joan Mitchell: "My Black Paintings …", exh. cat., Robert Miller Gallery, New York, 1994
Bill Scott, "In the eye of the tiger", *Art in America*, lxxxiii, March 1995, pp.70–77

Joan Mitchell first received critical acclaim during the 1950s as one of the second generation of Abstract Expressionists. Like her contemporaries Helen Frankenthaler (q.v.), Grace Hartigan (q.v.) and Alfred Leslie, Mitchell sought to extend and develop the abstract language of the older generation. A major aspect of Abstract Expressionism that became central to Mitchell's work was an exploration of the relationship between man and nature. Landscapes, in particular fields, water, land, trees and flowers, were the main inspiration for her paintings. Mitchell drew on her experience both of actual landscapes and of representations of nature in lyrical poetry, notably the work of William Wordsworth and Rainer Maria Rilke as well as contemporary verse by Frank O'Hara and Samuel Beckett, both of whom were her close friends. Although many of her images seem joyful, the predominant

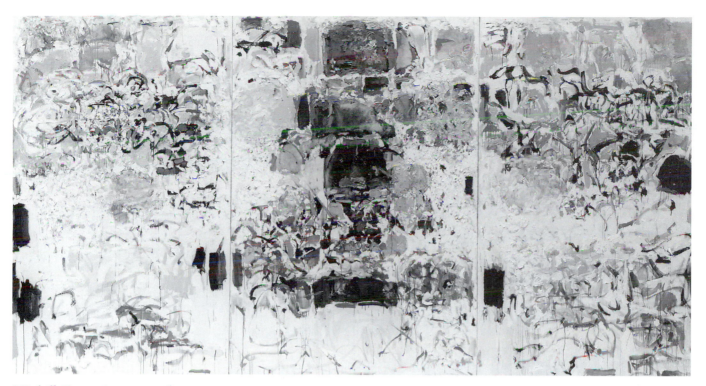

Mitchell: *Sans neige*, 1969; oil on canvas; 259.1 × 503.6 cm.; Carnegie Museum of Art, Pittsburgh

themes are death, loss and solitariness. Mitchell's work is distinctly autobiographical in the way in which it is invested with personal significance. Mitchell considered her painting as a dialogue between herself, the canvas and remembered sensations. Thus Mitchell's art is concerned with her "feelings" towards the subject and her memories of past experiences. The titles of the paintings, often given after the works were completed, allude to remembered experiences, people and places.

In 1950, after a year's stay in France, Mitchell returned to New York, where she met Franz Kline and Willem de Kooning, both of whom influenced her subsequent work. At the time Mitchell thought that being a female artist meant that it was unlikely that her work would be taken seriously. It is noteworthy, however, that she was one of the few women members of the exclusive Artists' Club, with Frankenthaler, Elaine de Kooning (q.v.) and Lee Krasner (q.v.). Although some of her work of this period reflected the urban environment in which she worked, there is an overriding preoccupation with what she has described as "remembered landscapes that I carry with me and remembered feelings of them" (Mitchell in Bernstock 1988, p.31). Characteristic of such work is *To the Harbormaster* (1957; Graham Gund Charitable Trust, Cambridge, MA), which was named after a poem of that title by Frank O'Hara. Mitchell associated large areas of water with Lake Michigan in Chicago where she had spent her childhood. The harbour represented security and calm, but also danger in a storm. The painting consists of short brush strokes that create a criss-cross web of thick impasto marks and drips. As in much of Mitchell's early work, the centre of the image is densely worked with a gradual thinning out towards the margins of the canvas. The contrasting colours, blue, cadmium red, green and crimson, are separated by blank canvas or

overpainted in white. Mitchell painted in oil on canvas and although the surface seems frenetic, the way in which the painting was made reveals the deliberation in her technique. In an interview with Irving Sandler, Mitchell described how she worked: "I paint from a distance. I decide what I'm going to do from a distance. The freedom in my work is quite controlled. I don't close my eyes and hope for the best ... I want to know what my brush is doing" (Sandler 1957, pp.46 and 69).

While on a trip to Paris in the summer of 1955, Mitchell met the painter Jean-Paul Riopelle, who was to be her companion until 1979. She divided her time between New York and Paris, and in 1959 acquired a studio on the rue Frémicourt. Mitchell described the subsequent images made in the early 1960s as "very violent and angry paintings" (Bernstock 1988, p.60). The cause of these feelings was complex, but centred on the death of her father in 1963 and her mother's prolonged illness with cancer from 1960 to 1967. Typical of such work is *Calvi* (1964; Robert Miller Gallery and Bernard Lennon Inc., New York), in which a central dark green mass dominates the image and alludes to organic forms, and the large surrounding area is blank or roughly painted in white with traces of colour underneath. The title refers to a place near Juan-les-Pins that Mitchell had visited on a sailing trip. In 1968 she settled permanently at the house she had purchased in the countryside at Vétheuil, north of Paris. She responded to her new environment by introducing intense and brilliant colours to her work. In *Sans neige* (1969; see illustration) the surface of the painting is heavily worked, emphasising the different paint texture in yellows, reds, greens and blues, with white impasto creating a diffused light.

Mitchell always worked on a grand scale using large, individual canvases and multiple canvases (*To the Harbormaster,* for instance, measures 193 × 299 cm.). During the early 1970s she embarked on a series of major triptychs. Typical of these works are the rectangular areas of saturated colour juxtaposed against veils of brushed and dripped paint that create an ambiguous space. Mitchell's use of the rectangle was influenced by the work of Hans Hofmann. In 1947 she had intended to study with Hofmann, but changed her mind after attending one of his classes, although she remained an admirer of his work. The three main themes of these works are beaches, fields and territories. The triptych *Field for Skyes* (1973; Hirshhorn Museum and Sculpture Garden, Smithsonian Institution, Washington, DC) contains green rectangles that both emphasise the flatness of the canvas surface and refer to the fields alongside the Seine at Vétheuil. The oppressive green and the title, however, refer to the death of one of her dogs, a Skye terrier.

Between late 1975 and 1984 Mitchell adopted a more all-over composition and her painting became increasingly lyrical in character. The rectangular shapes are gradually eliminated and replaced by short vertical or loosely criss-crossing marks. The work of this period has been compared to Monet's late images of waterlilies. Although Mitchell rejected any such similarity, her house at Vétheuil was situated on a hill overlooking a house in which Monet had lived and painted between 1878 and 1881. *Goodbye Door* (1980; Musée National d'Art Moderne, Centre Georges Pompidou, Paris) is a quadriptych in which a uniform thickness of paint covers the canvases in blues, greens and white. The title suggests Mitchell's continual preoccupation with the theme of death.

From 1985 onwards Mitchell struggled with mortality, both the prospect of her own death and the deaths of a number of close friends. Flowers, in particular sunflowers, and water are themes that are re-examined in her late work. In 1986 Mitchell explained to Yves Michaud: "Sunflowers are something I feel very intensely. They look so wonderful when young and they are so very moving when they are dying" (New York 1986, p.3). Mitchell's sombre images inspired by sunflowers are redolent with memories of the flowers she grew in her garden and those painted by van Gogh that she greatly admired. As Klaus Kertess observed: "in Mitchell's hands the very subject of sunflowers becomes a stunning *memento mori*" (Kertess 1992, p.100).

ROSEMARY HARRIS

Model, Lisette
Austrian photographer, 1901–1983

Born Elise Amélie Felicie Stern in Vienna, 10 November 1901 (family changed its name to Seybert, 1903). Studied music under Arnold Schoenberg, 1920. Moved to Paris and Nice with mother and sister Olga, 1926, and continued music and voice studies in Paris. Began to paint, 1932. Abandoned singing and music, and introduced to photography and darkroom techniques by Olga, 1933. Decided to become a professional photographer, 1933–4. Short apprenticeship with Florence Henri (q.v.), 1937. Married Russian Jewish painter Evsa Model in Paris, 1937; he died 1976. Emigrated to New York, October 1938; naturalised US citizen as Lisette Model, 1944. Freelance photographer for *Harper's Bazaar* and other publications, 1941–53. Special instructor in documentary photography at California School of Fine Arts, 1949. Taught at New School for Social Research, New York, 1951–82, and also privately. Recipient of Guggenheim fellowship, 1965; Creative Artists Public Service (CAPS) grant, 1973; honorary doctorate, New School for Social Research, New York, 1981; medal of the city of Paris, 1982. Honorary member, American Association of Magazine Photographers, 1968. Died in New York, 30 March 1983.

Selected Individual Exhibitions
Photo League, New York: 1941
Art Institute of Chicago: 1943
California Palace of the Legion of Honor, San Francisco: 1946
Museum of Modern Art, New York: 1948 (with Harry Callahan, Ted Croner and Bill Brandt)
Focus Gallery, San Francisco: 1975
Sander Gallery, Washington, DC: 1976
Galerie Zabriskie, Paris: 1977 (with Diane Arbus and Rosalind Solomon)
Center for Creative Photography, University of Arizona, Tucson: 1977
Vision Gallery, Boston: 1979
Ikona Gallery, Venice: 1980
Galerie Fiolet, Amsterdam: 1980
New Orleans Museum of Art: 1981 (touring retrospective)
Parsons Exhibition Center, New York: 1983
National Gallery of Canada, Ottawa: 1990–92 (touring retrospective)

Selected Writings
"On the firing line", *US Camera*, vii/7, 1944, p.51
"Picture as art: Instructor defines creative photography as scientific eye that captures life", *New York Times*, 9 December 1951, p.21
Essay in *The Snap-Shot*, ed. Jonathan Green, Millerton, NY: Aperture, 1974
Introduction in Charles Pratt, *The Garden and the Wilderness*, New York: Horizon, 1980

Bibliography
Lisette Model, Millerton, NY: Aperture, 1979 (preface by Berenice Abbott)
Shelley Rice, "Essential differences: A comparison of the portraits of Lisette Model and Diane Arbus", *Artforum*, xviii, May 1980, pp.66–71
David Vestal, "Lisette Model", *Popular Photography*, lxxxvi, May 1980, pp.114–19, 138–40
R.H. Cravens, "Notes for a portrait of Lisette Model", *Aperture*, no.86, 1982, pp.52–65
High Heels and Ground Glass: Pioneering Women Photographers, video, written and produced by Deborah Irmas and Barbara Kasten, New York: Filmmakers Library, c.1990
Lisette Model, exh. cat., National Gallery of Canada, Ottawa, and elsewhere, 1990 (contains extensive bibliography)
Judith Bell, "Lisette Model: The art of the split second", *Rangefinder*, xlii, January 1993, pp.40–50
Naomi Rosenblum, *A History of Women Photographers*, New York: Abbeville, 1994

Lisette Model Archives are in the National Gallery of Canada, Ottawa.

Throughout her career in photography the subject that consistently engaged Lisette Model was city dwellers in their natural habitat. Her images of people, rich or poor, were mordant, telling and frequently ironic. Only the creative – artists, actors, photographers and especially musicians – seem to have earned her admiration and escaped her sardonic scrutiny.

Model was born into a cultivated and prosperous family, and her first and enduring love was music. A serious music student first in Vienna (with Schoenberg) and later in Paris, Model took up photography rather late in life (1933–4) as a way "to make a living" (Vestal 1980, p.114). The war was approaching, her father had been Jewish, and she had no marketable skills. Apart from studying painting briefly in Paris, Model's training for a career in photography was informal and brief, and her teachers were all women. From her younger sister Olga, an amateur photographer, she learned darkroom techniques with the intention of doing laboratory work. From Rogi André, she learned never to photograph anything in which she was not passionately interested and also how to "see" Paris during their expeditions through the city's streets. In 1937 she also served a short apprenticeship with the photographer Florence Henri (q.v.).

Although always sensitive to formal and textural relationships, Model's real strengths were her trenchant and sobering insights into human nature, her eye for the telling incident, and her willingness to create images that were strong, and often ugly. Using a Leica or a Rolleiflex, she worked close to her subjects, which she chose viscerally and emotionally: "I select what I am attracted to", she stated, "I don't hesitate, question [or] analyze" (Ottawa 1990, p.46). Her negatives were the raw material out of which, through enlarging, cropping, burning or dodging, she created the final image.

Model's first important and stunningly assured series of photographs, *Promenade des Anglais* (1934–7), was of people observed on the boardwalk at Nice. Idling away leisure hours basking in the sun, her mainly bourgeois subjects seem, in varying degrees, ridiculous, self-indulgent and isolated. While never as corrosive an observer of humanity as George Grosz, she was none the less a biting satirist. In *Famous Gambler* (1934) a stylishly dressed woman sporting a jaunty straw hat is observed from behind; her silhouette, however, is mountainous. In another, *Lounging Man* (1934), a carefully dressed, bald and vaguely sinister man is seen slouching in his chair. Drowsy yet alert, he sizes up the photographer suspiciously through half-closed lids, like a turtle roused from its shell. The interplay between photographer and subject in this image is observed with obvious irritation by a smartly dressed woman sitting two chairs away – her newspaper reading has been disturbed.

Model's most productive decade was the 1940s, when she not only produced her most notable series of photographs – *Reflections, Running Legs, Lower East Side, Sammy's, Nick's* and *Gallaghers; Lighthouse Blind Workshop, St Regis Hotel, Fashion Show* and *Hotel Pierre* – but also won critical acclaim. Beaumont Newhall, curator of the newly formed Photography Department at the Museum of Modern Art, New York, purchased two of her prints. Her work also won many magazine commissions – Ralph Steiner, picture editor of *PM's Weekly*, published and promoted her work, as did Alexey Brodovitch, artistic director of *Harper's Bazaar*, where her anti-fashion images were in sharp contrast to those normally found in the pages of the chic fashion magazine. She also contributed to *Look, Vogue, US Camera* and *Cosmopolitan*.

The surreal conjunction of objects displayed in store windows, or combined with the forms reflected in them, intrigued Model, whether the store window belonged to Bonwit Teller or to a Lower East Side kosher butcher shop. Her resulting photographs – strange, haunting, sometimes amusing – comprise the *Reflection* series. In *Windows Bonwit Teller* (1939–40) a cigar-smoking businessman stands in front of the department store window. He is so engrossed in his newspaper that he is oblivious of everything else, including the coquettish siren call of the negligée-clad mannequin in the window behind him. In *Chicken and Glamour* (between 1939 and 1942) a plucked and very naked kosher chicken dangles in front of a cinema poster featuring James Cagney and Priscilla Lane. According to Model (*High Heels and Ground Glass* video, c.1990), her *Running Legs* series (1940–47) resulted after she pointed her camera down in an unsuccessful attempt to photograph New York sky-scrapers. The images in these uncharacteristically glamorous studies of feet and legs, taken at street level, capture the energy and excitement of constantly moving city crowds. Discovering that she had a talent for teaching and that she enjoyed doing it, Model taught photography at institutions (California School of Fine Arts and New School for Social Research) and privately, from 1940 until the year of her death. Among her most notable students were Diane Arbus (q.v.) and Rosalind Solomon.

Throughout her career Model produced many photographs of people who lived far outside society's norms – derelicts, dwarfs, the blind, the obese, transvestites, female impersonators – and she observed them with seeming objectivity and without pity. Her photographs also revealed that the wealthy and privileged of society could be equally freakish (*Mrs Cavanaugh and a Friend at an Opening of the Metropolitan Opera, NY, c.*1943). Model's work along these lines no doubt freed Diane Arbus to continue such explorations: Arbus's *Hermaphrodite and a Dog in a Carnival Trailer, Maryland* (1970), for example, seems to be a variation on Model's *Albert-Alberta, Hubert's Forty-Second Street Flea Circus, NYC* (1945). In the 1950s Model did a series of photographs of famous jazz musicians – Ella Fitzgerald, Erroll Garner, Bud Powell, Louis Armstrong, Horace Silver, Chico Hamilton, Percy Heath, Gerry Mulligan – shooting them while they were in the midst of performance and transported by their art. This series is among the most affirmative of Model's oeuvre and seems to suggest that, despite the fragile and ridiculous human condition she generally observed, some artists, through their ability to touch us deeply, can rise above that level. (All works cited are in the National Gallery of Canada, Ottawa.)

HELEN GOODMAN

Modersohn-Becker, Paula
German painter, 1876–1907

Born Paula Becker in Dresden, 8 February 1876. Moved with her family to Bremen, 1888. Took drawing lessons with the Bremen artist Wiegand, and attended classes at a London art school while staying with a relation, 1892. Teacher-training course at the Bremen Lehrerinnenseminar, 1893–5. Studied at the Zeichen- und Malschule des Vereins der Künstlerinnen und Kunstfreundinnen zu Berlin, Berlin, 1896–8. First visited Worpswede art colony, 1897; settled there, autumn 1898; met painter Otto Modersohn and Clara Rilke-Westhoff (q.v.). First trip to Paris, 1900; studied at Académie Colarossi and Ecole des Beaux-Arts; subsequent visits to Paris in 1903, 1905 and 1906. Married Modersohn, 1901; lived in Worpswede. Died in Worpswede of a heart attack, 21 November 1907, shortly after giving birth to a daughter.

Principal Exhibitions
Kunsthalle, Bremen: 1899, 1906 (both Worpswede artists exhibitions), 1908 (retrospective)

Selected Writings
Paula Modersohn-Becker in Briefen und Tagebüchern, ed. Günter Busch and Liselotte von Reinken, Frankfurt am Main: Fischer, 1979; as *Paula Modersohn-Becker: The Letters and Journals*, ed. Arthur S. Wensinger and Carole Clew Hoey, New York: Taplinger, 1983; revised edition, Evanston, IL: Northwestern University Press, 1990

The Letters and Journals of Paula Modersohn-Becker, ed. J. Diane Radycki, Metuchen, NJ: Scarecrow Press, 1980

"Lettres choisies (1900–1907), *Cahiers du Musée National d'Art Moderne*, no.10, 1982, pp.196–207

Bibliography

Gustav Pauli, *Paula Modersohn-Becker*, Berlin: Wolff, 1919; 3rd edition, 1934

Waldemar Augustiny, *Paula Modersohn-Becker*, Gütersloh: Mohn, 1960

—, *Paula Modersohn-Becker*, Hildesheim, 1971

Ellen C. Oppler, "Paula Modersohn-Becker: Some facts and legends", *Art Journal*, xxxv, Summer 1976, pp.364–9

Gillian Perry, *Paula Modersohn-Becker: Her Life and Work*, London: Women's Press, 1979

Christa Murken-Altrogge, *Paula Modersohn-Becker: Leben und Werk*, Cologne: DuMont, 1980

Günter Busch, *Paula Modersohn-Becker: Malerin, Zeichnerin*, Frankfurt am Main: Fischer, 1981

Griselda Pollock, "What's wrong with 'images of women'"?, *Framing Feminism*, ed. Rozsika Parker and Griselda Pollock, London and New York: Pandora, 1987

Christa Murken-Altrogge, *Paula Modersohn-Becker*, Cologne: DuMont, 1991

Mara R. Witzling, ed., *Voicing Our Visions: Writings by Women Artists*, New York: Universe, 1991; London: Women's Press, 1992

Diane Radycki, "Pretty/ugly: Morphing Paula Modersohn-Becker and Marie Laurencin", *Make: Magazine of Women's Art*, no.72, 1996, pp.19–21

Paula Modersohn-Becker is now perhaps best known for her powerful, monumental images of motherhood, painted in a style often closely associated with developments in early 20th-century French, rather than with contemporary German, modernism. Before her premature death in 1907 she made four trips to Paris, where she lived and worked for extended periods and became absorbed in the work of such Post-Impressionist painters as Gauguin and the Nabis, van Gogh and Cézanne. But Modersohn-Becker's aesthetic, iconographical and cultural interests also remained firmly rooted in the German environ-

ment in which she had lived and studied, especially the north German artists' colony of Worpswede, near Bremen.

In the 1890s a group of former art students from the Düsseldorf and Munich academies had settled in the village of Worpswede, then inhabited by peasant farmers and turf-cutters. In keeping with many other artistic movements flourishing in Germany at the time, this group of artists saw themselves as daring neo-romantics, seeking out "natural" subjects in the form of the indigenous peasant *Volk* in the local landscape. By the late 1890s, when Paula Becker first visited the village, these artists were mostly painting peasant and landscape subjects influenced by the work of Gustave Courbet and the French Barbizon painters. After establishing herself in the village in 1898 she studied under Fritz Mackensen, then well-known for his Courbet-influenced scenes of local peasant life. Partly under his influence, she became absorbed in the local imagery, drawing and painting many images of peasant women nursing their babies. Much of her work from this early period is characterised by a dark-toned, realistic technique, designed to evoke the harshness and poignancy of the "primitive" sources she was depicting. Modersohn-Becker's primitivism, her sense of this subject matter as somehow "other" in relation to her own sophisticated life, also involved a neo-romantic idealisation of the heroic purity of these peasant figures. In a diary entry for 25 October 1898 she wrote:

> I sketched a young mother with her child at her breast, sitting in a smoky hut. If only I could someday paint what I felt then! A sweet woman, an image of charity. She was nursing her big, year-old bambino, when with defiant eyes her four-year-old daughter snatched for her breast until she was given it. And the woman gave her life and her youth and her power to the child in utter simplicity, unaware that she was a heroine [quoted in Witzling 1991, p.193].

The cultural and artistic context provided by the artists colony of Worpswede was fraught with contradictions. Although some of the artistic interests that emerged (particularly in the work of Fritz Mackensen) encouraged a somewhat reactionary form of primitivism that exalted an essentially German peasant culture as a main source of artistic inspiration, there were other artists within the community whose less inward-looking ideas helped to nurture those of Modersohn-Becker. She developed a close friendship with Heinrich Vogeler, whose paintings and works in the applied arts were heavily influenced by the utopian socialist ideals of William Morris and the Arts and Crafts movement. In 1901 she married Otto Modersohn, a Worpswede landscape painter influenced by late 19th-century French landscape painting, in particular the legacy of the Barbizon painters, and who encouraged her own interest in developing a style of landscape painting loosely indebted to Impressionist techniques. At the end of the 19th century rural artists' communities (many of which were formed outside large German towns) provided women with a relatively tolerant social and professional atmosphere in which to work. While aspiring women artists were still handicapped by restricted access to educational opportunities and studio facilities in urban academic circles, within the less formal, generally more liberal environment of the artists' colony they were able to work and study alongside male artists.

Modersohn-Becker: *Self-Portrait with Amber Necklace*, 1906, oil; 61 × 50 cm.; Kunstmuseum, Basel

However, Modersohn-Becker's letters and diary entries suggest that she felt increasingly stifled by the personal and artistic relationships that she had formed in Worpswede, and yearned for the artistic stimulus of Paris. After her first two trips to Paris in 1900 and 1903, she sought increasingly to reduce her images to more monumental and simplified shapes, using flattened areas of bright colour. In 1903 she wrote in her diary: "A great simplicity of form is something marvelous. As far back as I can remember, I have tried to put the simplicity of nature into the heads that I was painting or drawing. Now I have a real sense of being able to learn from the heads of ancient sculpture" (*ibid.*, p.198). In her works from the period 1903 onwards Modersohn-Becker sought to put such ideas into practice, developing a form of primitivism derived from complex sources. In her *Poorhouse Woman in the Garden*, also titled *Poorhouse Woman with Glass Bowl* (repr. Perry 1979, pl. XV) she applies these techniques to a local Worpswede peasant subject. But her interpretation avoids the idealised, pseudo-religious earth mothers to be found in the work of some other Worpswede artists, notably Fritz Mackensen. She employs Gauguinesque simplifications, reducing the old woman's broad dimensions to flat areas of bright colour. As a result the figure appears both monumentalised and distorted, and is set against a decorative frieze of vertical flowers, giving the image a pattern-like quality. This peasant figure is thus removed from the realities of the local poor house (where Modersohn-Becker found many of her subjects) and has an ornamental, static appearance. In her attempt to combine a supposedly "primitive" subject matter with "primitive" techniques Modersohn-Becker created an ambiguous image of peasant life as remote and unworldly.

Modersohn-Becker's images of motherhood, particularly those produced during the last two years of her life, reveal a woman artist seeking to resolve some of the aesthetic, social and cultural contradictions that she confronted in her personal and professional life. The theme of the peasant woman was well established in European art as a whole, and in the work of the Worpswede group in particular, as a symbolic image for the representation of a "primitive" or natural life. Images of breast-feeding mothers recur in the work of such Worpswede artists as Mackensen, where they stand as potent metaphors for the "primitive" cycle of nature. Modersohn-Becker reworks these traditional symbolic associations in some of her images of peasant mothers, although she rejects the anecdotal realism and Impressionist-influenced styles of her Worpswede colleagues, and often combines the theme with that of the female nude. In her *Kneeling Mother with Child* (1907; Staatliche Museen Preussischer Kulturbesitz, Nationalgalerie, Berlin) a kneeling, breast-feeding mother is surrounded by fruit and plants, symbols of her fecundity. Although this work is also clearly influenced by Gauguinesque representations of the female nude that she had seen in Paris, this is not a sensual or erotic nude reminiscent of Gauguin's Tahitian works. Modersohn-Becker's figure has a heavily proportioned, monumental form with primitivised features; she suggests a powerful fecundity free of any suggestion of sexual availability. Her interest in this theme, and its monumental implications, are also related to more personal longings and fantasies. Her letters and diary entries reveal a woman who both grew increasingly disillusioned with her marriage, and who also

yearned for a somewhat idealised state of motherhood. In her *Self-Portrait on Her Wedding Anniversary* (1906; Sammlung Böttcherstrasse, Bremen) she portrays herself nude with a distended stomach as if pregnant. The work was painted many months before the conception of her only child, and represents a projection of her fantasy of herself as a fertile mother. While the fantasy was fulfilled with the birth of her daughter in November 1907, Modersohn-Becker's tragic death three weeks later has helped to give her interpretations of the theme of motherhood a poignant, almost mythical status.

Images of women, including the female nude, mother and child groups, portraits of women and self-portraits, feature prominently in Modersohn-Becker's work. While this choice of imagery may reveal the artist's preoccupation with the creative self as a woman, the predominance of certain images was also to do with the accessibility of subjects and models. Studies from the female nude formed an important part of the curriculum in the various French and German academies at which she studied. In Worpswede the models most readily available to her were the local women and their children, for most of the male community were working in the fields during the day.

Many of her mother and child compositions include still-life groups of fruit and flowers, where they are resonant with symbolic connotations of natural fecundity. But the still life became increasingly important as a genre in its own right in her work from 1903 onwards. Influenced by interpretations of the theme in the work of Post-Impressionist artists such as Cézanne, Emile Bernard and van Gogh, she became involved with the possibilities for formal expression that still-life subjects offered. She saw inanimate objects, such as fruit, flowers and jugs, as vehicles for her pursuit of "simplicity of form", for developing simplified compositional structures. In her writings she expresses a desire somehow to penetrate the inner qualities of an object through close observation. Such attitudes may have been informed by the ideas of the German poet Rainer Maria Rilke, with whom Modersohn-Becker became friendly. Influenced by Neo-romantic ideas, and by the work of Rodin (for whom Modersohn-Becker worked briefly as a secretary), Rilke evolved a theory of representation based on the notion of the intrinsic or "inner" meaning of objects, which could be revealed through the careful craftsmanship of the artist.

Modersohn-Becker's letters and diary entries have been seen as a kind of "confessional" within which she could make intimate disclosures about her personal struggles; they provided a space in which she could express her frustration in the face of conflicting demands of being a "woman" and an "artist" seeking a professional career. And the personal and aesthetic struggles that she describes are, of course, mediated by the different cultural contexts and discourses (both French and German) in which she participated. Her self-image as an artist (as expressed in her writings) is both steeped in Neo-romantic ideas about the artist's mission to reveal something deeper beneath the visible surfaces of objects and reveals an increasing concern with her need to study and learn from the work of modernist French painters. Her painted self-images suggest, however, a more ambivalent and even diffident approach to her status as a woman artist. In several self-portraits she paints herself nude with heavy dimensions and simplified forms, and places the figure boldly across the foreground space to suggest a monumental and powerful human presence, as in *Self-Portrait with Amber Necklace* (1906; see illustration). But these heroic, unerotic self-images are usually devoid of references to her role as artist, and may reveal the same conflict that she expressed in her writings. During her lifetime Modersohn-Becker sold only two or three paintings, a lack of professional success that must have affected her confidence and her self-image as an artist. In her *Self-Portrait with Amber Necklace,* then, the positive image that she projects is that of "woman" rather than "woman artist".

GILL PERRY

Modotti, Tina
Italian photographer, 1896–1942

Born in Udine, Italy, 16 August 1896. Joined father in California, 1913. Married the painter and poet Roubaix (Robo) de l'Abrie Richey, 1918; he died 1922. Moved to Mexico with Edward Weston, who taught her photography, 1923; stayed there after his return to USA in 1926; joined Mexican Communist Party, 1927; expelled from Mexico and moved to Germany, 1930. Gave up photography and worked for International Red Aid in Moscow, 1931–4, France, then Spain, under the *nom de guerre* María, 1935–9. Returned to Mexico City with Italian Communist Vittorio Vidali, 1939. Died in Mexico City, 5–6 January 1942.

Selected Individual Exhibitions
Aztec Land Shop, Mexico City: 1924 (with Edward Weston)
Museo del Estado, Guadalajara, Mexico: 1925 (with Edward Weston)
Sal de Arte, Mexico City: 1926 (with Edward Weston)
Biblioteca Nacional, Mexico City: 1929
Inez Amor Galerie de Arte, Mexico City: 1942 (memorial)

Selected Writings
"Sobre la fotografia/On photography", *Mexican Folkways*, v, October–December 1929, pp.196–8
The Letters from Tina Modotti to Edward Weston, ed. Amy Stark [Rule], Tucson: Center for Creative Photography, 1986

Bibliography
Carleton Beals, "Tina Modotti", *Creative Arts*, iv, February 1929, pp.xlvi–li
David Vestal, "Tina's trajectory", *Infinity*, xv, February 1966, pp.4–16
Mildred Constantine, *Tina Modotti: A Fragile Life: An Illustrated Biography*, New York: Paddington Press, 1975; revised edition, New York: Rizzoli, 1983
Maria Caronia and Vittorio Vidali, *Tina Modotti: Photographs*, Westbury, NY: Idea Editions, 1981 (Italian original, 1979)
Cubism and American Photography, 1910–1930, exh. cat., Sterling and Francine Clark Art Institute, Williams College, Williamstown, MA, 1981
Frida Kahlo and Tina Modotti, exh. cat., Whitechapel Art Gallery, London, and elsewhere, 1982
Herbert Molderings, "Tina Modotti: Fotografin und Agentin der GPU", *Kunstforum International*, lv, November 1982, pp.92–103
Edward Weston in Mexico, 1923–1926, exh. cat., San Francisco Museum of Modern Art and elsewhere, 1983
Robert D'Attilio, "Glittering traces of Tina Modotti", *Views* (Boston), vi/4, Summer 1985, pp.6–9
Amy Conger, "Tina Modotti and Edward Weston: A re-evaluation of their photography", *Edward Weston 100: Centennial Essays in Honor of Edward Weston*, Carmel, CA: Friends of Photography, 1986, pp.63–79
Christiane Barckhausen-Canale, *Auf den Spuren von Tina Modotti*, Cologne: Pahl-Rugenstein, 1988; as *Verdad y leyenda de Tina Modotti*, Havana: Casa de las Américas, 1989 (Spanish edition includes previously unpublished letters)
Reinhard Schultz, ed., *Tina Modotti: Photographien und Dokumente*, Berlin: Sozialarchiv, 1989
Modernidad y modernización en el arte mexicano, 1920–1960, exh. cat., Museo Nacional de Arte, Mexico City, 1991
Valentina Agostinis, ed., *Tina Modotti: Gli anni luminosi*, Pordenone: Biblioteca dell'Immagine, Cinemazero, 1992
Margaret Hooks, *Tina Modotti: Photographer and Revolutionary*, London and San Francisco: Pandora, 1993
Tina Modotti: Photographs, exh. cat., Philadelphia Museum of Art, and elsewhere, 1995 (contains extensive bibliography)

Tina Modotti was one of many expatriate artists and intellectuals who settled in Mexico during the early decades of the 20th century. Her photographs combine extraordinary formal clarity with incisive social content. Her style shares with other photographs of the period modernist elements that link it to the international phenomenon known as New Vision photography. Modotti's work marks the beginning of a modernist aesthetic in Mexico, but she tailored her vision of modernism to suit the circumstances at hand: she was not working near the metropolises of post-war Europe, but in an essentially agrarian Latin American country still coming to terms with the changes wrought by the Mexican Revolution.

Modotti went to Mexico in 1923 with the photographer Edward Weston and together they set up a photography studio (he left in 1926). She had gone to Mexico from California, where she had lived since emigrating from northern Italy in 1913. In San Francisco, she worked in the textile industry and then as a self-employed milliner. It was there that she began her acting career and received a favourable reception in the amateur Italian theatre. After her marriage to the poet and painter Roubaix de l'Abrie Richey in 1918 and their move to Los Angeles, Modotti landed roles in three films, starring in one (*The Tiger's Coat*), and modelled for a number of artists including the photographer Jane Reece. By early 1921 the Richeys had met Weston, who had a successful photographic portrait business. Under the influence of his partner, the photographer Margrethe Mather, Weston had begun to pursue modernist techniques.

In 1922 Modotti decided to become a photographer. Although she later credited Weston for having been her guide and initiator in photography (*The Letters from Tina Modotti to Edward Weston* 1986, p.55), there were a number of other relevant influences. Modotti's uncle, Pietro Modotti, ran a successful portrait studio and an influential school of photography in the town of Udine, her birthplace. Her father, too, had a short-lived photography studio when he first settled in San Francisco in 1907. Two tragedies also affected Modotti's resolution to become a photographer. Richey, who had gone to Mexico in advance of Modotti and Weston, perished within days of contracting smallpox; and a few weeks later her father died of stomach cancer. In addition, Modotti may have learned a great deal from her previous professions – acting and modelling. Working on the other side of the camera, both in

Modotti: *Tank No.1, Mexico*, 1927; gelatin silver print; 24.3 × 19.3 cm.; Metropolitan Museum of Art, New York / Ford Motor Co. Collection, Gift of Ford Motor Co. and John C. Waddell, 1987 (1987.1100.198)

moving and still pictures, she would have been introduced to the technical aspects of taking pictures and perhaps stimulated to think about such aesthetic issues as composition and tonality. Thus her resolution to become a photographer may have been a calculated decision to seize control of the gaze.

In Mexico Modotti learned photography from Weston, adopting many of his technical guidelines. Both photographers used large-format cameras. She used a 4 × 5-inch Corona, a stationary view camera that required a tripod, and later acquired a 3¹/₄ × 4¹/₄-inch Graflex, a hand-held, single-lens reflex camera. The precision of the Corona was ideal for formal portraiture and for documenting murals, activities by which Modotti supported herself during her photographic career, while the Graflex gave more flexibility and allowed for more spontaneous images. Yet Modotti, like Weston, considered that composing an image on ground glass and rigorous formal construction were of crucial importance. During this period, both artists used a contact method of printing, placing a negative directly on sensitised paper and exposing it to light.

Among Modotti's first photographs are still lifes. Like artists over the centuries, she used the genre to study formal issues – light, pattern, composition, tone – imbuing them with symbolic content. *Roses* (1924; Museum of Modern Art, New York), for example, is a sharply focused close-up of four white roses, the luminous petals of which animate the surface of the image. It functions, too, as a *memento mori*, a traditional role for the still-life genre. Modotti also made photographs of architectural elements, finding complicated spatial configurations with tonal gradations that demanded technical rigour. (This practice served her well later when she was photographing murals, the placement of which often involved considerable manipulation of her camera.) As a way of photographing, still life stayed with Modotti throughout her career.

Modotti approached her subjects with a modernist eye: novel, sometimes jarring vantage points, machine-age subject matter and the abstracting of space and form characteristic of New Vision practice are evident in her photographs. Her work shares with that of Weston aspects of American modernism, especially a formalism and emphasis on the materiality of the object depicted. But Modotti's photographic career evolved in conjunction with her activism. She melded a "straight" aesthetic similar in rigour to that of Weston with a distinctly social element that echoes the work of Germany's *Arbeiterfotograf* (Worker-Photograph) movement.

Modotti is allied with two strains of Mexican modernism, the mural movement, sometimes called the Mexican Renaissance, and the Movimiento Estridentista, the Mexican interpretation of Futurism. Adherents to both branches adhered to *Mexicanidad*, the principle based on the reclamation of Mexican art and culture as a visual resource. *Experiment in Related Form* (1924; Mills College Art Gallery, Oakland, CA) is an example of Modotti's aesthetic link with the Estridentistas. Its fractured surface and repetitive imagery (suggestive of mass production) render it emblematic of modernism.

Modotti enlisted her photographic skills to express her radicalism, and officially joined the Communist Party in 1927. Like her Mexican friends and colleagues, the muralists Diego Rivera, David Alfaro Siqueiros and José Clemente Orozco, she was inspired by the notion that art could educate and that the visual arts could be a catalyst for social and political changes. In her images of workers she eloquently put forth a political message. Her photographs of *campesinos* (farmers) and *obreros* (workers) offer a moving exegesis of Marxist doctrine, and present both the humanity of the people and their position at the heart of the Communist movement. In *Tank No.1, Mexico* (1927; see illustration) a worker seen from a dramatic worm's-eye view is highlighted by sunlight. The rivets that hold the structure together are emphasised, suggesting an analogous position of the worker within economic reform.

Modotti's choice of subject matter was provocative, even in the post-Revolutionary period. The government policies implemented in the 1920s, which proposed the formulation of a genuine Mexican art, were premised on aesthetising indigenous art to create the impression of a national culture. In this way the government hoped to make palatable to the middle classes policies of educational reforms designed for the lower and working classes, many of whom were of Indian descent. It is easy now to overlook the subversive power of Modotti's photographs and to miss the fact that images such as *Worker Reading "El Machete"* (1927; private collection, repr. Philadelphia 1995, pl.89) were seen as potent manifestos of revolt. The young *obrero* reading *El Machete* is a reminder that the Revolution's promise of universal literacy would be fulfilled only by the activism of the people. Modotti's photographs became more sharply critical of government policies that failed the objectives of the Revolution, and in 1930 she was deported as an undesirable alien. Within a year, she had abandoned her camera for the typewriter. For the next 12 years, Modotti worked for the International Red Aid, in Moscow, in France, and then in Spain, during the Civil War. Modotti returned to Mexico in 1939, where she died in January 1942.

SARAH M. LOWE

Moholy, Lucia
Czech photographer, 1894–1989

Born Lucia Schulz near Prague, 18 January 1894. German and English teacher and translator, 1912. Studied art history and philosophy at Prague University. Editor and journalist for publishers Kurt Wolff, Hyperion and Rowohlt, 1915–21. Married Hungarian artist László Moholy-Nagy, 1921; divorced 1929. Moved to Weimar, where Moholy-Nagy joined the Bauhaus, 1923. Apprenticeship at the photographic studio Eckner in Weimar, 1923–4. Studied at the Akademie für Graphische Künste und Buchgewerbe, Leipzig, 1925–6. Carried out architectural photography and design at the Bauhaus. Worked for the avant-garde journal *i-10*, 1926–8. Returned to Berlin, 1928. Head of photography department, Itten-Schule, Berlin, 1929–33. Emigrated to Britain, travelling via Prague, Vienna and Paris, 1933. Lecturer at London School of Printing and Graphic Arts, and Central School of Arts and Crafts, London, from 1934. Organiser of Manuscript Copying Programme, University of Cambridge, from 1940; head of the microfilm project of the Association of Special Libraries and Information Bureaux.

UNESCO commissioner for the documentation of the cultural heritage of the Middle East from 1946. Set up cultural-historical archives in Turkey, 1952–3. Moved to Switzerland, 1959. Fellow, Royal Photographic Society, 1948; honorary member, Association Internationale des Critiques d'Art (AICA) Section Suisse, 1975; member, European Society of the History of Photography, 1980. Died in Zollikon, Switzerland, 17 May 1989.

Principal Exhibitions

Individual
National Portrait Gallery, London: 1979
Galleria Milano, Milan: 1980
Galerie Renée Ziegler, Zürich: 1981
Gallery Pracapas, New York: 1984
Fotoforum, Bremen: 1988
Bauhaus-Archiv, Berlin: 1995 (retrospective)

Group
Kunstverein, Jena: 1928 (*Neue Wege der Photographie*)
Deutscher Werkbund, Stuttgart: 1929 (*Film und Foto*, touring)
Palais des Beaux-Arts, Brussels: 1932 (*Exposition internationale de la photographie*, touring)
Württembergischer Kunstverein, Stuttgart: 1968 (*50 Jahre Bauhaus*, touring), 1979 (*Film und Foto der 20er Jahre*, touring)
Art Institute of Chicago: 1976 (*Photographs from the Julien Levy Collection, Starting with Atget*)
Museum of Modern Art, San Francisco: 1980–82 (*Avant-Garde Photography in Germany, 1919–1939*, touring), 1987 (*Bauhaus Formmeisters*)
Fraenkel Gallery, San Francisco: 1981 (*Germany: The New Vision*)
Institut für Auslandsbeziehungen, Stuttgart: 1983 (*Bauhausfotografie*, touring)

Selected Writings
A Hundred Years of Photography, 1839–1939, Harmondsworth: Penguin, 1939
"Microphotography, 1835–1870–1944", *Discovery*, January 1944
"A few remarks on documentary reproduction in general and microfilm in particular", *Journal of Documentation*, i/1, 1945, pp.31–40
"Microfilm services and their application to scholarly study, scientific research, education and re-education in the post-War period: A suggestion with five appendices", submitted to the Conference of Allied Ministers of Education, August 1945
"Der Bauhausgedanke" *Blick in die Welt*, no.8, 1948, pp.30–31
"Die Kunst der Portraitphotographie", *Welt am Sonntag*, 5 December 1948
"Zu Photogrammen von Moholy-Nagy", *Ungegenständliche Photographie*, exh. cat., Gewerbemuseum, Basel, 1960
"Die Reprographie als Faktor in der Gesellschaftsbildung", *Bericht über den 1. Internationalen Kongress für Reprographie Köln, 14-19.10.1963*, ed. Ohmar Helwich, Darmstadt, 1964, pp.324–5
"Fragen der Interpretation", *Bauhaus and Bauhaus People*, ed. Eckhard Neumann, New York: Van Nostrand Reinhold, 1970, pp.169–78
Marginalien zu Moholy-Nagy, Krefeld: Scherpe, 1972
"Bauhaus im Rückblick", *Du*, no.433, March 1977, pp.50–65, 74
"The missing negatives", *British Journal of Photography*, no.130, 1983, pp.6–8, 18

Bibliography
Allan Porter, "Lucia Moholy", *Camera*, lvii, February 1978, pp.4–13
Avant-Garde Photography in Germany, 1919–1939, exh. cat., Museum of Modern Art, San Francisco, and elsewhere, 1980
Inge Bondi, "Modernist Lucia Moholy rediscovered", *Print Letter*, vi/3, 1981, pp.4–5
Margaret Harker, "From the margins to the centre: Lucia Moholy", *British Journal of Photography Annual 1982*, 1981, pp.46–55
Inge Bondi, "Lucia Moholy", *Contemporary Photographers*, ed. George Walsh, Colin Naylor and Michael Held, London: St James Press, 1982, pp.525–7
Bauhausfotografie, exh. cat., Institut für Auslandsbeziehungen, Stuttgart, and elsewhere, 1983
Rolf Sachsse, "Skizze zu Lucia Moholy", *Fotografie* (Göttingen), vii/23–4, 1983, pp.98–100
——, *Lucia Moholy*, Düsseldorf: Marzona, 1985 (contains extensive bibliography)
Sabine Hartmann, "Lucia Moholy: Fotografien für das Bauhaus", *Museumsjournal*, 3 February 1989, pp.42–3
Jeannine Fiedler, ed., *Photography at the Bauhaus*, Cambridge: Massachusetts Institute of Technology Press, 1990 (German original)
Anja Baumhoff, "Frauen und Foto am Bauhaus: Ein modernes Medium im Spannungsfeld von Geschlecht, Kunst und Technik", *Frauen Kunst Wissenschaft*, xiv, October 1992, pp.36–42
——, "Professionalisiering, Status und Geschlecht: Das Beispiel von Lucia Moholy am Bauhaus", *Wissenschaftliche Zeitschrift Hochschule für Architektur und Bauwesen Weimar*, xl/3, 1994, pp.3–5
Elke Eckert, *Bestandsverzeichnis zum Lucia Moholy-Archiv im Bauhaus-Archiv*, Berlin, 1994
Lucia Moholy: Bauhausfotografin, exh. cat., Bauhaus-Archiv, Berlin, 1995
Sabine Hartmann, "Lucia Moholy: Bauhausfotografin", *Museumsjournal*, 9 February 1995, pp.90–91

Lucia Moholy's hard-headed photographs of people and objects epitomised the Bauhaus between 1923 and 1928. In these pictures she not only documented works in the Bauhaus studios and, from 1926, the school buildings and master craftsmen's houses designed by Walter Gropius in Dessau, but also captured the teachers, students and friends of the Bauhaus itself in portrait series. Although she made an independent contribution to art and design at the Bauhaus with these photographs – one that partook of both the Neues Sehen (New Vision) and the Neue Sachlichkeit (New Objectivity) – at that time her works were regarded as mere "reproductions" that came into being in the shadow of her husband, the avant-garde Hungarian Constructivist artist László Moholy-Nagy. She saw herself "only" as a chronicler, not as an artist, and throughout her life she devoted herself, in the most diverse fields, to the question of "production-reproduction".

Moholy had already addressed this question in 1922 in a programmatic text that she co-wrote with Moholy-Nagy and which appeared in his name ("Produktion-reproduktion", *De Stijl*, July 1922, pp.98–100). In this article reproduction was described as a "virtuoso affair at best", whereas production (productive creation) was said to serve human development, and, because of this, "those appliances used so far for purposes of reproduction", such as photographs and film, should be expanded for the purposes of production. What is meant is an extension of technology from the dimension of the aesthetic and artistic to a purely practical application. Moholy herself defined her own later work as a photographer – above all at the Bauhaus – as a form of service, as she did her work on the Bauhaus books published by Moholy-Nagy and Gropius and a number of other texts by her husband, which she was meant to have formulated and reworked. Her name neither appeared by her photographs nor was she mentioned as a collaborator. Moholy herself emphasised again and again the insignificance

Moholy: *Bauhaus, Dessau, 1926*

of the rules of composition in photography and stressed the significance of that which is reproduced and mediated rather than its inherent form.

After Moholy had attended lectures on art history and philosophy – at first in her home town of Prague following her English teaching examinations – which introduced her to the empiro-critical approach of the Vienna School around Richard Avenarius and Ernst Mach, she worked as an editor for various publishing houses in Germany. With Moholy-Nagy, whom she had married at the beginning of 1921 in Berlin, she pursued the development of a new theory and practice in photography, also experimenting with the photogram and with photomontage. From these experiments there emerged the photogram *Double Portrait of László and Lucia* (1923; Bauhaus-Archiv, Berlin).

When Moholy-Nagy was asked to go to the Bauhaus in 1923, Moholy went with him as his wife, although she did not have her own contract of employment there. It was at the Bauhaus that she made her best-known group of works, which established her fame as an architectural photographer: the documentary photographs and the extensive series of pictures of the Bauhaus buildings in Dessau (see illustration). Each building was represented either frontally or from an angle of 45 degrees, mostly in diffused light, with the utmost objectivity and precision. Sections were sometimes given emphasis with obliquely falling sunlight. Panoramic views, medium shots of individual building complexes and façades, such as *Studio Façade*, as well as architectural details in close-up, such as *Studio House Balcony* (both 1926; Bauhaus-Archiv), were the usual features of her photographic approach. She took interior views of the master craftsmen's houses, such as the *Toilet Niche in the Guest Room* (1926; Bauhaus-Archiv), with the aim of demonstrating the way in which particular details were treated. The images convey an objectivity without any artistic claims: the subject itself was meant to be the main focus, not photography as a work of art. This is in contrast with the product photography of Hans Finsler – which also subscribed to Neue Sachlichkeit – in whose aestheticising photographs the object forms part of the composition. This is particularly true of Moholy's reproductions of works from the studio, such as the *Table Lamps by Jucker/Wagenfeld* (c.1924–5) and the *Teapot by Marianne Brandt* (1924; both Bauhaus-Archiv), which were not only shown in a Bauhaus sales department catalogue, but were also reproduced in newspaper supplements, magazines, in Bauhaus books, their own journal and other art and avant-garde publications.

Moholy later said of her portraits that she photographed people as if they were houses. Like her photographs of buildings, her portraits also gave the most objective portrayal possible of the subject; her concern was not the study of character, nor did she approach the problems in a purely photographic way. However, a shift in her reproductive work towards "productive creation" does become evident. Scientific documentary pictures were her starting point for each subject she took: a full-face photograph, another in profile, a view at an angle from above the forehead and hairline, and a three-quarters front view against the most neutral background possible. One of the best series is *Portraits of Florence Henri* (1927; Bauhaus-Archiv). She also made studies of hands, such as *Georg Muche's Hands* (c.1926; Bauhaus-Archiv). Although more clearly representative in character, Hugo Erfurth's

roughly contemporaneous portraits of the Bauhaus teachers show similarities in their objective stance.

In 1928 the Moholys left the Bauhaus and returned to Berlin. At first Moholy worked for her husband as a theatre and trade-fair photographer. After their separation in 1929, she lived with Theodor Neubauer, the Communist member of the Reichstag and later member of the resistance to the National Socialist regime, until his arrest by the Nazis in 1933. From this period, in which she was increasingly confronted with Germany's socio-political conditions, comes the impressive and very lively *Portrait Series of Clara Zetkin* (c.1929–30; Bauhaus-Archiv). From 1929 to 1931 she taught photography at Johannes Itten's private art school in Berlin, as a successor to Otto Umbehr (known as Umbo). Her classes focused on the technical, not the artistic principles of photography. At the same time she worked intensively on the theme of amateur photography, focusing her attention on travel scenes, people in everyday situations and landscape studies.

In 1933 Moholy fled across Europe to Britain, settling in London in the spring of 1934. There she quickly became a portraitist of prominent figures and produced conventional portraits of the British intelligentsia. Her documentary interests had to be pushed into the background. In addition, she prepared the publication on the cultural history of photography that she had long been planning. In the 1940s and 1950s she stopped working as a photographer, dedicating herself exclusively to documentary work, capturing cultural records on microfilm for various institutions and presenting this technique in numerous lectures and publications. From 1959 she worked in Zürich as a publisher of biographical collections, as an editor of the writings of Johannes Itten and as a correspondent for several English-speaking art journals – once again in a "reproductive" sense. She also wrote numerous critical articles on the Bauhaus from the viewpoint of a contemporary witness. Only in the 1970s and 1980s did Lucia Moholy receive wider acceptance as a photographer and as a critic, above all of the Bauhaus, which she regarded more as a school for a certain way of life than as an art school.

BRITTA KAISER-SCHUSTER

Moillon, Louise
French painter, 1609 or 1610–1696

Born in Paris, 1609 or 1610, to Nicolas Moillon (d. 1619), a painter and picture dealer, and his wife Marie Gilbert, the daughter of a goldsmith; Protestant family. In 1720 her mother married François Garnier, also a painter and picture dealer. Married Etienne Girardot de Chancourt, a Parisian wood merchant and Calvinist, 1640; three children; husband died before 23 January 1680. Died aged 86 in Paris, 1696.

Bibliography
Georges de Scudéry, *Le Cabinet de Mr de Scudéri gouverneur de Notre-Dame de la Garde*, 1646

E. Coyecque, "Notes sur divers peintres du XVIIe siècle", *Bulletin de la Société de l'Histoire de l'Art Français*, 1940, pp.76–82

Jacques Wilhelm, "Louise Moillon", *L'Oeil*, no.21, September 1956, pp.6–13

Michel Faré, *La Nature morte en France: Son histoire et son évolu-tion du XVIIe au XXe siècle*, 2 vols, Geneva, 1962

——, *Le Grand Siècle de la nature morte en France: Le XVIIe siècle*, Fribourg: Office du Livre, and Paris: Société Française du Livre, 1974

——, "Trois peintres de fruits du temps de Louis XIII", *Connaissance des Arts*, cclxxii, October 1974, pp.88–95

Women Artists, 1550–1950, exh. cat., Los Angeles County Museum of Art, and elsewhere, 1976

Charles Sterling, *Still Life Painting from Antiquity to the Twentieth Century*, revised edition, New York: Harper, 1981 (French origi-nal, 1952)

France in the Golden Age: Seventeenth-Century French Paintings in North American Collections, exh. cat., Grand Palais, Paris, and elsewhere, 1982

Christopher Wright, *The French Painters of the Seventeenth Century*, London: Orbis, and Boston: Little Brown, 1985

Michel and Fabrice Faré, "Louise Moillon, Les Girardot, marchands de bois parisiens et une oeuvre inédite de Louise Moillon", *Gazette des Beaux-Arts*, 6th series, cviii, 1986, pp.49–65

Grand Siècle: Peintures françaises du XVIIe siècle dans les collections publiques françaises, exh. cat., Musée des Beaux-Arts, Montreal, and elsewhere, 1993

Although Louise Moillon painted still lifes exclusively, her work cannot be associated with the humble subject matter that the French Académie Royale confined to the bottom of the artistic hierarchy, nor is it comparable to those paintings by young lady amateurs who became notorious in the 19th century for their still lifes. Instead, Moillon belonged to a circle of painters working in the Saint-Germain-des-Prés area of Paris that provided refuge for those from the southern Netherlands fleeing religious persecution. Both her father and her stepfather and several of her brothers and sisters were painters, and her work belonged to a recognisable artisanal tradition of still life. That is, it was produced for economic reasons and was not the "accomplishment" art that is often identified with women practitioners of the genre.

Stylistically, Moillon's work belongs to the convention of the "table-top" still life that was developed in the Saint-Germain-des-Prés quarter. *Still Life with Fruit and Asparagus* (Art Institute of Chicago), signed and dated 1630, is depicted as if seen from above, sloping towards the viewer and against an indistinct background. The fruit, basket and leaves are meticulously painted with great attention paid to the delineation of different textures. *Basket with Peaches and Grapes* (1631; see illustration) follows the same formula, with jewel-like fruits glowing against a murky background, and

Moillon: *Basket with Peaches and Grapes*, 1631; Staatliche Kunsthalle, Karlsruhe

trompe-l'oeil elements such as the leaves hanging over the edge of the table and the cut flesh of the peach revealing its inner texture. Combined with their small size, their simplicity and harmony, these works have been seen by some commentators as indicative of Moillon's Protestant faith and her celebration of *la vie silencieuse*. But the intimacy, the domestic subject matter and the absence of human models may be due as much to her gender and the craft tradition within which she worked. Although there are fewer works dating from after her marriage in 1640, the still life was the perfect subject for a woman with other domestic duties to practise at home, being small and needing no models. Other works, however, were larger and more clearly virtuoso demonstrations. *Still Life with Fruit and Vegetables* (Thyssen-Bornemisza Collection) is well over a metre in width and the customary apricots and plums in the basket on a stone shelf are joined by asparagus, artichokes and strawberries in a blue and white porcelain dish. As in all her works, the fruit is perfect, with none of the blemished, over-ripe fruit that Netherlandish artists depicted. Consequently, in Moillon's work there is little suggestion of any symbolic allusion to the frailty of human existence or of time passing: her still lifes embody perpetual present. If anything, Moillon's work suggests bourgeois comfort and plenty and there is little suggestion of frugality.

That Moillon was regarded as the equal of her male peers is demonstrated by Georges de Scudéry (1646), who placed her alongside the still-life painters Linard and Pierre van Boucle and compared all three with Michelangelo, Raphael and Titian. Clearly hyperbolic in tone, Scudéry's analogy highlights the distinction between the very public art of the Italian Renaissance that was to provide the model for the French Académie Royale and the private art of Moillon and those around her in the Saint-Germain-des-Prés area. After Jean François Félibien codified the hierarchy of the genres in the 1660s, still life was increasingly marginalised and seen as the perfect subject for the aspiring female artist, who was denied access to the higher genres because of their dependence on study from the model. Cathérine Duchemin, the first woman member of the Academy, was accepted in 1663 with a reception piece of flowers, and six years later Geneviève and Madeleine Boullogne were accepted with a collaborative still life that included an architectural backdrop and musical trophies. Well into the 19th century, women who wished for any success within the Academic system were more likely to be accepted if they produced still lifes or flower paintings. The stranglehold that the Académie Royale exercised on French artistic life and the constraint of the hierarchy of the genres meant, however, that the tradition of the perfectly crafted, intimate still life was replaced by much more literary and decorative works.

LESLEY STEVENSON

Moll, Marg
German sculptor and painter, 1884–1977

Born Margarethe Häffner in Mulhouse, Alsace, 2 August 1884. Studied under the painter Hans Völker in Wiesbaden, and attended the Städelsches Institut, Frankfurt am Main, 1903–5; studied painting under Oskar Moll in Bavaria, sculpture under Louise Schmidt in Frankfurt am Main, 1905. Went to Rome, 1905. Studied under Lovis Corinth in Berlin, 1906–7. Married Moll, professor at the Breslau Academy, 1906; two daughters. Studied at Académie Matisse, Paris, 1907–8; founded the Matisse School in Paris with Oskar Moll, 1908; studied under Fernand Léger in Paris, 1928. Lived in Berlin, 1908–19; Breslau, 1919–32; Berlin, 1934–52; Düsseldorf and Munich, from 1952. House in Berlin and much of work destroyed by bombing, 1943. Travelled in Europe and USA after husband's death in 1947; met Henry Moore in London, 1950. Member, Women's International Art Club, London, 1951; GEDOK (Gemeinschaft Deutscher und Österreichischer Künstlerinnen), 1930–70. Recipient of Groupe 1940 medal, Paris, 1940; medal of Women's International Art Club, 1951. Died in Munich, 1977.

Principal Exhibitions

Individual
Galerie Alfred Flechtheim, Berlin: 1931
Galerie Schüler, Berlin-Zehlendorf: 1947 (with Oskar Moll)
Kunstamt Tiergarten, Berlin: 1947, 1959, 1964
Leopold-Hoesch-Museum, Düren: 1949
Städtisches Kunstmuseum, Duisburg: 1958 (with Emy Roeder and Johanna Schütz-Wolff)

Group
Galerie Wolfgang Gurlitt, Berlin: 1914
Galerie von der Goltz, Munich: 1924
Grosse Berliner Kunstausstellung, Berlin: 1929
Novembergruppe, Berlin: 1929
Galerie Georges Petit, Paris: 1932
Kunstverein, Düsseldorf: 1935
Munich: 1937 (*Entartete Kunst*)
Städtisches Museum am Ostwall, Dortmund: 1950, 1954, 1961
National Eisteddfod, Wales: 1950
Haus am Tiergarten, Berlin: 1953, 1959
Kunstverein, Heidelberg: 1958

Selected Writings

Typescript autobiography, Moll-Archiv, Archiv für bildende Kunst, Germanisches Nationalmuseum, Nuremberg, no.1, 14d
"Unser gemeinsames Leben: Zum 90. Geburtstag Oskar Molls", *Die Kunst und das schöne Heim*, lxiii, 1964–5, pp.422–5

Bibliography

Max Osborn and Curt Glaser, Galerie Flechtheim exhibition reviews, *Berliner Börsencourier*, 1. supplement, no.21, 14 January 1931
Alfred Barr, Jr, *Matisse: His Art and His Public*, New York: Museum of Modern Art, 1951
Bonner Rundschau, 6 February 1954
Ernst Scheyer, *Die Kunstakademie Breslau und Oskar Moll*, Würzburg, 1961
John Anthony Thwaites, "Margarethe Moll", *Bulletin*, 24 March 1964 (New York Public Library Artists File, Cambridge, 1987–, microfiche no.M703)
Pariser Begegnungen, 1900–1945, exh. cat., Lehmbruck Museum, Duisburg, 1965
Brigitte Würtz, *Margarete Moll 85*, Düsseldorf, 1969
——, "Margarete Moll als Malerin", *Die Kunst und das schöne Heim*, lxxxi, 1969, pp.234–6, 398–400
——, "Die Bildhauerin und Malerin Marg Moll", brochure, Berlin: GEDOK, 1971 (in Bibliothek des Germanischen Nationalmuseums, Nuremberg, no.KK 93/v., 30 June 1971)

Margarete Moll: Bilder-Skulpturen-Skizzen, exh. cat., Düsseldorf, and elsewhere, 1974

H. Griesbach, "Zum Tode Margarete Molls", *Das Kunstwerk*, xxx/3, 1977, p.91

Das Verborgene Museum I: Dokumentation der Kunst von Frauen in Berliner öffentlichen Sammlungen, exh. cat., Akademie der Künste, Berlin, 1987

Dorothea Salzmann and Siegfried Salzmann, "Die Bildhauerin Marg Moll", *Matisse und seine deutschen Schüler*, exh. cat., Kaiserslauten, 1988, pp.103–6

Deutsche Bildhauer, 1900–1945: Entartet, exh. cat., Bremen and Duisburg, 1992

Erika Esau, "*Künstlerehepaar*: Ideal and reality", *Visions of the "Neue Frau": Women and the Visual Arts in Weimar Germany*, ed. Marsha Meskimmon and Shearer West, Aldershot: Scolar Press, 1995, pp.28–41

Erich Ranfft, "German women sculptors, 1918–1936: Gender differences and status", *ibid.*, pp.42–61

Moll: *Standing Woman with Jug*, 1928; height 54 cm.; Georg-Kolbe-Museum, Berlin

The revelatory moment in Margarethe (she was always known as Marg) Moll's life was her discovery of Matisse in Paris in 1907. For a young artist who had become a painter in Germany before modern art had reached the country, Matisse's brightly coloured canvases must have appeared astonishingly new and radical. Moll had studied first in Wiesbaden and Frankfurt am Main, and then at Lovis Corinth's famous school for women artists in Berlin. After marrying Oskar Moll in 1906 – many years later, she confessed that "he jokingly stated that he had to marry away the competition" (typescript autobiography) – she went with him to Paris, where the couple was instrumental, with the German artist Hans Purrmann, in establishing the Matisse School in Montparnasse. The school aimed at teaching and promoting the modernist aesthetic, especially that of Matisse, among visiting foreign artists. They became good friends with Matisse, who in 1908 painted a famous portrait of *Greta Moll* (National Gallery, London).

Marg Moll now began to concentrate on sculpture; she worked quite intensively with Matisse himself, perfecting a simplification of form using every kind of sculptural material. While she continued to paint throughout her life, she was the only sculptor of the Matisse group; as she later freely admitted, her decision to give up painting in favour of sculpture was to avoid any competition with her painter husband. By the time the Molls returned to Germany, where Oskar was appointed director of the Breslau Academy, Marg's sculptural style had moved from Matisse-like figurative works to the severely simple forms reminiscent of Constantin Brancusi, a modernist conception completely unknown in Germany at that time. At other times, she incorporated elements of German Expressionism and Bauhaus style, as she would have experienced them among the artists of the Breslau Academy.

The Molls were quite conscious of their mission as an artistic team, committed to the nurturing of a modernist vision in Germany. While Marg continued throughout her life to work as an active artist, she was also conscious of her role as "director's wife", which she saw as a means of spreading their aesthetic message. Their home was filled with the paintings of Matisse, Fernand Léger, Braque and Picasso; they frequently exhibited and lectured about their own collection, and their house became the centre of Breslau's artistic life.

In later interviews and her own writings, it is clear that Moll consciously maintained artistic independence from Oskar; while later their work was often exhibited together, her most significant early exhibitions were with other artists, most notably the Novembergruppe in Berlin, and with Oskar Schlemmer, a fellow Breslau artist, at the Galerie Flechtheim in 1931. Her works were bought by museums throughout Germany. In 1928, as she wrote in her autobiographical notes, she took an "Eheferien" – a vacation from marriage – and returned to Paris to work, most significantly with Léger. At this time, she also solidified her understanding of Brancusi and Zadkine; her *Standing Woman with Jug* (1928; see illustration) in brass exemplifies her experimental attempts to stress the medium itself through an analysis of simple forms and spatial relations, an attitude that she applied to all kinds of metals, as well as wood and even to mosaic friezes. She once told an interviewer: "Form! Form! I'm only concerned with form!" (quoted in Würtz 1971, p.8). It is telling that her pieces were included in the famous *Entartete Kunst* (Degenerate art) exhibition of 1937, in which the Nazis attempted to demonstrate the degeneracy and insanity of modern art. Consequently her works were removed from museums, many of them destroyed. While compelled to live in "internal exile" during World War II, the Molls were still able to build an ultra-modern house in Berlin designed by Hans Scharoun; it became, as one writer said, "an oasis of freedom" in wartime Germany. The house was destroyed during the bombing of Berlin in 1943, as were many of the Molls' works.

After the war and Oskar Moll's death in 1947, Marg Moll went to Britain, where she came to the attention of Henry Moore and Reg Butler; she exhibited there several times, before returning to Germany in 1951. Here she became increasingly involved in the activities of GEDOK, an organisation founded to aid women artists and to provide venues for exhibitions. At the age of 70 she travelled to America and gave a series of lectures on Matisse at Wayne State University in Detroit. During the 1950s most of her exhibitions were in conjunction with Oskar's colourful canvases, where her abstract sculptures would be juxtaposed with his paintings. On her 75th birthday in 1959 numerous congratulatory notes in newspapers and journals attest to her important role in furthering modern art in Germany, not only through her own work, but as a collector and advocate of modernist ideas. Of greatest interest in these laudatory essays is the recognition of her contribution to the cause of women artists, simply by remaining independent of her husband's style and through her continuous commitment to her own active artistic life. Comments made by Anna Klapheck about the artist's character could as easily apply to her artistic style: "An innate acerbity and unsentimentality, whereby she conceals her feelings, make her appear cooler than she actually is" (GEDOK statement for Moll's 75th birthday, 1959; in Moll-Archiv, Archiv für bildende Kunst, Nuremberg, no.1, 14d/37).

ERIKA ESAU

Morgan, Evelyn De *see* De Morgan

Morisot, Berthe

French painter, 1841–1895

Born in Bourges, 14 January 1841; father a government official. Settled in the Parisian suburb of Passy with her family, *c*.1852. Took drawing lessons from the academic painter Geoffroy Alphonse Chocarne, 1857, then studied under Joseph-Benoît Guichard of Lyons, a pupil of Ingres and Delacroix. Taught by Camille Corot, then by his pupil Achille-François Oudinot; also took lessons in sculpture from Aimé Millet. Introduced to Edouard Manet by Henri Fantin-Latour, *c*.1867–8. Travelled to the Pyrenees, 1862, to Normandy 1864; visited Madrid, 1872, England, 1875; spent summers in Pontoise and Brittany. Married Manet's brother Eugène, 1874; daughter born 1878; husband died 1892. Died in Passy, 2 March 1895.

Principal Exhibitions

Paris Salon: 1864–6, 1868, 1870, 1872–3
Impressionist group, Paris: 1874, 1876–7, 1880–82, 1886
Durand-Ruel Gallery, London: 1883
National Academy of Design, New York: 1886 (Impressionist group, special exhibition), 1887 (Impressionist group, organised by Paul Durand-Ruel)
Salon des XX, Brussels: 1887
Galerie Georges Petit, Paris: 1887 (*Exposition Internationale*)
Galerie Boussod et Valadon, Paris: 1892 (individual)
Salon de la Libre Esthétique, Brussels: 1894
Galerie Durand-Ruel, Paris: 1896 (retrospective)

Selected Writings

Correspondance de Berthe Morisot avec sa famille et ses amis, ed. Denis Rouart, Paris, 1950; as *The Correspondence of Berthe Morisot with Her Family and Friends: Manet, Puvis de Chavannes, Degas, Monet, Renoir and Mallarmé*, London, 1957; 2nd edition, 1959; with new introduction and notes by Kathleen Adler and Tamar Garb, London: Camden, 1986

Bibliography

Berthe Morisot (Mme Eugène Manet), 1841–1895, exh. cat., Paris, Galerie Durand-Ruel, 1896
Roger Marx, "Les femmes peintres et l'impressionisme: Berthe Morisot", *Gazette des Beaux-Arts*, 3rd series, xxxviii, 1907, pp.491–508
Armand Fourreau, *Berthe Morisot*, Paris: Rieder, 1925
Monique Angoulvent, *Berthe Morisot*, Paris: Morancé [1933]
Louis Rouart, *Berthe Morisot*, Paris, 1941
Rosamond Bernier, "Dans la lumière impressioniste", *L'Oeil*, no.53, May 1959, pp.38–47
Paul Valéry, *Degas, Manet, Morisot*, London: Routledge, and New York: Pantheon, 1960 (French original)
M.-L. Bataille and G. Wildenstein, *Berthe Morisot: Catalogue des peintures, pastels et aquarelles*, Paris: Les Beaux Arts, 1961
Philippe Huisman, *Morisot: Charmes*, Lausanne: International Art Books, 1962
John Rewald, *The History of Impressionism*, 4th edition, New York: Museum of Modern Art, and London: Secker and Warburg, 1973
Janine Bailly-Herzberg, "Les estampes de Berthe Morisot", *Gazette des Beaux-Arts*, 6th series, xciii, 1979, pp.215–27
Julie Manet, *Journal (1893–1899): Sa jeunesse parmi les peintres impressionistes et les hommes de lettres*, Paris: Klincksieck, 1979; as *Growing Up with the Impressionists: The Diary of Julie Manet*, London: Sotheby's Publications, 1987
Charlotte Yeldham, *Women Artists in Nineteenth-Century France and England*, 2 vols, New York: Garland, 1984
Alain Clairet, "'Le Cerisier' de Mézy", *L'Oeil*, no.358, May 1985, pp.48–51
Tamar Garb, *Women Impressionists*, Oxford: Phaidon, and New York: Rizzoli, 1986
The New Painting: Impressionism, 1874–1886, exh. cat., National Gallery of Art, Washington, DC, and elsewhere, 1986
Kathleen Adler and Tamar Garb, *Berthe Morisot*, Oxford: Phaidon, and Ithaca, NY: Cornell University Press, 1987

Beth Genné, "Two self-portraits by Berthe Morisot", *Psychoanalytic Perspectives on Art*, ed. Mary Mathews Gedo, ii, Hillsdale, NJ: Analytic Press, 1987, pp.133–70

Berthe Morisot: Impressionist, exh. cat., National Gallery of Art, Washington, DC, 1987

Robert L. Herbert, *Impressionism: Art, Leisure and Parisian Society*, New Haven and London: Yale University Press, 1988

Suzanne G. Lindsay, "Berthe Morisot and the poets: The visual language of woman", *Helicon Nine*, no.19, 1988, pp.8–17

Kathleen Adler, "The suburban, the modern and 'une dame de Passy'", *Oxford Art Journal*, xii/1, 1989, pp.3–13

Jean-Dominique Rey, *Berthe Morisot*, 2nd edition, Paris: Flammarion, 1989

T. J. Edelstein, ed., *Perspectives on Morisot*, New York: Hudson Hills Press, 1990

Anne Higonnet, *Berthe Morisot: A Biography*, New York: Harper, and London: Collins, 1990

Berthe Morisot (1841–1895), exh. cat., JPL Fine Arts, London, 1990

Anne Higonnet, *Berthe Morisot's Images of Women*, Cambridge, MA: Harvard University Press, 1992

Wendy Slatkin, ed., *The Voices of Women Artists*, Englewood Cliffs, NJ: Prentice Hall, 1993

Berthe Morisot's critical reputation has always been linked with Impressionism. Not only was she one of the founding and most consistent members of this exhibiting organisation in Paris in the 1870s and 1880s, her work came in the 1890s and subsequent French accounts of the period to stand for the purest and most essential embodiment of the Impressionist aesthetic. While British and American histories of the period all but ignored her contribution to Impressionism until the 1970s, when she was "rediscovered" in the wake of the feminist quest for "lost women artists", French accounts, from the 19th century onwards, afforded her a central place, but one that was circumscribed in highly gendered ways. Morisot came to stand as the quintessential "feminine" painter, one whose adherence to the "spontaneous", "superficial" art of "sensation" that Impressionism was seen to represent fulfilled the demands for the delicate, feminine sensibility deemed appropriate by 19th-century and subsequent French commentators. Unlike her "manly" contemporaries such as Rosa Bonheur (q.v.) and Suzanne Valadon (q.v.), widely seen to have reneged on their intuitive, feminine sensibilities, Morisot fulfilled these in her commitment to an art that celebrated physical sensation, spontaneity and unmediated response. Impressionism was seen as a feminine art, and a skilled woman artist such as Morisot was its most legitimate exponent. Morisot's reputation, although considerable in French art-historical accounts therefore, is based both upon a 19th-century notion of "femininity", and a particularly circumscribed understanding of Impressionism.

Morisot's fate in standard anglophone accounts of Impressionism was markedly different. If featured at all, she was most usually referred to as the pupil of Corot (with whom she briefly studied in 1862) or Manet (who was never in fact her teacher), and represented as a marginal if at all visible presence. John Rewald, the standard authority on Impressionism for decades, did not count her among the important "gang of four" – Monet, Renoir, Pissarro and Degas – who constituted, for him, the core Impressionist group. Such an exclusion is hard to justify, especially as Morisot was one of the most consistent participants in the Impressionist exhibitions and was included in seven out of the eight group shows organised between 1874 and 1886. What was more, Morisot, an

Morisot: *View of Paris from the Trocadéro*, 1872; oil on canvas; 45.9 × 81.4 cm.; Santa Barbara Museum, California, Gift of Mrs Hugh N. Kirkland

independently wealthy woman, helped to finance these ventures and was a key personality among the central participants in the group. Married to Eugène Manet, brother of Edouard Manet, the acknowledged mentor to all the younger Impressionists, friend and confidante of Renoir and Degas, referred to by Pissarro as "our old comrade" at the time of her death, and close friend of Stéphane Mallarmé, the Symbolist writer who wrote some of the most important 19th-century art criticism, Morisot was at the heart of progressive artistic and intellectual circles. An examination of her work reveals an artist committed to the naturalist principles of her cohort and a key player in the formation of a plein-air practice based upon the invention of a pictorial language that would be adequate to the recording of visual sensation and commensurate with a modern sensibility and modernist material self-consciousness.

Morisot was born in Bourges in 1841, the youngest of three sisters. Yves, the eldest, was born in 1838, and Edma, who also became an artist, was two years older than Berthe. She also had a younger brother, Tiburce. Their father was a high-ranking civil servant who moved the family to Passy, then still a village just outside Paris, later to become Paris's 16th *arrondissement*, when Morisot was eleven. She remained within the boundaries of Passy from then on for the remainder of her life. She was destined to live the life of any upper-middle-class French woman. Her early education followed the pattern set for young women of her class, and the painting lessons that she and her two sisters took formed part of the accepted grounding in the accomplishment arts without which no *bourgeoise* could be groomed and capable of making an eligible match. The young Morisot sisters were required to dabble in watercolours and sketching as they were required to learn to sew, play the piano and take an interest in fashion and personal adornment. To this end they were enrolled with an art master, Père Chocarne, who undertook to teach them drawing, an experience that they seem to have found dull and onerous. The oldest Morisot sister, Yves, was so put off by the experience that she gave up art altogether, but the two younger sisters were able to change teacher and became the pupils of the conservative painter and teacher, Joseph-Benoît Guichard. Horrified to find that he was dealing with two young ladies of talent, Guichard wrote to their mother:

> Considering the character of your daughters, my teaching will not endow them with minor drawing room accomplishments; they will become painters. Do you realize what this means? In the upper-class milieu to which you belong, this will be revolutionary, I might almost say catastrophic [*Correspondance*, Adler and Garb 1986, p.19].

To her credit, Mme Morisot was undaunted by this prospect and the Morisot girls were able to undertake a relatively serious training in the arts of painting and drawing.

All the official art schools were closed to women at this time, but wealthy women such as the Morisot sisters – unlike the majority of women – could benefit from private tuition. Privileged both materially and through the fact that they had enlightened parents, Berthe and Edma were afforded an unusually serious art education for their time, although they would never be given rigorous training in life drawing or classical culture as would have been the norm for contemporary male

students. Like all ambitious young artists, though, they were enrolled as copyists in the Louvre, where many aspirant women artists earned their living by copying famous works for provincial collections. It was here, too, that they made the acquaintance of many of the important younger generation of French artists such as Carolus-Duran (the fashionable portraitist whose wife was an accomplished painter and pastellist), Henri Fantin-Latour (painter and husband of the still-life painter Victoria Dubourg, q.v.) and Félix Bracquemond (engraver and future husband of the Impressionist painter Marie Bracquemond, q.v.) and began to imagine themselves as potential professional artists rather than as lady amateurs. Morisot was by now aware of the new, naturalist trends in contemporary art and intent on identifying herself with them. She had tired of her teacher Guichard whose teaching could not satisfy her new interests. Camille Corot, the most famous living naturalist landscapist had become a friend of the Morisot family and in 1862 gave Edma and Berthe some art lessons, fully initiating them into the rigours and procedures of plein-air painting. On Corot's recommendation, the sisters were taught by the landscapist Achille-François Oudinot. By the mid-1860s Morisot's apprenticeship was over and, like all young artists, she drew from her contemporaries and predecessors, learning from her peers and influencing them in turn. Probably the most important figure for her during the 1860s was the family friend Edouard Manet with whom she developed a close professional relationship, learning from him at the same time as developing her own painterly and light-filled style that would, in turn, influence the older artist and urge him in the direction of plein-air painting.

In 1864 both Berthe and Edma had works accepted at the Paris Salon, the most important annual exhibition of contemporary work, and they continued to exhibit regularly throughout the 1860s. Edma became engaged to a naval officer, Adolphe Pontillon, in 1867, and when she married him two years later she gave up painting, finding it impossible to combine the roles of professional artist and conventional wife. After the Franco-Prussian war and the Commune (1870–71), Berthe resumed her painting, and continued to submit works to the Salon. She was invited to join the artists planning a group exhibition, independent of the Salon, and in April 1874 her work was on view at the exhibition of the Société Anonyme des Artistes-Peintres, Sculpteurs, Graveurs etc., in the premises of the photographer Nadar on the boulevard des Capucines. This show became known as the first Impressionist exhibition. Morisot married Manet's brother Eugène in December 1874, and their only child, Julie, frequently the subject of her mother's paintings, was born on 14 November 1878.

Morisot remained loyal to the independent exhibitions, and never returned to the Salon. In 1887 her work was included in an International Exhibition organised by the dealer Georges Petit, as well as in his rival Paul Durand-Ruel's Impressionist exhibition in New York. Her first solo exhibition was held in 1892 at the premises of Boussod et Valadon. In 1894 the State made its first purchase of her work, *Jeune femme en toilette de bal* (Musée d'Orsay, Paris). This, like many of Morisot's works, was modelled in the family home. The model is depicted dressed in evening wear, but remains within the confines of the domestic interior. Many of Morisot's works use members of her family as models, and deal with the refined

Morisot: *Mme Pontillon (The Artist's Sister)*, 1871; Courtauld Institute Galleries, London

leisure pursuits of upper-middle-class women, their children and the domestic servants on whose labour this class depended. Morisot documented the phases of women's lives, starting with the infancy of her daughter, Julie, and showing her development as a young girl and an adolescent. She also represented her sisters during their confinements, producing some of the few portraits of pregnant women in 19th-century art. Her pastel portrait of Edma (*Mme Pontillon*, 1871; see illustration), her erstwhile companion and fellow painter, depicts her sister with arms characteristically resting on her swollen belly, once again ensconced within the family interior.

Morisot remained close to her Impressionist colleagues, particularly to Renoir, in the later years of her life. After her death in 1895, Camille Pissarro wrote to his son Lucien:

> You can hardly conceive how surprised we all were and how moved, too, by the disappearance of this distinguished woman, who had such a splendid feminine talent and who brought honour to our impressionist group which is vanishing – like all things. Poor Mme Morisot, the public hardly knows her!

The *View of Paris from the Trocadéro* (see illustration), probably painted in the summer of 1872, provides a useful example of Morisot's practice in both subject matter and technique. The view was one recommended in tourist guides, and very familiar to her, for the Morisot family home at this time was on the rue Franklin, adjacent to the gardens. The painting represents two women and a child on a path separated from the remainder of the grounds by a wooden barrier. Neither of the women is shown looking at the view of the city beyond. This view stretches beyond the immaculate lawns of the Trocadéro to the Seine and the Pont d'Iéna. Immediately beyond the river, to the right of the painting, is the empty space of the Champ de Mars, and beyond, on the horizon, various Paris landmarks can be identified, among them the Palais de l'Industrie, site of the annual Paris Salon, Sainte-Clotilde, Notre-Dame, Saint-Sulpice, the gilded dome of Les Invalides and, in the far distance, the dome of the Pantheon. The gardens of the Tuileries are visible on the extreme left of the painting.

The painting is unusual in its format, being almost twice as wide as it is high. The composition is a variant on one familiar in landscape painting, not only in the work of Corot but in 17th-century precedents, such as Claude and Poussin, with the figures on an elevated section in the foreground and a river leading the eye into the background. But Morisot makes this formula unrecognisable by the freedom with which the middle ground is painted, so that the effect is of a horizontal band, difficult to interpret, running across the painting. Details such as the carriages and figures are sketchily indicated, with no sense of preliminary drawing. Touches of colour – such as the red in the flower-beds to the right and the pink in the buildings on the far bank of the Seine – counter the sense of perspectival distance implied by the distant building, and emphasise the surface of the canvas.

Morisot painted a view of Paris restored to order after the events of the Franco-Prussian War, and especially of the Commune. In mid-May 1871, the year before the painting was executed, the Communards were in charge of the Trocadéro and the Versailles troops had commandeered most of Passy,

including the Morisots' home. Constant fire was exchanged between the Communards and the Versaillaises positioned in the Bois de Boulogne, and anyone standing in the position of the figures in this painting would have been caught in the crossfire. At the end of May, many of the public buildings in Paris were destroyed in fires, making the city appear, as Morisot's mother described it, "like a volcanic eruption". Nothing of this is visible in Morisot's painting, which represents Paris returned to order, all scars hidden. In this choice of subject matter, she shared a position with her fellow Impressionists, who also avoided any sites that bore visible traces of the events of the war and the Commune.

Morisot's choice of subject and vantage point is one that occurs frequently in her work. Most of her work represents the lives of women and children in the home, in areas such as Passy, or in places along the Normandy coast frequented by Parisians at leisure. Passy was the most village-like of the areas incorporated by Baron Haussmann in 1860 into the 20 *arrondissements* that make up Paris's administrative structure, and its residents clung to that village-like quality well into the 20th century, seeing their part of Paris as separate from the tumult of the city. This sense of separation is conveyed in Morisot's painting by the barrier of the fence and the sweep of the green lawns. Passy was by this date a suburb, growing rapidly in size, and emulating such London suburbs as Hampstead. It was differentiated from the centre of the city by being, during the day at least, largely a place for women and children, a place from which bourgeois men left to go to work in the heart of Paris. Morisot's painting shows this area as a woman's territory, a space in which women enjoyed a degree of freedom to visit friends and to walk with children. The literature on this painting continues to contrast it with Manet's earlier *View of the Exposition Universelle* (1867; Nasjonalgalleriet, Oslo), a painting to which it is related only by virtue of the fact that both are painted from the Trocadéro gardens. The repetition of this comparison indicates how difficult it is to evaluate Morisot, for she is constantly positioned in the literature of Impressionism in relation to her male colleagues, invariably in such a way as to diminish her achievement.

This painting was one of several that the dealer Paul Durand-Ruel bought from Morisot on consignment in February 1873. He paid 500 francs for it, and sold it, apparently on the same day, to the collector Ernest Hoschedé, one of the most committed collectors of Impressionist paintings at this date. Hoschedé paid Durand-Ruel 750 francs for the painting. It was then sold to the Romanian collector Georges de Bellio in 1876, immediately after the second independent group show, at the auction of Hoschedé's collection following the crash of his business.

In 1987 Mount Holyoke College Art Museum in association with the National Gallery of Art, Washington, DC, organised the exhibition *Berthe Morisot: Impressionist*. This exhibition, together with revisionist feminist scholarship of the period, made Morisot's oeuvre visible to an English-speaking public for the first time. During the past decade Morisot's achievement not only as an Impressionist but as a major woman artist of the modern period has been reassessed.

KATHLEEN ADLER and TAMAR GARB

Morreau, Jacqueline

American painter, 1926–

Born Jacqueline Segall in Milwaukee, Wisconsin, 1926. Studied at Chouinard Art Institute, Los Angeles, 1944–6; Jepson Art Institute under Rico Lebrun, 1946–9; Los Angeles City College and University of California Medical School, San Francisco, 1955–8 (diploma in medical illustration); graduate studies in etching at University of California, Berkeley, under Kathan Brown, 1962–3, and in San Francisco under Gordon Cook; studied lithography under Herb Fox at Stanhope Press, Boston, 1969. Moved to London, 1972. Studied theatre design at Royal Academy of Dramatic Art (RADA), London, 1989. Visiting lecturer in painting and drawing, Oxford Brookes University, Oxford, and professor of art, Regent's College, London, 1989. One child from first marriage born 1951. Married Patrick Morreau, 1959; son born 1960, two daughters born 1962 and 1964. Lives in London.

Selected Individual Exhibitions

Edna Stebbins Gallery, Cambridge, MA: 1970, 1972
Women's Arts Alliance, London: 1978
Pentonville Gallery, London: 1982
Art Space Gallery, London: 1986, 1988
Posterngate Gallery, City Museums and Art Galleries, Hull: 1988
Lyth Art Centre, Scotland: 1989
Odette Gilbert Gallery, London: 1990
Isis Gallery, Essex: 1992, 1994
Nuffield College, Oxford: 1993
Ferens Art Gallery, Hull: 1996

Selected Writings

Editor, *Women's Images of Men*, London and New York: Writers and Readers, 1985 (with Sarah Kent)
Jacqueline Morreau: Drawings and Graphics, Metuchen, NJ: Scarecrow Press, 1986 (introduction by Sarah Kent)
Jacqueline Morreau: Myth and Metaphor, London: Artemis, 1989 (introduction by Keith Wheldon)
The Sexual Imagination from Acker to Zola: A Feminist Companion, ed. Harriet Gilbert, London: Cape, 1993

Bibliography

Power Plays, exh. cat., Bluecoat Gallery, Liverpool, and Pentonville Gallery, London, 1983
Pandora's Box, exh. cat., Arnolfini Gallery, Bristol, 1984
Paradise Lost, exh. cat., Ikon Gallery, Birmingham, 1984
Women Live, video, ITV, 1986
Women in War and Peace, exh. cat., University of Houston, TX, 1986
Rozsika Parker and Griselda Pollock, *Framing Feminism: Art and the Women's Movement, 1970–85*, London: Pandora, 1987
Gill Saunders, *The Nude: A New Perspective*, London: Herbert, and New York: Harper, 1989
Keith Wheldon and others, *Americans Abroad*, Pontypool, Gwent: Archangel Press, 1989
Women and Water: Three Women, exh. cat., Odette Gilbert Gallery, London, 1989
Marks of Tradition, exh. cat., Museum of Modern Art, Oxford, 1990
Paradise Now: Jacqueline Morreau, exh. cat., Odette Gilbert Gallery, London, 1990
Beyond Reason, exh. cat., Battersea Arts Centre, London, 1991
Strategies for Women Artists, video, BBC Open University, 1992

Jacqueline Morreau's work as a feminist painter has involved the rewriting of narratives and myths central to the Western tradition from the perspective of a female subject. Her early training in traditional methods of figurative drawing and oil painting has never been abandoned but has steadily developed to exploit a "masterly" free-flowing line in drawing and a complex layering of colour in her oil paintings of figurative subjects.

Most of Morreau's work since 1972 has concentrated on several large cycles of mythic figures, which have formed the subject of her major exhibitions, particularly *Myth and Metaphor* and *Psyche and Eros*. In direct contrast to the general passivity and spectacle of "Woman" in classical Western allegories, Morreau's work places the desires, emotions and actions of her female figures in the foreground. She opens up a feminist reading because she provides a new point of identification for a female spectator with the actions of her chosen female subjects, Eve, Pandora, Persephone and Psyche. These are all myths in which the woman is blamed for creating new and more difficult states of being: specifically, banishment from the Garden of Eden (Eve); a world in which evil is set loose (Pandora); the creation of the seasons of winter and summer (Persephone); and the end of a blissful union between lovers because the woman seeks greater knowledge about her lover (Psyche). In each case the transformation and metamorphosis in women's lives is triggered by the highlighting of choices and actions within the composition. Morreau replaces the high drama of classical painting where "Woman" is seen as an object of sexual exchange between men – in Eve's case God and Adam, in Persephone's case Zeus and Hades – to focus on the woman herself and the changes wrought in her life. This focus serves to disrupt more traditional readings of the myth and story and initiates an elaborate spinning of meanings in terms of the association and identification on the part of the (female) spectator with the female character. The idea of the Fates as women who spin also became a subject in the mid-1980s. This deliberate shift in perspective, a disruption of accepted norms, underlies Morreau's work involvement in organising two major group exhibitions, *Women's Images of Men* and *Pandora's Box* in the 1980s. In the former, the way in which women looked at men reversed the normative expectation that art consists of men's images of women. In the latter, the depiction of Pandora as the "Woman" responsible for letting loose all the evils of the world was reread by women artists.

In Morreau's work the rewriting and rereading of myths become a vehicle of revelation about women's desires and psychology. Her paintings highlight conflicts engendered by emotion and reason in order to open up a space in which women's psychological dilemmas and choices and their resulting dramas can be seen in a direct figurative and expressive method. This is particularly true of her *Psyche and Eros* cycle (1985–95; e.g. *Disclosing Eros*, 1986; artist's collection) and the *Swimmers* series (1989–90; private collections, London, Chicago and Los Angeles). Morreau has also used the triptych form to represent not only different narrative elements but also to stress change and transformation, as in the *Persephone Triptych* (1982; Kouri Bank collection, CT), *Children's Crusade* and *Lessons of History* (1980–81 and 1987; both artist's collection). The latter two demonstrate her

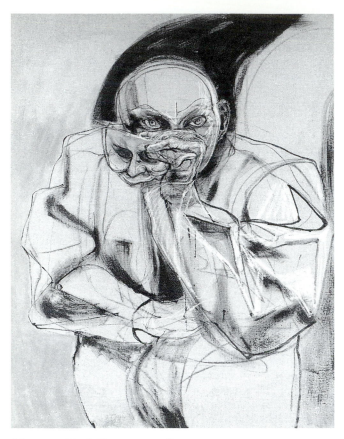

Morreau: *Mask II*, 1988; acrylic on canvas; 101.6 × 86.4 cm.

longstanding commitment against the horrors of war and the massacre of innocents (study for *Massacre of Innocents*, 1981; Arts Council Collection). In the 1960s she made a series of etchings (*Victims*; private collections, USA) about the horrors of the nuclear bombing of Hiroshima and Nagasaki. The triptych *Beyond Reason* (1991; artist's collection) was a response to the Gulf War and a reflection on Goya's late etching series. Her early interest in the expressionist tradition of Käthe Kollwitz (q.v.) and Max Beckmann, as well as such classical artists as Rubens, Rembrandt and Titian, remains an important set of reference points in her work. In the series of portraits on the *Divided Self*, she looks at the conflict between being a woman and an artist. In one work in this series (*Divided Self 3*, 1979; Cleveland Art Gallery, Middlesbrough) the woman artist stands on the opposite side of the river to a line of male artists (represented by images from their self-portraits). While the male artists hold in their hands at most only a paintbrush and have each other for company, the woman stands alone. Both her hands are full with a baby and her portfolio – literally her cultural baggage. The theme of internal conflict and a struggle between superficial appearance and underlying realities also emerges in a series of self-portraits collectively entitled *Mask* (1988; private collections, London; see illustration). Here the grimacing mask, the pleasing expression of woman, is removed to reveal a more determined and confrontational gaze.

In the *Bed* series of the mid-1990s Morreau abandoned her direct representation of the figure and began to explore the traces of human activity left behind in twisted draperies of a recently abandoned bed, the site of both sexuality and sleep. The environment, literally sea, sky and landscape, merges with this human trace to figure both sensuality and mood through the colour and atmospheric change shown. Dreams, acts of passion, the disruption or securing of sleep, hope and terror are all figured in these oils.

KATY DEEPWELL

Morris, May
British designer and craftworker, 1862–1938

Born Mary Morris in Bexleyheath, Kent, 25 March 1862, to the artist, designer and writer William Morris and his wife Jane Burden. Trained at the South Kensington School of Design, 1880–83. Subsequently joined father's firm of Morris & Co., founded 1862; appointed head of Embroidery Department, 1885; left the firm after her father's death in 1896. Married Henry Halliday Sparling, 1890, moving to Hammersmith, London; separated 1894; divorced 1899. Became an independent embroiderer and teacher, undertaking commissions and training private pupils as well as teaching at the Central School of Arts and Crafts, London (director of embroidery, 1899–1904; visitor, 1905–10). Visiting lecturer also at Birmingham and Leicester Schools of Art and Design. Lecture tour in USA, 1909–10. Contributed extensively to Arts and Crafts literature on embroidery practice and history. Involved in formation of Socialist League, 1884–5. Member, 1899, and committee member, 1905, Society for the Protection of Ancient Buildings. Founder of Women's Guild of Arts in emulation of all-male Art-Workers' Guild, 1907; served as president until her death. Member of Executive Committee, Arts and Crafts Exhibition Society, 1909–10. With furniture designer Ernest Gimson and Women's Guild of Arts, selected room displays for Arts and Crafts exhibition at Royal Academy, London, 1916. Retired to Kelmscott Manor, Oxfordshire, 1920s; active in community affairs, and in the opening of Kelmscott Memorial Hall for William Morris's centenary, 1934. Trips to Iceland, c.1924, 1926 and 1931. Died 16 October 1938.

Principal Exhibitions

Arts and Crafts Society of England, London: occasionally 1888–1931
33 Hertford Street, Mayfair, London: 1905 (with Katherine Adams)
Exposition Universelle de Gand, Ghent: 1913
Musée du Louvre, Paris: 1914 (*Arts décoratifs de Grande Bretagne et d'Irelande*)

Selected Writings

"Chain stitch embroidery", *Hobby Horse*, iii/12, 1888
"Materials" and "Colour", *Arts and Crafts Exhibition Society: Catalogue of the Third Exhibition*, exh. cat., New Gallery, London, 1890
"Embroidery", *Plain Handicrafts*, ed. A.H. Mackmurdo, London: Percival, 1892
Decorative Needlework, London: Hughes, 1893
"Of embroidery", "Of materials" and "Colour", *Arts and Crafts Essays*, New York: Scribner, and London: Rivington Percival, 1893; reprinted New York: Garland, 1977

"Of church embroidery", *Building News*, 13 October 1893–31 August 1894 (13 parts)

"Ancient Coptic textiles", *Architectural Review*, ii, 1894

"Mediaeval embroidery", *Journal of the Society of Arts*, xliii, 1895, pp.384–95

"Lady Griselda's dream", *Longman's Magazine*, xxxii, 1898 (one act play)

"Coptic textiles", *Architectural Review*, v, 1899, pp.274–87

"Pageantry and the masque", *Journal of the Society of Arts*, l, 1902, pp.670–74

White Lies: A Play, London: Chiswick Press, 1903

"Decorative art, 1800–1885", *Social England, 1801–1885*, vi, ed. H.D. Traill and J.S. Mann, London, 1904

"Opus anglicanum", *Burlington Magazine*, vi, 1905, pp.278–85, 440–48; vii, 1905, pp.54–64

Editor, *Collected Works of William Morris*, 24 vols, London: Longman, 1910–15; texts reprinted in *The Introductions to the Collected Works of William Morris*, ed. Joseph Riggs Dunlap, 2 vols, New York: Oriole Editions, 1973

Essay on embroidery in *International Exhibition Catalogue of British Arts and Crafts*, Exposition Universelle, Ghent, 1913

"William de Morgan", *Burlington Magazine*, xxxi, 1917, pp.77–83, 91–7

"Weaving and textile crafts", *Handicrafts and Reconstruction: Notes by Members of the Arts and Crafts Exhibition Society*, ed. J. Hogg, London: Arts and Crafts Exhibition Society, 1919

Editor, *William Morris: Artist, Writer, Socialist*, 2 vols, Oxford: Blackwell, 1936; New York: Russell and Russell, 1966

Bibliography

Anthea Callen, *Angel in the Studio: Women in the Arts and Crafts Movement, 1870–1914*, London: Astragal, 1979; as *Women Artists of the Arts and Crafts Movement, 1870–1914*, New York: Pantheon, 1979

Linda Parry, *William Morris Textiles*, London: Weidenfeld and Nicolson, and New York: Viking, 1983

Jan Marsh, *Jane and May Morris: A Biographical Story, 1839–1938*, London and New York: Pandora Press, 1986

The Art of Embroidery: May Morris, documentary film directed by Cathy Collis, Central Television, Birmingham, 1988

May Morris, 1862–1938, exh. cat., William Morris Gallery, Walthamstow, London, 1989

Marianne Carlano, "May Morris in context", *Early Modern Textiles: From Arts and Crafts to Art Deco*, exh. cat., Museum of Fine Arts, Boston, 1993, pp.10–27

May Morris's career in embroidery and design was shaped by her inheritance as the daughter of William and Jane Morris, her father being a leading designer in textiles and other applied arts in the period 1860–90, and her mother and aunt being skilled embroiderers involved in the production and management of the family firm. May showed an aptitude for art at an early age and studied at the South Kensington School before joining Morris & Co., where she designed "in the Morris style" mainly for needlework and wallpapers. One of her earliest pieces, a tablecloth (Kelmscott Manor, Oxfordshire) designed and made by herself and Marianne Collins in the 1880s, was a prize-winning exhibit at the Royal School of Needlework. An embroidered bag (William Morris Gallery, London) made by May and her sister Jenny to hold an illuminated psalter was shown at the Arts and Crafts Exhibition Society in 1899 and at the decorative arts exhibition in Paris in 1914. Larger designs include the *Orchard* or *Fruit Garden Portière* (c.1892; silks on silk damask; private collection, Britain) and the *Battye Hanging* (c.1900; silks on canvas; William Morris Gallery). The wool on linen curtains and

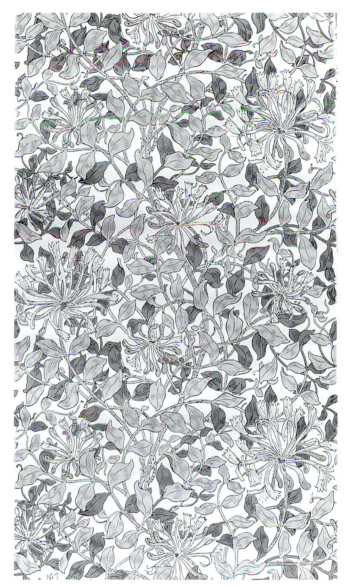

Morris: *Honeysuckle*, wallpaper for Morris & Co., 1883; William Morris Gallery, London

pelmet for her father's bed (Kelmscott Manor) were made in the Morris & Co. workshop and shown at the Arts and Crafts Exhibition of 1893. Other surviving samples of her work include the *Animal Cot Quilt* (c.1900; silks on linen; design in Victoria and Albert Museum, London) and the *Owl Bedspread* (c.1906; University of Central England, Birmingham), designed for the students at the Birmingham School of Art. (The main collections of the Morris family's work are in the William Morris Gallery and Victoria and Albert Museum, London, and at Kelmscott Manor, Oxfordshire; the Ashmolean Museum, Oxford, owns a large collection of her embroidery designs and pouncings; and a selection of her teaching materials is held by the Textile Department of the Birmingham City Art Gallery.)

Morris was much in demand both as a designer and a practitioner during the main years of the Arts and Crafts movement from the 1880s to World War I. As a designer she worked within the tradition established by Morris & Co., alongside other women such as Kate Faulkner, embroiderer Mary

Newill, bookbinder Katherine Adams and silversmith Georgina Cave Gaskin. She was also a close friend and colleague of many male Arts and Crafts designers. She typically produced flowing designs derived from natural forms, notably foliage and flowers, especially when intended for commercial and repeat production runs. For single commissions she favoured less symmetrical designs, tending also to leave more ground unfilled, with the unworked spaces irregularly incorporated into the designs. Frequently inscriptions are also employed, on scrolls and borders, in a manner that became characteristic of Arts and Crafts practice. In the years around 1900 Morris also produced Arts and Crafts jewellery (selection on display in Victoria and Albert Museum) and later in life worked on the loom, designing and weaving textiles, though few have survived.

Morris's position in the history of design is still somewhat difficult to assess, partly due to the low status of needle arts and the fugitive nature of its products. Sadly, the archives of the Women's Guild of Arts have also perished. From around 1885 to 1920, however, through her exhibits, essays and teaching, she was *faute de mieux* the premier theoretician of Arts and Crafts embroidery. Her design principles were based on traditional (i.e. pre-1800) methods, materials and colours, fine hand workmanship and fitness for function, whether for display, domestic or commercial use. She was therefore one of the chief exponents of Arts and Crafts design and practice, recognised as such in Britain, Europe and North America. But she was neither sufficiently innovative nor important to shape or advance the development of embroidery design beyond her own sphere, and thus remains a foremost practitioner rather than an influential designer. Politically, she was active in the Socialist League in the 1880s alongside her father, Eleanor Marx Aveling and others, and remained committed to socialist aims and to equality of the sexes, though tending to see feminist goals as falling within socialist ones. She had romantic hopes of dramatist George Bernard Shaw, but in 1890 married fellow-Socialist H.H. Sparling, whom she divorced in 1899, resuming her own name. Professionally modest and lacking in self-assertion, though renowned as a rigorous and opinionated employer and teacher, she devoted many of her later energies to preserving and promoting her father's work and fame, effectively and intentionally allowing his reputation to subsume and eclipse her own.

JAN MARSH

Morton, Ree

American artist, 1936–1977

Born Helen Marie Reilly in Ossining, New York, 3 August 1936. Studied nursing at Skidmore College, Saratoga Springs, New York, 1953–6. Married Ted Morton, 1956; three children (two daughters, one son), born 1957, 1960 and 1962; separated 1968, later divorced. Lived in Jacksonville, Florida, 1956–60; Saint Simons Island, Georgia, 1960–63; Norfolk, Virginia, 1963–5; Los Angeles, 1965; East Greenwich, Rhode Island, 1965–8; Horsham, Pennsylvania, 1968–70; New York, from 1972. Attended first art classes at Jacksonville

Museum, 1960; later studied at University of Rhode Island, Kingston, 1965–8 (BFA), and Tyler School of Art, Temple University, Philadelphia (MFA 1970). Visiting artist, School of the Art Institute of Chicago, 1974–5 and 1977; University of California, San Diego, 1975–6; School of Art and Design, California Institute of the Arts, Valencia, 1976. Participated in Biennial Exhibitions of Contemporary American Art, Whitney Museum of American Art, New York, 1973 and 1977. Recipient of Creative Artists Public Service (CAPS) grant, 1974; National Endowment for the Arts (NEA) grant, 1975. Died in Chicago after a road accident, 30 April 1977.

Selected Individual Exhibitions

Artists Space, New York: 1973
Whitney Museum of American Art, New York: 1974
South Street Seaport Museum, New York: 1975
Walter Kelley Gallery, Chicago: 1977
Santa Barbara Art Museum, University of California at Santa Barbara: 1977
New Museum, New York: 1980 (retrospective)

Selected Writings

"Places: Ree Morton", *Journal: Los Angeles Institute of Contemporary Art*, i, March 1976, pp.20–21
"Analects", *Individuals: Post-Movement Art in America*, ed. Alan Sondheim, New York: Dutton, 1977, pp.226–45

Bibliography

Lucy R. Lippard, "Ree Morton: At the still point of the turning world", *Artforum*, xii, December 1973, pp.48–50; reprinted in Lucy R. Lippard, *From the Center: Feminist Essays on Women's Art*, New York: Dutton, 1976
Lyn Blumenthal and Kate Hasfield, *Ree Morton*, taped interview, New York, 1974; published by Video Data Bank, School of the Art Institute of Chicago
Ree Morton, exh. cat., Whitney Museum of American Art, New York, 1974
Carol Squires, "Ree Morton: 'Antidotes for Madness'", *New Art Examiner*, ii, January 1975, p.4
Carter Ratcliff, "On contemporary primitivism", *Artforum*, xiv, November 1975, pp.57–65
Barbara Baracks, "Artpark: The new esthetic playground", *Artforum*, xv, November 1976, pp.28–33
Carol Squires, "Ree Morton, 1936–1977", *New Art Examiner*, iv, Summer 1977, pp.3, 23
Valentin Tatransky, "Ree Morton", *Arts Magazine*, lii, November 1977, pp.28–9
Ree Morton: Retrospective, 1971–1977, exh. cat., New Museum, New York, and elsewhere, 1980 (contains bibliography)
Brooks Adams, "Ree Morton and American landscape", *Arts Magazine*, liv, April 1980, pp.180–82
Mary Delahoyd, "Ree Morton", *Artforum*, xviii, May 1980, pp.60–65
Lisa Liebmann, "Innocence and irony: The art of Ree Morton", *Art in America*, lxix, January 1981, pp.88–95
Ree Morton: A New Acquisition – "Signs of Love", exh. brochure, Whitney Museum of American Art, New York, 1990
Cynthia Carlson, ed., "Three artists", *Art Journal*, liii, Summer 1993, pp.6–15

Although Ree Morton's artistic career spanned barely a decade, and few of her works survive, she is widely recognised for having made important contributions to the anti-formalist, expressive and painterly sculpture that developed in the USA from the mid-1960s alongside and contradicting the *a priori*

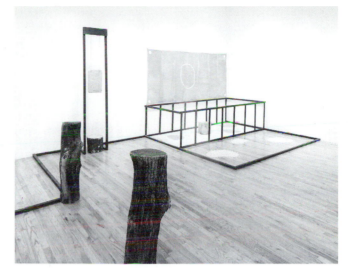

Morton: *Sister Perpetua's Lie*, two views of a part reinstallation, 1980, for a retrospective at the New Museum, New York; mixed media (first installed in 1973 at University of Pennsylvania, Philadelphia)

formalist concerns of Minimalism. For Morton, formal boundaries between painting, sculpture and even architecture were deliberately blurred as content deriving from personal concerns and from materials themselves began to determine a dynamic, dialectical way of working; the final form of the piece resulted from the "logic" of the process. As Morton said:

> I have things around, and then as I work, it's almost a kind of drawing process. It involves picking something up, placing it over there, looking at it, putting a third thing in, taking it out. It's a really physical manipulation of those things as lines or areas or zones or whatever they do ... [Blumenthal and Hasfield 1974, quoted in New York 1980].

Morton read voraciously. Her notebooks and journals are crammed with quotations from a variety of philosophic and literary sources that invite us to search for meanings in her pieces; yet specific meanings elude us. A work by Morton is open in its content: "Probably the only thing I absolutely insist on is that you can't see it wrong", she said (*ibid.*). In 1971 Morton began using branches, roots, rocks and paint to construct one spatial installation after another in her studio, often re-using components from one piece to construct a later work. Each work existed only long enough to be photographed before being dismantled. One of the simplest of these open "drawings", which engaged both floor and wall, was an untitled work of July 1971 (whereabouts unknown, repr. New York 1980, p.15) made of one branch, one rock and paint. The base of the branch was placed some distance from the wall and then leaned against it, thereby setting up a triangle further delineated by two dotted lines extending from each end of the branch to join at the base of the wall. Meanwhile, a rather large, porous rock, roughly pyramidal in shape, was placed in such a way as to create a second triangle on the floor when a dotted line joined branch, rock and intersected wall. With just two elements and dotted lines implicating the wall, Morton had created a pyramid of space. Most of her pieces, however, were more expansive in their occupation of space. A long branch might move diagonally to claim a large space occupied on the floor only by low-lying rocks, or a low wooden "house plan"; the wall might be engaged through simple drawings, or a piece of paper tacked up.

In such pieces one is pulled into a dramatic narrative: each element appears to act upon and receive action from fellow elements in a sculptural "play". Indeed, Morton has admitted that she has at times realised with shock that to her the elements are figures: "so what I do ... is let them be alive and see what happens, let them function as people without making them look like people" (quoted in Squires 1975, p.4). Such implied narrative was given a more overt form in Morton's most celebrated early piece, *Sister Perpetua's Lie* (1973; installation at the Institute of Contemporary Art, University of Pennsylvania, Philadelphia; partially reconstructed for Morton's retrospective at the New Museum, New York, in 1980; see illustration). Inspired by Raymond Roussel's disjunctive, surreal novel, *Impressions d'Afrique* (1910), Morton constructed three "situations", related to two walls and to each other by means of a "narrative path", black wooden strips that extend along the floor to connect the three units. Two tree stumps painted black stand at attention before a series of diagrams drawn on white sheets that Morton based on specific events from the novel. They frame a larger sheet of grey paper on which is quoted the passage: "To the question, 'Is this where the fugitives are hiding?' the nun, posted before her convent, persistently replied 'No' shaking her head from right to left after each deep peck of the winged creature". The diagrams and the verbal passage have no logical relation to each other – they are simply juxtaposed, as are events in Roussel's novel. Having read these messages, one changes orientation, turning 90 degrees with the black line as it moves along the base of the adjacent wall to the next "site". Here the line abruptly moves vertically to form a tall frame from which hangs a wooden tablet, suspended like a guillotine above a log slice painted red on top. Continuing along the wall to the third "site", the line forms a low rectangular cage with an open atrium before it. Placed on white paper covering the floor of the cage is another log slice, while its shape is painted in bloody red three times within the cage and chalked in white on the natural floor of the atrium. To the wall above the cage is stapled a grey canvas the size of the cage floor; on it, slightly off centre, the roughly circular shape of the log slice is repeated, this time in outline. The strict visual logic of repeated shapes and colours invites a meaningful narrative reading that is denied by the violent disjunction of the posted visual and verbal texts.

Through these works dating from 1971 to 1975, Morton, newly divorced, appears to have been discovering and staking out new kinds of space for a fiercely claimed, individual self. She discovered, however, that space can be claimed by psychological as well as physical means. In 1975 she made more than 100 nylon flags, each painted and appliquéd with images and the name of a person important to her life. These were flown above a 19th-century fishing schooner anchored on the East River in New York for her installation *Something in the Wind* (South Street Seaport Museum, New York). As she wrote: "It was a celebration for them, and a means of identifying and locating myself in the world by naming the persons who surround me" (*Attitudes Towards Space: Environmental Art*, exh. cat., Mount St Mary's Art Gallery, Los Angeles, 1977). Here we note a new twist to her interest in words: they can be made into emblems. Fascinated by the language of books about plants, she began making deliberately gaudy sculpture and banner-like wall hangings featuring isolated phrases such as "Fading Flowers", "Antidotes for Madness", "Terminal Clusters", using Celastic exuberantly coloured and moulded to form the curtains and swags that framed many of her last works. Playing on the notion of the frame as a window, Morton hung Celastic curtains over her series of paired oil paintings of seascapes with Rococo clouds and fish seen close up – as if one were peering through living-room windows at the two mutually exclusive perspectives (*Regional Paintings*, 1976; repr. New York 1980, p.57). Ree Morton's death in 1977 left many playful "dramas" unacted.

SUSAN HAVENS CALDWELL

Moser, Mary
British painter, 1744–1819

Born in London, 27 October 1744. Awarded special silver medal, Royal Society of Arts, London, 1759. Founder-member of the Royal Academy, 1769. Married Captain Hugh Lloyd, 1793. Died in London, 2 May 1819.

Principal Exhibitions

Society of Artists of Great Britain, London: 1760–64, 1766–8
Royal Academy, London: 1769–80, 1783–5, 1788–90, 1792, 1797–8, 1800, 1802

Bibliography

J.T. Smith, *Nollekens and His Times*, 2 vols, London, 1828; ed. Wilfred Whitten, 2 vols, London: Lane, 1920
Ellen C. Clayton, *English Female Artists*, 2 vols, London: Tinsley, 1876
Peter Mitchell, *Great Flower Painters: Four Centuries of Floral Art*, Woodstock, NY: Overlook Press, 1973
Women Artists, 1550–1950, exh. cat., Los Angeles County Museum of Art, and elsewhere, 1976
The Women's Art Show, 1550–1970, exh. cat., Castle Museum, Nottingham, 1982
Marcia Pointon, "Working, earning, bequeathing: Mary Grace and Mary Moser – 'paintresses'" (in preparation)

Mary Moser shared with Angelica Kauffman (q.v.) the distinction of being the only female founding members of the Royal Academy. She was a regular exhibitor at the Royal Academy, where she showed mostly flower paintings as well as a number of allegorical portraits and history subjects, until 1802. It is the flower-pieces on which her reputation rests.

Moser was the only daughter, and only surviving child, of George Michael Moser, a Swiss portraitist and goldsmith who settled in England (date unknown). He was a founding member of the Royal Society of Arts and, like her, a founder-member of the Royal Academy, and later its Keeper. Mary Moser's career was launched in 1759 when she won the silver medal in the class for Polite Arts at the Royal Society of Arts for a watercolour and gouache of flowers (which hangs today in the Society's rooms). She went on to exhibit at the Society of Artists of Great Britain, but withdrew from 1768, when she preferred to show her work at the Royal Academy. This move made it clear that her ambition was to succeed as a fine artist and not merely as a craft worker.

Moser's flower-pieces, which are mostly painted in oils or in watercolour and gouache, are competent but undistinguished. She produced delicately coloured and botanically accurate studies of individual flowers (the Victoria and Albert Museum, London, has seven watercolours of tulips) but the finished flower-pieces are painted in a flat, generalised ornamental style. She worked with a limited palette of rather dull tones in which a yellowish-buff predominates. A symbolic significance is often apparent in these pictures: six of the flower-pieces in the Broughton Collection at the Fitzwilliam Museum, Cambridge, represent signs of the zodiac, with appropriately seasonal flowers set in vases decorated with astrological motifs.

Her most impressive work is the decorative scheme she painted in the 1790s at Frogmore House, Windsor, for Queen Charlotte. Moser was already under the Queen's patronage when she undertook this commission: the Victoria and Albert Museum has a *Vase of Flowers* (see illustration), painted in tempera and dated 1764, that was once in Queen Charlotte's collection. The queen, a passionate devotee of botanical science, amassed botanical books and drawings, and a herbarium. The room at Frogmore, which combines floral decorations painted directly onto the walls with inset canvases, was designed to simulate a garden or conservatory complete with a *trompe-l'oeil* ceiling with an aperture open to a painted sky. Nollekens alleged that Moser was paid over £900 for these decorations.

Moser was professionally and financially successful, despite a career devoted to the flower-piece, which in Reynolds's hierarchy of genres was the most modest and minor. In 1797, however, she married Captain Hugh Lloyd, and subsequently painted only as an amateur, signing her works "Mary Lloyd". After 1802 she no longer exhibited, apparently because of failing eyesight.

GILL SAUNDERS

Moser: *Vase of Flowers*, 1764; tempera; Victoria and Albert Museum, London

Moses, Anna Mary Robertson [Grandma]

American painter, 1860–1961

Born Anna Mary Robertson in Greenwich, New York, 7 September 1860. Became a "hired girl" on a neighbouring farm, 1872, obtaining some education with the children of the family. Married Thomas Salmon Moses, 1887; ten children, five dying in infancy; husband died 1927. Lived and farmed in the Shenandoah Valley of Virginia, 1887–1905; purchased a farm in Eagle Bridge, New York, 1905. Painted first picture on a fireboard in her parlour, 1918; began to paint in earnest, c.1935. Displayed some work in Thomas's Drugstore in Hoosick Falls, New York, where it was seen by New York collector Louis J. Caldor, 1938. Three paintings included in *Contemporary Unknown American Painters* exhibition, Members Room, Museum of Modern Art, New York, 1939. Subsequently became well known through further exhibitions and publications. Paintings used for greeting cards by Hallmark from 1947. Recipient of many honours, including the Women's National Press Club award presented by President Harry S. Truman, 1949; honorary degrees from Russell Sage College, Troy, New York, 1949, and Moore Institute of Art, Philadelphia, 1951. The governor of New York, Nelson Rockefeller, proclaimed "Grandma Moses Day" on 7 September 1960 and again in 1961. Died in Hoosick Falls, New York, 13 December 1961.

Selected Individual Exhibitions

Galerie St Etienne, New York: 1940, 1944, 1947, 1948 (retrospective), 1951, 1953, 1955, 1957
Mt Holyoke College, South Hadley, MA: 1944–5 (touring)
Public Library, Manitowoc, WI: 1946–7 (touring)
Rockford Art Association, IL: 1947–8 (touring)
California Palace of the Legion of Honor, San Francisco: 1948, 1957
Phillips Gallery, Washington, DC: 1949
Neue Galerie, Vienna: 1950 (touring, organised by US Information Service)
William Rockhill Nelson Gallery of Art, Kansas City: 1951 (touring)
Art Gallery of Toronto: 1952
Syracuse Museum of Fine Arts, NY: 1952
Cedar Rapids Art Association, IO: 1952–3 (touring)
Santa Barbara Museum of Art, CA: 1953
Paula-Becker-Modersohn-Haus, Bremen: 1955–7 (touring)
Marquette University, Milwaukee: 1960–61 (*My Life's History*, touring, organised by Smithsonian Institution)

Selected Writings

My Life's History, ed. Otto Kallir, New York: Harper, and London: Deutsch, 1952

Bibliography

Sidney Janis, *They Taught Themselves: American Primitive Painters of the 20th Century*, New York: Dial Press, 1942
Otto Kallir, ed., *Grandma Moses: American Primitive*, New York: Dryden Press, 1946
Jean Lipman and Alice Winchester, *Primitive Painters in America, 1750–1950*, New York: Dodd Mead, 1950
Art and Life of Grandma Moses, exh. cat., Gallery of Modern Art, New York, 1969
Otto Kallir, *Grandma Moses*, New York: Abrams, 1973 (includes catalogue raisonné)
Grandma Moses: Anna Mary Robertson Moses (1860–1961), exh. cat., National Gallery of Art, Washington, DC, 1979
Jean McMahon Humez, "The life and art of Anna Mary Robertson Moses", *Woman's Art Journal*, i/2, 1980–81, pp.7–12
Jane Kallir, *Grandma Moses: The Artist Behind the Myth*, New York: Potter, 1982 (contains extensive bibliography)
The World of Grandma Moses, exh. cat., Museum of American Folk Art, New York, and elsewhere, 1984

Grandma Moses was a distinguished American folk artist who painted images of rural life, the life that she herself had known. With no formal training and beginning when she was in her seventies, she developed her style with great inventiveness. She used visual material at hand, such as greeting cards, magazine images, Currier and Ives prints, as well as observation of her surroundings and memories of her own life. She delighted in both immediate images and panoramic views and combined them in her paintings.

Source materials for the images have been documented by Jane Kallir (1982). Moses would clip or outline images of human figures or architecture and then incorporate them into her paintings. The figures are flat and abstract and placed generally in the fore- and middle ground of the painting in a decorative manner. They perform a variety of actions and are combined throughout into a number of vignettes that enrich the compositions. She would repeat poses and subjects, but always with changes of arrangement or differing combinations of images. A sense of space was achieved in the surrounding landscape with value, tonal and density variation. She studied nature directly, observing the colours to be found in the landscape. The technique for the landscape was impressionistic; that of the figures was flat and abstract. At times she used a method that owes a debt to "worsted" embroidery, a medium that Moses used early in her career. She would apply colours side by side "like strands of yarn" (*ibid.*, p.57).

Moses developed as an artist. Her ability to work with colours and with clippings of figures and structures improved consistently, as did her ability to capture weather and atmospheric conditions. *Hoosick Falls, New York in Winter* (1944; 50.8 × 60.9 cm.; Phillips Collection, Washington, DC) is one of her finest winter scenes. Storm clouds cover the delicately painted distant mountains. Houses, barns and churches fill the middle- and foreground of the scene. Crossing the icy blue river is a train contrasted with a nearby horse and buggy. *Apple Butter Making* (c.1947; see illustration) is a delightful study of her days in the Shenandoah Valley. The subjects of most of Moses's paintings can be traced to New York State, but some are drawn from her early years in Virginia. Moses generally labelled her paintings by their subject or location, such as the painting *Shenandoah Valley* (1961; repr. Kallir 1982, p.54). One of the houses the Moses family lived in, Dudley Place near the hamlet of Laurel Hill in northern Augusta County, Virginia, is included in *Apple Butter Making*, as well as vignettes concerned with picking apples, pealing, coring and cooking them, and putting the apple butter in casks. The fire, with its concentrated colour, is the focus at the centre of the painting. A woman in the foreground in a light mauve dress may represent Moses herself. The river, known locally as Middle River, and the distant fields and mountains provide the setting for the scene. Here, as elsewhere, the trees are created

Moses: *Apple Butter Making*, *c*.1947; oil on pressed wood; 41.9 × 60 cm; private collection

with dabs of colour while the figures are composed of flat colour shapes.

The decorative nature of Moses's work is especially apparent in her interiors. She preferred out-of-door scenes but there are a few "panoramic" interiors with many vignettes. *Quilting Bee* (1949; private collection, *ibid*., no.883) is dominated by the "piece-work" quilt and the dining table with place settings and food. Rich patterning is found throughout the space where men, women and children variously prepare food, including ice cream, visit each other and enjoy their pets. The arrangement of the vignettes is not dissimilar from the "piece-work" quilt. It is important to note the folklore content of the bee, which is well-recorded by Moses. Through the three large windows is a delicately painted hillscape.

In late works such as *Falling Leaves* (1961; Collection Walter K. Rush, *ibid*., no.1490) and *Deep Snow* (Collection Paul Simon, *ibid*., no.1486) the background is more narrow, less panoramic. Focusing on colour and working with impressionistic dabs of colour, she emphasises atmospheric effects. Some of the figures are rendered with a few strokes of colour, in a more fluid manner. Her last finished painting, *Rainbow* (1961; *ibid*., no.1511), is filled with colour and texture. She includes a figure in purple who seems to wave at the viewer and, in the distance, beneath the rainbow, is the white-steepled church found in many of her paintings. As was characteristic

of her later stylistic developments, the figures in *Rainbow* are composed of more fluid brush strokes, and her colour, while less true to nature, is exuberant in its more spontaneous expressionistic quality. From the mid-1930s until her death in 1961 Grandma Moses devoted herself to her art. Aided by such people as Otto Kallir and his Galerie St Etienne in New York, she presented a record of American rural life in a unique and enchanting style. Her paintings are truly landmarks in the history of American art.

MARTHA B. CALDWELL

Moss, Marlow

British painter, 1890–1958

Born Marjorie Jewell Moss in Richmond, Surrey, 29 May 1890. Attended St John's Wood School of Art, against the wishes of her wealthy family, *c*.1916–17; studied at Slade School of Fine Art, London, 1917–19. Moved to Cornwall, *c*.1919; subsequently returned to London and changed her name from Marjorie Jewell to Marlow; studied philosophy, literature, mathematics and the visual arts in British Museum Reading Room. Attended sculpture classes at Municipal

School of Art, Penzance, Cornwall, c.1924–6. Returned to London and began to paint, 1926. Decided to settle in Paris, 1927. Met Mondrian, 1929; in close contact with him until he left Paris in 1938; also studied at the Académie Moderne under Fernand Léger and Amadée Ozenfant. Founder-member, Abstraction-Création group, Paris, 1932. Escaped to Britain from the Netherlands, 1940; moved to Penzance, 1941; attended architecture courses. Entire early oeuvre destroyed in bombing of her house in Gauciel, near Evreux, 1944. Spent long periods in France from 1946. Member, Groupe Espace, Paris, 1951. Died in Penzance, 23 August 1958.

Principal Exhibitions

Salon des Surindépendants, Paris: 1931
Abstraction-Création group, Paris: 1932–6
Salon des Réalités Nouvelles, Paris: from 1946
Hanover Gallery, London: 1953, 1958 (both individual)
Stedelijk Museum, Amsterdam: 1962 (retrospective)

Bibliography

Marlow Moss: Sculpture, Paintings, exh. cat., Hanover Gallery, London, 1958
Marlow Moss, exh. cat., Stedelijk Museum, Amsterdam, 1962
Marlow Moss: Bilder, Konstruktionen, Zeichnungen, exh. cat., Galerie Gimpel & Hanover, Zürich, 1973
Women Artists, 1550–1950, exh. cat., Los Angeles County Museum of Art, and elsewhere, 1976
Abstraction-Création, 1931–1936, exh. cat., Westfälisches Landesmuseum, Münster, and Musée d'Art Moderne de la Ville de Paris, 1978
Randy Rosen, "Marlow Moss: Did she influence Mondrian's work of the thirties?", *Arts Magazine*, liii, April 1979, pp.163–5
L'altra metà dell'avanguardia, 1910–1940: Pittrici e scultrici nei movimenti delle avanguardie storiche, exh. cat., Palazzo Reale, Milan, and elsewhere, 1980
Florette Dijkstra, *Marlow Moss: Constructiviste and the Reconstruction Project*, Den Bosch: De Kleine Kapaciteit, 1995 (contains bibliography)

Correspondence with Paule Vézelay, 1954–6, courtesy of Mrs Sally Jarman, Paule Vézelay archives, c/o Tate Gallery Archives, London.

Together with Paule Vézelay (q.v.), Marlow Moss was a pioneering British painter in Paris in the heyday of 1930s abstraction: indeed her spiritual master, Piet Mondrian, suggested her as a founding member of the Abstraction-Création group. Her early loves had been the Dutch painters Rembrandt and van Gogh, who, like the French Impressionists, had been fundamentally concerned with representing light. Her early experiences in England, both personal and professional, were dispiriting; after severe tuberculosis, which cut short her promise as a pianist, and her father's death, she found her artistic ambitions thwarted by her family, which led to a definitive break with them. Like many contemporaries, she found the English art school teaching too old-fashioned, first at St John's Wood School of Art, then at the Slade. Her friend Antoinette H. Nijhoff, who promoted her work and contributed to the catalogue of Moss's Amsterdam retrospective of 1962, describes "a complete breakdown" due to "a shock of an emotional nature" that coincided with Moss's rejection of the Slade in 1919. She retreated to a lonely cottage in Cornwall "like a wounded animal" – only to be inspired and determined to pursue a creative life after reading a book on

Marie Curie, who would become a lifelong heroine. It was on returning to London that Moss not only changed her name from Marjorie Jewell to the sexually ambivalent "Marlow", but, like many women of the time, also cropped her hair and adopted the current *garçonne* look. Realising that in all matters but music she was "illiterate", she plunged herself into a strange period of voracious reading at the British Museum. (Moss's means of financial support at this time and afterwards remains unclear; one must suppose that she received some sort of allowance.) While there exist no further personal details either of Moss's crisis or its aftermath, this seems to have gone far beyond a question of fashion: later photographs of Moss seem to indicate a trans-sexuality that was part of the lesbian culture of "amazone" that developed in both Britain and France in the 1920s. Virginia Woolf's novel *Orlando* (1928) appeared a year before Joan Riviere's article "Womanliness as a masquerade" was published in the *International Journal of Psychoanalysis*. In France, Victor Margueritte's *La Garçonne* (1922, translated as *The Bachelor Girl*), a moralising tale of France's new *gamine* woman, was read by perhaps a quarter of the adult population, while Colette's *Ces plaisirs* (1932) deliberately recalled the notorious Welsh Ladies of Llangollen. In the Paris that Moss discovered in 1927, overt bisexuality or homosexuality was chic, and women became achievers: aviators, writers, painters, photographers; "Amazone" or "Américaine" – the terms were almost identical. With the low franc came such British women as Nancy Cunard and Eileen Agar (q.v.), complemented by the "Américaines" Gertrude Stein, Djuna Barnes, Lee Miller (q.v.) and Jean Heap. It is no coincidence that another Marjorie from Britain, Marjorie Watson-Williams, changed her name and identity at almost the same time to the ambivalent "Paule Vézelay". The two women would become friends. "I destroyed my old personality and created a new one", said Moss.

Although she worked in the Académie Moderne of the artists Fernand Léger and Amadée Ozenfant, neither of whom espoused a complete, geometric abstraction, it was Piet Mondrian who became Moss's "master". His uncompromising, rectilinear, primary colour abstractions offered Moss a credo that while ostensibly the most impersonal of receptacles for an art of space, light and colour, involved dimensions of fidelity and discipleship. In 1929 she painted her first neo-plastic composition, and the following year incorporated the curves introduced by Jean Hélion, particularly the use of the double line. Apparently, when Mondrian saw her work exhibited at the Salon des Surindépendants in 1931, he wrote a note asking for an explanation. Moss's considered reply – single lines split up the canvas, and make the composition static; the double or multiple line creates "a continuity of related and interrelated rhythm in space" – may, so Antoinette Nijhoff implies, have precipitated Mondrian's own compositions with double lines.

Strangely, Nijhoff records that Mondrian never revealed to Moss anything about his own technique, and that her own working methods – to achieve canvases that often looked almost identical to his own – were a result of trial and error. Although she read all the prerequisite mathematical treatises, such as Matila Ghyka's, was familiar with proportions such as the golden section, the "divine proportion", and worked meticulously with a ruler and mathematical proportions after her first preliminary sketches, her painted surfaces of superimposed thin coats of paint took months to perfect. First experimenting with a fine-weave linen, she progressed to a more coarsely-woven surface that gave her paint a different quality of mobility. Indeed, grounds were invented using different kinds of linen stuck together, where the use of white paint alone created paintings with a constructed, relief effect. And just as her compatriot Vézelay started making compositions with string – "lines in space" – in 1936 (going on to use freestanding curved wires), Moss sometimes replaced painted lines with thin plastic wire, or added cord to her canvases, replacing it later with very thick rope, painted white on white, although she finally reverted to black lines. Moss's white grounds were sometimes tinted with red, yellow or blue. As with Mondrian, her works had merely descriptive titles, such as *Composition with Double Line and Blue Surface* (1934), *White and Blue (with Red Cord)* (1935) and *White with Curved Cord* (1936; all Gemeentemuseum, Arnhem).

Moss became a founding member of the group Abstraction-Création in 1932, a period of expansion of international activity in geometric abstract art as recorded in the periodical *Abstraction-Création*, nos 1–5, which ran from 1932 to 1936. By issue no.4, of 1935, the editors concluded: "Thus, we can consider that 17 countries, outside France, are interested in abstract art and that Paris is the centre of the movement ...". Like Vézelay, Moss was at the heart of this exhilarating world of pioneer modernists and younger experimenters, although Nijhoff points out that she was never a pure cosmopolitan: like her experiences in Cornwall, her house at Gauciel, near Evreux, where she worked in France, offered a crucial contact with nature, and she was a committed gardener, entranced by the changing and shifting of forms, rather than their abstract fixity.

The outbreak of World War II heralded the liquidation of the School of Paris – in all its various manifestations. Artists returned to their home countries, sometimes with great difficulty, fled from persecution to a new life in America, or, more tragically, like Moss's contemporary, the abstract painter Otto Freundlich, died during deportation or in the concentration camps. Moss's great tragedy was not her condition as a spiritual exile in her native land – she managed to find a house in Cornwall and gathered new energy from architectural courses and three-dimensional experiments with metal constructions in steel and brass – but the loss of her work. She arrived in England with no paintings, books, materials or possessions; then learned that her house had been bombed, and its entire contents destroyed – all her art up to 1940, with the exception of works in transit or in private collections (14 canvases dated between 1931 and 1943 were shown at her Stedelijk Museum retrospective of 1962).

There was, of course, a community of artists in post-war Cornwall – besides the St Ives group (Ben Nicholson, Barbara Hepworth, q.v., etc.) and the second generation wave of painters such as Peter Lanyon, there were artists such as the female Surrealist painter and writer Ithell Colquhoun (q.v.). Moss's allegiances rested, however, with international abstraction; she turned a shack into a brilliant white studio, continued her abstract compositions and became an exhibiting member of the Groupe Espace formed in Paris in 1951, whose activities were co-ordinated in Britain by Vézelay from 1954. The group aspired to promote closer collaboration among architects, painters and sculptors, although it was, unfortunately, too fractional in Britain to be a success. However, the correspondence between Moss and Vézelay at this time demonstrates their shared concerns and a developing friendship: both were convinced that their British contemporaries lacked a committed approach to non-figurative abstract art (Moss wrote in the context of the first Mondrian retrospective in Britain, organised by William Sandberg at the Stedelijk Museum, Amsterdam, which toured to the Whitechapel Art Gallery, London, in 1955). In 1953 Moss held her first important exhibition at Erica Brausen's Hanover Gallery in London – a success that led to another offer of a show in 1958. Despite the fact that Moss could now return to Paris as her war damage claim had finally been met, she resolved to work fanatically for this second show: Nijhoff describes a "great breakthrough" in this period of her work, the most important development being six colour compositions that finally eliminated the black line and constructive scheme:

> Colour and colour alone ... determines construction, rhythm, harmony and the possibility of the limitless projection of this colour-spectacle beyond the canvas into space. She has succeeded in giving form to her obsession: "space, movement, light".

Moss fell ill two months after this second exhibition closed; it was fitting that as a "disciple who counted it an honour to be his follower", her retrospective exhibition followed Mondrian's at the Stedelijk Museum, Amsterdam, in 1962. Here, 46 paintings from 1931 to 1958, and 13 constructions, from 1943 to 1957 – ranging from a column in polished brass (1944) to spatial constructions in steel, an *Ovoid and Cylindrical Form on Pentagonal Wooden Base Painted White* (1956–7; repr. Dijkstra 1995, no.B15), and free reliefs in painted wood on aluminium, made in 1957, the year before her death – demonstrate the range and achievement of a pioneering British abstract artist, whose accomplishments now demand recognition.

SARAH WILSON

Motesiczky, Marie-Louise von

Austrian painter, 1906–1996

Born in Vienna, 24 October 1906. Left school at age 13 in order to study drawing; met Max Beckmann, c.1921; studied at the Städelschule, Frankfurt am Main, under Cissarz, 1925; worked in Paris, 1926; attended Max Beckmann's masterclass at the Städelschule, Frankfurt am Main, 1927–8. Left for the Netherlands with her mother after the German annexation of Austria, 1938; moved to London, 1939; lived in Amersham, Buckinghamshire, during World War II; settled in Hampstead, London, 1951. Recipient of Austrian Cross of Honour for Science and Art, first class, 1994. Died in London, 10 June 1996.

Principal Exhibitions

Individual

Kunsthandel Huize Esher Surrey, The Hague: 1939
Czechoslovak Institute, London: 1944 (with Mary Duras)
Städtische Galerie im Lenbachhaus, Munich: 1954 (with Erna Dinklage)
Kunstverein für die Rheinlande und Westfalen, Düsseldorf: 1955 (with Heinz May, Curt Beckmann and Hans van Breek)
Beaux Arts Gallery, London: 1960
Galerie der Wiener Secession, Vienna: 1966
Kunsthalle, Bremen: 1968
Goethe-Institut, London: 1985 (retrospective)
Fitzwilliam Museum, Cambridge: 1986
Royal Hospital, Kilmainham, Dublin: 1990
Österreichische Galerie, Vienna: 1994
Manchester City Art Gallery: 1994

Group

Kommunale Galerie im Refektorium des Karmeliterklosters, Frankfurt am Main: 1980 (*Max Beckmanns Frankfurter Schüler, 1925–1933*)
Orangerie des Schlosses Charlottenburg, Berlin: 1986 (*Kunst im Exil in Grossbritannien, 1933–45*, touring)
Kunstforum, Vienna: 1995 (*Die Neue Sachlichkeit in Österreich*)

Selected Writings

"Max Beckmann als Lehrer", *Frankfurter Allgemeine Zeitung*, 11 January 1964; abridged English version in *Artscribe*, no.47, July–August 1984, pp.50–53

Bibliography

J.P. Hodin, "Die Malerin Marie-Louise von Motesiczky", *Alte und Moderne Kunst*, no.89, 1966, pp.47–9
Marie-Louise von Motesiczky, exh. cat., Galerie der Wiener Secession, Vienna, 1966
Marie-Louise von Motesiczky: Paintings, Vienna 1925–London 1985, exh. cat., Goethe-Institut, London, 1985
Marina Vaizey, "The revelation of a dazzling talent", *Sunday Times*, 24 November 1985
John Russell Taylor, "Painting unparalleled for love and tender precision", *The Times*, 10 December 1985
"Es ist eigentlich ein Märchen", *Menschenbilder*, ed. Hubert Gaisbauer and Heinz Janisch, Vienna: ORF, 1992 (text of an interview broadcast on Austrian radio)
Marie-Louise von Motesiczky, exh. cat., Österreichische Galerie, Vienna, 1994
William Packer, "Beautiful in isolation", *Financial Times*, 21–2 May 1994

Although Viennese by birth, Marie-Louise von Motesiczky lived for the greater part of her life in London, and was one of the most distinguished of the German-speaking artists who had been forced into exile by the Nazis. She was a major figure, but has remained almost unknown, largely because of post-war neglect of German painting in Britain. Motesiczky was less prolific than either Kokoschka or Max Beckmann, but her best portraits can stand comparison with these two masters, who were both friends and supporters. Her own quite distinct contribution to 20th-century painting is a study of human character that she developed in small head studies, self-portraits and portraits, especially those of her mother in old age.

After leaving school at the age of 13, Motesiczky studied drawing in various Viennese art schools. At 14 her life and art were permanently affected by meeting Beckmann, who was a family friend. In Beckmann, with whom she later studied in Frankfurt, she recognised a force for renewal in painting, an artist whose work offered a more human model than the more popular Parisian masters. In the years before attending Beckmann's masterclass Motesiczky taught herself to paint and went abroad to concentrate on her work, to Frankfurt as well as to Paris, where she painted the *Workman, Paris* (1926; artist's estate), her first masterpiece.

In the 1930s the technical and moral influence of Beckmann outwardly dominated her work, but she already had an absolutely sure handling of her chosen genres, still life and portraiture. Her compositions show iconographic models drawn from historical as well as contemporary sources. Motesiczky's concentration on portraiture has nothing to do with working to commission but reflects her overriding interest, obsession almost, with the painting of character. *Workman, Paris* and *The Dwarf* (1928; artist's estate) are impressive, compassionate works, similar in spirit to the peasant portraits of Paula Modersohn-Becker (q.v.). Beckmann once compared the two artists.

Self-portraiture is an important theme: the early *Self-Portrait with Comb* (1926; Österreichische Galerie, Vienna), produced before her 20th birthday, shows the workings of a highly developed pictorial imagination. The act of introspection, brush and palette disguised as instruments of vanity, becomes an allegory of Motesiczky's state of mind. The full-length *At the Dressmaker's* (1930; Fitzwilliam Museum, Cambridge), also a self-portrait, is one of the first examples of an imaginative figure composition, based on portraits. These become more prevalent in the 1950s and are sometimes satirical. The portrait groups are unified by their involvement in a mysterious drama, sometimes closely touching Motesiczky's own life, and this gives her more affinity with an allegorist such as Jan Steen than a social observer such as Gainsborough.

By 1938, when she and her mother fled from Vienna, her style had moved on from the sculptural modelling and graphic shadows reflecting Beckmann's work of the 1920s. The freer use of paint and general feeling of spontaneity in works from this period (e.g. *Fire in July*, 1942; private collection; *Still Life with Apples*, 1942; private collection, Switzerland; *Countess with Plum*, 1944; artist's estate) have been attributed to the influence of Kokoschka, who became a close friend in London in the 1940s.

Motesiczky spent the war years in Amersham away from the bombing with her mother and their Austrian housekeeper. This was a period of isolation in which friendships developed with other members of the immigrant community. Kokoschka often came to visit the Motesiczkys, but the most important friendship was with the novelist Elias Canetti, who was also living in Amersham. Canetti's ideas about death may have influenced two paintings of very elderly sitters that prefigure the portraits of the artist's own mother in old age: the *Old Woman, Amersham* (1942) and *Father Milburn* (1958; both artist's estate), in whose house the Canettis lodged.

Motesiczky never sought commissions, and could never flatter a patron. Her sometimes surprising choice of sitters suggests a searching for impressive qualities among ordinary, care-worn people. Yet among her portraits there are paintings of important intellectuals, figures from Motesiczky's circle: *Iris Murdoch* (St Anne's College, Oxford), *Elias Canetti* (1992;

Motesiczky: *Henriette M.*, 1961; Manchester City Art Galleries

National Portrait Gallery, London), *Miriam Rothschild* (private collection), *Baron Philippe de Rothschild* (1986; Fitzwilliam Museum) and the art historians *Ludwig von Baldass* (private collection, Vienna) and *Benno Reifenberg* (1967; Städelsches Kunstinstitut, Frankfurt am Main).

By instinct Motesiczky was drawn to people. It is perhaps because of this instinctive focus that landscapes, of which she painted beautiful examples, are a rarity. One particularly fine example is *Finchley Road at Night* (1950; Stedelijk Museum, Amsterdam), a stagey painting, with dramatic lighting thrown by two street lamps, in which the protagonists are two cars racing out of town. In her still lifes Motesiczky explored more deeply the emblematic element that often features in the portraits. The still lifes yield glimpses of Motesiczky's creaturely pleasures: food in preparation, flowers brought in from the garden, personal possessions reflecting the presence of people in a room. Some seem to be part of the theme of autobiography that links several of the figure compositions. Some express unspoken wishes (*Beach Still Life*, 1944), or hint at

personal events (*Birthday*, 1962). One key painting is *Self-Portrait with Pears* (1965; Neue Galerie der Stadt Linz), in which the artist's face, reflected in a dressing-table mirror, actually becomes part of a still life. The juxtaposition of self and two pears is hard to interpret, but the *vanitas* connotation of the still-life genre, and of the mirror itself, is as powerful a guide to the meaning as the grey hair that frames the face of the artist nearing her 60th birthday.

By common agreement the most moving of all Motesiczky's portraits are the paintings of her mother, Henriette. This Viennese aristocrat, who lived to the age of 96, had been one of the artist's first models and became, as she grew older, a focus for an impressively dispassionate study of physical decay (*Old Song*, 1959; artist's estate; *Henriette M.*, 1961; see illustration; *Mother with Baton*, 1977; Arts Council Collection). It emerges from the many portraits for which Henriette posed that the relationship between mother and daughter was a vital element in the artist's development. One writer has compared the series, which continues to the moment of Henriette's death in 1978, to Rembrandt's paintings of Hendrieckje Stoffels. Motesiczky views her mother with an objectivity that is at times disturbing, yet there are light touches that convey the enduring warmth of the relationship. In several Henriette is seen with one of her dogs – of the same breed that she had kept since the days when she and her husband had hunted together. The hunting dog is a traditional attribute in formal portraiture, but in these paintings something deeper and more personal is intended (*From the Night into Day*, 1975; Tate Gallery, London). In fact the formal iconographic reference is a necessary restraint on emotion in these works. Like the crossing of boundaries between genres, the blending of humour with gravity is a defining characteristic of Motesiczky's work.

PETER BLACK

Mukhina, Vera (Ignatiyevna)
Russian sculptor, 1889–1953

Born in Riga, Latvia, 19 June 1889. Educated in Feodosiya in the Crimea, where she took lessons in drawing and landscape. Attended Konstantin Yuon's private art school in Moscow, *c*.1905; started courses in sculpture at Sinitsyna's studio, *c*.1908; worked in Ilya Mashkov's studio, 1911–12. Travelled to Paris, 1912; studied at Académie de la Grande Chaumière; took lessons from Emile-Antoine Bourdelle; met Ossip Zadkine and Jacques Lipchitz. Travelled with Lyubov Popova (q.v.) to Italy, 1914; returned to Russia at outbreak of World War I. Assistant to Alexandra Exter (q.v.) at the Chamber Theatre, Moscow, 1915–16. Worked on posters, magazine designs and monuments, increasingly turning to monumental sculpture, 1918–20s. Founder member, Monolit (Monolith) group of sculptors, 1919–20. Worked with Exter at the Atelier of Fashions, Moscow, 1923. Taught at Vkhutemas (Higher State Artistic and Technical Workshops), 1926–7; at Vkhutein (Higher State Artistic and Technical Institute), 1926–30. Designed porcelain and glassware, monuments and interiors, 1930s–1940s. Member, Chetyre Iskusstva (Four Arts Society), 1925; ORS (Society of Russian Sculptors), 1926. Academician of the USSR. Died in Moscow, 6 October 1953.

Principal Exhibitions

Monolit (Monolith) group: from 1919
Mir Iskusstva (World of Art), Moscow: 1921
Chetyre Iskusstva (Four Arts Society), Moscow: from 1925
Exposition Internationale des Arts Décoratifs et Industriels Modernes, Paris: 1925
Moscow: 1927 (*Jubilee Exhibition of the Arts of the Peoples of the USSR*), 1943 (with Lebedeva, Gerasimov, Deineka, Konchalovsky and Shmarinov)
Venice Biennale: 1928
State Russian Museum, Leningrad and Moscow: 1932–3 (*Artists of the RSFSR over 15 Years, 1917–1932*)
Exposition Internationale, Paris: 1937

Selected Writings

A Sculptor's Thoughts, Moscow: Foreign Languages Publishing House, n.d. (after 1953)

Bibliography

B. Ternovets, *V.I. Mukhina*, Moscow: Ogiz, 1937
R. Klimov, ed., *Mukhina*, 3 vols, Moscow: Iskusstvo, 1960
Trois sculpteurs soviétiques: A.S. Goloubkina, V.I. Moukhina, S.D. Lebedeva, exh. cat., Musée Rodin, Paris, 1971
O.P. Voronova, *V.I. Mukhina*, Moscow: Iskusstvo, 1976
Pyotr Suzdalev, *Vera Ignatiyevna Mukhina*, Moscow: Iskusstvo, 1981
I.A. Bashinskaya, *Vera Ignatiyevna Mukhina, 1889–1953*, Leningrad: Khudozhnik RSFSR, 1987
M. Kolesnikov, "Alexandra Exter i Vera Mukhina", *Panorama Iskusstv*, 1989, no.12, pp.89–110
Vera Ignatiyevna Mukhina, exh. cat., Tretyakov Gallery, Moscow, 1989
N.V. Voronov, *Vera Mukhina*, Moscow: Izobrazitelnoye iskusstvo, 1989
M.N. Yablonskaya, *Women Artists of Russia's New Age, 1900–1935*, New York: Rizzoli, and London: Thames and Hudson, 1990
Agitation zum Glück: Sowjetische Kunst der Stalinzeit, exh. cat., Documenta-Halle, Kassel, and elsewhere, 1993
Art and Power: Europe under the Dictators, 1930–1945, exh. cat., Hayward Gallery, London, 1995

With Anna Golubkina (q.v.) and Vera Isayeva, Mukhina was one of Russia's greatest sculptors and her influence on the course of Soviet sculpture was profound and permanent. While neither avant-garde nor highly experimental, Mukhina's sculpture demonstrates a strong confidence in the classical tradition and an artistic vitality that became especially appropriate to her interpretations of Socialist Realism. True, Mukhina's admiration of Rodin and Emile-Antoine Bourdelle left an imprint on her early figures, such as her cement portrait of *Alexander Vertepov* (1914; 32 × 18 × 33 cm.; Tretyakov Gallery, Moscow). With her friend Lyubov Popova (q.v.), Mukhina also investigated French Cubism in Paris, extending the new formal principles to sculptures such as *Pietà* (1916; destroyed) and to her dynamic costume designs (not realised) for several plays that Alexander Tairov prepared at his Chamber Theatre in the mid-1910s, such as *La Cena delle Beffe* and *The Rose and the Cross*. An assistant there to Alexandra Exter (q.v.), Mukhina took particular note of her subtle conception of volume and construction, mentioning later that "Exter exerted a deep influence on my entire life" (quoted in Voronova 1976, p.42). Later, in 1923, she worked with Exter and others at the Atelier of Fashions, Moscow, on dress designs and helped Exter with designs for the film *Aelita*, released in 1924.

Mukhina adjusted quickly to the demands of the October Revolution of 1917, producing relevant works such as her project for the *Flame of the Revolution* (1922–3; bronze; 104 × 60 × 60 cm.) and *Peasant Woman* (1927; bronze; 190 × 79 × 70 cm.; both Tretyakov Gallery, Moscow). Mukhina is now remembered for her documentary and often tendentious sculpture, reflecting her commitment to the new political ideology and to the fundamental tenets of Socialist Realism that required the artist to "depict reality in its revolutionary development" (extract from Andrei Zhdanov's speech at the First Congress of Soviet Writers, Moscow, 1934; translation in John E. Bowlt, ed., *Russian Art of the Avant-garde: Theory and Criticism, 1902–1934*, 2nd edition, London and New York: Thames and Hudson, 1988, p.293). Concealing her Cubo-Futurist flirtation, Mukhina brought an energy and clarity of message to her evocations of the Revolution and the Civil War. The grandeur of Mukhina's artistic vision appealed

Mukhina: *Industrial Worker and Collective Farm Girl* for the Soviet Pavilion at the Exposition Internationale, Paris, 1937; now Exhibition of Economic Achievements, Moscow to both the Party and the masses alike, ensuring her prestigious political commissions in the 1930s–50s, such as her figures for the Hotel Moscow (1930s), the buxom harvesters for the New Moscow River Bridge (1938) and her several responses to World War II, such as the bronze bust of *General Boris Yusupov* (1942; Tretyakov Gallery) and the group *We Demand Peace* (1950–51). Mukhina adjusted her artistic vision to the conventions of the Stalin style unabashedly, extending her love of the histrionic to her monumental busts and statues such as the famous *Industrial Worker and Collective Farm Girl* (see illustration), erected for the Exposition Internationale, Paris, in 1937. Towering above Boris Iofan's monumental Soviet Pavilion, the new Soviet man and woman, rendered in stainless steel, strode towards the bright future – and towards the Nazi eagle atop the German Pavilion directly opposite. Immediately, *Industrial Worker and Collective Farm Girl*, now in front of the permanent Exhibition of Economic Achievements in Moscow, became one of the most widely recognised symbols of the USSR and a model for many subsequent Soviet monuments.

But Mukhina conveyed individual moods and emotions as well as obvious political statements. Her statues of cultural heroes, from *Peter Tchaikovsky* (1945–53) to *Maxim Gorky* (1952) and the ballerina *Galina Ulanova* (1941; bronze; State Russian Museum, St Petersburg), testifying to an unhesitating mastery of volumetrical form, often show the sitter in a moment of deep concentration or lyrical inspiration; and Mukhina could also produce intimate and pensive sculpture such as her renderings of relatives and friends, including several heads of her husband, *Alexander Zamkov* (e.g. the bronze of 1918; State Russian Museum) and her son. Moreover, her interest in unexpected media such as glass and her numerous pencil and charcoal drawings show an aesthetic diversity and flexibility that are not always apparent from her more familiar public sculpture. Mukhina combined the need for historical accuracy with an impetuous fantasy, prompting the critic Boris Ternovets, Mukhina's old friend, to speak of her "vividness and expressivity of decorative invention" (Ternovets 1937, p.24).

JOHN E. BOWLT

Münter, Gabriele
German painter and printmaker, 1877–1962

Born in Berlin, 19 February 1877. Settled in Herford with her family, 1878; in Koblenz, 1884. Received first training in Düsseldorf in the studio of Ernst Bosch and later in the Damenschule (Ladies' School) of Willy Platz, 1897. Visited relatives in USA, 1898–1900. Attended beginners' classes of Maximilian Dasio at the Damenakademie des Münchener Künstlerinnenvereins, Munich, 1901; attended sculpture course under Wilhelm Hüsgen at the newly formed Phalanx school, 1901–2; established contact with the director, Wassily Kandinsky; attended a woodcut course with the graphic artist, Ernst Neumann, 1902–3. Start of intimate relationship with Kandinsky, 1902; travelled with him in Germany and abroad, to the Netherlands, North Africa, Italy and Brussels,

1904–5; resided with him in Paris and Sèvres, attending drawing classes at the Académie de la Grande Chaumière under Théophile Steinlen, 1906–7. Returned to Berlin and thereafter Munich, establishing contact with Russian artists Marianne Werefkin (q.v.) and Alexej Jawlensky, 1908. Founder member, Neue Künstlervereinigung München, 1909; seceded from the association, with Kandinsky and Franz Marc, to initiate Der Blaue Reiter, 1911. Increasing contact with art dealer Herwarth Walden, 1912–13. Travelled to Goldach in Switzerland at outbreak of World War I, and remained in Zürich when Kandinsky returned to Moscow, 1914. Established residence in Stockholm, 1915. Final visit of Kandinsky to Münter before his second marriage to Nina Andreyevskaya, 1916. Moved to Copenhagen, 1917. Returned to Germany, as artistic production continued to dwindle, 1920–22; made numerous short trips in Germany; in Cologne, started text "Beichte und Anklage" (completed 1928); settled in Berlin (until 1929) and joined the Reichsverband Bildender Künstler Deutschlands (German National Federation of Fine Artists), 1925. Made contact with the poet Eleonore Kalkowska and a circle from the Verein der Künstlerinnen zu Berlin, 1926. Trip to Paris, where she was joined by art historian Dr Johannes Eichner, 1929–30. Resided in Murnau with Eichner, 1933. Became a member of the newly formed Reichskammer der bildenden Künste (National Chamber of Visual Arts), 1934. Economic austerity and limited exhibiting outlets through association with "Degenerate Art", 1937–46. Recipient of Munich art prize for painting, 1956. Presented Kandinsky's early works and 25 of her own paintings to the Städtische Galerie im Lenbachhaus, Munich, 1957. Died in Murnau, 19 May 1962. Estate of writings, correspondence and works formed the Gabriele Münter- und Johannes Eichner-Stiftung at the Lenbachhaus, 1966.

Principal Exhibitions

Individual
Kunstsalon Lenoble, Cologne: 1908
Galerie Der Sturm, Berlin: 1913 (touring retrospective), 1915, 1917 (with Gösta Adrian-Nilsson and Paul Klee)
Carl Gummesons Konsthandel, Stockholm: 1916
Nya Konstgalleriet Ciacelli, Stockholm: 1917 (with Georg Pauli)
Den frie udstilling, Copenhagen: 1918
Ny Kunstsal, Copenhagen: 1919
Bremen: 1933–5 (touring retrospective)
Kunstverein Braunschweig: 1949–53 (touring)
Kestner-Gesellschaft, Hannover: 1951 (with Paula Modersohn-Becker)
Moderne Galerie Otto Stangl, Munich: 1954 (with Wassily Kandinsky and Franz Marc)
Städtische Galerie im Lenbachhaus, Munich: 1957 (with Wassily Kandinsky), 1962 (retrospective)
Dalzell Hatfield Galleries, Los Angeles: 1960 (with Wassily Kandinsky), 1963 (retrospective)
Marlborough Fine Art, London: 1960
Leonard Hutton Galleries, New York: 1961

Group
Salon des Indépendants, Paris: 1907–8, 1911–12
Salon d'Automne, Paris: 1907–10
Neue Künstlervereinigung München, Galerie Thannhauser, Munich: 1909, 1910
Isdebsky Salon, Odessa: 1910

Bubnovy valet (Jack/Knave of Diamonds), Moscow: 1910, 1912
Der Blaue Reiter, Galerie Thannhauser, Munich: 1911
Der Blaue Reiter, Kunsthandlung Hans Goltz, Munich, and Galerie
  Der Sturm, Berlin: 1912
Galerie Der Sturm, Berlin: 1913 (Erster Deutscher Herbstsalon)
Galerie Nierendorf, Berlin: 1927 (Die schaffende Frau in der bilden-
  den Kunst)
Galerie Rudolf Wiltschek, Berlin: 1930

Selected Writings

"Gabriele Münter über sich selbst", Das Kunstwerk, ii/7, 1948, p.25
"Bekenntnisse und Erinnerungen", Menschenbilder in Zeichnungen,
  ed. G.F. Hartlaub, Berlin, 1952
"Mein Bild Mann im Sessel", Die Kunst und das schöne Heim, li/2,
  1953, p.53
Wassily Kandinsky and Gabriele Münter: Letters and Reminiscences,
  1902–1914, ed. Annegret Hoberg, Munich: Prestel, 1994

Bibliography

Rheinisch-Westfälische Zeitung, 8 May 1910
Johannes Eichner, "Gabriele Münter: Das Werk von 1908–1933",
  Die Weltkunst, ix/22, 1935, p.2
Paul Ferdinand Schmidt, "Entdeckung einer Künstlerin",
  Wiesbadener Kurier, 4 October 1947
Hans Reetz, "Gabriele Münter: Eine Bahnbrecherin in moderner
  Kunst", Die Welt der Frau, April 1950, pp.4–5
Lilly Rydström-Wickelberg, "Gabriele Münter", Konstrevy, xxviii,
  1952, pp.216–20
Johannes Eichner, Kandinsky und Gabriele Münter: Von Ursprüngen
  moderner Kunst, Munich: Bruckmann, 1957
Hans Konrad Roethel, Gabriele Münter, Munich: Bruckmann, 1957
Maria-Dorothea Beck, "Vom frohen Tun: Die Malerin Gabriele
  Münter", Mädchenbildung und Frauenschaffen, ix, 1959, pp.1–10
Edouard Roditi, Dialogues on Art, London: Secker and Warburg,
  1960; New York: Horizon, 1961
Sabine Helms, Gabriele Münter: Das druckgraphische Werk,
  Sammlungskatalog 2, Städtische Galerie im Lenbachhaus,
  Munich, 1967
Peter Lahnstein, Gabriele Münter, Ettal: Buch Kunstverlag, 1971
Liselotte Erlanger, "Gabriele Münter: A lesser life?", Feminist Art
  Journal, iii/4, 1974–5, pp.11ff
Ursula Glatzel, Zur Bedeutung der Volkskunst beim Blauen Reiter,
  dissertation, Ludwig-Maximilians-Universität, Munich, 1975
Rosel Gollek, "Murnau im Voralpenland", Deutsche
  Künstlerkolonien und Künstlerorte, ed. Gerhard Wietek, Munich:
  Theimig, 1976, pp.178–87
Paul Vogt, Geschichte der deutschen Malerei im 20. Jahrhundert,
  Cologne: DuMont Schauberg, 1976
Anne Mochon, Gabriele Münter: Still-life, Folk Art and the Blaue
  Reiter, University of Massachusetts, Amherst, 1977
Erich Pfeiffer-Belli, Gabriele Münter: Zeichnungen und Aquarelle,
  Berlin: Mann, 1979
Brigitte M. Cole, Gabriele Münter and the Development of Her Early
  Murnau Style, dissertation, University of Texas, Arlington, 1980
Alessandra Comini, "State of the field, 1980: The woman artists of
  German Expressionism", Arts Magazine, lv, November 1980,
  pp.147–53
Gabriele Münter: Between Munich and Murnau, exh. cat., Busch-
  Reisinger Museum, Harvard University, Cambridge, MA, and
  elsewhere, 1980
Susan P. Bachrach, "A comparison of the early landscapes of Münter
  and Kandinsky, 1902–1910", Woman's Art Journal, ii/1, 1981,
  pp.21–4
Sara H. Gregg, "Gabriele Münter and Sweden: Interlude and separation", Arts Magazine, lv, May 1981, pp.116–19
Kenneth Lindsay, "Gabriele Münter and Wassily Kandinsky: What
  they meant to each other", Arts Magazine, lvi, December 1981,
  pp.56–62

Ellen Klausch, Frauenbilder im Werk Gabriele Münters, research
  paper, Berlin, 1987
Shulamith Behr, Women Expressionists, Oxford: Phaidon, and New
  York: Rizzoli, 1988
Gabriele Münter, exh. cat., Kunstverein Hamburg, and elsewhere,
  1988
Vivian Endicott Barnett, Kandinsky and Sweden, Malmö: Konsthall,
  and Stockholm: Moderna Museet, 1989
S. Heinlein, Gabriele Münter und Marianne Werefkin: Die Rollen
  zweier Frauen im "Blauen Reiter", MA thesis, Hamburg
  University, 1989
Johanna Werckmeister, "'Blauer Reiter' im Damensattel:
  Rezeptionsraster für eine Künstlerin", Kritische Berichte, xvii,
  1989, pp.70–77
Gisela Kleine, Gabriele Münter und Wassily Kandinsky: Biographie
  eines Paares, Frankfurt am Main: Insel, 1990
Andreas Hüneke, ed., Der Blaue Reiter: Dokumente einer geistigen
  Bewegung, Leipzig: Reclam, 1991
Sabine Windecker, Gabriele Münter: Eine Künstlerin aus dem Kreis
  des "Blauen Reiters", Berlin: Reimer, 1991
Shulamith Behr, "Leicestershire's new acquisition: Gabriele Münter's
  portrait of Anna [Roslund-]Aagaard", National Arts Collections
  Fund Review, London, 1992
Gabriele Münter, 1877–1962: Retrospektive, exh. cat., Städtische
  Galerie im Lenbachhaus, Munich, and elsewhere, 1992

Writings, correspondence and works are in the Gabriele Münter- und
Johannes Eichner-Stiftung, Städtische Galerie im Lenbachhaus,
Munich.

Gabriele Münter's contribution to early modernism has
received serious academic attention only in the last decade.
Moreover, art-historical narratives that have traditionally
consigned her role to that of "muse" or companion of Wassily
Kandinsky were clearly brought into question by the large
retrospective exhibition of 1992–3 that toured to Munich,
Frankfurt am Main, Stockholm and Berlin. The overall impact
of this spectacle of 160 paintings, 30 graphics and 60 drawings
allowed Münter's oeuvre to emerge forcefully from the shadow
of Kandinsky, who had been her tutor and lover between the
years 1902 and 1916.

As with most women practitioners, Münter's status was
problematic in relation to society in general and to the avant-
garde communities in which she worked. Münter was
descended from an upper-middle-class, Protestant background,
and the fact that she lived with a married, albeit separated
man, eleven years her senior, was distinctly unconventional for
the time. Moreover, she remained childless and career-orien-
tated, refusing to subordinate her aims to the success of the
relationship. In Münter's various self-portraits, the manner in
which she negotiated her self-identity testifies to the conflicts
engendered between societal constructions of the terms
"woman" and "artist" (see Behr in Munich 1992, pp.85–90).
Although she was an active contributor to and promoter of the
Neue Künstlervereinigung München (1909–12) and Blaue
Reiter (1912–14), the artist's ban on the publication of her
writings until 50 years after her death have made it difficult to
reconstruct her theoretical preoccupations. Abridged versions
of her correspondence and journals have recently been
published but, on the whole, art historians have assumed that
the lack of written testimony accounts for Münter's supposed
simplicity of character and intuitive directions in art.

On the whole, it is to Johannes Eichner that we owe the
dubious heritage of the elision between psychological charac-

ter and artistic production, between Münter's so-called naive temperament and "truly primitive" (*echte Primitive*) artistic statement, defined in opposition to Kandinsky's intellectual and spiritual contribution to the origins of modern art (Eichner 1957, pp.22 and 282). Münter herself contributed to this legend in her reminiscences ("Bekenntnisse und Erinnerungen", 1952) which recorded Kandinsky's observation:

> You are hopeless as a pupil. One cannot teach you anything. You can only do what you have inside you. You have everything instinctively [*alles von Natur*]. All I can do for you is to protect and cultivate your talent so that nothing false intervenes.

This must be one of the most frequently derided statements in the annals of feminist criticism due its patronising tone and determinist endorsement of the metaphors of woman as nature and instinct. Yet the myths of the "untutored", the "spontaneous" and "authentic" remained the hallmarks of Münter's reception, a state of affairs that continued unabated well into the 1970s (e.g. Vogt 1976, p.58; for a historiographic survey, see Windecker 1991). These values have to be assessed critically in relation to Münter's oeuvre and interpreted contextually, since such vitalist aspirations were important preoccupations of Expressionist artists at the time.

While anti-academicism may have been a feature of her mature works, this does not necessarily imply that Münter was unskilled; indeed, five sets of remarkable profile-head drawings, in pencil, survive from her school days. The six American sketchbooks, containing depictions of people, landscape and plants, reveal her ability to capture likeness and to distil the components of a scene with deft linear strokes and a minimum of subtle shading (e.g. *Aunt Lou in Plainview*, 1899; graphite on white paper; Städtische Galerie im Lenbachhaus, Munich, repr. Cambridge 1980, no.2). Interestingly, even when drawing from the nude model, Münter was far more comfortable when focusing on the salient contours of the pose than on the academic processes of shading and hatching (*Studies from the Model*, c.1902; Städtische Galerie im Lenbachhaus, repr. Munich 1992, fig.4).

Evidently, these skills were appropriate to her exploration of wood- and linocut technique, the processes of which received renewed attention and a growth in demand at the turn of the 19th and 20th centuries. As in the German Arts and Crafts movement (Jugendstil), which was particularly forceful in Munich, Münter endorsed the erosion between the fine and applied arts and a stylistic return to the handmade and non-mechanical rhythms of nature. Her colour linoleum print, the portrait of *Kandinsky* (1906; Leonard Hutton Galleries, New York, repr. Cambridge 1980, no.9), offsets a crisp bold silhouette against a background of simplified, organic shapes, delineated by contour. Already, during her stay in Paris, her woodcuts were deemed suitable for reproduction in the symbolist magazine *Les Tendances Nouvelles* (1906) and one of Münter's launching exhibitions in 1908 – at Friedrich Cohen's bookstore in Bonn – was exclusively devoted to her print production.

Although the mere existence of innumerable sketchbooks from all periods testifies to the artist's systematic reliance on preliminary studies for her final paintings, it is evident that Münter painted very quickly, often completing one or more large-format pictures in a single afternoon (see Hoberg 1994, letters dated 8 December 1910 and 12–13 December 1910, pp.97–9). Her initial training in the Phalanx school encouraged an interest in *in situ* landscape painting; on Kandinsky's advice, her early works (*Kandinsky Painting in the Landscape*, 1903; oil on canvas; Städtische Galerie im Lenbachhaus, repr. Munich 1992, no.5) rely on a limited colour range of yellows, greens and browns with extensive use of the palette knife. Her interpretation of this genre reached a climax in the Murnau period (see Hoberg in *ibid.*, pp.27–46) when, in the company of Kandinsky, Marianne Werefkin (q.v.) and Jawlensky, Münter's works abandoned the plein-air, Impressionist qualities of her Sèvres sojourn (*View from the Window in Sèvres*, 1906; oil on canvas; Städtische Galerie im Lenbachhaus, *ibid.*, no.18) to assume the values of synthetism. With their unusual palette of blue, green, yellow, pink with red for emphasis, the diverse surfaces and facture of Münter's Murnau vistas are bound together by strong contour, as in *Landscape with Hut in the Sunset* (1908; private collection, *ibid.*, no.47).

These small-scale oils on board, roughly 33 × 41 centimetres, served as an increasing stimulus for technical radicalism as the artist sought to negotiate a path between Jawlensky's Matisse-linked modernism and the inspiration of folk art. It is testimony to Münter's inventiveness that, even when interpreting similar motifs, the landscapes produced throughout her career – as when she returned to Murnau in the 1930s – always retain a freshness of the visual encounter and elements of surprise and pleasure for the viewer (*Street in Murnau*, 1931; private collection, *ibid.*, no.203). Less convincing, however, is the industrial landscape *Blue Excavator* (1935–6; oil on canvas; 60 × 90 cm.; Städtische Galerie im Lenbachhaus, *ibid.*, no.223), which arose from numerous sketches made of urban development at Olympiastrasse near Garmisch during the early years of the Third Reich. As part of a group of contributions to the travelling exhibition the *Streets of Adolf Hitler in Art* in 1936, these works testify to the invasiveness of official culture in prescribing stylistic limits and reducing the outlets for modern art.

According to Münter, it was Jawlensky who first drew her attention to Bavarian and Bohemian glass painting and the technique known as *Hinterglasmalerei* (painting behind glass). A substantial collection was owned by a local brewer in Murnau, Johann Kroetz (see Hoberg 1994, p.16, now in the town museum at Oberammergau). Münter started her own collection and copied traditional examples of this genre (e.g. *St Florian*, c.1909; repr. Munich 1992, p.253), acquiring the technique from Heinrich Rambold, a glass painter still active in Murnau. Notwithstanding the fact that the production of folk art had long been part of a thriving industry – stimulated by an expanding tourist economy in the region – the members of the Blaue Reiter group cherished the Neo-romantic belief in the innocent religiosity and naive originality of the artists.

In her *Still Life with St George* (1911; oil on board; Städtische Galerie im Lenbachhaus, *ibid.*, no.106) Münter combined a motley assortment of images: a statue of the Virgin, small crèche figurines from Oberammergau, a ceramic hen, a vase of flowers and, on the left-hand side, painted in a hazy aura, the glass-painting of St George. Divorced from their original location or narrative sequences, the votive objects are animated by inconsistent effects of lighting and invested with new mythic associations. Hence, in her appropriation of the methods and motifs of folk art, Münter implicated herself in the Western-based phenomenon of "modernist primitivism", a trend that transformed the inspiration of artefacts from so-called primitive societies into the departure for autonomous art.

In view of the perception of her work as aligned with nature, how could Münter's production escape critical understanding of women's creativity as remaining in the realm of matter, never capable of approaching male artists' sublimation of the "primitive" into high art? Invariably, she deployed such referents in ironic and potentially subversive depictions of the domestic, the private spheres of womanhood appropriated by male artists for modern subject matter. This is most apparent in Münter's more monumental works that portrayed her colleagues from the circles of the Neue Künstlervereinigung München and Blaue Reiter in rustic interiors, providing a subtle resonance between the rarefied atmosphere of intellectual discourse and the leisure activities of avant-garde communities. In works such as *Kandinsky at the Tea-Table* (1910; oil on board; Israel Museum, Jerusalem, *ibid.*, no.74) and *Kandinsky and Erma Bossi at the Table* (1912; oil on canvas; Städtische Galerie im Lenbachhaus, *ibid.*, no.113) Münter demonstrated her interest in juxtaposing animated still-life objects with figures, frozen in action, radically compressed in a two-dimensionalised space.

In *Man in Chair* (1913; oil on canvas; Bayerische Staatsgemäldessammlungen, Munich, *ibid.*, no.133) Paul Klee is portrayed wedged into an armchair set against an emerald-green rear wall of the Kandinsky and Münter apartment in Ainmillerstrasse, Munich. While his legs in white shimmering trousers are depicted folded sideways, the upper torso in a stiff black jacket is displayed frontally and comically. On the same level as his intense gaze, the dramatic arrangements of Bavarian *Hinterglasbilder* and folk-art figurines vie for the spectator's attention. Whether or not Münter was conscious of such inferences, the awkwardness of her sitters' countenances questions and subverts the assumption of masculine control of domestic and private spaces. It is interesting to note that Münter's correspondence reveals this paradoxical tension: an awareness of feminist ideas counteracted by an apparent obsession with domesticity: "Wanted to read in the afternoon – the philosophy of the feminist Lessing – a new book 'Weib, Frau, Dame' but the phonograph was going across the street ... – so I did some sewing and ironing – I always have my things quite tidy" (letter of 12–13 December 1910, Hoberg 1994, p.99).

Significantly, the women in her circle are interpreted far more sympathetically. This was particularly evident during the Scandinavian period (Annika Öhrner in Munich 1992, pp.67–84) when Münter depicted a series of women in interiors, focusing on the themes of isolation, illness and reverie. Unlike the primitivist and mystical undertones of her earlier compositions, these Swedish portraits focus attention on the contemplative mood, short hair-styles and reform dress of early 20th-century womanhood. Münter's friend Gertrude Holz served as the model for the pendant pieces *Reflection* (1917; oil on canvas; Städtische Galerie im Lenbachhaus, *ibid.*, no.154) and *Future (Woman in Stockholm)* (1917; Frank. E. Taplin, Jr, USA, *ibid.*, no.155). In both paintings the bust-

Münter: *Anna Roslund*, 1917; oil on canvas; 94 × 68 cm.

length figure is posed in front of a window, reinforcing the contrast between the external world and the confinement or seclusion of the interior setting. Strategic use of black and white contrasts with variations of the primary colours – red, yellow and blue – applied in broad, powerful strokes. Still-life objects are markedly more delineated than during the Murnau period but their forceful presence does not detract from the meditative atmosphere.

While these works were destined for the open market, Münter consistently sought portraiture commissions (see Behr 1992, pp.56–9). In the portrait of *Anna Roslund* (see illustration), painted in Copenhagen in 1917, Münter adopted a potent, three-quarter-length composition. Anna Roslund, the youngest sister of Nell Walden, was a writer and musician, and Münter represents her as a pipe-smoking, musing figure, an unconventional metaphor for creative womanhood. In declaring the confident independence of the "new woman", the bravura displayed in this work totally belies the biographical events of Münter's life at the time and alerts one to the dangers of assuming a conflation between the two.

During the 1920s Münter's ability to capture the essential features of a scene with immense economy of line coincided with the values of clarity given priority in Neue Sachlichkeit circles and in the advice offered by her mentor Johannes Eichner (see his letter of 29 September 1928 in Kleine 1990, p.563). In a work painted in Berlin entitled *Reflection II* (1928; oil on canvas; Städtische Galerie im Lenbachhaus, repr. Munich 1992, no.187) the full-length, seated figure is portrayed with crossed legs in profile while the upper part of the body faces the viewer, the head resting on her hands. Though there is an emphasis on two-dimensionality, the chair casts shadows within the shallow space as Münter explores the cubic volumes of the sitter in a range of red and ochre tonalities. This distillation of her painterly abilities needs to be viewed in the context of the crisis of Expressionism rather than as a withdrawal from the intensity of the earlier periods.

Although her works of the post-World War II period remained within the confines of the "lesser" genres – landscape, still life, interior scenes – it is necessary to reappraise Münter's transformation or disruption of figural and narrative material across the span of her oeuvre. Even her abstractions are quite remarkable for their independence from Kandinsky's methods, proclaiming distinctive gender differences with regard to their iconographic departure (see Heller in *ibid.*, pp.47–66). Methodologies that glibly assert the simplicity and "primitive" qualities of her production fail to do justice to their contingent and specific circumstances. Indeed, it is possible to observe that her images of the domestic and private realms were invested with the significance of contemporaneity, representing the equations between modern art and life.

SHULAMITH BEHR

Murray, Elizabeth

American painter, 1940–

Born in Chicago, Illinois, 1940. Studied at the School of the Art Institute of Chicago, 1958–62 (BFA); Mills College, Oakland, California, 1962–4 (MFA). Instructor, Rosary Hill College, Buffalo, 1965–7; Bard College, Annandale-on-Hudson, New York, 1974–5 and 1976–7; visiting instructor, Wayne State University, Detroit, 1975; California Institute of the Arts, Valencia, 1975–6; Art Institute of Chicago, 1975–6; instructor, Princeton University, 1977; Yale University, New Haven, 1978–9; lecturer, New York Studio School of Drawing, Painting and Sculpture, 1987. Married (1) sculptor Don Sunseri; one son; divorced; (2) poet Bob Holman, 1982; two daughters. Recipient of Walter M. Campana award, Art Institute of Chicago, 1982; American Academy and Institute of Arts and Letters award, New York, 1984; Skowhegan medal for painting, New York, 1986; Larry Aldrich prize in contemporary art, 1993; honorary doctorate, School of the Art Institute of Chicago, 1992; honorary degree, Rhode Island School of Design, Providence, 1993. Member, American Institute of Arts and Letters, 1992. Lives in New York.

Selected Individual Exhibitions

Paula Cooper Gallery, New York: 1976, 1978, 1981, 1983, 1984, 1987, 1988, 1989, 1990, 1992, 1994

Ohio State University Gallery of Fine Art, Columbus: 1978
Galerie Mukai, Tokyo: 1980, 1990
Carnegie-Mellon Art Gallery, Pittsburgh: 1986
Dallas Museum of Art: 1987–8 (touring retrospective)
University Art Museum, California State University, Long Beach: 1987 (*Centric 26*, touring)
San Francisco Museum of Modern Art: 1988
Mayor Rowan Gallery, London: 1989
Barbara Krakow Gallery, Boston: 1990–92 (touring)

Selected Writings

Notes for Fire and Rain, New York: Lapp Princess Press, 1981
"When is a painting finished?", ed. Paul Gardner, *Art News*, lxxxiv, November 1985, p.97

Bibliography

Early Works by Five Contemporary Artists, exh. cat., New Museum, New York, 1977
Donald B. Kuspit, "Elizabeth Murray's dandyish abstraction", *Artforum*, xvi, February 1978, pp.28–31
Jesse Murry, "Quintet: The romance of order and tension in five paintings by Elizabeth Murray", *Arts Magazine*, lv, May 1981, pp.102–5
Jacqueline Brody, "Elizabeth Murray, thinking in print: An interview", *Print Collector's Newsletter*, xiii, 1982, pp.74–7
Ronny H. Cohen, "Elizabeth Murray's colored space", *Artforum*, xxi, December 1982, pp.51–5
Robert James Coad, *Between Painting and Sculpture: A Study of the Work and Working Process of Lynda Benglis, Elizabeth Murray, Judy Pfaff and Gary Stephan*, PhD dissertation, New York University, 1984
Corinne Robins, *The Pluralist Era: American Art, 1968–1981*, New York: Harper, 1984
Joan Simon, "Mixing metaphors: Elizabeth Murray", *Art in America*, lxxii, April 1984, pp.140–47
Paul Gardner, "Elizabeth Murray shapes up", *Art News*, lxxxiii, September 1984, pp.46–55
Roberta Smith, "A three-sided argument", *Village Voice*, 30 October 1984, p.107
Elizabeth Murray: Drawings, 1980–1986, exh. cat., Carnegie-Mellon University Art Gallery, Pittsburgh, 1986
Richard S. Field and Ruth E. Fine, *A Graphic Muse: Prints by Contemporary American Women*, New York: Hudson Hills Press, 1987
Elizabeth Murray: Paintings and Drawings, exh. cat., Dallas Museum of Art, and elsewhere, 1987
Lilly Wei, "Talking abstract, pt 1", *Art in America*, lxxv, July 1987, pp.80–97
Ken Johnson, "Elizabeth Murray's new paintings", *Arts Magazine*, lxii, September 1987, pp.67–9
Robert Storr, "Shape shifter", *Art in America*, lxxvii, April 1989, pp.210–21, 275
Elizabeth Murray: Prints, 1979–1990, exh. cat., Barbara Krakow Gallery, Boston, and elsewhere, 1990
Recent Work by Elizabeth Murray, exh. cat., Wexner Center for the Arts, Ohio State University, Columbus, 1991
Corinne Robins, "Elizabeth Murray: Deconstructing our interiors", *Art Journal*, l, 1991, pp.57–9
Deborah Solomon, "Celebrating paint", *New York Times*, 31 March 1991, magazine section, pp.20–25, 40, 46
Brooks Adams, "Elizabeth Murray at Paula Cooper", *Art in America*, lxxx, December 1992, pp.110–11
Michael Kimmelman, "Looking for the magic in painting: At the Met with Elizabeth Murray", *New York Times*, 21 October 1994, pp.1, 28

Elizabeth Murray's paintings are rooted in the tradition of abstraction, but they remain connected to a peripheral brand

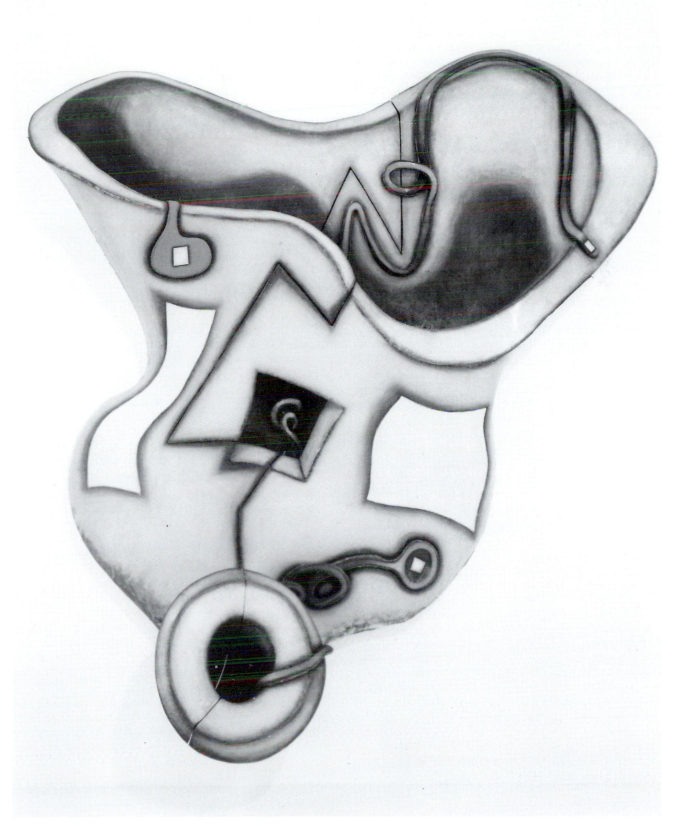

Murray: *Careless Love*, 1995–6; oil on shaped canvas with wood; 270.5 × 252.7 × 68.6 cm.; Collection National Gallery of Art, Washington, DC

of cryptic figuration. The transformations leading to the unique marriage of abstraction and figuration in her extraordinary conglomerates can be traced in her artistic development. She had a conventional artistic training at the School of the Art Institute of Chicago (1958–62), where she learned to paint figures and landscapes and to use colour theory. She was also influenced by modernist works in the Institute's collection, particularly the still lifes of Cézanne and the Cubist Juan Gris. Collectively this work was inspirational because of its spatial organisation, potent colour and incorporation of ordinary objects into abstract planes. The animation of Walt Disney provided an additional stimulus. During post-graduate studies at Mills College, near San Francisco, she became interested in Bosch, Max Beckmann, Chagall and Leon Golub. It is, however, Willem de Kooning whom she credits with showing her how to paint and to manipulate the canvas. The works of Frank Stella were also important. Mentally mining the solutions of modernist masters served her well in establishing her own distinct version of synthetic abstraction, a brash, punky style mixing high and low cultural references.

Murray's early paintings show a vitality of process akin to the art of Rauschenberg, Oldenburg and Jasper Johns. They are large and haunting, filled with floating ghouls and strange shapes. Using acrylics, she lavished thick paint on shaped canvases to which she added fragments of fabric and furniture. References from popular culture appear in the form of comic-strip characters. She was never part of Chicago's Hairy Who movement and, although her playful work hinting at a Surrealist sensibility certainly suggests a link to the Chicago Imagists, her automatism is derived from the structure of the shaped canvas and her own inventiveness, unhesitant and funky.

While teaching at a Catholic women's college in Buffalo, New York, in the mid-1960s, Murray explored sculpture, investigations that altered her aesthetic and became an integral part of her work. The years following her move to New York in 1967 were difficult, but it was also a period of tremendous growth. In 1971 she abandoned acrylic and decided to work instead with oil. The new paintings, drastically reduced in size, were filled with stick figures and bizarre imagery. The critical years of Murray's artistic exploration paralleled those of the "anti-painting" era, when the focus of the "cutting-edge" art world was on the impermanent, anti-object investigations of Post-Minimal and Conceptual artists. Murray was not deterred: "… I only wanted to paint and so I stuck with it!". During this period she examined painting as a viable medium and also her motives for persisting with it. Murray's first significant exposure in New York came in 1972 when she was invited to participate in the Painting Biennial at the Whitney Museum. That same year a Detroit collector, Jim Duffy, bought three paintings from her "alphabet series". She exhibited again at the Whitney in 1973, in *American Drawings, 1963–1973*. Such critical attention gave Murray the confidence to show her work to dealers, and in 1976 she had the first of many solo exhibitions at the Paula Cooper Gallery in New York.

In 1974 the direction of Murray's painting altered. The inauguration of her artistic maturing was signalled by the painting *One or Two Things* (1974), a square divided into a blaring red and moody aquamarine triangle with an orange dot at the centre. The scale is larger, there is a greater sense of assurance and inventiveness; colour becomes even more important, and its interaction with the symbols and planes led eventually to the shattering of the single canvas plane. Her transition from formalist to fantasist began in the mid-1970s, as biomorphic shapes infiltrated her cubist planes and geometric canvases.

Feeling that her work was becoming too formal, she introduced a new monumentality in paintings such as *Pink Spiral Leap* (1975). *Beginner* (1976; 304 × 304 cm.; Saatchi Collection, London, repr. Dallas 1987, p.27) is dominated by a mineral blue form resembling a profile face, animated by a violet, pretzel-like line. By 1977 her art had become even more outrageous, increasingly invaded by cartoony, imagistic characters. She participated in four major exhibitions that year: in New York at the Whitney, the Guggenheim and the New Museum; and in Chicago at the Museum of Contemporary Art. Although her paintings in this period still hung flat on the wall, the tension between the canvas frame and its compacted contents, evident in such works as *Tug* (1977), *Traveler's Dream* and *Parting and Together* (both 1978), soon led to her abandoning the rectangular support. Painting on an array of differently shaped surfaces which she loaded with fantastically coloured marks, Murray created powerful new works that were a disconcerting mix of electrifying shards and fragments. Her spirited style began to attract national attention, and critics recognised her contribution to a new kind of organic/geometric non-objective art, sometimes referred to as Neo-Abstraction.

In the 1980s Murray's reputation became firmly established in the USA. The biomorphic abstract forms of her earlier compositions were supplanted by recognisable images of cups, tables, telephones, shoes. Increasingly she physically fractured the canvas and accented the tension between the abstract and representational aspects, as in such works as *Breaking* (1980; Collection Paul and Camille Oliver-Hoffmann, *ibid.*, p.43) and *Painter's Progress* (1981; Museum of Modern Art, New York). From 1983 the formal strength and inventiveness of her paintings were derived from their content, which is often autobiographical. She achieved an original balance of vibrant colour and interactive geometric and organic shapes. In *Deeper than D* (1983; private collection, *ibid.*, p.67), for example, the introduction of a chair gives greater depth to the eccentric, torqued space of the shaped canvas.

Subsequently, Murray closed up her compositions, subdued her palette and pared down the narrative content. The zany character of her work becomes muted by a poignant, introspective quality in, for example, *Don't Be Cruel* (1985–6) and *Things To Come* (1986). In the looming shoe painting *Tomorrow* (1988) the mis-shapen transformation of an identifiable object simultaneously twists and stretches both the real and illusionist space. From the late 1980s her paintings became bigger, stranger and aggressively rowdier. The process of fragmentation led to the construction of pictorial structures that evince a spasmodic metamorphosis, pushing materials to extremes. Closer to sculpture than conventional paintings, they appear to be in a continuous state of flux, moving sideways and splitting apart. The viewer is challenged, invited to decipher the parts and to savour the experiences evoked. There is frustration in the dialogue, however, as Murray always seems to withhold significant clues to the completion of the puzzle.

Murray's art has been in more than 100 group exhibitions in the USA and Europe. An exhibition of her pastel drawings was held at the Carnegie-Mellon Art Gallery in Pittsburgh in 1986, and in 1987 a touring retrospective of her paintings and drawings was organised jointly by the Massachusetts Institute of Technology and the Dallas Museum of Art. Substantial catalogues were produced for both exhibitions. Her dynamically interwoven bolts of colour and discrete canvas segments create a psychologically active colour-space and semi-sculptural environment of intense expressive power. She is considered a master American painter of the late 20th century, whose works exude an air of mystery and a sensuous intelligence.

ELAINE A. KING

N

Nagel, Hanna

German painter, 1907–1975

Born in Heidelberg, 10 June 1907. Apprenticed to a bookbinder, 1924. Studied at the Karlsruhe Academy under Karl Hubbuch, Wilhelm Schnarrenberger, Hermann Gehri and Walter Conz, 1925–9; Berlin Academy under Emil Orlik and Hans Meid, 1929. Married Hans Fischer, 1931; daughter born 1938. Studied in Rome, 1933–6. Moved to Heidelberg, 1938. Recipient of Rome prize, 1933; Albrecht Dürer scholarship, 1935; Kassel prize and silver medal for graphic arts, Exposition Internationale, Paris, 1937; Drexel prize, Nuremberg, 1960. Member, Verein der Künstlerinnen zu Berlin, 1933–43. Died in Heidelberg, 15 March 1975.

Principal Exhibitions

Individual

Galerie Karl Buchholz, Berlin: 1938 (with Hans Fischer)
Kunsthalle, Regensburg: 1947
Heidelberger Kunstverein, Heidelberg: 1967 (retrospective)
Karl-Ernst-Osthaus Museum, Hagen: 1972
Städtische Museen, Freiburg: 1975

Group

Kunsthalle, Mannheim: 1931
Verein der Künstlerinnen zu Berlin: 1933, 1937, 1940, 1942, 1943
J. Lutz, Mannheim: 1935
Exposition Internationale, Paris: 1937
Stuttgart: 1959 (*Künstler gegen den Atomkrieg*, touring)

Selected Writings

Ich zeichne, weil es mein Leben ist, ed. Irene Fischer-Nagel, Karlsruhe: Braun, 1977

Bibliography

Ellen Schäfer, *Hanna Nagel: Fantasien über die Préludes von Chopin*, Wiesbaden, 1950
Eberhard Ruhmer, *Hanna Nagel*, Munich: Bruckmann, 1965
Hanna Nagel zum 60. Geburtstag, exh. cat., Heidelberger Kunstverein, Heidelberg, 1967
Hanna Nagel: Zeichnungen und Lithographien, exh. cat., Karl-Ernst-Osthaus Museum, Hagen, 1972
Rudolf Musik, "Hanna Nagel Zeichnerin und Illustratorin", *Illustration*, lxiii/3, 1975
Hanna Nagel: Das frühe Werk, exh. cat., Städtische Museen, Freiburg, 1975
Künstlerinnen international, 1877–1977, exh. cat., Schloss Charlottenburg, Berlin, 1977
Hanna Nagel: Frühe Arbeiten, 1926–1934, exh. cat., Galerie des Bezirksverbandes Bildender Künstler, Karlsruhe, 1981
Leo Mülfarth, "Die Graphikerin Hanna Nagel", *Ettlinger Hefte*, no.18, 1984
Profession ohne Tradition: 125 Jahre Verein der Berliner Künstlerinnen, exh. cat., Berlinische Galerie, Berlin, 1992
Sergiusz Michalski, *New Objectivity: Painting, Graphic Art and Photography in Weimar Germany, 1919–1933*, Cologne: Taschen, 1994 (German original, 1992)

By training Hanna Nagel may be classified as an artist of the Neue Sachlichkeit (New Objectivity). Yet she quite quickly moved away from the representation of reality, the painstaking description of detail, and found a pictorial language of her own (see Hans Pfannmüller in *Ansprache zur Eröffnung der Ausstellung Hanna Nagel*, exh. cat., Bruchsal, 1981), in which the expression of her inner emotional world, the fears, longings and dreams, determined the compositions of her drawings, lithographs, etchings and illustrations. Thus, after World War II she did not follow the preoccupation with abstract painting but devoted herself to the depiction of inner states. Rather than the representation of the everyday or the intellectual analysis of the world of objects, she considered her artistic task to lie in the intensification of feeling until its manifestation in a symbol.

Nagel's gift for drawing was evident early on. After an apprenticeship as a bookbinder, she enrolled at the Academy in Karlsruhe, which with Berlin, Munich, Cologne and Düsseldorf was one of the centres of Neue Sachlichkeit in the 1920s; artists active there included Wilhelm Schnarrenberger, Georg Scholz, Rudolf Schlichter and, of course, Karl Hubbuch. By the turn of the century the Academy already had a school of etching and a lithographic printing studio. The emphasis on drawing and graphic techniques undoubtedly determined Nagel's preference for these media. In addition to studying under Schnarrenberger, she was taught etching by Walter Conz and figure drawing by Hubbuch. Her relationship to Hubbuch was ambivalent. He influenced her choice of subject matter and formal design. A pen-and-ink drawing of 1930 (repr. *Ich zeichne ... 1977*) is indicative of their relationship: Nagel, with arms crossed and looking at the viewer, stands next to Hubbuch, who is drawing. Her future husband, Karl Fischer, stands at a distance from the two, his arms also crossed. In contrast to her work's formal similarities to Hubbuch's – its

Nagel: *Frau von Drukerpresse*

strong emphasis on the ugly, and the use of an elevated perspective – Nagel's subjects are viewed in a different way. Whereas Hubbuch's socially critical depictions caricature bourgeois or peasant life, her works have a strange presence of their own: figures isolated from any concrete, comprehensible surroundings – apparently represented realistically – who seem to represent an underlying social and personal reality (Michalski 1994). In Berlin, Nagel's teacher Emil Orlik saw her as the successor of Käthe Kollwitz (q.v.). Although Nagel represents social misery in some of her works, as for example the pen-and-ink drawing (1931; repr. "'Wem gehört die Welt': Kunst und Gesellschaft in der Weimarer Republik", *Neue Gesellschaft für Bildende Kunst*, 1977, pl.29) to paragraph 218 (the abortion law), it is always depicted as subjective suffering. Nevertheless, the two women had an amiable relationship: Kollwitz left Nagel her desk in the Academy studio when, as a "degenerate" artist, she could no longer work there (*Ich zeichne ...* 1977).

Nagel's most radical stylistic change began after her marriage to Fischer, when she increasingly concentrated on mediating her emotions in her works. Fish appear in her pictures as symbols of helplessness and fear, detached from the detailed representation of reality. Her works reflect her complex relationship with her husband.

Her use of symbols was further developed during her stay in

Rome, when the city itself was incorporated into her interior world. Thus a background of Roman architecture in a picture seems less a reference to the real location than an element of her imaginary world in which the innermost thoughts of the female figure, who dominates all her pictures, are brought to the surface. In the depiction of her marital relationship another layer of meaning is visible: the fundamental difference between man and woman. The compositions of many of her works are determined by this duality. Although the couples appear to be connected, they are distant from each other. The individuality of her work lies in her declared aim to capture this alienation so intensively that it is conveyed to the viewer:

> As different as a woman is from a man are the expressions of the soul. Accordingly, female art is something completely different from male art. It should be clearly visible in my works that they originate from a woman. Very few women achieve a real statement artistically – a statement that is so personal that the woman is visible in its creation. What matters to me is to draw the minute variations of female feelings, even those that have never yet been drawn by a woman [*ibid.*, p.34].

The depictions of the separateness of man and woman are interspersed with expressions of the intense desire to have children, which is also detectable in her drawings. Thus she explores the extremely ambivalent feelings of a woman who wants to fulfil more than one role: the difficulty of being woman, artist and mother and meeting the resulting demands. This conflict was intensified when Nagel became the family bread-winner. Afraid of being branded degenerate by the National Socialists, she suppressed her true artistic expressiveness in order not to lose commissions for illustrations, which were her livelihood. The situation was aggravated with the birth of her daughter Irene in 1938. The necessity to survive became part of her artistic existence, which she regretted but nevertheless accepted. Thus having been driven away from Berlin after the war, she earned her living with book illustrations and adult evening classes. She did not receive the longed-for professorship in Karlsruhe and did not want to accept one in East Berlin. There was also her alienation from abstract painting. Her depression was intensified when illness limited her ability to draw.

It was not only the threatening external situation that determined the sadness of her works. The symbols of the fish, the skull, the fool and the harlequin occur frequently in her pictures. The harlequin is always an ambivalent representation of menace and temptation. The fish, as the quintessence of fear, is "the expression of the material that never succeeds in 'reaching the moon'" (*idem*). She draws the fear of death, the mourning for unborn children, for the missing harmony in relationships and the lack of love. Her concern is to make visible the invisible world of feelings, sensations and associations. The feelings are visualised in her drawings. "I draw without sense or reason ... I draw as others are happy or sad" (*ibid.*, pp.34–5).

This is taken up in a drawing titled *Strange Dreams* (*ibid.*): a woman dressed as a nun stands in front of a brown background, arms stretched out, the left hand bandaged. She looks at the floor in front of her and not, as in most of Nagel's pictures, at the viewer. The figure of a huge fish with a skull, the empty eye sockets facing the viewer, breaks away from the black of her dress. For Nagel, intensity was everything.

Yet this resignation was balanced by her longing for beauty and harmony. She had had extensive training as a pianist, and immediately after World War II she created the *Chopin* cycle (Schäfer 1950) in which she visualised her musical sensations with symbolic female figures. The recurring loss of the imaginary world of beauty is visualised in her drawings. The immediacy of Nagel's inner world in composition and formal design led her to create her own pictorial language, which used symbols to give concrete expression to the undepictable portions of her imagination.

Most of Hanna Nagel's works are in the possession of her daughter, but there are examples in the Augustiner Museum and Museum für Neue Kunst, Freiburg; Germanisches Museum, Nuremberg; Stuttgarter Staatsgalerie, Stuttgart; Mannheimer Kunsthalle, Mannheim; and the Kunsthalle, Karlsruhe.

VERONIKA RÜTHER-WEISS

Nauen, Marie *see* Malachowski

Neel, Alice

American painter, 1900–1984

Born in Merion Square, Pennsylvania, 28 January 1900; grew up in Colwyn. Studied at Philadelphia School of Design for Women (now Moore College of Art), Philadelphia, 1921–5; attended Chester Springs summer school of the Pennsylvania Academy of the Fine Arts, 1924. Married Cuban artist Carlos Enriquez, and moved to Havana, Cuba, 1925; two daughters, born 1926 (d. 1927) and 1928; returned to New York, 1927; separated from husband, 1930; nervous breakdown, 1930–31. Moved to Greenwich Village, New York, with Kenneth Doolittle, 1932; he destroyed much of her work, 1934. Son by nightclub entertainer José Santiago born 1939. Met Marxist film-maker Sam Brody, 1940; separated soon after birth of son in 1941. Enrolled on Public Works of Art Project (PWAP), 1933; Works Progress Administration Federal Art Project (WPA/FAP) easel division, 1935. Recipient of Arts and Letters award, American Academy and Institute of Arts and Letters, 1969; honorary doctorate, Moore College of Art, 1971; National Women's Caucus for Art outstanding achievement award, 1979. Member, American Academy and Institute of Arts and Letters, 1976. Died 13 October 1984.

Selected Individual Exhibitions

Contemporary Arts Gallery, New York: 1938
Pinacotheca Gallery, New York: 1944
ACA Gallery, New York: 1950, 1954
New Playwrights Theater, New York: 1951
Graham Gallery, New York: 1963, 1966, 1968, 1970, 1973, 1976, 1977, 1978, 1980
Whitney Museum of American Art, New York: 1974 (retrospective)
Georgia Museum of Art, Athens: 1975 (retrospective)
Artemisia Gallery, Chicago: 1978
University of Bridgeport, CT, and Silvermine Guild of Artists: 1979 (retrospective)
Boston University Art Gallery: 1980
Artists Union, Moscow: 1981
Robert Miller Gallery, New York: 1982

Bibliography

Linda Nochlin, "Some women realist painters of the figure", *Arts Magazine*, xlviii, May 1974, pp.29–33; reprinted in *Women, Art and Power and Other Essays*, New York: Harper, 1988
Cindy Nemser, *Alice Neel: The Woman and Her Work*, Athens: Georgia Museum of Art, 1975
——, *Art Talk: Conversations with 12 Women Artists*, New York: Scribner, 1975
May Stevens, "The non-portraits of Alice Neel", *Women's Studies*, vi, 1978, pp.61–73
Barbaralee Diamonstein, *Inside New York's Art World*, New York: Rizzoli, 1979
Eleanor Munro, *Originals: American Women Artists*, New York: Simon and Schuster, 1979
Rita Mercedes, "Alice Neel", *Connoisseur*, ccviii, September 1981, pp.2–3 (interview)
Charlotte Streifer Rubinstein, *American Women Artists from Early Times to the Present*, Boston: Hall, 1982
Patricia Hills, *Alice Neel*, New York: Abrams, 1983
Alice Neel: Paintings, 1933–1982, exh. cat., Malone Art Gallery, Loyola Marymount University, Los Angeles, 1983
Ted Castle, "Alice Neel", *Artforum*, xxii, October 1983, pp.36–41 (interview)
Judith Higgins, "Alice Neel and the human comedy", *Art News*, lxxxiii, October 1984, pp.70–79
——, "Alice Neel, 1900–1984", *Art News*, lxxxiii, December 1984, p.14 (obituary)
Exterior/Interior: Alice Neel, exh. cat., Tufts University Art Gallery, Medford, MA, 1991
Marilyn Lincoln Board, "The legend of Alice Neel: Re-envisioning the Cinderella story", *Images of the Self as Female: The Achievement of Women Artists in Re-envisioning Feminine Identity*, ed. Kathryn N. Benzel and Lauren Pringle de la Vars, Lewiston, NY: Edwin Mellen Press, 1992
Pamela Allara, *Pictures of People: Alice Neel's American Portrait Gallery* (in preparation)

Alice Neel's career as a painter of portraits, still lifes, cityscapes and narrative scenes spanned over half a century. During that time she emerged from the fringes of the New York avant-garde of the 1920s and participated with other left-wing artists who worked on government projects during the Depression of the 1930s, while at the same time protesting against social conditions and the spread of international fascism. During World War II, struggling to get by in an apartment in Spanish Harlem, New York, and raising her two sons, she still continued to paint. She rarely exhibited during the 1940s and 1950s, but her career picked up as she was rediscovered, first by the Beat Generation of poets in the late 1950s, and later, in the 1970s, by the Women's Movement. When she died in 1984 she was riding the crest of interest in international neo-expressionism.

Neel was brought up in Colwyn, Pennsylvania, a small town that she found stifling. After holding down mundane clerical jobs as a teenager in Philadelphia, she determined to become an artist. Four years at the Philadelphia School of Design for Women (now Moore College of Art) solidified her

Neel: *Nude Self-Portrait*, 1980; oil on canvas; 139 × 100.6 cm.; National Portrait Gallery, Washington, DC

ambitions and provided her with the solid techniques to produce portraits and other pictures. At a summer school run by the Pennsylvania Academy of the Fine Arts she met and later married Carlos Enriquez, an upper-class Cuban painter. The young couple travelled to Havana in 1925 and spent two years there, where Neel exhibited with the Cuban avant-garde (Allara, book in preparation) and gave birth to her first daughter, Santillana. In 1927 Neel and Enriquez returned to New York to forge their painting careers. Santillana died that December from diphtheria, but another daughter, Isabella, was born the following November. In May 1930 Enriquez left with Isabella for Havana to raise funds from his family for a trip to Paris where they planned to live and paint. Instead, he left their daughter with Cuban relatives and went on alone to Paris. Virtually abandoned, Neel was torn by the contradictions in her life and suffered a nervous breakdown in August 1930. Briefly hospitalised, she was back home in Colwyn that winter and attempted suicide. Institutionalised in hospitals and a sanatorium for over six months, she gradually recovered her equilibrium and was released in September 1931.

In 1932 Neel moved to Greenwich Village with a sailor, Kenneth Doolittle, a jealous lover who later slashed many of her paintings. In contrast to Doolittle, another suitor, John Rothschild, lent her financial support and encouraged her art. She did a series of witty watercolours of herself and Rothschild in the hotel where they stayed on West 42nd Street, for example *Joie de Vivre* (1935; Yale University Art Gallery, New Haven).

During the early Depression years of the 1930s Neel, like many other out-of-work New York artists, signed up to work on the government art projects – first the Public Works of Art Project (PWAP) and later the Federal Art Project of the Works Progress Administration (WPA/FAP). During these years she painted unconventional portraits: *Joe Gould* (1933; artist's estate), in which the eccentric Gould is painted nude with five sets of genitals; *Kenneth Fearing* (1935; Museum of Modern Art, New York), with the poet surrounded by symbols of the Depression; and *Pat Whalen* (1935; Whitney Museum of American Art), in which the Communist labour organiser pounds his fist on a table upon which rests an issue of the *Daily Worker*, the newspaper of the Communist Party. Although unique in American painting, such portraits as *Max White* (1935; National Museum of American Art, Washington, DC) have a stylistic kinship to German portrait painters of the Neue Sachlichkeit (New Objectivity) of the 1920s.

In 1935 Neel met José Santiago, a charming Puerto Rican who played the guitar. She moved with him to Spanish Harlem in 1938 and a year later their son, Richard Neel, was born. Santiago moved out, and Neel became involved with Sam Brody, an intellectual and Communist documentary film-maker. Her son Hartley Stockton Neel was born in September 1941. Neel hung on to her government art job until 1943, when the WPA folded. During the 1940s and 1950s she painted her neighbours in Spanish Harlem and raised her two sons. Throughout this time she maintained her ties with left-wing artists and intellectuals. In 1949 Communist Party members were put on trial for violating the Smith Act, an act (later declared unconstitutional) that made it a crime merely to use the rhetoric of revolution against the US government. Neel attended the sessions of the trial and made drawings of the conservative Judge Medina and the State's star witness, Angela Calomaris. She also painted portraits of Communist Party organisers, such as *Mike Gold* and *Bill McKie*.

In December 1950 Neel had a major solo exhibition at the ACA Gallery in New York, and another in April 1951 at the New Playwrights Theatre. Mike Gold, editor of *Masses and Mainstream*, wrote a foreword for the catalogue of 1951 which said in part:

> Alice has for years lived with her children in a Harlem tenement. Her studio is the kitchen and her models the neighbors and the streets. She comes from an old Philadelphia family dating back to the Revolution. But her paintings reveal that here is her true family. In solitude and poverty, Alice has developed like a blade of grass between two city stones. She has become a superb craftsman, and the first clear and beautiful voice of Spanish Harlem. She reveals not only its desperate poverty, but its rich and generous soul ... ALICE NEEL is a pioneer of socialist realism in American painting.

The 24 paintings in the show included *Spanish Family*, *Investigation of Poverty of the Russell Sage Foundation* and *T.B. Harlem* (National Museum of Women in the Arts, Washington, DC). In 1954 Neel held a second exhibition at the ACA Gallery.

A turning point in her career occurred at the end of the 1950s. She began to see a psychologist who encouraged her to be more aggressive in advancing her own career and sending pictures to exhibitions. Encouraged, she contacted the poet Frank O'Hara and persuaded him to pose for her. In 1959 she was asked to play a part in the improvised avant-garde film made by Robert Frank and Al Leslie, *Pull My Daisy*, which also included the Beat Generation writers Allen Ginsberg, Gregory Corso and Jack Kerouac, and the artist Larry Rivers. At this time, her sons were off at college, and all her lovers had departed. Moreover, a woman friend, Muriel Bettancourt, offered to give her an annual stipend so that she would be free of financial worries. She then moved out of Spanish Harlem to 300 West 107th Street.

Neel's career blossomed during the 1960s and 1970s. In 1960 a reproduction of *Frank O'Hara, No.2* (1960; artist's estate) was published in *Art News*. The Graham Gallery, on Madison Avenue where other chic galleries were located, began to show her work in 1963. During the 1960s she painted portraits of art world personalities, such as the collectors *Stewart Mott*, *Arthur Bullowa* and *Walter Gutman*, the critics *Herbert Crehan* and *Henry Geldzahler*, the art dealer *Ellie Poindexter* and the artists *Robert Smithson*, *Milton Resnick*, *Pat Pasloff*, *Red Grooms*, *Mimi Gross* and *Geoffrey Hendricks*. She also turned her attention to her own sons – Richard and Hartley, their girlfriends and, later, their wives.

Neel's gallery of notables grew to include the Nobel Prize winner *Linus Pauling*, the composer *Aaron Copland*, the theatre producer *Joseph Papp*, the art historian *Linda Nochlin*, and further artists: *Duane Hanson*, *Andy Warhol*, *Marisol*, *Faith Ringgold* and *Benny Andrews*. But she also continued to paint neighbourhood people: the taxicab driver and black nationalist *Abdul Rahman*, the *Fuller Brush Man* and her cleaning woman, *Carmen*. Some of these portraits are sympathetically rendered (especially the portrayals of artists, art students and neighbourhood people), others are satirical (particularly the portraits of dealers, patrons, art critics and art historians), but all are painted with expressive candour. Like other artists, she needed, but often resented, the financial and psychological support of private patrons, dealers, art critics, curators, art historians and museum directors. Her ambivalence gave many of these portraits a power and tension, a love/hate nervousness.

One of her favourite ploys consisted in inviting art-world personalities into her studio and then asking them to disrobe so that she could paint them nude. Disarmed by her disingenuousness, they usually complied. Among her most notable nude portraits are those of the art critic *John Perreault*, painted as a frontal nude (1972; Whitney Museum of American Art, New York), and the critic *Cindy Nemser*, demurely covering her exposed breasts with her arms as she clasps the naked knee of her husband Chuck. Neel painted herself nude in 1980 (see illustration), with her flaccid body rolling out of a chair in which she sits, gripping brush with one hand and painting rag with another as she scrutinises the viewer and/or the mirror in which her image is reflected.

The sitters would make their own choices about clothes and body pose. But typically Neel would take over and rearrange them in order to heighten their expressive potential. Whether they timidly display their dimpled nude bodies or shroud themselves in protective layers of leather, wool and fur, Neel made certain that their hands, body pose and facial expression all contributed to the totality of the image – an image both specific and typical of their social class. From her brushes people emerged who seemed to reveal their inner lives through their self-posturing, their relationship to each other, either touching or separated in the double portraits, and their self-consciousness of the painter, staring back at Neel aggressively or pensively dreaming.

Her portraits of her own family members chart their emotional growth and the dynamics of family life. *Richard Neel* (1963) and *Hartley Neel* (1965) depict her two sons in the early years of manhood, direct and open to the viewer's observations. Some 15 years later – in *Hartley* of 1978 and *Richard in the Era of the Corporation* of 1979 – they had changed into professionals in mid-career, with Hartley going into radiology and Richard into corporate law. Neel commented that Richard's portrait of 1979 made her realise that the essence of the 1970s was the domination of American culture by business corporations. The bohemian mother had become ambivalent about the successes of her own sons.

Neel's paintings of Richard's wife, Nancy, are both specific portraits and expressive of women's lives in general. *Pregnant Woman* (1971; artist's estate) reveals Nancy swollen with the twins she will soon deliver. The masklike, expectant face stares impassively; her hands, irrelevant to her state of being, are hidden. Prominent are the rounded, brown-lined belly that contains the children, the buttocks that will release them to the world and the erect nipples ready to nurture them. Anticipation pervades the painting and points to its real subject – the process of human succession from generation to generation, Neel's own continuity with the future.

As early as the 1930s Neel had decided to paint the "human comedy", as Balzac had in his novels. By the 1970s she had a full cast of fascinating urban characters, to which she added in the early 1980s. She went on the lecture circuit with slides of her portraits. Looking like a bespectacled, kindly, white-haired grandmother, she amused her audience with outrageous remarks about her sitters' alleged sexual proclivities. In spite of Neel's own barely veiled misogyny, women art historians and critics enthusiastically organised shows of her work, invited her to campus art schools to speak and promoted her in the art magazines. She had become the paradigmatic "survivor" of the art world – a woman who had managed to achieve fame while raising children and enduring fickle men. And she did indeed achieve fame – finally, in her seventies. In 1976 Neel was elected to the prestigious American Academy and Institute of Arts and Letters; and in 1979 she was honoured by the National Women's Caucus for Art for outstanding achievement in art and received her award from none other than the President, Jimmy Carter, in the Oval Room of the White House. In 1984, only months before her death from cancer, she appeared on the Johnny Carson television show, regaling audiences across the nation with her stories, her portraits and her ambition to leave to posterity a gallery of American types from the late 20th century.

PATRICIA HILLS

Neilson Gray, Norah *see* Gray

Nelli, Plautilla
Italian painter, 1523–1588

Born Polissena Nelli, 1523, to Pietro di Luca Nelli, a Florentine patrician, and Maria di Biagio di Cristofano. Became a Dominican tertiary, as Suora Plautilla, at the convent of Santa Caterina di Siena, Florence, 1537; elected prioress by 1568. Died 1588.

Bibliography
Giorgio Vasari, *Le vite de' più eccellenti pittori, scultori ed architettori*, Florence, 1568; ed. Gaetano Milanesi, v, Florence: Sansoni, 1880, pp.79–80 (life of Properzia de' Rossi); as *Lives of the Most Eminent Painters, Sculptors and Architects*, 10 vols, London: Macmillan-Medici Society, 1912–15; reprinted New York: AMS, 1976

Ulrich Thieme and Felix Becker, *Allgemeines Lexikon der bildenden Künstler von der Antike bis zur Gegenwart*, xxv, Leipzig: Seeman, 1931

Giovanna Pierattini, "Suor Plautilla Nelli, pittrice domenicana", *Memorie Domenicane*, lv, 1938, pp.82–7, 168–71, 221–7, 292–7

Dizionario biografico italiano, vi, Rome: Istituto dell'Enciclopedia Italiana, 1964 (life of Camilla Bartolini-Rucellai)

Women Artists, 1550–1950, exh. cat., Los Angeles County Museum of Art, and elsewhere, 1976

Plautilla Nelli became a Dominican nun, as Suora Plautilla, at the convent of Santa Caterina di Siena, Florence, in 1537, and was elected prioress by 1568. This convent had been founded and built beside the male Dominican community of San Marco by Camilla Bartolini-Rucellai, called Suora Lucia, a passionate

Nelli: *Last Supper*, fresco; Santa Maria Novella, Florence

adherent of the Dominican friar Savonarola. The ethos of this community provided a nurturing environment for a woman with some artistic talent, because at its foundation Savonarola had recommended that the nuns should dedicate themselves to the arts of design, painting and modelling in order to be worthy of their keep and to encourage almsgiving. The fact that Plautilla's sister Costanza (Suor Petronella, another nun in the convent) composed a life of Savonarola suggests that the community maintained his ideals.

It has been speculated that Nelli was trained by male painters at San Marco, among whom was Fra Paolino da Pistoia, who had been an assistant to the Dominican painter Fra Bartolommeo (V. Marchese, *Memorie dei più insigni pittori scultori e architetti domenicani*, 2 vols, Bologna, 1878–9, ii, p.330). The methods of composition used by Fra Bartolommeo, which relied extensively on employing wax and plaster casts, and wax, wood and plaster figurines rather than live models would have suited Plautilla's training conditions. Since Vasari was able to list the contents of the convent's refectory, workroom and choir, it seems likely that Suor Plautilla's community, like many other Third Order convents dedicated to good works, was one that permitted some relaxation of the

rules of enclosure – in contrast to the stricter vows of the Second Orders – until 1575, when according to the *Memorie* of the convent and following the Tridentine decrees, complete enclosure was enforced. And while it is customary to single out Plautilla Nelli as a lone woman artist, her near-contemporary Serafino Razzi, writing in 1590, listed her pupils as Suore Prudenzia Cambi, Agata Traballesi and Maria Ruggeri, and Suora Veronica. He also described the sculpture of Suora Maurizia Niccolini and of his own sister, Suora Angelica Razzi.

Lay-women artists seem generally to have been restricted to portraiture, perhaps because in terms of early 16th-century Italian aesthetics portraits were considered as merely imitative of external reality, and therefore subordinate to the religious or historical narrative thought to require the highest creative and imaginative powers. In contrast, Plautilla's confinement in the convent meant that this type of secular representation was inappropriate. Instead, the Savonarolan injunction encouraged her to make large religious narrative paintings, while her own community exhibited her altarpieces in the public side of their church, guarded her reputation as a woman by the rules of enclosure, and dealt with her clients since all payments were made to the convent, rather than to the artist personally. In this unusually protective and encouraging environment, Plautilla Nelli produced a group of large altarpieces, as well as some small devotional pieces and illuminations.

According to Vasari she painted the following works: *Taking the Body of Christ for Burial with the Virgin Mary, the Three Marys, SS John the Evangelist and Peter, Nicodemus and Joseph of Arimathea*, formerly an altarpiece in the public area of the church of Santa Caterina di Siena, and now in San Marco, Florence (repr. *La chiesa e convento di San Marco a Firenze*, 2 vols, Florence, 1990, p.209, pl.38; the unusual inclusion of Peter in the scene suggests that this may have been a funerary altar for Nelli's father (Pietro) and mother (Maria), since the altar also honours Mary); the *Adoration of the Magi* (Regia Galleria, Parma; see Armando Quintavalle, *La Regia Galleria di Parma*, Rome, 1939, pp.318–19, no.158), also formerly an altarpiece in the public part of the church of Santa Caterina di Siena; and a *Last Supper* (see illustration), "with life-size figures", for the refectory of Santa Caterina di Siena, Florence, now on deposit in the cloister of Santa Maria Novella, Florence (recorded as untraced in Los Angeles 1976, p.21, note 44, where it is also reported that the painting had been photographed, Alinari 31081, in the Spanish Chapel of Santa Maria Novella).

Vasari lists further works, none of which has been identified: a *Madonna and Child with SS Thomas, Augustine, Mary Magdalene, Catherine of Siena, Agnes, Catherine of Alexandria and Lucy* in the nuns' choir of Santa Lucia, Pistoia; an *Annunciation* in the house of the wife of Signor Mondragone, Florence; an *Annunciation* in the house of Madonna Marietta de' Fedini, Florence; a *Madonna* in San Giovannino, Florence; predella scenes of the *Life of St Zenobius* in the Duomo (Santa Maria del Fiore), Florence; paintings for the workroom of the convent, and also for the director of the hospital of Lelmo di Balduccio; and a copy of Agnolo Bronzino's *Nativity of Christ*.

Padre Serafini Siepi (*Descrizione topologico-istorica della città di Perugia*, ii, Perugia, 1822, pp.516–17) records a *Pentecost* commissioned in 1554 by Guglielmo Pontano, a professor of law, as his funerary altarpiece, which is still in its original location in the left transept, beneath the organ, of San Domenico, Perugia – the patron's memorial is over the door to the left of the altar. This splendid large altarpiece includes two Dominican nuns, placed in the background in the centre, directly behind the Virgin Mary. Nelli further feminised the scene by the unusual inclusion of Mary Magdalene and another Mary on either side of the Virgin. Pentecost, the foundation of the Church's ministry to the world, was often shown as an all-male, apostolic event, but Plautilla put five women in the centre stage and placed the Apostles at the side, in two groups of six. She employed an austere architectural setting, reminiscent of Roman baths, with a barrel vault and a Tuscan order. The attribution of this painting to Nelli is confirmed in her contemporary obituary, written by Padre Modesto Biliotti.

[My thanks to Simon Tugwell of the Historical Institute, Rome, for his help in providing information for this article.]

CATHERINE KING

Nevelson, Louise
American sculptor, 1900–1988

Born Leah Berliawsky in Kiev, Russia, 23 September 1900, into a liberal Jewish family. Emigrated to USA with her family, settling in Rockland, Maine, 1905. Married ship owner Charles Nevelson and moved to New York, 1920; son born 1922; separated from husband 1931; later divorced. Studied painting and drawing under Theresa Bernstein and William Meyerowitz in New York, 1920; acting under Princess Norina Matchabelli at International Theater Arts Institute, 1926 (met Frederick Kiesler through Matchabelli). Studied under Kenneth Hayes Miller at the Art Students League, New York, 1929–30; under Hans Hofmann in Munich, 1931–2; also worked as a film extra in Vienna and Berlin, and spent time in Paris and Italy. Returned to New York, 1932; studied modern dance under Ellen Kearns, and worked briefly as assistant to Diego Rivera; studied sculpture with Chaim Gross, 1933. Included in *Young Sculptors* exhibition, arranged by the Secession Gallery at the Brooklyn Museum, New York, 1935. As part of the Works Progress Administration (WPA), taught art at the Educational Alliance School of Art, New York, 1937. Trips to Mexico, late 1940s. Studied printmaking at Stanley William Hayter's Atelier 17, New York, 1949; fellowships to Tamarind Workshop, Los Angeles, 1963 and 1967. Participated in National Council on Arts and Government, Washington, DC, 1965. Recipient of medal, MacDowell Colony, Peterborough, New Hampshire, 1969; Brandeis University Creative Arts award in sculpture, 1971; Skowhegan medal for sculpture, 1971; American Institute of Architects award, 1977; honorary doctorates from Western College for Women, Oxford, Ohio, 1966; Rutgers University, New Brunswick, 1972; Smith College, Northampton, Massachusetts, 1973; Hobart and William Smith Colleges, Geneva, New York, 1971; Columbia University, New York, 1977; Boston University, 1978. Chapter President, New York, 1957–9, and National President, 1962–4, Artists' Equity; first Vice-President, Federation of Modern Painters and Sculptors, 1962–4; Member, National Association of Women Artists and Sculptors' Guild. Died in New York, 17 April 1988.

Selected Individual Exhibitions
Karl Nierendorf Gallery, New York: 1941, 1942, 1944, 1946
Norlyst Gallery, New York: 1943
Grand Central Moderns Gallery, New York: 1956, 1958
Martha Jackson Gallery, New York: 1959, 1961, 1970
Galerie Daniel Cordier, Paris: 1960, 1961
Pace Gallery, New York: 1964, 1965, 1968, 1969, 1971, 1972, 1974, 1976, 1978, 1980, 1981, 1983, 1985, 1986, 1989
Kunsthalle, Bern: 1964
Galleria d'Arte Contemporanea, Turin: 1964
Whitney Museum of American Art, New York: 1967 (retrospective), 1970, 1980 (retrospective)
Rijksmuseum Kröller-Müller, Otterlo: 1969
Museum of Fine Arts, Houston: 1969 (retrospective)
University Art Museum, University of Texas at Austin: 1970
Walker Art Center, Minneapolis: 1973–5 (touring retrospective)
Musée d'Art Moderne de la Ville de Paris: 1974
Neue Nationalgalerie, Berlin: 1974
Storm King Art Center, Mountainville, NY: 1978
Phoenix Art Museum: 1980 (touring)

Galerie Claude Bernard, Paris: 1986
Solomon R. Guggenheim Museum, New York: 1986
List Visual Arts Center, Massachusetts Institute of Technology,
    Cambridge: 1986

Selected Writings

"Queen of the Black Black", *Art News*, lx, September 1961, pp.45ff
Dawns and Dusks, New York: Scribner, 1976 (with Diana
    MacKown)

Bibliography

"Louise Nevelson's debut", *Art Digest*, 1 October 1941, p.7
Hilton Kramer, "The sculpture of Louise Nevelson", *Arts Magazine*,
    June 1958, pp.26–9
Robert Rosenblum, "Louise Nevelson", *Artist's Yearbook*, Paris and
    New York, 1959, pp.136–9
Sixteen Americans, exh. cat., Museum of Modern Art, New York,
    1959
Dore Ashton, "USA: Louise Nevelson", *Cimaise*, April–June 1960,
    pp.26–36
The Art of Assemblage, exh. cat., Museum of Modern Art, New
    York, 1961
Cleve Gray, "Tamarind workshop", *Art in America*, li, October
    1963, p.98
John Canaday, "Art: Sculptures by Louise Nevelson", *New Yorker*,
    December 1964, pp.160–62
Louise Nevelson, exh. cat., Whitney Museum of American Art, New
    York, 1967
Robert Coates, "The art galleries: Sculpture at the Whitney", *New
    Yorker*, 7 January 1967, pp.84–6
Max Kozloff, "Art", *The Nation*, 10 April 1967, pp.477–88
Grégoire Müller, "A plastic presence", *Arts Magazine*, xliv,
    November 1969, pp.36–7
Germano Celant, *Louise Nevelson*, Milan: Fabbri, 1973
Nevelson Wood Sculpture, exh. cat., Walker Art Center, Minneapolis,
    1973
Arnold B. Glimcher, *Louise Nevelson*, 2nd edition, New York:
    Dutton, 1976
Louise Nevelson: Atmospheres and Environments, exh. cat., Whitney
    Museum of American Art, New York, 1980
Laurie Wilson, "Bride of the black moon: An iconographic study of
    the work of Louise Nevelson", *Arts Magazine*, liv, May 1980,
    pp.140–48
Robert Hughes, "Sculpture's queen bee", *Time*, 12 January 1981,
    pp.66–72
Jean Lipman, *Nevelson's World*, New York: Hudson Hills Press,
    1983
John Russell, "Louise Nevelson dies at 88: Enduring force in art
    world", *New York Times*, 18 April 1988
Amei Wallach, "I wanted the whole show: An appreciation of sculp-
    tor Louise Nevelson", *New York Newsday*, 19 April 1988
Louise Nevelson Remembered, exh. cat., Pace Gallery, New York,
    1989
Laurie Lisle, *Louise Nevelson: A Passionate Life*, New York: Summit,
    1990
Louise Nevelson, exh. cat., Palazzo delle Esposizioni, Rome, 1994

By the time Louise Nevelson became a recognised sculptor in
New York, she was 60 years old. She struggled to enter the
New York art world at a time when few women artists were
acknowledged, and none considered equal to men. Nevelson,
determined to make a name for herself, created an original
body of work and a career that made her one of the most
renowned artists of the 20th century.

A Russian Jew, Leah Berliawsky came to the USA at the age
of five, and was given a new name and forced to learn a new
language. Although she excelled in art classes early on, she had
a difficult childhood in Maine where anti-Semitism was prevalent. In 1920, to escape this provincial environment, she
married Charles Nevelson, a wealthy ship owner's son almost
15 years her senior. Her son Myron, known as Mike, was born
two years later. During the 1920s Nevelson lived as a wealthy
married woman in New York, taking art, voice, dance and
drama classes.

In Maine her father, who had owned a lumber business in
Russia, worked for a time as a junk peddler; later, when he
began to sell real estate, Louise would often accompany him,
discussing the architecture they encountered. Nevelson began
her art career as a painter, making forays into sculpture with a
variety of materials, preferring those such as clay that allowed
her to work quickly and spontaneously. But she was essentially
a collagist and continued to have the greatest affinity for wood.
Her large-scale walls reflect the teachings of Kenneth Hayes
Miller at the Art Students League, Hans Hofmann's school in
Munich, the murals of Diego Rivera at the New School, New
York, and the ideas of Frederick Kiesler. She was also influenced by the Pre-Columbian art and architecture that she saw
on trips to Central and South America and by Noguchi's
theatre designs and lunar landscapes.

Nevelson had her first solo show in New York at the
Nierendorf Gallery in 1941. Her individual works, such as
First Personage (1956; Brooklyn Museum, NY), a two-part
wood sculpture painted black, adopted the common Surrealist
vocabulary for sculpture that suggested figures without being
realistic. Nevelson's early personages owe much to the work of
Louise Bourgeois (q.v.). Other Surrealist-related titles refer to
kings, queens and moon gardens, themes found in the work of
Max Ernst and Alberto Giacometti, among others.

Nevelson developed her signature style in the years
1954–60 during the time when her house on 30th Street was
scheduled for demolition and after she moved downtown to
Spring Street in 1958. While scavenging the neighbourhood
that was being torn down to make way for a housing development (Kips Bay Plaza) she accumulated a mass of junk(ed)
materials and began filling boxes with her found objects. She
then stacked them against the walls of her studio in a manner
reminiscent of Kurt Schwitters.

Moon Garden + One, exhibited at the Grand Central
Moderns Gallery in 1958, was lit only by a few blue lights,
emphasising its uniform colour and theme. It was immediately
called an environment. *Sky Cathedral* (1958; Museum of
Modern Art, New York), originally part of this larger work, is
typical of Nevelson's best-known and most original sculpture.
The painted black structure with its various rectangular boxes
at first glance resembles a mysterious closet. Filled with objects
that appear both familiar and strange, it suggests a treasure
trove with a secret life of its own. Nevelson transformed both
her found objects (many pertaining to furniture) and the
modernist grid that contains them into a theatrical structure
that seems to emit a perpetually cryptic invitation to decipher
its enigmatic contents.

She went on to create room-size white environments, such
as *Dawn's Wedding Feast* (1959), first exhibited in the *Sixteen
Americans* exhibition at the Museum of Modern Art curated
by Dorothy Miller, and gold assembled sculptures such as the
Royal Tides series (see illustration), first exhibited at the
Martha Jackson Gallery in 1961. The white works create an

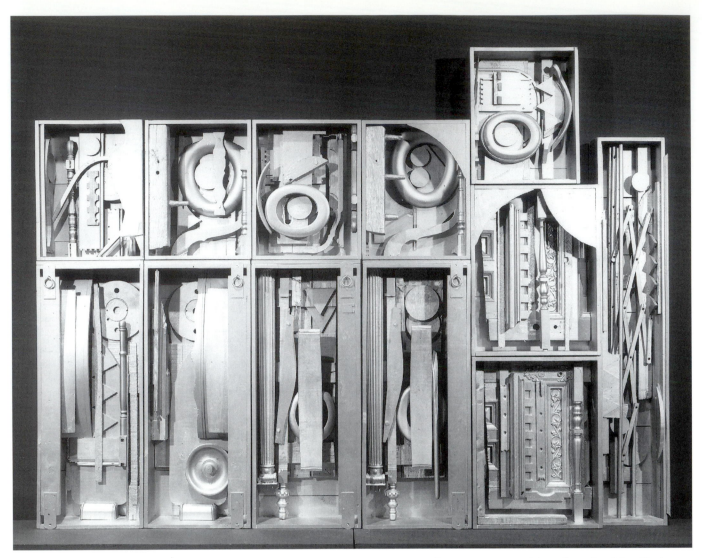

Nevelson: *Royal Tide II*, 1962–3; wood painted gold; 240 × 321.3 × 20.3 cm.; Whitney Museum of American Art, New York; gift of the artist

atmosphere of glaring stark purity, reflecting light rather than absorbing it as the black structures do. The gold pieces suggest ancient treasures, altars of some unspecified religion. Themes of royalty, death and marriage predominate, expressed most powerfully in the black wood environments that continue to evoke the strongest fascination, the deepest sense of mystery. Her friend, the artist Lucas Samaras, alluded to their covert sensual presence when he wrote at the time of her death: "The deep dark stark dangerous aroma of your work and passions continue to bedevil and caress me".

Nevelson was featured prominently in *The Art of Assemblage* at the Museum of Modern Art in 1961. This exhibition, according to its curator William Seitz, focused on objects that were "primarily assembled rather than painted, drawn, modeled, or carved" and composed entirely or in part of "preformed natural or manufactured materials, objects, or fragments not intended as art materials" (New York 1961). Nevelson was thus officially contextualised in a history of modern art that encompassed significant works by Picasso, the Italian Futurists, the Russian Constructivists, a number

of Dada and Surrealist artists including Duchamp, as well as by 19th-century American *trompe-l'oeil* painters such as John Haberle. Her place in the canon of modernism was assured.

In an interview of 1967 she expressed the hope that she might one day have enough money to build a museum for herself (as Noguchi and Warhol subsequently did). Although she never realised that ambition, she succeeded in a way that few women have. Nevelson was represented in the Whitney's American Art Annuals throughout the 1950s and 1960s, and in 1962 she was chosen to participate in the Venice Biennale. Her first major museum retrospective was held at the Whitney in 1967. Subsequent retrospectives were held at the Museum of Fine Arts in Houston (1969–70), the Walker Art Center in Minneapolis (1973–5) and again at the Whitney (1980).

Already in the mid-1950s when Nevelson began to exhibit her assemblages at Grand Central Moderns Gallery, she used unifying themes as well as colours, thereby pioneering the practice of gallery installations that would become the norm for Minimalist artists in the next decade and for others in the decades to come. *Mrs N's Palace* (1964–77) was a self-contained black wooden structure with a black mirror floor that expressed the sculptor's environmental sensibility. The viewer, always reflected back on herself, becomes a stand-in for the artist, for Nevelson implicitly was always at the centre of her work. But this walk-in palace, like Giacometti's tiny *Palace at 4 A.M.* (1932–3; Museum of Modern Art, New York) remains an enigma of mysterious reflections and shadows.

Nevelson also experimented with industrial materials. Her Plexiglas structures such as *Transparent Sculpture I* (1967–8; Albright-Knox Gallery, Buffalo) create a high-tech grid, suggestive of anonymous power stations. She was encouraged and sponsored by Arnold Glimcher, her dealer from 1961, to experiment with more permanent materials that would establish a place for her (and other Pace Gallery artists) in the growing field of public art. Nevelson worked with welders at the Lippincott foundry in Connecticut in a collage-like way, much as she did with her studio assistants using pieces of wood.

Her first public commission in Cor-ten steel was *Atmosphere and Environment X* (1969–70) for Princeton University. Among the first seven works purchased for the university's John B. Putnam, Jr, Memorial Collection, and the only work by a woman, it was sited adjacent to Firestone Library near the town's main street, ensuring public visibility within and outside the campus. The repetition of geometric shapes within a three-dimensional grid has a strong graphic presence but only hints at the depth and formal qualities of her wooden walls without their mystery.

The Princeton piece was the first of many public commissions for a variety of spaces. In 1977 she created a white wood installation at St Peter's Lutheran Church, Citicorp Center, Manhattan, and designed the vestments as well, making Nevelson one of the few 20th-century artists to design an entire chapel. Louise Nevelson Plaza in lower Manhattan, dedicated a year later in 1978 by Mayor Koch and David Rockefeller, chairman of the nearby Chase Manhattan Bank, reflected the degree of her success. When Nevelson viewed the site from above, she decided that she wanted to create sculptures to "appear to float like flags". *Shadows and Flags* includes seven welded black steel pieces, with vertical shafts as high as 21.3 metres.

Nevelson's striking appearance in her later years was as much a personal creation as her work, both concealing as much as they revealed. Her monumental sculpture, built of carefully selected and transformed scraps, suggested a secret language, a layered depth beneath an impenetrable surface. Painted black, sometimes reflected in mirrors, they suggested the darker side of life, the elusiveness of language and the power of scale and composition. Imposing order while suggesting chaos and mystery, Nevelson built her work as she had structured her life, with great drama, originality and determination. It was not by accident that her fame and reputation matched that of such renowned male 20th-century sculptors as Alexander Calder, Henry Moore and Noguchi. Late in life when an interviewer (Charles Kuralt) asked her how she maintained her pace and the quality of her work, Nevelson replied: "Look, dear, if you can walk you can dance".

HARRIET F. SENIE

Newbery, Jessie

British embroiderer, painter and designer, 1864–1948

Born Jessie Wylie Rowat in Paisley, Scotland, 28 May 1864; father a shawl manufacturer. Studied at Glasgow School of Art from 1884. Established class in embroidery at Glasgow School of Art, 1894; also held classes in mosaics, 1896–8, enamels, 1895–9, and book decoration, 1899; retired 1908. Married Francis ("Fra") H. Newbery, principal of Glasgow School of Art, 1889; two daughters, born 1890 and 1892. Organised *Ancient and Modern Embroidery and Needlecraft* exhibition at Glasgow School of Art, in aid of the Red Cross, 1916. Moved to Corfe Castle, Dorset, on husband's retirement in 1918. Recipient of bronze medal for stained-glass design, Department of Science and Art National Competition, 1889. Member, Glasgow Society of Lady Artists, early 1890s. Died 27 April 1948.

Principal Exhibitions

Paisley Art Institute: 1887–94
Glasgow Institute of the Fine Arts: 1892–1900
Arts and Crafts Exhibition Society, London: 1893, 1896
Scottish Society of Art Workers, Glasgow: 1899
Esposizione Internazionale d'Arte, Venice: 1899
International Exhibition, Glasgow: 1901
Esposizione Internazionale d'Arte Decorativa Moderna, Turin: 1902
Scottish Guild of Handicraft, Glasgow: from 1903
Musée du Louvre, Paris: 1914 (*Arts décoratifs de Grande Bretagne et d'Irelande*)

Bibliography

Gleeson White, "Some Glasgow designers and their work, III", *The Studio*, xii, 1897, pp.47–51
Margaret Swain, "Mrs Jessie R. Newbery (1864–1948)", *Embroidery*, no.24, 1973, pp.104–7
——, "Mrs Newbery's dress", *Costume*, xii, 1978, pp.64–73
Elizabeth F. Arthur, "Glasgow School of Art embroideries, 1894–1920", *Journal of the Decorative Arts Society, 1890–1940*, no.4, 1980, pp.18–25
Glasgow School of Art Embroidery, 1894–1920, exh. cat., Glasgow Museums and Art Gallery, 1980
A Centenary Exhibition to Celebrate the Founding of the Glasgow Society of Lady Artists in 1882, exh. cat., Collins Gallery, Glasgow, 1982
The Glasgow Style, 1890–1920, exh. cat., Glasgow Museums and Art Gallery, 1984
Jude Burkhauser, ed., *Glasgow Girls: Women in Art and Design, 1880–1920*, 2nd edition, Edinburgh: Canongate, and Cape May, NJ: Red Ochre, 1993
Deborah Cherry, *Painting Women: Victorian Women Artists*, London and New York: Routledge, 1993

According to a short article in the *Glasgow Evening News* (25 February 1913), Jessie Newbery's "strong personality" as well as her art work were "recognized far beyond Glasgow" where she was known as one of the city's most "interesting and picturesque figures in Art and social life". These claims were well founded. Newbery had begun her art education in Paisley, but by 1885 she had entered the Glasgow School of Art (GSA) where she was destined to achieve recognition not only as a student, but also as a teacher and as the founder of the embroidery department. While still a student, Newbery launched her career as an exhibiting artist when she had six pictures accepted by the Paisley Art Institute for their annual exhibition

Newbery: Embroidered corner of a cushion cover, detail of rose motif; *c*.1900; Victoria and Albert Museum, London

(1887). By 1889, when her student work was sent to South Kensington, Gleeson White, who would soon be editor of *The Studio*, praised Jessie Rowat's stained glass as "fresh, clever and pleasing" (*Scottish Art Review*, 1889, p.132). She continued to exhibit after her marriage to Francis Newbery, the recently appointed principal of the Glasgow School of Art, but during the 1890s her career shifted away from the production of landscapes, genre paintings and portraits, for example, *Sand Boat at Sannox* (1887; untraced), *Girl Knitting* (1893; private collection) and *White Cottage* (1899; untraced), to the decorative work for which she is better known. *Girl Knitting*, however, is well painted in the brightly coloured, loose brushwork style used by many Glaswegian painters of the era, and undoubtedly Jessie Newbery could have continued making pictures. Her work as a colourist remains to be researched and discussed.

By 1894 Newbery had established the embroidery department at the Glasgow School of Art, and she continued as a teacher of embroidery, enamelling and mosaic work until her retirement in 1908. During that time her work was widely exhibited in Glasgow and London as well as abroad. Half of one room at the Turin exhibition of modern decorative art (1902) was devoted to the embroidery of Newbery, Ann Macbeth and their students from the GSA; the floor was covered with an Axminster carpet designed by Newbery (*The Studio*, 1902, p.99). Her own designs reflected her concern for oppositions, for example: "of straight lines to curved; of horizontal to vertical; of purple to green, of green to blue" and for "beautifully shaped spaces", which were as important to her as the patterns themselves (Jessie Newbery as quoted in White 1897, p.48).

In addition, Newbery designed and made her own clothes, thereby turning herself into a work of art. Deborah Cherry argued for the spectatorship of this position as women partook of a "personal style" that was "organized and carried by the feminine body". According to Cherry, 19th-century women artists often "fashioned themselves as aesthetic objects, rearranging their appearance as spectacle and drawing on and feeding into high-cultural imagery" (Cherry 1993, p.89). Newbery's clothes were non-traditional and, if she arranged herself as "spectacle", she also encouraged freedom of movement and self-sufficiency: the making of one's own clothes and the ability to do this without ostentatious displays of wealth were priorities. She demanded a natural waist-line and simple materials. One might argue that Newbery challenged boundaries and, as Mary Blanchard suggested of other women in the "aesthetic movement", she may have helped to change "traditional concepts of the female as artistic object to the female as artistic subject" (Mary W. Blanchard, "Boundaries and the Victorian body", *American Historical Review*, February 1995, p.22). Newbery challenged class boundaries as well; she was "adamant that embroidery should be a form of art available to all social classes and that it could be worked as effectively on cheap as on expensive materials" (Glasgow 1980, p.4).

Thus, Newbery emphasised the "useful arts" and within the production of these arts, the rose motif became her "trademark" as, for example, on a cushion cover and on a collar and belt (*c*.1900; see illustration). Newbery's rose was frequently made with circles of pink linen and applied with a silk satin-stitch that indicated the pattern of the centre petals; this rose, perhaps the design that inspired the "Glasgow Rose", has been labelled as feminine and mystical. Recent interpretation has linked her work with genitalia symbolism (Burkhauser 1993, pp.102–5), but this kind of discussion underestimates Newbery's materialism, her commitment to socialism and her contribution to "community".

Newbery actively supported the Glasgow Society of Lady Artists, and sponsored many of her friends and students for membership of the Society, which provided an exhibiting venue as well as studio space for women artists. Called the "artistic suffragettes of twenty-five years standing" by a *Glasgow Herald* reporter in 1907, Newbery and her friends helped make suffrage banners and provided friendship and support to women competing in an art world that allowed them little room for advancement (for example, women could not join the segregated Glasgow Art Club at this time). Thus Jessie Newbery's commitment to art always exceeded the object: her legacy is one of producer, teacher and friend.

JANICE HELLAND

Ney, Elisabet
German sculptor, 1833–1907

Born Franciczka Bernardina Wilhelmina Elisabeth Ney (later spelled name Elisabet) in Münster, Westphalia, 26 January 1833; father a stonecarver. Studied at a private art school in Munich run by history painter Johann Baptiste Berdellé, 1852; first woman to attend sculpture class at Munich Academy, 1852–4 (diploma); studied in Berlin under sculptor Christian Daniel Rauch, 1854–5; subsequently admitted to Berlin Academy. Studio in Lagerhaus, Berlin. Visited London, 1863. Married physician Edmund Montgomery in Madeira, 1863; two sons, born 1871 and 1872, the elder dying in infancy. Lived in Madeira, then spent a year in Rome; visited the Austrian Tyrol, 1866; Munich, early 1868; Rome, Naples, Egypt and Greece, 1869. Left for USA with Montgomery, intending to establish a utopian colony, 1871. Initally settled in Thomasville, Georgia; moved to Liendo plantation, Waller County, Texas, 1873. Opened studio in Austin, Texas, 1892. Endeavoured to establish an "Academy of Liberal Arts" in Texas. Revisited Germany 1895, 1902 and 1903. Died in Austin, 29 June 1907.

Principal Exhibitions
Berlin Academy: 1856
Paris Salon: 1861
World's Columbian Exposition, Chicago: 1893
Louisiana Purchase Exposition, St Louis: 1904

Bibliography

Karl August Varnhagen von Ense, *Tagebücher*, Hamburg: Hoffmann und Campe, 1869

Sir John Simon, *Personal Recollections*, London: Sir John Simon, 1894

Herman Hüffer, *Lebenserinnerungen*, Berlin: Ernst Sieper, 1912

Nora Bickley, ed., *Letters from and to Joseph Joachim*, London: Macmillan, 1914; New York: Vienna House, 1972

Bride Taylor, *Elisabet Ney: Sculptor*, New York: Devin Adair, 1916

Jakob Baechtolds and Emil Ermatinger, eds, *Gottfried Kellers: Leben, Briefe und Tagebücher*, Stuttgart and Berlin: Cottassche Buchhandlung Nachfolger, 1925

Julia Wirth, *Julius Stockhausen: Der Sänger des deutschen Liedes*, Frankfurt am Main: Englert und Schlosser, 1927

Eugen Müller, *Elisabet Ney*, Leipzig: Koehler und Amelang, 1931

Jo van Ammers-Kuller, *Diana: Lebensgeschichte der Bildhauerin Elisabet Ney, 1833–1907*, Zürich: Sanssouci, 1960

J.W. Rutland, ed., *Sursum! Elisabet Ney in Texas*, Austin, TX: Hart Graphics and Office Centers, 1977

Sarah Lee Norman Wood, *The Heroic Image: Three Sculptures by Elisabet Ney*, MA thesis, University of Texas at Austin, 1986

Ursula Zehm, Karl Arndt and Jürgen Döring, "Plastische Porträts aus dem Besitz der Universität Göttingen", *Niederdeutsche Beiträge zur Kunstgeschichte*, xxv, 1986, pp.193–208

Renate Berger, *Und ich sehe nichts, nichts als die Malerei: Autobiographische Texte von Künstlerinnen des 18.–20. Jahrhunderts*, Frankfurt am Main: Fischer, 1987

Emily Fourmy Cutrer, *The Art of the Woman: The Life and Work of Elisabet Ney*, Lincoln: University of Nebraska Press, 1988 (includes extensive critical bibliography)

Brigitte Hüfler, "Zwölf Bildhauerinnen des 19. Jahrhunderts: Ein Beitrag zur Berliner Bildhauerschule", *Zeitschrift des Deutschen Vereins für Kunstwissenschaft*, xliii/2, 1989, pp.64–79 (special issue: *Malerei und Plastik vom späten 18. bis zum frühen 20. Jahrhundert*)

Charlotte Streifer Rubinstein, *American Women Sculptors*, Boston: Hall, 1990

Manuscript collections are in the Harry Ransom Humanities Research Center and Barker Texas History Center, University of Texas at Austin; Elisabet Ney Museum, Austin; Austin History Center of the Austin Public Library; and De Zavala Collection of the Texas State Archives.

"If you could only see Elisabet Ney, you would break your neck for her – she is incomparable!" a philosopher wrote to his publisher in 1860 (Berger 1987, p.113). One would not normally expect such enthusiasm for human beings – especially female ones – from Arthur Schopenhauer. Her bust of him (1859; Stadt- und Universitätsbibliothek, Frankfurt am Main, repr. Cutrer 1988, fig.6) came early on the young sculptor's path to fame. From the very beginning this descendant of the French Marshal Michel Ney, daughter of a stonecarver from Münster, broke new ground. After she had succeeded in studying at the Munich Academy, which was closed to women, she went to Berlin without her parents' knowledge and managed to get accepted as a pupil by one of the most significant sculptors in Germany, Christian Daniel Rauch. She thus entered the circle of Karl August Varnhagen von Ense, widower of Rahel Varnhagen.

Rauch belonged to a school that was partly Realist, partly Romantic. This movement was eventually to find itself in a broad Neo-classical current, via a renaissance of classical forms represented by Canova, Thorvaldsen and Houdon and influenced by Winckelmann. Commissions, given by scholars, politicians and rulers, were sustainable through personal recommendation and a far-reaching network of connections, from which Ney also profited. She was soon receiving important commissions, fulfilling her dream of meeting the great men of the world and sculpting busts of *Giuseppe Garibaldi* (1865; Fort Worth Art Museum, TX), *Otto von Bismarck* (1867; Elisabet Ney Museum, Austin, TX), distinguished scholars and artists such as *Jacob Grimm* (1858), *Friedrich Wöhler* (1868) and *Joseph Joachim* (1860; all Elisabet Ney Museum). These works paved the way for important connections (*King George V of Hannover*, 1859; Georg-August Universität, Göttingen), which eventually brought her to Munich, a cultural centre with unique opportunities for obtaining commissions. "This list of Ney's works reads like a *Who's Who* of European artistic, intellectual, and political life" (ibid., p.21). She had little time to reflect on the way in which she worked, however, and one danger soon became apparent: she had to find her way in isolation from her own generation, in constant contact with the older generation, who, like Schopenhauer, regarded her as a female curiosity and tolerated her as an "exception" because her abilities did not overstep the boundaries of conventional academicism. Like other women sculptors, she was hardly ever asked to create anything monumental; rather, busts and medallions that involved idealising the subject were what was demanded of her. The restrictions on women in a patriarchal society did not bother her at this time, however. Ney, too, could only conceive of the nationally or intellectually significant as being male, an attitude that she managed to suppress in the few works that she created for herself alone: examples are *Sursum or Genii of Mankind* (c.1863; private collection, *ibid.*, fig.17) and the over-life-size

Ney: *Lady Macbeth*, 1903; Elisabet Ney Museum, Austin, Texas

statue *Prometheus Bound* (1867; damaged; Elisabet Ney Museum), in which she had a critical look at Goethe and the role of the artist as the guardian of innovation, which is inseparable from rebellion.

At the age of 30 Ney married the Scottish physician and scholar Edmund Montgomery, on Madeira. As an opponent of marriage, she may not have acknowledged the marriage in public, but she did acknowledge him as "best friend", and this he remained until after her death 40 years later. It is thanks to him and a few of Ney's friends that her estate was preserved. In the 1860s she travelled to Britain, Egypt, Greece and Italy, but did not take advantage of the opportunity to make contact with the American women sculptors in Rome, the "white marmorean flock", Harriet Hosmer (q.v.) and others.

In 1868 Ney had to fight for the privilege of sculpting a life-size statue of *Ludwig II of Bavaria* (plaster; Elisabet Ney Museum), which required much patience, since one of the characteristics of great men seems to have been a lack of

knowledge as to the conditions for the creation of a work of sculpture. This difficulty was increased by the capriciousness and arrogance of the king. Postponements and painful interruptions led to a breach – with court life, with political involvement, and with Germany. The reasons for Ney's precipitant departure are still unknown. When she arrived in New York with Montgomery in 1871, she was 38 years old and determined to start afresh.

The couple eventually settled in Texas, but their plantation Liendo, in Hempstead, Texas, which was mainly supervised by Ney, soon turned out to be a loss-making enterprise. This motivated her in part to build a studio called Formosa in Austin, after a 20-year hiatus in her artistic work. She hoped to obtain commissions associated with the Texas Building at the World's Columbian Exposition in Chicago in 1893, or the fitting out of the Texas State Capitol in Austin and the National Statuary Hall in Washington, DC, with representations of the leaders of the state of Texas. There were several problems, however: she was living far from intellectual circles – Texas was hardly the centre of the artistic universe; she had very few educated and affluent patrons; and she was without the studio assistants that one could rely on in Europe. Only by sculpting representatives of the state of Texas would Ney be able to awaken an appreciation of her art. Ironically, despite the prejudice against female participation in the building of the state, it was through the Daughters of the Republic of Texas, a group of women who were culture bearers and organisers of the state's national representation, that Ney obtained the few commissions she did get, for statues of *Sam Houston* and *Stephen F. Austin* (both Texas State Capitol, University of Texas and Elisabet Ney Museum, Austin; United States Capitol, Washington, DC); even then, with all her debts, she had to pay out considerable sums of money in advance.

Ney's long isolation was broken only when she conceived of her studio in Austin, the capital of Texas, as a cultural centre, although she was at times mistrusted due to her unconventional appearance and energetic behaviour. After several trips to Europe to bring back her earlier works or translate them into marble (as, for example, the statue of *Ludwig II*), in order to legitimise herself as a sculptor with the American public, she began to realise that Texas was no longer a place of exile, but home. Nevertheless, her work did not receive the acclaim it deserved. This was partly because her public did not understand it and partly because, for a society that was seeking its own, new forms of representation, there was no appeal in an exponent of a Neo-classical style that had lost its adherents outside Europe.

There was one exception. Shortly before her death, Elisabet Ney dedicated herself to a theme that was outwardly literary but in fact drew together the sum of her ambitions, experiences and disappointments. In her life-size figure of *Lady Macbeth* (1903; Smithsonian Museum of American Art, Washington, DC; Elisabet Ney Museum and University of Texas; see illustration) she found not only a character but also a theme that could be understood immediately by women artists and friends in her area: a symbol of frontiers crossed, much longed for but only partially achieved. As a psychological portrait of her inner self the work not only reflects Ney's own conflicts but can also be seen as a renunciation of a woman's life permeated by conventions. She ended her career with a subject of her own choice, and probably for this reason her last work is the only one in which she overcame a Neo-classicism that had become formalised and fossilised. In this work, for all its simplicity and acerbity, she achieved for the first time a convincing fusion of symbolic content and psychological and romantic elements.

RENATE BERGER

Nicholson, Winifred

British painter, 1893–1981

Born Rosa Winifred Roberts in Oxford, 21 December 1893. Studied at Byam Shaw School of Art, London, c.1910–14 and 1918–19. Travelled to India, Ceylon and Burma, late 1919–early 1920. Married the artist Ben Nicholson, 1920; three children (two sons, one daughter), born 1927, 1929 and 1931; separated 1931; divorced 1938. Divided time between villa at Castagnola, near Lake Lugano, Italy, London and Cumberland, 1921–4, moving to Bankshead, Cumberland, in 1924. Also stayed in Isle of Wight, 1931–2, London, Paris and south of France, 1932–8; became a close friend of Piet Mondrian. Became a Christian Scientist, 1920s. Member of Seven and Five Society, 1926–35. Exhibited under the name Winifred Dacre, 1935–7. Spent war years in Cumberland. Made frequent trips to Hebrides and Scottish Isles, 1950s; visited Greece and North Africa, late 1960s. Died at Bankshead, 5 March 1981.

Selected Individual Exhibitions

Mayor Gallery, London: 1925
Beaux Arts Gallery, London: 1927
Lefevre Gallery, London: 1928 (with Ben Nicholson and Staite Murray), 1946 (with John Wells), 1949 (with Robert Macbryde and Robert Colquhoun), 1952
Leicester Galleries, London: 1930, 1936, 1954 (with Paule Vézelay)
Scottish Gallery, Edinburgh: 1953
Redfern Gallery, London: 1964
Crane Kalman Gallery, London: 1967, 1969, 1972, 1974, 1975, 1981
Abbot Hall Art Gallery, Kendal: 1969 (with Geoffrey Bennett), 1982 (retrospective)
LYC Museum and Art Gallery, Brampton, Cumberland: 1974, 1976, 1979, 1981
Third Eye Centre, Glasgow: 1979–80 (touring retrospective organised by Scottish Arts Council)
Tate Gallery, London: 1987 (retrospective)

Selected Writings

(as Winifred Dacre) "Unknown colour", *Circle: International Survey of Constructive Art*, ed. J.L. Martin and others, London: Faber, 1937
"Liberation of colour", *World Review*, December 1944, pp.29–40
"I like to have a picture in my room", *Christian Science Monitor*, 9 November 1954
"Mondrian in London: Reminiscences of Mondrian", *Studio International*, clxxii, 1966, pp.286–8
Flower Tales, Carlisle: LYC Museum Press, 1976
Unknown Colour: Paintings, Letters, Writings by Winifred Nicholson, ed. Andrew Nicholson, London: Faber, 1987 (includes contributions to *Christian Science Monitor*)

Bibliography

Mary Sorrell, "Winifred Nicholson", *The Studio*, cxlviii, 1954, pp.20–23
The Flowers of Winifred Nicholson, exh. cat., Crane Kalman Gallery, London, 1969
An Unknown Aspect of Winifred Nicholson: Abstract Paintings, 1920–1930, exh. cat., Crane Kalman Gallery, London, 1975
Winifred Nicholson: Paintings, 1900–1978, exh. cat., Third Eye Centre, Glasgow, and elsewhere, 1979
Donald Wilkinson, "A tribute to Winifred Nicholson", *Quarto: Abbot Hall Art Gallery Quarterly Bulletin*, xx, January 1983, pp.4–9
Jim Ede, *A Way of Life: Kettle's Yard*, Cambridge: Cambridge University Press, 1984
Kathleen Raine and John Lane, "Winifred Nicholson", *Temenos*, no.8, 1987, pp.164–80
Winifred Nicholson, exh. cat., Tate Gallery, London, 1987 (contains extensive bibliography and list of writings)
Robin Stemp, "Hidden colour: Winifred Nicholson", *Artist*, cii, October 1987, pp.31–3
Katy Deepwell, "Women in the Seven and Five Society", *Women Artists Slide Library Journal*, no.22, April–May 1988, pp.10–12
Teresa Grimes, Judith Collins and Oriana Baddeley, *Five Women Painters*, London: Lennard, 1989
A Painter's Place: Bankshead, Cumberland, 1924–31, exh. cat., Abbot Hall Art Gallery, Kendal, 1991
Charles Hall, "Art outside the Gallery", *Arts Review*, xliii, 6 September 1991, pp.450–51
Influence and Originality: Ivon Hitchens, Frances Hodgkins, Winifred Nicholson: Landscapes, c.1920–1950, exh. cat., Djanogly Art Gallery, University of Nottingham, and elsewhere, 1996

Winifred Nicholson is typically identified as the first wife of Ben Nicholson and as a painter of flower-pieces. This, however, is an inadequate assessment of an artist with a long and productive career spanning more than 60 years spent in Switzerland, London, Paris and Cumberland – of which her marriage consisted of eleven years – and who made elaborate and theorised explorations into colour. Her paintings, mostly oils and domestic in scale, between 50×50 and 75×75 centimetres, were not confined to flowers (traditionally regarded as a feminine and devalued genre) but embraced landscape *(The Island, St Ives*, 1928; Dartington Hall Trust; *Quai d'Auteuil*, 1932–3; National Museum of Wales, Cardiff), still life, domestic interiors and portraits of her children, family and friends (*Jake and Kate on the Isle of Wight*, 1931–2; City of Bristol Museum and Art Gallery; *Starry-Eyed*, 1927; artist's family), as well as an extensive period of experimentation with abstraction. She experimented in her portraits by introducing flattened, naive-style forms in often pastel-coloured compositions. In this respect she adopted the "primitivism" admired in the work of Alfred Wallis by her husband and other members of the Seven and Five Society.

For Nicholson, flowers were valued as exemplary of nature's most intense and unchanging colours. She developed a new kind of flower-piece in which the placing of flowers arranged in jugs or pots on a windowsill against a landscape succeeded in linking both interior and exterior views through carefully orchestrated colour compositions in a flattened, modernist painterly space (e.g. *Mughetti*, c.1922; private collection, repr. London 1987; *Cyclamen and Primula*, 1922; Kettle's Yard, Cambridge). It is this type of flower painting, developed from 1922, that formed the basis for her distinctive

Nicholson: *Quarante-huit, Quai d'Auteuil*, 1935; Tate Gallery, London

work in the period 1926–34 (*Primula*, 1928; Manchester City Art Galleries), and was central to the transformation of the Seven and Five Society from an *ad hoc* exhibiting group into one of the avant-garde groups in London. H.S. Ede's description of "beauty caught on the wing" (Ben Nicholson in letter to Mary Chamot, 23 May 1935, Tate Gallery Archive, London) characterises her work as much as that of her peers, Christopher Wood, Frances Hodgkins (q.v.), David Jones and Ben Nicholson, who all also experimented with this type of formal arrangement. Her work, however, has been more frequently discussed in terms of a personal and feminine sensibility, even earning her in the late 1920s the nickname "the female van Gogh", a form of compliment that ignores the strong affinities of her work with other male and female members of the Seven and Five, who were experimenting with the same motifs.

A move to Paris after her separation from Ben Nicholson provided Winifred with a new circle of friends in the Parisian avant-garde, including Piet Mondrian, César Domela, Jean Helion, Jean Arp and Sophie Taeuber-Arp (q.v.). She maintained her exhibiting links with London and a regular correspondence with Ben Nicholson after their divorce; he also came to Paris regularly to work and visit their children. Her explorations in abstraction in the mid- to late 1930s used still life as the point of departure and were by no means untypical of the Parisian avant-garde in this respect (e.g. *Abstract Sequence (Variation on Cyclamen and Primula)*, a series of gouache and pencil on paper variations; Redfern Gallery and Albemarle Gallery, London, and private collections). Nicholson's philosophy was expressed in her essay for *Circle* (1937), where she described modernist experimentation as releasing the possibility of a new dimension to colour beyond the known colour spectrum. The circle, presented as oval or ellipse, that is, as incomplete, remained central to the exploration of these ideas and colour arrangements (e.g. *Quarante-huit, Quai d'Auteuil*, 1935; see illustration). While colour, like music and mathematics, was for Nicholson a truly abstract art, she retained the idea that research into colour would reveal emotion rather than intellectual thought. Her interest in the possibilities of colour was at odds with the main development in Britain of theories of abstraction based on form and composition, where colour was subdued, eliminated to a "white light" or used only in primary combinations (as in the work of Ben Nicholson, Barbara Hepworth, q.v., and Henry Moore). She developed her theory of unknown and, as yet, unseen colour in later life through an analysis of the colour spectrum and an increasing interest in Christian Science, where colour harmonies/compositions were seen as a means of unlocking a mystical/religious truth behind appearances, providing contact with a spiritual life.

After 1945 Nicholson continued to experiment with colour arrangements using flower painting seen against a landscape, as in *Honeysuckle and Sweet Peas* (1945–6; Aberdeen Art Gallery), *Boothby Bank* (1946; Manchester City Art Galleries) and *Dawn on the Loire* (1949; British Council Collection). Her later works, particularly those painted in the Scottish islands, use the dispersion of light reflected from or refracted through objects – glasses, prisms, the colours emanating from the rainbow – rather than light falling on to or across objects (e.g. *Accord*, 1978, and *Sunroom*, 1980; both artist's family). In the late 1960s her friendship with Li Yuan Chia, a Chinese-born optical artist, resulted in his setting up a gallery near her home in Cumberland and a renewed interest in her rarely exhibited abstract work of the 1930s.

KATY DEEPWELL

Nilsson, Vera
Swedish painter, 1888–1979

Born in Jönköping, 1 June 1888. Trained as a drawing teacher at the Technical School, Stockholm, 1906–9; studied under Carl Wilhelmson at Valand Art School, Göteborg, 1910; under Henri Le Fauconnier at La Palette, Paris, 1911–12. In Paris, Brittany and Öland, Sweden, 1913–14; in Stockholm and Öland, 1914–16. Spent nine months in Spain, 1919–20. Worked in Paris, 1921–2 and winters 1922–5; daughter born there, 1922. Spent 1927–8 in Italy as recipient of Ester Lindahl travel award. Settled in Stockholm, 1928; usually spent summers in Öland. Trips to the USSR, 1933; Estonia, 1937. Returned to Paris, 1948–9, 1962, 1971 and 1976; made extended visit to Senegal, 1949–50; trips to New York and Martinique, 1966. Rarely exhibited or sold work. Recipient of Prins Eugen medal, 1948. Only woman member of the group Färg och Form (Colour and Form), constituted in 1932. Only woman member, Royal Academy of Fine Arts, Stockholm, 1954. Died in Stockholm, 13 May 1979.

Principal Exhibitions

Individual
Ovenlyssalen, Copenhagen: 1917 (with Mollie Faustman)
Konstnärhuset, Stockholm: 1933, 1948
Konsthallen, Göteborg: 1934
Göteborgs Konstmuseum, Göteborg: 1943 (with Mollie Faustman and Sigrid Hjertén)
Jönköpings Läns Museum, Jönköping: 1949
Royal Academy of Fine Arts, Stockholm: 1968, 1975 (touring retrospective)

Group
Liljevalchs Konsthall, Stockholm: 1918 (*Yngre svenska konstnärer* [Younger Swedish artists])
Flangen (Phalanx) group, Stockholm: 1922, 1925

Bibliography

Ingrid Rydbeck, "Vera Nilsson", *Konstrevy*, 1933
Erik Blomberg, "Nordisk konst i Mässhallen" [Nordic art in Mässhallen]", *Konstrevy*, 1939, pp.61–8 (special issue)
J.P. Hodin, "Vera Nilsson", *Paletten*, i, 1947
Karl Axel Arvidsson, "Mycket händer i Eskilstuna" [A lot happens in Eskilstuna], *Konstrevy*, 1955, pp.86–7
Elisabeth Lidén, *Expressionismen och Sverige* [Expressionism and Sweden], Lund, 1974
Catharina Nilsson, "Vera Nilsson och hennes fredssträvanden" [Vera Nilsson and her peace efforts], *Fred och Frihet*, iv, 1979
Beate Sydhoff, "De slutna rummen: Vera Nilsson's 'Händer' i Djurgårdsskolan, Eskilstuna" [The closed rooms: Vera Nilsson's "Hands" in school of Djurgården, Eskilstuna], *Konstverkens liv i offentlig miljö* [The art work in the public environment], Uddevalla: Sveriges Allmänna Konstförening, 1982, pp.83–7
Catharina Nilsson, *Vera Nilssons blad ur skissböcker, 1911–1979* [Sheets from Vera Nilsson's sketchbooks, 1911–1979], Stockholm, 1983
Ingrid Ingelman, "Women artists in Sweden: A two-front struggle", *Woman's Art Journal*, v/1, 1984, pp.1–7
Marit Werenskiold, *The Concept of Expressionism*, Oslo, 1984
Göran M. Silfverstolpe, *Vera Nilsson*, Uddevalla: Sveriges Allmänna Konstförening, 1986
Shulamith Behr, *Women Expressionists*, Oxford: Phaidon, and New York: Rizzoli, 1988
Marianne Nanne-Bråhammar, "Vera Nilsson: En bild måste vara sägande" [Vera Nilsson: A picture must be expressive], *Konstperspektiv*, no.4, 1990, pp.22–5
"Den otroliga verkligheten": 13 kvinnliga pionjärer ["The incredible reality": 13 women pioneers], exh. cat., Prins Eugens Waldermarsudde, Stockholm, and elsewhere, 1994

Only a few weeks before Vera Nilsson's death, at the age of 91, her last artistic work, *Fredskortet* (Card of Peace), was printed. On the card the text "KVINNOR" (Women) is printed in red, and "Stoppa upprustningarna" (Stop the re-armament) in black against a white background. Three large-scale women are placed frontally, their arms raised to complete a circle made up of similar female figures on a smaller scale. Moreover, the card was printed in Swedish, English and French. Nilsson personally travelled around in a taxi to distribute a number of the edition to museums. The rest were sold on behalf of the International Women's Association for Peace and Freedom.

It was symptomatic that Nilsson's last artistic involvement was concerned with peace, a subject that had preoccupied her deeply throughout her life. Yet she executed very few works with political and social subjects. It was not the choice of subject that determined the degree of involvement in Nilsson's art.

Nilsson was one of the many female artists who, often after pressure at home, trained as a teacher of drawing "for safety's sake". This training, together with a year in Göteborg, was her only formal artistic education in Sweden. It was therefore an even greater honour for Nilsson when she was chosen as the first woman member of the Royal Academy of Fine Arts. For her, this meant that she had the opportunity of influencing and fighting for the acceptance of more women at the Academy, as well as in other male-dominated artists' associations.

In 1911 Nilsson went to France, where she remained until the outbreak of World War I in 1914. She spent the war years in Copenhagen, where she made her exhibition debut in 1917. The French stay was the first of numerous longer foreign trips to continental Europe and Africa. During her travels she met many local people. They made a great impression on her and can be recognised as models for her art. In Paris she also met Nordic artists, many of whom were pupils at the Académie Matisse. Matisse himself did not teach at the school at the time Nilsson arrived in the city, but she nevertheless visited the school and never forgot the experience. She remembered a "'violet-pink studio', bright green doors and an Abyssinian model. God! How beautiful it was!" She chose instead to study

Nilsson: *Street in Malaga I*, 1920–21; oil on canvas; 106.5 × 71.5 cm.; Norrköpings Konstmuseum, Sweden

with Henri Le Fauconnier at La Palette. The fact that she was trained by a Cubist and not by Matisse was very significant for her art. Only drawings survive from these first years (she had left paintings behind at the outbreak of war, and when she returned to Paris after the war these had been lost). The drawings are executed in a Cubist spirit, both in the representation of space and in the treatment of form. But in her compositions and choice of subject – figures, street-scenes, landscapes – these drawings show that she had found her artistic identity.

One of Nilsson's earliest surviving paintings is *Street in Malaga* (1920–21; see illustration), which she executed in Paris on her return from a trip to Spain. The subject matter refers to something that she had herself witnessed, her usual practice. She described the work as follows: "The painting represents three homeless girls. The two faceless, elegant men who pass by represent people who passed by without bothering themselves about the children" (orally to the author). Nilsson depicted the girls in strong contrast to the men. The girls stand out like individuals, the men like anonymous figures who in shape and bearing lean more towards the city than towards the girls. In contrast, both compositionally and in their shape, the girls correspond more closely to the clouds of the background than to the men. In composition, as much as in the formal language and the handling of colour, Nilsson is here connected in a general way with Cubism. The classical spatial composition is abolished and, as in Cubism, the space shown is ambiguous and the depth of the painting is questioned. The strongly turned bodies of the dancing girls create a rhythm on the painting's surface. The colour scale throughout is warm, dominated by red and pink tones as well as black; elements of yellow and white are directly correlated to sources of light outside the painting.

Nilsson's artistry found its shape in the field of tension between Cubism and Expressionism. Works of both these movements as well as of El Greco, one of the old masters who enjoyed a revival during the 1910s, were on view at the *Sonderbund* exhibition in Cologne in 1912. Nilsson, a great admirer of El Greco's art, made sure that she went to this exhibition and, when visiting Spain a few years later, to Toledo. Even if *Street in Malaga* can be said to be a child of its time, it is significant for Nilsson's artistry. Its content and formal richness show an artistic maturity, whose fruits she was to reap at her first solo exhibition in Sweden in 1933; she was then 45 years old.

The 1920s were to be a rich decade for Nilsson. In 1922 her daughter Catharina was born in Paris, and she became a cherished and frequent subject. Nilsson's paintings of children have nothing sentimental about them. The portraits of her daughter say a lot not only about her, but also about children in general, for instance about moments of concentration or new achievements. Several of these paintings are in public collections, for example *The First Step* (1923; Prins Eugens Waldemarsudde, Stockholm), *Playmates* (1926; Göteborgs Konstmuseum, Göteborg) and *Soap Bubbles* (1927; Moderna Museet, Stockholm). Catharina's importance as a model diminished with the years, and thus also Nilsson's paintings of children.

At the beginning of the 1930s Nilsson worked intensively with colours. The year 1932 was a breakthrough one for her with colour: "I was aware myself of not having succeeded in making the chords of colour shine sufficiently" (orally to

author). So she painted, for example, some versions of her daughter in front of a window, as in *Blue and Red* (1932–3; Malmö Konstmuseum). In order to achieve this, she chose as her base colours red, blue and yellow as well as green. Black and white were not abolished from her palette, but had less priority during these years.

For an intellectual and radical person such as Nilsson, the 1930s was a decade of much anxiety and disappointment. Hitler's take-over of power in 1933, Italy's annexation of Abyssinia in 1936 and the Spanish Civil War led to a few different and strong paintings by her. The most interesting is *Money Against Life* (1938; Skövde Kulturhus), in which she attacks the capitalists, military and clergy who brought Franco and the Falangists to power. As an old friend of the "Spanish people", for whom she felt a great sympathy, she considered travelling to Spain as a free-lance correspondent, but this did not happen. She was moved by Picasso's *Guernica* when it was shown in Stockholm in 1938, but she missed the colour, stating in this context: "For me colour is expression". Although in a purely artistic way *Money Against Life* is not linked with *Guernica*, both are strongly expressive protest paintings directed against Franco's regime.

Nilsson's fear of an atomic war grew ever stronger over the years. During the latter part of the 1960s she executed a series of paintings, *In Error's Time* (one in Riksdagshuset, Stockholm; another in Eskilstuna Konstmuseum), which show our planet after an atomic war: the earth has cracked and is uninhabitable. Painted in rich colours, mainly in yellow, green, lilac, red, blue and various black tones, Nilsson here stretched the limits of the figurative towards a more abstract formal language.

Vera Nilsson's involvement with people and their condition was deep. She shared this with the central European Expressionists of the 1910s. Like them she wished to make paintings that were "more dynamic, more expressive" (told to author), a driving force that led her along new artistic paths throughout her life. (Examples of her work may be found in the Moderna Museet, Stockholm; Göteborgs Konstmuseum, Göteborg; Malmö Konstmuseum; and the Statens Museum for Kunst, Copenhagen.)

ELISABETH LIDÉN

Noack, Astrid (Marie Sophie)

Danish sculptor, 1888–1954

Born in Ribe, 30 January 1888. Moved to Copenhagen, 1902; apprenticed to a woodcarver in Vallekilde while studying under Ivar Bentsen at evening classes at the Technical School, 1906–10. Worked as a woodcarver under Joakim Skovgaard at Viborg Cathedral from 1912; subsequently as a restorer of church furniture at the Nationalmuseum, Copenhagen. Lived in Paris, 1920–32; studied under Danish sculptor Adam Fischer at Maison Watteau, the school for Nordic artists, 1926–7; subsequently taught there; also studied intermittently under Charles Despiau and Paul Cornet, c.1928–32. Returned to Copenhagen, 1932; made several further trips to Paris; visited Stockholm, 1947 and

1948. Member of Grønningen artists' group, 1935. Recipient of Eckersberg medal, 1940; Thorvaldsen medal, Copenhagen, 1954. Died 26 December 1954.

Principal Exhibitions

Individual
Kunstforeningen, Copenhagen: 1944
Svensk-Franska Konstgalleri, Stockholm: 1947

Group
Kunstnernes Efteraarsudstilling, "KE" (Artists' Autumn Salon), Copenhagen: 1915
Salon d'Automne, Paris: 1925
French section, Exposition Internationale des Arts Décoratifs et Industriels Modernes, Paris: 1925
Salon des Tuileries, Paris: 1930–31
Grønningen, Copenhagen: from 1933 (annuals)
Sommerudstilling (Summer Salon), Kunstmuseum, Copenhagen: 1941
Århus: 1941 (*Nordisk kunst* [Nordic art])
Oslo: 1946 (*Den officielle danske kunstudstilling* [Official Danish art exhibition])
Stockholm: 1948 (*Grønningen i Stockholm* [Grønningen in Stockholm])

Bibliography

Karl Madsen, "Anna Ancher", *Tilskueren*, i, 1936, pp.26–40
Haavard Rostrup, "Den danske bildhuggerinde Astrid Noack" [The Danish sculptress Astrid Noack], *Konstrevy*, no.2, 1939, pp.55–9
——, "Astrid Noacks monument for Anna Ancher", *Tilskueren*, ii, 1939, pp.187–97
Paul la Cour, "Astrid Noack", *Vor Tids Kunst*, no.37, 1943
——, *Et udvalg af billeder med indledende tekst af Paul la Cour* [A selection of pictures with a preface by Paul la Cour], Copenhagen: Naver, 1943
Erik Thommesen, "Astrid Noack i tidens kunst" [Astrid Noack in the context of the art of her time], *Signum: Tidsskrift for Moderne Kunst*, i/1, 1961, pp.41–7
Astrid Noack, Copenhagen: Astrid Noacks legatfond, 1964
Anna Ancher, Astrid Noack, exh. cat., Sophienholm, Lyngby, 1975
Hanne Pedersen, "Astrid Noack: Monument over Anna Ancher", *Kunst og Museum*, xx, 1987, pp.23–48

Astrid Noack was born in Ribe, an old Viking town near the western coast of the Jutland peninsula in Denmark. Towering above the small town that industrialisation had by-passed, and commanding the flat surrounding marshland, stands a medieval cathedral. Here Noack must have made herself familiar with some of the most exquisite Romanesque stone carvings in Scandinavia, and medieval sculpture came to be a lasting inspiration on her art. But when Noack left her home town at the young age of 14 in 1902, she was not an aspiring sculptor. She found her first employment in Copenhagen as a painter at the faience manufactory Aluminia, which produced mostly inexpensive, but often very well-designed tableware. In 1906 she began her apprenticeship as a woodcarver and in 1910 achieved her journeyman's probation. Noack started work at a furniture factory in Copenhagen but shortly afterwards made her first contacts with artists when she came to work as a woodcarver for Joakim Skovgaard, a Danish painter mainly active in the decoration of medieval cathedrals in Denmark and the once-Danish Scania in southern Sweden. At Viborg Cathedral in Jutland Skovgaard headed a workshop of woodcarvers and painters, among whom was another late-comer to the arts, Niels Larsen Stevns, whose tombstone

Noack: *Anna Ancher* monument; Collection of Skagens Museum, Denmark

Noack would make during the German occupation of Denmark. Her first artistic work was the carving of elaborate frames for Skovgaard's paintings of Pre-Raphaelite character, and from 1912 she was employed on the wooden ceiling of Viborg Cathedral. Her feeling for medieval sculpture was further developed when she started restoration work on altarpieces and pulpits for the Nationalmuseet of Denmark, but she was more than 30 years old when she finally decided to become an artist in her own right.

In 1920 she went to Paris to realise this ambition, in spite of having hardly any means to sustain herself abroad. She had to start factory work again, and also found employment in workshops producing "antique" furniture. In a memoir of Noack (Lyngby 1975) Gottfred Eickhoff, a fellow Danish sculptor, tells how she used acid as well as a shot-gun to simulate the work of woodworms. In 1926–7 she was taught by another Danish sculptor, Adam Fischer, a friend of Diego Rivera, at the Nordic artists' school, the Maison Watteau. The director of the school, the Swedish-born Lena Börjesson, let the impoverished Noack work as a model, a supervisor and finally as a teacher, at the same time as continuing her own studies with such French artists as Charles Despiau and Paul Cornet. Noack's courageous and upright character, as well as her willingness to share the little she had with others, in a true communistic spirit, made her a highly esteemed member of the artists' community. The French sculptor Jean Osouf and the Danish constructivist painter Georg Jacobsen became her friends, while Aristide Maillol was an important influence on her art.

Noack's first mature work is *Sitting Child*, modelled in 1922, which survives in a version of 1923, carved in mahogany (Aarhus Kunstmuseum, Århus). The small child (her short-lived, illegitimate son) still has a baby's plumpness and proportionately large head. As in most of Noack's sculpture, the work is characterised by a certain Archaic simplicity, and the frontality of the figure is stressed. She found her inspiration in Egyptian and early Greek art, as well as in the stone sculpture of the early and late Middle Ages. Noack worked exclusively with the human figure in full or bust length, preferably of women and children until quite late in her career (e.g. *Sleeping Baby*, 1936–7; plaster; Ribe Kunstmuseum). The period between her return from Paris in 1932 and World War II is distinguished by the creation of variations on the nude, female form in erect, straight-backed statues of a certain tender awkwardness (e.g. *Standing Woman*, teak wood; Göteborgs Konstmuseum, Göteborg). In spirit several of them are related to the Archaic *kore*, while others have the broad-shouldered stiffness of Egyptian wooden tomb figurines.

Noack's most important statue is the monument to the painter *Anna Ancher* (see illustration), placed in front of the house of Ancher and her painter-husband Michael in Skagen, also a museum dedicated to the painters of the Skagen artists' colony. Noack had not met Ancher (q.v.) in person, but recreated an image of the artist absorbed in transforming her impression of nature in a "yearning towards work", as Noack put it. Her aspiration was to convey the image of "what lies in the mind demanding expression and a form"; she saw Ancher's art as characterised by "intimacy and gentle experience". Hence Noack looked for inspiration in the fishermen's wives of Skagen, "upright and strong" (quoted in Lyngby 1975). In the full-length statue, which was cast in bronze and inaugurated

in 1939 (later replicas in Statens Museum for Kunst, Copenhagen; Louisiana Museum of Modern Art, Humlebæk; Openluchtmuseum voor Beeldhouwkunst Middelheim, Antwerp; and elsewhere), she portrayed Anna Ancher holding a sketchbook in her left hand and a pencil in her right, in a quiet implication of a walk. From the same year dates another full-length portrait of a female figure, the seated *Helen la Cour* (Statens Museum for Kunst).

During World War II Noack's sculpture came close to medieval religious art in such works as the relief *Shepherd and Sheep* (1941; plaster; Noack Foundation, Denmark) and a *Crucifixion* (plaster, 1943; old oak, 1943–6; Refugium, Løgumkloster), showing an entirely nude, male figure, which was conceived as a memorial to the war dead. Her last important work was another nude male figure, *Youth Planting a Tree* (1948–52; several versions, one in Louisiana Museum of Modern Art, Humlebæk). This sculpture of a young man, a reclining sheep at his left side, epitomises Noack's art: quiet earnestness and the awe of growing life.

CHARLOTTE CHRISTENSEN

Normand, Mrs Ernest *see* Rae

Nørregaard, Asta
Norwegian painter, 1853–1933

Born in Christiania (Oslo), 13 August 1853. Attended Knud Bergslien's painting academy, Christiania, c.1872–5; private student of Norwegian painter Eilif Peterssen in Munich, 1875–8; again studied in Christiania, and received Schäffer scholarship, 1877–9. Lived in Paris, 1879–85; studied under Léon Bonnat, Jean-Léon Gérôme and, for a short period, Jules Bastien-Lepage at Madame Trélat de Lavigne's Atelier pour Dames, 1879–81; also attended Académie Colarossi. Returned to Christiania, 1885, but made extended visits to France and Italy during the late 1880s, and lived in Rome, 1889–90. Ran small painting academy in Christiania, 1890–92. Awarded King's gold medal of merit, 1920. Died in Oslo, 23 March 1933.

Principal Exhibitions

Individual
Blomqvist, Christiania/Oslo: 1893, 1903, 1913, 1925

Group
Drammens Kunstforening (Art Association), Christiania: from 1879
Christiania Kunstforening (Art Association): from 1881 (outvoted 1883 and 1889)
Paris Salon: 1881–2
Høstutstillingen (Autumn Salon), Christiania: 1883–92, 1895–8
Christiania: 1883 (*Kunst- og industriutstilling* [National art exhibition]), 1914 (*Jubileumsutstilling, 1814–1914* [Jubilee exhibition])
Charlottenborg, Copenhagen: 1883 (*Den Nordiske udstilling* [Nordic exhibition]), 1884 (salon), 1888 (*Den Nordiske udstilling* [Nordic exhibition])
Exposition Universelle d'Anvers, Antwerp: 1885

Nørregaard: *In the Studio*, 1883; oil on canvas; 64.5 × 48 cm.; private collection, Oslo

Valand, Göteborg: 1886 (*Nordiska konstutställningen* [Nordic art exhibition])
Exposition Universelle, Paris: 1889
Minneapolis, USA: 1889 (*Norwegian Exhibition*)

Selected Writings
Portræter: I oliefarve, pastel og kul [Portraits: In oil, pastel and charcoal], 4 vols, Christiania, 1911

Bibliography
Jens Thiis, *Norske malere og billedhuggere* [Norwegian painters and sculptors], Bergen, i, 1904, p.132; ii, 1907, p.309
Anne Wichstrøm, "Asta Nørregaard og den unge Munch" [Asta Nørregaard and the young Munch], *Kunst og Kultur*, no.2, 1982, pp.66–77
——, *Kvinner ved staffeliet: Kvinnelige malere i Norge før 1900* [Women at the easel: Women painters in Norway before 1900], Oslo: Universitetsforlaget, 1983 (revised edition in preparation)
De drogo till Paris: Nordiska konstnärinnor på 1800-talet [They went to Paris: Nordic women artists in the 1880s], exh. cat., Liljevalchs Konsthall, Stockholm, 1988
Alessandra Comini, "Nordic luminism and the Scandinavian recasting of Impressionism", *World Impressionism: The International Movement, 1860–1920*, ed. Norma Broude, New York: Abrams, 1992, pp.274–313
Knut Berg, ed., *Norges malerkunst* [Norway's history of painting], i, Oslo, 1993
Anne Wichstrøm, "At century's end: Harriet Backer, Kitty Kielland, Asta Nørregaard", *At Century's End: Norwegian Artists and the Figurative Tradition, 1880/1990*, exh. cat, Henie-Onstad Art Center, Høvikodden, and National Museum of Women in the Arts, Washington, DC, 1995, pp.21–67

Asta Nørregaard was active as an artist in a rich and progressive period in Norwegian art. She was one of the many women painters who made a mark for themselves at a time when a national Norwegian school was established. She broke through during the 1880s with a varied activity in portraiture and genre painting. After 1890 she concentrated on portrait painting.

Already during her student years in Christiania (Oslo) and Munich her aim had been to become a portrait painter, and her earliest commissions were carried out in an unpretentious and realistic style. During the Munich years, however, when she studied alongside Harriet Backer (q.v.), among others, her repertoire was extended to include larger compositions as well, particularly genre pictures of a Late Romantic, slightly sentimental type. Her motifs were generally of children and women in Bavarian surroundings and landscapes. During that period she exhibited several pictures in Norwegian art associations.

During her years of study in Paris, Nørregaard established herself as an independent and mature artist. She was influenced by French academic realism through Jules Bastien-Lepage and Léon Bonnat, both of whom were her teachers. Bonnat's recommendation to let nature be master and to emphasise drawing over colour suited her well. Bonnat had great success as a portraitist of the upper classes, and as such he became a model for Nørregaard. There was great breadth in Nørregaard's development as a painter during the 1880s. As early as 1881 a large, religious composition, *Christ Is Coming!* (1881; private collection, repr. Wichstrøm 1983, p.97), was accepted by the Salon. There are other pictures with a religious content by her hand, but realistic genre paintings of French and Norwegian peasant women and children were to be more common. *Peasant Woman from Normandy* (1889; Nasjonalgalleriet, Oslo) is a contribution to French Salon realism. Nørregaard was influenced by plein-air painting and Impressionism, evident in, among others, *Music Interior* (?1885; Nasjonalgalleriet, Oslo). In addition to official portrait commissions (e.g. *Rector Sven Brun*, 1883; Holy Trinity, Oslo), she carried out charming informal portraits that look forward to her later portraiture, for example, *Maggie Plahte* (1881; private collection, repr. Wichstrøm 1995, cat.15). The self-portrait *In the Studio* (1883; see illustration) is a unique, self-conscious demonstration of the professionalism that Nørregaard attained during her years in Paris. She is surrounded by an altarpiece commission and a copy after Titian; in the corner is a chair with some drapery, ready to receive sitters. She demonstrates breadth and competence, and an academic understanding of space, treatment of light and figure representation. She masters it all. from the classical still life (the paint box) to the Impressionist technique in the autumn foliage outside the window.

During the 1880s Nørregaard exhibited in Norwegian and foreign exhibitions and attracted positive attention and good reviews. In 1890 there was a shift in her art; from then on she concentrated on portraiture. This shift can be connected to a study trip to Rome during the winter of 1889–90. The decision is symbolically confirmed in the elegant, but resigned *Self-Portrait* (1890; Oslo City Museum) painted during the Rome visit. In contrast with *In the Studio*, she now portrays herself as a fashionable society lady, on par with those who were, and in increasing numbers were to become, her sitters.

Nørregaard was entirely consumed by her role as a portrait painter of the upper classes. She carried out approximately 300 portraits in oil, pastel and charcoal, and in 1911 she published a sizeable catalogue of her own portraits. Her best period as a portraitist, when she received plentiful commissions from Oslo's upper-middle classes, lasted until 1905. Reasons for her success were her ability to create a likeness (she did not use photographs, which one might have suspected), moderate idealisation and individual characterisation. In the characterisation of her sitters there could be traces of both humour and irony. Her trademark, which earned her the designation "painter of fashion", was the excellent rendering of fashionable clothes and rich fabrics. The compositions are generally simple: the figure dominates the picture plane, and space and social circumstances are indicated with a single piece of furniture or object. Nørregaard often used patterned wallpapers or textiles for the background, or foliage and leaves as decorative elements. Her backgrounds can appear like stage-sets, on a par with those that portrait photographers used in their studios. There are examples in the Nasjonalgalleriet, Oslo.

Her speciality as a portrait painter was the use of pastel, and one of the first pastels she produced was a portrait of *Edvard Munch* (1855; Munch Museum, Oslo). It is a surprising fact that the young, radical Munch took time to sit for Nørregaard, who was by then already seen as a very conservative artist. Nørregaard has drawn a handsome young artist with a remote gaze, but clearly in a studious position. The most plausible background for the portrait is that the young Munch took lessons with Nørregaard. She had knowledge that was naturally attractive to young artists and not easily available in Oslo.

Nørregaard drew 60 pastel portraits during the period 1889–1905, many of them remarkably large. She often deviates from normal practice by using canvas as a support. She had acquired the pastel technique in Paris where it had become fashionable again around 1850. She did not, however, adopt the free pastel technique of the Impressionists, but used the traditional technique in which the colours are rubbed into each other in order to create gentle transitions. An original trait in her production is that the use of pastel was reserved for portraits of women and children, while serious, male captains of industry and men of science were rendered in oil (the portrait of *Edvard Munch* is an exception). The gentle quality of the pastel chalk was suited to the feminine and the childlike. At her best she achieved striking results, as in the portrait of *Elisabeth Fearnley* (1892; private collection, *ibid.*, p.36).

Asta Nørregaard was unusual in the context of Norwegian artistic life around 1900. Norwegian artists of the time were concerned to create a national art, but with her society portraits Nørregaard was related to an international trend. There was little tradition for portraiture in Norway, and she remained quite isolated as an artist and met with little understanding within her professional field. After 1890 she occasionally painted unpretentious landscapes and genre pictures in addition to portraits, demonstrating that she had retained her accomplishments from the 1880s.

ANNE WICHSTRØM

Nourse, Elizabeth

American painter, 1859–1938

Born in Mount Healthy, Ohio, 26 October 1859. Studied at McMicken School of Design, University of Cincinnati, 1874–81. Attended life classes at Art Students League, New York, under William Sartain, 1882. Joined the first life classes to be open to women at McMicken, 1885–6. Sailed for France with older sister Louise, 1887; studied at Académie Julian, Paris, under Gustave Boulanger and Jules Lefebvre. Lived in France with Louise for the rest of her life; exhibited widely in USA and Europe until her retirement in 1924. President, American Women's Art Association of Paris, 1899–1900. Associée, 1895, Sociétaire in drawing, pastel and watercolour, 1901, in oils, 1904, Société Nationale des Beaux-Arts, Paris; honorary member, Association of Women Painters and Sculptors (formerly Woman's Art Club), New York, 1914. Died in France, 8 October 1938.

Principal Exhibitions

Paris Salon: 1888–90
Royal Academy, London: 1889, 1892
Société Nationale des Beaux-Arts, Paris: 1890–1914, 1918–19, 1921
World's Columbian Exposition, Chicago: 1893 (medal)
Cincinnati Art Museum: 1893–4 (individual, touring)
Exposition Universelle, Paris: 1900 (silver medal)
Louisiana Purchase Exposition, St Louis: 1904 (silver medal)
Panama-Pacific Exposition, San Francisco: 1915 (gold medal)

Bibliography

Clara T. McChesney, "An American artist in Paris: Elizabeth Nourse", *Monthly Illustrator*, xiii/1, August 1896, pp.3–11

American Art Journal, i–xxx, 1898–1933

Clara Erskine Clement, *Women in the Fine Arts*, Boston: Houghton Mifflin, 1904; reprinted New York: Hacker, 1974

Edna Maria Clark, *Ohio Art and Artists*, Richmond, VA: Garrett and Massie, 1932

Alice Pike Barney: Paintings in Oil and Pastel, exh. cat., National Collection of Fine Arts, Washington, DC, 1957

The Golden Age: Cincinnati Painters of the Nineteenth Century Represented in the Cincinnati Art Museum, exh. cat., Cincinnati Art Museum, 1979

Charlotte Streifer Rubinstein, *American Women Artists from Early Times to the Present*, Boston: Hall, 1982

Elizabeth Nourse, 1859–1938: A Salon Career, exh. cat., National Museum of American Art, Smithsonian Institution, Washington, DC, and elsewhere, 1983 (includes extensive bibliography and catalogue raisonné)

In Pursuit of Beauty: Americans and the Aesthetic Movement, exh. cat., Metropolitan Museum of Art, New York, 1986

Elizabeth Nourse's parents both died in 1882, a year after she graduated from the McMicken School of Design, and she was required to support herself. She began by painting decorative oil panels and illuminating panels on furniture carved by her sister. Five years later, after the death of her twin sister, she left for Europe in the company of her older sister, Louise; they spent the rest of their lives in France with rare return visits to America.

In France, Nourse supported both herself and Louise through her work as a painter. For any artist this was a formidable task, for a woman it was even more difficult, but for a woman from a middle-class, Midwestern background it was particularly intimidating. Only a very few other American women had succeeded, and by and large they were helped by their families' position and connections. Nourse succeeded almost exclusively through her talent, commitment, determination and energies, supported only by her sister Louise and encouraged by a small group of friends from Cincinnati who visited her regularly in Paris and travelled with her during the summer. Her work was accepted by the all-male juries of the salons and international exhibitions, and received attention from male art critics. She was accorded considerable acclaim and honours as an artist, not merely as a woman artist, which is as she wanted it to be.

Most of Nourse's works are of women and children, but unlike those of Mary Cassatt (q.v.), she painted working-class, frequently peasant women, with great empathy. *Maternité* (1898; private collection, Cincinnati) shows a woman nursing her baby in a chair just outside her house – her dress, face and hands all reveal her to be a working woman. *Les Heures d'été* (1895; Newark Museum, NJ) depicts two peasant women in the Morbihan costume of Saint-Gildas-de-Rhuys in Brittany, sitting under a tree darning socks, the light coming from the side and filtering through the trees.

Nourse's domestic pictures often render the hardship and strength of peasant life observed on her many visits to Brittany and Normandy. Her interest in peasant themes was an extension of the simple rural subjects she had painted in the Midwest before leaving for Europe, and reflected her own values and view that beauty is to be found in the simplest

Nourse: *Interior, Closed Shutters*, 1910; oil on canvas; 100.5 × 100.5 cm.; Musée d'Orsay, Paris

aspects of daily life. Deep religious convictions led Nourse to many acts of personal charity and to an involvement in the lives of her models. She was able to paint urban and rural working people with a depth of understanding that few artists acquired – many saw them merely as picturesque figures. Of her painting *Le Repas en famille* (1891; untraced), for which she won a medal at the World's Columbian Exposition, Chicago, one critic wrote:

> Miss Nourse puts into these intimate little scenes the sentiments of goodness, of charity, of devotion and of thankfulness which she herself feels better than any one

else, and she reproduced them with an emotion that is always true and which communicates itself perfectly naturally, for she makes appeal to the best in each of us [*New York Herald* (Paris), 9 February 1910].

At a table are seated a family at their meagre meal of soup and bread. The table is placed in front of a bay window with light coming through and on to the white cloth. The mother leans over to help the baby seated on pillows on a chair; the older sister opposite the baby looks sadly at the mother; the father seems not to be part of the family, sitting as he does looking dejectedly into his bowl. Fine contrasts are drawn between the white cloth and plates, the dark crusty bread and the dark wood of the windows.

Nourse rarely painted specifically religious paintings but *Vendredi Saint* (1891; Union League Club, Chicago) is an exception, showing the traditional veneration of the Cross on Good Friday. She began the work in Paris, but altered the composition after a seven-month stay in Rome, which provided her with the opportunity to study Baroque art. She added a young kneeling girl to the foreground, a 17th-century device used to draw the viewer into the scene, and incorporated dramatic light effects.

In *La Rêverie* (1911; College-Conservatory of Music, University of Cincinnati) Nourse adopted a different subject, more akin to Cassatt. A young woman, dressed for early afternoon in a gossamer-patterned suit, stands over a round table on which is a fish bowl; the translucent bowl, angles and planes of light through the nearby window and patterns of colour and texture are skilfully handled. Her sister Louise was the model for the woman standing at a bureau, her back to the viewer, in *Interior, Closed Shutters* (1910; see illustration). The light comes in through the slats of the shutters behind her and is then reflected back from a mirror on the bureau, offering a wonderful play of repeat patterns. The woman is less a figure than a compositional element of form and dark colour. The work was purchased by the State from the Salon of 1910.

Nourse also departed from her usual subject matter during the period 1904–10, when she accepted a number of portrait commissions for fashionable clients in order to help pay her bills. Done often in pastels and showing her ability to capture expressions, they lack the obvious sympathy of her peasant women; instead, the women are often stiff and vacuous, held within a rigid set of expectations. At the same time these portraits exhibit a skilful handling of both the pastel and oil media, as well as revealing the artist's interest in light and colour.

Nourse was concerned not only with subject matter but also with the difficulties of portraying light accurately. Her early works, even of landscapes and outdoor scenes, look as though they were painted in the studio. But although never a follower of the Impressionists, as she began to spend more time in the countryside outside Paris, her palette took on a brighter quality and her technique became bolder. She painted in all seasons, at all times of day and night, indoors and out.

ELAINE HIRSCHL ELLIS

Nyman, Gunnel

Finnish glass artist and designer, 1909–1948

Born Gunnel Anita Gustafsson in Turku, 19 September 1909. Moved to Helsinki with her family, 1922. Studied furniture design at the Taideteollinen Korkeakoulu (Central School of the Industrial Arts), Helsinki, under Arttu Brummer, 1928–32. Married the Swede Gunnar Nyman, 1936; three daughters, born 1940, 1941 and 1945. Worked for Finnish glass manufacturers Riihimäki, 1932–47; Karhula, 1935–7; Nuutajärvi-Notsjö, 1946–8; Iittala, 1946–7; also designer for Oy Taito AB, manufacturer of lighting fixtures and articles in wrought metal, 1932–6; furniture designer for Oy Boman AB, 1936–8. Recipient of first prize, Finnish Society of Arts and Crafts lottery contest, 1932; third prize, 1933, second and third prizes, 1936, Riihimäki glass competition; second and third prizes, Karhula glass competition, 1936. Died in Helsinki, 7 October 1948.

Principal Exhibitions

Milan Triennale: 1933 (bronze medal), 1951 (gold medal, glass)
Exposition Internationale, Paris: 1937 (gold medal, glass; silver medal, furniture)
Museum of Applied Arts, Helsinki: 1938 (*Textil-möbler-glas* [Textiles, furniture, glass], with Dora Jung)
New York World's Fair: 1939
Nationalmuseum, Stockholm: 1941 (*Ny finsk konstindustri* [Finnish industrial arts])
Liljevalchs Konsthall, Stockholm: 1946 (*Nordiskt konsthantverk* [Nordic industrial arts])
Galleri Artek, Helsinki: 1947–8 (with Dora Jung, touring)
Århus, Denmark: 1947 (*Vort hjem* [Our home])
Nordiska Museet, Stockholm: 1948 (*Finlandia*)
Taidehalli Helsinki: 1948 (retrospective)

Selected Writings

"Lasi Glas Glass", *Ornamo*, 1949

Bibliography

Ornamo, Suomen koristetaiteilijain liito/Konstindustriförbundet i Finland årsböcker, i–xiv, 1927–54
Domus, Tidskrift för inredningskonst, konstindustri, måleri och skulptur, 1930–33
Applied Art in Finland: Les Arts appliqués en Finlande: Las artes utiles en Finlandia, Helsinki: Finnish Section of New York's World's Fair, 1939
Arttu Brummer, "Gunnel Nyman och finsk glaskonst" [Gunnel Nyman and Finnish glass art], *SvHOB*, no.6–7, 1947
Kerttu Niilonen, "Gunnel Nyman ja hänen lasitaiteensa" [Gunnel Nyman and her glass art], *Suomen Taiteen vuosikirja*, 1947
Dora Jung, "Gunnel Nyman", *Arina*, i, 1959
Kerttu Niilonen, *Finnish Glass*, Helsinki: Tammi, 1966
Scandinavian Modern Design, 1880–1980, exh. cat., Cooper-Hewitt Museum, New York, 1982
Suomen Lasimuseo [Finnish Glass Museum], exh. cat., Finnish Glass Museum, Riihimäki, 1983
The Modern Spirit: Glass from Finland, exh. cat., Cooper-Hewitt Museum, New York, and elsewhere, 1985
Marianne Aav and Kaj Kalin, *Form Finland* [Finnish form], Museum of Applied Arts Publication no.21, Helsinki, 1986
Gunnel Nyman, exh. cat., Finnish Glass Museum, Riihimäki, 1987
Jennifer Hawkins Opie, *Scandinavian Ceramics and Glass in the Twentieth Century*, London: Victoria and Albert Museum, and New York: Rizzoli, 1989

Gunnel Nyman is one of the pioneers of modern Finnish glass art. She became particularly well known in the 1940s for her introduction of a pure sculptural quality to Finnish glass design, which later, in the 1950s, became the trademark of the country's glassware. As a designer, Nyman was also an early exponent of mass-produced glassware. The bowls and vases she designed and made on a cottage industry basis in the 1930s may be seen as the first examples of series production in the Finnish glass industry. Nyman was originally trained as a furniture designer, and in the 1930s furniture and interior design formed an important part of her work. During the post-war period, however, right up to her early death, she dedicated herself almost exclusively to glass work. The characteristic mark of her production was a devoted attention to materials and the possibilities opened up by them, centring on glass, wood and silver.

Nyman's abundant furniture production of the 1930s embraces the ideals of the functionalism of the early 1930s, expressing itself in simple, standardised items. After the mid-1930s she broke away from functionalism and designed soft-lined furniture, representing the objective spirit of the times, in which there can be seen a clear relation to the work of the Swedish designer, Carl Malmsten. During the 1930s Nyman several times won the Finnish Industrial Art Society prize for her furniture designs, and from 1936 until 1938 worked as a designer for the firm of Oy Boman AB, well known for the high quality of its production. She achieved her most aesthetically pleasing results as a furniture designer with designs that were executed as high-level professional craftwork. In them the material came into its own, harmonising with a lyrical design-language that was favourable to it.

In the 1930s Nyman also worked as a producer of lighting and metal objects, and was one of the pioneer designers of the Finnish metalsmiths Oy Taito AB, making lighting and also silver articles intended mainly for ecclesiastical use. The design of lighting also involved an interest in glass as a material, and collaboration with the glassworks. Nyman's most noteworthy work of this period was the lighting of the Helsinki Swedish Theatre, done in collaboration with Taito's director, Paavo Tynell. The often classical design-language of Nyman's silver-work followed the Nordic ideals of the time. The same distinctly stylised line of classicism is also displayed in Nyman's commercial and ecclesiastical designs from the same period.

Nyman took up glass design with the encouragement of her teacher, Arttu Brummer. Brummer, who had acquired a legendary reputation at the Helsinki Central School of Industrial Arts as an instructor and interior designer, also began to design glassware himself, from the early 1930s onwards. The Finnish glassworks of the 1930s, inspired by Swedish glassware exhibition successes, had begun to realise the competitive value of design. In the 1930s and 1940s they did not yet employ designers on a permanent basis, but commissions were already building up as a result of competitions or the purchasing of individual patterns from the artists. Nyman's collaborative partners in the 1930s were Riihimäki glass and the Karhula glassworks. Her first glass items were the carafes and spirits glasses produced by Riihimäki. The items were again produced on a cottage industry basis in the 1930s from blown glass moulds, and they give a much heavier impression than Nyman's later productions.

In the 1930s Nyman also designed for Riihimäki a series of freely blown bowls and vases and Swedish-influenced glass objects decorated with engravings or sand blastings, the subjects of which were portrayals of Finnish folk life and scenes from biblical narrative. In collaboration with the Karhula glassworks she produced a series of bowls, vases and dishes, the most famous of which is the *Kalavati* (Fish plate; repr. Riihimäki 1987, no.40), made for the Paris Exposition Internationale of 1937. It anticipated the organic line for which Nyman became famous in the 1940s. Another of the principal lines of Nyman's later production had its antecedent

Nyman: *Serpentiini* crystal glass vase, 1946; Museum of Applied Arts, Helsinki

around this time. In addition to the pictorially decorated "epic" bowls, in 1941 Nyman produced the cut crystal dishes *Fasetti I* (Facet I; *ibid.*, no.43) and *Elisabeth* (*ibid.*, no.44), in which there are already pointers to the pure-lined sculptural quality that characterises several of her works of the late 1940s.

Nyman's strongest and most stylistically independent creative period was the last three years of her life, 1945–8. During that time she collaborated with three leading glass-works. For Riihimäki she designed both natural form-based soft-lined vases such as the *Kalla* (*ibid.*, no.49), *Simpukka* (Mussel; *ibid.*, no.50), *Näkki* (Water-spirit; *ibid.*, no.53) and *Koivikko* (*ibid.*, no.51) of 1946, and cut crystal bowls and vases. For Iittala she produced a series of cut crystal vases, several blown eggshell bowls and freely blown vases (*ibid.*). During her period of permanent employment at Nuutajärvi Glass she produced numerous utility series and blown bowls and vases (*ibid.*).

After 1945 Gunnel Nyman's ideas about the basis of glass design crystallised. Glass as a material fascinated her with its play of light and its momentarily occurring process of solidification of a flowing substance. She considered the chosen material to be the dominant factor in design, so determinative that the object could not be made from any other substance. The task of form, proportion and decoration was merely to emphasise the special qualities of the material. The prismlike refraction of light was emphasised in the bright cut crystal shapes. Her soft-lined bowl and vases, created in the spirit of the 1940s and often decorated with bubbles, serpentine filigree necklaces or frosting, frequently approach the most characteristic form of liquid material, the drop, as for example in the *Serpentiini* (Serpentine; see illustration), *Helminauha* (Pearl necklace; *ibid.*, no.102), *Shifonki* (Chiffon; *ibid.*, no.100) and *Sipuli* (Onion; *ibid.*, no.98) of 1947. The plasticity of thick glass, the decoration of the interior with bubbles, opal or frosted glass and the use of light and space in order to emphasise the form: all these are typical features of Nyman's production, and they also formed the basis for the development of modern Finnish glass art in the 1950s.

MARIANNE AAV

Nyström, Jenny

Swedish painter and illustrator, 1854–1946

Born in Kalmar, 13 June 1854. Studied at the Museum Design and Art School, Göteborg, 1868–70; Royal Academy of Fine Arts, Stockholm, 1873–81; Académie Julian and Académie Colarossi, Paris, 1882–6. Married Daniel Stoopendaal, 1887; son born 1893. Lived in Stockholm from 1886. Member, Konstnärsförbundet (Artist's Association), 1886–96. Died in Stockholm, 1946.

Principal Exhibitions

Student exhibition, Royal Academy of Fine Arts, Stockholm: 1881–2 (royal medal, with Richard Hall, 1881)
Sundsvall: 1882 (*Konstutställning, industriutställningen* [Art exhibition, industrial exhibition])
Paris Salon: 1884–5

Stockholm: 1885 (*Från Seinens strand* [From the shores of the Seine]), 1885 (*Opponenternas utställning* [Opponents' exhibition])
Valand, Göteborg: 1886 (*Nordisk konstutställningen* [Nordic art exhibition])
Blanchs konstsalong, Stockholm: 1886 (*Konstnärsförbundets utställning* [Artists' Association exhibition])
Konstföreningen för Södra Sverige (Art Society of Southern Sweden), Malmö: 1886, 1888, 1890, 1893, 1896
Konstnärsförbundet (Artists' Association), Stockholm: 1887
Sveriges allmänna konstförening (Sweden's Public Art Society), Stockholm: 1891, 1892 (both touring)
Artist's studio, Stockholm: 1896 (individual)

Selected Writings

"En Kalmarflicka" [A Kalmar girl], *Barndomslandet: Barndomsminnen av Jultomtens författare och konstnärer* [The land of childhood: Childhood memories by authors and artists of Father Christmas], Barnbiblioteket Saga, no.35, Stockholm, 1918
Några minnen [Some memories], Göteborg: Gamla Majpojkars, 1937

Bibliography

Ulla Ehrensvärd, *Gamla vykort: En bok för samlare* [Old picture postcards: A book for collectors], Stockholm: Bonnier, 1972
Karl Jäder and Astrid Jäder, *Jenny Nyström, den folkkära: En livsskildring* [Jenny Nyström, beloved by the people: Picture of a life], Stockholm: Gummesson, 1975
Barbro Werkmäster, "Barnkammarens konstnärer" [Artists of the nursery], *Kvinnor som konstnärer* [Women as artists], ed. Anna Lena Lindberg and Barbro Werkmäster, Stockholm: Liber. 1975
Ulla Ehrensvärd, *Den svenska tomten* [The Swedish brownie], Stockholm: Svenska Turistföreningens Publikation, 1979
Anders Neumüller, *God Jul: Svenska jultraditioner på helgkort från förr* [Happy Christmas: Swedish Christmas traditions on Christmas cards from earlier on], Stockholm: Bonnier, 1980
Ralph Herrmanns, *Ett år i Jenny Nyströms Sverige* [A year in Jenny Nyström's Sweden], Köping: Lindfors, 1983
Barbro Werkmäster, "'Gebietet barnavärlden' [The province of childhood]: The modern breakthrough in Scandinavian literature, 1870–1905", *IASS 1986*, ed. Bertil Nolin and Peter Forsgren, Göteborg, 1988
De drogo till Paris: Nordiska konstnärinnor på 1880-talet [They went to Paris: Nordic women artists in the 1880s], exh. cat., Liljevalchs Konsthall, Stockholm, 1988
Gunnel Forsberg Warringer, *Jenny Nyström: Konstnärinna* [Jenny Nyström: Artist], Kalmar: Kalmar Läns Museum, 1992

Jenny Nyström is one of the best known and beloved of Swedish artists. Her popularity is based primarily on her Christmas cards and her illustrations for children. Many of her cards are still in production and her illustrations are frequently reproduced both as postcards and in advertisements. From the turn of the 19th and 20th centuries, her artistic reputation among critics and artists gradually declined, mostly because of these countless cards, but since the 1970s her work has been increasingly appreciated and has risen in value. This is the result of many factors: the "discovery" of her watercolours and her early paintings and illustrations; a general interest in such realms as mass-media pictures, children's literature and folklore; and the expanding focus on the art of the 19th century and on women artists in general.

Nyström's family background influenced her career. She was born into a middle-class family – her father was a school-teacher and choir-master – and lived from the age of eight in Sweden's second town, Göteborg. Her artistic talent was

Nyström: *We Two*, 1895; oil on canvas; 71 × 82 cm.; Kalmar läns Museum, Sweden

noticed early and encouraged; patrons helped to promote her studies at the Royal Academy of Fine Arts in Stockholm, which had held a female class since 1864. At the Academy both teachers and colleagues regarded Nyström as one of the most gifted students. When she left Stockholm for further studies in Paris her decision was to be a painter, and during the next two decades she painted portraits, genre scenes and landscapes. She exhibited a self-portrait and a watercolour at the Paris Salon of 1884, and in 1885 a pastel of an old woman. During the 1880s she participated in several exhibitions in Sweden. At the Academy, Nyström had already reached maturity in the dominating academic style of classicism. Unlike many of her contemporary Swedish colleagues in Paris, she never gave up this style or developed it into other new styles, not even to Art Nouveau, a style that from the 1890s was frequently used in book illustration. Only her landscapes in watercolours give the impression of plein-air painting. Instead, she created a style of her own, based on traditional academic values such as perspective, solid form and outline drawing. Jenny Nyström became an illustrator, a Swedish pioneer in more than one sense. Altogether, she illustrated more than 1000 books and magazines.

Two self-portraits, from 1884 and 1895, can be interpreted as reflecting her choice of artistic career and its development. The first portrait differs in a significant way from other self-portraits of contemporary women artists. Although like many others Nyström depicted herself without artistic milieu or attributes, she added an unusual gesture and glance, and included contrary elements, although without any sense of conflict – the ambivalence of the portrait lies in the eyes of the beholder, not the painter's. The black silk dress is a sign of a middle-class woman, the ring on the bare left hand denotes an engaged woman. Contrarily, the fringe indicates freedom and modernity, and the hat and gloves the outdoors. The woman in the painting looks straight at the beholder with a slight mocking smile, her left hand on her hip in the position of a man of power; for a woman it can represent the pose of a variety singer. Thus the portrait shows the image of a respectable woman, and at the same time a woman on the stage attracting her audience. This audience was a new one historically, a mixture of the traditional cultivated *haute bourgeoisie* and the broad middle classes, both purchasers of public entertainment and, in Nyström's case, not only purchasers of easel paintings, but also buyers of illustrated publications for family reading. Nyström was one of the few artists who understood, accepted and exploited the new situation.

Coming from a non-affluent family, she had to earn her own living early on, which gave her a rather unusual characteristic for an artist – a go-ahead or entrepreneurial spirit. Her marriage to Daniel Stoopendaal was a step upwards socially, but it did not change her economic situation. Her husband never finished his medical studies, and she had to support him – and his life of pleasure. In 1884 she was unaware of these future problems; she painted herself in the guise of a successful painter, an established illustrator and a future doctor's wife, firmly intending to continue her artistic career. As can be seen in a gouache of 1887, she equipped her studio in Stockholm with all the props needed by a portraitist, genre painter and illustrator, such as palms, fans, draperies and a polar-bear-skin rug.

In 1895 Nyström portrayed herself close to her two-year-old son against a green background with flowers (see illustration) – an idealistic mother-and-child image from her own pictorial world, to be compared with the self-portraits of Elisabeth Vigée-Lebrun (q.v.) with her daughter of a century earlier. During the decade between these two self-portraits, Nyström had established herself, describing herself as a person who "successfully specialised in the realm of childhood".

Her career as an illustrator had already started when she was an art student in Stockholm. In 1875, on her own initiative, she illustrated her first book, *Lille Viggs äfventyr på julafton* (Little Vigg's adventure on Christmas Eve), written by the Swedish author Viktor Rydberg and previously published in serial form for a Göteborg newspaper. From 1880 to 1888 she was a contributor to the respected magazine *Ny Illustrerad Tidning*. Besides the many full-page genre pictures in this magazine she also drew report pictures, which was unusual for a woman. Perhaps to avoid the difficulty of being a woman working in a public milieu, some of these pictures were produced in collaboration with a female colleague, Ingeborg Westfelt, a unique co-operation at this time. In 1881, on Rydberg's request, Nyström illustrated his poem about an old goblin, a good-natured man with a long beard dressed in a grey costume of rough homespun cloth, who in the dark of the midwinter night gives a long philosophic monologue. In this illustration, Nyström formed the image of the Swedish *jultomten* (Father Christmas), half a wild goblin, half a domesticated brownie, figured as an old man – an image that she would popularise in numerous pictures.

From the beginning, Nyström was a very clever illustrator, and fully aware of the technical requirements of book reproduction, and eager to learn about new inventions. She was also aware of her public, and letters document how, introducing herself to a new publisher, she would stress those skills that were best suited to the taste of a particular audience. In some of her illustrated works intended for the drawing-room table, for example three collections of poems by C.D. Wirsén (1887–9), the motif, the pictures and the typographical composition form an aesthetic whole. In works for the general public, she stressed clarity of form and the emotionalism of the content.

Her most important achievement as an artist is in the sphere of children's literature. Together with Ottilia Adelborg, who made her debut in 1885, she was often referred to as the "children's artist". The 1880s were the breakthrough years in Sweden for children's literature. Women writers, many of them teachers, formed a new professional group, and Nyström illustrated a large number of their books. In 1882 she created the first Swedish picture book worth its name, *Barnkammarens bok* (Book of the nursery), with lithographic pictures in ten colours, and in 1886–7 she illustrated Johan Nordlander's *Svenska barnboken 1–2* (Swedish children's book), perhaps her most charming work.

Another important medium for illustrators was the many Christmas magazines, which were first published in the early 1890s. During her lifetime Nyström was responsible for the covers of about 250 magazines, and she also contributed full-page colour pictures and illustrations in black and white. It is possible to say that with her Christmas pictures Jenny Nyström helped to form the Swedish way of celebrating Christmas, with her images of sweet children dancing around a Christmas tree, gifts distributed by Father Christmas emerging from the depths of the forest, indoor and outdoor Christmas decorations, and so on. Her conception of Christmas also included Christmas cards, which she introduced into Sweden, paper decorations and tablecloths.

Nyström's best illustrations, especially those in black and white, date from the 1880s and 1890s. She applied her skill as an academically trained painter and draughtswoman on historical, anecdotal, landscape and portrait illustrations for a wide variety of literature. The 1880s mode of collage-formed illustrations also led her to combine elements from different genres in one picture, while the strict wood-engraving technique gave her pictures a distinct and authoritative form. As early as the 1880s, she combined her classicism with the harmony and idealism of such Renaissance painters as Raphael and the sentiment of 19th-century Romanticism. Again and again, Jenny Nyström depicted the ideal child and the ideal world, in many cases without being either sentimental or banal, which unfortunately the large number of commissions often pressurised her to be. Moreover, in her pictures, especially for the Christmas magazines, she also mixed elements from the whole gallery of art history without inhibition. On one example, the cover of a jubilee number of the Christmas magazine for children, *Jultomten*, in 1910, she placed a Father Christmas dressed in blue, with a pink Christian rose wreath around his red hood, on a golden throne decorated with Viking ornaments, a king's crown, Odin's ravens, a sunflower and lions – and the reader finds it quite in order.

With her middle-class background and being both a woman and an illustrator, Nyström belonged to the margins of the discourse of art history. This position can be of advantage, giving greater freedom to play and cross borders. She never became a modernist in a traditional sense, but she can be seen as an agent for modernity in her acceptance of the rules of the commercial mass-media world. In her illustrations, the sign of modern times lies in her way of borrowing and mixing elements from other pictures, even from her own, but also in her pictorial use of such inventions as telephones, cars and aeroplanes. Her classicism and the pictorial content of happy families, family feasts, agricultural life and nature scenes evoke good old times. This combination of modernity and traditionalism attracted – and still attracts – a broad audience. Jenny Nyström's pictures were accessible to all groups of society. Before World War II they were for many people in Sweden their main experience of art.

BARBRO WERKMÄSTER

O

Oakey, Maria *see* Dewing

Óbidos, Josefa de *see* Ayala

O'Keeffe, Georgia
American painter, 1887–1986

Born on a farm near Sun Prairie, Wisconsin, 15 November 1887. Studied at the School of the Art Institute of Chicago under John Vanderpoel, 1905–6; Art Students League, New York, under William Merritt Chase, F. Luis Mora and Kenyon Cox, 1907–8; Alon Bement's summer school at University of Virginia, Charlottesville, 1912 (assisted him in summers of 1913–16); Columbia University Teachers' College, New York, under Arthur Wesley Dow, 1914–16. Freelance commercial artist in Chicago, 1908–10. Taught art at Chatham Episcopal Institute, 1911–12; high school, Amarillo, Texas, 1912–14; Columbia College, South Carolina, 1915–16; West Texas State Normal College, Canyon, 1916–18. Met photographer Alfred Stieglitz in New York, 1916. Left teaching to pursue professional career as an artist in New York, 1918. Lived with Stieglitz from 1918; married him, 1924; he died 1946. Included in *Seven Americans* exhibition organised by Stieglitz, New York, 1925; *Paintings by Nineteen Living Americans*, the second exhibition at the newly opened Museum of Modern Art, New York, 1929. Settled in New Mexico, dividing time between Abiquiu and Ghost Ranch, 1949; subsequently also travelled widely. Lost central vision, 1970. Recipient of numerous awards and honours, including Creative Arts award, Brandeis University, 1963; gold medal for painting, National Institute of Arts and Letters, 1970; Medal of Freedom presented by President Gerald Ford, 1977; National Medal of Arts presented by President Ronald Reagan, 1985; honorary doctorates from College of William and Mary, Williamsburg, 1938; University of Wisconsin, Madison, 1942; Mount Holyoke College, South Hadley, Massachusetts, 1952; Mills College, Oakland, 1952; University of New Mexico, Albuquerque, 1964; Columbia University, New York, 1971; Brown University, Providence, Rhode Island, 1971; Minneapolis College of Art and Design, 1972; Harvard University, Cambridge, 1973; College of Santa Fe, 1977. Member, National Institute of Arts and Letters, 1949; American Academy of Arts and Letters, 1962; American Academy of Arts and Sciences, 1963; Benjamin Franklin fellow, Royal Society of Arts, London, 1969. Died in Santa Fe, New Mexico, 6 March 1986.

Selected Individual Exhibitions
291 Gallery, New York: 1917
Anderson Galleries, New York: 1923, 1924 (both organised by Alfred Stieglitz)
Intimate Gallery, New York: 1926, 1927, 1928, 1929
An American Place, New York: 1930, 1931, 1932, 1933, 1934, 1935, 1936, 1937, 1938, 1939, 1940, 1941, 1942, 1943, 1944, 1945, 1946, 1950
University of Minnesota, Minneapolis: 1937
College of William and Mary, Williamsburg, VA: 1938
Art Institute of Chicago: 1943 (retrospective)
Museum of Modern Art, New York: 1946 (retrospective)
Downtown Gallery, New York: 1952, 1955, 1957, 1958, 1961
Museum of Fine Arts, Dallas: 1953 (retrospective)
Worcester Art Museum, MA: 1960 (touring retrospective)
Amon Carter Museum of Western Art, Fort Worth, TX: 1966 (touring retrospective)
Whitney Museum of American Art, New York: 1970–71 (touring retrospective)
National Gallery of Art, Washington, DC: 1987 (touring retrospective)

Selected Writings
Some Memories of Drawings, ed. Doris Bry, Albuquerque: University of New Mexico Press, 1974
Georgia O'Keeffe, New York: Viking, 1976
"Introduction", *Georgia O'Keeffe: A Portrait by Alfred Stieglitz*, exh. cat., Metropolitan Museum of Art, New York, 1978

Bibliography
Georgia O'Keeffe, exh. cat., Art Institute of Chicago, 1943
Georgia O'Keeffe: Forty Years of Her Art, exh. cat., Worcester Art Museum, MA, 1960
Georgia O'Keeffe, exh. cat., Amon Carter Museum of Western Art, Fort Worth, 1966
Lisa Mintz Messinger, "Georgia O'Keeffe", *Metropolitan Museum of Art Bulletin*, xlii, Fall 1984 (entire issue)
Jan Garden Castro, *The Art and Life of Georgia O'Keeffe*, New York: Crown, 1985; London: Virago, 1986

Sasha Newman, *Georgia O'Keeffe*, Washington, DC: Phillips Collection, 1985

Georgia O'Keeffe: Works on Paper, exh. cat., Museum of New Mexico, Santa Fe, 1985

Laurie Lisle, *Portrait of an Artist: A Biography of Georgia O'Keeffe*, 2nd edition, Albuquerque: University of New Mexico Press, 1986; London: Heinemann, 1987

Georgia O'Keeffe: Art and Letters, exh. cat., National Gallery of Art, Washington, DC, and elsewhere, 1987 (contains extensive bibliography)

Lisa Mintz Messinger, *Georgia O'Keeffe*, New York: Thames and Hudson, 1988; London: Thames and Hudson, 1989

Anita Pollitzer, *A Woman on Paper: Georgia O'Keeffe*, New York: Simon and Schuster, 1988

Barbara Buhler Lynes, *O'Keeffe, Stieglitz and the Critics, 1916–1929*, Ann Arbor: University of Michigan Research Press, 1989 (contains extensive bibliography)

Roxana Robinson, *Georgia O'Keeffe: A Life*, New York: Harper, 1989; London: Bloomsbury, 1990

Georgia O'Keeffe: Paintings of Hawai'i, exh. cat., Honolulu Academy of Arts, 1990

Charles C. Eldredge, *Georgia O'Keeffe*, New York: Abrams, 1991

Sarah Whitaker Peters, *Becoming O'Keeffe: The Early Years*, New York: Abbeville, 1991 (contains extensive bibliography)

Mara R. Witzling, ed., *Voicing Our Visions: Writings by Women Artists*, New York: Universe, 1991; London: Women's Press, 1992

Alexandra Arrowsmith and Thomas West, eds, *Two Lives: Georgia O'Keeffe and Alfred Stieglitz: A Conversation in Paintings and Photographs*, New York: HarperCollins, 1992; London: Hale, 1993

Christopher Merrill and Ellen Bradbury, eds, *Georgia O'Keeffe as Icon*, Reading, MA: Addison Wesley, 1992

Christine Taylor Patten and Alvaro Cardona-Hine, *Miss O'Keeffe*, Albuquerque: University of New Mexico Press, 1992

Charles C. Eldredge, *Georgia O'Keeffe: American and Modern*, New Haven and London: Yale University Press, 1993

Barbara Buhler Lynes, *Georgia O'Keeffe*, New York: Rizzoli, 1993

——, *Georgia O'Keeffe: Catalogue Raisonné* (in preparation)

Georgia O'Keeffe first emerged as an innovative presence in 1916, when her charcoal drawings and watercolours were shown in New York. These abstractions drew on the natural world for their subjects, suggesting botanical forms, geological formations and fluid currents. The primary importance of the works, however, lay not in their images, or in the bold use of abstraction, but in their remarkable intimacy and emotion. O'Keeffe's ability to portray a private sensibility, one both vivid and powerful, would prove one of her greatest strengths and most important contributions.

O'Keeffe was one of the American modernists. Though based in New York, these painters were participants in the aesthetic revolution that began in Germany, with Kandinsky's call to abstraction. John Marin, Marsden Hartley, Arthur Dove, Charles Sheeler and O'Keeffe were all part of a circle dominated by the pioneering photographer and art dealer Alfred Stieglitz, who became O'Keeffe's husband.

O'Keeffe received a conservative education in art. She began at the Art Institute of Chicago in 1905, and went on to the Art Students League in New York two years later. These institutions taught through the imitation of classical and European masters. O'Keeffe became accomplished in the style of her teachers, but could see her way no further. "I began to realise that a lot of people had done this same kind of painting before I came along", she said, "I didn't think I could do it any better" (Katherine Kuh, *The Artist's Voice*, New York: Harper, 1962,

p.189). Around 1910 she gave up painting altogether, and resumed it only in 1912, when she encountered the theories of Arthur Wesley Dow, an influential teacher at Columbia University in New York. His approach, based on Oriental principles, required the creative participation of the student, instead of dutiful imitation.

In Europe, pictorial art had traditionally attempted to replicate the three-dimensional world through the use of modelling and perspective. Dow placed little value on the replication of three-dimensional reality, or on the separation between fine and decorative art. He held that pictorial art should create its own two-dimensional reality, and that this should be based on purely aesthetic principles. His approach to composition was abstract, and based on the use of three formal components – line, colour and *notan* (light and dark masses) – and five active principles, including repetition and symmetry. Dow's principles liberated O'Keeffe from conscientious imitation; they also gave her a theoretical basis for the emotional content in her work. In his textbook, *Composition*, Dow wrote: "It is not the province of the landscape painter, for example, to represent so much topography, but to express an emotion, and this he must do by art."

In 1915 O'Keeffe was teaching in South Carolina, isolated from the aesthetic ferment of New York. In late November she received a visit from Arthur Macmahon, the man at the centre of her emotional life. After this encounter, she worked for the next four weeks in a state of nearly ecstatic intensity. The combination of cultural isolation, emotional ferment and solitude produced a profound response. For the first time she was able to move beyond the conventions that had shaped her, and to translate her experience into what was finally and entirely her own work. The drawings of 1915–16 are charcoal abstractions. Typical of this series is *Special No.13* (Metropolitan Museum of Art, New York), in which rounded, bud-like forms nestle between a jagged silhouette and an undulating ripple. The work reveals both O'Keeffe's remarkable control of the medium and her highly personal approach to abstraction. The drawing is powerful in its confident line and its bold masses; it is also feminine, in its delicate forms, subtle undulations and sense of great and immanent tenderness. This paradoxical combination of power and femininity would reappear in O'Keeffe's work.

In 1916 O'Keeffe moved to Texas. In cultural isolation once again, she produced a powerful series in response to the wide-open prairie landscape. She continued to work in charcoal, but also began bold experiments in colour. The oils and watercolours of this period are small and semi-abstract. They are vividly hued, spatially disorienting, and pulsing with a sense of exultant liberation. In glowing, radiant colours O'Keeffe portrayed the Texas sky and its dramatic atmospherics: starlight, sunsets, sunrise. In these works she was experimenting with perspective and design, line and volume. In some of them the sophisticated manipulation of space makes it possible to read the works both as three-dimensional landscapes and as flat patterned abstractions. *Light Coming on the Plains III* (1917; Amon Carter Museum, Fort Worth) is a small watercolour from this period. A blue dome, its colour deepening upwards, arches nearly to the top of the paper. Below a low horizon lies a strip of blue darkness. From the centre of the horizon spreads a glow, a pale radiance. Here O'Keeffe's control of the medium is extraordinary. In this series the works are liquid, brilliant and fresh, done with great freedom and energy. With complete confidence the artist exploits the transparency and immediacy of watercolour, its potential for luminosity, its liquid, fluid qualities. Lucid, vivid and hauntingly pure, these works are direct translations of the landscape into O'Keeffe's aesthetic lexicon, as well as powerful renderings of the artist's emotional response to her subject.

In 1918 O'Keeffe returned to New York and began to investigate the possibilities of pure abstraction. Dow's approach made little distinction between objective and non-objective art, and O'Keeffe moved easily between the two. During the late 1910s and early 1920s she produced a number of large abstract oils. *Music – Pink and Blue I* (private collection, repr. *Georgia O'Keeffe* 1976), a large oil of 1919, consists of a trembling, lyrical arch of living tissue, formed by layers of rose and creams and giving on to a blue, limitless and ethereal space. O'Keeffe was profoundly engaged by colour, which was a crucial component of her work. She defied the convention that limited serious art to harsh or sombre palettes. On occasion, she revelled in warm, luscious, romantic hues, and the colours in this work are radiant and high-keyed. She did not confine herself to these colours, however: in *Red and Orange Streak* (1919; artist's estate, repr. Washington 1987, no.33) both the palette and the mood are different. Here the tones are rich and sombre, low-keyed and muted. A black background and sleek racing curve produce a futuristic vision of speed and space.

The early exhibitions of O'Keeffe's work (a group show at the 291 Gallery in 1916, and a solo one there in 1917) had commanded critical interest, and in 1921 both she and her work were on exhibition as subjects of Stieglitz's photographs. The sensuality of her work had not escaped notice. Now Stieglitz's photographs presented her both as an artist, with her work on display in the background, and also as a sensuous young woman, nude, her body on display. To her chagrin, O'Keeffe's sexuality became a matter of public speculation, a situation that would persist throughout her life.

In the early 1920s O'Keeffe executed a series of small experimental still lifes. These were based on Dow exercises, exploring the problems of mass, line and colour. The subjects were fruits, vegetables and leaves. The images were representational, though often the colours were not naturalistic. The forms were simplified, detail eliminated. Perspective was manipulated: depth was flattened and space compressed. Two-dimensional design took precedence over three-dimensional realism, and the result was clean stylised shapes and flat, unshaded masses in strong colour dynamics. In these works O'Keeffe revealed the influence of another member of the Stieglitz circle: the photographer Paul Strand, who had produced a series of brilliant abstract photographs in 1915. He exploited the mechanical manipulation that the camera lens makes possible, and through focusing, cropping, tilting and magnification, he transformed realistic subjects into pure abstractions. O'Keeffe had been struck by this approach, and now began to explore its possibilities. The process of magnification would become a brilliant and powerful component of her work. Whereas Strand had used this device to strip his subjects of identity, rendering their enlarged images as unidentifiable abstractions, O'Keeffe's use of magnification was entirely her own: she enlarged her subjects to intensify their specific identity, to increase their importance and to dramatise their emotional power. The subjects that she chose for this process were plant forms. Although she painted other botanical examples, the one she portrayed over and over again for more than a decade was the flower.

The series of magnified flowers is one of O'Keeffe's most powerful and perhaps the one for which she is best known. By her own account, this resulted from the consideration of two things: a small flower still life by Fantin-Latour, and the mood of speed and technological excitement that permeated New York at the time. Technology was the movement of the age, an exciting, limitless force based on logic. Its manifestations were dazzling: huge structures, blinding speed, unimaginable potency. By contrast, the small Fantin-Latour flower represented the force of nature: quiet, instinctive and intimate. O'Keeffe believed that nature was the equal of technology and made her flowers into potent presences: "I thought I'd make them big like the huge buildings going up. People will be startled – they'll *have* to look at them and they did" (Kuh *op. cit.* quoted in Robinson 1989).

O'Keeffe's statement resulted in a series of vivid and arresting pictures. *Black Iris III* (1926; Metropolitan Museum of Art) and *Red Poppy* (1927; private collection, repr. Washington 1987) are representative. In both these paintings, a voluptuous amplitude joins with a sense of overwhelming intimacy. The soft, yielding surfaces, the rapturous colours of the poppy, the subtle translucent veils of the iris and the hidden, vulnerable heart of both infuse these paintings with great dramatic depth. Again O'Keeffe produced images that were at once explicitly feminine and explicitly powerful.

The critical response to the flower paintings focused on sexuality. "The show", one critic wrote of her 1939 exhibition, "is one long, loud blast of sex..." (Lewis Mumford, quoted in Robinson 1989, p.282). The images of flowers, with their trembling, fragile layers of tissue, leading to a central, secret heart, were perceived as obvious references to female genitalia. This response was inevitable: Freud's theories of sexuality were popular topics in the artistic community, and O'Keeffe's work was a perfect target. Sex, like beauty, is in the eye of the beholder; the critic finished by admitting that "...perhaps only half the sex is on the walls; the rest is probably in me" (*idem*). He was right: in fact, O'Keeffe's flowers are botanically quite precise, and her pictures are no more prurient than the plants themselves. She used the flower as a metaphor for the emotional world, not the physical one. The statement they made was one of unsettling intimacy, powerful, bold and enchantingly beautiful. The notion of such an intimacy was disturbing to many viewers, and the insistent declaration of sexuality can be read as an attempt to deny the more profound, and truly unsettling nature of the work.

O'Keeffe and Stieglitz spent winters in Manhattan and summers at the Stieglitz family house in upstate New York. Increasingly, O'Keeffe felt stifled among the large clan, and in the summer of 1926 she left for four weeks alone in Maine. The result was a series of subdued but potent paintings, the most powerful of which are *Closed Clam Shell* and *Open Clam Shell* (private collections, repr. Washington 1987). In both these paintings the single magnified form, dignified and monumental, nearly fills the small rectangular canvas. The enlarged form in the modest space gives the subject a quiet and resonant

O'Keeffe: *Black Cross, New Mexico*, 1929; oil on canvas; 99 × 77.2 cm.; Art Institute of Chicago, Purchase Fund (1943.95)

presence. The power is emotional, as in the flower paintings, but the tone of the *Clam Shells* is very different. The palette is cool and muted, restricted entirely to neutral greys and whites. The shells themselves are smooth and hard, their surfaces impenetrable. In one the revealed opening is barely there; in the other it is inexorably shut in a cool line of denial. If the flower paintings suggest passionate vulnerability, the clam shells imply containment and prohibition, the closed and coupled self.

In 1926 O'Keeffe showed her first urban landscape. Previously, she had drawn exclusively on the natural world for subject matter; now she began to celebrate the smooth towering forms of the new skyscrapers (e.g. *City Night*, 1926; Minneapolis Institute of Arts). The simplification of the shapes and the sophisticated manipulation of perspective emphasise height and distance, giving the buildings dramatic monumentality. In these works atmospherics are as important as the buildings themselves: light, sky, wind, weather and darkness are all powerful compositional elements. O'Keeffe's reductive approach included not only the forms of the buildings but the idea of the city itself. The paintings contain no hint of the actual, messy, active life of the metropolis. They show only the sleek geometric buildings: no cars, no street life and, most strikingly, no people. This is true of almost the entire body of O'Keeffe's work: seldom did she portray a living creature. The animation is interior, however. Most of her works can be read as analogues of the human form or of the human heart; they body forth a powerful emotional state.

O'Keeffe spent the summer of 1929 in New Mexico, near Santa Fe, where she began to record the dry magical landscape. In *Black Cross, New Mexico* (1929; see illustration) the huge shape presses against the picture plane, sombre and threatening, a black symbol of prohibition. Oppressive, severe, it dominates the composition, nearly obliterating the earth and sky beyond it. The painting derives its formal strength from the powerful cruciform shape. Behind the inexorable black geometry of the cross, however, lies a countering force: voluptuous turbulence in the ripple of purple-red hills stretching out to the horizon. This is a recurrent theme in O'Keeffe's work: the dynamic juxtaposition of stern order and riotous passion.

In the early 1930s O'Keeffe began another great series: animal bones. "The bones seem to cut sharply to the center of something that is keenly alive on the desert even tho' it is vast and empty and untouchable – and knows no kindness with all its beauty" (*Georgia O'Keeffe*, exh. cat., An American Place, New York, 1939). In terms of composition, the bones are treated like the flowers: they are enlarged, centred, simplified, sometimes cropped. The mood and the palette are different, however: the bones are far cooler presences than the radiant flowers, more meditative, less demonstrative. They are closer in palette and mood to the muted, contained shells. The smooth osseous shapes, in O'Keeffe's hands, take on a mythic resonance. They suggest an interior strength, tranquil, remote and enduring. Their pearly forms gleam against flat fields of colour – sometimes the sky, sometimes the red hills, sometimes both, enigmatic and beautiful.

In late 1932 O'Keeffe developed severe psychological symptoms, and was hospitalised for a nervous breakdown in early 1933. She did not work again until early 1934. That year she returned to New Mexico, discovering the Abiquiu area, with its astonishing colours. The Abiquiu paintings are of mesas, cliffs and hills: soft collapsing forms, voluptuous run-offs of pink sandstone beneath high bluffs, round mounds of red siltstone. With their smooth curving forms, soft yielding sensuous shapes, lapped and folded layers and radiant rosy hues, they are strongly suggestive of the female body. The landscapes themselves seem animated, glowing with the artist's radiant response to this new world. From 1935 to 1946 O'Keeffe painted this lyrical landscape, celebrating the rich glowing colours, the pellucid light, the tender rounded hills and the endless and crystalline space (e.g. *Cliffs Beyond Abiquiu*, 1943; repr. *Georgia O'Keeffe* 1976).

O'Keeffe continued to paint animal skulls, their dry porous surfaces polished and smoothed by her brush. Calm, mystical and symmetrical, their shining iconic presences hang clean and centred against the picture plane, before the vast radiant space of New Mexico. In *From the Faraway Nearby* (1937; Metropolitan Museum of Art) a deer skull hangs serenely and mysteriously in the clear air, above a distant line of soft, pale, dreamlike hills. The antlers have been magically augmented; three tiers of them curve against the deepening blue of the sky. The painting reverberates with the combination of beauty, intimacy and haunting distance that characterises some of O'Keeffe's best work.

In the early 1940s O'Keeffe began a new bone series, focusing on the pelvis. This signalled a return to orificial imagery: "I like empty spaces", she said. "Holes can be very expressive" (Calvin Tomkins, "The rose in the eye looked pretty fine", *New Yorker*, 4 March 1974). In this series the bone is suspended against the sky, the ovoid shape central and dominant. The smooth white form is stark, at once abstract and realistic, set against a deep blue space. The paintings combine echoes of both birth and infinity; the sky behind the bones is clear and endless.

In 1946 Stieglitz died. O'Keeffe spent the next three years in New York, settling his estate and painting very little. In 1949 she moved to New Mexico for good and began painting again, but a change had taken place. After Stieglitz's death, O'Keeffe's work lost emotional content. Absent now were those qualities – yielding tenderness, turbulent passion, cold rage – that gave her earlier work such strength. During the 1950s she produced an austere series based on a rectangular wooden door in an adobe wall at Abiquiu. Large, handsome and implacable, the paintings contain a certain majesty, but little emotional power. What strength they have is purely formal. The moods and subjects of the works became increasingly remote. In 1958 she painted the beguiling *Ladder to the Moon* (artist's estate, repr. *Georgia O'Keeffe*, 1976), in which a ladder hangs diagonally and mysteriously against the deepening evening sky. This is an image of transition: the ladder is suspended half-way between earth and air, under a half-moon, at twilight. This strongly suggests the journey from earth to heaven; its psychological content is more spiritual than emotional.

O'Keeffe's last important works are the *Sky above Clouds* series of 1963–5. These enormous canvases are based on the view from an aeroplane. In *Sky above Clouds IV* (1965; Art Institute of Chicago) rows of small puffy white clouds are laid out schematically, in neat horizontal layers, beneath a tranquil sky. The shapes are rhythmic and repetitive, part of a strong decorative pattern. The scale is majestic. Ordered, peaceful and serene, the paintings suggest a sublime removal: there is no earth here, only sky. O'Keeffe lost her central vision in the early 1970s, and died in 1986.

Georgia O'Keeffe is one of the great artists of the 20th century. An early abstractionist, she explored formal and modernist concerns through her imaginative use of focus, scale and perspective. She was a breathtaking colourist, with a rich and vivid range of resonant hues. The greatest strength of O'Keeffe's work, however, lies in its emotional power. At a time when rage and coldness were fashionable, she was not afraid to paint passion, rapture and joy, as well as anger, resentment and withdrawal. The real subject of her paintings is the wide, intense, highly charged spectrum of emotion itself. It is for this remarkable contribution that we are most deeply indebted to her.

ROXANA ROBINSON

See also Training and Professionalism survey 10

Oosterwijck, Maria van
Dutch painter, 1630–1693

Born in Nootdorp, near Delft, 27 August 1630; father and grandfather both ministers in the Dutch Reformed Church. Moved to Amsterdam, 1672 or 1673. Never married, but brought up her orphaned nephew. Died in Uitdam, north of Amsterdam, 12 November 1693.

Bibliography

Jacob Campo Weyerman, *De levens-beschryvingen der Nederlantsche konstschilders en schilderessen* [Lives of the Netherlandish male and female painters], The Hague, 1729–69, ii, pp.262–5

Gerard de Lairesse, *Groot schilderboek* [Great book of painting], ii, 1740, p.360

Arnold Houbraken, *De groote schouburgh der Nederlantsche konstschilders en schilderessen* [The great theatre of Dutch male and female painters], 2nd edition, Amsterdam, 1753, ii, pp.214–18

Jean-Baptiste Descamps, "Marie van Oosterwyck/Eleve de David de Heem", *Vie des peintres flamands et hollandais*, ii, Marseille, 1842, pp.166–8

Johannes Immerzeel, "Oosterwijk, Maria van", *De levens en werken der Hollandische en Vlaamsche kunstschilders, beeldhouwers, graveurs en bouwmeesters, van het begin der vijftiende eeuw tot heden* [The lives and works of the Dutch and Flemish painters, sculptors, engravers and architects, from the beginning of the 15th century to the present], 3 vols, Amsterdam, 1842–3, ii, pp.280–28

Christiaan Kramm, *De levens en werken der Hollandsche en Vlaamsche kunstschilders, beeldhouwers, graveurs en bouwmeesters* [The lives and works of the Dutch and Flemish painters, sculptors, engravers and architects], iv, Amsterdam, 1859

A.L.G. Bosboom-Toussaint, *De bloemschilderes Maria van Oosterwijck* [The flower painter Maria van Oosterwijck], Leiden, 1862; reprinted in *Verzamelde werken van A.L.G. Bosboom-Toussaint* [Collected works of A.L.G. Bosboom-Toussaint], Rotterdam, 1899, pp.289–418

J.A. Worp, *De gedichten van Constantijn Huygens* [The poems of Constantijn Huygens], viii, Groningen, 1898 (contains poems relating to van Oosterwijck, pp.137 and 163)

Abraham Bredius, "Das Nachlass-Inventare von Juriaen Pool", *Künstler-Inventare: Urkunden zur Geschichte der holländischen kunst de XVIten, XVIIten und XVIIIten Jahrhunderts*, 8 vols, The Hague: Nijhoff, 1915–22, iv, p.1257

—, "Archiefsprokkelingen: Een en ander over Maria van Oosterwyck 'vermart Konstschilderesse'" [Gleanings from the archives: Assorted findings on Maria van Oosterwijck, "famous woman painter"], *Oud-Holland*, lii, 1935, pp.180–82

Remmit van Luttervelt, *Schilders van het stilleven* [Painters of still life], Naarden, 1947

Laurens J. Bol, *Holländische Maler des 17. Jahrhunderts nahe den Grossen Meistern: Landschaften und Stilleben*, Braunschweig: Klinkhardt und Biermann, 1969

Women Artists, 1550–1950, exh. cat., Los Angeles County Museum of Art, and elsewhere, 1976

Rosa Lindenburg, "Maria van Oosterwijck, 17th-century Dutch painter", *Woman Art*, ii/1, Fall 1977, p.17

Mary Ann Scott, *Dutch, Flemish and German Paintings in the Cincinnati Art Museum*, Cincinnati: Cincinnati Art Museum, 1987

Flowers and Nature: Netherlandish Flower Painting of Four Centuries, exh. cat., Nabio Museum of Art, Osaka, and elsewhere, 1990

Jan Davidsz. de Heem en zijn Kring [Jan Davidsz. de Heem and his circle], exh. cat., Centraal Museum, Utrecht, and Herzog Anton Ulrich-Museum, Braunschweig, 1991

Die Karl und Magdalene Haberstock-Stiftung, exh. cat., Munich and Augsburg, 1991

Paul Taylor, *Dutch Flower Painting*, New Haven and London: Yale University Press, 1995

Maria van Oosterwijck, the most highly esteemed Dutch woman artist before Rachel Ruysch (q.v.), was Holland's first internationally recognised woman artist. She painted still lifes exclusively. Her earliest-known dated work is from 1667, and her latest, 1689. According to Arnold Houbraken, her first biographer, she received painting instruction from "Jan Davidsz. de Heem of Utrecht", a crucial figure in the evolution of flower painting because of the way in which he combined the exuberance of Flemish still life with the naturalism of Dutch flower painting. Recent scholars have questioned Houbraken's statement since de Heem was residing in Antwerp during van Oosterwijck's youth. They have doubted that she ever actually had contact with him. Her understanding of his particular painterly conventions and techniques, however, suggests that she did study directly under him. De Heem probably began visiting the northern Netherlands again on a frequent basis around 1658, which seems to be the most logical time of contact with van Oosterwijck, particularly since de Heem did not develop the type of flower piece that influenced her until about 1650. In 1658 van Oosterwijck would have been 28, admittedly a late start for a painter, but presumably she would have studied with another master before de Heem. Houbraken stated that she showed talent at an early age, but provided no particulars.

Van Oosterwijck kept a painting studio in Delft until she moved to Amsterdam in 1672 or 1673. According to Houbraken, the flower painter Willem van Aelst visited her Delft studio and proposed marriage to her there. Not wanting to marry, but not wanting to hurt van Aelst's feelings by rejecting him outright, van Oosterwijck devised an agreement with her suitor, knowing that his restless temperament would prevent him from living up to it: if he painted every day for a year she would marry him. Since van Aelst's studio window was directly across the street from hers, van Oosterwijck, who worked religiously each day, was able to see whether or not he was at the easel. At the end of the year, when van Aelst came to claim her hand, she pointed out the large number of marks she had made on her window ledge, each one representing a day he had missed work. The tale appealed to the 19th-century novelist Bosboom-Toussaint, who transformed it into a theatrical historical romance with accompanying sketches by Willem Steelink. One illustration shows van Aelst on his knees in van Oosterwijck's studio, pleading with her as she turns away. Houbraken placed the marriage proposal episode in Delft, but it may well have occurred in Amsterdam where by 1676 the two painters lived opposite each other on the Nieuwe Keizersgracht (the reflection of a gabled house across the street in two of van Oosterwijck's paintings, in Städtische Kunstsammlungen, Augsburg, and Palazzo Pitti, Florence, may be a reference to van Aelst).

Curiously, the only contemporary documents that connect the two households record a conflict between them. The dispute arose when van Oosterwijck's housemaid, Geertje Pieters, went to van Aelst's house to retrieve a raincoat that her mistress had left there. Van Aelst's maid, Grietge, refused to hand over the coat and showered Pieters and van Oosterwijck with insults, calling them "beasts", "fat cows" and "sows", until a deputy sheriff arrived to break up the disturbance. Van Oosterwijck subsequently lodged formal complaints to the city when she and Pieters were threatened with physical assault by this same servant. From various sources we know that van Oosterwijck's relationship with her maid was unusually close. She even taught Pieters to paint in her manner, an act that became the subject of a poem by Constantijn Huygens in 1677. Pieters's only known flower-piece, featuring van Oosterwijck's trademark sunflower, is in the Fitzwilliam Museum, Cambridge.

Some writers have suggested that van Oosterwijck had some formal training with van Aelst, but this is unlikely. His work is more sumptuous than hers, with such props as silver vases and gold-fringed drapery, rather than the simple glass containers on naked stone or cold marble that van Oosterwijck preferred. What is more, the two artists knew each other at the point when they were already mature painters.

Van Oosterwijck's move to Amsterdam coincided with her increasing success in finding an international circle of wealthy, royal patrons. From the late 1660s until the 1680s, royal art collectors sought to include examples of her work in their galleries. After Louis XIV of France purchased one of her paintings, several other monarchs followed suit: William of Orange and Queen Mary (900 florins for one painting), Jan Sobieski known as August II, King of Poland (2400 Dordrecht guilders for three paintings), and the Elector of Saxony (two flower-pieces and one festoon for 1500 florins). Emperor Leopold of Austria and his wife were so delighted with the painting they purchased from her that they sent her portraits of themselves in frames encrusted with diamonds as a token of their esteem. Van Oosterwijck's success was rivalled by only one other female Dutch painter, Rachel Ruysch, but although van Oosterwijck worked for a greater number of monarchs, she never attained a formal court appointment. Houbraken described van Oosterwijck as unusually devout. She spent large amounts of money on charitable gestures. For example, on several occasions she purchased the freedom of Dutch soldiers who had been captured by Algerian pirates (as recorded in Amsterdam archival documents). The ransom she paid per person was fl. 750 – a considerable sum, equivalent to more than two years' salary of a tradesman in the period.

Houbraken reported that because Maria van Oosterwijck was an exceedingly slow, meticulous painter, works by her were rare. Today only about 20 are known, and most are flower (or flower with fruit) pieces. The lists of her works published in Thieme-Becker and Wurzbach are unreliable, as Ann Sutherland Harris has pointed out (Los Angeles 1976). Autograph paintings are housed in public collections at Augsburg (Städtische Kunstsammlungen), Cincinnati (Cincinnati Art Museum), Copenhagen (Statens Museum for Kunst), Dresden (Gemäldegalerie Alte Meister), Florence (Palazzo Pitti), The Hague (Mauritshuis), London (Kensington Palace, formerly in Hampton Court), Prague (National Gallery), Sacramento (Crocker Art Museum) and Vienna (Kunsthistorisches Museum).

In her work, van Oosterwijck used the artistic conventions developed by de Heem to achieve maximum naturalistic effect. She placed brightly illuminated floral arrangements against dark backgrounds, often within shallow stone niches, so that the shapes would stand in highest possible relief. She included a profusion of incidental insects and shiny water droplets among a great variety of flowers and leaves, to call attention to the carefully crafted spatial relationships existing between the individual elements. In contrast to de Heem, however, van Oosterwijck preferred a colour scheme of juxtaposed warm hues – reds, pinks, ochres, yellow-whites and, particularly, acidic yellow-oranges that would be highly discordant if they were not placed so artfully within her designs. Another preference was a heavy sunflower at the apex of a bouquet (Dresden and The Hague), as well as striped ribbon grasses hanging down in forked patterns to the left or right of a vase.

Van Oosterwijck painted on canvas, copper and panel, and usually signed her paintings with her full name on the edges of painted table tops. Her signatures are made to look as though they have been chiselled into the stone or marble. Perhaps the most memorable and poetic personal trademark in her still lifes is a butterfly – the *Vanessa atalanta*. It can be found in most of her major works, with its wings half spread, resting gently on a book (Kunsthistorisches Museum, Vienna), a ledge (Cincinnati Art Museum and Palazzo Pitti, Florence) or on a stem within a bouquet. Van Oosterwijck employed the "character" of the butterfly to lead the viewer into her paintings, and to direct attention to the heart of her artistic intention.

Van Oosterwijck's paintings seem to be particularly thoughtful and precise expressions of her deep religious beliefs. In the tradition of 17th-century Dutch still life, her works contain symbolic references to the vanity of earthly existence, the transience of all material things, and the need to attend to one's soul by dedicating one's life to God, for only through God can one's soul transcend the perishable world. Without labouring the point, van Oosterwijck would judiciously place an animated element or "protagonist" within the composition, which would then direct the gaze of the viewer to the heart of her message.

Two works stand out as particularly refined examples of these moral messages. The *Vanitas* painting dated 1668 (see illustration), which Harris identified as the work purchased by Leopold I (*ibid.*), depicts a thick, dog-eared tome entitled

Oosterwijck: *Vanitas*, 1668; Kunsthistorisches Museum, Vienna

Rekeningh ("reckoning") surrounded by examples of earthly vanity and transience: a skull, a bag of money, a half-eaten ear of corn, a globe, an hour-glass, books, flowers and a glass flask of *aqua vitae* reflecting a self-portrait of the artist at her easel. The Dutch word *Rekeningh* refers to the settling of an account, but in the context of this painting, the account is one's earthly life. The butterfly, the protagonist in the picture, rests on the title page of the book at the centre of the painting; it appears to be so light that it barely weighs down the sheet of paper it rests upon. Directly above its wing-tips are the words: *Wy Leeúen om te sterúen/En /Sterúen om te leeúen* ("We live to die and die to live"). They underline the fact that the butterfly symbolises both the Resurrection of Christ and that of the human soul on Judgement Day. This bitter-sweet quality found in van Oosterwijck's best works is seldom found in *vanitas* paintings by other artists of the period, who might pile mountains of skulls on a table in an effort to drive home their message.

The second work, a bouquet of flowers in a carved ivory vase (c.1670; Mauritshuis, The Hague), is crowned by a conspicuous sunflower in full bloom. The flower is so named because it turns its face towards the sun, a symbol for Christ or God. On the table next to the bouquet is the lid of the beaker, which has, as its finial, a striking figure of Venus, the pagan goddess of physical love. She seems to have been sharply interrupted while in the process of bathing. Her arm is still raised and her gaze is frozen on the head of the sunflower above, as though she has discovered a beauty that is much greater than her own. This interpretation is reinforced by the putti and satyrs at her feet and on the nearby vase who continue to play with a goat (Bacchus's mount) because they cannot see the divine light above.

The fact that van Oosterwijck remained unmarried without children, choosing instead to lead a quiet life painting highly finished floral bouquets, attracted attention. Early writers, who were struggling to find a way of dealing with the emerging phenomenon of the professional woman artist, generally did so by drawing moral parallels between traditional female virtues and the paintings that women produced. Being unmarried, however, van Oosterwijck did not neatly fit the model of devoted wife and mother. As a result, she never seems to emerge from these accounts as a truly three-dimensional personality; likewise, the very personal qualities of her work are, for the most part, left unexamined. (Those who wrote about Rachel Ruysch a generation later, on the other hand, had an easier time reconciling the artist's profession with her role as a wife and mother: Ruysch emerged as a delightful "Lady Bountiful" who painted cornucopias of fruit and flowers while producing ten children.) A great admirer of van Oosterwijck, the poet Dirk Schelte, for example, wrote a verse celebrating the incredible beauty both of the artist's painted bouquets and her personal character (i.e. chastity and religiosity) in 1673. An unusual double portrait attributed to Gerard de Lairesse (with Gooden and Fox Ltd, London, in 1958) pairs van Oosterwijck with Schelte and seems to illustrate the poem. Van Oosterwijck is posed rather awkwardly in the guise of a painter-muse, gazing at the poet with her brushes and palette in hand, inspiring him to write. The choice to show the unmarried van Oosterwijck with the married Schelte, in the intimate double portrait format usually reserved for married couples, was extremely bold. A more traditional portrait of the artist seated alone with her two interests, the Bible in her right hand and her palette in her left, was painted by Wallerant Vaillant in 1671 (Rijksmuseum, Amsterdam).

MARIANNE BERARDI

See also Guilds and the Open Market survey

Oppenheim, Meret

Swiss multi-media artist, 1913–1985

Born in Berlin-Charlottenburg, Germany, 6 October 1913; grew up in the Bernese part of the Canton Jura, and educated at various German and Swiss schools. Studied at the Kunstgewerbeschule, Basel, 1929–30; briefly attended the Académie de la Grande Chaumière, Paris, 1932. Met Jean Arp and Alberto Giacometti, and invited to exhibit with the Surrealists at the Salon des Surindépendants, Paris, 1933; participated in international Surrealist exhibitions in Copenhagen and Tenerife (1935), London and New York (1936) and Amsterdam (1938), and in the exhibition of fantastic furniture with Max Ernst, Leonor Fini and others at Galerie René Drouin et Leo Castelli, Paris, 1939. Returned to Basel, 1937; attended the Allgemeine Gewerbeschule for two years, supporting herself by restoring paintings. Entered a long depression. Associated with the Swiss Gruppe 33, and later Allianz (Union of Swiss Painters), officially becoming a member in 1948. Married Wolfgang la Roche, 1949; he died 1967. Entered a new phase of creativity in the mid-1950s, increasingly expanding her oeuvre to include writing. Recipient of Art Award, city of Basel, 1974; Grand art prize, city of Berlin, 1982. Died in Basel, 15 November 1985.

Selected Individual Exhibitions

Galerie Schulthess, Basel: 1936
Galerie d'Art Moderne, Basel: 1952
A l'étoile scellée, Paris: 1956
Galerie Riehentor, Basel: 1957, 1959
Galleria Schwarz, Milan: 1960
Galerie Gimpel und Hanover, Zürich: 1965
Moderna Museet, Stockholm: 1967 (retrospective)
Galerie Krebs, Bern: 1968
Wilhelm-Lehmbruck-Museum, Duisburg: 1972
Galerie Suzanne Visat, Paris: 1973
Galerie Renée Ziegler, Zürich: 1974
Museum der Stadt, Solothurn: 1974–5 (touring retrospective)
Galerie Levy, Hamburg: 1978
Galerie Edition Claude Givaudon, Geneva: 1981
Galerie nächst St Stephan, Vienna: 1982
Nantenshi Gallery, Tokyo: 1984
Musée d'Art Moderne de la Ville de Paris: 1984
Galerie Oestermalen, Stockholm: 1985
Institute of Contemporary Arts, London: 1989 (retrospective)

Selected Writings

"Enquêtes", *Le Surréalisme même*, no.3, 1957, pp.77, 82
"Enquêtes (le striptease)", *Le Surréalisme même*, no.5, 1959, p.58
"Meret Oppenheim spricht Meret Oppenheim: Man könnte sagen etwas stimme nicht", Gedichte, 1933–1969, tape recording, Cologne, 1973; 2nd edition, 1986
Speech given in Basel, 16 January 1975, on receiving the Art Award of the city of Basel, *Kunst-Bulletin des Schweizerischen Kunstvereins*, no.2, February 1975
"Entretien avec Daniel Boone", *L'Humidité*, no.23, 1976, pp.26–7
Sansibar, Basel: Fanal, 1981 (contains poems)
Caroline, Basel: Fanal, 1984
"Das Ende kann nur der Anfang sein", *Wissenschaft und Kunst*, ed. Paul Feyerabend and Christian Thomas, Zürich: Fachvereine, 1984, pp.243–50
Husch, husch, der schönste Vokal entleert sich: Gedichte, Zeichnungen, ed. Christiane Meyer-Thoss, Frankfurt am Main: Suhrkamp, 1984
Aufzeichnungen, 1928–1985: Träume, Bern and Berlin: Gachnang und Springer, 1986
Kaspar Hauser oder die Goldene Freiheit: Textvorlage für ein Drehbuch, Bern and Berlin: Gachnang und Springer, 1987

Bibliography

Lynne M. Tillmann, "'Don't cry…work'", *Art and Artists*, viii, October 1973, pp.22–7 (interview)

Valie Export, "Mögliche Fragen an Meret Oppenheim", *Magna: Feminismus, Kunst und Kreativität*, exh. cat., Galerie nächst St Stephan, Vienna, 1975

Josephine Withers, "The famous fur-lined teacup and the anonymous Meret Oppenheim", *Arts Magazine*, lii, November 1977, pp.88–93

Nicolas Calas, "Meret Oppenheim: Confrontations", *Artforum*, x, Summer 1978, pp.24–5

Ruth Henry, "Meret Oppenheim zum 70. Geburtstag", *Du: Die Kunstzeitschrift*, no.10, October 1983, pp.82–4 (interview)

Liliane Thorn, *Porträt der Künstlerin Meret Oppenheim*, video, RTL, 1984

Jaqueline Burckhardt, "The semantics of antics", *Parkett*, no.4, 1985, pp.22–33

Christiane Meyer-Thoss, "Poetry at work", *ibid.*, pp.34–45

Mary Ann Caws, "Ladies shot and painted: Female embodiment in Surrealist art", *The Female Body in Western Culture*, ed. Susan Rubin Suleiman, Cambridge, MA: Harvard University Press, 1986, pp.262–87

Meret Oppenheim: Legat an das Kunstmuseum Bern, exh. cat., Kunstmuseum, Bern, 1987

Pamela Robertson and Anselm Spoerri, *Imago: Meret Oppenheim*, film, 1988

Bice Curiger and others, *Meret Oppenheim: Defiance in the Face of Freedom*, Cambridge: Massachusetts Institute of Technology Press, 1989 (German original, 1982)

Stuart Morgan, *Meret Oppenheim: An Essay*, text published with 16 postcards of Meret Oppenheim's work in a velvet pocket on the occasion of an individual exhibition at the Institute of Contemporary Arts, London, 1989

Renée Riese Hubert, "From 'Déjeuner en Fourrure' to 'Caroline': Meret Oppenheim's chronicle of Surrealism", *Surrealism and Women*, ed. Mary Ann Caws and others, Cambridge: Massachusetts Institute of Technology Press, 1991, pp.37–49

Bettina Brandt, *The Coming of Age of the Child-Woman: Meret Oppenheim, Surrealism and Beyond*, PhD dissertation, Harvard University, 1993

Josef Helfenstein, *Meret Oppenheim und der Surrealismus*, Stuttgart: Hatje, 1993

Isabel Schulz, *Edelfuchs und Morgenrot: Studien zum Werk von Meret Oppenheim*, Munich: Silke Schreiber, 1993

Renée Riese Hubert, *Magnifying Mirrors: Women, Surrealism and Partnership*, Lincoln: University of Nebraska Press, 1994

Bettina Brandt, "Meret Oppenheims Inkognito: (De)maskierung und Reflexion in Meret Oppenheims Filmskript *Kaspar Hauser oder die Goldene Freiheit*", *Der Imaginierte Findling Studien zur Kaspar-Hauser Rezeption*, ed. Ulrich Struve, Heidelberg: Universitätsverlag C. Winter, 1995, pp.144–62

Meret Oppenheim's most frequently reproduced work, *A Demi-Tasse, Saucer and Spoon Covered in Chinese Gazelle Fur* (1936; Museum of Modern Art, New York), was the young artist's contribution to Alfred Barr's exhibition *Fantastic Art, Dada, Surrealism*, the first Surrealist show in the USA. The hairy lining transformed the ordinary teacup purchased at a Parisian department store into an exquisite Surrealist object; the unspoken invitation to bring one's lips to the fetishised vessel immediately provoked unfamiliar gastronomic and erotic associations. It was not until 1938 that André Breton christened the object *Le Déjeuner en fourrure* ("Luncheon in fur"). He chose the object's title as a play on Manet's famous painting *Le Déjeuner sur l'herbe* (1863; Musée d'Orsay, Paris), where fully clad male students lunch on the grass in the company of female nudes, and Sacher-Masoch's *Venus im Pelz* (1869), a *Bildungsroman* about a fur-wearing, whip-bearing woman, Wanda, and her slave, the narrator Severin. Treated increasingly cruelly, Severin finally loses his fascination with the submissive role when he is almost killed by Wanda and her latest conquest. Now opting for the dominator's role himself, he understands that "woman, as nature created her, is his enemy and can only be his slave or his dominatrix but never his companion". From the beginning, Oppenheim rejected Breton's title with its inherent repetition of unequal, patriarchal relations between the sexes, but the clever object, nevertheless, became canonised under the Surrealist leader's heading.

The most widely disseminated image of Oppenheim herself is not one of her own painted self-portraits but a famous Man Ray photograph entitled *Erotique voilée*, originally published in the Surrealist journal *Minotaure* in May 1934. Here the 20-year-old artist, standing nude behind a printing wheel, which simultaneously hides and covers her striking, partly blackened physique, is cast as Surrealism's latest muse: as *femme-enfant* or "child-woman" who enables the older, male Surrealist artists to go beyond the constraints of their bourgeois society. This particular Surrealist muse, a type predominant in the 1930s, was equipped with the power to transform sight into artistic vision, providing the male Surrealist artist with a convulsive image from which he subsequently constructed his work of art. She was the creative medium through which he channelled his own, otherwise difficult to access, artistic unconscious. In his riddle-ridden, often quoted invitation to Oppenheim's first solo exhibition in 1936, her former lover Max Ernst purposefully reinforced this child-woman image: "WOMAN IS A SANDWICH COVERED IN WHITE MARBLE. Who covers a soup spoon in precious fur? Little Meret. Who has outpaced us? Little Meret."

Initially, Oppenheim certainly profited from these personal and artistic connections with the more established Surrealist artists, but ultimately her uninhibited personality and the dramatic success of one particular work – the scandalous fur-lined teacup – created a persistent but all too narrow basis for her international fame.

Shortly before the outbreak of World War II, when a large number of Surrealists were getting ready to leave Paris, Oppenheim returned to Switzerland, where she soon lost faith in herself. She experienced an artistic and human crisis that lasted for almost 18 years. The artist herself once explicitly described this state of shattered self: "I felt as if millennia of discrimination against women were resting on my shoulders, as if embodied in my feelings of inferiority" (Curiger 1989). Oppenheim, who did not want to become known as the artist who lines things, progressed only slowly from enchanting muse and instant Surrealist hit to mature artist in her own right. Many of the works she created during her depression were destroyed by Oppenheim herself, reworked later or simply not shown to the public at all. Two of these works in particular show an increasingly de-stabilising, de-individualised image of the artist. Her oil painting *Stone-Woman* (1938; private collection, Bern, repr. Curiger 1989) depicts a female figure, made out of large boulders, resting at a stream with only her legs immersed in water, and in her drawing *Future Self-Portrait as an Old Woman* (1938; private collection, Basel, *ibid.*) the artist, at the age of 25, aged her features relentlessly to reflect accurately her inner state of mind. Oppenheim's self-questioning regarding the tension between woman as creative artist and

Oppenheim: *Ma gouvernante*, 1936; 14 × 21 × 33cm.; Moderna Museet, Stockholm

woman as subject on whose youthful body others had projected powerful and provocative images continued throughout her work. During these difficult years, Oppenheim studied the writings of Carl Gustav Jung intensively. His article "Woman in Europa" (1924) was especially influential on her artistic philosophy. Regretfully, this Jungian influence has led to certain simplified views on Oppenheim's works that unduly limit the perspective on her varied oeuvre.

Once her depression subsided, the artist, now in her early forties, rented a studio in Bern and designed masks and costumes for Picasso's *How to Catch Wishes by the Tail*. That same year she also created *Le Couple*, a pair of partially laced brown boots, grown together at the toes, with their leather tongues showing. Her work from this period is deeply connected to her earlier work, particularly in its relation to femininity and its constructions. In 1959 Oppenheim organised a banquet, served on the naked body of a female acquaintance and entitled *Spring-Feast*, for several of her intimate friends. Later that same year Breton asked the artist to contribute the *Feast* to the eighth *Exposition InteRnatiOnale du Surréalisme* (EROS) at the Galerie Cordier in Paris. For an enthusiastic public, Oppenheim's *tableau vivant* best captured the spirit of the shocking Surrealist exhibition as a whole. But Oppenheim, apprehensive about her participation early on, was annoyed when her private "feast for both men and women" was reduced to a voyeuristic spectacle where men once again could feast on the female body as a passive object of desire. This was the last time that the artist exhibited with the Surrealists; Oppenheim's work no longer had much in common with the latest generation of Surrealists.

A retrospective at the Moderna Museet in Stockholm in 1967 marked the beginning of the revival of interest in Oppenheim's work. A year or two later, she even made fun of her own "Luncheon in fur". She created the *Souvenir du Déjeuner en fourrure* (Museum of Modern Art, New York), a small, kitsch version of the famous original, explicitly undermining and cashing in on the continued marketability of her early signature work. By now her art had found a new public. At the age of 70 she was asked to participate in the Documenta at Kassel, the most significant European exhibition for contemporary art, organised every five years. There she displayed her latest works among those of 167, often significantly younger, post-modern colleagues. Meret Oppenheim's skilful undermining and ironic fetishisation of precisely those elements that have traditionally contributed to notions of "femininity" in art and society eventually gained the attention of such up-and-coming women artists as Valie Export, who recognised her as a role-model.

BETTINA BRANDT

Oppenheimer, Olga
German painter and graphic artist, 1886–1941

Born in Cologne, 9 July 1886, into a Jewish family. Studied in Munich and Dachau, 1907, then under Paul Sérusier in Paris, 1909. Opened studio and private art school, the Mal- und Zeichenschule Olga Oppenheimer, at the Gereonshaus, Cologne, 1909. Co-founder, Gereonsklub, Cologne, 1911. Married restaurant owner Adolf R. Worringer, 1913; two sons, born 1914 and 1916; divorced 1936. Ended artistic production, 1916. Committed to the Waldbreitbach sanatorium near Neuwied, 1918. Deported to Lublin concentration camp, Poland, 1941; died of "epidemic typhus", 4 July 1941.

Principal Exhibitions

Wallraf-Richartz-Museum, Cologne: 1910 (*Kölner Künstlerbund*), 1911 (*Graphik Kölner Künstler*)
Cologne Secession: 1912, 1913
Städtische Ausstellungshalle, Cologne: 1912 (*Sonderbundausstellung*)
Kunstsalon Friedrich Cohen, Bonn: 1913 (*Rheinische Expressionisten*)
International Exhibition of Modern Art, "Armory Show", New York: 1913 (touring)

Bibliography

Internationale Kunstausstellung des Sonderbundes Westdeutscher Kunstfreunde und Künstler zu Cöln 1912, Cologne, 1912
Georg Eugen Lüthgen, "Die Ausstellung der Kölner Sezession", *Deutsche Kunst und Dekoration*, xxx, 1912, pp.136–7
Elisabeth Erdmann-Macke, *Erinnerungen an August Macke*, Stuttgart, 1962
Wolfgang Macke, ed., *August Macke-Franz Marc*, Cologne, 1964
Die Rheinischen Expressionisten: August Macke und seine Malerfreunde, exh. cat., Städtisches Kunstmuseum, Bonn, and elsewhere, 1979
Max Ernst in Köln: Die rheinische Kunstszene bis 1922, exh. cat., Kölnischer Kunstverein, Cologne, 1980
Wulf Herzogenrath, "Die Tradition aktueller Kunstausstellungen in Köln", *Frühe Kölner Kunstausstellungen: Sonderbund 1912. Werkbund 1914. Pressa UDSSR 1928. Kommentarband zu den Nachdrucken der Ausstellungskataloge*, Cologne: Wienand, 1981, pp.12–19
Franz M. Jansen, *Von damals bis heute: Lebenserinnerungen*, Cologne, 1981
Ernst-Gerhard Güse, ed., *August Macke: Gemälde, Aquarelle, Zeichnungen*, Munich: Bruckmann, 1986
Werner Frese and Ernst-Gerhard Güse, eds, *August Macke: Briefe an Elisabeth und die Freunde*, Munich: Bruckmann, 1987
Shulamith Behr, *Women Expressionists*, Oxford: Phaidon, and New York: Rizzoli, 1988
Milton W. Brown, *The Story of the Armory Show*, 2nd edition, New York: Abbeville, 1988
Magdalena M. Möller, *August Macke*, Cologne: DuMont, 1988
Andreas Hüneke, ed., *Der Blaue Reiter: Dokumente einer geistigen Bewegung*, Leipzig: Reclam, 1991
Hildegard Reinhardt, "Olga Oppenheimer (1886–1941): Eine Kölner Malerin und Graphikerin", *Kölner Museums-Bulletin*, i, 1991, pp.19–32
——, "Olga Oppenheimer und die Kölner Sezession", *Wegweiser durch das jüdische Rheinland*, ed. Ludger Heid and Julius H. Schoeps, Berlin, 1992, pp.341–5
——, "Olga Oppenheimer und Emmy Worringer: Zwei Kölner Künstlerinnen zu Beginn des 20. Jahrhunderts", *Köln der Frauen*, ed. Irene Franken and Christiane Kling-Mathey, Cologne, 1992, pp.261–73
Jutta Dick and Marina Sassenberg, eds, *Jüdische Frauen im 19. und 20. Jahrhundert: Lexikon zu Leben und Werk*, Reinbek bei Hamburg: Rowohlt, 1993
Die Rheinischen Expressionisten, 1913: Der Schock der Moderne in Bonn, Schriftenreihe des Vereins August Macke-Haus, no.8, Bonn, 1993
Der Gereonsklub, 1911–1913: Europas Avantgarde im Rheinland, Schriftenreihe des Vereins August Macke-Haus, no.9, Bonn, 1993
Rheinische Expressionistinnen, Schriftenreihe des Vereins August Macke-Haus, no.10, Bonn, 1993

Olga Oppenheimer's artistic career was brief, lasting from 1907 to 1916, and the size of her oeuvre is not known. Only ten works survive, five of which are illustrations. These indicate that her subjects were mainly still lifes, figures and illustrations of literary sources. As most of her work is lost, probably destroyed, due to dramatic personal and political circumstances, it is difficult to assess her artistic standing. She was included in Shulamith Behr's *Women Expressionists* (1988), with Käthe Kollwitz (q.v.), Paula Modersohn-Becker (q.v.), Gabriele Münter (q.v.) and Marie von Malachowski (q.v.). Rather than Expressionist elements, however, her few surviving works show the influence of the Dachau circle and the Pont-Aven school.

The daughter of a fabric wholesaler, Max Oppenheimer, she studied first in Germany and then in Paris with Paul Sérusier, a companion of Gauguin in Pont-Aven, Brittany. In 1909 she established a studio in the Gereonshaus in Cologne, built by her father, as well as the Mal- und Zeichenschule Olga Oppenheimer. This studio was the first base of the Gereonsklub (1911–13), an "important emporium for modern art in Germany" (Joachim Heusinger von Waldegg) founded by Oppenheimer, Emmy Worringer and Franz M. Jansen. An exhibition and discussion forum, the Gereonsklub became a centre of contemporary avant-garde art in the Rhineland, presenting Der Blaue Reiter, Franz Marc, Paul Klee, Robert Delaunay and others for the first time in Cologne. It was probably through Emmy that she met the distinguished art-loving Worringer family, and in 1913 she married the restaurant owner Adolf R. Worringer.

Oppenheimer first showed her work in 1910 at the second exhibition of the Kölner Künstlerbund. The intense controversy surrounding this exhibition polarised the art community and led to the founding of the Cologne Secession. She participated in both the Secession exhibitions of 1912 and 1913, showing portraits and still lifes. Through the Gereonsklub, she was acquainted with Alfred Hagelstange, Alfred Flechtheim, August Macke, Karl Ernst Osthaus and Richart Reiche, the initiators of the important international *Sonderbund* exhibition in Cologne in 1912, in which, with Marie Laurencin (q.v.),

Oppenheimer: *Venice Motif*, 1907; woodcut; 11.5 × 11.5 cm.

Modersohn-Becker and others, she exhibited a still life (untraced). In 1913 she exhibited two still lifes (untraced) at the *Rheinische Expressionisten* exhibition organised by Macke and members of the Graurheindorfer circle at the Kunstsalon Cohen. Most sensational is her participation, as the only female German artist, in the Armory Show, which opened in New York in 1913 and toured to Chicago and Boston. There she showed a series of six woodcuts, *Van Zanten's Happy Time* (untraced), based on an extremely popular contemporary drop-out novel by Laurids Bruun, which was also treated by Max Pechstein, Georg Schrimpf and others.

Three woodcuts by Oppenheimer, *Harvest*, *Nude, Backview* and *Venice Motif* (all dated 1907; private collection, Milan), are inscribed Munich, Dachau and Venice respectively. The coloured woodcut genre scene *Harvest* depicts the bent figure of a gleaner and at the left two standing female figures wrapped in flowing robes and headscarves, the stylistic elements clearly derived from the Pont-Aven artists. Behind the three figures, who act as if they were on a stage, broad cornfields undulate up to the high horizon, marked by a frieze of tightly planted trees. The play of light and shadow modulates the dark, flat figures of the foreground as well as the bright fields. The right half of *Venice Motif* (see illustration) is marked by the rear view of a passer-by; the rest of the picture depicts slightly moving water, framed by numerous paths, stairs, walls and a bridge. Here, too, Oppenheimer concentrates on the exploration of light and dark tones, relinquishing strong contours for a more developed structuring of planes. The woodcut no doubt derives from a study trip to Venice that she probably made in 1907 from Munich or Dachau. The subject matter, formal composition and design of these prints, their strong contrasts of light and shade, distinct ornamental quality and two-dimensionality, indicate close links with artists of the Neue Dachauer, mainly Ludwig Dills, as well as with

those of the Munich magazine *Jugend*, founded in 1896 by Georg Hirth.

Through Sérusier, Oppenheimer became acquainted with Gauguin's style, and her *Portrait Study* (1913) and *Couple* (no date; both untraced, repr. *Die Rheinischen Expressionistinnen* 1993) reflect Sérusier's mediations of synthesism. Her artistic development, chiefly influenced by French avant-garde art, ended abruptly due to the onset of mental illness in 1916, during World War I. Committed to a sanatorium in 1918, she was deported in 1941 to Poland, where she died, presumably a victim of the National Socialist euthanasia programme.

Oppenheimer's posthumous rehabilitation began with two exhibitions: *Die Rheinischen Expressionisten: August Macke und seine Malerfreunde*, held in Bonn, Krefeld and Wuppertal in 1979, and *Max Ernst in Köln* in Cologne (1980). The August Macke-Haus in Bonn, dedicated to Expressionism in the Rhineland, honoured her work in three exhibitions: *Die Rheinischen Expressionisten 1913* (1993), *Der Gereonsklub (1911–13)* (1993) and *Rheinische Expressionistinnen* (1993–4).

HILDEGARD REINHARDT

Orléans, Princess Marie Christine d'

French amateur artist, 1813–1839

Born in Palermo, Sicily, 12 April 1813, the youngest daughter of Louis-Philippe, Duke of Orléans. Returned to France with her family, 1826; father crowned King of the French, 1830. Taught drawing and sculpture by the painter Ary Scheffer and studied sculpture under David d'Angers. Married Alexander Frederick William, Duke of Württemberg, 1837; son born 1837. Died in Pisa, Italy, 2 January 1839.

Selected Writings

Une correspondance inédite de la princesse Marie d'Orléans, duchesse de Wurtemberg, ed. Marthe Kolb, Paris: Boivin, 1937

Bibliography

Jules Janin, "La princesse Marie de Wurtemberg", *L'Artiste*, 2nd series, ii, 1839, pp.117–21
Trognon, *Notice sur la vie de Mme la princesse Marie d'Orléans, duchesse de Wurtemberg*, Paris, 1840
Harriet Grote, *Memoir of the Life of Ary Scheffer*, London, 1860
Catalogue des oeuvres de feu Barye, Hôtel Drouot, Paris, 1876
Luc-Benoist, *La Sculpture romantique*, Paris: Renaissance du Livre, 1928
Images de Jeanne d'Arc, exh. cat., Hôtel de la Monnai, Paris, 1979
The Romantics to Rodin: French Nineteenth-Century Sculpture from North American Collections, exh. cat., Los Angeles County Museum of Art, and elsewhere, 1980
Gert Schiff, "The sculpture of the 'Style Troubadour'", *Arts Magazine*, lviii, June 1984, pp.102–10
Un âge d'or des arts décoratifs, exh. cat., Grand Palais, Paris, 1991
Susan Waller, *Women Artists in the Modern Era: A Documentary History*, Metuchen, NJ: Scarecrow Press, 1991

In the July Monarchy, Princess Marie Christine d'Orléans, the youngest daughter of Louis-Philippe, King of the French, and Queen Marie-Amélie, embodied the ideal lady artist: pious,

Orléans: *Joan of Arc*, commissioned 1835; marble; Palais de Versailles, Paris

serious and earnest, she preferred elevated subjects and patriotic heroines.

Her education was typical of a woman of her class: she was watched over by a governess who had very strict standards of propriety and was given drawing lessons from a private instructor. The lessons she began at the age of 12 were with the distinguished German-born painter Ary Scheffer, who was a family friend. He later remembered that she refused to be confined to copying from prints or casts, which typically formed the most substantial part of the amateur artistic education of upper-middle-class women. Nevertheless, her lessons were firmly circumscribed by the conventions of ladylike behaviour, as Scheffer later recalled: "Restricted to the copying of draped figures (and these abundantly draped), the Princess remained of necessity unacquainted with the structure of the

human body" (Grote 1860, pp.40–41). She attempted historical compositions in watercolour, and in an effort to find a form that would challenge rather than frustrate her, Scheffer encouraged her to try sculpture: "a walk of art wherein I was equally unpractised with herself, and which therefore offered to both of us the attraction of novelty" (*ibid.*, p.42). She took to it readily, executing literary and historical subjects as bas-reliefs and works in the round. Scheffer sought out subjects suitable for a young princess; she particularly favoured themes from Goethe and Schiller, although she also completed a study of Charlotte Corday.

In 1835, when Louis-Philippe offered her the commission for a life-size sculpture of *Joan of Arc* (see illustration) after Jean-Jacques Pradier failed to provide the king with a satisfactory design, she accepted on the condition that if she produced a successful model it would be completed. With Scheffer's assistance, the princess produced a wax *maquette* for a sculpture that was executed by Auguste Trouchaud, the *practicien* who completed several works for her. Installed at the palace of Versailles, which Louis-Philippe had dedicated as a museum, it was her most important work and was reproduced in bronze for the town square of Orléans and in small casts by the Susse Frères foundry for private collections.

Joan of Arc had been a popular subject for paintings during the Restoration. The princess represented her dressed in armour, praying before leading French forces into battle against the English. She has set aside her helmet and gloves and stands with head bowed, holding her unsheathed sword over her breast. The introspective mood and medieval theme of the work has been linked to the Troubadour style, the precise and precious form of anecdotal history painting that flourished in the Empire and continued to be produced up to the Revolution of 1848. The figure's self-contained and pensive reverie contrasts markedly with the aggressive masculinity and extroverted gestures of the Horatii in Jacques-Louis David's *Oath of the Horatii* (1785; Louvre, Paris), which represented French patriotic ideals to an earlier generation. Scheffer called Princess Marie's *Joan of Arc* the finest modern sculpture at Versailles: "Not only does its impressive attitude, its simplicity and its distinctive feminine character contrast favourably with certain vulgar productions among which it stands, but it carries upon itself the stamp of the genius and the elevation of soul possessed by its author" (*ibid.*, pp.45–6).

In the princess's public image in France, her piety was conflated with her artistic identity. When Ary Scheffer – who recalled in his memoir that as a young girl she was spirited and headstrong – painted her portrait in 1833 (*Princess Marie d'Orléans*; Cleveland Museum of Art), he showed her seated pensively in her studio, which was said to be arranged for meditation as well as sculpture. She died of pulmonary disorder six years later, at the age of 25, two years after her marriage to the Duke of Württemberg, and was widely and publicly mourned in France. The art critic Jules Janin noted her intelligence, charm and modesty; the poet Alfred de Musset her piety, grace and modesty. Sébastien Delarue's commemorative statuette (repr. Los Angeles 1980, cat.110) represented her gazing heavenwards, with the fashionable narrow waist and sloping shoulders that characterise other figurines of famous personalities. Posthumously, in 1842, one of the princess's designs was completed as a collaborative work for the mausoleum of her brother the *Duc d'Orléans* (Chapelle Saint-Ferdinand, Neuilly), who was accidentally killed: Henri de Triquête completed the figure of the dead duke and Marie d'Orléans's kneeling angel was set at his head, gazing heaven-wards.

SUSAN WALLER

Orloff, Chana [Orlova, Khana]
Russian sculptor, 1888–1968

Born in Tsare-Konstantinovka, Ukraine, 12 July 1888. Moved with her family to Palestine, 1905. Travelled to Paris, 1910; already active as a sculptor. Enrolled at the Ecole Nationale des Arts Décoratifs, 1911; studied sculpture at the Académie Russe; soon established contact with Guillaume Apollinaire, Jean Cocteau, Max Jacob, Picasso and other bohemian artists and writers. Met Modigliani, 1912. Married the poet Ary Justman, 1916; one son; husband died 1918. Granted French citizenship, 1925. First trip to New York, 1928. Maintained an interest in Jewish cultural affairs, particularly in the establishment of a new museum in Tel Aviv, 1930s. Lived in Switzerland, 1943–5, then returned to Paris. Continued to work and travel, especially in Israel, until her death, exhibiting widely. Chevalier, Légion d'Honneur, 1925; Sociétaire, Salon d'Automne, Paris, 1925. Died in Tel Aviv, 18 December 1968.

Principal Exhibitions

Individual
Galerie Briant Robert, Paris: 1925
Galerie Druet, Paris: 1927
Weyhe Galleries, New York: 1929
Tel Aviv Museum of Art: 1935, 1949, 1952, 1961–2 (touring retrospective), 1969 (touring retrospective)
Galerie George Moos, Geneva: 1945
Galerie de France, Paris: 1946
Wildenstein Galleries, New York: c.1946
Herzliya Museum of Art, Israel: 1965

Group
Salon d'Automne, Paris: from 1913
Galerie Bernheim Jeune: 1915 (with Matisse, Rouault and van Dongen)
Salon des Indépendants, Paris: from 1918
Petit Palais, Paris: 1937 (*Les Maîtres de l'art indépendant*)

Bibliography

Léon Werth, *Chana Orloff*, Paris: Crès, 1927
Edouard des Courières, *Chana Orloff*, Paris: Gallimard, 1927
Haim Gamzu: *Chana Orloff*, Tel Aviv: Massada, 1951 (Hebrew text)
Chana Orloff (1888–1968): Exposition retrospective, exh. cat., Tel Aviv Museum of Art, and elsewhere, 1969
Chana Orloff: Sculptures et dessins, exh. cat., Musée Rodin, Paris, 1971
Haim Gamzu and others, *Chana Orloff*, Brescia: Shakespeare, 1980
Felix Marcilhac, *Chana Orloff*, Paris: Editions de l'amateur, 1991 (catalogue raisonné)

Born in the Ukraine into a Jewish family, Chana Orloff was one of several important sculptors who emigrated from the Russian Empire and Eastern Europe to Paris in the early 20th century, others being Alexander Archipenko, Jacques Lipchitz and Ossip Zadkine. While hardly nostalgic of her Ukrainian birthplace, Orloff maintained a lifelong allegiance to Israel, often sculpting Jewish friends, visiting Jerusalem and Tel Aviv, and designing monuments for several kibbutzim; after World War II she also received commissions for monuments honouring Jewish women and the Jewish resistance. Even so, Orloff

Orloff: *Bust of Rubin*, bronze; Brooklyn Museum, New York; Bequest of Frank E. Williams

was part of the international avant-garde in Paris in the 1910s and 1920s, counting Apollinaire, Foujita, Modigliani and Diego Rivera among her friends, and open to the many influences that coloured the artistic environment at that time – from Cézanne and Gauguin to African sculpture and Cubism. Elements of a moderate Cubism can be detected in several of her early portraits, such as *Eve* (1916; wood) and the *Jewish Painter* (1920; plaster), while Modigliani's melodious line recurs in *Head of a Woman* (1912; wood).

But in observing many methods, Orloff also developed her own style – what one critic has called "Expressionist Naturalism" (J. Cassou in Gamzu 1980, p.223) – that is, characterised by acuity of form and exaggeration of feature or accessory, such as a nose or a pair of spectacles. Sometimes the result borders on the grotesque or the satirical, as in the cement portrait of *Georges Lepape* (1924), and in all cases Orloff uses a single component to summarise the whole. The face or head is at the axis of Orloff's *oeuvre*, therefore, and for this reason she is remembered above all for her diverse portraits, from *Alexandre Mercereau* of 1922 to *Antoine Berheim* of 1926, from the *Rabbi* of 1930 to the portrait of the *Artist's Son* of 1939. This ability to see the general in the particular also extends to Orloff's remarkable renderings of birds and animals, almost psychological portraits that bring to mind the concurrent work of the Soviet animalists Ivan Efimov and Vasily Vatagin.

JOHN E. BOWLT

Osborn, Emily Mary
British painter, 1834–after 1908

Born 1834, the eldest child of an Essex clergyman; family moved to London from West Tilbury, 1848. Studied at Mr Dickinson's Academy, Maddox Street, London, under John Mogford, a minor landscape painter, then privately with James Matthew Leigh, portrait and history painter, at his home and at his gallery in Newman Street, London. Acquired a studio in London, c.1855; later also one in Glasgow. Signed petition demanding admission for women to Royal Academy Schools, 1859. Spent time working in Germany from 1861; visited Algeria, c.1881–2. Recipient of silver medal, Society for the Encouragement of the Fine Arts, 1862; first prize (60 guineas) for the best historical or figure subject at Crystal Palace Picture Gallery, 1864. Member, Society of Lady Artists. Never married but lived with her friend Miss Dunn. Died after 1908.

Principal Exhibitions
Royal Academy, London: 1851–67, 1870–73, 1875, 1877, 1880, 1884
British Institution, London: 1852–4, 1856
Society of British Artists, London: occasionally 1857–88 (silver medal 1862)
Dudley Gallery, London: 1872, 1877 (oil), 1889 (watercolour)
Society of Lady Artists, London: from 1875
Paris Salon: 1879, 1881
Grosvenor Gallery, London: 1882–4, 1887–8, 1890
Goupil Gallery, London: 1886 (individual)

New Gallery, London: from 1888
Society of Portrait Painters, London: 1896

Bibliography
James Dafforne, "British artists: Their style and character. lxxv: Emily Mary Osborn", *Art Journal*, 1864, pp.261–3
"Selected pictures: *God's Acre*", *Art Journal*, 1868, p.148
Ellen C. Clayton, *English Female Artists*, 2 vols, London: Tinsley, 1876
Jeremy Maas, *Victorian Painters*, London: Barrie and Rockliff, and New York: Putnam, 1969
Women Artists, 1550–1950, exh. cat., Los Angeles County Museum of Art, and elsewhere, 1976
Charlotte Yeldham, *Women Artists in Nineteenth-Century France and England*, 2 vols, New York: Garland, 1984
Pamela Gerrish Nunn, *Victorian Women Artists*, London: Women's Press, 1987
Deborah Cherry, *Painting Women: Victorian Women Artists*, London and New York: Routledge, 1993

Emily Mary Osborn was a Victorian genre painter who specialised in the theme of victimised and distressed young women. She could be described as the female equivalent of Richard Redgrave, a better known Victorian painter of tragic social themes, although there would appear to have been no connection between them. Osborn's best-known painting, *Nameless and Friendless* (1857; see illustration), which depicts an impoverished young female artist attempting to sell her work to a supercilious-looking art dealer, has in recent years become an icon of feminist art history. The picture contains subtle references to the plight of the single woman in search of employment: standing nervously twisting her ringless fingers as the dealer casts a judgemental eye over her work, she is as much an object of male scrutiny as her painting, as two men behind her appear to compare her with the short-skirted, bare-legged dancer in the print that they are examining. Like the governess, also a subject depicted by Osborn in 1860, the woman in *Nameless and Friendless* has been driven to exploit meagre skills acquired in girlhood, learned specifically to enhance her femininity, in order to pursue the unfeminine activity of earning her own living. For contemporary critics the picture told simply of the pathos of the unfortunate girl who "will doubtless have to retrace her steps through the pitiless rain to try her fortune elsewhere, and, not improbably, be compelled at last to leave her work in the hands of some pawnbroker for the advance of a small sum of money to support herself and her brother" (Dafforne 1864, p.261). There is a preparatory drawing for this painting in the Ashmolean Museum, Oxford, falsely signed "Millais".

In fact, Osborn herself was one of the more successful female artists of her day, winning wealthy patrons, selling pictures to Queen Victoria (*My Cottage Door*, 1855; *The Governess*, 1860; both Royal Collection; replica of *The Governess* in Yale Center for British Art, New Haven) and exhibiting regularly at the Royal Academy from the age of 17 in 1851 until 1884 when she was 50 years old. Also, her work regularly drew positive comment from the reviewers of the day. *The Governess*, for example, was described as a work of "rare power, the production of a comprehensive mind manifesting a thorough knowledge of the capabilities of Art" (*Art Journal*, 1860, p.170). The picture was exhibited with a quotation from

Osborn: *Nameless and Friendless*, 1857; private collection

Longfellow's poem "Evangeline", taken out of context, but pointing in an uplifting manner to the moral of the subject:

> Fair was she and young, but alas! before her extended
> Dreary, and vast, and silent, the desert of life, with its pathway
> Marked by the graves of those who had sorrowed and suffered before her.
> Sorrow and silence are strong, and patient endurance is godlike

In common with other British women artists of the mid- to late 19th century, Osborn displayed a predilection for female subjects expressing sadness and suffering. Often her pictures portray two young women, presumably sisters, facing adversity together. In *For the Last Time* (1864; 91.5 × 71.1 cm.; collection R.K.F. Brindley) two girls in mourning try to summon up the courage to enter the room where a parent or guardian lies dead. In *God's Acre* (in the possession of the publishers of the *Art Journal* in 1868), exhibited in Mr Wallis's Winter Exhibition in Pall Mall, London, in 1866, two young girls sheltering beneath a large red umbrella struggle across a snow-covered graveyard to place an ivy wreath upon their parents' grave. The *Art Journal* of 1868 offered subscribers an engraving of the picture by H. Bourne, in itself an indication of Osborn's popular success. The peasant dress of the children and the Continental style of the gravestones identify this as one of the works that Osborn produced in Germany, where she spent part of her career. *Half the World Knows Not How the Other Half Lives* (1864) deals with the poignant subject of the death of a child in a shoemaker's attic room and won Osborn first prize for historical painting in oils at the Crystal Palace.

Primarily a genre painter, often of works with genteel or whimsical titles – *Home Thoughts* (1851), *Pickles and Preserves* (1854), *Tough and Tender* (exh. Royal Academy 1859; silver medal, Society of British Artists, 1862), *Private and Confidential* and *Slow and Sure* (1863) – Osborn also took on lucrative portrait commissions. *Mrs Sturgis and Children* (1855; Collection Robert Peerling Coale, Chicago), which portrays a Bostonian family and was exhibited at the Royal Academy that year, earned Osborn 200 guineas, enough to pay for a new studio. She has posed the figures in an open-air seaside setting reminiscent of William Powell Frith's *Life at the Seaside (Ramsgate Sands)*, which won great attention at the

Royal Academy the previous year, an influence of which Osborn must have been aware. Another well-known Osborn portrait is of the founder of Girton College, Cambridge, *Barbara Leigh Smith Bodichon* (118 × 96 cm.; Girton College, Cambridge, presented in 1884). Osborn was one of the women artists associated with Bodichon's Langham Place Circle, publishers of the *English Woman's Journal* and campaigners for women's rights, and one of the 39 signatories of the letter of April 1859, sent to 40 Academicians and printed in *The Athenaeum*, which argued for women's access to the Royal Academy Schools.

Osborn painted a number of history pictures, the most notable of which is the *Escape of Lord Nithisdale* (sic) *from the Tower in 1716* (1861; oil on canvas; private collection, repr. Nunn 1987, fig.5), a subject suggested by an extract from a letter written by the Countess of Nithsdale to her sister Lady Mary Herbert, describing how her husband was smuggled out of prison in women's clothing. From the 1830s stories from Scottish history were popular with women artists, and this picture is extraordinary for the emphasis it puts on the heroism of the Countess, to whom the begowned Nithsdale clings, weak, frightened and dependent on his wife. The praise that met this picture was, as ever, accompanied by surprise at the achievement: "The subject of this picture is a bold one for a lady, and she has treated it with more strength and historical power than usually ascribed to her sex" (*Art Journal*, 1861, p.169).

Osborn's range included some literary subjects, such as *Isolde* and *Hero Worship in the Life of Johnson*, landscape – she had a one-woman show of landscape paintings of the Norfolk Broads at the Goupil Gallery in New Bond Street in 1886 – Algerian subjects (*An Algerian Mirror*, 1889) and an unusual picture of women workers, the *Bal Maidens* (1870s; 70 × 91 cm.; National Museum of Wales, Cardiff). The Bal Maidens were skilled surface workers in the Cornish tin mines, but Osborn conforms to Victorian notions of womanhood and does not show the women at work but presents them as neat, clean, orderly figures, unstained by the red tin ore, walking through a picturesque landscape.

JANE SELLARS

Ostroumova-Lebedeva, Anna
(Petrovna)

Russian painter and graphic artist, 1871–1955

Born Anna Petrovna Ostroumova in St Petersburg (later Petrograd/Leningrad), 5 May (Old Style calendar)/17 May (New Style calendar) 1871. Attended gymnasium and Stieglitz School of Technical Drawing, St Petersburg; entered the Academy of Arts, St Petersburg, studying painting under Ilya Repin, 1892; spent a year in Paris, studying at Académie Carmen Rossi under James McNeill Whistler, 1898–9; completed studies at St Petersburg Academy, 1900. Travelled widely and participated in exhibitions in Russia and abroad from 1900. Married the chemist Sergei Lebedev, 1905; he died 1934. People's Artist of the Russian Republic, 1951; active member, Academy of Arts, 1951. Died in Leningrad, 5 May 1955.

Principal Exhibitions

Individual
St Petersburg: 1911
Rumyantsev Museum, Moscow: 1916
Kazan: 1927
State Russian Museum, Leningrad: 1940
Society of Chamber Concerts, Leningrad: 1942

Group
Mir Iskusstva (World of Art), St Petersburg: 1900–24
Salon d'Automne, Paris: 1906 (*Exposition de l'art russe*)
SRKh (Union of Russian Artists), St Petersburg: 1906
Vienna Secession: 1908 (*Moderne russische Kunst*)
Makovsky Salon, St Petersburg: 1908–9
Izdebsky Salon, Odessa: 1909–10 (*International Exhibition*, touring)
SRKh (Union of Russian Artists), Kiev, Moscow and St Petersburg: 1910
Exposition Universelle, Brussels: 1910
Esposizione Internazionale, Rome: 1911
Petrograd: 1919 (*First State Free Exhibition of Painting*)
Galerie La Boétie, Paris: 1921 (*Artistes russes du Monde de l'Art*)
Grand Central Palace, New York: 1923–4 (*Russian Art*, touring)
Venice Biennale: 1924
Leningrad and Moscow: 1932–3 (*Artists of the RSFSR over 15 Years, 1917–1932*)
Moscow: 1939 (*All-Union Industry of Socialism*)

Selected Writings

Avtobiograficheskiye zapiski [Autobiographical notes], 3 vols, Leningrad, 1935–51; reprinted Moscow: Izobrazitelnoye Iskusstvo, 1974
Mastera iskusstva ob iskusstve [Masters of art on their art], ed. A.A. Fyodorov-Davydov and G.A. Nedoshivin, vii, Moscow: Iskusstvo, 1970, pp.373–97 (selections from diaries and letters)

Bibliography
A. Benois and S. Ernst, *Ostroumova-Lebedeva*, Moscow and Prague, n.d.
V. Kurbatov, *Peterburg: Khudozhestvenno-istoricheskiy ocherk i obzor khudozhestvennogo bogatstva stolitsy* [Petersburg: Art-historical essay and survey of artistic treasures of the capital], St Petersburg, 1913 (suite of 26 engravings)
V.N. Petrov and A.A. Sidorov, "Grafika", *Istoriya russkogo iskusstva* [History of Russian art], ed. I.E. Grabar, x/2, Moscow: Akademiya Nauk, 1969, pp.228–35
Vsevolod Petrov and Alexander Kamensky, *The World of Art Movement in Early 20th-Century Russia*, Leningrad: Aurora, 1991

Anna Ostroumova-Lebedeva was one of the artists who transformed engraving from a reproductive medium to an independent expressive art form. A pioneer in colour xylography and lithography, she was the first in Russia to combine aspects of European chiaroscuro prints and Japanese colour woodblocks to create her own style of colour engraving, and became best known for her landscapes and city vistas, especially of St Petersburg and Venice.

Anna was the second of six children in a prosperous St Petersburg family; her father worked in the Ministry of Finance. When Anna was five, their house burned down. Her mother saved the children by wrapping them in quilts and throwing them from the balcony into the garden, but Anna had nightmares, and hallucinations, even as an adult. She later believed that the early trauma had given her a strong attraction to bright colours (*Avtobiograficheskiye zapiski*, i, pp.30–31). She learned to read early and enjoyed drawing; at ten she entered a gymnasium. She had to leave school when diphtheria kept her in bed for months, but she amused herself by drawing and at 18 decided to attend the Central School of Technical Drawing, founded by Baron Stieglitz (Shtiglitz).

The school's director, the architect Maksimilian Mesmakher, taught preliminary classes to give pupils a sound foundation, and Ostroumova also learned about rendering architecture and ornamental detail from him. The well-known engraver Vasily Mate was her main instructor. Despite this good beginning, Ostroumova had doubts about an artistic career. She worried that her drawing was self-indulgent, but she had an urgent desire to create something that would endure after her death (*ibid.*, i, p.52). Her mother opposed her desire of entering the Academy of Arts, fearing that she would draw "naked men"; the rest of the family had little understanding of art. Her decision to take the entrance exam was a step towards autonomy and professional commitment.

At the time of her studies there (1892–6), Russia's "temple of art" was undergoing major reforms. Ostroumova's *Avtobiograficheskiye zapiski* record the atmosphere and activities in lively detail. There were few women students, Ostroumova noted, eight in her own class and a few others a year ahead (*ibid.*, i, p.61). Women had attended the Academy as auditors in the 1840s, but it was only in the 1890s that they were allowed to earn the official title of artist. In 1896 Ostroumova was admitted to the studio of Ilya Repin, a popular teacher who was instrumental in bringing about reforms. Her fellow-students Filip Malyavin and Konstantin Somov painted portraits of her (1896 and 1901; both State Russian Museum, St Petersburg). Like all students, she copied at the Hermitage, especially the works of Rembrandt, and she continued to work on her engraving with Vasily Mate. When he showed her some 16th-century chiaroscuro prints in 1898, Ostroumova was enthralled both by the technical aspects and by the dramatic effects of scale, perspective and stylisation.

Encouraged by Mate and Repin, Ostroumova went to Paris in 1898 to study under James McNeill Whistler at the Académie Carmen Rossi. It was a decisive encounter (*ibid.*, i, pp.146–62). Surprised by the rigid rules – everyone had to use the same size of palette, paint only with colours specified by Whistler himself and mix them according to a special formula – she decided "to submit completely" and acquire the Whistler system, although she reserved judgement as to whether or not it would suit her. She was soon convinced of Whistler's greatness, and was devastated when he looked at her study of a nude and exclaimed: "You can do nothing, you know nothing, I can't teach you!" But after some tutoring from Whistler's apprentice Inez Bates, she was singled out for praise. Ostroumova evidently made an impression on Whistler, because he invited her to come to New York with three other students and to work under his supervision. Although she was flattered by the invitation, she could not afford the trip and was genuinely homesick. Whistler regretted that she had studied for so short a time with him; he begged her to write, tell him about her progress and offered his advice whenever she needed it.

Ostroumova-Lebedeva: *Venice at Night*, 1914; woodcut

Apart from her classes at the Académie Carmen, Ostroumova attended the Académie Colarossi to draw from the model, and she studied the work of Albrecht Dürer, Italian chiaroscuro engraving, and Japanese colour woodcuts at the Bibliothèque Nationale. With Somov, Alexandre Benois and Evgeny Lansere, she visited museums and galleries, and often met her friends at the Benois home to discuss art and music; the circle became the core of the World of Art group. Ostroumova was closely involved with exhibitions and the journal *Mir iskusstva* (World of Art) from 1900, when she exhibited a suite of coloured engravings of landscapes. Each plate required two to four separate blocks, and the works showed Ostroumova's ability to synthesise an effect of nature, a quality, Benois wrote, that distinguished her from both the Impressionists and the Symbolists (Benois and Ernst, pp.14–15).

The city view was one of Ostroumova's major themes. She began with an architectural series to accompany Benois's article "Picturesque Petersburg" in *Mir iskusstva* (1901). Her series of 26 wood engravings (1913) for V. Kurbatov's book on the treasures of St Petersburg was acknowledged to be a masterpiece. She shared a love of historic St Petersburg with Benois, Lansere and Mstislav Dobuzhinsky, who all depicted the city and surrounding parks and palaces. While their prints and drawings were usually done for books or articles in *Mir iskusstva*, Ostroumova was a pioneer in the sphere of independent prints, meant to be displayed separately. Among her notable single plates are *New Holland* (1901; Pushkin Museum of Fine Arts, Moscow), *View of the Neva Through Columns of the Stock Exchange* (1908) and *Mining Institute* (1909; State Russian Museum). Her bold forms exploit the strong tonal contrasts of shadows cast by the slanting northern sunlight, juxtapositions of scale – with large architectural elements such as columns or parts of bridges depicted against distant embankments of the Neva – and emphatic contrasts between rectilinear buildings and the unfilled spaces of the river or sky. More akin to easel painting than to illustration dependent on a text, Ostroumova's works do not merely describe but convey atmosphere and mood, sometimes verging on Expressionism, as in the labyrinthine composition of masts and furled sails in *Petrograd, Rigging* (1917; Pushkin Museum of Fine Arts). The Musée du Luxembourg in Paris was the first to acquire her works in 1905; by 1911 her prints were in Rome, Prague, Dresden and Berlin. Russian museums were slow to act. The Tretyakov Gallery's acquisition committee regretted that they had no graphics department, but in 1916 the director of the Russian Museum, Dmitry Tolstoy, began the collection of original prints and wrote to Ostroumova about including her works (*ibid.*, ii, pp.329–30; iii, p.9).

Ostroumova's career took precedence over her personal life until 1905, when she married her cousin Sergei Lebedev, an organic chemist who later received distinguished honours. The political uprisings of 1905 aroused her liberal sympathies, and the brutal suppression by the government convinced her and many artists of the need to protest. With other World of Art members, she helped to found the satirical journal *Zhupel* (Bugbear), to which she contributed an engraving, *Sarcophagus*, commemorating the victims shot down by imperial troops on 9 January 1905. Ostroumova felt extreme pessimism at the defeat of liberal ideals.

She and her husband left Russia for extended travel in Europe. They were in Paris for the Salon d'Automne of 1906, when Diaghilev's exhibition of Russian art enjoyed tremendous critical success. Ostroumova showed 30 engravings, and she was one of seven Russians awarded honorary membership of the Salon. Travelling between 1906 and 1914, Ostroumova was only tangentially aware of the emerging radical avant-garde in Russia, and she was unprepared to recognise any value in non-figurative and formalist experiments. She herself, however, enjoyed increasing recognition, both in Europe and at home. In the autumn of 1916 the governing council of the Academy of Arts nominated her for the title of Academician. Conservatives protested against the awarding of the title to a woman and the subject was debated until a jurist noted that it was quite legal for women to become Academicians. Three other women, Zinaida Serebryakova (q.v.), Olga Della-vos Kardovskaya and A.P. Shneyder, were also nominated, and the vote was to be held at the meeting of October 1917. By a historical irony, the outbreak of the February Revolution cancelled the session.

Ostroumova greeted the Revolution with enthusiasm, but she also recorded the suffering in *Petrograd: Funeral of the Victims of the Revolution, 23 March 1917* (1917; State Russian Museum). The Civil War years were hard, but she was fortunate in being invited to teach at the newly organised

Institute of Photography and Phototechnology. She took part in the *First State Free Exhibition of Painting* at the former Winter Palace, but she judged that the array of 1000 works representing all tendencies had a confused and exhausting effect, and was sceptical about so-called leftist art (*ibid.*, iii, pp.35–9).

During the 1920s Ostroumova travelled to the Crimea and other parts of Russia. She participated in the important exhibition of Soviet art that opened in New York and toured to other American cities in 1924, and several foreign museums bought her work. In 1926 she went abroad for the first time since 1914, visiting Berlin to see graphic works by Emil Nolde, Ernst Barlach and Käthe Kollwitz (q.v.), which she thought "crude" but often original and beautiful (*ibid.*, iii, pp.104–5). She spent five weeks in Paris, studying contemporary French printmaking and visiting Russian expatriates, Benois, Bilibin, Serebryakova and others, but she never considered leaving her homeland.

The growing conservatism in the Soviet art establishment was not a threat, since Ostroumova's work was representational and technically fine. She took part in the encyclopedic exhibition, *Artists of the RSFSR over 15 years, 1917–1932*, with Leningrad artists representing the range of existing styles. After the death of her husband in 1934, she taught at the Academy of Arts for two years. She worked on her *Avtobiograficheskiye zapiski*, based on her diary and letters, and communicated the extremes of tension and depression experienced by everyone in Leningrad (*ibid.*, iii, pp.225–7). Despite all the difficulties, the director of the State Russian Museum, Nikolai Tsiganov, organised a large personal exhibition for Ostroumova in 1940, with 642 paintings, drawings, lithographs and engravings.

Ostroumova decided to stay in Leningrad when the city was surrounded by German troops in 1941 (*ibid.*, iii, pp.245–302). She described conditions during the siege, when people were seen taking corpses to the cemeteries. During the bombardment, Ostroumova kept writing her diary and worked on drawings and small engravings, until her hands could no longer function because of the cold. She compiled an album of wartime lithographs, and planned to take part in an exhibition honouring the Hero-City when the war was over. Her *Avtobiograficheskiye zapiski* end with the liberation of Leningrad on 27 January 1944. Ostroumova was revered by her younger colleagues as both an artist and a role model. In October 1943 members of the Central House of Art Workers in Moscow honoured Leningrad and Ostroumova herself as "a remarkable artist, a courageous woman and a genuine patriot" (*ibid.*, iii, p.340). In 1951 she was awarded the title of People's Artist of the Russian Republic, and was elected an active member of the Academy of Arts. She died at the age of 84.

ALISON HILTON

Overbeck, Gerta
German painter, 1898–1977

Born in Dortmund, 16 January 1898. Trained as a drawing teacher in Düsseldorf, 1915–18. Studied under Fritz

Burger-Mühlfeld at the Hannover Handwerker- und Kunstgewerbeschule, Hannover, 1919–22; met future members of the Hannover Neue Sachlichkeit group. Drawing teacher in Dortmund, 1922–31; professional artist in Hannover, 1931–8. Briefly married, 1937–8; one daughter. Returned to family home in Cappenberg near Lünen, 1938. Died in Lünen, 2 March 1977.

Principal Exhibitions

Grosse Westfälische Kunstausstellung, Dortmund: 1931
Herbstausstellung westfälischer Künstler, Dortmund: 1932
Herzog Anton Ulrich-Museum, Braunschweig: 1932 (*Die Neue Sachlichkeit in Hannover*)
Kunstverein Hannover: 1962 (*Die zwanziger Jahre in Hannover*)
Kunst- und Museumsverein, Wuppertal: 1967 (*Magischer Realismus in Deutschland, 1920–1933*)
Galerie Hasenclever, Munich: 1973 (*Realismus der zwanziger Jahre*)
Galerie von Abercron, Cologne: 1975 (*Neue Sachlichkeit: 12 Maler zwischen den Kriegen*)
Galerie Krokodil, Hamburg: 1976 (retrospective)

Selected Writings

"Industriebilder", *Der Wachsbogen*, vii–viii, 1932
"Der Blick durch die Wand", *Der Wachsbogen*, xi–xii, 1932, pp.11–13

Bibliography

George Pahl [Gustav Schenk], "Der Weg der jungen hannoverschen Maler", *Der Wachsbogen*, no.1, November 1931, p.4
——, "Die Situation der jungen Maler", *idem*
Werner Mirow, "Junge niedersächsische Kunst: Die Malerin Gerta Overbeck", *Hannoversches Tageblatt*, no.330, 29 November 1934, supplement *Kunst und Schriftum*, no.24
Die zwanziger Jahre in Hannover, exh. cat., Kunstverein Hannover, 1962
Wieland Schmied, *Neue Sachlichkeit und Magischer Realismus in Deutschland, 1918–1933*, Hannover: Fackelträger, 1969
Neue Sachlichkeit in Hannover, exh. cat., Kunstverein Hannover, 1974
Ursula Horn, "Zum Schaffen einer progressiven Künstlergruppe der zwanziger Jahre in Hannover", *Bildende Kunst*, xxiii, 1975, pp.172–6
Ursula Bode, "Sachlichkeit lag in der Luft: Zwanziger Jahre: Bilder einer Malprovinz", *Westermanns Monatshefte*, cxx/8, 1976, pp.34–43
Die zwanziger Jahre im Porträt: Porträts in Deutschland, 1918–1933, exh. cat., Rheinisches Landesmuseum, Bonn, 1976
Künstlerinnen international, 1877–1977, exh. cat., Schloss Charlottenburg, Berlin, 1977
Gottfried Sello, "Gerta Overbeck", *Brigitte*, no.10, 1978, p.375
Hildegard Reinhardt, "Gerta Overbeck (1898–1977): Eine westfälische Malerin der Neuen Sachlichkeit in Hannover", *Niederdeutsche Beiträge für Kunstgeschichte*, xviii, 1979, pp.225–48
——, "Gerta Overbeck: Malerin der Neuen Sachlichkeit", *Lady International*, xxviii, May 1979, p.4
——, "Gerta Overbeck: Späte Anerkennung", *Artis*, vii, July 1980, pp.18–19
Grethe Jürgens, Gerta Overbeck: Bilder der zwanziger Jahre, exh. cat., Bonner Kunstverein, Bonn, 1982
Domesticity and Dissent: The Role of Women Artists in Germany, 1918–1938, exh. cat., Leicester Museum and Art Gallery, and elsewhere, 1992
Marsha Meskimmon, *Women Artists and the Neue Sachlichkeit: Grethe Jürgens and Gerta Overbeck*, PhD dissertation, Leicester University, 1992
Marsha Meskimmon and Shearer West, eds, *Visions of the "Neue Frau": Women and the Visual Arts in Weimar Germany*, Aldershot: Scolar Press, 1995
Marsha Meskimmon, *The Art of Reflection: Women Artists' Self-Portraiture in the Twentieth Century*, London: Scarlet Press, and New York: Columbia University Press, 1996

Gerta Overbeck's best-known works are those she produced during the 1920s and 1930s while associated with the Hannoverian Neue Sachlichkeit (New Objectivity). Certainly, these were her most prolific years and after 1937 she went into partial retirement in Cappenberg by Lünen where she brought up her only child, a daughter. During the 1950s the artist took classes in glass painting and produced some small-scale religious works, but nothing comparable to her production during the years of the Weimar Republic.

Overbeck met the other students who would form the Hannover Neue Sachlichkeit group in the graphics class of Fritz Burger-Mühlfeld at the Hannover Handwerker- und Kunstgewerbeschule in 1919. This group, which included Grethe Jürgens (q.v.), Erich Wegner, Ernst Thoms and Hans Mertens, stood in opposition to the middle-class art politics of Hannover that clearly favoured abstraction. By affiliating themselves with realism and the local, working-class areas of the city, they developed a certain political viewpoint in their art.

Overbeck herself joined the Communist Party (KPD) briefly in the period and shared her fellow artists' commitment to anti-bourgeois art production. Her relationship to the group was modified, however, by the economic crises of the 1920s; in 1922 Overbeck moved to Dortmund to teach drawing because she could no longer support herself in Hannover. Although she remained in Dortmund until 1931, she suggested in later interviews that it was Hannover that was her artistic home. This distance, however, critically affected the work she produced and tended to marginalise her slightly from the Hannoverians (for example, she did not show with them until the early 1930s).

Unlike conservative, mercantile Hannover with its quaint "old town", Dortmund was in the centre of the industrial Ruhr, which, especially in the early 1920s, was an area of political upheaval. Overbeck was the only one of the Hannover group to represent workers' revolts and strike violence in her works: *Wounded Revolutionary* (1921; private collection, repr. Bonn 1982) and *Worker Revolt* (1922; private collection, repr. Meskimmon 1992). This more pointed political cast was not merely coincidental; neither was the fact that the industrial landscape became a major theme in her work at this time.

In Dortmund Overbeck lived with a mining family and experienced at first hand the industrial landscape of the Ruhr. Such works as *White House on the Slag-Heap* (c.1930; Galerie Krokodil, Hamburg) and *Industrial Landscape* (1927; private collection, *ibid.*) show the dominance of the heavy industries over the small communities in which the workers lived. Interestingly, however, Overbeck's industrial landscapes place the domestic situations of the workers and their families in the foreground. As a woman artist, her access to the spaces of industrialism would have been just these: the spaces of the domestic overshadowed by the machines, mills and refuse of industry.

In addition to her industrial landscapes, Overbeck's paintings, like those of her fellow Hannoverian artist Jürgens, frequently depicted the multi-faceted realms of women's outside work. In the *Rug Beaters* (1926) and *Servant Girl* (1929; both Galerie Krokodil) Overbeck represented the usually unseen activities of domestic servants. While the representation of women doing housework was relatively common in the period, it was far less usual to represent women who worked outside their own homes as domestic servants. Additionally, Overbeck produced a small sketch, *Prostitute* (1922; private collection, *ibid.*), which critically undercut the ubiquitous representations of prostitutes as symbols of urban decadence in the period. In her work Overbeck represented the prostitute during the day, in a chemist's shop, purchasing contraceptives (a large douche). This look at the prostitute as a worker, rather than a seductress or tragic figure, reinforces the fact that, as a woman artist, living in working-class neighbourhoods, Overbeck's experience of prostitution would not have been that of a male artist; she was not placed as a client, simultaneously appalled and attracted.

The *Self-Portrait at an Easel* (1936; private collection, repr. Meskimmon and West 1995) marks Overbeck's move into semi-retirement in Cappenberg. Having lived in Hannover from 1931 to 1938, taking an active part in the activities of the Neue Sachlichkeit group, including helping to print their short-lived journal *Der Wachsbogen*, her decision to have and bring up a child on her own necessitated a return to her family home. The self-portrait shows Overbeck pregnant and painting; it is a powerful statement about the difficulties of being both an artist and a mother, and the relationships between creativity and procreativity.

Overbeck's years in Dortmund and Hannover were her most prolific and the ones from which her best-known works derived. During the early 1930s she was most consistently shown and discussed as part of the Neue Sachlichkeit group. The Third Reich and World War II ended the activities of the Hannoverians for the most part, with Mertens dying in the war, Jürgens suffering emotional trauma and changing to abstraction in the 1950s and Overbeck leaving the area. Overbeck's later works tended mainly towards portraits of her daughter and grandchildren, some local landscapes and religious sketches. She adopted an interest in glass painting briefly, but did not produce many works in that medium. Because of the distance she had to maintain between herself and Hannover, until recently Overbeck remained the least-known, critically, of the Hannoverian circle.

MARSHA MESKIMMON

P

Paalen, Alice *see* Rahon

Pacheco, Ana Maria
Brazilian sculptor and graphic artist, 1943–

Born in Goiás, Brazil, 1943. Studied sculpture at University of Goiás (BA) and music at Federal University of Goiás (degree), 1960–64; music and education at University of Brazil, Rio de Janeiro, 1965. Lecturer, School of Fine Arts and School of Architecture, University of Goiás, and at Institute of Art, Federal University of Goiás, 1966–73. Represented Brazil at São Paulo Bienal, 1970. Awarded British Council scholarship to Slade School of Fine Art, London, 1973–5. Head of Fine Art, Norwich School of Art, Norfolk, 1985–9. Invited to become Associate Artist at National Gallery, London, 1996. Recipient of first prize, Goiás Bienal, 1970; prize, International Exhibition of Original Drawings, Rijeka, Yugoslavia, 1980; silver medal award, Europe prize for painting, Ostend, 1982; prize, Norwegian International Print Biennale, Fredrikstad, 1986; prize, Integrafik '87, East Germany, 1987. Lives in Kent, England.

Selected Individual Exhibitions
Ikon Gallery, Birmingham: 1983
International Contemporary Art Fair, London: 1985
Artsite Gallery, Bath: 1989–90 (touring)
Camden Arts Centre, London: 1991
Museum of Modern Art, Oxford: 1991
Trondhjems Kunstforening, Trondheim: 1992
Winchester Cathedral, Hampshire: 1992
Oslo Kunstforening, Oslo: 1993
Norwich Castle Museum, Norfolk: 1994
The Gas Hall, Birmingham Museum and Art Gallery: 1994
Print Fair, The Armory, New York: 1994
Pratt Contemporary Art, Ightham, Kent: 1994–5 (*Twenty Years of Printmaking*, touring retrospective)
City of Plymouth Museums and Art Gallery: 1995

Bibliography
Women's Images of Men, exh. cat., Institute of Contemporary Arts, London, 1980
Ana Maria Pacheco: Sculpture, Drawings, Prints, 1980–83, exh. cat., Ikon Gallery, Birmingham, 1983
Human Interest: Fifty Years of British Art about People, exh. cat., Cornerhouse, Manchester, 1985
Frances Carey, "The prints of Ana Maria Pacheco", *Print Quarterly*, v, 1988, pp.272–83
Sue Hubbard, "Visit to Ana Maria Pacheco", *Green Book*, iii/2, 1989, pp.44–9
Sean Kelly, Helen Boorman and Ian Starsmore, *Ana Maria Pacheco: Sculpture, Paintings, Drawings and Prints, 1980–1989*, Ightham, Kent: Pratt Contemporary Art, 1989
Ana Maria Pacheco: Twenty Years of Printmaking, exh. cat., Pratt Contemporary Art, Ightham, Kent, and elsewhere, 1994
Andrew Brighton: *Work by Ana Maria Pacheco*, Ightham, Kent: Pratt Contemporary Art, 1994
David Elliott and Paul Hills, *Ana Maria Pacheco: In Illo Tempore*, Ightham, Kent: Pratt Contemporary Art, 1994
Richard Noyce, "The theatre of Ana Maria Pacheco", *Printmaking Today*, iii/1, Spring 1994, pp.8–9
George Szirtes, "Rites and melodies: The work of Ana Maria Pacheco", *Contemporary Art*, ii/4, Winter 1994–5, pp.12–16

Ana Maria Pacheco is a Brazilian who came to Britain on a British Council scholarship in 1973, and studied at the Slade. There is a strong tradition of fantastical art in Latin America, underlaid by the starkly emotional religious art of the Iberian peninsula. Pacheco asserts that an influence which would of course be hard to discern in the European context is the 18th-century Brazilian sculptor, Alejadinho, of mixed Portuguese and Indian descent. Her own absorbing work, in which she has created a mesmerising and terrifying series of meditations on human character and emotion, on evil and goodness, suffering and redemption, is powerfully at variance with what has until recently been the comparative restraint of the British tradition. She portrays darker and more disturbing things than the British usually allow, and she is even-handed in the terrors and tribulations of men, women – and animals. In Pacheco's ambiguous, ambivalent crowds, the fundamental motif is vulnerability: the victims and the oppressed and the led are vulnerable, and so, curiously, are the leaders and the oppressors.

Formally, in Brazil, she studied art, education and music, and in her early twenties taught in fine art and architecture faculties before coming to Britain to study at the Slade at the age of 30, when the figurative sculptor Reg Butler was the most influential teacher there. Britain, long thought of as both literally and metaphorically insular, has been home to a

Ana Maria Pacheco: *The Longest Journey* (details), 1994; sculpture, polychromed wood; 320 cm. × 335 cm. × 1000 cm.; sited at The Gas Hall, Birmingham Museums and Art Gallery

significant number of artists from elsewhere who have made a vital contribution to the idioms and styles of "British" art; this has at times been strikingly so in sculpture. The reason this is little remarked on is that London, and Britain, unlike say New York, Berlin or Paris, has not been a focus for international influence in art. But, for example, in the 20th century the American Jacob Epstein and the Russian Naum Gabo were formative influences on British sculpture. The Brazilian-born Pacheco is a polymath: an extraordinarily gifted printmaker, draughtswoman, painter and sculptor. Her art has a distinct Latin American flavour, a kind of individual magic surrealism. The art is narrative, darkly humorous, savage and disturbing, as well as exploiting inventive flights of fancy. Her plots are her own, although sparked off by a profound interest in games, in folk and popular culture, as well as classical tales and the religious theme of suffering, perhaps rooted in her native Catholicism.

The strongest element in Pacheco's memorable and haunting imagery is the construction of mysterious and powerful narrative, in which her own cast of characters – poets, victims, acrobats, angels, manic animals and people – act out obscure rituals, or express more directly archetypal situations. The faces of her carved figures often have open mouths, with pearly rows of artificial teeth; their eyes too are artificial. A sculpture

some years in the making, *The Banquet* (exh. 1985), was characterised by her carved and painted wooden figures, stylised thickened torsos, heads with "real" teeth and inset eyes. The figures usually have no necks, the great heads rising straight from the shoulder. Pacheco is a carver, and this is true too of her intaglio prints; she is a superbly authoritative draughtswoman, convincing the spectator of the authority of her figures and their reality, in spite of the almost grotesque distortions many of them suffer. Her animals seem real, although rarely seen, if ever, in nature. Her figures on paper, and her sculptures in space, however, inhabit no landscape. They are always in limbo, and often dramatically seen in a kind of artificial twilight.

There is a medieval flavour to her work, a deliberate paring down to bulky figures with strong features. Much of her work is about individual pain, the strange beauty of suffering, while other aspects are concerned with conformity, combined with a sense of the stark savagery of man to man. In the presbytery aisle of Winchester Cathedral, in 1992, Pacheco showed her triptych of *John the Baptist*, two of the figures carved from wood, one from stone. *Man and His Sheep* was shown in St John's Roman Catholic Church, Bath. Here a man carries a sheep's head on a pole, like a wand; behind is a crowd of clothed people; are they too sheep in people's clothing? There is a strong religious theme in her work, not always so overtly Christian; but much of her work is irradiated by a sense of political oppression, of the torturer and the tortured. Her first piece of sculpture to be titled, *Some Exercise of Power* (1980), showed two besuited and bald men looking down, grinning slyly at a naked man lying on the floor, eyes barely open, mouth open in an astonished frozen circle: dead, dying, numb, suspended in limbo? *The Banquet* shows a group of people ferociously expressive of both detachment and involvement, four suited and bald men, standing in a line behind a table on which a naked man lies, head slightly raised. The terrible eyes of the clothed men feast on the naked body. "Little murders" Pacheco has said are the underside of so-called civilised life.

Many of Pacheco's prints are about relationships between suited men and small or large fantastical animals: threatening, enquiring, curious. There are in the sculptures classical allusions twisted topsy-turvy: the strange plumpness of the *Three Graces*, not entwined; one lies on a mattress, one sits, one stands. There are performances, pageants, carnivals; *The Acrobats* hang from their feet, entwined in rope as though upside down on a gibbet. Bodies in Pacheco's visual idiom are subtly distorted – the heads are often like masks, like great primitive carvings.

Pacheco is widely read, and she is fervent that all visual media are expressive of ideas; when she was the head of fine art at the Norwich School of Art she was as insistent that students read, go to lectures, understand complex theories, as on ardent student practice, particularly drawing. She herself is a fervent student of nothing less than the human condition, in both its grandest and most terrible aspects, enlivened by a strong and sly sense of humour and, paradoxically, an awkward grace.

MARINA VAIZEY

Pacheco, María Luisa

Bolivian painter and mixed-media artist, 1919–1982

Born María Luisa Dietrich Zalles in La Paz, 22 September 1919. Studied at Academia de Bellas Artes, La Paz, under Cecilio Guzmán de Rojas and Jorge de la Reza from 1934. Married Victor Pacheco Iturrizaga, 1939; daughter born 1940, son born 1943; divorced 1956. Illustrator for *La Razón* newspaper, La Paz, 1948–50; taught painting at Academia de Bellas Artes, La Paz, 1951 and 1953. Travelled to Spain on scholarship from Spanish Government; studied at the Academia de San Fernando, Madrid, and under Daniel Vásquez Díaz, 1951–2. Returned to La Paz, 1952; co-founder of the group Ocho Contemporáneos, La Paz, 1953. Moved to New York, 1956; worked as textile designer, 1959–60. Married Fred Bernard in New York, 1961; divorced 1975. Became US citizen, 1972. Recipient of first prize, "Pedro Domingo Murillo" Municipal Salon, La Paz, 1953; painting prize, Hispano-American Biennial of Havana, 1954; Guggenheim fellowships, 1958, 1959 and 1960; painting prize, São Paulo Bienal, 1959; annual prize for excellence in painting, University of San Andrés, La Paz, 1970. Died in New York, 21 April 1982.

Principal Exhibitions

Individual

Galería Nascimento, Santiago, Chile: 1953
Galería Plástica, Buenos Aires: 1954
Galería Sudamericana, New York: 1956, 1959
Pan-American Union, Washington, DC: 1957
Instituto de Arte Contemporáneo, Lima: 1961, 1966
Bolivian-German Institute, La Paz: 1962
Rose Fried Gallery, New York: 1962
Bertha Schaefer Gallery, New York: 1965
Sala Mendoza, Eugenio Mendoza Foundation, Caracas: 1968
Lee Ault Gallery, New York: 1971, 1974, 1977, 1980
Museo Nacional de Arte, La Paz: 1976 (retrospective)
Galería Buchholz, Bogotá: 1980
Museum of Modern Art of Latin America, Washington, DC: 1986 (retrospective)

Group

Centro Bolivano Americano, La Paz: 1953 (*Ocho pintores contemporáneos*)
São Paulo Bienal: 1953, 1955, 1959, 1961
Corcoran Gallery, Washington, DC: 1956 (*From Latin America*)
Bonino Gallery, New York: 1964 (*Magnet, New York*)
Solomon R. Guggenheim Museum, New York: 1965 (*The Emergent Decade: Latin American Painters and Paintings in the 1960s*, touring)
Yale University, New Haven: 1966 (*Art in Latin America since Independence*, touring)

Bibliography

"Ocho pintores contemporáneos", *El Diario* (La Paz), 22 March 1953
R.D., "María Luisa", *Art News*, lviii, March 1959
H.D.M., "María Luisa", *Arts Magazine*, March 1959
Javier Ugarte, "María Luisa Pacheco y la Pintura Abstracta", *Ultima Hora* (La Paz), 27 December 1961
José de Mesa and Teresa Gisbert, *Pintura contemporánea (1952–1962)*, La Paz: Presidencia de la República, 1962
Rigoberto Villarroel Claure, *Bolivia: Art in Latin America Today*, Washington, DC: Pan-American Union, 1963
Eleventh Exhibition of American Painting and Sculpture, exh. cat., Krannert Art Museum, University of Illinois, Champaign-Urbana, 1963
Roberto Guevara, "María Luisa Pacheco: Materia y representación", *El Nacional* (Caracas), 14 October 1968
Damián Bayón, *Aventura plástica de Hispanoamerica*, Mexico City: Fondo de Cultura Económica, 1974
María Luisa Pacheco: Exposición retrospectiva, exh. cat., Museo Nacional de Arte, La Paz, 1976
Rigoberto Villaroel Claure, *Teorías estéticas y otros estudios*, La Paz: Casa de la Cultura Franz Tamayo, 1976
Women Artists of Eastern Long Island, exh. cat., American Association of University Women, East Hampton, New York, 1979
Marta Traba, "Bolivia salida a Tierra", *Ultima Hora* (La Paz), 9 December 1980
Ernesto Volkening: "María Luisa Pacheco", *Eco* (Bogotá), June 1981
"María Pacheco Dies: Painter of abstracts of Andes childhood", *New York Times*, 23 April 1982
Guillermo Céspedes Rivera, "María Luisa Pacheco y la Danza de las Líneas", *Presencia Literaria* (La Paz), xxviii, 28 October 1984
Tribute to María Luisa Pacheco of Bolivia, 1919–1982, exh. cat., Museum of Modern Art of Latin America, Washington, DC, 1986 (Spanish version of essay by Félix Angel reprinted in *Arte en Colombia*, no.40, May 1989)
José Luis Gómez-Martínez, ed., *Bolivia, 1952–1986: Dieciseis ensayos sobre el período post revolucionario*, Athens: Georgia Center for Latin American Studies, 1986; La Paz: Ensayistas, 1987

Guillermo Francovich, *Los mitos profundos de Bolivia*, 2nd edition, La Paz: Los Amigos del Libro, 1987

Leopoldo Castedo, *Historia del arte iberoamericano, ii: Siglo XIX, siglo XX*, Madrid: Alianza, 1988

The Latin American Spirit: Art and Artists in the United States, 1920–1970, exh. cat., Bronx Museum, New York, 1988

Carlos Salazar Mostajo, *La pintura contemporánea de Bolivia: Ensayo histórico-crítico*, La Paz: Juventud, 1989

Pedro Querejazu, ed., *Pintura boliviana del siglo XX*, La Paz: Banco Hipotecario Nacional, 1989

Edward Lucie-Smith, *Latin American Art of the 20th Century*, London and New York: Thames and Hudson, 1993

María Luisa Pacheco: Pintora de los Andes, exh. cat., Museo Nacional de Arte, La Paz, 1993

Pedro Querejazu, "Identidad y expresión plástica en Bolivia, en el siglo XX", *Arte, historia e identidad en América: Visiones comparativas. XVII coloquio internacional de historia del arte, Universidad Nacional Autónoma de Mexico, Instituto de Investigaciones Estéticas, Mexico*, 1994, pp.507–22

Marta Traba, *Art of Latin America, 1900–1980*, Washington, DC: Inter-American Development Bank, 1994

María Luisa Pacheco was one of the first Bolivian artists to venture into abstraction in the 1950s, developing an individual style that was closely linked to Bolivia through its landscape and Pre-Hispanic past. Like all artists of her generation, Pacheco was trained under *Indigenismo*, the movement of the

María Luisa Pacheco: *Untitled*, 1966; oil and wood on canvas; 96.5 × 101.6 cm.; Archer M. Huntington Art Gallery, University of Texas at Austin; Gift of John and Barbara Duncan, 1971

1920s–50s in many Latin American countries that aimed to revindicate the Indian both culturally and socially. She shifted towards abstraction after her journey to Spain in 1951, the catalysts being the teaching of the Spanish artist Daniel Vásquez Díaz, who strengthened Pacheco's knowledge of Cubism (she had been introduced to it in a diluted form by Cecilio Guzmán de Rojas, her teacher at art school), and her contact with such Spanish avant-garde artists as Tápies. Pacheco became known during the 1950s, a period of great political and cultural turmoil in Bolivia. She belonged to the Generation of '52, a group of artists that arose after the National Revolution of 1952. *Indigenismo* had dominated the art scene since the 1920s and was still predominant. The new generation of artists split into two tendencies: a "social" one, committed to the Revolution and to the left; and an "abstract" one – to which Pacheco belonged – that sought to free their art from ideology and to integrate it with international art trends. Despite the strong opposition received from artists and public, who questioned their lack of political commitment and the value of abstract art as such, María Luisa Pacheco and the group of Ocho Contemporáneos to which she belonged succeeded in opening up Bolivian art to new possibilities. At the *Ocho pintores contemporáneos* show of 1953, Pacheco was described as "Cubist, Abstract Expressionist and influenced by Picasso" (Claure 1976, p.93). Despite the figurative nature of the subject matter in *Figure* (1956; oil on canvas; 78.8 × 58.7 cm.; María Clemencia Pacheco de Carpio collection, repr. Washington 1986, p.9), Pacheco's attempt at abstraction is clear, the fragmentation of planes being very close to Cubism. Some of Pacheco's subjects, such as the "Palliris" (mine women), were not entirely devoid of social concern. She was also interested in such Bolivian themes as Pre-Columbian idols, totems and mountains. Many of these subjects reappear in later stages of her work.

Pacheco settled in New York in 1956, when Abstract Expressionism was at its peak. Although the artist came under its influence, she continued working with Bolivian figurative references, as in *High Plateau* (1958; María Clemencia Pacheco de Carpio collection, *ibid.*, p.12). In the 1960s the artist moved into a total abstraction that bore some relation to Art Informel. By now she had become one of Bolivia's most important artists. She began experimenting with textures and materials, such as corrugated cardboard, sheets of plywood, papiers collés, wood, sands, pigments, and she glued these on to the canvas. In *Untitled* (1966; see illustration) the artist integrated long and triangular strips of wood diagonally on to the canvas, breaking up the stable horizontal composition and the edges of the picture. She would begin working out her ideas by sketching spontaneously, and at a second stage would structure a stable pictorial composition. *Petrous* (1965; Massachusetts Institute of Technology, Cambridge), a construction of articulated geometrical planes with strong contrasts of textures and earth-coloured areas, creates interesting pictorial tensions. The architectural character of Pacheco's pictures, and her emphasis on composition and structure, have been seen as partly determined by the artist's early contact with Pre-Hispanic Tiahuanaco and partly by the architectural discipline of her father, the architect Julio Maríaca Pando.

In the 1970s – and until her death – María Luisa Pacheco abandoned total abstraction for clear references to the landscape of the Bolivian Altiplano. *Sajama* (1978; mixed media on canvas; private collection, repr. Querejazu 1989, pl.106) and *Untitled* (c.1978; mixed media on canvas; private collection, New York, *ibid.*, pl.102) are in no way descriptive, but they are reminiscent of the dramatic scale and sculptural qualities of the Bolivian mountains. The vertical volumes, textures and luminosity are also reminiscent of this landscape; nevertheless the pictorial values can stand on their own. The *frisson* produced by the interplay between figuration and abstraction, between physical reality and the artist's subjectivity, is one of the most successful aspects of her work.

It has been widely debated whether or not María Luisa Pacheco was an abstract artist; whether or not her pictures represent or refer to the Bolivian landscape. The artist has been quoted as saying, in 1963: "Space is the reality that has to be fragmented and filled with subjective and intimate expressions of myself" (Washington 1986, p.8), in support of the argument that her work was fundamentally abstract. Even if Pacheco did not always attempt to "represent" the Bolivian landscape, many of her abstract shapes functioned as "plastic equivalents" (Rafael Squirru in Querejazu 1989, p.108). Another statement by the artist, 16 years later, provides a more definitive insight into Pacheco's work as a whole:

> ... the art of the Pre-Columbian artists remained fixed in my memory from my childhood on. At the same time I felt the strong magnet of the landscape of the Andes. During my art studies and experiences throughout the years, I learned to create an emotional, semi-abstract image of what I feel in front of the gigantic landscape and the ancient art of Bolivia [partially quoted in Washington 1986, p.8, and Querejazu 1989, p.312, with slight discrepancies; originally published in East Hampton 1979, p.21; this version has been slightly amended by the author].

In her last years Pacheco painted a series of almost monochrome white pictures. In *Triptych* (1980; INBO collection, La Paz) space and luminosity dominate a rhythmic composition; the landscape seems to have dematerialised in the transparency of the whites. María Luisa Pacheco died at the peak of her career. Although she lived in New York for more than 20 years and exhibited in numerous important exhibitions in the USA, she never belonged entirely to the North American art scene. Her work remained connected to Bolivia and achieved an indisputable celebrity in Latin America.

CECILIA FAJARDO HILL

Pane, Gina
French body artist and sculptor, 1939–1990

Born in Biarritz, 24 May 1939, to Italian parents; acquired French nationality, 1975. Lived in Turin, 1944–60; worked as an information-processor for IBM, 1959–60. Settled in Paris, 1960; studied at Ecole des Beaux-Arts and Atelier d'Art Sacré, Arnoldi, 1961–3. Opened performance studio at Centre Georges Pompidou, Paris, 1978. Taught painting at Ecole des Beaux-Arts, Le Mans, 1980. Died in Paris, 6 March 1990.

Selected Individual Exhibitions

Galerie Simone Heller, Paris: 1967
Tokyo Museum, Tokyo: 1968
Galleria Franzp, Turin: 1969
Galerie Rive-Droite, Paris: 1969, 1970
Galleria Diagramma, Milan, and LP, Turin: 1970
Galerie Isy Brachot, Brussels: 1978
Galerie Isy Brachot, Paris: 1980, 1983
Padiglione d'Arte Contemporanea, Milan: 1985
Musée d'Art Moderne, Villeneuve d'Asc: 1986
Kunst Station Sankt Peter, Cologne: 1989
Palau de la Virreina, Barcelona: 1990 (retrospective)
Centre d'Art Contemporain Passages, Cadran Solaire, Troyes: 1990
   (retrospective)

Selected Writings

"Gina Pane: Briser les servo-mécanismes", arTitudes, June 1972, p.6
"Le corps et son support image pour une communication non-
   linguistique", arTitudes, February–March 1973, p.8 (in English,
   p.10)

Bibliography

François Pluchart, "Agressions biologiques de Gina Pane", arTitudes,
   December 1971–January 1972, p.9 (in English, p.10)
Effie Stephano, "Performance of concern", Art and Artists, viii, April
   1973, pp.20–27 (interview)
——, "Paris", Art and Artists, ix, April 1974, pp.44–5
Lea Vergine, "Bodylanguage", Art and Artists, ix, September 1974,
   pp.22–7
Helena Kontová, "The wound as a sign: An encounter with Gina
   Pane", Flash Art, no.92–3, October–November 1979, pp.36–7
   (interview)
Gina Pane: Travail d'action, exh. cat., Galerie Isy Brachot, Paris,
   1980
Judith Barry and Sandy Flitterman, "Textual strategies: The politics
   of art-making", Screen, no.21, Summer 1980, pp.35–48
Mary Kelly, "Re-viewing modernist criticism", Screen, no.22,
   Autumn 1981, pp.41–62
Kirsten Martins, "Interview with Gina Pane", Performance: Another
   Dimension, Berlin: Frölich und Kaufmann, Künstlerhaus
   Bethanien, 1983, pp.153–7
Gina Pane: Partitions et dessins, exh. cat., Galerie Isy Brachot, Paris,
   1983
Gina Pane: Partitions, opere multimedia, 1984–85, exh. cat.,
   Padiglione d'Arte Contemporanea, Milan, 1986
Ezio Quarantelli, "Travels with St Francis", Contemporanea,
   November–December 1988, pp.44–7 (interview)
Liliana Albertazzi, "Gina Pane's Second Coming", ibid., pp.48–9
Kathy O'Dell, "The performance artist as masochistic woman", Arts
   Magazine, lxii, Summer 1988, pp.96–8
Gina Pane: La Chair ressuscitée, exh. cat., Kunst Station Sankt Peter,
   Cologne, 1989
Esther Ferrer, "The geography of the body", Lapiz, no.58, April
   1989, pp.36–41 (interview)
Catherine Lawless, "Entretien avec Gina Pane", Cahiers du Musée
   National d'Art Moderne, no.29, Autumn 1989, pp.97–104
Gina Pane, exh. cat., Palau de la Virreina, Barcelona, 1990
Gina Pane, exh. cat., Centre d'Art Contemporain Passages, Cadran
   Solaire, Troyes, 1990
Liliane Touraine, "Gina Pane, de la communication à la communion:
   Une esthétique du partage", Colóquio, Artes, no.90, 1991,
   pp.48–57
Kathy O'Dell, Toward a Theory of Performance Art: An
   Investigation of Its Sites, PhD dissertation, City University of New
   York, 1992

Gina Pane is best known as one of the few female body artists of the 1970s to use her body in her work in extreme ways, such as making small incisions in her flesh with a razor blade, lying on a metal bed over burning candles and stamping out small fires with her bare hands and feet. The often shocking nature of these performances – or "actions", as she preferred to call them – tended to overshadow Pane's work of the preceding and following decades, when she produced works using sculpture and/or photography prolifically. Throughout her career, however, the body – in either literal or conceptual form – was her main concern.

Soon after her formal training at the Ecole des Beaux-Arts in Paris, Pane began to feel constrained by the traditions of painting and in 1965 turned to making sculptures in which she "always left the interior space empty to allow the spectator to enter and circulate or sit down" (Stephano 1973, p.21). While able to make a place for the body in these works, Pane still felt the need to move beyond the aesthetic mandates of conventional media to more conceptually based work. The turning point came in 1968 after a mundane yet profound experience in which she observed that a pile of stones near a tree appeared to be "locked in the shade" (idem). In a poetic gesture, she simply moved them into the sun (1968; repr. Paris 1980). In another action, she attempted to bury a ray of sunshine. Such pieces commented on, according to Pane, "the problem of lack of sun in our cities" (Stephano 1973, p.21). These works led to others, still poetic, in which her body was more taxed – climbing a dangerously steep, sandy mountain to get to the sound of the forest above, or connecting an unfinished road to a finished one by laboriously laying large logs side by side (both 1970; repr. Paris 1980). Though documented photographically, these actions were carried out without an audience. In Hommage à une jeune drogue (1971), however, an audience was present. This was the next turning point in her career, especially since it was also the first piece in which she incurred an injury, a practice that would typify her body-art work of the 1970s.

Hommage à une jeune drogue was conducted in memory of a young drug addict who had overdosed. In the middle of a circle of audience members stood a pot of hot chocolate and a white towel. After reading a text about how the boy's parents restored order in their lives by returning to everyday rituals such as drinking hot chocolate every morning, Pane "washed" her hands in the scalding liquid. Audience members then participated in a discussion of drug addiction and related issues (Stephano 1973, p.21; Ferrer 1989, p.38). Pane's subsequent actions did not solicit audience participation, but did focus on social concerns, which she continued to emphasise by taking her body to extreme physical and psychological limits. In Escalade non anaesthesié (1971; see illustration) she climbed up and down an iron ladder, the rungs of which were affixed with sharp, pointed protrusions, stopping only when she could no longer endure the pain. Performed in her own studio, Pane wished to emphasise how artists are driven to get ahead and how they become anaesthetised in their efforts. "Here", she said, "I wanted to experience an ascent which wasn't anesthetized, where I would undergo a great deal of suffering and pain" (Stephano 1973, p.22).

Pane claimed that she was greatly influenced by political protests in Paris in May 1968, and by such international conflicts as the Vietnam War (Ferrer 1989, pp.37–8). In Nourriture-actualités télévisées-feu (1971; repr. Pluchart 1971) she force-fed herself and spat back up 600 grammes of raw

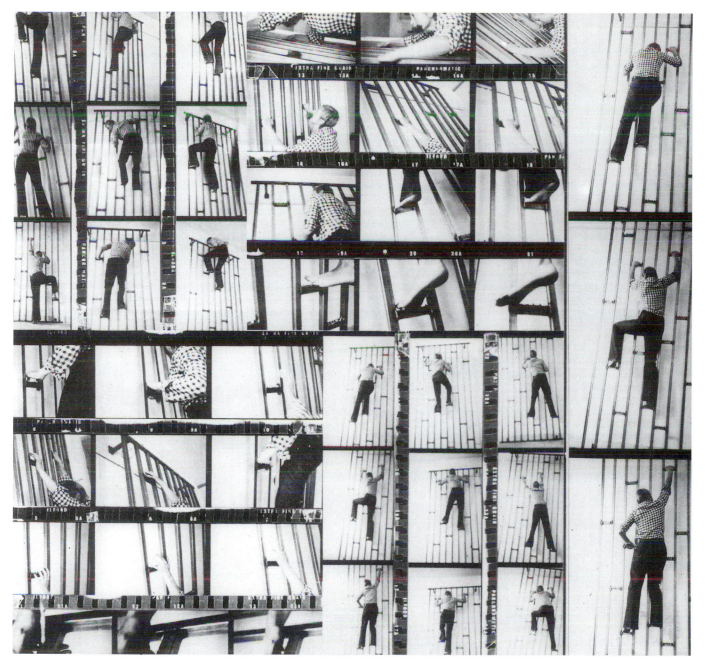

Pane: *Escalade non anaesthesié*, 1971; performance

ground meat, watched the nightly news on television as she stared past a nearly blinding light bulb, and extinguished flames with her bare hands and feet. After the performance, she said, people reported a heightened sensitivity. "Everyone there remarked: 'It's strange, we never felt or heard the news before. There's actually a war going on in Vietnam, unemployment everywhere'" (Stephano 1973, p.22).

It would appear that in the 1970s Pane was also influenced by the feminist movement. In *Psyché* (1974; repr. Barcelona 1990, p.69) she drew an image of her face on to a mirror with lipstick and eye make-up, then cut a small arc under each eyebrow with a razor blade (Stephano 1974, p.45). And in *Autoportrait(s)* (1973; repr. *arTitudes*, February–March 1973, cover and pp.7–14), after being suspended over burning

candles, she stood against a wall on to which slides of women applying nail polish were being projected, and made tiny incisions around her fingernails. By substituting her own blood for make-up and nail polish in these two pieces, she seemed to be pointing out the potentially painful vulnerability to which woman is subjected by conforming to (or being prone to, as symbolised by her prone position on the bed) patriarchal fashion standards. Despite these clear references to women's issues, Pane asserted that she "always felt and lived life as a human being, more than as female or male" (Ferrer 1989, p.40).

Feminist critics and historians have disagreed over the meaning of Pane's work of this period. Some believe that by counterposing pain and pleasure in her actions, Pane was reinforcing dualistic ideologies at the patriarchal base of Western metaphysics (Barry and Flitterman 1980, p.37). Others contend that pleasure was not part of Pane's work whatsoever. To imagine that Pane experienced pleasure in her actions, one historian feels, is to capitulate to the Freudian myth that all masochists enjoy suffering, a theory that lets observers of a self-imposed act of suffering off the hook from considering its more complex meanings, especially the ways in which observers themselves may be implicated in the act (O'Dell 1992, pp.107–9 and 396–7). Another critic argues that if Pane were playing with an opposition, it was not between pain and pleasure but the "aesthetics of lived experience ... [and] ... the object" (Kelly 1981, p.54).

Interestingly, it was to the object that Pane ultimately returned. After seriously injuring herself in 1980 in a rare attempt to repeat one of her actions (Ferrer 1989, p.38), she stopped performing and turned for the rest of her career to sculpture, sometimes incorporating photographs of her previous actions. *Un après-midi d'été à 16h30: Partition pour quatre jouets* (1983; Galerie Isy Brachot, Paris and Brussels) consists of a shelf of broken wine glasses and children's toys, above which is a string of photographs of an incision in Pane's flesh. A drop of blood dangles from the bottom of the incision. The illusion that the blood might fall into one of the chalice-like glasses converts the work into a kind of altarpiece.

Religious connotations became more overt in Pane's work after 1984, when she began to concentrate on the theme of saints and martyrs. Utilising materials such as iron, aluminium, wood, copper and glass – materials she considered analogous to human skin given their strength and fragility – she produced such works as *François d'Assise trois fois aux blessures stigmatisé (version 1)* (1985–7; Musée National d'Art Moderne, Centre Georges Pompidou, Paris). The piece consists of three panels, each a little over life-size, positioned horizontally above one another. The bottom two (rusted iron on the bottom, shiny metal in the middle) feature a raised imprint of a skeleton with circular imprints outlining areas of the chest, hands and feet inflicted with stigmata. The skeleton does not appear in the top panel (made of frosted glass), just the circular motifs. There is, however, an additional circle here, located where the head would have been. Perhaps Pane was suggesting that although the body dematerialises after death, memory of its suffering lives on in the mind of the observer.

Throughout Pane's career, whether she herself appeared in her work or not, her deepest commitment was to the concerns of the human body in relation to its social context. Even in her late work, as she said: "I am ... not interested in creating a hagiography. I place this work of the saints within current society, within our everyday life" (Quarantelli 1988, p.47).

KATHY O'DELL

Pape, Lygia
Brazilian artist, designer and film-maker, c.1930–

Born in Nova Friburgo, Rio de Janeiro, 7 April c.1930. Studied philosophy at Universidade Federal, Rio de Janeiro (BA). Taught Semiotics of Space in Faculdade de Arquitetura, Universidade Santa Ursula, Rio de Janeiro, 1972–85 (MA in philosophic aesthetics 1980). Appointed professor, Escola de Belas Artes, Universidade Federal, Rio de Janeiro, 1983. Founder-member of Grupo Frente, 1954–6, and Neoconcrete Grupo, 1959–61, both Rio de Janeiro. Worked with filmmakers of *Cinema Novo*, and designed letters, posters and displays, 1960s. Directed films in the 1970s. Recipient of first prize, Sul América, Brazil, 1952; citation, Salão Nacional de Arte Moderna, Rio de Janeiro, 1955; bronze medal, Salão de Arte Moderna, São Paulo, 1955; prize, Expo '67, Montreal, for film *La Nouvelle Création*, 1967; Guggenheim fellowship, 1980; Vitae Foundation fellowship, Brazil, and Mário Pedrosa prize, ABCA–AICA, for best national exhibition of the year, *Amazoninos*, Rio de Janeiro, 1990; best exhibition of 1991 at Instituto Brasil-Estados Unidos, Rio de Janeiro, 1992. Two daughters from marriage to Gunter Pape. Lives in Rio de Janeiro.

Selected Individual Exhibitions
Maison de France, Rio de Janeiro: 1975
Galeria Arte Global, São Paulo, and Museu de Arte Moderna, Rio de Janeiro: 1976
Pinacoteca do Estado, São Paulo: 1977
Hotel Meridien, Rio de Janeiro: 1979
Galeria do Centro Empresarial, Rio de Janeiro: 1984 (*O Olho do Guará*, touring)
Galeria Arte Espaço, Rio de Janeiro: 1985
Galeria Thomas Cohn, Rio de Janeiro: 1988, 1990
Galeria Instituto Cultural Brasil-Estados Unidos, Rio de Janeiro: 1991
Galeria Camargo Vilaça, São Paulo: 1992
Kunsthaus, Zürich: 1992
L'Onorabile Galleria, Milan: 1993
Museo Nacional de Belas Artes, São Paulo: 1994
Galeria Universidade do Espirito Santo, Brazil: 1995
São Paulo Bienal: 1995

Bibliography
Lygia Pape: 40 gravuras neoconcretas, exh. cat., Maison de France, Rio de Janeiro, 1975
Eat Me: A gula ou a luxúria?, exh. cat., Galeria Arte Global, São Paulo, and Museu de Arte Moderna, Rio de Janeiro, 1976
Mário Pedrosa and others, *Lygia Pape*, Rio de Janeiro: FUNARTE, 1983
Ronaldo Brito, *Neoconcretismo: Vértice e ruptura do projeto construtivo brasileiro*, Rio de Janeiro: FUNARTE/Instituto Nacional de Artes Plásticas, 1985
Fernando Cocchiarale and Anna Bella Geiger, *Abstracionismo: Geométrico e informal: A vanguarda brasileira nos anos cinqüenta*, Rio de Janeiro: FUNARTE/Instituto Nacional de Artes Plásticas, 1987
Art in Latin America: The Modern Era, 1820–1980, exh. cat., South Bank Centre, London, and elsewhere, 1989
Lygia Pape, exh. cat., Galeria Camargo Vilaça, São Paulo, 1992
Brasil: Segni d'arte: Libri e video, 1950–1993, exh. cat., Fondazione Scientifica Querini-Stampalia, Venice, and elsewhere, 1993
Ultramodern: The Art of Contemporay Brazil, exh. cat., National Museum of Women in the Arts, Washington, DC, 1993

Lygia Pape emerged as a significant Brazilian artist in the 1950s, a pioneer of Grupo Frente, the nucleus of the concretist art movement in Rio de Janeiro. Since then, she has always been at the centre of the Brazilian avant-garde, or one step ahead according to some critics (Paulo Herkenhoff in Washington 1993, p.40).

Pape has worked in diverse techniques and media, and there have been several breaks in her development. In her woodcuts of the early 1950s she explored ways in which the texture and marks of the wood introduced an organic quality into antiseptic geometric works, an exploration in advance of the constructive orthodoxy of the time. In the late 1950s and early 1960s, as a founder-member of Neo-concretism, she produced book art, objects, boxes and two Neo-concrete ballets (1958–9). She investigated viewer participation and introduced effects of light, colour and movement into art works. In the Neo-concrete ballet, geometric volumes of colour dance, propelled by human participants invisible to the public (repr. Brito 1985, p.86).

Following the dramatic events of the military take-over of Brazil in 1964 and after the dissolution of the Neo-concrete group, she began working with Brazilian avant-garde film-makers. In that context *Cinema Novo*, a type of documentary film focused on Brazilian socio-cultural identity mixed with an interest in linguistic and visual invention, emerged as a response to the urgent need to re-think the ethical and social dimensions of the aesthetic and the ever-problematic Brazilian identity. For Pape the rupture with traditional linguistic and artistic categories assumed an ethical meaning: "we were much more revolutionary than the traditional left-wing militant groups in their attempt to impose on the peasants a dogmatic programme of political awareness based on an intellectualised attitude and a theoretical approach totally distanced from the everyday life of the ordinary Brazilian people. We were the ones who climbed the mountains of Rio to hold meetings with the people in the slums" (interview with author, Rio de Janeiro, 25 October 1993).

In the late 1960s Pape was involved with process art and collective projects, works to be presented in the streets, in the slums, outside the traditional art environments. *O Divisor* (1968; artist's collection, repr. London 1989, p.281) is an enormous white cotton sheet (20 × 20 m.) with holes at mathematically determined intervals for people to insert their heads, so that from the top you see only the heads without the body and underneath only the body. It is a criticism of mechanised society, bureaucracy, a way of life that homogenises people, makes them all the same. Another work that was intended to awaken people to their own inner world and their identities was *Egg* (1968; artist's collection, repr. Pedrosa 1983, p.29). This piece comprises three cubic boxes (80 × 80 × 80 cm.) made of wood covered with plastic or paper so that people could go inside, rupture the plastic walls and emerge into the external space, experiencing a metaphorical rebirth.

In the 1970s Pape produced installations, environments and video art, returning to sculpture in the 1980s. This reflects the freedom and experimentation of her attitude towards art, which owes much to the Brazilian Trotskyist critic Mário Pedrosa. His famous phrase "art as an exercise of freedom" inspired Pape's generation. All her work is imbued with the poetry of life and sensuous physicality, from the woodcuts to the series of *Amazoninos* of the 1990s. Pape is a *carioca* (native of Rio) artist *par excellence*. Rio de Janeiro's dionysian natural and social environment is reflected through her work as a celebration of light, sensory energy and spirit of inventiveness. In her film *Catiti Catiti* (1978), which means "New Moon! Oh New Moon!" in the tupy-guarani language, Pape imagined the reaction of Pero Vaz de Caminha, chronicler of the Portuguese discovery of Brazil in 1500, arriving in Rio de Janeiro in the 1970s. It is a critical and ironic view of the coloniser towards the natives, which also refers to the anthropophagist theory of Oswald de Andrade, whose *Manifesto antropófago* (1928) advocated that the colonised should devour the culture of the coloniser, to absorb his power and transcend it.

But Pape's work has none of the connotations of fantastic art that might be expected from a South American artist. It presents a synthesis with Brazilian popular culture not as a narrative but as an energy that circulates, that nourishes her production. She gathers this energy as she moves around, from her home in the luxurious southern area of Rio, surrounded by trees and mountains, to the arid northern suburbs where she takes her students to experience the atmosphere of abundant life and the creativity of people who live in the slums. When she began working with film and video she felt that they were the ideal media for artists to gather ideas from real life: "it is reality itself that gives me material to work" (interview with author).

For the exhibition *Nova objectividade brasileira* (Museo de Arte Moderna, Rio de Janeiro, 1967) she produced two acrylic boxes (30 × 40 × 10 cm.) with mirrored bottoms. She filled one box with dead cockroaches, the other with live ants (repr. Pedrosa 1983, p.15). One represented the art of museums, she said, a rejection of collecting; the other, live art and the unpredictable behaviour of living things. The ants were fed on meat, and some even escaped into the museum. She said people were very shocked to look in the mirror and see their own image covered with cockroaches (interview with author).

Pape has long rejected the art world. Her first solo exhibition was held only in 1975, and she has made little attempt to sell her works, many of which have been seen only by friends at her home. In 1974 she created an installation, a topological proposition against violence, at CAYC (Centro de Arte y Communicación) in Buenos Aires, where a television circuit showed the same images inside and outside the gallery. Art and life should not be distinct; exterior and interior space should be the same; the sacred space of the art world should be abolished. Although Pape has never referred to these issues directly, it is arguable that if there is a narrative in her work, it is based on a sort of postmodern discourse, since she has touched on the questions of multi-culturalism, feminist and colonial discourses, not programatically or dogmatically but as a concern with the multiplicity of discourses (mass, popular, intellectual and so on) and ideas that permeate the contemporary world, particularly the fragmented cultural reality of such a country as Brazil. Her work is based on two axes: research into colours, colour as light and power irreducible either to nature or form on the one hand; and the recovery of popular aesthetics on the other – she believes that popular culture does not passively reproduce the hegemonic discourses but rather genuinely recycles them.

Pape says she is not a nihilist, and in fact her attitude is a very positive, absolutely modern one, in that her art is intended to provoke a response in people, to increase awareness, to interfere in life. Marcio Doctors characterised *displacement* as a central concept in her work. Displacement is not movement in itself but a "route of detours". It is a way of turning things upside down, inside out, to reveal their wholeness through their otherness. What Pape is against is all sorts of hegemonic discourse: political, cultural, artistic. Perhaps she inherited this combative attitude from the native Brazilians – a warrior spirit inherited from the black slaves and the Indians. For her, power comes from the most simple and natural aspects of life.

In her work *Eat Me: Gluttony or Lust* (1976) Pape presented objects as part of a symbolic universe considered feminine through the mythology of the feminine in the masculine discourse, to explore how the woman becomes a consumer object. She made several paper packs filled with lipsticks, face powder, pieces of hair, bottles of cheap cologne, little mirrors with erotic drawings, phrases collected from women's public lavatories, calendars showing naked women, etc ... to be sold in galleries (repr. Pedrosa 1983, pp.34–7). She was amazed at how street people came into the sophisticated gallery in São Paulo to buy these objects of seduction for the symbolic price of one *cruzeiro*, the lowest value note in Brazilian currency at the time. The gallery, however, closed the exhibition before the end (interview with author).

Pape considers herself a constructive artist, but the constructive aspects of her work are permeated with existential and phenomenological appeals. Since she co-founded the Neo-concrete group (1959–61) her work has followed the tendency to create abstract art as a vehicle for sensory and psychological experiences. She says that her geometry ought to be like that of the wisdom spiders, which can build invisible nests in the most precarious places without losing the intrinsic logic of their work.

Her Neo-concrete *Book of Creation* (1959; artist's collection, repr. London 1989, pp.270–71) was made of pieces of wood and cardboard painted in gouache, all 30 × 30 centimetres. She intended to tell the history of the creation of the universe by re-creating the non-verbal narrative visually, representing the archetypal ideas of time, cosmos, light, crops etc. Each piece, a "recasting of the creation story and early human discoveries, is a lucid geometric metaphor, it is also a set of manipulable models for the viewer to exercise his/her own creativity" (Guy Brett in *ibid.*, p.269).

In 1990 Pape returned to the idea developed in the *Book of Creation* in a series of metal wall sculptures (private collections, repr. São Paulo 1992) presented at her exhibition *Amazoninos* at the Galeria Thomas Cohn in Rio. These are conceived as *haikus*, Japanese poems based on a rigorous, complex structure that present a poetry of simplicity praising nature and the universe. Unlike the inorganic appearance that these large metal pieces should have, they refer rather to the organicity of unusual flowers that live in the Amazon river, aquatic plants, ephemeral flowers. Although they are enormous and heavy, they appear as if made of paper, and they have a subtle movement. Formed from basic shapes, the circle and the square, they do not suggest geometric rigidity. The vibrant colours – red or green, or orange and black, or pure black and white – are like a second element of the work, since their function is to deny its materiality, tricking the viewer's senses by playing with aspects of lightness and heaviness, emptiness and fullness, rigidity and flexibility.

As Herkenhoff observed, it would have been most interesting to see a discussion of Pape's work in Rosalind Krauss's book *Passages in Modern Sculpture* (New York: Viking, 1977): "Without such consideration ... any attempt to characterize the development of modern sculpture will be necessarily incomplete" (Herkenhoff in Washington 1993, p.43).

PAULA TERRA CABO

Parasole, Geronima Cagnaccia *see under* Parasole, Isabella Catanea

Parasole, Isabella [Elisabetta, Isabetta] Catanea
Italian printmaker, active 1585–1625

Active in Rome by 1585. Wife of the printmaker Leonardo Parasole, by whom she had two sons, Agostino, a lawyer, and Bernardino, a painter; husband died 1612. Died in Rome, 1625.

Bibliography
Giovanni Baglione, *Le vite de' pittori, scultori et architetti dal Pontificato di Gregorio XIII del 1572 in fino a' tempi di Papa Urbano Ottavo nel 1642*, Rome: Fei, 1642; reprinted Bologna: Forni, 1975–6
Charles LeBlanc, *Manuel de l'amateur d'estampes*, Paris, 1854–90, reprinted Amsterdam, 1971, ii, p.107
G.K. Nagler, *Die Monogrammisten*, 5 vols, Munich, 1858–79; reprinted Nieuwkoop, 1966
Elsa Ricci, ed., *Merletti e ricami della Aemilia ars*, Milan, 1929; reprinted Bologna: Bologna University Press, 1981
Arthur Lotz, *Bibliographie der Modelbücher*, Leipzig, 1933; reprinted Stuttgart: Hiersemann, 1963
A.M. Capecchi and others, *L'Accademia dei Lincei e la cultura Europea nel XVII secolo*, Rome, 1991

Isabella Parasole (also called Elisabetta and Isabetta) was a wood-engraver who worked in the late 16th and early 17th centuries, most famous for her publications of model books for lace designs that were copied by various publishers and reprinted several times throughout the first two decades of the 17th century. There was a busy market for books of needlework patterns, all of which (like calligraphy books) had to be printed with great detail in order to be useful. Although the embroidery guilds were largely made up of male needleworkers, these pattern books, which flourished from the 1520s to the 1640s, were most often dedicated to a female audience; men were rarely included in the introduction or title pages except as publishers. By 1600 Parasole was well known for her embroidery and lace designs, as is evident in the dedication of a new edition of her patterns published in Venice (*Pretiosa gemma delle virtuose donne*): "Knowing how much the work of Mrs Isabella Catanea Parasole has been accepted by the world, I have set myself to increasing it by many new works, different from the first ...". She designed and cut the patterns for six known model books, all catalogued by Lotz (1963): *Specchio delle virtuose donne* (Rome: Facchetti, 1595; Lotz 129a and c), *Studio delle virtuose dame* (Rome: Facchetti, 1597; Lotz 132), *Pretiosa gemma delle virtuose donne* (Rome: Gargano, 1598; Lotz 135a–c), *Fiori d'ogni virtu per le nobili et honeste matrone* (Rome: Facchetti, 1610; Lotz 143a), *Teatro delle nobili et virtuose donne* (Rome: Bona, 1616; Lotz 143b–f) and *Gemma pretiosa delle virtuose donne* (Rome: Facciotti, 1615; Lotz 146 a, b: later editions of *Specchio delle virtuose donne*). In a last, 1636, edition of the *Teatro* the publisher claimed to be reprinting the clever patterns by Parasole, "famous for such things among the ladies of Europe".

Unlike many previous model-book woodcarvers, Parasole used a dark background, letting the predominantly geometric patterns of the lace designs stand out in white, thus looking more like the filmy fabric itself. This was also an economical way of carving in terms of both labour and the longevity of the blocks: the designs could be cut directly into the block in the manner of drawing instead of carving out the wood from around the delicate lines, which left the complicated and delicate patterns raised and vulnerable to breakage during printing.

Parasole's background and training are unknown, although she calls herself "Romana" on the dedication page of the *Teatro delle nobili et virtuose donne*. She was married to the printmaker Leonardo Parasole and lived in their house near the Trevi fountain in Rome, in the same area as her publisher, Antonio Facchetti. Leonardo was one of four sons of a woodworker (Agostino Parasole di Sant'Angelo di Vissio) in the Via Giubbonari who made wooden clogs, drums and small boxes. The woodworkers decorated the outsides of the drums and the insides of the little wooden chests with prints they evidently made themselves: at the division of their inheritance Leonardo received the printing press and all the prints except those that, the agreement specified, were to be used for the drums and the boxes (G.L. Masetti-Zannini, *Stampatori e librai a Roma nella seconda metà del cinquecento*, Rome, 1980, pp.215ff). At the time of his father's death in 1585 Leonardo had already printed and made the illustrations for an elaborate herbal by Castor Durante (*Herbario nuovo di Castor Durante medico, et cittadino Romano*, Rome: Bericchia and Tornierij, 1585; text printed by Bartholomeo Bonfadino and Tito Diani) in which undertaking, Baglione says, he was aided by his wife Isabella. Neither of their names is mentioned in the herbal itself.

Isabella's son Bernardino was reported to have been a student of Giuseppe Cesari (Il Cavaliere d'Arpino), and made paintings for the Roman churches of San Crisogono and San Rocco. Parasole was also related by marriage to Geronima Cagnaccia Parasole (*c*.1569–8 July 1622), also a printmaker, who worked from designs by Antonio Tempesta (see the woodcut series of the *Life of St Antony*, Nagler 1858–79, iv, 3141) and whose portrait hangs in the Accademia di San Luca, Rome (G. Incisa della Rocchetta, *La collezione dei ritratti dell'Accademia di San Luca*, Rome, 1979, p.35, no.68, inv.625). She signed her prints PM and PMF, but although Nagler's assumption that this might mean "Parasole Moglie Fecit" may be correct, she was not the wife of Leonardo Parasole.

Baglione treats Parasole, Leonardo and Bernardino in a single *Life*, mentioning that Leonardo engraved in copper as well as wood, and engraved illustrations after drawings by Antonio Tempesta. He also mentions Isabella's lace and embroidery book with the copperplate frontispiece engraved by the printmaker and collector Francesco Villamena (*Teatro*

LAVORO DE PONTO INARIA.

Parasole: *Lavoro a Ponto in Aria*; from her book *Teatro delle nobili et virtuose donne*, 1616

delle nobili et virtuose donne), with whom the family had friendly and professional ties. It is Baglione who gives the information that Parasole was also involved in the illustration project for the herbal planned by Federico Cesi, founder of the Accademia Lincei. Cesi and the Academicians believed that graphic documentation was an important part of the scientific observation of nature (when the Academy member Johannes van Heck went on an exploratory voyage in 1604 he brought along a boy especially to engrave copperplates); Parasole's engagement in such a milieu must have stemmed from her experience with the Castor Durante herbal as well as from the minute engraving style she employed for the lace designs. Which of Cesi's projects she was involved in is unclear, since his books were finished years after they were first planned, and often in changed formats. But she has been most convincingly linked with the ambitious project of producing a printed and illustrated version of a colourful manuscript by the Spanish physician Francisco Hernandez. A copy of Hernandez's manuscript containing coloured illustrations of Mexican plant life had been brought to Naples from Spain, and in 1610 Cesi undertook to engrave and publish the drawings. It is known from a letter from Galileo to Cesi that the project was underway by 1611 (see Capecchi 1991). Parts of it were published as they were completed, therefore in 1613 a set of 68 woodcut prints of exotic plants, now in the Vatican Library (BAV, St Barb. N.VI.175), was offered to the Bishop of Bamburg, Goffredo Aschlausen. This work was finally published in 1651, after Cesi's death, as the *Rerum medicarum Novae Hispaniae thesaurus seu plantarum animalium mineralium mexicanorum historia ex Francisci Hernandez* (Rome, 1651), known as the *Tesoro messicano*. Among the other engravers who worked on the project were Niccolò Martini and Giovanni Giorgio Nuvolstella (see Baglione 1642; for Cesi and the *Tesoro messicano*, see Capecchi 1991).

Parasole's earliest known engraving work was the herbal for Castor Durante that she illustrated with her husband, and the success of that venture seems to have led her, in co-operation with her painter brother-in-law, to venture into lace-making books. Her skill at fine wood-carving, her connection with other engravers and her previous botanical experience made her suitable for the Cesi project, on the surface so different, and yet in terms of skill so similar to the lace patterns for which she is best known.

EVELYN LINCOLN

Parent, Mimi
Canadian painter, 1924–

Born in Montreal, 8 September 1924. Studied at the Ecole des Beaux-Arts, Montreal, under Alfred Pellan, 1942–7; met the painter-sculptor Jean Benoît and participated in Pellan's anti-academic riots. Expelled for misconduct with Benoît and others, 1947. Sold everything at first exhibition at Dominion Gallery, married Benoît and went with him to Paris on a French Government scholarship, 1948. Met André Breton and joined his Surrealist group, 1959; participated in most subsequent collective Surrealist exhibitions, including those at Galleria Schwarz, Milan (1960), Galerie de l'Oeil, Paris (1965), and in São Paulo (1967) and Prague (1968). Lives in Paris.

Selected Individual Exhibitions
Dominion Gallery, Montreal: 1948
Galerie Maya, Brussels: 1966
Galerie François Petit, Paris: 1984
Museum Bochum, Germany: 1984
Centre d'Art Contemporain, Noyers-sur-Serein: 1992 (*Sauvages des Villes – Sauvages des Iles*, with Jean Benoît, Fred Deux and Louis Pons)

Bibliography
André Breton, *Le Surréalisme et la peinture*, revised edition, Paris: Gallimard, 1965
Obliques, no.14–15, 1977 (special issue: *La Femme surréaliste*)
Mimi Parent, exh. cat., Galerie François Petit, Paris, 1984
Mimi Parent, exh. cat., Museum Bochum, 1984
André G. Bourassa, *Surréalisme et littérature québécoise*, Montreal: Les Herbes Rouges, 1986
La Femme et le surréalisme, exh. cat., Musée Cantonal des Beaux-Arts, Lausanne, 1987
Sauvages des Villes – Sauvages des Iles, exh. cat., Centre d'Art Contemporain, Noyers-sur-Serein, 1992

After learning a modernised approach to Fauvism under Alfred Pellan in the mid-1940s, as exemplified in her first significant picture, the oil *Little Pink Nude* (*c*.1947; artist's collection), it was with the move to France in 1948, and especially with the discovery of Surrealism ten years later, that Mimi Parent developed a unique painting technique of her own, so far rather inadequately described as *boîtes* ("boxes"). At once paintings, bas-reliefs, collages and assemblages, these works are first shaped out of plaster, then various objects are incorporated (Parent finds the latter at flea-markets or buys them from tramps); next, the whole structure is delicately painted, framed in wood and finally put behind a protective sheet of glass. The dreamlike effect of these paintings is unfortunately lost in flat reproductions, whereas the originals emanate a rare enchantment.

One of the most striking boxes, *Blue Space* (1991; artist's collection), represents an exquisite little mermaid swimming towards the viewer and emerging from a bluish land/seascape, bathed in a gentle light, presumably that of a delicately insinuated moon. To the mermaid's left, a blue-green pine forest gradually merges into the misty background and to the right, behind her, seemingly molten rocks, turning from blue to green as they cascade down into a fountain, level with the maiden. The picture exudes a supernatural, oneiric, almost Arthurian atmosphere, like a marine Brocéliande (the forest in Brittany where Tristram and Isolde wandered).

André Breton's fascination with Mimi Parent and her work associated her with the myth of the "femme enfant", or child-woman, one of the Surrealists' favourite images of woman, as represented by Lewis Carroll's Alice and by the mythical, serpent-tailed Mélusine. Parent seems to identify with this role in her work, where numerous semi-human Alice figures frequently appear. In *Goodbye Old World* (1991; private collection, repr. Noyers-sur-Serein 1992) such a girl-child is seen in back view, walking across broken glass or ice and holding on to the tail of a bird of prey; both appear to be striving towards a sky of more broken glass, beyond a toy town of coloured wooden houses. In the *Apple Thief* (1993; artist's collection) a doll (or is it a little girl?) in a Victorian dress sits Humpty-Dumpty-like on a wall, by the Wonderland gates of a fairy-tale mansion, with a dragon on its roof, spitting fire. Parent's dream-world, like that of Alice Rahon (q.v.), is often reached through the Looking Glass of a childlike imagination. A soft blue and/or green light blurs the carefully constructed shapes as they dissolve into the background and the differences between humans, animals and inanimate objects cease to exist. At the Surrealists' "Supreme Point", where reality meets and merges with secondary states, where the unconscious surfaces, new worlds appear and disappear, open and close, rise and disintegrate. The third stage of Freud's dream-work, representation, frequently manifests itself in Parent's work. Her "boxes" function like little theatres, staging spectacles from which the viewer, like the dreamer, must remain excluded.

Parent's beautifully drawn world is hardly reassuring. Her daring use of red, as in *Rape* (private collection, *ibid.*) and *Days and Nights* (1991; private collection, *ibid.*), comes across as rather ominous. Monsters more realistic and more ordinary than the dragon of the *Apple Thief* or the horse-woman of *La Belle Cheval* (1982; see illustration) – reminiscent of images by Leonora Carrington (q.v.) – can also seem more horrific, such as the rats climbing up to a woman's open window (the Freudian symbology could hardly be more obvious) in *Diane* (1977; private collection, repr. Noyers-sur-Serein 1992) or the giant crab in the foreground of *Rape*, fixing the spectator with tiny beady eyes and clasping a woman's boot in its cruel pincers. Seismatic fragmentation frequently occurs, as in *Adieu, vieux monde* and *Gold* (1990; private collection, repr. Galerie François Petit, Paris, 1984), which shows Atlas perched on the edge of an earthquake rift, his globe exploding into countless pieces on his very shoulder. Fetish objects abound, such as the balloon faces in *Family Spirit* (1982; private collection, *ibid.*), and a variety of phallic objects are included, such as giant fish, birds, plants, towers, large arms and lobster claws.

Mimi Parent has been at her most productive since the 1980s. Her early work from before the 1970s is not easily accessible, having been dispersed into private collections. She

Parent: *La Belle Cheval*, 1982; private collection

is typical of the later generation of women Surrealists in that she has remained faithful to the movement's ideology as represented by Breton's writings, thus regarding Surrealism as a poetic way of life, seeking to explore the mysteries of the unconscious, while at the same time developing her own, strong individual form of expression, independent of any group. In her case at least, a "child-woman" means a woman still in touch with the vivid imagination of her childhood. Like Annie LeBrun and various other younger women Surrealists, Parent feels that she came into her own through Surrealism and has little sympathy with feminist condemnations of the movement. The Surrealist antinomy and magical quality of Mimi Parent's art remains best described by the *phrase fusée* ("rocket or meteoric sentence") that Breton wrote about her in *Le Surréalisme et la peinture*: "In Mimi's thistle eyes Armide's gardens glow at midnight" (Breton 1965, p.391; my translation). Thistles combine floral beauty with the threat of their prickles, while the reference to Armide's gardens renders the miniature theatre aspect of Parent's "boxes" very well.

GEORGIANA M. M. COLVILE

Parlaghy(-Brachfeld), Vilma (Elisabeth)

Hungarian painter, 1863–1923

Born in Hajdu-Dorog, Haiducken, 15 April 1863. Moved to Budapest with her family, 1864. Studied drawing under Luigi Rostagni in Budapest, 1877; also gave public performances as a pianist. Made copies after paintings in the National Gallery, Budapest, and in museums in Florence, Italy. Moved to Munich with her family, 1880. Trip to Italy, Paris and the Netherlands, 1884. Studied under Wilhelm Dürr, Christian Roth, Eugen Quaglio and Franz von Lenbach in Munich, 1886–7; also advised by Leo Samberger. Moved to Berlin, 1887–8. Trip to Vienna to carry out portrait commissions, 1888–9. Married (1) lawyer Dr Karl Krüger, 1890; divorced 1895; (2) Prince Lwoff, 1899. Trips to USA, 1896 and 1899–1900. Moved to New York, 1905. Own castle on the French Riviera, 1912. Recipient of small gold medal, Berlin, 1890; large gold medal, Berlin Academy, 1894; gold medal for Art and Science, Company of the Order of the Württemberg Crown, 1896; large official State gold medal, Berlin, 1896. Officier, Société Nationale des Beaux-Arts, Paris, 1894; jury member, Grosse Berliner Kunstausstellung, Berlin, 1902; patron, American Museum of Natural History, New York. Died in New York, 28 August 1923.

Principal Exhibitions

Individual
Hamburg: 1892
Kunstsalon Schulte, Berlin: 1893
Privatausstellung Unter den Linden, Berlin: 1895
Marienbad: 1904
Plaza Hotel, New York: 1913
"Hall of Fame", Hotel Ritz Carlton, New York: 1923

Group
Internationale Kunstausstellung, Munich: 1883, 1885, 1894
Internationale Jubiläumsausstellung, Vienna: 1888
Berlin Academy: 1888, 1890–92
Grosse Berliner Kunstausstellung, Berlin: 1890–92, 1894–5, 1897, 1907
Paris Salon: 1892 (honourable mention), 1894 (honourable mention)
World's Columbian Exposition, Chicago: 1893 (gold medal)
Exposition Internationale d'Anvers, Antwerp: 1894
Kunstsalon Gurlitt, Berlin: 1895 (*Internationale Künstlerinnenausstellung*)
Kunstverein Hannover: 1896
Internationale Ausstellung des Vereins der Künstlerinnen und Kunstfreundinnen zu Berlin: 1898
Exposition Universelle, Paris: 1900

Bibliography

R., "Vilma Parlaghy", *Allgemeine Kunstchronik*, no.44, 1884, pp.875–6
C. Regnet, "Vilma Parlaghy", *Die Kunst in Österreich-Ungarn*, Vienna, 1884, pp.92–3
"Ein weiblicher Bildnismaler", *Allgemeine Kunstchronik: Illustrierte Zeitschrift für Kunst, Kunstgewerbe, Musik, Theater und Literatur*, xiii, 1889, pp.396–7
"Vilma Parlaghy über sich selbst", *Moderne Kunst: Illustrierte Monatsschrift*, v, 1890–91, n.p.
Dr v. Eyck, "Die Berliner Jury und das Parlagische Moltke-Bildnis", *Das Atelier*, i/17, 1 July 1891, pp.1–3
R.H., "Parlaghy-Ausstellung bei Schulte", *Das Atelier*, iii/59, 1893, p.5
D.R., "Zur Lage", *Das Atelier*, iv/18, 1894, pp.6–7
Georg Malkowsky, "Vilma Parlaghy", *Moderne Kunst: Illustrierte Monatsschrift*, ix, 1894–5
"Frau Parlaghy in Amerika", *Moderne Kunst: Illustrierte Zeitschrift*, x, 1895–6
Richard Wrede and Hans von Reinfels, *Das geistige Berlin*, i, Berlin, 1898, p.380
Jarno Jessen, "Meistermalerinnen der Gegenwart", *Moderne Kunst: Illustrierte Zeitschrift*, 1901–2, p.53
"Franz von Lenbach und die Parlaghi", *Vossische Zeitung: Königlich privilegirte Berlinische Zeitung*, no.232, Abendausgabe, 19 May 1904 (with account of the interview in the French journal *Gaulois*)
Anton Hirsch, *Die bildenden Künstlerinnen der Neuzeit*, Stuttgart, 1905
Otto Spengler, ed., *Das deutsche Element der Stadt New York: Biographisches Jahrbuch der Deutsch-Amerikaner New Yorks und Umgebung*, New York, 1913
George Leland Hunter, "A woman painter of great men", *International Studio*, li, 1914, pp.195–8
Oskar von Krücken and Imre Parlagi, eds, *Das geistige Ungarn*, Vienna and Leipzig: Braumuller, 1918
Ludwig Nissen, "Latest portrait of Theodore Roosevelt", *New York Times*, 8 February 1920
Das Verborgene Museum I: Dokumentation der Kunst von Frauen in Berliner öffentlichen Sammlungen, exh. cat., Akademie der Künste, Berlin, 1987
Petra Wilhelmy, *Der Berliner Salon im 19. Jahrhundert (1880–1914)*, Berlin: De Gruyter, 1989
Carola Muysers, "Warum gab es berühmte Künstlerinnen? Erfolge bildender Künstlerinnen der zweiten Hälfte des 19. Jahrhunderts", *Profession ohne Tradition: 125 Jahre Verein der Berliner Künstlerinnen*, exh. cat., Berlinische Galerie, Berlin, 1992, pp.21–34
Dietmar Fuhrmann and Klaus Jestaedt, "Der Auftrag: Zwischen freier Kunst und Erwerbstätigkeit", *ibid.*, pp.226–7, 431
Cornelius Steckner, "Die New Yorker Malerfürstin Vilma Princess Lwoff-Parlaghy", *Bilder aus der neuen und alten Welt: Die Sammlung des Diamantenhändlers Ludwig Nissen*, exh. cat., Schleswig-Holsteinisches Landesmuseum, Kloster Cismar, 1993, pp.34–42

Vilma Parlaghy was one of the most successful women artists of the German imperial period. With her multifarious activity in the art world she challenged the usual prejudices against women to such an extent that in reviews she was referred to as a "famous portrait painter" and only secondly as "female". Parlaghy proved her talent in 1875 with a copy of Titian's *St Mary Magdalene*, for which she received a fee of 500 gulden. Even Franz von Lenbach who did not normally take on students, let alone female ones, was convinced by her talent. The young Parlaghy executed such a convincing copy of Lenbach's study for the head of *Queen Marguerita of Italy* that he accepted her as his assistant.

Although her style of painting – painstakingly detailed, unidealised facial features on a dark background – resembles that of Lenbach, Parlaghy in contrast set great store by the accurate rendering of her sitter's hands, clothes and evidence of rank, as in the portraits of the Centre Party leader, *Ludwig Windthorst* (1890), and the Prussian Minister of Finance, *Johann von Miquel* (c.1891; both Niedersächsisches Landesmuseum, Hannover). In her career-minded manner, Parlaghy became an adept pupil of Lenbach, and she even surpassed him in her ability to attract portrait commissions from high-ranking figures. The young painter understood how to attract public attention to her artistic endeavours by capitalising on scandals: thus when she was refused permission to show her portrait of the Hungarian revolutionary *Lajos Kossuth* at the national exhibition in Budapest in 1884, Parlaghy exhibited it at a charity event instead. The picture was acquired by the Hungarian Independence Party for the sum of 1000 gulden and entered the Museum of Fine Art, Budapest, in 1908. The scandal brought Parlaghy numerous commissions from renowned figures in both Hungary and Vienna.

In Berlin the young artist was celebrated at a brilliant appearance at the Academy exhibition of 1890. The well-known critic Ludwig Pietsch valued her achievement in surpassing by far the dilettantism normally associated with women artists:

> An excellent portrait of the venerable Kossuth, her self-portrait – both life-size, … immediately procured a good place for her here. They leave no doubt that in this charming guest we were seeing much more than a talented, estimable, delightful dilettante, but rather an earnest and striving artist who should be taken seriously [*Vossische Zeitung*, 10 July 1890].

The picture of her *Mother* (1889; Nissenhaus-Nordfriesisches Museum, Husum), likewise shown at the exhibition, is among Parlaghy's best early works. The sparingly lit woman's face with its stern but noble features and the Venetian manner in which the body of the three-quarter figure seems to dissolve in shadows are striking.

A year later the artist benefited from a further scandal that was to help her gain the highest recognition. Her portrait of *Field Marshal Helmut Graf von Moltke* (1891; Nissenhaus-Nordfriesisches Museum), which she completed just five days before his death, was rejected by the jury of the Grosse Berliner Kunstausstellung. The picture was subsequently acquired by the Kaiser, Wilhelm II, who had it hung in the exhibition's Room of Honour. In this work, as in the portrait of *Bismarck* (1892; Nissenhaus-Nordfriesisches Museum), commissioned

Parlaghy: *Kaiser Wilhelm II*, 1895; oil on canvas; 132 × 90 cm.; Nationalgalerie, Berlin

by the Dutch industrialist van der Zypen, the difference between Parlaghy's and Lenbach's manner becomes clear. While the latter represented the Field Marshal and the Chancellor as individual figures, Parlaghy rendered both of the famous men in upright, princely poses. Lenbach worked with photographic reproductions on the canvas for his pictures, while in contrast Parlaghy employed a purely painterly technique. This is evident above all in Bismarck's facial features, in which the brush strokes have been left visible as intrinsically valuable.

From 1892 Parlaghy received patronage from the Kaiser, and she carried out a total of seven portraits of him. Her endeavours to depart from the pathos of the traditional ruler image through a balanced relationship between uniform, pose and individual expression, as for instance in the portrait illustrated here, did not meet with unanimous approval. On the occasion of the exhibition of a picture of the Emperor in the Kunstsalon Schulte in 1893 she was reproached: "… It has turned out as nothing more than a handsome man possessed of an approximate similarity to the Kaiser" (R.H. 1893). Despite such criticism, and although Parlaghy did not officially enjoy the status of court artist, the Kaiser's good will nevertheless assured her career – he even personally opened her big solo exhibition in 1895.

The artist's style did not undergo any great development before the turn of the 19th and 20th centuries. Her interest was focused on portraying the most influential figures in her unchanging portrait technique. Among her sitters in 1894 were *Leo Graf von Caprivi*, in 1896 *King Wilhelm of Württemberg*, *Tsar Nicholas of Russia*, *King Albert of Saxony*, *King Peter of Serbia*, *Graf von Eulenburg*, the *President of the Reichsbank, Koch*, *Emperor Franz Joseph of Austria*, *Ernst von Wildenbruch* and *Hermann Sudermann*, in 1901 *Professor Kuno Fischer* and the *Grand Duke of Baden* (all untraced).

With the move to America in 1905 Parlaghy succeeded in a second precipitous career. The great industrialist Andrew Carnegie brought the artist to New York where it was intended that she should produce portraits of famous Americans. Like Lenbach, Parlaghy made copies of her most important portrait commissions, which she exhibited as a collection in New York on several occasions. Preserved from this is a pastel of her American patron *Andrew Carnegie* (Nissenhaus-Nordfriesisches Museum), which displays a striking change of style. The half-length portrait of Carnegie, seated in an armchair looking up from a book, is composed with animated strokes. The realistic and sculptural facial features, rendered with finely drawn lines combined with soft pastel tones, create a contrast to the body, which is executed in diagrammatic flecks. Even more sketch-like are the pastel portraits of *Admiral Charles D. Sigsbee* (c.1907) and the sculptor *Daniel Chester French* (both Nissenhaus-Nordfriesisches Museum). Here Parlaghy heightened only the prominent features such as the chin, nose and brow with white in order to create an impression of three dimensions. In her oil painting the artist also turned towards looser brushwork. In the portrait of *Joseph Hodges Choate* (1914; Nissenhaus-Nordfriesisches Museum) she rendered the gown, hands and face of the judge in the same manner with rough brush strokes. President Theodore Roosevelt was among the important politicians, entrepreneurs, artists and poets whom Parlaghy portrayed. He was painted by her in a group portrait with the scientific explorer Anthony Fiala. Six weeks before Roosevelt's death in 1919 she painted a second picture, which was to be the last portrait of the President (untraced). Works by Parlaghy were sold at auction on 9 April 1924; a large number were acquired by Ludwig Nissen.

CAROLA MUYSERS

Pasch, Ulrica Fredrica
Swedish painter, 1735–1796

Baptised in Stockholm, 7 July 1735; daughter of the portrait painter Lorens Pasch the Elder, member of a well-known artistic dynasty, and his wife Anna Helena Beckman. Trained by her father. Never married. Member, Royal Academy of Painters and Sculptors (now Royal Academy of Fine Arts), Stockholm, 12 August 1773. Died in Stockholm, 2 April 1796.

Principal Exhibitions
Royal Academy of Painters and Sculptors, Stockholm: 1793, 1794

Bibliography
Thure Wennberg, *Minne af Ulrica Fredrica Pasch, Ledamot af Kongl. Målare- och Bildhuggare-Academien* [In memory of Ulrica Fredrica Pasch, Member of the Royal Academy of Painters and Sculptors], Stockholm, 1798

Ludvig Looström, *Den svenska Konstakademien under första århundradet af hennes tillvaro* [The Swedish Royal Academy of Fine Arts during its first century, 1735–1835], Stockholm: Looström, 1887

Vägledare till retrospektiva afdelningen på Svenska konstnärinnornas utställning [Guide to the retrospective section of the Swedish women artists' exhibition], exh. cat., Royal Academy of Fine Arts, Stockholm, 1911

Ludvig Looström, *Kungl. Akademiens för de fria konsterna samlingar af målning och skulptur* [The Royal Academy of Liberal Arts' collection of painting and sculpture], Stockholm, 1915

Sixten Strömbom, *Porträttmålaren Lorens Pasch d.y.: Hans liv och konst* [The portrait painter Lorens Pasch the Younger: His life and art], Stockholm: Norstedt, 1915

K.K. Meinander, *Porträtt i Finland före 1840-talet* [Portraits in Finland before the 1840s], Helsinki, 1931

Emil Hultmark, *Kungl. Akademiens för de fria konsterna utställningar, 1794–1887*, [Exhibitions of the Royal Academy of Liberal Arts, 1794–1887], Stockholm, 1935

Anna Lena Lindberg, "Stå på piedestal – eller konkurrera?" [Stand on a pedestal – or compete?], *Kvinnor som konstnärer* [Women as artists], ed. Anna Lena Lindberg and Barbro Werkmäster, Stockholm: Liber, 1975, pp.99–122

Britta Hammar, "Dräkter på porträtt" [Costumes in portraits], *Kulturen*, 1988, pp.86–94

Ulrica Fredrica Pasch, 1735–1796, exh. cat., Norrköpings Konstmuseum, Norrköping, and elsewhere, 1992

Anna Lena Lindberg, "Ulrica Fredrica Pasch and the 'Eternal Feminine'", *Woman's Art Journal*, xv/2, 1994–5, pp.3–8

Ulrica Fredrica Pasch och hennes samtid [Ulrica Fredrica Pasch and her contemporaries], exh. cat., Royal Academy of Fine Arts, Stockholm, 1996

Swedish art of the 18th century blossomed in contact with the art life of Europe, of which Paris was seen as the focus, although links with England were also important. The break-up of the guild tradition (when women could be trained in workshops) was hastened in 1773 when the Royal Academy of Painters and Sculptors (now the Royal Academy of Fine Arts) received its statutes from King Gustaf III and was definitively established. This transfer to institutional training signified that in Sweden, as elsewhere, women were excluded from art education and thereby indirectly from the expanding exhibition life and art market. Ulrica Fredrica Pasch's selection in 1773 as the only woman member of the Academy meant that she was likewise regarded as the first Swedish professional woman artist. The changed structure of the art world, however, itself put an end to a long tradition of professional women painters in Sweden, with such exponents as Anna Maria Ehrenstrahl (1666–1729) and Anna Maria Thelott (c.1683–1710), both of whom had been trained in their fathers' workshops.

Ulrica Fredrica Pasch was born into a well-known dynasty of artists: her great-grandfather, Danckwardt Pasch the Elder, a painter and alderman in Stockholm, had emigrated to Sweden from Lübeck at the end of the 17th century; her grandfather, Danckwardt the Younger, was also a painter, as were her uncle, the decorative painter Johan Pasch, and her father, the portrait painter Lorens Pasch the Elder. To what extent the

Pasch: *Self-Portrait*, late 1770s; Nationalmuseum, Stockholm

female members of the Pasch family collaborated in the craft workshops of the respective generations is, however, unclear. Ulrica Fredrica first trained with her father, together with her brother Lorens Pasch the Younger. The conventions of the time prevented her, but not her brother, from continuing her training abroad. Instead, she began her career as a professional artist by painting "regent tables", that is, a series of small copies after older royal portraits. Gradually, however, she began to portray live sitters. One of Pasch's earliest patrons was a now unknown noble lady, whose portrait hangs at the Kulturen, Lund. The sitter is dressed in the Swedish court dress of the period, a silk dress of light blue, with broad lace in flower patterns along the décolletage and lace frills on the sleeves. A date in the 1760s is indicated by the hairstyle, with its curls at the neck, and the arrangement of the silk cloak in Prussian blue. The artist's use of this newly released, artificially produced colour – and not the expensive ultramarine – shows that she, perhaps with her brother Lorens as intermediary, followed the latest developments in Europe. In any case her brother (who became director of the Academy in 1793) stated in a biography of Ulrica Fredrica (Strömbom 1915) that he had shared his acquired talents with her after returning to Stockholm in 1766, after 14 years of study (at the Royal Danish Academy of Fine Arts in Copenhagen and in Paris) and commissions abroad. Thereafter Lorens and Ulrica Fredrica worked together and shared their household with a younger sister, Hedvig Lovisa. Like their father, they worked mainly in oils.

Any mention of Ulrica Fredrica Pasch in the earlier art-historical literature gave a very biased picture of her capacities and influences. Only as a result of the research of the 1990s do we know that she had a very wide circle of patrons, drawn from the court, the nobility, the clergy, the growing middle class and even the peasantry. Like her father and brother, Pasch executed several portraits for patrons in Finland, which at that period belonged to Sweden. Apart from the above-mentioned female portrait, among her early paintings is the portrait of the spokesman for the peasants, *Josef Hansson* of Mossbo parish, dated 1766.

Pasch was also regularly engaged by the glamorous Gustavian cultural elite, painting portraits, for example, of the opera singer *Elisbeth Olin* (undated) and her husband *Carl Stenborg* (1785; both Kungliga Teatern, Stockholm), the poet and Marshal of the Realm *Johan Gabriel Oxenstierna* (1785; private collection) and such politicians as *Gustaf Adolf Reuterholm* (two portraits, 1776 and 1787; Gripsholm Castle). Reuterholm even commissioned Pasch to paint his entire family.

Baron Adolf Ludvig Stierneld was 25 years of age when Pasch painted him in Stockholm in August 1780 in his stark blue, so-called Swedish dress (Gripsholm Castle), two years after it was introduced by Gustaf III. Another male portrait, of the chemist *Torbern Bergman* (Gripsholm Castle), represents the sitter dressed in a similar way. The purpose of the dress reform, which was compulsory for all those, like Stierneld, who were attached to the Swedish court or, like Bergman, to the Academy of Sciences, was to check growing luxury and to stimulate national industry.

Pasch's portraits, including a series of charming representations of children, are immediate and realistic descriptions, constantly demonstrating her delight in colour and skill in the rendering of fabrics. Contrary to what had earlier been stated, an inventory taken before the exhibition of her work at Norrköping (1992) showed that she had as many male as female patrons.

A central work is Pasch's *Self-Portrait* (see illustration) from the late 1770s. The subject faces the viewer, her head slightly turned, but her eyes seemingly absorbed by something outside the picture. She wears a low-cut, rose-coloured silk dress with lace at the sleeves and a white tulle shawl, which she holds in her right hand. In the décolletage a few flowers, among them a rose, are attached to a yellow- and violet-striped silk ribbon tied in a bow. The artist has framed herself by an ideal landscape, with a tree to the left, a rose-tinted sky in the background and a faraway mountain on the horizon to the right. Such a composition, with a central figure set against an ideal landscape, was used frequently in the 18th century, and dates back at least as far as Leonardo da Vinci's *Mona Lisa* (Louvre, Paris).

Pasch's self-portrait differs in one important respect from those of other female artists of the time. Unlike the *Self-Portrait* (National Gallery, London) of Elisabeth Vigée-Lebrun, for example, where the artist shows herself with palette and brushes, thereby indicating her profession, here the artist holds her delicate shawl. This may be a compositional device, giving the hand a seemingly natural object to hold on to, or is her intention in fact similar to Vigée-Lebrun's? Pasch's painting is a reception piece, meant to hang in the Academy, where everybody knew that she was an artist. There was thus no need to emphasise her profession. Rather, she could demonstrate her ability to paint the shimmering silk of a dress, the transparency of the shawl, the freshness of the flowers, and to capture the likeness of her image as well as illustrate her knowledge of art traditions.

Most of Ulrica Fredrica Pasch's works are in private collections; the principal public collections of her paintings are the Royal Academy of Fine Arts and the Nationalmuseum, Stockholm; Gripsholm Castle; and the Museum of Foreign Art, Sinebrychoff, Helsinki.

ANNA LENA LINDBERG

See also Academies of Art survey

Passe, Magdalena van de
Dutch printmaker and draughtswoman, 1600–1637

Born in Cologne, 1600, the youngest of five children. Moved with her family to Utrecht, 1612. Trained by her father, the printmaker and publisher Crispijn van de Passe the Elder. Married Frederik van Bevervoordt, 1634; returned to her father's house after husband's death in 1636. Died in Utrecht, 1637.

Bibliography

Joachim von Sandrart, *L'Academia todesca della architectura, scultura e pittura: Oder Teutsche Academie der edlen Bau-, Bild- und*

Mahlerey-künste, i, Nuremberg, 1675; ed. A. R. Peltzer, Munich, 1925; reprinted Farnborough: Gregg, 1971

Christiaan Kramm, *De levens en werken der Hollandsche en Vlaamsche beeldhouwers, graveurs en bouwmeesters* [The lives and works of the Dutch and Flemish painters, sculptors, engravers and architects], ii, Amsterdam, 1859

Daniel Franken, *L'Oeuvre gravé des van de Passe*, Amsterdam, 1881

Charles Le Blanc, *Manuel de l'amateur d'estampes*, iii, Paris, 1888

P. Haverkorn van Rijsewijk, "De Nalatenschap van Crispiaen van de Pas den Oude" [The legacy of Crispiaen van de Pas the Elder], *Oud Holland*, x, 1892, pp.97–128

F. W. H. Hollstein, *Dutch and Flemish Etchings*, xvi, Amsterdam: Hertzberger, 1974

Hella Robels, *Niederländische Zeichnungen vom 15. bis 19. Jahrhundert im Wallraf-Richartz-Museum Köln*, Cologne: Das Museum, 1983

Katlijne van der Stighelen, *Anna Maria van Schurman (1607–1678) of "Hoe hooge dat een maeght kan in de konstel stijgen"* [Anna Maria van Schurman (1607–1678) or "How high a maid may rise in art"], Leuven: Universitaire Pers Leuven, 1987

Nadine Orenstein, "Who took the King of Sweden to bed?", *Print Quarterly*, viii, 1991, pp.44–7

Sabina Lessmann, "Zur Präsenz der Künstlerin Magdalena van de Passe", *Köln der Frauen*, ed. Irene Franken and Christiane Kling-Mathey, Cologne, 1992, pp.233–40

Magdalena van de Passe learned the trade of a graphic artist from her father, the copper engraver and publisher Crispijn van de Passe the Elder, who also taught his skills to Magdalena's three brothers Simon (b. 1595), Crispijn the Younger (b. 1597) and Willem (b. 1598). Unlike that of her sister Martha (b. 1594), Magdalena's training in drawing and copper engraving was not restricted to reproducing art work, but also allowed her to develop her own designs and style. While her brothers left Utrecht from 1616 onwards in order to find work in London and Paris, Magdalena carried on working in her father's workshops. All the work that can be ascribed to Magdalena today was published by her father, and all the extant dated prints were made between 1617 and 1634. It is not known whether she continued to work after her marriage in 1634, or whether she took up work again after her husband's death and her return to her father's house. The principal collections of her work are in the Rijksprentenkabinet, Rijksmuseum, Amsterdam, and the Wallraf-Richartz-Museum, Cologne.

The earliest dated drawings, three pictures of the *Sibyl* dated 1617, give an indication of the way in which the various members of the family worked together on an artistic project. Crispijn the Elder, Simon, Crispijn the Younger and Magdalena all worked on the *Sibyl* series, of which there are 12 altogether, and here their differing drawing styles are distinguishable. At the two extremes in this series lie Simon's hard, almost metallic line and Magdalena's soft light version. Apparently the workshop did not insist on laying down a standard style but allowed room for individuality, reflecting the distinctions between the artists. Noticeable characteristics of Magdalena's work are a preference for detail, lively line and pronounced chiaroscuro. Her work encompasses biblical and mythological scenes, symbolic representations, landscapes, architecture and portraits. There are copper engravings after Rembrandt, Adam Elsheimer, Rubens, Roelandt Savery, J. C. Pynes, Paul Bril, A. Willaert and also countless engravings after her father's

Passe: *Annunciation*, engraving; Rijksmuseum, Amsterdam, Graphic Collection

designs. Magdalena is credited by name as the engraver of these plates.

Gustus and *Auditus*, two pen-and-ink drawings signed by Magdalena, are sketches for the series the *Five Senses*. This was planned by Crispijn the Elder and engraved by Willem, who worked from Magdalena's sketches, as evidenced by the dots along the lines on the pictures. Tasks in the family business were accordingly divided up in various ways. The pen-and-ink drawings *Summer* and *Winter* in the series the *Four Seasons* were used by Magdalena herself to prepare the copper engravings. Her deviations from her father's designs again bear witness to her own creative ideas, which she was able to realise in the workshop.

The signatures on the above drawings are evidence both of her self-confidence as an artist and of the fact that she herself valued these drawings, which she produced as prototypes. There are also official mentions of Magdalena's role as an artist and active member of the workshop. A contract dated 1623 mentions a fee of 18 guilders to be paid to Magdalena by Hans Letoir for two drawings. An official letter dated 1636 gives Magdalena, who by then was already a widow, a claim on 1000 guilders that her father was to pass on to her for services rendered. This document does not detail whether these services included private and domestic tasks as well as artistic ones.

In light of the fact that only members of the Guild of St Luke could work as artists in Utrecht (Anna Maria van Schurman, q.v., is said to have been the only woman who was admitted to it), it is noteworthy that Magdalena van de Passe was able to ignore this. Apparently a family workshop offered sufficient protection here. Women, even when not organised according to the guilds, seem to have been accepted as exceptions to the rule. Their activities, however, were controlled and limited by guild regulations.

In 1630 Simon van de Passe finished an engraved portrait of his sister accompanied by Minerva and Pictura entitled *Magdalena de Pas Crispiana filia sculptrix celeberrima: Aet. 30* (Magdalena van de Passe, daughter of Crispijn, a most celebrated sculptress: aged 30). This, and the reference made by Joachim von Sandrart in his *Teutsche Academie*, bear witness to the artist's fame and recognition. Appreciative words about her are followed by an allusion to her brother Simon, who "was not inferior to his sister in his achievements", an inversion of the usual references to women in relation to male artists in art-historical texts.

Before 1623 Magdalena took on another task: the artistic training of Anna Maria van Schurman. These lessons brought two very different contemporaries together: on the one hand, Anna Maria van Schurman as the ideal embodiment of a female polymath, and on the other, Magdalena van de Passe as a specialist artist. Very few examples of the training of one woman artist by another have been handed down to us.

SABINA LESSMANN

Pauli, Hanna *see* Hirsch Pauli

Peale, Anna Claypoole, 1791–1878, and Sarah Miriam, 1800–1885
American painters

Daughters of Mary Claypoole, and of James Peale of Philadelphia, a miniature, still-life and portrait painter; uncle was the painter Charles Willson Peale. Other siblings, including sisters Margaretta Angelica (1795–1882) and Maria (1787–1866), were also painters.

Anna Claypoole Peale Born in Philadelphia, 6 March 1791. Trained by her father. Attended lectures on anatomy for artists at the College of Physicians, Philadelphia, 1819. Lived in Philadelphia, but painted in Washington, DC, late 1818–spring 1819; visited Washington again, 1820; also made annual trips to Baltimore, and painted briefly in Boston, 1821 and 1827, and New York. Married (1) Revd William Staughton, 27 August 1829; he died December 1829; (2) General William Duncan, 1841; he died 1864. Ceased professional activities after second marriage. Member, Pennsylvania Academy of the Fine Arts, Philadelphia, 1824. Died in Philadelphia, 25 December 1878.

Principal Exhibitions
Pennsylvania Academy of the Fine Arts, Philadelphia: 1811, 1814, 1817–32, 1835–8, 1840–42
Boston Athenaeum: 1828, 1831

Sarah Miriam Peale Born in Philadelphia, 19 May 1800. Trained by her father. Attended anatomy classes at College of Physicians, Philadelphia, with sister Anna, 1819. Travelled between Philadelphia and Baltimore with Anna, 1818–25, working in cousin Rembrandt Peale's Baltimore studio until 1822, and exhibiting work in his Museum. Lived in Baltimore, 1825–46, taking occasional trips to Washington, DC, to paint public figures. Resided in St Louis, 1847–77. Returned to Philadelphia, 1878. Member, Pennsylvania Academy of the Fine Arts, Philadelphia, 1824. Died in Philadelphia, 4 February 1885.

Principal Exhibitions
Pennsylvania Academy of the Fine Arts, Philadelphia: 1817–22, 1824–31
St Louis Agricultural and Mechanical Association: 1856 (diploma and prize), 1858, 1859 (first prize), 1860 (first prize), 1864 (first and second prizes), 1866, 1867 (two second prizes)
Missouri Historical Society, St Louis: 1872

Bibliography
Elizabeth Fries Ellet, *Women Artists in All Ages and Countries*, New York: Harper, 1859; London: Bentley, 1860
Anna Wells Rutledge, *Cumulative Record of Exhibition Catalogues: The Pennsylvania Academy of the Fine Arts, 1807–1870 …*, Philadelphia: American Philosophical Society, 1955
Rendezvous for Taste: Peale's Baltimore Museum, 1814 to 1830, exh. cat., Municipal Museum of the City of Baltimore, 1956
The Peale Family and Peale's Baltimore Museum, 1814–1830, exh. cat., Municipal Museum, Baltimore, 1965
Miss Sarah Miriam Peale, 1800–1885: Portraits and Still Life, exh. cat., Peale Museum, Baltimore, 1967
Lillian B. Miller, ed., *The Collected Papers of Charles Willson Peale and His Family*, microfiche, Millwood, NY: KTC Microform, 1980
Charlotte Streifer Rubinstein, *American Women Artists from Early Times to the Present*, Boston: Hall, 1982
Karen McCoskey Goering, "St Louis women artists, 1818–1945: An exhibition", *Gateway Heritage*, iii/1, Summer 1982, pp.14–21
Lincoln Bunce Spiess, "St Louis women artists in the mid-19th century", *Gateway Heritage*, iii/4, Spring 1983, pp.10–23
James L. Yarnall and William H. Gerdts, *The National Museum of American Art's Index to American Art Exhibition Catalogs from the Beginning through the 1876 Centennial Year*, Boston: Hall, 1987
Anne Sue Hirshorn, "Modes of accomplishment and fortune: Anna Claypoole, Margaretta and Sarah Miriam Peale", *Creation of a Legacy: The Peale Family, 1770–1870*, ed. Lillian B. Miller, New York: Abbeville, 1996
——, *Anna Claypoole Peale* (in preparation)

Unpublished correspondence, papers and catalogues of paintings are in the American Philosophical Society, Philadelphia (Peale-Sellers Papers); Archives of the Municipal Museum of the City of Baltimore (Peale Museum); Catalogue of American Portraits and Peale Family Papers office, National Portrait Gallery, Smithsonian Institution, Washington, DC; and Frick Art Reference Library, New York.

Born into a family of artists, Sarah Miriam Peale and her sister Anna Claypoole were introduced to painting at an early age by their father James Peale, a portraitist and still-life painter, whom they assisted with backgrounds and costume details. Anna reported that she would stand behind her father's chair "for hours and hours at a time watching James progress. He took great pains", she recalled, "in teaching her, pointing out the peculiar touches that produced his best effects by giving a

charm to the expression" (Ellet 1859, p.290). They were probably given the usual course of instruction for artists at the time,
with emphasis on drawing, the painting of still lifes and
copying. The James Peale family lived on an extremely limited
income, and at a young age Anna Claypoole worked at filling
in outlines of maps with delicate watercolour paint, colouring
engravings and, between 1805 and 1807, making an occasional copy of her father's miniature portraits at the request of
his patrons. With her sister Maria, she launched her public
career in 1811 with the exhibition of a painting of flowers at
the Pennsylvania Academy of the Fine Arts. However, it was
the delicate art of miniature painting – an art that was considered suitable for a genteel woman – that drew her to the life of
an artist; under her father's tutelage and assisted by her uncle,
Charles Willson Peale, Anna Claypoole began accepting
commissions for such portraits from 1814 on, her father relinquishing the market to her. Although still-life painting continued to command the attention of her older sister Maria and the
younger Margaretta (who occasionally exhibited still lifes – or,
infrequently, portraits – at the Pennsylvania Academy between
1828 and 1837, but who was essentially an amateur), from this
time Anna Claypoole concentrated her artistic attention on
miniature work.

Anna's miniatures followed her father's Federal style; lighter
in colour, more fluidly painted, her small watercolour portraits
on ivory were graceful and elegant. Praised for their "accuracy
and truth", clear and precise drawing, minute details of
costume and lively expression, such miniatures as *Miss
Susannah Williams* (1825; see illustration) responded directly
to the position of her sitters, in both their public and private
lives. Her miniature of *Major General Andrew Jackson* (1819;
Yale University Art Gallery, New Haven), for example, places
the soldier in a heroic setting, in recognition of his controversial but successful expedition in Florida against the Seminole
Indians, but Jackson as an individual remains remote and cold,
his gaze turned away from the viewer and his eyes veiled as he
contemplates a distant scene. Painted at the same time, her
miniature of *Senator Richard Mentor Johnson* (1819; Museum
of Fine Arts, Boston) is warmer, more informal, suggestive of a
close intimacy between the artist and the Kentucky colonel and
statesman, who was a friend of her family and, it would
appear, a suitor for a brief time during her Washington visit in
1819.

With the only interruption the brief interlude of her
marriage in 1829, Anna Claypoole Peale pursued an ambitious
artistic career. Her work reflected changing tastes in the miniature, which were manifested in particular in the work of such
Boston artists as Pamela Hill, Sarah Goodridge and her sister
Eliza Goodridge. From small delicately painted oval ivories,
framed in precious metals or stones, that could be carried or
worn, these artists, including Anna, began to favour larger
rectangular cabinet miniatures set in leather cases suitable for
display on a table top or for hanging on a wall. Instead of
presenting the sitter bust-size, her subjects, like others painted
in miniature during the 1820s and 1830s, began to be shown
in half-length, standing or sitting next to a table and framed by
draperies. As taste in the early Victorian period turned to
darker palettes, Anna also experimented with a richer, deeper
colouring. In response to the early Victorian interest in
European old masters and in art as an indication of cultivated

Anna Claypoole Peale: *Miss Susannah Williams*, 1825;
watercolour on ivory (miniature); Maryland Historical
Society, Baltimore

taste, she, too, turned to the making of copies, in watercolour
on ivory, of European works. Her copy of Guido Reni's
Beatrice Cenci (1829; untraced) suggests an ambition to create
imaginative art beyond the conventional portrait. During these
decades, Reni was one of the most popular 17th-century artists
in the USA, his *Sibyl* becoming the source of many a Victorian
"fancy piece". The story of Beatrice Cenci was also a popular
legend; it became the subject of Shelley's tragedy, *The Cenci*
(1819), of a painting by Thomas Sully in 1825 after Reni, and
of a sculpture by Harriet Hosmer (q.v.). Anna's choice of this
tragic heroine as a subject for a miniature suggests a deeper
side to the artist than is manifested in her charming, somewhat
shallow family miniatures, especially since it was painted soon
after the unhappy ending of her short marriage.

Like her sisters, Sarah Miriam Peale also began her artistic
career painting still life, but almost immediately turned to
portraiture. At the age of 17 she painted her first formal
portrait – a *Self-Portrait* (National Portrait Gallery,
Washington, DC) – which she exhibited in 1818 at the
Pennsylvania Academy to her uncle Charles Willson Peale's
praise that it was "wonderfully like". Although her uncle
reported in 1818 that Sarah was more interested in breaking
hearts than painting portraits, unlike her sister she did not
interrupt her career with marriage; instead, she remained, as
the *Missouri Republican* noted in 1877, "wedded to her art".

Sarah Miriam Peale is generally associated with Baltimore.
Here, she successfully competed for commissions with some of
the leading male artists of the time, and included among her
patrons members of the city's prosperous middle class – entire
families such as the William Jessops and visiting dignitaries

Sarah Miriam Peale: *Charles Levallen Jessop (Boy on a Rocking Horse)*, *c*.1840; private collection

such as the first Brazilian Chargé d'Affaires in the USA, *José Sylvestre Rabello* (1826; Brazilian Embassy, Washington, DC). Occasionally, she travelled to Washington, DC, to paint such public figures as the *Marquis de Lafayette* (1824–5; private collection) and, between 1841 and 1843, *Daniel Webster* (Mercantile Library, St Louis), *Abel P. Upshur* (Maryland Historical Society, Baltimore), *Congressman Henry Wise of Virginia* (Virginia Museum of Fine Arts, Richmond), *Congressman Caleb Cushing of Massachusetts* (untraced), *President John Tyler* (Historical Society of Pennsylvania, Philadelphia) and *Senator Thomas Hart Benton of Missouri* (Missouri Historical Society, St Louis). In 1847 Sarah Miriam accepted the invitation of some Missouri social and political leaders, including Nathaniel Childs, Trusten Polk and Senator L. F. Linn, to visit St Louis, where she remained for 30 years. Little is known about her life during this period, except that she was warmly welcomed in St Louis, a thriving community with a great interest in cultural activities and host to a number of artists. As in Baltimore, Sarah Miriam's patrons consisted of entire families, such as the Edward Armistead Owens family (three portraits, *c*.1857; private collection). In 1860 her portrait of *Edward William Johnston* (Mercantile Library of St Louis), a colonel in the Mexican War, was awarded the first premium at the St Louis Agricultural and Mechanical Association's fair. From 1859 Sarah Miriam painted primarily still lifes, exhibiting them successfully in the annual St Louis fairs and winning premiums. She returned to Philadelphia in 1878 and died there in 1885, the last member of the second generation of her painting family. One of America's first woman artists to earn professional recognition, she was also one of the first to maintain herself as an artist through a long lifetime.

As a result of her residency in Baltimore, many of Sarah Miriam Peale's Baltimore portraits have been mistakenly attributed to her cousin Rembrandt Peale, although her work is easily distinguished from his. Her portraits are firmly drawn, somewhat linear, and painted with a minimum of shadowing or chiaroscuro. She revelled in finely painted details of lace and fabrics, the use of accessories such as books, flowers or objects pertinent to the sitter's position, and rich colour and glazing that result in translucent, almost oily skin tones. Her sitters look lively and pleasant, and highly naturalistic. An occasional newspaper review of portraits painted in St Louis praised the "accuracy" of her likenesses and their "life like expression". Her portraits of children, such as *Charles Lavallen Jessop (Boy on a Rocking-Horse)* (*c*.1840; see illustration), are imaginatively and charmingly composed. Portraits of women painted during the 1820s and 1830s are enhanced by either a foreground still life or a landscape background; the subjects are elegantly costumed and wear beautifully painted shawls or transparent organdie bonnets. Sarah Miriam delighted in ornament, rich textures and elaborate patterns, as may be seen in the wedding portrait of her cousin, *Charlotte Ramsay Robinson* (*c*.1840; Peale Museum, Municipal Museum of Baltimore). Her male subjects appear dignified, intelligent and cheerful in simpler portraits that were considered more appropriate to their gender. Conservative and traditional, her portraits only occasionally suggest the spritely and independent personality described in her letters; one that does is *Veil of Mystery* (*c*.1830; Peale Museum), a romantic, sensuous and suggestive image composed around the same time that her sister Anna Claypoole was painting *Beatrice Cenci*.

During her lifetime Sarah Miriam painted at least 50 still lifes, not all of which have been located. Her earlier still lifes reflect the influence of her father James and cousin Raphaelle Peale; primarily depicting fruit composed on a strong diagonal and spilling out of a bowl on to a polished table top, they convey the luxuriance of American nature (e.g. *Still Life*, 1822; Richard York Gallery, New York). Her later still lifes are painted with a looser hand and stylistically reflect the changes that occurred in paintings of this genre in the mid-19th century under the influence of the American Pre-Raphaelites, who depicted flowers or fruit growing in their natural out-of-doors setting rather than artificially collected in containers indoors (e.g. *Cherries*, *c*.1860; private collection).

LILLIAN B. MILLER

Peeters, Clara
Flemish painter, active 1611–21

No certain details of her life are known. Possibly she was the Clara Peeters, daughter of Jan Peeters, who was baptised in St Walburgs, Antwerp, 15 May 1594. The same or another Clara Peeters married Hendrick Joossen in St Walburgs, 31 May 1639.

Bibliography

Women Artists, 1550–1950, exh. cat., Los Angeles County Museum of Art, and elsewhere, 1976

N.R.A. Vroom, *A Modest Message as Intimated by the Painters of the "Monochrome Banketje"*, 2 vols, Schiedam: Interbook International, 1980 (Dutch original, 1945)

Still-life in the Age of Rembrandt, exh. cat., Auckland City Art Gallery, 1982

De Rijkdom Verbeeld: Schatkamer van de Gouden Eeuw/A Prosperous Past: The Sumptuous Still Life in the Netherlands, 1600–1700, exh. cat., Stedelijk Museum Het Prinsenhof, Delft, and elsewhere, 1988

Celeste Brusati, "Stilled lives: Self-portraiture and self-reflection in seventeenth-century Netherlandish still-life painting", *Simiolus*, XX, 1990–91, pp.168–82

Pamela Hibbs Decoteau, *Clara Peeters, 1594–ca 1640, and the Development of Still-Life Painting in Northern Europe*, Lingen: Luca, 1992

Julie Berger Hochstrasser, *Life and Still Life: A Cultural Inquiry into Seventeenth-Century Dutch Still-Life Painting*, PhD dissertation, University of California, Berkeley, 1995

At the beginning of the 17th century in Europe, still life was just emerging as an independent genre in its own right, and Clara Peeters was playing a formative role in its development. Painting in the Netherlands, Peeters was among the originators of the finely detailed oil paintings of flowers, breakfasts and banquets, fish and game that proved so popular over the course of the century. Her earliest dated paintings, with the dates reading most probably 1607 and 1608, are small, intimate still lifes that set the tone for her production (repr. Decoteau 1992, pls 1 and 2). The motifs they present would recur in her work: glasses of wine, biscuits and sweets, oysters and shrimp, bread and fruit. The earlier picture (private collection, England) contains a biscuit in the shape of a *P* that may be self-referential; it is the first of many expressions of a subtle self-consciousness that distinguishes Peeters's art. Most notably, these compact compositions already differ from the more scattered lay-out and more distant, elevated viewpoint characteristic of other early still lifes of the laid table, such as those by the older Antwerp painter Osias Beert. Other early affinities of subject and technique suggest that Peeters may have studied under Beert, although surviving records do not list her as his pupil. But Beert's compositions were soon to appear old-fashioned, whereas Peeters's novel compositional instincts were borne out in the subsequent evolution of 17th-century Netherlandish still life.

Four larger, more elaborate paintings (*Game*, 51 × 71 cm.; *Dainties*, 52 × 73 cm.; *Fish*, 50 × 72 cm.; *Pie*, 55 × 73 cm.; all Prado, Madrid) masterfully summarise themes to which Peeters would return throughout her career. All signed and of nearly identical dimensions, they seem to have been produced as a group; three are dated, all 1611. One featuring a variety of dead birds is the earliest dated example of a "game piece" (unless one counts Jacopo de Barbari's Munich panel of 1504 which stands quite apart). Another focusing on freshly caught fish, shrimp, crabs and a strainer of artichokes presages numerous fish studies by Dutch painters. Peeters's characteristic linear articulation and hair-breadth brushwork detail every scale on the fish, every feather on the birds; in both pictures, closely clustered objects, viewed from a low vantage point, overlap to enhance the impression of depth, marking Peeters's

innovative approach to composition. The third Prado painting depicts a banquet laid on a fine damask tablecloth: delicacies such as an elaborate pie, citrus fruits, olives and boiled partridges are served up with fine tableware of silver and porcelain. In a central position at the front of the picture is a silver knife with adornments typical of the *bruidsmessen* (brides' knives) made by Antwerp goldsmiths between 1595 and 1600; along its edge the artist's name is clearly legible, depicted as if engraved there. Whether this was only a pictorial invention (Segal in Delft 1988) or a real object made and personalised for Peeters (Decoteau 1992) – a possibility supported by the fact that she depicted the same knife on several other occasions over a period of 20 years – the artist deploys it here as a distinctive means for signing her work. But a still more remarkable flourish of self-reflection appears in the fourth Prado painting. It combines a vase of flowers with a spread of costly tableware and dainty foods, centring on a finely wrought gilt goblet. Mirrored in the smooth nodes of the gold cup, Peeters has registered the reflection of herself at her easel. Her youthful face appears several times more on the polished surface of the pewter pitcher in the background on the right – and yet again on the lid of the stoneware jug in the fish piece.

These tiny reflections constitute an unusual kind of self-portrait: scarcely visible except under close scrutiny, they incorporate the working artist right into the still-life scenes she depicts. Heir to the sharply honed skills of her earlier Netherlandish predecessors, Peeters painted with oils to an intense level of illusionism. Jan van Eyck had similarly captured his reflection in miniature in the armour of St George in his *Virgin and Child with Canon van der Paele* (1436; Musée Communal, Bruges) – an image that Peeters may have seen (Brusati 1990–91). Her use of the device seems to invoke this heritage, claiming a place for herself within it. But Peeters was among the first painters to integrate such self-portraiture into the realm of still life – only one known example predates hers, an anonymous still life of 1538 (Kröller-Müller Museum, Otterlo) that she had probably not seen. Many other Netherlandish painters were later to incorporate reflected self-portraits into still lifes – Pieter Claesz, Jan de Heem, Abraham van Beyeren and others – often depicting one, occasionally two faces in a picture. But of the surviving examples, Peeters seems to have been the only one to repeat her likeness over and over within one image in this way, as if silently but perseveringly insisting that we cannot overlook the young woman who wields the brush. Rightly so: although in the 18th century still life became known as a woman's genre (a pejorative association reflecting unfavourable estimations of both women and still life), at this early juncture Peeters was the only Netherlandish woman whose name survives among a cast of men at work in this genre. Others followed later in the century – Margaretha de Heer (q.v.), Maria van Oosterwijck (q.v.), Rachel Ruysch (q.v.) – but Peeters had a seminal role.

From the prolific year of 1612 there are at least ten paintings from her hand, five of them dated; their innovations place Peeters at the forefront of the evolution of the genre. Most are flower paintings (all in private collections or untraced), in which Peeters begins to depart from the conventions of her contemporaries by trying out a more sparse, asymmetrical arrangement with fewer different species. Two of her three

Peeters: *Still Life*, 1612; Staatliche Kunsthalle, Karlsruhe

food paintings in this year are also signed and dated. Whether focusing on seafood and wine (Poltava Art Museum, Russia), herring, cherries and an artichoke (Richard Green Gallery, London), or gilt cup, sweets and a pomegranate (Richard Green Gallery), all intensify the compressed arrangement of her earliest "banquets". The latter two, of identical dimensions, may form pendants contrasting poor versus rich meals, or perhaps simply everyday versus festive fare; Peeters's face is vaguely visible again on the lid of the stoneware jug of the more "common" still life.

A masterpiece inscribed CLARA P. ANNO 1612 (see illustration) revisits the self-reflection exercise in a testimony both to Peeters's prodigious painterly skills and her irrepressible creative personality. It depicts an array of valuable things: gold coins and a golden chain, two extraordinary covered gilt goblets, a Chinese celadon bowl, exotic shells and a vase of rare flowers. The scene has been associated with *Wunderkammer* collections of rare and precious objects: even the blossoms, such as the tulip and the checkered fritillary, were coveted collectibles. Others have interpreted the fragile blooms and expensive display as a *vanitas* admonishing the ephemerality of worldly riches. But Peeters's reflected self-portraits add a unique twist to this image: on the smooth spots of the gilt goblet in the background, we detect again – and again and again, some eight times over – the tiny figure, seated at her easel, palette and brushes in hand, her position adjusted slightly each time for the angle of view. It is a record of patient observation that rewards careful looking, a display of meticulous crafting that rivals the skilful production of the precious objects she depicts (Brusati 1990–91). Peeters informs us in no uncertain terms who has produced the value of this painting. But more than mere self-promotion, these repeated self-reflections challenge the *vanitas* notion by reminding us that it is the unique ability of the artist to overcome the transience of fragile flowers, of earthly wealth, even of this youthful visage – by fixing them, triumphant against the ravages of time, in paint. It is all the more dramatic for the astonishing accomplishment displayed by this painter who, by all the accounts of the uncertain documentation, at the time was only 18 years old.

That scanty documentation is another element in the drama played out in these tiny self-portraits. We do not find Peeters inscribed into the Antwerp guild, though records for many applicable years are lost. Nor did art biographers of the period tell us of her life, despite the part her work clearly played in the course of Netherlandish painting. The only documents we have, about the Antwerp baptism of 1594 and the Antwerp marriage of 1639 of one Clara Peeters, are not even certainly about *this* Clara Peeters. If they are, they establish that her talents were precocious; yet a girl would have had to be exceptional to secure training at all in those days, and these youthful self-portraits do seem to correlate the age these documents indicate. Left as we are with little more than these pictures to inform us about their creator, the insistent painterly presence of these diminutive self-portraits becomes especially poignant.

To survey Peeters's oeuvre is to observe the careful arrangement and rearrangement of certain favoured subjects, masterfully rendered: a stack of cheeses, sometimes topped by a plate of butter pats, an artichoke halved to reveal the delicate patterns of its leaves and centre, whole shrimp with their hairlike antennae, plump red cherries, brittle pretzels, a plate of almonds and figs and raisins. Even the tableware becomes familiar; like many still-life colleagues during this period, Peeters studies the same objects over and over again, sometimes with slight variations. Her choices occasion virtuoso rendering of a wide variety of materials and textures: besides the faithful knife, the gilt goblets and the pewter pitcher, other repeated objects are too numerous to list exhaustively: a cylindrical silver salt-cellar, a certain stoneware jug, a patterned porcelain plate, a particular wicker basket, various distinctive wine-glasses. Her latest surviving dated work stands as an exception to this pattern: a painting on copper of the *Virgin and Child* within a floral wreath (1621; private collection, repr. Decoteau 1992). More representative is a large picture that inventories many of her chosen themes, combining flowers and fruit and other familiar subjects with the pitcher reflecting her face and the knife bearing her name (Ashmolean Museum, Oxford). Other undated paintings attributed to this decade for stylistic reasons include several more food paintings with cheeses or artichokes, and some variations on the theme of a pile of fresh fish eyed by a cat (one in the National Museum of Women in the Arts, Washington, DC). Four signed works probably from the 1630s consolidate the themes already put forward: a "cheesestack" that re-enlists the bridal knife, two fruit baskets with the nibbling monkeys popular in Flemish still life and another fish painting (all untraced). The panel-maker's initials marked on the back of this final piece date it probably after 1637, making it very likely the last of Peeters's surviving signed works.

Clara Peeters's influence was felt well beyond Antwerp, beyond the Southern Netherlands, in the Dutch Republic (the Northern Netherlands) and Germany. The several trips she was thought to have made from Antwerp north into Holland were an important bridge between the two creative centres. Her reduced format, low viewpoint and restricted palette provided impetus towards the monochrome style of such Haarlem painters as Nicolaes Gillis and Pieter Claesz. Peeters's hand is especially evident in Claesz's linear depictions of a few objects on a bare wood table in his "close-up" paintings of the 1620s – so much so that many attributions are disputed between the two artists. This situation is aggravated by their shared initials, as many paintings are monogrammed in ligature (C and P intertwined). In flower painting, her simplified bouquets predated Ambrosius Bosschaert's own adoption of more spacious arrangements, just as her work often anticipated that of Bosschaert's brother-in-law and follower Balthasar van der Ast early in his career. Banquet paintings by both the German Peter Binoit and the Fleming Artus Claessen directly echoed her work in style and motifs. Judging from the large number of paintings that have been attributed to her (particularly by Vroom) and the considerable circle of her influence (19 works have more recently been relegated to the "circle of Peeters" by Decoteau, with many more showing affinities), Clara Peeters was clearly neither minor nor unknown in her time. Decoteau pointed to the need to re-evaluate the extent of her influence and consider the possibility that she headed a small school. Her work demonstrates not only stylistic independence and painstaking technical achievement, but also a vital artistic personality. Besides putting forward her own visions of the possibilities of a new genre, Peeters devised ways to claim them as her own, leaving her mark on the history of still-life painting in the West.

JULIE BERGER HOCHSTRASSER

Peláez (del Casal), Amelia
Cuban draughtswoman, painter and ceramist,
1896–1968

Born in Yaguajay, Cuba, 5 January 1896. Moved with her family to Havana, 1915. Studied at Escuela de Bellas Artes de San Alejandro, Havana, 1916–24 and 1926–7; Art Students League, New York, 1924. Awarded Cuban government grant to study in France, 1927; attended art history and drawing courses at Académie de la Grande Chaumière, Ecole Nationale Supérieure des Beaux-Arts and Ecole du Louvre, Paris, 1928–31; studied at Académie Moderne under Alexandra Exter (q.v.), c.1930–34; also travelled extensively in Europe. Returned to Cuba and set up studio at her home in La Víbora, Havana, 1934. Concentrated on ceramic decoration and design, 1950–62, setting up a ceramic workshop in 1955; on murals, 1950–58. Recipient of prizes at Exposición Nacional de Pintura y Escultura, Havana, 1935, 1938, 1956 and 1959; first prize, Pintura moderna cubana, Galería Sudamericana, New York, 1956. Died in Havana, 8 April 1968.

Principal Exhibitions

Individual
Asociación de Pintores y Escultores, Havana: 1924 (with María Pepa Lamarque)
Galerie Zak, Paris: 1933
Lyceum, Havana: 1935, 1957, 1960 (retrospective), 1967
Círculo de Amigos de la Cultura Francesa, Havana: 1936 (with Carlos Enríquez and Domingo Ravenet)
Norte Gallery, New York: 1941
Institución Hispano-Cubana de Cultura, Havana: 1943 (retrospective)
Instituto Municipal de Cultura Marianao, Havana: 1959
Galería de la Habana, Havana: 1964
Museo de Arte Moderno, Bogotá: 1967
Museo Nacional, Palacio de Bellas Artes, Havana: 1968 (retrospective)

Group
Salon des Indépendants, Paris: 1934
Lyceum, Havana: 1936 (Exposición de pintura, with Victor Manuel, Carlos Enríquez and Domingo Ravenet), 1945 (5 Pintores), 1954 (Plástica cubana)
Centro de Dependientes, Havana: 1937 (Arte moderno)
Universidad de la Havana: 1940 (El arte en Cuba)
Museum of Modern Art, New York: 1944 (Modern Cuban Painters)
Pan-American Union, Washington, DC: 1946 (Cuban Modern Painting in Washington Collections), 1957 (4 Artists of the Americas, with Roberto Burle-Marx, Alexander Calder and Rufino Tamayo), 1959 (Contemporary Drawings from Latin America)
Liljevalchs Konsthall, Stockholm: 1949 (7 Kubanska malare [7 Cuban painters])
São Paulo Bienal: 1951, 1953, 1957, 1961, 1963
Venice Biennale: 1952
Galería Sudamericana, New York: 1956 (Pintura moderna cubana), 1957 (Five Women Painters from Latin America)

Solomon R. Guggenheim Museum, New York: 1957 (Guggenheim International Award, 1956)

Bibliography
Exposition Amelia Peláez del Casal, exh. cat., Galerie Zak, Paris, 1933
André Salmon, "Les Arts", Gringoire, 12 May 1933
Amelia Peláez, exh. cat., Lyceum, Havana, 1935
José Lezama Lima, "Amelia Peláez", El Arte en Cuba, Universidad de la Habana, 1940
David Alfaro Siqueiros, "Los artistas modernos cubanos", Ultra (Havana), xiv/83, July 1943, pp.36–9
Guy Pérez Cisneros, "Amelia Peláez o el Jardín de Penélope", Grafos Havanity, xiv/114, August 1943, pp.12–13
"Exposición Amelia Peláez", Ultra (Havana), September 1943
Jorge Mañach, "Amelia Peláez o el absolutismo plástico", Revista de la Habana, iii/13, September 1943, pp.32–8
José Gómez Sicre, Pintura cubana de hoy, Havana: Maria Luisa Gómez Mena, 1944
Alfred Barr, "Modern Cuban painters", Museum of Modern Art Bulletin, xi/5, April 1944, pp.2–7Robert Altman, "Ornamento y naturaleza muerta en la pintura de Amelia Peláez", Orígenes (Havana), Winter 1945, pp.7–14
4 Artists of the Americas: Roberto Burle-Marx, Alexander Calder, Amelia Peláez, Rufino Tamayo, exh. cat., Pan-American Union, Washington, DC, 1957
Alejo Carpentier, Amelia Peláez, Artes Plásticas, no.1, Havana: Dirección de Cultura del Ministerio de Educación, 1960
Loló de la Torriente, "El arte cubanísimo de Amelia Peláez", Bohemia (Havana), 7 September 1962
Graziella Pogolotti, "Amelia Peláez: Versión clásica del barroco cubano", Cuba, iv/33, January 1965, pp.34–45
Amelia Peláez: Exposición retrospectiva, exh. cat., Museo Nacional, Palacio de Bellas Artes, Havana, 1968
Alejandro G. Alonso, "Amelia Peláez y su magnificación de lo cotidiano, El Mundo: Suplemento Cultural (Havana), 22 December 1968, pp.6–8
Marisol Trujillo, Amelia Peláez, Comisión Nacional de la Unesco, Colección Pintura Cubana, Havana, 1973
Damián Bayón, Aventura plástica de Hispanoamerica, Mexico: Fondo de Cultura Económica, 1974
La gran pintora cubana Amelia Peláez, 1896–1968: Oleos, temperas, tintas, exh. cat., Museo de Arte Moderno, Mexico City, 1979
José Lezama Lima, "Amelia", Imagen y posibilidad, Havana: Letras Cubanas, 1981, pp.75–80 (reprinted from Oleos, témperas y dibujos de Amelia Peláez, exh. cat., Galería de la Habana, 1964, and La Gaceta de Cuba, no.38, 15 June 1964, pp.12–13)
Amelia Peláez: Dibujos, exh. cat., Museo de Arte Moderno, Universidad Nacional, Bogotá, 1987
José Seoane Gallo, Palmas reales en el sena, Havana: Letras Cubanas, 1987
Amelia Peláez, 1896–1968: A Retrospective/Una retrospectiva, exh. cat., Cuban Museum of Art and Culture, Miami, and elsewhere, 1988
The Latin American Spirit: Art and Artists in the United States, 1920–1970, exh. cat., Bronx Museum, New York, 1988
Bélgica Rodríguez, "Apuntes sobre Amelia Peláez y el arte latinoamericano", Plástica (San Juan, Puerto Rico), i/18, March 1988, pp.64–75
Art in Latin America: The Modern Era, 1820–1980, exh. cat., South Bank Centre, London, and elsewhere, 1989
Amelia Peláez: Exposición retrospectiva, 1924–1967: Oleos, témperas, dibujos y cerámica, exh. cat., Fundación Museo de Bellas Artes, Caracas, 1991
Edward Lucie-Smith, Latin American Art of the 20th Century, London and New York: Thames and Hudson, 1993
Juan A. Martínez, Cuban Art and National Identity: The Vanguardia Painters, 1927–1950, Gainesville: University Press of Florida, 1994

Marta Traba, *Art of Latin America, 1900–1980*, Washington, DC: Inter-American Development Bank, 1994

The importance of Amelia Peláez lies in the highly individual pictorial vocabulary that she created within Cuban modernism of the first half of the 20th century. In her art, Peláez achieved a new synthesis between certain aspects of Cuban cultural traditions and French modernist formal innovations, creating a modern national style that was at the same time universal.

Peláez belonged to a generation of Cuban "Vanguardia" painters that by the mid-1920s was reacting against the conservative practices of the Academy. Their fundamental concern was the need to create a national art that was at the same time universal. During the 1920s and early 1930s she did not participate actively in the Vanguardia agenda, but followed an independent but in many ways parallel path. Her paintings of the mid-1920s already show a rejection of the sentimental and anecdotal in favour of a more spontaneous and individual treatment of landscape, as in *Tree in the Cemetery* (1926; Museo Nacional de la Havana).

During the Paris years (1927–34) Peláez experimented extensively, producing a body of eclectic work. The teaching of the Russian Constructivist artist Alexandra Exter (q.v.) on composition, abstraction and colour theory was fundamental to her understanding of modernism. Peláez's grasp of Cubism, especially that of Picasso, Gris, Braque and Léger, and of the work of Matisse, gave her the formal language she needed to free herself from the constraints of naturalism and academicism. The ink drawing *Church* (1929; Museo Nacional de la Havana) is a schematic composition tending to abstraction; the planes are flattened and a thick, flowing black outline sketches in the church and the decorative elements dominating the scene. This drawing reveals a radical change in the artist's work and shows some of the elements that would characterise her mature style.

When Peláez returned to Cuba, she began to incorporate local "criollo" subject matter in her work: fruits, flowers and fish, and Cuban colonial and 19th-century architectural and ornamental elements – the wrought iron and carved wood of balconies, gates, fanlights and shutters, mosaics, stained-glass windows, chairs, tablecloths, lace, etc., considering them as representative of "Cubanía" (Cuban-ness; Seoane Gallo 1987). Peláez's interest in Cuban colonial architecture coincided with a general national concern for its preservation during the 1930s and 1940s. The tropical light also had a profound impact on her work, transforming the darker, sombre colours of the Parisian period into bright, contrasting areas of flat colour. In *Still Life in Red* (1938; Museum of Modern Art, New York) Peláez uses Cubist devices to create complex and ambiguous spatial effects. The flat, broken surfaces of the red mantelpiece rhyme with the central motif of a guanabana (local fruit); the open-window – a Cubist device – brings architecture into the picture, with intricate ironwork and exuberant greenery.

Peláez's work was dominated from this time by still lifes and figures of women in domestic settings; profuse decoration contrasted with solid, rigorous structure. Despite her subject matter being centred on the intimacy of the domestic sphere, her pictures are never anecdotal or sentimental, but abstracted or sublimated. Peláez belonged to an upper-class Creole family that retained old colonial values. She never married and her whole life was centred on her art. Her subject matter, particularly her women, belonged to the realm of her private life, rooted in the past, but her vocabulary was modern and experimental. (Peláez never painted male figures, with the exception, in the 1930s, of a series of papiers collés entitled *Card Players*, which were mostly a pretext for developing new plastic solutions.) In *The Balcony* (1942; Mr and Mrs Arturo Munder collection, Miami) two Picassoesque women are integrated into the decorative elements of the picture in a counterpoint between figuration and abstraction. The *Siesta* series of the 1940s (e.g. *Siesta*, 1941; Museo Nacional de la Havana) recalls Matisse's series of *Odalisques*, but the sensuality of Peláez's women is not studied or voyeuristic, but subtle, contained and natural. Between 1934 and 1945 Peláez also did illustrations for Cuban and Hispanic poetry (including *La Agonía de Petronio*, 1936, by her uncle Julián del Casal) and contributed drawings to literary and cultural magazines, especially *Orígenes*.

After 1940 ornament became the main structural element of her work, and sometimes also its subject, which has led to her style being characterised as "baroque". This term has been the cause of much dispute, because it had traditionally referred to a European style and period. The Cuban writer Alejo Carpentier has described "American baroque" as a particularly Cuban and American mode of life and art, vital, exuberant and ornamentally rich (for discussions of American baroque, see Alejo Carpentier, "La ciudad de las columnas" and "Problemática de la actual novela latinoamericana" in *Tientos y diferencias*, 1966, and Leonardo Acosta, *El barroco de indias y otros ensayos*, 1982). By this definition, some aspects of Peláez's style can be described as baroque. Works such as *Fishes* (1943; see illustration) show the artist's mature style: a stage-like setting, simultaneous arrangement of space and figures, formal tension, purified pictorial values, rhythms created by thick black organic lines on contrasting areas of flat colour, integration of architecture and stained-glass window, and profuse decoration. In *Still Life* (1945; private collection, Miami, repr. Miami 1988, p.86) Peláez has worked from the concrete to the abstract until ornamentation dominates the entire surface of the picture.

During the 1950s Peláez started working on ceramics, decorating traditional Cuban pottery and later designing her own works. At this time she received several commissions for ceramic public murals, one of the most important being the *Tiles Mural* for the Tribunal de Cuentas (now Ministry of Internal Affairs), Havana, in 1953. The nature of the surfaces of both pottery and tile murals led to important changes in her style, obliging her to simplify composition and favouring a tendency to greater abstraction.

Although many of her family left the country on the establishment of the Communist régime in 1959, Peláez decided to remain in Cuba and travelled abroad again only in 1966, for a cataract operation. In the 1960s she did some of her most interesting work. She returned to ideas and sketches of earlier years, and produced a series of almost monochrome still lifes, simplified and with a deep sense of balance, such as *Yellow Flowers* (1964; Museo Nacional de la Havana). In her last years she painted a series of works on paper in which the figurative motifs have disappeared. In the gouache *Untitled* (1966;

Peláez: *Fishes*, 1943; oil on canvas; 114.5 × 89.2 cm.; Museum of Modern Art, New York; Inter-American Fund

private collection, *ibid.*, p.95) the ornamental abstract motifs drawn with thick black lines on areas of flat colour create a dynamic and resolute composition. Peláez remained active until her death in 1968.

CECILIA FAJARDO HILL

Pepper, Beverly
American sculptor, 1924–

Born Beverly Stoll in Brooklyn, New York, 20 December 1924. Studied advertising and industrial design at Pratt Institute, Brooklyn, 1939–41 (BA), then worked as commercial art director for numerous advertising agencies, 1942–8; also attended classes at Art Students League and Brooklyn College, New York. Studied painting at Académie de la Grande Chaumière and under Fernand Léger and André Lhôte in Paris, 1949. Married writer and journalist Curtis Gordon "Bill" Pepper (second marriage), 1949; one daughter, one son (also one son from first marriage). Travelled widely before settling in Rome, *c.*1951; moved to Todi, Umbria, 1972. Recipient of gold medal and sculpture purchase award, Mostra Internazionale Fiorino, Italy, 1966; first prize and purchase award, Jacksonville Art Museum, Florida, 1970; National Endowment for the Arts (NEA) grants, 1975 and 1979; honorary doctorates from Pratt Institute, Brooklyn, 1982, and Maryland Institute College of Art, Baltimore, 1983; artist-in-residence, American Academy, Rome, 1986; professor emeritus, University of Perugia, 1987; Outstanding Achievement in the Visual Arts award, Women's Caucus for Art, 1994. Lives in New York and Gentile di Todi, Umbria, Italy.

Selected Individual Exhibitions
Barone Gallery, New York: 1954, 1956, 1958
Galleria dell'Obelisco, Rome: 1959
Galleria Pogliani, Rome: 1961
Marlborough Gallerie d'Arte, Rome: 1965, 1968, 1972
Marlborough-Gerson Gallery, New York: 1969–70 (touring)
Tyler School of Art, Temple University, Rome: 1973
André Emmerich Gallery, New York: 1975, 1977, 1979, 1982, 1983, 1984, 1986, 1987, 1988, 1989, 1990 (twice), 1991, 1993
San Francisco Museum of Art: 1975 (touring)
Sala delle Pietre, Todi, Umbria: 1979
Huntington Galleries, Huntington. WV, 1983
Albright-Knox Art Gallery, Buffalo, NY: 1986–7 (touring retrospective)
List Visual Arts Center, Massachusetts Institute of Technology, Cambridge: 1989
Metropolitan Museum of Art, New York: 1991

Selected Writings
"Space, time and nature in monumental sculpture", *Art Journal*, xxxvii, Spring 1978, p.251

Bibliography
Beverly Pepper: Recent Sculpture, exh. cat., Marlborough Gallery, New York, 1969
Beverly Pepper: Sculpture, 1971–1975, exh. cat., San Francisco Museum of Art, and elsewhere, 1975
Jan Butterfield, "Beverly Pepper: 'A space has many aspects'", *Arts Magazine*, l, September 1975, pp.91–4 (interview)
Eleanor Munro, *Originals: American Women Artists*, New York: Simon and Schuster, 1979
Beverly Pepper in Todi: Sculture nella Piazza, exh. cat., Sala delle Pietre, Todi, 1979
Margaret Sheffield, "Beverly Pepper's new sculpture", *Arts Magazine*, liv, September 1979, pp.172–3
Beverly Pepper: In Situ at the Huntington Galleries, exh. cat., Huntington Galleries, Huntington, WV, 1983
Will Ameringer, "The new sculpture of Beverly Pepper", *Arts Magazine*, lviii, October 1983, pp.108–9
Kenneth Baker, "Interconnections: Beverly Pepper", *Art in America*, lxxii, April 1984, pp.176–9
Beverly Pepper: Sculpture in Place, exh. cat., Albright-Knox Art Gallery, Buffalo, NY, and elsewhere, 1986
Beverly Pepper: Urban Altars and Ritual Sculpture, exh. cat., André Emmerich Gallery, New York, 1986
Barbara Rose, "A monumental vision", *Vogue*, March 1987, pp.484–7, 535
Gregory Galligan, "Beverly Pepper: Meditations out of callous steel", *Arts Magazine*, lxii, October 1987, pp.68–9
Deborah Solomon, "Woman of steel", *Art News*, lxxxvi, December 1987, pp.112–7
Walter Thompson, "Beverly Pepper: Dramas in space", *Arts Magazine*, lxii, Summer 1988, pp.52–5
John Beardsley, *Earthworks and Beyond: Contemporary Art in the Landscape*, revised edition, New York: Abbeville, 1989
Howard J. Smagula, *Currents: Contemporary Directions in the Visual Arts*, 2nd edition, Englewood Cliffs, NJ: Prentice Hall, 1989
Charlotte Streifer Rubinstein, *American Women Sculptors*, Boston: Hall, 1990
Duane Preble and Sara Preble, *Art Forms: An Introduction to the Visual Arts*, 5th edition, New York: HarperCollins, 1993

Born in Brooklyn, New York, Beverly Pepper received her early training at the Art Students League and Pratt Institute in industrial and advertising design. From 1942 to 1948 she worked as a highly successful advertising director, married and had a son. Then, becoming disenchanted with the commercial world, she turned to painting and, in 1948, after a divorce, left for Europe to study under Fernand Léger and André Lhôte. She married the journalist Bill Pepper and travelled widely in Europe and the Middle East before finally settling in Italy.

Pepper did not begin her sculpture career until she was 40. Invited to submit a welded sculpture to the exhibition *Sculture nelle città* in Spoleto, Italy, in 1962, she encountered the art concepts and technology that would transform her artistic medium from anguished abstract painting, in reaction to post-war experiences, to large-scale prismatic sculptures of enamelled steel. Her sculpture is a spectator art, built with the social intention of drawing the viewer into aesthetic and emotional confrontation with impressive and elegant sculptural forms. At Spoleto, Pepper assumed a direct personal role in the steel construction, made possible through training in welding and forging at a steel foundry. With a minimum of help, she worked in cutting and joining large-scale sheets of enamelled steel and, with the exception of *Amphisculpture*, assisted in working the bulldozer and cement mixer. In response to the concepts of classical art that she encountered in Italy, Pepper's imagery emerged as strikingly simple triangles and circles, adroitly integrated to create an immediate and uplifting visual impact.

Pepper: *Fallen Sky*, 1974; painted steel; Hirschhorn Museum of Art, Washington, DC

On-site sculpture, which was developed particularly in the 1960s and 1970s, placing large-scale, often abstract structures in outdoor settings, presents a diverse range of styles and concepts, from vast contrivances of steel beams to contoured terrains set with waterfalls and pools. Realities vary from the rigid and absolute to the ephemeral and self-destructive. They may stand apart, as minimal monoliths, separate from nature, or act as earth modulators, transient flags of nature's climatic cycles and geophysics. Pepper's on-site pieces exhibit a combination of both trends. Sturdy, permanent elements reflect natural transitory phenomena, yet invoke metaphors from history and prompt emotional reactions.

Fallen Sky (1974; see illustration) comprises several polished aluminium squares resting on each other in overlapping oblique patterns on a bed of natural pebbles within a square border. The reflections of sky captured in the squares are modulated through the criss-crossing of apertures to create interesting slanted designs. Rather than being directly tied into the ground, the piece's earth reference is made through the reflection of the pebbles in the polished surfaces of the squares.

Pepper's major piece, *Amphisculpture* (1974–7; 2.4 × 82 × 4.2 m.; repr. Rose 1987, p.486), was commissioned for the AT & T Office Building at Bedminster, New Jersey. It consists of a series of concentric rings of concrete embedded in the earth, interlocking with the terrace-like benches, the cement surfaces alternating with turf. The circular pattern is bisected by a wedge-shaped form that appears to ride lightly on the unit like folded wings, one wing extending over the rings to form a platform, reminiscent of the corridors of Greek theatres. But whereas in the ancient theatre the circular stage was situated in front of the semicircular auditorium, in Pepper's design the circular structure is extended around the back of the "stage", reinforcing the idea of the infinite. In addition to the formal references to Greek theatres, the notion of festival is symbolic in the rings themselves. Originating in the cycles of plays dedicated to Dionysus, god of wine, the circular area was devoted to ritual dancing and the joyous celebration of grape harvests. Instead of being made of transitory sculptural materials, as are many earthworks, *Amphisculpture* moderates the environmental conditions, rising out of winter snow, green turf turning to autumn brown, shifting sunlight slanting across the unit in varying shafts, marking the cycle of the seasons unchanged since the Dionysian pageants. All this is expressed in the clean-cut clarity of Greek concepts. As in the Greek theatre, spectators are invited to sit on the benches, to enjoy the changing aspects and the harmony of the total form.

Thel, constructed in September 1977 and comprising four pieces of enamelled steel, is situated in the grounds of Dartmouth College, Hanover, New Hampshire. Pepper's desire to create beautiful, social environments was realised in this multiple work on the campus lawn. Adjusted to the site for permanent emplacement, the smaller arrow segment is partly submerged in the ground, its flat surface ending in a point that directs the eye to the four smaller triangular shapes and then to the larger pristine triangular hood that projects boldly from the ground. The sharp slopes of the triangle, secured by two points at the rear, provide seating and shade for student relaxation, but do not intrude on the quality of the terrain, a response to the request of the concerned students who originally opposed the project. In fact, Pepper created a waffled interior in the larger form, of criss-cross ribs, which acts as seating support and provides visual contrast to the sheer outer surfaces of the sculpture. To enhance the sense of integration of the sculpture with the environment, one side of the large triangle is covered with turf. The transitory aspect of the work relies on movement around and in the structure, accented by the students' colourful clothing and varying positions both inside and out. As in other sculptures, *Thel* keeps time with the seasons, changing its impact from displaying its brilliant white slopes against the green lawns in summer, shimmering in soft moonlight at night or slicing up through the snow of winter.

Designed for the San Diego Federal Building, *Excalibur* (1976; 10.6 × 13.7 × 10.6 m.), in painted steel, consists of a series of triangular shapes. Three slanted shafts rising like sharks' teeth from a platform of steel seem to tug against their moorings. Two larger forms flare in classic simplicity from the front, balanced and held down by a third shape at the rear. It is an exuberant piece, yet full of elegance and tension. Pepper has achieved high acclaim for her monumental installations and has participated in major shows, such as the Venice Biennale in 1972. That same year she moved to Todi, where she resides in a 14th-century castle and maintains her own foundry.

JANET A. ANDERSON

Pereira, I(rene) Rice
American painter, 1902–1971

Born Irene M. Rice in Chelsea, Massachusetts, 5 August 1902. Attended evening classes at Art Students League, New York, studying under Richard Lahey and Jan Matulka, 1927–31. Travelled to Europe and Africa, 1931–2; possibly studied under Amédée Ozenfant at Académie Moderne, Paris. Taught painting and design synthesis for Design Laboratory, New York, 1936–9 (originally part of the Works Progress Administration Federal Art Project, WPA/FAP). Museum assistant, Museum of Non-Objective Painting, 1940–42.

Taught design at Pratt Institute, Brooklyn, 1942–3. Began Jungian psychoanalysis, 1948. Travelled to France, 1949. Moved to Salford, England, 1950. Returned to USA and taught at Ball State University, Muncie, Indiana, 1951. Spent time at MacDowell Colony, Peterborough, New Hampshire, 1953. Made frequent visits to Europe after 1960. Converted to Catholicism, 1963. Established I. Rice Pereira Foundation in New York, 1968. Moved to Spain after eviction from New York apartment, 1970. Married (1) painter and commercial artist Humberto Pereira, 1929; divorced 1938; (2) engineer and amateur photographer George Wellington Brown, 1942; divorced 1950; (3) Irish poet George Reavey, 1950; divorced 1959. Elected Life fellow, International Institute of Arts and Letters, Lindau-Bodensee, Germany, 1959. Recipient of honorary doctorate, L'Université Libre (Asie), Karachi, Pakistan, and International Federation of Scientific Research Societies of Europe, Asia, Africa and America, 1969. Died of emphysema in Marbella, Spain, 11 January 1971.

Principal Exhibitions

Individual
American Contemporary Arts (ACA) Gallery, New York: 1933, 1934, 1935, 1946, 1949
East River Gallery, New York: 1937
Howard University, Washington, DC: 1938
Julien Levy Gallery, New York: 1939
Museum of Non-Objective Painting, New York: 1940, 1942
Art of This Century Gallery, New York: 1944
San Francisco Museum of Art: 1947
Barnett Aden Gallery, Washington, DC: 1948
Whitney Museum of American Art, New York: 1953 (touring retrospective, with Loren MacIver)
Corcoran Gallery of Art, Washington, DC: 1956
Andrew Crispo Gallery, New York: 1976 (retrospective)

Group
Whitney Museum of American Art, New York: 1935 (*Abstract Art in America*)
Museum of Modern Art, New York: 1946 (*Fourteen Americans*, touring)
Metropolitan Museum of Art, New York: 1946 (*Advancing American Art*, touring)

Selected Writings
"Light and the new reality: A treatise on the metaphysics of light with a new aesthetic", New York, 1951; expanded and reprinted in *Palette*, Spring 1952, pp.2–11
The Transformation of "Nothing" and the Paradox of Space, New York: I. Rice Pereira, 1953
The Nature of Space: A Metaphysical and Aesthetic Inquiry, New York: I. Rice Pereira, 1956; reprinted Washington, DC: Corcoran Gallery of Art, 1968
The Lapis, New York: Wittenborn, 1957; reprinted Washington, DC: Corcoran Gallery of Art, 1970
Crystal of the Rose, New York: Nordness Gallery, 1959 (poems, with introductions by Lee Nordness and Ranjee Shahani)
The Finite Versus the Infinite, New York: I. Rice Pereira, 1959
The Transcendental Formal Logic of the Infinite: The Evolution of Cultural Forms, New York: I. Rice Pereira, 1966
The Poetics of the Form of Space, Light and the Infinite, New York: I. Rice Pereira, 1969

Bibliography
Elizabeth McCausland, "Alchemy and the artist: I. Rice Pereira", *Art in America*, xxxv, July 1947, pp.177–86

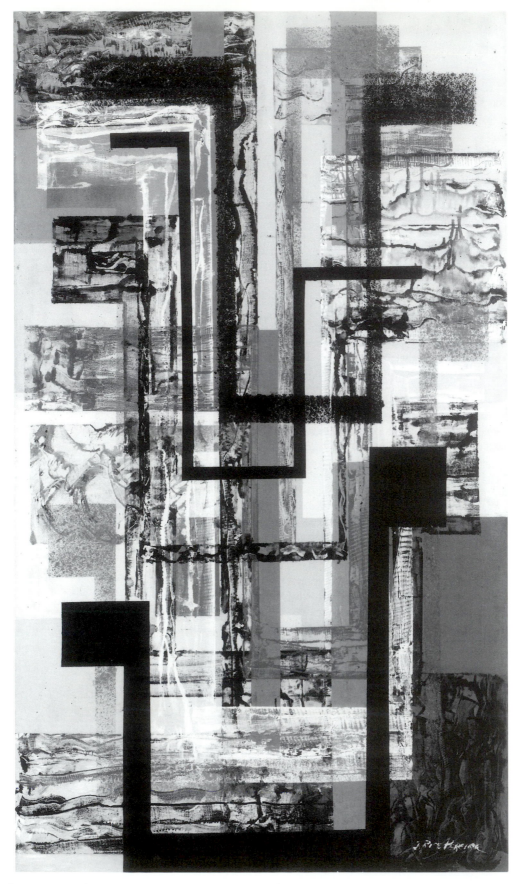

Pereira: *Pillar of Fire*, 1955; oil on canvas; San Antonio Museum of Art, Texas

Loren MacIver/I. Rice Pereira, exh. cat., Whitney Museum of American Art, New York, and elsewhere, 1953

James Harithas, "I. Rice Pereira: American painter-writer with bold solutions to old problems", *Vogue*, June 1970

I. Rice Pereira, exh. cat., Andrew Crispo Gallery, New York, 1976

Donald Miller, "The timeless landscape of I. Rice Pereira", *Arts Magazine*, liii, October 1978, pp.132–3

Therese Schwartz, "Demystifying Pereira", *Art in America*, lxvii, October 1979, pp.114–19

Judith K. Van Wagner, "I. Rice Pereira: Vision superseding style", *Woman's Art Journal*, i/1, 1980, pp.33–8

Irene Rice Pereira's Library: A Metaphysical Journey, exh. cat., National Museum of Women in the Arts, Washington, DC, 1988

Mara R. Witzling, ed., *Voicing Our Visions: Writings by Women Artists*, New York: Universe, 1991; London: Women's Press, 1992

Karen A. Bearor, *Irene Rice Pereira: Her Paintings and Philosophy*, Austin: University of Texas Press, 1993 (contains extensive bibliography and full exhibition list)

Irene Rice Pereira's Early Work: Embarking on an Eastward Journey, exh. cat., Lowe Art Museum, University of Miami, Coral Gables, 1994

In 1953 Irene Rice Pereira shared with Loren MacIver (q.v.) the honour of being the first living American woman to be given a retrospective at the Whitney Museum of American Art. Coming at the mid-point of a career spanning four decades, this show testified to her prominence in vanguard art movements of the time and capped a distinguished exhibition record that included solo and group shows at several of the most prominent Manhattan museums and galleries. Pereira became a pioneer in the use of glass as a painting support. Her most impressive works in this medium include *Shooting Stars* (1952; Metropolitan Museum of Art, New York), which is formed by two panes of corrugated glass suspended in a shadow-box frame over a panel. Each visual level is painted with opaque and translucent rectilinear forms that allow shadows and light to be cast into and reflected from the depths of the construction. The resulting effect is one of fugues of radiating colour and light, with geometric shapes appearing to surface within a rippling, aqueous matrix. Well-read in popular science and pseudo-science, idealist philosophy and Jungian psychology, the artist frequently related her works to the concept of a fluid and relational space-time continuum. She believed this cosmic continuum and the human psyche to be structurally isomorphic; thus these paintings also become metaphoric of the stratiform Jungian psyche. The visual synthesis of the physically discrete levels in these constructions is analogous to the process of individuation, which involves integrating the conscious, personal unconscious and collective unconscious of Jungian psychoanalysis. The mutable forms appearing to ascend from the interiors of paintings can then be interpreted as archetypes emerging from the depths of the collective unconscious.

If Pereira's geometric abstractions seemingly place her within a different artistic tradition from that of her Abstract Expressionist counterparts, her lifelong interest in subjectivity certainly places her within a similar philosophic one. While it is unclear when she became aware of Jung's writings (the earliest confirmed date is 1937), in the early 1930s she shared with her first husband, Humberto Pereira, an interest in the Faust legend – the structure of which Jung related to the process of individuation – and other mythical tales of spiritual quest and transformation. Such tales inform her paintings of machine and marine paraphernalia throughout this decade. These works are stylistically indebted to Synthetic Cubism; many of them are located in the Lowe Art Museum, University of Miami, Coral Gables, Florida, the largest single institutional holding of Pereira's paintings. Dabbling in social critique in 1936, when she became associated with leftist artist organisations in New York, Pereira offered an indictment of the impact of the machine on society in *Man and Machine* (first version, Lowe Art Museum; second version, University of Arizona Museum of Art).

The following year Pereira created her first abstractions, in which she explored the tactile and reflective properties of various materials, her investigations inspired by László Moholy-Nagy's book *The New Vision* (1930), based on Bauhaus studio practices. The Dessau Bauhaus was the pedagogical model for the Design Laboratory, a school of industrial design sponsored by the Works Progress Administration Federal Art Project in New York. Pereira was a member of the original faculty when it opened in 1936, and it was during her tenure there that she was also introduced to writings by Adolf von Hildebrand, Wilhelm Worringer, C. Howard Hinton and Sigfried Giedion. Texture and light are her main concerns in the abstract painting *White Rectangle No.1* (1938; Lowe Art Museum), which prefigures her first glass paintings of 1939 and 1940, the most successful of which is *Shadows with Painting* (1940; Museum of Modern Art, New York). Her earliest glass paintings are simple in construction, with only a single pane of flat window glass – painted in a style reminiscent of Josef Albers's abstract stained-glass designs of the Bauhaus era – suspended over a panel. These gradually evolved into the more complex glass paintings described above, which Pereira began to create during the mid-1940s.

In 1951 the artist began to publish philosophical essays infused with a light mysticism derived from her reading in 1950 of Richard Wilhelm's *The Secret of the Golden Flower*, a translation of an 8th-century Taoist-alchemical tract. With its introductory commentary written by Jung, this book is crucial to an understanding of Pereira's attempts to develop a philosophy reconciling the temporal and spiritual realms of existence with a system of graphic representation articulating a "circulation" of light. The circular path of light Pereira described in her first essay, "Light and the new reality" (1951), is metaphoric of Faust's chthonic descent and ascent and hence is also metaphoric of psychic individuation. Her third husband George Reavey, a poet and translator of Russian Symbolist literature who had been closely associated with Surrealist movements in London and Paris, encouraged her subsequent investigations into alchemy, mysticism and the occult. These interests are perhaps most evident in *The Lapis* (1957), which provides clues to understanding the angular U- and Z-shaped motifs appearing in canvases from the last two decades of her life, such as *Pillar of Fire* (1955; see illustration) and *Sphering the Turn* (1962; André Zarré Gallery, New York). Alchemical symbolism figures prominently in the poetry she wrote and published during these last two decades. It appears as well in the figurative gouache and ink drawings she created in leisure hours or as gifts for friends during the same period.

KAREN A. BEAROR

Perry, Lilla Cabot

American painter, 1848–1933

Born Lilla Cabot in Boston, Massachusetts, 13 January 1848. Married Professor Thomas Sergeant Perry, specialist in 18th-century English literature, 1874: three daughters, born 1876, 1880 and 1884; husband died 1928. Studied under Alfred Quentin Collins, summer 1884; under Robert Vonnoh and Dennis Miller Bunker at Cowles Art School, Boston, 1885–6. Accompanied husband to Paris, 1887–9. Studied at Académie Colarossi, Paris, 1887; Académie Julian, under Tony Robert-Fleury and Alfred Stevens, 1888–9; also studied under Fritz von Uhde in Munich, summer 1888, and visited Britain, Spain and Italy. Saw exhibition of Impressionist paintings by Monet at Galerie Georges Petit, 1889. Spent nine summers with her family in Giverny, renting a house close to Monet, 1889–1909. Promoted Impressionism in America by encouraging collectors and lecturing on Monet at Boston Art Students' Association (1894). Lived in Japan, 1898–1901, when her husband held a chair at Keiogijiku University, Tokyo. Spent less time abroad after 1912, working in Boston and at summer house in Hancock, New Hampshire. Also a poet. Founder-member, Guild of Boston Artists, 1914; member, Allied Artists Association, London; American Federation of Arts; International Society of Arts and Letters; League of American Artists; Société des Artistes Indépendants, Paris; Women's International Art Club; honorary member, Nippon Bijutsu-in Art Association, Tokyo. Died in Hancock, New Hampshire, 28 February 1933.

Principal Exhibitions

Individual

St Botolph Club, Boston: 1897
Tokyo, Japan: 1898
Copley Gallery, Boston: 1911
Twentieth Century Club, Boston: 1913
Guild of Boston Artists: 1915, 1917, 1920, 1922, 1924, 1927, 1929, 1931, 1934 (retrospective)
Braus Galleries, New York: 1922
Gordon Dunthorne, Washington, DC: 1927
Boston Art Club: 1933 (retrospective)

Group

Paris Salon: 1889
Massachusetts Charitable Mechanics' Association, Boston: 1893 (silver medal)
Woman's Building, World's Columbian Exposition, Chicago: 1893
Louisiana Purchase Exposition, St Louis: 1904 (bronze medal)
Panama-Pacific International Exposition, San Francisco: 1915 (bronze medal)

Selected Writings

The Heart of the Weed, Boston: Houghton Mifflin, 1886
"An informal talk given by Mrs T.S. Perry to the Boston Art Students' Association in the Life Class Room at the Museum of Fine Arts, Wednesday, January 24, 1894", Boston Art Students' Association
Impressions: A Book of Verse, Boston: Copeland and Day, 1898
From the Garden of Hellas: Translations into Verse from the Greek Anthology, Boston: Houghton Mifflin, 1904
The Jar of Dreams, Boston: Houghton Mifflin, 1923
"Reminiscences of Claude Monet from 1889 to 1909", *American Magazine of Art*, xviii, March 1927, pp.119–25

Bibliography

Carolyn Hilman and Jean Nutting Oliver, "Lilla Cabot Perry: Painter and poet", *American Magazine of Art*, xiv, 1923, pp.601–4
Memorial Exhibition of Paintings by Lilla Cabot Perry, exh. cat., Boston Art Club, 1933
Virginia Harlow, *Thomas Sergeant Perry: A Biography*, Durham, NC: Duke University Press, 1950
Lilla Cabot Perry: A Retrospective Exhibition, exh. cat., Currier Gallery of Art, Manchester, NH, and elsewhere, 1969
Women Artists, 1550–1950, exh. cat., Los Angeles County Museum of Art, and elsewhere, 1976
Bernice Kramer Leader, *The Boston Lady as a Work of Art: Paintings by the Boston School at the Turn of the Century*, PhD dissertation, Columbia University, 1980
Americans in Brittany and Normandy, 1860–1910, exh. cat., Phoenix Art Museum, AZ, 1982
Lilla Cabot Perry: Days to Remember, exh. cat., Santa Fe East Gallery, Santa Fe, 1983
Memories of Monet, documentary film based on the memoirs of Lilla Cabot Perry, Washington, DC, 1984 (Brown Distributors, Route 2, Box 718, Purcellville, VA 22132)
Lisa M. Ward, *Lilla Cabot Perry and the Emergence of the Professional Woman Artist*, MA thesis, University of Texas, Austin, 1985
Alessandra Comini and others, *National Museum of Women in the Arts: Selections from the Permanent Collection*, New York: Abrams, 1987
Lilla Cabot Perry: An American Impressionist, exh. cat., National Museum of Women in the Arts, Washington, DC, 1990 (contains bibliography)
Norma Broude, ed., *World Impressionism: The International Movement, 1860–1920*, New York: Abrams, 1992
William H. Gerdts, *Lasting Impressions: American Painters in France, 1865–1915*, Evanston, IL: Terra Foundation of Arts, 1992
——, *Masterworks of American Impressionism from the Pfeil Collection*, Alexandria, VA: Art Services International, 1992
——, *Monet's Giverny: Impressionist Colony*, New York: Abbeville, 1993
Revisiting the White City: American Art at the 1893 World's Fair, exh. cat., National Museum of American Art–National Portrait Gallery, Smithsonian Institution, Washington, DC, 1993

In the early years of her marriage to Thomas Sergeant Perry, Lilla Cabot was frequently in poor health, and throughout this period was sustained by writing poetry and doing translation work, all of which was published. Once restored to health, facing a choice between poetry and painting, she cast her lot firmly with the more active life of painting. Her daughters Margaret, Edith and Alice were the subjects of her early work. Only after their birth did Perry begin formal instruction, first with Alfred Quentin Collins in the summer of 1884 and then at the Cowles Art School, where by late 1885 she was being taught by Robert Vonnoh. Her third teacher, one of the first to work in Impressionist techniques, was Dennis Miller Bunker who had joined the School in 1885. These three had not only trained at the Académie Julian in Paris, but were all important portrait painters. By 1886 Perry intensified her instruction, knowing that the family would go to Paris the following year. Her husband's work as writer, editor and translator was a portable profession. Well before their departure from Boston, Lilla had the satisfaction of commercial success in her own chosen field.

Once in Paris, Perry enrolled at the Académie Colarossi. The next summer included two months studying in Munich with Fritz von Uhde, who told the Perrys of the new artists'

Perry: *Thomas Sergeant Perry*, exhibited 1889; oil on canvas; 81.3 × 64.8 cm.; private collection

colony in Giverny. In 1889 two of Perry's paintings were accepted by the Paris Salon de la Société des Artistes Français, one of *Edith Perry*, the other a portrait of her husband (see illustration). She became a pupil in the studio of Alfred Stevens and, in 1889, she saw the exhibition at Galerie Georges Petit of 145 of Monet's "impressions". Astonished by his work, the Perrys rented a house in Giverny for the summer, and later that year took back with them to Boston a painting by Monet for a relation.

Their close relationship with Monet grew in part because he was a strong family man. Most of that "first generation" of expatriates in Giverny were bachelors, somewhat more transient. The Perrys came five strong, and were to spend a total of nine summers there between 1889 and 1909. Monet did not take pupils (one myth about Perry is that she had been his pupil) but finding in Lilla an artist whose work closely paralleled his own beliefs, he advised her informally on her painting. Japan became another bond between them. Monet was one of the first French artists to discover Japanese prints, and Thomas Perry was the grand-nephew of Matthew Perry who had "opened" Japan to the West. Perry correspondence shows how protective the Perrys were of Monet's privacy. In the same way Lilla also avoided painting Giverny scenes that were too closely identified with him, although it was impossible to paint in Giverny without depicting the ubiquitous poplars and haystacks.

The first Perry stay in France ended in November 1889, after visits to Belgium and the Netherlands. Their two years had begun with a month in England, then six weeks in Spain, which Perry spent mainly in museums copying paintings. This was to be the established pattern in successive years. The family was back in France for only a part of 1891, but it included another summer at Giverny. Lilla's work that summer included interiors with her children, such as the meditative *Child in Window* (Collection Mr and Mrs T. Gordon Hutchinson), as well as radiant landscapes. *Landscape in Normandy* (Newark Museum, NJ) fairly hums with the energy from sunlit fields and sky.

The period in Boston between 1891 and their next trip to France in 1894 was a busy one for Perry. The Perrys had a life-long mission to help not only struggling artists, but also writers, poets and musicians. This included a meal, a bed, sometimes help in finding jobs, but most important, friendship and encouragement. Thomas had initiated a subscription in the 1880s to help Bernard Berenson, his former student, to study in Europe, and had also introduced him during the same period to Isabella Stewart Gardner (whose museum collection in later years was to be gathered largely under Berenson's tutelage). For Lilla in Boston a decade later, it meant helping to arrange an exhibit for Theodore Robinson and Theodore Wendel as she had earlier for John Leslie Breck. Back in France in the years 1894–7 – when the family rented "Le Hameau" next to the Monets during the summers – the Perrys met Pissarro and tried to help to find customers for his under-appreciated work. They even held weekly "at homes" during the Paris season primarily as a means to show Pissarro's work to visitors.

Japanese elements were popular in turn-of-the-century paintings, and Perry came by her own at first hand. In 1898 Thomas accepted a three-year contract to teach English at Keiogijiku University in Tokyo and Lilla took every advantage of the opportunity to paint that country's beauty. Of her 80 works done in Japan, 35 paintings of Mount Fuji were shown in a separate exhibit (e.g. *Fuji*, 1898–1901; Collection Edith M. Spenser, repr. Washington 1990, fig.15). In Perry's later portraits models often posed in kimonos. Direct Japanese influence in her painting is seen in her staccato, calligraphic rendering of bare branches or those of flowering fruit trees (*Road from Charleston to Savannah*; Collection Mrs Lilla Cabot Levitt, *ibid.*, pl.49).

In 1903 the Perrys bought a farm in Hancock, New Hampshire, later called "Flagstones" by Henry James. At first it was for summer vacations, but later the time spent there stretched to include more of the spring and autumn months. After Thomas Perry's death in 1928, Perry lived there all the year round. In Hancock she had a separate studio out in the meadow, heated by a wood stove. In their Boston house, built in 1879 (312 Marlborough Street), one can still see the top-floor studio window. Between 1910 and the end of her life Perry also had a studio in the Fenway Studios in Boston.

One "myth" that needs to be dispelled is that as a "Boston brahmin" Perry was not dependent on the sale of her paintings – her work was merely a genteel hobby. The reality is that Thomas's income from his books and articles and Harvard teaching never provided a secure income for the family, and that Lilla was pleased and proud to contribute to the family finances. Ironically, she was to profit from conservative Boston's alarm in the late 19th and early 20th centuries at the growing numbers of career women, resulting from the fact that Boston had lost more men in the Civil War than any other city in the country. The city became the base of the anti-suffrage movement. Artistically this resulted in a reaction to the still unsettling Impressionism and a return to paintings showing secure domestic scenes of women and children, tea parties, lap dogs – reassurance of stability and continuity. Perry capitalised on this trend, and her interior scenes of children, and of mothers and babies, were very popular, especially the series of more than a dozen canvases with blond young Hildegard as model. Her quiet scenes usually have a vitality and an immediacy not always typical of the Boston School (*White Bed Jacket*, c.1905; pastel; Hirsch and Adler Galleries Inc., New York, *ibid.*, fig.16).

It is not known whether Perry, most of whose work was in oil, ever received formal instruction in pastels, but from the start these had the skill and proficiency of her best work in oil. *Child in Kimono* (1898; Collection Edith M. Spenser, *ibid.*, pl.22), depicting Alice Perry, may be her earliest pastel. *White Bed Jacket* is another admirable example. In both media she also sought the added complexity offered by the rendering of lace, fur, satin, velvet and transparent fabrics. A good example of her proficiency here is *Lady with a Bowl of Violets* (National Museum of Women in the Arts, Washington, DC).

The pensive mood in Perry's work occasionally merges into melancholy (*Contemplation*, 1914; David Ramus Fine Arts, Atlanta). In contrast to the moods and emotions conveyed by some of her figures, however, Perry's landscapes have less complicated messages, and were usually painted for the sheer joy she found in the variety of the changing seasons and light – in France, Japan and New Hampshire (*State House, Boston*, 1910; private collection, *ibid.*, pl.43). Throughout the 30 years in Hancock, Perry painted freer, more impressionistic scenes than her Boston portrait commissions allowed. She painted the New Hampshire mountains at dawn, or sunset, in mist, or snow – her "snow scapes". And of course she took frequent advantage of the brilliant autumn colours. Like Monet, she was careful not to paint a particular scene beyond the changing light, but would rather put it aside and return to it only when the conditions were right. She also revelled in painting the plein-air figures that Monet had told her were her forte. Many Impressionist painters let their figures dissolve in the search for more important effects of light and colour, but not Perry. With her strong academic grounding in figure drawing and painting, she had an added interest as a surgeon's daughter in what lay beneath the surface. Her sketchbook of 1871 (Jay P. Moffat family archives; microfilm in Archives of American Art, Smithsonian Institution, New York and Washington, DC) shows detailed, labelled drawings of bones and muscles, in many poses.

During the Perrys' last stay in France, 1904–9, all but one summer was spent in Giverny. Rare among the artists who lived and worked in Giverny, Lilla Perry had spanned the years termed "first" and "second generation" there. Canvases of those last Giverny years are some of her surest Impressionist works. Among these are *Little Girl in a Lane* (1906–7; Collection James Holsaert heirs) and *Violoncellist* (1906–7; private collection, *ibid.*, pl.33), in which Edith Perry is depicted in plein air.

The period 1913–15 was one of great activity for Perry. She organised three exhibits of Boston women painters: in 1913 the City Art Museum in St Louis held *Some Boston Women Painters*; the following year she arranged *A Group of Boston Women* for the Detroit Institute of Arts; and finally, at Philip Hale's request, *Pictures by Women Painters* at the St Botolph Club, Boston, in 1915. In 1914 she was a founder member of the Guild of Boston Artists, and served as secretary until her husband's death in 1928. She held a number of solo shows there between 1915 and 1931.

A prolific painter for over half a century, painting was not only Perry's happy decision, her profession, at times her "bondage" (the commissioned portraits – the "bread and butter" work) but, at the end of her life, also her solace and release. Some of her very latest Hancock canvases show the freest Impressionist treatment of any of her work (*Mist on the Mountain*, 1931; Collection Easterly and Bayly, *ibid.*, pl.54). Mountains and trees disappear in snow and mist with a palette that contains all the remembered colours of her varied lifetime. Perry in her poetry had been able to write of the unseen. In her painting she was able to show what could not otherwise be described in words.

PAMELA DAWSON MOFFAT

Petherbridge, Deanna
British artist, 1939–

Born in Pretoria, South Africa, 1939. Studied fine art at University of the Witwatersrand, 1956–60, and taught art history there. Emigrated to Britain, 1960. Lived in Greece and travelled widely in North Africa, the Balkans and Middle East, late 1960s. Made first of three visits to India, studying temple architecture, 1979; returned under British Council sponsorship in 1985 and again in 1987 for an exhibition and lecture tour. Artist-in-residence, Manchester City Art Gallery, 1982. Work expanded to include lecturing and critical writing for art and architectural journals, radio and television, 1980s. Curated South Bank Centre touring exhibition, *The Primacy of Drawing*, 1991. Appointed professor of drawing, Royal College of Art, London, 1995. Commander, Order of the British Empire (CBE), 1996. Lives in London.

Selected Individual Exhibitions

Angela Flowers Gallery, London: 1973, 1980
Whitechapel Art Gallery, London: 1975
Manchester City Art Galleries: 1982–3 (touring retrospective)
Fischer Fine Art, London: 1987, 1990
Harris Museum and Art Gallery, Preston, Lancashire: 1987
India: 1987–8 (*Temples and Tenements*, touring, organised by British Council)
Bristol Museum and Art Gallery: 1991–2 (*Primacy of Drawing*, touring, organised by South Bank Centre)
British Council Gallery, Singapore: 1994–5 (*Drawing Allusions*, touring, organised by British Council)

Selected Writings

"On my architectonic drawings", *Leonardo*, x, 1977
Chapters in *Art Within Reach*, ed. Peter Townsend, London: Thames and Hudson, 1984
Editor, *Art for Architecture: A Handbook for Commissioning*, London: HMSO, 1987
"Battlepieces", *Architectural Design*, no.7, 1989
"Féminisme! C'est moi", *Art Monthly*, no.123, February 1989, pp.6–9
Art and Spatial Politics, Leeds: Centre for the Study of Sculpture in association with the Arts Council of England, 1994 (plenary session address, conference of the Association of Art Historians, Birmingham, 1994)
The Primacy of Drawing (in preparation)

Bibliography

The Iron Siege of Pavia and Other Drawings, exh. cat., Whitechapel Art Gallery, London, 1975
Hayward Annual '78, exh. cat., Arts Council of Great Britain, London, 1978
Deanna Petherbridge: Drawings, 1968–1982, exh. cat., Manchester City Art Galleries and elsewhere, 1982
Nicholas Orsini, *The Language of Drawing: Learning the Basic Elements*, New York: Doubleday, 1982
John McEwen, "Deanna Petherbridge: Drawings, 1968–82", *The Spectator*, 5 February 1983
——, "Deanna Petherbridge", *Art Monthly*, no.82, December 1984–January 1985
George Mitchell and others, *Temples and Tenements: The Indian Drawings of Deanna Petherbridge*, Calcutta: Seagull, 1987 (contains bibliography)
Philip Rawson, *Creative Design*, London: Macdonald Orbis, 1987; as *Design*, Englewood Cliffs, NJ: Prentice Hall, 1988
Margaret Garlake, "Petherbridge", *Art Monthly*, no.107, June 1987, pp.19–20
Themata: New Drawings by Deanna Petherbridge, exh. cat., Fischer Fine Art, London, 1990
Charlotte Du Cann, "Talking art: Charlotte Du Cann on artist Deanna Petherbridge", *The Guardian*, 17 January 1990
Katy Deepwell, "Themata: New drawings by Deanna Petherbridge", *Sp4rerib*, March 1990

Peter Dormer, "Blood, sweat and cheers: Bloodlines, a new work for the Royal Ballet", *Architects Journal*, xxiv, 12 December 1990, p.56

The Primacy of Drawing: An Artist's View, exh. cat., Bristol Museum and Art Gallery and South Bank Centre, 1991

Marina Vaizey, "Drawing up a new artistic agenda", *Sunday Times*, 1 October 1991

Anna Douglas, "Where do we draw the line?", *New Feminist Art Criticism*, ed. Katy Deepwell, Manchester: Manchester University Press, 1995

Deanna Petherbridge is an artist whose practice over some 30 years has been entirely devoted to drawing. Her work does not belong to any easily definable stylistic trend or school, but explores the social, political and emotional sub-text present in architectural form and has moved over the years from strictly geometrical architectonics to a more fluid use of imaginary architecture. Her architectural vocabulary has been developed from a variety of cultural and spiritual sources, ranging from the religious and vernacular traditions of Africa, Asia and the Middle East, to the analytical artists of the Renaissance. The emotional and political narratives that resonate through even the most abstracted and hieratic designs most often concern structures of aggression, ambiguity and contradiction. At different points in her career these have been interpreted as specific responses to political situations – South Africa, Vietnam, religious fundamentalism – but all her work contains a commentary on the psychological motivations within conflict. This can be read as strongly gendered, but while valid, forms only one element of Petherbridge's conception of humanity's several darker facets. In both subject matter and execution she explores essential systems of paradox – masculine/feminine, rigour/sensuality, form/chaos, abstraction/narrative – which frees her art from imitation, eclecticism or sterility.

Petherbridge's work of the 1960s was Abstract Expressionist; she produced large, shaped canvases that incorporated relief elements. In 1967 she moved to an island in the Cyclades. The effect of this new environment, particularly the intense light and austere Aegean architecture, was to introduce a formality to her work. She visited North Africa the following year to study vernacular architecture, particularly desert fortifications, and later continued her investigations into Eastern architecture and decorative traditions with travels to the Balkans and Turkey. By 1969 she had abandoned painting and sculpture altogether to concentrate on drawing. The rigour of a monochromatic medium had the effect of hardening the forms in her work, rendering surfaces metallic and accentuating the phallic-aggressive and visceral elements in her architectonic forms.

In 1971 Petherbridge was commissioned to create a large drawing for a lift/elevator shaft (private collection, repr. Manchester 1982, p.7). The work was composed on a grid structure of 5 centimetres, so that as the lift travelled slowly across the composition, its form, like music, unfurled rhythmically. Other work of the 1970s explored the dynamic tension of movement within restricted boundaries – roundels, lozenges and fortress forms. The *Curcurbitae* (gourd-shaped) series of 1973, *Ottoman* series of 1973–4 and *In the Seven Citadels* series of 1974 are strongly suggestive of a number of decorative forms belonging to different religions and media, most notably rose windows in Christian churches and Islamic decoration. Petherbridge's drawings are designed radially and to be hung any way up, and her technique highlights the tension between the viewer's simultaneous perception of both the drawing's construction – the carefully ruled and individually delineated lines – and the overall decorative pattern. The pattern itself refuses harmonious repetition, creating an internal dialogue of conflicting mutations within a rigid boundary in a graphic display of the drive for free expression. The sense of unease and aggression evoked encourages this construction of an emotional narrative, despite the minutely controlled abstraction.

Narrative is fully developed in Petherbridge's most acclaimed works of the period, the *Iron Siege of Pavia* (1973–5; private collection, USA, *ibid.*, p.5) and the *Concrete Armada* (1978; Manchester City Art Galleries). Both works are on a large scale and combine a number of perspectival systems – single point, isometric and vertical. The effect of the ambiguous viewpoints, the large areas of white and the composition's oscillation from recognisable form to abstraction, lend the scenes, particularly the first, a dreamlike quality where coherent narrative nevertheless resists attempts to rationalise. Petherbridge's own drawing technique encourages this sensation, for the drawing is begun at one edge of the paper and completed intuitively, without preliminary designs. Free from the suggestive qualities of colour, she concentrates on the emotive and ritualistic possibilities of the ruled line, constructing what she describes as "another reality, a personal cosmology … manipulated with exact intent" (London 1975). The *Iron Siege of Pavia* was inspired by a passage from the life of Charlemagne, with a central citadel simultaneously besieged from without and attacked from within. The *Concrete Armada* conjures scenes of World Wars I and II with references to barbed wire and gun placements on beaches. Action is frozen, whilst the chaos of war is evoked using imagined forms resonant of warfare from other cultures and centuries. The scope of these drawings recalls the great battle scenes of Paolo Uccello and Wyndham Lewis and the war machinery of Leonardo da Vinci.

In 1979, 1985 and 1987 Petherbridge travelled in India, studying both vernacular and temple architecture of the Hindu, Jain, Buddhist and Muslim faiths. The resulting work introduced a greater naturalism to structural forms, while repetition, displacement and partial articulation of elements – lintels, stairways, columns – continue to veil any single interpretation. This work also incorporates sepia washes and freehand drawing, which, unlike the metallic quality of earlier work, engineers discomfort by combining alien landscapes and material sensuality. *Become Enchanted on Seeing the Graceful Postures of Women* (1986; see illustration) illustrates this combination of textured shadow, ambivalent perspective and an emblematic use of rigid and sinuous elements.

Petherbridge's most recent work has fully introduced the figure to her interiors. Yet these abstracted, metallic people continue to explore violence, repression and alienation. Groups of men and women, sometimes children, are shown to provide each other and the viewer no comfort. Physical divisions dominate interiors and separate people. These variously seem to be signs for religion, patriarchy and political oppression. Recurring forms such as tables and chairs have their

Petherbridge: *Become Enchanted on Seeing the Graceful Postures of Women,* 1986; pen and brown ink on paper; 120 × 75 cm.; British Museum, London

hidden narratives of interrogation, hierarchy and dissection revealed. A work such as *Mary Approaching* (1989; repr. London 1990, p.14) carries all such narratives showing a diminutive female and baby alone in a spartan corridor approaching a group of men whose profession could be medical, legal, military or governmental but whose function is to examine, judge and dominate.

CARO HOWELL

Phalle, Niki de Saint *see* Saint Phalle

Phillips Fox, Ethel *see* Fox

Pickering, Evelyn *see* De Morgan

Pieters, Geertje *see under* Oosterwijck

Pigott, Gwyn Hanssen *see* Hanssen

Piattoli, Anna Bacherini *see* Copyists survey

Pindell, Howardena
American painter and mixed-media artist, 1943–

Born in Philadelphia, Pennsylvania, 14 April 1943. Studied at Boston University, 1961–5 (BFA), Yale University, 1965–7 (MFA). Exhibition assistant, 1967–9, curatorial assistant, 1969–71, and assistant curator, 1971–9, Museum of Modern Art, New York. Visiting artist, Skowhegan School of Painting and Sculpture, Maine, summer 1980; associate professor of art, 1979–84, and professor of art, 1984–present, State University of New York, Stony Brook; visiting artist, Vermont Studio School, Johnson, summer 1985. Six months study in Japan, 1981–2. Recipient of National Endowment for the Arts (NEA) grants, 1972 and 1983; Guggenheim fellowship, 1987; College Art Association Artist award for distinguished body of work, 1990; Artist award, Studio Museum in Harlem, 1994. Member, Board of Directors, College Art Association, 1981–5; member, International Association of Art Critics. Lives in New York.

Selected Individual Exhibitions
Rockefeller Memorial Galleries, Spellman College, Atlanta: 1971

AIR Gallery, New York: 1973, 1983
Kunstforeningen, Copenhagen: 1977 (touring)
Art Academy of Cincinnati: 1978
State University of New York, Stony Brook: 1979
Lerner-Heller Gallery, New York: 1980, 1981,
Trenton State College, NJ: 1980 (with Jack Witten)
Franklin Furnace, New York: 1981
Birmingham Museum of Art, AL: 1985
Studio Museum in Harlem, New York: 1986
Grand Rapids Arts Museum, MI: 1986
N'Namdi Gallery, Detroit: 1987
Cyrus Gallery, New York: 1989
Wadsworth Atheneum, Hartford, CT: 1989
Roland Gibson Gallery of Art, Potsdam, NY: 1992–5 (touring retrospective)

Selected Writings
"The aesthetics of texture in African adornment", *Beauty by Design: The Aesthetics of African Adornment*, exh. cat., African-American Institute, New York, 1984
"Art (world) and racism, testimony, documentation and statistics", *Third Text*, no.3–4, Spring–Summer 1988, p.157
"Art world racism: A documentation", *New Art Examiner*, xvi, March 1989, pp.32–6
"Breaking the silence", *New Art Examiner*, October 1990, pp.18–23; November 1990, pp.23–9, 50–51
"Some reminiscences", *M/E/A/N/I/N/G*, November 1991, pp.14–15
"Free, white and 21", *Third Text*, no.19, 1992, pp.30–39
"To extinguish once and for all the possibility of independent thought", *Spirit of January Monthly*, January–February 1992 (series)

Bibliography
Joyce Kozloff, ed., *Interview with Women in the Arts, Part 2*, New York: Tower Press, 1976
Contextures, exh. cat., Just Above Midtown Gallery, New York, 1978
Dialectics of Isolation: Third World Women Artists of the United States, exh. cat., AIR Gallery, New York, 1980
Judith Wilson, "Howardena Pindell", *Ms Magazine*, viii, May 1980, pp.66–70
Since the Harlem Renaissance: 50 Years of Afro-American Art, exh. cat., Center Gallery, Bucknell University, Lewisburg, PA, 1985
Howardena Pindell: Odyssey, exh. cat., Studio Museum in Harlem, New York, 1986
Howardena Pindell: Autobiography, exh. cat., Cyrus Gallery, New York, 1989
Making Their Mark: Women Artists Move into the Mainstream, 1970–85, exh. cat., Cincinnati Art Museum, and elsewhere, 1989
Lucy R. Lippard, *Mixed Blessings: New Art in a Multicultural America*, New York: Pantheon, 1990
Howardena Pindell: Paintings and Drawings: A Retrospective Exhibition, 1972–1992, exh. cat., Roland Gibson Gallery of Art, Potsdam, NY, and elsewhere, 1992
Mara R. Witzling, ed., *Voicing Today's Visions: Writings by Contemporary Women Artists*, New York: Universe, 1994

Since painting figuratively as an undergraduate, through the abstract minimalist forms influenced by Josef Albers during her graduate years at Yale University (1965–7), and via experiments in video, photography and mixed-media collage dating from the 1970s, Howardena Pindell has travelled varied stylistic worlds both literally and figuratively. Since travelling to Mexico in 1963, she has visited many regions and studied their cultures: Europe (Sweden, Denmark and France first in 1964), the Caribbean, India, Egypt and South America (Brazil in 1977). She spent seven months in Japan in 1981 after a first visit in 1979, and she has travelled widely in Africa, including Kenya, Ghana, Nigeria, the Ivory Coast and Senegal. The textures of Pindell's work communicate a sense of place, and the strong ethos of her mixed-media paintings – which incorporate everything from sequins and glitter to newspaper, from blood to perfume, from oil slick to photographs on handmade paper or stitched and sewn unstretched canvas – evoke the spirit of varied artistic traditions. Although many of her trips originated in curatorial projects – she began working in the Department of Prints and Illustrated Books of the Museum of Modern Art in 1967 – they have been preserved in the souvenir postcards collected along the way that became collage paintings in the 1980s, as for example *Autobiography: Japan (Kokuzo Bosatsu)* (1982; Heath Gallery, Atlanta).

During the 1970s Pindell's oeuvre hummed with the aesthetic tenor of the day – minimalist repetitive patterns and a mathematical resonance that prompt one to ponder her father's graduate degree in statistics (Holland Cotter in Potsdam 1992, p.10). (In later years, Pindell discovered a ledger page of her father's that she had coloured in the third grade, and her recent work still preserves in paint a repetitive yet organic comb-grid pattern.) Linda Goode-Bryant and Marcy S. Philips (New York 1978) labelled this phase of Pindell's career "Contexturalist" after her mixture of abstraction and conceptual systems – avenues that other artists felt they had to choose between, but which Pindell successfully managed to vault. Yet with their seemingly disorderly arrangement of patterns and the textured irregularity of handmade paper or sewn canvas, there is in these pieces a "deliberate challenge to the masculine rigors of quantification and classification that have for centuries dominated science and art" (Cotter in Potsdam 1992, p.11). Decoration and spirituality intertwine in her art – punctuated by four trips to India and captured in such essays as "The aesthetics of texture in African adornment" that she wrote for an exhibition at the African-American Institute in New York in 1984. "In Africa, the geometry and texture of the individual human body engages in an ever changing dialogue with the adornment selected by the wearer", Pindell observed:

> Placing the objects on zones of the body, the wearer is able to convey messages not only of beauty or sexual allure, but also of status, rank, age, tribal identification, and aesthetics, as well as of a state of mind or a desire to placate or seek protection from the environment [New York 1984, p.37].

While modernistic concerns with the self and the emotional journey of the spirit are pivotal to Pindell's art – as in the *Autobiography* series that she began in 1986 as a means of recovering memories lost after a near-fatal car crash in 1979, the same year that she joined the faculty of the State University of New York at Stony Brook, postmodern concerns with the social have taken on ever greater prominence. Both, however, have always been woven into her life and into her work. In the later 1960s Pindell aligned herself with the feminist movement, helping to found the AIR Gallery in New York. In the *Video Drawing* series of 1973–5 (artist's collection) she subtly tapped the tensions in American culture by pairing abstracted photographs of sports figures with lines of force and mathematical notation, hinting at both the social pressures on

athletes to perform and the ballet-like beauty of their movements. In 1980 she produced the video *Free, White and 21*. Here she wrapped herself in a white gauze, whitened her face and applied a blond wig as she voiced her own encounters with racism. The video parallels the works of her contemporary Adrian Piper.

In her seemingly abstract, kaleidoscopic paintings of the early 1970s a paper punch removed snippets of racist texts that had deep meaning for her as a woman, an African-American, and as an artist (*Parabia Text No.5*, 1974). Beginning in 1978, she created decorative, heavily impastoed surfaces on hand-sewn canvas that are closely allied to the Pattern and Decoration movement (*Feast Day of Iemanja II, December 31, 1980*; Studio Museum of Harlem). Yet text and language were always important and became increasingly so. In *Autobiography: Water/Ancestors/Middle Passage/Family Ghosts*

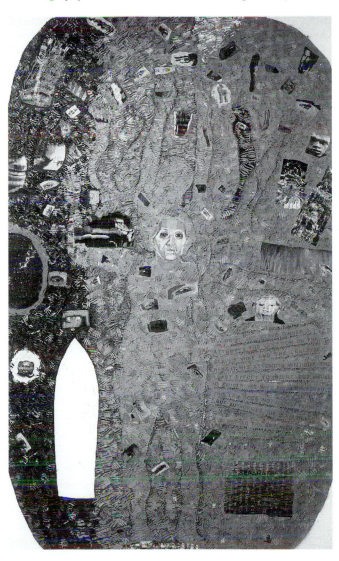

Pindell: *Autobiography: Water/Ancestors/Middle Passage/Family Ghosts*, 1988; acrylic, tempera, cattle markers, oil stick, paper, polymer, etc.; 118 × 71 cm.; Wadsworth Atheneum, Hartford, Connecticut; Ella Gallup Sumner and Mary Catlin Sumner Collection Fund; photo Josef Szaszfai

(1988; see illustration) a slave-trade law is partially embedded in the painting and the hold of a slave ship appears as a white silhouette at lower left. Apparently abstract, the monochromatic mixed-media painting *Separate but Equal: Apartheid* (1987; artist's collection) treats institutional racism and topical international issues. Phrases such as "DISAPPEARANCES" and "SOWETO" can be discerned in the black field, while "CRUEL" and "PROFIT" are faintly visible in white. Her carefully documented essays on racism in the art world and the situation of artists of colour have appeared in the *New Art Examiner*, and in 1988 she sent out on request a list of artists of colour in major New York galleries and museums. Later published in *Third Texts*, the accompanying documentation included damning comments from renowned art-world luminaries.

As Margaret Sheffield has observed, Pindell's art reveals an allusive, cultivated mind that fuses politics and poetic elegance (New York 1989). As an ensemble her works speak to the issues of later 20th-century art, mixing private, deeply emotional experiences with social and political issues, using organic and inorganic modes, texts and images; in both paintings and videos, handmade paper and souvenir photographs, she intertwines the spiritual and the mathematical, nature and technology, non-Western and Western historical references into works that are both personal and collective.

PHYLIS FLOYD

Pinney, Eunice
American amateur artist, 1770–1849

Born Eunice Griswold in Simsbury, Connecticut, 1770, into an upper-middle-class family. Married (1) Oliver Holcombe; two children; (2) Butler Pinney of Windsor, Connecticut, 1797; three children. Died in Simsbury, 1849.

Bibliography
Jean Lipman, "Eunice Pinney: An early Connecticut water-colorist", *Art Quarterly*, vi, 1943, pp.213–21

Mary Black and Jean Lipman, *American Folk Painting*, New York: Potter, 1966

Beatrix Rumford, ed., *American Folk Paintings: Paintings and Drawings other than Portraits from the Abby Aldrich Rockefeller Folk Art Center*, Boston: Little Brown, 1988

Important as an early American amateur watercolourist, Eunice Pinney seems to have begun painting after her children had grown up. More than 50 works have been assigned to her through signature or attribution, dating from 1809 to 1826. Pinney's watercolours are noteworthy for their wide range of subjects. Some are mourning pictures, increasingly common for the period; others include genre and landscape scenes. Many are taken from a remarkably broad sampling of late 18th-century literature, such as *Maria* (c.1810; Flint Institute of the Fine Arts) from Laurence Sterne's *Tristram Shandy* (completed 1767) and *A Sentimental Journey* (1768); *Lolotte and Werther* (1810; National Gallery of Art, Washington, DC) from Goethe's *Die Leiden des jungen Werthers* (1774); the *Cotter's Saturday Night* (c.1815; National Gallery of Art) from

Robert Burns's poem of the same title (1786); and *Valencourt and Emily* (undated; Abby Aldrich Rockefeller Folk Art Center, Williamsburg) from Ann Radcliffe's gothic romance *The Mysteries of Udolpho* (1794). Unusually for a naive artist, Pinney even tackled traditional "history" scenes, multi-figured compositions of Classical and religious subjects, such as *Hector and Achilles* (undated; Abby Aldrich Rockefeller Folk Art Center) and an *Ascension* (private collection). She also painted genre scenes, usually two figures in a landscape, which have been seen as allegorical. Her landscape scenes include the unusual subject *Old Newgate Prison* (private collection) in Granby, Connecticut.

Pinney's bold style has a peculiar charm. Her figures have the rubbery quality typical of an untrained artist, but often adventurous poses and composition give them a vivid energy or meaning. In *Plenty* (Jean Lipman collection), for instance, the woman raises one hand high and throws the other with an air of gay frivolity; in *Couple and Casualty* (see illustration) a man tumbles head over heels as his horse throws him right next to a courting couple. *Two Women* (c.1815; New York State Historical Association) depicts a static subject of two women seated at a table by a window, but the rigid formality of the design adds an air of tension.

It has been suggested that Pinney used engravings as a source on which to model her compositions, although for the most part specific sources have not yet been found. The fact that some of her characters wear 18th-century dress, although the watercolours were executed in the first decades of the 19th century, suggests older print sources. She consistently used painted or drawn oval frames in her watercolours that closely resemble those common in engravings. In one instance, at least, Pinney may have combined print sources, juxtaposing two different scenes for dramatic effect. The horseman in *Couple and Casualty* appears to derive from *Symptoms of Tumbling*, one in a series of British engravings entitled *Hints to Bad Horsemen*. It was reproduced as a textile pattern, probably Pinney's immediate source. The other half of the watercolour derives from an unidentified print.

Pinney's work attracted favourable attention early on in the modern reassessment of naive American art. The first (and only) monograph article on her attributed her artistic style to her age and station in life, and even to her personality, of which little is known. Pinney's style seemed "not only mature in its lusty vigor but actually more masculine than feminine". Its boldness was highlighted by comparison with the formulaic and sentimental works that became increasingly common in art instruction for girls and women in the 19th century. "A mature woman … she was endowed with a robust originality" in contrast with the "tentative, wobbly drawing, the stereotyped themes" of the "maiden-paintings" of "inexperienced schoolgirls" (Lipman 1943, pp.213 and 215). In fact, Pinney contributed directly to the growing conventions of "maiden paintings" and artistic training for women. Her daughter Minerva Emeline Bright taught at a school in Virginia, and Pinney often sent her advice and watercolours to use as models for copying. More recent work has focused on more specific characteristics of Pinney's style, but her work has maintained its appeal and its prominence in American naive art.

LESLIE REINHARDT

Pinney: *Couple and Casualty*, undated; watercolour; Abby Aldrich Rockefeller Folk Art Center, Williamsburg, Virginia

Pisan, Christine de *see* Women as Artists in the Middle Ages survey

Pleydell-Bouverie, Katharine

British potter, 1895–1985

Born at Coleshill, Berkshire, 7 June 1895. Studied at the Central School of Arts and Crafts, London, 1921–4. Joined Bernard Leach's pottery in St Ives, Cornwall, 1924. Set up Cole Pottery on family estate at Coleshill with Peter Mason, 1925; he left 1928. Partnership with Norah Braden (q.v.) at Coleshill, 1928–36. Work disrupted during World War II. Moved to Kilmington Manor, Wiltshire, after sale of Coleshill estate, 1946. Founder member, Craftsman Potters Association. Died at Kilmington Manor, January 1985.

Selected Writings

"Technical notes: Wood and vegetable ashes in stoneware glazes", *Ceramic Review*, no.5, 1970, p.7; no.6, 1970, p.14

"Michael Cardew: A personal account", *Ceramic Review*, no.20, 1973, pp.4–5; reprinted in *Michael Cardew: A Collection of Essays*, London: Crafts Advisory Committee, 1976

"Early days at St Ives", *Ceramic Review*, no.50, 1978, pp.25–9

"Ash glazes", *Ceramic Review*, no.51, 1978, p.30

Bibliography

W.A. Thorpe, "English stoneware pottery by Miss K. Pleydell-Bouverie and Miss D.K.N. Braden", *Artwork*, vi, 1930, pp.256–65

Ernest Marsh, "Studio potters of Coleshill: Miss K. Pleydell-Bouverie and Miss D.K.N. Braden", *Apollo*, xxxviii, 1943, pp.162–4

George Wingfield Digby, *The Work of the Modern Potter in England*, London: Murray, 1952

Muriel Rose, *Artist-Potters in England*, 2nd edition, London: Faber, 1970

Eileen Lewenstein and Emmanuel Cooper, "A visit to Katharine Pleydell-Bouverie", *Ceramic Review*, no.30, 1974, pp.4–6

Fiona Adamczewski, "Katharine Pleydell-Bouverie", *Crafts*, no.19, March–April 1976, pp.13–16

Thirties: British Art and Design Before the War, exh. cat., Arts Council of Great Britain, London, 1979

British 20th-Century Studio Ceramics, exh. cat., Christopher Wood Gallery, London, 1980

Katharine Pleydell-Bouverie, exh. cat., Crafts Study Centre, Holburne Museum, Bath, 1980

Isabelle Anscombe, *A Woman's Touch: Women in Design from 1860 to the Present Day*, London: Virago, and New York: Viking, 1984

David Leach, "Katharine Pleydell-Bouverie: A tribute", *Ceramic Review*, no.92, 1985, p.9

Barley Roscoe and Michael Casson, "Beano: A tribute", *Crafts*, no.75, July–August 1985, pp.36–9

Barley Roscoe and others, *Katharine Pleydell-Bouverie: A Potter's Life, 1895–1985*, London: Crafts Council, 1986

Barley Roscoe, "An earlier generation: Katharine Pleydell-Bouverie, 1895–1985", *Studio Pottery*, no.1, 1993, pp.31–5

Oliver Watson, *Studio Pottery: Twentieth-Century British Ceramics in the Victoria and Albert Museum Collection*, London: Phaidon,

1993 (originally published as *British Studio Pottery*, Oxford: Phaidon, 1990)

Pleydell-Bouverie's notes and glaze-books are kept at the Crafts Study Centre, Holburne Museum, Bath.

Katharine Pleydell-Bouverie (or Beano to her friends and Bina to her relatives) has been acclaimed as a pioneer in the field of 20th-century British studio pottery for her exhaustive study of vegetable ash glazes that enabled her to produce "... some of the loveliest glaze effects known to stoneware pottery, with their soft, luminous depths and matt surfaces in varied tones" (Digby 1952). From the beginning she maintained careful records of the recipes she devised, detailing firing temperatures and noting the results. These, as well as more than 40 pots spanning her career, she presented to the Crafts Study Centre, Holburne Museum, Bath (unless otherwise specified, all the pieces mentioned in this essay are in this collection).

During a long and active life that embraced more than 60 years of potting, Pleydell-Bouverie produced strong, functional wares focusing on series of vases, bottles and bowls. These could range in scale from c.2.5–5 centimetres for the smallest pots she used as glaze samples to over 30 centimetres in height for the larger bottles. All were numbered on the base so that they could be cross-referenced back to her notes. Shapes were simple and sometimes reminiscent of those found in Bronze Age British pottery, which she much admired. Brush decoration was seldom employed, but occasionally forms would be cut-sided, which often served to emphasise shape and show the glaze to advantage. Determined that her pots should be without pretension and in general daily use, she wanted her work "... to make people think, not of the Chinese, but of things like pebbles and shells and birds' eggs and the stones over which moss grows ... I do want the reaction of someone who sees flowers in my pots to be: 'That looks natural'" (letter from Katharine Pleydell-Bouverie to Bernard Leach dated 29 June 1930, published in Roscoe 1986). Quite apart from her glazed vases for flowers, Pleydell-Bouverie also produced a notable range of glazed stoneware flower-pots and saucers with combed decoration. Often made in graduated sets, there is a particularly fine, large individual planter with two handles dating from the 1930s in the Crafts Study Centre. This was the decade in which some of Pleydell-Bouverie's most notable work was produced, much of it in partnership with Norah Braden (q.v.), working from the pottery that Pleydell-Bouverie had established in 1925 at her family home at Coleshill, Berkshire. Here pots were fired either in reduction or oxidation in a wood-fired kiln in temperatures between 1250° and 1320°C. After World War II, Pleydell-Bouverie moved to Kilmington Manor, near Warminster, Wiltshire, and her work entered a second distinct phase with the installation of an oil-fired kiln in which pots were usually fired in reduction. Subsequently the third and final phase was marked in 1960, when she installed an electric kiln, which she continued to use for the rest of her life – firing her pots in oxidising atmospheres at temperatures under 1200°C.

Pleydell-Bouverie's interest in ceramics had first been aroused when she was in London in the early 1920s, when she saw some of the pots that Roger Fry had made for the Omega Workshops. Enthused, she joined a pottery class at the Central School, where Dora Billington was head of the ceramics department. Subsequently, an exhibition of Bernard Leach's work at the Paterson Gallery in Bond Street made a great impact on her. Leach had recently returned from Japan to set up his pottery on the outskirts of St Ives, Cornwall, with his great friend Shoji Hamada, and in 1924 Pleydell-Bouverie joined the pottery for a year. Michael Cardew was a fellow student as well as Ada Mason; Tsuronosuke Matsubayashi, known as Matsu, a Japanese potter with considerable technical knowledge, was also there, building Leach a three-chambered stoneware kiln. The following year Pleydell-Bouverie returned to Coleshill and, together with Mason, established her pottery at the Mill Cottage. Matsu designed a two-chambered wood-firing kiln for them and, encouraged by Leach, Pleydell-Bouverie turned her attention to ash glazes. She was the first to recognise that she was ideally placed to do so at Coleshill. Not only did the estate provide a wealth of trees, shrubs and plants with which to experiment, but there were also plentiful supplies of wood available for both ash and fuel, and five different types of throwable clay to be dug in the vicinity. Economically Pleydell-Bouverie was also at an advantage, since she had private means and was not financially dependent on selling her work, so could afford to experiment.

One of the first pieces she made at Coleshill was a heavy, spherical bottle with green-black glaze dating from 1925. Other early work includes two little sgraffito-decorated bottles quite unlike anything she was to make subsequently. Apart from impressing her own KPB seal on the base of her pots, Pleydell-Bouverie also employed a COLE seal until 1928. That year Mason left the pottery and Pleydell-Bouverie was joined by Norah Braden (who had also gone to the Central School and then to St Ives). Together they worked in close partnership for the next eight years, experimenting avidly and keeping detailed records. The subtleties of the glazes they obtained were legion and the series of plain and cut-sided bottles and bowls produced shows the wide variety of colours that could be obtained, such as white (apple, larch, walnut), blue (laurustinus, holly, hawthorne) and tawny yellow (chrysanthemum). Box-ash glaze was a particular favourite, often used in conjunction with a brown manganese splash and varying in colour from grey-blue to green. A series of large bottles glazed with box ash from the 1930s are among the finest examples of Pleydell-Bouverie's work. This was a most productive period and Pleydell-Bouverie and Braden regularly contributed to exhibitions in London and the annual exhibitions of the Red Rose Guild in Manchester.

Following Pleydell-Bouverie's move to Kilmington Manor in 1946, Norah Braden helped her to install an oil-fired kiln in the pottery she had established in the vast, dim barn adjoining the house. This marked a transition period and, at best, some of her pots equal those of the 1930s – for example, a tall bottle of 1955–6 with scotch-pine glaze and manganese splash in luminous grey-browns with a pink blush on one shoulder. In 1960 Pleydell-Bouverie decided to opt for an electric kiln and pots were now fired in lower temperatures in oxidising atmospheres. By careful mixing of oxides in basic wood-ash glazes, however, she still managed to produce apparently reduced effects reminiscent of the Coleshill days. Pots from this period were often cut or incised, for example a flared bowl of turquoise with cut-sided flame decoration around the form dating from 1980, and another bowl of the same year with curved incised lines radiating from the centre in thunder-blue glaze. The latter were both shown in a major retrospective of her work mounted at the Holburne Museum and Crafts Study Centre in 1980. Subsequently, in 1986, the Crafts Council in collaboration with the Crafts Study Centre published *Katharine Pleydell-Bouverie: A Potter's Life, 1895–1985*.

BARLEY ROSCOE

Polenova, Elena

Russian painter, graphic artist and craftworker, 1850–1898

Born in St Petersburg, 15 November (Old Style calendar)/27 November (New Style calendar) 1850; daughter of archaeologist Dmitry Polenov, sister of painter Vasily Polenov. Studied at the Drawing School of the Society for the Encouragement of the Arts, St Petersburg, 1863–7; studied in the studio of Charles Chaplin, Paris, 1869–70; scholarship to Paris, 1880; studied watercolour painting at the School of the Society for the Encouragement of the Arts, St Petersburg, 1880–82. Art teacher diploma, 1875; taught in secondary schools. Moved to Moscow, 1882. Co-organiser, Museum of Russian Folk Art, Abramtsevo, 1885. Artistic director of *kustar* (folk art) workshops, Abramtsevo, 1885–93 (head of wood-working workshop). Organiser of "Ceramics Thursdays", Abramtsevo, from 1888. Designer for Solomenko embroidery workshops, Tambov province, from 1895. Member, Moscow Association of Artists, 1893. Organiser of *Popular-Historical Exhibition*, Moscow, 1893. In Paris 1897–8, as organiser of Russian applied arts section for the Exposition Universelle of 1900. Died of a brain tumour in Moscow, 7 November (Old Style calendar)/19 November (New Style calendar) 1898. Polenova prize inaugurated for young Russian artists to travel abroad, 1902.

Principal Exhibitions

Peredvizhniki (Wanderers): from 1889
MTKh (Moscow Association of Artists): from 1894
Nizhny Novgorod: 1896 (*All-Russian Arts and Industry*)
Mir Iskusstva (World of Art), St Petersburg: 1899 (retrospective)
Moscow: 1902 (retrospective)

Selected Writings

Voyna gribov [War of the mushrooms], Moscow 1889
Russkiye narodniye skazki i pribytka [Stories and sayings of the Russian people], Moscow 1906

Bibliography

"E.D. Polenova", *Mir iskusstva*, ii/18–19, 1899, pp.97–120
V. Stasov, "E.D. Polenova", *Iskusstvo i khudozhestvennaya promyshlennost* [Art and industry], 1899, no.13, pp.1–49
E. Sakharova, *E.D. Polenova*, Moscow, 1952
——, *V.D. Polenov, E.D. Polenova: Khronika semi khudozhnikov* [V.D. Polenov, E.D. Polenova: A chronicle of a family of artists], Moscow, 1964
H. Beloglazova, *V.D. and E.D. Polenovy v Abramtseve* [V.D. and E.D. Polenov at Abramtsevo], Leningrad, 1980
Russian Stage Design: Scenic Innovation, 1900–1930, from the Collection of Mr and Mrs Nikita D. Lobanov-Rostovsky, exh. cat., Mississippi Museum of Art, Jackson, 1982
Wendy R. Salmond, *Arts and Crafts in Late Imperial Russia: Reviving the Kustar Art Industries, 1870–1917*, New York and London: Cambridge University Press, 1996

"An outstanding and talented woman, she was one of the most important representatives of modern Russian art and her role in the history of our painting is of great significance and meaning"; "Elena Polenova is the supreme artist"; "without Polenova's experiments there can be no question that Bilibin's series of folk tales and legends would not have been created"; "her influence is impossible to exaggerate"; "she was the first to realise that the decorative art of a country should express popular thought in popular language ... She led the way, and gradually became the guiding and informing spirit of a small group of Muscovite artists". From obituaries written by supporters of the antagonistic Wanderers and World of Art groups, through the championing by a leader of the St Petersburg avant-garde, to her acknowledged pre-eminence with contemporary Western critics, Soviet historians and recent Western commentators, the place of Polenova at the forefront of the modern movement in Russian art has never been questioned. For she was a dominant force, most particularly in the quest for a synthetic art that fused national traits with inner experience. This led to a "Polenova school", which expressed unities of artistic self and folk culture through various forms of severe stylisation, and included Vrubel, Malyutin, Zinoviev, Roerich, Golovin, Stelletsky, Marya Yakunchikova (q.v.) and Elena Guro (q.v.).

Polenova was trained as a ceramist and watercolourist in the studios of St Petersburg and Paris, and her early approach to landscape and genre painting revealed an association with the lyrical realist manner of her elder brother, Vasily Polenov, as well as an interest in fabled and ancient worlds, derived from her parents – her mother was a children's writer, her father an archaeologist. Thus while she painted Moscow street scenes and studies of local nature, as *On the Edge of the Forest (Water Lilies)* (1885; History, Art and Literature Museum, Abramtsevo), she could also depict an organ-grinder, a nursery, Prince Boris before his murder and an *Icon-Painting Workshop of the 16th Century* (1887; Tretyakov Gallery, Moscow), all with an intimate delicacy.

This attraction to past traditions and myths led Polenova, like her mentor and colleague Viktor Vasnetsov, to abandon the hierarchical distinctions between the fine and applied arts, as well as to resuscitate and reinterpret Russian folk forms for the modern age and client. Besides painting, her activities embraced graphic art, woodwork, ceramics and embroidery design. In addition, in 1885, she created Russia's first museum of folk art at the Mamontov's estate of Abramtsevo outside Moscow. The diverse application of her energies meant that she was able to establish the new focus on vernacular ceramics at the Abramtsevo artists' colony, while being in charge of the new wood-carving workshop there from 1885. The broad success of her brand of revivalist modernism was such that she assumed a leading role in organising the displays of the Russian crafts section at the seminal *All-Russian Arts and Industry* exhibition at Nizhny Novgorod (1896) and the Paris Exposition Universelle of 1900.

Polenova: *Ivanusha-Durachok*, early 1890s; published in the periodical *Iskusstvo i khudozhestvennaya promyshlennost*, xiii, 1899, opposite p.16

Polenova led the way in Neo-Russian furniture design and decoration, adapting the form of wooden cupboards, chairs, tables and doors from the crude but practical geometricised forms of peasant objects from across Russia. These she combined with starkly stylised and simplified painted dandelion, camomile, strawberry, tulip, horse or *sirin* bird motifs in red, green and blue, and occasionally gold. In addition, she incorporated a mixture of incised and relief-carved motifs, either abstract geometrical or representative of flora and fauna. These were transferred from items including distaffs, beetles, salt cellars, horsecart backboards and hut window casings, for example, *Apothecary Cupboard* (1885–90) and *Fairy-Tale Door* (1891–3; both History, Art and Literature Museum). Her work, with its market-conscious synthesis of artfully extrapolated and exaggerated naive qualities, was created by the boy apprentices brought to study in her Abramtsevo workshop to ensure the survival of the traditions.

Polenova's attempt to convey with originality the poetic, primal relationship of the Russian folk with Russian nature was emphatically expressed in her graphic work. This she divided into two cycles: *Abramtsevo* (mid- to late 1880s) and *Kostroma* (late 1880s–early 1890s). In these she created an integrated form of text and illustration that was unprecedented in Russian children's books. She created picture-booklets in which the most expressive, vital elements from tales she had recorded herself, or which were well known, were manifested in visual and handwritten form. The first series comprised animalist, primitive images with fantastic landscapes revealing national identity through a composite of Russian architectural forms and decorative motifs, Abramtsevo scenes and local flora, fauna and fungi, as in the *War of Mushrooms* (1886; History, Art and Literature Museum). The second cycle contained more human figures and a bolder, calligraphic line, as demonstrated in *Synko Filippko* (early 1890s; Tretyakov Gallery) and *Ivanushka-Durachok* (early 1890s; see illustration). The conception indicated an awareness of Walter Crane's "toy books".

Probably the fullest embodiment of Polenova's approach was the Neo-Russian dining room she designed, and which was completed by Golovin after her death, for the Yakunchikov family mansion at Nara near Moscow (1897). For this she projected numerous painted and embroidered panels, the furniture, carpet, tiled stove, heavily carved door and all the other objects, most of which were made at Abramtsevo. Every surface appeared covered in boldly stylised organic motifs, some painted in bright, unmixed colours. The appearance of the embroidered panels, which included images of a firebird, swan maiden, forest ferns and fungi, followed from Polenova's involvement in the mid-1890s in the new Solomenko embroidery workshops and her creation of a massive *Firebird* panel for the workshops' display at the Nizhny Novgorod exhibition. The contemporary critic Alexandre Benois described the interior as "the complete decorative scheme for a fantastic fairytale, full of talent yet wild".

JEREMY HOWARD

See also Training and Professionalism survey 7

Pompadour, Marquise de *see* Amateur Artists and Printmakers surveys

Popova, Lyubov (Sergeyevna)
Russian painter and designer, 1889–1924

Born on the family estate at Krasnovidova, near the village of Ivanovskoye, Moscow province, 24 April (Old Style calendar)/7 May (New Style calendar) 1889. Studied at the Yalta gymnasium, 1902–6; Arsenev gymnasium, Moscow, 1906; A.S. Alferov's School, Moscow, 1906–8 (degree in literature); studied in studio of Impressionist painter Stanislav Zhukovsky, 1907; studios of Konstantin Yuon and Ivan Dudin, Moscow, 1908–9; "The Tower" studio, Moscow, 1912; La Palette, Paris, 1912–13; studio of Vladimir Tatlin, Moscow, 1914–16. Visited Italy, 1910; France and Italy with Vera Mukhina (q.v.), 1914. Taught at Svomas (State Free Art Studios), Moscow, 1918–20; Vkhutemas (Higher State

Artistic and Technical Workshops), Moscow, 1920–24; GVTM (Higher State Theatrical Workshops), 1921–2; also taught a course for Proletkult, Moscow, 1924. Member, Inkhuk (Institute of Artistic Culture), 1920–24. Married art historian Boris von Eding, March 1918; son born November 1918; husband died of typhus, 1919. Died in Moscow, 25 May 1924.

Principal Exhibitions

Bubnovy valet (Jack/Knave of Diamonds), Moscow: 1914, 1916
Petrograd: 1915 (*Tramway V: First Futurist Exhibition of Paintings*), 1915 (*0.10 [Zero-Ten]: Last Futurist Exhibition of Paintings*)
Moscow: 1916 (*Futurist Exhibition: The Store*), 1918 (*First Exhibition of Paintings by the Professional Union of Artists in Moscow*), 1918 (*Fifth State Exhibition*), 1919 (*Tenth State Exhibition: Non-Objective Creation and Suprematism*), 1921 (*5 × 5 = 25*, with Rodchenko, Stepanova, Exter and Vesnin)
Galerie van Diemen, Berlin: 1922–3 (*Erste russische Kunstausstellung*, touring)
Museum of Decorative Painting, Moscow: 1923 (*Moscow's Theatrical and Decorative Art, 1918–1923*)
Stroganov Institute, Moscow: 1924 (retrospective)

Selected Writings

Untitled text in *Katalog desyatoy gosudarstvennoy vystavki* [Catalogue of the Tenth State Exhibition], exh. cat., VTsVB IZO Narkompros, Moscow, 1919, p.22
Untitled text in *5 × 5 = 25*, exh. cat., Moscow, 1921
"Poyasnitelnaya zapiska k postanovke 'Zemlya dybom' v teatre Meyerkholda" [Explanatory note on the production of "The Earth in Turmoil at Meyerkhold's Theatre"], *Lef*, no.4, 1924, p.44

Bibliography

Katalog posmertnoy vystavki khudozhnika konstruktora L.S. Popovoy, 1889–1924 [Catalogue of posthumous exhibition of the artist-constructor L.S. Popova, 1889–1924], exh. cat., Stroganov Institute, Moscow, 1924
Künstlerinnen der russischen Avantgarde/Women Artists of the Russian Avant-Garde, 1910–1930, exh. cat., Galerie Gmurzynska, Cologne, 1979
Angelica Zander Rudenstine, ed., *The George Costakis Collection: Russian Avant-Garde Art*, New York: Abrams, and London: Thames and Hudson, 1981
Christina Lodder, *Russian Constructivism*, New Haven and London: Yale University Press, 1983
Liubov Popova: Spatial Force Constructions, 1921–1922, exh. cat., Rachel Adler Gallery, New York, 1985
Art into Life: Russian Constructivism, 1914–1932, New York: Rizzoli, 1990
Briony Fer, "What's in a line? Gender and modernity", *Oxford Art Journal*, xiii, 1990, pp.77–88
L.S. Popova, 1889–1924: Katalog vystavki proizvedeniy k stoletiyu so dnya rozhdeniya [L.S. Popova, 1889–1924: Catalogue of the exhibition of works marking the centenary of her birth], exh. cat., Tretyakov Gallery, Moscow, 1990
Dmitri V. Sarabianov and Natalia L. Adaskina, *Popova*, New York, Abrams, and London: Thames and Hudson, 1990 (Russian original)
M.N. Yablonskaya, *Women Artists of Russia's New Age, 1900–1935*, New York: Rizzoli, and London: Thames and Hudson, 1990
Liubov Popova, exh. cat., Museum of Modern Art, New York, and elsewhere, 1991
Dmitry Sarabyanov, *Lyubov Popova: Zhivopis–Novaya Galereya XX veka* [Lyubov Popova: New Gallery paintings of the 20th century], Moscow: Galart, 1994

Lyubov Popova first came to prominence in the mid-1910s as an artist within the Russian Cubo-Futurist movement, exploring the potential overlay between the ideas of Futurism and the formal language of Cubism. She subsequently played an important role in elaborating the non-objective language of Suprematism and in developing the theory and practice of Constructivism. In 1924 her artistic evolution was summarised:

> A Cubist period (the problem of form) was followed by a Futurist period (the problem of movement and colour) and the principle of abstracting the parts of an object was followed logically and inevitably by the abstraction of the object itself. The problem of representation was replaced by the problem of the construction of form and line (Post-Cubism) and colour (Suprematism). In 1917 her revolutionary tendencies came to the fore ... The most productive period of Popova's career took place in the years 1921–24 [Moscow 1924, p.6].

Popova's early training was rooted in Impressionism, Post-Impressionism and the work of Cézanne, as can be seen in such paintings as *Still Life* (1907–8; George Costakis Collection). She also admired the innovative works of Mikhail Vrubel, which she saw in Kiev in 1909, and Giotto's frescoes, which she studied in Italy in 1910. Like many of her generation, she was inspired by the traditional arts and architecture of her homeland and between 1910 and 1911 visited important ancient cities such as Novgorod, Pskov, Yaroslavl and Suzdal. In the early 1910s she produced several drawings in the spirit and style of Neo-primitivism, using motifs and stylistic features derived from ancient Russian icon painting (e.g. *Adoration of the Infant Christ*, early 1910s; Tretyakov Gallery, Moscow).

Although Popova was aware of modern Western developments through journals, temporary exhibitions and permanent collections such as that of Shchukin in Moscow, she became more familiar with contemporary ideas when she spent the winter of 1912–13 in Paris. There she worked at La Palette under the direction of Jean Metzinger and Henri Le Fauconnier and visited the studios of Alexander Archipenko and Ossip Zadkine. This close contact with Cubism was matched by a growing knowledge of Futurist theory and practice, and it seems likely that she saw Umberto Boccioni's Parisian exhibition of July 1913. In Popova's figure paintings of 1913–14, such as *Figure + House + Space* (State Russian Museum, St Petersburg), the various parts of the female body are translated into cuboid and conical elements, while the joints are rendered as open circular forms. Lines extend from these shapes to relate them to the surrounding spatial environment. While the formal language is indebted to Analytical Cubism, Popova's title pays homage to Umberto Boccioni's painting *Head + House + Light* of 1912. In early 1914 her brightly coloured compositions became flatter, the objects became more fragmented, and a greater unity was established between the dislocated elements and the grounds (e.g. *Objects from a Dyer's Shop (Early Morning)*, 1914; Museum of Modern Art, New York).

After Popova studied at "The Tower" in 1912, she became associated with such artists as Vladimir Tatlin and Nadezhda Udaltsova (q.v.) and in January 1914 she made her exhibition debut with the Knave (or Jack) of Diamonds group. She revisited France and Italy in the summer of 1914. During 1914–15

Popova: *Painterly Architectonic*, 1918; watercolour and gouache; Yale University Art Gallery, New Haven; Gift from the Estate of Katherine S. Dreier

Popova experimented intensely with the possibilities of the Cubo-Futurist idiom and produced her own personal variations. In *Travelling Woman* (1915; Costakis Collection) Futurist devices, such as lines of force and sequential repetition of elements, are combined with features derived from Cubism, such as dislocation, restrained tonalities and lettering, to evoke the sensation of movement and the experience of travelling through time and geographical space.

In 1915 Popova also started to experiment with collage and to produce three-dimensional reliefs (in her terms "plastic paintings"), such as *Jug on a Table, Relief* (Tretyakov Gallery). This comprises found elements (the table leg), lettering ("2 lir") and heavily worked textures. The forms of the jug are translated into boldly curving sheets of card which are heavily painted and protrude dramatically from the ground plane while evoking the forms of the jug as seen from various viewpoints. Although Popova's reliefs were undoubtedly inspired by Tatlin's example and display a similar interest in textures and the spatial extension of the object, they are clearly distinct from the "culture of materials" that Tatlin developed and according to which the material determines the form. Even Popova's most abstract relief (repr. Moscow 1924) suggests that she was more interested in painted texture (and such pictorial elements as wallpaper) than in the sculptural potential and surface qualities of materials such as wood, metal and glass. Popova showed *Jug* and other reliefs at the *0.10* exhibition (December 1915, Petrograd), where Kazimir Malevich launched his Suprematist paintings of coloured geometric forms on white grounds.

Subsequently, in November 1916, Popova exhibited six non-objective paintings under the title of *Zhivopisnaya arkhitektonika*, which has been translated variously as *Pictorial* or *Painterly Architectonic* or *Architectonics*. These works consisted of coloured planes overlaid in fairly dense, centralised compositions against plain grounds. These retained some relationship to collage, but were evidently also influenced by Suprematism. During the winter of 1916–17 Popova belonged to Malevich's circle and was involved in creating various designs for the group's magazine *Supremus*, which was never published. In 1917 and 1918 she continued to develop her *Pictorial Architectonics*, producing paintings that evoke a greater sense of spatial dynamism by concentrating on large, diagonally intersecting planes of modulated colour (e.g. *Painterly Architectonic*, 1918; see illustration). In March 1918 she married the art historian Boris von Eding and in November gave birth to a son. While staying at Rostov on Don during the summer and autumn of 1919, her husband died of typhus and Popova became seriously ill. Not surprisingly, Popova did not produce many paintings between late 1918 and late 1919.

During the Civil War (1918–20) Popova executed some work for the Fine Arts Section (IZO) within the People's Commissariat of Enlightenment (Narkompros), designing propaganda posters (for campaigns such as that against illiteracy) and producing decorations for the revolutionary festivals. In April 1919 she collaborated with the artist and architect Alexander Vesnin on decorating the building of the Moscow Soviet for May Day. Two years later, in May 1921, they worked together with the writer Ivan Aksyonov and the producer Vsevolod Meyerkhold on the staging of a mass festival to be held in Moscow in honour of the Third International.

The cast of thousands was to have moved from the "Capitalist Fortress", the city of the past, which was rendered predominantly as a conglomeration of closed cuboid volumes, towards the "City of the Future". The latter was built of far more curving and transparent, open-work constructions, reminiscent of advanced engineering structures such as bridges and cranes and echoing the technological language of iron girders and glazed volumes, which Tatlin had celebrated in his *Model for a Monument to the Third International* of 1920. Popova and Vesnin produced models, but the project was cancelled at a late stage for financial reasons.

In 1918 Popova joined the staff of the Svomas (State Free Art Studios) and she continued to teach there when it changed into the Vkhutemas. She helped to organise the structure of the Basic Course and taught a course on colour construction that formed part of its syllabus. A member of the Inkhuk (Institute of Artistic Culture) from May 1920, Popova initially worked with Wassily Kandinsky in the Section of Monumental Art. She then helped to formulate the programme of the General Working Group of Objective Analysis, participating actively in the discussions of spring 1921 that sought to define the distinction between concepts of composition and construction. This important debate led to the formation of the Working Group of Constructivists (also known as the First Working Group of Constructivists) in March 1921. These artists denied the validity of art as an autonomous activity and instead wished to participate in the construction of the new socialist society by designing everyday objects, which could be mass-produced by industry. Popova did not join this group initially, but allied herself with the Working Group of Objectivists which included Vesnin, Udaltsova and Alexander Drevin and which met for the first time on 15 April 1921. Popova continued to contribute to Inkhuk meetings and in September 1922 she presented a paper concerning her design for Meyerkhold's production of Fernand Crommelynck's farce, *The Magnanimous Cuckold* of April 1922. She also participated in the debate concerning how art should be taught, producing a paper "Toward the question of the new methods in our art school", which was clearly based on her own pedagogical experience.

In September 1921 Popova collaborated with Alexander Rodchenko and Varvara Stepanova (q.v.), founder members of the Constructivist group, Vesnin and Alexandra Exter (q.v.) in the important exhibition 5 × 5 = 25 in Moscow. The five artists each contributed five works. Popova's exhibits were entitled *Experiments with Pictorial Force Structures*. This marks the first appearance of Popova's *Space-Force Constructions* or *Prostranstvenno-silovoye postroyeniye*, which she continued to produce until 1922. These were often drawn in paint directly on to unsized wood. The compositions were built up of intersecting and overlapping lines of varying thicknesses which created structural and spatial tensions (e.g. *Space-Force Construction*, 1921; Tretyakov Gallery). The title was also applied to works that incorporated arcing or circular lines and were more obviously dynamic in intention (e.g. *Space-Force Construction*, 1921; Costakis Collection). The statement that Popova produced in the 5 x 5 = 25 catalogue indicated that she had rejected easel painting as the ultimate aim of artistic activity and that henceforth she intended to direct her artistic skills towards more immediately utilitarian objectives. She wrote that the paintings exhibited "are to be regarded only as series of preparatory experiments towards concrete material constructions." From this point onwards Popova became directly involved with more functional design work.

In 1921 Meyerkhold invited Popova to teach a course on the "Analysis of the elements of material design" at his Higher State Theatrical Workshops (or GVTM) in Moscow. Building on this experience, in 1922 she designed the sets and costumes for Meyerkhold's production of *The Magnanimous Cuckold*, transforming the watermill of the action into a multi-levelled, skeletal machine that consisted of staircases, shoots and rotating wheels. She dressed the actors in plain coloured overalls (production clothing or *prozodezhda*), which, she explained, were conceived as prototypes for industrial or working clothing in the real world. This treatment complemented Meyerkhold's acting style, which combined mechanised movements with the gestures of the *commedia dell'arte*. The production was widely regarded as the first application of Constructivist principles to theatrical design. In 1923 her set for Sergei Tretyakov's reworking of Marcel Martinet's play *The Earth in Turmoil* approached the industrial object from a rather more pragmatic standpoint. The set was based on a gantry crane and the costumes and properties were not new artistic prototypes devised by the artist, but were selected from already existing mass-produced objects. Popova also devised a large number of political slogans for the production.

In early 1924 Popova and Stepanova started to work as fabric designers at the First Textile Print Factory in Moscow, which had previously been known as the Emil Tsindel Factory. In accordance with the machine aesthetic that the Constructivists embraced and the mechanical nature of industrial manufacture, Popova and Stepanova considered that the replacement of traditional floral and plant patterns with geometrically based designs was an essential pre-requisite for the rationalisation of textile production and clothing design. By manipulating a small number of simple geometric forms and primary colours, they produced a vast array of exciting designs, some of which went into mass production. At this time Popova also worked on dress designs, sometimes using her own fabrics, so that the pattern emphasised the dress's functional and structural elements.

Popova contributed texts and reproductions to the avant-garde magazine *Lef* (Left Front of the Arts), which was founded by Vladimir Mayakovsky in 1923. She also produced a large number of graphic designs for various projects, including banners, wall labels, musical scores and journals (e.g. *The Cinema* (*Kino*), *c*.1922; Costakis Collection). In spring 1924 she started teaching courses on stage design at Proletkult; a few months later, Popova caught scarlet fever from her son and died on 25 May.

CHRISTINA LODDER

Potter, Beatrix
British painter and illustrator, 1866–1943

Born in South Kensington, London, 28 July 1866; father a prosperous businessman and lawyer. Spent childhood summers in Scotland and Lake District. Studied art under a Miss Cameron, 1878–83; received Art Student's Certificate, Science and Art Department of the Committee of the Council on Education, 1881; also advised by John Everett Millais, a family friend. First children's book, *The Tale of Peter Rabbit*, published by Frederick Warne in 1902. Purchased Hill Top Farm, Sawrey, Westmorland, after the death of her fiancé, Norman Warne, in 1905. Married local solicitor William Heelis, 1913; moved to Castle Cottage and began sheep rearing. Died in Sawrey, 22 December 1943. Bequeathed lands in Lake District to National Trust.

Selected Writings
Peter Rabbit series, from 1900 (for children)
The Journal of Beatrix Potter, from 1881 to 1897, ed. Leslie Linder, London and New York: Warne, 1966
Dear Ivy, Dear June: Letters from Beatrix Potter, ed. Margaret Crawford Maloney, Toronto: Other Press, 1977
Beatrix Potter's Americans: Selected Letters, ed. Jane Crowell Morse, Boston: Horn Book, 1981; London: Warne, 1982
The World of Peter Rabbit, London and New York: Warne, 1987 (collection)

Bibliography
Marcus Crouch, *Beatrix Potter*, London: Bodley Head, 1960; New York: Walck, 1961

Beatrix Potter, 1866–1943, exh. cat., National Book League, London, 1966

Anne Carroll Moore, Enid Linder and Leslie Linder, *The Art of Beatrix Potter*, revised edition, London and New York: Warne, 1972

Leslie Linder, *The History of the Tale of Peter Rabbit*, London: Warne, 1976

Margaret Lane, *The Magic Years of Beatrix Potter*, London and New York: Warne, 1978

Ulla Hyde Parker, *Cousin Beatie: A Memory of Beatrix Potter*, London: Warne, 1981

Margaret Lane, *The Tale of Beatrix Potter: A Biography*, revised edition, London and New York: Warne, 1985

Anne Stevenson Hobbs and Joyce Irene Whalley, eds, *Beatrix Potter: The Victoria and Albert Collection*, London: Victoria and Albert Museum, 1985; New York: Warne, 1986

Ann Wilsher, "The Potters and photography", *History of Photography*, ix, 1985, pp.223–5

Elizabeth Battrick, *The Real World of Beatrix Potter*, Norwich: Jarrold, 1986

Judy Taylor, *Beatrix Potter: Artist, Storyteller and Countrywoman*, London and New York: Warne, 1986

Beatrix Potter, 1866–1943: The Artist and Her World, exh. cat., Tate Gallery, London, 1987

Leslie Linder, ed., *A History of the Writings of Beatrix Potter Including Unpublished Work*, 2nd edition, London and New York: Warne, 1987

W. R. Mitchell, *Beatrix Potter Remembered*, Lancaster: Dalesman Books, 1987

Judy Taylor, *That Naughty Rabbit: Beatrix Potter and Peter Rabbit*, London and New York: Warne, 1987

Joyce Irene Whalley and Wynne K. Bartlett, *Beatrix Potter's Derwentwater Sketchbook*, London: Warne, 1988

Anne Stevenson Hobbs, *Beatrix Potter's Art: Paintings and Drawings*, London: Warne, 1989

Catherine J. Golden, "Beatrix Potter: Naturalist artist", *Woman's Art Journal*, xi/1, 1990, pp.16–20

——, "Retrieving Beatrix Potter's revision process", *Victorian Authors and Their Works: Revision Motivations and Modes*, ed. Judith Kennedy, Athens: Ohio University Press, 1991, pp.28–40

Eileen Jay, Mary Noble and Anne Stevenson Hobbs, *A Victorian Naturalist: Beatrix Potter's Drawings from the Armitt Collection*, London: Warne, 1992

Beatrix Potter is best known as the author-illustrator of the *Peter Rabbit* tales, but this series of 23 "little books" published by Warne from 1902 overshadows her achievements as a naturalist artist. Potter's first ambition was to have her works accepted by the leading organisation of British natural scientists, the Linnaean Society in London. In 1896 she presented her specialised fungi and mushroom studies to the botanists and director of the Royal Botanic Gardens at Kew. Potter's work was dismissed because of her gender and her age. Some of her studies illustrated theories drawn from independently conducted experiments; for example, she drew lichens as dual organisms, a theory in advance of the Kew authorities that was later proved correct. In light of this rejection, Potter laid aside her original ambition and became a successful author-illustrator. At the turn of the century, female authorship was no longer an anomaly, and book illustration, a "lesser art", offered women unprecedented opportunities for illustrating texts for women and children. Potter's book illustrations follow in the best English watercolour tradition associated with the illustrators Randolph Caldecott (her most obvious guide) and Walter Crane. Although she was appreciated as an author-illustrator in her own times, in recent years there has been extensive critical interest in Potter's art and accomplishments.

From the age of eight, Potter studied the animals, insects, plants, fungi, flora and fossils that she and her brother Bertram collected during family holidays in Scotland and the Lake District. They smuggled rabbits, hedgehogs, bats and owls into the upper-floor nursery of their London home, and secretly skinned and boiled dead birds, rabbits and even a fox to articulate the skeletons for Potter's anatomical drawings. Potter had little formal art training (the family engaged governesses and occasional art teachers), but the entire Potter family was part of the contemporary art world, both as patrons and practitioners. John Everett Millais, a close family friend, offered Potter artistic advice and complimented her skill in observation. The Art Student's Certificate that she received from the Science and Art Department of the Committee of the Council on Education in 1881 affirmed her skill in freehand and model drawing, practical geometry and linear perspective.

Potter's famous first story about a playful rabbit

Beatrix Potter: *Fungus Study, Gomphidius glutinosus,* 1894; Armitt Trust, Ambleside

adventuring in Mr McGregor's garden began as a "picture letter" (as Potter called it) to the son of her former governess, Annie Carter Moore. Aware of the growing market for children's books, Potter revised the picture letter (dated 4 September 1893) for publication, expanding the plot and adding illustrations. Although this was the first picture letter that Potter turned into a story, it is but one of many she wrote in the 1890s that reveal her gifts as a storyteller and observer of the natural world. Consciously following in the tradition of Crane, Caldecott and medieval illuminators, Potter carefully co-ordinated text and illustration. Drawing from live models, she also drew inspiration from her portfolios of natural history studies. For example, still lifes of mushrooms, rose hips and fungi re-emerge as authentic woodland details in the illustrations for *The Tale of Squirrel Nutkin* (1903), and studies of waterlilies, beetles and frogs inform her illustrations for *The Tale of Mr Jeremy Fisher* (1906). Although her lifelong publishers Warne were critical of her human figures, they praised her skill in drawing flora, fauna, landscape and animals, which she sustained even in those illustrations that place animal characters in human settings. Potter's renderings of rabbits, squirrels, frogs and hedgehogs convey an anatomical accuracy paralleling that of Rosa Bonheur (q.v.).

Frogs and hedgehogs seem unlikely choices for storybook characters, but Potter was unusual in her ability to realise the charms of all animal behaviour. Her illustrations blend scientific precision with a fanciful quality, also found in Caldecott's drawings of animals in clothes. Potter never used clothing to disguise the animal nature of her characters. Rather, she used it symbolically; for example, Peter's blue jacket, which he loses in Mr McGregor's garden, comes to symbolise his mischievousness and becomes this character's trademark. Typically, Potter began her book illustrations as rough pencil sketches pasted into the corners of paper-covered exercise books. From these she made detailed pen-and-ink drawings to which she added watercolour wash. In her early colour designs, such as those for greeting cards (1890), she used a fairly dry brush technique particularly suited to rendering the fur of small animals. Over the years, she developed a fluid illustrative style and relied more heavily on colour wash. In her few later books (e.g. *The Tale of Little Pig Robinson*, 1930) she combined pen-and-ink illustrations with colour plates. She insisted that her picture books be reasonably priced, amply illustrated and small enough to fit into a child's hand.

The years 1901 to 1913 mark Potter's most fruitful period as an illustrator: she produced 19 picture books. The success of her first books brought her financial independence. In 1905 she purchased Hill Top Farm and eventually settled in the Lake District, where she set many of her tales. In 1913, following her marriage to William Heelis, she wrote only an occasional story, and her interests turned to breeding livestock and conservation. On her death, she bequeathed 4000 acres in the Lake District to the National Trust, preserving the landscape that had inspired many of her endearing illustrations.

Today, Potter's picture books are children's classics. In the 1960s the quality of her naturalist studies was finally recognised when the mycologist W.P.K. Findlay used 59 of Potter's watercolours to illustrate his natural history, *Wayside and Woodland Fungi*, (London: Warne, 1967). More recently, Eileen Jay, Mary Noble and Anne Stevenson Hobbs have urged reappraisal of Potter's scientific and artistic accomplishments in *A Victorian Naturalist* (1992). Potter had wished for such recognition from the scientific community during her lifetime, yet in her children's tales she was a naturalist artist, making fitting her inclusion in this collection of leading women artists.

Major collections of Potter's naturalist art and book illustrations can be found in the Victoria and Albert Museum and Tate Gallery, London; Armitt Trust, Ambleside; the National Trust; Frederick Warne Archive; Beatrix Potter Gallery, Hawkshead; Royal Botanic Gardens, Kew; and Free Library of Philadelphia.

CATHERINE J. GOLDEN

Potter, Bessie Onahotema *see* Vonnoh

Potter, Mary
British painter, 1900–1981

Born Marian Anderson Attenborough in Beckenham, Kent, 9 April 1900. Attended Beckenham School of Art, 1916–18. Won exhibition to Royal College of Art, London, 1918, but instead used it to obtain bursary to Slade School of Fine Art, London; studied there under Henry Tonks and Wilson Steer, 1918–29. Taught at Eastbourne School of Art, 1920; opened studio in Fitzroy Street, London, 1921; also travelled in Italy and France. Member, Seven and Five Society, London, 1920. Exhibited at New English Art Club, London, 1920; with London Group from 1927. Married writer Stephen Potter, 1927; two sons, born 1928 and 1931; divorced 1955. Settled in Aldeburgh, Suffolk, 1951; opened studio at Red House, 1963. Prizewinner, John Moore's Exhibition, Liverpool, 1981. Officer, Order of the British Empire (OBE), 1979. Died 14 September 1981.

Selected Individual Exhibitions
Bloomsbury Gallery, London: 1931
Redfern Gallery, London: 1934 (with Edna Clarke Hall), 1949
Tooth's Gallery, London: 1936, 1946
Leicester Galleries, London: 1951, 1953, 1954, 1957, 1961, 1963
The Minories, Colchester: 1961 (retrospective), 1979
Whitechapel Art Gallery, London: 1964 (touring retrospective)
New Art Centre, London: 1967, 1969, 1972, 1974, 1976
Oxford Gallery, Oxford: 1968
Aldeburgh Festival, Suffolk: 1969, 1976, 1980
Tate Gallery, London: 1980
Serpentine Gallery, London: 1981 (touring retrospective, organised by Arts Council of Great Britain)

Bibliography
Mary Potter: Paintings, 1938–64, exh. cat., Whitechapel Art Gallery, London, 1964
Frances Spalding, "Mary Potter", *Studio International*, cxciii, 1977, pp.183–4
Mary Potter, exh. cat., Aldeburgh Festival, Suffolk, 1980
Mary Potter: Paintings, 1922–80, exh. cat., Arts Council of Great Britain, London, 1981
The Times, 16 September 1981, p.12 (obituary)

Mary Potter, exh. cat., New Art Centre, London, 1986
Mary Potter, 1900–1981: A Selective Retrospective, exh. cat., Oriel 31 Gallery, Newtown, Powys, and elsewhere, 1989
Marina Vaizey, "Mary Potter: 'A very English artist'", *Green Book*, iii/3, 1989, pp.26–8

Mary Potter was a delicate, romantic, allusive painter who in her best work combined a poetic feeling for landscape, particularly that of the austere, cold, bleak, beautiful and light-filled North Sea coast of Suffolk. The peculiar quality of the sky over water also influenced her work all her life, as she moved from living by the Thames in Chiswick to Harley Street near Regent's Park in London, with its ornamental waters and canals. After the end, by divorce, of her 27-year marriage to Stephen Potter, a producer for the British Broadcasting Corporation and the author of *Gamesmanship*, *Oneupmanship* and other books of that genre, Mary Potter moved from river to sea, finally living near the sea in Suffolk. Estuary and coast were to inform the subjects of her painting. Her house there, the Red House, was to become the home of her great friends the composer Benjamin Britten and the singer Peter Pears, founders of the Aldeburgh Festival. As her

commitment to her art progressed and advanced, so her imagery became more abstract, oriental in feeling in its dispersion of objects in space, yet still referential in its suggestions of observed reality.

Mary Potter came from a middle-class family and was brought up in Beckenham. She trained at the Slade, part of the University of London, and an older art school where women had always had their place, even if not entirely free of prejudice. The Bloomsbury painter Carrington (q.v.) had also trained there, as had Gwen John (q.v.) and Edna Clarke Hall (q.v.), the last also an under-rated artist. Yet even her most eminent patrons in later life could damn her with faint praise: here is Kenneth Clark, Lord Clark of Civilisation as he was nicknamed after his television series on the history of Western culture: "They [Mary Potter's paintings] discover in nature moments which seem to be both permanent and exceptional, and record them with, apparently, no fuss." If by "no fuss" is meant a subtle and pervasive attention to essentials, then the comment is accurate and full of insight. For it is insight that Potter possessed in abundance. Clark also suggested that it would be "a mistake to bring the heavy engines of analysis and

Mary Potter: *East Coast Window*, 1959; oil on canvas; 17 × 91.5 cm.; Tate Gallery, London

interpretation to bear on Mary Potter's pictures", which again has a patronising tinge; but the art historian Frances Spalding commented that: "It is indeed the kind of painting that begins where words end." Myfanwy Piper, librettist for Benjamin Britten, wife to the artist John Piper, described the still calm of Mary Potter's painting as "a kind of suspended extension of the moment".

Potter's technique was as original as her vision; she mixed beeswax with the paint, making it chalky, almost matte, and detested varnish; this may be because a soft, changing light typical of England, where at twilight forms merge, was among the visual things that interested her, rather than sharp edges and a raking light. Almost equally she found it difficult, even impossible to think of frames for her paintings, preferring them just to hang on the walls unframed. Her watercolours, small in scale, were conventionally mounted and framed. She first visited Venice and Greece when already in her fifties and sixties: her sensibility was not Mediterranean, not the bright, even, harsh blue light of the south, but the silvery grey ambiguous light of the north. She worked her paintings over and over, layering the direct observation from her drawings and tiny watercolours with memory. There is an anecdote of Potter rushing past a friend in Aldeburgh just as a dramatic storm was about to break; she had not taken in the storm, just the changing light, perfect for the appearance of a puddle of water she wanted to sketch, and was running into the storm.

Her art was known to a small circle of devoted friends and admirers; she could be a gifted portrait painter, and indeed did paint, among others, *Imogen Holst* in an affecting portrait that now hangs in the Maltings, Snape, the concert hall of the Aldeburgh Festival. But she found the genre too rigid: likenesses – at which she was gifted – restricted her own personal style. She was part of no group of artists; she had briefly joined the Seven and Five Group in 1920, but after that had worked in increasing isolation. Although her work is in the Tate Gallery, London, and other major British galleries, her special contribution to the art of landscape and the domestic interior will become increasingly recognised for its refinement, delicacy yet resolute strength. During her 30 years in Aldeburgh, her style became looser, her references to the observed world more oblique. Her repertoire of pale colours is particularly individual, reminiscent of the colours of plants seen in shadowy light and the grey sea under a grey sky, softly sparkling. While her work always has an echo of recognisable form, hers is a representational idiom in which the phrase "less means more" takes on a particular meaning, expressive of the emotional reticence of this most affecting of artists.

MARINA VAIZEY

Poupelet, Jane
French sculptor, 1878–1932

Born in Saint-Paul-Lizonne, Dordogne, 19 April 1878. Moved to Paris independently of her family, 1896. Studied at the Ecole des Beaux-Arts, Bordeaux (teaching diploma in drawing). Rejected academic ethos of Académie Julian, Paris, and studied instead under the sculptor Lucien Schnegg.

Visited Italy on a state scholarship, 1905. Invited to exhibit with Rodin as member of Société Nouvelle at Galerie Georges Petit, Paris, 1909–14. Independent studio in Montparnasse, Paris. Exhibited with several associations of women artists: Les Quelques, Les Unes Internationales and Le Lyceum, Paris, and American Associations of Women Painters and Sculptors, New York. Belonged to association of professional women, militating for political rights, education and employment. Worked on the Medical Surgery for the American Red Cross during World War I; health permanently damaged. Recipient of Whitney Hoff award, 1911; American Women Painters and Sculptors prize, 1918. Sociétaire, 1910, and president, Jury of Sculpture, 1921, Société Nationale des Beaux-Arts; founder member, Salon des Tuileries, Paris, 1923. Chevalier, Légion d'Honneur, 1928. Died in Paris after an operation, 18 November 1932.

Principal Exhibitions

Individual
Gallery T.B. Star, New York: 1914
Goupil Gallery, New York: 1916 (with Janet Scudder)
Rüch Gallery, New York: 1924
Galerie Bernier, Paris: 1928, 1930, 1938 (retrospective)
Montross Gallery, New York: 1928, 1931
Brooklyn Museum, NY: 1933 (retrospective)

Group
Société Nationale des Beaux-Arts, Paris: 1904–14, 1920–22
Salon d'Automne, Paris: 1904, 1907–8
La Jeune Peinture Française, Paris: 1920–26
Salon des Tuileries, Paris: 1923–31

Bibliography

Maurice Guillemot, "Jane Poupelet", *Art et Décoration*, xxxiv, 1913, pp.51–6
Janet Scudder, "A great French sculptress", *Harpers Weekly*, 8 April 1916, p.370, and *Current Opinion*, xl, 1916, pp.430–31
André Salmon, *La Jeune Peinture française*, Paris: Société des Trente, 1919
H. Martinie, "Jane Poupelet", *Art et Décoration*, xlvi, 1924, pp.87–96
Janet Scudder, *Modeling My Life*, New York: Harcourt Brace, 1925
Jane Poupelet, exh. cat., Galerie Bernier, Paris, 1928
A. Henri Martinie, *La Sculpture au XXe*, Paris, 1928
Charles Kunstler, *Jane Poupelet*, Paris: Crès, 1930
E[lizabeth] H[amelin], "Jane Poupelet, sculptor", *Brooklyn Museum Quarterly*, xx/2, 1933, pp.53–6
Vincent Wapler, *Jane Poupelet sculpteur: Mémoire de maîtrise*, Lille: Université de Lille, 1973 (catalogue raisonné)
La Bande à Schnegg, exh. cat., Musée Bourdelle, Paris, 1974
Claudine Mitchell, *Inventaires des plâtres du Studio Jane Poupelet*, Mont-de-Marsan: Musée Despiau-Wlerick, Donjon Lacataye, 1992
La Sculpture du XXème siècle dans les Musées du Nord et du Pas de Calais, exh. cat., Calais, 1992

The female nudes that Jane Poupelet designed in the period 1907–12 ensured her a position of eminence in the French establishment until the late 1930s. They also won her a committed international audience of professional women. Her career opened in 1904 with *Funeral of a Child in Dordogne* (plaster; Musée de Périgueux), a serial sculpture that contrasts social types from rural France beside a thoughtful female figure at the centre of the procession. The study of classical art in

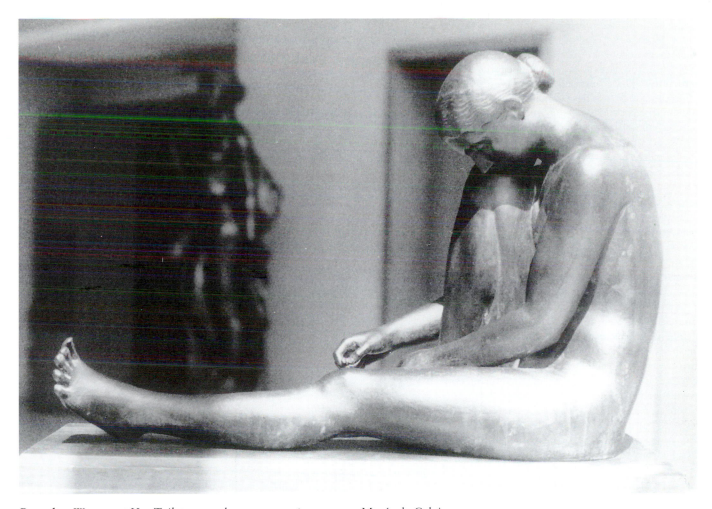

Poupelet: *Woman at Her Toilet*, 1910; bronze; 42 × 61 × 23 cm.; Musée de Calais

Italy in 1905 confirmed her interest in the non-narrative female nude. The bronze *Woman at Her Toilet* (State purchase of 1910; see illustration) became the focus of interest on the part of critics who, like Louis Vauxcelles, advocated a formalism that need not lead to abstraction.

Formal issues were also conceptual issues for Poupelet in her attempt to unify the intellectual and the physical in an image of women who would be self-contained and yet endowed with the muscular body and intellectual power that women needed to act in the public sphere. What is emphasised in *Woman at Her Toilet* is the physical presence of the muscular body – the long thigh pressing against the plinth of the sculpture. By positioning one leg folded against the breast and the arms in front of the genitalia, Poupelet ensured that from any viewpoint certain sections of female anatomy escape the beholder's gaze, thus representing the sexual dimension as guarded and within the control of the female subject: with the stability and self-containment of its formal structure, the lowered head, the eyes closed and lips mute, the work conveys a mental climate of poise and inner concentration. *Woman Mirroring Herself in the Water* (1910; plaster; private collection, repr. Mitchell 1992, JP 05–8) reverses the myth of Narcissus by showing a female figure in the posture of a runner getting ready for a race, turned towards the world of action and competition. *Before the Wave* (1912; bronze; private

collection, repr. Wapler 1973, no.45), featuring a woman in another athletic posture, crouching on both her knees, challenges the tradition of erotic art in its very tension, resilience and awkwardness of construct. The two sculptures convey an image of women conspicuously enjoying the free exercise of their bodies, unconcerned by the gaze of masculine sexual desire.

As was the case for many women at the time, the experience of World War I deeply affected Poupelet, leaving her uncertain as to the social status and purposes of art practice. Her "war effort" consisted in fabricating facial masks for gravely mutilated soldiers, a practice that the American sculptor Ann Ladd had set up in Paris in 1918; Poupelet was still working for the Hospital of Val de Grâce in 1920. Her one certainty rested with a decision not to put the female nude at the service of monumental art that cemented dominant or nationalist ideologies.

Influenced by contemporary issues within the French feminist movement, the pre-war nudes formed part of a collective endeavour for women to gain control over the physical realities of their bodies. They have no counterpart in Poupelet's work of the 1920s. Her new design of 1923, *Sleeping Woman* (plaster; private collection, repr. Mitchell 1992, JP 32–5), integrates some of the compositional devices of *Woman Mirroring Herself in the Water*, only to negate its optimism as the female figure is positioned lying on her side, across a tomb-like rectangular block, eyes closed and hands in a position of prayer. There was no public space for this project for a monument to women in the oppressive regime of post-war "national reconstruction". There followed *Meditation* (1924; bronze; private collection, repr. Wapler 1973, no.62), which challenges the ideologies developed around Rodin's *Thinker* by showing the seated female figure supporting one cheek against her closed hands.

Poupelet's creative practice after 1923 took place essentially in the medium of drawing, experimenting with diverse techniques from the continuous outline evolved from the use of tracing paper to ink wash in the Chinese tradition, dividing her subjects between the female nude and animals observed on her farm in the Dordogne. Her interest now turned to the female body as affected by maternity and the ageing process. Objects of an active exhibition policy on her part, these drawings were shown at the Galerie Bernier in Paris and Montross Gallery in New York.

Another aspect of Poupelet's work was the sculpture of domestic and farm animals displaying compact surfaces and geometricised designs. Drawn from her interest in Greek, Egyptian and Oriental sculptures, most of these were designed before 1911. Commercialised, they continued to prove a regular, if small, source of income throughout the 1920s, particularly from her American clients (examples of her animal bronzes, *Rabbit*, *Cat*, *Young Donkey*, *Cock* and *Goose*, in Musée National d'Art Moderne, Paris; Art Institute of Chicago; Musée des Beaux-Arts, Calais; Musée du Périgord, Périgueux).

Poupelet's artistic reputation and public image in the 1920s rested with the recasting and international display of pre-World War I designs, in particular *Woman Placing Her Foot in the Water*, modelled in 1912 (1923; bronze; one cast in Art Institute of Chicago, donation of George Porter, one of Poupelet's regular clients; another in Musée du Périgord) and *Woman Torso* purchased by the Brooklyn Museum, New York, in 1921, a reworking of her *Seated Woman* of 1913, the head and the arms now severed.

Poupelet maintained an independent practice with a studio in Montparnasse, held administrative positions in the French establishment and enjoyed the apparent freedom to decide what her art practice should be like. Specialising in small-scale works enabled her to keep much of the process of making a sculpture in the control of her own hands. She did her own chiselling and developed unique techniques for bronze patina. To her female audience, and in the perspective of women's struggle to achieve recognition in the field of culture, the way in which Poupelet conducted her career set a model to follow: "In a period when women were beginning to turn to art seriously as a vocation, she stands prominent for sincerity of purpose and successful achievement" testified Elizabeth Hamelin on the occasion of the Brooklyn retrospective (1933). Her career in the USA had been mostly promoted by a network of professional women she had met in Paris, including the American sculptor Janet Scudder (q.v.), who in 1913 negotiated the purchase of *Woman at Her Toilet* by the Metropolitan Museum of Art, New York. In the French cultural establishment Poupelet's female nudes were not expected to signify beyond their rigorous and harmonious constructs. To her

female audience they symbolised a state of existence where women could enact their aspiration for emancipation. Thus Poupelet's works operate a duality of meaning that make them even more in danger of being misunderstood today.

CLAUDINE MITCHELL

Povorina, Alexandra
Russian painter, 1885–1963

Born in St Petersburg, 26 February 1885. Moved to Munich to study under the Hungarian painter Simon Hollósy, 1903. Lived in Paris from 1911. Taught art classes in Vyatka, Russia, 1913. Returned to Paris, then moved to Hamburg at the outbreak of World War I. Married German painter Friedrich Ahlers-Hestermann; daughter born 1919. Stayed in Ascona, Switzerland, 1924–5. Moved from Hamburg to Cologne, 1928. Founder member of Imaginisten group, Cologne; member of Deutscher Künstlerbund and Abstraction-Création group, Paris. Banned from exhibiting by the National Socialists. Moved to Berlin, 1939. Lecturer at Hochschule für Angewandte Kunst, Berlin Weissensee, 1947–52. Died in Berlin, 23 December 1963.

Principal Exhibitions

Individual
Galerie Becker-Newman, Cologne: 1930
Provinzialmuseum, Hannover: 1932
Kunstverein, Hamburg: 1932 (with Naum Slatzky)
Haus am Waldsee, Berlin: 1961
Haus am Lützowplatz, Berlin: 1966 (retrospective)

Group
Galerie Commeter, Hamburg: 1915, 1916, 1918 (*Neue Gruppe Hamburg*)
Hamburg Secession: from 1920
Kunstverein, Hamburg: 1921 (*Deutsche Künstlerbund*), 1945 (*I. Nachkriegsausstellung der Hamburger Sezession*)
Deutscher Künstlerbund, Cologne: 1929
Nassauischer Kunstverein, Wiesbaden: 1932 (*Zeichen und Bilder*)
Salon des Surindépendants, Paris: 1933
Abstraction-Création group, Paris: 1933, 1935
Museum Folkwang, Essen: 1933 (*Zeichen und Bilder*, closed by the National Socialists)
Künstlerbund, Berlin: 1951

Selected Writings
"Manuskript der Rechtfertigungsrede vor dem Vorstand der GEDOK vermutlich von 1933", manuscript, Collection Tatiana Ahlers-Hestermann, Hamburg

Bibliography

"Programm der Imaginisten", probably 1931–2, Collection Tatiana Ahlers-Hestermann, Hamburg
"Manuskript des Vorworts der Ausstellung von A. Povòrina und N. Slatzky in Hamburg 1932", Collection Tatiana Ahlers-Hestermann, Hamburg
Friedrich Ahlers-Hestermann, *Pause vor dem dritten Akt*, Hamburg: Mann, 1949
Franz Roh, *"Entartete" Kunst: Kunstbarbarei im Dritten Reich*, Hannover: Fackelträger, 1962

Alexandra Povòrina, Alma del Banco, Anita Rée, exh. cat., Kunsthaus, Hamburg, 1966

Alexandra Povòrina: Gemälde und Collagen, 1913–1960, exh. cat., Haus am Lützowplatz, Berlin, 1966

Friedrich Ahlers-Hestermann, Alexandra Povòrina-Hestermann, Tatiana Ahlers-Hestermann, exh. cat., Städtisches Museum, Flensburg, 1969

Vom Dadamax bis zum Grüngürtel: Köln in den zwanziger Jahren, exh. cat., Kölner Kunsthalle, Cologne, 1975

Der Anteil der Frau an der Kunst der 20er Jahre, exh. cat., Galerie Pels-Leusden, Berlin, 1977

Künstlerinnen international, 1877–1977, exh. cat., Schloss Charlottenburg, Berlin, 1977

Abstraction-Création, 1931–1936, exh. cat., Westfälisches Landesmuseum für Kunst- und Kulturgeschichte, Münster, and elsewhere, 1978

Anke Manigold, *Der Hamburger Maler Friedrich Ahlers-Hestermann (1883–1973)*, Hamburg: Verein für Hamburgische Geschichte, 1986

Isabel Schulz, *Die Frau als Künstlerin: Über das Leben und Werk von Künstlerinnen früher und heute*, Hamburg: Museumspädagogischer Dienst Hamburg, 1986

Das Verborgene Museum I: Dokumentation der Kunst von Frauen in Berliner öffentlichen Sammlungen, exh. cat., Akademie der Künste, Berlin, 1987

Künstlerinnen der Hamburger Sezession, 1919–1933: Alma del Banco, Dorothea Maetzel-Johannsen, Alexandra Povòrina, Anita Rée, Gretchen Wohlwill, exh. cat., Patriotische Gesellschaft von 1765, Hamburg, 1988

Anke Münster, "Alexandra Povòrina und Lotte B. Prechner: Zwei Künstlerinnen im Köln der 20er Jahre", *Kölner Museums-Bulletin: Berichte und Forschungen aus den Museen der Stadt Köln*, i, 1994, pp.28–35

With Julius Bissier, Ernst-Wilhelm Nay and Otto Ritschl, Povorina was one of the artists who turned to abstract painting in Germany a few years before the National Socialists seized power. Distancing herself from the "rational, intellectual abstraction" of Constructivism, she wanted to create pictures that "renouncing objective appearance, depict fantastic, self-contained creatures whose meaning is not completely graspable, whose shape reveals an imaginative world with its own laws". Thus, an unknown writer (1931–2; typescript, private

Povorina: *Still Life with Plaster Head*, 1930; oil on wood; 81 × 105 cm.; Nationalgalerie, Berlin

collection) described the artistic objective of the group Imaginisten to which Povorina belonged. She was also a member of the Paris artists' group Abstraction-Création.

As Povorina's earliest extant works date from 1913, nothing survives from her upbringing in St Petersburg or from her studies in Munich with Simon Hollósy. And due to the loss of her works in 1914, it is not possible to document her stay in Paris, which she considered very important for her artistic development. There she had contact with Alexander Archipenko, Mossei Kogan and her studio neighbour Constantin Brancusi. At the "Russian studio" of the painter Marya Vassilyeva she met her future husband, Friedrich Ahlers-Hestermann, a painter from Hamburg. With the outbreak of World War I she followed him to Germany.

The couple lived in Hamburg from 1914 to 1928, where they were among the founding members of the Hamburg Secession and participated regularly in exhibitions. Povorina was in close contact with the artists Gretchen Wohlwill, Alma del Banco and Anita Rée (q.v.). In 1915 she painted a portrait of *Anita Rée* (Schleswig-Holsteinisches Landesmuseum, Schloss Gottdorf). Her work from this period shows her connection with French painting, especially the work of Cézanne. During trips in the summer she experimented with landscapes, for example *Landscape with Red House* (1915) and *Houses on the River* (1921; both Hamburger Kunsthalle), most of which treat the connection between nature and the presence of humans. Houses, ships or people working are recurring motifs, and individual forms are clearly demarcated by dark contours. The harmony of form and colour she sought is particularly evident in *Blankenese* (1919; Altonaer Museum, Hamburg).

Like many artists, Povorina and her husband painted portraits to support themselves through the post-war economic difficulties. Hanseatic collectors regularly bought their work, and a few examples remain in private collections, but many were lost when German Jews had to emigrate in 1933. Still lifes also played an important role in Povorina's work, and they mark her slow move towards abstract painting from 1928. She regarded still lifes as arrangements of form and colour rather than as depictions of objects, for example *Still Life with Plaster Head* (1930; see illustration) and *Still Life* (1930; Hamburger Kunsthalle). The influences of Picasso and Braque are clear in this phase.

The development of Povorina's art was accompanied by enormous productivity and widespread recognition. Her first solo exhibition was held in 1930 at the Galerie Becker-Newman in Cologne, and two years later Alexander Dorner presented her work at the Provinzialmuseum in Hannover. As a member of artists' groups including Deutscher Kunstlerbund, Imaginisten and Abstraction-Création, she contributed increasingly to exhibitions in this period.

Povorina explored possibilities between abstraction and realism, and symbolic form, colour combinations and figurative works were of equal importance. She sought to create a pictorial language for the depiction of the emotions and forces that she called the essential, a search that linked her to such painters as Fritz Winter and Ernst-Wilhelm Nay. An example of her use of figurative elements in abstract works is the study (1930; Sprengel Museum, Hannover) for the painting *Dancing Goblin*, which was bought by the Provinzialmuseum in Hannover but disappeared after it was confiscated as degenerate by the National Socialists. By contrast, in the oil painting *Dark Force* (1933; Sprengel Museum), created during the Nazis' seizure of power, she concentrated solely on effects of colour, line and plane.

In internal exile, with no possibility of exhibiting, Povorina stopped painting between about 1937 and 1945, contributing to the family's support with prints on cloth. Despite health problems, she entered a new artistically productive phase after the war, resuming the formal language she had developed in the early 1930s. She exhibited regularly but without the success she had experienced before 1933 and that was being enjoyed by Nay, Werner and Winter. In her later works figurative elements, especially the human body, are found only rarely, and there is a significant intensification of colour, as in *Beach Vision* (1949; private collection, repr. Berlin 1966, frontispiece) and *Plants* (1956; Berlinische Galerie).

Towards the end of the 1950s illness forced Povorina to give up painting and she returned to the collage technique she had first tried in the 1930s. Using charcoal, pastel and watercolour on various papers, she created a last group of works that often seem more delicate and lyrical than her paintings, for example *On Blue-Green* (undated, *ibid.*, no.73). Three years after her death she was honoured with a solo exhibition in Berlin.

ANKE MÜNSTER

Prechner, Lotte B.
German graphic artist, painter and sculptor, 1877–1967

Born Lotte Stein in Ückermünde, Pomerania, 1 June 1877, into a Jewish family. Studied philosophy in Berlin. From *c*.1900, studied art at the Damenakademie des Münchener Künstlerinnenvereins under Ludwig Herterich; Académie Julian and Académie Colarossi in Paris; Kunstgewerbeschule in Cologne and Düsseldorf. Moved to Cologne. Marriage to dentist Dr Hermann Prechner, *c*.1905–10; one daughter. War artist in Belgium, 1915. Lived in Cologne with art historian Professor Walter Bombe, then went with him to Paris, 1926–7; subsequent trips with Bombe to Berlin, Budapest, Vienna, Prague and Rome; emigrated to Belgium, 1936. Lived in Brussels and Portici, near Naples, after World War II. Member, Das Junge Rheinland and Rheinische Secession. Died in Portici, 10 October 1967.

Principal Exhibitions
Kölnischer Kunstverein, Cologne: 1916, 1918
   (*Weihnachtsausstellung*), 1921 (*Kölner Künstlerbund*), 1923,
   1930 (*Kölner Künstler*)
Leopold-Hoesch Museum, Düren: 1918
Städtisches Museum Villa Obernier, Bonn: 1918
Kunstgewerbemuseum, Cologne: 1918 (*Vereinigung zur
   Unterstützung notleidender Künstler*)
Suermond Museum, Aachen: 1920
Weimarischer Kunstverein, Weimar: 1920
Badischer Kunstverein, Karlsruhe: 1921, 1924, 1925
Kunsthalle, Düsseldorf: 1921, 1927, 1928 (all *Das Junge Rheinland*),
   1929 (*Rheinische Sezession*)
Münchener Kunstverein, Munich: 1921

Nassauischer Kunstverein, Wiesbaden: 1922, 1923
Grosse Berliner Kunstausstellung, Berlin: 1922, 1929
Grosse Kunstausstellung, Düsseldorf: 1926
Kunstverein für Böhmen, Prague: 1927
Verein der Künstlerinnen zu Berlin: 1929 (*Die Frau von heute*), 1930
Kunstverein Hannover: 1954 (*Arbeit, Soziales, Beruf in der Kunst*)

Selected Writings

"Flächenholzschnitt und Linoleumschnitt", *Die Kunstschule*, no.5, 1928, pp.133–9
"Malversuche", *Die Kunstschule*, no.11, 1928, pp.343–5
"Der Maler und sein Modell", *Die Bergstadt*, ii, 1929, pp.236–43
"Poesie in Prosa", Recklinghausen, 1975

Bibliography

Walter Bombe, "Von neuer Graphik", *Westdeutsche Wochenschrift*, no.3, 1921, pp.35–7
Otto Brües, "Lotte B. Prechners Holzschnitte", *Westdeutsche Wochenschrift für Deutsche Kunst*, no.14, 1922, pp.265–71
Max Osborn and others, *Handbuch des Kunstmarktes: Kunstadressbuch*, Berlin, 1926
Das Buch der lebenden deutschen Künstler, Altertumssforscher, Kunstgelehrten, Kunstwissenschaftler und Kunstschriftsteller, ii of *Dresslers Kunsthandbuch*, Berlin, 1930
Robert Delevoy, "Les gravures de Lotte B. Prechner", *Savoir et Beauté*, no.12, Brussels, 1938, pp.433–5
Mario Marchi, "Lotte B. Prechner", *Savoir et Beauté*, no.6, Brussels, 1938, pp.222–3
Werner Doede, *Lotte B. Prechner*, Recklinghausen, 1966
Joachim Heusinger von Waldegg, "Engagement für Unterprivilegierte: Nachlass Lotte B. Prechner", *Das Rheinische Landesmuseum Bonn: Berichte aus der Arbeit des Museums*, iv, 1974, pp.57–8
Profession ohne Tradition: 125 Jahre Verein Berliner Künstlerinnen, exh. cat., Berlinische Galerie, Berlin, 1992
Rheinische Expressionistinnen, Schriftenreihe Verein August Macke Haus, no.10, Bonn, 1993
"Unbekannte Druckgraphik des Rheinischen Expressionismus: Texte und Kurzbiographien zur Ausstellung", typescript, August Macke Haus, Bonn, 1993
Anke Münster, "Alexandra Povórina und Lotte B. Prechner: Zwei Künstlerinnen im Köln der 20er Jahre", *Kölner Museums-Bulletin: Berichte und Forschungen aus den Museen der Stadt Köln*, i, 1994, pp.28–35

Lotte B. Prechner's main artistic production was the socially critical graphic work she began directly after World War I. Here she assimilated the misery of refugees that she had experienced as a war artist in the German-occupied parts of Belgium as well as the post-war upheaval of Germany. In 1918–19 she created a large series of woodcuts and linocuts depicting strikes, refugees, Gypsy families and city scenes. The formal concentration characteristic of these works was achieved by an Expressionist reduction of artistic means. With extreme simplification, she used rough drawing to develop her subject matter from the contrast of pure black and white. This condensed formal language is clearly illustrated in her linocut *Impending Strike* (*c*.1920; Rheinisches Landesmuseum, Bonn): the row of rebels is indicated by a single closed black form that moves towards an archway across a sparingly defined street. The group seems anonymous, a moving mass that cannot be stopped. As in other works, the focus is not on the demonstration as a political revolt but as a threatening, yet fascinating incident. In the linocut *Strike II* (*c*.1920; Rheinisches Landesmuseum) the impression of determination is increased

Prechner: *Strike*, *c*.1920; woodcut; 17 × 15.2 cm.; Rheinisches Landesmuseum, Bonn

by the more frontal position of the demonstration, forced forward by the framing rows of houses.

Although Prechner did not take an overtly political stance, her works capture the historical and social atmosphere of the post-war period in Germany. Instead of analysing social grievances, she was mainly interested in the portrayal of the existential situation and human fate, as in the linocuts *Emigrant*, *Feeling Safe* and *Rest on the Flight* (*c*.1920; both Rheinisches Landesmuseum). In such works as the woodcut *Sick Child* (*c*.1920; Rheinisches Landesmuseum) and the linocut *Gypsy Child* (*c*.1920; Bibliothèque royale Albert 1er, Brussels) she gave a sympathetic portrayal of outsiders and the underprivileged.

In contrast to the depiction of expulsion, imprisonment and social exclusion, Prechner portrayed the family, mainly the intimacy between mother and child. Without idealisation, the affection of the mother remains a constant, independent of class or adverse situations. She treated this subject archetypally in the linocut *Pietà* (*c*.1920; Bibliothèque royale Albert 1er) and topically in the linocut *Gypsy Family* (*c*.1920; Rheinisches Landesmuseum): in the midst of threat and homelessness the child finds protection and security with the mother.

With these works Prechner established herself in the art market and obtained significant success. The Wallraf-Richartz-Museum in Cologne bought six linocuts from this series in 1921. She also sold graphic works in 1922 through Johanna Ey, the well-known dealer of Das Junge Rheinland gallery. Works were bought by the Leopold-Hoesch-Museum, Düren (1920), the Staatliche Zeichenakademie, Hanau (1921), and the Moderne Galerie, Prague (1927). Her graphic works from this period illustrated two important essays by Bombe (1921) and Brües (1922). She was stimulated by contact with other artists associated with Das Junge Rheinland, notably Frans Masereel and Otto Dix, who painted her portrait in watercolour (1924; Herzog Anton Ulrich-Museum, Braunschweig).

Prechner's early work, up to 1918, is stylistically heterogeneous. It consists largely of copper- or zinc-plate etchings, the majority showing landscapes around Cologne or the Lower Rhine, or genre scenes. The high quality is already evident in such works as *Trees and House, Banks of the Rhine* and *Country Fair* (all before 1918; Rheinisches Landesmuseum). In another series, for example *Mother with Two Children* (before 1918; Rheinisches Landesmuseum), she reworked the formal possibilities of Art Nouveau. In some etchings, such as *At the Market Café* (before 1918; Rheinisches Landesmuseum), she experimented with illustration and caricature.

Other than graphic works, only a few paintings survive from this early period: landscapes influenced by Impressionism, an early *Self-Portrait in Profile* of c.1900 and a *Portrait of the Father* of c.1905 (both oil on canvas; Rheinisches Landesmuseum). She continued her landscape painting in the 1920s, referring to the socio-critical subjects of the graphic work, but also developing new themes linked to the painting of the Neue Sachlichkeit (New Objectivity; *Jazz Dancer*, 1929; oil on canvas; Rheinisches Landesmuseum).

Prechner's painting *Epoch* (1928; oil on canvas; Friedrich-Ebert-Stiftung, Bonn) was exhibited with great success at the Grosse Berliner Kunstausstellung of 1929. Conceived as a collage, it deals with world political situations, illuminated through associative elements and language contractions. In its analysis of the *Zeitgeist* several layers of meaning overlap, from discussions of daily politics and the Kellogg Pact (1928) to the replacement of religions by totalitarian political systems. After Berlin, the painting was exhibited in Brussels, Cologne, Düsseldorf, Munich, Prague, Stuttgart and Vienna. It was also published in *Querschnitt*, a leading contemporary art magazine edited by Alfred Flechtheim. With this, Prechner's popularity reached a second peak.

At the end of the 1920s Prechner began making sculpture. These were mainly small-scale plaster casts that were usually executed in stone, sometimes in bronze or wood. Thematically, they refer to her graphic work, with subjects such as *Prisoners*, *Workers* and *Mother with Two Children*. Formally, the concentrated effect of her sculptures also relates to her graphic works, for example the strength of the group surging forward in *Struggle for Existence* (1931; Friedrich-Ebert-Stiftung, Bonn) or the massive figure of the *Seated Mother and Children* (c.1937; untraced), imparting a sense of peace and safety.

Prechner and her family had to leave Germany in 1936–7 due to the increasing National Socialist threat to her as a Jew. Her watercolour *The Stricken* (1923; Museum Ludwig, Cologne) was confiscated as degenerate from the Wallraf-Richartz-Museum in 1937. The family settled in Brussels. Although she received some attention there through two articles in the magazine *Savoir et Beauté*, and her complete graphic work was purchased by the Bibliothèque royale Albert 1er in Brussels, her work was largely ignored until after her death. After the war, she spent her last years in Portici, near Naples, and in Brussels, mainly painting landscapes; this was a period of artistic isolation.

MARTINA PADBERG

Preindlsberger, Marianne *see* Stokes

Preston, Margaret
Australian painter and printmaker, 1875–1963

Born Margaret Rose McPherson (later also used spelling MacPherson) in Port Adelaide, 29 April 1875. Attended classes in W. Lister Lister's Angel Place studio, Sydney, 1888. Studied at the National Gallery School, Melbourne, under Frederick McCubbin, 1893–4, and Bernard Hall, 1896–7 (honourable mention, painting and life school, and one year studentship); Adelaide School of Design under H.P. Gill, and Hans Heysen's life drawing class, 1898. Taught at studio in Adelaide, 1899–1912, except for a trip to Europe after mother's death, 1904–6 (attended classes at the Damenakademie des Münchener Künstlerinnenvereins, Munich, studied in Paris and visited Spain). Visited Europe again, 1912–19, staying in France and Britain; studied pottery at Camberwell School of Arts and Crafts, London, and taught crafts at Seale-Hayne Neurological Military Hospital, Devon. Married company director William G. Preston in Adelaide, 1919; moved to Mosman, Sydney, 1920. Subsequently travelled widely, both in Australia and abroad, visiting the Far East, New Zealand, Pacific Islands, North and South America, Middle East and Europe. Fellow, South Australian Society of Arts, 1911; Royal Art Society, 1923. Died in Mosman, 28 May 1963.

Principal Exhibitions

Individual
Preece's Gallery, Adelaide: 1919 (with Gladys Reynell)
Grosvenor Galleries, Sydney: 1925 (with Thea Proctor), 1929
Macquarie Galleries, Sydney: 1936, 1953
Art Gallery of New South Wales, Sydney: 1942 (retrospective, with William Dobell), 1959 (retrospective)

Group
South Australian Society of Arts, Adelaide: 1895–1914, 1936, 1951, 1956
Société Nationale des Beaux-Arts, Paris: 1905–6, 1913–14
Royal Art Society of New South Wales, Sydney: 1910–22, 1951
New English Art Club, London: 1913–18
Society of Women Artists, London: 1913–18
Society of Artists of New South Wales, Sydney: 1922–60
Royal Academy, London: 1923 (*Works by Australian Artists*)
Australian Art Association, Melbourne: 1923–33
Contemporary Group, Sydney: 1924–36
Roerich Museum, New York: 1930 (*First Contemporary All Australian Art Exhibition*)
Australian Pavilion, Exposition Internationale, Paris: 1937 (silver medal)
Art Gallery of New South Wales, Sydney: 1938 (*150 Years of Australian Art*), 1946 (*Exhibition of Australian Women Artists*)
Australian Academy of the Arts: 1938–43
Yale University Art Museum, New Haven: 1941–2 (*Art of Australia, 1788–1941*, touring)
Contemporary Art Society (Australia): 1942–55
Musée d'Art Moderne, Paris: 1946 (UNESCO, *Exposition internationale d'art moderne*)

Selected Writings

Letter to Norman Carter, 18 August 1913, Norman Carter Papers, Mitchell Library, Sydney, MS 471/1

"Why I became a convert to modern art", *Home* (Sydney), iv/2, June 1923, p.20

"Away with poker-worked kookaburras and gumleaves", *Sunday Pictorial* (Sydney), 6 April 1930, p.22

"New developments in Australian art", *Australia National Journal*, ii/6, 1941, pp.12–13

"The orientation of art in the post-war Pacific", *Society of Artists Book 1942*, Sydney: Ure Smith, 1942, pp.7–9

Bibliography

"The art of Margaret Preston", *Art in Australia*, 3rd series, no.22, December 1927 (special issue; includes Preston's autobiography, "From eggs to electrolux")

Sydney Ure Smith and Leon Gellert, *Margaret Preston's Recent Works*, Sydney: Art in Australia, 1929

Basil Burdett, "Australian art today", *The Studio*, cxv, 1938, pp.3–18

Exhibition of Australian Women Artists, exh. cat., Art Gallery of New South Wales, Sydney, 1946

Sydney Ure Smith, ed., *Margaret Preston's Monotypes*, Sydney: Ure Smith, 1949

Joyce Burn Glen, "Outback yields art: Preston painting famous", *Christian Science Monitor*, January 1954, p.6

Leon Gellert, "Margaret Preston was one of the greats", *Daily Telegraph* (Sydney), 8 January 1967, p.14

Humphrey McQueen, *The Black Swan of Trespass: The Emergence of Modernist Painting in Australia to 1944*, Sydney: Alternative Publishing, 1979

The Art of Margaret Preston, exh. cat., Art Gallery of South Australia, Adelaide, and elsewhere, 1980

Janine Burke, *Australian Women Artists, 1840–1940*, Collingwood, Victoria: Greenhouse, 1980

Margaret Preston: The Art of Constant Rearrangement, exh. cat., Art Gallery of New South Wales, Sydney, 1985

Roger Butler, *The Prints of Margaret Preston: A Catalogue Raisonné*, Canberra: Australian National Gallery/Melbourne: Oxford University Press, 1987 (includes extensive bibliography and reprints of articles by Margaret Preston)

Ian North, "Aboriginal orientation", *Creating Australia: 200 Years of Art*, exh. cat., Art Gallery of South Australia, Adelaide, 1988, pp.142–3

Jeanette Hoorn, "Women make Modernism", *Strange Women: Essays in Art and Gender*, ed. Jeanette Hoorn, Melbourne: Melbourne University Press, 1994, pp.9–27

Anne Stephens, "Margaret Preston", *Heritage: The National Women's Art Book*, ed. Joan Kerr, Sydney: Dictionary of Australian Artists/Craftsman House, 1995

As a modernist innovator in Sydney, Margaret Preston enjoyed a degree of influence often denied to female contemporaries in Europe. The magazine *Art in Australia* devoted a special issue to her in 1927, two monographs were published in her lifetime (1929 and 1949) and two retrospective exhibitions were held at the Art Gallery of New South Wales, Sydney (1942 and 1959). She was the first woman to be included in the Art Gallery's collection of self-portraits commissioned from distinguished Australian artists. Her *Self-Portrait* (1930; see illustration) shows a woman with a sober, astute gaze, sporting a fashionable hairstyle and a 1920s shift dress; beside her are Australian wildflowers, her favoured subject at this time.

Characteristically, she did not disguise the narcissistic aspects of her early artistic ambitions. In her autobiography "From eggs to electrolux" she describes how she watched students painting at the Art Gallery and wanted to become

herself a focus of the visitors' gaze. Male contemporaries complained bitterly about her "vanity" and "jealousy". Some colleagues, the writer Ian Mudie and his circle, attempted to exploit her self-regard by enlisting her in various projects in order to tap into her popularity with critics and the public. An alternative reading is that Preston's confidence in her abilities disturbed male artists, who comforted themselves by invoking stereotypical female qualities of vanity and foolishness. Yet many of the conservative artists who objected to her assertiveness also owned works by her. Her acute consciousness of professionalism as a central issue, beyond gender, derived from her training with Bernard Hall at the National Gallery School in Melbourne. Other female students, including Alice Bale, shared this confidence without, however, responding to modernism.

Preston's studies in Melbourne were interrupted by her father's terminal illness. She returned to Adelaide and supported her mother for nearly two years, before re-enrolling in 1896. Perhaps this early experience of the uncertainty of Victorian middle-class life, when the breadwinner was incapacitated, impressed upon her the necessity of self-reliance. After completing art school, she tried to establish herself in Adelaide, where she was considered prickly and unconventional, and in 1911 was expelled from the Art Society of South Australia by eminent male artists. She did, however, receive important commissions, such as a portrait of the political reformer *Catherine Helen Spence*, and was employed to buy art for the Art Gallery of South Australia. The early figurative works she exhibited in Adelaide, documented in photographs, appear to be deliberately ungainly and un-dainty. Most notable were a portrait filled with the vast hips and stomach of an old man and a study of a girl in a white dress, in which the physical clumsiness of the child was emphasised rather than the romantic clichés usually associated with such images. Preston taught to raise money for study overseas, and for two extended periods she lived abroad with female companions: Bessie Davidson in 1904–6 and Gladys Reynell in 1912–19. During her studies in Munich, on her first trip to Europe, she was disconcerted to encounter contemporary art. Decades later, her writings vividly express her confusion and shock at seeing the works of Theodor Heine at the Secession of 1904.

Rumours that Preston was a lesbian were particularly persistent, but they may reflect the standard Australian response to strong, competent, independent women. She presented herself as very happily married and extremely dependent in an interview (*Sunday Herald*, Sydney, 20 September 1953). Marriage gave her the financial security to take up a central position in Sydney art circles. It freed her from the pressures of the marketplace and enabled her to travel frequently, to South and North America, Africa, Asia and Europe, creating a glamorous media persona for herself.

During World War I Preston gained attention from British critics when she exhibited, as Margaret MacPherson, with the Society of Women Artists. Her works were described as "the chief feature of the exhibition ... delicate colour and well balanced design" (Frank Rutter, *Sunday Times*, 6 February 1916, p.4). Elements later identified with her printmaking appeared in wartime still lifes such as *Flowers* (1917; National Gallery of Australia, Canberra): the rigid design with each petal a cog or ratchet in an intersecting framework; the

Preston: *Self-Portrait*, 1930; oil on canvas; 61 × 50.8 cm.; Art Gallery of New South Wales, Sydney; Gift of the artist at the request of the Trustees, 1930

cloisonnist colour shining out from black line work. Even the gleaming silver and steel industrial surfaces of her Léger-inspired still-lifes of the late 1920s are prefigured in her English flower-pieces: note the handling of the coffee pot in the right of *Still Life No.2* (1915; repr. Sotheby's Melbourne, May 1991), especially the abstraction of the reflections through grey tones.

Preston's detailed letters praise artists she admired in this period (*c.*1910–20), including Matisse, Gauguin and Stanley Spencer, but their influence is not discernible in her slightly decorative Impressionism. Pale tonality, bravura handling of white-on-white in sunlight, was her preoccupation (*Still Life with Teapot and Daisies*, *c.*1915; Art Gallery of New South Wales). This interest continued until the late 1920s, when she turned briefly to streamlining and industrialisation. She soon returned to themes from nature, specifically Australian flowers, using a more restricted palette and a looser plein-air style in certain flower-pieces of the mid-1930s. Other works, such as *West Australian Gum Blossoms* (1928; Art Gallery of New South Wales) and *Eucalyptus* (1928; Art Gallery of West Australia) were as stark as her outstanding crockery still life *Implement Blue* (1927; Art Gallery of New South Wales). In the later 1930s the influence of aboriginal rock art and bark painting brought a new sense of linear formality to her work.

A small corpus of etchings was produced around 1916. Conventional, picturesque rural scenes, they are among Preston's rare lapses in originality during her prolific career. Etching was not a congenial medium, unlike the woodblock print with which she is so associated in Australia. She claimed to have made wood engravings as early as 1904 in Munich, although no documentation has been found. Her woodcuts included landscapes, still lifes and figurative subjects, ranging from traditional floral styles, European and Australian, to Art Deco, Primitivism and Expressionism. Her skill with the woodcut is equally evident in decorative alphabets or large, flamboyant compositions such as *Wheelflowers* (1929) and *Bird of Paradise* (1925; both National Gallery of Australia and other collections). By the early 1940s muscle strain forced her to abandon woodcut and she turned to masonite cuts, mono-typing and screen printing, including designs for commercial textiles, before settling on stencil prints for the last two decades of her life.

Preston's writings are a significant oeuvre; few Australian artists mapped the intellectual framework of their art with such lucid and far-ranging texts. Consistent themes are nationalism in art and the development of an indigenous Australian style. Her writings on travel, design and fashion, witty and provocative, intensified her artistic and social influence in Sydney before World War II. She lectured frequently, and in 1938 presented an art history course at the Art Gallery of New South Wales, sponsored by the Carnegie Corporation.

In the late 1930s Preston discussed Surrealism in her lectures. She later repudiated the engaging, somewhat camp Sydney Surrealism, the "charm school", in favour of left-wing Sydney modernist factions of the 1940s. Similarly, she moved in the 1940s from the right-wing nationalism of the "Jindyworobak" intellectuals to the writings of the left-wing Australian art historian Bernard Smith, attracted by his *Place, Taste and Tradition* (1945). However, she found in Surrealism keys to an appropriate response to wartime Australia: *Japanese Submarine Exhibition* (1942; Art Gallery of New South

Wales), *Tank Traps* (1943; Mornington Peninsula Arts Centre) and the *Children's Corner at the Zoo* (*c.*1944; Art Gallery of New South Wales; all oil on canvas). The last, almost whimsical and childlike, is undercut by a consciousness of the grotesque treatment of performing animals. *Tank Traps*, inspired by the stark geometrical outlines of concrete defence works on a beach, is perhaps her closest approach to pure abstraction.

Chinese art inspired Preston's outstanding landscapes of the early 1940s, linking the viewpoint from an aeroplane with the use of a rising perspective from Chinese landscape painting. The Chinese use of schemas and representative formulae in traditional landscape painting seemed to fascinate her, as did the importance of perception rather than direct representation. Her "Chinese" landscapes still display the earths and ochres of her "Australian" palette and the "Aboriginal" rhythmic patterning within clearly articulated areas of the compositions. These landscapes were structured, while her still lifes became ragged, casual in their design, until the 1950s, when both stencil prints and oils depict diverse objects scattered across table tops: *Sea Shells and Bowl of Flowers* (1955; oil on canvas; Cruthers Collection, Perth), *Sea Flowers* (1953; stencil print; Christie's Melbourne, April 1994). The overall compositions, with their loose horizontal spread, recall her paintings from World War I; some of the objects may be identical. The randomness of these 1950s still lifes represents the purging of "period style" and a degree of "feminine" decoration from the early compositions.

Preston achieved some international exposure in the late 1930s and early 1940s. A landscape featured on the cover of *The Studio* (October 1942). In 1937 she won a silver medal at the Paris Exposition Internationale. In 1939 a series of wild-flower paintings was featured on Australia's "moderne" exhibition stand at the New York World's Fair, and the pictures remained in American public collections. A similar series was commissioned for the P&O liner *Orcades*. Arnold Haskell and Somerset Maugham were impressed by the work of the "unfamiliar" artist. She wrote on Aboriginal art for the exhibition *Art of Australia, 1788–1941*, which toured North America, and a major landscape from the exhibition was bought for the Yale University Art Gallery, New Haven. Her international status suffered subsequently, as outstanding works by her in overseas collections were de-accessioned and sent back to Australia.

Informed by early 20th-century Primitivism, Preston was largely responsible for introducing the influence of Aboriginal art to contemporary design, just as her floral woodcuts allied hard-edge 1920s modernism and Australian flora. Until the late 1920s, Australian Aboriginal art and craft tended to be regarded by whites as anthropological detritus. By the 1930s Aboriginal motifs proliferated in graphic arts, porcelain and fabric designs, in an Australian version of Art Deco, while Aboriginal residents were still denied the vote.

Preston's Aboriginal themes must be assessed in terms of this cultural morality. According to some writers, it is naive to regard white women as tactful colonisers in contrast to insensitive, rapacious male settlers. Roger Butler suggests, however, that Preston, through extensive field trips and consultation with anthropologists, approached a subtler understanding of Aboriginal social, ritual and spiritual values in art. Issues of colonisation and cultural assimilation are touched on in *Aboriginal Flowers* (1928; oil on canvas; Art Gallery of South Australia), which depicts not real flowers but anemones made from feathers by Aboriginal women. This craft, like shell work an adaptation by Aboriginal women of Victorian fancywork, offered a neat conceit for Preston, as the stylisation of the artificial flowers was akin to the ordered geometry she imposed on flowers in paintings and prints. She appreciated the creativity of Aboriginal women, and she raised their status by donating carvings by two Aboriginal women to the Art Gallery of New South Wales. Her late treatments of biblical themes, personified by Aboriginal Australians, can be seen as politically provocative in the context of the widespread racism of the 1950s.

Preston's essay "New developments in Australian art" (1941) idealises Australian Aboriginals as avant-garde-literate noble savages. A "fine simple art" was produced by the intuitive natural modernist "with his mind's eye … A camera-mind produced a camera picture, and this type of mentality has never belonged to the aboriginal". She discusses astutely the symbolic and totemic nature of representation in Aboriginal art. While decrying plagiarism, she advised white artists to emulate the aims and outlook of Aboriginal artists. Her innocent advocacy of Aboriginal art is alien to contemporary postcolonialism, but it has not diminished regard for her. A singular status was first posited for her by Humphrey MacQueen in *The Black Swan of Trespass* (1979). Three other major monographs on her art make her the best-documented Australian woman artist. Research, particularly by Roger Butler, has established a complex outline of her personality and achievements. Margaret Preston is undoubtedly the one Australian woman artist who is widely recognised by the general public.

JULIET PEERS

Prinner, Hans Anton

Hungarian sculptor and printmaker, 1902–1983

Born in Budapest, 31 December 1902. Entered School of Fine Arts, Budapest, 1920. Moved to France, 1927. Studied engraving under Stanley William Hayter at Atelier 17, Paris, 1935. Left Paris for the "Tapis vert" in Vallauris, against the advice of artist friends, 1950. Returned to Paris, 1964. Died in Paris, 1983.

Principal Exhibitions

Individual
Galerie Pierre, Paris: 1945, 1948
Galerie Katia Granoff, Paris: 1962
Galerie Yvonne Lambert, Paris: 1965
Galerie Charley Chevalier, Paris: 1971
Librarie Pluriel, Montparnasse, Paris: 1974
Librarie du Pot d'Etain, Paris: 1976
Galerie Meyer Bugel, Paris: 1985 (retrospective)

Group
Galerie Pierre Loeb, Paris: 1930
Galerie René Drouin, Paris: 1945 (*Sculpture d'aujourd'hui*)

Bibliography

Anton Prinner, 1902–1983, exh. cat., Galerie Meyer Bugel, Paris, 1985

Hans Anton Prinner trained in Budapest before moving to Paris in the late 1920s. At the height of the period of the Abstraction-Création international abstract movement in Paris, her Constructivist sculpture used strong geometric forms and, unusually, the motif of concentric circles, also echoed in her geometric painting of the period. The impact of Surrealism, however, is visible in the very fine engravings she made, first at Stanley William Hayter's celebrated Atelier 17; a sexuality and distortion reminiscent of the work of Salvador Dalí is visible in the drawing *War and Peace* (1942). In 1937 Prinner abandoned Constructivism and turned to figurative sculpture, with the ambiguously titled *Bull Woman*, of granite.

Why did Prinner disguise her true sex? Her present dealer, Marion Meyer, declared: "Because there were no great female sculptors, he repressed his femininity to become a great sculptor. He wanted to be 'he'". While Prinner appears in photographs, with the dealer Pierre Loeb, for example, in a sexless sweater, trousers and beret, and was often photographed smoking a pipe, the issue of female sexuality is a constant in her work. An undated autobiographical account, "Paris, 1927" (where finally she meets a fellow Hungarian artist, Arpad Szenes, partner of Maria Elena Vieira da Silva, is rescued from work in a doll factory and meets Picasso), has its own extraordinary tale of hesitation and disgust in front of the steps of the mandatory brothel. Most violent and disturbing are the engravings she made to illustrate her own remarkable text, "La Femme tondue", a poem of February 1946. De Gaulle had finally granted Frenchwomen the vote in 1944 in recognition of their indispensable role as workers and often as Resistance fighters during the war. The recognition at this late date of women's legitimate aspiration to the "Droits de l'homme" must be contrasted with the savage treatment of female "collaborators" during the "épuration" period. Paraded, shaved and tarred, they were denounced by women as viciously as by men – a ritualised vengeance, doubtless the most naked expression of France's profound humiliation during the war. Prinner's poem "La Femme tondue" echoed the litany of insults: " – Salope! – Putain! – Charogne! – Fumier! – Dégueulasse! – Ordure! – Regarde-la!" (– Whore! – Tart! – Carcass! – Piece of shit! – Disgusting! – Look at her!). The shaved woman of Prinner's title replies: "Remember, Humanity, that I am your work, that you have made me in your image." The poem's form, a tribunal recalling the trial of Joan of Arc, expresses a sado-masochistic rage, echoed by the artist's stylised engravings.

Prinner's female figures in plaster and wood often have smooth, hairless heads, but *Woman with Plait* of 1939, her first work in wood, depicting a woman braiding her hair, shows a particular tenderness: the move from plaster to warm-toned, beautifully caressed and polished wood was also significant. Prinner's second set of engravings, *Le Livre des morts* (1947), edited by Jean Godet and based on the ancient Egyptian Book of the Dead, demonstrates conclusively the influence of Egyptian art in her sculpture, already apparent from 1940, with the use of low relief, a strong frontality and bilateral symmetry, and spread-out, almost moonlike faces, reminiscent of depictions of Hathor, goddess of music. (One should recall that the Egyptian department in the Louvre was one of the very few not to be evacuated during the war, and an essential influence on the post-war sculpture of Prinner's contemporary, Alberto Giacometti.) The curious half-height scale of many works is also reminiscent of Egyptian sculptures, as is, of course, her nomenclature for a process of printing directly from sometimes abstract engravings made on paper, "papyrogravure" (in October 1949 her apocalypse engravings executed in the "papyrogravure" process were presented to the public in a lecture at the Librairie La Hune). Inscriptions on Prinner's sculpture and engravings give certain pieces a magical and fetishistic quality (one may compare them to the "magic" aspects of the work of Victor Brauner, her contemporary from the Romanian school of Paris, who also made small, sexually ambiguous and smooth-headed sculptures); in particular one should mention the sensual and delightful large-scale, generally female chess pieces created in an edition of eleven for Editions Marcel Zerbib, Paris, between 1946 and 1948, most of which, alas, are lost.

"I am inexistentialist!", Prinner declared, confidently asserting the necessity of philosophical contraries. Her sexual identity remained a well-kept secret, in the British periodical *Horizon*, for example, which profiled her in the mid-1940s. Her oeuvre is varied, beautiful, strange and sensually finished; her output (including pieces in bronze) was not comparable with that of Germaine Richier (q.v.), for instance, despite her rare monumental pieces three or four metres high (e.g. the wooden sculpture, *Man*). A friend of the Parisian cognoscenti of the day, Arpad Szenes, Vieira da Silva, Picasso, Pierre Loeb, André Breton, Jean Paulhan and Jacques Prévert, Prinner created for herself the typical life of a School of Paris sculptor. "Our epoch is branded by red-hot irons with the word 'success'", she declared. She was resolutely masculine until the end, and her last years were destitute. Prinner, indefatigable, fragile, determined, deserves to be rediscovered.

SARAH WILSON

Procter, Dod

British painter, 1892–1972

Born Doris Shaw in London, 1892. Moved to Newlyn, Cornwall, to study at Stanhope Forbes's School, 1907; met other artists including Laura Knight (q.v.), Harold Knight, Winifred Tennyson Jesse, Ernest Procter and Gluck (q.v.). Studied at Académie Colarossi, Paris, 1910. Exhibited at Royal Academy, London, from 1916. Married Ernest Procter, 1911; son born 1913; husband died 1935. Lived in Newlyn, but often travelled abroad: Burma, 1920–21; Tenerife, Canary Islands, 1938–9 and 1946; Basutoland, South Africa, 1948–9; Jamaica, 1953, 1956, 1958 and 1961; Tanzania, 1964; also visited Scilly Isles, 1945. Associate, 1934, and member, 1942, Royal Academy, London; member, Royal West of England Academy, Bristol, 1956. Died 31 July 1972.

Selected Individual Exhibitions

Fine Art Society, London: 1913, 1974 (retrospective, with Ernest Procter)
Leicester Galleries, London: 1913, 1925, 1927, 1929, 1935 (all with Ernest Procter); 1932, 1942, 1945 (all solo)
Manchester City Art Gallery: 1927–9 (touring, with Ernest Procter, organised by the *Daily Mail*; venues included *Aquitania* and *Berengaria*, liners on the New York crossing)
Birmingham City Art Gallery: 1928 (with Ernest Procter)
Carl Fischer Gallery, London: 1936
Adams Gallery, London: 1948

Bibliography

Frank Rutter, *Evolution in Modern Art*, New York: Dial Press, 1926; revised edition, London: Harrap, 1932
M. Chamot, "Ernest and Dod Procter", *Apollo*, vi, 1927, pp.248–52
Anthony Bertram, "Contemporary British painting: Dod Procter", *The Studio*, xcvii, 1929, pp.92–7
Laura Knight, *Oil Paint and Grease Paint: Autobiography of Laura Knight*, London: Nicholson and Watson, and New York: Macmillan, 1936
Frank Rutter, *Modern Masterpieces: An Outline of Modern Art*, London: Newnes, 1940
J. Wood Palmer, "The Procters: Ernest and Dod", *The Studio*, cxxxii, 1946, pp.43–7
Laura Knight, *The Magic of a Line: The Autobiography of Laura Knight*, London: Kimber, 1965
Dod Procter, RA, and Ernest Procter, ARA, exh. cat., Fine Art Society, London, 1974
Painting in Newlyn, 1880–1930, exh. cat., Barbican Art Gallery, London, 1985
Katy Deepwell, "Almost unknown: Royal Academy women", *Women Artists Slide Library Journal*, no.19, October–November 1987, pp.6–8
Dod Procter, RA, 1892–1972, Ernest Procter, ARA, 1886–1935, exh. cat., Walker Art Gallery, Liverpool, and elsewhere, 1990
Katy Deepwell, "Dod Procter (1892–1972)", *Women's Art Magazine*, no.34, May–June 1990, pp.19–20
Paddy Kitchen, "Free expressions", *Country Life*, clxxxiv, 19 July 1990, pp.124–5

Dod Procter has the distinction of being the second woman to be elected Royal Academician (the third Associate member) since the 18th century. Her life was not full of dramatic incident but was marked by consistent output and a regular pattern of exhibition from 1916 to 1969. Like Laura Knight (q.v.), her fellow Academician, she was part of a distinctive group of painters who had lived and worked in Newlyn, Cornwall, in the 1910s, most of whom gained honours within the Royal Academy in the 1920s and 1930s, for example, Ernest Procter, Harold Knight and Alfred J. Munnings. Unlike Laura Knight, Dod Procter was not elected to the Council, nor did she seek to gain any special privileges within the Royal Academy (for example, attendance at the Academicians' Banquet, which remained barred to women until 1968), other than sending in her paintings on a regular basis. On her election to Associate membership in 1934, the *Sunday Times* (April 1934) declared that she was "one of the few modern artists whose reputation has been made on the walls of the Royal Academy". Although this exaggerates the case, because she had many solo exhibitions at the Leicester Galleries, Procter was widely celebrated for producing a synthesis of what had been perceived as two irreconcilable opposites: the academic and the modern. To academics, she reinvigorated the tradition of academic painting with a renewed attention to the

Procter: *Morning*, 1926; Tate Gallery, London

principles of modern painting, highlighting formal design and close tonal harmonies in her compositions. To modernists, she was an artist who had learned the lessons of Cubism because she simplified forms, used precise colour arrangements and her approach to her chosen subjects emphasised psychology rather than narrative.

Procter's first exhibited works were flower studies (exh. RA 1916–17). From the 1920s onwards, her works appear divided evenly between portraits of young women and children (e.g. *Girl in Blue*,1925; Laing Art Gallery, Newcastle upon Tyne; *Girl in White*, 1923; City Museum and Art Gallery, Stoke-on-Trent; *Pearl Necklace*, 1932–41; Royal Academy, London), flower paintings and still lifes (e.g. *Anemones*, 1936–7; Williamson Art Gallery and Museum, Birkenhead; *Flowers on a Chair*, c.1950; Royal West of England Academy, Bristol), and landscapes and views from or of domestic settings (e.g. *Early Morning, Newlyn*, c.1925–6; Glynn Vivian Art Gallery, Swansea; *Kitchen at Myrtle Cottage*, 1935; *The Orchard*, 1934; both Chantrey Bequest purchases, Tate Gallery, London). It was, however, her figure studies made during the 1920s that attracted considerable critical attention, for instance, *Model Resting* (1924; Pyms Gallery, London), *Clara* (1927; City Museum and Art Gallery, Stoke-on-Trent) and *The Bather* (c.1929–30; Oldham Art Gallery).

Debate about the academic and/or modern qualities of Dod's work is centred on the critical reception of two works, *The Model* (private collection, repr. Liverpool 1990), first shown in 1925 at the Royal Academy, and *Morning* (1926; see illustration), which created a huge media sensation when first exhibited in 1927 at the Royal Academy and was purchased for the nation by the *Daily Mail*. *Morning* represents a scene in the stark bedroom of a typical young working woman (the model was Cissie Barnes), modestly dressed and half-asleep as daylight breaks, lighting her room with a cool blue light. The

painting, read as a psychological portrait of exhaustion after an honest day's toil combined with optimism for the new day, was sensationally treated by the newspapers as a portrait of modern life. Anthony Bertram felt that both works were "the finest work that has yet been done by a woman painter" because "although Mrs Procter represents accurately, conforming to the foot-rule in which the academic mind takes so great a delight, she is essentially a modern painter" (Bertram 1929, p.92). Frank Rutter declared: "she has created a new vision of the human figure which amounts to the invention of a twentieth century style in portraiture" by virtue of "an extraordinary powerful and personal sense of form" (Rutter 1940, p.275). In *Evolution in Modern Art* (1926) Rutter linked these works to those of William Roberts and Wadsworth, noting their common descent in formal terms from Cézanne and Picasso. *Morning* was sent on a much advertised national tour of 22 British cities (1927–9) and two ocean liners on the New York crossing, alongside other paintings and drawings by both Ernest and Dod Procter.

Although she exhibited jointly with her husband until his death in 1935, Procter's works are radically different from his. While Dod concentrated on figure drawing, Ernest developed large decorative compositions, classical academic allegories and, later, paintings of religious subjects. In 1920 both the Procters were commissioned to decorate Kokine Palace in Rangoon, Burma, for the Chinese millionaire, Ching Tsong, their only collaborative venture. From this trip, Dod developed an interest in painting native children (e.g. *Burmese Children by the Irrawaddy*, c.1920; Atkinson Art Gallery, Southport), and after 1938 she began to travel abroad on a regular basis, painting both landscapes and children, particularly in Africa (Masai children in *African Head*, Plymouth Museum and Art Gallery) and Jamaica (*Jamaican Girl in Red*, c.1956–7; private collection, repr. Liverpool 1990). After 1934 her painting style changed, showing a move away from the tightly orchestrated tonal compositions that had won her great critical recognition into a looser, more painterly, Post-Impressionist style, although she continued to produce portraits of women and girls (e.g. *Aunt Lilla*, 1943; Newlyn Orion, Penzance; *Shelagh among the Ferns*, 1935; private collection, *ibid.*).

KATY DEEPWELL

Properzia de' Rossi *see* Rossi

Purser, Sarah
Irish painter, 1848–1943

Born in Dún Laoghaire, Co. Dublin, 22 March 1848; grew up in Dungarvan, Co. Waterford. Educated at a private finishing school in Montmirail, Switzerland, 1861–3. Studied at Dublin School of Art, 1872–8; Académie Julian, Paris, 1878–9; further frequent visits to France, 1880–1938. Studio in Dublin from 1881. Visited Balkans and Near East, 1902; Prague, Vienna, Berlin and Munich, 1913; Italy, 1930. Invited to open exhibition of Neo-Impressionist painting, Galerie Bernheim Jeune, Paris, 1909. Founder, An Túr Gloine (Tower of Glass), Dublin, 1903; Friends of the National Collections of Ireland, 1924; Purser-Griffith scholarship in history of art at Trinity College and University College, Dublin, 1933. Founder member, Dublin Art Club, 1886; only woman member of organising committee, Art Loan Exhibition, Dublin, 1899. Member, Mansion House committee for Provision of a Municipal Gallery, Dublin, 1912; Board of Governors and Guardians, National Gallery of Ireland, Dublin, 1914–43. Honorary member, 1890, first woman Associate member, 1923, and first woman member, 1924, Royal Hibernian Academy. Died in Dublin, 7 August 1943.

Principal Exhibitions
Royal Hibernian Academy, Dublin: 1872, 1878–99, 1901, 1903–16, 1918, 1921, 1923, 1925–8
Liverpool Autumn Exhibition: 1883
Royal Academy, London: 1885–6
Dublin Art Club: 1886–9, 1891–5
Grosvenor Gallery, London: 1886
New Gallery, London: 1892, 1896, 1899
Guildhall, London: 1904 (*Works by Irish Painters*)
Franco-British Exhibition, London: 1908
Whitechapel Art Gallery, London: 1913 (*Irish Art*)
Galerie Barbazanges, Paris: 1922 (*L'Art irlandais*)
Engineers Hall, Dublin: 1923 (retrospective)
Palais des Beaux-Arts, Brussels: 1930 (*L'Art irlandais*)

Selected Writings
"French and English pictures in Dublin", *Art Journal*, 1899, pp.155–6
"At the loan collection", *Daily Express* (Dublin), 25 April 1899 (fictive dialogue)
"In a Dublin parlour", *The Leader* (Dublin), 17 and 24 November and 8 December 1900 (dialogues)

Foreword, *Catalogue: A Loan Collection of Pictures*, exh. cat., Dublin, 1901
"Art and Ireland", *Freeman's Journal* (Dublin), 11 August 1906
"Municipal Gallery of Modern Art", *Irish Times*, 15 January 1908
"The Lane pictures and the new gallery", *Irish Times*, 6 July 1928

Bibliography
Le Journal de Marie Bashkirtseff, ed. A. Theuriet, 2 vols, Paris, 1887; as *The Journal of Marie Bashkirtseff*, London: Cassell, 1890; ed. Rozsika Parker and Griselda Pollock, London: Virago, 1985
L.M. Little, "A new art in Ireland", *Irish Packet*, i/22, 1904
Stephen Gwynn, *Experiences of a Literary Man*, London: Butterworth, 1926
An Túr Gloine: Twenty-Fifth Anniversary Celebration, Dublin, 1929
Beatrice (Lady) Glenavy, *"Today We Will Only Gossip"*, London: Constable, 1964
Elizabeth Coxhead, *Daughters of Erin: Five Women of the Irish Renaissance*, London: Secker and Warburg, 1965
John O'Grady, "Sarah H. Purser", *Capuchin Annual*, 1977, pp.89–104
Anne Crookshank and the Knight of Glin, *The Painters of Ireland, c.1660–1920*, London: Barrie and Jenkins, 1978
Irish Women Artists from the Eighteenth Century to the Present Day, exh. cat., National Gallery of Ireland, Dublin, and elsewhere, 1987
Nicola Gordon Bowe, David Caron and Michael Wynne, *Gazetteer of Irish Stained Glass*, Dublin: Irish Academic Press, 1988
Sarah Purser, RHA: Drawings and Watercolours, exh. cat., Gorry Gallery, Dublin, 1993
John O'Grady, *The Life and Work of Sarah Purser*, Dublin: Four Courts Press, 1996

Purser Papers are in the Manuscripts Department, National Library of Ireland, Dublin.

When Sarah Purser began exhibiting in 1872, art training in Ireland was problematic; the Royal Hibernian Academy Schools excluded women students, and the formerly vibrant Royal Dublin Society School languished under an arid syllabus dictated from Kensington in London. Paris beckoned, and in 1878 Purser arrived to study at the Académie Julian. From there she sent *A Fellow Citizen* (untraced) to the Royal Hibernian Academy in 1879, catching the attention of reviewers who thought it novel in style and content. They describe a plein-air picture with an urchin theme, a pictorial formula popularised at recent Salons by Jules Bastien-Lepage. Modern, but not riskily avant-garde, this mode enthralled Purser's fellow-students and friends Louise Breslau (q.v.) and Marie Bashkirtseff (q.v.), whose *Journal* mentions the Irish "peintre et philosophe". Purser absorbed contemporary French art, particularly admiring Puvis de Chavannes and Degas, and adopting a bold *au premier coup* technique. The atmosphere of her circle suffuses *Le Petit Déjeuner* (1880–81; see illustration), a moody little picture for which a Parisian friend posed.

Settled again in Dublin, Purser kept up to date by visiting the Salon annually, viewing London exhibitions en route. Through the early 1880s she painted each summer on the coast of Co. Cork, her plein-air peasant subjects finding favour with Irish exhibiting bodies, gaining good reviews and selling well. *Fishwives Gossiping* (1881; private collection, repr. O'Grady 1996) is sunny, ably composed and briskly handled; the larger *Raking in Seaweed on the South Coast* (1883; City Art Gallery, Limerick) depicts foul-weather toil. Reviewers enthused about the vigour and modernity of Purser's genre work, noting

Purser: *Le Petit Déjeuner*, 1880–81; oil on canvas; 35 × 27 cm.; National Gallery of Ireland, Dublin

stylistic links to French paintings at the Royal Hibernian Academy. The *Gardener's Daughter* (1886; Georgetown University, Washington, DC) emphasises the connection; the near-life-size "little French girl" with "merry brown eyes" in sabots and "white linen cap and blue blouse" delighted reviewers, who declared the "artistic treatment of the cabbage garden … a revelation … a wealth of colour and tone".

Purser's ability to catch likeness impressed commentators from 1881, and in 1883 one critic pronounced her life-size, three-quarter-length *Samuel Haughton* (Trinity College Dublin) "by common consent the portrait of the year" at the Royal Hibernian Academy. Purser began accepting portrait work throughout Ireland and Britain. Her life-size, full-length double portrait of the younger children of Sir Robert Sheffield Bt of London (private collection, *ibid*.), shown at the Royal Academy in 1885, has a splendid panache. Purser's London exhibits in 1886 were a Scots viscountess at the Royal Academy, and an Anglo-American author at the Grosvenor Gallery (both untraced).

By then her professional repute, keen mind and sense of Irishness had made her a personality in Dublin cultural and nationalistic circles. "Her studio at Harcourt Terrace was a place where a young man thought it a great privilege to have his wits sharpened" (Gwynn 1926). When the Viceroy of Ireland commissioned her to portray his children in 1888, his choice reflected her position as the country's foremost portraitist. Her success finally shamed the Royal Hibernian Academy – which did not admit women to its professional ranks – into granting her Honorary membership, with what she called the "slender privileges" of HRHA status.

Purser had continued to paint genre: *The Coopers' Shop at James's Gate Brewery* (1889; Guinness Museum, Dublin) is a busy industrial scene, boldly designed. She commented on deprivation: *Penny Dinners in Kevin Street – The Boys' Table* (untraced, repr. O'Grady 1996) was hailed at the Royal Hibernian Academy of 1891 as social truth, though the drear charity kitchen is enlivened by a wittily observed confrontation between two urchins. Two pictures of 1894 treat maternity in poverty: *Mother and Child with a Young Woman* (Hugh Lane Municipal Gallery of Modern Art, Dublin) and *An Irish Idyll* (Ulster Museum, Belfast) appeared respectively at the Dublin Art Club and Royal Hibernian Academy exhibitions. The last title derives from Jane Barlow's popular book *Irish Idylls*. At Purser's suggestion, Barlow and she collaborated from 1897 on illustrated tales of peasant life, four being published in Christmas issues of the national co-operative movement's *Irish Homestead*. This journal also reproduced three Purser subject pictures and her sensitive *Jane Barlow* (1894; Hugh Lane Municipal Gallery of Modern Art). Meanwhile Purser created superb pastels of *W.B. Yeats* and *Maud Gonne* (both 1898; Hugh Lane Municipal Gallery of Modern Art).

Purser's knowledge of modern art and acquaintance with such masters as Jean Louis Forain and Degas gained her a seat on the Executive of the 1899 Dublin exhibition of recent French and British paintings, and involved her particularly with lenders of works by Manet, Monet and Degas. The show occasioned her first published writings: a critique in the London *Art Journal*, and a newspaper piece in the form of a dialogue among fictive visitors at the show, a device allowing Purser to air her advanced views on art. She used the same format a year later in polemical articles about unjust neglect of living Irish artists, not least by the churches, which spent large sums importing costly but inferior art and craftwork. She redressed one injustice single-handedly, organising their first exhibition for Nathaniel Hone and John Butler Yeats RHA in 1901. That year she painted *Circus Encampment* (private collection, repr. O'Grady 1996), a gem-like evocation of summer joys.

When Purser founded An Túr Gloine (Tower of Glass) to further the ideal of national self-sufficiency in stained glass, she had perforce to employ an expert from abroad to initiate the Irish artist-craftworkers. Yet the studio's first window, *Naomh Andris* (Gaelic: St Andrew; 1903; Laban church, Co. Galway), reflects Purser's own figural and narrative style, which dominates her little window *Breandán Naomhtha ar an muir* (Gaelic: Holy Brendan on the sea; 1903; Cathedral of St Brendan, Loughrea, Co. Galway). Purser stopped designing glass as she increasingly undertook public commitments in art affairs. But she continued painting, and began receiving invitations to contribute to representative shows of Irish art abroad. She still kept up to date; the invitation in 1909 to open a Neo-Impressionist exhibition in Paris was acknowledgement of her modernity.

Her palette brightened through the second decade of the 20th century. This trend marks her first portrait of *Roger Casement* (1914; National Gallery of Ireland) but has freer expression in such landscapes as *Kerry Blue* (1920; private collection, *ibid*.). Then in 1923 she arranged her only solo show, with pictures spanning a half century. Paintings that had made her reputation in the 1880s hung with profound new works such as the *Sad Girl* (National Gallery of Ireland), luscious *Dahlias* (private collection, *ibid*.) and the sparkling *Little Regatta – Howth* (untraced, *ibid*.). The exhibition was an unqualified critical success. Purser continued producing, and the life-size, half-length *Kathleen* (1935; private collection, *ibid*.), her last dated painting, is a characteristically strong genre piece of undiminished verve.

JOHN N. O'GRADY

Q–R

Quick-to-See Smith, Jaune *see* Smith

Rae, Henrietta
British painter, 1859–1928

Born in Hammersmith, London, 30 December 1859; father a civil servant, mother a gifted amateur musician. Studied at Queen's Square (later Female) School of Art, London, 1871–3; studied independently in British Museum and attended evening classes at Heatherly's School of Art, 1874–7; attended Royal Academy Schools, 1877–84. Exhibited widely in London and the provinces, 1879–1922. Married the artist Ernest Normand, 1884; son born 1886, daughter born 1893; husband died 1923. Lived in Kensington, London; studio in Norwood from 1893. Studied in Paris at Académie Julian under Benjamin-Constant and Jules Lefèbvre, and in Grez-par-Nemours, 1890. Visited Italy, 1896. Supported the campaign for women's suffrage. First woman to serve as member of hanging committee, Liverpool Autumn Exhibition, 1893; president, Women's Art Section, *Victorian Exhibition*, 1897. Member, Society of Women Artists, 1905. Died 26 March 1928.

Principal Exhibitions
Society of British Artists, London: 1879–82
Royal Academy, London: 1880–1919
Grosvenor Gallery, London: 1885, 1888–9
Exposition Universelle, Paris: 1889 (honourable mention)
Institute of Painters in Oil, London: 1891–5
World's Columbian Exposition, Chicago: 1893 (medal)
Doré Gallery, London: 1895 (with Ernest Normand)
Earl's Court, London: 1897 (*Victorian Exhibition*)
Louisiana Purchase Exposition, St Louis: 1904

Bibliography
Frank Rinder, "Henrietta Rae – Mrs Ernest Normand", *Art Journal*, 1901, pp.303–7
Arthur Fish, *Henrietta Rae (Mrs Ernest Normand)*, London: Cassell, 1905
Great Victorian Pictures: Their Paths to Fame, exh. cat., Arts Council of Great Britain, London, 1978
Deborah Cherry, *Painting Women: Victorian Women Artists*, London and New York: Routledge, 1993

Pamela Gerrish Nunn, *Problem Pictures: Women and Men in Victorian Painting*, Aldershot: Scolar Press, 1995

Henrietta Rae (later Mrs Normand) was one of the foremost female artists of late Victorian and Edwardian Britain. She was the most prominent woman artist in the classical revival that dominated British art in the last two decades of the 19th century, and the most important female painter of the nude in the pre-modern period. Rae's oeuvre exemplifies the opportunity and the ambition characteristic of the second generation of Victorian women artists, who, after 1860, enjoyed access to the Royal Academy Schools and acceptance as a fact of British cultural life, albeit a still controversial one.

Rae was intended by her mother for a musical career, and thus was a late starter in painting. Her career was marked from the beginning by determination: she was the first female student to be accepted at Heatherly's, the foremost preparatory school for the Royal Academy Schools, and she was accepted into the Schools on her sixth attempt. From her earliest exhibited works, shown while she was still attending the Schools, she painted on a large scale, taking the full-length female figure as her primary motif and the highest genres as her arena: literature, mythology, history. Her subjects ranged from Tennyson, Shakespeare (*Ophelia*, 1890; see illustration) and Keats through Greek mythology (*Eurydice Sinking back to Hades*, 1887; untraced, repr. Fish 1905) to imaginative, pseudo-literary or pseudo-classical figures (*Spring Blossoms*, 1893; David Messum Gallery, London). She was greatly influenced in her participation in the classical revival by the most successful of her male contemporaries and President of the Royal Academy, Frederic Leighton, and her work was often said to be a weak imitation of his. Although her principal works often used the female nude, as did Leighton's, her typical work compares more nearly with less distinguished men of her time, such as Arthur Hacker.

A study trip to France with her husband in 1890, spent at the Académie Julian and other Paris studios and in the rural colony of Grez-par-Nemours, resulted in a new painterliness that moderated the previous academicism of Rae's work, attracting criticism from conservatives for slovenliness. While she continued to mine evergreen literary sources for heroines such as *Ophelia*, *Mariana* (1892; untraced) and *Isabella* (1896; untraced, *ibid.*), the themes and motifs that Rae took from classicism's repertoire were given poetical and rhetorical rather

Rae: *Ophelia*, 1890; Walker Art Gallery, Liverpool

than dramatic treatment, and her occasional attempts to incorporate action, as in *Apollo and Daphne* (1895; untraced, repr. *Royal Academy Pictures*), were not critically successful. Her depiction of men was also particularly rebuffed. Her most ambitious mythological composition, the huge *Psyche Before the Throne of Venus* (1894; untraced, repr. London 1978), represented a passage in William Morris's version of the nymph's story that necessitated more than a dozen full-length figures. Although dismissed by critics as pretty and therefore effete, it entered one of the most important collections of contemporary art (McCulloch). Despite critical carping, Rae consistently sold her paintings – *Ophelia* was purchased by the Liverpool Corporation in 1890. Although many works have now disappeared from view, inhibiting an appraisal of her technical excellence, many are known in engraved or photographic form through Fish's biography published with the artist's co-operation in 1905.

As the first female artist to represent the naked body regularly, Rae – known generally by her maiden name throughout her career – was often cited in the controversy about the nude in art that raged in Britain from 1885 to the end of the 19th century. Much of her use of the female nude looks naive to a 20th-century feminist eye in its acceptance of the erotic strategies of the work of her male contemporaries. Some of her images have a conspicuously lubricious character (*Loot*, 1903–4; untraced, repr. Fish 1905) and in this respect are indistinguishable from the more offensive nudes of her mentors.

Rae's only piece of public art, the fresco in the Richard Whittington cycle at the Royal Exchange, London, which she completed in 1900, was untypical of her oeuvre and, after the turn of the century, portraits of aristocrats and public servants leavened her output of subject pictures. She continued to exhibit at the Royal Academy and in provincial cities until 1922.

PAMELA GERRISH NUNN

Rahon, Alice
French painter and poet, 1904–1987

Born Alice Marie Yvonne Philippot in Chenecey-Buillon, Doubs, 8 June 1904; grew up in Paris. Married Austrian painter Wolfgang Paalen, 1934. Joined André Breton's Surrealist group with Paalen. Wrote poetry under the name of Alice Paalen. Sailed to India with Valentine Penrose after affair with Picasso, 1936. Emigrated to Mexico, travelling via west coast of Canada and USA and studying Native American art, 1939. Participated in international Surrealist exhibition, Mexico City, 1940; subsequently became full-time painter, writing only intermittently after 1941. Contributed to Paalen's journal *Dyn*, 1942–5. Amicable divorce from Paalen, late 1940s; adopted mother's maiden name of Rahon. Married American decorator Edward FitzGerald. Led increasingly retired life in San Angel, a suburb of Mexico City, after Paalen's suicide (1959) and divorce from FitzGerald (c.1960). Ceased painting in mid-1970s. Died in Mexico, 1987.

Selected Individual Exhibitions
Galería de Arte Mexicano, Mexico City: 1944, 1945, 1946, 1951
Stendhal Art Gallery, Los Angeles: 1945
Art of This Century, New York: 1945
Caresse Crosby Gallery, Washington, DC: 1945
Art Institute, San Francisco: 1945, 1953
Willard Gallery, New York: 1948, 1951, 1955
Galerie de la Cour d'Ingres, Paris: 1955
Galería El Eco, Mexico City: 1956, 1965
Galería Antonio Souza, Mexico City: 1957, 1959, 1960, 1962, 1963, 1964
Galería IFAL, Mexico City: 1958, 1965
Worth Avenue Gallery, Palm Beach: 1961
Louisiana Gallery, Houston: 1962
Galería Juliana Larsson, Beirut: 1962
Galería Misrachi, Mexico City: 1967
Palacio de Bellas Artes, Mexico City: 1986 (retrospective)

Selected Writings
(as Alice Paalen)
A même la terre, Paris: Editions Surréalistes, 1936 (poems)
Sablier couché, Paris: Sagesse, 1938 (poems)
Noir Animal, Mexico City: Larue, 1941
Text in *Pleine marge*, no.4, December 1986, pp.19–28

Bibliography
Jacqueline Johnson, "Exposition Alice Paalen", *Dyn*, no.7, 1945, p.23
Alice Rahon, exh. cat., Galerie de la Cour d'Ingres, Paris, 1955
Anaïs Nin, *Diary*, iv, 1944–1947, New York: Harcourt Brace, 1971; as *Journal*, iv, London: Owen, 1972
Whitney Chadwick, *Women Artists and the Surrealist Movement*, Boston: Little Brown, and London: Thames and Hudson, 1985
Alice Rahon: Exposición antológica, exh. cat., Palacio de Bellas Artes, Mexico City, 1986
La Femme et le surréalisme, exh. cat., Musée Cantonal des Beaux-Arts, Lausanne, 1987
La mujer en Mexico/Women in Mexico, exh. cat., National Academy of Design, New York, and elsewhere, 1990
Nancy Deffebach, "Alice Rahon: Poems of light and shadow: Painting in free verse", *OnTheBus*, nos.8–9, 1991, pp.171–96 (expanded version of "Alice Rahon: Paintings in free verse", *Latin American Art*, ii, Summer 1990, pp.43–7)
Renée Riese Hubert, *Magnifying Mirrors: Women, Surrealism and Partnership*, Lincoln: University of Nebraska Press, 1994
Georgiana M.M. Colvile, "Through an hour-glass lightly: Valentine Penrose and Alice Rahon-Paalen", *Reconceptions: Reading Modern French Poetry*, ed. Russell King and Bernard McGuirk, Nottingham Monographs in the Humanities, 1996, pp.81–112

For the catalogue of her exhibition at the Willard Gallery in New York in 1951, Alice Rahon wrote a poetic text defining her aspirations towards a magical, ethereal world only to be reached through painting:

> In earliest times painting was magical; it was a key to the invisible. In those days the value of a work lay in its power of conjuration, a power that talent alone could not achieve. Like the shaman, the sibyl and the wizard, the painter had to make himself humble, so that he could share in the manifestation of spirits and forms … Perhaps we have seen the Emerald City in some faraway dream that belongs to the common emotional fund of man. Entering by the gate of the Seven Colors, we travel along the Rainbow.

As a child, Rahon spent holidays in Brittany and liked to tell people that she was a native of that region; Celtic landscapes and folk tales inspired her painting, as they did that of the half-Irish Leonora Carrington (q.v.). Other crucial influences were a visit to the prehistoric caves of Altamira in Spain with Wolfgang Paalen in 1933, and their journey through the Pacific Northwest in 1939, when they discovered Native American art, masks and totem poles, as well as a close association with André Breton's Surrealist group in the mid-1930s and finally the revelation of India with Valentine Penrose in 1936. Thus, when the poet Alice Paalen later settled in Mexico for the rest of her life, decided to become a painter and to adopt her mother's maiden name of Rahon, her canvases reflected a blend of prehistoric cave-painting and petroglyphs, primitive art, exotic memories of the Orient, supernatural Celtic lore and the Surrealist quest for oneiric, magical, mad, invisible states. The title of her second poetry collection, *Sablier couché* (1938), predicts her passage from one art to another, much like Breton's "communicating vessels" of dream and reality. In her article on Rahon (1991) Nancy Deffebach pointed out the close correspondences between the early poetry and the painting that followed. The poems are full of colours and other visual elements. The first collection, *A même la terre* (1936), opens with what appears to be an ironic self-portrait: "A woman who was beautiful/one day/took off her face/her head became smooth/blind and deaf/sheltered from mirror's traps/and love's glances …" (translated by Vanina Deler and Nancy Deffebach). These lines are especially representative of the work of several women Surrealists (Claude Cahun, Kay Sage, Toyen, Frida Kahlo, Bona, all q.v., and Marianne van Hirtum) who frequently produced pictorial and literary (self-)portraits of faceless women as reflecting their search for an identity.

At the same time, as Deffebach also indicated, Rahon never turned away from Surrealism the way most of the other women artists did, and seemed to accept the "femme-enfant" or child-woman image so frequently projected on to their partners by the mainstream, male Surrealists. In fact, Rahon's only *Self-Portrait* (1951; see illustration) depicts her as the namesake she liked to cultivate – Lewis Carroll's Alice: she has a schematic clown's face depicted against a double background,

Rahon: *Self-Portrait*, 1951

first a geometric Wonderland in bright hues, including the White Rabbit, a green town and various card or chess symbols, behind which a dark-blue nocturnal sky in Surrealist fashion simultaneously features sun and moon, the latter both full and a thin crescent.

Rahon's paintings often seem to point to rites of passage. One of the first, the *Smile of Death*, a gouache produced in 1939 (private collection, Mexico, repr. Deffebach 1991), figures in *Dyn* (no.1, April–May 1942) with a three-line poem, listed in the contents as "Tableau-poème" and reversely entitled "Poème-tableau". The poem's title, "Le sourire de la mort", becomes clearer through the picture, in which the grinning face of Death with black features against a red and orange background can also be read as little men getting in and out of a boat, etched in petroglyph style. This oxymoronic piece captures the macabre humour of Mexico, combining it with Breton's notion of black humour.

Max Ernst's picture *Alice's Friends* (1957; Fondation des Treilles Tourtour) appears to be a tribute to Rahon as well as to Carroll's heroine – it is even executed in Rahon's style, representing a proliferation of animals, as though in a Mexican jungle, against a blurred blue background: mostly birds, including a toucan, with a large cat in the centre. All her life Rahon loved, protected and painted animals. Her home in San Angel was full of stray cats and she was able to produce enough cat pictures for a full show in 1957. Her magical, multi-coloured canvas with a typical luminous blue background, *Toucan and the Rainbow* (1967; private collection, Mexico, repr. Deffebach 1991), was a tribute to her late friend and former husband Wolfgang Paalen. The same year she painted *Man Crossed by a River* (ibid.) as a tribute to André Breton, probably referring to the bridge into Transylvania, where the vampires came to meet Murnau's hero in the film *Nosferatu the Vampire* (1921), evoked by Breton in *Les Vases communicants* (1932) and transposed by Rahon in *Noir Animal*: "Sometimes I built bridges to the other side/ but my phantom life/ I have left at the gates of childhood" (my translation). The *Ballad of Frida Kahlo* (1956–66; private collection, Mexico, repr. Deffebach 1991), one of Rahon's best works, combines a series of miniature schematised vignettes related to Kahlo's life and work, against a glowing background of the same blue as Frida's Coyoacan house, where she was born and died.

In her semi-abstract landscapes and indeed in most of her pictures, Rahon used some of the Surrealist "automatic" techniques, such as Ernst's *frottage* and Paalen's *fumage*; she also tended to privilege the oneiric colours blue and green, blue being connected with imagination and the other side of the mirror, green representing the plant world, regeneration, life's awakening, strength and hope, as well as the secret fire and the unifying principle of nature for the Alchemists (see Jean Chevalier and Alain Gheerbrandt, *Dictionnaire des symboles*, Paris: Laffont, 1982). *Out of Africa* (1945; oil on canvas; private collection, repr. New York 1990) suggests a boat in the foreground and a distant city against a dark-green nocturnal background scattered with tiny black Klee-like figures and forms. Basically non-figurative, *Fortunate Islands* (1959; oil on canvas; private collection, ibid.) splurges blue and green with a few yellowish brown patches – probably islands in a tropical sea – with subtle reflections rippling across the blue expanse.

Rahon also absorbed the culture of her adopted country, Mexico. She wrote a poem to the mountain Ixtaccihuatl and many of her plastic works refer to Mexican landscapes or legends, as in the humorous oil *The God Ebecatl Meeting a Woman* (1955; private collection, ibid.): the blurred, semi-geometric figures in brown, red and yellow, joined by stick-like arms, stand out against a bright aquamarine sea, with a boat on the horizon. The dots and stripes vaguely constituting the characters come close to Joan Miró's technique, which, like Paul Klee's style, often influenced Rahon. She also created various Surrealist objects, generally inspired by Native American artefacts.

Rahon's last painting, aptly named *A Giant Called Solitude* (1975; oil and sand on canvas; private collection, Mexico City), an ominous blue female figure towering over a town, echoes the loneliness, isolation and depression of the final years, when nearly all her friends had died. Except for the ultimate retrospective, her numerous exhibitions came to an abrupt end in 1967. Alice Rahon is still remembered and respected as an important Surrealist painter in Mexico, but she seems to have been forgotten in Europe, even in France, where Breton once helped her publish her first poems. In her diary, Anaïs Nin conveys the specular and spectacular osmosis between the younger Rahon's radiant, vital beauty and the enchanting quality of her work: "Her smile and her expression are dazzling, dazzling with spirit, wit, life … Her paintings are completely drawn from subterranean worlds, while her descriptions of Mexico are violent with color, drama and joy" (Nin 1971, p.58).

GEORGIANA M.M. COLVILE

Rainer, Yvonne
American choreographer and film-maker, 1934–

Born in San Francisco, California, 1934. Moved to New York, 1956; trained as a modern dancer from 1957; studied under Martha Graham and Merce Cunningham, 1960–67. Began to choreograph her own work, 1960. Founder-member, Judson Dance Theater, New York, 1962. Presented choreography throughout the USA and Europe, 1962–75, notably on Broadway, 1969, in Scandinavia, London, Germany and Italy, 1964–72, and at the Festival d'Automne, Paris, 1972. Began to integrate short films into her performances, 1968; made complete transition to film-making by 1975. Recipient of Guggenheim fellowships, 1969 and 1988; National Endowment for the Arts (NEA) grants, 1972, 1974, 1983, 1985, 1988, 1990 and 1995; Creative Artist Public Service (CAPS) grants, 1973 and 1975; Deutscher Akademischer Austauschdienst (DAAD) grant, 1976; Rockefeller Foundation grant, 1988 and 1990; Special Achievement award, Los Angeles Film Critics Association, for *Journeys from Berlin/1971* (1980, co-produced with the British Film Institute); James D. Phelan award in Filmmaking, 1990; Geyer Werke prize at the International Documentary Film Festival, Munich, for *Privilege* (1990), 1991; honorary doctorates from Massachusetts College of Art, Boston, 1988; Rhode Island School of Design, Providence, 1988; School of the Art Institute of Chicago, 1993; California Institute of the Arts, Valencia, 1993. Member, American Film Institute, 1995. Lives in New York.

Selected Writings

"Don't give the game away", *Arts*, xli, April 1967, pp.44–5
Yvonne Rainer: Work, 1961–1973, Halifax: Press of Nova Scotia College of Art and Design, and New York: New York University Press, 1974
"More kicking and screaming from the narrative front/backwater", *Wide-Angle*, vii/1–2, 1985, pp.8–12
The Films of Yvonne Rainer, Bloomington: Indiana University Press, 1989
"Narrative in the (dis)service of identity: Fragments toward a performed lecture dealing with menopause, race, gender and other uneasy bedfellows in the cinematic sheets: Or, how do you begin to think of yourself as a lesbian-and-white when you had just about gotten used to the idea of being an 'A-woman'", *Review of Japanese Culture and Society*, iv, December 1991, pp.46–52

Bibliography

Willoughby Sharp and Liza Bear, "The performer as a persona: An interview with Yvonne Rainer", *Avalanche*, no.5, Summer 1972, pp.46–59
Stephen Koch, "Performance: A conversation", *Artforum*, xi, December 1972, pp.53–8
Annette Michelson, "Yvonne Rainer", *Artforum*, xii, January 1974, pp.57–63; February 1974, pp.30–35
Lucy R. Lippard, "Yvonne Rainer on feminism and her film", *Feminist Art Journal*, iv, Summer 1975, pp.5–11; reprinted in Lucy R. Lippard, *From the Center*, New York: Dutton, 1976
—, "Talking pictures, silent words: Yvonne Rainer's recent movies", *Art in America*, lxv, May–June 1977, pp.86–90
Sally Banes, *Terpsichore in Sneakers: Post-Modern Dance*, Boston: Houghton Mifflin, 1980
Profile, iv/5, Fall 1984 (entire issue)
Robert Storr, "The theoretical come-on", *Art in America*, lxxiv, April 1986, pp.158–65
Ginette Vincendeau, "The man who envied women: Interview with Yvonne Rainer", *Screen*, xxviii, Autumn 1987, pp.54–6
Marianne Goldberg, "The body, discourse and *The Man Who Envied Women*", *Women and Performance*, iii/2, 1987–8, pp.97–102
Peggy Phelan, "Feminist theory, poststructuralism and performance", *Drama Review*, xxxii, Spring 1988, pp.107–27
Berenice Raynaud, "L'ancien et le romantisme de toujours chez les indépendants)", *Cahiers du Cinema*, no.437, November 1990, pp.4–6
Connie Richards, "Films of Yvonne Rainer: Approaches to feminine filmmaking", *Feminisms*, iv, March 1991, pp.17–19
Michele Wallace, "Multiculturalism and oppositionality", *Afterimage*, xix, October 1991, pp.6–9
Scott MacDonald, "Demystifying the female body", *Film Quarterly*, xlv, Fall 1991, pp.18–32
Shelley Green, *Radical Juxtaposition: The Films of Yvonne Rainer*, Metuchen, NJ: Scarecrow, 1994
"Questions of feminism: 25 responses", *October*, no.71, Winter 1995, p.37

Yvonne Rainer's career as a dancer and choreographer began in the early 1960s in New York, where she contributed to the development of a radical modern dance at once analytic, objective and aleatory. She studied with Merce Cunningham from 1960 to 1967, and worked with Robert Dunn, Trisha Brown, Simone Forti and others at what became the Judson Dance Theater between 1961 and 1963. Her *Terrain* (Judson Memorial Church, 28–9 April 1963) was a controlled improvisation in five sections for six performers, lasting one and a half hours. In the first section, "Diagonal", the dancers moved through the performance space using prescribed movements executed according to a complex set of rules; the order in which the activities would occur was contingent upon choices made by the performers during the piece. Some sections were set to music, such as "Duet", performed by Trisha Brown and Rainer, while others were played out against recited texts, as in "Solo Section". *Terrain* emphasised the process of the dance performance and signalled Rainer's concern to question the relationship between performer, performance and audience.

Like Brown and Forti, Rainer critically examined the traditional language of modern dance by using vernacular movement as the basis of her choreography. Rainer's *Trio A*, originally the first part of a larger composition, *The Mind Is a Muscle* (Judson Church, 10 January 1966), consisted of a series of movements, equally weighted and performed without affect by three people simultaneously. The gestures are matter-of-fact, rather than illusionistic or miming, and because none is highlighted by an excess of energy, there is no sense of narrative. The viewer's desire to look at and identify with the dancers is frustrated by the performers, who avert their gazes from the audience. Rainer contributed *Trio A* to the Judson Flag Show, an exhibition organised by the Guerrilla Art Action Group at the Judson Church in November 1970, to protest against the arrests of people accused of desecrating the American flag, under the Flag Desecration Law of 1967. The performers tied flags around their necks and disrobed to dance in the nude, making of the highly abstract and self-reflexive piece a statement against repression and censorship.

The three issues central to *Trio A*, illusion, narrative and the relationship of performer and audience, are articulated in the films Rainer made beginning in 1972. Because dance exists in real time and space, demonstrating its literalness by emphasising duration, gesture is ultimately limited. Film permits space and time to be manipulated and offers more room to explore the complexities of the issues that Rainer finds compelling.

Lives of Performers (1972; all films distributed by Zeitgeist Films, New York) opens with a sequence of dancers in rehearsal, executing movements according to the directions of the off-screen choreographer; the film's roots are in another dance, *Grand Union Dreams* (Emmanuel Midtown YM-YWHA, New York, 16 May 1971). Rainer seems at pains not to seduce the viewer: the close framing of the performers and the choreographer's equivocation make it difficult to decipher the meaning of the scene. The gender differences of the dancers are down-played, which will undercut the emotional content of the apparent narrative. That story about the off-stage romances of the performers is further subverted by the use of voice-overs of the performers and Rainer commenting on the action on screen, often in self-conscious or uninflected voices. The film ends as abruptly and arbitrarily as it began, with a series of tableaux that mimic film stills from G. W. Pabst's *Pandora's Box* (1928). The reference to this film, which starred Louise Brooks as a *femme fatale* who meets her end at the hands of Jack the Ripper, makes clear that Rainer is critically examining the representation of women in film by denying the viewer the visual pleasure he or she expects from narrative cinema.

Rainer: Still from *Privilege*, showing Gabriella Farrar, 1990; Zeitgeist Films, New York

Rainer's *This Is the Story of a Woman Who ...* (1974) deconstructs narrative strategies by multiplying them. The narrative is acted out, or adumbrated through inter-titles. Two male-female pairs of actors play the main roles, making it difficult to decide whether one or two stories are being told. In a central sequence, Rainer appropriates stills from Alfred Hitchcock's *Psycho* (1960), the shower scene in which the character played by Janet Leigh is murdered. B. Ruby Rich points out that Hitchcock's film transgressed the rules of the suspense genre in killing off a leading character before the end of the film, and that by making reference to it Rainer legitimises her subversion of narrative (*The Films of Yvonne Rainer* 1989, p.8). That narrative conventions and the denial of subjectivity to women in film go hand in hand is reiterated in a long, discomforting scene in which the camera slowly zooms in on the pubic region of one of the female leads as a man slowly pulls down her undergarments, then tracks back as the garments are replaced. Throughout, the man holds the camera/viewer's gaze unwaveringly, implicating the audience in the objectification of the woman's body.

Rainer made two more films in the 1970s: *Kristina Talking Pictures* (1976) and *Journeys from Berlin/1971* (1980). She said of her first four films that she focused on the production and frustration of narrative at the expense of plot and character development, but that as she became more interested in political and theoretical texts as material, it seemed necessary to couch those interests in a clearer narrative structure. For her political message to come across, she translates it into personal terms by permitting the viewer to identify somehow with the film.

In *The Man Who Envied Women* (1985) Michel Foucault's theory of power and feminist film theories are critically examined. The central character, Jack, is played by two actors. His ex-lover, Trisha, never appears on screen but is present on the soundtrack commenting on the action, invisible to the gaze that is central to so many feminist analyses of film. The central scene occurs between Jack and Jackie (a *femme fatale* figure) in a hallway during a party. Their movements articulate a seduction, but their words are at cross-purposes: his speech quotes Foucault, hers a feminist text by the Australian Meaghan Morris. At the same time, however, Marianne Goldberg argues that the viewer's gaze is finally satisfied with Jackie's appearance, which figures the attraction and repulsion of sexual difference embodied in the woman.

Feminist theory, articulated in the mainstream by white, middle-class women, is questioned in Rainer's film *Privilege* (1990; see illustration), by her incorporation of issues touching on race, class, age and sexuality. Rainer's *alter ego* is a black woman, Yvonne Washington, who interviews Jenny about her experience with menopause for a documentary. In the course of the interview, Jenny relates her memories of living in a lower-class, racially-mixed neighbourhood, including an incident in which one of her neighbours is raped. Jenny's intervention in the subsequent events, in which she identifies the attacker as black and exaggerates what she knows in order to incriminate him, is exposed through Yvonne's interrogation as determined by her race and class. This is a feminist film in the best sense, at once politically engaged and self-critical.

MARGO HOBBS THOMPSON

Rama, (Olga) Carol
Italian painter, 1918–

Born in Turin, 18 September 1918, into an old and wealthy family. Artistic development alongside such figures as Massimo Mila and Albino Galvano. Member of MAC (Movimento Arte Concreta) group, 1950s. Has always stayed in the Turin region, working in a studio in Via Napione, on the banks of the Po.

Selected Individual Exhibitions
Galleria Faber, Turin: 1945
Galleria il Bosco, Turin: 1947
Galleria Art Club, Rome: 1948
Galleria Salto, Milan: 1955
Galleria La Bussola, Turin: 1959
Galleria La Carabaga, Genoa: 1964
Galleria Stampatori, Turin: 1964
Museo Civico, Pistoia: 1965
Galleria Lutrin, Lione: 1966
Galleria Numero, Rome: 1967
Galleria il Fauno, Turin: 1974
Galleria Anselmino, Milan: 1976
Galleria il Capricorno, Venice: 1976
Galleria Weber, Turin: 1978
Galleria Salzano, Turin: 1980 (retrospective), 1986, 1990
Sagrato del Duomo, Comune di Milano, Milan: 1985 (retrospective)
Galleria dell'Oca, Rome: 1987 (retrospective)
Casa del Mantegna, Mantua: 1988
Circolo degli Artisti, Turin: 1989

Bibliography
Carol Rama, exh. cat., Galleria Stampatori, Turin, 1964
L'altra metà dell'avanguardia, 1910–1940: Pittrici e scultrici nei movimenti delle avanguardie storiche, exh. cat., Palazzo Reale, Milan, and elsewhere, 1980
Carol Rama: Acquarelli, 1939–1941, exh. cat., Galleria Salzano, Turin, 1980
Carol Rama, exh. cat., Comune di Milano, Milan, 1985
Carol Rama: Opere dal 1937 al 1987, exh. cat., Galleria dell'Oca, Rome, 1987
Carol Rama, exh. cat., Casa del Mantegna, Mantua, 1988
Paolo Fossati, Carol Rama, Turin: Allemandi, 1989
Corrado Levi, "Well-defined and vulnerable organisms: The art of Carol Rama", Arts Magazine, lxv, January 1991, pp.54–7
A. Bonito Oliva, Carol Rama dal presente al passato, 1994–1936, Milan: Bocca, 1994

A central figure in the Italian transavanguardia (a movement in which the artist aims to free him or herself from tradition and previous experience), over a long career Carol Rama has shown herself to be a strange and audacious painter, who employs both abstract and figurative means, moving from one technique to another, to take art beyond the realm of rationality and to challenge accepted values.

Her career began in the early 1930s with drawings, watercolours and a few oil paintings that were almost incredible for the indecency of their subject matter. Rama thus not only contravened the rules of figurative art of the time, which was still grounded in the academic tradition and tended towards Social Realism, but also upset the conventional order of middle-class Turin. Many works of this period, such as Grandmother Carolina (1936; repr. Fossati 1989, pl.1), Little Brooms (1937; repr. Milan 1980) and Work 15, False Teeth (repr. Fossati 1989, pl.7), were not shown to the public until 1979, at the Galleria Martano, Turin. There was, however, a show of them in 1945, at the Galleria Faber, Turin, but this was closed due to censorship problems.

Just before the outbreak of World War II, in 1939, Rama painted Glass Bubbles (ibid., pl.8), in which the colours are applied with a palette knife, with unusual brutalism. She defines her work of the 1930s as the use of familiar images from the domestic sphere, where "objects – memory – fetishes" and figurative ghosts alternate in an anxious and obsessive way. She expresses "things one cannot say, things one cannot do" – the contents of the Freudian Id. Critics have seen a bloody aggressiveness in these feminine obscenities, composed of young women in wheelchairs, or mysterious and lascivious victims crowned with floral garlands – ironically very Victorian. But a love for life itself is also present: Rama depicts rejected objects and situations – mutilations, protheses, razors and urinals – precisely because she loves them, because they carry her back to the world of her childhood. They are symbols that appeal to the instinctive and the visceral: themes and motifs endowed with erotic and subversive charge.

In the period immediately following World War II, Rama participated more intensively in solo, group, national and international exhibitions. She took an interest in engraving, and the resulting series, Of the Parks (ibid., pp.11, 14 and 15), depicts figurative "presences", grotesque phantoms of a tragic and visionary reality, executed roughly, with desecrated forms. In the 1950s, impelled to experiment, Rama belonged to the Turin section of MAC (Movimento Arte Concreta). In a series of independent works she passed into an abstract phase, painting canvases in which quadrangular forms, both regular and irregular (e.g. rhomboids and lozenges), float on lunar backgrounds, giving life to a mysterious cosmography, as in the painting Untitled (1953; ibid., pl.20).

By contrast, in the 1960s Rama created a series of Bricolages (Do-it-yourself works; ibid., pls 24 and 28), inserting into the marks of coloured paint diverse, sometimes "organic" materials: needles, teeth, nails, even glass eyes. Rama described these disconcerting and corrosive works herself: "I put them [there] with rage[,] those nails should scratch" (ibid.). The artist wishes to do harm to others and perhaps also to herself, thereby annulling the aestheticism of art. We find ourselves confronted by an extravagant and ironic neo-Dadaism: the new, free outpouring of the painter's moods makes her abstractions as "alarming as a nightmare", according to Natalia Aspesi ("L'incubo dell'occhio di vetro", La Repubblica, 14 June 1985).

In the 1970s Rama sought further formal solutions, though still in the abstract sphere: the coloured marks disappear and the monochrome surfaces highlight the objects, generally old car or bicycle tyres, symbols of suffering humanity or rejection: the old worn rubber tyres in *War Is Abstract* (1970; repr. Fossati 1989, pl.34) become a metaphor of life lived. Subsequently, in the 1980s, Rama returned to the ambiguous and disturbing themes of her youth: monstrous and deformed images of luciferian angels, of sadistic and ironic toads, of chimeras and winged beings that change into mutilated women in a variety of brilliant colours, now on supports of old land registry cards or graph paper, as in *Maps and Pictures* (1983; ibid., pl.52).

A new appreciation of Rama's work and artistic value occurred in the 1980s, when her paintings began to be deciphered as containers – of things, presences and diverse forms – in which the colours have a significant value, space is manipulated in different ways and new materials and controversial themes are explored, always with the awareness that unity and equilibrium cannot be restored to art. As one critic declared, Rama's long apprenticeship of introspection brought forth a "nomadic fragmentism" that documents the crises of the expressive possibilities of contemporary art. The manipulation of banal objects in her watercolours reveals the fantasy and magic that are hidden under the appearance of things; sexual symbols cause the emotions and libido to prevail over the sense of reality. The use of extraordinary, impertinent and challenging materials permits Rama to follow at the same time her aggressive timidity and her sincere impudence: "I paint to heal myself, I speak of healing for having fornicated in the world of fears without limitations" (Rome 1987, p.34); thus Carol Rama has accepted her destiny, whether as a woman or as an artist in a productive career and in a reality of solitude in which she refines her pictorial practice through continual conflict.

LUCIA CAPPELLOZZA

Ramshaw, Wendy
British artist jeweller, 1939–

Born in Sunderland, Co. Durham, 1939. Trained in illustration and fabric design at the College of Art and Industrial Design, Newcastle upon Tyne, 1956–60. Studied for art teacher's diploma at Reading University, where she began to experiment with jewellery, 1960–61. Post-graduate residency at the Central School of Arts and Crafts, London. Artist in residence, Western Australian Institute of Technology, Perth, 1978. Visiting artist, Glass Department, Royal College of Art, 1986. Married David Watkins, 1962; two children, born 1967 and 1974. Recipient of De Beers "Diamonds Today" prize, 1970; Council of Industrial Design award, 1972; Johnson Matthey award for Platinum Jewellery, 1974; World Crafts Council diploma, Ontario, 1974; Crafts Advisory Committee bursary, 1974; De Beers Diamond International award, 1975; Crafts Council research grant, 1984; Winston Churchill Memorial Trust travelling fellowship, 1993. Officer, Order of the British Empire (OBE), 1993; Lady Liveryman of the Worshipful Company of Goldsmiths, 1986; Fellow of the Society of Industrial Artists and Designers. Lives in London.

Selected Individual Exhibitions
Pace Gallery, London: 1970
Oxford Gallery, Oxford: 1971
Goldsmiths' Hall, London: 1972 (with David Watkins)
Scottish Arts Council, Edinburgh: 1975 (touring)
Festival of Perth Exhibition, Western Australian Institute of Technology: 1978
National Gallery of Victoria, Melbourne: 1978
Galerie Am Graben, Vienna: 1980
Helen Drutt Gallery, Philadelphia: 1981
Victoria and Albert Museum, London: 1982
Princessehof Museum, Netherlands: 1983, 1988
Ontario Crafts Council, Canada: 1985
Electrum Gallery, London: 1986
Schmuckmuseum, Pforzheim: 1987 (with David Watkins)
Goldschmiedehaus, Hanau: 1987
Hand and Spirit Gallery, Scottsdale, AZ: 1988
Stafford Art Gallery, Staffordshire: 1988
Galerie Atrium at Basel "Art" Museum: 1988
Scottish Gallery, Edinburgh: 1989–90 (touring, with David Watkins, organised by British Council)
Royal Festival Hall, London: 1990
Musée d'Art Moderne et d'Art Contemporain, Nice: 1993 (with David Watkins)

Selected Writings
"Wendy Ramshaw: Artist jeweller", *Jewellery Studies*, iv, 1990, pp.73–83
"Picasso's ladies", *Antique Collector*, lxi, March 1990, pp.58–61

Bibliography
Jewellery in Europe, exh. cat., Scottish Arts Council, Edinburgh, 1975
Ralph Turner, "Two British jewelers: Wendy Ramshaw – David Watkins", *American Craft*, xl, October–November 1980, pp.18–21
Wendy Ramshaw, exh. cat., Victoria and Albert Museum, London, 1982
Barbara Cartlidge, *Twentieth-Century Jewelry*, New York: Abrams, 1985
Peter Dormer and Bob Cramp, *Wendy Ramshaw*, Leeuwarden, 1989
Helen Craven, "Sources of inspiration", *Crafts*, no.106, September–October 1990, pp.40–43
Peter Dormer and Ralph Turner, *The New Jewelry: Trends and Traditions*, 2nd edition, New York: Thames and Hudson, 1994
David Watkins, *The Best in Contemporary Jewellery*, London: Batsford, 1994
Ruth Pavey, "Commissions: St John's College, Oxford", *Crafts*, no.131, November–December 1994, pp.14–17
Helen Drutt English and Peter Dormer, *Jewelry of Our Time: Art, Ornament and Obsession*, London: Thames and Hudson, and New York: Rizzoli, 1995
Schmuckkunst der moderne Grossbritannien, exh. cat., Landesmuseum, Mainz, 1995
Shining Through, exh. cat., Crafts Council, London, 1995

Wendy Ramshaw established her reputation as a central figure in the British artist-jewellery movement at the beginning of the 1970s. This was an exciting time in modern jewellery, when traditional materials and concepts of adornment were being challenged by young, radical craftsmen and women, such as those featured in the touring exhibition *Jewellery in Europe* organised by the Scottish Arts Council in 1975. Since then,

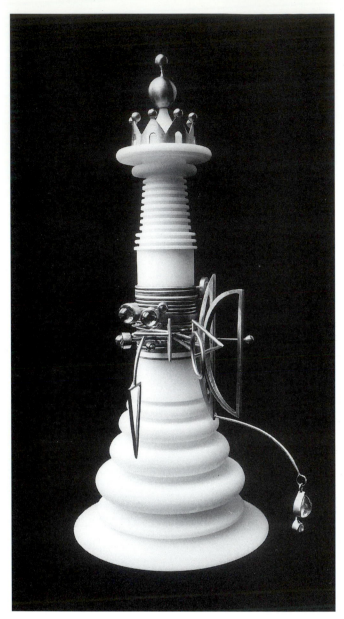

Ramshaw: *White Queen Ring Set,* 1976; yellow gold and semi-precious stones on white plexiglass stand

Ramshaw's work has continued to challenge the accepted conventions and to contribute to the international debate over the nature of jewellery. While the work of some of her contemporaries has become increasingly theoretical and esoteric, she has remained committed to the principle that jewellery should be wearable.

Her first commercial jewellery, made with David Watkins in 1964, was a range of fashion jewellery that they called *Optik Art.* It was made of brightly coloured Perspex decorated with geometric patterns influenced by the Op Art movement. There followed *Something Special,* an ephemeral collection of vibrantly coloured paper jewellery that was bought flat and assembled by the wearer. Both collections were sold anonymously, but were an auspicious beginning, being promoted by the Council of Industrial Design in London and sold in boutiques and department stores as far apart as London and Japan. By 1967 Ramshaw was exhibiting silver jewellery, and from 1969 she concentrated full-time on jewellery.

The principal influences evident in her work are industrial design and modernism, and her distinctive style is characterised by the interplay of simple geometric forms and the precise lines of lathe-turned metal. In 1975 she described her jewellery as "linear drawings conceived to be worn" (Edinburgh 1975, p.42). Twenty years later she wrote: "I like to think of jewellery as a language, a means of communicating ideas and feelings ... as a kind of music to delight the eye", and that in terms of design theories: "excitement comes from a simple form repeated to make a complex whole" (London 1995). These principles – fluidity, simplicity, controlled regularity and the exploration of the linear within a three-dimensional form – are evident throughout her work, giving a common identity and unity to pieces made over several decades.

The intellectual arguments underlying her work are matched by the highest levels of technical sophistication. Surface textures are smooth and polished, and the different elements of a piece are combined with seamless precision. While some of her contemporaries have rejected the use of precious metals and gemstones, she has continued to draw on a wide range of materials, both traditional and new. She is not bound by their intrinsic value and has proved herself equally accomplished working with acrylic and feathers as with gold and diamonds. Decoration is minimal, but colour is often introduced, either with domed cabochon stones or with parallel stripes of coloured enamel. In both materials the chosen colours are kept separate within their defined areas, acting as separate units within the design.

Ramshaw's most distinctive innovation is the ring set, made up of a collection of individual co-ordinated rings that are then combined in different arrangements by the wearer. They range from small groups with plain geometric bezels in different-coloured alloys to those set with contrasting colours of gemstones or shapes of diamonds. Some elements might extend far beyond the line of the finger – projecting up like a tower, reaching across the other fingers at a tangent or forming a large disc of concentric circles. Each set has a separate identity and the more important ones are named. They are made with minaret-shaped display stands of turned nickel, brass or acrylic, so that they may be enjoyed as sculpture when not being worn.

Ramshaw sees the participation of the wearer as an important aspect of her jewellery and many designs have an intrinsic flexibility that leaves the ultimate creative choice to the wearer. Whether with ring sets or with pendant elements hanging from a rigid wire necklet, she provides an exciting balance of ingredients from which the wearer must choose, thereby contributing their own personality and preferences to the appearance of the piece. Of such a piece she wrote: "the way in which others may organise it is an open-ended extension of its use" (London 1982). Immense variety is in theory possible: when the ring set *White Queen Number 1* was exhibited in 1975, it was accompanied by a computer print-out that proved that the 16 rings could be worn in 513,397,635,499,186,271,110,570,940,162 different arrangements.

In 1978 Ramshaw and David Watkins visited Australia as artists-in-residence at the Western Australian Institute of

Technology in Perth. Here the influence of Aboriginal art led to experiments with assemblage jewellery, using motifs as talismans. At this time porcelain and slender emu feathers first appeared in her work. On her return to Britain the use of ceramics was further developed through a major collaborative project with the manufacturers Wedgwood, the results of which were shown at an exhibition at the Victoria and Albert Museum in 1982. Angular and spherical beads of jasper-ware (a dense, vitrified stoneware with similar properties to porcelain) were turned on a lathe identical to the one that had been installed by Josiah Wedgwood in 1763. The beads were grouped into columns on vertical nickel alloy wires to make totem-pole pendants, or threaded on circlets to make necklaces. Shades of blue, black and white were the principal colours used. Mottling could be achieved by combining granules of different colours, while cutting through a contrasting coloured slip gave bolder effects. Wedgwood's famous black basalt was made into arrowhead shapes and used to decorate pins. Both one-off and multiple-production pieces were made.

From 1988 Ramshaw has been engaged on a major series of jewels called *Picasso's Ladies*, each piece inspired by one of the many portraits Picasso painted of women. The first pieces in the series were exhibited by the British Council in 1989–90, when her mastery of line, form and colour and the imaginative treatment of well-known images made clear the appropriateness of the venture. The overlapping, quasi-geometric forms of Cubism were abstracted and transformed by Ramshaw into new, three-dimensional works in turned metal, while line drawings received a flatter treatment in oxidised silver wire. Dramatic painted stripes were echoed in bands of bright enamel or acrylic, while cabochon moonstones and aquamarines were used to convey a softer palette. Some of the jewels take the form of ring sets, some of neck-pieces and others of complete parures.

Two more recent ironwork commissions have prompted work on a much larger, architectural scale: a gate made for St John's College, Oxford (completed 1993), and a large grille for the Victoria and Albert Museum, London (completed 1997). These explore linear themes closely related to those in her jewellery and they indicate an impressive ability to work in widely differing scales.

There are examples of Ramshaw's work in the Stedelijk Museum, Amsterdam; National Museum of Scotland, Edinburgh; Crafts Council Collection and Victoria and Albert Museum, London; Museum of Modern Art, Kyoto; and the Philadelphia Museum of Art.

CLARE PHILLIPS

Rappard, Clara von

Swiss painter and graphic artist, 1857–1912

Born in Wabern, Bern, 19 May 1857. Took first drawing lessons with Döme Skutzesky in Venice, 1868; subsequently studied drawing under Heinrich Dreber in Rome, 1869–75; life drawing under Eduard August Lürssen in Berlin, 1869–71, and Heinrich Gerhardt in Rome, 1870–72; portrait painting under Friedrich August Kaulbach in Hannover,

1873–5; attended Karl Gussow's women's class in Berlin, 1875–85. Also studied portrait painting under Christian Roth and etching under Ludwig von Gleichen-Reisswurm on extended visits to Munich during 1880s. Advised by Arnold Böcklin, Adolf Menzel and Paul Meyerheim. Made numerous trips to Italy, France and Britain; visited the Balkans, Istanbul and Black Sea, 1874. Increasing back problems from 1893; ceased work years before her death. Member, Verein der Künstlerinnen und Kunstfreundinnen zu Berlin; Münchner Künstlergenossenschaft (Munich Artists Association); Münchner Radierclub (Munich Etching Club). Died in Bern, 12 January 1912.

Principal Exhibitions

Individual
Salon Schulte, Berlin: 1894
Kunsthalle, Bremen: 1894
Kunstverein Hannover: 1894
Kupferstichkabinett des Städtischen Museums, Magdeburg: 1894
Kunstmuseum, Bern: 1896, 1912 (retrospective)

Group
Schweizer Turnusausstellung: 1885, 1890, 1893, 1896, 1897, 1900
Internationale Jahresausstellung, Münchner Künstlergenossenschaft: 1888, 1893, 1898
Paris Salon: 1890
German Exhibition, London: 1892 (second-class gold medal)
Albrecht Dürer-Verein, Nuremberg: 1892
Woman's Building, World's Columbian Exposition, Chicago: 1893
Verein der Künstlerinnen und Kunstfreundinnen zu Berlin: 1898, 1901
International Exhibition of Women Artists, London: 1900 (large gold medal)
Bernische Malerinnen, Bern: 1905
Bern section, Gesellschaft Schweizer Malerinnen und Bildhauerinnen, Bern: 1910

Selected Writings

"Orientreise eines deutschen Backfisches in Tagebuchblättern", *Sonntagsblatt des Bundes*, 1905, pp.73–5, 81–3, 89–91, 97–100, 105–8, 113–15, 121–3, 129–32, 137–40, 149–54

Bibliography

Adolf Frey, "Clara von Rappard", *Die Schweiz*, i, 1898–9, pp.395–403
"Unsere Bilder", *Das Hardermannli*, v, 1906, pp.123–4
Clara von Rappard, exh. cat., Kunstmuseum, Bern, 1912
"Eine schweizer Künstlerin am Hoffest: Aus dem unveröffentlichten Tagebuch von Clara von Rappard", *Die Schweiz*, xiv, 1912, pp.471–4
Jules Coulin, *Clara von Rappard*, Basel, 1920
——, "Politik und Lebensweisheiten in den Tagebüchern einer Malerin", *Wissen und Leben*, xiii, 1920, pp.603–9
——, "Arnold Böcklin in Clara von Rappards Aufzeichnungen", *Neue Zürcher Zeitung*, no.561, 4 April 1920
——, "Clara von Rappard bei Adolf Menzel", *Sonntagsblatt der Basler Nachrichten*, xiv/16, 18 April 1920, p.64
M. R., "Clara von Rappard: Das Leben einer Malerin", *Die Garbe*, iv, 1921, pp.432–30
Emmy Marti, "Clara von Rappard: Das Lebensbild einer Künstlerin", *Das Hardermannli*, xxxiv, 1935, pp.209–16; xxxv, 1936, pp.1–2
"Mich interessiert das Licht, Clara von Rappard: Wabern 1857–Bern 1912", *Berner Zeitung*, 21 July 1984

Renate Berger, "Und ich sehe nichts als die Malerei", *Autobiographische Texte von Künstlerinnen des 18.–20. Jahrhunderts*, Frankfurt am Main: Fischer, 1987, p.404

Hans Rudolf Hubler, "Für eine fast vergessene schweizer Malerin", *Der Bund*, no.27, 3 July 1992

Carola Muysers, "Warum gab es berühmte Künstlerinnen? Erfolge bildender Künstlerinnen der zweiten Hälfte des 19. Jahrhunderts", *Profession ohne Tradition: 125 Jahre Verein der Berliner Künstlerinnen*, exh. cat., Berlinische Galerie, Berlin, 1992, pp.21–34

——, "Zu den Werken der Malerin Clara von Rappard (1857–1912) im Kunstmuseum Bern", *Berner Kunstmitteilungen*, no.299, March–April 1995, pp.9–21

During her lifetime Clara von Rappard was considered the "most important woman artist" in Switzerland (Frey 1898). Her career developed in marked contrast to the usual limitations imposed on women artists at this time. The artist's first intensive steps forward were indebted to the freethinking attitude of her parents – the German revolutionary, jurist and scientist Konrad von Rappard and his wife Albertine (née Engell). Annual extended stays in Italy and Berlin served as a constant professional training programme for the budding painter.

Between 1871 and 1873 Rappard executed pencil illustrations for Tennyson's "Lady Godiva" and "Enoch Arden" (with texts translated by her father) and to Paul Heyse's "L'Arrabiata". Her conception of landscape and figures was indebted to the Romantic tradition and reveals the influence of Heinrich Dreber. At the suggestion of Adolph Menzel, whom Rappard met in Berlin for the first time in 1871, she turned her attention to the study of nature. Her parents' involvement with German and Swiss liberals stimulated her to undertake portrait painting. Her studies and sketches of the meetings of the free-thinkers in her family home, the Villa Rugen in Interlaken, were followed by commissioned works, for example the portraits of *Grafen von Reichenbach* (1876), the journalist *Julius Hausmann* (1877), the parliamentarian *Löwe-Calbe* (1885) and the industrialist *Henry Simon* (1887; all untraced).

Rappard soon developed an independent style in portrait painting. After her father's death in 1881, but also in the preceding years, portrait commissions formed part of her professional work. Karl Gussow's method of composing the head in flecks of light and shadow like a mosaic is clearly apparent in the numerous portraits she executed from 1875. Her early portraits, such as the one of her father (1878; private collection), are distinguished by the sitter's frontal, eye-level viewpoint and large areas of light and shadow contrasts. The later portraits, such as the those of a *Clergyman* (private collection), *Baroness von Fabrice* (1885) and *Self-Portrait in White* (1890; both Kunstmuseum, Bern), are characterised more by the striking exploration and detailed treatment of light than by plasticity and realism.

On a visit to the Paris Salon in 1885, Rappard realised that her fascination with the effects of light and shade was shared by many other artists. During these years she turned increasingly towards direct observation from nature, and painted plein-air portraits in light colours with looser brush strokes and coloured shadows, for example *Marie and Edith Hilty in Rugenpark, Interlaken* (1882; private collection), *Miss Hardy on the Rose Terrace in Rugen* (1883) and *Married Couple Beneath Roses* (1886; both Kunstmuseum, Bern). Rappard's interest in the direct translation of the observed,

Rappard: *Brahmin Souls*, 1885; oil on canvas; 80.5 × 139 cm.; Kunstmuseum, Bern

notwithstanding the appearance of the individual sitters, finally led to her own characteristic, modern style of portraiture. In the *Artist's Mother in front of the Blue Curtain* (1886), *Spotlight, Knitting Mother* (1890; both Kunstmuseum, Bern) and portrait of *Albertine von Rappard Knitting* (private collection) the incidence of light determines colour, form and the structure of the objects. Thus the blue curtain in the first painting, the brown dress and the brown background in *Spotlight*, and the red sofa in the last are entirely dissolved by light, whereas the firm and sculptural substance of the mother's face and hands is enhanced.

Rappard did not gain independence in landscape painting until very much later. Her first oil paintings with mountain motifs date from the middle of the 1880s. In such works as the *Jungfrau* (private collection) and *Jungfrau in Fog* (1891; Kunstmuseum, Bern) she explored momentary atmospheric conditions. The mountains appear as if dissected by streams of light flowing from fields of refracted sun rays on snow; in *Jungfrau in Fog* light and darker cloud particles provide additional structure to the mountain peak. The return to nature that in 1892 Rappard explicitly declared as the ideal for her art led her to a landscape style that became increasingly adjusted to the single value of colour and form. After 1900 she executed several watercolours whose stark colour contrasts announced an expressive painting style. As a result of illness, however, she was unable fully to exploit this stage of her artistic evolution.

The artist herself considered the portfolio entitled *Studies and Fantasies* (1897; Bruckmann publishers, Munich; Kunstmuseum, Bern; private collection) as the essence of her talent. The 18 graphic works contained in it reveal themes that derive from her innermost artistic and social beliefs. Thus the cycle *Guilt* is devoted to the progress of a murderer: before the deed he ascends with flying grace to the highest honour, but finally, shipwrecked and dying, he atones for his sins. The four masterly composed black chalk drawings are invested with Rappard's belief in the inevitability of fate, which was related to the naturalistic principles of Zola and Dostoevsky. In *Flying Thoughts* the artist used two motifs: a girl with wings reading at a table with books, superimposed on a coastal scene with sailing ships. Here the discovery of a motif specific to the written word has been rendered pictorially – an artistic self-expression comparable only to Max Klinger's.

The tendency to the fantastic is also inherent in Rappard's painting. Such works as *Brahmin Souls* (1885; see illustration), *Archangel in the Clouds* (1887), *Enigma of Life, Improvisations* (1890) and *Light and Shadow* (1896; study and oil painting; all Kunstmuseum, Bern) point in the direction of symbolism and ambiguity. The composition of these pictures is based on the dualism of light and shadow in which the figures are immersed. The way in which the dragon in *Brahmin Souls* bears the facial features of the artist remains unique in the history of modern self-portraiture. The other works also depict real-life characters, mostly her mother and both her aunts, as fantasy figures. With her fusion of naturalism with visionary imaginings, Clara von Rappard stands next to Böcklin, at the beginning of Swiss modernism. (In 1996 the Gesellschaft Clara von Rappard was founded in Freiburg, Switzerland.)

CAROLA MUYSERS

Raverat, Gwen
British printmaker, painter and illustrator, 1885–1957

Born Gwendolen Mary Darwin at Newnham Grange (now Darwin College), Cambridge, 26 August 1885, to Sir George Darwin, Plumian Professor of Astronomy and Experimental Philosophy at Cambridge, and Maud Du Puy; granddaughter of Charles Darwin. Visited Rembrandt exhibition in Amsterdam, 1898. Studied at Slade School of Fine Art, London, 1908–11; self-taught in wood-engraving. Married artist Jacques Raverat, 1911; two daughters, born 1916 and 1919. Lived in Le Havre, France, then moved to Weston, near Baldock, 1915; moved to Vence, France, on account of husband's health (disseminated sclerosis), 1920; returned to England after his death, 1925. Settled at the Old Rectory, Harlton, Cambridgeshire, 1928; moved to Cambridge during World War II. Art critic for *Time and Tide*, 1929–40; produced drawings and wood-engravings for Cambridge University Press, Faber and Faber and other publishers, 1932–52; abandoned engraving after a stroke, 1951. Founder-member, Society of Wood Engravers, 1920; Associate member, 1920, and member, 1920, Royal Society of Painter-Etchers and Engravers. Died in Cambridge, 11 February 1957.

Principal Exhibitions
Friday Club, London: from 1910
New English Art Club, London: from 1913
Society of Wood Engravers, London: from 1920
Royal Society of Painter-Etchers and Engravers, London: from 1920
Thomas Agnew & Sons, London: 1959 (touring retrospective)

Selected Writings
Period Piece: A Cambridge Childhood, London: Faber, 1952

Bibliography
M.C. Salaman, *Modern Woodcuts and Lithographs by British and French Artists*, London and New York: Studio, 1919
Herbert Furst, ed., *Modern Woodcutters, i: Gwendolen Raverat*, London: Morland Press, 1920
John Gould Fletcher, "The woodcuts of Gwendolen Raverat", *Print Collector's Quarterly*, xviii, 1931, pp.330–50
The Times, 13 February 1957 (obituary)
Reynolds Stone, *The Wood Engravings of Gwen Raverat*, London: Faber, 1959; 2nd edition ed. by Simon Brett, Cambridge: Silent, 1989
Cambridge Review, 23 January 1960
Gwendolen Mary Raverat RE, exh. cat., Manor Gallery, Royston, Herts, 1987
Patricia Jaffé, *Women Engravers*, London: Virago, 1988
Gwen and Jacques Raverat: Paintings and Wood-Engravings, exh. cat., University of Lancaster Library, 1989 (contains extensive bibliography and list of contributions to *Time and Tide*)
Joanna Selborne and Lindsay Newman, eds, *Gwen Raverat: Wood Engraver*, Fleece Press, 1996

Light on a landscape or figures seen from an unusual viewpoint, translated into wood-engraving, sounds unspectacular, but Gwen Raverat's skill in matching medium with vision sets her in the forefront of 20th-century printmakers. A subject and its translation into engraving by this artist seem as one, just as her insistence that, in books, illustration and text should be an entity. The rise of photogravure and new forms of commercial

Raverat: *Clare Bridge*, 1935; wood engraving; Fitzwilliam Museum, Cambridge

printing towards the end of the 19th century prompted artists to return to the medium of printmaking for its own sake – this is manifested most notably in the resurgence of wood-engraving in the first 40 years of the 20th century. It was fortunate that Raverat flourished at this time.

The springboard for Raverat's inspiration was the familiar place. As a member of the Darwin family, growing up in Cambridge, with holidays at Down House, Kent, the home of her famous grandfather, the late Charles Darwin, Gwen stored up images in her mind. It is this love that Raverat described in *Period Piece* (1952):

> Long after I have forgotten all my human loves, I shall still remember the smell of a gooseberry leaf, or the feel of the wet grass on my bare feet; or the pebbles in the path. In the long run it is this feeling that makes life worth living, this which is the driving force behind the artist's need to create.

After visiting Amsterdam at the age of 13, Raverat was deeply impressed by Rembrandt and his engravings; her other hero was the 18th-century engraver Thomas Bewick. Since childhood a sketchbook was always in her pocket and, through her life, her skill was acquired by constant practice and radical revision when re-cutting blocks for engravings. Her mother was a close friend of the American artist Cecilia Beaux (q.v.), who came to stay with the family in Cambridge when Gwen was a child – this may well have been her first contact with a professional woman artist (information courtesy Tara L. Tappert).

Although Raverat trained at the Slade School, she did not learn wood-engraving there. Apart from some help from the wood-engraver Elinor (Monsell), who had married her cousin Bernard Darwin, she appears to have been self-taught – unlike the women engravers from 1912 onwards who worked under the tuition of Noel Rooke at the Central School of Arts and Crafts. The earliest engravings by Raverat date from 1909, and by the end of her life she had recorded 569 prints. Early engravings are of ballad subjects with a ghostly theme, such as *Clerk Saunders* and *Fair Margaret's Ghost* (both 1909), in which drama is created by the effect of light. Other prints invite us to question the story behind the image, as in *The Philosopher* (1922), where a face looks through a window at an old man crouched over his books, and *David Old* (1921), where David in bed is viewed from behind his head while he gazes at the naked Bathsheba.

Raverat also collaborated with her husband Jacques, whom she had married in 1911; the prints were drawn by Jacques and engraved by Gwen. The linear figures and religious subject matter of the joint engravings *Pietà* (1912) and the *Prodigal Son* (1914) show some similarities with the work of Eric Gill. By contrast Gwen's own engravings of *Gypsies* (1910) and the *Bolshevist Agent* (1920) are larger and more boldly cut, with more natural figures.

Raverat's first published engravings appeared in a book of poems by her cousin, Frances Cornford, *Spring Morning* (1915). These eight, almost postage-stamp-sized works depict lyrical landscapes, an outline of trees lit by sun or moonlight, with perhaps one small figure. The grandeur of trees and light offsets the actual size of the work. Because she felt so strongly about the importance of harmonising the two components, the artist is said to have been unhappy about the placing of the engravings in the text in the printing of this book.

In 1920 Jacques Raverat's illness led to the couple's move to Vence, France; they now had two daughters and Gwen remained at the hub of family life while working on her woodblocks. The engravings made in France are chiefly landscape views of Vence market places, effective in their portrayal of the brilliance of southern light. Other prints are of rather sinister groups of elderly black-clad figures used later in her illustrations for children's books. The heat caused the splitting of several of Raverat's woodblocks. Tragically, the French climate did not improve Jacques's health and he died in 1925. Virginia Woolf wrote to Gwen in April of that year: "Jacques' death will probably make you, because it will so intensify everything …" (*The Letters of Virginia Woolf*, ed. Nigel Nicolson and Joanne Trautmann, London: Hogarth Press, and New York: Harcourt Brace, 1977, iii, 8 April 1925, p.177).

The striking head of *Jacques Raverat*, completed before his death, is one of the very few portrait engravings by Raverat – he is looking alert, the contours delicately engraved on the long face. The other portrait is of her contemporary and friend *Rupert Brooke*, engraved on the title page of *The Collected Poems of Rupert Brooke* (1919; drawing for this portrait, 1910, in National Portrait Gallery, London, as is Raverat's drawing on canvas of her father, *Sir George Howard Darwin*).

In the 1930s Raverat became widely known when her engravings were published as book illustrations. Of her childhood the artist has said "my mind was full of dreams" (*Period Piece*) and in her illustrations for children's books she drew on imaginary and remembered images. She illustrated Kenneth Grahame's *The Cambridge Book of Poetry for Children* (1932) with tiny engravings of the widest variety of subjects from historical to fantastical. Illustrations for many other children's books followed, most importantly *The Runaway* by Elizabeth Anna Hart (1936). Generally the artist was commissioned by commercial publishers, but an exception was the Ashendene Press who published Longus's *Les Amours pastorales de Daphnis et Chloé* (1933) with 28 engravings by Raverat; these works, showing graceful nudes in harmony both with their pastoral setting and the text, met with acclaim. Raverat's knowledge of East Anglian country life is shown in her illustrations for A.G. Street's *Farmer's Glory* (1934); if, perhaps, she was uneasy about engraving large animals on a small scale she solved this by viewpoint, so only a row of cows' tails and their shed are visible. Also on a pastoral theme, Raverat made six engravings for the London Omnibus Company's *Little Rivers of London's Country* (1929).

Raverat was innovative in her use of colour in some of her illustrations, particularly those for H.A. Wedgwood's *The Bird Talisman: An Eastern Tale* (1939), with its haunting image of an Eastern figure sitting on a flying carpet being drawn by huge black birds. Separate blocks were cut for each colour. Compared with a decorative use of colour in the published work, Raverat's single colour engravings are chiefly landscapes, in which the colour is muted and very subtle.

Raverat is now popularly known as the author of *Period Piece*, but as an artist she will be remembered for her wood-engraving; *The Fen* (1935) and *Clare Bridge* (1935; see illustration) are just two of so many memorable prints. An almost complete collection of Raverat's prints, as well as many of the original woodblocks, are in the Fitzwilliam Museum, Cambridge; there is a large collection of engravings in the Victoria and Albert Museum, London; some prints and a woodblock are in the British Museum, London.

SARAH WIMBUSH

Read, Katharine
British painter, 1723–1778

Born in Dundee, Scotland, 1723, to Alexander Read and his wife Elizabeth, daughter of Sir John Wedderburn Bt. Studied pastel painting under Maurice Quentin de la Tour in Paris after 1745; stayed in Rome, 1751–3. Set up studio in London, 1753. Elected honorary member, Incorporated Society, 1769. Sailed for Madras, India, with her niece Helena Beatson, 1777. Made a will, 29 June 1778; left for England and died on board ship, 13 or 15 December 1778.

Principal Exhibitions
Society of Artists of Great Britain, London: 1760, 1766–72
Free Society of Artists, London: 1761–5, 1768–9, 1779
Royal Academy, London: 1773–4, 1776

Bibliography
Edward Edwards, *Anecdotes of Painters*, London: Leigh and Sotheby, 1808
Elizabeth Fries Ellet, *Women Artists in All Ages and Countries*, New York: Harper, 1859; 2nd edition, London: Bentley, 1860
Ellen C. Clayton, *English Female Artists*, 2 vols, London: Tinsley, 1876
A.R. Ellis, ed., *The Early Diary of Frances Burney, 1768–78*, 2 vols, London: Bell, 1889
A.F. Steaurt, "Miss Katherine [sic] Read: Court paintress", *Scottish Historical Review*, ii, 1904, pp.38–46
R.M. Sée, *English Pastels, 1750–1830*, London: Bell, 1911
Sir William Foster, "British artists in India, 1760–1820", *Walpole Society*, xix, 1930–31, pp.1–88
Lady Victoria Manners, "Catherine [sic] Read: The 'English Rosalba'", *Connoisseur*, lxxxviii, 1931, pp.376–86; lxxxix, 1932, pp.35–40, 171–8
Mildred Archer, *India and British Portraiture, 1770–1825*, London and New York: Sotheby Parke Bernet, 1979

Katharine Read was the fifth of 13 children of a merchant from Dundee, Alexander Read, who had joined the land-owning classes on his marriage to Elizabeth Wedderburn. The family were both financially secure and had strong Jacobite connections, two contributing factors that made it possible for Katharine to become an artist. The transition from middle-class "young lady" to trainee professional artist is not documented. However, as drawing lessons formed an important part of the training for "young ladies", it seems likely that Read must have demonstrated strong abilities, and her subsequent contact with the engraver Robert Strange suggests that she may have shared with him the same art teacher in Edinburgh. Thus, in 1745 (the year of the failed Jacobite Rebellion), Katharine Read was still unmarried – and at the age of 22 was no doubt considered a confirmed spinster by society's standards – but she showed considerable artistic talent. It was therefore expedient to send her to Paris to train under the artist Maurice Quentin de la Tour.

The pastel medium came into fashion in Paris with the arrival of Rosalba Carriera (q.v.) in 1720. Her success encouraged La Tour to take up the technique, and by the time of Read's apprenticeship he had become the leading pastel painter of the day and portraitist to the royal family of France. Read's selection of the pastel medium was probably a case of social necessity and financial astuteness. Pastel painting, or crayon painting as it was known in Britain, was considered a "feminine" medium, due to the often cited "delicacy" of touch required when applying the pigment, and the general smallness of scale of works due partly to the medium's inherent fragility. In terms of financial astuteness, while London abounded in portrait painters in oil, pastel – or crayon – painters were much rarer, thus suggesting a market waiting to be exploited. As Read said in a letter from Italy to her brother, Alexander, in 1751: "I hear my old master La Tour is in London where I

Read: *Mrs Eva Garrick*, pastel; Victoria and Albert Museum, London

don't doubt of his getting money by his great merit and great price … however I could have wished he had staid at home."

From 1751 to 1753 Katharine Read stayed in Rome, hopeful that her training in France would enable her to consolidate her position as a professional artist back in Britain. In 1752 she wrote to her brother Alexander: "… as I have staid one year in Rome for Improvement, I must certainly stay in it another for Name, and then you'll see I'll top it with the best of them." She used her time in Rome to establish a clientele not only from the Italian aristocracy, but also from the British nobility visiting Rome on the Grand Tour. On her return to Britain in 1753, Read set up her studio in London. For the next 20 years she was one of the most fashionable crayon painters in the city, painting not only members of the royal family (such as *Queen Charlotte*, in 1761 and 1763), but also members of the aristocracy and Scottish nobility as well as famous people of the day, such as the actor *David Garrick* and his wife *Eva*. Eva is portrayed vividly in one portrait (see illustration), dressed in a Gypsy-style costume, staring confidently out of the picture, her face turned in a typical three-quarter view towards the viewer.

Her success as a crayon painter did not confine Read to this medium. She also painted in oil, as can be seen in her portrait of the *Countess of Sussex* (Ranger's House, London). This three-quarter-length portrait shows the sitter posing in an ermine cloak, against a background of classical pillar and velvet curtain. The casualness of the pose and the inclusion of a pillar – a decorative element usually ascribed to grand-manner portraits of men – gives the work a slightly stronger edge than the figure-hugging clothes and languorously draped arms suggest.

Read's sitters were essentially women and children. The translucent, smudged effect of the crayon medium was considered to suit the subject matter, and the small scale of crayon paintings gave a suggestion of intimacy and informality. Crayon was a modest medium, not for grand-scale portraits and thus deemed well suited to women, as can be seen in Read's portrait of *Lady Shelbourne and Her Son, Lord Fitzmaurice* (Bowood House, Wiltshire). Although Read is often referred to as the "English Rosalba", the comparison is misleading and limiting. She did copy works after Rosalba Carriera, but she cited La Tour as her "model among all portrait painters" and described the Italian artist Guido Reni as "my favourite master". Carriera was a figurehead for all crayon painters of the period, not just Katharine Read.

Read's studio appears to have functioned in a similar way to those of other fashionable artists of the time, who often held "open house" to clients and potential clients from the respectable to the not-so-respectable, providing a spectacle not unlike a visit to the theatre. Fanny Burney (*Early Diary of Frances Burney, 1768–78*) cites a visit to Read's studio directly after a visit to Sir Joshua Reynolds's. Studio visits were a social activity; it was, for example, through illicit meetings at Read's studio that Lady Susan Fox-Strangways was able to cultivate her romance with the actor William O'Brien.

Read's trip to India in 1777 at the age of 54 was a search for a new, and less competitive market, as well as the opportunity to find a suitable match for her niece, Helena Beatson. It appears that her popularity was waning at this time, although Burney described her in 1774 as "Miss Reid [sic], the

celebrated paintress". She continued in a less flattering vein, however: "… she is so very deaf, that it is a fatigue to attempt [conversing] with her. She is most exceedingly ugly, and of a very melancholy, or rather discontented humour …" (*ibid.*). This flippancy does not do justice to the overwhelming achievement of a woman who spent at least 20 years as a professional artist and whose artistic output amounts to more than 200 attributed works, nearly all of which are in private collections.

Dorcas Taylor

Ream, Vinnie
American sculptor, 1847–1914

Born in Madison, Wisconsin, September 1847; father a government surveyor. Attended the Academy at Christian College, Columbia, 1857–8, after the family's move to Missouri. Settled in Washington, DC, with her family, who opened a boarding house, 1861; worked as a postal clerk to supplement their modest income. Apprenticed to sculptor Clark Mills, c.1863. Received commission from Congress to sculpt Abraham Lincoln, 1866; left for Italy to have the work carved in marble, 1869, accompanied by her parents, who depended on her for support. Studied briefly under Léon Bonnat in Paris, then under Luigi Majoli in Rome, opening a studio on Via San Basilio. Returned to Washington, 1871. Married Lieutenant Richard L. Hoxie, 1878; son born 1883. Moved with Hoxie on his transferral from Washington to Montgomery, Alabama, 1884, then to various other posts until his retirement, as Brigadier-General, in 1908; subsequently divided time between Washington, Iowa City and Miami. Died in Washington, DC, 14 November 1914.

Principal Exhibitions

Grand Exhibition of National Industries, American Institute, New York: 1871
Exposition and Industrial Fair of Kings County, Brooklyn, NY: 1871
Louisville Industrial Exposition: 1874
Centennial Exposition, Philadelphia: 1876
Woman's Building, World's Columbian Exposition, Chicago: 1893

Bibliography
Harold E. Miner, "Vinnie and her friends", undated manuscript, Archives of American Art, film roll 297

Richard L. Hoxie, *Vinnie Ream*, Washington, DC: Gibson, 1908

Charles E. Fairman, *Art and Artists of the Capitol of the United States*, Washington, DC: Government Printing Office, 1927

Maude E. Griffin, "Vinnie Ream: Portrait of a sculptor", *Missouri Historical Review*, lvi, April 1962, pp.230–43

Gordon Langley Hall, *Vinnie Ream: The Story of the Girl Who Sculptured Lincoln*, New York: Holt Rinehart, 1963

Carolyn Berry Becker, "Vinnie Ream: Portrait of a young sculptor", *Feminist Art Journal*, v, Fall 1976, pp.29–31

Ruth L. Bohan, "The Farragut monument: A decade of art and politics, 1871–1881", *Records of the Columbia Historical Society of Washington, DC, 1973–1974*, 1976, pp.209–43

Art and the United States Capitol, Washington, DC: Government Printing Office, 1978

Harold Holzer and Lloyd Ostendorf, "Sculptures of Abraham Lincoln from life", *Magazine Antiques*, cxiii, 1978, pp.382–93

Ream: *Abraham Lincoln*, 1871; marble; US Capitol, Washington, DC

Joan A. Lemp, "Vinnie Ream and Abraham Lincoln", *Woman's Art Journal*, vi/2, 1985, pp.24–9

Charlotte Streifer Rubinstein, *American Women Sculptors*, Boston: Hall, 1990

Glenn V. Sherwood, "A labor of love: The life and art of Vinnie Ream", manuscript, Historical Society of Washington, DC, 1991

Vinnie Ream and Richard L. Hoxie Papers are in the Manuscript Division, Library of Congress, Washington, DC.

Vinnie Ream was one of the generation of pioneering American women sculptors that also included Harriet Hosmer (q.v.) and Emma Stebbins (q.v.). She was not a prolific artist, however, and her reputation rests on fewer than a dozen sculptures; the locations of other objects recorded in literature are not known. Her artistic career was closely tied not only to the political life in Washington, DC, but also to her ability to meet and charm those in positions of power. While she had detractors, such as the columnist Jane Grey Swisshelm, she counted among her friends and supporters many in positions of political and social influence. The literature on Ream leaves little doubt of her youthful beauty and her powers of persuasion with men; her coquettish manner was apparently disarming.

The American Civil War left profound scars on the citizens of the country, and in April 1865 the tragedy deepened when President Abraham Lincoln was assassinated. The general consensus in Washington was that Lincoln's memory should be honoured by Congress with a statue placed in the Capitol. Ream's winning the commission against such artists as Hosmer is a fascinating tale of political manoeuvring and intrigue; such powerful men as President Andrew Johnson, General Ulysses S. Grant and Representative Thaddeus Stevens all came to her assistance, supporting her in the face of much opposition on account of her youth and inexperience. When she was awarded the contract in 1866, she became the first woman artist to receive a sculptural commission from Congress.

Although the details are unclear, it is generally accepted that Vinnie Ream had modelled Lincoln's bust shortly before his death. Following the practice of the day, after Ream's model was approved by the Secretary of the Interior, she took it to Carrara in Italy to be carved in marble. While Horatio Greenough's marble statue of *George Washington* (1833–41; Smithsonian Institution, Washington, DC) was based on 19th-century reconstructions of Phidias' *Zeus*, Ream chose to follow the growing tendency of representing her standing *Abraham Lincoln* (1871; see illustration) in contemporary dress, with the cloak serving to give mass to the form in the manner of Neo-classical draperies. Although the pose is a stock one, there is an easy grace to the figure that softens the realism of the face (there is a marble bust-length version of the subject at Cornell University, Ithaca). It was only with Augustus Saint-Gaudens and Daniel Chester French that Lincoln received a profoundly new interpretation.

One of Ream's finest statues is the marble *Sappho* (c.1870; National Museum of American Art, Washington, DC). Her representation of the Greek poetess demonstrates the continuing influence of Neo-classicism in the American sculptural tradition. Some years earlier, the young American artist Edward Bartholomew had sculpted a marble *Sappho* (c.1856; Wadsworth Atheneum, Hartford, CT) in Rome, but it is uncertain that Ream knew his work (according to Lemp 1985, p.28,

she had seen another version of *Sappho* in London). Other ideal subjects in a Neo-classical manner by Ream are *Spirit of the Carnival* and *Passion Flower* (both State Historical Society of Wisconsin, Madison). *The West* (c.1870; Wisconsin state capitol, Madison), which was exhibited in Chicago in 1893, is an idealised allegorical female figure bearing symbols representing the cultivation of the American West. Western expansion was a significant theme of 19th-century American art; at the US Capitol Ream would have seen such works as Thomas Crawford's Senate pediment sculpture, *Progress of Civilization* (1863), and Emanuel Leutze's mural in the House wing, *Westward the Course of Empire Takes Its Way* (1862).

Ream's success with *Lincoln* led to a second commission from Congress for a monument dedicated to the naval hero Admiral David G. Farragut, who was famous for the bloodless capture of New Orleans in 1862 and for his action at Mobile Bay in 1864. Shortly after Farragut's death in 1870, Ream sculpted his portrait using photographs provided by his widow. The award of this governmental commission was a long-drawn-out affair, but Ream finally prevailed, thanks in large part to such influential friends as General William Tecumseh Sherman and Mrs Farragut. She signed a contract in 1875, although the monument was not completed until 1881. Ream's bronze figure (Farragut Square, Washington, DC) stands atop a multi-tiered granite base; the Admiral is depicted with a marine glass in his hands and his left foot resting on a block and tackle. Although the monument to Farragut is perhaps Ream's most ambitious undertaking – and it is certainly a credible piece of public sculpture – in the end it must stand comparison with Augustus Saint-Gaudens's great bronze *Farragut Monument* of 1879–80 in New York.

Vinnie Ream had enjoyed a meteoric rise in Washington society, and was often the focus of attention in social columns. Following her marriage to Lieutenant Richard L. Hoxie, and the completion of the *Farragut Monument*, she seems almost to have abandoned sculpture for two decades. During these years she devoted her energies to social and charitable activities and to her music – she was a talented musician, and she sang in addition to playing several instruments. The demands of Hoxie's military career kept the couple away from Washington for many years, but around 1903 Ream developed a renewed interest in sculpture.

In 1906 the Iowa General Assembly approved an act for her to execute a statue of *Samuel J. Kirkwood* for the US Capitol. Kirkwood's political achievements included serving as a US Senator and as Secretary of the Interior under President Garfield. The statue does not advance Ream's reputation, although it is typical of the many sculptures of public officials in contemporary dress that fill the halls of Congress. On the other hand, her bronze statue of *Sequoya* (US Capitol, Washington, DC), which was commissioned by Oklahoma in 1912, is notable for its graceful forms and facile surface textures. The statue, which was left unfinished at her death, was completed by George J. Zolnay. The sculpture is a fitting tribute to Ream's interest in the struggle of Native Americans throughout her life. Sequoya (Sequoia), a Cherokee born in Tennessee c.1760, developed an alphabet that taught his people to read and write.

Although the romantic details of Vinnie Ream's life dominate the literature regarding her, her artistic achievements should not be negated. Not only did she help open the way for women to receive public commissions, but as a Midwesterner she successfully competed against the Eastern art establishment. Stylistically, her sculpture is an interesting, if not unique assimilation of lingering Neo-classicism and emerging realism.

KENT AHRENS

Redpath, Anne
British painter, 1895–1965

Born in Hawick, Galashiels, 29 March 1895; father the tweed designer Thomas Redpath. Studied at Edinburgh College of Art, 1913–19 (diploma and postgraduate year); trained as an art teacher at Moray House College of Education, Edinburgh, 1913–17. Visited Brussels, Bruges, Paris, Siena and Florence on a travelling scholarship, 1919. Lived in France after marriage to James Beattie Michie, an architect with the War Graves Commission, 1920; three sons; husband died 1958. Returned home to Hawick, 1934. Settled in Edinburgh, 1949; often travelled abroad. Recipient of honorary doctorate, University of Edinburgh, 1955. Professional member, Society of Scottish Artists, 1934; member, 1939, and president, 1944–7, Scottish Society of Women Artists; member, Royal Society of British Artists, 1946–53; Royal Institute of Oil Painters, 1948; associate member, Royal Society of Painters in Watercolour, 1962. Associate member, 1947, and member, 1952, Royal Scottish Academy; member, Royal West of England Academy, Bristol, 1957; Associate, Royal Academy, 1960. Officer, Order of the British Empire (OBE), 1955. Died in Edinburgh, 7 January 1965.

Selected Individual Exhibitions

Saint-Omer, France: 1921
Casino, Saint-Raphaël: 1928
Gordon Small Gallery, Edinburgh: 1947
Scottish Gallery, Edinburgh: 1950, 1953, 1957, 1960, 1963
Lefevre Gallery, London: 1952, 1959, 1962, 1964
Royal West of England Academy, Bristol: 1956
Danish Institute, Edinburgh: 1958
Stone Gallery, Newcastle upon Tyne: 1961
Festival Exhibition, Edinburgh: 1963 (*Four Scottish Painters*, with William MacTaggart, Robin Philipson and Joan Eardley, organised by Arts Council of Great Britain, Scottish Committee)
Arts Council of Great Britain, Scottish Committee, Edinburgh: 1965 (touring retrospective)

Bibliography

R.H. Westwater, "Anne Redpath", *Scottish Art Review*, v/3, 1955, pp.11–14, 33
T. Elder Dickson, "Anne Redpath", *The Studio*, clix, 1960, pp.86–9
Felix McCullough, "Anne Redpath", *Scottish Art Review*, ix/2, 1963, pp.15–18
Anne Redpath: Memorial Exhibition, exh. cat., Scottish Committee of the Arts Council of Great Britain, 1965
George Bruce, *Anne Redpath*, Edinburgh: Edinburgh University Press, 1974
Anne Redpath, 1895–1965: All the Works in the Collection, exh. cat., Scottish National Gallery of Modern Art, Edinburgh, 1975
Anne Redpath, 1895–1965: Her Life and Work, exh. cat., Bourne Fine Art, Edinburgh, 1989 (contains bibliography)
Scottish Art since 1900, exh. cat., Scottish National Gallery of Modern Art, Edinburgh, and elsewhere, 1989

Anne Redpath was the eldest of a triumvirate of Scottish women artists who were at the forefront of post-war Scottish painting, the others being Joan Eardley (q.v.) and Elizabeth Blackadder (q.v.). She was born in the Scottish Borders, which, while they have a rich literary tradition, have not produced many well-known painters. Her father was a textile designer in Hawick, and Redpath in later life said: "I do with a spot of red or yellow in a harmony of grey what my father did in his tweeds". She flourished at the Edinburgh College of Art, where she enrolled in 1913 despite parental opposition. Her reputation as the most promising student of her year was confirmed when she won a major travelling scholarship in her final year (1919). She set off for the Continent and was much influenced by the 14th-century frescoes of the Lorenzetti brothers in the Palazzo Pubblico, Siena, where sophisticated and exquisite technique is allied to a simple, powerful vision. Thirty years later she was to acknowledge early Italian painting as the greatest single influence on her work. Her ability mentally to file away visual experiences for indefinite periods was one of the strengths of her artistic sensibility.

She married the architect James Michie and his work took them in 1920 to northern France. This area had been the painting ground where S.J. Peploe and J.D. Fergusson, the Scottish Colourists, found so much inspiration. In the 15 years that she lived there, however, Redpath became thoroughly immersed in the responsibilities of bringing up her three children and found no time and perhaps little inclination for painting. It was not until her family's return to Scotland in 1934, her marriage effectively over, that she returned to full-time painting. In 1961, referring to her time in France, Redpath said:

> Whatever I did for my home was creative but I never ceased to be a painter – I have a painter's mind. Were the choice to be made again, there would not be any division in my mind: my family would come first. However, I always had a rather guilty conscience. I always knew I would come back to painting.

It was not until 1942 that the painter found the confidence that her brilliant student days had promised. It was at this time that she painted what is probably her masterpiece, *Indian Rug (Red Slippers)* (1942; see illustration). While indebted to Matisse for the Fauvist red of the chair and the slippers and the flat patterns of the rug, the painterly enjoyment of pigment and impasto and the use of whites and greys as a contrast to the strong colours are characteristic of Redpath's work.

In 1944 Redpath was elected president of the Scottish Society of Women Artists. Founded in Edinburgh in the 1920s, the Society gave women painters the showcase they felt they were being denied by the Royal Scottish Academy. During Redpath's presidency, younger painters were encouraged and members' paintings were no longer accepted automatically but were judged against the standards set by a nucleus of artists. In later years Redpath changed her opinion about the practice of women exhibiting collectively. She told Sydney Goodsir Smith that it was as silly "as would be a special exhibition by men over six feet tall taking size fourteen shoes". She held strong, reasoned opinions on other painters and could express her views in an articulate and unpretentious manner. Her admira-

Redpath: *Indian Rug (Red Slippers)*, c.1942; oil on plywood; 73.9 × 96.1 cm.; Scottish National Gallery of Modern Art, Edinburgh

tion for such contemporaries as Joan Eardley, Robin Philipson and Willie Gillies was not uncritical. She was uneasy with Eardley's use of materials such as sand, newspaper and grasses; this offended her own belief in truth to materials and she doubted its long-term value. The approach of Redpath, the intellectual, contemplative artist, who created a work of art to be treasured, is in marked contrast to that of Eardley, the highly charged expressionist artist, who employed whatever materials were to hand, and painted for the here and now.

During the 1950s Redpath took several trips abroad. New and exotic surroundings became the source of her inspiration and a catalyst for the development of both technique and subject matter. Although Redpath returned from her continental expeditions brimming with ideas for landscapes, street scenes and church interiors, as many as half the paintings that she exhibited throughout the 1950s were still lifes, featuring objects on a table, plants and flowers. Redpath arranged her still lifes on the floor, making the viewer more aware of the form of the objects – a vase or a teacup appear much rounder when viewed from above. Instead of ellipses, one sees circles.

This is an exploration of form and not merely a mannerism. Redpath was able to paint a perfectly modelled object with no trace of highlights or exaggerated shadows.

On painting trips to Fife in the late 1950s she used to curse the bright sunny days, declaring that strong sunlight destroyed form and local colour. She preferred dull weather with no shadows, when colour becomes a property of form and not of light. She was developing an essentially intellectual approach to painting. A great deal more thought than actual activity was going into her oil paintings. The gouaches and colour notes would be executed quickly, on the spot, in order to capture the "essentials", but the painting of the oil itself is reminiscent of the description of Cézanne at work – several minutes between each brush stroke, occupied by the painter staring at his subject.

Further confirmation of this contemplative approach is found in the short film of Redpath produced by the BBC in 1963: "… sometimes I just simply see the picture without having anything actual in front of me. I see it as a completed picture and that means that half the picture is done for me. I see it in colour and shape." Redpath worried that she would become old-fashioned. She witnessed a "happening" in Edinburgh in the late 1950s, where an artist was doing some action painting that included all sorts of random ways of putting paint on canvas short of riding a bicycle over it. According to friends, the subsequent loosening of her technique was not unconnected with that experience. Her concern with keeping up to date with the latest techniques did not mean that she was prepared to compromise on sound and correct methods. She used "degreasing", which involved putting the paint on blotting-paper to drain out the poppy oil and give it a dry, chalky appearance. She hardly ever varnished her oil paintings, preferring to see them "in the raw". For this reason the exhibition oils were always under glass. Another of her methods for getting texture and rough surface was to scour the paint with what was described as a small piece of chain-mail. Individual, adventurous, colourful and independent, Redpath's art was an extension of her personality and the same descriptions apply to both. When she died, at the age of 69, her painting was as fresh and inventive as ever.

PATRICK BOURNE

Rée, Anita
German painter, 1885–1933

Born in Hamburg, 9 February 1885. Studied in Hamburg under Arthur Siebelist, 1905–10; shared studio with Franz Nölken and Friedrich Ahlers-Hestermann from 1910; studied in Paris under Fernand Léger, 1912. Freelance artist in Hamburg from 1913. Founder-member, Hamburg Secession, 1919. Study trip to Positano, Italy, 1922–5. Moved to Sylt, 1932. Committed suicide in Kampen, Sylt, 12 December 1933.

Principal Exhibitions

Individual
Kunsthaus Lochte, Hamburg: 1919
Schabbelhaus, Lübeck: 1921
Galerie Commeter, Hamburg: 1922, 1925
Versmannshaus, Hamburg: 1926
Kabinett Kunde, Hamburg: 1927

Group
Galerie Commeter, Hamburg: 1913
Kunsthalle, Hamburg: 1917–19, 1923–4
Premier Salon International d'Art, Geneva: 1920
Grosse Kunstausstellung, Dresden: 1921
Liljevalchs Konsthall, Stockholm: 1922 (*Nyare tysk konst* [Recent German art]), 1930 (*Tysk konst under tva sekler* [German art over two centuries])
Albrecht Dürer-Verein und Kunstverein, Nuremberg: 1927
Galerie Neumann and Galerie Nierendorf, Berlin: 1928
Kunsthalle, Göteborg: 1931
Kunstverein, Hamburg: 1932

Bibliography
Alexandra Povòrina, *Alma del Banco, Anita Rée*, exh. cat., Kunsthaus, Hamburg, 1966
Carl Georg Heise and Hildegard Heise, eds, *Anita Rée: Ein Gedenkbuch von ihren Freunden*, Hamburg, c.1968
Claudia Heuer, *Anita Rée: Hamburg, 1885–1933: Ein vorläufiges Werkverzeichnis*, MA thesis, Universität Regensburg, 1982
Maike Bruhns, "Anita Rée und Carl Einstein: Nachrichten aus dem Nachlass einer Malerin", *Kritische Berichte*, xiii/4, 1985, pp.26–8
——, *Anita Rée: Leben und Werk einer Hamburger Malerin, 1885–1933*, Hamburg: Verein für Hamburgische Geschichte, 1986
Künstlerinnen der Hamburger Sezession, 1919–1933: Alma del Banco, Dorothea Maetzel-Johannsen, Alexandra Povòrina, Anita Rée, Gretchen Wohlwill, exh. cat., Patriotische Gesellschaft von 1765, Hamburg, 1988
Die jüdischen Maler der Hamburgischen Sezession, exh. cat., Altonaer Museum, Hamburg, 1989

Manuscript collection is in the Archiv der Kunsthalle, Hamburg.

Anita Rée's work is largely unknown to the general public, although she was one of the early representatives of the Neue Sachlichkeit (New Objectivity) in the 1920s and contributed substantially to the development of modern painting in Germany. Her main subjects were portraits and figures, mostly of women and children.

After studying plein-air painting in Hamburg with Arthur Siebelist, she left to share a studio with his former pupils Friedrich Ahlers-Hestermann and Franz Nölken. They had studied with Matisse in Paris and introduced Rée to French painting. Disappointed by her relationship with Nölken, Rée went to Paris herself in 1912–13 to study painting with Fernand Léger. Again in Hamburg, she worked independently, living in modest economic circumstances. She used the simplified painting technique she had learned in Paris in depictions of Agnes, the Rée family's domestic servant (*Agnes II*, 1913; oil on canvas; private collection, Frankfurt am Main, repr. Bruhns 1986). The "statuesque repose" of the figure is characteristic of this series and of almost all her later works. Fear, insecurity, hunger and misery are expressed in her depictions of figures reflecting World War I (*Blowing Bubbles*, before 1919; destr. 1943; *Pierrot*, before 1920; untraced, *ibid.*; *Blue Woman*, 1919; private collection, Hamburg, *ibid.*; all oil on canvas). In the circle of Margit Durrieu, Pauli or Ida Dehmel she met patrons and artists including Gretchen Wohlwill, Alma del Banco and Franz Radziwill and made a name for herself as a portraitist of Hamburg society. A founder and jury member of the Hamburg Secession, to which she belonged until its dissolution in 1933, she sharpened her critical sense confronting contemporary artistic movements, mainly Expressionism, with which she experimented in her own work (*Incubus & Primus in amicia*, no date; pen, ink and watercolour; Galerie Herold, Hamburg).

From 1922 to 1925 Rée lived in Italy, in Positano, a fishing village on the mountainous Amalfi coast, whose picturesque romanticism exerted a magical attraction for German artists in the 1920s. The landscape, the light and the cubist southern architecture, which accorded with her preference for geometrical compositions, changed her painting (*Bridge near Positano*, 1922–5; watercolour; Museen für Kunst- und Kulturgeschichte, Lübeck). In her treatments of Italian subjects she repeatedly juxtaposed the irregularity of nature with the strict geometry of architecture, and takes up the metaphysical in her cityscapes (*Casa Ferdinando con Città Morta* and *White Trees*; both 1922–5; oil on canvas; untraced, *ibid.*): "Her Positano is a magic, secretive experience in which the exterior

Rée: *Teresina*, 1922–5; Hamburger Kunsthalle, Hamburg

appearance of the objects reflects time, culture and not least nature" (*ibid.*, p.88). According to contemporary art critics she was one of the "major modern German painters" (*ibid.*, p.105). The most important phase of her artistic development occurred during her stay in Positano when her personal "neo-objective" style matured (*Teresina*, 1922–5; see illustration). She described it as the happiest period of her life.

A crucial factor for this was her relationship with the artist and bookseller Gottfried Selle, whom she met in Positano. Like all her relationships with men, this one failed, soon after her return to Hamburg in 1925. Although Rée never commented openly on this, a homoerotic interest in women is suggested in such pictures as *Couple/Two Roman Heads* (1922–5; oil; untraced, *ibid.*) and *Vision of St Antony of Padua* (1930; two panels, oil on wood; private collection).

In Hamburg Rée taught painting and executed portraits of public personalities. Despite well-paid commissions, her living and working conditions deteriorated. The commission for the monumental mural *Wise and Foolish Virgins* (1929; Staatliche Hauswirtschafts- und Gewerbeschule, Uferstrasse, Hamburg; destr. 1937) proved an additional physical and psychic strain. It initiated her occupation with themes from the Old Testament, which culminated in the triptych for the church of Saint Ansgar.

In spite of her artistic success, Rée was unable to find a close personal relationship and suffered from loneliness. After a last failed relationship with the Hamburg merchant Carl Vorwerk, she fled to Sylt in 1932. Fear and loneliness are evident in her self-portraits from this period (*Self-Portrait*, 1930; oil on canvas, Hamburger Kunsthalle, Hamburg; *Self, Half Facing Left with Earring*, 1932–3; private collection, Hamburg, *ibid.*). From 1916, and especially after her flight from Hamburg, she contemplated suicide. Her Sylt landscapes devoid of people and her depictions of distressed animals (*Flock of Starving Sheep in the Snow*; watercolour; private collection, Hamburg, *ibid.*) are considered to be cryptic psychogrammes. Her feeling of threat became concrete in 1933 with the seizure of power by the National Socialists, who termed her art "degenerate" and would have persecuted her for being Jewish. Rée did not have the strength to emigrate, and she committed suicide.

Marina Sassenberg

Reeves, Ruth
American textile artist, 1892–1966

Born in Redlands, California, 14 July 1892. Studied at Pratt Institute, Brooklyn, New York, 1910–11; California School of Design, San Francisco, 1911–13; Art Students League, New York, 1913–15; Académie Moderne, Paris, intermittently 1922–8. Worked as a batik artist and as designer and illustrator for the trade paper *Women's Wear* in New York, London and Paris, 1917–28. Began printing and exhibiting textiles, 1928. Trip to Guatemala, 1934. National co-ordinator, *Index of American Design*, 1936. Married Donald Baker, 1922 (second marriage); three daughters, born 1924, 1928 and 1932. Recipient of Guggenheim fellowship, 1940. Lived in India from 1956. Died in New Delhi, 23 December 1966.

Principal Exhibitions
American Designers Gallery, New York: 1928, 1929
Rhoss Museum, Göteborg: 1930 (*Amerikansk konstslojd* [American handicrafts])
American Federation of Art: 1930 (*Decorative Metals and Cotton Textiles*, touring)
W. & J. Sloane Company, New York: 1930 (*Contemporary Textiles*, touring)
Minneapolis Institute of Arts: 1930 (individual)
American Union of Decorative Artists (AUDAC), Brooklyn Museum, NY: 1931 (*Modern Industrial and Creative Art*)
M.H. de Young Museum, San Francisco: 1932 (individual)
RCA Building, New York: 1935 (*Guatemalan Exhibition of Textiles and Costumes Collected by Miss Ruth Reeves*, touring)
Addison Gallery, Andover, MA: 1947 (*Textile Panorama*)

Selected Writings
"The modern designer's 'primitive' sources", *Baltimore Museum of Art Quarterly*, iii, Spring 1938, pp.2–10
"Art forms in architecture: Murals", *Architectural Record*, lxxxviii, October 1940, pp.73–6
"Pre-Columbian fabrics of Peru", *Magazine of Art*, xlii, March 1949, pp.103–7
Cire-perdue Casting in India, New Delhi: Crafts Museum, 1962

Bibliography
Exhibition of Contemporary Textiles, exh. cat., W. & J. Sloane Company, New York, 1930
Stark Young, "Decorative textiles by Ruth Reeves", *American Magazine of Art*, no.22, January 1931, pp.31–3
Blanche Naylor, "Textiles derived from paintings", *Design*, no.33, February 1932, pp.214–19
Guatemalan Exhibition of Textiles and Costumes Collected by Miss Ruth Reeves under the Auspices of Carnegie Institution of Washington, exh. cat., RCA Building, New York, and elsewhere, 1935
Harry V. Anderson, "Ruth Reeves", *Design*, no.35, March 1936, pp.24–6, 39
At Home in Manhattan: Modern Decorative Arts, 1925 to the Depression, exh. cat., Yale University Art Gallery, New Haven, 1983
Alastair Duncan, *American Art Deco*, New York: Abrams, and London: Thames and Hudson, 1986
Mary Schoeser, *Fabrics and Wallpapers*, New York: Dutton, and London: Bell and Hyman, 1986
Nicola J. Shilliam, "Emerging identity: American textile artists in the early twentieth century", *Early Modern Textiles: From Arts and Crafts to Art Deco*, exh. cat., Museum of Fine Arts, Boston, 1993, pp.28–44
Whitney Blausen, "Ruth Reeves: A pioneer in American Design", *Surface Design Journal*, xix, Winter 1995, pp.5–6, 36

Ruth Reeves was perhaps the most prominent textile artist to work in the USA between the late 1920s and the mid-1950s, breaking new ground in textile printing and design. In the 1920s she was among the first to explore the possibilities of hand-screen printing with vat dyes when both the technique and the medium were all but unknown and considered highly experimental. Her advances were not, however, confined to the technical.

Reeves trained as a painter and lithographer. When she began to print on cloth, she brought a painter's sensibility to a field that was considered an artistic backwater, not worthy of serious consideration. The first public exhibition of Reeves's prints was held in 1928 at the American Designers Gallery in New York. With her colleagues Henry Varnum Poor, Ilonka

Karasz, Donald Deskey and Paul Frankl, Reeves was a founding member of this co-operative gallery, established to provide a showcase for American artists working in the modern style.

Reeves: *Manhattan*, 1930; textile; Victoria and Albert Museum, London

Not since the batik revival of the late 1910s had contemporary textiles been presented as works of art. The design press took notice.

Reeves's work of the 1920s and early 1930s was invariably described by critics as witty, modern and above all as being truly representative of the American experience. Some of her most successful pieces incorporate vignettes from her own life or from the lives of her neighbours. *American Scene* (1930; Victoria and Albert Museum, London; Yale University Art Gallery, New Haven) contains images of a leisurely summer afternoon: a couple plays tennis; children swim in a pond; games of chess and bridge progress; Reeves and her family sit at a table, listening to the radio, or perhaps anticipating the Sunday roast. The autobiographical *South Mountain* (1928; repr. *Home and Field*, October 1930, p.54) is a modern, slightly tongue-in-cheek version of a *toile de Jouy*. A pot-bellied stove warms the kitchen where Reeves's infant daughter has her bath; two older children watch, awaiting their turn; Reeves's husband bathes the child, while Reeves herself looks on, bemused.

Throughout the 1920s critics debated whether a country of immigrants could possibly have a cohesive national style. Reeves glorified and romanticised the so-called American way of life during a period when profound national self-doubt lay just beneath a surface of jingoistic chauvinism. Moreover, at a time when textiles for interiors were largely confined to silk brocades and damasks for the wealthy and floral cretonnes for the rest, Reeves provided a refreshing alternative.

One of Reeves's best known and most widely published designs is *Manhattan* (1930; Victoria and Albert Museum; Whitworth Gallery, Manchester; Yale University Art Gallery; see illustration), commissioned by the W. & J. Sloane Company. *Manhattan* vibrates with energy, incorporating steam ships, aeroplanes and soaring views of skyscrapers, the quintessential symbol of American design and know-how. Here again, Reeves drew her inspiration from the world around her. In this respect she may have been influenced by Kenneth Hayes Miller, her former teacher at the Art Students League. Miller, whose other students included Reginald Marsh, Isabel Bishop (q.v.) and Edward Hopper, encouraged his students to research and record the contemporary scene. It was a lesson that Reeves learned well.

From 1922 to 1928 Reeves lived and worked in Paris, where she studied under Fernand Léger. His influence, as well as that of other contemporary French painters, can be seen in *Figures with Still Life* (1930; Victoria and Albert Museum; Cooper Hewitt Museum, New York; Yale University Art Gallery) and *Petit Dejeuner* and *Carneval* (both 1929; Yale University Art Gallery). Both *Figures with Still Life* and *Carneval* were conceived as pictorial wall hangings, meant to complement the modern furnishings and interiors designed by Deskey and Frankl. Such design journals as the *American Magazine of Art*, *Design* and *Good Furniture and Decoration* credited Reeves with bridging the gap between the fine and decorative arts. They all regularly reviewed her progress. That Reeves considered herself a modernist is without question, although she more often simply referred to herself as a contemporary American designer. She abhorred the textile industry's practice of reproducing historical designs that she felt had no meaning for the present. She saw herself as an artist whose experimental work in a contemporary idiom set a higher standard for the industry.

Reeves worked simultaneously in a variety of styles throughout her career. Her designs of 1932 for the interior of Radio City Music Hall, the wall covering for the main auditorium (Radio City Music Hall, Rockefeller Center, New York) and carpet for the grand foyer (Radio City Music Hall; Cooper-Hewitt Museum, New York), are superb examples of American Art Deco design. *Overlooking Kingston* (1934; Helen Louise Allen Textile Collection, University of Wisconsin, Madison; Cleveland Museum of Art) is one of five in a series of *Hudson River Prints*. Here Reeves used the Hudson River school of landscape painting as a point of departure for a group of semi-abstract pictorial textiles.

In 1934 Reeves was appointed a Carnegie Traveling Fellow to Guatemala. On her return to New York she exhibited a large collection of primarily abstract and geometric designs inspired by the textile traditions of highland Guatemala. In her introduction to the catalogue she expressed her conviction that the role of the artist is to make a deeply felt, personal response to one's source material. Reeves wrote frequently about the principles of good design, and this was a point she made again and again.

Ruth Reeves continued to be a leading textile designer throughout the 1940s and into the 1950s. Fashions in design change, however – the 1950s brought a new interest in the structure of cloth and in texture rather than pattern. Ruth Reeves turned 64 in 1956; she might have contemplated retirement. Instead, she applied to the Fulbright Foundation for a year's research in India to document vanishing craft techniques. The year turned into ten. She became Honorary Advisor to the office of the Registrar General of India, a position she held until her death in 1966.

WHITNEY BLAUSEN

Regina
Italian sculptor and graphic artist, 1894–1974

Born Regina Prassede Cassolo in Mede Lomellina, Pavia, 21 May 1894. Educated at a convent school in Pavia after father's early death; concentrated on music studies. Took a diploma at the Accademia di Brera, Milan; subsequently studied under the sculptor Giovanni Alloati in Turin. Married figurative painter Luigi Bracchi, c.1940. Lived in Milan until her death, 14 September 1974.

Principal Exhibitions

Individual
Galleria del Senato, Milan: 1931 (with Luigi Bracchi)
Libreria Salto, Milan: 1951
Mede Lomellina, Pavia: 1976 (retrospective)

Group
Palazzo della Permanente, Milan: 1928 (*Mostra regionale d'arte lombarda*)
Venice Biennale: 1934, 1936, 1938, 1940
Quadriennale d'Arte Contemporanea, Rome: 1935, 1939
Milan Triennale: 1936, 1951
Galleria Bompiani, Milan: 1951 (*Mostra storica dell'astrattismo*)

Libreria Salto, Milan: 1951 (*MAC e MAC Espace*)
Saletta dell'Elicottero, Milan: 1952 (*Materie plastiche in forme concrete*)
Galleria Gissi, Turin: 1952 (*Pittori concreti di Milano e Torino*)
Studio B, Milan: 1953 (*Mostra del MAC*)
Galleria del Fiore, Milan: 1955 (*MAC-Espace: Esperimenti sintesi delle arti*)
Parc de Saint-Cloud, Paris: 1955 (*Groupe Espace*)
Galleria Schettini, Milan: 1957 (*MAC: Rassegna nazionale di arte concreta*)
Galleria d'Arte di Brera, Milan: 1959 (*La donna nell'arte contemporanea*)
Galleria Minima, Milan: 1963 (*Proposta per un'evidenza dell'astrattismo italiano*)
Palazzo Sormani, Milan: 1969 (*F.T. Marinetti ed il Futurismo*)
Galleria Blu, Milan: 1970 (*Aeropittura futurista*)
Museo Poldi Pezzoli, Milan: 1972 (*Milano 70/70: Un secolo d'arte*)

Bibliography
Vanny Scheiwiller, *Regina*, Milan: All'insegna del pesce d'oro, 1971
Regina: Una scultrice d'avanguardia, exh. cat., Mede Lomellina, Pavia, 1976
Simone Weller, *Il complesso di Michelangelo*, Pollenza: La Nuova Foglia, 1976
Continuità dell'avanguardia in Italia, 2: Regina (1894–1974), exh. cat., Galleria Civica, Modena, 1979
L'altra metà dell'avanguardia, 1910–1940: Pittrici e scultrici nei movimenti delle avanguardie storiche, exh. cat., Palazzo Reale, Milan, and elsewhere, 1980
C. Belli, *Regina, nove sculture, quindici poesie inedite*, Milan: All'insegna del pesce d'oro, 1983
Regina: Sculture e disegni, exh. cat., Kooh-I-Noor Circolo Culturale, Milan, 1985
M. Barry Katz, "The women of Futurism", *Woman's Art Journal*, vii/2, 1986–7, pp.3–13
Costruzioni di luce, exh. cat., Casa del Mantegna, Mantua, 1990
S. Weller, "Lo spazio in Regina", *Noi donne*, 1990, pp.84–6
Regina, exh. cat., Castello, Sartirana Lomellina, 1991

A free spirit, released from the excessive compositional subtlety typical of the post-war period, Regina herself defined her artistic journey with a few words: "To look, to think ... it is always the true that inspires me with a more or less distant echo" (Scheiwiller 1971).

Some critics have seen Regina's first works, of the 1920s, as cautious, quasi-academic tests of plasticity, in which a conscientious naturalism is prominent, a result of her training in Turin and Milan, about which very little is known. This is apparent in *Heads* (1925–30; plaster; Comune di Mede Lomellina, Pavia). At the same time they recognise an approach to the work of Brancusi, particularly in the adherence to a new use of volume, essential and sculptural, as demonstrated in the delightful sculpture *Canary* (1925–30; plaster; Comune di Mede Lomellina). During these years Regina began to experiment with new materials and techniques that resulted in a lightening of her work, as demonstrated in the elegant line and freer, more sparingly-placed forms of some bas-reliefs, which emphasise her poetic sensibility.

It was the following decade, however, that marked the artist's maturity. Regina's rejection of traditional models and her willingness to experiment led her to invent light, airy forms, executed in slender sheet-metal, the profiles cut, etched, removed, folded or drilled – fragile figures occupying a realm between dream, memory and the observation of the everyday, a whole world between irony and fairy-tale, the whimsical forms created from plaster, yellow sandpaper, porcelain, rope, net or celluloid. Silvana Sinisi perceptively compared Regina's new working methods with "the dressmaker who tacks (bastes) the model" (Mantua 1990, p.8).

Unusual methods, uncommon materials: it is difficult to define Regina's relationship to the avant-garde; but her experiments undoubtedly emphasise an urgent need for renewal and modernity, demands that drove her to adhere to the precepts of Second Futurism. Forms such as *Aero-Sensitivity* and *Aviator's Lover* (both 1935; aluminium; Comune di Mede Lomellina) render in sculpture the sensations of a poetic moment for which traditional artistic language is inadequate.

Regina's works from this time must be seen in contexts that derive from Umberto Boccioni, from primitivism and from Cubism. This is demonstrated by her montages of sheets of aluminium, although her solutions, as in *Abyssinian Women* (1935; paper and pins; other versions in iron and aluminium; private collections), are nevertheless independent, spontaneous and very personal. In the mid-1930s Regina arrived at witty and elegant neo-Dadaist experiments, such as *Polenta and Fish* and *Happy Tree* (repr. Sartirana Lomellina 1991, pp.23 and 26), but, struck by her own audacity or perhaps by some criticism, she destroyed the works, and now only photographs remain.

In spite of the fact that Regina was influenced by Futurism – her works show clear references to the sculpture of Mino Rosso and to the painting of Fillia – and had even formally joined the Movement in 1934, signing, in the periodical *Sant'Elia*, the Manifesto for the 25th, her contacts with it were sometimes painful, and on an interior level she always remained on the margins of the movement. Although fascinated by the "cine-panoramic sense of flight" and "the intoxication of space and air", she interpreted these in a minimalist form. Her other artistic activities – she executed costumes for the avant-garde Teatro Arcimboldi in Milan, as well as models and masks, and produced a short abstract film – are also reflected in studies, in paper and in drawing, as in *Projects for the Land of the Blind* (1935; private collection, *ibid.*, p.60), and by her restless search for new expressive forms.

At the end of the 1930s Regina approached abstraction, although she was too independent to imitate the rigorous formalism of Piet Mondrian and Theo van Doesburg. Instead, her starting point was the careful observation of reality, and although the geometrical element seems to predominate, she always remained faithful to the rendering of natural forms, as exemplified by *Flower* (1947; plaster; Comune di Mede Lomellina) and *Spatial Sculpture* (1947; plaster, and later copy in marble; private collection, *ibid.*).

Soon after this, however, Regina freed herself from thematic superimpositions, allowing an attraction to a more geometric formalism. Her natural destination was the Milanese movement of MAC (Movimento Arte Concreta), founded in 1948 by Atanasio Soldati, Bruno Munari, Gillo Dorfles and Monnet. Here she could sharpen her research into formal purity and could reinvigorate her work with the use of new materials, from Plexiglas to Perspex to laminated plastics, participating in the first of the "Syntheses of the Arts" exhibitions, *Materie plastiche in forme concrete*, in 1952. This was the period of her structures in Plexiglas – white or transparent, yellow or green-blue – a material that permits new chromatic effects and compositions in which the object is dematerialised. The artist produced sharp and precise structures, which she transferred also into other, more traditional materials: plaster (*Sputnik*, 1952; private collection, *ibid.*, p.77), iron (*Structures*, 1953; private collection, *ibid.*, p.76) and marble (*Little Theatre*, 1954; private collection, repr. Scheiwiller 1971). In these last works Regina's dominant concern – the relationship between form and space – is emphasised. Lightweight structures are animated and revolve according to the vibrations of the atmosphere, and are modified and reinvented by light. She thus exploited the transparency of the medium and perceptual phenomena, affirming: "my structures almost always have an unstable equilibrium". Subsequently, in the years 1960–70, she turned to themes of space, such as astronauts, realised with a clarity and rigour through the intelligent application of her feeling for geometry.

Regina is also important for her drawings (Comune di Mede Lomellina), in which she demonstrated a multitude of interests and original starting points: from her drawings of the 1940s, in which she sought to discover the "geometry of flowers"; to her kinetic drawings of the 1950s, preparations for sculpture; to her drawing-collages of the 1960s, using luminous paper; to the famous ones expressing the sounds of the countryside; and to those of the late 1960s on shiny or graph paper studying the language of canaries – all demonstrate a passionate experimentalism.

It is almost impossible to draw an unambiguous conclusion about Regina's personality and work. One could remember either the coherence or the unpredictability of her character; her imaginative sensitivity that was always linked to the real and the everyday; the original solutions and the unusual manual handling of the materials. It is apt, in closing, to quote her: "I have always been in the avant-garde, at least in the way I think; since I was a young girl I had so much faith in progress that I was convinced I would not die. Even today, the hope remains ..." (Scheiwiller 1971, p.7). A large collection of Regina's works and drawings was left to the Comune of Mede Lomellina by Regina's husband, and this now constitutes a permanent display.

LUCIA CAPPELLOZZA

Rego, Paula (Figueiroa)
Portuguese painter and printmaker, 1935–

Born in Lisbon, 26 January 1935. Extra-mural student at Slade School of Fine Art, London, 1952–6. Lived in Ericeira, Portugal, with painter Victor Willing, 1957–62; married him, 1959; three children (one son, two daughters) born 1956, 1959 and 1961; husband died 1988. Divided time between London and Portugal, 1962–75; settled in London, 1976. Selected by Roland Penrose for inclusion in *Six Artists* exhibition at Institute of Contemporary Arts, London, 1965. Represented Portugal, 1969 and 1976, and Britain, 1985, São Paulo Bienal. Visiting lecturer in painting, Slade School of Fine Art, 1983; Senior fellow, Royal College of Art, London, 1989; first National Gallery Associate Artist, 1990. Recipient

Rego: *Joseph's Dream*, 1990; acrylic on paper on canvas; 183 × 122 cm.; private collection

of honorary degree, Winchester School of Art, 1992. Lives in London.

Selected Individual Exhibitions

Sociedade Nacional de Belas-Artes, Lisbon: 1965
Galeria III, Lisbon: 1978, 1989, 1990
AIR Gallery, London: 1981
Edward Totah Gallery, London: 1982–3 (*Girl and Dog*, touring), 1984, 1985, 1987
Art Palace, New York: 1985
Fundação Calouste Gulbenkian, Lisbon, and Serpentine Gallery, London: 1988 (retrospective)
Marlborough Graphics Gallery, London: 1989, 1992
Galeria III, ARCO, Madrid: 1989
British Council touring exhibition in Europe: 1990–91 (*Nursery Rhymes*)
South Bank Centre, London: 1990–92 (*Nursery Rhymes*, touring)
National Gallery, London: 1991–2 (*Tales from the National Gallery*, touring)
Marlborough Fine Art, London: 1992, 1994

Bibliography

Andrea Hill, "Paula Rego", *Artscribe*, no.37, October 1982, pp.33–7
Paula Rego: Paintings, 1984–5, exh. cat., Edward Totah Gallery, London, 1985
Paula Rego, exh. cat., Fundação Calouste Gulbenkian, Lisbon, and Serpentine Gallery, London, 1988
Sarah Kent, "Rego's girls", *Art in America*, lxxvii, 1989, pp.158–63, 205
Alberto de Lacerda, "Paula Rego e Londres", *Colóquio, Artes*, no.83, 1989, pp.18–23
Paula Rego: The Nursery Rhymes, exh. cat., South Bank Centre, London, and elsewhere, 1990
Sanda Miller, "Paula Rego's *Nursery Rhymes*", *Print Quarterly*, viii, 1991, pp.53–60
Hector Obalk, *Paula Rego*, Kyoto: Kyoto Shoin, 1991
Paula Rego: Tales from the National Gallery, exh. cat., National Gallery, London, and elsewhere, 1991
John McEwen, *Paula Rego*, New York: Rizzoli, 1992; London: Phaidon, 1993 (contains bibliography)
Paula Rego: Peter Pan and Other Stories, exh. cat., Marlborough Fine Art, London, 1992
Ruth Rosengarten, "Tales from the National Gallery: A reading of four recent works by Paula Rego", *London Magazine*, xxxii/9–10, 1992–3, pp.62–76
Paula Rego: Dog Woman, exh. cat., Marlborough Fine Art, London, 1994
Marina Warner, ed., *Nursery Rhymes*, London: Thames and Hudson, 1994
—, ed., *Wonder Tales*, London: Chatto and Windus, 1994

Paula Rego first received widespread critical attention at the time of her first important solo exhibition in London, held at the Serpentine Gallery in 1988. Most comment was because her paintings were uncompromisingly figurative, not simply in a representational sense, but also in a narrative one. For decades, the idea that paintings could be used to tell stories had been seen as a kind of treason against the modernist cause, yet this exhibition included large-scale works with a traditional illusionistic picture space, which represented characters who were taking part in a story. This was at a time when painting was dominated by the so-called Neo-expressionists, such as Georg Baselitz and Jack Clemente, who were being seen as the successors to the "old guard", those figurative painters grouped around the senior figure of Francis Bacon. Compared to these artists, the spatial and narrative clarity of Rego's work

was as unexpected as it was impressive, demonstrating that an artist was under no obligation to be constrained by fashionable dictates.

Rego was born into an affluent Portuguese family in Lisbon. Memories of her childhood, of being brought up as a girl in a male-dominated Roman Catholic society, and of being looked after by servants, were to be of crucial importance to her work. She attended an English school in Portugal, after which she was sent to a finishing school in Kent, England, from which she discharged herself at the age of 17. That same year, 1952, she became a student at the Slade School of Fine Art, where she met and fell in love with fellow student Victor Willing, who was married, and in 1956 their first child was born. After Willing obtained a divorce, they married in 1959. Her work at this time shows strong affinities with Picasso, Joan Miró and especially Jean Dubuffet, whose Art Brut she found particularly exciting. *Salazar Vomiting the Homeland* (Fundação Calouste Gulbenkian, Lisbon) of 1960 has similarities with Picasso's *Dream and Lie of Franco*, with scrawly and expressive biomorphic figures in a political allegory (Salazar was Portugal's right-wing dictator, who was to be overthrown in a bloodless revolution in 1975).

In 1961 Rego had her first professional success. The Gulbenkian Foundation in Lisbon selected three collages for their exhibition *Segunda exposição de artes plásticas*. Collage was an important technique for her at this time: the artist would cut up her own drawings and paintings and rearrange them to make new work. In 1962 she was awarded a two-year Gulbenkian scholarship, living with her husband in Portugal during the summer and in London for the rest of the year. In 1965 she had her first solo exhibition, at the Sociedade Nacional de Belas-Artes, Lisbon, where she was recognised as being one of Portugal's most important artists. *Stray Dogs (The Dogs of Barcelona)* (repr. McEwen 1992, pl.67) was a central work, inspired by a report that the authorities of Barcelona had decided to rid the city of its stray dogs by feeding them with poisoned meat. Executed in collage and oil on canvas, the picture writhes with action, with shapes and forms that evoke grotesquely distorted animals and giant flies. At 1.85 metres across, the work has the scale of a mural. The coarseness and rawness of its appearance owes more to graffiti than to any fine art tradition. Asked in an interview to explain her artistic line of descent, she replied that she could see none: "The reason is perhaps that I get inspiration from things that have nothing to do with painting: caricatures, items from newspapers, sights in the street, proverbs, nursery rhymes, children's games and songs, nightmares, desires, terrors."

In 1969, when she represented Portugal at the São Paolo Bienal, collage was still her favoured way of working. By the early 1970s she had begun to work in the more direct medium of gouache, producing a series of works entitled *Contos populares portuguêsas*, which were inspired by Portuguese folktales. The most notable development is that the figures and characters, rather than deriving from Dubuffet or Miró, are now immediately accessible to an audience unfamiliar with the artistic conventions of the 20th century. For example, *Two Men Separated by a River of Blood* (1975; *ibid.*, pl.85) shows two tall cliffs. On top of each sits a man, one of whom is blindfolded. Beneath them and between them a red river flows towards a distant horizon. The picture space perhaps owes something to Salvador Dalí, with Rego turning her back on the pictorial conventions of modernism that had dictated the appearance of her earlier work.

The break was not immediate, however, for several powerful collages were produced during the late 1970s and early 1980s, among them the *Annunciation* of 1981 (*ibid.*, pl.90), a traditional theme that has the archangel Gabriel pieced together as a nightmarish monster. The much smaller *Red Monkey* paintings, which were started in the same year, were of much greater significance. Made in acrylic on paper, they show a series of animals, including a lion, a bear, a rabbit and the red monkey himself, who enact a series of stories, with titles such as the *Red Monkey Beats His Wife* and *Wife Cuts Off Red Monkey's Tail* (*ibid.*, pls 96 and 97). The animals take on human characteristics, combining comic behaviour with alarming violence.

A series of much larger sized works followed, made in acrylic on paper laid down on canvas. These included the *Opera* series, where stories from the opera provided subjects of conflict, desire and human emotions, which were represented with caricatured animals and humans. Finally, there is the *Proles' Wall* (1984; Fundação Calouste Gulbenkian), over 12 m. long and covered with literally hundreds of characters, including dogs, bears, camels and flamingos, acting out comedies and tragedies, including rape, murder and decapitation. Rego's fascination with complex, even chaotic compositions continued with the *Vivian Girls* paintings of 1984 (*ibid.*, pls 126–8, 130). The idea came from her interest in the work of Henry Darger, a Chicago hospital orderly, whose "outsider" novel about a gang of unruly and subversive girls living on a planet ruled by soldiers had been recently discovered after his death.

Tragically, Rego's husband Vic had been diagnosed in 1967 as suffering from multiple sclerosis. During the mid-1980s he became progressively more disabled and Rego spent more and more time nursing him. This period in her life is represented by a series of extremely personal works, with the group title of *Girl and Dog* (*ibid.*). These are acrylic paintings on paper that show a young girl looking after a dog, feeding it, washing it, shaving it. Vic died in 1988, earlier in the year of the Serpentine exhibition, which finally established Rego's reputation as an artist of great originality, conviction and force. The *Red Monkey* and *Girl and Dog* series were shown, as well as several powerful and large-scale works, such as *Little Murderess* (1987; *ibid.*, pl.154), the *Cadet and His Sister* (1988; *ibid.*, pl.160) and *Soldier's Daughter* (1987; *ibid.*, pl.159). These showed a move away from the caricature style of the *Proles' Wall* and the *Vivian Girls* by featuring figures that had all been drawn from life in the studio. The drawings were then used to make the final paintings, where the figures engage with one another in complex and subtle dramas. The theme of powerful women is common to them all. The soldier's daughter plucks a dead goose, the cadet's sister ties his shoelace for him, a policeman's daughter cleans her father's boot with her arm thrust symbolically inside it. The figures are squat and stocky, suggestive of physical, sexual and psychological power.

Rego's continuing success was marked by the purchase of *The Dance* (1989) by the Tate Gallery, London. This painting, romantic, wistful and nostalgic, was started before her husband's death and completed afterwards. She was then invited by the National Gallery in London to become its first Associate Artist, with the brief of making work directly inspired by the old masters in the Gallery's collection. Given a studio on the premises, she at first found this a daunting prospect, not least of being a woman suddenly placed among an almost exclusively masculine tradition, but the works produced during this time confirmed her ever-growing status. *Joseph's Dream* (1990; see illustration), for example, is a reworking of a 17th-century altarpiece, the *Vision of St Joseph* by Philippe de Champaigne, and can be interpreted as an allegory of a female artist in a man's world. A version of Champaigne's painting is on an easel, in an unfinished state, only now being painted by a female artist, who has firmly blocked in the archangel Gabriel and lightly indicated the Virgin Mary. Rego replaced the Joseph of the original picture by the heavy form of a sleeping man. The small image behind his head shows a rhino with its horn removed, symbolic of his powerlessness. The woman artist seems to receive her inspiration and power from the angel she has just painted and is completely in control, having claimed as her own the production of a man and repainted it for her own purposes.

Also resulting from Rego's time as the National Gallery Associate Artist is a three-part work, displayed as a mural, entitled *Crivelli's Garden*. This was painted for the Gallery's new Sainsbury Wing Restaurant, which opened in 1991. The three paintings hang together and appear to be one continuous work. A traditional Renaissance perspective scheme is used, into which are placed many of the characters who may be found in Italian Renaissance altarpieces, notably those by Carlo Crivelli. Rego playfully imagined them as existing in Crivelli's garden, where he could go and find the ones that he needed to paint in his pictures. Some of these figures are depicted as real, some exist as sculptures in the garden and others are represented on illusionistically painted tiles. These *azulejos* are a popular and ancient Portuguese folk art. Portugal has no "high art" tradition but is rich in folk art, the directness and immediacy of which has always been an important influence on Rego. The common theme that Rego depicts in *Crivelli's Garden* is that of the triumphant woman. St Catherine triumphs over the man who persecuted her, a heavy figure of Delilah crouches over the defeated Samson, a young Judith drops what the viewer imagines to be the severed head of Holofernes into a bag held by her maid. Images from Classical mythology also appear. Diana has transformed Actaeon into a stag, and Odysseus' men have been turned into pigs by the enchantress Circe. One whole panel is devoted to the Virgin Mary. A modern version of the Visitation is painted, as the young Virgin is whispered to by St Elizabeth. Behind them, on the blue *azulejos*, are shown many other traditional scenes from the life of the Virgin. But perhaps the point of these scenes is that Christ is nowhere represented. Mary, the virgin mother, is the crucial figure. After the clarity of the National Gallery work, Rego experienced the desire to regain some of the disjointed and chaotic qualities of her earlier work. Pictures such as *Caritas* are once again jammed with incident but now the figures originate in drawings made from models.

Rego is also highly active as a printmaker. Her *Nursery Rhymes* series reinterpreted traditional English children's themes such as *Baa Baa Black Sheep* and *Little Miss Muffet* into scenes of sinister and frightening implications, and after she finished her time at the National Gallery, she produced a series of etchings on the subject of *Peter Pan*. A change in medium resulted in a set of large drawings in coloured pastel, entitled *Dog Woman*, which were shown in 1994. This is a series of individual studies, made from life, with the model acting in various roles: for example, scavenging or preening. Many are deeply disturbing and can be understood as studies in mental illness that have a precedent in the work of Géricault; others are symbolic of the everyday lives of women, and although no men are seen, their presence and the effect they can have on women's lives are strongly implied.

COLIN WIGGINS

Remedios *see* Varo

Reynolds, Frances *see* Academies of Art survey

Rice, Anne Estelle
American painter and illustrator, 1877–1959

Born in Conshohocken, Pennsylvania, 11 June 1877. Received general degree and certificate in decorative painting and applied design from School of Industrial Art of the Pennsylvania Museum, Philadelphia, 1897; studied at Pennsylvania Academy of the Fine Arts, first terms of 1899–1900 and 1902–3. Active as a magazine illustrator in Philadelphia, c.1897–1905. In Paris, 1905–13; produced illustrations for fashion commentary and Wanamaker advertising in the Philadelphia *North American* and for Wanamaker magazine *La Dernière Heure à Paris*. Member of J.D. Fergusson's circle from 1907. Drawings published in British magazine *Rhythm*, 1911–13. Settled in London after marriage to critic O. Raymond Drey, 1913; son born 1919. Sociétaire, 1910, and juror, 1912, Salon d'Automne, Paris. Died in London, 20 September 1959.

Principal Exhibitions
Salon d'Automne, Paris: 1908–13
Pennsylvania Academy of the Fine Arts, Philadelphia (watercolour): 1909
Salon de la Union Internationale des Beaux-Arts, des Lettres, des Sciences et de l'Industrie, Paris: 1910
Salon des Indépendants, Paris: 1911–12
Women's International Art Club, Grafton Galleries, London: 1911
London Salon of the Allied Artists Association: 1911–13, 1917
Baillie Gallery, London: 1911, 1913 (both individual)
Cologne Sonderbund: 1912 (special section devoted to *Rhythm* artists)
Stafford Gallery, London: 1912 (*Rhythm* group)
Leeds City Arts Club: 1913 (*Post-Impressionism*)
Doré Galleries, London: 1913 (*Post-Impressionist and Futurist Exhibition*)
Society of Independent Artists, New York: 1917
London Group: 1924, 1926, 1952
Leicester Gallery, London: 1944–55
Middleton Hall, University of Hull: 1969 (touring retrospective)

Selected Writings
"Les Ballets Russes", *Rhythm*, ii, August 1912, pp.106–10
"Memories of Katherine Mansfield", *Adam: International Review*, 1963–5, pp.76–85 (article completed 1959)

Bibliography
Holbrook Jackson, "'Personal expression in paint': The work of Estelle Rice", *Black and White*, 11 March 1911, pp.340–41
Michael T.H. Sadler, "Fauvism and a Fauve", *Rhythm*, i, Summer 1911, pp.14–18
Huntly Carter, *The New Spirit in Drama and Art*, London: Frank Palmer, 1912; New York: Kennerley, 1913
"Tis" [Charles Mariott], "About Anne Estelle Rice", *Colour*, xi, August 1919, pp.2–6
Anne Estelle Rice (1879–1959), exh. cat., Middleton Hall, University of Hull, and elsewhere, 1969
Malcolm Easton, "The meaning of 'rhythm'", *Apollo*, lxxxix, 1969, p.235
——, "The art of Anne Estelle Rice", *Connoisseur*, clxxii, December 1969, pp.300–04
Anne Estelle Rice, exh. cat., Annexe Gallery, London, 1978
Colour, Rhythm and Dance: Paintings and Drawings by J.D. Fergusson and His Circle in Paris, exh. cat., Glasgow Art Gallery and Museum, and elsewhere, 1985
Carol A. Nathanson, "Anne Estelle Rice: Theodore Dreiser's 'Ellen Adams Wrynn'", *Woman's Art Journal*, xiii/2, 1992–3, pp.3–11
Anne Estelle Rice, exh. cat., Emscote Lawn, Warwick, 1995

Anne Estelle Rice created a body of Fauve work that attracted considerable critical attention in Britain and France before World War I. Before the late 1970s, her efforts were largely overlooked, despite increasing attention paid to a wide range of early abstractionists and women artists in general. This neglect can be traced both to the loss of a large portion of important earlier paintings and to perceptions of her contribution based largely on her post-Paris activity, particularly the late paintings of the 1940s and 1950s that comprise the bulk of her work to have come on the art market. This late work reflects many of Rice's original concerns as an artist and is in general very finely executed, but is not as avant-garde as her earlier painting.

After gaining a degree from the School of Industrial Art of the Pennsylvania Museum in 1897, Rice established herself in Philadelphia as an illustrator, while pursuing additional coursework at the Pennsylvania Academy. Rice's illustrations appeared in a number of popular journals, including the *Saturday Evening Post*, for which she created three cover designs, coveted work for any illustrator. The flat tones and emphatic contours of her work – lazily rhythmic or full of restless movement – drew on varied sources, including the art of Kate Greenaway (q.v.), Walter Crane and Alphonse Mucha and the noted Philadelphia illustrators Jessie Willcox Smith, Violet Oakley and Elizabeth Shippen Green. On assignment in Paris from late 1905 for the *North American*, Rice regularly sent back inventive drawings that illustrate fashion commentary written by Elizabeth Dryden. Many of the illustrations are poster-like, several containing newsprint backgrounds and overlapped planes that anticipate Cubist collage.

Rice: *Twilight*, 1910; oil on board; 33.7 × 41.3 cm.; collection of the artist's family, London

After meeting the Scottish artists J.D. Fergusson and S.J. Peploe in 1907, Rice became a member of Fergusson's Anglo-American circle in Paris and increasingly turned her attention to painting. Like her mentor Fergusson, with whom she also developed a romantic relationship, Rice depicted French and Mediterranean harbour and resort scenes and the activity in Parisian parks and cafés, as well as still-life subjects. In the early oils *Five o'clock Tea* (private collection, Hampshire) and *By the Sea, Saint-Georges-de-Didonne, France* (Timothy Hobson collection, Somerset), both of 1907–8, Rice follows Fergusson's lead, drawing inspiration from Manet and Impressionism to paint in a broken, sketchy manner, with whites, pastels and a few notes of vibrant colour deployed against darkened areas. By 1909 both artists had come fully under the influence of Post-Impressionist and Fauve art and were working with flattened, simplified forms and a more brilliant palette. In *Barges* (1910–11; artist's family collection, London) boats with electric red contours and interior planes of intense blue, green and rose stand out against a backdrop of opalescent water. The abstracted natural forms and decorative patterning in Rice's Paris paintings and illustrations often appear as circles, arcs or other curvilinear shapes. Ovals describe foliage in *Station at Montgeron* (1908 or 1909; private collection, London, repr. *Anne Estelle Rice*, exh. cat., Browse & Darby, London, 1980, cover), an oil that also reveals Rice's admiration (shared by Fergusson) for Cézanne's art in its thinly painted, patchy planes. Many of Rice's paintings were worked up from sketchbook drawings in conté crayon. Their bold, calligraphic contour lines and energetic hatching are reflected in the active brushwork of the paintings.

Rice's love of vibrant colour and decoratively repeated shapes, encouraged by her applied arts training and work in fashion illustration, was reinforced by contact with the extravagant costumes and decor of the Ballets Russes, which performed in Paris from 1909. Rice's fascination with the Ballets' romantic subjects also emerges in depictions of exotic women, nude or semi-nude, that she and Fergusson created from around 1910. Although clearly influenced by the seductive women of Symbolist art, figures in the drawing *Schéhérazade* (1911; repr. Sadler 1911, p.15) and the paintings *Nicoline* (1910–11; untraced, repr. as *Study* in Carter 1912, opposite p.44) and *A Bowl of Fruit* (1911; private collection, repr. Christie's, London, 6 November 1981, p.70) reflect Rice's personal belief in the primacy of the sensual. Gazing levelly at the viewer and smiling slightly, these women display directness and confidence, traits very much part of Rice's own nature. In 1912 Rice wrote an article on Diaghilev's troupe for *Rhythm*, the British "little magazine" to which she regularly contributed illustrations and of which Fergusson was art editor. Rice's expressionist viewpoint emerges clearly in this essay in which she emphasises the symbolic, emotive value of colours, shapes and linear rhythms.

Although Rice's art shows a strong kinship to that of Fergusson, her work distinguishes itself in a number of important respects, particularly from around 1910. Rice's palette gives a more central place to saturated primary and secondary colours, which she uses to structure striking warm/cool oppositions. Shapes in her work are simpler, more expansive and more often located close to the picture plane, features apparent in such paintings as *In the Harbour* (1910–11; untraced, repr. Jackson 1911, p.340), *Twilight* (1910; see illustration) and *Moonlight in the Harbour* (1910–11; artist's family collection). The writer Theodore Dreiser, in his story "Ellen Adams Wrynn", a fictionalised portrait of Rice and her relationship with Fergusson, emphasises the bolder look of Rice's art.

In late 1913 Rice married the British art and drama critic O. Raymond Drey and settled permanently in London. On the strength of her exhibition record in both Paris (where she had become a Sociétaire of the Salon d'Automne) and London, completion of a set of murals (now destroyed) for the Philadelphia Wanamaker's store and international press coverage of her work, including positive response by such British critics as Huntly Carter, Charles Lewis Hind and Frank Rutter, Rice anticipated continuing success. However, her career stagnated, with the exception of commissions to illustrate two de luxe limited editions of poetry for Cyril Beaumont's private press – one being D.H. Lawrence's *Bay* (1919) – and to create set and costume designs for two notable theatrical productions of the 1930s (*Jolly Roger*, a comic opera starring George Robey, opening in London at the Savoy Theatre in 1933, and *Basalik*, a drama starring Paul Robeson and presented at the Arts Theatre Club, London, in 1935). In an early effort to re-establish herself, Rice had returned to the USA in the winter of 1914–15, bringing with her the greater part of her Paris production. Not only did her stay in New York fail to produce significant results but, having difficulty in paying to transport the work back, she was forced to leave a great many paintings behind. Never retrieved by the artist, those works remain untraced (apart from eleven oils located by her widower in the late 1960s and a further seven paintings discovered in 1996).

The diminishment of Rice's career is attributable to several factors. She had arrived in Britain on the eve of World War I, at a time of decreasing opportunities for sales and exhibitions for artists. At the end of the war, Rice, then 42, had an infant son to look after. His care and the management of her home consumed much of her time and energy. In addition, after coming to Britain, Rice worked independently of any supportive artists' group, while her earlier association with Fergusson's circle earned her antagonism from the powerful Bloomsbury set. Her son grown up, from the 1940s she began exhibiting with greater frequency, primarily in group summer shows.

Such paintings as *The Sisters* (1913–14; Geoffrey Hassell collection, Cheltenham), which Rice produced around the time she settled in England, show increasing interest in Cubism, especially the colouristic, narrative-oriented type practised by the Gleizes-Metzinger circle. In work of the later 1910s to the mid-1920s, such as the portrait of *Katherine Mansfield* (1918; Te Papa Tongarewa Museum, Wellington, New Zealand) and *A Merry-Go-Round* (c.1924; private collection, repr. Hull 1969, no.12), Rice largely abandoned the planarities of Cubism but retained its geometric stylisations, creating delicately linear work very much in keeping with contemporary Art Deco aesthetics yet also expressing her personal taste for the decorative. From the later 1920s Rice returned to freer, more textured paint application. Colours, while more naturalistic than earlier, remain strikingly vivid, especially in the exuberant flower still lifes that Rice painted partly in reaction to the absence of sustained light and warmth in England, the subject of constant comment in her letters. Both interior subjects and landscape paintings from the mid-1940s and the 1950s – the latter including numerous Breton subjects from holidays in France – contain passages of roughly scumbled paint and forms delineated in an abrupt, stabbed-in style. A feeling of impatience pervades these works, of which a Breton beach scene painted around 1950–55 offers a good example (private collection, London, repr. Sotheby's, Glasgow, 7 February 1989, p.73). Rather than exploring her subject, it is as if Rice wishes to render what she already knows exists within it.

CAROL A. NATHANSON

Richier, Germaine

French sculptor, 1902–1959

Born in Grans, Bouches-du-Rhône, 16 September 1902. Entered the Ecole des Beaux-Arts, Montpellier, studying under Guigues, a former pupil of Rodin, 1920. Moved to Paris and became sole student of the sculptor Emile Bourdelle, 1926. Married (1) Swiss sculptor Otto Bänninger, 1926; divorced 1954; (2) poet René de Solier, 1954. Studio in Paris from 1930. Trips to Pompeii, 1935; Czechoslovakia, 1938. In Zürich at outbreak of World War II; decided to stay in Switzerland for the duration of the war, supporting herself by teaching. Divided time between France and Switzerland, 1946; then returned to Paris. Exhibited at New York World's Fair, 1939; Salon de Mai, Paris, 1947; Venice Biennale, 1950, 1952 and 1954. Recipient of Prix Blumenthal, 1936; medal of honour, Exposition Internationale, Paris, 1937; first prize for sculpture, São Paulo Bienal, 1951; Grand Prix, Exposition Universelle et Internationale, Brussels, 1958. Died in Montpellier, 31 July 1959.

Selected Individual Exhibitions
Galerie Max Kaganovitch, Paris: 1934
Kunstmuseum, Winterthur: 1942
Anglo-French Art Centre, London: 1947 (retrospective)
Galerie Maeght, Paris: 1948
Hanover Gallery, London: 1955
Musée National d'Art Moderne, Paris: 1956 (retrospective)
Martha Jackson Gallery, New York: 1957
Musée Picasso, Antibes: 1959 (retrospective)

Bibliography
Germaine Richier, exh. cat., Musée National d'Art Moderne, Paris, 1956
Aftermath: New Images of Man, 1945–1954, exh. cat., Barbican Art Gallery, London, 1982
Paris Post-War: Art and Existentialism, 1945–1955, exh. cat., Tate Gallery, London, 1993
Germaine Richier: Rétrospective, exh. cat., Fondation Maeght, Saint-Paul de Vence, 1996 (contains extensive bibliography)

Germaine Richier is perhaps the most powerful French sculptor in bronze of the 20th century. Astonishingly, after her retrospective of 1959 at the Musée Picasso, Antibes, her work was not revealed in full to an international public until the major retrospective of 1996 at the Fondation Maeght, Saint-Paul.

Richier insisted on a traditional training in a métier where her great precursor was Camille Claudel (q.v.); at first, at the Ecole de Beaux-Arts in Montpellier, she worked under Rodin's disciple and assistant Guigues; then in 1926 she went to Paris, and, through sheer perseverance and strength of character, insisted on becoming the only student of Rodin's successor, Emile Bourdelle – a man with links to Provence. During the pre-war period, already acknowleged as a successful professional artist, she made many talented portrait busts including that of *Françoise Cachin-Signac*, granddaughter of Paul Signac and later director of the Musées de France. None was so surprising, however, as a bust of *c*.1934 (repr. Saint-Paul 1996, no.1), in which all personal traits are masked with insect-like scales, anticipating not only her metamorphic mode of the 1940s but a fencer's mask (see *Woman Fencer*, 1943; *ibid.*, no.10).

The pure traditions of monumental sculpture with which she wished to be affiliated, in the line of Rodin and Bourdelle, was modified, in Richier's case, through her anti-Parisian, Provençal link with nature. This became particularly pronounced in her mature work, after World War II, in great contrast to her contemporary Alberto Giacometti, retrospectively the rival whose fame has unjustly eclipsed her reputation. His art, originating in Surrealism, was poised in the 1940s between existentialist tragedy and a sophisticated, urban absurd. His work of this period represented the body as attenuated almost to nothing – a thread of upright metal; or, to read his work more topically, a concentration camp survivor. In contrast, the most powerful – and fleshy – of Richier's male figures, *The Storm* (1948; Louisiana Museum of Modern Art, Humlebaek), used the very model, Nardone, now an old man, who had posed in his youth for Rodin's nude *Balzac* – the very paradigm of male potency and creativity. His female complement, *Hurricane Woman* (*L'Ouragane*) (1948–9; Louisiana Museum of Modern Art), actually subverted the gender of the masculine word "l'ouragan" in French, so that despite the show of strength and equality in Richier's work, its

Richier: *Le Diabolo*, 1950; bronze; Musée National d'Art Moderne, Centre Georges Pompidou, Paris

"femaleness" was often directly challenging. Just as Richier would work with Rodin's models, she also worked with his foundries, Rodier, Valsuani and Susse, and embraced both the hard physical labour and the Vulcanic imagery of worker with metal and fire. While the imagery of death in Giacometti's emaciated figures was perhaps starker than Richier's, her relationship to the male and female body and to issues of sexuality and death is equally fascinating. It is to Richier, rather than to Giacometti, that the tradition of post-war sculpture owes its characteristically "brutalised" surfaces, along with the configurations that would be baptised in Britain, after her London retrospective of 1947, as "the geometry of fear". Her scarified surfaces and the deathlike ugliness of some of her female creations countered notions of sculptural beauty with intimations of deformity and mutilation. Yet a unifying totality in tension with a totalising sense of desire in her work conformed perfectly to Sartre's later definition of the Beautiful.

Richier created explicit metaphors of nature's physical invasion of sculpture. In *The Forest* (1946; Fondation Marguerite et Aimé Maeght, Saint-Paul) a disturbing metamorphosis occurs: Richier cast twigs and branches as arms and limbs; leaves were pressed into the wet clay to leave their silhouettes prior to casting. Nature invaded the monument – and the monument would find its home in nature, leaving Giacometti's city square. *Praying Mantis* (1946) represents, upright and deathlike, the insect celebrated by the Surrealists as a token of female sexual power: she devours the male after copulation. Figures such as *The Ant* (1953) evoke both creativity and entrapment with their weblike imagery – ambivalently always, because the spinner, one of the three Fates, is a primeval image of female power. In the aftermath of the death camps and Hiroshima, the idea of a reversal of evolution, the degenerating of the human through mammal and bat to bird and insect forms, was a powerful metaphor in Richier's work, not only of nature, but of regression to a more bestial universe.

It was this element of regression and decay that caused fear and repulsion in Richier's *Crucifix* for the church of Assy in 1950. The Dominicans created a modern, ecumenical church for this sanatorium village in the Haute-Savoie, which involved courageous avant-garde commissions for church decoration from a spectrum of modern artists. On a poetic and etymological level, the fusion of body and bark in Richier's *Crucifix* evoked the metamorphosis of event to symbol. Yet Fernand Léger's magnificent mosaic portals were dubbed a blasphemy; Richier's *Crucifix* caused a riot. The so-called Angers tract was issued by the right-wing Integrists entitled "God shall not thus be mocked". It juxtaposed Richier's work with a typical head of Christ captioned "The Face of Christ? No!" "A scandal for Christian piety". The work was finally removed by the Bishop of Annecy. The Vatican launched an explicit attack in 1951.

After the Assy scandal Richier continued to work and exhibit through the 1950s. In contrast with the spikiness of the insect women, certain works achieved a solemn and monumental dignity. They remained deeply rooted in Richier's homeland of Provence, using objects found on the land and the seashore: *Shepherd of the Lands* (1951; Louisiana Museum of Modern Art) has his face made from a brick pierced and rubbed smooth by the sea. Richier's collaborations, with Hans Hartung, Zao Wou-ki, and in particular with Maria Elena Vieira da Silva (q.v.), the most important woman painter in the School of Paris, gave her work a new dimension, in which the notion of sculptural patina and base extended to embrace a painted enamel background. *Spinning Top/La Toupie*, which she made with Vieira da Silva, means equally in French "old frump" – the "woman" issue was never far away, despite Richier's evident prowess in her arduous and masculine métier. An expensive métier, too, but Richier was fiercely independent, and throughout her career supported herself by teaching when necessary. "Equality of achievement" was the yardstick for the talented woman in the early 1940s: for Simone Weil as farmworker, member of the Resistance and religious mystic, for Simone de Beauvoir in her novels, travelogues and scholarship, notably *The Second Sex* (1949), as for Richier in sculpture. Richier's sexuality in conjunction with her work challenged and disturbed conventional notions. Francis Ponge, the critic of Fautrier and Dubuffet, wrote in the special number of *Derrière le Miroir* (no.13, 1948) that accompanied Richier's show at the Galerie Maeght: "I dare not pronounce the word 'virility' as regards her work, although that's the most appropriate term." "Le sculpteur", "L'artiste" (both masculine

nouns) and Richier's "unfeminine" working ski outfit are balanced against "this universe, where woman is sovereign, which returns to origins", a clear case of confusion surrounding the classical dichotomy: male creativity versus female nature. André Pieyre de Mandiargues, the Provence-based, Surrealist-affiliated writer and follower of the Marquis de Sade, used sadism as a metaphor for Richier the sculptor, who kneads, twists, breaks, pokes and scratches prior to the "orgasm" of consummation between artist and sculpture as the work is deemed finished. He invoked Otto Weiniger's theories of the sadist who ornaments and then strips sculptures to humiliate them – but then hastened to make a compensatory statement: "I've never known a woman so good, so discreet, full of spiritual bounty, a force of nature" ("La main déchaînée", *Le Disque Vert*, no.3, 1953).

Richier's lack of the reputation she deserves beyond France (although complicated by litigation after her death) is not unconnected with the ambiguous reactions that her oeuvre provoked in critics. In contrast to Giacometti, whose works were not shown to a French public until 1951, Richier had become, by 1950, the focus of national controversy with her scarred, eroded *Crucifix* for the church of Assy. A comparison of the exhibiting history of the two artists between 1935 and 1955 would establish Richier's greater contemporary reputation without doubt. Her work never became a commodity, a matter for financial speculation. To what extent was the contrary true of Giacometti, precisely because of the myth-making process that would link him so inextricably with the existentialist writings of Sartre? The fact that, unlike Giacometti, Richier had an immediate posterity in the School of London sculptors, and in the work of César in France, bears a more eloquent witness to her fecundity than any uncomfortable contemporary praise.

The awkward, scratched surfaces of Richier's *Young Girl with a Diabolo*, the informal nudes, together with work by her contemporaries – Jean Fautrier's scarred and iridescent *Hostage* paintings and sculptures or Jean Dubuffet's females such as *Olympia*, literally gouged into the *matière* of his canvases – must read "against" the frou-frou of the New Look, the "Miss Tabou" beauty contests in Saint-Germain-des-Prés, the historical costume dramas in the theatres and the cinema, the taste for a "fantastic forties", all of which played their role in characterising the reborn *Femme française*. Richier's uncompromising toughness and her disturbingly hard, spiky, metamorphic imagery contrasts with the extreme delicacy of the much smaller-scale work she made at the end of her life – possibly when she knew that she had cancer and was unable to continue working on large pieces at the foundry – the tiny figures based on cuttlefish carving, often with a golden finish; the sacred works, such as the model for cathedral doors, which aligns her work with such Catholic contemporaries as Lucio Fontana; the tremendous exuberance of the polychromed works, kept a secret for so many years, which, surprisingly, look forward to the colourful sculpture of Niki de Saint-Phalle (q.v.). The exhaustive history of Germaine Richier's life and work presented in the Fondation Maeght catalogue of 1996 at last reveals the true stature of this major woman artist.

SARAH WILSON

Rie, Lucie
British potter, 1902–1995

Born Lucie Gompertz in Vienna, 16 March 1902. Studied ceramics at the Kunstgewerbeschule, Vienna, under Michael Powolny, 1922–6. Married Hans Rie, 1926; divorced 1940. Emigrated to Britain, settling in London, 1938; later naturalised. Visited Bernard Leach at Shinner's Bridge Pottery, Dartington, Devon, 1939. Worked for the Bimini glass jewellery and button workshop during World War II. Operated own button-making business and pottery in London, 1945. Shared workshop in Albion Mews, London, with Hans Coper, 1947–58. Taught part-time at Camberwell School of Arts and Crafts, London, 1960–71; also visiting lecturer at Royal College of Art, London, and Bristol College of Art. Recipient of gold medals at Exposition Universelle, Brussels, 1935, Milan Triennale, 1936, and International Exhibition, Munich, 1954; honorary doctorates from Royal College of Art, London, 1969, and Heriot-Watt University, Edinburgh, 1992. Officer (OBE), 1968, Commander, 1981 (CBE), and Dame Commander (DBE), 1991, Order of the British Empire. Died in London, 1 April 1995.

Selected Individual Exhibitions
Berkeley Galleries, London: 1949, 1950 (with Hans Coper), 1951 (with Hans Coper), 1953 (with Hans Coper), 1956 (with Hans Coper), 1960, 1966
Bonnier's Gallery, New York: 1954
Röhsska Konstslöjdmuseet, Göteborg: 1955 (with Hans Coper)
University of Minnesota, Minneapolis: 1957 (with Hans Coper)
Museum Boymans-van Beuningen, Rotterdam: 1967 (with Hans Coper, touring)
Arts Council Gallery, London: 1967 (touring retrospective)
Museum für Kunst und Gewerbe, Hamburg: 1972 (with Hans Coper)
Hetjens Museum, Düsseldorf: 1979
Sainsbury Centre for Visual Arts, Norwich: 1981–2 (touring retrospective)
Peter Dingley Gallery, Stratford-upon-Avon: 1983
Fischer Fine Art, London: 1984 (with Hans Coper)
Galerie Besson, London: 1988 (retrospective), 1990, 1991 (with Hans Coper)
Sogetsu-Kai Foundation, Tokyo: 1989 (*Issey Miyake Meets Lucie Rie*, touring)
Crafts Council Gallery, London: 1992 (retrospective)
Metropolitan Museum of Art, New York: 1994 (with Hans Coper)
Barbican Art Gallery, London: 1997 (retrospective, with Hans Coper)

Bibliography
George Wingfield Digby, *The Work of the Modern Potter in England*, London: Murray, 1952
Dora Billington, "The younger English potters", *The Studio*, cxlv, 1953, pp.78–85
Michael Casson, *Pottery in Britain Today*, London: Tiranti, and New York: Transatlantic Arts, 1967
Lucie Rie, exh. cat., Arts Council Gallery, London, and elsewhere, 1967 (contains bibliography)
Muriel Rose, *Artist Potters in England*, 2nd edition, London: Faber, 1970
Lucie Rie–Hans Coper: Keramik, exh. cat., Museum für Kunst und Gewerbe, Hamburg, 1972
Tony Birks, *The Art of the Modern Potter*, 2nd edition, London: Country Life, 1976; New York: Van Nostrand Reinhold, 1977
British 20th-Century Studio Ceramics, exh. cat., Christopher Wood Gallery, London, 1980
Emmanuel Cooper, "Lucie Rie: Potter", *Ceramic Review*, no.72, 1981, pp.4–9
John Houston, ed., *Lucie Rie: A Survey of Her Life and Work*, London: Crafts Council, 1981 (contains extensive bibliography)
Sheila Hale, "Simple genius: Lucie Rie's pots are high art", *Connoisseur*, cxxv, June 1985, pp.126–30
Issey Miyake Meets Lucie Rie, exh. cat., Sogetsu-Kai Foundation, Tokyo, and elsewhere, 1989
Emmanuel Cooper, "Lucie Rie", *Ceramic Review*, no.134, 1992, pp.26–31
Lucie Rie, exh. cat., Crafts Council Gallery, London, 1992
Oliver Watson, *Studio Pottery: Twentieth-Century British Ceramics in the Victoria and Albert Museum Collection*, London: Phaidon, 1993 (originally published as *British Studio Pottery*, Oxford: Phaidon, 1990)
Tony Birks, *Lucie Rie: An Illustrated Biography*, 2nd edition, Marston Magna: Marston House, 1994 (contains bibliography)
Emmanuel Cooper, "Lucie Rie's notebooks", *Ceramic Review*, no.150, 1994, pp.28–37
Amy Shelton, "Lucie Rie", *Studio Pottery*, no.7, 1994, pp.30–35
"Dame Lucie Rie: Tributes", *Ceramic Review*, no.154, 1995, pp.8–21
Obituaries in *Daily Telegraph*, 3 April 1995; *The Independent*, 3 April 1995; *The Times*, 3 April 1995; *Crafts*, no.134, May–June 1995
Tanya Harrod and others, "Dame Lucie Rie, 1902–1995", *Crafts*, no.135, July–August 1995, pp.42–7
Lucie Rie and Hans Coper: Potters in Parallel, exh. cat., Barbican Art Gallery, London, 1997

Born into an upper-middle-class Viennese family with intellectual interests, Lucie Rie toured Europe with her antiquarian uncle Alexander Wolf before entering the Kunstgewerbeschule, Vienna, at the age of 20. Her studies under Michael Powolny involved exhaustive glaze trials that were to prove the foundation of her later reputation as an exciting potter in control of fantastic colours and textures. As a young woman, married in 1926 to Hans Rie (a manager in a hat factory), Lucie Rie made pots on a wheel set up in her immaculate architect-designed apartment in Vienna (examples from this period may be seen in the Victoria and Albert Museum, London). In 1938 she and her husband came to Britain with very few possessions – refugees from Nazi domination. Hans Rie left for the USA, but Lucie was determined to stay in London, renting a small mews house near Hyde Park in which to recreate her workshop and home. At the outset she asked Bernard Leach (then potting at Dartington in Devon) for advice, and visited him for four days' "tuition". Irrespective of the obvious differences in their work, their subsequent friendship and mutual admiration became an important factor in Rie's development in England.

During the war years Rie was forced to abandon pottery for work in a glass studio, followed by the manufacture of clay buttons and accessories for the clothing trade, in her own workshop. It was not until 1947 that she was able to devote herself to her chosen craft, working long hours in her studio and rarely leaving London. At first the workshop produced thrown earthenware cups and saucers, stylish and simple, glazed in black on the outside and white on the inside. From 1946 she was assisted by the young German refugee, Hans Coper, and from late 1948, as a result of the installation of a reliable new kiln, they worked together on a range of stoneware pots for the table. Rie also introduced porcelain to her workshop for the first time at this date.

Rie: Bottle, vase and dish, 1972; coarse dark stoneware with spirally thrown glaze; Crafts Council, London

Exhibitions in London followed swiftly; the first shows were held at the Berkeley Galleries and pots could always be purchased from the select craft shop Primavera. Throughout the 1950s and 1960s output was made up of tea, coffee and breakfast sets, cleanly thrown and coloured in monochrome, and individual porcelain bowls and bottles, often exploiting *sgraffito* (scratched) decoration in radiating lines. The strong graphic sensibility of Rie's work can be seen at its best in pots from these two decades, when her physical skill and strength were at their zenith.

In her maturity, during the 1970s and early 1980s, abstract elements of colour and texture dominated Rie's work, although she continued to make forms that were essentially useful containers, such as vases and bowls. Glazes of piercingly bright colours, or of bubbling, erupting and pitted surfaces, were combined with shiny, matt or even metallic finishes in a group of clearly identifiable "Rie" shapes. These include the bottle-vase with its tall, flared neck, shaped like a trumpet, the conical bowl, the footed bowl and the essential cylinder or beaker. The work was not without grit: rugged furrowed and flattened-sided pots, and those deeply colour-stained or scored into are also prized; they show Rie in command of a battery of clays, body stains and glazes that she enjoyed manipulating.

The inspiration for Rie's pots came from the process of their making and the results were often much more flamboyant than these processes, the rigorous persona of the maker or her meticulously kept environment would suggest. Her reputation was constantly high, as witnessed by regular showings in Britain and abroad. Recognition by major bodies came first in 1967, when the Arts Council of Great Britain organised a solo retrospective show at its London gallery. This was followed by another in 1981 at the Sainsbury Centre for Visual Arts, Norwich, which toured to the Victoria and Albert Museum, London. In 1991 Lucie Rie was created a DBE, an honour never before granted to a potter.

Although Rie had many imitators, especially potters emulating her glazes, for which they regularly sought the recipes, she had no pupil-followers as such. She did not find teaching a rewarding experience. Working in solitude, as she did for most of her career, or seeing friends in very small groups, suited Lucie Rie best. The major collections of Rie's work are at the Crafts Council, London; Highcross House, Dartington, Devon; Holburne Museum and Crafts Study Centre, Bath; Paisley Museum and Art Gallery, Scotland; and the Victoria and Albert Museum, London. After her death, Stoke-on-Trent City Museum and Art Gallery was given the contents of Rie's studio, including potter's wheels, tools, aprons, a small kiln, tables, chairs and shelving; the intention is to install the studio permanently in the ceramics gallery.

MARGOT COATTS

Riley, Bridget
British painter, 1931–

Born in London, 25 April 1931. Studied at Goldsmiths' College School of Art, London, under Sam Rabin, 1949–52; Royal College of Art, London, 1952–5 (ARCA); Thubron's summer school, Norfolk, under Maurice de Sausmarez, 1959. Travelled to Italy with de Sausmarez, summer 1960. Worked for J. Walter Thompson Advertising Agency, 1958–9; part-time lecturer at Loughborough College of Art, Leicestershire, 1959–61, Hornsey College of Art, London, 1960, and Croydon School of Art, Surrey, 1962–4. Spent time in Vaucluse, France, from 1961, building a studio there in 1970s. Travelled widely, making frequent trips to continental Europe with Robert Kudielka, 1971–5, and visiting USA, India, Far East and Australasia. Included in *The Responsive Eye* exhibition, Museum of Modern Art, New York, 1965. Co-founder, with Peter Sedgley, of SPACE, a scheme for the organisation of studios for artists, 1969. Trustee of National Gallery, London, 1981–8. Recipient of prize, John Moore's Exhibition, Liverpool, 1963; International prize for painting (the first woman), Venice Biennale, 1968; Ohara Museum prize, International Prints Biennale, Tokyo, 1972; gold medal, Grafik Biennale, Norway, 1980; honorary doctorates from University of Manchester, 1976; University of Ulster, 1986; University of Oxford, 1993. Commander, Order of the British Empire (CBE), 1972. Lives in London and Cornwall.

Selected Individual Exhibitions
Gallery One, London: 1962, 1963
Richard Feigen Gallery, New York: 1965, 1966, 1967, 1968
British Pavilion, Venice Biennale: 1968 (with Phillip King, touring)
Rowan Gallery, London: 1969, 1971, 1972, 1975, 1976, 1981
Kunstverein Hannover: 1970–71 (touring retrospective)
Arts Council of Great Britain, 1973 (touring), 1980–82 (touring), 1984–5 (*Working with Colour*, touring)
Sidney Janis Gallery, New York: 1975, 1978, 1990
Coventry Gallery, Sydney: 1976
Minami Gallery, Tokyo: 1977
Albright-Knox Art Gallery, Buffalo, NY: 1978–80 (touring retrospective, organised by British Council)
Australian Galleries, Melbourne: 1979
Nishimura Gallery, Tokyo: 1983, 1990
Juda Rowan Gallery, London: 1983
Royal Institute of British Architects, London: 1984
Galerie Reckermann, Cologne: 1984
Galerie und Edition Schegl, Zürich: 1987, 1989
Mayor Rowan Gallery, London: 1987, 1989
Kunsthalle, Nuremberg: 1992–3 (touring)
Karsten Schubert, London: 1992, 1993, 1994, 1996
Tate Gallery, London: 1994

Selected Writings
"The hermaphrodite", *Art and Sexual Politics*, ed. Thomas B. Hess and Elizabeth C. Baker, New York: Macmillan, 1973

"A decoration for the Royal Liverpool Hospital", *Transactions 7*, Royal Institute of Architects, iv/1, 20th Century Series, 1985
"The artist's eye: Seurat", *Modern Painters*, iv/2, 1991, pp.10–14
"Continuing", *Ready Steady Go: Paintings of the Sixties from the Arts Council Collection*, exh. cat., South Bank Centre, London, 1992

Bibliography
Michael Compton, *Optical and Kinetic Art*, London: Tate Gallery, 1967
David Sylvester, "Bridget Riley interviewed", *Studio International*, clxxiii, 1967, pp.132–5
Bridget Riley, exh. cat., Kunstverein Hannover, 1970
Maurice de Sausmarez, *Bridget Riley*, London: Studio Vista, and Greenwich, CT: New York Graphic Society, 1970
Robert Melville. "An art without accidents", *New Statesman*, 23 July 1971
Bridget Riley: Paintings and Drawings, 1961–73, exh. cat., Arts Council of Great Britain, London, 1973
John Rothenstein, *Modern English Painters: Wood to Hockney*, London: Macdonald, 1974
John A. Walker, *Art since Pop*, London: Thames and Hudson, 1975; Woodbury, NY: Barron's, 1978
Hugh Adams, *Art of the Sixties*, Oxford: Phaidon, 1978
Bridget Riley: Works, 1959–78, exh. cat., Albright-Knox Art Gallery, Buffalo, NY, and elsewhere, 1978 (contains bibliography)
J.G. Harper, *Product and Response: The Painting of Bridget Riley*, PhD dissertation, University of London, Courtauld Institute of Art, 1982
Working with Colour: Recent Paintings and Studies by Bridget Riley, exh. cat., Arts Council of Great Britain, London, 1984
"Bridget Riley", *The Great Artists: Their Lives, Works and Inspiration*, iv: *20th century*, London, 1986
Karina Türr, "Jenseits von Op Art? Uberlegungen zu Farbstreifen Bridget Rileys", *Pantheon*, xliv, 1986, pp.157–63, 204–5 (with English summary)
The Artist's Eye: Bridget Riley: An Exhibition of National Gallery Paintings Selected by the Artist, exh. cat., National Gallery, London, 1989
The Experience of Painting: Eight Modern Artists, exh. cat., South Bank Centre, London, 1989
Bridget Riley, exh. cat., Sidney Janis Gallery, New York, 1990
Robert Hughes, *The Shock of the New*, 2nd edition, London: Thames and Hudson, and New York: Knopf, 1991
Bridget Riley: Painting, 1982–92, exh. cat., Kunsthalle, Nuremberg, and elsewhere, 1992 (contains bibliography)
The Sixties Art Scene in London, exh. cat., Barbican Art Gallery, London, 1993
Robert Kudielka, ed., *Bridget Riley: Dialogues on Art*, London: Zwemmer, 1995
Edward Lucie-Smith, *Movements in Art since 1945*, 4th edition, London: Thames and Hudson, 1995

Bridget Riley's work is routinely but somewhat narrowly characterised as Op Art; although she would not disclaim such a label for her early work, she has resisted the limitations it would impose on her, laying claim instead to an art that "engages the whole personality" and expects a similar total response from its audience. Certainly the linking thread that runs through from the earliest black-and-white pieces to the coloured syncopations of the 1980s and 1990s is one of perception and the sensations of seeing. As the critic Robert Melville wrote in 1971: "No painter, dead or alive, has ever made us more aware of our eyes than Bridget Riley". Riley has never studied optics, and her works are not optically mechanical. Rather they are dramatic exercises in generating visual sensations, though as she says: "not to the exclusion of

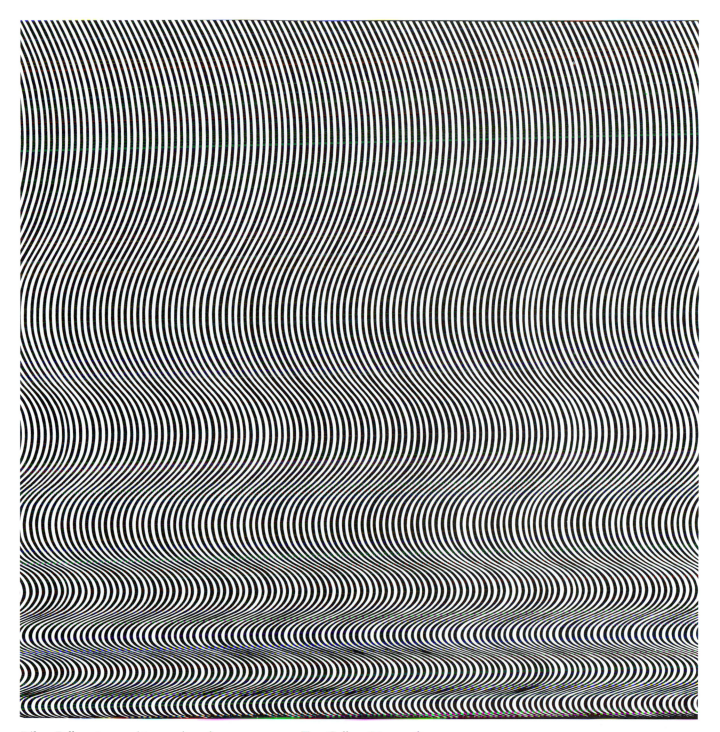

Riley: *Fall*, 1963; emulsion on board; 141 × 140 cm.; Tate Gallery, Liverpool

emotion". Indeed she has said that one of her aims is that these two responses – the visual and the emotional – "shall be experienced as *one and the same*". More than most, her work is diminished and distorted by reproduction because the sensation it delivers is dependent on an exact concatenation of elements that must be experienced full-scale.

Despite their precision and geometric formality, the compositional structures of her work, and the tonal relationships within them, are not arrived at solely by logic or calculation; intuition plays an important role in ensuring a free play of elements, and a resistance to predictable sequences, logical progressions. Musical analogies are often aptly used to describe and explain her work: from the first she has been concerned with modulation, progression, rhythm, changes in tempo, consonance and dissonance, pause and flow. Throughout her career Riley has eschewed the autographic mark and the distraction of extraneous allusion by employing assistants to paint the final work on canvas following her precise instructions. She composes by means of drawings and watercolours, including full-size cartoons, and latterly by organising cut-out coloured shapes in infinitely variable "patterns". This method of working has the effect of distancing her from the physical character of the work, while not reducing the process to the purely mechanical. Every decision with regard to scale, interval, colour and format is hers alone. Like an architect, she designs every detail of the whole and then directs its realisation.

A student at Goldsmiths' College, and then at the Royal College of Art, it took Riley a long time to find her direction as a painter. The experiments with perception that characterise Futurism and Divisionism interested her to the extent that she sought out works by Gino Severini and Giacomo Balla and copied works by Georges Seurat. She also experimented with a Neo-impressionist style, culminating in *Pink Landscape* (private collection, London), a subject drawn in the hills around Siena during an Italian tour with the painter and art scholar Maurice de Sausmarez in 1960. Of this painting David Thompson later wrote:

> [it is] already concerned with a kind of optical situation which constantly recurs in her later work – that of a dominant formal pattern under pressure of disintegration … As a painting about making pure colour convey visual shimmer, it is a direct precursor of *Late Morning* (1967–8) [quoted in de Sausmarez 1970].

A personal and artistic crisis later that year led her to repeated attempts to paint one last, black picture; from this originate her first black-and-white works, which are clearly related to contemporary Hard Edge painting (e.g. *Kiss*, 1960–61; Bryan Robertson, London), but rapidly developed into a personal pictorial language. These pictures of the early 1960s have titles such as *Shift* (1963), *Shiver* (1964) and *Static I* (1966) that announce quite directly a concern with visual sensation, but imply too a physical dimension to the passive act of seeing. These apparently simple compositions are a remarkably sophisticated synthesis of mathematical concepts.

Riley's work has always drawn much of its strength from her deliberate economy of means. The paintings of the early 1960s use relatively few structural ideas, such as modulation of contrasted forms, displacement in an otherwise rhythmical progression, a shifting centre within a circular form and dramatic tensions in zigzag patterns. A pivotal work in Riley's development is *Fall* (1963; see illustration). The sense of movement here derives not from a shifting progression of forms but from the cumulative repetition of a single curving line. Repetition and reiteration become the dominant structural devices by which Riley organises her canvases. It is in these black-and-white paintings, and notably in *Fall*, that a particular visual phenomenon becomes apparent. Anton Ehrenzweig, well-known for his work on the psychoanalysis of aural and visual perception, observed of Riley's pictures of this period that "strangely iridescent disembodied colours … begin to play around the centres of maximum tension".

Riley's "star" status was established with the exhibition *The Responsive Eye* at the Museum of Modern Art in New York, in January 1965. It included two works, *Current*, which was used for the cover of the catalogue, and *Hesitate*. Concurrently she had a sell-out show at the Richard Feigen Gallery, also in New York. The "Op Art" pictures became synonymous with 1960s style and were ruthlessly plagiarised by fashion and advertising.

A period of transition from 1965 to 1967 was marked by the introduction of "coloured" greys into her paintings; polarities of "warm" and "cold" in these greys herald the eventual adoption of colour. Titles, in Riley's work, are always pertinent – the process of composition in these paintings, and their effects on the viewer, are signalled by such titles as *Arrest*, *Drift* and *Deny*. Of *Deny II* (Chase Manhattan Bank, New York), Riley has said she intended: "To oppose a structural movement with a tonal movement, to release increased colour through reducing the tonal contrast" (Sylvester 1967). In fact the picture sets up a remarkably complex sequence of oppositional forces, subtly deployed: warm is pitched against cold, fast against slow, as the grid of forms rises and falls, ebbs and flows, diagonally left to right and from top to bottom.

A move into pure colour occurred in 1967 with *Chant* (Collection Hoh, Germany) and *Late Morning* (Tate Gallery, London). Red and blue replace the warm and cold greys. *Chant* is a seminal example of Riley's spare use of pure colour to create complex visual effects. Red and blue stripes – red surrounding blue, blue surrounding red – alternate across the canvas; the width of the bands increases and decreases while the white intervals between them remain constant. The picture seems to radiate coloured light, an effect that arises from the fact that colours bordering white may either fuse or induce contrasting colours. This spilling-over of colour is known as adjacent colour-spread. Much of Riley's work has explored this propensity, with her choice of colours designed to induce these effects, for example, the orange, violet and green of *Orient I*. Less dominant colours – cerise, turquoise, olive – can be exploited for their susceptibility to a shifting identity. Many of the gouache studies of 1969–70 use the stripe format to explore the potential of such colour combinations.

Chant was one of the pictures shown at the Venice Biennale in 1968 when Riley was one of the two artists chosen to represent Britain; she became the first woman ever to win the International prize for painting. During this period, continuing until the early 1970s, she produced those works for which she is perhaps best known: the "stripe" paintings, which use a classically simple form to explore colour relationships. She has described the rationale behind the structures of her work and the relation between form and colour. The complex forms and energies of the earlier work could be fully expressed only by simplifying colour to black and white, with occasional grey sequences, whereas "colour energies need a virtually neutral vehicle if they are to develop uninhibited" (London 1973, p.10). She found this vehicle in the repeated stripe. The vertical stripe continued to be the organising element of Riley's compositions, though in the early 1970s she extended her formal means with such devices as the "twisted" stripes in *Zing I* (1971; private collection, Switzerland) and the undulating curves of *Gala* (1974; private collection, Barbados) and *Rill* (1976; private collection, Cincinnati). In the late 1970s Riley progressively eliminated the white ground, as in *Aurulum* (1977; private collection), with its sequence of five pale colours – blue, pink, yellow, violet, green. The apotheosis of this is reached in the *Song of Orpheus* series of 1978 in which the colours seem almost to disappear.

Subsequent work continued to explore the problem of how to approach colour. A major touring retrospective took place in 1978–80, taking in the USA, Australia and Japan. Riley herself travelled extensively at this time, working meanwhile on a sequence of lyrical "curve" paintings. The next stage was inspired by the remembered colours seen during a visit to Egypt in 1979–80. Freely reconstructing the strong colours of this "Egyptian palette", Riley resumed the simple formal structure of the earlier "stripe" paintings in order to focus on the density of the colours themselves. Other sources in European, and especially Venetian painting became the object of study for colour theory and practice. In 1981 she was appointed a Trustee of the National Gallery, London, where in 1989 she curated one in the series of shows *The Artist's Eye*, which was pertinently subtitled "The Colour Connection". Riley's career has been single-minded in its devotion to painting. Although she has also made prints, her work outside the studio and the gallery has been infrequent: it includes a mural for the Royal Liverpool Hospital in 1983, and stage-set designs for the Ballet Rambert's *Colour Moves* at the Edinburgh Festival the same year.

Sensation became the basis for Riley's changes in the pictorial structure in the years 1980 to 1985: initially black bands articulate the colour orchestration in such works as *Luxor* (1982; Glasgow Art Gallery and Museum), *Summer's Field* (1982; Kunsthalle, Nuremberg) and *Serenissima* (1982; private collection); this device is then discarded for *Greensleeves* (1983) and *Cherry Autumn* (1983; private collection); in *Coxcomb* (1984) lilac is substituted for white; and finally such structural supports are abandoned altogether in *Saraband* (1985) and *Burnished Sky* (1985; private collection). Colour is finally released from the control exerted by the armature of pauses and intervals of black or white. *Cherry Autumn* is the key picture of this period because it predicts a later re-orientation. Riley's initial interest in the chromatic aspect of colour's energy was superseded by the realisation that colour's true potential, for painting, was spatial, or as she prefers to call it, "plastic". In other words, it is not an illusionistic pictorial space in the usual sense, but an unstable and shifting property of colours that fluctuates between them. Experiments in 1984 and 1985 at her studio in Vaucluse made it clear that this "plasticity" could not be developed by means of vertical stripes; thus in 1986 her work took a radical new direction with the balance of the pictorial space disrupted by the introduction of a dynamic diagonal. The building block of the paintings is no longer the stripe but a slanted rectangle. By using these interlocking shapes she was able to subvert the insistent vertical of the stripe while not wholly abandoning it as a compositional device. Although still concerned with sensation, these paintings allow themselves the luxury of a referential dimension, to emotion and to landscape. Colour and form in these latest works offer an expressive complexity that Riley experiences as positive and forward-looking but also open-ended: *From Here* (1994) is both a confident assertion of arrival and vantage, and an honest admission of uncertainty as in "where do we go ...?"

GILL SAUNDERS

Rilke-Westhoff, Clara
German sculptor and painter, 1878–1954

Born Clara Westhoff in Bremen, 21 November 1878. Studied at Fchr/Schmid-Reutte private art school, Munich, 1895–8; studied under Bernhard Buttersack in Heimhausen near Munich, 1897; Fritz Mackensen in Worpswede, 1898; Max Klinger in Leipzig, 1899; studied in Paris at Académie Julian, Ecole des Beaux-Arts and in Rodin's studio, 1899–1900; also studied under Arthur Segal in Berlin. First visited Worpswede art colony, 1898. Married poet Rainer Maria Rilke, April 1901; daughter born December 1901; separated from husband; he died 1926. Often travelled abroad: Paris, 1902, 1905, 1908–9 and 1913; Rome, 1903–4; Denmark and Sweden, 1904; Egypt, 1907. Resided in Worpswede, Bremen and Berlin; lived in Munich, 1911–19; in Fischerhude from 1919. Died in Fischerhude, 9 March 1954.

Principal Exhibitions

Individual
Graphisches Kabinett, Bremen: 1939, 1948, 1955 (retrospective)
Galerie Schwoon, Oldenburg: 1949 (with Paula Modersohn-Becker)
Galerie Kunstschau, Fischerhude: 1963 (retrospective)

Group
Kunsthalle, Bremen: 1899, 1901, 1902, 1905, 1910, 1912, 1927, 1948, 1950
Deutsche Kunstausstellung, Dresden: 1899
Internationale Kunstausstellung, Dresden: 1901
Vienna Secession: 1902
Kunstsalon Heller, Vienna: 1912
Galerie Caspari, Munich: 1913
Münchener Neue Secession, Munich: 1918
Graphisches Kabinett, Bremen: 1924–5, 1932–3, 1937–8, 1940–43 (annuals), 1941 (*GEDOK-Ausstellung*)
Hannover: 1927 (*95. Grosse Kunstausstellung*), 1937 (*GEDOK-Ausstellung*)
Museum Folkwang, Essen: 1928 (*Kunst und Technik*)
Haus der Deutschen Kunst, Munich: 1937 (*Grosse Deutsche Kunstausstellung*)
Schloss Celle: 1940 (*Kunstausstellung Osthannoverscher Maler*)
Schloss Schönhausen, Berlin: 1942

Selected Writings
Text in *Paula Modersohn-Becker: Ein Buch der Freundschaft*, ed. Rolf Hetsch, Berlin: Rembrandt, 1932, pp.42–52
Editor, *Letters on Cézanne* by Rainer Maria Rilke, New York: Fromm International, 1985; London: Cape, 1988 (German original, 1952)

Bibliography
Worpswede: Aus der Frühzeit der Künstlerkolonie, exh. cat., Kunsthalle, Bremen, 1970
Clara Rilke-Westhoff: Plastiken, Zeichnungen, Gemälde, exh. cat., Galerie Cohrs-Zirus, Worpswede, 1979
Worpswede: Eine deutsche Künstlerkolonie um 1900: 150 Werke aus dem Besitz der Kunsthalle Bremen, exh. cat., Kunsthalle, Bremen, 1980
Marina Sauer, *Die Bildhauerin Clara Rilke-Westhoff, 1878–1954: Leben und Werk*, Bremen: Hauschild, 1986 (includes catalogue raisonné)
Sigrid Weltge-Wortmann, *Die Ersten Maler in Worpswede*, 2nd edition, Worpswede: Worpsweder Verlag, 1987
Die Bildhauerin Clara Rilke-Westhoff, 1878–1954, exh. cat., Museum Langenargen am Bodensee, 1988

Rilke-Westhoff: *Gerhardt Hauptmann*, 1910; bronze; height 37 cm.; Kunsthalle, Bremen

Clara Rilke-Westhoff's beginnings presaged a brilliant future. Supported by parents and mentored by celebrated teachers, she developed into a sculptor of unusual talent whose work was critically acclaimed in exhibitions. At the age of 18 the determined, strong-willed student described herself as an "emancipated *fin-de-siècle* female", secure enough to enter a then male-dominated branch of the arts. Yet life and art commingled to the detriment of the latter. As the wife of the celebrated poet Rainer Maria Rilke, she slowly subverted her own inclinations, never to realise her full potential.

In 1895, when women were still barred from academies, Clara Rilke-Westhoff enrolled at the private Fehr/Schmid-Reutte School in Munich. She was quick to grasp the financial and qualitative inequities of gender-based instruction, against which she rebelled unsuccessfully. A serious student, she took advantage of the first-rate museums of the vibrant metropolis and visited the Munich Secession and the international Glaspalast exhibition, at which a group of landscape painters from the artist colony of Worpswede had received critical acclaim. Its leader, Fritz Mackensen, would become her teacher three years later.

Rilke-Westhoff moved to Worpswede in 1898, and followed Mackensen's advice to concentrate on sculpture rather than painting. Her first work, a plaster bust of *A Peasant Woman*, clearly demonstrates her independent vision and style. Devoid of the idealising tendencies of her teacher, Rilke-Westhoff portrayed rural hardship and old age in an almost brutal, starkly realistic, yet empathetic manner. A bronze portrait of *Paula Modersohn-Becker*, a fellow-student with whom she formed a close friendship, followed. The thrusting, fluid movement of the head – a good likeness – captured her friend's inquisitive intensity perfectly. A recommendation from Mackensen enabled Rilke-Westhoff to study with Max Klinger in Leipzig, who instructed her in marble techniques. Impressed by her talent, individual style and stamina, Klinger and his colleague Carl Seffner advised against a return to Worpswede, suggesting instead anatomy studies at academies that accepted women. Courses at a variety of schools in Paris, including the Académie Julian and the Ecole des Beaux-Arts, followed, and Max Klinger's endorsement opened the doors to Rodin's studio and the master's coveted corrections.

Concentrated work marked her return to Worpswede in 1900, the year Rainer Maria Rilke arrived from Russia. It was the poet's first encounter with the visual arts. Enchanted by the "sisters of his soul", as he called Clara Rilke-Westhoff and Paula Modersohn-Becker (q.v.), he was drawn to the free and independent spirit of the young sculptor. Their marriage in the spring of 1901 was a turning point in Rilke-Westhoff's life. The immediate withdrawal from her Worpswede friends was based on Rilke's claim of solitude for his work. Over the years she adopted the role of acquiescent wife that Rilke had demanded and yet resented. *Siblings*, *Woman with Child* and two busts, *Rainer Maria Rilke* (Rilke-Archiv, Gernsbach) and *Heinrich Vogeler* (Kunsthalle, Bremen), were completed during their first year together. The portraits appear inner-directed through pose and physiognomy, heightened by subtly modelled surfaces of fleeting light and shadow.

Rilke-Westhoff's contact with Rodin, although frequently interrupted by long absences from Paris, spanned a period of 13 years. She was Rodin's student in 1900, 1902 and again in 1905, when her husband became Rodin's private secretary. In 1908 and 1909 she worked in his atelier. In 1913 the Mannheim Kunsthalle commissioned Rilke-Westhoff to sculpt a portrait of Rodin. Although he initially agreed, the project did not materialise. Rodin repeatedly praised Rilke-Westhoff's work as among the best he had seen. His influence is clearly evident in several early bronzes, especially a group of nude children. Rilke-Westhoff's light-reflecting surfaces are, however, less dramatic and smoother than those of Rodin and her sculptures seem inward-directed and self-contained. Whether standing, crouching or sitting, each figure is a small world unto itself, an island of being. Extraneous or realistic detail, so evident in her early work, has been eliminated. Other works, such as a *Peasant Woman Holding a Child*, a *Nude* and a *Dancer* convey the essence of physical and spiritual consciousness.

Despite the birth of a daughter, the Rilke household was dissolved a year after their marriage and a decade of long separations, restless wandering and financial hardships followed. Lack of funds also derailed the divorce proceedings that Rilke-Westhoff initiated in 1911. For many years the poet was unable to support his family, yet always solicited friends to secure work for his wife. These commissions, frequently executed in exchange for the sitters' hospitality, rarely ameliorated her difficulties, although, through exhibitions, they contributed to Rilke-Westhoff's reputation as one of the finest portraitists of her time. The Rilkes maintained an active correspondence until the poet's death and remained lifelong friends.

In a portrait bust of the German writer *Gerhardt Hauptmann* (1910; see illustration) Rilke-Westhoff embarked on a new simplification of style. This is also evident in such portraits as *Ricarda Huch* (1912), *Kurt Wolfskehl* (1913), *Elisabeth von Hellingrath* (1914), *Alfred Schuler* (1923) and *Rudolf Alexander Schröder* (1930s; Kunsthalle, Bremen). All extraneous surface detail is eliminated in favour of an expressive force emanating solely from Rilke-Westhoff's keen insight into the human psyche and her ability to make manifest the interior world of her sitters. A posthumous portrait of *Rainer Maria Rilke* (1936; Kunsthalle, Bremen) emits, in its extreme economy, the spirituality of other-worldly realms. Much of Rilke-Westhoff's work remains in private collections, even more has been lost or is unaccounted for.

When Clara Rilke-Westhoff realised that her career was turning away from its hopeful beginnings she painted her only self-portrait, an image of sorrow and resignation. Paula Modersohn-Becker's portrait of 1905 confirms the wrenching despair of her once dynamic, spirited and energetic friend. After years of professional and personal struggle, of uprootedness and financial crisis, Rilke-Westhoff settled in the small northern village of Fischerhude, not far from Worpswede. Increasingly she turned to painting, this time not of people but of the flat, luminous northern landscape where she finally found peace. Clara Rilke-Westhoff belonged to a generation of women who ventured into new territory but whose unquestionable talent could not yet be accommodated by the art world or society, and sometimes not even by themselves.

SIGRID WORTMANN WELTGE

Ringgold, Faith

American mixed-media artist and writer, 1930–

Born Faith Jones in Harlem, New York, 8 October 1930. Studied at City College of New York (BS 1955; MA in art 1959). Married (1) jazz pianist Robert Earl Wallace, 1950; two daughters, born 1950; divorced 1956; (2) Burdette Ringgold, 1962. Travelled to Europe for the first time, 1961, to Africa, 1976. Art teacher in New York City public schools, 1955–73; lecturer, Bank Street College Graduate School, New York, 1970–80; visiting professor, 1984, and professor of art, from 1985, University of California, San Diego; subsequently divided time between California and New York. Recipient of Creative Artists Public Service (CAPS) grant, 1971; National Endowment for the Arts (NEA) grants, 1978 and 1989; Wonder Woman award, Warner Communications, 1983; Guggenheim fellowship, 1987; Napouli Foundation award, France, 1990; Artist of the Year, Studio Museum in Harlem, 1991; Coretta Scott King award, for children's book, 1991; Arts International award, 1992; honorary doctorates from Moore College of Art, Philadelphia, 1986; College of Wooster, Ohio, 1987; Massachusetts College of Art, Boston, 1991; City College of New York, 1991; Brockport State University, New York, 1992; California College of Arts and Crafts, Oakland, 1993; Rhode Island School of Design, Providence, 1994. Lives in Englewood, New Jersey.

Selected Individual Exhibitions

Spectrum Gallery, New York: 1967, 1970
Jane Voorhees Zimmerli Gallery, Rutgers University, NJ: 1973 (retrospective)
Summit Gallery, New York: 1979
Museum of African and African-American Art, Buffalo, NY: 1980
Studio Museum in Harlem, New York: 1984 (retrospective)
College of Wooster Art Museum, OH: 1985
Baltimore Museum of Art: 1987
Bernice Steinbaum Gallery, New York: 1987, 1988
Fine Arts Museum of Long Island, Hempstead, NY: 1990–93 (touring retrospective)
Saint Louis Art Museum, MO: 1994, 1995

Selected Writings

"The politics of culture: Black, white, male, female", *Women Artists' News*, vi, Summer 1980, pp.20–19, 13
"Being my own woman", *Confirmation: An Anthology of Africanamerican Women*, ed. Amiri and Amina Baraka, New York: Morrow, 1983
Tar Beach, New York: Crown, 1991 (for children)
"Those cookin' up ideas for freedom take heed: Only a watched pot boils", *Art Journal*, l, Fall 1991, pp.84–6
Aunt Harriet's Underground Railroad in the Sky, New York: Crown, 1992 (for children)
The French Collection, Part 1, New York: Being My Own Woman Press, 1992
Dinner at Aunt Connie's House, New York: Hyperion, 1993 (for children)
We Flew Over the Bridge: The Memoirs of Faith Ringgold, Boston: Little Brown, 1995

Bibliography

Elton C. Fax, *Seventeen Black Artists*, New York: Dodd Mead, 1971
Lucy R. Lippard, "Faith Ringgold flying her own flag", *Ms*, v, July 1976, pp.34–9
Eleanor Munro, *Originals: American Women Artists*, New York: Simon and Schuster, 1979
Faith Ringgold: Twenty Years of Painting, Sculpture and Performance (1963–1983), exh. cat., Studio Museum in Harlem, New York, 1984
Faith Ringgold: Painting, Sculpture and Performance, exh. cat., College of Wooster Art Museum, OH, 1985
Faith Ringgold, Change: Painted Story Quilts, exh. cat., Bernice Steinbaum Gallery, New York, 1987
Thalia Gouma-Peterson, "Faith Ringgold's narrative quilts", *Arts Magazine*, lxi, January 1987, pp.64–9
Freida High Tesfagiorgis, "Afrofemcentrism and its fruition in the art of Elizabeth Catlett and Faith Ringgold", *SAGE*, iv, Spring 1987, pp.25–32
Lowery Sims, "Aspects of performance in the works of Black American women artists", *Feminist Art Criticism*, ed. Arlene Raven, Cassandra L. Langer and Joanna Frueh, Ann Arbor: UMI Research Press, 1988, pp.207–25
Judy Seigel, "Faith Ringgold: What do black women want?", *Women Artists' News*, xiii, Summer 1988, pp.5–6
Lucy R. Lippard, *Mixed Blessings: New Art in a Multicultural America*, New York: Pantheon, 1990
Faith Ringgold: A 25 Year Survey, exh. cat., Fine Arts Museum of Long Island, Hempstead, NY, and elsewhere, 1990
Faith Ringgold: The Last Story Quilt, created and produced by Linda Freeman, L and S Video Enterprises, Inc., 1991 (video)
Mara R. Witzling, ed., *Voicing Our Visions: Writings by Women Artists*, New York: Universe, 1991; London: Women's Press, 1992

Wendy Slatkin, ed., *The Voices of Women Artists*, Englewood Cliffs, NJ: Prentice Hall, 1993
Norma Broude and Mary D. Garrard, eds, *The Power of Feminist Art: The American Movement of the 1970s*, New York: Abrams, and London: Thames and Hudson, 1994
Melody Graulich and Mara R. Witzling, "The freedom to say what she pleases: A conversation with Faith Ringgold", *NWSA Journal*, vi, Spring 1994, pp.1–27

Faith Ringgold successfully merges the Western art tradition in which she was trained with the pictorial and narrative traditions of her African-American heritage. Ringgold has asserted that she did not want to achieve artistic success at the expense of "one iota of my blackness, or my femaleness, or my humanity" (Hempstead 1990, p.23), a goal that she has met successfully. First trained as a painter, Ringgold began using stitched fabric to make figures, which she then engaged in performances. Over the years, her need to articulate her stories expanded, resulting in her creation of text-and-image "story quilts" for which she writes original narratives. Ringgold is also noted as a writer. In 1977 she began writing her autobiography, "Being my own woman", which was published in 1995 as *We Flew Over the Bridge* and, since 1989, she has written and illustrated several children's books.

Ringgold remembers the Harlem of her childhood as a culturally rich community. Living close to her extended family, she heard fascinating stories and reminiscences that they traded back and forth. Their neighbours and friends in the elegant Sugar Hill section of Harlem were among the most distinguished black political and cultural figures of the generation. As a child, Ringgold was frequently bed-ridden with asthma, and artistic creation became one of her favourite escapes from the boredom of illness. She was aware in her early teens of her special talent, and by her senior year in high school had decided that she wanted to become an artist.

Ringgold's formal study of art began in 1948 when she enrolled in the City College of New York as an art education major, specialising in painting. In 1950 she married the jazz pianist Robert Earl Wallace and had two daughters, eleven months apart, before the year was out. She graduated from City College in 1955 with a degree in art education and began an 18-year career teaching art in the New York public schools. Ringgold did not begin to define herself as an artist, however, until the early 1960s. She completed her master's degree in 1959, and in 1961 she took an important trip to Europe to see the art that she had studied. On her return to the USA, she claimed her former dining room as studio space, an important gesture that established art-making as a major priority in her life. Shortly thereafter, her first marriage having ended, she married Burdette Ringgold, in 1962.

It was at this time that Ringgold began to work towards finding a way to create images of black people that were acceptable to her. She felt that she had to go beyond her education, which taught art through copying the "masters" of the Western tradition. She began to seek models that would allow her to create more vital images, and found inspiration in Cubism and African art. "Instead of looking to Greece, I looked to Africa", she once said. By the later 1960s Ringgold had developed a mature style characterised by bold, flat colours and abstracted forms. This style is evident in works belonging to her *American People* series and most particularly in such paintings as the *Flag Is Bleeding* (1967; Bernice Steinbaum Gallery, New York) and *Die* (1967). In their accessible imagery, the American flag, for instance, these works bear a resemblance to works of the Pop Art movement that was in its heyday at that time, but Ringgold imbued the popular icons with political meaning, commenting on the violence of race relations in the USA. In 1971 she helped to found Where We At, an organisation of black artists.

During the next decade Ringgold began to work with three-dimensional forms executed in fabric. After seeing an exhibition of Tibetan *tankas* in Amsterdam, she decided to mount her paintings on "soft frames" to make them easier to transport. She also began a series called the *Family of Woman*, fiercely haunting masks, their mouths open to allow them to speak, of mixed media, animated with fabric bodies. While working on these pieces she collaborated with her mother, Willi Posey, a seamstress who had by then become a fabric designer. Ringgold recounts that she had taught such African crafts as beading and mask-making for some time before she realised that she could use these techniques in her own work. Giving herself permission to deviate from Western traditions, by incorporating in her own work elements from her African cultural heritage and her mother's art, Ringgold was able to take an important step closer to her goal of expressing her inner vision. By the mid-1970s Ringgold was animating the characters she created, at first stuffing the bodies to give them greater dimension, as in her "bag" couple, Zora and Fish. She then moved to making environmental performance pieces, employing characters she created. The *Wake and Resurrection of the Bi-Centennial Negro* (1976; Bernice Steinbaum Gallery), for example, dealt with the devastating impact of drugs on the lives of black people. In these performances she also collaborated with her daughter, the writer Michele Wallace. Ringgold took a further significant step in 1973 when she resigned from her teaching position in the New York schools in order to devote her energies exclusively to her artistic career.

In the 1980s Ringgold achieved a breakthrough to her greatest artistic achievement to date, in the conception of the "story quilt". She created her first quilt for a project conceived by Charlotte Robinson, entitled *The Artist and the Quilt*, which brought together quilts made by 18 women artists who usually worked in "high art" media. Ringgold collaborated with her mother on *Echoes of Harlem* (1980; Philip Morris Companies, Inc.), portraying in paint the faces of people she had known, while Posey used traditional quilting techniques to sew the finished piece. Although this was their last collaboration (Posey died in 1981), the work provided the catalyst for Ringgold's subsequent artistic development. During the next decade Ringgold executed numerous story quilts: at first, she made single works, such as *Who's Afraid of Aunt Jemima?* (1983; Fred Collins, Brooklyn, NY), but later went on to make multiple-quilt series that elaborated intricately plotted stories, such as her five-quilt sequence, the *Bitter Nest* (1988; Bernice Steinbaum Gallery). While the first quilts were built from individually painted "pieces", her subsequent quilts were made by framing a central painted panel with quilted fabric. As she herself has noted, the story quilts were a vehicle for bringing together the characters she had created in her earlier masks and performance pieces. Each quilt is narrated by a woman, articulating a point of view that is decidedly female. Their

Ringgold: *French Collection I: No.8, On the Beach at St Tropez*, begun 1991; pieced fabric border; 188 × 233.7 cm.; artist's collection

scenarios and characters are diverse – a slave born on the crossing from Africa to America, a pious woman from the South, an affluent black alumna of Williams College in Massachusetts, as well as many voices from Harlem. Ringgold wrote all the stories for her quilts herself, with the exception of the narrative material on the *Purple Quilt* (1986; Bernice Steinbaum Gallery), which is derived from Alice Walker's book *The Color Purple*. Their narrative structure derives from her family's oral tradition of story-telling, which Ringgold has claimed as a major influence in her life. Thalia Gouma-Peterson has suggested that some of Ringgold's quilt stories are related to the African "dilemma tale" in which a problem is posed but inconclusively resolved, forcing the viewer/reader to confront ambiguity ("Modern dilemma tales" in Hempstead 1990).

With eight quilts in Part I and four in Part II, the *French Collection* (begun 1991; see illustration) is her most complex and ambitious work to date, a *Kunstlerroman* in quilts in which Ringgold inserts an African-American presence into the tradition of Parisian modernism in which she was trained. Her protagonist is a young African-American woman, Willia Marie Simone, who goes to Paris to study art in the 1920s. Each quilt presents a fictional gathering of a cast of characters interpolated with at least one "masterpiece" of the Euro-centric tradition. In the first quilt of the series, the three daughters of Willia's friend go dancing at the Louvre (also the name of the quilt) in front of the *Mona Lisa*. In the *Picnic at Giverny* Willia paints a group of contemporary feminists who sit in Monet's famous garden. The series explores themes related to being a woman artist, especially one of African-American heritage, in the bastion of male artistic hegemony. Through Willia, Ringgold asserts that, rather than being models and muses, women can be the speaking subjects of their lives. In *Sunflower Quilting Bee at Arles* (private collection) the National Sunflower Quilters, female African-American freedom fighters, gather in van Gogh's sunflower fields, saying: "Now we can do our real quilting, our real art – making this world piece up right" (*The French Collection* 1992, p.24).

Ringgold's use of the quilting medium shows her awareness of traditional African quilting methods and her sensitivity to the significance that quilts have had in women's lives. She allows black women to speak with authority in their own voices, to tell their own stories, bypassing the stereotypes of the dominant culture, thus giving them power and centrality. Freida High Tesfagiorgis has described Ringgold as an "Afrofemcentrist", because her art consistently and centrally shows black, female subjects and conveys black women's realities. Perhaps the greatest significance of the story quilts is the challenge that they present to the assumptions regarding the traditionally separate realms of crafts and fine art. Since the 19th century, women have used quilts to express the truths about their lives, whether through the vaguely referential symbolic language of pattern or through more directly representative means. The very fabrics used for quilts often have meaning to their makers, and quilts are used to mark events of importance, such as engagements and births. Like those quilts produced from within the crafts tradition, Ringgold's quilts maintain those connections to women's lives. Yet Ringgold is an artist trained in the fine art tradition; she exhibits her quilts in art galleries, not at craft fairs, and they are bought by museums. The quilts thus cross the borders between cultural and artistic traditions; as objects and in the stories they tell, they have many meanings.

Ringgold has also reiterated her affirmative vision in several award-winning books which she both wrote and illustrated. The first, *Tar Beach* (1991), based on her story quilt *Tar Beach* (1988; Solomon R. Guggenheim Museum, New York), shows tenement dwellers on a hot summer night picnicking on the roof, the only "beach" they can afford to visit. It echoes African folk stories about people who fly, with its protagonist, eight-year-old Cassie Louise Lightfoot, flying over the George Washington Bridge and claiming it as her own, and concludes: "anyone can fly". In Ringgold's second book, *Aunt Harriet's Underground Railroad in the Sky* (1992), the first written especially for children, Cassie and her little brother Bebe encounter Harriet Tubman. Her third book, *Dinner at Aunt Connie's House* (1993), a revision of another story quilt, *Dinner Quilt*, introduces children to other heroic African-American women, "sheroes" as Ringgold calls them.

MARA R. WITZLING

See also Training and Professionalism survey 10

Ritsema, Coba

Dutch painter, 1876–1961

Born Jacoba Johanna Ritsema in Haarlem, 26 June 1876, daughter of the painter and printmaker Coenraad Ritsema, sister of landscape artist Jacob Ritsema. Attended evening classes in drawing at the Kunstnijverheidschool (Technical School) in Haarlem from the age of 12, eventually becoming a full-time student there, 1891–3. Studied at the Rijksacademie (Royal Academy), Amsterdam, under August Allebé, 1893–7. Member of a group of eight women artists dubbed the Amsterdam Joffers. Set up as a painter in Haarlem, 1897. Rented a studio on the Singel in Amsterdam, 1899–1958; initially commuted from Haarlem; settled permanently in Amsterdam only after her mother's death in 1922. Member of the artists' society Arti et Amicitiae, and of Sint Lucasgilde (Guild of St Luke), both in Amsterdam, 1900. Recipient of silver medals, city of Amsterdam, 1912 and 1923; gold medal from HM the Queen, Netherlands, 1918; Rembrandt prize for entire oeuvre, city of Leiden, 1958. Knight of Orange Nassau, 1935. Moved into an Amsterdam nursing home in 1958. Died 13 December 1961.

Principal Exhibitions

Individual
Charlottenborg, Copenhagen: 1916
Gallery Buffa, Amsterdam: 1924, 1935
Gallery De Bois, Haarlem: 1928
Pictura, Dordrecht: 1929
Gallery Bennewitz, The Hague: 1942
Stedelijk Museum, Amsterdam: 1946
Frans Halsmuseum, Haarlem: 1951
De Lakenhal, Leiden: 1958

Group
Arti et Amicitiae, Amsterdam: occasionally 1900–61 (Willink van Collen prize 1900, gold medal 1917)
Sint Lucas, Amsterdam: occasionally 1900–61 (Sint Lucas prize 1937)
Exposition Universelle et Internationale, Brussels: 1910 (bronze medal)
Stedelijk Museum, Amsterdam: 1912, 1932 (both *Internationale tentoonstelling van levende meesters* [International exhibition of contemporary masters]), 1917, 1942 (both *Hollandsche kunstenaarskring* [Dutch artists circle]), 1948–50 (*Amsterdamse schilders van nu* [Amsterdam painters of today], annuals)
Amsterdamse Joffers, Netherlands: 1926, 1937, 1940, 1946, 1950, 1958
Rotterdamse Kunstring [Rotterdam Art Circle]: 1926 (*De Amsterdamse schilderessen* [Amsterdam women painters])
Venice Biennale: 1932
Exposition Internationale, Paris: 1937 (diploma of honour)

Bibliography
Albertine de Haas, "Coba Ritsema", *Onze·Kunst*, xii/9, September 1913
Adriaan Venema, *De Amsterdamse Joffers* [The Amsterdam Ladies], Baarn: Wereldvenster, 1977
Bloemen uit de kelder [Flowers from the cellar], exh. cat., Gemeentemuseum, Arnhem, 1989

Coba Ritsema belongs to the first generation of Dutch women artists that was able to receive a thorough professional training. By the end of the 19th century academies were increasingly admitting women, a situation of which Ritsema took advantage. Her teachers at the Amsterdam Academy were impressed by her command of form, sense of colour and outstanding feeling for composition, qualities that she developed over the years. She attained a level of professional ability that, by her own account, she would never have achieved without an academic training, despite the fact that her father and brother were also artists. It was above all Professor August Allebé, a pedagogue of the old school, who put Ritsema on the right track. Allebé, himself a painter, demanded "keen observation" and "sober, modest realism" from his pupils. These were Ritsema's guiding principles, though her brushwork became freer over

Ritsema: *Studio, Sitting Girl*, exhibited 1910; oil on canvas; 74 × 50 cm.; Haags Gemeentemuseum, The Hague

the years, and her recording of impressions more spontaneous. When she was 23 she fitted up her own studio in the heart of Amsterdam and went there to paint portraits and still lifes in an impressionistic style. During her successful career she produced only a limited number of works.

At the Academy Ritsema came to know other women students, and formed lifelong friendships with them: Marie van Regteren Altena, Jo Stumpff (who married the painter Marius Bauer in 1902) and Lizzy Ansingh. After leaving the Academy, this group joined forces with a further four women who were already practising artists: Ans van den Berg, Nelly Bodenheim, Jacoba Surie and Betsy Osieck (who married H.K. Westendorp in 1917). These women, with a few exceptions, all came from well-to-do families, had all been to the Amsterdam Academy and around 1900 had all set up their own studios in the city. They had agreed to meet regularly for Sunday afternoons at the house of Lizzy Ansingh's aunt, the portrait painter Thérèse Schwartze (q.v.). At this time women artists were still not welcome at the artists' association Arti et Amicitiae. Schwartze, a painter of established reputation who maintained contact with painters of The Hague school and artists of her own generation, may be seen as the group's supervisor. Like Ritsema, she attached the greatest importance to ability. The group of friends discussed each other's work critically, exhibited at the same galleries and had joint exhibitions. In 1912 the well-known Dutch art critic Albert Plasschaert nicknamed them the "Amsterdamse Joffers". According to Ansingh, Ritsema was "the greatest talent"; her touch of the brush in handling paint was also the most energetic. She was consequently one of the sustaining forces of the Amsterdamse Joffers, who were described and criticised as a group.

At the time that Ritsema was beginning to paint independently, the work of the Amsterdam Impressionists was attracting a good deal of attention. Ritsema maintained amicable professional contact with their most important representative, George H. Breitner. She caused the same warm, glowing Amsterdam light that Breitner captured in his townscapes to fall over the still lifes that she painted in her studio. At the exhibitions of Arti et Amicitiae she encountered the work of the French Impressionists for the first time, but by her own admission it was the paintings of Edouard Manet that made the deepest and most lasting impression on her. She did not look for new influences from among her contemporaries.

Like many other women painters, Ritsema tended not to date her works, making it very difficult to establish a precise chronology for them. Hence the portraits will be discussed first, and then the still lifes. After her time at the Academy Ritsema began to paint fairly small-scale portraits of girls from the Jordaan district of Amsterdam. *Head of a Girl* (31 × 23 cm.; Stedelijk Museum, Amsterdam) is a striking example. Unlike many of her contemporaries, she portrays her subjects not picturesquely but with their heads in characteristic attitudes. In this first phase of her career her work is modest in tone, but in *Girl with a Beret* (Stedelijk Museum) she succeeds in recording her impressions with great immediacy. The little *Girl with Toothache* (private collection, repr. Venema 1977, p.97) makes its impact by means of warm colouring against a dark background, free and vigorous brush strokes in, for example, the white cloth around the girl's head, and the introverted expression of her face. In the *Artist's Mother*

(1899; Dienst Verspreide Rijkscollecties, The Hague) Ritsema's mother poses in an armchair before her daughter, who paints her frontally, and in magisterial attitude.

Ritsema's reputation was established in 1910, when her *Studio, Sitting Girl* (see illustration) won a prize at the Brussels Exposition. This work shows how her colours had grown lighter and more refined in their harmonies over the years, and that she was still capable of creating a well-ordered composition, no matter how complex, in this case assisted by the warm light that pours into the room. Although the brushwork is spontaneous, the firm delineation of forms also contributes to the arrangement of space. The girl sits on a folding chair with her back turned to the spectator, a pose that Ritsema used on several occasions. She had painted the folding chair before, at the beginning of her career, in *Green Chair* (Stedelijk Museum), but a comparison of this work with *Studio, Sitting Girl* highlights Ritsema's artistic development: besides its greater technical accomplishment, the brushwork of the later painting is no longer precise but free and vigorous, the tonalities are brighter and the colours more varied. The late *Girl with a Mirror* (private collection, *ibid.*, p.113) was praised by contemporaries. Although the subject might lend itself to a saccharine treatment, Ritsema, characteristically, portrays the girl in direct and restrained fashion, though her white dress is exuberantly painted. Selective highlights intensify the poetic atmosphere. The combination of restraint and exuberance is typical of Ritsema's work. There are no known self-portraits by her.

The early *Still Life with Bottles* (private collection, *ibid.*, p.96) possesses the realism and modest colouring characteristic of the first part of Ritsema's career, and shows that she already had excellent command of the representation of material substances, though at this stage was able to make only scant use of the broad brush stroke. Like her later figure paintings, such still lifes as *Peonies* (Haags Gemeentemuseum, The Hague; Boijmans Van Beuningen Museum, Rotterdam) are full of exuberance. In them Ritsema could give her painter's temperament free rein. She produced several of these flower paintings, whose lucid and expansive compositions are full of colour nuances. *Blue Feather* (Stedelijk Museum) demonstrates a nonchalant excess. In *Rose Azalea* (private collection, repr. Arnhem 1989, fig.5) Ritsema seems to be setting down a shout of joy on to the canvas. Her style here is not very far removed from non-figurative forms of expression. Her pastels, for example *The Breakfast* (Stedelijk Museum De Lakenhal, Leiden), are more light-hearted in tone than her paintings.

Throughout her life Ritsema exhibited regularly and with success in group exhibitions at home and abroad, and was granted solo exhibitions and awards. Her still lifes and portraits easily found a market, but in spite of this she remained above all true to herself. Her painting style provoked observations such as the description of the "masculine enunciation of form" that underpinned "her feminine sense of the magnificence and grace of materials and colours", and the reference to "a typically female virtuosity with colour". In 1977, in his book *De Amsterdamse Joffers*, Venema was still speaking of the "really feminine tact" with which Ritsema's compositions were arranged.

ROSELLA M. HUBER-SPANIER

Rivera, Frida *see* Kahlo

Robertson, Christina
British painter, 1796–1854

Born Christina Saunders in Kinghorn, Fife, 17 December 1796. Little is known of her early life and artistic training. Established in the Marylebone district of London as a professional miniaturist, sharing a studio with her uncle, the Scottish portraitist George Saunders, by 1823. Married artist James Robertson, 1822; several children, of whom only four, two sons, two daughters, survived to adulthood; taught her daughters Agnes and Mary to paint. Trips to Paris from the mid-1830s. Travelled to St Petersburg, 1839; patronised by the Russian Imperial family. Back in London by 15 December 1841. Returned to St Petersburg, late 1840s. Honorary member, Royal Scottish Academy, 1829; Imperial Academy of Arts, St Petersburg, 1841. Died in St Petersburg, 30 April 1854.

Principal Exhibitions
Royal Academy, London: 1823–39, 1841–4
Society of British Artists, London: 1824–36, 1838–9, 1847
Royal Scottish Academy, Edinburgh: 1829–31, 1834, 1839, 1845
British Institution, London: 1833–5, 1838–9, 1847

Bibliography
John Burke, *The Portrait Gallery of Distinguished Females, Including the Courts of George IV and William IV*, 2 vols, London, 1833
Ellen C. Clayton, *English Female Artists*, 2 vols, London: Tinsley, 1876
M.D. Buturlin, *Zapiski* [Notes], Moscow: Russkiy Arkhiv, 1901, iii, p.451
Alan Bird, "A painter of the Russian aristocracy", *Country Life*, clxi, 6 January 1977, pp.32–3
Larissa A. Dukelskaya and Elizaveta Renne, *British Painting from 16th to 19th Centuries: Catalogue of Western European Painting*, Florence, 1990
Elizaveta Renne, "A British portraitist in Imperial Russia", *Apollo*, cxlii, September 1995, pp.43–5
Christina Robertson: A Scottish Portraitist at the Russian Court, exh. cat., City of Edinburgh Museums and Galleries, Edinburgh, 1996

Although she was a particularly fashionable and popular portraitist in her day, as well as a prolific exhibitor at the major London exhibiting institutions, and distinguished with honorary memberships of the Imperial Academy of Arts in St Petersburg (1841) and the Royal Scottish Academy in Edinburgh (1829), where she stands out historically as the first female honorary member, Christina Robertson suffered an extreme lack of critical attention after her death. This lack was properly redressed only when the first solo exhibition of her work was held in Edinburgh in 1996.

She began her career as a miniaturist; many of her ivories are large and rectangular in format, depicting the sitter half, three-quarter or full length, such as her *Self-Portrait* (c.1822; Victoria and Albert Museum, London), and her earliest known work, the double portrait of *The Hon. Clementina Elizabeth Drummond-Burrell and Her Sister* (Grimsthorpe and Drummond Castle Trust), which is signed and dated 1819. Her

sitters were mainly drawn from the British aristocracy and landed gentry and included a significant number of Scots, such as the Hon. William Adam, Lord Chief Commissioner for the Jury Court of Scotland, the Marchioness of Lothian and the Duke and Duchess of Buccleuch. One of her most important early commissions was to paint miniature portraits of *Hugh, 3rd Duke of Northumberland* and his wife, *Charlotte Florentia* (Duke of Northumberland, Alnwick Castle). The artist published an engraving from the Duke's portrait, presumably as a means of publicity; engravings from many of her miniature portraits of society beauties appeared in contemporary albums and journals, such as John Burke's *Portrait Gallery of Distinguished Females* (1833), *La Belle Assemblée* and the *Book of Beauty*.

Her account book (Library, Victoria and Albert Museum) demonstrates the high prices she charged her clients and is a valuable record of her sitters. Her clientele became more cosmopolitan in the mid-1830s when she began to visit Paris, where she painted, among others, the *Comtesse de Noailles* and *Monsieur Adolphe Thiers* (1838), the eminent statesman and historian. It was in Paris that she first came into contact with her Russian clients. Her account book for 1837 includes mention of Princess Wittgenstein and of the Countesses Zavadovsky and Patoski. Some of these noble ladies from the highest echelons of St Petersburg society and close to the Imperial family no doubt recommended her to the Russian court. Robertson may have been in St Petersburg by September 1839, although this cannot be verified. She did, however, take part in the autumn exhibition at the Imperial Academy of Arts that year. In the exhibition review an unknown Russian art critic noted:

> … the best portrait of all those exhibited at the Academy, however, is a portrait of a woman in a white satin dress playing the organ. This might confidently be placed alongside Rembrandt, and it would lose little from such a dangerous comparison. What a bold, powerful brush! How all is simple, natural, how alien to artificiality! What superb colouring! And who would have thought all this is the work of a weak woman's hand! or more correctly, only a woman could paint this: a man would not be capable of so much feeling … It is immediately clear that Mrs Robertson is an Englishwoman, that she was brought up in the traditions of sublime portrait painting …

Robertson's popularity in Russia must have grown particularly after she painted the whole of the Imperial family, including Tsar Nicholas I. She painted his portrait in 1840 and although its whereabouts are unknown, a lithograph by Maurin and published by LeMercier in Paris gives an idea of the original work. Robertson was awarded Honorary Membership of the Academy of Arts in the following year for her portraits of the Empress, Alexandra Fyodorovna, and three of her daughters (Hermitage, St Petersburg), which were exhibited at the Academy in 1841. It is interesting that in Russia she began to paint large, formal State portraits in oil on canvas; these tend to lose the quality and charm of her earlier miniature portraits, in which the faces are very delicately and finely drawn and in which she displays a talent for rendering different textures of satin, velvet and lace. Her portraits are often

Christina Robertson: *Children with a Parrot*, 1850; oil on canvas; 112 × 104 cm.; Hermitage Museum, St Petersburg

flattering. With Karl von Steuben, H. Vernet and J.D. Court, Robertson was the most popular and highly paid portraitist in St Petersburg. Her clients included the Yusupovs, the Baryatinskys, the Orlov-Davydovs, the Shuvalovs, the Sheremetyevs, Belosel'skys and the Bobrinskys (paintings kept in collections throughout Russia and the CIS, including the State Hermitage Museum and State Russian Museum, St Petersburg, and the major state museums in Moscow, Stavropol', Omsk, Voronezh, Alupka, Simferopol and Tashkent). Her contemporary popularity was demonstrated by Buturlin (1901), who commented: "for two or three years she won from her fellow artists almost all their practice. It was the fashion among the Petersburg nobility of the time to have their portraits painted by this foreign artist who charged unheard of prices."

At the end of 1841 Christina Robertson returned to Britain where she continued to paint and exhibit her work. Although she still painted miniatures on ivory during this period, most of the paintings she now exhibited were oils on canvas, often small cabinet pieces depicting full-length figures in an interior, which were well received in the contemporary press. She returned to Russia, however, some time at the end of the 1840s; all of the paintings from this second prolonged stay in Russia date from the years 1849–52. Although Robertson was essentially a portraitist, she did exhibit a genre scene of the *Meeting of the Earl of Leicester and Amy Robsart* at the British Institution in 1847. The picture, now lost, is known through a copy on porcelain (Hermitage) by Ilya Artemyev.

ELIZAVETA RENNE

Robertson, Suze
Dutch painter, 1855–1922

Born in The Hague, 17 December 1855. Studied at the Academie voor Beeldende Kunsten (Academy of Fine Arts), The Hague, 1874–7 (bronze and silver medals 1876, teaching certificate 1877). Subsequently taught drawing at a girls' secondary school in Rotterdam, attending evening life classes at the Rotterdam Academy. Studied art privately under Petrus van der Velden in The Hague, 1880–82. Took up another teaching appointment in Amsterdam, 1882; attended evening classes at the Rijksacademie (Royal Academy), Amsterdam. Gave up teaching to pursue a professional career as a painter and moved back to The Hague, 1883. Married painter Richard Bisschop, 1892; daughter born 1894. Reduced painting activity for nine years after birth of daughter, although gave drawing lessons to maintain the family income. Member of the Nederlandse Etsclub (Dutch Etching Club) and the Pulchri Studio, Amsterdam, where she took part in drawing evenings with Georg Hendrik Breitner, Willem Bastiaan Tholen and De Zwart. Died 18 October 1922.

Principal Exhibitions
International Colonial Exhibition, Amsterdam: 1883
Arti et Amicitiae, Amsterdam: occasionally 1886–1914
Pulchri Studio, The Hague: occasionally 1888–1922 (annuals), 1921 (individual), 1924 (retrospective)
Exposition Triennale et Jubilaire des Beaux-Arts, Antwerp: 1888
Paris: 1891 (*Maîtres hollandais*)
De Hollandsche Teekenmaatschappij [Dutch Society of Draughtsmen], The Hague: occasionally 1893–1922
Exposition Universelle, Paris: 1900 (gold medal)
International Exhibition of Women's Art, London: 1900 (gold medal)
Louisiana Purchase Exposition, St Louis: 1904 (bronze medal)
Sint Lucas, Amsterdam: occasionally 1904–22
Arnhem: 1905 (*Levende meesters* [Contemporary masters], gold medal)
Rotterdamse Kunstkring, Rotterdam: 1905 (individual)
Exposition Universelle et Internationale, Brussels: 1910
Exposición Internacional del Cenario, Buenos Aires: 1910 (bronze medal)
Exposición Internacional de Arte, Barcelona: 1911 (silver medal)
Internationale Kunstausstellung, Munich: 1913 (gold medal)
Maatschappij voor Beeldende Kunsten, Amsterdam: 1921 (individual)

Bibliography
G.H. Marius, "Suze Robertson", *Onze Kunst*, vi, 1906, pp.181–8
H.P. Bremmer, *Beeldende Kunst*, 1917, nos 7–9; 1927, no.9; 1928, no.6; 1933, no.1
N. van Harpen, *Menschen die ik gekend heb* [People I have known], Rotterdam, 1928, pp.26–33
A.M. Hammacher, *Beeldende Kunst*, no.9, 1941
Suze Robertson, exh. cat., Gemeentemuseum, The Hague, and Stedelijk Museum, Amsterdam, 1955
Suze Robertson, exh. cat., Gemeentemuseum, The Hague, 1984
Bloemen uit de kelder [Flowers from the cellar], exh. cat., Gemeentemuseum, Arnhem, 1989
De schilders van Tachtig: Nederlandse schilderkunst, 1880–1895 [Painters of the 1880s: Dutch painting], exh. cat., Waanders Uitgevers, Zwolle, and elsewhere, 1991

Suze Robertson was the first Dutch woman to be allowed to draw from the nude model at the Academy (of Rotterdam). It

Suze Robertson: *Display of Old Things*, *c.*1900; oil on canvas; 112 × 104 cm; Haags Gemeentemuseum, The Hague

was 1877. In that year she gained her secondary school teaching certificate in drawing after two years of classical training at The Hague Academy. She distinguished herself there from the beginning, and won two silver medals and one bronze. Even at that stage she had her own distinctive way of approaching a subject. On leaving the Academy, Robertson earned her keep by giving drawing lessons, first in Rotterdam and then in Amsterdam, while also attending lessons at the academies there. Between 1880 and 1882 she took private lessons from Petrus van der Velden, and under his influence embarked on her career. Many painters were then still working in the style of The Hague school, which had flourished around 1870 but which in the 1880s was slowly being superseded by new movements, such as Amsterdam Impressionism and later Symbolism. Like such Hague school painters as Jozef Israels, van der Velden painted naturalistic representations of peasants and fishermen in interior settings, but his style was rougher and broader than theirs (according to a letter of 1883 by van Gogh). Robertson saw van Gogh's work in the 1890s, and was full of admiration for it. Another revolutionary figure of the time was George H. Breitner, generally considered to be an Amsterdam Impressionist. Robertson had come to know Breitner during her time at The Hague Academy, where he had been a fellow pupil, and she afterwards maintained professional contact with him.

Robertson found her own way in the new movement. Through her use of colour and her bold brushwork she developed an expressive style. Her palette is warm and restrained, dark in tone; her compositions are well ordered and likewise restrained; and the surfaces of her paintings are often irregular, due to working over the underpainting several times. Her oeuvre as a whole is characterised by a spontaneous method of working, though one that also involves careful preparation.

In the autumn of 1883 Robertson decided to work independently in The Hague. From 1885 until around 1903 she sold work at group exhibitions, such as those organised for their members by the Pulchri Studio in The Hague and by Arti et Amicitiae in Amsterdam. Although more than 600 works could be shown at one time on these occasions, Robertson's paintings stood out. By the end of the 1890s a handful of dealers had begun to be interested in her work, and she also took part in exhibitions abroad, receiving awards on several occasions. In 1905 she had her first and immediately successful solo exhibition, consisting of 93 paintings, watercolours, pastels and black chalk drawings – both new and previously sold works. Despite their modernity, her work was sold by dealers, mostly to collectors.

Because Robertson rarely dated her work, it is not possible to establish a reliable chronology. She nearly always signed her work, resolutely and in full, as "Suze Robertson", even after her marriage. While studying with van der Velden, she painted mostly still lifes and heads. In 1883 she successfully submitted a *Vegetable Still Life* (Haags Gemeentemuseum, The Hague) to an international exhibition in Amsterdam. The composition of this early work is already broad and clearly ordered, but it still belongs in the tradition of The Hague school. On this occasion Robertson used what was for her a fairly large canvas, namely 75 × 85 centimetres. Most of her paintings are somewhat smaller in format. *Still Life with Onions and a Pewter Dish* (1885–90; repr. exh. cat., Borzo Gallery, Den Bosch, 1976, fig.4) is still rather academic and has a light background, but *Still Life with Vegetables, Pewter Dish and Pickling-Bottle* (Stedelijk Museum, Amsterdam) already has much of her own style: the foreground and table-top are relatively light in contrast to the fairly dark background, and the composition is relieved by the use of brilliant, but generally quite small highlights. There are several of these still lifes of pickling bottles and fruit in the Haags Gemeentemuseum; of these, *Still Life with Apples and a Bottle* (between 1905 and 1910) and *Corner of the Studio* (c.1900) attract special attention.

In the 1880s Robertson produced a handful of robustly painted self-portraits (1883; *ibid*., fig. 1, and Haags Gemeentemuseum), in which the face is lit up against a dark background, and the attitude and expression are determined. She also painted various nude studies at this time, such as *Lena* (Dordrechts Museum), for which she won a gold medal at the International Exhibition of Women's Art in London, and semi-draped studies, such as *Nude Boy* – exceptional in her oeuvre, since she always painted women – *Nellie* and other, later works (all Haags Gemeentemuseum). The girls seem shy at having to pose under Robertson's close scrutiny. In *Display of Old Things* (c.1900; see illustration) she portrayed, in her characteristic style, her nursemaid, Pietje, who also appears in *Pietje in a Farm-Style Chair* (after 1900; Haags Gemeentemuseum), a painting suffused with her personal symbolism. Besides young girls, Robertson on many occasions painted a single old woman at work, as in *Washing the Dishes* and *Bleaching Lawn* (both between 1898 and 1903; Haags Gemeentemuseum), in which a stooping woman spreads white cloths on green grass, and, after 1905, *Peeling Potatoes* (Haags Gemeentemuseum; Rijksmuseum Kröller-Müller, Otterlo) and *At the Wash Tub* (Haags Gemeentemuseum). She also painted women at the spinning wheel, a favourite subject of the time, in many variations, for instance, *Women at the Spinning Wheel* (Haags Gemeentemuseum). A comparison between a watercolour of this subject by Robertson and a similar drawing by Albert Neuhuys (chapter entitled "De macht der taal", Arnhem 1989) reveals that Robertson presents an old women marked by daily cares and absorbed in her work, while Neuhuys depicts a young and graceful woman. Her work stems from an intense concern; his from tender feeling. In 1919 a critic described Robertson in this connection as a "painter of pure, feminine sentiment". Her "profound inner feeling" was interpreted as typically feminine. On the other hand her "visions of misery", namely her renderings with powerful touches of sturdy old working women were criticised as masculine. The portrait of an *Old Woman*, also called *Hanne* (before 1909; Rijksmuseum Kröller-Müller), one of her mature works, is a lucid and impassioned depiction of the subject, which calls van Gogh to mind.

In the 1890s Robertson began to produce various paintings of Dutch fishing villages, scenes of houses with white gables, in which a woman is nearly always at work. These include *Village Scene* (Haags Gemeentemuseum) and *The White House*

(Haags Gemeentemuseum; Rijksmuseum Kröller-Müller). From 1914 the accent began to fall on drawing, though Robertson had made charcoal drawings and watercolours throughout her career. The Rijksmuseum Kröller-Müller in Otterlo owns many sketches and fully worked drawings, for example *Negroes*. There are also numerous drawings and watercolours in the Haags Gemeentemuseum, The Hague. In addition, Robertson produced splendid watercolours, such as *Corner of the Studio* (1898–1901; Rijksmuseum H.W. Mesdag, The Hague). A pastel of a seated nude girl is in the Gemeentemuseum, Arnhem.

Robertson belonged to the same generation as Thérèse Schwartze (q.v.), who enjoyed a considerable contemporary reputation; but while Robertson made a living from her work, she did not become wealthy from it. She was too much ahead of her time and, unlike Schwartze, did not make concessions to the market. At present the positions are reversed, and Robertson's work is the more highly acclaimed.

ROSELLA M. HUBER-SPANIER

Robineau, Adelaide Alsop
American ceramist, 1865–1929

Born Adelaide Beers Alsop in Middletown, Connecticut, 9 April 1865. Married Frenchman Samuel Robineau in New York, 1899; one son, born 1900, two daughters, born 1902 and 1906. Co-founder, with her husband, 1899, and editor, 1899–1928, of the Arts and Crafts magazine *Keramic Studio* (title changed to *Design*, 1924). Moved to Syracuse, New York, 1901. Began making art porcelains in her pottery in Syracuse, 1903. Worked with the French ceramist Taxile Doat at the Art Academy (part of the American Woman's League), University City, Missouri, 1909–10. Returned to Syracuse, 1911; ran Arts and Crafts summer schools at her home, 1912–14. Recipient of honorary doctorate in ceramic science, Syracuse University, 1917. Joined the staff of Syracuse University, 1921. Died of cancer in Syracuse, 18 February 1929.

Principal Exhibitions

Esposizione Internazionale, Turin: 1911 (with American Woman's League; grand prix)
Panama-Pacific International Exposition, San Francisco: 1915 (Grand prize)
Metropolitan Museum of Art, New York: 1929 (retrospective)

Bibliography

Irene Sargent, "An American maker of hard porcelain: Adelaide Alsop Robineau", *Keystone*, xxvii, June 1906, pp.921–4
Frederick H. Rhead, "Adelaide Alsop Robineau, maker of porcelains", *Potter*, i, February 1917, pp.81–8
A Memorial Exhibition of Porcelain and Stoneware by Adelaide Alsop Robineau, exh. cat., Metropolitan Museum of Art, New York, 1929
Frederick Hurten Rhead, "Chats on pottery", *Potters Herald* (East Liverpool, OH), 1934–5, passim
Carlton Atherton, "Adelaide Alsop Robineau", unpublished memoir, c.1935; Robineau Archive, Everson Museum of Art, Syracuse, NY

Robert W. Blasberg, "American art porcelain: The work of Adelaide Alsop Robineau", *Spinning Wheel*, April 1971, pp.40–42

Anthea Callen, *Angel in the Studio: Women in the Arts and Crafts Movement, 1870–1914*, London: Astragal, 1979; as *Women Artists of the Arts and Crafts Movement*, New York: Pantheon, 1979

Peg Weiss, ed., *Adelaide Alsop Robineau: Glory in Porcelain*, Syracuse, NY: Syracuse University Press, 1981 (contains extensive bibliography)

Martin Eidelberg, "Apotheosis of the toiler", *American Craft*, xli, December 1981–January 1982, pp.2–5

Jane Perkins Claney, "Edwin Atlee Barber and the Robineaus: Correspondence, 1901–1916", *Tiller*, November–December 1982, pp.31–54

Barbara Perry, ed., *American Ceramics: The Collection of the Everson Museum of Art*, New York: Rizzoli, 1989

When she died in 1929 Adelaide Alsop Robineau was regarded as one of America's most distinguished ceramists, her art porcelains evoking, in the words of her assistant Carlton Atherton, "a feeling of awe and wonder". Initially a water-colourist and miniaturist, she turned to china painting and then, around 1903, she began making art porcelains. Robineau was largely self-taught, but her work developed rapidly and her incised and glazed wares were considered among the most beautiful pieces ever produced.

Robineau had taught herself china painting in the 1880s to provide additional income for her family. Although she worked successfully in this competitive field for some 20 years, she never achieved any particular prominence. Then in 1899 she married Samuel Robineau, a Frenchman living in New York, and within weeks they had launched *Keramic Studio*, an Arts and Crafts orientated monthly intended "for the designer, potter, decorator, firer". This magazine was to provide the Robineaus with an income for years to come. Robineau herself took on the editorship, contributing written material and publishing many of her own designs, which often reflected the current vogue for Art Nouveau. These were frequently adapted from such European publications as *The Studio*, *Art et Décoration* and *Dekorative Vorbilder*.

Robineau, encouraged by her husband, now became interested in making porcelains. Her new ambition may have been stimulated by an article she had published in *Keramic Studio* on the Paris Exposition Universelle of 1900, where the Scandinavian potteries in particular had put on notable shows of porcelain, and where there had been striking displays of crystalline glazes. In 1901 the Robineaus moved to Syracuse, a centre of the American Arts and Crafts movement and an ideal environment for the development of Robineau's ideas. She still practised her china painting, but in 1903, in search of instruction on the making of porcelains, she attended the short summer course at Alfred University run by a British potter, Charles Binns. That same year Samuel Robineau obtained a treatise on porcelain-making from the Sèvres ceramist Taxile Doat. Translated by Robineau himself, it appeared in *Keramic Studio* as a series of didactic articles under the title "*Grand feu* ceramics".

Adelaide Robineau now began to make porcelains in earnest, undertaking all the processes herself – designing, making the pots, choosing the composition of the bodies and the glazes, carrying out the decorations and overseeing the firing. Switching from china painting to making porcelains was

Robineau: *Scarab Vase*, 1910; Everson Museum of Art, Syracuse

not an easy option and was "about as rational and as possible as a vocational change ... from dentistry to cello playing", as her friend the Anglo-American potter Frederick Hurten Rhead observed (*Potters Herald*, 9 May 1935). Robineau was able to meet this challenge because she was "the possessor of a remarkably placid and tranquil mind together with a patient and gentle obstinacy or determination which no influence could affect" (*idem*). She made rapid progress and by 1904 had produced her first successful crystalline glaze.

The next year Robineau began carving, or excising, the porcelain. It is for this decorative method that she is best known. An excised design is formed on the ware by gradually scraping away the background until the ornament stands out in relief, a particularly difficult operation on porcelain, which has to be worked when dry. Robineau used only one tool, a very sharp point, which also made the work extremely slow, requiring "inexhaustible, consistent and tranquil patience" (Rhead 1917, p.87). She seems to have positively welcomed the difficulties, as excising was the method that pleased and suited her best. She even preferred excising to another highly skilled decorative process, *pâte-sur-pâte*, "not only", as she explained, "because it is more artistic, but also because it is more difficult" (*Panama-Pacific Exposition, Robineau Porcelains*, 1915, n.p.).

Robineau's early carved, as well as her rare incised designs, relied heavily on motifs from her pottery painting days. A vase decorated in 1905 with carved dragonflies (private collection, New Brunswick), for instance, was based on a design that had appeared in *Art et Décoration*, and the ships she excised on another piece made the same year, the *Viking Ship Vase* (Everson Museum of Art, Syracuse), were adapted from a *Dekorative Vorbilder* design of 1901. Standing 18.4 centimetres high, this piece was decorated in blue, green and brown glazes. Incised decoration appears on another work in the Everson Museum, the *Poppy Vase* of 1910. This has inlaid slips of blue, pink and olive and a white crystalline glaze and may owe something to Japanese prints.

In 1909 the Robineaus and Frederick Hurten Rhead joined the Ceramics Division of the Art Academy at the People's University, Missouri. The University, a part of the American Woman's League, was the brain child of the entrepreneur Edward G. Lewis and he had persuaded the Sèvres ceramist Taxile Doat to head the Division. The project was fatally flawed, but for a period in 1910 some prestigious work was produced. It was here that Robineau made her most famous piece, the *Scarab Vase* (see illustration), the excised work taking her 1000 hours and the glazing a further week. Its motif was the sacred Egyptian beetle, and on the underside she cut the words "Apotheosis of the Toiler". The "Toiler" here referred not only to her own labours on the vase but to the scarab as a symbol of rebirth and resurrection. Another work completed in 1910, the *Pastoral Vase* (National Museum of American History, Smithsonian Institution, Washington, DC), was made by Robineau for her daughter Priscilla. The pastoral theme combined an overall pattern of excised daisies with satyr masks executed in *pâte-sur-pâte*, a rare instance of her use of this technique.

After World War I, Robineau was invited to join the staff of Syracuse University, where her teaching inspired a generation of students. During the last decade of her life she also produced some of her most original work. She was, for instance, intent on reproducing works and glazes that had been perfected by the Chinese. Among these glazes were flambés that have been compared with the finest Chinese oxbloods. She also developed some unusual crystalline glazes, ranging from pale pinks and lavenders to a deep rose red, colours considered by some to be almost impossible to achieve (Weiss 1981, p.151). Other notable achievements were her eggshell bowls, made to what Atherton described as "an unbelievable thinness". These were extremely difficult to work and in the event only three were completed, one of which, the largest and best, was broken when Robineau allowed it to drop. Asked by Rhead how long it would take her to replace it, she replied "that she had no intention of ever attempting another eggshell piece of that size. She had succeeded in making a perfect piece of this type and that was that!" (*Potters Herald*, 24 October 1935). The Metropolitan Museum of Art in New York owns one of the two survivors, a piece completed in 1924 with pierced and excised floral decoration.

Robineau herself knew the value of her work, though during her lifetime it never fetched its true worth. After her death the Metropolitan Museum paid her the tribute of mounting a retrospective exhibition "to the memory of one who may with every reason be called a master craftsman".

BERNARD BUMPUS

Robinson, Annie *see* Swynnerton

Robusti, Marietta
Italian painter, *c.*1552 or 1560–1590

Born in Venice, *c.*1552 or 1560; father the painter Jacopo Robusti, known as Tintoretto. Married a goldsmith, Mario Augusta. Died in Venice, 1590; buried in Santa Maria dell'Orto.

Bibliography
Carlo Ridolfi, *Vita de G. Robusti, detto il Tintoretto*, Venice, 1642; as *The Life of Tintoretto and of His Children Domenico and Marietta*, University Park and London: Pennsylvania State University Press, 1984
Adolfo Venturi, *Storia dell'arte italiana*, ix, Milan: Electa, 1901
Evelyn Phillipps, *Tintoretto*, London: Methuen, 1911
E. Tietze-Conrat, "Marietta, fille du Tintoret: Peintre de portraits", *Gazette des Beaux-Arts*, 6th series, xii, 1934, pp.258–62
Hans Tietze, *Tintoretto: The Paintings and Drawings*, London: Phaidon, 1948
Eric Newton, *Tintoretto*, London: Longman, 1952
Rodolfo Pallucchini and Paola Rossi, *Tintoretto: L'opera completa*, 2 vols, Venice: Alfieri, 1974–82
Francesco Valcanover, *Tintoretto*, New York: Abrams, 1985
Whitney Chadwick, *Women, Art and Society*, New York and London: Thames and Hudson, 1990; revised edition, 1996

Only a handful of women artists had successful careers during the Renaissance. These women were either born into noble families, and had the means and social connections to pursue

Robusti (attrib.): *Old Man with Boy*, *c.*1585; Kunsthistorisches Museum, Vienna

careers in the arts, or, as demonstrated in the case of the 16th-century Venetian painter Marietta Robusti, they were born into the family trade. Marietta was an active contributor throughout her lifetime in the workshop of her father, Jacopo Robusti (known as Tintoretto), and was renowned in her own right for her work as a portraitist. According to her 17th-century biographer, Carlo Ridolfi, she was trained by Tintoretto in "design and colour, whence later she painted such works that men were amazed by her lively talent"; her "special gift" was "knowing how to paint portraits well". Ridolfi records that she portrayed many noble Venetian men and women, as well as the goldsmith friends of her husband. He noted her portrait of the long-bearded *Marco dei Vescovi*, which was still in the possession of the Tintoretto family, along with that of his son, Pietro, and also mentions a portrait of *Jacopo Strada* (untraced), the antiquarian of the Emperor Maximilian, who presented it to his patron. To date, however, only one work has been attributed to Robusti alone, the portrait of an *Old Man with Boy* (c.1585; see illustration). For years the work was considered to be one of Tintoretto's finest portraits, but according to Tietze-Conrat (1934) it bears Robusti's monogram, and should be considered as autograph (some subsequent scholars, however, have questioned his reading of the monogram). A high level of training is evident in the sophisticated handling of the paint, the keenly observed characterisation and the contrast of the two states of youth and old age.

Unfortunately, to date no documentation has emerged to clarify the various roles played by family members in Tintoretto's workshop; any attempt to create an artistic identity for Robusti has rested exclusively on stylistic evidence. It is known that she worked for her father for about 15 years, and that her fame as a portraitist spread as far afield as Spain and Austria. She was invited first to the court of Emperor Maximilian, and later to work for Philip II of Spain. Her father, however, refused to allow her to leave his workshop, and she remained in Venice until her death in 1590.

The first attempt to identify works that might have been produced by her was undertaken by Adolfo Venturi (1901); he considered her work to display a "sentimental femininity, a womanly grace that is strained and resolute". His views are not generally accepted by modern scholars. In the 1940s Hans Tietze created the art-historical category of the "Tintorettesque style", in an attempt to reconcile the tremendously varied output of Tintoretto's studio. He chose not to identify specific works, which might have been created by different individuals in the workshop; instead, he promoted the belief that Tintoretto "used his own works to educate his assistants, until their manner of seeing and depicting approximated to his own". Thus, the artistic identities of individual contributors to Tintoretto's works were subsumed within a larger, corporate whole ruled by the master.

Later in the 20th century, such scholars as Valcanover, Pallucchini and Rossi continued to follow this hierarchical and conservative view of Tintoretto's workshop, relying on traditional art-historical constructions of artistic genius. For instance, it is reasonable to assume that Marietta contributed to the creation of large altarpieces, as well as being a skilled portraitist: this was normal practice in Renaissance family workshops. It is assumed by these scholars that she and her brother Domenico would have been assigned the less important parts of the painting, leaving the more important parts of the work to the master, her father. Such a hierarchical view of artistic production has been criticised by more recent scholars, however. It seems evident that the notion of the genius of her father Tintoretto, who is claimed to have done the highest quality work and left the more mundane areas to the lesser individuals in his workshop, has tended to obscure Marietta's contribution to Venetian painting; however, more work remains to be done on this subject.

According to Ridolfi, Marietta also displayed excellent skills in music and deportment; he placed her among the most illustrious women of all time, comparing her to famous women in antiquity. His work is indebted to earlier debates on the ideal of femininity during the Renaissance. This debate had begun in earnest around 1528, in Baldassare Castiglione's *Book of the Courtier*; according to such writers as Castiglione and the Florentine artist Giorgio Vasari, women artists were considered to be exceptional within society, their talent legitimised because of its combination with other, "feminine" virtues. Ridolfi's life of Marietta continues this tradition into the next century: she is especially praised by him for her virtuous conduct and unusually brilliant mind. Although impossible to verify, Ridolfi also mentions that she dressed as a boy and accompanied her father everywhere, suggesting that she had to flout social conventions to succeed in her art.

During the 19th century, the biography of Marietta Robusti inspired Romantic painters and authors to create paintings, a novel and several plays based on her life, which focused on her presumed filial devotion and tragic early death: she became a model of the demure, long-suffering heroine, who inspires the men in her life – first, her father Tintoretto, and later, in the play by Luigi Marta, the 16th-century Venetian painter Paolo Veronese – to new creative heights. As Chadwick has indicated (1990), this treatment of her life diminished her role as an artistic producer in her own right, by denying her individuality and treating her only in relation to male creativity. Hopefully, continued research on this artist will extend the rather limited view we currently have of her achievements.

CATHERINE HARDING

Rockburne, Dorothea

Canadian artist, 1934–

Born in Montreal, Quebec, 1934. Studied at Ecole des Beaux-Arts, Montreal, 1947–50; Black Mountain College, North Carolina, 1951–6 (BFA). Brief marriage; one daughter. Taught art theory, School of Visual Arts, New York. Visiting artist, Skowhegan School of Painting and Sculpture, Maine, 1984; Milton and Sally Avery Distinguished Professor, Bard College, Annandale-on-Hudson, New York, 1986; artist-in-residence, American Academy in Rome, 1991. Recipient of Witowsky award, Art Institute of Chicago, 1972; Guggenheim fellowship, 1972; National Endowment for the Arts (NEA) grant, 1974; Brandeis University Creative Arts award, 1985. Lives in New York.

Selected Individual Exhibitions

Bykert Gallery, New York: 1970, 1972, 1973
Sonnabend Gallery, Paris: 1971
Galleria Toselli, Milan: 1972, 1973, 1974
Lisson Gallery, London: 1973
Galleria Schema, Florence: 1973, 1975, 1992
John Weber Gallery, New York: 1976, 1978
Xavier Fourcade, New York: 1980, 1982, 1985, 1986
David Bellman Gallery, Toronto: 1980
Museum of Modern Art, New York: 1980
Galleriet, Lund, Sweden: 1983
Arts Club of Chicago: 1987
André Emmerich Gallery, New York: 1988, 1989, 1990, 1991, 1992, 1994
Rose Art Museum, Brandeis University, Waltham, MA: 1989 (retrospective)

Selected Writings

"Notes to myself on drawing", *Flash Art*, April 1974, p.66
"Putting together thoughts on the new painting", *Artforum*, xxiii, October 1984, pp.72–5
"Special issue: Drawing in the '80s", *White Walls: A Magazine of Writing by Artists*, Spring 1986, p.51

Bibliography

Jennifer Licht, "An interview with Dorothea Rockburne", *Artforum*, x, March 1972, pp.34–6
——, "Work and method", *Art and Artists*, vi, March 1972, pp.32–5 (interview)
Roberta Olson, "An interview with Dorothea Rockburne", *Art in America*, lxvi, November–December 1978, pp.141–5
Kenneth Baker, "Dorothea Rockburne's 'Egyptian paintings'", *Artforum*, xix, April 1981, pp.24–5
Robert Storr, "Painterly operations", *Art in America*, lxxiv, February 1986, pp.84–9
John Gruen, "Dorothea Rockburne's unanswered questions", *Art News*, lxxxv, March 1986, pp.97–101
——, "Artist's dialogue: Dorothea Rockburne: A beckoning stillness", *Architectural Digest*, February 1987, pp.40–47
Dorothea Rockburne: Pascal and Other Concerns, exh. cat., André Emmerich Gallery, New York, 1988
John Loughery, "Dorothea Rockburne", *Arts Magazine*, lxii, May 1988, p.92
Dorothea Rockburne, exh. cat., Rose Art Museum, Brandeis University, Waltham, MA, 1989
John Gruen, *The Artist Observed: 28 Interviews with Contemporary Artists, 1972–1979*, Chicago: a Capella, 1991
Murray Pomerance, "Dorothea Rockburne's quantum leap", *Canadian Art*, x, Fall 1993, pp.48–51
Lilly Wei, "Dorothy Rockburne: Stargazer", *Art in America*, lxxxii, October 1994, pp.110–13

At Black Mountain College, where she studied under Max Dehn and Merce Cunningham, with colleagues who included the painters Robert Rauschenberg and Cy Twombly, Dorothea Rockburne was taught to experiment and to question limits. She is among the artists of the 1970s who challenged the canons of modernism and altered the course of art. Her work has been associated with Minimalism, Post-Minimalism and Conceptual Art; her recent wall paintings approach installation art. Although her aesthetic explorations have contributed significantly to the discourse of painting, her work defies simple classification. By its nature abstract, her art conveys no message, yet its conceptual basis prevents it from being either painting or sculpture. She is primarily concerned with aesthetic issues and uses an intellectual structure of logic to convey her rigorous concepts and discoveries. In recent years she has allowed an interaction of chance, intuition and mystery to fuse with the pervasive logical structure.

Rockburne's early work grew out of a conceptually based, non-gestural abstract language. Unlike the works of many Conceptual artists, who espoused "visual indifference" based on Marcel Duchamp's theories of the primacy of the idea over the object, her constructions had a seductive visual authority as well as an intellectual rigour. Attracted by the nature of mathematics to predetermine spatial relationships, she studied Boolean algebra, set theory, the Fibonacci series, the golden section, as well as logic. In 1970, at the time of her first solo exhibition in New York, at the Bykert Gallery, her works were informed particularly by the ideas of Ludwig Wittgenstein and Edmund Husserl. In *Levelling* (1970; oil on paper and chipboard) a dramatic effect is achieved by the interplay of the materials and the repeated geometric shapes.

During the 1970s Rockburne investigated set series and systems of mathematics as well as the nature of art, questioning the self-sufficiency of drawing. Her drawings were never intended as mark-making, but instead expose the inherent relationships between object and material. Such examples as *Drawing Which Makes Itself* (1973) and *Square Separated by Parallelogram with Diamond* (1974) give concrete visual form to theoretical concepts of mathematics and set theory. The fold, introduced in the former, remained an essential element in her investigations. In 1974–6 she made a series of shaped canvases based on the proportion known as the golden section. Her simple aesthetic vocabulary consists of light, surface and form, which are incorporated into the materials: paper, pencil, oil, conte, gesso and linen.

The *Arena* series, inspired by the colours of Giotto's frescoes in the Arena Chapel in Padua, provide a bridge between the *Golden Section Paintings* and the *Egyptian Paintings*, produced in 1979–80. *Arena IV* (1978; see illustration) embodies mathematical determinants interacting with curves drawn on translucent vellum in pure red, yellow, green and blue. These series are among Rockburne's most elegant and rigorous works, in which her visual and formal vocabulary of light, surface, form and logic was crystallised. Contradictions are presented in the construction *Egyptian Painting, Stele* (1980; artist's collection, repr. Waltham 1989): it is balanced yet asymmetrical, static yet shifting, exposed yet with parts hidden; boundaries are defined, yet the change is suggested by the interrelationship of parts.

Rockburne exploits the potential of painting and drawing through elegantly layered and folded shapes that resemble Japanese origami. Pure colour, albeit restricted, is an important element, penetrating and activating the geometric planes. Inspiration came from the 16th-century Mannerist painter Pontormo, she revealed in an interview: "Instead of seeing Pontormo as someone reacting against Classical art, I see him as an artist looking for and finding deeper meaning."

In the early 1970s Rockburne began to achieve international recognition. She won awards and fellowships, and was included in such exhibitions as Documenta V in Kassel, Germany (1972), *Eight Contemporary Artists* at the Museum of Modern Art, New York (1974), and the Whitney Museum of American Art Biennial (1979). Most women artists in this period were engaged with feminist issues, but Rockburne's

Rockburne: *Arena IV*, 1978; vellum paper, coloured pencil; 138.4 × 119.4 cm.

exploration of structuring systems was shared by some female colleagues including Agnes Denes, Jackie Ferrara (q.v.) and Agnes Martin (q.v.). However, the artist who worked most closely along the lines of Rockburne was Mel Bochner.

In the early 1980s, with the dramatic revival of figurative painting in Europe and the USA, Rockburne entered an intense period of reflection, questioning the very definition of abstract art. *White Angel No.2* (1981) shares characteristics with the *Egyptian* series, but her reductivist vision is extended in pristine white tones and more complicated folds. The interacting planes engage in a silent dialogue with the light and contours of the paper and board. In further transformations, her work became darker and bolder, with geometry and colour dissolving the boundaries between figure and ground, as in *Two Angels, 100 Years* (1984; Collection Mr and Mrs Walter N. Thayer, *ibid.*). Matisse had long influenced Rockburne, and the use of intensified colour and concentrated geometric shapes gave a new sense of movement and gesture to these compositions. Despite the shift in critical interest away from abstract and conceptual work, Rockburne's work continued to be widely exhibited and acclaimed, culminating in her ten-year retrospective at Brandeis University in 1989.

By the mid-1980s Rockburne had initiated another investigation, based on the ideas of the 17th-century French philosopher and mathematician Blaise Pascal. Her work became more moody and romantic, her marks more gestural. Musical influences are indicated by such titles as *Mozart Upsidedown and Backward* (1985–6). Her vehicle remained the geometric motif, but issues of time, atmosphere and light became significant. In 1988, after exhibiting *Pascal and Other Concerns*, she began a new series titled *Cut-Ins*, in which references to Matisse and Pontormo are combined with her own visual language. The emotive energy and brilliant colour of this series demonstrate her ability to make powerful and expressive works. Contradiction abounds in these squares defined by convex and concave brush strokes. The use of micro-thin white outlines around certain areas accents the unfolding geometric drama. The series represents a synthesis of logic with chance and spontaneity. In works including *Glory of Doubt* (1988–9) she achieved order, elegance and a seductive intensity.

In another pivotal period, 1990–91, Rockburne moved away from strict geometric structural organisation. Sharply defined circular shapes radiate from a churning red and yellow interior space in *Intimate Act* (1990), suggesting a metamorphosis from solid to liquid. Yet another evolution is evident in *Ship Curves No.5* (1991): mysterious colour fields are bombarded by atom-like shapes, and the composition is cut by diagonal lines. Order and chaos co-exist in this layering of the fields of colour against the precise suspended lines.

Rockburne's mural installations of the 1990s are among her most awesome creations, and they represent a kind of quantum leap, visually and intellectually. Her concepts could no longer be contained by paper or linen and her work could not remain detached from its architectural environment. The scale is vastly enlarged in the *Roman Wall Paintings*, executed directly on the walls of the André Emmerich Gallery, New York, in 1992. In 1993 she created a spectacular pair of frescoes for Philip Johnson's Sony USA building in New York. An energised, vibrating competition appears to take place between the monumentality of the fantastic architecture and the exploding colours and forms of Rockburne's murals. Titled *Northern Sky* and *Southern Sky*, the paintings are a homage to the electro-magnetic fields at the North and South Poles. Despite the intense colours and leaping arabesque forms, the chapel-like setting invites reflection. One of the catalysts for this new direction was a complex formula to clarify chance by the French fractal geometer Benoit Mandelbrot. Mandelbrot's concepts provided her with another language for expressing her ideas about the cosmos.

Shortly after the Sony murals, Rockburne created the colossal series *Painting from Nature* (1993) that occupied five walls of the Emmerich Gallery. In *Starpath* (1993) carefully calculated orbits reach across adjacent walls. Brilliant yellow suns frame the corner walls, as intersecting comet tails arch across an expanse of deep ocean blue. *Dividing (the Water under the Firmament from the Water above the Firmament)* (1993) is one of her most spectacular performances to date, with a seductive power reminiscent of her meticulous wall drawings of the early 1970s. Contrasting planes of information are depicted, and the painterly and the structural, the emotive and the rational come into focus. Rockburne's recent mural installations suggest that, far from relying on successful formulas from the past, she may create works that are still more complicated and powerful.

ELAINE A. KING

Roeder, Emy

German sculptor and draughtswoman, 1890–1971

Born in Würzburg, 30 January 1890. Studied under the sculptor Arthur Schleglmünig in Würzburg, 1908–10; studied at the Munich Academy, 1910–11, then in Darmstadt under Bernhard Hoetger, 1912–14. Moved to Berlin, 1915; member of Freie Secession, 1918; founder member, Novembergruppe zu Berlin, 1919. Married sculptor Herbert Garbe, 1920; he died 1945. First woman Meisterschülerin (master student) of sculpture at Berlin Academy, under Hugo Lederer, 1920–25. Learned woodcarving in Oberammergau, c.1920–21. Stayed in Paris, 1923; Rome and Paris, 1933–5. Moved to Florence, Italy, 1937. Banned from exhibiting under the National Socialists, 1937–45. Arrested in Italy as a German national and interned, 1944–5. Lived in Rome and surrounding area, 1945–9. Returned to Germany, July 1949. Taught at Landeskunstschule, Mainz, 1950–53. Studio in Aibling, Bavaria, from 1959. Frequent travels abroad, 1954–67. Recipient of numerous awards including Rohr prize, Berlin Academy, 1920; prize of the city of Cologne, 1929; Villa Romana prize, 1936; prize of the city of Berlin, 1953; art prize, state of Rheinland-Pfalz, 1956; art prize, state of Nordrhein-Westfalen, 1960; Great Distinguished Service Cross, Federal Republic of Germany, 1960; art prize, city of Würzburg, 1966. Member, Verein der Berliner Künstlerinnen, 1927–30. Died in Mainz, 7 February 1971.

Principal Exhibitions

Individual
Galerie Goldschmidt und Wallerstein, Berlin: 1922, 1925
Galerie Möller and Galerie Nierendorf, Berlin: 1927

Berlin Secession: 1931
Städtische Kunsthalle, Mannheim: 1950
Kestner-Gesellschaft, Hannover: 1953
Hessisches Landesmuseum, Darmstadt: 1958
Städtisches Kunstmuseum, Duisburg: 1958 (with Marg Moll and
   Johanna Schütz-Wolff)
Singener Kunstausstellung, Singen: 1962 (special exhibition, with H.
   Purrmann)
Kunstkabinett Hannah Bekker vom Rath, Frankfurt am Main: 1965
Städtische Galerie, Würzburg: 1969 (touring)

Group
Freie Secession, Berlin: 1918–19, 1923
Novembergruppe, Berlin: 1919–21, 1929
Anderson Galleries, New York: 1923 (*A Collection of Modern
   German Art*)
Juryfreie Kunstschau, Berlin: 1929
Haus der Juryfreien, Berlin: 1931 (*Frauen in Not*, touring)
Munich: 1937 (*Entartete Kunst*)
Deutscher Künstlerbund, Berlin: 1951
Kestner-Gesellschaft, Hannover: 1951 (*Deutsche Bildhauer der
   Gegenwart*), 1954

Bibliography

Adolf Behne, "Graphik und Plastik von Mitgliedern der
   Novembergruppe Berlin", *Menschen*, ii/14, December 1919,
   pp.1–2, 48–9
Alfred Kuhn, "Emy Roeder: Über das Formproblem der Plastik", *Der
   Cicerone*, xii, 1920, pp.423–35
Peter Leu, *Führer durch die Abteilung der Novembergruppe:
   Kunstausstellung, Berlin, 1920*, Berlin-Friedenau:
   Novembergruppe [1920]
Alfred Kuhn, *Emy Roeder*, Junge Kunst, xviii, Leipzig: Klinkardt und
   Biermann, 1921
——, *Die neuere Plastik von Achtzehnhundert bis zur Gegenwart*,
   Munich: Delphin, 1921
K[arl] Sch[effler], "Ausstellungen Berlin", *Kunst und Künstler*, xxi/2,
   1922, p.68
Willi Wolfradt, "Umschau-Ausstellungen", *Das Kunstblatt*, vi, 1922,
   p.503
A[lfred] K[uhn], "Berliner Ausstellungen", *Der Cicerone*, xix, 1927,
   pp.676, 705–7
Hans Hildebrandt, *Die Frau als Künstlerin*, Berlin: Rudolf Mosse,
   1928
Viktor Wallerstein, "Zeichnungen der Bildhauerin Emy Roeder", *Das
   Kunstblatt*, xiv, 1930, pp.205–7
"Zwei Bildnerinnen über ihr Schaffen", *Koralle*, new series, iv, 31
   January 1936, pp.156–7 (includes statement by Roeder)
Alfred Hentzen, *Deutsche Bildhauer der Gegenwart*, 2nd edition,
   Berlin: Rembrandt, 1937
Friedrich Gerke, *Emy Roeder: Werkbiographie (mit Gesamtkatalog
   der Bildwerke und Zeichnungen)*, Wiesbaden: Steiner, 1963 (cata-
   logue raisonné of sculptures and drawings)
Helga Kliemann, *Die Novembergruppe*, Berlin: Mann, 1969
Emy Roeder: Bildwerke, Handzeichnungen, exh. cat., Städtische
   Galerie, Würzburg, 1981
Ulrike Evers, *Deutsche Künstlerinnen des 20. Jahrhunderts: Malerei,
   Bildhauerei, Tapisserie*, Hamburg: Schultheis, 1983 (contains
   extensive bibliography)
*Das Verborgene Museum I: Dokumentation der Kunst von Frauen in
   Berliner öffentlichen Sammlungen*, exh. cat., Akademie der
   Künste, Berlin, 1987
Emy Roeder, 1890–1971: Akzente, exh. cat., Städtische Galerie,
   Würzburg, and elsewhere, 1989
Entartete Beeldhouwkunst: Duitse Beeldhouwers, 1900–1945
   [Degenerate sculpture: German sculptors, 1900–1945], exh. cat.,
   Commanderie van St Jan, Nijmegen, and elsewhere, 1991
Magdalena Bushart, "Der Formsinn des Weibes: Bildhauerinnen in
   den zwanziger und dreissiger Jahren", *Profession ohne Tradition:
125 Jahre Verein der Berliner Künstlerinnen*, exh. cat., Berlinische
   Galerie, Berlin, 1992, pp.135–50
Erich Ranfft, "Expressionist sculpture, *c.*1910–30, and the signifi-
   cance of its dual architectural/ideological frame", *Expressionism
   Reassessed*, ed. Shulamith Behr and others, Manchester:
   Manchester University Press, 1993, pp.65–79
——, "German women sculptors, 1918–1936: Gender differences and
   status", *Visions of the "Neue Frau": Women and the Visual Arts
   in Weimar Germany*, ed. Marsha Meskimmon and Shearer West,
   Aldershot: Scolar Press, 1995, pp.42–61
Elizabeth Tumasonis, "The sculpture of Emy Roeder: Expressionism
   and beyond", *Woman's Art Journal*, xviii/1, 1997, pp.20–25

Emy Roeder was one of Germany's most important modern
sculptors of the 20th century. Her production of more than
100 sculptures was complemented by an output of several
hundred finished drawings. Her artistic career spanned more
than five decades, beginning with her growing prominence
while based in Berlin during the Weimar Republic, from 1919
until the early 1930s. Roeder's status placed her in the
company of the most famous Weimar women sculptors – Milly
Steger (q.v.), Renée Sintenis (q.v.) and Käthe Kollwitz (q.v.).

Central to Roeder's sculptures and drawings were the
female figure and themes of childhood, adolescence, pregnancy
and motherhood. Also significant were her depictions of
animals and her portraits. Her sculptural production consisted
mainly of free-standing pieces under 50 centimetres in height,
reliefs of an area under 35×35 centimetres, and portrait busts
in life-size proportions. After 1930 most of her works were
cast in bronze (unless otherwise indicated, all works listed
below are of this medium). The finished drawings, begun as a
main preoccupation after 1925, were made from black or red
chalk or pencil. They are typically line drawings with shading
along the contours. The Städtische Galerie in Würzburg
possesses the most comprehensive collection of sculptures and
drawings by Roeder.

Roeder's first years as a professional artist were marked by
her evocative contributions to German Expressionist sculpture
before *c.*1923. Early on she was heavily influenced by
Bernhard Hoetger, her former teacher. His eclectic use of
historicising and exotic motifs was echoed, for example, in
Roeder's set of five figural groups comprising the *Manger*
(1916; terracotta; private collection, Mainz, repr. Kuhn 1920,
p.431), which synthesises Egyptian, Near Eastern and Oriental
sources into a Christian theme. Roeder's Expressionism after
1918 was motivated by her involvement in the Berlin
Novembergruppe and by the post-war "ecstasy" of Christian
religious and spiritual expression. In this milieu she worked
closely with the sculptor Herbert Garbe, whom she married in
1920.

Roeder's pivotal sculpture was the frontally posed, half-
figure of *Pregnant Woman* (1919; terracotta; 80.5cm.?; repr.
Ranfft 1993, p.72, and Ranfft 1995, pl.6, front and side
views), which she produced in the village of Fischerhude, near
Bremen. Roeder wrote that she felt "the cosmic of all being"
(quoted in Kuhn, *Emy Roeder*, 1921, p.15) in the experience
of pregnancy and motherhood among the peasant women and
animals. Roeder's romanticisation of Fischerhude was not
unlike the sentiments of Paula Modersohn-Becker (q.v.) for
Worpswede. Within Expressionist ideology, *Pregnant Woman*
had a spatial and ritualistic presence: "Her hands lie protecting

Roeder: *Manger Relief*, 1920; wood; Robert Gore Rifkind Collection, Beverly Hills, California

the cathedral body which carries a Saviour" (Kuhn, *Die neuere Plastik ...*, 1921, p.105). Roeder's communion with Fischerhude also inspired her first animal sculptures, such as *Mare and Foal* (1919; Nationalgalerie, Staatliche Museen zu Berlin).

Pregnant Woman was followed by a "life-cycle" of female figures, such as *Embryo* (1919; artificial stone; repr. Kuhn, *Emy Roeder*, 1921, pl.22) and *Family* (1920; wood; repr. Tumasonis 1997, fig.4), which strongly suggests the matriarchal grouping of a grandmother holding her pregnant daughter and infant. These figures are delineated in reductivist and angular shapes that are compressed into an overall relief-like surface. In its showing at the Novembergruppe exhibition of 1920, it was described as "the very embodiment of the spiritual" (Leu [1920], p.17). *Family* was also an example of Roeder's participation in the Expressionist vogue for carving in wood, which she learned in 1920 in Oberammergau from Bavarian artisans: for instance, *Manger Relief* (1920; see illustration), whose angularity and harsh diagonals (akin to Expressionist woodcuts) imbue the religious scene with "ecstatic" resonance, while *Praying Boy* (1921; 98.5 cm.; Städtische Galerie, Würzburg) presents solidity of form and smoothened surfaces, under the influence of Ernst Barlach.

From 1925 until the late 1930s Roeder continued to preoccupy herself with the female figure and portray those individuals with whom she shared a close connection, especially the poorest of the city and country (such as farmers and Gypsies). Unlike Käthe Kollwitz or Katharina Heise (q.v.), she did not seek to make social or political statements. Her sculptures during the late 1920s did, however, express degrees of pathos and empathy. These works were marked by more naturalistic handling of form and detail, such as *Head of the Girl Else* (1929–30; artificial stone; Städtische Galerie, Würzburg) and the highly emotive *Heads of Children* (1928; artificial stone; Nationalgalerie, Staatliche Museen zu Berlin), which depicts the upper torso of a boy holding the head of his sister in his arms. Thereafter Roeder simplified her sculptures and concentrated on rounded contours, which were indebted to the classicising influence of Aristide Maillol (e.g. *Seated Young Woman with Towel*, 1937; *Girl Friends*, 1940–41; both Städtische Galerie, Würzburg).

Roeder enjoyed far greater support than her husband during the Weimar years, which had much to do with the assertion of her feminine identity in the critical reception: "the man [Garbe], the larger intellect, the woman, the even deeper artist" (Kuhn 1927, p.676). The sincerity of her conviction was often noted, as she is "the intense woman who works seriously" (1927) and "belongs to the most endearing of creative female personalities in the world" (1936; both quoted in Ranfft 1995, p.50). Hers was a maternal image conflated by the early 1930s with women's dominant media image of domesticity. In contrast, Roeder's "sensitivity" was seen as a disadvantage when compared to the "masculine strength" of Milly Steger.

After World War II Roeder drew inspiration from her period of internment at Padula (1944–5): each of the four reliefs of *Padula* (I, II and III of 1945–6, V of 1949; all Städtische Galerie, Würzburg) depicts three young nude women in the camp's showers, their bodies and arms moving gracefully under the downpour of water. Roeder then undertook numerous two- and three-dimensional representations of animals, such as the sculptures *Two Sheep with Lamb Resting* (1946–7) and *Pair of Resting Goats* (1958; both Städtische Galerie, Würzburg). These works are characterised by reductive, planar forms with angular contours. Such qualities were taken to an extreme flatness in the relief *Cows in the Rain* (1962; 47 × 34.5 cm.; Städtische Galerie, Würzburg), in which Roeder has simply "etched" the design on to the surface.

In the 1960s Roeder began anew to sculpt and draw representations of women, especially Moslem women. Her sculpted figures featured elongated bodies with slender limbs and a simplification of form and detail through the suggestion of their enveloping clothing (e.g. *Tunisian Women Beggars*, 1971; Städtische Galerie, Würzburg). This period was also marked by two monumental, over-life-size sculptures: the seated woman of *Tripoli III* (1963) and the *Standing Woman from Tripoli* (1967; both Städtische Galerie, Würzburg).

Portrait busts continued to be an important preoccupation; the best known are those of Roeder's old artist friends, *Erich Heckel* (1951–2), *Hans Purrmann* (1950–1; both Städtische Galerie, Würzburg) and *Karl Schmidt-Rottluff* (1955–6; Brücke Museum, Berlin; Städtische Galerie, Würzburg). More remarkable were Roeder's self-portraits, in two busts of 1958 and 1964 (both Städtische Galerie, Würzburg) and in more than ten drawings in black chalk, beginning in 1965 (average size 47 × 35 cm.; all Städtische Galerie, Würzburg). Inviting comparisons to the sculpted self-portrait (1926–36; bronze) by Käthe Kollwitz, Roeder's bust of 1964

is a powerfully honest statement of old age and physical decay. Roeder did not shrink from the depiction of the wrinkles lining her forehead, cheeks, and the papery flesh of her throat. Yet it is clear that they were made by laughter as well as by care. The corners of the eyes are crinkled; the mouth is curved in a faint smile, wry and self-mocking [Tumasonis 1997].

ERICH RANFFT

Roghman, Geertruydt [Giertje]
Dutch printmaker, 1625–after 1651

Baptised in the Nieuwe Kerk, Amsterdam, 19 October 1625, eldest child of Hendrik Lambertsz. Roghman, engraver and apprentice of Harmen Jansz. Muller, and Maritje Saverij, who came from a family of artists in Courtrai. Worked in the family workshop in Amsterdam with her father, brother Roelant and sister Magdalena. Never married. Last documented March 1651; deceased by December 1657.

Bibliography

Arnold Houbraken, *De Groote Schouburgh der nederlantsche konstschilders en schilderessen* [The great theatre of Dutch male and female painters], iii, Amsterdam, 1721

F.W.H. Hollstein, *Dutch and Flemish Etchings, Engravings and Woodcuts*, xx, Amsterdam: van Gendt, 1949

Margarita Russell, "The women painters in Houbraken's Groote Schouburgh", *Woman's Art Journal*, ii/1, 1981, pp.7–11

W. T. Kloek, *De Kasteeltekeningen van Roeland Roghman* [The Castle drawings of Roeland Roghman], ii, Canaletto: Alphen aan den Rijn, 1990

Martha Moffitt Peacock, "Geertruydt Roghman and the female perspective in 17th-century Dutch genre imagery", *Woman's Art Journal*, xiv/2, 1993–4, pp.3–10

Like many female artists of the 17th century, Geertruydt Roghman was born into an artistic heritage. With her father, her brother Roelant and sister Magdalena, she was part of a family workshop whose major production was in the field of printmaking. In connection with this role, Roghman spent much of her time engraving or etching the designs of other artists. In particular, she made a number of prints after the landscape drawings of her brother. While these images gave her little chance for experimentation, a series of domestic genre scenes that she designed and engraved demonstrates her unique approach, in both composition and mood, to a ubiquitous 17th-century Dutch subject.

It is likely that Roghman's earliest extant work is an engraved portrait (1647; Rijksprentenkabinet, Amsterdam) after a lost painting by Paulus Moreelse of her great-uncle Roelant Saverij, painter to Emperor Rudolph II. It is a portrait in the manner of her father's work, and is accompanied by a eulogising verse signed by him. Although no other works by Roghman are dated, it may be that an engraved copy (Rijksprentenkabinet) in reverse of Aegidius Sadeler's print after Tintoretto's *Massacre of the Innocents* also belongs to this early period, in which she copied the works of other artists. The copy is quite accurately handled, but she makes the significant alteration of writing out the biblical text in Dutch rather than Latin. This penchant for the common and ordinary permeates all of Roghman's works.

This characteristic is very evident in a series of 14 landscape prints done after drawings by her brother. The series, *Plaisante lantschappen ofte vermakelijcke gesichten na t'leven* (Pleasant landscapes or entertaining/enjoyable views after life/nature; *c.*1645–8; Rijksprentenkabinet), is typical of a formula developed earlier on by the artist and publisher Claes Jansz. Visscher (who also published this series). After the title plate, which indicates Roelant as the inventor of the scenes, views from the districts around Amsterdam are depicted with identifying inscriptions. In addition to landmarks such as churches, these prints contain many commonplace genre activities and details. While there is some question regarding the etching of these prints, most scholars attribute it to Roghman, due to the careful technique, resembling engraving. This is supported by the existence of one other landscape etching, *House [Castle] at Zuylen* (after 1652; Rijksprentenkabinet), in which the inscription identifies Roghman as the etcher after a design by Roelant. As in the previous series, a number of genre details – figures gathered around a sketching artist and water fowl – have been added to the foreground. In this particular case (and perhaps by association with the previous series) we can assume that these humanising details were added by Roghman, because of their absence in the still-extant preliminary drawing by Roelant.

It is possible that Roghman was given more significant credit in the *Zuylen* print than in the earlier landscape series because she had established, by then, an artistic reputation of her own, through her domestic series. These prints, designed and engraved by Roghman, were published twice, and are unique as subjects in printmaking. Although the engravings

Roghman: *Woman Scouring Metalware*, engraving; Rijksmuseum, Amsterdam

depict well-known conventions in contemporary painting – *Two Women Sewing*, *Woman with Vanitas Objects*, *Pancake Baker*, *Woman Spinning*, *Woman Scouring Metalware* (*c.*1650; Rijksprentenkabinet) – they portray the women in a much less anecdotal or didactic fashion than other depictions of the themes.

The final print in the series, *Woman Scouring Metalware* (see illustration), demonstrates Roghman's distinctly different interpretation of the subject. Dutch images of the 17th century depicting women scouring metalware in the kitchen almost always contained sexual innuendo. At times the erotic anecdote was acted out in theatrical fashion (usually between a maid and her master), while elsewhere it was only humorously indicated through the use of sexual metaphors handled by bawdy, grinning females. In contrast to such images, Roghman's maidservant is decidedly non-sexual. From a surprising and innovative back view (common to three of the prints), she does not tempt the viewer with her gaze, smile or décolletage. She scrubs away vigorously at her burdensome task, creating an unposed slice-of-life effect. As in the other scenes, Roghman concentrates exclusively on the common yet monumental figure, her work and the tools specific to it.

Such an altering of artistic conventions suggests that Roghman saw these domestic images in a different light from many of her male predecessors. It appears that she viewed such scenes as reflections of a new interest in women and their domain that bestowed a greater importance on the roles of women. One other work that indicates the significance

Roghman attributed to these figures is her only extant drawing. It depicts a *Female Artist* (*c.*1650; private collection, repr. *Bernard Houthakker, Old Master Drawings*, sale cat. 253, 1975), drawing with charcoal in the same (reversed) pose of the profile needlewoman in the first scene of the print series. Both females, whether sewing or drawing, are intent on their work, as if they are tasks of great significance. Just as Roghman gained a certain amount of power and reputation through her skill as an artist, other women in this middle-class society achieved status through their skilful management of home, children and servants.

Although recently the trend in feminist studies has been to treat women artists in a gender-less fashion, the art of Roghman indicates that abandonment of a gendered approach altogether is problematic. Roghman's images demonstrate how significant the female experience was to these innovative views of a 17th-century woman's world. Post-structuralist methods, however, are also necessary in order to understand fully Roghman and the role her art played in gender relationships of the 17th century. Not all male artists of the period, for example, treated women in a moralising or titillating fashion. Like Roghman, many males treat the depicted women in domestic genre sympathetically – as subjects busy with their own pursuits, rather than as objects for the male gaze. Many male artists seem to have been influenced towards this more sympathetic view in part because of their contact with Roghman's prints, and the opportunity they provided to view women through the eyes of a woman. The several back and lost-profile views of women at fireplaces or windows in barren settings by Jacobus Vrel and Esaias Boursse post-date and are obviously influenced by Roghman's scenes. Specifically, Caspar Netscher's *Lacemaker* (1662; Wallace Collection, London) with its barren setting, sparse still-life objects and seated, lost-profile figure appears indebted to Roghman's *Woman Spinning*. And, finally, it might be suggested that either directly or indirectly the domestic images of Johannes Vermeer, Pieter de Hooch and Pieter Janssens Elinga that concentrate on singular females busy at their domestic tasks owe something to the quiet, dignified and powerful females of Geertruydt Roghman's vision.

MARTHA MOFFITT PEACOCK

Roldán, Luisa (Ignacia)

Spanish sculptor, 1652–1706

Born in Seville, 1652, to the sculptor Pedro Roldán and his wife Teresa de Ortega y Villavicencio; at least two of her siblings, María Josefa and Francisca, mother of the sculptor Pedro Duque Cornejo, were also sculptors. Trained by her father; married, against his wishes, a sculptor, Luis Antonio de los Arcos Navarro, 1671; seven children, of whom at least two survived infancy. In Cádiz, 1684–7. Moved to Madrid, 1688/9; named "Sculptor to the Bedchamber" (*Escultora de Cámara*) by Charles II, 1692; appointed "Sculptor to the King" by Philip V, 1701; subsequently signed herself "escultora de su Magestad". Accademica di Merito, Accademia di San Luca, Rome, 1706. Died in Madrid, 10 January 1706.

Bibliography

Juan Agustín Ceán Bermúdez, *Diccionario histórico de los más illustres profesores de las bellas artes en España*, 6 vols, Madrid, 1800

María Elena Gómez Moreno, *Escultura del siglo XVII*, xvi of *Ars Hispaniae: Historia universal del arte Hispánica*, 22 vols, Madrid: Plus-Ultra, 1947–77

E. Sánchez Corbacho, *Pedro Roldán y sus discípulos*, Seville, 1950

Beatrice Gilman Proske, "Luisa Roldán at Madrid", *Connoisseur*, clv, 1964, pp.126–32, 199–203, 269–73

Domingo Sánchez-Mesa Martin, "Nuevas obras de Luisa Roldán y José Risueño en Londres y Granada", *Archivo Español de Arte*, xl, 1967, pp.325–31

Jorge Bernales Bellesteros, *Pedro Roldán: Maestro de escultura (1624–1699)*, Seville: Arte Hispalense, 1973

María Victoria Garciá Olloqui, *La Roldana: Escultora de Cámara*, Seville: Arte Hispalense, 1977

Antonio Palomino, *Lives of the Eminent Spanish Painters and Sculptors*, Cambridge and New York: Cambridge University Press, 1987 (Spanish original, 1724)

Catherine Hall-van den Elsen, "Una valoración de dos obras en terracota de Luisa Roldán", *Goya*, no.209, 1989, pp.291–5

——, "Una obra inédita de Luisa Roldán", *Archivo Hispalense*, no.221, 1989, pp.205–8

Domingo Sánchez-Mesa Martin, *El arte del barroco*, vii of *Historia del arte en Andalucia*, Seville: Gever, 1991

Catherine Hall-van den Elsen, *The Life and Work of the Sevillian Sculptor Luisa Roldán, with a Catalogue Raisonné*, PhD dissertation, La Trobe University, Melbourne, 1992

Very little is known about Luisa Roldán's life and work, and many details of her life remain obscured beneath a mist of conjecture. Identification of her early work, done while she was attached to her father's studio, has been hindered by the enormous output of her father's workshop, one of the largest in Seville during the second half of the 17th century.

After her marriage to Luis Antonio de los Arcos in 1671, Roldán began to work independently of her father, completing life-sized figures in polychromed wood for the commissions for multi-figure processional Holy Week floats representing the *Passion*, which her husband received from Sevillian brotherhoods. These were initially inspired by her training in her father's studio but reveal her steady progression from his didactic approach to the single standing figure towards a more dynamic, High Baroque sentiment, perhaps under the influence of Juan de Valdes Leal, her sister's godfather. Two early figures, the thieves from the float of the *Exaltation of the Cross* (1678–9; Santa Catalina, Seville), reveal Roldán's mastery of the male nude – an exceptional skill for a female in 17th-century Spain – which must have been acquired in her father's studio. As with a number of works included in commissions signed by Roldán's husband, attribution of these figures is based on stylistic evidence, since she rarely signed a wooden sculpture.

Recognition of her independence from her famous father was confirmed when she spent time in the city of Cádiz from 1684 to 1687. The free-standing *Ecce Homo* (1684; see illustration), a recently identified sculpture in Cádiz Cathedral, is a typical example of her work of this period. The moment portrayed is immediately after the scourging and mocking of Christ by the Roman soldiers. The body of Christ is very slender, with the bones appearing to press almost through the skin. This is most noticeable at the collar-bone, the upper ribs and the left hip, seen beneath the abdominal cavity. The veins of the arms, forearms and hands are emphasised and the hands are finely sculpted and appear almost skeletal. Christ's face is gaunt, his mouth half open with exhaustion. Delicately traced eyebrows emphasise translucent eyelids and an elongated nose. The neck is slender, revealing veins beneath the surface of the skin. This innovative work foreshadows the advances Roldán would make during her next period, where rather than being content with modest success close to her home town, she would reveal both the complexity and individuality of her talents. Sometime in 1689 Roldán travelled to Madrid with her husband and the two or three surviving children of the seven she bore. After establishing herself in the court city, possibly with the assistance of a Sevillian noble, in 1692 she received the title of Sculptor to the Bedchamber of King Charles II.

The most significant difference between the market for sculpture in Seville and that in Madrid was the less prestigious role accorded in the capital to sculptors, who still retained the rank of tradesmen. Royal taste in public sculpture, influenced by Italian theorists, favoured marble over wood. There were fewer opportunities open to sculptors in Madrid to display their work. The importance of processional images to Sevillian religious life guaranteed their authors publicity. Madrid society, however, placed less importance on sculpture as a vehicle for disclosing the mysteries of faith, and painting remained the preferred medium for many patrons.

As a sculptor at the Spanish court, Roldán was one of a number of artists and writers whose work reflects the struggle to maintain confidence in Spain, when the political and social currents in Madrid were anything but reassuring. In a court full of political and moral uncertainties, great reliance was placed on the Church for assurances of the righteousness of basic articles of faith. Together with the glorification of the Virgin Mary and reminders of the inescapable presence of death, they occupied an important place in Spanish culture as stimuli for artistic endeavour. Roldán interpreted the themes of the day with an immediacy conveyed by the three-dimensionality of her medium that was unavailable to court painters, limited by the surfaces of their canvases. The first work in wood that she executed specifically for King Charles in 1692 was the over-life-size *St Michael and the Devil* (1692; El Escorial Monastery, Madrid). The figure of St Michael continues the pattern of innovation initiated by Roldán four years earlier in Cádiz. Added to this is a new, vital sense of movement intrinsic to Madrid art of the period that was often ignored by sculptors of her father's school, where sculpture served a didactic rather than a rhetorical purpose. The work is signed by both Roldán and her husband's younger brother Tomás Antonio de los Arcos, a painter of sculpture who regularly worked with Roldán.

In the same year as the *St Michael* Roldán sculpted in wood the head and hands of a *St Clare* for a royal convent in Murcia. Now lost, the figure was designed to hold a monstrance in accordance with the saint's traditional iconography. Like St Michael, St Clare was an important figure in late 17th-century Spain, famed for her legendary use of the Eucharist in the defence of the city of Assisi when it was under attack by the Saracens. For the anxious Spaniards of the late 17th century, St Clare's victory was a commentary on the triumph of Catholicism over Protestantism.

Roldán: *Ecce Homo*, 1684; Cádiz Cathedral

Despite her membership of one of Seville's most prolific families of sculptors in wood, and continuing to produce wooden sculptures throughout her life, Roldán is now known principally for her work in terracotta. She began producing terracotta sculptures – images of the Virgin Mary and the Christ Child, measuring approximately 40 × 50 centimetres – soon after her arrival in Madrid. These intimate works are characterised by simplicity and warmth, which are conveyed by the cherubs, animals and plants that adorn the scenes. One of her earliest works in terracotta, the *Virgin and Child with St John the Baptist* (1691; Martin D'Arcy Gallery, Loyola University, Chicago) is a typical example of Roldán's iconographically simple works, which associate an intimate familial scene and an admonition of its sanctity by its reference to the Holy Family.

Many of her more elaborate terracotta works are more iconographically complex than is generally acknowledged. When read in the light of the 17th-century Spanish literary tradition, in which image and symbol are interpreted as a single unit, these sculptures present a compelling reaffirmation of the strength of the Catholic faith. One of the most iconographically complex of all of Roldán's terracotta groups is the work known as the *Death of Mary Magdalene* (c.1697; Hispanic Society, New York). The work is composed of the reclining figure of the Magdalene attended by angels and cherubs. Among the animals and plants depicted are an owl, a rabbit nibbling at a clump of blue and white irises, a scourge, a skull resting on a book and below that a salamander and a snake. The salamander and the snake placed beneath the Magdalene suggest a more significant iconological role than has previously been attributed to them. The salamander is a symbol of chastity and among its mythical powers is the ability to withstand and even to extinguish fire. The placing of these two animals beneath the figure of the Magdalene is indicative of their relevance to the theme of repentance. The snake, symbol of the fires of Hell, is placed next to the animal capable of withstanding the flames. The salamander here symbolises spiritual salvation, as recounted in Isaiah 43:1–3. The conflict between sin and salvation represented by the snake and the salamander can be related to the conflict between lust and chastity that is symbolised in this work by the rabbit and the irises. By placing the symbols relating to the life of the penitent saint directly beneath her reclining body, Roldán reminds us that the Magdalene has triumphed over lust and the flames of passion. Her salvation has been achieved through withdrawal from society (the owl) and repentance (the scourge, the skull and the book).

The power with which Roldán was able to convey the strength of Spain's religious conviction in over-life-size sculptures belies the tendency of writers to cast her in a mould of helpless subservience. Like Ceán Bermúdez, who in 1800 saw Roldán's terracotta works as appropriate to the delicacy of her gender (*delicadeza de su sexo*), some have had difficulty in reconciling their image of a female artist with the force of her work in wood. It is, however, not surprising that until the age of 40 Roldán confined her artistic output to a medium with which she had grown up. Her family, her friends and the godparents of her children were all involved in different stages of the production of wooden figures as sculptors, joiners, painters and gilders. While those sculptures reflect both her roots in the Sevillian Holy Week tradition and, in her later work, the ethos of Madrid's golden age of painting, her terracotta groups respond to a quieter faith, where miracles reward the saintly deeds of the protagonists. Delicate workmanship attracts the lingering gaze of the viewer, who must contemplate the image for protracted periods of time in order to comprehend the often complex message contained within the group. The intimate contact the viewer is required to have with the works recalls immediately the art of Murillo and Zurbarán in Seville, as well as that of Claudio Coello and Mateo Cerezo in Madrid. The elaborate details reveal Roldán's affinity with contemporary painting rather than wooden sculpture, which as a medium was still confined to the representation of grandiloquent figures of saints and kings. The pastel colours employed in the polychromy of her terracotta works reflect a concern for subtle harmonies of tone that were not adopted in Spain until the establishment of porcelain factories in the second quarter of the 18th century.

Luisa Roldán sought and received recognition in her home town, in the important cathedral city of Cádiz, in the Royal Palace, in the household of at least one noble patron and, on the day she died, from the Roman Accademia di San Luca, which honoured her with the title of Accademica di Merito on 10 January 1706. This final honour was substantially more than any received from the prestigious academy by contemporary Spanish painters. Roldán's place in history should not be confined to a final paragraph of a book on the golden age of Spanish sculpture. Her work is the manifestation of a truly Spanish tradition, and she should be accorded a place among the leading artists of her time.

CATHERINE HALL-VAN DEN ELSEN

See also Court Artists survey

Romer, Louise *see* Jopling

Ronner-Knip, Henriëtte
Dutch painter, 1821–1909

Born Henriëtte Knip in Amsterdam, 31 May 1821, into an artistic family. Studied under her father, the landscape painter Josephus Augustus Knip. Lived in France with her family until 1827, then in The Hague; moved to Brabant in 1833; to Brussels after her father's death in 1847. Married Feico Ronner, 1850; six children, of whom Alfred Ronner, born 1852, became a draughtsman and illustrator, and Henriëtte Emma Alice Ronner, born 1857, became a flower painter. Exhibited widely, receiving gold and silver medals. Member, Arti et Amicitiae, Amsterdam; Pulchri Studio, The Hague; Société d'Artistes Belges; Cercle Artistique et Littéraire de Bruxelles; Société Belge des Aquarellistes, Brussels. In the election of committee members intended to establish female counterparts of the French Academy, she ended in the first five with around 2000 votes. Knight of the Order of Leopold I, Belgium, 1887 (one of the few women to be so honoured); Knight of the Order of Orange-Nassau, Netherlands, 1901. Died in Brussels, 2 March 1909.

Principal Exhibitions

Internationale Kunstausstellung, Düsseldorf: 1836
Levende Meesters [Contemporary masters], Amsterdam: 1838–1909
Arti et Amicitiae, Amsterdam: 1840–1909
Paris Salon: 1845, 1859, 1867, 1870, 1880, 1883–9
Triennial Salon, Brussels, Antwerp and Ghent: 1853–1907
International Exhibition, London: 1862, 1871
Fine Art Society, London: 1890 (individual)
Royal Academy, London: 1891, 1894–1903
Goupil Gallery, London: 1892 (individual)
Galerie Goupil, Paris: 1901 (individual)

Bibliography

E. Baes, "Exposition des tableaux par Mme Ronner", *Journal des Beaux-Arts*, xxix, 1887, p.187
J. Gram, *Henriëtte Ronner en hare katjes* [Henriëtte Ronner and her little cats], Leiden: Sijthof, 1891
M.H. Spielman, *Henriëtte Ronner: The Painter of Cat Life and Cat Character*, London: Cassell, 1892
J. Gram, *Henriëtte Ronner en hare kunst* [Henriëtte Ronner and her art], Leiden, 1893 (French original)
Emile Wesley, "Henriëtte Ronner", *Elseviers Geïllustreerd Maandschrift*, i, 1893, pp.349–64
Max Rooses, ed., *Dutch Painters of the Nineteenth Century*, i, London: Sampson Low Marston, 1898 (Dutch original)

Ronner-Knip: *Three Against One*, 1868; 82 × 127.5 cm.; Rijksmuseum, Amsterdam

P. Leautaud, *Wat betreft katten: Met vierentwintig tekeningen van Henriëtte Ronner* [Concerning cats: With twenty-four drawings by Henriëtte Ronner], Amsterdam, 1970

J. A. Knip (1777–1847), exh. cat., Noordbrabants Museum, 's-Hertogenbosch, 1977

Germaine Greer, *The Obstacle Race: The Fortunes of Women Painters and Their Work*, London: Secker and Warburg, and New York: Farrar Straus, 1979

B. Honders, "Hondenleed en Kattenpret: Henriëtte Ronner-Knip" [Dog sorrow and cat fun: Henriëtte Ronner-Knip], *Tableau*, no.55, 1981, pp.52–7

De familie Knip: Drie generaties kunstenaars uit Noord-Brabant [The Knip family: Three generations of artists from North Brabant], exh. cat., Noordbrabants Museum, 's-Hertogenbosch, 1988

Harry J. Kraaij, *Lazy Cats and Playful Kittens: Life and Work of Henriëtte Ronner-Knip (1821–1909)* (in preparation)

According to her early biographer Emile Wesley (1893), Henriëtte Ronner-Knip began painting when she was eleven years old, when she received an easel as a birthday present. Before that time, however, she had already copied many studies and sketches from her father, Josephus Augustus Knip. The greater part of her childhood drawings that are known (Rijksprentenkabinet, Amsterdam; acquired 1994) originated during her stay in France (1822–7), where her father was active as a painter and teacher in Paris and elsewhere.

Around 1833, after settling in Beek near Nijmegen and later in 's-Hertogenbosch in Brabant, she began to work from nature. Most works from this period are lost or in private collections, but several are reproduced in 's-Hertogenbosch 1988; from these, it appears that during this period she painted such wide-ranging subjects as pastoral landscapes, castles, farms, genre scenes and portraits. Already in 1842 her painting *People Leaving a Church in Brabant* was reproduced as a lithograph in the Dutch art periodical *De Kunstkronijk*.

When her father went blind in 1832, the talented Ronner-Knip had to provide the income for her family with her artistic production. Shortly afterwards she sold a painting to Crown Prince Willem II, representing his farm in Tilburg and signed with her brother August, and she made her debut at the annual art exhibition in Düsseldorf (1836). To avoid confusion with her aunt Henriëtte Geertruij Knip, she signed her name in full, with her last name in capital letters, usually placed obliquely underneath her first name.

Ronner-Knip had a love of animals, and she applied herself more and more in her meadow landscapes to views of cows, horses, sheep and birds. Her style at this point was very precise, with great attention to detail, for example in the vegetation. Through this and also through the predominance of dark colours, these works show the influence of the classicistic landscapes of her father. Around 1845 Ronner-Knip specialised in animal scenes with representations of dogs, usually hunting dogs in forest and heath landscapes. With her accomplished painting technique, balanced compositions and large formats, she had begun to receive critical praise during this period.

In 1850 she left for Brussels with her husband Feico Ronner, who was four years her elder. Six children were soon born, and since her husband was sickly, she was once again responsible for the family income. Moreover, biographers make mention of a family member, probably her nephew the painter Henri Knip, who appears to have been a financial liability to the young family. These difficulties are reflected in the generally sombre mood of the works from this period. Often she painted animals that steal each other's food, or scenes with aggressive dogs, such as the three savage dogs up against a spitting cat in *Three Against One* (1868; see illustration). In these works and in those of the period that followed she employed a less smooth technique, with a pastier application of paint.

Ronner's images with dog-carts, a means of transport that was used frequently in the 19th century by less well-to-do farmers and peddlers, have a more tragic Romantic feeling. An especially splendid example is *Death of a Friend* (1860; Musée des Beaux-Arts, Brussels), in which a sand porter weeps beside his dead, still straining dog, who has collapsed under the heavy load. This work received critical praise at the International Exhibition in London for its non-academic dark colours and its large format, but it was untraced for a long time after Ronner's death. Ronner's fame spread and she received an increasing number of commissions. In this way she came to paint portraits of dogs belonging to the Queen of the Belgians and to the Countess of Flanders.

Around 1870 she shifted her choice of subject matter to cats, which were being kept in increasing numbers as house pets. She established herself with the art-buying urban middle classes with this theme. In similarly dark colours she painted sleepy cats and playful kittens in richly decorated interiors. Through the incorporation of Japanese elements and Chinoiserie she often achieves a charming reflection of the period of the 1880s and 1890s. Not infrequently, she used moralising titles that allude to the human world.

Ronner-Knip reaped very great success with her cat paintings, which were sought-after. In response, her production greatly increased. She made a watercolour or oil sketch from every painting, to avoid repetition and to be able to detect forgeries. With the rise of modernism, however, she encountered a good deal of adverse comment. Her work was found uninspiring and conservative. It was possibly as a result of these comments that she lightened up her palette and broke away from such carefully arranged compositions.

HARRY J. KRAAIJ

Roosenboom, Margaretha

Dutch painter, 1843–1896

Born in The Hague, 24 October 1843. Received first lessons from her father, Nicolaas J. Roosenboom, a landscape painter. Spent youth in The Hague and Brussels. Studied for some years with her maternal grandfather, landscape painter Andreas Schelfhout, in The Hague, from 1867. Moved to Hilversum, 1887; lived with a cousin, Maria van Wielik, and Maria's husband, painter Johannes Gijsbertus Vogel; three years later moved with the household to Voorburg, where her cousin died in 1892. Married Vogel 11 months later. Died 26 December 1896.

Principal Exhibitions

Pulchri Studio, The Hague: from 1859
Weltausstellung, Vienna: 1873 (gold medal)
Arti et Amicitiae, Amsterdam: 1880 (*Levende meesters* [Contemporary masters])
International Colonial Exhibition, Amsterdam: 1883 (gold medal)
Exposition Universelle d'Anvers, Antwerp: 1885
Fine Art Society, London: 1890
World's Columbian Exposition, Chicago: 1893 (gold medal)
Galerie Biesing, The Hague: 1898 (retrospective, with Johannes Gijsbertus Vogel)

Bibliography

Margaretha Vogel-Roosenboom en den Heer J.G. Vogel, exh. cat., Galerie Biesing, The Hague, 1898
J. Gram, "Johannes Gijsbertus Vogel", *Elseviers Tijdschrift*, February 1902, pp.82–3
H.P. Bremmer, ed., *Beeldende Kunst*, iii/11, no.85, 1915–16, pp.126–7
H.E. van Gelder, "Een kunstzinnige Haagse familie" [An artistic Hague family], *Die Haghe*, 1950, pp.12–20
Bloemen uit de kelder [Flowers from the cellar], exh. cat., Gemeentemuseum, Arnhem, 1989
De schilders van tachtig: Nederlandse schilderkunst, 1880–1895 [Painters of the 1880s: Dutch painting], exh. cat., Waanders Uitgevers, Zwolle, and elsewhere, 1991

Margaretha Roosenboom came from a family with painters on both sides. She was therefore able, even from childhood, to develop her talent with the benefit of professional training. At the age of 16 she showed work at the well-known exhibitions organised in The Hague by the artists' association Pulchri Studio. She continued to enter her paintings and watercolours – mostly still lifes of flowers – for these exhibitions throughout her life, and won numerous prizes. Through them she became so well known that her work sold regularly. She was also a much respected teacher.

Roosenboom first received lessons from her father Nicolaas J. Roosenboom, a landscape painter, and then, from the age of 24, had painting lessons from her maternal grandfather, the Romanticist Andreas Schelfhout. She was therefore brought up in the tradition of Dutch Romanticism. Her still lifes display a refined use of colour, a command of form and a strong sense of composition, usually with a diagonal emphasis. Afterwards Roosenboom distanced herself firmly from the customs and conventions of her own time.

Even by the time of the Dutch golden age of the 17th century, flower painting was a flourishing genre, and one considered to be a suitable occupation for women. Anna Janssens, active in the middle of the 17th century, depicted flowers in a detailed and naturalistic manner, "after the life"; Rachel Ruysch (q.v.) and later Margareta Haverman (q.v.) painted luxurious arrangements, with sinuous lines and strong chiaroscuro. The flower painting of the first half of the 19th century by George J.J. van Os and others depicted elegant, artificial and extravagant arrangements. Gerardine Jacoba van de Sande Backhuyzen returned to a more naturalistic manner. Roosenboom, who knew the latter's work, took her artless, unaffected style of flower painting further. After her, Sina Mesdag-van Houten and Anna Abrahamsz. produced Impressionist flower paintings.

Roosenboom's style marks a distinct development in flower painting. She sought a greater naturalism and simplicity of

Roosenboom: *White Roses*, oil on canvas; 72 × 54.5 cm.; Haags Gemeentemuseum, The Hague

expression than did her 19th-century predecessors, and paid less attention to detail. However, she painted neither from her first impressions, nor depicted flowers out of doors. One of the ways in which she simplified flower painting was to restrict herself to just a few species; very often she chose roses – creamy white or pale pink rather than red. No reference to love seems to be intended in these. By the third quarter of the 19th century flower paintings had virtually lost their symbolic significance and had become purely decorative. In 1902 a critic described her paintings as "sensitive, harmonious colour-poems". The soft colouring of the flowers shows up against the green of the leaves and the greenish-beige tints of the background. Her work is lyrical in tone.

Roosenboom considered the still-life *Cauliflower and Endive* (Rijksmuseum Hendrik Willem Mesdag, The Hague) to be a study. It was shown for the first time in the posthumous exhibition of her work in 1898, when it was praised and recognised as occupying a special position in her oeuvre. The brush strokes with which the leaves, in all their subtleties of colour, are rendered, are more than usually vigorous. No other vegetable still life by Roosenboom is known, although there is a *Still Life with Strawberries in a White Dish* in the Rijksmuseum, Amsterdam. *Still Life with Flowers* (Gemeentemuseum, Arnhem), though very finely painted, is at first sight one of her conventional paintings of mainly roses, with some ivy and a dead branch, all lying on the ground

against a wall in such a way as to create a diagonal composition. Striking, however, are the references in the painting to transitoriness (the dead branch and the roses in all stages of bloom), given that most of her flower-pieces testify primarily to the principle of art for art's sake. Moreover, the signature in this work is remarkable, not only because Roosenboom wrote it in full (it was her custom to use the abbreviated "Margt." for her first name), but also because, rather than running horizontally in the bottom left-hand corner, it follows the diagonal line of the dead branch precisely. Did Roosenboom imply by this that she did not expect to grow old? She died at the age of 53, as a result of injuries sustained in a fall.

In many of Roosenboom's still lifes the flowers are not arranged in a vase, as for example in *Still Life with Roses and a Guitar* (Rijksdienst Beeldende Kunst, The Hague), for which she won a gold medal, *Flowers* (Koninklijk Museum for Schone Kunsten, Antwerp) and *White Flowers on a Stone Tablet* (private collection, repr. Arnhem 1989, fig.54). In these paintings the composition is looser than in those described above; the flowers and leaves are placed at a variety of angles, but their forms are still graceful and clear, filled in with tiny touches of paint in subtle nuances of colour. The paint of the backgrounds is very thinly applied. The size of these paintings varies from 60 × 120 to 29.5 × 46 centimetres. The works in which flowers are depicted in a vase, often a brown pitcher, are some of the most distinctive of her oeuvre, for example *White Azalea* (Centraal Museum, Utrecht), *White Roses* (see illustration), *Peonies in an Earthenware Pitcher* (1890; private collection, *ibid.*, fig.49) – one of her few dated works – and the watercolour *Vase of Roses* (Rijksprentenkabinet, Amsterdam). The transparency of the petals, the effects of light and shade, the solidity of the compositions and the brushwork, besides those qualities named above, have ensured that Roosenboom's work, both in her own lifetime and up to the present day, has enjoyed the attention of critics, dealers and collectors. In Roosenboom's lifetime, critics at home and abroad (Brussels, London) praised her work in their writings, not only for its grace and warmth of colour – qualities that were thought to correspond to female nature – but also because some of them at least recognised her artistry and the powerful vision of her subject matter. Thanks to these latter qualities Margaretha Roosenboom's work makes a genuine contribution to the development of flower painting.

ROSELLA M. HUBER-SPANIER

Rosalba *see* Carriera

Rosler, Martha
American artist, 1943–

Born in New York, 1943. Studied at Brooklyn College, City University of New York (BA 1965); University of California, San Diego (MFA 1974). Recipient of National Endowment for the Arts (NEA) grants, 1975, 1976 (art critics fellowship),

1980, 1983 and 1994; honourable mention (second prize), best documentary, for *Born to be Sold*, Atlanta Film and Video Festival, 1989. Member, Advisory Task Force to the Society for Photographic Education, 1980–82; Photography Fellowships panel, National Endowment for the Arts, Washington, DC, 1982; Board of Directors, Association for Independent Video and Film, 1982–4; New Arts Fellowship panel, Artists' Foundation of Massachusetts, Boston, 1985; Editorial board, *Old Westbury Review*, 1985–7; External Review panel, Visual Art Department, University of Massachusetts, Boston, 1987; Board of Directors, Media Alliance, 1990–92. Professor of visual art, Rutgers University, New Brunswick, New Jersey. Lives in Brooklyn, New York.

Selected Individual Exhibitions

Long Beach Museum of Art, CA: 1977
Whitney Museum of American Art, New York: 1977
Institute of Contemporary Arts, London: 1979, 1983 (both video)
A-Space, Toronto: 1980
University Art Museum, University of California, Berkeley: 1980
Institute of Contemporary Art, Boston: 1987 (video)
Dia Art Foundation, New York: 1989
Museum of Modern Art, Oxford: 1990 (*Housing Is a Human Right*, touring)
Simon Watson Gallery, New York: 1991
Jay Gorney Modern Art, New York: 1993
Contemporary Arts Center, Cincinnati: 1994
San Francisco Museum of Modern Art: 1995 (installation in *Public Information: Desire, Disaster, Document* exhibition)

Selected Writings

"Untitled", *Los Angeles Institute of Contemporary Art Journal*, no.4, February 1975, p.34
"The private and public: Feminist art in California", *Artforum*, xvi, September 1977, pp.66–74
"A new-found career", *Journal: A Contemporary Art Magazine*, no.16, October–November 1977, pp.40–45; reprinted in *ibid.*, no.40, Fall 1984, pp.48–53
Service: A Trilogy on Colonization, New York: Printed Matter, 1978 (in English and Spanish)
"For an art against the mythology of everyday life", *Journal: Southern California Art Magazine*, no.23, June–July 1979, pp.12–15; no.24, September–October 1979, p.72
3 Works: Critical Essays on Photography and Photographs, Halifax: Nova Scotia College of Art and Design Press, 1981
"Watchwords of the eighties", *High Performance*, vi/2, 1983, pp.67, 87
If You Lived Here: The City in Art, Theory and Social Activism, ed. Brian Wallis, Seattle: Bay Press, 1991
"In the place of the public: Observations of a traveller", *The Invisible in Architecture*, ed. Ole Bouman and Roemer van Toorn, London: Academy, and New York: St Martin's Press, 1994; longer version entitled "In the place of the public: Observations of a frequent flier", *Assemblage* (in preparation)
"Video: Shedding the utopian moment", *The Block Reader in Visual Culture*, London and New York: Routledge, 1996, pp.258–78

Bibliography

Lucy R. Lippard, "Caring: Five political artists", *Studio International*, cxciii, 1977, pp.197–203
Ruth Askey, "Martha Rosler's video", *Artweek*, 4 June 1977
Carrie Rickey, "Return to sender", *Village Voice*, 14 August 1978
Amy Taubin, "And what is a fact anyway? (on a tape by Martha Rosler)", *Millennium Film Journal*, nos 4–5, Summer–Fall 1979
Issue: Social Strategies for Women Artists, exh. cat., Institute of Contemporary Arts, London, 1980
Jane Weinstock, "Interview with Martha Rosler", *October*, no.17, Summer 1981
Bruce Barber and Serge Guilbaut, "Interview with Martha Rosler", *Parachute*, October 1981
Martha Gever, "An interview with Martha Rosler", *Afterimage*, ix, October 1981, pp.10–17
Benjamin H.D. Buchloh, "Allegorical procedures: Appropriation and montage in contemporary art", *Artforum*, xxi, September 1982, pp.43–56
Craig Owens, "The discourse of others: Feminism and postmodernism", *The Anti-Aesthetic: Essays on Postmodern Culture*, ed. Hal Foster, Port Townsend, WA: Bay Press, 1983; London: Pluto, 1985
Moira Roth, *The Amazing Decade: Women and Performance Art in America, 1970–1980*, Los Angeles: Astro Artz, 1983
Lucy R. Lippard, *Get the Message: A Decade of Art for Social Change*, New York: Dutton, 1984
Benjamin H.D. Buchloh, "From gadget video to agit video: Some notes on four recent video works", *Art Journal*, xlv, Fall 1985, pp.217–27
Donald Kuspit, "The art of memory/the loss of history", *Artforum*, xxiv, March 1986, pp.120–21
Steve Edwards, "Secrets from the street and other stores", *Ten 8*, no.35, 1989–90, pp.36–43 (interview)
Brian Wallis, "Living room war", *Art in America*, lxxx, February 1992, pp.104–7
Laura Cottingham, "Crossing borders", *Frieze*, no.13, November–December 1993, pp.52–5
Martha Rosler: In the Place of the Public, exh. brochure, Contemporary Arts Center, Cincinnati, 1994
Val Williams, *Warworks: Women, Photography and the Iconography of War*, London: Virago, 1994
Marjorie Welish, "Word into image: Robert Barry, Martha Rosler, Nancy Spero", *Bomb*, Spring 1994, pp.36–44 (interview)
Joan Seeman-Robinson, "Martha Rosler", *Artforum*, xxxiii, January 1995, p.90

Martha Rosler was among the artists of the 1970s who abandoned traditional media and turned instead to technology, perceiving its potential for conveying more intensely and expressively the complex layers of contemporary life. Over two decades she has produced a consequential body of work in photography, performance, art criticism and video. She has consistently produced critically arresting pieces that raise questions about human vulnerability within the social system. Content, rather than formal or material issues, is always the primary concern, and she demands that the viewer spend time deciphering her social messages. Unlike the work of modernists who strove to present universal truths and positive resolutions, Rosler's media-generated imagery is full of contradictions and ambiguities; it invites the viewer to ask questions about media information and its portrayal of the reality we live in.

Although today Rosler is known for her videos and conceptual photographic installations, she first trained as a painter. What she desired to communicate through her art required more than traditional materials could provide, however, and by using mixed media she brought together text, visual elements and real time, as well as finding her artistic voice. Issues associated with food, motherhood, domesticity, sex and career inform her earlier conceptual pieces, books, performances and videos. The idiosyncratic nature of her art grew from the climate of feminism in the early 1970s, her experiences as a single parent and her interest in alternative forms of art that transcend commodification. Like other women artists of that era, she called for a new, non-hierarchical theory of culture. Her mixed-media work cuts across varied disciplines, and her art is observant about everyday conduct.

Since the early 1970s Rosler has been analysing social systems. Viewers are required to find the connections between the multiple elements and references presented. Her work is intended to expose the subliminal power relationships innate in all social structures, especially the capitalist society of the USA. In her examination of various organisations and institutions, she gives a voice to the powerless, questions the status quo and aspires to raise our consciousness about social injustice by revealing the aggregate of sub-texts that inform media dissimulation. When what she produces is perceived as difficult, often it is the directness and simplicity of the work that prevent the viewer from immediately grasping her intended message.

Like much of the work of Hans Haacke, who also analyses social structures, Rosler's art can be classified as political. However, it is never "politically correct" in the sense of the trendy political art of the 1990s. Hers is a pro-active art, not merely a veneer of fashionable reactionary ideology. One of her earliest political works was a series of photomontages entitled *Bringing the War Home* (1967–72), in which she used an amalgam of imagery to confront the Vietnam war, juxtaposing war scenes with ordinary American interiors. It was included in the British touring exhibition *War Works* of the early 1990s, and was shown at the Victoria and Albert Museum in London.

Rosler has used feminist criticism as a tool to understand the patriarchal forces controlling the media and other forms of cultural production. The female body became significant as a subject in her live performances and videos. She sees attitudes to the body as essential to the control and oppression of women in society and recognises that women are treated as objects everywhere, from advertising to the doctor's examining room. Rosler is central to a group of women artists who began focusing on events that affect the lives of women of all races and classes. In *Vital Statistics of a Citizen, Simply Obtained*, performed live at the University of California, San Diego, in 1973, Rosler plays the naked character coldly interrogated by a clothed male examiner as he measures her. It is a straightforward piece that is not intended to entertain but to raise the viewer's consciousness. This simplicity and directness are evident in all Rosler's videos and photographs. She plays the protagonist in many of her videos and performances.

Rosler identified food as an important theme in the lives of women and as playing a role in differentiating class and social rank. Many of her early performances took place in the kitchen or dealt with women's "service" relationship to food and men, and her important videos on this theme include *A Budding Gourmet* (1974) and *Semiotics of the Kitchen* (1975). Food is also the central subject of her postcard novels of the 1970s titled *A Budding Gourmet, McTowers Maid, Tijuana Maid*. Both *Semiotics of the Kitchen* and *Vital Statistics* are considered classic feminist videos and continue to be viewed and discussed. Her controversial video *Born to be Sold (Baby M)*, which had its première at the 1988 Video Festival of the American Film Institute in Los Angeles, is a raw social commentary on surrogate motherhood and the politics of power.

The street and public places where large numbers of people gather have been sites for several significant projects. *The Bowery*, considered one of Rosler's critical works, juxtaposes black-and-white photographs of Manhattan's skid row with clichés used to describe alcoholics and alcoholism. It opens a window on a closed class that mainstream society is programmed to fear and loathe. In 1980, with a hand-held Super-8 camera, Rosler shot *Secrets from the Street: No Disclosure* while driving around the Mission District of San Francisco, capturing the tension between bourgeois society and street culture. The single-channel video *If It's Too Bad To Be True, It Could Be Disinformation* (1985) debunks the world of network news transmission. A tranquil gallery space was transformed into a mock airport terminal in her site installation *In the Place of the Public* at Jay Gorney Modern Art, New York (1993). Using text, audio speakers and large colour photographs of airport interiors, she revealed the sterility of airport environments and how people become curiously abstracted in public places. Visual elements and text work together in her systemic critique of a capitalist social institution that has become an arena for products, money and illusions.

Although Rosler's work has never been aligned with the mainstream art world, she was recognised very early on for her unique artistic voice, critical thinking and contributions to the discourse on media art. She has received several awards from the National Endowment for the Arts, including an artist's fellowship (1975), a critic's fellowship (1976) and one for photography (1994). Her impressive body of critical writings and catalogue essays spans a diverse range of topics including feminism, post-modernism, digital photography, the history of photography, media and video. Her writings have been influential for critics and artists as well as for the discourse of critical theory. She has had more than 50 solo exhibitions, selected screenings, installations and performances at venues in the USA and Europe, and in 1981 *Watchwords of the Eighties* was performed at Documenta VII in Kassel, Germany. Her videos and photographs are in about 75 public collections around the world. Rosler's art functions as an informational, intellectual puzzle that demands the viewer's active participation to decipher. Her use of language is not intentionally explicit, it serves as clues and is always deliberately related to all the components in her multitudinous constructions.

ELAINE A. KING

Rossetti, Elizabeth Eleanor *see* Siddal

Rossetti, Lucy *see* Brown

Rossi, Properzia de'
Italian sculptor, active 1514–29

Born in Bologna, *c.*1490 (cited as aged 25 in a document of 1515); father a Bolognese citizen and the son of a notary. Brought before the Bologna tribunal on several occasions to

Rossi: *Joseph Fleeing Potiphar's Wife, c.1525–6*; bas relief; Museo di San Petronio, Bologna

answer charges of disorderly conduct, 1520–21; again in 1525, accused of throwing paint in the face of another artist. Employed by the Fabbrica di San Petronio, Bologna, 1525–6. Patient in the Ospedale di San Giobbe, Bologna, April 1529. Dead by February 1530 (Vasari).

Bibliography

Giorgio Vasari, *Le vite de' più eccellenti architettori, pittori et scultori italiani, da Cimabue insine à tempi nostri*, 1550, ed. Luciano Bellosi and Also Rossi, Turin: Einaudi, 1986, pp.728–31

——, *Le vite de' più eccellenti pittori et scultori ed architettori*, Florence, 1568; ed. Gaetano Milanesi, v, Florence: Sansoni, 1880, pp.73–81; as *Lives of the Most Eminent Painters, Sculptors and Architects*, 10 vols, London: Macmillan-Medici Society, 1912–15; reprinted New York: AMS, 1976

Antonio Saffi, *Della vita e delle opere di Maria de' Russi scultrice bolognese: Discorso all'Accademia di Belle Arti in Bologna, detto il 22 giugno 1830*, Bologna, 1832

Michelangelo Gualandi, "Memorie intorno a Properzia de' Rossi scultrice bolognese", *L'Osservatorio*, nos 33, 34 and 35, Bologna, 1851

Ottavio Mazzoni-Toselli, *Racconti storici estratti dall'Archivio Criminale di Bologna*, ii, Bologna: Chierici, 1868

Laura M. Ragg, *The Women Artists of Bologna*, London: Methuen, 1907

I.B. Supino, *Le sculture delle porte di S. Petronio in Bologna*, Florence: Istituto Micrografico Italiano, 1914

Vera Fortunati Pietrantonio, "Per una storia della presenza femminile nella vita artistica del cinquecento bolognese: Properzia De Rossi, 'schultrice'", *Carrobbio*, vii, 1981, pp.167–77

Fredrika H. Jacobs, "The construction of a life: Madonna Properzia De' Rossi 'schultrice bolognese'", *Word & Image*, ix, 1993, pp.122–32

With the exception of several payment records and some documents in the Archivio Criminale, Bologna, few facts are known about Properzia de' Rossi. The principal source of information about the sculptor comes from the first and second editions of Giorgio Vasari's *Vite* (1550 and 1568). Subsequent writers, such as Raffaello Borghini (*Il Riposo*, 1584) and Antonio Saffi (1832), did little more than to repeat information stated by Vasari.

Vasari reported that de' Rossi's earliest works were carvings of peach stones. The one described by him, a cluster of eleven stones intricately carved with scenes of the *Passion* and images of martyrs, all of which were set within a silver filigree coat-of-arms of the Grassi family of Bologna, is still extant (Museo Civico Medievale, Bologna). A similar carving, but rendered from a cherry stone (Museo degli Argenti, Palazzo Pitti, Florence), was first attributed to de' Rossi by Gaetano Milanesi in his edition of Vasari's *Vite*. Such carvings reflect the popularity of objects deemed "marvels" for their artistic virtuosity that were being assembled in *Kunst- und Wunderkammern* throughout 16th-century Europe.

The Grassi heraldic device was not de' Rossi's only commission from Bolognese nobility. Vasari reported that she carved in marble a portrait bust of *Conte Guido Peppoli* (Museo di San Petronio, Bologna) to demonstrate her mastery of the medium in the hope of securing work on the decorative project for the church of San Petronio. Given the influential role played by Guido's son Alessandro Peppoli in the awarding of commissions for this project, and considering the appearance

of de' Rossi's name in Fabbrica records from 1525, there is little reason to question Vasari on this point.

On 15 January and 5 April 1526 two other sculptors engaged on the San Petronio façade, Tribolo and Alfonso Lombardi, were paid for "models made by Propertia". Several months later, on 4 August, the balance of her account for carvings of two sibyls, at least two angels and a "panel" (*quadro*) was settled for 40 lire. While the earlier payment records indicate that de' Rossi was not paid directly, the amount she received is commensurate with the compensation given to her male peers. Vasari is responsible for identifying the *quadro* in question, a relief depicting *Joseph Fleeing Potiphar's Wife* (see illustration). The muscular figure types and classicising profiles bear a striking resemblance to Raphael's rendition of the story in the Vatican Logge, Rome, an image subsequently engraved by Marcantonio Raimondi (*c*.1517; National Gallery of Art, Washington, DC). Since in the second edition of the *Vite* Vasari notes his acquisition of "some very good [pen] drawings" by de' Rossi's hand "copied from works by Raphael", it is likely that her conception of classical form owes a debt to artistic developments in Rome during the 1510s. Accepted as an autograph work, *Joseph Fleeing Potiphar's Wife* is the measure for identifying de' Rossi's hand elsewhere on San Petronio's façade. *Potiphar's Wife Accusing Joseph* seems a plausible candidate. It is not clear which of the many sibyls and angels flanking and surrounding the portals might be attributed to her. What, if any, effect de' Rossi's confrontations with Bologna's civil and criminal justice authorities in 1525 had on her relationship with the Fabbrica is uncertain, but her name disappears from the records after the payment of 4 August 1526, with the sole exception of being listed as a patient in the Ospedale di San Giobbe, a hospital reserved for indigents, in April 1529. Although Vasari says that she spent her last years working in engraving, no works in this medium have been attributed to her.

FREDRIKA H. JACOBS

Rothenberg, Susan
American painter and graphic artist, 1945–

Born in Buffalo, New York, 20 January 1945. Studied at Cornell University, Ithaca, sculpture, 1962–5, painting, 1967 (BFA); Corcoran School of Art and George Washington University, Washington, DC, 1967. Settled in New York, 1969. Worked as assistant to Nancy Graves (q.v.) and Joan Jonas (q.v.), 1970. Married (1) George Trakas, 1971; daughter born 1972; divorced 1979; (2) Bruce Nauman, 1989. Moved to New Mexico, 1990. Recipient of Creative Artists Public Service (CAPS) grant, 1976; National Endowment for the Arts (NEA) grant, 1979; Guggenheim fellowship, 1980; American Academy and Institute of Arts and Letters award, 1983; Grand prix, International Biennial of Graphic Art, Yugoslavia, 1985. Member, American Academy and Institute of Arts and Letters, 1990. Lives in New Mexico.

Selected Individual Exhibitions
Willard Gallery, New York: 1976, 1977, 1979, 1981, 1983, 1985

University Art Museum, University of California, Berkeley: 1978
Mayor Gallery, London: 1980 (touring)
Kunsthalle, Basel: 1981–2 (touring, with Robert Moskowitz and Julian Schnabel)
Stedelijk Museum, Amsterdam: 1982
Los Angeles County Museum of Art: 1983–5 (touring)
Barbara Krakow Gallery, Boston: 1984 (touring)
University Art Museum, California State Center, Long Beach: 1985 (*Centric 13*, touring)
Phillips Collection, Washington, DC: 1985–6 (touring)
Sperone Westwater, New York: 1987, 1990
Baltimore Museum of Art: 1988
Albright-Knox Art Gallery, Buffalo, NY: 1992–4 (touring retrospective)

Bibliography

Roberta Smith, "The abstract image", *Art in America*, lxvii, March–April 1979, pp.102–5
Susan Rothenberg, exh. cat., Kunsthalle, Basel, 1981
Bice Curiger, "Robert Moskowitz, Susan Rothenberg, Julian Schnabel", *Flash Art*, no.106, 1982, p.60
Susan Rothenberg: Recente schilderijen/Recent Paintings, exh. cat., Stedelijk Museum, Amsterdam, 1982
Carter Ratcliff and others, "Expressionism today: An artists' symposium", *Art in America*, lxx, December 1982, pp.58–75, 139
Robert Storr, "Spooks and floats", *Art in America*, lxxi, May 1983, pp.153–9
Lisbet Nilson, "Susan Rothenberg: 'Every brushstroke is a surprise'", *Art News*, lxxxiii, February 1984, pp.46–54
Hayden Herrera, "In a class by herself", *Connoisseur*, ccxiv, April 1984, pp.112–17
Susan Rothenberg, exh. cat., Phillips Collection, Washington, DC, and elsewhere, 1985
Rachel Robertson Maxwell, *Susan Rothenberg: The Prints: A Catalogue Raisonné*, Philadelphia: Maxwell [1987]
Carter Ratcliff, "Artist's catalogue: Susan Rothenberg: Images on the edge of abstraction", *Architectural Digest*, December 1987, pp.52–62
Susan Rothenberg: 15 år – en överblick/15 Years – a Survey, exh. cat., Rooseum, Malmö, 1990
Ellen Handy, "Mysteries of motion: Recent paintings by Susan Rothenberg", lxiv, *Arts Magazine*, May 1990, pp.70–74
Joan Simon, *Susan Rothenberg*, New York: Abrams, 1991
Susan Rothenberg: Paintings and Drawings, exh. cat., Albright-Knox Art Gallery, Buffalo, NY, and elsewhere, 1992

Susan Rothenberg entered the New York art world in the mid-1970s with a series of paintings whose central protagonist was a horse. Iconic images inflected by autobiographical innuendo, the horse pictures issued out of a mélange of possibilities that animated the downtown art scene. While identified early on as a "New Image" painter and subsequently, during the 1980s, as a "Neo-Expressionist", Rothenberg has persistently forged her own path, drawing ideas from her immediate environment and using these as a basis for painting that mines the gap between abstraction and figuration.

Rothenberg's first artistic efforts were informed by Minimalism and Post-Minimalism, process and performance art. Eventually she focused on painting, and her early involvement with dance and performance brought a wider perspective to her work. So did her assistantship to the sculptor Nancy Graves (q.v.), whose emphasis on process and the literalness of materials and content (Rothenberg helped to fabricate bones and fossils for one of Graves's elaborate installations) provided an ideological springboard. By the early 1970s painting was once again on the rise. Like many of her peers, Rothenberg took certain cues from Post-Minimalism – an emphasis on formal process and procedures, anti-illusionism and literalness – but at the same time she sought greater content. Something as mundane as a horse provided a host of possibilities. She told her biographer Joan Simon:

> The horse was a vehicle for me. I think in the same way Jasper Johns had to use his imagery … it was a surrogate

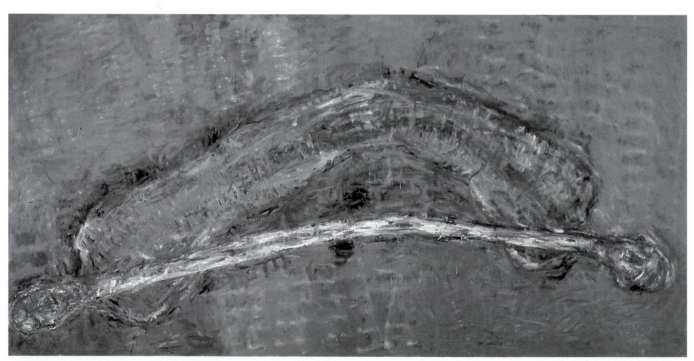

Rothenberg: *Bone Heads*, 1989–90; oil on canvas; 195.6 × 386 cm.; Eli Broad Family Foundation, Santa Monica, California

for dealing with a human being, but at the same time it was neutral enough and I had no emotional relationship to horses, so it really was a powerful object that divided asymmetrically but seemed to present a solid symmetrical presence [Simon 1991, p.29].

In some of the first "horse" pictures – *Triphammer Bridge* (1974; collection Edward R. Broida Trust, repr. Simon 1991, p.31); *Butterfly* (1976; collection Maggie Trakas, *ibid.*, p.53); *Double Measure* (1977; collection Miani Johnson/Willard Gallery, New York, *ibid.*, p.56) – formal devices, such as criss-crossing diagonals or a vertical zip that bifurcate the composition, tend to stabilise, and in the process neutralise, a psychological dimension. But as time goes on, as the motif undergoes transformations affected by personal circumstances, compositions become progressively more dramatic. *Squeeze* (1978–9; collection Frances and John Bowes, *ibid.*, p.69), *For the Light* (1978–9; Whitney Museum of American Art, New York) and *Tattoo* (1979; Walker Art Center, Minneapolis) are poignant analogues for pain, displacement and fragmentation. These provocative images, exhibited at the Willard Gallery in 1979, not only extended the motif spatially and emotionally, but their critical reception propelled the artist into an international arena.

The first horse picture began as a sketch, an unpretentious doodle on canvas. Rothenberg's creative process generally involves sketching on an intimate scale, where intuitive strokes can be tested, varied and, if necessary, purged. Drawing is her crucible for potential ideas, or, as Michael Auping put it: "drawing is the preconscious seedbed of her imagery" (Buffalo 1992, p.23). Painting poses its own formal challenges, empirically tackled from canvas to canvas. As a series nears completion, drawing provides a transition, a fluid means of questing once again into the unknown.

What had been her signature image for about six years suddenly "ran out", which is how the artist described the phasing out of the horse in her subsequent work. Although aspects of the motif would reappear in her painting in the 1990s (recapitulation is a strong part of Rothenberg's sensibility), by the end of the 1970s she was primed for change. By this time, too, her technique had become more painterly and her images more eccentric. *Blue Body* (1980–81; Eli and Edythe L. Broad Collection, repr. Simon 1991, p.79) and *White Mountain* (1980–81; collection Courtney and Steven Ross, *idem*) lead to a series of anguished "Heads and Hands" – some of the last works she executed in acrylic and Flashe before taking up oil paint in the summer of 1981.

Painting in oil enhanced the depth and texture of Rothenberg's work and allowed for more subtle modulations of light. Some of Rothenberg's first oils – *The Creek* (1981–2; Stedelijk Museum, Amsterdam) and *Two Rays* (1981; collection Douglas S. Cramer, Los Angeles, *ibid.*, p.97) – were based on things she saw in her Long Island backyard. A monumental picture such as *Withall* (1982; Stedelijk Museum) is a culminating arena for motifs – head and hand, swan, sailing boat, figures – that characterise the work up to this point. Personal rather than cultural, intimate rather than histrionic, Rothenberg's forms have intrinsic meaning. And as her technique grew bolder and more assertive, she never relinquished her rapport with painting as an intuitive exploration of the self.

For this reason, among others, Rothenberg's association with Neo-Expressionism, a transcultural *Zeitgeist* that bonded artists as diverse as Julian Schnabel, David Salle, Sandro Chia, Francesco Clemente, George Baselitz and Anslem Kiefer, in retrospect seems a curatorial concession rather than a legitimate connection. Whereas Neo-Expressionists tended to paint grand themes, historical and apocalyptic, with a bravura befitting their content, Rothenberg consistently strove to simplify her means. If Neo-Expressionists preferred subjects gleaned from culture, Rothenberg drew hers from personal experiences.

Rothenberg aspires to monumental painting without melodrama. During the 1980s her cast of characters included dancers, spinners, bikers, jugglers and vaulters (*Vaulting*, 1986–7; Cleveland Museum of Art). She began each canvas as though starting from ground zero, building up paint into swirling images of motion and speed, sequential actions unfolding as though through time. Since her marriage to Bruce Nauman (1989) and move to New Mexico, she has continued in this direction, introducing, in such works as *Blue U-Turn* (1989; F. Ross Collection, Switzerland, *ibid.*, p.163) and *Bone Heads* (1989–90; see illustration), a more overt and autobiographical figuration. Never one to limit her options, Rothenberg remains open to all possibilities as potential ideas for painting.

DOUGLAS DREISHPOON

Rowe, Louise *see* Jopling

Rozanova, Olga (Vladimirovna)

Russian painter, printmaker, designer and poet, 1886–1918

Born in Melenki, near Vladimir, 22 June (Old Style calendar)/4 July (New Style calendar) 1886; father police chief Vladimir Rozanov. Studied art in Moscow at the private Bolshakov School of Painting and Sculpture, 1904–9; also took classes in Konstantin Yuon's studio. Joined Soyuz molodyozhi (Union of Youth), and moved to St Petersburg, 1911; began to participate regularly in their half-yearly exhibitions and to contribute to the journal of the same name; wrote Union of Youth manifesto, 1913. From 1913 worked on many book-design projects with Futurist poet Alexei Kruchyonykh, who became her companion; they never married, due to their anarchic beliefs. Member of Kazimir Malevich's group Supremus, 1916–17. Active after the Revolution in the organisation of the first professional union of Russian artists, 1917–18, and joined IZO, Narkompros (Fine Arts Section, People's Commissariat of Enlightenment). Died from diphtheria in Moscow, 7 November 1918.

Principal Exhibitions

Soyuz molodyozhi (Union of Youth), St Petersburg: 1911–13

Galleria Sprovieri, Roma: 1914 (*Libera mostra internazionale futurista di pittura e scultura*)
Petrograd: 1915 (*Tramway V: First Futurist Exhibition of Paintings*), 1915 (*0.10 [Zero-Ten]: Last Futurist Exhibition of Paintings*)
Bubnovy valet (Jack/Knave of Diamonds), Moscow: 1917
Moscow: 1917 (*Verbovka: Contemporary Applied Art*), 1918 (*First Exhibition of Paintings by the Professional Union of Artists of Moscow*), 1918 (retrospective)

Selected Writings

"Cubism, Futurism, Suprematism", *Von der Malerei zum Design*, exh. cat., Cologne, 1981
"The bases of the New Creation", *Russian Art of the Avant-garde: Theory and Criticism, 1902–1934*, ed. John E. Bowlt, 2nd edition, London and New York: Thames and Hudson, 1988
"Manifest soyuza molodyozhi" [Manifesto of the Union of Youth] and "Kubizm, Futurizm, Suprematizm", *Neizvestniy Russkiy Avangard* [The unknown Russian avant-garde], ed. A. Sarabyanov and Nina Guryanova. Moscow, 1992

Bibliography

Pervaya gosudarstvennaya vystavka: Posmertnaya vystavka kartin, etyudov, eskizov i risunkov O.V. Rozanovoy [First State exhibition: Posthumous exhibition of paintings, studies, sketches and drawings by O.V. Rozanova], exh. cat., Moscow, 1918
Varst (V. Stepanova), "O vystavke Rozanovoy" [On Rozanova's exhibition], *Iskusstvo*, no.4, 22 February 1919
A. Efros, "O. Rozanova", *Profili*, Moscow, 1930, pp.228–9
Camilla Gray, *The Great Experiment: Russian Art, 1863–1922*, London: Thames and Hudson, and New York: Abrams, 1962
Nikolai Khardzhiyev, ed., *K istoriy russkogo avangarda/The Russian Avant-Garde*, Stockholm: Hylaea, 1976
Künstlerinnen der russischen Avantgarde/Women Artists of the Russian Avant-Garde, 1910–1930, exh. cat., Galerie Gmurzynska, Cologne, 1979
Angelica Zander Rudenstine, ed., *The George Costakis Collection: Russian Avant-Garde Art*, New York: Abrams, and London: Thames and Hudson, 1981
Gerald Janacek, *The Look of Russian Literature: Avant-Garde Visual Experiments, 1900–1930*, Princeton: Princeton University Press, 1984
Vera Terechina, "Majakowski und Rosanowa", *Bildende Kunst*, no.11, 1988, pp.499–501
Nina Guryanova, "Na puti k novomu iskusstvu: Olga Rozanova" [Towards the new art: Olga Rozanova], *Iskusstvo*, no.1, 1989
Charlotte Humphreys, *Cubo-Futurism in Russia, 1912–1922: The Transformation of a Painterly Style*, PhD dissertation, University of St Andrews, 1989
E.F. Kovtun, *Russkaya futuristicheskaya kniga* [The Russian Futurist book], Moscow: Kniga, 1989
V. Terekhina, "O.V. Rozanova", *Panorama iskusstv*, xi, Moscow, 1989, pp.38–62
M.N. Yablonskaya, *Women Artists of Russia's New Age, 1900–1935*, New York: Rizzoli, and London: Thames and Hudson, 1990
Olga Rozanova, exh. cat., Moscow, 1992
John E. Bowlt and N. Misler, *The Thyssen-Bornemisza Collection: Twentieth-Century Russian and East European Painting*, New York, 1993
L'Avant-garde russe, 1905–1925, exh. cat., Musée des Beaux-Arts, Nantes, and elsewhere, 1993
Nina Guryanova, "Olga Rozanova: Colore libero", *Art e Dossier*, no.85, December 1993, pp.37–43
——, "Suprematism and transrational poetry", *Elementa*, i, 1994, pp.369–83

The direction of Russian avant-garde art – with its characteristic traits of constant renewal, bold experimentation and negation of previous traditions – was fully reflected in Rozanova's painting, poetry and theoretical articles. Her complicated daily life hurtled through war, revolution, disorder, poverty and, at times, extreme isolation and incomprehension. During her artistic training in Konstantin Yuon's studio, she created several works in Post-Impressionist and Neo-primitivist styles, but soon went over to the Cubist and Futurist trends. From the very beginning of her mature artistic career (which lasted only eight years) Rozanova preferred abstract compositions, based on dynamics, interactions of colour and discordant linear rhythms, which were created, as it were, "in a single breath", in contrast to the plot-oriented scenes and "literariness" of traditional Russian art. She often experimented with new painterly techniques and genres. Futuristic works by Rozanova (who never travelled outside Russia) were so unusual and innovative that they were introduced in the Russian section of the first Futurist exhibition in Rome in 1914 alongside paintings by Alexandra Exter (q.v.) and sculpture by Alexander Archipenko, who were both already well known in Europe. During the next four years Kazimir Malevich, Mayakovsky, Khlebnikov, Rodchenko and Lyubov Popova (q.v.) were among Rozanova's friends and collaborators.

From 1911 to 1914 Rozanova was a leading member of the Union of Youth, one of the first associations of avant-garde artists in Russia, located in St Petersburg. Among the participants were Pavel Filonov, Malevich and David Burlyuk, who worked in the so-called Cubo-Futurist style. During these years, the most fruitful of her career, Rozanova moved gradually from early Neo-primitivist still lifes and portraits, such as *Still Life* (1912–13; Saratov State Art Museum), *Blue Vase with Flowers* (1912; State Russian Museum, St Petersburg) and *Woman in a Pink Dress (Portrait of A.V. Rozanova, Sister of the Artist)* (1911–12; Ekaterinburg Museum of Fine Arts; all oil on canvas), towards the new Futurist dynamism and expressiveness of abstraction with scenes of the industrial city and its spiritual disharmony. Her best compositions in this genre – *Embankment* (Thyssen-Bornemisza Collection), *City (Industrial Landscape)* (Historical Museum, Slobodskoy), *The Port* (untraced), *Man in the Street* (Thyssen-Bornemisza Collection), *Construction Work* (Samara Art Museum; all 1913; oil on canvas) and *Fire in the City* (1914; oil on tinplate; Samara Art Museum) – are characterised by rich surface texture, a combination of a light point touch with an energetic, wide brush stroke, and the striking application of a black line or contour, creating a strong feeling of dissonance.

Suprematist abstraction was already anticipated in Rozanova's canvases of 1914–15, such as *Playing Cards (Series)* (1915), *Metronome* (1915; Tretyakov Gallery, Moscow), *Writing Desk* (1915; State Russian Museum, St Petersburg; all oil on canvas) and *Workbox* (1915; oil and collage with lace on canvas; Tretyakov Gallery). These works display a painterly construction composed of colour planes that served as a background for "random" highlighted objects or details. The purely Cubo-Futurist "intonation" of the street scene, which stressed dynamism and simultaneity, is no longer present. On the contrary, these constructions can be seen as a kind of hypothetical "picture" or rebus offered to the viewer. As a rule, the isolated sign, or object, or signboard, etc., "torn off" from its usual context, becomes a requisite attribute of such compositions, and the irrational laws of construction for such painterly texts were in many ways identical to the laws

Rozanova: *City Landscape*, 1913; lithograph

governing the construction of the new transrational poetry, created by the Russian Futurists.

Rozanova's powerful lyrical sense and ability to improvise marked her out from the start as an independent talent. As Alexei Kruchyonykh noted in one of his books: "Rozanova knows how to introduce feminine cunning into all the 'horrors of Cubism', which is so startlingly unexpected that it confuses many people." Rozanova's graphic work suited itself perfectly to the style, intonation and internal logic of verse by Kruchyonykh, who was also the inventor and theoretician of the transrational (*zaum*) language. In 1913 he published his famous manifesto *The Word as Such*, in which he proclaimed "a new verbal form", "a language lacking a determinate rational meaning". The artistic and personal ties between Rozanova and Kruchyonykh were most fruitful, and resulted in the creation of the unique style of Russian Futurist books. *Vzorval* (Explodity), in which Rozanova's lithographs appear alongside works by Malevich and Natalya Goncharova (q.v.), *Utinoye*

gnezdyshko … durnykh slov (A duck's nest … of dirty words), *Igra v adu* (A game in hell), *Te li le* (Te li le) and others were produced in 1913–14. *Te li le* was made in the genre of "colourful auto-writing" invented by Rozanova, an early virtuoso demonstration of visual poetry, in which line was the equivalent of the word, and colour the equivalent of sound.

In 1915–16 Rozanova and Kruchyonykh created a new version of the Futurist book by using collages made from coloured paper. Rozanova employed this technique in designing a book by Kruchyonykh and Alyagrov (pseudonym for Roman Jakobson), *Zaumnaya Gniga* (Transrational book; 1915), and a portfolio of verse by Kruchyonykh entitled *Voyna* (War; 1916), which contained colour linocuts and collages. Rozanova was so enthusiastic about transrational poetry that she began to compose verse influenced by Kruchyonykh's work. Kruchyonykh, in his turn, applied himself to visual art, and under Rozanova's guidance created some collages, publishing them in his album *Vselenskaya voyna* (Universal war; 1916). In the preface to this edition he declared "transrational" (here in the sense of abstract) painting to be the winner, and wrote: "it was Rozanova, who first gave examples of the style that now is given the inexpressive name of Suprematism by other artists ... Transrational language, of which I am the first representative, gives its hand to transrational painting." During this period, Rozanova arrived at abstraction: through the medium of coloured-paper collage she was able to solve purely painterly issues, similar to those with which Malevich was dealing in his Suprematist compositions.

Malevich greatly appreciated Rozanova's painting of this period, and in a polemic recognised her as "the only true Suprematist". In such sophisticated abstract paintings as *Suprematism* (State Russian Museum), *Suprematism* (Tretyakov Gallery) and *Suprematism: Flight of the Aeroplane* (Samara Art Museum; all 1916; oil on canvas) Rozanova reveals the discordant concordance of coloured planes through the effects of their interaction and the rhythm that had been liberated from objectivity. In 1916–18 she worked in close collaboration with Malevich, as a member of his group Supremus and secretary-editor of their magazine.

From the beginning of her artistic career, colour was Rozanova's main concern – in theory, and in practical experimentation with new ideas of colour schemes. In 1916–17 she tried to formulate her own concept on this matter in the article "Kubizm, Futurizm, Suprematizm". She created her own variant of Suprematism (defined as *tsvetopis*), in which the emphasis moved from form and painterly texture to the spiritual, mystical qualities of colour and its interconnection with light. One of the best examples of this style is *Green Stripe* (1917; Costakis Collection; another version of the same title in Rostov Museum), once part of triptych (the other two canvases, *Purple Stripe* and *Yellow Stripe*, are untraced and probably destroyed), as well as *Non-Objective Composition* (1917; Simbirsk Art Museum). At the same time Rozanova was considering some of the projects involving the projection of strong light into the open space of the Moscow stadium. Her ideas influenced Rodchenko, who created a whole series of compositions named *tsvetopis* in 1918–19.

The last year of Rozanova's life, 1918, was dedicated not only to painting but also to social action: she wrote several polemical articles on the poetics of anarchy in art in the newspaper *Anarkhiya* (Anarchy), closed by the Bolsheviks at the end of that year.

One of the most original, fascinating and distinguished artists of the Russian avant-garde of the 1910s, Rozanova is still not well known. Her premature death in 1918 prevented her from receiving the place in history that belongs to her: after her death, her paintings shared the fate of avant-garde art after the Revolution, when masterpieces by Kandinsky, Malevich and Chagall were sent to provincial museums, many of them to be destroyed in the 1930s. Almost all of Rozanova's archive was destroyed during the Russian Civil War. As a result, for many years her name was a mere "legend" for scholars. It was only in the 1970s that her "rebirth" began: some of her articles on art were translated into English for the first time, and her paintings began to be shown in various exhibitions of the Russian avant-garde. The Futurist books and paintings by Rozanova have found their places in such world-famous collections as the State Russian Museum, St Petersburg;

Tretyakov Gallery, Moscow; Thyssen-Bornemisza Collection; Galerie Gmurzynska and Ludwig Museum, Germany; Marinetti Collection, Rome; and the Russian avant-garde collection of the late George Costakis, to whom belongs the following words about Rozanova's work:

> Shortly after the end of the Second World War, by accident, I encountered some avant-garde art. The painting I saw first was done in 1917, yet it might easily have been a revolutionary work of about 1950. Indeed it might almost have been mistaken for a canvas by Barnett Newman, who, to be sure, had no knowledge of its existence. Olga Rozanova was the artist, and she died in 1918. It was her work that opened my eyes to the existence and compelling power of the avant-garde [Rudenstine 1981].

NINA GURYANOVA

Rude, Sophie
French painter, 1797–1867

Born Sophie Frémiet in Dijon, 15 June 1797. Moved to Brussels with her family, 1816. Studied under Anatole Devosge in Dijon and Jacques-Louis David in Brussels. Married sculptor François Rude in Brussels, 1821; one son, born 1823 (d. 1830); husband died 1855. Moved to Paris, 1830. Died in Paris, 4 December 1867.

Principal Exhibitions
Brussels Salon: 1818, 1821
Salon d'Anvers, Antwerp: 1819
Ghent Salon: 1820 (medal of honour), 1824 (medal of honour), 1826
Lille Salon: 1825 (bronze medal)
Paris Salon: occasionally 1827–67 (second class medal 1833)
Société des Amis des Arts, Dijon: 1837, 1849, 1858

Bibliography
Louis de Bast, *Annales du Salon de Gand*, Ghent: Goesin, 1823, pl.20
Charles Lenormand, *Les Artistes contemporains, ii: Salon of 1833*, p.193
Jules David, *Le Peintre Louis David: Souvenirs et documents inédits*, 2 vols, Paris: Havard, 1880–82
Louis de Fourcard, *François Rude, sculpteur: Ses oeuvres et son temps*, Paris: Librairie de l'Art, 1904
P. Quatré, "Portraits de François Rude et de Mme Rude au Musée de Dijon", *Annales de Bourgogne*, xxvii/2, 1955, pp.114–15
Catalogues des peintures françaises, Dijon: Musée des Beaux-Arts, 1968
Monique Geiger, "Quelques femmes peintres de Dijon au XIXe siècle", *Mémoires de l'Académie des Sciences, Arts et Belles-Lettres de Dijon*, cxxvii, 1983–4, pp.214–29
Dominique Vautier, "Sophie Rude", *Autour de Neo-classicisme en Belgique*, exh. cat., Musée d'Ixelles, Brussels, 1985, pp.252–4
Monique Geiger, "Sophie Rude (1797–1867): Une élève de David et son évolution artistique (avec essai de catalogue de son oeuvre)", *Bulletin de la Société de l'Histoire de l'Art Français*, 1987, 1989, pp.167–90

Although Sophie Frémiet pursued a long and successful painting career, first in Belgium and then in Paris, exhibiting

Rude: *Ariadne Abandoned on the Isle of Naxos*, 1826; Musée des Beaux-Arts, Dijon

regularly at the Salons until her death, and was a highly esteemed pupil and collaborator of Jacques-Louis David, her work was virtually unknown until Monique Geiger published the first broad study of the artist's oeuvre in 1989. As is so often the case with women artists, Rude had previously appeared only as a minor character in discussions of the lives and work of her teacher David, and her famous husband, the sculptor François Rude. She is not even included in the exhaustive list of David's pupils by Delecluze.

Sophie Frémiet was born into an artistically cultivated family in Dijon in 1797. Her mother Sophie Monnier was the daughter of the Dijon engraver Louis-Gabriel Monnier, who became the first conservateur of the Musée de Dijon in 1799. Her father Louis Frémiet, a government official and later a journalist, was a close friend of François Devosge, founder of the Ecole de Dessin in Dijon. François's son Anatole Devosge was Sophie's first teacher, and her earliest known work is a drawing (c.1815; Musée des Beaux-Arts, Dijon) after his painting *Hercules and Phillo*. After the fall of Napoleon in 1815, her father, an ardent Bonapartist, was forced to leave France for Belgium, where he was joined by his family, including Sophie, in 1816. Settling in Brussels, Sophie Frémiet became a

pupil of David, now also in exile in Brussels, and, over the next several years, made several copies of his works, beginning with *Cupid and Psyche* (1817; untraced). In 1818 she made her public début at the Brussels Salon with two portraits, also now lost. The following year she exhibited *A Sacred Reading* (repr. Geiger 1989, fig.2) at the Salon d'Anvers. This accomplished, if somewhat eclectic work, which combines Italian idealisation with northern naturalism, echoes the half-length format and even the figures of David's *Wrath of Achilles* (repr. Antoine Schnapper, *David*, New York: Alpine Fine Arts, 1980, pl.188), a work that Frémiet had copied at David's request. David's influence continues in her painting *La Belle Anthia* (private collection, repr. Geiger 1989, fig.3), with which she competed for the grand prix and won a medal of honour at the Ghent Salon in 1820, and for which she received her first critical acclaim. This work and associated correspondence reveal Frémiet as a talented and ambitious 23-year-old artist who aspired to be a history painter, the height of the profession so difficult for women to attain, while also pursuing the more traditional female career path as a portraitist. The work, although somewhat unresolved in composition, contains all the Neo-classical essentials: an elevated Classical theme enacted by a protagonist dressed and posed *all'antica*. The landscape setting with an ancient temple in the distance departs from the usual interior setting.

In 1821 Frémiet married the sculptor François Rude, who had been a family friend during her days in Dijon, and in 1823 their son Louis-Amédée was born. It is evident that Rude's close relationship with David continued, since she painted a copy, signed by David, of his *Farewell of Telemachus and Eucharis* (private collection, repr. Schnapper, *op. cit.*, pl.187) for the printer Didot in 1822. Rude exhibited regularly at Salons in Brussels and Ghent and, from 1827, in Paris, focusing on portraiture, particularly of family members, but also exhibiting religious and history paintings. Her portraits, such as that of her father *Louis Frémiet* (Musée des Beaux-Arts, Dijon), reveal careful observation and a straightforward, unidealised approach similar to that of David. In fact, David's signed portrait of *Wolf* (Louvre, Paris) is now at least partially attributed to Rude on the basis of a contemporary account. In 1824–5 she was commissioned to paint 13 allegorical figures on glass for the bookcases of the library of the Duke of Arenberg (four, representing *Law*, *Medicine*, *Geography* and *Geometry*, in Palais d'Egmont, Brussels). At about the same time she painted a series of decorative panels of the *Seasons*, now lost, for the Château de Tervuren. In 1826 she exhibited a religious subject and an ambitious history painting, *Ariadne Abandoned on the Isle of Naxos* (1826; see illustration), at the Ghent Salon. The work is striking for its elegant and accomplished female nude, an unusual subject for a female artist, its strong emotional expressiveness and its luminous landscape setting in a grotto by the sea. As is typical in her works, the protagonist is a woman.

By 1827–8 the Rudes were frequently in Paris, settling there by 1830, the year of their child's death. In 1831, at her second Paris Salon, Sophie Rude exhibited the Raphaelesque *Sleep of the Virgin*, also called *Holy Family* (Musée des Beaux-Arts, Dijon), a subject so original that this was its first appearance at the 19th-century Salons. In addition to exhibiting portraits on a regular basis, she abandoned Neo-classicism to paint subjects drawn from British and French history. Such Romantic historicising works in the Troubadour genre were immensely popular by the 1830s, when Rude made her debut in this genre with *Charles I, King of England, Bidding Farewell to His Children* (private collection, repr. Geiger 1989, fig.9), which won a second-class medal at the Paris Salon of 1833. The work, which was reproduced in a lithograph by Lion, was bought by the Minister of Commerce and given, for services rendered, to Guizot, a minister and ambassador under Louis-Philippe. Among her essays in this genre were a scene from the War of the Fronde, exhibited in 1836, and a scene of the Revolt at Bruges in 1436 (Musée des Beaux-Arts, Dijon), exhibited at the Salon of 1841, each of which is characterised by rich, historically evocative settings, multi-figured compositions and dramatic actions (*ibid.*, figs 10–11).

Rude's many portraits painted and exhibited between 1830 and 1850 include a fine *Self-Portrait* (Musée des Beaux-Arts, Dijon) and a portrait of her husband *François Rude* (Musée Royaux des Beaux-Arts de Belgique, Brussels), both probably executed in 1842, the latter reminiscent of Renaissance portraiture. In 1849 she sent five works, now lost, to the exhibition of the Société des Amis des Arts of Dijon. Several artists

in the exhibition are listed as "pupils of Madame Rude", including Madame Sophie Aizelin, indicating that Rude was also important as a teacher. After her husband's death in 1855, she received a pension from the state and continued to exhibit at the Salons until her death.

MARTIN ROSENBERG

Rue, Lizinka *see* Mirbel

Ruysch, Anna *see under* Ruysch, Rachel

Ruysch, Rachel
Dutch painter, 1664–1750

Born in The Hague; baptised in the Groote Kerk, 3 June 1664; father the eminent scientist Frederik Ruysch; maternal grandfather Pieter Post, architect to the Dutch stadhouder. Moved to Amsterdam with her family, 1667. Studied under the flower painter Willem van Aelst. Married portrait painter Juriaen Pool II, 1693; ten children, none of whom became painters, born 1695–1711. Both Ruysch and her husband became guild members in The Hague. Court painter to the Elector Palatine, Johann Wilhelm, in Düsseldorf, 1708–16. Died in Amsterdam, 12 October 1750.

Bibliography

Jan van Gool, *De nieuwe schouburg der Nederlandsche kunstschilders en schilderessen* [The new theatre of Netherlandish male and female painters], i, The Hague, 1750; reprinted Soest, 1971, pp.210–33

Jean-Baptiste Descamps, *La Vie des peintres flamands, allemands et hollandais*, iii, Paris, 1760

John Smith, *A Catalogue Raisonné of the Works of the Most Eminent Dutch, Flemish and French Painters*, vi, London, 1835; reprinted 1908

Abraham Bredius, "Das Nachlass-Inventare von Juriaen Pool", *Künstler-Inventare: Urkunden zur Geschichte der holländischen Kunst des XVIten, XVIIten und XVIIIten Jahrhunderts*, 8 vols, The Hague: Nijhoff, 1915–22, v, pp.1203–9

Cornelis Hofstede de Groot, *Beschreibendes und kritisches Verzeichnis der Werke des hervorragensten holländischen Maler des XVII. Jahrhunderts*, x, Esslingen, 1928, pp.309–31

Maurice H. Grant, *Rachel Ruysch, 1664–1750*, Leigh-on-Sea: Lewis, 1956

Werner Timm, "Bemerkungen zu einem Stilleben von Rachel Ruysch" [Remarks on a still life by Rachel Ruysch], *Oud-Holland*, lxxvii, 1962, pp.137–8

Jaromir Síp, "Notities bij het stilleven van Rachel Ruysch" [Notes on the still life by Rachel Ruysch], *Nederlands Kunsthistorisch Jaarboek*, xix, 1968, pp.157–70

Peter Mitchell, *European Flower Painters*, London: A. & C. Black, 1973

Women Artists, 1550–1950, exh. cat., Los Angeles County Museum of Art, and elsewhere, 1976

A Flowery Past: A Survey of Dutch and Flemish Painting from 1600 until the Present, exh. cat., Kunsthandel P. de Boer, Amsterdam, and Noordbrabants Museum, 's-Hertogenbosch, 1982

Yvonne Friedrichs, "Adriaen van der Werff und Rachel Ruysch: Zwei Hofmaler des Kürfursten Johann Wilhelm von der Pfalz in Düsseldorf", *Weltkunst*, vi, 1984, pp.712–15

Marianne Berardi, "The nature pieces of Rachel Ruysch", *Porticus*, x–xi, 1987–8, pp.2–15

Stillevens uit de Gouden Eeuw/Still Life Paintings from the Golden Age, exh. cat., Museum Boymans-van Beuningen, Rotterdam, 1989

Jan Davidsz. de Heem en zijn Kring [Jan Davidsz. de Heem and his circle], exh. cat., Centraal Museum, Utrecht, and Herzog Anton Ulrich-Museum, Braunschweig, 1991

Die Karl und Magdalene Haberstock-Stiftung, exh. cat., Munich and Augsburg, 1991

Mauritshuis in Bloei: Boeketten uit de Gouden Eeuw/Mauritshuis in Bloom: Bouquets from the Golden Age, exh. cat., Zwolle and The Hague, 1992

Renate Trnek, "Ruysch, Rachel," *Die holländischen Gemälde des 17. Jahrhunderts in der Gemälde-Galerie der Akademie der Bildenden Künste in Wien*, Vienna: Bohlau, 1992, pp.333–42

Erika Gemar-Koeltzsch, *Luca Bild-Lexikon: Holländische Stillebenmaler des 17. Jahrhundert*, iii, Lingen: Luca, 1995

Wiepke Loos and others, *The Age of Elegance: Paintings from the Rijksmuseum in Amsterdam, 1700–1800*, Amsterdam: Rijksmuseum, 1995

Paul Taylor, *Dutch Flower Painting, 1600–1720*, New Haven and London: Yale University Press, 1995

Rachel Ruysch was the most celebrated Dutch woman artist of the 17th and 18th centuries, and enjoyed a long and prosperous life as one of Holland's most esteemed flower painters (her main artistic rival was Jan van Huysum). Her career intersected with the lives of scientists, artists, wealthy Dutch merchants, powerful politicians and an international group of aristocratic patrons, creating a fascinating web of cross-disciplinary influences.

Archival records suggest that Ruysch lived in Amsterdam, the commercial capital of Holland, for all but the first three years of her life – initially in her parents' house on the Bloemgracht (flower canal), and from the time of her marriage until her death on the nearby Wolvenstraat. Her lucrative artistic career spanned more than 65 years, and she continued to paint well into her eighties. Her earliest dated work, a floral festoon (private collection, New York), is from 1681; her latest, companion paintings of nosegays (Musée des Beaux-Arts, Lille) are dated 1747.

Ruysch owed part of her professional success to her father, a man of astonishing energy and one of the most remarkable scientists of his time. Over a 90-year lifespan, Frederik Ruysch catalogued the Amsterdam botanical garden, which he expanded to the richest in the world; developed new techniques of obstetrics; invented an improved embalming fluid and method of surgical injection; and created the first natural history museum in Europe in a few rented rooms on the Nieuwezijds Achterburgwal – while simultaneously engaging in heated disputes with hostile religious figures and rival scientists, and corresponding with Sir Isaac Newton and Marcello Malpighi, among others. Like his daughter, he was also a shrewd entrepreneur, amassing a sizeable fortune from his scientific work, and gaining patrons from as far away as Russia, where he drew support from Peter the Great. Contemporary sources show that Dr Ruysch drew his family

into his scientific adventures, particularly the preservation and display of rare specimens – a new art form of its own. In his cabinets, embalmed hydrocephalic children, wrapped in their own intestines, and other such wonders were arranged like *tableaux vivants* – playing instruments and engaging in other lifelike activities. Rachel Ruysch's woodland still-life paintings of *c.*1683–9, in which fire-breathing lizards are juxtaposed with accurately observed grasses and bindweeds, exhibit a similar mixture of science and fantasy, didacticism and entertainment. Clearly, Rachel's childhood experience in preparing specimens schooled her in the theatrics of visual arrangement.

At the age of 15, Ruysch studied with the noted flower painter Willem van Aelst. Once launched, her career followed a logical course. She seems to have set clearly defined artistic problems for herself, mastered them with a single-minded focus and then moved on to a new set of challenges. Generally, she tended to concentrate on a particular type of still life, or a specific way of composing it, for a period of five to seven years before shifting to something new. Throughout her career, however, she remained focused on fruit, flowers and nature pieces, never seeming to deviate from that speciality into other genres of still life, such as breakfast, *vanitas*, banquet, kitchen and hunting pieces. It is particularly interesting that she seems to have had no interest in painting game pieces despite her familiarity with zoology and her teacher van Aelst's reputation for painting exquisite trophies of the hunt. Her nature pieces differ from those of her male contemporaries because the violent encounters she depicts between insects and reptiles never seem to result in dead animals.

Ruysch spent approximately the first decade of her career (*c.*1679–91) painting a wider variety of still life than she did at any other point in her life. She painted floral garlands and flower and fruit festoons against dark backgrounds and shallow niches (National Gallery, Prague); nature pieces with mossy banks, caves and dark woodland pools in the manner of both Otto Marseus van Schrieck (Glasgow Art Gallery and Museum; University of Rostock; Fitzwilliam Museum, Cambridge; Gemäldegalerie Alte Meister, Dresden; National Gallery, Prague) and Jan Davidsz. de Heem (Schloss Wilhelmshöhe, Kassel; Memorial Art Gallery, University of Rochester, NY; Museum Boijmans Van Beuningen, Rotterdam); fruit still lifes with peaches and grapes on a simple marble ledge (ex-Christie's, New York, 12 January 1996, lot 96); and small bouquets of flowers in blown-glass goblets or vases placed on a ledge (Hamburger Kunsthalle, Hamburg), sometimes with gold-fringed velvet cloths nearby. These paintings imitated the work of van Aelst and his colleagues quite closely, but showed Ruysch's great skill in designing a range of compositions and rendering a wide variety of textures. She also learned to paint landscape as a back-drop for her outdoor still lifes, but these glimpses of scenery are seldom as convincing as the still lifes in front of them, and often have the feeling of a natural history diorama.

Being a woman presented serious obstacles to the next phase of Ruysch's career. She was not admitted to the Amsterdam painters' guild, which did not accept women to its membership, and consequently she could not sell her works as an independent artist. This probably explains why, for approximately five years from 1690 to 1695, her paintings were quite modest in scale and in subject. In this period, Ruysch seems to have devoted her efforts to painting small-scale nosegays, which often contain about a dozen varieties of common garden flowers. She presented these intimate bouquets rather casually on a marble or stone ledge, against plain dark backgrounds (Fitzwilliam Museum; Gemäldegalerie Alte Meister, Dresden; Hamburger Kunsthalle; Victoria and Albert Museum, London; Norton Simon Museum, Pasadena). Van Aelst also painted this type of composition, but chose larger, more formal flowers such as roses for his bouquets, and rendered them in a harder manner with cooler hues. By contrast, Ruysch's nosegays include not only roses but columbine and snapdragons, and often use field grasses and garden herbs (ribbon grass and rue are favourites) to create a web of graceful linear rhythms that soften the edges of the bouquet. The overall effect is wistfully romantic. Her bouquets appear to have been discarded absent-mindedly, the stems of the flowers often falling in all directions, since the string that bound them has slipped away. During the last half of the 1690s Ruysch painted traditional arrangements of flowers in a glass vase, but designed them along an S-curve from lower left to upper right (Städelsches Kunstinstitut und Städtische Galerie, Frankfurt am Main) and suffused them in a smoky atmosphere. Sometimes Ruysch introduced a landscape element or glimpse of sky into the dark backgrounds, which recalled her work with nature pieces from the previous decade (Musée Thomas Henry, Cherbourg). The asymmetry of these bouquets, with their snipped-off central blossom, also had its roots in van Aelst's floral arrangements.

In 1701 Ruysch and her husband became members of the painters' guild in The Hague, where women were welcome. Interestingly, at this point Ruysch's sex became an asset rather than a detriment to her career. Having been not only much better trained and educated than most women artists of the period – who seldom rose above the rank of amateur – but also more thoroughly schooled in flower painting than many men, she became a "celebrity". In less flattering terms, she was a "curiosity", who reached the pinnacle of success in a discipline in which there were no models for women. During her years in the guild at The Hague, Ruysch began to paint her first major flower-pieces, which she sold to an international group of patrons. These paintings feature spectacular horticultural specimens, including varieties that the Dutch had only recently begun to hybridise. Ruysch organised the flowers comprising these bouquets within a pronounced triangular geometry. The largest, most striking blossoms are pushed forward to define the surface of the triangle and are painted as though under a spotlight. During this period, Ruysch frequently placed a piece of fruit, and sometimes a fallen blossom, on the table top beside the vase. Perhaps her most exquisite work from the guild years, and unquestionably her finest painting in an American museum, is the flower-piece with an aubergine on a ledge (1704; see illustration), recently acquired by the Detroit Institute of Arts.

From 1707 Ruysch began to paint ambitious outdoor fruit pieces as pendants to her prize floral bouquets, and such pendants became one of her specialities after she gained court patronage. She invariably placed a bounty of cultivated fruit in a setting rather incongruous for such unnaturally occurring produce – in deep woodlands usually in front of a cave. The idea for this subject derives from paintings by Abraham Mignon, which are in turn derived from compositions by Jan

Davidsz. de Heem. Although Ruysch adapted Mignon's general subject matter, probably from first-hand knowledge of his paintings, her displays are none the less significantly different in appearance and probably in intention. Mignon, a devoutly religious man, described each piece of fruit with strong outline and full illumination, as if each specimen rested clearly in the light of religious truth. In Ruysch's work, by contrast, the fruit seems to be a more ambiguous emblem of the overwhelming variety, abundance and mystery of nature. Consequently, her fruit scenes exist in a kind of murky, somewhat forbidding half-light. In a painting of 1714 (Städtische Kunstsammlungen, Augsburg) she combined both a harvest of fruit and an overflowing basket of flowers within a single canvas, creating one of her most sumptuous outdoor compositions.

Ruysch's skill was such that in 1708 she was offered an appointment as court painter in Düsseldorf by the Elector Palatine, Johann Wilhelm, an admirer of the *fijnschilder* technique (a detailed and polished method of painting). The Elector bought everything that Ruysch produced over a four-year period (1710–13), and sent two of her paintings (Uffizi, Florence) to his Medici in-laws in Florence as a gift.

Ruysch's flower-pieces of the Düsseldorf period maintain the dark backgrounds of her earlier work. She moved away from bouquets of triangular shape, however, preferring rounder arrangements centred on a bright triad of blossoms, usually roses. In an effort to create more graceful, natural-looking compositions, she often surrounded her bright centres with smaller, more delicate flowers that let the darkness sift through them to form a rather ambiguous perimeter to the arrangement. Ruysch would then place a few large dramatic blossoms at the outer edge. These perimeter accents vary from painting to painting, but generally consist of African marigolds, flamed tulips, sunflowers, a cluster of primroses, a cabbage rose and a passion flower (Alte Pinakothek, Munich; Rijksmuseum, Amsterdam).

After the death of the Elector (1716) until 1723, Ruysch continued to paint fruit and flower pieces, often on a somewhat less grand scale, for patrons in the Netherlands and abroad. Her work became increasingly refined, with the central core of the bouquet growing in density and becoming a more sculptural mass of blossoms. In 1723 Ruysch, her husband and their son Georgio won the Holland jackpot of 60,000 florins, a windfall that seems to have led to a substantial drop in Ruysch's productivity as a painter for approximately one decade. From the mid-1720s to 1730s no known works survive, although there are several paintings from these years attributed to Ruysch in old sale catalogues and inventories.

By the 1720s the trend in flower painting had begun to shift away from the darker backgrounds favoured by Ruysch, which ultimately depend upon the work of painters from the previous generation, such as Jan Davidsz. de Heem and Willem van Aelst. Taste began to favour lighter backgrounds and more pastel hues, a trend that Ruysch herself never entirely followed, although her few surviving works from the years 1739, 1741, 1742 and 1743 show a tentative move in that direction. Jan van Huysum set the model for this brighter style, which carried flower painting into the late 18th century. During the last five years of her life, from 1745 onwards, although her eyesight and steadiness of hand were clearly failing, Ruysch again

Ruysch: *Flowers in a Glass Vase*, 1704; oil on canvas; 83 × 66 cm.; Detroit Institute of Arts; Founders Society Purchase, aided by various funds and donors

began to produce paintings with some frequency. These nosegays are similiar in composition to those that she produced in the 1690s but with much less sure draughtsmanship.

By the time of her death, Ruysch's career had been celebrated in published biographies and poems and her paintings sold for prices in excess of 1000 guilders, equalled by only half a dozen other Dutch painters. Her first biographer, Jan van Gool, visited the elderly Ruysch for an interview in her home two years before her death and found it remarkable that she was still at work. Impressed with Ruysch as both a personality and artist of great achievement, van Gool devoted one of the longest biographies in *De nieuwe schouburg* to her. The *bloem-schilderesse* herself was memorialised in several portraits by other artists, including works by Juriaen Pool II (Stadtmuseum, Düsseldorf; Museum Boijmans Van Beuningen; Stedelijk Museum "De Lakenhal", Leiden), Aert Schouman (Rijksmuseum), Arnold Houbraken (etching after Schouman published in van Gool's biography of her), Godfried Schalcken (Cheltenham Art Gallery and Museums), Ludolf Bakhuysen (Hermitage, St Petersburg) and Michiel van Musscher (private collection, London). Ruysch's fame remained unparalleled by any woman artist until Elisabeth Vigée-Lebrun (q.v.).

Approximately 100 paintings by Ruysch are known to survive today, although records of paintings sold during her lifetime suggest that she produced nearly twice that number, averaging about three per year. She worked primarily on canvas, but occasionally produced works on panel and copper. Throughout her career, Ruysch maintained her maiden name and usually signed her paintings in full in the lower right or left corner, often dating them as well. Her signature changed over the years, from a large, highly calligraphic script with strong flourishes to one that was increasingly smaller and simplified. The signatures on her late works from the 1740s are an exception, for they are proportionally quite large for the paintings, and often include the artist's age – almost as a symbol of pride that she was still at the easel.

Many of Ruysch's finest and most ambitious paintings are preserved in German museums, having come from the collection of her work in the Elector Palatine's Düsseldorf gallery. No drawings by Ruysch's hand have yet been securely identified, although like many other flower painters of the period she doubtless kept sketchbooks containing studies of individual blossoms. Michiel van Musscher's portrait of Rachel Ruysch from 1692 (noted above), which depicts the artist in her studio preparing to paint a flower-piece, implies just this. Before her are a bouquet of live flowers as well as three pattern or sketch-books – suggesting that she worked both from nature and from reference drawings made after nature. On 25 January 1751, three months after Ruysch's death, an anonymous collection of prints, drawings and rarities was sold through a book dealer in Amsterdam. The sale included 12 sheets of flower drawings described as being by Ruysch. These items may well have included some of Ruysch's own artistic reference material that her descendants (who were not painters) disposed of after her death.

Like numerous Dutch artists of the period, Ruysch may have occasionally collaborated with other painters. She is known to have contributed the floral bouquet to her husband's painting of their family group in 1716 (Stadtmuseum,

Düsseldorf). She apparently had no students outside her family. She probably taught her sister Anna Elisabeth (1666–after 1741) as well as her father to paint. Recent scholarship suggests that Anna Ruysch was probably more prolific than previously supposed, and may well have studied directly with van Aelst, and Ernst Stuven, a German painter who trained with van Aelst, though these facts are not recorded. A nature piece bearing her signature (Staatliche Kunsthalle, Karlsruhe) copies a composition by Mignon (Musées royaux des Beaux-Arts de Belgique, Brussels). A bouquet of flowers in a footed vase in the Musée des Beaux-Arts, Rouen, which has a false Rachel Ruysch signature, is probably also by Anna Ruysch.

Ruysch's highly refined technique and the linear grace of her arrangements continued to be prized by collectors long after her death. Artists working in Germany, where Ruysch's best works were most numerous, often copied and mimicked her style well into the 18th century, even though the blonder tonalities were in vogue at the time. Her work seems to have had a particular attraction for other women flower painters. Jacobea Nikkelen, a pupil of Herman van der Mijn, who also worked at the court in Düsseldorf, produced bouquets with rather compact arrangements and low centres of gravity, reflecting Ruysch's manner. Interestingly, Ruysch's particular aesthetic seems to have skipped a generation, resurfacing in the mid-19th century. At that point, Victorian still-life painters began to employ many of her motifs: discarded nosegays on a slab, a bouquet of flowers left negligently in a wood, or a drama between weak and strong creatures (a theme that took on new meanings in the light of Darwinian theory). It is also striking that Ruysch's paintings entered British collections in great quantity during the Victorian period.

MARIANNE BERARDI

See also Court Artists survey

Rydingsvard, Ursula von *see* von Rydingsvard

Ryggen, Hannah
Norwegian textile artist, 1894–1970

Born Hannah Jönsson in Malmö, Sweden, 21 March 1894. Schoolteacher. Evening studies at the Technical School, Lund, under Danish painter Fredrik Krebs, 1918–22; also studied old masters in Dresden, 1922, and Paris, 1947. Married Norwegian painter Hans Ryggen, 1923; one daughter; husband died 1956. Moved to a farmhouse in Ørlandet, Trondheimsfjord, Norway, and started tapestry weaving career, 1924. In Copenhagen, 1946–7. Moved to Trondheim, 1957. Recipient of Prins Eugen gold medal, Sweden, 1959; government artist's income, 1961. Member, Royal Academy of Fine Arts, Stockholm, 1962; Royal Order of St Olav, 1965. Died in Trondheim, 2 February 1970.

Selected Individual Exhibitions

Trondhjems Kunstforening, Trondheim: 1933, 1937, 1945, 1952, 1963

Kunstnerforbundet, Oslo: 1935, 1939, 1946, 1949, 1961, 1963

Danske Kunstindustrimuseum, Copenhagen: 1946

Röhsska Museet, Göteborg: 1948

Malmö Museum: 1948, 1951

Kunstforeningen, Drammen and Hamar: 1950

Kunstforeningen, Bergen: 1952

Kunstnernes Hus, Oslo: 1953

Nordenfjeldske Kunstindustrimuseum, Trondheim: 1961, 1968, 1970

Moderna Museet, Stockholm: 1962

Venice Biennale: 1964 (Norwegian representative)

Bibliography

Tora Sandal, *Billedveversken Hannah Ryggen* [The tapestry weaver Hannah Ryggen], *Nordenfjeldske Kunstindustrimuseum Årbok* (Trondheim), 1946, pp.58–107

Leif Østby, "Hannah Ryggen", *Kunst og Kultur*, xxx, 1947, pp.57–9

Hannah Ryggen, exh. cat., Lunds Konsthall, 1972

Hjørdis Danbolt, *Hannah Ryggen: Norske klassikere* [Hannah Ryggen: Norwegian classics], Oslo: Tiden, 1985

Albert Steen, *Hannah Ryggen: En dikter i veven* [Hannah Ryggen: A poet in the weave], Oslo: Kunstindustrimuseet, 1986 (with English summary)

Hannah Ryggen, 100 år [Hannah Ryggen, 100 years], exh. cat., Vikingsbergs Konstmuseum, Hälsingborg, 1994

When Hannah Ryggen exhibited her tapestries at the Kunstnerforbundet in Oslo in 1939, the public discovered the artist that she was for the first time. Her woven pictures caused a sensation. She wove a commentary on the world, politics and war, and related them to the common people. She continued in the best weaving tradition of the Middle Ages and combined it with the message of her time from the viewpoint of her own life. Her message was unsentimental: "The all important and most precious thing to mankind is free thought and man's individual life" (Steen 1986). Her visionary art had a force beyond the daily struggle of existence.

Hannah Jönsson was born in Malmö, in the south of Sweden, and qualified as a teacher. She also studied painting. She met the Norwegian painter Hans Ryggen in Dresden, on a study tour in 1922. After their marriage in 1923 they moved to his home district near Trondheim. They lived as farmers, and had one daughter; Hans painted in his spare time, mostly landscapes and flowers. Hannah started her weaving career during the long dark winters – she had been aware of the technique since meeting her husband in 1922. Weaving has always been the work of women in the countryside – the Viking women wove as did the women of the Middle Ages. Ryggen continued this tradition, but she did it her own way. Her lack of special training in weaving gave her a unique freedom. Her weavings were not just for use in the household, but have a message of timeless value.

Ryggen's pictorial tapestries fascinate with their expression of ruthless frankness and aggression; they show her technical skill and wild imagination. She very rarely worked from sketches or cartoons, but started with her idea right on to the loom and created all the weaving through her imagination. She wove in the *haute-lisse* technique, which meant that she could see no more than 1.4–1.5 metres of what she had done, before rolling that part of the weave over the bar. She was a great story-teller, and worked on a large scale. She was fired by anger, and she used it (Hälsingborg 1994).

Ryggen's information about the world came from the Oslo daily paper *Dagbladet* and from the radio. For example, in the hanging rug *Blood in the Grass* (1966; Vestlandske Kunstindustrimuseum, Bergen) she reflected on the Vietnam war, and in *Spania* (Kunstindustrimuseum, Oslo), as early as 1938, on the Spanish Civil War. She was troubled by what she read and saw in the paper and this tapestry was her protest against the war. The two opposing Spanish factions are woven in the middle of an almost square tapestry (193 × 226 cm.), with Franco in blue-black behind the cross-design to the left and the bright, naked and bleeding republican to the right against a background of red drops of blood. Although Ryggen lived far away in the north without electric light – the farm was not supplied with electricity until 1945 – she was not only aware of but interested and engaged in the life of ordinary people. The tapestry *Spania* was later shown at the Venice Biennale of 1964, and still, after 28 years, its message was felt – the Spanish representative protested and wanted the tapestry taken down.

Ryggen was a contemporary artist with biting comments on her own time, but she also had a warm and humorous side. She prepared, dyed and wove the wool herself. In 1963 she wove a self-portrait called *Pot Blue* (Nasjonalgalleriet, Oslo; 122 × 83 cm.), in which she "is playing at the loom to pass a drab Easter Holiday". That is typical of her. She worked at the loom during the winters and used the summers to take care of the farm and to collect wild flowers to dye her homespun wool.

Her pot-blue colour has its own story. Ryggen loved this blue colour, but it was hard to obtain. She needed genuine indigo from India and urine from men who had been drinking a lot of beer. The use of urine was not exceptional, but its derivation from beer to get her own special blue colour was Ryggen's invention. The urine had to be kept warm for days to facilitate the fermentation process before the indigo was added. After a few days she could test the dyeing bath. The wool should be very green in colour when emerging from the bath, turning into blue in the air. If this did not happen it meant that the dyeing bath was too cold, and Ryggen had to start all over again.

In 1966, at the age of 71, Ryggen accepted a commission to weave a picture tapestry for Oslo University. She was free to choose whatever subject she wanted. She made *Trollveggen* (Magic wall). In the middle is a representation of science. A man is lecturing and sows the seeds of knowledge into the hearts of his students. At the sides are comments on the effects of teaching; in between are criticisms of tendencies found in contemporary art and music. On each side are woven scenes portraying loneliness and decay. The pot-blue colour of the background unifies the tapestry, despite its size (1.9 × 7.2 m.) and division into five parts. Using the same pot-blue background colour, Ryggen wove a protest against the Norwegian endorsement of NATO. The tapestry *Christmas Doubts* (1956; Nordenfjeldske Kunstindustrimuseum, Trondheim) shows on the right a well-dressed Norwegian man in actual size. The artist is giving him a helping hand as he goes on his way to demonstrate against the heads of NATO on the left of the weaving. It is naive but clear in its message, and made with a

Ryggen: *Karsten in the Weavers' Heaven*, 1962; Nationalmuseum, Stockholm

weaving. It is naive but clear in its message, and made with a great deal of humour.

During World War II Ryggen's husband Hans was imprisoned by the Germans. In 1945 she depicted this situation in *Grini* (the name of the prison; Trondhjems Kunstforening, Trondheim). Made in colours of red and brown, the weaving shows the painter seated in the middle of the tapestry dressed in prison garments marked with his number, 13243. He is painting death's-head signs for the Germans while dreaming of the horrors of the war and his homecoming. In 1936, already aware of the fascist and Nazi movements, Ryggen made the tapestry *Dead Dreams* (Nordenfjeldske Kunstindustrimuseum; 225 × 272 cm.) in colours of black, grey, brown and off-white. It is a prophecy of the horrors of fascism and Nazism with prisoners in jail, blood and swastikas: "I named it *Dead Dreams*, since all dreams will turn into dead dreams", she said.

Hannah Ryggen's first known tapestry dates from 1922. She worked in the Gobelin technique with wool. She was inspired by nature, her family and her engagement with the conditions of humankind. She has shown to later generations that traditional weaving can indeed be contemporary art, when made by a very individual artist.

LENA HOLGER

S

Saar, Betye
American sculptor, 1926–

Born Betye Irene Maze in Los Angeles, 30 July 1926; grew up in Pasadena, California. Studied at University of California, Los Angeles (BA 1949); California State University, Long Beach, 1958–62; University of Southern California, Los Angeles, 1962; California State University, Northridge, 1966; American Film Institute, Los Angeles, 1972. Married artist Richard W. Saar, 1952; three daughters (one the artist Alison Saar born 1956); divorced 1968. Instructor in art, California State University, Hayward, 1971, Northridge, 1973–4; Otis Art Institute, Los Angeles, 1976–83; lecturer and freelance designer for films, 1970–75; costume designer, Inner City Cultural Center, Napa Valley Theatre Company, 1968–73. Recipient of National Endowment for the Arts (NEA) grants, 1974 and 1984; J. Paul Getty fellowship, 1990; Guggenheim fellowship, 1991; James Van Der Zee grant, 1992; Fresno Art Museum Distinguished Artist award, California, 1993. Member, Los Angeles Institute of Contemporary Art. Lives in Los Angeles.

Selected Individual Exhibitions
Multi-Cul Gallery, Los Angeles: 1972
Berkeley Art Center, CA: 1973
Fine Arts Gallery, California State University, Los Angeles: 1973
Whitney Museum of American Art, New York: 1975
Wadsworth Atheneum, Hartford, CT: 1976
San Francisco Museum of Modern Art: 1977 (with Marie Johnson)
Studio Museum in Harlem, New York: 1980
Museum of Contemporary Art, Los Angeles: 1984, 1990
List Visual Arts Center, Massachusetts Institute of Technology, Cambridge: 1987
Wight Art Gallery, University of California, Los Angeles: 1990–91 (with Alison Saar, touring)
Objects Gallery, Chicago: 1991
Joseloff Gallery, University of Hartford, CT: 1992
University of Colorado Art Galleries, Boulder: 1992
Fresno Art Museum, CA: 1993
Santa Monica Museum of Art, CA: 1994
Exhibits USA: 1995 (*Personal Icons*, touring)

Bibliography
Betye Saar, exh. cat., Whitney Museum of American Art, New York, 1975
Cindy Nemser, "Conversation with Betye Saar", *Feminist Art Journal*, iv, Winter 1975–6, pp.19–24
Channing Johnson, "Betye Saar's 'Hoodoo' World of Art", *Essence*, March 1976, pp.84–5
Ishmael Reed, *Shrovetide in Old New Orleans*, New York: Doubleday, 1978
Phylis Floyd, "An interview with Betye Saar", *Kresge Art Museum Bulletin*, vii, 1979, pp.1–11
Eleanor Munro, *Originals: American Women Artists*, New York: Simon and Schuster, 1979
Houston Conwill, "Interview with Betye Saar", *Black Art: An International Quarterly*, iii/1, 1980, pp.4–15
Rituals: The Art of Betye Saar, exh. cat., Studio Museum in Harlem, New York, 1980
Crystal Britton, "Interview: Betye Saar", *Art Papers*, v, September–October 1981, pp.8–9
Gretchen Erskine Woelfle, "On the edge: Betye Saar, personal time travels", *Fiberarts*, ix, July–August 1982, pp.56–60
Betye Saar, exh. cat., Museum of Contemporary Art, Los Angeles, 1984
Betye Saar: Resurrection: Site Installations, 1977 to 1987, exh. cat., Art Gallery, California State University, Fullerton, 1988
Making Their Mark: Women Artists Move into the Mainstream, exh. cat., Cincinnati Art Museum, and elsewhere, 1989
Lilly Wei, "The peripatetic artist: 14 statements: Betye Saar", *Art in America*, lxxvii, July 1989, p.135
Lucy R. Lippard, *Mixed Blessings: New Art in a Multicultural America*, New York: Pantheon, 1990
Charlotte Streifer Rubinstein, *American Women Sculptors*, Boston: Hall, 1990
Secrets, Dialogues, Revelations: The Art of Betye and Alison Saar, exh. cat., Wight Art Gallery, University of California, Los Angeles, and elsewhere, 1990
Jon Etra, "Family ties", *Art News*, xc, May 1991, pp.128–33
M.J. Hewitt, "Betye Saar: An interview", *International African American Artist*, x/2, 1993, pp.7–15
Betye Saar: Secret Heart, exh. cat., Fresno Art Museum, CA, 1993
Lizzetta LeFalle-Collins, *The Art of Betye Saar and John Outtenbridge: The Poetics of Politics, Iconography and Spirituality*, Washington, DC: United States Information Agency, 1994
Betye Saar: Personal Icons, exh. cat., Exhibits USA, 1995

Growing up in Pasadena during the 1930s, Betye Saar often walked with her grandmother to see Simon Rodia craft mosaic and wire, broken bottles, mirrors and shells into his famous Watts Towers in Los Angeles. The experience sensitised her to the transformative power of artefacts, which, thanks to the ingenuity of folk artists, can become mysterious and magical works of art. Saar was first trained as a commercial artist and graphic designer, and she enjoyed a successful career in these

Saar: *Cryptic Confessions: The Answer*, 1988; mixed media; Kresge Art Museum, East Lansing; Michigan State University purchase, funded by the Office of the Vice-President for Research and Graduate Studies

fields while bringing up her three children. (Her daughter Alison is also a renowned artist, and once took a seminar that her mother taught at the Otis Art Institute.) Although she thought of herself as a painter, in 1966 Betye saw a retrospective exhibition of Joseph Cornell and was struck by the possibilities of assemblage. She was also spurred to experiment with mixed-media, perhaps unconsciously influenced by the southern California art scene, where assemblage dominated the art of the 1960s, best represented by the work of Ed Kienholz. Frequent excursions to natural history museums also fortified Saar's interest in the expressive language of artefacts.

In 1966 she created *Mystic Window for Leo* (artist's collection), the first of her so-called window assemblages, which reveal her ongoing concerns with history – here family history – and with the type of seeing that art makes possible. "The window", says Saar, "is a way of traveling from one level of consciousness to another, like the physical looking into the spiritual" (Los Angeles 1984, p.11). Betye studied diverse occult and spiritual traditions – voodoo and shamanism, phrenology and palmistry – and their symbols regularly appear in her work.

During the later 1960s and early 1970s, as the cries of the Civil Rights movement resonated in the background, Saar answered by again recalling history, this time the history of African-Americans, whose stereotypical images had been woven into the fabric of the majority culture. (Extensive and thought-provoking evaluation by both women and artists of colour, their place in art, culture and society, took centre stage in critical discussions of American art during these years. In southern California, projects such as Womanhouse in central Los Angeles and reformations in art instruction and criticism, as reflected in the program at the California Institute of the Arts in Valencia, resulted from such discussions. Although Saar was not directly involved with these groups, she felt their impact.) The assassination of Martin Luther King in 1968 convinced her to forgo the more autobiographical "windows" to produce boxes or "coffins", such as the *Liberation of Aunt Jemima* (1972; University of California Art Museum, Berkeley) and *Is Jim Crow Really Dead?* (1972; Dr Janice C. Johnson Collection, Los Angeles), which she acknowledges reflected the anger she felt at having been excluded from the political realm as well as the art world: "When I look back on it, I think I was angry" (Nemser 1975, p.20).

Although she softened her tone in the mid-1970s and the message seemingly became more subtle, Saar's later assemblages bespoke ongoing concerns with content and with history. "The content of my art", Saar wrote, "has progressed from ancestral history (ritual works), to family history (nostalgic works) to personal history ... My concerns, however, remain the same: the recycling and transformation of materials, the quality of texture, form, pattern, a sense of beauty, and mystery" (Los Angeles 1984, p.8). In the series entitled *Mojotech*, a centrepiece in her more recent work, symbols, artefacts and stories from both the mainstream Western culture as well as ancient traditions, such as those of Africa, Egypt and Mexico, express her fascination with systems of spirituality and technology, as well as the conflicts that invariably arise between them. Inspiration to pursue the theme came in part from a residency at the Massachusetts Institute of Technology in 1987, but the immediate trigger was the film *The Gods*

Must Be Crazy. One can imagine that the sight of Simon Rodia using mirror, glass and wire to create his "fairy tale palace" in Watts also had a nascent impact. "Mojos combine mystical symbols with natural objects ... Each Mojo is constructed with a particular essence to act as its protective charm" (Johnson 1976, p.85). *Cryptic Confession: The Question* (1988; private collection), which is nearly identical to its counterpart *Cryptic Confessions: The Answer* (1988; see illustration), both belong to this group. Resembling ancient Persian miniatures, *Cryptic Confessions* are dominated by scarabs, *milagros*, Egyptian figurines and computer boards – prevalent in the second-hand shops of southern California where Saar seeks her source materials and which she first used for an assemblage in 1975 (*Samadhi*; High Museum, Atlanta). A rich blue ground, nearly universally associated with spirituality, she notes, dominates the two assemblages.

Throughout her career, Saar has resurrected found materials for altars (*Indigo Mercy*, 1976; Studio Museum in Harlem, New York), collages, murals and, since the late 1970s, installations. Among these, the *House of Gris Gris* (1988) was conceived in collaboration with her daughter, Alison, for a joint exhibition curated by the Wight Art Gallery of the University of California, Los Angeles, whose tour included a showing at the Museum of Contemporary Art in Chicago. While Saar uses found objects, each element, she explains, is selected for its "ancestral, ritual, autobiographical, nostalgic and historical aura". Individual elements embody their own histories, but they also take on a life and metaphysical meaning in combination with other materials. This resurrection and transformation, the mystery and magic they evoke, form the basis of Betye Saar's work.

PHYLIS FLOYD

Sage, Kay
American painter, 1898–1963

Born Katherine Linn Sage in Albany, New York, 25 June 1898; father a wealthy senator. Lived with her mother after parents' separation in 1900, attending a variety of schools in Europe and USA. Attended classes at Corcoran School of Art, Washington, DC, and worked as translator for Censorship Bureau, New York, during World War I. Studied painting and drawing at British School and Scuola Libera delle Belle Arti, Rome, 1920. Married Prince Ranieri di San Faustino, 1925; lived in Rome and Rapallo until divorce, 1935. Moved to Paris, 1937; discovered by the Surrealists after exhibiting a single painting at the Salon des Surindépendants. Returned to New York after outbreak of World War II and helped a number of Surrealists to escape there. Exhibited with the Surrealists in New York (1942) and Paris (1947). Married painter Yves Tanguy, 1940. Moved to Woodbury, Connecticut, 1941. Became reclusive after Tanguy's death in 1955. Stopped painting due to failing eyesight, 1958. Attempted suicide, 1959. Shot herself in Woodbury, 8 January 1963.

Selected Individual Exhibitions

Galleria del Milione, Milan: 1936
Pierre Matisse Gallery, New York: 1940
San Francisco Museum of Art: 1941
Julien Levy Gallery, New York: 1944, 1947
Catherine Viviano Gallery, New York: 1950, 1952, 1956, 1958,
    1960 (retrospective), 1961
Galleria dell'Obelisco, Rome: 1953
Galerie Nina Dausset, Paris: 1953
Wadsworth Atheneum, Hartford, CT: 1954 (with Yves Tanguy)
Herbert F. Johnson Museum of Art, Cornell University, Ithaca, NY:
    1977 (touring retrospective)

Selected Writings

"China eggs", manuscript, 1955, Archives of American Art,
    Washington, DC (autobiography)
Demain, Monsieur Silber, Paris: Seghers, 1957 (collected poems)
The More I Wonder, New York: Bookman, 1957 (poems)
Faut dire c'qui est, Paris: Debresse-Poésie, 1959 (poems)
Mordicus, Paris: Benoît, 1962
Yves Tanguy: Un recueil de ses oeuvres, New York: Matisse, 1963

Bibliography

Yves Tanguy, Kay Sage, exh. cat., Wadsworth Atheneum, Hartford,
    CT, 1954
Kay Sage: Retrospective Exhibition, 1937–1958, exh. cat., Catherine
    Viviano Gallery, New York, 1960
Kay Sage, 1898–1963, exh. cat., Herbert F. Johnson Museum of Art,
    Cornell University, Ithaca, NY, and elsewhere, 1977
Charlotte Streifer Rubinstein, *American Women Artists from Early
    Times to the Present*, Boston: Hall, 1982
Stephen R. Miller, "The Surrealist imagery of Kay Sage", *Art
    International*, xxvi, September–October 1983, pp.32–47, 54–6
Whitney Chadwick, *Women Artists and the Surrealist Movement*,
    Boston: Little Brown, and London: Thames and Hudson, 1985
La Femme et le surréalisme, exh. cat., Musée Cantonal des Beaux-
    Arts, Lausanne, 1987
Mary Ann Caws, Rudolf E. Kuenzli and Gwen Raaberg, eds,
    Surrealism and Women, Cambridge: Massachusetts Institute of
    Technology Press, 1991
Mara R. Witzling, ed., *Voicing Our Visions: Writings by Women
    Artists*, New York: Universe, 1991; London: Women's Press, 1992
Judith D. Suther, "Separate studios: Kay Sage and Yves Tanguy",
    Significant Others: Creativity and Intimate Partnership, ed.
    Whitney Chadwick and Isabelle de Courtivron, New York and
    London: Thames and Hudson, 1993, pp.136–53
Renée Riese Hubert, *Magnifying Mirrors: Women, Surrealism and
    Partnership*, Lincoln: University of Nebraska Press, 1994
Judith D. Suther, *Kay Sage: Solitary Surrealist* (in preparation)

Kay Sage was one of the few women artists to be officially designated as a participant in the Surrealist movement by André Breton, the group's leader (Charles Henri Ford, "Interview with André Breton", *View*, no.7–8, October–November 1941). However, her association with the Surrealists and marriage to the painter Yves Tanguy occurred well after the collective formulation of Surrealist doctrines. The influences of Giorgio de Chirico and Tanguy are immediately identifiable in her paintings, yet Sage's mature vocabulary of architectural scaffolding set in barren landscapes infused with a disquieting melancholy is intensely personal and entirely her own.

Sage studied drawing briefly at the Corcoran School of Art in 1919 before moving to Italy the following year. In Rome she enrolled in classes at the British School and Scuola Libera delle Belle Arti but took little interest in formal training. *Young Girl*

in Orange Dress (c.1920; Mattatuck Museum, Waterbury, CT), one of the few known paintings from this period, is a standard academic portrait bearing a marked resemblance to the artist. Certainly the girl's sad, pensive expression conjures the psychological discomfort and loneliness expressed so forcefully in Sage's later imagined landscapes and poetry. Sage soon joined Onorato Carlandi, an older artist, on his weekly informal painting excursions to the countryside, producing realistic views of rolling hillsides (*Landscape with Poplar*, 1923; *Landscape with Five Trees*, 1923; both Mattatuck Museum). She considered the expansive horizons envisioned in her Surrealist canvases as originating from these early experiences: "I think my perspective idea of distance and going away is from my formative years in the Roman Campagna. There is always that long road and the feeling it gives that it goes a long way, and living near the Mediterranean, the sea and boats, the feeling of the sun" (Julien Levy, "Tanguy, Connecticut, Sage", *Art News*, liii, September 1954, p.27).

Sage rarely painted during the years of her marriage to an Italian prince, but in 1936, only one year after separating from her husband, she held her first solo exhibition at the Galleria del Milione in Milan. It included geometric abstract paintings, of which few survive. One transitional work, *Untitled* (c.1930; Collection Daniel Filipacchi), marks a significant departure from the landscapes of the early 1920s, with its Cubist rooftops composed of jutting diagonals and horizontals. In place of the conventional device of trees uniting fore- and background, a monolithic building rises incongruously from amidst the low houses; the mountains are reduced to an undulating line across a blank sky. A non-representational idiom of overlapping geometric forms is adopted in *Vorticist* (c.1935; Mattatuck Museum), a small oil on panel. Ezra Pound, a friend of Sage's, may have introduced her to Vorticism, and perhaps even encouraged her to resume painting (Miller 1983, p.33).

Following Sage's move to Paris in 1937, the considerable impact of de Chirico is evident in the gradual evolution from abstraction to dreamscapes occupied by mysterious objects with elusive meanings. This shift is illustrated in *Afterwards* (1937; Colorado Springs Fine Arts Center), in which slatted shapes of varying sizes appear stacked haphazardly at an exaggeratedly tilted perspective. Slight shadows, a muted palette and minute, precise brushwork together lend a connotation of eerie stillness to what is still an abstract composition. Further configurations of geometric forms are placed in undefined settings with greater contrasts of light and dark (*Untitled*, c.1938, Collection Herbert B. Palmer; *Sempre*, 1938; repr. New York 1960, no.2). As a result, the objects exist in a space that seems simultaneously recognisable and ambiguous. Around 1940, Sage bought de Chirico's *Torment of the Poet* (1940). Her iconography of the late 1930s–early 1940s is primarily borrowed, though altered, from the Italian metaphysical painter, as Sage sought her own distinctive voice. It includes the egg, sloping ramp and arched doorway (*A Little Later*, 1938; Denver Art Museum; *My Room Has Two Doors*, 1939; Mattatuck Museum), distant diagonally cast shadows (*I Have No Shadow*, 1940; Worcester Art Museum, MA) and figures shrouded in drapery (*Near the Five Corners*, 1943; *ibid*, no.13; *The Hidden Letter*, 1944; Fine Arts Museums of San Francisco; *I Saw Three Cities*, 1944; Princeton University Art Museum).

Sage: *Tomorrow Is Never*, 1955; oil on canvas; 96.2 × 136.7 cm.; Metropolitan Museum of Art, New York; Arthur H. Hearn Fund, 1955

During her first year in Paris, Sage became acquainted with Surrealism and was especially impressed by the work of Tanguy. She met Tanguy, as well as Breton and other Surrealist colleagues, in the autumn of 1938. With the outbreak of World War II, Sage returned to New York, followed by Tanguy, and they married. These developments in Sage's personal life pertain directly to the formal path taken in her art, since Tanguy's stylistic influence would prove crucial both as inspiration and as catalyst for determining an individualistic course. Her concern that her work should not be perceived as derivative even made her reluctant to exhibit with Tanguy. In a joint interview in 1954, Sage remarked: "We are really concealed from each other in our work. He doesn't know what picture I am painting – although I take more interest in his than he does in mine – naturally" (Hartford 1954, pp.24–5).

Sage's paintings of the mid-1940s until Tanguy's death in 1955 are ultimately her strongest, for in them she realised her signature imagery. Already in works such as *Danger, Construction Ahead* (1940; Yale University Art Gallery, New Haven), *At the Appointed Time* (1942; Newark Museum) and *In the Third Sleep* (1944; Art Institute of Chicago) she created desolate vistas inhabited by angular, unidentifiable shapes concealed beneath drapery. While possessing similarities to

Tanguy's meticulous depictions of vast plains peopled with imaginary forms, where Tanguy's figuration is biomorphic, Sage's remains decidedly non-organic, differentiating it from popular Surrealist imagery. Beginning with *Bounded on the West by the Land under Water* (1946; University of Michigan Museum of Art), scaffolding appears in her pictures; subsequently, architectural structures become a constant theme. These constructions are rearranged in a multitude of ways, but the external attributes of each silent landscape – parched beneath a blank sky illuminated by an unseen source, and painted in cool tones of silvery blue, ochre, grey and pale green – express an interior mental state of bleak isolation. An underlying sense of tragedy prevails throughout. In *All Soundings Are Referred to High Water* (1947; Davison Art Center, Wesleyan University), *The Instant* (1949; Mattatuck Museum) and *Unusual Thursday* (1951; repr. New York 1960, no.35) the scaffolding lies dismantled in the foreground, both leading the viewer in and acting as barrier. Intermittently, drapery softens the harsh edges of forms. Interlocking slats obliterate all traces of the human face in *Small Portrait* (1950; Vassar College Art Gallery, Poughkeepsie, NY), with only reddish blond hair hinting at a female identity. In fact, this is one of two rare self-portraits. The thin latticework might combine with heavy upright boards (*Third Paragraph*, 1953; Mattatuck Museum), rest against a receding line of massive blocks (*No Passing*, 1954; Whitney Museum of American Art, New York) or be erected as a tower (*Hyphen*, 1954; Metropolitan Museum of Art, New York; *Tomorrow Is Never*, 1955; see illustration). Close-range perspectives from within the scaffolding in *Day Without Name* (1955; Collection Mr and Mrs Lee Ault, New York) and *A Bird in the Room* (1955; Cleveland Museum of Art) exude a particularly haunting element of confrontation. Unusually, both depict night scenes, which adds to the sinister effect; in the former, two rows of white cloths sway slightly; in the latter, rocks drip from vines like dead foliage. *Le Passage* (1956; Collection Mrs Wirt Davis II, Dallas), the second self-portrait, is anomalous within this period because it conveys the human figure and lacks scaffolding. The figure, shown from behind, hides her face and naked breasts as she pulls her hair forward, thereby denying typical aspects of feminine portraiture. Removed beyond a border of razor-like rocks, she connects with the distant faceted terrain, avoiding the observer's scrutiny and indicating the artist's barred encounter with her self.

Sage was diagnosed with cataracts in 1956, and her late works reflect her fear of no longer being able to paint. Titles become more literal and associative. A succession of empty frames or easels in *The Answer Is No* (1958; Collection Alexandra Darrow) evoke a mournful gathering of canvases never to be realised. Viewed from above, the stacked easels in *Watching the Clock* (1958; Museum of Modern Art, New York) fill the entire picture plane. On its completion, Sage had two bullet holes shot through this canvas, inviting speculation over the meaning of this gesture as Surrealist irreverence for the work of art or a chilling premonition of her suicide by gunshot to the heart. Among Sage's last works are small watercolour collages resembling rock formations, suggesting that her failing vision prompted a more intimate examination of landscape (*Blue Wind*, 1958; Collection Alexandra Darrow; *The Great Impossible*, 1961; Museum of Modern Art).

After Tanguy's death, Sage published four volumes of poetry characterised by a detached fatalism that not only mirrors the depression to which she had succumbed, but also parallels the harsh, disturbing world represented in her paintings of the previous 15 years. Writing "I have built a tower on despair/You hear nothing in it, there is nothing to see" (from "Tower", 1957), Sage could be describing her spare structures devoid of human presence.

When Breton first saw Sage's painting in 1938 he assumed its tense, calculated air must have been created by a man. Indeed, her work opposes the Surrealist analogy of the fertile earth to the nurturing, life-affirming female nature. Unlike other women artists associated with Surrealism, she avoided autobiographical and organic content, preferring the cryptic. Sage came into her own as a painter relatively late, drawing upon the language of Surrealism only in her forties. Although she embraced its penchant for enigmatic titles and the dislocation of dreams, the austerity of Sage's vision corresponds powerfully to her own feelings of alienation, setting her apart from her contemporaries.

MARY CHAN

Saint Phalle, Niki de
French painter and sculptor, 1930–

Born Catherine Marie-Agnès Fal de Saint Phalle in Neuilly-sur-Seine, 29 October 1930. Worked as a fashion model, appearing in *Vogue*, *Harper's Bazaar* and *Life* magazines, 1948–9. Married US marine Harry Mathews (later a novelist and poet), 1950; daughter born 1951, son born 1955; divorced 1960. Lived in Cambridge, Massachusetts, 1950–52, then returned to Paris. Studied drama at Ecole de la rue Blanche, 1952–3. Hospitalised after a nervous breakdown, 1953. Lived with Nouveau Réaliste artist Jean Tinguely from 1960; married him, 1971; he died 1991. Joined Nouveaux Réalistes group, Paris, 1961. Suffered a pulmonary abscess, which led to hospitalisation, 1974; ill for four years after an attack of rheumatoid arthritis in 1982. Lives in France and USA.

Selected Individual Exhibitions
Galerie J, Paris: 1961
Galerie Rive Droite, Paris: 1962
Alexander Iolas Gallery, New York: 1962 (with Jean Larcade), 1965, 1966, 1967
Hanover Gallery, London: 1964, 1968, 1969
Stedelijk Museum, Amsterdam: 1967 (*Les Nanas au pouvoir*, touring)
Gimpel Fils, London: 1972, 1982, 1985, 1988, 1991
Gimpel and Weitzenhoffer Gallery, New York: 1973, 1977, 1979–82 (*Monumental Projects*, touring), 1982, 1985, 1990
Musée National d'Art Moderne, Centre Georges Pompidou, Paris: 1980–81 (touring retrospective)
Kunsthalle der Hypo-Kulturstiftung, Munich: 1987
Nassau County Museum of Fine Art, Roslyn, NY: 1987 (retrospective)
Galerie de France and JGM Galerie, Paris: 1989, 1990
Kunst- und Ausstellungshalle der Bundesrepublik Deutschland, Bonn: 1992–3 (touring retrospective)

Bibliography
Richard Roud, "Taboo or not Taboo", *The Guardian*, 6 April 1973 (Arts section)
Niki de Saint Phalle: Exposition retrospective, exh. cat., Musée National d'Art Moderne, Centre Georges Pompidou, Paris, and elsewhere, 1980
1960: Les Nouveaux Réalistes, exh. cat., Musée d'Art Moderne de la Ville de Paris, 1986
Les Années 60: L'Object – sculpture, exh. cat., JGM Galerie, Paris, 1990
Jean-Paul Ameline, *Les Nouveaux Réalistes*, Paris: Centre Georges Pompidou, 1992
Niki de Saint Phalle, exh. cat., Kunst- und Ausstellungshalle der Bundesrepublik Deutschland, Bonn, and elsewhere, 1992 (contains extensive bibliography)
Phyllis Braff, "Nanas, guns and gardens", *Art in America*, lxxx, December 1992, pp.102–7
Mary Blum, "Niki de Saint Phalle: Bursting out of the frame", *International Herald Tribune*, 21 June 1993
Barbara Jones, *Images of the Body*, MA thesis, University of East London, 1994
Joanna Thornberry, *Niki de Saint Phalle: Tirs and Trangressions*, MA thesis, Courtauld Institute of Art, University of London, 1995

Niki de Saint Phalle has produced a prolific body of work that spans oil painting, assemblage, performance art, film, sculpture and even architecture. Her art, in its diversity, thus defies easy categorisation. Saint Phalle turned to art after a nervous breakdown that led to hospitalisation and electro-shock treatment in 1953. She has never received any form of artistic training and as an auto-didact she likens herself to primitive man who was also unable to draw in three dimensions. Although she identifies herself with "outsider art" such as Art Brut, she does not associate herself directly with any sort of movement and is instead desirous to remain outside the realms of high art tradition.

Her early oil paintings, for example *Round Room* (1956; repr. Bonn 1992, p.191), illustrate this primitive quality. They are garishly coloured and executed with childlike simplicity. Despite their fairy-tale subject matter, their fragmented surfaces and thick impasto brushwork create a sense of disorder and confusion. They can be considered as a visual expression of the mental turmoil that led to her nervous breakdown. The fragmentation of these oil paintings became three dimensional in Saint Phalle's first assemblages. Influenced by the international emergence of Neo-dadaism, an art form that appropriated and extended the metaphor of Marcel Duchamp's ready-made, Saint Phalle began to fix real objects such as knives, scissors and guns to the surface of the canvas embedding them in thick, uneven plaster; the result: bleak, threatening and surreal landscapes exemplified by *Bouche d'incendie* (1959; *ibid.*, p.195).

In 1961 the inherent violence of the oil paintings and assemblages became explicit when Saint Phalle created her first "tirs" or shooting paintings (1961–3). For these "tirs" Saint Phalle constructed reliefs with a profusion of different found objects and sealed sachets containing paints of different colours, or sometimes food such as eggs and spaghetti, and then painted the whole thing white. The finished assemblage was then hung and bullets fired into it, bursting the sachets, which would splatter and seep paint over the work. Despite this aggressive and apparently nihilistic gesture, Saint Phalle's purpose was in fact positive; the gun shot did not symbolise death but instead a point of departure. Her ultimate message, implicit within the "tirs", was creation through destruction. Saint Phalle's "tirs", although initially abstract, gradually became more explicitly religious and political, illustrated by the works *Khrushchev and Kennedy* (1962; JGM Galerie, Paris) and *Autel, noir et blanc* (1962; Collection Alexandre Iolas, Athens).

It was Saint Phalle's use of the found object and her Neo-dadaist tendencies that brought her to the attention of Pierre Restany, the art critic and leader of the Nouveaux Réalistes, who asked her to join the group in 1961. Saint Phalle's profound exploration of contemporary society differs, however, from the group's concern with an art form that communicated the look of contemporary society often without questioning its basis. Perhaps as a consequence Saint Phalle has remained a somewhat marginal figure within the group.

In 1963 Saint Phalle began making relief assemblages and free-standing sculptures that focused upon women's roles in contemporary society. Subjects such as brides, mothers and whores recurred. These works, constructed with chicken wire, papier-mâché, textiles, plastic dolls and animals, represent the female body in a form of grotesque realism. In creating these works Saint Phalle aimed to expose the horror of the roles that a patriarchal society demanded of women. This is clearly

illustrated by the horrific birthing scene *L'Accouchement en rose* (1963–4; Moderna Museet, Stockholm) and *La Mariée et le cheval* (1963–4; *ibid.*, p.219).

The disappearance of the more gruesome assemblages from Saint Phalle's oeuvre marked the arrival of the "nanas" in 1965 and a more optimistic phase in her work. The "nana", from Parisian slang for "chick" or "babe", was inspired by Larry Rivers's drawings of his pregnant wife. These three-dimensional sculptures are large, round and fun, for example, *Upside-Down Nana* (1967; Clarice Rivers Collection) and *Black Venus*, also titled *Miss Black Power* (1965–7; see illustration). Unlike the amputated forms of Saint Phalle's earlier

Saint Phalle: *Black Venus*, also titled *Miss Black Power*, 1965–7; painted polyester; 279.4 × 38.9 × 61 cm.; Whitney Museum of American Art, New York; Gift of the Howard and Jean Lipman Foundation Inc.

female assemblages, the "nanas" are whole, smooth and brightly painted; they glory in their feminine bodies, in their sexuality and physicality. The "nanas" marked a new period of contentment for Saint Phalle who described them as a way "of 'blowing out' into my own feminity and liberation which was suppressed for so many years" (unpublished interview). The "nana" also inspired Saint Phalle's first architectural venture, a collaborative piece entitled *La Hon* (which means "she" in Swedish), which was constructed in the Moderna Museet, Stockholm, in 1966 (*ibid.*, pp.60–71). Unlike the earlier "nanas", which merely suggested sexual penetration, this monumental "nana" (24.9 × 9.1 × 6 m.) was literally penetrable through a vaginal portal. Features inside the huge reclining figure included a planetarium in the left breast and a milk bar in the right.

Saint Phalle's interest in building and shaping space evinced by *La Hon* is further exemplified by her numerous architectural projects, which include for example *Golem* (1972; Jerusalem), a children's playhouse, and *Le Temple idéal* (1990; Nîmes), a house of worship for all denominations. Marking the world with a place of her own had been an obsession of Saint Phalle's since seeing Antonio Gaudí's Parc Güell in Barcelona in 1955 and finds its fullest realisation in her monumental Giardino del Tarocchi (1978–94; *ibid.*, pp.108–23) in Tuscany. This sculpture park or garden takes the 22 major Arcana of the tarot pack as its theme. Each tarot card is represented by an individual sculpture/building constructed in metal, concrete and ceramics and decorated with mosaics of mirrored glass, which, in reflecting the light and the landscape, unite the sculpture with its surroundings. The garden thus functions as a continual dialogue between architecture and nature, a place of escape and calm meditation.

Although the Giardino del Tarocchi has occupied much of Saint Phalle's time and energy since the late 1970s, she has continued to produce numerous individual pieces. For example the "skinny" sculptures that she started in 1979 are figures that, as the name suggests, literally exist as lines in space, exemplified by *La Déesse de la lumière* (1980; *ibid.*, p.248). They contrast dramatically with the solidity and corporeality of works such as the "nanas", expressing their life force not through weighty flesh but instead through space. As Saint Phalle emphasises: "The skinnys breathe. They are air sculptures" (exh. cat., Gimpel Fils, London, 1982). Saint Phalle's highly finished bronze sculptures of the 1990s, based on Egyptian gods and goddesses such as *Anubis* (1990; JGM Galerie), not only demonstrate the diversity of her materials but also her artistic development from the aggressive, crude debris constructions of the early 1960s. Saint Phalle's most recent artistic ventures are the "Tableaux éclatées", for example *Méta-Tinguely* (1992; artist's collection), created as a homage to her late husband, the artist and designer Jean Tinguely. The collage elements on these canvases are operated by photo-electric cells that break apart as the spectator approaches and then regroup. They symbolise the movement from chaos to order, from destruction to creation, echoing the ideas initially explored in the "tirs".

It is through film that Saint Phalle has created some of her most controversial work, developing the socially exploratory nature of the "tirs". For example, her film *Daddy – A Bedtime Story* (1972–3) is a subversive and pornographic work that explores incest, transvestism, lesbianism and patricide. Like the "tirs" the film functions as an exhortation, revealing human evil in order to effect its positive transformation (see Thornberry 1995).

JOANNA THORNBERRY

Salmenhaara, Kyllikki
Finnish ceramist and glass designer, 1915–1981

Born 1915. Studied in the department of ceramics, Taideteollinen Keskuskoulu (Central School of the Industrial Arts), Helsinki, 1938–43; studied at the Saxbo pottery, Denmark, under Natalie Krebs, 1946; New York State College of Ceramics at Alfred University, 1956 (ASLA Fulbright scholarship); study trip to Spain and Portugal, 1960. Worked at Kauklahti glassworks, 1943–6; Sakari Vapaavuori ceramic studio, Helsinki, 1946–7; Arabia ceramics factory, Helsinki, 1947–61. Teaching consultant, Ceramic Training Institute, China Productivity and Trade Center, Taiwan, and initiator of the School for Ceramics and adviser for the ceramic industry in Taiwan, 1961–3. Teacher and head of department, ceramics department, Taideteollinen Oppilaitos (Institute of Applied Arts), Helsinki, 1963–73; chief instructor of ceramics, Taideteollinen Korkeakoulu (Central School of Industrial Design), 1973–81. Lecture tours and designer in the USA, Canada and Japan, 1956–76. Recipient of diploma of honour, Syracuse, New York, 1958; Pro Finlandia medal, 1961; Finnish Cultural Foundation grants, 1967 and 1969; State prize for industrial art (for the book *Keramiikka*), Finland, 1975; prize of honour, Finnish Cultural Foundation, 1981. Died 1981.

Principal Exhibitions

Individual
Arabia Showroom, Helsinki: 1952, 1957
Museum of Applied Arts, Helsinki: 1979
Hetjens-Museum Deutsches Keramikmuseum, Düsseldorf: 1986–7 (touring retrospective, organised by the Museum of Applied Arts, Helsinki)

Group
Milan Triennale: 1951 (silver medal), 1954 (diploma of honour), 1957 (grand prix), 1960 (gold medal)
USA: 1954–7 (*Design in Scandinavia*, touring)
Hälsingborg: 1955 (*H 55*)
Exposition Universelle et Internationale (Expo '58), Brussels: 1958
Zürich, Amsterdam and London: 1961 (*Finlandia*)
Exposition Universelle et Internationale (Expo '67), Montreal: 1967
Röhsska Konstslöjdmuseet, Göteborg: 1977 (*100-år Finsk konstindustri* [100 years of Finnish industrial art])
Centre Georges Pompidou, Paris: 1978 (*Metamorphoses finlandaises*)

Selected Writings

"Ajatuksia keramiikasta" [Thoughts about ceramics], *Arkkitehti*, no.6, 1955
Keramiikka, Massat, Lasitukset, Työtavat [Ceramics, mixes, glazes and working practices], Helsinki: Otava, 1974; 2nd edition, 1983

Bibliography

"X Triennale Milanossa", *Keramiikka ja lasi*, no.4, 1954

Oili Mäki, *Finnish Designers of Today*, Helsinki: Söderström, 1954

Brita Korkkinen, *Savi elää* [Clay lives], *Aikamme*, no.12, 1956

Annikki Toikka-Karvonen, "Kyllikki Salmenhaaren uutta kerami-ikkaa", *Helsingin Sanomat*, 31 March 1957

"Arabia: Posliinin maailmanmerkki" [Arabia: World-mark of porcelain], *Keramiikka ja lasi*, no.3, 1958

Pirkko Aro, *Arabia Design*, Helsinki: Otava, 1959

Armi Ratia, ed., *The Ornamo Book of Finnish Design*, Helsinki: Society of Decorative Artists Ornamo, 1962

Anita Karhunen, "Yliopettajana Taiwanilla" [As a senior teacher in Taiwan], *Muoto*, no.1, 1980

Ritva Lundsten, "Purjeet lähtee" [Sails to go], *Suomen Kuvalehti*, 31 July 1981

Scandinavian Modern Design, 1880–1980, exh. cat., Cooper-Hewitt Museum, New York, 1982

Heikki Hyvönen, *Suomalaista keramiikkaa* [Finnish ceramic art], Porvoo, 1983

Marianne Aav and Kaj Kalin, *Form Finland* [Finnish form], Museum of Applied Arts Publication no.21, Helsinki, 1986

Kyllikki Salmenhaara, 1915–1981, exh. cat., Hetjens-Museum Deutsches Keramikmuseum, Düsseldorf, Museum of Applied Arts, Helsinki, and elsewhere, 1986

Marjut Kumela and others, *Arabia*, Helsinki: Oy Wärtsilä Ab Arabia, 1987

Jennifer Hawkins Opie, *Scandinavian Ceramics and Glass in the Twentieth Century*, London: Victoria and Albert Museum, and New York: Rizzoli, 1989

Salmenhaara: *Arabia* ceramic bowl and bottles, 1959–60; Museum of Applied Arts, Helsinki

Kyllikki Salmenhaara belongs to the generation of Finnish decorative artists that elevated Finland's design reputation to a world plane after World War II. Her own career as a ceramic artist is clearly divided into two parts: the strongly creative period she spent as an artist at the Arabia ceramics works (1947–61), and her work as a teacher of ceramics, which began in the 1960s and continued until her death, forming her reputation as one of the most highly regarded teachers in her field. The essence of Salmenhaara's work as a ceramic artist is characterised by a thorough grounding in solid professional craftsmanship and a knowledge of materials.

During Salmenhaara's student years, in the 1930s and 1940s, the teaching of ceramics was for the most part concerned with the development of an aesthetic sense of form that involved the use of ready-made materials. Impelled by a lack of knowledge, during her student years Salmenhaara had already begun to make her own experiments in mixing and glazing. Before starting work as an artist at Arabia, she had also managed to gain some additional knowledge of materials in Denmark, where she worked as a student in the ceramics workshop of Natalie Krebs, whose stoneware production was based on a sound knowledge of materials and technical skill, which took as its example the classical ceramic art of China, in particular that of the Song dynasty. From Krebs, who had received a training in chemistry, Salmenhaara was also able to learn about the development of copper and iron glazes.

At the Arabia works, unlike her colleagues, Salmenhaara made glazes for her own use right from the outset. Her early Arabia production comprises small, hand-turned, thin-walled bowls and bell-shaped vases or bottles, the bark-like surfaces of which are emphasised by splashes of oxide (Arabia Museum and Museum of Applied Arts, Helsinki). The bottles and vases were successfully exhibited in 1951 and 1954 at the Milan Triennale. The ASLA travel stipend that Salmenhaara received in order to visit the USA in 1956 played an important role in her subsequent development. The acquaintance that she made with American ceramic art and Abstract Expressionism and the new dimensions she encountered freed Salmenhaara from the constriction of simplified forms. At her solo exhibition of 1957 in Helsinki she showed utility ceramics containing hand-turned chamotte made from a stoneware mix. Another novel functional starting point was her use of feldspar glaze.

In addition to developing a knowledge of materials, Salmenhaara still aspired to develop her ceramic skill towards a perfection based in Japanese Zen Buddhism. In her opinion, the good ceramic artist was a master of his or her craft to such an extent that he or she no longer needed to pay attention to the process of creation – rather, the art works would come into being of their own accord. Her critical examination of her own production was aided by photographs of all the works she produced. A master demonstration of her skill as a ceramic artist may be seen in the so-called Flying Saucers that she produced at the end of the 1950s. They contain a tension between a narrow base and a saucer-like, expanding body. Among other works of the late 1950s and early 1960s are elegant pots and high-necked, high-based ball-shaped bowls. Their forms, which derive from age-old object types, and their glaze-less surface structure, recalling rock that has been weathered and baked by the sun for millennia, give these works an ageless, eternal feel. To the refined and often seemingly anaemic decorative ceramics of the early 1960s Salmenhaara brought powerful, luxuriantly coloured objects that derive from an innovative full-bloodedness, close to the soil. As a ceramic artist, Salmenhaara grew principally famous as a producer of unique, one-off works. She produced commercial designs on only a few occasions: the coffee cups she made for Arabia in 1957, which were lifelessly refined and straight-lined in the style of the period, and the soft-toned, brush-stroke-decorated rustic Whispering Pines dinner service she designed in 1968 for the American firm, Iron Mountain Stoneware.

Salmenhaara's career as an artist at Arabia was interrupted in 1961; it was followed by 20 years of continuous work as a teacher, first in Taiwan and from 1963 at the Helsinki Institute of Applied Arts (later the Central School of Industrial Design) where she made a radical reform of teaching methods. As in her own production, in her teaching Salmenhaara laid emphasis on the importance of technical skill and a knowledge of materials as a prerequisite of all creation. She took local traditions and materials as a starting-point in her instruction, and encouraged her young ceramic artists to look for the possibilities offered by the clay of their own districts, as distinct from the low-fired, red-burning clay traditionally used in Finland during the preliminary stages of ceramics teaching. In her work as a teacher, Salmenhaara continued her experiments in glazing and materials, and in 1974 she published her textbook on ceramics, mixes, glazes and working practices. Salmenhaara's influence on the ceramic art of Finland during the past few decades is undisputed. By inculcating in her students a readiness for independent work, she played an important role in the revival of Finnish ceramics during the 1970s and in the establishment of numerous private ceramics studios.

Being unable to undertake lathe-work, Salmenhaara had already at the beginning of her teaching years opted for moulding or rolling as a working technique. In the 1960s and 1970s she produced round-lined cups and jugs made of red-burning clay and stoneware, in the surfaces of which she experimented with various glazes. But the most famous of Salmenhaara's late works are the *kietaisut*, or "wrap-arounds" produced by rolling. Some of the windings were like billowing sails, others resembled pieces of bark and some were like paper cones wrapped into a roll. She herself liked to call them "letters", ceramic messages that each person may interpret as he or she wishes. The name "wrap-around" also expresses the ostensible ease with which the objects came into being. At last the artist had attained her aspiration of having the art works create themselves. The last "wrap-arounds", which date from 1980, are pure white, and monumental in their simplicity.

Apart from the museums in Helsinki cited above, examples of Salmenhaara's work may be found in the Stedelijk Museum, Amsterdam; Museo Internazionale delle Ceramiche, Faenza; Badisches Landesmuseum, Karlsruhe; Württembergisches Landesmuseum, Stuttgart; and the Victoria and Albert Museum, London.

MARIANNE AAV

Salomon, Charlotte

German painter and graphic artist, 1917–1943

Born in Berlin-Charlottenburg, 16 April 1917. Studied applied art under Erich Böhm at Vereinigte Staatsschulen für freie und angewandte Kunst (United State Schools for Free and Applied Art), Berlin; studied illustration and drawing under Ludwig Bartning, 1936–8. Emigrated to Villefranche-sur-Mer, France, 1939. Interned for one month in a camp for the imprisonment of foreign Jews in Gurs, Pyrenees, 1940. Married Austrian-Jewish emigrant Alexander Nagler, May 1943. Deported to Auschwitz, 21 September 1943; last recorded on arrival there, 7 October 1943.

Selected Writings

Leben? oder Theater? Ein autobiographisches Singspiel in 769 Bildern, ed. Judith Herzberg, Cologne, 1981; as *Charlotte: Life? or Theater?*, New York: Viking, and London: Allen Lane, 1981

Bibliography
Paul Tillich and Emil Straus, *Charlotte: A Diary in Pictures*, New York: Harcourt Brace, and London: Collins, 1963

Susanne Hassenkamp, "Das Leben malen, um es zu bewahren", *Art*, no.6, 1981, pp.70–85

Katja Reichenfeld, "Leben? oder Theater? Regie: Charlotte Salomon", *Jong Holland*, iv, 1981, pp.20–29

Dalia Elbaum, "Esthetische analyse van het werk van Charlotte Salomon: Leben? oder Theater?" in exh. cat., Bibliothèque royale Albert 1er, Brussels, 1982, pp.24–33

Susanna Partsch, "Charlotte Salomon: Anmerkungen zu einem Zyklus", *Kritische Berichte*, x/4, 1982, pp.49–56

Christine Fischer-Defoy, ed., *Charlotte Salomon: Leben? oder Theater? Das "Lebensbild" einer jüdischen Malerin aus Berlin, 1917–1943: Bilder und Spuren, Notizen, Gespräche, Dokumente*, Schriftenreihe der Akademie der Künste, xviii, Berlin, 1986

Mary Lowenthal Felstiner, "Engendering an autobiography in art: Charlotte Salomon's 'Life? or Theater?'", *Revealing Lives: Autobiography, Biography and Gender*, ed. Susan Groag Bell and Marilyn Yalom, Albany: State University of New York Press, 1990, pp.183–92

Charlotte Salomon: Life? or Theatre?, exh. cat., Joods Historisch Museum, Amsterdam, 1992

Charlotte Salomon: Vie? ou théatre?, exh. cat., Musée National d'Art Moderne, Centre Georges Pompidou, Paris, 1992

Friedrich Rothe, "Lotte Laserstein und Charlotte Salomon: Zwei künstlerische Entwicklungen unter den Bedingungen der NS-Zeit", *Profession ohne Tradition: 125 Jahre Verein der Berliner Künstlerinnen*, exh. cat., Berlinische Galerie, Berlin, 1992, pp.151–8

Sabine Dahmen, *Bilder von Liebe und Tod in Charlotte Salomons "Leben? oder Theater?"*, MA thesis, Universität Bonn, 1994

Mary Lowenthal Felstiner, *To Paint Her Life: Charlotte Salomon in the Nazi Era*, New York: HarperCollins, 1994

In addition to self-portraits, landscape studies and graphic works, Charlotte Salomon left a work that is unique in the history of painting. Created at night during her exile in France, *Leben? oder Theater?* is a series of 769 gouaches synthesising painting, literature and music in a range of styles from medieval manuscript illumination to Expressionist elements and cinematographic techniques. In the first third she wrote the texts in pencil on parchment paper and placed them over the matching gouaches. These texts consist of dialogues and comments as well as musical quotations from popular operas and songs, which intensify the already dense narrative atmosphere of the gouaches. References to an aria from *Carmen* or *Orpheus and Eurydice* or a line from Rilke or Goethe's *Faust* convey the artist's unspoken thoughts or feelings. From the second third onwards the texts are written directly on the gouaches and thus become an integral part. A few weeks after its completion and shortly before she was deported to

Salomon: From *Leben? oder Theater?*, 1940–42; gouache; Collection Jewish Historical Museum, Amsterdam

Auschwitz, Salomon gave the work to the doctor of Villefranche-sur-Mer, reportedly saying: "Take good care of it. It is my whole life ...".

Leben? oder Theater? does have pronounced autobiographical features, although its division into acts and scenes like a classical play distances it from the artist. She described and painted her life in retrospect: the childhood in Berlin dominated by the loss of her mother, her intense, secret love for her father's second wife, Paula Lindberg, a famous opera singer whom he married in 1930. She depicted the seizure of power by the National Socialists on 30 January 1933 in impressive compositions, while in the same period she covered several hundred pages with images of her second intense insecure love, for her stepmother's singing teacher, Alfred Wolfsohn, who was also a passionate admirer of the singer. Everybody who appears in the play was given a name imitative of sound: the diva is "Paulinka Bimbam", the ever-penniless Wolfsohn is "Amadeus Daberlohn", a German term referring to his financial misery.

In January 1939 Salomon left Germany to join her grandparents in the south of France. The following year her grandmother committed suicide, and only after this event did she learn that her mother had not in fact died of influenza, but that she too had killed herself. This traumatic news gave her the urge either to take her own life "or to undertake something extraordinarily crazy" (*Leben? oder Theater?*, p.777). This explanation for the "crazy undertaking" is given on one of the last sheets of the cycle, at the end of which the viewer/reader is asked to return to the beginning. Here again, the third gouache shows a stage with the curtain up, introduces the figures, and the tragic "play" of persecution, love and death can start anew.

Leben? oder Theater? is of singular importance because at that time all art in Germany was censored by the National Socialist regime. Yet, in the face of this terror, the loss of so many loved ones and the knowledge that her own death was imminent, the young artist created a life's work in a very brief period. In 769 sheets she moved from a detailed narrative to an extremely gestural, expressive, even forceful and liberating pictorial language with which she challenged all the injustice she had endured and all that awaited her.

As the epilogue of the work is roughly foreshadowed in its prologue – the transformation of her experience of the fear of death and suicide, the conscious will to create – it can be assumed that a concept informed the creation of all the parts. This is shown by the numerous cross-connections evident to the attentive viewer in sheets from different parts of the work: for example, the depiction of a woman lying on the floor in a pool of blood refers to the suicide of her mother (p.32) and her grandmother (p.748).

In the isolation of exile, Salomon cast off the academic norms she had been taught at art school and created an individual style of great authenticity, which in its combination of writing and pictures seems immensely modern. The work depicts interiors, streets, sometimes landscapes, but mainly people in their complicated entanglements of life and love. Although the pictures are figurative, they are never realistic; on the contrary, the sheets of the epilogue tend towards abstraction, when for example the cross-hatched blue lines and brown dots represent planes dropping bombs and the horror of war.

Leben? oder Theater? was created in the exceptional situation of exile, when in two years of intensive, even manic work Salomon struggled to produce a painted autobiography. Its quality and fascination stem from the tension of the different styles, the dynamic relationship of text and picture and the great variety of themes with which she treated openly and sensitively subjects that are often taboo in art, such as female homosexuality and suicide. Her exemplary depiction of the systematic destruction of Jewish culture is important not least because it prevents viewers from suppressing, or even forgetting, the Holocaust.

Salomon always remembered Wolfsohn's farewell words to her, in her play attributed to Amadeus Daberlohn: he begged her "not to forget that I love life and have a very positive attitude to it. To love life completely, it may be necessary to encompass and understand its other side, death, as well. Never forget that I believe in you" (*ibid.*, pp.665–6). These words became a magic formula for the artist, lending her the strength to overcome the thought of suicide and to venture without compromise into the depths of her life: despite all the pain and loss, to paint and write of her childhood and years as a young Jew in a time of racial hatred. At the end of *Leben? oder Theater?* she wrote: "And she saw with daydreaming eyes all the beauty surrounding her, saw the sea, felt the sun and knew: she had to disappear for some time from the human surface and to sacrifice much for it – in order to create her world anew from the depth" (*ibid.*, pp.782–3).

SABINE DAHMEN

Sánchez, Josefa

Spanish painter, active 1639–49

Bibliography

E. Tormo, "La Inmaculada y el arte español", *Boletin de la Sociedad Española de Excursiones*, xxii, 1914, pp.176–218

Emilio Orozco Diaz, *Temas del barroco de poesía y pintura*, Granada: Universidad de Granada, 1947

Manuel Sanchez Camargo, *La muerte y la pintura española*, Madrid: Nacional, 1954

J. de Mesa and T. Gisbert, "Una pintora española del siglo XVII: Josefa Sánchez", *Archivo Español del Arte*, iv, 1970, pp.93–5

Diego Angulo, *Pintura española del siglo XVII*, Madrid: Plus-Ultra, 1971

Diego Angulo and Alfonso E. Pérez Sánchez, *La escuela toledana de la primera mitad del siglo XVII*, Madrid, 1972

José Camon Aznar, *La pintura española del siglo XVII*, Madrid: Espasa-Calpe, 1977

Jonathan Brown, *Images and Ideas in Seventeenth-Century Spanish Painting*, Princeton: Princeton University Press, 1978

Angela Franco, "Un crucifijo de la pintora Josefa Sánchez", *Reales Sitios*, no.66, 1980, pp.65–7

Alfonso E. Pérez Sánchez, "Las mujeres 'pintoras' en España", *La imagen de la mujer en el arte español: Actas de las terceras jornadas de investigación interdisciplinaria*, Madrid: Universidad Autónoma de Madrid, 1984, pp.73–86

Crucis mysterium, exh. cat., Diócesis de Segovia, Segovia, 1990

There is very little documentation on the painter Josefa Sánchez, and her dates of birth and death as well as her place of residence are unknown. There is no reference to her in any dictionary of art from the time or from later periods, although a Jesualda Sánchez appears in some of them – she had an open studio in Valencia in the 17th century, but she is now known to be a different painter, unrelated to Josefa Sánchez. The only documentation that exists is in the form of three works that have recently been located. In 1970 a signed and dated painted *Crucifixion* made of wood was discovered in the Convent of San Antonio el Real de Segovia, providing the first historical evidence of Sánchez's existence. Later, in 1980, Angela Franco made known the existence of a second signed and dated *Crucifixion* (Museo de Artes Decorativas, Madrid). In 1990 the Diocese of Segovia organised an exhibition of religious art in which a *Crucifixion* signed by a Josefa Sánchez was exhibited, dated to the 16th century. Stylistic similarities with the former *Crucifixions* confirm, however, that this piece should be dated to the first third of the 17th century and that the artist is the same. There are thus three known works preserved by Josefa Sánchez.

As all biographical data is missing, it is not known exactly where Sánchez produced her work. She probably lived and worked in Castile – possibly in the province of Segovia – because her painting clearly belongs to the Castilian school, and was active in the mid-17th century, as is known from the date of the *Crucifixions*. She appears to have been dedicated to the religious life, as is deduced from her signature. Some works are signed D. Maria Josepha Sánchez; in others, the initials D.M.R. precede her name – these probably mean "De" (of) or "Doña" (Lady) "Madre Reverenda" (Reverend Mother) or "Muy Reverenda" (Very Reverend). This is the interpretation of the majority of contemporary historians. Sánchez's work undoubtedly falls within the Castilian school of Mannerism, and in particular the Christ figures painted by Sánchez are clearly related to those executed by Luis Tristán, El Greco's most talented disciple.

The first of the three *Crucifixions* discovered is the one preserved in the Convent of San Antonio el Real de Segovia, dated 1639. This work, like the others, was undoubtedly an object of personal devotion, as was common in the 17th century. This can be deduced above all from its size (29.5 × 52.9 cm.), but also because next to the image of the Son is that of the Immaculate Conception. Both motifs enjoyed great devotional importance during the Mannerist period and later during the Baroque, and the joining of the two, while not very common, may be explained by the fact that the piece was conceived as an object of personal prayer and meditation.

As Angulo and Pérez Sánchez have pointed out, Luis Tristán usually painted two types of Christ: a dead Christ, with the head down, and a live Christ, looking upwards with a body that naturally has more animation than that of the former. Josefa Sánchez also followed these two types, usually the second, as in this case. The crucified figure is treated with a naturalism that already belongs to the second third of the 17th century, with a clear interest in chiaroscuro that is undoubtedly influenced by Jacopo Bassano. The colours of the flesh are golden and ochre, contrasting with the shadows of the background. As in the case of Luis Tristán, both the face and the body are stylised and carefully painted, with a notable interest in anatomy, contradicting once more the notion that women painters have not been concerned with capturing the characteristics of the human figure. The loin-cloth enables the painter to create a light-toned focus in contrast to the golden flesh

tones, as well as demonstrating her Mannerist virtuosity in the depiction of the folds of the cloth. The figure of the Immaculate Virgin, located beneath the principal motif, is far more detailed than the crucified figure. It seems as if the painter paid greater attention to capturing all the nuances of the figure, an interest in the fine drawing of the golden hair, of the halo, of the cape trimmed with pearls and in the folds of the tunic. This is in notable contrast to the execution of the Christ figure, which appears more natural, more in harmony with the latest style of Mannerism than the Virgin, whose representation, although more accomplished, is nevertheless more archaic. Lastly, a small skull appears at the feet of the Virgin, alluding to Calvary.

The *Crucifixion* in the Museo de Artes Decorativas in Madrid is dated 1649 and is thus ten years later than the previous one; it is without doubt the most outstanding of Sánchez's known works. It belongs to a similar type of private devotional object of reduced dimensions (48 × 28 cm.), although there are differences between this and the previous *Crucifixion*: it is smaller and simpler, lacking an image of the Immaculate Virgin, and in the lower part of the cross is a simple skull, magnificently painted and of great realism, which refers both to ancient representations of Calvary as well as to the vanity of earthly life. The greatest similarity between the two works is clearly the Christ figure, which in both has three nails. The face is also turned up towards the sky with an expression of sweetness that is nevertheless marked with physical pain and exhaustion. The expressiveness is moving, in accordance with the traditions of the time – the mid-17th century – when religious images made maximum use of their emotional charge with the aim of moving the faithful to prayer and penitence. In this context, the enormous influence of the *Spiritual Exercises* of St Ignatius Loyola should be remembered, which analysed each step of the life of Christ, dwelling on the dramatic and theatrical aspect – in the Baroque meaning of the words – of each one. The writings were used as a daily spiritual guide and were an important source of iconographic models in Spain. As has justly been observed, the texts of St Ignatius had a greater influence on this type of ascetic-naturalistic Christ as depicted by painters such as Josefa Sánchez – who in turn used the model of Luis Tristán – than the mystical type painted by El Greco.

In the third *Crucifixion* by Sánchez, preserved in the Convento de las Madres Dominicas, Segovia, Christ is already dead, with closed eyes and the face vanquished by pain. Again there are three nails but the body is less contorted than those of the other *Crucifixions*, with less attention paid to anatomy. The overall composition is more hieratic, giving it a much more archaic appearance. Below the crucified figure the Immaculate Virgin is represented in a simpler manner: she is kneeling in an attitude of prayer, dressed in a simple white tunic, and her divine character is shown by the fact that she rests her knees on a ball of fire, the symbolic representation of the universe. Overall, this painting is the least successful of the three, the most hieratic, with less stylised figures. It is thus logical to conclude that it was executed before the other two. Despite this, the work, like the others, is of a great quality and beauty, explaining why all the surviving *Crucifixions* by Josefa Sánchez are signed, indicating that the artist must have enjoyed a certain prestige and reputation in her time: and it is also these signatures that have enabled these works to be rescued from anonymity.

KARINA MAROTTA PERAMOS

Sandrart, Susanna Maria von

German printmaker and draughtswoman, 1658–1716

Born in Nuremberg, 8 August 1658, to Jacob von Sandrart and Regina Christina (née Eimmart). Trained by her father and by her great-uncle, Joachim von Sandrart. Married (1) painter Johan Paul Auer, 1683; he died 1687; (2) bookseller Wolfgang Moritz Endter, 1695. Died in Nuremberg, 20 December 1716.

Selected Writings

Editor, *Auserlesenes Hand-Buch für Gottseelige Krancke und Sterbende ...*, Nuremberg, 1719 (collection of texts, religious verse and prayers)

Bibliography

Joachim von Sandrart, *L'Academia todesca della architectura, scultura e pittura: Oder Teutsche Academie der edlen Bau-, Bild- und Mahlerey-künste*, ii, Nuremberg, 1679; ed. A.R. Peltzer, Munich, 1925; reprinted Farnborough: Gregg, 1971

Johann Gabriel Doppelmayr, *Historische Nachricht von den Nürnbergischen Mathematicis und Künstlern*, Nuremberg, 1730

Georg Andreas Will, *Nürnbergisches Gelehrtenlexikon oder Beschreibung aller Nürnbergischen Gelehrten beyderley Geschlechtes nach Ihrem Leben: Verdiensten und Schrifften*, iii, Nuremberg: Altdorf, 1757

Ignaz Emanuel Wessely, *Kunstübende Frauen*, Leipzig, 1884

Barock in Nürnberg, 1600–1750, exh. cat., Germanisches Nationalmuseum, Nuremberg, 1962

Lore Sporhan-Krempel, "Susanna Maria von Sandrart und ihre Familie", *Archiv für Geschichte des Buchwesens*, xxi, 1980, pp.966–1003

Jean M. Woods and Maria Fürstenwald, *Schriftstellerinnen, Künstlerinnen und gelehrte Frauen des deutschen Barock*, Stuttgart, 1984

Sabina Lessmann, *Susanna Maria von Sandrart: Arbeitsbedingungen einer Nürnberger Graphikerin im 17. Jahrhundert*, Hildesheim: Olms, 1991

——, "Susanna Maria von Sandrart: Women artists in 17th-century Nürnberg", *Woman's Art Journal*, xiv/1, 1993, pp.10–14

Susanna Maria von Sandrart developed within the family firm into a competent and recognised artist. Her artistic development was influenced not only by the family workshop and art trade but also by the considerable number of women within the Sandrart family circle who were active in various areas. Moreover, the town of Nuremberg, as a "free imperial city" without guilds, enabled local women to work in the workshops, to become qualified, and to increase the profits of family businesses.

Sandrart produced hundreds of drawings, copper engravings and etchings. Her work was published both singly and as a series by her father's publishing house, as contributions to Joachim von Sandrart's *Teutsche Academie* and *Iconologia deorum*, and as book illustrations for other publishing houses. It appeared in Bibles, in stories about sea voyages and in religious and edifying tales. Her subject matter ranged from portraits, landscapes, town views, maps, animals and religious, mythological and allegorical scenes to nudes and life studies (see illustration). She produced countless series of drawings – usually a set of six that were designed to be hung together. Among others, these show costumes after Nicolas and Robert Bonnart; Roman fountains after Johann Baptista Falda; ornaments after Hubertus Quellinus and Paul Androuet Du Cerceau; vases, altars and decorations after Jean Le Pautre; and flowers after Nicolaus Guillaume de La Fleur. Following demand and contemporary taste, she also engraved pictures after Antonio Tempesta, Ludovico and Annibale Carracci, Pietro da Cortona, Guido Reni and Gérard de Lairesse. Further works show pieces by Oliviero Gatti, Simon Vouet, Sebastian Bourdon and Johann Franz Ermels, and there are also 14 representations of Raphael's *Psyche* frescoes in the Villa Farnesina, Rome.

Shortly before her death, Sandrart had one copy of each of her printed works and of the drawings she had produced in charcoal, red chalk, pencil and indian ink bound into a folio volume (Germanisches Nationalmuseum, Nuremberg). This brings together nearly all her work, with the exception of a few copper engravings and the drawings that she gave away as presents. It is painstakingly bound in leather and furnished with metal fastenings, and contains a foreword by the artist's second husband, Wolfgang Moritz Endter, as well as hand-written texts by Sandrart that give information about her artistic activities, her themes and her personal situation. The artist has added religious verses to some of the pictures in her own handwriting. The volume gives an insight into the artistic development of an illustrator of reproductions in the 17th century. Because not only the high-quality later published works but also the early practice sheets and private sketches have been preserved, the artist's development can be precisely followed.

Sandrart's subject matter and techniques correspond exactly to Joachim von Sandrart's ideas on artistic education, as set out in his *Teutsche Academie*. He divides the tuition into three stages: copying from drawings (two-dimensional models), copying from classical statues (three-dimensional models) and drawing from life. Susanna Maria von Sandrart's work appears to reflect these stages: there are practice drawings of other artists' work; there are antique plaster models; there are drawings of animals, landscapes, Mediterranean ruins, studies of heads and hands, and nudes, including some of male models. All her work, however, consists of copies of other artists' drawings. Her education did not include drawings from original statues, or from animal corpses; she did not make study trips to far-away countries or take part in sessions drawing from models. The "Painters' Academy" founded by Jacob and Joachim von Sandrart was a recognised meeting place for artists and art lovers, and drawing from live models was available there. Although these meetings are known to have taken place in Susanna's home from 1662 onwards, women were not allowed to attend. Thus she was forced to rely on the output of her male colleagues, which she could then copy. It is clear from this that the taboo for a female artist was not in the drawing of naked male models, but in the actual attendance at life classes and the direct observation of the nude body.

Sandrart's artistic education took place before her first marriage in 1683. Her second productive phase was during her

Sandrart: *Male Nude*, drawing; Germanisches Nationalmuseum, Nuremberg

widowhood, from 1687 to 1695. She produced virtually nothing during her years of marriage, when her commercial work was suspended completely. The fact that her first husband was a painter and her second a bookseller and publisher did not further her artistic career. She nevertheless spoke of her art with great pride, writing in her folio volume:

> Myself Susanna Maria, daughter of the deceased Jacob von Sandrart, though taught by my now deceased mother from an early age to do domestic and other work, had an inclination also to draw, making in idle times the drawings presented in this book, begun also by my own impulse to etch in copper. When my late father saw that I held a natural inclination for this occupation, he encouraged me and gave me copper to train, at least those copper works which he could use for his art trade. This work was interrupted when I was married in 1683 to my first husband Johan Paul Auer. After his early death, when I had been married only four years and ten weeks, I had the advantage that I could support my father's and my brother's work so I could earn my living and was not a burden to anyone. All the copper etchings in this book were made by myself, most of them while I was a widow. In 1695 I was married for a second time – because of divine guidance and my parents' advice – to the widower Wolfgang Moritz Endter; I had to stop my occupation then because of the extensive housework.

> Nearly all I produced I collected in this book to see what I did in my youth and especially in my seven years of widowhood. This book I gave my dearest husband Wolfgang Moritz Endter for my kind memory wishing him benevolence for body and soul.

Many things attest to the regard in which Susanna Maria von Sandrart was held, and to the recognition she enjoyed: Joachim von Sandrart's mention of her in his *Teutsche Academie*, her admittance to the ranks of significant artists in contemporary publications, the production of a framed portrait of the artist as an epitaph (bequeathed to the city of Nuremberg by Wolfgang Moritz Endter) and, last but not least, the folio volume, which was also given to the city of Nuremberg.

SABINA LESSMANN

Santos Torroella, Angeles

Spanish painter, 1912–

Born in Port Bou, Girona, 1912; sister of art critic Rafael Santos Torroella. Moved to Seville as a child, and later to Valladolid, where she formed friendships with local intellectuals. Took private painting classes in Valladolid with Italian artist Cellino Perotti. Pursued an active artistic career after her success at the Salón de Otoño, Madrid, in 1929. Married painter Emilio Grau Sala, 1935; one son, the painter Julián Grau Santos. Moved to Paris in 1936, after the outbreak of the Spanish Civil War. Painted privately after her marriage, but started showing new work again in the mid-1960s. Returned to Spain after husband's death in 1975; subsequently divided her time between Sitges in Catalonia and Madrid.

Principal Exhibitions

Individual
Ateneo, Valladolid: 1929
Lyceum Club Femenino, Madrid: 1929
Círculo de Bellas Artes, Madrid: 1931
Casino de Bellas Artes, San Sebastián: 1931
Galería Estilo, Madrid: 1943
Sala Parés, Barcelona: 1974, 1980
Galería Juan Gris, Madrid: 1988

Group
Municipal de Valladolid: 1927
Salón de Otoño, Madrid: 1929, 1930 (individual room)
Carnegie Institute, Pittsburgh: 1930, 1932
Circulo de Bellas Artes, Madrid: 1931
Exposición de Artistas Ibéricos, Oslo: 1931
Exposición de la Sociedad de Artistas Ibéricos, Copenhagen and
     Berlin: 1933
Venice Biennale: 1936
Madrid: 1936 (Arte español contemporáneo, touring)
Exposición Nacional de Bellas Artes, Madrid: 1942
Galería Multitud, Madrid: 1975 (El surrealismo en España)
Galería Anne Barchot, Madrid: 1975 (Pintoras en España)
Centro Cultural Conde Duque, Madrid: 1984 (Mujeres en el arte
     español)
Centro Cultural Santa Mónica, Barcelona: 1988 (Surrealismo a
     Catalunya, 1924–36)

Bibliography

J. Arroyo, "La pintura de Angelita Santos", Meseta (supplement),
     Valladolid, 1929
Ramón Gómez de la Serna, "La genial pintora Angeles Santos, inco-
     municada en un sanatorio", La Gaceta Literaria, 1 April 1930
R. Santos Torroella, "Angelita (Recuerdo)", El Noticiero Universal, 4
     October 1967
J.R. Jimenez, Españoles de tres mundos (Angeles Santos), Madrid,
     1969
J. Gigh, "Arte y artistas: El retorno de Angeles Santos", La
     Vanguardia Española, 19 November 1969
Angeles Santos: Acuarelas y dibujos, exh. cat., Sala Parés, Barcelona,
     1974
F. Gutierrez, "Angeles Santos en la Sala Parés", La Vanguardia
     Española, 16 March 1974
A. Gonzalez Garcia and F. Calvo Serraller, Surrealismo en España,
     Madrid, 1975
Raul Chavarri, Artistas contemporáneas en España, Madrid: Gavar,
     1976
M. Vayreda i Trullol, "Quatre obres d'Angels Santos", Pintors surre-
     alistes de l'Empordá, ed. R. Santos Torroella, Girona, 1977
Angeles Santos, exh. cat., Galería Alençon, Madrid, 1982
Rosa Agenjo Bosch, Angeles Santos, PhD dissertation, Faculty of Fine
     Arts, Barcelona, 1986
Lucia Garcia de Carpi, La pintura surrealista española (1924–1936),
     Madrid: ISTMO, 1986
F. Rivas and others, Angeles Santos, Madrid, 1987
J.M. Bonet, "Angeles Santos: Un retrato", Guadalimar, no.95, 1988
Surrealismo a Catalunya, 1924–36, exh. cat., Centro Cultural Santa
     Mónica, Barcelona, 1988
J.M. Bonet, "La pintora catalana Angels Santos ...", Diario 16, 18
     January 1988
M.A. Trenas, "Pinto exclusivamente para mí ...", La Vanguardia, 29
     January 1988
Francisco Calvo Serraller, ed., Enciclopedia del arte español del siglo
     XX, i: Artistas, Madrid, 1991
Valeriano Bozal, Pintura y escultura españolas del siglo XX
     (1900–1936), Madrid: Espasa-Calpe, 1992
Catálogo Museo Nacional Centro de Arte Reina Sofia, Madrid, 1992
Vinyet Panyella, Angeles Santos, Barcelona, 1992

The artistic career of Angeles Santos started early and developed surprisingly. Her outstanding drawing abilities led her father to guide her towards art, encouraged by the nuns at the college at which she studied. Her position as a child who was both extremely gifted in art and ingenuous influenced her relationship with intellectual circles as well as the critical reception of her later work. It could be said that Santos had a peculiar relationship with intellectuals because, as her talent revealed itself when she was still very young, they did not really take her as seriously as might have been expected given the extremely high quality of her work. This problem is also one shared by other women artists associated with the avant-garde in the 20th century. Proof of this, for instance, is the sensitive article that Ramón Gómez de la Serna wrote about her in 1930, when Santos was interned in a rest house by her father, who was no doubt alarmed by what he considered to be the emotional and artistic excesses of his daughter. On this occasion – one more episode in the hazardous existence that the artist was obliged to live – the writer published the article in defence of the brilliant adolescent that was suffering the effects of the same retrograde society in which Salvador Dalí was thrown out of his father's house and Tina Modotti (q.v.) was tormented in Paris.

Santos's first solo exhibition took place at the Ateneo, Valladolid, when she was 17 years old. The exhibition immediately caused a stir in the small Castilian town and the painter became part of the fertile local intellectual circle. Various articles about her appeared in the Meseta magazine, the town's most avant-garde literary and artistic medium, closely linked to Madrid's Gaceta Literaria. That same year she exhibited A World (1929; see illustration) at the capital's Salón de Otoño and the artist became the discovery of the year – as the artist Maruja Mallo (q.v.) had been the previous one. Her work caused such a sensation that in the Salón de Otoño of 1930 she was given a whole room to herself, an honour that had previously been awarded only to the most esteemed artists, such as Eduardo Rosales.

The individual nature of Santos's work can be perceived from the start in the fact that she represented the concerns of modernity without being aware of them; in other words, her painting is unconsciously Surrealist. The image of a re-created world is given form in her works, with apparent reality subverted in a way that is both effective and natural. Her inspiration was not drawn from theories – the study of the avant-garde – but rather from her own inner life. In one sense, Santos is tangible proof that Surrealism was a sincere attitude, a necessary rupture with tradition that manifested itself spontaneously in a young spirit. In fact, there is also a relationship between the vicissitudes of Santos's life and her temporary

Santos Torroella: *A World*, 1929; Museo Nacional Centro de Arte Reina Sofía, Madrid

adherence to Surrealism, in the sense in which her meeting with the avant-garde took place at a particular moment in her life, during her adolescence, that coincided with a personal necessity to break down barriers, to transcend her situation as an educated young lady in a small provincial town. Because of this, the painter's early works subtly reflect the anxiety of a constricted world, the uneasiness of first youth, the torment of an intense inner life. Her pictures seem to be the result of a need to express a vital anxiety. Furthermore, in her letters to Ramón Gómez de la Serna, the artist gave vent to her desire for freedom: "... and afterwards I will go into the countryside, running away from those who want to turn me into a tame animal."

Santos's attitude towards painting is very intimate. The artist has stated several times that she has always painted for herself and even that the enthusiastic criticism written about her has never affected her, as she lived out her experiences within her own world, in domestic surroundings from which she extracted the everyday themes of her pictures or her personal dreams. In this sense, it should be pointed out that Santos's works exude a timelessness that belongs to an extremely complex inner world. Time is suspended in Santos's pictures and simultaneously becomes infinite, as in some of Giorgio de Chirico's works. Her most emblematic work is the aforementioned *A World*, in which characteristic elements of her early paintings (never really abandoned) are present, with the artist starting from a minute observation of reality – extreme detail that in one way is close to that of children's drawings. She elevated this realism to the realm of the absurd, a cubic planet, while at the same time imbuing the work with profound symbolism and metaphors – the mother, giver of life, women/angels who are lighting the stars, inspired by the verses of Juan Ramón Jiménez – and worrying extra-terrestrial beings, like wire.

It is difficult to apply a label to Santos's work, as strictly speaking only *A World* can be considered to be Surrealist. In this same year the artist was producing other works, such as *The Land* (1929; 76 × 86cm.; artist's collection), which conjure up an oneirical vision of the universe close to the symbolism of Odilon Redon. Like the previous work, *The Land* is a personal re-creation of the universe in which reality is touched by a sense of magic, of the unreal. In the same manner, her fine work *The Gathering* (1930; 130 × 193 cm.; Museo Nacional Centro de Arte Reina Sofía, Madrid) depicts an intimate female world in which reality acquires a timeless character. Widely dispersed over the surface of the canvas, Santos places three female figures with bored and simultaneously disturbing looks, unconsciously reminiscent of the tedium of life that is also present in the paintings of Otto Dix.

Angeles Santos, however, clearly always had classical leanings. Among her preferred artists are Raphael, Velázquez, Pierre Bonnard and Edouard Vuillard, and it was to these artists that the painter gradually drew closer in her later work (all in the possession of the artist or her family, or in private collections). She admits that the realist painting of her husband, Grau Sala, had a decisive influence on her, so much so that in coming into contact with his paintings she discovered new worlds and came to despise her own earlier production. Furthermore, the difficult life she led and her inner contortions seem to have disappeared in her later works, in which the intimate nature of domestic subjects continues to be evident, but is now treated with a fragility and a poetry removed from the heart-rending lyricism of the 1930s. As she has declared, French Impressionism was a very important influence on her work during the years she lived in Paris, and has continued to influence her. One of her most recent works, the decoration of the church of La Visitación, Las Rozas, Madrid (1992), inspired in its "predella" by Fra Angelico, follows this poetic realism. In works dating from the 1960s onwards, the image of the window appears frequently, of a world seen from one's own room, with timidity and discretion, silencing – in a very feminine way – her youthful rebellious nature.

KARINA MAROTTA PERAMOS

Savage, Augusta
American sculptor, 1892–1962

Born Augusta Christine Fells in Green Cove Springs, Florida, 29 February 1892. Married (1) John T. Moore, 1907; daughter born 1908; husband died a few years later; (2) James Savage c.1915; divorced early 1920s; (3) Robert L. Poston, 1923; he died 1924. Moved to West Palm Beach with her family, 1915. Moved to Jacksonville, Florida, 1919; to New York, 1921. Studied at Cooper Union, New York, 1921–3; also attended Women's Art School. Studied in Paris, funded by two Julius Rosenwald fellowships, 1930–32; studied at Académie de la Grande Chaumière under Félix Benneteau-Desgrois and later Charles Despiau; then eight-month study tour in France, Belgium and Germany funded by Carnegie Foundation grant. Established Savage Studio of Arts and Crafts, New York, 1932. Organised a group of young intellectuals, the Vanguard, 1933. First black member, National Association of Women Painters and Sculptors, 1934. Assistant supervisor, Works Progress Administration Federal Art Projects (WPA/FAP), 1936. First director, Harlem Community Art Center, 1937. Director, Salon of Contemporary Negro Art in Harlem, 1939. Recipient of silver medal, Women's Service League of Brooklyn, 1939. Retired to Saugerties in the Catskill Mountains, New York, 1945. Died in the Bronx, New York, 26 March 1962.

Principal Exhibitions
Douglas High School, Baltimore: 1926
Salon d'Automne, Paris: 1930–31
Spring Salon, American Art Anderson Galleries, New York: 1932
Argent Galleries, New York: 1934, 1938 (both group), 1939 (individual)
New York World's Fair: 1939
Tanner Art Galleries, Chicago: 1940 (*American Negro Exposition*)

Selected Writings
"An autobiography", *The Crisis*, xxxvi, August 1929, p.257

Bibliography
Maxine Block, ed., "Augusta Savage", *Current Biography*, New York: Wilson, 1941
De Witt S. Dykes, Jr, "Augusta Christine Savage", *Notable American Women, the Modern Period: A Biographical Dictionary*, ed. Barbara Sicherman and Carol Hurd Green, Cambridge, MA: Harvard University Press, 1980, pp.627–9
Augusta Savage and the Art Schools of Harlem, exh. cat., Schomburg Center for Research in Black Culture, New York Public Library, 1988
Against the Odds: African-American Artists and the Harmon Foundation, exh. cat., Newark Museum, NJ, 1990
Charlotte Streifer Rubinstein, *American Women Sculptors*, Boston: Hall, 1990
Romare Bearden and Harry Henderson, *A History of African-American Artists from 1792 to the Present*, New York: Pantheon, 1993
Deirdre Bibby, "Augusta Savage", *Black Women in America: An Historical Encyclopedia*, ii, ed. Darlene Clark Hine, Elsa Barkley Brown and Rosalyn Terborg-Penn, New York: Carlson, 1993
Three Generations of African-American Women Sculptors: A Study in Paradox, exh. cat., Afro-American Historical and Cultural Museum, Philadelphia, 1996

The standing of Augusta Savage in the world of 20th-century American art rests as much on the role she played during the 1930s in teaching young African-American artists, promoting their art, fighting racism in the art world and being a forceful presence in the Harlem community of New York as on her actual sculptural production which, although often beautifully conceived and executed, never exceeded more than a few dozen pieces. Specific information about Savage's early marriages and her primary school and art education are sketchy at best, and brief biographies written during her own lifetime, while stressing her triumphs over adversity, often contradict one another. De Witt S. Dykes, Jr (1980) made the first attempt to sort through the rich archives at the Schomburg Center for Research in Black Culture, a branch of the New York Public Library, and to use the files of Savage's daughter to establish the actual birth date. And when Deirdre L. Bibby organised the exhibition *Augusta Savage and the Art Schools of Harlem* (1988) for the Schomburg Center, further biographical puzzles became untangled, with Bibby's essay and the chronology prepared by Juanita Marie Holland, based on scrapbooks held by Savage's family. The essay that best captures the personality and fighting spirit of Savage was written by the artist Romare Bearden and completed by Harry Henderson after Bearden's death in 1988. As a close friend of her students during the 1930s, Bearden appreciated the very real struggles that Savage confronted as she developed from a poor, black Southern child into the dynamic presence that dominated the Harlem art world.

The incidents that recur in the early biographies and newspaper stories emphasise the poverty and racism that she continuously had to overcome, her perseverance and the instant recognition of her talent by people with the means to help her. Born the seventh child in a poor, African-American family of 14 children, at the age of 15 Savage married John T. Moore and gave birth to her only child, Irene Connie Moore. When her husband died, she rejoined her family with her child; and in 1915 they all moved to West Palm Beach. In one account Savage recalled that her religious father, a part-time Methodist preacher who supported the large family with carpentry, fishing and farming, "almost whipped all the art" out of her, because he disapproved of the "graven images" she had created as a child from the clay she found near her home (Bearden and Henderson 1993, p.168). Another tells how a high school principal introduced her to a local potter, who gave her 25 pounds of clay. Thus encouraged, she modelled an image of the Virgin Mary and a horse, which won the admiration of the principal and prompted him to employ her to teach a class in modelling for a dollar a day (New York 1988, p.12). Another opportunity came when George Graham Currie, superintendent of the West Palm Beach County Fair in 1919, urged her to enter her work. Her sculpture met with enthusiasm, and she received a special prize of $25, as well as $175 from the fair-going public eager to help her budding career (Dykes 1980, p.627). After a brief sojourn in Jacksonville, Florida, where she had unrealistically hoped to earn a living with portrait commissions from the black middle class, she moved on to New York in 1921. She left behind her second husband, James Savage, a carpenter, whom she subsequently divorced (New York 1988, p.12). Like many young African-American women with single-minded ambitions and a supportive family, she left her daughter behind with her parents when she moved to New York to make her fortune.

Possessing a letter of introduction from Currie, Savage called on the sculptor Solon Borglum, a founder of the School of American Sculpture in New York. Realising that her poverty precluded her paying the tuition fees, he directed her to Kate Reynolds, the director of Cooper Union, an endowed art school without fees to students (*ibid.*, p.13). Once enrolled at Cooper Union, Savage studied under George Brewster and moved rapidly through her studies, while supporting herself with part-time jobs (Bearden and Henderson 1993, p.169). But racism impeded her opportunities. In 1923 she entered a competition for a summer scholarship to an art school located at Fontainebleau, outside Paris. Although accepted, her scholarship was withdrawn by the judges to appease white Southern girls who also planned to attend the school. Savage challenged the judges; she told the *New York World* (20 May 1923):

> My brother was good enough to be accepted in one of the regiments that saw service in France during the war, but it seems his sister is not good enough to be a guest of the country for which he fought … How am I to compete with other American artists if I am not to be given the same opportunity? [quoted in Bearden and Henderson 1993, p.170].

Although both black and white intellectuals mounted a protest against the racist decision, the judges would not waver, with the exception of the sculptor Hermon A. MacNeil, who promptly invited Savage to study with him that summer.

Savage's assertiveness was not surprising, given her personality as well as the climate of quiet but firm protest then developing among the black intelligentsia. Many of them, like Savage, had moved to New York in the early 1920s as part of the "great migration" – a voluntary relocation of two million African Americans during and after World War I from the South in search of well-paid jobs and opportunities in the northern cities of Chicago, Detroit and New York. Harlem – that area of Manhattan north of Central Park – became one of the destinations of these migrants. In the 1920s Marcus Garvey

Savage: Augusta Savage at work in her studio, inscribed "to George Harris, with sincere appreciation, Augusta Savage, Nov 1961"; Photographs and Prints Division, Schomburg Center for Research in Black Culture, New York Public Library

and his Universal Negro Improvement Association preached self-esteem and independence for blacks. W.E.B. Du Bois, editor of *The Crisis*, the journal of the National Association for the Advancement of Colored People, urged young writers and artists to develop their minds; he felt that the "talented tenth" would counter racist stereotypes. By the mid-1920s musicians, poets, novelists and other intellectuals had created what came to be known as the New Negro Movement, or the Harlem Renaissance. Savage quickly found a place in these circles. The branch library in Harlem commissioned her to model a portrait bust of *Du Bois* (untraced); another commission set her to work on a bust of *Garvey* (repr. Bearden and Henderson 1993, p.171). Through this commission she met and married one of Garvey's chief lieutenants, Robert L. Poston. Although Poston died a few months later, she remained a lifelong black nationalist.

In 1925 Du Bois attempted to raise funds for Savage to study in Rome, but the funds fell short of realistic living expenses. Her own earnings went to support her parents, who eventually moved in with her. Four years later, however, the directors of the Julius Rosenwald Fund were so impressed with *Gamin* (1929; Schomburg Center for Research in Black Culture, New York), a sculptured bust of her nephew as a cocky African-American street kid, that they awarded her a year-long fellowship (renewed for a second year) for study in France.

On her return to New York in 1932, she was confronted with the economic Depression that had gripped the country. Both the Argent Galleries and the Art-Anderson Galleries accepted her work, and she secured some portrait commissions, but she felt that young black artists needed her help. She opened the Savage Studio of Arts and Crafts, in a basement apartment on West 143rd Street, and obtained a grant of $1500 from the Carnegie Foundation to teach art to children. Her adult students included Norman Lewis, William Artis, Ernest Crichlow, Elton C. Fax and later Gwendolyn Knight. In 1934 her exhibition at the Argent Galleries led to an invitation to join the National Association of Women Painters and Sculptors, the first African American to be so honoured.

In 1933 Savage organised a group, the Vanguard, which supported progressive causes (*ibid.*, p.15), and also participated with her colleagues in creating the Harlem Artists Guild, which held exhibitions at the Harlem branch of the Young Men's Christian Association (YMCA). She pressed the government to support the arts, and in 1936 she became an assistant supervisor for the Federal Art Project of the Works Progress Administration, which employed destitute artists in exchange for their participating on mural projects, painting easel pictures for schools and hospitals, producing posters and teaching at community centres. In this position she made sure that young black artists, such as Jacob Lawrence, were taken on. When in December 1937 the WPA's Harlem Community Art Center opened with great fanfare (which included an official visit from Eleanor Roosevelt), Savage became its first director.

That same month she received the commission from the board of design of the New York World's Fair to sculpt a work "symbolic of the unique contribution made by the American Negro to the world's music, particularly in song" (*New York Times*, 9 December 1937). Taking a leave of absence from the Harlem Community Art Center, she worked on *The Harp*, which was installed in the courtyard of the Contemporary Arts Building for the duration of the Fair (1939–40). More than 4.87 metres tall, made of plaster painted black, *The Harp* depicted African-American singers in choir robes as the strings of a harp, while the forearm and cupped hand of the Creator formed its base. Kneeling in front, an African-American man stretches out his arms as he holds a plaque inscribed with musical notes from James Weldon Johnson's famous anthem "Lift Every Voice and Sing". Because funds for bronze casting could not be raised, *The Harp* was destroyed at the conclusion of the Fair; but a small bronze replica, *Lift Every Voice and Sing* (1939; Schomburg Center), survives.

Savage continued to be active in artists' organisations and for a brief period ran a private art gallery, the Salon of Contemporary Negro Art, but her own artistic output was slim. The expense of bronze casting no doubt held her back. She eschewed the innovations of modernism (including modernism's indebtedness to African art forms) in favour of a soft naturalistic style, particularly for her portraits. *Gamin* is considered her *chef d'oeuvre*, because it ushered in a period when the frank portrayal of African-American physiognomy spurred other artists to infuse racial pride into their own work.

During the late 1930s, when private patronage barely existed, and when exhibitions of her work did not bring her the critical acclaim she felt she deserved, Savage decided to leave Harlem. In the early 1940s she moved to Saugerties, and lived in isolation from the New York art world for most of the last 17 years of her life. During the 1930s, however, there was probably no other artist in Harlem with quite the single-minded force of Savage. Because of her and the young artists she mentored, the Harlem Renaissance of the visual arts, unlike the literary arts, can be said to have flourished well into the 1940s.

PATRICIA HILLS

Schapiro, Miriam

American multi-media artist, 1923–

Born in Toronto, Canada, 15 November 1923; grew up in New York. Studied at Museum of Modern Art and attended Federal Art Project classes, 1937–41; studied at Hunter College, New York, 1943; University of Iowa, Iowa City, 1943–9 (BA 1945; MA 1947, MFA 1949). Married artist Paul Brach, 1946; son born 1955. Lived in Columbia, Missouri, working as children's art teacher, 1950–52; in New York, 1952–67. Instructor, Parsons School of Design, New York, and visiting lecturer, Connecticut College for Women, New London, 1966–7. Moved to La Jolla, California, with family, 1967; taught at University of California, San Diego, 1967–9. Faculty member, California Institute of the Arts, Valencia, 1970; co-director, with Judy Chicago (q.v.), Feminist Art Program, 1971 (sole director 1973). Co-founder, Los Angeles Institute of Contemporary Art, 1974. Returned to New York, 1975. Co-founder of the feminist journal *Heresies*, 1976; founder-member of Feminist Art Institute, New York, 1977. Recipient of Ford Foundation grant for printmaking, Tamarind Lithography Workshop, 1964 (with Paul Brach); National Endowment for the Arts (NEA) grant, 1976; Guggenheim fellowship, 1987; honors award, Women's Caucus for Art, 1988; honors award, National Association of Schools of Art and Design (NASAD), 1992; honorary doctorates from College of Wooster, Ohio, 1983; California College of Arts and Crafts, Oakland, 1989; Minneapolis College of Art and Design, 1994. Member of advisory board, Women's Caucus for Art; College Art Association (former director); associate member, Heresies Collective. Lives in New York.

Selected Individual Exhibitions

André Emmerich Gallery, New York: 1958, 1960, 1961, 1963, 1967, 1969, 1971, 1973, 1976, 1977

Skidmore College, Saratoga Springs, NY: 1964

Lyman Allen Museum, New London, CT: 1966 (touring retrospective)

Newport Harbor Art Museum, CA: 1969 (retrospective, with Paul Brach)

Comsky Gallery, Los Angeles: 1974, 1975

Mandeville Art Gallery, University of California at San Diego: 1975

Allen Memorial Art Museum, Oberlin College, Oberlin, OH: 1977–9 (*Femmages*, touring)

Lerner-Heller Gallery, New York: 1979, 1980

Galerie Marcel Liatowitsch, Basel: 1979

Barbara Gladstone Gallery, New York: 1980, 1981, 1982

College of Wooster Art Museum, Wooster, OH: 1980–82 (touring retrospective)

Galerie Rudolf Zwirner, Cologne: 1981

Dart Gallery, Chicago: 1984

Bernice Steinbaum Gallery, New York: 1986, 1988, 1990, 1991

Guild Hall Museum, East Hampton, NY: 1992

ARC Gallery, Chicago: 1993

Steinbaum Krauss Gallery, New York: 1994

Selected Writings

"The education of women as artists: Project Womanhouse", *Art Journal*, xxxi, 1972, pp.268–70

"Female imagery", *Womanspace Journal*, i/1, Summer 1973, pp.11–17 (with Judy Chicago)

Editor, *Anonymous Was a Woman*, Valencia: California Institute of the Arts, 1974

"Notes from a conversation on art, feminism and work", *Working It Out*, ed. Sara Ruddick and Pamela Daniels, New York: Pantheon, 1977, pp.283–305

"Waste not/want not: Femmage", *Heresies*, no.4, Winter 1978, pp.66–9 (with Melissa Meyer); reprinted in *Collage: Critical Views*, ed. Katherine Hoffman, Ann Arbor: UMI Research Press, 1989, pp.295–315

"Recalling Womanhouse", *Women's Studies Quarterly*, xv, Spring–Summer 1987, pp.25–30

"Cunts/quilts/consciousness", *Heresies*, no.24, 1989, pp.6–13 (with Faith Wilding)

Rondo: An Artist Book, San Francisco: Bedford Arts Press, 1990

Bibliography

Paul Brach and Miriam Schapiro: Paintings and Graphic Works, exh. cat., Newport Harbor Art Museum, Newport Beach, CA, 1969

Linda Nochlin, "Miriam Schapiro: Recent work", *Arts Magazine*, xlviii, November 1973, pp.38–41

Miriam Schapiro: The Shrine, the Computer and the Dollhouse, exh. cat., Mandeville Art Gallery, University of California at San Diego, La Jolla, 1975

Jeff Perrone, "Approaching the decorative", *Artforum*, xv, December 1976, pp.26–30

Mary Stofflet, "Miriam Schapiro", *Arts Magazine*, li, May 1977, p.12

Donald Kuspit, "Interview with Miriam Schapiro", *Art in America*, lxv, September 1977, p.83

Eleanor Munro, *Originals: American Women Artists*, New York: Simon and Schuster, 1979

John Perreault, "The new decorativeness", *Portfolio*, June–July 1979, pp.46–51

Jim Collins and Glenn B. Opitz, eds, *Women Artists in America*, revised edition, Poughkeepsie, NY: Apollo, 1980

Miriam Schapiro: A Retrospective, 1953-1980, exh. cat., College of Wooster Art Museum, Wooster, OH, and elsewhere, 1980

Norma Broude, "Miriam Schapiro and 'femmage': Reflections on the conflict between decoration and abstraction in twentieth-century art", *Arts Magazine*, liv, February 1980, pp.83–7; reprinted in *Feminism and Art History: Questioning the Litany*, ed. Norma Broude and Mary D. Garrard, New York: Harper, 1982, pp.315–29

Charlotte Streifer Rubinstein, *American Women Artists from Early Times to the Present*, Boston: Hall, 1982

Elizabeth Frank, "Miriam Schapiro: Formal sentiments", *Art in America*, lxx, May 1982, pp.106–11

Paula Bradley, *Miriam Schapiro: The Feminist Transformation of an Avant-Garde Artist*, PhD dissertation, University of North Carolina, Chapel Hill, 1983

Charlotte Robinson, ed., *The Artist and the Quilt*, New York: Knopf, 1983

Miriam Schapiro: Femmages, 1971-1985, exh. cat., Brentwood Gallery, St Louis, 1985

Katherine M. Duncan, "The early work of Miriam Schapiro: The beginnings of reconciliation between the artist and the woman", *Athanor*, v, 1986, pp.43–51

"I'm Dancing as Fast as I Can": New Paintings by Miriam Schapiro, exh. cat., Bernice Steinbaum Gallery, New York, 1986

Thalia Gouma-Peterson, "The theater of life and illusion in Miriam Schapiro's recent work", *Arts Magazine*, lx, March 1986, pp.38–43

Susan Gill, "From 'femmage' to figuration", *Art News*, lxxxv, April 1986, pp.94–101

Christy Sheffield Sanford and Enid Shomer, "An interview with Miriam Schapiro", *Women Artists News*, xi, Spring 1986, pp.22–6

Daniel Wheeler, *Art since Mid-Century: 1945 to the Present*, Englewood Cliffs, NJ: Prentice Hall, and London: Thames and Hudson, 1991

Norma Broude and Mary D. Garrard, eds, *The Power of Feminist Art: The American Movement of the 1970s*, New York: Abrams, and London: Thames and Hudson, 1994

Miriam Schapiro's Collaboration Series: "Mother Russia", exh. cat., Steinbaum Krauss Gallery, New York, 1994

Lucy R. Lippard, *The Pink Glass Swan: Selected Essays on Feminist Art*, New York: New Press, 1995

Wendy Slatkin, *Women Artists in History: From Antiquity to the Present*, 3rd edition, Englewood Cliffs, NJ: Prentice Hall, 1997

Typically identified as a feminist artist whose art is described as "decorative", Miriam Schapiro's recent work has concentrated on explorations of larger questions of how artists relate to their immediate society. One of the first artists to investigate the potential of non-traditional materials, she adapted the visual language of Abstract Expressionism to her increasingly strong statements about issues of particular concern to women artists working in an artistic tradition established by men. Schapiro's art offers a profoundly human social statement that inevitably raises it above the level of mere feminist expression.

Beginning her career during the 1950s when Abstract Expressionism dominated Western art, Schapiro explored both

Schapiro: *Anatomy of a Kimono*, installation view, 1975–6; acrylic and patterned fabric on canvas; 200 × 1590 cm.; Courtesy Galerie Bischofberger, Zürich

figural and landscape themes in the context of this avant-garde style. She was an acknowledged member of the "second generation" of the New York School, and her paintings *Bouquet*, *Idyll No.1* and *Idyll No.2* were included in the *New Talent* exhibition in 1957 at the Museum of Modern Art, New York. At her first solo show at the prestigious André Emmerich Gallery in 1958, she exhibited *By the Sea*, *Nightwood* and *Fanfare*. This was followed in 1960 by a second solo show of Abstract Expressionist paintings of film stars and tropical gardens at the same gallery. That same year she was included in the *Woman Artists* exhibition at Dord Fitz Gallery, Texas, with 19 artists including Elaine de Kooning (q.v.), Helen Frankenthaler (q.v.) and Louise Nevelson (q.v.).

During the late 1960s, and coinciding with the early stages of the women's movement, Schapiro immersed herself and her art in feminist purpose. Her large painting *OX* (1967; Museum of Contemporary Art, Los Angeles) became the banner for the Women's Movement in California where she and her husband were teaching at the University of San Diego. Thalia Gouma-Peterson explained that the "O", the nucleus of *OX*, is the egg transformed into an octagon, exposing its own cavity and extending dynamically outwards in the outstretched limbs of the "X" (Wooster 1980). Schapiro herself considered this painting to be the final resolution of her identity crisis and formal proclamation that a woman is capable of male-associated assertiveness and logical reasoning in a woman's body.

Schapiro was among the first artists to recognise the artistic potential of the computer, producing Hard Edge computerised paintings that communicated her newly awakened feminist intentions effectively. In 1970 she collaborated with the physicist David Nalibof to program perspective images into a computer, creating forms reminiscent of *OX* and later described by Barbara Rose as "abstract illusionism". The result was a series of large (1.02 × 1.27 m.) computerised images painted in enamel on magna on canvas.

In 1971 Schapiro was appointed, with Judy Chicago, to teach at the California Institute of the Arts where the two artists exchanged ideas, initiated the Feminist Art Program and collaborated with students and several other Los Angeles artists to produce *Womanhouse* (1972; Institute of the Arts, Valencia). This project consisted of converting an abandoned house into a space in which feelings, fantasies and fears about being women who were also artists could be expressed in visual terms. The house was designed to embody all the diverse ideas of the artists who worked on it, and it included works in the tradition of crafts, quilts and other examples of the anonymous expressions created by women throughout history. The challenge for women artists during this period of embryonic feminism was to expand the definitions of art by exploring alternative approaches and by experimenting with materials from the domestic realm instead of traditional oil paint on canvas or bronze sculpture. She asserted that feminism had taught her not to worry about what she was "allowed" or "not allowed" to do.

Aligned with the *Womanhouse* project, Schapiro and Sherry Brody worked on the *Dollhouse* (1972; artist's collection), a miniature three-dimensional construction with six rooms, each of which contained a specific political message. The form of the dollhouse, chosen for its insignificance, provided an arena in which to explore the symbol of house as woman and to connect the triviality of interior decoration with artistic purposes. The *Dollhouse*, too, was a mixed-media construction that included a variety of non-art materials. In her unabashed use of fabric, wood and paper, and techniques that included stitching and pasting, Schapiro contributed to the ever-widening range of artistic approaches.

In 1975 Schapiro returned to New York where she continued to make statements about women's issues with complex collages in which she included a wide range of materials. The large *Anatomy of a Kimono* (1975–6; see illustration) is an example of the bold imagery that came out of her association with West Coast artists with feminist concerns. *Anatomy of a Kimono*, an architectural construction combining fabric collage and painting, developed from the earlier "Femmages" that emphasised themes and materials associated primarily with women.

Schapiro defined collage, explored during the early 20th century by Pablo Picasso, Wassily Kandinsky and Henri

Matisse, as "pictures assembled from assorted materials". Femmage, she asserted, described the activity, appropriated by modernist artists, that women had practised for centuries as quilting, brocade, appliqué and embroidery. By working with fabric swatches and embroidery techniques, Schapiro established a connection with a tradition that preceded modernist collage and one that is more authentic to purposes shared by many contemporary women artists. In *Anatomy of a Kimono*, for example, she employed monumental scale to emphasise ideas previously dismissed as irrelevant to mainstream artistic developments. Women, Schapiro believes, have always been creative and able to "make something out of nothing", but the results of their efforts have rarely been valued. Schapiro's femmage aesthetic is demonstrated in the large *Barcelona Fan* (1979; 1.83 × 3.66 m.; Howard Kalka and Stephen M. Jacobson), a fan-shaped canvas as support for acrylic paint and sheer fabric. *Wonderland* (1983; 2.5 × 4 m.; Bernice Steinbaum Gallery, New York) is an even more complex acrylic and fabric collage on canvas that combines old Australian needlework, crocheted aprons and embroidered handkerchiefs.

When a search for reproductions of the work of women artists in history for her *Collaboration* series (1974) yielded only a few examples by artists such as Angelica Kauffman (q.v.), Mary Cassatt (q.v.) and Berthe Morisot (q.v.), Schapiro realised that most women artists had been excluded from the art-historical record. Textbooks used for survey classes in art history rarely, if ever, introduced women artists to beginning students. Infuriated, she raised the issue with the board of the College Art Association, of which she was a member, arguing effectively for awareness of the need for wider historical coverage. She has also served on the governing board of the Women's Caucus for Art, is a founding member of the Feminist Art Institute in New York, and has lectured widely on feminist issues and feminist education at conferences, colleges, universities and for various professional associations. Later work includes *Wonderland* (1983; Bernice Steinbaum Gallery), an acrylic and fabric collage on canvas. In this, and other works, she continues to explore the additive and inclusive methods that emerged during the collaborations of the 1970s but that became cool and austere in works such as *Heartland* (1985; Bernice Steinbaum Gallery). During her career, Miriam Schapiro has successfully synthesised abstraction and feminist iconography to comment on the history of civilisation from a fresh perspective.

MARY F. FRANCEY

Schendel, Mira (Hargersheimer)
Brazilian artist, 1919–1988

Born in Zürich, Switzerland, 1919; later became a Brazilian citizen. Studied philosophy in Milan, where her family had moved when she was a child. Began to concentrate seriously on art in 1949, after moving to Pôrto Alegre, southern Brazil; encouraged to paint by artist Sérgio Camargo. Moved to São Paulo, 1952, but remained detached from Brazilian Constructivist movement. Recipient of first prize, Salón de Arte Moderno, El Salvador, 1953; gold medal, New Delhi

Triennial, India, 1971; best object of the year, Associação Paulista de Criticos de Arte, São Paulo, 1973; acquisition prizes at Salão de Arte Moderna, São Paulo, 1963, and São Paulo Bienal, 1967 and 1969. Died in São Paulo, 1988.

Selected Individual Exhibitions
Museu de Arte Moderna, São Paulo: 1954
Galeria Adorno, Rio de Janeiro: 1960
Galeria Selearte, São Paulo: 1962
Galeria São Luis, São Paulo: 1963
Galeria Astréia, São Paulo: 1964
Petit Galerie, Rio de Janeiro: 1965
Museu de Arte Moderna, Rio de Janeiro: 1966
Signals Gallery, London: 1966
Galeria Bucholz, Lisbon: 1966
Technische Hochschule, Stuttgart: 1967
Gromholt Galleri, Oslo: 1968
St Stephan Gallerie, Vienna: 1968
Gallerie bei Minoritensaal, Graz: 1969
Galeria Ralph Camargo, São Paulo: 1972
Brazilian-American Cultural Institute, Washington, DC: 1973
Schmidtbank-Galerie, Nuremberg: 1974
Gabinete de Artes Gráficas, São Paulo: 1975
Galeria Cosme Velho, São Paulo: 1978, 1980
Galeria Luisa Strina, São Paulo: 1981, 1983
Paulo Figueiredo Galeria de Arte, São Paulo: 1982, 1985
GB Arte, Rio de Janeiro: 1982
Gabinete de Arte Raquel Arnaud, São Paulo: 1987
São Paulo Bienal: 1994 (retrospective)

Bibliography
David Medalla, *Signals Newsbulletin*, London, 1966
Aracy Amaral, "Mira Schendel: Os cadernos", *Arte e meio artístico (1961–1981): Entre a feijoada e o x-burguer*, São Paulo: Nobel, 1982, pp.183–5
Mira Schendel, exh. cat., Paulo Figueiredo Galeria de Arte, São Paulo, 1982
Mira Schendel: Pinturas recentes, exh. cat., Paulo Figueiredo Galeria de Arte, São Paulo, 1985
Modernidade: Art brésilien du 20e siècle, exh. cat., Musée d'Art Moderne de la Ville de Paris, 1987
Projeto arte brasileira: Abstração geométrica 2, Rio de Janeiro: FUNARTE/Instituto Nacional de Artes Plásticas, 1988
Art in Latin America: The Modern Era, 1820–1980, exh. cat., South Bank Centre, London, and elsewhere, 1989
Mira Schendel, exh. cat., Museu de Arte Contemporânea, Universidade de São Paulo, 1990
Brasil: Segni d'arte: Libri e video, 1950–1993, exh. cat., Fondazione Scientifica Querini-Stampalia, Venice, and elsewhere, 1993
Latin American Artists of the Twentieth Century, exh. cat., Museum of Modern Art, New York, 1993
Ultramodern: The Art of Contemporary Brazil, exh. cat., National Museum of Women in the Arts, Washington, DC, 1993
Mira Schendel, unpublished exh. cat., São Paulo Bienal, 1994

Personally reserved and solitary as an artist, Mira Schendel did not belong to the Brazilian avant-garde Concretist or Neo-concretist movements, although her name is often linked to both. Her work touched on many of the themes explored by these groups, such as space-time, the status of the object and spectator participation. The development of her work from painting to sculpture, to objects, to installations, to demateri-alised art parallels that of other Brazilian artists, but it assumed a distinctive position. Little has been written about Schendel mainly because conceptual work by South American artists is often seen as derivative of New York and Europe, rather than

Schendel: *Droguinhas (Little Scraps, Nothings, Junk)*, 1964–5; knotted Japanese rice paper; left, diameter 28 cm., right (detail), 90 × 90 cm. (approx); Collection Guy Brett, London

as part of a strong indigenous intellectual avant-garde (Sterling in Washington 1993, p.12; Amaral in New York 1993, p.97).

Schendel, whose reading included Heidegger, Kierkegaard and Hermann Schmitz, began studying philosophy in Milan where her family moved when she was a child. She established herself as an artist in Brazil in the 1950s, living most of the time in São Paulo, where she produced her major works. She lived briefly in London in 1966, where she had a solo exhibition at the short-lived Signals gallery, directed by Paul Keeler and David Medalla.

The works of the early 1950s were simultaneously rigorous and speculative, precise and spontaneous, geometrical yet with an expressive character. They were constructions that escaped from the geometric constraints we expect from orthodox Constructivism. Their rigour is not geometric but conceptual. They have a sense of order, but an unorthodox order that cannot be totally separated from an existential perception of the world and its forms. Her search for order is quite distinct from the positivist rationalism of the São Paulo Concretists in this period.

Schendel was one of the first Brazilian artists to explore the passage from planar to spatial, adding a third dimension to her paintings (*Untitled*, 1954; Collection Adolpho Leirner, repr. *Projeto arte brasileira* 1988, p.35). The meticulously treated surface in subtle sombre colours interacts with the abstract geometric forms that project into space. The physicality of

Schendel's works, her use of materials including earth, rice paper, acrylic, plaster and wood, differs from that of such Neo-concrete artists as Lygia Clark (q.v.) and Lygia Pape (q.v.). Her reduction of the visual elements (colour, line, space, shape) is balanced by a scrupulous surface treatment, and she explored the relations of equivalence (tension, intensity, rhythm and amplitude) to reduce language to the elemental. As in oriental philosophy, signs become more expressive and meaningful in their bareness than the elaborations of conventional rhetoric. The ultimate reduction of language, Schendel's poetry is a poetry of silence.

A large series of works on rice paper produced in the mid-1960s marked a turning point for Schendel. They are a kind of monotype, produced by using a stylus to mark the surface of the extremely fragile paper, which is then "printed" on a metal or glass plate covered by paint (private collections, repr. London 1989, pp.274–5; New York 1993, p.327).

The imposition of the narrative on viewers, inviting them to make their own process of discovery through the immateriality of the exquisitely subtle drawings, reached its peak in *Droguinhas* (private collections, repr. London 1989, p.275; New York 1993, p.327; see illustration), a series of ephemeral sculptures. The *Droguinhas* ("little nothings") could be seen as an expression of Schendel's adherence to the philosophy of Heidegger, imbued with an existential anguish that cannot be "separated from an extremely subtle social viewpoint". They could be seen as a silent response to the ideology of progress that moved both the frenetic, turbulent, mechanised life of São Paulo and the military dictatorship imposed on the Brazilians in 1964. *Droga* is an "irate and depreciative term for an undesired thing or situation, something irritating", although its diminutive form, *Droguinha*, has connotations of something of no importance. The significance of these sculptures is in their precarious, fragile and ephemeral character. They are like open propositions whose physicality and presence are merely an excuse to bring the viewer to interact with them, to rearrange them in infinite ways, as one chooses (Herkenhoff in Washington 1993, pp.48–50).

Another series from the 1960s, the *Cadernos* ("notebooks"; private collections, repr. Venice 1993, p.33) are almost indescribable. Schendel created an individual syntax based on psychoanalysis and philosophy, logic and intuition, metaphysics and mathematics, and presented it through her multisensorial – visual and tactile – notebooks. The *Cadernos* are made of rectangular or square sheets of paper bound with plastic-coated coloured cardboards. She used paper of different textures, thicknesses, degrees of transparency and qualities – card, tracing paper, chrome-coated paper – and some are perforated, offering multiple views through the pages. The viewer is intended to browse through these little treasures, to participate in the play proposed by the artist, to discover the particular logic/illogic of each notebook. The words and graphic signs never make figurative references, they are mental signs, although visible – letraset letters and numbers, a fusion of thought and image. The choice of materials is also based on individual themes: "e and é" (*and* and *being*); "n = 0"; "p that becomes q". What is emphasised in these works is the concept "that represents a reality, but it is not a mirror" (Schendel in Amaral 1982).

Also in the 1960s she produced the *Objetos graficos*, drawings placed between two acrylic plates; the *Trenzinhos* (Small trains), an extended wire with sheets of rice paper fastened to a stick (private collections, repr. Medalla 1966); and the *Ondas paradas de probabilidade* (Waves of probability paralysed in the air), an installation of very thin nylon wires that hung from ceiling to floor (São Paulo Bienal 1969). In the 1970s she made a new edition of the *Objetos graficos*, using white letraset letters applied to acrylic circles hanging from the ceiling (*Circular Graphic*, Collection Ricardo Takeschi Akagawa, repr. Washington 1993, p.49).

From the mid-1970s Schendel resumed drawing and the use of colour and created small pieces (*Untitled*, 1973; mixed media; Collection Gilberto Chateaubriand; *Small Bits Series*, 1972; mixed media on rice paper; Collection Ada C. Dub Schendel Bento, *ibid.*, p.50). Subsequently, she changed medium and dimension to work on huge paintings, returning to some of the ideas from earlier works. During this period she made a series of paintings in tempera with gold (1979–86); *Sarafos* ("slats", from 1987), a series using brick dust; and an unfinished series *Mais ou menos frutas*. Also in the 1980s she worked on a series of visual interpretations of the *I Ching*.

Schendel's trajectory, from her first paintings in the 1950s, through the rice-paper drawings, the ephemeral paper sculptures, the notebooks, paper objects, graphic objects in space and the installations of the 1960s, to her resumption of painting in the 1980s is a philosophical exploration of the limits of art, presented through a dialectic that re-affirms art while appearing to deny it, to explore the limited horizons of the art of the past within the new unlimited horizon of art. Referring to her work *Cantos dos Jovens – a proposito de Stockhausen* (1964; VII Bienal of São Paulo), Schendel said:

> ... asceticism is always presented to us as something detached from the world. However, there are different kinds of asceticism, such as the tantra asceticism, for example, which is extremely sensuous and sensorial ... A good example of this is Stockhausen's work, in which you find an extraordinary restraint, but at the end of the piece a cosmic explosion occurs [Schendel quoted in São Paulo 1994, from "Interview with Jorge Guinle", 1981].

PAULA TERRA CABO

Schjerfbeck, Helene
Finnish painter, 1862–1946

Born Helena Sofia Schjerfbeck in Helsinki, 10 July 1862; later changed the spelling of her name from Helena to Helene. Hip injury at the age of four; suffered from ill health for the rest of her life. Studied at the Finnish Art Society drawing school, Helsinki, 1873–7 (scholarship 1877); Adolf von Becker's private art academy, Helsinki, 1877–9. Recipient of Finnish Imperial Senate travel grant, 1880; scholarship, 1881. Studied at Académie Colarossi, Paris, under Gustave Courtois and others, 1881–4; copied paintings in the Louvre, particularly works by Velázquez; lived and studied in France and Britain during most of the 1880s, spending time at the artists' colonies at Concarneau and Pont-Aven, Brittany, and St Ives, Cornwall; also visited Italy and St Petersburg. Taught painting at the Finnish Art Society drawing school, Helsinki, 1892–1902 (resigned because of failing health). Stayed in Florence, Italy, 1894. Lived in Hyvinkää, 1902–25; Tammisaari, 1925–41. Between 1939 and 1944 moved to several different places in southern Finland due to the Winter War and World War II. Moved to Saltsjöbaden, near Stockholm, February 1944. Recipient of Finnish State second prize in genre painting, 1882 and 1886; Order of the White Rose of Finland, 1920; Artists and Writers Foundation pension, 1921. Foreign member of the Academy of Free Arts, Royal Academy of Fine Arts, Stockholm, 1942. Died at Saltsjöbaden, 23 January 1946; buried in Helsinki.

Principal Exhibitions

Individual

Stenman Gallery, Helsinki: 1917
Liljevalchs Konsthall, Stockholm: 1934 (with Hannes Autere, Marcus Collin and T.K. Sallinen)
Stenmans Galleri, Stockholm: 1937, 1938, 1939, 1940, 1942, 1944, 1946 (touring retrospective)

Group

Finnish Art Society, Helsinki: occasionally 1879–1946 (third prize 1879)
Paris Salon: 1883–4, 1888
Exposition Universelle, Paris: 1889 (first-class bronze medal)
Institute of Painters in Oils, London: 1889
Turku Art Society: occasionally 1891–1941

Ateneum, Helsinki: 1905 (women artists)
Friends of Finnish Handicraft: 1905, 1908–9, 1911
Malmö: 1914 (*Baltiska utställningen* [Baltic exposition])
Liljevalchs Konsthall, Stockholm: 1916 (*Finsk konst* [Finnish art]),
    1929 (*Finlands nutida konst* [Contemporary Finnish art])

Selected Writings

"Helene Schjerfbeck: Seitsemän kirjettä Maria Wiikille" [Helene
    Schjerfbeck: Seven letters to Maria Wiik], ed. Kaarina Calonius,
    Suomen taiteen vuosikirja 1946 [Yearbook of Finnish Art 1946],
    Poorvoo, 1946, pp.48–69

Bibliography

H. Ahtela [Einar Reuter], *Helena Schjerfbeck*, Helsinki, 1917
Helena Schjerfbeck, 1879–1917, exh. cat., Stenman Gallery, Helsinki,
    1917
Helena Westermarck, *Mina levnadsminnen* [My memoirs], Åbo, 1941
Hanna and Eilif Appelberg, *Helene Schjerfbeck: En biografisk
    konturteckning* [Helene Schjerfbeck: A biographical outline],
    Helsinki, 1949
H. Ahtela [Einar Reuter], *Helena Schjerfbeck: Kamppailu kauneud-
    esta* [Helena Schjerfbeck: The struggle for beauty], Porvoo:
    Söderström, 1951; Swedish edition, Stockholm: Rabén & Sjögren,
    1953
John Boulton Smith, *The Golden Age of Finnish Art: Art Nouveau
    and the National Spirit*, 2nd edition, Helsinki: Otava, 1985
*Dreams of a Summer Night: Scandinavian Painting at the Turn of the
    Century*, exh. cat., Arts Council of Great Britain, London, 1986
Lena Holger, *Helene Schjerfbeck: Liv och konstnärskap* [Helene
    Schjerfbeck: Life and art), Stockholm: Ekdahl, Pettersson &
    Winbladh, 1987
Riitta Konttinen, "Finska konstnärinnors, 1880-tal: Ljus, luft och
    färg" [Finnish women artists in the 1880s: Light, air and colour],
    De drogo till Paris: Nordiska konstnärinnor på 1880-talet [They
    went to Paris: Nordic women artists in the 1880s], exh. cat.,
    Liljevalchs Konsthall, Stockholm, 1988, pp.220–53
——, *Suomalaisia naistaiteilijointa 1880-luvulta* [Finnish women
    artists in the 1880s], Helsinki, 1988
Kirk Varnedoe, *Northern Light: Nordic Art at the Turn of the
    Century*, New Haven and London: Yale University Press, 1988
Denise Delouche, "Helene Schjerfbeck: Les funérailles à Pont-Aven,
    1884", *Artistes étrangers à Pont-Aven, Concarneau et autres lieux
    de Bretagne*, Rennes, 1989
Helene Schjerfbeck: Finland's Modernist Rediscovered, exh. cat.,
    Finnish National Gallery Ateneum, Helsinki, Phillips Collection,
    Washington, DC, and elsewhere, 1992
Lena Holger, *Helene Schjerfbeck: Teckningar och akvareller* [Helene
    Schjerfbeck: Drawings and watercolours], Stockholm, 1994
Michelle Facos, "Helene Schjerfbeck's self-portraits: Revelation and
    dissimulation", *Woman's Art Journal*, xvi/1, 1995, pp.12–17

Schjerfbeck: *Self-Portrait with Palette*, 1937; Moderna
Museet, Stockholm

The Finnish artist Helene Schjerfbeck is one of the links in the
enormous transformation that took place in art at the turn of
the 19th and 20th centuries, from realism to modernism and
abstraction. She started her training as an artist at a very early
age. In 1873 she entered the drawing school in Helsinki aged
eleven, some six or seven years younger than the other pupils,
and soon became the best of them. Her family could not afford
her education, but she received a grant. At the age of 16 she
won a prize at the annual exhibition. Her first known *Self-
Portrait* (Museet Ett Hem, Turku), a black-and-white crayon
drawing of 1878, belongs to this period. It shows a curly-
haired, good-looking girl. Schjerfbeck's talented and strong
pencil work is already apparent.

Schjerfbeck shows how art can be non-realistic without
compromising naturalism. Beginning in the 1880s, using

French subjects, Schjerfbeck followed naturalism, which
focuses on the personal rather than the general, but she
tempered it with the outlines of modern art. In all her portraits
the spiritual dimensions of the human mind are made visible,
as in the boy *Woodcutter II* (1911; Turun Taidemuseo, Turku)
and *Stubborn Girl* of 1939. Schjerfbeck painted her sitters as if
the light were coming from inside them, as if they were their
own lamps. Her technique minimalises. She takes more and
more details away, yet there is still a sense of growth in what
is left. The series of self-portraits painted between 1942 and
1945, when she was in her old age, is particularly raw and
gripping – she painted these images as if to surprise even
herself.

With the economic development and internationalisation of
the Nordic countries at the turn of the 19th and 20th centuries,
art and women's education became acceptable, and Finnish
women were the first in Europe to be enfranchised (1906). This
was accompanied by a demand for freedom in all areas of life
– in society, in religion and in dress. Women cut their hair,
shortened their skirts to the knee and even wore trousers. This
is not to say that everyone did, nor that Schjerfbeck did – she
was brought up two generations earlier – but these things now
became possible, and gave both society and art a certain
freedom. In Nordic literature these social changes first became
apparent in works by the Danish literary critic Georg Brandes
and by his friend the Swedish writer Ernst Ahlgren, a pseudonym for Victoria Benedictsson, in her novels *Pengar* (Money;
1885) and *Fru Marianne* (Mrs Marianne; 1887); in Norway by

Henrik Ibsen's *Et dukkehjem* (A doll's house; 1879) and in Sweden by August Strindberg's *Ett drömspel* (A dream play; 1902). They all discussed the status of women in society, fought against conservatism and declared that women had a right to their own intellectual opinions and, at least in theory, to work with equal status to men, especially in the arts.

Schjerfbeck read these books and started a series of portraits of working women, with whom she wished to identify. The first of these, *The Seamstress* (1903–5; Ateneum, Helsinki), shows a seated woman, painted in sharp profile, taking a rest from her work. She is dressed in black, in contrast to the red of the rocking chair. The pause from work is almost over, and the figure is preparing to rise. Schjerfbeck's concept of modernism was simplicity. She formed no details if her eye did not register them when she first conceived of her idea. She focused on her subject, saw the basic concept of the form and noticed the crucial details – which is why her model here is equipped with a pair of scissors, the seamstress's tool, hanging on a green band from her waist. Later, in 1927, when she made a second free version of *The Seamstress* (private collection, Finland), Schjerfbeck narrowed her interest to the sitter's face and upper body, painting a half-length portrait. Her focus had changed, and women had obtained some rights in society as well. She concentrated her attention on problems of form, as Picasso, for example, had done ten years earlier, showing that she was well aware of the discourses in European art. The same process, focused on line and form, is also apparent when in 1927 she made a second version of her colouristic and sensitive *Convalescent* (first version, 1888; Ateneum; second version, private collection, Sweden). The first version, her best-known painting from her realist period, was exhibited at the Paris Salon of 1888 and the Exposition Universelle of 1889. By the time she made the second version, she was more than 60 years old, free in her mind and at last accepted as an artist by the art world. When her mother died in 1923 Schjerfbeck was also free to move, and from 1925 lived by the sea in the small town of Tammisaari (Ekenäs); for the first time she had her own studio.

Schjerfbeck is best known for her self-portraits, her still lifes and to some extent for her landscape paintings. These were all ordinary subjects for an artist of the time, but are different when interpreted by Schjerfbeck's sensitive talent. She would use still-life motifs to find out what time did to the shape and colour of a fruit or a flower. In *Market Apple* (1927; private collection, Finland) she painted a red volume on a green surface, two complementary colours, so that the apple looks as if it is flying. In *Lemons in a Wooden Bowl* (1934–44; private collection, Sweden) the motifs appear to be suspended on the canvas, while in *Still Life in Green* (1932; Ateneum) some pears are turning black because the painting took too long – the putrefaction process had already started. Schjerfbeck's still lifes are sensual, fresh and exquisite.

In the years around 1900 Finland was struggling for autonomy in the face of pressure from the Russian government. In countries with low populations women as well as men are resources in the fight for independence. Strong women artists, such as Schjerfbeck's closest friend Helena Westermarck, also a writer and champion of women's rights, played a prominent role. In Brittany Schjerfbeck captured the sitter's strong character in the expressionistic *Helena Westermarck in Profile*

(1884; Gösta Serlachiuksen Taidemuseo, Mänttä), painted in plein air. In 1907 Westermarck bought Schjerfbeck's painting of an *Old Woman* (1905; private collection, Finland), in which the artist gave a personal face to the fighting spirit of a proud Finnish woman, a mother and grandmother, sitting upright in front of the woods. But Schjerfbeck herself was not active in the women's rights movement. Her letters show that although she did have some reflections on the subject, what she wanted most was to be accepted as an independent artist by her family, her friends and the Finnish art world. But it was not until 1915 that the Finnish Art Society commissioned her self-portrait for their collection (*Self-Portrait with Black Background*, 1915; Ateneum; repr. Facos 1995, cover).

Schjerfbeck had close friendships with three women artists, whom she called "my painting sisters". All three – Maria Wiik (q.v.), Ada Thilén and Westermarck – had Swedish as their mother tongue, and they derived strength from each other. They met at the Finnish Art Society drawing school and from time to time a pair of them would share a studio in France or Finland and make study trips together. None of them was married. It was not that Schjerfbeck did not like men – in her twenties she had been engaged to a British painter, and there were later two other serious relationships with men – but she decided to live alone, even if this decision was not entirely her own. In 1918, when she was 54, she painted in light colours a portrait of *The Sailor*, a young, muscular and good-looking man wearing a tight shirt and bearing a cautious smile. The model was the writer and artist Einar Reuter, with whom she stayed friends all her life. As early as 1888 she had written to Wiik about being an artist and being married: "They say she had to marry because she did not get on with her painting. If only being alone would help!" (Åbo Akademi, Turku). Schjerfbeck could not compromise, and her love for art dictated her priorities.

The painting sisters got to know other women artists, particularly in Paris, and visited them in their home countries, which introduced them to new ideas. Thilén, for example, painted in Norway with the Norwegian artist Kitty Kielland (q.v.), and Schjerfbeck went to England with the Austrian painter Marianne Stokes (q.v.). She also portrayed Stokes at the Académie Colarossi in Paris, with the light on her back and her hair formed into a halo (1881; *Two Profiles*; Ateneum). In 1889 Wiik followed Schjerfbeck to England, where they used the same old woman as a model, Schjerfbeck in *Autumn Rose* and Wiik in *Out in the World* (both Ateneum). The women all travelled a great deal, and in 1894 Schjerfbeck stayed in Florence, where she studied the work of Italian Renaissance painters and of Titian, and shared a studio for some months with another Finnish painter, Ellen Thesleff (q.v.), in the cloister of San Marco. They studied Fra Angelico's frescoes and were both influenced by the Symbolist movement. Schjerfbeck's awareness of the special Italian silver light is seen in *Fiesole Landscape* (private collection, Finland).

Some years later Schjerfbeck painted *Old Manor House* (1901; Åbo Konstmuseum, Turku), one of her few paintings in the Symbolist style. By that time she had nearly finished her teaching career at her old drawing school in Helsinki, which had reduced her own painting opportunities. She meant a great deal to some of her pupils, notably Sigrid Schauman, but she had little influence on the younger generation until after the 1930s.

From 1900 Schjerfbeck stayed in Finland, until she was forced to go to Sweden in 1944, as a result of World War II. In 1913 she was visited by the Finnish-Swedish art dealer Gösta Stenman, who organised her first solo exhibition in 1917 in Helsinki, but she was not well known until he presented her work to a wider public, starting in Sweden in 1937. In 1938–9, on Stenman's initiative, she made six lithographic prints, her only ones, incorporating motifs from her paintings.

Schjerfbeck developed an ascetic and almost abstract style in contact with the traditions of European modernism, known to her after the turn of the century only through magazines, art books and the reports of friends. She painted mostly in a soft and temperate, but fastidious, colouring, with a strong outline, pointing to the essentials in the work. During her lifetime Schjerfbeck was overshadowed by such male artists as the Finnish painters Albert Edelfelt, for a time also her teacher, and Akseli Gallen-Kallela, whose work was more nationalistic in character. Today her work, with that of the Norwegian Expressionist artist Edvard Munch, is considered to be the most important in Nordic art. Schjerfbeck is represented in a number of Finnish museums, as well as, in Scandinavia, the Nasjonalgalleriet, Oslo; Göteborgs Konstmuseum, Göteborg; Malmö Museum; Moderna Museet and Nationalmuseum, Stockholm.

LENA HOLGER

Schneemann, Carolee
American artist, 1939–

Born in Fox Chase, Pennsylvania, 12 October 1939. Studied at Universidad de Puebla, Mexico; New School for Social Research, New York; Columbia University School of Painting and Sculpture, New York; Bard College, Annandale-on-Hudson (BA); University of Illinois, Urbana (MFA). Settled in New York, 1962. Founder-director, Kinetic Theater movement and design workshops, New York, 1963–8; founder-member, International-Local group, New York, 1976. Taught at University of Illinois, Urbana, 1961–2; artist-in-residence, Colby College, Waterville, Maine, 1968; Dartington College, Totnes, Devon, 1972. Recipient of National Endowment for the Arts (NEA) grants, 1974, 1977, 1978 and 1983; Creative Artists Public Service (CAPS) grant, 1978; Guggenheim fellowship, 1993. Lives in New York.

Principal Exhibitions

Individual
Artist's Studio, New York: 1962, 1963, 1964
University Art Museum, University of California, Berkeley: 1974
Galerie De Appel, Amsterdam: 1979
Real Art Ways, Hartford, CT: 1981
Max Hutchinson Gallery, New York: 1982, 1983, 1985
New Music America, Miami: 1988
Emily Harvey Gallery, New York: 1990
Penine Hart Gallery, New York: 1994
Kunstraum, Vienna: 1995
New Museum of Contemporary Art, New York: 1996 (retrospective)

Group
Sculpture Center, New York: 1984 (Sound Art)
Milwaukee Art Museum: 1995 (Neo-Dada: Redefining Art, touring)

Selected Writings
Parts of a Body House Book, Cullompton, Devon: Beau Geste Press, 1972
Cézanne: She Was a Great Painter: Essays on History, Sexuality and Naming: Unbroken Words to Women, New Paltz, NY: Trespuss Press, 1975
Cézanne: She Was a Great Painter: The Second Book, January 1975: Unbroken Words to Women, Sexuality Creativity Language Art History, New Paltz, NY: Trespuss Press, 1975
Up To and Including Her Limits, privately printed, 1978
More than Meat Joy: Complete Performance Works and Selected Writings, ed. Bruce McPherson, New Paltz, NY: Documentext, 1979
The Recent History and Destruction of Lebanon: A Research Extract, privately printed, 1983
Carolee Schneemann: Early and Recent Work, New Paltz, NY: Documentext, 1983
"The obscene body/politic", Art Journal, l, Winter 1991, pp.28–35

Bibliography
Ann Sargent-Wooster, "Carolee Schneemann", Artforum, xiv, May 1976, pp.73–4
Ted Castle, "Carolee Schneemann: The woman who uses her body as her art", Artforum, xix, November 1980, pp.64–70
Daniel Cameron, "Object vs. persona: The early work of Carolee Schneemann", Arts Magazine, lvii, May 1983, pp.122–5
Scott Macdonald, "The men cooperated", Afterimage, xii, April 1985, pp.12–15
Udo Kultermann, "Die Performance-Art von Carolee Schneemann", Idea: Jahrbuch der Hamburger Kunsthalle, vi, 1987, pp.141–51
Barbara Smith, "On the body as material", Artweek, xxi, 4 October 1990, pp.24–5 (interview)
Andrea Juro and V. Vale, eds, Angry Women, San Francisco: Re/Search, 1991
Johannes Birringer, "Imprints and re-visions: Carolee Schneemann's visual archeology", Performance Art Journal, June 1993, pp.31–46
Norma Broude and Mary D. Garrard, eds, The Power of Feminist Art: The American Movement of the 1970s, New York: Abrams, and London: Thames and Hudson, 1994
Joanna Frueh, "The erotic as social security", Art Journal, liii/1, 1994, pp.66–72
Jay Murphy, Imaging Erotics: The Body Politics of Carolee Schneemann (in preparation)

A few memorable images from Carolee Schneemann's work of the 1960s and 1970s normally represent her oeuvre in overviews of the avant-garde work of that time: a naked, body-painted Schneemann boldly staring into the camera, ensconced in a multi-media environment, in Eye Body (1963; see illustration); Schneemann and other barely clad performers rolling about with chicken carcasses in Meat Joy (1964); Schneemann, again naked and body-painted, gradually un-twining a delicate paper scroll from her vagina, in Interior Scroll (1975). These and other works assure her place as a pioneering and influential figure in body art, performance art and experimental film.

Schneemann had been painting in a loosely expressionistic style before arriving in New York in 1962. Through the mid-1960s her paintings evolved into painted collages, boxed constructions and even kinetic works, whose complex surfaces have been compared to contemporary work by Robert

Schneemann: *Eye Body: 36 Transformative Actions for Camera*, 1963; performance: instantaneous interactions with paint, glue, fur, feathers, garden snakes, glass, plastic, etc.; photos on black-and-white 35 mm. film

Rauschenberg. They also bear the imprint of Joseph Cornell, whom she eventually met. The representative *Native Beauties* (1962–4; artist's collection), a collaged and constructed diptych, juxtaposes images of a Senegalese woman and Schneemann on a beach towel, with bits of driftwood, pebbles, glass and painted areas added.

Schneemann's breakthrough work *Eye Body* (1963) occurred when she felt the need to add her own body to an extensive loft environment of mirrors, rope, plastic and other materials, in a private performance recorded by a photographer. Of her painted body, she later wrote that it was both "erotic, sexual, desired, desiring" and also "written over in a text of stroke and gesture discovered by my creative female will" (*More than Meat Joy* 1979, p.52). The work's title, "Eye Body", nicely condenses a sense, running through much of her work, of the importance of a (specifically female) sensuous self-awareness as an instrument of knowing.

Meanwhile, Schneemann had already begun taking part in the fertile performance experimentation centred on the Judson Dance Theater. She participated in works with Robert Morris and Claes Oldenberg, and was choreographing works for groups of performers, including Yvonne Rainer (q.v.), Deborah Hay, Dorothea Rockburne (q.v.) and others, as early as 1962 (*Glass Environment for Sound and Motion*, Living Theater). *Meat Joy* (1964), the most shocking and ambitious of her large performances, was performed in Paris, London (its only all-nude performance) and New York. Conceived as having "the character of an erotic rite: excessive, indulgent, a celebration of flesh as material" (*ibid.*, p.63), the work involved its nine performers in planned but improvisational encounters with piles of shredded paper, flashlights, dead fish, chickens, chains of sausages and buckets of paint.

Schneemann began making films during this time, as well as incorporating film in some performances. *Viet-Flakes* (1965; distributed by Film-Makers Cooperative, New York) montaged and altered photographs from the Vietnam War; the performance *Snows* (New York, 1967) combined film clips, music and performers on a bright white stage to explore again the costs of that war. *Fuses* (1967; distributed by Film-Makers Cooperative) is a landmark erotic film by a woman artist. Observer and participant, Schneemann used a hand-held camera to film herself and her then-husband, James Tenney, making love; she then subjected the film to heat, acid, paint and scratching, a disordering and dismemberment analogous to the intensity of subjective sexual experience.

Two major performance works involved suspended bodies. In *Water Light/Water Needle* (1966) Schneemann and several other performers travelled along ropes suspended across the performance space. In *Up To And Including Her Limits* (first performed in New York, 1973) Schneemann dangled and swung, nude, in a leather harness, creating random markings on a papered stage. Daniel Cameron's observations apply well to such works: "She projects toward the viewer an intensely intimate persona, and then intercepts it with a formalized and/or chance activity that allows one to see the artist, as it were, through a screen of materiality" (Cameron 1983, p.125). *Interior Scroll* (1975), in which Schneemann read from a scroll while pulling it from her vagina, engaged a number of concepts: her own theory of "vulvic space", the sense of knowledge emerging from the body, and the symbology of the serpent.

Although Schneemann associated and performed with participants in the major performance movements of that time – Alan Kaprow and other makers of Happenings, the Vienna Group and Fluxus – she often felt isolated, unsupported in her own work, even rebuffed. Her relationship with Fluxus was particularly rocky. A work that she directed for Kaprow, part of Charlotte Moorman's New York Avant Garde Festival (*Push and Pull*, 1965), degenerated into chaos, damaging the theatre and ending with police intervention. Shortly after *Meat Joy* was performed, the Fluxus founder George Maciunas circulated a letter, warning that Schneemann was not to be considered a Fluxus artist, because of her eroticism and baroque tendencies. The unacknowledged sexism underlying such difficulties has been partly redressed by her inclusion in numerous recent retrospectives and anthologies devoted to Fluxus activity.

Although she abandoned large-scale performance in the mid-1970s, Schneemann has continued to produce mixed-media environmental works and performances that expand on her continuing themes. *Fresh Blood – A Dream Morphology* (1981–7) offered, through live performance and slide images, an exploration of menstruation, as multi-layered symbol and experience. *War Mop* (1986; artist's collection) responded to the civil war in Lebanon, with a motorised mop striking a television monitor playing images from the war. In *Cycladic Imprints* (1988; artist's collection, repr. David Joselit, "Projected identities", *Art in America*, lxxix, November 1991, p.120), with motorised violins and projected images of stringed instruments, Cycladic sculptures, hourglass-shaped objects, female bodies and genitals, Schneemann ironically reclaimed the Surrealist icon of woman-as-instrument. Her *Mortal Coils* (1994; artist's collection, repr. *Artforum*, xxxiii, September 1994, p.109), a kinetic and projected environment of similar scope, acted as a memorial, with images and written reminiscences of dead friends and colleagues, slithering motorised ropes as mortal coils and images of her own body.

Schneemann has written extensively and articulately about her work and other issues, notably in her compilation *More than Meat Joy* (1979). Her insistence on the interconnected validity of her "creative female will" and sexuality as a mode of perception and experience has under-girded a body of work that remains both disturbing and powerful.

MIRIAM SEIDEL

Schurman, Anna Maria van
Netherlandish amateur artist, 1607–1678

Born in Cologne, 1607, to Frederik van Schurman of Antwerp and his wife Eva von Harff de Dreiborn. Moved to Utrecht with her family, *c.*1616. Included in the register of the Guild of St Luke in Utrecht, 1643. Lived in Cologne, 1653–*c.*1655, then in the countryside near Vianen. Back in Utrecht by 1660; became a follower of the Protestant preacher Jean de Labadie; joined the Labadist community in Amsterdam, *c.*1669; moved with the community to Herford in Westphalia, then Altona and later Wieuwerd in Friesland. Died in Wieuwerd, 4 May 1678.

Selected Writings

De vitae humanae termino, Leiden, 1639; Paris, 1646

Dissertatio de ingenii muliebris ad doctrinam et meliores litteras aptitudine, Leiden: Elzevir, 1641; English edition as *The Learned Maid; or, Whether a Maid May Be a Scholar?*, London, 1659

Opuscula hebraeca, graeca, latina, gallica: Prosaica et metrica, Leiden: Elzevir, 1642; Utrecht, 1652; London, 1649; revised edition ed. Dorothea Loeber, Leipzig, 1749

Eukleria, seu melioris partis electio, Altona, 1673; Amsterdam: Van de Velde, 1684; reprinted Leeuwarden: De Tille, 1978

Bibliography

Una Birch, *Anna van Schurman: Artist, Scholar, Saint*, London: Longman, 1909

Katlijne Van der Stighelen, *Anna Maria van Schurman (1607–1678) of "Hoe hooge dat een maeght kan in de konsten stijgen"* [Anna Maria van Schurman (1607–1678) or "How high a maid may rise in art"], Louvain: Universitaire Pers Leuven, 1987

Mirjam de Baar and others, eds, *Choosing the Better Part: Anna Maria van Schurman, 1607–1678*, Dordrecht: Kluwer Academic Publishers, 1996 (Dutch original, 1992)

Commanding in her lifetime such titles as "Wonder of the Upper World", "The Tenth Muse", "Gabenzelt" and "La Célèbre", Anna Maria van Schurman enjoyed a Europe-wide reputation as a phenomenon of female talent. Besides her proficiency in a range of artistic media and her musical and poetic abilities, she was renowned for her knowledge of ancient and modern languages and for her scholarship in general, numbering among her acquaintance such intellectuals as Constantijn Huygens and Descartes. Her artistic output is perhaps best understood as one aspect of this many-sided virtuosity. Despite a brief period of training, she seems never to have worked as a professional artist. Instead her art functioned as part of a complex construction of herself as multi-talented, a construction that may be seen as a deliberate assertion of the possibility of female equality in all branches of the arts and sciences, and which reflects the arguments of her treatise, the *Dissertatio* (1641), for the inclusion of women in higher education and for their suitability for scientific study. This multiplicity also extended to her artistic oeuvre as a single element within that self-construction: although it consists almost entirely of portraits and self-portraits, of similar format, these are executed in a spectacular variety of media.

In *Eukleria*, a kind of "spiritual autobiography" written late in life, van Schurman claims to have had no artistic training. It seems, however, that in her youth she was apprenticed for a time to the engraver Magdalena van der Passe (q.v.). Despite her description in the *Eukleria* of the admiration shown her work by Gerrit van Honthorst, and the suggestion by subsequent writers that she may have studied at his Utrecht academy, which, according to Roger de Piles, accepted women students, there is no evidence of any direct contact between Honthorst and van Schurman.

Her earliest dated works, two small portraits in oil on panel ('t Coopmanshûs, Franeker), probably of her brothers Hendrik Frederik and Johan Gotschalk van Schurman, are of 1623 and 1624 respectively. Her most productive period, however, was the 1630s and 1640s. Her inclusion in the members' register of the Utrecht Guild of St Luke in 1643 as "artist, sculptor and engraver" thus comes near the end of her artistic career. Although it would seem to imply that she was then working professionally, she appears to have had no other links with the guild and did not pay yearly contributions. It is therefore more than likely that this registration was honorary, reflecting her position of esteem within the city – a position that van Schurman herself cultivated. Known as the "Star of Utrecht", she characterised herself as one of its wonders. The anonymous engraved portrait of her in Jacob Cats's *Werelts begin midden en eynde, besloten in den trou-ringh, met den proef-steen van den selven* (The beginning, middle and end of the world, contained in the wedding ring, with the proving-stone of the selves; Dordrecht, 1637), which he dedicated to her, follows her own design and shows her in front of a window through which may be seen the tower of Utrecht's famous cathedral. This juxtaposition both posits her as an equivalent attraction and advertises her presence in the city – with topographical

Schurman: *Self-Portrait at 25*, 1633; etching; Rijksmuseum, Amsterdam

accuracy, since the van Schurman house was in the Domskerkhof.

Prestigious visitors to this house, including Louise-Maria de Gonzaga, Queen of Poland (1645), and Christina of Sweden (*c*.1651), testify to van Schurman's contemporary fame. During these visits to the "Pinacoteca Schurmannae" they witnessed the Tenth Muse herself, admired the fruits of her talents and saw those talents in action: contemporary sources confirm that it was her custom to make portraits of visitors. Besides such visitors, family and friends were both the viewers and the subjects of her works, almost all of which are portraits. Her etched portrait of *Gisbert Voet* (1647; Rijksprentenkabinet, Rijksmuseum, Amsterdam; Historisch Museum, Rotterdam) is characteristic of her works, being modest in scale and format, with the subject shown bust-length and in three-quarter profile, without hands. This practice of using associates as models may be partly ascribed to convenience. It is also possible, however, to see van Schurman's decision to represent individuals with whom she enjoyed a familial or amicable, rather than a merely commercial relationship as a deliberate attempt to emphasise her artistic activity as the exercise of a liberal art, not just the fulfilment of a financial contract.

Van Schurman's many self-portraits may be placed within a tradition of self-portraiture by women artists that included, in the Netherlands, Catharina van Hemessen (q.v.) and Judith Leyster (q.v.). This tradition may have depended in part on the prototype of Iaia, one of the women artists named by Pliny, who describes her as painting her own portrait with the aid of a mirror. In this context, van Schurman's self-portrayal, for example the signed and dated etching, *Self-Portrait at 25* (1633; see illustration), the inscription of which refers pointedly to its own making, may be seen as the defining gesture of the woman artist. At a period when only certain human qualities were considered to justify portrayal, it also constitutes a repeated assertion of herself as a woman of exceptional knowledge and talent.

Van Schurman was proficient in an extraordinary variety of media, producing portraits in oil, gouache, graphite and pastel, engraved and etched portraits and portraits modelled in wax and carved in ivory and boxwood. Her pastel *Self-Portrait* of 1640 ('t Coopmanshûs, Franeker) is the earliest known example of this technique in the Netherlands. She was also skilled in activities more commonly practised by women of good family: embroidery, calligraphy, paper cut-outs and glass engraving. These forays into an unusually broad range of techniques may be interpreted as an attempt to demonstrate a many-sided virtuosity, and as a way of claiming some kind of mastery over the world. In the 1640s van Schurman's artistic output declined considerably, probably as a result of her developing interest in theological issues and her commitment to a religious life.

KATE BOMFORD

See also Amateur Artists survey

Schwabacher, Ethel

American painter, 1903–1984

Born Ethel Kremer in New York, 20 May 1903. Studied at the Art Students League, New York, 1918–27. Studied sculpture under Anna Hyatt Huntington (q.v.), summer 1927; began to paint that year, studying under Max Weber. Independent study in France and Austria, 1928–34; studied under Arshile Gorky in New York, 1934–5. Married lawyer Wolfgang S. Schwabacher, 1935; daughter born 1936, son born 1941; husband died 1951. First included in Whitney Museum of American Art group exhibition, 1947. Lived in New York until her death, 25 November 1984.

Selected Individual Exhibitions

Georgette Passedoit Gallery, New York: 1935, 1947
Betty Parsons Gallery, New York: 1953, 1956, 1957, 1960, 1962
Women's City Club, New York: 1955
Greenross Gallery, New York: 1964
Gallery 219, State University of New York, Buffalo: 1972
Bodley Gallery, New York: 1976
Jane Voorhees Zimmerli Art Museum, Rutgers University, New Brunswick, NJ: 1987 (touring retrospective)

Selected Writings

Foreword, *Arshile Gorky Memorial Exhibition*, exh. cat., Whitney Museum of American Art, New York, 1951
Arshile Gorky, New York: Whitney Museum-Macmillan, 1957
"Formal definitions and myths in my paintings", *Leonardo*, vi, 1973, pp.53–5

Hungry for Light: The Journal of Ethel Schwabacher, ed. Brenda S. Webster and Judith Emlyn Johnson, Bloomington: Indiana University Press, 1993

Bibliography

Ethel Schwabacher: Pastels and Oils, exh. brochure, Passedoit Gallery, New York, 1947
Schwabacher: Paintings and Glass Collages, 1951–1953, exh. brochure, Betty Parsons Gallery, New York, 1953
Nature in Abstraction, exh. cat., Whitney Museum of American Art, New York, and elsewhere, 1958
Ethel Schwabacher: Pastels of People, exh. brochure, Bodley Gallery, New York, 1976
Ethel Schwabacher: A Retrospective Exhibition, exh. cat., Jane Voorhees Zimmerli Art Museum, Rutgers University, New Brunswick, and elsewhere, 1987
Ruth Bass, "Ethel Schwabacher", *Art News*, lxxxvi, December 1987, p.162
Abstract Expressionism: Other Dimensions, exh. cat., Jane Voorhees Zimmerli Art Museum, Rutgers University, New Brunswick, and elsewhere, 1989
Ethel Schwabacher: Abstract Expressionist Works, exh. brochure, Gallery Schlesinger, New York, 1989
Judith E. Johnson, Jayne L. Walker and Brenda S. Webster, "Ethel Schwabacher: The lyric/epic and the personal", *Woman's Art Journal*, x/1, 1989, pp.3–9
Ronny Cohen, "Ethel Schwabacher", *Artforum*, xxviii, November 1989, p.153
Whitney Chadwick, *Women, Art and Society*, London and New York: Thames and Hudson, 1990; revised edition, 1996
Jeffrey Berman, "'One's effort to find a little truth': Ethel Schwabacher's artistic and psychoanalytic odyssey", *Psychoanalytic Review*, lxxviii, 1991, pp.607–27
Judith E. Bernstock, *Under the Spell of Orpheus: The Persistence of a Myth in Twentieth-Century Art*, Carbondale: Southern Illinois University Press, 1991
Estella Lauter, "Women as mythmakers revisited", *Quadrant*, xxiii/1, 1991, pp.35–51
April Kingsley, *The Turning Point: The Abstract Expressionists and the Transformation of American Art*, New York: Simon and Schuster, 1992
Elizabeth Shostak, "Portrait of the artist", *Women's Review of Books*, x/12, September 1993, pp.28–9 (review of *Hungry for Light*)

Ethel Schwabacher Papers are in the Archives of American Art, Smithsonian Institution, Washington, DC.

Ethel Schwabacher was a first-generation Abstract Expressionist artist who exhibited at the Georgette Passedoit Gallery in New York in the 1940s and at the Betty Parsons Gallery in the 1950s with such Abstract Expressionists as Jackson Pollock and Mark Rothko. Her work, which is as layered in meaning as it is rich in colour, provides a key to an understanding of underlying gender issues in the formative years of the New York School.

A student of Arshile Gorky in the mid-1930s and later his biographer, Schwabacher was led by him to experience Surrealism as freedom – freedom from the purely conscious. In the late 1940s, under Gorky's influence, Schwabacher did a series of paintings of cows, bulls and peacocks that she thought of as Surrealist and whose "unusual combinations of animals and flowers" she stressed. There is a complex interplay of nature and association in these canvases. In one painting of cows and bulls, *Untitled* (1945–9; San Francisco Museum of Modern Art), two animals are visible, indicated by part of the

Schwabacher: *Woman III*, 1951; oil on canvas; 91.4 × 76.2 cm.

udders on the left and hind legs on the right. Suggestions of other animals abound and intermingle freely with the richly and expressively coloured canvas (Mona Hadler in New Brunswick 1987, p.5)

Emerging from the yoke of Gorky, Schwabacher did a group of paintings in the early 1950s entitled *Women*. In this series she addressed the theme of birth, which she saw as providing an opportunity to express her conception of "femininity triumphant". These paintings are larger and more roughly painted than the canvases that precede them. In a work such as *Woman III* (1951; see illustration) Schwabacher attempted to express the intensity of her vision of the power of woman's experience, using a limited reference to the body combined with energetic Abstract Expressionist brush strokes and vivid colour (*ibid.*, p.6). Schwabacher's paintings point to an understanding of the differing relationships of male and female Abstract Expressionists to the issue of "nature". They form a provocative foil to De Kooning's well-known images of women of the same time (Chadwick 1990, p.307).

The period from the mid-1950s to the early 1960s was a fertile one for Schwabacher: it was then that she painted such canvases as *Warm Rain III* (1960; Collection Christopher C. Schwabacher) and *Wild Honey* (1961; artist's estate). These paintings, like the work of other artists from the 1950s that have been called Abstract Impressionist, are often suggestive of nature. In them, after years of work, she mastered a language to convey her vision. It is here, with a mingling of memory and perception, expressed through swift brush strokes and suggestive colour, that Schwabacher achieved what she called her "paradise of the real".

During the 1960s Schwabacher risked her growing recognition by shifting her focus from abstraction to mythology (Greta Berman in New Brunswick 1987, pp.13–20). Although she worked independently, her art joins the recent tradition of women artists and poets who have reinterpreted the Bible and mythology from a feminist perspective. In 1974 she wrote of Adam and Eve in a private journal: "She gave up a rib to make a penis. But, she will 'possess' the penis – through love – And yet that was the sin?" She turned again to the theme that year with a watercolour, *Creation of Adam out of Eve's Rib* (artist's estate). Schwabacher often mused, visually and verbally, on the relationship of Orpheus and Eurydice with its complex interplay of art and love, masculinity and femininity. Major paintings from this period include the large *Orpheus and Eurydice I* (1969; Jane Voorhees Zimmerli Art Museum, Rutgers University, New Brunswick). She saw Orpheus as androgynous and admitted to an identification with both Orpheus and Eurydice (Hadler in *ibid.*, p.5; Berman in *ibid.*, pp.17–18; Bernstock 1991, p.160). In this, as with her earlier conflations of bulls, cows and flowers, which she described as the co-existence of the masculine with the feminine, she adds another example of the complex androgynous identification of the woman artist.

In the later decades of her life Schwabacher suffered from severe arthritis. Her physical pain, like that of Frida Kahlo (q.v.), must have contributed to the added intensity of the visual imagery of her late small drawings. Slowly losing the ability to paint, she turned to her journals, which, from 1967 to 1980, increasingly became the focus of her artistic life. Schwabacher was a masterful writer, and her journals have

been likened to those of Virginia Woolf in their depiction of the growth and education of the female artist (Berman 1991, p.608). Analyses of myths and paintings coincide with probings into her childhood unearthed by years of psychoanalysis. She had understood well the Surrealists' emphasis on the unconscious, for she had a lifelong, passionate interest in psychoanalysis and Freud. She entered analysis in New York in the 1920s but she soon applied to the source, travelling to Vienna in 1928. In Vienna Schwabacher was in analysis for a period of time with Helene Deutsch, who had already written on the psychology of women. After her husband's death in 1951, Schwabacher re-entered what was to become decades of analysis with Marianne Kris, wife of Ernst Kris who had written his *Psychoanalytic Explorations in Art* in 1952. Her relationship with Kris forms a subtext of the journals, while she attempts to define on a broader level the "I am" of the woman artist. These journals provide a rich source of psychological insight into the origins of creativity in the woman artist (Webster introduction to *Hungry for Light*, p.xviii).

MONA HADLER

Schwartze, Thérèse
Dutch painter, 1851–1918

Born in Amsterdam, 22 December 1851; father the portrait painter Johann Georg Schwartze; sister the sculptor Georgine Schwartze. First taught by her father. Studied in Munich under Gabriel Max, Franz von Lenbach and Karl von Piloty, 1875–6. Trips to Paris, 1878, 1879 and 1884; studied under Jean Jacques Henner, Jules Breton and Madeleine Lemaire (q.v.). Married editor Anton van Duyl, 1906. Taught pupils at her Amsterdam studio, which also became the meeting place for the group of women artists known as the Amsterdam Joffers. Member of the artists' society Arti et Amicitiae, Amsterdam; Pulchri Studio; Haagschen Kunst Kring, The Hague; honorary member, Rotterdam Teekenmaatschapph (Rotterdam Drawing Society). Recipient of gold medal, Artists Association, Amsterdam. Knight of Orange-Nassau, 1892. Died in Amsterdam, 23 December 1918.

Principal Exhibitions

Individual
Frans Buffa & Zonen, Amsterdam: 1880, 1907, 1915
Panoramagebouw, Amsterdam: 1890
Kunstzaal Kleykamp, The Hague: 1915
Arti et Amicitiae, Amsterdam: 1915 (*Na 100 Jaar* [After 100 years], Schwartze family)
Stedelijk Museum, Amsterdam: 1919 (retrospective)

Group
Paris Salon: from 1878 (honourable mention 1884, gold medal 1889)
Royal Academy, London: 1885
Exposition Universelle, Paris: 1889 (silver medal), 1900 (silver medal)
Internationale Ausstellung, Munich: 1890 (gold medal)
Kunstsalon Gurlitt, Berlin: 1891, 1895 (both *Internationale Künstlerinnenausstellung*)
World's Columbian Exposition, Chicago: 1893
Verein der Künstlerinnen und Kunstfreundinnen zu Berlin: 1898 (*Internationale Künstlerinnenausstellung*)

International Exposition, Barcelona: 1898 (first class gold medal)
Louisiana Purchase Exposition, St Louis: 1904 (gold medal)
Rotterdam: 1917 (*Levende meesters* [Contemporary masters])

Bibliography

H. Leonardsz, "Thérèse Schwartze", *Elsevier's Geïllustreerd Maandschrift*, ii/3, Amsterdam, 1892, pp.1–26

Anton Hirsch, *Die bildenden Künstlerinnen der Neuzeit*, Stuttgart: Enke, 1905

Walter Shaw Sparrow, *Women Painters of the World*, London: Hodder and Stoughton, 1905; reprinted New York: Hacker, 1976

F.M. Lurasco, *Onze moderne meesters*, Amsterdam, 1907

Bice Viallet, "Una pittrice olandese: Teresa Schwartze", *Vita d'Arte*, xiii, 1914, pp.205–10

G.H. Marius, *De Hollandsche schilderkunst in de negentiende eeuw*, 2nd edition, The Hague, 1920; as *Dutch Painters of the 19th Century*, Woodbridge, Suffolk: Antique Collectors' Club, 1974

Wilhelm Martin, *Thérèse van Duyl-Schwartze, 1851–1918: Een gedenkboek* [Thérèse van Duyl-Schwartze, 1851–1918: A memorial book], Amsterdam: Scheltema & Holkma, 1920

A.C.A. Plasschaert, *Korte geschiedenis der Hollandsche schilderkunst* [Short history of painting in Holland], Amsterdam, 1923

H. van Hall, *Repertorium voor de geschiedenis der Nederlandsche schilder- en graveerkunst sedert het begin der 12de eeuw tot het eind van 1932* [Index for the history of Netherlandish painting and printmaking from the beginning of the 12th century to the end of 1932], 2 vols, The Hague, 1935–6

——, *Portretten van Nederlandse beeldende kunstenaars/Portraits of Dutch Painters and Other Artists of the Low Countries*, Amsterdam, 1963

J. de Kleyn, "Over enkele portretten die Thérèse Schwartze van haar nichtje Lizzy Ansingh maakte" [On several portraits that Thérèse Schwartze made of her niece Lizzy Ansingh], *Antiek*, ii, 1967–8, pp.302–11

Adriaan Venema, *De Amsterdamse Joffers* [The Amsterdam Joffers], Baam: Wereldvenster, 1977

Lisbeth Brandt-Corstius, "Schildern uit liefhebberij" [Painting as a hobby], *Openbaar Kunstbezit*, no.22, 4 November 1978, pp.158–67

W.F. van Eekelen, *Het grafisch werk van Thérèse Schwartze: Inleiding en oeuvrekatalogus* [The graphic work of Thérèse Schwartze: Introduction and catalogue raisonné], Kunst Laaf, 1983

Bloemen uit de Kelder [Flowers from the cellar], exh. cat., Gemeentemuseum, Arnhem, 1989

Thérèse Schwartze, 1851–1918: Portreet van een gevierd schilder [Thérèse Schwartze, 1851–1918: Portrait of a celebrated painter], exh. cat., Het Zeister Slot, Zeist, 1989

Mieke Gerritsen Kloppenburg and Henriette Coppes Heerlen, *De kunst van het beschudde bestaan: Vijf schilderessen aan het begin van deze eeuw* [The art of the shaken existence: Five women painters at the beginning of this century], De Voorstad, 1991

De schilders van tachtig: Nederlandse schilderkunst, 1880–1895 [The painters of the eighties: Netherlandish painting, 1880–1895], exh. cat., Waanders Uitgevers, Zwolle, and elsewhere, 1991

Profession ohne Tradition: 125 Jahre Verein der Berliner Künstlerinnen, exh. cat., Berlinische Galerie, Berlin, 1992

When Thérèse Schwartze embarked on her career, Dutch portrait painting was at a low ebb. This would partly account for her rapid ascendancy to a position as one of Holland's most important portrait painters, despite all the disadvantages for women artists. From the age of ten, encouraged by her father, she staunchly pursued her desire for artistic training. The portrait of *Dr J. L. Dusseau* (1870; Rijksmuseum, Amsterdam) still owes a debt to the tradition of miniature painting in its delicate, smooth rendering. The sitter's clothes – black jacket, cravat and white shirt – are executed in just as much detail as the carefully modelled face. The less than idealised face with its expression of tension reveals the young artist's interest in realistic interpretation.

After the death of her father in 1874, Thérèse Schwartze finished his portrait commissions and went to Munich. That year, 1875–6, had a decisive influence on her style. Although as a woman she was barred from studying at the Academy, she managed to obtain excellent artistic guidance from Gabriel Max, Karl von Piloty and Franz von Lenbach. The last, who was a celebrated portrait painter of leading figures in the German Empire, became Thérèse Schwartze's exemplar. Following his advice she made copies after Velázquez and Rubens in the Alte Pinakothek.

After her return to the Dutch capital Schwartze obtained numerous portrait commissions from distinguished Amsterdam families through the intervention of the Mayor of Tienhoven. Her experiences in Munich led her to imitate the patina of old master paintings in her works in order to give her sitters an obvious historical aspect. In 1881 she obtained a commission to paint the portrait of the Dutch queen, *Emma*, and in 1887 another for a portrait in pastel of *Princess Wilhelmina* (both untraced). Following these commissions the artist steadfastly continued her training on trips to Berlin, Vienna, Dresden, Kassel, Munich, London and Hamburg. Her first trip to Paris in 1878 was not to leave a lasting impression, but the subsequent extended visits there in 1879 and 1884 influenced her artistic development quite considerably.

Her contact with Impressionism left Schwartze with a personal portrait style in which she would model the face and hands finely and in contrast depict clothes and other objects in the picture with rough brush strokes. A particularly good example of this is the portrait of the Commander-in-Chief of the South African Republic, *Piet J. Jonbert* (1890; Rijksmuseum). Thérèse Schwartze rendered the uniform with its sash and braiding with a lively brush stroke that is not constrained to the plastic form, thus loosening up the rigid formality of the portrait. Such unpretentious intimacy with her sitters produced interesting results, as in the manner in which the artist depicted *Maria Elisabeth Georgina* (1902; Rijksmuseum), sitting astride a chair, her right side at an angle supported by the chair's arm and the left half of her face strongly shaded. Her clothes are merely indicated with dashing brush strokes and even the usual fine modelling of the face has been waived by the artist. But in spite of this technique the reflective expression of the sitter is clearly captured.

From 1885 onwards Thérèse Schwartze carried out numerous portraits in pastel. The soft graphic effect of this technique enticed her into drawing society ladies and children in the manner of a courtly portrait tradition with enlarged eyes, miniature mouths and elongated fingers. The pastel portraits, as, for instance, those of *Amelia Blisa van Leeuwen* (1900), *Alida Elisabeth Greves* (1889) and *Marie Catherine Josephina Jordan* (1902; all Rijksmuseum), are considerably inferior to Schwartze's usual realism and keen experimentation in their concentration on the depiction of costly clothes and jewels as well as fulsome, expressionless facial features.

Concurrently with the commissioned works, Schwartze also executed a number of genre paintings. The works, *Three Girls in an Amsterdam Orphanage* (1885; Rijksmuseum), *Lutheran Communicants* (1894; Stedelijk Museum, Amsterdam) and

Schwartze: *My House Companions*, 1916; oil; 190 × 230 cm.; Stedelijk Museum De Lakenhal, Leiden

Five Orphan Girls from the Amsterdam Maagdenhuis (1888; Museum Boijmans Van Beuningen, Rotterdam), give an insight into Holland's Protestant life. Schwartze caught the young orphan girls and the faithful at particular moments – for instance, sitting by a table or in church at confirmation. Thus she created as her themes variations on sitting positions, from profile, facing the spectator to three-quarter view, as well as the various activities – reading, knitting, praying and listening – with the corresponding facial expressions and poses. Both the plain and uniform clothes that Schwartze reproduced with her fine technique and the innocent expressions on the girls' faces invoke the moral character of these works.

Schwartze's fame reached its peak between 1880 and 1890. Nevertheless, works of great stylistic variety were produced by her during her later years. In the group portrait *A.M. Otrop-Hanlo with Her Children* (1906; Centraal Museum, Utrecht) she rendered the six members of the family in the brown tones of old master portraiture. Particularly lively are the five children who cling to the mother in moving postures, or else hold on to her hands. The fabric of the creased clothes and the

bonnets glimmers patchily in the subdued light. *My House Companions* (1916; see illustration) is a most uncompromising group portrait. Here Schwartze distinctly composed the character of the individual sitters. Thus on the left at the edge of the picture is the shaded profile of the artist's sister, Georgine Schwartze, seated in an attitude of refusal, and to her right her mother, Theresia Ansingh-Schwartze, in a standing pose and puritanical dress with a cap and hands folded across each other; in the centre A.C.G. van Duyl looks up from a book with a stern expression and to his right stands the upright and imposing figure of Thérèse Ansingh, against whom her daughter, Lizzy Ansingh, leans. Apart from the last two figures, the characters are perceived as in individual portraits, and have no relationship to one another. Schwartze has abandoned the concept of a typical family portrait in favour of the individuals.

Thérèse Schwartze was among the most successful women artists of the 19th century. She left behind her three houses on the Prinsengracht in Amsterdam and a personal fortune of one million gulden. In 1887 she was invited to include her portrait in the gallery of artists' self-portraits in the Uffizi, Florence. In this portrait (1888) she presents herself with palette and brush in her right hand while shading her eyes with her left, as though contemplating a motif in the far distance. Out of this striking and dominant image speaks her simple maxim: "Painting is looking", to which she remained faithful until her death.

CAROLA MUYSERS

Scott, Kathleen
British sculptor, 1878–1947

Born Edith Agnes Kathleen Bruce in Carlton-in-Lindrick, Nottinghamshire, 27 March 1878. Orphaned early and brought up in Edinburgh by her great-uncle, W.F. Skene, Historiographer Royal of Scotland. Studied sculpture at Slade School of Fine Art, London, 1899; Académie Colarossi, Paris, 1901–6; met Rodin. Relief worker in the Balkans, 1903; spent several months in Italy recovering from typhoid. Settled in London with a studio in Belgravia, 1906. Married (1) Antarctic explorer Captain Robert Falcon Scott, 1908; son Peter, naturalist and painter, born 1909; husband died 1912; (2) Sir Edward Hilton Young MP (later Baron Kennet of the Dene), 1922; son Wayland born 1923. Lived in Great Yarmouth, Norfolk, and London. Travelled around the world. Associate member, 1928, first woman member of Council, 1937, and Fellow, 1946, Royal Society of British Sculptors. Died in London, 25 July 1947.

Principal Exhibitions

Grafton Gallery, London: 1912 (Women's Work)
Royal Academy, London: from 1913
Whitechapel Art Gallery, London: 1922 (Modern British Art)
Paris Salon: 1923 (medal of honour), 1925
International Society, Grosvenor Galleries, London: 1923
Greatorex Gallery, London: 1927, 1928 (individual), 1929
Fine Art Society, London: 1934 (individual)
Heal's Mansard Gallery, London: 1947 (retrospective)

Selected Writings

Letters from Turkey, Being Glimpses of Macedonian Misery, Nottingham: Saxton, 1907 (with Rosslyn Bruce)
Self-Portrait of an Artist, London: Murray, 1949

Bibliography

"Pater Patriae", Illustrated London News, 23 March 1935, p.183
Stephen Gwynn, ed., Homage: A Book of Sculpture, London: Bles, 1938
The Times, 26 July 1947, p.6 (obituary)
Geoffrey Dearmer, "Kennet, Kathleen", The Dictionary of National Biography, 1941–1950, ed. L.G. Wickham Legg and E.T. Williams, London: Oxford University Press, 1959, pp.447–9
Elspeth Huxley, Scott of the Antarctic, London: Weidenfeld and Nicolson, 1977; New York: Atheneum, 1978
Sculpture in Britain Between the Wars, exh. cat., Fine Art Society, London, 1986
Philip Attwood, "Kathleen Scott: The sculptor as medallist", British Numismatic Journal, lx, 1990, pp.121–9
Louisa Young, A Great Task of Happiness: The Life of Kathleen Scott, London: Macmillan, 1995

Kathleen Scott documented the eminent British men of her time in bronze. She studied sculpture at the Slade from 1899 and then for five years at the Académie Colarossi in Paris. She knew Rodin socially and possibly studied under him: "he would flatter me and my work", she said, but her work was clearly influenced by him in its lively surfaces that reflect the light. Her male figures may have been influenced by the New Sculptors, but her sculpture shows no other obvious 20th-century influence. A competent, not innovative sculptor, perfectly of her time, Scott met the demand for heroic public statues, portraiture and war memorials.

From 1906 to 1907 she had a studio in Belgravia, London, where she made portraits of young men, but although she had a gift for such work, she sold none. She also worked on groups including babies, which held some sentimental fascination for her, but none has survived in public collections. In 1908 she married the explorer Robert Falcon Scott and her son Peter was born the following year. She went on to produce sculpture prolifically throughout her life, constantly agonising about the conflict between work and the demands of a family. She was attractive to men, and as Scott's widow, and later a politician's wife and socialite, she was surrounded by heroic, powerful and interesting men, of whom she would make portraits. Scott rarely portrayed women – not for her the Victorian role of the woman sculptor who left the heroic male figures to the men. She hated categorisation as a woman artist, yet it was a women's exhibition at the Grafton Gallery (1912) that gave the first impetus to her career, providing her with commissions, including that for a series of bishops for Winchester College Chapel, Hampshire.

A very fine portraitist, Scott achieved a likeness easily; a bust might be finished and ready for the foundry in two hours. That of Lord Reading (National Portrait Gallery, London), exhibited at the Royal Academy in 1926, was produced in India when he was Viceroy from two daylight and two gaslight sittings. Thus her portraits do not look laboured, and she avoided the blandness of some previous portraitists. One of Scott's most successful sculptures is the portrait of George Bernard Shaw (Russell Cotes Art Gallery, Bournemouth), shown at the Royal Academy in 1940. Shaw is depicted almost half length, his hands holding his head in an expressive gesture, reflecting the writer's anguish in producing his art. In her struggle to produce a good likeness and also a great and enduring work, Scott almost always worked from the model: "How shocked Rodin would be", she commented when she was unable to do so; she resorted to photographs only when this was unavoidable. During World War I she was offered the work of making models of men wounded in the face, for plastic surgeons. She signed up for the same work in 1939, when sculpture seemed too irrelevant.

Scott was already established as a sculptor of statues to the famous dead before her husband's death in 1912 (her statue of C.S. Rolls, the first Englishman to fly the channel, was unveiled on Dover Promenade in 1911). She may have dealt with her grief by working on his statue, for which there could be no more suitably qualified sculptor; it is perhaps her most significant work. The bronze statue of Scott (see illustration) was unveiled in Waterloo Place, London, on 11 November 1915, by the First Lord of the Admiralty, and a marble version of it in Christchurch, New Zealand, in 1917. The unveiling of

Scott: *Captain R. F. Scott, RN*, completed 1915; Waterloo Place, London

these memorials to the heroic Scott was a national morale booster, a vital part of the war effort. Scott is represented in authentic Antarctic kit, ski sticks in his extended, thickly gloved hand. The broad, simple modelling of the costume imparts a modern appearance. In the New Zealand version the use of marble seems appropriate, as if carved out of the very element in which Scott perished, but this was occasioned by the lack of bronze foundries in the country. Scott, the modeller, carved the marble from the roughly prepared block with apparent ease, not changing the design to suit the medium, except that the marble figure was equipped with a wooden ski stick, whereas in the bronze version the stick is an integral part of the sculpture. The lack of cluttering plaques also adds to the clarity of design of the New Zealand version. Although the site in Christchurch conceals Scott's better view (the left, in Kathleen's opinion), he faces north, as he would have done on his return from the Pole, symbolically a better aspect. In 1927 the Swedish sculptor Milles told Kathleen that he liked her Scott figure better than anything in London, and Gleichen (*London's Open-Air Statuary*, 1928) observed: "It is a pity that the sculptor does not give us more of her work".

Scott was perhaps innovative in her robust enthusiasm, as a woman artist, for the male nude, which she considered her serious, not bread-and-butter work. She never compromised the heroism and idealism of her subjects by portraying them in fashionable garments; functional clothing or none – the figure needed no embellishment. Scott's nudes are realistically modelled, neither sensuous nor sentimental, but wiry, perhaps due to her preference for or the availability of undernourished models, and often in difficult poses. Several served as war memorials. In 1934 she presented *These Had Most to Give*, a life-size bronze of 1919, to the Scott Institute, Cambridge, as a memorial to the young. The work had been exhibited at the Royal Academy and Wembley in 1923, and received a medal of honour at the Paris Salon. Her youths reach idealistically towards a higher purpose, understating the sacrifice of which she must have been keenly aware. Appropriately, her bronze medallion on her own memorial at West Overton Church, Wiltshire, shows a nude angel with uplifted arms.

ANDREA GARRIHY

Scudder, Janet

American sculptor, 1867–1940

Born Netta Scudder in Terre Haute, Indiana, 27 October 1867. Attended classes at Rose Polytechnic Institute, Terre Haute, then studied at Cincinnati Academy of Art, 1887–90; Académie Colarossi, Paris, 1894–6. Worked as assistant to Lorado Taft for Chicago Exposition of 1893, and subsequently as assistant to Frederick MacMonnies in Paris. Returned to New York in 1896, but continued to spend much time in France. Visited Italy, 1899–1900; China and Japan, 1901. Member, National Sculpture Society, USA; associate member, National Academy of Design, New York, 1920. Chevalier, Légion d'Honneur, France, 1925. Died in Rockport, Massachusetts, 9 June 1940.

Principal Exhibitions

Individual
Theodore B. Starr, New York: 1912, 1913
Goupil Gallery, New York: 1916 (with Jane Poupelet)
Gorham Galleries, New York: 1918
Ferargil Galleries, New York: 1926

Group
World's Columbian Exposition, Chicago: 1893 (bronze medal)
Paris Salon: from 1899 (honourable mention 1911)
Louisiana Purchase Exposition, St Louis: 1904 (bronze medal)
Panama-Pacific International Exposition, San Francisco: 1915 (silver medal)
Amsterdam: 1928 (Olympiad medal)
Exposition Internationale, Paris: 1937 (silver medal)

Selected Writings
"The art student in Paris", *Metropolitan Magazine*, v, April 1897, pp.239–44
"Janet Scudder tells why so few women are sculptors", *New York Times*, 18 February 1912, magazine section, p.13
Modeling My Life, New York: Harcourt Brace, 1925

Bibliography
Leila Mechlin, "Janet Scudder, sculptor", *International Studio*, xxxix, 1910, pp.lxxxi–lxxxviii
"Sculpture by Janet Scudder", *New York Times*, 9 November 1913, magazine section, p.15
"Janet Scudder, sculptor, dies, 66", *New York Times*, 11 June 1940, p.25
Mary E. Warlick, *Janet Scudder and the Beaux-Arts Tradition in American Garden Sculpture*, MA thesis, State University of New York, Binghamton, 1976
The Woman Sculptor: Malvina Hoffman and Her Contemporaries, exh. cat., Berry-Hill Galleries, New York, 1984
Janis Conner and Joel Rosenkranz, *Rediscoveries in American Sculpture: Studio Works, 1893–1939*, Austin: University of Texas Press, 1989
Charlotte Streifer Rubinstein, *American Women Sculptors*, Boston: Hall, 1990
Wendy Slatkin, *The Voices of Women Artists*, Englewood Cliffs, NJ: Prentice Hall, 1993

Janet Scudder was a successful woman sculptor in an age when that was a rarity. She found her métier as a sculptor of garden fountains and statues after visiting Italy in 1899, and thereafter pursued a career providing garden ornaments for wealthy American clients. By combining her talent with sheer determination and focusing on a particular niche in the decorative market, she overcame a background of poverty and the prevalent prejudice against women to become celebrated in her field both in the USA and France.

Born into a large family in the American Midwest, Scudder showed an early aptitude for drawing and before leaving high school attended Saturday classes at the local art institute. At the age of 18 she left Terre Haute for good, studying at the Cincinnati Academy of Art, where she was encouraged by one of her instructors, the Italian-born Louis Rebisso (her name "Janet" derives from that time because the registrar protested that her original name, Netta, was not a real one). Money was a problem and during her years of study she was supported by a brother who invited her to join him in Chicago when she completed her course. Scudder's first job there was making architectural decorations in a wood-carving factory. This was the first time she encountered gender discrimination; only men

Scudder: *Frog Fountain*, 1901; bronze; height 95.3 cm.;
Metropolitan Museum of Art, New York; Rogers Fund 1906
(06.967)

were permitted to join the woodcarvers' union and she was
forced to resign. Shortly afterwards she obtained a position as
studio assistant to Lorado Taft, who was engaged in work for
the World's Columbian Exposition of 1893, and became one of
his "White Rabbits" (the name came from a chance remark
made by the director of the fair to Taft that he could employ
anyone, even white rabbits, so long as the work was completed
on time). Scudder and the other women earned a respectable
$5 a day for their work. In addition to enlarging work for
various buildings and statues, Scudder was given two sculptures of her own to model.

At the Exposition Scudder first saw the work of Frederick
MacMonnies and determined to study with him. She used the
money she earned to buy a ticket to France, arriving in 1894
accompanied by Taft's sister Zulime. Eventually MacMonnies
agreed to take her on as an assistant, assigning her work on
figures for the Library of Congress and West Point. After two
years she returned to New York where she experienced
extreme poverty. A chance encounter with a friend led to a

commission of $750 to provide the seal for the New York Bar
Association. Despite this, she was still unable to obtain a position as studio assistant and supported herself by making
portrait medallions (examples on store in Metropolitan
Museum of Art, New York), memorial plaques and funerary
urns. In 1898 she returned to Paris, where she renewed her
contact with MacMonnies and continued to supply medallions
and plaques, although she was discontented with this type of
work. In her autobiography of 1925 she stated that she was
determined not to

> add to this obsession of male egotism that is ruining
> every city in the US with rows of hideous statues of men
> – men – men – each one uglier than the other – standing,
> sitting, riding horseback – every one of them pompously
> convinced that he is decorating the landscape [*Modeling
> My Life* 1925, p.155].

The discovery of Italian Renaissance sculpture on her trip to
Italy in the winter of 1899–1900 led to a dramatic change in
content and style. She was struck by the use of bronze statues
as focal points in the design of houses and determined: "Even
if I had to die in a poorhouse… my work should please and
amuse the world … My work was going to decorate spots,
make people feel cheerful and gay – nothing more!" (*ibid.*,
p.165). It is ironic that this was so alien to her character that
her friend Gertrude Stein would later comment: "There are
only two perfectly solemn things on earth, the doughboy and
Janet Scudder" (*Selected Writings of Gertrude Stein*, ed. Carl
Van Vechten, New York: Random House, 1946, p.255).

The first work modelled after Scudder's Italian trip proved
to be the most important: *Frog Fountain* (1901; see illustration), in which a young boy in a playful pose reacts to water
sprayed on him by three open-mouthed frogs. The child is
plump and happy and with this carefree subject Scudder aimed
to attract a new clientele. The strategy was successful, and in
1901 the second cast of *Frog Fountain* was seen in New York
by the architect Stanford White who bought it for his own
home. Thereafter White provided commissions for Scudder
regularly until his murder in 1906. By then Scudder was established as a supplier of garden statuary and fountains for the
rich and famous, including members of the Rockefeller family.
In addition she also undertook more serious commissions
including the figure of *Japanese Art* (1908) for the façade of
the Brooklyn Institute of Arts and Sciences (now Brooklyn
Museum, NY). Although Scudder was influenced by the sculpture she saw in Italy, it should be noted that *Frog Fountain* also
owes much to her mentor MacMonnies. A later work, *Tortoise
Fountain* (1906; Brook Green Gardens, Murrells Inlet, SC), is
also a hybrid of these two influences.

By 1912 Scudder was well-respected enough to warrant
virtually a full-page article in the *New York Times* in which she
explained that there are few women sculptors "because they
[women] do not approach the subject of the profession seriously enough … I believe that sculpture is a much more scientific pursuit than painting, as scientific as music". She deplored
the contemporary preoccupation with novelty, commenting: "I
think too much stress is laid in America on the fact of being
original … Why not be interested in doing a beautiful thing
just because it is beautiful?" She also expressed firm views on
the status of women artists:

Women are comparatively new in this profession, but there is really no sex in art, nor should there be. For that reason I condemn "Women Art Exhibits," so called. If a work is good it is good; if bad, bad, and it makes no difference whether it is created by a person in a smock and trousers or one in blouse and skirt.

The years before the 1920s were Scudder's zenith, but although she worked successfully until her death some of the spontaneity was missing. Her later creations became stylised and almost lifeless in comparison with her earlier works. For 40 years Scudder commuted between France and the USA, undertaking commissions and exhibiting in both countries. During World War I she assisted the French Red Cross, lent her house to the YMCA and entertained French troops; for these activities she was made a Chevalier of the Légion d'Honneur in 1925.

MIRIAM KRAMER

Scultori, Diana *see* Mantuana

Seidler, Louise (Caroline Sophie)
German painter, 1786–1866

Born in Jena, 15 May 1786. Took private drawing lessons with the sculptor Friedrich Wilhelm Doell in Gotha, 1800–03; lessons in pastel painting with Jakob W. Christian Roux in Jena, 1805–6; studied privately under academicians Christian L. Vogel and Gerhard von Kügelgen in Dresden, 1810–14. Further studies at the Munich Academy, 1817–18; also studied in Rome, 1818–20 and 1821–3, and Florence, 1820–21. Lived in Weimar, 1823–66; stayed in Paris, 1826; made second trip to Italy, 1832–3; further travels in connection with exhibitions, visits to artists and portrait commissions to Berlin, Frankfurt am Main, Konstanz (Constance), Zürich, Vienna and elsewhere. Appointed drawing teacher to the princesses of Sachsen-Weimar, 1823; curator of the painting gallery in Weimar, 1824 (received official acknowledgement for her work there, 1834); court painter at Sachsen-Weimar, 1835. Recipient of gold medal for civilian merit in art and science, Sachsen-Weimar, 1843. Remained unmarried; friendships with Goethe and his family, the philosopher Friedrich Wilhelm von Schelling and the artists Philipp Veit, Caspar Schinz, Marie Ellenrieder (q.v.) and Angelika Facius, among others. Went blind in later years; Facius remained at her side until her death. Died in Weimar, 7 October 1866.

Principal Exhibitions

Weimar Academy: 1805, 1811–12, 1814, 1821, 1823–7, 1829, 1833–7, 1840, 1842
Berlin Academy: 1814, 1832
Dresden Academy: 1821, 1824, 1829–30, 1832–3, 1836, 1841, 1845

Selected Writings

Köpfe aus Gemälden vorzüglicher Meister nach sorgfältig auf den Originalen durchgezeichneten Umrissen in der Sammlung von
Louise Seidler: Zum Gebrauch für Zeichenschüler lith. von J.J. Schmeller, Weimar, 1836
Erinnerungen und Leben der Malerin Louise Seidler: Selbstbiographie, ed. Hermann Uhde, Berlin, 1874; revised editions, 1875 and 1922; abridged edition, Weimar, 1964

Bibliography
Bilderchronik des sächsischen Kunstvereins, 9 vols, Dresden, 1828–36
Adolf Schoell, *Weimars Merkwürdigkeiten einst und jetzt*, Weimar, 1847
Ernst Guhl, *Die Frauen in der Kunstgeschichte*, Berlin, 1858
Hermann Grimm, "Goethe und Louise Seidler", *Preussische Jahrbücher*, xxxiii/1, 1874
Friedrich von Boetticher, *Malerwerke des 19. Jahrhunderts*, ii/2, 1901
Friedrich Noack, *Das Deutschtum in Rom*, 1927; reprinted Aalen: Scientia, 2 vols, 1974
Ottilie von Goethe, *Tagebücher und Briefe*, ed. Heinz Blum, Vienna, 1962
Martin Franke, "Die Malerin Louise Seidler", *Bildende Kunst*, no.11, 1986
Helene M. Kastinger Riley, *Die weibliche Muse*, Columbia, SC: Camden House, 1986 (with list of works)
Edith Krull, *Women in Art*, London: Studio Vista, 1989 (German original, 1984)
Bettina Baumgärtel, "Mehr als hübsche Talente", *Kunst und Antiquitäten*, no.5, 1994, pp.8–13
Bärbel Kovalevski, "Goethe: Förderer und Modell von Malerinnen", *HB – Kunstführer Thüringen*, no.57, 1995

As a young girl in her home town of Jena, Louise Seidler had access to the important circle of early Romanticism through her contacts with the families of Schelling, Tieck, Schlegel, Gries and Frommann. With their poetry readings, discussions of literary translations from Spanish and English, as well as music and lectures, these houses resembled an academic school for literature, art and aesthetics. In 1807 Seidler became engaged to a French physician, Geoffrey, who was killed two years later in Spain. Thereupon she decided to devote her life solely to the arts. Among her friends in Dresden were the painters Caspar David Friedrich, Georg Friedrich Kersting, Anton Graff and the female miniature painter Doris Stock. In 1810–11 she received two important commissions: the portrait of *Johann Wolfgang von Goethe* (Goethe-Nationalmuseum, Weimar), which she painted that winter while living in Goethe's house, and the portrait of the natural scientist *Bernhard von Lindenau* (Staatliches Lindenau-Museum, Altenburg). The portrait of *Goethe* is an impressive psychological study focusing on the head of the sitter in close-up, whereas the half-length portrait of *Lindenau* is a painting in a classicist style with a wide landscape background. These portraits, as well as other commissions for the dukes and their families in Weimar and Gotha, were executed by Seidler in pastel, a medium she had skilfully mastered. Instructed by her Dresden teachers, she also learned the technique of oil painting, in which she copied paintings by Carlo Dolci, van Dyck and the Carracci, among others.

In 1817 Seidler became the first woman in Germany to receive a scholarship to study at the Munich Academy. She also obtained letters of recommendation for admission to the Academy from the dukes of Sachsen-Weimar and Gotha-Altenburg. At the Academy there was a bias towards the classicist views of the director Langer, who, however, also

ST. ELISABETH ALLMOSEN AUSTHEILEND.

Dem Königlich Preußischen Geheimen-Staats-Rath Ritter des Königlich Preußischen rothen Adler Ordens Herrn Niebuhr und der Frau Margaretha Niebuhr aus innigstem Dankgefühl und treuster Anhänglichkeit gewidmet von der Verfasserin

Seidler: *St Elisabeth*, 1827; lithograph; Kupferstichkabinett, Berlin, Preussische Kulturbesitz

encouraged a thorough study of nature. Seidler was sympathetic towards advocates of the Romantic school, such as Heinrich Hess, who demanded that a work of art possess both emotion and "soul". A further scholarship made it possible for her to continue her studies in Italy. For five years she lived and worked in Rome in the circle of artists that included Julius Schnorr von Carolsfeld, Philipp Veit, Anton Koch, Friedrich Overbeck, Wilhelm Schadow and Bertel Thorvaldsen. In the last year of her stay in Italy, Marie Ellenrieder (q.v.) arrived in Rome. Seidler became an indispensable friend to the sensitive and partially deaf Ellenrieder. They shared the view that the main purpose of art was to serve religion, and thus regarded the work of the Nazarenes as an appropriate model.

In 1819 Seidler exhibited in Rome a half-length portrait of her friend *Fanny Caspar* (untraced; wood engraving in *Illustrierte Zeitung*, Leipzig, 3 July 1875), which she had painted under Thorvaldsen's tutelage. Historic Rome is shown in the background. Compared with the portraits of 1810–11, this work shows a definite strengthening of form due to more a emphatic drawing technique. In 1820, in Rome, Prince Friedrich von Gotha commissioned two portraits of himself from Seidler as well as a devotional painting entitled *Mary with the Sleeping Christ Child and Three Angels: Faith, Hope and Love* (Schlossmuseum, Gotha). In this extraordinary example of her work, which is clearly influenced by Raphael, Seidler achieved a combination of clear drawing, refined colouring and profound emotion; the result is quite different from Overbeck's cool and unsensual works. Seidler's historical compositions are related to works by Carolsfeld, to whom she felt especially close because of their common Protestant faith, surrounded as they were in Rome by the Nazarenes who were converting to Catholicism.

While in Italy Seidler became adept at copying Raphael's paintings. Her copies were particularly admired by art lovers and two were acquired by the Prussian king in 1822 (*The Violinist*, Stiftung Schlösser und Gärten Potsdam-Sanssouci, Potsdam; *Madonna with the Goldfinch*, Staatliche Kunstsammlungen zu Weimar, Schlossmuseum, Weimar). Such copies, which were highly regarded and attracted higher sums than original works by contemporary painters, enabled Seidler to feel free of her "apprenticeship" (*Erinnerungen und Leben* 1874, p.379). She returned to Weimar with numerous sketches of Italian life and landscapes, tracings of famous paintings and studies of the Florentine school (Goethe-Nationalmuseum and Staatliche Museen, Weimar).

When she returned to Weimar in 1823, Seidler worked as a drawing teacher and curator of the ducal painting gallery, and was also an active member of the Saxon art world. At the same time she carried out numerous portrait commissions and worked intensively on new compositions as a history painter. Her close relationship with Goethe until his death in 1832 restricted her artistic freedom and development, however: his influence as patron and superior was all-powerful, not only affecting her intentions as a curator but also the subject matter of her paintings. He was an opponent of the Nazarene direction in art, with which Seidler was clearly associated, as can be seen in her painting of *St Elisabeth* (1822; untraced; for lithograph, see illustration). *Painting and Poetry* (1831; untraced; engraving in Kupferstichkabinett, Dresden), on the other hand,

was commissioned by Goethe and executed by Seidler in a classicist style. According to Goethe's ideas, in this painting she was supposed to depict the "lasting" and the "fleeting", which the "highly esteemed painter" did to his satisfaction.

Seidler's other main works, such as the altarpiece of *Christ the Merciful* (1829) for Sehestedt church near Rendsburg/ Schleswig and the painting of *St Elisabeth of Thüringen* (1822–6; untraced), show the influence of the Nazarenes. St Elisabeth, a contemporary of Francis of Assisi, practised both charity and spiritual care, but traditional paintings of her were restricted to representations of her almsgiving. The look and hand movement between Elisabeth and an inquiring woman underline spiritual care as a new element in the depiction of this saint, due to Seidler. The painting was commissioned by the Grand Duke of Sachsen-Weimar and was brought – with public support – to Wartburg near Eisenach, the saint's former home as countess (*Landgräfin*) of Thüringen. Like other artists of the time, Seidler also took literary models as themes for her paintings. The *Knight Toggenburg* (1836; untraced; engraving in Kupferstichkabinett, Dresden), based on a ballad by Schiller, and *Odysseus and the Sirens* (1834; Staatliche Kunstsammlungen, Weimar) were both particularly praised by contemporary critics.

Although Seidler continued to demonstrate her abilities in further paintings after 1840, their themes tell of her increasing loneliness and renunciation (*Pilgrim*, 1841; untraced; drawing in Staatliche Kunstsammlungen, Weimar). This development can be seen in a fine drawing of 1849 (Kupferstichkabinett, Dresden) that shows a young woman, her arms crossed over her chest and with a crown of thorns on her loose hair, standing barefoot on thorn branches under a crucifix. Underneath, an inscription by the artist reads: "In memory of the days of hard struggle". The circumstances behind this drawing were probably the changes in public taste, changes within Seidler's circle of friends and her increasing blindness. Around the middle of the 19th century neither the classicist nor the Romantic style was in vogue, and thus recognition through new commissions failed to materialise. This was of as much concern to Seidler as to her friends from Dresden, Caspar David Friedrich, Ferdinand Hartmann and others.

As a portrait painter, Seidler had worked in the genres of single, group and child portraiture, where she combined exploration of character with idealisation, in accordance with the Nazarenes' views on portrait painting (*Margarete Niebuhr*, Rome, 1822; Goethe-Nationalmuseum, Weimar; *Frau Gogel*, c.1822; three-quarter-length with landscape background; Historisches Museum, Frankfurt am Main; *Spiegel Sisters*, c.1824; Goethe-Museum, Düsseldorf). In later years Seidler tended towards the realistic Biedermeier portrait (four portraits in Goethe-Haus, Frankfurt am Main; a full-length portrait in an interior of the theologian *Marezoll*, 1826; Friedenskirche, Jena), seen also in a portrait drawing of *Gisela von Armin* (Staatliche Kunstsammlungen, Weimar). Given the overlapping effects of her classicist training, the influence of Goethe and her early adoption of Romantic ideas, Seidler's history paintings are best described as Romantic Classicism.

BAERBEL KOVALEVSKI

Serebryakova, Zinaida (Evgenevna)
Russian painter, 1884–1967

Born Zinaida Evgenevna Lansere on the family estate of Neskuchnoye, near Kharkov, 28 November (Old Style calendar)/10 December (New Style calendar) 1884; grew up in St Petersburg. Studied at Tenisheva School under Ilya Repin, 1901; visited Italy, 1902–3; studied under the portrait painter Osip Braz, 1903–5; studied at the Académie de la Grande Chaumière, Paris, 1905–6. Married writer and railway engineer Boris Serebryakov, 1905; four children, born 1906, 1907, 1912 and 1915. Lived at Neskuchnoye. Joined Mir Iskusstva (World of Art) group, 1906. Nominated for rank of Academician, Petrograd Academy of Arts, 1916. Left Neskuchnoye after home burned (1918) and husband died of typhus (1919); moved to Petrograd and worked in IZO (Fine Arts Section) of Narkompros (People's Commissariat of Enlightenment), 1920. Went to Paris to fulfil a commission, 1924; never returned to Russia. Travelled and painted in England, Brittany and North Africa. Lived in Paris until her death, 19 September 1967.

Principal Exhibitions

SRKh (Union of Russian Artists), St Petersburg: 1910
St Petersburg/Petrograd: 1910 (*The Contemporary Female Portrait*), 1918 (*Russian Countryside*)
Mir Iskusstva (World of Art): 1910–13, 1922, 1924
Kharkov Soviet Worker Deputies, Kharkov: 1919 (*First Exhibition of the Arts*)
House of Arts, Petrograd: 1920
Tretyakov Gallery, Moscow: 1924 (*The Peasant in Russian Painting*)
Galerie Charpentier, Paris: 1927 (individual)
Union of Artists of the USSR, Moscow: 1965–6 (touring retrospective)

Bibliography

V. Dmitriyev, "Khudozhnitsy" [Women artists], *Apollon*, 1917, nos 8–10
Sergei Ernst, *Z.E. Serebryakova*, Petrograd: Akvilon, 1922
Zinaida Serebryakova: Vystavka proizvedeniy iz muzeyev i chastnykh sobraniy [Zinaida Serebryakova: Exhibition of works from museums and private collections], exh. cat., Union of Artists of the USSR, Moscow, and elsewhere, 1965
Alexandre Benois, "Zinaida Serebryakova", *Aleksandr Benua razmyshlayet* [Alexandre Benois reflects], Moscow: Nauka, 1968, pp.219–22
V. Lapshin, *Serebryakova*, Moscow: Sovetsky Khudozhnik, 1969
Aleksei Savinov, *Zinaida Serebryakova*, Leningrad: Khudozhnik RSFSR, 1973
V.P. Knyazeva, *Zinaida Evgenevna Serebryakova*, Moscow: Izobrazitelnoye Iskusstvo, 1979
Alison Hilton, "Zinaida Serebriakova", *Woman's Art Journal*, iii/2, 1982–3, pp.32–5
M.N. Yablonskaya, *Women Artists of Russia's New Age, 1900–1935*, New York: Rizzoli, and London: Thames and Hudson, 1990
Vsevolod Petrov and Alexander Kamensky, *The World of Art Movement in Early 20th-Century Russia*, Leningrad: Aurora, 1991

Zinaida Serebryakova's paintings reflect none of the tumult of the Russian avant-garde era. Fascinated with the human figure and dedicated to careful observation and fresh rendering of her perceptions, before the Bolshevik Revolution of 1917 she was acclaimed for her portraits and her large-scale paintings of nudes and of peasants at work or at rest. After leaving the country to pursue career prospects, she became a reluctant exile in Paris for almost half her life, but she always identified her art as Russian. Neither allied with avant-garde abstraction nor with Socialist Realism, Serebryakova worked in near isolation, concentrating on a limited range of subjects and formal problems.

She was born on the estate of Neskuchnoye, near the provincial city of Kharkov. Her father Evgeny Lansere was a sculptor known for lively bronze figures of Cossack horsemen; one brother became a painter and graphic artist, the other an architect. Her mother Ekaterina Lansere, a painter, came from the Benua (Benois) family, whose members included an architect, a composer and the artist Alexandre Benois, a founder of the World of Art group. After her father's death in 1886, her mother took the young children to live in the Benois household in St Petersburg, where they all began to draw and grew accustomed to the presence of painters, musicians, writers and other figures in the art world.

At the age of 17 Zinaida Lansere began her formal art training at the school founded by Princess Marya Tenisheva and directed by the realist painter Ilya Repin; she studied with the portraitist Osip Braz for two years, and spent several months in Italy. After her marriage to Boris Serebryakov in 1905, she went to Paris to study at the Académie de la Grande Chaumière. Her notes and copies of paintings show an interest in the works of Titian, Rubens and Rembrandt, Watteau and Fragonard, Renoir, Monet and Degas. When she returned to St Petersburg in 1906, she joined the cosmopolitan World of Art group. Benois, Sergei Diaghilev, Leon Bakst, Konstantin Somov, her brother Evgeny Lansere and other founders of the World of Art believed that direct interaction between Russian and European artists was essential to break down provincialism and invigorate contemporary art. Their journal, exhibitions and Diaghilev's opera and ballet productions emphasised aesthetic values rather than content; international in spirit, they also fostered appreciation of the distinctiveness of Russian culture. Serebryakova shared the group's standards of artistic quality and admiration for a timeless concept of beauty, but she was not interested in the historicism and stylisation of much of their work. She decided to live at Neskuchnoye, and to bring up her four children in the country while focusing her art on the activities of rural life. She corresponded with her brother and uncle, made several trips to St Petersburg and abroad, and generally stayed in touch with artistic events, but her paintings display a serenity that might have been hard to achieve in the capital.

Her portraits, landscapes and studies of peasants show Serebryakova's ability to clarify the chief features of a place or a person and to integrate figures with their settings. Her best-known work, *Self-Portrait at the Dressing Table* (1909; see illustration), was admired for its originality and lack of pretension. It came about casually, when the artist was snowed-in at Neskuchnoye with no other models, and began painting her reflection along with all the trifles, as she said, that made up her intimate environment. The painting is structured so that every part of the composition contains elements that parallel those in other sections: the delicate toiletries in the foreground have simpler echoes in the wash-basin, jug and mirror in the background, and the lace-trimmed dresser-scarf picks up the

Serebryakova: *Self-Portrait at the Dressing Table*, 1909; Tretyakov Gallery, Moscow

textures of the pillow-case and the nightshirt. The creamy tint of the walls, bedspread and chemise draws the scene together, while the verticals of the candle and its reflection reinforce the painted frame of the mirror, just inside the edge of the canvas. In contrast, the action of the arms brushing the thick dark hair and the parallel diagonals of the hat-pins create an energetic hub at the very centre of the picture, drawing the viewer's eyes to the oblique glance of the reflected artist. In 1910 Serebryakova sent the painting to the Union of Russian Artists' exhibition in St Petersburg, where it was purchased by the Tretyakov Gallery, a remarkable success for a young artist's first show.

At the Table (1914; Tretyakov Gallery, Moscow) combines the strong framework of the table with the apparent spontaneity of the children, who seem to look up questioningly at an adult. A close viewpoint and lack of horizon also convey a sense of familiarity in Peasants at Dinner (1914; State Russian Museum, St Petersburg), showing a woman and a man preparing for their noon meal. The large-scale figure composition In the Bathhouse (1913; Tretyakov Gallery) could be classified as genre, but it comes closer to a rhythmic choreography of nude bodies arranged in distinct planes across the composition. The steamy atmosphere and natural postures in the study (1913; State Russian Museum) are absent in the almost manneristic final version. In two large outdoor scenes, Harvest (1915; Art Gallery, Odessa) and Bleaching Linen (1917; Tretyakov Gallery), the statuesque figures of peasant women seem stilled in a moment of purely aesthetic balance, rather than captured in the midst of activity. These works, with their low viewpoints, monumentality and harmony, testify to Serebryakova's productive study of High Renaissance art. Her affinity for the Renaissance was most apparent in a mural project for the Kazan Railway Station in Moscow. The project was not realised, but her tempera studies for the lunettes survive (1916; Tretyakov Gallery). Four female nudes personifying Persia, Siam, Turkey and India and two odalisques exemplify the decorative tendency of her work, while their complex crouching poses are reminiscent of Michelangelo's ignudi.

Within a decade of finishing her studies, Serebryakova had achieved success and recognition by her peers. In the autumn of 1916 the council of the Academy of Arts took the first step in recognising the achievements of women by recommending that the title of Academician be awarded to Serebryakova and three other women artists, Anna Ostroumova-Lebedeva (q.v.), Olga Della-vos Kardovskaya and A.P. Shneyder (hitherto, Artist of the Third Rank was the highest title that women could earn). Ironically, the session of the Academy at which the final vote would take place was cancelled because of the outbreak of the February Revolution in 1917.

Soon after the October Revolution, Serebryakova's life changed abruptly. A fire destroyed her house and many of her paintings in 1918, and a year later her husband died of typhus. She found a temporary job at the Kharkov Archaeological Museum, but it was a difficult time, and a painting of her children entitled House of Cards (1919; State Russian Museum) conveys the family's uncertainty. They moved to the Benua home in 1920, and Serebryakova found new subjects in the theatre and ballet. She watched rehearsals and drew pencil and pastel studies of dancers, emphasising the difficult poses of trained bodies and playing with the effects of mirror reflections, oblique angles and the interactions of figures with the surrounding space.

Serebryakova worked in the IZO (Fine Arts Section) of Narkompros (People's Commissariat of Enlightenment), but she did not expect regular employment, and in 1924 she decided to accept a commission in Paris. Circumstances forced her to remain abroad, but she made no effort to become part of the Russian émigré circle in Paris, a group that included Natalya Goncharova (q.v.), Larionov and other members of the former avant-garde. She took part in few exhibitions and felt alienated from the arguments of the contemporary art world. She travelled to Morocco and Algeria, to Britain and Brittany, and continued to paint landscapes, portraits and decorative compositions, with a strong feeling for visual rhythm. In 1955 she sent some of her best works to Soviet museums, and in 1965–6 a retrospective exhibition of her work was held in Moscow, Kiev and Leningrad. A year later she died in Paris.

Serebryakova remained a figurative artist throughout her life. She never felt that she was limited in copying nature, and did not question the validity of realism. Like her World of Art colleagues, she emphasised aesthetic values, and she regarded the extreme formalist experiments of Goncharova, Lyubov Popova (q.v.), Kazimir Malevich and other avant-garde contemporaries as a denial of those values. Although she experienced privations during the Revolution and Civil War, and in the long years of isolation abroad, Serebryakova did not allow the circumstances to disturb the essential harmony of her art.

ALISON HILTON

Sharples, Ellen Wallace, 1769–1849, and Rolinda, 1793–1838
British painters

Ellen Wallace Sharples Born 1769, possibly in Bath, Somerset, into a Quaker family. Studied drawing under James Sharples in Bath. Married him, c.1787; son James born c.1788, daughter Rolinda born 1793; also a stepson, Felix, from husband's previous marriage; all three children became artists. In USA with family, c.1794–1801 and 1809–11. Settled in Clifton, Bristol, with Rolinda and James after husband's death in New York (1811). Founder, Bristol Academy for the Promotion of the Arts (now Royal West of England Academy), to which she bequeathed most of her estate and the family's work. Died in Bristol, 1849.

Principal Exhibitions
Royal Academy, London: 1807

Rolinda Sharples Born 1793, probably in Bath. Studied briefly under Philip Reinagle in London, 1814 and 1820. Honorary member, Society of British Artists, 1828–40. Died of breast cancer in Bristol, 1838.

Principal Exhibitions
Royal Academy, London: 1820, 1822, 1824
Carlisle Academy: 1824–6, 1830

Society of British Artists, London: 1825–8, 1830–31, 1834, 1836
Liverpool Academy: 1827–9
Bristol Society of Artists: 1827, 1834
Royal Hibernian Academy, Dublin: 1829
Bristol Institution: 1829

Bibliography

Elizabeth Bryant Johnston, *Original Portraits of Washington, Including Statues, Monuments and Medals*, Boston: Osgood, 1882

Richard C. Tuckett, *The Bristol Academy for the Promotion of the Fine Arts*, Bristol: Harmon, 1899

Richard Quick, *Sharples Collection of Pastel Portraits and Oil Paintings*, Bristol: Bristol Art Gallery, 1910

Theodore Bolton, *Early American Portrait Painters in Miniature*, New York: Sherman, 1921

——, "James Sharples", *Art in America*, xi, 1923, pp.137–43

Katharine McCook Knox, *The Sharples: Their Portraits of George Washington and His Contemporaries*, New Haven: Yale University Press, 1930; reprinted New York: Kennedy Graphics, 1972

Arnold Wilson, "Rolinda Sharples and her family", *Country Life*, cxliii, 4 January 1968, pp.26–8

——, "The Sharples family of painters", *Magazine Antiques*, c, 1971, pp.740–43

Robert Erwin Jones, "Portraits of Benjamin Rush MD by his contemporaries", *Magazine Antiques*, cviii, 1975, pp.94–113

John C. Milley, "Thoughts on the attribution of Sharples pastels", *University Hospital, 1975 Antiques Show*, Philadelphia, 1975, pp.59–62

Karen Petersen and J.J. Wilson, *Women Artists: Recognition and Reappraisal*, New York: Harper, 1976; London: Women's Press, 1978

K.K. Yung and Mary Pettman, eds, *National Portrait Gallery: Complete Illustrated Catalogue, 1856–1979*, London, National Portrait Gallery, 1981

Charlotte Streifer Rubinstein, *American Women Artists from Early Times to the Present*, Boston: Hall, 1982

Charlotte Yeldham, *Women Artists in Nineteenth-Century France and England*, i, New York: Garland, 1984

Pamela Gerrish Nunn, *Victorian Women Artists*, London: Women's Press, 1987

Sally Davies, *Rolinda Sharples*, Women Artists Slide Library, London, c.1989

——, "Rolinda Sharples", *Women Artists Slide Library Journal*, no.28, 1989, p.24

Nancy G. Heller, *Women Artists: An Illustrated History*, 2nd edition, New York: Abbeville, 1991

Susan Waller, *Women Artists in the Modern Era: A Documentary History*, Metuchen, NJ: Scarecrow Press, 1991

British Paintings, 1500–1850, sale cat., Sotheby's, London, 15 July 1992, lot 85

Kathryn Metz, "Ellen and Rolinda Sharples: Mother and daughter painters", *Woman's Art Journal*, xvi/1, 1995, pp.3–11

Unpublished diary, 1803–36, of Ellen and Rolinda Sharples is in the Bristol Reference Library; typescripts of the diary are in the Sharples Archives, Bristol City Museum and Art Gallery, and the Frick Art Reference Library, New York (as well as Sharples study photographs); the Catalog of American Portraits is in the National Portrait Gallery, Washington, DC.

Working at the turn of the 18th and 19th centuries in both Britain and the USA, in the tradition of family artist practice, Ellen Sharples was one of a relatively small number of women to achieve professional status. Her portraits, in pastel and watercolour miniatures on ivory, show careful attention to detail and expression, and their warm colours and soft, illuminating light provide sympathetic interpretations of her subjects. She received her only known training from James Sharples before their marriage. During their family's first sojourn in the USA in the 1790s, where they were itinerant artists, Ellen began to copy pastel portraits in the same small formats as her husband's originals. She also did skilled needlework, as demonstrated by four examples of her silk embroidery in the City of Bristol Museum and Art Gallery.

Ellen Sharples wrote in her diary that she had learned drawing "as an ornament for amusement", which she put "to a useful purpose" by copying her husband's portraits of such notables as George Washington, James Madison and their wives, diplomats such as Talleyrand, writers and scientists. James Sharples's portraits were in great demand for their straightforward, accurate portrayals, and Ellen's copies were considered equal to the originals and priced the same. She must have done many, especially as her husband became involved in unremunerative mechanical inventions. At least six of the many pastel copies of *George Washington* done by the family from James's two originals have been attributed to Ellen (three in private collections; the others in Allentown Museum, PA; Yale University Art Museum, New Haven – given by Washington to a contemporary who recorded that the portrait was "by Mrs Sharples from an original by Mr Sharples" (quoted in Knox 1930) – National Gallery of Art, London, repr. *Connoisseur*, US edition, April 1941, cover). These pastels show the typical family format: bust or waist-length profile or three-quarter view, with the head and body developed in layers of pigment applied with a brush to resemble painting, with increasingly deep tones and fine detail in facial features and wig texture; the background and lower sections of the dress painted in freer, broader, more obvious strokes. Ellen also did a remarkable silk embroidery portrait of *Washington* (c.1796; Mount Vernon) based on these pastel portraits, with similar attention to detail and character.

During the 1800s Ellen Sharples did miniature copies in watercolour on ivory, a medium that James did not use. Examples include *Dr Priestley*, *George Washington* and *General Alexander Hamilton* (c.1804), *Sir Joseph Banks* (c.1803) and *North American Indian* (1808; all City of Bristol Museum and Art Gallery); all are known to be copies of her husband's portraits except the last, which is from an unknown source and unusual in the family's work in its dignified, three-quarter-length pose and fuller landscape background. On the basis of diary notations and style, the portrait copy of *Benjamin Rush* (1805), a noted physician, humanitarian and an early advocate of education for women, and of the writer *Charles Brockden Brown* (1810; both Independence Historical Park, Philadelphia) have been attributed to Ellen. Another portrait copy attributed to her, *Joseph Priestley* (c.1794; National Portrait Gallery, London), illustrates her fine, sympathetic portrayal and warm palette. Ellen also undertook original portrait commissions in both miniatures and pastel, but of the 18 portraits done from life noted in her diary, including original miniatures of her husband and children, only the first pastel has been located: *Arthur M. Browne, MP* (1803; City of Bristol Museum and Art Gallery). Informed by her miniatures, the face and figure are carefully rendered with close attention to the sitter's expression and presence. The success of this portrait led to further requests for original portraits from life.

After 1810 Ellen did not mention her own work, focusing

Rolinda Sharples: *Clifton Racecourse*, 1830–36; City of Bristol Museum and Art Gallery

instead on Rolinda, for whom she was an important mentor (she later transcribed Rolinda's diary notations and incorporated them with her own into a single volume). Rolinda Sharples received her only known art training outside the family with Philip Reinagle in London, known for his portraits, animal paintings, landscapes and copies of Dutch masters. She worked on a larger scale than her mother, employing a fuller palette in oil on panel and canvas, and progressing to more natural and varied poses. From individual portraits she expanded into figure groups, genre and narrative paintings, becoming one of the first British women artists to depict contemporary events. She also painted flowers and shells. Although the diary mentions about 70 portraits in oil, pastel or miniature, as well as various copies and pencil studies, only 15 of these have been located, mostly small in size, and most in the City of Bristol Museum and Art Gallery. They include a *Self-Portrait*, a portrait of *Ellen Sharples*, a double portrait of the *Artist and Her Mother* (c.1816), which shows the proud mother regarding her daughter working at the easel on a genre scene, surrounded by framed paintings, and *Madame Catalini* (1814 or 1821), the famous Italian soprano. Both the latter works are rich in colour and illumination, and natural in expression and modelling. There is also a three-quarter-length life-size portrait of *Ellen Sharples* in the Royal West of England Academy, Bristol.

The first of Rolinda's group paintings, *Cloakroom, the Clifton Assembly Rooms* (c.1817–18; City of Bristol Museum and Art Gallery), with its portraits of Bristol society members, attracted local attention. The diary reveals her diligent work habits and early-morning site drawings for verisimilitude for her first exterior scene, *A Market* (begun 1816; untraced). The animated figures in the painting received favourable reviews at her first Royal Academy exhibition in 1820, and led to a painting commission when exhibited at the Society of British Artists in 1825. *Rownham Ferry* (exh. Royal Academy 1822; ex-Sotheby's, London, 15 July 1992, lot 85) shows a development to a more complex composition with deeper space, a background of buildings, hills and cliffs, and groups of figures in boats and on shore merged with contrasting lights and darks.

Rolinda attained her mature style in *Stoppage of the Bank* (1825–7; City of Bristol Museum and Art Gallery, repr. *Money: From Cowrie Shells to Credit Cards*, exh. cat., British Museum, London, 1986), which depicted the Bristol Bullion Bank failure of 1822. Groups of figures are shown in various states of alarm in a stage-like space that extends into a receding city street and landscape, with sunlight shining through gathering clouds. The warm earth tones are enriched with colour accents and light. The painting was favourably reviewed in the Society of British Artists exhibition of 1827, and invitations to exhibit it followed from Liverpool, Leeds,

Birmingham and the Bristol Institution. As in some of her other paintings, *St James's Fair* (1823–5; Dibick Hall, Durham) and *Village Gossips* (c.1828; City of Bristol Museum and Art Gallery), the facial expressions and interaction among the figures and with the surrounding environment reflect influences from the genre paintings of the Bristol artist Edward Bird and such Dutch painters as Adriaen van Ostade.

The Bristol riots of 1831 were a reaction to inefficient local government and demand for parliamentary reform. Sharples joined the throng at the subsequent trial of the commander of the local troops, Colonel Brereton, who had refused to use force to stop the rioters without an order from the aldermen. Her work on the *Trial of Colonel Brereton after the Bristol Riots* (1832–4; City of Bristol Museum and Art Gallery) involved hours of sketching during the trial and subsequent individual sittings. The painting, nearly 1.8 metres long, contains more than 100 portraits. With evident sympathy for the Colonel, who committed suicide two days after the trial began, Sharples depicted him as a young man although he was 50 at the time. She worked on the painting almost every day during the two years it took to complete it, while also maintaining her portrait practice. It was exhibited at the Bristol Society of Artists and the Society of British Artists in 1834, and remains an important visual document of a critical episode in the city's history. Many of Sharples's friends sat for the figures in *Clifton Racecourse* (1830–36; see illustration), her most complex and expansive composition. The vast scene, immersed in light, shows influences from Dutch genre and English landscape painting. Completed at the peak of her career, two years before her premature death from cancer, this last-known painting is a further example of her ambition and development in subject matter not yet deemed acceptable for most women artists to pursue.

KATHRYN METZ

See also Copyists survey

Shchekatikhina-Pototskaya, Aleksandra (Vasilevna)

Russian ceramist and designer, 1892–1967

Born Aleksandra Vasilevna Shchekotikhina in the Ukraine, 1892, into a family of Old Believers. Studied in the Drawing School of the Society for the Encouragement of the Arts, St Petersburg/Petrograd, under Nicholas Roerich and Ivan Bilibin, 1908–15; sent on a tour of northern Russia with Marya Lebedeva, 1910; to Greece, Italy and France, 1913; while in Paris, studied at Académie Ranson under Maurice Denis, Félix Vallotton and Paul Sérusier. Designed costumes and stage sets for opera and ballet, 1912–20; executed designs for the State Porcelain Factory, Petrograd, 1918–23. Married Nikolai Pototsky, 1915; one son; husband died 1920; married the artist Ivan Bilibin, 1923; adopted the spelling Shchekatikhina-Pototskaya, late 1920s; husband died in siege of Leningrad, 1942. Visited Egypt, Ethiopia and the Near East, 1923. Lived in Paris, working as an illustrator and stage designer, 1925–36. Worked under Suetin at the

Lomonosov Porcelain Factory, Leningrad, 1937–53. Died in Leningrad, 1967.

Principal Exhibitions

Individual
Galerie Druet, Paris: 1926
Amsterdam: 1929 (with Ivan Bilibin)
Leningrad: 1955

Group
Mir Iskusstva (World of Art): from 1915
Petrograd: 1919 (*First State Free Art Exhibition*)
Exposition Internationale des Arts Décoratifs et Industriels Modernes, Paris: 1925 (gold medal)
State Russian Museum, Leningrad: 1927 (*Russian Porcelain*)
Art and Design Exhibition, Monza: 1927 (diploma of honour)
Leningrad and Moscow: 1932–3 (*Artists of the RSFSR over 15 Years, 1917–1932*)

Bibliography

A. Rusakova, "Zhizneradostnoye iskusstvo" [Cheerful art]", *Neva*, 1955, no.5
Aleksandra Vasilevna Shchekotikhina-Pototskaya, exh. cat., Leningrad, 1955; published Leningrad, 1958
V. Noskovich, "A. V. Shchekotikhina-Pototskaya", *Iskusstvo*, 1956, no.1
——, *A.V. Shchekotikhina-Pototskaya*, Leningrad, 1959
M.N. Pototsky, *Dyadya Vanya* [Uncle Vanya], Leningrad, 1970
I. Ya. Bilibin, 1876–1942, A.V. Shchekotikhina-Pototskaya, 1892–1967, exh. cat., Leningrad, 1977
Art into Production: Soviet Textiles, Fashion and Ceramics, 1917–1935, exh. cat., Museum of Modern Art, Oxford, 1984
Nina Lobanov-Rostovsky, *Revolutionary Ceramics: Soviet Porcelain, 1917–1927*, London: Studio Vista, and New York: Rizzoli, 1990
De grote utopie/Die grosse Utopie/The Great Utopia, exh. cat., Stedelijk Museum, Amsterdam, and elsewhere, 1992
Agitation zum Glück: Sowjetische Kunst der Stalinzeit, exh. cat., Documenta-Halle, Kassel, and elsewhere, 1993

Aleksandra Shchekatikhina-Pototskaya played a major role in the popularisation of ceramics in the early Soviet period, using folk motifs and subjects with an understanding that helped her to achieve the underlying political goal of making both fine and applied art accessible to the masses.

Her childhood in the Ukraine, where her deeply Orthodox grandfather painted eggs, icons and miniatures, and her grandmother produced traditional embroidered designs, gave her an instinctive feel for folk art and motifs that was to be evident throughout her career. Her initial desire was to move away from her folk roots, but she failed to gain entrance to the Academy of Arts in St Petersburg. In 1908, however, she entered the Drawing School of the Society for the Encouragement of the Arts, where a radical change in staff in 1906, inspired partly by the widespread Russian Revival movement, had brought in Nicholas Roerich as director and Ivan Bilibin as teacher. The Russian Revivalists, however, largely products of a different social background, had an ethnographic interest in folk art and consciously sought to "learn" and apply its lessons, while Shchekatikhina-Pototskaya sought to acquire the artistic means to express and extend her inherent understanding of it. Thus, in 1913, she travelled to Greece, Italy and France, spending several months studying at the Académie Ranson in Paris under Maurice Denis and Félix Vallotton. Like the avant-garde artists Mikhail Larionov and Natalya

Goncharova (q.v.), and in contrast to the refined artists of the Mir Iskusstva (World of Art) movement, she sought not to perfect folk art, but to present it with all its naïvety and imperfections. Here the expressionism of Roerich was more important than the precise, pedantic approach of Bilibin, but she remained largely untouched by the former's literary symbolism and rationalism, just as she was interested in the naivety of provincial icons rather than in their mysticism.

She collaborated with Roerich and Bilibin on theatre designs and she produced book and magazine illustrations, occasionally exhibiting her drawings and paintings with the World of Art group. The Revolution of 1917, however, was radically to change the way she worked, for in 1918 the Petrograd (former Imperial, later Lomonosov) Porcelain Manufactory set up a special painting section under Sergei Chekhonin, and Shchekatikhina-Pototskaya was one of the 25 artists taken on, with the aim of producing objects not for the middle classes or the aristocracy, but for the people.

This was very much to her taste, particularly with her tendency towards expressive decoration rather than works with a theoretical, intellectual basis, and in the first two years she covered cups, saucers and plates with pictures of village weddings and folk tales. The intense colour contrasts of these early works were clearly derived from the cheap popular Russian print known as *lubok*. Her small statuette of the *Snow Maiden* was produced for many years. But while she was to be awarded medals at the Exposition Internationale des Arts Décoratifs et Industriels Modernes in Paris in 1925, in view of her later work we see that the agit-porcelain (plates and objects with revolutionary symbols and slogans, for example the plates *Petrograd: Revolution Square* and *Commissar*) that she produced in the early 1920s represented a diversion from what really interested her, and even those pieces that used folk-style paintings (*Village* cups) or subjects from fairy tales (*Snow Maiden* coffee service) reveal that she did not in these first years pay much attention to the relationship between the object as a sculptural form and the surface decoration, with the latter seeming to be in conflict with the restrictive edge of the plate or cup. This was a problem in the work of many artists at the factory at the time, as they were initially forced to use forms left over from pre-Revolutionary "bourgeois" products, often totally unsuited to the new approach.

Bilibin had moved to Egypt in 1920, and in 1923 Shchekatikhina-Pototskaya joined him and there they were married. The difference in the works that they both produced in Egypt reveal how far removed they were in their art, but Bilibin's documentary precision and calm observation had some influence on her mixed planes and generalised forms, as became increasingly clear over the next decade. Their move to Paris in 1925 was apparently initially motivated by the Exposition Internationale, which in turn led to a one-woman show of her paintings, watercolours and porcelain at the Galerie Druet in 1926, and to participation in the Salons d'Automne. With Bilibin she made many trips to the south of France, producing still lifes that reveal an increasing tendency towards the decorative rather than expressive use of colour. This became noticeable in the vast number of porcelain pieces she produced in Paris, for Sèvres and other manufacturers, in which her colours became more restrained and severe, with a more painterly approach to subjects, as on her plates with depictions of bulls and rams. She also visited Maurice Denis in Brittany in 1927, and his muted tones and silhouetted figures contributed to this tendency in her work, although in some ways she was closer to Pierre Bonnard in her desire to achieve a decorative effect. By the early 1930s she was using only two or three colours in her simple, unfussy, round plates. The conflict between surface and space, contour and volume, which can be seen in her paintings, particularly the still lifes, was a means of resolving that seen earlier in her paintings on porcelain, and in her new pieces the painting had more relation to the object. The favoured motifs of this time were animals and fruits, and fish, first seen on a dish produced in 1926, became a recurring theme. She continued to design clothes and produce illustrations, as well as working in the theatre, but these remained secondary to her ceramics and porcelain.

In 1936 the family moved back to the Soviet Union, and Shchekatikhina-Pototskaya returned to the flourishing Lomonosov Factory, where the former Suprematist Nikolai Suetin was now in charge, and the emphasis was on producing designs for mass production. In the first few years she also produced her first serious sculptural pieces, albeit still in a naïve, folk style, and the beloved fish, birds and fruit of the Paris years take on three-dimensional form (*Carp* salad dish, *Duck* butter dish).

Shchekatikhina-Pototskaya's subject matter was inevitably affected by the war and the siege of Leningrad, during which her husband died of starvation, and she produced a series of vases with images of Russian historical heroes, such as *Alexander Nevsky* (1942) and *Dmitry Donskoy* (1943; both produced 1946). Once again, where the subject matter was the result of political dictates, the result was less successful, but once the war was over and she returned to the production of bowls and containers in the shape of fruits and animals (*Pepper* butter dish, 1948), a new severity and coherence made itself felt, a balance between form and decoration and a greater understanding of the difference between the painting of sculptural pieces and the flat decoration of ordinary round plates, cups and saucers, even when using traditional Russian motifs, as in the *Golden Cockerel* tea service of 1949. During the 1940s and 1950s her works largely set the agenda in the factory, whose products since her death have proved the earlier debt to her in their relatively unadventurous approach or dependence on her designs. Major collections containing examples of porcelain pieces, as well as drawings and paintings, include the Bilibin and Shchekatikhina-Pototskaya Museum in Ivangorod, Russia, and the Lomonosov Porcelain Factory, St Petersburg.

CATHERINE PHILLIPS

Sher-Gil, Amrita
Indian painter, 1913–1941

Born in Budapest, Hungary, 30 January 1913, to an Indian father and Hungarian mother. Returned to India with her family, 1921, settling in Simla. Visited Italy, 1923–4. Studied art in Paris, 1929–34, first at Académie de la Grande Chaumière under Pierre Vaillant, then at the Ecole Nationale

Sher-Gil: *The Banana Sellers*

des Beaux-Arts under Lucien Simon. Returned to India, November 1934; toured South India, 1936. Married a cousin, Dr Victor Egan, in Hungary, 1938; returned to India with him, settling on family estate at Saraya, Gorakhpur, 1939. Associée, Grand Salon, Paris. Died in Lahore, 5 December 1941.

Principal Exhibitions

Simla Fine Art Society, India: from 1935
Fine Arts Society, New Delhi: 1936
Faletti's Hotel, Lahore: 1937 (individual)
All India Fine Arts and Crafts Society: 1938
Punjab Literary League Hall: 1941 (retrospective)

Bibliography

Karl Khandalavah, *Amrita Sher-Gil*, Bombay: New Book Company, 1944
A.S. Raman, "The present art of India", *The Studio*, cxlii, 1951, pp.97–105
H. Goetz, "Amrita Sher-Gil", *The Studio*, cl, 1955, pp.50–51
R. de Loyola Furtado, *Three Painters*, New Delhi: Dhoomimal Ramchand, 1960
Baldoon Dhingra, *Sher-Gil*, New Delhi: Lalit Kala Akademi, 1965
Marg, xxv, March 1972 (entire issue)
Chintamani Vyas, *Amrita Sher-Gil*, Amritsar: Punjab Academy of Fine Arts and Crafts, 1982 (contains bibliography)
Six Indian Painters, exh. cat., Tate Gallery, London, 1982
N. Iqbal Singh, *Amrita Sher-Gil: A Biography*, New Delhi: Vikas, 1984
Mulk Raj Anand, *Amrita Sher-Gil*, New Delhi: National Gallery of Modern Art, 1989

An ancient culture in the process of change is how Alan Bowness, then director of the Tate Gallery, introduced a show of six contemporary Indian painters chosen by the British painter Howard Hodgkin in 1982. Of the six, Amrita Sher-Gil was the only woman, and again perhaps unusually was herself half-Hungarian, and was to marry a Hungarian. Her father came from a prominent Punjabi family; a scholar, he married a Hungarian pianist, whose brother was also a scholar of India. Her early childhood was spent in the Europe of World War I, but the family moved to India when she was eight; she was to return to Europe to study art in Paris, and then came back to India, where she visited some of the best-known sites of Indian sculpture and temple art, including Ellora and Ajanta, and studied Mughal miniatures. She was already celebrated when she lived in Lahore in the last few months of her life; she was to die at the age of 28.

Sher-Gil's subject matter was based on observation, of village life, of musicians, of children, of young women. The Indian tradition is neither realistic nor naturalistic, but is figurative and representational, if often in fantastical and magical mode. It is this that affected Sher-Gil's painting; her experience of India ante-dated Indian independence (1947) and her experience of Europe was not only in time of war, but also, in the 1930s, at a time when the existing empires had not been dismantled – and extreme prescience would have been needed to see how rapidly the European empires were to dissolve in the period after World War II.

So Sher-Gil's painting was practised in a society that in some respects was still profoundly colonial, and yet which also had a strong caste system of its own. In Indian painting the adoption of abstraction, in particular Abstract Expressionist idioms, was to come in the post-war period, although traditional schools of painting have also been kept. It was Sher-Gil's gift to take something of the delicacy pertinent to, say, the fantastical worlds of Paul Klee, and the kind of brilliant colour that we may associate with Kandinsky, and use the skills and freedoms of European modernism to see again her India: the family estate, the life of the villages, rural moments and rural landscapes. Her work was small in scale, but not miniature; and her subjects were based on her observations of many levels of society. These are fiery yet tender paintings, serene yet pulsating with a curious vitality. And they are certainly special: occasionally quaint, but not folkloric; rather they have a quality of haunting evocation of a life that was both familiar and alien to the artist. She admired Gauguin, an artist who had also painted societies that were exotic to him, from rural France to the South Seas. Amrita Sher-Gil, some of whose delicate yet strong paintings are on view in the National Gallery of Modern Art in Delhi, has no international reputation, but is a minor legend in the history of Indian art.

MARINA VAIZEY

Siddal, Elizabeth Eleanor
British painter, 1829–1862

Born Elizabeth Eleanor Siddall in London, 25 July 1829, to an artisan cutler and retailer originally from Sheffield and his London-born wife; signed her work Siddal by 1855. Became artist's model, 1850; began relationship with Dante Gabriel Rossetti c.1852; also taught by him. Received financial help from John Ruskin, 1855–7; travelled to Paris and Nice at his expense, partly for health reasons, winter 1855–6. Took classes at Sheffield School of Art, c.1857. Married Rossetti in Hastings, 1860; still-born daughter born 1861. Died from a laudanum overdose in London, 11 February 1862 (coroner returned verdict of accidental death).

Principal Exhibitions

Pre-Raphaelite group, 4 Russell Place, London: 1857
National Academy of Design, New York: 1857–8 (*American Exhibition of British Art*, touring)

Selected Writings

Verse in *The New Oxford Book of Victorian Verse*, ed. Christopher Ricks, Oxford and New York: Oxford University Press, 1987

Bibliography

W.M. Rossetti, "Dante Rossetti and Elizabeth Siddal", *Burlington Magazine*, i, 1903, pp.273–95
Violet Hunt, *The Wife of Rossetti: Her Life and Death*, London: Lane, and New York: Dutton, 1932
Eleonore Reichert, *Elizabeth Eleanor Siddal: Leben und Werk einer viktorianischen Malerin*, PhD dissertation, Universität Giessen, 1972
Roger C. Lewis and Mark Samuels Lasner, *Poems and Drawings of Elizabeth Siddal*, Wolfville, Nova Scotia: Wombat Press, 1978
Joanna Banham and Jennifer Harris, eds, *William Morris and the Middle Ages: A Collection of Essays*, Manchester: Manchester University Press, 1984

Deborah Cherry and Griselda Pollock, "Woman as sign in Pre-Raphaelite literature: A study of the representation of Elizabeth Siddal", *Art History*, vii, 1984, pp.206–27

The Pre-Raphaelites, exh. cat., Tate Gallery, London, 1984

Charlotte Yeldham, *Women Artists in Nineteenth-Century England and France*, 2 vols, New York: Garland, 1984

Alicia Craig Faxon, *Dante Gabriel Rossetti*, Oxford: Phaidon, 1989

Jan Marsh, *The Legend of Elizabeth Siddal*, London: Quartet, 1989

Jan Marsh and Pamela Gerrish Nunn, *Women Artists and the Pre-Raphaelite Movement*, London: Virago, 1989

Susan P. Casteras, *English Pre-Raphaelitism and Its Reception in America in the Nineteenth Century*, Rutherford, NJ: Fairleigh Dickinson University Press, 1990

Elizabeth Siddall, 1859–1862: Pre-Raphaelite Artist, exh. cat., Ruskin Gallery, Sheffield, 1991 (contains poems by Siddal and bibliography)

Deborah Cherry, *Painting Women: Victorian Women Artists*, London and New York: Routledge, 1993

Beth Harris, *"For the Needle She?": Images of the Seamstress in the 1840s*, PhD dissertation, City University of New York, Graduate Center (in preparation)

Nothing is known of Elizabeth Eleanor Siddall's early education or training, but she is believed to have worked in the fashion trade as a dressmaker/milliner. One account claims that she showed her first designs to the director of the School of Design and was then introduced to his son, Walter Howell Deverell, associate of the Pre-Raphaelite Brotherhood, for whom she sat as a model for Viola in *Twelfth Night* (1850). Thereafter she sat to William Holman Hunt for Sylvia in *Two Gentlemen of Verona* (1851) and to John Everett Millais for *Ophelia* (1852) before exciting the particular attention of Dante Gabriel Rossetti, whose unofficial pupil she became. In 1855 Rossetti showed her work to John Ruskin, who provided financial support that enabled Siddal (as she now signed herself) to purchase colours – up to this point her work was entirely in pencil or ink (with the exception of a self-portrait in oils) – and also to travel. She spent the winter of 1855–6 in Paris and Nice, though no trace of this is visible in her work. Her subjects were typically Pre-Raphaelite and "poetic" – illustrations to works by Shakespeare, Keats, Tennyson and Browning and to Walter Scott's *Minstrelsy of the Scottish Border*, as well as Christian themes such as the Nativity and the Virgin and Child. She made her exhibition debut in 1857, with the independent Pre-Raphaelite group show organised by Ford Madox Brown, to which Siddal sent three watercolours, her self-portrait and four studies. The watercolour *Clerk Saunders* (1857; Fitzwilliam Museum, Cambridge) was sold to Charles Eliot Norton of Boston and was included in an exhibition of British art that toured the USA later that same year. Siddal herself went to Sheffield at this period, studying at the local School of Art under director Young Mitchell, and then to Derbyshire. In the spring of 1860, after an estrangement, she and Rossetti were finally married and settled in London.

During her decade as an artist, Siddal produced more than 100 paintings and drawings (Faxon 1989). She was essentially self-taught, yet while her preliminary sketches are often crude, the finished works possess "great imaginative and evocative power". Her earliest dated works are the *Lady of Shalott* (signed and dated 15 December 1853; pencil, pen and ink; Jeremy Maas, London) and the *Self-Portrait* (inscribed "EES 1853–4"; oil; private collection, Britain, repr. Cherry 1993). There followed two ink drawings, *Lovers Listening to Music*

Siddal: *Pippa Passes*, 1854; drawing; Ashmolean Museum, Oxford

and *Pippa Passes* (1854; see illustration). Finished watercolours include the *Ladies' Lament from Sir Patrick Spens* (inscribed "EES/56"; Tate Gallery, London), *Lady Clare* (inscribed "EES/57"; private collection, Britain, repr. London 1984, no.222), *Clerk Saunders* (inscribed "EES 1857"; Fitzwilliam Museum) and *Before the Battle* or *Lady Affixing Pennant to Knight's Spear* (c.1858–9; Tate Gallery). Her subjects remained imaginary and "medieval" in the Victorian sense, and on a small scale, reflecting her lack of resources, but also as if in emulation of medieval illumination. Her figures possess a similar anatomical stiffness, combined with Romantic intensity of expression and composition. Because of her relationship with Rossetti, it has been frequently claimed that her work is an awkward imitation of his, or that he "customarily" assisted with her painting. Of this there is little evidence apart from a jointly signed watercolour that once belonged to Ruskin, *Sir Galahad and the Holy Grail* (1857; inscribed "EES inv EES & DGR del"; private collection, *ibid.*, no.217). Rather, it would seem that something of the studied simplicity of Rossetti's works of the mid-1850s, such as *Arthur's Tomb* (1854) and the *Wedding of St George* (1857), was borrowed from the genuine naivety that Siddal's work had in common with medieval art. In this sense, she can be termed a "true Pre-Raphaelite". Algernon Charles Swinburne commented on her originality of style, adding: "Gabriel's influence and example [were] not more perceptible than her own independence and freshness of inspiration" (quoted in W.M. Rossetti, *Some Reminiscences*, i, London, 1906, p.195).

After Siddal's death from an opiate overdose in 1862, Rossetti collected all her works, including fragments, and had the studies and sketches photographed for a memorial album (copy in Fitzwilliam Museum; original glass negatives in Ashmolean Museum), from which her working practices and ambitions can be reconstructed. Due to lack of exhibition, her work virtually vanished from view and public knowledge for over a century, until such feminist scholars as Deborah Cherry began to rediscover its existence and re-instate Siddal in the ranks of art history. Before this she was known chiefly for Millais's *Ophelia* and as Rossetti's model and muse, with whom he buried and later exhumed his poems. In the Tate

Gallery's Pre-Raphaelite exhibition of 1984 she was represented by the *Lady of Shalott*, *Sir Galahad and the Holy Grail* and *Lady Clare*. Of the last, Cherry wrote:

> The watercolour represents two women. They are constructed in difference to each other through the production of daughter/mother, lady/servant, youth/age as poles of contrast ... The relationship of these two, which has the potential to disrupt heterosexual romantic love and which has diverted dynastic succession, is here presented as one of conflict, difference and divided interests. The drawing of the figures and the originality of the architectural space oppose Renaissance notions of anatomy and perspective which were enshrined in academic traditions [and are to be] understood as calculated strategies in the production of "medievalness" [Cherry in London 1984, no.222].

In 1991 Siddal was the subject of a solo show at the Ruskin Gallery, Sheffield, where 34 works were exhibited, as well as some 20 photographs and other items.

JAN MARSH

Sintenis, Renée

German sculptor and graphic artist, 1888–1965

Born Renate Alice Sintenis in Glatz, Silesia, 20 March 1888. Studied at the Stuttgart art school, then at the Kunstgewerbeschule, Berlin, 1908–12. Married painter and graphic artist Emil Rudolf Weiss, 1917. First female sculptor to become a member of the Prussian Academy, 1931 (resigned 28 February 1934 under growing Nazi pressure). Studio destroyed by bombing, 1944. Professor at the Berlin Academy, 1948–55. Recipient of Olympia prize for *Runner Nurmi*, 1932; art prize of the city of Berlin, 1948; Order "Pour le Mérite", 1952; Great Distinguished Service Cross of the Federal Republic of Germany, 1953. Died in Berlin, 22 April 1965.

Principal Exhibitions

Individual

Galerie Alfred Flechtheim, Düsseldorf: 1920 (with Otto Waetjen and Paul Grosch)
Weyhe Gallery, New York: 1921, 1928
Galerie Alfred Flechtheim, Berlin: 1925 (with Marie Laurencin), 1930 (with Marie Laurencin, Martel Schwichtenberg and Alexandra Exter)
Galerie Barbazanges, Paris: 1927, 1928
Galerie George Bernheim, Paris: 1929
Ausstellungsraum Karl Buchholz, Berlin: 1935 (with Alfred Partikel)
Buchholz Gallery, New York: 1939, 1940
Magistrat von Gross-Berlin (Haus Braasch), Berlin: 1949 (with Richard Scheibe)
Kasseler Kunstverein, Kassel: 1950 (*Berliner Künstler*, with Georg Tappert and Heinrich Graf von Luckner)
Galerie Axel Vömel, Düsseldorf: 1952, 1956, 1965
Gallery Wittenborn, New York: 1957
Städtisches Museum, Mülheim an der Ruhr: 1962

Group

Berlin Secession, Berlin: 1915, 1927 (*Sport*), 1930 (*Plastik-Ausstellung*)
Galerie Alfred Flechtheim, Berlin: 1922 (*Das Schwedische Ballett*), 1932 (*111 Porträts*)
Kestner-Gesellschaft, Hannover: 1931 (*Tiere in der Kunst*)
Museum of Modern Art, New York: 1931 (*Modern German Painting and Sculpture*)
Museum der Bildenden Künste, Leipzig: 1963 (*Sport in der bildenden Kunst*)

Bibliography

Marie Laurencin, Renée Sintenis, exh. cat., Galerie Alfred Flechtheim, Berlin, 1925
René Crevel and Georg Biermann, *Renée Sintenis*, Junge Kunst, lvii, Berlin: Klinkhardt und Biermann, 1930
Hanna Kiel, ed., *Renée Sintenis*, Berlin: Rembrandt, 1935
Renée Sintenis: Neuere Bronzen und Graphik, exh. cat., Karl Buchholz, Berlin, 1935
Rudolf Hagelstange and others, *Renée Sintenis*, Berlin: Aufbau, 1947
Adolf Jannasch, *Renée Sintenis*, Potsdam, 1949
Berliner Künstler: Malerei, Grafik, Plastik, exh. cat., Kasseler Kunstverein, Kassel, 1950
Bildhauer-Meisterwerke der Galerie Alex Vömel, exh. cat., Galerie Alex Vömel, Düsseldorf, 1954
Ausstellung Galerie Alex Vömel, exh. cat., Galerie Alex Vömel, Düsseldorf, 1956
Hanna Kiel, *Renée Sintenis*, Berlin: Rembrandt, 1956
Friedrich Terveen, *Renée Sintenis zeichnet und modelliert ein Fohlen*, Göttingen, 1957
Renée Sintenis, Johann Michael Wilm, exh. cat., Städtische Kunstsammlungen, Lindau-Bregenz, 1961
Gert von der Osten, *Plastik des 20. Jahrhunderts in Deutschland, Österreich und der Schweiz*, Königstein im Taunus, 1962
Renée Sintenis: Plastiken, Zeichnungen, Druckgraphik, exh. cat., Georg-Kolbe-Museum, Berlin, and elsewhere, 1983
Britta E. Buhlmann, *Renée Sintenis: Werkmonographie der Skulpturen*, Darmstadt: Wissenschaftliche Buchgesellschaft, 1987
Entartete Beeldhouwkunst: Duitse Beeldhouwers, 1900–1945 [Degenerate sculpture: German sculptors, 1900–1945], exh. cat., Commanderie van St Jan, Nijmegen, and elsewhere, 1991
Erich Ranfft, "German women sculptors, 1918–1936: Gender differences and status", *Visions of the "Neue Frau": Women and the Visual Arts in Weimar Germany*, ed. Marsha Meskimmon and Shearer West, Aldershot: Scolar Press, 1995, pp.42–61

One of the best-known female German sculptors of the 20th century, Renée Sintenis experienced her first success in 1915, when she exhibited at the Berlin Secession and Rainer Maria Rilke became her patron. Her work was handled by, among others, Alfred Flechtheim, one of the most important dealers of the later 1920s, who had good connections abroad. Sintenis treated contemporary themes and made small-scale works that were favoured by patrons. In 1931 she participated in the seminal exhibition *Modern German Painting and Sculpture* at the Museum of Modern Art in New York, and she was included in Alfred Hentzen's important publication *Deutsche Bildhauer der Gegenwart* (1934, pp.60–62).

Sintenis never worked directly from nature, because she claimed this spoiled the overall impression with a plethora of detail (Kiel 1935, p.19). Nevertheless, her sculptures are the essence of her experience and observation, based on meticulous studies of nature, but done from memory. The materials she used permitted spontaneity: clay for life-size works and black refractory wax for small-scale ones, for which the rigidity of the material provided a clear outline and precision of detail. Later, these were cast in bronze or silver.

Sintenis was most famous for her sculptures of animals: young, lively, innocent, clumsy, playful, comical, often grotesquely disproportioned horses, ponies, donkeys, calves, dogs, bears, deer and elephants. Captured in their characteristic movements, they portray the typical in the individual subject. She was interested in expressing the instinctive life of animals, their helplessness, wantonness, insecurity and loneliness, without humanising them.

Anatomical accuracy was not her prime objective, and the stretched legs of *Frolicsome Foal* (1925; bronze; Bayerische Staatsgemäldesammlung, Munich), which express energy and rhythm, mix description and artificiality. In *Rearing Foal* (1915; bronze; Nationalgalerie, Berlin) and *Jumping Shetland Pony* (1933; bronze; Noack Foundry, Berlin; collection Dr Maria Lex, Berlin) movement equals love of life. She developed certain types. The archetypal static standing *Foal* (1915; bronze, clay; Bayerische Staatsgemäldesammlung) is developed in the less fleshy *Scratching Foal* (1918; bronze; Bayerische Staatsgemäldesammlung; Städelsches Kunstinstitut, Frankfurt am Main) and *Foal Looking Back* (1919; bronze; Noack Foundry, Berlin; collection Frau Colzman, Langenberg), also anatomically distinct and the first to turn its head. This posture is further investigated in *Lying Foal* (1932; bronze; Hermann-Hinrich Reemtsma Collection, Hamburg) and *Foal Looking Back* (1951; bronze; private collection, Koblenz, repr. Buhlmann 1987, p.231), in which the spatial impact derives from the extreme turn of the slender neck.

Sintenis's most important large-scale commission was *Daphne* (1930; bronze, clay; Wallraf-Richartz-Museum, Cologne; Museum of Modern Art, New York), based on the bronze maquette *Small Daphne* of 1918. It illustrates the legend from Ovid's *Metamorphoses* in which the nymph Daphne, fleeing the advances of Apollo, prayed for help from her father, the river god Peneus, who changed her into a laurel tree. This process of self-abnegation and surrender is shown in Sintenis's work, with the body of Daphne beginning to lose human proportions in the transition from woman to tree: the head bowed in fear, her extremely slim figure grows towards the sky, the arms resembling branches swaying in the wind.

A gradual distancing from self-idealisation and stylisation is evident in Sintenis's self-portraits. The earliest example (1914; repr. Kiel 1935, p.94), an etching of "classical anonymity" (R.W. Schnell, "Die Künstlerin Renée Sintenis", *Bildende Kunst*, no.3, 1958, p.202), shows a profile with clear, simple features, a pronounced nose, an introverted gaze and an altogether feminine expression. Softness gradually disappears in the sombre, contemplative terracotta *Self-Portrait* (1915; repr. Kiel 1935, p.9), a face like an antique mask, with a smooth, youthful surface. The process is further developed in the bronze *Self-Portrait* (1931; Tate Gallery, London): broad cheekbones and a markedly fine chin convey an impression of austerity, and deep wrinkles stress her age. Rather than depict herself with the conventional attributes of a woman, she analysed her individuality and produced this rather prim masculine image, corresponding to the sportive ideals of the time. In a *Self-Portrait* of 1944–5 (bronze, concrete, clay; Nationalgalerie, Berlin) the device of the mask is not used to hide the true self, but to symbolise a person who bears the

Sintenis: *Runner Nurmi*, 1926; Nationalgalerie, Berlin

marks of suffering and war yet keeps a distance from the viewer and does not seek compassion. This silent, mourning face transforms Sintenis's personal experience into a universal depiction of the tragic end of old Europe. Ursel Berger called it "Germany after the War".

In her portraits Sintenis strove to reach beyond external appearance, to depict the inner truth of the sitter with psychological empathy and to find the universally valid. The rough surface and sketch-like modelling of her portrait of a poet friend *Joachim Ringelnatz* (1923; stucco, clay, bronze, stone; Nationalgalerie, Berlin) stresses his unusual physiognomy, vulnerability, mental agility and conflicting moods, as well as identifying him as a prototypical bohemian. In the portrait of *Ludwig Klages* (1932; terracotta; repr. Buhlmann 1987, p.151), a philosopher and psychologist, many layers of clay and a high forehead define him as a person whose work is mental.

There was a growing interest in sport in the 1920s and an increasing commercialisation of sportsmen as "mass idols". Sintenis, who was a passionate horsewoman, combined her artistic intuition and expert knowledge in works on sport themes. Her sports figures skilfully capture the phenomenon of dramatic movement, yet the three-dimensionality inevitably gives a sense of statis and compactness. The Finnish runner Paavo Nurmi, who won four gold medals at the Paris Olympics in 1924, was the subject of one such work. But *Runner Nurmi* (1926; see illustration) is more than a portrait; in the carefully observed physiognomy, posture and running style, it is the embodiment of a runner *per se*. The force of the forward thrust is emphasised by the tension of the muscles, the energetic vibration of the whole body and the enormous stride.

A rare work by Sintenis that combines animals and humans is *Polo Player II* (1929; bronze; Nationalgalerie, Berlin), in which conscious and unconscious movement unites in a "drama of harmony" (Schnell *op. cit.*, p.203). Sintenis captured the elusive moment between the two movements: his mallet raised to strike, the rider keeps a delicate balance on the galloping horse.

Originally apolitical, Sintenis came to reject the Nazi regime, which she expressed by abstaining from official glorification of the State. Attempts to force her resignation from her post at the Academy were finally successful in 1934. Although several of her works were removed from museums and public collections, she was not considered sufficiently noisome for the Nazis to deny her the right to exhibit or exclude her from the Reich Chamber of Culture. Preferring to depict young creatures, who were not yet marked by socialisation and history, Sintenis deliberately refused to participate in contemporary political events.

INES SCHLENKER

Sirani, Elisabetta

Italian painter and printmaker, 1638–1665

Born in Bologna, 8 January 1638, daughter of the painter Giovan Andrea Sirani, assistant to Guido Reni; her two sisters Barbara and Anna Maria were also painters. Trained by her father. Lived in Bologna all her life. Member of Accademia di San Luca, Rome. Buried in San Domenico, Bologna, 29 August 1665 (maid accused of poisoning her, but autopsy revealed perforated stomach ulcers).

Bibliography

Luigi Picinardi, *La poesia muta celebrata dalla pittrice loquaci applausi di nobili ingegneri al pinnello immortale della Signorina Elisabetta Sirani pittrice bolognese*, Bologna, 1666 (funeral oration, as "Il pennello lagrimato …", 1665, reprinted in Malvasia 1678)

Carlo Cesare Malvasia, *Felsina pittrice: Vite de' pittori bolognesi*, ii, Bologna, 1678, pp.385–407 (contains "Nota delle pitture fatte da me, Elisabetta Sirani", pp.393–6)

Luigi Crespi, *Vite de' pittori bolognese*, Rome, 1769 (as third volume of Malvasia 1678)

G. Giordani, *Notizie delle donne pittrici di Bologna*, Bologna, 1832

Ottavio Mazzoni-Toselli, *Di Elisabetta Sirani pittrice bolognese e del supposto veneficazione credeesi morta*, Bologna, 1833

Domenico Vaccolini, *Biografia di Elis. Sirani scritta dal Prof. D. Vaccolini*, Rome, 1844

Carolina Bonafede, *Cenni biografici e ritratti d'insigni donne bolognese raccolti dagli storici più accreditati*, Bologna, 1845

Andrea Bianchini, *Prove legali sull'avvelenamente della celebre pittrice bolognese, Elisabetta Sirani, emergenti dal relativo processo*, Bologna, 1854

——, *Il processo di avvelenamento fatto 1665–66 in Bologna contro Lucia Tolomelli per la morte di Elisabetta Sirani*, Bologna, 1904

Laura M. Ragg, *The Women Artists of Bologna*, London: Methuen, 1907

Evelyn Foster Edwards, "Elisabetta Sirani", *Art in America*, xvii, August 1929, pp.242–6

Otto Kurz, *Bolognese Drawings in the Royal Library at Windsor Castle*, London, 1955

G. Baldi, *La farmacia nella breve mortale malattia della pittrice bolognese Elisabetta Sirani*, Pisa, 1958

Andrea Emiliani, "Giovan Andrea ed Elisabetta Sirani", *Maestri della pittura del Seicento emiliano*, exh. cat., Palazzo dell'Archiginnasio, Bologna, 1959, pp.140–45

Women Artists, 1550–1950, exh. cat., Los Angeles County Museum of Art, and elsewhere, 1976

P. Bellini, "Elisabetta Sirani: Catalogue des gravures", *Nouvelles de L'Estampe*, November–December 1976, pp.7–12

Fiorella Frisoni, "La vera Sirani", *Paragone*, xxix/335, 1978, pp.3–18

Germaine Greer, *The Obstacle Race: The Fortunes of Women Painters and Their Work*, London: Secker and Warburg, and New York: Farrar Straus, 1979

Edward Goldberg, *Patterns in Late Medici Art Patronage*, Princeton: Princeton University Press, 1983

Elisabetta Landi and Massimo Pirondini, "Elisabetta Sirani", *Arte emiliana dalle raccolte storiche al nuovo collezionismo*, ed. G. Manni, E. Negro and M. Pirondini, Modena: Artioli, 1989, pp.108–11

Fiorella Frisoni, "Elisabetta Sirani", *La Scuola di Guido Reni*, ed. Emilio Negro and Massimo Pirondini, Modena, 1992

Adelina Modesti, "Elisabetta Sirani 'Pittrice eroina': A portrait of the artist as a young woman", *Identità ed appartenza: Donne e relazioni di genere dal mondo classico all'età contemporanea. Acts of the First International Congress of the Italian Society of Women Historians: Rimini*, 1995

In Counter- and post-Reformation Bologna an unprecedented number of women became professional artists; among these, Elisabetta Sirani, like Lavinia Fontana (q.v.), gained international recognition. As a young girl, Sirani was apprenticed to her father Giovan Andrea Sirani at the insistence of the critic Malvasia, who noticed her precocious drawing talent. She is often regarded as a mere imitator of her father's master, Guido Reni, but she produced more than 200 works in a career of only 13 years, and her achievements deserve closer attention. She was a full member of the Accademia di San Luca in Rome, although she never left her home town of Bologna, where she was the centre of an artistic circle. A master by the age of 19, she ran the Sirani workshop, which included her sisters Barbara and Anna Maria, and supported the whole family when her father was no longer able to paint. She also established an art school for young girls and, in addition to her sisters, her pupils are said to have included Teresa Muratori, Vincenza Franchi, Lucrezia Bianchi, Antonia Pinelli, Maria Oriana Galli Bibiena, Veronica Fontana, Lucrezia Scarfaglia, Camilla Lanteri, Caterina Mongardi, Teresa Maria Coriolani, Ginevra Cantofoli, Vincenza Fabbri and Giovan Battista

Sirani: *Judith Triumphant*, 1658; Burghley House Collection, Stamford

Zanichelli (most from artists' families), as well as the noblewomen Caterina Pepoli and Maria Elena Panzacchi, all of whom worked professionally at some point.

The literature about Sirani is extensive but largely hagiographic, depicting her as a romantic heroine. Typical of this mythologising tendency is Luigi Picinardi's oration at her state funeral, in which he referred to her as "the glory of the female sex"; while Malvasia praised her "extraordinary moral virtue … modesty and inimitable goodness". Her attested beauty and "femininity" ensured that Sirani conformed to the female ideal specified in Renaissance treatises. As a professional painter, unmarried and childless, she also fitted the model of the virtuous noble artist described by Leon Battista Alberti and Giorgio Vasari and epitomised by Raphael. Her works, like Raphael's, were believed to reflect the beauty of her character. Since both the muse of painting and its allegorical personification were female, Sirani could represent both the beauty of womanhood and the perfection of art (see her self-portraits, e.g. as *La Pittura*; Pinacoteca Nazionale, Bologna).

Unlike the paintings of her near contemporary Artemisia Gentileschi (q.v.), which often subvert traditional notions of femininity, Sirani's works do not challenge the male symbolic order, a factor that undoubtedly contributed considerably to her popularity and critical success. Interpreting established artistic models and iconographic traditions in a more personal and intimate manner, she executed mythological works, allegorical scenes and *vanitas*, portraits and large-scale history paintings, both religious and classical (e.g. *Judith Triumphant*, 1658; see illustration; *Portia Wounding Her Thigh*, signed and dated 1664; ex-Wildenstein Collection, New York). The main subjects of her oeuvre, however, are the Holy Family and the Virgin and Child, from one of her earliest public commissions, the *Madonna of the Rosary* (1657; Parish Church, Coscogno), to the numerous small paintings on canvas and copper she produced for private devotional use (e.g. *Madonna of the Girdle* for the Marchese Cospi, 1663; Parish Church, Bagnarola di Budrio). In her last painting, a portrait of *Anna Maria Ranuzzi as Charity* (signed and dated 1665; Cassa di Risparmio, Bologna), the relationship between mother and children is presented in the refined manner of Reni, but with a greater naturalism typical of Emilia, the half-length figures filling the composition and emphasising the closeness of the family group. The representation of maternal love as the Christian virtue of charity gives a spiritual dimension to this secular portrait. A sense of immediacy and intimacy is also seen in Sirani's depictions of the Holy Family in everyday domestic situations to accord with Counter-Reformation devotional requirements (*Madonna of the Swaddling Clothes*, signed and dated 1665; private collection, Madrid, repr. Frisoni 1978, fig.26).

In particular Sirani developed a new iconography of the Virgin and Child with St John the Baptist, presenting the cousins as ordinary playful children (e.g. *Christ Child and Young St John the Baptist*, signed and dated 1661; private collection, repr. Manni, Negro and Pirondini 1989, fig.79), with the Virgin as a more accessible earthly figure wearing the turban of Bolognese peasant women rather than the traditional veil (e.g. two versions of *Virgin and Child with the Young St John*, both 1664; Cassa di Risparmio, Cesena; Museo Civico, Pesaro). Her depictions of children are especially notable:

Vincenzo Ranuzzi as Cupid (signed and dated 1663; National Gallery, Warsaw), *Sleeping Infant Christ* (Fondazione Querini-Stampalia, Venice) and the cherubs and angels of numerous altarpieces (e.g. *St Antony with the Christ Child*, 1662; Pinacoteca Nazionale, Bologna). The sentimentality and soft *colorito* of these images recall the work of Sirani's Spanish contemporary Murillo. Another favoured subject was the *Penitent Magdalene* (e.g. signed and dated 1660; Pinacoteca Nazionale, Bologna), associated with Guido Reni.

The most important sources for Sirani's life and work are the writings of the critic and historian Conte Carlo Cesare Malvasia, who was a close family friend. In his famous two-volume work, *Felsina pittrice: Vite de' pittori bolognesi* (1678), he included "Nota delle pitture fatte da me Elisabetta Sirani", an incomplete inventory list of c.182 works painted by Elisabetta between the age of 17 and her death, as well as a eulogy to her, the "Pittrice Eroina" of Bolognese painting. In this first text promoting a Bolognese school of painting, Malvasia aimed to redress the central Italian bias of Vasari's *Lives* (1550 and 1568), presenting Reni as Bologna's most important and influential artist. It is in this context of the articulation of a specifically Bolognese artistic identity (that was increasingly identified with the school of Reni), which challenged the hegemony of the central Italian art promoted by Vasari, that Sirani's work should be considered. Having learned the elegant Renian classical *maniera* from her father, Reni's foremost assistant, Sirani was primarily responsible for passing on Reni's legacy to the latter half of the 17th century.

An extremely fashionable artist, Sirani had a coterie of aristocratic patrons cultivated by her protective father and influential family friends. Documents indicate that her patrons and collectors included many of the most prominent Bolognese families as well as representatives of other social levels: friends, the fishmonger, her music teacher and doctor, clergymen and members of the nobility and royalty, such as the King of Poland. Although she never travelled, her reputation and fame spread far beyond Bologna, with nobility from all over Europe coming to watch her work, as noted by Sirani in her diary entries and confirmed by early sources.

Her fame was based on her prodigious talent, her deft touch and masterly handling of paint, and her skill as a portraitist, especially of women. Contemporaries often stressed her painterly skills and virtuoso brushwork, associating her with Venetian *colorito* rather than central Italian *disegno*. In her drawing style as well she rejected the Vasarian model of finely studied preliminary drawings for paintings, preferring the Venetian use of wash sketches made with a few quick brush strokes. Such a bold, freely sketched drawing style, which differs from 17th-century Bolognese practice (usually more detailed and linear, in pen and black chalk), seems to have been her own invention and was used only by artists she influenced, such as Zani. The apparent effortlessness of her *maniera*, akin to the studied spontaneity of Rubens, can be seen for example in such passages as Anna Maria Ranuzzi's sleeve, the opalescent flesh of her favoured subjects, young children, and the fine modelling and delicate facial features of her madonnas, saints and sibyls.

According to Malvasia, Sirani aimed at developing an individual style, and he cited her largest and most important public commission, the *Baptism of Christ* (signed and dated 1657; La

Certosa, Bologna) as evidence of her "genius/invenzione". He claims that immediately on receiving the commission, Sirani, then age 19, dashed off her "concetto" for the composition in a brush-wash sketch (Albertina, Vienna). This confirms that she created her own designs and did not merely copy the compositions of others, a criticism often directed against women artists. Because of her painterly skills and invention she was said to have "acquired the virile sex" (Picinardi); this is also demonstrated by the association of her work with traditionally male artistic concepts such as "genius" and "invention". Considered the equal of any male artist, she was compared with masculine ideals and judged by male aesthetic standards.

More recent writers have rightly attempted to extract the "true" Sirani from her identity as a follower of Reni, arguing that she developed a distinct personal style independent of his, in order to give her work credibility. Yet it also must be remembered that her professional standing and popularity were due precisely to the fact that she was considered the "second Guido". Unlike her father, Sirani consciously modelled herself on Reni: her appropriation of his style and iconography, which she transformed in her original compositions into a warmer and more intimate and naturalistic form of his academic classicism, appears to have been a carefully considered career choice. Malvasia lamented that her father, in his determination to develop a distinctive style of his own, lost an opportunity to share in Reni's glory and remained a mediocre artist.

Although her work is now less valued than that of the great Guido, Sirani was perhaps more marketable to the majority of collectors. Many of her patrons were members of the Bolognese middle class, who could not afford an original Reni and wished to possess the next best thing: a copy or a work in a similar style inspired by his iconography of swooning saints and beautiful madonnas. Current research confirms Sirani as one of the most commissioned and collected artists among Reni's followers. According to archival sources, many Bolognese collections included at least one work by her, which was often the only painting listed by title and singled out for comment, and among the highest valued (c.300–500 lira, as opposed to 100 lira for the majority of works cited in inventories).

To own a "Sirana" was highly prized until the late 19th century, when the Bolognese school fell out of favour with critics such as Ruskin and Baudelaire and her works were regarded as typifying the school's less glorious aspects: its lack of perfection in design and its vigorous new deep colouring. By the early 20th century her work – and by implication Reni's – was considered of little artistic value, judging by an exhibition catalogue entry of 1924 in which it was dismissed as "tired and pallid imitations of the most tired and pallid manner of Guido Reni" (*La pittura italiana del Seicento e del Settecento alla mostra di Palazzo Pitti*, Milan-Rome, 1924, p.81).

While some of Sirani's paintings are of extremely high quality (*Anna Maria Ranuzzi*, *St Antony with the Infant Christ*, *Portia*, *Baptism of Christ*) and show her compositional skill in dealing with crowd scenes on a grand scale, with an appropriate variety of gestures, poses and emotions, her oeuvre is inconsistent in quality, style and type. Her popularity and fame may seem incomprehensible, since collectively the work does not represent a "great" talent, yet many are probably workshop pieces, produced by her assistants to satisfy high public demand. In 17th-century workshops, copying the master's work was one method of training apprentices. It was normal practice for the master to create the concept and design and for assistants either to work on sections of the painting, leaving important areas such as the figures and faces to be completed by the master (considered an "original"), or to complete the whole painting themselves (a work of the pupil "after" the master, for example Ginevra Cantofoli's altarpiece of the *Last Supper* for San Procolo, based on a design by her teacher Sirani). Artistic collaboration appears to have been quite common: Sirani is known to have worked with her father, with Lorenzo Loli, and with Teresa Maria Coriolani.

While contemporaries were sometimes critical of Sirani, they did value her as an artist in her own right: her portrait was painted a number of times (e.g. by her sister Barbara Borgognoli and Lorenzo Loli) and her paintings were copied and reproduced as prints by other artists (e.g. Bartolommeo Zanichelli and Loli). The cycle of copying extended from Reni to his students and followers, of whom a select few were themselves copied, with Sirani the principal disseminator of his style. From Malvasia onwards, in critical attempts to establish an artistic identity and cultural authority for the Bolognese school of painting Sirani has been cited as exemplifying its particular qualities: sweetness, naturalism, refined and erudite elegance, virtuoso brushwork, subtlety of expression and sensual colour. Both in artistic discourse and in the popular imagination Sirani represented the success that women could achieve with natural talent, diligence and skills cultivated through sound workshop training (albeit without life drawing).

ADELINA MODESTI

See also Printmakers survey

Sjöö, Monica
Swedish painter, 1938–

Born in Härnösand, Ångermanland, northern Sweden, 31 December 1938. Met silversmith Stevan Trickey in Paris, 1957; married him in Sweden and moved to Bristol, England; three sons (eldest died of cancer, 1987; youngest killed in a road accident, 1985). Made and designed jewellery with Trickey while studying sculpture and etching part-time at Bristol Academy of Art, 1958–63. Studied theatre design at Bristol Old Vic Theatre School, 1964. Subsequently lived in Sweden for two years, returning to Bristol in 1967. Active in the feminist movement from the late 1960s. Lived in Pembrokeshire, Wales, early 1980s. Lives in Bristol.

Principal Exhibitions
Galleri Karlsson, Stockholm: 1967 (individual)
Woodstock Gallery, London: 1971 (*First Women's Art Exhibition*)
Swiss Cottage Library, London: 1973 (*Five Women Artists: Images of Womanpower*)
Konsthall, Lund, Sweden: 1974–5 (*Kvinnoliv* [Women's lives], with Anna Sjödahl, touring)
Kulturhuset, Stockholm: 1975–6 (*Kvinnfolk* [Womenfolk], touring)

Ibis Gallery, Leamington Spa: 1978–87 (*Women Magic: Celebrating the Goddess Within Us*, touring)
Mostyn Arts Gallery, Llandudno: 1984–5 (*Women Artists in Wales*, touring)
Assembly Rooms, Glastonbury: 1989 (*The Goddess Re-emerging*)
Gaia Gallery, Berkeley, CA: 1990 (*Stones and the Goddess*, with Chris Castle)
Goddess and Green Man Gallery, Glastonbury: 1992 (individual)
City Museum and Art Gallery, Plymouth: 1994 (*With Your Own Face On*)

Selected Writings

The Ancient Religion of the Great Cosmic Mother of All, edited and extended by Barbara Mor, Trondheim, Norway: Rainbow Press, 1981; revised as *The Great Cosmic Mother: Rediscovering the Religion of the Earth*, San Francisco: Harper, 1987; 2nd edition, 1991
"Journey into darkness", *Glancing Fires: An Investigation into Women's Creativity*, ed. Lesley Saunders, London: Women's Press, 1987
"Tested by the dark/light mother of the other world", *Voices of the Goddess: A Chorus of Sibyls*, ed. Caitlin Matthews, Wellingborough: Aquarian Press, 1990, pp.124–49
New Age or Armageddon: The Goddess or the Gurus? Towards a Feminist Vision of the Future, London: Women's Press, 1992
"Thoughts inspired by reading *Gender and Genius: Towards a Feminist Aesthetic* by Christine Battersby and *Voicing Our Visions: Writings by Women Artists* edited by Mara R. Witzling", *From the Flames*, vii, Autumn 1992, pp.28–32

Bibliography

Rozsika Parker and Griselda Pollock, *Framing Feminism: Art and the Women's Movement, 1970–85*, London and New York: Pandora Press, 1987
Hilary Robinson, ed., *Visibly Female: Feminism and Art: An Anthology*, London: Camden Press, 1987; New York: Universe, 1988
Gloria Feman Orenstein, *The Reflowering of the Goddess*, New York: Pergamon Press, 1990
Michael Tucker, *Dreaming with Open Eyes: The Shamanic Spirit in Twentieth-Century Art and Culture*, London: Aquarian, and San Francisco: Harper, 1992
Mara R. Witzling, ed., *Voicing Today's Visions: Writings by Contemporary Women Artists*, New York: Universe, 1994

Monica Sjöö's numerous images of strong, powerful female figures express her deep belief in the Ancient Mother and Earth Spirit as a source of rejuvenating energy that has been denied by centuries of patriarchal culture but to which we humans must return if we are to survive. A self-taught artist, Sjöö was born in Sweden but spent most of her adult life living and working in Britain. A leading figure in the international Goddess movement, Sjöö is also a prolific writer, the author of two books and numerous articles and poems, most notably *The Great Cosmic Mother*, co-authored with the American poet Barbara Mor. Both her written work and her visual art are inspired by her contact with the Goddess as manifest in visions and dreams and experienced at sacred places.

Sjöö was the only child of two struggling artists who had met while attending art school in Stockholm. Her parents separated when she was three and from then on she lived with her mother, spending summers on the Swedish coast with her father. When Sjöö was 16 she decided that she wanted to be an artist herself, and she supported herself as an artist's model. In 1957, while travelling with a friend, she met a young silver-smith in Paris and, when she became pregnant, married him and moved with him to Bristol, England, his home town. With the exception of two years when she returned to Sweden in the mid-1960s and several years in the mid-1980s when she lived in Wales, she has lived in Bristol ever since. During her first five years there, Sjöö designed jewellery, while pursuing part-time studies in sculpture and painting at the Bristol Academy of Art. In 1964, during her studies at the Bristol Old Vic Theatre School, she first encountered Brechtian theatre, an important influence on her subsequent artistic development.

After her return from Sweden to England in 1967, Sjöö became involved with the women's movement. She began exhibiting her work in group shows with other women artists, culminating in an exhibition at the Swiss Cottage Library, *Five Women Artists: Images of Womanpower*. In 1973 she was accused of "obscenity and blasphemy" for her monumental painting *God Giving Birth* (1968; see illustration), a large female figure of indeterminate race depicted in the midst of the birth process. Viewed by Sjöö as a "sacred painting", it was inspired by the home birth of her second son in 1961, which she describes as her first mystical experience of the Great Mother's power. During the 1970s Sjöö participated in *Kvinnoliv*, an ongoing, touring exhibition that was shown in various Scandinavian venues, and in *Kvinnfolk*.

Another transformative experience in Sjöö's life that had an important impact on her art work occurred in 1978 when she felt the tangible presence of the Goddess at ancient worship sites around Avebury, Wiltshire, and at New Grange, Ireland. Since that time, she has made pilgrimages to various ancient sacred sites (stone circles, mounds, holy wells) in Britain, Brittany, Crete and Malta. Between 1978 and 1987 she participated in *Women Magic: Celebrating the Goddess Within Us*, which toured to numerous British and Continental cities. Sjöö's paintings from this period (artist's collection) reflect her mystical interactions with the earth, focusing on landscapes of the many holy sites she visited and their inhabitation with figural expressions of the Goddess.

The increasing success that Sjöö enjoyed in her professional life in the 1980s was accompanied by intense personal pain. Her works were included in other exhibitions besides the still-travelling *Women Magic*, and she gave presentations at several spiritual workshops. Additionally, she had reached a mature point in her artistic style. The illusion of well-being was abruptly shattered in August 1985 when Sjöö's 15-year-old son, Leif, was hit by a car while on holiday in southern France. His death plunged her into a state of despair, which intensified shortly thereafter when she learned that her eldest son, Sean, was suffering from cancer, from which he died in July 1987. Sjöö experienced a devastating period in which she felt that she could not go on. She has now integrated those experiences with a renewed sense of the preciousness of life, as expressed in some of her most powerful paintings, *Lament for My Young Son* (1985) and *My Sons in the Spirit World/Spiderwoman* (1989; both artist's collection). Her paintings have been shown in several exhibitions since the late 1980s, including *The Goddess Re-emerging* (1989), *Stones and the Goddess* (1990) and *With Your Own Face On* (1994).

Sjöö considers herself a shaman and painting a "shamanistic act, a spiritual activity". For Sjöö there is an identification between the ecstasy of artistic creation and the evocation of the

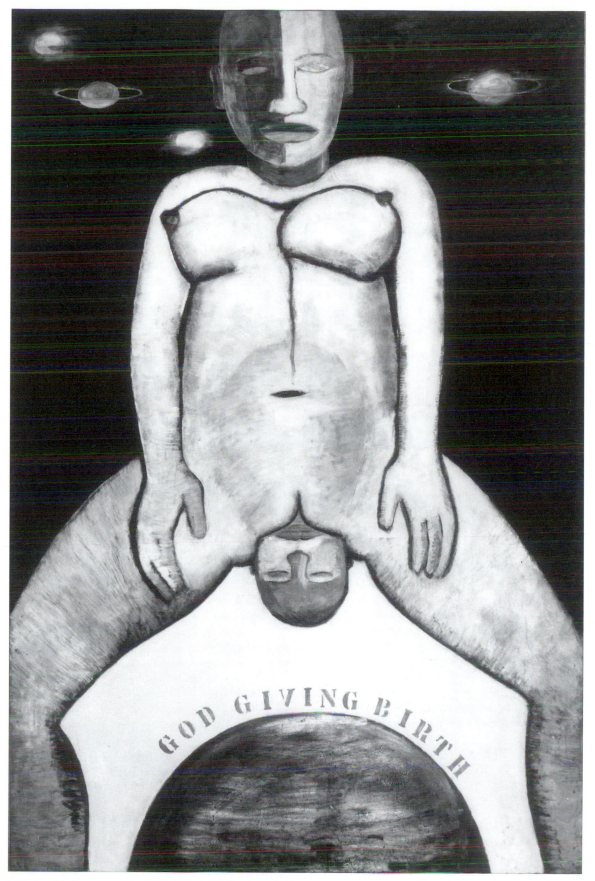

Sjöö: *God Giving Birth*, 1968; Museum Anna Nordlander, Skellefteå, Sweden

Goddess's presence, as there is with some other women artists, including Mary Beth Edelson (q.v.), Buffie Johnson and Ana Mendieta. As Gloria Feman Orenstein (1990) has pointed out, in her paintings Monica Sjöö has created a "contemporary iconography for the Great Cosmic Mother". Drawing upon goddesses of many cultures who have spoken to her in dreams and visions, Sjöö has created images of female strength to empower contemporary women to reclaim both the earth and women's bodies from their subjugated position in the dominant culture.

MARA R. WITZLING

Skulme, Marta

Latvian sculptor, 1890–1962

Born Marta Liepiņa in Malpils, a settlement 60 km. east of Riga, 13 May 1890; father a teacher and landowner, and organiser of local cultural activities. Attended evening drawing classes at Riga Art School, 1913; studied at Kazan Art School, 1913–14; at Mikhail Bernshtein's Art School and in the sculpture studio of Leonid Sherwood (Leonty Shervud), Petrograd, 1916–18; studied privately under Professor Peter Bromirsky in Moscow, 1918. Returned to Latvia, autumn 1918. Married painter and theatre designer Oto Skulme, 1920; one daughter, the painter Džemma Skulme, born 1925. Study tours to Berlin and Dresden, 1922, to Paris, 1929 and 1937. Recipient of first and second prizes, Freedom Monument competition, Riga, 1924 (with sculptor Kārlis Zāle); Cultural Foundation prize, Latvia, 1934. Member, Riga Artists Group, 1922–40; Artists Union of Latvia, 1945–62. Died in Riga, 3 January 1962.

Principal Exhibitions

Arts Salon, Latvian Telegraph Agency (LETA), Riga: 1920 (*Common Exhibition of Sculptures and Paintings by Six Artists*)
Riga Artists Group: 1923–38
Riga: 1928 (*Latvian Art*), 1942 (*Art Exhibition*), 1943 (*Latvian Art*), 1945 (*Women Artists of Soviet Latvia*), 1945 (*Artists of Soviet Latvia*), 1949 (*Latvian Soviet Art*, touring), 1952 (*Artists of Soviet Latvia*), 1958 (*Works of Sculptors of the Lithuanian SSR, Estonian SSR and Latvian SSR*)
Oslo: 1933–9 (*Latvian Art*, European touring)
Exposition Universelle et Internationale, Brussels: 1935
Cultural Foundation of Latvia, Riga: 1935–6 (*Second Exhibition of Latvian Art*, touring), 1936–7 (*Third Exhibition of Latvian Art*, touring), 1937–9 (*Fourth Exhibition of Latvian Art*, touring)
Common Exhibition of the Works of Latvian Artists, Riga: 1939, 1954
Common Exhibition of the Works of Latvian Artists Dedicated to the Anniversaries of Soviet Latvia and the October Socialist Revolution, Riga: 1945, 1947, 1949, 1950, 1951, 1955, 1957, 1960
Moscow: 1953 (*Artists of the Lithuanian SSR, Estonian SSR and Latvian SSR*), 1955 (*Fine Art of the Latvian SSR: The Decade of Latvian Art and Literature*)
Latvian State Museum of Fine Art, Riga: 1969 (retrospective)

Bibliography

Uga Skulme, "R. Sutas glezna *Zemnieki* un M. Liepiņas-Skulmes veidojumi" [R. Suta's painting *Peasants* and M. Liepiņa-Skulme's sculptures], *Daugava*, 1939, no.3, pp.291–3
Marta Skulme, exh. cat., Latvian State Museum of Fine Art, Riga, 1969
Ilga Straume, "Pirmās latviešu tēlnieces peimiņai" [In memoriam of the first Latvian sculptress], *Art Almanac: Latviešu tēlotāja māksla* [Latvian fine art], Riga, 1970, pp.182–8
Ruta Čaupova, "Marta Skulme", *Portrets Latviešu tēlniecpība* [The portrait in Latvian sculpture], Riga, 1981, pp.68–70, 85
Ojārs Ābols, "Marta Skulme", *Latviešu tēlniecības vecmeistari* [Latvian sculptors of the older generation], Riga, 1982, pp.65–6
Ruta Čaupova, "Tēlnieciba", *Latviešu tēlotāja māksla, 1860–1940* [Sculpture: Latvian fine art, 1860–1940], Riga: Latvian Academy of Sciences, 1986, pp.181–279
——, "Die lettische Bildhauerei: Tendenzen des konstruktiven Antzatzes", *Unerwartete Begegnung lettische Avangarde, 1910–1935: Der Beitrag Lettlands zur Kunst der europäischen Moderne*, exh. cat., Staatlichen Kunsthalle, Berlin, and elsewhere, 1990, pp.85–91
Marta Skulme 100, memorial booklet, Riga: Latvijas Mākslinieku savienība, 1990
Ruta Čaupova, *Marta Skulme: Tēlnieciba* [Marta Skulme: Sculpture monograph], Riga: Zinātne, 1992

Marta Skulme was the only woman artist in Latvia working in sculpture in the early 1920s, and she became one of the leading Latvian sculptors of the inter-war period. Her early works were semi-abstract Constructivist and Cubist, but from the mid-1920s she developed her own monumental figurative style, based on a profound integrity of structure, form and feeling. Her searching intuition was directed at exposing the archetypal roots of being, at finding the spiritual and formal power inherent in sculpture itself. Unlike other, more rationally minded Latvian sculptors, she persistently elaborated her instinctively rich and delicate sensual feeling for the natural growth of forms. She had an innate feeling for the primeval vitality of life and form and also a respect for structure. Her works include simple, powerful heads in granite and plaster; seated or standing female figures in granite, bronze and plaster; numerous intimate, expressive compositions of nudes, groups of two or three figures in bronze or plaster; semi-abstract or figurative relief compositions; and several projects for monuments. Her personal experiences during World War I (her parents spent the war as refugees in Galicina, near Moscow, and her father died soon after his return to Latvia) created an inner tension and a deep spirituality that appeared in her works as a strong feeling for the existential stoicism of man. Her search for an ethnic and feminine identity is expressed in skilfully modified universal and individual images.

During her training under V. Bogatiryev at the Kazan Art School and under Leonid Sherwood (Leonty Shervud) and Mikhail Bernshtein in Petrograd, Skulme learned to model and to render figures realistically, but her vision as a sculptor was little influenced by her teachers. At Bernshtein's Art School, famous for its tolerance of modern trends, she experienced creative freedom and the spread of Cubist, Futurist and Constructivist ideas.

Skulme returned to Latvia in 1918. In 1919–20, at her parents' country house in Mālpils, she carved several abstract architectural sculptures in wood (untraced; a photograph shows one, a column reminiscent of Latvian peasant architecture). Only one small polychromed wooden sculpture has survived from the early period, *My Family* (1920; Džemma Skulme collection). The pithiness of her early style shows the influence of African wooden sculpture, which was an important source for modern Latvian artists. (The Latvian artist V.I. Matvejs's book about African art published in 1919 was a modernists' handbook.)

In 1920, after her marriage, Skulme settled in Riga, where her husband earned their living as a set designer at the Art Theatre (Dailes Teātris). She received no commissions and devoted herself to developing her creative ideas. In the early 1920s she made several semi-abstract plaster reliefs entitled "constructive sculptures". These were lost in the 1950s when they had to be hidden from Soviet officials; one was reconstructed by I. Dobičins (1992; State Museum of Fine Art, Riga). Her first major sculpture in the round was the heavily built seated figure *Guitar Player* (1921; bronze cast 1964; State Museum of Fine Art). Seeking her own interpretation of Synthetic Cubism, she learned to concentrate the gravitational energy of volume and mass, using simplified, strictly defined planes and avoiding narrative or naturalistic elements.

Skulme visited Berlin in 1922 for the *Erste russische Kunstausstellung*. The Riga Artists' Group, to which she belonged, had regular contact in the 1920s with Le Corbusier, Jacques Lipchitz, Amédée Ozenfant and others connected with the magazine *L'Esprit Nouveau*. Like many modern sculptors, she was drawn to primitive art, the art of remote periods and civilisations. Her close personal links with the Latvian peasant world and tradition was one of the essential sources of her inspiration. Skulme executed the first of her typical small-scale monumental sculptures in 1923, a standing figure of a female in national costume, *Tautu Meita* (State Museum of Fine Art). She later created many small or medium-sized figurative compositions of women and girls in Latvian costume. Some of these symbolic images were intended to be enlarged for outdoor monuments, but she did not receive commissions for such intimate and informal subjects and it was difficult for her to compete with male colleagues in organising the technical processes for making large-scale sculpture. In 1924 she shared first and second prize with the well-known Latvian monumental sculptor Kārlis Zāle in the competition to design the *Freedom Monument* in Riga (his design was executed in 1935). In a portrait head, *Janītis* (1926; Džemma Skulme collection), she created a clear and powerful formal concept of an individualised image. Her awareness of the geometric aspects of formal relations had reached a delicate balance and she had turned to firmly rounded volumes and smooth surfaces. The powerful gravitational vitality of her mature style is characterised by such works as *Woman's Head* or *Large Head* (two versions: toned plaster, 1928; granite, 1933; both Džemma Skulme collection) and a seated figure *A Woman from Vidzeme* (1933; see illustration). Like other Latvian sculptors, she was inspired by the magnificent granite sculptures of Ancient Egypt. She shared themes and stylistic tendencies with the Latvian sculptors T. Zaļkalns and E. Melderis. In an international context, the primeval vitality of her expression is comparable with the archetypal consciousness embodied in the female heads of Marino Marini and in the early works of Henry Moore and Barbara Hepworth (q.v.).

In the 1930s Skulme's heads and figurative compositions

Skulme: *A Woman from Vidzeme*, 1933; granite; 75 × 43 × 53 cm.; State Museum of Art, Riga

took on a pictorial quality, and she turned to expressive poses and gestures. After her trips to Paris (1929, 1937), Maillol's influence is evident in some of her nudes. She deliberately avoided the classicising tendencies of the 1930s, remaining faithful to her heavy accumulated forms and archaic expressiveness. In the post-war years of the Soviet period, Skulme, like all Latvian sculptors, suffered from the conflict of her aesthetic ideals with official dogmatic restrictions. The dull, photographic, illustrative naturalism that was the only acceptable form of artistic expression was completely alien to her, but official requirements had to be taken into account if she wished to exhibit. During her later years a certain dualism was evident in her work for the first time, and several officially commissioned portrait busts show a pedantic naturalism. At the same time she created absolutely sincere expressive compositions, which she was unable to exhibit. One of these, a group of tragic, falling and rising figures entitled *Composition for a Monument* (1947; Džemma Skulme collection), shows the tragedy of mass suffering and the spirit of resistance. Marta Skulme was the first Latvian sculptor to express this 20th-century theme. The first solo retrospective of her work was not held until 1969, at the State Museum of Fine Art, Riga.

RUTA ČAUPOVA

Sleigh, Sylvia
British painter, 1916–

Born in Llandudno, Wales, 8 May 1916. Studied at Brighton School of Art, Sussex, 1933–7; University of London Extra-Mural Department (diploma 1947). Married art critic Lawrence Alloway, 1954; he died 1990. Moved to USA, 1961. Edith Kreeger Wolf distinguished professor, Northwestern University, Evanston, Illinois, 1977; visiting assistant professor, State University of New York, Stony Brook, 1978; instructor, New School of Social Research, New York, 1974–7 and 1978–80; visiting artist, Baldwin Seminar, Oberlin College, Ohio, 1982. Recipient of National Endowment for the Arts (NEA) grant, 1982; Pollock-Krasner Foundation award, 1985. Lives in New York.

Selected Individual Exhibitions
Bennington College, Bennington, VT: 1963
SoHo 20 Gallery, New York: 1973, 1980, 1985
AIR Gallery, New York: 1974, 1976, 1978
Mabel Smith Douglass Library, Rutgers University, New Brunswick, NJ: 1974
Wadsworth Atheneum, Hartford, CT: 1976
Zaks Gallery, Chicago: 1976, 1985
Ohio State University, Columbus: 1976
Everson Museum of Art, Syracuse, NY: 1976 (*Paintings by Three American Realists*, with Alice Neel and May Stevens)
G.W. Einstein Co. Inc., New York: 1980, 1983, 1985
Gallery 210, University of Missouri, St Louis: 1981
Milwaukee Art Museum: 1990 (*Invitation to a Voyage and Other Works*, touring)
Stiebel Modern, New York: 1992 (retrospective), 1994

Bibliography
Linda Nochlin, "Some women realists: Painters of the figure", *Arts Magazine*, xlviii, May 1974, pp.29–33
Gerrit Henry, "The artist and the face: A modern American sampling", *Art in America*, lxiii, January–February 1975, pp.34–41
Lisa Tickner, "The body politic: Female sexuality and women artists since 1970", *Art History*, i, 1978, pp.237–51
Margaret Walters, *The Nude Male: A New Perspective*, New York and London: Paddington, 1978
Deborah Schwartz, "An interview with Sylvia Sleigh", *Arts and Sciences*, Spring 1978, pp.11–15
Kevin Eckstrom, *Images of Men in the Paintings of Sylvia Sleigh*, MA thesis, Indiana University, 1980
Sylvia Sleigh: Recent Paintings, exh. cat., G.W. Einstein Co. Inc., New York, 1980
Alessandra Comini, "Art history, revisionism and some holy cows", *Arts Magazine*, liv, June 1980, pp.96–100
Charlotte Streifer Rubinstein, *American Women Artists from Early Times to the Present*, Boston: Hall, 1982

Sleigh: *Philip Golub Reclining*, December 1971; oil on canvas; 101.6 × 144 cm.; Milwaukee Art Museum

Gerrit Henry, "Sylvia Sleigh at G.W. Einstein", *Art in America*, lxxi, Summer 1983, pp.158–9

Joanna Frueh, "Chicago: Sylvia Sleigh at Zaks", *Art in America*, lxxiv, January 1986, pp.143–5

Betty Ann Brown and Arlene Raven, *Exposures: Women and Their Art*, Pasadena, CA: New Sage Press, 1989

Sylvia Sleigh: Invitation to a Voyage and Other Works, exh. cat., Milwaukee Art Museum, and elsewhere, 1990

John Loughery, "Sylvia Sleigh: Invitation to a voyage and other works", *Woman's Art Journal*, xii/1, 1991, pp.69–71

The Sixties Art Scene in London, exh. cat., Barbican Art Gallery, London, 1993

Ken Johnson, "Sylvia Sleigh at Stiebel Modern", *Art in America*, xii, December 1994, p.98

Sylvia Sleigh is a portrait painter. "Even if I paint a leaf, it should be a portrait", she once asserted to Arlene Raven, "It is my belief that if we could all appreciate every living thing in detail, we would be kinder and better to one another" (Brown and Raven 1989, p.68). Sleigh is perhaps best known for her nude portraits of men. Many of these are single figure studies. *Philip Golub Reclining* (1971; see illustration), which quotes the *Toilet of Venus* (1651; National Gallery, London) by Velázquez, is remarkable because of its gender inversion, that is, its unsettling presentation of a male figure laid out on a bed to receive the erotic gaze our culture has usually directed at women. It is also remarkable in its studied refusal of prettied idealisation. While nude females are often distanced and objectified in order to receive the gaze (to become sex "objects", as it were), Golub, the son of the artists Nancy Spero (q.v.) and Leon Golub, is presented as a unique and known individual, fully human and fully vulnerable. In 1973 Sleigh painted the *Turkish Bath* (artist's collection), a large group portrait inspired by Ingres's depiction of harem women (1863; Louvre, Paris). Again, Sleigh not only reversed gender, thus challenging the cultural expectations of the eroticised gaze, she also presented known individuals rather than idealised or stereotyped "objects". One of the men in the *Turkish Bath* is Lawrence Alloway, a renowned critic and the artist's husband.

Alloway and Sleigh emigrated from Britain to the USA in 1961. Sleigh was soon swept into the feminist art movement. She founded, joined and became active in several artists' groups, including the Ad Hoc Women Artists Committee, Women in the Arts, SoHo 20 and the AIR Cooperative Gallery. Sleigh's portraits of the members of SoHo 20 (1974; University of Missouri at St. Louis) and of the AIR Gallery (1977; artist's collection) remain important documents of the New York women's art movement. The 20 women of the AIR Gallery are clustered in a three-tiered composition that unfolds towards the viewer. The women settle into comfortable and companionable conversation among themselves and, it seems, with the viewer, in a manner reminiscent of Rembrandt's group portraits.

Sleigh's group portraits are, in a sense, her rewriting of art history. For centuries, European academies valued history painting above all other genres. Barred from anatomy classes, women could not receive the training necessary for complex compositions involving numerous human figures. To develop her own history paintings, and to work directly with nude models, is to assert that women certainly have the capacity – the vision and the skills – to produce the art that history denied them. Sleigh never merely quotes the works of old masters, but always transforms them into contemporary terms that are idiosyncratically her own. *Venus and Mars* (1976; Milwaukee Museum of Art) presents portraits of Maureen Connor and Paul Rosano (one of Sleigh's favourite sitters) in positions that echo Botticelli's early Renaissance painting of the Classical gods (National Gallery, London). The specificity of Connor's fashionable attire, carefully painted features and alert expression lift her out of allegory into individuality. Rosano, on the other hand, is nude except for cut-off jeans and appears to sleep while the artist immortalises him. Here Sleigh inverts the traditional bipolar opposition that links male with active (which has been valued historically) and female with passive (devalued historically). In grappling with archetypes and challenging the unexamined assumptions on which we all too often build our identities, Sleigh uses portraiture to explore the meaning of human subjectivity.

While Sleigh has often worked on a large scale – many of her nudes are somewhat larger than life-size – her largest work is *Invitation to a Voyage* (1984; artist's collection), an immense mural consisting of 14 oil-on-canvas panels, each 2.4 × 1.5 metres, which wraps around a room and was originally exhibited at the Milwaukee Museum of Art. Inspired by the French writer Baudelaire's poem, Sleigh depicted a group of her contemporaries picnicking at the edge of the Hudson River. Behind them stands Bannerman's Island Arsenal, which Sleigh romanticises as a Claudian "enchanted castle". Artists, writers and other friends stroll through the radiant landscape, frozen by the timelessness of paint into what the art critic Ken Johnson has referred to as Sleigh's "persuasive marriage of the actual and the numinous" (Johnson 1994).

BETTY ANN BROWN

Sligh, Clarissa

American photographer and installation artist, 1939–

Born in Washington, DC, 30 August 1939. Studied at Hampton Institute, Virginia (BS 1961); Howard University, Washington, DC (BFA 1972); Skowhegan School of Art, Maine, 1972; University of Pennsylvania, Philadelphia (MBA 1973); International Center of Photography, New York, 1979–80. Part-time research assistant, Philadelphia Federal Reserve Bank and Wharton Entrepreneurial Center, 1972–3; financial analyst, Mobil Oil Corporation, New York, 1974–5; and Goldman, Sachs and Company, New York, 1975–84; computer programmer, National Aeronautics and Space Administration's Manned Space Flight Program, Maryland, and Price Williams and Associates, 1962–72. Visual arts instructor, City College of New York, 1986–7; visiting artist faculty, Minneapolis College of Art and Design, 1988–9; arts instructor, Lower Eastside Printshop, New York, 1988–90; Dayton Hudson distinguished visiting artist and teacher, Carleton College, Northfield, Minnesota, 1992. Recipient of National Endowment for the Arts (NEA) grant, 1988; New York State Council on the Arts Visual Artists Sponsored Work Project award, 1990; Artiste en France fellowship, Greater New York Links and French Government, 1992; International Center of Photography Annual Infinity award,

1995. Board member, National Women's Caucus for Art of the College Art Association, 1991–2; Printed Matter and Visual Studies Workshop, 1991–4. Has one daughter. Lives in New York.

Selected Individual Exhibitions
CEPA Satellite Space, Buffalo, NY: 1987
White Columns, New York: 1990
Washington Project for the Arts, Washington, DC: 1991
Center for Photography in Woodstock, NY: 1992
Art in General, New York: 1992
Afro-American Historical and Cultural Museum, Philadelphia: 1993
Toronto Photographers Workshop, Toronto: 1994
Galerie Junge Kunst, Trier: 1995

Selected Writings
Reading Dick and Jane with Me, New York: privately printed, 1989
"On being an American black student", *Heresies*, vii/1, 1990
"Witness to dissent: It wasn't Little Rock", *Ikon*, no.12–13, 1992
"Home truths", *What Can a Woman Do with a Camera?*, ed. Jo Spence and Joan Solomon, London: Scarlet Press, 1995
"Reliving my mother's struggle", *Liberating Memory: Our Work and Our Working-Class Consciousness*, ed. Janet Zandy, New Brunswick: Rutgers University Press, 1995

Bibliography
Constructed Images: New Photography, exh. cat., Schomburg Center, New York Public Library, and elsewhere, 1989
Naomi Rosenblum, *World History of Photography*, 2nd edition, New York: Abbeville, 1989
Deborah Willis-Thomas, *An Illustrated Bio-Bibliography of Black Photographers, 1940–1988*, New York: Garland, 1989
Convergence: 8 Photographers, exh. cat., Photographic Resource Center and Visual Studies Workshop, 1990
Ann R. Langdon, *Women Visual Artists You Might Like to Know*, New Haven: Women in the Arts, 1990
Lucy R. Lippard, *Mixed Blessings: New Art in a Multicultural America*, New York: Pantheon, 1990
Words and Images with a Message, exh. cat., Women's Studio Workshop, Rosendale, NY, 1990
Clarissa Sligh: The Presence of Memory, exh. cat., Robert B. Menschel Photography Gallery, Syracuse University, NY, 1991
Clarissa Sligh: Witness to Dissent: Remembrance and Struggle, installation brochure, Washington Project for the Arts, Washington, DC, 1991
Crossing Over/Changing Places, exh. cat., Print Club, Philadelphia, and elsewhere, 1991
Bridges and Boundaries: African Americans and American Jews, exh. cat., Jewish Museum at New York Historical Society, and elsewhere, 1992
Alice R. George and others, *Flesh and Blood: Photographers' Images of Their Own Families*, New York: Picture Project, and Manchester: Cornerhouse, 1992
Malcolm X: Man, Ideal, Icon, installation brochure, Walker Art Center, Minneapolis, 1992
Prisoners of War: In My Native Land/On Foreign Soil, exh. cat., Parsons School of Design, New York, 1992
Personal Narratives: Women Photographers of Color, exh. cat., Southeastern Center for Contemporary Art, Winston-Salem, NC, 1993
The Subject of Rape, exh. cat., Whitney Museum of American Art, New York, 1993
Imagining Families: Images and Voices, exh. cat., National African American Museum Project, Smithsonian Institution, Washington, DC, 1994
Multiple World: An International Survey of Artists' Books, exh. cat., Atlanta College of Art Gallery, 1994
Naomi Rosenblum, *A History of Women Photographers*, New York: Abbeville, 1994
Melissa Harris, ed., *On Location with Henri Cartier-Bresson, Graciela Iturbide, Barbara Kruger, Sally Mann, Andres Serrano, Clarissa Sligh*, New York: Aperture Foundation, 1995
Make Yourself at Home: Race, Ethnicity and the American Family, exh. cat., Atlanta College of Art Gallery, 1995

In the brief period from 1984, Clarissa Sligh has amassed a body of photographic collage constructions whose content bears witness to the confrontation between American democratic ideals and the history of enslavement. During the turbulent era of the American civil rights movement, she was one of many black children involved in the school desegregation crisis of the 1950s. Memory and the child's voice reverberate in her photographic collages, artist books and installations. In her early works of the 1980s she combined negatives to create works that include writing ("mark-making") and drawing with a centrepiece of the photograph-as-artefact (interview with artist, 21 June 1995). Using the text – visual and written – as a forum for shattering taboos and silences about the commodification of the black and/or female body, she made a personal and historical inquiry into the affective domain where such dramatic events as abuse, racism and sexism are treated courageously in *Witness to Dissent: Memory, Yearning and Struggle*, a series of site-specific installations at the Washington Project for the Arts (1991) and Art in General in New York (1992). She expresses memories of terror and powerlessness in assembling and re-framing photographs of desegregation in Virginia in the 1960s ("Witness to dissent", 1992, p.115).

With a photographic palette limited to black, white and van-dyke brown, Sligh experimented with methods of photography and printing to perfect a documentary technique to fit the epic form of her dense narratives on African-American cultural life and the American political landscape. During a residency at Pyramid Atlantic in Maryland, she collaborated with the master printer Susan Rostow on *What's Happening with Momma?* (1988; see illustration), an artist's book of interconnected paper row houses with triangular roofs containing family photographs and commentary. An attempt "to connect to who she was" in the photographs, the work represents the interface between myth and public opinion as a site of self-censorship (see artist's commentary in Philadelphia 1991). By the late 1980s, when field research was popularised by artists of colour to formulate ideas and images, Sligh used conversation, reading and questionnaires to collect data for the content of her works. She employed this scrapbook approach in *Momma*, a photographic technique in which reshoots, reprints and rewrites are a means for self-reconstruction, healing and discovery about experiences unique to the Black tradition. Portions of the *Witness* series (*Untitled, Witness to Dissent: Remembrance and Struggle*) were also produced at Pyramid Atlantic in collaboration with the master printer and paper maker Helen C. Frederick. The work is a pulp painting on hand-made cotton and abaca paper, executed by pouring liquid pulp on to wet paper, creating the effect of a print. The series toured the USA and Europe under the 1992 Arts in America Program of the United States Information Agency.

Sligh's works have become integral to the lived histories of women who have experienced abuse, as in her cyanotypes *Seeking Comfort, I Suck My Thumb* (1989) and *Wonderful*

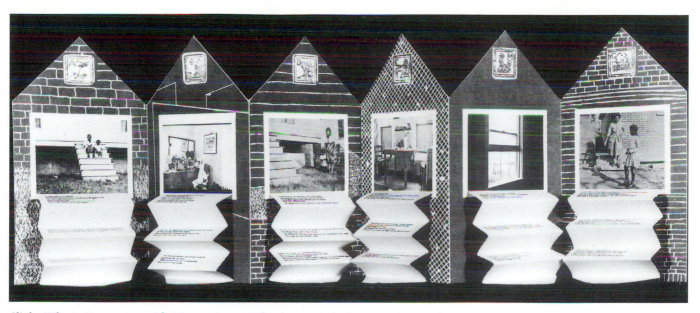

Sligh: *What's Happening with Momma?*, 1988; book, van Dyke brown print (inside); 27.9 × 91.4 cm.

Uncle (1988), the latter a van-dyke brown print in which text surrounds a girl alienated by sexuality, hypocrisy and power within the presumed safety of the family. She revisited these disjunctive emotions in *Seeking Comfort*, retreating to a metaphor of juvenile security in the visual space while her mind journeys to the dangerous and fearsome moments of childhood.

The late 1980s were a turning point for Sligh, marking a transition from her career as a financial analyst and computer programmer. Her work with the Women's Caucus for Art introduced her to exhibition organising in 1986, initially as East Coast co-ordinator and co-curator of the *Coast to Coast: National Women Artists of Color Book Project* and exhibition. In 1988 she was national co-ordinator and co-curator of the *Coast to Coast* initiative, which opened at Diverse Works in Houston in conjunction with the Women's Caucus for Art annual national conference, and toured to nine sites nationally. Two commissions established her as an installation artist. In 1992 she collaborated with the artist Carole Byard on the Walker Art Center group exhibition *Malcolm X: Man, Ideal, Icon*, which travelled to the Institute of Contemporary Art in Boston in 1993. Their *EHM (El-Haj Malik)* was a site-specific work in which images and artefacts associated with the assassinated American hero addressed both the spiritual and materialist commercialisation of Malcolm X. At the end of the 1980s Sligh was occupied with lectures and panel discussions, and in 1995 she was the keynote speaker at the annual conference of the Society for Photographic Education in Atlanta, which established her as a spokesperson for the use of photography as interactive narrative documentary art. Her work is in major private and public collections including the Museum of Modern Art and Schomburg Center for Research in Black Culture, New York Public Library, New York; National Museum of Women in the Arts and Corcoran Gallery of Art, Washington, DC; Museum of Fine Arts, Boston; George Eastman House, Rochester, New York; and the National Gallery of Australia, Canberra.

Sligh's work exemplifies and parallels late 20th-century debates on the role of the arts in the formation of cultural identity and its relationship to nationalism, gender and politics. Riding this wave, she employed an artistic practice that weaves the personal, the political, the public and the private, using the photograph as a means of indictment and liberation. In both technique and imagery Sligh surpasses the photo-realist tradition, featuring autobiography and sacrificing personal privacy as a way into the collective unconscious of civil rights activism and feminist social action, and as a way out of personal isolation.

ROBIN M. CHANDLER

Slott-Møller, Agnes
Danish painter, 1862–1937

Born Agnes Rambusch in Copenhagen, 10 June 1862; father a high-ranking naval officer. Studied at Vilhelm Klein's School of Drawing and Applied Art for Women, Copenhagen, 1878–85; studied under Peder Severin Krøyer, winter 1885–6; Harald Slott-Møller, from 1886. Married Slott-Møller, 1888. Travelled with husband to Germany, Italy and France, 1888–9; France, 1895; Britain, France and Germany, 1896; London, winter 1897–8; Britain, winter 1899–1900; Italy, spring 1900 and 1904; Austria and Italy, 1910; Norway, 1915. Founder member, Den frie udstilling (Free exhibition), Copenhagen, 1891. Recipient of Eckersberg medal, Copenhagen, 1906. Died 11 June 1937.

Principal Exhibitions
Charlottenborg, Copenhagen: occasionally 1885–1935
Den frie udstilling (Free exhibition), Copenhagen: 1891–2, 1894–7, 1899–1900
World's Columbian Exposition, Chicago: 1893
Royal Academy, London: 1897
Exposition Universelle, Paris: 1900

Den frie udstillingsbygning, Copenhagen: 1920 (*Kvindelige kunstneres retrospektive udstilling* [Women artists' retrospective])
Venice Biennale: 1932

Selected Writings
Article in *Tilskueren*, i, 1910, pp.331–50 (autobiography)
Text in *Berlingske Tidende*, 13 September 1929
Folkevise Billeder [Folk-ballad pictures], 1932

Bibliography
Viggo Stuckenberg, article in *Kunst*, i, 1899
William Sharp, article in *Magazine of Art*, xxiv, 1900, pp.289–95
C.A. Been and E. Hannover, eds, *Danmarks Malerkunst* [Denmark's
painting], ii, 1903
Holger Jerrild, article in *Gads danske Magasin*, 1932, pp.225–33
"Harald og Agnes Slott-Møller", *Små Kunstbøger*, no.23, 1934
Else Kai Sass, text in *Kvinden i Danmark* [The woman in Denmark],
1940, pp.726–7
Den frieskvindelige kunstnere, 1891 [Den frie's women artists, 1891],
exh. cat., Kvindemuseet, Århus, and Skagens Museum, Skagen,
1991

Agnes Slott-Møller is best known for her fanciful depictions of subjects from Danish folklore and history. After attending the School of Drawing and Applied Art for Women in Copenhagen, she studied privately with the naturalists Peder Severin Krøyer and Harald Slott-Møller. Under their tutelage she practised plein-air painting of landscape and genre subjects. Although Harald, whom she married in 1888, was one of the leading proponents of Naturalism in Denmark during the 1880s, both artists shifted their approach under the influence of Symbolism.

An important early influence on Slott-Møller was the Pre-Raphaelite Brotherhood; she shared their interest in historical and literary themes and their pursuit of a linear style with crisp contours and saturated colours. Although the first of her many visits to Britain occurred only in 1896, Pre-Raphaelite images were readily available in periodicals of the time such as *The Studio*, to which she subscribed. Another important influence on Slott-Møller's work was early Italian Renaissance painting, popular at the time among artists seeking a simplified linear style devoid of unnecessary narrative or descriptive detail. Slott-Møller travelled to Italy often after her initial visit in 1888–9. She was particularly impressed by Fra Angelico's decorations in the monastery of San Marco, Florence, and their simple beauty found their way into her own work.

Slott-Møller's attraction to Danish history (e.g. *Death of Queen Dagmar*, 1896; Rodkilde High School, Rodkilde) and folk tales as sources of inspiration was a result of the Romantic nationalism pervading Danish intellectual circles at the time. While its roots lay in the late 18th century, the forced cession of Norway from Denmark to Sweden in 1815, and the loss of the provinces of Schleswig and Holstein in the 1850s, generated patriotic fervour in Denmark. If geographical boundaries were not the defining feature of a nation, then what was? The answer provided by Hans Christian Andersen and others was language, culture and tradition. Slott-Møller was among those who sought to promote consciousness of a Danish national identity through the vehicle of collective myth and history.

Slott-Møller, her husband and other Danish painters embraced Symbolism in the 1890s as a means of expressing ineffable ideas about nation, culture and personal experience.

Slott-Møller: *Aage and Else*, 1902; South Jylland Art Museum, Denmark

Paul Gauguin was an important influence on them, since he frequently visited Copenhagen during the 1880s with his Danish wife, Mette. The simplified forms, saturated colours and distilled compositions of his post-1888 Synthetist painting offered to Scandinavian painters a language of expression they found appropriate to their new painterly goals. The conceptual shift from Naturalism to Symbolism was prepared for Slott-Møller and other Danes by their compatriot, the writer Georg Brandes. He viewed Symbolism not as a rejection of Naturalism but rather as a broadening of its imperative to represent "nature through a temperament". He argued that memory and emotion filtered all experience, and that this was the proper subject matter for painting. Slott-Møller's fairy-tale imagery speaks of an idyllic world generated by the imagination, but evocative of a distant, collective memory. Among these works are *Niels Ebbesen* (1893; Randers Kunstmuseum, Randers), *Kaas Manor in Saling* (1895; Hirschprung Collection, Copenhagen), *Aage and Else* (1902; see illustration) and *Knight and Maiden* (1903; Holger Drachmann collection).

MICHELLE FACOS

Smith, Barbara Leigh *see* Bodichon

Smith, Grace Cossington
Australian painter, 1892–1984

Born Grace Smith at "Cossington", Neutral Bay, Sydney, 22 April 1892. Took drawing lessons at Anthony Dattilo-Rubbo's atelier, Rowe Street, Sydney, 1910–11. Travelled to Britain with her sister Mabel, attending classes at Winchester School of Art, 1912. Spent three months at Speck near Stettin, Germany, 1913. Returned to Sydney, resuming studies under Dattilo-Rubbo, 1914. Lived in Turramurra, with studio at parents' home. Taught at Turramurra Boys College from 1927. Sailed for England, December 1948; travelled to Italy, 1949; returned to Sydney, February 1951. Member, Society of Artists, Sydney, 1947. Officer, Order of the British Empire (OBE), 1973; Order of Australia, 1983. Died in Roseville, 20 December 1984.

Principal Exhibitions

Individual

Grosvenor Galleries, Sydney: 1928
Macquarie Galleries, Sydney: 1932, 1937, 1939, 1942 (with Enid Cambridge), 1945, 1947, 1951, 1952, 1964, 1967, 1968, 1970, 1972, 1974, 1975, 1976, 1977
Walkers Galleries, London: 1932 (with Lionel and Mrs Crawshaw)
Johnstone Gallery, Brisbane: 1952
Pioneer Contemporaries, Sydney: 1960 (with Roland Wakelin and Roy de Maistre)
Art Gallery of New South Wales, Sydney: 1973–4 (touring retrospective)
Macquarie Galleries, Canberra: 1975

Group

Royal Art Society of New South Wales, Sydney: 1915–23, 1925, 1927
Society of Artists, Sydney: occasionally 1919–65
Contemporary Group, Sydney: 1929, 1932–6, 1938–47, 1950–53, 1955–7, 1959
Group of Seven, Macquarie Galleries, Sydney: 1930
Art Gallery of New South Wales, Sydney: 1938 (*150 Years of Australian Art*)
Australian Academy of Art, Sydney and Melbourne: 1938–40

Bibliography

Thea Proctor, "Modern art in Sydney", *Art in Australia*, 3rd series, no.73, November 1938, pp.24–30
Daniel Thomas, "Grace Cossington Smith", *Art and Australia*, iv, 1967, pp.300–09
Grace Cossington Smith, exh. cat., Art Gallery of New South Wales, Sydney, and elsewhere, 1973
Ruth Brack, "Grace Cossington Smith and the motif of the 'bridge'", *Studies in Australian Art*, ed. Ann Galbally and Margaret Plant, Melbourne: University of Melbourne Department of Fine Arts, 1978, pp.91–8
Bruce James, *Grace Cossington Smith*, Sydney: Craftsman House, 1990 (contains extensive bibliography)
Bethia Foott, *Ethel and the Governors' General*, Sydney: Rainforest, 1992
Daniel Thomas, *Grace Cossington Smith: A Life from Drawings in the Collection of the National Gallery of Australia*, Canberra: National Gallery of Australia, 1993

Grace Cossington Smith's early work, the *Sock Knitter* (1915; Art Gallery of New South Wales, Sydney), a painting of her sister, Madge, knitting socks for the troops in World War I, established her as one of Australia's first Post-Impressionist artists. The bold use of large areas of colour, the flattened perspective, the decorative patterned background – a youthful, but intelligent response to the viewing of reproductions of the work of Matisse, Cézanne and the Camden Town Group painters – had hitherto not been seen in Australian art. The

painting foreshadowed Smith's later oeuvre, a foray into dramatic interpretations of modernity and then, later, a combination of exciting and original technique with gentle, domestic subject matter.

Smith's introduction to Post-Impressionist styles was through the atelier of Anthony Dattilo-Rubbo where she studied intermittently from 1910 to 1927. The Italian-trained Dattilo-Rubbo facilitated an absorption of modernist ideas and techniques in his students by providing information on European styles by way of magazines, reproductions of European works brought back by travelling students, his own interest in colour, and his spirited defence of his students' work when it was challenged by the exhibition committees of the Royal Art Society and the Society of Artists. Under his tutelage Smith produced such works as *Still Life* (c.1915; University of Sydney) and *The Reader* (c.1915; Art Gallery of New South Wales), which are indicative of the prevailing influence of British Post-Impressionism in their bright but tonal colours, short visible brush strokes and attention to the flat character of the picture plane. Smith remarked at this time that she could not bear a "pulled down ... slithery, slimy" stroke but instead sought a paint texture that was "crumbly" and "dry", and that she was concerned with the relation of forms to each other (Thomas 1993, pp.18–19).

Smith reflected Dattilo-Rubbo's interest in social realist work in a series of paintings including *Strike* (c.1917; Newcastle Region Art Gallery), *Reinforcements: Troops Marching* (c.1917) and *Rushing* (c.1922; both Art Gallery of New South Wales), which depict scenes of war-time and post war-time Sydney. The works, however, lack sympathy. Crowds are depicted as faceless and milling, and are indicative of Smith's conservative political attitude, which was at such odds with her adventurous painting techniques: "I am cured forever of any democratic feelings ... They [the crowds] swagger about with their hats on one side, chewing and laughing and lolling" (Grace Cossington Smith, letter to Mary Cunningham, 12 December 1917, quoted in James 1990, p.42). *Centre of a City* (1925; John Fairfax Group Ltd, Sydney) shows groups of people submerged in darkness while in the upper half of the painting the buildings are bathed in sunlight and backed by the sky, a glowing aura of uplifted brush strokes.

In the mid-1920s Smith's work became too adventurous even for Dattilo-Rubbo. Somewhat isolated by an unsympathetic Sydney art world that viewed her as an amateur painter rather than a committed professional artist and often rejected her works from art society exhibitions, and by a family that though supportive lacked understanding of her art, Smith was to benefit greatly from the interest of Ethel Anderson. Anderson, an artist and writer, provided encouragement by way of writing articles about the artist's work, discussing her aims, opening exhibitions and, in the 1940s, lobbying the Art Gallery of New South Wales to accept a gift of a painting by the artist – the first to enter its collection.

This appreciation of her achievements gave Smith the confidence to create her most daring and exciting works, those of the late 1920s. Works such as *Trees* (c.1926; Newcastle Region Art Gallery) shimmer with the movement of short patterned brush strokes that make up complex but almost insubstantial forms, the dazzling slivers of unpainted white canvas and bright colours. These works are essentially formal exercises in

Grace Cossington Smith: *Curve of the Bridge*, 1928–9; oil on cardboard; 110.5 × 82.5 cm.; Art Gallery of New South Wales, Sydney; purchased by the Art Gallery Society of New South Wales and James Fairfax, 1991

paint application. Other works such as *Eastern Road, Turramurra* (c.1926; National Gallery of Australia, Canberra) are not only modernist in their formal qualities but, with the depiction of a swath of roadway and telegraph poles triumphantly cutting through the bushland around Sydney, celebrate modernisation and suburbanisation.

These works were a prelude to Smith's series of paintings and drawings of the movements of people and machines in the city, and led on to a group of major works: paintings and drawings of the construction of the Sydney Harbour Bridge from 1928 to 1931. The best known of these, the *Bridge in Curve* (1930; National Gallery of Victoria, Melbourne) and *Curve of the Bridge* (1928–9; see illustration), show the artist's ability to capture the excitement and majesty of the building project in her use of dynamic angles and lively, almost sketchy paint application. In the former work, the heroic symbolism of the joining arch is emphasised by a surrounding radiant halo of light; in the latter, the mightiness and exhilaration of the rising structure is shown in the overwhelming and disorienting perspective.

The death of her parents in the 1930s and a move from her garden-shed studio to one inside the family home, Cossington at Turramurra, inspired works more genteel in subject matter, but at the same time vigorous consolidations of her explorations of style and technique. In works such as *Sea Wave (Sea)* (1931; private collection, repr. James 1990, p.88) the artist has used her now characteristic blocky brush stroke to build up a subtle and evocative depiction of flowing forms. Flower studies such as *Landscape with Flowering Peach* (c.1933; Shepparton Art Gallery) and *Wildflowers* (1940; Art Gallery of New South Wales), on the other hand, show the artist's ability to imbue the delicate, soft flower forms with as much architectonic interest as the complex steel structure of the Harbour Bridge. A depiction of a department store tea room, *Lacquer Room* (1935–6; Art Gallery of New South Wales), not only gives a glimpse of the artist's own social life but also captures the essence of Henri Bergson's Vitalism (influential generally in Australian art at this time) in the vibrancy of the contrasting red chairs and green tables. The interest in Art Deco, electricity, health and hygiene, fashion and the growing social freedom of women visible in the work are signs of modernity.

The artist's oeuvre culminated in a large body of sophisticated but more introspective works depicting the interior of her home, and ranging over 30 years from the 1940s to the 1970s. These works combine Smith's life-time interests: her closely knit family background, her piety, her role as an independent woman artist and her interest in modern art. Typical of these works, *Interior with Wardrobe Mirror* (1955; Art Gallery of New South Wales) shows a paint surface composed entirely of the artist's identifying, identically sized square brush strokes of bright, pure-hued paint. The picture is geometrically divided by the rectangular shapes of the wardrobe shelves, the doors, the floor rug, the shelves of the bookcase and the picture rail. On one level the work could be read as a purely abstract exercise. The decorative quality of the colour and paint application evoke Matisse's interiors and exploration of colour and form. Its subject matter – a room interior, an open wardrobe, a mirror reflecting the view of the garden and street beyond a window – is, however, a metaphysical study of interior and exterior, private and public, internal and external.

Light is depicted in the room metaphorically through the mirrored reflection and physically by the bright colour and broken brush stroke. The painting is characteristic of Smith's spirituality, painting style and subject matter. Interviewed by Hazel de Berg in 1965 she said of her painting: "I use squares [her brush strokes] because I feel in that way that light can be put into colour". She described her work as "expressing form in colour. Colour vibrant with light – but containing this other, silent quality which is unconscious, and belongs to all things created" (Hazel de Berg, taped interview with the artist, 16 August 1965; National Library of Australia, Canberra).

HEATHER JOHNSON

Smith, Jaune Quick-to-See

American painter and mixed-media artist, 1940–

Born in St Ignatius, Flathead Indian Reservation, Montana, 15 January 1940, a Native American of Salish, French-Cree and Shoshone heritage. Studied at Framingham State College, Massachusetts (BA in art education 1976); University of New Mexico, Albuquerque (MFA 1980). Recipient of Purchase award, Academy of Arts and Letters, New York, 1987; Fellowship award, Western States Art Foundation, 1988; Association of American Cultures Arts Service award, 1990; honorary doctorate, Minneapolis College of Art and Design, 1992. Honorary professor, Beaumont Chair, Washington University, St Louis, 1989. Lives in Corrales, New Mexico.

Selected Individual Exhibitions

Kornblee Gallery, New York: 1979
University of Pittsburgh: 1980
Marilyn Butler Gallery, Santa Fe: 1983, 1985, 1987, 1988
Galerie Akmak, Berlin: 1983
Bernice Steinbaum Gallery, New York: 1983, 1985, 1987, 1990
Washington State Arts Commission: 1984 (*Flathead Wellspring*, touring)
Peter Stremmel Gallery, Reno, NV: 1985
Yellowstone Art Center, Billings, MT: 1986
Cambridge Multi-Cultural Art Center, MA: 1989
California State University, Long Beach: 1989
Anne Reed Gallery, Sun Valley, ID: 1991
Steinbaum Krauss Gallery, New York: 1992
Chrysler Museum, Norfolk, VA: 1993 (touring)

Bibliography

Jamake Highwater, *The Sweet Grass Lives On: Fifty Contemporary North American Indian Artists*, New York: Crowell, 1980
Laurel Reuter, "Jaune Quick-to-See Smith", *Artspace*, June 1980
Ronny Cohen, "Jaune Quick-to-See Smith at Kornblee", *Art in America*, March 1980, pp.116–17
Edwin C. Wade and Rennard Strickland, *Magic Images: Contemporary Native American Art*, Norman: University of Oklahoma Press, 1981
Deborah C. Phillips, "Jaune Quick-to-See Smith", *Art News*, lxxxii, October 1983, p.93
Ruth Bass, "Jaune Quick-to-See Smith", *Art News*, lxxxiii, March 1984, p.224
Women of Sweetgrass, Cedar and Sage, exh. cat., Gallery of the American Indian Community House, New York, 1985
Gregory Galligan, "Jaune Quick-to-See Smith: Crossing the great divide", *Arts Magazine*, lx, January 1986, pp.54–5

—, "Jaune Quick-to-See Smith: Racing with the moon", *Arts Magazine*, lxi, January 1987, pp.82–3

Committed to Print: Social and Political Themes in Recent American Printed Art, exh. cat., Museum of Modern Art, New York, 1988

Betty Ann Brown, "Review shorts", *Artweek*, xx, 21 October 1989, pp.11–12

The Decade Show, exh. cat., The New Museum, New York, 1990

Lucy R. Lippard, *Mixed Blessings: New Art in a Multicultural America*, New York: Pantheon, 1990

Shared Visions: Native American Painters and Sculptors in the Twentieth Century, exh. cat., Heard Museum, Phoenix, and elsewhere, 1991

Melanie Herzog, "Building bridges across cultures: Jaune Quick-to-See Smith", *School Arts*, xcii, October 1992, pp.31–4

Jenifer P. Borum, "Jaune Quick-to-See Smith: Steinbaum Krauss Gallery", *Artforum*, xxxi, January 1993, pp.87–8

Lawrence Abbott, ed., *I Stand in the Center of the Good: Interviews with Contemporary Native American Artists*, Lincoln: University of Nebraska Press, 1994

Over the past 20 years, Jaune Quick-to-See Smith has earned a position as one of the best known Native American artists of her generation. She enjoys a substantial international reputation not only for her well-honed and powerful art but also for her work as a curator, lecturer and environmental activist. Her wide-reaching career has established Smith as an eloquent and effective spokesperson for contemporary Native American perspectives and values in a world that is increasingly aware of its multi-cultural base.

Smith's journey to her achievements might well be termed an odyssey in which the time frame shifts back and forth. Hers was a childhood that established a firm hold on traditional Native American values; it was followed by a formal Euro-American art education that engaged her for 22 years, and a belated art career that places her between modernism and post-modernism. Smith's essential identity and consistent point of reference is her childhood experience on the Flathead Reservation of the Confederated Salish and Kootenai tribes of southwestern Montana, where she acquired a traditional sensitivity to the land and the animals and people who are one with it. Smith aspired to be an artist from early childhood, and her education was spread across a generation of dramatic change in Native American art. When she studied art in the 1960s and 1970s, her role models were such artists as Oscar Howe, Allan Houser and Fritz Scholder, who took their native heritage into the mainstream. By the time Smith received her MFA degree from the University of New Mexico in 1980, she was a member of a substantial group of Native American artists with university educations, strong personal styles and increasing access to the art establishment. Artists such as Smith, George Longfish and Hachivi Edgar Heap of Birds have been aggressive on political issues ranging from social conditions on the reservation to the exploitation of the environment. Accordingly, Smith and others have been characterised as post-modern both for their political content, coming as it does from a minority cultural perspective, and formally because of the ease with which they appropriate the modernist idiom and merge it with their native tradition and intent.

Early in her studies, Smith faced discouragement when advised by a teacher not to consider an art career because that was only for men. The pain of this comment struck deeply, but she eventually found encouragement through women teachers and students as the women's movement grew in the 1970s.

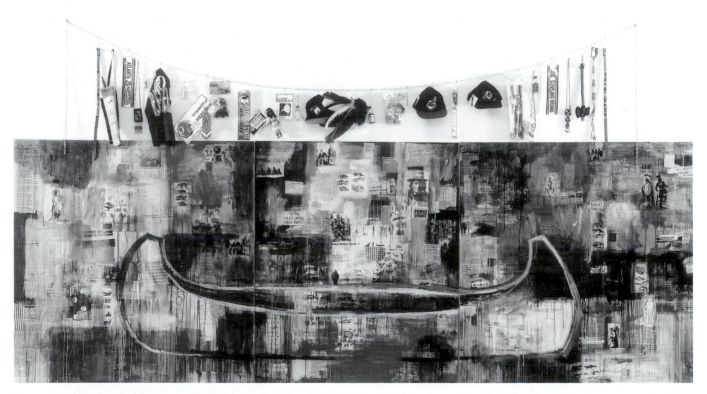

Jaune Quick-to-See Smith: *Trade (Gifts for Trading Land with White People)*, 1992; triptych, oil and collage on canvas, mixed media; 152.4 × 431.8 cm.; Chrysler Museum of Art, Norfolk, Virginia

Smith was likewise frustrated by a lack of critical responsiveness to Native American artists who were dismissed for mixing abstraction with tribal motifs, even though this was an accepted vocabulary for other modernists. In fact, she states that throughout her years of college education "it wasn't acceptable to show any ethnicity in my work" and that her professors "taught from a perspective that was all white, Eurocentric, and male" (Abbott 1994, p.216). These experiences helped to galvanise Smith's outspoken activism on women's and Native American issues. She began drawing as a child, an activity encouraged by her father, and she began formal art education in 1958.

From the beginning Smith had a strong interest in the environment, and landscape became a consistent feature of her work. Her view of the land was a gentle one, a land inhabited by plants, insects, animals and people, a perspective that she considers to be inherently Native American and highly positive. In the mid-1970s she painted on unstretched canvases loosely resembling hides in a style marked by muted colour and minimal design (e.g. *Ronan Robe* series). Her career took off in 1979 when she participated in two exhibitions in New York: a group show at the Droll/Kolbert Gallery and a two-artist show at the Kornblee Gallery. The works in these exhibitions were from her *Wallowa Waterhole* series inspired by readings about Chief Joseph (e.g. *Kalispell No.2*, 1979; pastel on paper; repr. Cohen 1980). Smith says that in this series she "developed a language that has sustained me to this day. Picto figures of humans and animals emerged" (Abbott 1994, p.213). Works of this period are lyrical, combining figurative and abstract images in a fragmented narrative. Pictograph-like outlines of horses and stick-figure men are given a modernist feeling through compositional devices reminiscent of such modern artists as Paul Klee and Joan Mirò. An example of work in this style is the pastel *Porcupine Ridge Series, No.35* (1979; Laurel Reuter Collection, ND). In the early 1980s Smith continued working on landscapes with animals in series such as *Red Lake*. Soon she had developed a sophisticated and integrated style merging landscapes with pictographic symbolism with a powerful personal expressiveness and modern quality, well represented by *Herding* (1985; Bernice Steinbaum Gallery, New York).

A series of paintings executed in 1986–7 and inspired by efforts to save the petrographics on a lava escarpment west of Albuquerque, New Mexico, propelled Smith into greater environmental activism. Works in this series became bolder with strong movement and large shapes based on pictographs. In 1989 she began a series of paintings based on Chief Seattle's environmental speech of 1854. In these paintings she incorporated words and attached objects – small found materials such as tin cans – to the painted surface. This trend towards a stronger mixed-media approach continued into the 1990s with increasingly direct messages about threats to the environment, for example, *Rain* (1991; Heard Museum, Phoenix, AZ). Smith's response to the Columbus Quincentenary produced such works as *Trade (Gifts for Trading Land with White People)* (1992; see illustration). Of this strongly political piece, which features a row of items such as Washington Redskin caps and plastic tomahawks, Smith said that if it could speak, it might say "why won't you consider trading the land we handed over to you for these silly trinkets that so honor us?

Sound like a bad deal? Well, that's the deal you gave us" (Arlene Hirschfelder, *Artists and Craftspeople*, New York: Facts on File, 1994, p.115).

Critical response to Smith has been fairly consistent and generally quite positive. From the earliest reviews of her work, authors have made the most of Smith's self-proclaimed goal to bridge the Native American and Euro-American cultures. Like other artists before her, she is positive about connecting the traditional and contemporary worlds. Much was made by commentators in the early and mid-1980s of Smith's synthesis of Euro-American art education and her American Indian heritage. Critics found in her affinity with Willem de Kooning, Mirò, Klee, Franz Marc and Robert Rauschenberg a reaffirmation of the mainstream. They made much of the compatibility of traditional Native American art and modern abstraction, and to be sure, the similarity is not missed on the artist. By the late 1980s, such terms as neo-expressionist were left behind when referring to Smith, and she is increasingly discussed in terms of how she fits with post-modernism. Her overt and aggressive political messages and the directness of her mixed-media technique place her squarely in the forefront of Native American post-modernism.

JOHN A. DAY

Smith, Pamela Colman

American painter and printmaker, 1878–1951

Born in London, 16 February 1878; grew up in Manchester and in Kingston, Jamaica. Studied at Pratt Institute, New York, 1893–7; accompanied Lyceum Theatre Company on some of its provincial tours. Freelance book illustrator in New York, 1898–9. Returned to England after being orphaned, 1899. Lived in household of actress Ellen Terry; had first vision while listening to music there, Christmas 1900. Joined Isis-Urania Temple of the Hermetic Order of the Golden Dawn, London, and became member of Irish Literary Society, c.1901. Co-authored *A Broad Sheet* with Jack B. Yeats, 1901–2; founded and edited *Green Sheaf* journal, 1903–4; founded Green Sheaf Press, 1905. Opened shop for sale of prints, 1904 (closed by 1906). Working as professional storyteller by 1903, telling Anglo-Irish and Afro-Jamaican tales. Joined the Masquers, a theatre group organised by Walter Crane, 1903; also active in Yeats's Stage Society; joined Edith Craig's feminist theatre group, the Pioneer Players, c.1911 (appointed to Advisory Council 1915). Member of Alfred Stieglitz's Photo-Secession group, New York, 1909–10. Converted to Catholicism, 1911. Purchased house, "Parc Garland", on the Lizard, Cornwall, establishing chapel and rest-home for priests, c.1918. Moved to Bude, Cornwall, 1941. Member, Royal Society of Arts, 1941. Died 18 September 1951.

Principal Exhibitions

Baillie Gallery, London: 1905–17
291 Gallery, New York: 1907, 1908, 1909 (all individual)
Berlin Photographic Company, New York: 1912
Exposition Universelle de Gand, Ghent: 1913

Musée du Louvre, Paris: 1914 (*Arts décoratifs de Grande Bretagne et d'Irlande*)

Selected Writings

"Two negro stories from Jamaica", *Journal of American Folklore*, xxxv, 1896, p.278

Annancy Stories, New York: Russell, 1899

Chim-Chim: Folk Stories from Jamaica, London: Green Sheaf Press, 1905

"A protest against fear", *Craftsman*, xi, 1907, p.728

"Should the art student think?", *Craftsman*, xiv, 1908, pp.417–18

"Music made visible", *Illustrated London News*, clxx, 1927, pp.258–60 (with the Hon. Mrs Forbes-Sempill)

Bibliography

Arthur Ransome, *Bohemia in London*, London: Chapman and Hall, and New York: Dodd Mead, 1907

"Pictured music", *Current Literature*, xlv, 1908, pp.174–7

Benjamin De Casseres, "Pamela Colman Smith", *Camera Work*, July 1909, pp.18–20

M. Irwin Macdonald, "The fairy faith and pictured music of Pamela Colman Smith", *The Craftsman*, xxiii, 1912, pp.20–34

Gertrude Moakley, "The Waite-Smith 'Tarot': A footnote to 'The Waste Land'", *Bulletin of the New York Public Library*, lviii, 1954, pp.471–5

——, "Introduction", in Arthur Edward Waite, *The Pictorial Key to the Tarot*, New Hyde Park, NY: University Books, 1959

Martha B. Caldwell, "Pamela Colman Smith: A search", *Southeastern College Art Conference Review*, vii, Fall 1974, pp.33–8

To All Believers: The Art of Pamela Colman Smith, exh. cat., Delaware Art Museum, Wilmington, and elsewhere, 1975

William Innes Homer, *Alfred Stieglitz and the American Avant-Garde*, Boston: New York Graphic Society, and London: Secker and Warburg, 1977

Pamela Colman Smith, exh. cat., McMaster University, Hamilton, Ontario, 1977

Melinda Boyd Parsons, "Mysticism in London", *The Spritual Image in Modern Art*, ed. Kathleen Regier, Wheaton, IL: Theosophical Publishing, 1987, pp.73–101

Lisa Tickner, *The Spectacle of Women: Imagery of the Suffrage Campaign, 1907–1914*, London: Chatto and Windus, 1987; Chicago: University of Chicago Press, 1988

Melinda Boyd Parsons, "Theatrical productions, symphonic music and the rise of 'musical painting' in the late 19th century", *Nineteenth-Century Studies*, i, Spring 1989, pp.49–72

Stuart R. Kaplan, *The Encyclopedia of Tarot*, New York: US Games Systems, 1990

Katharine Cockin, "New light on Edith Craig", *Theatre Notebook*, xlv, 1991, pp.132–43

Melinda Boyd Parsons, "Pamela Colman Smith and Alfred Stieglitz: Modernism et '291'", *History of Photography*, xx, 1993, pp.285–92

In 1907 the New York photographer Alfred Stieglitz exhibited 72 watercolours by Pamela Colman Smith, a mystical painter and printmaker of mixed Anglo-American and Afro-Caribbean origin, deeply committed to socialism and feminism. Smith said that her images of goddesses, folkloric heroes, star-crossed lovers and occult symbols "came to her" as visions to music and that she painted them "automatically" – that is, in a trance-state, without conscious control. Both her automatism and exotic subjects drew huge crowds to the gallery, sparking rave reviews.

Yet these small, lyrically Art Nouveau watercolours, for example *Blue Cat (Schumann's "Carnivale")* (see illustration),

Untitled (Self-Portrait with Water-Folk) and *Beethoven Sonata No.11* (all *c*.1907; Beinecke Rare Book and Manuscript Library, Yale University, New Haven), were more mediated than Smith claimed, their iconography influenced by literature and folklore (Yeats's poems, theatrical productions by Henry Irving and Ellen Terry, Anglo-Irish and Afro-Jamaican folklore, etc.) and by mystical texts she read as a member of the Rosicrucian Hermetic Order of the Golden Dawn. Yet the paintings also contain subtle feminist/socialist "messages" about women's independence and agency – indeed, Smith's aggressive goddesses, androgynous fairies and nature-spirits inhabit a world of far greater gender equity than her own.

It was to lend authority to these messages, drawing viewers into contemplating their meaning without conscious awareness of their political radicalism, that Smith claimed only to paint what was revealed in visions. She developed this strategy during her childhood in Manchester (then a hotbed of spiritualism closely linked with socialist/feminist agitation) by watching female "mediums" veil their own political views in the authority of "spirit-voices from beyond", thus articulating ideas women were normally barred from discussing.

Smith adapted this strategic indirection in early illustrated books and prints and by 1900 had garnered a reputation as one of America's most "advanced" illustrators as, for example, in *Annancy Stories* (1899; Schomburg Center for the Study of Black Culture), *The Golden Vanity and the Green Bed* (1899; Philadelphia Museum of Art) and *Widdicombe Fair* (1899; Library of Congress, Washington, DC). Created in an innovative printmaking technique combining mechanical reproduction with areas of hand-stencilling, these works were influenced stylistically by Smith's studies at the Pratt Institute with Arthur Dow. Dow's interest in Gauguin, Whistler and Japanese art fostered his belief that painting was "visual music": its forms could be manipulated, like musical tones, to increase the emotionalism and abstraction of the resulting image. Because "musical painting" rejected visual mimesis, it was regarded by avant-garde artists and critics as transcendent and anti-materialist – hence its appeal to a socialist-mystic like Smith.

Smith developed Dow's Synthetist style with brilliant colour and energetic line perfectly suited to her folkloric and theatrical subjects. At the time folk studies were new, and the so-called "primitive purity" of pre-modern folk cultures seemed an appropriate model for reforming over-civilised Euro-American society. Radical critics such as De Casseres thus perceived a political component in Smith's folkloric subjects. Yet these images were also encoded with feminist messages (generally ignored – or not perceived – by reviewers). In *Annancy Stories*, for instance, which were based on Jamaican folk tales and Afro-Christian religion, Smith countered Anglo-Jamaican racism and sexism by consistently depicting Obeah magicians as women (most such sorcerers were men), also using formal manipulations to give greater visual presence to her Afro-Jamaican figures than their white cohorts. Likewise, in her print *Macbeth, Act I* (1898; repr. Wilmington 1975), Smith empowered women by reversing male and female roles; thus in giving Lady Macbeth the role of Shakespeare's Macbeth, Smith was commenting on contemporaneous debate over theatrical cross-dressing and "proper" roles for actresses.

In London, by 1899, Smith collaborated on stage-sets, theatrical souvenirs and costuming projects with W.B. Yeats,

Pamela Colman Smith: *Blue Cat (Schumann's "Carnivale")*, *c.*1907; Beinecke Rare Book and Manuscript Library, Yale University, New Haven

A.W. Pinero (*Trelawny of the Wells*, 1899; New York Public Library), Bernard Shaw, Gordon Craig, Walter Crane and, at the Lyceum Theatre, with Henry Irving, Bram Stoker and Ellen Terry (*Sir Henry Irving and Miss Ellen Terry ...*, 1899; Ellen Terry Memorial Museum; costume sketches of various dates in Victoria and Albert Museum, London, and Ellen Terry Memorial Museum).

Smith supported herself with publishing projects and professional story-telling. In 1901–2 she collaborated with Jack Yeats on *A Broad Sheet* (Museum of Fine Arts, Boston), illustrating Irish supernatural tales in prints of vivid hue and lyrical line. The following year she founded and edited a journal, the *Green Sheaf* (Firestone Library, Princeton University), publishing work by the Yeatses, Lady Gregory, John Masefield, Æ (George William Russell), J.M. Synge and others. Smith's own *Green-Sheaf* illustrations varied between her early Synthetist style and the looser style of her visionary paintings (which had begun in 1900).

The works for which Smith is best known today are her lithographs for the occult scholar A.E. Waite's Tarot deck (1909; Victoria and Albert Museum; reprints through US Games Systems Inc.), a type of card used since the Renaissance for occult divination. While to some extent Smith's drawings necessarily reflect traditional Tarot iconography, she also said that she "saw" certain images in visions; in addition, the cards refer to contemporaneous feminist and suffrage agitation in their depiction of "female kings" and women warriors. This iconographic device was influenced by Smith's involvement, from 1909, with London's Suffrage Atelier and (after 1911) the Pioneer Players, a feminist theatre group founded by Edith Craig, Ellen Terry's politically radical lesbian daughter. Smith designed the logo for the Pioneer Players (Edith Craig Collection; National Trust, Smallhythe) and created a number of suffrage posters in a restrained, black-and-white drawing style quite unlike her earlier work (Fawcett Archives, Guildhall University, London).

After Smith's conversion to Catholicism in 1911, she dedicated her life to the renewal of religious art, using an innovative combination of visionary, "musical" automatism and Catholic imagery – as, for instance, in her version of Paul Claudel's *Way of the Cross* (London: Art and Book Co., 1917), *An Early English Nativity Play* (1919; Enthoven Theatre

Collection, Victoria and Albert Museum) and her ink drawing *Light of the World* (before 1921; repr. *Illustrated London News*, 12 February 1921). Other visionary watercolours, painted in a delicate, atmospheric style, use moody landscape motifs to convey a generalised sense of the difficulty of spiritual pilgrimage, for example *Aria in G, Bach* (1913), *O Pines of Sister Pines* (1943) and *Duet, Stravinsky* (1946; all repr. Kaplan 1990).

Smith's claim to visionary automatism sparked public interest and brought her exhibitions and commissions in her lifetime, yet subsequently this worked against her: in particular, the lack of conscious aesthetic control implied by automatism, viewed as "feminine" passivity, contributed to her neglect by modernist critics and historians. Only now, in the context of feminist post-modernism, has the significance of Smith's art – with its politics and emphasis on visionary inspiration, collaborative creativity and traditional religion and folk-belief – become clear.

MELINDA BOYD PARSONS

Snyder, Joan

American painter and mixed-media artist, 1940–

Born in Highland Park, New Jersey, 16 April 1940. Studied at Douglass College (AB in sociology 1962) and Rutgers University (MFA 1966), both in New Brunswick. Moved to New York, 1967; to Eastport, New York, 1985. Taught at State University of New York, Stony Brook, 1967–9; Yale University, New Haven, 1974; University of California, Irvine, 1975; San Francisco Art Institute, 1976; Princeton University, 1975–7; Parsons School of Design, New York, 1992–3. Married Laurence Fink, 1969; daughter born 1979; divorced. Recipient of National Endowment for the Arts (NEA) grant, 1974; Guggenheim fellowship, 1981. Lives in Brooklyn, New York.

Selected Individual Exhibitions

Paley & Lowe, New York: 1970, 1971, 1973
Los Angeles Institute of Contemporary Art: 1976
Neuberger Museum, State University of New York at Purchase: 1978
Hamilton Gallery of Contemporary Art, New York: 1978, 1982
WARM, Minneapolis: 1979 (touring)
San Francisco Art Institute: 1979–80 (touring)
Wadsworth Atheneum, Hartford, CT: 1981
Nielsen Gallery, Boston: 1981, 1983, 1986, 1991, 1992, 1993, 1994
Hirschl and Adler Modern, New York: 1985, 1988, 1990, 1992, 1994
David Winton Bell Gallery, Brown University, Providence, RI: 1988–9 (*Joan Snyder Collects Joan Snyder*, touring)
Allentown Art Museum, PA: 1993
Rose Art Museum, Brandeis University, Waltham, MA: 1994 (retrospective)

Selected Writings

"Passages", *Modern Painters*, iv, Autumn 1991, pp.48–9

Bibliography

Marcia Tucker, "The anatomy of a stroke: Recent paintings by Joan Snyder", *Artforum*, ix, May 1971, pp.42–5

Joan Snyder: Seven Years of Work, exh. cat., Neuberger Museum, State University of New York at Purchase, 1978
Joan Snyder at WARM: A Women's Collective Art Space, exh. cat., Women's Art Registry of Minnesota, Minneapolis, and elsewhere, 1979
Gerrit Henry, "Joan Snyder", *Art in America*, lxx, Summer 1982, pp.141–2
Carter Ratcliff and others, "Expressionism today: An artists' symposium", *Art in America*, lxx, December 1982, pp.58–75, 139
Joan Snyder, exh. cat., Hirschl and Adler Modern, New York, 1985
Paul Gardner, "When is a painting finished?", *Art News*, lxxxiv, November 1985, pp.89–100
Gerrit Henry, "Joan Snyder: True grit", *Art in America*, lxxiv, February 1986, pp.96–101
Jed Perl, "Houses, fields, gardens, hills", *New Criterion*, February 1986
Susan Gill, "Painting from the heart", *Art News*, lxxxvi, April 1987, pp.128–35
Joan Snyder Collects Joan Snyder, exh. cat., David Winton Bell Gallery, Brown University, Providence, RI, and elsewhere, 1988
Joan Snyder, exh. cat., Hirschl and Adler Modern, New York, 1990
Joan Snyder, exh. cat., Nielsen Gallery, Boston, 1991
Joan Snyder: Works with Paper, exh. cat., Allentown Art Museum, PA, 1993
Joan Snyder: Painter, 1969 to Now, exh. cat., Rose Art Museum, Brandeis University, Waltham, MA, 1994
Donald Kuspit, "Joan Snyder", *Artforum*, xxxii, Summer 1994, pp.92–3
Bill Jones, "Painting the haunted pool", *Art in America*, lxxxii, October 1994, pp.120–23, 157

Joan Snyder discovered painting in 1962 while she was a student at Douglass College in New Brunswick, New Jersey. It was an epiphanous experience: "... when I started to paint, it was like speaking for the first time. I mean, I felt like my whole life, I had never spoken. I had never been heard. I had never said anything that had any meaning. When I started painting, it was like I was speaking for the first time" (Minneapolis 1979, p.16). The discovery also entailed what might be called a spiritual conversion, as the following statement indicates: "...my painting is my religion. It's the altar that I go to and it's where I face myself and find out who I am ... And you make offerings at the altar. At some level you give generously" (Boston 1991, n.p.).

Snyder realised her initial maturity at the end of the 1960s in a series of pictures that became known as her stroke paintings, the first of which was *Lines and Strokes* (1969; artist's collection). It consists of eight horizontal swathes of colour, each spreading more than less from one side of the canvas support to the other, each resembling the horizon line in a landscape image. But landscape is not what the picture is about. Stacked as they are, each laden with a distinctly expressive energy, the lines and strokes refer to nothing outside themselves, nothing, that is, except the fundamental urge to make an expressive mark and thereby take possession of a space. Thick and thin, large and small, transparent, opaque, elegant, rough-hewn, brushed on, squeezed from the tube, carefully controlled and impulsively splotched, the strokes deconstruct the medium, resulting in an impressive painting primer that reveals Snyder personalising her medium and finding her voice. In the stroke paintings, we see her learning to speak visually.

The stroke paintings were well received and deeply satisfying, but Snyder herself was not finally satisfied by them: "They were easy, I could do them in two days ... Everybody loved

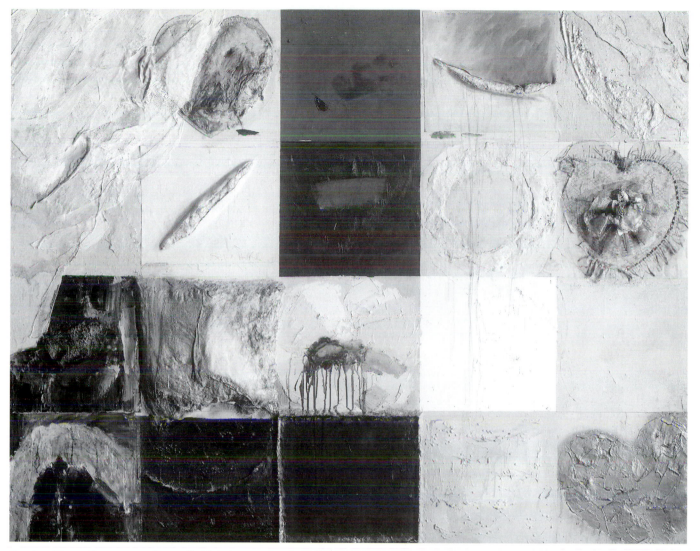

Snyder: *Heart-On*, 1975; oil, acrylic, fabric, etc.; 182.8 × 243.8 cm.; Metropolitan Museum of Art, New York; Gift of Mr and Mrs Donald Rugoff, 1981 (1981.199)

them, and I stopped doing them. I had to change ... I had nowhere to go but into my own past, into my own iconography ... and that is what I did" (Purchase 1978, pp.2 and 20). In paintings such as *Flesh/Art* (1973–4; artist's collection) and *Heart-On* (1975; see illustration) she began to explore that personal iconography, which consisted of images of the female body, childlike drawings of houses and landscape spaces, handwritten diaristic notes and a wide range of challenging and funky collage elements such as fabric, papier-mâché, wallpaper and linoleum. In addition, she adopted new and unconventional techniques that entailed slashing, stuffing and sewing the canvas, engaging it as an active and physical entity instead of a merely passive and accommodating support. In emphasising her experience of being in the world, Snyder's work became personal in a new way, the way not of a reductive abstraction but of an embracing feminism that she was instrumental in forging. She thus became in the 1970s a model for ambitious women artists of her generation and a leading example of their innovative approaches to thinking about and making art.

Expressive landscapes were among the images that Snyder produced when she began painting, and she often returned to landscape in her paintings of the 1980s. Pictures such as *Beanfield with Music* (1984; First Church of Christ Scientist, Boston), *Waiting for a Miracle (for John and Nina)* (1986; Collection Mr and Mrs Gifford Phillips, New York) and *Ode to the Pumpkin Field* (1986–7; Twin Farms Collection, Barnard, VT) are typically expansive and physical, incorporating a variety of materials and offering a wide range of feelings associated with space and light and colour, the changing seasons, dormancy, rebirth, flowering, abundance. More often than not the images ascend and spread across the entire surface, rising before us without horizons, as if limitless, their presentation suggesting that we might be lying face down in these landscapes, embracing them, one with them. The erotic equation of landscape and the human body represents a theme that Snyder first entertained as a young artist in the 1960s and occasionally explored from a feminist perspective, graphically, with frustration and anger, during the decade that followed (e.g. *Nude in Landscape*, 1977; Parrish Art Museum, Southampton, NY). When she returned to it in the 1980s, she did so with the full powers of a mature painter and with a clearly more resolved and optimistic vision: "I painted sacred fields, serene fields, fields of moons, moons in mud, and cantatas. This work reflects all of my moods, my sorrows, losses and struggles, and a peace that has finally come into my life" (New York 1990, p.5).

In more recent works Snyder's concerns have broadened further. *Women in Camps* (1988; Collection Mr and Mrs Richard Albright, Wayland, MA) summons the grim memory of the Holocaust through haunting photographs of its victims, while *Journey of the Souls* (1993; private collection, Boston), its centre black and vast and impenetrable, refers to the frightening tragedy of AIDS. Such pictures take us to a new level of global concern, and in this they embody the values and aims of a second generation of feminist artists, a generation for whom Snyder's vision is as much a model today as it was for her contemporaries more than two decades ago.

CARL BELZ

Sobrino, Cecilia and María *see* Convents survey

Solomon, Rebecca

British painter, 1832–1886

Born in London, 26 September 1832, into a large Jewish family. Attended Spitalfields School of Design with older brother Abraham. Exhibited widely in London and the provinces, 1850–74. Assisted painters Thomas Faed, William Frith, John Phillip and John Everett Millais, 1850s–60s. Travelled abroad with younger brother Simeon, c.1857; to Italy with him, 1865–6. Worked as a graphic artist for illustrated papers, 1860s. Died after being run over by a hansom cab in the Euston Road, London, 20 November 1886.

Principal Exhibitions

British Institution, London: 1850–54, 1866
Royal Academy, London: 1852, 1854–65, 1867, 1869
International Exhibition, London: 1862
Dudley Gallery, London: 1865–9, 1871
Society of Lady Artists, London: 1874

Bibliography

Ellen C. Clayton, *English Female Artists*, 2 vols, London: Tinsley, 1876
Pamela Gerrish Nunn, "Rebecca Solomon: Painting and drama", *Theatrephile*, ii/8, 1985, pp.3–4
Solomon: A Family of Painters, exh. cat., Geffrye Museum, London, and elsewhere, 1985
Lynda Nead, *Myths of Sexuality: Representations of Women in Victorian Britain*, Oxford: Blackwell, 1988
Pamela Gerrish Nunn, "Rebecca Solomon's 'A Young Teacher'", *Burlington Magazine*, cxxx, 1988, pp.769–70
Deborah Cherry, *Painting Women: Victorian Women Artists*, London and New York: Routledge, 1993

Rebecca Solomon is one of a handful of successful Jewish artists to practise in Victorian Britain, and the middle member of a unique trio of sibling artists: her older brother Abraham and her younger brother Simeon were also professional painters. Her career shows that by the middle of the 19th century it had become possible for women to carry on a professional painting practice, earning a living and making a name, though not necessarily breaking new ground or allying themselves with any particular school or style.

Like Abraham, in whose home she lived and by whom she was partially trained, Rebecca Solomon served the mainstream public with medium-size paintings of moral and sentimental themes with figures in modern or historical dress. Essaying subjects of interest to the contemporary middle class, such as *The Governess* (1854; see illustration) and the *Story of Balaclava* (1855; ex-Leicester Galleries, London), though with a keen eye for a female point of view of those topics, she produced paintings that did the rounds of the London and provincial exhibitions. Her subject matter reflects the range of mainstream taste, though her work was frequently accused, with Abraham's, of vulgarity, and her technical excellence was uneven. Her biggest successes were with paintings that fell within the higher genres of history or literature, *Peg Woffington's First Visit to Triplet* (1860; untraced, repr. London 1985) and *Fugitive Royalists* (1862; untraced, *ibid.*). Both works use ingredients – several figures in an interior, connected by a presumed narrative of some complexity and shown in a moment of emotional drama – that the artist employed successfully on several other occasions, as in *Behind the Curtain* (1858; private collection, *ibid.*) and *A Plea for Mercy* (*Sweet Mercy Is Nobility's True Badge*) (1865; Geffrye Museum, London).

Financial difficulties in the mid-1860s after Abraham's unexpected death in 1862 led to her having to supplement her original work with assisting several popular painters known to her through Abraham and with illustrations for middle-class periodicals such as *London Society* and *Churchman's Family Magazine*. She may have worked also as an artist's model at this time, and began to produce and exhibit watercolours as well as oil paintings. She took up residence with her younger brother Simeon, whose wild social life was in marked contrast to her alleged religious observance. Simeon's connections with the circle of Dante Gabriel Rossetti brought both siblings in touch with second-wave Pre-Raphaelitism and Aestheticism, stylistic trends that can be seen in *Primavera* (1864; private collection, Japan) and *Wounded Dove* (1866; University College of Wales, Aberystwyth). Since none of the artist's late work is presently traced, it is difficult to know if she persisted in this vein.

It is possible that Simeon's covert homosexuality, which led eventually to his prosecution and ostracism from artistic circles, hampered Rebecca's professional standing from the late 1860s. Equally, it was suggested after her death that she became an alcoholic in her mature years. Like Abraham but in marked contrast to Simeon, Rebecca made little reference to her Jewishness in her painting. Titles of works exhibited after 1866 (e.g. *Giovannina, Rome*, 1867; untraced) indicate a body of work resulting from the artist's travels in Italy as well as a continued appeal to the literary element of mainstream taste (e.g. *Helena and Hermia*, 1869; untraced) Overall, Solomon's

Solomon: *The Governess*, 1854; oil on canvas; 66 × 86.4 cm.; Yale Center for British Art, New Haven / Edmund J. and Suzanne McCormick Collection

oeuvre represents vividly the struggle of a working woman artist of the mid-19th century to compete with her male contemporaries in an increasingly commodified art market.

PAMELA GERRISH NUNN

Spartali, Marie
British painter, 1843–1927

Born in Middlesex, 10 March 1843; father a merchant and Greek consul-general in London. Well-educated at home in classical and foreign languages. Became pupil of Ford Madox Brown, 1864, and close friend of his daughter Lucy (q.v.); sat for Brown as well as for Dante Gabriel Rossetti and Edward Burne-Jones; photographed by Julia Margaret Cameron (q.v.). Married William James Stillman, widower and former American consul in Greece, 1871; one son, one daughter.

Settled in Florence, 1878, then in Rome when Stillman was appointed The Times correspondent for Italy and Greece (lived in England, 1883–5). Returned home to Surrey, England, on Stillman's retirement in 1898. Also visited USA. Daughter Effie and stepdaughter Lisa were also artists. Died 6 March 1927.

Principal Exhibitions

Dudley Gallery, London: 1867–73, 1875–8 (watercolour), 1872 (black-and-white)
Society of Female Artists, London: 1869
Royal Academy, London: 1870, 1873, 1875–7
Society of British Artists, London: 1874
National Academy of Design, New York: 1875
American Society of Painters in Water Color, New York: 1877–8, 1883–4
Grosvenor Gallery, London: 1877, 1879–85, 1887
New Society of Painters in Watercolour, London: 1886–7
New Gallery, London: 1888–99
Curtis and Cameron, Boston: 1903 (individual)
Oehme Galleries, New York: 1908 (individual)

Spartali: *Childhood of St Cecilia*, 1884

Bibliography

William Michael Rossetti and others, *English Painters of the Present Day*, London: Seeley Jackson, 1871

Ellen C. Clayton, *English Female Artists*, 2 vols, London: Tinsley, 1876

Clara Erskine Clement and Laurence Hutton, *Artists of the Nineteenth Century and Their Work*, 2 vols, Boston: Houghton Osgood, and London: Trübner, 1879; reprinted New York: Arno Press, 1969

Percy Bate, *The English Pre-Raphaelite Painters: Their Associates and Successors*, London: Bell, 1899; reprinted New York: Books for Libraries, 1970

William Michael Rossetti, *Some Reminiscences*, 2 vols, London: Brown Langham, and New York: Scribner, 1906

The Pre-Raphaelite Era, 1848–1914, exh. cat., Delaware Art Museum, Wilmington, 1976

Charlotte Yeldham, *Women Artists in Nineteenth-Century France and England*, 2 vols, New York: Garland, 1984

The Last Romantics: The Romantic Tradition in British Art: Burne-Jones to Stanley Spencer, exh. cat., Barbican Art Gallery, London, 1989

Jan Marsh and Pamela Gerrish Nunn, *Women Artists and the Pre-Raphaelite Movement*, London: Virago, 1989

Rowland Elzea, "Marie Stillman in the United States: Two exhibitions, 1908 and 1982", *Journal of Pre-Raphaelite and Aesthetic Studies*, ii, Spring 1989, pp.56–72

Deborah Cherry, *Painting Women: Victorian Women Artists*, London and New York: Routledge, 1993

The daughter of a wealthy businessman and the honorary Greek consul, Marie Spartali was a member of the cultured Anglo-Greek community in Britain, which included such important art patrons as the Ionides family. She trained in the studio of Ford Madox Brown, an associate of the Pre-Raphaelite Brotherhood, alongside Lucy Madox Brown (q.v.) and Catherine Madox Brown, later Hueffer. She was also a friend of Dante Gabriel Rossetti, for whom she occasionally modelled, of William and Jane Morris, and of Edward Burne-Jones, and thus personally and artistically linked to the Pre-Raphaelite circle, whose style she adopted as her own. Her artistic career was opposed by her father, who regarded professional status as socially demeaning; when she sold an early painting to Frederick Leyland MP, her father argued that she should make it a gift. He also opposed her marriage to W.J. Stillman, a penniless widower with three children and no income; for economic reasons she painted for exhibition and sale, sending regularly to shows in London, Manchester, Liverpool and North America, and for the same reason her oeuvre contains a high proportion of attractively saleable subjects as well as more serious and ambitious pieces. Her subjects are mainly poetic and imaginative (figures in landscape, etc.), or the single female heads favoured by patrons, but flower pictures, portraits and landscapes (British and Italian) also feature. Her work is in a typically Pre-Raphaelite dense watercolour with body colour, on a medium-sized scale, and is characterised by a soft touch and delicate drawing, together with a fine sense of colour and atmosphere that harmonises with late Pre-Raphaelite and Aesthetic practice.

Spartali's first works are more angular and "primitive" in style, and the themes display a political aspect in keeping with the artist's Greek ancestry: an early work exhibited in London and Liverpool in 1867 showed Antigone performing the burial rites for her brother in defiance of Creon's edict, which relates to the contemporary Cretan uprising against Ottoman rule. In several other subjects she showed an awareness of gender that belies her later reputation for prettiness; among these are *Corinna* (1867; untraced), the legendary founder of poetry, and *Procne in Search of Philomela* (exh. Society of Female Artists 1869; untraced). In 1875 she sent two "elaborately finished" watercolours on Arthurian themes (previously shown at the Royal Academy) to the National Academy of Design in New York, where their imaginative and intellectual charm was noted by Henry James, who identified Spartali as a "profound colourist", heir to the traditions and temper of the Pre-Raphaelite Brotherhood, and in her own right as "a spontaneous, sincere, naive Pre-Raphaelite" (*Galaxy*, July 1875). Delicacy is not necessarily naivety, however, and Spartali's sustained and varied output argues against her association with amateurism and imitation. Stylistically she owed most to Madox Brown, Burne-Jones and to a lesser extent Rossetti, whose influence on her work has been exaggerated due to her habit of choosing topics from his verse translations of Italian literature. These and related sources form the subjects of several of her larger works, including the *Enchanted Garden* (1889; Pre-Raphaelite Inc.) on a theme from Boccaccio, and *Mandetta of Toulouse* (1903; National Trust, Wightwick Manor, Wolverhampton), a Petrarchan subject set in the ancient church of La Daurade. She was equally successful with single or paired figures, and sensitive depictions of children. One recently rediscovered work in the Virgin and Child mode is the *Childhood of St Cecilia* (1884; see illustration).

In her lifetime Spartali's reputation was steady amid the middle ranks of artists loosely associated with Aestheticism. Thus, for example, the *Art Journal* of July 1873: "Mrs Stillman has brought imagination to her work. These vistas of garden landscape are conceived in the spirit of romantic luxuriance, when the beauty of each separate flower was a delight. The figures, too, have a grace that belongs properly to art." After her death, her work vanished from view, together with much 19th-century art, only to be rediscovered in the 1970s and 1980s with the renewed interest in Pre-Raphaelitism, although she has suffered from gender bias (John Christian, in London 1989, refers to the artist as "Marie" and describes her "hesitant drawing and gently lyrical vision"). Other writers have generally identified her by reference to Rossetti's studies of her head, and therefore as a typical Pre-Raphaelite beauty or "stunner", often omitting all mention of her artistic career. The largest collection of Spartali's work is in the Delaware Art Museum, Wilmington; a smaller selection is at Wightwick Manor, Wolverhampton (National Trust), and the Walker Art Gallery, Liverpool. Other works are in private hands and several known titles remain unlocated.

JAN MARSH

Spence, Jo
British photographer, 1934–1992

Born in South Woodford, Essex, 15 June 1934. Attended secretarial college, 1948–50. Secretary and assistant in PhotoCoverage commercial studio, 1951–62; assistant, secretary and printer to Canadian advertising photographer Walter Curtin, 1962–4; farm secretary, 1965. Own photographic studio, Joanne Spence Associates, in Hampstead, London, 1967–74. Abandoned commercial work for radical documentary photography, 1973. Co-founder, with photographer Terry Dennett, of Photography Workshop, 1974. Subsequently helped to set up photography collective, the Hackney Flashers, 1975, and started *Camerawork* magazine, 1976. Degree course in film and photographic arts at Polytechnic of Central London (now University of Westminster), attending classes with Victor Burgin, 1979–82 (BA). Breast cancer diagnosed, 1982; with Rosy Martin and others, developed photo therapy, an alternative treatment of the emotional aspects of cancer, 1984–9. Toured Australia, Canada and USA, 1990. Chronic lymphatic leukaemia diagnosed, 1990. Married David Roberts (second marriage), 1992. Died in London, 24 June 1992.

Principal Exhibitions

Shaw Theatre, London: 1976 (*Children Photographed*, touring)
Massachusetts Institute of Technology, Cambridge: 1983 (*Re-modelling Photohistory*, with Terry Dennett, touring)
Cockpit Gallery, London: 1985 (*The Picture of Health?*, organised by Photography Workshop, touring)
Photography Workshop, London: 1985 (*Photo Therapy Road Show*, with Rosy Martin, touring)
Cambridge Darkroom, Cambridge: 1985 (touring retrospective)
National Portrait Gallery, London: 1987 (*Staging the Self: Self-Portrait Photography, 1840–1980s*)
Miriam and Ira Wallach Art Gallery, Columbia University, New York: 1988 (*Sexual Difference: Both Sides of the Camera*, with Terry Dennett)
Metropolitan Museum of Photography, Tokyo: 1990 (*Exploring the Unknown Self*)
Australia and USA: 1990–91 (*Jo Spence: Collaborative Works*, touring)
McLellan Galleries, Glasgow: 1991 (*Narratives of Dis-ease: Ritualised Procedures*, with Tim Sheard; touring, organised by Photography Workshop)
Leeds City Art Gallery: 1991 (*Missing Persons/Damaged Lives*, touring)
Museet for Fotokunst, Odense: 1992 (*Real Stories: The Crisis Project: Scenes of the Crime*, with Terry Dennett, touring)
South Bank Centre, London, and Impressions Gallery, York: 1994–5 (touring retrospective)

Selected Writings

"The politics of photography", *Camerawork*, no.1, 1976; reprinted in *British Journal of Photography*, 26 March 1976
Photography, London: Macdonald, 1977 (with Richard Greenhill and Maggie Murray)
"Photography, ideology and education", *Screen Education*, no.21, 1977 (with Terry Dennett)
"What do people do all day? Class and gender in images of women", *Screen Education*, no.29, Winter 1978–9; reprinted in *In Whose Image? Writings on Media Sexism*, ed. Kath Davies and Julienne Dickey, London: Women's Press, 1986
Editor, *Photography/Politics: One*, London: Photography Workshop, 1979 (with Terry Dennett, David Evars and Sylvia Gohl)
"Remodelling photo-history: A collaboration between two photographers", *Ten 8*, no.9, 1982 (with Terry Dennett)
Editor, *Photography/Politics: Two*, London: Comedia, 1986 (with Patricia Holland and Simon Watney)
Putting Myself in the Picture: A Political, Personal and Photographic Autobiography, London: Camden Press, 1986; Seattle: Real Comet, 1988

"The picture of health", *Spare Rib*, no.163, February 1986; no.165, April 1986
"Re-working the family album", *Media Education*, no.12, 1990
Editor, *Family Snaps: The Meanings of Domestic Photography*, London: Virago, 1991 (with Patricia Holland)
The Creatures Time Forgot: Photography and Disability Imagery, London and New York: Routledge, 1992 (with David Hevey and Jessica Evans)
Cultural Sniping: The Art of Transgression, ed. Jo Stanley, London and New York: Routledge, 1995 (anthology of writings)
What Can a Woman Do with a Camera? London: Scarlet Press, 1995 (with Joan Solomon)

Bibliography

Three Perspectives on Photography, exh. cat., Hayward Gallery, London, 1979
John Roberts, "Jo Spence", *Art Monthly*, no.87, June 1985, pp.6–8
Matter of Facts: Photographie art contemporain en Grande-Bretagne, exh. cat., Musée des Beaux-Arts, Nantes, and elsewhere, 1988
John Roberts, *Postmodernism, Politics and Art*, Manchester: Manchester University Press, 1990
Jan Zita Grover, "Photo therapy: Shame and the minefields of memory", *Afterimage*, xviii, Summer 1990, pp.14–18
—, "The artist and illness", *Artpaper*, xi, January 1992, pp.11–13 (interview)
David Hevey, "Marks of struggle", *Women's Art Magazine*, no.47, July–August 1992, pp.8–11 (interview)
Jane Brettle, Val Williams and Rosy Martin, "Putting us all in the picture: Jo Spence", *Women's Art Magazine*, no.48, September–October 1992, pp.14–15
Hilary Robinson, "Jo Spence, 1934–1992", *Portfolio Magazine*, no.15, Winter 1992, pp.15–16
Rosy Martin, "Putting us all in the picture: The work of Jo Spence", *Camera Austria*, no.43–4, 1993, pp.42–55
—, "Home truths? Phototherapy, memory and identity", *Artpaper*, xii, March 1993, pp.7–9
Jo Spence: Matters of Concern: Collaborative Images, 1982–1992, exh. cat., South Bank Centre, London, Impressions Gallery, York, and elsewhere, 1994

The Jo Spence Memorial Archive is c/o Terry Dennett, 152 Upper Street (Rear Entrance), London N1 1RA; telephone/fax 0171 359-9064.

Jo Spence was a feminist photographer, writer and theorist. She was born in London in 1934 and her childhood was marked by her experience of evacuation during World War II and a transient early existence: she had moved home eleven times and been to six different schools by the time she was ten. In later years much of her photographic work reflected upon the role that these early experiences had had on the formation of her subjectivity and identity as a working-class woman. She left school at the age of 13, and trained to become a secretary. Her first encounter with photography was while she was employed as a shorthand typist and bookkeeper in a small commercial photographers in London. She soon purchased her own camera and began on the career that was to mark her as one of the most important and influential photographers of her time.

Initially she started with small commissions, weddings and portraits, for family and friends, but moved on to develop a professional commercial career, specialising at one stage in the production of portfolios for actors and models. She also cited her year as assistant to the Canadian advertising photographer Walter Curtin and her work for a Fleet Street photographer, where she was taught picture editing skills, as influential on her

Spence: *Eight and a Half Months; Five Hundred and Twenty-Eight Months Later,* from *The Family Album,* 1939–1979; Jo Spence/Terry Dennett, 1979

developing career and later work. These formative years in commercial photography were to have a profound effect and influence on her later experimental and artistic photographic work. Her later work returns to these earlier commercial experiences to interrogate the conventions and hidden meanings involved within traditional commercial images.

Spence's transition away from commercial photography began in the early 1970s when she became involved in the vibrant socialist and feminist movements of the period, and her photographic style changed dramatically. She destroyed most of her earlier commercial work, explaining later that she was ashamed "ideologically speaking" of what she had been doing. Her work now took on the campaigning and tendentious style of the documentary photograph. She became involved in a number of campaigns ranging from a photographic exhibition on children's rights to documenting a Gypsy literacy project. As her experience of documentary photography developed, however, she found herself increasingly questioning the power relationship involved in the taking of such photographs and the ways in which those depicted were shown. It was during this time that she met her fellow photographer and lifelong friend Terry Dennett. In the mid-1970s Jo Spence's work began to take up clearly identifiable feminist politics and concerns. She began to show her photographs in the feminist publication *Spare Rib* and to work on her contribution for a feminist photographic exhibition that documented the invisible and hidden work of working-class women, titled *Women and Work*.

In 1974, with Terry Dennett, she helped to found the photographic project Photography Workshop. This became an important educational, research, publishing and resource centre for many photographers, photographic groups and projects. Spence became a member of one such group initiated by the Photography Workshop, the Hackney Flashers Collective. The Hackney Flashers was a socialist, feminist group that employed photography to campaign on issues of importance for working-class women. During this time Spence also became interested in radical anti-realist photographic artists, such as John Hartfield, and radical anti-realist strategies from the theatre as proposed by the theorist Bertolt Brecht. These theories help clarify her increasing disillusionment with the traditional documentary form. Her transition away from the use of photography as a reflection of reality to a more questioning style of photomontage can be traced between her work for the exhibition *Women and Work* and the later Hackney Flashers show *Who's Holding the Baby?* (1979).

In 1975 Photography Workshop temporarily merged with a gallery, the Half Moon, to form the Half Moon Photography Workshop, which began to publish the radical photographic magazine *Camerawork*. After disagreements, however, Dennett and Spence parted company with this new group and moved into self-publishing, producing the two influential photographic publications *Photography/Politics: One* (1979) and *Photography/Politics: Two* (1986). This involvement in publishing helped to convince Spence of the importance of contributing critical writing alongside her photographic work, and she went on to write several books and publish numerous articles. In 1979 she enrolled for a full-time degree course at the Polytechnic of Central London, where she encountered the ideas and support of the respected photographic theorist Victor

Burgin. In this year she produced one of her most impressive photographic installations: *The Family Album* (see illustration). This installation took as its starting point her own family album; by combining images and text she called into question the role that family photographs had played in forming her own subjectivity and identity. This early critical work on the family album was to have a significant influence on the work of many of her contemporaries. Moreover, this initial investigation of the dual identities of both gender and class was to become a central concern in her later work.

In 1982 Spence's life changed drastically when she was diagnosed with breast cancer. This news and her subsequent experiences of the medical treatment for cancer became a strong theme in her photographic work. During this period she also began to train as an art therapist; once again Spence combined this training with her past interest in the theories surrounding radical theatre to initiate a new photographic practice: photo therapy. Alongside the feminist photographer Rosy Martin she devised a way of using photography as a form of personal therapy – as she described it: "literally using photography to heal ourselves". In a collectively produced touring exhibition, *The Picture of Health* (1985), Spence combined documentary-style photographs, experimental photo-therapy images and image-text pieces to produce a powerful critique of the power relationships involved within traditional medical institutions and their treatment of breast cancer. Through her "invention" of photo therapy, Spence's work returned, once again, to the hidden and repressed elements of her family album. Photo therapy was employed as an empowering tool – where past repressed feelings, experiences and memories could be made visible by re-staging them in front of the camera.

Spence was still working with Terry Dennett on an exhibition of photographic work titled the *Final Project: A Photofantasy and Phototherapeutic Exploration of Life and Death* when she died of leukaemia. In this exhibition she aimed to challenge one of the most hidden and taboo subjects in Western culture: death itself. Finally becoming too weak to use her camera, she returned to older images and earlier work and reused them to develop yet another photographic technique, which she named photo fantasy.

Jo Spence was an influential and inspirational feminist photographer. Throughout her life she made a formidable contribution to the development of feminist photographic theory and practice. Her work was never safe, static or conventional but was always pushing the boundaries and potential of the photographic medium to its very limits. She died in the Marie Curie Hospice in London shortly after her 58th birthday.

SARAH EDGE

Spencer, Lilly Martin
American painter, 1822–1902

Born Angélique Marie Martin in Exeter, England, 26 November 1822, to French parents; nicknamed Lilly. Emigrated to USA with her family, 1830; grew up in Marietta, Ohio. Moved to Cincinnati with her father to pursue a professional career in art, 1841; studied briefly under the portrait painter John Insco Williams, 1842. Married Benjamin Rush Spencer, 1844; first of 13 children born 1845; husband died 1890. Moved to New York, 1848; attended evening drawing classes at National Academy of Design. Sold first paintings to the Western Art Union, Cincinnati, 1847, to the American Art-Union, New York, 1848, to the Cosmopolitan Art Association, New York, 1855. Moved to Newark, New Jersey, 1858; took a studio on Broadway, New York, 1867; moved to Highland, New York, 1879; returned to New York, 1900. Honorary member, National Academy of Design, 1850. Died in New York, 22 May 1902.

Principal Exhibitions

Rectory of St Luke's Episcopal Church, Marietta, OH: 1841 (individual)
Western Art Union, Cincinnati: 1847
American Art-Union, New York: 1848
National Academy of Design, New York: from 1848
Cosmopolitan Art Association, New York: 1855
Great Central Fair, Philadelphia: 1864
Women's Pavilion, Centennial Exposition, Philadelphia: 1876

Bibliography

Henrietta A. Hadery, "Mrs Lilly M. Spencer", *Sartain's Union Magazine*, ix, August 1851, pp.152–4
Elsie F. Freivogel, "Lilly Martin Spencer: Feminist without politics", *Archives of American Art Journal*, xii/4, 1972, pp.9–14
Lilly Martin Spencer, 1822–1902: The Joys of Sentiment, exh. cat., National Collection of Fine Arts, Smithsonian Institution, Washington, DC, 1973 (contains extensive bibliography)
Robin Bolton-Smith and Douglas Hyland, "*Baby Chicks*: The sentimental brush of Lilly Martin Spencer", *Register of the Spencer Museum of Art, University of Kansas*, v, Spring 1982, pp.80–93
Helen S. Langa, "Lilly Martin Spencer: Genre, aesthetics and gender in the work of a mid-nineteenth century American woman artist", *Athanor*, ix, 1990, pp.37–45
Elizabeth Johns, *American Genre Painting: The Politics of Everyday Life*, New Haven and London: Yale University Press, 1991
David M. Lubin, *Picturing a Nation: Art and Social Change in Nineteenth-Century America*, New Haven and London: Yale University Press, 1994

Manuscript collection is in the Archives of American Art, Washington, DC.

Lilly Martin Spencer is distinguished as one of the few American women artists of the 1840s and 1850s who had a successful career as a popular artist and who also had a large family. She was initially encouraged to achieve in her art and compete with mainstream male artists largely because of her enlightened parents, Angélique and Giles Martin, French socialists who came to America with hopes of organising a communal society following the ideas of Charles Fourier. Her father brought her as a teenager from the small community in Marietta, Ohio, where they lived, to the bustling city of Cincinnati, and there secured professional instruction for her while he supported them both with his tutoring. Furthermore, her husband, Benjamin Rush Spencer, also fostered her art ambitions, even devoting his own time and energies to assume the responsibilities of household manager and carer of their 13 children, of whom seven reached adulthood.

From the beginning of her career, Spencer painted spirited genre scenes inspired by her own domestic experiences. These proved popular with the Western Art Union, based in Cincinnati, which showed eight of her paintings at its first exhibition in 1847. Seeking career opportunities for Lilly, the family moved to New York in 1848, by then the art centre of the USA. In New York she perfected her craft and regularly exhibited at the National Academy of Design, the American Art-Union and the Cosmopolitan Art Association. William Schaus published many of her paintings as popular lithographs that found an audience in Europe as well as America. During the following ten years her reputation grew, although finances were often tight for the expanding family. Her ambitions and hardships are chronicled in a series of moving letters to her mother, now on file in the Archives of American Art (Washington, DC). Finally, in 1858, the Spencers moved across the Hudson River to Newark, New Jersey, where they rented a home from her patron Marcus L. Ward, but her career never prospered there as it had in New York.

Spencer painted her best work in the late 1840s and 1850s. She focused on women and children in domestic situations, but also painted "fancy pictures" of young girls and boys looking sweet and coquettish. The usual sentimental message is the devotion of mothers to their children. In *Domestic Happiness* (subtitle *"Hush: Don't Wake Them"*, alternative title *Domestic Felicity*, 1849; see illustration) she celebrates familial love by representing a father and mother gazing down lovingly at their baby and toddler asleep on a bed, arms intertwined. The hand of the mother reaches up to her husband to quiet his own gestures towards the two children; hence, the mother's dominance within the painting symbolically parallels Spencer's control as a painter constructing her own idealised images of women as the agents of domestic bliss. In *"This Little Pig Went to Market"* (1857; oil on composition board; Campus Martius Museum, Marietta, OH) a doll-like mother tweaks the toes of her laughing baby in the privacy of the nursery. A review in the December 1859 issue of the *Cosmopolitan Art Journal* offered typical praise: "We have here Mrs Spencer in her best mood … The expression is very happy; the story is read at a glance. The detail is worked in with wondrous ease and beauty. Mrs Spencer elaborates, but never crowds her canvas. In this fine work all her best characteristics appear" (quoted in Washington 1973, p.169). When painting such pictures Spencer would have used herself and her own children as models. Her portrait skills are also evident in paintings she did of the children of Marcus Ward.

However, in kitchen scenes, such as *"Shake Hands?"* (1854; oil on canvas; Ohio Historical Center, Columbus), Spencer showed the humorous side of her art. Here a female servant, looking up from kneading dough, teasingly offers a flour-covered hand to the viewer. In *Young Husband: First Marketing* (1854; oil on canvas; private collection, repr. Washington 1973) Spencer pokes fun at the novice husband, hurrying along a rainy city street and unable to manage both the umbrella and the groceries and poultry spilling out of his market basket on to a wet pavement. The situations of her genre subjects tend to be unique in the history of 19th-century art, primarily because they so clearly suggest a woman's point of view about domestic life and even, at times, suggest a sinister or subversive sub-text. Although her lack of mastery of

Spencer: *Domestic Happiness: "Hush Don't Wake Them"*, 1849; oil on canvas; 141 × 114.9 cm.; Detroit Institute of Arts; Bequest of Dr and Mrs James Cleland, Jr

human anatomy is evident, she generally paints with a rich palette of jewel-like tones – ruby, emerald and sapphire colours – and with deft strokes detailing the fabrics of clothing and emphasising the succulence of fruits and vegetables. The retrospective exhibition of Spencer's work at the National Museum of American Art in 1973, with its catalogue that reproduced all her known paintings and drawings, revived interest in her work and made clear the parallels to the sentimental women's literature of the mid-19th century.

PATRICIA HILLS

Spero, Nancy
American artist, 1926–

Born in Cleveland, Ohio, 24 August 1926. Studied at University of Colorado, Boulder, 1944–5; School of the Art Institute of Chicago, 1945–9 (BFA); Ecole des Beaux-Arts and Atelier André Lhôte, Paris, 1949–50. Apprenticeship in scene design, Ivoryton Summer Theatre, Connecticut, 1950. Married artist Leon Golub, 1951; three sons, born 1953, 1954 and 1961. Lived in New York, 1950–51; Chicago, 1951–6; Ischia and Florence, Italy, 1956–7; Bloomington, Indiana, 1957–9; Paris, 1959–64; New York, from 1964. Joined Art Workers Coalition (AWC), 1968–9; Women Artists in Revolution (WAR), 1969; Ad Hoc Committee of Women Artists, 1970. Founder-member of AIR Gallery, New York, 1972. Recipient of Creative Artists Public Service (CAPS) grant, New York State Council of the Arts, 1976; National Endowment for the Arts (NEA) grant, 1977; NARAL/NY Pro-Choice Media award, 1995; Skowhegan medal for works on paper, 1995; Hiroshima art prize, Japan, 1996; honorary doctorate, School of the Art Institute of Chicago, 1991. Lives in New York.

Selected Individual Exhibitions
Galerie Breteau, Paris: 1962, 1965, 1968
Rhona Hoffman Gallery, Chicago: 1983, 1988
Riverside Studios, London: 1984
Burnett Miller Gallery, Los Angeles: 1985
Galerie Barbara Gross, Munich: 1986, 1991, 1995
Josh Baer Gallery, New York: 1986, 1987, 1988, 1989, 1993
Institute of Contemporary Arts, London: 1987 (touring retrospective)
Museum of Contemporary Art, Los Angeles: 1989
Schirn Kunsthalle, Frankfurt am Main: 1989
Haus am Waldsee, Berlin: 1990 (touring)
Galerie Montenay, Paris: 1990
Glyptothek am Königplatz, Munich: 1991
Galleria Stefania Miscetti, Rome: 1991
Ulmer Museum, Ulm: 1992 (retrospective)
National Gallery of Canada, Ottawa: 1993
Konsthall, Malmö: 1994
List Visual Arts Center, Massachusetts Institute of Technology, Cambridge: 1994 (with Leon Golub)
American Center, Paris: 1995 (with Leon Golub)
Vancouver Art Gallery: 1996
Hiroshima City Museum of Contemporary Art: 1996 (with Leon Golub)

Selected Writings
"Ende", *Women's Studies*, vi, 1978, pp.3–11

"The discovered uncovered", *M/E/A/N/I/N/G*, no.2, November 1987, p.32
"Sky Goddess: Egyptian acrobat", *Artforum*, xxvii, March 1988, pp.103–5
"Tracing Ana Mendieta", *Artforum*, xxx, April 1992, pp.75–7

Bibliography
Corinne Robbins, "Nancy Spero: 'Political' artist and the nightmare", *Feminist Art Journal*, Spring 1975, pp.19–22, 48
——, "Words and images through time: The art of Nancy Spero", *Arts Magazine*, liv, December 1979, pp.103–5
Donald B. Kuspit, "From existence to essence: Nancy Spero", *Art in America*, lxxii, January 1984, pp.88–96
Nancy Spero, exh. cat., Institute of Contemporary Arts, London, and elsewhere, 1987
Nancy Spero: Works since 1950, exh. cat., Everson Museum of Art, Syracuse, NY, and elsewhere, 1987
Tamar Garb, "Nancy Spero interviewed", *Artscribe International*, Summer 1987, pp.58–62
Jeanne Siegel, "Nancy Spero: Woman as protagonist (interview)", *Arts Magazine*, lxii, September 1987, pp.10–13
Jean Fulten, "A feminist resolution: The art of Nancy Spero", *New Art Examiner*, xvi/1, 1989, pp.32–5
Elizabeth Ann Dobie, "Interweaving feminist frameworks", *Journal of Aesthetics and Art Criticism*, xlviii, 1990, pp.381–94
Nancy Spero: Bilder, 1958–1990, exh. cat., Haus am Waldsee, Berlin, and elsewhere, 1990
Pamela Wye, "Freedom of movement: Nancy Spero's site paintings", *Arts Magazine*, lxv, October 1990, pp.54–8
Josephine Withers, "Nancy Spero's American-born Sheela-na-gig", *Feminist Studies*, xvii/1, 1991, pp.51–6
Jon Bird, Jo Anna Isaak and Sylvère Lotringer, *Nancy Spero*, London: Phaidon, 1996

In 1972, after two years, Nancy Spero completed the *Codex Artaud*, a work that in both form and content became the basis for her subsequent practice. *Codex Artaud* comprises 33 panels of collaged images and texts on hand-made English Bodleian paper, French vellum and Japanese rice paper, each section varying in length from 1.2 to 7.6 metres, the width (approximately 0.6 m.) being determined by the dimensions of each individual piece of paper. Spero has adhered predominantly to the horizontal format of the scroll ever since, although since the mid-1980s she has produced occasional vertical works or "Totems". The only significant deviation from this structure occurred in her development of a technique for direct printing on to interior and exterior wall surfaces in her installations from 1987 onwards. In the early 1980s the wood-backed zinc plates used for printing on to paper were supplemented by pliable polymer plates allowing the image to be reproduced also on uneven surfaces, as with *Re-Birth of Venus* (1989; see illustration) on the curved interior walls and columns of the Schirn Kunsthalle, Frankfurt am Main, and *Minerva, Sky Goddess* (1991) on the roof and parapet walls of the Circulo de Bellas Artes, Madrid.

Spero trained at the Art Institute of Chicago, where she met her husband, the painter Leon Golub, and through the 1950s she produced a series of figurative paintings on the themes of lovers, prostitutes, maternity and family groups. In these powerfully expressive works, named the *Black Paris Paintings* after the five-year period the family spent in Europe, she introduced disturbing references to grotesque, nightmarish and fantastic forms in a tonal range that darkened to the point where the image barely emerged from the ground. Returning to

Spero: *Re-Birth of Venus* (detail), 1989

New York in 1964, Spero continued painting but finally abandoned the medium two years later. The *War Series* followed: small-scale works on paper that employed a ferocious imaging of the Vietnam War as phallic power – helicopters and bombs ejaculating and defecating on to helpless victims with scrawled texts drawn from the official and media statements that disavowed the reality of American aggression.

The works of this period also carried the signs of Spero's increasing sense of alienation from the institutional structures of the art world – an experience of marginality and exclusion historically enacted on the grounds of gender and race. Blocked and silenced at almost every point as a woman artist whose work was primarily figurative and political, Spero turned to the tortured prose of the French poet Antonin Artaud as an analogous reference point for her own angry isolation. Artaud's desire to escape the body, made acute by the physical and emotional effects of his incarceration in the asylum at Rodez, erupts in the fractured materiality of a language pervaded by metaphors of separation and loss. Through Artaud Spero found a voice that, as her anger became politicised and historicised in the context of the Women's Movement, became a feminist voice committed to re-visioning the representation of the female body, not as the Other of the male, but as a sexual, maternal and active imaginary body dancing between the lines of histories and cultures.

With *Torture of Women* (1976; length 3.8 m.; National Gallery of Canada, Ottawa) Spero decided to concentrate solely upon representations of the female while extending the theme of language, and thus subjectivity, under duress – at the moments when the body is experienced in its extreme states as abjection or "jouissance". *Torture of Women* documents accounts of torture taken from Amnesty International. Each obscene case history is accompanied by a bestiary of fantastic and mythological creatures and figures; the pathology of oppression is given its archaic expression in the Babylonian

creation myth of the battle between Marduk, the sun-god, and Tiamat, the original mother-goddess. This epic functions in *Torture of Women* not only as the symbolic representation of violence against all women, but also signifies the scope of the scrolls interspersing and repeating images from different histories, traditions and cultures, in extended and accumulative visual narratives, to displace any notion of a fixed feminine Other.

Two further major works followed: the monumental *Notes in Time on Women* (1979; 0.5 × 68.6 m.) and *The First Language* (1981; 0.5 × 57.9 m.). *Notes in Time on Women* juxtaposes images of women from prehistory to the present with the "official" texts of patriarchal culture extracted from literature, philosophy, journalism and the media. Cavorting female figures run and dance over and between the lines of print, a carnivalesque subversion by the painted and hand-printed active female bodies of the way woman is spoken of in male discourse. *Notes in Time on Women* is both document and archive; a narrativisation of the social and historical concept of woman placed "in parenthesis" by a mocking and empowered feminine presence. Formal allusions range from Egyptian wall paintings and papyrus, the Bayeux Tapestry (first seen by Spero when it was exhibited in Chicago in the 1950s), to the rebellious scrawls of urban graffiti. Reversing the usual text/image relationship where it is the literary that anchors the visual, these images up-end and fragment the discourse of power of masculine authorities. In *The First Language* Spero introduced a contemporary woman combing her hair, a Roman stone monument of a matron, a Japanese doll alongside recycled images introduced in *Torture of Women*: a roller-skating Artemis (who "heals women's pain"), the Venus of Willendorf juxtaposed with repeated hand-stamped adaptations of the Egyptian sky-goddess and protectress, Nut. It is the female body's expressive potential that articulates a semiotics of gesture and activity, a choreographic unfolding of women's experience from victimisation to celebration privileging the maternal as a place of origin.

Paralleling her interest in the work of French feminist critical theory, particularly Julia Kristeva's notion of a semiotic "chora" as the reinscription of the maternal in the body of the text and Hélène Cixous's argument for an "écriture féminine", Spero suggested that her work could be seen as the possibility of a "peinture féminine". Through the 1980s the carnivalesque aspect, of a joyful assertion of women's sexuality and pleasure, floods the scrolls with ecstatic figures celebrating rhythmical movement in upbeat colour and tonal relations. In *Sky Goddess* (1985; 0.5 × 13.7 m.) the repeated image of the Goddess (an amalgamation of the Roman wolf nurturing the infants Romulus and Remus with the Egyptian Nut) arches over, and is interspersed with, the repeated profile of Athena, alongside schematic and abstracted dancing figures derived from Aboriginal and prehistoric sources, the whole movement concluded and then returned with the image of a Vietnamese woman, an upright, sprightly walking figure – a survivor.

Towards the end of the 1980s Spero's delineation of internal space – the gaps or "silences" between the active forms, and the external dimension – the lateral (or vertical in the case of the *Totems*) spread of the scroll across the wall, took a different turn in the installations that freed the figure–ground relation from the constraints of a framing-edge. In such works

as *Waterworks* (1988), *To Soar III* (1991; Harold Washington Library, Chicago), *Minerva, Sky Goddess* (1991; Circulo de Bellas Artes, Madrid), *Ballade von der "Judenhure" Marie Sanders* (1991; Wuppertal), *Première* (1993; Ronacher Theatre, Vienne) and *To the Revolution* (1994; American Center, Paris) Spero's unbounded female figures, intermingling the mythological and the fantastic with the social and historically specific, feminise the architectural space itself. In *Vulture Goddess*, an installation at the Institute of Contemporary Art, Philadelphia (1991), the Celtic goddess of fertility and destruction – Sheela-na-Gig – defiantly displays her vagina/womb in an extended "chorus line" from the overhead beams, whereas in *To Soar I* (1988; Museum of Contemporary Art, Los Angeles) a line of dildo dancers gleefully run along the base of a wall and vanish round a corner – figures defiantly "out-of-place", defying the gaze and appearing where least expected. *Black and the Red III* (1994; Konsthall, Malmö), a scroll 60.9 metres long comprising 22 panels of dense overprinting, mixes familiar cross-cultural and historical figures from Spero's lexicon (which now approximates more than 300 individual female images) with references to heraldry, the abstract patterning of Greek vase painting and the grids of Minimal art. Interspersing vibrant areas of colour saturation within an overall scheme of red, black, gold and white vertical and horizontal squares and divisions, the textual density and surface presence here replace the open spacing and muted palette of earlier works. Interweaving the archaic with the contemporary, the mythological with the social, absence and void with density and presence, Spero's practice represents a choreographing of the liberated female body in new spatial configurations and relations in which women can act as subjects.

JON BIRD

St Leger Eberle, Mary Abastenia *see* Eberle

Starr, Louisa

British painter, 1845–1909

Born in Philadelphia, Pennsylvania, 26 November 1845, the only child of a well-to-do Anglo-Italian family. Emigrated with parents to Britain, 1858. Studied at Heatherley's School of Art, London, and subsequently at the Royal Academy Schools, 1862–7 (gold medal for copying 1865, gold medal for history painting 1867). Independent study in northern Italy, 1868; became engaged to a cousin, Enrico Canziani. Married Canziani, 1882; daughter Estella, also an artist, born 1887. Exhibited under married name from 1885. Became involved in campaigns for dress reform and against cruelty to animals and birds, late 1880s. President, Art Section, International Congress of Women, London, 1889; gave address on "The spirit of purity in art". Also gave address on "Women's work in art" at World's Columbian Exposition, Chicago, 1893. Member, Society of Women Artists, 1894. Died in London, 25 May 1909.

Principal Exhibitions

Royal Academy, London: 1863, 1866–96, 1898–1902, 1905–9
Society of Female Artists, London: 1869–73
Grosvenor Gallery, London: 1879–82, 1884
New Gallery, London: 1888–90, 1905
Woman's Building, World's Columbian Exposition, Chicago: 1893
Louisiana Purchase Exposition, St Louis: 1904

Bibliography

Estella Canziani, *Round About Three Palace Green*, London: Methuen, 1939
Pamela Gerrish Nunn, *Canvassing: Recollections by Six Victorian Women Artists*, London: Camden, 1986
Jane Sellars, *Women's Works: Paintings, Drawings, Prints and Sculpture by Women*, Liverpool: National Museums and Galleries on Merseyside, 1988

Louisa Starr holds a historic position as the first woman to gain medals for excellence from the Royal Academy Schools. She bears comparison with her contemporary, the Impressionist painter Mary Cassatt (q.v.), as a woman who brought an American independence of spirit to a European artistic career.

Although she emerged into the public eye in 1867 as a potential history painter with her prize-winning *David Brought Before Saul* (untraced), in her early professional years Starr exhibited a wide variety of figure paintings including fancy pictures such as the *Pet of the Brigands* (1867; untraced), literary subjects corresponding with contemporary taste such as *La Penserosa* (1867; untraced), *Mariana* (1868; untraced) and *Undine* (1870; ex-Queensland Art Gallery, Brisbane) and portraits. She gradually made portraiture her speciality. Although female artists always found it easier to attract commissions for the portrayal of children and women, Starr showed herself just as capable of male portraiture (*Brian Hodgson*, 1872; National Portrait Gallery, London), and the realism of her likenesses was often commented on. Her sitters included many members of the liberal aristocracy (*Margaret Rose, Countess of Euston*, 1880; Euston Hall) and contemporary artistic circles, as well as friends (such as the sitters in *Buttercups*, 1893; Cheltenham Art Gallery). She was capable of setting sitters in their own domestic interiors or outdoors, though in the latter case she painted the background in plein air while adding the figure in the studio (*Kathleen and Marianne Sheppard*, 1888; see illustration). She was equally adept at small-scale and life-size portraiture. Her works were shown regularly until her death in London at the Royal Academy, the New Gallery, the Society of Female Artists and in provincial cities. In 1872 *Sintram*, a scene of filial piety from a tale by Friedrich de la Motte Fouqué, one of the artist's favourite literary sources, was purchased by the Liverpool Corporation.

Starr's personal sympathies were engaged by middle-class reform movements such as the campaigns for female suffrage and dress reform and the Society for the Protection of Birds, and it can be suspected that, had she been less dependent on painting for a living, social problems might have dominated her subject matter. Her early *Hardly Earned* (1875; untraced, repr. *Illustrated London News*, 1875) and late *Cold Spring (The Alien)* (1906; Aberdeen Art Gallery) indicate the liberalism and feminism that, in the event, surfaced more clearly in

Starr: *Kathleen and Mary Anne Sheppard*, 1888; Russell-Cotes Art Gallery and Museum, Bournemouth

her personal than her professional life. She directed her daughter to follow in her own footsteps, and Estella Canziani became a popular illustrator and watercolourist of the early 20th century, as well as her mother's biographer.

PAMELA GERRISH NUNN

Stebbins, Emma

American sculptor, 1815–1882

Born in New York, 1 September 1815; father a wealthy banker. Taught by painter Henry Inman and sculptor Edward Brackett; exhibited as an amateur artist; elected Associate member, National Academy of Design, New York, 1842. First trip to Rome, meeting actress Charlotte Cushman and sculptor Harriet Hosmer (q.v.), winter 1856–7; settled in Rome, embarking on professional career as a sculptor, 1857; studied under American sculptor Paul Akers. Returned permanently to USA and abandoned sculpture, 1870; lived with Cushman in Newport, Rhode Island, until the latter's death in 1876. Died in New York, 25 October 1882.

Principal Exhibitions

National Academy of Design, New York: 1843–4
Artists' Fund Society, Philadelphia: 1845, 1847
Pennsylvania Academy of the Fine Arts, Philadelphia: 1847
Goupil Gallery, New York: 1861 (individual)

Selected Writings

Editor, *Charlotte Cushman: Her Letters and Memories of Her Life*, Boston: Houghton Osgood, 1878; reprinted New York: Blom, 1972

Bibliography

Elizabeth Fries Ellet, *Women Artists in All Ages and Countries*, New York: Harper, 1859

Henry T. Tuckerman, *Book of the Artists: American Artist Life*, New York: Putnam, 1867; reprinted New York: Carr, 1966

Clara Erskine Clement and Laurence Hutton, *Artists of the Nineteenth Century and Their Work*, 2 vols, Boston: Houghton Osgood, and London: Trübner, 1879; reprinted New York: Arno Press, 1969

Mary Stebbins Garland, "Notes on the art life of Emma Stebbins", manuscript, 1888, New York Public Library

Clara Erskine Clement, *Women in the Fine Arts*, Boston: Houghton Mifflin, 1904; reprinted New York: Hacker, 1974

The White Marmorean Flock: Nineteenth-Century American Women Neoclassical Sculptors, exh. cat., Vassar College Art Gallery, Poughkeepsie, NY, 1972

John Stephens Crawford, "The Classical orator in nineteenth century American sculpture", *American Art Journal*, vi, November 1974, pp.56–72

Wayne Craven, *Sculpture in America*, 2nd edition, Newark: University of Delaware Press, 1984

Sara Foose Parrott, "Networking in Italy: Charlotte Cushman and 'The White Marmorean Flock'", *Women's Studies*, xiv, 1988, pp.305–38

Charlotte Streifer Rubinstein, *American Women Sculptors*, Boston: Hall, 1990

Nancy G. Heller, *Women Artists: An Illustrated History*, 2nd edition, New York: Abbeville, 1991

Dolly Sherwood, *Harriet Hosmer: American Sculptor, 1830–1908*, Columbia: University of Missouri Press, 1991

Elizabeth Milroy, "The public career of Emma Stebbins: Work in marble", *Archives of American Art Journal*, xxxiii/3, 1993, pp.2–12

The Emma Stebbins scrapbook is in the Archives of American Art, Smithsonian Institution, Washington, DC.

Although Emma Stebbins had already spent nearly 20 years in the study of drawing, painting and pastels, and had been elected an associate member of the National Academy of Design (1842), where she had exhibited her paintings – largely copies of old master paintings and portraits – she was still considered an amateur artist when in 1856 she went to Rome. It took only six months in Rome to change both Stebbins's direction and investment in her art. A friendship with the established sculptor Harriet Hosmer (q.v.) and with the actress Charlotte Cushman encouraged Stebbins to settle permanently in Rome to pursue sculpture professionally. Like most of the early American women sculptors in the city, Stebbins enjoyed the full support of her family, both financially and morally, in her undertaking.

Hosmer introduced Stebbins to the sculptors John Gibson and Paul Akers; the latter was to become Stebbins's teacher in Rome, the former was Hosmer's. Gibson played an important role for Stebbins by commissioning her first full-scale sculpture in marble, the *Lotus Eater* (1857–60; untraced, repr. Milroy 1993, p.2) after Tennyson's treatment of the Homeric theme. An adaptation of the Capitoline *Faun* (or Satyr) of Praxiteles, which simultaneously inspired the novel *The Marble Faun* by Stebbins's friend, Nathaniel Hawthorne, the *Lotus Eater* is early evidence of Stebbins's close study of Classical models. The expression and downward gaze indicate that the figure is lost in thought, dreaming of his "... island home/... far beyond the wave". The modern figure assumes a more stable pose than its ancient model, with the languor of a dreamer rather than the energy of a faun. Stebbins has successfully negotiated the awkward fig leaf, ubiquitous in Vatican collections, by employing the figure's right hand to hold a lotus branch across the genital region. Like most of Stebbins's works, the *Lotus Eater* was conceived as a "table-top" marble piece, only 71 centimetres high.

The Capitoline *Faun* remained an important model for Stebbins, later informing her figure, *Commerce: The Sailor* of 1859, commissioned by the coal tycoon, Charles Heckscher, with a companion figure, *Industry: The Miner* (both Heckscher Museum, Huntington, NY). In *Commerce* Stebbins rejected Classical nudity in favour of modern dress. *Industry: The Miner* also follows a freely adapted ancient model, the *Doryphorus* of Polykleitos from Pompeii, which Stebbins could have seen during her visit to Naples in 1857 (*ibid.*, note 22). The *Industry* and *Commerce* figures were highly praised at their first New York exhibition by the Goupil firm in January 1861. The felicitous combination of ancient structures with contemporary detailing and subject matter appealed to a nationalistic and modernist taste, and indicates an early movement away from strict Neo-classicism in American sculpture. A reviewer for the *New York Times*, after complimenting Stebbins's "laborious, earnest accuracy", notwithstanding her gender, praised the *Industry* and *Commerce* figures in particular:

> The whole spirit of American labor, honest, fearless, young, high-spirited yet manly, dignified, respectful and self-respecting, speaks in these stately and graceful figures. Modern in face as in costume though they be, the antique art itself revives in the typical beauty which breathes from them. For they have grown up, not out of a sentiment only, but out of a serious and sustained study of anatomy, which indicates itself in the masterly poise and harmonized vigor of the figures [quoted in Milroy 1993, pp.6–7].

There is, however, no record of Stebbins's ever having studied anatomy on a medical level as did her peers Anne Whitney (q.v.) and Harriet Hosmer. The "serious study" that this reviewer commends in Stebbins's case was primarily of ancient and contemporary models.

In 1863 Charlotte Cushman, and perhaps Stebbins as well, was present at the excavation of the *Augustus of Prima Porta*, described by Stebbins in Cushman's biography as the "last and finest portrait statue of the Vatican" (*Charlotte Cushman* 1878, p.138). The following year Stebbins completed her first and only portrait statue in bronze, *Horace Mann* (see illustration), now in front of the State Capitol of Boston. While the *Mann* figure is not directly inspired by the *Augustus*, her comment does indicate awareness of the importance of the orator in ancient art. In his discussion of 19th-century study of this figure, Crawford (1974) noted that both ancient literary sources, such as Quintilian's *Institutio Oratoria*, and Classical statuary informed the self-styling of 19th-century orators. The educator *Horace Mann* seems to have been inspired by a statue of an unknown orator of the 1st century AD in the Museo Nazionale, Naples. The hand position of the *Horace Mann* repeats that of the Naples orator almost exactly, in turn described in very precise terms in Quintilian's discussion of the correct gestures for the *narratio* or "statement of facts" moment of the oration.

Today Stebbins's most remembered works are her monumental fountain in Central Park, New York, the *Angel of the*

Stebbins: *Horace Mann*, 1864; bronze statue; State Capitol, Boston, Massachusetts

Waters or *Bethesda Fountain*, unveiled in 1873, and a life-sized marble statue of *Christopher Columbus* (1863–6; in front of Brooklyn Civic Center, NY), yet these were entirely atypical of the artist's production. Most of her works were marble "table-top" pieces, under 100 centimetres in height (others included: *Samuel*, 1868; Chrysler Museum, Norfolk, VA; *Sandalphon*, 1862; copy of 1866 in E.P. Richardson Collection; *Joseph* as a young boy, 1862; commissioned by Samuel Courtauld; and *Satan*, 1862; untraced). Milroy reported that Stebbins's extreme perfectionism and fear of being accused of not having produced her own work deterred her from employing artisans to assist her in the carving of her works (Milroy 1993, p.10). Much to the dismay of her companion Charlotte Cushman, Stebbins would exhaust herself and damage her health in insisting on carving her pieces herself.

In her bust of *Charlotte Cushman* (1859; Handel and Haydn Society, Boston) Stebbins again seems to be working within a classical tradition of realistic portraiture, perhaps studied in the extensive collection of Roman Republican and Imperial busts in the Vatican museums. Cushman was not considered an example of conventional female beauty in the 19th century, and presented particular challenges to the idealising tendencies of the Neo-classical style. Stebbins's bust combines the clear-eyed realism of the Republican style with an engaging infusion of the actress's personality. (A fascinating comparison can be made between this severely realistic bust, Stebbins's romantically idealised bust of the model *Nanna Risi* as *Roma* (c.1860–70; Museum of Fine Arts, Boston) and Anne Whitney's portrayal of *Roma* as an old beggar woman from a Hellenistic model.) The natural severity of Cushman's features is emphasised by the deep carving of her coiffure and sudden transitions between light and shadow, playfully contrasting with the softness of the modelling of the shallow dip between the brow, the depressions that define the cheeks and the creases at the corners of the mouth. The eyebrows are both strictly uniform in their symmetry and realistically rendered in their texture, belying the puffiness of the soft skin beneath the eyes. A contemporary critic wrote that Stebbins's bust of the famous actress was "full, not of the fame which flickers and burns into life on the stage, but of the enduring qualities which make fame worth having when it is won" ("Recent works of American artists", *op. cit.*, quoted in *ibid.*, p.7).

NANCY PROCTOR

Steger, Milly
German sculptor, 1881–1948

Born in Rheinberg, near Moers, 15 June 1881. Studied at the Kunstgewerbeschule, Elberfeld, then in the private studio of Karl Janssen in Düsseldorf, 1901–c.1905. Visited Florence, Paris and Belgium. Studied under Georg Kolbe in Berlin. Moved to Hagen, 1910; city sculptor of Hagen, 1914. Moved to Berlin and took over Georg Kolbe's studio, 1917. Head of sculpture class at the Zeichen- und Malschule des Vereins der Künstlerinnen zu Berlin from 1929. Several works declared "degenerate" and confiscated by the National Socialists, 1937. Apartment, studio and numerous works destroyed by bombing, 1943. Recipient of fourth prize and honourable mention, Olympic Art Competition, Berlin, 1936; Villa Romana prize, 1938 (with Georg Kolbe). Member, Arbeitsrat für Kunst (Workers Council of Art), Berlin, 1918–19; Berlin Secession, 1931. Member, 1927–43, member of executive committee, 1927–32, honorary president, 1932–43, and honorary member, 1943, Verein der Künstlerinnen zu Berlin; honorary member, 1945, and member of honorary executive committee, 1948, Deutscher Demokratischer Frauenbund (German Democratic League of Women). Died in Berlin, 31 October 1948.

Principal Exhibitions

Individual
Prussian Academy, Berlin: 1922
Verein der Künstlerinnen zu Berlin, Galerie Archivarion, Berlin: 1949 (retrospective)

Group
Berlin Secession: 1909, 1935
Sonderbund, Düsseldorf: 1910
Internationale Ausstellung des Sonderbundes, Cologne: 1912
Museum Folkwang, Hagen: 1913 (*Hagener Künstler*), 1921 (*Die Künstler um Karl Ernst Osthaus*)
Deutscher Werkbund, Cologne: 1914

Kunsthalle, Mannheim: 1914 (*Plastiken neuzeitlicher Bildhauer*)
Freie Secession, Berlin: 1920
Grosse Berliner Kunstausstellung, Berlin: 1921
Galerie Alfred Flechtheim, Berlin: 1922 (*Frauen*)
Verein der Künstlerinnen zu Berlin: 1927–34, 1937, 1940, 1942–3
    (annuals), 1929 (*Die Frau von heute*), 1930 (*Das Kind*)
Prussian Academy, Berlin: 1931
Frühjahrsausstellung, Hannover: 1933
Ausstellung des deutschen Künstlerbundes im Kunstverein Hamburg:
    1936 (*Malerei und Plastik in Deutschland 1936*)
Museumsverein, Hannover: 1936
Verein der Künstlerinnen zu Berlin and Lyzeum-Club, Galerie von der
    Heyde, Berlin: 1939
Gäste des Vereins Berliner Künstler, Berlin: 1941
Hilfswerk für deutsche bildende Kunst in der NS-Volkswohlfahrt,
    Berlin: 1941
Berliner Zeughaus, Berlin: 1946 (*Erste deutsche Kunstausstellung*)

Selected Writings

"Antwort", *Ja! Stimmen des Arbeitsrates für Kunst in Berlin*, Berlin,
    1919, p.65
"Begegnung mit Minne", *Kunst der Zeit*, ii/5–6, 1928–9, pp.108–9

Bibliography

Festschrift zur Einweihung des Hagener Stadttheaters, Hagen, 1911
Hans Hildebrandt, "Milly Steger", *Das Kunstblatt*, ii, 1918,
    pp.372–6
Alfred Kuhn, "Milly Steger", *Deutsche Kunst und Dekoration*, xxvi,
    1922–3, pp.198–200
Karl Scheffler, "Ausstellungsrezensionen", *Kunst und Künstler*,
    no.21, 1923, p.68
Otto Grautoff, "Milly Steger", *Die Kunst für Alle*, xli, 1926,
    pp.321–8
Hans Hildebrandt, *Die Frau als Künstlerin*, Berlin: Rudolf Mosse,
    1928
Paul Ferdinand Schmidt, "Milly Steger", *Der Kunstwanderer*,
    September 1931–August 1932, pp.241–3
Thorwald, "Milly Steger", *Kunst der Nation*, ii/14, July 1934, p.2
Fritz Nemitz, "Milly Steger", *Die Kunst für Alle*, l, October 1934,
    pp.10–15
Gertrud Richert, "Milly Steger in Memoriam", *Berliner
    Künstlerinnen- und Milly-Steger-Gedächtnis-Ausstellung*, Berlin,
    1949, p.5
Anna Christa Funk, "Die Bildhauerin Milly Steger in Hagen",
    Hagener Heimatkalender, Hagen, 1970, pp.121–4
Herta Hesse Frielinghaus and others, *Karl Ernst Osthaus: Leben und
    Werk*, Recklinghausen: Bongers, 1971
Milly Steger, 1881–1948, exh. cat., Karl Ernst Osthaus-Museum,
    Hagen, 1981
Ulrike Evers, *Deutsche Künstlerinnen des 20. Jahrhunderts: Malerei,
    Bildhauerei, Tapisserie*, Hamburg: Schultheis, 1983
German Expressionist Sculpture, exh. cat., Los Angeles County
    Museum of Art and elsewhere, 1983
*Das Verborgene Museum I: Dokumentation der Kunst von Frauen in
    Berliner öffentlichen Sammlungen*, exh. cat., Akademie der
    Künste, Berlin, 1987
Werner Gerber, *Hagener Bohème: Menschen um Osthaus*, Hagen,
    1990
Entartete Beeldhouwkunst: Duitse Beeldhouwers, 1900–1945
    [Degenerate sculpture: German sculptors, 1900–1945], exh. cat.,
    Commanderie van St Jan, Nijmegen, and elsewhere, 1991
Magdalena Bushart, "Der Formsinn des Weibes: Bildhauerinnen in
    den zwanziger und dreissiger Jahren", *Profession ohne Tradition:
    125 Jahre Verein der Berliner Künstlerinnen*, exh. cat., Berlinische
    Galerie, Berlin, 1992, pp.135–50
Birgit Schulte, "Milly Steger: Stadtbildhauerin von Hagen", *Hagener
    Impuls*, no.8, September 1994, pp.27–36
Erich Ranfft, "German women sculptors, 1918–1936: Gender differ-
    ences and status", *Visions of the "Neue Frau": Women and the
    Visual Arts in Weimar Germany*, ed. Marsha Meskimmon and
    Shearer West, Aldershot: Scolar Press, 1995, pp.42–61

Manuscript collections are in the Archiv des Vereins der Berliner
Künstlerinnen, Berlin, and the Karl Ernst Osthaus-Archiv, Hagen.

Milly Steger was one of the first woman artists to obtain public commissions for architectural sculptures. In the early 1920s she was invariably included in texts on contemporary sculpture, and some critics considered her the most important female sculptor in Germany (Scheffler 1923, Thorwald 1934). In 1932, with Ernst Barlach and Wilhelm Lehmbruck, she was cited in *Knaurs Konversationslexikon* as an exemplary sculptor of the 20th century.

From the beginning of her career, Steger was concerned with pure form, infused with her interest in architectonic structuring. She treated specified subjects only exceptionally, as in the religious works from the 1930s onwards. Her female figures and groups of figures have terse, generic titles: *Woman*, *Girl*, *Torso*, *Group*. The poses are standing, striding, kneeling and feature every kind of movement. In addition to working in wood and bronze, she carved even the hardest stone herself in order to retain the evidence of her own hand.

Very little of her work before 1910 survives. Apart from Georg Kolbe, the crucial influences on her early work were Maillol and Bernhard Hoetger, with their full understanding of the figure. Her career was established with the move to Hagen, at the invitation of Karl Ernst Osthaus, founder of the Folkwang Museum. She created her first large architectural sculpture for this Westphalian industrial town: four over-life-size, column-like, nude female figures in sandstone for the façade of the theatre (1911; Stadttheater Hagen). Without attributes or symbolic-allegorical meaning, the nudes created a scandal that made the young artist known in Germany. The figures were saved only after a campaign of support by Osthaus.

Despite serious controversies, Steger was appointed the city sculptor of Hagen in 1914 and was employed for public commissions. She designed a series of colossal panthers above the entrance to the new town hall (1914; destroyed World War II, repr. Gerber 1990, p.25), as well as an oval relief of *Dancers* (destroyed, repr. Klaus-Jürgen Sembach, *Henry van de Velde*, London: Thames and Hudson, and New York: Rizzoli, 1989) for the theatre of the Deutsche Werkbundausstellung in Cologne, built by Henry van de Velde. Steger's plaster models (destroyed, repr. Schulte 1994, p.32) for two life-size bronze figures (unexecuted) intended for portal niches at the Folkwang Museum were exhibited in the Hagen Room, arranged by Osthaus, at the Werkbundausstellung. For her own house, built by Jan Mathieu Lauweriks, at the Hagen artists' colony of Eppenhausen, she designed a façade relief of a caryatid supporting the balcony (1911; Am Stirnband, Hagen). In Jan Thorn-Prikker's house at Eppenhausen, she executed an overmantel relief that recalls the Cologne theatre relief: three female nudes fill the oval with flowing dance movements (1910; Am Stirnband, Hagen).

The essential character of Steger's later works, its expressive gesture, is already discernible from 1910. This is largely attributable to the influence of Expressionism. Lightness and

Steger: *Sitting Woman*, *c*.1930; height 43 cm.; Karl Ernst Osthaus-Museum, Hagen

movement took the place of mass. The figures, composed of geometrical structures, are complexly intertwined, the faces are introverted and melancholy. The combination of strict composition and strong expressiveness characterises Steger's works from 1917 to the early 1920s. The nearly life-size *Rising Youth* (*c*.1919; wood; Städtische Galerie und Städelsches Kunstinstitut, Frankfurt am Main) is constructed from relating horizontals, verticals and diagonals. This close connection of expressive, stylised imitation and gestures is also visible in *Female Half-Figure* (*c*.1920; coloured plaster; Karl Ernst Osthaus-Museum, Hagen), in which spiritualised expression is pushed to its limits. More space is required by the tragic Old Testament figure *Jephtah's Daughter* (1919; bronze; private collection, repr. Hagen 1981), whose energised body language

reflects contemporary expressive dance. Material weight is removed, and the fine-limbed, nearly life-size dancer is defined by the opposition of flowing arched forms. Steger understood the self-willed dynamism of her figures as the expression of emotions.

A change in style to a greater emphasis on the dynamic element, which occurred around 1920, is linked to Steger's move to Berlin. The war had prevented the realisation of other public commissions in Hagen, and her plan to establish a workshop for tombstones and monuments had failed due to lack of investment. This forced her return to Berlin in 1917. There, lacking public commissions, she executed mainly free-standing figures and portraits, and these required a different concept from architectural sculpture. Another stylistic change, replacing the Expressionist phase, began in 1922–3. It is clearly visible in the small sculpture *Sitting Woman* (*c*.1930; see illustration). Steger increasingly made reference to natural forms, and her figures gained weight. Although strong torsion and gestural language are still of central importance, the figure's emotional language is expressed in a more controlled movement. Extreme postures correspond to such attributes and titles as *The Lament, The Lonely, The Pensive*. The figures remain under-life-size, as in *The Austere* (1928; bronze; Märkisches Museum, Berlin) and *My Ball* (1932; bronze; untraced, repr. Bushart 1992, p.139).

In 1929, when mixed classes for life-drawing and sculpture were introduced at the school of the Unterrichtsanstalt des Vereins der Berliner Künstlerinnen, Steger ran them, one of the first female artists to teach male students. Steger appears to have worked relatively undisturbed after the National Socialists seized power in 1933. She accepted a few public commissions, such as works for the Olympic Games of 1936 (*Boy Playing Ball*) and 1940 (*Relief with Rowers*; both untraced). To some extent her late work could be seen to reflect contemporary taste in art, for example *Woman Carrying a Jug* (*c*.1940; untraced, *ibid.*, p.140). Yet, *Woman Striding/Woman Carrying a Jug I* (1934; bronze; private collection, repr. Nijmegen 1991, p.243) was confiscated as "degenerate" from the Staatliche Museen, Berlin, in 1937; six works by Steger were on the list of works confiscated.

After a year's stay in Florence in 1938, in connection with the Villa Romana prize, Steger executed several small marble groups employing the *non finito*, with figures against a deliberately unfinished background, for example *Naiads* (after 1940; marble; Nationalgalerie, Berlin) and *Two Sisters* (1946; marble; private collection, repr. Hagen 1981, no.18). The sorrowful experiences of war are reflected in two late works, *Pietà 45* (1945; spruce; private collection, *ibid.*, no.16) and *In Memoriam* (*c*.1945; marble; untraced, repr. Richert 1949).

With her male clothes and manners, Steger throughout her life reinforced the legend of her innate male genius that was created about her in the writings of critics and reviewers. By presenting herself in this way, the renowned sculptor, an acknowledged outsider, united her emancipation from the traditional role of the female artist with an adaptation to the male domain she had conquered.

BIRGIT SCHULTE

Steir, Pat

American painter, 1940–

Born Patricia Iris Sukoneck in Newark, New Jersey, 10 April
1940. Studied at Pratt Institute, Brooklyn, 1956–8 (graphic
art); Boston University, 1958–60; Pratt Institute, 1960–62
(BFA 1961). Married (1) Merle Steir, late 1950s; divorced; (2)
Dutch publisher Joost Elffers, 1985. Art Director, Harper and
Row, New York, c.1968–70. Taught at Parsons School of
Design, New York, Princeton University and Hunter College,
New York, 1970–73; California Institute of Arts, Los
Angeles, 1973–5. Travelled in USA and Europe, 1975–8.
Founder-member of *Printed Matter* and *Heresies* magazines,
New York, 1975; also worked on *Semiotext* magazine.
Recipient of National Endowment for the Arts (NEA) grant,
1974; Guggenheim fellowship, 1982; honorary doctorate,
Pratt Institute, Brooklyn, 1991. Lives in New York and
Amsterdam.

Selected Individual Exhibitions

Terry Dintenfass Gallery, New York: 1964
Corcoran Gallery of Art, Washington, DC: 1973
Galerie Farideh Cadot, Paris: 1976, 1978, 1979, 1980, 1981, 1982
Droll/Kolbert Gallery, New York: 1978, 1980
Galerie d'Art Contemporain, Geneva: 1980
Contemporary Arts Museum, Houston, TX: 1983 (*Arbitrary Order*, touring)
Spencer Museum of Art, University of Kansas, Lawrence: 1983 (*Form, Illusion, Myth*, touring)
Brooklyn Museum, NY: 1984–8 (*Brueghel Series*, touring), 1992
Galerie Eric Franck, Geneva: 1985, 1987, 1989
Dallas Museum of Art: 1986
New Museum of Contemporary Art, New York: 1987
M. Knoedler Gallery, New York: 1987, 1988
Rijksmuseum Vincent van Gogh, Amsterdam: 1987
Baltimore Museum of Art: 1987
Cabinet des Estampes, Musée d'Art et d'Histoire, Geneva: 1988–9 (touring)
Musée d'Art Contemporain, Lyon: 1990
Robert Miller Gallery, New York: 1990, 1995
Galerie Franck + Schulte, Berlin: 1991, 1993
Guild Hall Museum, East Hampton, NY: 1993
Irish Museum of Modern Art, Dublin: 1994

Selected Writings

Rome Poem: Short Stories and Love Songs, Paris: Farideh Cadot
Gallery, 1977

Bibliography

Marcia Tucker, "Pat Steir: 'The thing itself, made by me'", *Art in America*, lxi, January–February 1973, pp.70–74
Ted Castle, "Pat Steir and the science of the admirable", *Artforum*, xx, May 1982, pp.47–55
Carter Ratcliff and others, "Expressionism today: An artists' symposium", *Art in America*, lxx, December 1982, pp.58–75, 139
Arbitrary Order: Paintings by Pat Steir, exh. cat., Contemporary Arts Museum, Houston, 1983
Form, Illusion, Myth: Prints and Drawings of Pat Steir, exh. cat., Spencer Museum of Art, University of Kansas, Lawrence, and elsewhere, 1983
Pat Steir: The Brueghel Series (a Vanitas of Style), exh. cat., Brooklyn Museum, NY, and elsewhere, 1984
Ted Castle, "Pat Steir: Ways of marking", *Art in America*, lxxii, Summer 1984, pp.124–9
New Work on Paper III, exh. cat., Museum of Modern Art, New York, 1985
Stuart Greenspan, "Pat Steir: The *Brueghel Series (a Vanitas of Style)*", *Art & Auction*, vii, February 1985, pp.56–9
Paul Gardner, "Pat Steir: Seeing through the eyes of others", *Art News*, lxxxiv, November 1985, pp.80–88
Carter Ratcliff, *Pat Steir: Paintings*, New York: Abrams, 1986 (contains extensive bibliography)
Nancy Princenthal, "The self in parts", *Art in America*, lxxv, November 1987, pp.170–73
Pat Steir: Gravures/Prints, 1976–1988, exh. cat., Cabinet des Estampes, Musée d'Art et d'Histoire, Geneva, and elsewhere, 1988
Pat Steir, exh. cat., Musée d'Art Contemporain, Lyon, 1990
Constance Lewallen, "Interview with Pat Steir, San Francisco, November 1990", *View (Oakland)*, vii/6, 1991 (entire issue)
Pat Steir, exh. cat., Guild Hall Museum, East Hampton, NY, 1993
Thomas McEvilley, *Pat Steir*, New York: Abrams, 1995

For Pat Steir, the process of art-making entails ongoing research and self-discovery. Primarily a painter, Steir also works extensively in drawing and prints. In the mid-1970s she began analysing the styles of other artists within her art and since then has established a "living relationship with art history" in numerous series of works (Gardner 1985, p.88). Through her exploration of past representational practices, Steir maintains faith in the power of the artist's gesture or mark to contribute to the continuum of human expression.

While studying at the Pratt Institute under Richard Lindner, Steir worked in a figurative vein. She later attributed her many self-portraits and images of women to self-absorption and a grappling with the predicament of a woman artist emerging at a time when men, particularly the Abstract Expressionists, dominated the art scene. In these paintings, the woman faces conflict: in *Woman Running Into and Away From Her Dreams* (1958; repr. Ratcliff 1986, no.5) she runs towards a palette of abstract drips, tripping on a large mask while ghostly female faces loom in the background. Influenced by the Jungian notion of universal symbols, the puppet-like figures are archetypes of the naturally evolved artist on whom Steir fashioned herself (*Woman Looking at Her Reflection*, 1960; destroyed, *ibid.*, no.8; and *Sideways Crying Lady*, 1961; Collection Nancy Grossman).

Two animalistic guardians flanking the central panel in the triptych *Altar* (1968–9; *ibid.*, no.18) represent the last of Steir's mythically symbolic figures. She even regarded the middle panel as a gateway to a new direction in her art. With *Bird* (1969; *ibid.*, no.20), Steir returned to painting after a six-month hiatus working in publishing, travelling and taking up photography. In this canvas of a bird on a grey field with strips of blue sky visible beyond wooden boards, she abandons the literalness of autobiographical subject matter and for the first time transposes the irrationality of experience into private signs arranged on the painted surface.

Ending her isolation from the contemporary art world, Steir produced a number of grid paintings inspired by Agnes Martin (q.v.) (*Looking for the Mountain*, 1971; National Museum of American Art, Smithsonian Institution, Washington, DC; *Way to New Jersey*, 1971; Whitney Museum of American Art, New York; *The Four Directions of Time/No.2: Entropy*, 1972; Dallas Museum of Fine Arts). Painterly landscape motifs overlay the grids, often with the addition of single images of

Steir: *The Brueghel Series (A Vanitas of Style) (for Jurgen Glaesemer)*, 1982–4; oil on canvas; 72.3 × 57.2 cm.; Kunstmuseum, Bern

flowers or words, reflecting Conceptualist systems of mapping and naming.

Most of the large-scale *Breadfruit* (1973; Collection Martin Melzer, New York) is composed of wide black strokes dripping on to the lower border. In the upper left, in white, the numeral 1 is followed by a scribbled line, 2 by a thick horizontal stroke and, in the lower right, 3 accompanies a blooming flower. Steir's simplification of painting to line, colour and texture alongside the resultant pictorial representation led to paintings of flowers crossed out (*As I Am Forgotten*, 1974; Honolulu Academy of Arts; *Word Unspoken*, 1974; private collection, Chicago, *ibid.*, no.45; and *Word Unheard*, 1974; Albright-Knox Art Gallery, Buffalo). By slashing an X through the flower, Steir negates its illusionistic beauty and thereby rids it of its iconic status.

For two years Steir stopped painting, contemplating her ideas solely through drawing and printmaking and introducing a multi-panelled format that reappears in her canvases (*Rose Nose*, 1974; four-part drawing; Fourcade Droll Inc., New York). In 1975 she toured European museums, where she was particularly affected by the paintings of Rembrandt, Manet and Courbet, which subsequently changed her attitude towards her own art: "I had been immersed in questions of my own existence before. Now I saw myself, my art, in relation to other artists, the past, the culture. I made a subject of the myths that society develops from the illusions of art" (*ibid.*, p.54). *Rembrandt's Hairline No.1* (1978; Collection Jean Paul Jungo, Morges, Switzerland), the first canvas to originate from this experience, initiated several similar compositions: a square framed within a square, containing a single brush stroke at its centre (*Van Gogh/Goya*, 1978; Sydney and Frances Lewis Foundation, Richmond, VA; *Black and White Painting (After Pollock)*, 1979; artist's collection; *American Painting (Homage to De Kooning)*, 1979; private collection, Colts Neck, NJ, *ibid.*, no.73). The scribbled lines composing the hair in a Rembrandt self-portrait had struck Steir as akin to the modernist reduction of painting to line and colour, thus prompting the recognition that all art work is both rooted in the present of its creation and inexorably linked with the past.

There followed beautifully lush, three-panelled flower and tree paintings executed in rich reds, pinks, purples and blues (*Joost's Carnation Landscape*, 1981; Collection Sydney and Frances Lewis, Richmond, VA; *Blue Iris on Blue Background*, 1983; Collection Mr and Mrs Lewis Silberman, Coconut Grove, FL; *Pink Chrysanthemum*, 1984; private collection, *ibid.*, no.95; *Morning Tree*, 1983; Joslyn Art Museum, Omaha; *Red Tree, Blue Sky, Blue Water*, 1984; private collection, Netherlands, *ibid.*, no.105). The progression of each panel gradually magnifies the motif as the mode of representation evolves from realistic to abstract, paralleling the sequential development of styles in art history.

The *Brueghel Series* (1982–4; see illustration) marks the culmination of Steir's art-historical quotations, preceded by two monochrome versions (Collections American Express Company and Agnes Gund) and numerous studies. Taking a poster of a 17th-century still life of a vase of flowers by Jan Brueghel the Elder, Steir divided the image into a 64-part grid and then painted each section in the style of a different artist, ranging from the 14th century to the 20th. Through this ambitious undertaking – the painting of the history of Western

painting – Steir reaffirms the continuity of visual culture while inserting herself within it.

In 1984–5 Steir made drawings based on the images of waves in Courbet paintings and Japanese prints, particularly the famous Hokusai woodcut, as well as on a Rilke poem that reads: "For beauty is nothing but the beginning of terror … which we are still just able to endure … every angel is terrified". Her mother's death, as if she were "engulfed by a wave and washed away" (East Hampton 1993) also affected this thematic choice. Blue and black arcs made with sweeping arm gestures fill the length of the large scroll-like drawings (*Untitled [After Courbet and Hiroshige]*, 1985; Museum of Modern Art, New York). Waves painted in the manner of various artists following Courbet incorporate a lineage of quotations (*Winter: The Wave After Courbet As Though Painted by an Italian Baroque Painter*, 1985, repr. *Art in America*, July 1986, p.113; *Spring: The Wave As Though Painted by Ensor*, 1986; repr. East Hampton 1993). *The Moon and the Wave* tondos (1986–7; *ibid.*) reinforce the movement of water through their circular formats. From the waves came a series of paintings and etchings of waterfalls drawing on the legacies of Chinese ink landscapes and Abstract Expressionism (*Beloved Ghost Waterfall/Beijing*, 1990; coloured woodblock print on rice paper; *Small Vertical Falls*, 1991; aquatint etching; both repr. *View*, 1990, pp.26 and 37). The first paintings are serene meditations in black and white (*Primary Amsterdam Waterfall*, 1990; *Waterfall for a Mature Bride*, 1990; both repr. *Pat Steir: Waterfalls*, exh. cat., Robert Miller Gallery, New York, 1990). Streams of pigment down the canvases ending in splashes of tossed paint imitate the rushing flow of water. A second group adds dual colour, one for ground, the other for splashes. In *Dragon Waterfall* (1992; repr. East Hampton 1993) bright orange cascades over an equally vibrant field of red, emphasising the dynamic gestural technique.

Steir also created site-specific installations surrounding the viewer with large-scale images. For *Self-Portrait* (1987; New Museum of Contemporary Art; and 1991; MacKenzie Art Gallery, Saskatchewan), slides taken from 15th- to 19th-century physiognomy studies, notably Dürer's analysis of human proportion, were projected and traced on to the gallery walls, producing a surreal environment of multiple eyes, ears, noses and mouths, each some two metres high. By rendering supposedly universal human features, Steir leaves her own subjective imprint on the history of visual perception. In *The Heartline* (1992; Centre National d'Art Contemporain de Grenoble; and 1993; Galerie Franck + Schulte, Berlin) symbols from different cultures – some ritualistic, like the Celtic cross, others personal, like the waterfall – were formed by a single line that connected each image, linking their histories and magical meanings.

More recently, Steir has resumed the waterfalls, expanding the colour scheme and varying the rhythms of splattered paint (*Wintertide, Japanese Waterfall*, 1994; *Coastal Winter, China Waterfall*, 1994; *Red, Pink and Blue Waterfall*, 1994; all repr. *Pat Steir: About Waterfalls*, exh. cat., Anders Tornberg Gallery, Lund, 1994). In these elegantly beautiful works, the drip signifies both water and icon of modernism; figuration and abstraction merge.

Steir desires that her works be seen not as copies or appropriations of past art, but rather as interpretations. Her intellectual preoccupations with style are ruminations over the complex, interrelated acts of representing and perceiving; her art is an attempt to understand the role of artists, most importantly herself, within the broader context of cultural history.

MARY CHAN

Stepanova, Varvara (Fyodorovna)

Russian painter and designer, 1894–1958

Born in Kovno (now Kaunas), Lithuania, 9 October (Old Style calendar)/21 October (New Style calendar) 1894. Studied at Kovno gymnasium, graduating in 1910; Kazan Art School, 1910–13; Stroganov School of Applied Art, Moscow, 1913–14; studied in the studios of Konstantin Yuon, Ivan Dudin and Leblanc, Moscow, 1915–17. Assistant director, Art and Literature Section of IZO, Narkompros (Fine Arts Section, People's Commissariat of Enlightenment), 1919–20. Taught at the Krupskaya Academy for Communist Education, 1920–25; Vkhutemas (Higher State Artistic and Technical Workshops), Moscow, 1924–5. Member, Inkhuk (Institute of Artistic Culture), Moscow, 1920–23. Met Alexander Rodchenko at the Kazan' Art School; lived with him from 1916; one daughter; Rodchenko died 1956. Died in Moscow, 20 May 1958.

Principal Exhibitions

Moscow: 1918 (*Fifth State Exhibition*), 1919 (*Tenth State Exhibition: Non-Objective Creation and Suprematism*), 1920 (*Nineteenth State Exhibition*), 1921 (*5 x 5 = 25*, with Rodchenko, Popova, Exter and Vesnin), 1928 (*The Everyday Soviet Textile*), 1930 (*First Exhibition of the October Group*)
Galerie van Diemen, Berlin: 1922–3 (*Erste russische Kunstausstellung*, touring)
Museum of Decorative Painting, Moscow: 1923 (*Moscow's Theatrical and Decorative Art, 1918–1923*)
Venice Biennale: 1924
Exposition Internationale des Arts Décoratifs et Industriels Modernes, Paris: 1925
Academy of Arts, Leningrad: 1927 (*Graphic Art in the USSR, 1917–1927*)
State Tretyakov Gallery, Moscow: 1927 (*Russian Drawing During the Ten Years since the October Revolution*)
Cologne: 1928 (*International Pressa Exhibition*)
Park of Culture and Rest, Moscow: 1929 (*First Exhibition of Theatrical and Decorative Art*)
Petit Palais, Paris: 1931 (*International Exhibition of the Art of the Book*)
Historical Museum, Moscow: 1933 (*Artists of the Soviet Theatre over 17 Years, 1917–1934*)

Selected Writings

V. Agarykh [V. Stepanova], "O vystavlennykh grafikakh: Bespredmetnoye tvorchestvo" [About the graphic works on display: Non-objective creation], *Katalog desyatoy gosudarstvennoy vystavki: Bespredmetnoye tvorchestvo i suprematizm* [Catalogue of the Tenth State Exhibition: Non-Objective Creation and Suprematism], Moscow, 1919, pp.5–9
Untitled text in *5 x 5 = 25*, exh. cat., Moscow, 1921

Varst [V. Stepanova], "Kostyum segodnyashnego dnya prozodezhda" [The costume of the present day is working clothing], *Lef*, no.2, 1923, pp.65–8
Varst [V. Stepanova], "O rabotakh konstruktivistskoy molodyozhi" [Concerning the work of Young Constructivists], *Lef*, no.3, 1923, pp.53–6
Varst [V. Stepanova], "Rabochiy Klub: Konstruktivist A.M. Rodchenko" [The Workers' Club: The Constructivist A.M. Rodchenko], *Sovremennaya arkhitektura*, no.1, 1926, p.36
"Ot kostyuma k risunku i tkani" [From costume to drawing and the fabric], *Vechernaya Moskva*, no.49, 1929, p.3
Chelovek ne mozhet zhit bez chuda: Pisma, Poeticheskiye opyty, Zapiski khudozhnitsy [Man cannot live without miracles: Letters, poetical experiments, the artist's notes], Moscow: Izdaltelstvo Sfera, 1994

Bibliography

E. Kovtun, "Varvara Stepanova's anti-book", *Von der Flache zum Raum: Russland, 1916–1924/From Surface to Space: Russia, 1916–1924*, Cologne: Galerie Gmurzynska, 1974, pp.269–84
Varvara Fyodorovna Stepanova, 1894–1958, exh. cat., Kostroma Regional Museum of Fine Arts, 1975
Künstlerinnen der russischen Avantgarde/Women Artists of the Russian Avant-Garde, 1910–1930, exh. cat., Galerie Gmurzynska, Cologne, 1979
Angelica Zander Rudenstine, ed., *The George Costakis Collection: Russian Avant-Garde Art*, New York: Abrams, and London: Thames and Hudson, 1981
Christina Lodder, *Russian Constructivism*, New Haven and London: Yale University Press, 1983
Rodcenko e Stepanova: Alle origini del Costruttivismo, Milan: Electa, 1984
Alexander Lavrentiev, *Varvara Stepanova: A Constructivist Life*, ed. John E. Bowlt, Cambridge: Massachusetts Institute of Technology Press, and London: Thames and Hudson, 1988 (Russian original)
Art into Life: Russian Constructivism, 1914–1932, exh. cat., Henry Art Gallery, University of Washington, Seattle, 1990
M.N. Yablonskaya, *Women Artists of Russia's New Age, 1900–1935*, New York: Rizzoli, and London: Thames and Hudson, 1990
The Future Is Our Only Goal: Aleksander M. Rodchenko, Varvara F. Stepanova, exh. cat., Österreichisches Museum für angewandte Kunst, Vienna, and elsewhere, 1991

Varvara Stepanova produced some innovative work synthesising poetry and painting in the late 1910s, and from 1921 onwards played an important role in developing the theory and practice of Constructivism, notably in the areas of theatrical, costume and typographical design. From the very beginning her career was closely bound up with that of her husband, the artist Alexander Rodchenko, whom she met at the Kazan Art School around 1911.

In 1917, under the influence of the artist Olga Rozanova (q.v.), Stepanova began to write transrational poetry (*zaum*). Between 1918 and 1919 she produced a series of illustrated, collaged and handwritten books such as *Rtny khomle*, *Zigra ar*, *Globolkim*, *Gaust chaba* and *Toft*, which she categorised as "visual poetry" and "colour script graphics". In these she integrated words, phrases and lines of poetry into colourful non-objective configurations of lines and shapes, using words as pictorial elements and experimenting with collage.

She was an active participant in artistic life during the revolutionary period, working as assistant director of the Art and Literature Section of IZO, Narkompros (Fine Arts Section of the People's Commissariat of Enlightenment, 1919–20) and

Stepanova: *Figure with Drum*, 1921; Alexander Laurentiev Collection

sitting on the council of representatives of the Union of Art Workers at IZO (1920–22). She also taught at the Krupskaya Communist Academy (1920–25), and in 1925 arranged a book evening there. A member of Moscow's Inkhuk (Institute of Artistic Culture), 1920–23, Stepanova was secretary to the Group for Objective Analysis (1920–21) and contributed to the discussions in spring 1921 that sought to define the distinction between concepts of composition and construction. As a result she, Aleksei Gan and Rodchenko founded the Working Group of Constructivists (also known as the First Working Group of Constructivists) in March 1921. The group denied the validity of art as an autonomous activity, wanting to participate in the construction of a socialist society by designing everyday objects that could be mass produced. In December 1922 Stepanova contributed a paper "On Constructivism" to Inkhuk.

In September 1921 Stepanova collaborated with Rodchenko, Lyubov Popova (q.v.), Alexander Vesnin and Alexandra Exter (q.v.) in the important exhibition 5 × 5 = 25 in Moscow. The five artists each contributed five works. Stepanova exhibited paintings based on the mechanical and geometrical analysis of the human body (e.g. *Two Figures*, 1920; Costakis Collection). In these works, which she had started making in 1919, the figure is translated into flat geometric shapes, which are organised into almost abstract compositions (e.g. *Figure with Drum*, 1921; see illustration). The forms are imbued with a certain irregularity that is complemented by the rough textures of the painted surface. Stepanova stated in the catalogue that "Technology and industry have presented art with the problem of construction as effective action, not contemplative figuration". She subsequently used a similar, but more precise geometry for drawings and woodcuts of human figures and celebrities such as Charlie Chaplin, some of which in 1922 she contributed to Aleksei Gan's film and photographic magazine *Film-Fot*.

In 1922 Stepanova designed the set and costumes for Vsevolod Meyerkhold's production of Sukhovo-Kobylin's play *The Death of Tarelkin*. She devised a series of acting apparatuses comprising collapsible structures (made from standard planks used as slats and painted white), which reinforced the action of the play and could be adapted to perform several functions. The costumes consisted of geometrically articulated overalls (working clothes or *prozodezhda*), which were sewn in two contrasting colours to identify the actors and emphasise their movements.

In early 1924 Stepanova and Popova started to work as fabric designers at the First Textile Print Factory in Moscow (formerly the Emil Tsindel Factory). In accordance with the Constructivists' machine aesthetic and the nature of industrial manufacture, Stepanova and Popova argued that geometrically based designs had to replace traditional floral and plant patterns as part of the total rationalisation of the textile and clothing industries. By manipulating simple geometric forms and primary colours, Stepanova created 150 designs, of which 20 were actually manufactured. She also became involved with the theoretical and practical problems of dress design, particularly working clothing and sports clothing (*sportodezhda*).

Stepanova contributed articles and illustrations to the journal *Lef* and *New Lef* (1923–7). In 1925 she began to design posters with Vladimir Mayakovsky (e.g. the *Literate*

Man Improves the Peasant Economy, 1925). From the mid-1920s onwards she tended to concentrate almost exclusively on typographical and graphic design, producing covers and lay-outs for such magazines as *Sovetskoye Kino* (Soviet cinema), *Kniga i revolyutsiya* (Book and Revolution), *Sovremennaya arkhitektura* (Contemporary architecture) and *Krasnoye studenchestvo* (Red students). In the 1930s she collaborated with Rodchenko on Soviet propaganda publications such as *SSSR na stroyke* (USSR in construction; e.g. no.12, 1935, on parachuting; no.8, 1936, on the wood industry; and no.7, 1940, on Mayakovsky). They also worked together on large illustrated books such as *Desyatet Uzbekistana* (Ten years of Uzbekistan; 1934) and *Pervaya Konnaya* (First cavalry; 1938). Stepanova remained active in these areas during the 1940s and 1950s, when she was involved on the design of such magazines as *Sovetskaya zhenshchina* (Soviet woman; 1945–6) and albums including the *Moskovsky metro* (Moscow Metro; 1953). She returned briefly to painting in the late 1930s, when she produced some landscapes and still lifes (e.g. *Cabbage and Onions*, 1939; artist's family collection).

CHRISTINA LODDER

Stephens, Alice Barber
American painter, illustrator and graphic artist, 1858–1932

Born Alice Barber near Salem, New Jersey, 1 July 1858. Studied at Philadelphia School of Design for Women (now Moore College of Art), 1869–79; Pennsylvania Academy of the Fine Arts, Philadelphia, under Thomas Eakins, 1876–7 and 1879–81; Académie Julian, Paris, under Tony Robert-Fleury, 1886–7; Académie Colarossi, Paris, 1887. Worked as a wood-engraver and illustrator from 1873, and solely as an illustrator by 1884; also active as a painter from 1880. Contributed to numerous publications from 1878, including *Scribner's Monthly*, *Harper's Young People*, *Harper's Bazar*, *Harper's New Monthly Magazine*, *Century Illustrated Monthly*, *Cosmopolitan*, *Harper's Round Table*, *Collier's Weekly*, *Woman's Home Companion*, *New Idea Woman's Magazine*, *Ladies' Home Journal*, *Delineator*, *McCall's*, *Reader* and *Country Gentleman*; publishers included Houghton Mifflin, from 1901; Harper, New York, from 1903; and Little Brown, Boston, from 1904. Taught drawing and painting from life, crayon portraiture and illustration at the Philadelphia School of Design for Women, 1889–93. Married painter Charles Hallowell Stephens, 1890; son born 1893; husband died 1931. Founder member of The Plastic Club, Philadelphia (an art club for women), and Fellowship of the Pennsylvania Academy of the Fine Arts, 1897. Member, Society of American Wood Engravers; New Century Club. Moved to Rose Valley, Pennsylvania, 1904. Died in Philadelphia after a stroke, 13 July 1932.

Principal Exhibitions
Boston Art Club: 1880–86 (annuals), 1895 (*Original Drawings by Famous Illustrators*)

Pennsylvania Academy of the Fine Arts, Philadelphia: 1881–90
   (Mary Smith prize 1890)
Museum of Fine Arts, Boston: 1881 (*American Engravings on Wood*)
Salmagundi Club, New York: 1881–3 (black and white)
Philadelphia Society of Artists: 1881–3
Paris Salon: 1887
Art Gallery and Woman's Building, World's Columbian Exposition,
   Chicago: 1893 (honourable mention)
Cotton States International Exposition, Atlanta: 1895 (bronze medal)
The Plastic Club, Philadelphia: 1898 (individual), 1929 (retrospective)
Earls Court, London: 1899 (*Women's Work*, gold medal)
Exposition Universelle, Paris: 1900 (bronze medal)

Bibliography

Frederick W. Webber, "A clever woman illustrator", *Quarterly Illustrator*, i, 1893, pp.174–80
"Alice Barber Stephens, illustrator", *Woman's Progress*, November 1893, p.49
Esther Singleton, "Book illustrators, xv: Alice Barber Stephens", *Book Buyer*, xii, August 1895, pp.392–4
Aimée Tourgée, "A clever woman artist", *Art Interchange*, xxxix, October 1897, pp.74–5
Regina Armstrong, "Representative American women illustrators", *Critic*, xxxvii, July 1900, pp.43–54
Elizabeth Lore North, "Women illustrators of child life", *Outlook*, lxxviii, 1 October 1904, pp.271–80
Julius Moritzen, "Some women illustrators", *Twentieth Century Home*, December 1904, p.46
"Alice Barber Stephens", *Art Digest*, vi, 1 August 1932, p.6 (obituary)
"Alice Barber Stephens", *Art News*, xxx, 13 August 1932, p.8 (obituary)
The American Personality: The Artist-Illustrator of Life in the United States, 1860–1930, exh. cat., Grunwald Center for the Graphic Arts, University of California at Los Angeles, and elsewhere, 1976
Alice Barber Stephens: A Pioneer Woman Illustrator, exh. cat., Brandywine River Museum, Chadds Ford, PA, 1984
Helen Goodman, "Alice Barber Stephens, illustrator", *Arts Magazine*, lviii, January 1984, pp.126–9
—, "Alice Barber Stephens", *American Artist*, xlviii, April 1984, pp.46–9

Unpublished correspondence is in the Archives of American Art, Smithsonian Institution, Washington, DC; an illustration scrapbook is in the Art Division, New York Public Library; original drawings and paintings are in the Brandywine River Museum, Chadds Ford, PA; original drawings are in the Library of Congress, Washington, DC.

The wood-engraving skills that Alice Barber Stephens learned at the Philadelphia School of Design for Women were the basis for the linear qualities of her drawing style for many years. She developed a more painterly style as a result of her studies with Thomas Eakins at the Pennsylvania Academy of the Fine Arts. Stephens illustrated romances, mysteries and adventures, but as women have often been encouraged to adopt work related to their image as mothers, she became best known for her illustrations for children's literature. Stylistically, Stephens's illustrations reflect the changing technology of reproducing images as well as her observations of other artists' work.

In the late 1860s and 1870s she learned to draw in pen and ink using traditional linear and hatching methods, because linear work was easily translated into wood-engraving. As staff wood-engraver for *Women's Words* in the late 1870s, Stephens both drew and engraved her illustrations. Her portraits for the series "Eminent Women of the Past" are tightly drawn,

Stephens: *Piano Lesson*, engraving in *Harper's Young People*, 1 May 1888

detailed busts constructed with varying parallel lines, some broken, much as in traditional copper engraving. She experimented with slightly fluid lines and some cross-hatching in her more ambitious, half-length portrait of the German writer *Wilhelmine von Hillern* for the front page of the July 1877 edition.

Because Stephens felt that wood-engraving was confining, she entered evening classes at the Pennsylvania Academy in 1876 to study painting. Eakins, her instructor, was teaching modern French methods of painting directly from nature. Stephens learned his naturalistic techniques by painting, rather than drawing, directly from the nude model. From Eakins she probably also learned photography, which she used as a tool for composition and studying light effects. She began to paint as well as draw her illustrations. She has become particularly well known for her gouache of the *Women's Life Class* (1879; for illustration, see p.135), which accompanied a story on art schools in Philadelphia for *Scribner's Monthly* in September 1879. She also engraved the scene on wood, which required more effort than merely copying the lines on to a block – she used extremely fine, closely drawn parallel lines to create varying shades of grey to model the figures and reproduce the tones of the gouache.

By 1880 Stephens had opened her own studio and taught wood-engraving, executed illustration and wood-engraving commissions, and painted. Her work for *Our Continent* magazine in the early 1880s included drawing and wood engraving landscapes, genre scenes and architectural views. She varied her engraving style to suit the subject. Often her engravings of her own drawings are spontaneous and free, especially landscapes, in which she portrayed naturalistic effects of light with economic and sketchy line work. In contrast, for the cover story for a memorial to Stephen Girard, a mariner and merchant, in the issue of 20 June 1883, she used a dry, traditional approach of simple parallel lines and cross-hatching.

Stephens's commissions for *Harper's Young People* of the mid-1880s were extremely detailed yet freely drawn pen-and-ink illustrations, such as the *Piano Lesson* (see illustration) for Lucy C. Lillie's "The household of Glen Holly" in the issue of 1 May 1888. Similar drawings for children's fiction by the well-known authors Louisa May Alcott and Kate Douglas Wiggin helped to build her reputation as one of the publisher's best artists.

In 1886–7 Stephens studied in Europe, where she viewed the new Impressionism and the work of artists participating in the Arts and Crafts movement. On her return she increasingly painted out-of-doors. Later, in an interview with Bertha Mahony and Elinor Whitney for *Contemporary Illustrators of Children's Books* (Boston, 1930), Stephens said that she wanted to capture the "pitch of color, in the swift impressionistic manner. ... I was hungry to use color and the brush; and it strengthened the illustrating". She subsequently worked more frequently in oil, exhibiting paintings at the Pennsylvania Academy and in large national exhibitions.

By 1889 photographic methods made it possible to reproduce illustrations directly. Photogravure could capture the actual qualities of the media and of the artist's hand in charcoal, colour crayon, oil, gouache and watercolour, giving the artist increased flexibility and freedom. Stephens used the painterly materials, especially washes, to create stronger, more dramatic images that particularly attracted viewers' attention with luminous sensations of colour even when reproduced in half-tone. A particularly fine example of her naturalistic style used to depict indoor light is *Buying Christmas Presents* (1895; Library of Congress), which she painted in watercolour and gouache for *Harper's Weekly*.

The Arts and Crafts movement became an influence on Stephens's style around 1900. She flattened space and adopted decorative effects. For years she had articulated her figures with soft outline or with thicker engraving strokes to simulate an outline, but during the period 1904–5 she outlined her forms with the strong, sinuous line used by Art Nouveau artists. She then filled in the forms using oil, watercolour or charcoal. Until 1911 she continued to use linear qualities of the decorative style in such works as *I First Saw the Children with Their Mother* (1906 for *Harper's Monthly*; Library of Congress), in which she filled the forms with colour crayon. With its close-up, cut composition, *I First Saw the Children* also demonstrates how Stephens was sometimes inspired by photography.

Stephens was frequently referred to as one of America's leading illustrators, although she was usually evaluated in the context of women's work and singled out as an exemplary "woman artist". In an article for the *Quarterly Illustrator*, Frederick Webber wrote: "she stands with the foremost women painters and illustrators of the country". He claimed that she and other women were adept at illustration because they had "more delicate sensibilities and ... natural love of the beautiful ... a closer sympathy with nature and life, and a quicker perception of the poetic element" (Webber 1893). Even women writers with deeply internalised sexism, such as Esther Singleton and Elizabeth Lore North, stereotyped and trivialised women. In the *Book Buyer* (1895) Singleton wrote that Stephens "... is one of the few women who knows how to draw and who recognizes the intense importance of form and line and shading". For "Women illustrators of child life" North (1904) remarked that Stephens's work was "entirely free from prettiness or sentimentality". Julius Moritzen (1904) wrote that she ranked "with a class of illustrators who know no fashion, no vagary in art. E.A. Abbey, Smedley, Frost and those akin to them ... the aristocracy of the profession ... her presence there is an honor to her sex as well". After years of having her work or reviews of it segregated by sex, she asked the critic and former student Aimée Tourgée: "Why woman? ... If I do clever work, why not let it go at that? Can't they judge me as an artist, not as a woman?" (Tourgée 1897, p.75). Yet, as a founding member of The Plastic Club and a participating member of the New Century Club, she closely identified with and enthusiastically supported women in the arts.

PHYLLIS PEET

Stern, Irma

South African painter and graphic artist, 1894–1966

Born in Schweizer-Reneke, Transvaal, 2 October 1894, into a prosperous German-Jewish immigrant family. Spent only about eight years in South Africa before 1920, due to the Boer War and World War I. Stayed mainly in Berlin during school years, 1901–12; studied at a private art school in Berlin, 1912–13, then at the Grossherzogliche Sächsische Hochschule für Bildende Kunst, Weimar, under Fritz Mackensen and Gari Melchers, intermittently 1913–14; subsequently studied under Martin Brandenburg in Berlin. Met painter Max Pechstein, 1917. Participated in Freie Secession exhibitions, 1918 and 1920; founder-member of Novembergruppe. Returned to South Africa, 1920; lived and worked at "The Firs", Cape Town, from 1927 until her death. Close contact with Jewish intelligentsia in Cape Town; friendships with Jewish intellectuals Roza von Gelderen and Hilda Purwitzky, among others. Married former tutor Dr Johannes Prinz, professor of German at University of Cape Town, 1926; divorced 1935. Travelled extensively in South Africa, and visited other parts of Africa; long stays in Germany, with trips to other European countries, 1923–4, 1926–7, 1929–30 and 1931–2; trip to the Netherlands, Britain and Italy, studying fresco technique in Fiesole, 1937–8; long periods of study in Madeira, 1931, 1950 and 1963; several trips to Europe after World War II. Recipient of diploma of honour, Exposition Internationale des Beaux-Arts, Bordeaux, 1927; Cape Tercentenary Matteno grant for outstanding work, 1959; regional award, Guggenheim International art prize, 1960; Oppenheimer award for best painting, *Art South Africa Exhibition Today*, Durban Art Gallery, 1963; medal of honour for painting, South African Academy, 1965. Member, Frauenkunstverband, Berlin; South African Society of Arts (SASA), 1931. Died in Cape Town, 23 August 1966. House with works and extensive art collection dedicated to "the encouragement and promotion of Fine Arts within and outside the Republic of South Africa"; became Irma Stern Museum in 1972.

Principal Exhibitions

Individual

Galerie Gurlitt, Berlin: 1919, 1923, 1927, 1930
Ashbey's Galleries, Cape Town: 1922, 1926, 1929, 1932
Galerie Goldschmidt, Frankfurt am Main: 1923, 1925, 1929
Galerie Billiet-Vorms, Paris: 1927, 1929, 1932
Kestner-Gesellschaft, Hannover: 1929
Galerie Kleikamp, The Hague: 1930, 1932, 1935, 1937
Foyles Gallery, London: 1932
Gainsborough Gallery, Johannesburg: 1940, 1942, 1947, 1949, 1951, 1956
Argus Gallery, Cape Town: 1941, 1942, 1943, 1944, 1945, 1946, 1947, 1948
Galerie Wildenstein, Paris: 1947
Association of Arts, Cape Town: 1949, 1950, 1951, 1952, 1953, 1954, 1955, 1956, 1957, 1958, 1961, 1963, 1964
Galerie André Weil, Paris: 1953, 1965
Galerie Wolfgang Gurlitt, Munich: 1955, 1960
Galerie Wasmuth, Berlin, and Stadtgalerie, Linz: 1956
Grosvenor Gallery, London: 1967 (retrospective)

Group

Freie Secession, Berlin: 1918, 1920
Grosse Berliner Kunstausstellung, Berlin: 1929, 1930
International Jewish Exhibition, Zürich: 1929
Tate Gallery, London: 1948 (*Overseas Exhibition of South African Art*)
Venice Biennale: 1950, 1952, 1954, 1958

Selected Writings

"How I began to paint", *Cape Argus*, 12 June 1926
"Was eine Malerin in Afrika sah", *Frau und Gegenwart*, no.16, 1927
"Irma Stern and her work", *South African Life and the Woman's Forum*, 7 December 1933
"My amazing models", *Day Express*, 8 November 1936
"Bazaar of Zanzibar", *The Pictorial*, 1939
Congo, Pretoria: Van Schaik, 1943
Zanzibar, Pretoria: Van Schaik, 1948
"My aim in art", *NCW News*, November 1955
Paradise: The Journal and Letters (1917–1933) of Irma Stern, ed. Neville Dubow, Diep River: Chameleon Press, 1991

Bibliography

Max Osborn, *Irma Stern*, Reihe Junge Kunst, li, Leipzig: Klinkhardt und Bierman, 1927
Joseph Sachs, *Irma Stern and the Spirit of Africa*, Pretoria: Van Schaik, 1942
A.C. Bouman, *Painters of South Africa*, Cape Town: HAUM, 1949
Joan Rebecca Hurwitz, *Irma Stern: South African Artist: A Bibliography*, Johannesburg: University of the Witwatersrand, 1968
Esmé Berman, *Art and Artists of South Africa*, Cape Town: Balkema, 1970
Neville Dubow, *Irma Stern*, Cape Town: Struik, 1974
Liliana Daneel, *South African Guide to Sources on Irma Stern*, Pretoria: Centre for Art Historical Research, South African Institute for Language, Literature and Arts, Human Sciences Research Council, 1981
Reinhild Kauenhoven Janzen, "African art in Cape Town: Where is it, what is it? Irma Stern's African art collection in context", *Quarterly Bulletin* (South African National Gallery), xv, 1983, pp.1–7
Esmé Berman, *Painting in South Africa*, Johannesburg: Southern, 1993
Karel Schoeman, *Irma Stern: The Early Years, 1894–1933*, Cape Town: South African Library, 1994
Marion Arnold, *Irma Stern: A Feast for the Eye*, Vlaeberg, SA: Fernwood Press, 1995
Irma Stern und der Expressionismus: Afrika und Europa: Bilder und Zeichnungen bis 1945, exh. cat., Kunsthalle Bielefeld, 1996

Irma Stern was, and probably still is, the best known of all South African artists, although she is little known in Europe today. She trained and first exhibited in Berlin. In 1920 she returned to Cape Town, where she had her first exhibition in South Africa in 1922. She spent the rest of her life in Cape Town, interrupted by stays in Europe and travels in Africa. Yearly exhibitions and reviews brought her to the attention of the public. Her travels, her house and extensive art collection, the sales of her pictures and, not least, her imposing appearance were commented on by the media, making her a central, often controversial figure in the cultural life of the country.

Stern's extensive oeuvre – more than 800 paintings so far identified, innumerable drawings, watercolours and prints, as well as sculptures and ceramic works – bears witness to her significance. Her former house in Cape Town is now a museum housing both her own works and her art collection, which includes masterpieces of Central African art as well as European medieval sculptures, Renaissance furniture, small Egyptian and Greek sculptures, Russian icons and Chinese porcelain and stoneware. Her life and work testify to her continuing search for cultural, ethnic and sexual identities or differences and to her attempts to promote cultural exchange between Europe and Africa.

Stern's thinking and work began from a critique of the civilisation that had prevailed in Europe since industrialisation and which had intensified during World War I. As Gauguin and the Expressionist artists Emil Nolde and Max Pechstein had done in the South Seas, in Africa she wanted to return to the origins, and sought those places "unspoilt by civilization" and "native life in all its beauty and splendour" ("Irma Stern and her work", 1933). Until about 1933 her work concerned the depiction of different worlds – the people and ways of life in Europe and various regions of South Africa – at first in a naturalistic-impressionistic formal vocabulary (until *c*.1916) and then starting from a German Expressionist style. She visited other African countries and acquainted herself with their artistic practices, integrating the crafts in particular into her own work, either as frame or background. In her books *Congo* (1943) and *Zanzibar* (1948) and in at least two exhibitions in Johannesburg and Paris, she presented her art alongside works from Central Africa and Zanzibar. Her house remains a testament to her vision of an artistic practice that unites all mankind and epochs.

In the history of art in South Africa, Stern is regarded as the artist who introduced the country to post-World War I

Stern: *Two Harlots, Madeira*, 1932; Rembrandt van Rijn Art Foundation, Collection Mrs Huberte Rupert, Stellenbosch, Republic of South Africa

European avant-garde painting, which she developed into her own formal vocabulary, as did Maggie Laubser, who returned a few years later. Stern's artistic development took place in Germany and was influenced by a number of factors: nostalgia for her South African homeland; encounters with European culture through travel and in the intellectual, artistic atmosphere of her sophisticated, assimilated middle-class Jewish relations in Berlin; and revolutionary thought during and after the war. These factors caused her to rebel against conventions that, as a woman, she found restricting both in Imperial Germany and in the colonial society of South Africa. Her diaries as a young woman (South African Library, Cape Town), the list of books she read and the stage productions she saw, the journal she wrote and illustrated (1919–23; Irma Stern Museum), and the article "How I began to paint" (1926) all demonstrate how aware she was, often plagued with self-doubt, that her desire to study art was moulded by her diverse experiences.

The discrimination against women who sought artistic training preoccupied Stern from an early age. She began her studies at a private art school in Berlin, but at the age of 17 she moved to the Grossherzogliche Sächsische Hochschule für Bildende Kunst in Weimar where a special class existed for women. Her early work is largely concerned with the conventional academic subject matter of landscapes, nudes, portraits and still lifes (e.g. *Village Street*, 1914; *Nude Study*, 1916; both Irma Stern Museum; *Green Apples*, 1916; Johannesburg Art Gallery), but there are also studies and portraits of people from South Africa (e.g. *Tswana Child*, 1913; Irma Stern Museum).

Above all, it was the suffering of women and children in World War I that led Stern beyond the themes and techniques of the academic tradition. This is evident in the small half-length portrait of a girl disturbed by the war, holding a bunch of wild flowers, later called *Eternal Child* (1916; Rupert Family Foundation for the Arts, Stellenbosch), which is reminiscent of works by Paula Modersohn-Becker (q.v.). A crucial event in Stern's early career was meeting the painter Max Pechstein, who was by then already successful. Stern told him about South Africa, particularly about its Stone Age rockscape art, and she sent him a large rock with engravings on it. Pechstein encouraged her desire to paint and to use her experience of South Africa. He selected the work for her first solo exhibition, in 1919 at the renowned Galerie Gurlitt, Berlin, all of which included genres and motifs from both Europe and South Africa: 34 paintings and 70 drawings and watercolours.

Stern also represented her bonds with two very different cultures in an explicit way in her two portfolio works of 1920, both published in Berlin. In *Visionen, Zehn Steinzeichnungen* (Irma Stern Museum), which is based on a story by Turgenev, she shows her familiarity with European literature and with the tension of modern urban civilisation, a tension that is echoed in the characteristic nervous, linear drawing style of the lithographs, reminiscent of pen-and-ink drawings. The portfolio *Dumela Morena: Bilder aus Afrika* (Irma Stern Museum) presents "Pictures from Africa" as idylls with naked figures in the open countryside, as well as lithographs resembling large-scale charcoal drawings.

In this portfolio work and in the early paintings from Berlin with motifs from Africa (*Stone Chopper*, 1920; Rupert Family Foundation for the Arts) Stern broke with the depictions allied to ethnographic illustrations traditionally made by white South African artists of non-whites; the break was even more radical in her work of the 1920s after her return to South Africa. She did this primarily with her drawings and paintings of the coloured inhabitants of Natal, Zululand, Swaziland, Pondoland and Cape Town's Malai Quarter, which idealised the life of the "uncivilised". Often, as in the large vertical format oil paintings *Beer Dance* (1922; South Africa House, London) and *The Hunt* (1926; Irma Stern Museum), she depicts men or women in a group, bound to their surroundings and filling the picture space. She gets close to her subjects, characterising them as dignified, sometimes also melancholic creatures of nature; she uses stylised, simplified forms in the Expressionist-Cubist idiom and powerful colours as a means of achieving empathy with the attitude and rhythm of the figures she represents. Unlike earlier white South African artists, she sought close contact with the people she wished to portray, travelling to them and trying to share their lives. In her pictures and writings she recorded her experiences with diverse types of people and individuals (*Three Swazi Girls*, 1925; Irma Stern Museum; *Malai Mother and Child*, 1928; *Pondo Woman*, 1929; both Pretoria Art Museum; *Swazi Girls*, 1931; South African National Gallery, Cape Town), the landscapes in which they lived (*Umgababa*, 1922; Irma Stern Museum), their ways of life and her own enthusiasm for the "naturalness" and "beauty" of these strangers.

In Europe, both sides of Stern's artistic work were seen. The first book on the artist was published in Germany in 1927 in the series Junge Kunst, which already included publications on Pechstein, Modersohn-Becker and Picasso. In this book, the renowned Berlin critic Max Osborn emphasised the interest of this "artist nourished by all the potions of occidental culture" in the life close to nature and the unspoilt way of life in her African homeland. He verified the authenticity of Stern's experiences by reprinting a long diary entry on her adventures in Umgababa. In the same year Stern was awarded a prize in Bordeaux for a "European" painting, *Children* (1924; Rupert Family Foundation for the Arts). In South Africa, however, what were called her "native studies" were intensely controversial. For this reason, in South Africa she did not exhibit her large compositions with scenes from African life ("Irma Stern and her work", 1933), but only smaller works on this theme, as well as landscapes (e.g. *Level Crossing*, 1924; South African National Gallery), still lifes (e.g. *Fish God*, 1924; Rupert Family Foundation for the Arts) and, chiefly, portraits of white friends and intellectuals (e.g. *Dr Louis Herman*, 1922; *Roza von Gelderen*, 1929; both Irma Stern Museum).

In the 1930s and 1940s Stern moved towards a method of working and representation that departed further and further from the abstraction and generalisation of Expressionism. The Madeira pictures from the early 1930s – such as *Blind Boy* (1931; private collection, London), *Two Harlots, Madeira* (1932; see illustration) and *Butcher's Shop* (1932; Kunsthalle, Bielefeld) – are sensitive psychological studies in a new representational idiom with a more complex pictorial structure, painted with an impasto, iridescent vividness and with vibrating, short brush strokes. The exceptional, the individual, the vivid in colour and form become her subject, not only in the impressive, rich still-life paintings with flowers (e.g. *Still Life with Magnolias*, 1935; Durban Art Gallery; *Still Life with*

Magnolias, 1936; *Still Life with Chrysanthemum*, 1937; both Rupert Family Foundation for the Arts), but also in portraits of friends and relations (e.g. *Lippy*, 1944; Irma Stern Museum; *Young Girl*, 1944; Johannesburg Art Gallery) and in landscapes (*Lake Kivu, Congo*, 1946; South African National Gallery).

The figurative work from the Congo of the 1940s (e.g. *Azande Musicians*, 1942; private collection; *Manbetu Bride*, 1947; private collection) and particularly those from Zanzibar (*Arab Group, Zanzibar*; *Ramadan*; both 1945; Rupert Family Foundation for the Arts; *Rich Old Arab*, 1945; Irma Stern Museum; *Arab Women Dance*, 1945; private collection; *Golden Shawl*, 1945; South African National Gallery), with the still lifes, are regarded in South Africa as the high points of Stern's work. According to her own statements, she found the timeless beauty of Egyptian queens in the figures from the Congo "the quintessence of beauty"; in Zanzibar she discovered the "spiritual world", where nearly all the people she portrays appear to be tranquil. These spiritual powers are also "a truth from early times and handed down from age to age, a worship of spiritual forces ... which are the roots of a work of art" ("My aim in art", 1955). She often portrayed her figures individually or in pairs, as half-figures that filled the canvas in deep, radiantly warm yellow-orange-red colours on a monochrome ground that appears to transport them away from reality. The pictures are framed by elaborate wood-carvings by local craftsmen, which link the figures to their home country and local traditions in an almost magical way.

Stern's idealising picture of an "unspoilt" Africa was destroyed forever by the clashes during the de-colonialisation after World War II and by the increase in military conflicts in Africa, particularly in the Congo. She continued to work tirelessly, but now only very occasionally painted in Africa, exclusively in the South African regions. Europe was accessible once more, but hopes that there was increasing interest in art from Africa, whether by her or traditional artists, were only partially fulfilled. From the mid-1950s representational art was less and less in demand in Europe in general and in a West Germany moulded by the East-West conflict in particular. Stern's works were exhibited most frequently in Britain, also in Germany and France, but she was now shown as a South African who had brought modern painting to the "colonies". She was even described as an English figurative painter in the 1958 edition of Vollmer, a well-known German dictionary of artists. From the early 1950s Stern made almost annual visits to southern Europe, attending cultural events, but mainly painting, often in the south of Spain. After a phase of painting religious themes, she orientated herself with the European masters Picasso and Matisse and the beauty of their use of linear forms. Strictly rejecting abstract painting, she experimented with new media, techniques and forms of representation. Speed, almost haste, is now characteristic of her landscapes, most painted in one go (*Spanish Landscape*, 1961; Irma Stern Museum), her still lifes (*Arum Lilies*, 1951; South African National Gallery; *Still Life with Apples*, 1959; Humphreys Art Gallery, Kimberley), portraits and group scenes such as *Olive Pickers* (1963; Irma Stern Museum) and *Bathers* (1965; Rupert Family Foundation for the Arts).

In South Africa Stern was respected and feared. Her works were still occasionally attacked by the political authorities because of her sympathetic portrayals of people of colour. This may explain why, despite her high reputation, relatively few of her works are in public collections there. She won various prizes, such as the Oppenheimer award, for the *Water Drawer* (private collection) in 1963, and above all she represented South Africa on many occasions at the Venice Biennale and other international exhibitions. Under the increasingly restrictive system of apartheid, she seemed to be a guarantor for cosmopolitan attitudes and liberality – and also apparently for official cultural and educational policy, because she did not explicitly question the thought and control structures of colonialism and paternalism. Under the changed political circumstances, Stern's contradictory attempts to move between the worlds of Europe and Africa and to produce an art that embraced all cultures met no response. However, this idea remains visible and alive in the Irma Stern Museum.

IRENE BELOW

Stettheimer, Florine

American painter, 1871–1944

Born in Rochester, New York, 29 August 1871. Studied at Art Students League, New York, 1892–5. Moved to Europe with her mother and sisters Ettie and Carrie, 1906; toured Italy, Germany, France and Switzerland; studied art in Berlin, Munich and Stuttgart, and lived in Paris; visited Esposizione Internazionale, Venice, 1909. Returned to New York, 1914. Moved to studio apartment in Beaux Arts Building after mother's death in 1935. Died in New York, 11 May 1944.

Principal Exhibitions

M. Knoedler & Co., New York: 1916 (individual)
Society of Independent Artists, New York: 1917–26
Carnegie International Exhibition, Pittsburgh: 1924
Art Institute of Chicago: 1925 (*Modern Decorative Art*, annual)
Arts Council of the City of New York: 1929 (*One Hundred Important Paintings by Living American Artists*)
American Society of Painters, Sculptors and Gravers: from 1932
Museum of Modern Art, New York: 1930 (*Three American Romantic Painters*), 1932 (*Modern Works of Art*), 1942 (*Twentieth-Century Portraits*), 1946 (retrospective)
Whitney Museum of American Art, New York: 1932 (*First Biennial Exhibition of Contemporary American Painting*)

Selected Writings

Crystal Flowers, ed. Ettie Stettheimer, New York: privately printed, 1949

Bibliography

Adolfo Best-Maugard, *A Method for Creative Design*, New York: Knopf, 1926
Florine Stettheimer, exh. cat., Museum of Modern Art, New York, 1946
Parker Tyler, *Florine Stettheimer: A Life in Art*, New York: Farrar Straus, 1963
Anthony Bower, "Florine Stettheimer", *Art in America*, lii/2, 1964, pp.88–93
Women Artists, 1550–1950, exh. cat., Los Angeles County Museum of Art, and elsewhere, 1976
Barbara Zucker, "An 'autobiography' of visual poems", *Art News*, lxxvi, February 1977, pp.68–73

Florine Stettheimer: Still Lifes, Portraits and Pageants, 1910 to 1942, exh. cat., Institute of Contemporary Art, Boston, and elsewhere, 1980

Linda Nochlin, "Florine Stettheimer: Rococo subversive", *Art in America*, lxviii, September 1980, pp.64–83

Charlotte Streifer Rubinstein, *American Women Artists from Early Times to the Present*, Boston: Hall, 1982

Donna Graves, "'In spite of alien temperature and alien insistence': Emily Dickinson and Florine Stettheimer", *Woman's Art Journal*, iii/2, 1982–3, pp.21–7

Barbara Heins, *Florine Stettheimer and the Avant-garde American Portrait*, PhD dissertation, Yale University, 1986

Susan Waller, *Women Artists in the Modern Era: A Documentary History*, Metuchen, NJ: Scarecrow Press, 1991

Eleanor Heartney, "Saints, esthetes and hustlers: Florine Stettheimer", *Art News*, xc, May 1991, pp.95–6

Jerry Saltz, "Twilight of the Gods", *Arts Magazine*, lxvi, March 1992, pp.21–2

Roberta Smith, "Very rich hours of Florine Stettheimer", *New York Times*, 10 October 1993, p.39

Barbara J. Bloemink, *The Life and Art of Florine Stettheimer*, New Haven and London: Yale University Press, 1995

Florine Stettheimer: Manhattan Fantastica, exh. cat., Whitney Museum of American Art, New York, 1995

Manuscript collection is in the Rare Books Room, Columbia University, New York.

Florine Stettheimer was an American original whose work cannot be placed into any category. Although she was academically trained, in mid-life she adopted her own unique style, rejecting almost everything she had studied or seen. The new style was deliberately naive, the figures weightless and flat, and the perspective unconventional. In lively colours, with wit and humour, she portrayed members of her own family and the New York art world.

Born into old money wealth, Florine never had to earn a living. She lived with her mother and her two elegant sisters, Carrie and Ettie. They followed intellectual and cultural pursuits, Florine studying painting and Ettie philosophy. Father seems to have long since vanished. Florine received sound academic training. At the Art Students League, she studied under Kenyon Cox and Robert Henri, painting the customary nudes, still lifes, landscapes and portraits. Admiration for John Singer Sargent influenced her portraits, and Chinese and Japanese art, her flowers. Her work was well executed but unremarkable. In Europe, she studied at academies in Berlin, Stuttgart and Munich. She also travelled extensively, becoming familiar with the Symbolist painters Klimt and Hodler, and with the Impressionists, Fauves and Nabis in Paris. Diaghilev's Ballets Russes made a great impression, and later paintings reflect its influence. She began to move away from the academic style, searching for something more personal and feminine, foreshadowed in *Spring Figure* (1907; Columbia University, New York), where Spring is personified as a young girl garlanded with flowers.

With the outbreak of World War I, the Stettheimers returned to New York. There they established a salon, which soon attracted their many friends in the art world: Marsden Hartley, Marcel Duchamp, Alfred Stieglitz, Virgil Thomson and the critic Henry McBride. Florine sketched her illustrious guests and painted from the sketches the following day; conversation pieces, she called them. She had not yet arrived at her mature style, but new themes and devices were evident.

Family Portrait No.1 (1915; Columbia University), for example, is viewed from above, the figures flattened, white pigment applied with a palette knife to heighten the colours, and open brushwork for the details.

In 1916 Stettheimer was persuaded to hold a solo exhibition at Knoedler's gallery in New York, but stipulated that she would arrange the installation. She wanted to recreate the environment in which the paintings had been completed – her own bedroom. Gallery walls were draped in white muslin, and the white and gold of her bed canopy duplicated. The show was not a success, and was largely ignored by the critics. After this disappointment, apart from some unjuried group shows, Stettheimer did not exhibit again. The failure helped to convince her to seek personal expression in her own way. With *Heat* (1918; Brooklyn Museum, NY) and *Lake Placid* (1919; Boston Museum of Fine Arts) she reached her mature style.

Growth continued in the 1920s. *Asbury Park South* (1920; Fisk University, Nashville), a study of a segregated New Jersey beach, was influenced by the Harlem Renaissance. Adolfo Best-Maugard introduced her to his aesthetic system of seven basic forms (*A Method of Creative Design*, 1926). Duchamp made her aware of Surrealism and Dada. She enjoyed folk art and began the use of unorthodox materials: gold, silver tassels, velvets, paste jewels and putty soaked with oil pigments. The portraits done in this period are lively, whimsical and reveal the essence of the sitter. Among the best are *Henry McBride* (1922; Smith College Museum of Art, Northampton, MA), *Portrait of My Mother* (1925; collection Mrs Julius Ochs Adler) and *Ettie, Carrie* and *Portrait of Myself* (all 1923; Columbia University). *Family Portrait No.2* (1933; Museum of Modern Art, New York) shows the family in their New York apartment, with Florine's personal motif of flowers climaxed by a huge, three-part bouquet and a selective panorama of Manhattan outside. Other pictures from this period show feminine themes, *Spring Sale at Bendels* (1922; Philadelphia Museum of Art) and *Beauty Contest* (1924; Wadsworth Atheneum, Hartford, CT). In 1934 Virgil Thomson persuaded Stettheimer to design the costumes, sets and lighting for an opera he had composed with a libretto by Gertrude Stein, *Four Saints in Three Acts*. The black singers were drenched in white light, and the costumes of brilliant colours were fashioned out of cellophane, seashells, feathers and lace. Both opera and set met with critical acclaim on Broadway, and Stettheimer, greatly encouraged, used some of the ideas in later paintings.

Stettheimer's most important works are the four "cathedral" paintings, *Cathedral of Broadway* (c.1929), *Cathedral of Fifth Avenue* (c.1931), *Cathedral of Wall Street* (c.1939) and *Cathedral of Art* (c.1942; all Metropolitan Museum of Art), left unfinished at her death. Each celebrates and satirises some aspect of the New York social and cultural scene. They are packed with action, peopled by her family and friends and mix reality with fantasy. *Cathedral of Fifth Avenue* features a society wedding, the marriage of money and power; the Rolls-Royce has a dollar sign on its grill, and Tiffany's name blazes in the sky. In *Cathedral of Wall Street*, a surprised George Washington finds himself with Rockefeller, the Roosevelts, the American eagle and the Salvation Army. *Cathedral of Art* (see illustration) shows the power-brokers of the art world with the paintings, artists and admiring public. The scene of action is the grand staircase of the Metropolitan Museum. Baby Art is

Stettheimer: *Cathedral of Art*, c.1942; unfinished; oil on canvas; Metropolitan Museum of Art, New York; Gift of Ettie Stettheimer, 1953

in the foreground; portraits walk out of their frames, dealers clutch their wares, critics give the go-ahead and avid photographers swarm around. Stettheimer was part of these worlds, and she admired and criticised them all.

After her mother's death in 1935, Stettheimer moved into the Beaux Arts studios at Bryant Park. There she continued her salon, fusing life and art, and working on her cathedrals until her death. Art dealers were beginning to be interested in her, but it was too late. Florine Stettheimer was a free and ultra-feminine spirit who loved and satirised a small privileged society in New York, and its cultural and economic institutions. Her decorative, *faux-naïf* style with its radiant colour and light and feminist themes were not appreciated during her lifetime, but a memorial exhibit of her paintings was held at the Museum of Modern Art in 1946. Her poems, not meant for publication, were collected by Ettie and published under the title *Crystal Flowers* (1949). Her paintings are now in many museums and there is a resurgence of interest in her.

PATRICIA BRAUCH

Stevens, May

American painter, 1924–

Born in Quincy, near Boston, Massachusetts, 9 June 1924. Studied at Massachusetts College of Art, Boston (BFA 1946); Art Students League, New York, 1948; Académie Julian, Paris, 1948–9. Married painter Rudolf Baranik, 1948; son born 1948 (d. 1981). Taught at School of Visual Arts, New York, from 1961 (faculty member 1964); visiting artist, Syracuse University, New York, 1975; Rhode Island School of Design, Providence, 1977; Oberlin College, Ohio, 1988; distinguished visiting professor, California State University, Long Beach, 1990; faculty member, Skowhegan School of Painting and Sculpture, Maine, 1992. Co-founder of the feminist journal *Heresies*, New York, 1976. Recipient of Childe Hassam purchase awards, National Institute of Arts and Letters, 1968, 1969 and 1975; Creative Artists Public Service (CAPS) grant, New York State Council for the Arts, 1974; National Endowment for the Arts (NEA) grant, 1983; Guggenheim fellowship, 1986; Lifetime Achievement award, Women's Caucus for the Arts, 1990. Member, College Art Association. Lives in New York.

Selected Individual Exhibitions

Galerie Huit, Paris: 1951
ACA Gallery, New York: 1957
Roko Gallery, New York: 1963 (*Freedom Riders*, touring), 1968
Herbert F. Johnson Museum, Cornell University, Ithaca, NY: 1973
Douglass College, New Brunswick, NJ: 1974
SoHo 20, New York: 1974
Lerner-Heller Gallery, New York: 1975, 1976, 1978, 1981
Everson Museum, Syracuse, NY: 1976 (*Three American Realists*, with Alice Neel and Sylvia Sleigh)
Boston University Art Gallery: 1984–5 (*Ordinary, Extraordinary: A Summation, 1977–1984*, touring)
New Museum of Contemporary Art, New York: 1988
Orchard Gallery, Derry, Northern Ireland: 1988
Olin Gallery, Kenyon College, Gambier, OH: 1988
Herter Gallery, University of Massachusetts, Amherst: 1991
Colorado University Art Galleries, Boulder: 1993
Exit Art Gallery, New York: 1994 (*In Words*, with Rudolf Baranik)
Mary Ryan Gallery, New York: 1996

Selected Writings

Ordinary, Extraordinary, New York: privately printed, 1980
In Words, New York: privately printed, 1994 (with Rudolf Baranik)

Bibliography

Cindy Nemser, "Conversations with May Stevens", *Feminist Art Journal*, iii, Winter 1974–5, pp.4–7
Lucy R. Lippard, *From the Center: Feminist Essays on Women's Art*, New York: Dutton, 1976
Moira Roth, "Visions and re-visions: Rosa Luxemburg and the artist's mother", *Artforum*, xix, November 1980, pp.36–9; reprinted in Boston 1984
Lisa Tickner, "May Stevens", *Block*, no.5, 1981, pp.28–33; reprinted in Boston 1984 and *The Block Reader in Visual Culture*, London and New York: Routledge, 1996
May Stevens: Ordinary, Extraordinary: A Summation, 1977–1984, exh. cat., Boston University Art Gallery, and elsewhere, 1984
Hilary Robinson, ed., *Visibly Female: Feminism and Art: An Anthology*, London: Camden, 1987; New York: Universe, 1988
Patricia Mathews, "A dialogue of silence: May Stevens' *Ordinary, Extraordinary*, 1977–1986", *Art Criticism*, iii, Fall 1987, pp.34–42
Josephine Withers, "Revisioning our foremothers: Reflections on the Ordinary, Extraordinary art of May Stevens", *Feminist Studies*, xiii, Fall 1987, pp.485–512
May Stevens: One Plus or Minus One, exh. cat., Orchard Gallery, Derry, 1988
Rosa, Alice: Ordinary – Extraordinary, exh. cat., Olin Gallery, Kenyon College, Gambier, OH, 1988
Carol Jacobsen, "Two lives: Ordinary/Extraordinary", *Art in America*, lxxvii, February 1989, pp.152–7, 183, 185
Lois Tarlow, "Profile: May Stevens", *Art New England*, xii, February 1991, pp.7–9
May Stevens, exh. cat., Colorado University Art Galleries, Boulder, 1993
Norma Broude and Mary D. Garrard, eds, *The Power of Feminist Art: The American Movement of the 1970s*, New York: Abrams, and London: Thames and Hudson, 1994
Mara R. Witzling, ed., *Voicing Today's Visions: Writings by Contemporary Women Artists*, New York: Universe, 1994
Patricia Hills, "May Stevens: Painting history as lived, feminist experience", *Redefining American History Painting*, ed. Patricia M. Burnham and Lucretia Hoover Giese, New York and Cambridge: Cambridge University Press, 1995, pp.310–30, 383–7

May Stevens has held a central position within the New York art scene of activist artists since the early 1960s. Her career trajectory touches down on many of the art-and-politics events of the past three decades. In 1966 she, with Rudolf Baranik, Leon Golub, Nancy Spero (q.v.), Denise Levertov, Mitchell Goodman and Irving Petlin, organised Artists and Writers Protest Against the War in Vietnam, which in 1967 sponsored an "Angry Arts Week" – one of the earliest artists' organised protests against American involvement in the Vietnam War. In 1967 she contributed to the *Collage of Indignation* exhibition at the Loeb Student Center at New York University. She became active in feminist circles in the early 1970s, and in 1976 joined a group of New York women to found *Heresies*, a collaborative publishing venture. During 1992 and 1993 she was active in WAC – Women's Action Coalition.

Throughout her career her activist social concerns as well as her own working-class background have influenced her

Stevens: *Mysteries and Politics*, 1978; acrylic on canvas; 198.1 × 365.8 cm.; the figures represented, clockwise from bottom left, are: Betsy Damon as the Seven-Thousand-Year-Old Woman, Pat Steir, Mary Beth Edelson as the Great Goddess, Alice Stevens holding her first child, Poppy Johnson holding her twins Mira and Bran, Carol Duncan, Patricia Hills pregnant with Andrew Whitfield, May Stevens with her back turned, Suzanne Harris seated in front of the large head of Rosa Luxemburg, Amy Sillman and Elizabeth Weatherford standing on the right, and Joan Snyder, pregnant with Molly Fink, seated on a folding chair; Collection of San Francisco Museum of Modern Art

figurative work. In the 1960s she painted works inspired by the "Freedom Riders" – the northern Civil Rights workers who went to the South to work on voter registration campaigns; Martin Luther King, Jr wrote a foreword to the catalogue of a touring exhibition of her *Freedom Riders* paintings, which opened at the Roko Gallery in New York in 1963. In the late 1960s, as the Vietnam War escalated, she created for her paintings "Big Daddy", an iconic image of American racism and militarism. Although originally based on her own, working-class father, the figure – a middle-aged, spectacled, faintly grinning and balding male, often nude and often seated with a bulldog cradled in his lap – grew into a universalised figure, authoritarian, patriarchal. For the *Big Daddy* series she used a flat, poster style, painting in either acrylic on canvas or gouache on paper, with red, white and cobalt blue predominating, as in *Big Daddy Paper Doll* (1970; acrylic on canvas; Brooklyn Museum, NY).

By the mid-1970s the "Big Daddy" figure gave way to three large paintings (all acrylic on canvas, 182 × 304 cm.) on the theme of the artist in her studio: *Artist's Studio (After Courbet)* (1975; private collection, St Louis), *SoHo Women Artists* (1977–8; National Museum of Women in the Arts, Washington, DC) and *Mysteries and Politics* (1978; see illustration). Working out her ideas in these three works and their studies, she realised that she was not only drawing on the tradition of group portraiture (as Rembrandt and Courbet had

done before) but infusing that tradition with the history of which she had become a part, that of contemporary feminists attempting to integrate the demands of family, radical politics and artistic creativity (Hills 1995, p.310). The flat poster style gave way to a more subtle and nuanced chiaroscuro combined with an aesthetic of montage.

In 1976 she embarked on another series, one that grew out of the images she used for two montages published as a two-page spread in the feminist journal *Heresies*, pairing the Polish Communist Rosa Luxemburg, who with Karl Liebknecht had founded the German Communist Party in 1918, with her own mother Alice Stevens, a working-class housewife from Quincy, Massachusetts. Through a dozen small mixed-media works and many large paintings, known as the *Ordinary/Extraordinary* series, she contrasted the lives of her mother (then living in a nursing home outside Boston) and her Communist heroine. The theme of her mother and Luxemburg provided the issues for Stevens to explore the implications of the social constructions of gender and class. Recalling this series, she wrote in September 1995:

> I asked myself what was the reach possible to a woman of that time and class. What avenues could she walk? What doors open? What thoughts think? What actions take? Blocked, where could she turn?
>
> The politics of women's lives in any given historical period: Could this woman have been more than she was?

Is it possible to understand what/who she was? How she felt? Was sexuality open to her? Did she choose the life she lived? Did she wish to alter it? Was she able to make changes?

Immigrants both living in a world not ready for them. Each was out of place. Each was killed for not fitting in. Alice's world made her gentle, defenseless. Rosa's world made her powerful, then punished her for moving toward the fulfillment of that power. Alice's world destroyed her gentleness, that was not malleable, could not toughen.

Rosa Luxemburg and Alice Stevens, workers both, frustrated as lovers and mothers; one fulfilled as thinker, fighter, leader; the other here fulfilled in this tribute, as mother [letter to author, 10 September 1995].

Stevens transformed the two figures into universal symbols: Alice Stevens's oblivion represents the fate of many working-class women who stifle their own intellectual interests and sink into the tedium of housekeeping. In *Go Gentle* (1983; acrylic on canvas; Museum of Fine Arts, Boston) earlier flat, photographic images of a girl, and then a woman, who might have had the potential to shape her life, contrast with a heavy-set, richly painted image of an older Alice, confused even by the most quotidian routines. By contrast *Procession* (1983; acrylic on canvas; Metropolitan Museum of Art, New York) represents a demonstration of people marching on the anniversary of Luxemburg's and Leibknecht's deaths. The reproduction of Luxemburg's face, on a placard held high by one of the marchers, dominates the scene and proclaims that Luxemburg, after death, had grown into an international heroine.

In a series of collages and small paintings done in the late 1980s Stevens drew on the imagery of a photographic project done by her son, Steven Baranik, who died in the early 1980s. That imagery was of burning horses (actually toy plastic horses that melted as they burned and which Stevens's husband, Rudolf Baranik, had also explored in his art) and symbolised the nature of representation – with elusive images of memories disappearing into the recesses of abstraction, of colour and of shadow.

In the early 1990s Stevens increasingly incorporated words into her paintings. Earlier, in *Voices* (1983; acrylic on canvas; artist's collection) from the *Ordinary/Extraordinary* series, Stevens had included layers of words spread across the canvas in the space above the coffins of Luxemburg and Leibknecht carried along during the martyrs' funeral procession; the words were those of Luxemburg. With *Sea of Words* (1991; acrylic on canvas; artist's collection) four small rowing boats with figures float across a sea of words excerpted from the writings of Virginia Woolf and Julia Kristeva. Subsequent paintings focused on young prostitutes walking the streets, women prisoners exercising in a yard or women scullers on a river. In all of these Stevens uses a limited palette of gold, silver, black, blue and green, as she merges words and elusive figures. Thus, Stevens maintains a political consciousness through oblique and subtle imagery that evokes both personal and collective memories.

PATRICIA HILLS

Stillman, Mrs W. J. *see* Spartali

Stoddart, Margaret Olrog
New Zealand painter, 1865–1934

Born in Diamond Harbour, Canterbury, New Zealand, 3 October 1865. Studied intermittently at Canterbury College School of Art, Christchurch, 1882–90. Visited Australia, 1894. Lived in Europe, 1898–1906; studied in Britain and France under Norman Garstin, Louis Grier and Charles Lasal. Lived with her mother and sisters after return to New Zealand in 1906. Visited Australia and Tahiti, 1924(?). Member of National Art Association of New Zealand and Christchurch Women's Club; Vice-president, Canterbury Society of Arts and Society for Imperial Culture. Died in Hanmer, 10 December 1934.

Principal Exhibitions
Canterbury Society of Arts, Christchurch: occasionally 1883–1934 (annuals), 1928 (retrospective)
James Peele's studio, Melbourne: 1894 (individual)
Royal Birmingham Society of Artists: 1898–9
Royal Institute of Painters in Watercolour, London: 1899
Royal Society of British Artists, London: 1899–1900
Paris Salon: 1902–4, 1909–10, 1912–14, 1923, 1925–8, 1930
Baillie Gallery, London: 1902, 1906
Société Nationale des Beaux-Arts, Paris: 1905–6
Royal Academy, London: 1906
Society of Women Artists, London: 1906

Bibliography
The Argus (Melbourne), 21 August 1894, p.5
"Art and artists", *Sunday Times* (London), 12 October 1902, p.6
"Art in Europe", *Press* (Christchurch), 11 February 1907, p.8
Sydney Lough Thompson and James Shelley, "Miss M.O. Stoddart", *Art in New Zealand*, viii/2, December 1935, pp.99–101
E.H. McCormick, *Letters and Art in New Zealand*, Wellington: Department of Internal Affairs, 1940
Barbara Harper, *Petticoat Pioneers: South Island Women of the Colonial Era*, Wellington: Reed, 1980
Julie King, "Margaret Stoddart: Landscapes of a Canterbury flower painter", *Art New Zealand*, no.31, 1984, pp.46–9
Anne Kirker, *New Zealand Women Artists: A Survey of 150 Years*, 2nd edition, Tortola, BVI: Craftsman House, 1993
Marion Whybrow, *St Ives, 1883–1993: Portrait of an Art Colony*, Woodbridge, Suffolk: Antique Collectors' Club, 1994

Margaret Stoddart belonged to the first generation of artists born in New Zealand and, by establishing herself as a professional painter, contributed to the advancement of women's participation in art in the late 19th and early 20th centuries. She was fortunate to belong to an enterprising and educated family who supported her ambitions, and to grow up when art institutions were in place in the colony. Her early development was shaped by women's artistic culture, and it was as a botanical and flower painter that she gained a reputation in the 1880s and 1890s. Her interest in plein-air painting was stimulated by the arrival in 1889 of James McLachlan Nairn, an artist from the Glasgow School, and in 1894 by a visit to Australia, where she was introduced to the work of the Heidelberg School. In 1906 Stoddart returned home from her

Stoddart: *In the Mackenzie Country*, 1930; Robert McDougall Art Gallery, Christchurch, New Zealand

sojourn in Europe with a new interest in landscape. While she continued to exhibit flower painting with great success, it was also as a landscapist in Impressionist and regional painting that she made her contribution to art in New Zealand.

Stoddart inherited a privileged position in society and a keen interest in natural history and the arts. After attending the Canterbury College School of Art she made a determined effort to establish herself as an artist and exhibited regularly throughout the colony. In 1894, with the influential support of the Australian flower painter Ellis Rowan, she held a successful exhibition in Melbourne. Her painting of native plants and wildflowers was situated within a widespread interest in the Victorian period in botanical discovery, and her search for specimens took her on expeditions to the New Zealand Alps and in 1886 and 1891 to the Chatham Islands. More concerned with artistic effect than botanical correctness, Stoddart progressed from traditional watercolour techniques and carefully drawn detail to free brushwork, opaque paints and bold, close-up compositions. From the 1890s she specialised in arrangements of garden flowers set against a plain background, seen in *Primroses and Apple Blossom* (1891; University of Canterbury, Christchurch). Although her compositions remained unchanged, she developed an increasingly fluent treatment of media and captured a range of impressionist and decorative effects, as in *Roses (White)* (1924; Museum of New Zealand, Te Papa Tongarewa, Wellington).

In 1898 Stoddart arrived in Europe, travelling to Norway (where her mother's family lived) and along established sketching routes through France, Switzerland and Italy. During her time away, she studied with Norman Garstin, Louis Grier and Charles Lasal. Like her contemporaries, Frances Hodgkins (q.v.) and Dorothy Kate Richmond, she spent time in Cornwall and the three women met there in 1902. Based at St Ives, an artists' colony and a centre for English Impressionism, Stoddart concentrated on landscape painting and experimented with various watercolour techniques. A review, possibly by Frank Rutter, of an exhibition at the Baillie Gallery in 1902, compared her work to that of Robert Allan and E.A. Waterlow, promising that she needed only to add "... the

impressionism of Arthur Melville to go very far indeed, and in her best work there is promise that these further achievements are within her essential gifts" (*Sunday Times*, 12 October 1902, p.6). Her accomplished technique is seen in *Spring Blossom (A Cornish Orchard)* (1906; Dunedin Public Art Gallery), where she exploited watercolour for its painterly and expressive effects, using wet washes, varied brushwork and enlivening the surface with light splashes of white gouache. She showed widely during her nine years away, and before leaving England in 1906 exhibited 39 works at the Baillie Gallery and had a painting accepted at the Royal Academy. This constituted success viewed from New Zealand at this time.

The immediate results of working abroad were seen in Stoddart's expressive technique and in the selection of Impressionist themes, including gardens, spring blossom and autumnal change. In *Old Homestead, Diamond Harbour* (1913; Robert McDougall Art Gallery, Christchurch) she used a variety of brushwork to suggest the luxuriant natural growth overtaking a pioneer cottage. Her practice as a flower painter gave her an appreciation of the connection between plants and places, which had a special bearing on the representation of her surroundings. Stoddart practised what might be termed a feminised landscape, in which she expressed her apprehension at the vividness and variety of nature in a rapidly changing environment. From the 1920s she concentrated on the native landscape and gained a significant place in regional painting for her representation of the vegetation and distinctive characteristics of Canterbury and the South Island – scrub, tussock, mountain and plains (*In the Mackenzie Country*, 1930; see illustration). Her flower painting had enormous popular appeal throughout her life, and in 1940, six years after her death, E.H. McCormick observed: "Miss Stoddart's roses have become part of the tradition of New Zealand painting ..." (McCormick 1940, p.159).

JULIE KING

Stokes, Marianne
Austrian painter, 1855–1927

Born Marianne Preindlsberger in Graz in the region of Styria, South Austria, 1855. Studied at the Graz Academy, then Munich Academy under Professor von Lindschmidt. In Paris by 1880; won silver medal, Académie Colarossi, 1882; also studied under Paul Colin, Gustave Courtois and Dagnan-Bouveret. Subsequently worked in Concarneau, Brittany, influenced by Bastien-Lepage and met painter Adrian Stokes. Married Stokes and moved to Britain, 1884; lived in St Ives, Cornwall, for several years from 1887, also retaining a London address; travelled widely, including trips to Pont-Aven, Brittany, 1885; Paris, 1885–6; artists' colony in Skagen, Denmark; Italy, 1891; Austria, 1891 and 1913–14; the Netherlands, 1899–1900; Hungary, c.1905–9. Associate member, Royal Society of Painters in Watercolour, 1887; Society of Women Artists, 1887; Royal Watercolour Society, 1923; member, New English Art Club, 1887; Society of Painters in Tempera, 1905. Died in London, 13 August 1927.

Principal Exhibitions

Paris Salon: 1884 (honourable mention)
Royal Academy, London: occasionally 1884–1926
Liverpool Autumn Exhibition: occasionally 1886–1927
New English Art Club, London: from 1888
Grosvenor Gallery, London: 1889–90
Dowdeswell Gallery, London: 1891 (with Newlyn School)
Woman's Building, World's Columbian Exposition, Chicago: 1893
  (medal)
New Gallery, London: from 1896
Fine Art Society, London: 1900 (*Dutch Life and Landscape*, with
  Adrian Stokes)
Leicester Galleries, London: 1907 (with Adrian Stokes)
Lanham's Gallery, London: 1927 (*St Ives Artists*)

Bibliography

Maud Howe Elliott, ed., *Art and Handicraft in the Woman's Building
  of the World's Columbian Exposition, Chicago, 1893*, Chicago:
  Rand McNally, 1893
Helene L. Postlethwaite, "Some noted women painters", *Magazine of
  Art*, 1895, pp.17–22
Harriet Ford, "The work of Mrs Adrian Stokes", *The Studio*, xix,
  1900, pp.149–56
Wilfrid Meynell, "Mr and Mrs Adrian Stokes", *Art Journal*, 1900,
  pp.193–8
Alice Meynell, "Mrs Adrian Stokes", *Magazine of Art*, 1901,
  pp.241–6
Aymer Vallance, "The revival of tempera painting", *The Studio*, xxiii,
  1901, p.155
Walter Shaw Sparrow, *Women Painters of the World*, London:
  Hodder and Stoughton, and New York: Stokes, 1905; reprinted
  New York: Hacker, 1976
Adrian Stokes, *Hungary*, London: A. & C. Black, 1909 (illustrations
  by Marianne and Adrian Stokes)
Connoisseur, lxxix, 1927, p.127 (obituary)
Jeanne Madeline Weimann, *The Fair Women*, Chicago: Academy,
  1981
Magdalen Evans, *Marianne Stokes*, thesis, 1987, Walker Art Gallery
  archives, Liverpool
Pamela Gerrish Nunn, *Victorian Women Artists*, London: Women's
  Press, 1987
Jane Sellars, *Women's Works: Paintings, Drawings, Prints and
  Sculpture by Women*, Liverpool: National Museums and Galleries
  on Merseyside, 1988
*The Last Romantics: The Romantic Tradition in British Art: Burne-
  Jones to Stanley Spencer*, exh. cat., Barbican Art Gallery, London,
  1989
Deborah Cherry, *Painting Women: Victorian Women Artists*, London
  and New York: Routledge, 1993

Marianne Stokes was a prolific and hard-working painter, an Austrian who based herself in England after her marriage to the British artist Adrian Stokes in 1884. Although she engaged closely with English artistic circles, Stokes's art was much influenced by the many working visits she made to other European countries throughout her life. She was a painter in oils, tempera and watercolour, of religious subjects, medieval legend, fairy tales, portraits and especially pictures of children. In common with many accomplished female painters of children, for example Mary Cassatt (q.v.), Stokes had no children of her own. Her first success, which won an honourable mention at the Paris Salon in 1884, was *A Parting* (1884; 59 × 79.3 cm.; Walker Art Gallery, Liverpool), a touching study of a child bidding farewell to a trussed calf, ready for despatch to the market. This picture is painted with thick, buttery, square-brushed strokes of oil paint, displaying a

Stokes: *Candlemas Day*, 1901; Tate Gallery, London

rendition of the effects of light she learned from working in the open air alongside other artists drawn to the cool, clear natural light of Pont-Aven in Brittany, where Marianne Preindlsberger went after studying in Munich and Paris and where she met her future husband, the artist Adrian Stokes.

After they left France, the couple migrated from one artists' colony to another, keeping a studio in St Ives in Cornwall as well as a London address. In St Ives in the 1880s it was the bond of the French influence, especially of Bastien-Lepage, that drew artists such as Elizabeth Adela Forbes (q.v.) and Alexander Stanhope Forbes, George Clausen, Henry La Thangue and T.C. Gotch together. *Polishing Pans* (1888; 59 × 79.3 cm.; Walker Art Gallery), Stokes's first exhibited work at the New English Art Club, simultaneously a sensitive portrayal of childhood and a masterly study of reflected light, is painted in the manner of the St Ives and Newlyn schools. From the beginning of the 1890s, however, Stokes's style and subject matter changed significantly. The artist's devout Catholicism, her love of the rituals of the Church and a feeling for religious mysticism, combined with her discovery of the Italian Primitives on a first visit to Italy in 1891, turned her towards religious subjects. At about the same time she read Christine Herringham's translation of Cennino Cennini's treatise on painting, in which the description of the process of tempera painting caused her eventually to make the break from oil paint. Her work moved towards the simplicity and purity of early Italian art with her adoption of a decorative manner and handling of paint.

The quintessential Stokes image is of a serene female figure with bowed head, generally engrossed in an attitude of prayer whether the subject is religious or secular, as in *Candlemas Day* (1901; see illustration). The usually rural settings for her figures eschew any connection with contemporary life, drawing on Stokes's first-hand studies of peasant communities, particularly in the Tyrol and in the Netherlands, and her knowledge of Italian art. The interest in light that preoccupied the artist in Brittany and in Cornwall remained throughout her life, but she moved away from a concern with natural light and its effects towards a more symbolist approach. In her paintings of the 1890s, for example, *Light of Lights* (exh. Grosvenor Gallery 1890), *Hail Mary* (1891), which won a medal at the World's Columbian Exposition in Chicago, and *Angels Entertaining the Holy Child* (1893; 160 × 175 cm.; Pyms Gallery, London), all oil on canvas, Stokes first sought to portray the effect of the aureole of holiness surrounding her figures, yet retaining much of her academic-realist style.

From the late 1890s, as her tempera technique developed, Stokes's work became idiomatically primitive. Painting in tempera is an exacting discipline – Stokes herself remarked that "An impatient nature will never find its best medium in tempera" (Vallance 1901) – and the artist was universally admired for her mastery of it. Walter Shaw Sparrow wrote: "Mrs Marianne Stokes is made of sterner stuff. She has worked of late in the most stern and stubborn medium, tempera, and small things of hers in various exhibitions attract one always with the desire to know more of her attractive work" (Sparrow 1905, p.72).

Medieval romantic subjects began to feature in her work, such as *The Page* (exh. New Gallery 1896; tempera; 101.6 × 96.5 cm.; private collection), a subject inspired by lines from a poem by Heinrich Heine. The poet and art critic Wilfrid Meynell admired the lady in the picture for her "clear, round-browed Piero della Francesca profile, with delicately hollow eyes, expressive of some threat of evil destiny" (Meynell 1900, p.198) and Harriet Ford described how "each line in the Queen and the Page carries its full force of spiritual significance" (Ford 1900, p.156). From Malory, a familiar Pre-Raphaelite source, Stokes took the story of *Aucassin and Nicolette* (exh. New Gallery and Liverpool 1898); from Tennyson's *Idylls of the King*, *Tristram's Death* (1902); and, inspired by Maeterlinck's play *Pelléas et Mélisande*, she painted the mournful figure of *Melisande* (1903; tempera; private collection) sitting by a stream. Clearly, there is a debt to Pre-Raphaelitism in this choice of medieval theme, jewel-like colour and sharply drawn detail, and also to the *fin-de-siècle* Victorian passion for chivalric tales. The move away from the modernist interest in painterly texture and natural light towards a medieval romantic subject matter and a Pre-Raphaelite style of execution is the most extraordinary feature of Stokes's art. Hence her inclusion in the exhibition *The Last Romantics* at the Barbican Art Gallery (1989), alongside second-generation Pre-Raphaelite disciples of Burne-Jones and the Slade School Symbolists, such as Augustus John and Stanley Spencer.

Stokes also made occasional forays into the kind of subject matter favoured by the Belgian Symbolists, such as Fernand Khnopff, Xavier Mellery and Emile Fabry, as in *Death and the Maiden* (1908; Musée d'Orsay, Paris). When she was in her mid-forties, a childhood influence from German culture returned to absorb Stokes's work, and from 1900 to 1915 she painted a series of uncommissioned works illustrating the Grimms' *Fairy Tales*, including *Jug of Tears* (exh. New Gallery 1901; tempera), *Princess on the Glass Mountain* (exh. Royal Academy 1914) and *Little Brother, Little Sister* (exh. Fine Art Society 1900; all untraced). This last picture was executed in *gesso grosso*, a technique Stokes discovered around this time, which has the appearance of fresco painting on a rough plaster wall. It was shown at a joint exhibition with her husband entitled *Dutch Life and Landscape*, the fruits of their labours during visits to the Netherlands. While Adrian Stokes concentrated on the landscape, Marianne's pictures were largely depictions of young girls in Dutch peasant costume, such as *A Council* and *The Accident*. Travels around Hungary also led to joint projects – an exhibition at the Leicester Galleries in 1907 and a book written by Adrian Stokes with illustrations by husband and wife (1909), again showing Marianne's interest in the traditional costumes of women and children, and in the religious rituals of the place.

Marianne Stokes's obituary in the *Connoisseur* (1927) described her as an artist who

... specialised in figure and fancy subjects, which she depicted with both refinement and charm. Generally, her work was permeated with a poetic feeling that testified no less to her imaginative faculty than did her technique to her sensitive skill as a painter.

JANE SELLARS

Stölzl, Gunta

German weaver and textile designer, 1897–1983

Born in Munich, 5 March 1897. Studied ceramics and decorative and glass painting at the Kunstgewerbeschule, Munich, 1914–16; worked as a Red Cross nurse, 1916–18; resumed studies at the Kunstgewerbeschule, 1919. Student at Bauhaus, Weimar, 1919–25 (journeyman's diploma 1922); assisted Johannes Itten in establishing Ontos Weaving Workshop near Zürich, 1925. Appointed technical director, 1925, and junior master, 1927, Weaving Workshop, Bauhaus, Dessau. Participated in 13 Bauhaus-related national and international group exhibitions, 1922–31. Married Palestinian architect Arieh Sharon, losing German citizenship, 1929; daughter born 1929; divorced 1936. Forced to resign post as director of Weaving Workshop, 1931. Established S-P-H Stoffe, a handweaving studio (with Gertrud Preiswerk and Heinrich-Otto Hürlimann) in Zürich, 1931; closed 1933. Joined Swiss Werkbund, 1932. Founded S+H Stoffe with Hürlimann, 1935. Established Handweberei (Handweaving Studio) Flora and joined Gesellschaft Schweizer Malerinnen, Bildhauerinnen und Kunstgewerblerinnen (Society of Swiss Women Painters, Sculptors and Craftsmen), 1937. Participated in interior scheme design of Swiss Pavilion, Lyon, 1941. Married Willy Stadler and acquired Swiss citizenship, 1942; daughter born 1943. Dissolved handweaving business and executed only tapestries after c.1967. Weavings purchased by Museum of Modern Art, New York, and Busch-Reisinger Museum, Cambridge, Massachusetts, 1949–63; fabrics and designs purchased by Victoria and

Albert Museum, London, 1967–9. Died in Zürich, 22 April 1983.

Selected Individual Exhibitions
Lyzeumclub, Zürich: 1970
Paulus-Akademie, Zürich: 1971, 1980
Bauhaus-Archiv, Berlin: 1976, 1987 (touring retrospective)

Selected Writings
"Weberei am Bauhaus", *Buch- und Weberkunst*, no.7, 1926, p.405
"Die Entwicklung der Bauhausweberei", *Bauhaus-Zeitschrift für Bau und Gestaltung*, no.2, July 1931
"Textilien im Innenraum", *Schweizer Monatszeitschrift für Architektur, Kunst und künstlerisches Gewerbe*, 1936, p.379
"Abschied von Klee", *Werk*, no.9, 1940
Text in *Über die Bauhaus-Weberei*, exh. cat., Goppinger-Galerie, Frankfurt am Main, 1964, p.110
"In der Textilwerkstatt des Bauhauses 1919 bis 1931", *Werk*, lv, 1968, pp.744–8
"Fünf Jahre Bauhaus: Grundlage für eine fünfzigjährige Freundschaft", *Benita Koch-Otte: Vom Geheimnis der Farbe*, exh. cat., Bauhaus-Archiv, Bethel and Berlin, 1972

Bibliography

Staatliches Bauhaus Weimar, 1919 bis 1923, Weimar: Bauhaus, 1923
Neue Arbeiten der Bauhauswerkstätten, no.7, Munich: Albert Langen, 1925
Wall Hangings, 2 vols, exh. cat., Museum of Modern Art, New York, 1969
Mildred Constantine and J.L. Larsen, *Beyond Craft: The Art Fabric*, New York: Van Nostrand Reinhold, 1973
Hans M. Wingler, *The Bauhaus: Weimar Dessau Berlin Chicago*, 3rd edition, Cambridge: Massachusetts Institute of Technology Press, 1976
Frank Whitford, *Bauhaus*, London: Thames and Hudson, 1984
Gillian Naylor, *The Bauhaus Reassessed: Sources and Design Theory*, New York: Dutton, and London: Herbert Press, 1985
La tessitura del bauhaus, 1919/1933, nelle collezioni della Repubblica Democratica Tedesca, Venice: Marsilio, 1985
The Bauhaus Weaving Workshop: Source and Influence for American Textiles, exh. cat., Philadelphia College of Textiles and Science, 1987
Gunta Stölzl: Weberei am Bauhaus und aus eigener Werkstatt, Bauhaus Archiv, Berlin: Kupfergraben, 1987
Bauhaus: Masters and Students, exh. cat., Barry Friedman, New York, 1988
Magdalena Droste, *Bauhaus, 1919–1933*, Bauhaus Archiv, Cologne: Taschen, 1990
Eckhard Neumann, ed., *Bauhaus and Bauhaus People*, New York: Van Nostrand Reinhold, and London: Chapman and Hall, 1993
Sigrid Wortmann Weltge, *Bauhaus Textiles: Women Artists and the Weaving Workshop*, London: Thames and Hudson, 1993; as *Women's Work: Textile Art from the Bauhaus*, San Francisco: Chronicle, 1993

Gunta Stölzl, the only female faculty member of the Bauhaus, was one of the foremost weavers and textile designers of the 20th century. Like other women students entering the Bauhaus in its founding year, she was attracted by the egalitarian principles stated in its manifesto. That these were at once disregarded was due to the unexpectedly large number of applicants who were directed into a separate Women's Department. Within a year, the scope of opportunity narrowed further when the Weaving Workshop became the sole repository for female students. Its development into one of the most successful workshops was due to Stölzl's leadership.

Stölzl studied decorative painting and ceramics at the Kunstgewerbeschule in Munich from 1914 to 1916. For the last two years of World War I she served as a Red Cross nurse behind the front lines, resuming her education in 1919 first in Munich and then at the Bauhaus in Weimar. Just as Walter Gropius believed that only the *Gesamtkunstwerk* (total work of art) could redeem society, so he envisaged a Bauhaus-trained design professional to be fully conversant in a craft as well as in the theories of design and art. Teachers capable of imparting such all-encompassing knowledge did not yet exist, and workshops, the corner-stone of Bauhaus education, were therefore staffed by both a form and a craft master. Since none was able to teach weaving, students were essentially left to their own devices.

A determined Stölzl, having discovered her unusual affinity for textiles, set out to master the medium. Although she was an auto-didact, her progress was remarkably quick, and the Bauhaus supported her in taking courses in weave and dye technology at a professional textile school in Krefeld. This enabled her to instruct her fellow students and assume responsibility for the workshop itself. Stölzl's early textiles convey the exuberance of experimentation encouraged by the Weimar Bauhaus (1919–25). After 1925 they reflect the institution's turn towards the unity of art and technology. This evolution, analogous to the development of the Weaving Workshop itself, is evident in her collaboration with Marcel Breuer. Breuer's *African* chair (1921; destroyed), a romantic evocation of primitive art, served as Stölzl's loom for a colourful tapestry directly woven on to its rough-hewn frame. Breuer's next chair (Bauhaus Archiv Museum für Gestaltung, Berlin), although still a one-of-a-kind object, looks decidedly modern, not least because the colours of Stölzl's interlaced straps incline towards those of De Stijl. In 1926, when Breuer's tubular steel frames aligned themselves with industrial design, Stölzl's functional covers broke equally new ground, both technically and aesthetically.

The ease with which Stölzl mastered completely divergent aspects of textile design is a hallmark of her career. One of her signature pieces, the *Slit Tapestry* (1926; Bauhaus Archiv Museum für Gestaltung), although executed in the time-honoured Gobelin technique, endowed the medium with a vibrant, contemporary pictorial language. This holds true for one of her finest Jacquard hangings *5 Chöre* (1928; see illustration), with which she proved unequivocally that the mechanism of the industrial loom can be harnessed into communicating the rhythms of colour abstraction. Designs on paper for these and other hangings are works of art in themselves and show her mastery of watercolour, gouache, collage and mixed media. Inspired by the Bauhaus painters, especially Paul Klee, who was close to the weavers, Stölzl executed exquisite works on paper throughout her career.

Stölzl passed her journeyman's examination in 1922 and became technical director of the Weaving Workshop after the Bauhaus's move to Dessau in 1925. She was appointed junior master in 1927. In addition to administrative duties she continued to teach, establish contacts with mills and set up marketing schemes. She also revised the curriculum to implement the new policy of designing for industry. Under her direction, she and other members of the Weaving Workshop developed industrial prototypes classified as structural fabrics. These

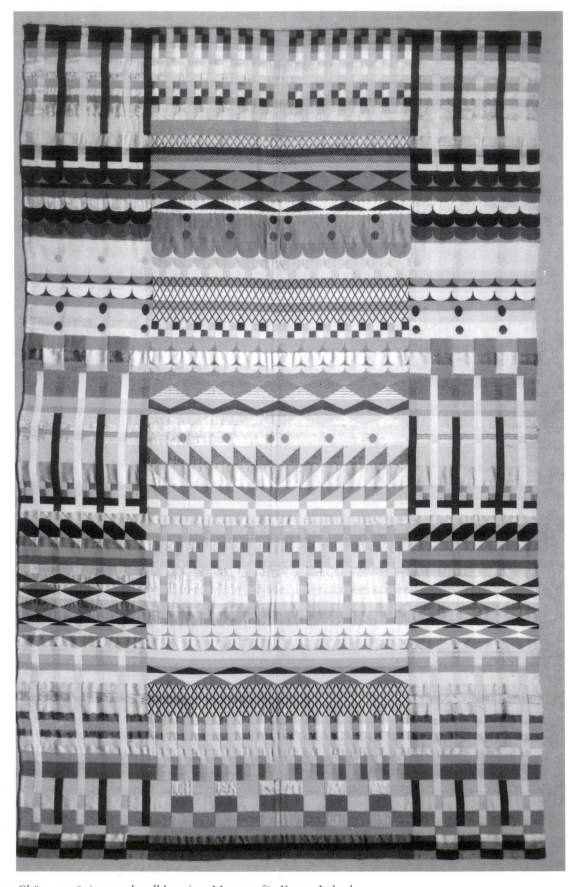

Stölzl: *5 Chöre*, 1928; jacquard wall hanging; Museum für Kunst, Lubeck

derived their visual interest not from pictorial motifs but rather from the construction of the weave and from the property of the material itself. Fabrics were designed to blend into the modern interior. As draperies they became part of the architectural scheme; as partners of new industrial products – car, train and aeroplane seats or radio covers – they integrated themselves unobtrusively. Their end use was carefully researched, taking into account easy maintenance, light and sound reflection or non-flammability. In addition, these fabrics pioneered the use of new materials such as raffia, bast and cellophane (samples in the Bauhaus-Archiv Museum für Gestaltung and the Busch-Reisinger Museum, Cambridge, MA) yet, despite their contemporary look, they were not meant as personal statements but rather as the expression of their age. The July 1931 issue of *bauhaus* magazine carried an article by Stölzl in which she eloquently described the evolution of these textiles.

After her forced resignation from the Bauhaus and emigration to Switzerland, Gunta Stölzl continued to work, often in difficult circumstances, as a hand-weaver and as a designer for industry. Her enthusiasm for weaving never abated nor did her desire to explore its myriad possibilities. As the sole woman among the Bauhaus masters, she had advanced a little-regarded workshop into becoming one of the most respected. Likewise, she never wavered in her belief that textiles should be integral to 20th-century design. The enormous influence of Bauhaus textiles world-wide, developed under her leadership, has vindicated her faith. During the last years of her life, Stölzl came full circle. After years of production weaving she turned once again to tapestry, creating hangings of great subtlety and textural beauty. Gropius's vision of the *Gesamtkunstwerk* and the ideal balance of manual and mental creativity found its perfect embodiment in Stölzl's career: she understood it, she taught it and she lived by it.

SIGRID WORTMANN WELTGE

Strauss-Likarz, Maria *see* Likarz-Strauss

Stryjeńska, Zofia

Polish painter, graphic artist and designer, 1891–1976

Born Zofia Lubańska in Kraków, 13 May 1891. Studied drawing under Celestyn Czynciel in Kraków, then attended Leonard Stroynowski's school until its closure in 1909; subsequently studied drawing, painting and decorative arts under Jan Bukowski at Maria Niedzielska's school. Left for Munich dressed as a boy and with her brother's passport, intending to apply to the Munich Academy, 1911; accepted out of 200 applicants; studied drawing under Ritter von Hacki, painting under Hugo von Habermann, anatomy under Frantz Burhard. Married (1) architect Karol Stryjeński, 1916; three children; divorced; (2) Artur Socha, an actor, 1929; marriage soon dissolved. Member of Rytm, the Institute of Fine Arts in Kraków, and Warsztaty Krakowskie and Ład, both co-operatives/societies of applied arts. Recipient of gold medal, Society

for the Encouragement of Fine Arts, Warsaw, 1921; diploma di partecipazione, Seconda Fiera Internazionale del Libro, Florence, 1925; diploma for graphic design, Nemzeti Salon, Budapest, 1926; diploma of correspondent Der Verein "Deutsche Buchkünstler", Leipzig, 1927; great gold medal, Poznań, 1929; Polonia Restituta Order, 1930; silver medal, Academy of Literature, Padua, 1932; gold academic wreath, Polish Academy of Literature, Warsaw, 1936; Alfred Jurzykowski Foundation award, New York, 1972. Légion d'Honneur, France, 1925. Died in Geneva, 28 February 1976.

Principal Exhibitions

Individual
Society for the Encouragement of Fine Arts, Warsaw: 1924, 1926
Salon Sztuki Czeslaw Garliński, Warsaw: 1924
Society of the Friends of Fine Art, Kraków: 1928
Phillips Salon, Warsaw: 1930
City Museum of Artistic Industry, Lwów: 1932
Berlin and Munich: 1935 (organised by Instytut Propagandy Sztuki)

Group
Society for the Encouragement of Fine Arts, Warsaw: 1912, 1915, 1919, 1921 (gold medal), 1923–4, 1928
Exposition Internationale des Arts Décoratifs et Industriels Modernes, Paris: 1925 (four gold medals)
Esposizione Internazionale d'Arte Sacra Cristiana Moderna, Padua: 1932 (silver medal)
Venice Biennale: 1932 (gold medal)

Selected Writings

Chleb prawieże powszedni: Pamiętnik [Nearly daily bread: The diary], ed. Maria Grońska, 2 vols, Warsaw, 1995

Bibliography

Katalog wystawy zbiorowej prac Z. Stryjeńskiej w salonach Towarzystwa Zachęty Sztuk Pięknych w Warszawie [Catalogue of the exhibition of the collective works of Z. Stryjeńska at the Salons of the Zachęta Association of Fine Arts in Warsaw], exh. cat., Warsaw, 1919
Przewodnik Towarzystwa Zachęty Sztuk Pięknych No.13, Wystawà kolekcji prac Stryjeńskiej Zofii [A guide to the Zachęta Association of Fine Arts, no.13, exhibitions of the collection of works of Zofia Stryjeńska], exh. cat., Warsaw, 1926
Artur Shroeder, "Zofia Stryjeńska: Z okazji wystawy w krakowskim Pałacu Sztuki" [Zofia Stryjeńska: On the occasion of the exhibition in the Kraków Palace of Art], *Sztuki Piękne*, 1927–8, pp.161–72
Mieczyslaw Wallis, "Zofia Stryjeńska jako ilustratorka" [Zofia Stryjeńska as an illustrator], *ibid.*, pp.172–87
Thadee Seweryn and others, *The Polish Peasants' Costumes*, Nice: Szwedzicki, 1939
Eugene Kusielewicz, *Treasured Polish Christmas Customs and Traditions: Carols, Decorations and a Christmas Play*, 3rd edition, Minneapolis, 1974
Alicja Okońska, *Malarki polskie* [Polish women painters], Warsaw, 1976
Dorota Suchocka, "O sukcesie Zofii Stryjeńskiej" [Zofia Stryjeńska's success], *Biuletyn Historii Sztuki*, xliii, 1981, pp.411–36 (with French summary)
Irene Huml, *Polska sztuka stosowana XX wieku* [Polish applied art of the 20th century], Warsaw, 1987
Artystki polskie [Polish women artists], exh. cat., National Museum, Warsaw, 1991
Maria Grońska, *Zofia Stryjeńska*, Wrocław: Zakład Narodowy im Ossolińskich, 1991 (with English summary)

Polish Women Artists and the Avant-Garde: Voices of Freedom, exh. cat., National Museum of Women in the Arts, Washington, DC, 1991

Maria Grońska, *Grafika w książce, tece i albumie* [Graphic art in book, portfolio and sketchbook], Warsaw, 1994

Słownik biograficzny teatru polskiego [Biographical dictionary of the Polish theatre], ii, Warsaw, 1994

Zofia Stryjeńska's artistic personality was formed in Kraków, where Młoda Polska (Young Poland) was most active. It is believed that she was influenced by Stanisław Wyspianski, a prominent member of the movement, who idealised the Lech, or early Slavonic traditions of Poland, and considered that the peasant class represented the Polish nation in its purity. His work was known for its flat areas of colour, the influence of Japanese art and for the use of Art Nouveau line. Although these elements form part of Stryjeńska's style, she never considered the Lech tradition as the pure source of nationalism, and in her diary does not recognise any influence from Wyspianski. Her line, which initially was somewhat Cubist, became fluid and did not relate to Art Nouveau. She is also related to the Formists who emerged out of Młoda Polska, and who also wanted to create a national Polish style, but through direct contact with folk art, especially that of Podhale.

Stryjeńska soon established her independence as an artist. In 1912 she exhibited a cycle of 18 *Polish Fables Based on Folk Tales*, inspired by medieval illuminations, but already containing elements of her mature style, such as a love of the fantastic and of Polish history, dynamism, theatrical composition, simplified form, flat areas of colour separated by prominent line and a wealth of ornamentation. In 1917 she created a cycle of 15 lithographs of two and three tones, *Slavic Gods*, based on Slavic mythology as related in early chronicles, but interpreted in her own imaginative and fantastic manner. She created both lithographs, printed in 1918 by Warsztaty Krakowskie, and large cartoons (National Museum, Warsaw) for frescoes she executed in Kraków, in the rooms of Warsztaty Krakowskie in the Museum of Industry and in Baszta Senatorska in the Wawel Royal Castle. Stryjeńska's ability to adapt a design to architectural decoration culminated in 1919 in a fresco frieze in the Warsaw residence of Zdzisław Kalinowski. The only surviving example of her architectural decoration is on a house on the corner of Rynek Starego Miasta (Square of the Old Town) and Świętojańska Street in Warsaw; both the buildings and Stryjeńska's energetic dancing girls on a bright green background were reconstructed in 1953 after being destroyed in World War II.

In the five-picture cycle of *Pascha* (Song of Resurrection; 1918) Stryjeńska combined Christian iconography with Lech myth and folk art. In the watercolour and tempera *Meeting with the Mother* (see illustration) the youthful, blond Christ is based on a Slavic prototype, his barefoot Mother is an old Polish peasant woman dressed in a fantastic folk costume, and the Apostles sport peasants' garments. It is no coincidence that the cycle was executed at the time of Poland's independence after World War I – Christ's Resurrection parallels that of Poland. The composition is concentrated on the picture plane, the figures are simplified and almost subordinated to the brilliant colours and light emanating from Christ, and the subject competes with the fantastic ornamental headdresses and vegetation. As in all Stryjeńska's work, the interpretation is personal; in the *Three Marys* and *Noli me tangere* Mary Magdalene wears contemporary dress, her hair of the same colour as Stryjeńska's.

Stryjeńska's style culminated in the six decorative panels in tempera on canvas representing the *Seasons*, which decorated the walls of the Polish Pavilion at the Paris exhibition of 1925 (the designs were also executed as tapestries and shown in a textile exhibition at the Louvre in 1927). The series depicts allegories of the Labours of the Months, two to each panel, the elements drawn from Polish folklore. A photograph of one panel, *January and February*, survives, as do the schemes for all six panels, in watercolour and pencil on paper (all National Museum). Stryjeńska's stylisation and simplification of form here reaches its apogee: line plays an important role; the colours are strong and flat; the figures are dynamic, in motion, and reflect the artist's love of narrative and humour. The panels formed an organic unit with the pavilion architecture, designed by Józef Czajkowski, who also received the Grand Prix, and with Karol Stryjeński's furniture.

In *Polish Dances* (1927) and *Music of Podhale* (1930; both watercolour and tempera) Stryjeńska represented regional Polish dances in authentic costumes. She captured the music and rhythm of dance with contagious dynamism and energy; her mastery of the body's motion as it responds to music demonstrates both her familiarity with dance and her complete control of human anatomy. By now her line is more fluid, and in *Music of Podhale* there is a note of romanticism in the representation of the Podhale landscape. Stryjeńska's representations of Polish dance have not been surpassed. They became very popular, and were endlessly reproduced on posters, postcards, ornamental dishes, toys and even candy wrappers.

Book illustration forms an important aspect of Stryjeńska's oeuvre. In 1921 Karol Stryjeński formed Fala, a publishing house for her book illustrations. Among the books published by Fala and illustrated by Stryjeńska are Ronsard's *Sixteen Love Sonnets*, Ignacy Krasicki's *Monachomachia* (1922) and Kazimierz Tetmajer's *Jak baba diabła wyonacyła* (How a woman tricked the devil). The illustrations of the latter two works are humorous, full of verve and life, like the artist's personality. The publications were so successful that special editions of Stryjeńska's work, including *Polish Dances* and *Polish Costumes*, were published by Jakub Mortkowicz. In 1926, in collaboration with Warsztaty Krakowskie, Stryjeńska illustrated Szymanowicz's *Sielanki* (Pastorals). In 1929 she created illustrations for *Music of Podhale*, a major ethnographic work by Stanisław Mierczyński with an introduction by the composer Karol Szymanowski. The illustrations stress the spirit of the mountaineers, their personalities, costumes and the landscape, with all of which she was familiar. They were so effective that in 1933 they were published in Lwów by Książnica Atlas as *Tatry i górale: 9 ilustracji z dzieła Stanisław Mierczyńskiego Muzyka Podhala* (The Tatras and the mountaineers: 9 illustrations from the work of Stanislaw Mierczynski: The music of the Tatra highlands).

Stryjeńska was also a notable stage and costume designer. As early as 1917 she choreographed a pantomime, *Bajki o Maćku Piecuchu i pannie Gapiomile królewnie* (Tales about Maciek Piecuch and the maiden princess Gapiomila), for which she also designed the sets and costumes. She received high praise for her later stage designs and costumes. Among

Stryjeńska: *Meeting with the Mother*, 1918; watercolour; National Museum, Warsaw

these are her projects for productions directed by Towarzystwo Słowackiego of works by Juliusz Słowacki, one of Poland's most eminent romantic poets – *Promienie FF* (Rays; 1 October 1921) and *Balladyna* (20 June 1927) – and Karol Szymanowski's *Harnasie* (Chief brigands of the Tatras), staged on 1 October 1938 at the Great Theatre, Warsaw. A simplified version of the last was presented by Polski Balet Reprezentacyjny (Representational Polish Ballet) in Theatre Mogadur, Paris, in February 1939 (17 costume projects are preserved in Muzeum Teatralne, Warsaw). Stryjeńska's costumes, stylised versions of those of the Podhale highlanders, with all foreign influences eliminated, were effective on stage and seen as representative of the spirit of the region. In the Muzeum Teatralne are two watercolours of her costume designs for two characters in *Turandot*. Both are based on Chinese prototypes, but subordinated to Stryjeńska's refined sense of design, rich patterning and colour juxtapositions.

Stryjeńska was also an active member of Warsztaty Krakowskie, whose aim was to unify the arts. Her lithographs at the Exhibition of Furniture in the Kraków Palace of Art in 1918, and her decorative panels at the Paris exhibition of 1925, formed an integral and organic part of the architecture and furnishings. She also designed a kilim for the Paris exhibition showing strong Cubist influence, adapted to its decorative function. In her other tapestries, however, she created delicate repetitive motifs derived from nature. Her work in the applied arts was very influential on post-war Polish fibre art.

In 1946, after the Communist take-over of Poland, Stryjeńska left with her children for Switzerland. The government retaliated by obliterating her name from catalogues of museum collections and only negative articles about her were published. The regime still continued to reproduce her works, but without paying her for the right, and selling them at a great profit. Only after Poland regained democratic government in 1989 was Maria Grońska allowed to publish a brief monograph on the artist. Stryjeńska's diary, which was in the possession of her son Jan, a professor of architecture at Geneva University, was published in 1995. It reveals Stryjeńska's emotional and artistic life, her despair at the Allies' failure to prevent Poland becoming a satellite of the USSR, her inability to produce paintings without a studio, without financial security and in failing health. In exile, Stryjeńska's great talent lay dormant, but the enormous oeuvre produced by her before World War II is ample testimony to it.

DANUTA BATORSKA

Stuart, Louisa Anne *see* Waterford

Stuart, Michelle
American artist, 1933–

Born in Los Angeles, California, 1933. Visited Mexico, 1950. Studied at Chouinard Art Institute, Los Angeles, 1951–2, then worked part-time as topographical draughtswoman for the Army Corps of Engineers. Briefly attended Instituto de Bellas Artes, Mexico City, 1953, leaving to join team of Diego Rivera's apprentices. Married a Spanish artist and lived in Europe, primarily Paris, 1953–6 (later divorced). Settled in New York, 1957; attended classes at New School for Social Research, 1958–60. Subsequently travelled widely. Taught and held several visiting artist positions during 1970s, notably at Pratt Institute, Brooklyn; Parsons School of Design, Fordham University and School of the Visual Arts, New York; and several campuses of State University of New York. Founder-member of feminist journal *Heresies*, 1976; also helped to create Women's Art Registry, New York. Recipient of MacDowell Colony fellowship, 1974; Ford Foundation-Tamarind Institute grant, 1974; National Endowment for the Arts (NEA) grants, 1974, 1977, 1980 and 1989; Creative Artists Public Service (CAPS) grant, New York State, 1974; Guggenheim fellowship, 1975; New York Foundation for the Arts fellowship, 1987; New York City Art Commission award for excellence in design, 1990; Purchase award, American Academy and Institute of Arts and Letters, 1992. Member, National Academy of Design, 1996. Lives in New York City and Amagansett, New York.

Selected Individual Exhibitions
Douglass College, Rutgers University, New Brunswick: 1973
Max Hutchinson Gallery, New York: 1974, 1975, 1976
Galerie Farideh Cadot, Paris: 1976, 1978
Williams College Museum of Art, Williamstown, MA: 1977
Hayden Gallery, Massachusetts Institute of Technology, Cambridge: 1977
Centre des Arts Plastiques Contemporains, Bordeaux: 1978
Institute of Contemporary Arts, London: 1979
Galleriet Anders Tornberg, Lund: 1980, 1983, 1987, 1995
Walker Art Center, Minneapolis: 1983
Neuberger Museum, Purchase, NY: 1984
Ueda Gallery, Tokyo: 1984, 1987
Hillwood Art Gallery, C.W. Post Campus, Long Island University, Greenvale, NY: 1985 (*Voyages*, touring)
Arts Club of Chicago: 1986
Van Straaten Gallery, Chicago: 1988
Rose Art Museum, Brandeis University, Waltham, MA: 1988 (touring)
Fawbush Gallery, New York: 1989, 1992, 1994

Selected Writings
The Fall, New York: Printed Matter, 1976 (prose poem)
From the Silent Garden, Williamstown, MA: Williams College, 1979 (introduction by Lucy R. Lippard)

Bibliography
Lawrence Alloway, "Michelle Stuart: A fabric of significations", *Artforum*, xii, January 1974, pp.64–5
Corinne Robins, "Michelle Stuart: The mapping of myth and time", *Arts Magazine*, li, December 1976, pp.83–5
Lucy R. Lippard, "A new landscape art", *Ms*, April 1977
Strata: Nancy Graves, Eva Hesse, Michelle Stuart, Jackie Winsor, exh. cat., Vancouver Art Gallery, 1977
William Wilson, "Michelle Stuart's 'Green River Massachusetts, Variations': The mapping of time, place and season in books without words", *Print Collector's Newsletter*, viii, 1977, pp.135–6
Lucy R. Lippard, "Strata: Nancy Graves, Eva Hesse, Michelle Stuart, Jackie Winsor", *Vanguard*, vi, October 1977, pp.17–18
Michelle Stuart: Paperwork, exh. cat., Institute of Contemporary Arts, London, 1979
Eleanor Munro: *Originals: American Women Artists*, New York: Simon and Schuster, 1979
Corinne Robins, "The paper surfaces of Michelle Stuart: Traces of matter = marks of light", *Art International*, xxiii, November–December 1979, pp.62–0
Roger Lipsey, "Michelle Stuart: A decade of work", *Arts Magazine*, lvi, April 1982, pp.110–11
Lucy R. Lippard, *Overlay: Contemporary Art and the Art of Prehistory*, New York: Pantheon, 1983
Michelle Stuart: Voyages, exh. cat., Hillwood Art Gallery, C.W. Post Campus, Long Island University, Greenvale, NY, and elsewhere, 1985
Michelle Stuart: Essence of Place: Paintings, Objects and Drawings for the Earth, exh. cat., Arts Club of Chicago, 1986
Paper Now: Bent, Molded and Manipulated, exh. cat., Cleveland Museum of Art, 1986
Elizabeth Duvert, "With stone, star and earth: The presence of the archaic in the landscape visions of Georgia O'Keeffe, Nancy Holt and Michelle Stuart", *The Desert Is No Lady: Southwestern Landscapes in Women's Writing and Art*, ed. Vera Norwood and Janice Monk, New Haven and London: Yale University Press, 1987, pp.197–222
Stephen Westfall, "Melancholy mapping", *Art in America*, lxxv, February 1987, pp.104–9
Gerrit Henry, "Michelle Stuart: Navigating coincidence", *Print Collector's Newsletter*, xviii, 1988, pp.193–5
Carey Lovelace, "Michelle Stuart's *Silent Gardens*", *Arts Magazine*, lxiii, September 1988, pp.76–9
Michelle Stuart: Place and Time, exh. cat., Walker Art Center, Minneapolis, 1989
Susan Tallman, "Paper, precious paper", *Arts Magazine*, lxv, May 1991, pp.25–6
Breakdown, exh. cat., Rose Art Museum, Brandeis University, Waltham, MA, 1992
Susan L. Stoops, "Michelle Stuart: A personal archaeology", *Woman's Art Journal*, xiv/2, 1993–4, pp.17–21

Michelle Stuart has been preoccupied both with earth processes and with our relationships to them since she was very young. She grew up with geological surveys and water-table charts because her father was a water-rights engineer. In the early 1950s she worked as a cartographer for the Army Corps of Engineers in Los Angeles. In the late 1960s she began a series of drawings based on NASA photographs of the moon's surface. From an early age she travelled widely, studying archaeological sites, indigenous cultures, prehistoric petroglyphs and, always, land formations and native vegetation. She keeps meticulous journals that provide "field notes" on specific sites – photographs, descriptions (which include her own experiences at the site) and samples of earth. These journals must be considered as part of her art work. The artist's mapping, charting and sampling of specific sites evoke the geologist, the cartographer or the archaeologist. Stuart, however, *participates* with natural elements at the sites she investigates; she does not dominate them.

Although she had her first one-woman exhibition in Paris in 1955, and subsequently showed frequently in New York, Stuart began to receive critical attention only in the 1970s, when pluralism and feminism opened up a broader array of critical issues and art forms. A series of graphite drawings (most of them numbered rather than titled), presented in a one-woman exhibition at Rutgers University in 1973, drew the attention of Lawrence Alloway, partly because of their large formats (3.65 × 1.52 m., 2.74 × 1.52 m.) – the scale of paintings rather than drawings. Alloway (1974) related them also to sculpture, in that the papers curled a little "according to the paper's memory of earlier rolling during the work process", and continued downwards to roll forward from the wall into the viewer's space. From a distance the drawings present an all-over, non-hierarchical but modulated image; up close they reveal minute details of various earth surfaces, due to her technique, which Max Ernst once named *frottage*. Working on a table, rolling up the larger drawings as she progressed, she rubbed a block of graphite over a surface of sand or small rocks, sprinkling or brushing on graphite powder and using different grades of pencil, an eraser and at times an ink wash to produce additional subtleties of surface. Some of these surfaces are subdivided by means of drawn lines at regular intervals. Such impersonal measuring devices, like grids, which she had learned from her experience as a cartographer, apply metaphorically the restraints of culture to nature's chaos. Culture, however, never gains the upper hand, but rather a balance is achieved. Such visual reconciliation of nature and culture is an important element in the meaning of most of Stuart's art works.

In 1972 Stuart began to make what she called "paper scrolls". To make these very large scrolls she expended tremendous physical effort, shovelling earth from a chosen site, breaking down rocks and pounding the residues into handmade rag paper, rubbing the dust into the paper and burnishing it with her hand. The process, she points out, is a natural one: in nature, time is a continuous breaking down. *Sayerville Strata* (1976; muslin-mounted rag paper and earth; Max Hutchinson Gallery, New York) is a particularly breath-taking example of the beauty of this technique. Four large panels (together 1.57 × 3.66 m.) present the colours of four different strata of the earth – literal manifestations of geological time. The panels are experienced as four luminous fields of colour, from warm tan to rich coral. Stuart herself has said that the earth-impressed paper "feels like skin, the most delicate, soft, and warmest of surfaces" (quoted in London 1979).

On a more intimate scale than the paper scrolls are Stuart's "rock books", the pages of which are made by the same process of rubbing in earth, or by covering them with graphite or paint, or coating them with wax and then incising them. These books without written text refer none the less to culture, to its duration, traces of what man has created, which Stuart compares to the traces of time left in and on the earth itself. *Book of the Library near Zagora* (1983; handmade paper, earth and hydrocol; repr. Cleveland 1986, fig.27) evokes the artist's memory of a library on the edge of the Sahara Desert where ancient manuscripts of extremely fragile condition are stored in an adobe building without air conditioning. The clay-coloured book has congealed into an impenetrable lumpish mass tied with a cord, embodying the magic of the archaeological site.

Stuart's large earthwork of 1979, *Stone Alignments/Solstice Cairns*, was laid out in Oregon on the Rowena Plateau, which

Stuart: *Book of the Stone*, 1984–5; earth from site (Changu Narain Temple Complex, Nepal), wax, linen, paper; ten pages, 22.9 × 22.9 × 6.4 cm

overlooks the Columbia River Gorge. It comprises 3400 boulders gathered from the foot of Mount Hood, some 50 kilometres away. Its wheel shape is punctuated by four stone cairns that align with the summer solstice and, by uncanny chance, also with an island in the river below, formerly a sacred burial site of Indians (Lippard 1983, pp.111–12). Below the cairns, Stuart buried mementoes from sites that she had visited across the globe.

A favourite medium for the last few years has been encaustic, a beeswax and resin mixture that Stuart works extensively, layering it, chipping it, covering portions with earth, as she embeds into its surface plants, flowers and other objects found in a particular region. *Paradisi* (1985–7; encaustic, pigment, plants and flowers; Max Protetch Gallery, New York, repr. Westfall 1987) is atypical with regard to its site – the New York metropolitan area. It is a gigantic painting, more than 4.88 × 10 metres (16 × 33 feet), made up of 628 panels, each 0.3 metres (1 foot) square. In these paintings, then, she continues to construct according to a grid. Here the grid evokes our way of looking: separate glances are inventoried and combined to present an overall impression of the colours and textures of a particular site. One looks with fresh eyes even at New York City. The range of these encaustic paintings presents an amazing array of colours.

Although her observations and methods approach those of both the archaeologist and the primitive worker of rituals, Stuart is also involved poetically with each site. Speaking about the Southwest landscape that inspired *Red ... Earth ... Dream Wall of the Big House*, one of eight paintings that make up *Silent Gardens* (1984–7), she said: "When I traveled through that vast space dreaming about beginnings I was shaping and being shaped by my landscape" (*From the Silent Garden* 1979).

SUSAN HAVENS CALDWELL

Sutherland, Jane
Australian painter, 1853–1928

Born in New York, 26 December 1853, to George Sutherland, woodcarver, and his wife Jane, both from Glasgow. Emigrated with her family to Australia via Scotland, 1864, moving from Sydney to Melbourne in 1870. Attended National Gallery School, Melbourne, 1871–5, 1877 and 1882–6 (prize 1883); one of the few women protesters during the Gallery School dispute of the late 1870s. First woman member of the Buonarotti Society, an art and literary society in Melbourne, 1884; first female councillor of the Victorian Artists Society, Melbourne, 1900. Suffered a stroke, *c*.1899. Ceased working *c*.1912 after the death of her brother William, who had driven her to sketching sites. Lived with her sisters in Kew, Melbourne, until her death, 25 July 1928.

Principal Exhibitions
Victorian Academy of the Arts, Melbourne: 1878
Australian Artists Association, Melbourne: 1887
Victorian Artists Society, Melbourne: 1888–1912

Bibliography
Sutherland, exh. cat., College of the Arts, Melbourne, 1977
Frances Lindsay, "Jane Sutherland", *Lip*, 1978–9, pp.12–15
Janine Burke, *Australian Women Artists, 1840–1940*, Collingwood, Victoria: Greenhouse, 1980
Golden Summers: Heidelberg and Beyond, exh. cat., National Gallery of Victoria, Melbourne, and elsewhere, 1986
Australian Watercolours, 1802–1926, in the National Gallery of Victoria, exh. cat., National Gallery of Victoria, Melbourne, 1991
Sue Rowley, "The journey's end: Women's mobility and containment", *Australian Cultural History*, x, 1991
Completing the Picture: Women Artists and the Heidelberg Era, exh. cat., Artmoves, Hawthorn East, and elsewhere, 1992
Juliet Peers, *What No Man Had Ever Done Before ...*, Melbourne: Dawn Revival Press, 1992
——, "The tribe of Mary Jane Hicks: Imaging women through the Mount Rennie rape case, 1886", *Australian Cultural History*, xii, 1993, pp.127–44
Mary Eagle and John Jones, *A Story of Australian Painting*, Sydney: Macmillan, 1994
Jane Clark and Juliet Peers, "Jane Sutherland", *Heritage: The National Women's Art Book*, ed. Joan Kerr, Sydney: Dictionary of Australian Artists/Craftsman House, 1995

In the mid- to late 1880s, without access to European training, several Melbourne artists learned plein-air painting by working with colleagues who had direct experience of French and British avant-garde art. This practical experience, combined with information from overseas publications and rare importations of progressive European works, led to the development of an Australian version of plein-air painting. Jane Sutherland was the most acclaimed female artist associated with this movement. Her considerable abilities were confirmed by her rapid transition from tightly painted silver-toned works inspired by Bastien Lepage with anecdotal incident ordered in a vertical format, as in *Obstruction Box Hill* (1887; Ballarat Fine Art Gallery), to a looser, freer style with more allusive subject matter. She began to reduce landscape to a series of regressing horizontal striations, as in her first fully developed work, *Numb Fingers Working On, Though the Eye of Morn Is Yet Bedimmed with Tears* (1888; National Gallery of Victoria, Melbourne). Her stylistic development paralleled that of other Melbourne plein-air painters, who had used similar tight vertical formats *c*.1886–7, although she is persistently treated as imitative and derivative of her male colleagues in histories of Australian art.

On the Last Tramp (1899; private collection, Western Australia) confirmed Sutherland's interest in the key nationalist themes that engaged self-consciously avant-garde Australian artists of the late 19th century. Her subject, an itinerant tramp or swagman on a country road, is depicted in an open landscape painted in clear pinks, blues and ochres, reflecting her enduring interest in colour. This new spaciousness developed throughout her landscapes in the 1890s, moving from a decorative spatial arrangement, as in *Mushroom Gatherers* (1895; see illustration), to a French-based realist orientation in *A Cabbage Patch* (1896; National Gallery of Australia, Canberra), to the *Harvest Field* (1897; private collection), which evoked the Australian canon of grandiose, sun-filled landscapes. *Harvest Field* was probably the last significant landscape she painted before a stroke impeded her professional activities.

Sutherland's ambition encompassed the Australian avant-garde preoccupation with landscape and rural labour. Her practice as a landscape artist is significant in local discourse and in relation to the overviews of white Australian art that have been formed overseas. For much of the 20th century, foreign commentators have echoed Australian critics in validating landscape art as "authentically" Australian. Sutherland's focus on landscape and labour sets her apart from the better-known French and American female Impressionists, who painted interiors and scenes of middle-class life.

The interpretation of plein air developed by Sutherland was original in the Australian context. Colours were brushed broadly over a warm, cinnamon-coloured ground, which was revealed in areas to form part of the composition, bypassing "finish" as a sign of her anti-academicism. In the late 1880s short, broken brush strokes created a flicking, feathery impressionistic effect. Consistent with Australian plein-air practice in the 1880s, she generally mixed her colours on the palette, apart from occasional accents of pure red or blue. In the 1890s her brush strokes became smoother, though still scumbled over a visible ground. Her definition of foliage was less meticulous than that of contemporaries who used asymmetrical friezelike devices borrowed from Anglo-Japanese design. *A Cabbage Patch* (1896) features palette knife work in its broad slabs of paint. The use of pure colour and the blending of colours on the canvas suggest that there was a more accurate knowledge of major French Impressionists in Melbourne by the mid-1890s. As well as reflecting the work of Australian artists returned from France, the pale blue-green colour scheme of *A Cabbage Patch* can be traced in her work from 1889.

Sutherland: *Mushroom Gatherers*, 1895; oil on canvas; 41.6 × 99.3 cm.; National Gallery of Victoria, Melbourne; Presented by Dr Margaret Sutherland, 1972

Sutherland, who was the daughter of a carver of figure-heads, never fitted the image of the "lady painter", and her work is not restricted to the stereotypical "women's work" defined by Australian critics of the period. Her working life was substantially played out in isolated or anomalous positions and shadowed by her deviation from accepted patterns. She was never part of fashionable female exhibition circles, but "respectability" required her to return home at night instead of staying at the bohemian painting camps organised by male colleagues.

The position of women in advanced art circles in Melbourne was difficult. On at least three occasions in the 1880s prominent artists protested when public competitions were won by women rather than men, identifying female botanical and academic artists as inimical to progressive art practice. In technique and subject, Sutherland was allied with a faction frankly antipathetic to women artists. Rather than painting intimate idylls of family and motherhood, associating herself as a sister/participant, she often represented rural workers, young women and children, with a distant, godlike eye. Her subjects frequently were shown engaged in work, their backs turned to the viewer, without eye contact, and their lack of awareness of the viewer's gaze emphasises the mood of stealth. Her motivation for such work is not known, but their scrutiny of woman and landscape resonates with the obsession with violent crimes against women in Australia in the 1880s and 1890s.

Sutherland was sustained by her socially ambitious family. Intellectual and cultural ability, rather than money or political power, enabled the Sutherlands to change class and mix with Melbourne's academic and artistic elite. Possibly because of their singular status, the family remained self-reflexive, dependent on one another for stimulation and encouragement, which was exacerbated by the poor health of several members. The family expressed the nascent Australian nationalism through their expeditions in the bush and interest in native flora. This familial recreation translated easily into Sutherland's adoption of the plein-air landscapes of the Australian professional mainstream, forging a sense of national identity in the late 19th century.

Only in the pastels produced after her stroke *c.*1899 did Sutherland conform to some extent to contemporary notions of "feminine" expression in art. Domestic scenes, studies of her nieces at play and portraits of adolescents with soulful eyes, inspired by popular Edwardian illustrators such as Harrison Fisher (e.g. *Blue and Gold*, *c.*1905; National Gallery of Victoria), appear in her later oeuvre. Generally smaller in scale, with tighter handling, these works still feature heightened colours. The inclusion of factories and industrial skylines in her views of the Yarra River (e.g. *Kew Landscape*, *c.*1905; Ballarat Fine Art Gallery; *Yarra River*, *c.*1910; ex-Sotheby's Australia, April 1995, lot 392) indicates that her instincts for realism and social commentary were never entirely subsumed in the Australian convention of picturesque landscape painting. Direct references to urban sites are uncommon in the paintings of Australian women in this period.

The critical discussion of Sutherland in Australia in the 1960s and 1970s reflected a reluctance to grant women's painting equal esteem to men's. Her symbolic importance in Australian male-centric histories is incalculable. She most closely followed the admired male aesthetic, but also defined for conservatives the marginal place of women, a faint silver mirror, reflecting male pre-eminence and the female predilection for weaker expression. Studying a wide range of her works reveals that the gap between Sutherland and her male peers is narrower than is indicated in mainstream Australian art history. She was praised more fully in the 1890s than in the contentious atmosphere of her second period of fame, beginning in the 1960s. According to the Melbourne *Argus* of 29 March 1890, Sutherland's works were "racy of the Australian soil and climate" and bore "the stamp of veracity and sincerity".

JULIET PEERS

Sveinsdóttir, Júlíana
Icelandic painter and textile artist, 1889–1966

Born in the Westmann Islands, off the south coast of Iceland, 31 July 1889. Studied painting at the Royal Danish Academy of Fine Arts, Copenhagen, 1912–17. Taught drawing and weaving in Copenhagen, 1917–27. Study tours to Italy, 1926, 1932 and 1934. Studied mural painting and fresco technique at the Royal Danish Academy, 1927–31. Spent most of her adult life in Denmark. Member of the Danish Kammeraterne (Comrades) group, 1960–66. Jury member, Charlottenborg exhibitions, Copenhagen, 1941–9. Recipient of Alfred Benzon prize, 1943; Eckersbergs medal, 1947; gold medal, Milan Triennale, 1951. Died in Copenhagen, 17 April 1966.

Selected Individual Exhibitions

KFUM (YMCA) House, Westmann Islands: 1926
Den Frie, Copenhagen: 1927
Bergstadastræti 72, Reykjavík: 1929
Bachs Kunsthandel, Copenhagen: 1943
Listamannaskálinn, Reykjavík: 1949
National Gallery of Iceland, Reykjavík: 1957 (retrospective)
Kunstforeningen, Copenhagen: 1963 (retrospective)
Kjarvalsstadir, Reykjavík: 1974 (retrospective)

Bibliography

Georg Gretor, *Islands Kultur und seine junge Malerei*, Jena, 1928
Kristján Fridriksson, ed., *Islensk myndlist* [Icelandic art], Reykjavík, 1943
Karid Lund, "Júlíana Sveinsdóttir", *Håndarbejdets Fremme*, no.7, 1946, pp.97–103
Elof Risebye, "Júlíana Sveinsdóttir: En islandsk malerinde i Danmark" [Júlíana Sveinsdóttir: An Icelandic painter in Denmark], *Samleren*, 1946, pp.44–8
Ellen Marie Magerøy, "Navn og retninger i Islands malerkunst" [Names and directions in Icelandic painting], *Kunst og Kultur*, xxxiv, 1951, pp.1–24
Björn Th. Björnsson, *Islensk myndlist á 19. og 20. öld* [Icelandic art in the 19th and 20th centuries], i, Reykjavík: Helgafell, 1964
—, *Júlíana Sveinsdóttir*, Reykjavík: Kjarvalsstadir, 1974
Adalsteinn Ingólfsson, *Kristín Jónsdóttir*, Reykjavík, 1987
Aldarspegill, *Icelandic Works in the National Gallery of Iceland, 1900–1987*, Reykjavík, 1988
Júlíana Sveinsdóttir: Landslagsmyndir [Júlíana Sveinsdóttir: Landscapes], exh. cat., National Gallery of Iceland, Reykjavík, 1989 (with English summary)

Júlíana Sveinsdóttir was one of the pioneers of modern Icelandic landscape painting. She and her contemporary Kristín Jónsdóttir were the first Icelandic women to become professional artists. Although she lived abroad for most of her adult life, she always drew nourishment – both spiritual and artistic – from her Icelandic roots. Her works are a lyrical personal interpretation of the magnificence of nature. Examples are to be found in the National Gallery of Iceland, Reykjavík, as well as in the collection of Leifur Sveinsson, Reykjavík.

Sveinsdóttir began her career as a naturalistic landscape painter with Romantic inclinations (*Eiríksjökull*, 1921; Reykjavík Municipal Art Museum). In the 1920s she was to some extent influenced by the Icelandic landscape painter Jón Stefánsson, who emphasised the value of firm composition and formal clarity. In the late 1920s Sveinsdóttir underwent a period of intense self-questioning. After a study tour to Italy in 1926, her search resulted in her enrolling again at the Academy, this time to learn mural painting and fresco technique in order to fulfil her need for a more tactile and textural expression. Her teacher there, Elof Risebye, a former fellow student, whose lyrical and sensitive art is mainly characterised by a religious mysticism, became a close friend. Although Risebye had no stylistic influence on Sveinsdóttir's work, he undoubtedly influenced her way of thinking and was moreover able to nurture certain characteristics of hers that were to become the corner-stone of her art, not least her lyrical and introspective approach to nature. Under Risebye's influence she also started painting interiors, window scenes and still lifes with flowers (*White Jar and a Book*, 1948; Collection Leifur Sveinsson, Reykjavík). Concentrating on pure still lifes with bowl and jars (*Black Bowl*, 1957; National Gallery of Iceland), she simplified the forms and excluded all extraneous features. It seems that she had more emotional distance from these inanimate but formally strong objects than from the landscape. In her still lifes, she succeeds in distancing herself from the visible reality that was beginning to inhibit her creativity, and also adopts a more subjective, painterly approach. Early on Sveinsdóttir also developed an aptitude for portraits and became one of Iceland's finest portrait painters. Throughout her life she made a series of interesting self-portraits (*Self-Portrait*, 1925; Collection Sveinn Björnsson, Hafnarfjördur).

From the middle of the 1930s onwards one may detect a steady development in Sveinsdóttir's art. Earlier she had used colour graduations (dark colours – brown, blue, rust red) and brushwork to differentiate between forms. In her painting *Mount Hekla* (1936; Collection Knútur Björnsson, Reykjavík) outlines are no longer used to separate the planes. Instead the fields of colour are softly brushed together, allowing Sveinsdóttir to demonstrate her sensitivity to the interaction of colour and light. She interprets the unreal, almost dream-like colour spectrum of the Icelandic landscape with warm lyricism. The expansive and horizontal planes of colour create an impression of calm majesty. She sometimes painted many versions of the same subject over a limited period of time. At a first glance, they seem almost identical, but closer inspection reveals subtle variations in colour. Sveinsdóttir obviously learned a great deal from Danish art, naturally enough, since she lived in Denmark for decades and participated in the art life of the country. Her preference seems to have been for the so-called Bornholm painters. The island of Bornholm, bathed in the reflected light of the Baltic sea, which changes to every colour, may have reminded Sveinsdóttir of her birthplace.

Although Sveinsdóttir originally started weaving in the 1920s as a means of earning her living, she always seems to have looked on it as an artistic medium, fit to be shown alongside her paintings. In her textiles she used Icelandic wool that she dyed herself, using plants that she collected during her summer visits to Iceland. Her textiles were proof that Icelandic wool could be used in textiles of high quality. She used an abstract formal language in her textiles, geometric as well as biomorphic, and consistently stressed the flatness of the woven surface. She had more freedom of expression in her textiles than in her paintings, since textile art, though based on firm rules, does not have as strong a tradition behind it as painting. Weaving demanded a degree of formal simplification and

Sveinsdóttir: *From the Westmann Islands,* 1946; oil; 82 × 90 cm.; National Gallery of Iceland, Reykjavík

concentration that helped Sveinsdóttir to discard some of the constraints of naturalism. Her textiles no doubt influenced the development of her paintings, steering her towards simple forms and a lively surface texture.

This influence can be best seen in Sveinsdóttir's paintings from her birthplace, the Westmann Islands. After World War II, Sveinsdóttir visited the islands in the summer of 1946. According to the artist, this trip was a watershed in her life and art, in that it made her tackle her art with a new seriousness: "I feel that I saw the Westmann Islands from the painter's point of view for the first time in 1946" (*Morgunbladid,* 11 September 1957). The islands were to become a kind of leit-motif in her art and a very important influence on her artistic development. Sveinsdóttir, however, did not paint the cliffs and mountains as such, but rather the continuous assault of the waves, their ceaseless movement and the way they reflect the ebb and flow of life: "There is something very human about the sea. It is constantly changing, just as we are" (*idem*). In her later paintings from the Westmann Islands, such as *Home Rock in the Sunshine* (1954; Collection Sverrir Sigurdsson, Seltjarnarnes), she narrows her focus and builds up massive forms that dominate the picture plane. Features such as the black lava, deep-blue sea and the sun-drenched brown cliffs with their soft grassy knolls become parts of a near-abstract structure. In one of her last paintings, *Still Life* (Collection Sveinn Björnsson, Hafnarfjördur), painted in 1965, a year before she died, she moves still further towards simplification and demonstrates how masterfully she reduced her means to the bare but profound essentials. The picture consists of basic geometric shapes, sphere and cube, but through drawing and shading Sveinsdóttir also creates a traditional three-dimensional effect.

HRAFNHILDUR SCHRAM

Swanwick, Betty

British painter, illustrator and designer, 1915–1989

Born Ada Elizabeth Swanwick in Forest Hill, London, 22 May 1915. Studied at Goldsmiths' College School of Art, London, 1931–4, continuing part-time after winning scholarships to Central School of Arts and Crafts and Royal College of Art; studied simultanously at all three, 1934–6. Joined teaching staff of Goldsmiths', 1936; head of Design School, 1948–69; also taught occasionally at Royal Academy Schools, Royal College of Art and Central School of Arts and Crafts. Member, Society of Mural Painters, 1937; Society of Industrial Artists, 1960–61; Royal Watercolour Society, 1976. Associate, 1972, and member, 1979, Royal Academy. Granted civil list pension by the Queen, 1983. Died in Tunbridge Wells, Kent, 22 May 1989.

Principal Exhibitions

Exposition Internationale, Paris: 1937 (diploma)
Leicester Galleries, London: 1947
Little Gallery, London: c.1950 (individual)
Royal Academy, London: 1965–88 (annuals), 1977 (*British Painting, 1952–1977*)

Selected Writings

The Cross Purposes: A Coloured Novelette, London: Editions Poetry, 1945
Hoodwinked, London: Barker, 1957 (novel)
Beauty and the Burglar, London: Barker, 1958 (novel)
Essay on toy theatres in *Handbook of Crafts*, ed. Griselda Lewis, London: Hulton, 1960

Bibliography

Lesley Blanch, "Constructive eccentrics or three proper cautions", *Vogue*, 8 February 1939
The Observer, 19 February 1950
Harold F. Hutchison and others, *London Transport Posters*, London: Transport Board, 1963
The Observer (magazine supplement), 29 May 1977
Leonie Grayeff, "In the mind's eye", *The Artist*, xcvii, December 1982, pp.16–19, 36
Lord Rossmore, "The contemporary work of Betty Swanwick RA: Studies and drawings", *Country Bazaar*, iii/4, Summer 1985, pp.21–40
Stephen Gardiner, "Betty Swanwick, obituary", *Modern Painters*, ii/3, 1989, pp.128–9
Brian Murphy, *The Art of Betty Swanwick RA*, Oxford: Oxford Polytechnic, 1989
Oliver Green, *Underground Art: London Transport Posters, 1908 to the Present*, London: Studio Vista, 1990
Watercolours, Drawings and Paintings from the Studio of the Late Betty Swanwick, sales cat., Bonhams, Knightsbridge, London, 31 January 1990
Paddy Rossmore, "Earth and imagination", *Resurgence*, no.139, March–April 1990, pp.31–3
——, "Betty Swanwick: Another world", *The Artist*, cv, June 1990, pp.42–4
The Illustrators: The British Art of Illustration, 1800–1991, exh. cat., Chris Beetles, London, 1991

Betty Swanwick entered Goldsmiths' College School of Art during its golden period. She had drawn since childhood, with pencils salvaged from shipwrecks by her mother, who came from the Scilly Isles. Her precocity, graphic invention and wit brought commissions while a student. Like a milliner trying out hats, Swanwick was painter, designer, writer and illustrator, toy theatre producer, collagist and mural painter. Her images were used for advertising, greeting cards, book jackets, illustrations for magazines, printed patterns for needlework, ceramic tiles, hand-painted chocolate boxes (Bendicks of Mayfair) and posters. Most famously, she was selected by Frank Pick of the London Transport Passenger Board to design nine posters (1936–54; Victoria and Albert Museum, London), including two panel posters, for the historic advertising campaign that transformed the London Underground. Later clients included Shell-Mex, Fisons Fertilisers and the Brighton Furniture Co. (*Right Chair for the Occasion*, 1982; private collection, repr. Murphy 1989, p.6). She painted several murals, beginning with a scheme for the Rocket Restaurant on the South Bank, London (Festival of Britain, 1951). Her London scenes of Pearly Kings and Queens brought her commissions from a theatre (designs submitted to the Lyric, Hammersmith) and hospitals (1960; Evelina Children's Hospital) and election to the Society of Mural Painters. Her gift for devising complicated figure compositions (*Battle Scene*, 1966–7; National Portrait Gallery, London) was put to use in her work as a theatre director, and the plays she wrote for Goldsmiths' Toy Theatre were said to have genius in their production and a magical intensity.

While painting she was also writing. Swanwick's first fiction was *The Cross Purposes* (1945); thereafter she wrote and/or illustrated nine books and continued to design book jackets and illustrate magazines until the 1970s (*Country Fair*, *The Strand*, *The Mirror*). These pictures resembled the curious tableaux of the celebrated taxidermist Walter Potter, a world where animals masqueraded as people, gently satirising their foibles. A wily crocodile, painted in "Woolworth's brightest and best paints" (*Vogue*, c.1938), gives a crystal-ball reading to an impressionable sheep (*Fortune Teller*, c.1957; private collection, repr. Rossmore, *The Artist*, 1990). Swanwick's anthropomorphism appears quaint, but it has an undercurrent, as John Betjeman observed when reviewing her novel *Hoodwinked* (1957): "... strange, startling, funny and with a weird beauty. Not the Victorian pastiche it seems to be at first glance" (note on dust jacket). Animals were essential to Swanwick's life, and her pets – Jobo the African Grey parrot, Little Nell the cavalier spaniel, Olly the dachshund, Louis and Sasha the pugs and a Burmese cat named Bewick – appear in her work; birds act as messengers, dogs guide the blind (*Parliament of the Yard*, 1985; private collection, repr. *The Royal Academy Illustrated*, 1986; *Borders of Sleep*, 1984; private collection, repr. Murphy 1989, p.17). Swanwick described herself as "part of the small tradition of English painting that is a bit eccentric, a little odd and a little visionary" (*ibid.*, p.5). She owned a Punch cartoon by Dickie Doyle; "Catastrophe in a Minute" by Louis Wain; a

Swanwick: *Pandora's Box*, 1979; watercolour; private collection, Royal Academy, London

Chaplinesque clown with a bird's head by Marc Chagall; a facsimile of a Samuel Palmer sketchbook and botanical prints by Thornton.

Swanwick rose to become head of the Design School at Goldsmiths' in 1948, spending 33 years coaching pupils in illustration, while proving the connections between commercial and fine art by continuing her own work. The retirement in 1958 of the principal, Clive Gardiner, also a practising artist and Swanwick's friend and mentor, coincided with the era of abstraction, which she called the "Dark Ages". Her classes dwindled and she felt increasingly obsolete. But the anti-art movement, as she saw it, created the vortex in which she produced haunting inner visions. Swanwick's early work, albeit distinctive, bore scant resemblance to her flowering in her mid-forties – the transformation was astonishing.

She lived an intense and spiritual life that nevertheless remained rooted. Pictures of the 1960s expressed a gamut of attitudes and emotions: terror, flight, sorrow and joy. Some, such as *The Bed* (1968; private collection, repr. *Royal Academy Illustrated*, 1968), fixed on the union of luckless lovers, fraught with sexual tensions. By the mid-1970s the prevalent atmosphere in Swanwick's work was concord and expressed the contentment she felt (*Still Voice in the Wilderness*, 1979; private collection, repr. Murphy 1989). Lovers found their satisfaction and, in the lines of Marlowe's poem "The Passionate Shepherd to his Love", the pleasures were "proved" (*Walk to the Paradise Garden*, 1981; private collection, repr. Rossmore, *The Artist*, 1990; also inspired by an interlude from Delius's *A Village Romeo and Juliet*).

Inspiration for Swanwick's other-worldly, narrative pictures was drawn not only from poetry (*In Country Sleep*, 1982; private collection; inspired by Dylan Thomas's poem of the same title), the evocative parables of the New Testament (*Mustard Seed*, 1982; private collection, repr. Rossmore, *The Artist*, 1990) and mythology (*Pandora's Box*, 1979; see illustration), but also music (*Celia's Holiday*, 1984; private collection, repr. Murphy 1989, p.18), a concern for the environment (*Lost Wilderness*, 1975; repr. Rossmore, *Resurgence*, 1990) and her own mental visions (*Labyrinthine Ways*, 1977; private collection, *ibid.*). She was fascinated by outsiders; immigrants (*The Departure*, also called *The Flight*, 1967; private collection), punks and gardeners (*Primavera and the Sleeping Gardener*, 1978; diploma work, Royal Academy, London), fishermen, musicians (*Louis Armstrong with His Trumpet*, 1987; *Black Shepherd*, private collection, repr. Murphy 1989, p.3) and tramps (*The Folly*, 1983; *ibid.*, p.4), as well as maidens in diaphanous garments (see the ghostly Angelica Kauffman, alongside Reynolds, chosen for the poster advertising the Royal Academy summer exhibition of 1974; Royal Academy, London).

Swanwick re-fashioned the human form, what she called "taking liberties" (Grayeff 1982), and her appreciation of Botticelli and Picasso can be seen in her own distorted inventions. Swanwick's figures have exceptionally bright eyes (*Sightless Man*, 1973; private collection, repr. Murphy 1989, p.10), magnificent feet (she was referred to as "the best boot drawer in England", Grayeff 1982) and wonderfully expressive bodies, like great oaks in a gale that none the less move with the fluidity of swimmers. Absolute reality was essential to her but she was not beyond painting two left feet (*The Footbath*, 1987; repr. Murphy 1989, frontispiece) or too few legs. She wrote: "There is nothing extra in those pictures that is of no consequence. I have to be most economical and spare myself nothing. I have to put everything exactly right" (Grayeff 1982). Over the years she gathered references, making detailed studies of hands, plants, animals, objects and places, such as the ruins of Bayham Abbey, Sussex, to capture the mystery that existed there (*Key of the Kingdom*, 1985; ex-Bonhams Studio Sale 1990).

On average a picture took 150 to 200 hours to complete and went through several stages, beginning with a very free drawing, called a "rough rough", using a variety of pencils and Imperial size paper (22×30 inches, 56×76 cm.). From the moment the first mark was made, that mark had a voice. The "rough rough" was then clarified ("rough") and finally honed (sometimes enlarged by squaring up). The completed drawing was composed of high points rather than a single focal point, full of small, lovely details, providing clues to the tensions within the piece. From 1971 Swanwick used these drawings as cartoons for her watercolours, by transferring the outlines on a light box, keeping them alongside to aid painting tonal values. She chose watercolour, the most luminous medium. Gum arabic was used to harden the surface of the paper and paint applied in many layers over several weeks, during which time she would select an anchor in the picture and bring one section to completion.

Swanwick was an artist of great humility (her rule of thumb for pricing her work was to multiply the number of hours she had spent by the hourly rate earned by a bus driver) and relative obscurity. Until the 1980s virtually nothing was written about her, and she was never affiliated to any gallery. From 1965, however, she exhibited at the Royal Academy (sending two or three works annually, then her full entitlement of six once elected an Associate in 1972). By the 1980s practically everything she made was sold before it was shown; for many, Swanwick's imaginative fantasies were the most memorable. She avoided publicity but achieved fame none the less. Denton Welch, with whom she had shared a painting space at Goldsmiths', thought her one of the most uniquely talented of their generation, and re-created her in the thinly disguised characters, Betsy (*A Voice Through a Cloud*, 1950) and Fat Bertha Swan (*A Party*, 1951; published in *A Last Sheaf*). *The Dream* (1973; private collection, repr. Grayeff 1982) inspired a song on the Genesis album *Selling England by the Pound*, and was used for its cover.

Swanwick's last works were increasingly ethereal, achieving a highly distinctive, evanescent complexity of colour akin to the delicate hues of tropical fruits and the phosphorescence of deep sea fishes. Her penultimate painting, *Fields of Ennor* (1989; private collection, repr. *Royal Academy Illustrated*, 1989), in which Scillonians harvest paper whites (doubling as a rendition of Persephone snatched away by Hades), achieved a harmonic symphony of balance and colour. It is one of her finest achievements.

JANE HILL

Swanzy, Mary
Irish painter, 1882–1978

Born in Dublin, 15 February 1882; father the eye surgeon Sir
Henry Swanzy. Educated at Alexandra College, Dublin, Lycée
Versailles and in Freiburg, Germany. Studied art in Dublin
under Mary Manning and John Butler Yeats, and under the
sculptor John Hughes at the Metropolitan School of Art; in
Paris, 1905–6, in various studios including that of Lucien
Simon; also attended Académie de la Grande Chaumière and
Académie Colarossi. Studio at 18 Nassau Street, Dublin,
from 1908, 9 Garville Avenue, Rathgar, 1918. Travelled to
Italy and France. Joined her sister in relief work with the
Protestant Mission in the Balkans, 1921–2. Travelled to
Hawaii, Samoa and USA, 1923–4, returning to Ireland in
February 1925. Settled in Blackheath, London, but returned
to Dublin for three years during World War II; also spent
time in France. Committee member, Salon des Indépendants,
Paris, 1920; member, Society of Dublin Painters, 1920.
Honorary member, Royal Hibernian Academy, 1949. Died in
London, 7 July 1978.

Principal Exhibitions

Individual
Mills' Hall, Dublin: 1913, 1919
Dublin Painters' Gallery: 1920 (with Clare Marsh), 1943
Cross Roads Studios and elsewhere, Honolulu: 1924
Art Club Gallery, Santa Barbara, CA: 1925
Galerie Bernheim Jeune, Paris: 1925
Mespil House, Dublin (Sarah Purser's home): 1932
Reid and Lefevre Galleries, London: 1934
St George's Gallery, London: 1947
Hugh Lane Municipal Gallery of Modern Art, Dublin: 1968 (retro-
    spective)
Dawson Gallery, Dublin: 1974, 1976

Group
Royal Hibernian Academy, Dublin: occasionally 1905–77
Salon des Indépendants, Paris: 1914, 1918, 1923, 1926, 1934
Society of Sculptors, Painters and Gravers, London: 1916
Women's International Art Club, London: 1929
Irish Exhibition of Living Art: 1943
St George's Gallery, London: 1946 (with Vlaminck, Chagall, Braque
    and Henry Moore)

Bibliography

Mary Swanzy: Retrospective Exhibition, exh. cat., Hugh Lane
    Municipal Gallery of Modern Art, Dublin, 1968
Fionnuala Brennan, *Mary Swanzy, 1882–1978*, BA thesis, Trinity
    College, Dublin, 1983
*The Irish Impressionists: Irish Artists in France and Belgium,
    1850–1914*, exh. cat., National Gallery of Ireland, Dublin, 1984
Mary Swanzy, HRHA (1882–1978), exh. cat., Pyms Gallery, London,
    1986
Irish Women Artists from the Eighteenth Century to the Present Day,
    exh. cat., National Gallery of Art, Dublin, and elsewhere, 1987
Mary Swanzy, HRHA (1882–1978), exh. cat., Pyms Gallery, London,
    1989 (contains bibliography)
Kenneth McConkey, *A Free Spirit: Irish Art, 1860–1960*,
    Woodbridge, Suffolk: Antique Collectors' Club-Pyms Gallery,
    1990
S.B. Kennedy, *Irish Art and Modernism, 1880–1950*, Belfast:
    Institute for Irish Studies, 1991

Swanzy: *Samoan Scene*, c.1923–4; oil on canvas; 152 ×
92 cm.; Allied Irish Bank Art Collection, AIB Group, Dublin

Mary Swanzy belongs to the first generation of women artists
to introduce modernism to Ireland. Studying in Paris in the
early 20th century, she became familiar with new ideas of
abstraction based on Cubism, Fauvism and Orphism, and with
Mainie Jellett (q.v.) and others, she spread these ideas through
the Dublin Painters' Society.

Swanzy began her career as a portraitist in the conservative
tradition of the Royal Hibernian Academy and artists such as
John Butler Yeats, but she very quickly found new ideas, especially from Fauvism and Cubism, during her studies in Paris in
1905 and 1906. Her portraiture and style remained largely
traditional, however, until 1914, when, exhibiting at the Salon
des Indépendants in Paris, strong influences from both Cubism
and from the Orphism of Robert Delaunay become apparent.
Young Woman with Flowers (c.1914; 76 × 152.5 cm.; private
collection, repr. Dublin 1987, pl.23) is one of her early efforts
at Cubism. The face of the girl is surrounded by shafts of light,
arabesque flowers and broad curving areas of colour. From the
same period and close to Delaunay's work is *Futuristic Study*

with *Skyscrapers and Propellers* (c.1914; repr. London 1986, pp.41–2). Although she continued working in a Cubist manner, Swanzy turned more to landscapes, some influenced by Cézanne. Most are lyrical, displaying delicate, decorative forms and a fascination with light effects. Many were done in Provence with characteristic fields and hill-top villages. Throughout Swanzy's career her work showed strong ties to French art, both in style and locale of subject.

In the 1920s Swanzy ventured to different lands. After the murder of a cousin by the IRA in 1920, she travelled to Yugoslavia and Czechoslovakia and found rural life and landscapes to paint (e.g. *Village with Roof of Church and Green Hills*, c.1919–20; repr. London 1986, p.65). These works were drawn or painted boldly with crayons or oil paints using very bright, Fauve-like colours (e.g. *Twisted Tree Against Red Houses*, ibid., p.51). Her travels in the Pacific resulted in scenes of Hawaii and Samoa that show a joyful responsiveness to the richness of the scenery. The sunlit tropical pool and bathers of *Samoan Scene* (c.1923–4; see illustration) are not only enjoyed by the viewer but also by the native spectator in the left foreground. Using oil on canvas, Swanzy delighted in the shapes and colours of the flowers, fruits and parrots. The boldly modelled and painted figure, material and roots give way to foliage treated in flat planes and with impressionistic dabs of colour. The parrots and coconuts add to the richness of the colour, and the distant mountain serves as a foil to the lush and patterned palm and banana trees.

Symbolic or visionary art appears dominant from the late 1930s onwards. Initially, Swanzy's subjects reflect the upheaval of war, death and destruction. Generally she uses a dark palette and adds glazes for a denser surface. Dating to the early 1940s, the oil painting *The Message* (Hugh Lane Municipal Gallery of Modern Art, Dublin) has clear religious references with a Madonna-like figure contrasted with shepherds who seem boorish and ignorant. Another painting of the same period, *Allegorical Figure* (1942; Jorgensen Gallery, Dublin), has rich warm colours and many flowers but none the less a sense of sadness pervades the scene. A head crowned with a laurel wreath holds flowers and looks downwards. White lilies in a vase, set against a background of richly coloured flowers, dominate the centre of the painting. In the lower left corner is a dark form – perhaps a hand between breasts. The pervasive mood is one of mourning.

Swanzy's late paintings are more serene and full of personal symbolism. Clowns, birds, lovers, all done with a rich palette, place her within the traditions of the School of Paris. *Gardener and the Bluebird* (1965; private collection, repr. Dublin 1987, p.146) is an idyllic scene with a gardener whistling to a singing bluebird, the distant landscape evoking images of Italy.

Swanzy began her career as an eclectic artist responding to the styles of art she found in Paris, but her later art, certainly from the period of the Samoan paintings onwards, is very personal. Strength of composition, a sure sense of appropriate and rich colour and the ability to put paint on a canvas beautifully are intrinsic qualities of her art; her later works display a personal symbolism that challenges the spectator. At her best she produced some truly outstanding works. Swanzy lived or travelled abroad most of her life, and for 25 years did not exhibit her work in Ireland. Then in 1968 a large retrospective was arranged by Irish admirers of her work at the Municipal Gallery of Modern Art, Dublin, which brought this artist to the attention of the Irish public. It was followed by other exhibitions in Dublin, securing for Mary Swanzy an important place in Irish art.

MARTHA B. CALDWELL

Swynnerton, Annie
British painter, 1844–1933

Born Annie Louisa Robinson in Kersal, Manchester, 1844; father a solicitor. Studied at Manchester School of Art; Académie Julian, Paris; and in Rome. Co-founder, with Susan Isabel Dacre, of the Manchester Society of Women Painters, 1879. Married sculptor Joseph William Swynnerton, 1883; lived in Rome until his death in 1910. Member, Society of Women Artists, 1887; Royal Society of Portrait Painters, 1891; New English Art Club, 1909; International Society of Sculptors, Painters and Gravers. Associate, Royal Academy, 1922 (first woman member since the 18th century). Died in Hayling Island, near Portsmouth, 24 October 1933.

Principal Exhibitions
Liverpool Autumn Exhibition: occasionally 1878–1934
Royal Academy, London: 1879–86, 1902, 1906–9, 1912–14, 1920–33
Grosvenor Gallery, London: 1882–7
New Gallery, London: c.1890
World's Columbian Exposition, Chicago: 1893
Manchester City Art Gallery: 1923 (individual)

Bibliography
Walter Shaw Sparrow, *Women Painters of the World*, London: Hodder and Stoughton, and New York: Stokes, 1905; reprinted New York: Hacker, 1976
Paintings by Mrs Swynnerton, ARA, exh. cat., Manchester City Art Gallery, 1923
Art News, xxxii/4, 28 October 1933, p.10 (obituary)
Gladys Storey, *Dickens and Daughter*, London: Muller, 1939; reprinted New York: Haskell House, 1971, pp.201–4
Concise Catalogue of British Paintings, i, Manchester City Art Galleries, 1976
Jane Sellars, *Women's Works: Paintings, Drawings, Prints and Sculpture by Women*, Liverpool: National Museums and Galleries on Merseyside, 1988
Deborah Cherry, *Painting Women: Victorian Women Artists*, London and New York: Routledge, 1993

Annie Swynnerton was a painter of allegorical and symbolical figure subjects, portraits, pictures of children and landscape. She showed early artistic promise, and as a girl painted watercolours to supplement her family's meagre income. Swynnerton lived until the age of 90, producing much work throughout her long working life. She is remarkable for the admiration she drew from fellow artists, whose support ensured healthy sales for her pictures and the recognition she deserved. In 1922, backed by Sir George Clausen and John Singer Sargent, she won the distinction of becoming the first female Associate member of the Royal Academy since Mary Moser (q.v.) and Angelica Kauffman (q.v.) at its foundation in 1768. Her backers also enabled Swynnerton's representation in

Swynnerton: *Sense of Sight*, 1895; oil on canvas; 87.3 × 101 cm.; Walker Art Gallery, Liverpool

major collections: Clausen, by purchasing her painting *New-Risen Hope* in 1906 and presenting it to the National Gallery of Victoria, Melbourne, Australia, and Sargent by gifting *The Oreads*, a group of sea nymphs, to the Tate Gallery, London, in 1922. The Chantrey Bequest purchased three further Swynnerton pictures for the Tate: a second version of *New-Risen Hope* (1924), *The Convalescent* (1929) and a portrait of *Dame Millicent Fawcett* (1930).

Although she did not spend a great deal of her life there, Swynnerton is closely associated with the city of Manchester where she was born. There are 16 of her oil paintings in the Manchester City Art Galleries, including a portrait of *The Reverend William Gaskell* (1879), husband of the novelist Elizabeth Gaskell, *Illusions*, a portrait of a little girl in medieval costume, *An Italian Mother and Child* (1886), one of many figure subjects painted in Rome, *The Dreamer* (1887), a head-and-shoulders portrait of a beautiful dark-haired, Italian-looking girl holding knitting wool and needles, in fact painted on the Isle of Man, the *Town of Siena*, one of a number of Italian views, and a striking portrait of her artist friend *Susan Isabel Dacre* (1880), which is affectionately inscribed "A mon amie".

Swynnerton's friendship with Dacre is significant, not only because they worked together in Paris, Rome and London during the early part of their careers, but also because together they established the Manchester Society of Women Painters in 1879. In the late 19th century Manchester was a city of some cultural status, confirmed by the Art Treasures Exhibition of 1857, the Royal Jubilee Exhibition of 1887 and the Autumn shows of the Manchester Royal Institution, but civic power excluded women. Swynnerton and Dacre formed the Society for Women Painters in order to give women artists the advantages for study and recognition that were denied to them. They organised exhibitions in 1880, 1882 and 1883, set up life classes and organised art administration for women in the city. Otherwise, Manchester women artists were confined to the "Lady Exhibitors" section of the Manchester Academy for Fine Arts; they were not allowed to become full members until 1884.

Swynnerton and Dacre were active campaigners for women's rights – they were among the 100 women artists included in the 2000 signatories of the Declaration in Favour of Women's Suffrage of 1889. As Deborah Cherry has commented, Swynnerton's image of Dacre, with her unkempt hair, anxious expression and plain gown, is an unusually realistic and truthful view of a working woman artist, intended above all as a token of the friendship between the two women (Cherry 1993, p.52).

In 1895 Swynnerton also penetrated another male bastion of the art establishment by becoming the second woman, after Henrietta Rae (q.v.), to be elected a member of the Hanging Committee of the Liverpool Autumn Exhibition held at the Walker Art Gallery, to which she was herself a frequent contributor . The Committee not only selected works for the annual show, but it also advised on the purchase of pictures from it for the Walker's permanent collection. Swynnerton is represented at Liverpool by an allegorical picture, *Sense of Sight* (1895; see illustration), which personifies sight in the form of a half-length, winged female figure with huge blue eyes, looking dramatically upwards towards the light. This type of female figure, sometimes a child, representing some abstract quality, was a popular Swynnerton subject. Other examples include *Southing of the Sun* (1911; 111 × 88.9 cm.; Manchester City Art Galleries), titled after a line in a poem by Emerson and depicting a peasant woman, her hands open-palmed, striding in the sunlit landscape of Nemi in Italy.

The artistic influences on Swynnerton were varied. For nearly 30 years her main residence was in Italy, and from Italian art and landscape she learned a sense of space and light and a grasp of form that is almost sculptural. Christie's catalogue of Swynnerton's studio sale, held early in 1934, the year after her death, includes works by the Italian masters Guercino and Zuccarelli, as well as faience, marble and bronze sculpture, wood carvings, Flemish tapestry and Persian rugs. Her painting style also has some debt to British contemporaries, particularly G.F. Watts and Edward Burne-Jones, to whom she was introduced by Elizabeth Gaskell. According to Lawrence Haward, who wrote the eulogy to Swynnerton that introduces the catalogue for the exhibition held at Manchester City Art Gallery ten years before her death: "Miss Gaskell's introduction to Burne-Jones Mrs Swynnerton regards in fact as the turning point in her life" (Manchester 1923). In her numerous landscapes, painted mostly in Britain and in Italy around Rome and in Tuscany, there is evidence of the influence of the French Impressionists. Her landscape subjects include *Carricky Bay, Isle of Man* (1923; collection Mrs Charles Hunter), *Sabine Mountains from Tusculum* (1923; collection Mrs George Garrett) and views of Capri.

Swynnerton also earned her living from portraiture, and her subjects included *Henry James* (untraced), *Mr Stanley Baldwin, Uncle of the Premier* (1923; collection C. F. Brockbank), *Count Zouboff*, her husband *Joseph William Swynnerton*, *Rhoda Garrett* and *Louisa Garrett Anderson CBE* (all untraced). She was herself painted in a double portrait by her friend John Singer Sargent, posing with one of her most generous patrons Mrs Charles Hunter, sister of the composer Ethel Smyth. She painted many portraits of children. One of her subjects (*Evelyn, Daughter of Vernon Bellhouse*, 1911; untraced) recalled sitting for Swynnerton at the Bellhouse home in Alderley Edge, Cheshire:

My father invited her to stay with us and I can remember her smoking a cigar. She didn't finish the painting while she was with us but she took my dress away with her, and the couch I'm sitting on belonged to the artist J.S. Sargent, a friend of hers ... She was a splendid old lady and told me the most fascinating stories, hence my wide-eyed stare [Priscilla Hodgson, "Myself when young", Cheshire Life, October 1982].

In common with other women painters of her day, however, most of all Swynnerton painted pictures of women, both as portraits and as symbolic figures. For the Woman's Building at the World's Columbian Exposition in Chicago in 1893, Swynnerton exhibited a picture of *Florence Nightingale at Scutari Hospital*, flanked by two paintings, one of a mother and child and the other of a young woman caring for an older woman, denoting the care of women for the weak and helpless (all untraced). Her most unusual female subject is an image of a woman worker, the *Factory Girl's Tryst* (Salford Museum and Art Gallery), exhibited at the Royal Academy in 1881.

Towards the end of her long, hard-working life, Swynnerton won some laurels not always bestowed on women painters: her membership of the Royal Academy, a solo exhibition at a major provincial gallery and the praise of the critics. Her obituary in *The Times* summed up her achievement with the word "vitality", and described her painting as an expression of "youngness of heart, joy in life, and reckless abandonment to the appeal of light and colour".

JANE SELLARS

T

Taeuber-Arp, Sophie

Swiss artist and designer, 1889–1943

Born Sophie Henriette Taeuber (or Täuber) in Davos, 19 January 1889; father German, mother Swiss. Studied textile design at the Gewerbeschule, Sankt Gallen, 1908–10. Studied in experimental art studio of Walter von Debschitz in Munich, 1911–12 and 1913–14; attended the Kunstgewerbeschule, Hamburg, 1912–13. Became a member of the Schweizerischer Werkbund, 1915. Met artist Jean Arp, 1915; married him, 1922. Active member of Dada group in Zürich, 1916–19. Professor of textile design, Kunstgewerbeschule, Zürich, 1916–29. Served on jury of Swiss section for the Exposition Internationale des Arts Décoratifs et Industriels Modernes, Paris, 1925. Visited Italy, 1925. Became French citizen with Arp, 1926. Moved to Meudon-Val-Fleury, near Paris, 1928. Exhibited at the Salon des Surindépendants, Paris, 1929–30. Member of Cercle et Carré group founded by Michel Seuphor and Torrès-Garcia, Paris, 1930; Abstraction-Création group, Paris, 1931–4; Allianz (union of Swiss painters), Zürich, 1937–43. Participated in international Surrealist exhibitions in London (1936), New York (1936), Paris (1938) and Amsterdam (1938). Founder and editor of the journal *Plastique*, 1937–9. Stayed in Grasse with Arp and their friends Sonia Delaunay (q.v.) and Alberto Magnelli, 1941–2. Died in Zürich as the result of an accident, 13 January 1943.

Selected Individual Exhibitions

Libraire La Mésange, Strasbourg: 1928 (*Projets de l'Aubette et oeuvres d'Arp, Taeuber, van Doesburg*)

Galerie des Cahiers d'Art, Paris: 1934 (with Jean Arp, Nicolas Ghika and Jean Hélion)

Galerie Delcourt, Paris: 1937 (with Georges Vantongerloo)

Galerie Jeanne Bucher, Paris: 1939 (with Jean Arp)

Selected Writings

"Bemerkungen über den Unterricht im ornamentalen Entwerfen", *Korrespondenzblatt des Schweiz. Vereins der Gewerbe- und Hauswirtschaftslehrerinnen*, no.11–12, 31 December 1922, pp.156–9

Anleitung zum Unterricht im Zeichnen für Textile Berufe, Zürich, 1927 (with Blanche Gauchat)

Bibliography

Georg Schmidt, ed., *Sophie Taeuber-Arp*, Basel: Holbein, 1948 (includes catalogue raisonné by Hugo Weber)

Margit Staber, *Sophie Taeuber-Arp*, Lausanne: Rencontre, 1970

Elsa Honig Fine, *Women and Art: A History of Women Painters and Sculptors from the Renaissance to the 20th Century*, Montclair, NJ: Allanheld and Schram, and London: Prior, 1978

Germaine Greer, *The Obstacle Race: The Fortunes of Women Painters and Their Work*, London: Secker and Warburg, and New York: Farrar Straus, 1979

Joan M. Marter, "Three women artists married to early modernists: Sonia Delaunay-Terk, Sophie Taüber-Arp and Marguerite Thompson Zorach", *Arts Magazine*, liv, September 1979, pp.88–95

Sophie Taeuber-Arp, exh. cat., Museum of Modern Art, New York, and elsewhere, 1981

Sophie Taeuber-Arp, exh. cat., Museo Communale, Ascona, 1983

Hans Arp und Sophie Taeuber-Arp: Die Elemente der Bilder und Bücher, exh. cat., Herzog August Bibliothek, Wolfenbüttel, 1988

Serge Faucherau, *Arp*, New York: Rizzoli, 1988; London: Academy, 1989

Sophie Taeuber, Hans Arp: Künstlerpaare – Künstlerfreunde/Dialogues d'artistes – résonances, exh. cat., Kunstmuseum, Bern, and elsewhere, 1988

Sophie Taeuber, exh. cat., Musée d'Art Moderne de la Ville de Paris, and elsewhere, 1989 (contains exhibition list and extensive bibliography)

Sophie Taeuber-Arp: Zum 100 Geburtstag, exh. cat., Aargauer Kunsthaus, Aargau, and elsewhere, 1989

Sophie Taeuber-Arp, Hans Arp: Besonderheiten eines Zweiklangs, exh. cat., Staatliche Kunstsammlungen Albertinum, Dresden, 1991

Angela Thomas, *Mit unverstelltem Blick: Bericht zu drei Künstlerinnen: Anna Baumann-Kienast, Alis Guggenheim, Sophie Taeuber-Arp*, Bern: Benteli, 1991

Sophie Taeuber-Arp, 1889–1943, exh. cat., Bahnhof Roldandseck, and elsewhere, 1993

Renée Riese Hubert, "Sophie Taeuber and Hans Arp: A community of two", *Art Journal*, lii, Winter 1993, pp.25–32

——, *Magnifying Mirrors: Women, Surrealism and Partnership*, Lincoln: University of Nebraska Press, 1994

"One views with amazement the range of media to which Sophie Taeuber-Arp adapted her decorative genius, whether it be at l'Aubette, in her weaving, embroidery, marionettes, stage décor, furniture design, stained glass, collage, wood reliefs, or even in dancing and publishing" attests Germaine Greer in her volume on the obstacles faced by women artists. In the same paragraph, Greer laments that Taeuber's sculptor husband Jean Arp is treated as a "more significant figure...although it is perfectly well known that the innovative qualities of [his] work owed a great deal to the fruitful vision of [Taeuber]" (Greer 1979, p.43).

Sophie Taeuber was teaching applied arts and studying dance in Zürich when Jean Arp moved there in 1915 to avoid being drafted by the German army. He called their meeting "the main event of my life" and never stopped emphasising Taeuber's merits or the manner in which she influenced him. "It was Sophie who, by the example of her work and her life, both of them bathed in clarity, showed me the right way. In her world, the high and the low, the light and the dark, the eternal and the ephemeral, are balanced in perfect equilibrium" (quoted in Fauchereau 1988, p.11).

By 1916 the two artists were not only a couple, they were also members of the group that met in Hugo Ball's Cabaret Voltaire to found the Dada art movement. Dada began in Zürich largely in response to the horrors of World War I. "After the carnage, we are left with hope for a purified humanity", wrote the poet Tristan Tzara in the Dada Manifesto of 1918. Dada stressed humour and absurdity, spontaneity and chance. It debunked both conventional art media and traditional arts institutions as it celebrated a merging of the performing, literary and visual arts. Taeuber had already embraced most of these values by the time she met Arp. She composed in fabric and thread as easily as in wood and pigment, had disdain for paintings in oil on canvas, and often preferred dancing to drawing. Her dancing was a major contribution to the interdisciplinary pursuits of Swiss Dada: the entry in Hugo Ball's journal of 29 March 1917 tells of an "abstract dance" that Taeuber executed to one of his poems, wearing a mask by Arp.

Taeuber and Arp embarked on a shared life of collaboration, "in duo", as they said.

Sophie Taeuber and I had decided to renounce completely the use of oil colors in our compositions. We wanted to avoid any references to the paintings which seemed to us characteristic of a pretentious and ostentatious world. In 1916, Sophie Taeuber and I began to work together on large compositions in fabric and paper. I embroidered with Sophie Taeuber's help a series of vertical and horizontal configurations ... In the years during which we worked exclusively with new materials, I made embroidery and configurations in paper and in fabric, and it affected us like a sort of purification, like spiritual exercises, so that finally we rediscovered painting in its original state of purity [ibid., p.12].

Such purity can be seen in their *Amphora* (1917; Foundation Arp, Clamart), in which the two artists created a refined wooden sculpture by affixing one goblet atop another so as to establish rhythmic vertical symmetry and graceful horizontal balance.

Taeuber was a pioneer of geometric abstraction (although, with Arp, she preferred the term "concretion", since neither was "abstracting" from any objective source). As early as 1915, Arp wrote of their collaboration that they worked with "the simplest forms, using painting, embroidery and pasted paper. They were probably the first manifestations of their kind, pictures that were their own reality, without meaning or cerebral intentions. We rejected everything in the nature of a copy or a description, in order to give free flow to what was elemental and spontaneous" (quoted in Fine 1978, p.173). While Arp's sculpture soon moved into its characteristic biomorphic mode, Taeuber maintained a preference for the rectilinear that led to affinities with Constructivism. Fine asserted that the "pulsating rhythms and movements of [Taeuber's] 'taches quadrangulaires' of the 1920s anticipated Mondrian's 'Broadway Boogie-Woogie' (1942) by almost twenty years" (ibid., p.174). In 1926–7 Taeuber collaborated with the De Stijl painter Theo van Doesburg to design the "boldly geometric" interior of the Café l'Aubette in Strasbourg. She then designed the studio-house that she shared with Arp in Meudon-Val-Fleury, in an enclave of Clamart. In 1929 she and Arp joined the Cercle et Carré group of Constructivist artists (in spite of the fact that Arp had already established ties with the Surrealists). Both were members of Abstraction-Création group; both worked on the writing staff of the *Abstraction-Création* journal. In 1937 Taeuber began publishing the Constructivist magazine *Plastique*, but due to the outbreak of World War ll could produce only five issues.

Immediately before the war, Taeuber and Arp collaborated on the book *Muscheln und Schrime* (Meudon-Val-Fleury, 1939). Renée Riese Hubert noted that the title was a surrealistic allusion to "chance encounters à la Lautréamont between a shell (not a sewing machine) and an umbrella", adding that the text and image were related as music and dance: Taeuber's drawings were "essentially a subdued and intermittent musical accompaniment" to Arp's poems (Hubert 1993, p.30). In one of the drawings, six similar curvilinear forms drift down the white page, like a scattering of shells or petals over open space. In another, seven varied forms cluster in vertical parade. Rounded contours on one side form rhythmic counterpoint to opposing straight edges (repr. Hubert 1993, figs 3 and 4). Taeuber's *Parasols* (1938; Rijksmuseum Kröller-Müller, Otterlo), created during the period of collaboration on the book, is a large wooden panel on which jigsaw-like cut-outs seem to tumble from chaos into precarious stasis. Gentle curves are answered by angles and planes in a satisfying but never static dialogue. The artist continued similar work in Meudon until the arrival of the Nazis forced her to flee with Arp to Grasse, where they were joined by their old friend Sonia Delaunay (q.v.), and they all worked on a collective series of lithographs there. In 1942 the couple took refuge in Zürich. The following year, Taeuber died in a freak accident at the home of the sculptor Max Bill. Arp was so devastated by her death that he retired for a period to a Dominican friary. When he emerged, he continued their collaboration by tearing Sophie's drawings into patches of paper and arranging them "by chance" on to his own collages (see especially his *Collage of a Torn Drawing by Sophie Taeuber*, 1946; van Doesburg Estate, The Hague).

BETTY ANN BROWN

Tait, Agnes
American painter and graphic artist, 1894–1981

Born in Greenwich Village, New York City, 14 June 1894. Studied at the National Academy of Design, New York, under Charles L. Hinton, Francis Jones and Leon Kroll, 1908–18 (Hollgarten prizes for painting and composition, Suydam bronze medal for life drawing). Visited Paris for the first time, studying at Ecole des Beaux-Arts, 1927; travelled to the West Indies, 1929. Married journalist William L. McNulty, 1933; he died 1952. Joined Public Works of Art Project (PWAP) as an easel painter, 1934. Lived in Providence, Rhode Island, 1937–41. Moved to Santa Fe, New Mexico, 1941; subsequently visited Mexico, 1951, Italy, 1960, and Ireland, 1961. Died in Santa Fe, 23 August 1981.

Principal Exhibitions

Individual
Dudensing Galleries, New York: 1928 (with Jo Cantine and Jean Paul Slusser)
Ferargil Galleries, New York: 1932, 1945
Fine Arts Museum of New Mexico, Santa Fe: 1945–7 (touring)
Roosevelt County Fine Arts Society, Eastern New Mexico College, Portales: 1946
Art Alliance Office in Prince Plaza, Santa Fe: 1951
Art Gallery of New Mexico, Santa Fe: 1953
Farmington, NM: 1954
Patio Gallery, Knopp-Hunter shop, Santa Fe: 1956
Albany Institute of History and Art, NY: 1958
Eleanor Bedell at The Shop, Santa Fe: 1963
Arvada Center for the Arts and Humanities, Arvada, CO: 1984 (touring retrospective)

Group
Corcoran Gallery of Art, Washington, DC: 1934 (National Exhibition of Art by the Public Works of Art Project)
Museum of Modern Art, New York: 1937 (New Horizons in American Art)
New York World's Fair: 1939
Argent Galleries, New York: 1940 (Women Artists)
Library of Congress, Washington, DC: 1943 (First National Exhibition of Prints)

Bibliography

Judith Kaye Read, "Agnes Tait in Santa Fe", Art Digest, no.29, March 1945, p.18
Women Artists, 1550–1950, exh. cat., Los Angeles County Museum of Art, and elsewhere, 1976
The Life and Times of Agnes Tait, 1894–1981, exh. cat., Arvada Center for the Arts and Humanities, Arvada, CO, and elsewhere, 1984
Lydia M. Peña, "In the American scene: The life and times of Agnes Tait", Woman's Art Journal, v/1, 1984, pp.35–9

The work of Agnes Tait received considerable attention in New York during the 1930s and in New Mexico in the 1940s and 1950s, yet she is little known today. She painted landscapes, cats and people; she was a muralist and decorator, a pen-and-ink artist, lithographer and book illustrator. Whatever the medium, Tait focused on the noble, the majestic, the pastoral – romantic sentiments that made her seem hopelessly old-fashioned when modernism took hold of American art after World War II.

Tait's early paintings, according to a review of an exhibition of her works at the Dudensing Galleries, New York, betrayed the influence of the Pre-Raphaelite school (New York Times, May 1928). But although the themes of the paintings on display (Girls and Doves, Pretty Creatures, La Blonde au Bois; all untraced) may have been borrowed from the Pre-Raphaelites, their simplicity and suppressed detail are more akin to works by the early Italian painters Giotto, Duccio and Simone Martini. In The Bride (1928; untraced, repr. Arvada 1984, p.14) a slender, imaginary figure, unconventionally attired in garlands of waxy flowers, is set off by a bay of deepest blue, with mauve rocks in the far distance. This painting was selected for the first annual exhibition at the Art Institute of Chicago (1928), and was reproduced in the Chicago Evening Post; the caption noted that it had been accorded "much popular admiration" at the show (16 December 1928).

In the summer of 1928 Tait was represented in the first exhibition of the newly formed Cooperstown Art Association and was commissioned by the association's founder, Dr Henry Sam Fenimore Cooper, to paint a mural in his summer home. A painting exhibited at the Brownell Lambertson Galleries, New York, attracted the attention of an executive from the United Fruit Company, who offered her a trip to Jamaica, Haiti and the surrounding islands in return for a screen – incorporating bananas – for his office. In addition to exhibiting paintings and prints of the islands at the Brownell Lambertson Galleries, Tait also began portrait work, and prepared for a show of notables at the Ferargil Galleries, painting Lewis Mumford and Lawrence Dennis, whom she described as "a controversial political figure". The exhibition, which opened in December 1932, received some critical attention. A critic for the New York Times found her work "happily free from affected style" and painted in a "direct and informal" mode. The review commented on her "light, fresh color", which seemed "particularly adapted to children's portraits, which she paints with sympathy but without sentimentality" (New York Times, quoted in Art Digest, January 1933).

In 1934 Tait joined the Public Works of Art Project (PWAP), which represented the earliest massive New Deal relief and patronage effort on behalf of destitute artists. Her most celebrated painting, Skating in Central Park (1934; see illustration), responds to the guidelines given to the artists, to depict an aspect of the "American Scene". The picture, which combines the styles of American primitive art with that of Pieter Breughel the Elder, depicts a winter landscape that is eloquent with bare trees and small, bustling, darkly clothed figures and skaters playing hockey on a frozen pond in the background. The picture captures a brisk, cold feeling of a winter day similar to that pervading Breughel's Return of the Hunters (1565; Kunsthistorisches Museum, Vienna). The narrative flavour of Skating in Central Park links Tait with the main current of American genre painting buried by the impact of the Armory Show of 1913, but revived during the Depression. The work paved the way for her further involvement in New Deal art projects, with both murals and prints. She prepared a number of lithographs for the Treasury Department, including Seals (Metropolitan Museum of Art), which was shown at the Metropolitan Museum of Art in 1936. Here she combined realism with abstraction to create a private

Tait: *Skating in Central Park*, 1934; Denver Public Library

fantasy world. That same year Tait collaborated with a team of artists charged with painting a mural for Bellevue Hospital, a psychiatric facility in New York. Unlike so many Federal Art Project paintings, which portrayed people at work, Tait chose the theme *Summer Holidays*, depicting families at play (mural now covered over). Sketches submitted to earlier mural competitions of the Treasury Department Section of Fine Arts brought her a commission to decorate the US Post Office in Laurinburg, North Carolina. The mural, *Fruits of the Land* (1941; National Museum of American Art, Smithsonian Institution, Washington, DC), celebrates the three basic crops – cantaloupes, watermelons and cotton – harvested in North Carolina at that time. At the centre of the composition is a large chinaberry tree, its height curtailed by the ceiling edge. Resting in the shade of the tree is a semicircular group echoing the shape of the foliage: a mother feeds her son, a young man fingers an accordian and children play. Making an even larger semicircular sweep are field workers gathering the crops.

Tait's travels in the West Indies are recorded in a number of lithographs, including *Trinidad Singers* (c.1937; repr. Arvada 1984, p.33), depicting the art of catching hens and later published in the *New York Times* (20 February 1944), and *Dominique* (1937; New York Public Library), which was exhibited at the *Women Artists* show at the Argent Galleries, New York, in 1940, and chosen to illustrate the review in the *Art Digest* (January 1940). In 1943 Tait's lithograph *El Cristo*

Rey (repr. Arvada 1984, p.82) was selected for the first *National Exhibition of Prints* at the Library of Congress, while *Survivors* (c.1941; Library of Congress, Washington, DC) was included in the touring print exhibition of 1943, *America in the War, the Artists for Victory*. The theme of survival in *Survivors* is generalised – there is no indication of time, place or specific disaster – and the benevolence of nature and healing factor of human relationships are emphasised. The church dominating the village serves as a symbol of faith, and the child greeting the group disembarking from the boat stands for a "ray of hope", according to the artist.

In 1945 Tait had two solo exhibitions, one at the Fine Arts Museum of New Mexico, which toured to several Southwestern cities, and one at the Ferargil Galleries, New York. The latter, which featured landscapes of Santa Fe and its environs, was widely reviewed. The critic for *Art News* commented on the uneven skill of Tait's work, noting that she was evidently seeking to "expand, by experimentation, both her technique and subject matter. ... At her best, she captures in sharp point drawing and high key colors the character of the region around Taos and Santa Fe, and gives us in a half-naturalistic, half-romantic style the subject's charm" (1 March 1945). The "unevenness" perceived by this viewer continued to be apparent in Tait's work as she became increasingly preoccupied with caring for her sister Anita, who had spinal meningitis, then her husband's illness and finally her own.

Tait also gained a reputation as an illustrator. In December 1945 *Household* magazine featured *Christmastide in New Mexico* as a cover illustration, but her big break came in 1947, when Lippincott asked her to illustrate Johanna Spyri's *Heidi* (1948). Tait was also a painter of cats, which she considered an escape from the more exacting task of painting humans. After a brief trip to Mexico in 1951, and an exhibition at the Art Alliance of the Mexican paintings, portraits and cat paintings, Tait went to New York to complete several portrait commissions. In 1952 she received two mural commissions, one from Via Coeli, a rehabilitation centre for priests in Jemez Springs, New Mexico, the other from the First National Bank in Santa Fe. These murals, like *Fruits of the Land*, were painted on canvas and adhered to the wall with linoleum paste. Their whereabouts are currently unknown.

While negotiating an exhibit at the Albany Institute of History and Art, Tait wrote to the director: "The only thing is to avoid the suggestion that I'm a 'regional' painter. Living in Santa Fe is for me a matter of circumstance – not of importance in my work. People do like to label me, and I just don't fit it any category" (14 July 1958). It was around this time that Tait became disenchanted with Santa Fe and its museum; according to a former museum employee, she "was not particularly in sympathy with the new art" (interview with Thelma Robinson, Santa Fe, 3 January 1978).

In the oil paintings from her Southwestern periods, such as *Taos Pueblo* (*c*.1950; repr. Arvada 1984, p.84), the high noon light emphasises the vibrant colours – golden browns, blue-greens and reds – and heightens the importance of the "little people" who dominated her work throughout her 60 years as an exhibiting artist. Eliminating detail, she emphasised people's dignity. The pueblo looms large against the holy mountain: "the majesty of that scene has brushed off on the people who live there". There are no signs of poverty or decay to mar the cleanliness and purity of the scene. And this was Tait's view of the world, as earlier reflected in the wartime lithograph *Survivors* – she always saw the "ray of hope".

LYDIA M. PEÑA

Tanguy, Kay Sage *see* Sage

Tanning, Dorothea

American painter, sculptor and graphic artist, 1910–

Born in Galesburg, Illinois, 25 August 1910. Worked part-time at Galesburg Public Library after leaving school at age 16. Studied at Knox College, Galesburg, 1928–30, then for two weeks at the Art Institute of Chicago. Moved to New York, 1936, supporting herself by various draughtswoman jobs in advertising. Left for Paris, August 1939, hoping to meet the Surrealists, who were no longer in France; took last boat back to New York before outbreak of World War II. Met Surrealist art dealer Julien Levy and through him Max Ernst, 1942. Married Ernst in a double ceremony with Man Ray and Juliet Browner in Beverly Hills, 1946. Exhibited with the Surrealists at Galerie Maeght, Paris, 1947. Lived in Sedona, Arizona, then in Provence and Paris until Ernst's death in 1976. Returned to USA, 1980. Lives in New York.

Selected Individual Exhibitions
Julien Levy Gallery, New York: 1944
Galerie Les Pas Perdus, Paris: 1950
Alexandre Iolas Gallery, New York: 1953
Galerie Furstenberg, Paris: 1954
Musée des Beaux-Arts, Tours: 1956 (*Trois peintres américains*, with Max Ernst and Man Ray)
Galerie Edouard Loeb, Paris: 1959
Galerie Der Spiegel, Cologne: 1963
Galerie d'Art Moderne, Basel: 1966
Casino Communal, Knokke-le-Zoute: 1967 (retrospective)
Le Point Cardinal, Paris: 1970
Centre National d'Art Contemporain, Paris: 1974 (retrospective)
Gimpel and Weitzenhoffer Gallery, New York: 1979
Stephen Schlesinger Gallery, New York: 1989
Nahan Contemporary, New York: 1990
New York Public Library: 1992 (retrospective)
Konsthall, Malmö: 1993

Selected Writings
Abyss, New York: Standard Editions, 1977 (novel, written 1947)
Birthday, Santa Monica, CA: Lapis Press, 1986 (autobiography)

Bibliography
The Astonished Gaze, film by Jean Desvilles, Paris, 1959
Alain Bosquet, *Dorothea Tanning: Peintures récentes*, Paris: Galerie Mouradian et Valloton, 1962
——, *La Peinture de Dorothea Tanning*, Paris: Pauvert, 1966
Dorothea Tanning: Oeuvre, exh. cat., Centre National d'Art Contemporain, Paris, 1974
Cindy Nemser, "'In her own image'", *Feminist Art Journal*, iii/1, Spring 1974, pp.11–18
Linda Nochlin, "Dorothea Tanning at the CNAC", *Art in America*, lxii, November–December 1974, p.128
Alain Jouffroy, "Dorothea Tanning: Le chavirement dans la joie", *XX siècle*, no.43, December 1974, pp.60–68
Gilles Plazy, *Dorothea Tanning*, Paris: Filipacchi, 1976
Daniel Abadie and others, *Dorothea Tanning: Essais, lettres, poèmes et témoignages*, Paris: XXe Siècle, 1977
Peter Schamoni, *Insomnias*, film, 1978 (on Tanning's paintings)
Dorothea Tanning: 10 Recent Paintings and a Biography, exh. cat., Gimpel and Weitzenhoffer, New York, 1979
Dorothea Tanning: Paintings, exh. cat., Stephen Mazoh Gallery, New York, 1983
Ann Gibson, "Dorothea Tanning: The impassioned double entendre", *Arts Magazine*, lviii, September 1983, pp.102–33
Whitney Chadwick, *Women Artists and the Surrealist Movement*, Boston: Little Brown, and London: Thames and Hudson, 1985
La Femme et le surréalisme, exh. cat., Musée Cantonal des Beaux-Arts Lausanne, 1987
Dorothea Tanning: On Paper, 1948–1986, exh. cat., Kent Fine Art, New York, 1987
Eleven Paintings by Dorothea Tanning, exh. cat., Kent Fine Art, New York, 1988
Dorothea Tanning: Between Lives: Works on Paper, exh. cat., Runkel-Hue-Williams, London, 1989
Dorothea Tanning: Hail, Delirium! A Catalogue Raisonné of the Artist's Illustrated Books and Prints, 1942–1991, exh. cat., New York Public Library, 1992

Creating visionary drawings since childhood as an escape from her uneventful early life in Illinois, Dorothea Tanning discovered Surrealism at the landmark exhibition *Fantastic Art, Dada, Surrealism* held at the Museum of Modern Art in New York in 1936. The movement's enthusiastic embrace of the marvellous in art and life helped Tanning to confirm and contextualise her own artistic direction. Her association with the exiled European Surrealists in New York a few years later, however, and in particular her long marriage to Max Ernst, compromised her career. Eclipsed from art history until 1966 when the first monograph on her work was published, Tanning's oeuvre is generally understood nowadays as directly inspired by Surrealist automatic procedures. Although Tanning acknowledges her continued affinity with the works of her old Surrealist friends and acquaintances, her recurrent portrayal of the female body, whether in symbiotic merger or in violent separation towards autonomy, deliberately transcends the traditional image of woman as portrayed in Surrealism.

Tanning, unlike most other women artists who joined the Surrealists in the 1930s and 1940s, did not fit the mould of the typical Surrealist *femme-enfant*, or "child-woman". The 32-year-old American artist had already established herself as a painter of noteworthy individuality when she encountered Ernst through her art dealer Julien Levy. A self-portrait from this period, in which the artist – bare-breasted with a winged lemur at her naked feet – opens a door that reveals endless corridors of more unlocked doorways, reflects Tanning's growing confidence in her private painterly explorations. It was Ernst who christened this oil painting *Birthday* (1942; artist's collection), a title that Tanning later recycled for her autobiography in memory of her dead husband.

During the 1940s Tanning created some of the most meticulously rendered images of the Surrealist movement. In *Children's Games* (1942; collection Preminger, New York) and *Eine kleine Nachtmusik* (1944; collection Penrose, Britain) unkempt girls in ragged clothes play in formalised corridors containing magical doorways. These female models of almost perfect behaviour seem to be acting out their young erotic fantasies in a rebellious self-exploration that threatens to overthrow the existing social order. In her novel *Abyss* (written in 1947 but not published until 1977) Tanning revisited this theme once more. In an attempt to regain access to the childhood world of "perpetual astonishment" and "incomparable secrets", Albert Exodus, a painter who does not paint, is drawn into the fascinating realm of the young and beautiful Destina Meridian. Unfortunately, his path crosses Destina's destructive quest for a new trophy to include in her memory box.

Until the 1950s, Tanning's paintings such as *Palaestra* (1947; collection Filipacchi), *Interior with Sudden Joy* (1951; private collection, USA, repr. Bosquet 1962) and *Guest Room* (1950–52; private collection, Belgium, *ibid.*) continued to focus on tantalising childhood obsessions. From 1952 onwards, while not abandoning this subject matter, Tanning relinquished the exactitude of the first Surrealist period and opted for a surer, freer form; she created a world of soft sensual shapes in perpetual interplay. The paintings of the 1950s and 1960s, directly affected by Tanning's recent ballet designs for George Balanchine (*Night Shadow*, 1946, and *Bayou*, 1952), John Cranko (*The Witch*, 1950), Ruthanna Boris (*Will-o'-the Wisp*, 1953) and Jean-Louis Barrault (*Judith*, 1961; all untraced), contain a greater sense of movement, both of materials and of the body. In *The Ill-Forgotten* (1955; collec-

tion Rosalind and Melvin Jakobs), *Insomnia* (1957) and *Two-Words* (1963; both collection Cavalio, New York) figures interweave to the point of mutation, hinting at the sheer infinite number of possible constructions. Tanning herself once described this conceptual change to Alain Jouffroy in an interview in the 1970s:

> In the first years, I was painting *our* side of the mirror – the mirror for me is a door – but I think that I've gone over, to a place where one no longer faces identities at all. One looks at them somewhat obliquely, slyly. To capture the moment, to *accept* it with all its complex identities [Jouffroy 1974].

When Tanning began sculpting in 1969 she ignored such traditional materials as bronze, marble, terracotta and wood and turned instead to upholstery and needlework to create an original series of soft sculptures. Earlier that year, while listening to Karlheinz Stockhausen's electronic piece *Hymnen* at the Maison de la Radio, the artist had actually seen her future soft sculptures in a vision. In her autobiography she described suddenly noticing "spinning among the unearthly sounds...earthy even organic shapes that I would make, had to make, out of cloth and wool...fugacious, they would be, and fragile, to please their creator and survivor". From 1969 until 1974 Tanning moulded, with the aid of her sewing machine, twisting anthropomorphous figures in tweeds and rose-coloured fabrics, sometimes growing out of a wall, or a piece of furniture. In 1974 at a retrospective at the Centre National d'Art Contemporain in Paris some of these soft sculptures were arranged in a hotel room that Tanning had created for this purpose; the *Hôtel du Pavot (Poppy Hotel), Room 202*, is now part of the permanent collection of the Centre Georges Pompidou, Paris.

The exhibition at the New York Public Library in 1992 drew overdue attention to 50 years of Dorothea Tanning's graphic work. She produced most of her lithographs with Pierre Chave, many intended to illustrate books for old friends from the Surrealist days. In her more than 100 prints, produced with Georges Visat, the artist turned once again to the female body in perpetual metamorphosis. Continuously shifting her modes of creativity, Tanning frankly challenges her public to solve her latest artistic riddles:

> We leave enigmas lying around, signs to be read ranging from knife-edge to nebulae-pleas for guesses. Having posed our riddle we hide behind a tree or a gallery wall and wait for a sign. Even a firefly radiance. We have time enough but we wait rather anxiously for a pair of eyes, any eyes, to flash pulsations to a mind, any mind that will take us on with our visual propositions.

BETTINA BRANDT

Tawney, Lenore
American artist, 1907–

Born in Lorain, Ohio, 10 May 1907. Attended evening classes at the School of the Art Institute of Chicago while working as a proof-reader, 1927–42. Married George

Tawney, 1941; he died 1943. Studied art at University of
Illinois, Champaign-Urbana, 1943–5. Studied at the Institute
of Design, Chicago, under László Moholy-Nagy, Alexander
Archipenko and Emerson Woelffer, 1946–7; continued studies
in Archipenko's studio, Woodstock, New York, 1947–8.
Toured Europe and North Africa and lived in Paris, 1949–51.
Studied tapestry weaving under Martta Taipale at Penland
School of Crafts, North Carolina, 1954; experimented with
open-warp weavings, 1955. Toured Greece and the Near
East, 1956; moved to New York, 1957. Studied gauze weave
under Lili Blumenau and Jacquard mechanism at Textile
Institute, Philadelphia, and travelled to Peru and Bolivia,
1960–64. Subsequently travelled throughout the Far East,
with long stays in India. Artist-in-residence, University of
Notre Dame, Indiana, and at Fabric Workshop, Philadelphia;
distinguished lecturer, University of Arizona, Tucson, from
1978. Fellow, American Craft Council, 1975. Recipient of
National Endowment for the Arts (NEA) grant, 1979;
Outstanding Achievement in the Visual Arts award, Women's
Caucus for Art, 1983; gold medal, American Crafts Council,
1987. Lives in New York.

Selected Individual Exhibitions
Staten Island Museum, New York: 1961
Art Institute of Chicago: 1962
Pennsylvania Academy of the Fine Arts, Philadelphia: 1970
California State University, Fullerton: 1975
Hadler Galleries, New York: 1978
New Jersey State Museum, Trenton: 1979
Tacoma Art Museum, WA: 1981
Musée des Arts Décoratifs, Paris: 1981
Mokotoff Gallery, New York: 1985, 1986
American Craft Museum, New York: 1990–91 (touring retrospective)
Delaware Arts Center Gallery, Narrowsburg, NY: 1991
Maryland Institute College of Art, Baltimore: 1992
Tenri Gallery, New York: 1994
Stedelijk Museum, Amsterdam: 1996

Bibliography
Ruth Kaufman, *The New American Tapestry*, New York: Reinhold,
   1968
Wall Hangings, exh. cat., Museum of Modern Art, New York, 1969
Lee Nordness, *Objects: USA*, Chicago: Johnson, and London:
   Thames and Hudson, 1970
Mildred Constantine and Jack Lenor Larsen, *Beyond Craft: The Art
   Fabric*, New York: Van Nostrand Reinhold, 1972
André Kuenzi, *La Nouvelle Tapisserie*, Geneva: Bonvent, 1973
Lenore Tawney: A Personal World, exh. cat., Brookfield Craft Center,
   CT, 1978
Eleanor Munro, *Originals: American Women Artists*, New York:
   Simon and Schuster, 1979
Weich und Plastisch: Soft-Art, exh. cat., Kunsthaus, Zürich, 1979
Mildred Constantine and Jack Lenor Larsen, *The Art Fabric:
   Mainstream*, New York: Van Nostrand Reinhold, 1981
Gerrit Henry, "Cloudworks and collage", *Art in America*, lxxiv, June
   1986, pp.116–21
Lenore Tawney: A Retrospective, exh. cat., American Craft Museum,
   New York, and elsewhere, 1990
Sigrid Wortmann Weltge, *Bauhaus Textiles: Women Artists and the
   Weaving Workshop*, London: Thames and Hudson, 1993; as
   Women's Work: Textile Art from the Bauhaus, San Francisco:
   Chronicle, 1993

Lenore Tawney's career defies easy classification. Her work in
clay, fibre, woven forms, collage, assemblage, drawing,

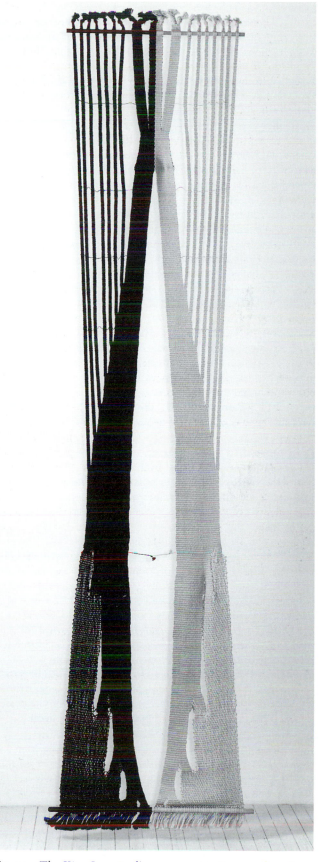

Tawney: *The King I,* 1962; linen; 375.9 × 78.7 cm.; American
Craft Museum, New York

painting and sculpture has been consistently in the avant-garde. Tawney's genius lies in her autonomy and emancipation from prescribed boundaries and her challenge to art historical categories. Teachers such as László Moholy-Nagy, Emerson Woelffer, Marli Ehrman, Martta Taipale and Alexander Archipenko encouraged this independence but in the end it was she who developed and articulated new forms of artistic expression.

Tawney's early career as a weaver coincided with a revival of the craft in the 1950s. The term fibre art had not yet been coined but "the new tapestry" emerged both in the USA and in Europe, especially Eastern Europe. Pictorial weaving ceded to iconographic abstraction. Disregarding traditional Gobelin techniques, weavers began to emphasise the autonomy of the individual thread and the integrity of textural surfaces or the sculptural possibilities inherent in fibres. Tawney contributed a number of ground-breaking hangings. In *Bound Man* (1957; American Craft Museum, New York) the gravity and downward pull of an abstracted figure strains the fragility of the sheer background, producing a tension that confronts the viewer with the tenuousness of life itself. In such works as *Jupiter* (1959; American Craft Museum) and *Triune* (1961; Metropolitan Museum of Art, New York) Tawney manipulated visibly floating, exposed yarns achieving shimmering, impressionistic colour effects. These early weavings approached the medium in a completely non-traditional, almost painterly way. Threads, normally hidden, asserted themselves as pure colour or calligraphic lines across exposed backgrounds, revealing Tawney's sure hand, so evident in many of her preparatory drawings.

In the early 1960s Tawney's work was informed by her studies of two diametrically opposed forms of manipulating fibres, the gauzes of ancient Peru and the technical possibilities inherent in the industrial Jacquard loom. Both advanced her art in new directions. A series of india ink drawings on graph paper reflect the intricate cord system of the Jacquard loom and convey, despite their precision, a luminous, hovering quality. At the same time Tawney experimented with weavings liberated from the concept of loom-controlled rectangles and arrived at her "woven forms", which pioneered shaped contours in the fibre arts. Hangings such as *The River* (1961; Museum of Modern Art, New York) and *Black Woven Form (Fountain)* (1966; American Craft Museum) departed radically from traditional weaving. Abandoning colour and iconography, Tawney constructed her open, slit pieces from natural or black linen and hung them away from the wall. Thus liberated, they asserted themselves as independent entities, penetrating and sharing the same space as the viewer. Some were imposing in size, others of almost miniature proportions, all heralded the dawn of a new era in the fibre arts.

Although Tawney used her New York studio as a base, her travels from the mid-1960s onwards took her across Europe, the Middle East and India. Her art increasingly reflected her involvement in Eastern thought and meditation. Works on paper explored her preoccupation with the circle in the square, with scrolls and ancient manuscripts, finely drawn lines and hand-written texts. Strips of old documents, laid out like warp and weft, remained flat or burst into dimension-revealing objects such as birds' eggs, bones and feathers. Tawney continued to develop these collages in subsequent decades, but unlike

those of Schwitters, whom she acknowledged in her collage *Schwitters' Smile* (1985; artist's collection), hers are not an amalgam of society's detritus. They are instead exquisitely painted surfaces on which writings resembling runic scripts and mysterious objects are carefully balanced. In *Chalcid* (1966) and *Round and Square* (1966; both artist's collection) Tawney combined old manuscripts with precisely drawn lines, wrestling with a language of geometric form reminiscent of the explorations of early Renaissance masters.

Some of Tawney's densely woven squares reveal perfect circles of open slits, partially covered with manuscript papers (*Waters above the Firmament*, 1976; Art Institute of Chicago). Others convey their strength through monochrome colour alone, broken by back light penetrating through the slits (*In Fields of Light*, 1975, and *Red Sea*, 1974; both artist's collection). This ease of crossing from one medium to the other is also evident in a series depicting the American flag. Such works on paper as *Adulterated Flag* (1975) find their counterpart in weavings with superimposed manuscript paper (*Untitled*, 1974; both artist's collection).

In 1976 Tawney abandoned loom-woven constructions but continued to work in fibre. In her *Cloud Series* (*Cloud Series IV*, 1977–8; Santa Rosa Federal Building, CA; *Cloud Series VI*, 1981; Frank J. Lausche State Office Building, Cleveland; *Cloud Series VII*, 1983; Connecticut State University, Danbury) she tied thousands of individual threads into painted canvas backings that were then suspended from the ceiling. These environments, often of enormous size, are powerful yet ethereal and are best described as movements in space. If her *Cloud Series* are monumental, her torn and painted paper constructions (*Far Off, Most Secret, Inviolate Rose*, 1986; artist's collection) are intimate encounters, their subtle vibration and fluttering occasioned by the viewer's proximity.

Throughout her career Tawney has worked in three-dimensional form, which she prefers to call assemblage rather than sculpture. Boxes, frames and cages contain found objects, carefully strung fibres, eggs, bones, feathers and vials. Some containers are covered with manuscripts and open up like books to reveal the secrets of the past (*Médecins Anciens, Materia Medica*, 1966; artist's collection) or treasures found in attics. A delicately painted glove cradled within a musical score evokes the vitality of bygone years (*Birth*, 1970; artist's collection). Is *Cello Lady at Eighty-Seven* (1994; artist's collection) a self-portrait of Tawney? A large wooden mannequin, covered with manuscripts, is seated in a chair holding a hollow cello bursting with a lifetime of accumulated writings and ideas.

Lenore Tawney has participated in important avant-garde exhibitions, both in Europe (the Lausanne Biennale and the Milan Triennale) and in major museums in the USA. Her contribution to art has been acknowledged by commissions from the public, private and religious sectors. Although the nature of her work is meditative it has been consistently on the cutting edge. She uses words and graphics as spiritual communication, not as echoes of a media-crazed environment. Through her unique vision, her unwavering integrity as an artist and her pioneering spirit, Tawney has brought closer disparate branches of the arts, tradition and avant-garde, East and West.

SIGRID WORTMANN WELTGE

Tchalenko, Janice

British potter and ceramic designer, 1942–

Born in Rugby, Warwickshire, 5 April 1942. Worked as a clerical officer in the Foreign Office, London, after leaving school. Married John Tchalenko, 1964; son born 1977. Studied at Putney School of Art, London, 1964–7 (diploma). Workshop assistant and part-time teacher, 1967–9; attended Workshop Pottery course at Harrow School of Art, 1969–71. Set up workshop in East Dulwich, London, with the aid of a Crafts Council grant, 1971; moved workshop to Camberwell, London, 1988. Taught part-time at Camberwell School of Arts and Crafts, London, 1972–87. Tutor at Royal College of Art, London, from 1981. Designer for Dart Pottery, Devon, from c.1984. Visited Goa You porcelain factory, Jiangsu province, China, to design new products, 1991. Recipient of first prize for Dart design, Manchester prize for Art in Production, 1988; joint winner, with Dart Pottery, of BBC Radio 4 Enterprise award, 1988. Appointed curator of British Council's *British Ceramics* Indian tour (1991), 1989. Member, Craftsmen Potters Association and Contemporary Applied Arts. Fellow, Royal College of Art, London, 1987. Lives in London.

Selected Individual Exhibitions

Atmosphere Gallery, London: 1981
Crafts Council Shop, Victoria and Albert Museum, London: 1981, 1982 (with weaver John Hinchcliffe), 1990 (with Richard Wentworth)
Bohun Gallery, Henley-on-Thames: 1983, 1987 (with painter David Remfry)
Blum Helman, New York: 1985 (with Betty Woodman and Mary Heilman)
Kunstformen Jetz, Salzburg: 1986 (with Alison Britton)
Scottish Gallery, Edinburgh: 1989
Nationalmuseum, Stockholm: 1990
Ruskin Craft Gallery, Sheffield: 1992 (touring retrospective)
Victoria and Albert Museum, London: 1993

Bibliography

Emmanuel Cooper, "Janice Tchalenko", *Ceramic Review*, no.80, 1983, pp.21–5
Peter Dormer, "Tchalenko, eclectic", *Crafts*, no.72, January–February 1985, pp.16–17, 59
Tanya Harrod, "Design and production: Janice Tchalenko and Dart pottery", *The Harrow Connection*, exh. cat., Northern Centre for Contemporary Art, Sunderland, and elsewhere, 1989, pp.74–6
Emmanuel Cooper, "Table talk", *Crafts*, no.107, November–December 1990, pp.22–6
Colours of the Earth (Twentieth-Century British Ceramics), exh. cat., British Council, 1991
"Talking pots: Janice Tchalenko and Jane Hamlyn", *Ceramic Review*, no.135, 1992, pp.13–16
John Tchalenko and Oliver Watson, *Janice Tchalenko: Ceramics in Studio*, London: Bellew, 1992
Oliver Watson, *Studio Pottery: Twentieth-Century British Ceramics in the Victoria and Albert Museum Collection*, London: Phaidon, 1993 (originally published as *British Studio Pottery*, Oxford: Phaidon, 1990)

Potter and designer, Janice Tchalenko combines in her work an acute understanding of the needs of applied art with the sensitivity and knowledge of the maker. Her work is characterised by an ever-changing response to a growing awareness of the craft, and how, in its many forms, it can be incorporated into the lives of ordinary people. In addition to being a highly skilled maker, Tchalenko has an ability to set up creative collaborations with artists from other disciplines as well as with industry, to develop shapes and decoration that move in fresh directions, exploring different forms and attracting new audiences.

Tchalenko studied pottery at a time when the idea of self-sufficiency and hand-made functional work appeared as an attractive alternative to the growing materialism and anonymity of the booming 1960s. Inspiration came from the work of the artisan, country potter, and from the ideas and methods of Bernard Leach. Trained as a potter on the craft-oriented, workshop-based studio pottery course at Harrow School of Art, Tchalenko acquired the basic skills of throwing and firing with formidable ease. Determined to compete in this male-dominated course, she set out to throw as quickly and easily as the male students, often outstripping them in accuracy and speed. Tchalenko subsequently chose to set up her studio in London rather than in a rural retreat, a destination favoured by many of her fellow potters, so identifying with the sophistication of metropolitan culture. During the 1970s, under the influence of such potters as Leach, Richard Batterham and Michael Casson, she produced a range of kitchenware. Shapes included pestle and mortars, colanders, teapots and nesting bowls as well as "medieval jugs", all thrown on the wheel, glazed with muted "natural" coloured glazes and fired to stoneware temperatures in a reduction kiln.

A John Ruskin bursary in 1979 provided an opportunity to rethink the forms she was making. The enthusiasm for neutral colours and plain rather than decorated pots was being challenged by an interest in colour and pattern, and more assertive forms. Tchalenko simplified her shapes, making the jug, for example, an inverted cone with straight sides, with a thin rather than chunky rim, and handles that were obviously attached rather than appearing to grow out of the form. Teapots were given a simple rounded form with a short stubby spout. For the first time Tchalenko used decoration, opting for trailed glaze on a white background to achieve maximum brightness. The results were fresh, modern and exciting, in keeping with ceramics that appeared to reflect the times in which they were made rather than looking back to earlier periods or other cultures. Patterns were based on flowers, fish and foliage, but rendered in a semi-abstract form well integrated with the shape.

The move was an unqualified success. A collaboration with the textile maker John Hinchcliffe encouraged Tchalenko to look at patterns on fabric and to see how such designs could be applied on three-dimensional objects. In addition to the glaze trailed techniques, she experimented with stencils and sponge decoration (good examples in the Victoria and Albert Museum, London). At the invitation of Next Interiors, she designed a range of three shapes that were produced in Stoke-on-Trent, in earthenware, and sold at low cost in the Next stores.

In the mid-1980s, a collaboration with the Dart Pottery Workshop (now Dartington Pottery) enabled her to give up making functional pots, leaving her free to make her own individual vessel forms and to concentrate on designing in collaboration with industry. For Dart, she designed a range of table-

Tchalenko: Stoneware vases, *c.*1990

ware based on her own shapes with patterns of abstracted flowers and foliage that could be easily repeated. Characteristically, Tchalenko spent long periods at Dartington developing and refining the range to ensure that the pieces could be made, and that a high quality of work was maintained. Several ranges were designed, all characteristic of Tchalenko's clear ideas about how form and pattern could work together.

Other collaborations included fabrics for the Designers Guild and, with Roger Law, a series of forms for the satirical television show *Spitting Image*. These pots, based on the concept of the Seven Deadly Sins, included fantastic caricatured animals satirising their characteristics. In 1991 Tchalenko worked with a factory in China to design a range of pots. She then collaborated with Royal Doulton to revive their range of reduction-fired flambé lustrewares, and designed pieces for the new Collectors Club at Poole Pottery. Her work is well represented in the Aberystwyth Art Centre, Crafts Council Collection, Manchester City Art Galleries and Victoria and Albert Museum, London.

In her individual pieces, Tchalenko abandoned tablewares in favour of vessel forms and sculpture. Jugs, often with strongly articulated shapes with flowing decoration (as, for example, in *Two Jugs*; private collection), oval dishes and bowls offered the greatest opportunity for the use of rich colours, which, as Tchalenko says, have a painterly feel. One of her most ambitious projects was working with the sculptor Richard Wentworth to produce a series of wave-like forms, some covered with nails, that are sensual and seductive as well as sharp and repellent.

Janice Tchalenko has broadened and extended the work of the artist-potter and the designer, raising fundamental questions about the perceived divisions between art, craft and design. As a potter, she has a unique and deep understanding of her chosen material, and uses this as a basis for her designs, which are produced as objects rather than drawings. She has also liberated the craft from its narrow role of conventionally-made utilitarian pots in favour of a free, inventive use of shapes and decoration. Ceramics will never be the same again.

EMMANUEL COOPER

Teerlinc, Levina
South Netherlandish painter, *c.*1510/20–1576

Born Levina Bening between 1510 and 1520, the eldest of five daughters of the Bruges illuminator Simon Bening and his wife Catherine Stroo. Married George Teerlinc of

Blanckenberghe before 1545; one son, Marcus. In England, at the court of Henry VIII, in 1546; subsequently court painter to Edward VI, Mary I and Elizabeth I; received annual payments of £40, from 1547 to 1576. Died in London, 1576.

Bibliography

Lodovico Guicciardini, *Descrittione di tutti i paesi bassi, altrimenti detti Germania Inferiore*, Antwerp, 1567; 2nd edition, 1588

Biographie universelle de Belgique, 16 vols, Brussels, 1866–1986, i, pp.158–9

W.H.J. Weale, "Simon Binnink, miniaturist", *Burlington Magazine*, vii, 1906, pp.355–6

Simone Bergmans, "The miniatures of Levina Teerlinc", *Burlington Magazine*, lxiv, 1934, pp.232–6

Erna Auerbach, *Tudor Artists: A Study of Painters in the Royal Service and of Portraiture on Illuminated Documents from the Accession of Henry VIII to the Death of Elizabeth I*, London: Athlone Press, 1954

Women Artists, 1550–1950, exh. cat., Los Angeles County Museum of Art, and elsewhere, 1976

Roy Strong, *The English Renaissance Miniature*, London and New York: Thames and Hudson, 1983

Catherine King, "Looking a sight: Sixteenth-century portraits of women artists", *Zeitschrift für Kunstgeschichte*, lviii, 1995, pp.381–406

Levina Teerlinc came from a family with the greatest pictorial skills, being the granddaughter of Catherine van der Goes (sister or niece of Hugo van der Goes) and of Alexander Bening. It seems likely that she was trained by her father, Simon Bening, who was one of the most successful illuminators in Bruges and who is also thought to have worked in England. By 1545 she had married George Teerlinc of Blanckenberghe, and in 1546 both she and her husband are recorded in England. She enjoyed a successful career as court painter to the Tudor monarchs Henry VIII, Edward VI, Mary I and Elizabeth I, with an annuity of £40, but Lodovico Guicciardini (1567, p.100) was the sole historian to note her profession in print.

Between 1551 and the year of her death in 1576, a succession of documents records Teerlinc's creation of miniature portraits for the monarchs. She painted various portraits of *Elizabeth I*: in 1559, 1562 and 1563 (the last two "with other personages"), 1564 (on a Royal Progress), 1567 (a full-length portrait), 1568 ("with Knights of the Order"), 1575 ("with other personages") and 1576. She also painted a portrait of the queen, perhaps not a miniature, as *Princess Elizabeth* (1551). In 1553 she painted a small picture of the *Trinity* for Mary I. She also did a painting of a house "with certain personages" (1565).

In addition, the existence of a *Self-Portrait* by Teerlinc is documented in the inventory of the possessions of the Italian miniaturist Giulio Clovio, a member of the Farnese household in Rome, at his death in 1578: "a little round box with the portrait of Livinia, miniaturist to the Queen of England" (A. Bertolotti, "Don Giulio Clovio: Principe dei miniatori", *Atti e memorie delle RR Deputazione di Storia Patria per le Provincie dell'Emilia*, vii/2, 1881, p.274). This has been linked with a letter written around 1561 by Clovio to an unnamed, non-Italian female miniaturist, thanking her for sending him her miniature portrait (Julius von Schlosser, "Two portrait miniatures from Castle Ambras", *Burlington Magazine*, xli, 1922, pp.197–200; the full text of the letter, which was found by

Guglielmo Della Valle in a bunch including one dated 1561, is in his edition of Giorgio Vasari's *Vite de' più eccellenti pittori, scultori ed architetti*, 11 vols, 1791–4, x, pp.354–5). Clovio sent Teerlinc an example of his work in return, and it appears that both artists saw themselves as engaging in the activity of exchanging examples of their skills with eminent practitioners in distant areas, as took place between Raphael and Dürer, and Raphael and Francia (King 1996).

Teerlinc and her husband George became salaried members of the royal entourage in 1546 – she being officially attached to "the privye chamber of the Quenes Majestie" – and in 1547 she was one of four painters working for Henry VIII, alongside three men: Bartholomew Penne, Anthony Toho and Nicholas of Modena. During the reign of Edward VI she returned to the Netherlands and bore her only child – a son named Marcus – at Calais, before crossing to England. In 1556 George Teerlinc rented a house in Stepney, London, and in 1559, when Levina was given an annuity of £40 for life by Queen Elizabeth, the family were living in London at Stratford le Bowe. In 1566 the Teerlincs became English subjects. Ten years later, in 1576, Levina died in Stepney, where George had built a house valued at £500. On her death her husband returned to the Netherlands.

Because of the high salary she received over three decades, and the fact that she followed in the footsteps of Luca Hornebolte and Hans Holbein as a court painter, it has been surmised that Teerlinc must have invented major elements in the political iconography of the Tudor monarchs, such as the Great Seal of Elizabeth I, and other early portraits of Elizabeth close to the period of her coronation, and that as a skilled miniaturist she would have been the obvious person to have instructed Nicholas Hilliard. To date, however, no inscribed extant works have been identified, but it seems likely that eventually some secure pictures by Teerlinc will be discovered.

Roy Strong (1983) discusses several possible attributed works, including some woodcuts and the Great Seal of England following the designs of Teerlinc. They include: a miniature portrait of *Princess Elizabeth*, "Aged 18" (1550; Yale Center for British Art, New Haven); a manuscript illumination of Mary I healing a man of scrofula for *Certain Prayers To Be Used by the Queen* (1553–8; Westminster Cathedral Library, London); an indenture for establishing the Poor Knights of Windsor (30 August 1559; Public Record Office, London, E36/277); and miniatures on vellum of *Catherine Grey, Countess of Hereford* (c.1555–60; Victoria and Albert Museum, London), *Elizabeth I Performing Maundy Ceremonies* (c.1565; Countess Beauchamp, Madresfield Court), *Elizabeth I* (1565; Royal Collection), *Portrait of an Unknown Man* (inscribed "aged 27"; 1569; Countess Beauchamp, Madresfield Court) and *Portrait of an Unknown Man* (inscribed "Che io sono inteso"; 1569; Waddesdon Manor, National Trust).

CATHERINE KING

See also Court Artists survey

ter Borch, Gesina *see* Borch

Therbusch, Anna Dorothea *see* Lisiewska-Therbusch

Thesleff, Ellen

Finnish painter and graphic artist, 1869–1954

Born in Helsinki, 5 October 1869. Attended school in Kuopio. Studied at Adolf von Becker's academy, Helsinki, 1885–7; Finnish Art Society drawing school, Helsinki, 1887–9; Gunnar Berndtson's private academy, Helsinki, 1889–91; Académie Colarossi, Paris, under Gustave Courtois and Pascal Dagnan-Bouveret, 1891–2. In Paris, 1893–4 and 1899–1900; in Italy, 1894–1916 and 1920–39; usually spent winters in Florence, summers in Murole, Finland. Member of Septem group, 1912. Died in Helsinki, 12 January 1954.

Principal Exhibitions

Finnish Artists' Association, Helsinki: 1891–5
Stockholm: 1897 (*Allmänna konst- och industriutställningen* [Universal art and industry exhibition])
Exposition Universelle, Paris: 1900 (first-class bronze medal)
Graphic Exhibition, Moscow: 1916
Finnish Art Exhibition, Petrograd: 1917
Konstsalongen, Helsinki: 1919 (woodcuts)
Liljevalchs Konsthall, Stockholm: 1929 (*Finlands nutida konst* [Contemporary Finnish art])
Nationalmuseum, Stockholm: 1944 (*Finsk nutidskonst* [Contemporary Finnish art])
Helsinki Art Hall: 1946 (Finnish Art Society centenary)

Selected Writings

Dikter och tankar [Poems and thoughts], Helsinki, 1954

Bibliography

Walter Shaw Sparrow, *Women Painters of the World*, London: Hodder and Stoughton, and New York: Stokes, 1905; reprinted New York: Hacker, 1976
Bulletin of the Cleveland Museum of Art, xiv, 1927
Leonard Bäcksbacka, *Ellen Thesleff*, Helsinki, 1955
Salme Sarajas-Korte, *Suomen varhaissymbolismi ja sen lähteet:Tutkielma Suomen maalaustiteesta, 1891–95* [Early Symbolism in Finland: A study of Finnish painting, 1891–95], Helsinki: Otava, 1966; Swedish edition as *Vid symbolismens källor* [At the source of Symbolism], Jakobstad, 1981
Ellen Thesleff, exh. cat., Ateneumin Taidemuseo, Helsinki, 1969
Markku Lahti, "Arvoitus Ellen Thesleff – Gordon Craig" [The mystery of Ellen Thesleff and Gordon Craig], *Art Museum of Ateneum Bulletin*, xviii, 1973 (also in Swedish, and with English summary)
Målarinnor från Finland/Seitsemän suomalaista taiteilijaa [Women painters from Finland], exh. cat., Nationalmuseum, Stockholm, and elsewhere, 1981
Dreams of a Summer Night: Scandinavian Painting at the Turn of the Century, exh. cat., Arts Council of Great Britain, 1986
Kirk Varnedoe, *Northern Light: Nordic Art at the Turn of the Century*, New Haven and London: Yale University Press, 1988
Salme Sarajas-Korte, "Ellen Thesleffin, 1890-luku", [Ellen Thesleff in the 1890s], *Ars: Suomen*, iv, 1989
——, *Helene Schjerfbeckin ja Ellen Thesleffin 1900-luku* [Helene Schjerfbeck and Ellen Thesleff in the 1900s], *Ars: Suomen*, v, 1990
Leena Ahtola-Moorhouse, "Löydetty Arkadia" [Arcadia discovered], *Taide*, xxxi/1, 1991, pp.45–8
Eeva Kilpi, *Ellen Thesleff: Laula rakkaudesta: Valikolma neljästä runokokoelmasta*, Helsinki: WSOY, 1991

In 1909 Ellen Thesleff wrote: "I lie deep in the sand so my heart can listen to the heartbeat of the globe, and with that rhythm I grasp colours and lines, feeling secure and free. I do not know what the result will be, but in any case it will be something wonderful." She was a painter and poet throughout her life, her family supporting her artistic ambitions. She grew up with the Symbolists and studied under the Finnish painter Gunnar Berndtson. Like several other Finnish women painters, she studied in Paris, at the Académie Colarossi from 1891. She was inspired by the French Symbolist painter Eugène Carrière, but although her works show a similarly reduced palette and the expression of airy plastic forms created by light, her technique is quite different from his. Whereas Thesleff would always add lines and paint, Carrière wiped them off. Thesleff was the first Finnish artist to paint a Symbolist work, the portrait of her sister *Thyra Elisabeth* (1892; Helsinki City Art Museum). By then she wanted her paintings to be free from realism, and have more of the curved lines of Art Nouveau. In the 1890s her portraits and landscapes were painted in dark colours, but she endeavoured to express the soul's beauty through her art.

In the Nordic countries the climate is hard to endure, with winter days that are very dark, dry and cold. But suddenly in summer outdoor life can carry on through day and night. Thesleff caught that feeling of being free and independent in the open air in the painting *Echo* (1890–91; private collection, Helsinki), which she painted before her studies abroad. *Echo* shows a girl in profile with open mouth calling or perhaps singing. True to its time, the girl in the foreground is dressed in a white blouse down to her hips. The girl's head is painted against a luminous sky and the white of her blouse contrasts with the dark forest in the background. It is a vision of youth and its uncurbed strength, which also finds a parallel in the contemporary political situation, when Finland was struggling for independence from a powerful Russia. The painting was well received when it was shown at the first exhibition of the Finnish Artists' Association in the autumn of 1891, and it was bought by the exhibition committee.

In 1894–5, on her first visit to Florence, Thesleff drew a self-portrait in full face, composed of thousands of pencil lines, a grey vision in a dreamy but clear mood (see illustration). It looks as if the artist saw her face through a hazy glass and suddenly there was a clear spot over the centre. Thesleff's touch is both light and precise, and creates the impression of a clairvoyant's vision. Some Finnish friends of hers, the artists Ada Thilén and Helene Schjerfbeck (q.v.), also came to Florence. In the spring of 1894 Thesleff and Schjerfbeck worked together in the monastery of San Marco, copying Fra Angelico's frescoes. Thesleff's favourite Italian masters were Fra Angelico and Botticelli, with their clear, light colours, and Leonardo da Vinci, with his strong compositions. She was also inspired by theosophy, then a topical subject.

In 1906 Thesleff met the British theatre designer, writer and graphic artist Gordon Craig in Florence. He was a strong personality, and lived a long and bohemian life – he had 16

Thesleff: *Self-Portrait*, 1894–5; pencil and wash; 31.5 × 23.5 cm.; Museum of Finnish Art Ateneum, Helsinki

children by 11 different women, one of them the dancer Isadora Duncan. Thesleff's meeting with Craig led to a lifelong friendship, no children, but a correspondence comprising hundreds of letters. And, what is even more important, it started Thesleff's career as a graphic artist, an important complement to her work as a painter. She began to do woodcuts in 1907, initially working under Craig's influence. Her woodcut *Marionettes* (1907) was published in the journal *The Mask* in 1908. She made studies – drawings and colour notes – of the figures in the Museo Civico, Venice, both of plates with old woodcuts and of small marionette figures. In a letter of the same year she mentions this woodcut as being one of her best from the period. *Marionettes* used traditional methods, but Thesleff later tried experimental techniques of her own. She printed several colours simultaneously from the same plate and would even add colours to the print afterwards. Her monotypes were airy, often with bright, but light colours, and looked like paintings. The woodcut technique showed her the way to the unexpected and she used mild colours to create a rare lyricism.

In 1916 Thesleff wrote about her works: "No theories, no form, just colour". She worked with these ideas throughout her life. During the inter-war years she continued to live in both Italy and Finland. During World War II she stayed at home, visiting Stockholm in 1944, when she took part in the exhibition of *Finsk nutidskonst* (contemporary Finnish art).

LENA HOLGER

Thomas, Alma W.
American painter, 1891–1978

Born in Columbus, Georgia, 22 September 1891. Moved with her family to Washington, DC, 1907; lived in the same house for the rest of her life. Studied art at Armstrong Technical High School, Washington, DC (graduated 1911); Miner Teachers Normal School, Washington, DC, 1911–13 (teaching certificate); taught art at Thomas Garrett Settlement House, Wilmington, Delaware, 1915–21; studied at Howard University, Washington, DC, 1921–4 (first graduate of its art department, BS 1924). Taught art at Shaw Junior High School, Washington, DC, 1924–60; meanwhile graduated MA in art education from Teachers College, Columbia University, New York, 1934; director of the School Arts League Project, Washington, DC, 1936–9; studied painting at American University, Washington, DC, 1950–60, and in Europe (1958); taught Sunday art class for neighbourhood children at Uplift House, Washington, DC, 1964–6. Cofounder of Kappa Mu Honorary Society at Howard University; was the first African-American woman to have a solo exhibition at the Whitney Museum; worked in the US State Department's Art in Embassies program. Recipient of first prize for oil paintings, art fair sponsored by US Department of Commerce, 1939; Purchase prize, Howard University, 1963; Two Thousand Women of Achievement award, 1972; International Women's Year award, 1976. Named on Honor Roll of Distinguished Women by National Association of Colored Women's Clubs, 1962. Member,

Watercolour Society, Washington, DC. Invited to exhibit her paintings at the White House, Washington, DC, 1969, 1970 and 1977. Died in Washington, DC, 24 February 1978.

Selected Individual Exhibitions
Bennett College, Greensboro, NC: 1959 (touring, organised by College Arts Service, Washington, DC)
Dupont Theater Art Gallery, Washington, DC: 1960, 1961, 1962
Gallery of Art, Howard University, Washington, DC: 1966 (retrospective), 1975
Franz Bader Gallery, Washington, DC: 1968, 1970, 1974
Carl Van Vechten Gallery of Fine Arts, Fisk University, Nashville: 1971
Whitney Museum of American Art, New York: 1972
Corcoran Gallery of Art, Washington, DC: 1972 (retrospective)
Studio Museum in Harlem, New York: 1973
Martha Jackson Gallery, New York: 1973
H.C. Taylor Art Gallery, North Carolina Agricultural and Technical State University, Greensboro: 1976
Martha Jackson West Gallery, New York: 1976
National Museum of American Art, Smithsonian Institution, Washington, DC: 1981 (retrospective)

Bibliography
Alma W. Thomas: A Retrospective Exhibition (1959–1966), exh. cat., Gallery of Art, Howard University, Washington, DC, 1966
J. Edward Atkinson, ed., *Black Dimensions in Contemporary American Art*, New York: New American Library, 1971
Alma W. Thomas, exh. cat., Whitney Museum of American Art, 1972
Alma W. Thomas: Retrospective Exhibition, exh. cat., Corcoran Gallery of Art, Washington DC, 1972
Elsa Honig Fine, *The Afro-American Artist: A Search for Identity*, New York: Holt Rinehart, 1973
Grace Glueck, "Art: Studio Museum exhibits Alma Thomas", *New York Times*, 20 October 1973
Alma W. Thomas: Recent Paintings, exh. cat., Gallery of Art, Howard University, Washington, DC, 1975
Benjamin Forgey, "The Corcoran Biennial: A generational split", *Art News*, lxxvi, May 1977, pp.106–14
Eleanor Munro, *Originals: American Women Artists*, New York: Simon and Schuster, 1979
J. Wilson, "Alma Thomas: A one-woman art movement", *Ms*, no.7, February 1979, pp.59–61
Forever Free: Art by African-American Women, 1862–1980, exh. cat., Illinois State University, Normal, and elsewhere, 1980
A Life in Art: Alma Thomas, 1891–1978, exh. cat., National Museum of American Art, Smithsonian Institution, Washington, DC, 1981
J. Maurice Thomas, ed., *Alma Thomas Album*, Washington, DC: National Museum of American Art, Smithsonian Institution, 1981
Charlotte Moser, "Alma Thomas", *Art News*, lxxxi, May 1982, p.142
Janet Kutner, "Artist: Alma Thomas", *Dallas Morning News*, 13 February 1987
Romare Bearden and Harry Henderson, *A History of African-American Artists from 1792 to the Present*, New York: Pantheon, 1993

Alma W. Thomas Papers are on deposit at the Archives of American Art, Smithsonian Institution, Washington, DC.

In the late 1960s Alma Thomas developed a lyrical, colour-filled and movement-infused approach to abstraction. Although often associated with the so-called Washington Color School, Thomas's art is distinctive, retaining strong ties to the real world, even when the paintings appear non-

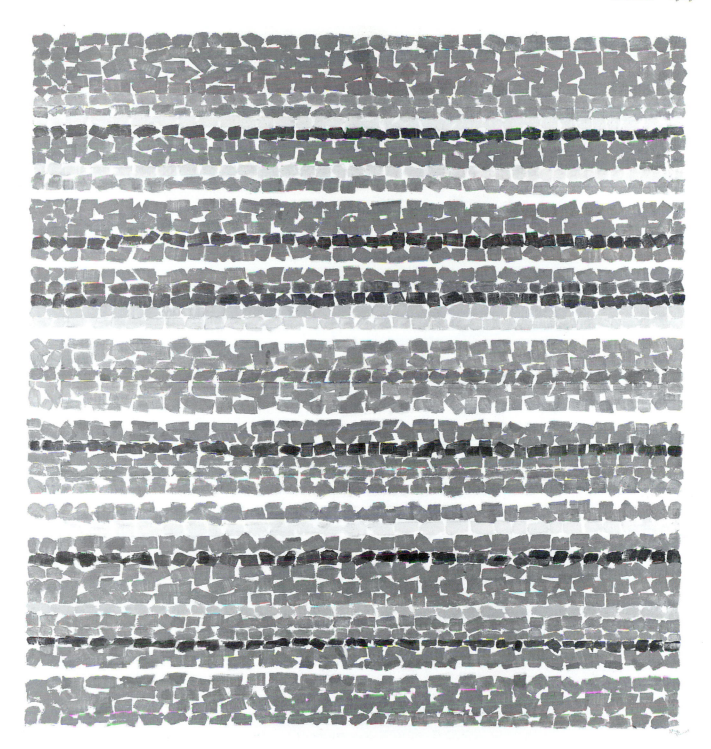

Thomas: *Light Blue Nursery*, 1968; acrylic on canvas; 124.4 × 121.5 cm.; National Museum of American Art, Washington, DC

representational. Her work – which can be found in the permanent collections of numerous major museums – is particularly remarkable considering that, unlike her mostly white, male counterparts, Thomas was a black woman from the segregated South, who supported herself as a schoolteacher for four decades, only becoming a full-time painter at the age of 69. Deciding that her single-minded approach to life precluded having both a family and a career, Thomas opted for the latter and, after moving with her parents and sisters from Georgia to

Washington, DC, earned a certificate for teaching art in the public schools. From then on, she developed a reputation for demanding hard work and high standards from both her students and herself; and Thomas always continued painting.

The work that survives from her years at Howard University consists of competent and conventional still lifes painted in oil on canvas and realistic clay portrait busts (repr. Washington 1981). But a number of connections that Thomas made at Howard spurred her interest in abstraction, for example her friendship with Lois Mailou Jones (q.v.), a painting teacher at Howard who had studied in Paris. Thomas was strongly influenced by the ideas of James V. Herring, who had established the Art Department at Howard and who co-founded the Barnett-Aden Gallery, one of the first in Washington to exhibit contemporary art, in 1943. As that gallery's first vice-president, Thomas became familiar with many of the artists it represented, including Hans Hofmann, Gene Davis, Jacob Kainen and Jones. During her summers at Columbia University, she visited the galleries that featured avant-garde work, such as Alfred Stieglitz's An American Place.

Another important factor in Thomas's move towards abstraction was her experience at the American University. Although she was 60 when she enrolled there, the paintings that she produced under Joseph Summerford, Robert Gates and Kainen clearly demonstrate her eagerness to experiment with several different modernist approaches. Thomas's *Still Life with Corn* (c.1954; Collection Max Robinson, Chicago) owes much of its stylisation, flat patterning and heavy outlines to the art of Henri Matisse; her *Untitled* painting of 1958 (Collection Harold Hart, New York) is clearly related to the system of rectangular colour patches developed by Hofmann; and *Blue Night (At Sea)* (1959; Collection John Maurice Thomas, Washington, DC) is a solid example of Abstract Expressionism. As Thomas neared the end of her teaching career, she achieved two long-standing artistic goals: her first trip to Europe, in 1958, and her first solo exhibition, held the following year.

Thomas's breakthrough as a painter occurred in 1966, when she was offered a retrospective at Howard University. As the artist has explained, for this event she wanted to produce a body of work different from anything she had exhibited before. At this time Thomas developed her signature format: large canvases filled with dense, irregular patterns of thick colourful brush marks of acrylic paint. Typically, Thomas's mature paintings lack a central focus or references to specific subject matter. What makes these works so exciting are the spaces between the coloured marks, the syncopated rhythms they convey, and the vividness of the white canvas or under-painted tones that shine through. Good examples are *Antares* (1972), *Aquatic Gardens* (1973; both National Museum of American Art, Smithsonian Institution, Washington, DC) and *Light Blue Nursery* (1968; see illustration).

Over the years critics have pointed out numerous parallels between Thomas's mature paintings and the works of other artists. Her emphasis on dash-like marks of colour has an obvious relationship to the pointillist technique of such 19th-century French artists as Georges Seurat – and, indeed, Thomas did study colour theory. But whereas the Frenchman's minuscule dots combine to give the illusion of different colours, Thomas's short brush strokes remain separate and distinct. More importantly, Seurat's dots produce the effect of solid, unmoving forms, while Thomas's pictures scintillate. Her work is much closer to Impressionism – especially the late series of Claude Monet. Just as the French master spent many of his later years painting variations on his favourite themes (haystacks, cathedral façades, waterlilies), so Thomas, late in life, concentrated on producing multiple versions of her best-loved subjects: leaves blowing in the wind, rivers splashing over rocks, flower petals falling to the ground. These images, which Thomas called her "Earth Paintings", do not specifically describe leaves, water or flowers. In fact without their evocative titles (*Wind and Crepe Myrtle Concerto, Scarlet Sage Dancing a Whirling Dervish*), their subjects would be difficult to guess. The varied moods of these paintings, however, created by the artist's skilful choice of tonal and spatial variations, often suggest their relationship to natural phenomena. There are also a number of paintings with surprisingly legible subjects, notably *Launch Pad* (1970; National Air and Space Museum, Smithsonian Institution), that reflect the artist's interest in the Apollo space programme.

Much of Thomas's mature painting draws on specific visual memories: childhood recollections of the flora and the spectacular sunsets viewed from her family's hill-top Georgia home. In Washington, much of her inspiration came from the flower garden and, especially, the big holly tree outside the living-room window of the house on 15th Street, NW, where she lived for 57 years. Possible sources for other aspects of Thomas's art abound. Many writers compare her work with Byzantine mosaics, which she saw on her many museum visits. The artist often commented that her appreciation of colour was partly due to the vivid hues of the clothing that her mother used to sew. But most often Thomas's work is discussed in relationship to the Washington Color School, a diverse group of painters, including Gene Davis and Kenneth Noland, who lived in the Baltimore-Washington area, producing large-scale, colourful abstractions, and who came to prominence in the 1960s. Clearly, there are resemblances between Thomas's art and theirs; *A Joyful Song of Spring* (1968; Collection Mr and Mrs Jacob Kainen, Chevy Chase, MD), for example, is made up of concentric coloured circles, as are many of Noland's pictures, and *Light Blue Nursery* (cited above) is one of her numerous "stripe" paintings – a format for which Davis became famous. But these resemblances are only superficial. Thomas's paintings lack the sense of mechanical precision so central to Davis's work. Instead of using masking tape to achieve crisp edges between her forms, she painted free-hand, using watercolour sketches and faint pencil lines as her guide; in many respects her work is closer to the hard-edge but humorous abstractions of Larry Poons. The artist whose work comes closest in spirit to Thomas's is the Abstract Expressionist Joan Mitchell (q.v.). Although Mitchell's technique is quite different, she too spent the last part of her life painting enormous, essentially abstract canvases inspired by the landscapes she knew best.

As a black artist living in Washington during the 1960s and 1970s, Thomas was inevitably criticised for the absence of political references in her paintings. Yet Thomas was a committed activist throughout her life; at the age of 75, despite severe arthritis and the demands of her career, she was still teaching weekly classes for local children in Anacostia, one of the city's most impoverished neighbourhoods. A truly indomitable woman, two years after breaking her hip, Thomas finished one of her largest works, the triptych entitled *Red Azaleas Singing and Dancing Rock and Roll Music* (1976; 1.8 × 3.4 m.; acrylic on canvas; National Museum of American Art).

NANCY G. HELLER

Thompson, Elizabeth *see* Butler

Thornycroft, Mary
British sculptor, 1809–1895

Born Mary Francis in Thornham, Norfolk, 21 May 1809. Trained by her father, the sculptor John Francis. Married one of his pupils, Thomas Thornycroft, 1840; seven children born 1841–53, of whom Alyce, Helen, Theresa and Hamo became artists; husband died 1885. Lived in London; in Rome, studying under John Gibson, 1842–3. Appointed to teach sculpture to the royal princesses, 1867. Died 1895.

Principal Exhibitions
Royal Academy, London: 1834–40, 1844, 1847–50, 1852–73, 1875, 1877
British Institution, London: 1840, 1845–64
Exposition Universelle, Paris: 1855

Bibliography
Clara Erskine Clement and Laurence Hutton, *Artists of the Nineteenth Century and Their Work*, 2 vols, Boston: Houghton Osgood, and London: Trübner, 1879; reprinted New York: Arno Press, 1969

F.G. Stephens, "The late Mrs Mary Thornycroft", *Magazine of Art*, xviii, 1895, pp.305–7

Mrs Fenwick-Miller, "The ladies' column", *Illustrated London News*, 16 February 1895

Emilie Isobel Barrington, "Mrs Mary Thornycroft", *Spectator*, 23 February 1895, pp.263–4

Elfrida Thornycroft, *Bronze and Steel: Life of Thomas Thornycroft, Sculptor and Engineer*, Long Compton: King Stone Press, 1932

Elfrida Manning, *Marble and Bronze: The Art and Life of Hamo Thornycroft*, London: Trefoil, 1982

Pamela Gerrish Nunn, *Victorian Women Artists*, London: Women's Press, 1987

Penny McCracken, "Sculptor Mary Thornycroft and her artist children", *Woman's Art Journal*, xvii/2, 1996–7, pp.3–8

Documents, correspondence and diaries are in the Thornycroft Archive, Henry Moore Centre for the Study of Sculpture, Leeds.

Mary Thornycroft was trained in the studio of her father, the sculptor John Francis, and exhibited at the Royal Academy from 1834 (she was the only woman exhibitor in 1837). Although these early career advantages were offset by her marriage and by the birth of seven children, she continued to sculpt into her eighties. In 1842 Mary went with her husband Thomas Thornycroft to Rome, where she impressed John Gibson, leader of the colony of British sculptors there, with her *Sleeping Child* (that or a similar figure was used on the *Martin* tomb at Ledbury, Herefordshire). Gibson recommended her to Queen Victoria as better able to execute portraits of the royal children than himself. Back in London, Thornycroft was commissioned to portray the children as the *Four Seasons*, beginning with Princess Alice, aged one, as *Spring* in 1845 (Royal Collection, Osborne, Isle of Wight). These so pleased the royal patrons that she was commissioned to portray four generations of the royal family, and was given her own rooms in Windsor Castle for the purpose, becoming the principal bread-winner of her family. Her last piece, exhibited at the Royal Academy in 1877, was the *Duchess of Edinburgh* (Royal Collection, Buckingham Palace, London). Although Thornycroft was fortunate in that the queen's patronage kept her constantly employed, she was left with neither time nor incentive to develop her talents and extend her repertoire; thus the artistic fashions of the day passed her by.

Thornycroft was a competent portraitist in the classical tradition, whose talent might have benefited from a more thorough study from life, then generally unavailable to women. Her *Skipping Girl* (untraced), exhibited at the Exposition Universelle, Paris, in 1855, was admired by the critic Jerichau as "one of the six most beautiful statues in the world" (Thornycroft 1932, p.55); a replica in bronze was made for Albert, the Prince Consort. But while Thornycroft enjoyed great popular success with her portraits of the rich and the royal, mainly women and children, she did not acquire the renown of the male sculptors who received the "important" commissions for heroic and equestrian statues. While the statues of *Charles I* and *James I* at the Old Bailey, London, have been attributed to both Thomas and Mary, she may have been more instrumental in the production of other statues by her husband and son Hamo than has been acknowledged. Elfrida Manning considered Mary to be a sculptor of equal worth to her husband, and, according to a studio assistant, she was his superior, because "Her heart was in it". In the family sculpture workshop, where each member contributed his or her own particular skills, Mary's speciality was portraiture, at which she excelled. An expert and delicate carver, she still had to put up with Thomas physically correcting her work. There is no evidence, however, that Mary worked on Thomas's large *Boadicea* (1902; Westminster Bridge, London), left unfinished at his death, although it has been claimed elsewhere that she did. Other works by Mary Thornycroft include a full-length figure of *Lady Braye* reclining on her monument in Stamford Church, Lincolnshire (1862), with her dog at her feet, and a bust of *Melpomene*, the Muse of Tragedy, exhibited at the Royal Academy in 1872; her other contributions to the *Poet's Fountain* (1875; Park Lane, London; demolished 1949) are documented in Hamo's journal (Thornycroft Archive, Leeds).

According to Mrs Fenwick-Miller (1895), one of the most interesting pieces entrusted to Mary Thornycroft was a marble bust of *Alderman Pochin* (Collection Lord Aberconway, Bodnant) for Salford Corporation. The bust, exhibited at the Royal Academy in 1870, shows Pochin wearing his chain of office. The eyes are incised, and not left classically blank as in most of the artist's earlier works, demonstrating a more naturalistic influence in her work.

More typical are Thornycroft's portraits of the royal children that adorn the drawing room of Osborne House, Isle of Wight. Elfrida Thornycroft (1932) wrote: "Her child portraits were graceful without ever being merely sentimental and there is character as well as charm in her Princess Beatrice in a Nautilus Shell of 1858". *Princess Beatrice (Osborne House)* (see illustration) was one of many of Thornycroft's sculptures given as Christmas and birthday presents from Prince Albert to the queen; she gave the work high praise when she received it at Christmas 1858. The sculpture also received the distinction of being reproduced as a Minton porcelain figure (City Museum, Stoke-on-Trent). The conventional rendering of the princesses as passive symbolic figures representing *Peace* and

Thornycroft: *Princess Beatrice (Osborne House)*, 1858;
Royal Collection © Her Majesty Queen Elizabeth II

Plenty is no less surprising than that of the young princes in the active roles of half-naked *Fisher Boy* and *Hunter*. These works were reproduced in the *Art Journal* (1864), which considered them suitable for reproduction in Parian ware, while engravings of Thornycroft's statues were popular in gift albums of the day. A macabre example of her work at Osborne is the collection of marble hands and feet of the young princes and princesses, whose names and ages were inscribed on the stumps. Casts of Mary's own hand were kept by the Thornycroft family.

An unsigned late painting, probably by her daughter Alyce (*c.*1890; ex-Phillips, Bath, 31 October 1994, lot 317), shows Mary with a small clay sculpture in hand, her thumb turned back from modelling. She would say: "I cannot be happy without a piece of clay to play with". She taught sculpture to Princess Louise, and passed on her enthusiasm for the art to her daughters and especially to her son Hamo, exhorting him to "stick to the clay, my boy" and not to dissipate his energy on other activities, as perhaps she and his father had.

ANDREA GARRIHY

Ticho, Anna
Israeli graphic artist and painter, 1894–1980

Born in Brünn, Austria (now Brno, Czech Republic), 1894. Moved to Vienna, 1904. Enrolled at Kunstschule, Vienna, 1909. Moved to Jerusalem and married a cousin, Dr Albert Ticho, 1912; he died 1960. Lived in Damascus, where husband served as medical officer in Austrian army, 1917–19. Returned to Jerusalem, 1919. Co-founder of the New Bezalel School, 1935. Participated in Venice Biennale, 1953. Recipient of City of Jerusalem art prize, 1965; Sandberg prize, Israel Museum, 1975; Israel prize, 1980. Honorary citizen of Jerusalem, 1970. Died in Jerusalem, 1 March 1980.

Selected Individual Exhibitions

Stematsky Gallery, Jerusalem: 1934
Passedoit Gallery, New York: 1953
Bezalel National Museum, Jerusalem: 1959, 1963
Stedelijk Museum, Amsterdam: 1959
Baltimore Museum of Art: 1962
Museum of Modern Art, Haifa: 1962
Art Institute of Chicago: 1964
Museum Boymans-van Beuningen, Rotterdam: 1964
Dreitzer Gallery, Brandeis University, Waltham, MA: 1967
Israel Museum, Jerusalem: 1968, 1973, 1978, 1981 (memorial)
Jewish Museum, New York: 1969
Ashmolean Museum, Oxford: 1972
Tel Aviv Museum: 1974, 1978

Bibliography

Max Eisler, *Anna Ticho: Jerusalem, 12 Facsimile Plates*, Vienna: Gerlach und Wiedling, 1951
Elisheva Cohen, *Jerusalem Landscapes: Drawings and Watercolours*, London: Lund Humphries, 1971
Anna Ticho, exh. cat., Israel Museum, Jerusalem, 1973
Jerusalem Landscapes, exh. cat., Tel Aviv Museum, 1974
Yona Fischer, ed., *Anna Ticho: Sketches, 1918–1975*, Jerusalem: Israel Museum, 1976
Elisheva Cohen, *Anah Ticho*, Jerusalem: Keter, 1986
Irit Salmon, *Ticho House*, Jerusalem: Israel Museum, 1994

Anna Ticho is one of Israel's most celebrated and well-loved artists, best known for her landscape drawings of Jerusalem and the Judaean Hills, but who also produced numerous portraits and flower studies. Her romantic choice of subject matter – ruins, barren hills, wrinkled old men and women, gnarled, ancient olive trees and wilting flowers – all allude to the effects of the passing of time. Although she was involved with the Bezalel Art School in Jerusalem, and was partly responsible for its reopening in 1935, she never attempted to assimilate the Middle Eastern stylistic trends that were advocated by this institution. Nor did she follow any other movement, or belong to any other group. Instead, it was the art of Vienna, the city in which she lived from 1904 to 1912, and in which she received her only formal art training, that shaped her artistic taste. The memories of the paintings and more particularly the drawings by the old masters that she had seen in Viennese museums and galleries influenced her work strongly, as did the work of Gustav Klimt and Egon Schiele.

When Ticho went to Jerusalem in 1912 she was at first too overwhelmed to draw:

Ticho: *Jerusalem*, 1940; drawing; Rijksmuseum, Amsterdam

When I came to Israel, I was impressed by the grandeur of the scenery, the bare hills, the large ancient olive trees and the clefted slopes...the sense of solemnity and eternity...I was dumbfounded and overcome with emotion, and could not work" [interview with the artist quoted in Salmon 1994, p.18].

Early drawings that were still in her studio at her death are cautious and tentative, testifying to the awe in which she held her new home. Ticho first produced pencil drawings showing Jerusalem's Old City, such as the *Old City of Jerusalem* (1927; Israel Museum, Jerusalem). She often sketched the views from roof-tops, drawing the city from above, so that the roofs and turrets of the city filled up the paper, leaving little or no room for the sky. Her drawings are usually devoid of figures and of any anecdotal detail; instead she concentrated on accurately depicting the buildings of the city, and paid careful attention to details such as their odd windows and irregular walls. Other drawings of this period show similarly accurate and detailed depictions of Jericho and Tiberias.

As she gained confidence in her work, Ticho experimented with different drawing materials, and found that she was particularly well suited to using charcoal, which enabled her to produce strong contrasts between light and shade. Her drawings became larger, and buildings interested her less than the bare hills surrounding the city. *Jerusalem* (1940; see illustration) is as minutely worked as her earlier drawings, but here she pays more attention to natural than to the man-made aspects of the landscape. Thus a large tree dominates the foreground, and in the distance we see the slopes of the surrounding hills, while the Dome of the Rock is placed well to the side.

During this period Ticho worked for much of the day in her husband's eye clinic, and would often use the patients as models for portrait sketches. She preferred to draw the elderly, and placed great emphasis on strong facial expressions and gesturing hands, paying homage to the Expressionist portraits of Klimt and Schiele. In order to not to make them into genre drawings, she avoided placing her models in specific settings and instead drew them against a blank background, as can be seen in *Study of an Old Yemenite Woman* (c.1950; Israel Museum). She also drew careful studies of flowers and thistles. For her large-scale drawings, Ticho produced numerous sketches, using felt-tip pens regularly, but also working in pencil and pen and ink. She studied her subject from many different angles in order to arrive at a unified and carefully structured composition. Throughout her life, she made sketches of nudes, regarding this as an indispensable form of practice.

In the 1940s Ticho painted some landscapes in oils, but was not drawn to the possibilities of working in colour in this medium. The paintings are almost all monochrome and very graphic in nature. She did, however, work in watercolour and gouache, painting mainly flowers. She also painted watercolours of Jericho and Tiberias, as well as some portraits, but rarely depicted Jerusalem in this medium, preferring to render the city's scenery in black and white, which she felt better suited its special character and colour scheme. In the 1960s and 1970s she returned to the subject of flowers, producing a series of watercolours that differ from earlier works by their free use of brush stroke, bright colours and coloured wash in the background.

In the 1950s the Tichos purchased a home at Motza in the Judaean Hills near Jerusalem, and from then on Ticho concentrated on depicting this scenery. The deterioration in her husband's health, however, led to her abandoning her practice of working from nature. She instead worked in her studio, either drawing from photographs or from memory. This brought about a marked change in her style. No longer close to the subject of her drawings, she began to depict the Jerusalem landscape in a freer mode, which sometimes almost gave way to abstraction. She began the works with a series of broken lines that she gradually built up into a recognisable landscape. The stimulus to produce these works came from within: "I gradually strove to turn my back on observed nature and find sources of inspiration also from within my soul – to grasp the spiritual essence of this grand and eternal landscape" (quoted in Salmon 1994, p.20).

After her husband's death in 1960, Ticho was able to devote herself fully to her art, and travelled around Israel to visit and draw new sites in the Negev Desert and around the Dead Sea. In the 1970s she began to use pastels, adding colour to her Jerusalem landscapes for the first time, albeit working in a very limited range of earth colours. She took an interest in portraying the landscape in different weather conditions, as in *Autumn Landscape* (1973) and *Passing Cloud* (1975; both Israel Museum). She continued to work until her death in 1980. Ticho bequeathed her Jerusalem home to the Israel Museum, which has converted it into a museum annexe where her work is on permanent display.

JULIA WEINER

Tilsa *see* Tsuchiya

Tintoretto, Marietta *see* Robusti

Toorop, Charley
Dutch painter, 1891–1955

Born Annie Caroline Pontifex Toorop in Katwijk, 24 March 1891. Trained by her father, the painter Jan Toorop. Married Henk Fernhout, 1912; two sons, born 1912 (the painter Edgar Fernhout) and 1913, daughter born 1916. Settled in Bergen, North Holland, 1912; moved to Laren, North Holland, 1915. Separated from Fernhout and moved to Utrecht, then Amsterdam, 1917. Frequent trips to Paris from 1918; knew Mondrian. Visited the Borinage mining district of Belgium, 1922. Worked on her studio-house, "De Vlerken", in Bergen, with the architect Piet Kramer, from 1921. Lived in Amsterdam, 1926–30; co-founded Filmliga (Film League) and met Joris Ivens. Organised exhibitions at the Stedelijk Museum, Amsterdam, with the architect J.J.P. Oud, 1928 and 1929. Studio in Paris, 1930; trip to Berlin, 1931. Settled in "De Vlerken", 1932. Died in Bergen, 6 November 1955.

Principal Exhibitions

Individual

Gallery Gerbrands, Utrecht: 1922, 1931

Stedelijk Museum, Amsterdam: 1927

Gallery d'Audretsch, The Hague: 1931, 1935

Palais des Beaux-Arts, Brussels: 1933

Gallery G.J. Nieuwenhuizen Segaar, The Hague: 1934, 1937 (*Drie Generaties* [Three generations], with Jan Toorop and Edgar Fernhout), 1939, 1945

Haags Gemeentemuseum, The Hague: 1951 (touring retrospective)

Hammer Galleries, New York: 1952

Amersfoortse Gemeenschap, Amersfoort: 1953

Gallery Huinck and Scherjon, Amsterdam: 1954

Group

Stedelijk Museum, Amsterdam: 1916–37

Venice Biennale: 1938

Kunsthalle, Bern: 1950 (*Fünf holländische Maler*)

Bibliography

H.P. Bremmer, *Beeldende Kunst*, ix, 1922, pp.57–64; xx, 1933, pp.13, 54 and 63 (in addition, at least one reproduction and comments in all volumes, 1918–37)

A.M. Hammacher, "Charley Toorop", *Beeldende Kunst*, xxvii, 1940, pp.25–32

Charley Toorop, exh. cat., Haags Gemeentemuseum, The Hague, and elsewhere, 1951

A.M. Hammacher, *Charley Toorop: Een beschouwing van haar leven en werk* [Charley Toorop: A study of her life and work], Rotterdam: Brussel, 1952

Nico J. Brederoo, *Charley Toorop: Leven en werken* [Charley Toorop: Life and work], Amsterdam: Meulenhoff, 1982 (contains bibliography)

Charley Toorop, exh. cat., Centraal Museum, Utrecht, 1982

Carel Blotkamp, "Charley Toorop over De Stijl" [Charley Toorop on De Stijl], *Jong Holland*, vi/2, 1990, pp.14–15 (with English summary)

Met verve [With verve], exh. cat., Stichting Amazone, Amsterdam, 1991

De maaltijd der vrienden [The meal with friends], exh. cat., Het Huis Kranenburgh, Bergen, North Holland, 1994

Charley Toorop: Werken in de verzameling [Charley Toorop: Works in the collection], exh. cat., Rijksmuseum Kröller-Müller, Otterlo, 1995

Charley Toorop has left behind an oeuvre that is impressive in both extent and power. Around 400 oil paintings, 120 drawings and 15 prints by her are currently in Dutch museums and private collections. Nearly one-third of these are portraits, of which many are self- and group portraits. Toorop also produced numerous still lifes (some of them churned out for dealers), besides townscapes, a few café interiors and subjects such as her garden, flowering orchards and plants. She was a well-known painter in her lifetime, and her reputation has survived up to the present day.

At around the age of 18 Toorop indicated that she wanted to become a painter. Her father Jan Toorop, one of the best-known Dutch artists at the turn of the century (his reputation is still high today), maintained many contacts with other artists, so Toorop came into contact from an early age with a circle of male and female painters, including Piet Mondrian, with whom she remained friends, Jacoba van Heemskerck (q.v.) and Jan Sluyters. Luminism and theosophy were important influences for painters at the time, as was the Parisian avant-garde. The Toorop family spent several summers at Domburg, on the island of Walcheren. At this early stage (1911), Toorop was already exhibiting in her father's exhibition room ("Het paviljoentje") there, next to many younger and older painters of repute, and, as a result, her work came to be shown elsewhere. She had learned the principles of painting from her father, who continued to advise and assist her. Thanks to her forceful personality, she nevertheless found her own direction. The fact of being a woman did not deter her from practising the profession, although bringing up three young children on her own certainly presented problems.

Toorop's earliest portraits, which date from c.1913, were painted under the influence of spiritualist ideas, for example the portrait of her baby son *John Fernhout* (1913; private collection, repr. Utrecht 1982, no.20). *Lighthouse at Evening* (1915; Rijksmuseum Kröller-Müller, Otterlo) shows clear signs of Symbolism. The spiritual element in her work began to fade after 1921, when she fell under the influence of painters from the Bergen school. This group painted in a style that had both Expressionist and Cubist elements, in which forms were emphasised by their contours. Moreover, she was also fascinated by the work of Vincent van Gogh, in particular his "profound, stark love of reality", as she recounted in an interview in 1953. In 1922 she went to the mining region of the Borinage in Belgium – as van Gogh had done 44 years earlier; her work from that time includes two double portraits of a mother and daughter: *The Owner and Her Daughter* (1922; Rijksmuseum Kröller-Müller) and *Two Women Miners* (1922; Dienst Verspreide Rijkscollecties, The Hague). In these works Toorop felt that she had achieved the kind of expression that she wanted. The figures are large and positioned in the foreground. No contact is implied between the sitters, but each woman is clearly individualised, not "prettified" but keenly observed. Other paintings show a similar desire to portray Toorop's vision of things without "a blurring of the fierce and direct beauty of life", as she described it in an interview of 1951. These Borinage works reveal a strongly personal approach. Her portrait of patients from a lunatic asylum, *The Imbeciles* (1924; Stedelijk Museum, Amsterdam), shows Toorop at her best; the two seated women, rendered with a greater plasticity than in the earlier portraits, are expressively painted. In this period she also received more and more portrait commissions from well-to-do clients. These were executed in a realistic manner, with little detail, and include her portrait of *Plasschaert* (1927; Stedelijk Museum). A striking aspect of Toorop's portraits is that she frequently depicts her subjects almost frontally; the viewer is thus directly confronted by the results of her acute observation.

After 1924 Toorop several times turned to social realism, as in the *Boarding House* (1928; Stedelijk van Abbemuseum, Eindhoven) and *Bistro, Paris* (1931; Centraal Museum, Utrecht), both produced during one of her sojourns in France. It is more than likely that the influence of the German movement Neue Sachlichkeit (New Objectivity) had its effect on her, since she maintained an awareness of avant-garde art. At the exhibition *Socialistische kunst heden* (Socialist art today) at the Stedelijk Museum in Amsterdam (1930) she showed *Five Zeeland Peasants* (1930; Centraal Museum); the middle peasant of the five, large in stature, is shown half-length and frontally, and as if seen through a sharply focused camera lens. *Musicians and Dancing Peasants* (1927; Rijksmuseum Kröller-

Beuningen, Rotterdam), a monumental group portrait, depicts some of her artist friends, among them Gerrit Rietveld of the De Stijl group and the sculptor John Rädecker. Toorop intended *Recumbent Medusa* (1938–9; Stedelijk Museum) and *Medusa Puts Out to Sea* (1941; Rijksmuseum Kröller-Müller) as laments. Her consciousness of the threat of Nazism produced this vision of beauty deceived. Medusa's head, painted after a plaster model (Toorop always used models), is beautiful and powerful, but it is as if her soul has taken temporary shelter elsewhere. The war years are reflected in *Still Life with White Jug* (private collection, *ibid.*, no.334), which bears the pointed subtitle *Meal Without Friends*. Its clearly constructed composition, characteristic of her still lifes after 1930, is brightened by the light effects and the decorative contour lines. The inner truth with which Toorop painted here comes more powerfully than ever to the fore. *Clown* (1941; Rijksmuseum Kröller-Müller) and *Female Worker among the Ruins* (1943; Stedelijk Museum) were painted after the destruction of Rotterdam in 1940.

Three Generations (see illustration) is one of her last monumental canvases. She had worked on it, with interruptions, since 1941; it was eventually completed in 1950. At the upper left she painted the bronze mask made by John Rädecker after a photograph of her father, in the background at the right her son, the painter Edgar Fernhout, and in the middle herself. The work exudes a compelling power. It is the fourth from the last in the impressive series of around 35 painted and drawn self-portraits. Throughout her life she subjected herself to an unsparing scrutiny, and painted herself in many guises: open, as in *Self-Portrait Against a Wall* (1925; Museum Boijmans Van Beuningen); self-assured, as in *Self-Portrait Standing with a Palette* (1933); with a sorrowful expression, as in *Self-Portrait with a Palette* (1952; both Haags Gemeentemuseum); and *Self-Portrait with Almost Drawn Curtain* (1955; Stedelijk Museum, Alkmaar), painted when she felt herself to be at the end of her life, and capable only of looking back. Toorop was a free spirit who showed no desire to belong to a specific school. Her work is of a distinctive and penetrating expressive realism.

ROSELLA M. HUBER-SPANIER

Toorop: *Three Generations*, 1941–50; oil on canvas; 200 × 121 cm.; Museum Boijmans Van Beuningen, Rotterdam

Müller) reveals the influence of film even more clearly. Toorop's still lifes, most of them larger than 50 × 50 centimetres, follow a similar progression to her portraits, moving from an Expressionist style with Cubist elements to a sturdy and powerful realism, for example *Flowers* (1919; Dordrechts Museum, Dordrecht), *Vase of Flowers Before a Stone Wall* (1924; repr. Utrecht 1982, no.249) and *Still Life with Horse's Skull* (1929; Rijksmuseum Kröller-Müller).

The years between 1930 and the outbreak of World War II were Toorop's most prolific period, and the one in which she produced her mature work; later, her health began to deteriorate. She continued to practise in different genres, to receive portrait commissions and to sell work through dealers. She carried out a number of large-scale projects, among them *Cheese Market at Alkmaar* (1933; 150 × 179 cm.; Stedelijk Museum). These have a deep emotional resonance. Another project, *Meal with Friends* (1933; Museum Boijmans Van

Toyen
Czech painter, 1902–1980

Born Maria Cerminová in Prague, 21 September 1902. Attended the School of Applied Arts, Prague, 1919–20. Met painter Jindřich Štyrský in Yugoslavia, 1922; took part in formation of Czech avant-garde group Devětsil, 1920; exhibited with the group, 1923. Moved to Paris with Štyrský, 1925; returned to Prague, 1928/9. Began transition to Surrealism, 1929. Co-founder and member of Surrealist group in Prague, 1934; participated in International Surrealist exhibitions in Tenerife (1935), London (1936), Tokyo (1937), Paris (1938) and Amsterdam (1938). Forced underground by the German occupation of Czechoslovakia, 1939. Left for Paris with poet Jindřich Heisler, 1947; joined André Breton's

Surrealist group; exhibited with the Surrealists in Paris and Prague, 1947. Died in Paris, November 1980.

Selected Individual Exhibitions
Galerie d'Art Contemporain, Paris: 1926 (with Jindřich Štyrský)
Galerie Vavin, Paris: 1927 (with Jindřich Štyrský)
Prague: 1938 (with Jindřich Štyrský, touring)
Topicuv Salon, Prague: 1945
Galerie Denise René, Paris: 1947
Galerie "A l'étoile scellée", Paris: 1953, 1955
Galerie Furstenberg, Paris: 1958
Galerie Raymond Cordier, Paris: 1960, 1962
Moravská Galerie, Brno: 1966–7 (with Jindřich Štyrský, touring)
Alternativi Attuali 3, L'Aquila, Italy: 1968 (with Jindřich Štyrský, retrospective)
Musée National d'Art Moderne, Centre Georges Pompidou, Paris: 1982 (retrospective, with Jindřich Štyrský and Jindřich Heisler)

Bibliography

Vítezslav Nezval and Karel Teige, *Štyrský a Toyen*, Prague: Borovy, 1938
André Breton, Jindřich Heisler and Benjamin Péret, *Toyen*, Paris: Sokolova, 1953
Štyrský a Toyen, 1921–1945, exh. cat., Moravská Galerie, Brno, 1966
Annie Le Brun, *Sur-le-champ*, Paris: Editions Surréalistes, 1967
Radovan Ivsic, *Toyen*, Paris: Filippachi, 1974
Künstlerinnen international, 1877–1977, exh. cat., Schloss Charlottenburg, Berlin, 1977
Obliques, no.14–15, 1977 (special issue: *La Femme surréaliste*)
André Breton, *Le Surréalisme et la peinture*, 2nd edition, Paris: Gallimard, 1979
L'altra metà dell'avanguardia, 1910–1940: Pittrici e scultrici nei movimenti delle avanguardie storiche, exh. cat., Palazzo Reale, Milan, and elsewhere, 1980
David Meyer, "Le surréalisme tchèque", *Cahiers du Musée National d'Art Moderne*, lxxxii, 1982, pp.279–95
Štyrský, Toyen, Heisler, exh. cat., Musée National d'Art Moderne, Centre Georges Pompidou, Paris, 1982
Whitney Chadwick, *Women Artists and the Surrealist Movement*, Boston: Little Brown, and London: Thames and Hudson, 1985
Ragnar von Holten, *Toyen: Katalogredaktor*, Stockholm: Moderna Museet, 1985
La Femme et le surréalisme, exh. cat., Musée Cantonal des Beaux-Arts, Lausanne, 1987
Whitney Chadwick, "Toyen: Toward a revolutionary art in Prague and Paris", *Symposium*, xlii, 1989, pp.276–95
Grit Wendelberger, "Rätsel und Phantome", *Bildende Kunst*, no.5, 1989, pp.31–2
George Melly, *Paris and the Surrealists*, New York and London: Thames and Hudson, 1991
Renée Riese Hubert, *Magnifying Mirrors: Women, Surrealism and Partnership*, Lincoln: University of Nebraska Press, 1994

The women artists included among the Surrealists are surprisingly numerous. The Czech painter Toyen, among the least spoken of, is surely one of the most interesting: a "fine and underrated painter", George Melly called her, in his *Paris and the Surrealists* (1991). She, like Benjamin Péret, remained faithful to the ideas and spirit of Surrealism until her end. She had lived in Paris from 1925 to 1928, exhibiting with her companion Jindřich Štyrský. In 1934 she co-founded the Czech Surrealist group with Štyrský and Karel Teige, with whom she welcomed André Breton and Paul Eluard in Prague the following year. Originally an anarchist, she translated the revolutionary writings of Arthur Rimbaud, Lautréamont, Alfred Jarry

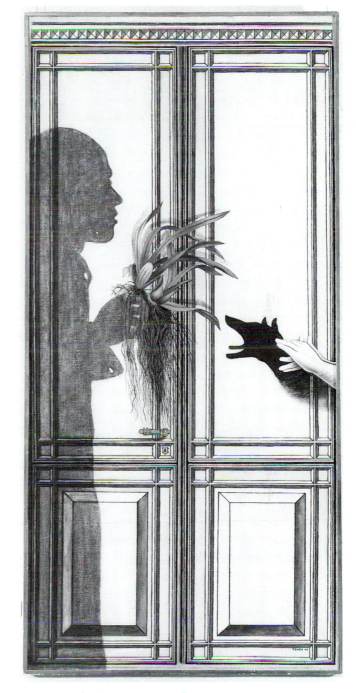

Toyen: *Myth of Light*, 1946; oil on canvas; 160 × 75 cm.; Moderna Museet, Stockholm

and Guillaume Apollinaire into Czech. With Jindřich Heisler, she published a collection of assemblages. During the Nazi raids, he hid in her bathroom for four years; they settled in Paris as political refugees in 1947.

Toyen is known for her images of the body, as in *Magnetic Woman* (1934; collection Bernard Galateau), where a tree limb is placed alongside the torso of a woman, divided in places like the bark of a tree trunk, both of these objects cast against a background of streaked blue, uneven like the bark/flesh. Many of her most imaginative pieces deal with the relations between the human body and nature.

The terribleness of war is foretold and reflected upon, its waste, its desolate figures and emptied constructions, dead birds and human body parts, architectural ruins and stripped tree trunks, in the series *Rifle Range* (1939–44; collection Radovan Ivsic), with its imprisoning images and its desolation. The same irregularities and upsets, undoing any smooth rendering, mental or artistic, of the painted objects, are to be found in Toyen's *Tremor in the Crystal* of 1946, where an earthquake has dislodged boulders and a church steeple extends diagonally to the top of the picture, but upon whose white front there is a clock face with no hands. Time has stopped – only its traces remain. Nothing is whole, even or static in this painting, which Breton would call "a universe of fissures".

Many are the objects projecting fright in Toyen's work: an eagle filling up the entire picture frame and resting its human hands upon shards of glass protruding from a wall marks *Dangerous Hour* (1942; Galerie A.F. Petit, Paris). One of her most haunting canvases, *Myth of Light* (1946; see illustration), projects, against a door frame, the shadow of a Native American holding out what looks like a yucca plant, its roots streaming down and its leaves stretching over the vertical upright in the centre, towards a wolf's head also projected as a shadow by two white-gloved hands. The wolf's open mouth reaches for the leaves held out, in a vaguely threatening attitude, so that a tension is established between natural animality and figurality on the one hand, and artistic craft on the other, between shadow and substance. Finally, the strong diagonal of the line reading down from top left to middle right, from the profiled shadow of human head/real plant/profiled shadow of wolf's head/real hands is balanced by the uprights of the Indian figure and the central division of the door. The painting has a quite extraordinary power, its shadows, substance and continuity projected as both linear and natural: plant, animal, human figure. Toyen's conceptions were intensely complicated, more so than the majority of Surrealist artists of either gender. Elsewhere, a sleep-walking child clutching a butterfly net stands with her back to us, facing the horizon, bodiless under her open dress (*The Sleeper*, 1937).

Toyen's face "medalled in nobility" and her eyes like "beaches of light" were as moving to Breton as her work: "luminous as her heart and still crossed by sombre predictions". It is in his "Introduction to the work of Toyen" (1953) that Breton importantly explains how, since photography and film have undermined the notion of imitative art, painting must now of necessity become visionary. And, he says, Toyen's work becomes progressively more serene, both in its drawing and its constructions, such as the cycle *Neither Wings nor Stones: Wings and Stones* of 1949, and the very beautiful cascade of hair and water in *The Somnambulist* (1958; Collection Charles Silbermann), about which he wrote in his most moving prose poems: "It's for you that my head bends back under the high radar of the comb. Meeting you, I go forward between the light and the shadow: do with me what you won't wish ..." (1958).

MARY ANN CAWS

Traquair, Phoebe
Irish artist, designer and craft worker, 1852–1936

Born Phoebe Anna Moss in Dublin, 24 May 1852. Studied at Royal Dublin Society design school, c.1869–72. Married Scots palaeontologist Ramsay Traquair, 1873; two sons, born 1874 and 1875, one daughter, born 1879; husband died 1912. Lived in Edinburgh after marriage. First woman honorary member, Royal Scottish Academy, 1920. Died in Edinburgh, 4 August 1936.

Principal Exhibitions
World's Columbian Exposition, Chicago: 1893
Arts and Crafts Society of Ireland, Dublin: 1895, 1904
Guild of Women-Binders, London: from 1898
Scottish Guild of Handicraft, Glasgow: 1898
Arts and Crafts Exhibition Society, London: 1899, 1903, 1906
Exposition Universelle, Paris: 1900 (with Guild of Women-Binders)
Royal Scottish Academy, Edinburgh: from 1902
Louisiana Purchase Exposition, St Louis: 1904

Bibliography
Gerard Baldwin Brown, "Some recent efforts in mural decoration", *Scottish Arts Review*, January 1889, pp.225–8
Margaret Armour, "Beautiful modern manuscripts", *The Studio*, 1897, pp.47–55 (special winter issue)
—, "Mural decoration in Scotland", *The Studio*, x, 1897, pp.100–06
"A Scottish lady decorator: Mrs Traquair", *Scots Pictorial*, 7 May 1898, p.10
Esther Wood, "British tooled bookbindings and their designers", *The Studio*, 1899–1900, pp.38–47 (special winter issue: *Modern Bookbindings and Their Designers*)
James Caw, "The art work of Mrs Traquair", *Art Journal*, 1900, pp.143–8
G.A. Anstruther, ed., *The Bindings of Tomorrow: A Record of the Work of the Guild of Women-Binders and of the Hampstead Bindery*, London: Guild of Women-Binders, 1902
A.F. Morris, "A versatile art worker: Mrs Traquair", *The Studio*, xxxiv, 1905, pp.339–45
Barbara Morris, "Some early embroideries of Mrs Phoebe Traquair", *Embroidery*, 1966, pp.49–53 (Diamond Jubilee edition)
Anthea Callen, *Angel in the Studio: Women in the Arts and Crafts Movement, 1870–1914*, London: Astragal, 1979; as *Women Artists of the Arts and Crafts Movement, 1870–1914*, New York: Pantheon, 1979
Arts and Crafts in Edinburgh, 1880–1930, exh. cat., Edinburgh College of Art, 1985
Elizabeth Skeoch Cumming, *Phoebe Anna Traquair HRSA (1852–1936) and Her Contribution to Arts and Crafts in Edinburgh*, PhD dissertation, University of Edinburgh, 1987
Elizabeth Cumming, "A note on Phoebe Traquair and an Edinburgh Dante", *Edinburgh Review*, 1992, pp.143–9
Phoebe Anna Traquair, 1852–1936, exh. cat., Scottish National Portrait Gallery, Edinburgh, 1993 (contains bibliography)
Nicola Gordon Bowe and Elizabeth Cumming, *The Arts and Crafts Movements in Dublin and Edinburgh* (in preparation)

In the 1890s and 1900s Phoebe Traquair was the leading artist and craft worker of the Arts and Crafts movement in Scotland. Working in a diverse range of media, from mural decoration to easel painting, manuscript illumination to book tooling, and from embroidery to enamel work, she produced a substantial corpus of work that was exhibited world-wide and at the time was noted by critics in Edinburgh and London to be romantic in its treatment of literary subjects and unique in the artist's use of colour and texture. More recently she has been recognised as Scotland's first professional woman artist. Her work is in the collections of the Victoria and Albert Museum, London, and the Royal Museum of Scotland, Edinburgh.

Phoebe Anna Moss was born into the heart of middle-class Ireland. Many members of her family, including her father, were distinguished surgeons and medical practitioners. Her earliest work reflected this inheritance: from the early 1870s she produced highly detailed scientific drawings of fossil fish to illustrate the scientific research papers of the Royal Dublin Society curator (and her future husband), Ramsay Traquair. Dublin also offered rich opportunities for her to study museum and library collections. The combined use of colour and pattern to convey spiritual values in such medieval manuscripts as the Book of Kells (Trinity College Library, Dublin) engaged her attention from an early age and was subsequently to inform much of her work in the course of a long and prolific career.

On arrival in Edinburgh in 1874, Traquair first worked in the field of domestic embroidery, which she worked in a simple style using crewel techniques. Surviving examples (Victoria and Albert Museum, London), however, give little indication of the rich imagination and technical bravura found in her subsequent embroideries. For the first ten years of marriage she devoted her energies to bringing up her children, but by the mid-1880s she was determined to widen her vision beyond household duties. Gradually her social circle expanded to include some of the leading thinkers in Edinburgh – men such as John Miller Gray (later the first curator of the Scottish National Portrait Gallery), the botanist, critic, social reformer and environmentalist Patrick Geddes, and the art historian Gerard Baldwin Brown – who not only introduced her to the ideas and poetry of Rossetti and Tennyson, Blake and Dante, but also individually helped engineer the launch of her career.

Traquair's first professional commission came through the Edinburgh Social Union, a philanthropic body spearheaded by Geddes. For the Union she decorated the tiny mortuary chapel of the Royal Edinburgh Hospital for Sick Children (1885–6). Here, on walls measuring 2.3 × 1.5 metres, she combined the aesthetics of medieval manuscripts with a style much indebted to late Pre-Raphaelitism. She used vivid blues, reds and gold leaf, and the decoration was described by Baldwin Brown in the *Scottish Art Review* as "a piece of illumination enlarged". The central theme of Christian redemption introduced here was one that would be used many times over the following 30 years.

While engaged on this first commission, Traquair started the first of her ambitious panels of "artistic embroidery". An early series of three panels was worked on the theme of the *Salvation of Mankind* (1886–93; City of Edinburgh Museums and Art Galleries). When the suite was shown in Dublin in 1895, a critic commented on the "broadness of treatment, decorative feeling, colour and dexterity in dealing with a difficult material" (William Hunt in *Journal and Proceedings of the Arts and Crafts Society of Ireland*, 1896, p.26). Each measuring over 1.8 metres in height, these embroideries neatly illustrate her stylistic development over a seven-year period. The density of the Aesthetic figural imagery of the central panel (*Angel of Redemption and Purification*, 1886–7), with its undercurrent of medieval and Morrisian naturalism, contrasts dramatically with the simpler design of the two side panels (*Souls of the Blest*, 1889–91, and *Souls Waiting on Earth*, 1891–3). This early panel shows a similar intensity of design and imagery to a series of illuminated manuscripts produced in 1887 (private collections) when Traquair was in correspondence with John Ruskin, who lent her medieval manuscripts from his Brantwood library, and in turn admired her efforts.

In the 1890s the inspiration for Traquair's work continued to range widely from Blake and Rossetti to medieval manuscripts and textiles. Her work, however, had its own distinctive, strong identity and she pursued a personal Symbolist language expressed through a form of decorative realism. This is most obvious in her decoration of two Edinburgh buildings: the Song School at St Mary's Cathedral (1888–92) and the Catholic Apostolic Church (1893–1901). Combining portraiture with imaginative concepts, the Song School scheme was called "fresh and modern" by a London critic. The Catholic Apostolic Church decoration more obviously reflects the influence of the paintings of Botticelli and Fra Angelico, which Traquair had viewed in Florence in 1889 and 1895, and realised her primary goal of uniting the fine and decorative arts. Inspired by Renaissance ideals, Traquair here used gesso and gold leaf to give texture to the surfaces, but experimentation with the medium resulted in an original method designed to withstand (unsuccessfully) the Scottish climate: she diluted the oils with turpentine, blended beeswax with it and coated the surface with a beeswax varnish. Illuminated manuscripts of this decade, such as Elizabeth Barrett Browning's *Sonnets from the Portuguese* (1892–7; National Library of Scotland, Edinburgh), were also inspired in technique and style by Italian examples of the early Renaissance.

Recognition by London critics encouraged Traquair to produce some of her most confident and finest work during this decade. While decorating the Catholic Apostolic Church, she stitched a suite of four embroideries on the same theme of the *Progress of a Soul* (1893–1902; see illustration), in which choice and imaginative use of traditional and modern stitches and of colour are united with powerful imagery to produce some of the finest textiles of the Arts and Crafts movement. The iconography represents the drama of a soul's development through life, from innocence through experience to ultimate salvation at the point of death. This romantic subject, at once personal and universal, may have been originally inspired by Walter Pater's tale of Denys l'Auxerrois in *Imaginary Portraits*, but it also includes iconographic references to Apollo, Orpheus and the innocent Parsifal. The underlying message supplied by Traquair, a committed Christian, was again that of man's redemption through the grace of God.

This theme continued to inform Traquair's work in a variety of media in the 1890s and 1900s. Working alongside a group of women binders who included Annie Macdonald and Jessie McGibbon at the Dean Studio in Edinburgh's West End, Traquair produced not only some of her finest manuscripts but blind-tooled and embossed, almost sculpted, monochrome leather book covers. From 1901, however, she learned the rudiments of a fashionable medium, enamelling, from Lady Gibson Carmichael, who had studied the craft in London with Alexander Fisher. Their designs were in part inspired by the

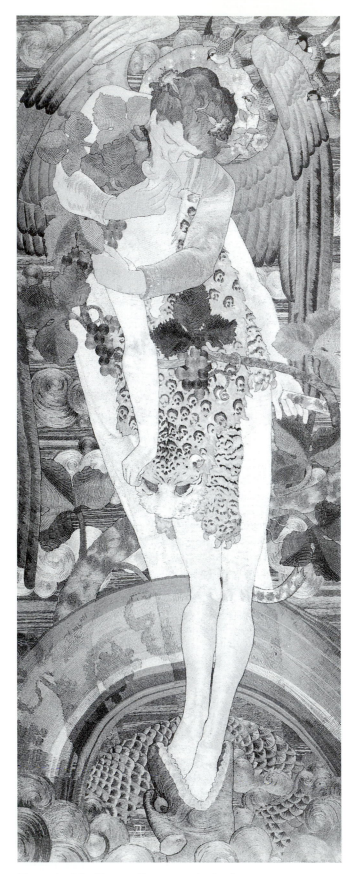

Traquair: *The Victory (Progress of a Soul)*, 1893–1902; embroidery; National Gallery of Scotland, Edinburgh

medieval collections formed by Lady Carmichael's husband, Sir Thomas Gibson Carmichael. Enamelling quickly became Traquair's favoured small-scale colour craft. Here, as in illumination and mural decoration, she was able, in the true Arts and Crafts spirit, to reunite art and design. With mural painting Traquair had wrestled with the difficulties of translating small-scale designs to an "epic" architectural context, but with manuscripts and now enamels she encountered no such problem. In letters written in the 1900s to Percy Nobbs, a young architect and friend of her elder son Ramsay, she referred to such pieces as "little lyrics", commenting that these could produce "bits of lovely colour quite beautiful in themselves".

Traquair's interest in colour, always present in her work, became dominant in her work of the 1900s. When an enamelled triptych of the *Red Cross Knight* (1905; private collection, repr. *The Studio*, xxxvii, 1906, p.213) – a subject celebrating the victory of good over evil – was shown at the Arts and Crafts Exhibition Society in London in 1906, *The Studio* was quick to refer to "the charm of colour...[that] turns this triptych into a pleasant and effective, even noble, decoration" (*ibid.*, p.214). The colours she employed in enamelled jewellery, caskets and triptychs – medieval forms so well suited to the medium – were quite different from those of Fisher and his pupils. The green of land, the ultramarine of sea and the amber of an autumn sunset were conveyed in a manner that was at once harmonious and powerful. Traquair's enamels illustrated narrative scenes in which angels rescued or comforted mortals: at times sentiment was avoided only through inventive exploration of the material. Uniquely, Traquair added tiny slivers of foil to the flux to reflect light and to add texture to the surface.

Although mural decoration was primarily a craft of the 1880s and 1890s, Traquair produced two late schemes for buildings in England. The first, for the tiny church of St Peter in the village of Clayworth, Nottinghamshire (1904–5), was painted over two summers and combined portraiture with a representation of an angel choir. The other commission took her three summers to complete: painted in the apse of Detmar Blow's Manners chapel at Thorney Hill in the New Forest, Hampshire, between 1920 and 1922 it was virtually her swan-song. By the mid-1920s, with failing eyesight, Traquair had abandoned enamelling and once more took up the craft of domestic embroidery. Her career had turned almost full circle. Her achievements had been many, however, and her obituaries were fullsome in their praise. According to one, she was "a little woman and sparely built but overflowing with nervous energy, her artistic activities were remarkable both in extent and quality" (*The Times*, 6 August 1936).

ELIZABETH CUMMING

Treu, Katrina *see* Court Artists survey

Trumbull, Alice *see* Mason

Tryggvadóttir, Nína

Icelandic painter and stained glass artist, 1913–1968

Born in Seydisfjördur, 16 March 1913. Studied at the Royal Danish Academy of Fine Arts, Copenhagen, 1935–9. Lived in Paris, 1939. Studied at the Arts Students League, New York, under Morris Kantor and Hans Hofmann, 1943–6; designed set and costumes for Stravinsky's *Soldier's Tale* at the Macmillan Theatre, Columbia University, 1946. Wrote and illustrated children's books from 1946. Exhibited with the September Show group, Reykjavík, 1947. Married medical scientist and painter Alfred L. Copley (pseudonym Alcopley), 1949; daughter born 1951. Settled in Paris with her family, 1952; participated in Salons des Réalités Nouvelles, 1953–6. Moved to London, 1957, to New York, 1959. Died in New York, 18 June 1968.

Selected Individual Exhibitions

Gardastraeti 17, Reykjavík: 1942
New Art Circle, J.B. Neumann Gallery, New York: 1945, 1948
Artists Gallery, Reykjavík: 1946, 1963 (with Alcopley)
Friends of Arts Salon, Reykjavík: 1952
Galerie Colette Allendy, Paris: 1954
Galerie Aujourd'hui, Palais des Beaux-Arts, Brussels: 1955
Galerie Birch, Copenhagen: 1955
Kunstforeningen, Oslo: 1955
National Library of Iceland, Reykjavík: 1956
Galerie Arnaud, Paris: 1957
Galerie La Roue, Paris: 1958
Drian Gallery, London: 1959
Rose Fried Gallery, New York: 1961
Round Room, National Museum, Reykjavík: 1967
National Gallery of Iceland, Reykjavík: 1974 (retrospective)

Selected Writings

"Painting through light with colored glass", *Leonardo*, i, 1968, pp.25–35

Bibliography

R.V. Gindertael, "Nína Tryggvadóttir met dans ses peintures la limpidité de son air natal", *Les Beaux-Arts* (Brussels), no.679, 1955
Michel Seuphor, *Dictionary of Abstract Painting*, London: Methuen, 1958 (French original, 1957)
Jo Schreiter, "Die Glasmalerei unseres Jahrhunderts", *Das Kunstwerk*, xii/5–6, 1958
Vitraux de Tryggvadóttir, exh. cat., Gallerie La Roue, Paris, 1958
J.P. Hodin, "Nína Tryggvadóttir", *Quadrum*, vi, 1959, pp.162–3
Lawrence Campbell, "Nína Tryggvadóttir", *Craft Horizons*, xxii, November–December 1962, pp.24–7, 52
Jules Langsner, *Nína Tryggvadóttir and Alcopley*, Oslo, 1963
Halldór Laxness, "Nína Tryggvadóttir in memoriam", *Yfirskyggdir stadir* [Overshadowed places], Reykjavík: Helgafell, 1971
Björn Th. Björnsson, *Íslensk myndlist* [Icelandic pictorial art], ii, Reykjavík: Helgafell, 1973
Nína Tryggvadóttir, 1913–1968, exh. cat., National Gallery of Iceland, Reykjavík, 1974
Halldór Laxness and Hrafnhildur Schram, "Nína Tryggvadóttir: Serenity and power", *Iceland Review*, 1982
N. Tryggvadóttir: Nature Abstractions, 1957–1967, exh. cat., National Gallery of Iceland, Reykjavík, 1995

At the end of World War II Icelandic art students who had sought education in the USA or continental Europe returned home. They all seemed convinced that art would capture the spiritual content of the time only if its features were totally changed. Nina Tryggvadóttir was one of the young art students who in 1947 formed the group September Show, which was to secure the place of abstraction within the Icelandic visual arts. Thereafter, most artists differentiated between abstract and figurative art, a way of thinking that remained very persistent. After a period of experimentation with a flat, semi-Cubist framework, as in *On the Way* (1946; National Gallery of Iceland, Reykjavík), where some traces of the original model, a woman, are still discernible, although the figure has been broken down into geometric planes and rounded forms, Tryggvadóttir exhibited *Composition* (1947; National Gallery of Iceland) at the first September Show. Here she has cleared the canvas of any figurative matter; the demarcated colour planes merge with the background and form a kind of diamond pattern on the two-dimensional surface. By 1949 Tryggvadóttir had developed a style of concise, highly textured, almost sculptural planes and warm colours.

From the very beginning it was obvious that Tryggvadóttir possessed an intuitive understanding of structure and knew how to pare down her paintings to the bare essentials. These gifts are nowhere more apparent than in the portraits of her artist and writer friends that she painted in Iceland during the war (*Halldór Laxness*, 1940; Art Museum of the Labour Union, Reykjavík). Approaching her subjects with the same pictorial sensibility as if she were painting still lifes, she first drew the facial features, then simplified, compressed and eliminated all superfluous details, leaving exactly what she needed and nothing more. Yet these are not portraits in the traditional sense that require only a likeness, but strong personal statements by which the artist stylises the personal traits of the sitter to her own liking. These portraits are distinctive and without parallel in Icelandic art.

After the end of World War II Tryggvadóttir worked with collage and papier collés. While waiting in Iceland for a visa to the USA, she exhibited in 1952 more than 30 collages, made of multi-coloured paper, pasted on white sheets, with black lines drawn in, connecting and enclosing the bold colour planes. These were strictly geometric works, yet the feeling of nature was strong and Tryggvadóttir called them "mostly landscapes". According to her own comments she had sought this form of expression "to clean her palette". When settling in Paris in 1952, inspired by the Gothic cathedrals of France, she found a way to develop the collages further through the medium of stained glass. From 1953, when she started working in the Oidtmann stained-glass workshop in Linnich, Germany, and until her death, she devoted as much time to her stained-glass designs as to her paintings.

Tryggvadóttir and her artist-husband Alcopley showed their works with the group Réalités Nouvelles during their years in Paris, and the first part of this period falls within Tryggvadóttir's geometric phase. *Composition* (1954; National Gallery of Iceland) is built up of square forms or variations thereof, connected with ties or elongated points in clear, unmixed colours of black, white and red. Tryggvadóttir, however, wrenches her squares out of the strict pattern of the school, and they are subject to no law other than her emotions, but they never became patterned – her strong lyrical bent saw

Tryggvadóttir: *Eruption*, 1964; oil; 131.5 × 105 cm.; National Gallery of Iceland, Reykjavík

to that. Nor did she ever unequivocally embrace the geometric doctrine – she always retained a link to the organic form of nature.

In 1955–6 Tryggvadóttir's forms began to free themselves from the bonds that kept them linked to the two-dimensional canvas. They acquired a more organic shape, creating motion on the pictorial surface by cutting into, or overlapping each other. The earth colours – brown, yellow and green – also underscore the connection with nature (*Abstraction*, 1955; Collection Una Dóra Copley, New York). She described these works in an interview as "Icelandic landscapes". The artist's comments over the years indicate that she was always dependent on the Icelandic landscape. In her abstractions of 1960–64 (*Eruption*, 1964; see illustration) the massive block forms are large and forceful. They are thrown about the canvas, frequently with such explosive power that their rhythm continued far outside the limits of the picture. Her style of painting became more concise, and yet softer, through her use of a spatula to spread the colours in large sweeps. In this way she was able to interpret the natural phenomena of her homeland – basalt columns, waterfalls and rainfalls – in her work in a convincing manner. Her style has been referred to as "abstract impressionism".

Tryggvadóttir's reliance on Icelandic natural imagery increased with time, although she lived mostly abroad, in Paris, London and New York, from 1952 until her death in 1968. Her main works are to be found in the National Gallery of Iceland, Reykjavík, and in the collection of her daughter, Una Dóra Copley, New York.

HRAFNHILDUR SCHRAM

Tsuchiya, Tilsa

Peruvian painter, 1932–1984

Born María Tilsa Tsuchiya Castillo in Supe, Peru, 24 September 1932. Studied at Escuela Nacional de Bellas Artes, Lima, 1954–9; studied humanities at the Sorbonne, and painting and printmaking at the Ecole des Beaux-Arts, Paris, 1960–64. Married Charles Mercier Midelet in Paris, 1963; one son; separated from husband, 1973. Returned to Lima, 1966; established studio Shangri-La and began collaboration with artist José Tola. Chosen to represent Peru at São Paulo Bienal, 1979. Recipient of Segundo Premio Municipal de Pintura, Lima, 1957; Gran Premio, Escuela Nacional de Bellas Artes, Lima, 1959; Premio Francisco Laso, Lima, 1968; Premio Bienal "Technoquímica", Lima, 1970. Died in Lima, 23 September 1984.

Selected Individual Exhibitions

Instituto de Arte Contemporáneo, Lima: 1959, 1968, 1970
Galerie Cimaise, Paris: 1966
Galería Carlos Rodríguez Saavedra, Lima: 1972
Galería Ars Concentra, Lima: 1975
Galería Astrolabio, Lima: 1976
Galería Enrique Camino Brent, Lima: 1980
Sala de Arte Petroperú, Lima: 1984 (retrospective)

Bibliography

Tilsa: XV Bienal de São Paulo, exh. cat., Instituto Nacional de Cultura, Lima, 1979

Jorge Eduardo Wuffarden, *Tilsa Tsuchiya,* Lima: Banco Popular del Perú, 1981

Art of the Fantastic: Latin America, 1920–1987, exh. cat., Indianapolis Museum of Art, and elsewhere, 1987

Oriana Baddeley and Valerie Fraser, *Drawing the Line: Art and Cultural Identity in Contemporary Latin America*, London and New York: Verso, 1989

Edouardo Moll, *Tilsa Tsuchiya*, Lima: Navarrete, 1991

Edward Lucie-Smith, *Latin American Art of the 20th Century*, London and New York: Thames and Hudson, 1993

Tilsa Tsuchiya is respected in Peru as one of the most original painters of the rich world of legend and myth that has resided in the Andes for centuries. Combining the European experience of Surrealism with that of her own unique mixture of Chinese, Japanese and Peruvian heritage, Tilsa, as she was affectionately known, created exquisite canvases of lush surfaces and meticulous details. As a student at the Escuela Nacional de Bellas Artes in Lima in the mid-1950s, she learned about the dominant trends of modernism, including Abstract Expressionism, as well as the realistic and sensitive depictions favoured by the *indigenismo* movement that had an impact in many areas of Latin America with large indigenous populations. The *indigenismo* writers and artists celebrated the dignity of the native people, often looking to the Mexican muralists for inspiration. One of the foremost proponents of *indigenismo* was José Sabogal, teacher and later director at the Escuela Nacional, who had a profound effect on the curriculum by the time Tilsa was in attendance there. The school emphasised nationalistic themes based on nativist subjects.

Even before the sojourn in Paris in the early 1960s that marks her artistic advancement to a mature style, Tilsa was already experimenting with poetic re-evaluations of the formal qualities of her compositions in such works as *Bodegón* (1959; private collection) and *Table in a Landscape* (1960; private collection). The subject of the *bodegón*, still-life arrangements of bottles, flowers and simplified objects on tables, occupied her throughout her career and with these compositions it is possible to trace the evolution of her painterly style from the depiction of real objects to those totally from her imagination. Beginning with items placed in careful relationships and depicted as flat areas of muted tonalities, the *bodegón* quickly lost definition as an ordinary grouping of household jars and pitchers and assumed a shadowy quality, lending an air of mystery to the most banal of subjects. Mysterious interplays of shape and form, both real and imagined, are characteristic of her mature work, and evident in *Bodegón* (1965; private collection) and *Domestic Fellowship* (1966; private collection). On her return from Paris and classes in figure drawing, the *bodegón* was supplanted by surreal compositions featuring armless figures and mythical landscapes inspired by the Andes, as seen in *Personage* and *Landscape and Figures* (both 1970; private collection, Lima). Her encounter with Surrealism, already in its last phase in Paris, liberated her work from its formalist and academic restrictions and brought forth the world of shadows and mystery that seemed to have been lurking in her psyche from the very beginning. The return to Peru with new confidence in the technical and conceptual

Tsuchiya: *Machu Picchu*, 1974; oil on canvas; 130 × 97 cm.; Collection Rafael Lemor, Lima, Peru

aspects of painting allowed her to embark on a series of works commemorating Andean art and culture with images that appear as ancient as the stories that inspired their very existence.

Although Tilsa never claimed to be re-interpreting or depicting actual myths or personages, a knowledge of pre-Inca and Inca mythology and objects of the archaeological record informed her work. Ever since the discovery of Machu Picchu in 1911, the Inca Empire has fascinated Peruvians and foreigners alike. For Peruvians, the amazing city in the clouds was a unique part of their history that was admired throughout the world. As the subject of her painting *Machu Picchu* (1970; see illustration), the city named after the two mountain peaks that overlook and protect the site emerges from the clouds. An armless figure perches between the dark peaks upon a ritual altar of stone in the shape of a coiled snake, a reference to the sacred environment of the city and the great carving skills of the Andean people who created their first deities of stone. In Quechua legend, rocks and other natural phenomena are sacred objects called *wak'as*. Demanding offerings to assure their beneficence, the *wak'as* are physical and spiritual embodiments of an ancient system of beliefs that persists to this day among the indigenous people. Dominating the pantheon of nature gods and goddesses, the Great Earth Mother, Pachamama, is responsible for fertility and the cycle of life and death. The armless females that float in Tilsa's imaginary world pay tribute to her power and that of the spirits, the *apus*, that dwell in her domain.

In 1976 Tilsa began a series of works honouring the rich tradition of myths and legends in the Andes and the oneiric spirits who dwell in the high peaks and in the desolate sands of the desert, home to people long gone but remembered by the wealth of artefacts found in archaeological excavations. Borrowing design elements of flat and sinuous patterns and demonic figures combining animal, bird and human forms from their stone carvings, textiles and ceramics, she composed images of strange females perched in trees, flying with the wind and occupying rugged mountain landscapes. Women assume mythic power in such works as *Myth of the Tree* (1976; collection Oscar Berckemeyer P.H., Galería Camino Brent, Lima) and *Myth of the Warrior* (1976; private collection, Lima). They emerge from the mist of an imaginary setting reminiscent of the cloud patterns hovering above pristine oriental landscapes, and the vaporous and mysterious shadows that shroud Inca cities built high in the Andes. It is this combination of stylistic and symbolic devices cultivated from the variety of sources that are very much part of her own heritage and feminine intellectual experience that distinguishes the work of Tilsa Tsuchiya. More than a surreal rendering of indigenous subjects, her paintings draw upon the legends of the past to visualise a world of dreams beyond the imagination.

CAROL DAMIAN

Twamley, Louisa Anne *see* Meredith

U–V

Udaltsova, Nadezhda (Andreyevna)

Russian painter, draughtswoman and textile designer, 1886–1961

Born in Orel, 29 December 1885 (Old Style calendar)/10 January 1886 (New Style calendar); father the General of Gendarmerie, Andrei Prudkovsky. Moved to Moscow with her family, 1892; educated at a private high school for girls from aristocratic families. Attended classes in Konstantin Yuon's studio, and met Lyubov Popova (q.v.) and Vera Mukhina (q.v.). Married A.D. Udaltsov, 1908; separated after 1917. Continued her artistic education in Paris, 1912; with Popova, studied at La Palette under Henri Le Fauconnier and Jean Metzinger. Returned to Moscow, 1913. Member of Kazimir Malevich's group Supremus, 1916–17. After the Revolution, became active in the organisation of the first professional union of Russian artists, 1917–19, and joined IZO, Narkompros (Fine Arts Section, People's Commissariat of Enlightenment). Taught painting and textile design at Vkhutemas (Higher State Artistic and Technical Workshops), and Vkhutein (Higher State Artistic and Technical Institute), Moscow, 1920–30. Member of Inkhuk (Institute of Artistic Culture), Moscow, 1920–21. Explored the Russian frontiers – Ural and Altai – and worked in Armenia with her second husband, painter Alexander Drevin, late 1920s–early 1930s; son born 1921; husband executed 1938. Died in Moscow, 25 January 1961.

Principal Exhibitions

Individual
Russian Museum, Leningrad: 1928 (with Alexander Drevin)
Central Club of Artists, Moscow: 1965 (retrospective)

Group
Bubnovy valet (Jack/Knave of Diamonds), Moscow: 1914, 1917
Petrograd: 1915 (*Tramway V: First Futurist Exhibition of Paintings*), 1915 (*0.10 [Zero-Ten]: Last Futurist Exhibition of Paintings*)
Moscow: 1917 (*Verbovka: Contemporary Applied Art*), 1918 (*First Exhibition of Paintings by the Professional Union of Artists in Moscow*)
Galerie van Diemen, Berlin: 1922–3 (*Erste russische Kunstausstellung*, touring)

Selected Writings
Zhizn russkoy kubistki: Dnevniki, stati, vospominaniya [Life of a Russian Cubist woman artist: Diaries, articles, memoirs], Moscow: "RA", 1994

Bibliography

V. Denisov, "Moskovskiye zhivopistsy v Leningrade" [Moscow painters in Leningrad], *Zhizn iskusstva*, no.8, 1928, pp.6–7
O. Beskin, *Formalizm v iskusstve* [Formalism in art], Moscow, 1933
Camilla Gray, *The Great Experiment: Russian Art, 1863–1922*, London: Thames and Hudson, and New York: Abrams, 1962
J.-P. Bouillon, "Le cubisme et l'avant-garde russe", *Actes du première colloque d'histoire de l'art contemporain: Université de Saint-Étienne, 1973*, pp.153–223
Kazimir Malevich, *The Artist, Infinity, Suprematism: Unpublished Writings, 1913–1933*, ed. Troels Andersen, Copenhagen: Borgen, 1978
Künstlerinnen der russischen Avantgarde/Women Artists of the Russian Avant-Garde, 1910–1930, exh. cat., Galerie Gmurzynska, Cologne, 1979
Angelica Zander Rudenstine, ed., *The George Costakis Collection: Russian Avant-Garde Art*, New York: Abrams, and London: Thames and Hudson, 1981
E. Zavadskaya, "Moy drug zhivopisets N.A. Udaltsova" [My friend, the painter N.A. Udaltsova], *Tvorchestvo*, no.10, 1986, pp.27–8
M.N. Yablonskaya, *Women Artists of Russia's New Age, 1900–1935*, New York: Rizzoli, and London: Thames and Hudson, 1990
Alexander Drevin, Nadezhda Udaltsova, exh. cat., Union of Soviet Artists Gallery, Moscow, 1991
De grote utopie/Die grosse Utopie/The Great Utopia, exh. cat., Stedelijk Museum, Amsterdam, and elsewhere, 1992
I. Schlagheck, "Geniale Tochter der russische Revolution", *Art*, no.3, March 1992, pp.32–47

Nadezhda Udaltsova's first artistic endeavours date from her early childhood as part of a large, aristocratic and cultured family in the ancient city of Orel, under the guidance of her well-educated, gentle mother, Vera Choglokova, who was descended from one of Russia's oldest noble families. The entire collection of Udaltsova's first drawings, made in coloured pencils, was carefully kept in her archive through revolutions and two world wars. In 1905 she entered the studio of the prominent Russian painter Konstantin Yuon. After looking at her childhood drawings, one of the instructors there told Udaltsova that she was already complete as an artist and that she merely needed to find herself in art. "My art is my life. That is true. I am an artist not only deeply inside my 'ego' and not only for myself – I am an artist. How many years I was afraid to call myself an artist. It is necessary to find the joy and goodness in everything. To live in joy, to love and to create in joy" (*Zhizn russkoy kubistki … 1994*, p.28). These words, written ten years later, in 1916, became an artistic and personal

Udaltsova: *At the Piano*, 1914–15; Yale University Art Gallery, New Haven; Gift of Collection Société Anonyme

motto that Udaltsova retained throughout her long and dramatic life, a life as full of joy as of suffering and struggle, which is so beautifully reflected in her recently published diaries.

After Udaltsova realised that Yuon's traditional method of painting differed from her own feelings and innovative ideas concerning art, she moved to the studio of the Hungarian artist Carol Kish, which was oriented towards the Munich school of Art Nouveau. On several occasions in 1911 she visited the Free Collective Studio, the Tower (*Bashnya*), where she became friendly with such leaders of the Russian avant-garde as Natalya Goncharova (q.v.), Mikhail Larionov, Vladimir Tatlin and Lyubov Popova (q.v.), who had just started her artistic career. In 1912, with Popova, Udaltsova went to Paris to study painting at La Palette, in the studios of the Cubist artists Henri Le Fauconnier and Jean Metzinger, which was very popular among Russian students. She was already familiar with European art: she had visited the famous Dresden Gallery in Germany in 1908, and a visit to Shchukin's private collection of French modernism in Moscow had introduced her to the work of Cézanne, Matisse, Gauguin, van Gogh and Picasso. But, according to her own later recollection, it was Paris that left the greatest impact on her life and career. Her one year there, spent entirely dedicated to art, made her aware for the first time of her unique creative individuality.

Initially, Udaltsova thought that Cubism was just another style, another method and school, but it became her passion. She was fascinated by its strong painterly structure and its reserved colour scale combined with the deep rational logic of the compositions. From that time she became an artist who was always searching for a logical explanation of phenomena and for a mathematically calculated rational sense of harmony. Her distaste for Eastern art seems shocking for the period; it was then extremely fashionable among young modernists. Anything even vaguely mystical, visionary or sublime seemed unacceptable to her; instead, she was drawn towards clarity and rationality with a materialistic approach. Udaltsova achieved fast progress in her artistic studies in Paris, but she still did not participate in exhibitions there and composed no outstanding works in France. Only after returning to Russia in 1913 was she able to release all her new experiences gained in Europe.

Soon after her return Udaltsova worked for a while in Tatlin's studio in Moscow, and in 1914 she decided to exhibit for the first time with the Jack of Diamonds group. During the next three or four years she created her best Cubist and abstract compositions, including such masterpieces of the Russian avant-garde as *Cubist Composition* (1915; State Russian Museum, St Petersburg), *Violin* (1914–15; Tretyakov Gallery, Moscow), *At the Piano* (1914–15; see illustration) and *Musical Instruments* (1915; State Russian Museum), in which she gracefully explored the theme of music and musical harmony, one of the most typical of Cubist subjects; *Red Nude* (1915; Rostovo-Yaroslavl Art Museum, Rostov), with its rich, deep texture of different tones of red and grey; *Restaurant* (1915; State Russian Museum), with its reminiscences of Paris; and *Kitchen* (1915; State Russian Museum; all oil on canvas). The quiet harmony of the very simple still life in the last work recalls the traditions of French classicism rather than Cubism. Udaltsova was the most "classicist" and traditional in spirit of

the Russian avant-garde artists of her generation. In her diaries she mentions, on the same page and sometimes in the same paragraph, Veronese, Titian and Poussin, Cézanne, Matisse and Picasso. In her diary she confessed that in 1915 the most influential and strong artistic experiences for her were from icons, in which she, like Malevich, saw "autonomous form thrown into space" (*Zhizn russkoy kubistki...* 1994, p.28).

Udaltsova's works of 1915–17 were executed in different styles and genres, ranging from Cubism to Suprematism, from painting to the applied arts and theatre design. Her main interest was in mastering the painterly texture, and sometimes, as in *Blue Jar* (1915; Tretyakov Gallery), the flat painterly surface is almost transformed into relief by the use of a heavy impasto. Some of her abstract compositions of the same period are known by her title *Non-Objective Studies in Texture*.

Towards the end of 1915 and early 1916 Udaltsova experienced the strong and extensive influence of Malevich's Suprematism. She joined his group, but although she created a series of small-scale Suprematist compositions in watercolour and gouache, she never applied this style to her oil painting. These compositions (most were created as sketches for embroidery designs) are very different from Malevich's idea of Suprematism – they are still strongly linked to the Cubist tradition of depicting and analysing objects, and sometimes she called them "Plane (two–dimensional) Cubism".

Like most artists of the Russian avant-garde, Udaltsova welcomed the October Revolution and collaborated with the new government, participating in different committees on art and education and other organisational activities. In 1918 she was offered a teaching position at the newly organised Free Artistic State Studio, and between 1920 and 1930 was a professor at Vkhutemas (Higher State Artistic and Technical Workshops) and later Vkhutein (Higher State Artistic and Technical Institute).

In 1921, with her husband, the artist Alexander Drevin, she left Inkhuk (Institute of Artistic Culture), disagreeing in principle with its new orientation towards Constructivism and "productive" (or "industrial") art, proclaimed by her former comrades Rodchenko, Stepanova, Popova and others. Udaltsova and Drevin returned to traditional easel painting, hoping to collaborate with the former members of the Jack of Diamonds, the Russian "Cézannists" Ilya Mashkov, Aristarkh Lentulov and Pyotr Konchalovsky. In the 1920s Udaltsova finally abandoned abstract art, turning again to Cézanne and his principles of composition, and finding new inspiration in nature.

Udaltsova's favourite genres in the late 1920s to 1940s were still life and landscape. In the 1920s and early 1930s she created three large series of landscapes, travelling with Drevin in the most distinctive parts of the Soviet Union – ancient Armenia and the wild regions of Altai and Ural:

My own creative exertion (tension) gave way to passive meditation, experience of the surrounding nature, study of nature. Life in the city passed during the winter and in the summer we lived in the countryside with the wild and rural untouched nature. Ural with its mountains and dales, with its fast river Chusova, bears in the pine woods, greying cliffs, blue forests and blazing sunsets, villages on river banks, the melodic speech of women and children – all that was reflected in my landscapes of the time. Colour was the main structural element in my compositions. This trip...changed my work dramatically [Moscow 1991, p.92].

This new turn in her work towards compositional structure built on perspective and colour, though still interpreted in a dry and rational rather than emotional manner, is seen at its best in such compositions as *Ural, Forest* (1926; Tretyakov Gallery), *Ural: In the Mountains* (1927; State Russian Museum), in most of the *Altai* series (artist's family collection, Moscow), in *Armenia: Landscape with Figures* (1933; Tretyakov Gallery) and *In the Garden: Village, Armenia* (1933; Tretyakov Gallery; all oil on canvas).

The crucial change in Udaltsova's career occurred after Drevin was arrested and executed in 1938. As the wife of a victim of Stalin's regime, Udaltsova was ostracised. Her own life was in danger, and it was very difficult for her to sell any work. Despite the danger, she hid and saved all of Drevin's paintings left in his studio. During World War II she remained in Moscow, working intensively. She painted realistic portraits of war heroes, but mostly still lifes. The most expressive in its solemn simplicity, *Still Life: Bread (During the War)* (1942; State Russian Museum), is one of the highlights of her late period. Among others are *Mimosa on a White Tablecloth* (1948; State Russian Museum), *Autumn: Onion in the Bowl* (1952; Tretyakov Gallery) and *Kitchen Table* (1960; State Russian Museum).

In the late 1940s, however, Udaltsova's art and personality were again under officially sanctioned attack by Soviet art critics, who accused her of "formalism in painting" and "worshipping Western culture". Udaltsova's painterly realism of her late period never went along with the official principles of Socialist Realism. Her realistic style was influenced by the Renaissance masters and by French painting of the 19th and 20th centuries, was inspired by meditations on nature, and always existed outside the strict laws of Soviet ideology.

NINA GURYANOVA

Uranga, Remedios *see* Varo

Valadon, Suzanne

French painter and graphic artist, 1865–1938

Born Marie-Clementine Valadon in Bessines-sur-Gartempe, Haute Vienne, 23 September 1865, the illegitimate daughter of a sewing maid; grew up in Montmartre, Paris. Began working as an artist's model, c.1880. Son Maurice Valadon (the artist Maurice Utrillo) born 1883; Spanish journalist Miquel Utrillo y Molins claimed to be his father, 1891. Affair with composer Erik Satie, 1893. Married a well-to-do clerk, Paul Mousis, 1896; separated 1909; divorced. Lived with painter André Utter from 1909; married him, 1914. Bought château at Saint-Bernard in the Saône valley, 1923; subsequently divided time between Saint-Bernard and Paris. Exhibited at Société Nationale des Beaux-Arts, 1894; Salon

d'Automne from 1909; Salon des Indépendants from 1911; Salon des Femmes Artistes Modernes, 1933–8, all in Paris. Sociétaire, Salon d'Automne, 1920; member, Femmes Artistes Modernes, 1933. Died in Paris, 7 April 1938.

Selected Individual Exhibitions
Galerie Clovis Sagot, Paris: 1911
Galerie Berthe Weill, Paris: 1915 (with André Utter), 1921 (with Utrillo), 1922 (twice, both with Utrillo), 1927 (retrospective), 1928
John Levy Gallery, Paris: 1921
Galerie Dalpayat, Limoges: 1922 (with André Utter and Utrillo)
Galerie Bernheim-Jeune, Paris: 1923 (with Utrillo), 1925 (with André Utter and Utrillo)
Galerie des Archers, Lyon: 1928
Galerie Bernier, Paris: 1929 (twice), 1937, 1939 (retrospective)
Galerie au Portique, Paris: 1931, 1932
Galerie le Centaure, Brussels: 1931 (retrospective)
Moos Gallery, Geneva: 1932 (with André Utter and Utrillo)
Galerie Georges Petit, Paris: 1932 (retrospective)

Selected Writings
Suzanne Valadon par elle-même, Paris: Promothée, 1939 (with Germain Bazin)

Bibliography
André Tabarant, "Suzanne Valadon et ses souvenirs de modèle", *Bulletin de la Vie Artistique*, 15 December 1921, pp.626–9
Robert Rey, *Suzanne Valadon*, Paris: Nouvelle Revue Française, 1922
Adolf Basler, *Suzanne Valadon*, Paris: Crès, 1929
Suzanne Valadon, exh. cat., Galerie Georges Petit, Paris, 1932
Jean Bouret, *Suzanne Valadon*, Paris: Pétridès, 1947
Robert Beachboard, *La Trinité maudite: Valadon, Utter, Utrillo*, Paris: Amiot-Dumont, 1952
John Storm, *The Valadon Drama: The Life of Suzanne Valadon*, New York: Dutton, 1958; as *The Valadon Story*, London: Longman, 1959
Suzanne Valadon, exh. cat., Musée National d'Art Moderne, Paris, 1967
Paul Pétridès, *L'Oeuvre complet de Suzanne Valadon*, Paris: Compagnie Française des Arts Graphiques, 1971
Jeanine Warnod, *Suzanne Valadon*, New York: Crown, 1981 (French original)
Sarah Bayliss, *Utrillo's Mother*, London: Pandora, 1987; New Brunswick, NJ: Rutgers University Press, 1989
Rosemary Betterton, "How do women look? The female nude in the work of Suzanne Valadon", *Looking On: Images of Femininity in the Visual Arts and Media*, ed. Rosemary Betterton, London and New York: Pandora, 1987, pp.217–34 (expanded version of article first published in *Feminist Review*, no.19, March 1985)
Patricia Mathews, "Returning the gaze: Diverse representations of the nude in the art of Suzanne Valadon", *Art Bulletin*, lxxiii, 1991, pp.415–30
Thérèse Diamand Rosinsky, *Suzanne Valadon*, New York: Universe, 1994
Gill Perry, *Women Artists and the Parisian Avant-Garde*, Manchester: Manchester University Press, and New York: St Martin's Press, 1995
Suzanne Valadon, exh. cat., Fondation Pierre Gianadda, Martigny, 1996
June Rose, *Mistress of Montmartre: A Life of Suzanne Valadon*, London: Cohen, 1997

Suzanne Valadon is now one of the best documented French women artists of the early 20th century, and her work has aroused much interest among feminist art historians, especially her bold, unconventional images of women and the female

Valadon: *The Future Unveiled; or, The Fortune-Teller*, 1912; oil on canvas; 130 × 163 cm.; Musée du Petit Palais, Geneva

nude. Much has been written about Valadon's working-class background as the illegitimate daughter of a domestic worker, and her early art "training" in Montmartre. Without the means to pay for tuition in an art academy (many of which charged higher fees for women than for men), Valadon was partly self-taught, and gained early experience of the Parisian art world on the streets of Montmartre – in the studios where her mother worked as a cleaner, and from the artists for whom she posed from the age of 15 to 28. These included Puvis de Chavannes, Pierre-Auguste Renoir and Toulouse-Lautrec, more academic artists such as Jean-Jacques Henner and Hector Leroux, and the Realist painter Giuseppe de Nittis. Her early interest in drawing was encouraged by her friendship with Edgar Degas, who bought many of her sketches. He also taught her the technique of soft-ground etching in 1895, and over the next 20 years Valadon worked extensively on soft-ground etchings, lithographs and drawings, many of which she subsequently destroyed. Her subjects included adolescent girls and boys, for which her son Maurice Utrillo was often the model, and women and girls engaged in their toilette, a theme that echoes some of the so-called modern-life subjects of Degas

and Toulouse-Lautrec. But unlike the more voyeuristic images of women bathing by these better-established male painters, Valadon's works on this theme are characterised by a strong, almost severe use of line, and candid, sometimes awkward images of bathing women and children. The harshness of her linear style and imagery led some critics to describe her works as "virile" or somehow uncharacteristic of "feminine" art (the paradigmatic example of which was generally seen to be the art of Marie Laurencin, q.v.). Such critical assumptions continued to feature in reviews of Valadon's graphic and painted work throughout her career.

She did not take up painting seriously until around 1909, and during the years leading up to the outbreak of World War I produced a series of large-scale allegorical works, several of which were shown at the Salon d'Automne and the Salon des Indépendants. These include *Joy of Life* (1911; Metropolitan Museum of Art, New York) and *The Future Unveiled; or, The Fortune-Teller* (1912; see illustration). These are both works in which the nude incorporates a wide range of literal and symbolic possibilities of meaning. Both rework iconographical conventions for the representation of the female nude: in the

Joy of Life Valadon reworks the popular bathers-in-nature theme, recalling Matisse's famous painting of 1906 with the same title; and in *The Future Unveiled* she produces an image reminiscent of the traditional "odalisque" theme in which a milky-white female body reclines horizontally across the canvas space. But both works offer possibilities for more diverse narrative interpretations. In *Joy of Life* Valadon employs a variety of seemingly unconnected poses, based on art-historical precedents, for her female protagonists, who are watched by a nude male spectator on the right (for whom her partner André Utter was the model). These female figures seem strangely separate from each other, from the male viewer and from the nature that surrounds them. Far from evoking a utopian harmony of woman and nature suggested by, for example, Matisse or Gauguin, Valadon's robust and sharply outlined women suggest a more ambiguous, dislocated relationship with both nature and the male spectator.

The Future Unveiled reveals even more complex layers of narrative and allegorical meaning. It combines the conventions of "odalisque" painting with the allegory of the card player who foretells the future as she holds up the queen of diamonds. Patricia Mathews (1991) has argued that the "symbolism of the queen of diamonds held in the hand of the fortune-teller directly related the allegory to the reading of the odalisque as a sexualized body. The card connecting the two women's bodies is a sign for the feminine principle, of physicality and the senses, and of money matters. In conjunction with the four kings in the circular arrangement of cards, it evokes a prostitute or courtesan". She suggests that the painting could thus be seen to lead to a moralising reading of the nude, as it both implicates the folly of indulgence in card-games and fortune-telling, an activity usually performed by Gypsies, and the eroticism of the courtesan. But Valadon's mode of representing this female nude could also be seen to undermine the conventional associations of the odalisque theme. The woman does not assume a passive reclining pose but seems to be actively engaged with the fortune-teller. Moreover, her heavy, sharply defined body lacks the sensual eroticism associated with 19th-century interpretations of the theme.

Valadon's interest in the nude was not confined to studies of the female body, although her painted male nudes were produced mostly for her large-scale historical and allegorical works from the period 1909–14, when she used Utter as her model. Even her male nudes were seen to disrupt convention, for she was not permitted to show her *Adam and Eve* of 1909 (Musée National d'Art Moderne, Centre Georges Pompidou, Paris) in the Salon des Indépendants of 1920 until she had painted vine leaves over Adam's genitalia. After Utter was called up on military service in 1914, depictions of the male nude disappear from her work, an absence that coincided with a move away from Valadon's ambitious, large-scale exhibition pieces.

Tensions and contradictions in both the sexual and narrative meanings of her work are also evident in some of her less ambitious, more intimate portraits of (sometimes nude) women and men that she continued to produce during the 1920s and 1930s. After receiving a contract from the dealer Bernheim Jeune in 1924 she enjoyed one of the most successful periods of her career, and gained an international reputation. Like many women artists who worked outside the established avant-garde groups of the time, she tended to be represented as an "independent" artist on the fringes of the broadly labelled "School of Paris". Her resistance to – and reworkings of – both academic and avant-garde conventions for representing the female nude have encouraged interest in her work within recent feminist art history. It has been argued that many of her images of women signal a form of resistance to some of the dominant representations of female sexuality in early 20th-century Western art. Many of her nudes painted from the 1910s onwards are heavily proportioned and sometimes awkwardly posed. They are conspicuously at odds with the svelte, elongated adolescent body that became the ideal "feminine" type to be found in the imagery of both popular and "high" art (see, for example, the imagery of women in the work of Laurencin and van Dongen) in the 1920s. In, for example, her *Nude with Striped Coverlet* (1922; Musée d'Art Moderne de la Ville de Paris) and *Reclining Nude* (1928; Metropolitan Museum of Art) she uses strong outlines reminiscent of her earlier drawings, rich colour, and places the figures boldly across the foreground picture plane to suggest a powerful yet unerotic presence. *Reclining Nude* appears to undermine the conventions of passive, erotic display associated with the "odalisque" pose in that the woman literally shields her body; it is closed to a voyeuristic gaze.

Valadon's ability to produce some unconventional images of the female nude has been partly explained with reference to her unusual class position and background. Most successful women artists of her period came from middle-class backgrounds that could provide economic support for an art training and an often risky professional life. Unconstrained by an academic training, she may have felt better able to break with artistic conventions. Moreover, her experiences as a model may have encouraged her interest in the theme of the female nude, and enabled her to approach it from the position of a woman's experience of her own body. Unusually for a woman artist, she produced several nude self-portraits, which provide self-images from different periods of her career. These are unselfconscious images, boldly painted and free from any suggestion of "feminine" softness or available sexuality. Many of the later self-portraits reveal a frank representation of the artist's ageing in the depiction of precisely those parts of the female anatomy that could signify the ideal of youthful "feminine" beauty. She bravely depicts fallen breasts and jowls, and heavy drooping eyes, but with an air of resignation and acceptance, signified by the addition of a necklace and make-up (e.g. *Portrait with Bare Breasts*, 1931; private collection, repr. Rosinsky 1994, p.83).

Although she is better known for her portraits and studies of the female nude, still-life and landscape paintings formed an important part of Valadon's artistic output in the 1920s and 1930s. Her first known landscapes date from the 1910s, and include a series of views of the rue Cortot in Montmartre, where she lived and worked between 1914 and 1926. Scenes of Montmartre were also the subject of many of Utrillo's works from this period, which were in great demand in the 1920s, and which may have inhibited her own interest in this genre. Still lifes, especially flower paintings, began to appear in her work from around 1900. The reason that the genre does not appear earlier is probably because she had little experience of still-life painting while working as an artist's model. Thérèse Diamand Rosinsky has argued:

As a model she never observed the artists for whom she posed painting still lifes. Therefore, she had no first-hand observation of the subject and might have thought it an unimportant genre. The images she saw on the posters, in newspaper cartoons and even the illustrations in teaching manuals focused on the human figure and physiognomy [*ibid.*, p.109].

The genre was popular with clients and patrons, however, and flower paintings feature prominently in her work from the 1920s, when they often include many personalised references. She frequently dedicated such works to close friends for whom she included inscriptions on the back of the frame, or flowers chosen for their symbolic significance. Many contemporary critics emphasised the gendered associations of this genre, seeing flower painting as a relatively superficial or "feminine" subject matter, without intellectual meaning and thus best suited to women painters. Yet flower paintings and still lifes are among the most complex of Valadon's works, often replete with symbolic meanings, personal references and possible narratives. For example, in her *Still Life with Violin* (1928; Musée d'Art Moderne de la Ville de Paris) she employs an elaborate composition dominated by a violin, its case, rich folds of red drapery and a dog-eared paperback, with flowers in a pitcher and large pot in the background. As a backdrop to these objects, she includes an autobiographical reference by reproducing the corner of her large exhibition piece *Casting of the Net* of 1914. This corner shows only the thighs and legs of her male protagonists, for whom she had used Utter as a model, with Valadon's signature and date written across the lower torso of the right-hand figure.

Although Valadon's work has recently been reassessed in terms of the unconventional imagery of women and feminine sexuality that it demonstrates, she did not espouse any feminist causes, and was sceptical of organised feminism. Such organisations were viewed with suspicion by many liberal political and social groups during the first few decades of the 20th century, despite the increasing public interest in "the woman question". Like many women painters of her era, Valadon saw herself as an "independent", engaged with a more personal aesthetic agenda and working separately from those avant-garde interests that have shaped most histories of modernism. While this representation provides a convenient framework within which to explain her position within the art history of the period, much work still remains to be done on the complex relationship of her art to the styles and culture of the early 20th-century avant-garde.

GILL PERRY

Vallain, Nanine

French painter, active 1785–1810

Details of family and early life unknown. Studied under Joseph-Benoît Suvée and Jacques Louis David. Married M. Pietre by 1793; lived in rue Thibaut-au-Dé, Paris. Joined the Commune Générale des Arts, a revolutionary group of artists opposed to the Académie Royale, October 1793. Date of death unknown.

Principal Exhibitions

Exposition de la Jeunesse, Paris: 1785, 1787, 1788
Paris Salon: 1793, 1795, 1806, 1808, 1810
Jacobin Club, Paris: 1794

Bibliography

"Collections des pièces sur les beaux-arts imprimées et manuscrites, recueillies par P.-J. Mariette, C.-N. Cochin et M. Deloynes", Deloynes Collection, Paris, Bibliothèque Nationale, 1745–1881
Women Artists, 1550–1950, exh. cat., Los Angeles County Museum of Art, and elsewhere, 1976
Vivian Cameron, *Woman as Image and Image-Maker in Paris During the French Revolution*, PhD dissertation, Yale University, New Haven, 1983
Philippe Bordes and Régis Michel, eds, *Aux armes et aux arts! Les Arts de la Révolution, 1789–1799*, Paris: Biro, 1988
La Révolution française et l'Europe, 1789–1799, exh. cat., Grand Palais, Paris, 1989
Philippe Bordes and Patrick Jager, *Découverte peinture: Nanine Vallain*, Château de Vizille: Musée de la Révolution Française, 1992 (museum brochure)

Nanine Vallain's first recognition came from the critics in 1785 when she exhibited at the Exposition de la Jeunesse in Paris. A critic from the *Mercure de France* wrote of her work that it contained spirit and truth, promising much for her future artistic career. Two years later she exhibited a study of a female allegorical figure entitled *L'Etude* (untraced) and was praised for her firm handling, sophistication, harmony and agreeable colour and brushwork (Deloynes Collection, xiv, no.347). One of these contemporary critics also commented on Vallain's youth. Most of her works at this time were portraits, very much in keeping with the prevailing trend for women artists.

During the time of her first exhibitions at the Place Dauphine, Vallain was also a pupil of the prominent artists Joseph-Benoît Suvée and Jacques-Louis David. Her career continued to evolve, culminating in the painting of *Liberty* (1793–4; see illustration). Now more assured, she broadened her range beyond portraits to include such allegorical works, meeting the challenges of the day set by artistic competitions. She was clearly an ambitious painter, eager to extend the boundaries of her repertoire.

Liberty exemplifies this. A woman in Classical dress, a blue tunic and dark yellow skirt, is seated at the centre of the painting. In her right hand she grasps a scroll of the declaration of the Rights of Man while in her left she holds a pike upon which a red Phrygian cap, a symbol of liberty, is placed. At her feet lie a broken crown and chains, representative of the fall of monarchy. The fasces, appropriated at this time as an emblem of unity, are situated beneath an urn on which are inscribed the words: "To our brothers who died for her". The sense of human loss, suggested by the urn and its inscription, is reinforced by the mortuary crown of yew branches. These various symbols represent the different components of Republican history and ideology. Liberty is triumphant but demands sacrifice. The eternal yet grave nature of this triumph is expressed through the pyramidical structure behind the seated figure. Liberty is unadorned, her simplicity being part of her attraction and strength. Indeed her posture, drapery, dress and demeanour are reminiscent of Vallain's teacher Suvée's *Cornelia, Mother of the Gracchi* (1790–95; Louvre, Paris; Bordes and Jager 1992). Liberty, like Cornelia, sits upright,

Vallain: *Liberty*, 1793–4; Musée du Louvre, Paris (painting damaged)

steadfast and full of resolve. As a personification of Republican France, she is surrounded by symbols, but not overshadowed by them. The painting was hung in the Jacobin Club in Paris until it was removed in 1795, after the fall of Robespierre. This painting by a woman artist of a powerful female allegorical figure was thus exhibited within the context of a predominantly male public-political space. It is not known whether *Liberty* was commissioned or donated, but it must surely be viewed as a testament not only to Vallain's artistic preferences for allegorical scenes, but also her political motivations.

Praised for its potential in 1785, by the 1800s Vallain's work was poorly received (*Le Pausanias français*, Deloynes Collection, xxxix, no.1053). Between the years 1796 and 1805 she did not exhibit. It is perhaps significant that this gap occurred at a time when the rights of women were diminishing and their visibility in public life was increasingly frowned upon. At the Salons of 1806, 1808 and 1810 she exhibited numerous portraits and the paintings *Sappho Singing a Hymn to Love*, *Cain Fleeing with His Family after the Death of Abel* and *Tirzan, Wife of Abel, Crying on the Tomb of Her Spouse and Imploring Mercury* (all untraced). The only known portrait from this time is *Portrait of a Woman* (National Gallery of Ireland, Dublin). So although Vallain continued to paint portraits, it is her allegorical and biblical compositions that distinguish her place in women's art history of the late 18th and early 19th centuries.

UTE KREBS and ESMÉ WARD

Vallayer-Coster, Anne
French painter, 1744–1818

Born Anne Vallayer in Gobelins, 21 December 1744; father a goldsmith at the royal tapestry manufactory. Moved to central Paris with her family, 1757. Nothing known of her training. Elected member of the Académie Royale, 1770. Granted title "painter to the queen", 1780. Allocated lodgings in the Louvre, 1781. Married lawyer Jean-Pierre-Silvestre Coster, 1781. Died in Paris, 28 February 1818.

Principal Exhibitions

Paris Salon: 1771, 1773, 1775, 1777, 1779, 1781, 1783, 1785, 1787, 1789, 1795, 1798, 1800–02, 1804, 1810, 1817

Bibliography

Marianne Michel, "A propos d'un tableau retrouvé de Vallayer-Coster", *Bulletin de la Société de l'Histoire de l'Art Français*, 1965, 1966, pp.185–90

Denis Diderot, *Salons*, ed. Jean Seznec and Jean Adhémar, iv, Oxford: Clarendon Press, 1967

Marianne Roland Michel, *Anne Vallayer-Coster, 1744–1818*, Paris: CIL, 1970

Les Femmes peintres au XVIIIe siècle, exh. cat., Musée Goya, Castres, 1973

French Painting, 1774–1830: The Age of Revolution, exh. cat., Grand Palais, Paris, and elsewhere, 1974

Women Artists, 1550–1950, exh. cat., Los Angeles County Museum of Art, and elsewhere, 1976

Chardin and the Still-Life Tradition in France, exh. cat., Cleveland Museum of Art, 1979

Charles Sterling, *Still-Life Painting from Antiquity to the Twentieth Century*, New York: Harper, 1981 (French original, 1952)

Anne Vallayer was born at the royal tapestry manufactury of the Gobelins. In 1757 her father, Joseph Vallayer, having gained his mastership as a goldsmith, opened his own studio in Paris where he held the Royal Privilege for the production of military medals and the cross of the Order of St Louis. This background may help to account for the royal favour and aristocratic patronage that Vallayer-Coster was to enjoy during her career as a painter and it may also account for her admittance into the Académie Royale at the early age of 26, a month after the appointment of Jean-Baptiste Pierre, who may have been a family friend, as First Painter to the King. Anne Vallayer took the name Vallayer-Coster after her marriage in 1781 to Jean-Pierre-Silvestre Coster, an *avocat* to the Parlement of Paris and a member of a noble family of financiers and courtiers. The marriage took place at Versailles and the marriage contract includes the signature of Queen Marie-Antoinette.

Although the basic components of Vallayer-Coster's art did not vary much, her output was not restricted to paintings of still life and flowers. She produced miniatures, large decorative panels of animals and trophies of the hunt, painted *trompe-l'oeil* bas reliefs of fictive plaster sculpture and full-size portraits, including the one of the Royal medal-maker *Roettiers* (1777; Musée de Versailles). Her portraits were, however, harshly criticised by contemporary writers and she stopped producing them after 1789. She may well have suffered from the scathing comparisons that were made between her work in this genre and that of her fellow women academicians, the specialist portrait painters, Elisabeth Vigée-Lebrun (q.v.) and Adélaïde Labille-Guiard (q.v.).

It was as a painter of still life that Vallayer-Coster first achieved prominence. Somewhat exceptionally, she was approved and received into the Academy on the same day, 28 July 1770, on the basis of two imposing public pieces of virtuoso painting, *Allegory of the Arts* (1769) and *Instruments of Music* (1770; both Louvre, Paris). These subjects had been painted by Chardin and, superficially, the compositions might seem to follow the lead he had set. In manner and technique they are, however, quite different. Texture, colour and the application of paint are rich, sensuously tactile and serve to embellish the richness of the visual display. The table on which the instruments of music have been carefully posed is covered by a rich green velvet cloth fringed with a gold tassel. Against a mottled grey-brown background, the range of assorted instruments creates strong diagonals and forcefully curved forms in space. The lute, resting vertically against the pulpit and with a light blue ribbon loosely knotted round the pegs of its sound board, shows the confident marks of an individual, personal and creative contribution to the genre.

Vallayer-Coster first exhibited flower paintings at the Salon of 1775 at a time when she was cultivating a wealthy and aristocratic clientele and during the most prolific and successful decade of her career. A fine example of this type of work is her *Vase of Flowers and Shell* (1780; see illustration). In the centre of the oval canvas a lavish bunch of fresh flowers has been arranged in a bronze-mounted blue vase that rests on a grey stone ledge. To the left of the vase lies a shell providing an obvious and exotic contrast in shape, form and colour. The

Vallayer-Coster: *Vase of Flowers and Shell*, 1780; oil on canvas; 50.2 × 38.1 cm.; Metropolitan Museum of Art, New York; Gift of J. Pierpont Morgan, 1906

juxtaposition of animate and inanimate objects creates much visual interest and also reflects contemporary interest in the cataloguing and recording of botanical specimens. The objects exist as isolated in themselves but are displayed so as to contribute to the unity and harmony of the composition as a whole. A cool and distanced observation of detail has been combined with a lively handling of the coloured pigment. The subtle variations and tonalities achieve the palpable effect of pastel in oil paint – a proto-Impressionist technique that precedes the flower paintings of Henri Fantin-Latour.

Vallayer-Coster was always firmly attached to the aristocratic tastes of her noble patrons. These patrons included some of the highest in the land. In 1781 she finally obtained lodgings in the Louvre through the personal interventions of the First Painter to the King, Pierre, the Director General of the King's Buildings, the Comte d'Angiviller and the queen, Marie-Antoinette. A clear mark of the queen's favour is the listing of her painting of a Vestal Virgin as belonging to the queen in the Salon catalogue of 1779. Other purchasers of her paintings included the Prince de Conti, the Comte de Merle and the Marquis and Marquise de Créqui. These patrons were courtiers of the noblest of ranks, but her works were also collected by other persons of influence and important State officials such as, for instance, M. Beaujon, Councillor of State, Receiver General to the Finances of the Generality of Rouen and Honorary Treasurer to the royal and military Order of St Louis (Roland Michel 1970, p.50).

The forms and content of Vallayer-Coster's finely crafted bravura paintings show little thematic or stylistic evolution, in spite of the turbulent times through which she lived and the high-minded Neo-classical innovations of Jacques-Louis David and his school. The same compositional patterns and motifs occur again and again, although there are subtle variations of arrangement and of detail. Dead game hang down; red coral, exotic shells and madrepore come to be juxtaposed with a small plaster statuette of an antique female deity, a bronze mounted blue vase; against a mottled grey-brown background a pink ham with a knife sticking out is set against a broken bread roll; peaches or apples are piled up into pyramids; a wicker basket is filled to overflowing with vine leaves and bunches of grapes. The elongated forms of bunches of radishes, round porcelain tea sets, glasses of water, nuts are all used in a variety of combinations so as to create sumptuous pictorial effects. *Still Life with Game* (1782) and *Lobster, Silver Tureen, Fruit and Bread on a Table* (1781; both Museum of Art, Toledo) were exhibited in the Salon of 1783 as the property of Girardot de Marigny. They form pendants; the game is strung up to hang down from a tree in the open air while the pink, cooked lobster dominates the interior scene of the richly laden table. Such subjects were not generally the province of women artists, and contemporary Salon critics such as Denis Diderot and Louis Petit de Bachaumont almost always remarked on Vallayer-Coster's achievements as a woman in a genre that was held to be the preserve of men. She was, however, much more harshly criticised for her portrait painting, especially for those she exhibited at the Salon of 1785. About a now lost portrait of an anonymous bishop, Bachaumont noted that it was vexing to see Vallayer-Coster abandon still life where she had superiority for portraiture where she was inferior to her female rivals and that the bishop looked shameful in his corner (*Mémoires secrets, deuxième lettre*, 22 September 1785). These comments are revealing for the implied comparison with Vigée-Lebrun and Labille-Guiard, for the increasing importance of the Salon and the positioning of a work of art within the Salon hang as a marker of public opinion, and for notions of genre hierarchy and of hierarchies in general at this time.

Vallayer-Coster returned to the subject of still life with a lobster in the last painting she exhibited at the Paris Salon, *A Table with Lobster, Different Fruits, Game etc.* (1817; Mobilier National, Paris). Her picture-making was far removed from the smooth finish and emblematic symbolism of a 17th-century Dutch *vanitas* painting, yet in this last Salon piece, which she appears to have donated to the king, a spray of white lilies, emblem of the now-restored Bourbon monarchy, has been carefully isolated out. The painting as a whole still serves, though, as a forceful summation of much of the oeuvre of Vallayer-Coster and of the taste and luxury, before the Revolution, of her rich patrons, which she, faithfully and with much loyalty, celebrated.

VALERIE MAINZ

van de Passe, Magdalena *see* Passe

Vanderbilt, Gertrude Whitney *see* Whitney

van Heemskerck, Jacoba *see* Heemskerck

van Hemessen, Catharina *see* Hemessen

van Oosterwijck, Maria *see* Oosterwijck

van Schurman, Anna Maria *see* Schurman

Varo, Remedios
Spanish painter, 1908–1963

Born in Anglés, Spain, 16 December 1908. Settled in Madrid with her family, 1917. Studied at Academia de San Fernando, Madrid, 1924–30. Married (1) painter Gerardo Lizarraga, 1930; separated 1936; (2) Surrealist poet Benjamin Péret, 1940s; separated 1947; (3) businessman Walter Gruen, 1952. Lived in Barcelona, 1932–7; moved to Paris and joined the Surrealists, 1937; settled in Mexico, 1941; became close friend of Leonora Carrington (q.v.); active in the group of European exile artists. Died in Mexico City, 8 October 1963.

Principal Exhibitions
Academia de San Fernando, Madrid: 1934
Glorieta Catalonia-Librería, Barcelona: 1936 (*Lógicofobista*)
London Gallery, London: 1937 (*Surrealist Objects and Poems*)
Nippon Salon, Tokyo: 1937 (*Exposition internationale du surréalisme*)
Galería de Arte Mexicano, Mexico City: 1940 (*Exposición internacional del surrealismo*, touring)
Galerie Maeght, Paris: 1947 (*Le Surréalisme en 1947*)
Galería Diana, Mexico City: 1955 (group), 1956 (individual)
Galería de Arte Contemporáneo, Mexico City: 1956 (*Salon Frida Kahlo*)
Galerías Excelsior, Mexico City: 1958 (*Salon de la plástica femenina*), 1959
INBA, Mexico City: 1960 (*Bienial: Pintura mexicana*)
Instituto de Arte Contemporáneo, Mexico City: 1961 (*Pintura mexicana contemporánea de la Galería de Antonio Souza de México*)
Museo Nacional de Arte Moderno, Mexico City: 1961 (*El retrato mexicano contemporáneo*)
Galería Juan Martín, Mexico City: 1961 (group), 1962 (individual)
Instituto Nacional de Bellas Artes, Mexico City: 1964 (retrospective)

Selected Writings
De homo Rodans, Mexico City: Calli-Nova, 1970 (under pseudonym Halikcio von Fuhrangschmidt)
Cartas, sueños y otros textos, ed. Isabel Castells, Mexico: Universidad Autónoma de Tlaxcala, 1994

Bibliography
Dictionnaire abrégé du surréalisme, Paris: Galerie Beaux-Arts, 1938
International Exhibition of Surrealism, exh. cat., Galería de Arte Mexicano, Mexico City, 1940
Edouard Jaguer, *Remedios Varo*, Paris: Filippachi, 1963 (contains numerous illustrations)
La obra de Remedios Varo, exh. cat., Instituto Nacional de Bellas Artes, Mexico City, 1964
Octavio Paz and Roger Caillois, *Remedios Varo*, Mexico City: Era, 1966
Ida Rodriguez Prampolini, *El surrealismo y el arte fantástico de México*, Mexico City: Universidad Nacional Autónoma de México, 1969
Obra de Remedios Varo, 1913/1963, exh. cat., Museo de Arte Moderno, Mexico City, 1971
Karen Petersen and J.J. Wilson, *Women Artists: Recognition and Reappraisal*, New York: Harper, 1976; London: Women's Press, 1978
Obliques, no.14–15, 1977 (special issue: *La Femme surréaliste*)
L'altra metà dell'avanguardia, 1910–1940: Pittrici e scultrici nei movimenti delle avanguardie storiche, exh. cat., Palazzo Reale, Milan, and elsewhere, 1980
Remedios Varo, 1913–1963, exh. cat., Museo de Arte Moderno, Mexico City, 1983
Artistic Collaboration in the Twentieth Century, exh. cat., Hirshhorn Museum, Washington, DC, 1984
Estella Lauter, *Women as Mythmakers: Poetry and Visual Art by Twentieth-Century Women*, Bloomington: Indiana University Press, 1984
Whitney Chadwick, *Women Artists and the Surrealist Movement*, London: Thames and Hudson, and Boston: Little Brown, 1985
Science in Surrealism: The Art of Remedios Varo, exh. cat., New York Academy of Sciences, 1986
Janet A. Kaplan, "Art essay: Remedios Varo", *Feminist Studies*, xiii/1, 1987
Remedios Varo, exh. cat., Fundación Banco Exterior, Madrid, 1988
Surrealismo a Catalunya, 1924–36, exh. cat., Centro Cultural Santa Mónica, Barcelona, 1988
Georgiana M. M. Colvile, "Beauty and/is the beast: Animal symbology in the work of Leonora Carrington, Remedios Varo and Leonor Fini", *Surrealism and Women*, ed. Mary Ann Caws and others, Cambridge: Massachusetts Institute of Technology Press, 1991, pp.159–81
Remedios Varo: Arte y literatura, exh. cat., Museo de Teruel, Spain, 1991
Renée Riese Hubert, *Magnifying Mirrors: Women, Surrealism and Partnership*, Lincoln: University of Nebraska Press, 1994
Janet A. Kaplan, *Unexpected Journeys: The Art and Life of Remedios Varo*, 2nd edition, New York: Abbeville, 1994 (contains extensive bibliography and illustrations)
Remedios Varo, 1908–1963, exh. cat., Museo de Arte Moderno, Mexico City, 1994
Ricardo Ovalle and others, *Remedios Varo: Catalogo Razonado*, Mexico City: ERA, 1994 (contains numerous illustrations)
Deborah J. Haynes, "The art of Remedios Varo: Issues of gender ambiguity and religious meaning", *Woman's Art Journal*, xvi/1, 1995, pp.26–32

Péret-Varo Papers are in the International Rescue Committee Archives, State University of New York, Albany; Péret Letters are in the Trotsky archives, Harvard University, Cambridge, Massachusetts; Varo Papers are in the Water Gruen archive, Mexico City.

The painter Remedios Varo was born in Spain, worked in France and gained renown after settling in Mexico. She was part of many worlds: Catholic convent schools and the Fine Arts Academy of Madrid as a young student; the artistic vanguard of Barcelona during the years of the Spanish

Varo: *Embroidering Earth's Mantle*, 1961

Republic; the Parisian Surrealist group (including the French poet Benjamin Péret, who became the second of her three husbands), with whom she exhibited early experimental work, most notable among them a little oil on copper, *Double Agent* (1936; Isidore Ducasse Fine Arts, New York, repr. Kaplan 1994, p.49); the chaos of wartime Marseille and Casablanca, where she sought to arrange the many documents needed to escape from the Nazis; and finally, the hospitable refuge of Mexico where she created her mature work. Varo's startling and distinctive paintings were greeted with such resounding critical and popular success in Mexico that from her first solo exhibition in 1956 she had to establish waiting lists for her many eager patrons.

Dead of a heart attack at the age of 55, Varo left an innovative legacy of mature paintings, produced in the short span of ten years, which retains a significant position in 20th-century Mexican art. Her earlier work has recently been recognised as well, both that done in Paris and that from her earlier association with the avant-garde of pre-Civil War Barcelona. Among the most widely exhibited of these are a series of remarkable collages, including the *Anatomy Lesson* (1935; Marcel Jean,

Paris, *ibid.*, p.41), and composite images created collaboratively from chance associations, as in *Cadavre exquis* (1935; Museum of Modern Art, New York, *ibid.*, p.39) – works that speak of the importance of Spain's cultural contributions to the development of modernism in Europe.

Throughout Varo's work modernism is worked out in the kitchen and the parlour, where images and ideas are brewed and stewed and cooked and knitted and embroidered. Slyly shifting the Surrealist stage from the boudoir to the kitchen, she established culinary activities as a particularly potent site for experimentation in the occult, undertaking investigations that ranged from infamous experiments with farcical recipes to serious study of alchemy, science, magic, mysticism and the occult. In *Embroidering Earth's Mantle* (1961; see illustration) the art of needlework, long used as a means of acculturation for docile femininity, is transformed into a god-like act of creation and a site of subversive empowerment. Spilling forth from tower battlements is the fabric of the world, created by sequestered schoolgirls working with materials distilled in an alchemical alembic. Their embroidered cosmology, including a landscape of houses, ponds, streams and boats, is "women's work", here presented as an incantatory process that initiates transformation of the marvellous from the mundane. In many of Varo's works female characters employ alchemical methods, as in *Creation of the Birds* (1958; private collection, *ibid.*, p.180), where a female owl artist/musician uses a palette of materials synthesised through a process of alchemical distillation to create that most highly prized of magical creations, an image that comes to life, here a drawn bird that takes flight out of a window.

In Varo's fantastically constructed universe, the properties of the organic and inorganic, the scientific and magical, the natural and technological, interchange and overlap. Peopled by insect geologists (*Discovery of a Mutant Geologist*, 1961), wood nymph musicians (*Solar Music*, 1955; private collection, *ibid.*, p.127) and enchanted astronomers (*Revelation; or, The Clockmaker*, 1955; private collection, *ibid.*, p.175), it is a world that challenges preconceived assumptions about how things ought to work. In *Unexpected Presence* (1959; private collection, *ibid.*, p.158) chairbacks open to reveal human faces; in *Emerging Light* (1962; private collection, *ibid.*, p.165) bodies emerge from behind walls; in *Useless Science or the Alchemist* (1955; private collection, *ibid.*, p.126) the hard is made pliable; in *Toward the Tower* (1961; private collection, *ibid.*, p.19) the soft stiffens; and in *Farewell* (1958; private collection, *ibid.*, p.209) bodies and their shadows become interchangeable. Inspired by images from Bosch, Goya and El Greco that she had studied at the Prado in Madrid as well as the Romanesque Catalan frescoes, medieval and Renaissance architecture and veiled women of North Africa that she had seen in her early years of family travel, Varo created a world alive with the possible, the incantatory and the magical, set in the everyday.

While Surrealism was the movement within which Varo developed, the work she produced in her Mexican years is marked by an ironic, even taunting ambivalence towards Surrealist theory and practice, particularly pointed in its critique around issues related to women. Central to this stance is a challenge to authority or, in terms derived from one of Varo's paintings, a "dropping of the father". In *Woman Leaving the Psychoanalyst* (1961; private collection, *ibid.*, p.154) – rather than the son's transgression that was the Oedipal stock-in-trade of the male Surrealists – it is a daughter who, on leaving the offices of Dr FJA (representing Freud, Jung and Adler), proceeds, quite literally, to drop the head of her father into a nearby well, claiming her independence through this psychological rite of passage. Throughout her work Varo offered an alternative iconography specifically counter to the orthodoxies of male-defined Surrealist theory with its proscribed and limited role for woman as muse to male creativity. Transferring power across gender lines and conferring heroic authority on women, Varo's work is based on woman's psychology and experiences in which her access to the marvellous relies on the self as active agent.

In many paintings Varo adopted a strategy of transposition of traditionally male mythic heroes into female form. A female Minotaur holds a magical key before a mysterious floating keyhole (*Minotaur*, 1959; private collection, *ibid.*, p.184); a female Pan in the form of a woodland nymph with owlish eyes and feathery body plays a double reed (*Troubador*, 1959; private collection, *ibid.*, p.192); there is even a female Ulysses

setting off in a waistcoat to explore uncharted waters (*Exploration of the Sources of the Orinoco River*, 1959; private collection, *ibid.*, p.168). Although many of the characters in Varo's paintings are androgynous or asexual, in these mythological transformations she was careful to delineate the female anatomy of her heroines.

Throughout her finely wrought compositions Varo's style carries a nostalgic echo of the illuminated manuscript, that document of obsessive belief in the transformative power of seeing the whole world in the finest moment of detail. In works such as *Mimesis* (1960; private collection, *ibid.*, p.159) she employed old master techniques of glazing and varnishing, perfected through her years of rigorous training, to create paintings, often, as here, in oil on masonite, that are masterfully rendered and painstakingly executed. Theatrical in her miniaturist vision, she created carefully constructed narrative tableaux as doll's house-like stage sets, here the fairy-tale world of a woman, immobilised in an armchair, whose skin has taken on the pallor of its fleur-de-lis upholstery, her feet and hands turned to wood. Just as fairy tales have long been used to encode subversive knowledge, so Varo used her fabulist style as a form of masking and masquerade, as a ploy to belie the power of her critique, here directed towards the condition of women whose vitality has been enervated by domestic isolation. In both style and content, Varo's work offers a strong subversive voice within the Surrealist idiom, a subtle but forceful alternative presented from a distinctly female perspective.

JANET A. KAPLAN

Vasegaard, Gertrud

Danish potter and ceramic designer, 1913–

Born Gertrud Hjorth in Rønne, Bornholm, 23 February 1913. Studied at the Kunsthåndværkerskolen (School for Applied Arts), Copenhagen, including studio experience with Arne Bang, Axel Salto and Bode Willumsen, 1930–32. Worked with Olga Jensen in her studio, 1933. Established a workshop with her sister, Lisbet Hjorth (later Lisbet Munch-Petersen), in Gudhjem, 1933–7. Married Sigurd Vasegaard, 1935; daughter Myre, also a potter, born 1936. Worked at own studio in Holkadalen, Bornholm, 1938–48; spent winter months at Bing & Grøndahl Porcelain Manufactory, Copenhagen, returning to Holkadalen in summers of 1945–8. Artist-in-residence at Bing & Grøndahl, 1949–59. Freelance work for Royal Copenhagen Porcelain Manufactory, 1959–75. Shared studio in Frederiksberg with Myre from 1959. Lives in Copenhagen.

Principal Exhibitions

Individual
Clausens Kunsthandel: 1976, 1978, 1983
Kunstindustrimuseet, Copenhagen: 1984 (retrospective)

Group
Milan Triennale: 1951, 1957 (gold medal)
USA: 1954–7 (*Design in Scandinavia*, touring)
Musée du Louvre, Paris: 1958 (*Formes scandinaves*)

Liljevalchs Konsthall, Stockholm: 1959 (*Dansk form og miljø* [Danish form and environment])

Metropolitan Museum of Art, New York: 1960 (*Arts of Denmark*)

Victoria and Albert Museum, London: 1968 (*Two Centuries of Danish Design*)

Groninger Museum voor Stad en Lande, Groningen: 1968 (*Deense kunstnijverheid* [Danish applied art])

Museum Boymans-van Beuningen, Rotterdam: 1976 (*Acht deense ceramisten* [Eight Danish ceramists])

Nationalmuseum, Stockholm: 1981 (*Danskt 50-tal* [Danish 1950s])

Palmer Museum of Art, Pennsylvania State University, University Park: 1981 (*Danish Ceramic Design*)

Cooper-Hewitt Museum, New York: 1982 (*Scandinavian Modern, 1880–1980*)

Kunstindustrimuseet, Copenhagen: 1990 (*Brændpunkter: Dansk keramik, 1890–1990* [Firing points in Danish ceramics, 1890–1990])

Bibliography

Skandinavische Keramik: Sammlung Thiemann, Hamburg, exh. cat., Focke Museum, Bremen, 1972

Erik Lassen, *En Københavnsk porcelansfabriks kistorie Bing & Grøndahl, 1853–1978* [The history of a Copenhagen porcelain manufactory: Bing & Grøndahl, 1853–1978], Copenhagen, 1978

Danish Ceramic Design, exh. cat., Palmer Museum of Art, Pennsylvania State University, University Park, 1981

Danskt 50-tal [Danish 1950s], exh. cat., Nationalmuseum, Stockholm, 1981

Bredo L. Grandjean, *Kongelig Dansk Porcelain, 1884–1980* [Royal Danish Porcelain, 1884–1980], Copenhagen, 1983

Bo Gyllensvärd, *Gustaf VI Adolfs: Samling af dansk og svensk stentøj* [Gustave VI Adolf's collection of Danish and Swedish stoneware], Copenhagen: Bing & Grøndahl, 1983

H. V. F. Winstone, *Royal Copenhagen*, London: Stacey, 1984

Vibeke Woldbye, *Gertrud Vasegaard keramiske arbejder, 1930–1984* [Gertrud Vasegaard ceramic works, 1930–1984], Stockholm: Nationalmuseum, 1985

Jennifer Hawkins Opie, *Scandinavian Ceramics and Glass in the Twentieth Century*, London: Victoria and Albert Museum, 1989

Brændpunkter: I dansk keramik, 1890–1990 [Firing points in Danish ceramics], exh. cat., Kunstindustrimuseet, Copenhagen, 1990

Dansk keramik 1991: Arbejder fra 22 værksteder Århus Kunstforening af 1847 [Works from 22 workshops, Århus Art Association of 1847], exh. cat., Århus Kunstbygning, Aarhus, 1991

Danish Ceramics/Deense keramiek, exh. cat., Boymans-van Beuningen Museum, Rotterdam, 1995

The studio that Gertrud Vasegaard has shared with her daughter Myre since 1959 is part of a substantial early 19th-century farm complex in Frederiksberg, a municipality bordering and hardly distinguishable from Denmark's capital, Copenhagen. The building was in a rural setting when it was built, and even today, after entering the tranquil cobblestoned courtyard outside the place where the artist works and lives, one exchanges the bustle of the late 20th century for a quieter, saner milieu. The setting and sense of place are not unlike the studio of Lucie Rie (q.v.) in the quiet mews off Bayswater Road in London, and one is struck with another parallel – the Danish potter is dressed entirely in white.

The matt surfaces of Vasegaard's studio, with its scrubbed and bleached wooden surfaces, the white walls and white fabrics at the windows, are an ideal setting for the five or six glazed works of ceramic art that might be found there at any one time. The writer has made several visits to her studio and each time has been struck by the authority of the work confronted. The lines are simple, the glazes subtle, the decoration, when it occurs, tends to be a repeated motif that with each viewing takes on a greater complexity. It is not surprising to learn that the objects viewed are the survivors of the hammer, which demolishes those pieces that fail to live up to Vasegaard's exacting standards.

Everything was in place for Gertrud Hjorth to learn the potter's skills at an early age. She was born into a family of potters in Rønne on the island of Bornholm. The Hjorth Terra Cotta Factory founded by her grandfather, Lauritz Adolph, in 1859 and under the direction of her father, Hans, was the environment of her childhood and she began her apprenticeship decorating ceramics at the family factory at the age of 14. Her subsequent studies in Copenhagen included practical experience in the studios of Arne Bang, Axel Salto, Bode Willumsen and Olga Jensen. In 1933 she joined her sister Lisbet, also a distinguished potter, in setting up a joint workshop in the picturesque fishing port of Gudhjem on the east coast of Bornholm. After her marriage to Sigurd Vasegaard and the birth of her daughter, she established her own studio in Holkadalen, maintaining it for ten years. She spent several winters in the studios of the Bing & Grøndahl Porcelain Manufactory in Copenhagen, a prelude to her employment as a full-time artist-in-residence there in 1949.

The years at Bing & Grøndahl witnessed a very important development in Vasegaard's art as she investigated and mastered the properties of high-fire stoneware and porcelain. Her sense and command of form and integration of surface decor were faultless and became the crowning achievement of those years. She worked with Aksel Rode, artistic consultant to the factory and an instructor at the Royal Academy of Fine Arts, in the pursuit of glazes and underglaze pigments for the high-fire media of her factory pots. It seems safe to say that her most spectacular unique works in that decade were decorated with repeated motifs in underglaze blue. Handled with complete authority, this became one of the hallmarks of "Danish Modern" so successfully exported to Europe and America in the two decades following World War II. But underglaze blue was not her only decor. A broad palette of colours, including celadons, amber and complex greys, was developed for single colour wares or combination surfaces. Increasingly, those surfaces were punctuated by random dark-brown spots occasioned by the addition of granules of ferrous oxide to the clay. She was not alone in using this technique but, as in so many aspects of her work, her handling of it became another part of her signature quality.

In 1958 the artist designed a tea set for commercial production by Bing & Grøndahl. Eschewing the temptation of relating shapes that are part of something called a "set", Vasegaard endeavoured to design each element as the most satisfying form she could envision for its function. Hence, the teapot is hexagonal, the milk jug is round, the cake plate is octagonal, the tea caddy is a flattened ovoid. The cups lack handles and are of two types deriving from the traditional Chinese winter and summer tea bowls. This beautiful group of objects is held together by a rich, cream-coloured glaze edged in matt burnt orange.

It would be impossible to comment on the many shapes that Vasegaard has produced, but a particular form deserves special comment. From 1971 through much of the 1980s she created

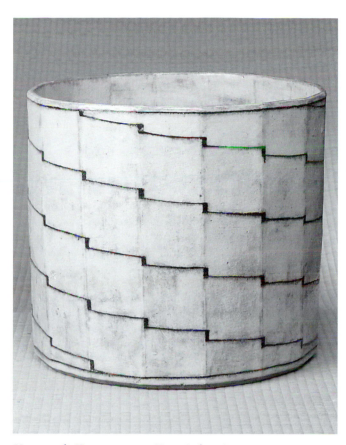

Vasegaard: *Kumme*, 1978; Kunstindustrimuseum, Copenhagen

a number of large structured vessels that she termed *kumme* (a word not easily translated into English but a reasonable equivalent might be "cistern"). The *kumme* are large, straight-sided vessels, sometimes cylindrical but mostly polygonal, ranging up to 45 centimetres in height. Because the diameters of these vessels are similar to their heights, there is a monumental quality about them. These arresting pieces are mostly decorated with some version of Vasegaard's "staircase" pattern with black slip inlaid under a warm, clear glaze; once seen, they are impossible to forget.

Three dinner services for the Royal Copenhagen Porcelain Manufactory were undertaken from her studio. The first two were put into production in 1961 following two years of preparation. *Gemina*, a service of 35 pieces, was hand-painted in underglaze blue featuring twin elements spaced twice in each band, a double twin as it were. *Gemma* is a service of 32 pieces all in white with a stamped, centred design based on a quartered rhombus enclosed in a circle. The quartered rhombus has recurred in unique works since the early 1950s and surfaces again in underglaze blue on the teapot of *Gemina*. In 1975, for the 200th anniversary of the factory, the *Capella* service was commissioned. It was kept to 16 pieces, several of which had more than one use – the saucer, for instance, has no well for the cup and could be used as a small plate. The colour for the set is a pale celadon and the artist arranged to have tiny granules of ferrous oxide in the glaze to provide a subtle, random pattern of fine dark flecks, her ultimate "signature", and her crowning achievement as a designer.

Gertrud Vasegaard, now in her eighties, continues to make works of depth and subtlety. She leaves a legacy for many who own elements of her production pieces as well as for those fortunate few who have unique works from this artist's hands. Both may sense a rare insight into the character of a remarkable artist potter, in their handling and viewing. The principal collections of Vasegaard's work are in the Kunstindustrimuseet and Statens Museum for Kunst, Copenhagen; Louisiana Museum, Humlebæk; Nationalmuseum, Stockholm; Museum Boijmans Van Beuningen, Rotterdam; Palmer Museum of Art, University Park, Pennsylvania; and the Victoria and Albert Museum, London.

WILLIAM HULL

Velarde, Pablita

American painter, 1918–

Born in Santa Clara, New Mexico, 19 September 1918, into a Pueblo Indian family; Indian name "Golden Dawn". Boarded at St Catherine's Mission School, Santa Fe, after mother's early death, then studied at Santa Fe Indian School under Dorothy Dunn, 1932–6. Returned to Santa Clara, 1936; taught crafts part-time at elementary school. Participated in Federal Art Project, 1939–40. Married Anglo-American policeman Herb Hardin, 1942; daughter Helen born 1943, son Herbert born 1944 (both became artists); divorced 1959. Moved to Albuquerque, 1947; returned to Santa Clara, 1960s. Recipient of first prize, Indian Market, Santa Fe, 1938; Grand Purchase award, annual American Indian Artists' Exhibition, Philbrook Art Center, Tulsa, 1953; first prize, Gallup Inter-Tribal Ceremonial, 1954; Palmes d'Académiques award, French government, 1954; first prize, Museum of New Mexico Annual Exhibition of Indian Paintings, 1957; best painting, Cherokee National Museum, Trail of Tears Art Show, 1967; Waite-Phillips award, Philbrook Art Center, 1968; first award, Scottsdale Native American Indian Cultural Foundation Arts and Crafts competition, 1970; Governor's award for Excellence in the Visual Arts, 1977; honorary doctorate, University of New Mexico, Albuquerque, 1978; Erna Fergusson award, New Mexico Folklore Society, 1981; first place, 1986, 1987 and 1989, special award, 1991, best in traditional painting, 1988, 1989 and 1991, and Helen Hardin award for Creative Excellence, 1989, 1990 and 1992, Northern Pueblos Annual Artists' and Craftsmen's Show; Women's Caucus for the Arts award, 1990. Honoured as a "living treasure", Santa Fe, 1988. Lives in Albuquerque, New Mexico.

Principal Exhibitions

Corcoran Gallery of Art, Washington, DC: 1934 (*Public Works of Art Project*)
Denver Art Museum: 1954 (*Annual Indian Artists' Exhibition*)
M.H. de Young Memorial Museum, San Francisco: 1955
Philbrook Art Center, Tulsa: 1955
Hall of Ethnology, Museum of New Mexico, Santa Fe: 1957
California Palace of the Legion of Honor, San Francisco: 1958
Heard Museum, Phoenix: 1966
Museum of Albuquerque: 1976 (*Women of New Mexico*)

Indian Pueblo Cultural Center, Albuquerque: 1976, 1992
National Museum of Women in the Arts, Washington, DC: 1990
Bandelier National Monument, Los Alamos: 1992
Wheelwright Museum of the American Indian, Santa Fe: 1993 (retrospective)

Selected Writings
Old Father: The Story-Teller, Globe, AZ: King, 1960

Bibliography
W. Thetford LeViness, "Pablita Velarde: Pueblo painter", *American Artist*, xxix, April 1965, pp.40–45, 76–8
Mary Carroll Nelson, *Pablita Velarde*, Minneapolis: Dillon Press, 1971
Clara Lee Tanner, *Southwest Indian Painting*, 2nd edition, Tucson: University of Arizona Press, 1973
100 Years of Native American Painting, exh. cat., Oklahoma Museum of Art, Oklahoma City, 1978
Magic Images: Contemporary Native American Art, exh. cat., Philbrook Art Center, Tulsa, 1981
Mara R. Witzling, ed., *Voicing Our Visions: Writings by Women Artists*, New York: Universe, 1991; London: Women's Press, 1992
Betty LaDuke, *Women Artists: Multi-Cultural Visions*, Trenton, NJ: Red Sea Press, 1992
"Woman's Work": The Art of Pablita Velarde, exh. cat., Wheelwright Museum of the American Indian, Santa Fe, 1993
Sally Hyer, "Pablita Velarde: Woman's work", *Southwest Art*, xxii, March 1993, pp.80–85

In 1932 Pablita Velarde, then 14 years of age, arrived at the Santa Fe Indian School to become the first full-time female student in Dorothy Dunn's art classes. Dunn, who came from the Art Institute of Chicago, initiated the first officially sanctioned art programme in an Indian school, which came to be known as the Studio. Operating under Dunn's guidance, between 1932 and 1937 the alumni of the Studio constituted the foundation for the Indian easel-painting tradition. Velarde and her classmates, who included Oscar Howe, Allan Houser and Cecil Dick, were at the forefront of a generation of Native American artists who benefited from a growing public interest in Indian art.

Velarde was an outstanding student and received much encouragement and support from Dunn. In 1933 she exhibited an oil mural at the *Century of Progress Exhibit* in Chicago and, by the time she graduated in 1936, her work had been shown in several major museums. Thus launched on a promising course, the artist never wavered from her career and by the early 1960s was among the most celebrated Indian artists of the Southwest and perhaps the best-known Native American woman painter. Like many of the Indian artists of her generation, Velarde's roots in the Studio exercised a strong influence on her career as a whole. By the late 1950s the Santa Fe style inspired by the Studio had become entrenched and was subject to growing criticism as repetitive and clichéd. To a greater or lesser degree Velarde's generation began experimenting with new styles, but the cutting edge of Indian fine art began to shift to the younger artists.

One unique aspect of Velarde's career lies in her position as a woman in Pueblo culture. Born in Santa Clara Pueblo, New Mexico, in 1918, she faced values and traditions that held that

Velarde: *Koshares of Taos*, 1946; Philbrook Museum of Art, Tulsa

the proper place for a woman was as mother and housewife and that painting was man's work. Fortunately, her resolve to be an artist was reinforced early on by Tonita Peña, the first female Pueblo representational painter, who came to the Santa Fe Indian School to paint murals for the Works Progress Administration (WPA). Peña encouraged Velarde to pursue an art career and served as an inspiration for the young artist. Due perhaps to the early taunting of male students at Santa Fe, Velarde took special pleasure in her growing critical success and felt especially vindicated when she was the first woman to receive the Grand Purchase award at the Philbrook Art Center's Annual American Indian Artists' Exhibition in 1953.

Velarde came from a strongly traditional background, and it is the stories and experiences of Pueblo life that provide the subject of her art. First-hand knowledge and research combine to give her an authoritative and instinctive grasp of this life. She sees herself and her art as a bridge between native traditions and the contemporary world. Describing herself as a story-teller, it has been Velarde's lifelong quest to preserve the customs, legends and beliefs of her people in a manner that will communicate their power and vitality to an Anglo world. Perhaps no single effort characterises her artistic purpose better than her illustrated book *Old Father* of 1960, which recounts six traditional oral legends of her people.

At the Santa Fe Indian School Velarde began to draw Pueblo subject matter, and this penchant was reinforced in Dorothy Dunn's classes. Rather than teaching academic art, Dunn exhorted her students to seek their inspiration in tribal sources and to draw from memory rather than nature. She also encouraged them to study Indian art of the past. In response, Velarde's paintings focused on representations of the daily life of the Santa Clara Pueblo executed largely in casein and tempera (e.g. *Santa Clara Women Before the Altar*, c.1933; Museum of New Mexico, Museum of Indian Art and Culture). She also participated in mural projects that introduced her to the medium of "earth painting", in which various colours of earth are mixed with water and glue to make paint. The style of Velarde's paintings at this time was characterised by bilateral symmetry, strong outlines, flat colours, little or no illusionism, frozen action and attention to detail.

Between 1938 and 1948 she completed one of her most significant works: a series of 84 painted backdrops for museum cases at the Bandelier National Monument in Frijoles Canyon, New Mexico. Commissioned as a WPA project to provide interpretative illustrations of Pueblo life, the series offers a unique opportunity to assess Velarde's stylistic development and represents her coming of age as an artist. The early works of the series, produced in 1939–40, are relatively sketchy and proportionally awkward, while those painted in its second phase (1946–8) are well composed, surely drawn and more complex in colour. What is most remarkable about these paintings is the wealth of authoritative information that they provide on Pueblo life, symbolism and ceremony. A good example of her work at the beginning of the project is *Animal Dance, Santa Clara Pueblo* (1939–40). While not a part of the Bandelier series, the painting *Koshares of Taos* (1946; see illustration) typifies the sophistication acquired by the artist as she perfected her version of the Santa Fe style in the later 1940s.

In the 1960s Velarde, a successful and celebrated artist, returned to the Santa Clara Pueblo to refresh her contact with the oral traditions of her people. She also began extensive work with the earth paintings, which still continues. Inspired by ancient paintings on Kiva walls and pottery designs, Velarde explored more symbolic and abstract work such as *Thunder Knives* (1957; Museum of Indian Arts and Culture). By the time she painted *How the Skunk Got His Scent* (1990; R. Dunning and N. Correll Collection), the artist had further personalised her style to feature more highly animated compositions with rhythmic patterns and rich detail put to the service of recounting Tewa mythology and legend.

Pablita Velarde's artistic career is a rich and varied one. Her art has constantly demonstrated greater sophistication born of the practice of her profession, a willingness to experiment and a receptivity to change. From beginning to end, however, her strengths have been consistent: a passionate engagement in the heritage of her people and an aesthetic that celebrates narrative description with an emphasis on detail and pattern.

JOHN A. DAY

Vézelay, Paule
British painter, sculptor and designer, 1892–1984

Born Marjorie Watson-Williams in Clifton, Bristol, 14 May 1892. Studied at Bristol Municipal School of Art, 1909–12. Moved to London, 1912; studied briefly at Slade School of Fine Art, then at London School of Art under *Punch* illustrator George Belcher, 1912–14; also attended evening classes in lithography at Chelsea Polytechnic. First visited Paris, 1920; spent six months in Austria, 1922. Organised the exhibition *Pictures, Sculpture and Pottery by Some British Artists of Today* at the Lefevre Gallery, London, 1925. Settled in Paris, changing name to Paule Vézelay, 1926. Lived with Surrealist painter André Masson, 1929–32. Returned home to Bristol, 1939; settled in London, 1944. Exhibited most years at Salon des Surindépendants, Paris, 1929–37; Salon des Réalités Nouvelles, Paris, 1946–51. Member of London Group, 1922–33; Abstraction-Création, Paris, 1934; Artists' International Association, 1944–7; Salon des Réalités Nouvelles, 1946; Groupe Espace, 1953 (set up British branch, 1954; President of British branch, 1957). Member, 1949, and Fellow, 1958, Society of Industrial Artists (as illustrator and textile designer). Died 20 March 1984.

Selected Individual Exhibitions
Galerie Georges Giroux, Brussels: 1920 (with Gustave de Smet)
Galerie des Feuillets d'Art, Paris: 1920
Galerie Louis Manteau, Brussels: 1924
Lefevre Gallery, London: 1928, 1936, 1942
Galerie Vavin-Raspail, Paris: 1930
Galerie Jeanne Bucher, Paris: 1934, 1937, 1946
Galerie Colette Allendy, Paris: 1946 (retrospective), 1950
Gimpel Fils, London: 1950
Leicester Galleries, London: 1954 (with Winifred Nicholson)
Grosvenor Gallery, London: 1968 (retrospective)
Zabriskie Gallery, New York: 1980 (retrospective)
Tate Gallery, London: 1983 (retrospective)

Selected Writings

(as M. Watson-Williams)

Contributions to *Drawing and Design*, no.29, September 1917,
pp.100–01; no.32, December 1917, pp.34–5; no.33, January
1918, pp.58–9; no.34, February 1918, pp.80–81; no.35, March
1918, pp.104–5; no.36, April 1918, pp.134–5; new series, no.24,
April 1922, pp.818–21

(as Paule Vézelay)

"Juan Gris", *Artwork*, iv, 1928, pp.258–61

"On children's drawings", *Horizon*, x, 1944, pp.109–13

"Imagination, mathématique et equilibre", invitation sheet to Paule
Vézelay's exhibition at Galerie Colette Allendy, Paris, 1946

"Jean Arp", *World Review*, September 1949, pp.61–4

"Comment on lines in space", unpublished article, January 1964;
abridged version published in *The Tate Gallery Report, 1963–64*,
p.45

Bibliography

Michel Seuphor, "Paule Vézelay", *L'Art d'aujourd'hui*, 5th series,
no.8, December 1954, p.12

Charles Spencer, "Talking to Paule Vézelay", *London Magazine*, n.s.,
viii, October 1968, pp.69–75

Abstraction-Création, 1931–1936, exh. cat., Westfälisches
Landesmuseum, Münster, and Musée d'Art Moderne de la Ville
de Paris, 1978

Paule Vézelay, exh. cat., Tate Gallery, London, 1983

Leonie Caldecott, ed., *Women of Our Century*, London: Ariel
Books/British Broadcasting Corporation, 1984 (interview with
Germaine Greer)

Paule Vézelay: Paintings and Constructions, exh. cat., Annely Juda
Fine Art, London, 1987

Paule Vézelay, 1892–1984: Early Work, 1909–1939, exh. cat.,
Michael Parkin Fine Art, London, 1988

Paule Vézelay: Imagination, Mathematics, Balance, exh. cat.,
Zabriskie Gallery, New York, 1988

Paule Vézelay, 1892–1984: Master of Line, exh. cat., England and
Co., London, 1988

*Paule Vézelay and André Masson: Paintings and Works on Paper,
1928–1934*, exh. cat., England and Co., London, 1989

Paule Vézelay, 1892–1984, exh. cat., England and Co., London, 1993

Paule Vézelay/Hans Arp: The Enchantments of Purity, exh. brochure,
Centre for the Study of Sculpture, Leeds, 1995

Paule Vézelay archives are c/o Tate Gallery Archives, London.

Paule Vézelay may be considered Britain's first abstract artist.
She started her career, however, as Marjorie Watson-Williams
and came from Bristol, where she had been born to a distinguished medical family in 1892. She determined to be an artist,
moving from the Bristol Municipal School of Art to an exhilarating pre-war London where "Futurism and Ragtime danced
together, unchaperoned" in 1912. As M. Watson-Williams, she
established her reputation as an illustrator of delicacy and wit,
under the aegis of George Belcher, the *Punch* artist; she immediately abandoned the Slade, although her first oils demonstrated the influence of Sickert. Whistler's example inspired her
to adopt a butterfly-like monogram, intertwining "M" and
"W" – the first step towards a new identity.

Three artists were important for Vézelay before her meeting
with Jean Arp: the Belgians Léon and Gustave de Smet, and the
Surrealist André Masson. Léon de Smet, for whom Paule
posed, arrived in London in 1914 and was soon moving in the
intellectual circle of the writer John Galsworthy. His amorous
persistence, Vézelay claimed, drove her to Paris in 1920.
Subsequently her friendship with his brother Gustave developed; his *mâtelot* sailor themes and zigzag motifs were echoed

in some of her paintings. They held a joint exhibition at the
Galerie Georges Giroux in Brussels in 1920. The de Smets'
encouragement was important, leading to Vézelay's exhibition
at the Galerie Louis Manteau in Brussels in 1924. In October
1920, however, Marjorie Watson-Williams held her first Paris
exhibition at the Galerie des Feuillets d'Art. Formal debts were
now to Degas and to Bonnard; but it was through her visits to
the Cirque Medrano, much-beloved by Picasso and
Archipenko, that the motif of the tightrope dancer entered her
work, anticipating the boxed lines and wires in space that
would constitute perhaps her most original contribution as an
artist working in three dimensions.

"Paule Vézelay", the name she took in 1926, was both
poetic and evocative, a homage to the superb Romanesque
church at Vézelay, and ambiguous in its resonances: this was
the era of the liberated *garçonne* and the name "Paule" feminised the sometimes useful disguise of a masculine-sounding
name. (A similar indeterminacy surrounds the name of
Marlow Moss, q.v., who later became very friendly with
Paule.) Vézelay found many dedicated and delightful female
colleagues at the Salon des Surindépendants where she exhibited from 1929 to 1937, such as Christine Boumeester, Maria
Elena Vieira da Silva (q.v.), Marlow Moss and, of course,
Sophie Taeuber-Arp (q.v.).

Although Vézelay claimed in retrospect: "I was producing
pure abstract art from 1928" (the year when in fact she turned
to Juan Gris's Cubism), one must consider the Surrealist interlude that was so important for her work. In 1929 she fell in
love with the prominent Surrealist André Masson. The couple
were almost married: Vézelay experienced the most intense
happiness and despair at this time. The influence upon her
work was direct: the tightrope "lines in space" in still essentially figurative works became marked by Masson's more flamboyant *écriture*, while, inevitably, Vézelay was drawn into the
intense, sexually exploratory, and with Masson often violent
arena of Surrealism. It was an ultimately tragic affair: another
fresh start was necessary.

Vézelay's membership of the international abstract group
Abstraction-Création from 1934 can thus be seen as a deliberate change of allegiance and of artistic direction, although,
ironically, it was via Arp that she unsuccessfully attempted to
show in the International Surrealist Exhibition in London in
1936. Transitional works reveal the influence of Giacometti's
drawings of sculptures, some imaginary, some realised, the
famous "Objets mobiles et muets" published in *Le Surréalisme
au service de la révolution* in 1931. Giacometti's biomorphic
forms here display a sexual thrust whose malevolence,
however, is entirely absent in Vézelay's floating, biomorphic
shapes. Arp's biomorphic work, always sensuous, is often
humorous; his formal jokes retain the complex spirit of Dada
that Vézelay, always serious, would never emulate. Her paintings such as *Triangles and Tubes* of 1932 (repr. London 1989,
no.18) show the move not only towards a more geometric art,
in which emotions are sublimated into a world of purer forms,
but towards an art in which the confusion on a two-dimensional surface of flat versus shaded, three-dimensional shapes
again shows her developing instinct for sculpture. Recent work
was shown at the important Galerie Jeanne Bucher (with two
books illustrated by the Surrealist Kurt Seligmann) in February
and March 1934.

By this time Vézelay had met Arp; his studio was surely a revelation: his reliefs and sculptures, the interrelationship of forms, space and materials, his lightness and liberty – all would find their echo in Vézelay's developing three-dimensional work. Despite the fact that Sophie Taeuber-Arp's studio was discreetly hidden one floor above her husband's (she appeared to be the model wife), the friendship with Sophie, too – indeed Vézelay's perception of the couple's working relationship – was as important as meeting Arp himself. By the late 1930s, Sophie Taeuber's work was rigorously geometric – circles, squares, oblongs, triangles – but the sinuous, curving lines to which Vézelay later replied with her coloured wires in space expressed a grace and *joie de vivre* inspired by dance. There is no doubt that this new double friendship was a tremendous catalyst for Vézelay's work. Arp's ability to mingle the geometric world of modernism with the shapes and forms of the natural world, together with the tenderness of his approach, struck chords in the heart of the Englishwoman deprived of her national landscapes. As Vézelay recalled:

In 1935 I made my first constructions in three dimensions by using a small box in which I composed dried leaves, fishing lines and dry flies, sand and pebbles. This small and unimportant construction enticed me in 1936 to compose with white string stretched over canvas, and to make a collage with black-and-white forms on a black background, over which white cotton lines were stretched from point to point above the collage in the space beneath. I made other constructions which were included under the title of "Recherches en trois dimensions" at the Galerie Jeanne Bucher exhibition in 1937 ... Such constructions with lines in space, as well as some drawings, certainly show an absorbing interest in space, and it was in 1935 that I began making sculpture in plaster, which increased my knowledge of form and its relation to space. Such forms, especially spheres and circles, are static, consequently they have a stabilising power in composition ... [*Tate Gallery Illustrated Catalogue of Acquisitions, 1974–6*, p.160].

Because of the evolution of Arp's sculptures from his painted reliefs, much freestanding work had been made in painted wood: thus Vézelay was not inhibited by the difficulties and the mystique of direct carving in stone, as she might have been in Britain at the time. Her sculpture is not so humorous as that of the former Dadaist, and it has a quieter purity: fish and leaf shapes are unashamedly representative, while the abstract *Garden* (repr. Leeds 1995), in the mode of Art Deco jardinières, was filled with sand and shells, starfish and seaweed. An immensely impressive list of international artists attended Vézelay's exhibition at the Galerie Jeanne Bucher in 1937; this was, undoubtedly, the summit of her career; in May 1939 Arp and Sophie Taeuber held a joint exhibition at the gallery. Vézelay joined the couple in the *Réalités nouvelles* exhibition at the Galerie Charpentier later in the year, which heralded the post-war Salon of the same name. In 1938 she exhibited with Arp, César Domela, Kandinsky, Alberto Magnelli, Jacques Seligmann and Taeuber-Arp at the Galleria del Milione in Milan. In August 1939 she joined the Arps and François Arp's family in Maja-Sacher's Villa Santez-Gwen at Saint-Cast, Brittany. When war was declared, Taeuber-Arp's abstract works were full of foreboding, with titles such as *Lines Lost in a Chaotic Background*: Vézelay had no option but to return to Britain, where her flying forms in space soon metamorphosed into menacing barrage balloons.

Abstraction was relaunched in Paris in 1945 at the Galerie René Drouin where Taeuber-Arp, Kandinsky, Mondrian and Klee were all commemorated at the exhibition *Art Concret*. The following year, the Salon des Réalités Nouvelles became the forum for a new generation of international abstract artists. Vézelay was elected a member in 1946; she returned to Paris for an exhibition at the Galerie Jeanne Bucher in May–June 1946. Besides the tragic death of Sophie Taeuber-Arp in 1943, she had now to bear the death from cancer of her dealer Jeanne Bucher; a bohemian life in Paris was no longer financially viable or even desirable, despite her move to the avant-garde Galerie Colette Allendy, where she held an important retrospective. Her prose piece, "Imagination, mathématique et equilibre", published on this occasion (*Paule Vézelay: Oeuvres de 1926 à 1946*, exh. leaflet, Galerie Colette Allendy, Paris, 1946), is far more confident and mature than her poem to Arp, "With no power for words", written in August 1939, with its explicitly Kantian balancing of reason, will and desire; it corresponds to the control of the new boxed work with curved and coloured wires, although the shadows that are part of these works insist, as always, upon fragility and the ephemeral.

For Vézelay, Arp's studios at Meudon, outside Paris, and in Ascona near Locarno in Switzerland, became havens: yet she refused his proposal of marriage, fearing the enforced domesticity and role of amanuensis that it would entail. The relationship with Arp continued, both tense and tender. Vézelay worked energetically and creatively in London despite disappointments. She joined Groupe Espace in 1953, becoming its British president four years later, but her hopes for collaborations between abstract artists and architects were thwarted by the boycott in Britain of such powerful figures as Henry Moore. She made textile designs for Metz of Amsterdam and Heal's of London, in which her shapes and lines in space became mobile patterns on beautiful curtains. Only in the 1960s was Vézelay able to think of casting her work in bronze, but the experiments were disappointing. Despite a Leicester Galleries exhibition in 1954, *Lines in Space and Their Shadows*, and a Grovesnor Gallery retrospective in 1968, recognition was not really forthcoming until Vézelay's first solo show in New York in 1980 and the Tate Gallery retrospective of 1983. Subsequently, feminists such as Germaine Greer have become interested in her work; Greer interviewed Vézelay for the BBC *Women of Our Century* programme in 1984.

While Vézelay's life as a woman artist is exemplary, her output was relatively small; its influences, while transformed with sensitivity and flair, are evident – she was privileged to have such an intimate dialogue with the pioneers of first-generation modernism, such as Masson and Arp, when her individual circumstances could never have matched the historical conjunctions that formed their art. Sadly, she antagonised powerful younger groups of artists with her claims to priority, in particular the grouping of Henry Moore, Barbara Hepworth (q.v.), Ben Nicholson and Herbert Read; it was not until the 1980s that her reputation was consolidated.

SARAH WILSON

Vieira da Silva, Maria Elena
Portuguese painter, 1908–1992

Born in Lisbon, 13 June 1908. Studied drawing under Emilia Santos Braga, painting under Armando Lucena, professor at the Academia de Belas-Artes, Lisbon, 1919–27; sculpture under Antoine Bourdelle at Académie de la Grande Chaumière, Paris, 1928–9; engraving under Stanley William Hayter at Atelier 17, Paris. Exhibited at Salon des Surindépendants, Paris, 1930. Married Hungarian painter Arpad Szenes, 1930; he died 1985. Lived in Paris, 1929–39; Lisbon, 1935–6 and 1939–40; Brazil, 1940–47; Paris from 1947. Naturalised French citizen, 1956. Recipient of Acquisition prize, 1953, and Grand International prize, 1962, São Paulo Bienal; Tapestry prize, University of Basel, 1954; Grand Prix National des Arts, Paris, 1963; Grand Crois de Santiago da Espada, Lisbon, 1977; Grand Prix Florence Gould, Académie des Beaux-Arts, Paris, 1986; Grand Prix Antena 1, Lisbon, 1986; Gra-Cruz da Ordem da Liberdade du Portugal, 1988; Ordre du Mérite, Paris, 1988. Chevalier, 1960, and Commandeur, 1962, Ordre des Arts et Lettres, Paris; Member, Academy of Arts, Lisbon, 1970; Chevalier, Légion d'Honneur, France, 1979; Member, Académie des Sciences, des Arts et des Lettres, Paris, 1984; honorary member, Royal Academy, London, and Art Gallery of Ontario, Canada, 1988. Fundação Arpad Szenes-Vieira da Silva founded in Lisbon, 1989. Died in Paris, 6 March 1992.

Selected Individual Exhibitions

Galerie Jeanne Bucher, Paris: 1933, 1937, 1939, 1947, 1951, 1960, 1963, 1967, 1969, 1971, 1976, 1982, 1986
Galeri UP, Lisbon: 1935
Museo Nacional de Belas Artes, Rio de Janeiro: 1942
Palacio Municipal, Belo Horizonte, Brazil: 1946 (with Arpad Szenes)
Marian Willard Gallery, New York: 1946
Galerie Pierre, Paris: 1949, 1951, 1955
Galerie Blanche, Stockholm: 1950
Redfern Gallery, London: 1952
Cadby Birch Gallery, New York: 1953
Stedelijk Museum, Amsterdam: 1955 (with Germaine Richier)
Kestner-Gesellschaft, Hannover: 1958 (touring retrospective)
Knoedler Gallery, New York: 1961, 1963, 1966, 1971
Phillips Art Gallery, Washington, DC: 1961, 1963
Kunsthalle, Mannheim: 1961
Musée de Peinture et de Sculpture, Grenoble, and Museo Civico, Turin: 1964 (retrospective)
Albert Loeb Gallery, New York: 1965
Musée National d'Art Moderne, Paris: 1969–70 (touring retrospective)
Musée Fabre, Montpellier: 1971 (retrospective)
Galerie Artel, Geneva: 1974
Musée d'Art Moderne de la Ville de Paris: 1977 (touring retrospective)
Nordjyllands Kunstmuseum, Ålborg, Denmark: 1978 (retrospective)
Galerie EMI-Valentim de Carvalho, Lisbon: 1984 (with Arpad Szenes)
Artcurial, Paris: 1986
Fondation Calouste Gulbenkian, Lisbon: 1988 (touring)
Fondation Juan March, Madrid: 1991 (retrospective)

Bibliography

Pierre Descargues, Vieira da Silva, Paris: Presses Littéraires de France, 1949
René de Solier, Vieira da Silva, Paris: Fall, 1956
José-Augusto França, Vieira da Silva, Lisbon: Artis, 1958
Guy Weelen, Vieira da Silva, Paris: Hazan, 1960
Vieira da Silva, exh. cat., Galerie Jeanne Bucher, Paris, 1967
Dora Vallier, Vieira da Silva: La Peinture de Vieira da Silva: Chemins d'approche, Geneva: Weber, 1971
Mario de Oliveira, 3 ensaios: Vieira da Silva e sua pintura, Braga: Pax, 1972
Guy Weelen, Vieira da Silva, Paris: Hazan, 1973
Antoine Terrasse, L'Univers de Vieira da Silva, Paris: Scrépel, 1977
Guy Weelen, Vieira da Silva: Les Estampes, 1926–1976, Paris: Arts et Métiers Graphiques, Paris, 1977
Agustina Bessa-Luis, Longas dias têm cem anos: Presença de Vieira da Silva, Lisbon: Imprensa Nacional-Casa da Moeda, 1978
Jean Laude, "Vieira da Silva", Cimaise, no.145, 1978
Anne Philipe, L'Eclat de la lumière: Entretiens avec Marie-Hélène Vieira da Silva et Arpad Szenes, Paris: Gallimard, 1978
Jacques Lassaigne and Guy Weelen, Vieira da Silva, New York: Rizzoli, 1979 (French original)
Dora Vallier, Vieira da Silva: Chemins d'approche, Paris: Galilée, 1982
Michel Butor, Vieira da Silva: Peintures, Paris: L'autre Musée, 1983
Guy Weelen, Vieira da Silva: Oeuvres sur papier, Paris: La Différence, 1983
Mário Cesariny, Vieira da Silva, Arpad Szenes ou o Castelo Surrealista, Lisbon: Assirio e Alvim, 1984
Vieira da Silva, exh. cat., Fondation Calouste Gulbenkian, Lisbon, and Galeries nationales du Grand Palais, Paris, 1988
Vieira da Silva/Arpad Szenes, exh. cat., Casa de Serralves, Porto, 1989
Vieira da Silva, exh. cat., Fondation Juan March, Madrid, 1991
Jean-Luc Daval, Jean-François Jaeger and Guy Weelen, Vieira da Silva, 2 vols, Geneva: Skira, 1994 (contains catalogue raisonné)

"In front of the paintings of Vieira da Silva", wrote the Portuguese critic Mario de Oliveira, "the viewer experiences a reality that unites the work and its exterior, for we are ourselves transported into the desired space automatically" (Oliveira 1972). The "desired space" (o espaço desejado) is an ambiguous phrase. Desired by whom? By the painting itself, as appears to be Oliveira's meaning, rather than by the viewer or the artist as subjects? It is certainly a task of the work of art to assign the viewer to his or her proper place in the aesthetic relation, and it is the task of painting to orient the spectator and establish the point from which the logic of its organisation is produced and disclosed. And indeed it would be also correct to point out that a curious longing for a "home", a space of rest and repose, seems to inhabit the expressive depths of Vieira da Silva's works, these paintings obsessed with the recurrence of the void, with the mapping of tangible and intangible distances, reflecting the artist's quest for a place in the work itself as if denied or dissatisfied with a home in reality.

Maria Elena Vieira da Silva was born in Portugal in the early decades of the 20th century, and her life and career encompassed two continents, and the cities of Lisbon, Rio de Janiero and Paris. The displacements of the formative and early professional years followed those of her childhood when she travelled with her family to Britain, France and Switzerland (where her father died in 1911). Music and the visual arts were her first interests, which led, after beginning studies in the visual arts in Portugal, to a first period in Paris, from 1928 (studies with Bourdelle, later with Léger, Despiau and Bissière), with intervals in Lisbon in 1935 and 1939, and interrupted by the outbreak of World War II. From 1940 to 1946 she lived in Rio de Janeiro, returning to Paris in 1947. The period after the

Vieira da Silva: *Disaster (War)*, 1942; Musée National d'Art Moderne, Centre Georges Pompidou, Paris

war coincided with the final evolution of her mature style and her participation in the developments of modern French painting, a period of formation of abstract art in France with the contributions of artists as diverse as the German-born Hartung, the Canadian Riopelle, the Russians Lanskoy and Poliakoff, the Chinese Zao Wou-ki, to name a few, as well as the Frenchmen Soulages, Manessier, Le Moal, among others. Vieira da Silva was a central figure in this "internationalised" period of the School of Paris, which was also the last international diffusion of "French-Parisian" art.

An interest in sculpture, which she studied with Bourdelle and Despiau, and the creation of textile and tapestry designs early in her career indicate the practical beginnings of two main elements of her paintings: the methodic construction of surfaces by the accumulation of small visual units and lines, and the preoccupation with space depiction and space creation on the flat surface of the canvas. The organisation of space is the main element in *Atelier* (Fundação Arpad Szenes-Maria

Elena Vieira da Silva, Lisbon, repr. Daval, Jaeger and Weelen 1994, no.176), painted in Lisbon in 1934. The multiplication of geometric surface elements creates figures and ground, and guides the eye towards the depths of space, doubling the depths of human suffering in *Disaster (War)* (1942; see illustration). A further development of these elements is given by *Card Players* (1947–8; private collection, France, *ibid.*, no.593). Something of the graphic, linear, dynamic and surface elements of Duchamp's early "abstract" paintings (nudes, card players) are echoed in Vieira da Silva's works – as well as, on a different level, the methodic and inspired geometry of the works of Torres Garcia (whose simplicity of form, clarity and vigorous optimism, however, are very distant from the Portuguese artist). Also combined with these elements is present also the specific recognition by the artist of the fragility of the painted surface, as if to indicate the travail of patience, love and loss that characterise the adventure of creation.

Vieira da Silva's mature works reflect the investigation of

the transitions from interior to exterior space (*Three Windows*, 1972–3; Alice Pauli, Lausanne, *ibid.*, no.2681) while the patient accumulation of graphic marks, lines and colours creates imaginary vistas (*The Awakening*, 1973; *ibid.*, no.2658) and imaginary cities (*New Amsterdam II*, 1970; private collection, Portugal, *ibid.*, no.2343). Or she presents, by the repetitive and, at times, painful weaving of marks and colours on the canvas surface, textures that stand for the "flesh" of the painted object itself (*L'Herbe*, 1973; private collection, Switzerland, *ibid.*, no.2661; *Library in Malraux*, 1974; private collection, France, *ibid.*, no.2730).

And yet, for all their accumulated elements, graphic dislocations and the apparent dynamism of their imaginary displacements, integrations and disintegrations of sites and spaces, in the end the paintings of Vieira da Silva convey the feeling of a silent return to self. This, perhaps more than the allusions to the popular and decorative art of the Portuguese *azulejos* and the occasional landscapes or cityscape drawings of Portugal, indicates a specific cultural sensibility at work beyond the elegant expressions of the visual culture of modern French art. The space in Vieira da Silva is the mask of the self, the mirror of the primary, internal space of the subject. A subjective space that reflects something of the interiority, of the self-absorbed, meditative aspects of the *alma portuguesa* (Portuguese soul).

MARCELO LIMA

Vigée-Lebrun, Elisabeth

French painter, 1755–1842

Born Marie Louise Elisabeth Vigée in Paris, 16 April 1755. Trained by her father, a portrait painter, and by Gabriel Briard. Established as a professional portrait painter by 1770; elected member of the Académie de Saint-Luc, Paris, 1774. Married painter and art dealer Jean-Baptiste-Pierre Lebrun, 1776; daughter born 1780 (d. 1819); divorced 1794. Elected member of Académie Royale de Peinture et de Sculpture, Paris, 31 May 1783. Left Paris for Rome with daughter, October 1789; elected member of the Accademia di San Luca, Rome, April 1790; stayed in Rome until April 1792, making three trips to Naples. On homeward journey through Italy, learned that her name was on the proscribed list of exiles in Paris, and decided to go to Vienna instead. Lived in Vienna until April 1795, then went to St Petersburg, Russia; stayed in Moscow, winter 1800–01; left St Petersburg in spring 1801; spent six months in Berlin before returning to Paris in January 1802. Stayed in London, 1803–5; visited Switzerland, 1807 and 1808. Divided time between country retreat at Louveciennes and Paris from 1809. Member of the academies of Paris, Rome, Parma, Bologna, St Petersburg, Berlin, Geneva, Rouen, Avignon and Vaucluse. Died in Paris, 29 May 1842.

Principal Exhibitions

Académie de Saint-Luc, Paris: 1774
Salon de la Correspondance, Paris: 1779, 1781–3
Paris Salon: 1783, 1785, 1787, 1789, 1791, 1798, 1802, 1817, 1824

Selected Writings

Souvenirs de Mme Louise-Elisabeth Vigée Lebrun, 3 vols, Paris: Fournier, 1835–7

Memoirs of Madame Vigée Lebrun, ed. Lionel Strachey, New York: Doubleday, 1903; London: Grant Richards, 1904; abridged edition with introduction by John Russell, New York: Braziller, 1989

Souvenirs, ed. Claudine Herrmann, 2 vols, Paris: Des Femmes, 1984

The Memoirs of Elisabeth Vigée-Le Brun, ed. Siân Evans, Bloomington: Indiana University Press, and London: Camden, 1989

Bibliography

Jean-Baptiste-Pierre Le Brun, *Précis historique de la vie de la citoyenne Lebrun, peintre*, Paris: Lebrun, 1794

J. T. L. F. Tripier Le Franc, *Notice sur la vie et les ouvrages de Mme Lebrun*, Paris, 1828

Charles Blanc, "Elisabeth Vigée-Lebrun", *Histoire des peintres de toutes les écoles*, ed. Charles Blanc, 14 vols, Paris: Renouard, 1861–76

Charles Pillet, *Madame Vigée-Lebrun*, Paris: Librairie de l'Art, 1890

Pierre de Nolhac, *Madame Vigée-Lebrun: Peintre de la reine Marie-Antoinette, 1755–1842*, Paris: Goupil, 1908; revised 1912

Louis Hautecoeur, *Madame Vigée-Lebrun*, Paris: Laurens, 1914

W. H. Helm, *Vigée-Lebrun: Her Life, Works and Friendships*, London: Hutchinson, and Boston: Small Maynard, 1915

André Blum, *Madame Vigée-Lebrun: Peintre des grandes dames du XVIIIe siècle*, Paris: Piazza, 1919

Lada Nikolénko, "The Russian portraits of Madame Vigée-Lebrun", *Gazette des Beaux-Arts*, 6th series, lxx, 1967, pp.91–120

Anne-Marie Passez, *Adélaïde Labille-Guiard (1749–1803): Biographie et catalogue raisonné de son oeuvre*, Paris: Arts et Métiers Graphiques, 1973

Women Artists, 1550–1950, exh. cat., Los Angeles County Museum of Art, and elsewhere, 1976

Andrzej Ryszkiewicz, "Les portraits polonais de Madame Vigée-Lebrun", *Bulletin du Musée National de Varsovie*, xx, 1979, pp.16–42

Joseph Baillio, "Le dossier d'une oeuvre d'actualité politique: *Marie-Antoinette et ses enfants par Mme Vigée LeBrun*", *L'Oeil*, no.308, March 1981, pp.34–41, 74–5; no.310, May 1981, pp.52–61, 90–91

Jean Owens Schaefer, "The souvenirs of Elizabeth Vigée-Lebrun: The self-imaging of the artist and the woman", *International Journal of Women's Studies*, iv, 1981, pp.35–49

Joseph Baillio, "Quelques peintures réattribuées à Vigée-Le Brun", *Gazette des Beaux-Arts*, 6th series, xcix, 1982, pp.13–26 (with English summary)

Elisabeth-Louise Vigée-Le Brun, exh. cat., Kimbell Art Museum, Fort Worth, TX, 1982

H. T. Douwes Dekker, "Gli autoritratti di Elisabeth Vigée-Lebrun (1755–1842)", *Antichità Viva*, xxii/4, 1983, pp.31–5

Paula Radisich, "Qui peut définer les femmes? Vigée-Lebrun's portraits of an artist", *Eighteenth-Century Studies*, xxv, 1992, pp.441–68

Susan Sontag, *The Volcano Lover: A Romance*, New York: Farrar Straus, and London: Cape, 1992

Mary Sheriff, "Woman? hermaphrodite? history painter? On the self-imaging of Elisabeth Vigée-Lebrun", *The Eighteenth Century: Theory and Interpretation*, xxxv, Spring 1994, pp.3–28

——, "The immodesty of her sex: Elisabeth Vigée-Lebrun in 1783", *The Consumption of Culture in the Early Modern Period*, ed. Ann Bermingham and John Brewer, London and New York: Routledge, 1995, pp.455–88

——, *The Exceptional Woman: Elisabeth Vigée-Lebrun and the Cultural Politics of Art*, Chicago: Chicago University Press, 1996 (contains extensive bibliography)

Elisabeth Vigée-Lebrun's life and work are split by that great cultural and political divide known as the French Revolution. She was born in Paris in 1755 and died there in 1842, but she spent the years between 1789 and 1802 in exile. Her close association with Queen Marie-Antoinette and her protégés made the artist a target for political pamphleteers, and she left France with the first wave of émigrés in 1789. Only a petition signed by 255 artists in 1801 opened the way for her repatriation. If Vigée-Lebrun's reputation was first secured in the French capital as the queen's painter, her career after 1789 was marked by travel from court to court and country to country. Even after her return to Paris in 1802, the artist continued her peripatetic life, making trips to Britain, Switzerland, Belgium and throughout France. These travels she recorded in her *Souvenirs*, published between 1835 and 1837.

The *Souvenirs* are filled with anecdotes of the artist's life before the Revolution, as well as accounts of her travels during and after her exile. Not only is it uncertain how much of the text she actually wrote, but her "memories" often depend on what others said about her, and her writing transcribes word for word flattering poems, letters and reviews. These representations, as well as the standard tropes of artistic biography and the myths of the painter's imagination, are fundamental to her *Souvenirs*. She inserted into these ready-made stories the events – remembered, fantasised or constructed – of her own life, and published this highly mediated self-representation under her name as her authorised biography. The *Souvenirs*, then, are not a factual record of her life, but a self-projection, an image as crafted as those she projected in her paintings.

The daughter of a guild painter, Louis Vigée, and a hairdresser, Jeanne Messin, Elisabeth Vigée-Lebrun did not come from an exalted social rank or wealth, but neither did she come from the poor or dispossessed. Luck of birth positioned her so she might have a chance, even if her sex made the odds of actually having one, let alone successfully seizing it, quite small. Her father taught her the trade at home, a mode of training typical for women, and she continued her education with the academic artist Gabriel Briard. From the start, Elisabeth Vigée seems to have managed her career astutely, and by 1770 she was establishing herself as a portrait painter. At 19 the artist belonged to the guild (the Académie de Saint-Luc de Paris), and she showed at its exhibition in 1774, receiving very favourable notices in the press. She married the painter and art dealer Jean-Baptiste-Pierre Lebrun in 1776, a marriage that facilitated her study of art and travel abroad. By 1780 she had the support of influential patrons, such as the Comte de Vaudreuil and the finance minister Calonne, whom she entertained at suppers. She became, most importantly, a favoured painter of Marie-Antoinette.

The path that Vigée-Lebrun took was the one that led to noble patrons and royal favour, a path familiar to French artists for more than a century. She pursued her ambitions according to the particular circumstances of the arts and the structures governing their practice. When the Revolution came, however, it would not have been easy for her to change course. Not only did she draw her clients from the aristocracy and well-to-do, but Vigée-Lebrun was the only artist working for the crown who was calumniated in print. A highly visible public woman competing directly with men, Vigée-Lebrun was a perfect target for the fears of de-differentiation and feminisation that were played out most dramatically in the revolutionary period. In pursuing government commissions and royal favour before the Revolution, however, Vigée-Lebrun walked that well-travelled path a bit differently from her male colleagues. For them, admission into the Academy or its schools usually preceded royal favour. In her case, royal favour secured her acceptance into the privileged body of artists on 31 May 1783. That acceptance was one of the most unusual and most contested on record.

The basic story line of the controversy surrounding Vigée-Lebrun's admission is simple: because she was married to an art dealer, the Academy, represented by its Director, the Comte d'Angiviller, held her in violation of the statute forbidding artists from engaging in commerce. The reason recorded in the official records of the Academy (the *Procès verbaux*) is as follows:

> Madame Lebrun, wife of an art dealer, is very talented and would have long ago been elected to the Academy were it not for the commerce of her husband. It is said, and I believe it, that she does not mix in commerce, but in France a wife has no other station [*état*] than that of her husband.

Vigée-Lebrun's status as an art dealer's wife necessitated an exception to the statute, which the king ordered at the request of the queen. The Academy had no choice but to admit her, and on the same day also received Adélaïde Labille-Guiard (q.v.), whose acceptance as a portrait painter it conducted and recorded according to established practice. The academicians compensated themselves, however, for the forced admission by obtaining from the King an order limiting the number of women to four (since Mme Vien and Anne Vallayer-Coster, q.v., were already academicians, there were precisely four women in the Academy at the time). D'Angiviller justified the order by reasoning:

> this number is sufficient to honour their talent; women can not be useful to the progress of the arts because the modesty of their sex forbids them from being able to study after nature and in the public school established and founded by Your Majesty.

What the Director meant by progress of the arts is the progress of history painting, the grand genre he sought to revive as an instrument of state. Women could not be useful to the arts because theoretically and practically they were barred from practising as history painters. Not only were their mental talents believed inadequate, but they could attend neither the Academy's life drawing classes nor other essential training sessions (in perspective, anatomy, history). Vigée-Lebrun, however, gave the lie to d'Angiviller's claim of women's uselessness in choosing her reception piece. Because she was admitted to the Academy in such an unusual way, on the day of her acceptance the artist presented no work by which the academicians could classify her as practising a particular genre. They asked her to bring to the next meeting some painting that could stand as her reception piece. As Vigée-Lebrun was best known as a portrait painter, the Academy probably anticipated that she would bring a portrait. Thwarting this expectation, she presented instead *Peace Bringing Back Abundance* (1780; 102 × 132 cm.; Louvre, Paris), an allegorical history painting. The Academy never officially recognised this work and never

Vigée-Lebrun: *Self-Portrait in a Straw Hat*, exhibited Salon of 1783; National Gallery, London

positioned her within a rank or genre, but when the painting appeared in the Salon the following autumn it was listed in the guide and discussed in the press as her reception piece.

In *Peace Bringing Back Abundance* Vigée-Lebrun capitalised on the elements of history painting that did provide openings for women. Within the allegorical tradition, the idealised female body was used to represent any number of abstract ideas, and often made to stand for virtues that in the "real world" were not ordinarily ascribed to women or gendered as feminine. Those history paintings that featured the female body opened possibilities for women artists who could draw "after Nature" either by using themselves or their female friends or servants as models. In two other history paintings exhibited at the same Salon – *Juno Borrowing the Belt of Venus* and *Venus Binding Cupid's Wings* (both untraced) – and in works shown in 1785, most notably *Bacchante* (Musée Nissim de Camondo, Paris) – the artist took advantage of changes in history painting that marked the first half of the 18th century when mythological subjects of the type popularised by Boucher featured the female body. Such subjects met the criteria for history paintings in that they were drawn from literature and mythology, and demanded that the painter visualise an event, idealise the figures, imagine their passions and choose the most appropriate artistic language. By 1783, however, some Salon critics and academic officials argued that such unedifying subjects debased history painting, eschewing its moral, serious (masculine) side and cultivating its erotic, frivolous (feminine) side. Indeed, d'Angiviller designed his reform of history painting to rescue the highest genre from the depths into which it had allegedly fallen in the hands of such painters as Boucher. Although most of Vigée-Lebrun's images could be compared to Boucher's mythologies, *Peace and Abundance* invoked a tradition of earlier royalist iconography, a tradition that in d'Angiviller's terms *could* be useful to the progress of the arts.

In *Peace and Abundance* Vigée-Lebrun deploys a standard monarchical iconography in a theme previously used for Academy reception pieces. In this iconography, Abundance is represented as a woman holding a cornucopia filled with nature's bounty, even though she is meant to refer to the financial abundance that will accrue to the arts with renewed patronage after a period of military outlay. Painted in 1780, Vigée-Lebrun's work anticipates the end of French expenditures for the American Revolution, which would bring back abundance to the arts in the sense of providing money to continue d'Angiviller's projects. Three years later, when the work appeared at the Salon, Vigée-Lebrun's contemporaries took it as a comment on the reign of Louis XVI, for the treaty ending France's involvement in the American War of Independence was signed in that year.

Salon criticism in 1783 was preoccupied with the unprecedented appearance of works by four women. Vigée-Lebrun's paintings inevitably garnered the most discussion, and much of it focused on her attempts to become a history painter. The most pointed of these addressed not a history painting, but her *Self-Portrait in a Straw Hat* (private collection; autograph copy in National Gallery, London; see illustration). Published under the name Coup de Patte, this commentary presented itself as the conversation of a painter, poet and musician. The trio pauses before Vigée-Lebrun's self-portrait and the musician

asks whom the work represents. The painter explains that the work is a self-portrait. "Indeed! this pretty person has painted herself!" exclaims the surprised poet. The painter, however, is troubled because the figure's hair is a little négligé. The musician takes this as a sign that she has the "taste" of great artists not focused on mundane details. Addressing himself to the painter, the musician asks: "Is she a history painter?" And the painter replies:

> No. The arms, the head, the heart of women lack the essential qualities to follow men into the lofty region of the fine arts. If nature could produce one of them capable of this great effort, it would be a monstrosity, the more shocking because there would be an inevitable opposition between her physical and mental/moral (*morale*) existence. A woman who would have all the passions of a man is really an impossible man. So the vast field of history, which is filled with vigorously passioned objects, is closed to those who would not know how to bring to it all the expressions of vigour [Coup de Patte (pseud.), *Le Triumvirat des arts ...*, Paris, 1783, p.27].

The hermaphrodite is the governing image throughout this passage. In characterising the woman history painter as a monstrosity, the text evokes the long history of considering the hermaphrodite among the mistakes of nature. As the woman history painter, Vigée-Lebrun tried to assume a man's role; if her imitation were possible, it would produce an impossible opposition between her physical and mental-moral existence. A woman who had the force to produce significant works of art would be neither woman nor man, but impossible man.

Although within the context of the Salon Vigée-Lebrun's self-image evoked the woman history painter as monstrous hermaphrodite, it also offered its viewers other associations. Based on Rubens's *Chapeau de Paille* (1620–25: National Gallery, London), the self-portrait presents Vigée-Lebrun as both beautiful woman and accomplished artist. The painting by Rubens was well-known as an excellent model for depicting beauty, but one that presented to the artist who imitated it difficult problems of colouring and light effects. Vigée-Lebrun takes up the artistic challenge but separates herself from both Rubens's beautiful model and her later *semblables* who devised their masquerade costumes after the dress shown in Rubens's painting. Vigée-Lebrun's costume – a dress *en chemise* and straw hat – evokes that sported by fashionable women of the 1780s and particularly associated with the queen and her circle at Trianon.

Vigée-Lebrun's self-image, like the one she would make in 1790 (Uffizi, Florence) for the Grand Duke of Tuscany's gallery of artists' self-portraits, advertises her association with Marie-Antoinette. Her position as a favoured painter to the queen had been won partly by social contacts, but more significantly by the approval of the queen's mother, the Habsburg empress Maria Teresa. As her correspondence indicates, throughout the 1770s Maria Teresa was exasperated by her search for an official portrait of her daughter that pleased her. When Vigée-Lebrun's portrait of the queen in her official court dress (Kunsthistorisches Museum, Vienna) arrived in Vienna in April 1779, the empress, who was finally satisfied, wrote: "Your large portrait pleases me! [The Prince de] Ligne has found it resembling, but it is enough for me that it represents your face,

Vigée-Lebrun: *Marie-Antoinette with Her Children*, exhibited Salon of 1787; Palais de Versailles, Paris

with which I am quite happy" (letter from Maria Teresa to Marie-Antoinette, 1 April 1779).

Vigée-Lebrun was called on over the years to make many images of the queen. The most famous was the portrait of *Marie-Antoinette with Her Children* (see illustration), a piece of royal propaganda calculated to present the queen in a positive light. The image is significant not only because executed on a monumental scale, but also as the first and only work from Vigée-Lebrun commissioned through official channels – through the Bâtiments du Roi. In fact, this portrait was the only work in the 18th century that the Bâtiments commissioned from a woman. Thoroughly politicised, the image appeared at the Salon of 1787, where it was praised by royalist supporters and denounced by many oppositional critics. Less obviously political, but more controversial, was the image of the queen *en chemise* shown four years earlier (private collection, Germany; autograph copy, National Gallery of Art, Washington, DC). This portrait so outraged a segment of the public that Vigée-Lebrun was forced to remove it from the Salon. What shocked that public was the costume *en chemise*.

Imported from England in the 1780s, the robe *en chemise* was made from sheer white muslin fastened down the back and caught at the waist with a sash. The underskirt and corset, which ordinarily showed through the transparent muslin, were often of blue or pink silk, as in Vigée-Lebrun's *Self-Portrait* shown in 1783. Although the style was immensely popular in Britain, where it suggested the "natural woman", in France formalities of court made it less acceptable. For public appearances the *robe en chemise* was considered immodest, even though it revealed far less of the body than traditional court dresses. More significantly, the portrait *en chemise* shows Marie-Antoinette not as the king's consort, or in relation to a position at court, but as the queen of Trianon, her private domain in the grounds of Versailles. Indeed, the dress *en chemise* signalled the circle of women that Marie-Antoinette drew around her at Trianon, and whom libels such as the *Portefeuille d'un talon rouge* characterised as the "tribades of Trianon". In fact, slurs directed at Vigée-Lebrun's portrait articulated the most common themes of the libels emanating from the court: the queen's foreign character, her extravagant spending and uncontrolled sexuality. The portrait opened itself to these libels not simply because it showed Marie-Antoinette *en chemise* but because it showed the queen in an official public setting – the king's art exhibition – in a private role. If at the Salon of 1783 Vigée-Lebrun claimed a public role as a history painter, she allowed the queen the right to pose publicly as a private individual.

Although she aspired to a public role, it is as a painter of private individuals that Vigée-Lebrun has become best known. During her lifetime she was sought precisely because she made pleasing images of women both as society ladies and good mothers. Her most convincing works of the first sort include the *Lady Folding a Letter* (1784; Toledo Museum of Art, OH) and the portraits of the *Duchesse de Polignac* (1783; National Trust, Waddesdon Manor) and *Marquise de Jaucourt* (1789; Metropolitan Museum of Art, New York); and among her most striking representations of motherhood are the portrait of the *Marquise de Pezé and the Marquise de Rouget with Her Two Children* (1787; National Gallery of Art, Washington,

DC) and her self-portrait called *Maternal Tenderness* (1787; Louvre); the last was Vigée-Lebrun's most popular painting at the Salon of 1787, and critics praised the work lavishly for the sentiment it expressed. The artist also represented women in coquettish allegorical disguise, as in the portrait of the *Duchesse de Gramont as a Grape Gatherer* (1784; Nelson-Atkins Museum of Art, Kansas City). Although reputed to be a painter of women, Vigée-Lebrun throughout her career executed compelling, lively and original portraits of men, as her images of *Alexandre Charles Emmanuel de Crussol-Florensac* (1787; Metropolitan Museum of Art), *Hubert Robert* (1787; Louvre) and the *Count Shuvaloff* (North Carolina Museum of Art, Raleigh) so well demonstrate.

Indeed, Vigée-Lebrun worked for private patrons both in France before the Revolution and during her years of exile. Her years of exile, moreover, repeatedly challenged her to locate new clients, establish new studios and find her place in social and artistic circles as she moved from Italy to Germany to Austria to Russia. Her works during these years sometimes repeat paradigms that she had already established in France; for example, her portrait of Marie-Antoinette's sister, *Marie-Thérèse* (Musée Condé, Chantilly), painted in Italy in 1790, strongly recalls in costume, pose and bearing her images of the French queen, while her portrait of the *Princess A.P. Golitsyna with Her Son* (Pushkin Museum, Moscow), executed in Vienna in 1794, is modelled on the highly succesful *Maternal Tenderness*. Other images made in France are reconstituted for elite women of all nationalities for whom it was fashionable to masquerade in the imagined dress of a culture thought exotic. With some changes here and there, the *Portrait of a Lady* (1789; National Gallery of Art, Washington, DC), which shows a turbaned woman in costume *à la turque* seated on a divan, her right arm bent and resting on a pillow, her left arm extended, becomes her image of the *Comtesse Skavronskaia* (Musée Jacquemart-André, Paris), painted in Naples in 1790. In addition to repeating these portrait-types while in exile, Vigée-Lebrun also established more "modern" sorts of representations, some of which had been presaged by work in France.

By 1790 many of her portraits were set out of doors, and early on Vigée-Lebrun worked with a type that would become a norm in later Romantic portrait painting. Her portrait of the *Comtesse de Buquoi* (1793; Minneapolis Art Institute), for example, positions the sitter on a hillock in an autumnal landscape suggestive of scenery along the Danube, and her earlier portrait of *Madame du Barry* (1789; Musée Lambinet, Versailles) shows the ageing royal mistress reading in an overgrown garden setting. With works such as the portraits of *Countess Golovine* (c.1798; Barber Institute of Fine Arts, University of Birmingham) and *Varvara Ivanovna Narishkine* (1800; Gallery of Fine Arts, Columbus, OH), Vigée-Lebrun also developed the close-up portrait focused on the sitter's intense gaze and expression, a type that became popular in the first half of the 19th century.

Vigée-Lebrun's most ambitious "romantic" portrait, however, is her representation of Madame de Staël as the title character of her novel *Corinne; ou, L'Italie* (1807). The peripatetic Vigée-Lebrun journeyed to Switzerland (one of many trips after her repatriation), to Madame de Staël's château at Coppet, to render her subject from life. In the final portrait

(1808; Musée d'Art et d'Histoire, Geneva) Madame de Staël plays the improvisational poet-sibyl Corinne in the midst of an inspired performance. The work evokes a specific moment in the story when Corinne performs an improvisation in the Neapolitan countryside, but it also represents the dramatic tensions evident in the novel. Like her character Corinne, the expressive Madame de Staël embodies what much late 18th-century thinking conceptualised as a natural, sublime force – a singular genius.

Madame de Staël as Corinne is one of Vigée-Lebrun's most challenging works, and the challenge comes not only from showing a female poet in conventions usually reserved for the male genius (and especially Homer and Ossian), but also – and perhaps more forcefully – from offering viewers a flawed and expressive Madame de Staël where they expect a perfect and idealised woman. Vigée-Lebrun presents the sitter as a monumental figure with sculptural limbs, large, expressive features – and a markedly individualised physiognomy that is distinctly unlike the one Staël gives the beautiful Corinne. In the face of Corinne, Vigée-Lebrun's portrait suggests that Staël could have a profound influence on her audience, on her culture, even on history, without that quintessential signifier of femininity. Moreover, Vigée-Lebrun's monumental portrait reveals the effect of situating a woman in the pantheon of genius. This representation unmasks, without perhaps realising it, those grand illusions that have seemed natural idealisations when donned by men and ridiculous vanities when worn by women. Those illusions are not only inscribed on the sitter; they also mark the artist who conceptualised the image.

Vigée-Lebrun's portrait of Staël, like her struggle with the Academy and her reception by Salon critics, makes visible the barriers that prevented women who practised the arts at an extraordinary level of achievement from positioning themselves in the canon of great masters. For better or worse, their work could only spur other exceptional women. The father of Rosa Bonheur (q.v.) challenged his daughter not to compete with Poussin or David, but to surpass the most talented woman painter – Elisabeth Vigée-Lebrun.

MARY D. SHERIFF

See also Academies of Art survey

Vigri, Caterina [St Catherine of Bologna]

Italian painter and illuminator, *c*.1413–1463

Born in Bologna, *c*.1413; grew up in Ferrara. Entered Corpus Christi, Ferrara, a convent of Poor Clares, *c*.1427; professed *c*.1429–30. Appointed abbess of Corpus Domini, Bologna, 1456. Died in Bologna, 9 March 1463. Canonised 1712.

Selected Writings

Le sette armi spirituali (completed after 1456), ed. S. d'Aurizio, Bologna, 1981

Le sette armi spirituali (completed after 1456), ed. Cecilia Foletti, Padua: Antenore, 1985

Bibliography

Illuminata Bembo, *Lo specchio di illuminazione* (15th century), ed. S. d'Aurizio, Bologna, 1983

G.B. Melloni, *Atti o memorie degli uomini illustri in santità nati, o morti in Bologna*, i and iii, Bologna, 1818

I.B. Supino, *L'arte nelle chiese di Bologna, secoli XV–XVI*, ii, Bologna, 1838

Laura M. Ragg, *The Women Artists of Bologna*, London: Methuen, 1907

P. Lucius M. Nuñez OFM, "Descriptio breviarii manuscripti S. Catharinae Bononiensis O.S.CL", *Archivum Franciscanum Historicum*, iv, 1911, pp.732–47

La santa nella storia, nelle lettere e nell'arte, Bologna: Garagnani, 1912

F. Wormald, "A saint identified in a Lee picture", *Journal of the Warburg and Courtauld Institutes*, xxv, 1962, pp.129–30

R. Ricciardi, *Santa Caterina da Bologna*, Padua, 1963

Serena Spanò, "Per uno studio su Caterina da Bologna", *Studi Mediaevali*, 3rd series, xii, 1971, pp.713–59

Teodosio Lombardi, *I francescani a Ferrara*, iv, Bologna, 1975

Serena Spanò Martinelli, "La Biblioteca del 'Corpus Domini' bolognese: L'inconsueto spaccato di una cultura monastica femminile", *Bibliofilia*, lxxxviii, 1986, pp.1–23

J. Berrigan, "Catherine of Bologna: Franciscan mystic", *Women Writers of the Renaissance and Reformation*, ed. Katharina M. Wilson, Athens: University of Georgia Press, 1987, pp.81–95

F. Cardini, "Santa Caterina da Bologna e il trattato *Le sette armi spirituali*", *Studi Francescane*, lxxxvi, 1989, pp.53–64

Jeryldene M. Wood, *Women, Art and Spirituality: The Poor Clares of Early Modern Italy*, Cambridge: Cambridge University Press, 1996

Known to posterity as St Catherine of Bologna, Caterina Vigri actually spent most of her life in Ferrara. While she was born in Bologna and died there in 1463, she lived in Ferrara from early childhood until 1456 when she became abbess at the Corpus Domini, a Bolognese convent of Poor Clares. According to her first biographer Sister Illuminata Bembo, who knew the saint from about 1432, her father Giovanni Vigri was employed at the court of Niccolò d'Este in Ferrara, and Catherine served as a lady-in-waiting to Niccolò's daughter Margarita (Bembo 1983, p.100). After Margarita's marriage in 1427, Catherine entered a house of Poor Clares at Ferrara, the Corpus Christi, where she professed her vows *c*.1429–30 (for a recent study of the saint's life and writings, see *Le sette armi spirituali*, ed. Foletti 1985, pp.1–76). A series of visions and ecstasies established her reputation for sanctity; several of these were incorporated into her treatise *Le sette armi spirituali*, which was completed after her transfer to the Corpus Domini in Bologna and made public only on her deathbed.

Eighteen days after Catherine's burial, a sweet odour emanating from her grave led to the exhumation of her corpse. Probably sketched at this time, a portrait attributed to Bembo records the pale, ascetic features of the abbess (chalk and gold on paper; Corpus Domini, Bologna, repr. Ricciardi 1963, fig.12). A popular cult soon developed around Catherine's incorrupt body, which was exhibited to visitors at the nun's communion window in the Corpus Domini until the construction of a separate chapel (see Wormald 1962, p.129). The present Cappella della Santa in the same church dates to the late 17th century, when the chamber was remodelled in anticipation of Catherine's long-awaited canonisation in 1712.

Whether Catherine received her artistic training at court or in the convent is uncertain. Bembo claimed that she was educated at the d'Este court; like other upper-class young women of this era, she would have studied grammar, history, poetry, scripture, Latin, some rhetoric and perhaps music (she played a small violin) and drawing (see M. King and A. Rabil, *Her Immaculate Hand*, Binghamton, NY, 1983, p.15). Yet it may well be that Catherine learned her craft in the scriptorium of the Corpus Christi; for according to Bembo, she chanted poems of her own composition as she painted numerous images of the swaddled Infant Christ on the walls of the convent. These murals are lost, but some sense of their appearance can be gleaned from the haloed *bambini* drawn in the margins of the breviary decorated during this period (c.1438–52; conserved as a relic in Cappella della Santa, Corpus Domini, Bologna, repr. *La Santa nella storia* 1912, p.57), and from a painted wooden plaque of the Christ Child wrapped in rich fabric (c.1456–63; Corpus Domini, repr. *Le sette armi spirituali*, ed. d'Aurizio 1981).

St Catherine's artistic practice cannot be separated from her experiences as a nun and a mystic, or from her work as a writer and a musician. She did not pursue a "professional" career like her contemporary, the Dominican friar Fra Angelico, who often worked on projects outside his friary in Florence. As a nun cloistered in an Observant Franciscan convent that followed a strict interpretation of St Clare's monastic rule, Catherine's activities were restricted. Her production cannot be evaluated by the criteria developed for male artists because she remained essentially an "amateur" painter: she did not undergo an apprenticeship, oversee a workshop or participate in ambitious commissions. Her style does not evolve; it retains the same direct and somewhat naive character throughout her career. Her oeuvre is relatively limited: four independent paintings (two on paper and two on panel); an illumination in *Le sette armi spirituali*, and the many decorated pages of her 519-page breviary; and the wooden *Christ Child* (the *St Ursula and Four Saints* formerly attributed to her in the Accademia, Venice, is now listed as workshop of Giovanni Bellini). Although Catherine was later named the patron saint of painters in Bologna, it is unclear whether her paintings were seen by outsiders during her lifetime. As far as we know, she did not create altarpieces for the public space of the Poor Clares' churches at either Ferrara or Bologna; she provided instead personal works for herself and her sisters.

St Catherine's art is best considered as a devotional activity akin to prayer. Bembo discloses that the abbess prayed and shed tears as she worked on her breviary, and that spiritual edification rather than artistic decoration was her purpose. The merging of text and image in the breviary fosters "the memory of the sweet Jesus", as on folio 10r, where the head of Christ appears in the capital letter of "Fratres" and a boy Christ in the V of "Verbum", as well as a chalice and host emerging at the centre of the simple foliage enframing the page (repr. *La santa nella storia* 1912, p.51). On the page for the feast of her patron saint, Catherine of Alexandria, the crowned head of the virgin-martyr in the capital letter of "Deus" resembles a 15th-century lady more than the Early Christian queen famed for her mystical marriage with Christ (fol.465r; repr. Nuñez 1911, p.746), and annotations referring to the "Most happy spouse of Christ" express the abbess's identification

Vigri: *Virgin and Child*; Convent of Corpus Domini, Bologna

with her namesake. Catherine's approach fuses painting, writing and spirituality, as on the vellum sheet inserted in *Le sette armi spirituali* (after fol.49v; Corpus Domini, repr. d'Aurizio 1981), where yearning for mystical union with Jesus informs the historiated capital letter of "Deus". There the tiny Poor Clare (perhaps a self-portrait) gazing at the Crucified Saviour offers a visual parallel to a line in one of Catherine's poems: "O sweet Fruit of Mary, when I am finally lost in You, making melody within your side …".

Despite the vivid recollections of visions in *Le sette armi spirituali*, Catherine does not reproduce specific mystical events in her visual art. Her paintings focus on the epiphanies experienced during ecstasy (especially the doctrine of the Incarnation, which was clarified for her in a vision) and thereby function as devotional guides to assist spiritual enlightenment. The medium, small scale and delicate brushwork of her paintings promote personal study and meditation. In her *Redeemer* (tempera on paper; Corpus Domini, repr. Ricciardi 1963, fig.4) roundels containing the angel Gabriel and the Annunciate Virgin denote the Incarnate Christ, who stands below blessing with one hand and displaying an open book with the other. Encircled by golden rays and attired in a white dalmatic sprinkled with gold stars, the Redeemer embodies the light of wisdom inscribed on his book: "In me is all the grace of the way and of the truth; in me is all hope of life and of virtue" (Ecclesiasticus, xxiv:25).

The lavish gold, bright colours and flat, stylised figures of Catherine's paintings indicate that even after three decades of claustration she continued to assimilate memories of secular life into her monastic experience. The affection shared by Mary and Christ in a half-length *Virgin and Child* (see illustration) charms in spite of the awkward anatomies; indeed, the courtly elegance of the panel resembles the Gothic style of the north Italian artists Pisanello and Jacopo Bellini, who worked for the d'Este in the first half of the 15th century.

Catherine's paintings offer a glimpse of female monastic attitudes towards the visual arts in early modern Italy. Exhibited in the Cappella della Santa, her *Madonna del Pomo* (repr. *Le sette armi spirituali*, ed. d'Aurizio 1981) represents Mary and her Son garbed in expensive brocade and wearing gold crowns. The paradoxical juxtaposition of their royal splendour and the humble brown habit worn by the miraculously preserved Catherine intimates that through their denial of material comforts in this life, the nuns hoped to enjoy eternal bliss in a celestial court.

JERYLDENE M. WOOD

Visscher, Anna Roemersdochter, 1584–1651, and Maria Tesselschade, 1592–1649
Dutch amateur artists

Anna Roemersdochter Visscher Born in Amsterdam, 1584, eldest daughter of Roemer Pieterszoon Visscher, merchant and man of letters, and of Aefgen Jansdochter Onderwater. Married Dominicus Boot van Wesel, 11 February 1624; two sons. Converted to Catholicism with her husband, c.1640. Died in Amsterdam, 6 December 1651.

Maria Tesselschade Visscher Born 25 March 1592. Married naval officer Allert Janszoon Crombalch, 20 November 1623; husband and eldest daughter both died 29 May 1634. Converted to Catholicism shortly after 1640. Buried 24 June 1649.

(A third sister, Truyte Visscher, who was four years younger than Anna, was also active in the arts before her marriage to a brewer, Claes van Buyl, in 1609.)

Bibliography

J. Scheltema, *Anna en Maria Tesselschade, de dochters van Roemer Visscher*, Amsterdam, 1808

D. H. de Castro, "Eén en ander over glasgravure" [Glass-engraving miscellanea], *Oud-Holland*, i, 1883, pp.290–91

R. Schmidt, "Die gerissenen und puynktierten Holländischen Gläser", *Der Cicerone*, iii, 1911, pp.817–29

F. Hudig, "Graveerwerk van Anna Roemers Visscher" [The engraved work of Anna Roemers Visscher], *Oud-Holland*, xli, 1923–4, pp.175–83

M. Sauerlandt, "Ein Roemer von Anna Roemers Visscher im Museum für Kunst und Gewerbe in Hamburg", *Oud-Holland*, xlii, 1925, pp.109–10

Maurits Sabbe, "De Antwerpsche vriendenkring van Anna Roemers Visscher" [Anna Roemers Visscher's Antwerp circle], *Plantin de Moretussen en hun kring: Verspreide opstellen door Dr Maurits Sabbe* [The Moretuses and their circle: Miscellaneous essays by Dr Maurits Sabbe], Brussels: Kryn, 1926, pp.53–73

M. Pelliot, "Verres gravés au diamant", *Gazette des Beaux-Arts*, lxxii, 1930, pp.318–19

——, "Verres hollandais", *Revue de l'Art Ancien et Moderne*, lxx, 1936, pp.80–83

A. van Buchell, *Notae quotidianae*, 3rd series, lxx, 1940, p.71

M. A. Heukensfeldt-Jansen, "Noord-Nederlandsch glas van de 17e en 18e eeuw" [Northern Netherlandish glass of the 17th and 18th centuries], *Historia*, x, 1944, pp.241–50

I. Schlosser, *Das Glas: Ein Handbuch für Sammler und Liebhaber, Bibliothek für Kunst und Antiquitätenfreunde*, xxxvi, Braunschweig, 1965

Letter-Juweel [Letter-jewel], facsimile, ed. E. W. de Kruyter, Amsterdam, 1971

M. A. Schenkeveld-van der Dussen, "Anna Roemers Visscher: De tiende van de negen, de vierde van de drie" [Anna Roemers Visscher: The tenth of the nine, the fourth of the three], *Jaarboek van de Maatschappij der Nederlandse Letterkunde (1979–1980)*, Leiden, 1981, pp.3–14

Katlijne Van der Stighelen, "Anna Maria van Schurman 'die de wetenschap had, met eenen diamant op het glas geestig te schrijven'" [Anna Maria van Schurman, "who knew how to write wittily on glass with a diamond"], *Antiek*, xix, 1985, pp.513–23

——, *Anna Maria van Schurman (1607–1678) of "Hoe hooge dat een maeght kan in de konsten stijgen"* [Anna Maria van Schurman (1607–1678) or "How high a maid may rise in art"], Louvain: Universitaire Pers Leuven, 1987

F. G. A. M. Smit, "Anna Roemers and Maria Tesselschade and their engravings on glass", manuscript, Peterborough, 1990

Mieke Smits-Veldt, *Maria Tesselschade: Leven met talent en vriendschap* [Maria Tesselschade: A life of talent and friendship], Zutphen, 1994

A. Agnes Sneller and Olga van Marion, eds, *De gedichten van Tesselschade Roemers* [The verses on Tesselschade's Roemers], Hilversum, 1994

Of the three Visscher sisters, it is Anna and Tesselschade who are still remembered as women of exceptional ability. In December 1612 the polyglot Ernst Brinck visited the "Roemerhuis" in Amsterdam. He wrote: "Ro[e]mer ... has three daughters, all of whom have many accomplishments, being expert in music, painting, glass-cutting or engraving, composing verses and devising emblems. They do all kinds of embroidery and can also swim well ...". From a purely artistic point of view, Anna Roemers was the most productive. As early as 1599, one of her works had become the subject of a eulogy, namely the sonnet by the Hoorn physician P. Hogerbeerts: "To Little Anna Roemers on the horn of plenty with the motto 'Obedientibus ...'".

We do not know the medium in which this cornucopia was executed, though the sonnet gives us some idea of her artistic activity at what was a fairly young age. Of the sisters' education nothing is known, but from their early adulthood their talent for poetry, knowledge of languages (Anna knew French, Italian and Latin), musical abilities and skill of hand seem to have attracted attention. The techniques they used were those commonly practised by amateurs, such as calligraphy (on paper and glass) and embroidery. In 1620 Rubens dedicated an engraving by Lucas Vorsterman after his own version of the "chaste Susanna" to Anna, for which she thanked him with a poem. In a poem of 1623 Joost van den Vondel observed that in Anna's house paintings from her hand were also to be seen. None of these survive, though examples of her works in lesser genres are preserved. Anna attributed her reputation above all to contact with the eminent men of letters who were also associates of her father. In 1616 Daniël Heinsius dedicated a eulogy to her: "Goddess, born by the waters of the Amstel, dearly beloved of Phoebus, the elect of Pallas, Born I suppose, and many so believe, not from your mother's womb, but from your father's head", lines that imply wonder at the coincidence of femininity on the one hand and of art and learning on the other. A similar note of wonder is to be found in the dedication to Jacob Cats's *Maechden-plicht* (A Maiden's Duty) of 1618, in which she is described as virtuous, honourable and a talented artist, and is dubbed "the tenth of the nine Muses".

A year later, in *Silenus Alcibiadis*, Cats explicitly praised her poetry and calligraphy. In the same year, 1619, Constantijn Huygens also made the sisters' acquaintance. On 3 May 1619 he wrote a little poem: "On the diamond stylus of Miss Anna Roemers". Two years later Pieter Cornelisz. Hooft, sheriff of Muiden, wrote a poem on the same theme: "You take delight in stippling glass with a diamond …", comparing her work with that of butterflies. Both before and after her marriage glass engraving was the technique to which Anna most applied herself. That she continued her artistic activity after her marriage is confirmed by a competition held by the "Nederduytsche Academie" in 1630, in which the first prize was a *princenroemer* "On which Pallas [alias Anna Visscher] with her diamond engraved the marshal of the land …". Balthasar Moretus, in a letter to Bartholomeus de los Rios of 4 November 1640, remarked of Anna "… nam et scribere et pingere accurate novit" (she renewed both calligraphy and painting). Her fame continued unabated, as is evident from the presentation to her, on 14 November 1643, of a silver dish from the Antwerp magistrature, as thanks for an engraved chalice and a laudatory poem that she had dedicated to the city.

The only works by Anna Visscher that survive and that can be ascribed to her with certainty are four glasses with calligraphic inscriptions. The Rijksmusem has a green *roemer* with the inscription "TO Constantinus Huÿgens", a second green *roemer* (see illustration) with the Italian inscription "Bella DORI gentil (…)" and a *berkemeier* inscribed "Vincens tui". The Museum für Kunst und Gewerbe in Hamburg has a *berkemeier* with the inscription "Enough is better than too much". In addition to these are a few glasses whose present whereabouts are unknown. A further example, a *roemer* with the inscription "Pacifici Beati Sunt", formerly in the Museum Boijmans Van Beuningen, Rotterdam, was broken in 1939. Besides these, 20 literary references to examples of her glass calligraphy are known. Anna Visscher's merit lies chiefly in her introduction of a more naturalistic style of ornament that is mostly derived from botanical manuals. It seems that she was also the first in the Netherlands to apply the technique of stipple-engraving to glass, a technical innovation whose chief contribution was the creation of new possibilities for the representation of areas of shade. Around 1640 she and her husband converted to Catholicism, which to some extent distanced them from the milieu they had hitherto frequented.

Literary sources also make it possible to connect about a dozen glasses with Maria Tesselschade Visscher, who may have learned the technique from her sister. On the occasion of her marriage to the naval officer Allert Janszoon Crombalch in 1623, Pieter Corneliszoon Hooft composed the following lines: "When she takes up the diamond and makes a scratch with it, The dumb glass speaks". As yet only two glasses can be traced. The Rijksmuseum has a green *roemer* with the calligraphic inscription "A demain les affaires", as well as a second *roemer* bearing the quotation "Sic soleo amicos". In May 1637 Caspar Barlaeus remarked in a letter to Hooft that he rated Tessel's

Visscher: A light green *roemer* with Italian inscription; Rijksmuseum, Amsterdam

intellect above that of Anna Maria van Schurman (q.v.): unlike the latter, she did not smell of "schoolmastering". Shortly after 1640, Tessel, like Anna, converted to Catholicism.

The young women were brought up in the spirit of the Renaissance, in which painting, drawing, embroidery and calligraphy on paper, parchment or glass were seen as specifically feminine techniques. The activities in which they engaged were those of the amateur, having no professional end but developed rather as "leisure-pursuits". In this respect the sisters' manual skills may be usefully compared with their musical education. Anna played the flute, lute and perhaps also the viola da gamba; Maria Tesselschade played the lute, viola de gamba and harpsichord, and was particularly celebrated for her singing.

KATLIJNE VAN DER STIGHELEN

von Malachowski, Marie *see* Malachowski

von Motesiczky, Marie-Louise *see* Motesiczky

Vonnoh, Bessie Onahotema Potter
American sculptor, 1872–1955

Born Bessie Onahotema Potter in St Louis, Missouri, 17 August 1872; grew up in Chicago. Studied at the Art Institute of Chicago under Lorado Taft, 1886 and 1889–91. Opened own studio in Chicago, 1894. Visited Paris, meeting Rodin, 1895. Married painter Robert Vonnoh, 1899; he died 1933. Lived in New York, also spending time at summer house in Lyme, Connecticut, and in Grez-sur-Loing, south of Paris. Married urologist Edward Keyes, 1948; he died 1949. Member, National Sculpture Society, 1899; Society of American Artists, 1904; National Institute of Arts and Letters, 1931. Associate member, 1906 (first woman sculptor), and member, 1921, National Academy of Design. Died in New York, 8 March 1955.

Principal Exhibitions

Art Institute of Chicago: occasionally 1891–1939 (annuals), 1914 (individual)
Society of American Artists, New York: occasionally 1894–1904 (Julia A. Shaw memorial prize 1904)
National Sculpture Society, New York: 1895, 1898, 1908 (Baltimore), 1923, 1929 (San Francisco)
Exposition Universelle, Paris: 1900 (bronze medal)
Pan-American Exposition, Buffalo, NY: 1901 (honourable mention)
Louisiana Purchase Exposition, St Louis: 1904 (gold medal)
National Academy of Design, New York: occasionally 1905–1945 (Elizabeth N. Watrous gold medal 1921)
Corcoran Gallery of Art, Washington, DC: 1910, 1919 (both individual)
Brooklyn Institute of Arts and Sciences (now Brooklyn Museum), NY: 1913 (individual)
Montross Galleries, New York: 1913 (with Robert Vonnoh)
Panama-Pacific International Exposition, San Francisco: 1915 (silver medal)

Selected Writings

"Tears and laughter caught in bronze", The Delineator, cvii, October 1925, pp.8–9, 78, 80, 82

Bibliography

Arthur Hoeber, "A new note in American sculpture: Statuettes by Bessie Potter", Century Magazine, liv, 1897, pp.732–5
Lucy Monroe, "Bessie Potter", Brush and Pencil, ii, April 1898, pp.29–36
Elizabeth Anna Semple, "The art of Bessie Potter Vonnoh", Pictorial Review, xii, April 1911, pp.12–13
Janis Conner and Joel Rosenkranz, Rediscoveries in American Sculpture: Studio Works, 1893–1939, Austin: University of Texas Press, 1989
Charlotte Streifer Rubinstein, American Women Sculptors, Boston: Hall, 1990
Julie Aronson, Bessie Potter Vonnoh (1872–1955) and Small Bronze Sculpture in America, PhD dissertation, University of Delaware, Newark, 1995

A collection of the artist's papers is in the Archives of American Art, Smithsonian Institution, Washington, DC.

Although she belonged to a generation of sculptors who generally aspired to create ambitious monumental public sculpture, Bessie Onahotema Potter Vonnoh opted instead for an individual career path. Determined to create art that would speak a universal language, she pursued themes that appealed to a broad audience and produced sculpture for the home at a price middle-class patrons could afford. Her efforts coincided neatly with those of the National Sculpture Society, founded in 1893 with the express aim of popularising sculpture among a mass audience to encourage patronage and cultivate an appreciation of sculpture.

Vonnoh's studies at the Art Institute of Chicago under the French-trained Lorado Taft and her employment as his assistant on the sculpture of the World's Columbian Exposition of 1893 provided a thorough education in current Beaux-Arts methods and theories. Although trained to sculpt full-size works, Vonnoh soon discovered an exceptional penchant for modelling on an intimate scale. Inspired by freely executed bronzes by Paul Troubetzkoy in the Italian display at the Fair, Vonnoh began modelling portrait statuettes of friends, which, although nearly all untraced, are thought to have measured from about 35 to 48 centimetres in height. The artist had these statuettes cast only in plaster then tinted them with colours; the sole located example, An American Girl (1895; Amon Carter Museum, Fort Worth, TX), a casually seated figure of a young woman in contemporary dress, is gently coloured pale mauve with rose madder. Even Vonnoh's early works, such as this one, reveal her characteristically fluid, lively and delicate modelling. The painter Jean-François Raffaelli dubbed her "an impressionist in plaster" both for her modelling, which is more suggestive than descriptive, and for her adoption of the everyday themes preferred by the Impressionist painters. She later claimed: "What I wanted was to look for beauty in the everyday world, to catch the joy and swing of modern American life, using the methods of the Greeks but not their subject-matter" ("Tears and laughter caught in bronze", 1925, p.9).

In 1896, one year after her first trip to Paris, Vonnoh created A Young Mother (see illustration), the sculpture that announced her maturity and firmly secured her reputation. A rendering of a mother in a rocking chair cradling her slumbering infant, the intimate group is rich in observed details such as the dropping of the dozing baby's head heavily against the mother's arm. Critics admired Vonnoh's sculpture for its air of frank truthfulness. The turn of the mother's head and the direction of her gaze as it tenderly rests upon her child evoke a sensation of serene harmony, enhanced by the graceful and uninterrupted flow of lines and forms. First cast in bronze by the Henry-Bonnard Bronze Company in 1899, A Young Mother was among the first of Vonnoh's works to be produced in multiple versions and would remain among the artist's most popular sculptures.

The universal nature of the age-old theme of motherhood held a powerful attraction for Vonnoh. Deemed the leading American sculptor of the subject, she explored maternity further in Motherhood (Pennsylvania Academy of the Fine Arts, Philadelphia) and Enthroned (Corcoran Gallery of Art, Washington, DC), both dating from 1902. In each sculpture a mother is surrounded by three children of differing ages, suggesting progressive phases of childhood. Compositions such as these demonstrate Vonnoh's remarkable ability to create an impression of monumentality in works of small size.

Throughout her career, Vonnoh maintained a fascination with dance. In 1897 she modelled the popular Girl Dancing (Metropolitan Museum of Art), a figure of a young woman in early 19th-century costume engaged in social dancing with an

Vonnoh was one of a number of artists at the turn of the century to alert Americans to the beauty of small bronze sculpture. Her most significant contribution was in her perceptive and nuanced renderings of contemporary women and children. As American women sculptors continued to encounter difficulties in breaking into the male arena of the monument, the efforts of pioneers such as Bessie Vonnoh and Janet Scudder (q.v.) made the fields of small bronzes and garden statuary ones in which women could enjoy successful careers as sculptors.

JULIE ARONSON

von Rappard, Clara *see* Rappard

von Rydingsvard, Ursula
American sculptor, 1942–

Born in Deensen, Germany, 26 July 1942. Emigrated to USA with her family, 1950, settling in Plainfield, Connecticut. Studied at University of New Hampshire, Durham, 1960–62; University of Miami, Coral Gables, 1962–5 (BA, MA); University of California, Berkeley, 1969–70; Columbia University, New York, 1973–5 (MFA). Subsequently assistant professor, Pratt Institute, Brooklyn, New York, 1978–82; instructor, School of Visual Arts, New York, 1981–2; assistant professor, Fordham University, Bronx, 1980–82; associate professor, Yale University, New Haven, 1982–6; professor of sculpture, graduate division, School of Visual Arts, 1986. Married Paul Greengard, 1985 (second marriage); one daughter from previous marriage born 1969. Recipient of National Endowment for the Arts (NEA) grants, 1979 and 1986; Creative Artists Public Service (CAPS) grant, 1980; Guggenheim fellowship, 1983; honorary doctorate, Maryland Institute College of Art, Baltimore, 1991; Sculpture award, American Academy of Arts and Letters, 1994. Lives in New York.

Selected Individual Exhibitions
55 Mercer, New York: 1977, 1979, 1980
Rosa Esman Gallery, New York: 1981, 1982
Hillwood Art Gallery, Long Island University, Greenvale, NY: 1985 (with Judith Murray)
Laumeier Sculpture Park, St Louis: 1988, 1990 (with Vito Acconci)
Exit Art, New York: 1988
Cranbrook Art Museum, Bloomfield Hills, MI: 1989
Capp Street Project, San Francisco: 1990
Lorence Monk Gallery, New York: 1990, 1991
Centre for Contemporary Art, Ujazdowski Castle, Warsaw, Poland: 1992
Storm King Art Center, Mountainville, NY: 1992
Galerie Lelong, New York: 1994
Weatherspoon Art Gallery, Greensboro, NC: 1994

Selected Writings
"Thoughts about my work", *Issue: A Journal for Artists*, vi, Spring 1986, pp.45–7

Vonnoh: *A Young Mother*, 1896; bronze; Metropolitan Museum of Art, New York, Rogers Fund, 1906

unseen partner. The sculptor would become increasingly preoccupied with the movement of the uncorseted female body, portraying women in clinging draperies in works such as *The Dance* (c.1909; Corcoran Gallery of Art) and later nude, as in the group of three dancers entitled *Allegresse* (1920; Detroit Institute of Arts). Vonnoh's portrayals of dance contributed to the frequent comparison of her sculpture to the Tanagra figurines of Hellenistic Greece, small terracotta statuettes of women, often shown dancing.

Taking advantage of the demand for art to adorn the estates of wealthy Americans, in 1913 Vonnoh created her first garden sculpture, *Water Lilies* (Brookgreen Gardens, SC), a charming figure of a pert little girl perched on a rock and grasping a drooping water lily. The production of garden statuary became her principal occupation in the 1920s. A close friend to several of the foremost natural scientists in the country, Vonnoh was commissioned by the National Audubon Society to create a fountain for a bird sanctuary in honour of Theodore Roosevelt at Oyster Bay, New York (1923–7). Her composition consists of two children – a young boy seated at the feet of a standing girl with willowy proportions – offering food and drink to animals and birds. She designed a similar pairing of figures for the *Frances Hodgson Burnett Memorial* (1926–37) in Central Park, New York, but with a vague mythological reference to a young nymph and piping Pan. These two important commissions served as the culmination of Vonnoh's long career.

Bibliography

Ursula von Rydingsvard, exh. cat., Bette Stoler Gallery, New York, 1984

Judith Murray: Painting/Ursula von Rydingsvard: Sculpture, exh. cat., Hillwood Art Gallery, Long Island University, Greenvale, NY, 1985

Home Show, exh. cat., Santa Barbara Contemporary Arts Forum, CA, 1988

Ursula von Rydingsvard, exh. cat., Exit Art, New York, 1988

Avis Berman, "Ursula von Rydingsvard: Life under siege", *Art News*, lxxxvii, December 1988, pp.97–8

Ursula von Rydingsvard, exh. cat., Cranbrook Art Museum, Bloomfield Hills, MI, 1989

Jill Viney, "A rich, redemptive journey", *Sculpture*, viii, November–December 1989, pp.32–25

Out of Wood: Recent Sculpture, exh. cat., Whitney Museum of American Art, New York, 1990

Charlotte Streifer Rubinstein, *American Women Sculptors*, Boston: Hall, 1990

Ursula von Rydingsvard and Vito Acconci: Sculpture at Laumeier, exh. cat., Laumeier Sculpture Park, St Louis, 1990

Ursula von Rydingsvard: Sculpture, exh. cat., Centre for Contemporary Art, Ujazdowski Castle, Warsaw, Poland, 1992

Ursula von Rydingsvard: Sculpture, exh. cat., Storm King Art Center, Mountainville, NY, 1992

David Levi Strauss, "Sculpture as refuge", *Art in America*, lxxxi, February 1993, pp.88–93, 125

Eight Contemporary Sculptors: Beyond Nature: Wood into Art, exh. cat., Lowe Art Museum, Miami, 1994

Visions of America: Landscape as Metaphor in the Late Twentieth Century, exh. cat., Denver Art Museum, 1994

For more than 20 years, Ursula von Rydingsvard has explored the contradictory sensations of loss and sustenance and confinement and protection through monumental abstract sculptures of carved wood. Her work, which is characterised by architectural references, vigorously tactile surfaces and slow, laborious techniques, was seen at first as a reaction to the impersonality and perfect finish of Minimalism. Today, however, von Rydingsvard's sculptures are credited as "psychological and historical events" (Michael Brenson in Mountainville 1992, p.19) in their own right, chronicling the intimate drama of connections between generations of families and the emotional attachments to one's earliest environment. Von Rydingsvard was born to Polish parents in Germany, where her family spent the years 1942–50 in forced-labour and refugee camps before emigrating to the USA. Her objects and structures, which recall barns, barracks and tools, also evoke pews, altarpieces and other features of churches – the dominant images from her years as a displaced person in an occupied country. Yet these works, while brooding and sombre, are oddly comforting, haunting rather than despairing, stoic rather than sentimental. In constructions that enclose space, and so render a hostile world inhabitable, von Rydingsvard suggests how pain is mastered by endurance and close human ties.

In undergraduate and graduate school, von Rydingsvard studied painting and design. At Columbia University she studied with the painter and sculptor Ronald Bladen, whom she credits as an important influence on her life and work. Under Bladen's tutelage, von Rydingsvard fused sheets of welded steel with small steel beads made from heating a rod and dripping it on to the sheets as it melted. Perhaps the most significant aspect of this period was von Rydingsvard's discovery of a craft-oriented process for manipulating an industrial material and giving it a rich, hand-worked texture: she pierced the sheets with holes, sewed them together and shined them.

In 1975 a friend gave von Rydingsvard some cedar beams, and she used them to make a sculpture combining steel and wood. Working with wood was not only a revelation for her, but a way to by-pass Minimalism, a movement then in its heyday, but one that she distrusted because of its confidence in the artist's supreme ability to strip an object of its associations. "The Minimalists", she has stated, "were too antiseptic and too elegant ... for me. I wanted something that was more vernacular ... I like more the carnal, the physical presence of something rather than the implications of the presence" (Berman 1988, p.98).

Since 1975, beams of milled cedar ranging from 8 to 24 feet (2.43 to 7.3 m.) in length have been von Rydingsvard's primary medium. She stacks individual pieces into blocks and then carves, grinds, chisels, cuts, laminates, layers, glues, paints, stains or rubs the wood with graphite, using determinedly traditional tools: a circular hand-held saw, a circular grinder, a wood chisel and a mallet. Accordingly, her sculptures look scarred and furrowed, as if formed over a long period of time and then eroded. Von Rydingsvard considers her first mature work to be *Song of a Saint (Eulalia)* (1979; dismantled), a scattered procession of totem-like poles fabricated for an outdoor installation at Artpark in Lewiston, New York. (Despite her dissatisfaction with the philosophical assertions of Minimalism, von Rydingsvard has retained its emphasis on the rhythmic repetition of basic elements.) The installation marked the first time she was aware of making a physical impact on people with her sculpture. Von Rydingsvard has frequently worked outdoors on an ambitious scale ever since, saying: "I love working with the land, making relationships between my piece and the curves of ... [the] earth" (Maureen Megerian in Mountainville 1992, p.9).

Wood was the also the key to unlocking the autobiographical contents that von Rydingsvard needed to express: the sensations and images of her childhood in eastern Europe during and after World War II. Although von Rydingsvard's sculptures are never figurative, they allude to the human presence as much as they do to ploughed landscapes and vernacular architecture. *Ignatz Comes Home* (1986; artist's collection) is a hut-like structure that was occasioned by her father's leaving nursing home for a visit. The sculpture was based on the type of house he and his ancestors made with their own hands: the built environment stands in for human effort and creativity. Similarly, *Zakopane* (1987; artist's collection), named for a town in southeastern Poland, resembles a choir stall in a rural church and distills the artist's recollection of rows upon rows of peasant women praying intensely at Mass.

The steady interplay between sadness and solace that has been a hallmark of von Rydingsvard's work is amply demonstrated in *Untitled* (1988–9; see illustration), a group of 45 hollowed-out boxes commissioned for Laumeier Sculpture Park in St Louis, Missouri. The rectangular cedar tubs are laid out in five rows of nine, reminiscent of a barracks. The repetition is meant to convey the sense of marginalisation and sameness that von Rydingsvard links to the atmosphere of displaced persons' camps. If the exteriors of the boxes signal feelings of containment, the interiors speak of individuality. Each carved-out space can hide or cradle anyone who might climb in, and

von Rydingsvard: *Untitled*, 1988–9; Laumeier Sculpture Park, St Louis

these mini-sanctuaries are chopped and hacked with a rugged-ness contrasting with the smooth outer shell. Von Rydingsvard has said:

> Within this regimented grid the energetic excavation of the inside of these chambers is an effort toward fighting anonymity and establishing an identity in a place where one has little control over what happens in the future. It's the condition that a child finds itself in when it is in a system which it did not make, yet must exist in that system and find its own way. As aggressive as those inte-riors are, there is something that feels very human, very comforting – you can save yourself through making your own mark on the anonymous surface of life [unpublished interview with author, 1989].

In the early 1990s von Rydingsvard's sculpture became less overtly derived from the uncertainties of her childhood. She has drawn more on Greek sculpture as well as on non-Western sources of art, such as Oceanic and African art, in works suggesting boats, masks, bowls and ancient implements. She retains, however, the introspection and gravity of her earlier vision through her continued engagement with vernacular structures and their relationship to the land, the dignity of peasant culture, and the tools of the pre-industrial age.

AVIS BERMAN

von Sandrart, Susanna Maria *see* Sandrart

von Wiegand, Charmion

American painter, 1900–1983

Born in Chicago, Illinois, 1900; grew up in San Francisco. Attended Barnard College, Columbia University School of Journalism and Columbia University, New York. Began paint-ing, 1926. Moscow correspondent for Hearst newspapers, 1929–32. Married Joseph Freeman, novelist and journalist, 1932 (second marriage). Lived in New York. Editor of *Art Front*, the magazine of the Artists Union; wrote publicity for the Federal Art Project (FAP), and articles and art criticism for left-wing journal *New Masses* and other publications. Met Mondrian, 1941; wrote first American essay on his work and edited his writings in English. Associate member, 1941, member, 1947, and president, 1951–3, American Abstract Artists (AAA). Recipient of first prize, National Religious Art exhibition, Cranbrook Academy of Arts, Michigan, 1969; Hassam and Speicher Fund Purchase award, American Academy of Arts and Letters, 1980; honor award, National

Women's Caucus for Art, 1982. Died in New York, June 1983.

Selected Individual Exhibitions

Rose Fried Gallery ("The Pinacotheca"), New York: 1947, 1948
Saidenberg Gallery, New York: 1952
Howard Wise Gallery, New York: 1961 (retrospective), 1963, 1965
Richard Gray Gallery, Chicago: 1964
University of Texas Art Museum, Austin: 1969
Birmingham Art Museum, AL: 1970
Galleria Fiamma Vigo, Rome and Venice: 1973
Annely Juda Fine Art, London: 1974 (retrospective)
Noah Goldowsky Gallery, New York: 1974
Museum of Fine Arts, Springfield, MA: 1975
Marilyn Pearl Gallery, New York: 1978, 1981
Bass Museum of Art, Miami Beach: 1982 (retrospective)

Selected Writings

Masters of Abstract Art, exh. cat., New Art Center, New York, 1942 (editor, with Stephan C. Lion)
"The meaning of Mondrian", *Journal of Aesthetics and Art Criticism*, ii/8, 1943, pp.62–70
"The Russian arts", *Encyclopedia of the Arts*, ed. D.D. Runes and H.G. Schrickel, New York: Philosophical Library, 1945
"The oriental tradition and abstract art", *The World of Abstract Art*, New York: Wittenborn, 1957, pp.55–68
"The vision of Mark Tobey", *Arts Magazine*, xxxiii, September 1959, pp.34–41
"Georges Vantongerloo", *Arts Magazine*, xxxiv, September 1960, pp.40–45
"Mondrian: A memoir of his New York period", *Arts Yearbook*, no.4, New York: Art Digest, 1961, p.57
"Introduction", *The Art of Tibet*, New York: American Federation of Arts, 1969
"The Adamantine way", *Art News*, April 1969, pp.38–41

Bibliography

Paul Cummings "Charmion von Wiegand", unpublished interview transcript, Archives of American Art, Smithsonian Institution, Washington, DC, 9 October 1958
Virginia Pitts Rembert, *Mondrian, America and American Painting*, PhD dissertation, Columbia University, New York, 1970
Three American Purists: Mason/Miles/von Wiegand, exh. cat., Museum of Fine Arts, Springfield, MA, 1975
Paris – New York, exh. cat., Musée National d'Art Moderne, Centre Georges Pompidou, Paris, 1977
The Circle of Charmion von Wiegand, documentary film, narrated and produced by Ce Roser, 1978
Constructivism and the Geometric Tradition: Selections from the McCrory Corporation Collection, exh. cat., Albright-Knox Art Gallery, Buffalo, and elsewhere, 1979
Mondrian and Neo-Plasticism in America, exh. cat., Yale University Art Gallery, New Haven, 1979
Charmion von Wiegand: Her Art and Life, exh. cat., Bass Museum of Art, Miami Beach, 1982
Virginia Pitts Rembert, "Charmion von Wiegand's way beyond Mondrian", *Woman's Art Journal*, iv/2, 1983–4, pp.30–34
Charmion von Wiegand: In Search of the Spiritual, exh. cat., Hartford Art School, West Hartford, and University of Hartford, CT, 1993

The legacy of Charmion von Wiegand is one of writer, editor, advocate and artist. Following in the footsteps of her father, a foreign news correspondent, she initially pursued a career as a journalist, but eventually left the Columbia University School of Journalism to pursue the study of art history and archaeology at Columbia. In 1926 von Wiegand began painting

von Wiegand: *White, Red and Blue Planes*, 1952; gouache and graphite on matte board; 33 × 33 cm.; Collection of Elton and Penny Yasuna

seriously while undergoing psychoanalysis. In her Greenwich Village studio she painted expressionist, religiously inspired works. Since she had no formal training she relied on the advice of painter friends, Joseph Stella and Jules Pascin. Between 1929 and 1932, while living in Moscow as a newspaper correspondent, von Wiegand also painted landscapes. On her return to New York she married the novelist Joseph Freeman, co-founder of the left-wing journal *New Masses*, and later of the *Partisan Review*, and continued her writing activities. At the same time a growing passion for abstract art led her to review the first American Abstract Artists (AAA) exhibition in 1937.

Von Wiegand's attraction to the practitioners and social philosophies of abstract art prompted her to seek out Piet Mondrian, who had arrived in New York in October 1940. In the spring of 1941 the American artist Carl Holty, a friend of von Wiegand's, arranged for her to meet Mondrian. By that summer she was spending several days each week with him, preparing an article (later published in the *Journal of Aesthetics*), editing his essays in English for publication and studying his paintings.

Von Wiegand's writing and painting informed and influenced each other. In 1941 she joined the AAA as an associate member, exhibiting in their annual shows from 1947, even heading the organisation from 1951 to 1953. She edited the catalogue for the *Masters of Abstract Art* exhibition, which included works by both American and European artists. Her dual role as artist and advocate was best demonstrated in 1947 when she both exhibited in her first solo show at the renowned Rose Fried Gallery, "The Pinacotheca", and organised a Kurt Schwitters exhibition there.

Her mature style began in the mid-1940s after her intensive study of the principles of Neo-plasticism with Mondrian, as demonstrated in her large paintings of that time, which merged biomorphic forms into orthogonal abstract compositions (*Telescopic Forms*, 1945; gouache on paper; 49.5 × 38.1 cm.; Collection Lehman American Express). Freely drawn shapes joined rectangles that enclosed an array of personal symbols, as in *Individual Worlds* (1947; oil on canvas; 76.2 × 63.5 cm.; Collection Barbara Millhouse, New York). Her artistic method, incorporating art-historical references, personal memories and creative invention, was best typified in her collage experiments of the same period, which utilised oriental papers from the Chinatown of her youth, allusions to the work of Schwitters and actual bus transfers (*Melodic Tapestry No.70*, 1948; collage; Museum of Fine Arts, Springfield, MA). While small gouaches were initially prepared as studies for larger works, they eventually assumed an independent identity and characterise some of the artist's best works. Their scale allowed her a sense of free play, evident in her work with collage but missing from the larger paintings (*Study for City Lights*, 1946; gouache on board; private collection, repr. Miami Beach 1982, p.12; *White, Red and Blue Planes*, 1952; see illustration).

Von Wiegand's strict adherence to Mondrian's approach is last strongly felt in a series of works from 1949 that feature rectangles of primary colours juxtaposed like a mosaic against a white ground in a chequer pattern (*Radiating Plane*, 1949; oil on canvas; 88.9 × 63.5 cm.; Grey Art Gallery and Study Center, New York University). While it was Mondrian's formal style that greatly influenced her work, it was also his reliance on theosophical teachings and writings that fascinated von Wiegand. Eventually she conducted her own study of Eastern art and religion, finding much in Tibetan art especially to inform her work.

Slowly, von Wiegand found aspects of Mondrian's style confining and began to seek other artistic strategies capable of a greater degree of expression. She expanded her colour to include high key tones that she believed reflected the reconciliation of opposites. Her study of the *I Ching* inspired forms based on the logarithmic spirals that she believed embodied the law of change. The five symbolic colours of Tibetan art led her to create her own seven-tone scale (*Yin-Yang with 8 Triagrams*, undated; gouache on paper; artist's estate, *ibid.*, p.39). Her experiments with colour modulation produced a series of magic square paintings from 1960 in which number arrangements were transferred into carefully ordered tones, such as the gouache *Magic Square No.138* (1960; private collection). Non-Western cultures – including Chinese, Egyptian, Indian and Tibetan – continued to provide the impetus for von Wiegand's work until her death in 1983. The late work maintains her steadfast devotion to the spiritual possibilities of art (*Offering to the Adi Buddha Amoghasiddha*, 1966–7; oil on canvas; Archer M. Huntington Gallery, University of Texas, Austin).

Von Wiegand's work, both as a disciple of Mondrian and as a student of Eastern philosophies, combined her respect for a strict formal order with a profound philosophical root. Throughout her artistic career she believed that abstract art provided the means for mankind to overcome its materialistic nature. Her assimilation of Eastern thought did not lead her to reject her previous work with Mondrian, but rather extended it for the purpose of creating a new, universal art.

AMY J. WOLF

Vorobyov, Marevna *see* Marevna

Walker, Ethel

British painter and sculptor, 1861–1951

Born in Edinburgh, 9 June 1861. Moved with her family to Wimbledon, London, 1870. Attended Ridley School of Art in her late twenties. Visited Madrid, making copies of Velázquez in the Prado, 1884; saw Manet exhibition and met George Moore in Paris on return journey. Studied at Putney School of Art, then Westminster School of Art under Fred Brown. Attended Slade School of Fine Art, London, 1899–1901, 1912–13, and 1921–2; studied sculpture under James Harvard Thomas, c.1912. Exhibited at Royal Academy from 1898, New English Art Club from 1899, Women's International Art Club from 1900, all in London. Attended the Friday Club organised by Vanessa Bell (q.v.) in Bloomsbury, London, 1916. Divided time between Cheyne Walk, London, and cottage in Robin Hood's Bay, Yorkshire, c.1917–51, moving to Buckinghamshire to escape bombing, 1941–2. Represented Britain at Venice Biennale, 1930 and 1932. Recipient of de Lazlo medal, Royal Society of British Artists, 1949. Honorary president, Women's International Art Club, 1932–51. Member, New English Art Club, 1900; Royal Society of British Artists, 1932; Royal Society of Portrait Painters, 1933; London Group, 1936; Society of Mural Painters, 1947. Associate, Royal Academy, 1940. Commander (CBE), 1938, and Dame Commander (DBE), 1943, Order of the British Empire. Died in London in difficult economic circumstances, 2 March 1951.

Selected Individual Exhibitions

Goupil Gallery, London: 1924 (with Charles Ginner and Louise Pickard)

Redfern Gallery, London: 1927

Leicester Galleries, London: 1929, 1947

Lefevre Galleries, London: 1931, 1933, 1935, 1939, 1940 (with Katherine Church), 1942, 1949

Wildenstein's, London: 1936

Little Burlington Galleries, London: 1937

Rotherham Museum and Art Gallery: 1943

Thomas Agnew and Sons, London: 1947

Tate Gallery, London: 1952 (retrospective, with Gwen John and Frances Hodgkins)

Bibliography

Grace English, "Ethel Walker", unpublished monograph, Tate Gallery Archives, n.d.

George Moore, *Hail and Farewell*, 3 vols, London: Heinemann, 1911–14; reprinted 1933 (Walker cited under pseudonym; her best friend Clare Christian as "Stella")

Mary Chamot, "Ethel Walker", *Apollo*, xiii, 1931, pp.307–8

——, "Paintings by Ethel Walker", *Country Life*, lxxvii, 26 January 1935, pp.98–9

——, *Modern Painting in England*, London: Country Life, and New York: Scribner, 1937

Mary Sorrell, "Dame Ethel Walker, ARA", *Apollo*, xlv, 1947, pp.119–21

John Rothenstein, *Modern English Painters: Sickert to Smith*, London: Eyre and Spottiswoode, 1952

Ethel Walker, Frances Hodgkins and Gwen John, exh. cat., Tate Gallery, London, 1952

Katy Deepwell, "The memorial exhibition of Ethel Walker, Gwen John and Frances Hodgkins", *Women Artists' Slide Library Journal*, no.16, April–May 1987, pp.5–6

Germaine Greer, *Slade School Women*, film, 1990

Justine Kenyon, "Ethel Walker (1861–1951): In pursuit of heaven", *Women's Art Magazine*, no.47, July–August 1992, pp.17–19

Katy Deepwell, "A fair field and no favour: Women artists in Britain between the two world wars", *This Working Day World: Social, Political and Cultural History of Women's Lives, 1914–45*, ed. Sybil Oldfield, London: Taylor and Francis, 1994, pp.141–55

Ethel Walker was widely celebrated as Britain's leading woman Impressionist painter in the inter-war years, but she received very belated recognition for her achievements in her lifetime. At her death in 1951, she bequeathed a large body of important works from her studio to the Tate Gallery, London (the Chantrey Bequest had already purchased a number of paintings in 1931). To date, in spite of several academic theses in the 1980s, there have been no catalogue raisonnés or full biographies published of this outstanding artist, unlike those that have secured the reputations of her immediate male peers, Augustus John, Frederick Brown, Wilson Steer and Walter Sickert – all of whom championed her work.

Walker began exhibiting at the age of 37, and her first major success came with the portrait of *Angela* (1900; repr. Rothenstein 1952) – a Whistlerian study of a girl in a white dress with one arm resting against a mantelpiece – exhibited at the New English Art Club (NEAC), where she was promptly elected a member (see also other early portraits, *The Hon. Mrs Adams*, c.1901; Tate Gallery; *Forgotten Melody*, 1902; Laing

Walker: *Zone of Hate*, 1914–15; Tate Gallery, London

Art Gallery, Newcastle upon Tyne). Walker was one of the few women artists to be elected a member of the NEAC (only seven women were elected to its 40-strong membership between 1886 and 1918), and this in spite of the fact that women artists were exhibiting in increasing numbers at the NEAC's annual open exhibitions (forming 40 per cent of the total exhibitors in the inter-war years). Many women exhibitors at the NEAC also showed with the newly formed Women's International Art Club (1900), to which Walker was elected honorary president in 1932. She was one of a group of women painters, largely but not exclusively single, who had trained at the Slade and exhibited at the NEAC and who were known as the Cheyne Walkers, because they lived and worked in Cheyne Walk, Chelsea (the others included Beatrice Bland, Fairlie Harmar (Viscountess Harberton), Louise Pickard and Josephine Mason).

Walker exhibited her portraits, seascapes, still lifes, flower paintings and nudes regularly at the Royal Academy, the NEAC and the Women's International Art Club from 1900 to the 1940s (*Prize Bouquet with Grapes*, 1936; York City Art

Gallery). She was, however, one of the last of 40 NEAC members (including two other women) to be elected to the ranks of the Royal Academy in the years 1918–40. Her decision to return to art school in the 1910s and 1920s, in spite of her success in group exhibitions, was unusual, but in each case she developed her skills, studying sculpture, printmaking and returning to an underlying enthusiasm, drawing and painting from the model (*Aspiration*; pencil drawing; Courtauld Institute of Art, London). She moved from a style heavily influenced by Whistler and Manet (*On the Balcony*; Leeds City Art Gallery; *A Symphony in Bronze and Silver*; Birmingham City Art Gallery) to looser and more expressive paint work, evident in her portraits (*Lucien Pissarro*; Scottish National Gallery of Modern Art, Edinburgh) and flower paintings of the inter-war years (*Bouquet of Flowers*, 1938–9; Manchester City Art Galleries).

Walker's large-scale imaginative compositions represent a synthesis of the Slade's mixture of finely executed life drawing combined with Impressionist-painting techniques, a bright palette of colours and Classical, allegorical and biblical themes (e.g. *Nausicaa*, Tate Gallery; *The Four Seasons*, Musée d'Art Moderne de la Ville de Paris; *Wooing of Lilith*, Boijmans Van Beuningen Museum, Rotterdam; *Decoration: Morning*, c.1936; York City Art Gallery). *Zone of Hate* (1914–15; see illustration) is an explicitly anti-war statement in which a centrally placed earth mother mourns the loss of life in front of the gods of war, greed and revenge, surrounded by a chorus of aggressive youths and grieving women. Its companion piece, *Zone of Love* (1930–32; Tate Gallery), sets out an idyllic world in which women commune together with nature and music while man, represented by a small Adam-like figure playing pipes, remains exiled from this community on a distant slope. Women feature strongly in her imaginative compositions, particularly her fascination with Lilith, the first Eve, who was cast into exile, and the story of Nausicaa, deserted by her lover, and in her portraits (e.g. *Vanessa* [Bell] 1937; *Miss Jean Werner Laurie*, 1927–8; both Tate Gallery; *Self-Portrait*, National Portrait Gallery, London; *Eileen*, 1931; Manchester City Art Galleries).

Many first-hand accounts exist of Walker's reputedly eccentric character and lifestyle, her pithy wit (usually at a man's expense), her confidence in her own reputation and abilities combined with "furious energy". John Rothenstein wrote: "when we consider her character, her freedom from ordinary conventions, her fanatical independence, her habit of uttering her uncensored thoughts and her domineering ways, it is perhaps odd that she led so tranquil a life" (*ibid.*, p.72). She had several close, probably lesbian, relationships with other women, including Clare Christian, with whom she lived for 15 years, but for most of her adult life she appears to have lived alone.

Her sea pieces, executed on painting trips to her cottage, The White Gate, in Robin's Hood Bay, Yorkshire, deal evocatively with the impression of light, mood and atmosphere between sea and sky (*October Morning*, c.1938; Royal Collection; *An August Morning*, 1938; Manchester City Art Galleries; *September Morning*, Leicester City Art Gallery; *Landscape at Robin Hood's Bay*, 1945; York City Art Gallery).

KATY DEEPWELL

WalkingStick, Kay
American painter, 1935–

Born in Syracuse, New York, 2 March 1935. Studied at Beaver College, Glenside, Pennsylvania (BFA 1959); Pratt Institute, Brooklyn, New York (MFA 1975). Assistant professor of art, Cornell University, Ithaca, 1988–90 and from 1992; State University of New York, Stony Brook, 1990–92; visiting artist, Vermont Studio Center, Johnson, 1995. Artist-in-residence at MacDowell Colony, Peterborough, New Hampshire, 1970–71; Yaddo Artists' Colony, Saratoga Springs, New York, 1976; William Flanagan Memorial Creative Persons Center, Albee Foundation, Montauk, New York, 1983; Rockefeller Conference and Study Center, Bellagio, Italy, 1992. Recipient of National Endowment for the Arts (NEA) grant, 1983; Joan Mitchell Foundation award, 1995; National Honor award for Achievement in the Arts, Women's Caucus for Art, 1996. Member of Cherokee Nation of Oklahoma. Lives in Ithaca, New York.

Selected Individual Exhibitions
SoHo Center for the Visual Arts, New York: 1976
Bertha Urdang Gallery, New York: 1978, 1981, 1984
M-13 Gallery, New York: 1987, 1990
Wenger Gallery, Los Angeles: 1988
Hillwood Art Museum, Long Island University, Brookville, NY: 1991 (touring retrospective)
Elaine Horwitch Gallery, Scottsdale, AZ: 1991
Galerie Calumet, Heidelberg, Germany: 1993
June Kelly Gallery, New York: 1994

Selected Writings
"Democracy, Inc.: Kay WalkingStick on Indian law", *Artforum*, xxx, November 1991, pp.20–21
"Native American art in the postmodern era", *Art Journal*, li, Fall 1992, pp.15–17 (guest editor, with Jackson Rushing)

Bibliography
Contemporary Native American Art, exh. cat., Gardiner Art Gallery, Oklahoma State University, Stillwater, and elsewhere, 1983
Signale: Indianischer Kunstler, exh. cat., Gallery Akmak, Berlin, and elsewhere, 1984
Pat Malarcher, "The meaning of 'duality' in art", *New York Times*, 22 December 1985
The Painting and Sculpture Collection: Acquisitions since 1972, Buffalo, NY: Albright-Knox Art Gallery, 1987
We the People, exh. cat., Artists Space, New York, 1987
Judy Kay Collischan van Wagner, *Lines of Vision: Drawings by Contemporary Women*, New York: Hudson Hills Press, 1989
Kellie Jones, "Kay WalkingStick", *Village Voice*, 16 May 1989
The Decade Show: Frameworks of Identity in the 1980s, exh. cat., New Museum of Contemporary Art, New York, and elsewhere, 1990
Lucy R. Lippard, *Mixed Blessings: New Art in a Multicultural America*, New York: Pantheon, 1990
Phyllis Braff, "A special regard for nature's forces", *New York Times*, 14 April 1990
Kay WalkingStick: Paintings, 1974–1990, exh. cat., Hillwood Art Museum of Long Island University, Brookville, NY, and elsewhere, 1991
Shared Visions: Native American Painters and Sculptors in the Twentieth Century, exh. cat., Heard Museum, Phoenix, and elsewhere, 1991

Land, Spirit, Power: First Nations at the National Gallery of Canada, exh. cat., National Gallery of Canada, Ottawa, and elsewhere, 1992

Nicole Vogtlin, "Landschaften und deren Spiegelbilder", *Rhein-Neckar-Main*, 7 April 1993

Robin Lawrence, "Native tradition spoken in language of post-modernism", *The Weekend Sun/Saturday Review* (Vancouver), 31 December 1993

Lawrence Abbott, ed., *I Stand in the Center of the Good: Interviews with Contemporary Native American Artists*, Lincoln: University of Nebraska Press, 1994

Erin Valentino, "Mistaken identity: Between death and pleasure in the art of Kay WalkingStick", *Third Text*, no.26, Spring 1994, pp.61–73

H.W. Janson, *History of Art*, 5th edition, revised by Anthony F. Janson, New York: Abrams, 1995

Richard Vine, "Kay WalkingStick", *Art in America*, lxxxiii, January 1995, p.106

Anne Barclay Morgan, "Kay WalkingStick", *Art Papers*, November–December 1995, pp.12–15

The art of Kay WalkingStick expresses issues of duality and complexity, especially as those issues derive from personal experience and identity. Her paintings of the 1980s and 1990s have usually contained two distinct components that speak to both estrangement or separateness and reconciliation or unification. The role of nature is paramount in her art. While her imagery is concerned in part with primal forces, her style – which has been described as both Neo-abstract and Neo-expressionist – is a sophisticated, informed one that uses a highly developed formal language to deal with fundamental, mythic matters. At times, her work has made direct statements about the situation, past and present, of Native Americans.

WalkingStick was the daughter of a Cherokee father and a European-American mother. Although there was little direct contact with her father and his culture (based in Tahlequah, Oklahoma) during her childhood, her Native American heritage was impressed upon her by her mother and siblings. Her primary experience growing up was the dominant white culture of New York State, and only in adulthood did she come to terms with and begin to express the Native American aspect of her heritage. After receiving a BFA in 1959, she delayed graduate school to raise her family, receiving a MFA from the Pratt Institute in 1975. During those years, she dealt with realist treatments of the nude, then in the early 1970s produced a series of "apron" paintings with hand-applied markings that indicated her shift towards abstraction as well as a new approach to the process of painting.

Her first major artistic statement about her Cherokee heritage, *Messages to Papa* (artist's collection), came in 1975. The new piece was both object and experience: the interior of a conical tipi form large enough to contain only the artist was hung with feathers and paper strips on which were written "messages" in the Cherokee language. (The Cherokee was unique among the tribes in the USA in that one of its members, Sequoyah, developed a syllabary specifically for their language.) Describing the construction of this sculpture as a "ritual activity", WalkingStick used wooden poles and canvas that she sewed and then painted with brightly coloured abstractions. Although the tipi was not used by the Cherokee (their origins were in the mountains and woodlands of the southeastern USA; the tipi is a Plains dwelling form), she recognised that the tipi was "a symbol of the Native Americans to non-Native Americans" (quoted in Valentino 1994, p.64).

In subsequent work she continued to explore imagery that spoke of both aspects of her heritage and that, in addition, developed further layers of meaning. The arcing forms found in both the apron paintings and *Messages to Papa* were developed in several ways, especially in the 36-piece *Chief Joseph* series (*c.*1974–7; artist's collection). Other paintings used a variety of linear forms such as a single line or an equilateral cross. The restraint and deliberation of these poised

WalkingStick: *Four Directions: Stillness*, 1994; acrylic, wax, oil on canvas; 91.4 × 182.9 cm.

compositions were balanced by the earthiness and emotion of the process. Precise lines were incised into a deep impasto so that layers of colour were revealed. The surface was worked by hand, added to and reworked again until it literally built up its own history, at the same time suggesting markings on an ancient surface. In much of her work, the use of her own hands in applying and manipulating the material has been a central technique for WalkingStick. In 1983 she stated: "I apply the paint (acrylic and wax) with my hands to give the painting energy, excitement and a 'handedness'; the paint is dense; it is layered, scratched, and scraped" (Stillwater 1983). Later on, she elaborated: "I redraw, repaint, repeat, and layer until the painting seems to me to reach a kind of significant level of meaning. The message is as much in the paint as in the imagery" (Brookville 1991, p.34).

In the mid-1980s WalkingStick embarked on a long series of two-panelled paintings in which one side carries abstract, emblematic, usually geometric shapes while the other is a recognisable but highly expressionist depiction of land features such as a river, waterfall or rocky cliffs, as in *Four Directions: Stillness* (1994; see illustration), *On the Edge* (1989) and *Remnant of Cataclysm* (1992; all artist's collection). Both sides are thickly painted and often presented on deep frames so that they have a strong, three-dimensional presence. WalkingStick has explained that these paintings are seated in her own identity as a bi-racial woman in the dominant white culture. In her writings she has noted the "double life" of many Indians who draw on tribal identities as well as experiences in the broader culture. Her paintings give form to such notions of separateness but at the same time speak to the possibility of transcendence and unity. In these searches and struggles, the role of land is seminal, as WalkingStick has explained: "The two portions represent two kinds of knowledge of the earth. One is visual, immediate and particular, the other is spiritual, long-term, and non-specific" ("Native American art in the postmodern era", 1992). Retaining the idea of the sacredness of the land that is a tenet in tribal beliefs, WalkingStick joins it to contemporary ecological concerns, both personal and societal. This inclusionary quality is typical of the multi-layered nature of her work both in imagery and technique. In a statement of 1991 WalkingStick discussed the purpose of her work and the role of duality in that purpose:

My paintings show two different perceptions of the world in two different methods of painting: to some viewers these are diametrically opposed methods. Yet, I believe in the possibility of unity, of wholeness. My goal is to make meaningful, intuitive connections between these different, but mythically related, views [Brookville 1991, p.34].

In other work of the 1990s WalkingStick has dealt with Native American issues, including historical events such as the Massacre at Wounded Knee (*The Wizard Speaks, the Cavalry Listens, December 29th, 1890*, 1992; artist's collection). She has used her personal history in a book of drawing and commentary, *Talking Leaves* (1993; artist's collection), in which she records and reflects upon offensive and presumptuous remarks made to her over the years about being an Indian. She is a prominent spokesperson on matters concerning Native American artists and served as co-editor of the College Art Association *Art Journal* issue on "Recent Native American art" (Fall 1992). She has taught at colleges, universities and museums and is currently Associate Professor of Art at Cornell University.

LEA ROSSON DELONG

Walton, Cecile
British painter and illustrator, 1891–1956

Born in Glasgow, 22 March 1891. Grew up in London; later moved with her family to Edinburgh. Attended a few classes at Edinburgh College of Art, then spent a year in Paris, 1908–9, studying at Académie de la Grande Chaumière and at La Palette; also visited Florence. Married painter Eric Robertson, 1914; two sons; separated from husband 1923; later divorced. Joined the re-formed Edinburgh Group, 1919. Visited Dorothy Johnstone (q.v.) in Vienna, summer 1923. Spent a few years in Cambridge, working for Tyrone Guthrie at the Festival Theatre. Returned to Edinburgh in 1933, to organise BBC's Scottish Children's Hour. Married Gordon Gildard, 1936; divorced 1945. Settled in Kirkcudbright. Died in Edinburgh, 26 April 1956.

Principal Exhibitions
Royal Scottish Academy, Edinburgh: occasionally 1909–54 (Guthrie award 1921)
Royal Academy, London: 1913–14, 1920–23
New Gallery, Edinburgh: 1919–21 (with Edinburgh Group)
Edinburgh: 1924 (with Dorothy Johnstone)

Bibliography
E.A. Taylor, "The Edinburgh Group", *The Studio*, lxxix, 1920, pp.88–98
Jessica Walker Stephens, "Cecile Walton and Dorothy Johnstone", *The Studio*, lxxxviii, 1924, pp.80–87
The Edinburgh Group, exh. cat., City Art Museum, Edinburgh, and elsewhere, 1983
The Last Romantics: The Romantic Tradition in British Art: Burne-Jones to Stanley Spencer, exh. cat., Barbican Art Gallery, London, 1989
Scottish Art since 1900, exh. cat., Scottish National Gallery of Modern Art, Edinburgh, and elsewhere, 1989
Duncan Macmillan, *Scottish Art, 1460–1990*, Edinburgh: Mainstream, 1990
John Kemplay, *The Two Companions: The Story of Two Scottish Artists, Eric Robertson and Cecile Walton*, Edinburgh: Crowhurst, 1991
Emmanuel Cooper, *The Sexual Perspective: Homosexuality and Art in the Last 100 Years in the West*, 2nd edition, London and New York: Routledge, 1994
Duncan Macmillan, *Scottish Art in the Twentieth Century*, Edinburgh: Mainstream, 1994

Cecile Walton was born in Glasgow in 1891. Her father, the painter E.A. Walton, was one of the "Glasgow Boys", but when she was a child her family moved to London. There they lived latterly in Cheyne Walk, Chelsea, where Whistler became a neighbour, and when still young Walton was on friendly terms with him and with such painters as James Guthrie, James Pryde and Arthur Melville. She was precocious and as a child

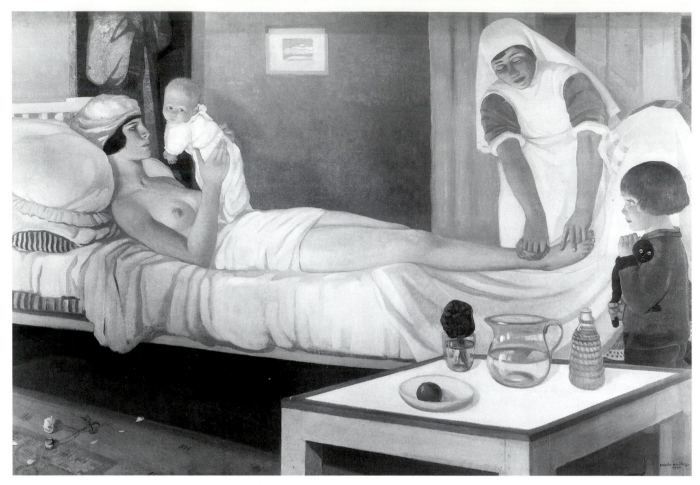

Walton: *Romance*, 1921; Scottish National Portrait Gallery, Edinburgh

her drawing style was already highly accomplished, but in spite of the company she kept, her leaning was always towards the Pre-Raphaelites and Puvis de Chavannes rather than the Impressionists. Around 1904 or 1905, however, the family moved back to Scotland, settling in Edinburgh. There Walton attended classes at the Edinburgh College of Art. At the age of 17 she went to Paris to study, attending the drawing classes at La Grande Chaumière and then, after a brief return to Edinburgh, at the atelier of La Palette. Jessie M. King (q.v.), whom she met in Paris, was an early influence on her work. King introduced her to pen and ink, and in 1911 her first book illustrations, to Hans Christian Andersen's *Fairy Tales*, were published. Using the pen and ink technique, they reveal the importance of the older artist's example. Thereafter Walton produced illustrated books occasionally throughout her life, five in all, including more fairy tales in *Polish Fairy Tales* (1920).

In Edinburgh the Symbolist painter John Duncan became a friend and was an important influence on her painting. He was the only teacher at the Edinburgh College of Art whom she really admired and he confirmed her leaning towards a rather Pre-Raphaelite style based on drawing. She inherited something of his Symbolism. She never adopted its poetic and metaphysical complexity, but she did develop a style that, like his, is characterised by light tonality and sharp clear line. This is seen, for instance, in a beautiful double portrait of two of her

friends, *Eric Robertson and Mary Newbery* (c.1912; private collection), reclining in the open air. Her friendship with Mary Newbery, daughter of Fra Newbery, principal of the Glasgow School of Art, was a link to the Glasgow circle of Charles Rennie Mackintosh and Margaret Macdonald (q.v.). In 1914 she married Robertson who was also a pupil of Duncan. He had a somewhat doubtful reputation, both for his free living and for the erotic character of his art, which had caused John Duncan to break with him. Not surprisingly, the marriage was against her parents' wishes. Indeed they had sent her away to Italy in order to try to end the relationship. While there she took the opportunity to try fresco painting, but remained undeflected in her purpose of marriage. In 1919, with Dorothy Johnstone (q.v.), another close friend and a fellow student whom she had met through Duncan, and Mary Newbery, she joined the Edinburgh Group, a small exhibiting society of young artists formed before World War I. She had already shown with them in 1914. Robertson was a founder member.

In 1921 Walton won the Royal Scottish Academy's top prize, the Guthrie award, for her painting *To Nobody Knows Where* (untraced). The award had been instituted only two years earlier in 1919 and she was the first woman to win it. Her picture is of a group of children – it is clearly pointed out that they are of different races – moving through a landscape in a kind of happy version of the Pied Piper's procession. Her marriage proved stormy and ended in 1923; the couple divorced a few years later. They had two children and one of Walton's finest paintings, *Romance* (1921; see illustration), is a self-portrait that shows her in bed, half nude, with Edward, her new-born, second child in her arms. This remarkable image challenges the conventional iconography of the female nude and boldly combines the traditional imagery of mother and child with the nudity of Manet's *Olympia*. In 1924 she had a joint exhibition in Edinburgh with Dorothy Johnstone and around this time she painted a large mural, *Suffer Little Children* (Piccadilly Gallery, London), for the Children's Village in Humbie, near Edinburgh. Children are the most frequent theme of her painting and she also carried out two murals for the children's department of a shop in Edinburgh. The disruption of her private life affected her painting, however, and her best work belongs to these early years.

Leaving Edinburgh to seek a new direction, Walton worked for four years as a theatre designer with Tyrone Guthrie at the Festival Theatre in Cambridge and at the end of that period returned to Scotland in 1933 to start the BBC's Scottish Children's Hour, a post for which she was invited to apply and to which she was appointed by the BBC director-general John Reith himself. In 1936 she married Gordon Gildard, but in 1945 this second marriage also ended in divorce. During the last few years of her life she returned to art, publishing book illustrations in 1949 and in 1954, but in her painting she could not recapture the freshness of her earlier work. She died in Edinburgh in 1956.

DUNCAN MACMILLAN

Ward, Henrietta (Mary Ada)

British painter, 1832–1924

Born in London, 1 June 1832, into a family of artists. Taught drawing by her mother, Mary Webb, and from 1843 by future husband Edward Matthew Ward. Married Ward, causing family estrangement, 1848; eight children. Attended art classes at Sass's, then lectures at the Royal Academy; own studio at home at 33 Harewood Square, London. Taught various royal children after 1854, when living near Windsor. Set up art school for girls after husband's death in 1879, in order to support her family. Signed petition for the admission of women to the Royal Academy Schools, 1859. Honorary member, Society of Female Artists, 1877; member of Central Committee of the National Society for Women's Suffrage, 1897. Died 12 July 1924.

Principal Exhibitions

Royal Academy, London: occasionally 1846–1921
Society of Female (later Lady) Artists, London: occasionally 1857–83
Dudley Gallery, London (oil): 1872

Selected Writings

Mrs E.M. Ward's Reminiscences, ed. Elliott O'Donnell, London: Pitman, 1911
Memories of Ninety Years, ed. Isabel McAllister, London: Hutchinson, 1924; New York: Holt, 1925

Bibliography

James Dafforne, "British artists: Their style and character, lxxvii: Henrietta Ward (Mrs E.M. Ward)", *Art Journal*, 1864, pp.357–9
Sarah Tytler, *Modern Painters and Their Paintings*, London: Strahan, 1873; Boston: Roberts, 1874
Ellen C. Clayton, *English Female Artists*, 2 vols, London: Tinsley, 1876
Clara Erskine Clement and Laurence Hutton, *Artists of the Nineteenth Century and Their Work*, 2 vols, Boston: Houghton Osgood, and London: Trübner, 1879; reprinted New York: Arno Press, 1969
R.W. Maude, "Mrs E.M. Ward: 'Royalties as Artists'", *Strand Magazine*, xvi, October 1898, pp.366–71
Connoisseur, lxx, 1924, p.57 (obituary)
Pamela Gerrish Nunn, "The case history of a woman artist: Henrietta Ward", *Art History*, i, 1978, pp.293–308
Charlotte Yeldham, *Women Artists in Nineteenth-Century France and England*, 2 vols, New York: Garland, 1984
Pamela Gerrish Nunn, ed., *Canvassing Women: Recollections by Six Victorian Women Artists*, London: Camden, 1986
——, *Victorian Women Artists*, London: Women's Press, 1987
Paula Gillett, *The Victorian Painter's World*, New Brunswick, NJ: Rutgers University Press, and Gloucester: Sutton, 1990
Deborah Cherry, *Painting Women: Victorian Women Artists*, London and New York: Routledge, 1993

Henrietta Ward was a prolific and successful Victorian painter of historical subjects with a domestic flavour. In her own long lifetime she saw her work win royal patronage and critical acclaim, and then go completely out of fashion. Today few of her pictures can be located, although her subjects are well recorded in contemporary reviews, the exhibition records of the Royal Academy and elsewhere, and in her own memoirs, *Reminiscences* (1911), which were more or less republished in *Memories of Ninety Years* in the year of her sparsely recorded death.

Born into a dynasty of British artists (grandfather James Ward, RA, father George Raphael Ward, a painter and engraver, and mother Mary Webb, a miniature painter) and married to the artist Edward Matthew Ward, Henrietta enjoyed both the educational advantages and suffered the public disadvantages of her connections. Ward's work was never reviewed without some comparative reference to her male relatives, especially as her husband also specialised in historical genre painting. Henrietta Ward feminised her art, preferring female protagonists and often concentrating on the depiction of emotions, for which reasons she was seen by some to be domesticating history. Much of her work emphasised female virtues and the happiness of family life. For example, in *George III and His Family at Windsor* (1872; see illustration), exhibited at the Royal Academy as *The Queen's Lodge, Windsor in 1786*, she shows a visit paid by the artist Mary Delany (q.v.) to the king and queen. Ward depicts a scene of domestic tranquillity, with the queen and lady artist engaged in conversation while the king plays on the floor with Princess Amelia and the other royal children paint and draw at the table. This work, because of its theme and compositional similarity, could have been intended as a companion piece to E.M. Ward's picture of the *Royal Family of France* (1872; Harris Museum and Art Gallery, Preston), which shows the disruption of a happy family brought about by Revolution.

In the 1850s Ward specialised in domestic scenes for which her own home life, servants included, was the model. The

Ward: *George III and His Family at Windsor*, 1872; oil on canvas; 118 × 133.3 cm.; Walker Art Gallery, Liverpool

Wards lived near Windsor, so that her husband could work on his royal commissions. Queen Victoria and Prince Albert visited the artists in their studios and Henrietta's paintings and drawings of her own brood won her a number of commissions to paint the royal children. Ward writes frankly about her own domestic arrangements in *Memories*, in which she describes a harmonious working partnership, but with the business and housekeeping responsibilities falling heavily on to her shoulders. Although she praises her husband for his "broadmindedness" in allowing his wife to be a career woman, it would appear from her account of daily life in the Ward household, where both had their studios, that his work was rarely interrupted while she was often faced with "some knotty problem that could only be solved by the mistress of the house". She often used her own children as models in her domestic subject pictures, such as *Morning Lesson* (1855), *The Bath* (1858), *A First Step in Life* (1871) and *God Save the Queen* (1857; repr. *Art Journal*, 1875). This was a sometimes hazardous practice,

such as the occasion recorded by Ward when her two-year-old daughter, modelling for *The Birthday*, "industriously removed all my painting, having vigorously rubbed it all over with a paint rag" while the artist's back was turned.

In the 1860s Ward shifted her interest from purely domestic subjects to depictions of women in history. Her particular source was Agnes Strickland's book *The Lives of the Queens of Scotland* (1850), in which she found the basis for her paintings of women of courage, fortitude and assertive action. At the Royal Academy in 1863 she exhibited *Queen Mary Quitted Stirling Castle on the Morning of Wednesday, April 23...*, in which the scene is set in the nursery at Stirling Castle, with the dignified figure of Mary Queen of Scots standing over the cradle of her sleeping child as she prepares to leave and meet her unhappy fate. Celebrated by the critics as "thoroughly a woman's subject, which a woman's heart and hand may best understand and paint" (*Illustrated London News*, 11 July 1863), this work is now lost, as is the case with much of

Ward's oeuvre. Ward's history pictures, meticulously researched in details of costume and setting, focused on her heroines in the roles of wife and mother, but never to detract from their dignity and courage. Other subjects include *Scene at the Louvre in 1649: The Despair of Henrietta Maria at the Death of Her Husband Charles I* (1862), *Sion House, 1553* (1868), an episode in the life of Lady Jane Grey, *Scene from the Childhood of the Old Pretender* (1869), *Defence of Latham House* (1874), which records the cool heroism of the Countess of Derby and her daughters when her house was under siege, and *Princess Charlotte of Wales* (1877), chronicling the princess's motherly kindness to a wounded waif. French history was also a popular source for Ward, for example *Scene from the Childhood of Joan of Arc* (1867) and *First Interview of the Divorced Empress Josephine with the King of Rome* (1870).

The Victorian picture-viewing public expected history painters to provide them with a readable narrative and complete historical accuracy. In her autobiography Ward recorded one occasion on which the pursuit of artistic truth almost put her life in danger. Engaged in an unchaperoned sitting with a soldier-model for *Scene from the Camp at Chobham, in the Encampment of the 79th Highlanders* (1854) – her husband out of earshot in his own studio – she was alarmed to realise that the queen's piper model had been drinking, and even more horrified when he lunged at her with a knife. Ward remained calm, the soldier collapsed after his frenzy and the picture was rewarded with a fine review in the *Art Journal* (1854, p.170).

From more recent history, Ward took the subject of one of her best-known works, *Newgate 1818* (1876; original probably in the USA; replica of 1895 in Friends' House, London), in which she depicts Elizabeth Fry, the great Quaker philanthropist, conducting her young friend Mary Sanderson around the grim female prison. Ward professed great admiration for Fry, describing her as a woman who "was determined to probe the depths of humanity's miseries, not from any curiosity, but because she had realised the truth of vital Christianity".

The death of her husband in 1879 left Ward in her late forties with a family to support on her own. Like many other women artists in her situation she turned to teaching to boost her income, opening an art school for girls in 1880, much patronised by royalty and the aristocracy and with distinguished visiting teachers such as Sir Lawrence Alma-Tadema, Marcus Stone, William Powell Frith and Sir Luke Fildes. Ward's own daughters, Eva, Flora, Beatrice and Enid, studied with her and themselves became artists. Despite Ward's own steely professionalism, on the whole her pupils were confirmed amateurs in search of no more than an attractive feminine accomplishment. The work of running the school prevented Ward from exhibiting so often and, in the latter part of her life, her art out of fashion, she turned to landscape and domestic scenes.

Ward was one of the few Victorian women artists to find success, albeit in constant comparison with that of her male family members, within the art establishment. She exhibited regularly at the Royal Academy for much of her life (her drawing of *Elizabeth Woodville Parting from the Duke of York* was accepted when she was only 14; collection of artist's descendants), and supported the Society of Female Artists by

showing her studies and sketches there from 1857. Although many of her most significant works are now inaccessible, her painting *Palissy the Potter* (1866) is in Leicester City Art Galleries, and *Chatterton* (1873), one of a number of scenes from the lives of poets, is in Bristol City Museum and Art Gallery. Although criticism of Ward constantly noted the "feminine" defects of her art, equally her skills of pictorial composition and her natural figure relationships were always admired. Speaking for herself, Ward wrote: "personally I feel that the RA-ship should be open to women equally with men, for there is no sex in Art, and it is pure selfishness that has excluded women from this honour, with the exception of Mary Moser and Angelika Kauffmann".

JANE SELLARS

Wärff, Ann *see* Wolff

Warrick, Meta Vaux *see* Fuller

Waterford, Louisa, Marchioness of
British amateur artist, 1818–1891

Born Louisa Anne Stuart in Paris, 14 April 1818, to Sir Charles Stuart (created Lord Stuart de Rothesay 1828), a British diplomat, and Lady Elizabeth Yorke, daughter of the Earl and Countess of Hardwicke. Returned to England with her family, 1824; spent two further years in Paris, 1828–30; subsequently settled at Highcliffe, Hampshire (now Dorset). Presented at Court, 1835. Married Henry de la Poer Beresford, 3rd Marquess of Waterford, 1842; no children. Lived at Curraghmore, Co. Waterford, Ireland, until husband's death in 1859, then moved to Ford, Northumberland. Inherited Highcliffe at her mother's death in 1867; subsequently spent summers there. Began correspondence with Ruskin, 1853. Patroness, 1865, and honorary member, 1887, Society of Female (later Lady) Artists. Died at Ford, 12 May 1891.

Principal Exhibitions
Grosvenor Gallery, London: 1878–82
Society of Lady Artists, London: 1886–7, 1890
Dudley Gallery, London: 1887, 1889
8 Carlton House Terrace, London: 1892, 1910 (both retrospectives)
Royal Academy, London: 1893 (retrospective)

Selected Writings
"Recollections up to the age of twelve", *Highcliffe Parish Magazine*, n.d.

Bibliography
Fine Arts Quarterly Review, ii, 1864, p.198
Ellen C. Clayton, *English Female Artists*, 2 vols, London: Tinsley, 1876

Berwick Advertiser, 15 May 1891 (obituary)

Charles Stuart, *A Short Sketch of the Life of Louisa, Marchioness of Waterford*, London, 1892

Exhibition of Works by the Old Masters...Including a Collection of Watercolour Drawings etc. by William Blake, Edward Calvert, Samuel Palmer and Louisa, Marchioness of Waterford, exh. cat., Royal Academy, London, 1893

Augustus Hare, *The Story of Two Noble Lives, Being Memorials of Charlotte, Countess Canning, and Louisa, Marchioness of Waterford*, 3 vols, London: Allen, and New York: Randolph, 1893

Hastings M. Neville, *Under a Border Tower: Sketches and Memories of Ford Castle, Northumberland*, Newcastle upon Tyne: Mawson, 1896

Walter Shaw Sparrow, *Women Painters of the World*, London: Hodder and Stoughton, and New York: Stokes, 1905; reprinted New York: Hacker, 1976

Catalogue of the Loan Exhibition of Watercolour Paintings by Louisa, Marchioness of Waterford, with a Short Memoir Written in 1892, exh. cat., 8 Carlton House Terrace, London, 1910

Mrs Steuart Erskine, "The drawings of Lady Waterford", *The Studio*, xlix, 1910, pp.283–6

Virginia Surtees, ed., *Sublime and Instructive: Letters from John Ruskin to Louisa, Marchioness of Waterford, Anna Blunden and Ellen Heaton*, London: Joseph, 1972

Germaine Greer, *The Obstacle Race: The Fortunes of Women Painters and Their Work*, London: Secker and Warburg, and New York: Farrar Straus, 1979

The Lady Waterford Hall, Ford, Northumberland, Ford: The Trustees of Lady Waterford Hall, 1980

Pamela Gerrish Nunn, "Ruskin's patronage of women artists", *Woman's Art Journal*, ii/2, 1981–2, pp.8–13

Lady Waterford Centenary Exhibition, exh. cat., Lady Waterford Hall, Ford, Northumberland, 1983

Charlotte Yeldham, *Women Artists in Nineteenth-Century France and England*, 2 vols, New York: Garland, 1984

Irish Women Artists from the Eighteenth Century to the Present Day, exh. cat., National Gallery of Ireland, Dublin, and elsewhere, 1987

Pamela Gerrish Nunn, *Victorian Women Artists*, London: Women's Press, 1987

Michael Joicey, *Louisa Anne, Marchioness of Waterford: A Look at Her Life and a Guide to the Murals Painted by Her at Ford, Northumberland*, Ford: Trustees of Lady Waterford Hall, 1991

Clarissa Campbell Orr, ed., *Women in the Victorian Art World*, Manchester: Manchester University Press, 1995

Louisa Stuart, later Marchioness of Waterford, was a self-taught artist who devoted her artistic activities to supporting her religious convictions and to fulfilling the social obligations expected of an aristocratic woman in the Victorian era. Her life was perceived to be a reflection of model Christian virtue, and commemorated by two biographies, by Augustus Hare (1893) and Hastings M. Neville (1896). Her artistic achievement accounted for a great part of her renown, and during her lifetime such leading figures as Sir Edwin Landseer, Dante Gabriel Rossetti, Sir Edward Burne-Jones, George Frederick Watts and John Ruskin took a lively interest in her work. She worked principally in watercolour, and the most ambitious artistic endeavour she undertook was the mural scheme of biblical subjects for the school at Ford, Northumberland. Her painting was admired for the originality of conception, for the sense of the monumental and for the individual use of colour, which prompted comparison with Venetian painting. In 1895 the president of the Dudley Gallery, Walter Severn, praised her "lovely" sketches "which will long continue to lighten up

many a drawing room and boudoir like settings of gems and precious stones on the wall" (Neville 1896, p.84), and the posthumous exhibitions of her work attracted a number of complimentary reviews in the press.

She demonstrated an early aptitude for treating figures, and her predilection for the monumental was displayed in the designs for coloured glass that she and her elder sister Charlotte – (later Charlotte Canning, also a renowned artist) – contributed to the improvements made at Highcliffe. In 1835 she was presented at Court and, celebrated for her beauty, sat for Hayter, for the sculptor Boehm and for Sir Francis Grant, who painted a full-length portrait of her (National Portrait Gallery, London). Watts, a particular admirer, painted her in profile and was to design the headstone for her grave at Ford. She maintained close connections at Court throughout her life, and in 1890 presented Queen Victoria with a picture she had admired, entitled *Relentless Time* (repr. Yeldham 1984, fig.121).

After her marriage in 1842, she and her husband divided their time between the ancestral estates in Co. Waterford, Ireland, with its seat at Curraghmore, and those centred on Ford, Northumberland. They were renowned for their encouragement of agriculture and industries and for their concern to improve social welfare, particularly during the Irish famine of the 1840s. Louisa designed six stained-glass windows for the church at Curraghmore (1842–3) and in 1849 her illustrations for the ballad *Babes in the Wood* were published anonymously (London: Cundell, 1849; 2nd edition 1863). After the sudden death of her husband in 1859, Lady Waterford continued to manage the estate of Ford, now her principal home. She restored Ford Castle, eliminating "gingerbread Gothic" in order to return it to the "appearance of an ancient building" (Hare 1893, vol.iii), and rebuilt the village on a new site, with a commemorative fountain to designs by Gilbert Scott. In 1862 she started on her "great experiment" to decorate the school at Ford with "frescoes" – in fact, paintings on paper stretched on wooden frames. The theme of virtue in childhood governs the selection of subjects from the Old and New Testaments. On the west and east walls respectively are large-scale representations of *Jesus Blessing the Children* and *Jesus Among the Doctors* (see illustration). The nine Old Testament subjects on the north wall are set in triangular-shaped lunettes bearing relevant biblical texts, flanked by medallions with monochrome figures set against decorative treatments of flora and fauna. In between the lower windows of the south wall are representations of the *Saviour Jesus as a Child*, the teaching of the scriptures to children from a text from Timothy, and figures of SS John the Evangelist and John the Baptist in simulated architectural niches.

Always acutely self-critical and aware of her lack of professional instruction, Lady Waterford relied on Ruskin for critical endorsement of her work. He visited Ford early in 1864, but while he admired her colouring, he found the scheme lacking in exactitude. In response, she applied herself more methodically to her work and was to describe how she spent several months in copying a print after Jan van Eyck. While Ruskin's recommendations were not entirely compatible with her artistic intuition, the interest he took in her art strengthened her resolve and attracted much notoriety to the scheme. The larger scale and more ambitious compositions of the New Testament

Waterford: Interior of the school at Ford, showing *Jesus Among the Doctors*, c.1862; Lady Waterford Hall, Ford, Northumberland; Ford and Etal Estates, Northumberland

subjects, undertaken after the Old Testament series was completed (by 1870), are not, however, obviously due to Ruskin's intervention.

Louisa had an unerring sense of draughtsmanship and her surviving notebooks reveal her facility for capturing rapid impressions in outline with pencil or pen. With pen and wash she was able to emphasise her competence at modelling, giving her figures a characteristic sculptural monumentality. She stressed that direct observation of nature and its colours was the principal source of her art, and the fact that her figures were based on people she knew. She underestimated the strength of the impressions that Italian painting made on her visual memory, gained from printed sources and from her visits to Italy between 1837 and 1867, and which is evident in compositional quotations. Although Louisa's painting has been grouped with that of the Pre-Raphaelites on the basis of its literary motive and inculcated moral, her critical response to their art reflects her intuitive affinity for classical values and she hoped that their art would become beautiful after passing through "all their phases of ugliness first" (*ibid.*, i, p.247).

The anonymous introduction to the catalogue of the exhibition of Lady Waterford's work in 1910 assessed her art in terms of the achievement of an amateur, as the "work of a lady whose life was not especially devoted to art" but for whom "painting was the expression of her inner life". Louisa's religious convictions were deeply held, and she never wavered in the view of her talent as a gift from God that was to be perfected and "fructified in God's service". She extinguished any personal gratification that her art might bring her, writing shortly after her marriage: "I do *love* my art (dare I call it mine?)" (*ibid.*, i, p.397) and elsewhere: "The love of art must not be treated as a sin. All that is great and beautiful comes from God and to God it should return" (*ibid.*, i, p.346). She directed the ambition she had to "do a great work" into the scheme for the school at Ford. She quoted the case of Marie Bashkirtseff (q.v.) as an example of the futility of seeking earthly success. Her only regret was her lack of professional instruction, and she criticised the scheme at Ford for the lack of preparatory consideration: "nothing was ever done with so little arrangement or propriety – alas! alas!" (*ibid.*, iii, p.362).

The extent to which Louisa received encouragement in the development of her art from her social peers needs clarification. The exceptional quality of her talent was recognised but valued less highly than the other accomplishments expected from an aristocrat's wife. A letter to their mother from her sister Charlotte after a visit to Curraghmore in November 1842 elaborates on the comforts that Louisa was introducing to her new home, but makes only a brief reference to her artistic activity, observing simply that Louisa was engaged in "a few drawings but very good ones – of the *Babes in the Wood*". The initiative that the publication of these drawings represents may be indicative, so soon after her marriage, of the interest taken in Louisa's art by her husband. Although she sent work to private and institutional exhibitions, her chief artistic concern was for the scheme at Ford, and despite the acclaim of her as an artist of the first rank she chose to remain identified with the norms ascribed to the amateur.

CLAIRE A. A. BRISBY

Watson, Caroline
British printmaker, 1760 or 1761–1814

Born in London, 1760 or 1761; daughter of printmaker James Watson. Appointed Engraver to Queen Charlotte, 1785. Died in Pimlico, London, 10 June 1814.

Bibliography

G. Goodwin, *Thomas Watson, James Watson and Elizabeth Judkins*, London: Bullen, 1904

Freeman O'Donoghue and Henry M. Hake, *Catalogue of Engraved British Portraits...in the British Museum*, 6 vols, London, 1908–25

Gerald Eades Bentley, *Blake Records*, Oxford: Clarendon Press, 1969

Richard and Maria Cosway: Regency Artists of Taste and Fashion, exh. cat., Scottish National Portrait Gallery, Edinburgh, and National Portrait Gallery, London, 1995

Caroline Watson, stipple engraver, primarily of portraits, engraved two or three plates a year between 1780 and 1810, and was the only Englishwoman to have had an extended career as an independent engraver in 18th-century Britain. Other women certainly worked as professional engravers, but they all belonged to families headed by male engravers. It is true that Watson's father, James, was an engraver, but he worked exclusively in mezzotint, whereas his daughter worked primarily in stipple, the technique that suddenly became fashionable in the mid-1770s with the demand for "furniture prints" after pictures and drawings by Angelica Kauffman (q.v.) and others; the prints, generally ovals or circles, were often printed in red or in colours and close-framed in gilt. James Watson had done well enough to retire to Welwyn in Hertfordshire by 1781.

It is not known who taught Watson to engrave in the new technique, but she was signing plates by 1780 and soon began working for the leading print publisher John Boydell, for whom her father had engraved many plates. In 1781 Boydell published her *Boy and Dog* after a painting by Murillo, the first of at least seven plates by her that he issued. Another early

Watson: *The Winter Day*, aquatint after a drawing by Maria Cosway, illustrating a poem by Mary Robinson (published by Ackermann, 1804)

commission was from the painter Robert Edge Pine to engrave his pictures of Shakespearian scenes of which he held a special exhibition; these were unusual in being imaginative depictions rather than stage scenes. Pine's venture failed and the plates, such as Watson's *Miranda* (1782), were bought by Boydell, who soon after developed Pine's idea and launched his Shakespeare Gallery.

Perhaps because she was seen as a woman on her own, Watson attracted support from a number of influential people. Her father engraved many pictures by Sir Joshua Reynolds, who was one of the first to help Watson's career, allowing her to engrave and publish two pictures in his possession: in 1788 *St Matthew* after Rubens, and in 1786 a miniature of the poet *John Milton*. In the inscription on the latter Reynolds praises the way in which she had preserved the likeness with "the utmost exactness". The extreme delicacy of her modelling was well suited to the reproduction of miniatures and she engraved at least 20, including seven after Samuel Shelley.

In the 1780s Watson herself published a number of prints from Fitzroy Street, London, where she probably lived with her

barrister brother. It is possible that she had the help of her father with print selling; he was living with her at the time of his death in 1790. Her reputation increased rapidly, not least because of her appointment as Engraver to Queen Charlotte in 1785; she had engraved a portrait of *Prince William* for Boydell in 1781, and in 1786 engraved portraits by Hoppner of the princesses *Sophia* and *Mary*, which she published with dedications to the king and queen. This appointment seems to have brought prestige rather than employment from the queen, who had begun to collect prints, and no doubt her example encouraged others to buy Watson's productions. A more valuable association was the one she formed with the diplomat and collector Lord Mountstuart, later 4th Earl and 1st Marquess of Bute, and his wife; for the rest of her career she engraved pictures and family portraits belonging to the Bute family. Some of these plates have her name as publisher, but they were probably more in the nature of private plates, with the family paying handsomely for copies to distribute to friends and relations.

The end of the 1780s, when the print market was buoyant,

must have been the busiest period of Watson's career. According to the *Monthly Magazine* (1803, p.48), it was at the specific request of Reynolds that she engraved a large plate of the *Death of Cardinal Beaufort*, the picture he painted for Boydell's Shakespeare Gallery, of which proofs were published in 1790. It was unfortunate for her that this was such an unsatisfactory picture; alterations had to be made to the print in order to make it less ludicrous. During the 1790s Watson published very few prints herself; this may have been because of the difficulties that any sole engraver had in distributing prints, but it was also probably because the print market contracted as a result of hostilities with France. Instead Watson began to engrave plates for the printseller Molteno, and she also began to work for the book trade. In 1804 Ackermann published a set of 12 aquatints by her after drawings by Maria Cosway (q.v.) illustrating Mary Robinson's poem *The Winter Day* (see illustration). This appears to be her only major project in aquatint, and the etched outlines give the subjects a vivacity that was not obtainable with the softness of stipple. The next major commission that she secured was for seven plates in William Hayley's *Life of William Cowper*, published in 1809. Despite the adverse views expressed by the sculptor John Flaxman about Watson's abilities (Flaxman to Hayley, 16 June 1804), Hayley was keen to employ her; another friend, who had heard she was in need of work, visited her on Hayley's behalf in Furnival's Inn Court, Holborn, and reported that he "found her a very interesting, diffident woman ... Her reputation is so high, & her powers of art so delightful, that I rejoice you have employed her" (John Carr to Hayley, 28 March 1805, quoted in Bentley 1969, p.161). This work was the last major undertaking she finished; her health began to deteriorate, her output dropped off after 1810 and she did not entirely complete her last plate, the *Annunciation* by Murillo in the Bute collection at Luton Hoo, Bedfordshire.

DAVID ALEXANDER

Waugh, Edna *see* Clarke Hall

Wautier, Michaelina *see* Woutier

Wayne, June

American printmaker, painter and tapestry designer, 1918–

Born June Claire in Chicago, Illinois, 7 March 1918. Invited to paint in Mexico by Mexican Department of Public Education, 1936. Worked for Modern Gallery at Marshall Field and Company, Chicago, 1937–8. Easel painter with Works Progress Administration Federal Art Project (WPA/FAP), Chicago, 1938. Designer of accessories in New York fashion industry, 1939. Trained as a production illustrator at California Institute of Technology, Los Angeles, 1943.

Daughter by first husband born 1944. Staff writer, WGN radio, Chicago, 1943–4. Settled in Los Angeles, 1945. Began to make lithographs, working with printer Lynton Kistler, 1948. Worked in Paris with printer Marcel Durassier, 1957–8. Founder, 1960, and director, 1960–70, Tamarind Lithography Workshop, Los Angeles (transferred to University of New Mexico, Albuquerque, and renamed Tamarind Institute, 1970). Academy Award (Oscar) nomination for documentary film *Four Stones for Kanemitsu* (1974). Recipient of Woman of the Year award, *Los Angeles Times*, 1952; National Endowment for the Arts (NEA) grant, 1980; Citation for Distinguished Contributions to the Visual Arts, National Association of Schools of Art and Design, 1990; Printmaker Emeritus, Southern Graphics Print Council, Knoxville, 1994; honorary doctorates from International College, London/Los Angeles, 1976; Atlanta College of Fine Arts, 1988; California College of Arts and Crafts, Oakland, 1988; Moore College of Art and Design, Philadelphia, 1991; Rhode Island School of Design, Providence, 1994. Honorary faculty, California State University, Northridge, 1994. Commendations by the City of Los Angeles, 1970–84. Lives in Los Angeles.

Selected Individual Exhibitions

Palacio de Bellas Artes, Mexico City: 1936
Santa Barbara Museum of Art, CA: 1950, 1953, 1958
San Francisco Museum of Art: 1950
Art Institute of Chicago: 1952
M.H. de Young Memorial Museum, San Francisco: 1956
California Palace of the Legion of Honor (Achenbach Foundation), San Francisco: 1958
Los Angeles County Museum of Art: 1959
Art Museum of the University of New Mexico, Albuquerque: 1968
Cincinnati Art Museum: 1969
Grunwald Center for the Graphic Arts, University of California, Los Angeles: 1971
Municipal Art Gallery, Los Angeles: 1973
La Demeure Gallery, Paris: 1975
Art '76, Basel: 1976
Les Premontres, Nancy: 1977–80 (touring)
San Diego Art Museum: 1981–3 (*Dorothy Series*, touring, organised by Western Association of Art Museums)
Fresno Art Museum, CA: 1988 (*Djuna Set*, touring retrospective)
Macquarie Galleries, Sydney, and National Gallery of Australia, Canberra: 1989 (touring)
Knoxville Museum of Art, TN: 1995
Skirball Museum of Art, Los Angeles: 1996
Neuberger Museum, Purchase, NY: 1997 (touring retrospective)

Selected Writings

Foundation Gamesmanship, 1966
New Careers in the Arts, 1966
About Tamarind, 1969
Preface, *The Tamarind Book of Lithography: Art and Technique*, 1971
Foreword, *Sex Differentials in Art Exhibition Reviews: A Statistical Study*, 1972
"On originality", *Print Collector's Newsletter*, iii, 1972, pp.28–9
"The male artist as stereotypical female", *College Art Journal*, xxxii, 1973, pp.414–6; reprinted in *Art News*, lxxii, December 1973, pp.41–2, and elsewhere
"The tradition of narrative tapestry", *Craft Horizons*, xxxvi, August 1974, pp.26–9, 49
"The creative process: Artists, carpenters and the Flat Earth Society", *Craft Horizons*, xxxvi, October 1976, pp.30–31, 64–7

Avant-Garde Mindset in the Artist's Studio, 1987 (written 1985, presented at Hofstra University 1986)
Making Art in the 1980s: A Hard Choice, 1987 (ancillary to *Avant-garde Mindset in the Artist's Studio*, 1987)
"Broken stones and whooping cranes: Thoughts of a wilful artist", *Tamarind Papers*, xiii, 1990, pp.16–27, 94
Rapture and the Bends: Essays by June Wayne (in preparation)

Bibliography

Mary W. Baskett, *The Art of June Wayne*, New York: Abrams, 1968
June Wayne: An Exhibition of Paintings, Tapestries, Lithographs, exh. cat., Municipal Art Gallery, Los Angeles, 1973
June Wayne: An Exhibition of Lithographs and Tapestries, exh. cat., Muckenthaler Cultural Center, Fullerton, CA, 1974
Eleanor Munro, *Originals: American Women Artists*, New York: Simon and Schuster, 1979
Arlene Raven, "*Cognitos*: June Wayne's new paintings", *Arts Magazine*, lix, October 1984, pp.119–21
June Wayne: The Djuna Set, exh. cat., Fresno Art Museum, CA, and elsewhere, 1988
Pat Gilmour, "A love affair with lithography: The prints of June Wayne", *Print Quarterly*, ix, 1992, pp.142–76 (contains catalogue raisonné)
June Wayne: A Retrospective, exh. cat., Neuberger Museum of Art, Purchase, NY, and elsewhere, 1997
Pat Gilmour, *June Wayne: Catalogue Raisonné* (in preparation)

June Wayne's international reputation rests not only on her work as a painter, tapestry designer and innovative graphic artist, but also on the intelligence with which she changed the ecology for artists' prints. Realising that stone lithography was dying out in the USA, she conceived a programme for its restoration, persuaded the Arts and Humanities Division of the Ford Foundation to back it, and founded and ran the resultant Tamarind Lithography Workshop from 1960 until 1970. By ending the secrecy surrounding the lithographic process, introducing it to artists of every aesthetic persuasion and by training printers, Wayne not only transformed American printmaking, but radically affected it elsewhere as well.

Brought up in Chicago, Wayne was always determined to become an artist, although the only schooling she ever received was at the children's classes of the Art Institute. She dropped out of school at 15, and by the age of 18 had already mounted two solo exhibitions under her given names, June Claire. The first, in 1935 – a quarter of a century before Pop Art – featured watercolours influenced by the three-colour process dots in comic strips, and resulted in an invitation to work and exhibit in Mexico City. In 1938 she became an easel painter with the WPA Federal Art Project in Chicago, choosing mills, factories and the Chicago River as subjects, and mixing with an influential circle of musicians, writers and scientists. In 1939 she continued to paint while working as an ornament designer for the fashion industry in New York.

War took her to California where she studied production illustration, making three-dimensional drawings from aeroplane blueprints. This led her to investigate the point at which the laws of perspective broke down. In 1948 Wayne took up lithography in the hope that it would give her a new slant on compositions dealing with focal and peripheral vision, suggested by driving through a Los Angeles tunnel at night. In the prophetic lithograph *Strange Moon* (1951; Gilmour 1992, G12) she determined the spectator's eye path by moving a floating disc across a field like an expanded chequer-board.

The work anticipated the Optical Art movement, which was not launched in New York until more than a decade later. Since she did not subscribe to the contemporary rejection of narrative, Wayne also enjoyed inventing pictorial characters. Her painting *The Sanctified* (1950; oil and wax on canvas; Palm Springs Desert Museum, CA), for example, pokes fun at sanctimonious people, obliquely referring to a male artist in her community. As with other paintings of the period, the idea was also realised as a lithograph. During the early 1950s Wayne's thematically related prints, paintings and drawings were exhibited in several solo shows on the West Coast, and in 1952 she won the *Los Angeles Times* Woman of the Year award for modern art. In addition to taking numerous print prizes in juried exhibitions of the 1950s, she was one of several artists selected to represent the USA at the São Paulo Bienal in 1955 and at the Tate Gallery, London, a year later.

When Wayne first worked with the Los Angeles printer Lynton Kistler, he still offered stone lithography to artists, and she became so enamoured of the process that by the mid-1950s she had already collaborated with him on some 40 editions. Around 1956, however, Kistler abandoned stone because of an allergy to its chemicals. Consequently, Wayne's *Fable Series*, stemming from Abraham Kaplan's irreverent adaptations of Bible stories, had to be drawn on metal plates for the offset press. As lithography was by now as important to her as painting and she felt that the only other artists' lithographer in the USA had considerable limitations, Wayne left for Paris early in 1957, to work with Marcel Durassier.

In 1990 Wayne, a gifted writer, immortalised Durassier in the article "Broken stones and whooping cranes", which includes one of the most memorable descriptions of a printer in the English language. She tells how the Frenchman, initially opposed to her unconventional methods, was eventually won over by the originality of her washes for a series of prints inspired by the English Metaphysical poet John Donne. The prints prepared the ground for a book based on Donne's *Songs & Sonets* (*ibid*., G66), which she made in an intense marathon lasting from mid-October until the New Year, during a second French sojourn in 1958. Exhibited early in 1959 at the Los Angeles County Museum, Wayne's book was hailed as one of the first *livres d'artiste* to be made by an American – let alone by an American woman.

Songs & Sonets also played its part in the conception of Tamarind. Just before leaving for France to work on it with Durassier, Wayne pointed out to W. McNeil Lowry of the Ford Foundation that she now had to go to Europe to make lithographs, and suggested that the Foundation should do something for all artists by restoring the dying art. When Wayne returned with her book, Lowry recognised her as a person who would carry through whatever she undertook, and he eventually secured over $2 million to fund the workshop she proposed, as long as she agreed to direct it herself. Her plan for Tamarind proved so sound that not only were numerous artists introduced to the process but, in 1983, a journal recorded that there were now 163 print workshops spread across 25 states (Lisa Peters, "Print workshops USA: A listing", *Print Collector's Newsletter*, viii, 1983, pp.201–6).

Although Wayne continued to make prints while she was running Tamarind – the title of one of her masterpieces, *At Last a Thousand* (1965; Gilmour 1992, G82), refers to the

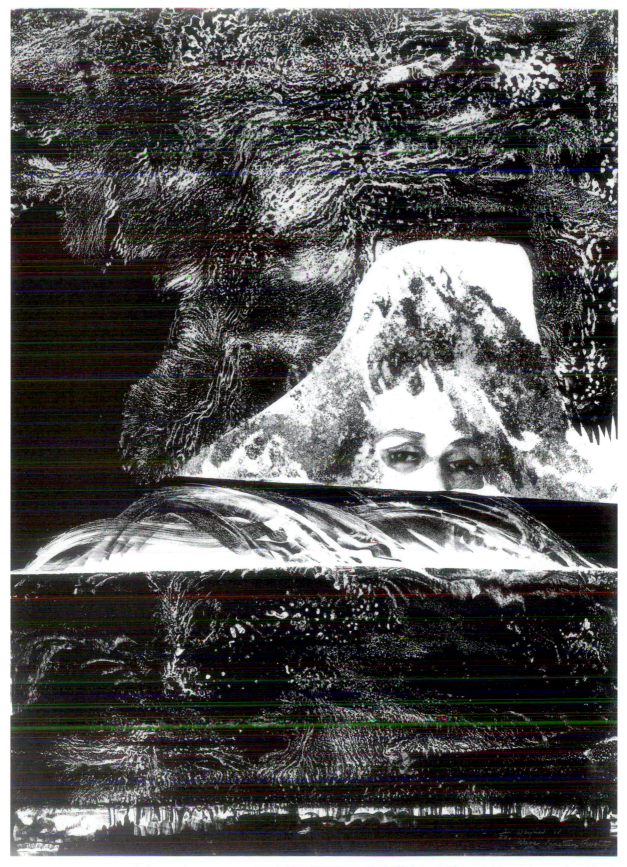

Wayne: *Wave 1920*, 1968–70; lithograph; 84.5 × 61.3 cm.; bleed image on Zerkall Copperplate Deluxe paper; printed by Serge Lozingot, TLW Los Angeles in black and warm black, from a drawing on zinc transferred to stone; 41 impressions

number assigned to the lithograph by the workshop – her duties allowed little time for her own work. So she returned to it with relief in 1970 after transferring Tamarind to the University of New Mexico. In her first lithographic self-portrait *Wave 1920* (1968–70; see illustration), transitional to a series on tidal waves and other natural forces, she looks out from under an engulfing wall of water formed by one of her characteristic washes on zinc.

Wayne took up a number of feminist themes in the 1970s, including several sheets of the *Burning Helix* series honouring Rosalind Franklin, the X-ray crystallographer central to the cracking of the genetic code. She also completed the *Dorothy Series*, an affectionate and moving portfolio of 20 colour lithographs dealing with the predicament of women as expressed through the life of her mother, Dorothy Kline, who had died just before Tamarind opened. Because her parents parted when she was a baby, Wayne was brought up in a matriarchal household, cared for by her widowed grandmother while her divorced mother worked as a corset saleswoman to support the family. Wayne brought her mother to life with the documents, photographs and other artefacts associated with her, and the suite enjoyed great popular success when it toured the USA during the 1980s, and is still frequently exhibited. One of its spin-offs was the witty *Next of Skin* series, featuring both male and female undergarments – among them a delicate brassière entitled *A Little Nothing* (ibid., G192) and a green silk *Jock for Cocktails* (ibid., G200), replete with prancing unicorns.

These figurative suites were somewhat tangential to Wayne's abstract work, much of which now turned to science for inspiration. The *Burning Helix* lithographs became cartoons for a magisterial series of tapestries on a grand scale, woven in France and toured extensively through Europe. *Verdict* (ibid., G101/II), some three metres high, was suggested by the colour state of a print in which the helical staircase revealed by Franklin had become a twisted strand of beads. Living in Los Angeles, Wayne was ideally placed to indulge her growing fascination for "the ineffably beautiful but hostile wilderness of astrophysical space", and her work on the subject moved into high gear in the second half of the 1970s when she employed the Tamarind-trained Edward Hamilton as her personal printer. Creating minimalist striations from the subtle oxidation patterns formed on zinc, Wayne used them as a paradigm for solar winds that blow from dying stars with great fury, furnishing the elements from which everything is made. The irreproducible *Silent Wind* (ibid., G135), suggesting an intricate and fragile network of fissured skin, is a monochrome masterpiece of the period, while the *Stellar Winds* series, in which the white of the paper functions as light, was the first of several portfolios on the astrophysical theme, completed in 1979. During the 1980s Wayne's daily collaboration with Hamilton was increasingly concerned with vivid colour. Vast distances and luminescent gases were cleverly evoked in the five sheets of *Solar Flares* (1983), conjuring up the heat and light of the sun, while in the nine gorgeous lithographs of *My Palomar* (1984), a square, ambiguously alternating detail and field, is tracked through interstellar space.

In the second half of the 1980s Wayne again forged links between media when she worked on the *Cognitos* reliefs, suggesting complex planetary topographies. Ink on paper, judiciously printed with a subtle range of greys, cleverly mimics the icy brilliance of reliefs clothed in silver leaf, while in other innovatory hybrids three-dimensional silver elements are collaged on to black lithographic fields.

Despite this intense aesthetic activity, Wayne has always found time to rally forces or address an issue. While with the WPA, she testified before a Congressional Committee in Washington, DC, petitioning for continued support for the arts. In the 1950s she took part in the "You and Modern Art" programmes set up by the critic Jules Langsner after an episode in which the Los Angeles City Council maintained that modern art was a Communist conspiracy. In 1972 and 1973 she ran the celebrated Joan of Art seminars to help women artists realise their full potential. And, periodically, she has defended the National Endowment for the Arts when it has been attacked, or raised the alarm when taxation issues threatened artists with bankruptcy. She has also been a witty and mordant analyst of her profession, notably in "The male artist as stereotypical female" (1973) and "The creative process: Artists, carpenters and the Flat Earth Society" (1976). Both urged artists to place more faith in their intellects and to spend less time cultivating "the divine flame that gets one invited to dinner".

In 1989 Wayne closed down her own press in order to spend more time on paintings and collages for the *Djuna Set*, first shown in a major retrospective at the Fresno Museum in 1988. Although she has made fewer lithographs since then, a tiny etching of 1888 by the Belgian artist, James Ensor, sparked a new print series. Ensor had depicted himself as a skeleton, entitling the work *Mon portrait en 2060*. Wayne appropriated the image for a lithograph, added her own skeleton and a couple of California palms, and called the new composition *Nos portraits en 1960* (Gilmour 1992, G274). Meanwhile she is adding new paintings to the *Djuna Set* in preparation for a major retrospective of all media in 1997, organised by the Neuberger Museum.

Wayne's prints are held by most major museums in the USA including the Achenbach Foundation for Graphic Arts, San Francisco; Grunwald Center for the Graphic Arts, Los Angeles; Los Angeles County Museum of Art; Museum of Modern Art, New York; National Gallery of Art, Washington, DC; and the Museums of American Art and American History at the Smithsonian Institution, Washington, DC. They can also be seen at the Bibliothèque Nationale, Paris; Bibliothèque royale Albert Ier, Brussels; British Museum, London; and the National Gallery of Australia, Canberra.

PAT GILMOUR

Wegmann, Bertha
Danish painter, 1847–1926

Born in Soglio, Graubunden, Switzerland, 16 December 1847. Moved with her parents to Copenhagen, 1853. Studied drawing under Frederik Ferdinand Helsted, painting under Frederik Christian Lund and Heinrich Buntzen. Lived in Munich, 1867–81; studied painting under Wilhelm Lindenschmidt and Eduard Kurzbauer. Returned to Copenhagen, 1882. Trips to Paris and Brittany in 1881–2, 1884, 1886 and 1888–9; also studied in Florence. Recipient

Wegmann: *Jeanne Bauck*, 1881; oil on canvas; 106 × 85 cm.; Nationalmuseum, Stockholm

of Thorvaldsen medal, Copenhagen, 1883. Member of the Plenum Assembly (Plenarforsamling), Royal Danish Academy of Fine Arts, Copenhagen, 1883 (only female member). Died in Copenhagen, 22 February 1926.

Principal Exhibitions

Charlottenborg, Copenhagen: occasionally 1873–1926 (salons; first-place gold medals 1892 and 1896), 1883 (*Den Nordiske udstilling* [Nordic exhibition]), 1888 (*Den Nordiske udstilling* [Nordic exhibition]), 1926 (retrospective)

Paris Salon: 1880 (honourable mention), 1882 (gold medal)

Exposition Universelle, Paris: 1889 (silver medal), 1900 (silver medal)

World's Columbian Exposition, Chicago: 1893

Industriforeningen, Copenhagen: 1895 (*Kvindernes udstilling – fra fortid til nutid* [Women's exhibition – from the past to the present])

Den frie udstillingsbygning, Copenhagen: 1920 (*Kvindelige kunstneres retrospektive udstilling* [Women artists' retrospective])

Bibliography

S. Müller, *Nyere dansk malerkunst* [More recent Danish painting], 1884

C.A. Been, *Danmarks malerkunst* [Denmark's painting], Copenhagen: Det Nordiske Forlag, 1902

"Bertha Wegmann", *Illustreret Tidende*, no.63, 1917, pp.437–8

Bertha Wegmanns mindendstilling [Bertha Wegmann's commemorative exhibition], exh. cat., Charlottenborg, Copenhagen, 1926

Knud Voss, *Dansk kunsthistorie, billedkunst og skulptur: Friluftsstudie og virkelighed skildring, 1850–1900* [Danish art history, painting and sculpture: Open-air study and depiction of reality, 1850–1900], Copenhagen: Politikens Forlag, 1974

Hans Edvard Norregard-Nielsen, *Dansk kunst* [Danish art], ii, Gyldendal, 1987

De drogo till Paris: Nordiska konstnärinnor på 1880-talet [They went to Paris: Nordic women artists in the 1880s], exh. cat., Liljevalchs Konsthall, Stockholm, 1988

Alessandra Comini, "Nordic luminism and the Scandinavian recasting of Impressionism", *World Impressionism: The International Movement, 1860–1920*, ed. Norma Broude, New York: Abrams, 1992, pp.274–313

Bertha Wegmann painted portraits at a time when portraiture was one of the few artistic avenues in which women artists could make a living. Her impressionistically brushed depictions of men and women were portraits of the model as well as of the artist herself. Critics commented on her ability to capture the individual character of each sitter.

Wegmann emigrated from Switzerland to Copenhagen with her parents when she was only five. The death of her mother, when Wegmann was ten, was influential on her later choice of subjects: throughout her career she painted many canvases depicting mothers and children. Because there were no official art schools in Copenhagen that women could attend until the establishment of the Drawing School for Women in 1876 and the Art School for Women in 1888, most aspiring female artists studied privately. Wegmann studied first at Frederik Ferdinand Helsted's private drawing school, then with Frederik Christian Lund, who, as Wegmann bitterly recalled, verbally abused his female students.

Her father arranged for friends to sponsor her studies in Munich from 1867 to 1881. During the Munich period her palette was dark, although her portraits showed a lively, fresh interpretation of personalities. While studying in Munich she met the painter Jeanna Bauck, with whom she painted and

travelled over the following years. Moving to Paris in 1881, both Wegmann and Bauck became influenced by the modified, genre-based Impressionism of Jules Bastien-Lepage, who influenced the work of a number of the Nordic painters living in Paris during the 1870s and 1880s. Wegmann's canvases painted in Paris, exemplified by the portrait of *Jeanna Bauck* (1881; see illustration), lightened in colour and human interest. Over the space of a year she painted more than 20 portraits of Bauck. *Fru Seekamp, the Painter's Sister* (1880; Statens Museum for Kunst, Copenhagen) was not only placed in the Paris Salon of 1882, but received a gold medal there.

Wegmann became the first woman artist to be invited to show work in the Danish Academy's plein-air collection; and in 1883 was invited to be a member of the Academy and later a member of the jury for their exhibitions at the Charlottenborg Palace. In 1895 she helped to organise Denmark's first "Women's exhibition".

Although portraiture was the staple of her career, Wegmann also painted many canvases depicting still-life compositions and genre scenes (e.g. *Still Life*, 1883; *Mother and Child*; both Nationalmuseum, Stockholm). Her portraits, such as those of *Professor Julius Thomsen* (1897; Copenhagen University), the sculptor *August Saabye* (1903; private collection) and *Director Edouard Suenson* (1903; Frederiksborg Castle), chronicled the cultural elite of Copenhagen's academic and artistic communities.

MARY TOWLEY SWANSON

Weisberg, Ruth

American painter, draughtswoman and printmaker, 1942–

Born in Chicago, 31 July 1942. Enrolled at University of Michigan, Ann Arbor, 1959, then left to study painting and printmaking at Accademia delle Belle Arti, Perugia, Italy, 1960–62 (laurea). Studied at University of Michigan, 1963–5 (BA, MFA). Worked in Paris with Stanley William Hayter at Atelier 17, 1964 and 1965. Married research psychologist Kelyn Roberts, 1966 (second marriage); daughter born 1973, son born 1977. Lived in Ann Arbor and taught at Eastern Michigan University, Ypsilanti, 1966–9; moved to Santa Monica, California, 1969. Taught at University of Southern California, Los Angeles, from 1970 (full professor 1980). Contributor to *Artweek* from 1975. Founder, Southern California Chapter, Women's Caucus for Art, 1976. Recipient of Ford Foundation grant, 1969; Vesta award, Women's Building, Los Angeles, 1984; Phi Beta Kappa Faculty Recognition award for creative work, University of Southern California, 1986; National Women's Caucus for Art Mid-Career Achievement award, 1987; University of Michigan School of Art outstanding alumni award, 1987 and 1992; Distinguished Artist award, Fresno Art Museum, California, 1990; National Endowment of the Humanities Summer Seminar award, 1994. Visiting artist, American Academy in Rome, 1992 and 1994. President, College Art Association, 1990–92. Lives in Santa Monica, California.

Weisberg: *The Basin II*, 1990; monotype; 64.8 × 50.8 cm.

Selected Individual Exhibitions

Alice Simsar Gallery, Ann Arbor, MI: 1968, 1969, 1972, 1974, 1977, 1988, 1992

Municipal Art Gallery, Oslo: 1972

University of Southern California, Los Angeles: 1972, 1986 (*A Circle of Life*, touring)

Union Gallery, Arizona State University, Tempe: 1976

Oglethorpe University, Atlanta: 1978

Hunter Art Gallery, Hunter College, New York: 1978

Los Angeles Municipal Art Gallery, Barnsdall Park: 1979

Judah L. Magnes Museum, Berkeley, CA: 1981

Jack Rutberg Fine Arts, Los Angeles: 1983, 1985, 1988, 1991, 1993, 1995

Philadelphia Print Club, Philadelphia: 1985

Joseph Gallery, Hebrew Union College, New York: 1987–9 (*The Scroll*, touring)

Associated American Artists, New York: 1987, 1990

Jean Paul Slusser Gallery, University of Michigan, Ann Arbor: 1988–9 (touring retrospective)

Fresno Art Museum, CA: 1990 (retrospective), 1994 (*Sisters and Brothers*, touring)

Gwenda Jay Gallery, Chicago: 1991, 1992, 1995

Temple University, Rome: 1994

Selected Writings

The Shtetl: A Journey and a Memorial, Santa Monica, CA: Kelyn Press, 1971 (limited edition)

Bibliography

Ruth Weisberg: Survey Exhibition, 1971–79, exh. cat., Los Angeles Municipal Art Gallery, Barnsdall Park, 1979

Ruth Weisberg, exh. cat., Judah L. Magnes Museum, Berkeley, CA, 1981

Melinda Wortz, "Ruth Weisberg", *Art News*, lxxxiii, January 1984, pp.112–13

Gilah Yelin Hirsch, "Ruth Weisberg: Transcendance of time through persistence of imagery", *Woman's Art Journal*, vi/2, 1985–6, pp.41–5

A Circle of Life, exh. cat., Fisher Gallery, University of Southern California, Los Angeles, and elsewhere, 1986

Peter Clothier, "Ruth Weisberg at USC", *Art in America*, lxxiv, April 1986, pp.197–8

The Scroll, exh. cat., Joseph Gallery, Hebrew Union College, New York, and elsewhere, 1987

Ruth Weisberg: Paintings, Drawings, Prints, 1968–1988, exh. cat., Jean Paul Slusser Gallery, University of Michigan, Ann Arbor, and elsewhere, 1988

Thalia Gouma-Peterson, "Passages in cyclical time: Ruth Weisberg's *Scroll*", *Arts Magazine*, lxii, February 1988, pp.56–9

Betty Ann Brown and Arlene Raven, *Exposures: Women and Their Art*, Pasadena, CA: NewSage Press, 1989

Ruth Weisberg Prints: Mid-Life Catalogue Raisonné, 1961–1990, exh. cat., Fresno Art Museum, CA, 1990

Judith Hoffberg and June Wayne, "Ruth Weisberg prints", *Tamarind Papers*, xiv, 1991–2, pp.83–4

Ruth Weisberg feels the rush of time. She is very aware of the past and of the fleeting moment she occupies in the present. Her prints, paintings and performances record her passions, memories, dreams; they are eternal images of the ephemeral.

In the 1970s personal narrative became an imperative as feminist and post-structuralist theory gave artists permission to reveal more and more of themselves in their works. Weisberg, who had anticipated this movement with autobiographical representations from as early as the 1960s (e.g. *In the Mirror*, 1969; oil on canvas; artist's collection; *Deposition*, 1969; mixed-media drawing; Whitney Museum of American Art, New York), committed herself to an ongoing exploration of her identity as woman, as artist, as Jew. As she continues to situate herself, her friends and her family in radiant pictorial tableaux, Weisberg's works echo the writings of the American transcendentalist philosopher Ralph Waldo Emerson, who asserted: "All history becomes subjective; in other words, there is properly no History, only Biography" (*Emerson's Essays*, New York: Harper, 1926).

In the early 1980s Weisberg worked on a cycle of eleven paintings (with numerous related drawings and lithographs) entitled *A Circle of Life*. The *Circle* explores the timeless but temporally bound themes of birth, growth, transformation and transition in shimmering veils of translucent colour that appear to blend the amber and aqua of fire and water. Although Weisberg bases her compositions on traditional academic drawing, her silken curtains of light and deep cavernous shadows give her paintings a poetic quality that is quite modern. Because the artist combines images from different places and times in single framed segments and juxtaposes scenes that are neither logically nor narratively linked, she eludes any linear or illustrative mode. First exhibited at the University of Southern California where Weisberg was professor of art, the *Circle* then toured to the Hewlett Gallery of Carnegie-Mellon University, Pittsburgh. *Circle and Leave* from the cycle is now in the collection of the National Museum of Women in the Arts, Washington, DC, and the related *Passage* lithograph is in the Whitney Museum of American Art, New York.

Weisberg's innovative compositions have often been fuelled by her willingness to deal with issues of transcendence and spirituality, in many cases, but not always, through Judaism. *The Scroll* (1986–7; length 28.6 m.; Skirball Cultural Center of Hebrew Union College) is a drawing that depicts a life's journey blended with biblical story and Jewish history. Weisberg has worked for years with Rabbi Laura Geller (rabbi of the Temple Emmanuel Reformed Synagogue in Beverly Hills, and the only female rabbi of a major synagogue in the USA) to write the austere patriarchy out of Judaism; the artist uses the Torah to illuminate her own life and to link it to that of all Jews. Read from right to left, the monumental *Scroll* establishes a compelling and rhythmic counterpoint that pauses at poignant moments of individual emphasis then accelerates through dense, cascading waves of humanity in order to meld the personal with the universal.

Weisberg has long considered the relationship of the viewer to her art work. Her consciousness of the physicality and perceptions of the viewer merged with her experiences as a performance artist (she began performing in the late 1960s with the Fluxus-influenced Once Group in Ann Arbor) to lead her to create installations that invite viewers to enter and be enveloped by imagery. Weisberg's installation *Isaac's Heirs* (artist's collection), created for the *Utopian Dialogues* exhibition at the Los Angeles Municipal Art Gallery in 1993, is structured around the passport of her grandfather Isaac Herbst, who came to the USA from Poland and was co-founder of the utopian community of Clarion in Utah in 1911. When Clarion failed in 1915, Herbst moved to Salt Lake City, then Chicago. In 1929 he travelled to Russia to found Biro-Bidzhan, a second community based on his radical political ideals of social justice, collectivity and a Jewish homeland. Flanking large images of the accordion-folded pages of Herbst's passport are portraits of Weisberg and her mother Theresa, seated at a kitchen table discussing their family history. A carefully edited tape-recording of their conversations about Herbst and about Theresa's early life at Clarion whispers the story to viewers who enter the embrace of the paintings. Weisberg's large-scale work *Sisters and Brothers* (1994; Jack Rutberg Fine Arts, Los Angeles) consists of 14 paintings in a tent-like steel structure 3.96 metres high and 5.49 metres in diameter. Mixing biblical and contemporary references, *Sisters and Brothers* invites viewers to construct their own narratives about conflicts, struggles and reconciliations between siblings.

Weisberg is a committed and accomplished activist for the arts in general and for women in the arts in particular. In 1981 she and the feminist performance artist Suzanne Lacy organised a protest at the sexist and racist exhibition record of the Los Angeles County Museum of Art, focusing on that year's *Museum as Site* exhibition that included only two women artists and no artists of colour. Weisberg founded the Southern California Chapter of Women's Caucus for Art in 1976 and has received many awards and honours. She was the first woman artist to hold the position of President of the College Art Association, and has written more than 55 articles, reviews and catalogue essays.

Emerson wrote: "All inquiry into antiquity...is the desire to do away this wild, savage, and preposterous There or Then, and introduce in its place the Here and the Now. It is to banish the *not me* and supply the *me*. It is to abolish difference and restore unity" (*Emerson's Essays*, New York: Harper, 1926, p.6). Ruth Weisberg's art, as it incorporates her own face and body into scenes of art and family history, of Jewish ritual and of the life cycles of Everywoman, gives concrete visual form to the historical inquiry about which Emerson speculated. Weisberg's art seeks "to abolish difference and restore unity".

BETTY ANN BROWN

Weiss, Rosario

Spanish painter and printmaker, 1814–1843

Born in Madrid, 2 October 1814. Studied under the painter Francisco de Goya between the ages of seven and fifteen; under the architect Tiburcio Pérez, 1823–4. Further studies under Goya in Burdeos, 1824–8; also studied under M. Vernet and later Pier Lacour, Director of the Burdeos Academy. Returned to Madrid, 1833; made a living as a copyist. Appointed drawing instructor to Queen Isabel II, 18 January 1842. Recipient of silver medal, Sociedad Filomática de Burdeos. Academician of merit, Real Academia de San Fernando, 1840. Died in Madrid, July 1843.

Principal Exhibitions

Real Academia de San Fernando, Madrid: 1835–42

Bibliography

D.F.A. Rascon, "Rosario Weiss", *Gaceta del Gobierno*, 20 September 1843

"Rosario Weiss", *Semanario Pintoresco Español*, 26 November 1843
Vicente Díaz Canseco, *Diccionario biográfico universal de mujeres célebres*, 3 vols, Madrid, 1844–5
José Parada y Santín, *Las pintoras españolas: Boceto histórico-biográfico y artístico*, Madrid, 1902 (preface by Avilés y Merino)
Colección de cuatrocientas cuarenta y nueve reproducciones de cuadros, dibujos y agua fuertes de Don Francisco de Goya precedidos de un epistolario del gran pintor y de las Noticias biográficas publicadas por don Francisco Zapater y Gómez, Madrid: Saturnino Calleja, 1924
Enrique Lafuente Ferrari, *Antecedentes, coincidencias e influencias del arte de Goya*, Madrid: Sociedad Española de Amigos del Arte, 1947
J. López Rey, "Goya and his pupil Maria del Rosario Weiss", *Gazette des Beaux-Arts*, 6th series, xlvii, May–June 1956, pp.251–84
Carmen G. Pérez-Neu, *Galería universal de pintoras*, Madrid: Nacional, 1964
Manuel Ossorio y Bernard, *Galería biográfica de artistas españoles del siglo XIX*, Madrid: Libreria Gaudi, 1975
Germaine Greer, *The Obstacle Race: The Fortunes of Women Painters and Their Work*, London: Secker and Warburg, and New York: Farrar Straus, 1979
Juan Carrete, *El grabado en España (siglos XIX y XX)*, Summa Artis, xxxii, Madrid: Espasa-Calpe, 1988
María Elena Gómez Moreno, *Pintura y escultura españolas del siglo XIX*, Summa Artis, xxxv/1, Madrid: Espasa-Calpe, 1993

Rosario Weiss is a paradigm of several inescapable obstacles in the careers of female artists: a disciple rather than an artist, an imitator rather than a creator, she put her talent to the service of technique and even worked on the falsification of paintings. Because of this, very few examples of works attributed to her survive and contemporary critics have underrated her through the always problematic comparison with her teacher and, in all likelihood, father, Francisco de Goya.

As in the cases of many other women artists, serious problems make it difficult today to judge the true artistic merit of Weiss's work. On the one hand, the painter appears as the young artist to whom Goya referred as "possibly the greatest phenomenon there will be in the world for such a young girl" (*Colección de cuatrocientas cuarenta y nueve reproducciones... 1924*, p.54). Vicente Díaz Canseco wrote that she could have executed "works that would have been as immortal as those painted by Murillo, Velázquez and Herrera" (Díaz Canseco 1844–5, p.641); even in 1902 José Parada y Santín considered her to be an impassioned and cultivated artist. Those who have studied Goya in the 20th century, however, have not viewed Weiss in so positive a light. Lafuente Ferrari, seeking the heritage of Goya's genius in Weiss, reached unfavourable conclusions, while López Rey considered her work to be merely an appendix to Goya's late work. Gómez Moreno seems to have been disillusioned with Weiss's later development. There can be two possible readings of the adverse development of Weiss's critical fortune: either an excess of gallantry in 19th-century criticism has de-contextualised her work, or else the present loss of most of it prohibits a correct evaluation, which is based instead excessively on the artist's personal relationship with Goya.

According to statements in his biography, Goya began to teach Rosario when she was scarcely seven years old; to do so, he would draw "small figures, groups and caricatures of things that might catch her attention" on sheets of paper, which she would copy, frequently on the back of his drawings. For Greer

Weiss: *Self-Portrait*, Biblioteca Nacional, Madrid

(1979), such a teaching method signified the invasion of a child's mind by a powerful artistic figure who configured the painter's graphic language. Weiss's later teaching by Lacour was also based on the imitation of models. Several drawings from this period attributed to the artist are preserved in the Hispanic Society of New York, as well as others in the Biblioteca Nacional, the Prado and the Museo Lázaro Galdiano, Madrid, and the Museo Diocesano, Girona (see López Rey 1956). On her return to Madrid, Weiss's skill in imitating the great masters opened up a market for her producing copies of works by Leonardo da Vinci, Andrea del Sarto, Titian, Goya and Murillo; she even made a living from faking pictures. Nevertheless, one of her own creations sent to the Sociedad Filomática of Burdeos won her a silver medal and suggests a creativity that was never fully exploited. She executed important work as a draughtswoman and printmaker, although she greatly disliked the failure of lithography to reproduce the quality and details of her drawings. The high quality and precision of her printmaking can be appreciated in her copies of other paintings such as the reproduction of Goya's portrait of *Vicente López* (Biblioteca Nacional, Madrid) and that of the *Dukes of San Fernando* (Colección Antonio, Correa), painted by Rafael Tejeo. Outstanding among Weiss's drawings are two *Self-Portraits*, the portrait of the landlord Romanos for the fourth edition of *Escenas Matritenses*, the *Wet-Nurse* for the Liceo Artístico y Literario and the portraits of *Manuela Oreiro* and *Zorilla* (all Biblioteca Nacional). She also illustrated Manuela de Andueza's *Isla de Cuba pintoresca* (Biblioteca Nacional) and painted a *Praying Virgin* (Museo de la Real Academia de Bellas Artes de San Fernando, Madrid).

RUTH PÉREZ ANTELO

Welles, Clara Pauline Barck
American silversmith, 1868–1965

Born Clara Pauline Barck in Oregon, 1868. Studied under Louis J. Millet at the School of the Art Institute of Chicago, graduating in 1900. Opened shop to sell burnt leatherwork and weavings in Chicago, 1900. Married amateur metalworker George S. Welles, 1905. Founded Kalo Art-Craft community for metalsmithing in Park Ridge, Illinois, and opened a Chicago showroom, 1905; established a retail outlet in New York, 1914–18. Teacher and designer for Kalo community and shop, 1905–40. Retired to Mission Hills, near San Diego, California, 1940. Turned business over to four employees, 1959 (shop closed 1970). Died 1965.

Principal Exhibitions
Art Institute of Chicago: occasionally 1902–21
Metropolitan Museum of Art, New York: 1937

Bibliography
Robert Judson Clark, ed., *The Arts and Crafts Movement in America, 1876–1916*, Princeton: Princeton University Press, 1972

Sharon S. Darling, *Chicago Metalsmiths: An Illustrated History*, Chicago: Chicago Historical Society, 1977

Erne R. Frueh and Florence Frueh, "Clara Barck Welles and her Kalo silverware", *Antiques Journal*, xxxiii, May 1978, pp.12–15, 48

Anthea Callen, *Angel in the Studio: Women in the Arts and Crafts Movement, 1870–1914*, London: Astragal, 1979; as *Women Artists of the Arts and Crafts Movement, 1870–1914*, New York: Pantheon, 1979

Wendy Kaplan, ed., *Encyclopedia of Arts and Crafts*, New York: Dutton, and London: Headline, 1989

Reflections: Arts and Crafts Metalwork in England and the United States, exh. cat., Kurland-Zabor, New York, 1990

Elizabeth Cumming and Wendy Kaplan, *The Arts and Crafts Movement*, London and New York: Thames and Hudson, 1991

The Ideal Home, 1900–1920, exh. cat., American Craft Museum, New York, 1993

Elyse Zorn Karlin, *Jewelry and Metalwork in the Arts and Crafts Tradition*, Atglen, PA: Schiffer, 1993

It was not at random that Clara Barck Welles chose the name "Kalo" for the silversmithing shop she opened in Chicago in the early 20th century – Kalo means beautiful in Greek and beauty is what she strove for in her work. Welles is still an important name in the history of American metalsmithing, and she is probably the most important of all American women silversmiths. Growing up in Chicago, she came of age just as the Arts and Crafts movement had made its way from Britain to the USA. With its many residents who were interested in social, educational and aesthetic reform, Chicago was a particularly receptive city to the ideals of the movement. Through her studies at the Art Institute of Chicago and her exposure to lectures by such British Arts and Crafts luminaries as C.R. Ashbee, Welles entered her profession with a desire to create objects that were completely hand-made and of "honest construction". This goal symbolised a return to earlier times before the advent of machines in silversmithing and jewellery-making. Almost single-handedly, Welles created a renaissance of silversmithing in Chicago. Her work, however, like that of most American silversmiths of the Arts and Crafts period, differed from British work in one important way – whereas Welles began with sheets of metal that had been rolled out of

Welles: *Bowl*, Kalo shop, Park Ridge, Illinois, 1905–14; silver; height 8.3 cm.; diameter of top, 8.3 cm.; Art Institute of Chicago; Restricted gift of Mr and Mrs Robert A. Kubicek, 1988.443

an ingot by machine, her British counterparts did their work entirely by hand. To Welles, the importance of the enterprise lay in the originality of the design and her love for her work, which began for her when a piece of silver started to be raised from the sheet of metal. She was also a perfectionist who required the same from the silversmiths who executed her designs, and the quality of the pieces that came out of her shop remains today as testament to these high standards.

Early in her career Welles and her "Kalo girls" (the young girls who helped to execute items from her designs) worked in copper, making simple trays, bowls, bookends and desk accessories. These early copper pieces are quite rare, because not many were made. Before long Welles was lining the bowls with silver, leading her into real silversmithing, which was to become her métier. One example from the period 1905–14 is a copper bowl with a silver lining and an applied "S" on the outside (Chicago Historical Society). Originally, it may have been accompanied by a silver fork and spoon to form a salad set (Darling 1977, p.45).

Welles specialised in the design of tableware. The early pieces were often somewhat angular, and set with cabochon stones (frequently green in colour) in the manner of work produced by Ashbee and the Guild of Handicraft. As her design sense evolved, she moved into a softer, more rounded look, which although embarked on originally to give physical strength to her silver creations became her signature in style as well. Items designed by Welles were extremely popular in her time, and are highly coveted by collectors today for their "classic simplicity", which was no doubt influenced by the characteristic austerity of early American silver. Her designs, executed by many important silversmiths who were apprenticed and worked for her, were always beautifully crafted and expertly finished. They featured visible hammer marks – a trademark of the Arts and Crafts movement.

While her silver pieces were simply decorated with only an applied rim or applied monogram, they were at the same time extremely sophisticated. Many were purchased by wealthy Chicago citizens and other prominent Americans. A fine example is a partly flared silver bowl on a circular foot with the applied initials "C de M C" (Kurland-Zabor Gallery, New York). The bowl is believed to have been made for the American film director Cecil B. de Mille and his wife Constance and given to them on their wedding anniversary in 1927 (New York 1990, p.41). The variety of items designed by Welles and produced by the Kalo shop was endless, ranging from flatware and serving pieces for the table to christening items, letter openers, picture frames, calling-card cases and boxes. Items could be bought from stock but many were also custom-made. Jewellery also became an important part of Welles's design repertoire. The range of items produced included necklaces, bracelets, rings, earrings, watch chains and fobs, stickpins, cufflinks, belt buckles and brooches. Like the silver domestic items, the jewellery was usually quite simple in nature, often decorated with images of native American flowers, such as the poppy, pansy, and lily-of-the-valley, or fruits, as on her well-known cherry pins (repr. Darling 1977, p.51). Pearls and semi-precious stones, including opals, moonstone, garnet, lapis lazuli, amethyst, jade and bloodstone, were set into some of her jewellery. Later designs, after 1920, exhibit a strong Nordic influence, particularly that of Georg Jensen, due to the fact that Welles employed a number of talented Nordic silversmiths in the shop. Although most of her jewellery was wrought in silver, some gold work was executed as well.

The Chicago Historical Society has more than 300 drawings of items designed by Welles in its collection, as well as examples of her work. Many pieces of Kalo table items and jewellery survive today in private collections, and on storage at several museums. The Art Institute of Chicago has a number of pieces, including a simple silver bowl (see illustration), made between 1905 and 1914, a silver pitcher with the initial "F" applied to it, and a silver pin with an enamel setting. The survival of such pieces is in perfect harmony with the Kalo motto: Beautiful, useful, "enduring".

ELYSE ZORN KARLIN

Wells, Joanna Boyce *see* Boyce

Werefkin, Marianne
Russian painter, 1860–1938

Born in Tula, 29 August 1860, into a military family. Received drawing lessons from a woman Academy instructor, 1874. Trained in portrait painting by the Warsaw-based artist P. Heinemann in Lublin, Poland, 1876. Studio established in summer residence "Gut Blagodat" in Kovno (now Kaunas), Lithuania, 1879. Became a private student of Ilya Repin, 1880. Trained under Illarion Pryanishnikov at the Moscow

Academy, 1883. Moved to St Petersburg, 1886. Right hand injured in a shooting accident, 1888. Met the artist Alexej Jawlensky, 1891. Inherited an annuity on the death of father, enabling her to move to Munich with Jawlensky, 1896; devoted herself to developing Jawlensky's career for the next ten years. Founded the St Luke Artists Association, which held meetings at her Munich residence, 1897. Visited Venice with Jawlensky and other Russian painters from Anton Ažbè's studio, 1899. Started journal *Lettres à un inconnu* (completed 1905) and travelled to Russia, 1901–2. Visited Normandy and Paris with Jawlensky and was impressed by work of Neo-Impressionists and van Gogh, 1903. Accompanied Jawlensky on extended trip to Brittany, Paris, Provence and Switzerland, visiting the artist Ferdinand Hodler, 1905. Under the impact of the French avant-garde, began to sketch again, 1906. Visit of the Nabis Jan Verkade and Paul Sérusier to studio, 1907. Painted alongside Jawlensky, Gabriele Münter (q.v.) and Kandinsky in Murnau, 1908–10. Founder member, Neue Künstlervereinigung München, 1909; left the association after publication of Otto Fischer's book *Das Neue Bild* to participate in exhibitions of Der Blaue Reiter, 1912. Extended visit to Russia, 1914; emigrated to St Prex, Switzerland, at outbreak of World War I. Established contact with exponents of Dada and attended sessions of the Cabaret Voltaire in Zürich; cessation of payment of tsarist pension after the October Revolution, 1917. Settled in Ascona, Switzerland, 1918. Returned to Munich to arrange storage of possessions and paintings, 1920. Separated from Jawlensky, 1922. With seven other artists, founded the group Der grosse Bär in Ascona, 1924. Visited major sites of Italy, 1926. Died 6 February 1938; buried according to Russian Orthodox rites.

Principal Exhibitions

Neue Künstlervereinigung München, Galerie Thannhauser, Munich: 1909–11
Galerie Der Sturm, Berlin: 1912 (*Der Blaue Reiter*), 1913 (*Erster deutscher Herbstsalon*), 1914 (with Jacoba van Heemskerck)
Sonderbund, Cologne: 1912
Kunstsalon Wolfsberg, Zürich: 1919 (with Alexej Jawlensky, Arthur Segal and Robert Genin)
Venice Biennale: 1920
Kunsthalle, Bern: 1925 (*Der grosse Bär*)
Galerie Nierendorf, Berlin: 1928 (with Christian Rohlfs, Karl Schmidt-Rottluff and Der grosse Bär, touring)

Selected Writings

Briefe an einen Unbekannten 1901–1905, ed. Clemens Weiler, Cologne: DuMont Schauberg, 1960
"Lettres à un inconnu, 1901–1905", *Voicing Our Visions: Writings by Women Artists*, ed. Mara R. Witzling, New York: Universe, 1991; London: Women's Press, 1992, pp.132–46

Bibliography

Otto Fischer, *Das Neue Bild*, Munich: Delphin, 1912
Gustav Pauli, *Erinnerungen aus sieben Jahrzehnten*, Tübingen: Wunderlich, 1936
F. Stöckli, *Marianne Werefkin, Otillie Roederstein, Hans Brühlmann*, Zürich: Kunsthaus, 1938
Marianne Werefkin, 1860–1938, exh. cat., Städtisches Museum, Wiesbaden, 1958
Elisabeth Erdmann-Macke, *Erinnerung an August Macke*, Stuttgart: Kohlhammer, 1962
Jelena Hahl-Koch, "Marianne Werefkin und der russische Symbolismus: Studien zur Ästhetik und Kunsttheorie", *Slavistische Beiträge*, xxiv, 1967
Rosel Gollek, *Der Blaue Reiter im Lenbachhaus München: Katalog der Sammlung in der Städtischen Galerie*, Munich: Prestel, 1974; 4th edition, 1988
Monte Verità: Berg der Wahrheit, exh. cat., Gemeindemuseum, Ascona, and Kunsthaus, Zürich, 1978
Alessandra Comini, "State of the field, 1980: The woman artists of German Expressionism", *Arts Magazine*, lv, November 1980, pp.147–53
Marianne Werefkin: Gemälde und Skizzen, exh. cat., Städtische Museum, Wiesbaden, 1980
Renate Berger, *Malerinnen auf dem Weg ins 20. Jahrhundert: Kunstgeschichte als Sozialgeschichte*, Cologne: DuMont, 1982
Ulrike Evers, *Deutsche Künstlerinnen des 20. Jahrhunderts: Malerei, Bildhauerei, Tapisserie*, Hamburg: Schultheis, 1983
Bernd Fäthke, "Die Werefkin im Profil", *Alexej Jawlensky, 1864–1941*, exh. cat., Städtische Galerie im Lenbachhaus, Munich, 1983, pp.67–71
B. Weidle (Pörtener), *Die Malerin Marianne Werefkin in München (1896–1914) und ihr Beitrag zur Entstehung der abstrakter Malerei in Deutschland*, MA thesis, Bonn University, 1986
Shulamith Behr, *Women Expressionists*, Oxford: Phaidon, and New York: Rizzoli, 1988
Marianne Werefkin: Leben und Werk, 1860–1938, exh. cat., Museo Comunale d'Arte Moderna, Ascona, and elsewhere, 1988
S. Heinlein, *Gabriele Münter und Marianne Werefkin: Die Rollen zweier Frauen im "Blauen Reiter"*, MA thesis, Hamburg University, 1989
C. Ashjian, *Primitivism and Modernity in Marianne Werefkin's 1907–1914 Works*, MA thesis, Courtauld Institute of Art, University of London, 1992
Bernd Fäthke, "Die Wiedergeburt der 'Blaue Reiter – Reiterin' in Berlin: Von der Diskriminierung der Frau in der Kunst am Beispiel Marianne Werefkin", *Profession ohne Tradition: 125 Jahre Verein der Berliner Künstlerinnen*, exh. cat., Berlinische Galerie, Berlin, 1992, pp.237–48

While Marianne Werefkin's pivotal role within Munich-based Expressionism was acknowledged by contemporary commentators, her contribution has been woefully neglected in accounts of early modernism. In post-World War II Germany her works surfaced publicly at an exhibition in Wiesbaden in 1958. Interestingly, however, she was excluded from the ambitious exhibition *Women Artists, 1550–1950* at the Los Angeles County Museum of Art in 1976 and only mentioned in passing in the accompanying catalogue (p.282). This possibly attests to the difficulty of contextualising her production in relation to either German or Russian avant-garde art and yet, even in a ground-breaking article of 1980, Alessandra Comini queried whether Werefkin's work measured up to that of her fellow Russians Alexej Jawlensky and Wassily Kandinsky (Comini 1980, p.147).

Surprisingly, then, unlike other women practitioners in her circle such as Gabriele Münter (q.v.) and Erma Bossi, Werefkin's intellectual preoccupations have received far more focused attention than her artistic abilities. In comparison to their training in Germany, women artists were not excluded from academies in Russia, and Werefkin's confident interaction in public life was considered unusual in the Munich context (Pauli 1936, p.264). By virtue of her family's military background and her independent means, she was accorded aristocratic status and was indubitably the initiator of cultural discourse at the salons organised at her Giselastrasse residence in Schwabing.

To date, however, there has been no comprehensive publication of Werefkin's writings, notes or reminiscences. In 1960 Clemens Weiler published an abridged German translation of her diaries, *Lettres à un inconnu*, 1901–5, in which he stressed Werefkin's direct influence on Kandinsky's theoretical formulations and move towards abstraction (Weiler 1960, p.71). By 1967 serious academic attention was paid to the artist's Russian symbolist heritage in Jelena Hahl-Koch's doctoral dissertation and subsequent publications. This was supplemented by Bernd Fäthke's findings on the significance of French symbolist theory to Werefkin's early intellectual maturity; titles, excerpts and commentaries on key authors and poets (Rimbaud, Mallarmé, Verlaine, Baudelaire and Edgar Allan Poe) were listed in a notebook dating from 1889 (Wiesbaden 1980, p.7). Since 1970 Fäthke and his wife have been responsible for initiating a Werefkin Archive of source material and documentation and his publication accompanying the major retrospective of her works in 1988 (Munich, Hannover and Ascona) is enriched by quotations from primary evidence; these, however, are invariably undated and unclassified.

Werefkin chose to write her journals in French, the language of elite circles in tsarist Russia. The manner of addressing the inner, unique self (*Letters to an Unknown*) acknowledges the impact of Charles Baudelaire's intimate journals *Mon coeur mis à nu* ("My heart laid bare", 1869), but Werefkin's interest in the divided being is compounded by her awareness of societal constructions of the terms "woman" and "artist": "Am I a true artist? Yes, yes, yes. Am I a woman? Alas, yes, yes, yes. Are the two able to work as a pair? No, no, no" (vol.i: abridged English translation in Witzling 1991, p.136). Hence, while the journals record the private frustrations caused by her lack of personal creative fulfilment and domestic trauma, they also divulge a calculated attempt to construct an artistic personality. In this she was informed by Nietzsche's beliefs – she read his *Birth of Tragedy* (1872) in 1900 – in the visionary role of the artist and the salvationary power of art to transform society (Weidle 1986, pp.60–64). Werefkin's aspirations to this status are well conveyed in her *Self-Portrait* of *c*.1910 (tempera on board; Städtische Galerie im Lenbachhaus, Munich, repr. Behr 1988, pl.6), which radiates the intensity of her personality, the startling colour of the piercing red eyes investing the image with prophetic qualities.

It is therefore understandable that in her journal Werefkin declared the autonomy of art from imitating nature: "Art is a Weltanschauung...which finds its expression in those forms, which inspire its technical means: sound, colour, form, line, word" (vol.ii: abridged German translation in Hahl-Koch 1967, p.94). This prescription for abstraction, transmitted in a forceful declamatory style, places Werefkin's journals at the forefront of Expressionist treatises and indicates that her formulations were intended for a wider and initiated audience. It was not without some familiarity with her writings that Otto Fischer could claim: "For this spiritual woman, art is the essential expression of an inner life, that is totally accessible...possibly only to those tuned to the same pitch. The large gouaches that she paints are for her the confessions of a journal" (Fischer 1912, p.42). Evidently, by 1912, critical reception had

little difficulty in accepting Werefkin's "visionary" status even though she had devoted herself exclusively to nurturing Jawlensky's artistic talent between 1896 and 1906.

The lack of consistency in Werefkin's development as a painter can be attributed to this hiatus in her career, to the complexity of her situation as a Russian expatriate in Munich and Switzerland and to her unsystematic practice. Her major paintings were left undated and unsigned, while her studies were only occasionally dated. For various reasons, Werefkin did not have access to her pre-1914 Russian and Munich oeuvre which was only retrieved by her close friend in Ascona, Ernst Alfred Aye, after her death (see Fäthke 1992, pp.247–8). There is no catalogue raisonné of her works and the mostly uncatalogued state of her sketchbooks prevents systematic examination of her production. One can, however, distinguish the major features of her thematic departures, process and style from a chronological breakdown of her output in the three geographic locations: Russia (1880–96), Munich (1906–14) and Ascona (1918–38).

Werefkin's concern for figure painting was inherited from her training with Pryanishnikov in Moscow and Repin in St Petersburg. As members of the Wanderers (*Peredvizhniki*), a realist movement associated with radical social comment, their iconography included portraiture, landscape and depictions of peasant life. Werefkin's early oils on canvases, focusing on depictions derived from her domestic and military environment, reveal a considerable talent in capturing likeness within an overall monumentality of form. The formal qualities of the ambitious, full-length portrait of her *Father's Orderly* (1883) and bust-length portrait of her *Mother* (1886; both collection of Dr C. Artzibushev, Odessa/Florida, repr. Ascona 1988, pls 1 and 2) rely on a tradition of Dutch and Spanish naturalism. Employing a limited tonal palette, Werefkin highlights the facial and gestural characterisation against a neutral background, seizing on the impact of red for dramatic detail.

Her paintings of the 1890s confirm that the permanent crippling of her right-hand thumb and index finger in 1888 represented more of a challenge than a threat to her career. She continued to portray figural types – Jews, peasants, servants – drawn from the margins of society that she encountered at the Werefkin summer estate in Kovno, Lithuania. In the painting *Jewish Day-Labourer* (*c*.1890; oil on canvas; private collection, *ibid.*, fig.27) Werefkin attempted to reach beyond the tattered shabbiness of the man's attire in representing the quiet dignity of the bearded worker. Abandoning the tight control of realistic modelling, her brushwork became looser and less descriptive, allowing the figure to emerge more effectively from an atmospheric background. She received positive endorsement of her progress when her works were exhibited with the Wanderers in St Petersburg in 1891; comparing the impact to that of Velázquez, Repin admired the freedom of the modelling and expressive forcefulness of the portraits (Fäthke in Ascona 1988, pp.30–31). It is worth noting, however, that photographs of Werefkin's studio in St Petersburg (*ibid.*, fig.30) indicate that she was a prolific artist and adept at painting studies of the nude, still-life, landscape and multi-figured compositions.

Werefkin began sketching in 1906 after spending approximately a decade in Munich. By the time that she resumed painting, she revised her understanding of what constituted

Werefkin: *Black Women*, 1909; gouache over graphite on board; 72.5 × 111.5 cm.; Sprengel Museum, Hannover

high art. She abandoned the earthy tonalities and medium of oil painting on canvas, favouring the primary significance of colours and quicker drying processes of a mixed technique: watercolour, gouache and/or tempera on paper or board. It would be misleading to suggest that she was working in a more *alla prima*, intuitive style, since Werefkin always retained a complex method of producing ink and graphite sketches or fully developed studies in colour before executing final paintings. Undoubtedly, the impact of her second visit to Paris in 1905 and viewing of the launch exhibition of the Salon d'Automne confirmed her theoretical departure from naturalistic form and colour. Indeed, Werefkin proclaimed: "I went to France for a year, started everything afresh and in a few months I had found the direction that I am now going in" (quotation undated; Stöckli 1938, p.5). Werefkin's subject matter embraced modern experience, and her work of this period expresses the city/country paradigm and other issues that were fiercely debated in the cultural politics of the 1900s (see Ashjian 1992, pp.21, 38–9).

Equating the spectacles of Paris and Munich, Werefkin declared in her journal:

> The everyday man relishes life and it is always the same to him, if he wanders on the Parisian boulevard or drinks beer in the Munich Hofbräu. The life he creates around himself, is always the same. Here and there more sociable or elegant, here and there stiffer and more boring for the most part though always the same [quotation undated; Fäthke in Ascona 1988, p.80].

Inspired by the works of Toulouse-Lautrec, the Nabis and Intimists, she pursued themes of modernity derived from the extremes of social entertainment, from sophisticated salon, ballroom and soirée interiors (Behr 1988, pp.28 and 40) to scenes from popular culture – the circus, cabaret and low life (for Werefkin's role as *flâneuse*, see Ashjian 1992, p.24). The uniformity engendered by urban capitalism is most suitably portrayed in the tempera on board *In the Café* (1909; Fondazione Marianne Werefkin, Ascona, repr. Ascona 1988, pl.32). The rhythmic positioning of the four male figures close to the picture plane, in a frieze-like arrangement, is complemented by a sinuous flow of contour that defines the downcast facial expressions and hand movements. A symbolist use of blue dominates the composition, from the dark shapes of the figures to the transparency of the table top, relieved only by the pastel shades of green and pink in the wine glasses.

Werefkin's distinctive stylistic and thematic interests are equally pronounced in her country works; her concern for social topics was unusual both in the context of the Neue Künstlervereinigung München and in relation to the Murnau works produced by Jawlensky, Kandinsky and Münter between 1908 and 1910. In its focus on genre-like detail of costume and daily ritual, *The Washerwomen* (1909; tempera on paper mounted on board; 50.5 × 60 cm.; Städtische Galerie im Lenbachhaus, repr. Behr 1988, pl.3) has much in common with the paintings of the school of Pont-Aven, Brittany. In other works on this theme, however, as in the larger scale *Black Women* (1909; see illustration), the depiction of processions of darkly clad women, burdened by white bundles, indicate a less-than-idealised commentary on peasant life in the changing economy of the region. The stylising process is more accentuated, and dramatic use is made of silhouette, spatial distortion and mood-evoking coloration.

The encroachment of industrialisation on the traditionally romantic, Alpine setting is consistently dealt with in Werefkin's Murnau landscapes. In *Roof-tile Factory* (1910; tempera on board; 105 × 80 cm.; Museum Wiesbaden, repr. Behr 1988, pl.11) the tall smokestack of the factory in Oberau competes with the mountain peaks, while a peasant portrayed in the foreground appears displaced in this compressed and unstable composition. Yet, as in the paintings of the community of artists in the Blaue Reiter, Werefkin was not immune to investing nature with mystical and spiritual importance. The iconic value of the motifs and verticality of the composition in the *Red Tree* (1910; tempera on board; 76 × 57 cm.; Fondazione Marianne Werefkin, *ibid.*, pl.8) belie its source of inspiration in a Japanese print by Hokusai, *Pine in front of Mount Fuji* (1835; repr. Ascona 1988, fig.150). The dominating, blue ice-capped mountain, vivid red foliage of the centrally placed tree, the seated contemplative figure and thatched chapel suggest a hermetic reading of the visual components. Moreover, Werefkin dismissed plein-airism (local colour has been heavily overpainted and obscured in this painting), focusing attention on the emotional and expressive power of the colours. Recognising the value of these ideas, Franz Marc communicated to Maria Franck in a letter of 12 December 1910: "Miss Werefkin said ... that colour is totally different [to illumination] and has little to do with light."

In Ascona Werefkin entered into the spirit of the international artistic community and her anthroposophist leanings became more pronounced. Mystical and religious associations were prevalent in her themes and titles and, as in her Murnau works, the motifs of steep mountain ranges and hill-top villages of the Italian-Swiss Alps were employed as systematic metaphors for spiritual evocation. In the painting *Sacred Fire* (1919; tempera on board; 74 × 56 cm.; Fondazione Marianne Werefkin, *ibid.*, pl.90) Werefkin exploits the use of rhythmic, organic line and a harmony of red colours to sweep the eye towards the centrally placed summit, haloed by stars and luminosity.

Interestingly, the artist does not allow one to forget the centres of metropolitan power even at a distance from the materialism of city life. In a painting entitled *The Victor* (c.1929; tempera on board; 68 × 96 cm.; Fondazione Marianne Werefkin, *ibid.*, pl.99) a train track penetrates the idyll, as cranes load quarried stone on to the rail cars, threatening the anthropomorphically shaped, cowering images of the mountain range. Ceaselessly exploring variations of facture and colour orchestration, Werefkin invested each of her mature paintings with a power of suggestion, imagination and mystery. As one cannot say this of the late works of many avant-garde male painters who reach the age of 78, it is evident that a more rigorous contextual study of her contribution is both urgent and overdue.

SHULAMITH BEHR

Westhoff, Clara *see* Rilke-Westhoff

Wheeler, Candace
American embroiderer and designer, 1827–1923

Born Candace Thurber in Delhi, New York, 1827; father a farmer, Presbyterian deacon and abolitionist. Married stockbroker Thomas M. Wheeler, 1844; four children, including painter and textile designer Dora (born 1856). Moved to Brooklyn, New York, after marriage; to Hollis, Long Island, 1854. Studied painting in Europe, 1860s. Visited Philadelphia Centennial Exposition and saw work of the Royal School of Art Needlework, 1876. Co-founder and vice-president, Society of Decorative Art of New York City, 1877; founder, Woman's Exchange, for the sale of crafts and foodstuffs, 1878. Partner and textile specialist of Associated Artists, 1879–83; continued to produce textiles under the name Associated Artists after dissolution of original partnership, 1883–1907. Designed wallpapers for Warren, Fuller and Company from 1881; textiles for Cheney Brothers, Connecticut, from c.1884. Colour (i.e. interior) director for Woman's Building and director of Bureau of Applied Arts for State of New York display, World's Columbian Exposition, Chicago, 1893. Awarded first prize, Society of Decorative Art of New York City, 1879. Died in New York, 5 August 1923.

Principal Exhibitions
World's Columbian Exposition, Chicago: 1893

Selected Writings
Editor, *Columbia's Emblem: Indian Corn: A Garland of Tributes*, Boston: Houghton Mifflin, 1893
Editor, *Household Art*, New York: Harper, 1893
"Applied arts in the Woman's Building", *Art and Handicraft in the Woman's Building of the World's Columbian Exposition, Chicago, 1893*, ed. Maud Howe Elliott, Chicago and New York: Rand McNally, 1894, pp.59–67
"Decorative art", *Architectural Record*, iv, 1895, pp.409–13
"Art education for women", *Outlook*, lv, 2 January 1897, pp.81–7
Content in a Garden, Boston: Houghton Mifflin, 1901
How to Make Rugs, New York: Doubleday, 1902
Principles of Home Decoration with Practical Examples, New York: Doubleday, 1903
Yesterdays in a Busy Life, New York: Harper, 1918 (autobiography)
The Development of Embroidery in America, New York: Harper, 1921

Bibliography
Constance Cary Harrison, *Woman's Handiwork in Modern Homes*, New York: Scribner, 1881
——, "Some work of the Associated Artists", *Harper's New Monthly Magazine*, lxix, August 1884, pp.343–51
Wilson H. Faude, "Associated Artists and the American renaissance in the decorative arts", *Winterthur Portfolio*, x, 1975, pp.101–30
——, "Candace Wheeler: Textile designer", *Magazine Antiques*, cxii, 1977, pp.258–61
Karal Ann Marling, "Portrait of the artist as a young woman: Miss Dora Wheeler", *Bulletin of the Cleveland Museum of Art*, lxv, February 1978, pp.46–57
Anthea Callen, *Angel in the Studio: Women in the Arts and Crafts Movement, 1870–1914*, London: Astragal, 1979; as *Women*

Artists of the Arts and Crafts Movement, 1870–1914, New York: Pantheon, 1979

Virginia Williams, "Candace Wheeler: Textile designer for Associated Artists", *Nineteenth Century*, vi, Summer 1980, pp.60–61

Jeanne Madeline Weimann, *The Fair Women*, Chicago: Academy, 1981

Isabelle Anscombe, *A Woman's Touch: Women in Design from 1860 to the Present Day*, London: Virago, and New York: Viking, 1984

In Pursuit of Beauty: Americans and the Aesthetic Movement, exh. cat., Metropolitan Museum of Art, New York, 1986 (contains bibliography)

Lamia Doumato, *Candace Wheeler and Elsie de Wolfe: A Bibliography*, Monticello, IL: Vance, 1989

Gillian Moss, "Textiles of the American Arts and Crafts movement", *William Morris and the Arts and Crafts Movement: A Sourcebook*, ed. Linda Parry, London: Studio, 1989, pp.16–22

Susan Waller, *Women Artists in the Modern Era: A Documentary History*, Metuchen, NJ: Scarecrow, 1991

Candace Wheeler's 45-year career as artist and writer began when she was 50 years of age, and well established as a wealthy society matron in New York. The Royal School of Art Needlework (London) exhibit in the Main Building of the Philadelphia Centennial Exposition in 1876 provided the impetus for the activities of the rest of her life. The exhibit, a

Wheeler: *Consider the Lillies of the Field*, portières, exhibited 1879; Mark Twain House, Hartford, Connecticut

set of British art needlework pieces based on designs inspired by William Morris and others, was a revelation to American needleworkers who were immersed in Berlin woolwork and other "fancy work" of the period. Wheeler, whose motives were charitable as well as artistic, was also impressed with the Royal School's scheme for assisting impoverished gentlewomen who were in need of remunerative work but limited by social custom from seeking employment. Wheeler saw art needle-work as a means of providing work for seamstresses displaced by mechanisation and as an opportunity to improve artistic taste among the needleworkers of America.

Her first attempt at organisation, the Society of Decorative Art of New York City (1877), was an amalgamation of socialites and artist advisers. Although it proved a successful model for similar societies in other American cities, its artistic goals were not as successful. Americans did not care for British designs and, having a less sophisticated art tradition, tended to produce work that failed to meet the standards of the socialites who selected work for the Society's sales. Wheeler was forced to resign when she formed the Woman's Exchange, deemed by her associates to be a competing organisation. She took advantage of her disaffiliation, however, to enter her wool and silk embroidered and painted velvet portières based on British examples, *Consider the Lillies of the Field* (see illustration), in the Society's competition of 1879 and took first prize.

In 1879 she took the unusual step for a woman of that period of going into business with three men. She joined Louis Comfort Tiffany, Samuel Colman and Lockwood de Forest as textile specialist in their interior decorating firm, Associated Artists, a group now recognised as a major influence in the American Aesthetic movement. Their first commission, an embroidered drop-curtain for the new Madison Square Theatre in New York, was designed by the partners and executed under Wheeler's direction. The curtain, a realistic landscape in velvet and silks, was unfortunately burned on 26 February 1880 in a gas-lighting accident during the theatre's first season (it was replaced with a copy that has not survived). Wheeler's work as textile designer for Associated Artists during this period included decoration of the 7th Regiment Armory in New York (1880–81), the Mark Twain house in Hartford (1881) and redecoration of the White House in Washington, DC (1882–3).

Although textiles were Wheeler's major interest, she ventured into wallpaper design for a competition sponsored by the firm of Warren, Fuller and Company in October 1881. She and her students submitted designs and swept the four prizes, with Wheeler taking first for her bees and honeycomb pattern. Some of Wheeler's designs were used by Cheney Brothers, a large silk manufacturer of Manchester and Hartford, Connecticut. She did a series of designs based on American flora and fauna including a popular carp pattern and a bees and honeycomb design similar to her prize-winning wallpaper pattern. Much of her work drew on British and Japanese prece-dents. She also greatly admired the work of Walter Crane and the British pre-Raphaelite painters. Because she wanted her fabric designs to be affordable by less affluent consumers, she had them printed on cotton as well as silk. Representative samples of her work are now in the Metropolitan Museum of Art, New York, and the Mark Twain Memorial.

In 1883 the Associated Artists firm was dissolved by mutual agreement. Tiffany's group, Louis C. Tiffany and Company, moved into Art Nouveau and became one of the leading expo-nents of the Art Nouveau style in America. Wheeler retained the name of Associated Artists and stayed with the naturalistic plant and animal forms that had characterised her work from the beginning. She rejected the British embroidery designs of the South Kensington school as too conventional and pursued pictorial representations as being more typically American. She continued as director of Associated Artists until shortly before 1900 when her son, Dunham Wheeler, took over. The firm produced textiles until 1907.

Wheeler and her associates experimented with needle-weaving, a technique that simulated tapestry weaving. In 1883 she patented an "American tapestry" method combining embroidery with weaving on a silk canvas. The tapestries included portraits and copies of other works of art, in particu-lar a copy of Raphael's tapestry cartoon, the *Miraculous Draught of Fishes* (c.1519; Victoria and Albert Museum, London), executed by the staff of Associated Artists in the 1880s. It was greatly admired, and exhibited at the Chicago World's Columbian Exposition in 1893.

The major appointment of Wheeler's career was that of colour director of the Woman's Building at the World's Columbian Exposition. The idea of a Woman's Building had been put forward by Mrs Potter Palmer of Chicago and others who felt that women's achievements would be overshadowed if they were placed with those of men in exhibits dispersed throughout the fair. Wheeler was in charge of the interior deco-ration of the building, particularly the New York State Room, a library devoted to books written by women. Her responsibil-ities included selecting art works for the many national and state exhibits. The great success of the Woman's Building lay in the overwhelming impression created by an entire building of exhibits devoted to women's achievements.

Wheeler wrote prolifically on interior decoration and related topics. Of her books, *The Development of Embroidery in America* (1921), published when she was 94, is the best known. It has more significance as the pioneering work on the history of American needlework than as a scholarly study. Although it has some value for its description of extant pieces, the text was not well researched, and contains many historical inaccuracies.

CONSTANCE A. FAIRCHILD

Whitney, Anne
American sculptor, 1821–1915

Born in Watertown, Massachusetts, 2 September 1821, into a family of Liberal Unitarians; worked for social justice all her life. Contributed poetry to *Harper's*, the *Atlantic Monthly* and other magazines from 1847. Turned to a career in sculp-ture, c.1857. Attended Pennsylvania Academy of the Fine Arts, Philadelphia, 1860, then studied anatomy at a hospital in Brooklyn, New York. Studied under William Rimmer in Boston, 1862–4. Stayed in Rome, 1867–71; trip to Florence and Paris, 1875–6. Won national competition for anonymous entry for a memorial sculpture of abolitionist Clark Sumner, 1875; denied commission when judges found out she was a woman. Taught modelling at Wellesley College, Massachusetts, spring 1885. Had lifelong friend and companion Adeline Manning. Died in Boston, 23 January 1915.

Principal Exhibitions
Centennial Exposition, Philadelphia: 1876
Woman's Building, World's Columbian Exposition, Chicago: 1893

Selected Writings
Poems, New York: Appleton, 1859

Bibliography
Henry T. Tuckerman, *Book of the Artists: American Artist Life*, New York: Putnam, 1867; reprinted New York: Carr, 1966

Mary A. Livermore, "Anne Whitney", *Our Famous Women*, ed. H.B. Stowe and R.T. Cooke, Hartford, CT: Worthington, 1884, pp.674ff

Clara Erskine Clement, *Women in the Fine Arts*, Boston: Houghton Mifflin, 1904; reprinted New York: Hacker, 1974

Elizabeth Rogers Payne, "Anne Whitney, sculptor", *Art Quarterly*, xxv, 1962, pp.244–61

Margaret Farrand Thorp, *The Literary Sculptors*, Durham, NC: Duke University Press, 1965

Elizabeth Rogers Payne, "Anne Whitney: Art and social justice", *Massachusetts Quarterly*, xxv, 1971, pp.245–60

The White Marmorean Flock: Nineteenth-Century American Women Neoclassical Sculptors, exh. cat., Vassar College Art Gallery, Poughkeepsie, NY, 1972

Karen Petersen and J.J. Wilson, *Women Artists: Recognition and Reappraisal*, New York: Harper, 1976; London: Women's Press, 1978

Wayne Craven, *Sculpture in America*, 2nd edition, Newark: University of Delaware Press, 1984

Liana Borghi, "Anne Whitney: Letters home", *Rivista di Studi Anglo-Americani*, iii/4–5, 1984–5, pp.115–21

American Women Artists, 1830–1930, exh. cat., National Museum of Women in the Arts, Washington, DC, 1987

Charlotte Streifer Rubinstein, *American Women Sculptors*, Boston: Hall, 1990

Dolly Sherwood, *Harriet Hosmer: American Sculptor, 1830–1908*, Columbia: University of Missouri Press, 1991

The Lure of Italy: American Artists and the Italian Experience, 1760–1914, exh. cat., Museum of Fine Arts, Boston, 1992

Anne Whitney Papers are in the Wellesley College Archives, Wellesley, Massachusetts.

Although she began her career relatively late in comparison with her peers, at the age of 34, Anne Whitney produced an extraordinarily large oeuvre in her 93 years, installing her last public commission, the monumental bronze of *Charles Sumner*, in Harvard Square, Cambridge, Massachusetts, at the age of 81. From a wealthy and politically progressive family, Whitney was able to concentrate on producing works that reflected her personal and political interests, unhindered by excessive concern for the saleability of her sculptures. She spurned the lucrative portrait-bust industry at the beginning of her career, and criticised the sculptor Harriet Hosmer (q.v.) for diminishing the integrity of the original art object by reproducing her popular figures in large quantities. Further, her early training in anatomy and sculpture with the artist and physician William Rimmer, a true maverick and author of some of the most interesting and anomalous works of the

period, provided early encouragement for Whitney's innovative works.

Her first full-figure work was a life-sized *Lady Godiva* (private collection, Dallas), after Tennyson, completed in marble in 1862. The same year she began a full-figure, life-sized male nude, reworked during her first visit to Rome as the *Lotus Eater* (1867; destroyed; similar plaster statuette at Whitney Farm, Shelburne, NH; cf. Emma Stebbins's eponymous work of 1857–60), also after Tennyson's poem on the Homeric theme. Whitney quickly passed to more overtly political works. In 1864 she sculpted *Africa*, a reclining female figure shown "waking from the sleep of slavery". The theme was intended as an abolitionist one, although it also evokes 19th-century calls by American and British travellers to Rome for "Rome to awake" and cast off the mental and spiritual shackles imposed on the city's inhabitants by the papal regime; thus today the *Africa* may seem problematic in terms of where it places the responsibility for "submission" to slavery, and liberation from it. The work, now destroyed but surviving in photographs (repr. Payne 1971), was a powerful re-writing of the *grand odalisque* form, with thick, highly textured locks of hair pulled to the back of the figure's head and deeply set eyes under a strong brow ridge that resist the idealising tendencies and Anglo-Saxon imperative of the Neo-classical style. Nevertheless, after seeing the figure on exhibit at the National Academy of Design, New York, Colonel Thomas Wentworth Higginson, leader of the first black regiment during the Civil War, wrote to Whitney suggesting that the features of the figure were not African enough. Whitney did try to alter them, but was not satisfied with the results and destroyed the plaster original after her return from Europe, a loss that she later regretted.

When Whitney arrived in Rome in 1867, the rest of Italy had been united under the constitutional monarchy of Victor Emmanuel for some six years. Rome itself, however, was being uneasily defended by the troops of Napoleon III as the last papal stronghold. Whitney's response to the fraught political situation in 1869 was one of her strongest works, an allegory of Rome – *Roma* – in the form of a life-sized seated bronze of an old beggar woman, weakly holding a permit to beg in her left hand, as two coins drop from her right (see illustration for first bronze casting of the figure; at least one more bronze, one marble and two plaster versions were made, all untraced). Along the hem of her skirt are relief medallions of Rome's most famous sculptural works – the *Apollo Belvedere*, the *Laocoön*, the *Dying Gaul/Gladiator*, *Hercules* – and, originally, a portrait of *Cardinal Antonelli*, generally considered responsible for the worst of the papal government's abuses. When the portrait was recognised and destruction of the work threatened, Whitney had it smuggled to Florence, whence it was shipped to the USA. She eventually replaced the Antonelli portrait with a triple mitre.

In her *Roma* Whitney makes reference to a long tradition not only of representing cities with female allegorical figures, but also of representing Rome as a broken pauper woman, a figure that first appears in the Middle Ages after the sack of Rome (my thanks to Dr Paul Gwynne for this note). Manuscript engravings of this figure could have been on display in the Vatican Library among other collections open to Whitney in Rome. But the most direct influence on Whitney's

Anne Whitney: *Roma*, 1890; bronze; 68.6 × 39.4 × 53.3 cm.; Davis Museum and Cultural Center, Wellesley College, Wellesley, Massachusetts

figure seems to have been the sculpture of an old "drunken" woman of the 2nd century BC after an original attributed to Myron of Thebes in the Capitoline Museums (another copy in Glyptothek, Munich). Adopting the realistic portraiture and tormented drapery of the Capitoline sculpture, the *Roma* is a figure not only representative of a perceived decay of Rome, but also sensitive to the particular plight of the poor and the aged in difficult economic and political times.

A later bronze work sculpted in Paris in 1875, *Le Modèle* (Museum of Fine Arts, Boston), representing the turbaned head of a wrinkled woman, again focuses attention specifically on the condition of poor and ageing women. Today we can read the title of this work as a striking reference to the artist's position in the socio-economic hierarchy with respect to the model. Mary A. Livermore, Whitney's first biographer in *Our Famous Women* (1884), recognised an allegory for France in *Le Modèle*, writing: "Whatever the idea of the artist, this bronze head fitly symbolizes France – broken by revolutions, worn out by war, overcome by domestic violence, degraded by submission to a despotism under the name of a republic – desiring only rest" (quoted in Payne 1971). Both *Le Modèle* and *Roma* were exhibited to critical acclaim at the Philadelphia Centennial Exposition in 1876.

Another important work on the theme of social justice was a statuette of the Haitian revolutionary leader, *Toussaint L'Ouverture* (exh. c.1872–3; untraced, repr. Payne 1971). The figure, with now undeniably African features, is portrayed seated on a stone block in prison. Wearing only loose knee-breeches, he leans forward on his right leg to point with his right arm to an inscription on the plinth, "Dieu se charge", while his left arm and leg pull back in a dynamic, apparently unstable pose. The figure, far from "awakening from the sleep of slavery", seems ready to leap up at any moment to pursue the future that is fixed by his unwavering gaze.

Examples of portraiture, particularly of abolitionist and feminist leaders, increase in the latter part of Whitney's oeuvre. They range from the celebrated case of the Charles Sumner public monument commission, which Whitney won in a blind competition but was later rejected because of her gender, to a long series of busts of social reformers and friends of the artist (original Sumner plaster competition model in Watertown Free Public Library, Watertown, MA). She also received public commissions for monumental bronzes of *Samuel Adams* (commissioned 1873, completed 1876; Statuary Hall, US Capitol, Washington, DC; and in front of Faneuil Hall, Boston) and *Leif Ericson* (Commonwealth Avenue, Boston). Whitney designed at least two fountains, one of *Shakespeare: A Midsummer Night's Dream* (1897; plaster model in Watertown Public Library), and the other of a child angel playing in calla lily leaves (1885). This bronze, *Angel Fountain* or *Calla Lily Fountain*, was installed in a traffic island in West Newton, Massachusetts, and is the subject of a heroic campaign on the part of the community to save the work and the artist from obscurity.

NANCY PROCTOR

Whitney, Gertrude Vanderbilt

American sculptor and patron, 1875–1942

Born in New York, 9 January 1875, to the financier and philanthropist Cornelius Vanderbilt and his wife Alice Claypoole Gwynne. Married financier and sportsman Harry Payne Whitney, 1896; three children; husband died 1930. Advised by the artist Howard Cushing, 1898–1903; studied under Norwegian sculptor Hendrik Christian Andersen, and travelled in Europe; established studio in New York and studied sculpture under James Earle Fraser and at the Art Students League. Opened MacDougal Alley studio in Greenwich Village, New York, 1907; resided in Paris as student of Andrew O'Connor, Jr, 1909–14, receiving private criticism from Rodin. Won open competition for *Titanic* memorial, 1914. During World War I, founded, equipped and maintained American Ambulance Hospital at Jouilly, France. As patron, from 1907 on, exhibited works by contemporary

American artists in MacDougal Alley studio; founded Whitney Studio Club to provide exhibition space for American artists, 1918. Established Whitney Museum of American Art, New York (opened 1931), after the Metropolitan Museum refused her collection of contemporary American art. Supported Society of Independent Artists (1917) for 15 years and *The Arts*, a leading liberal art magazine of the 1920s. Patron of the Metropolitan Opera, New York; provided funds for the Whitney Wing of the American Museum of Natural History, New York. Recipient of Médaille de la Reconnaissance, Government of France, 1922; Grand Cross, Order of King Alfonso of Spain, 1922; medal, American Art Dealers Association, 1932; medal, National Sculpture Society, 1940; honorary degrees from New York University, 1922; Tufts College, Medford, Massachusetts, 1924; Rutgers University, New Brunswick, New Jersey, 1934; Russell Sage College, Troy, New York, 1940. Associate, National Academy of Design, New York, 1940; member, American Federation of Arts and Association of Women Painters and Sculptors. Died in New York, 18 April 1942.

Principal Exhibitions

Individual
Galerie Georges Petit, Paris: 1921
Thomas McLean Gallery, London: 1921 ·
Wildenstein Galleries, New York: 1923 (retrospective)
Galeries Durand-Ruel, Paris: 1924
M. Knoedler and Co., New York: 1936 (touring)
Whitney Museum of American Art, New York: 1943 (retrospective)

Group
Pan-American Exposition, Buffalo: 1901
Paris Salon: 1913 (honourable mention)
National Arts Club, New York: 1914 (prize)
Panama-Pacific International Exposition, San Francisco: 1915 (bronze medal)
Art Association of Newport, RI: 1916
Palace of Fine Arts, San Francisco Art Association: 1917
New York Society of Architects: 1922 (medal)
New York World's Fair: 1939

Selected Writings
"The end of America's apprenticeship", *Arts and Decoration*, xiii, 1920, pp.150–51

Bibliography
Guy Pène du Bois, "Mrs Whitney's journey in art", *International Studio*, lxxvi, 1923, pp.351–4
Memorial Exhibition: Gertrude Vanderbilt Whitney, exh. cat., Whitney Museum of American Art, New York, 1943
Margaret Breuning, "Gertrude Vanderbilt Whitney's sculpture", *Magazine of Art*, xxxvi, February 1943, pp.62–5
Juliana Force and American Art: A Memorial Exhibition, exh. cat. Whitney Museum of American Art, New York, 1949
The Whitney Museum and Its Collection, exh. cat. Whitney Museum of American Art, New York, 1954
Daty Haly, *History of the Whitney Museum*, PhD dissertation, New York University, 1960
Edward T. James, Janet Wilson James and Paul S. Boyer, eds, *Notable American Women, 1607–1950*, Cambridge, MA: Harvard University Press, 1971
200 Years of American Sculpture, exh. cat. Whitney Museum of American Art, New York, 1976
B.H. Friedman, *Gertrude Vanderbilt Whitney: A Biography*, Garden City, NY: Doubleday, 1978

Mahonri Sharp Young, "Gertrude Vanderbilt Whitney", *Apollo*, cxi, 1980, pp.58–9
Charlotte Streifer Rubinstein, *American Women Artists from Early Times to the Present*, Boston: Hall, 1982
Rebecca Wright Bilbo, *Gertrude Vanderbilt Whitney: Patron of the American Realists*, MA thesis, University of Cincinnati, 1985
Janis Conner and Joel Rosenkranz, *Rediscoveries in American Sculpture: Studio Works, 1893–1939*, Austin: University of Texas Press, 1989

Unpublished correspondence, diaries, writings, newspaper clippings, magazine articles, exhibition catalogues, photographs and files of Whitney's paintings and research materials are in the Whitney Museum of American Art; the Gertrude Vanderbilt Whitney Papers are in the Archives of American Art, Smithsonian Institution, Washington, DC; see also the Inventory of American Sculpture, National Museum of American Art, Smithsonian Institution, Washington, DC.

Gertrude Vanderbilt Whitney's art interests developed after her marriage, when she and her husband occupied his family's mansion in New York, which was filled with Renaissance tapestries, French antique furniture and old master paintings. She became interested in acquiring American art after commissioning stained-glass windows from John La Farge and purchasing three of his Japanese watercolours in 1898. Desiring active work and cultural stimulation, she decided to pursue her studies in France where she came under the influence of Rodin, who was attracted to her marble group *Paganism* (1907; Whitney Museum of American Art, New York), modelled, presumably, according to his theories. In the following years, Rodin continued to influence the practice of her art, as in *Wherefore* (1910; Art Institute of Chicago), originally called *Man on a Rock*, which shows his influence both in subject and handling of surface. But Whitney's technique did not emulate Rodin's subtle modelling – for the most part it was developed independently, following her earlier ideas and training.

Whitney's interest in ideal or allegorical subjects, such as *Aspiration* (1900), was derived in part from the work of the American sculptor Daniel Chester French. This was a traditionally modelled sculpture; its theme was repeated in many works that followed, such as the dramatic *St Nazaire* (1924; Saint-Nazaire, France; bombed during World War II) and *Spirit of Flight* (1938; exh. New York World's Fair, 1939; working model, Whitney Museum of American Art). During World War I Whitney founded and maintained the American Ambulance Hospital at Jouilly, France, and her subsequent war sculptures (models in Whitney Museum of American Art) reveal how much these war experiences influenced her work. Highly realistic, they depart from her earlier – more decorative – work in their directness and emotional expression (1921; Washington Heights, Inwood, NY; 1924; Saint-Nazaire, France). Filled with symbolic details but naturalistic in the rendering of forms, they convey both the tragedy of war and its heroism. Similarly, her large monument to *Christopher Columbus* (1928–9) at the harbour at Palos, Spain, was designed to express "man's courage and faith in the eternal conquest of the unknown" (New York 1943, p.4). With their emphasis on the moral spirit of the country, democratic heroes and idealism, these public monuments reflect the prevailing nationalism of the period as, for example, the monumental *Titanic Memorial* in Waterfront Park, Washington, DC, a prestigious commission of 1914, and *Fountain* (1910; McGill University, Montreal). Whitney's smaller works, such as *Boy with Parrot* (1905; Whitney Museum of American Art), *Spanish Peasant* (1912; Metropolitan Museum of Art, New York), *Gwendolyn* (1934) and *Woman and Child* (1935; both Whitney Museum of American Art) are more individual expressions, full of personal feeling and free of heavy symbolism. Her monument to *Peter Stuyvesant* (1938; Stuyvesant Square, New York) shows her strength in rendering the human figure and expressing emotion through gesture.

Whitney's support of American independent artists in the early 20th century by providing them with exhibition space in her Whitney Studio Club and buying their works brought her under the influence of such realists as Robert Henri, members of the "Ashcan" School and artists who rebelled against the strictures of the National Academy of Design. Their aesthetic of social realism appears in such works as *Unemployed* (1932; Whitney Museum of American Art) and *Woman and Child*. Whitney also collected works by such European masters as Picasso, Duchamp and Braque. Her founding of the Whitney Museum of American Art in 1931 represents the culmination of her efforts to bring contemporary art to the wider public and promote the artists' cause through a sequence of clubs and galleries; the museum, an enormously influential force in American art, was Gertrude Vanderbilt Whitney's greatest personal achievement.

LILLIAN B. MILLER

Wieland, Joyce

Canadian painter, film-maker and multi-media artist, 1931–

Born in Toronto, 30 June 1931. Studied at the Central Technical School, Toronto, under Carl Schaeffer, Doris McCarthy and Bob Ross. Married artist Michael Snow, 1956; divorced. Animator, Graphic Films, Toronto, 1957–9. Lived in New York, 1962–71. Instructor, Nova Scotia College of Art and Design, 1971; San Francisco Art Institute, 1985–6; artist-in-residence, University of Toronto, Architecture School, 1988–9. Recipient of Canada Council grants, 1966, 1968, 1984 and 1986; second prize, Ann Arbor Film Festival, for *A & B in Ontario*, 1986; Canada Council Victor M. Staunton award, 1972; Toronto Arts award, 1987; YWCA Woman of Distinction award, 1987. Member, Royal Academy, London, 1973. Officer, Order of Canada, 1983. Ceased working when affected by Alzheimer's disease, c.1990. Lives in Toronto.

Selected Individual Exhibitions

Isaacs Gallery, Toronto: 1960, 1962, 1963, 1967, 1972, 1974, 1981, 1983
Hart House Gallery, University of Toronto: 1962 (with Michael Snow, touring)
Museum of Modern Art, New York: 1968, 1969
Vancouver Art Gallery: 1968 (retrospective)
Glendon College Art Gallery, York University, Toronto: 1969 (retrospective)
National Gallery of Canada, Ottawa: 1971, 1978 (touring)
Pauline McGibbon Cultural Centre, Toronto: 1979
Powerhouse Gallery, Montreal: 1980 (with Judy Chicago)
Forest City Gallery, London, Ontario: 1982 (touring)
Concordia University, Montreal: 1985
Alma Gallery, Toronto: 1986
Art Gallery of Ontario, Toronto: 1987–8 (touring retrospective)
Canada House Gallery, London: 1988
Agnes Etherington Art Centre, Queen's University, Kingston, Ontario: 1995

Bibliography

Michel Sanouillet, "The sign of Dada", *Canadian Art*, xix, March–April 1962, p.111
Jonathan Holstein, "New York's vitality tonic for Canadian artists", *Canadian Art*, xxi, September–October 1964, pp.270–79
Barrie Hale, "Joyce Wieland: Artist, Canadian, soft, tough woman!", *The Telegram* (Toronto), 11 March 1967
P. Adams Sitney, "There is only one Joyce", *Artscanada*, April 1970, pp.43–5
True Patriot Love/Véritable amour patriotique: Joyce Wieland, exh. cat., National Gallery of Canada, Ottawa, 1971
Hugo McPherson, "Wieland: An epiphany of north", *Artscanada*, xxviii, August–September 1971, pp.17–27
Regina Cornwell, "True patriot love: The films of Joyce Wieland", *Artforum*, x, September 1971, pp.36–40
Toronto Painting, 1953–1965, exh. cat., National Gallery of Canada, Ottawa, 1972
William J. Withrow, *Contemporary Canadian Painting*, Toronto: McClelland and Stewart, 1972
Kay Armatage, "Kay Armatage interviews Joyce Wieland", *Take One*, iii, February 1972, pp.23–5
Joyce Wieland: Drawings for "The Far Shore", exh. cat., National Gallery of Canada, Ottawa, 1978
Lauren Rabinovitz, "Issues of feminist aesthetics: Judy Chicago and Joyce Wieland", *Woman's Art Journal*, i/2, 1980–81, pp.38–41
——, "An interview with Joyce Wieland", *Afterimage*, viii, May 1981, pp.8–12
Martha Fleming, "Joyce Wieland", *Parachute*, no.23, Summer 1981, p.45
Lauren Rabinovitz, "The development of feminist strategies in the experimental films of Joyce Wieland", *Film Reader 5*, Evanston, IL: Northwestern University Press, 1982, pp.132–9
Toronto Painting of the 1960s, exh. cat., Art Gallery of Ontario, Toronto, 1983
John Porter, "Artists discovering film: Post-war Toronto", *Vanguard*, xiii, 1984, pp.24–6
Toronto Painting '84, exh. cat., Art Gallery of Ontario, Toronto, 1984
Cache du Cinéma: Discovering Toronto Filmmakers, exh. cat., Funnel Experimental Film Theater, 1985
Joyce Wieland: A Decade of Painting, exh. cat., Concordia University, Montreal, 1985
Kass Banning, "Textual excess in Joyce Wieland's *Hand-Tinting*", *Cine-Action*, no.5, May 1986
Kay Armatage, *Artist on Fire: The Work of Joyce Wieland*, documentary film, Toronto: Canadian Filmmakers Distribution Centre, and New York: Women Make Movies, 1987
Kass Banning, "The mummification of mommy: Joyce Wieland as the Art Gallery of Ontario's first living other", *C Magazine*, no.13, 1987, pp.32–9; reprinted in *Sightlines: Reading Contemporary Canadian Art*, ed. Jessica Bradley and Lesley Johnstone, Montreal: Artextes, 1994
Joyce Wieland, exh. cat., Art Gallery of Ontario, Toronto, and elsewhere, 1987 (contains extensive bibliography)
Kay Armatage, "The feminine body: Joyce Wieland's *Water Sark*", *Canadian Women's Studies/Cahiers de la Femme*, viii, Spring 1987, pp.84–8
Susan M. Crean, "Notes from the language of emotion: A conversation with Joyce Wieland", *Canadian Art*, Spring 1987, pp.64–5

Jay Scott, "Full circle: True patriot womanhood: The thirty year passage of Joyce Wieland", *ibid.*, Spring 1987, pp.56–63

Kay Armatage, "Joyce Wieland: Feminist documentary and the body of work", *Canadian Journal of Political and Social Theory*, xiii/1–2, 1989

Linda Hutcheon, *Splitting Images: Contemporary Canadian Ironies*, Toronto: Oxford University Press, 1991

Lauren Rabinovitz, *Points of Resistance: Women, Power and Politics in the New York Avant-Garde Cinema, 1943–71*, Urbana: University of Illinois Press, 1991

Joyce Wieland: Twilit Record of Romantic Love, exh. cat., Agnes Etherington Art Centre, Queen's University, Kingston, Ontario, 1995

Joyce Wieland is one of the most prominent artists of her generation in Canada, and one of the earliest women to develop an art practice deliberately woman-centred and political in its concerns. In the heyday of Pop Art she asserted a female viewpoint on eroticism and on the sexual body, and drew not only on mass media but on women's traditions of creativity. She has worked collaboratively with other women artists and craft workers, and since the 1970s has focused increasingly on political issues. Her art, however, has never been didactic. Throughout her career Wieland has cultivated a sensibility that revels in humorous playfulness and a baroque exuberance of colour and of sensuous reference to the physical world. With her constant attention to the formal possibilities of her media and to the social nature of sign systems, her persistent concern with embodiments of a feminine desire and her courage to work outside current fashions, Wieland has produced a body of work that remains compelling, if often controversial, to younger feminist artists and critics.

Born in Toronto to English immigrant working-class parents, and orphaned young, Wieland moved directly from the art department of the Central Technical School, Toronto, to work for commercial art and advertising companies, including Graphic Films, a commercial company whose director George Dunning later made the Beatles' film *Yellow Submarine*. Here she learned film animation techniques and story-boarding, and met a lively group of fellow artists, including Michael Snow, whom she would marry in 1956. Wieland drew on this experience as she joined a generation of Toronto artists who inherited the formal legacy of the Canadian Abstract Expressionist-inspired Painters Eleven, while opening their art to the imagery of urban consumer culture under the stimulus of Dada, Surrealism and Pop Art.

The remarkable body of painting that Wieland produced during the years 1956–66, the first decade of her artistic career, has been discussed by Sandra Paikowsky (Montreal 1985). Her earliest figure paintings proclaimed her admiration for the work of Willem de Kooning (*Morning*, 1956; oil on canvas; repr. Montreal 1985, p.16). She made several series of informal, playful drawings of nude lovers, responding to Picasso's erotica, but focusing on the male as love object, or wryly noting women's vulnerability in the power structure of the heterosexual couple (Allen in Kingston 1995, pp.6–10). From 1959 Wieland developed a distinctive abstract language in which coloured shapes, suggestive of anatomical fragments or organic forms, cluster together or disperse as areas of brushed pigment over richly stained grounds (see *Redgasm*, 1960; oil on canvas; repr. Montreal 1985, p.19). Working often on a very large scale, Wieland went beyond conventional sexual symbols to evoke the rhythms of sexual intercourse and the cycles of female sexuality through large spontaneously drawn circular forms, loops and paint splashes. She also made lyrical collages of found materials that referred abstractly to water and sky, breasts, belly and penis, to sexual activity and to nature eroticised (*Summer Blues – Ball*, 1961; mixed media; *ibid.*, p.29).

From 1962 to 1971 Wieland lived and worked in New York with Michael Snow. Experimental film now became a major part of their output, as they became members of the "New York underground" of independent film-makers around Jonas Mekas, organiser of the Film-Makers' Cooperative and Cinematheque. Wieland collaborated with a number of its members (notably Hollis Frampton, Shirley Clarke, George and Mike Kuchar), and delighted in the freedom offered by the deliberately primitive "home-movie" aesthetic. Unfortunately, Mekas would exclude her from his Anthology Film Archives set up in 1970, in marked contrast to the treatment given to Snow, whose films became classics of the structural film movement (Rabinovitz in Toronto 1987, pp.166–7).

Wieland's early New York works in film, painting and multi-media introduced a woman's voice into an aesthetic current that explored the vernacular of commercial imagery and the mass media's fascination with eroticism and sensational disasters. The film *Patriotism, Part II* (1964; 16 mm., 5 minutes, silent, colour), with its Pop imagery of hot dogs, cigarettes and aeroplanes, parodied "a world ruled by the phallus", while *Water Sark* (1964–5; 16 mm., 14 minutes, colour) explored "a woman's familiar domestic space as the site for feminine self-discovery...the kitchen table as domestic altar and a world of aesthetic beauty" (Rabinovitz in *ibid.*, p.120). In *Hand Tinting* (1967–8; 16 mm., 5½ minutes, colour) Wieland used footage she had shot for a film, commissioned by Xerox, about a Job Corps Center for young women. She turned this into an abstract and rhythmic study of their gestures, expressions and movements, using repetition and reversal of short sequences of incomplete action, and varying sections by using negative prints, or dyeing or puncturing the film. Recent critics have found specifically feminist textual qualities in Wieland's manipulations. For Kass Banning, *Hand Tinting* displays "an unspeakable excess, a space of contradiction, an inscription of difference, through the rhythmic play not only of the female forms which shape the image but of the rhythmic oscillation of the film material itself..." (cited in Armatage, "The feminine body", 1987, p.84). Armatage finds in *Water Sark*, with its refractions of water, breast and mirror captured through circling and evasive movement, Wieland's "'discovery' of the feminine body", and a mode that "bears close links with and certainly shares the significance of what we have come to know as *l'écriture feminine*" (idem).

In her New York paintings and assemblages Wieland employed the sequential units of the story-board and the film-frame as a structural grid. The pervasive sexual imagery is sometimes humorous; sometimes lyrical, as in *Nature Mixes* (1963; oil on canvas; repr. Toronto 1987, pl.38) where a hand metamorphoses into a flower and then into a limp penis; and sometimes playfully parodic, in the scenes of romantic encounter of the *First Integrated Film with a Short on Sailing* (1963; oil on canvas; *ibid.*, p.49). In several paintings a distant sailboat or ocean liner moves erratically through the frames to

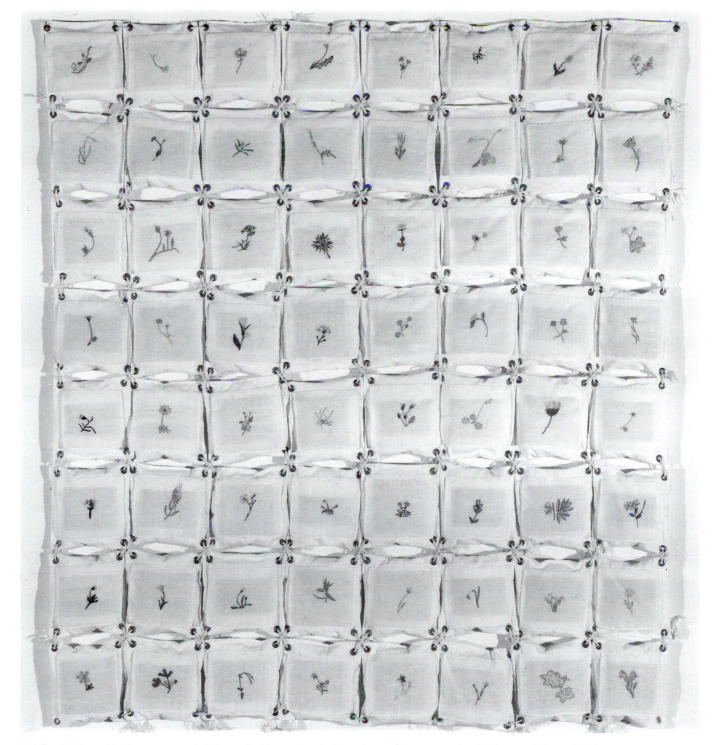

Wieland: *Water Quilt*, 1970–71; fabric, emboidery thread, thread, metal grommets, braided rope, ink on fabric; 121.9 × 121 cm.; Art Gallery of Ontario; purchased with assistance from Wintario, 1977

end in a sudden sinking, or aeroplanes cross blue skies and plummet to earth. Wieland's assemblages of 1964–5 used discarded wooden boxes as framing units in which phallic planes and boats (children's toys) appear in counterpoint with articles coded as feminine. The lipstick-stained coffee cups and heart-shaped bodice of a red ball-gown pegged on a washing line in *Cooling Room II* (1964; mixed media construction;

National Gallery of Canada, Ottawa), for example, are suggestively juxtaposed with a crashed toy aeroplane, and with an ocean liner represented by a red plastic bath toy.

From 1966 Wieland turned to women's craft traditions, designing sewn images in the form of quilts executed by her sister Joan Stewart, and composing wall hangings or "home totems" of vertically arranged pouches and frames that she made of coloured transparent celluloid, stuffed with cotton wads or found objects and images. Their imagery paid fond or ironic homage to the dominance of the cine camera and the news media in current consciousness. At a time of political upheaval in the USA, triggered by the Vietnam war and by racial and social conflicts, Wieland increasingly incorporated political references in her assemblages – press reports and photographs of the Vietnam war in *N.U.C.* (1966; mixed media; *ibid.*, p.67) and images of the American, British and Canadian flags that question the ethics of patriotic identification. In the film *Rat Life and Diet in North America* (1968; 16 mm., 14 minutes, colour) Wieland deals with the exodus of draft resisters to Canada. The protagonists, a group of pet gerbils in a Beatrix Potter-like narrative, flee from terror and confinement to idyllic flower-festivals and organic gardening in Canada. Wieland's treatment ironically combines the pleasures and playfulness of a children's tale with allusions to the fears and desires of the contemporary world.

From 1967 Wieland turned to issues of Canadian identity and politics. Her interest was triggered by a number of factors: distress at the invisibility of Canada in the USA; the mood of Canadian national celebration and self-examination unleashed by the Canadian Centennial in 1967; and the vexed problems of Quebec separatism and of American domination of the Canadian economy. A rail trip across Canada for a retrospective of her work at the Vancouver Art Gallery triggered her major film *Reason over Passion/La Raison avant la passion* (1967–9; 16 mm., 90 minutes, colour). This is a romantic-ironic exploration of the Canadian landscape and of national icons such as the flag (instituted in 1964) and the image of Pierre Trudeau, whose election as Prime Minister at the Liberal leadership convention of April 1968 appears as a balletic, dream-like freeze frame sequence at the centre of the film. Using a hand-held camera, Wieland crosses the country from sea to sea, shooting from the train and through the windscreen of a car, provoking visual discoveries through the physical constraints, accidents and perceptions of a particular journey. The resulting footage is re-filmed and rendered more abstract, structured into segments punctuated with regular electronic beeps, while Trudeau's catchword "reason over passion" appears superimposed at the centre of the screen in endless computer-generated permutations.

In 1971 Wieland was the first woman artist to be invited to mount a large solo exhibition at the National Gallery of Canada. As she worked on this, relations between Quebec and the rest of Canada were polarised by the FLQ terrorist kidnappings. Wieland turned the show into an affirmation of Canadian national identity and of its defining symbols, titling it *True Patriot Love* from the words of the Canadian national anthem. Echoing the earlier Canadianism of the Group of Seven, whom she admired, Wieland emphasised imagery of the wilderness, now endangered, and of the Arctic. She constructed an Arctic environment with fir trees and hatchling Canada geese, and an "Arctic Passion Cake", whose sugar-icing landscape held a female personification of "the Spirit of Canada suckling the French- and English-Canadian beavers" and a polar bear, mortally wounded by hunters. A large number of quilted, knitted and embroidered works were executed for her by women craft experts, their content asserting the French, English and aboriginal presences in Canadian

history and culture, through works such as *Montcalm's Last Letter/Wolfe's Last Letter* (1971; embroidery on cloth; repr. Toronto 1987, pl.54) and *Eskimo Song: The Great Sea* (1970–71; cloth assemblage; Canada Council Art Bank). While her work was highly sophisticated in its use of formal structure and its concern with the implications of symbol systems, Wieland sought to overcome the alienation of the public from avant-garde art by involving collaborators, by using down-to-earth media, and by addressing issues of common concern, often inspired by the political critiques published at that time by members of the socialist Waffle Group. An example is *Water Quilt* (1970–71; see illustration). Wieland's political activism was further seen in her work for CAR, the Canadian artists' union, and in strikingly idiosyncratic political films such as *Solidarity* (1973; 16 mm., 11 minutes, colour), which records a rally of striking women factory workers while the camera allows us to see only the protagonists' feet, and *Pierre Vallières* (1972; 16 mm., 45 minutes, colour), an interview with the Quebec nationalist and socialist leader, in which the sole image is a close-up of the speaker's active mouth with the English subtitles to his text. In 1976 Wieland embodied her nationalist and ecological themes, with qualified success, in a full-length commercial feature film, *The Far Shore* (35 mm.; 106 minutes, black and white).

During the 1980s Wieland again turned her attention to painting and drawing, working in coloured pencils, in water-colour and oil, and appropriating what she found most eloquent in the artistic traditions of the West, particularly in the painting and music of the Baroque period. Her allegorical images offer glimpsed intuitions of transcendence, showing humans, animals and fragments of the Canadian landscape infused with energy and harmonised by freely brushed lines and patches of radiant prismatic colour. The eroticism in Wieland's work of the early 1960s re-emerges as a vital force that is shown pervading not only human life but the growth of plants and the movement of the elements, for example in *Victory of Venus* (1981; coloured pencil on paper; *ibid.*, p.94). She has cited the mystical writings of Teilhard de Chardin and of Hildegard of Bingen (q.v.) as inspiration for her attempts to picture a redemptive mode of emotional experience. This imagery has distressed some feminist observers in its turn away from immediate political issues, while others have seen in it "a tenacious expression of faith in love" in the face of the contemporary "eviction of love from social discourse" (Fleming 1981; Allen in Kingston 1995, p.13).

GERTA MORAY

Wieselthier, Vally
Austrian ceramist, 1895–1945

Born Valerie Wieselthier in Vienna, 25 May 1895. Studied at the Kunstschule für Frauen und Mädchen; then at the Kunstgewerbeschule, Vienna, under Michael Powolny and Josef Hoffmann, 1914–20. Joined the Wiener Werkstätte at Hoffmann's invitation, 1919; left Werkstätte to establish private workshop, the Keramische Werkstätte Vally Wieselthier, 1922. Sold business to Werkstätte and became director of its ceramic department, 1927. Stayed in USA for 18 months, 1928–9. Founder-member of Contempora, a co-operative group in New York, 1929. Emigrated to USA, 1932; worked as a designer for Sebring Pottery, Ohio, then settled in New York. Died in New York, 1 September 1945.

Principal Exhibitions

Kunstschau, Vienna: 1920
Deutsche Gewerbeschau, Munich: 1922
Haus Werkbund, Frankfurt am Main: 1923
Exposition Internationale des Arts Décoratifs et Industriels Modernes, Paris: 1925 (gold and silver medals)
The Hague: 1927
Metropolitan Museum of Art, New York: 1928 (*International Exhibition of Ceramic Art*, touring, organised by American Federation of Arts)
National Ceramic Exhibition, Museum of Fine Arts, Syracuse, NY: 1933, 1938, 1940–41
New York World's Fair: 1939

Selected Writings

"Ceramics", *Design*, xxxi, November 1929, pp.101–2
"Studying art in Vienna: A brief autobiography", *Arts and Decoration*, xliii, February 1936, pp.28–9, 46

Bibliography

"Vally Wieselthier Ausstellung in New York", *Deutsche Kunst und Dekoration*, lxiv, 1929, pp.38–46
Alfr. Wenzel, "Neue Terrakotten von Vally Wieselthier", *Deutsche Kunst und Dekoration*, lxvii, 1931, pp.390–98
Waltraud Neuwirth, *Die Keramik der Wiener Werkstätte*, i: *Originalkeramiken, 1920–1931*, Vienna: Neuwirth, 1981
The Diversions of Keramos: American Clay Sculpture, 1925–1950, exh. cat., Everson Museum of Art, Syracuse, NY, and elsewhere, 1983
Isabelle Anscombe, *A Woman's Touch: Women in Design from 1860 to the Present Day*, London: Virago, and New York: Viking, 1984
Waltraud Neuwirth, *Wiener Werkstätte: Avantgarde, Art Déco, Industrial Design*, Vienna: Neuwirth, 1984
Werner J. Schweiger, *Wiener Werkstätte: Designs in Vienna, 1903–1932*, New York: Abbeville, and London: Thames and Hudson, 1984 (German original, 1982)
Jane Kallir, *Viennese Design and the Wiener Werkstätte*, New York: Braziller, and London: Thames and Hudson, 1986
Elaine Levin, "Vally Wieselthier/Susi Singer", *American Craft*, xlvi, December 1986–January 1987, pp.46–51
Barbara Perry, ed., *American Ceramics: The Collection of the Everson Museum of Art*, New York: Rizzoli, 1989
Susan Waller, *Women Artists in the Modern Era: A Documentary History*, Metuchen, NJ: Scarecrow Press, 1991
Angela Volker, *Textiles of the Wiener Werkstätte, 1910–1932*, London: Thames and Hudson, 1994; as *The Wiener Werkstätte Textiles*, New York: Rizzoli, 1994 (German original, 1990)

In the decades between the two world wars, Vally Wieselthier's witty and exuberant ceramic figures, with their disregard of traditional techniques and standards of finish, dismayed such Austrian purists as the architect and designer Adolf Loos and fascinated American ceramists.

Wieselthier's middle-class Viennese family did not think it appropriate for a young woman to attend art school, but after two years at the stylish Kunstschule für Frauen und Mädchen, she arranged to take the exam for the more professional Kunstgewerbeschule without their permission and was admitted. During her studies there she worked on wallpaper, glass and fabric designs. When she saw a friend working with clay, she became fascinated with ceramics and studied under Michael Powolny. Wieselthier's work came to the attention of Josef Hoffmann, who regularly encouraged outstanding students to join the Wiener Werkstätte, the co-operative design workshops that he had founded in 1903 with Koloman Moser.

Wieselthier spent the years 1919–22 working for the workshop. She was one of a number of women who in the years following World War I displaced men in the Wiener Werkstätte: in 1920 there were 19 women among the 23 designers. Since the luxury materials that had characterised the Werkstätte's early production had become scarce during the war years, these designers turned to cheaper materials, creating light-hearted, witty and fashionable designs that were well received in the growing affluence of the 1920s. The sculptural and functional ceramics of Wieselthier and Susi Singer combined a spontaneous, expressionist handling of the clay and bright, freely applied glazes. Function was less important than style, and the finely wrought and polished porcelain surfaces of earlier Werkstätte ceramics – including that of Powolny – were rejected for rough modelling and splashed-on glazes. This exuberance was called frivolous and degenerate by Loos, a respected architect and designer, who banned "feminine" ornamentation – he argued that it marked the destructive influence of the consumer's poor taste – from his own work.

Unhappy with administrative changes made in the Werkstätte in 1922, Wieselthier established her own workshop: the Keramische Werkstätte Vally Wieselthier. In an earthenware vase of 1923 (Everson Museum of Art, Syracuse, NY) the plasticity of the clay is emphasised by twisted ribbons of clay that serve as handles and throwing marks that drag across the body. Loosely applied glazes contribute to the sense of spontaneity. Wieselthier's work was well received at the Haus Werkbund Fair in Frankfurt in 1923, and in 1925 she won silver and gold medals at the Paris Exposition. Although in 1927 she was invited to return to the Wiener Werkstätte as director of ceramics, she remained only briefly. The warm reception that Wiener Werkstätte works had received at the American Federation of Arts *International Exhibition of Ceramic Art*, which opened at the Metropolitan Museum of Art in New York and toured to other North American cities in 1928, suggested that there was an audience and a market for her work in the USA.

In 1929 Wieselthier joined Contempora, a collaborative group in New York that included Rockwell Kent, Paul Poiret and Bruno Paul, and exhibited a collection of vases, busts of women and full-scale nude figures (repr. Levin 1987, p.49, and "Vally Wieselthier Ausstellung in New York", 1929). The life-size figures were assembled from thrown forms: Wieselthier believed that all clay works grew from the concept of the pot. Slabbed and coiled clay was added to form waves of fabric and curls of hair. All were roughly modelled, with the seams allowed to show, and brightly glazed. The slim proportions of the kneeling or standing figures, their bobbed hair, plucked eyebrows, rosebud mouths and bright orange rouged cheeks suggest the exhilaration and freedom of the stylish young women – the flappers – of the 1920s, but their nudity and the deer and dogs that often accompany them evoke classical Greek sculpture of nymphs and goddesses. Her figures were used as garden decorations and in window displays of depart-

Wieselthier: *Taming the Unicorn*, 1946; stoneware; Everson Museum of Art, Syracuse

ment stores: Wieselthier remembered a few years later that as a child she had been fascinated by fashion illustrations of women in beautiful clothes that she copied from magazines.

Wieselthier remained in the USA for 18 months, completing bronze elevator doors for the Squibb Building in Pittsburgh and several other commissions. The figures she exhibited in 1930 were more elegant than exuberant: she left the terracotta surface unglazed and gave the sculptural forms an added refinement (repr. Wenzel 1931). R. Guy Cowan, the director of Cowan Pottery in Cleveland – who had already encouraged several American ceramists to study in Austria – hoped to employ Wieselthier, but his pottery closed in 1932. When Wieselthier returned to the USA in 1932 to stay, she worked briefly in Sebring Pottery in Ohio before establishing herself in New York.

Wieselthier believed ceramics to be one of the arts that "have no deep message to give the world save that of their own beauty and the artist's joy in making, intimate arts that make life gayer and yet have all the seriousness of a thing that is felt intensely and worked out with the utmost care" (quoted in Anscombe 1984, p.108). Her interest in the expressive qualities of clay and the potential of colour set an important example for American ceramists who were accustomed to traditional moulding techniques for creating sculptural works. Her fountains and tabletop sculptures were exhibited at the

National Ceramic Exhibitions at the Everson Museum in Syracuse and other exhibitions, and her witty and casual Viennese style made a strong impression on the figurative ceramic tradition in the USA.

SUSAN WALLER

Wiik, Maria
Finnish painter, 1853–1928

Born in Helsinki, 2 August 1853. Attended Adolf von Becker's academy, Helsinki, 1873; Finnish Art Society school, Helsinki, 1874–5; studied privately under Severin Falkman in Helsinki, 1874–5; studied at Académie Julian, Paris, under Tony Robert-Fleury, 1875–6 and 1877–80. Taught at the Finnish Art Society drawing school, 1880–81. Painted in Paris and Helsinki, 1881–2; Helsinki, Paris, Concarneau and Pont-Aven, Brittany, 1883–4; Finland, 1885–8; Normandy, 1886; worked under Puvis de Chavannes in Bouvet's studio, Paris, and in St Ives, Cornwall, 1889. Lived in Helsinki, making trips to Italy, 1895, Norway, 1898, 1911, 1913 and 1914, Paris, 1905, and Switzerland, 1908. Died in Helsinki, 19 June 1928.

Principal Exhibitions
Finnish Art Society, Helsinki: 1878, 1880–88, 1891–1903, 1905–6, 1908–10, 1916, 1919, 1922, 1924
Paris Salon: 1880–81, 1883–4
House of Nobility, Helsinki: 1885 (special exhibition of Finnish art, honourable mention)
Exposition Universelle, Paris: 1900 (bronze medal)
Ateneum, Helsinki: 1905 (women artists)
Finnish Artists Exhibition Hall, Helsinki: 1929 (retrospective)

Bibliography
L. Wennervirta, *Finlands konst: Från förhistorisk tid till våra dagar* [Finland's art: From prehistoric times to the present], Stockholm: Bokforlaget Natur och Kultur, 1926

Helena Westermarck, *Tre konstnärinnor: Fanny Churberg, Maria Wiik och Sigrid af Forselles* [Three women artists: Fanny Churberg, Maria Wiik and Sigrid af Forselles], Helsinki: Söderström, Förlagsaktiebolag, 1937

Onni Okkonen, *Finnish Art*, Helsinki: Werner Söderström Osakeyhtio, 1946

Pia Katerma, *Maria Wiik*, Helsinki: Werner Söderström Osakeyhtio, 1954

Målarinnor från Finland/Seitsemän Suomalaista Taiteilijaa [Women painters from Finland], exh. cat., Nationalmuseum, Stockholm, and elsewhere, 1981

Mildred Ratia, "Helena Schjerfbeck ja Maria Wiik in Janakkalan kesa 1885" [Helena Schjerfbeck and Maria Wiik and the Janakkala summer of 1885], *Janakkala ennen ja nyt* [Janakkala before now], 1982

1880-årene i nordisk maleri [The 1880s in Nordic painting], exh. cat., Nasjonalgalleriet, Oslo, and elsewhere, 1985

Sixten Ringbom, *Konsten i Finland* [Art in Finland], 2nd edition, Helsinki, 1987

Riitta Konttinen, "Finska konstnärinnors, 1880-tal: Ljus, luft och färg" [Finnish women artists in the 1880s: Light, air and colour], *De drogo till Paris: Nordiska konstnärinnor på 1880-talet* [They went to Paris: Nordic women artists in the 1880s], exh. cat., Liljevalchs Konsthall, Stockholm, 1988, pp.220–53

Wiik: *Out into the World*, 1889; Museum of Finnish Art Ateneum, Helsinki

Salme Sarajas-Korte, "Maalaustaide 1880-luvulla-ulkoilmarealismi" [The art of painting in the 1880s: Outdoor realism], *Ars Suomen Taide*, iv, 1989, pp.201–53

Riitta Konttinen, *Totuus enemmän kuin kauneus: Naistaiteilija, realismi ja naturalismi, 1880-luvulla: Amelie Lundahl, Maria Wiik, Helena Westermarck, Helene Schjerfbeck ja Elin Danielson* [Truth before beauty: The woman artist, realism and naturalism in the 1880s...], Helsinki: Otava, 1991

Taiteilijasisaria [Painting sisters], exh. cat., Jarvenpaa Community Hall, Finland, 1994

In a letter to her parents written in Paris in December 1875, Maria Wiik exclaimed that the best Christmas gift she had received was an accolade, "Cela va bien", from her teacher Tony Robert-Fleury, who had stopped to compliment her on a drawing. Wiik studied at the Académie Julian from early morning until the evening hours, retaining this focused dedication to her painting until the end of her life. Wiik's academic training in Paris, combined with her ability to catch the psychological as well as physical likeness in portraiture, enabled the young artist to support herself as a painter from the mid-1880s, an unusual situation for any Finnish artist in that period, let alone a woman. Contemporary critics considered her to be the best portraitist of her time.

Wiik was the first of the core group of leading Finnish women painters of the 1880s (among them Helene Schjerfbeck, Amelie Lundahl, Helena Westermarck and Elin Danielsson) to study in Paris. She travelled to Paris in the autumn of 1875, accompanied by her sister, Hilda, who later became a textile artist. Both daughters had benefited from the cultural environment created by their parents, architect Johan Wiik and Gustava Meyer. As daughters of the Swedish-speaking Finnish middle class, they had sufficient financial and official backing to consider careers in art. In 1874 Wiik entered the Finnish Art Society drawing school in Helsinki, originally founded in 1847. Not segregated in classes as were the sexes in the other European academies, both men and women drew together from draped models in the Helsinki school.

Throughout the latter decades of the 19th century women art students also entered the yearly exhibitions of the Finnish Art Society in substantial numbers, many winning prizes alongside their male colleagues. The first accolade that Wiik received from Finnish critics related to five figure studies entered in the Art Society exhibition of 1878, which C.G. Estlander described in *Finsk Tidskrift* as "clearly excellent". Wiik, moreover, won honourable mentions for portraits of *Marietta* (1880) and *Hilda Wiik* (1881; Ateneum, Helsinki) in the special exhibition of Finnish art at the House of Nobility, arranged by the Senate and honouring the visit of the Russian royal family. The portrait of *Hilda Wiik* had been shown at the Paris Salon of 1881, a considerable achievement for a painter at the start of her career. Her portraits, however, were not singled out in Axel Berndtson's official criticism of the exhibition of 1885, but were grouped instead with women's work as a whole, which according to Berndtson tended towards the new realist style rather than a more academically grounded foundation. In contrast, Berndtson wrote individual reviews on men's work in the exhibition. Fifty years later, the critic and former "painting sister" Westermarck wrote that the portrait of *Hilda Wiik* was a remarkable character study, painted with restrained colours symbolic of an elegant, yet tension-filled atmosphere (Westermarck 1937).

During the 1880s, a period of strong creativity for Wiik, she submitted several canvases depicting Breton women and children to the annual exhibitions of the Finnish Art Society. Finnish critics typically assigned them to women's concerns. Wiik, however, who experimented with Impressionist colour and light during this period in her numerous genre scenes (e.g. *Breton Children*, 1880; Ateneum; *Out into the World*, 1889; see illustration; *At Home*, 1894; private collection, *ibid.*), implied that the content of her canvases related directly to the concern of French naturalism to depict the working classes and daily life, not to a maternal feeling for subject matter. Like three of her "painting sisters", Wiik never married but painted domestic scenes because these environments were a natural part of her middle-class existence.

Wiik determined to re-invigorate her subject matter and use of colour in 1889 after several years of concentrating on painting portraits. With her Finnish colleague Helene Schjerfbeck (q.v.), she studied under the French painter Puvis de Chavannes in Paris in 1889. Both in Paris and later that summer in St Ives, Cornwall, she painted with Schjerfbeck. In fact portraits of the same child, *Girl with Pussy Willows* (1886; private collection, Helsinki) by Schjerfbeck and *A Girl's Head* (1886; private collection, Jyvaskyla) by Wiik, document the use of similar types of models by both artists during the several summers they painted together in France and Finland. *Out into the World* supposedly represents the change in her painting resulting from the summer study in St Ives and the more symbolistic influence of Puvis de Chavannes. Its austere, geometric surfaces appear bathed in an overall grey light. The narrative depicts a young girl about to enter into the working world while her grandmother sits with an open Bible, warily acknowledging the continuity of one generation of women passing on physical responsibilities to the next. Referred to by critics as Wiik's most important work, it presaged more symbolic illustrations and genre scenes that often juxtaposed members of the older generation, usually old women, with those of a younger one, as in *Fru Sorg* (1903; private collection, Helsinki).

Portraiture was Wiik's primary vocation. Two well-known works were an official portrait of *B.O. Schauman* (1888), superintendent of the Finnish Art Society, and of the singer *Ida Basilier-Magelsen* (1887; both Ateneum) for the Finnish theatre. Her portraits of the leading members of Finnish society, viewed as cultural documents of the 1890s and early 20th century, were often commissioned by academic institutions, such as that of *Dr P. Nordmann* (1916) for the Friends of the Swedish Folk Schools and the teacher *Anna Blomqvist* (1911) for the Swedish Girls' High School.

Although Gösta Stenman, the gallery director who managed the career of Helene Schjerfbeck, attempted to arrange solo exhibitions for Wiik in 1917 and again in 1919, the painter was a very private person and insisted that she was too critical of her own work to see it exhibited together. In 1922 she received a special invitation to participate in the Finnish Art Society exhibition, and showed 17 canvases at the exhibition of 1924. Five years before her death, the Finnish government gave her a pension in recognition of her status as a painter.

MARY TOWLEY SWANSON

Wilke, Hannah
American performance artist, 1940–1993

Born Arlene Hannah Butler in New York, 7 March 1940; Wilke was first husband's name. Studied sculpture at Tyler School of Fine Arts, Temple University, Philadelphia (BS, BFA 1961). Instructor in sculpture at School of Visual Arts, New York, from 1974. Recipient of Creative Artists Public Service (CAPS) grant, 1973; National Endowment for the Arts (NEA) grants, 1976, 1979, 1980 and 1987; Guggenheim fellowship, 1982; Pollock-Krasner Foundation grants, 1987 and 1992; International Association of Art Critics (United States Section) First Place award for Best Show in an Art Gallery at Ronald Feldman Gallery, 1993. Died of cancer, 28 January 1993.

Selected Individual Exhibitions

Margo Leavin Gallery, Los Angeles: 1972, 1974, 1976
Ronald Feldman Fine Arts, New York: 1972, 1974, 1975, 1978, 1984, 1989, 1994
Galerie Gerald Piltzer, Paris: 1975
Fine Arts Gallery, University of California at Irvine: 1976
Marianne Deson Gallery, Chicago: 1977
PS 1, Institute for Art and Urban Resources, Long Island City, NY: 1978
Washington Project for the Arts, Washington, DC: 1979
Joseph Gross Gallery, University of Arizona, Tucson: 1984
Gallery 210, University of Missouri, St Louis: 1989 (touring retrospective)
Genovese Graphics Gallery, Boston: 1990

Bibliography

Judith Tannenbaum, "Hannah Wilke", *Arts Magazine*, xlviii, May 1974, p.62
Cindy Nemser, "Four artists of sensuality", *Arts Magazine*, xlix, March 1975, pp.73–5
Mark Savitt, "Hannah Wilke: The pleasure principle", *Arts Magazine*, l, September 1975, pp.56–7
Lucy R. Lippard, "The pains and pleasures of rebirth: Women's body art", *Art in America*, lxiv, May–June 1976, pp.73–81; reprinted in Lucy R. Lippard, *Through the Center: Feminist Essays on Women's Art*, New York: Dutton, 1976
Avis Berman, "A decade of progress, but could a female Chardin make a living?", *Art News*, lxxix, October 1980, pp.73–9
Moira Roth, *The Amazing Decade: Women and Performance Art in America, 1970–1980*, Los Angeles: Astro Artz, 1983
Lowery Sims, "Body politics: Hannah Wilke and Kaylynn Sullivan", *Art and Ideology*, exh. cat., New Museum of Contemporary Art, New York, 1984, pp.45–56, 69–71
Marvin Jones, "Hannah Wilke's art, politics, religion and feminism", *New Common Good*, May 1985, pp.1, 9–11
Judy Siegel, "Between the censor and the muse? Hannah Wilke: Censoring the muse?", *Women Artists News*, xi, Winter 1986–7, pp.4, 47–8
Hannah Wilke: A Retrospective, exh. cat., Gallery 210, University of Missouri, St Louis, 1989
Debra Wacks, *Feminism/Humanism in Hannah Wilke's SOS: Starification Object Series*, MA thesis, Institute of Fine Arts, New York University, 1992
Intra-Venus: Hannah Wilke, exh. cat., Ronald Feldman Fine Arts, New York, 1994
Anette Kubitza, "Hannah Wilke: Bildervollständiger und unvollständiger Schönheit", *Frauen Kunst Wissenschaft*, no.17, May 1994, pp.72–91
Lucy R. Lippard, *The Pink Glass Swan: Selected Essays on Feminist Art*, New York: New Press, 1995

Life, Walter Benjamin observed, acquires definable meaning only at and through death. Hannah Wilke's final exhibition, *Intra-Venus* (1994), was a dramatic instance of the power of the last act radically to rewrite the meaning of an entire life's opus. Yet when her earlier work is looked at through the retrospective lens of the last exhibition, it seems to be part of a continuum that leads with all the economy and precision of a Greek tragedy to this particular climax. Shown posthumously, *Intra-Venus* documents, in 13 larger-than-life photographs set out like the stations of the Cross, Wilke's confrontation with her own death from lymphoma (see illustration). In her signature style of humorous, self-assured exhibitionist, she plays all her roles, including her last – the grotesque dying crone. Bald, naked, bloated, scarred by chemotherapy and bone-marrow treatments, hooked to I.V. tubes, Wilke runs through her repertoire of poses, from the calendar girl of 1954, taken when she was 14, to the uncannily prophetic image of herself with make-believe scars juxtaposed with her mother's cancer-mutilated body in the *So Help Me Hannah Series* (1978–81; artist's estate). Whether she assumes the beatitude of the Virgin Mary with downcast eyes and bent head shrouded in a blue shawl, or clowns such as Carmen Miranda, balancing a bouquet of plastic flowers on her head, the humour of Wilke's last performance is the clearest example we are likely to get of what Freud calls the "triumph of narcissism". "Humour", Freud realised, "has something liberating about it...something of grandeur and elevation. The grandeur in it clearly lies in *the triumph of narcissism*, the victorious assertion of the ego's invulnerability. The ego refuses to be distressed by the provocations of reality, to let itself be compelled to suffer."

Narcissistic indulgence and exhibitionism were frequent criticisms levelled against Wilke's work throughout her life. Perhaps it is only now, when her last performance is over, that we come to understand the function of narcissism. This was a woman who could manipulate herself endlessly, who displayed a liberated sensuality, who maintained a primary narcissism (the one characteristic that Freud stated women have and men lack). Her power was seen as a threat, which she played upon in all her works. Wilke exemplified perfectly the Lacanian proposition that the woman does not exist, that femininity itself is a series of masquerades. Insofar as Wilke would enter the frame of a particular fantasy of womanhood she embodied pathological enjoyment; but she would always "traverse" the fantasy, always go too far.

In *Hannah Wilke: Super-T-Art* (1974; artist's estate) she photographs herself in a progression of 20 poses through which she transforms herself from martyred saint, hands held outwards as if to reveal stigmata, to burlesque dancer doing a seductive striptease, and finally to the crucified Christ, the drapery from the striptease now wrapped as a simple loincloth. The sexualised image of the female is ultimately consigned to the conventions of masculine visual pleasure or martyrdom. By making a display of her figurative death Wilke suggests that there is a price to be paid for this spectacular ruse.

All of Wilke's work insists that gender and sexuality are indeterminate processes of signification inscribed on the surface of the body. Throughout her career she used her own body as a sculptural element, presenting it as an object in the interplay of libidinal and economic forces. In a video

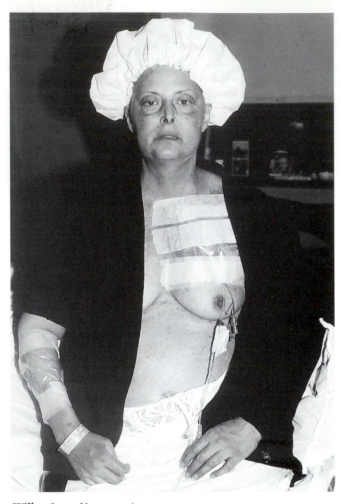

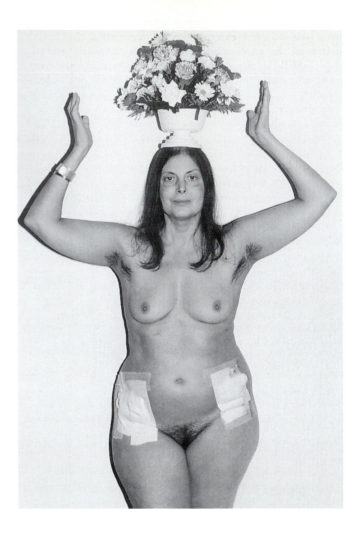

Wilke: *Intra-Venus*, series, 1992–3

performance of 1977 entitled *Intercourse with...* her naked torso is inscribed with other people's names – lovers, friends, those who made an impact on her – implying that all inter-course, all language, represents loss or damage to the body. In *Exchange Values (Marx)* (1978–84; artist's estate) she poses precariously on top of the wheels and pistons of an air compressor tank labelled "Exchange Values", her body is liter-ally caught up in the mechanism of exchange, like Charlie Chaplin in the factory scene in *Modern Times*. In *Give: Hannah Wilke Can – A Living Sculpture Needs to Make a Living* (1978; artist's estate) she sets herself up like a street beggar or someone soliciting donations for a charity: on the label of the donation cans spread about her is her own image in an ambiguous pose of religious/erotic martyrdom or ecstasy. The commodification of her body-as-image is how she makes her living, and she makes the audience acknowledge that economic reality. In *SOS: Starification Object Series* (1974–5; artist's collection) her body is scarred with wads of chewing gum shaped in the form of female genitalia. The "plastic" nature of these vulvae shows how attempts to render woman's sexuality visible ultimately consign it to the artificial while at the same time suggesting that what we can objectify (either aesthetically or medically) as woman's sexual anatomy is purely a construct. Each frame figures her in some stereotypi-cally feminine pose: a cowgirl, a vamp, a film star, an Islamic woman wearing headgear and veil. Even the deification of the movie "stars" asserts that an intelligible system of signification of sexuality is achieved only through performative violence. Female sexuality is made visible only through starification /scarification; ultimately it leads to her call for help – "SOS".

When the masquerade of femininity began to fail, as it did towards the end of Wilke's life, she, with her usual intrepid *élan*, persisted in it to the very end, forcing the viewer to accompany her to its radical conclusion. What is so threaten-ing about the *femme fatale*, the ambiguous woman capable of many disguises, is not that she is so immersed in disguise and deception, but rather, as Slavoj Zizek has argued, that she will go too far, reveal what he terms "the real", accept without reserve her own non-existence, the imminence of her own death (Slavoj Zizek, *Looking Awry: An Introduction to Jacques Lacan Through Popular Culture*, Cambridge: Massachusetts Institute of Technology Press, 1991, p.66). Hannah Wilke is just such a *femme fatale*, the narcissistic woman who does not cede her desire, a subject fully assuming her own fate. Her work is triumphant, not because she wins the battle, either with identities' undoing or with death; it is triumphant in her challenge to society's obsession with masking, with the denial of lack and loss, in her willingness to look steadily at the "disappearance that everybody denies".

Wilke's work is an extraordinary synthesis of sensuous,

body-based material explorations of femininity, theoretical critiques of the production of art and gender, and feminist activism. Wilke's "signature", vaginal imagery, and her daring performances using her own body were central to the development of the feminist movement in the 1970s. Her critique of the stereotypic images of women in the media; her exploration of the masquerade of femininity, her deconstructive use of language; her humour, particularly her Duchampian puns; and her insights into the gender bias inherent in art production, even in such seemingly "neutral" art movements as Conceptualism and Minimalism, have made her work the precursor of a great deal of the art produced by women artists working in the 1980s, such as Barbara Kruger (q.v.), Cindy Sherman and the performance artists Karen Finley and Annie Sprinkle. In her straightforward account of disease and the process of dying, she is sister to Nancy Fried and Jo Spence (q.v.).

As a sculptor, painter, photographer, performer and installation artist, Wilke was involved in a number of art movements, including Abstract Expressionism, Minimalism, Conceptualism and Post-modernism and, of course, the Feminist Art Movement. She experimented with an array of media including clay, oil paint, latex, watercolours, family photos, postcards, videotape, chewing gum and laundry lint as well as Marcel Duchamp's *Large Glass*. Her extensive art production combined with her contributions to the fields of art, politics, sexuality and prejudice against women made her one of the leading feminist theoreticians and activists of her day.

JO ANNA ISAAK

Williams, Evelyn

British painter and sculptor, 1929–

Born in London, 1929. Studied at St Martin's School of Art, London, 1944–7; Royal College of Art, London, 1947–50 (first-class diploma and E.Q. Henriques prize for drawing). Recipient of first prize for sculpture, John Moore's Exhibition, Liverpool, 1961. Participated in Cleveland Drawing Biennale, 1975 and 1979. Lives in Cardiff.

Selected Individual Exhibitions

Whitechapel Art Gallery, London: 1972 (retrospective)
Monika Kinley, London: 1983
Riverside Studios, London: 1984
Ikon Gallery, Birmingham: 1985 (touring)
Prema Arts Centre, Uley, Gloucestershire: 1988
Arts Council Gallery, Belfast: 1989
Graves Art Gallery, Sheffield, and Chapter, Cardiff: 1990
Mead Gallery, University of Warwick: 1994 (*Antinomies*, touring)
Manchester City Art Galleries: 1996

Bibliography

Evelyn Williams: A Retrospective Exhibition, 1945–72, exh. cat., Whitechapel Art Gallery, London, 1972
Women's Images of Men, exh. cat., Institute of Contemporary Arts, London, 1980
Hayward Annual 1982: British Drawing, exh. cat., Hayward Gallery, London, 1982
Evelyn Williams, exh. cat., Riverside Studios, London, 1984
What's New in the Arts Council Collection: A Touring Exhibition of a Selection of Purchases from 1983–84, exh. cat., Arts Council of Great Britain, London, 1984
M. Beaumont, "Evelyn Williams", *Arts Review*, xxxvi, 3 August 1984, p.386
Human Interest, exh. cat., Cornerhouse, Manchester, 1985
Piranesi's Prisons, exh. cat., Graves Art Gallery, Sheffield, 1988
S. Cawkwell, "Out of the archive: Evelyn Williams", *Women Artists Slide Library Journal*, no.24, August–September 1988, pp.18–19
Evelyn Williams, exh. cat., Arts Council Gallery, Belfast, 1989
John McEwen, "Interview", *The Independent*, 20 January 1990 (magazine supplement)
Antinomies: Works by Evelyn Williams, exh. cat., Mead Gallery, University of Warwick, and elsewhere, 1994
Evelyn Williams: Encounters Paintings, 1992–1996, exh. cat., Manchester City Art Galleries, 1996

"My work comes from my life, shaped, nourished and determined by events and accidental happenings, misfortunes and relationships. If I could use words or sing songs, there would be no need to paint pictures." Evelyn Williams's notes, extracted from various studio workbooks kept over recent years, have emerged in publications accompanying exhibitions in 1990 and 1994 as a self-critical foil to the work and personal commentary on her artistic production. Her work embraces insight and melancholic truths. It deals in particularities – triggered by things seen (*Catching the Thief*, 1984; painted relief; private collection), newspaper reports (*Burning Man*, 1985; painted relief; artist's collection), universal visions and recurrent, obstinate, waking dreams: affective images that can startle with qualities of both wit and fear. It can be unsettling as well as affirmatory for the viewer. Such combinations of qualities and difficulties in relating Williams neatly to the taxonomy of post-war British art probably lie behind her remaining under-represented in British public collections. Critical attention gathered momentum only in the 1990s.

As an artist her professional beginnings are indicative of the isolated and paradoxical position she has come to occupy. She trained in the immediate post-war years when the male-dominated ethos of the art schools was bolstered by young artists whose early training had been interrupted by the war and in many cases active service. Williams's actual generation is that of John Bratby, Derrick Greaves, Jack Smith and the returners from war, Edward Middleditch and George Fullard. Hers is also the generation of Leon Kossoff and Frank Auerbach. Of the women artists of her generation, both Sandra Blow (q.v.) and Bridget Riley (q.v.) emerged in the 1960s as equally single-minded and culturally broadly based abstract as opposed to figurative artists. Williams points to there being few role models for women artists in her day. Her career has had to accommodate home-making, children, men and relationships, all of which, over time, have also nurtured her perceptions, subject matter and ambitions for a personal art. Her will power for her art led her into a monumental facture not as a young artist but as a middle-aged one. She can be seen as isolated as a woman artist in her generation and isolated in her concern for the power of an inner reality to translate itself into a realised form.

Williams's recorded judgement of her teachers at the Royal College and before that – from the age of 14 at St Martin's School of Art – is harsh, for they appear to have valued

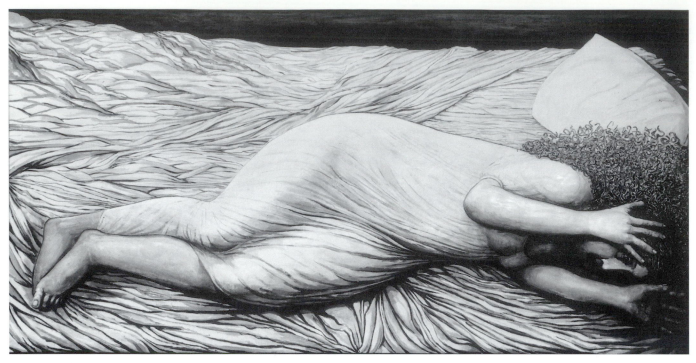

Williams: *All Night Through*, 1984; painted relief, 143 × 266 cm.; New Hall, Cambridge

qualities of execution rather than image and yet there are some plausible affiliations with artists such as Carel Weight. Looking back beyond Weight, the artist would acknowledge an abiding fascination for Stanley Spencer's created world. Ten years after college and her idiosyncratic position there, her emergence in the public domain was no less ambiguous. In the John Moore's Liverpool Exhibition of 1961 she entered two large-scale heads in a papier-mâché collage technique (National Museums and Galleries on Merseyside). The work was entered in the painting section and yet awarded first prize in sculpture by the jury, prompting a furore among the sculptors and a continuing problematic categorisation for Williams's work – which went on to take the form of wax models, painted relief sculpture, boxed works and drawings and paintings retaining a sculptural feel.

The deep roots of Williams's themes and images are vested in her experience of life and particularly by feelings of isolation and fears as well as the predicaments of the couple and the individual made visible in touching, tender, witty and at times brutally honest ways. She experienced an extraordinary sense of isolation from an early age. Following advice from Bertrand Russell to her parents, she was placed, aged three, at A. S. Neill's Summerhill school. This freedom and experimentation in a grown-up childhood led her to a sense of deprivation, withdrawal within herself and a paralysis of her will rather than its responsible emancipation.

Her career was initially side-tracked into being that of a portraitist of children. Hugh Casson commissioned her to paint his children and this led to other commissions. The Moore's prize showed her breaking into the monumental and startling area that she has continued to occupy. The developments from this work largely involved the fragility and translucency of wax modelled in its own right. These now appear a necessary passage to her natural imagery. With a painter's

training she began to embark on these pieces, which began to be sizeable and were models if not sculptures – wax allowed also for an element of built-in colour. These works formed by touch defy touch in the spectator – they also have ambiguities inherent in their doll-like appearance.

Throughout the unfolding of her media and subject matter there has been a constant interest in drawing. Her drawing can have a Kollwitz-like naturalism or can explore the coming into being of her individual characteristic human forms. She will explore how her creations behave. These creations have never taken on the over-generalised sameness of the monolithic sculptures of Elisabeth Frink (q.v.). They remain intensely individual even when configured in a crowd. In the late 1970s and early 1980s the properties of an Italian modelling material allowed the artist to develop her imagery in large-scale reliefs. These are weighty works in all senses. Their colours remain predominantly earth colours and bleached whites. High key colour is actually painful to the eyes of this artist – who traces some of the dulling sense of monochromatic landscape back to the childhood evacuation of Summerhill to North Wales. The painted reliefs of these years produced some of her most monumental and yet individual statements of the human condition, both in single figure pieces, such as *All Night Through* (1984; see illustration), and a massing of humanity in plight: *The Valley* (1984; artist's collection) and *Out of the Forest* (1979; Sheffield City Art Galleries). Configurations of people are paralleled in another constant of the work, a sort of sub-set perhaps undertaken as an escape from the demands of figuring people, where the artist explores some full burgeoning natural forms. The profusion and unfolding rhythms of nature have been explored in a series of decorative and yet oppressive flower pieces.

Manipulation of the large-scale heavy reliefs, a form that Williams had found in her fiftieth year, entailed enormous physical demands on the artist. She carried on working with this material into the second half of the 1980s. The reliefs became too difficult to manoeuvre in the studio, but scale persisted and a series of large-scale drawings incorporating astonishing, witty and moving mind's-eye images of relationships, physically figured, resulted: *Loving Couples, Fleeing Couples* and *The Family* (all 1988; watercolour ink and white on paper; artist's collection). These are some of Williams's most potent works, combining the sculptural qualities of the painted reliefs with a distillation of her imagery. Their strangeness and haunting qualities in some ways make her harder to categorise in critical debate and more easy to equate with the psychotic qualities of much Outsider Art. Also emerging in these works are Williams's affinity with Gothic and early Renaissance art.

A long meditation on the qualities of some early Renaissance artists, Masaccio and Piero della Francesca, informs her work from *Out of the Garden* (1989) onwards. The reliefs may have marked the most dramatic of her statements but the work has continued to evolve based on simple things found out in the course of constant work. Works of the 1990s are modest, intense paintings of figures and faces seen close to – summations of the woman's and the couple's life cycle with references back to the studies for *All Night Through*. Many of her images have been stubbornly recurrent – returning to her consciousness perennially. Sometimes the works have used the subtle changes between two images to convey the sense of moment.

Examples of Williams's work may be found in the Arts Council Collection, England; Sheffield City Art Galleries; Victoria and Albert Museum, London; and New Hall, Cambridge. Major touring exhibitions have brought her work to an increasing public; significantly, Christine Battersby's essay in the catalogue accompanying the *Antinomies* touring exhibition of 1994 explored for the first time the clear territory of the female sublime revealed in Evelyn Williams's work in terms freed from the male concepts of the sublime that have characterised art since the late 18th century's definitions of such an aesthetic.

DAVID ALSTON

Winsor, Jackie
American sculptor, 1941–

Born Vera Jacqueline Winsor in St John's, Newfoundland, Canada, 20 October 1941. Moved with her family to Boston, Massachusetts, 1952. Studied at Yale Summer School of Art and Music, New Haven, 1964; Massachusetts College of Art, Boston (BFA 1965); Douglass College, Rutgers University, New Brunswick (MFA 1967). Married Keith Sonnier, 1965; divorced 1978. Moved to New York, 1967. Member of the faculty, School of Visual Arts, New York. Recipient of Creative Artists Public Service (CAPS) grant, 1973; National Endowment for the Arts (NEA) grants, 1974, 1977 and 1984; Louis Comfort Tiffany grant, 1977; Guggenheim fellowship, 1978; Brandeis University Creative Artists award, 1979; honorary doctorate, University of Newfoundland;

honoree, Sculpture Center, New York, 1995; honored alumni, Massachusetts College of Art, Boston, 1996. Lives in New York.

Selected Individual Exhibitions
Douglass College Gallery, New Brunswick, NJ: 1968
Paula Cooper Gallery, New York: 1973, 1976, 1982, 1983, 1986, 1989, 1992
Contemporary Arts Center, Cincinnati: 1976–7 (touring)
Museum of Modern Art, New York: 1979 (touring)
Hayden Gallery, Massachusetts Institute of Technology, Cambridge: 1983 (with Barry Ledoux)
Margo Leavin Gallery, Los Angeles: 1987
Milwaukee Art Museum, Milwaukee: 1991–3 (touring)

Bibliography
Liza Bear, "An interview with Jackie Winsor", *Avalanche*, vii, Spring 1972, pp.10–17
Lucy R. Lippard, "Jackie Winsor", *Artforum*, xii, February 1974, pp.56–8; reprinted in Lucy R. Lippard, *From the Center: Feminist Essays on Women's Art*, New York: Dutton, 1976
Jackie Winsor: Sculpture, exh. cat., Contemporary Arts Center, Cincinnati, and elsewhere, 1976
Strata: Nancy Graves, Eva Hesse, Michelle Stuart, Jackie Winsor, exh. cat., Vancouver Art Gallery, 1977
Roberta Smith, "Winsor-built", *Art in America*, lxv, January–February 1977, pp.118–20
Robert Pincus-Witten, "Winsor knots: The sculpture of Jackie Winsor", *Arts Magazine*, li, June 1977, pp.127–33
Eleanor Munro, *Originals: American Women Artists*, New York: Simon and Schuster, 1979
Jackie Winsor, exh. cat., Museum of Modern Art, New York, and elsewhere, 1979
John Gruen, "Jackie Winsor: Eloquence of a Yankee pioneer", *Art News*, lxxviii, March 1979, pp.57–60
Craig Gholson, "More than minimal Jackie Winsor", *Interview*, April 1979, pp.62–4
Jackie Winsor/Barry Ledoux: Sculpture, exh. cat., Hayden Gallery, Massachusetts Institute of Technology, Cambridge, 1983
Corinne Robins, *The Pluralist Era: American Art, 1968–1981*, New York: Harper, 1984
Howard J. Smagula, *Currents: Contemporary Directions in the Visual Arts*, 2nd edition, Englewood Cliffs, NJ: Prentice Hall, 1989
Charlotte Streifer Rubinstein, *American Women Sculptors*, Boston: Hall, 1990
John Gruen, *The Artist Observed: 28 Interviews with Contemporary Artists*, Chicago: A Capella, 1991
Jackie Winsor, exh. cat., Milwaukee Art Museum, Milwaukee, and elsewhere, 1991
Margot Mifflin, "Jackie Winsor: Pieces of life", *Art News*, xci, Summer 1992, pp.100–05

Jackie Winsor's sculptures, weighty, ascetic and elegant, have made her one of the major figures of the post-Minimalist generation of artists who came of age in the late 1960s. Known chiefly for her permutations of the cube form, achieved through various labour-intensive processes, Winsor has actually progressed through numerous forms while pursuing her remarkably consistent concerns with weight, density and interiority versus exteriority. Devoting herself to the often dauntingly repetitive tasks involved in the creation of each piece, she has produced a "small body of perfect work" (Peter Schjeldahl in Milwaukee 1991, p.13), comprising some 75 sculptures made between 1967 and 1991.

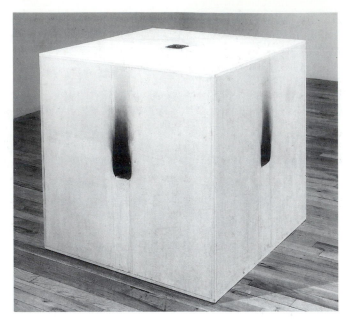

Winsor: *Burnt Paper Piece*, 1981–2; wood, hydrostone, paper reams; 81.6 cm. square

Born into the rural environment of St John's, Newfoundland, in 1941, Winsor learned carpentry as a child. Although her family moved to Boston in 1952, she has returned to Newfoundland regularly since then. She studied painting at the Massachusetts College of Art, Boston; during a summer spent at the Yale Summer School in New Haven, she took up photography, concentrating on self-contained natural forms. By the time she earned her BFA in 1965, she had abandoned painting altogether. Winsor then entered the MFA programme at Douglass College, Rutgers University, where she met Keith Sonnier (they were married from 1965 to 1978) and Joan Snyder (q.v.). She began making sculpture at Rutgers, experimenting with resins, rubbers and metal. One work paired two masonite cubes covered in industrial rubber, with hair-like, curling metal strips surrounding them (*Untitled*, 1967; destroyed).

Winsor moved to New York in 1967. Partly due to safety concerns, she abandoned resins, working with rubber sheeting, tubes, cord and hair, materials favoured in this period by such artists as Eva Hesse (q.v.). Thick cables of rope led her to *Rope Trick* (1967–8; artist's collection), considered her first mature work. The column of thick rope, 188 centimetres high, stands freely, thanks to a metal rod inside. She worked on these brutish physical rope pieces – coiled circles, arches and chunks – throughout the early 1970s.

By 1968 Winsor had joined the Ad Hoc Women Artists Committee, a burgeoning group offering information and support within the male-dominated art world of that time. There she met Mary Miss (q.v.), Jackie Ferrara (q.v.) and the critic Lucy Lippard, a co-founder of the group, who included Winsor in a number of shows she curated. In addition to these artists, Winsor associated during this period with Richard Serra and Gordon Matta-Clark, both of whom were then exploring Process Art. But more than any sculptor, the artist who most impressed her at that time was Yvonne Rainer (q.v.). Winsor has acknowledged the influence of Rainer's movement work, particularly the lecture/performance *The Mind Is a Muscle* (1968), for its restraint and internal focus. In 1971 Winsor produced her only performance, *Up and/or Down*, involving a thick rope being pulled through a hole in the gallery floor by a man, who then slowly lowered the rope over a woman lying on the floor below.

In 1973 Winsor had her first solo show at the Paula Cooper Gallery, showing sculptures made from wood, logs and twine unbraided from her thick rope. Many of these works both employed and subverted the Minimalist grid with these powerful natural materials; an example is *Bound Square* (1972; ht 193 cm.; Museum of Modern Art, New York), whose square of massive logs is softened by thick hemp bindings at each corner. Winsor produced her only outdoor, site-specific works, incorporating living trees, during this period.

Her first cube pieces (1974–5) were constructed of strips of pine, 2.54 centimetres square, in grid formations. The cube, a Minimalist icon, would hold her attention for the next ten years. While her cubes became solid and thick – constructed of such materials as plywood, sheetrock (wallboard), cement and reclaimed wood from her loft – they were never impenetrable. Small windows cut into each face allowed limited visual access to their interior spaces. Between 1977 and 1982 Winsor created three cube works that together provided a dramatic, even apocalyptic coda to her process explorations. For *Burnt Piece* (1977–8; Museum of Modern Art) she laid alternate layers of wood and cement over a wire-mesh frame; burning the piece over a bonfire destroyed the wood, leaving a charred and honeycombed concrete surface. The 50 vari-coloured coats of paint she applied to the inside and outside of *Painted Piece* (1979–80; Milwaukee Art Museum) were partially revealed after the cube was dragged along the sidewalk on each face. With *Exploded Piece* (1980–82; private collection, repr. Milwaukee 1991, p.81) chance overcame her obsessive planning and facture, as a police bomb squad inadvertently exploded a work that was meant to be imploded with its exterior left intact (she subsequently restored it to its cubic form).

Winsor has spoken of the sense of potential energy she wished her works to project. With this culmination of her cube series, she seemed to be releasing that energy, like some hands-on, idiosyncratic physicist. These works also take their place in a developing allegory of the relationship of self and other that has been noted in her work. Earlier works contain hidden, secret layers; the boxes too have their private facets, but quietly (except for *Exploded Piece*) reveal their often contrasting interiors to the interested observer. She developed this leitmotif of hiding and revelation throughout the mid-1980s with a series of technically dazzling combinations of cubes and spheroids, one shape often nesting inside the other.

Winsor's series of truncated stepped pyramids and modestly scaled *Inset Wall Pieces*, begun in 1988 and all executed in acrylic-modified cement (e.g. *Inset Wall Piece*, 1990; Solomon R. Guggenheim Museum, New York), opened a new vantage-point on her themes. The steps of the pyramids, and the facets of the wall pieces receding into the wall, surround deeply saturated square pools of colour: red, blue or black. Here, interiority is revealed, and a serenity hinted at earlier is frankly embodied.

MIRIAM SEIDEL

Wolff, Ann
Swedish glass artist, painter and graphic artist, 1937–

Born Ann Schaefer in Lübeck, Germany, 27 February 1937.
Studied visual communication under Thomas Maldonado at
Hochschule für Gestaltung, Ulm, 1956–9. Married glass
designer Göran Wärff, 1960; three daughters, born 1961,
1963 and 1971; divorced 1971. Began professional career
under the name Ann Wärff; changed surname to Wolff, 1985.
Glass designer, Pukebergs Glasbruk, Nybro, Sweden,
1960–64; Kosta Boda, Sweden, 1964–78. Guest teacher in
various schools and academies in Europe, Japan and USA
from 1974. Guest lecturer in USA, giving workshops at
California College of Arts and Crafts, Oakland; California
State University, Fullerton; Vanderbilt University, Nashville;
Penland School of Crafts, 1976. Guest professor and faculty
member, Pilchuck Glass Center (later School), Standwood,
Washington, 1977, 1979, 1984, 1986 and 1995. Established
the glass studio Stenhytta in Transjö, Kosta, Sweden, with
Wilke Adolffson, 1978; closed 1983. Co-founder, 1982, and
director, 1982–4, of the glass studio Transjö Kulturarbetare i
Glas. Involvement in graphics, painting and sculpture from
1982. Independent artist in Berlin from 1990. Professor of
design at Hochschule für Bildende Künste, Hamburg, from
1993. Recipient of Lunningpriset (for Scandinavia), 1968;
first prize, Coburger Glaspreis, 1977; first and third prizes,
Centralschweizer Glaspreis, Switzerland, 1980; award of
honour, Internationale Glaskunst 81, Kassel, 1981; glass
prize, World's Crafts Exhibition, Bratislava, 1984; gold
medal, Bayerischer Staatspreis, Munich, 1988. Lives in
Hamburg and Berlin, Germany, and in Gotland and Transjö,
Sweden.

Selected Individual Exhibitions
Varbergs Museum, Sweden: 1966, 1984
Norrköpings Museum, Sweden: 1967
Galerie Wulff, Helsinki: 1968
Galerie Doktor Glas, Stockholm: 1976, 1979, 1984, 1987
Galerie SM, Frankfurt am Main: 1978
Yamaha, Kyoto, Japan: 1980
Heller Gallery, New York: 1982, 1987
Ivor Kurland Gallery, Los Angeles: 1983, 1987
Holsten Galleries, Palm Beach, FL: 1983, 1986
Galerie Lietzow, Berlin: 1984
Maurice Littleton Gallery, Washington, DC: 1985
Gotlands Fornsal, Visby, Sweden: 1986
Stockholm Art Fair: 1988
Chicago Art Fair: 1989, 1994
Konstmuseum, Visby: 1990
Musée Château d'Annecy, France: 1990
Noah's Art Space, Tokyo: 1992
Arts Découverts, Palais Royal, Paris: 1992
Gamla Riksbanken, Vänersborg, Sweden: 1994
Heller Gallery, Palm Beach, FL: 1995
Gösta Werner Museum, Simrishamm, Sweden: 1995

Selected Writings
"Selbstmord eines Glashauses/Suicide of a glasshouse", *Neues
Glas/New Glass*, February 1990, pp.70–72

Bibliography
K. Moriyama, "Glass windows designed by Ann Wärff", *Japan
Interior Design*, no.214, 1977
—, "Work by Ann Wärff", *Japan Interior Design*, no.234, 1978
Michael Taylor, "Svenskt Glas [Swedish glass]", *Glass Studio*, i,
January–February 1978, pp.18–23
Bertil Palmquist, *I Glasrike* [In the realm of glass], Lund, 1979
K. Moriyama, "Two women designers from Sweden", *Graphic
Design* (Tokyo), no.73, 1979, pp.77–80
Mailis Stensman, "Kvinnobilder i glas [Images of women in glass]",
Form, lxxv/6, 1979, pp.8–10
Ruby Bernstein and Caryl Hansen, "Ann Wärff", *Glass Art Society
Journal*, v, 1980, pp.8–10
J. Schou-Christensen, "Der Grosse Aufbruch: Europäische Glaskunst
seit 1945", *Neues Glas*, 1980, p.3
Klaus Moje, "Das Pilchuck glass center", *ibid*, p.20
Lena Boëthius, "Formrevy: Mästelig teknik och rikt uttryck" [Form
revue: Masterful techniques and rich expression], *Form*, lxxvii/5,
1981, p.32
Märit Ehn, "Ny glasglädje från Stenhytta [New glass joy from
Stenhytta]", *Form*, lxxviii/4, 1982, p.51
Hans Frode, "Ann Wärff", *New Work*, Spring 1982, pp.8–9
David A. Fryxell, "Art by design", *Horizon*, xxv, July 1982,
pp.20–28
Mailis Stensman, "Glas: Ett material för offentlig miljö" [Glass: A
material for public buildings], *Statens Konstråd*, iv, November
1982, p.2
Sylvia Girard, "Ann Wärff", *Revue de la Céramique et du Verre*,
no.10, 1983, pp.34–5
Åke Huldt, "The design and the artist: A talk with Ann Wärff",
American Craft, xliii, April–May 1983, pp.38–41
Ann Wolff, exh. cat., Malmö, 1984
Lena Gyllenpalm, "Formkrönikan 1983" [Chronicle of forms, 1983],
Form, lxxx/1, 1984, pp.26–9
Christiane Sellner, *Geschichte des Studioglases*, 1984
Verena Tafel, "Entdeckung und Veränderung/Discoveries and
changes: Neue Arbeiten von Ann Wolff/New works by Ann
Wolff", *Neues Glass/New Glass*, 1986, pp.258–64
—, *Ann Wolff: A Signal Had To Be Given*, Transjö, 1986
Ann Wolff: Fornsalens Bildstenshall [Ann Wolff in the hall of Viking
stone sculpture], exh. cat., Gotlands Fornsal, Visby, 1986
Ann Wolff, exh. cat., Galerie Doktor Glas, Stockholm, 1987
Ann Wolff, exh. cat., Musée Château d'Annecy, France, 1990
Kuroki Rika, "Ann Wolff: In search of truth", *Glassworks*,
November 1993, pp.12–17
A New Century in European Design, exh. cat., Tokyo, and else-
where, 1994

For 20 years Ann Wolff's artistic career was chiefly characterised by her work as an internationally recognised, award-
winning glass artist. Her name at that time, Ann Wärff, was
virtually a synonym for Swedish glass design. From the very
beginning, her spherical, intensely coloured, narrative-poetic
objects formed milestones of a new artistic consciousness in
glass art (examples in the Corning Museum of Glass and
Metropolitan Museum, New York; Stedelijk Museum,
Amsterdam; Hokkaido Museum, Sapporo; Victoria and Albert
Museum, London; Kestner Museum, Hannover; Museum für
Kunst und Gewerbe, Hamburg; and the art collections of Veste
Coburg, Germany). In the mid-1980s the artist began purposefully to expand the spectrum of her forms of expression: etchings, watercolours, drawings, oil paintings and glass sculptures
were new techniques that provided her with further possibilities for plumbing the depths of the central theme of her work,
namely the facets of human – and particularly of womankind's
– existence. With her transformation from industrial designer
to free artist, with the moving of her place of work from the
glassworks to the studio, came a change of name as well: Ann
Wärff became Ann Wolff.

Wolff: *The Duckbill-Goddess*, 1986; sculpture; height 56 cm.

Through all of Wolff's work there runs, like a connecting thread, a deeply felt impulse to express, by means of objective, figurative representation, the spanning of existence between two poles, the ambivalence inherent in all things and both the separation and simultaneity of two principles. Already in her glass works of the 1960s, Wolff experimented with new techniques; she revolutionised the melting process in order to make tangible the phenomenon of the enclosure and the disclosure of space. To give just one example, *Snowball* (1978), an organic-seeming, transparent glass sculpture that holds a night-light – which is still a classic and a big seller for the internationally famous Swedish glassworks Kosta Boda – was invented through her experiments with contrasts: hot molten glass versus the cold snow of a Nordic winter. With her husband Göran Wärff, during her years at Kosta Boda, she carried out designs for industrially manufactured mass-produced items until 1971. At the same time she consistently pursued the development of her own artistic work.

In the early 1970s the first works in glass using cold techniques appeared. From 1973 Wolff began using etching techniques in her own studio in the Kosta plant and from 1975 she also used the sand-blasting process in order to attain altered structures in the glass and to enable it to become the image-carrier for her narratives. Her great "material discipline", to use one of her own expressions, her technique of combining line and brush etching (whereby she first paints with hot wax on extremely thin but strongly coloured overlay and underlay glass and then places the prepared piece in hydrofluoric acid), with which Wolff is able to intensify the material's properties of ambiguity and transparency still further, makes the artist one of the pioneers in her field. The visions – recorded as designs on gleaming receptacles (bowls and vases) and on glass windows, or cut as glass reliefs – repeat motifs such as scissors, teacups, teapots and also a hare. By repetition, the objects of daily life appear isolated and magnified; they seem to have grown from the collective unconsciousness and attain the character of symbols, of archetypes, metaphors often for the fate, the function, the enchainment and entanglement of womankind.

By the mid-1970s her artistic breakthrough had taken place. In 1976 she began lecturing at American universities, and was stimulated by an interchange of ideas with Marvin Lipovsky and Erwin Eisch. Since 1977 she has lectured regularly at the centre of the "glass movement" in the USA, the Pilchuck Glass School in Washington State. In 1977 she emerged as the winner of the Coburg Glass prize from among 194 submitted works by artists from 19 European countries. Her works were exhibited in more than 20 museum collections.

Her departure from Kosta Boda and the foundation of her own enterprise, the glassworks studio Stenhytta, which she built with Wilke Adolfsson (one of the most renowned masters of glass-making from the Orrefors glassworks) as a meeting place for the international glass world in 1978, gave Wolff the artistic freedom to pursue her own path in a consistent way. Her style changed and the expressive elements were intensified. The forms on glass walls appear drawn out, angular, spindly. Dramatic events in whose midst women and symbols of the feminine are placed; scenes full of ambiguity, labyrinths, places of battle between the male and the female, are to be found in the images on the objects, which are given poetic, enigmatic titles: *Secret Fliers of the Night*, *This Is the Willow Witch's Shopping Bag*, *Number Two* (Victoria and Albert Museum, London), *Glass Art in Space: The Trouble-Makers Are at it Again* (Museum Veste Coburg). The conflict inherent in the content finds its formal correspondence in the technical possibilities of the working of the glass, with its overlapping and overlaying of layers of colour.

In the 1980s the large Swedish architectural commissions increased, such as the fashioning of a glass wall for the parish rooms in Nybro (1981), for the foyer in the government building in Kalmar (1981), large-format room decorations in the old people's home in Knivsta, in the library in Trelleborg, in the concert hall in Vaxjo (1992). The last to be completed was the altar window of the medieval church at Ödestugu near Jönköping (1993).

In 1982, the year in which Wolff founded a second glassworks studio with the name Transjö Kulturarbetare i Glas, she experimented for the first time with making prints from glass with Harvey Littleton in Spruce Pine, North Carolina, a year after she had ventured – with drawings that had no immediate connection with her working of glass – to take her first steps towards the fine arts. In 1985 she began to paint in water-colours at her summer residence in Gotland; she soon mastered the technique of colour etching, step by step she tested material after material, from pastel to charcoal drawing, from wood to clay. She simultaneously reduced her iconography, concentrating on the symbolic vocabulary, first of all on paper and then emulating this on glass as well. Where once the narrative emerged as the dominant element of the image, heads and bodies now fill the image-space: layered glasses with a distinctive physiognomy and corporeality. In place of description, sentimental value – expression – enters more and more. In order to intensify this, Wolff searches for the appropriate form: glass windows whose leading no longer follows the standard rectangle; glass sculptures formed at the pipe; tentacles that came into being through collaboration with Dirk Bimberg.

The year 1990 marked a further turning point in Wolff's life and work. Having returned to Germany, she first of all withdrew to a Cologne studio and occupied herself with the study of art history; the works of Jan van Eyck, Vincent van Gogh and Paul Cézanne all stimulated her. The results – large format, gestural, layered charcoal and pastel drawings, often in pure black; painted and also collaged sheets of glass revolving around their central theme of inner and outer identity, the twin-like double figure, the polarity of being – were exhibited in Annecy. At the same time she publicly declared in the journal *New Glass* (February 1990) her break-out from the "dead-end street" of an exclusive restriction to one material, the "imprisoning by glass" and the "self-isolation" of glass art, and proclaimed her "disobedience to material" to be a "material waywardness as the start of a change to the immediate". Her recent development has led her towards sculptural works with glass. In Czech glassworks she produces double-sided sculptures of heads using the traditional ovencasting technique.

VERENA TAFEL

Worringer, Marta

German graphic artist and painter, 1881–1965

Born Marta Schmitz in Cologne, 16 January 1881. Educated at boarding school in Belgium, 1897–8. Received private art tuition from Wilhelm Spatz, a professor at the Düsseldorf Academy, 1899. Continued studies in Munich. Married art historian Wilhelm Worringer, 1907; three daughters (eldest died of jaundice in 1934); husband died 1965. Lived in Bern, Switzerland, 1910–14, then settled in Bonn. Member of Das Junge Rheinland group and second Cologne Secession, but rarely exhibited after 1919. Moved to Königsberg (now Kaliningrad, Russian Federation) where her husband had been offered a professorship, 1928; studied at the Königsberg Academy under Professor Burmann. Fled to Berlin with her family, leaving her work behind, 1944; fled from Halle in the Russian sector to Munich, 1950; lived in difficult economic circumstances. Died in Munich, 27 October 1965.

Principal Exhibitions

Salon d'Automne, Paris: 1911
Galerie Flechtheim, Düsseldorf: 1919 (*Frauen*)
Grosse Kunstausstellung, Düsseldorf: 1920
Kaufhaus Tietz, Düsseldorf: 1922 (*Internationale Kunstausstellung*)
Graphikausstellung, Hagen: 1922
Kölnischer Kunstverein, Cologne: 1924 (*Kölner Künstler*)
Städtisches Museum, Villa Obernier, Bonn: 1925
Cologne Secession: 1926

Bibliography

Otto Grauthoff, "Der Pariser Herbstsalon", *Der Cicerone*, iii, 1911, pp.834–6
Rudolf Uebe, "Inhalt und Ausdruck: Bemerkungen zum Thema Fantastik und Groteske im Graphischen", *Hellweg*, no.45, 1922, pp.870–74
"Marta Worringer", *Bonner Zeitung*, 8 August 1928
"Marta Worringer", *Deutsche Reichszeitung*, 8 August 1928
Anke Münster, "Künstlerinnen in Köln und Düsseldorf von 1918 bis 1933", typescript, Giessen, 1991
Ernst Moritz Engert, *Bonner Köpfe und Theater*, Schriftenreihe des August Macke Haus, no.6 Bonn, 1992
Der Gereonsclub, 1911–1913, Schriftenreihe Verein August Macke Haus, no.9, Bonn, 1993
Rheinische Expressionistinnen, Schriftenreihe Verein August Macke Haus, no.10, Bonn, 1993

From the few works of hers that are still extant – due to losses in World War II, only ten works from the period up to 1933 have as yet been authenticated – it is clear that Marta Worringer was one of the independent artistic personalities of the first half of the 20th century. A few pictures in art journals, various book illustrations and photographs of her work confirm the individual stamp of her representation of figures and places in the second phase of Expressionist art in Germany.

Worringer kept her art in the background of her life because of her family situation. She had three daughters and ran a traditional household, and out of respect for her husband's work hesitated to let her work appear in public. She was married to the art historian Wilhelm Worringer, who found particular approval within the circles of modern artists. She is known to have participated in exhibitions on only eight occasions, including the Paris Salon d'Automne in 1911 and the *Internationale Kunstausstellung* of 1922 in Düsseldorf.

Worringer was in close contact with the artists who after 1911 in Cologne set themselves up as the Gereonsclub for contemporary art of all types. August Macke was among the leading lights of the Gereonsclub, whose members also included Olga Oppenheimer (q.v.), Franz M. Jansen and Marta's sister-in-law Emmy Worringer. In 1912 Macke had brought the first touring exhibition of Der Blauer Reiter to Cologne. Marta Worringer also belonged to the group of artists known as Das Junge Rheinland, which from 1919 onwards brought the modern forces of the Rhineland area together. Because Worringer did not have her own studio until 1928, she at first concentrated on printmaking and embroidered pictures. As a means of expression of equal worth to painting, this skilled craft work is a very important part of her oeuvre. The extant prints and embroideries show the extravagant figures characteristic of the artist and the pictures have an ornamental structure. One of the earliest surviving pieces of silk embroidery is *Stadtpark* (c.1920; private collection, repr.

Worringer: *Silent Ones*, 1920; Stadtmuseum, Düsseldorf

Rheinische Expressionistinnen 1993, p.158). As can also be seen in the pen drawing *Miners' Wives in Dortmund Outside a Mine on the Occasion of a Mining Disaster* (c.1925; Kunstmuseum, Bonn), Worringer's figures are long and narrow with distorted faces and ill-proportioned bodies. Contemporary critics pointed out more than once the ugliness and almost repellent aspect of these deformed people. Industrial motifs in the background emphasise the despair of the miners' wives. This also occurs in other works. In her choice of motifs, Worringer shows a particular interest in representing the fate of women. In 1925 she created a profile of the grief-stricken wife of the pawnbroker, the main character in Fyodor Dostoevsky's *The Gentle Woman*, shown in 15 pen drawings. Loneliness and sorrow are recurring themes in Worringer's work. Like countless other women artists of the first half of the 20th century, Worringer's regard for the work of Käthe Kollwitz (q.v.) is reflected in her choice of subject matter.

From around 1920 Worringer's figures and objects relate to the outer limits of the whole composition, as in the lithograph *Silent Ones* (1920; see illustration). The ornamental shapes are broken open by the complexity of the composition and the differing scales of the figures and objects. The separate elements of the picture are so closely linked to one another that a contemporary review by Rudolf Uebe referred to the objects as having "sweated together". The resulting crystalline structure of the picture, in which objects appear like facets from the outer form, is particularly clear in the lithograph *Suburb* (1920; Stadtmuseum, Düsseldorf). In the succeeding years Worringer's work concentrated more and more on individuals. As in the pen drawing *The Doctor* (1925) and in the tempera work *Mother* (1926; both Kunstmuseum, Bonn), the figures come to the front of the picture plane, directly facing the observer with their fear and sorrow.

When Worringer obtained her first studio in Königsberg, at the age of 47, she concentrated increasingly on oil painting. These are now known only from photographs, which show her paintings to have been almost exclusively portraits. One photograph shows the artist's *Self-Portrait* (1935; *ibid.*, p.140), which is clearly reminiscent of the approach of Käthe Kollwitz. Because Worringer's work appeared in public only rarely, the seizing of power and the cultural policies of the National Socialists did not represent any direct threat to her. From 1933 onwards, she carried on working in secret. A few prints, now in private ownership, document her rejection of despotism. Towards the end of the 1930s they show lonely, persecuted people, also frequently women surrounded by the sick and dying. In these pictures Worringer stayed stylistically and thematically true to herself.

When she fled from Königsberg in 1944, Worringer had to leave almost all her work behind – three decades of it. Other works were abandoned when she fled the Russian-occupied zone six years later; thus most of her life's work was lost. Yet the artist carried on working in Munich when she was over 70 years old. As at the beginning of her career, she occupied herself mainly with printmaking and embroidery, in which mythological and religious motifs are predominant. She stopped taking part in exhibitions, however, and there are no examples of her later work in public collections.

ANKE MÜNSTER

Woutier [Wautier, Woutiers], Michaelina
Flemish painter, active 1642–59

Dates of birth and death unknown. Active in Mons, Belgium, and still unmarried in 1659.

Bibliography

Günther Heinz, "Studien über Jan van den Hoecke und die Malerei der Niederländer in Wien", *Jahrbuch der Kunsthistorischen Sammlungen in Wien*, lxiii, 1967, pp.109–64

Edith Krull, *Women in the Arts*, London: Studio Vista, 1986 (German original)

Katlijne van der Stighelen, "'Une robustesse bien extraordinaire chez une femme': De schilderijen van Michaelina Woutiers" ["Truly extraordinary strength in a woman": The paintings of Michaelina Woutiers], *Vrouw en kunst/Woman and Art*, Antwerp, 1997

Few biographical details about this artist are known, but it is certain that she came from or worked in the town of Mons, Belgium, and in 1659 was still unmarried. Between 1642 and 1659 she made at least nine paintings, which were exceptional in many respects. She did not limit herself to portraits and genre pieces but also painted an ambitious history piece as well

Woutier: *Annunciation*, 1659; Musée Promenade de Marly-le-Roi, Louveciennes

Pardo in Paris. There is also a pendant to this painting with the same theme.

Four paintings attributable to Michaelina Woutier are cited in the above-mentioned inventory of Leopold-Wilhelm (all Kunsthistorisches Museum, Vienna). The inventory date of 1659 thus provides a *terminus ante quem* for the date of their execution. There are three half-length images of male saints: two of *St Joachim* and one of *St Joseph*. They strike one as naturalistic character heads, provided with attributes but without haloes. The fourth and most impressive work is a canvas of a large bacchanalian procession in the open air, with more than a dozen half-naked protagonists. The composition is Italianate in inspiration but Flemish in its powers of observation of the figures, which are occasionally reminiscent of those of Anthony van Dyck. The *bacchante* who appears at the far right of the picture plane holding a thyrsos in her hand is almost certainly a self-portrait. The woman looks out directly at the viewer, and the portrait-like characteristics of the face are unmistakable. Self-portraits of women artists in the form of a *portrait historié* are, as far as we know, rare in the Western pictorial tradition. The integration of a self-portrait in a mythological and thus "heathen" picture may even be unique in the context of the South Netherlandish Counter-Reformation.

Woutier's last known work is an *Annunciation* (see illustration), originally from the church of St Vigor in Marly. Until 1977 the *Annunciation* was attributed to the French painter Pierre Bedeau but upon restoration (1985) the signature "Michaelina Wautier fecit 1659" was revealed.

The exceptional nature of the compositions, which show the influence of French classicism as well as Italian and Flemish work, has often in the past hindered their accurate attribution. In this sense Woutier is a victim of her own versatility. No other woman from this period succeeded in realising comparable pictorial quality in such very diverse genres. As a person she remains – apart from the presumed self-portrait in the *Bacchanale* in Vienna – elusive. Her signed work comprises the enduring proof of her exceptional artistic activity.

KATLIJNE VAN DER STIGHELEN

as a monumental religious composition. The most important source of information is provided by the inventory of the paintings of Archduke Leopold-Wilhelm, who was established in Vienna in 1659 and who had no less than four works by her hand in his collection. Nothing is known of Woutier's training, but she was probably related to Charles (or Karel) Wautier (or Woutier(s)), who was active in Antwerp around the middle of the 17th century. He painted, among others, a portrait of the Bergen abbot *Jacques Neutre*, dated 1663 (Musée des Beaux-Arts, Mons).

The earliest known work by Woutier is a print after a lost portrait of the *maître de camp général* Cantelmo. The inscription reads: "Michaelina Woutiers pinxit, Paull. Pontius fecit exc. et dedicavit, 1643". A second work, a life-sized portrait of an unidentified man, signed and dated "Michaelina Woutier 1646", is found in the Musées royaux d'Art et d'Histoire, Brussels. The physiognomic type is mercilessly realistic and the palette used for the costumes makes the work colouristically appealing.

In 1960, on the occasion of the exhibition *Bloem en tuin in de Vlaamse kunst* (Flower and garden in Flemish art) in Ghent, a descriptive flower-piece was shown; the garland, painted on panel, is signed "Michaelina Woutiers fecit 1652". The painting was then (1960) in the collection of the art dealer Benito

Wren, Denise

British potter, 1891–1979

Born Denise Kate Tuckfield in Albany, Western Australia, 7 January 1891; settled in Surrey, England, with her family, 1900. Studied design at Kingston-upon-Thames School of Art, Surrey, under Archibald Knox, 1907–12. Co-founder, Knox Guild of Design and Craft, Kingston-upon-Thames, 1912; exhibited with the Guild from 1914. Married Henry Wren, 1915; daughter Rosemary, also a potter, born 1922; husband died 1947. Built house (Potters Croft) and workshop at Oxshott, Surrey, and attended pottery evening classes at Camberwell School of Arts and Crafts, London, under Henry Hopkins, c.1920. Taught two-week summer schools at Oxshott, 1922–c.1950; evening classes at Teddington School of Art, 1924–6; also in other schools and training colleges. With Henry Wren, ran annual Artist-Craftsman exhibitions at

Central Hall, Westminster, 1923–38. Ceased potting temporarily during World War II. Daughter Rosemary joined pottery full-time, 1950. Moved Oxshott Pottery to Easterbrook Farm, Hittisleigh, near Exeter, Devon, 1978. Died in Exminster, Devon, May 1979.

Selected Individual Exhibitions
Craftsmen Potters Association, London: 1960, 1964
Berkeley Galleries, London: 1960 (with Rosemary Wren)
Crafts Study Centre, Holburne Museum, Bath: 1984 (*The Oxshott Pottery*, retrospective)

Selected Writings
Handcraft Pottery for Workshop and School, London: Pitman, 1928 (with Henry Wren)
Raffia: Methods and Suggestions for Work, London: Pitman, 1929 (with Louisa Begg); 2nd edition, 1952
"Playful basketry", *Simple Basketry for Homes and Schools*, ed. Mabel Roffey, London: Pitman, 1930
Pottery: The Finger-Built Methods, London: Pitman, 1932 (with Henry Wren)
Pottery Making: Making Pots, and Building and Firing Small Kilns, London: Pitman, 1952 (with Rosemary Wren)

Bibliography
Michael Casson, *Pottery in Britain Today*, London: Tiranti, and New York: Transatlantic Arts, 1967
Muriel Rose, *Artist Potters in England*, 2nd edition, London: Faber, 1970
Rosemary Wren, "Denise K. Wren: Sixty-one years a potter", *Ceramic Review*, no.15, 1972, pp.12–13
Ceramic Review, no.59, 1979, p.38 (obituary)
British 20th-Century Studio Ceramics, exh. cat., Christopher Wood Gallery, London, 1980
Margot Coatts, "Denise and Henry Wren: Pioneer potters", *Ceramic Review*, no.87, 1984, pp.22–4
The Oxshott Pottery, exh. cat., Crafts Study Centre, Bath, 1984 (contains extended chronology and bibliography)
Oliver Watson, *Studio Pottery: Twentieth-Century British Ceramics in the Victoria and Albert Museum Collection*, London: Phaidon, 1993 (originally published as *British Studio Pottery*, Oxford: Phaidon, 1990)

Denise Wren came to prominence in the crafts in the 1960s when, at over 70, her pots in salt-glazed stoneware received acclaim and popularity. These pots show her lifelong adaptable approach to constructing forms in clay, and especially her interest in firing. She was also a recognised expert in designing and building small kilns for use by studio potters.

Born in Western Australia into a family of pioneers (her father was an inventor), Denise Wren moved to England as a child. She received a formative art education at Kingston School of Art, where her most revered teacher was Archibald Knox, the noted designer of Liberty metalwork in the Celtic Revival style, which is often associated with Art Nouveau. From Knox, Wren learned to hand-build pots using coils of clay, which she had to fire at a local brickworks because there was no proper pottery course taught at Kingston (or at any British art school) at the time. Only one unglazed pot from this Kingston period remains (Holburne Museum, Bath).

Wren dismissed herself from art school in 1912, following Knox's sudden and contentious resignation; she founded immediately, in his honour, a group studio for women called the Knox Guild of Design and Craft. Here she worked as potter, artist in illumination and private teacher. The Guild gave up its premises in Kingston-upon-Thames during wartime in 1915, but members continued to exhibit under its name until 1935, moving after 1920 from Kingston-upon-Thames Art Gallery to the Whitechapel Art Gallery, London. Coincidentally, 1915 was the year Denise married Henry Wren.

In 1920 the Wrens designed and built a house with workshops called Potters Croft at Oxshott in Surrey. Here they founded the Oxshott Pottery and, for two decades, Wren made and sold individual "pots for flowers". They were made in earthenware and coloured with plain slips and glazes; Wren preferred this varied activity to the more common production of tableware. She also taught pottery in schools and colleges around the country and organised summer courses at her own workshop. Many student-teachers and artist-potters from Britain and abroad went to learn about hand-building and throwing, and about firing kilns especially. Wren prepared and circulated constructional drawings and instructions for several types of kiln and a kick wheel; these could be supplied by post and many went abroad to educational institutions and missions.

During the 1920s Wren contributed articles on practical education in the crafts to newspapers and periodicals; she published *Handcraft Pottery* with Henry Wren in 1928, and in 1932 *Pottery: The Finger-Built Methods*, designing her own book jackets. Late in the 1930s, however, her attention was diverted from pottery to printed textiles and she began to sell painted designs to British firms including Liberty and Tootal. For the war effort, when shortages of materials prevented craft workers from carrying on, she ran a local garden and smallholding scheme at Oxshott, and also bred bees and goats. After World War II she resumed work as a potter and teacher and in 1952 her daughter Rosemary Wren, a graduate of the Royal College of Art, moved into her own workshop at Potters Croft.

The approach to hand-building that Denise Wren had developed by this time was in advance of many other studio potters. She had turned a classroom exercise into an expressive medium that, in her hands, gradually became more and more tactile. Wren allowed the indentations of her fingers in the clay to remain in an undisguised state and, in addition, used various seals and gouges to mark the surface. Her "paper-bag" and "cactus" pots and planters dating from this period are typical.

When, by the end of the 1950s, there was a reliable salt-glaze kiln in use at Oxshott, developed by Rosemary, Denise Wren was beginning to produce modelled elephants, about 25 centimetres long. She had an enormous love and respect for these magnificent creatures and spent her last potting decade, 1965–75, making them almost exclusively. The character of the elephants was intensified by materials of monochrome colours; the animals were made either in salt-glazed or unglazed stoneware, the latter fired in sawdust to produce black shadows and hollows that heightened the expression of the sculptural marks.

Outside the workshop Denise Wren exhibited regularly, at first with the Knox Guild, then from 1923 she took a leading part in the Artist-Craftsman exhibitions, held in the Horticultural Halls, London, and arranged by Henry Wren. These large gatherings were the originators of the modern craft fair, where makers stood alongside and sold from their stands.

She also exhibited at British Empire Exhibitions, in 1923 in a caravan under her own name, and in 1924 in a hut with future members of the Artist-Craftsman exhibitions (information courtesy of Rosemary Wren, 19 December 1995). With the advent of the Craftsmen Potters Association in the late 1950s, Denise Wren's salt-glazed stoneware was included in several exhibitions, together with her craggy modelled elephants. In 1984 she was the subject of a retrospective exhibition in Bath. Her works may be seen at the Holburne Museum and Crafts Study Centre, Bath; Kingston-upon-Thames Museum and Heritage Centre; and the Victoria and Albert Museum, London.

MARGOT COATTS

Y

Yakunchikova(-Weber), Marya
Russian painter and graphic artist, 1870–1902

Born in Wiesbaden, Germany, 19 January 1870. Grew up in Moscow. Studied privately under N.A. Martynov from 1883; attended the Moscow School of Painting, Sculpture and Architecture as an unregistered student, 1885; took evening classes with Elena Polenova (q.v.), 1886–9. Began to form a collection of folk art, 1887–9. Travelled to Austria and Italy, 1888; France and Germany, 1889; studied at Académie Julian, Paris, 1889–90; subsequently spent long spells in Paris. Organised an exhibition of applied art by women artists in Paris, 1894. Married physician L.N. Weber, 1896; two sons. Directed the Abramtsevo embroidery workshops after Polenova's death in 1898, and continued her work on the section of Russian applied arts for the Exposition Universelle, Paris, 1900. Died of tuberculosis in Chêne Bougerie, Switzerland, 14 December 1902.

Principal Exhibitions
Mir Iskusstva (World of Art): 1899–1902
Moscow: 1905 (retrospective)

Bibliography
N. Polenova, *Marya Vasilevna Yakunchikova*, Moscow, 1905
E. Sakharova, *V.D. Polenov, E.D. Polenova: Khronika semi khudozhnikov* [V.D. Polenov, E.D. Polenova: A chronicle of a family of artists], Moscow, 1964
Wendy Salmond, "The Solomenko embroidery workshops", *Journal of Decorative and Propaganda Arts*, Summer 1987, pp.126–43
M.N. Yablonskaya, *Women Artists of Russia's New Age, 1900–1935*, New York: Rizzoli, and London: Thames and Hudson, 1990

In the late 1890s Marya Yakunchikova rose to prominence in Russian art as a leading symbolist painter, graphic artist and designer. She then revealed her ability to blend universalism with nationalism, and idealism with intimism, in a variety of soulscapes, be they oil, colour engraved, poker-work or appliqué linen panels. This syncretist trend, in which Yakunchikova appeared as the second Russian woman artist after Elena Polenova (q.v.), her mentor and close friend, was supported by the milieu in which she grew up – the circles of artists who gathered on the Mamontovs' estate at Abramtsevo and at the Polenov family home in Moscow. There, such artists

as the landscapists Isaak Levitan and Konstantin Korovin encouraged a poetic, mystical response to organic nature and a particular reverence for the Russian countryside that Yakunchikova was to forge into a powerful, personal visual expression in her mature period.

Unable to complete her studies at the Moscow School of Painting, Sculpture and Architecture due to tuberculosis, Yakunchikova moved to Paris in 1889 and enrolled at the Académie Julian, thereby following in the footsteps of her consumptive compatriot Marie Bashkirtseff (q.v.). Like her predecessor she was to begin in Paris to express a melancholic vision of the world in which the pathos of fragile, ephemeral life was pungently, though distinctively, revealed. This characterises her painting *Reflections of an Intimate World* (1894; I.S. Weber Collection, Chêne Bougerie, Switzerland), with its symbolic juxtaposition of the physical and spiritual through the depiction of a room in evening light and the reflection of a contemplative young woman in the window.

In her search for an appropriate creative language that would at once be personal and universal, Yakunchikova turned away from narrative description to generalised forms iterated in a bold range of colours. These she abstracted from her local environment or from her childhood memories – her country home, garden, forest or the Bois de Boulogne with its serpentine banks and swans. Often she would convey the conjunction of architecture and landscape, as in *From the Window of an Old House* (1897; see illustration), which depicted the long, uninterrupted vista from the family mansion at Vvedenskoye near Zvenigorod, with the Corinthian-style columns of the porch. The loosely defined natural forms, the cracked plaster and vegetal capitals suggest the transience of all things, man-made or organic, evoking a nostalgic delicacy that was to characterise the contemporary work of the disabled Borisov-Musatov.

Passing, decay and human frailty were to be consistent characteristics of Yakunchikova's work, whether an image of a candle flame caught in the breeze, a cross above a well on the Yakunchikov estate at Nara outside Moscow, or a little girl lost in a forest. The last was the subject of a large linen appliqué panel, the *Lost Child* (c.1899; I.S. Weber Collection), shown at the Paris Exposition Universelle in 1900. A small barefoot girl is depicted amid the stylised cut-outs of the green and brown forest vegetation, having been lured off her path by the malicious wood goblin (*leshiy*) of Russian folklore. The girl

Yakunchikova: *From the Window of an Old House*, 1897; Tretyakov Gallery, Moscow

appears to be a young representation of Yakunchikova, in keeping with the suggestions of self-portrait that were evoked in *Reflections of an Intimate World* as well as in the etching *The Unattainable* (late 1890s; repr. in *Vesy*, 1, 1905), with its finely linear image of a young woman with arms stretched vainly aloft while a group of swallows circles around her. A similarly introspective self-portrayal is evident in *Terror* (*c*.1894; Polenov Museum, Tarusa), which, under the influence of her teacher Eugène Delâtre, she also made as an engraving in green, violet and blue. Here, however, there is greater angst as the girl rushes headlong from the starlit, shadowy woods, her hand clasped to her cheek in apparent paraphrase of Edvard Munch's *The Scream* (1893).

Yakunchikova's febrile concern with recording impressions and inner experience before they slipped away for ever, which was probably encouraged by her marriage to a neuropathologist (Lev Weber) as well as her illness, could be expressed in dichotomic images that spoke of far-away reverie or close-up studies of details of life. The latter could be caught with Japonist intimacy, particularly in her poker-work, which included subjects such as the oar of a rowing boat surrounded by water-lilies, and a vase of flowers on a window-sill juxtaposed with part of a fir tree, as in *The Window* (1896; Tretyakov Gallery). Although a sense of elegy is still to be sensed in these intimist works, it is inner vitality rather than decay that frequently dominates, something that is also to be felt in her emblematic cover for the *Mir iskusstva* (World of Art) magazine (1899, nos 13–24). In this symbolist conglomeration, Yakunchikova asymmetrically fused stylised juniper berries, ancient Cyrillic orthography, a white swan with spreading wings facing the evening star, and fir trees whose tops are formed of a variety of Christian crosses.

The combination of the ancient and the modern, like the individual and the national, was continually confronted by Yakunchikova, whether in her promotion of folk art, her reinterpretation of traditional Russian *naboyka* prints with their primitive designs of forest fruits, foliage and birds, or in her contribution of furniture, textiles and toys to the Russian crafts

section at the Paris exhibition of 1900. In addition, she was also active in the promotion of women's art, as seen in her organisation of a women's exhibition in Paris in 1894, her liberal approach being conditioned by her association with such progressive groups as the Abramtsevo colony, the World of Art and the 36 Artists group.

JEREMY HOWARD

Yermolayeva, Vera (Mikhaylovna)
Russian painter and graphic artist, 1893–1938

Born in Petrovsk, Saratov province, 1893. Graduated from secondary school in St Petersburg, *c*.1912. Studied in the studio of Mikhail Bernshtein, where she met members of Mikhail Larionov's group. Associated with Soyuz molodyozhi (Union of Youth) and made contact with Kazimir Malevich and Mikhail Matyushin. Visited France, Switzerland and Britain. Graduated from the Archaeological Institute, Petrograd, 1917. Member of IZO Narkompros (Fine Arts Section, Commissariat of the Enlightenment), Petrograd, 1918. Active in the resurgence of artistic life in Petrograd; worked at the City Museum, 1918–19; took up the preservation of painted shop signs, publishing an influential article in *Iskusstvo kommuny*; also organised a publishing house, *Segodnya* (Today), which brought out books illustrated with hand-coloured linocuts. Rector of Vitebsk School of Applied Art, 1919–22; invited Malevich to teach. Founder member of Unovis (Affirmers of the New Art) group. Returned to Petrograd, 1923; became head of the colour laboratory at Ginkhuk (State Institute of Artistic Culture) until 1926. Worked on children's magazines and books published by the State Publishing House, Detgiz, 1920s. Imprisoned with four colleagues in December 1934 during the Stalinist purges following the assassination of Kirov. Became seriously ill, 1936; died in Karaganda, Khazakhstan, 1938.

Principal Exhibitions

Unovis (Affirmers of the New Art), Vitebsk and Moscow: 1920–21
Van Diemen Gallery, Berlin: 1922–3 (*Erste russische Kunstausstellung*, touring)
Leningrad: 1925 (*Five Years of Leningrad Painters*), 1932 (*Artists of the RSFSR over 15 Years, 1917–32*)

Selected Writings

"Peterburgskiye vyveski" [St Petersburg signs], *Iskusstvo kommuny*, 26 January 1919

Bibliography

E.F. Kovtun, "Khudzhnik detskoy knigi Vera Yermolayeva" [The children's book illustrator Vera Yermolayeva], *Detskaya literatura* [Literature for children], no.2, Moscow, 1971
B.D. Souris, "Stranitsa khudozhestvenoy zhizni v Rossiy v 1917" [A page of Russian artistic life in 1917], *Iskusstvo*, 1972, no.4, pp.62–7
E.F. Kovtun, "Khudozhnitsa knigi Vera Mikhaylovna Yermolayeva" [The book illustrator Vera Yermolayeva], *Iskusstvo knigi*, ed. D. Shmarinov and others, no.8, Moscow, 1975, pp.68–81
John E. Bowlt, "Malevich and his students", *Soviet Union*, v/2, 1978, pp.256–86

Künstlerinnen der russischen Avantgarde/Women Artists of the Russian Avant-Garde, 1910–1930, exh. cat., Galerie Gmurzynska, Cologne, 1979

Paris-Moscou, 1900–1930, exh. cat., Centre Georges Pompidou, Paris, 1979

The Avant-Garde in Russia, 1910–1930: New Perspectives, exh. cat., Los Angeles County Museum of Art, and elsewhere, 1980

Andrei Nakov, *Abstrait/Concret: Art non-objectif russe et polonais*, Paris: Transédition, 1981

Russian Stage Design: Scenic Innovation, 1900–1930, from the Collection of Mr and Mrs Nikita D. Lobanov-Rostovsky, exh. cat., Mississippi Museum of Art, Jackson, 1982

M. German and others, *Zhivopis Gosudarstveniy Russkiy Muzey, 1920–1930* [Paintings from the State Russian Museum, 1920–1930], Moscow: Sovetskiy Khudozhnik, 1989

Yevgeny Kovtun and Alla Povelikhina, *Russian Painted Shop Signs and Avant-Garde Artists*, Leningrad: Aurora, 1991

Yelena Yasen, "The development of children's book illustration in post-revolutionary Russia", *Design Issues*, viii, 1991, pp.57–66

Soviet Socialist Realist Painting, 1930s–1960s, exh. cat., Museum of Modern Art, Oxford, 1992

Vera Yermolayeva is often seen in terms of her participation in and assimilation of the various artistic cultures of the Revolutionary period in Russia. She does more than merely reflect the stylistic obsessions of her contemporaries, however. The range of her interests and skills was to make her contribution to Russian art unique and influential, if only in relation to her role in preserving the painted street signs of St Petersburg and her use of such folk idioms in her illustrations to children's books.

In the popular print *The Cockerel* (1918; see illustration), for example, her approach is distinct from that of her contemporary, Mikhail Larionov. A comparison with his *Cockerel* (1912; Tretyakov Gallery, Moscow, repr. Paris 1979, p.121) demonstrates her distance from his "Rayist" or "Rayonist" experiments (*luchizm*). Although both are indebted to "primitivist" forms, Yermolayeva has based her design more obviously on the painted shop sign and the *lubok* (traditional print). A clear link can be made, for example, with the *Tale of the Cock and the Fox* (1852; copper engraving; State Russian Museum, St Petersburg), where a central iconic image dominates the scene, while side partitions explore the narrative. There is a deliberate irregularity to the partitions, emphasising the hand-made character of the print. Where Larionov's image has almost disappeared in sophisticated Futurist abstractions of colour and line, Yermolayeva's object remains intact, and vital to the message and function of the print. Yermolayeva's early linocut covers for children's books reveal an individual approach to the functions of the genre. The easily readable, childlike imagery and lay-out are eminently suited to the *Segodnya* children's book project, as in the cover for Vengrov's book *Mishata* (Little mice) of 1918 (repr. Kovtun and Povelikhina 1991, illustration 243).

Yermolayeva's article on St Petersburg signs for *Iskusstvo kommuny* (1919), so influential on the preservation of these contemporary popular art forms, is a significant indicator of her own beliefs and working methods. She stresses simplicity and directness, with individuality subordinated to the demands of the text and the medium. Her cover illustration for an edition of Walt Whitman's "Pioneers! O Pioneers!" (1918; hand-coloured linocut; State Russian Museum, *ibid.*, illustration 244) shows her ability to translate the dynamic rhythms

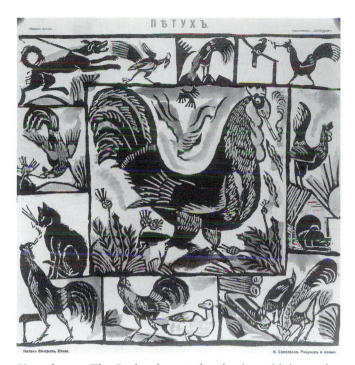

Yermolayeva: *The Cockerel*, 1918; hand-coloured lithograph; State Russian Museum, St Petersburg

of Whitman's free verse into dramatic line and colour. In comparison, her illustrations to Mayakovsky's *Misteriya-buff* (Mystery-Bouffe) of the same year adopt a more abstract and appropriately Futurist dynamic (repr. Kovtun 1975, p.69).

When in 1919 Yermolayeva went to Vitebsk, she initiated a period of intense and productive activity. Her invitation to Kazimir Malevich meant that Suprematism would inevitably become the dominant artistic mode, and her contributions show that she had clearly understood its formal language and essential ideas. Her well-known designs for Matyushin's opera *Victory over the Sun* of February 1920 are still in line with Malevich's original sets and costumes of 1913 (see, for example, *Stage Design for Action II*, first reproduced in the almanac *Unovis* (Vitebsk), no.1, 1920; woodcut with water-colour additions, Museum of Modern Art, New York, repr. Los Angeles 1980, illustration 47; untraced woodcut, repr. Jackson 1982, illustration 77). On the same day as the re-staging of *Victory over the Sun*, a Suprematist ballet was performed, to which Yermolayeva contributed another abstracted stage design, also printed in *Unovis*, no.1 (private collection, Russia, repr. Nakov 1981, p.61). Her schematic diagrams and designs are entirely suited to the Futurist/Suprematist idiom of both opera and ballet. It is significant that her linocuts for sets and costumes were shown at the *Erste russische Kunstausstellung* exhibition in Berlin as prototypes of the new artistic language. Her participation in the drawing up of the Unovis group's programme with six other key members (including Malevich, El Lissitzky and Nina Kogan) is another indication of her formative influence on its ideas.

The Vitebsk "renaissance" ended as abruptly as it had begun with the departure of Malevich, Yermolayeva and their followers for Petrograd in 1923. Yermolayeva's control of the colour laboratory at Ginkhuk (State Institute of Artistic Culture) in the years 1923–6 was to provide her with more opportunities for scientific investigations, and she continued to encourage debate on the relationship between form and colour and their practical application.

Throughout the 1920s she illustrated children's books and was very active in Detgiz (the State Children's Book Publishing House) from 1925 to 1934. She took part in editing and illustrating children's monthly magazines such as *Vorobey* (Sparrow) and *Novy Robinzon* (New Robinson) and later *Yozh* (Hedgehog). Her work, with its imaginative approach, was a strong influence both on her contemporaries and on future children's books. A radical organisation of spatial construction in relation to meaning made the books both appealing and instructive, for example, *Zaychik* (Little hare) of 1923, *Top Top Top* of 1925 and *Ivan Ivanich Samovar* of 1930 (all repr. Kovtun 1975, pp.70–73 and 75–7). The relationship with folk art is still apparent. Yermolayeva's best books combine text and image in an attractive fusion, with appropriate illustrations. With Lev Yudin she worked on a new type of children's "play-book", *Kto kovo* (Who will win?) and *Bumaga i nozhnitsy* (Paper and scissors) among others, and she illustrated Krylov's fables, always working from keenly observed, simple images, freshly attuned to each book and thus never repetitive (e.g. Krylov's *Martyshka i Ochki* [The monkey and the spectacles] of 1929). Between 1929 and 1931 many of her illustrated books went into second and third editions.

In 1928 she travelled to the Barents Sea, where her feeling for the sublimity of the elements was eventually revealed in her paintings of the 1930s. Her gouaches of 1928 already had a sensitivity to colour that some relate to early contacts with Larionov, but which overall show how the various complex artistic cultures in which she had been involved had become fused. The influence of Braque is apparent in such paintings as *The Accordionist* but, as Kovtun and Povelikhina (1991, p.159) have pointed out, the legacy of street signs is also clear. From about 1934 a series of still lifes and epic themes began to obsess her. Many are sharply distinguished from previous works in their reduction of colour, but intensity of expression remains, for example, in the illustrations to Cervantes's *Don Quixote* (1933–4; gouache, St Petersburg; repr. German 1989, pl.245). Difficult as it is to communicate deep philosophical meanings through pictorial means, she does convey expressive power through brushwork. It is possible to see the realisation of her encounter with natural forces on the trip to the Barents Sea in late works such as the illustrations to Lucretius' *De rerum natura*, for example, *Lucretius Greeting the Sun* (1934; gouache and pencil; St Petersburg, *ibid.*, pl.246). These, however, were not officially approved themes. Her decision to concentrate on the practicalities of book illustration may well have been influenced by the dominance of AKhRR (the Association of Artists of Revolutionary Russia), particularly after an article denouncing Malevich and colleagues in 1926. She wrote mournfully to Larionov in Paris: "AKhRR is taking over completely. AKhRR art is the official art" (quoted in Oxford 1992, p.10).

SARA M. DODD

Z

Zámečniková, Dana
Czech painter and glass artist, 1945–

Born in Prague, 24 March 1945. Studied at the Technical University, Prague, 1962–8; Academy of Applied Arts, Prague, 1969–72. Freelance artist in Prague from 1972; also an interior designer. Married glass artist Marian Karel, 1978; daughter born 1982. Recipient of special prize, Graphisch-plastische Darstellung, Kassel, 1981; International Juried Art Competition, New York, 1985; gold medal, Kristallnacht competition, American Interfaith Institute, Philadelphia, 1991; grand prize, Kanazawa '92, Japan, 1992. Member, Prague Glass Association, from 1990; Glass Art Society, Corning, New York, from 1991. Lives in Prague.

Selected Individual Exhibitions
Galerie Theatre v Nerudovce, Prague: 1980
Galerie Karolina, Prague: 1981
Heller Gallery, New York: 1984, 1986, 1987, 1989, 1991 (with Marian Karel)
Galerie Edith Gottschalk, Frankfurt am Main: 1985
Galerie L, Hamburg: 1986
Galerie Semafor, Prague: 1987
Galerie Nakama, Tokyo: 1988 (with Marian Karel and Vladimír Kopecký), 1992 (with Marian Karel)
Galerie Clara Scremini, Paris: 1988 (with Marian Karel), 1990
Galerie Gottschalk-Betz, Frankfurt am Main: 1990 (with Stanislav Libenský and Jaroslavá Brychtová)
San Francisco State University: 1992
Galerie Nova Siň, Prague: 1994

Bibliography
Glaskunst '81: Internationale Ausstellung zur Studioglasbewegung der Gegenwart, exh. cat., Orangerie, Kassel, 1981
Kristían Suda, "Raum des Spiels, Spiel des Raums: Glasobjekte von Dana Zámečniková", Glasrevue, no.5, 1982, pp.24–8
— , "Spiel im Raum, Raum im Spiel", Neues Glas, no.4, 1984, pp.187–91
Zweiter Coburger Glaspreis für moderne Glasgestaltung in Europa, 1985, exh. cat., Kunstsammlungen der Veste, Coburg, 1985
Susanne Frantz, Contemporary Glass: A World Survey from the Corning Museum of Glass, New York: Abrams, 1989
Ferdinand Hampson, Joanne B. Murphy and John Lawson, Glass: State of the Art, ii, Huntington Woods, MI: Johnston [1989]
Dan Klein, Glass: A Contemporary Art, New York: Rizzoli, and London: Collins, 1989
Verres de Bohème, 1400–1989: Chefs d'oeuvre des musées de Tchéchoslovaquie, exh. cat., Musée des Arts Décoratifs, Paris, 1989
Dana Zámečniková: Oeuvres, exh. cat., Galerie Clara Scremini, Paris, 1990
Neues Glas in Europa: 50 Künstler, 50 Konzepte, exh. cat., Kunstmuseum, Düsseldorf, 1990
Prague Glass Prize '91/Sklářská cena Praha '91, exh. cat., Mánes, Prague, 1991
Le Verre: Exposition internationale de verre contemporain, exh. cat., Espace Duchamp-Villon, Centre Saint-Sever, Rouen, 1991
Catherine Vaudour, L'Art du verre contemporain, Paris, 1993
Susanne Frantz, Seven Glass Sculptures, Corning, NY, 1994
Dana Zámečniková, exh. cat., Galerie Nova Siň, Prague, 1994
World Glass Now, '94, exh. cat., Hokkaido Museum of Modern Art, Sapporo, and elsewhere, 1994
Prostor světlo sklo [Space light plan], exh. cat., Míčovna Pražského Hradu, Prague, 1995

Dana Zámečnikova is one of the most internationally renowned glass artists now at work. She occupies a special position in contemporary Czech glass art – she was the first of the post-war generation of glass artists to come from another academic discipline, and she works with glass in a very unconventional way. Normally, the course of studies in glass design that was developed after World War I in Czechoslovakia was based on an inherited tradition of glass craftsmanship that was perfected technically and artistically at a technical college for glass. After graduation, the most talented students went on to study for a diploma at the Academy of Applied Arts in Prague, which in addition to providing a training in the fine arts – painting, drawing and sculpture – also taught industrial design. Building on the basis of this consistent, specialised training, the glass art scene in Czechoslovakia – which sets the tone internationally – was able to develop. In contrast to this, Zámečnikova's artistic personality was formed by academic training only. Her work is included in the collections of the Corning Museum of Glass, New York; Musée des Art Décoratifs, Lausanne; Victoria and Albert Museum, London; Musée des Arts Décoratifs, Paris; Museum of Applied Arts, Prague; and the Hokkaido Museum of Modern Art, Sapporo, Japan.

Zámečnikova's artistic work aimed to combine classical drawing and painting with the medium of glass; glass was at first the three-dimensional vehicle for the image and then, in her work after 1986, a sculptural element in its own right.

Zámečniková: *Behind the Looking-Glass*, 1994; artist's collection, Prague

Starting from the principles of set design, in 1980 the artist began creating glass paintings in the form of display cases, whose unmistakable artistic language presents the figure in surrealist alienation and both painting and drawing in three-dimensional layers. The glass paintings consist of several sheets of glass behind one another; they have a matt finish and are painted cold with oil, pastel and house paints or are engraved with a flexible drive (an electric motor combined with a flexible cable, with a handpiece housing the bearings, chuck, burrs and wheels for engraving). The perspective in the drawing, which suggests three-dimensionality, is intensified through the layering of the sheets of glass, creating an illusionistic extension of the depicted space. The surface is roughened by hand to a matt finish – for greater durability – using etching or emery paper, and the marks of this process correspond to the gestural quality of the painting.

Reality and imagination overlap on many levels in Zámečniková's work. Depictions of theatrical scenes or scenes from everyday life, dreams and memories are interwoven with each other in ever new, mostly surrealistic contexts. Personal experience is pondered on, reappraised and recreated in a more or less encoded manner and ultimately a universally valid form. The complex messages of the paintings touch mental and spiritual planes whose presence is perceptible but not always interpretable. Thus the first glass paintings, which appear superficially vivacious, funny or ironic, confront emptiness, loneliness and depression at the same time; the borders between laughter and screaming, composure and torment are porous in the artist's depiction of spiritual wounds. Woman, her point of view and her feelings – without any feminist claims being made – shape Zámečniková's whole body of work. In this context, the accompanying motif of the man, particularly in works after 1988, is the trigger mechanism of emotions or conflicts that call assumptions into question or arouse fundamental fears.

Since 1986 Zámečniková has been working on large-scale groups of sculptures that are composed of sheet-glass elements combined with other materials. They contain almost life-size figures cut from sheets of glass, which the artist leaves with sharp, ridged edges, giving an aggressive impression. The artist has also painted on paper since 1988 (when she contributed to the glass symposium in Nový Bor), and the paper is enclosed between sheets of glass. Ominous themes such as falling, decay and loss come to the fore, painted in an expressive, restless characteristic style, which is accentuated with aggressive red and yellow tones. The male and female motifs are once again accompanied by animal motifs, such as hares, domestic and big cats, dogs and fish. With the exception of the dog motif, they

Sassenberg, Marina PhD Student, University of Potsdam, Germany. Author of *Jüdische Frauen im 19. und 20. Jahrhundert* (with Jutta Dick, 1993). **Essays:** Berend-Corinth; Rée.

Saunders, Gill Curator of Documentation, Collection of Prints, Drawings and Paintings, Victoria and Albert Museum, London. Author of *The Nude: A New Perspective* (1989), *Recording Britain: A Pictorial Domesday of Pre-War Britain* (with David Mellor and Patrick Wright, 1990) and *Picturing Plants: An Analytical History of Botanical Illustration* (1995). **Essays:** Moser; Riley.

Scales, Alette Rye Freelance lecturer and linguist. **Essay:** Ancher.

Schlenker, Ines PhD candidate, Courtauld Institute of Art, University of London. **Essays:** Caspar-Filser; Meidner; Sintenis.

Schmitt, Eva Freelance writer. Contributor to *Glas-Kunst-Handwerk, 1970–1945* (catalogue, 1989), *Margret Winnecke* (1989), *Jiří Harcuba* (1990), *Rosemarie Lierke* (1991), *Glas, 1945–1991* (1991) and *Glas: Historismus-Jugendstil-Zwanziger Jahre* (1995), and to the journals *Neues Glas, Kunst und Antiquitäten* and *Glaswelt*. **Essays:** Brychtová; Zámečniková.

Schoeneck, Edith Freelance art historian. Author of *Anna Rosina Lisiewska-Matthieu-de Gasc* (dissertation, in preparation); contributor to *Arx, Burgen und Schlösser in Bayern Österreich und Südtirol* (1994). **Essays:** Lisiewska; Lisiewska-Therbusch.

Schoeser, Mary Consultant Archivist and Curator based in Britain. Author of *Marianne Straub* (1984), *Influential Europeans* (catalogue, 1992) and *International Textile Design* (1995). Contributor to *The Lancashire Cotton Industry* (1996) and *Founders of Modern Craft* (1997).

Schram, Hrafnhildur Director, National Einar Jonsson Gallery, Reykjavík, Iceland. Author of *Ásgrimur Jonsson: The Painter* (1986) and contributor to the *Yearbook of the National Gallery of Iceland* and *Iceland Review*. **Essays:** Sveinsdóttir; Tryggvadóttir.

Schulte, Birgit Curator at the Karl Ernst Osthaus-Museum, Hagen, Germany. Author of catalogues on *Christian Rohlfs* (1989), *Eberhard Viegener* (1990), *Ruth Biller* (1990), *Henry van de Velde* (1992), *Emil Rudolf Weiss* (1992), *Druckgrafik des Expressionismus* (1993), *Bruno Taut* (1994), *Egon Wilden* (1994), *Milly Steger* (1994) and *Herbert Bardenheuer* (1995); contributor to *Das Kunstwerk*. **Essay:** Steger.

Seidel, Miriam Philadelphia corresponding editor, *Art in America*. Contributor to *Art in America*, *New Art Examiner* and *Philadelphia Inquirer*. **Essays:** Schneemann; Winsor.

Sellars, Jane Curator, Harewood House Trust, Leeds. Author of *Women's Works: Paintings, Drawings, Prints and Sculpture by Women* (1988) and *The Art of the Brontës* (with Christine

Alexander, 1995). Contributor to the periodicals *Feminist Art News, Transactions of the Brontë Society, Museums Journal* and *Art Review*. **Essays:** De Morgan; Kemp-Welch; Osborn; Stokes; Swynnerton; Ward.

Senie, Harriet F. Director of Museum Studies and Professor of Art History, City College, City University of New York. Author of *Contemporary Public Sculpture: Tradition, Transformation and Controversy* (1992). Co-editor of *Critical Issues in Public Art* (1992); contributor to *Encyclopedia of New York City* (1995) and to *Art Journal* and *Art News*. **Essay:** Nevelson.

Sharp, Jane A. Assistant Professor of Art History, University of Maryland, College Park. Contributor to *The Great Utopia: The Russian Soviet Avant-Garde, 1915–1932* (catalogue, 1992), *Sexuality and the Body in Russian Culture* (1993) and *Nathalie Gontcharova, Michel Larionov* (catalogue, 1995). **Essay:** Dymshits-Tolstaya.

Sheriff, Mary D. Professor, University of North Carolina, Chapel Hill. Author of *Fragonard: Art and Eroticism* (1990) and *The Exceptional Woman: Elisabeth Vigée-Lebrun and the Cultural Politics of Art* (1996). Co-editor of *Eighteenth Century Studies*. **Essays:** Collot; Gérard; Lemoine; Vigée-Lebrun; Academies of Art survey (with Anna Lena Lindberg and Wendy Wassyng Roworth).

Shilliam, Nicola J. Assistant Curator, Textile and Costume Collection, Department of European Decorative Arts and Sculpture, Museum of Fine Arts, Boston. Author of *Early Modern Textiles: From Arts and Crafts to Art Deco* (with Marianne Carlano, 1993). Contributor to the periodicals *Magazine Antiques, Textile and Text* and *Journal of the Museum of Fine Arts, Boston*. **Essay:** Zorach.

Shirley, Pippa Assistant Curator, Metalwork, Silver and Jewellery Department, Victoria and Albert Museum, London. **Essays:** Courtauld; Emes.

Slatkin, Wendy Associate Professor of Art History, University of Redlands, California. Author of *Women Artists in History* (1985, 1990 and 1997) and *The Voices of Women Artists* (1993). Contributor to *Woman's Art Journal, College Art Journal, Arts Magazine* and *Gazette des Beaux-Arts*. **Essay:** Falkenstein.

Sloan, Kim Assistant Keeper, Department of Prints and Drawings, British Museum, London. Author of *Vases and Volcanoes: Sir William Hamilton and His Collection* (with Ian Jenkins, 1996). Contributor to *The Poetry of Landscape* (1987) and *Victorian Painting in the Beaverbrook Art Gallery* (1989), and to the *Burlington Magazine*. Editor, to 1992, of the *Brinsley Ford Dictionary of British and Irish Travellers on the Grand Tour*. **Essay:** Anne Forbes.

Smailes, Helen E. Assistant Keeper, British Art, National Gallery of Scotland, Edinburgh. Author of *Scottish Empire* (1981), *A Portrait Gallery for Scotland: The Foundation, Architecture and Mural Decoration of the Scottish National*

Portrait Gallery, 1882–1906 (1985), *John Zephaniah Bell, 1794–1883* (1990) and *Kenneth MacLeay, 1802–78* (1992). Contributor to the catalogues *France in the National Galleries of Scotland* (1985), *A Celebration of Mary, Queen of Scots: The Queen's Image* (1987), *Virtue and Vision: Sculpture in Scotland, 1540–1990* (1991) and *Hidden Assets: Scottish Paintings from the Flemings Collection* (1995). Contributor to *Photographic Collector*, *Burlington Magazine*, *Journal of the History of Collections* and *Book of the Old Edinburgh Club*. **Essay:** Grant.

Smart, Mary Consultant. Author of *A Flight with Fame: The Life and Art of Fredrick MacMonnies* (1996) and contributor to the *Woman's Art Journal*. **Essay:** MacMonnies.

Smith, Elizabeth A.T. Curator, Museum of Contemporary Art, Los Angeles; Adjunct Professor, School of Fine Arts, University of Southern California, Los Angeles. Editor of the catalogues *Rebecca Horn: Diving Through "Buster's Bedroom"* (1990), *Blueprints for Modern Living: History and Legacy of the Case Study Houses* (1989) and *Urban Revisions: Current Projects for the Public Realm* (1994). **Essay:** Bontecou.

Smith, Richard J. Freelance researcher. Author of a forthcoming biography and catalogue raisonné on Margaret Carpenter; contributor to the *Hatcher Review*. **Essay:** Carpenter.

Somerville, John Fine art consultant and Honorary Keeper, Burghley House, Stamford. Author of *Italian Paintings from Burghley House* (with Hugh Brigstocke, 1995). Formerly Director of Sotheby's. **Essay:** Caffi.

Spadaro, Domenica Lecturer at the Politecnico in Milan, Italy. **Essay:** Galizia (with Flavio Caroli).

Spivey, Virginia B. Graduate student, Case Western Reserve University, Cleveland. **Essay:** Antin.

Stevenson, Lesley Senior Lecturer, Thames Valley University, London. **Essays:** Dubourg; Moillon.

Stighelen, Katlijne Van der Member of the faculty, Catholic University, Leuven, Belgium. Author of *Anna Maria van Schurman (1607–1678) of "Hoe hooge dat een maeght kan in de konsten stijgen"* (1987), *De portretten van Cornelis de Vos* (1990) and many articles and catalogue essays on Flemish and Netherlandish art. Co-editor of *Pictura nova*, a series on Flemish painting and drawing. **Essays:** Heer; Visscher; Woutier; Amateur Artists survey (16th and 17th centuries).

Stober, Karin Scientific employee, University of Karlsruhe. Contributor to *Buchobjekte* (catalogue, 1980), *Von allen Seiten betrachtet: 4 Heiligenfiguren von Ignaz Günther* (catalogue, 1988), *Klar und lichtvoll wie eine Regel: Planstädte der Neuzeit* (catalogue, 1990), *Mitteilungsblatt des Ministeriums für Kultus und Wissenschaft* (1990), *"...und hat als Weib unglaubliches Talent" (Goethe): Angelika Kauffmann (1741–1807), Marie Ellenrieder (1791–1863)* (catalogue, 1992), *Palmanova–Fortezza d'Europa, 1593-1993* (catalogue, 1993), *Handbuch der deutschen Kunstdenkmäler* (1993) and

Faszination eines Klosters: 750 Jahre Kloster Lichtenthal (catalogue, 1995), and to *Studi Piemontesi*. **Essay:** Ellenrieder.

Swanson, Mary Towley Associate Professor, University of St Thomas, St Paul, Minnesota. **Essays:** Wegmann; Wiik.

Sykora, Katharina Professor of Art History, University of Bochum, Germany. Co-editor of the feminist art journal *Frauen-Kunst-Wissenschaft* (1984–94) and of *Die Neue Frau* (1993). Author of *Das Phänomen des Seriellen in der Kunst* (1983) and *Weiblichkeit-Metropole-Moderne: Ernst Ludwig Kirchners Strassenbilder* (1995). **Essay:** Bergmann-Michel.

Tafel, Verena Art historian and journalist; head of Public Relations Department, Hochschule der Künste, Berlin. Author of numerous articles on contemporary artists and historical aspects of art collecting and dealing. **Essay:** Wolff.

Tanner, Ailsa Art historian. Contributor to *Glasgow Girls: Women in Art and Design, 1880–1920* (1990 and 1993). **Essays:** Gray; MacNicol.

Tappert, Tara Leigh Independent scholar. Author of *The Emmets: A Generation of Gifted Women* (1993) and *Out of the Background: Cecilia Beaux and the Art of Portraiture* (in preparation). Contributor to *Revivals! Diverse Traditions, 1920–1945* (1994), *Craft in the Machine Age: European Influence on American Modernism, 1920–45* (1995) and to *Women's Studies: An Interdisciplinary Journal*. **Essay:** Beaux.

Taylor, Dorcas Curatorial assistant, Centre for the Study of Sculpture, Henry Moore Institute, Leeds, and graduate student researching Katharine Read and professional women artists in 18th-century Britain at the University of Manchester. Author of *Michael Kidner: Making Maps, Looking for Landmarks* (1997); contributor to the *Encyclopedia of Interior Design* (1997). **Essay:** Read.

Terra Cabo, Paula PhD candidate, Department of Art Theory and History, University of Essex, Colchester. Author of *Casa França-Brasil* (1991) and contributor to *Hélio Oiticica* (catalogue, 1992) and to *The Independent* newspaper. **Essays:** Clark; Pape; Schendel.

Thiemann, Birgit PhD candidate; assistant editor, *Allgemeines Künstlerlexikon*, Leipzig. Contributor to *Avantgarde in Aschaffenburg* (catalogue, 1993), *Spanien im Blick: Spanische Reiseberichte* (1995), *Allgemeines Künstlerlexikon* and to the journal *Frauen-Kunst-Wissenschaft*. **Essay:** Lassnig.

Thomas, Alison Lecturer, Cambridge Centre for Sixth Form Studies. Author of *Edna Clarke Hall, 1879–1979: Watercolours and Drawings* (catalogue, 1985) and *Portraits of Women: Gwen John and Her Forgotten Contemporaries* (1994); contributor to *Antiques Collector*. **Essay:** Clarke Hall.

Thompson, Margo Hobbs PhD candidate, Art History Department, Northwestern University, Evanston, Illinois. **Essays:** Benglis; Miss; Rainer.

Thornberry, Joanna Exhibitions Assistant, Anthony D'Offay Gallery, London. **Essay:** Saint Phalle.

Thue, Anniken Director, Oslo Museum of Applied Art. Author of *Frida Hansen: En europeer i norsk tekstilkunst omkring 1900* (1986) and numerous articles on Norwegian historicism and contemporary Norwegian arts and crafts. **Essay:** Hansen.

Vaizey, Marina. Editor of Publications, National Art Collections Fund. Author of *100 Masterpieces of Painting* (1980), *The Artist as Photographer* (1982), *Peter Blake* (1985), *Christo* (1990) and *Christiane Kubrick* (1990). Contributor to *Connoisseur*, *Art International*, *Antique Collector*, *New Statesman*, *Times Literary Supplement*, *Times Educational Supplement*, *Tatler*, *Vogue*, *The Sunday Times* and other periodicals. **Essays:** Cameron; Ana Maria Pacheco; Mary Potter; Sher-Gil.

Wacks, Debra PhD candidate in Art History, Graduate Center, City University of New York. **Essay:** Chryssa.

Walker, Neil Keeper of Fine Art, Nottingham Castle Museum and Art Gallery. Contributor to *Richard Parkes Bonington, Paul Sanby: Wegbereiter der Aquarellmalerei* (catalogue, 1989) and *The Staithes Group* (catalogue, 1993). **Essay:** Knight.

Waller, Susan PhD candidate in art history, Northwestern University, Evanston, Illinois. Author of *Women Artists in the Modern Era* (1991); contributor to *Women Artists News* and *Woman's Art Journal*. **Essays:** Bonheur; Demont-Breton; Grotell; Orléans; Wieselthier.

Ward, Esmé Freelance gallery and museum educator. Contributor to *Dulwich Picture Gallery Children's Art Book* (1997) and *Dulwich Picture Gallery Activity Book* (1997). **Essays:** Duparc; Vallain (both with Ute Krebs).

Ward-Jackson, Philip Deputy Librarian, Conway Library, Courtauld Institute of Art, University of London. Contributor to *Burlington Magazine*, *Journal of the Warburg and Courtauld Institutes*, *Revue de L'Art* and *Journal of the Church Monuments Society*.

Warwick, Genevieve Lecturer, Courtauld Institute of Art, University of London. Contributor to the journals *Word and Image*, *Master Drawings*, *Art Bulletin* and to the *CIHA Conference Proceedings* (1996).

Weaver, Cynthia R. Senior Lecturer, History of Dress and Textiles, University of Central England, Birmingham. Contributor to *Enid Marx and Her Circle* (catalogue, 1992) and to the periodicals *Antique Collecting*, *Journal of Design History* and *Newsletter of Design History Society*. **Essay:** Marx.

Weber, Michelle L. Research Assistant, Library and Research Center, National Museum of Women in the Arts, Washington, DC. **Essay:** General bibliography.

Weibull, Nina Curator of the Stockholm University Art Collection; editor of *Divan*. Co-author of *Channa Bankier* (1994) and *Liv Derkert* (1994); contributor to the catalogues *Carlssons* (1995), *Liljevalchs* (1995) and *Sigrid Hjertén* (1995). **Essay:** Hjertén.

Weiner, Julia Curator, Ben Uri Art Society, London. Contributor to *Jewish Artists: The Ben Uri Collection* (1994) and to the journals *AJA Review*, *Manna*, *Jewish Chronicle* and *Jewish Quarterly*. **Essay:** Ticho.

Weltge, Sigrid Wortmann Professor, History of Art and Design, Philadelphia College of Textiles. Author of *Die Ersten Maler in Worpswede* (1979 and 1987), *Bauhaus Textiles: Women Artists and the Weaving Workshop* (1993) and *Women's Work: Textile Art from the Bauhaus* (1993). Contributor to *International Dictionary of Women Artists Born Before 1900* (1985), *The Bauhaus Weaving Workshop: Source and Influence for American Textiles* (catalogue, 1987) and *Sonja Flavin: Weavings and Computer Drawings* (catalogue, 1989). Contributor to the journals *Tiller*, *Update*, *Women's Studies Quarterly*, *Portfolio*, *Interweave Magazine*, *Arts Exchange Magazine* and *Women's Caucus for Art News*. **Essays:** Rilke-Westhoff; Stölzl; Tawney.

Welu, James A. Director, Worcester Art Museum, Worcester, Massachusetts. Contributor to the catalogues *Seventeenth-Century Dutch Painting: Raising the Curtain on New England Private Collections* (1979), *The Collector's Cabinet: Flemish Paintings from New England Private Collections* (1983) and *Judith Leyster: A Dutch Master and Her World* (1993), and to the journal *Art Bulletin*. **Essay:** Leyster.

Werkmäster, Barbro Author, art critic and Senior Lecturer in Art History, Uppsala University. Author of *Frihet jämlikhet systerskap* (with Maud Hägg, 1971), *Kvinnor och sex* (with Maud Hägg, 1973), *Bilden som Handling* (with J. Rosell, 1984), *Möte med bilderboken* (with Lena Kåreland, 1985), *Anna Nordlander och hennes samtid* (1993) and *Livsvandring i tre akter* (with Lena Kåreland, 1994). Editor of *Kvinnor som konstnärer* (with Anna Lena Lindberg, 1975). Contributor to *Kvinnor och skapande* (1983) and *Visual Paraphrases: Studies in Mass Media Imagery* (1984) and to the periodicals *Författaren*, *Hertha*, *Konsthistorisk Tidskrift*, *Kvinnovetenskaplig Tidskrift*, *Ord & Bild*, *Paletten*, *Phaedrus* and *Valör*. **Essay:** Nyström.

Weston, Helen Senior Lecturer, History of Art Department, University College, London. Contributor to *Burlington Magazine*, *Oxford Art Journal*, *Art Monthly* and *RES: Journal of Anthropology and Aesthetics*. **Essay:** Mayer.

Wichstrøm, Anne Professor of Art, University of Oslo. Author of *Kvinner ved staffeliet: Kvinnelige malere i Norge før 1900* (1983) and *Oda Krohg: Et kunstnerliv* (1988). Contributor to the catalogues *De drogo till Paris: Nordiska konstnärinnor på 1880-talet* (1988) and *At Century's End: Norwegian Artists and the Figurative Tradition, 1880/1990* (1995), and to the periodicals *Kunst og Kultur* and *Woman's Art Journal*. **Essay:** Nørregaard.

Wiggins, Colin Member of the Education Department, National Gallery, London. Author of *Working After the Masters: Frank Auerbach and the National Gallery* (1995) and *Now We are 64: Peter Blake at the National Gallery* (1996). Contributor to *Paula Rego: Tales from the National Gallery* (catalogue, 1991). **Essay:** Rego.

Wilson, Beth Elaine Adjunct Professor, State University of New York at New Paltz. Contributor to *Geometries of Color: American Post-Painterly Abstraction* (catalogue, 1991), and to the journals *Arts Magazine, Tema Celeste* and *FAD Magazine.* Text editor, *Blind Spot* photography magazine. **Essay:** Bourke-White.

Wilson, Sarah Lecturer in 20th-Century Art, Courtauld Institute of Art, University of London. Author of *Matisse* (1992), *Max Ernst* (1994), *When Modernism Failed: Art and Politics of the Left in France, 1935–1955* (in preparation) and *Intellectual Revolution: Art and Politics in France, 1958–1981* (in preparation). Contributor to *Orlan* (1996), *Critical Introductions to Art: Portraiture* (1996), *Face à l'histoire* (1996) and *Rrose is a Rrose is a Rrose: Gender Performance in Photography* (catalogue, 1997). **Essays:** Goldschmidt; Khodossievitch; Lansiaux; Moss; Prinner; Richier; Vézelay; Training and Professionalism survey: France, 20th century (with Gill Perry).

Wimbush, Sarah Assistant, Photographic Survey Department, Courtauld Institute of Art, University of London. **Essay:** Raverat.

Winnan, Audur H. Author of *Wanda Gág: A Catalogue Raisonné of the Prints* (1993). **Essay:** Gág.

Witzling, Mara R. Professor, Art History and Women's Studies, University of New Hampshire, Durham. Author of *Voicing Our Visions* (1991), *Mary Cassatt: A Private World* (1991) and *Voicing Today's Visions* (1994); contributor to *Woman's Art Journal* and *NWSA Journal.* **Essays:** Chase-Riboud; Flack; Ringgold; Sjöö; Feminism and Women Artists survey.

Wolf, Amy J. Independent art dealer specialising in 20th-century art. Curator of the exhibitions *New York Society of Women Artists, 1925* (1987) and *Significant Others: Artist Wives of Artists* (1993). **Essays:** Greene; von Wiegand.

Wood, Jeryldene M. Assistant Professor of Art History, University of Illinois, Urbana. Author of *Women, Art and Spirituality: The Poor Clares of Early Modern Italy* (1996) and contributor to the periodicals *Konsthistorisk Tidskrift, Art History* and *Renaissance Quarterly.* **Essay:** Vigri.

Yarrington, Alison Senior Lecturer, History of Art, Leicester University. Author of *The Commemoration of the Hero, 1800–1864* (1988). Editor of *Reflections of Revolution: Images of Romanticism* (with Kelvin D. Everest, 1993) and *An Edition of the Ledger of Sir Francis Chantrey, RA, at the Royal Academy, 1809–1841* (with others, 1994). Contributor to *Art and Artists: Painters, Sculptors, Terms and Techniques* (1981), *The Thames and Hudson Encyclopedia of British Art* (1985) and *Patronage and Practice: Sculpture on Merseyside* (1989), and to the journals *Art History, Parametro* and *Women's Art Magazine.* **Essays:** Damer; Hosmer.

Yeldham, Charlotte Independent scholar. Author of *Women Artists in Nineteenth-Century France and England* (1984) and *Margaret Gillies, RWS: Unitarian Painter of Mind and Emotion, 1803–1887* (1997). **Essay:** Gillies.

Zerbi, Myriam Art historian and journalist. Author of *Una scultrice contemporanea* (1990), *Venezia nel 1700* (1992), *Chiese di Venezia* (1993) and *Cavalli di S. Marco* (1995); contributor to the periodicals *Civiltà Mantovana, Alma Roma, Nuova Venezia, Tribuna, Mattino* and *Arrivederci.* **Essay:** Fetti.

PHOTOGRAPHIC
ACKNOWLEDGMENTS

The Publisher, the editor and the picture researchers would like to thank all the organisations, agencies and individuals who have kindly provided photographic material and given permission for the use of the illustrations in this book. The locations of works are given in the captions. All illustrations are reproduced by courtesy and by kind permission of the sources given in the captions, and of the following:

© the Artist: All artists' copyright in their works is acknowledged

© DACS, London 1997: 162; 208; 292; 312; 363; 400; 422; 446; 453; 472; 522; 595; 621; 630; 698; 716; 742; 797; 799; 807; 832; 840; 854; 920; 931; 961; 999; 1047; 1142; 1186; 1214; 1223; 1233; 1271; 1332; 1370; 1371; 1385; 1401
© DACS London / ADAGP Paris 1997: 287; 1051; 1162
© DACS London / ARS New York 1997: 141
© DACS London / VAGA New York: 242; 299; 607; 734; 921; 1433
© DACS / VIS-ART: 1453

ACA Galleries, New York / Munich: 646; (Tar Beach 1988) 1173
Alexander & Bonin, New York: 913; 985
Alinari: 189; 1011; 1200
Alinari-Giraudon: 536
American Craft Museum, New York (photo: George Erml): 1355
André Emmerich Gallery, New York / Sotheby's: 1186
© Ann M. Mills: 1286
Annely Juda Gallery, London: 408
© Anthony D'Offay Gallery, London: 237
Archer M. Huntington Art Gallery, University of Texas at Austin (photo: George Holmes): 1062
© Armitt Trust, Ambleside: 1109
Arquivo Nacional de Fotografia, Instituto Português de Museus: 203
Art First, Cork Street, London: 215
Art Gallery of Ontario, Toronto: (photo: Carlo Catenazzi) 352; (photo: Larry Ostrom) 1453
photo © 1996 Art Institute of Chicago. All Rights Reserved: 1040; 1441
Art Resource, New York: 322; 455; 1008; 1363
Artcurial Gallery (photo J. Hyde): 472

Arts Council Collection, Hayward Gallery, London: 205; (photo: John R. Freeman & Co.) 461

Battaglini-Giraudon: 571
Bauhaus Archiv, Berlin: 312; (© Dr F. Karsten, London) 971
Bayerische Staatsgemäldesammlungen, Munich: 346
Beacon Hill Fine Art, New York: 1416
Bibliothèque Nationale, Paris / Warburg Institute, London: 677
Bildarchiv Foto Marburg: 576
Board of Trustees of the National Museums and Galleries on Merseyside: 187; 317; 540; 755; 1130; 1347; 1426
Board of Trustees of the Victoria and Albert Museum, London: 6; 227; 414; 429; 497; 503; 529; 569; 584; 987; 1016; 1153; 1144
Bradford Art Galleries and Museums: 638
Brewster Arts Ltd, New York: 363
photo: Bridgeman Art Library: 1306

© Carolee Schneemann, photo by Erro: 1245
© Charlotte Salomon Foundation: 1227
© Christopher Schwabacher, New York: 1249
photo © A. C. Cooper: 251
photo: Claudine Mitchell: 376
photo: Conway Library, Courtauld Institute of Art, London: 411; 917; 1254
photo: Courtauld Institute of Art, London: 360; 451; 1053; 1267; 1273
Central Art Archives, Helsinki: 113; 393; 1361; 1457
Central St Martin's, Art and Design Archive, London: 407
Ceramic Review: 311; 714; 1358
Christopher Wood, London: 280
Chrysler Museum of Art, Norfolk, VA / © Steinbaum Krauss Gallery, New York: 1288
Ciardi-Duprè family, Villa Duprè, Fiesole (photo: Nancy Proctor): 478
City of Aberdeen Art Gallery and Museums Collections: 895

photo: Vince Wade: 600

Waddington Galleries, London: 854

Warsaw National Museum (photo: H. Romanowski): 256; 260; 1335

Washburn Galleries, New York (photo: Nathan Rabin): 441

photo © 1996 Whitney Museum of American Art, New York: 141; 265; 921; 1223

A. Wilson, Leicestershire: 533

By kind permission of the Winn Family, Nostell Priory (Lord St Oswald): 767

recall inner images that spring from the creative process. Along with their psychological interpretation as ambiguous instinct symbols, they also embody the victim and aggressor types. The frequently used motif of the dog, for the most part a symbol of loyalty and the guardian and guider of souls, has quite concrete links with the artist's everyday life, because she usually keeps two large dogs. One striking motif of the early 1990s is a large fish, which is also found as a significant figure in the three-dimensional, sculptural group *Behind the Looking-Glass* (1994; see illustration) and in *Theatrum Mundi* (1992–3). The trigger and source of inspiration for *Behind the Looking-Glass* was Lewis Carroll's *Through the Looking-Glass* (1871). The complex theme of "theatre" as a mirror-image of life, taken up by the artist again and again, is treated in the group *Theatrum Mundi*. This work was one of the commissions given by the glassworks Corning Inc. to seven internationally recognised artists for the interior of its new administration building in Corning, New York. In both works, the accented colourful fish as a mute creature signifies the presence of latent vital energies.

The cat, on the other hand, appears in the installation *Behind the Mirror* as a static guardian figure in the form of a mummy, akin to the Egyptian burial objects that were intended to attract the protection of the goddesses Isis and Bastet. Comparable quotations from famous works of art, such as the Venus of Willendorf and Ingres's *Turkish Bath* (1863), have been repeatedly situated by Zámečniková in new contexts of meaning in recent years and integrated into her work as signs of cultural recollection. To call these works post-modern would not, however, do justice to their complexity, because it would bring only one of their many facets to the fore. The artist's work is based on the way she is affected as a person and on her own sensitive and watchful treatment of internal and external images.

In a project for an exhibition in Prague in 1995, which includes a wall 6 metres in length with openwork figures, the artist replaced glass, the material that had been familiar to her for 15 years, with an acrylic glass material that was technically more suited to the work. This step beyond the "specifics of glass design" had already been predicted in 1982 by Kristián Suda, the first writer to deal with Zámečniková's work.

EVA SCHMITT

Zeisel, Eva
Hungarian ceramist and designer, 1906–

Born Eva Polanyi Stricker in Budapest, 11 November 1906. Studied at the Royal Academy of Fine Arts, Budapest, 1923–4; apprenticed to traditional potter Jakob Karapancisk, 1924–5. Started own pottery in Budapest, 1925–6; designer for Kispester Pottery, Budapest, 1926–7; Hansa Kunstkeramik, Hamburg, 1927–8; Schramberger Majolika Fabrik, Schramberg, 1928–30; freelance designer for Carstens Gesellschaft, and painted in a studio rented by her family in Berlin, 1930–32; designer for Lomonosov factory, Leningrad, 1932–4; Dulevo factory, Moscow, 1934–7. Married lawyer and sociologist Hans Zeisel, 1938; daughter born 1941, son born 1944. Emigrated to USA and settled in New York,

1938. Ceramics instructor, Pratt Institute, Brooklyn, 1939–53. Freelance designer in USA for diverse companies including Bay Ridge Specialty Company, Trenton, New Jersey, from 1938; Sears, Roebuck and Co., from *c*.1940; Castleton China Company of New Castle, Pennsylvania, from *c*.1940; Red Wing Pottery, Minnesota, from *c*.1946; Riverside Ceramic Company, 1946–7; General Mills, *c*.1948; Hall China of East Liverpool, Ohio, 1951–6; Bryce Brothers, 1952–3; Hyalyn Porcelain Company, North Carolina, from 1963; designer for European companies Rosenthal, Selb, Bavaria, Germany, from 1957; Mancioli, Montelupo, Italy, from 1958; Zsolnai, Pécs, Hungary, from 1983; Kispester Pottery, Budapest, from 1983. Recipient of National Endowment for the Arts (NEA) senior fellowship, 1983. Lives in New York.

Principal Exhibitions
Museum of Modern Art, New York: 1946 (*Modern China: New Designs by Eva Zeisel Produced by Castleton China*)
Le Château Dufresne, Musée des Arts Décoratifs, Montreal: 1984–5 (touring retrospective, organised by Smithsonian Institution, Washington, DC)
Iparművészeti Múzeum, Budapest: 1987 (retrospective)

Selected Writings
"Die Künstlerin hat das Wort", *Das Schaulade*, viii, February 1932, pp.173–4
"Grimasy bezvkusitsy na farfore" [Grimaces of bad taste on porcelain], *Lyogkaya industriya*, 4 April 1936
"Ceramic design at Pratt Institute", *China, Glass and Lamps*, lix, June 1940, pp.20–21
"Dinnerware from Pratt Institute", *China, Glass and Lamps*, lx, June 1941, pp.58–9
"Subtleties of plastic design in ceramics", *Interiors*, ci, November 1941, pp.53–5, 68–71
"Ceramic design for replacement", *China, Glass and Lamps*, lxi, May 1942, pp.12, 24
"Some problems of dinnerware design", *Ceramic Age*, xl, July 1942, pp.3–10
"Design techniques for war-ware conducted by Donald R. Dohner", *Interiors*, cii, July 1943, pp.36–9
"Are handles necessary?", *Department Store Economist*, viii, July 1945, pp.97, 112
"How to make designs 'different'", *Crockery and Glass Journal*, cxxxvii, September 1945, pp.36–7
"Can Dun's rate the designer", *Retailing: Home Furnishings*, xviii, 30 May 1946, p.24
"On designing for industry", *Interiors*, cv, July 1946, pp.76, 130–32
"Registering a new trend", *Everyday Art Quarterly*, Fall 1946, pp.1–2
"Decorations grow to Fine Arts level" in "Designs for living in America", *Crockery and Glass Journal*, clxii, February 1958, p.40
"Foreword" in Brent C. Brolin and Jean Richards, *Sourcebook of Architectural Ornament*, New York: Van Nostrand Reinhold, 1982, pp.6–7

Bibliography
Sarah Bodine, "Eva Zeisel: Humanistic design for mass production", *American Ceramics*, iii/3, 1984, pp.26–37
Eva Zeisel: Designer for Industry, exh. cat., Le Château Dufresne, Musée des Arts Décoratifs, Montreal, Smithsonian Institution, Washington, DC, and elsewhere, 1984
Eva Zeisel: A Modern Amerikai Keramika Úttörője, Budapest, New York, exh. cat., Iparművészeti Múzeum, Budapest, 1987

Eva Zeisel is acknowledged to be one of the most creative and influential designers in the field of industrial design. Her reputation rests mainly on her designs for ceramics, particularly those developed in post-war America for the tableware industry. These won critical acclaim and proved to be a popular commercial success. Working as a freelance designer, she was able to synthesise and refine the European stylistic influences of her youth to evolve witty, sophisticated but functional products and tailor them for a range of manufacturers with differing requirements and expectations. Her designs, and those of the designer Russell Wright, were crucial to the development of a contemporary style in the 1950s by English ceramic factories such as W.R. Midwinter and J. & G. Meakin.

Her apprenticeship with a traditional Hungarian potter in 1924, to learn the basis of the ceramic processes, marked the beginning of Zeisel's association with ceramics. After six months she set up her own pottery, producing pots that were largely in a local folk style but showed evidence of an appreciation of the work of the Wiener Werkstätte. This was borne out by her designs for the Kipester Pottery. Her later pre-war work in Germany and Russia confirmed the ability to absorb prevailing aesthetic and theoretical idioms and to synthesise their elements within her own designs. In the table services and ornamental wares she designed for Schramberger Majolika Fabrik, with their highly functional, geometric shapes and sparse decoration, the influence of the Bauhaus, the Deutscher Werkbund and the modern movement in architecture has been leavened by the inventiveness of her vision. It was not until she was establishing herself as a freelance designer and teacher in America, however, that her most characteristic and individual style evolved.

The streamlined *Stratoware* designed for Sears, Roebuck and Co. and her prototype service *Utility* had already brought her to the notice of the art establishment, and she was recommended by the Director of the Museum of Modern Art in New York to act as a designer for a dinner service that was to be approved by the Museum. Made by the Castleton China Company, the *Museum* service showed that she had moved away from her earlier stylistic influences that had been to some extent replaced by the fluid organic shapes popularised by the work of such European artists as the architect and designer Alvar Aalto and the Surrealist Joan Miró. Zeisel's conception of the style could be refined and elegant, as in her designs for *Museum*, or less formal and more robust, as her *Town and Country* service for the Red Wing Pottery demonstrates. These commissions won their designer critical and public acclaim. In 1947 she set up a design studio staffed by some of her students from the Pratt Institute and set out to fulfil the large number of requests for designs from the ceramic industry as well as designing for plastic, glass and stainless steel. Her most popular shape range for a ceramic service, *Tomorrow's Classic*, was produced for Hall China in 1950.

With *Tomorrow's Classic* and her designs for *Hallcraft/Century*, which were released on the market in 1956, Zeisel had translated and refined the organic, curving shape to an ultimate expression of functional but elegant relationship of flowing line and mass. Her daring approach to form and search for a modern idiom in traditional tableware can be found in the dinner plates that evolve from the usual round shape to oval platters and finally, in *Hallcraft/Century*, to

tear-shaped dishes with graceful "petal tipped" raised ends as handles. Although at their best in pure white unadorned porcelain, the wares were often produced with patterns designed by Zeisel and her studio to meet the perceived demand of the market.

Throughout the 1950s, designing for other media such as glass continued to occupy her. The table glass produced in collaboration with Bryce Brothers was created to complement the service *Tomorrow's Classic*. Her work at the time entailed a great deal of travelling as she would go to the factories that were making her commissions to supervise the production, or to meetings to discuss design details with clients and assist with the marketing process. By the late 1950s the American ceramic industry was in decline and Zeisel began to find clients abroad. Her most interesting designs, which continue her concern with bold, fluent shapes, were made by the Mancioli pottery in Italy. These were not put into production, but her designs for the Rosenthal factory in Germany in 1957 were a commercial success. The *Eva* range of wares are, however, less exciting than her previous work. Her last major American ceramic commission for the Hyalyn Porcelain Company used rich coloured glazes to suggest the effect of studio pottery, although the shapes are characteristic of her earlier work. From the mid-1960s Zeisel turned her energies away from design to writing, but she did undertake the occasional challenge, and in the 1980s returned to Hungary to experiment with new forms and glazes.

Examples of the pieces described here can be seen in major British and American collections of ceramics, such as the Victoria and Albert Museum, London, and the Museum of Modern Art, New York.

ANN EATWELL

Zorach, Marguerite Thompson
American painter and textile artist, 1887–1968

Born Marguerite Thompson in Santa Rosa, California, 25 September 1887; grew up in Fresno, California. Enrolled at Stanford University, autumn 1908, but left to accompany her aunt on a trip to Paris; saw paintings by the Fauves at Salon d'Automne; met Gertrude Stein, Pablo Picasso and Ossip Zadkine. Toured Europe, 1908–11. Studied painting at La Palette, Paris, 1911; painted in southern France with Jessica Dismorr (q.v.), summers 1910–11. Travelled to Near and Far East, 1911–12; returned to USA, 1912. Married artist William Zorach in New York, 1912; son born 1915, daughter born 1917; husband died 1966. Lived in New York; later resided mainly in Robinhood Cove, Maine, spending winters in Brooklyn. Taught at the Modern Art School, New York, 1915–16. Founder and first president, New York Society of Women Artists, 1925. Visiting artist (with William) at Skowhegan School of Painting and Sculpture, Maine, summers 1946–66; member of board of governors, 1960–68. Recipient of silver medal, California Palace of the Legion of Honor, 1919; honorary doctorate, Bates College, Lewiston, Maine, 1964. Died in Brooklyn, New York, 27 June 1968.

Principal Exhibitions

Individual

Royar Galleries, Los Angeles: 1912

Playhouse, Cleveland: 1913 (with William Zorach)

Charles Daniel Gallery, New York: 1915–16 (touring), 1916, 1918 (all with William Zorach)

Tenth Street studio (Zorach studio), New York: 1918, 1919 (both with William Zorach)

Dayton Museum of Arts, OH: 1922 (with William Zorach)

Montross Gallery, New York: 1923 (touring)

Downtown Gallery, New York: 1928, 1930, 1934

Brummer Gallery, New York: 1935 (retrospective)

Knoedler Galleries, New York: 1944

California Palace of the Legion of Honor, San Francisco: 1946 (with William Zorach)

Kraushaar Galleries, New York: 1953, 1957, 1962, 1968

Colby College Art Museum, ME: 1968–9 (touring retrospective, with William Zorach)

Group

American Women's Art Association, Paris: 1910

Salon des Indépendants, Paris: 1911

Salon d'Automne, Paris: 1911

International Exhibition of Modern Art, "Armory Show", New York: 1913

Panama-Pacific International Exhibition, San Francisco: 1915

Anderson Galleries, New York: 1916 (*Forum Exhibition of Modern American Painters*)

Society of Independent Artists, New York: 1917

Whitney Museum of American Art, New York: 1932 (annuals)

Selected Writings

"When is an American artist?", *Space*, i, March 1930, pp.28–30

"A painter turns craftsman", *Craft Horizons*, iv, February 1945, pp.2–3

"Embroidery as art", *Art in America*, xliv, Fall 1956, pp.48–51, 66–7

Bibliography

Marya Mannes, "The embroideries of Marguerite Zorach", *International Studio*, xcv, March 1930, pp.29–33

"Mrs Zorach's new art, pictures in wool, make bow at exhibition here", *New York Herald Tribune*, 23 October 1935

Louis M. Starr, "Reminiscences of William Zorach", typescript, Butler Library, Columbia University Oral History Collection, New York, 1957 (includes interviews with Marguerite Zorach, pp.247–83)

William Zorach, *Art Is My Life: The Autobiography*, Cleveland: World Publishing, 1967

Marguerite Zorach: The Early Years, 1908–1920, exh. cat., National Collection of Fine Arts, Smithsonian Institution, Washington, DC, and elsewhere, 1973

Roberta K. Tarbell, "Early paintings by Marguerite Thompson Zorach", *American Art Review*, l, March–April 1974, pp.43–57

Joan M. Marter, "Three women artists married to early modernists: Sonia Delaunay-Terk, Sophie Taüber-Arp and Marguerite Thompson Zorach", *Arts Magazine*, liv, September 1979, pp.88–95

William and Marguerite Zorach: The Maine Years, exh. cat., William A. Farnsworth Library and Art Museum, Rockland, ME, and elsewhere, 1980

Charlotte Streifer Rubinstein, *American Women Artists from Early Times to the Present*, Boston: Hall, 1982

Marguerite and William Zorach: The Cubist Years, 1915–1918, exh. cat., Currier Gallery of Art, Manchester, NH, and elsewhere, 1987

Companions in Art: William and Marguerite Zorach, exh. cat., Williams College Museum of Art, Williamstown, MA, 1991

Marguerite Zorach: Cubism and Beyond, exh. cat., Kraushaar Galleries, New York, 1991

Susan Waller, *Women Artists in the Modern Era: A Documentary History*, Metuchen, NJ: Scarecrow Press, 1991

Nicola J. Shilliam, "Emerging identity: American textile artists in the early twentieth century", *Early Modern Textiles: From Arts and Crafts to Art Deco*, exh. cat., Museum of Fine Arts, Boston, 1993, pp.28–44

Hazel Clark, "The textile art of Marguerite Zorach", *Woman's Art Journal*, xvi/1, 1995, pp.18–25

Marguerite Zorach Papers are in the Library of Congress manuscript division and Archives of American Art, Washington, DC.

Marguerite Thompson Zorach was one of a small group of American artists who brought modernism to New York in the early 20th century. In her work, much of which still remains in private collections, she bridged the conventional divisions between the so-called fine and decorative arts. Throughout her long career as a painter, printmaker, woodcarver and textile artist, Zorach's subject matter – human figures, animals, idyllic sea- and landscapes – was a celebration of everyday life interpreted through a sophisticated synthesis of modern styles. Yet, like her contemporary Sonia Delaunay (q.v.), Zorach explored some of her main artistic themes and theories through the medium of textiles, which conventional art historians have tended to hold in lower esteem.

Marguerite Thompson's early work was deeply influenced by her travels abroad in Europe and the Far East. At the invitation of an aunt living in Paris, she abandoned her studies at Stanford University to study art in France. Based in Paris from 1908 to 1911, she visited much of western Europe, including Belgium, the Netherlands, Italy and Germany, where she viewed some of the most recent developments in modern art, as well as painting and sketching from nature. In 1911 she studied painting under John Duncan Fergusson and Jacques-Emile Blanche at La Palette, an informal, progressive Parisian art school that attracted many foreign students, including William Zorach, her future husband. The expressive use of colour and vigorous brushwork of her early paintings, such as *Café in Arles* (1911; private collection, repr. Washington 1973, p.25), reflected her admiration for the Fauves, especially Matisse, and her interest in the early work of the Cubists. Before returning to the USA in 1912, she spent seven months travelling through Egypt, Palestine, India, Burma, Malaysia, Indonesia, China, Korea and Japan, painting, sketching and making notes. These experiences provided the inspiration for many of her later works, including textiles. In works such as *Judea Hill in Palestine* (1911; private collection, *ibid.*, p.27), a landscape composed of bands of flattened forms and abstracted shapes outlined in blue, in the Fauve manner, she interpreted an exotic landscape in the style she had evolved in Paris.

On her return to California, she spent two months in the Sierra Mountains, where, inspired by the beauty of the rugged landscape, she produced a series of boldly executed paintings, including *Man Among the Redwoods* (1912; private collection, *ibid.* p.33), and delicate calligraphic drawings, reminiscent of Japanese scroll paintings. In late 1912 she moved to New York, married William Zorach and established what the Zorachs referred to as their "Post Impressionist" studio. In the 1910s both artists were at the forefront of American

Zorach: *Embroidered Panel* (joined side panels from bedspread), 1925–8; polychrome wool embroidered on linen; 137.2 × 228.6 cm.; Museum of Fine Arts, Boston; Frank B. Bemis Fund

modernism, exhibiting paintings at the Armory Show, where Marguerite Zorach's Fauvist portrait of a woman (untraced) received the distinction of being vilified in the conventional art press. The Zorachs lived and worked mainly in New York, but spent summers in the country, where Marguerite Zorach sought rejuvenation through her contact with nature. Between 1915 and 1920 she experimented with Cubist devices, including faceted planes, in such paintings as the *Deserted Mill* (1917; private collection, repr. Manchester 1987, p.24) and *Sunrise – Moonset, Provincetown* (1916; Nebraska Art Association, Lincoln).

Around 1913 Zorach began to make pictorial embroideries, which she referred to as embroidered tapestries. She wrote:

In 1912 when I returned from Paris full of enthusiasm over the world of lively color the Fauves had discovered, paint seemed dull and inadequate to me. The wealth of beautiful and brilliant color available in woolen yarns so fascinated me that I tried to paint my pictures in wool. … But almost immediately they became divorced from the painting viewpoint and developed life and form in their own medium. Yet were I not a painter my embroideries would never be what they are or have the stature that they possess ["Embroidery as art", 1956, p.48].

In her first embroideries, Zorach often reinterpreted works that she had already executed in paint, for example an embroidery entitled *The Sea* (1917–18; private collection, repr. Washington 1973, p.12) was based on a picture known as *The Swimmers* (1917; private collection). William Zorach collaborated on some of these early projects, including *The Sea* and *Maine Islands* (1919; National Museum of American Art, Smithsonian Institution, Washington, DC), and the two artists often shared motifs in their works in different media. In the later embroideries only portions or particular motifs related to existing paintings or sketches. Marguerite Zorach's working method was to make only the simplest sketch of the forms on the fabric before working them up freely in brightly hued wool yarns, without the use of an embroidery frame, in inventive stitches that created a rich surface texture resembling brush strokes. Zorach's textiles, with their rhythmical compositional devices, flat patterning and expressive use of non-naturalistic colour, were the ideal medium for her art of this time. They appear to have been better received than her paintings of the same period. One critic wrote: "It happens that many who reject cubist art in painting accept it readily enough in decorative productions, and so more unanimous praise is heard for the Zorach rugs and embroideries than for the pictures."

Zorach concentrated on the creation of textiles throughout the 1910s and 1920s, when she divided her time between art and her young family. In these works she explored the familiar connotations of traditional domestic textiles, such as the 18th-century embroidered pictures, bedcovers and later hooked rugs that were beginning to become highly collectible as American folk art. Yet her textiles also reveal her experience of European modernism, as is evident in a hooked rug with a figure of a reclining nude in the style of Matisse (*c.*1925; private collection, repr. Rockland 1980, p.15). In common with other young American textile designers in this period, Zorach was also interested in ancient and non-European sources of design. She was one of the first Americans to practise batik, a resist-dyeing technique, primarily used to decorate fabrics, that she probably learned during her visit to Indonesia, where she acquired batik-making implements. Although Zorach's batiks won prizes in the Art Alliance of America's competitions of 1916–20, which were intended to attract the attention of progressive textile manufacturers, her designs do not appear to have been produced industrially. Some of her batiks were made into artistic dress, such as a silk scarf with horses and nude riders (c.1918; Museum of Fine Arts, Boston). Others functioned as decorative wall hangings, for example, a set of three hangings (1918–20; Metropolitan Museum of Art, New York) with stylised nudes and animals reminiscent of African sculpture that Zorach and other artists interested in Cubism studied. Zorach exhibited batiks with her paintings in 1919 at the height of the fashion for batiks in New York.

Although Zorach made decorative textiles and dress for her own and her family's use, she was also commissioned to make textiles by collectors of modern art. Major patrons were Helen and Lathrop Brown, for whom she made many items, including an embroidered bedcover (1925–8; see illustration). The cover is decorated with whimsical figures of God and angels and scenes from Provincetown, where the Zorachs worked with the Provincetown Players, an avant-garde theatre group, in 1916 and 1921–3, and the Browns summered in the seaside community of artists. Embroidered portraits of other patrons included that of the *Jonas Family* (1925–6; private collection, repr. Mannes 1930, p.32) and the *Family of John D. Rockefeller, Jr, Seal Harbor, Maine* (1929–32; private collection, repr. "Embroidery as art". 1956, facing p.67). These pictorial embroideries, with iconic figures piled against a high horizon line, were executed in a denser manner than the bedcovers, the stitches almost entirely covering the linen ground fabric. Reviewers of the major retrospective of most of the embroideries at the Brummer Gallery in 1935 generally concurred with a critic who wrote: "She has never before approached, in any medium, the quality of work she now publishes" (H[enry] McB[ride], "Mrs Zorach steps forward", *New York Sun*, 26 October 1935).

Zorach continued to paint throughout her life, and after 1923, when the Zorachs purchased a house in Maine, local landscapes and characters, such as *Maine Sheriff* (1930; Whitney Museum of American Art, New York), featured prominently in her paintings. Powerful portraits, such as *Guy Lowe – The Last of Lowe's Point, Maine* (1928; private collection, repr. New York 1991), with their flattened forms and deliberate naïveté to emphasise character traits, suggest the influence of American folk painting on her work of this period. Some of the last embroideries that she executed were family portraits, including *Robinhood Farm, Georgetown Island, Maine* (1937; private collection, repr. Rockland 1980, p.19), depictions of her children, Tessim Zorach and Dahlov Ipcar with their families in domestic settings, both executed in the 1940s, and the retrospective *My Home in Fresno Around the Year 1900* (1949; National Museum of American Art). Having made more than 20 embroidered pictures and four bedcovers, Zorach was forced to abandon the more exacting work of embroidery completely in 1953 as a result of an eye condition, but was still able to paint, teach and exhibit into the 1960s. In

her later paintings, which were mainly landscapes, Zorach's palette became purer, almost acidic, as is evident in *Maine Fishing Village* (1950; private collection, *ibid.*, p.26).

NICOLA J. SHILLIAM

Zürn, Unica
German artist and writer, 1916–1970

Born in Grunewald, Berlin, 6 July 1916. Worked for Universum-Film AG (UFA), Berlin, as secretary, editor, archivist and artistic adviser, 1933–mid-1940s. Married Eric Laupenmühlen, 1942; daughter born 1943, son born 1945; divorced 1949; lost custody of children. Began career as a creative writer for German and Swiss magazines. Met the artist Hans Bellmer in Berlin, and moved with him to Paris, where she met the Surrealists, 1953. First nervous breakdown, 1957; subsequent internments of varying lengths in psychiatric hospital of Sainte-Anne, Paris. Committed suicide in Paris, 19 October 1970.

Principal Exhibitions
Galerie Le Soleil dans la Tête, Paris: 1953, 1957 (both individual)
Galerie Daniel Cordier, Paris: 1959 (*EROS: Exposition inteRnatiOnale du Surréalisme*)
Galerie Point Cardinal, Paris: 1962, 1964 (both individual)
Galerie Dieter Brunsberg, Hannover: 1967 (with Hans Bellmer)
Galerie Werner Kunze, Berlin: 1975 (retrospective)

Selected Writings
Hexentexte, Berlin: Galerie Springer, 1954 (appendix by Hans Bellmer); as *Oracles et Spectacles*, Paris: Visat, 1967
Der Mann in Jasmin, 1965; as *L'Homme jasmin*, Paris: Gallimard, 1971; as *The Man of Jasmine*, London: Atlas, 1994
Dunkler Frühling, Hamburg: Merlin, 1969; as *Sombre printemps*, ed. Ruth Henry and Robert Valanay, Paris: Belfond, 1971
Gesamtausgabe, Berlin: Brinkmann und Böse, 1988
The House of Illnesses, London: Atlas, 1993
Lettres au Docteur Ferdière, Paris: Séguier, 1994 (with Hans Bellmer)

Bibliography
Obliques, 1975 (special issue: Hans Bellmer)
Obliques, no.14–15, 1977 (special issue: *La Femme surréaliste*)
Jean-François Rabain, "Le démembrement de la figure chez Bellmer, Zürn, Schreber", *Confrontation*, Autumn 1980
Peter Webb and Robert Short, *Hans Bellmer*, London: Quartet, 1985
Luce Irigaray, "Une lacune natale", *Le Nouveau Commerce*, no.62–3, Autumn 1985, pp.39–45
Renée Riese Hubert, "Portrait d'Unica Zürn en anagramme", *Pleine Marge*, no.7, June 1988, pp.61–73
Leonora Carrington, *The House of Fear*, New York: Dutton, 1988; London: Virago, 1989
John M. MacGregor, *The Discovery of the Art of the Insane*, Princeton: Princeton University Press, 1989
Thérèse Lichtenstein, "Behind closed doors", *Artforum*, xxix, March 1991, pp.119–22
Renée Riese Hubert, *Magnifying Mirrors: Women, Surrealism and Partnership*, Lincoln: University of Nebraska Press, 1994

Unica Zürn does not fit easily into the category of Woman-Surrealist. She was the muse and obsession of the Surrealist artist Hans Bellmer for the last two decades of his life; she was

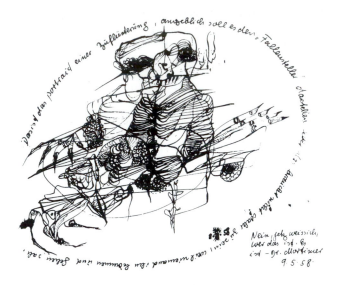

Zürn: *Portrait of a Whispered Message*, from *The House of Illnesses*, 1958

a *Nadja retrouvée* in the eyes of André Breton; she did practise Surrealist "psychic automatism" in her automatic writing and drawing. Such aspects of her career seem to locate her within the genre of the *femme-enfant* ("child-woman"), but Zürn's is a difficult case because her art is inseparable from – indeed interdependent with – her mental instability. Her most creative periods were also her most schizophrenic. The Surrealists, ever since their first Manifesto of 1924, had a highly romanticised concept of insanity, but for Zürn the imagined became the real "whether she wants it or not ... the most incredible, hitherto unseen things become reality ..." (*The Man of Jasmine* 1994, pp.32–3). Zürn, not unlike Antonin Artaud before her, was "adopted" by the Surrealists, who "heralded the benefits that would accrue from unlocking the gates of reason, and ignored the abominations" (Susan Sontag, "Artaud", *Antonin Artaud: Selected Writings*, New York: Farrar Straus, 1976, p.xxvi).

Zürn's career began in the field of film in 1933, working for Universum-Film AG in Berlin, seemingly unaware of Nazi atrocities and only finding out the truth late in the war. It was not until the end of her marriage in 1949 that she began her life as an artist, writing short stories and radio plays for newspapers and journals, and painting in a fluid, automatic style, already coined – unknown to her – as the technique of "chance" or "decalomania" by the Surrealists in Paris. Zürn's writings were consistently haunted by a father figure, an ethereal presence whom she referred to as the "Man of Jasmine". He symbolised both her creative side and her mental instability; when she felt his presence she was enraptured and dominated by a faceless force: "Someone travelled inside me, crossing from one side to the other ... From his gaze the circle closes around me" (*The Man of Jasmine* 1994, p.26). Several figures represented this force for Zürn: Herman Melville, Henri Michaux, Hans Bellmer. It was Bellmer, whom Zürn met and became infatuated with in Berlin in 1953, who played the greatest role in her career, however, and who introduced her to the Surrealists in Paris that year.

The anagram provides the best key to Zürn's work (examples were published in *Panorama*, *Panderma* and *Der Monat*,

1959–61). In 1953 she produced both her first written anagram-poems and her first collection of anagram-drawings (i.e. automatic drawings that also involved a subversion of signs). The written and drawn are inseparable in Zürn's work, for in the mode of Art Brut she etched and erased lines, whether figurative or linguistic, filling up every section of paper with a fragmentary collage of bizarre sparks of thought. This link between writing and drawing had been celebrated by Breton in his essay "Le Message automatique" (1934), wherein Surrealism was discussed alongside the iconography of the insane/schizophrenic (André Breton, *Oeuvres complètes*, ed. Marguerite Bonnet and others, i, Paris: Gallimard, 1988). In his preface to Zürn's *Hexentexte* of 1954 Bellmer also romanticised this word-image interplay peculiar to the anagram as one born of "a violent, paradoxical conflict, a conflict that presupposes the need for the greatest strain of the imaginative will and at the same time insists on the exclusion of all preconceived intention" (*Obliques* 1975, p.111; my translation).

Working in indian ink on paper, Zürn would begin with one blot and end up with a fusion of forms, hybrids of self and subconscious portraits, as in her illustrations in *The House of Illnesses*. Here the narrative is both linguistic and formalistic. We read of a Dr Mortimer, Zürn's imagined personal death who has the bearing of an army (Nazi?) officer and who denies her any hope or traditional last wish. His presence and his effect on Zürn's persecuted mind come across not from her brief narration of this encounter, but from her accompanying image: *Portrait of a Whispered Message* (see illustration). Here art and psychosis merge in a frenzy of black ink strokes that build up a hawk-like portrait of prey. We see that the artist herself only read this image when it had been completed, writing around its form on 8 May 1958: "This is the portrait of a whispered message; apparently it represents 'the trapper', but that must not necessarily be true because no one saw him come or go." The following day she added: "No, now I know who it is – it's Dr Mortimer".

This hawk-like form recurs in her imagery when she describes her enemy in *The Man of Jasmine* (1994, p.30) as one who "describes circles" preying over her, the "masochistic chicken" and portraying him, Phoenix-like, stealing her heart in *The House of Illnesses* (1993, p.20). Hers is not an inner bestiary, however, like that of her Surrealist counterpart Leonora Carrington (q.v.). Zürn dissolves rather than seeks a mythical identity (cf. Leonora Carrington's *The House of Fear* with *The House of Illnesses*). While Carrington found refuge in Shamanism and the occult, Zürn denied herself spiritual recompense and throughout her periods of breakdown continued to be plagued with images of death, torture and murder.

Two biographical factors contributed to this obsession and the resultant iconography: the loss of her children and maternal identity (on her divorce in 1949 and the subsequent abortions she chose to have), and the loss of a sense of national (i.e. German) identity. Both crises, personal and political, led to a guilt in Zürn that could not be exorcised: hence her foetal-like self-portraits and embryo-faces and her militant enemies. As she wrote herself: "I am obsessed by faces when I draw" (*The Man of Jasmine* 1994, p.40). She feared men in white coats, suspecting that they wanted to torture her "here on this bed" because she came from "the race which had set up the concentration camps" (*ibid.*, p.137).

This schizophrenic approach is constant in all Zürn's art: she both creates in a frenzy and analyses her inner and outer self. This automatic delirium was embraced by the Surrealists who invited her to exhibit with them (albeit in the section "Invention neuve" with the visionary artist Friedrich Schröder Sonnenstern) in 1959 at Galerie Daniel Cordier, Paris. Her ink drawing *Zoobiologie* (repr. *Exposition internationale du surréalisme, 1959–1960*, exh. cat., Galerie Daniel Cordier, Paris, 1959, p.116) embodies a nest of chimerical beasts, with bird legs, sagging breasts, male and female heads, and scribbled words – a fantastic creature that may be compared to Henri Michaux's *Meidosems* (1948).

Most recent interpretations of Zürn's work have misread this complex woman as a failed woman. She has been simplistically dismissed as a protégée of Bellmer (Webb and Short 1985), and as a woman who failed to be both a woman and an artist, lacking both a female and/or an artistic identity. The latter critique, by Luce Irigaray (1985), argues that Zürn's lack of an "ideal self" and the fragmentary nature of her imagery is due to the fact that she is lost in a metaphorical "passage between her selves", that her imagery represents a nostalgia for a "self", a body threshold. Yet Surrealism, especially in postwar Paris, was no longer searching for this mythological self, it focused on the experience of experiencing (see Maurice Blanchot, "Le demain joueur", *Nouvelle Revue Française*, April 1967, pp.863–88). Jean Schuster identified this shift as consciously pessimistic: "at the present time its main ambition is to establish a balance between revolt and despair" (Jean Schuster, *Entretiens sur le surréalisme*, ed. F. Alquié, The Hague: Mouton, 1968).

Zürn's "plight" was not one of a miscarried identity, of a loss of the female self, of a "failure to be born". Rather in accepting her self as a medium between the supposedly sane and insane universes, Zürn accepted that at times she felt "ashamed that she herself is a woman", that she is mad "she takes it quite for granted – she likes this word: crazy" (*Man of Jasmine*, 1994, pp.144 and 42). She gave a voice to Artaud's assertion, that the artist, or in this case the woman-artist, is inevitably suicided by society.

On 19 October 1970 Zürn threw herself from the sixth floor of the apartment she had shared for 17 years with Bellmer in Paris. The previous day she had been released from Sainte-Anne psychiatric clinic in Paris and had visited Bellmer only to find that he was determined to end their relationship. In "Le Printemps noir" she had described a childhood vision of her own suicide: "'It is finished', she says in a quiet voice and she feels herself already dead before her feet leave the window-sill. She falls on her head and breaks her neck". Ruth Henry, her close friend, concluded: "For her, who no longer had the will to live, wakefulness had become intolerable. The Black Spring of the little girl had become her life and her suicide hers" (Ruth Henry, "Le printemps noir d'Unica", *Obliques* 1977, p.259; my translation). In her poem of 1965, "Das leben, ein schlechter Traum" (Life is a bad dream), however, Zürn had also foretold this final departure, one that pushed the paradigm of the creative subject to its ultimate foreclosure: "I break everything in the middle: nose,/belly, right arm,/ Miserable list/of love! Martyr! Oh the glow/of the pale dream – it laughed/at me, life deceiver,/and provided nothing. Poor soul" (translated in Hubert 1994, p.145).

ALYCE MAHON

See also Bona

NOTES ON ADVISERS
AND CONTRIBUTORS

Aagerstoun, Mary Jo Graduate teaching assistant in the Doctoral Program in the History of Art, University of Maryland, College Park. Editor of *Women and Business Ownership: An Annotated Bibliography* (1986). Contributor to an exhibition catalogue on works by Klumpke from the Mueller Collection, Arizona State University (1993), and author of *Anna Klumpke* (MA thesis, 1994). **Essay:** Klumpke.

Aav, Marianne Curator, Museum of Applied Arts, Helsinki. **Essays:** Nyman; Salmenhaara.

Abdy, Jane Art dealer and writer. Author of *The French Poster* (1969), *The Souls* (with Charlotte Gere, 1984) and various articles for the *Financial Times*, *Apollo* and *Christie's Yearbook*. **Essay:** Bernhardt.

Adler, Kathleen Head of Education, National Gallery, London. Author of *Manet* (1986), *Berthe Morisot* (with Tamar Garb, 1987) and *Unknown Impressionists* (1988); editor of *The Body Imaged: The Human Form and Visual Culture since the Renaissance* (with Marcia Pointon, 1993). Book review editor, *Art History* (1991–5). **Essay:** Morisot (with Tamar Garb).

Ahrens, Kent Director, Kennedy Museum of American Art, Ohio University, Athens. Contributor to the catalogues *Drawings and Watercolors by Truman Seymour (1824–1891)* (1986), *Oils and Watercolors by Edward D. Boit* (1990) and *Cyrus E. Dallin: His Small Bronzes and Plasters* (1995), and to the journals *Wadsworth Atheneum Bulletin*, *Antiques*, *American Art Journal* and *Woman's Art Journal*. **Essays:** Frishmuth; Ream.

Alexander, David Independent scholar. Author of *Painters and Engraving: The Reproductive Print from Hogarth to Wilkie* (with Richard T. Godfrey, catalogue, 1980); contributor to *Affecting Moments* (catalogue, 1993). Member of the editorial board for the journal *Print Quarterly*. **Essays:** Beauclerk; Watson; Printmakers survey.

Alston, David Keeper of Art, National Museums and Galleries of Wales, Cardiff. Author of *Under the Cover of Darkness: Night Prints* (1986) and *Piranesi's Prisons: A Perspective* (1987); contributor to *David contre David* (1993). Founder editor of *Oxford Art Journal*. **Essay:** Williams.

Anderson, Janet A. Professor of Art History, University of Wisconsin, Whitewater. Author of *Women in the Fine Arts: A Bibliography and Illustration Guide* (1991) and *Pedro de Mena: Spanish Sculptor* (in preparation). **Essays:** Hoffman; Pepper.

Anderson, Janice Graduate student, Concordia University, Montreal. **Essays:** Hambling; Hicks.

Antelo, Ruth Pérez PhD candidate. Contributor to *Las mujeres en Andalucia*, *Revista da comision Galega do V Centenario* and *Goya*. **Essays:** Beer; Brockmann; Weiss.

Arnold, Bruce Literary editor, political columnist and art critic of the *Irish Independent* newspaper. Author of numerous books including *A Concise History of Irish Art* (1969), *Orpen: Mirror to an Age* (1981), *The Art Atlas of Britain and Ireland* (1991), *William Orpen* (1991) and *Mainie Jellett and the Modern Movement in Ireland* (1991); maker of the film *To Make It Live: Mainie Jellett, 1897–1944*. **Essay:** Jellett.

Aronson, Julie Assistant Curator of American Art, Nelson-Atkins Museum of Art, Kansas City. Author of *Bessie Potter Vonnoh (1872–1955) and Small Bronze Sculpture in America* (PhD dissertation, 1995); contributor to *American Naive Paintings* (1992). **Essays:** Eberle; Vonnoh.

Baden Fuller, Kate Glass artist and lecturer for the National Association of Fine and Decorative Arts, UK. **Essay:** Hobson.

Barton, Christina Curator, Contemporary New Zealand Art, Museum of New Zealand Te Papa Tongarewa, Wellington. Author of *Louise Henderson: The Cubist Years* (1991); co-editor of *Antic* magazine (1988–90) and *Alter/Image: Feminism and Representation in New Zealand Art, 1973–1993* (1993). **Essays:** Henderson; Lynn.

Batorska, Danuta Associate Professor of Art History, University of Houston. Author of *Giovanni Francesco Grimaldi* (in preparation). Contributor to the journals *Antichità Viva*, *Master Drawings*, *Paragone*, *Polish Heritage*, *Perspectives*, *Woman's Art Journal*, *Polish Review* and *Art Journal*. **Essays:** Beyer; Bilińska-Bohdanowicz; Boznańska; Stryjeńska.

Bearor, Karen A. Associate Professor, Florida State University, Tallahassee. Author of *Irene Rice Pereira: Her Paintings and Philosophy* (1993) and *Irene Rice Pereira's Early Work: Embarking on an Eastward Journey* (1994). **Essay:** Pereira.

Beckers, Marion Business manager and editor, Das Verborgene Museum, Berlin. Author, with Elisabeth Moortgat, of *Russland 1932/33* (1988), *Lotte Jacobi, 1896–1990* (1990), *Eva Besnyö: Photographs, 1930–1989* (catalogue, 1991) and *Atelier Lotte Jacobi: Berlin New York* (1997). Contributor to *Else Thalemann: Industrie und Pflanzenphotographien der 20er und 30er Jahre* (catalogue, 1993), *Jüdische Frauen im 19. und 20. Jahrhundert* (1993) and *Fotografieren hiess steilnehmen* (catalogue, 1994), and to the journal *Frauen-Kunst-Wissenschaft*. **Essay:** Jacobi.

Behr, Shulamith Bosch Lecturer in 20th-Century German Art, Courtauld Institute of Art, University of London. Author of *Women Expressionists* (1988), *Conrad Felixmüller: Works on Paper* (catalogue, 1994), *Women and Expressionist Culture* (in preparation); co-editor of *Expressionism Reassessed* (1993); contributor to *Gabriele Münter, 1877–1962: Retrospektive* (catalogue, 1992), *Sigrid Hjertén* (catalogue, 1995), *Visions of the "Neue Frau": Women and the Visual Arts in Weimar Germany* (1995) and to the journals *Art History*, *Burlington Magazine*, *National Arts Collection Fund: Annual Review* and *Oxford Art Journal*. **Essays:** Münter; Heemskerck; Werefkin.

Below, Irene Professor of Art History and Women's Studies, Oberstufenkolleg, University of Bielefeld, Germany. Co-editor of *Die schönen Zeiten sind vorbei, die schönen Zeiten hat es nie gegeben: Ästhetische Kultur von unten an einer Reforminstitution* (1984) and *Es gab nicht nur das Bauhaus: Wohnen und Haushalten Dessauer Siedlungen der 20er Jahre* (1994). Co-author, *Irma Stern und der Expressionismus: Afrika und Europa: Bilder und Zeichnungen bis 1945* (catalogue, 1996). Editor of *Kunstwissenschaft und Kunstvermittlung* (1974) and contributor to the journals *Kritische Berichte* and *Frauenkunst Wissenschaft*. **Essay:** Stern.

Belz, Carl Director, Rose Art Museum, Brandeis University, Waltham, Massachusetts. Contributor to the catalogues *Frank Stella: Metallic Reliefs* (1978), *Frankenthaler: The 1950s* (1981), *William Beckman and Gregory Gillespie* (1984), *Katherine Porter: Paintings, 1969–1984* (1985), *Stephen Antonakos: Neons and Drawings* (1986), *Jake Berthot* (1988), *Stanley Boxer, 45 Years* (1992) and *Joan Snyder, Painter: 1969 to Now* (1994). **Essay:** Snyder.

Berardi, Marianne Independent scholar. Author of *Catlin's Indians: The Kemper Portfolio* (1990) and *Under the Influence: The Students of Thomas Hart Benton* (1993). Contributor to *Sculpture by Women in the Eighties* (catalogue, 1985), *Mel Bochner: Paintings and Drawings, 1973–1985* (1985), *Memorial Art Gallery: An Introduction to the Collection* (1988), *American Paintings in the Collection of the Carnegie Museum of Art* (1992), *American Drawings and Watercolors from the Kansas City Region* (1992) and *Women's Studies Encyclopedia* (in preparation), and to the journal *Porticus*. **Essays:** Haverman; Oosterwijck; Ruysch.

Berger, Renate Professor of Art History, Hochschule der Künste, Berlin. Author of *Malerinnen auf dem Weg ins 20. Jahrhundert: Kunstgeschichte als Sozialgeschichte* (1982) and *"Und ich sehe nichts, nichts als die Malerei": Autobiographische Texte von Künstlerinnen des 18.–20. Jahrhunderts* (1987). Editor of *Camille Claudel, 1864–1943* (catalogue, 1990). Co-editor of *Weiblichkeit und Tod in der Literatur* (1987) and *Frauen-Kunst-Geschichte, Forschungsgruppe Marburg, Feministische Bibliographie zur Kunst- und Kulturgeschichte von Frauen* (1993). Contributor to *Die Weibliche und die Männliche Linie* (1993). **Essays:** Ney; Training and Professionalism survey: Germany, Austria and Switzerland.

Berman, Avis Independent writer and art historian. Author of *Rebels on Eighth Street: Juliana Force and the Whitney Museum of American Art* (1990) and *James McNeill Whistler* (1993); co-author of *Jacob Kainen* (catalogue, 1993). Contributor to *The Old Guard and the Avant-Garde: Modernism in Chicago* (1990), the inaugural catalogue for the Andy Warhol Museum (1994), *Notable American Women, American National Biography*, and to the *New York Times, Smithsonian, Apollo, Art News, Boston Globe, Art in America, Antiques, Archives of American Art, Art and Antiques* and *Architectural Digest*. **Essay:** von Rydingsvard.

Bessis, Henriette Art historian. Author of *Marcello Sculpteur* (catalogue, 1980), *Marcello: Adèle d'Affry, duchesse Castiglione Colonna* (catalogue, 1980), *Le Romantisme dans la peinture française (1820–1870)* (1982). Co-editor of *Tout l'œuvre peint de Delacroix* (1984) and *George Sand: Questions d'art et de littérature* (1991). **Essays:** Halicka; Marcello.

Bird, Jon Reader in Visual Culture, Middlesex University. Co-author of *Nancy Spero* (1996). Co-editor of *Mapping the Futures: Local Cultures, Global Change* (1993), *Traveller's Tales: Narratives of Home and Displacement* (1994), *The Block Reader in Visual Culture* (1996) and *FutureNatural: Nature, Science, Culture* (1996). Contributor to the journals *Art in America, Block, New Socialist, Artscribe International, Art Monthly, Control Magazine, Frameworks Journal* and *Studio International*. **Essays:** Bourgeois; Spero.

Black, Emily Cataloguer, Old Master Paintings Department, Sotheby's, London. Contributor to *The Dictionary of Art* (1996). **Essay:** Maron-Mengs.

Black, Peter Art historian. Author of *The Prints of Stanley William Hayter: A Complete Catalogue* (1992); editor of *Geoffrey Clarke: Symbols for Man* (1995). Contributor to the journal *Print Quarterly*. **Essay:** Motesiczky.

Blausen, Whitney Adjunct Professor, New York University. Contributor to *Dictionnaire de la mode au XXe siècle* (1994), *Contemporary Fashion* (1995), *Fifty American Designers* (in preparation) and to the periodicals *Surface Design Journal, Fiber Arts* and *Theatre Crafts International*. **Essay:** Reeves.

Bloem, Marja Curator, Stedelijk Museum, Amsterdam. Contributor to *Agnes Martin: Prints and Drawings* (catalogue, 1991), *Rini Hurkmans* (catalogue, 1991), *Lood om Oud ijzer* (1992), *Sadness, Sluices, Mermaids, Delay* (catalogue, 1994), *De lijmstokman* (1995) and to the periodicals *Museumjournaal* and *Forum International*. **Essays:** Darboven; Agnes Martin.

Bolte, Ulrike Art historian. Co-editor of *Frauen-Kunst-Wissenschaft* (1987–9); contributor to *Allgemeines Künstlerlexikon*. **Essay:** Chéron.

Bomford, Kate Currently studying for a PhD on English and Flemish 17th-century friendship portraiture at the Courtauld Institute of Art, London; has worked at the Dulwich Picture Gallery, the Wallace Collection and the University College Art Collections, London. **Essay:** Schurman.

Boström, Antonia Curatorial Intern, Detroit Institute of Arts. Contributor to the journals *Burlington Magazine, Apollo, Sculpture Journal* and *Nederlands Kunsthistorisch Jaarboek*. Member of the editorial board of the *Sculpture Journal*. **Essay:** Hydman-Vallien.

Bourne, Patrick Art dealer and editor at Atelier Books, Edinburgh. Author of *Anne Redpath: Her Life and Works*

(1989) and *The Clydesdale Bank Collection* (1991). **Essay:** Redpath.

Bowe, Nicola Gordon Lecturer and art and design historian. Author of *Harry Clarke* (1979), *20th-Century Irish Stained Glass* (1983), *Harry Clarke: His Graphic Art* (1983), *The Dublin Arts and Crafts Movement* (1985), *Cork Glass Art* (1986), *The Life and Work of Harry Clarke* (1989), *My Tender Shell: Maud Cotter* (1991) and *The Arts and Crafts Movements in Dublin and Edinburgh* (with Elizabeth Cumming, in preparation). Editor of *A Gazetteer of Irish Stained Glass* (1988) and *Art and the National Dream: The Search for Vernacular Expression in Turn of the Century Design* (1993). Contributor to a wide variety of journals. **Essay:** Geddes.

Bowlt, John E. Professor, Department of Slavic Languages and Literature, University of Southern California, Los Angeles. Author of *Russian Avant-Garde: Theory and Criticism, 1902–34* (1988), *20th-Century Russian and East European Painting* (with Nicoletta Misler, 1993), *Artists of the Russian Theater* (in Russian, 1994) and *The Salon Album of Vera Stravinsky* (1995). Contributor to the *Journal of Decorative and Propaganda Arts*. Member of the editorial board of *Experiment: A Journal of Russian Culture*. **Essays:** Delaunay; Exter; Mukhina; Orloff.

Boydell, Christine Senior Lecturer in Design History, University of Central Lancashire, Preston. Contributor to *A View from the Interior: Feminism, Women and Design* (1989), and to the *Decorative Arts Society Journal* and the *Journal of Design History*. **Essay:** Dorn.

Brandt, Bettina Visiting Assistant Professor of German Studies, Columbia University, New York. Contributor to *Der Imaginierte Findling: Studien zur Kaspar-Hauser-Rezeption* (1995). Co-editor, *Tijdschrift voor Vrouwenstudies*. **Essays:** Oppenheim; Tanning.

Brauch, Patricia Associate Librarian for Information Services, Brooklyn College of the City University of New York. Contributor to *Magazines for Libraries* (1986 and 1988), *Books for College Libraries* (1988), *Reference Librarian* (1988), *Research Guide to American Historical Biography* (1990), *St James Guide to Biography* (1991) and *Dictionary of American Biography*. **Essay:** Stettheimer.

Brisby, Clare A.A. Researcher and lecturer. **Essay:** Waterford.

Brooke, Xanthe Curator, European Fine Art, Walker Art Gallery, Liverpool. Author of *Murillo in Focus* (1990), *Lady Lever Art Gallery: Catalogue of Embroideries* (1992) and *Face to Face: Three Centuries of Artists' Self-Portraiture* (1994). **Essay:** Ayala de Óbidos.

Brown, Betty Ann Art historian, critic and curator; Professor, Department of Art, California State University, Northridge. Author of *Exposures: Women and Their Art* (with Arlene Raven, 1989), *Roland Reiss: A Seventeen Year Survey* (1991) and *Communitas: The Feminist Art of Community Building* (1992). Contributor to *Behind the Mask in Mexico* (1988), *Smoke and Mist: Mesoamerican Studies in Memory of Thelma D. Sullivan* (1988), *Californian Women Artists* (1989) and *Forty Years of California Assemblage* (catalogue, 1989). Contributor to *Art Scene, Arts Magazine, Los Angeles Reader, New Art Examiner, InSpain* and *Artweek*. Founding editor of *Visions: The Los Angeles Art Quarterly*. **Essays:** Cunningham; Hammond; Kozloff; Lundeberg; Sleigh; Taeuber-Arp; Weisberg.

Bruce, Candice Curator, Australian Art, Queensland Art Gallery, Brisbane. Author of *Eugen von Guerard: A German Romantic in the Antipodes* (1980). Contributor to *Australian Dictionary of Biography* (1985), *First Views of Australia* (1987), *Impressions of Woollahra Past and Present* (1988), *Dictionary of Australian Artists, Painters, Sketchers, Photographers and Engravers to 1870* (1992), *Heritage: The National Women's Art Book* (1995) and to the journal *Art and Australia*. **Essays:** Beckett; Ironside; Meredith.

Buchanan, William Art historian. Author of *Joan Eardley* (1976) and *The Art of the Photographer: J. Craig Annan, 1864–1946* (1992); editor of *J. Craig Annan: Selected Texts and Bibliography* (1994). Contributor to *Japonisme in Art* (1980), *A Companion to Scottish Culture* (1981), *The Golden Age of British Photography, 1839–1900* (1984), *British Photography in the Nineteenth Century* (1989) and *Photography 1900* (1993). Contributor to *The Listener, Scottish Art Review, Art and Artists, Photographic Collector, Arts Review Year Book, History of Photography* and *Scottish Photography Bulletin*. **Essay:** Eardley.

Buckland, Georgina Freelance writer. **Essay:** Hiller.

Budick, Ariella Adjunct Professor, Department of Fine Arts, New York University. Contributor to the journal *History of Photography*. **Essay:** Arbus.

Bumpus, Bernard Ceramic historian. Author of *Charlotte Rhead: Potter and Designer* (1988) and *Pâte-sur-Pâte: The Art of Ceramic Relief Decoration, 1849–1992* (1992). Contributor to *Rhead: Artists and Potters* (catalogue, 1986), *The Rheads of Staffordshire* (catalogue, 1989) and to the periodicals *Antique Collector, Decorative Arts Society Journal, Dossier de l'Art, Sèvres, Arts Ceramica, Arts and Crafts, Collector's World* and *Antique Dealer and Collector's Guide*. **Essays:** Escallier; Robineau.

Bumpus, Judith Art historian. Author of *Graham Clarke* (as Clare Sydney, 1985), *Flower Painting* (as Clare Sydney, 1986), *Elizabeth Blackadder* (1988), *Van Gogh's Flowers* (1989) and *Impressionist Gardens* (1990). Contributor to the journals *Art and Artists, Art Review, Contemporary Art, Royal Academy Magazine* and *Kew Magazine*. **Essays:** Ayres; Blackadder; Blow; Clough.

Burke, Janine Writer. Author of *Australian Women Artists, 1840–1940* (1980), *Joy Hester* (1983), *Field of Vision, A Decade of Change: Women's Art in the 70s* (1990) and *Dear Sun: The Letters of Joy Hester and Sunday Reed* (1995), and of fiction. Contributor to the journals *Art International*, *Art and Text*, *Art in Australia*, *Art Monthly*, *Art Network*, *Australian Book Review*, *Lip*, *Meanjin*, *Overland* and *Island*. **Essay:** Hester.

Caldwell, Martha B. Professor of Art History, James Madison University, Harrisonburg, Virginia. Contributor to *Alfred Bossom's American Architecture, 1903–1926* (1984). **Essays:** McGuinness; Moses; Swanzy.

Caldwell, Susan Havens Associate Professor, School of Art, University of Oklahoma, Norman. Author of *Domus feminis: Royal Leonese Women and San Isidoro in León* (in preparation). Contributor to *Folk Art in Oklahoma* (catalogue, 1981), *Ken D. Little: Catalogue of Works* (1983), *Songs of Glory: Medieval Art from 900–1500* (1985), *Contemporary Masterworks* (1991) and to the periodicals *Woman's Art Journal*, *Art Voices*, *Art Voices (South)*, *ArtCraft* and *Art History*. **Essays:** Morton; Stuart.

Cameron, Vivian P. Independent scholar. Author of *Woman as Image and Image-Maker in Paris During the French Revolution* (PhD dissertation, 1983). Contributor to *Eroticism and the Body Politic*, *College Art Journal*, *Woman's Art Journal* and *Studies in Eighteenth-Century Culture*. **Essays:** Auzou; Benoist; Capet; Labille-Guiard.

Camiz, Franca Trinchieri Adjunct Professor in Art History, Rome campuses of Trinity College (Hartford, Connecticut) and Temple University (Philadelphia). Contributor to *Picturing Women in Renaissance and Baroque Italy* (in preparation) and to the journals *Artibus et Historiae*, *Burlington Magazine*, *Metropolitan Museum Journal*, *Ricerche in Storia dell'Arte*, *Imago Musicae* and *Bollettino d'Arte*. **Essays:** Croce; Dominici; Ginnasi.

Cappellozza, Lucia Teacher of art history, Milan. Contributor to *Bijoux* (1995) and *Libri e documenti* (in preparation). **Essays:** Benedetta; Rama; Regina.

Carmean, E.A., Jr Director, Memphis Brooks Museum of Art, Memphis. Author of *Helen Frankenthaler: A Paintings Retrospective* (catalogue, 1989) and catalogues on David Smith, Robert Motherwell, Picasso, Mondrian and other artists. Contributor to the journals *Art Présent*, *Separata*, *Macula*, *Art in America*, *Art International*, *Arts* and *Studio International*. **Essays:** Frankenthaler; Graves.

Caroli, Flavio Professor of the History of Art, Politecnico, Milan. Author of *Sofonisba Anguissola e le sue sorelle* (1987), *Fede Galizia* (1989 and 1991) and numerous other publications. **Essay:** Galizia (with Domenica Spadaro).

Carr, Annemarie Weyl Professor and Chair of Art History, Southern Methodist University, Dallas. Author of *Byzantine Illumination, 1150–1250: The Study of a Provincial Tradition* (1987) and *A Masterpiece of Byzantine Art Recovered: The Thirteenth-Century Murals of Lysi, Cyprus* (1991), and numerous articles and papers on Byzantine art. Editor of *Gesta* (1994-7). **Essay:** Women as Artists in the Middle Ages survey.

Casteras, Susan P. Member of the department of Art History, University of Washington, Seattle. Author of *The Victorian Cult of Childhood* (1986), *Images of Victorian Womanhood in English Art* (1987), *English Pre-Raphaelitism and Its Reception in America in the 19th Century* (1990), *Pocket Cathedrals: Pre-Raphaelite Book Illustration* (1991) and *James Smetham: Artist, Author, Pre-Raphaelite Associate* (1995); co-author of *Richard Redgrave* (1988), *Breaking the Rules: Audrey Flack: A Retrospective, 1950–1990* (catalogue, 1992), *A Struggle for Fame: Victorian Women Artists and Authors* (catalogue, 1994) and *Pre-Raphaelite Art and Its European Context* (1995). Co-editor of *The Grosvenor Gallery: A Palace of Art in Victorian England* (1996). **Essays:** Anderson; Boyce; Eakins; Hale; Marisol; Merritt.

Čaupova, Ruta Senior researcher, Institute of Literature, Folklore and Art of the Latvian Academy of Sciences, Riga; Vice-President of the Artists' Union of Latvia. Author of *The Portrait in Latvian Sculpture* (in Latvian, 1981) and *Marta Skulme: Telnieciba* (1992). Contributor to *Unerwartete Begegnung lettische Avangarde, 1910–1935* (catalogue, 1990) and to the journals *Scientific Magazine*, *Latvijas Zinatries Akademijas Vestis* and *Mausea*. **Essay:** Skulme.

Caviness, Madeline H. Mary Richardson Professor and Professor of Art History, Tufts University, Medford, Massachusetts. Author of *The Early Stained Glass of Canterbury Cathedral, ca.1175–1220* (1977), *The Windows of Christ Church Cathedral, Canterbury* (1981), *Stained Glass Before 1540: An Annotated Bibliography* (1983) and *Sumptuous Arts at the Royal Abbeys in Reims and Braine* (1990). Editor of *Medieval and Renaissance Stained Glass from New England Collections* (catalogue, 1978) and *Studies in Medieval Stained Glass* (1985). Contributor to *Stained Glass Windows* (1993), *Women's Literary and Artistic Patronage in the Middle Ages* (1996), *Translation Theory and Practice in the Middle Ages* (1997) and to the periodicals *Art Bulletin*, *La Revue de l'Art*, *Journal of the Warburg and Courtauld Institutes*, *Antiquaries Journal*, *Österreichische Zeitschrift für Kunst und Denkmalpflege*, *Walpole Society Publications*, *Gesta* and *Speculum*. **Essay:** Hildegard of Bingen.

Caws, Mary Ann Distinguished Professor of English, French and Comparative Literature, Graduate School, City University of New York. Author of *The Eye in the Text* (1980), *Reading Frames in Modern Fiction* (1985), *The Art of Interference* (1989), *Women of Bloomsbury* (1990) and *Robert Motherwell: What Art Holds* (1996). Editor of *Surrealism and Women* (with others, 1991) and *Joseph Cornell's Theater of the Mind* (1993). **Essays:** Bell; Toyen.

Chan, Mary Curatorial assistant, Department of Drawings, Museum of Modern Art, New York. **Essays:** Lim; Sage; Steir.

Chandler, Robin M. Assistant Professor, Northeastern University, Boston, and artist. Contributor to *African American Women: A Biographical Directory* (1993), *A Very Strange Society? Comparative Perspectives on South Africa* (in preparation) and to the journals *International Review of African-American Art*, *American Political Science Review*,

Journal of Arts Management, Law and Society, Third Text and *Black Issues in Higher Education.* **Essays:** Fuller; Sligh.

Cheney, Liana De Girolami Professor of Art History and Chair of Art Department, University of Massachusetts, Lowell. Author of *Religious Architecture of Lowell* (1984), *The Paintings of the Casa Vasari* (1985), *Quattrocento Neoplatonism and Medici Humanism in Botticelli's Mythological Paintings* (1985), *Andrea del Verrocchio's Celebration, 1435–1488* (1990), *Pre-Raphaelitism and Medievalism in the Arts* (1992), *Symbols of Vanitas in the Arts, Literature and Music* (1992) and *Readings in Italian Mannerism* (1995). Contributor to the periodicals *Emblematica, Woman's Art Journal, Italian Culture, Studies in Iconography, Sixteenth-Century Journal, Artibus et Historiae* and *Journal of Pre-Raphaelite Studies.* **Essay:** Longhi.

Cherdron, Anja PhD candidate, University of Oldenburg, Germany. Contributor to *Emy Roeder, 1890–1971* (catalogue, 1989). **Essay:** Cauer.

Christensen, Charlotte Curator, Museum of Danish National History, Hillerød. Contributor to *Weltgeltung und Regionalität: Nordeuropa um 1900* (1992), *Nationalencyclopedien* (Sweden), *Danmarks Nationalencyklopædi* and *Danish National Biography*, and to the journals *Sicilia, Konsthistorisk Tidskrift, Hoogsteder-Naumann Mercury* and *Apollo.* **Essays:** Beskow; Carl Nielsen; Clausen; Ferlov; Krohg; Jerichau Baumann; Lindegren; Noack; Training and Professionalism survey: Nordic countries.

Clark, Hazel Head, School of Design, Hong Kong Polytechnic University. Contributor to *Women Designing: Redefining Design in Britain Between the Wars* (1994) and to the journals *Arts Textrina* and *Journal of the Decorative Arts Society.* **Essay:** Clissold.

Clark, Trinkett Curator of Twentieth-Century Art, Chrysler Museum of Art, Norfolk, Virginia. Author of *The Drawings of David Smith* (1985) and *Land Ho! The Mythical World of Rodney Alan Greenblat* (1992). Has organised and written brochures for the *Parameters* exhibition series since 1991. **Essay:** Buchanan.

Clegg, Sue Principal Lecturer, Leeds Metropolitan University. Contributor to *International Socialism Journal, Radical Philosophy* and *Journal of Graduate Education.* **Essay:** Lessore (with Sylvia Gosden).

Coatts, Margot Exhibition curator and writer. Author of *A Weaver's Life: Ethel Mairet* (1983), *The Oxshot Pottery* (catalogue, 1984), *Heywood Sumner* (1986), *Lucie Rie* (1992), *Robert Weldy* (1995) and *Marianne de Trey* (1995). Features writer for the periodical *Crafts* and Associate Editor of *Craft History* (1989–91). **Essays:** Rie; Wren.

Coleby, Nicola Senior Exhibitions Officer, Brighton Museum and Art Gallery. Co-author of *The Blue Guide to Mexico* (1997); contributor to *Brighton Revealed Through Artists'*

Eyes, 1760–1960 (1995) and to *The Dictionary of Art* (1996). Specialist in Latin American art.

Collins, Judith Assistant Keeper, Modern Collection, Tate Gallery, London.

Colvile, Georgiana M.M. Professor of French Film and Comparative Literature, University of Colorado, Boulder. Author of *Vers un langage des arts autour des années vingt* (1977), *Beyond and Beneath the Mantle: On Thomas Pynchon's The Crying of Lot 49* (1988), *Blaise Cendrars, Ecrivain Protéiforme* (1994) and of many articles on French, American and Canadian literature, film and painting, with emphasis on Surrealism and women. Editor of *Women's Voices from the Other Americas* (1995) and *Cendrars, la Provence et la Seduction du Sud* (with Monique Chefdor, 1996). **Essays:** Bona; Carrington; Fini; Parent; Rahon.

Cooper, Emmanuel Writer. Author of *A History of World Pottery* (1988), *The Sexual Perspective: Homosexuality and Art in the Last 100 Years in the West* (2nd edition, 1994) and *Fully Exposed: The Male Nude in Photography* (2nd edition, 1995). Contributor to the journals *Time Out, Creative Camera* and *Crafts Magazine.* Co-editor of *Ceramic Review.* **Essays:** Barton; Braden; Duckworth; Hanssen Pigott; Hoy; Lempicka; Lowndes; Tchalenko.

Crabbe, John Freelance author and consultant. Author of *Hi-Fi in the Home* (1973), *Hector Berlioz: Rational Romantic* (1980) and *Beethoven's Empire of the Mind* (1982). Contributor to the journals *Apollo, Women Artists Slide Library Journal, Country Life* and *Watercolours and Drawings.* **Essay:** Bodichon.

Cropper, Elizabeth Professor, History of Art, Johns Hopkins University, Baltimore. Author of *Pietro Testa, 1612–1650: Prints and Drawings* (catalogue, 1988) and *Nicolas Poussin: Friendship and the Love of Painting* (with Charles Dempsey, 1996). **Essay:** Gentileschi.

Crowley, Bridget Freelance lecturer, National Gallery, London, and other collections. **Essay:** Frink.

Cumming, Elizabeth Lecturer in Design History, Edinburgh College of Art. Author of *The Arts and Crafts Movement* (with Wendy Kaplan, 1991), *Glasgow 1900: Art and Design* (1992), *Phoebe Anna Traquair, 1852–1936* (1993) and *The Arts and Crafts Movements in Dublin and Edinburgh* (with Nicola Gordon Bowe, in preparation). **Essay:** Traquair.

Curtis, Penelope Curator, Henry Moore Institute, Leeds. Author of *Julius Gonzalez: Sculptures and Drawings* (catalogue, 1990) and *Barbara Hepworth: A Retrospective* (catalogue, 1994); contributor to *Archives de l'Art Français, Woman's Art Journal* and *Gazette des Beaux-Arts.* **Essay:** Hepworth.

Dahmen, Sabine Doctoral candidate, Bonn University. Author of MA thesis on Charlotte Salomon. **Essay:** Salomon.

Damian, Carol Assistant Professor, Art History, Florida International University, Coral Gables. Author of *The Virgin of the Andes: Art and Ritual in Colonial Cuzco* (1995). Editor of *Tribal Arts Newsletter*. **Essays:** Amaral; Forner; Izquierdo; Tsuchiya.

Danilowitz, Brenda Curator, Josef and Anni Albers Foundation, Orange, Connecticut. Author of *Josef Albers at Marfa* (1991); contributor to *Josef Albers Photographien, 1928–55* (1991) and *Constance Stuart Larrabee: Adventures with a Camera* (catalogue, 1995). Contributor to the journal *African Arts*. **Essays:** Albers; Matthiasdóttir.

Day, John A. Dean, College of Fine Arts, University of South Dakota, Vermillion. Contributor to *Understanding Undergraduate Education* (1990) and to the journals *Plains Anthropologist, Southwest Art, Choice* and *Caduces*. **Essays:** Jaune Quick-to-See Smith; Velarde.

Deepwell, Katy Trustee of Women's Art Library, London (Chair, 1990–94). Author of *Ten Decades: Careers of Ten Women Artists Born 1897–1906* (catalogue, 1992); editor of *New Feminist Art Criticism: Critical Strategies* (1995) and *Women and Modernism* (in preparation). Contributor to *Women's Art Magazine*. **Essays:** Agar; Colquhoun; Dismorr; Gosse; Hermes; Morreau; Nicholson; Procter; Walker; Training and Professionalism survey: Britain and Ireland, 20th century.

DeLong, Lea Rosson Adjunct Professor, Drake University, Des Moines, Iowa. Author of *Nature's Forms/Nature's Forces: The Art of Alexandre Hogue* (1984) and *New Deal Art of the Upper Midwest* (1988). Contributor to *Chemistry Imagined: Reflections on Science* (1993) and to the *Woman's Art Journal*. **Essay:** WalkingStick.

de Montfort, Patricia Research assistant, Centre for Whistler Studies, University of Glasgow. Author of *The Patons: An Artistic Family* (catalogue, 1993) and contributor to *Inferno: St Andrew's Journal of Art History*. **Essay:** Alma-Tadema.

Derrey-Capon, Danielle Attaché, Centre International pour l'Etude du XIXè siècle, Musées royaux des Beaux-Arts de Belgique, Brussels. Author of *A.W. Finch, 1854–1930* (catalogue, 1992) and *Henri Evenepoel, 1872–1899* (catalogue, 1994); co-author of *Felicien Rops* (1984), *L'Inventaire de la peinture moderne des MRBAB* (catalogue, 1984) and *Fernand Khnopff* (catalogue, 1987). Contributor to *1893: L'Europe des peintres* (catalogue, 1993), *Impressionism to Symbolism* (catalogue, 1994), *The Dictionary of Art* (1996) and *Biographie nationale belge*. **Essay:** Boch.

Dick, Jutta PhD candidate, University of Potsdam, Germany. Author of *Jüdische Frauen im 19. und 20. Jahrhundert* (with Marina Sassenberg, 1993). **Essay:** Biermann.

Diego, Estrella de Professor of Contemporary Art History, Universidad Complutense, Madrid. Author of *La mujer y la pintura del XIX español* (1987), *El andrógino sexuado: Eternos ideales, nuevas estrategias de género* (1992) and

Leonardo (1994). Contributor to the journals *Lápiz, Revista de Occidente, La Balsa de la Medusa, ArtPress, Art Journal, Contemporanea* and *Art Magazine*. **Essays:** Mallo; Training and Professionalism survey: Spain.

Diethe, Carol Reader in European Cultural History, Middlesex University, London. Author of *Aspects of Distorted Sexual Attitudes in German Expressionist Drama* (1988) and *Nietzsche's Women: Beyond the Whip* (1996). Translator of *On the Genealogy of Mortality* by Nietzsche (1994); guest editor, Nietzsche edition of *German Life and Letters* (October 1995). **Essay:** Lasker-Schüler.

Diggory, Terence Professor of English, Skidmore College, Saratoga Springs, New York. Author of *William Carlos Williams and the Ethics of Painting* (1991) and *Grace Hartigan and the Poets: Paintings and Prints* (catalogue, 1993). Contributor to *Art Journal*. **Essay:** Hartigan.

Dodd, Sara M. Open University tutor, West Yorkshire. Contributor to *The Yorkshire Coast* (1991) and *Women in the Victorian Art World* (1995). **Essay:** Yermolayeva.

Doherty, Claire Exhibitions co-ordinator, Ikon Gallery, Birmingham. Contributor to *Re-Presenting Barbara Hepworth* (1996) and to the journal *Untitled*. **Essay:** Messager.

Dougherty, Siobhan Research Assistant, Scottish National Gallery of Modern Art, Edinburgh. **Essay:** Lijn.

Doumato, Lamia Head of Research Services, National Gallery of Art, Washington, DC. Author of *Architecture and Women: A Bibliography Documenting Women Architects* (1988). Contributor to the *International Dictionary of Women Artists Born Before 1900* (1985), *Architecture: A Place for Women* (1989) and to the periodicals *Art Documentation, Choice, Oxford Art Journal* and *Architecture*. **Essay:** Dewing.

Dreishpoon, Douglas Curator of Collections, Weatherspoon Art Gallery, University of North Carolina at Greensboro. Contributor to *Art Journal* and *Art News*. **Essays:** Abakanowicz; Hesse; Rothenberg.

Dumas, Charles Chief Curator, RKD (Netherlands Institute for Art History), The Hague. Author of several books, including *Haagse stadsgezichten, 1550–1800: Topgrafische schilderijen van het Haags Historische Museum* (1991) and *Kleur en Raffinement: Tekeningen uit de Unicorno Collectie* (catalogue, 1994). Co-editor of *The Hague School: Dutch Masters of the 19th Century* (catalogue, 1983). Contributor to *In het zadel: Het Nederlands ruiterportret van 1550 tot 1900* (catalogue, 1979) and to the journals *Antiek, Burlington Magazine, Jaarboek Die Haghe, Pulchri, RKD Bulletin* and *Vereniging Rembrandt*. **Essay:** La Fargue.

Dunn, Marilyn Associate Professor of Fine Arts, Loyola University, Chicago. Contributor to the periodicals *Art Bulletin, Burlington Magazine, Antologia di Belle Arti* and *Römisches Jahrbuch der Bibliotheca Hertziana*. **Essay:** Convents survey (After the Council of Trent).

du Pont, Diana C. Curator of 20th-Century Art, Santa Barbara Museum of Art, California. Author of the catalogues *San Francisco Museum of Modern Art: The Painting and Sculpture Collection* (1985), *Pedro Mayer: Photographs of Latin America* (1987), *Photography: A Facet of Modernism* (1987), *External Encounters, Internal Imaginings* (1990), *Florence Henri* (1991), *Centric 42: Lorrie Novak* (1991), *Centric 45: Eugenia Vargas* (1991), *Centric 46: Betty Goodwin* (1992), *Modern Dance as Muse: The Art of Françoise Gilot* (1992), *Dialogue: The Art of Elsa Rady and Robert Mapplethorpe* (1993) and *Point Counter Point: Two Views of Twentieth-Century Latin American Art* (1995). **Essay:** Henri.

Eastmond, Elizabeth Senior Lecturer, Art History, University of Auckland. Author of *Women and the Arts in New Zealand: Forty Works, 1936–86* (with Merimeri Penfold, 1986) and *Frances Hodgkins: Paintings and Drawings* (with Iain Buchanan and Michael Dunn, 1994). **Essays:** Angus; Hodgkins.

Eatwell, Ann Assistant Curator, Metalwork, Silver and Jewellery Department, Victoria and Albert Museum, London. Contributor to *Women in the Victorian Art World* (1995) and *Silver* (1996). **Essays:** Bateman; Cooper; Godfrey; Zeisel.

Edge, Sarah Exhibition organiser and performance artist; Lecturer in Media Studies, University of Ulster, Coleraine. Contributor to the journals *Feminist Review*, *Women's Art Magazine* and *Film Ireland*. Member of editorial board, *Irish Journal of Feminist Studies*. **Essay:** Spence.

Elliott, Bridget Associate Professor of Visual Arts, University of Western Ontario, London. Author of *Women Artists and Writers: Modernist (Im)positionings* (with Jo-Ann Wallace, 1994); contributor to *On Your Left: New Historical Materialism in the 1990s* (1996) and to the periodicals *Genders*, *Feminist Review*, *Feminist Art News*, *Victorian Studies*, *Oxford Art Journal* and *Art History*. **Essay:** Modernism and Women Artists survey.

Ellis, Elaine Hirschl President, Arts and Crafts Tours, USA. Contributor to *In the Arts and Crafts Style* (1992) and to the journals *Arts and Crafts Quarterly* and *Arts and Crafts Quarterly Symposium*. Curator of an exhibition on Gustav Stickley (1982). **Essays:** Brown; Nourse.

Esau, Erika Lecturer, Art History, Australian National University, Canberra. Contributor to *Pre-Modern Art of Vienna, 1848–1898* (1987), *German Expressionism at Lawrence University: The La Vera Pohl Collection* (1988), *Visions of the "Neue Frau": Women and the Visual Arts in Weimar Germany* (1995) and to the *Australian Journal of Art*. Editor, *Art Documentation* (1982–5) and *Australian Art Association Newsletter* (1991–3). **Essays:** Hasse; Moll.

Evans, Michael Fellow of the Warburg Institute, University of London. Author of *Medieval Drawings* (1969), *Herrad of Hohenbourg: Hortus Deliciarum* (with Rosalie Green and others, 1979) and *Basic Grammar for Medieval and Renaissance Studies* (1995). Contributor to *Studies in Church History: Subsidia. I: Medieval Women* (1978), *Manuscripts in the Fifty Years after the Invention of Printing* (1983), *Sight and Insight: Essays on Art and Culture in Honour of E.H. Gombrich at 85* (1994) and to the periodicals *Architectural Association Quarterly*, *Source: Notes on the History of Art* and *Journal of the Warburg and Courtauld Institutes*. **Essay:** Herrad.

Fabiankowitsch, Gabriele Curator in the Educational Department, Österreichisches Museum für angewandte Kunst, Vienna; assistant in the Wiener Werkstätte Archive. **Essays:** Baudisch; Flögl; Likarz-Strauss.

Facos, Michelle Assistant Professor, History of Art, Indiana University, Bloomington. Contributor to *Domesticity and Modernism* (1995) and to the journals *Gazette des Beaux-Arts*, *Arts Magazine*, *Zeitschrift für Kunstgeschichte*, *Konsthistorisk Tidskrift* and *Woman's Art Journal*. **Essays:** Backer; Hirsch Pauli; Jobs; Kielland; Slott-Møller.

Fahlman, Betsy Associate Professor of Art History, Arizona State University, Tempe. Author of *Pennsylvania Modern: Charles Demuth of Lancaster* (1983), *The Spirit of the South: The Sculpture of Alexander Galt* (1992) and *John Ferguson Weir: The Labor of Art* (in preparation). **Essay:** Lange.

Fairchild, Constance A. Assistant Professor of Library Administration (Emerita), University of Illinois, Urbana. Contributor to *American Mass Market Magazines* (1990) and *Reference and Information Services: An Introduction* (2nd edition, 1995). Book reviewer in decorative arts for *Library Journal*. **Essay:** Wheeler.

Faxon, Alicia Craig Rhode Island Regional Editor of *Art New England* and Professor of Art History (Emerita), Simmons College, Boston. Author of *The Prints of Jean-Louis Forain: A Catalogue Raisonné* (1982), *Jean-Louis Forain: Artist, Realist, Humanist* (1982) and *Dante Gabriel Rossetti* (1989). Editor of *Pilgrims and Pioneers: New England Women in the Arts* (with Sylvia Moore, 1987) and contributor to the periodicals *Art Bulletin*, *Master Drawings*, *Metropolitan Museum of Art Journal*, *Journal of Pre-Raphaelite Studies* and *Art New England*. **Essays:** Hawarden; Jones.

Fidell-Beaufort, Madeleine Senior Lecturer, Art History, American University of Paris. Author of *Daubigny* (with Janine Bailly-Herzberg, 1975); editor of *The Diaries, 1871–1882, of Samuel Putnam Avery, Art Dealer* (with Herbert L. Kleinfield and Jeanne K. Welcher, 1979). Contributor to *Jules Breton and the French Rural Tradition* (catalogue, 1982), *Le Commerce de l'art de la Renaissance à nos jours* (1992) and to the periodicals *Oxford Art Journal*, *Confrontation*, *Ecrire*, *Publier*, *Lire Les Correspondences*, *Archives of American Art Journal*, *Gazette des Beaux-Arts*, *Bulletin of the Detroit Institute of Fine Arts* and *Nouvelle de l'Estampe*. **Essay:** Gardner.

Floyd, Phylis Associate Professor, Michigan State University, East Lansing. Author of *The Prints of Frank Stella: A Catalogue Raisonné* (with Richard Axsom, 1983). Contributor to *Treasures of the Hood Museum of Art* (1985), *The Prints of Ellsworth Kelly: A Catalogue Raisonné* (1987), *The Ivan Albright Collection* (catalogue, 1988), *St James Guide to Biography* (1991), *The Dictionary of Art* (1996) and to the journals *Kresge Art Museum Bulletin* and *Art Bulletin*. **Essays:** Kruger; Pindell; Saar.

Foley, Jeana K. Curatorial Assistant, Department of Photographs, National Portrait Gallery, Smithsonian Institution, Washington, DC. Author of thesis on the photography of Lee Miller, University of North Carolina (1995). **Essay:** Miller.

Francey, Mary F. Associate Professor of Art History and Associate Dean, College of Fine Arts, University of Utah, Boise. Author of *Depression Printmakers as Workers: Re-Defining Traditional Interpretations* (1988) and *American Women at Work: Prints by Women Artists of the 1930s* (1991). Contributor to *Dutch Art: An Encyclopedia* (1997). **Essays:** de Kooning; Mangold; Schapiro.

Friello, Kathleen M. Independent art historian. **Essays:** Kruglikova; Lebedeva.

Gantefűhrer, Anne Art historian, associated with the August Sander Archiv, Bonn. Contributor to *Eugène Druet, 1868–1916* (catalogue, 1993) and *Licht und Schatten: Rodin-Photographien von Eugène Druet* (catalogue, 1994), and to the periodical *Berliner Museen*. **Essay:** Kobro.

Garb, Tamar Reader in History of Art, University College, London. Author of *Women Impressionists* (1986), *Berthe Morisot* (with Kathleen Adler, 1987) and *Sisters of the Brush* (1994). Review editor, *Oxford Art Journal*. **Essays:** Bashkirtseff; Bertaux; Bracquemond; Morisot (with Kathleen Adler).

Garrihy, Andrea Sculptor, writer and lecturer. Contributor to *Feminist Art News*, *Fan* and *Circumspice*. **Essays:** Scott; Thornycroft.

Gellman, Lola B. Professor and Chair, Department of Art and Photography, Queensborough Community College, City University of New York. Editor of *Women's Studies and the Arts* (with Elsa Honig Fine and Judy Loeb, 1978). Contributor to *Outside the City Limits: Landscape by New York City Artists* (catalogue, 1977) and to the journals *Burlington Magazine*, *Women's Studies in Art and Art History* and *Simiolus*. Member of the Editorial Board, *Woman's Art Journal*. **Essay:** Hemessen.

Giacometti, Margherita Freelance art historian. Contributor to the catalogues *Drawings from Venice: Masterworks from the Museo Correr* (1985), *Italian Art in the 20th Century* (1989), *I Tiepolo e il Settecento Vincentino* (1990), *The Glory of Venice* (1994) and to the journals *Art Newspaper* and *RA Magazine*. **Essay:** Carriera.

Gill, Linda Freelance writer and editor. Author of *Gretchen Albrecht* (1991) and editor of *Letters of Frances Hodgkins* (1993). **Essay:** Albrecht.

Gilmour, Pat Visiting Professor, University of East London. Author of *Modern Prints* (1970), *Henry Moore: Graphics in the Making* (1975), *Artists at Curwen* (1977), *Artists in Print* (1981), *Ken Tyler, Master Printer* (1986), *Lasting Impressions: Lithography as Art* (1988) and *The Prints of June Wayne: A Catalogue Raisonné* (in preparation). Contributor to *The Woodblock and the Artist: Shiko Munakata* (1991) and to the journals *Print Quarterly*, *Print Collector's Newsletter* and *Tamarind Papers*. **Essay:** Wayne.

Goldberg, Deborah A. PhD candidate, Institute of Fine Arts, New York University; lecturer at the Museum of Modern Art and the Metropolitan Museum of Art, New York, and educational consultant, Storm King Art Center, Mountainville, New York. Author of *Alexander Archipenko: The Sculptor as Printmaker* (1990) and contributor to the journals *Apollo*, *New Art Examiner* and *Print Collector's Newsletter*. **Essay:** MacIver.

Golden, Catherine J. Associate Professor of English, Skidmore College, Saratoga Springs, New York. Editor of *The Captive Imagination: A Casebook on "The Yellow Wallpaper"* (1992) and contributor to the journals *Victorian Poetry*, *Victorian Studies*, *Victorian Periodicals Review*, *CEA Critic*, *Profession 95*, *Salmagundi* and *Woman's Art Journal*. **Essay:** Beatrix Potter.

Goldman, Saundra. PhD candidate, University of Texas at Austin. Author of *Gender: Fact or Fiction?* (catalogue, 1992); contributor to *Anne Wallace: Into the Light* (catalogue, 1992) and to the journals *Art News*, *New Art Examiner*, *Art Papers* and *Drama Review*. **Essay:** Jonas.

Goodman, Helen Lecturer, Fashion Institute of Technology, New York. Author of *The Art of Rose O'Neill* (catalogue, 1989); contributor to the periodicals *Arts Magazine*, *American Artist*, *History of Photography* and *Woman's Art Journal*. **Essays:** Dahl-Wolfe; Johnston; Model.

Goring, Elizabeth Curator, Department of History and Applied Art, National Museums of Scotland, Edinburgh. Committee member, Society of Jewellery Historians; formerly reviews editor, *Jewellery Studies*. **Essay:** Flöckinger.

Gosden, Sylvia Formerly part-time counsellor and tutor, Open University, and part-time lecturer in History of Art, Harrogate College of Art and Technology. **Essay:** Lessore (with Sue Clegg).

Govier, Louise PhD candidate, University College, London, and part-time lecturer. Contributor to the *Art Quarterly of the Art Collections Fund*. **Essay:** Bouliar.

Grace, Trudie Adjunct Assistant Professor of Art History, Fashion Institute of Technology, New York; Director, Visual

Arts Program, New York State Council on the Arts. Contributor to the *Art Journal*. **Essays:** Ferrara; Fish.

Grieco, Sara F. Matthews Member of the Syracuse in Italy Program, Florence. Co-editor of *Picturing Women in Renaissance and Baroque Italy* (in preparation).

Grove, Jeffrey D. Assistant Curator, Akron Art Museum, Ohio, and PhD candidate, Case Western Reserve University, Cleveland. Co-author of *Lee Krasner: A Catalogue Raisonné* (1995). Contributor to *Ohio Selections X* (catalogue, 1991) and *Creating in a Crisis: Making Art in the Age of AIDS* (catalogue, 1994). **Essay:** Krasner.

Guryanova, Nina Lecturer, Columbia University, New York. Author of *Russian Futurists and Their Books* (1993). Contributor to *Unknown Russian Avant-Garde* (1992) and to the journals *Elementa, Russian Literature, Art e Dossier* and *Iskusstvo*. **Essays:** Rozanova; Udaltsova.

Hadler, Mona Associate Professor, Brooklyn College and the Graduate Center of the City University of New York. Contributor to *Ethel Schwabacher: A Retrospective Exhibition* (catalogue, 1987) and to the periodicals *Art Journal, Arts Magazine, Metropolitan Museum Journal* and *Source: Notes on the History of Art*. **Essay:** Schwabacher.

Hall-van den Elsen, Catherine Independent scholar. Contributor to *Archivo Hispalense, Boletín del Museo e Instituto Camón Aznar, Goya* and *Revista de Arte*. **Essay:** Roldán.

Halliwell, Lesley Lecturer, Cambridge Regional College, and artist. **Essay:** Jaray.

Harding, Catherine Assistant Professor, University of Victoria, British Columbia. Contributor to *Florence and Italy: Renaissance Studies in Honour of Nicolai Rubenstein* (1988) and to *Dumbarton Oaks Papers*. Member of advisory board, *Racar*. **Essay:** Robusti.

Harriman, Helga H. Associate Professor of History, Oklahoma State University, Stillwater. Author of *Women in the Western Heritage* (1995). **Essay:** Blau.

Harris, Beth Curatorial assistant, Galerie St Etienne, New York, and Adjunct Assistant Professor, Fashion Institute of Technology, New York. **Essay:** Blunden.

Harris, Rosemary Curator, NatWest Group Art Collection, London. Contributor to *Tate Gallery Illustrated Catalogue of Acquisitions, 1982–84* (1986), *Tate Gallery Illustrated Catalogue of Acquisitions, 1984–86* (1989), *Within These Shores: A Selection of Works from the Chantrey Bequest* (catalogue, 1989) and the *Guinness Encyclopedia* (1990). **Essays:** Mary Martin; Mitchell.

Hayden, Ruth Author of *Mrs Delany: Her Life and Her Flowers* (1980; 2nd edition, as *Mrs Delany's Flower Collages*, 1993). **Essay:** Delany.

Heer, Lisa Independent scholar. Author of *Problems in Copies: The Production, Consumption and Criticism of Copies after the Old Masters in Eighteenth-Century England* (PhD dissertation, 1995). **Essays:** Amateur Artists (18th and 19th centuries) and Copyists surveys.

Helland, Janice Associate Professor of Art History, Concordia University, Montreal. Author of *The Studios of Frances and Margaret Macdonald* (1995). Contributor to *Glasgow Girls: Women in Art and Design, 1880–1920* (1990 and 1993), *Charles Rennie Mackintosh* (1996) and the periodicals *Art History* and *Woman's Art Journal*. **Essays:** Elizabeth Forbes; King; Frances Macdonald; Margaret Macdonald; Newbery.

Heller, Nancy G. Associate Professor of Humanities, University of the Arts, Philadelphia. Author of *The Regionalists* (with Julia Williams, 1976) and *Women Artists: An Illustrated History* (2nd edition, 1991); editor of *North American Women Artists of the 20th Century: A Biographical Dictionary* (with Jules Heller, 1995). Contributor to the journals *Arts, American Ceramics, Art News, Philadelphia Inquirer, Washington Post, Sculpture Magazine* and *Museum & Arts Washington*. **Essays:** Bartlett; Thomas.

Hill, Cecilia Fajardo PhD student in contemporary Latin American Art, University of Essex, Colchester. Contributor to *Alfredo Ramírez Lira* (catalogue, 1990) and *Roberto Burlemarx* (catalogue, 1991). **Essays:** María Luisa Pacheco; Peláez.

Hill, Jane Freelance writer, lecturer and consultant. Author of *The Art of Dora Carrington* (1994) and curator of *Dora Carrington: A Retrospective* (London, 1995). Contributor to the journals *World of Interiors* and *The Artist*. **Essays:** Carrington; Swanwick.

Hill, Mike Director, Brontë Parsonage Museum, Haworth, Yorkshire. **Essay:** Fritsch.

Hills, Patricia Professor of Art History, Boston University. Author of *The Painters' America: Rural and Urban Life, 1810–1910* (1974), *Turn of the Century America: Paintings, Graphics, Photographs, 1890–1910* (1977), *Alice Neel* (1983), *John Singer Sargent* (1986) and *Stuart Davis* (1996). Co-editor of *Eastman Johnson* (1972) and contributor to *Oxford Art Journal* and *Art New England*. **Essays:** Catlett; Neel; Savage; Spencer; Stevens.

Hilton, Alison Associate Professor, Fine Arts Department, Georgetown University, Washington, DC. Author of *New Art from the Soviet Union: The Known and the Unknown* (with Norton Dodge, 1977), *Kasimir Malevich* (1992) and *Russian Folk Art* (1995). Contributor to the periodicals *Art Bulletin, Art Journal, Art in America, Arts Magazine, Art News, Woman's Art Journal, Studies in Iconography, Journal of Decorative and Propaganda Arts* and *Slavica Tamperensia*. **Essays:** Golubkina; Ostroumova-Lebedeva; Serebryakova.

Hochstrasser, Julie Berger Independent scholar. Author of *Life and Still Life: A Cultural Inquiry into Seventeenth-*

Century Dutch Still-Life Painting (PhD dissertation, 1995). Contributor to *Center 12: Record of Activities and Research Reports June 1991–May 1992*, National Gallery of Art, Washington, DC (1992) and *Dutch Art: An Encyclopedia* (1997). **Essay:** Peeters.

Holger, Lena   Chief Curator, Nationalmuseum, Stockholm. Author of *Helene Schjerfbeck: Liv och konstnärskap* (1987), *Helene Schjerfbeck* (catalogue, 1994), *Åsa Herrgård, Sculptor* (1994) and *Bo Andersson, Sculptor* (1995). **Essays:** Churberg; Cronqvist; Ryggen; Schjerfbeck; Thesleff.

Hooker, Denise   Author of *Nina Hamnett: Queen of Bohemia* (1986) and editor of *Art of the Western World* (1989). Series consultant to Channel 4/WNET television series *Art of the Western World*. **Essay:** Hamnett.

Howard, Jeremy   Lecturer, University of St Andrews, Scotland. Author of *The Union of Youth: An Artists' Society of the Russian Avant-Garde* (1992) and *Art Nouveau: International and National Styles in Europe* (1996). **Essays:** Guro; Makovskaya-Luksch; Polenova; Yakunchikova.

Howell, Caro   Member of the Education Department, Tate Gallery, London. **Essay:** Petherbridge.

Huber-Spanier, Rosella M.   Art teacher. Author of *Over moderne kunst* (1994); contributor to *Bloemen uit de kelder* (catalogue, 1989). **Essays:** De Graag; Ritsema; Suze Robertson; Roosenboom; Toorop; Training and Professionalism survey: The Netherlands.

Hull, William   Director Emeritus, Palmer Museum of Art, Pennsylvania State University. Contributor to *Danish Ceramic Design* (catalogue, 1981). **Essays:** Eriksen; Vasegaard.

Huneault, Kristina   PhD candidate, University of Manchester. Contributor to *Journal of Canadian Art History*. **Essay:** Greenaway.

Hurtado, Shannon Hunter   PhD candidate, University of Manitoba, Canada. Contributor to *Canadian Journal of History*. **Essay:** Durant.

Hylton, Jane   Curator of Australian art, Art Gallery of South Australia, Adelaide. Author of *Ivor Francis: An Adelaide Modernist* (1987), *Adelaide Angries: South Australian Painting of the 1940s* (catalogue, 1989), *Colonial Sisters: Martha Berkeley and Theresa Walker* (1994), *David Dallwitz* (1994), *South Australian Women Artists: Paintings from the 1890s–1940s* (1994) and *Australian Colonial Art, 1800-1900* (with Ron Radford, 1995). **Essay:** Black.

Isaak, Jo Anna   Professor of Art History, Hobart and William Smith Colleges, Geneva, New York. Author of *The Ruin of Representation in Modernist Art and Texts* (1986), *Laughter Ten Years After* (1995) and *Feminism and Contemporary Art: The Revolutionary Power of Women's Laughter* (1996). Co-author of *Nancy Spero* (1996). Contributor to *Heresies: A Feminist Publication on Art and Politics*. **Essay:** Wilke.

Iversen, Margaret   Reader, Department of Art History and Theory, University of Essex, Colchester. Author of *Alois Riegl: Art History and Theory* (1993); contributor to the journals *Psychoanalysis and Art History* and *Art History*. **Essay:** Kelly.

Jacobs, Fredrika H.   Associate Professor, Virginia Commonwealth University, Richmond. Contributor to *Word and Image*, *Renaissance Quarterly*, *Art Bulletin* and *Artibus et Historiae*. **Essays:** Anguissola; Rossi.

Jacobs, Lynn F.   Assistant Professor of Art, University of Arkansas, Fayetteville. Author of *The South Netherlandish Carved Altarpiece* (in preparation); contributor to *Art Bulletin*, *Zeitschrift für Kunstgeschichte* and *J. Paul Getty Museum Journal*. **Essay:** Guilds and the Open Market survey (15th and 16th centuries).

Johns, Christopher M.S.   Associate Professor of Art History, University of Virginia, Charlottesville; Fellow, American Academy in Rome. Author of *Papal Art and Cultural Politics: Rome in the Age of Clement XI* (1993). Advisory editor for *Art History* and *Eighteenth-Century Studies*. **Essay:** Benincampi.

Johnson, Cecile Soliz   Sculpture Fellow, Faculty of Art, Design and Engineering, University of Wales, Cardiff. Contributor to *The Dictionary of Art* (1996). **Essay:** Celmins.

Johnson, Deborah Jean   Associate Professor of Art and Art History, Providence College, Rhode Island. Author of *Mabel Ducasse: Artist, Critic, Woman of Her Time* (1991) and *Joe Norman: Fantasia Del Tugurio* (1992). Editor of *A Century of Black Photographers* (1983) and *Students on Gender* (1994 and 1995). Contributor to the catalogues *Whistler to Weidenaar: American Prints, 1870–1950* (1987), *The Rise of Landscape Painting in France: Corot to Monet* (1991), *Roberta Paul* (1991) and *Joseph Norman* (1991), and to the periodicals *Burlington Magazine*, *Photographic InSight*, *Mosaic*, *Choice* and *Source: Notes on the History of Art*. **Essay:** Training and Professionalism survey: North America, 20th century.

Johnson, Heather   Lecturer, writer and art historian. Author of *Roy De Maistre: The Australian Years* (1988) and *Roy De Maistre: The English Years* (1995). Contributor to *Art and Australia* and *Australian Journal of Art*. **Essay:** Grace Cossington Smith.

Johnston, Alexa M.   Principal Curator, Auckland City Art Gallery. Author of books in the series *Aspects of New Zealand Art: Sculpture 1 and 2* (1986), *Colin McCahon: Gates and Journeys* (1988), *Alexis Hunter: Fears, Dreams and Desires* (1989) and *The 1950s Show* (1993). **Essay:** Macalister.

Jones, Amelia   Member of the Department of History of Art, University of California, Riverside. Author of *Postmodernism and the En-Gendering of Marcel Duchamp* (1994); editor of *Sexual Politics: Judy Chicago's Dinner Party in Feminist Art History* (1996). Contributor to the journals *Art History*, *Camera Obscura*, *Art+Text* and *Artscribe*. **Essay:** Chicago.

Jones, Ann Exhibition organiser, National Touring Exhibitions at the Hayward Gallery, London. Exhibitions organised include *Medardo Rosso*, *Josef Albers* and *Recent British Sculpture*; curated the New Hall collection of women's art, Cambridge. **Essays:** Fell; Koenig.

Kaiser-Schuster, Britta Museum Assistant, Bauhaus-Archiv, Berlin. Author of *Kunstkarikatur im Deutschen Kaiserreich* (doctoral thesis, 1992) and *Das frühe Bauhaus und Johannes Itten* (1994), of catalogue essays on the Bauhaus and articles in the periodicals *Neues Glas* and *Museumsjournal*. **Essays:** Brandt; Moholy.

Kaplan, Janet A. Professor of Art History and Chair of Liberal Arts, Moore College of Art and Design, Philadelphia. Author of *Unexpected Journeys: The Art and Life of Remedios Varo* (1988 and 1994). Contributor to *Women Artists in History: From Antiquity to the 20th Century* (1985), *A Woman's Thesaurus: An Index of Language Used to Describe and Locate Information About Women* (1989), *Mexican Journeys: Myth, Magic and Mummies* (catalogue, 1990), *Artists Choose Artists* (catalogue, 1991), *Beyond Aesthetics: Artworks of Conscience* (catalogue, 1991) and *Remedios Varo: Catalogo Razonado* (1994). Contributor to the periodicals *Woman's Art Journal*, *Feminist Studies*, *Art News*, *Choice*, *Times Higher Education Supplement*, *New Statesman and Society* and *M/E/A/N/I/N/G*. **Essay:** Varo.

Karlin, Elyse Zorn Freelance writer. Author of *Children Figurines of Bisque and Chinawares, 1850–1950* (1991) and *Jewelry and Metalwork in the Arts and Crafts Tradition* (1993). Contributor to *Collectors, Clocks and Jewelry Magazine*, *Heritage Magazine* and *Society of Jewelry Historians USA Newsletter*. **Essay:** Welles.

Kennedy, S.B. Head of Fine and Applied Art, Ulster Museum, Belfast. Author of *Paul Henry* (1991), *Irish Art and Modernism, 1880–1950* (1991) and *Frank McKelvey, RHA, RUA: A Painter in His Time* (1993). Contributor to the journals *Art about Ireland*, *Irish Arts Review*, *CIRCA*, *British Journal of Aesthetics* and *Burlington Magazine*. **Essays:** Guinness; Hamilton; Henry; Hone; Madden.

Kettering, Alison McNeil Professor of Art History, Carleton College, Northfield, Minnesota. Author of *The Dutch Arcadia: Pastoral Art and Its Audience in the Golden Age* (1983) and *Drawings from the Ter Borch Studio Estate in the Rijksmuseum* (1988). Contributor to the journal *Art History*. **Essay:** Borch.

King, Catherine Head of Art History, Open University, Milton Keynes. Author of *Gender and Art in Renaissance Italy, c.1300–c.1570* (1997); editor of *Women as Consumers and Users of Art and Architecture in the Italian Renaissance* (in preparation). Contributor to the periodicals *Journal of the Warburg and Courtauld Institutes*, *Wiener Jahrbuch für Kunstgeschichte*, *Zeitschrift für Kunstgeschichte*, *Gazette des Beaux-Arts*, *Pantheon*, *Art Christiana* and *Renaissance Studies*. **Essays:** Claxton; Nelli; Teerlinc.

King, Elaine A. Associate Professor of Critical Theory and Art History, Carnegie Mellon University, Pittsburgh. Contributor to *Beyond Walls and Wars: Art, Politics and Multiculturalism* (1992), *The Architect's Dream* (catalogue, 1993), *Peggy Cyphers: Lexicon of Paradise* (catalogue, 1993), *Alfred DeCredico: Drawings, 1985-1993* (catalogue, 1994), *Light Into Art: From Video to Virtual Reality* (1994), *The Figure as Fiction* (catalogue, 1994) and *The Post-Modern Enigma: Who and What Is Killing Art?* (1995). **Essays:** Abbott; Murray; Rockburne; Rosler.

King, Julie Senior Lecturer in Art History, University of Canterbury, Christchurch. Contributor to *The Book of New Zealand Women: Ko Kui Ma Te Kaupapa* (1991) and co-editor of *Spiral 7: A Collection of Lesbian Art and Writing from Aoteoroa* (1992). Contributor to the *Bulletin of New Zealand Art History* and *Art New Zealand*. **Essays:** Browne; Fahey; Stoddart.

Kirker, Anne Curator of Prints, Drawings and Photographs, Queensland Art Gallery, Brisbane. Author of *Being and Nothingness: Bea Maddock: Work from Three Decades* (with Roger Butler, 1992) and *New Zealand Women Artists: A Survey of 150 Years* (1993). **Essays:** Binns; Maddock; Training and Professionalism survey: Australasia (with Juliet Peers).

Kloek, Els Member of the Faculteit der Letteren, University of Utrecht, Netherlands. Co-editor of *Women of the Golden Age* (1994); contributor to *Judith Leyster: A Dutch Master and Her World* (catalogue, 1993). **Essay:** Guilds and the Open Market survey (17th and 18th centuries).

Knox, George Professor Emeritus, University of British Columbia, Vancouver. Author of *Giambattista and Domenico Tiepolo: The Chalk Drawings* (1980), *Giambattista Piazzetta, 1682–1754* (1992) and *Antonio Pellegrini, 1675–1741* (1995). **Essay:** Lama.

Kovalevski, Baerbel Teacher at the Hochschule der Künste, Berlin. Author of *Bau-u-Kulturgeschichte Schloss Güstrow, 1556–1603* (1972), *Denkmale der Stadt Güstrow* (1976–83); contributor to *Keramikfreunde der Schweiz* (1994–5). **Essays:** Bardua; Seidler.

Kraaij, Harry J. Art historian and head of Bureau A tot Z, Amsterdam. Author of *Charles Leickert (1816–1907): Painter of the Dutch Landscape* (1995), *Ary Schefferfons* (1996) and *Lazy Cats and Playful Kittens: Life and Work of Henriëtte Ronner-Knip (1821–1909)* (in preparation). **Essay:** Ronner-Knip.

Kramer, Miriam Freelance writer. **Essay:** Scudder.

Krebs, Ute Picture researcher, AKG London. **Essays:** Duparc; Vallain (both with Esmé Ward).

Lambertson, John P. Assistant Professor of Art History, University of New Hampshire at Manchester. **Essay:** Mirbel.

Langdale, Cecily Partner, Davis & Langdale Co. Inc., New York. Author of *Gwen John: Paintings and Drawings from the Collection of John Quinn and Others* (catalogue, with Betsy G. Fryberger, 1982), *Monotypes by Maurice Prendergast in the Terra Museum of Art* (1984), *Gwen John: An Interior Life* (with David Fraser Jenkins, 1985) and *Gwen John: With a Catalogue Raisonné of the Paintings and a Selection of the Drawings* (1987). Contributor to the *Dictionary of National Biography* and to the journals *Drawing*, *Connoisseur* and *Antiques*. **Essay:** John.

Lemny, Doïna Art Historian at Musée National d'Art Moderne, Centre Georges Pompidou, Paris. Author of *Brancusi: L'Inventeur de la sculpture moderne* (with Marielle Tabart, 1995). Contributor to the journal *Sculpt'âge* and to the magazine of the Centre Georges Pompidou. **Essay:** Dumitrescu.

Lessmann, Sabina Curator, Kunstmuseum, Bonn. Author of *Selbst-Akt: Frauenaktdarstellungen* (1990), *Susanna Maria von Sandrart* (1991), *Das Bewusstsein hat immer einen Leib: Fotografische Selbstbildnisse* (1992) and *Weiblichkeit ist Maskerade: Fotografien von M. Astfalck: Victor und Gertrud Arndt* (1994); contributor to *Woman's Art Journal*. **Essays:** Passe; Sandrart.

Lewis, Mary Tompkins Visiting Assistant Professor, Trinity College, Hartford, Connecticut. Author of *Cézanne's Early Imagery* (1989); contributor to *Cézanne: The Early Years, 1858–1872* (1988) and to the *Art Journal*. **Essay:** Gonzalès.

Lidén, Elisabeth Curator, Millesgården, Stockholm. Author of *Albin Amelin* (1975), *Between Water and Heaven: Carl Milles' Search for American Commissions* (1986) and *Kalle Hedberg* (1989); contributor to the journal *Konsten i Sverige*. **Essay:** Nilsson.

Lima, Marcelo Assistant Professor, Visual Arts Department, Sangamon State University, Springfield, Illinois. Contributor to the journals *New Art Examiner*, *Psychohistory Review* and *Revista do Museu de Arte Contemporanea*. **Essays:** Malfatti; Vieira da Silva.

Lincoln, Evelyn Assistant Professor of the History of Art, Brown University, Providence, Rhode Island. Author of *Art in Transition: Post Impressionist Prints and Drawings from the Achenbach Foundation for Graphic Arts* (with Robert Flynn Jonson, 1988). Contributor to *Art History*. **Essays:** Mantuana; Parasole.

Lindberg, Anna Lena Assistant Professor, University of Lund, Sweden. Editor of *Kvinnor som konstnärer* (with Barbro Werkmäster, 1975). Author of *Studentlitteratur* (1991). Contributor to *Ulrica Fredrica Pasch, 1735–1796* (catalogue, 1992), *Ulrica Fredrica Pasch och hennes samtid* (catalogue, 1996) and to the *Woman's Art Journal*. **Essays:** Pasch; Academies of Art survey (with Wendy Wassyng Roworth and Mary D. Sheriff).

Lloyd, Stephen Assistant Keeper, Scottish National Portrait Gallery, Edinburgh. Editor of *Richard and Maria Cosway:*

Regency Artists of Taste and Fashion (catalogue, 1995). Contributor to *Journal of Anglo-Italian Studies*. **Essay:** Cosway.

Lobstein, Dominique Archivist, Musée d'Orsay, Paris. Author of *Au temps de l'impressionisme* (1994). **Essays:** Abbéma; Breslau; Lemaire.

Lodder, Christina Reader in Art History, University of St Andrews, Scotland. Author of *Russian Constructivism* (1983) and *Russian Painting of the Avant-Garde, 1906–1924* (1993); co-author of *Catalogue Raisonné of the Constructions and Sculptures of Naum Gabo: Sixty Years of Constructivism* (1985). Contributor to *Art into Life: Russian Constructivism, 1914–1932* (1990), *The Great Utopia: The Russian Soviet Avant-Garde, 1915–1932* (catalogue, 1992) and *The Avant-Garde Frontier: Russia Meets the West, 1910–1930* (1992). **Essays:** Popova; Stepanova.

Lowe, Sarah M. Independent curator and writer. Author of *Frida Kahlo* (1991), *Consuelo Kanaga: An American Photographer* (with Barbara Head Millstein, 1992), *Tina Modotti: Photographs* (catalogue, 1995) and *The Diary of Frida Kahlo: An Intimate Self Portrait* (1995). Contributor to the catalogues *Herman Cherry: Monotypes* (1985) and *The House That Jack Built: The Politics of Domesticity* (1987), and to the journals *History of Photography* and *Center Quarterly*. **Essays:** Kahlo; Modotti.

Lucchesi, Joe PhD candidate and instructor, University of North Carolina, Chapel Hill. **Essays:** Brooks; Gluck.

Luckyj, Natalie Associate Professor, Art History, Carleton University, Ottawa. Author of the catalogues *From Women's Eyes: Women Painters in Canada* (with Dorothy Farr, 1975), *Visions and Victories: 10 Canadian Women Artists, 1914–1945* (1983) and *Prudence Heward* (1984). **Essay:** Training and Professionalism survey: North America, 19th century: Canada.

Ludwig, Heidrun Museums assistant. Author of *Nürnberger naturgeschichtliche Malerei im 17. und 18. Jahrhundert* (PhD dissertation, 1993). Contributor to *Der Franken Rom: Nürnbergs Blütezeit in der zweiten Hälfte des 17. Jahrhunderts* (1995) and *Archives of Natural History*. **Essays:** Dietzsch; Merian.

MacDonald, Margaret F. Research Fellow, Centre for Whistler Studies, University of Glasgow. Author of *The Paintings of J. McN. Whistler* (with others, 1980), *James McNeill Whistler* (with Richard Dorment, catalogue, 1995) and *James McNeill Whistler: Drawings, Watercolours and Pastels* (1995); editor of *Whistler's Mother's Cookbook* (1979). **Essay:** Jopling.

McGreevy, Linda F. Associate Professor of Art History and Criticism, Old Dominion University, Norfolk, Virginia. Author of *The Life and Works of Otto Dix: German Critical Realist* (1981) and articles for *Arts*, *Art Papers* and other journals. **Essays:** Applebroog; Edelson.

MacKenzie, Catherine Chair, Department of Art History, Concordia University, Montreal. Previously editor of *University Art Association of Canada Women's Caucus Newsletter*. Essays: Bishop; Bloch; Greenwood; Mason.

Macmillan, Duncan Professor, History of Scottish Art, University of Edinburgh. Author of *Painting in Scotland: The Golden Age* (1986), *Scottish Art, 1460–1990* (1990) and *Scottish Art in the 20th Century* (1994). Essays: Johnstone; Walton.

Maharaj, Sarat Reader in History of Art, Goldsmiths' College, London. Contributor to *The Duchamp Effect* (1996). Member of the editorial board of the journals *Third Text* and *Art History*. Essay: Donagh.

Mahon, Alyce PhD candidate (post-war Surrealism in Paris), Courtauld Institute of Art, London. Essays: Hugo; Maar; Zürn.

Mainz, Valerie Associate Lecturer, Fine Art Department, University of Leeds. Contributor to *The Dictionary of Art* (1996), *The Companion Encyclopaedia to the Making of Western Art* and to the journal *Interfaces*. Essays: Charpentier; Loir; Vallayer-Coster; Court Artists survey.

Markhof, Marietta Mautner Curator for 20th-century international art, Albertina, Vienna. Author of the catalogues *Kunst der letzten 30 Jahre* (1979), *Künstlerinnen* (1983), *Wiener Kinetismus* (1983), *Erika Giovanna Klien, 1900–1957* (1987) and *The Life and Work of Erika Giovanna Klien* (1989); contributor to *Franz Cizek: Pionier der Kunsterziehung* (catalogue, 1985), *Die Ungewisse Hoffnung: Österreichische Malerei und Graphik zwischen 1918 und 1938* (1993) and to the journal *Bildende Kunst*. Essay: Klien.

Marsh, Jan Writer and independent scholar. Author of *Pre-Raphaelite Sisterhood* (1985), *Women Artists and the Pre-Raphaelite Movement* (with Pamela Gerrish Nunn, 1989) and *Bloomsbury Women* (1995); contributor to *Women in the Victorian Art World* (1995). Curator of exhibitions on May Morris (1988) and Elizabeth Siddal (1991). Essays: Brickdale; Bunce; Morris; Siddal; Spartali.

Marsteller, Nancy-Clay PhD candidate, Case Western Reserve University, Cleveland. Assistant Professor at Our Lady of Holy Cross College, New Orleans, and lecturer at Cleveland Museum of Art. Essay: Allingham.

Marter, Joan M. Professor of Art History, Rutgers University, New Brunswick, New Jersey. Author of *Alexander Calder* (1991) and *Theodore Roszak: The Drawings* (1992). Contributor to the catalogues *Vanguard American Sculpture, 1913–1939* (1979), *Beyond the Plane: American Constructions, 1930–1965* (1983) and *Dorothy Dehner, Sixty Years of Art* (1993). Guest editor of a sculpture issue of *Art Journal* (1994). Essay: Dehner.

Martin, Brenda Researcher, Dorich House Project for Kingston University, Surrey. Essay: Gordine.

Mathews, Nancy Mowll Eugénie Prendergast Curator, Williams College Museum of Art, Williamstown, Massachusetts. Author of *Cassatt and Her Circle: Selected Letters* (1984), *Mary Cassatt* (1987), *Mary Cassatt: The Color Prints* (1989), *Maurice Prendergast* (1990) and *Mary Cassatt: A Life* (1994); contributor to *Maurice Brazil Prendergast, Charles Prendergast: A Catalogue Raisonné* (1990). Essays: Cassatt; Training and Professionalism surveys: France, 19th century; North America, 19th century.

Mellamphy, Janelle Graduate student, Concordia University, Montreal. Essay: Accardi.

Meskimmon, Marsha Lecturer in History of Art and Design, Staffordshire University. Author of *Domesticity and Dissent: The Role of Women Artists in Germany, 1918–1938* (with Martin Davies, 1992) and *The Art of Reflection: Women Artists' Self-Portraiture in the Twentieth Century* (1996). Editor of *Visions of the "Neue Frau": Women and the Visual Arts in Weimar Germany* (with Shearer West, 1995). Essays: Grundig; Höch; Jürgens; Laserstein; Mammen; Overbeck.

Metz, Kathryn Professor Emerita of Art, University of California, Santa Cruz; painter and printmaker. Contributor to the journals *Arts and Architecture*, *California Printmaker* and *Woman's Art Journal*. Essay: Sharples.

Michaels, Barbara L. Art historian, writer and lecturer. Author of *Gertrude Käsebier: The Photographer and Her Photographs* (1992) and contributor to the journals *Art Bulletin*, *History of Photography*, *Afterimage* and *New York Times*. Series Editor, Perspectives on Photography, Cambridge University Press. Essay: Käsebier.

Miller, Lillian B. Historian of American Culture, Smithsonian Institution, and Editor, The Peale Family Papers, National Portrait Gallery, Washington, DC. Author of *Patrons and Patriotism: The Encouragement of Fine Arts in the United States, 1790–1860* (1966, 1974) and *In Pursuit of Fame: Rembrandt Peale, 1778–1860* (1992); editor of *The Collected Papers of Charles Willson Peale and His Family* (microfiche edition, 1980; book edition, 1983–). Essay: Peale; Gertrude Vanderbilt Whitney.

Mitchell, Claudine Associate Lecturer, University of Leeds. Author of *Auguste Rodin* (in preparation); contributor to *On the Brink? Women Sculptors in Yorkshire* (1992), *Reflections of Revolution* (1993) and to the journals *Art History* and *Feminist Review*. Essays: Cazin; Claudel; Poupelet.

Modesti, Adelina Lecturer, History and Theory of Art, Gippsland School of Art, Monash University, Australia. Co-author of *Art in Diversity* (1988); contributor to *Pilgrimage: Works by Julie Adams, Kaye Green and Susan Purdy* (catalogue, 1991), *David Hazelwood "Collages"* (catalogue, 1993), *Identità ed appartenza: Donne e relazioni di genere dal mondo classico all'età contemporanea* (1995) and to the journal *Arts Gippsland*. Essay: Sirani.

Moffat, Pamela Dawson Art historian. Contributor to *Lilla Cabot Perry: An American Impressionist* (catalogue, 1990). **Essay:** Perry.

Monahan, Laurie J. Doctoral candidate, Harvard University, Cambridge, Massachusetts. Author of articles on Surrealism, Claude Cahun, Matisse and Robert Rauschenberg. **Essay:** Cahun.

Moray, Gerta Associate Professor of Fine Art, University of Guelph, Ontario. Author of *Mary Pratt* (with Sandra Gwynn, 1989) and *Northwest Coast Native Culture and the Early Indian Paintings of Emily Carr, 1899–1913* (PhD dissertation, 1993); contributor to *Textual Studies in Canada*. **Essays:** Carr; Wieland.

Morrison, John Lecturer in History of Art, Aberdeen University. Contributor to *Jong Holland* and *Journal of the History of Collections*. **Essay:** Barns-Graham.

Mulley, Elizabeth PhD candidate in art history and part-time lecturer at McGill University, Montreal. Contributor to *Journal of Canadian Art History*. **Essay:** Garzoni.

Münster, Anke Art historian. Contributor to *Rheinische Expressionistinnen* (1993) and to the periodicals *Kunstforum Gummersbach* and *Kölner Museums-Bulletin*. **Essays:** Brück; Kerkovius; Malachowski; Povorina; Worringer.

Murphy, Caroline P. Author of *Lavinia Fontana: An Artist and Her Society in Late Sixteenth-Century Bologna* (PhD dissertation, 1996); contributor to *Women of the Golden Age* (1994) and *Picturing Women in Renaissance and Baroque Italy* (in preparation). **Essay:** Fontana.

Murray, Joan Director, Robert McLaughlin Gallery, Oshawa, Ontario. Author of *The Beginning of Vision: The Drawings of Lawren S. Harris* (with R. Fulford, 1982), *The Best of the Group of Seven* (1984, 1993), *Daffodils in Winter: The Life and Letters of Pegi Nicol MacLeod* (1984), *The Last Buffalo: The Story of Frederick Arthur Verner* (1984), *The Best Contemporary Canadian Art* (1987), *Northern Lights: Masterpieces of Tom Thomson and the Group of Seven* (1994), *Tom Thomson: The Last Spring* (1994), *Tom Thomson: Design for a Canadian Hero* (1995) and *Confessions of a Curator: Adventures in Canadian Art* (in preparation). Contributor to *Canadian Art*, *Canadian Forum*, *Descant*, *Horizon Canada*, *Journal of Canadian Art History* and *Maclean's*. **Essays:** Luke; Isabel McLaughlin.

Muysers, Carola PhD candidate, Dresden. Contributor to *Blickwechsel: Konstruktion von Männlichkeit und Weiblichkeit in Kunst und Kunstgeschichte* (1989), *Vereins der Berliner Künstlerinnen* (catalogue, 1990), *Profession ohne Tradition: 125 Jahre Verein der Berliner Künstlerinnen* (catalogue, 1992) and to the journals *Frauen Kunst Wissenschaftsrundbrief*, *Berner Kunstmitteilungen* and *Feministische Studien*. **Essays:** Parlaghy; Rappard; Schwartze.

Nathanson, Carol A. Associate Professor of Art History, Wright State University, Fairborn, Ohio. Contributor to *Women's Rites of Passage: Telling the Story* (catalogue, 1995) and to the *Cleveland Museum of Art Bulletin*, *American Art Journal*, *Archives of American Art Journal* and *Woman's Art Journal*. **Essay:** Rice.

Necol, Jane Adjunct Lecturer, Department of Art, Brooklyn College, New York. Contributor to *Art in America*. **Essays:** Jaudon; Martins.

Nunn, Pamela Gerrish Senior Lecturer, School of Fine Arts, University of Canterbury, Christchurch, New Zealand. Author of *Canvassing Women: Recollections by Six Victorian Women Artists* (1986), *Victorian Women Artists* (1987) and *Women Artists and the Pre-Raphaelite Movement* (with Jan Marsh, 1989). **Essays:** Butler; Rae; Solomon; Starr; Training and Professionalism survey: Britain and Ireland, 19th century.

O'Dell, Kathy Assistant Professor of Art History and Theory, University of Maryland, Baltimore County. Contributor to *Illuminating Video: An Essential Guide to Video Art* (1990) and to the journals *Lusitania* and *Arts Magazine*. **Essay:** Pane.

O'Grady, John N. Lecturer in the History of Art, University College, Dublin. Author of *The Life and Work of Sarah Purser* (1996); contributor to *The Dictionary of Art* (1996) and to the journals *Capuchin Annual*, *Gazette des Beaux-Arts* and *Italia Stampa*. **Essay:** Purser.

Öhrner, Annika Curator of Riksutställningar (Swedish Travelling Exhibitions). Contributor to *Porträtt, porträtt, studier i Statens porträttsamling på Gripsholm* (1987), *Den goda fröken och huset* (1989), *Fogelstadkvinnor: En porträttutställning Gripsholms slott* (1990) and *Gabriele Münter, 1877–1962: Retrospektive* (catalogue, 1992), and to the journals *Dagens Nyheter*, *INDEX/Contemporary Scandinavian Images*, *Tidskriften 90* and *Kvinnovetenskaplig Tidskrift*. **Essays:** Derkert; Klint.

Opie, Jennifer Hawkins Deputy Curator, Ceramics and Glass Department, Victoria and Albert Museum, London. Author of *The Poole Potteries* (1980), *19th-Century European and American Art and Design* (1987) and *Scandinavia: Ceramics and Glass in the Twentieth Century* (1989). Editor of *Thirties: British Art and Design Before the War* (catalogue, 1979). Contributor to *British Art and Design* (1983), *William Morris* (1996) and *Glass* (1997).

Orenstein, Gloria F. Professor of Comparative Literature and Women's Studies, University of Southern California, Los Angeles. Author of *The Theater of the Marvelous: Surrealism and the Contemporary Stage* (1975), *The Reflowering of the Goddess* (1990) and *Multi-Cultural Celebrations: The Paintings of Betty LaDuke, 1971–1992* (1993). Editor of *Reweaving the World: The Emergence of Ecofeminism* (with Irene Diamond, 1990). **Essay:** LaDuke.

Padberg, Martina Art historian, based in Bonn. **Essay:** Prechner.

Parsons, Melinda Boyd Associate Professor, History of Art, University of Memphis. Author of *Visionary Experience, Automatism and Issues of Authority in Modern Art: The Case of Pamela Colman Smith* (in preparation); contributor to *The Spiritual Image in Modern Art* (1987) and to the journals *Nineteenth-Century Studies* and *History of Photography*. **Essay**: Pamela Colman Smith.

Parton, Anthony Director, Hatton Gallery, University of Newcastle upon Tyne. Author of *Mikhail Larionov and the Russian Avant-Garde* (1993); contributor to *Nathalie Gontcharova, Michel Larionov* (catalogue, 1995); editor and translator of *Women Artists of Russia's New Age, 1900–1935* by M.N. Yablonskaya (1990). **Essay**: Goncharova.

Patton, Pamela A. Assistant Professor of Art History and Curator of Spanish Art, Southern Methodist University, Dallas. Contributor to the periodicals *Burlington Magazine*, *Gesta*, *Goya* and *Source: Notes on the History of Art*. **Essays**: Díaz; Ende.

Peacock, Martha Moffitt Assistant Professor, Brigham Young University, Provo, Utah. Editor of *Rembrandt as Printmaker: An Exhibition at Brigham Young University* (catalogue, 1988) and contributor to the periodicals *Woman's Art Journal*, *Dutch Crossing* and *Konsthistorisk Tidskrift*. **Essay**: Roghman.

Peers, Juliet Lecturer, Art and Design History, RMIT, Melbourne. Author of *Completing the Picture: Women Artists and the Heidelberg Era* (with Victoria Hammond, 1992), *More Than Just Gumtrees: A Personal, Social and Artistic History of the Melbourne Society of Women Painters and Sculptors* (1993), *A l'ombre des jeunes filles et des fleurs: A Guide to Women Artists in the Benalla Art Gallery Collection, pre-1960* (catalogue, 1995). Contributor to *Pre-Raphaelite Sculpture* (1991) and *Heritage: The National Women's Art Book* (1995). Editor of the *Women's Art Register*, Melbourne. **Essays**: Fox; Preston; Sutherland; Training and Professionalism survey: Australasia (with Anne Kirker).

Peet, Phyllis Director/Professor of Women's Programs and Women's Studies, Monterey Peninsula College, Monterey, California. Author of *American Women of the Etching Revival* (catalogue, 1988), *American Paintings and Sculpture in the Collection of the High Museum of Art, Atlanta* (with Donelson Hoopes and Judy Larson, 1994). Contributor to *Life Sources: Multiple Visions* (catalogue, 1990), several reference books and *American Society of Wood Engravers Journal*, *Woman's Art Journal*, *Journal of the Print World* and *Imprint*. **Essays**: Mary Louise McLaughlin; Stephens.

Peña, Lydia M. Professor of Art History, Regis University, Denver. Author of *The Life and Times of Agnes Tait, 1894–1981* (catalogue, 1984) and contributor to the *Woman's Art Journal*. **Essay**: Tait.

Peramos, Karina Marotta Art historian. Author of several catalogue essays and of articles in *Tiempo y Forma*, *La Balsa de la Medusa*, *Tacho* and *Nike*. **Essays**: Francés y Arribas; Sánchez; Santos Torroella.

Perry, Gill Senior Lecturer in Art History, Open University, Milton Keynes. Author of *Paula Modersohn-Becker: Her Life and Work* (1979) and *Women Artists and the Parisian Avant-Garde* (1995). Co-editor of *Femininity and Masculinity in 18th-Century Art and Culture* (1994). Contributor to *Primitivism, Cubism Abstraction: The Early Twentieth Century* (1993). Reviews editor for the journal *Art History*. **Essays**: Blanchard; Charmy; Laurencin; Marevna; Marval; Modersohn-Becker; Valadon; Training and Professionalism survey: France, 20th century (with Sarah Wilson).

Phillips, Catherine Freelance translator/Russian specialist. Contributor to *The Medieval Treasury: The Art of the Middle Ages in the Victoria and Albert Museum* (1986), *Blackwell Encyclopedia of Jewish Culture* (1989) and various travel guides to Russia. **Essays**: Danko; Shchekatikhina-Pototskaya.

Phillips, Clare Assistant Curator, Department of Metalwork, Silver and Jewellery, Victoria and Albert Museum, London. Author of *Jewelry: From Antiquity to Its Present State* (1996). Contributor to *St Cuthbert, His Cult and His Community to AD 1200* (1989) and *The Illustrated History of Textiles* (1991). **Essay**: Ramshaw.

Pollock, Griselda Professor of Social and Critical Histories of Art, University of Leeds. Author of *Old Mistresses: Women, Art and Ideology* (with Rozsika Parker, 1981), *Framing Feminism: Art and the Women's Movement, 1970–1985* (with Rozsika Parker, 1987), *Vision and Difference: Femininity, Feminism and the Histories of Art* (1988) and *Avant-Garde Gambits: 1888–1893: Gender and the Colour of Art History* (1992); editor of *Dealing with Degas* (with Richard Kendall, 1992).

Potter-Hennessey, Pamela Professor, Art History, University of Maryland, College Park. Contributor to *Proceedings: Emerging Scholars Symposium* (1996) and *American Art*. **Essay**: Huntington.

Powers, Alan Librarian, Prince of Wales's Institute of Architecture, London. Author of *Shop Fronts* (1989), *Oliver Hill: Architect and Lover of Life, 1887–1968* (1989) and *Modern Block-Printed Textiles* (1992); contributor to *The Last Romantics: The Romantic Tradition in British Art: Burne-Jones to Stanley Spencer* (catalogue, 1989). **Essay**: Florence.

Prelinger, Elizabeth Associate Professor and Chair, Department of Art, Music and Theatre, Georgetown University, Washington, DC. Author of *Edvard Munch: Master Printmaker* (1983) and *Käthe Kollwitz* (catalogue, 1992); contributor to *Seymour Slive Festschrift* (1995) and the journal *Print Quarterly*. **Essay**: Kollwitz.

Proctor, Nancy Art history lecturer, Saint Mary's College, Rome Program; PhD candidate, University of Leeds. Author of articles on American women sculptors in Rome, Mary Kelly and Frank Faulkner. Also experimental film-maker, with exhibitions in Leeds and São Paolo. **Essays**: Duprè; Fauveau; Lewis; Stebbins; Anne Whitney; Training and Professionalism survey: Italy.

Ranfft, Erich   Henry Moore Scholar in the Study of Sculpture, Department of Fine Art, University of Leeds. Co-editor of *Sculpture and Its Reproductions* (in preparation); contributor to *Expressionism Reassessed* (1993), *Visions of the "Neue Frau": Women and the Visual Arts in Weimar Germany* (1995), *The Dictionary of Art* (1996) and to the journals *Art History*, *Burlington Magazine* and *Women's Art Magazine*. **Essays:** Forster; Heise; Roeder.

Reese, Beate   Wissenschaftliche Mitarbeitein, Städliche Galerie Würzburg. Contributor to *Eva Niestrath: Werke* (catalogue, 1993), *Denkräume zwischen Kunst und Wissenschaft* (1993) and to the journal *Kritische Berichte*. **Essay:** Horn.

Reeve, Christopher   Keeper of Fine and Decorative Art, St Edmundsbury Borough Council, Suffolk. Author of *Something to Splash About: Sybil Andrews in Suffolk* (1991) and *Mrs Mary Beale, Paintress* (catalogue, 1994); contributor to the *Burlington Magazine*. **Essays:** Beale; Mellis.

Reinhardt, Hildegard   Freelance art historian and translator. Contributor to the catalogues *Gustav Wunderwald* (1982), *Lea Grundig* (1981), *Grethe Jürgens, Gerta Overbeck: Bilder der zwanziger Jahr* (1982), *Jeanne Mammen* (1981), *Marta Hegemann* (1990), *Hermine Overbeck* (1991), *Jeanne Mammen* (1991), *Der Gereonsklub, 1911–1913* (1993), *Rheinische Expressionistinnen* (1993) and *Profession ohne Tradition: 125 Jahre Verein der Berliner Künstlerinnen* (1993), and to the journals *Kölner Museums-Bulletin*, *Hessische Heimat*, *Niederdeutsche Beiträge für Kunstgeschichte* and *Bonner Geschichtsblätter*. **Essays:** Lohse-Wächtler; Oppenheimer.

Reinhardt, Leslie   Editorial Assistant, The Peale Family Papers, National Portrait Gallery, Washington, DC. Contributor to *American Paintings of the Eighteenth Century* (1995) and to the *Art Bulletin*. **Essay:** Pinney.

Renne, Elizaveta   Curator of British and Scandinavian Painting in the State Hermitage, St Petersburg, Russia. Co-author of *British Painting from 16th to 19th Centuries: Catalogue of Western European Painting* (1990) and *Christina Robertson: A Scottish Portraitist at the Russian Court* (catalogue, 1996); contributor to the periodicals of the State Hermitage and to *Apollo* and the *National Museum Bulletin* (Stockholm). **Essay:** Christina Robertson.

Riding, Jacqueline   Assistant Curator, Palace of Westminster, London. Co-author of *Art in Parliament: The Permanent Collection of the House of Commons* (1996); contributor to the *Encyclopedia of Interior Design* (1997). **Essay:** Duncombe.

Roberts, Ann   Associate Professor, Lake Forest College, Illinois. Contributor to *Creative Women in Medieval and Early Modern Italy* (1994) and to the periodicals *Art Bulletin*, *Zeitschrift für Kunstgeschichte* and *Burlington Magazine*. **Essay:** Convents survey (Before the Council of Trent).

Robinson, Roxana   Writer. Author of *Georgia O'Keeffe: A Life* (1989) and fiction. Contributor to *Arthur Dove* (1984), *William Harnett* (1992) and to *Arts Magazine*, *Art News* and *American Art and Antiques*. **Essay:** O'Keeffe.

Roscoe, Barley   Curator, Holburne Museum and Crafts Study Centre, Bath. Contributor to *Women and Craft* (1986), *Katharine Pleydell-Bouverie: A Potter's Life, 1895–1985* (catalogue, 1986), *Arts and Crafts in the Cotswolds* (1993) and to the periodicals *Crafts*, *Ceramic Review*, *Ceramic Monthly*, *Studio Pottery* and *Journal for Art and Design Education*. **Essay:** Pleydell-Bouverie.

Rose, Peter   Lecturer and writer. Author of *George Tinworth* (1982) and *Hannah Barlow: A Pioneer Doulton Artist, 1815–1916* (1985); contributor to the *Royal Doulton International Collectors' Club Magazine*. Former chairman of the Decorative Arts Society. **Essay:** Barlow.

Rosenberg, Martin   Professor of Art History, University of Nebraska at Omaha. Author of *Raphael and France: The Artist as Paradigm and Symbol* (1995); contributor to *Art Journal*, *Eighteenth-Century Studies*, *Bulletin of the Allen Memorial Art Museum* and *Journal of European Studies*. **Essay:** Rude.

Rothstein, N. K. A.   Retired curator, formerly with the Department of Textiles, Victoria and Albert Museum, London. Author of *Silk Designs of the Eighteenth Century in the Collection of the Victoria and Albert Museum* (1990); editor of *Barbara Johnson's Album of Fashion and Fabrics* (1987). Contributor to *Textiles in Trade*, a conference of the Textile Society of America (1990), *Les Filières de la soie lyonnaise* (1991), *La seta in Europa secc. XIII–XX* (1993) and the journals *CIETA Bulletin*, *Proceedings of the Huguenot Society* and *Textile History*. **Essay:** Garthwaite.

Roworth, Wendy Wassyng   Professor of Art History, University of Rhode Island, Providence. Author of *"Pictor Succensor": A Study of Salvator Rosa as Satirist, Cynic and Painter* (1978); editor of *Angelica Kauffman: A Continental Artist in Georgian England* (1992). Contributor to *Eighteenth-Century Women and the Arts* (1988), *Femininity and Masculinity in Eighteenth-Century Art and Culture* (1994) and to the periodicals *Burlington Magazine*, *Art Bulletin*, *Metropolitan Museum Journal*, *Muse* and *The Seventeenth Century*. **Essays:** Kauffman; Academies of Art survey (with Anna Lena Lindberg and Mary D. Sheriff).

Rüther-Weiss, Veronika   Publishing assistant. Contributor to *Ethnologie und Interdisziplinarität im Ethnologie, Entwicklung und der Sozio-Kulturelle Kontext*. **Essay:** Nagel.

Salmond, Wendy R.   Associate Professor and Chair, Department of Art, Chapman University, Orange, California. Author of *Arts and Crafts in Late Imperial Russia: Reviving the Kustar Art Industries, 1870–1917* (1996) and contributor to the journals *Decorative and Propaganda Arts* and *Studies in Decorative Arts*. **Essay:** Training and Professionalism survey: Russia.